CONSERVATION DIRECTORY

49TH EDITION

The Guide to Worldwide Environmental Organizations

Bill Street, *Editor*

ISLAND PRESS

Washington • Covelo • London

Copyright © 2004 Island Press

ISBN 1-55963-415-4

All rights reserved under International and Pan-American Copyright Conventions. No part of this book may be reproduced in any form or by any means without permission in writing from the publisher: Island Press, 1718 Connecticut Avenue, N.W., Suite 300, Washington, DC 20009.

ISLAND PRESS is a trademark of The Center for Resource Economics.

NATIONAL WILDLIFE FEDERATION
11100 Wildlife Center Drive • Reston • VA 20190-5362
www.nwf.org

The mission of the National Wildlife Federation is to educate, inspire, and assist individuals and organizations of diverse cultures to conserve wildlife and other natural resources, and to protect the Earth's environment in order to achieve a peaceful, equitable, and sustainable future.

The *Conservation Directory* is published as a public service. Organizations are included on the basis of their stated objectives and other information provided. Inclusion does not imply confirmation of the information nor does it imply any endorsement of the organizations listed by the National Wildlife Federation.

To purchase the *Conservation Directory*, call Island Press at (800) 828-1302. If you have any general questions about the *Conservation Directory*, call the National Wildlife Federation at (703) 438-6000. To update your listing, please visit our Web site at www.nwf.org.

Library of Congress Cataloging-in-Publication Data is available on file. British Cataloguing-in-Publication Data is also available.

Printed on recycled, acid-free paper containing a minimum of 30 percent postconsumer recycled content.

Manufactured in the United States of America

09 08 07 06 05 04 03   8 7 6 5 4 3 2 1

LETTER FROM THE EDITOR

Dear Conservation Directory Reader:

The National Wildlife Federation is pleased to present the 49th edition of the *Conservation Directory*. The National Wildlife Federation is the only conservation education organization currently providing an annually updated directory of conservation organizations.

Since its debut in 1955, the information contained in this publication has helped a wide variety of people. Over the years we have heard from research scientists, professional resource managers, wildlife biologists, non-profit groups and their staff members, citizen activists, librarians, and students looking for internships and other job opportunities who have found what they were looking for within these pages. We sincerely hope that this will be your experience as well.

The *2004 Conservation Directory*, by its very nature, displays constant growth and change in natural resource-related organizations, both private and governmental. When the first directory was published, it was only one-fourth the size it is today. In many ways, pages added over the years track the popular development of personal commitment to environmental stewardship in America.

This commitment is what the National Wildlife Federation is all about and we will be satisfied if our publication helps you to make a vital contact in your search to contribute to this essential stewardship ethic.

NWF is proud to have Island Press as the publisher of the *Conservation Directory*. It is only fitting that this valuable resource is published by a leader in environmental publications. I also wish to thank Artech Group, Inc. for their expertise in the design and editing of this Directory.

As always, we welcome your comments, suggestions, additions, or corrections for next year's edition. You may visit the online *Conservation Directory* at **www.nwf.org/conservationdirectory** and update your organization's information automatically.

Sincerely,

Bill Street
Senior Director of Education
National Wildlife Federation

National Wildlife Federation Executive Staff

Lawrence J. Amon, *Acting President & Chief Executive Officer*
Eileen Morgan Johnson, *General Counsel*
Wayne Schmidt, *Board Relations Director*

Vice Presidents and Senior Staff: Jessie A. Brinkley, Gabriela Chavarria, Dan Chu, Robert S. Ertter, R. Montgomery Fischer, Carole S. Fox, Douglas B. Inkley, Patricia J. Key, Jaime Berman Matyas, Thomas F. McGuire, Susan Rieff

National Wildlife Productions: Christopher N. Palmer, *President & CEO*

eNature.com, Inc.: Chris Krueger, *President*

Past President: Mark Van Putten

Conservation Directory Editorial and Production Staff

Bill Street, *Editor and Senior Director of Education Programs*
Robert Goldman, *Assistant Editor*
Serge Visaggio, *Assistant Editor*
Laura Hickey, *Senior Director of Production*
Guy Williams, *Senior Director of Community Education*
Eliza Russell, *Manager of Volunteer Programs*
Jo Sorrell, *Manager of Promotions*
Renay Galati, *Acquisitions Manager*
Ian Mishalove, *Technical Director, Activism Development*
Sean Conaton, *Email & Online Marketing Manager, Membership*
Julie Mascatello, *Sr. Systems Analyst*
Heather Meese, *Program Assistant*
Marieke Beltman, *Habitat Ambassador Assistant*
Van Foster, *Volunteer*

TABLE OF CONTENTS

National Wildlife Federation Affiliate Organizations vi

MEMBERS OF U.S. CONGRESS 1

U.S. FEDERAL AND INTERNATIONAL GOVERNMENT AGENCIES 16
Includes Departments of the Executive Branch, Independent Agencies, Commissions,
Canadian Federal Government Agencies, and other International Government Agencies

STATE AND PROVINCIAL GOVERNMENT AGENCIES 132
Includes U.S. State and Canadian Provincial Government Agencies

NON-GOVERNMENTAL NON-PROFIT ORGANIZATIONS 241
Includes United States and International Organizations not affiliated with government agencies

NON-GOVERNMENTAL FOR-PROFIT ORGANIZATIONS 563
Includes United States and International Organizations not affiliated with government agencies

EDUCATIONAL INSTITUTIONS 572
Colleges and universities with conservation and environmental studies programs

INDICES
ORGANIZATION NAME INDEX 629
This is a quick and easy way to locate an organization. The index includes the name of every
organization included in the directory in alphabetical order with the corresponding page number.

KEYWORD INDEX 657
This useful reference tool lists various subject areas and gives the name of those organizations
whose work is related to that keyword. Index citations contain page numbers.

STAFF NAME INDEX 724
The Conservation Directory is very helpful if you know the name of an individual involved with an
organization but do not know the specific name of the organization. This index lists all individuals cited
in directory listings. Each citation contains the individual's name and page numbers where it appears.

GEOGRAPHIC INDEX 760
This index lists agencies and organizations by geographic regions. It is a great way to locate
organizations that can be found in a certain state or province.

NWF AFFILIATES

National Wildlife Federation Affiliates are autonomous, statewide organizations that support the purposes and objectives of the National Wildlife Federation. Each affiliate is governed by its own board of directors and develops its own membership on a local level. Affiliates provide NWF with an organized grassroots network nationwide. The elected delegates from the state affiliates determine the conservation policy for NWF through a resolution process at the NWF annual meeting. The delegates also elect NWF's chair, vice chairs, and 13 regional directors. Detailed descriptions can be found in the non-governmental organization section.

ALABAMA WILDLIFE FEDERATION
3050 Lanark Rd., P.O. Box 1339
Millbrook, AL 36054-0029
phone: (334) 285-4550
fax: (334) 285-4959
email: alabamawf@mindspring.com
web: www.alawild.org

ARIZONA WILDLIFE FEDERATION
751 S. Holmes Rd.
Apache Junction, AZ 85219-8871
phone: (602) 644-0077
fax: (480) 644-0078
email: awf@azwildlife.org
web: www.primenet.com/~awf

ARKANSAS WILDLIFE FEDERATION
9700 N. Rodney Parham Road, Suite I-2
Little Rock, AR 72227-6212
phone: (501) 224-9200
fax: (501) 224-9214
email: arkwildlifefed@aristotle.net
web: www.arkansaswildlifefederation.org

PLANNING AND CONSERVATION LEAGUE
926 J Street, Suite 612
Sacramento, CA 95814-2707
phone: (916) 444-8726
fax: (916) 448-1789
email: pclmail@pcl.org
web: www.pcl.org/pcl

COLORADO WILDLIFE FEDERATION
445 Union Blvd, #302B
Lakewood, CO 80228-1237
phone: (303) 987-0400
fax: (303) 987-0200
email: cwf@coloradowildlife.org
web: www.coloradowildlife.org

CONNECTICUT FOREST AND PARK ASSOCIATION, INC.
16 Meriden Road
Rockfall, CT 06481-2945
phone: (860) 346-2372
fax: (860) 347-7463
email: conn.forest.assoc@snet.net
web: www.ctwoodlands.org

DELAWARE NATURE SOCIETY
P.O. Box 700, 3511 Barley Mill Rd.
Hockessin, DE 19707-0700
phone: (302) 239-2334
fax: (302) 239-2473
email: ashland@dca.net
web: www.dca.net/naturesociety

FLORIDA WILDLIFE FEDERATION
P.O. Box 6870
Tallahassee, FL 32314-6870
phone: (850) 656-7113
fax: (850) 942-4431
email: wildfed@aol.com
web: www.ssnow.com/fwf/org.htm

GEORGIA WILDLIFE FEDERATION
11600 Hazelbrand Road
Covington, GA 30014-1059
phone: (770) 787-7887
fax: (770) 787-9229
email: gwf@gwf.org
web: www.gwf.org

CONSERVATION COUNCIL FOR HAWAII
P.O. Box 2923
Honolulu, HI 96802-2923
phone: (808) 968-6360
fax: (808) 968-0896
email: cch@aloha.net
web: www.conservation-hawaii.org

IDAHO WILDLIFE FEDERATION
P.O. Box 6426
Boise, ID 83707-6426
phone: (208) 342-7055
fax: (208) 342-7097
email: iwfboise@micron.net
web: www.idahowildlife.org

PRAIRIE RIVERS NETWORK
809 South Fifth Street
Champaign, IL 61820
phone: (217) 344-2371
fax: (217) 344-2381
email: robmoore@prairierivers.org
web: www.prairierivers.org

INDIANA WILDLIFE FEDERATION
950 North Rangeline Rd., Suite A
Carmel, IN 46032-1315
phone: (317) 571-1220
fax: (317) 571-1223
email: iwf@indy.net
web: www.indianawildlife.org

IOWA WILDLIFE FEDERATION
P.O. Box 3332
Des Moines, IA 50316-0332
phone: (319) 624-3107

KANSAS WILDLIFE FEDERATION
P.O. Box 8237
Wichita, KS 67208-0237

LEAGUE OF KENTUCKY SPORTSMEN, INC.
P.O. Box 8527
Lexington, KY 40533-8527
phone: (606) 635-8896
fax: (606) 635-8896
email: kysportsmen@kih.net
web: www.loks.org

LOUISIANA WILDLIFE FEDERATION, INC.
P.O. Box 65239
Baton Rouge, LA 70896-5239
phone: (225) 344-6707
fax: (225) 344-6707
email: lawildfed@aol.com

NATURAL RESOURCES COUNCIL OF MAINE
3 Wade Street
Augusta, ME 04330-6318
phone: (207) 622-3101
fax: (207) 622-4343
email: nrcm@nrcm.org
web: www.maineenvironment.org

ENVIRONMENTAL LEAGUE OF MASSACHUSETTS
14 Beacon Street, Suite 714
Boston, MA 02108-3704
phone: (617) 742-2553
fax: (617) 742-9656
email: elm@environmentalleague.org
web: www.environmentalleague.org

MICHIGAN UNITED CONSERVATION CLUBS, INC.
2101 Wood St., P.O. Box 30235
Lansing, MI 48912-3728
phone: (517) 371-1041
fax: (517) 371-1505
email: mucc@mucc.org
web: www.mucc.org

MINNESOTA CONSERVATION FEDERATION
551 South Snelling Avenue, Suite B
St. Paul, MN 55116-1584
phone: (612) 690-3077
fax: (612) 690-3077
email: mncf@mtn.org
web: www.mncf.org

MISSISSIPPI WILDLIFE FEDERATION
855 S. Pear Orchard Road, Suite 500
Ridgeland, MS 39157-5138
phone: (601) 206-5703
fax: (601) 206-5705
email: mwf@netdoor.com
web: www.mswildlife.org

CONSERVATION FEDERATION OF MISSOURI
728 West Main Street
Jefferson City, MO 65101-1534
phone: (573) 634-2322
fax: (573) 634-8205
email: confedmo@socket.net
web: www.confedmo.org

MONTANA WILDLIFE FEDERATION
P.O. Box 1175
Helena, MT 59624-1175
phone: (406) 458-0227
fax: (406) 458-0373
email: mwf@mtwf.org
web: www.montanawildlife.com

NEBRASKA WILDLIFE FEDERATION, INC.
P.O. Box 81437
Lincoln, NE 68501-1437
phone: (402) 994-2001
fax: (402) 994-2021
email: nebraskawildlife@alltel.net

NEVADA WILDLIFE FEDERATION, INC.
P.O. Box 71238
Reno, NV 89570
phone: (775) 885-7965
fax: (775) 885-0405
email: nvwf@nvwf.org
web: www.nvwf.org

NEW HAMPSHIRE WILDLIFE FEDERATION
54 Portsmouth Street
Concord, NH 03301-5486
phone: (603) 224-5953
fax: (603) 226-7147
email: nhwf@aol.com
web: www.nhwf.org

NEW MEXICO WILDLIFE FEDERATION, INC.
2921 Carlisle Blvd. NE
Albuquerque, NM 87110-2865
phone: (505) 299-5404

ENVIRONMENTAL ADVOCATES
353 Hamilton Street
Albany, NY 12210-1709
phone: (518) 462-5526
fax: (518) 427-0381
email: info@envadvocates.org
web: www.emvadvocates.org

NORTH CAROLINA WILDLIFE FEDERATION
1024 Washington St., P.O. Box 10626
Raleigh, NC 27605-0626
phone: (919) 833-1923
fax: (919) 829-1192
email: ncwf_chuck@mindspring.com
web: www.ncwildlifefed.org

NORTH DAKOTA WILDLIFE FEDERATION
P.O. Box 7248
Bismarck, ND 58507-7248
phone: (701) 845-0812
fax: (701) 222-0334
email: ndwf@gcentral.com
web: www.ndwf.org

LEAGUE OF OHIO SPORTSMEN
642 W. Broad Street
Columbus, OH 43215-2750
phone: (614) 224-8970
email: info@leaugeofohiosportsmen.org
web: www.leagueofohiosportsmen.org

OKLAHOMA WILDLIFE FEDERATION
P.O. Box 60126
Oklahoma City, OK 73146-0126
phone: (405) 521-9270
fax: (405) 521-9270
email: owf@nstar.net
(405) 524-7009
web: www.okwildlife.org

PENNSYLVANIA FEDERATION OF SPORTSMEN'S CLUBS
2426 N. Second Street
Harrisburg, PA 17110-1104
phone: (717) 232-3480
fax: (717) 231-3524
email: pawild@paonline.com
web: www.pfsc.org

PUERTO RICO ORNITHOLOGICAL SOCIETY
P.O. Box 195166
San Juan, PR 00919
phone: (787) 720-1868
email: sopi@gruposyahoo.com
www.avesdepuertorico.com

ENVIRONMENT COUNCIL OF RHODE ISLAND
P.O. Box 9061
Providence, RI 02940-9061
phone: (401) 621-8048
fax: (401) 331-5266
email: environmentcouncil@earthlink.net
web: www.environmentcouncilri.org

SOUTH CAROLINA WILDLIFE FEDERATION
2711 Middleburg Drive, Suite 104
Columbia, SC 29204-2413
phone: (803) 256-0670
fax: (803) 256-0690
email: mail@scwf.org
web: www.scwf.org

SOUTH DAKOTA WILDLIFE FEDERATION
P.O. Box 7075
Pierre, SD 57501-7075
phone: (605) 224-7524
fax: (605) 224-7524
email: sdwf@sbtc.net
web: www.sdwf.org

TENNESSEE CONSERVATION LEAGUE
300 Orlando Avenue
Nashville, TN 37209-3257
phone: (615) 353-1133
fax: (615) 353-0083
email: tcl@conservetn.com
web: www.conservetn.com

TEXAS COMMITTEE ON NATURAL RESOURCES
3532 Bee Caves Rd., Ste. 110
Austin, TX 78746-5466
phone: (512) 441-1122
fax: (214) 265-1260
email: tconr@eden.com
web: www.eden.com

UTAH WILDLIFE FEDERATION
P.O. Box 526367
Salt Lake City, UT 84152-6367
phone: (801) 487-1946
fax: (801) 773-0412
email: uwfhall@xmission.com

VERMONT NATURAL RESOURCES COUNCIL
9 Bailey Avenue
Montpelier, VT 05602-2152
phone: (802) 223-2328
fax: (802) 223-0287
email: info@vnrc.org
web: www.vnrc.org

VIRGIN ISLANDS CONSERVATION SOCIETY, INC.
Arawak Building, Suite 3, Gallows Bay
Christiansted, VI 00820
phone: (340) 773-1989
fax: (340) 773-7545
email: sea@viaccess.net
www.ecani.com/environassoc

WASHINGTON WILDLIFE FEDERATION
P.O. Box 1966
Olympia, WA 98507-1966
phone: (360) 705 1903
email: wwf@washingtonwildlife.org
web: www.washingtonwildlife.org

WEST VIRGINIA WILDLIFE FEDERATION, INC.
P.O. Box 275
Paden City, WV 26159-0275
phone: (304) 445-6401
fax: (304) 445-6401
email: pleinbach@aol.com
www.wvwf.org

WISCONSIN WILDLIFE FEDERATION, INC.
720 St. Croix St., Suite 101
Prescott, WI 54021-1454
phone: (715) 262-9279
fax: (920) 235-6030
email: wiwf@execpc.com
web: www.easy-axcess.com/wwf

WYOMING WILDLIFE FEDERATION
P.O. Box 106
Cheyenne, WY 82003-0106
phone: (307) 637-5433
fax: (307) 637-6629
email: admin@wyomingwildlife.org
web: www.wyomingwildlifc.org

MEMBERS OF U.S. CONGRESS

Updated as of September 1, 2003

ALABAMA

Senators:

Jeff Sessions
  Phone: 202-224-4124   Fax: 202-224-3149
  E-mail: senator@sessions.senate.gov
  Website: www.sessions.senate.gov

Richard Shelby
  Phone: 202-224-5744   Fax: 202-224-3416
  E-mail: senator@shelby.senate.gov
  Website: www.shelby.senate.gov

Representatives:

Jo Bonner
  Phone: 202-225-4931   Fax: 202-225-0562
  Website: www.house.gov/callahan

Terry Everett
  Phone: 202-225-2901   Fax: 202-225-8913
  Website: www.hillsource.gov/everett

Michael D. Rogers
  Phone: 202-225-3261   Fax: 202-226-8485
  E-mail: mike.rogersal03@mail.house.gov
  Website: www.house.gov/mike-rogers

Robert B. Aderholt
  Phone: 202-225-4876   Fax: 202-225-5587
  E-mail: robert.@mail.house.gov
  Website: www.house.gov/aderholt

Robert E. "Bud" Cramer Jr.
  Phone: 202-225-4801   Fax: 202-225-4392
  E-mail: budmail@mail.house.gov
  Website: www.house.gov/cramer

Spencer Bachus
  Phone: 202-225-4921   Fax: 202-225-2082
  Website: www.house.gov/bachus

Artur Davis
  Phone: 202-225-2665   Fax: 202-226-9567
  Website: www.house.gov/arturdavis

ALASKA

Senators:

Ted Stevens
  Phone: 202-224-3004   Fax: 202-224-2354
  Website: www.stevens.senate.gov

Lisa Murkowski
  Phone: 202-224-6665   Fax: 202-224-5301
  E-mail: email@murkowski.senate.gov
  Website: www.murkowski.senate.gov

Representatives:

Don Young
  Phone: 202-225-5765   Fax: 202-225-0425
  E-mail: don.young@mail.house.gov
  Website: www.house.gov/donyoung

ARIZONA

Senators:

John McCain
  Phone: 202-224-2235   Fax: 202-228-2862
  E-mail: john_mccain@mccain.senate.gov
  Website: www.mccain.senate.gov

Jon L. Kyl
  Phone: 202-224-4521   Fax: 202-224-2207
  Website: www.kyl.senate.gov

Representatives:

Rick Renzi
  Phone: 202-225-2315   Fax: 202-226-9739
  E-mail: rick.renzi@mail.house.gov
  Website: www.house.gov/renzi

Trent Franks
  Phone: 202-225-4576   Fax: 202-225-6328
  Website: www.house.gov/franks

John B. Shadegg
  Phone: 202-225-3361   Fax: 202-225-3462
  Website: www.johnshadegg.house.gov

Ed Pastor
  Phone: 202-225-4065   Fax: 202-225-1655
  Website: www.house.gov/pastor

J.D. Hayworth
  Phone: 202-225-2190   Fax: 202-225-3263
  E-mail: jdhayworth@mail.house.gov
  Website: www.house.gov/hayworth

Jeff Flake
  Phone: 202-225-2635   Fax: 202-226-4386
  E-mail: jeff.flake@mail.house.gov
  Website: www.house.gov/flake

Raul Grijalva
  Phone: 202-225-2435   Fax: 202-226-6846
  Website: www.house.gov/grijalva

Jim Kolbe
  Phone: 202-225-2542   Fax: 202-225-0378
  Website: www.house.gov/kolbe

ARKANSAS

Senators:

Blanche L. Lincoln
  Phone: 202-224-4843   Fax: 202-228-1371
  Website: www.llncoln.senate.gov

Mark Pryor
  Phone: 202-224-2353   Fax: 202-228-0908
  E-mail: mark.pryor@pryor.senate.gov
  Website: www.pryor.senate.gov

Representatives:

Marion Berry
  Phone: 202-225-4076   Fax: 202-225-5602
  Website: www.house.gov/berry

Vic Snyder
  Phone: 202-225-2506   Fax: 202-225-5903
  E-mail: snyder.congress@mail.house.gov
  Website: www.house.gov/snyder

John Boozman
  Phone: 202-225-4301   Fax: 202-225-5713
  Website: www.house.gov/boozman

Mike Ross
  Phone: 202-225-3772   Fax: 202-225-1314
  E-mail: mike.ross@mail.house.gov
  Website: www.house.gov/ross

CALIFORNIA

Senators:

Dianne Feinstein
  Phone: 202-224-3841   Fax: 202-228-3954
  Website: www.feinstein.senate.gov

Barbara Boxer
  Phone: 202-224-3553   Fax: 415-956-6701
  Website: www.boxer.senate.gov

Representatives:

Mike Thompson
  Phone: 202-225-3311   Fax: 202-225-4335
  Website: www.house.gov/mthompson

Wally Herger
  Phone: 202-225-3076
  Website: www.house.gov/herger

Doug Ose
  Phone: 202-225-5716   Fax: 202-226-1298
  Website: www.house.gov/ose

John T. Doolittle
  Phone: 202-225-2511   Fax: 202-225-5444
  Website: www.house.gov/doolittle

Robert T. Matsui
  Phone: 202-225-7163   Fax: 202-225-0566
  Website: www.house.gov/matsui

MEMBERS OF U.S. CONGRESS

Lynn Woolsey
  Phone: 202-225-5161   Fax: 202-225-5163
  Website: www.house.gov/woolsey
George Miller
  Phone: 202-225-2095   Fax: 202-225-5609
  E-mail: george.miller@mail.house.gov
  Website: www.house.gov/georgemiller
Nancy Pelosi
  Phone: 202-225-4965   Fax: 202-225-8259
  E-mail: sf.nancy@mail.house.gov
  Website: www.house.gov/pelosi
Barbara Lee
  Phone: 202-225-2661   Fax: 202-225-9817
  E-mail: barbara.lee@mail.house.gov
  Website: www.house.gov/lee
Ellen O. Tauscher
  Phone: 202-225-1880   Fax: 202-225-5914
  Website: www.house.gov/tauscher
Richard Pombo
  Phone: 202-225-1947   Fax: 202-225-0861
  E-mail: rpombo@mail.house.gov
  Website: www.house.gov/pombo
Tom Lantos
  Phone: 202-225-3531   Fax: 202-226-9789
  Website: www.house.gov/lantos
Fortney H. "Pete" Stark
  Phone: 202-225-5065   Fax: 202-226-3805
  Website: www.house.gov/stark
Anna Eshoo
  Phone: 202-225-8104   Fax: 202-225-8890
  Website: www.house.gov/eshoo
Michael M. Honda
  Phone: 202-225-2631   Fax: 202-225-2699
  E-mail: mike.honda@mail.house.gov
  Website: www.house.gov/honda
Zoe Lofgren
  Phone: 202-225-3072   Fax: 202-225-3336
  E-mail: zoe.lofgren@mail.house.gov
  Website: www.zoelofgren.house.gov
Sam Farr
  Phone: 202-225-2861   Fax: 202-225-6791
  Website: www.house.gov/farr
Dennis Cardoza
  Phone: 202-225-6131   Fax: 202-225-0819
  Website: www.house.gov/cardoza
George P. Randovich
  Phone: 202-225-4540   Fax: 202-225-3402
  Website: www.radanovich.house.gov
Calvin Dooley
  Phone: 202-225-3341   Fax: 202-225-9308
  Website: www.dooley.house.gov
Devin Nunes
  Phone: 202-225-2523 Fax: 202-225-3404
  Website: www.nunes.house.gov
William M. Thomas
  Phone: 202-225-2915   Fax: 202-225-8798
  E-mail: bill.thomas@mail.house.gov
  Website: www.house.gov/billthomas
Lois Capps
  Phone: 202-225-3601   Fax: 202-225-5632
  Website: www.house.gov/capps
Elton Gallegly
  Phone: 202-225-5811   Fax: 202-225-1100
  Website: www.house.gov/gallegly
Howard "Buck" McKeon
  Phone: 202-225-1956   Fax: 202-226-0683
  E-mail: tellbuck@mail.house.gov
  Website: www.house.gov/mckeon
David Dreier
  Phone: 202-225-2305   Fax: 202-225-7018
  Website: www.dreier.house.gov

Brad Sherman
  Phone: 202-225-5911   Fax: 202-225-5879
  Website: www.house.gov/sherman
Howard L. Berman
  Phone: 202-225-4695   Fax: 202-225-3196
  E-mail: howard.berman@mail.house.gov
  Website: www.house.gov/berman
Adam Schiff
  Phone: 202-225-4176   Fax: 202-225-5828
  Website: www.house.gov/schiff
Henry A. Waxman
  Phone: 202-225-3976   Fax: 202-225-4099
  Website: www.house.gov/waxman
Xavier Becerra
  Phone: 202-225-6235   Fax: 202-225-2202
  Website: www.house.gov/becerra
Hilda L. Solis
  Phone: 202-225-5464   Fax: 202-225-5467
  E-mail: hilda@mail.house.gov
  Website: www.house.gov/solis
Diane Watson
  Phone: 202-225-7084   Fax: 202-225-2422
  E-mail: diane.watson@mail.house.gov
  Website: www.house.gov/watson
Lucille Roybal-Allard
  Phone: 202-225-1766   Fax: 202-226-0350
  Website: www.house.gov/roybal-allard
Maxine Waters
  Phone: 202-225-2201   Fax: 202-225-7854
  Website: www.house.gov/waters
Jane F. Harman
  Phone: 202-225-8220   Fax: 202-226-7290
  Website: www.house.gov/harman
Juanita Millender-McDonald
  Phone: 202-225-7924   Fax: 202-225-7926
  E-mail: millender.mcdonald@mail.house.gov
  Website: www.house.gov/millender-mcdonald
Grace F. Napolitano
  Phone: 202-225-5256   Fax: 202-225-0027
  Website: www.napolitano.house.gov
Linda T. Sanchez
  Phone: 202-225-6676   Fax: 202-226-1012
  Website: www.house.gov/lindasanchez
Edward Royce
  Phone: 202-225-4111   Fax: 202-226-0335
  Website: www.house.gov/royce
Jerry Lewis
  Phone: 202-225-5861   Fax: 202-225-6498
  Website: www.house.gov/jerrylewis
Gary G. Miller
  Phone: 202-225-3201   Fax: 202-226-6962
  E-mail: publicca41@mail.house.gov
  Website: www.house.gov/garymiller
Joe Baca
  Phone: 202-225-6161   Fax: 202-225-8671
  E-mail: cong.baca@mail.house.gov
  Website: www.house.gov/baca
Ken Calvert
  Phone: 202-225-1986   Fax: 202-225-2004
  Website: www.house.gov/calvert
Mary Bono
  Phone: 202-225-5330   Fax: 202-225-2961
  Website: www.house.gov/bono
Dana Rohrabacher
  Phone: 202-225-2415   Fax: 202-225-0145
  E-mail: dana@mail.house.gov
  Website: www.house.gov/rohrabacher
Loretta L. Sanchez
  Phone: 202-225-2965   Fax: 202-225-5859
  E-mail: loretta@mail.house.gov
  Website: www.house.gov/sanchez

MEMBERS OF U.S. CONGRESS

Christopher Cox
  Phone: 202-225-5611   Fax: 202-225-9177
  E-mail: christopher.cox@mail.house.gov
  Website: cox.house.gov
Darrell Issa
  Phone: 202-225-3906   Fax: 202-225-3303
  Website: www.issa.house.gov
Randy "Duke" Cunningham
  Phone: 202-225-5452   Fax: 202-225-2558
  Website: www.house.gov/cunningham
Bob Filner
  Phone: 202-225-8045   Fax: 202-225-9073
  Website: www.house.gov/filner
Duncan Hunter
  Phone: 202-225-5672   Fax: 202-225-0235
  Website: www.house.gov/hunter
Susan A. Davis
  Phone: 202-225-2040   Fax: 202-225-2948
  E-mail: susan.davis@mail.house.gov
  Website: www.house.gov/susandavis

COLORADO

Senators:

Ben Nighthorse Campbell
  Phone: 202-224-5852   Fax: 202-228-4609
  Website: www.campbell.senate.gov
Wayne Allard
  Phone: 202-224-5941   Fax: 202-224-6471
  Website: www.allard.senate.gov

Representatives:

Diana L. DeGette
  Phone: 202-225-4431   Fax: 202-225-5657
  E-mail: degette@mail.house.gov
  Website: www.house.gov/degette
Mark Udall
  Phone: 202-225-2161   Fax: 202-226-7840
  Website: www.house.gov/markudall
Scott McInnis
  Phone: 202-225-4761   Fax: 202-226-0622
  Website: www.house.gov/mcinnis
Marilyn Musgrave
  Phone: 202-225-4676   Fax: 202-225-5870
  E-mail: rep.musgrave@mail.house.gov
  Website: www.house.gov/musgrave
Joel Hefley
  Phone: 202-225-4422   Fax: 202-225-1942
  Website: www.house.gov/hefley
Thomas G. Tancredo
  Phone: 202-225-7882   Fax: 202-226-4623
  E-mail: tom.tancredo@mail.house.gov
  Website: www.house.gov/tancredo
Bob Beauprez
  Phone: 202-225-2645   Fax: 202-225-5278
  Website: www.house.gov/beauprez

CONNECTICUT

Senators:

Christopher J. Dodd
  Phone: 202-224-2823   Fax: 202-224-1083
  Website: www.dodd.senate.gov
Joseph I. Lieberman
  Phone: 202-224-4041   Fax: 202-224-9750
  Website: www.lieberman.senate.gov

Representatives:

John B. Larson
  Phone: 202-225-2265   Fax: 202-225-1031
  Website: www.house.gov/larson
Robert R. Simmons
  Phone: 202-225-2076   Fax: 202-225-4977
  Website: www.house.gov/simmons
Rosa DeLauro
  Phone: 202-225-3661   Fax: 202-225-4890
  Website: www.house.gov/delauro
Christopher Shays
  Phone: 202-225-5541   Fax: 202-225-9629
  E-mail: rep.shays@mail.house.gov
  Website: www.house.gov/shays
Nancy L. Johnson
  Phone: 202-225-4476   Fax: 202-225-4488
  Website: www.house.gov/nancyjohnson

DELAWARE

Senators:

Joseph R. Biden Jr.
  Phone: 202-224-5402   Fax: 202-224-0139
  E-mail: senator@biden.senate.gov
  Website: www.biden.senate.gov
Thomas R. Carper
  Phone: 202-224-2441   Fax: 202-228-2190
  Website: carper.senate.gov

Representatives:

Michael Castle
  Phone: 202-225-4165   Fax: 202-225-2291
  Website: www.house.gov/castle

FLORIDA

Senators:

Bob Graham
  Phone: 202-224-3041   Fax: 202-224-2237
  Website: www.graham.senate.gov
Bill Nelson
  Phone: 202-224-5274   Fax: 202-228-2183
  E-mail: senator@billnelson.senate.gov
  Website: www.billnelson.senate.gov

Representatives:

Jeff Miller
  Phone: 202-225-4136   Fax: 202-225-3414
  Website: www.house.gov/jeffmiller
F. Allen Boyd Jr.
  Phone: 202-225-5235   Fax: 202-225-5615
  Website: www.house.gov/boyd
Corrine Brown
  Phone: 202-225-0123   Fax: 202-225-2256
  Website: www.house.gov/corrinebrown
Ander Crenshaw
  Phone: 202-225-2501   Fax: 202-225-2504
  Website: www.crenshaw.house.gov
Ginny Brown-Waite
  Phone: 202-225-1002   Fax: 202-226-6559
  Website: www.house.gov/brown-waite
Cliff Stearns
  Phone: 202-225-5744   Fax: 202-225-3973
  Website: www.house.gov/stearns
John Mica
  Phone: 202-225-4035   Fax: 202-226-0821
  E-mail: john.mica@mail.house.gov
  Website: www.house.gov/mica
Ric Keller
  Phone: 202-225-2176   Fax: 202-225-0999
  Website: www.house.gov/keller
Michael Bilirakis
  Phone: 202-225-5755   Fax: 202-225-4085
  Website: www.house.gov/bilirakis
C.W. "Bill" Young
  Phone: 202-225-5961   Fax: 202-225-9764
  E-mail: bill.young@mail.house.gov
  Website: www.house.gov/young

Jim Davis
　　Phone: 202-225-3376　　Fax: 202-225-5652
　　Website: www.house.gov/jimdavis
Adam Putnam
　　Phone: 202-225-1252　　Fax: 202-226-0585
　　Website: www.house.gov/putnam
Katherine Harris
　　Phone: 202-225-5015　　Fax: 202-226-0828
　　E-mail: katherine.harris@mail.house.gov
　　Website: www.house.gov/harris
Porter J. Goss
　　Phone: 202-225-2536　　Fax: 202-225-6820
　　E-mail: porter.goss@mail.house.gov
　　Website: www.portergoss.house.gov
Dave Weldon
　　Phone: 202-225-3671　　Fax: 202-225-3516
　　Website: www.house.gov/weldon
Mark Foley
　　Phone: 202-225-5792　　Fax: 202-225-3132
　　Website: www.house.gov/foley
Kendrick B. Meek
　　Phone: 202-225-4506　　Fax: 202-226-0777
　　Website: www.house.gov/kenmeek
Ileana Ros-Lehtinen
　　Phone: 202-225-3931　　Fax: 202-225-5620
　　Website: www.house.gov/ros-lehtinen
Robert I. Wexler
　　Phone: 202-225-3001　　Fax: 202-225-5974
　　Website: www.house.gov/wexler
Peter Deutsch
　　Phone: 202-225-7931　　Fax: 202-225-8456
　　Website: www.house.gov/deutsch
Lincoln Diaz-Balart
　　Phone: 202-225-4211　　Fax: 202-225-8576
　　Website: www.house.gov/diaz-balart
E. Clay Shaw Jr.
　　Phone: 202-225-3026　　Fax: 202-225-8398
　　Website: www.house.gov/shaw
Alcee L. Hastings
　　Phone: 202-225-1313　　Fax: 202-225-1171
　　E-mail: alcee.pubhastings@mail.house.gov
　　Website: www.house.gov/alceehastings
Tom Feeney
　　Phone: 202-225-2706　　Fax: 202-226-6299
　　E-mail: tom.feeney@mail.house.gov
　　Website: www.house.gov/feeney
Mario Diaz-Balart
　　Phone: 202-225-2778　　Fax: 202-226-0346
　　Website: www.house.gov/mariodiaz-balart

GEORGIA

Senators:

Zell B. Miller
　　Phone: 202-224-3643　　Fax: 202-228-2090
　　Website: www.miller.senate.gov
Saxby Chambliss
　　Phone: 202-224-3521　　Fax: 202-224-0103
　　E-mail: saxby.chambliss@chambliss.senate.gov
　　Website: www.chambliss.senate.gov

Representatives:

Jack Kingston
　　Phone: 202-225-5831　　Fax: 202-226-2269
　　E-mail: jack.kingston@mail.house.gov
　　Website: www.house.gov/kingston
Sanford Bishop, Jr.
　　Phone: 202-225-3631　　Fax: 202-225-2203
　　E-mail: bishop.email@mail.house.gov
　　Website: www.house.gov/bishop

Jim Marshall
　　Phone: 202-225-6531　　Fax: 202-225-3013
　　E-mail: jim.marshall@mail.house.gov
　　Website: www.house.gov/marshall
Denise L. Majette
　　Phone: 202-225-1605　　Fax: 202-226-0691
　　Website: www.house.gov/majette
John Lewis
　　Phone: 202-225-3801　　Fax: 202-225-0351
　　E-mail: john.lewis@mail.house.gov
　　Website: www.house.gov/johnlewis
Johnny Isakson
　　Phone: 202-225-4501　　Fax: 202-225-4656
　　E-mail: ga06@mail.house.gov
　　Website: www.isakson.house.gov
John Linder
　　Phone: 202-225-4272　　Fax: 202-225-4696
　　E-mail: john.linder@mail.house.gov
　　Website: www.house.gov/linder
Michael "Mac" Collins
　　Phone: 202-225-5901　　Fax: 202-225-2515
　　Website: www.house.gov/maccollins
Charles Norwood
　　Phone: 202-225-4101　　Fax: 202-226-0776
　　Website: www.house.gov/norwood
Nathan Deal
　　Phone: 202-225-5211　　Fax: 202-225-8272
　　Website: www.house.gov/deal
Phil Gingrey
　　Phone: 202-225-2931 Fax: 202-225-2944
　　E-mail: gingrey.ga@mail.house.gov
　　Website: www.house.gov/gingrey
Max Burns
　　Phone: 202-225-2823 Fax: 202-225-3377
　　E-mail: max.burns@mail.house.gov
　　Website: www.house.gov/burns
David Scott
　　Phone: 202-225-2939 Fax: 202-225-4628
　　Website: www.house.gov/davidscott

HAWAII

Senators:

Daniel K. Inouye
　　Phone: 202-224-3934　　Fax: 202-224-6747
　　Website: www.inouye.senate.gov
Daniel K. Akaka
　　Phone: 202-224-6361　　Fax: 202-224-2126
　　E-mail: senator@akaka.senate.gov
　　Website: www.akaka.senate.gov

Representatives:

Neil Abercrombie
　　Phone: 202-225-2726　　Fax: 202-225-4580
　　E-mail: neil.abercrombie@mail.house.gov
　　Website: www.house.gov/abercrombie
Ed Case
　　Phone: 202-225-4906　　Fax: 202-225-4987
　　E-mail: ed.case@mail.house.gov
　　Website: www.house.gov/case

IDAHO

Senators:

Larry E. Craig
　　Phone: 202-224-2752　　Fax: 202-228-1067
　　Website: www.craig.senate.gov
Michael D. Crapo
　　Phone: 202-224-6142　　Fax: 202-228-1375
　　Website: www.crapo.senate.gov

MEMBERS OF U.S. CONGRESS

Representatives:

C.L. "Butch" Otter
   Phone: 202-225-6611   Fax: 202-225-3029
   E-mail: butch.otter@mail.house.gov
   Website: www.house.gov/otter

Mike Simpson
   Phone: 202-225-5531   Fax: 202-225-8216
   Website: www.house.gov/simpson

ILLINOIS

Senators:

Richard J. Durbin
   Phone: 202-224-2152   Fax: 202-228-0400
   E-mail: dick@durbin.senate.gov
   Website: www.durbin.senate.gov

Peter G. Fitzgerald
   Phone: 202-224-2854   Fax: 202-228-1372
   Website: www.fitzgerald.senate.gov

Representatives:

Bobby L. Rush
   Phone: 202-225-4372   Fax: 202-226-0333
   Website: www.house.gov/rush

Jesse L. Jackson, Jr.
   Phone: 202-225-0773   Fax: 202-225-0899
   E-mail: jjackson@jessejacksonjr.org
   Website: www.jessejacksonjr.org

William O. Lipinski
   Phone: 202-225-5701   Fax: 202-225-1012
   Website: www.house.gov/lipinski

Luis V. Gutierrez
   Phone: 202-225-8203   Fax: 202-225-7810
   Website: www.luisgutierrez.house.gov

Rahm Emanuel
   Phone: 202-225-4061   Fax: 202-225-5603
   Website: www.house.gov/emanuel

Henry J. Hyde
   Phone: 202-225-4561   Fax: 202-225-1166
   Website: www.house.gov/hyde

Danny K. Davis
   Phone: 202-225-5006   Fax: 202-225-5641
   Website: www.house.gov/davis

Philip M. Crane
   Phone: 202-225-3711   Fax: 202-225-7830
   Website: www.house.gov/crane

Janice D. Schakowsky
   Phone: 202-225-2111   Fax: 202-226-6090
   E-mail: jan.schakowsky@mail.house.gov
   Website: www.house.gov/schakowsky

Mark S. Kirk
   Phone: 202-225-4835   Fax: 202-225-0837
   E-mail: rep.kirk@mail.house.gov
   Website: www.house.gov/kirk

Jerry Weller
   Phone: 202-225-3635   Fax: 202-225-3521
   Website: www.house.gov/weller

Jerry F. Costello
   Phone: 202-225-5661   Fax: 202-225-0285
   Website: www.house.gov/costello

Judy Biggert
   Phone: 202-225-3515   Fax: 202-225-9420
   Website: www.judybiggert.house.gov

J. Dennis Hastert
   Phone: 202-225-2976   Fax: 202-225-0697
   E-mail: dhastert@mail.house.gov
   Website: www.house.gov/hastert

Timothy V. Johnson
   Phone: 202-225-2371   Fax: 202-226-0791
   Website: www.house.gov/timjohnson

Donald A. Manzullo
   Phone: 202-225-5676   Fax: 202-225-5284
   Website: www.manzullo.house.gov

Lane Evans
   Phone: 202-225-5905   Fax: 202-225-5396
   E-mail: lane.evans@mail.house.gov
   Website: www.house.gov/evans

Ray LaHood
   Phone: 202-225-6201   Fax: 202-225-9249
   Website: www.house.gov/lahood

John M. Shimkus
   Phone: 202-225-5271   Fax: 202-225-5880
   Website: www.house.gov/shimkus

INDIANA

Senators:

Richard G. Lugar
   Phone: 202-224-4814   Fax: 202-228-0360
   E-mail: senator_lugar@lugar.senate.gov
   Website: www.lugar.senate.gov

Evan Bayh
   Phone: 202-224-5623   Fax: 202-228-1377
   Website: www.bayh.senate.gov

Representatives:

Peter J. Visclosky
   Phone: 202-225-2461   Fax: 202-225-2493
   Website: www.house.gov/visclosky

Chris Chocola
   Phone: 202-225-39-15   Fax: 202-225-6798
   Website: www.house.gov/chocola

Mark Souder
   Phone: 202-225-4436   Fax: 202-225-3479
   E-mail: souder@mail.house.gov
   Website: www.house.gov/souder

Steve Buyer
   Phone: 202-225-5037   Fax: 202-225-2267
   Website: www.house.gov/buyer

Dan Burton
   Phone: 202-225-2276   Fax: 202-225-0016
   Website: www.house.gov/burton

Mike Pence
   Phone: 202-225-3021   Fax: 202-225-3382
   E-mail: mike.pence@mail.house.gov
   Website: www.mikepence.house.gov

Julia M. Carson
   Phone: 202-225-4011   Fax: 202-225-5633
   E-mail: rep.carson@mail.house.gov
   Website: www.juliacarson.house.gov

John N. Hostettler
   Phone: 202-225-4636   Fax: 202-225-3284
   E-mail: john.hostettler@mail.house.gov
   Website: www.house.gov/hostettler

Baron Hill
   Phone: 202-225-5315   Fax: 202-226-6866
   Website: www.house.gov/baronhill

IOWA

Senators:

Charles E. Grassley
   Phone: 202-224-3744   Fax: 202-224-6020
   Website: www.grassley.senate.gov

Tom Harkin
   Phone: 202-224-3254   Fax: 202-224-9369
   E-mail: tom_harkin@harkin.senate.gov
   Website: www.harkin.senate.gov

Representatives:

Jim Nussle
   Phone: 202-225-2911   Fax: 202-225-9129
   E-mail: nussleia@mail.house.gov
   Website: www.nussle.house.gov

Jim Leach
Phone: 202-225-6576   Fax: 202-226-1278
E-mail: talk2jim@mail.house.gov
Website: www.house.gov/leach

Leonard L. Boswell
Phone: 202-225-3806   Fax: 202-225-5608
E-mail: rep.boswell.ia03@mail.house.gov
Website: www.house.gov/boswell

Tom Latham
Phone: 202-225-5476   Fax: 202-225-3301
E-mail: latham.ia05@mail.house.gov
Website: www.house.gov/latham

Steve King
Phone: 202-225-4426   Fax: 202-225-3193
Website: www.house.gov/steveking

KANSAS

Senators:

Sam Brownback
Phone: 202-224-6521   Fax: 202-228-1265
Website: www.brownback.senate.gov

Pat Roberts
Phone: 202-224-4774   Fax: 202-224-3514
Website: www.roberts.senate.gov

Representatives:

Jerry Moran
Phone: 202-225-2715   Fax: 202-225-5124
E-mail: jerry.moran@mail.house.gov
Website: www.house.gov/moranks01

Jim R. Ryun
Phone: 202-225-6601   Fax: 202-225-7986
Website: www.ryun.house.gov

Dennis Moore
Phone: 202-225-2865   Fax: 202-225-2807
Website: www.house.gov/moore

Todd Tiahrt
Phone: 202-225-6216   Fax: 202-225-3489
Website: www.house.gov/tiahrt

KENTUCKY

Senators:

Mitch McConnell
Phone: 202-224-2541   Fax: 202-224-2499
E-mail: senator@mcconnell.senate.gov
Website: www.mcconnell.senate.gov

Jim Bunning
Phone: 202-224-4343   Fax: 202-228-1373
Website: www.bunning.senate.gov

Representatives:

Edward Whitfield
Phone: 202-225-3115   Fax: 202-225-3547
Website: www.house.gov/whitfield

Ron Lewis
Phone: 202-225-3501   Fax: 202-226-2019
E-mail: ron.lewis@mail.house.gov
Website: www.house.gov/ronlewis

Anne M. Northup
Phone: 202-225-5401   Fax: 202-225-5776
E-mail: rep.northup@mail.house.gov
Website: www.northup.house.gov

Ken R. Lucas
Phone: 202-225-3465   Fax: 202-225-0003
Website: www.house.gov/kenlucas

Harold Rogers
Phone: 202-225-4601   Fax: 202-225-0940
E-mail: talk2hal@mail.house.gov
Website: www.house.gov/rogers

Ernest Lee Fletcher
Phone: 202-225-4706   Fax: 202-225-2122
Website: www.house.gov/fletcher

LOUISIANA

Senators:

John B. Breaux
Phone: 202-224-4623   Fax: 202-228-2577
Website: www.breaux.senate.gov

Mary Landrieu
Phone: 202-224-5824   Fax: 202-224-9735
Website: www.landrieu.senate.gov

Representatives:

David Vitter
Phone: 202-225-3015   Fax: 202-225-0739
E-mail: david.vitter@mail.house.gov
Website: www.vitter.house.gov

William J. Jefferson
Phone: 202-225-6636   Fax: 202-225-1988
E-mail: jeffersonmc@mail.house.gov
Website: www.house.gov/jefferson

W.J. "Billy" Tauzin
Phone: 202-225-4031   Fax: 202-225-0563
Website: www.house.gov/tauzin

Jim McCrery
Phone: 202-225-2777   Fax: 202-225-8039
Website: www.house.gov/mccrery

Rodney Alexander
Phone: 202-225-8490   Fax: 202-225-5639
Website: www.house.gov/alexander

Richard H. Baker
Phone: 202-225-3901   Fax: 202-225-7313
Website: www.house.gov/baker

Chris John
Phone: 202-225-2031   Fax: 202-225-5724
Website: www.house.gov/john

MAINE

Senators:

Olympia J. Snowe
Phone: 202-224-5344   Fax: 202-224-1946
E-mail: olympia@snowe.senate.gov
Website: www.snowe.senate.gov

Susan M. Collins
Phone: 202-224-2523   Fax: 202-224-2693
E-mail: senator@collins.senate.gov
Website: www.collins.senate.gov

Representatives:

Thomas H. Allen
Phone: 202-225-6116   Fax: 202-225-5590
E-mail: rep.tomallen@mail.house.gov
Website: www.tomallen.house.gov

Michael H. Michaud
Phone: 202-225-6306   Fax: 202-225-2943
E-mail: rep.mikemichaud@mail.house.gov
Website: www.house.gov/michaud

MARYLAND

Senators:

Paul S. Sarbanes
Phone: 202-224-4524   Fax: 202-224-1651
Website: www.sarbanes.senate.gov

Barbara A. Mikulski
Phone: 202-224-4654   Fax: 202-224-8858
Website: www.mikulski.senate.gov

Representatives:

Wayne Gilchrest
Phone: 202-225-5311   Fax: 202-225-0254
E-mail: wgilchrest@mail.house.gov
Website: www.house.gov/gilchrest

MEMBERS OF U.S. CONGRESS

C.A. "Dutch" Ruppersberger
  Phone: 202-225-3061 Fax: 202-225-3094
  E-mail: dutch.ruppersberger@mail.house.gov
  Website: www.house.gov/ruppersberger

Benjamin L. Cardin
  Phone: 202-225-4016 Fax: 202-225-9219
  E-mail: rep.cardin@mail.house.gov
  Website: www.house.gov/cardin

Albert Wynn
  Phone: 202-225-8699 Fax: 202-225-8714
  Website: www.wynn.house.gov

Steny H. Hoyer
  Phone: 202-225-4131 Fax: 202-225-4300
  Website: www.hoyer.house.gov

Roscoe Bartlett
  Phone: 202-225-2721 Fax: 202-225-2193
  Website: www.bartlett.house.gov

Elijah Cummings
  Phone: 202-225-4741 Fax: 202-225-3178
  Website: www.house.gov/cummings

Chris Van Hollen, Jr.
  Phone: 202-225-5341 Fax: 202-225-0375
  E-mail: chris.vanhollen@mail.house.gov
  Website: www.house.gov/vanhollen

MASSACHUSETTS

Senators:

Edward M. Kennedy
  Phone: 202-224-4543 Fax: 202-224-2417
  Website: www.kennedy.senate.gov

John F. Kerry
  Phone: 202-224-2742 Fax: 202-224-8525
  E-mail: john_kerry@kerry.senate.gov
  Website: www.kerry.senate.gov

Representatives:

John W. Olver
  Phone: 202-225-5335 Fax: 202-226-1224
  Website: www.house.gov/olver

Richard E. Neal
  Phone: 202-225-5601 Fax: 202-225-8112
  Website: www.house.gov/neal

James P. McGovern
  Phone: 202-225-6101 Fax: 202-225-5759
  Website: www.house.gov/mcgovern

Barney Frank
  Phone: 202-225-5931 Fax: 202-225-0182
  Website: www.house.gov/frank

Marty Meehan
  Phone: 202-225-3411 Fax: 202-226-0771
  Website: www.house.gov/meehan

John F. Tierney
  Phone: 202-225-8020 Fax: 202-225-5915
  Website: www.house.gov/tierney

Edward J. Markey
  Phone: 202-225-2836 Fax: 202-226-0092
  Website: www.house.gov/markey

Michael Capuano
  Phone: 202-225-5111 Fax: 202-225-9322
  Website: www.house.gov/capuano

Stephen F. Lynch
  Phone: 202-225-8273 Fax: 202-225-3984
  E-mail: stephen.lynch@mail.house.gov
  Website: www.house.gov/lynch

William Delahunt
  Phone: 202-225-3111 Fax: 202-225-5658
  E-mail: william.delahunt@mail.house.gov
  Website: www.house.gov/delahunt

MICHIGAN

Senators:

Carl Levin
  Phone: 202-224-6221 Fax: 202-224-1388
  E-mail: senator2@levin.senate.gov
  Website: www.levin.senate.gov

Debbie A. Stabenow
  Phone: 202-224-4822 Fax: 202-228-0325
  E-mail: senator@stabenow.senate.gov
  Website: www.stabenow.senate.gov

Representatives:

Bart Stupak
  Phone: 202-225-4735 Fax: 202-225-4744
  E-mail: stupak@mail.house.gov
  Website: www.house.gov/stupak

Peter Hoekstra
  Phone: 202-225-4401 Fax: 202-226-0779
  E-mail: tellhoek@mail.house.gov
  Website: www.house.gov/hoekstra

Vernon Ehlers
  Phone: 202-225-3831 Fax: 202-225-5144
  Website: www.house.gov/ehlers

Dave Camp
  Phone: 202-225-3561 Fax: 202-225-9679
  Website: www.house.gov/camp

Dale E. Kildee
  Phone: 202-225-3611 Fax: 202-225-6393
  E-mail: dkildee@mail.house.gov
  Website: www.house.gov/kildee

Fred Upton
  Phone: 202-225-3761 Fax: 202-225-4986
  E-mail: tellupton@mail.house.gov
  Website: www.house.gov/upton

Nick Smith
  Phone: 202-225-6276 Fax: 202-225-6281
  Website: www.house.gov/nicksmith

Michael J. Rogers
  Phone: 202-225-4872 Fax: 202-225-5820
  Website: www.house.gov/mikerogers

Joseph Knollenberg
  Phone: 202-225-5802 Fax: 202-226-2356
  E-mail: rep.knollenberg@mail.house.gov
  Website: www.house.gov/knollenberg

Candice Miller
  Phone: 202-225-2106 Fax: 202-226-1169
  E-mail: mi10.wyr@mail.house.gov
  Website: www.house.gov/candicemiller

Thaddeus G. McCotter
  Phone: 202-225-8171 Fax: 202-225-2667
  Website: www.house.gov/mccotter

Sander M. Levin
  Phone: 202-225-4961 Fax: 202-226-1033
  E-mail: slevin@mail.house.gov
  Website: www.house.gov/levin

Carolyn C. Kilpatrick
  Phone: 202-225-2261 Fax: 202-225-5730
  E-mail: carolyn.cheeks.kilpatrick@mail.house.gov
  Website: www.house.gov/kilpatrick

John Conyers Jr.
  Phone: 202-225-5126 Fax: 202-225-0072
  E-mail: john.conyers@mail.house.gov
  Website: www.house.gov/conyers

John D. Dingell
  Phone: 202-225-4071 Fax: 202-226-0371
  Website: www.house.gov/dingell

MINNESOTA

Senators:

Mark Dayton
   Phone: 202-224-3244   Fax: 202-228-2186
   Website: www.dayton.senate.gov

Norm Coleman
   Phone: 202-224-5641   Fax: 202-224-1152
   E-mail: opinion@coleman.senate.gov
   Website: www.coleman.senate.gov

Representatives:

Gil Gutknecht
   Phone: 202-225-2472   Fax: 202-225-3246
   E-mail: gil@mail.house.gov
   Website: www.gil.house.gov

John Kline
   Phone: 202-225-2271 Fax: 202-225-2595
   E-mail: john.kline@mail.house.gov
   Website: www.house.gov/kline

Jim Ramstad
   Phone: 202-225-2871   Fax: 202-225-6351
   E-mail: mn03@mail.house.gov
   Website: www.house.gov/ramstad

Betty McCollum
   Phone: 202-225-6631   Fax: 202-225-1968
   Website: www.house.gov/mccollum

Martin Olav Sabo
   Phone: 202-225-4755   Fax: 202-225-4886
   Website: www.house.gov/sabo

Mark R. Kennedy
   Phone: 202-225-2331   Fax: 202-225-6475
   E-mail: mark.kennedy@mail.house.gov
   Website: www.markkennedy.house.gov

Collin Peterson
   Phone: 202-225-2165   Fax: 202-225-1593
   Website: www.collinpeterson.house.gov

James L. Oberstar
   Phone: 202-225-6211   Fax: 202-225-0699
   Website: www.house.gov/oberstar

MISSISSIPPI

Senators:

Thad Cochran
   Phone: 202-224-5054   Fax: 202-224-9450
   Website: www.cochran.senate.gov

Trent Lott
   Phone: 202-224-6253   Fax: 202-224-2262
   E-mail: senatorlott@lott.senate.gov
   Website: www.lott.senate.gov

Representatives:

Roger F. Wicker
   Phone: 202-225-4306   Fax: 202-225-3549
   E-mail: roger.wicker@mail.house.gov
   Website: www.house.gov/wicker

Bennie G. Thompson
   Phone: 202-225-5876   Fax: 202-225-5898
   E-mail: thompsonms2nd@mail.house.gov
   Website: www.house.gov/thompson

Charles "Chip" Pickering Jr.
   Phone: 202-225-5031   Fax: 202-225-5797
   Website: www.house.gov/pickering

Gene Taylor
   Phone: 202-225-5772   Fax: 202-225-7074
   Website: www.house.gov/genetaylor

MISSOURI

Senators:

Christopher S. "Kit" Bond
   Phone: 202-224-5721   Fax: 202-224-8149
   E-mail: kit_bond@bond.senate.gov
   Website: www.bond.senate.gov

Jim Talent
   Phone: 202-224-6154   Fax: 202-228-1518
   Website: www.talent.senate.gov

Representatives:

William L. Clay, Jr.
   Phone: 202-225-2406   Fax: 202-225-1725
   Website: www.house.gov/clay

Todd Akin
   Phone: 202-225-2561   Fax: 202-225-2563
   E-mail: rep.akin@mail.house.gov
   Website: www.house.gov/akin

Richard A. Gephardt
   Phone: 202-225-2671   Fax: 202-225-7452
   E-mail: gephardt@mail.house.gov
   Website: dickgephardt.house.gov

Ike Skelton
   Phone: 202-225-2876   Fax: 202-225-2695
   Website: www.house.gov/skelton

Karen McCarthy
   Phone: 202-225-4535   Fax: 202-225-4403
   Website: www.mccarthy.house.gov

Samuel B. Graves
   Phone: 202-225-7041   Fax: 202-225-8221
   E-mail: sam.graves@mail.house.gov
   Website: www.house.gov/graves

Roy Blunt
   Phone: 202-225-6536   Fax: 202-225-5604
   E-mail: blunt@mail.house.gov
   Website: www.house.gov/blunt

Jo Ann H. Emerson
   Phone: 202-225-4404   Fax: 202-226-0326
   Website: www.house.gov/emerson

Kenny C. Hulshof
   Phone: 202-225-2956   Fax: 202-225-5712
   Website: www.house.gov/hulshof

MONTANA

Senators:

Max Baucus
   Phone: 202-224-2651   Fax: 202-228-3687
   Website: www.baucus.senate.gov

Conrad Burns
   Phone: 202-224-2644   Fax: 202-224-8594
   Website: www.burns.senate.gov

Representative:

Dennis Rehberg
   Phone: 202-225-3211   Fax: 202-225-5687
   Website: www.house.gov/rehberg

NEBRASKA

Senators:

Chuck Hagel
   Phone: 202-224-4224   Fax: 202-224-5213
   Website: www.hagel.senate.gov

Ben Nelson
   Phone: 202-224-6551   Fax: 202-228-0012
   E-mail: senator@bennelson.senate.gov
   Website: www.bennelson.senate.gov

Representatives:

Doug Bereuter
   Phone: 202-225-4806   Fax: 202-225-5686
   Website: www.house.gov/bereuter

Lee Terry
   Phone: 202-225-4155   Fax: 202-226-5452
   E-mail: talk2lee@mail.house.gov
   Website: www.leeterry.house.gov

Tom Osborne
   Phone: 202-225-6435   Fax: 202-226-1385
   Website: www.house.gov/osborne

MEMBERS OF U.S. CONGRESS

NEVADA

Senators:

Harry Reid
　Phone: 202-224-3542　　Fax: 202-224-7327
　Website: www.reid.senate.gov

John Ensign
　Phone: 202-224-6244　　Fax: 202-228-2193
　Website: www.ensign.senate.gov

Representatives:

Shelley Berkley
　Phone: 202-225-5965　　Fax: 202-225-3119
　E-mail: shelley.berkley@mail.house.gov
　Website: www.house.gov/berkley

James A. Gibbons
　Phone: 202-225-6155　　Fax: 202-225-5679
　E-mail: mail.gibbons@mail.house.gov
　Website: www.house.gov/gibbons

Jon C. Porter
　Phone: 202-225-3252　Fax: 202-225-2185
　Website: www.house.gov/porter

NEW HAMPSHIRE

Senators:

Judd Gregg
　Phone: 202-224-3324　　Fax: 202-224-4952
　E-mail: mailbox@gregg.senate.gov
　Website: www.gregg.senate.gov

John E. Sununu
　Phone: 202-224-2841　　Fax: 202-228-4131
　E-mail: mailbox@sununu.senate.gov
　Website: www.sununu.senate.gov

Representatives:

Jeb Bradley
　Phone: 202-225-5456　　Fax: 202-225-5822
　Website: www.house.gov/bradley

Charles Bass
　Phone: 202-225-5206　　Fax: 202-225-2946
　E-mail: cbass@mail.house.gov
　Website: www.house.gov/bass

NEW JERSEY

Senators:

Frank R. Lautenberg
　Phone: 202-224-3224　　Fax: 202-228-4054
　E-mail: frank_lautenberg@lautenberg.senate.gov
　Website: www.lautenberg.senate.gov

Jon Corzine
　Phone: 202-224-4744　　Fax: 202-228-2197
　Website: www.corzine.senate.gov

Representatives:

Robert E. Andrews
　Phone: 202-225-6501　　Fax: 202-225-6583
　E-mail: rob.andrews@mail.house.gov
　Website: www.house.gov/andrews

Frank A. LoBiondo
　Phone: 202-225-6572　　Fax: 202-225-3318
　E-mail: lobiondo@mail.house.gov
　Website: www.house.gov/lobiondo

Jim Saxton
　Phone: 202-225-4765　　Fax: 202-225-0778
　Website: www.house.gov/saxton

Christopher H. Smith
　Phone: 202-225-3765　　Fax: 202-225-7768
　Website: www.house.gov/chrissmith

Scott Garrett
　Phone: 202-225-4465　　Fax: 202-225-9048
　Website: www.house.gov/garrett

Frank Pallone, Jr.
　Phone: 202-225-4671　　Fax: 202-225-9665
　E-mail: frank.pallone@mail.house.gov
　Website: www.house.gov/pallone

Michael A. Ferguson
　Phone: 202-225-5361　　Fax: 202-225-9460
　Website: www.house.gov/ferguson

Bill Pascrell, Jr.
　Phone: 202-225-5751　　Fax: 202-225-5782
　Website: www.pascrell.house.gov

Steven R. Rothman
　Phone: 202-225-5061　　Fax: 202-225-5851
　Website: www.rothman.house.gov

Donald M. Payne
　Phone: 202-225-3436　　Fax: 202-225-4160
　Website: www.house.gov/payne

Rodney Frelinghuysen
　Phone: 202-225-5034　　Fax: 202-225-3186
　E-mail: rodney.frelinghuysen@mail.house.gov
　Website: www.house.gov/frelinghuysen

Rush Holt
　Phone: 202-225-5801　　Fax: 202-225-6025
　Website: www.holt.house.gov

Robert Menendez
　Phone: 202-225-7919　　Fax: 202-226-0792
　E-mail: menendez@mail.house.gov
　Website: www.menendez.house.gov

NEW MEXICO

Senators:

Pete V. Domenici
　Phone: 202-224-6621　　Fax: 202-228-0900
　Website: www.domenici.senate.gov

Jeff Bingaman
　Phone: 202-224-5521　　Fax: 202-224-2852
　E-mail: senator_bingaman@bingaman.senate.gov
　Website: www. bingaman.senate.gov

Representatives:

Heather A. Wilson
　Phone: 202-225-6316　　Fax: 202-225-4975
　E-mail: ask.heather@mail.house.gov
　Website: www.wilson.house.gov

Steve Pearce
　Phone: 202-225-2365　　Fax: 202-225-9599
　Website: www.house.gov/pearce

Tom Udall
　Phone: 202-225-6190　　Fax: 202-226-1331
　Website: www.house.gov/tomudall

NEW YORK

Senators:

Charles E. Schumer
　Phone: 202-224-6542　　Fax: 202-228-3027
　Website: www.schumer.senate.gov

Hillary Rodham Clinton
　Phone: 202-224-4451　　Fax: 202-228-0282
　Website: www.clinton.senate.gov

Representatives:

Tim Bishop
　Phone: 202-225-3826　　Fax: 202-225-3143
　Website: www.house.gov/timbishop

Steve J. Israel
　Phone: 202-225-3335　　Fax: 202-225-4669
　Website: www.house.gov/israel

Peter King
　Phone: 202-225-7896　　Fax: 202-226-2279
　E-mail: peter.king@mail.house.gov
　Website: www.house.gov/peteking

Carolyn McCarthy
　Phone: 202-225-5516　　Fax: 202-225-5758
　Website: www.house.gov/carolynmccarthy

Gary L. Ackerman
    Phone: 202-225-2601   Fax: 202-225-1589
    E-mail: gary_ackerman@mail.house.gov
    Website: www.house.gov/ackerman
Gregory W. Meeks
    Phone: 202-225-3461   Fax: 202-226-4169
    E-mail: congmeeks@mail.house.gov
    Website: www.house.gov/meeks
Joseph Crowley
    Phone: 202-225-3965   Fax: 202-225-1909
    E-mail: write2joecrowley@mail.house.gov
    Website: www.crowley.house.gov
Jerrold Nadler
    Phone: 202-225-5635   Fax: 202-225-6923
    E-mail: jerrold.nadler@mail.house.gov
    Website: www.house.gov/nadler
Anthony D. Weiner
    Phone: 202-225-6616   Fax: 202-226-7253
    E-mail: weiner@mail.house.gov
    Website: www.house.gov/weiner
Edolphus Towns
    Phone: 202-225-5936   Fax: 202-225-1018
    E-mail: edolphus.towns@mail.house.gov
    Website: www.house.gov/towns
Major R. Owens
    Phone: 202-225-6231   Fax: 202-226-0112
    Website: www.house.gov/owens
Nydia Velazquez
    Phone: 202-225-2361   Fax: 202-226-0327
    E-mail: nydia.velazquez@mail.house.gov
    Website: www.house.gov/velazquez
Vito Fossella
    Phone: 202-225-3371   Fax: 202-226-1272
    E-mail: vito.fossella@mail.house.gov
    Website: www.house.gov/fossella
Carolyn Maloney
    Phone: 202-225-7944   Fax: 202-225-4709
    E-mail: rep.carolyn.maloney@mail.house.gov
    Website: www.house.gov/maloney
Charles B. Rangel
    Phone: 202-225-4365   Fax: 202-225-0816
    Website: www.house.gov/rangel
Jose E. Serrano
    Phone: 202-225-4361   Fax: 202-225-6001
    E-mail: jserrano@mail.house.gov
    Website: www.house.gov/serrano
Eliot Engel
    Phone: 202-225-2464   Fax: 202-225-5513
    Website: www.house.gov/engel
Nita M. Lowey
    Phone: 202-225-6506   Fax: 202-225-0546
    E-mail: nita.lowey@mail.house.gov
    Website: www.house.gov/lowey
Sue W. Kelly
    Phone: 202-225-5441   Fax: 202-225-3289
    Website: www.house.gov/suekelly
John E. Sweeney
    Phone: 202-225-5614   Fax: 202-225-6234
    Website: www.house.gov/sweeney
Michael R. McNulty
    Phone: 202-225-5076   Fax: 202-225-5077
    E-mail: mike.mcnulty@mail.house.gov
    Website: www.house.gov/mcnulty
Maurice Hinchey
    Phone: 202-225-6335   Fax: 202-226-0774
    Website: www.house.gov/hinchey
John McHugh
    Phone: 202-225-4611   Fax: 202-226-0621
    Website: www.house.gov/mchugh

Sherwood L. Boehlert
    Phone: 202-225-3665   Fax: 202-225-1891
    E-mail: rep.boehlert@mail.house.gov
    Website: www.house.gov/boehlert
James T. Walsh
    Phone: 202-225-3701   Fax: 202-225-4042
    E-mail: rep.james.walsh@mail.house.gov
    Website: www.house.gov/walsh
Thomas Reynolds
    Phone: 202-225-5265   Fax: 202-225-5910
    Website: www.house.gov/reynolds
Jack Quinn
    Phone: 202-225-3306   Fax: 202-226-0347
    Website: www.house.gov/quinn
Louise McIntosh Slaughter
    Phone: 202-225-3615   Fax: 202-225-7822
    E-mail: louiseny@mail.house.gov
    Website: www.house.gov/slaughter
Amory Houghton Jr.
    Phone: 202-225-3161   Fax: 202-225-5574
    Website: www.houghton.house.gov

NORTH CAROLINA

Senators:
John R. Edwards
    Phone: 202-224-3154   Fax: 202-228-1374
    Website: www.edwards.senate.gov
Elizabeth Dole
    Phone: 202-224-6342   Fax: 202-224-1100
    Website: www.dole.senate.gov

Representatives:
Frank W. Ballance, Jr.
    Phone: 202-225-3101   Fax: 202-225-3354
    E-mail: frank.ballance@mail.house.gov
    Website: www.house.gov/ballance
Bob Etheridge
    Phone: 202-225-4531   Fax: 202-225-5662
    Website: www.house.gov/etheridge
Walter Jones Jr.
    Phone: 202-225-3415   Fax: 202-225-3286
    E-mail: congjones@mail.house.gov
    Website: www.house.gov/jones
David E. Price
    Phone: 202-225-1784   Fax: 202-225-2014
    Website: www.house.gov/price
Richard Burr
    Phone: 202-225-2071   Fax: 202-225-2995
    E-mail: richard.burrnc05@mail.house.gov
    Website: www.house.gov/burr
Howard Coble
    Phone: 202-225-3065   Fax: 202-225-8611
    E-mail: howard.coble@mail.house.gov
    Website: www.house.gov/coble
Mike McIntyre
    Phone: 202-225-2731   Fax: 202-225-5773
    Website: www.house.gov/mcintyre
Robin Hayes
    Phone: 202-225-3715   Fax: 202-225-4036
    Website: www.hayes.house.gov
Sue Myrick
    Phone: 202-225-1976   Fax: 202-225-3389
    E-mail: myrick@mail.house.gov
    Website: www.myrick.house.gov
Cass Ballenger
    Phone: 202-225-2576   Fax: 202-225-0316
    E-mail: cass.ballenger@mail.house.gov
    Website: www.ballenger.house.gov
Charles H. Taylor
    Phone: 202-225-6401   Fax: 202-226-6422
    Website: www.house.gov/charlestaylor

MEMBERS OF U.S. CONGRESS

Melvin L. Watt
 Phone: 202-225-1510   Fax: 202-225-1512
 E-mail: nc12.public@mail.house.gov
 Website: www.house.gov/watt

Brad Miller
 Phone: 202-225-3032   Fax: 202-225-0181
 Website: www.house.gov/bradmiller

NORTH DAKOTA

Senators:

Kent Conrad
 Phone: 202-224-2043   Fax: 202-224-7776
 E-mail: senator@conrad.senate.gov
 Website: www.conrad.senate.gov

Byron L. Dorgan
 Phone: 202-224-2551   Fax: 202-224-1193
 E-mail: senator@dorgan.senate.gov
 Website: www.dorgan.senate.gov

Representatives:

Earl Pomeroy
 Phone: 202-225-2611   Fax: 202-226-0893
 E-mail: rep.earl.pomeroy@mail.house.gov
 Website: www.house.gov/pomeroy

OHIO

Senators:

Mike DeWine
 Phone: 202-224-2315   Fax: 202-224-6519
 E-mail: senator_dewine@dewine.senate.gov
 Website: www.dewine.senate.gov

George V. Voinovich
 Phone: 202-224-3353   Fax: 202-228-1382
 Website: www.voinovich.senate.gov

Representatives:

Steve Chabot
 Phone: 202-225-2216   Fax: 202-225-3012
 Website: www.house.gov/chabot

Rob J. Portman
 Phone: 202-225-3164   Fax: 202-225-1992
 E-mail: portmail@mail.house.gov
 Website: www.house.gov/portman

Michael Turner
 Phone: 202-225-6465   Fax: 202-225-6754
 E-mail: oh03.wyr@mail.house.gov
 Website: www.house.gov/miketurner

Michael G. Oxley
 Phone: 202-225-2676   Fax: 202-226-0577
 Website: www.house.gov/oxley

Paul E. Gillmor
 Phone: 202-225-6405   Fax: 202-225-1985
 Website: www.gillmor.house.gov

Ted Strickland
 Phone: 202-225-5705   Fax: 202-225-5907
 Website: www.house.gov/strickland

David Hobson
 Phone: 202-225-4324   Fax: 202-225-1984
 Website: www.house.gov/hobson

John A. Boehner
 Phone: 202-225-6205   Fax: 202-225-0704
 E-mail: john.boehner@mail.house.gov
 Website: www.johnboehner.house.gov

Marcy Kaptur
 Phone: 202-225-4146   Fax: 202-225-7711
 E-mail: rep.kaptur@mail.house.gov
 Website: www.house.gov/kaptur

Dennis J. Kucinich
 Phone: 202-225-5871   Fax: 202-225-5745
 Website: www.house.gov/kucinch

Stephanie Tubbs Jones
 Phone: 202-225-7032   Fax: 202-225-1339
 E-mail: stephanie.tubbs.jones@mail.house.gov
 Website: www.house.gov/tubbsjones

Patrick J. Tiberi
 Phone: 202-225-5355   Fax: 202-226-4523
 Website: www.house.gov/tiberi

Sherrod Brown
 Phone: 202-225-3401   Fax: 202-225-2266
 E-mail: sherrod@mail.house.gov
 Website: www.house.gov/sherrodbrown

Steven C. LaTourette
 Phone: 202-225-5731   Fax: 202-225-3307
 Website: www.house.gov/latourette

Deborah Pryce
 Phone: 202-225-2015   Fax: 202-225-3529
 E-mail: pryce.oh15@mail.house.gov
 Website: www.house.gov/pryce

Ralph Regula
 Phone: 202-225-3876   Fax: 202-225-3059
 Website: www.house.gov/regula

Tim Ryan
 Phone: 202-225-5261   Fax: 202-225-3719
 E-mail: tim.ryan@mail.house.gov
 Website: www.house.gov/timryan

Bob Ney
 Phone: 202-225-6265   Fax: 202-225-3394
 E-mail: bobney@mail.house.gov
 Website: www.house.gov/ney

OKLAHOMA

Senators:

Don Nickles
 Phone: 202-224-5754   Fax: 202-224-6008
 Website: www.nickles.senate.gov

James M. Inhofe
 Phone: 202-224-4721   Fax: 202-228-0380
 Website: www.inhofe.senate.gov

Representatives:

John Sullivan
 Phone: 202-225-2211   Fax: 202-225-9187
 E-mail: ok01.sullivan@mail.house.gov
 Website: www.sullivan.house.gov

Brad Carson
 Phone: 202-225-2701   Fax: 202-225-3038
 E-mail: brad.carson@mail.house.gov
 Website: www.carson.house.gov

Frank D. Lucas
 Phone: 202-225-5565   Fax: 202-225-8698
 E-mail: replucas@mail.house.gov
 Website: www.house.gov/lucas

Tom Cole
 Phone: 202-225-6165   Fax: 202-225-3512
 E-mail: tom.cole@mail.house.gov
 Website: www.house.gov/cole

Ernest Istook Jr.
 Phone: 202-225-2132   Fax: 202-226-1463
 E-mail: istook@mail.house.gov
 Website: www.house.gov/istook

OREGON

Senators:

Ron Wyden
 Phone: 202-224-5244   Fax: 202-228-2717
 Website: www.wyden.senate.gov

Gordon Smith
 Phone: 202-224-3753   Fax: 202-228-3997
 Website: www.gsmith.senate.gov

Representatives:

David Wu
 Phone: 202-225-0855   Fax: 202-225-9497
 Website: www.house.gov/wu

Greg Walden
Phone: 202-225-6730 Fax: 202-225-5774
E-mail: greg.walden@mail.house.gov
Website: www.house.gov/walden

Earl Blumenauer
Phone: 202-225-4811 Fax: 202-225-8941
Website: www.house.gov/blumenauer

Peter A. DeFazio
Phone: 202-225-6416 Fax: 202-225-0032
Website: www.house.gov/defazio

Darlene Hooley
Phone: 202-225-5711 Fax: 202-225-5699
Website: www.house.gov/hooley

PENNSYLVANIA

Senators:

Arlen Specter
Phone: 202-224-4254 Fax: 202-228-1229
E-mail: arlen_specter@specter.senate.gov
Website: www.specter.senate.gov

Rick Santorum
Phone: 202-224-6324 Fax: 202-228-0604
Website: www.santorum.senate.gov

Representatives:

Robert A. Brady
Phone: 202-225-4731 Fax: 202-225-0088
E-mail: robert.a.brady@mail.house.gov
Website: www.house.gov/robertbrady

Chaka Fattah
Phone: 202-225-4001 Fax: 202-225-5392
Website: www.house.gov/fattah

Philip S. English
Phone: 202-225-5406 Fax: 202-225-3103
Website: www.house.gov/english

Melissa A. Hart
Phone: 202-225-2565 Fax: 202-226-2274
Website: www.house.gov/hart

John E. Peterson
Phone: 202-225-5121 Fax: 202-225-5796
E-mail: john.peterson@mail.house.gov
Website: www.house.gov/johnpeterson

Jim Gerlach
Phone: 202-225-4315 Fax: 202-225-8440
Website: www.house.gov/gerlach

Curt Weldon
Phone: 202-225-2011 Fax: 202-225-8137
E-mail: curtpa07@mail.house.gov
Website: www.house.gov/curtweldon

Jim Greenwood
Phone: 202-225-4276 Fax: 202-225-9511
Website: www.house.gov/greenwood

Bill Shuster
Phone: 202-225-2431 Fax: 202-225-2486
Website: www.house.gov/shuster

Don Sherwood
Phone: 202-225-3731 Fax: 202-225-9594
Website: www.house.gov/sherwood

Paul E. Kanjorski
Phone: 202-225-6511 Fax: 202-225-0764
E-mail: paul.kanjorski@mail.house.gov
Website: www.house.gov/kanjorski

John P. Murtha
Phone: 202-225-2065 Fax: 202-225-5709
E-mail: murtha@mail.house.gov
Website: www.house.gov/murtha

Joseph M. Hoeffel III
Phone: 202-225-6111 Fax: 202-226-0611
Website: www.hoeffel.house.gov

Mike Doyle
Phone: 202-225-2135 Fax: 202-225-3084
E-mail: rep.doyle@mail.house.gov
Website: www.house.gov/doyle

Pat Toomey
Phone: 202-225-6411 Fax: 202-226-0778
E-mail: rep.toomey.pa15@mail.house.gov
Website: www.house.gov/toomey

Joseph R. Pitts
Phone: 202-225-2411 Fax: 202-225-2013
Website: www.house.gov/pitts

Tim Holden
Phone: 202-225-5546 Fax: 202-226-0996
Website: www.house.gov/holden

Timothy F. Murphy
Phone: 202-225-2301 Fax: 202-225-1844
E-mail: murphy@mail.house.gov
Website: www.house.gov/murphy

Todd R. Platts
Phone: 202-225-5836 Fax: 202-226-1000
Website: www.house.gov/platts

RHODE ISLAND

Senators:

Jack Reed
Phone: 202-224-4642 Fax: 202-224-4680
Website: www.reed.senate.gov

Lincoln D. Chafee
Phone: 202-224-2921 Fax: 202-228-2853
Website: www.chafee.senate.gov

Representatives:

Patrick J. Kennedy
Phone: 202-225-4911 Fax: 202-225-3290
E-mail: patrick.kennedy@mail.house.gov
Website: www.house.gov/patrickkennedy

James R. Langevin
Phone: 202-225-2735 Fax: 202-225-5976
E-mail: james.langevin@mail.house.gov
Website: www.house.gov/langevin

SOUTH CAROLINA

Senators:

Ernest F. Hollings
Phone: 202-224-6121 Fax: 202-224-4293
Website: www.hollings.senate.gov

Lindsey O. Graham
Phone: 202-224-5972 Fax: 202-224-1189
Website: www.lgraham.senate.gov

Representatives:

Henry E. Brown, Jr.
Phone: 202-225-3176 Fax: 202-225-3407
E-mail: writehenrybrown@mail.house.gov
Website: www.house.gov/henrybrown

Joe Wilson
Phone: 202-225-2452 Fax: 202-225-2455
E-mail: joe.wilson@mail.house.gov
Website: www.house.gov/joewilson

J. Gresham Barrett
Phone: 202-225-5301 Fax: 202-225-3216
Website: www.house.gov/barrett

Jim DeMint
Phone: 202-225-6030 Fax: 202-226-1177
E-mail: jim.demint@mail.house.gov
Website: www.demint.house.gov

John M. Spratt, Jr.
Phone: 202-225-5501 Fax: 202-225-0464
Website: www.house.gov/spratt

MEMBERS OF U.S. CONGRESS

James Clyburn
    Phone: 202-225-3315   Fax: 202-225-2313
    E-mail: jclyburn@mail.house.gov
    Website: www.house.gov/clyburn

SOUTH DAKOTA

Senators:

Thomas A. Daschle
    Phone: 202-224-2321   Fax: 202-224-6603
    Website: wwwdaschle.senate.gov

Tim Johnson
    Phone: 202-224-5842   Fax: 202-228-5765
    Website: www.johnson.senate.gov

Representatives:

William J. Janklow
    Phone: 202-225-2801   Fax: 202-225-5823
    Website: www.housae.gov/janklow

TENNESSEE

Senators:

Bill Frist
    Phone: 202-224-3344   Fax: 202-228-1264
    Website: www.frist.senate.gov

Lamar Alexander
    Phone: 202-224-4944   Fax: 202-228-3398
    Website: www.alexander.senate.gov

Representatives:

William L. Jenkins
    Phone: 202-225-6356   Fax: 202-225-5714
    Website: www.house.gov/jenkins

John J. Duncan, Jr.
    Phone: 202-225-5435   Fax: 202-225-6440
    Website: www.house.gov/duncan

Zach Wamp
    Phone: 202-225-3271   Fax: 202-225-3494
    Website: www.house.gov/wamp

Lincoln Davis
    Phone: 202-225-6831   Fax: 202-226-5172
    Website: www.house.gov/lincolndavis

Jim Cooper
    Phone: 202-225-4311   Fax: 202-226-1035
    E-mail: jim.cooper@mail.house.gov
    Website: www.house.gov/cooper

Bart Gordon
    Phone: 202-225-4231   Fax: 202-225-6887
    Website: www.house.gov/gordon

Marsha Blackburn
    Phone: 202-225-2811   Fax: 202-225-3004
    Website: www.house.gov/blackburn

John S. Tanner
    Phone: 202-225-4714   Fax: 202-225-1765
    Website: www,house.gov/tanner

Harold E. Ford, Jr.
    Phone: 202-225-3265   Fax: 202-225-5663
    E-mail: rep.harold.ford.jr.@mail.house.gov
    Website: www.house.gov/ford

TEXAS

Senators:

Kay Bailey Hutchison
    Phone: 202-224-5922   Fax: 202-224-0776
    Website: www.hutchison.senate.gov

John Cornyn
    Phone: 202-224-2934   Fax: 202-228-2856
    Website: www.cornyn.senate.gov

Representatives:

Max A. Sandlin, Jr.
    Phone: 202-225-3035   Fax: 202-225-5866
    Website: www.house.gov/sandlin

Jim Turner
    Phone: 202-225-2401   Fax: 202-225-5955
    Website: www.house.gov/turner

Sam Johnson
    Phone: 202-225-4201   Fax: 202-225-1485
    Website: www.samjohnson.house.gov

Ralph M. Hall
    Phone: 202-225-6673   Fax: 202-225-3332
    E-mail: rmhall@mail.house.gov
    Website: www.house.gov/ralphhall

Jeb Hensarling
    Phone: 202-225-3484   Fax: 202-226-4888
    Website: www.house.gov/hensarling

Joe Barton
    Phone: 202-225-2002   Fax: 202-225-3052
    Website: www.joebarton.house.gov

John A. Culberson
    Phone: 202-225-2571   Fax: 202-225-4381
    Website: www.house.gov/culberson

Kevin P. Brady
    Phone: 202-225-4901   Fax: 202-225-5524
    Website: www.house.gov/brady

Nicholas V. Lampson
    Phone: 202-225-6565   Fax: 202-225-5547
    Website: www.house.gov/lampson

Lloyd Doggett
    Phone: 202-225-4865   Fax: 202-225-3073
    E-mail: lloyd.doggett@mail.house.gov
    Website: www.house.gov/doggett

Chet Edwards
    Phone: 202-225-6105   Fax: 202-225-0350
    Website: www.house.gov/edwards

Kay Granger
    Phone: 202-225-5071   Fax: 202-225-5683
    E-mail: texas.granger@mail.house.gov
    Website: www.kaygranger.house.gov

Willliam "Mac" Thornberry
    Phone: 202-225-3706   Fax: 202-225-3486
    Website: www.house.gov/thornberry

Ron E. Paul
    Phone: 202-225-2831   Fax: 202-226-6288
    Website: www.house.gov/paul

Ruben E. Hinojosa
    Phone: 202-225-2531   Fax: 202-225-5688
    E-mail: rep.hinojosa@mail.house.gov
    Website: www.house.gov/hinojosa

Silvestre Reyes
    Phone: 202-225-4831   Fax: 202-225-2016
    E-mail: talk2silver@mail.house.gov
    Website: www.house.gov/reyes

Charles W. Stenholm
    Phone: 202-225-6605   Fax: 202-225-2234
    Website: www.hosue.gov/stenholm

Sheila Jackson Lee
    Phone: 202-225-3816   Fax: 202-225-3317
    E-mail: tx18@mail.house.gov
    Website: www.house.gov/jacksonlee

Larry Combest
    Phone: 202-225-4005   Fax: 202-225-9615
    Website: www.house.gov/combest

Charles A. Gonzalez
    Phone: 202-225-3236   Fax: 202-225-1915
    Website: www.house.gov/gonzalez

Lamar S. Smith
    Phone: 202-225-4236   Fax: 202-225-8628
    Website: www.lamarsmith.house.gov

Tom DeLay
    Phone: 202-225-5951   Fax: 202-225-5241
    Website: www.tomdelay.house.gov

Henry Bonilla
   Phone: 202-225-4511   Fax: 202-225-2237
   Website: www.house.gov/bonilla
Martin Frost
   Phone: 202-225-3605   Fax: 202-225-4951
   Website: www.house.gov/frost
Chris Bell
   Phone: 202-225-7508   Fax: 202-225-2947
   Website: www.house.gov/bell
Michael C. Burgess
   Phone: 202-225-7772   Fax: 202-225-2919
   Website: www.house.gov/burgess
Solomon P. Ortiz
   Phone: 202-225-7742   Fax: 202-226-1134
   Website: www.house.gov/ortiz
Ciro D. Rodriguez
   Phone: 202-225-1640   Fax: 202-225-1641
   Website: www.house.gov/rodriguez
Gene Green
   Phone: 202-225-1688   Fax: 202-225-9903
   Website: www.house.gov/green
Eddie Bernice Johnson
   Phone: 202-225-8885   Fax: 202-226-1477
   E-mail: rep.e.b.johnson@mail.house.gov
   Website: www.house.gov/ebjohnson
John R. Carter
   Phone: 202-225-3864   Fax: 202-225-5886
   Website: www.house.gov/carter
Pete Sessions
   Phone: 202-225-2231   Fax: 202-225-5878
   E-mail: petes@mail.house.gov
   Website: www.house.gov/sessions

UTAH

Senators:
Orrin G. Hatch
   Phone: 202-224-5251   Fax: 202-224-6331
   Website: www.hatch.senate.gov
Robert Bennett
   Phone: 202-224-5444   Fax: 202-228-1168
   Website: www.bennett.senate.gov

Representatives:
Rob Bishop
   Phone: 202-225-0453   Fax: 202-225-5857
   Website: www.house.gov/robbishop
Jim Matheson
   Phone: 202-225-3011   Fax: 202-225-5638
   E-mail: jim.matheson@mail.house.gov
   Website: www.matheson.house.gov
Chris Cannon
   Phone: 202-225-7751   Fax: 202-225-5629
   E-mail: cannon.ut03@mail.house.gov
   Website: www.house.gov/cannon

VERMONT

Senators:
Patrick J. Leahy
   Phone: 202-224-4242   Fax: 202-224-3479
   Website: www.leahy.senate.gov
James M. Jeffords
   Phone: 202-224-5141   Fax: 202-228-0776
   Website: www.jeffords.senate.gov

Representative:
Bernard Sanders
   Phone: 202-225-4115   Fax: 202-225-6790
   E-mail: bernie@mail.house.gov
   Website: www.bernie.house.gov

VIRGINIA

Senators:
John W. Warner
   Phone: 202-224-2023   Fax: 202-224-6295
   Website: www.warner.senate.gov
George Allen
   Phone: 202-224-4024   Fax: 202-224-5432
   Website: www.allen.senate.gov

Representatives:
Jo Ann S. Davis
   Phone: 202-225-4261   Fax: 202-225-4382
   Website: www.house.gov/joanndavis
Edward L. Schrock
   Phone: 202-225-4215   Fax: 202-225-4218
   Website: www.schrock.house.gov
Bobby Scott
   Phone: 202-225-8351   Fax: 202-225-8354
   E-mail: bobby.scott@mail.house.gov
   Website: www.house.gov/scott
Randy Forbes
   Phone: 202-225-6365   Fax: 202-226-1170
   Website: www.house.gov/forbes
Virgil H. Goode, Jr.
   Phone: 202-225-4711   Fax: 202-225-5681
   Website: www.house.gov/goode
Bob Goodlatte
   Phone: 202-225-5431   Fax: 202-225-9681
   E-mail: talk2bob@mail.house.gov
   Website: www.house.gov/goodlatte
Eric I. Cantor
   Phone: 202-225-2815   Fax: 202-225-0011
   Website: www.cantor.house.gov
James P. Moran
   Phone: 202-225-4376   Fax: 202-225-0017
   Website: www.house.gov/moran
Rick Boucher
   Phone: 202-225-3861   Fax: 202-225-0442
   E-mail: ninthnet@mail.house.gov
   Website: www.house.gov/boucher
Frank R. Wolf
   Phone: 202-225-5136   Fax: 202-225-0437
   Website: www.house.gov/wolf
Thomas M. Davis III
   Phone: 202-225-1492   Fax: 202-225-3071
   E-mail: tom.davis@mail.house.gov
   Website: www.house.gov/tomdavis

WASHINGTON

Senators:
Patty Murray
   Phone: 202-224-2621   Fax: 202-224-0238
   E-mail: senator_murray@murray.senate.gov
   Website: www.murray.senate.gov
Maria Cantwell
   Phone: 202-224-3441   Fax: 202-228-0514
   Website: www.cantwell.senate.gov

Representatives:
Jay Inslee
   Phone: 202-225-6311   Fax: 202-226-1606
   Website: www.house.gov/inslee
Rick R. Larsen
   Phone: 202-225-2605   Fax: 202-225-4420
   E-mail: rick.larsen@mail.house.gov
   Website: www.house.gov/larsen
Brian Baird
   Phone: 202-225-3536   Fax: 202-225-3478
   Website: www.house.gov/baird

MEMBERS OF U.S. CONGRESS

Doc Hastings
  Phone: 202-225-5816   Fax: 202-225-3251
  Website: www.house.gov/dochastings
George R. Nethercutt, Jr.
  Phone: 202-225-2006   Fax: 202-225-3392
  Website: www.house.gov/nethercutt
Norman D. Dicks
  Phone: 202-225-5916   Fax: 202-226-1176
  Website: www.house.gov/dicks
Jim McDermott
  Phone: 202-225-3106   Fax: 202-225-6197
  Website: www.house.gov/mcdermott
Jennifer Dunn
  Phone: 202-225-7761   Fax: 202-225-8673
  E-mail: dunnwa08@mail.house.gov
  Website: www.house.gov/dunn
Adam Smith
  Phone: 202-225-8901   Fax: 202-225-5893
  E-mail: adam.smith@mail.house.gov
  Website: www.house.gov/adamsmith

WEST VIRGINIA

Senators:
Robert C. Byrd
  Phone: 202-224-3954   Fax: 202-228-0002
  E-mail: senator_byrd@byrd.senate.gov
  Website: www.byrd.senate.gov
John D. Rockefeller
  Phone: 202-224-6472   Fax: 202-224-7665
  E-mail: senator@rockefeller.senate.gov
  Website: www.rockefeller.senate.gov

Representatives:
Alan B. Mollohan
  Phone: 202-225-4172   Fax: 202-225-7564
  Website: www.house.gov/mollohan
Shelley Moore Capito
  Phone: 202-225-2711   Fax: 202-225-7856
  Website: www.house.gov/capito
Nick J. Rahall II
  Phone: 202-225-3452   Fax: 202-225-9061
  E-mail: nrahall@mail.house.gov
  Website: www.house.gov/rahall

WISCONSIN

Senators:
Herbert H. Kohl
  Phone: 202-224-5653   Fax: 202-224-9787
  E-mail: senator_kohl@kohl.senate.gov
  Website: www.kohl.senate.gov
Russ Feingold
  Phone: 202-224-5323   Fax: 202-224-2725
  Website: www.feingold.senate.gov

Representatives:
Paul D. Ryan
  Phone: 202-225-3031   Fax: 202-225-3393
  Website: www.house.gov/ryan
Tammy Baldwin
  Phone: 202-225-2906   Fax: 202-225-6942
  E-mail: tammy.baldwin@mail.house.gov
  Website: www.tammybaldwin.house.gov
Ron J. Kind
  Phone: 202-225-5506   Fax: 202-225-5739
  Website: www.house.gov/kind
Jerry Kleczka
  Phone: 202-225-4572   Fax: 202-225-8135
  Website: www.house.gov/kleczka
F. James Sensenbrenner, Jr.
  Phone: 202-225-5101   Fax: 202-225-3190
  E-mail: sensenbrenner@mail.house.gov
  Website: www.house.gov/sensenbrenner

Thomas E. Petri
  Phone: 202-225-2476   Fax: 202-225-2356
  Website: www.house.gov/petri
David R. Obey
  Phone: 202-225-3365
  Website: www.house.gov/obey
Mark Green
  Phone: 202-225-5665   Fax: 202-225-5729
  E-mail: mark.green@mail.house.gov
  Website: www.house.gov/markgreen

WYOMING

Senators:
Craig Thomas
  Phone: 202-224-6441   Fax: 202-224-1724
  Website: www.thomas.senate.gov
Michael B. Enzi
  Phone: 202-224-3424   Fax: 202-228-0359
  E-mail: senator@enzi.senate.gov
  Website: www.enzi.senate.gov

Representative:
Barbara Cubin
  Phone: 202-225-2311   Fax: 202-225-3057
  Website: www.house.gov/cubin

AMERICAN SAMOA

Representative:
Eni F.H. Faleomavaega
  Phone: 202-225-8577   Fax: 202-225-8757
  E-mail: faleomavaega@mail.house.gov
  Website: www.house.gov/faleomavaega

GUAM

Representative:
Madeleine Z. Bordallo
  Phone: 202-225-1188   Fax: 202-226-0341
  E-mail: madeleine.bordallo@mail.house.gov
  Website: www.house.gov/bordallo

PUERTO RICO

Representative:
Anibal Acevedo-Vila
  Phone: 202-225-2615   Fax: 202-225-2154
  E-mail: anibal@mail.house.gov
  Website: www.house.gov/acevedo-vila

VIRGIN ISLANDS

Representative:
Donna M. Christian-Christensen
  Phone: 202-225-1790   Fax: 202-225-5517
  E-mail: donna.christensen@mail.house.gov
  Website: www.house.gov/christian-christensen

HOUSE COMMITTEES

SEE U.S. FEDERAL AND INTERNATIONAL GOVERNMENT AGENCIES

SENATE COMMITTEES

SEE U.S. FEDERAL AND INTERNATIONAL GOVERNMENT AGENCIES

U.S. FEDERAL AND INTERNATIONAL GOVERNMENT AGENCIES

A

ADVISORY COUNCIL ON HISTORIC PRESERVATION
1100 Pennsylvania Avenue NW, #809
The Old Post Office Building
Washington, DC 20004 United States
Phone: 202-606-8503   Fax: 202-606-8672
E-mail: achp@achp.gov
Website: www.achp.gov

Membership: 1–100
Scope: National
Description: An independent federal agency, the Council is the primary policy advisor to the President and Congress on historic preservation matters and guides, and other federal agencies to ensure their actions do not result in unnecessary harm to the nation's historic properties. The Council, established by the National Historic Preservation Act of 1966, is made up of the heads of seven federal departments whose actions regularly affect historic properties.
Keyword(s): Land Issues, Pollution (general), Public Health, Reduce/Reuse/Recycle
Contact(s):
John Fowler, Executive Director

ALBERTA ENVIRONMENTAL CONSERVATION SERVICE
PRAIRIE AND NORTHERN REGION
CANADIAN WILDLIFE SERVICE
4999-98th Ave.
Edmonton, T6B 2X3 Alberta Canada
Phone: 780-951-8853   Fax: 780-495-2615
Website: www.ec.gc.ca

Membership: 1–100
Scope: Regional
Contact(s):
Gerald McKeating, Regional Director

APPALACHIAN REGIONAL COMMISSION
1666 Connecticut Ave., NW, Suite 700
Washington, DC 20009 United States
Phone: 202-884-7700   Fax: 202-884-7691
Website: www.arc.gov

Founded: 1965
Membership: 1–100
Scope: Regional
Description: To promote economic and human development in the 13-state Appalachian region and to provide a framework for joint federal and state efforts. Includes 406 counties in Alabama, Georgia, Kentucky, Maryland, Mississippi, New York, North Carolina, Ohio, Pennsylvania, South Carolina, Tennessee, Virginia and West Virginia.
Publication(s): Appalachia-Quarterly
Contact(s):
Tom Hunter, Executive Director; 202-884-7700
Michael Kiernan, Public Information; 202-884-7771
Paul Patton, States Co-Chairman
Bill Walker, States Washington Representative; 202-884-7746
Jesse White, Federal Co-Chairman; 202-884-7660

B

BRITISH COLUMBIA ENVIRONMENTAL CONSERVATION SERVICE
PACIFIC AND YUKON REGION: ENVIRONMENT CANADA
201401 Burrard Street
Vancouver, V6C 3S5 British Columbia Canada
Phone: 604-664-4065   Fax: 604-664-9190
Website: www.ec.gc.ca

Contact(s):
Don Fast, Regional Director, Acting

C

C AND O CANAL NATIONAL HISTORICAL PARK
NATURAL RESOURCES DIVISION
1850 Dual Highway Suite 100
Hagerstown, MD 21740 United States
Phone: 301-739-4200   Fax: 301-739-5275
E-mail: CHOH_Superintendent@nps.gov
Website: www.nps.gov/choh/

CALIFORNIA COOPERATIVE FISHERY RESEARCH UNIT (USGS)
CO-OP FISH UNIT
Humboldt State University
1 Harpst Street
Arcata, CA 95521 United States
Phone: 707-826-3268   Fax: 707-826-3269
E-mail: cuca@humboldt.edu
Website: www.humboldt.edu/~cuca

Founded: 1967
Membership: 1–100
Scope: National
Description: A cooperative research and education group consisting of Humboldt State Univ., Calif. Dept. of Fish and Game and U.S. Geological Survey.
Publication(s): See publication website
Keyword(s): Ecosystems (precious), Water Habitats & Quality
Contact(s):
Walter Duffy, Leader; 707-826-5644; wgd7001@humboldt.edu
Kenneth Cummins, Senior Advisory Scientist; kenwcummins@aol.com
Margaret Wilzbach, Assistant Leader; 707-826-5645; paw7002@humboldt.edu

CANADIAN FOREST SERVICE NATURAL RESOURCES CANADA
PACIFIC FORESTRY CENTRE
506 W. Burnside Rd.
Victoria, V8Z 1M5 British Columbia Canada
Phone: 250-363-0600   Fax: 250-363-0775
Website: www.NRCan.gc.ca/cfs

Description: CFS promotes sustainable development of Canada's forests and competitiveness of the Canadian forest sector for the well-being of present and future generations of Canadians. The CFS also establishes links with other non-governmental organizations to better address issues such as international trade, market access and the sustainable management of forests world-wide.
Contact(s):
Paul Addison, Director General; 506 West Burnside Rd., Victoria, British Columbia V8Z 1M5; 604-363-0608; Fax: 604-363-6088
Jacques Carette, Director General of Policy, Planning and International Affairs; 613-947-9100; Fax: 613-947-9038
Boyd Case, Director General; 5320 122 St., Edmonton, Alberta T6H 3S5; 403-435-7202; Fax: 403-435-7396
Doug Ketcheson, Director General for Industry, Economics and Programs Branch; 613-947-9052; Fax: 613-947-9038
Ed Kondo, Director General; P.O. Box 490, 1219 Queen St. East, Sault Ste. Marie, Ontario P6A 5M7; 705-949-9461; ext. 2039; Fax: 705-759-5714
Normand Lafreniere, Director General; 1055 du P.E.P.S. St., P.O. Box 3800, Sainte-Foy, Quebec G1V-4C7; 418-648-3957; Fax: 418-648-7317
Sylvie Letellier, Director of Communications and Executive Services; 613-947-7404; Fax: 613-947-7396
Gordon Miller, Director General of Science Branch; 613-947-8984; Fax: 613-947-9090

Gerrit Van Raalte, Director General; P.O. Box 4000, Regent St., Fredericton, New Brunswick E3B 5P7; 506-452-3508; Fax: 506-452-3140
Sylvia Frehner, Manager of Sector Human Resources Unit; 613-947-7386; Fax: 613-947-7409
Yvan Hardy, Assistant Deputy Minister of Canadian Forest Service; 613-947-7400; Fax: 613-947-7395
Anne McLellan, Minister; 613-996-2007; Fax: 613-996-4516
Jean McLoskey, Deputy Minister; 613-992-3456; Fax: 613-992-3828

CANADIAN WILDLIFE SERVICE
3rd Fl., Place Vincent Massey, 351 St. Joseph Blvd.
Hull, K1A 0H3 Quebec Canada
Phone: 819-997-1301   Fax: 819-953-7177
Membership: 1–100
Scope: Regional
Publication(s): The Canadian Field Naturalist
Contact(s):
David Brackett, Director General; 019-997-1301; Fax. 819-953-7177

CANADIAN WILDLIFE SERVICE
ENVIRONMENT CANADA
Ottawa, K1A 0H3 Ontario Canada
Phone: 819-997-1095   Fax: 819-997-2754
Website: www.cws-scf.ec.gc.ca/
Description: Canadian Wildlife Service is a federal agency devoted to the protection and management of migratory birds and nationally important wildlife habitat, endangered species, research on nationally important wildlife issues, control of international trade in endangered species, and international treaties.
Publication(s): Full list of publications is available on the organization's website.
Contact(s):
Ken Sato, Director General; 819-953-8065; Fax: 819-994-2724

COLUMBIA RIVER INTER-TRIBAL FISH COMMISSION
729 NE Oregon, Suite 200
Portland, OR 97232 United States
Phone: 503-238-0667   Fax: 503-235-4228
Website: www.critfc.org
Founded: 1977
Scope: Regional
Description: The Commission was formed to return salmon to Columbia basin rivers and to protect the Indian tribes' treaty-reserved fishing rights.
Contact(s):
Olney Patt, Jr., Executive Director

COLUMBIA RIVER INTER-TRIBAL FISH COMMISSION
STREAMNET LIBRARY
729 NE Oregon St., Suite 190
Portland, OR 97232 United States
Phone: 503-731-1304   Fax: 503-731-1260
E-mail: fishmail@critfc.org
Website: www.fishlib.org
Description: The StreamNet Library is a cooperative venture of the region's fish and wildlife agencies and tribes and serves these organizations. It is a fisheries and aquatic species library emphasizing management and restoration of the Columbia River salmon and sturgeon, providing data and data services. Open to the public.
Keyword(s): Wildlife & Species

Contact(s):
David Liberty, Library Technician; libd@critfc.org
Laurie Nock, Assistant Librarian; nocl@critfc.org
Lenora Ofterdahl, Head Librarian; oftl@critfc.org

CONSERVATION COUNCIL OF WESTERN AUSTRALIA, INC.
City West Lotteries House
2 Delhi St.
West Perth, West Australia, 6005 Australia
Phone: 08-9420-7266   Fax: 08-9420-7273
E-mail: conswa@conservationwa.asn.au
Website: www.conservationwa.asn.au/
Founded: 1970
Membership: 101–1,000
Scope: State
Description: To promote the cause of conservation and environmentalism throughout the state of Western Australia; and to serve as a liaison to other bodies dealing with conservation and environmental issues.
Contact(s):
Rachel Siewert, Contact

CZECH REPUBLIC MINISTRY OF THE ENVIRONMENT
Vrsovicka 65
100 10 Prague 10, Czech Rep
Phone: 420-2-6712-2769   Fax: 420-2-6731-0370
E-mail: roudna@env.cz
Contact(s):
Peter Roth, Chairman; roth@env.cz
Milena Roudna, Minister; roudna@env.cz

CZECH REPUBLIC MINISTRY OF THE ENVIRONMENT
ENVIRONMENTAL COMMISSION
Academy of Sciences of The Czech Republic, Narodni 3
11720 Praha 1, Czech Rep
Phone: 420-2-2420538   Fax: 420-2-24220944
E-mail: info@env.cz
Contact(s):
Milos Kuzvart, Secretary; petr.kuzvart@enc.cz

D

DELAWARE RIVER BASIN COMMISSION
P.O. Box 7360
West Trenton, NJ 08628-0360 United States
Phone: 009-883-9500, ext. 200   Fax: 609-883-9522
E-mail: drbc@drbc.state.nj.us
Website: www.drbc.net
Founded: 1961
Membership: 1–100
Scope: Regional
Description: Delaware River Basin Commission (DRBC) is an interstate/federal compact organization managing water resources without regard to political boundaries. The basin includes area in NY, NJ, PA & DE. DRBC adopts and promotes "uniform and coordinated policies for water conservation, control, use, and management in the basin." Priorities include: PCB TMDL-Delaware Estuary; anti-deg. program; fair allocation of water, and comprehensive water resources plan.
Publication(s): Administrative Manual and Water Code, Water Resources Program, Annual Report, Delaware River Basin Compact
Contact(s):
Carol Collier, Executive Director
Christopher Roberts, Public Information Officer

E

EGYPTIAN ENVIRONMENTAL AFFAIRS AGENCY
30, Misr Helwan St., Maadi
Cairo, Egypt
Phone: 25256442　　　　　Fax: 02-525-6451

Publication(s): Annual Report, EAS, National Workplan and Law

Contact(s):
Nadia Ebeid, H.E. Minister
Nirvana Khadr; 025256447

ENVIRONMENT CANADA
351 St. Joseph Boulevard
Hull, K1A 0H3 Quebec Canada
Website: www.ec.ga.ca

Description: Purpose is to formulate and take action to meet threats to environment arising through adverse impacts of human activities. Priority responsibilities include toxic chemicals, acid rain ozone depletion, urban smog, and the ongoing management of concerns such as hazardous wastes.

Contact(s):
David Anderson, Minister of the Environment; 819-997-1441; David.Anderson@ec.ga.ca

ENVIRONMENTAL CONSERVATION SERVICE
1 Place Vincent Massey
351 St. Joseph Blvd.
Hull, K1A 0H3 Quebec Canada
Phone: 819-994-4750　　　　　Fax: 819-997-1541
Website: www.infolane.ec.gc.ca

Membership: 1–100
Scope: International

Description: In Environmental Conservation Service (ECS) our goal is to ensure that future generations of Canadians inherit a natural environment as rich as the one we enjoy today. We work with many partners—individual Canadians, environmental and community groups, aboriginal peoples, industry, other levels of government, and international organizations. We provide information on the natural environment to Canadians.

Contact(s):
Ken Sato, Director General; 819-953-8065; Fax: 819-994-2724
Karen Brown, Assistant Deputy Minister; 819-997-2161; Fax: 819-997-1541

ENVIRONMENTAL CONSERVATION SERVICE
ATLANTIC REGION ENVIRONMENT CANADA
17 Waterfowl Lane
Sackville, E4L 4N1 New Brunswick Canada
Phone: 506-364-5044　　　　　Fax: 506-364-5062
E-mail: nature@ec.gc.ca
Website: www.ec.gc.ca

Scope: International

Contact(s):
George Finney, Regional Director

ENVIRONMENTAL PROTECTION AGENCY
1200 Pennsylvania Ave. NW
Washington, DC 20460 United States
Phone: 202-564-0241　　　　　Fax: 202-564-4613
Website: www.epa.gov

Membership: 10,001–100,000
Scope: State

Description: The Environmental Protection Agency (EPA) was established as an independent agency in the Executive Branch of the U.S. Government, pursuant to Reorganization Plan No. 3 of 1970, effective December 2, 1970. EPA endeavors to achieve systematic control and abatement of pollution, by properly administering and integrating a variety of research, monitoring, standard-setting, and enforcement activities.

Contact(s):
Donald Barnes, Science Advisory Board Director; 202-260-4125
Jeanette Brown, Small & Disadvantaged Business Utilization Director; 202-260-4100
Jay Benforado, Associate Administrator for Reinvention, Acting; 202-260-1849
Joseph Crapa, Associate Administrator (Congressional & Intergovernmental); 202-260-5200
Linda Fisher, Deputy Administrator
Scott Fulton, General Counsel, Acting; 202-260-8064
Sallyanne Harper, Chief Financial Officer, Acting; 202-260-1151
W. Ryan, Comptroller; 202-260-9674
Nikki Tinsley, Inspector General, Acting; 202-260-3137
Loretta Ucelli, Associate Administrator (Communications, Education & Media); 202-260-9828

ENVIRONMENTAL PROTECTION AGENCY
AIR AND RADIATION
1200 Pennsylvania Ave. NW
Washington, DC 20460 United States
Phone: 202-564-4700
Website: www.epa.gov/air

Founded: 1973
Scope: Local, State, Regional, National, International

Description: The Office of Air and Radiation develops national programs, technical policies, and regulations for controlling air pollution and radiation exposure. OAR is concerned with pollution prevention, indoor and outdoor air quality, industrial air pollution, pollution from vehicles and engines, radon, acid rain, stratospheric ozone depletion, and radiation protection.

Keyword(s): Air Quality/Atmosphere, Climate Change, Development/Developing Countries, Ecosystems (precious), Energy, Ethics/Environmental Justice, Pollution (general), Public Health, Transportation

Contact(s):
Elizabeth Cotsworth, Radiation and Indoor Air Director, Acting; 202-564-9320
Brian McLean, Atmospheric Programs Director; 202-564-9081
Margo Oge, Office of Transportation and Air Quality; 202-564-1682
Steve Page, Air Quality Planning and Standards Director; 919-541-5618
Robert Brenner, Deputy Administrator; 202-564-7400
Jeffrey Holmstead, Assistant Administrator; 202-564-7400

ENVIRONMENTAL PROTECTION AGENCY
REGION 1 (CT, ME, MA, NH, RI, VT)
1 Congress Street, Suite 1100
Boston, MA 02114-2023 United States
Phone: 617-918-1111
Website: www.epa.gov/region01

Contact(s):
John Devillars, Regional Administrator; 617-918-1010

ENVIRONMENTAL PROTECTION AGENCY
REGION 2 (NJ, NY, PR, VI)
290 Broadway
New York, NY 10007-1866 United States
Phone: 212-637-3000　　　　　Fax: 212-637-5046
Website: www.epa.gov/region02

Founded: 1970
Scope: Local, State, Regional, National, International

Description: This regional office of the U.S. Environmental Protection Agency serves New Jersey, New York, Puerto Rico, the U.S. Virgin Islands and the seven federally recognized Tribal Nations located within the region.

Contact(s):
Jane Kenny, Regional Administrator; 212-367-5000
William Muszynski, Deputy Regional Administrator

U.S. FEDERAL AND INTERNATIONAL GOVERNMENT AGENCIES – F

ENVIRONMENTAL PROTECTION AGENCY
REGION 3 (DE, DC, MD, PA, VA, WV)
1650 Arch St.
Philadelphia, PA 19103 United States
Phone: 215-814-5000   Fax: 215-814-5103
Website: www.epa.gov/region03/
Membership: 1,001–10,000
Scope: Regional
Contact(s):
   Donald Welsh, Regional Administrator

ENVIRONMENTAL PROTECTION AGENCY
REGION 4 (AL, FL, GA, KY, MS, NC, SC, TN)
61 Forsyth St., S.W.
Atlanta, GA 30303 United States
Phone: 404-562-9900   Fax: 404-562-8174
Website: www.epa.gov/region04
Membership: 1,001–10,000
Scope: Regional
Contact(s):
   Stanley Meiburg, Contact

ENVIRONMENTAL PROTECTION AGENCY
REGION 5 (IL, IN, MI, NM, OH, WI)
77 West Jackson Blvd.
Chicago, IL 60604 3507 United States
Phone: 312-353-2000   Fax: 312-353-1120
Website: www.epa.gov/region05/
Scope: Regional
Contact(s):
   Thomas Skinner, Regional Administrator
   David Ulrich, Deputy Regional Administrator; 312-886-3000

ENVIRONMENTAL PROTECTION AGENCY
REGION 6 (AR, LA, NM, OK, TX)
Fountain Place, 12th Fl., Suite 1200, 1445 Ross Ave.
Dallas, TX 75202-2733 United States
Phone: 214-665-6444   Fax: 214-665-8072
Website: www.epa.gov/region06/
Membership: 101–1,000
Scope: International
Contact(s):
   Gregg Cooke, Regional Adminstrator; 214-665-2100

ENVIRONMENTAL PROTECTION AGENCY
REGION 7 (KS, MO, NE)
901 N. 5th St.
Kansas City, KS 66101 United States
Phone: 913-551-7003
Website: www.epa.gov/region07/
Membership: 101–1,000
Scope: Regional
Contact(s):
   William Rice, Regional Administrator

ENVIRONMENTAL PROTECTION AGENCY
REGION 8 (CO, MT, ND, SD, UT, WY)
999 18th St. Suite 300
8-RA
Denver, CO 80202-2466 United States
Phone: 303-312-6312   Fax: 303-312-6882
Website: www.epa.gov/region08/
Membership: 101–1,000
Scope: Regional
Contact(s):
   Jack McGraw, Regional Administrator (Acting)

ENVIRONMENTAL PROTECTION AGENCY
REGION 9 (GU, AS, NV, HI, CA, AZ)
75 Hawthorne Street
San Francisco, CA 94105 United States
Phone: 415-744-1702
Website: www.epa.gov/region09/
Scope: International
Contact(s):
   Laura Yoshii, Regional Administrator; yoshii.laura@epa.gov

ENVIRONMENTAL PROTECTION AGENCY
REGION 10 (WA, OR, ID, AK)
PUBLIC ENVIRONMENTAL RESOURCE CENTER
1200 Sixth Ave.
CEC-124
Seattle, WA 98101 United States
Phone: 206-553-1200   Fax: 206-553-0149
E-mail: epa-seattle@epamail.epa.gov
Website: www.epa.gov/region10/
Founded: 1970
Membership: 101–1,000
Scope: Local, State, Regional, National, International
Description: Responsible for implementing federal programs in Alaska, Oregon, Idaho and Washington.
Keyword(s): Agriculture/Farming, Air Quality/Atmosphere, Ecosystems (precious), Ethics/Environmental Justice, Forests/Forestry, Oceans/Coasts/Beaches, Pollution (general), Public Health, Reduce/Reuse/Recycle, Water Habitats & Quality
Contact(s):
   L. Iani, Regional Administrator; 206-553-1234

ENVIRONMENTAL PROTECTION AGENCY
SOLID WASTE AND EMERGENCY RESPONSE
1200 Pennsylvania Avenue NW
Washington, DC 20460 United States
Phone: 202-564-4700
Website: www.epa.gov/swerrins
Contact(s):
   Elizabeth Cotsworth, Solid Waste Director, Acting; 703-308-8895
   Walter Kovalick, Technology Innovation Director; 703-603-9910
   Stephen Luftig, Director Emergency and Remedial Response; 703-603-8960
   James Makris, Chief Preparedness and Prevention Director; 202-260-8600
   Timothy Fields, Assistant Administrator, Acting; 202-260-4610

F

FISH AND WILDLIFE REFERENCE SERVICE
KRA CORPORATION
5430 Grosvenor Lane, Suite 110
Bethesda, MD 20814 United States
Phone: 001-492-0403   Fax: 301-564-4059
E-mail: fw9_fa_reference_service@fws.gov
Website: fa.r9.fws.gov/r9fwrs/
Founded: 1965
Membership: 10,001–100,000
Scope: National
Description: Produces "Fish and Wildlife Reference Service Databases", bibliographic database of primarily state fish and wildlife agency research reports; some USFWS publications; COOP Unit Theses and dissertations and some USGS publications.
Publication(s): FWRS Quarterly Newsletter
Keyword(s): Wildlife & Species

U.S. FEDERAL AND INTERNATIONAL GOVERNMENT AGENCIES – F

Contact(s):
   Paul Wilson, Project Manager; 800-582-3421; Fax: 301-564-4059; paul_wilson@fws.gov
   Geoffrey Yeadon, Senior Indexer; 800-582-3421; Fax: 301-564-4059; geoffrey_yeadon@fws.gov

FISHERIES AND OCEANS CANADA
COMMUNICATIONS DIRECTORATE
200 Kent St.
Ottawa, K1A 0E6 Ontario Canada
Phone: 613-993-0999   Fax: 613-990-1866
E-mail: info@dfo-mpo.gc.ca
Website: www.dfo-mpo.gc.ca
Scope: Local, Regional, National
Description: The Communications Branch houses the Department's expertise in internal and external communications. Communications advisors meet regularly with internal clients to discuss their communication objectives and to recommend appropriate strategies and tools for effective communication.
Contact(s):
   Paul Schubert, Director General; 613-993-0989

FISHERIES AND OCEANS CANADA
FISHERIES AND MANAGEMENT
200 Kent St., 13th Floor Station 13228
Ottawa, K1A 0E6 Ontario Canada
Phone: 613-993-0999   Fax: 613-990-1866
E-mail: info@dfo-mpo.gc.ca
Website: www.dfo-mpo.gc.ca
Contact(s):
   Mike Alexander, Director General: Aboriginal Affairs; 613-993-8598
   David Balfour, Director General: Program Planning and Coordination; 613-993-2574
   David Bezan, Director General: Resource Management; 613-990-0189
   Dennis Brock, Director General: Conservation and Protection; 613-990-6012
   Earl Wiseman, Director General: International; 613-993-1873
   Pat Chamut, Assistant Deputy Minister; 613-990-9864
   Paul Sprout, Associate Assistant Deputy Minister; 613-990-7203

G

GENERAL SERVICES ADMINISTRATION
GSA Building
1800 F Street NW
Washington, DC 20405 United States
Phone: 202-501-1231
Website: www.gsa.gov
Description: Concerned with the conveyance of surplus real property for wildlife conservation purposes to the Secretary of Interior or to a state, pursuant to Public Law 537, 80th Congress.
Contact(s):
   John Martin, Director of Redeployment Services Division/Property Disposal; 202-501-4671
   Ronald Rice, Director of Program Development and Outreach; 202-501-0052
   David Barram, Administrator

GEORGIA COOPERATIVE FISH AND WILDLIFE RESEARCH UNIT (USDI)
University of Georgia
Warnell School of Forest Resources
Athens, GA 30602-2152 United States
Phone: 706-542-5260   Fax: 706-542-8356
E-mail: coopunit@smokey.forestry.uga.edu
Website: www.uga.edu/~gacoop
Founded: 1984
Membership: 1–100
Scope: State
Description: The Unit is supported by the Biological Resources Division, USGS; Georgia Department of Natural Resources; and the Wildlife Management Institute; and the University of Georgia. Fisheries and wildlife research, graduate education and training, technical assistance, and extension are the main missions of the Unit.
Keyword(s): Land Issues, Water Habitats & Quality, Wildlife & Species
Contact(s):
   Michael Conroy, Assistant Unit Leader Wildlife
   Cecil Jennings, Unit Leader
   James Peterson, Assistant Unit Leader, Fisheries

GREAT LAKES FISHERY COMMISSION
2100 Commonwealth Blvd.
Suite 100
Ann Arbor, MI 48105 United States
Phone: 734-662-3209   Fax: 734-741-2010
E-mail: info@glfc.org
Website: www.glfc.org
Founded: 1956
Scope: International
Description: The 1955 Canada-U.S. Convention on Great Lakes Fisheries established the Commission to advise governments on ways to improve the fisheries, to develop and coordinate fishery research programs, to develop measures and implement programs to manage sea lamprey, and to improve and perpetuate fishery resources.
Publication(s): Misc. Publications, Special Publication Series, Technical Report Series, Great Lakes Invader, Fact Sheet Series, Brochure about Sea Lamprey Control
Contact(s):
   Chris Goddard, Executive Secretary; cgoddard@glfc.org

GREAT LAKES INDIAN FISH AND WILDLIFE COMMISSION
P.O. Box 9
Odanah, WI 54861 United States
Phone: 715-682-6619   Fax: 715-682-9294
E-mail: jgilbert@glifwc.org
Website: www.glifwc.org
Founded: 1983
Description: Provide biological, enforcement, and legal services to our member tribes in matters related to off-reservation treaty gathering rights in Wisconsin, Michigan, and Minnesota.
Publication(s): Technical reports, Masinaigan
Contact(s):
   Gerald Deperry, Deputy Administrator
   Tom Maulson, Chairman of the Board
   James Schlender, Executive Administrator

GULF STATES MARINE FISHERIES COMMISSION
P.O. Box 726
Ocean Springs, MS 39566-0726 United States
Phone: 228-875-5912   Fax: 228-875-6604
E-mail: lsimpson@gsmfc.org
Website: www.gsmfc.org
Founded: 1949
Membership: 1–100
Scope: State, Regional, National
Description: The GSMFC is an interstate compact of the states of Alabama, Florida, Louisiana, Mississippi, and Texas. The compact was authorized by the U.S. Congress. The Commission has 15 commissioners. The purpose of the Commission is to promote better utilization of the fisheries, marine, shell, and anadromous, of the seaboard of the Gulf of

Mexico by cooperative programs for the promotion and protection of such fisheries and the prevention of the physical waste of the fisheries from any cause.

Publication(s): Publications on line

Contact(s):
Larry Simpson, Executive Director
Ronald Lukens, Assistant Director
Mike Ray, Chairman

H

HELSINKI COMMISSION/ BALTIC MARINE ENVIRONMENT PROTECTION COMMISSION
Katajanokanlaituri 6 B FIN-00160
Helsinki, 00160 Finland
Phone: 358-9-6220220   Fax: 358-9-62202239
E-mail: helcom@helcom.fi
Website: www.helcom.fi

Founded: 1980
Scope: International
Description: To protect the marine environment of the Baltic Sea from all sources of pollution.
Publication(s): Baltic Sea Environment Proceedings (BSEP)
Keyword(s): Agriculture/Farming, Ecosystems (precious), Executive/Legislative/Judicial Reform, Land Issues, Oceans/Coasts/Beaches, Pollution (general), Transportation, Water Habitats & Quality, Wildlife & Species

Contact(s):
Anne Brusendorff, Professional Secretary
Kaj Forsius, Professional Secretary
Claus Hagebro, Professional Secretary
Ulrike Hassink, Information Officer
Ritva Kostakow-Kampe, Administrative Officer
Juha-Markku LeppSnen, Professional Secretary

HOUSE COMMITTEE ON AGRICULTURE
DEPARTMENT OPERATIONS, OVERSIGHT, NUTRITION AND FORESTRY; GENERAL FARM COMMODITIES, RESOURCE CONSERVATION AND CREDIT; LIVESTOCK AND HORTICULTURE; RISK MANAGEMENT, RESEARCH AND SPECIALTY CROPS
Rm. 1301, Longworth House Office Bldg.
Washington, DC 20515 United States
Phone: 202-225-2171   Fax: 202-225-0917
E-mail: agriculture@mail.house.gov
Website: www.agriculture.house.gov

Founded: 1820
Membership: 1–100
Scope: National
Description: Adulteration of seeds, insect pests, and protection of birds and animals in forest reserves; agriculture generally; agricultural and industrial chemistry; agricultural colleges and experiment stations; agricultural economics and research; agricultural education extension services; agricultural production and marketing and stabilization of prices of agricultural products; animal industry and diseases of animals; crop insurance and soil conservation; dairy industry; and more.

Contact(s):
Larry Combest, Chair

HOUSE COMMITTEE ON APPROPRIATIONS
AGRICULTURE, RURAL DEVELOPMENT, FOOD AND DRUG ADMINISTRATION; COMMERCE, JUSTICE, STATE, AND JUDICIARY; DISTRICT OF COLUMBIA ENERGY AND WATER DEVELOPMENT; FOREIGN OPERATIONS, EXPORT FINANCING, AND RELATED PROGRAMS; INTERIOR; LABOR, HEALTH AND HUMAN SERVICES
Rm. H-218, Capitol Bldg.
Washington, DC 20515 United States
Phone: 202-225-2771
Website: www.house.gov/appropriations

Membership: 1–100
Scope: National
Description: Consists of 60 members: Appropriation of the revenue for the support of the government, rescissions of appropriations contained in appropriation acts, and transfers of unexpended balances.

Contact(s):
Bill Young, Chair

HOUSE COMMITTEE ON EDUCATION AND THE WORKFORCE
2181 Rayburn House Office Bldg.
Washington, DC 20515 United States
Phone: 202-225-4527   Fax: 202-225-9571
E-mail: sharongrey@mail.house.gov
Website: http://edwrkforce.house.gov

Membership: 1–100
Scope: National
Description: Jurisdiction: Measures relating to education or labor generally; child labor; Gallaudet College; Howard University; convict labor and the entry of goods made by convicts into interstate commerce; labor standards; labor statistics; mediation and arbitration of labor disputes; regulation or prevention of importation of foreign laborers under contract; food programs for children in schools; United States Employees' Compensation Commission; vocational rehabilitation; wages and hours of labor; etc.

Contact(s):
John Boehner, Chairman; 202-225-6205

HOUSE COMMITTEE ON ENERGY AND COMMERCE
TELECOMMUNICATIONS, TRADE, AND CONSUMER PROTECTION; FINANCE AND HAZARDOUS MATERIALS; HEALTH AND ENVIRONMENT; ENERGY AND POWER; OVERSIGHT AND INVESTIGATIONS
2125 Rayburn House Office Bldg.
Washington, DC 20515 United States
Phone: 202-225-2927   Fax: 202-225-1919
Website: http://energycommerce.house.gov

Membership: 101–1,000
Scope: National
Description: Jurisdiction: Interstate and foreign commerce generally; national energy policy generally; measures relating to the exploration, production, storage, supply, marketing, pricing, and regulation of energy resources, including all fossil fuels, solar energy, and other unconventional or renewable energy resources; measures relating to the conservation of energy resources; measures relating to the commercial application of energy technology; and more.

Contact(s):
Dave Marventano, Chief of Staff
James Barnette, General Counsel
Billy Tauzin, Chair

HOUSE COMMITTEE ON INTERNATIONAL RELATIONS
AFRICA; ASIA AND THE PACIFIC; THE WESTERN HEMISPHERE; INTERNATIONAL ECONOMIC POLICY AND TRADE; INTERNATIONAL OPERATIONS AND HUMAN RIGHTS
2170 Rayburn House Office Bldg.
Washington, DC 20515 United States
Phone: 202-225-5021   Fax: 202-225-0225
E-mail: hirc@mail.house.gov
Website: www.house.gov/hyde

Membership: 1–100
Scope: National

Description: Jurisdiction: Foreign policy; international economic and environmental policy; international conferences and congresses; United Nations organizations; fishing agreements; nuclear export policy.
Contact(s):
Henry Hyde, Chairman

HOUSE COMMITTEE ON RESOURCES
Rm. 1324, Longworth House Office Bldg.
Washington, DC 20515 United States
Phone: 202-225-2761
Website: www.house.gov/resources/

Scope: National
Description: Consists of 52 members: Forest reserves and national parks created from the public domain; national parks lands; forfeiture of land grants and alien ownership, including alien ownership of mineral lands; geological survey; interstate compacts relating to apportionment of waters for irrigation purposes; irrigation and reclamation, including water supply for reclamation projects, and easements on public lands for irrigation projects, and acquisition of private lands.
Contact(s):
Allen Freemyer, Chief of Staff
James Hansen, Chair

HOUSE COMMITTEE ON RULES
Capitol Bldg.
H-312
Washington, DC 20515 United States
Phone: 202-225-9191   Fax: 202-225-6763
Website: www.house.gov/rules

Membership: 1–100
Scope: National
Description: Consists of 13 members: Grants rules outlining conditions for floor debate on legislation reported by regular standing committees, which includes granting emergency waivers under the Congressional Budget Act of 1974; also has legislative authority to create committees, change the rules of the House, and provide order of business of the House.
Contact(s):
David Drier, Chair
Porter Gross, Vice Chair

HOUSE COMMITTEE ON TRANSPORTATION AND INFRASTRUCTURE
Rm. 2163 Rayburn House Office Bldg.
Washington, DC 20515 United States
Phone: 202-225-4472   Fax: 202-226-1270
E-mail: dara.schlieker@mail.house.gov
Website: www.house.gov/transportation/democrats/

Membership: 1–100
Scope: National
Description: Consists of 73 members.
Keyword(s): Air Quality/Atmosphere, Energy, Land Issues, Oceans/Coasts/Beaches, Pollution (general), Sprawl/Urban Planning, Transportation, Water Habitats & Quality
Contact(s):
Don Young, Chairman

INSTITUTO NACIONAL DE BIODIVERSIDAD (INBIO)
Apdo. #22-3100
Santo Domingo, Costa Rica
Phone: 5062440690   Fax: 5062442816
E-mail: inbioparque@inbio.ac.cr
Website: www.inbio.ac.cr

Founded: 1989
Description: INBIO is conducting a biodiversity inventory in Costa Rica's protected areas. Through this knowledge, society will be able to appreciate and value the resources contained in the wildlands, and use this information in a sustainable manner.
Publication(s): Mariposas Heliconius de Costa Rica, Guia de Aves de Costa Rica, Biodiversidad de Costa Rica: Lecturas para Ecoturistas, Biodiversity Prospecting
Contact(s):
Rodrigo Gamez, General Director; rgamez@inbio.ac.cr
Ana Gueuvara, Prospecting Coordinator; agueuvara@inbio.ac.cr
Eric Mata, Management Coordinator; emata@inbio.ac.cr
Vanessa Matamorros, Public Relations; vmatamorros@inbio.ac.cr
Alfio Piva, Deputy Director; apiva@inbio.ac.cr
Sonia Rojas, Biodiversity Education; srojas@inbio.ac.cr
Jesus Ugalde, Biodiversity Inventory; jugalde@inbio.ac.cr
Natalia Zamora, Biodiversity & Garden; nzamora@inbio.ac.cr
Karla Zanabria, Communications; kzanabria@inbio.ac.cr

INTERNATIONAL BOUNDARY AND WATER COMMISSION, UNITED STATES AND MEXICO
UNITED STATES SECTION
4171 North Mesa Street, Suite C-100
El Paso, TX 79902 United States
Phone: 915-832-4175   Fax: 915-832-4195
E-mail: sallyspener@ibwc.state.gov
Website: www.ibwc.state.gov

Founded: 1889
Scope: Regional, International
Description: International commission of the United States and Mexican governments. Responsible for applying the boundary and water treaties between the two countries. The Commission is involved in water quality and water quantity issues.
Keyword(s): Development/Developing Countries, Recreation/Ecotourism, Water Habitats & Quality

INTERNATIONAL JOINT COMMISSION
CANADIAN SECTION
234 Laurier Ave. W., 22nd Floor
Ottawa, K1P 6K6 Ontario Canada
Phone: 613-995-2984   Fax: 613-993-5583
Website: www.ijc.org

Membership: 1–100
Scope: International
Publication(s): Focus
Contact(s):
Mary Gusella, Chairman, Canadian Section

INTERNATIONAL JOINT COMMISSION
GREAT LAKES REGIONAL OFFICE
100 Ouellette Ave.
8th Floor
Windsor, N9A 6T3 Ontario Canada
Phone: 519-257-6700   Fax: 519-257-6740
E-mail: commission@windsor.ijc.org
Website: www.ijc.org

Founded: 1909
Scope: Regional
Description: The IJC prevents and resolves disputes between the U.S. and Canada under the 1909 Boundary Waters Treaty and persues the common good of both countries as an independent advisor to the two governments. It assists them in the protection of the transboundary environment including the implementation of the Great Lakes Water Quality Agreement and improvement of transboundary air quality. It alerts the government to emerging issues along the boundary that may give rise to bilateral disputes.
Publication(s): Focus (newsletter), Biennial Reports
Contact(s):
Jennifer Day, Director of Public Affairs

INTERNATIONAL JOINT COMMISSION
UNITED STATES SECTION
1250 23rd St., NW, Suite 100
Washington, DC 20037 United States
Phone: 202-736-9000　　　Fax: 202-467-0746
E-mail: Commission@washington.ijc.org
Website: www.ijc.org

Founded: 1909
Membership: 1–100
Scope: International
Description: Established by the Boundary Waters Treaty of 1909 to prevent and resolve disputes regarding the use of the waters on the U.S.- Canadian Boundary, and to act as an independent advisor on issues referred by both countries. Regional office monitors, evaluates, and reports on compliance with the Great Lakes Water Quality Agreement of November 22, 1978. Commission functions in quasi-judicial, investigative, and coordination capacities.
Publication(s): Biennial Report Great Lakes Water Quality, Focus, quarterly newsletter
Keyword(s): Agriculture/Farming, Air Quality/Atmosphere, Climate Change, Oceans/Coasts/Beaches, Pollution (general), Public Health, Sprawl/Urban Planning, Water Habitats & Quality
Contact(s):
  Herb Gray, Canadian Section Chair; 613-995-2984; Commission@ottawa.ijc.org
  Dennis Schornack, U.S. Section Chair; 202-736-9000; Commission@washington.ijc.org
  Gail Krantzberg, Director, Regional Office; 100 Ouellette Ave., 8th Floor, Windsor, Ontario N9A 6T3; 519-257-6700; Fax: 519-257-6740
  Frank Bevacqua, Public Information Officer; 202-736-9024; Fax: 202-467-0746; bevacquaf@washington.ijc.org
  Murray Clamen, Canadian Section Secretary; 234 Laurier Ave. West, 22nd Floor, Ottawa, Ontario K1P 6K6; 613-995-2984
  Jennifer Day, Public Information Officer; 313-226-2170; ext. 6733; Fax: 519-257-6740; DayJ@windsor.ijc.org.

INTERNATIONAL PACIFIC HALIBUT COMMISSION
P.O. Box 95009
Seattle, WA 98145-2009 United States
Phone: 206-634-1838　　　Fax: 206-632-2983
Website: www.iphc.washington.edu

Founded: 1923
Scope: International
Description: Scientific investigation and management of the Pacific halibut resource. Established by a convention between Canada and the United States.
Keyword(s): Oceans/Coasts/Beaches
Contact(s):
  Bruce Leaman, Executive Director; 206-634-1838; Fax: 206-632-2983; bruce@iphc.washington.edu

INTERNATIONAL WHALING COMMISSION
The Red House 135 Station Rd.
Impington, Cambridge+132, CB4 9NP United Kingdom
Phone: 01223-233971　　　Fax: 01223-232876
E-mail: iwcoffice@compuserve.com

Founded: 1946
Description: Established under the International Convention for the Regulation of Whaling in 1946 to provide for the conservation of whale stocks and the orderly development of the whaling industry. Member Nations: USA, Antigua and Barbuda, Argentina, Australia, Austria, Brazil, Chile, People's Republic of China, Costa Rica, Denmark, Dominica, Finland, France, Germany, Grenada, India, Ireland, Italy, Japan, Kenya, Republic of Korea, Mexico, Monaco, Netherlands, New Zealand, Norway, Oman, Peru, and other.
Publication(s): International Journal of Cetacean Research and Management, Special Issues Series on specialist cetacean subjects, Annual reports of the Commission (including reports and papers of the Scientific Committee)
Contact(s):
  J. Baker, U.S. Commissioner; U.S. Department of Commerce, Rm. 5128, Herbert C. Hoover Bldg., 14th and Constitution Ave., NW, Washington, DC 20230
  M. Canny, Chairman, Ireland
  Bo Fernholm, Vice Chairman, Sweden
  R. Gambell, Secretary, Cambridge
  M. Harvey, Executive Officer, Cambridge

INTERSTATE COMMISSION ON THE POTOMAC RIVER BASIN
6110 Executive Blvd., Suite 300
Rockville, MD 20852-3903 United States
Phone: 301-984-1908　　　Fax: 301-984-5841
E-mail: info@ICPRB.org
Website: www.potomacriver.org

Founded: 1940
Scope: Regional
Description: Interstate compact, established by Maryland, Pennsylvania, Virginia, West Virginia, and the District of Columbia. Coordinates, tabulates, and summarizes existing data on condition of streams in Potomac Watershed; promotes uniform legislation; disseminates information; cooperates in studies; promotes coordination of program in Basin states. Areas of interest are water quality, water supply, and land resources associated with the Potomac and its tributaries.
Publication(s): In the Anacostia Watershed, Potomac Basin Reporter
Contact(s):
  Joseph Hoffman, Executive Director
  James Cummins, Associate Director of Living Resources
  Curtis Dalpra, Communications Manager
  Carlton Haywood, Associate Director of Water Quality

M

MARINE MAMMAL COMMISSION
4340 East-West Highway
Room 905
Bethesda, MD 20814 United States
Phone: 301-504-0087　　　Fax: 301-504-0099
E-mail: mmc@mmc.gov

Founded: 1972
Scope: State, Regional, National, International
Description: Established by the Marine Mammal Protection Act of 1972, P.L. 92-522, the Marine Mammal Commission, in consultation with its Committee of Scientific Advisors on Marine Mammals, periodically reviews the status of marine mammal populations; manages a research program concerned with their conservation; and develops, reviews, and makes recommendations on federal activities and policies which affect the protection and conservation of marine mammals.
Publication(s): Research Reports, Annual Report
Keyword(s): Ecosystems (precious), Oceans/Coasts/Beaches, Wildlife & Species
Contact(s):
  David Cottingham, Executive Director; 301-504-0087; Fax: 301-504-0099; dcottingham@mmc.gov
  Timothy Ragen, Scientific Program Director
  Michael Gosliner, General Counsel
  David Laist, Policy and Program Analyst

MIGRATORY BIRD CONSERVATION COMMISSION
1849 C St., NW (ARL SQ. 622)
Washington, DC 20240 United States
Phone: 703-358-1716　　　Fax: 703-358-2223
E-mail: Jeffrey-M-Donahoe@fws.gov

Founded: 1929
Membership: 1–100
Scope: National
Description: Considers, passes upon, and fixes the prices for lands recommended by the Secretary of the Interior for purchase or lease by him under the Migratory Bird Conservation Act of February 18, 1929, as amended, as migratory bird refuges in the National Wildlife Refuge System.
Contact(s):
Jeffery Donahoe, Secretary; 703-358-1716; Fax: 703-358-2223

MINNESOTA-WISCONSIN BOUNDARY AREA COMMISSION
619 2nd St.
Hudson, WI 54016 United States
Phone: 651-436-7131   Fax: 715-386-9571
E-mail: mwbac@mwbac.org
Website: www.mwbac.org
Founded: 1965
Membership: 1–100
Scope: Regional
Description: To conduct studies, develop recommendations, and coordinate planning for protection, use, and development in the public interest of lands, river valleys, and waters that form the boundary between Minnesota and Wisconsin, principally on the St. Croix and Mississippi rivers.
Publication(s): River Steward Journal
Contact(s):
Robin Grawe, Mississippi Valley Director
Buck Malick, Executive Director
Rosetta Herricks, Office Manager
Judith Olson, Secretary

N

NATIONAL AGRICULTURAL LIBRARY
10301 Baltimore Ave.
Beltsville, MD 20705 United States
Phone: 301-504-5755   Fax: 301-504-6927
E-mail: agref@nal.usda.gov
Website: www.nal.usda.gov
Founded: 1862
Membership: 1–100
Scope: National, International
Description: Produces "Agricola", a database of bibliographic citations covering all aspects of agricultural and food sciences, including natural resources, animal welfare, pollution, pesticides and land and water management. The database has over 4 million records.

NATIONAL SCIENCE FOUNDATION
4201 Wilson Blvd.
Arlington, VA 22230 United States
Phone: 703-292-5111
E-mail: info@nsf.gov
Website: www.nsf.gov
Founded: 1950
Description: Responsible for the support of science and engineering research and the development of science education programs. Policy is set by the National Science Board, which is composed of 24 part-time members appointed by the President, with the consent of the Senate, and includes the Director of the Foundation.
Publication(s): Where Discoveries Begin, NSF in a Changing World: The National Science Foundation Strategic Plan, Grant Proposal Guide, Guide to Programs
Contact(s):
Rita Colwell, Director; 703-306-1000
Julia Moore, Director of Office of Legislative and Public Affairs; 703-306-1070
Stephanie Bianchi, Head Librarian; 703-306-0658
Joseph Bordogna, Deputy Director; 703-306-1000
Eamon Kelly, Chairman of National Science Board; 703-306-2000

NATIONAL TRANSPORTATION SAFETY BOARD
490 L'Enfant Plaza East, SW
Washington, DC 20594 United States
Phone: 202-314-6000   Fax: 202-314-6148
Website: www.ntsb.gov
Scope: National
Description: The Safety Board is an independent federal accident investigation agency. The Board's mission is to determine the "probable cause" of transportation accidents and to formulate safety recommendations to improve transportation safety.
Contact(s):
Ron Battocchi, Director, Office of General Counsel
Jamie Finch, Director, Office of Government, Public, and Family Affairs

NORTH AMERICAN DEVELOPMENT BANK
NADB
203 South St. Mary's
Suite 300
San Antonio, TX 78205 United States
Phone: 210-231-8000   Fax: 210-231-6232
E-mail: webmaster@nadb.org
Website: www.nadb.org
Founded: 1993
Scope: Local, State, Regional, International
Description: The NADB is an international financial institution established and capitalized in equal parts by the U.S. and Mexico for the purpose of financing environmental infrastructure projects. All NADB-financed environmental projects must be certified by the BECC, be related to potable water supply, wastewater treatment or municipal solid waste management and be located within the border region, defined as 100 km. (62 miles) north and south of the international boundary between the two countries.
Publication(s): BECC-NADB Quarterly Status Reports, U.S. Mexico 5-Year Outlook 2001 Edition, NADB Annual Reports
Keyword(s): Air Quality/Atmosphere, Development/Developing Countries, Energy, Finance/Banking/Trade, Pollution (general), Public Health, Reduce/Reuse/Recycle, Water Habitats & Quality
Contact(s):
Raul Rodriguez, Managing Director; 210-231-8000; Fax: 210-231-6232
Jorge Garcias, Deputy Managing Director; 210-231-8000; Fax: 21-231-6232
Suzanne Gallagher, Director of Program Development; 210-231-8000; Fax: 210-231-6232; sgallagher@nadb.org
Armando Perez-Gea, Director of Project Development; 210-231-8000; Fax: 210-231-6232; aperez-gea@nadb.org

NORTH AMERICAN WETLANDS CONSERVATION COUNCIL
UNITED STATES DEPARTMENT OF THE INTERIOR
UNITED STATES FISH AND WILDLIFE SERVICE
DIVISION OF BIRD HABITAT CONSERVATION
4401 North Fairfax Dr.
Mail Stop MBSP 4501-4075
Arlington, VA 22203 United States
Phone: 703-358-1784   Fax: 703-358-2282
E-mail: birdhabitat@fws.gov
Website: www.birdhabitat.fws.gov
Founded: 1989
Scope: Local, State, Regional, National, International
Description: On behalf of the Secretary of the Interior, The North American Wetlands Conservation Council encourages public-private partnerships to conserve wetland ecosystems for

waterfowl, other migratory birds, fish, and wildlife. Grant projects with a 1-1 match are funded to acquire, restore, and enhance wetlands and associated habitats in Canada, the U.S., and Mexico.

Publication(s): "Birdscapes", Progress Report 2000-2001

Keyword(s): Oceans/Coasts/Beaches, Public Lands/Greenspace, Water Habitats & Quality, Wildlife & Species

Contact(s):
- John Berry, Member; National Fish and Wildlife Foundation, 1120 Connecticut Avenue, NW, Suite 900, Washington, DC 20036; 202-857-0166; Fax: 202-857-0162; berry@nfwf.org
- John Cooper, Vice-Chair; South Dakota Game & Fish, 7 Parks Department, 523 East Capitol, Pierre, SD 57501-3182; 605-773-3387; Fax: 605-773-7201; john.cooper@state.sd.us
- Michael Dennis, Esq., Member; The Nature Conservancy, 4245 North Fairfax Drive, Suite 100, Arlington, VA 22203; 703-841-5318; Fax: 703-841-8796
- Jean Hocker, Member; 20 West Chapman Street, Alexandria, VA 22301; 703-683-0506; Fax: 703-683-4940; jean@hockers.com
- Wayne MacCallum, Member; Massachusetts Division of Fisheries and Wildlife, 1 Rabbit Hill Road, Westborough, MA 01581; 508-792-7270; ext. 143; Fax: 508-792-7275; wayne.maccallum@state.ma.us
- Steve Miller, Member; Wisconsin Dept. of National Resources, Madison, WI 53707; 608-266-5782; Fax: 608-266-6983; millesw@dnr.state.wi.us
- David Nomsen, Alternate Member; Pheasants Forever, Inc, 2101 Ridgewood Drive, Alexandria, MN 56308; 320-763-6103; Fax: 320-763-6103; pfnomsen@rea-alp.com
- Duane Shroufe, Chairperson; Arizona Game and Fish Department, 2221 West Greenway Road, Phoenix, AZ 85023-4399; 602-789-3278; Fax: 602789-3299; dshroufe@gf.state.az.us
- David Smith, Council Coordinator & Division Chief; U.S. Fish & Wildlife Service, 4401 North Fairfax Drive,, Mail Stop 4501-4075, Arlington, VA 22203; 703-358-1784; Fax: 703-358-2282; david_a_smith@fws.gov
- W. Wentz, Member; Ducks Unlimited, Inc., One Waterfowl Way, Memphis, TN 38120-2351; 901-758-3784; Fax: 901-758-3855; awentz@ducks.org
- Steve Williams, Member; U.S. Fish & Wildlife Service, Department of the Interior, 1849 C Street, NW, Washington, DC 20240-0001; 202-208-4717; Fax: 202-208-6965; Steven_A_Williams@fws.gov

NORTH PACIFIC ANADROMOUS FISH COMMISSION
889 W. Pender Street, Suite 502
Vancouver, V6C 3B2 British Columbia Canada
Phone: 604-775-5550   Fax: 604-775-5577
E-mail: secretariat@npafc.org
Website: www.npafc.org

Founded: 1993
Membership: 1–100
Scope: International

Description: Established by a Convention between Canada, Japan, Russia, and the U.S. for the conservation of the anadromous fish resources of the North Pacific Ocean.

Publication(s): North Pacific Anadromous Commission newsletter

Contact(s):
- Anatoly Makoedov Dr., President
- Koji Imamura, Vice President, Russia
- Vladimir Fedorenko, Executive Director

NORTHEAST ATLANTIC FISHERIES COMMISSION
22 Berners St.
London, WIP 4DY United Kingdom
Phone: 0207-631-0016   Fax: 2076369225
E-mail: info@neafc.org

Founded: 1980

Description: To promote the conservation and optimum utilization of the fishery resources of the northeast Atlantic, within a framework appropriate to the regime of extended coastal state jurisdiction over fisheries, and to encourage international cooperation and consultation with respect to these resources.

Publication(s): Handbook of Basic Texts, Annual Report

Contact(s):
- O. Tougaard, President
- E. Lemche, Vice President
- V. Sokolov, Vice President
- Sigmund Engesaeter, Secretary

NORTHEASTERN FOREST FIRE PROTECTION COMMISSION
36 Roslyn Ave.
Warner, NH 03278-4021 United States
Phone: 603-456-3474   Fax: 603-456-3474
Website: www.nffpc.com

Membership: 1,001–10,000
Scope: International

Description: International forest fire protection mutual aid organization composed of three commissioners each from CT, ME, MA, NH, RI, VT, NY, and the Canadian Provinces of Quebec, New Brunswick, and Nova Scotia plus New England national forests (Green Mountain and White Mountain). Uniform fire organization planning and suppression technique training carried out annually by the members. The Northeastern Interstate Forest Fire Protection Compact is the governing document that established the organization.

Contact(s):
- Clark Davis, Executive Director; 36 Roslyn Ave., Warner, NH 03278-4021; 603-456-3474

NUCLEAR REGULATORY COMMISSION
2120 L Street
Washington, DC 20555 United States
Phone: 301-415-8200
E-mail: opa@nrc.gov
Website: www.nrc.gov

Founded: 1975
Scope: National

Description: Five-member commission responsible for regulating all commercial uses of nuclear energy to protect the health and safety of the public and the environment.

Keyword(s): Energy

Contact(s):
- William Beecher, Director, Office of Public Affairs; 301-415-8200
- Paul Bird, Director, Office of Personnel; 301-415-7516
- Bruce Boger, Director, Division of Reactor Controls and Human Factors; 301-415-1004
- Guy Caputo, Director, Office of Investigations; 301-415-2373
- Frank Congel, Director of Incident Response Division; 301-415-7476
- Donald Cool, Director, Division of Industrial and Medical Nuclear Safety; 301-415-7197
- John Cordes, Director, Office of Commission Appellate Adjudication; 301-415-1600
- Gerald Cranford, Director, Office of Information Resources Management; 301-415-7585
- Lloyd Donnelly, Director, Financial Management, Procurement, Administration; 301-415-5828
- Francis Gillespie, Director, Division of Inspection and Support Programs; 301-415-1275
- John Greeves, Director, Division of Waste Management; 301-415-7358
- Brian Grimes, Director; 301-415-1193
- Edward Halman, Associate Director, Contract, Security, F01 and Publications; 301-415-7305
- M. Hodges, Director, Division of Systems Technology; 301-415-5728

Gary Holahan, Director, Division of Systems Safety and Analysis; 301-415-2884
Edward Jordan, Director, Office for Analysis and Evaluation of Operations; 301-415-7472
John Larkins, Executive Director; 301-415-7360
James Lieberman, Director, Office of Enforcement; 301-415-2741
John Linehan, Director, Program Management, Policy and Analysis; 301-415-7780
Irene Little, Director, Office of Small Business and Civil Rights; 301-415-7380
Paul Lohaus, Director; 301-415-2326
Thomas Martian, Deputy Director, Division of Reactor Programs; 301-415-1199
James Milhoan, Deputy Executive Director, Nuclear Reactor Regulation; 301-415-1705
Frank Miraglia, Director of Office of Nuclear Reactor Regulation; 301-415-1270
Bill Morris, Director, Division of Regulatory Applications; 301-415-6207
David Morrison, Director, Office of Nuclear Regulatory Research; 301-415-6641
Carl Paperiello, Director, Office of Nuclear Material Safety and Safeguards; 301-415-7800
Kenneth Raglin, Director of Technical Training Division; 423-855-6500
Dennis Rathbun, Director, Office of Congressional Affairs; 301-415-1776
C. Rossi, Director, Safety Programs Division; 301-415-7499
Lawrence Shao, Director, Division of Engineering Technology; 301-415-5678
Brian Sheron, Director, Division of Engineering; 301-415-2722
Carlton Stoiber, Director, Office of International Programs; 301-415-1780
James Taylor, Executive Director, Operations; 301-415-1700
Elizabeth Teneyck, Director, Division of Fuel Cycle Safety and Safeguards; 301-415-7212
Hugh Thompson, Deputy Executive Director, Nuclear Materials, Safety; 301-504-1713
William Travers, Director of Spent Fuel Project Office; 301-415-8500
Richard Bangart, Deputy Director of Office of State Programs; 301-415-3340
Hubert Bell, Inspector General; 301-415-5930
Stephen Burns, Asst. General Counsel (Hearing, Enforcement & Administration); 301-415-1740
Leonard Callan, Regional Administrator, Region 4; 611 Ryan Plaza Dr., Suite. 4000, Arlington, TX 76011-8064; 817-860-8225
Samuel Collins, Deputy; 817-860-8226
B. Cotter, Chief Administrative Judge and Chairman of Atomic Safety; 301-415-7450
Karen Cyr, General Counsel; 301-415-1743
Greta Dirus, Commissioner; 301-415-1820
Stewart Ebneter, Regional Administrator, Region 2; 101 Marietta St., Suite 2900, Atlanta, GA 30323-0199; 404-331-5500
Roger Fortuna, Deputy Director; 301-415-3476
Jesse Funches, Deputy Controller; 301-415-7322
Elizabeth Hayden, Deputy Director; 301-415-8200
John Hoyle, Secretary of the Commission; 301-415-1969
Shirley Jackson, Chairman; 301-415-1820
William Kane, Deputy; 610-337-5340
Malcolm Knapp, Deputy Director; 301-415-8468
Arnold Levin, Deputy Director of Licensing Support Systems Administrator; 301-415-7458
Martin Malsch, Deputy General Counsel; 301-415-1740
James McDermott, Deputy Director; 301-415-7516
Richard Meserve, Chairman of Commission
Hubert Miller, Regional Administrator, Region 1; 475 Allendale Rd., King of Prussia, PA 19406-1415; 610-337-5299
Patricia Norry, Associate Director of Office of Administration; 301-415-7443
William Olmstead, Licensing and Regulation; 301-415-1740
Paul Pomeroy, Vice Chairman; 301-415-7360
Linda Portner, Associate Director; 301-415-1776
Luis Reyes, Deputy; 404-331-5610
Kenneth Rogers, Commissioner; 301-415-1855
Denwood Ross, Deputy Director; 301-415-7473
Ronald Scroggins, Deputy Chief Financial Officer/Controller; 301-415-7501
Robert Seale, Vice Chairman; 301-415-7360
Frederick Shon, Deputy Chief Administrative Judge; 301-415-7468
Themis Speis, Deputy Director; 301-415-6802
Michael Springer, Associate Director of Facilities and Property Management; 301-415-8080
Martin Steindler, Chairman of Advisory Committee on Nuclear Waste; 301-415-7360
Ashok Thadani, Associate Director, Insp. and Tech. Review; 301-415-1274
Roy Zimmerman, Associate Director of Projects; 301-415-1284

O

OHIO RIVER VALLEY WATER SANITATION COMMISSION
5735 Kellogg Ave.
Cincinnati, OH 45228-1112 United States
Phone: 513-231-7719 Fax: 513-231-7761
E-mail: info@orsanco.org
Website: www.orsanco.org

Founded: 1948

Scope: State, Regional

Description: An interstate agency representing Illinois, Indiana, Kentucky, New York, Ohio, Pennsylvania, Virginia, and West Virginia for control of water pollution in the Ohio River Valley Compact District.

Publication(s): Ohio River Fish Populations; and other, Annual Report, ORSANCO Quality Monitor; Publications of general or technical interest.

Contact(s):
Alan Vicory, Executive Director and Chief Engineer
Jeanne Ison, Public Information Programs Manager
Rhonda Barnes-Cloth, Communications Coordinator

ONTARIO DEPARTMENT OF FISHERIES AND OCEANS
CANADA DIVISION
200 Kent St. Centennial Towers, 13th Floor
Ottawa, K1A 0E6 Ontario Canada
Phone: 613-993-0999 Fax: 613-990-1866
Website: www.dfo-mpo.gc.ca

Scope: National

Description: Fisheries and Oceans Canada is responsible for policies and programs in support of Canada's economic, ecological, and scientific interests in oceans and inland water; and for safe, effective and environmentally sound marine services responsive to the needs of Canadians in a global economy.

Contact(s):
Herb Dhaliwal, Minister; 613-992-3474
Wayne Wouters, Deputy Minister; 613-993-2200

ONTARIO DEPARTMENT OF FISHERIES AND OCEANS
CANADIAN COAST GUARD
200 Kent St.
Ottawa, K1A 0E6 Ontario Canada
Phone: 613-998-1571 Fax: 613-990-2780
Website: www.ccg-gcc.gc.ca

Membership: 101–1,000

Scope: International

U.S. FEDERAL AND INTERNATIONAL GOVERNMENT AGENCIES – P

Contact(s):
- Dave Faulkner, Director General: Integrated Technical Support; 613-998-1638; Fax: 613-993-5333
- Charles Gadula, Director of Fleet; 613-993-1849; gadulac@dfo-mpo.gc.ca
- Debra Normoyle, Director General: Marine Programs; 613-990-5508; Fax: 613-991-4982
- Anne O'Toole, Director General: Integrated Business Management; 613-998-1440; Fax: 613-990-3480
- John Adams, Assistant Deputy Minister, Marine Services/Commissioner; 613-998-1571; Fax: 613-990-2780
- Guy Bujold, Deputy Commissioner; 613-998-1570; Fax: 613-990-2780

ONTARIO DEPARTMENT OF FISHERIES AND OCEANS
CORPORATE SERVICES
200 Kent St.
Ottawa, K1A 0E6 Ontario Canada
Phone: 613-993-0868   Fax: 613-990-3604
Website: www.intra.dfo-mpo.gc.ca/index.htm

Membership: 101–1,000
Scope: National

Contact(s):
- Robert Bergeron, Director General: Small Craft Harbours; 613-993-1037
- Yves Dupuis, Director General: Human Resources; 613-990-0023
- Mike Hawkes, Director General: Finance and Administration; 613-993-9372
- Paul Hession, Director General: IT; 613-993-2051
- Donna Petrachenko, Assistant Deputy Minister; 613-993-0868

ONTARIO DEPARTMENT OF FISHERIES AND OCEANS
LEGAL SERVICES
200 Kent St.
Ottawa, K1A 0E6 Ontario Canada
Phone: 613-993-0966
Website: www.dfo-mpo.gc.ca

Scope: National
Description: Canadian Government

ONTARIO DEPARTMENT OF FISHERIES AND OCEANS
OCEANS
200 Kent St.
Ottawa, K1A 0E6 Ontario Canada
Phone: 613-993-0850-000   Fax: 613-990-2768
Website: www.intra.dfo-mpo.gc.ca

Contact(s):
- Paul Cuillerier, Director General: Habitat Management & Environmental Sciences; 613-991-1280
- Daniel McDougall, Director General: Oceans Directorate; 613-990-0001
- Matthew King, Assistant Deputy Minister; 613-993-0850

ONTARIO DEPARTMENT OF FISHERIES AND OCEANS
POLICY
200 Kent St.
Ottawa, K1A 0E6 Ontario Canada
Phone: 613-993-1808   Fax: 613-993-6958

Membership: 1–100
Scope: National

Contact(s):
- Sharon Ashley, Director General: Policy, Coordination & Liaison; 613-990-0007
- Lori Ridgeway, Director General: Economic & Policy Analysis; 613-993-1914
- Paul Thompson, Director General: Strategic Priorities & Planning; 613-990-0146
- Richard Wex, Director General: Office of Sustainable Aquaculture; 613-993-1872
- Liseanne Forand, Assistant Deputy Minister; 613-993-1808

ONTARIO DEPARTMENT OF FISHERIES AND OCEANS
SCIENCE
615 Booth Street
Ottawa, K1A 0E6 Ontario Canada
Phone: 613-990-5123   Fax: 613-990-5113
Website: www.intra.dfo-mpo.gc.ca

Scope: National

Contact(s):
- Serge Labonte, Director General: Fisheries & Biodiversity Science Directorate; 613-990-9082
- Elizabeth Marsollier, Director General: Ocean & Aquaculture Science Directorate; 613-990-0271
- Tony O'Connor, Director General: Canadian Hydrography Services; 613-995-4413
- Brian Wilson, Director General: Program Planning & Coordination; 613-990-0149
- John Davis, Assistant Deputy Minister; 613-990-5123

P

PACIFIC SALMON COMMISSION
1155 Robson St., Suite 600
Vancouver, V6E 1B5 British Columbia Canada
Phone: 604-684-8081   Fax: 604-666-8707
Website: www.psc.org

Membership: 1–100
Scope: International
Description: Charged with implementation of the Pacific Salmon Treaty signed by Canada and the United States in 1985, the Commission provides regulatory advice and recommendations to the U.S. and Canada relative to their management of salmon originating in one country, but subject to interception by the other. The Commission is also charged with conserving Pacific Salmon stocks in order to achieve optimum production.

Contact(s):
- Don Kowal, Executive Secretary

PACIFIC STATES MARINE FISHERIES COMMISSION
45 SE 82nd Dr., Suite 100
Gladstone, OR 97027-2522 United States
Phone: 503-650-5400   Fax: 503-650-5426
Website: www.psmfc.org

Founded: 1947
Membership: 1–100
Scope: State
Description: The Commission serves the Pacific states of Alaska, California, Idaho, Oregon, and Washington to promote conservation, development and management of marine and anadromous fisheries of mutual concern through a coordinated regional approach to fisheries research, monitoring, and utilization. Activities focus on multistate databases, interjurisdiction fishery management plans, marine debris, saving fisheries habitat, and marine mammal/fishery interactions.

Contact(s):
- Randy Fisher, Executive Director

PEACE CORPS
1111 20th St., NW
Washington, DC 20526 United States
Phone: 202-692-2100
E-mail: volunteer@peacecorps.gov
Website: www.peacecorps.gov

Founded: 1961

Membership: 1,001–10,000
Scope: International
Description: The Peace Corps was established in 1961. More than 165,000 Americans have joined the Peace Corps and have served in 135 countries. The Peace Corps has three goals: to help the people of interested countries in meeting their need for trained men and women; to help promote a better understanding of Americans on the part of the peoples served; and to help promote a better understanding of other peoples on the part of Americans.
Publication(s): The Peace Corps Times
Contact(s):
Charles Baquet, Acting Director; 202-692-2100

PEACE CORPS
ECUADOR
Avenida 6 de Diciembre 2269
Quito, Ecuador
Phone: 5932561224
E-mail: fgarces@ec.peacecorps.gov
Founded: 1960
Description: Peace Corps Ecuador provides technical assistance and cultural exchange in rural communites, through conservation NGO's and government agencies. Technical assistance is provided in the fields of EE, Agroforestry, and Conservation of Protected Areas.
Publication(s): Remedios Naturales Contra Plagas, Algunes alternativas para el desarrallo, Agroforesteria en los Audes del Ecuador
Contact(s):
Francisco Garces, Natural Resources Program Director; 593-256-1224; fgarces@ec.peacecorps.gov
Marcy Kelly, Peace Corps Ecuador Director; 593-256-1224; mkelly@ec.peacecorps.gov
Tim Criste, Program and Training Officer; 593-256-1224; tcriste@ec.peacecorps.gov

Q

QUEBEC DEPARTMENT OF CANADIAN HERITAGE
PORTFOLIO AND CORPORATE AFFAIRS
15 Eddy St. Room 12B 22
Hull, K1A 0M5 Quebec Canada
Phone: 819-994-3046   Fax: 819-953-4796
Scope: National
Contact(s):
Yazmime Laroche, Assistant Deputy Minister; 819-994-3046

QUEBEC ENVIRONMENTAL CONSERVATION SERVICE
ECOSYSTEM AND ENVIRONMENTAL RESOURCES DIRECTORATE
7th Fl., Place Vincent Massey, 351 St. Joseph Blvd.
Hull, K1A 0H3 Quebec Canada
Phone: 819-997-5674   Fax: 819-994-2541
Scope: International
Contact(s):
Jennifer Moore, Director General; 819-997-5674; Fax: 819-994-2541

QUEBEC ENVIRONMENTAL CONSERVATION SERVICE
QUEBEC REGION ENVIRONMENT CANADA
Canadian Wildlife Service, 1141 Route de l'Eglise, P.O. Box 10100, 9th Floor
Sainte-Foy, G1V 4H5 Quebec Canada
Phone: 418-648-2543   Fax: 418-649-6475
Contact(s):
Albin Tramblay, Regional Director; 418-648-7808

S

SENATE COMMITTEE ON APPROPRIATIONS
S128, Capitol Bldg.
Washington, DC 20510 United States
Phone: 202-224-7292   Fax: 202-224-8553
Website: www.appropriations.senate.gov
Scope: National
Description: Concerned with all proposed legislation, messages, petitions, memorials, and other matters relating to appropriation of the revenue for the support of the federal government.
Contact(s):
Terry Sauvain, Staff Director
Robert Byrd, Chairman

SENATE COMMITTEE ON AGRICULTURE, NUTRITION, AND FORESTRY
PRODUCTION AND PRICE COMPETITIVENESS; MARKETING, INSPECTION, AND PRODUCT PROMOTION; FORESTRY, CONSERVATION, AND RURAL REVITALIZATION; RESEARCH, NUTRITION, AND GENERAL LEGISLATION
Rm. 328-A, Russell Building
Washington, DC 20510 United States
Phone: 202-224-2035
Website: www.senate.gov/~agriculture
Scope: National
Description: Concerned with agriculture and agricultural commodities; inspection of livestock, meat, and agricultural products; animal industry and diseases; pests and pesticides; agricultural extension services and experiment stations; forestry in general and forest reserves and wilderness areas other than those created from the public domain; agricultural economics and research; human nutrition; home economics; farm credit and farm security; rural development, rural electrification and watersheds; etc.
Contact(s):
Keith Luse, Minority Staff Director
Mark Halverson, Chief of Staff
Tom Harkin, Chairman
David Johnson, Counsel
Richard Lugar, Ranking Republican Member
Robert Sturm, Chief Clerk

SENATE COMMITTEE ON COMMERCE, SCIENCE, AND TRANSPORTATION
AVIATION; COMMUNICATIONS; CONSUMER AFFAIRS, FOREIGN COMMERCE AND TOURISM; SCIENCE, TECHNOLOGY, AND SPACE; SURFACE TRANSPORTATION AND MERCHANT MARINE; OCEANS AND FISHERIES
U.S. Senate SD508 Dirksen Office Building
Washington, DC 20510 United States
Phone: 202-224-1251   Fax: 202-224-1259
Website: www.senate.gov/~commerce/
Description: Concerned with interstate commerce; transportation; regulation of interstate common carriers, including railroads, buses, trucks, vessels, pipelines, and civil aviation; merchant marine and navigation; marine and ocean navigation, safety and transportation, including navigational aspects of deepwater ports; Coast Guard; inland waterways, except construction; communications; regulation of consumer products and services, except for credit, financial services, and housing; the Panama Canal; etc.
Contact(s):
Fritz Hollings, Ranking Member
John McCain, Chairman

SENATE COMMITTEE ON ENERGY AND NATURAL RESOURCES
Rm. SD-364 Dirksen Bldg.
Washington, DC 20510 United States
Phone: 202-224-4971   Fax: 202-224-6163

Membership: 1–100
Scope: National
Description: Concerned with the comprehensive study and review of matters relating to energy and resources development. Jursdiction: Coal production, distribution, and utilization; energy policy; energy regulation and conservation; energy related aspects of deepwater ports; energy research and development; extraction of minerals from oceans and Outer Continental Shelf lands; hydroelectric power, irrigation, and reclamation; mining education and research; mining, mineral lands, mining claims; etc.

Contact(s):
Frank Murkowski, Chair

SENATE COMMITTEE ON ENVIRONMENT AND PUBLIC WORKS
TRANSPORTATION AND INFRASTRUCTURE; SUPERFUND; WASTE CONTROL AND RISK ASSESSMENT; CLEAN AIR, WETLANDS, PRIVATE PROPERTY, AND NUCLEAR SAFETY; DRINKING WATER, FISHERIES, AND WILDLIFE
Dirksen Bldg.
Washington, DC 20510 United States
Phone: 202-224-6176   Fax: 202-228-2040
E-mail: alicia_buller@epw.senate.gov
Website: http://epw.senate.gov

Membership: 1–100
Scope: National
Description: Committee on Environment and Public Works, to which shall be referred all proposed legislation, messages, petitions, memorials, and other matters relating to the following subjects: environmental policy; environmental research and development; ocean dumping; fisheries and wildlife; environmental aspects of Outer Continental Shelf lands; solid waste disposal and recycling; environmental effects of toxic substances, other than pesticides; water resources; etc.

Contact(s):
James Inhofe, Chairman
Jim Jeffords, Ranking Member

SENATE COMMITTEE ON FOREIGN RELATIONS
AFRICAN AFFAIRS; EAST ASIAN AND PACIFIC AFFAIRS; EUROPEAN AFFAIRS; INTERNATIONAL ECONOMIC POLICY, EXPORT AND TRADE PROMOTION; INTERNATIONAL OPERATIONS; NEAR EASTERN AND SOUTH ASIAN AFFAIRS; WESTERN HEMISPHERE, PEACE CORPS, NARCOTICS AND TERRORISM
U.S. Senate
Washington, DC 20510-6225 United States
Phone: 202-224-4651   Fax: 202-228-1608
Website: www.foreign.state.gov

Membership: 1–100
Scope: National
Description: Jurisdiction: Foreign and national security policy; international treaties, conferences, and congresses; World Bank and International Monetary Fund; oceans and international environmental and scientific affairs; humanitarian assistance and hunger; and United Nations and its affiliated organizations.

Contact(s):
Sam Brownback, Chair, Subcommittee on Near Eastern and South Asian Affairs
Christopher Dodd, Chair, Subcommittee on Western Hemisphere, Peace Corps, Narco
Bill Frist, Chair, Subcommittee on African Affairs
Rod Grams, Chair, Subcommittee on International Operations
Chuck Hagel, Chair, Subcommittee on International Economic Policy, Export

SENATE COMMITTEE ON HEALTH, EDUCATION, LABOR, AND PENSIONS
AGING; CHILDREN, FAMILY, DRUGS, AND ALCOHOLISM; EDUCATION, ARTS, AND HUMANITIES; EMPLOYMENT AND PRODUCTIVITY; HANDICAPPED; LABOR
SD-428 Dirksen Bldg.
Washington, DC 20510 United States
Phone: 202-224-6770   Fax: 202-224-6510
E-mail: greggstaff@labor.senate.gov
Website: health.senate.gov/

Contact(s):
Judd Gregg, Chairman
Ted Kennedy, Ranking Member

SOUTH ATLANTIC FISHERY MANAGEMENT COUNCIL
One Southpark Circle
Charleston, SC 29407-4699 United States
Phone: 843-571-4366   Fax: 843-769-4520
E-mail: safmc@safmc.net
Website: www.safmc.net

Founded: 1976
Membership: 1–100
Scope: Regional
Description: Responsible for the conservation and management of fish stocks within the 200-mile limit (federal waters) of the Atlantic off the coasts of North Carolina, South Carolina, Georgia, and Florida.
Publication(s): South Atlantic Update, Fishery Management Plans
Keyword(s): Oceans/Coasts/Beaches, Wildlife & Species

Contact(s):
Robert Mahood, Executive Director
Fulton Love, Chairman

SOUTH DAKOTA COOPERATIVE FISH AND WILDLIFE RESEARCH UNIT (USDI-USGS)
Department of Wildlife and Fisheries Sciences
P.O. Box 2140B
South Dakota State University
Brookings, SD 57007 United States
Phone: 605-688-6121   Fax: 605-688-4515
E-mail: charles_berry@sdstate.edu
Website: wfs.sdstate.edu

Founded: 1963
Scope: Local, State, Regional, National, International
Description: Conducts fish and wildlife research and provides educational experiences for fishery and wildlife biologists. Cooperators: South Dakota Department of Game, Fish and Parks, South Dakota State University, US Geological Survey, USDI, and Wildlife Management Institute.

Contact(s):
Charles Berry, Leader; 605-688-6121; Fax: 605-688-4515; charles_berry@sdstate.edu
Steven Chipps, Assistant Leader for Fisheries; steven_chipps@sdstate.edu
Kenneth Higgins, Assistant Leader for Wildlife; kenneth_higgins@sdstate.edu

SUSQUEHANNA RIVER BASIN COMMISSION
1721 N. Front St.
Harrisburg, PA 17102 United States
Phone: 717-238-0422   Fax: 717-238-2436
E-mail: srbc@srbc.net
Website: www.srbc.net

Founded: 1970
Scope: Local, State, Regional
Description: The Susquehanna River Basin Commission (SRBC) is a federal-interstate compact commission which covers parts of New York, Pennsylvania and Maryland within the Susquehanna watershed. SRBC's mission is to enhance the public welfare through comprehensive planning, allocation and management of the water resources of the watershed.
Publication(s): Susquehanna Guardian (newsletter), Annual Report
Keyword(s): Pollution (general), Recreation/Ecotourism, Water Habitats & Quality
Contact(s):
Thomas Beauduy, Deputy Director
Paul Swartz, Executive Director; 1721 N. Front St., Harrisburg, PA 17102; 717-238-0422

SWAZILAND ENVIRONMENT AUTHORITY (SEA)
Ministry of Natural Resources Building
Mbabane, Swaziland
Phone: 2684041719
Founded: 1993
Description: SEA is the responsible government agency for environmental management in Swaziland (policy, EIA, legislation, monitoring, developing standards, environmental ed/public awareness)
Publication(s): Environment Management Act, Solid Waste Regulations, etc., Swaziland's Environment Action Plan
Contact(s):
J. Vilakati, Director; 268-404-1719
Irma Allen, Chair/Board; 268-404-1719; Fax: 268-518-6284; szallen@iafrica.sz
Stephen Zuke, Senior Environmental Officer; 268-404-1719

T

TANZANIA COASTAL MANAGEMENT PARTNERSHIP
Haile Selassie St., P.O. Box 71886
Dar Es Salaam, Tanzania
Phone: 255-51-667589   Fax: 255-51-668611
E-mail: gluhikula@epog.or.tz
Description: Integrated coastal management policy process in Tanzania.
Keyword(s): Oceans/Coasts/Beaches
Contact(s):
G. Luhikula, Contact

TENNESSEE VALLEY AUTHORITY
400 W. Summit Hill Dr.
Knoxville, TN 37902-1499 United States
Phone: 865-632-2101
E-mail: tvainfo@tva.gov
Website: www.tva.gov
Founded: 1933
Scope: Regional
Description: TVA was created by an Act of Congress for the regional development of the Tennessee Valley region in Tennessee, Kentucky, Mississippi, Alabama, Virginia, Georgia, and North Carolina. In 1964, TVA opened Land Between the Lakes as a national demonstration project for outdoor recreation, environmental education, and resource management.
Publication(s): Recreation on TVA Lakes, RiverPulse, various others on different subjects
Keyword(s): Air Quality/Atmosphere, Energy, Forests/Forestry, Land Issues, Pollution (general), Recreation/Ecotourism, Water Habitats & Quality, Wildlife & Species

TENNESSEE VALLEY AUTHORITY
MUSCLE SHOALS TECHNICAL LIBRARY
CTR 1E
P.O.Box 1010
Muscle Shoals, AL 35662-1010 United States
Phone: 256-386-2872
E-mail: whclark@tva.gov
Scope: Local, State, Regional, National
Description: We are a technical library which specializes in environmental research.

TENNESSEE VALLEY AUTHORITY
RESEARCH LIBRARY, KNOXVILLE AND CHATTANOOGA
400 W. Summit Hill Dr., ET PC
Knoxville, TN 37902-1499 United States
Phone: 865-632-3464
E-mail: corplibknox@tva.gov
Website: www.tva.gov
Founded: 1933
Scope: Local, State, Regional, National, International
Description: TVA achieves excellence in public service for the good of the people of the Tennessee Valley by supporting sustainable economic development, supplying affordable, reliable power, and managing a thriving river system. TVA's Knoxville and Chattanooga libraries support the agency's mission by providing research services and access to engineering, environmental and historical materials.

TEXAS COOPERATIVE FISH AND WILDLIFE RESEARCH UNIT
Texas Tech. University
P.O. Box 42120
Lubbock, TX 79409-2120 United States
Phone: 806-742-2851   Fax: 806-742-2946
E-mail: txcoop@hobbes.tcru.ttu.edu
Website: www.tcru.ttu.edu/tcru/
Founded: 1988
Membership: 1–100
Scope: Local, State, Regional, National, International
Description: To conduct research, train graduate students, and provide technical assistance in the maintenance and management of fish and wildlife biodiversity, biological informatics, wetland ecology, molecular (genetic) biology, aquatic and wildlife ecology, general and reproductive physiology, and fish culture using the technical expertise of three federal staff members and collaborators.
Publication(s): Webpage at www.tcru.ttu.edu/tcru/
Keyword(s): Agriculture/Farming, Ecosystems (precious), Energy, Land Issues, Pollution (general), Public Health, Reduce/Reuse/Recycle, Sprawl/Urban Planning, Wildlife & Species
Contact(s):
Clint Boal, Assistant Leader - Wildlife; 806-742-2851; Fax: 806-742-2946
Nick Parker, Leader; 806-742-2851; Fax: 806-742-2946
Reynaldo Patino, Assistant Leader - Fisheries; 806-742-2851; Fax: 806-742-2946

U

UNITED NATIONS RESEARCH INSTITUTE FOR SOCIAL DEVELOPMENT (UNRISD)
Palais des Nations, CH 1211
Geneva 10, Switzerland
Phone: 41-22-798-8400   Fax: 41-22-740-0791
E-mail: info@UNRISD.org
Website: www.unrisd.org
Founded: 1963

Description: UNRISD is an autonomous agency that researches the social dimensions of contemporary development problems. The Institute provides governments, development agencies, grassroots organizations, and scholars with a better understanding of how development policies and processes of economic, social, and environmental change affect different social groups. UNRISD promotes original research and strengthens research capacity in developing countries.

Publication(s): Discussion Papers, Focus on Integrating Gender into The Politics of Development, The Challenge of Peace, UNRISD News

Keyword(s): Agriculture/Farming, Development/Developing Countries, Forests/Forestry, Land Issues, Reduce/Reuse/Recycle, Sprawl/Urban Planning, Wildlife & Species

Contact(s):
Dharam Ghai, Director

UNITED STATES COUNCIL ON ENVIRONMENTAL QUALITY
722 Jackson Pl., NW
Washington, DC 20503 United States
Phone: 202-456-6224   Fax: 202-456-2710
Website: www.eop.gov/ceq

Founded: 1970
Membership: 1–100
Scope: International
Description: CEQ serves as the source of environmental expertise and policy analysis for the President and other organizations within the Executive Office of the President, and provides for coordination between departments and agencies. It is also charged with implementing statutory or regulatory requirements and programs.
Publication(s): CEQ Annual Report
Contact(s):
Philip Cooney, Chief of Staff
Dave Anderson, Associate Director Congressional Affairs
Cameron Bailey, Special Assistant
Dinah Bear, General Counsel
Jim Connaughton, Chairman
Bill Leary, Associate Director for Natural Resources
Elizabeth Slotpe, Associate Director
V. Stevens, Associate Director
Sam Thurstrom, Associate Director of Communications

UNITED STATES DEPARTMENT OF AGRICULTURE
1400 Independence Ave. SW
Washington, DC 20250 United States
Phone: 202-720-8732   Fax: 202-690-3605
Website: www.oig.usda.gov

Founded: 1862
Scope: National
Description: Created by Congress to acquire and disperse "useful" information on subjects connected with agriculture in the most general and comprehensive sense of that word, and to procure, propagate, and distribute among the people new and valuable seeds and plants. Today, in addition to managing the national forests and grasslands, USDA manages a variety of research, regulatory, domestic and foreign marketing, food and nutrition, and many other programs.
Contact(s):
Ann Veneman, Secretary, Department of Agriculture

UNITED STATES DEPARTMENT OF AGRICULTURE
AGRICULTURAL RESEARCH SERVICE
1400 Independence Ave., SW, Suite 302A
Washington, DC 20250 United States
Phone: 202-720-3656   Fax: 202-720-5427
Website: www.ars.usda.gov

Scope: Local, Regional
Description: Conducts research in natural resources, plant sciences, animal sciences, food sciences and human nutrition.
Contact(s):
Dwayne Buxton, Deputy Administrator; 301-504-5084
Allen Dedrick, Associate Deputy Administrator for Natural Resources and Sustainable Agricultural Systems; 301-504-7987
Floyd Horn, Administrator; 202-720-3656
Edward Knipling, Associate Administrator; 202-720-3658
Caird Rexroad, Associate Deputy Administrator for Animal Production, Product Value, and Safety; 202-720-3658
Judith St. John, Associate Deputy Administrator for Crop Production, Product Value, and Safety; 301-504-6252

UNITED STATES DEPARTMENT OF AGRICULTURE
ANIMAL AND PLANT HEALTH INSPECTION SERVICE
ANIMAL CARE
4700 River Road, Unit 84
Riverdale, MD 20737-0123 United States
Phone: 301-734-4980   Fax: 301-734-4978
E-mail: ace@usda.gov
Website: www.aphif.usda.gov/ac

Membership: 1–100
Scope: Local, Regional, National
Description: Investigates and prosecutes violations of federal laws governing the movement of animals and plants between states or into and out of the United States and regulates the humane care and treatment of warmblooded animals used for purposes of research or exhibition, for sale as pets at the wholesale level, or transported in commerce.
Publication(s): List of Licensed Dealers, List of Licensed Exhibitors, List of Registered Research Facilities
Contact(s):
W. Dehaven, Deputy Administrator for Animal Care; 301-734-4980
Richard Watkins, Assistant Deputy Administrator for Animal Care; 301-734-7833

UNITED STATES DEPARTMENT OF AGRICULTURE
ANIMAL AND PLANT HEALTH INSPECTION SERVICE
ANIMAL CARE CENTRAL REGIONAL OFFICE
P.O. Box 915004
Ft. Worth, TX 76115-9104 United States
Phone: 817-885-6923   Fax: 817-885-6017
E-mail: ace@usda.gov
Website: www.aphis.usda.gov/ac

Membership: 1–100
Scope: National
Contact(s):
Walter Christensen, Assistant Regional Director

UNITED STATES DEPARTMENT OF AGRICULTURE
ANIMAL AND PLANT HEALTH INSPECTION SERVICE
ANIMAL CARE EASTERN REGIONAL OFFICE
920 Main Campus Drive, Suite 200
Raleigh, NC 27606 United States
Phone: 919-716-5532   Fax: 919-716-5696
E-mail: ace@usda.gov
Website: www.aphis.usda.gov/ac

Membership: 1–100
Scope: Regional
Contact(s):
Elizabeth Goldentyer, Regional Director

UNITED STATES DEPARTMENT OF AGRICULTURE
ANIMAL AND PLANT HEALTH INSPECTION SERVICE
ANIMAL CARE WESTERN REGIONAL OFFICE
9580 Micron Ave., Suite J
Sacramento, CA 95827-2623 United States
Phone: 916-857-6205 Fax: 916-857-6212
Website: www.aphis.usda.gov/ac

Contact(s):
Robert Gibbons, Regional Director; 916-857-6205

UNITED STATES DEPARTMENT OF AGRICULTURE
ANIMAL AND PLANT HEALTH INSPECTION SERVICE
INTERNATIONAL SERVICES ASIA AND PACIFIC OFFICE
USDA, APHIS, IS American Embassy, Tokyo Unit 45004, Box 226 APO AP
Tokyo, 96337-5004 Japan
Phone: 81332245457 Fax: 81332245291

Contact(s):
Gary Green, Regional Director

UNITED STATES DEPARTMENT OF AGRICULTURE
ANIMAL AND PLANT HEALTH INSPECTION SERVICE
INTERNATIONAL SERVICES CENTRAL AMERICA, CARIBBEAN AND PANAMA OFFICE
USDA-APHIS-IS, American Embassy, Guatemala, Unit 3319
APO, 34024-3319 United States
Phone: 502-331-2036

UNITED STATES DEPARTMENT OF AGRICULTURE
ANIMAL AND PLANT HEALTH INSPECTION SERVICE
INTERNATIONAL SERVICES EUROPE, AFRICA, RUSSIA, NEAR EAST OFFICE
USDA-APHIS-IS FAS-USEU, PSC 82, Box 002
APO, 9724 United States
Phone: 322-508-2762

UNITED STATES DEPARTMENT OF AGRICULTURE
ANIMAL AND PLANT HEALTH INSPECTION SERVICE
INTERNATIONAL SERVICES MEXICO OFFICE
USDA-APHIS-IS, P.O. Box 3087
Laredo, TX 78044 United States

Contact(s):
Gordon Tween, Regional Director

UNITED STATES DEPARTMENT OF AGRICULTURE
ANIMAL AND PLANT HEALTH INSPECTION SERVICE
INTERNATIONAL SERVICES SCREWWORM ERADICATION PROGRAM OFFICE
USDA-APHIS-IS, P.O. Box 3087
Laredo, TX 78044 United States

Contact(s):
John Wyss, Regional Director

UNITED STATES DEPARTMENT OF AGRICULTURE
ANIMAL AND PLANT HEALTH INSPECTION SERVICE
INTERNATIONAL SERVICES SOUTH AMERICA
OFFICE: USDA/APHIS
American Embassy Santiago, Unit 4113
APO, NY 34033 United States
Phone: 562-638-1989

UNITED STATES DEPARTMENT OF AGRICULTURE
ANIMAL AND PLANT HEALTH INSPECTION SERVICE
NATIONAL WILDLIFE RESEARCH CENTER
4101 LaPorte Avenue
Fort Collins, CO 80521 United States
Phone: 970-266-6000 Fax: 970-266-6032
E-mail: nwrc@aphis.usda.gov
Website: www.aphis.usda.gov/ws/nwrc

Description: The U.S. Department of Agriculture's National Wildlife Research Center is the federal institution devoted to resolving problems caused by the interaction of wild animals and society. The Center applies scientific expertise to the development of practical methods to resolve these problems and to maintain the quality of the environments shared with wildlife.

Contact(s):
Richard Curnow, Director
John Kinsella, Regional Director; Fax: 919-716-5626; john.s.kinsella@usda.gov

UNITED STATES DEPARTMENT OF AGRICULTURE
ANIMAL AND PLANT HEALTH INSPECTION SERVICE
PLANT PROTECTION AND QUARANTINE
302E JL Whitten Building
Washington, DC 20250 United States
Phone: 202-720-5601 Fax: 202-690-0472
Website: www.aphis.usda.gov/ppq/

Description: Regulates the importation of plants, plant products, and animal products from foreign countries. Regulates the movement of such products between U.S. possessions and the mainland and the importation and interstate movement of plant pests. Inspects and certifies plants and plant products for export. Administers cooperative programs with states to control and eradicate insects, diseases, weeds, and nematodes of economic importance.

Contact(s):
Richard Dunkle, Deputy Administrator; 202-720-5601; Richard.L.Dunkle@usda.gov

UNITED STATES DEPARTMENT OF AGRICULTURE
ANIMAL AND PLANT HEALTH INSPECTION SERVICE
VETERINARY SERVICES
4700 River Road
Riverdale, MD 20737 United States
Phone: 301-734-8093
Website: www.aphis.usda.gov

Description: Regulates the importation of animals, animal semen, embryos, and animal products from foreign countries and the interstate movement of animals. Inspects and certifies animals for export. Administers cooperative federal-state programs to control and eradicate animal pests and diseases. Provides laboratory support for animal health programs and diagnostic referral assistance for private and state laboratories.

Contact(s):
Joseph Annelli, Chief Staff Veterinarian; 301-734-8073; joseph.f.annelli@usda.gov
Gary Colgrove, Assistant Director; 301-734-4356; gary.s.colgrove@usda.gov
Alfonso Torres, Deputy Administrator for Veterinary Services; 202-720-5193; alfonso.torres@usda.gov

UNITED STATES DEPARTMENT OF AGRICULTURE
COOPERATIVE STATE RESEARCH, EDUCATION, EXTENSION SERVICE (CSREES)
NATURAL RESOURCES AND ENVIRONMENT (NRE)
Mail Stop 2210
1400 Independence Ave., SW
Washington, DC 20250-2210 United States
Phone: 202-401-4555 Fax: 202-401-1706
Website: www.reeusda.gov/nre/index.htm

Scope: Local, State, Regional, National

Description: NRE provides leadership and administers research, education, and extension programs that ensure the efficient use and conservation of the Nation's natural resources and protection of the environment.

Keyword(s): Air Quality/Atmosphere, Climate Change, Ecosystems (precious), Forests/Forestry, Water Habitats & Quality, Wildlife & Species

Contact(s):
 Larry Biles, National Program Leader, Forestry Management; 202-401-4926; lbiles@csrees.usda.gov
 Catalino Blanche, National Program Leader, Forest Biology; 202-401-4190; cblanche@csrees.usda.gov
 John Buckhouse, National Program Leader, Rangeland Resources; 541-737-1629; Fax: 541-737-0504; john.c.buckhouse@oregonstate.edu
 Greg Crosby, National Program Leader, Sustainable Development; 202-401-6050; gcrosby@csrees.usda.gov
 Jane Dodds, Environmental Affairs, ANR Forum Network; 202-401-4044; jdodds@csrees.usda.gov
 Lisa Duriancik, Program Specialist, Natural Resources and Environment; 202-401-4141; lduriancik@csrees.usda.gov
 Raymond Knighton, National Program Leader, Air Quality; 202-401-6417; rknighton@csrees.usda.gov
 Dan Kugler, Deputy Administrator; dkugler@csrees.usda.gov
 Agnes Lamar, Program Analyst, Natural Resources and Environment; 202-401-4318; alamar@csrees.usda.gov
 Bruce Menzel, National Program Leader, Fisheries and Wildlife; 202-401-5016; bmenzel@csrees.usda.gov
 Eric Norland, National Program Leader, Forest Biology; 202-401-5971; enorland@csrees.usda.gov
 Michael O'Neill, National Program Leader, Water Quality; 202-205-5952; moneill@csrees.usda.gov
 Christy Pereira, Program Specialist, Natural Resources and Environment; 202-401-6444; cpereira@csrees.usda.gov
 Mary Rozum, National Program Leader, Conservation and Nutrient Mgmt.; 202-401-4533; mrozum@csrees.usda.gov

UNITED STATES DEPARTMENT OF AGRICULTURE
ECONOMIC RESEARCH CENTER
1800 M St., NW
Washington, DC 20036 United States
Phone: 202-694-5050 Fax: 202-694-5734
Website: www.ers.usda.gov

Scope: Regional

Description: Provides a program of agricultural, economic, and social research and analysis, statistical programs, technical consultation, planning assistance, and associated services. Conducts research and staff work relating to natural resources and environmental quality, including supplies, uses, and projected future requirements for land and water; effects of environmental quality improvement measures on agricultural production and agricultural resource use; and more.

Publication(s): Various research monographs, conservation, agricultural inputs, pest control

Contact(s):
 Paul Chen, Director of Information Services Division
 Adrie Custer, Director of Publication Services Branch
 Kitty Smith, Director of Resource Economics Division
 Susan Offutt, Administrator

UNITED STATES DEPARTMENT OF AGRICULTURE
FARM SERVICE AGENCY (FSA)
CONSERVATION AND ENVIRONMENTAL PROGRAMS DIVISION
USDA/FSA/CEPD/STOP 0513
1400 Independence Ave., S.W.
Washington, DC 20250-0513 United States
Phone: 202-720-6221 Fax: 202-720-4619
Website: www.fsa.usda.gov

Founded: 1936
Membership: 10,001–100,000
Scope: National

Description: Formerly known as Agricultural Stabilization and Conservation Service. Administers the following: Conservation Reserve Program, Conservation Reserve Enhancement Program, Emergency Conservation Program, various commodity and farm loan programs, production flexibility contracts, and various farm loan and disaster assistance programs.

Keyword(s): Agriculture/Farming, Air Quality/Atmosphere, Climate Change, Ecosystems (precious), Energy, Water Habitats & Quality, Wildlife & Species

Contact(s):
 Grady Bilberry, Director of Price Support Division
 Diane Sharp, Director of Production, Emergencies and Compliance Division
 Robert Stephenson, Director, Conservation and Environmental Programs
 Tade Sullivan, Director of Public Affairs
 Carolyn Cooksie, Deputy Administrator for Farm Loan Programs
 James Little, Acting Administrator
 Larry Mitchell, Deputy Administrator for Farm Programs

UNITED STATES DEPARTMENT OF AGRICULTURE
FOREST SERVICE
P.O. Box 96090
Washington, DC 20090-6090 United States
Phone: 202-205-8333 Fax: 202-205-1599
Website: www.fs.fed.us

Scope: National

Description: Administers National Forests and National Grasslands and is responsible for the management of their resources. Cooperates with federal and state officials in the enforcement of game laws on the National Forests and in the development and maintenance of wildlife resources; cooperates with the state and private owners in the application of sound forest management practices, in protection of forest lands against fire, insects, diseases, and in the distribution of planting stock.

Publication(s): See publications on website

Contact(s):
 Hilda Diaz-Stero, Director of Pacific SW Research Station Region 5; 202-205-1491
 Kathy Gause, Civil Rights Director; 202-205-1585
 Phil Janik, Director of Wildlife, Fish, Water & Air Research; 202-205-1661
 George Lennon, Director of Office Communications; 202-205-8333
 Randy Phillips, Executive Director of Forest County Payments Advisory Committee; 202-205-1663
 Michael Rains, Director North East Research Station; 202-205-1657
 Dale Bosworth, Chief; 202-205-1661
 Paul Brouha, Associate Deputy National Forest System; 202-205-1465
 Sally Collins, Deputy Chief for Natural Resources; 202-205-1465

Jim Furnish, Deputy National Forest System; 202-205-1523
Vincette Goerl, Chief Financial Officer; 202-205-1784
Robert Lewis, Deputy Research and Development; 202-205-1665
Valdis Mezainis, International Programs; 202-205-1650
Clyde Thompson, Business Operations; 202-205-1707
Bill Wasley, Law Enforcement and Investigations; 703-605-4690
Barbara Weber, Associate Deputy Research and Development; 202-205-1702

UNITED STATES DEPARTMENT OF AGRICULTURE
FOREST SERVICE
ALLEGHENY NATIONAL FOREST
222 Liberty St., Box 847
Warren, PA 16365 United States
Phone: 814-723-5150   Fax: 814-726-1465
E-mail: r9_allegheny_nf@fs.fed.us
Website: www.fs.fed.us/r9/allegheny
Membership: 101–1,000
Scope: Regional, National
Description: Managing the resources of the Allegheny National Forest
Keyword(s): Ecosystems (precious), Forests/Forestry

UNITED STATES DEPARTMENT OF AGRICULTURE
FOREST SERVICE
ANGELES NATIONAL FORESTS
701 N. Santa Anita Ave.
Arcadia, CA 91006-2725 United States
Phone: 626-574-1613   Fax: 626-574-5233
Scope: Regional

UNITED STATES DEPARTMENT OF AGRICULTURE
FOREST SERVICE
ANGELINA, DAVY CROCKETT, SABINE AND SAM HOUSTON NATIONAL FOREST
National Forest in Texas, Homer Garrison Federal Bldg., 701 N. 1st St.
Lufkin, TX 75901 United States
Phone: 936-897-1068   Fax: 936-897-3406
Website: www.southernregion.fs.fed.us/texas
Scope: Regional

UNITED STATES DEPARTMENT OF AGRICULTURE
FOREST SERVICE
ANGELINA NATIONAL FOREST
111 Walnut Ridge Rd.
Zavalla, TX 75980 United States
Phone: 936-897-1068   Fax: 936-897-3406
Website: www.southernregion.fs.fed.us/texas
Scope: Local, State
Description: Angelina National Forest within the National Forests and Grasslands of Texas
Keyword(s): Ecosystems (precious), Forests/Forestry, Water Habitats & Quality, Wildlife & Species

UNITED STATES DEPARTMENT OF AGRICULTURE
FOREST SERVICE
APACHE-SITGREAVES NATIONAL FOREST
Federal Bldg., Box 640
Springville, AZ 85938 United States
Phone: 928-333-4301   Fax: 928-333-6357
Scope: Regional

UNITED STATES DEPARTMENT OF AGRICULTURE
FOREST SERVICE
ARAPAHO AND ROOSEVELT NATIONAL FORESTS
240 W. Prospect St.
Fort Collins, CO 80526 United States
Phone: 970-498-1064   Fax: 970-498-1328
Scope: Regional

UNITED STATES DEPARTMENT OF AGRICULTURE
FOREST SERVICE
ASHLEY NATIONAL FOREST
355 N. Vernal Ave.
Vernal, UT 84078 United States
Phone: 435-789-1181   Fax: 435-781-5142
Website: www.fs.fed.us/r4/ashley/ - 5k
Scope: Regional

UNITED STATES DEPARTMENT OF AGRICULTURE
FOREST SERVICE
BEAVERHEAD—DEERLODGE NATIONAL FOREST
420 Barrett St.
Dillon, MT 59725-3572 United States
Phone: 406-683-3900
Scope: Regional

UNITED STATES DEPARTMENT OF AGRICULTURE
FOREST SERVICE
BIENVILLE, DELTA, DESOTO, HOLLY SPRINGS, HOMOCHITTO, AND TOMBIGBEE NATIONAL FORESTS
National Forests in Mississippi
100 W. Capital St., Ste. 1141
Jackson, MS 39269-1199 United States
Phone: 601-965-4391   Fax: 601-965-5519
Website: www.fs.fed.us/r8/miss
Scope: Regional

UNITED STATES DEPARTMENT OF AGRICULTURE
FOREST SERVICE
BIGHORN NATIONAL FOREST
2013 Eastside 2nd St
Sheridan, WY 82801 United States
Phone: 307-674-2600   Fax: 307-674-2668
E-mail: mailroom_r2_bighorn@fs.fed.us
Website: www.fs.fed.us/r2/bighorn
Scope: Regional

UNITED STATES DEPARTMENT OF AGRICULTURE
FOREST SERVICE
BITTERROOT NATIONAL FOREST
1801 N. 1st St.
Hamilton, MT 59840 United States
Phone: 406-363-7100
Scope: Regional

UNITED STATES DEPARTMENT OF AGRICULTURE
FOREST SERVICE
BLACK HILLS NATIONAL FOREST
25041 N. Highway 16
Custer, SD 57730-7239 United States
Phone: 605-673-9200   Fax: 605-673-9350
E-mail: mailroom_r2_black_hills@fs.fed.us
Website: www.fs.fed.us/r2/blackhills
Scope: Regional

U.S. FEDERAL AND INTERNATIONAL GOVERNMENT AGENCIES – U

UNITED STATES DEPARTMENT OF AGRICULTURE
FOREST SERVICE
BOISE NATIONAL FOREST
1249 S. Vinnell Way, Ste. 200
Boise, ID 83709 United States
Phone: 208-373-4100   Fax: 208-373-4201
Website: www.fs.fed.us/r4/boise/
Scope: Regional

UNITED STATES DEPARTMENT OF AGRICULTURE
FOREST SERVICE
BRIDGER-TETON NATIONAL FOREST
P.O. Box 1888
Jackson, WY 83001 United States
Phone: 307-739-5500   Fax: 307-739-5503
E-mail: r4_b-t_info@fs.fed.us
Website: www.fs.fed.us/btnf/
Scope: Regional

UNITED STATES DEPARTMENT OF AGRICULTURE
FOREST SERVICE
BUFFALO GAP NATIONAL GRASSLAND
WALL RANGER DISTRICT / NATIONAL GRASSLANDS VISITOR CENTER
708 Main St., P.O. Box 425
Wall, SD 57790 United States
Phone: 605-279-2125
Scope: Regional

UNITED STATES DEPARTMENT OF AGRICULTURE
FOREST SERVICE
BUFFALO GAP NATIONAL GRASSLAND, FALL RIVER RANGER DISTRICT
P.O. Box 732
1801 Highway 18 Bypass
Hot Springs, SD 57747 United States
Phone: 605-745-4107
Scope: Local, State, Regional
Description: District office Buffalo Gap National Grasslands, Nebraska National Forest, U. S. Forest Service

UNITED STATES DEPARTMENT OF AGRICULTURE
FOREST SERVICE
BUTTE VALLEY NATIONAL GRASSLAND
Goosenest Ranger District
37805 Highway 97
Macdoel, CA 96058 United States
Phone: 530-398-4391
Scope: Regional

UNITED STATES DEPARTMENT OF AGRICULTURE
FOREST SERVICE
CARIBBEAN NATIONAL FOREST
HC 01, Box 13490
Rio Grande, PR 00745-9625 United States
Phone: 787-888-1810   Fax: 787-888-5622
Website: www.r8web.com/caribbean/
Scope: Regional

UNITED STATES DEPARTMENT OF AGRICULTURE
FOREST SERVICE
CARIBOU—TARGHEE NATIONAL FOREST
1405 Hollipark Drive
Idaho Falls, ID 83401 United States
Phone: 208-524-7500   Fax: 208-557-5826
Website: www.fs.fed.us/r4/caribou-targhee
Scope: Regional

UNITED STATES DEPARTMENT OF AGRICULTURE
FOREST SERVICE
CARSON NATIONAL FOREST
Fed. Bldg., 208 Cruz Alta Rd., Box 558
Taos, NM 87571 United States
Phone: 505-758-6200   Fax: 505-758-6213
Scope: Regional

UNITED STATES DEPARTMENT OF AGRICULTURE
FOREST SERVICE
CEDAR RIVER / GRAND RIVER NATIONAL GRASSLAND
1005 5th Ave. W., P.O. Box 390
Lemmon, SD 57638 United States
Phone: 605-374-3592
Scope: Regional

UNITED STATES DEPARTMENT OF AGRICULTURE
FOREST SERVICE
CHATTAHOOCHEE AND OCONEE NATIONAL FORESTS
1755 Cleveland Hwy.
Gainesville, GA 30501 United States
Phone: 770-297-3000   Fax: 770-297-3011
Website: www.fs.fed.us/conf/
Scope: State
Description: Government Agency - Natural Resource Management

UNITED STATES DEPARTMENT OF AGRICULTURE
FOREST SERVICE
CHEQUAMEGON—NICOLET NATIONAL FOREST
1170 4th Ave., S.
Park Falls, WI 54552 United States
Phone: 715-762-2461   Fax: 715-762-5179
E-mail: dmklein@fs.fed.us
Website: www.fs.fed.us/r9/cnn
Scope: Regional
Contact(s):
  Anne Archie

UNITED STATES DEPARTMENT OF AGRICULTURE
FOREST SERVICE
CHEROKEE NATIONAL FOREST
P.O. Box 2010
Cleveland, TN 37320 United States
Phone: 423-476-9700
E-mail: mailroom_r8_cherokee_@fs.fed.us
Website: www.southernregion.fs.fed.us/cherokee
Scope: Regional

UNITED STATES DEPARTMENT OF AGRICULTURE
FOREST SERVICE
CHEYENNE NATIONAL GRASSLAND
Box 946
Lisbon, ND 58054 United States
Phone: 701-683-4342
Scope: Regional
Contact(s):
  Coleen Rufsvold, Manager; 701-683-4342; crufsvold@fs.fed.us

UNITED STATES DEPARTMENT OF AGRICULTURE
FOREST SERVICE
CHIPPEWA NATIONAL FOREST
200 Ash Ave., NW
Cass Lake, MN 56633 United States
Phone: 218-335-8600   Fax: 218-335-8632
E-mail: chippewapublic@fs.fed.us
Website: www.fs.fed.us/r9/chippewa/
Scope: Regional

UNITED STATES DEPARTMENT OF AGRICULTURE
FOREST SERVICE
CHUGACH NATIONAL FOREST
3301 C Street, Suite 300
Anchorage, AK 99503-3998 United States
Phone: 907-743-9500   Fax: 907-743-9476
E-mail: mailroom_r10_chugach@fs.fed.us
Website: www.fs.fed.us/r10/chugach/
Scope: Regional

UNITED STATES DEPARTMENT OF AGRICULTURE
FOREST SERVICE
CIBOLA NATIONAL FOREST
2113 Osuna Rd. NE, Ste. A
Albuquerque, NM 87111–1001 United States
Phone: 505-346-3900   Fax: 505-346-3901
Scope: Regional

UNITED STATES DEPARTMENT OF AGRICULTURE
FOREST SERVICE
CIMARRON NATIONAL GRASSLAND
242 Hwy. 56 E., P.O. Box 300
Elkhart, KS 67950 United States
Phone: 620-697-4621   Fax: 620-697-4340
Website: www.fs.fed.us/r2/psicc/cim/index.shtml
Scope: Regional
Description: National Grassland management

UNITED STATES DEPARTMENT OF AGRICULTURE
FOREST SERVICE
CLEARWATER NATIONAL FOREST
12730 Highway 12
Orofino, ID 83544 United States
Phone: 208-476-4541   Fax: 208-476-8329
Scope: Regional

UNITED STATES DEPARTMENT OF AGRICULTURE
FOREST SERVICE
CLEVELAND NATIONAL FOREST
10845 Rancho Bernardo Road, Suite 200
San Diego, CA 92127 United States
Phone: 858-674-2901   Fax: 858-673-6192
Scope: Regional

UNITED STATES DEPARTMENT OF AGRICULTURE
FOREST SERVICE
COCONINO NATIONAL FOREST
2323 E. Greenlaw Ln.
Flagstaff, AZ 86004 United States
Phone: 928-527-3600   Fax: 928-527-3620
E-mail: sharper@fs.fed.us
Website: www.fs.fed.us/r3/coconino
Founded: 1908
Scope: Regional
Description: USDA, Forest Service, National Forest

UNITED STATES DEPARTMENT OF AGRICULTURE
FOREST SERVICE
COLVILLE NATIONAL FOREST
716 S. Main
Colville, WA 99114 United States
Phone: 509-684-7000
Website: www.fs.fed.us/r6/colville
Scope: Regional

UNITED STATES DEPARTMENT OF AGRICULTURE
FOREST SERVICE
COMANCHE NATIONAL GRASSLAND
27204 Hwy. 287, P.O. Box 127
Springfield, CO 81073 United States
Phone: 719-553-1400
Scope: Regional
Contact(s):
  Ben Garcia, Manager; 719-523-6591; bgarcia02@fs.fed.us

UNITED STATES DEPARTMENT OF AGRICULTURE
FOREST SERVICE
CORONADO NATIONAL FOREST
300 W. Congress St
Tucson, AZ 85701 United States
Phone: 520-670-4552   Fax: 520-670-4567
Scope: Regional

UNITED STATES DEPARTMENT OF AGRICULTURE
FOREST SERVICE
CROATAN, NANTAHALA, PISGAH AND UWHARRIE NATIONAL FORESTS
National Forests in North Carolina, P.O. Box 2750
Asheville, NC 28802 United States
Phone: 828-257-4200   Fax: 828-257-4263
E-mail: mailroom_r8_north_carolina@fs.fed.us
Website: www.cs.unca.edu/nfsnc
Scope: National, International
Description: National Forests
Contact(s):
  Larry Hayden, Ecosystems & Planning Staff Officer; 828-257-4200; ext. 864; Fax: 828-257-4263

U.S. FEDERAL AND INTERNATIONAL GOVERNMENT AGENCIES – U

UNITED STATES DEPARTMENT OF AGRICULTURE
FOREST SERVICE
CROOKED RIVER NATIONAL GRASSLAND
813 SW Highway 97
Madras, OR 97741 United States
Phone: 541-475-9272

Scope: Local, Regional
Keyword(s): Agriculture/Farming, Ecosystems (precious), Forests/Forestry, Land Issues, Recreation/Ecotourism, Water Habitats & Quality, Wildlife & Species
Contact(s):
  Robert Rock, District Manager
  Glenn Adams, Rangeland Management Specialist
  Anne Alford, Wildlife Biologist

UNITED STATES DEPARTMENT OF AGRICULTURE
FOREST SERVICE
CURLEW NATIONAL GRASSLAND
1405 Hollipark Drive
Idaho Falls, ID 83252 United States
Phone: 208-524-7500
Website: www.fs.fed.us/r4/caribou/

Scope: Regional

UNITED STATES DEPARTMENT OF AGRICULTURE
FOREST SERVICE
CUSTER NATIONAL FOREST
P.O. Box 50760
Billings, MT 59105 United States
Phone: 406-657-6200   Fax: 406-657-6222

Scope: Regional

UNITED STATES DEPARTMENT OF AGRICULTURE
FOREST SERVICE
DANIEL BOONE NATIONAL FOREST
1700 Bypass Rd.
Winchester, KY 40391 United States
Phone: 859-745-3100   Fax: 859-744-1568
Website: www.southernregion.fs.fed.us/boone

Scope: Local, State, Regional, National
Description: Located in the mountains of eastern Kentucky, the Daniel Boone National Forest encompasses almost 700,000 acres of land. The land is gnerally rugged and characterized by steep forested ridges, narrow valleys, and over 3,400 miles of cliffline. The Forest contains two large lakes, many rivers and streams, two wilderness areas and the 269-mile Sheltowee Trace National Recreation Trail that extends across the length of the forest.

UNITED STATES DEPARTMENT OF AGRICULTURE
FOREST SERVICE
DESCHUTES NATIONAL FOREST
1645 Highway 20 East
Bend, OR 97701 United States
Phone: 541-388-2715

Scope: Regional

UNITED STATES DEPARTMENT OF AGRICULTURE
FOREST SERVICE
DIXIE NATIONAL FOREST
Supervisor's Office
1789 Wedgewood Lane
Cedar City, UT 84720 United States
Phone: 435-865-3701
E-mail: jmgreen@fs.fed.us
Website: www.fs.fed.us/dxnf

Scope: Regional

UNITED STATES DEPARTMENT OF AGRICULTURE
FOREST SERVICE
ELDORADO NATIONAL FOREST
100 Forni Rd.
Placerville, CA 95667 United States
Phone: 530-622-5061   Fax: 530-621-5297
Website: www.fs.fed.us/r5

Scope: Regional

UNITED STATES DEPARTMENT OF AGRICULTURE
FOREST SERVICE
FINGER LAKES NATIONAL FOREST
5218 State Route 414
Hector, NY 14841 United States
Phone: 607-546-4470   Fax: 607-546-4474
Website: www.fs.fed.us/r9/gmfl

Founded: 1958
Scope: Local, State, Regional, National, International
Description: The mission of the Finger Lakes National Forest is to sustain, protect and enhance forest ecosystems. We understand that our greatest asset is the land, our greatest strength is our work force, and we will strive to gain public understanding, trust, and confidence in all that we do through demonstration and education.
Keyword(s): Forests/Forestry
Contact(s):
  Paul Brewster, Forest Supervisor; 802-747-6704; Fax: 802-747-6766; pbrewster@fs.fed.us
  Michael Dockry, Forest Planner; 607-546-4470; ext. 316; Fax: 607-546-4474; mdockry@fs.fed.us
  Martha Twarkins, Hector District Ranger; 607-546-4470; ext. 314; Fax: 607-546-4474; mtwarkins@fs.fed.us

UNITED STATES DEPARTMENT OF AGRICULTURE
FOREST SERVICE
FISHLAKE NATIONAL FOREST
115 East 900 North
Richfield, UT 84701 United States
Phone: 435-896-9233

Scope: Regional
Contact(s):
  May Erickson, Manager; 435-896-1001; mcerickson@fs.fed.us

UNITED STATES DEPARTMENT OF AGRICULTURE
FOREST SERVICE
FLATHEAD NATIONAL FOREST
1935 3rd. Ave., E.
Kalispell, MT 59901 United States
Phone: 406-758-5251
Website: www.fs.fed.us/r1/flathead

Founded: 1905
Membership: 101–1,000
Scope: State
Description: Manage the Flathead National Forest

UNITED STATES DEPARTMENT OF AGRICULTURE
FOREST SERVICE
FORT PIERRE NATIONAL GRASSLAND
124 South Euclid Ave., P.O. Box 417
Pierre, SD 57501 United States
Phone: 605-224-5517   Fax: 605-224-6517
Website: www.fs.fed.us/r2/nebraska
Scope: Regional
Contact(s):
Anthony Detoy; 605-224-5517; adetoy@fs.fed.us

UNITED STATES DEPARTMENT OF AGRICULTURE
FOREST SERVICE
FRANCIS MARION AND SUMTER NATIONAL FOREST
4931 Broad River Rd.
Columbia, SC 29212-3530 United States
Phone: 803-561-4000   Fax: 803-561-4004
E-mail: gewhite@fs.fed.us
Website: www.fs.fed.us/r8/fms
Scope: Local, State, Regional, National
Description: Natural Resource

UNITED STATES DEPARTMENT OF AGRICULTURE
FOREST SERVICE
FREMONT NATIONAL FOREST
1301 S. G St.
Lakeview, OR 97630 United States
Phone: 541-947-2151
Scope: Regional

UNITED STATES DEPARTMENT OF AGRICULTURE
FOREST SERVICE
GALLATIN NATIONAL FOREST
10 E. Babcock Ave., Federal Bldg., Box 130
Bozeman, MT 59771 United States
Phone: 406-587-6701   Fax: 406-587-6758
Scope: Regional
Contact(s):
Becki Heath, Forest Supervisor
Rich Inman, Deputy Forest Supervisor

UNITED STATES DEPARTMENT OF AGRICULTURE
FOREST SERVICE
GEORGE WASHINGTON AND JEFFERSON NATIONAL FORESTS
5162 Valleypointe Pkwy.
Roanoke, VA 24019 United States
Phone: 540-265-5100
Website: www.southernregion.fs.fed.us/gwj/
Scope: Regional
Description: Manage 1.8 million acres of National Forest land in Virginia and West Virginia.

UNITED STATES DEPARTMENT OF AGRICULTURE
FOREST SERVICE
GIFFORD PINCHOT NATIONAL FOREST
10600 N.E. 51st Circle
Vancouver, WA 98682 United States
Phone: 360-891-5000   Fax: 360-891-5045
E-mail: r6_gp_forest@fs.fed.us
Website: www.fs.fed.us/gpnf
Scope: Regional

UNITED STATES DEPARTMENT OF AGRICULTURE
FOREST SERVICE
GILA NATIONAL FOREST
3005 E. Camino del Bosque
Silver City, NM 88061 United States
Phone: 505-388-8201   Fax: 505-388-8204
E-mail: jprislan@fs.fed.us
Website: www.fs.fed.us/r3/gila
Founded: 1905
Scope: National
Description: The Gila National Forest is part of the Southwestern Region of National Forests and Grasslands
Keyword(s): Air Quality/Atmosphere, Ecosystems (precious), Forests/Forestry, Land Issues, Public Lands/Greenspace, Recreation/Ecotourism, Water Habitats & Quality, Wildlife & Species

UNITED STATES DEPARTMENT OF AGRICULTURE
FOREST SERVICE
GRAND MESA, UNCOMPAHGRE AND GUNNISON NATIONAL FORESTS
2250 Highway 50
Delta, CO 81416 United States
Phone: 970-874-6600   Fax: 970-874-6698
Scope: Regional

UNITED STATES DEPARTMENT OF AGRICULTURE
FOREST SERVICE
GREEN MOUNTAIN NATIONAL FOREST
231 N. Main Street
Rutland, VT 05701 United States
Phone: 802-747-6700   Fax: 802-747-6766
Website: www.fs.fed.us/r9/gmfl
Founded: 1932
Scope: Local, State, Regional, National, International
Description: The mission of the Green Mountain National Forest is to sustain, protect and enhance forest ecosystems. We understand that our greatest asset is the land, our greatest strength is our work force, and we will strive to gain public understanding, trust, and confidence in all that we do through demonstration and education.
Keyword(s): Air Quality/Atmosphere, Development/Developing Countries, Ecosystems (precious), Forests/Forestry, Land Issues, Pollution (general), Public Lands/Greenspace, Reduce/Reuse/Recycle, Water Habitats & Quality
Contact(s):
Paul Brewster, Forest Supervisor; 802-747-6704; Fax: 802-747-6766; pbrewster@fs.fed.us
Kathleen Diehl, Public Affairs Officer; 802-747-6709; Fax: 802-747-6766; kdiehl@fs.fed.us
Melissa Reichert, Forest Planner; 802-747-6754; Fax: 802-747-6766; mmreichert@fs.fed.us

UNITED STATES DEPARTMENT OF AGRICULTURE
FOREST SERVICE
HELENA NATIONAL FOREST
2880 Skyway Dr.
Helena, MT 59602 United States
Phone: 406-449-5201   Fax: 406-449-5436

U.S. FEDERAL AND INTERNATIONAL GOVERNMENT AGENCIES – U

UNITED STATES DEPARTMENT OF AGRICULTURE
FOREST SERVICE
HIAWATHA NATIONAL FOREST
2727 N. Lincoln Rd.
Escanaba, MI 49829 United States
Phone: 906-786-4062
Scope: Regional

UNITED STATES DEPARTMENT OF AGRICULTURE
FOREST SERVICE
HOOSIER NATIONAL FOREST
811 Constitution Ave.
Bedford, IN 47421 United States
Phone: 812-275-5987   Fax: 812-279-3423
Scope: Regional

UNITED STATES DEPARTMENT OF AGRICULTURE
FOREST SERVICE
HUMBOLDT—TOIYABE NATIONAL FOREST
1200 Franklin Way
Sparks, NV 89512 United States
Phone: 775-331-5301   Fax: 775-355-5349
Scope: Regional

UNITED STATES DEPARTMENT OF AGRICULTURE
FOREST SERVICE
HURON-MANISTEE NATIONAL FOREST
1755 S. Mitchell St.
Cadillac, MI 49601 United States
Phone: 231-775-2421   Fax: 231-775-5551
Scope: Regional

UNITED STATES DEPARTMENT OF AGRICULTURE
FOREST SERVICE
IDAHO PANHANDLE NATIONAL FORESTS
3815 Schreiber Way
Coeur d'Alene, ID 83815-8863 United States
Phone: 208-765-7223   Fax: 208-765-7307
Website: fs.fed.us/ipns

UNITED STATES DEPARTMENT OF AGRICULTURE
FOREST SERVICE
INYO NATIONAL FOREST
351 Pacu Lane
Bishop, CA 93514 United States
Phone: 760-873-2400   Fax: 760-873-2458
E-mail: mail_inyo@fs.fed.us
Website: www.fs.fed.us/r5/inyo
Membership: 101–1,000
Scope: Regional

UNITED STATES DEPARTMENT OF AGRICULTURE
FOREST SERVICE
KAIBAB NATIONAL FOREST
800 South 6th St.
Williams, AZ 86046 United States
Phone: 928-635-2681   Fax: 928-635-8208
Website: fs.sed.us/r3/kai
Scope: Regional
Contact(s):
  Mike Williams, Director; 928-635-2681

UNITED STATES DEPARTMENT OF AGRICULTURE
FOREST SERVICE
KIOW / RITA BLANCA NATIONAL GRASSLAND
714 Main St.
Clayton, NM 88415 United States
Phone: 505-374-9652
Website: www.fs.fed.us/r3/cibloa
Scope: Regional

UNITED STATES DEPARTMENT OF AGRICULTURE
FOREST SERVICE
KISATCHIE NATIONAL FOREST
2500 Shreveport Hwy.
Pineville, LA 71360 United States
Phone: 318-473-7160   Fax: 318-473-7117
Scope: Regional

UNITED STATES DEPARTMENT OF AGRICULTURE
FOREST SERVICE
KLAMATH NATIONAL FOREST
1312 Fairlane Rd.
Eureka, CA 96097 United States
Phone: 530-842-6131   Fax: 530-841-4571
Website: r5.fs.fed.us
Scope: Regional

UNITED STATES DEPARTMENT OF AGRICULTURE
FOREST SERVICE
KOOTENAI NATIONAL FOREST
1101 Highway 2 W
Libby, MT 59923 United States
Phone: 406-293-6211   Fax: 406-283-7709
Scope: Regional

UNITED STATES DEPARTMENT OF AGRICULTURE
FOREST SERVICE
LAKE TAHOE BASIN MANAGEMENT UNIT
870 Emerald Bay Rd., Ste. 1
South Lake Tahoe, CA 96150 United States
Phone: 530-573-2600   Fax: 530-573-2780
Scope: Regional

UNITED STATES DEPARTMENT OF AGRICULTURE
FOREST SERVICE
LEWIS AND CLARK NATIONAL FOREST
Box 869, 1101 15th St., N.
Great Falls, MT 59403 United States
Phone: 406-791-7700   Fax: 406-731-5302
Scope: Regional

UNITED STATES DEPARTMENT OF AGRICULTURE
FOREST SERVICE
LINCOLN NATIONAL FOREST
Fed. Bldg., 1101 New York Ave.
Alamogordo, NM 88310-6992 United States
Phone: 505-434-7200
Scope: Regional

UNITED STATES DEPARTMENT OF AGRICULTURE
FOREST SERVICE
LITTLE MISSOURI NATIONAL FOREST, MCKENZIE RANGER DISTRICT
1901 S. Main Street
Watford City, ND 58854 United States
Phone: 701-842-2393
Scope: Regional
Contact(s):
Frank Guzman; 701-842-2393; fguzman@fs.fed.us

UNITED STATES DEPARTMENT OF AGRICULTURE
FOREST SERVICE
LITTLE MISSOURI NATIONAL GRASSLANDS, MEDORA RANGER DISTRICT
161 21st St. W.
Dickinson, ND 58601 United States
Phone: 701-225-5151
Website: www.fs.fed.us/r1/dakotaprairie
Scope: Regional

UNITED STATES DEPARTMENT OF AGRICULTURE
FOREST SERVICE
LOLO NATIONAL FOREST
Bldg. 24, Ft. Missoula
Missoula, MT 59801 United States
Phone: 406-329-3797
Scope: Regional

UNITED STATES DEPARTMENT OF AGRICULTURE
FOREST SERVICE
LOS PADRES NATIONAL FOREST
6755 Hollister Avenue
Suite 150
Goleta, CA 93117 United States
Phone: 805-968-6640
Website: www.fs.fed.us/r5/lospadres
Scope: Regional
Description: 1.75 million acre national forest in the central coastal mountains of California. Five ranger districts with offices in King City, Santa Maria, Santa Barbara, Ojai and Frazier Park, CA. Forest Supervisor's Office is in Goleta, CA. Forest consists of a wide variety of landscapes and habitats from coastal, to oak savannah and high elevation conifer forest, to arid badlands.
Keyword(s): Ecosystems (precious), Energy, Oceans/Coasts/Beaches, Recreation/Ecotourism, Water Habitats & Quality, Wildlife & Species
Contact(s):
Maeton Freel, Wildlife Biologist; 805-961-5764; mfreel@fs.fed.us
Jeff Saley, Human Resource/Volunteer Program Coordinator; 805-961-5771; jsaley@fs.fed.us
Rich Tobin, Director of Conservation Partnerships; 805-961-5748; rtobin@fs.fed.us

UNITED STATES DEPARTMENT OF AGRICULTURE
FOREST SERVICE
LYNDON B. JOHNSON / CADDO NATIONAL FOREST
1400 N. US. 81/287 Hwy., P.O. Box 507
Decatur, TX 76234 United States
Phone: 940-627-5475
Website: southernregion.fs.fed.us.fordtexas.com
Scope: Regional

Contact(s):
Tim Crooks; 940-627-5475; jcrooks@fs.fed.us

UNITED STATES DEPARTMENT OF AGRICULTURE
FOREST SERVICE
MALHEUR NATIONAL FOREST
431 Patterson Bridge Rd.
P.O. Box 909
John Day, OR 97845 United States
Phone: 541-575-1731
Website: www.fs.fed.us/r6/malheur
Scope: Regional

UNITED STATES DEPARTMENT OF AGRICULTURE
FOREST SERVICE
MANTI-LASAL NATIONAL FOREST
599 West Price River Dr.
Price, UT 84501 United States
Phone: 435-637-2817   Fax: 435-637-4940
Website: www.fs.fed.us/r4/mantilasal/
Scope: Regional

UNITED STATES DEPARTMENT OF AGRICULTURE
FOREST SERVICE
MARK TWAIN NATIONAL FOREST
410 Fairgrounds Rd.
Rolla, MO 65401 United States
Phone: 573-364-4621
Website: www.fs.fed.us/r9/marktwain/
Scope: Regional

UNITED STATES DEPARTMENT OF AGRICULTURE
FOREST SERVICE
MCCLELLAN CREEK/BLACK KETTLE NATIONAL GRASSLAND
Rt. 1, Box 55B
Cheyenne, OK 73628 United States
Phone: 580-497-2143
Website: www.fs.fed.us/r3/cibloa
Scope: Regional
Contact(s):
Bryan Hajny, Wildlife Biologist; 580-497-2143; bhajny@fs.fed.us

UNITED STATES DEPARTMENT OF AGRICULTURE
FOREST SERVICE
MEDICINE BOW-ROUTT NATIONAL FOREST
2468 Jackson St.
Laramie, WY 82070-6535 United States
Phone: 307-745-2300   Fax: 307-745-2398
Website: www.fs.fed.us/r2/mbr/
Scope: Regional

UNITED STATES DEPARTMENT OF AGRICULTURE
FOREST SERVICE
MENDOCINO NATIONAL FOREST
825 N. Humboldt Ave.
Willows, CA 95988 United States
Phone: 530-233-5811
Scope: Regional

U.S. FEDERAL AND INTERNATIONAL GOVERNMENT AGENCIES – U

UNITED STATES DEPARTMENT OF AGRICULTURE
FOREST SERVICE
MODOC NATIONAL FOREST
800 W. 12th St.
Alturas, CA 96101 United States
Phone: 530-233-5811   Fax: 530-233-8709
Scope: Regional

UNITED STATES DEPARTMENT OF AGRICULTURE
FOREST SERVICE
MONONGAHELA NATIONAL FOREST
USDA Bldg., 200 Sycamore St.
Elkins, WV 26241-3962 United States
Phone: 304-636-1800
Scope: Regional
Description: USDA Forest Service

UNITED STATES DEPARTMENT OF AGRICULTURE
FOREST SERVICE
MT. HOOD NATIONAL FOREST
2955 Division St.
Gresham, OR 97030 United States
Phone: 503-668-1700
Scope: Regional

UNITED STATES DEPARTMENT OF AGRICULTURE
FOREST SERVICE
NATIONAL FORESTS IN ALABAMA
2946 Chestnut St.
Montgomery, AL 36107 United States
Phone: 334-832-4470
Scope: Regional

UNITED STATES DEPARTMENT OF AGRICULTURE
FOREST SERVICE
NATIONAL FORESTS IN FLORIDA
325 John Knox Rd., Ste. F-100
Tallahassee, FL 32303 United States
Phone: 850-523-8500   Fax: 850-523-8543
Scope: State, Regional
Description: Manages the 3 national forests in Florida
Contact(s):
  Marsha Kearney, Forest Supervisor

UNITED STATES DEPARTMENT OF AGRICULTURE
FOREST SERVICE
NEBRASKA NATIONAL FOREST
125 N. Main St.
Chadron, NE 69337 United States
Phone: 308-432-0300
Scope: Regional

UNITED STATES DEPARTMENT OF AGRICULTURE
FOREST SERVICE
NEZ PERCE NATIONAL FOREST
Rt. 2, Box 475
Grangeville, ID 83530 United States
Phone: 208-983-1950   Fax: 208-983-4099
Website: www.fs.fed.us/r1/nezperce
Founded: 1906
Membership: 101–1,000
Scope: Regional
Description: USDA Forest Service Northern Region, Nez Perce National Forest, Forest Supervisor's Office
Keyword(s): Ecosystems (precious), Forests/Forestry, Land Issues, Public Lands/Greenspace, Recreation/Ecotourism, Water Habitats & Quality, Wildlife & Species
Contact(s):
  Laura Smith, Public Affairs Officer; 208-983-1950; ext. 4102; lasmith@fs.fed.us

UNITED STATES DEPARTMENT OF AGRICULTURE
FOREST SERVICE
NORTH CENTRAL RESEARCH STATION
1992 Folwell Ave.
St. Paul, MN 55108 United States
Phone: 651-649-5000   Fax: 651-649-5285
Website: www.ncrs.fs.fed.us
Scope: Local, State, Regional, National, International
Description: The Station, part of the Forest Service's Research & Development branch, employs 45 scientists and more than 200 technical and support people located in 7 Midwestern states. The Station strives to enhance the quality of people's lives by providing the knowledge and tools to help people make informed choices about natural resources. We supply the scientific and technical foundation for actions that ensure clean air, sparkling water, rich soil, healthy economies, and a diverse living landscape.
Contact(s):
  Linda Donoghue, Director

UNITED STATES DEPARTMENT OF AGRICULTURE
FOREST SERVICE
NORTHEASTERN RESEARCH STATION
100 Matsonford Rd., 5 Radnor Corporate Center, Suite 200
Radnor, PA 19087-4585 United States
Phone: 610-975-4017
Contact(s):
  Bob Eav, Director

UNITED STATES DEPARTMENT OF AGRICULTURE
FOREST SERVICE
OCHOCO NATIONAL FOREST
3160 N.E. 3rd Street
Prineville, OR 97754 United States
Phone: 541-416-6500   Fax: 541-416-6695
E-mail: bjensen01@fs.fed.us
Website: www.fs.fed.us/r6/centraloregon
Scope: Regional

UNITED STATES DEPARTMENT OF AGRICULTURE
FOREST SERVICE
OGLALA NATIONAL GRASSLAND
16524 Hwy. 385
Chadron, NE 69337 United States
Phone: 308-432-4475
Scope: Regional

UNITED STATES DEPARTMENT OF AGRICULTURE
FOREST SERVICE
OKANOGAN NATIONAL FOREST
1240 S. Second
Okanogan, WA 98840 United States
Phone: 509-826-3275
Scope: Regional

UNITED STATES DEPARTMENT OF AGRICULTURE
FOREST SERVICE
OLYMPIC NATIONAL FOREST
1835 Blacklake Blvd., SW
Olympia, WA 98512 United States
Phone: 360-956-2402
E-mail: Mailroom_R6_olympic@fs.fed.us
Scope: Regional

UNITED STATES DEPARTMENT OF AGRICULTURE
FOREST SERVICE
OTTAWA NATIONAL FOREST
E 6248 US Hwy. 2
Ironwood, MI 49938 United States
Phone: 906-932-1330   Fax: 906-932-0122
Scope: Regional

UNITED STATES DEPARTMENT OF AGRICULTURE
FOREST SERVICE
OUACHITA NATIONAL FOREST
Box 1270, Federal Bldg.
Hot Springs National Park, AR 71902 United States
Phone: 501-321-5202   Fax: 501-321-5353
Website: www.fs.fed.us/oonf/ouachita.htm
Founded: 1890
Scope: Regional
Contact(s):
  Maureen Hyzer, Deputy Supervisor; 501-321-5202

UNITED STATES DEPARTMENT OF AGRICULTURE
FOREST SERVICE
OZARK—ST. FRANCIS NATIONAL FOREST
605 West Main St.
Russellville, AR 72801 United States
Phone: 479-968-2354   Fax: 479-964-7255
E-mail: r8.ozark.forinfo@fs.fed.us
Website: www.fs.fed.us/oonf/ozark/index.html
Scope: Regional

UNITED STATES DEPARTMENT OF AGRICULTURE
FOREST SERVICE
PACIFIC NORTHWEST RESEARCH STATION
P.O. Box 3890
Portland, OR 97208 United States
Phone: 503-808-2592   Fax: 503-808-2130
E-mail: desmith@fs.fed.us
Website: www.fs.fed.us/pnw
Contact(s):
  Robert Szaro, Director; 503-808-2100

UNITED STATES DEPARTMENT OF AGRICULTURE
FOREST SERVICE
PACIFIC SOUTHWEST RESEARCH STATION
P.O. Box 245
Berkeley, CA 94701 United States
Phone: 510-559-6300   Fax: 510-559-6440
E-mail: psw_webmaster@fs.fed.us
Website: www.fs.fed.us/psw
Scope: National
Publication(s): See publications on website
Contact(s):
  Garland Mason, Director, Acting

UNITED STATES DEPARTMENT OF AGRICULTURE
FOREST SERVICE
PAWNEE NATIONAL GRASSLAND
660 O St.
Greeley, CO 80631 United States
Phone: 970-353-5004
Scope: Regional
Description: Responsible for the management of the 193,000 acre Pawnee National Grassland located in Northeast Colorado.
Keyword(s): Agriculture/Farming, Ecosystems (precious), Energy, Forests/Forestry, Land Issues, Public Lands/Greenspace, Recreation/Ecotourism, Water Habitats & Quality, Wildlife & Species
Contact(s):
  Steve Currey, Manager; 970-353-5004; scurrey@fs.fed.us
  Beth Humphrey, Wildlife Biologist; 970-346-5004; ehumphrey@fs.fed.us
  Maggie Marston, Range Staff; 970-346-5008; mmarston@fs.fed.us
  John Oppenlander, Minerals Staff; 970-346-5005; joppenlander@fs.fed.us

UNITED STATES DEPARTMENT OF AGRICULTURE
FOREST SERVICE
PAYETTE NATIONAL FOREST
Payette National Forest, Box 1026
P.O. Box 1026
McCall, ID 83638 United States
Phone: 208-634-0700
Scope: Regional

UNITED STATES DEPARTMENT OF AGRICULTURE
FOREST SERVICE
PIKE AND SAN ISABEL NATIONAL FORESTS
2840 Kachina Dr.
Pueblo, CO 81008 United States
Phone: 719-553-1400

UNITED STATES DEPARTMENT OF AGRICULTURE
FOREST SERVICE
PLUMAS NATIONAL FOREST
159 Lawrence St., Box 11500
Quincy, CA 95971 United States
Phone: 530-283-2050   Fax: 530-283-7746
Scope: Regional

UNITED STATES DEPARTMENT OF AGRICULTURE
FOREST SERVICE
PRESCOTT NATIONAL FOREST
344 S. Cortez Street
Prescott, AZ 86303 United States
Phone: 928-443-8000   Fax: 928-443-8008
Website: www.fs.fed.us/r3/prescott
Founded: 1898
Scope: Regional
Description: The Prescott National Forest lies in west Central Arizona. Total acreage is approximately 1.25 million acres. At the lowest elevation, the vegetation is of the Sonoran Desert type. As the elevation rises, chaparral becomes common, followed by pinon pine and juniper. Above that, ponderosa pine dominates. The forest offers many activities including hiking, mountain biking, camping, wildlife viewing, OHV use, hunting and fishing to name just a few.
Keyword(s): Forests/Forestry

UNITED STATES DEPARTMENT OF AGRICULTURE
FOREST SERVICE
REGION 01 (NORTHERN)
200 E. Broadway, P.O. Box 7669
Missoula, MT 59807 United States
Phone: 406-329-3316 Fax: 406-329-3411
Website: www.fs.fed.us/r1
Founded: 1905
Scope: National
Description: Land Management Agency
Contact(s):
   Brad Powell, Regional Forester

UNITED STATES DEPARTMENT OF AGRICULTURE
FOREST SERVICE
REGION 02 (ROCKY MOUNTAIN)
P.O. Box 25127
Lakewood, CO 80225 United States
Phone: 303-275-5450
Website: www.fs.fed.us/r2
Membership: 101–1,000
Scope: Regional
Contact(s):
   Rick Cables, Regional Forester

UNITED STATES DEPARTMENT OF AGRICULTURE
FOREST SERVICE
REGION 03 (SOUTHWESTERN)
333 Broadway S.E.
Albuquerque, NM 87102 United States
Phone: 505-842-3300 Fax: 505-842-3110
Website: www.fs.fed.us/r3
Contact(s):
   Eleanor Towns, Regional Forester

UNITED STATES DEPARTMENT OF AGRICULTURE
FOREST SERVICE
REGION 04 (INTERMOUNTAIN)
Federal Office Bldg. 324, 25th St.
Ogden, UT 84401 United States
Phone: 801-625-5605 Fax: 801-625-5359
Website: www.fs.fed.us/r4
Scope: Regional
Contact(s):
   Jack Troyer, Regional Forester
   Glenna Prevado, Assistant

UNITED STATES DEPARTMENT OF AGRICULTURE
FOREST SERVICE
REGION 05 (PACIFIC SOUTHWEST)
Mare Island, 1323 Club Dr.
Vallejo, CA 94592 United States
Phone: 707-562-9000
Website: www.fs.fed.us/r5
Scope: State
Description: The Pacific Southwest Region of the USDA Forest Service manages 18 National Forests, covering over 20 million acres, in California.
Contact(s):
   Bradley Powell, Regional Forester

UNITED STATES DEPARTMENT OF AGRICULTURE
FOREST SERVICE
REGION 06 (PACIFIC NORTHWEST)
333 SW 1st Ave.
Portland, OR 97208 United States
Phone: 503-808-2200
Website: www.fs.fed.us/r6
Scope: Regional
Contact(s):
   Harvey Forsgren, Regional Forester

UNITED STATES DEPARTMENT OF AGRICULTURE
FOREST SERVICE
REGION 08 (SOUTHERN)
1720 Peachtree Rd., NW,
Atlanta, GA 30309 United States
Phone: 404-347-4178 Fax: 404-347-4821
Website: www.fs.fed.us/r8
Scope: Regional
Description: Oversees the care & management of 13.5 million acres of national forest (NF) lands in the Southeast. These NF treasures stretch across 13 southern states & PR. They offer a wide array of natural resources, recreation & outdoor opportunities. Charged with caring for the land & serving people, the Forest Service is one of the World's premier conservation organizations of natural resource and forestry professionals. The agency supports a number of cooperative forestry programs & incentives.
Contact(s):
   Robert Jacobs, Regional Forester; 1720 Peachtree Rd., Rm 760S, Atlanta, GA 30309; 404-347-4177; Fax: 404-347-4821
   Ken Arney, Deputy Regional Forester, State & Private Forestry; 404-347-4177; Fax: 404-347-4821
   Roberta Moltzen, Deputy Regional Forester, Natural Resources; 404-347-4177; Fax: 404-347-4821
   Robert Pierson, Deputy Regional Forester, Operations; 404-347-4177; Fax: 404-347-4821

UNITED STATES DEPARTMENT OF AGRICULTURE
FOREST SERVICE
REGION 09 (EASTERN)
310 W. Wisconsin Ave., Suite 580
Milwaukee, WI 53203 United States
Phone: 414-297-3600 Fax: 414-297-3778
Website: www.fs.fed.us/r9
Scope: State
Contact(s):
   Robert Jacobs, Regional Forester

UNITED STATES DEPARTMENT OF AGRICULTURE
FOREST SERVICE
REGION 10 (ALASKA)
P.O. Box 21628
709 W. 9th St.
Juneau, AK 99802-1628 United States
Phone: 907-586-8863 Fax: 907-586-7840
Website: www.fs.fed.us/r10
Scope: Regional
Contact(s):
   Paul Forward, Acting Regional Forester

UNITED STATES DEPARTMENT OF AGRICULTURE
FOREST SERVICE
RIO GRANDE NATIONAL FOREST
1803 West Highway 160
Monte Vista, CO 81144 United States
Phone: 719-852-5941
Scope: Regional

UNITED STATES DEPARTMENT OF AGRICULTURE
FOREST SERVICE
ROCKY MOUNTAIN RESEARCH STATION
2150 Centre Ave., Bldg. A
Suite 376
Ft. Collins, CO 80526-2098 United States
Phone: 970-295-5926   Fax: 970-295-5927
Website: www.fs.fed.us/rm
Membership: 101–1,000
Scope: Local, State, Regional, National, International
Description: The Rocky Mountain Research Station develops scientific information and technology to improve management, protection, and use of the forests and rangelands. Research is designed to meet the needs of National Forest managers, Federal and State agencies, public and private organizations, academic institutes, industry, and individuals.
Keyword(s): Air Quality/Atmosphere, Climate Change, Ecosystems (precious), Forests/Forestry, Land Issues, Pollution (general), Public Lands/Greenspace, Recreation/ Ecotourism, Water Habitats & Quality, Wildlife & Species
Contact(s):
   Marcia Patton-Mallory, Director; 970-295-5925; Fax: 970-295-5927; mpattonmallory@fs.fed.us

UNITED STATES DEPARTMENT OF AGRICULTURE
FOREST SERVICE
ROGUE RIVER NATIONAL FOREST
Fed. Bldg., 333 W. 8th St., Box 520
Medford, OR 97501 United States
Phone: 541-776-3600
Scope: Regional

UNITED STATES DEPARTMENT OF AGRICULTURE
FOREST SERVICE
ROUTT NATIONAL FOREST
925 Wiess Dr.
Steamboat Springs, CO 80487-9550 United States
Phone: 970-879-1870
Scope: Local

UNITED STATES DEPARTMENT OF AGRICULTURE
FOREST SERVICE
SALMON-CHALLIS NATIONAL FOREST
50 Highway 93 South
Salmon, ID 83467 United States
Phone: 208-756-5100
Scope: Regional

UNITED STATES DEPARTMENT OF AGRICULTURE
FOREST SERVICE
SAN BERNARDINO NATIONAL FOREST
1824 S. Commercenter Cir.
San Bernardino, CA 92408 United States
Phone: 909-383-5588   Fax: 909-383-5770
Scope: Regional

UNITED STATES DEPARTMENT OF AGRICULTURE
FOREST SERVICE
SAN JUAN NATIONAL FOREST
San Juan Public Land Center
Federal Bldg., 15 Burnett Court
Durango, CO 81301-3647 United States
Phone: 970-247-4874
Scope: Regional

UNITED STATES DEPARTMENT OF AGRICULTURE
FOREST SERVICE
SANTA FE NATIONAL FOREST
1220 St. Francis Dr.
Santa Fe, NM 87504 United States
Phone: 505-438-7834   Fax: 505-438-7834
Website: www.fs.fed.us/r3/sfe/
Scope: Regional

UNITED STATES DEPARTMENT OF AGRICULTURE
FOREST SERVICE
SAWTOOTH NATIONAL FOREST
2647 Kimberly Rd., East
Twin Falls, ID 83301-7976 United States
Phone: 208-737-3200   Fax: 208-737-3236
Scope: Regional

UNITED STATES DEPARTMENT OF AGRICULTURE
FOREST SERVICE
SEQUOIA NATIONAL FOREST
900 W. Grand Ave.
Porterville, CA 93257 United States
Phone: 559-784-1500   Fax: 559-781-4744
Scope: Regional

UNITED STATES DEPARTMENT OF AGRICULTURE
FOREST SERVICE
SHASTA-TRINITY NATIONAL FOREST
2400 Washington Ave.
Redding, CA 96001 United States
Phone: 530-244-2978   Fax: 530-242-2233
Scope: Local
Description: Federal Agency managing the Shasta-Trinity National Forest

UNITED STATES DEPARTMENT OF AGRICULTURE
FOREST SERVICE
SHAWNEE NATIONAL FOREST
50 Hwy. 145 South
Harrisburg, IL 62946 United States
Phone: 618-253-7114   Fax: 618-253-1060
E-mail: mailroom_r9_shawnee@fs.fed.us
Website: www.fs.fed.us/r9/shawnee/
Founded: 1933
Scope: Regional

UNITED STATES DEPARTMENT OF AGRICULTURE
FOREST SERVICE
SHOSHONE NATIONAL FOREST
808 Meadow Ln.
Cody, WY 82414-4516 United States
Phone: 307-527-6241   Fax: 307-578-1212
Website: www.fs.fed.us/r2/shoshone/

Scope: Regional
Contact(s):
  Rebecca Aus, Manager; 307-527-6241; raus@fs.fed.us

UNITED STATES DEPARTMENT OF AGRICULTURE
FOREST SERVICE
SIERRA NATIONAL FOREST
1600 Tollhouse Rd.
Clovis, CA 93611 United States
Phone: 559-297-0706, ext. 4800   Fax: 559-294-4809
Scope: Regional

UNITED STATES DEPARTMENT OF AGRICULTURE
FOREST SERVICE
SISKIYOU NATIONAL FOREST
Box 440
Grants Pass, OR 97528 United States
Phone: 541-471-6500
Website: www.fs.fed.us/r6/siskiyou
Scope: Regional

UNITED STATES DEPARTMENT OF AGRICULTURE
FOREST SERVICE
SIUSLAW NATIONAL FOREST
P.O. Box 1148
Corvallis, OR 97339 United States
Phone: 541-750-7000   Fax: 541-750-7234
Website: www.fs.fed.us/r6/siuslaw
Scope: Regional
Keyword(s): Agriculture/Farming, Air Quality/Atmosphere, Ecosystems (precious), Forests/Forestry, Land Issues, Oceans/Coasts/Beaches, Recreation/Ecotourism, Water Habitats & Quality, Wildlife & Species

UNITED STATES DEPARTMENT OF AGRICULTURE
FOREST SERVICE
SIX RIVERS NATIONAL FOREST
1330 Bayshore Way
Eureka, CA 95501 United States
Phone: 707-442-1721
Website: www.fs.fed.us/r5/sixrivers
Scope: Regional

UNITED STATES DEPARTMENT OF AGRICULTURE
FOREST SERVICE
SOUTHERN RESEARCH STATION
P.O. Box 2750
160 A Zillicoa St.
Asheville, NC 28802 United States
Phone: 828-257-4200   Fax: 828-257-4263
E-mail: mailroom_r8_north_carolina@fs.fed.us
Website: www.cs.unca.edu/nfsnc
Scope: State
Contact(s):
  Rob McClanahan, Forest Wildlife Biologist

UNITED STATES DEPARTMENT OF AGRICULTURE
FOREST SERVICE
STANISLAUS NATIONAL FOREST
19777 Greenley Rd.
Sonora, CA 95370 United States
Phone: 209-532-3671   Fax: 209-533-1890
Website: www.fs.fed.us/r5/stanislaus
Scope: Regional

UNITED STATES DEPARTMENT OF AGRICULTURE
FOREST SERVICE
SUPERIOR NATIONAL FOREST
8901 Grand Avenue Place
Duluth, MN 55808-1102 United States
Phone: 218-626-4300
Website: www.superiornationalforest.org
Scope: Regional

UNITED STATES DEPARTMENT OF AGRICULTURE
FOREST SERVICE
TAHOE NATIONAL FOREST
631 Coyote St.
Nevada City, CA 95959-6003 United States
Phone: 530-265-4531   Fax: 530-478-6109
Website: www.fs.fed.us/r5/tahoe
Scope: Regional

UNITED STATES DEPARTMENT OF AGRICULTURE
FOREST SERVICE
THUNDER BASIN NATIONAL GRASSLANDS
2250 East Richards
Douglas, WY 82633 United States
Phone: 307-358-4690
Website: www.fs.fed.us/r2/mbr
Scope: Regional
Contact(s):
  Norman Wagoner, District Ranger; 307-358-4690

UNITED STATES DEPARTMENT OF AGRICULTURE
FOREST SERVICE
TONGASS NATIONAL FOREST
SITKA OFFICE
204 Siginaka Way
Sitka, AK 99835-7316 United States
Phone: 907-747-6671   Fax: 907-747-4331
Website: www.fs.fed.us/r10/tongass/
Scope: Regional
Description: Manages land and resources of the Tongass National Forest

UNITED STATES DEPARTMENT OF AGRICULTURE
FOREST SERVICE
TONGASS-KETCHIKAN AREA NATIONAL FOREST
Federal Bldg.
648 Mission St.
Ketchikan, AK 99901-6591 United States
Phone: 907-225-3101   Fax: 907-228-6215
E-mail: mjjones@fs.fed.us
Website: www.fs.fed.us/r10/tongass
Scope: Regional

UNITED STATES DEPARTMENT OF AGRICULTURE
FOREST SERVICE
TONGASS-PETERSBURG OFFICE NATIONAL FOREST
Box 309
15 North 12th
Petersburg, AK 99833-0309 United States
Phone: 907-772-3841   Fax: 907-772-5895
E-mail: mjjones@fs.fed.us
Website: www.fs.fed.us/r10/tongass/
Scope: Regional
Description: Land and resource management agency

UNITED STATES DEPARTMENT OF AGRICULTURE
FOREST SERVICE
TONTO NATIONAL FOREST
2324 E. McDowell Rd.
Phoenix, AZ 85006 United States
Phone: 602-225-5200   Fax: 602-225-5295
Scope: Regional

UNITED STATES DEPARTMENT OF AGRICULTURE
FOREST SERVICE
UINTA NATIONAL FOREST
88 West 100 North
Provo, UT 84601 United States
Phone: 801-342-5100
E-mail: %20abauer01@fs.fed.us
Website: www.fs.fed.us/r4/uinta
Scope: Regional
Contact(s):
   Peter Karp, Manager; 801-342-5100; peterkarp@fs.fed.us

UNITED STATES DEPARTMENT OF AGRICULTURE
FOREST SERVICE
UMATILLA NATIONAL FOREST
2517 SW Hailey Ave.
Pendleton, OR 97801 United States
Phone: 541-278-3716
Website: www.fs.fed.us/r6/uma
Scope: Regional

UNITED STATES DEPARTMENT OF AGRICULTURE
FOREST SERVICE
UMPQUA NATIONAL FOREST
2900 Stewart Parkway
Roseburg, OR 97470 United States
Phone: 541-672-6601   Fax: 541-957-3495
Website: www.or.blm.gov/roseburg
Scope: Regional

UNITED STATES DEPARTMENT OF AGRICULTURE
FOREST SERVICE
WALLOWA WHITMAN NATIONAL FORESTS
Box 907/1550 Dewey
Baker City, OR 97814 United States
Phone: 541-523-6391
Website: www.fs.fed.us/r6/w-w
Scope: Regional

UNITED STATES DEPARTMENT OF AGRICULTURE
FOREST SERVICE
WASATCH-CACHE NATIONAL FOREST
8236 Federal Bldg., 125 S. State St.
Salt Lake City, UT 84138 United States
Phone: 801-524-3900
E-mail: %20kfcoleman@fs.fed.us
Website: www.fs.fed.us/wcnf
Scope: Regional

UNITED STATES DEPARTMENT OF AGRICULTURE
FOREST SERVICE
WAYNE NATIONAL FOREST
13700 U.S. Highway 33
Nelsonville, OH 45764-9552 United States
Phone: 740-753-0101   Fax: 740-753-0118
Scope: Regional

UNITED STATES DEPARTMENT OF AGRICULTURE
FOREST SERVICE
WENATCHEE NATIONAL FOREST
215 Melody Lane
Wenatchee, WA 98801 United States
Phone: 509-662-4335   Fax: 509-662-4368
Website: www.fs.fed.us/r6/wenatchee/
Scope: Regional

UNITED STATES DEPARTMENT OF AGRICULTURE
FOREST SERVICE
WHITE MOUNTAIN NATIONAL FOREST
719 North Main Street
Laconia, NH 03241 United States
Phone: 603-528-8721   Fax: 603-528-8722
Website: www.fs.fed.us/r9/white
Scope: Regional

UNITED STATES DEPARTMENT OF AGRICULTURE
FOREST SERVICE
WHITE RIVER NATIONAL FOREST
Old Federal Bldg., P.O. Box 948
Glenwood Springs, CO 81602 United States
Phone: 970-945-2521   Fax: 970-945-3266
Scope: Regional

UNITED STATES DEPARTMENT OF AGRICULTURE
FOREST SERVICE
WILLAMETTE NATIONAL FOREST
Box 10607
Eugene, OR 97440 United States
Phone: 541-465-6521   Fax: 541-225-6222
Website: www.fs.fed.us/r6/willamette
Scope: Regional

UNITED STATES DEPARTMENT OF AGRICULTURE
FOREST SERVICE
WINEMA NATIONAL FOREST
2819 Dahlia
Klamath Falls, OR 97601 United States
Phone: 541-883-6714   Fax: 541-883-6709
Website: www.fs.fed.us/r6/winema
Scope: Regional

UNITED STATES DEPARTMENT OF AGRICULTURE
NATURAL RESOURCES CONSERVATION SERVICE
USDA-NRCS
1400 Independence Ave. SW
P.O. Box 2890
Washington, DC 20013 United States
Phone: 202-720-3210   Fax: 202-720-1564
Website: www.nrcs.usda.gov
Founded: 1935
Scope: National
Description: (formerly Soil Conservation Service) NRCS provides leadership in a partnership effort to help people conserve, maintain, and improve our natural resources and environment. NRCS is the technical delivery arm for conservation of the United States Department of Agriculture. It provides technical assistance and conservation programs through a unique

U.S. FEDERAL AND INTERNATIONAL GOVERNMENT AGENCIES – U

partnership with America's conservation districts, state agencies and others.

Contact(s):

Terry Bish, Director, Conservation Communications Staff; Room 6121-S, Washington, DC 20013

Renae Anderson, WI Public Affairs Specialist; 6515 Watts Rd., Suite 200, Madison, WI 53719-2726; 608-276-8732; Fax: 608-276-5890; randerso@wi.nrcs.usda.gov

Nancy Atkinson, WY Public Affairs Specialist; Federal Office Bldg., 100 East B St., Room 3124, Casper, WY 82601; 307-261-6482; Fax: 307-261-6490; nla@wy.nrcs.usda.gov

Petra Barnes, CO Public Affairs Specialist; 655 Parfet St., Rm. E 200C, Lakewood, CO 80215-5517; 303-236-2886; ext. 216; Fax: 303-236-2896; pbarnes@co.nrcs.usda.gov

Lynn Betts, IA Public Affairs Specialist; 693 Federal Bldg., 210 Walnut St., Des Moines, IA 50309-2180; 515-284-4262; Fax: 515-284-4394; lynn.betts@ia.nrcs.usda.gov

Chris Bieker, WA Public Affairs Specialist; Rock Pointe Tower 2, Suite 150, West 316 Boone Ave., Spokane, WA 99201-2348; 509-323-2912; Fax: 509-323-2909; cbieker@wa.nrcs.usda.gov

Larry Blick, TN Public Affairs Specialist; 675 U.S. Courthouse, 801 Broadway St., Nashville, TN 37203-3878; 615-736-5490; Fax: 615-736-7764; lblick@tn.nrcs.usda.gov

Herb Bourque, LA Public Affairs Specialist; 3737 Government St., Alexandria, LA 71302-3727; 318-473-7762; Fax: 318-473-7682; hbourque@laso2.la.nrcs.usda.gov

Anita Brown, CA Public Affairs Specialist; 2121-C 2nd St., Suite 102, Davis, CA 95616-5475; 530-792-5644; Fax: 530-792-5791; anita.brown@ca.usda.gov

Harold Bryant, TX Public Affairs Specialist; W.R. Poage Federal Bldg., 101 S. Main St., Temple, TX 76501-7682; 254-742-9811; Fax: 254-742-9819; hbryant@tx.nrcs.usda.gov

Paige Buck, IL Public Affairs Specialist; 1902 Fox Dr., Champaign, IL 61820-7335; 217-398-5273; Fax: 217-398-5310; paige.mitchell@il.nrcs.usda.gov

Kathy Carpenter, NY Public Affairs Specialist; 441 S. Salina Street, Suite 354, Syracuse, NY 13202; 315-477-6524; kathy.carpenter@ny.nrcs.usda.gov

Sonja Coderre, AR Public Affairs Specialist; Federal Office Bldg., Rm. 5404, 700 W. Capitol Ave., Little Rock, AR 72201-3228; 501-301-3133; Fax: 501-301-3189; scoderre@ar.usda.gov

Jeanne Comerford, RI Public Affairs Specialist; 60 Quaker Ln., Suite 46, Warwick, RI 02886-0111; 401-828-1300; Fax: 401-828-0433; jcomerford@ri.nrcs.usda.gov

Christina Coulon, MI Public Affairs Specialist; 1405 S. Harrison Rd., Rm. 101, East Lansing, MI 48823-5243; 517-337-6701; Fax: 517-337-0905; ccoulon@miso.mi.nrcs.usda.gov

Arlene Deutscher, ND Public Affairs Specialist; Federal Bldg., 220 E. Rosser Ave., Rm. 278, 220 E. Rosser Ave., Bismarck, ND 58502-1458; 701-250-4768; Fax: 701-250-4778; ajd@nd.nrcs.usda.gov

Carol Donzella, CT Public Affairs Specialist; 344 Merrow Rd., Tolland, CT 06084; 203-787-0390; caroldonzella@ct.usda.gov

Becky Fraticelli, Puerto Rico Public Affairs Specialist; IBM Bldg., 6th Flr., 654 Munoz Rivera Ave., Hato Rey, PR 00918-7013; 787-766-5206; ext. 236; Fax: 787-766-5987; becky@pr.nrcs.usda.gov

Joyce Hawkins, Program Assistant; Room 6121-S, Washington, DC 20013; 202-720-3210; Fax: 202-720-1564; joyce.hawkins@usda.gov

Anne Hillard, VT Public Affairs Specialist; 69 Union St., Winooski, VT 05404-1999; 802-951-6796; Fax: 802-951-6327; ahillard@vt.nrcs.usda.gov

Carol Hollingsworth, MD Public Affairs Specialist; John Hanson Business Center, 339 Busch's Frontage Rd., Suite 30, Annapolis, MD 21401-5534; 410-757-0861; ext. 313; Fax: 410-757-0687; carol.hollingsworth@md.usda.gov

Lynn Howell, HI Public Affairs Specialist; 300 Ala Moana Blvd., Rm. 4316, Honolulu, HI 96850-0002; 808-541-2600; Fax: 808-541-2652; lhowell@hi.nrcs.usda.gov

Lois Jackson, KY Public Affairs Specialist; 771 Corporate Dr., Suite 110, Lexington, KY 40503-5479; 606-224-7372; Fax: 606-224-7399; ljackson@kystate.ky.nrcs.usda.gov

Betty Joubert, NM Public Affairs Specialist; 6200 Jefferson St., NE, Suite 305, Albuquerque, NM 87109-3734; 505-761-4406; Fax: 505-761-4463; betty.joubert@nm.nrcs.usda.gov

Norm Klopfenstein, MO Public Affairs Specialist; Parkade Center, Suite 250, 601 Business Loop, 70 West, Columbia, MO 65203-2546; 573-876-0911; Fax: 573-876-0913; normk@mo.nrcs.usda.gov

Wendi Kroll, MA Public Affairs Specialist; 451 West St., Amherst, MA 01002-2995; 413-253-4351; Fax: 413-253-4375; wkroll@ma.nrcs.usda.gov

Irene Lieberman, NJ Public Affairs Specialist; 1370 Hamilton St., Somerset, NJ 08873-3157; 732-246-1171, ext. 124; Fax: 732-246-2358; ilieberman@nj.nrcs.usda.gov

Jeanine May, MS Public Affairs Specialist; Federal Bldg., Suite 1321, 100 W. Capitol St., Jackson, MS 39269-1399; 601-965-4337; Fax: 601-965-4536; jbm@ms.nrcs.usda.gov

Michael McGovern, IN Public Affairs Specialist; 6013 Lakeside Blvd., Indianapolis, IN 46278-2933; 317-290-3222; ext. 324; Fax: 317-290-3225; mmcgover@in.nrcs.usda.gov

Pat McGrane, NE Public Affairs Specialist; Federal Bldg., Rm. 152, 100 Centennial Mall, N., Lincoln, NE 68508-3866, 402-437-5328; Fax: 402-437-5327; pat.mcgrane@ne.usda.gov

Mary McQuinn, AZ Public Affairs Specialist; 3003 N. Central Ave., Suite 800, Phoenix, AZ 85012-2945; 602-280-8778; Fax: 602-280-8809; mmcquinn@az.nrcs.usda.gov

Stacy Mitchell, PA Public Affairs Specialist; One Credit Union Pl., Suite 340, Harrisburg, PA 17110-2993; 717-237-2208; Fax: 717-237-2238; smitchell@pa.nrcs.usda.gov

Laura Morton, NH Public Affairs Specialist; Federal Bldg. 2 Madbury Rd., Durham, NH 03824; 732-246-1171

Marie Mundheim, Pacific Basin Public Affairs Specialist; 671-472-7490; ext. 21; Fax: 671-472-7298; pacbas@ite.net

Gayle Norman, OR Public Affairs Specialist; 101 SW Main Street, Suite 1300, Portland, OR 97204-3221; 503-414-3236; Fax: 503-414-3101; gnorman@or.nrcs.usda.gov

Sharon Norris, ID Public Affairs Specialist; 3244 Elder St., Room 124, Boise, ID 83705-4711; 208-378-5725; Fax: 208-378-5735; snorris@id.nrcs.usda.gov

Pat Paul, VA Public Affairs Specialist; Culpeper Bldg., 1606 Santa Rosa Rd., Suite 209, Richmond, VA 23229-5014; 804-287-1681; Fax: 804-287-1737; ppaul@va.nrcs.usda.gov

Paul Petrichenko, DE Public Affairs Specialist; 1203 College Park Dr., Suite 101, Dover, DE 19904-8713; 302-678-4178; Fax: 302-678-0843; ppetrichencko@de.nrcs.usda.gov

Dwain Phillips, OK Public Affairs Specialist; 100 USDA Agriculture Center Bldg., Suite 203, Stillwater, OK 74074-2624; 405-742-1243, Fax: 405-742-1201; dwain.phillip@ok.usda.gov

Sylvia Rainford, MN Public Affairs Specialist; 600 Farm Credit Services Bldg., 375 Jackson St., St. Paul, MN 55101-1854; 612-602-7859; Fax: 612-602-7914; str@mn.nrcs.usda.gov

Peg Reese, WV Public Affairs Specialist; 75 High St., Rm. 301, Morgantown, WV 26505; 304-291-4152; ext. 168; Fax: 304-291-4628; preese@wv.nrcs.usda.gov

Mary Schaffer, KS Public Affairs Specialist; 760 S. Broadway, Salina, KS 67401; 785-823-4571; Fax: 785-823-4540; mary.shaffer@ks.nrcs.usda.gov

Andrew Smith, NC Public Affairs Specialist; 4405 Bland Rd., Suite 205, Raleigh, NC 27609-6293; 919-873-2107; Fax: 919-873-2156; asmith@nc.nrcs.usda.gov

Dorothy Staley, FL Public Affairs Specialist; 2614 NW 43rd St., Gainesville, FL 32606-6611; 352-338-9565; Fax: 352-338-9574; dstaley@fl.nrcs.usda.gov

Elaine Tremble, ME Public Affairs Specialist; 5 Godfrey Dr.,

Orono, ME 04473; 207-866-7241; Fax: 207-866-7262; etremble@me.nrcs.usda.gov

Lori Valdez, MT Public Affairs Specialist; Federal Bldg., Rm. 443, 10 E. Babcock St., Bozeman, MT 59715-4704; 406-587-6842; Fax: 406-587-6761; lvaldez@mt.nrcs.usda.gov

Liz Warner, NV Public Affairs Specialist; 5301 Langley Ln., Bldg. F, Suite 201, Reno, NV 89511; 775-784-5288; Fax: 702-784-5939; ewarner@nv.nrcs.usda.gov

Joyce Watkins, SD Public Affairs Specialist; 200 4th St., SW, Federal Bldg., Huron, SD 57350-2475; 605-352-1228; Fax: 605-352-1261; joyce.watkins@sdso1.sd.nrcs.usda.gov

UNITED STATES DEPARTMENT OF AGRICULTURE
RESEARCH EDUCATION AND ECONOMICS
1400 Independence Ave., SW Room 216-W
Washington, DC 20250-0110 United States
Phone: 202-720-5923 Fax: 202-690-2842
Website: www.usda.gov

Membership: 1–100
Scope: National
Contact(s):
Joseph Jen, Under Secretary

UNITED STATES DEPARTMENT OF AGRICULTURE
RESEARCH EDUCATION AND ECONOMICS
ARS BELTSVILLE AREA
10300 Baltimore, Rm. 223, B-003 BARC-West
Beltsville, MD 20705 United States
Phone: 301-504-6078 Fax: 301-504-5863
Website: www.ba.ars.usda.gov

Scope: National
Contact(s):
Phyllis Johnson, Area Director
Ronald Korcak, Associate Area Director

UNITED STATES DEPARTMENT OF AGRICULTURE
RESEARCH EDUCATION AND ECONOMICS
ARS MID SOUTH OFFICE
P.O. Box 225
Stoneville, MS 38776 United States
Phone: 662-686-5265 Fax: 662-686-5459
E-mail: atucker@ars.usda.gov
Website: www.ars.usda.gov

Membership: 101–1,000
Scope: Regional
Contact(s):
Edgar King, Area Director

UNITED STATES DEPARTMENT OF AGRICULTURE
RESEARCH EDUCATION AND ECONOMICS
ARS MIDWEST OFFICE
1815 N. University St.
Peoria, IL 61604 United States
Phone: 309-681-6602 Fax: 309-681-6684
Website: www.mva.arf.usda.gov

Membership: 1–100
Scope: Regional
Publication(s): Midwest Area Research Highlights 2000
Contact(s):
Adrianna Hewings, Area Director

UNITED STATES DEPARTMENT OF AGRICULTURE
RESEARCH EDUCATION AND ECONOMICS
ARS NORTH ATLANTIC OFFICE
600 E. Mermaid Ln.
Windmoor, PA 19038 United States
Phone: 215-233-6593 Fax: 215-233-6719
Website: naa.ars.usda.gov

Membership: 101–1,000
Scope: National
Contact(s):
Wilda Martinez, Area Director

UNITED STATES DEPARTMENT OF AGRICULTURE
RESEARCH EDUCATION AND ECONOMICS
ARS NORTHERN PLAINS AREA OFFICE
1201 Oakridge Dr.
Suite 150
Fort Collins, CO 80525-5562 United States
Phone: 970-229-5500 Fax: 970-229-5565
Website: www.npa.ars.usda.gov

Membership: 1–100
Scope: State, National
Description: Agricultural Research
Contact(s):
Wilbert Blackburn, Area Director

UNITED STATES DEPARTMENT OF AGRICULTURE
RESEARCH EDUCATION AND ECONOMICS
ARS PACIFIC WEST AREA
800 Buchanan St.
Albany, CA 94710 United States
Phone: 510-559-6060 Fax: 510-559-5779
E-mail: abetschart@pw.ars.usda.gov
Website: www.pwa.ars.usda.gov

Founded: 1890
Membership: 1,001–10,000
Scope: National, International
Description: The USDA ARS Pacific West Area consists of 52 Research Programs in the eight western states of AK, AR, CA, HI, ID, NV, OR and WA. Research is conducted by some 1400 employees at 25 centers. The $145 million budget is appropriated by the U.S.Congress. Research projects are issue-driven and the outcome of the research is directed to the customers and beneficiaries through technology transfer. Scientific excellence with impact is the hallmark of USDA ARS research in the Pacific West Area.
Contact(s):
A. Betschart, Area Director

UNITED STATES DEPARTMENT OF AGRICULTURE
RESEARCH EDUCATION AND ECONOMICS
ARS SOUTH ATLANTIC OFFICE
Russell Agr. Res. Center, P.O. Box 5677
College Station Rd.
Athens, GA 30604-5677 United States
Phone: 706-546-3311 Fax: 706-546-3398
Website: saa.ars.usda.gov

Contact(s):
Karl Narang, Area Director

UNITED STATES DEPARTMENT OF AGRICULTURE
RESEARCH EDUCATION AND ECONOMICS
ARS SOUTHERN PLAINS OFFICE
7607 Eastmark Dr., Suite 230
College Station, TX 77840 United States

U.S. FEDERAL AND INTERNATIONAL GOVERNMENT AGENCIES – U

UNITED STATES DEPARTMENT OF AGRICULTURE
RESEARCH EDUCATION AND ECONOMICS
COOPERATIVE STATE RESEARCH, EDUCATION, AND EXTENSION SERVICE
1400 Independence Ave., SW., 305A
Washington, DC 20250 United States
Phone: 202-720-7441   Fax: 202-720-8987
Website: www.reeusda.gov

Description: The Cooperative State Research, Education, and Extension Service links the research and education resources and programs of the U.S. Department of Agriculture and works with land-grant institutions in each state, territory, and the District of Columbia.

Contact(s):
George Cooper, Deputy Administrator for Partnerships; 202-720-5623; george.cooper@usda.gov
Jane Coulter, Deputy Administrator for Science and Education Resources Dev; 202-720-3377
Colien Hefferan, Administrator; 202-720-7441; colien.hefferan@usda.gov
Alma Hobbs, Deputy Administrator for Families 4-H and Nutrition; 202-720-2908; alma.hobbs@usda.gov
Sally Rockey, Deputy Administrator for Competitive Research Grants and Awa; 202-401-1761

UNITED STATES DEPARTMENT OF COMMERCE
Herbert C. Hoover Bldg., Rm. 5610, 14th St. and Constitution Ave., NW
Washington, DC 20230 United States
Phone: 202-219-3605   Fax: 202-482-5168
Website: www.doc.gov

Scope: International
Description: The Department of Commerce promotes job creation, economic growth, sustainable development, and improved living standards for all Americans, by working in partnership with business, universities, communities, and workers.

Contact(s):
Sam Bodman, Deputy Secretary
Donald Evans, Secretary; 202-482-4883

UNITED STATES DEPARTMENT OF COMMERCE
ECONOMIC DEVELOPMENT ADMINISTRATION
Department of Commerce
Herbert C. Hoover Bldg.
14th St. and Constitution Ave., NW
Washington, DC 20230 United States
Phone: 202-482-5081   Fax: 202-273-4701
E-mail: edawebmaster@eda.eoc.gov
Website: www.doc.gov/eda

Scope: National
Description: Conducts programs to help stimulate private enterprise and create permanent jobs in economically distressed areas of the Nation. Provides public works grants and planning and technical assistance in areas with high unemployment or low median family income.

Contact(s):
David Sampson, Assistant Secretary

UNITED STATES DEPARTMENT OF COMMERCE
NATIONAL OCEANIC AND ATMOSPHERIC ADMINISTRATION
Herbert C. Hoover Bldg., Rm. 5128
14th and Constitution Ave., NW
Washington, DC 20230 United States
Phone: 202-482-2636   Fax: 202-408-9674
Website: www.noaa.gov

Founded: 1970
Membership: 1–100
Scope: Regional
Description: NOAA was created within the Department of Commerce to promote global environmental stewardship and to describe and predict changes in the Earth's environment. NOAA conducts oceanic and atmospheric research; maintains environmental databases and disseminates environmental information products; manages living marine resources and the marine environment; and operates environmental satellites, ships, aircraft, and buoys.

Contact(s):
Scott Gudes, Deputy Under Secretary; 202-482-4569

UNITED STATES DEPARTMENT OF COMMERCE
NATIONAL OCEANIC AND ATMOSPHERIC ADMINISTRATION
ACE BASIN NATIONAL ESTUARINE RESEARCH RESERVE
South Carolina Department of Natural Resources, P.O. Box 12559
Charleston, SC 29412 United States
Phone: 803-762-5062   Fax: 803-762-5412
E-mail: Theresa.Eisenman@noaa.gov
Website: www.dnr.state.sc.us

Scope: Regional

UNITED STATES DEPARTMENT OF COMMERCE
NATIONAL OCEANIC AND ATMOSPHERIC ADMINISTRATION
APALACHICOLA NATIONAL ESTUARINE RESEARCH RESERVE
Department of Environmental Protection, 350 Carroll St.
Eastpoint, FL 32328 United States
Phone: 850-670-4783   Fax: 850-670-4324
Website: www.ocrm.nos.noaa.gov/nerr/reserves/nerrapalachicola.html

Scope: Regional

UNITED STATES DEPARTMENT OF COMMERCE
NATIONAL OCEANIC AND ATMOSPHERIC ADMINISTRATION
CHANNEL ISLANDS NATIONAL MARINE SANCTUARY
113 Harbor Way
Santa Barbara, CA 93109 United States
Phone: 805-966-7107   Fax: 805-568-1582
E-mail: channelislands@noaa.gov
Website: www.channelislands.noaa.gov

Founded: 1980
Scope: Regional

UNITED STATES DEPARTMENT OF COMMERCE
NATIONAL OCEANIC AND ATMOSPHERIC ADMINISTRATION
CHESAPEAKE BAY NATIONAL ESTUARINE RESEARCH RESERVE
MARYLAND OFFICE
Department of Natural Resources, Tawes State Office Bldg., E-2, 580 Taylor Ave.
Annapolis, MD 21401 United States
Phone: 410-260-8730   Fax: 410-260-8739
Website: www.dnr.state.md.us

Scope: Regional

UNITED STATES DEPARTMENT OF COMMERCE
NATIONAL OCEANIC AND ATMOSPHERIC ADMINISTRATION
CHESAPEAKE BAY NATIONAL ESTUARINE RESEARCH RESERVE
VIRGINIA OFFICE
Virginia Institute of Marine Science
P.O. Box 1346
Greate Road
Gloucester Point, VA 23062 United States
Phone: 804-684-7135   Fax: 804-684-7120
E-mail: cbnerr@vims.edu
Website: www.vims.edu/cbnerr

Founded: 1991
Scope: Local, State, Regional, National
Description: CBNERRVA strives to be a national leader in demonstrating how science, education and coastal resource stewardship can solve coastal management problems and improve the awareness and understanding of estuaries. Our Reserve system located along the York River estuary is a key resource that supports all aspects of Reserve activities. Reserve components include Sweet Hall Marsh, Taskinas Creek, Catlett Island, and Goodwin Islands.
Keyword(s): Ecosystems (precious), Oceans/Coasts/Beaches, Water Habitats & Quality

UNITED STATES DEPARTMENT OF COMMERCE
NATIONAL OCEANIC AND ATMOSPHERIC ADMINISTRATION
CORDELL BANK NATIONAL MARINE SANCTUARY
P.O. Box 159
Olema, CA 94950 United States
Phone: 415-663-0314   Fax: 415-663-0315
E-mail: cordellbank@noaa.gov
Website: www.sanctuaries.nos.noaa.gov/oms/omscordell/omscordellvisit.html

Founded: 1989
Scope: Regional
Description: Cordell Bank National Marine Sanctuary is one of 13 National Marine Sanctuaries in the United States and 1 of 4 sanctuaries in California. Cordell Bank is an underwater rocky reef environment offshore of Point Reyes, CA. The habitat is a destination feeding ground for highly migratory marine mammals and seabirds, as well as being a lush feeding ground for resident fish and inverterbrates. The Sanctuary conducts research to gain a better understanding of this unique offshore ecosystem.

UNITED STATES DEPARTMENT OF COMMERCE
NATIONAL OCEANIC AND ATMOSPHERIC ADMINISTRATION
DELAWARE NATIONAL ESTUARINE RESEARCH RESERVE
818 Kitts Hummock Rd.
Dover, DE 19011 United States
Phone: 302-739-3436   Fax: 302-739-3446
Website: www.dnrec.state.de.us/DNREC2000/Divisions/Soil/DNERR

Founded: 1993
Scope: Local, State, Regional, National, International
Description: The DNERR's mission is to preserve and manage the natural resources within the Reserve as a place for research, to provide education and outreach programs that promote better understanding of Delaware's estuarine and coastal areas, and to promote informed coastal decision-making.
Keyword(s): Ecosystems (precious), Land Issues, Oceans/Coasts/Beaches, Public Lands/Greenspace, Recreation/Ecotourism, Sprawl/Urban Planning, Water Habitats & Quality, Wildlife & Species

Contact(s):
Mark Del Vecchio, Reserve Manager; 302-739-3436, ext. 11; Fax: 302-739-3446; mark.delvecchio@state.de.us
Katy Lamborn, Education Coordinator; 302-739-3436, ext. 20; Fax: 302-739-3446; katy.lamborn@state.de.us
Robert Scarborough, Research Coordinator; 302-739-3436; ext. 14; Fax: 302-739-3446; bob.scarborough@state.de.us

UNITED STATES DEPARTMENT OF COMMERCE
NATIONAL OCEANIC AND ATMOSPHERIC ADMINISTRATION
FLORIDA KEYS NATIONAL MARINE SANCTUARY
P.O. Box 500368, 5550 Overseas Hwy.
Marathon, FL 33050 United States
Phone: 305-743-2437   Fax: 305-743-2357
E-mail: floridakeys@noaa.gov
Website: www.fknms.nos.noaa.gov/

Scope: Regional

UNITED STATES DEPARTMENT OF COMMERCE
NATIONAL OCEANIC AND ATMOSPHERIC ADMINISTRATION
FLOWER GARDEN BANKS NATIONAL MARINE SANCTUARY
1200 Briarcrest, Suite 4000
Bryan, TX 77802 United States
Phone: 979-846-5942   Fax: 979-846-5959
E-mail: flowergarden@noaa.gov
Website: www.flowergarden.nos.noaa.gov

Founded: 1992
Scope: Regional
Description: Mission is to serve as trustee for the Flower Garden Banks National Marine Sanctuary in conserving, protecting, and enhancing the marine biodiversity, ecological integrity and cultural legacy.
Publication(s): 100 Common Fishes
Keyword(s): Ecosystems (precious), Oceans/Coasts/Beaches

UNITED STATES DEPARTMENT OF COMMERCE
NATIONAL OCEANIC AND ATMOSPHERIC ADMINISTRATION
GRAY'S REEF NATIONAL MARINE SANCTUARY
10 Ocean Science Cir.
Savannah, GA 31411 United States
Phone: 912-598-2345
Website: www.graysreef.nos.noaa.gov

Founded: 1981
Scope: Local, State, Regional, National, International
Description: Marine protected area
Keyword(s): Ecosystems (precious), Oceans/Coasts/Beaches, Water Habitats & Quality, Wildlife & Species

UNITED STATES DEPARTMENT OF COMMERCE
NATIONAL OCEANIC AND ATMOSPHERIC ADMINISTRATION
GREAT BAY NATIONAL ESTUARINE RESEARCH RESERVE
Department of Fish and Game, 225 Main St
Durham, NH 03824 United States
Phone: 603-868-1095   Fax: 603-868-3305
E-mail: rmjohnston@starband.net

Scope: Regional

UNITED STATES DEPARTMENT OF COMMERCE
NATIONAL OCEANIC AND ATMOSPHERIC ADMINISTRATION
GULF OF FARALLONES NATIONAL MARINE SANCTUARY
Fort Mason Building 201
San Francisco, CA 94123 United States

Phone: 415-561-6622   Fax: 415-561-6616
E-mail: farallones@noaa.gov
Website: farallones.nos.noaa.gov
Founded: 1981
Scope: Regional, National
Description: The Gulf of the Farallones National Marine Sanctuary was designated to protect the unique marine wildlife and habitats off the California coast west of San Francisco. The Sanctuary encompasses 948 square nautical miles of open ocean and the nearshore waters of Bodega Bay, Tomales Bay, Estero Americano, Estero de San Antonio, and Bolinas Lagoon. National Marine Sanctuaries are administered by the National Oceanic and Atmospheric Administration (NOAA).
Publication(s): Beyond the Golden Gate, Hydrosphere
Keyword(s): Ecosystems (precious), Oceans/Coasts/Beaches, Recreation/Ecotourism, Water Habitats & Quality, Wildlife & Species
Contact(s):
Edward Ueber, Sanctuary Manager; 415-561-6622
Mary Jane Schramm, Public Information Officer; 415-561-6622; ext. 205; Fax: 415-561-6616; maryjane.schramm@noaa.gov

UNITED STATES DEPARTMENT OF COMMERCE
NATIONAL OCEANIC AND ATMOSPHERIC ADMINISTRATION
HAWAIIAN ISLANDS HUMPBACK WHALE NATIONAL SANCTUARY
726 South Kihei Road
Kihei, HI 96753 United States
Phone: 808-879-2818   Fax: 808-874-3815
E-mail: hihumpbackwhale@noaa.gov
Website: http://hawaiihumpbackwhale.noaa.gov/
Founded: 1997
Scope: Regional, National
Description: One of 13 marine sanctuaries. Mission is to protect the humpback whale and its Hawaiian habitat.

UNITED STATES DEPARTMENT OF COMMERCE
NATIONAL OCEANIC AND ATMOSPHERIC ADMINISTRATION
HUDSON RIVER NATIONAL ESTUARINE RESEARCH RESERVE
c/o Bard College Field Station, Annandale-on-Hudson
Annandale, NY 12504 United States
Phone: 845-758-7010   Fax: 845-758-7033
E-mail: hrnerr@gw.dec.state.ny.us
Website: www.dec.state.ny.us
Scope: Regional

UNITED STATES DEPARTMENT OF COMMERCE
NATIONAL OCEANIC AND ATMOSPHERIC ADMINISTRATION
JACQUES COUSTEAU NATIONAL ESTUARINE RESEARCH RESERVE INSTITUTE OF MARINE AND COASTAL SCIENCES
71 Dudley Road
New Brunswick, NJ 08901 United States
Phone: 732-932-6555   Fax: 732-932-8578
Website: http://marine.rutgers.edu/pt/home.htm
Scope: Regional
Description: The JCNERR program goals are to (1) ensure a stable environment for research through long-term protection of the NERR resources; (2) address coastal management issues indentified as significant through coordinated estuarine research within the system; (3) enhance the public awareness and understanding of estuarine areas; (4) conduct and coordinate estuarine research within the system, gathering and making available information necessary for improving understanding and management of estuarine areas.

UNITED STATES DEPARTMENT OF COMMERCE
NATIONAL OCEANIC AND ATMOSPHERIC ADMINISTRATION
JOBOS BAY NATIONAL ESTUARINE RESEARCH RESERVE
Department of Natural Resources, Call Box B
Aquirre, PR 00704 United States
Phone: 787-853-4617   Fax: 787-853-4618
Website: www.ocrm.nos.noaa.gov/nerr/reserves/nerrjobos.html
Scope: Regional

UNITED STATES DEPARTMENT OF COMMERCE
NATIONAL OCEANIC AND ATMOSPHERIC ADMINISTRATION
KACHEMAK BAY NATIONAL ESTUARINE RESEARCH RESERVE
2181 Kachemak Drive
Homer, AK 99603 United States
Phone: 907-235-6377   Fax: 907-267-4794
E-mail: kbrr@fishgame.state.ak.us
Website: www.kbayrr.org
Scope: Regional

UNITED STATES DEPARTMENT OF COMMERCE
NATIONAL OCEANIC AND ATMOSPHERIC ADMINISTRATION
MONITOR NATIONAL MARINE SANCTUARY
c/o the Mariners' Museum, 100 Museum Dr.
Newport News, VA 23606 United States
Phone: 757-599-3122   Fax: 757-591-7353
E-mail: monitor@noaa.gov
Website: monitor.nos.noaa.gov/
Scope: Regional

UNITED STATES DEPARTMENT OF COMMERCE
NATIONAL OCEANIC AND ATMOSPHERIC ADMINISTRATION
MONTEREY BAY NATIONAL MARINE SANCTUARY
299 Foam St., Suite D
Monterey, CA 93940 United States
Phone: 831-647-4201   Fax: 831-647-4250
E-mail: montereybay@noaa.gov
Website: www.sanctuaries.nos.noaa.gov/oms/omsmonterey/omsmontereyvisit.html
Founded: 1992
Scope: Regional

UNITED STATES DEPARTMENT OF COMMERCE
NATIONAL OCEANIC AND ATMOSPHERIC ADMINISTRATION
NARRAGANSETT BAY NATIONAL ESTUARINE RESEARCH RESERVE
Department of Environmental Management, 55 South Reserve Dr.
Prudence Island, RI 02872 United States
Phone: 401-683-6780   Fax: 401-682-1936
E-mail: roger.green@noaa.gov
Website: www.ocrm.nos.noaa.gov//nerr
Scope: Regional

UNITED STATES DEPARTMENT OF COMMERCE
NATIONAL OCEANIC AND ATMOSPHERIC ADMINISTRATION
NATIONAL ENVIRONMENTAL SATELLITE, DATA, AND INFORMATION SERVICE
1335 East-West Highway
Silver Spring, MD 20910-3284 United States
Phone: 301-713-3578 Fax: 301-713-1249
Website: www.noaa.gov

Scope: State

Description: Manages satellites which observe the natural variability of the global Earth systems - the ocean, atmosphere, features of the solid earth, and the near-space system.

Contact(s):
Gregory Withee, Assistant Administrator; 301-713-3578; ext. 101; Fax: 301-713-1249; greg.withee@noaa.gov

UNITED STATES DEPARTMENT OF COMMERCE
NATIONAL OCEANIC AND ATMOSPHERIC ADMINISTRATION
NATIONAL MARINE FISHERIES SERVICE
Silver Spring Metro Center 3, 1315 East-West Hwy.
Silver Spring, MD 20910 United States
Phone: 301-713-2239 Fax: 301-703-1940
Website: www.nmfs.noaa.gov

Founded: 1871
Membership: 1,001–10,000
Scope: Local, State, Regional, National, International

Description: Provides management, research, and services for the protection and rational use of living marine resources for their aesthetic, economic, and recreational value. Determines the consequences of the natural environment and human activities on living marine resources and provides knowledge and services to achieve efficient and judicious domestic and international management, use, and conservation of the resources.

Publication(s): Publications on line

Contact(s):
Donald Knowles, Senior Advisor for Intergovernmental Programs; 301-713-2239; Fax: 301-713-1940; don.knowles@noaa.gov
Rebecca Lent, Deputy Assistant Administrator for Regulatory Programs; 301-713-2239; Fax: 301-713-1940; rebecca.lent@noaa.gov
John Oliver, Deputy Assistant Administrator for Operations; 301-713-2239; Fax: 301-713-1940; john.oliver@noaa.gov
Michael Sissenwine, Director, Scientific Programs and Chief Science Advisor; 301-713-2239; Fax: 301-713-1940; michael.sissenwine@noaa.gov
Gloria Thompson, Special Assistant; 301-713-2239; Fax: 301-713-1940; gloria.thompson@noaa.gov
William Hogarth, Assistant Administrator; 301-713-2239; Fax: 301-713-1940; bill.hogarth@noaa.gov

UNITED STATES DEPARTMENT OF COMMERCE
NATIONAL OCEANIC AND ATMOSPHERIC ADMINISTRATION
NATIONAL OCEAN SERVICE
COASTAL SERVICES CENTER
2234 South Hobson Avenue
Charleston, SC 29405 United States
Phone: 843-740-1200 Fax: 843-740-1224
Website: www.csc.noaa.gov

Founded: 1984
Scope: Local, State, Regional, National, International

Description: A product and service organization for state coastal resource management programs. Emphasis areas include data, coastal hazards, smart growth, and habitat management.

UNITED STATES DEPARTMENT OF COMMERCE
NATIONAL OCEANIC AND ATMOSPHERIC ADMINISTRATION
NATIONAL WEATHER SERVICE
Silver Spring Metro Center 2, 1325 East-West Hwy.
Silver Spring, MD 20910 United States
Phone: 301-713-0689 Fax: 301-713-0662
Website: www.nws.noaa.gov

Scope: Local, Regional

Description: Observes, describes, and predicts the natural variability of the atmosphere, and to some extent the ocean and the earth, in order to protect life and property and enhance the national economy.

Contact(s):
Robert Burpee, Director of National Hurricane Center; 305-229-4470
John Kelly, Director and Assistant Administrator for Weather Service
Jerry McCall, Director of National Data Buoy Center; 601-688-2800
Ronald McPherson, Director of National Centers for Environmental Prediction; 301-713-8016
Frederick Ostby, Director of Severe Storm Forecast Center; 816-426-5922
Richard Augulis, National Weather Service Central Region; 816-426-5400
Louis Boezi, Deputy Assistant Administrator for Modernization; 301-713-0397
Randee Exter, Public Affairs Officer of Weather; 301-713-0622
John Forsing, National Weather Service Eastern Region; 516-244-0100
Richard Hagemeyer, National Weather Service Pacific Region; 808-541-1641
Harry Hassel, Southern Region; 817-334-2651
Richard Hutcheon, National Weather Service Alaska Region; 907-271-5136
Thomas Potter, National Weather Service Western Region; 801-524-5122
Susan Zevin, Deputy Assistant Administrator for Operations; 301-713-0711

UNITED STATES DEPARTMENT OF COMMERCE
NATIONAL OCEANIC AND ATMOSPHERIC ADMINISTRATION
NORTH CAROLINA NATIONAL ESTUARINE RESEARCH RESERVE
5600 Marvin Moss Lane
Wilmington, NC 28409 United States
Phone: 910-962-2470 Fax: 910-962-2410
Website: www.ncnerr.org

Membership: 1–100
Scope: Regional

Description: Manages forest site thats encompasses 10,000 acres. Research, education, and compatible recreational uses are explored.

UNITED STATES DEPARTMENT OF COMMERCE
NATIONAL OCEANIC AND ATMOSPHERIC ADMINISTRATION
NORTH INLET NATIONAL ESTUARINE RESEARCH RESERVE
Winyah Bay NERR, Baruch Marine Field Lab, P.O. Box 1630
Georgetown, SC 29442 United States
Phone: 843-546-3623 Fax: 843-546-1632
Website: baruch.sc.edu/bmfl

Scope: Regional

UNITED STATES DEPARTMENT OF COMMERCE
NATIONAL OCEANIC AND ATMOSPHERIC ADMINISTRATION
OFFICE OF GLOBAL PROGRAM
1100 Wayne Ave.
Silver Spring, MD 20910 United States
Phone: 301-427-2089 Fax: 301-427-2222
Website: www.ogp.noaa.gov

Scope: State

Description: Provides the primary focus for coordination with national and international scientific communities in the areas of global warming, Tropical Oceans and Global Atmosphere Project, and worldwide climate research.

Contact(s):
   J. Hall, Director; 301-427-2089

UNITED STATES DEPARTMENT OF COMMERCE
NATIONAL OCEANIC AND ATMOSPHERIC ADMINISTRATION
OFFICE OF OCEANIC AND ATMOSPHERIC RESEARCH
Silver Spring Metro Center 3, 1315 East-West Hwy.
Silver Spring, MD 20910 United States
Phone: 301-713-2458 Fax: 301-713-0163
Website: www.oar.noaa.gov

Membership: 101–1,000
Scope: International

Description: Conducts environmental research in the oceans, atmosphere, and space. Administers the National Sea Grant College Program, which provides grants to academic institutions for research, education, and advisory/extension services in the marine environment.

Keyword(s): Air Quality/Atmosphere, Climate Change

Contact(s):
   Ronald Baird, Director of National Sea Grant College Program of Extension; 301-713-2448
   Barbara Moore, Director of National Undersea Research Program; 301-713-2427
   David Evans, Assistant Administrator; David.Evans@noaa.gov
   Louisa Koch, Deputy Assistant Administrator
   Dane Konop, Public Affairs Officer; 301-713-2483
   Maryann Whitcomb, Resource Management; 301-713-2454

UNITED STATES DEPARTMENT OF COMMERCE
NATIONAL OCEANIC AND ATMOSPHERIC ADMINISTRATION
OLD WOMAN CREEK NATIONAL ESTUARINE RESEARCH RESERVE
2514 Cleveland Rd., East
Huron, OH 44839 United States
Phone: 419-433-4601 Fax: 419-433-2851

Scope: Regional

UNITED STATES DEPARTMENT OF COMMERCE
NATIONAL OCEANIC AND ATMOSPHERIC ADMINISTRATION
OLYMPIC COAST NATIONAL MARINE SANCTUARY
138 W. First St.
Port Angeles, WA 98362-2600 United States
Phone: 360-457-6622

Scope: Regional

UNITED STATES DEPARTMENT OF COMMERCE
NATIONAL OCEANIC AND ATMOSPHERIC ADMINISTRATION
PADILLA BAY NATIONAL ESTUARINE RESEARCH RESERVE
10441 Bayview-Edison Rd.
Mt. Vernon, WA 98273-9668 United States
Phone: 360-428-1558 Fax: 360-428-1491
E-mail: alex@padillabay.gov
Website: www.padillabay.gov

Founded: 1980
Scope: Regional

Description: One of 25 National Estuarine Research Reserves, Padilla Bay is set aside for research and education about eelgrass in the Puget Sound region.

Keyword(s): Ecosystems (precious), Oceans/Coasts/Beaches, Water Habitats & Quality

UNITED STATES DEPARTMENT OF COMMERCE
NATIONAL OCEANIC AND ATMOSPHERIC ADMINISTRATION
ROOKERY BAY NATIONAL ESTUARINE RESEARCH RESERVE
Department of Environmental Protection
300 Tower Road
Naples, FL 34113 United States
Phone: 239-417-6310 Fax: 239-417-6315
Website: www.ocrm.nos.noaa.gov/nerr/programs.html

Founded: 1972
Membership: 101–1,000
Scope: Regional

Description: Coastal stewards of 110,000 acres, providing science-based data for more informed coastal decisions.

Keyword(s): Ecosystems (precious), Forests/Forestry, Land Issues, Oceans/Coasts/Beaches, Public Lands/Greenspace, Recreation/Ecotourism, Water Habitats & Quality, Wildlife & Species

Contact(s):
   Gary Lytton, Administrator

UNITED STATES DEPARTMENT OF COMMERCE
NATIONAL OCEANIC AND ATMOSPHERIC ADMINISTRATION
SAPELO ISLAND NATIONAL ESTUARINE RESEARCH RESERVE
P.O. Box 15
Sapelo Island, GA 31327 United States
Phone: 912-485-2251 Fax: 912-485-2141

Scope: Regional

UNITED STATES DEPARTMENT OF COMMERCE
NATIONAL OCEANIC AND ATMOSPHERIC ADMINISTRATION
SEA GRANT PROGRAM - ALABAMA
Mississippi and Alabama Sea Grant Consortium
Caylor Bldg., Gulf Coast Research Lab.
P.O. Box 7000
Ocean Springs, MS 39566-7000 United States
Phone: 228-875-9341 Fax: 228-875-0528
Website: www.masgc.org

Membership: 1–100
Scope: State

Contact(s):
   Richard Wallace, Coordinator and Extension Marine Specialist; Alabama Sea Grant Extension Program: 4170 Commanders Dr., Mobile, AL 36615; 334-438-5690; Fax: 334-438-5670

UNITED STATES DEPARTMENT OF COMMERCE
NATIONAL OCEANIC AND ATMOSPHERIC ADMINISTRATION
SEA GRANT PROGRAM - ALASKA
UNIVERSITY OF ALASKA
P.O. Box 755040
Fairbanks, AK 99775-5040 United States
Phone: 907-474-7086 Fax: 907-474-6285
E-mail: fygrant@uaf.edu
Website: www.uaf.edu/seagrant/

Scope: State

Description: A state/federal partnership administered by the National Oceanic and Atmospheric Administration and the

University of Alaska that sponsors and conducts marine research, graduate education, marine industry advisory services, and formal and nonformal public education aimed at promoting the wise use and conservation of Alaska's coastal and marine resources.

Publication(s): Free catalog, posters, videos, SeaWeek Curriculum Series, Biennial Program Report, Management Strategies for Exploited Fish Populations, Guide to Marine Mammals of Alaska

Keyword(s): Oceans/Coasts/Beaches, Wildlife & Species

Contact(s):
Ronald Dearborn, Director; fnrkd@uaf.edu
Donald Kramer, Director of Marine Advisory Program; University of Alaska, Carlton Trust Bldg., Suite 110, 2221 E. Northern Lights Blvd., Anchorage, AK 99508-4140; 907-274-9691; Fax: 907-277-5242; afdek@uaa.alaska.edu
Kurt Byers, Communications Manager; Alaska Sea Grant College Program, University of Alaska, P.O. Box 755040, Fairbanks, AK 99775-5040; 907-474-6702; fnkmb1@uaf.edu
Sue Keller, Publications Manager; P.O. Box 755040, Fairbanks, AK 99775-5040; 907-474-6703; fnsk@uaf.edu
Sherri Pristash, Publications Manager; 888-789-0090; fypubs@uaf.edu

UNITED STATES DEPARTMENT OF COMMERCE
NATIONAL OCEANIC AND ATMOSPHERIC ADMINISTRATION
SEA GRANT PROGRAM - CALIFORNIA
UNIVERSITY OF CALIFORNIA
9500 Gilman Drive
La Jolla, CA 92093-0232 United States
Phone: 858-534-4440   Fax: 858-534-2231
E-mail: caseagrant@ucsd.edu
Website: www-csgc.ucsd.edu/

Scope: Local, State, Regional

Description: A university-based program of marine research, extension services, and education that contributes to the growing body of knowledge about coastal and marine resources. Through its extension and communications components, transfers information and technology to industry, government, and the public.

Publication(s): Bight Bulletin / Boletin de la Cuenca, Publication List, Sea Grant News, Program Directory

Keyword(s): Oceans/Coasts/Beaches, Water Habitats & Quality

Contact(s):
Linda Duguay, Director, USC Sea Grant Program; University of Southern California, University Park, Los Angeles, CA 90089-0373; 213-740-1961; Fax: 213-740-5936; seagrant@usc.edu
Russell Moll, Director; California Sea Grant, University of California, 9500 Gilman Drive, La Jolla, CA 92093-0232; 858-534-4440; Fax: 858-534-2231
Judy Lemus, Leader, and Associate; USC Sea Grant Program Marine Advisory Service, University of Southern California, University Park, Los Angeles, CA 90089-0373; 213-740-1965; Fax: 213-740-5936
Paul Olin, Interim Extension Leader; Sea Grant Extension, UC Cooperative Extension, 2604 Ventura Avenue, Room 100, Santa Rosa, CA 95403; 707-565-2621; Fax: 707-565-2623

UNITED STATES DEPARTMENT OF COMMERCE
NATIONAL OCEANIC AND ATMOSPHERIC ADMINISTRATION
SEA GRANT PROGRAM - CONNECTICUT
UNIVERSITY OF CONNECTICUT
1080 Shennecossett Rd.
Groton, CT 06340-6048 United States
Phone: 860-405-9110   Fax: 860-405-9109
E-mail: vanpatte@uconnvm.uconn.edu
Website: www.seagrant.uconn.edu

Founded: 1988
Membership: 1–100
Scope: Local, State, Regional, National, International

Description: Connecticut Sea Grant is part of the National Sea Grant network. Sea Grant is implemented through the National Oceanic and Atmospheric Administration (NOAA) and is a partnership with the State's Sea Grant College, in our case the University of Connecticut. Our mission is to foster the wise use and conservation of coastal and marine resources through research, outreach and education. We produce educational programs and resources, mostly specific to the Long Island Sound region.

Publication(s): Aquatic Nuisance Species booklets, LIS Lobster Research Summary, Wrack Lines, Sound Facts (Long Island Sound)

Keyword(s): Agriculture/Farming, Air Quality/Atmosphere, Climate Change, Development/Developing Countries, Ecosystems (precious), Land Issues, Oceans/Coasts/Beaches, Pollution (general), Public Health, Sprawl/Urban Planning, Water Habitats & Quality, Wildlife & Species

Contact(s):
Edward Monahan, Director; 860-405-9110; Fax: 860-405-9109; sgoadm01@uconnvm.uconn.edu
Nancy Balcom, Extension Leader; 860-405-9127; Fax: 860-405-9109; nancy.balcom@uconn.edu
Peg Van Patten, Communications Director; 860-405-9141; Fax: 860-405-9109; vanpatte@uconnvm.uconn.edu

UNITED STATES DEPARTMENT OF COMMERCE
NATIONAL OCEANIC AND ATMOSPHERIC ADMINISTRATION
SEA GRANT PROGRAM - DELAWARE
UNIVERSITY OF DELAWARE
College of Marine Studies
Marine Public Education Office
222 S. Chapel Street, Rm. 103
Newark, DE 19716-3530 United States
Phone: 302-831-8083   Fax: 302-831-2005
E-mail: marinecom@udel.edu
Website: www.ocean.udel.edu/seagrant/

Founded: 1968
Scope: Local, State, Regional, National

Description: The University of Delaware Sea Grant College Program conducts research, education, and outreach projects to help people from all walks of life wisely use, manage, and conserve Delaware's ocean and coastal resources. The program is a partnership involving the National Sea Grant College Program in the National Oceanic and Atmospheric Administration (NOAA), U.S. Department of Commerce; the State of Delaware; and the University of Delaware.

Publication(s): Publications Catalog

Keyword(s): Agriculture/Farming, Ecosystems (precious), Oceans/Coasts/Beaches, Pollution (general), Recreation/Ecotourism, Transportation, Water Habitats & Quality, Wildlife & Species

Contact(s):
David McCarren, Executive Director; University of Delaware, College of Marine Studies, 118 Robinson Hall, Newark, DE 19716-3501; 302-831-8255; Fax: 302-831-1487; mccarren@udel.edu
Carolyn Thoroughgood, Director; University of Delaware, College of Marine Studies, 111 Robinson Hall, Newark, DE 19716-3501; 302-831-2841; Fax: 302-831-4389; ctgood@udel.edu
Tracey Bryant, Communications Director; University of Delaware, Marine Public Education Office, 222 S. Chapel Street, Rm. 103, Newark, DE 19716-3530; 302-831-8185; Fax: 302-831-2005; tbryant@udel.edu
James Falk, MAS Director; University of Delaware, Sea Grant College Program, 700 Pilottown Road, 204H Cannon Lab, Lewes, DE 19958; 302-645-4235; Fax: 302-645-4213; jfalk@udel.edu

U.S. FEDERAL AND INTERNATIONAL GOVERNMENT AGENCIES – U

UNITED STATES DEPARTMENT OF COMMERCE
NATIONAL OCEANIC AND ATMOSPHERIC ADMINISTRATION
SEA GRANT PROGRAM - FLORIDA
UNIVERSITY OF FLORIDA
P.O. Box 110400
Gainesville, FL 32611-0400 United States
Phone: 352-392-5870   Fax: 352-392-5113
Website: www.flseagrant.org

Founded: 1972
Scope: State
Description: A statewide university-based program of coastal and ocean research, education, and public service to enhance productivity, conservation, and long-term use and management of marine systems and resources.
Publication(s): Listing of various publications available
Keyword(s): Agriculture/Farming, Ecosystems (precious), Oceans/Coasts/Beaches, Sprawl/Urban Planning, Water Habitats & Quality
Contact(s):
 James Cato, Director: Florida Sea Grant College Program; jcato@mail.ifas.ufl.edu
 William Seaman, Associate Director: Florida Sea Grant College Program; seaman@mail.ifas.ufl.edu
 Michael Spranger, Assistant Dean and Coordinator: Sea Grant Extension Program; P.O. Box 110405, University of Florida, Gainesville, FL 32611-0405; 352-392-1837; msspranger@mail.ifas.ufl.edu

UNITED STATES DEPARTMENT OF COMMERCE
NATIONAL OCEANIC AND ATMOSPHERIC ADMINISTRATION
SEA GRANT PROGRAM - GEORGIA
UNIVERSITY OF GEORGIA
Marine Sciences Bldg.
Rm. 220
Athens, GA 30602-3636 United States
Phone: 706-542-5954   Fax: 706-542-3652
Website: www.marsci.uga.edu/gaseagrant

Founded: 1971
Scope: State, Regional
Description: A part of the National Sea Grant College Program, the Georgia program fosters the sustainable development and environmental stewardship of the nation's marine resources. It is a competitive grant program funding applied marine research, education, and advisory service projects at universities in Georgia.
Keyword(s): Development/Developing Countries, Oceans/Coasts/Beaches, Reduce/Reuse/Recycle
Contact(s):
 Mac Rawson, Director, Sea Grant College Program; mrawson@arches.uga.edu
 Randy Walker, Marine Extension; 706-542-5956; rwalker@arches.uga.edu
 David Bryant, Communicator
 Keith Gates, Leader, Marine Advisory Service

UNITED STATES DEPARTMENT OF COMMERCE
NATIONAL OCEANIC AND ATMOSPHERIC ADMINISTRATION
SEA GRANT PROGRAM - HAWAII
UNIVERSITY OF HAWAII
2525 Correa Rd., HIG 238
Honolulu, HI 96822 United States
Phone: 808-956-7031   Fax: 808-956-3014
E-mail: seagrant@soest.hawaii.edu
Website: www.soest.hawaii.edu/seagrant/

Founded: 1968
Membership: 1–100
Scope: International
Description: The University of Hawaii Sea Grant College Program supports research projects in coastal and marine-related areas. Its extension service has agents and specialists located in Honolulu, Maui, the Big Island of Hawaii, Kauai, and American Samoa. Agents help marine users benefit from the Sea Grant-supported research, especially in the areas of commercial and recreational fishing, aquaculture, coastal nearshore resources, marine recreation and tourism development, marine biotechnology.
Contact(s):
 Mary Donohue, Associate Director: Sea Grant College Progam
 E. Gordon Grau, Director: Sea Grant College Program; sg-dir@soest.hawaii.edu
 Dr. Richard Brock, Sea Grant Extension Leader
 Mary Donohue, Acting Director of Communications Program; 808-956-2414; Fax: 808-956-2880
 Richard Brock, Fisheries Extension Specialist; 808-956-2859; Fax: 808-956-2858
 Valerie Franck, Hanauma Bay Educational Program Outreach Coordinator; 808-397-5840; Fax: 808-395-0468
 Alan Kam, Fisheries Extension Agent; 808-956-2865; Fax: 808-956-2858
 Elizabeth Kumabe, Regional Environmental Education Specialist; 808-956-2860; Fax: 808-956-2858
 Peter Rappa, Coastal Resource Management Extension Agent; 808-956-2868; Fax: 808-956-2858
 Clyde Tamaru, Aquaculture Extension Specialist; 808-956-2869; Fax: 808-956-2858
 Christine Woolaway, Coastal Recreation & Tourism Extension Agent; 808-956-2872; Fax: 808-956-2858

UNITED STATES DEPARTMENT OF COMMERCE
NATIONAL OCEANIC AND ATMOSPHERIC ADMINISTRATION
SEA GRANT PROGRAM - ILLINOIS-INDIANA
UNIVERSITY OF ILLINOIS
1101 W. Peabody, Rm. 350
Urbana, IL 61801 United States
Phone: 217-333-6444   Fax: 217-333-8046
Website: www.iisgcp.org

Membership: 1–100
Scope: Local, State, Regional, National
Description: Illinois-Indiana Sea Grant College Program fosters the creation and stewardship of an enhanced and sustainable environment and economy along Southern Lake Michigan and in the Great Lakes region through research, education, and outreach.
Keyword(s): Land Issues, Oceans/Coasts/Beaches, Pollution (general), Public Health, Public Lands/Greenspace, Sprawl/Urban Planning
Contact(s):
 Richard Warner, Director; University of Illinois, 350 NSRC, 1101 W. Peabody, Urbana, IL 61801; 217-333-6444; dickw@uiuc.edu
 Patrice Charlebois, Biological Resources Specialist; Lake Michigan Biological Station, Illinois Natural History Survey, 400 17th Street, Zion, IL 60099; 847-872-0140; Fax: 847-872-8679; charlebo@uiuc.edu
 Leslie Dorworth, Aquatic Ecology Specialist; Purdue University, Calumet, Department of Biology, Hammond, IN 46323-2094; 219-989-2726; Fax: 219-989-2130; dorworth@calumet.purdue.edu
 Martin Jaffe, Coastal Business & Environmental Interim Specialist; University of Illinois Chicago, Great Cities Institute (MC348), 412 South Peoria Street, Suite 400, Chicago, IL 60607-7067; 312-996-2178; Fax: 312-413-2314; mjaffe@uiuc.edu
 Robert McCormick, Planning with POWER Coordinator; Purdue University, 1200 Forest Products Building, West Lafayette, IN 47907; 765-494-3627; Fax: 765-496-6026; rmccormick@fnr.purdue.edu

Brian Miller, Associate Director and Outreach Coordinator; Purdue University, 1200 Forest Products Building, West Lafayette, IN 47907-1200; 765-494-3573; Fax: 765-496-6026; bmiller@fnr.purdue.edu

Robin Goettel, Communications Coordinator; University of Illinois, 63 Mumford Hall, Urbana, IL 61801; 217-333-9448; Fax: 217-333-2614; goettel@uiuc.edu

UNITED STATES DEPARTMENT OF COMMERCE
NATIONAL OCEANIC AND ATMOSPHERIC ADMINISTRATION
SEA GRANT PROGRAM - LOUISIANA
LOUISIANA STATE UNIVERSITY
Baton Rouge, LA 70803 United States
Phone: 225-578-6710   Fax: 225-578-6331
Website: www.laseagrant.org/

Founded: 1968
Scope: National
Description: The Louisiana Sea Grant College Program is a research, education, and public service organization supported by federal, state, and private sector funds. The Program provides the knowledge, trained personnel, and public awareness needed to wisely and effectively develop and manage coastal and marine areas and resources in a manner that will assure sustainable economic and societal benefits.
Publication(s): Coast and Sea: Marine and Coastal Research in Louisiana's Universities
Keyword(s): Development/Developing Countries, Oceans/Coasts/Beaches, Recreation/Ecotourism, Reduce/Reuse/Recycle, Water Habitats & Quality
Contact(s):
Jack Vanlopik, Executive Director; Louisiana State University, 239 Sea Grant Building, Baton Rouge, LA 70803; 225-578-6710; Fax: 225-578-6331; jvl@lsu.edu

Marilyn Barrett-O'Leary, Communications Coordinator; Louisiana Sea Grant College Program, Louisiana State University, 103 Sea Grant Building, Baton Rouge, LA 70803; 225-578-6349; moleary@lsu.edu

Ronald Becker, Associate Director; Louisiana Sea Grant College Program, Louisiana State University, 232 Sea Grant Building, Baton Rouge, LA 70803; 225-578-6345; rbecker@lsu.edu

Michael Liffmann, Associate Director; 225-578-6290; mikelif@lsu.edu

UNITED STATES DEPARTMENT OF COMMERCE
NATIONAL OCEANIC AND ATMOSPHERIC ADMINISTRATION
SEA GRANT PROGRAM - MAINE
UNIVERSITY OF MAINE
5715 Coburn Hall #14
Orono, ME 04469-5715 United States
Phone: 207-581-1435   Fax: 207-581-1426
E-mail: umseagrant@umain.edu
Website: www.seagrant.umaine.edu

Membership: 1–100
Scope: National
Description: Part of a national network funding reasearch on marine issues.
Keyword(s): Oceans/Coasts/Beaches, Water Habitats & Quality, Wildlife & Species
Contact(s):
Paul Anderson, Director; 207-581-1435; Fax: 207-581-1426; panderson@maine.edu

Paul Anderson, Director & Marine Extension Leader; 207-581-1422; panderson@maine.edu

Chris Bartlett, Finfish Aquaculture Specialist; Marine Technology Center, Washington County Technical College, 16 Deep Cove Road, Eastport, ME 04631-0618; 207-853-2518; Fax: 207-853-0940; chris.bartlett@umit.maine.edu

Dana Morse, Extension Associate, Darling Marine Center; Clarks Cove, Walpole, ME 04573; 207-563-3146; ext. 205; Fax: 207-563-3119; dana.l.morse@umit.maine.edu

Natalie Springuel, Extension Associate

Kristen Whiting-Grant, Extension Agent; Wells Reserve, 342 Laudholm Farm Rd., Wells, ME 04090; 207-646-1555; Fax: 207-646-2930; kristen.whiting-grant@maine.edu

UNITED STATES DEPARTMENT OF COMMERCE
NATIONAL OCEANIC AND ATMOSPHERIC ADMINISTRATION
SEA GRANT PROGRAM - MARYLAND
UNIVERSITY OF MARYLAND
4321 Hartwick Rd.
Suite 300
College Park, MD 20740 United States
Phone: 301-403-4220   Fax: 301-403-4255
Website: www.mdsg.umd.edu/

Founded: 1977
Membership: 1–100
Scope: National
Description: Maryland Sea Grant supports marine research, education, and outreach activities, especially in connection with the Chesapeake Bay. It currently supports research at four of the region's marine laboratories, and on the campuses of the University System of Maryland, the Johns Hopkins University, and other institutions of higher learning.
Publication(s): Chesapeake Quarterly, Maryland Marine Notes, Maryland Sea Grant Books and Videos, Watershed, Aquafarmer - quarterly newsletters
Keyword(s): Oceans/Coasts/Beaches, Public Health, Water Habitats & Quality, Wildlife & Species
Contact(s):
Jonathan Kramer, Director; 301-403-4220; ext. 10; Fax: 301-403-4255; kramer@mdsg.umd.edu

Jack Greer, Assistant Director; 301-403-4220; ext. 18; Fax: 301-403-4255

UNITED STATES DEPARTMENT OF COMMERCE
NATIONAL OCEANIC AND ATMOSPHERIC ADMINISTRATION
SEA GRANT PROGRAM - MASSACHUSETTS
MASSACHUSETTS INSTITUTE OF TECHNOLOGY
E38-330, 292 Main St.
Cambridge, MA 02139-9910 United States
Phone: 617-253-7131   Fax: 617-258-5730
Website: www.mit.edu/seagrant/

Scope: National
Contact(s):
Chrys Chryssostomidis, Director; chrys@deslab.mit.edu

UNITED STATES DEPARTMENT OF COMMERCE
NATIONAL OCEANIC AND ATMOSPHERIC ADMINISTRATION
SEA GRANT PROGRAM - MASSACHUSETTS
WOODS HOLE OCEANOGRAPHIC INSTITUTION
193 Oyster Pond Rd.
Mail Stop #2
Woods Hole, MA 02543-1525 United States
Phone: 508-289-2398   Fax: 508-457-2172
E-mail: seagrant@whoi.edu
Website: www.whoi.edu/seagrant/

Founded: 1973
Scope: National
Description: The WHOI Sea Grant Program supports research, education, and advisory projects to promote the wise use and understanding of ocean and coastal resources for the public benefit. It is part of the National Sea Grant College Program of the National Oceanic and Atmospheric Administration, a network of 30 individual programs located in each of the

coastal and Great Lakes states to foster cooperation among government, academia, and industry.

Keyword(s): Agriculture/Farming, Ecosystems (precious), Oceans/Coasts/Beaches, Wildlife & Species

Contact(s):
Judith McDowell, Director; 508-289-2557; jmcdowell@whoi.edu
Katherine Madin, Educator; 508-289-3639; Fax: 508-457-2172; kmadin@whoi.edu
James O'Connell, Coastal Processes Specialist; 508-289-2993; Fax: 508-457-2172; joconnell@whoi.edu
Tracey Crago, Communicator; 508-289-2665; tcrago@whoi.edu
Sheri Derosa, Program Assistant; 508-289-2398; sderosa@whoi.edu
Bill Walton, Fisheries Aquaculture Specialist; CCCE/Barnstable Cty., P.O. Box 367, Barnstable, MA 02630; 508-830-6478; Fax: 508-362-4518; wwalton@whoi.edu

UNITED STATES DEPARTMENT OF COMMERCE
NATIONAL OCEANIC AND ATMOSPHERIC ADMINISTRATION
SEA GRANT PROGRAM - MICHIGAN
MICHIGAN STATE UNIVERSITY
One Great Lakes Plaza
401 E. Liberty Ste. 330
Ann Arbor, MI 48104-2298 United States
Phone: 734-763-1437   Fax: 734-647-0768
Website: www.miseagrant.umich.edu

Founded: 1969
Membership: 1–100
Scope: Local, State, Regional, National
Description: To promote the understanding and wise use of the Great Lakes through research, education and extension.

Contact(s):
George Carignan, Director; Michigan Sea Grant College Program, One Great Lakes Plaza, 401 E. Liberty Ste. 330, Ann Arbor, MI 48104-2298; 734-763-1437; Fax: 734-647-0768; carignan@umich.edu
Jennifer Read, Assistant Director; 734-936-3622; Fax: 734-647-0768; jenread@umich.edu
Dave Brenner, Web Designer; 734-764-2421; Fax: 734-647-0768
Joyce Daniels, Editor; 734-617-0766; Fax: 734-647-0768; joydan@umich.edu
Minuet Henderson, Publications Assistant; 734-764-1118; Fax: 734-647-0768; minti@umich.edu
Elizabeth Laporte, Communication Coordinator; 734-647-0767; Fax: 734-647-0768; elzblap@umich.edu
Elyse Larsen, Fiscal Officer; 734-763-1438; Fax: 734-647-0768; elarsen@umich.edu
John Schwartz, Program Leader: Sea Grant Extension; Michigan Sea Grant College Program, 334 Natural Resources Bldg., Michigan State University, East Lansing, MI 48824; 517-355-9637; Fax: 517-353-6496; schwartj@msue.msu.edu
William Taylor, Associate Director; Michigan Sea Grant College Program, 13 Natural Resources Bldg., Michigan State University, East Lansing, MI 48824; 517-355-0233; taylorw@msu.edu

UNITED STATES DEPARTMENT OF COMMERCE
NATIONAL OCEANIC AND ATMOSPHERIC ADMINISTRATION
SEA GRANT PROGRAM - MINNESOTA
UNIVERSITY OF MINNESOTA
208 Washburn Hall
2305 E. 5th St.
Duluth, MN 55812-1445 United States
Phone: 218-726-8106   Fax: 218-726-6556
E-mail: seagrant@umn.edu
Website: www.seagrant.umn.edu

Membership: 1–100
Scope: State
Description: A statewide program that supports research, outreach, and educational programs related to Lake Superior and Minnesota's inland waters. Research areas include: water quality, fisheries, biotechnology, aquaculture, exotic species, and coastal tourism.

Publication(s): Seiche, The Newsletter, see publication web site
Keyword(s): Development/Developing Countries, Oceans/Coasts/Beaches, Public Health, Water Habitats & Quality, Wildlife & Species

Contact(s):
Carl Richards, Director; crichard@d.umn.edu
Doug Jensen, Coordinator, Exotic Species Information Center; 218-726-8712; djensen1@d.umn.edu
Sharon Moen, Editor; 218-726-6195; smoen@d.umn.edu

UNITED STATES DEPARTMENT OF COMMERCE
NATIONAL OCEANIC AND ATMOSPHERIC ADMINISTRATION
SEA GRANT PROGRAM - MISSISSIPPI-ALABAMA CONSORTIUM
MISSISSIPPI-ALABAMA SEA GRANT CONSORTIUM
Caylor Bldg., Gulf Coast Research Laboratory
P.O. Box 7000
Ocean Springs, MS 39566-7000 United States
Phone: 228-818-8836   Fax: 228-818-8841
Website: www.masgc.org

Scope: State
Contact(s):
Ladon Swann, Director; swanndl@auburn.edu

UNITED STATES DEPARTMENT OF COMMERCE
NATIONAL OCEANIC AND ATMOSPHERIC ADMINISTRATION
SEA GRANT PROGRAM - NEW HAMPSHIRE
UNIVERSITY OF NEW HAMPSHIRE
Kingman Farm
Durham, NH 03824-3512 United States
Phone: 603-749-1565   Fax: 603-743-3997
Website: www.seagrant.unh.edu

Scope: National
Keyword(s): Development/Developing Countries, Oceans/Coasts/Beaches, Recreation/Ecotourism, Reduce/Reuse/Recycle, Water Habitats & Quality, Wildlife & Species

Contact(s):
Ann Bucklin, Director; 603-862-0122; acb@cisunix.unh.edu
Steve Adams, Coordinator, Communications; steve.adams@unh.edu
Brian Doyle, Associate Director and Program Leader; brian.doyle@unh.edu

UNITED STATES DEPARTMENT OF COMMERCE
NATIONAL OCEANIC AND ATMOSPHERIC ADMINISTRATION
SEA GRANT PROGRAM - NEW JERSEY
NEW JERSEY MARINE SCIENCES CONSORTIUM
Bldg. 22
Fort Hancock, NJ 07732 United States
Phone: 732-872-1300   Fax: 732-291-4483
E-mail: kkosko@njmsc.org
Website: www.njmsc.org/Sea_Grant/Main_Page.htm

Description: The New Jersey Marine Sciences Consortium is an alliance of 29 institutions from New Jersey, New York, and Pennsylvania formed for the purposes of conducting sponsored research in marine and coastal sciences, technology development through group action; and assembling material resources which lie beyond the capabilities of the individual

member institutions. The consortium manages the Sea Grant College Program and the Sea Grant Extension Program.
Keyword(s): Oceans/Coasts/Beaches, Water Habitats & Quality
Contact(s):
Eleanor Bochenek, Associate Sea Grant Director/Sea Grant Extension Director; Eleanor@njmsc.org
Michael Weinstein, Director; mikew@njmsc.org

UNITED STATES DEPARTMENT OF COMMERCE
NATIONAL OCEANIC AND ATMOSPHERIC ADMINISTRATION
SEA GRANT PROGRAM - NEW YORK
SUNY AT STONY BROOK
121 Discovery Hall
Stony Brook University
Stony Brook, NY 11794-5001 United States
Phone: 631-632-6905   Fax: 631-632-6917
E-mail: NYSeaGrant@notes.cc.sunysb.edu
Website: www.nyseagrant.org
Founded: 1971
Membership: 1–100
Scope: Local, State, Regional, National
Description: A cooperative program of the State University of New York and Cornell University fostering the wise use and development of coastal resources through research grants, extension advisory services, education, training, and informational materials.
Keyword(s): Climate Change, Oceans/Coasts/Beaches, Recreation/Ecotourism, Sprawl/Urban Planning, Water Habitats & Quality, Wildlife & Species
Contact(s):
Jack Mattice, Director; 121 Discovery Hall, Stony Brook University, Stony Brook, NY 11794-5001; 631-632-6905; Fax: 631-632-6917; Jack.Mattice@stonybrook.edu
Dale Baker, Associate Director and Program Leader; New York Sea Grant, 348 Roberts Hall, Cornell University, Ithaca, NY 14853-4203; 607-255-2832; Fax: 607-255-2812; drb17@cornell.edu
Barbara Branca, Communicator; 115 Discovery Hall, Stony Brook University, Stony Brook, NY 11794-5001; 631-632-6956; Fax: 631-632-6917; Barbara.Branca@stonybrook.edu
Paul Focazio, Assistant Communicator; 115 Discovery Hall, Stony Brook University, Stony Brook, NY 11794-5001; 631-632-6910; Fax: 631-632-6917; Paul.Focazio@stonybrook.edu
Robert Kent, Marine Program Coordinator; New York Sea Grant, Cornell University Research and Extension Center, 3059 Sound Ave., Riverhead, NY 11901-1098; 631-727-3910; Fax: 631-369-5944; rjk13@cornell.edu
Stefanie Massucci, Fiscal Officer of New York Sea Grant; 121 Discovery Hall, Stony Brook University, Stony Brook, NY 11794-5001; 631-632-6905; Fax: 631-632-6917; smassucci@sunysb.edu
Cornelia Schlenk, Assistant Director; 121 Discovery Hall, Stony Brook University, Stony Brook, NY 11794-5001; 631-632-6905; Fax: 631-632-6917; Cornelia.Schlenk@stonybrook.edu
David White, Great Lakes Program Coordinator; New York Sea Grant, SUNY College at Oswego, Oswego, NY 13126-3599; 315-312-3042; Fax: 315-312-2954; dgw9@cornell.edu

UNITED STATES DEPARTMENT OF COMMERCE
NATIONAL OCEANIC AND ATMOSPHERIC ADMINISTRATION
SEA GRANT PROGRAM - NORTH CAROLINA
NORTH CAROLINA STATE UNIVERSITY
Box 8605
100B 1911 Bldg.
Raleigh, NC 27695-8605 United States
Phone: 919-515-2454   Fax: 919-515-7095
Website: www.ncseagrant.org
Scope: State
Publication(s): Marine Extension News, Water Wise, Coast Watch
Keyword(s): Agriculture/Farming, Oceans/Coasts/Beaches, Recreation/Ecotourism, Water Habitats & Quality, Wildlife & Species
Contact(s):
Ronald Hodson, Director; ronald_hodson@ncsu.edu
Jack Thigpen, Extension Director
Katie Mosher, Assistant Director for Communications
Steve Rebach, Associate Director

UNITED STATES DEPARTMENT OF COMMERCE
NATIONAL OCEANIC AND ATMOSPHERIC ADMINISTRATION
SEA GRANT PROGRAM - OHIO
1314 Kinnear Rd.
Columbus, OH 43212-1194 United States
Phone: 614-292-8949   Fax: 614-292-4364
Website: www.sg.ohio-state.edu/
Founded: 1977
Membership: 1–100
Scope: State, Regional
Description: The Ohio Sea Grant College Program is dedicated to the goal of promoting the understanding and management, development, utilization, and conservation of ocean, coastal, and Great Lakes resources, specifically Lake Erie, through research, education, outreach, and communications. The program is administrated by The Ohio State University. Stone Laboratory is Ohio's biological field station located on Gibraltar Island at Put-in-Bay, Ohio.
Publication(s): Twine Line
Keyword(s): Agriculture/Farming, Climate Change, Oceans/Coasts/Beaches, Pollution (general), Public Lands/Greenspace, Recreation/Ecotourism, Reduce/Reuse/Recycle, Sprawl/Urban Planning, Water Habitats & Quality, Wildlife & Species
Contact(s):
Jeffrey Reutter, Director; reutter.1@osu.edu

UNITED STATES DEPARTMENT OF COMMERCE
NATIONAL OCEANIC AND ATMOSPHERIC ADMINISTRATION
SEA GRANT PROGRAM - OREGON
OREGON STATE UNIVERSITY
500 322 Kerr Administration Bldg.
Corvallis, OR 97331-2131 United States
Phone: 541-737-2714   Fax: 541-737-7958
E-mail: seagrant.admin@orst.edu
Website: seagrant.orst.edu/
Scope: State
Description: Oregon Sea Grant takes an integrated approach to addressing the problems and opportunities of Oregon's marine resources through three related primary activities—research, education, and extension services. Oregon Sea Grant responds to the needs of ocean users.
Publication(s): Catalogue available upon request from Sea Grant Communications.
Keyword(s): Oceans/Coasts/Beaches, Public Health, Wildlife & Species
Contact(s):
Robert Malouf, Program Director; maloufr@ccmail.orst.edu
Jan Auyong, Assistant Director for Programs; jan.auyong@orst.edu
Joseph Cone, Assistant Director for Communications; 402 Kerr Admin. Bldg. OSU, Corvallis, OR 97331-2134; 541-737-2716; Fax: 541-737-7958; joe.cone@orst.edu

Jay Rasmussen, Extension Program Leader; Hatfield Marine Science Center, 2030 S. Marine Science Dr., Newport, OR 97365; 541-867-0370; Fax: 541-867-0369; jay.rasmussen@hmsc.orst.edu

UNITED STATES DEPARTMENT OF COMMERCE
NATIONAL OCEANIC AND ATMOSPHERIC ADMINISTRATION
SEA GRANT PROGRAM - PUERTO RICO
UNIVERSITY OF PUERTO RICO
UPRM P.O. Box 9011
Mayaguez, PR 00681 United States
Phone: 787-832-3585   Fax: 787-265-2880
Website: http://seagrant.uprm.edu/seagrant/main.html

Founded: 1985
Scope: International
Description: Promote marine education activities among pre-college teachers and students. Faciliate interdisciplinary teaching and learning experience using the marine environment as a resource.
Publication(s): The Boletin Marino, Seagrant in the Caribbean
Keyword(s): Oceans/Coasts/Beaches, Water Habitats & Quality, Wildlife & Species
Contact(s):
Manuel Valdes Pizzini, Director of UPR Sea Grant College Program; 787-832-3585; Fax: 787-265-2880; ma_valdes@rumac.uprm.edu

UNITED STATES DEPARTMENT OF COMMERCE
NATIONAL OCEANIC AND ATMOSPHERIC ADMINISTRATION
SEA GRANT PROGRAM - RHODE ISLAND
UNIVERSITY OF RHODE ISLAND COASTAL INSTITUTE
Narragansett Bay Campus
Narragansett, RI 02882-1197 United States
Phone: 401-874-6842   Fax: 401-874-6817
E-mail: allard@gso.uri.edu
Website: seagrant.gso.uri.edu/

Scope: Local, State, Regional, National
Description: The Rhode Island Sea Grant College Program conducts research and outreach on important marine issues. Outreach topics include coastal management and fisheries, aquaculture, and seafood safety.
Keyword(s): Ecosystems (precious), Oceans/Coasts/Beaches, Public Lands/Greenspace, Sprawl/Urban Planning, Water Habitats & Quality, Wildlife & Species
Contact(s):
Barry Costa-Pierce, Director
Malia Schwartz, Communications Director; 401-874-6842

UNITED STATES DEPARTMENT OF COMMERCE
NATIONAL OCEANIC AND ATMOSPHERIC ADMINISTRATION
SEA GRANT PROGRAM - SOUTH CAROLINA
SC Sea Grant Consortium
287 Meeting Street
Charleston, SC 29401 United States
Phone: 843-727-2078   Fax: 843-727-2080
Website: www.scseagrant.org

Membership: 1–100
Scope: National
Description: A Universtiy-based state agency that supports research, education and outreach to conserve coastal and marine reserves and provide economic oppurtunities for the cities of South Carolina and the region.
Publication(s): Coastal Heritage, coastal hazard information, aquaculture handbooks, marine education publications and slide presentations, extension materials, Inside SeaGrant
Keyword(s): Development/Developing Countries, Oceans/Coasts/Beaches, Water Habitats & Quality, Wildlife & Species

Contact(s):
Linda Blackwell, Director of Communications; blackwlj@musc.edu
M. Devoe, Executive Director; devoemr@musc.edu
Bob Bacon, Extension Program Leader; baconrh@musc.edu
Elaine Knight, Assistant Director; knightel@musc.edu

UNITED STATES DEPARTMENT OF COMMERCE
NATIONAL OCEANIC AND ATMOSPHERIC ADMINISTRATION
SEA GRANT PROGRAM - TEXAS
TEXAS A & M UNIVERSITY
2700 Earl Rudder Freeway South
Suite 1800
College Station, TX 77845 United States
Phone: 979-845-3854   Fax: 979-845-7525
E-mail: egraham@neo.tamu.edu
Website: texas-sea-grant.tamu.edu/

Scope: State, National
Publication(s): Texas Shores, Marine Education
Keyword(s): Agriculture/Farming, Ethics/Environmental Justice, Land Issues, Oceans/Coasts/Beaches, Reduce/Reuse/Recycle, Water Habitats & Quality, Wildlife & Species
Contact(s):
Robert Stickney, Director; 2700 Earl Rudder Frwy. S., Suite 1800, College Station, TX 77845; 979-845-3854; Fax: 979-845-7525; stickne@unix.tamu.edu
Amy Broussard, Associate Director, Marine Information Service; 2700 Earl Rudder Frwy. S, Suite 1800, College Station, TX 77845; 979-862-3767; Fax: 979-845-7525; abrouss@unix.tamu.edu
Jim Hiney, Editor, Texas Shores Magazine; 2700 Earl Rudder Frwy. S, Suite 1800, College Station, TX 77845; 409-862-3773; Fax: 409-862-3786; bohiney@unix.tamu.edu
Russell Miget, Marine Advisory Service; Texas A&M University, Natural Resources Center, 6300 Ocean Dr., Suite 2800, Corpus Christi, TX 78412; 361-825-3460; Fax: 361-825-3465; rmiget@falcon.tamucc.edu

UNITED STATES DEPARTMENT OF COMMERCE
NATIONAL OCEANIC AND ATMOSPHERIC ADMINISTRATION
SEA GRANT PROGRAM - VIRGINIA
UNIVERSITY OF VIRGINIA
Virginia Graduate Marine Science Consortium
170 Rugby Rd.
Madison House
Charlottesville, VA 22903 United States
Phone: 804-924-5065   Fax: 804-982-3694
E-mail: phf7b@virginia.edu
Website: www.virginia.edu/virginia-sea-grant/

Scope: State
Keyword(s): Oceans/Coasts/Beaches, Reduce/Reuse/Recycle, Water Habitats & Quality
Contact(s):
William Rickards, Director; rickards@virginia.edu
William Dupaul, Staff of Marine Advisory Program; Virginia Institute of Marine Science, Gloucester Point, VA 23062; 804-684-7163

UNITED STATES DEPARTMENT OF COMMERCE
NATIONAL OCEANIC AND ATMOSPHERIC ADMINISTRATION
SEA GRANT PROGRAM - WASHINGTON
3716 Brooklyn Ave., NE
Seattle, WA 98105-6716 United States
Phone: 206-543-6600   Fax: 206-685-0380
E-mail: seagrant@u.washington.edu
Website: www.wsg.washington.edu/

Founded: 1971

Scope: State

Description: Since 1968, Washington Sea Grant Program has supported research, advisory, and communication activities for the benefit of marine resources, users, and communities. It is part of a national network of universities meeting the changing environmental and economic needs of people in our coastal and Great Lakes regions.

Publication(s): El Nino North: Nino Effects in the Eastern Subarctic Pacific Ocean, Guide to Manila Clam Culture in Washington, Shape and Form of Puget Sound, The, Ocean Ecology of North Pacific Salmonids

Keyword(s): Development/Developing Countries, Oceans/Coasts/Beaches, Public Health, Water Habitats & Quality, Wildlife & Species

Contact(s):
Louie Echols, Director; echols@u.washington.edu
Melissa O'Neill, Communications Manager; 206-685-9215; Fax: 206-685-0380; nboneill@u.washington.edu
Susan Cook, Publications Coordinator/Web Master; 206-685-2606; Fax: 206-685-0380
Andrea Copping, Assistant Director; 206-685-8209

UNITED STATES DEPARTMENT OF COMMERCE
NATIONAL OCEANIC AND ATMOSPHERIC ADMINISTRATION
SOUTH SLOUGH NATIONAL ESTUARINE RESEARCH RESERVE
P.O. Box 5417
Charleston, OR 97420 United States
Phone: 541-888-5558   Fax: 541-888-5559
E-mail: katherine.andreasen@state.or.us
Website: southsloughestuary.org

Founded: 1974

Scope: Local, State, Regional, National, International

Description: The mission of the South Slough National Estuarine Research Reserve is to improve the understanding and stewardship of Pacific Northwest estuaries and coastal watersheds.

UNITED STATES DEPARTMENT OF COMMERCE
NATIONAL OCEANIC AND ATMOSPHERIC ADMINISTRATION
STELLWAGEN BANK NATIONAL MARINE SANCTUARY
175 Edward Foster Rd.
Scituate, MA 02066 United States
Phone: 781-545-8026   Fax: 781-545-8036
E-mail: stellwagen@noaa.gov
Website: www.stellwagen.nos.noaa.gov

Founded: 1992

Scope: Regional

Description: New England's only National Marine Sanctuary

Keyword(s): Ecosystems (precious), Oceans/Coasts/Beaches, Recreation/Ecotourism

UNITED STATES DEPARTMENT OF COMMERCE
NATIONAL OCEANIC AND ATMOSPHERIC ADMINISTRATION
TIJUANA RIVER NATIONAL ESTUARINE RESEARCH RESERVE
301 Caspian Way
Imperial Beach, CA 91932 United States
Phone: 619-575-3613   Fax: 619-575-6913
E-mail: trnerr@ixpres.com
Website: www.tijuanaestuary.com

Founded: 1982

Scope: Regional, International

Description: The Tijuana River NERR emcompasses 2500 acres of protected southern California wetland, upland and riparian habitat and is located on the U.S./Mexico border. It includes Border Field State Park and Tijuana Slough National Wildlife Refuge and is jointly managed by California State Parks and U.S. Fish & Wildlife Service with additional support from NOAA. It is home to over 300 species of birds and 7 endangered species. The Visitor Center is open from 10-5 seven days a week.

UNITED STATES DEPARTMENT OF COMMERCE
NATIONAL OCEANIC AND ATMOSPHERIC ADMINISTRATION
WAQUOIT BAY NATIONAL ESTUARINE RESEARCH RESERVE
Department of Environmental Management, P.O. Box 3092
Waquoit, MA 02536 United States
Phone: 508-457-0495   Fax: 617-727-5537
E-mail: waquoit.bay@state.ma.us
Website: www.waquoitbayreserve.org

Scope: Regional

Description: Our mission is to work with commmunities to provide and promote improved understanding and management of coastal resources through integrated programs of research, education and stewardship.

UNITED STATES DEPARTMENT OF COMMERCE
NATIONAL OCEANIC AND ATMOSPHERIC ADMINISTRATION
WEEKS BAY NATIONAL ESTUARINE RESEARCH RESERVE
11300 U.S. Highway 98
Fairhope, AL 36532 United States
Phone: 251-928-9792   Fax: 251-928-1792

Scope: Regional

Contact(s):
L. Adams; 251-928-9792

UNITED STATES DEPARTMENT OF COMMERCE
NATIONAL OCEANIC AND ATMOSPHERIC ADMINISTRATION
WELLS NATIONAL ESTUARINE RESEARCH RESERVE
342 Laudholm Farm Rd.
Wells, ME 04090 United States
Phone: 207-646-1555   Fax: 207-646-2930
Website: www.wellsreserve.org

Founded: 1984

Membership: 1,001–10,000

Scope: Regional

Description: Research, education, and stewardship on behalf of coastal environments around the Gulf of Maine. Housed at historic Laudholm Farm.

Publication(s): Watermark Newsletter, Coastal Resource Library

Keyword(s): Agriculture/Farming, Climate Change, Ecosystems (precious), Land Issues, Oceans/Coasts/Beaches, Pollution (general), Public Health, Recreation/Ecotourism, Sprawl/Urban Planning, Water Habitats & Quality, Wildlife & Species

Contact(s):
Paul Dest, Manager
Michele Dionne, Research Coordinator
Laura Lubelczyk, Education Coordinator
Tin Smith, Stewardship Coordinator

UNITED STATES DEPARTMENT OF DEFENSE
The Pentagon, Office of the Secretary, 3400 Defense Pentagon
Washington, DC 20301-3400 United States
Phone: 703-697-9846	Fax: 703-693-7011
Website: www.denix.osd.mil

Scope: International

Description: Responsible for the security of the U.S. by establishing policies and procedures relating to national defense. The Department of Defense conducts programs to prevent pollution, enhance the environment, and conserve the natural and cultural resources on military lands.

Publication(s): DOD Commanders' Guide to Biodiversity, Legacy Resource Management Program Report to Congress, Cultural Resources in the Department of Defense, Natural Resources in the Department of Defense

Contact(s):
Sarah Hagan, Key Contact

UNITED STATES DEPARTMENT OF DEFENSE
AIR FORCE
CENTER FOR ENVIRONMENTAL EXCELLENCE
HQ-AFCEE
3300 Sidney Brooks
Brooks AFB, TX 78235-5112 United States
Phone: 210-536-3823	Fax: 210-536-3890
E-mail: afcee.webmaster@brooks.af.mil
Website: www.afcee.brooks.af.mil/

Scope: National, International

Description: Provides program and project support for Air Force installations worldwide.

Contact(s):
Edward Bakunas, Chief, Program Support Division; 210-536-3334; ed.bakunas@brooks.af.mil
Mary Anderson, Botanist; 210-536-3808; mary.anderson@brooks.af.mil
Daniel Friese, Natural Resource Specialist; 210-536-3823; daniel.friese@brooks.af.mil
Kevin Porteck, Forester; 210-536-5631; kevin.porteck@brooks.af.mil

UNITED STATES DEPARTMENT OF DEFENSE
AIR FORCE, 43RD AIRLIFT WING
POPE AFB, NC
43 CES/CEV
560 Interceptor Rd.
Pope AFB, NC 28308 United States
Phone: 910-394-4195
Website: www.pope.af.mil

Membership: 1–100
Scope: Local

Description: Pope Air Force Base Environmental Flight Supports the 43rd Airlift Wing with Environmental Programs including Mandatory Recycling, Stormwater Management, Review of Construction Projects, Pollution Prevention, Installation Restoration (Cleanup of Sites/Soils), Asbestos and Lead-based Paint Abatement Programs, Tanks, Spill Response, Natural Resources, Historic Properties, Hazardous Wastes, and NEPA.

Keyword(s): Air Quality/Atmosphere, Ecosystems (precious), Land Issues, Pollution (general), Public Health, Recreation/Ecotourism, Reduce/Reuse/Recycle, Water Habitats & Quality, Wildlife & Species

Contact(s):
Viola Walker, Natural/Cultural Resources Manager; 910-394-4195

UNITED STATES DEPARTMENT OF DEFENSE
AIR FORCE MAJOR AIR COMMANDS
AFBCA/EV HEADQUARTERS
Air Force Real Property
1700 N. Moore St., Ste. 2300
Arlington, VA 22209-2802 United States
Phone: 703-696-5536	Fax: 703-696-8833
E-mail: jerry.cleaver@afrpa.pentagon.af.mil

Contact(s):
Jerry Cleaver, Conservation Manager; HQ AFBCA/EV, 1700 N. Moore St., Ste. 2300, Arlington, VA 22209-2802; 703-696-5536

UNITED STATES DEPARTMENT OF DEFENSE
AIR FORCE MAJOR AIR COMMANDS
AFSOC/EV HEADQUARTERS
HQ AFSOC/EV, 427 Cody Ave.
Hurlburt Field, FL 32544 United States
Phone: 850-884-2260	Fax: 850-884-5982

Scope: International

Contact(s):
Michael Applegate, Natural Resource Manager and Entomologist; 850-884-2562

UNITED STATES DEPARTMENT OF DEFENSE
AIR FORCE MAJOR AIR COMMANDS
AIR MOBILITY COMMAND (AMC)
CIVIL ENGINEERING/ENVIRONMENTAL PROGRAMS DIVISION
HQ AMC/CEVP,
507 Symington Drive
Scott AFB, IL 62225-5022 United States
Phone: 618-229-0842	Fax: 618-229-0257
E-mail: will.summers@scott.af.mil
Website: https://amc.af.mil/ce/cev/index.cfm

Founded: 1947
Membership: 101–1,000
Scope: Local, State, Regional, National

Description: U.S. Air Force Air Mobility Command natural resources manager is a function of the Environmental Programs Division which oversees natural resources management on twelve USAF military bases and related outlying airfields and airspace.

Keyword(s): Agriculture/Farming, Ecosystems (precious), Forests/Forestry, Land Issues, Oceans/Coasts/Beaches, Pollution (general), Public Lands/Greenspace, Recreation/Ecotourism, Water Habitats & Quality, Wildlife & Species

Contact(s):
William Summers, Natural Resources Manager, HQ AMC/CEVP

UNITED STATES DEPARTMENT OF DEFENSE
AIR FORCE MAJOR AIR COMMANDS
ANDREWS AFB, MD
3500 Fetchet Ave.
Andrews AFB, MD 20331-5157 United States
Phone: 301-836-8798

Contact(s):
Pat Richerson, Natural Resources Manager, HQ ANG/CEVP

UNITED STATES DEPARTMENT OF DEFENSE
AIR FORCE MAJOR AIR COMMANDS
BOLLING AFB, DC
3700 Brookley Ave.
Washington, DC 20332 United States
Phone: 202-767-8600	Fax: 202-767-1160

Contact(s):
Mark Dickerson, Chief of Environmental Planning Branch

UNITED STATES DEPARTMENT OF DEFENSE
AIR FORCE MAJOR AIR COMMANDS
GERMANY AFB
Unit 3050, Box 10
APO, AE, 09094-5010 Germany
Phone: 011-49-6371-47-6482

Contact(s):
Edwin Worth, Natural/Cultural Resources Manager, HQ USAFE/CEVP

UNITED STATES DEPARTMENT OF DEFENSE
AIR FORCE MAJOR AIR COMMANDS
KIRTLAND AFB, NM
9700 Avenue G S.E.
Suite 266
Kirtland AFB, NM 87117-5671 United States
Phone: 505-846-5674   Fax: 505-846-0684

Contact(s):
Peter Windler, Chief, USAF Bash Team

UNITED STATES DEPARTMENT OF DEFENSE
AIR FORCE MAJOR AIR COMMANDS
LANGLEY AFB, VA
129 Andrews St., Suite 102, Major Air Commands
Langley AFB, VA 23665-2769 United States
Phone: 757-764-9338
Website: www.acc.af.mil/

Scope: Regional
Description: Provide natural resource conservation leadership to 18 AF installations, protecting threatened and endangered species, migratory birds, neotropical birds in an ecoystem management approach.

Contact(s):
Roy Barker, Natural Resources Manager, HQ ACC/CEVA

UNITED STATES DEPARTMENT OF DEFENSE
AIR FORCE MAJOR AIR COMMANDS
PETERSON AFB, CO
150 Vandenberg St., Suite 1105
Peterson AFB, CO 80914-4150 United States
Phone: 719-554-9915   Fax: 719-554-3849

Scope: Local, State, Regional, National, International
Description: AFSPC is a Major Command with over 14 installations in the U.S. and overseas.
Keyword(s): Agriculture/Farming, Ecosystems (precious), Forests/Forestry, Land Issues, Oceans/Coasts/Beaches, Public Lands/Greenspace, Recreation/Ecotourism, Sprawl/Urban Planning, Water Habitats & Quality, Wildlife & Species

Contact(s):
Stanley Rogers, Natural Resources Manager, HQ AFSPC/CEVP; stanley.rogers@peterson.af.mil

UNITED STATES DEPARTMENT OF DEFENSE
AIR FORCE MAJOR AIR COMMANDS
RANDOLPH AFB, TX
266 F St., West, Bldg. 901
Randolph AFB, TX 78150-4321 United States
Phone: 210-652-3959
Website: www.aetc.randolph.af.mil/

Contact(s):
Carl Lahser, Natural Resources Manager, HQ AETC/CEV

UNITED STATES DEPARTMENT OF DEFENSE
AIR FORCE MAJOR AIR COMMANDS
ROBINS AFB, GA
155 Richard Ray Blvd.
Robins AFB, GA 31098-1635 United States

UNITED STATES DEPARTMENT OF DEFENSE
AIR FORCE MAJOR AIR COMMANDS
SPECIAL OPERATIONS COMMAND
Building 90333
427 Cody Avenue
Suite 225
Hurlburt Field, FL 32404 United States
Phone: 850-884-2977   Fax: 850-884-5982
E-mail: ronald.nasca@hurlburt.af.mil
Website: www.hurlburt.af.mil

Founded: 1990
Membership: 1,001–10,000
Scope: Local, International
Description: Hurlburt Field, home of the AF Special Operations Command

Contact(s):
Philip Pruit, Natural Resources Manager; 850-884-4651

UNITED STATES DEPARTMENT OF DEFENSE
AIR FORCE MAJOR AIR COMMANDS
USAF ACADEMY
8120 Edgerton Dr., Suite 40
USAF Academy, CO 80840-2400 United States
Phone: 719-333-3308   Fax: 719-333-3337
E-mail: brian.mihlbachler@usafa.af.mil
Website: www.usafa.af.mil

Scope: Local, Regional
Description: Range, Wildlife, and Forestry Management

Contact(s):
Brian Mihlbachler, Natural Resource Planner A/CEVP; 719-333-3308; Fax: 719-333-3337; brian.mihlbachler@usafa.af.mil
Jim McDermott, Natural Resource Planner; 719-333-3308; Fax: 719-333-3337; james.mcdermott@usafa.af.mil

UNITED STATES DEPARTMENT OF DEFENSE
AIR FORCE MAJOR AIR COMMANDS
USAF/ILEV HEADQUARTERS
Environmental Division, HQ USAF/ILEV, 1260 Air Force Pentagon
Washington, DC 20330-1260 United States
Phone: 703-604-0632   Fax: 703-604-3740

Scope: National
Description: A comprehensive natural resources conservation program focusing on fish and wildlife management, forestry, outdoor recreation, and soil and water conservation has been conducted on Air Force lands since the mid-1950's. Current policy requires all installations with significant land and water resources to develop integrated natural resource management plans as part of the base comprehensive planning process.

Contact(s):
Alan Holck, Natural and Cultural Resources Program Manager

UNITED STATES DEPARTMENT OF DEFENSE
AIR FORCE MAJOR AIR COMMANDS
WRIGHT PATTERSON AFB, OH
HQ AFMC/CEVQ
4225 Logistics Ave., Rm. A128
Wright Patterson AFB, OH 45433-5747 United States
Phone: 937-656-1409   Fax: 937-587-5875
E-mail: mike.cornelius@wpafb.af.mil
Website: https://www.afmc-mil.wpafb.af.mil/HQ-AFMC/CE/

Scope: National
Description: Provides natural resources program and budget support for AFMC installations.

Contact(s):
Mike Cornelius, Natural Resources Manager; HQ AFMC/CEVQ,

U.S. FEDERAL AND INTERNATIONAL GOVERNMENT AGENCIES – U

UNITED STATES DEPARTMENT OF DEFENSE
AIR FORCE MAJOR U.S. INSTALLATIONS
ALTUS AFB, OK
97 CES/CEV
607 South First Street
Altus AFB, OK 73523-5106 United States
Phone: 580-481-7606
E-mail: carl.lahser@randolph.af.mil
Contact(s):
Jim Bellon, Natural Resources Manager; 580-481-7606

UNITED STATES DEPARTMENT OF DEFENSE
AIR FORCE MAJOR U.S. INSTALLATIONS
ANDERSON AFB, GUAM, UNITED STATES
Contact(s):
Heidi Hirsh, Natural Resources Manager; 671-366-2549

UNITED STATES DEPARTMENT OF DEFENSE
AIR FORCE MAJOR U.S. INSTALLATIONS
ANDREWS AFB, MD, UNITED STATES
Contact(s):
Carol Devier-Heemey, Cultural/Natural Resources Manager; 301-981-2579

UNITED STATES DEPARTMENT OF DEFENSE
AIR FORCE MAJOR U.S. INSTALLATIONS
ARNOLD AFB, TN, UNITED STATES
Contact(s):
Clark Brandon, Natural/Cultural Resources Manager; 615-454-7115

UNITED STATES DEPARTMENT OF DEFENSE
AIR FORCE MAJOR U.S. INSTALLATIONS
AVON PARK AFB, FL, UNITED STATES
Contact(s):
Paul Ebersbach, Chief of Conservation Programs; 941-452-7119, ext. 301

UNITED STATES DEPARTMENT OF DEFENSE
AIR FORCE MAJOR U.S. INSTALLATIONS
BARKSDALE AFB, LA
6141 Range Road, 71110 United States
Phone: 318-456-1981   Fax: 318-456-1321
E-mail: mark.gates@barksdale.af.mil
Contact(s):
Bruce Holland, Natural Resources Manager; 318-456-1981

UNITED STATES DEPARTMENT OF DEFENSE
AIR FORCE MAJOR U.S. INSTALLATIONS
BEALE AFB, CA, UNITED STATES
Contact(s):
Kristen Christopherson, Natural Resouces Manager; 916-634-2643

UNITED STATES DEPARTMENT OF DEFENSE
AIR FORCE MAJOR U.S. INSTALLATIONS
BOLLING AFB, DC, UNITED STATES
Contact(s):
Fioravante Gaetano, Natural Resources Manager; 202-767-8603

UNITED STATES DEPARTMENT OF DEFENSE
AIR FORCE MAJOR U.S. INSTALLATIONS
BROOKS AFB, TX, UNITED STATES
Contact(s):
Hamid Kamalpour, Natural Resources Manager; 210-536-6703

UNITED STATES DEPARTMENT OF DEFENSE
AIR FORCE MAJOR U.S. INSTALLATIONS
CANNON AFB, NM, UNITED STATES
Contact(s):
Rick Crow, Cultural/Natural Resources Manager; 505-784-6383

UNITED STATES DEPARTMENT OF DEFENSE
AIR FORCE MAJOR U.S. INSTALLATIONS
CHARLESTON AFB, SC
437 CES/CEVP
100 West Stewart Avenue
Charleston, SC 29404 United States
Contact(s):
Al Urrutia, Cultural/Natural Resources Manager; 843-963-4978

UNITED STATES DEPARTMENT OF DEFENSE
AIR FORCE MAJOR U.S. INSTALLATIONS
COLUMBUS AFB, MS
14 CES/CEV
555 Simler Boulevard
Columbus AFB, MS 39701-6010 United States
Contact(s):
Ryan Nelson, Cultural/Natural Resources Manager; 601-434-7315

UNITED STATES DEPARTMENT OF DEFENSE
AIR FORCE MAJOR U.S. INSTALLATIONS
DAVIS-MONTHAN AFB, AZ, UNITED STATES
Contact(s):
Gwen Lisa, Cultural/Natural Resources Manager; 520-228-3215

UNITED STATES DEPARTMENT OF DEFENSE
AIR FORCE MAJOR U.S. INSTALLATIONS
DOVER AFB, DE
600 Chevron Avenue
Dover, DE 19902 United States
Phone: 302-677-6820   Fax: 302-677-4754
Contact(s):
Charles Mikula, Cultural/Natural Resources Manager; 302-677-6820

UNITED STATES DEPARTMENT OF DEFENSE
AIR FORCE MAJOR U.S. INSTALLATIONS
DYESS AFB, TX UNITED STATES
Phone: 915-696-5049   Fax: 915-696-2899
Website: https://www.mil.dyess.af.mil
Contact(s):
Jim Robertson, Cultural/Natural Resources Director

UNITED STATES DEPARTMENT OF DEFENSE
AIR FORCE MAJOR U.S. INSTALLATIONS
EDWARDS AFB, CA, UNITED STATES
Contact(s):
Mark Hagan, Natural Resources Manager; 805-277-1418

UNITED STATES DEPARTMENT OF DEFENSE
AIR FORCE MAJOR U.S. INSTALLATIONS
EGLIN AIR FORCE BASE
NATURAL RESOURCE MANAGEMENT UNIT
Jackson Guard
107 Highway 85N
Niceville, FL 32578 United States
Phone: 850-882-4164, ext. 301   Fax: 850-882-5321
Founded: 1945
Scope: Local, State, Regional, National

Description: Natural Resource managers for 464,000 acre Eglin AFB, one of The Nature Conservancy's hotspots of national biodiversity. Natural Resource managers sections cover Forestry, Fire and Wildlife.

Keyword(s): Ecosystems (precious), Forests/Forestry, Public Lands/Greenspace, Recreation/Ecotourism, Water Habitats & Quality, Wildlife & Species

UNITED STATES DEPARTMENT OF DEFENSE
AIR FORCE MAJOR U.S. INSTALLATIONS
EIELSON AFB, AK, UNITED STATES

Contact(s):
Gerald Von Rueden, Natural Resources Manager; 907-377-5182

UNITED STATES DEPARTMENT OF DEFENSE
AIR FORCE MAJOR U.S. INSTALLATIONS
ELLSWORTH AFB, SD, UNITED STATES

Contact(s):
Jim Stengler, Cultural/Natural Resources Manager; 605-385-6677

UNITED STATES DEPARTMENT OF DEFENSE
AIR FORCE MAJOR U.S. INSTALLATIONS
ELMENDORF AFB, AK
3CES/CEVP
6326 Arctic Warrior Drive
Elmendorf AFB, AK, 99506-3240 United States

Contact(s):
Alan Richmond, Natural Resources Manager; 907-552-1609

UNITED STATES DEPARTMENT OF DEFENSE
AIR FORCE MAJOR U.S. INSTALLATIONS
F.E. WARREN AFB, WY
300 Vefle Dr. @600
F.E. Warren AFB, WY 82005 United States
Phone: 307-773-5494   Fax: 307-773-2322

Contact(s):
Catherine Pazenti, Natural Resources Manager; 307-773-5494

UNITED STATES DEPARTMENT OF DEFENSE
AIR FORCE MAJOR U.S. INSTALLATIONS
FAIRCHILD AFB, WA, UNITED STATES

Contact(s):
Gerald Johnson, Natural Resources Manager; 509-247-2313

UNITED STATES DEPARTMENT OF DEFENSE
AIR FORCE MAJOR U.S. INSTALLATIONS
GOODFELLOW AFB, TX
17 CES/CEV
460 Kearney Boulevard
Goodfellow AFB, TX 37608-4122 United States

Contact(s):
Lyndal Fisher, Natural Resources Manager; 915-654-3451

UNITED STATES DEPARTMENT OF DEFENSE
AIR FORCE MAJOR U.S. INSTALLATIONS
GRAND FORKS AFB, ND, UNITED STATES

UNITED STATES DEPARTMENT OF DEFENSE
AIR FORCE MAJOR U.S. INSTALLATIONS
HANSCOM AFB, MA, UNITED STATES

Contact(s):
Don Morris, Natural Resources Manager; 617-377-4667

UNITED STATES DEPARTMENT OF DEFENSE
AIR FORCE MAJOR U.S. INSTALLATIONS
HICKAM AFB, HI, UNITED STATES

Contact(s):
Gary O'Donnell, Natural Resources Manager; 808-449-9695; ext. 205

UNITED STATES DEPARTMENT OF DEFENSE
AIR FORCE MAJOR U.S. INSTALLATIONS
HILL AFB, UT, UNITED STATES
Phone: 801-777-4618

Contact(s):
Marcus Blood, Cultural/Natural Resources Manager; 801-777-4618

UNITED STATES DEPARTMENT OF DEFENSE
AIR FORCE MAJOR U.S. INSTALLATIONS
HOLLOMAN AFB, NM, UNITED STATES

Contact(s):
Hildy Reiser, Natural Resources Manager; 505-475-3931

UNITED STATES DEPARTMENT OF DEFENSE
AIR FORCE MAJOR U.S. INSTALLATIONS
HURLBURT FIELD, FL, UNITED STATES
Phone: 850-884-7921   Fax: 850-884-2580
E-mail: philip.pruit@hulburt.af.mil

Contact(s):
Philip Pruit, Natural/Cultural Resources Manager; 850-884-4651

UNITED STATES DEPARTMENT OF DEFENSE
AIR FORCE MAJOR U.S. INSTALLATIONS
KEESLER AFB, MS
81 CES/CEV
508 L Street
Keesler AFB, MS 39534-2115 United States
Phone: 228-377-2489   Fax: 228-377-2749

Contact(s):
George Daniels, Natural Resources Manager; 228-377-2489

UNITED STATES DEPARTMENT OF DEFENSE
AIR FORCE MAJOR U.S. INSTALLATIONS
KIRTLAND AFB, NM UNITED STATES
Phone: 505-280-7604

Contact(s):
Bob Dow, Natural Resources Manager; 505-280-7604

UNITED STATES DEPARTMENT OF DEFENSE
AIR FORCE MAJOR U.S. INSTALLATIONS
LACKLAND AFB, TX, UNITED STATES
Phone: 210-671-4843

Contact(s):
Robert Johnson, Natural Resources Manager; 210-671-4843

UNITED STATES DEPARTMENT OF DEFENSE
AIR FORCE MAJOR U.S. INSTALLATIONS
LANGLEY AFB, VA UNITED STATES
Phone: 757-764-1090

Contact(s):
Patsy Kerr, Natural Resources Manager; 757-764-1090

UNITED STATES DEPARTMENT OF DEFENSE
AIR FORCE MAJOR U.S. INSTALLATIONS
LAUGHLIN AFB, TX
47 CES/CEV
251 Fourth Street
Laughlin AFB, TX 78843-5143 United States
Phone: 830-298-5063

Contact(s):
Jadee Bell, Natural Resources Manager; 830-298-4298

U.S. FEDERAL AND INTERNATIONAL GOVERNMENT AGENCIES – U

UNITED STATES DEPARTMENT OF DEFENSE
AIR FORCE MAJOR U.S. INSTALLATIONS
LITTLE ROCK AFB, AR
314 CES/CEV
528 Thomas Avenue
Little Rock AFB, AR 72099-4987 United States
Phone: 501-987-3681

Contact(s):
James Popham, Cultural/Natural Resources Manager; 501-987-3681

UNITED STATES DEPARTMENT OF DEFENSE
AIR FORCE MAJOR U.S. INSTALLATIONS
LUKE AFB (AND THE BARRY M. GOLDWATER AFR), AZ
56 CES/CEV
13970 Lightning
Luke AFB, AZ 85309-1149 United States
Phone: 623-856-3823

Contact(s):
Robert Barry, Chief of Conservation Programs; 623-856-3823; ext. 242

UNITED STATES DEPARTMENT OF DEFENSE
AIR FORCE MAJOR U.S. INSTALLATIONS
MACDILL AFB, FL
Jason Kirkpatrick
2610 Pink Flamingo Avenue
MacDill AFB, FL 33621 United States
Phone: 813-828-0459

Scope: Local
Description: Natural/Cultural Resources Program for MacDill AFB. Responsible for environmental compliance, and protection/improvement of natural and cultural resources on base.
Keyword(s): Air Quality/Atmosphere, Ecosystems (precious), Ethics/Environmental Justice, Pollution (general), Reduce/Reuse/Recycle, Water Habitats & Quality, Wildlife & Species

Contact(s):
Jason Kirkpatrick, Conservation Program Manager; 813-828-0459; Fax: 813-828-2212
Jeff Sprinkmann, Natural Resources Manager; 813-828-0460

UNITED STATES DEPARTMENT OF DEFENSE
AIR FORCE MAJOR U.S. INSTALLATIONS
MALMSTROM AFB, MT UNITED STATES
Phone: 406-731-6438

Contact(s):
Rudy Berzuh, Cultural/Natural Resources Manager; 406-731-6437

UNITED STATES DEPARTMENT OF DEFENSE
AIR FORCE MAJOR U.S. INSTALLATIONS
MAXWELL AFB, AL
MSD/CEV
400 Cannon Street
Maxwell AFB, AL 36112-6523 United States
Phone: 334-953-5757   Fax: 334-953-5360

Contact(s):
Ruth Vandiver, Natural Resources Manager; 334-953-3892

UNITED STATES DEPARTMENT OF DEFENSE
AIR FORCE MAJOR U.S. INSTALLATIONS
MCCHORD AFB, WA
62 CES/CEVN
555 A Street
McChord AFB, WA 98438 United States
Phone: 253-982-3913

Scope: Local

Contact(s):
Valerie Elliott, Natural Resources Manager

UNITED STATES DEPARTMENT OF DEFENSE
AIR FORCE MAJOR U.S. INSTALLATIONS
MCCLELLAN AFB, CA UNITED STATES
Phone: 916-643-1742

Contact(s):
Molly Enloe, Natural Resources Manager; 919-643-1742

UNITED STATES DEPARTMENT OF DEFENSE
AIR FORCE MAJOR U.S. INSTALLATIONS
MCCONNELL AFB, KS UNITED STATES
Phone: 316-759-3884

Contact(s):
John Hafker, Cultural/Natural Resources Manager; 316-759-3884

UNITED STATES DEPARTMENT OF DEFENSE
AIR FORCE MAJOR U.S. INSTALLATIONS
MCGUIRE AFB, NJ, UNITED STATES

UNITED STATES DEPARTMENT OF DEFENSE
AIR FORCE MAJOR U.S. INSTALLATIONS
MOODY AFB, GA
347 CES/CEVA
3485 Georgia Street
Moody AFB, GA 31699-1707 United States
Phone: 229-257-5881   Fax: 229-257-5811
E-mail: gregory.lee@moody.af.mil

Scope: Local, State, Regional, National
Description: The Environmental Flight at Moody AFB is charged with the professional stewardship of the natural resources entrusted to the installation.

Contact(s):
Gregory Lee, Natural Resources Manager; 229-257-5881; Fax: 229-257-5811; gregory.lee@moody.af.mil

UNITED STATES DEPARTMENT OF DEFENSE
AIR FORCE MAJOR U.S. INSTALLATIONS
MOUNTAIN HOME AFB, ID 83648 UNITED STATES
Phone: 208-828-6351

Scope: Local
Description: Home of the 366th Fighter Wing

Contact(s):
Angelia Martin, Chief, Conservation; 208-828-6351

UNITED STATES DEPARTMENT OF DEFENSE
AIR FORCE MAJOR U.S. INSTALLATIONS
NELLIS AFB, NV
99 CES/CEVN
4349 Duffer Drive
Suite 1601
Nellis AFB, NV 89191 United States
Phone: 702-652-3173   Fax: 702-652-2021
E-mail: Shelia.Amos@Nellis.af.mil
Website: www.Nellis.af.mil

Founded: 1988
Scope: Local, State
Description: Conservation Team responsible for the compliance of Federal, state and local environmental laws on 2.9 million acres of land in Nevada

Contact(s):
Shelia Amos, Natural Resources Manager; 702-652-3173; Fax: 702-652-2021; Shelia.Amos@Nellis.af.mil
Bill Sandeen, Land Manager; 702-652-2834; Fax: 702-652-2021; William.Sandeen@Nellis.af.mil
Deborah Stockdale, Chief, Conservation; 702-652-6106; Fax: 702-652-2021; Deborah.Stockdale@Nellis.af.mil

UNITED STATES DEPARTMENT OF DEFENSE
AIR FORCE MAJOR U.S. INSTALLATIONS
OFFUT AFB, NE
CES/CEV
106 Peacekeeper Dr. #2N3
Offut AFB, NE 68113 United States
Contact(s):
  Gene Svensen, Cultural/Natural Resource Manager; 402-294-7619

UNITED STATES DEPARTMENT OF DEFENSE
AIR FORCE MAJOR U.S. INSTALLATIONS
PATRICK AFB, FL UNITED STATES
Phone: 321-494-7288
Contact(s):
  Mike Camardese, Cultural/Natural Resources Manager; 321-853-0910

UNITED STATES DEPARTMENT OF DEFENSE
AIR FORCE MAJOR U.S. INSTALLATIONS
PETERSON AFB, CO UNITED STATES
Phone: 719-554-9915
Contact(s):
  Dan Rogers, Natural Resource Manager

UNITED STATES DEPARTMENT OF DEFENSE
AIR FORCE MAJOR U.S. INSTALLATIONS
RANDOLPH AFB, TX
12 CES/CEV
1651 Fifth Street West
Randolph AFB, TX 78150-4513 United States
Phone: 210-652-4668   Fax: 210-652-3685
Contact(s):
  Catherine Vornberg, Natural Resources Manager; 210-652-4668

UNITED STATES DEPARTMENT OF DEFENSE
AIR FORCE MAJOR U.S. INSTALLATIONS
REMOTE SITES (611 SUPPORT GROUP), AK, UNITED STATES
Contact(s):
  Gene Augustine, Natural Resources Manager; 907-552-0788

UNITED STATES DEPARTMENT OF DEFENSE
AIR FORCE MAJOR U.S. INSTALLATIONS
SCOTT AFB, IL
375th CES/CEV
702 Hangar Rd #52
Scott AFB, IL 62225-5035 United States
Phone: 618-256-2092   Fax: 618-256-5934
Contact(s):
  William Calvert, Cultural/Natural Resources Manager; 618-256-2092

UNITED STATES DEPARTMENT OF DEFENSE
AIR FORCE MAJOR U.S. INSTALLATIONS
SEYMOUR JOHNSON AFB (AND DARE COUNTY AFR), NC UNITED STATES
Phone: 919-722-5173
Contact(s):
  Brian Henderson, Cultural/Natural Resources Manager; 919-722-5173

UNITED STATES DEPARTMENT OF DEFENSE
AIR FORCE MAJOR U.S. INSTALLATIONS
SHAW AFB, SC, UNITED STATES
Contact(s):
  Terry Madewell, Cultural/Natural Resources Manager; 803-895-5193

UNITED STATES DEPARTMENT OF DEFENSE
AIR FORCE MAJOR U.S. INSTALLATIONS
SHEPPARD AFB, TX
82 CES/CEV
231 Ninth Street
Sheppard AFB, TX, 76311-3333 United States
Phone: 940-676-5698
Contact(s):
  Tim Hunter, Cultural/Natural Resources Manager; 940-676-5698

UNITED STATES DEPARTMENT OF DEFENSE
AIR FORCE MAJOR U.S. INSTALLATIONS
SHRIEVER AFB, CO UNITED STATES
Phone: 719-567-3360
Contact(s):
  Melissa Trenchik, Natural Resource Manager

UNITED STATES DEPARTMENT OF DEFENSE
AIR FORCE MAJOR U.S. INSTALLATIONS
TINKER AFB, OK, UNITED STATES
Contact(s):
  John Krupovage, Natural Resources Manager; 405-734-3093

UNITED STATES DEPARTMENT OF DEFENSE
AIR FORCE MAJOR U.S. INSTALLATIONS
TRAVIS AFB, CA UNITED STATES
Phone: 707-424-7515
Contact(s):
  Robert Holmes, Natural Resources Manager

UNITED STATES DEPARTMENT OF DEFENSE
AIR FORCE MAJOR U.S. INSTALLATIONS
TYNDALL AFB, FL
325 CES/CEVN
119 Alabama Avenue
Tyndall AFB, FL 32403-5014 United States
Phone: 850-283-2641
Contact(s):
  Bob Bates, Natural Resources Manager; 850-283-2641

UNITED STATES DEPARTMENT OF DEFENSE
AIR FORCE MAJOR U.S. INSTALLATIONS
VANCE AFB, OK UNITED STATES
Contact(s):
  Mark Buthman, Cultural/Natural Resources Manager

UNITED STATES DEPARTMENT OF DEFENSE
AIR FORCE MAJOR U.S. INSTALLATIONS
VANDENBERG AFB, CA UNITED STATES
Contact(s):
  Allan Naydol, Natural Resources Manager

UNITED STATES DEPARTMENT OF DEFENSE
AIR FORCE MAJOR U.S. INSTALLATIONS
WHITEMAN AFB, MO UNITED STATES
Contact(s):
  Neil Bass, Cultural/Natural Resources Manager
  Angela Corson, Natural Resources Manager

UNITED STATES DEPARTMENT OF DEFENSE
AIR FORCE MAJOR U.S. INSTALLATIONS
WRIGHT-PATTERSON AFB, OH
88SBW/EMO
Wright-Patterson AFB, OH 45433 United States
Phone: 937-257-5535, ext. 262
Contact(s):
  Terri Lucas, Natural Resources Planner; 937-257-5535; ext. 262

UNITED STATES DEPARTMENT OF DEFENSE
ARMY
Pentagon Environmental Dept.
Washington, DC 20310 United States
Phone: 703-695-7824　　　　Fax: 703-693-8149
Scope: State
Contact(s):
　Raymond Fatz, Deputy Assistant Secretary of the Army, Environment of Safety; 703-695-7824
　Phil Huber, Assistant for Environmental Quality; 703-614-9555

UNITED STATES DEPARTMENT OF DEFENSE
ARMY CORPS OF ENGINEERS
HEADQUARTERS
441 G St.
Washington, DC 20314-1000 United States
Phone: 202-761-0001
Website: www.usace.army.mil
Founded: 1775
Membership: 10,001–100,000
Scope: Local, State, Regional, National, International
Description: The mission of the Corps of Engineers is to provide quality, responsive engineering and environmental services to the nation. The Corps plans, designs, builds, and operates water resources and other civil works projects. The Corps designs and manages the construction of military facilities and activities for the Army and Air Force and provides design and construction management support for other defense and federal agencies.
Keyword(s): Development/Developing Countries, Energy, Oceans/Coasts/Beaches, Pollution (general), Public Health, Public Lands/Greenspace, Recreation/Ecotourism, Reduce/Reuse/Recycle, Transportation, Water Habitats & Quality, Wildlife & Species
Contact(s):
　John Bellinger, Endangered Species/NEPA Coordinator; 202-761-0166
　Darrell Lewis, Chief, Natural Resources; 202-761-0247
　Robert Mirelson, Chief, Public Affairs; 202-761-0010
　Paul Rubenstein, Cultural Resources Coordinator; 202-761-1257
　Lloyd Saunders, Executive Secretary, Environmental Advisory Board; 202-761-8731
　Robert Soots, Chief, Office of Environmental Policy; 703-428-6491
　John Studt, Chief, Regulatory; 202-761-1785
　Timothy Toplisek, Fish and Wildlife Coordinator; 202-761-1789
　James Wolcott, Chief, Environmental Compliance; 202-761-0200

UNITED STATES DEPARTMENT OF DEFENSE
ARMY CORPS OF ENGINEERS
ALASKA ENGINEER DISTRICT
Anchorage, AK 99506-0898 United States
Phone: 907-753-2520　　　　Fax: 907-753-2526
Website: www.poa.usace.army.mil
Membership: 101–1,000
Scope: National

UNITED STATES DEPARTMENT OF DEFENSE
ARMY CORPS OF ENGINEERS
ALBUQUERQUE ENGINEER DISTRICT
4101 Jefferson Plaza NE
Albuquerque, NM 87109-3435 United States
Phone: 505-342-3116　　　　Fax: 505-342-3199
Membership: 101–1,000
Scope: National

UNITED STATES DEPARTMENT OF DEFENSE
ARMY CORPS OF ENGINEERS
ALEXANDRIA ENGINEER DISTRICT
7701 Telegraph Rd.
Alexandria, VA 22315-3864 United States
Phone: 703-428-6600　　　　Fax: 703-428-8154
Website: www.tech.army.mil
Membership: 101–1,000
Scope: National

UNITED STATES DEPARTMENT OF DEFENSE
ARMY CORPS OF ENGINEERS
ALEXANDRIA ENGINEER DISTRICT
7701 Telegraph Road, Casey Building
Alexandria, VA 22315-3868 United States
Phone: 703-428-8250　　　　Fax: 703-428-8171
Website: www.iwr.usce.army.mil
Membership: 101–1,000
Scope: State

UNITED STATES DEPARTMENT OF DEFENSE
ARMY CORPS OF ENGINEERS
BALTIMORE ENGINEER DISTRICT
P.O. Box 1715
Baltimore, MD 21203 United States
Phone: 410-962-2809　　　　Fax: 410-962-3660
Website: www.nab.usace.army.mil/
Membership: 1,001–10,000
Scope: International
Description: Through the execution of Military, Civil Works and Support for Others programs, Baltimore District provides design, engineering, construction, environmental and real estate expertise to a variety of important projects and customers. This support spans across five states, the District of Columbia, overseas, and across the Susquehanna, Potomac and Chesapeake Bay watersheds
Publication(s): The Constellation
Keyword(s): Ecosystems (precious), Oceans/Coasts/Beaches, Recreation/Ecotourism, Water Habitats & Quality
Contact(s):
　Charles Flala, District Engineer

UNITED STATES DEPARTMENT OF DEFENSE
ARMY CORPS OF ENGINEERS
BUFFALO ENGINEER DISTRICT
1776 Niagara Street
Buffalo, NY 14207-3199 United States
Phone: 716-879-4200　　　　Fax: 716-879-4195
Website: www.lrb.usace.army.mil
Scope: State
Contact(s):
　Nancy Sticht, Public Affairs Officer; 716-879-4410; nancy.j.sticht@usace.army.mil

UNITED STATES DEPARTMENT OF DEFENSE
ARMY CORPS OF ENGINEERS
CHAMPAIGN ENGINEER DISTRICT
P.O. Box 9005
Champaign, IL 61826-9005 United States
Phone: 217-373-7201　　　　Fax: 217-373-7222
Website: www.cecer.army.mil
Membership: 101–1,000
Scope: International

UNITED STATES DEPARTMENT OF DEFENSE
ARMY CORPS OF ENGINEERS
CHARLESTON ENGINEER DISTRICT
69 A Hagood Ave
Charleston, SC 29403-5107 United States
Phone: 843-329-8000

Contact(s):
Peter Mueller

UNITED STATES DEPARTMENT OF DEFENSE
ARMY CORPS OF ENGINEERS
CHICAGO ENGINEER DISTRICT
111 N. Canal Street, Suite 600
Chicago, IL 60606-7206 United States
Phone: 312-846-5330   Fax: 312-353-2525
Website: www.lrc.usace.army.mil

Founded: 1833
Membership: 101–1,000
Scope: Local, Regional, National
Description: The Chicago District has been serving the people of the Chicago metropolitan area since 1833, with expertise in the fields of inland navigation, flood damage reduction, environmental protection and restoration, construction management, watershed management and natural disaster response.

Contact(s):
Mark Roncoli, District Commander

UNITED STATES DEPARTMENT OF DEFENSE
ARMY CORPS OF ENGINEERS
DETROIT ENGINEER DISTRICT
P.O. Box 1027
Detroit, MI 48231-1027 United States
Phone: 313-226-6762   Fax: 313-226-6009

Membership: 101–1,000
Scope: State

Contact(s):
Richard Polo, Commander & District Engineer

UNITED STATES DEPARTMENT OF DEFENSE
ARMY CORPS OF ENGINEERS
FORT WORTH ENGINEER DISTRICT
Fort Worth, TX 76102-0300 United States
Phone: 817-978-2300   Fax: 817-978-3311
Website: www.usace.army.mil

Membership: 101–1,000
Scope: Regional

UNITED STATES DEPARTMENT OF DEFENSE
ARMY CORPS OF ENGINEERS
GALVESTON ENGINEER DISTRICT
P.O. Box 1229
Galveston, TX 77553-1229 United States
Phone: 409-766-3001   Fax: 409-766-3951
Website: www.usace.army.mil

Membership: 101–1,000
Scope: Local
Description: The Galveston District deals with environmental, operation & maintenance, regulatory, engineering and construction issues.
Keyword(s): Ecosystems (precious), Oceans/Coasts/Beaches, Recreation/Ecotourism, Water Habitats & Quality, Wildlife & Species

Contact(s):
Mary Ann Patlan, Secretary

UNITED STATES DEPARTMENT OF DEFENSE
ARMY CORPS OF ENGINEERS
GREAT LAKES AND OHIO ENGINEER DISTRICT
P.O. Box 1159
Cincinnati, OH 45201-1159 United States
Phone: 513-684-3002   Fax: 513-684-2085
E-mail: celrd-de@usace.army.mil
Website: www.lrd.usace.army.mil

Founded: 1774
Membership: 1,001–10,000
Scope: Local, State, Regional, National, International
Description: The world's premier public engineering organization responding to our nation's needs in peace and war. Striving to achieve Environmental Sustainability, recognizing the interdependence of life and the physical environment, seeking balance and synergy among human development activities and natural systems and building and sharing an integrated scientific, economic and social knowledge base that supports a greater understanding of the environment and impacts of our work.

Contact(s):
Steven Hawkins, Division Commander of the Great Lakes & Ohio River

UNITED STATES DEPARTMENT OF DEFENSE
ARMY CORPS OF ENGINEERS
HANOVER ENGINEER DISTRICT
72 Lyme Road
Hanover, NH 03755-1290 United States
Phone: 603-646-4200   Fax: 603-646-4178
Website: www.crrel.usace.army.mil

Membership: 101–1,000
Scope: International
Publication(s): Technical Reports

Contact(s):
Barbara Sotirin, Director; 603-646-4200

UNITED STATES DEPARTMENT OF DEFENSE
ARMY CORPS OF ENGINEERS
HONOLULU ENGINEER DISTRICT
Building 230
Fort Shafter, HI 96858-5440 United States
Phone: 808-438-1069   Fax: 808-438-8351
Website: www.poh.usace.army.mil

Membership: 101–1,000
Scope: State

Contact(s):
Alex Skinner, Executive Assistant

UNITED STATES DEPARTMENT OF DEFENSE
ARMY CORPS OF ENGINEERS
HUNTINGTON ENGINEER DISTRICT
502 8th Street
Huntington, WV 25701-2070 United States
Phone: 304-529-5395   Fax: 304-529-5591
Website: www.intra.lrh.usace.army.mil

Membership: 101–1,000
Scope: Regional

Contact(s):
John Ridenburg, Colonel

UNITED STATES DEPARTMENT OF DEFENSE
ARMY CORPS OF ENGINEERS
JACKSONVILLE ENGINEER DISTRICT
P.O. Box 4970
Jacksonville, FL 32232-0019 United States
Phone: 904-232-2241   Fax: 904-232-1213

Membership: 101–1,000
Scope: State

Contact(s):
James May, District Engineer

U.S. FEDERAL AND INTERNATIONAL GOVERNMENT AGENCIES – U

UNITED STATES DEPARTMENT OF DEFENSE
ARMY CORPS OF ENGINEERS
KANSAS CITY ENGINEER DISTRICT
601 E. 12th Street
Kansas City, MO 64106-2896 United States
Phone: 816-983-3201   Fax: 806-426-5575
Membership: 101–1,000
Scope: Regional

UNITED STATES DEPARTMENT OF DEFENSE
ARMY CORPS OF ENGINEERS
LITTLE ROCK ENGINEER DISTRICT
P.O. Box 867
Little Rock, AR 72203-0867 United States
Phone: 501-324-5531   Fax: 501-324-6968
Website: www.swl.usace.army.mil
Membership: 101–1,000
Scope: Regional
Contact(s):
  Dale Leggett, Chief Natural Resources Branch

UNITED STATES DEPARTMENT OF DEFENSE
ARMY CORPS OF ENGINEERS
LOS ANGELES ENGINEER DISTRICT
P.O. Box 532711
Los Angeles, CA 90053-2325 United States
Phone: 213-452-3840   Fax: 213-452-4219
E-mail: publicaffairs-spl@usace.army.mil
Website: www.spl.usace.army.mil
Scope: Local, State, Regional
Description: Environmental Resources Branch
Contact(s):
  Paul Rose, Chief of Environmental Resources Branch; 213-452-3840; Fax: 213-452-4219; prose@spl.usace.army.mil

UNITED STATES DEPARTMENT OF DEFENSE
ARMY CORPS OF ENGINEERS
LOUISVILLE ENGINEER DISTRICT
P.O. Box 59
Louisville, KY 40201-0059 United States
Phone: 502-315-6768   Fax: 502-315-6771
E-mail: LRL-Pagemaster-PA@lrl02.usace.army.mil
Website: www.lrl.usace.army.mil/
Scope: Local, State, Regional, National
Description: The U.S. Army Corps of Engineers, Louisville District, has a civil mission in Indiana, Kentucky and Ohio. The military mission also includes Michigan and Illinois. The District's civil mission includes navigation, flood reduction, regulatory and emergency response. The military mission includes military construction, world-wide support for the Army Reserve Centers and environmental cleanup up at Formerly Used Defense Sites and military sites under the Installation Restoration Program.

UNITED STATES DEPARTMENT OF DEFENSE
ARMY CORPS OF ENGINEERS
MEMPHIS ENGINEER DISTRICT
167 N. Main Street, Rm. B202 Attn: Environmental Branch
Memphis, TN 38103-1894 United States
Phone: 901-544-3221   Fax: 901-544-3955
Scope: International

UNITED STATES DEPARTMENT OF DEFENSE
ARMY CORPS OF ENGINEERS
MISSISSIPPI VALLEY ENGINEER DIVISION
Vicksburg, MS 39181-0080 United States
Phone: 601-634-5750   Fax: 601-634-5666
E-mail: cemvd-de@mvd02.usace.army.mil
Website: www.mvd.usace.army.mil

Membership: 101–1,000
Scope: National
Contact(s):
  Patti Beard, Executive Secretary

UNITED STATES DEPARTMENT OF DEFENSE
ARMY CORPS OF ENGINEERS
MOBILE ENGINEER DISTRICT
P.O. Box 2288
Mobile, AL 36628-0001 United States
Phone: 334-690-2511   Fax: 334-690-2525
Website: www.sam.usace.army.mil
Scope: National
Contact(s):
  Janet Shelby, Public Affairs Specialist

UNITED STATES DEPARTMENT OF DEFENSE
ARMY CORPS OF ENGINEERS
NASHVILLE ENGINEER DISTRICT
P.O. Box 1070
Nashville, TN 37202-1070 United States
Phone: 615-736-7161   Fax: 615-736-7065
E-mail: edward.m.evans@usace.army.mil
Website: www.lrn.usace.army.mil
Founded: 1888
Membership: 101–1,000
Scope: Regional
Description: Covers 59,000 square miles and parts of seven states throughout the Cumberland and Tennessee River basins for navigation, hydropower, flood control, recreation, and environmental stewardship.
Publication(s): Navigation Maps & Charts
Keyword(s): Energy, Land Issues, Public Lands/Greenspace, Recreation/Ecotourism
Contact(s):
  Byron Jorns, District Engineer; P.O. Box 1070, Nashville, TN 37202-1070

UNITED STATES DEPARTMENT OF DEFENSE
ARMY CORPS OF ENGINEERS
NEW ENGLAND DISTRICT
696 Virginia Rd.
Concord, MA 01742-2751 United States
Phone: 978-318-8237   Fax: 978-318-8850
E-mail: sally.m.rigione@usace.army.mil
Website: www.nae.usace.army.mil
Founded: 1775
Membership: 10,001–100,000
Scope: Local, State, Regional, National
Description: The Corps helps manage & protect our country's water resources, reduce flood damage, facilitate navigation in rivers & harbors, protect wetlands, provide outdoor recreation, conserve & safeguard environment. Along the 6,100 miles of New England coastline, Corps built 11 deep-water ports, 174 commercial & recreational harbors, 46 shore protection projects. The approximately 55,400 miles of inland rivers & streams have 22 Corps projects built on their banks, preserving & protecting public property.
Keyword(s): Development/Developing Countries, Energy, Oceans/Coasts/Beaches, Pollution (general), Public Health, Public Lands/Greenspace, Recreation/Ecotourism, Reduce/Reuse/Recycle, Transportation, Water Habitats & Quality, Wildlife & Species
Contact(s):
  Colonel Thomas Koning, Commander and District Engineer; 978-318-8220; thomas.l.koning.COL@usace.army.mil
  William Scully, Deputy District Engineer (Project Management); 978-318-8230; william.c.scully@usace.army.mil
  Richard Carlson, Chief, Construction/Operations Division; 978-318-8321; richard.c.carlson@usace.army.mil

David Dulong, Chief, Engineering/Planning Division; 978-318-8500; david.l.dulong@usace.army.mil
Christine Godfrey, Chief, Regulatory Division; 978-318-8673; christine.a.godfrey@usace.army.mil
Robert Byrne, Chief, Programs Branch; 978-318-8509; robert.h.byrne@usace.army.mil
William Hubbard, Chief, Environmental Resources Section; 978-318-8552; Fax: 978-318-8560; william.a.hubbard@usace.army.mil
John Kennelly, Chief, Planning Branch; 978-318-8505; john.r.kennelly@usace.army.mil
Larry Rosenberg, Chief, Public Affairs; 978-318-8657; Fax: 978-318-8850; larry.b.rosenberg@usace.army.mil

UNITED STATES DEPARTMENT OF DEFENSE
ARMY CORPS OF ENGINEERS
NEW ORLEANS ENGINEER DISTRICT
New Orleans, LA 70160-0267 United States
Phone: 504-862-2204   Fax: 504-862-1259
E-mail: cemvn-de@mvn02.usace.army.mil
Website: www.mvn02.usace.army.mil

Membership: 1,001–10,000
Scope: Regional

UNITED STATES DEPARTMENT OF DEFENSE
ARMY CORPS OF ENGINEERS
NEW YORK ENGINEER DISTRICT.
Jacob K. Javits Federal Building
26 Federal Plaza, Room 2109
New York, NY 10278-0090 United States
Phone: 212-264-0100   Fax: 212-264-5947
Website: www.nan.usace.army.mil

Membership: 101–1,000
Scope: Local, State, Regional, National
Description: Federal agency

UNITED STATES DEPARTMENT OF DEFENSE
ARMY CORPS OF ENGINEERS
NORFOLK ENGINEER DISTRICT
Waterfield Building, 803 Front Street
Norfolk, VA 23510-1096 United States
Phone: 757-441-7601   Fax: 757-441-7678
E-mail: neo@usace.army.mil
Website: www.nao.usace.army.mil

Membership: 101–1,000
Scope: Regional
Contact(s):
Bob Hume, Chief Regulatory Branch

UNITED STATES DEPARTMENT OF DEFENSE
ARMY CORPS OF ENGINEERS
NORTH ATLANTIC ENGINEER DISTRICT
Fort Hamilton Military Community
General Lee Ave.
Building 302
Brooklyn, NY 11252-6000 United States
Phone: 718-765-7018   Fax: 718-765-7173
E-mail: david.j.lipsky@usace.army.mil
Website: www.nad.usace.army.mil

Founded: 1775
Membership: 1,001–10,000
Scope: Regional
Description: The North Atlantic Division of the U.S. Army Corps of Engineers is made up of about 4,000 team members in six districts and a division HQ. We plan, design and build for the Army and Air Force in the northeastern states and Europe. Our districts develop and manage water resources, in addition to protecting and restoring the environment. When asked, we work for other federal, state and local agencies and foreign nations.

UNITED STATES DEPARTMENT OF DEFENSE
ARMY CORPS OF ENGINEERS
NORTHWESTERN DIVISION
Regional Headquarters, P.O. Box 4626
Portland, OR 97208-4626 United States
Phone: 503-808-3700   Fax: 503-808-3706

UNITED STATES DEPARTMENT OF DEFENSE
ARMY CORPS OF ENGINEERS
OMAHA ENGINEER DISTRICT
106 S. 15th St.
Omaha, NE 68102-1618 United States
Phone: 402-221-3900   Fax: 402-221-4886
E-mail: candace.m.gorton@usace.army.mil
Website: https://w3.nwo.usace.army.mil/

Founded: 1775
Membership: 1,001–10,000
Scope: National
Description: The Omaha District is the Corps' largest district. Its boundaries encompass all or parts of 10 states covering more than 700,000 square miles of land. Three major missions include civil works, military construction, and environmental remediation.
Keyword(s): Ecosystems (precious), Energy, Ethics/Environmental Justice, Land Issues, Pollution (general), Public Lands/Greenspace, Recreation/Ecotourism, Water Habitats & Quality, Wildlife & Species
Contact(s):
Kurt Ubbelohde, District Engineer; 402-221-3900; kurt.f.ubbelohde@usace.army.mil
Thomas Fleeger, Chief, Operations Division; 402-221-4135; Fax: 402-221-4230; thomas.w.fleeger@usace.army.mil
Candace Gorton, Chief, Environmental/Economic/Cultural Resources Section; 402-221-4575; Fax: 402-221-4886; candace.m.gorton@usace.army.mil
Ralph Roza, Chief, Planning Branch; 402-221-4574; Fax: 402-221-4886; ralph.r.roza@usace.army.mil
Kathryn Schenk, Chief, Regulatory Branch; 402-221-4211; Fax: 402-221-4939; kathryn.m.schenk@usace.army.mil

UNITED STATES DEPARTMENT OF DEFENSE
ARMY CORPS OF ENGINEERS
PACIFIC OCEAN ENGINEER DISTRICT
Building 525
Fort Shafter, HI 96858-5440 United States
Phone: 808-438-1500   Fax: 808-438-8387

Membership: 1–100
Scope: Regional
Contact(s):
Frank Oliva, Key Contact

UNITED STATES DEPARTMENT OF DEFENSE
ARMY CORPS OF ENGINEERS
PHILADELPHIA DISTRICT
Wanamaker Building
100 Penn Square East
Philadelphia, PA 19107-3390 United States
Phone: 215-656-6515   Fax: 215-656-6820
E-mail: webmaster@nap02.usace.army.mil
Website: www.nap.usace.army.mil

Founded: 1775
Membership: 10,001–100,000
Scope: National, International
Description: Federal engineering and project management agency.
Publication(s): District Observer
Keyword(s): Ecosystems (precious), Oceans/Coasts/Beaches, Recreation/Ecotourism, Transportation, Water Habitats & Quality, Wildlife & Species

Contact(s):
Timothy Brown, District Commander
John Vickers, Deputy District Commander

UNITED STATES DEPARTMENT OF DEFENSE
ARMY CORPS OF ENGINEERS
PITTSBURGH ENGINEER DISTRICT
U.S. Army Corps of Engineers
William S. Moorhead Fed. Bldg.
1000 Liberty Avenue
Pittsburgh, PA 15222-4186 United States
Phone: 412-395-7103 Fax: 412-644-4093
Website: www.lrp.usace.army.mil/
Membership: 101–1,000
Scope: Regional
Description: The Pittsburgh District maintains and operates 23 locks and dams and 16 reservoir projects, and oversees 42 local flood protection projects in PA, OH, NY, WV and MD. With over 100 years of experience, Pittsburgh District has developed expertise in the fields of inland navigation and flood control, environmental protection and restoration, construction management, recreation, watershed management, water supply, water quality, acid mine drainage remediation and natural disaster response.
Keyword(s): Ecosystems (precious), Recreation/Ecotourism, Transportation, Water Habitats & Quality, Wildlife & Species
Contact(s):
Richard Dowling, Public Affairs Officer; 412-395-7501; lrp.webinquiries@usace.army.mil

UNITED STATES DEPARTMENT OF DEFENSE
ARMY CORPS OF ENGINEERS
PORTLAND ENGINEER DISTRICT
P.O. Box 2946
Portland, OR 97208-2946 United States
Phone: 503-808-4500 Fax: 503-808-4505

UNITED STATES DEPARTMENT OF DEFENSE
ARMY CORPS OF ENGINEERS
ROCK ISLAND ENGINEER DISTRICT
Clock Tower Building
Rodman Avenue
P.O. Box 2004
Rock Island, IL 61204-2004 United States
Phone: 309-794-5759 Fax: 309-794-5807
E-mail: mvr@usace.army.mil
Website: www.mvr.usace.army.mil
Scope: State, Regional
Contact(s):
Bob Romic, Key Contact

UNITED STATES DEPARTMENT OF DEFENSE
ARMY CORPS OF ENGINEERS
SACRAMENTO ENGINEER DISTRICT
1325 J Street
Sacramento, CA 95814-2922 United States
Phone: 916-557-7490 Fax: 916-557-7859

UNITED STATES DEPARTMENT OF DEFENSE
ARMY CORPS OF ENGINEERS
SAN FRANCISCO ENGINEER DISTRICT
333 Market Street
San Francisco, CA 94105-2195 United States
Phone: 415-977-8500 Fax: 415-977-8524
Contact(s):
Timothy O'Rourke, LTC

UNITED STATES DEPARTMENT OF DEFENSE
ARMY CORPS OF ENGINEERS
SEATTLE ENGINEER DISTRICT
4735 East Marginal Way South
Seattle, WA 98134-2385 United States
Phone: 206-764-3690 Fax: 206-764-6544
E-mail: paoteam@usace.army.mil
Website: www.nws.usace.army.mil/index.cfm
Membership: 101–1,000
Scope: Regional
Publication(s): Flagship

UNITED STATES DEPARTMENT OF DEFENSE
ARMY CORPS OF ENGINEERS
SOUTH ATLANTIC ENGINEER DISTRICT
Room 9M15, 60 Forsyth Street, SW
Atlanta, GA 30303-8801 United States
Phone: 404-562-5003 Fax: 404-562-5002
Membership: 101–1,000
Scope: Regional

UNITED STATES DEPARTMENT OF DEFENSE
ARMY CORPS OF ENGINEERS
SOUTH PACIFIC ENGINEER DISTRICT
333 Market Street, Room 1101
San Francisco, CA 94105-2195 United States
Phone: 415-977-8001 Fax: 415-977-8316

UNITED STATES DEPARTMENT OF DEFENSE
ARMY CORPS OF ENGINEERS
SOUTHWESTERN ENGINEER DISTRICT
1100 Commerce Street
Dallas, TX 75242-0216 United States
Phone: 214-767-2502 Fax: 214-767-6499
Scope: National

UNITED STATES DEPARTMENT OF DEFENSE
ARMY CORPS OF ENGINEERS
ST. LOUIS ENGINEER DISTRICT
1222 Spruce Street
St. Louis, MO 63103-2833 United States
Phone: 314-331-8010 Fax: 314-331-8770
Website: www.mvs.usce.army.mil
Membership: 101–1,000
Scope: National
Contact(s):
Linda Collins, Executive Secretary

UNITED STATES DEPARTMENT OF DEFENSE
ARMY CORPS OF ENGINEERS
ST. PAUL ENGINEER DISTRICT
Army Corps of Engineers Centre, 190 5th Street East
St. Paul, MN 55101-1638 United States
Phone: 651-290-5300 Fax: 651-290-5256
Website: www.mvp.usace.army.mil
Membership: 101–1,000
Scope: Regional
Description: Federal government

UNITED STATES DEPARTMENT OF DEFENSE
ARMY CORPS OF ENGINEERS
TULSA ENGINEER DISTRICT
1645 South 101st East Avenue
Tulsa, OK 74128-4609 United States
Phone: 918-669-7201 Fax: 918-669-7207
E-mail: stephen.l.nolen@usace.army.mil
Website: www.swt.usafe.army.mil
Membership: 101–1,000
Scope: National

UNITED STATES DEPARTMENT OF DEFENSE
ARMY CORPS OF ENGINEERS
VICKSBURG ENGINEER DISTRICT
4155 Clay Street
Vicksburg, MS 39183 United States
Phone: 601-631-5010   Fax: 601-631-5296
Website: www.usace.army.mil

Membership: 101–1,000
Scope: National

UNITED STATES DEPARTMENT OF DEFENSE
ARMY CORPS OF ENGINEERS
VICKSBURG ENGINEER DISTRICT
3909 Halls Ferry Road
Vicksburg, MS 39180-6199 United States
Phone: 601-634-2000   Fax: 601-634-2388
E-mail: james.r.houston@erdc.usace.army.mil
Website: www.erdc.usace.army.mil

Founded: 1929
Membership: 1,001–10,000
Scope: National
Description: All of the research and development laboratories of the Corps of Engineers
Keyword(s): Climate Change, Ecosystems (precious), Oceans/Coasts/Beaches, Water Habitats & Quality, Wildlife & Species
Contact(s):
Dr. James Houston, Director
Edwin Theriot, Director, Environmental Laboratory; 601-634-2678; edwin.a.theriot@erdc.usace.army.mil

UNITED STATES DEPARTMENT OF DEFENSE
ARMY CORPS OF ENGINEERS
WALLA WALLA ENGINEER DISTRICT
201 North 3rd Avenue
Walla Walla, WA 99362-1876 United States
Phone: 509-527-7700   Fax: 509-527-7804

UNITED STATES DEPARTMENT OF DEFENSE
ARMY CORPS OF ENGINEERS
WILMINGTON ENGINEER DISTRICT
P.O. Box 1890
Wilmington, NC 28402-1890 United States
Phone: 910-251-4501   Fax: 910-251-4185
Website: www.saw.usace.army.mil

Membership: 101–1,000
Scope: State
Publication(s): Wilmington District Newsletter
Contact(s):
Penny Schmidt, Chief of Public Affairs

UNITED STATES DEPARTMENT OF DEFENSE
ARMY ENGINEER RESEARCH AND DEVELOPMENT CENTER
Champaign, IL 61826-9005 United States
Phone: 217-352-6511   Fax: 217-373-7222

Founded: 1969
Scope: National
Description: CERL conducts research on infrastructure and environmental problems facing the operations of military facilities. CERL also conducts research on innovative materials and engineering procedures; energy reduction measures and equipment; management systems; air and water pollution; environmental compliance; and natural resource management.
Publication(s): The Cutting Edge, Index to Publications, CERL Abstracts
Contact(s):
Dana Finney, Champaign Public Affairs

UNITED STATES DEPARTMENT OF DEFENSE
ARMY FORCES COMMAND
Forester, HQ USAFORSCOM
Attn: AFEN-EN (Mr. Cannon)
1777 Hardee Ave, SW
Fort McPherson, GA 30330-1062 United States
Phone: 404-464-5762   Fax: 404-464-7827
E-mail: cannons@forscom.army.mil

Membership: 1–100
Scope: National
Description: Administer evvironmental policy and budgets for selected Army installaitons across the country.
Keyword(s): Agriculture/Farming, Air Quality/Atmosphere, Ecosystems (precious), Forests/Forestry, Land Issues, Pollution (general), Public Lands/Greenspace, Recreation/Ecotourism, Reduce/Reuse/Recycle, Sprawl/Urban Planning, Water Habitats & Quality, Wildlife & Speci
Contact(s):
Albert Bivings, Wildlife Biologist; bivingsb@forscom.army.mil
Stuart Cannon, Forester

UNITED STATES DEPARTMENT OF DEFENSE
ARMY MATERIEL COMMAND
5001 Eisenhower Ave.
Alexandria, VA 22333-0001 United States

Contact(s):
Billye Haslett, Land Manager of Blue-Grass Army Depot; 606-625-6669
Ken Knouf, Natural Resources Manager of Jefferson Proving Ground, Indiana; 812-273-7436
Randy Quinn, Natural Resources Manager of Letterkenny Army Depot, Ohio; 717-267-8438
Bob Speaker, Natural Resources Manager of Savanna Army Depot, Illinois; 815-273-8533
James Bailey, Wildlife Biologist of U.S. Army Aberdeen Proving Ground, Maryland; 410-278-6748
William Burns, Forester of Anniston Army Depot, Alabama; 205-235-4217
Robert Burton, Archeologist of White Sands Missile Range, New Mexico; 505-678-8731
Richard Clewell, Natural Resources Specialist, Installations and Services Act; 309-782-8252
Tom Coleman, Agronomist of Red River Army Depot, Texas; 903-334-2385
Jesse Horton, Forester of Redstone Arsenal Support Activity, Alabama; 205-876-3122
Junior Kerns, Wildlife Biologist of Yuma Proving Ground, Arizona; 602-328-2148
John Martin, Chief of Conservation and Preservation of Dugway Proving Ground; 801-831-2986
Timothy McNamara, Environmental Protection Specialist of U.S. Army Aberdeen Proving Ground, Maryland; Directorate of Safety, Health and Environment; 410-278-5622
Valerie Morrill, Wildlife Biologist of Yuma Proving Ground, Arizona; 602-328-2244
Patrick Morrow, Wildlife Biologist of White Sands Missile Range, New Mexico; 505-678-7095
Bennie Murray, Forester, Chief Land Manager of Red River Army Depot, Texas; 903-334-2379
James Pottie, Wildlife Biologist of U.S. Army Aberdeen Proving Ground, Maryland; 410-278-6772
Terry Ruth, Forester of Red River Army Depot, Texas; 903-334-2379
Abdul Shiek, Entomologist of U.S. Army Aberdeen Proving Ground, Maryland; 410-278-3303
Roger Stoflet, Forester of U.S. Army Aberdeen Proving Ground, Maryland; 410-278-4915
Daisan Taylor, Wildlife Biologist of White Sands Missile Range, New Mexico; 505-678-6140
Tom Vorac, Forester, Installations and Services Activity, Illinois; 309-782-4062

U.S. FEDERAL AND INTERNATIONAL GOVERNMENT AGENCIES – U

Mason Walker, Project Engineer of Tooele Army Depot, Utah; 801-833-2891
Steve Wampler, Environmental Protection Specialist of U.S. Army Aberdeen Proving Ground, Maryland; Directorate of Safety, Health and Environment; 410-671-4843
Bob Wardwell, Agronomist of U.S. Army Research Laboratory, Maryland; 301-394-1060

UNITED STATES DEPARTMENT OF DEFENSE
ARMY MILITARY ACADEMY
NATURAL RESOURCES BRANCH
DHPW
U.S. Military Academy
West Point, NY 10996-1592 United States
Phone: 845-938-2314   Fax: 845-938-2324

Membership: 1–100
Scope: Local
Description: Natural resources management on the 16,000-acre West Point Military Reservation
Keyword(s): Ecosystems (precious), Forests/Forestry, Water Habitats & Quality, Wildlife & Species
Contact(s):
Catherine Coleman, ITAM Program Manager; 1 Bn, 1 Inf, US Military Academy, West Point, NY 10996; 845-938-5453; Catherine.Coleman@usma.army.mil
James Beemer, Fish and Wildlife Biologist; 845-938-3857; Fax: 845-938-2324; yj6936@exmail.usma.army.mil
Joe Deschenes, Branch Chief and Forester; 845-938-2314; Fax: 845-938-2324; Joseph.Deschenes@usma.army.mil
Robert Jones, Agronomist; 845-938-6789

UNITED STATES DEPARTMENT OF DEFENSE
ARMY TRAINING AND DOCTRINE COMMAND
ATBO-SE
Fort Monroe, VA 23651 United States
Contact(s):
Ron Levy, Director of Environment of Fort McClellan; 205-848-3539
Charles Ford, Chief Natural Resources Manager of Fort Benning; 706-544-7319
Don Hack, Natural Resources Manager of Navajo Depot Activity; 602-774-7161; oxt. 274
Mark Imlay, Natural Resources Manager of Army National Guard Bureau; 703-756-5794
Ronald Moore, Natural Resources Manager of Camp Atterbury; 812-526-1250
Bob Anderson, Natural Resources Specialist; 804-727-2077
Dave Apsley, Forester of Fort Knox; 502-624-8147
Edna Barber, Environmental Officer of U.S. Army Military District of Washington; 202-690-3015
Joyce Beelman, Environmental Protection Specialist of Fort Greeley; 907-451-2141
Scott Belfit, Natural Resources Team of U.S. Army Environmental Center; 410-612-6831
Kenneth Boyd, Wildlife Biologist of Fort Gordon; 706-791-2403
Allen Braswell, Forester of Fort Gordon; 706-791-2327
Patrick Ching, Agronomist of Schofield Barracks; 808-655-6383
Bob Coleman, Chief Environment Branch of Fort Chaffee; 501-484-2516
Marie Cottrell, Archeologist; 804-727-2389
Doug Dasher, Environmental Protection Specialist of Fort Greeley; 907-451-2172
Bob Decker, Natural Resources Team of U.S. Army Environmental Center; 410-612-6831
Glen Degarmo, Archeologist of Fort Bliss; 915-568-5140
Joe Deschenes, Chief of Natural Resources of U.S. Military Academy; 914-938-2314
Chris Dunn, Entomologist of Fort Benning; 706-545-3224
Mark Dutton, Chief of Natural Resources of DA Headquarters; 803-751-4103
Al Freeland, Chief Environmental Management Division of Fort Knox; 502-624-3629
Brad Fristoe, Environmental Protection Specialist of Fort Greeley; 907-451-2159
Bill Garland, Forester of Fort McClellan; 205-848-3758
Bill Gates, Wildlife Biologist of DA Headquarters; 803-751-4793
Hershel Gaw, Forester of Military Traffic Management Command; 919-457-8292
Tom Glueck, Wildlife Biologist of Fort Leonard Wood; 314-596-0871
William Gossweiler, Wildlife Biologist of Fort Richardson; 907-384-3017
Jack Greenlee, Forester of Fort Benning; 706-544-7319
Stuart Hayashi, Entomologist of Headquarters of U.S. Army Pacific; 808-438-2180
William Herb, Natural Resources Team of U.S. Army Environmental Center; 410-671-1234
Lawrence Hirai, Environmental Protection Specialist of Headquarters of U.S. Army; 808-438-8997
Mike Hudson, Forester of Fort Belvoir; 703-806-4007
Wayne Johndrown, Natural Resources Specialist of Fort Chaffee; 501-484-2231
Robert Jones, Agronomist of U.S. Military Academy, Natural Resources Branch; 914-938-3467
Dorothy Keough, Acting Chief of Environmental and Natural Resources Division; 703-806-4007
Robert King, Wildlife Biologist of Fort Benning; 706-544-7319
Pamela Klinger, Natural Resources Team of U.S. Army Environmental Center; 410-612-6832
James Loewen, Biologist of Fort Lee; 804-734-5080
Paul Lukowski, Archeologist of Fort Bliss; 915-568-6999
James McCracken, Biologist of DA Headquarters; 803-751-4622
Kevin McCurdy, Biological Tech./Game Warden of Fort Sill; 405-351-4324
Robert Mcguire, Chief of Environmental Resources Management of Army National Guard Bureau; 703-756-5794
Roger Meyers, Wildlife Biologist of Fort Dix; 609-562-2040
John Miller, Forester of Information Systems Command; 602-533-7083
James Murphy, Agronomist of U.S. Army Military District of Washington; 202-696-3815
Marvin Myers, Agronomist of Fort Leonard Wood; 314-596-0871
Matt Nowak, Forester of Fort Leavenworth; 913-684-2749
Luther Owen, Natural Resources Specialist of Fort McClellan; 205-848-5663
Delarie Parmer, Agronomist of Fort Rucker; 205-255-9363
William Pittman, Agronomist of Health Services Command; 512-221-4411
Bill Quirk, Environmental Specialist of Fort Richardson; 907-384-3021
Clark Reames, Wildlife Biologist of Fort Chaffee; 501-484-2231
Tony Rizzio, Forester of Fort Eustis; 804-878-4152
Mark Salley, Environmental Protection Specialist of Schofield Barracks; 808-656-2878
John Schenck, Entomologist of Fort Eustis; 804-878-2585
Eric Seaborn, Natural Resources Team of U.S. Army Environmental Center; 410-612-6833
Steve Sekscienski, Natural Resources Team of U.S. Army Environmental Center; 410-612-6832
Thomas Shafer, Chief of Environment of Fort Benjamin Harrison; 317-549-5386
Donald Sheroan, Wildlife Biologist Tech. of Fort Knox; 502-624-7373
Bob Shuffield, Forester of Fort Rucker; 205-255-9368
Roger Smith, Agronomist of Fort Dix; 609-562-2040
Sheridan Stone, Wildlife Biologist of Information Systems Command; 602-538-7340
Gene Stout, Chief of Natural/Environmental Resources of Fort Sill; 405-351-4324

Jerry Sturdy, Chief Natural Resources Section of Fort Chaffee; 501-484-2231
Joe Tarnopol, Entomologist of U.S. Army Military District of Washington; 202-475-1003
Donald Teig, Entomologist; 804-727-2366
Steve Thurman, Forester of Fort Leonard Wood; 314-596-0871
Robert Turnbow, Entomologist of Fort Rucker; 205-255-3710
Kevin Von Finger, Ecologist of Fort Bliss; 915-568-7031
Glen Wampler, Fish and Wildlife Administrator of Fort Sill; 405-442-8111
Steve Willard, Chief of Environmental and Natural Resources of Fort Gordon; 706-791-2403
Jerry Williamson, Natural Resources Team of U.S. Army Environmental Center; 410-612-6833

UNITED STATES DEPARTMENT OF DEFENSE
ARMY TRAINING AND DOCTRINE COMMAND
Department of the Army, HQ TRADOC, ATBO-SE, Environmental Division
Fort Monroe, VA 23651 United States

Description: Manages conservation programs for 2 million acres at 16 Army installations nationwide. It also provides for compliance with federal, state, and local environmental regulations.

Publication(s): Endangered Species Law Sourcebook, Army Leader's Guide to NEPA, Historic Preservation Sourcebook

Contact(s):
Robert Anderson, Natural Resources Specialist; 757-727-2077
Jack Damron, NEPA Consultant; 757-727-4135
Frances Doyle
John Esson, NEPA Consultant; 757-727-3335
Shawn Holsinger, Conservation and Analysis Branch; 757-727-3045
Jim White, NEPA Consultant; 757-727-5896

UNITED STATES DEPARTMENT OF DEFENSE
ASSISTANT CHIEF OF STAFF FOR INSTALLATION MANAGEMENT, OFFICE OF THE DIRECTOR OF ENVIRONMENTAL PROGRAMS, AND CONSERVATION TEAM
Attn: DAIM-ED-N, 600 Army Pentagon
Washington, DC 20310-0600 United States
Website: www.hqda.army.mil/acsimweb/homepage.shtml

Description: Natural and cultural resources professionals are responsible for the management of approximately 12 million acres of land on Army military installations. Management objectives include: Compliance with environmental laws, conservation and protection of resources, support to the military mission uses of the land, and contributions to programs which support the public needs. Resources managed include: Land, forest, wildlife, soils, vegetation, and historical and archaeological sites.

Contact(s):
Bob Decker, Natural Resources Specialist; 703-693-0673
Joe Dudley, Conservation Specialist; 703-693-9423
Vic Diersing, Conservation Team Leader; 703-693-0677
Lee Foster, Cultural Resources Specialist; 703-693-0675
Bill Woodson, Natural Resource Specialist; 703-693-0680

UNITED STATES DEPARTMENT OF DEFENSE
HQ PACAF/CEVQ
HICKAM AFB, HI
25 E St. # D306
Hickam AFB, HI 96853-5412 United States
Phone: 808-449-9695   Fax: 808-448-4209
E-mail: pacf.csv@exchange.hickam.af.mil
Website: www.hqpacif.af.mil/ce/cevindx/cevindx.htm

Membership: 1–100
Scope: National

Contact(s):
Arthur Buckman, Natural Resources Manager, HQ PACAF/CEVEP

UNITED STATES DEPARTMENT OF DEFENSE
MARINE CORPS
Headquarters, U.S. Marine Corps
2 Navy Annex, Room 3109
Washington, DC 20380-1775 United States
Phone: 703-695-8240, ext. 3339   Fax: 703-695-8550
E-mail: hirshh@hqmc.usmc.mil
Website: www.usmc.mil

Founded: 1775
Membership: 1–100
Scope: Local, State, Regional, National, International
Description: The Marine Corps, as America's premier crisis response force, trains as it fights. Accordingly, Marine Corps cultural and natural resources managers provide and maintain a variety of landscapes to support military training, while protecting and preserving the cultural and natural resources the American people cherish for their intrinsic value.
Keyword(s): Agriculture/Farming, Air Quality/Atmosphere, Climate Change, Ecosystems (precious), Forests/Forestry, Land Issues, Oceans/Coasts/Beaches, Pollution (general), Public Lands/Greenspace, Recreation/Ecotourism, Reduce/Reuse/Recycle, Sprawl/Urban Planning

Contact(s):
Jim Omans, Head of Natural Resources Section; 703-695-8232

UNITED STATES DEPARTMENT OF DEFENSE
MARINE CORPS INSTALLATIONS, UNITED STATES

Contact(s):
Lupe Armas, MCB Camp Pendleton, CA: Head of Environmental Management Department; 619-725-3561
Mark Brannan, MCAS Cherry Point, NC: Head of Environmental Department
Bruce Frizzell, MCCDC Quantico, VA: Head of Environmental Management Department; 703-640-4030
Alice Howard, MCAS Beaufort, SC: Head of Environmental Management Department; 803-522-7370
Roy Madden, MCAGCC Twentynine Palms, CA: Head of Natural Resources Branch; 619-830-5719
Johnsie Nabors, MCRD Parris Island, SC: Head of Environmental Management Department; 803-525-2779
Jerry Palmer, MCLB Albany, GA: Head of Environmental Management Department; 912-439-6261
Ron Pearce, MCAS Yuma, AZ: Head of Natural Resources Branch; 802-341-3318
Jack Stormo, MCLB Barstow, CA: Head of Environmental Management Department; 619-577-6111
Bob Warren, MCB Camp Lejeune, NC: Head of Environmental Management Department; 910-451-5003

UNITED STATES DEPARTMENT OF DEFENSE
NAVY
1000 Navy Pentagon, Department of the Navy
Washington, DC 20350-1000 United States
Website: www.navy.mil

Description: The mission of the Navy is to maintain, train, and equip combat-ready Naval forces capable of winning wars, deterring aggression and maintaining freedom of the seas.

Contact(s):
Gordon England, Secretary
Susan Livingstone, Under Secretary

UNITED STATES DEPARTMENT OF DEFENSE
OFFICE OF THE CIVIL ENGINEER
AF/ILE, 1260 Air Force Pentagon
Washington, DC 20330-1260 United States
Phone: 703-604-0632   Fax: 703-604-1812

UNITED STATES DEPARTMENT OF EDUCATION
400 Maryland Ave., SW
Washington, DC 20202-0498 United States
Phone: 202-401-3000   Fax: 202-401-0048
E-mail: customerservice@inet.ed.gov
Website: www.ed.gov

Contact(s):
Roderick Paige, Secretary; 202-401-3000

UNITED STATES DEPARTMENT OF ENERGY
Forrestal Bldg., 1000 Independence Ave., SW
Washington, DC 20585 United States
Phone: 202-586-5575   Fax: 202-586-4403
Website: www.energy.gov

Description: Provides the framework for a comprehensive and balanced national energy strategy through the coordination and administration of the energy functions of the federal government. The department is responsible for research, development, and demonstration of energy technology; the marketing of federal power; energy conservation programs; the nuclear weapons program; energy regulatory programs; and a central energy data collection and analysis program.

Publication(s): Assessment of Costs and Benefits of Flexible and Alternative Fuel Use in the United States Transportation Sector, Report to the Congress of the United States: Limiting New Greenhouse Gas Emissions in the United States

UNITED STATES DEPARTMENT OF ENERGY
CARBON DIOXIDE INFORMATION ANALYSIS CENTER
OAK RIDGE NATIONAL LABORATORY
Oak Ridge National Laboratory, P.O. Box 2008 MS-6335
Oak Ridge, TN 37831-6335 United States
Phone: 865-574-0390   Fax: 865-574-2232
E-mail: cdiac@ornl.gov
Website: http://cdiac.ornl.gov/

Founded: 1982
Membership: 1–100
Scope: International
Description: The Carbon Dioxide Information Analysis Center (CDIAC) provides data and information support for the United States Department of Energy's global change research program and makes these data and information products available to a multidisciplinary community of researchers, policymakers, and educators at no cost.
Publication(s): CDIAC Communications, Trends Online, Annual Report
Keyword(s): Air Quality/Atmosphere, Climate Change

Contact(s):
Robert Cushman, Director; 865-574-4791, Fax: 865-574-2232; cushmanrm@ornl.gov
Sonja Jones, Information Services; 865-574-3645; Fax: 865-574-2232; cdiac@ornl.gov

UNITED STATES DEPARTMENT OF ENERGY
FEDERAL ENERGY REGULATORY COMMISSION
888 First Street, NE
Washington, DC 20426 United States
Phone: 202-502-6088
Website: www.ferc.gov

Founded: 1977
Membership: 1,001–10,000
Scope: National
Description: The Federal Energy Regulatory Commission regulates the interstate aspects of the electric power and natural gas industries and establishes rates for transporting oil by pipeline. The Commission issues and enforces licenses for construction and operation of nonfederal hydroelectric power projects. The FERC also advises federal agencies on the merits of proposed federal multiple-purpose water development projects.

Contact(s):
Shelton Cannon, Director of Electric Power Regulation; 202-208-1200
Thomas Herlihy, Director and Chief Financial Officer of Finance, Accounting; 202-208-0300
Kevin Madden, Director of Pipeline Regulation; 202-208-0700
Richard O'Neill, Director of Economic Policy; 202-208-0100
Carol Sampson, Director of Hydropower Licensing; 202-219-2700
Rebecca Schaffer, Director of Office of External Affairs; 202-208-0004
Virginia Strasser, Director of Office of Administrative Litigation; 202-219-2600
Vicky Bailey, Commissioner; 202-208-0388
David Boergers, Secretary; 202-208-0400
Linda Breathitt, Commissioner; 202-208-0377
Curtis Herbert, Commissioner; 202-208-0601
Thomas Herlihy, Chief Information Officer, Acting; 202-208-1055
James Hoecker, Chair; 202-208-0000
William Massey, Commissioner; 202-208-0366
Douglas Smith, General Counsel; 202-208-1000
Curtis Wagner, Chief Administrative Law Judge; 202-219-2500

UNITED STATES DEPARTMENT OF HEALTH AND HUMAN SERVICES
200 Independence Ave., SW
Washington, DC 20201 United States
Phone: 202-690-7000   Fax: 202-690-7203
Website: www.hhs.gov

Scope: National
Description: The Department of Health and Human Services is the United States government's principal agency for protecting the health of all Americans and providing essential human services, especially for those who are least able to help themselves.

Contact(s):
Robert Wood, Chief of Staff; 202-690-7431
Tommy Thompson, Secretary; 202-690-7000

UNITED STATES DEPARTMENT OF HEALTH AND HUMAN SERVICES
FOOD AND DRUG ADMINISTRATION
5600 Fishers Ln.
Rockville, MD 20857 United States
Phone: 410-433-1544
Website: www.fda.gov

Description: Protects the health of American consumers by enforcing federal laws which require that foods must be safe, pure, and wholesome; human and veterinary drugs, biologics, and therapeutic devices must be safe and effective; cosmetics and radiation-emitting products must be harmless; and that all these products must be honestly and informatively labeled and packaged.

Contact(s):
Betsy Adams, Director of Press Relations for Staff of Office of Public Affairs; 410-443-4177
D. Burlington, Director; 410-443-4690
Mary Danello, Director; 410-443-1565
Rosamelia de la Rocha, Director of Office of Equal Employment and Civil Rights; 410-443-5541
Marlene Haffner, Director of Office of Orphan Products Development
Joseph Levitt, Director of Office of Executive Operations; 410-443-5004
Gerald Meyer, Director; 410-443-2894
Henry Miller, Director of Office of Biotechnology; 410-443-7573
Bernard Schwetz, Director; 501-543-7517
Fred Shank, Director; 202-205-4850
Richard Teske, Director; 410-594-1740
Randolph Wykoff, Director of Aids Coordination Staff

Kathryn Zoon, Director; 410-496-3556
Ronald Chesemore, Associate Commissioner for Regulatory Affairs; 410-433-1594
Paul Coppinger, Associate Commissioner for Planning and Evaluation; 410-433-4230
R. Grant, Associate Commissioner for Consumer Affairs; 410-443-5006
Sharon Holston, Associate Commissioner for Management and Operations; 410-443-3370
Jack Martin, Special Assistant to the Commissioner for Program Policy; 410-443-6776
Stuart Nightingale, Associate Commissioner for Health Affairs; 410-433-6143
James O'Hara, Associate Commissioner for Public Affairs; 410-443-1130
Amanda Pedersen, Ombudsman; 410-443-1306
Mary Porter, Chief Counsel for Office of General Counsel; 410-443-4370
Carol Scheman, Deputy Commissioner for External Affairs; 410-443-2400
Michael Taylor, Deputy Commissioner for Policy; 410-443-2854
Dianne Thompson, Associate Commissioner for Legislative Affairs; 410-443-3793
Mary Veverka, Deputy Commissioner for Management and Systems; 410-443-1263

UNITED STATES DEPARTMENT OF HOMELAND SECURITY
CUSTOMS AND BORDER PROTECTION
EAST TEXAS CMC
2323 S. Shepard St., Suite 1200
Houston, TX 77019 United States
Phone: 713-387-7200 Fax: 713-387-7202
Contact(s):
John Babb, Director

UNITED STATES DEPARTMENT OF HOMELAND SECURITY
CUSTOMS AND BORDER PROTECTION
GULF CMC
423 Canal St.
New Orleans, LA 70130 United States
Phone: 504-670-2404 Fax: 504-670-2286
Membership: 101–1,000
Scope: Regional
Contact(s):
Leticia Moran, Director

UNITED STATES DEPARTMENT OF HOMELAND SECURITY
CUSTOMS AND BORDER PROTECTION
MID-AMERICA CMC
610 S. Canal St., Suite 900
Chicago, IL 60607 United States
Phone: 312-983-9100 Fax: 312-886-4921
Website: www.dhs.gov
Membership: 101–1,000
Scope: Regional
Description: Law enforcement: We are the guardians of our Nation's borders. We are America's frontline. We safeguard the American homeland at and beyond our borders. We protect the American public against terrorists and the instruments of terror. We steadfastly enforce the laws of the United States while fostering our Nation's economic security through lawful international trade and travel. We serve the American public with vigilance, integrity and professionalism.

UNITED STATES DEPARTMENT OF HOMELAND SECURITY
CUSTOMS AND BORDER PROTECTION
NEW YORK CMC
One Penn Plaza, 11th Floor
New York, NY 10119 United States
Phone: 646-733-3100 Fax: 646-733-3245
Website: www.customs.treas.gov
Membership: 1,001–10,000
Scope: International

UNITED STATES DEPARTMENT OF HOMELAND SECURITY
CUSTOMS AND BORDER PROTECTION
NORTH ATLANTIC CMC
10 Causeway St.
Boston, MA 02222-1056 United States
Phone: 617-565-6200 Fax: 617-565-6277
Website: www.dhs.gov
Scope: International
Description: Import/Immigration and certain Argiculture requirements
Keyword(s): Agriculture/Farming
Contact(s):
Philip Spayd, Director

UNITED STATES DEPARTMENT OF HOMELAND SECURITY
CUSTOMS AND BORDER PROTECTION
OFFICE OF PUBLIC AFFAIRS
1300 Pennsylvania Ave., NW,
Washington, DC 20229 United States
Phone: 202-354-1000 Fax: 202-927-1393
Website: www.cbp.gov
Founded: 2003
Membership: 10,001–100,000
Scope: National, International
Description: Customs and Border Protection is responsible for the enforcement of the U.S. laws regarding the importation and exportation of injurious and endangered species both plant and animal.
Publication(s): US Customs Today - Monthly Newsletter
Keyword(s): Wildlife & Species
Contact(s):
Robert Bonner, Commissioner
Ben Devane, Special Agent in Charge, Acting
Allan Doody, Special Agent in Charge
Bobby Fernandez, Special Agent in Charge, Acting
Frank Figueroa, Special Agent in Charge, Acting
Gary Hillberry, Special Agent in Charge
Ken Kilroy, Special Agent in Charge
James Lewis, Special Agent in Charge, Acting
Leonard Lindheim, Special Agent in Charge
Bruce Murray, Special Agent in Charge, Acting
Charlie Simonsen, Special Agent in Charge
Jeremiah Sullivan, Special Agent in Charge
Bonni Tischler, Assistant Commissioner for Office of Field Operations; 202-927-0100
Awilda Villafane, Special Agent in Charge, Acting; 555 E. River Rd., Tucson, AZ 85704
Gary Waugh, Special Agent in Charge
Joe Webber, Special Agent in Charge, Acting

UNITED STATES DEPARTMENT OF HOMELAND SECURITY
CUSTOMS AND BORDER PROTECTION
SOUTH FLORIDA CMC
909 SE 1st Ave.
Miami, FL 33131 United States
Phone: 305-810-5120 Fax: 305-810-5143

UNITED STATES DEPARTMENT OF HOMELAND SECURITY
CUSTOMS AND BORDER PROTECTION
SOUTH PACIFIC CMC
One World Trade Center, P.O. Box 32639
Long Beach, CA 90831 United States
Phone: 562-980-3100   Fax: 562-980-3107

Scope: National

Contact(s):
Audrey Adams, Director

UNITED STATES DEPARTMENT OF HOUSING AND URBAN DEVELOPMENT
HUD Bldg., 451 7th St., SW
Washington, DC 20410 United States
Phone: 202-708-1600
Website: www.hud.gov

Scope: National

Contact(s):
Philip Musser, Chief of Staff; 202-708-2236
Vicker Meadows, General Deputy Assistant Secretary for Administration; 202-708-0940
Kenneth Donohue Sr., Inspector General; 202-708-0430
Michael Liu, Assistant Secretary for Public & Indian Housing; 202-708-0950
Mel Martinez, Secretary; 202-708-0417
John Weicher, Assistant Secretary; 202-708-3600

UNITED STATES DEPARTMENT OF JUSTICE
ENVIRONMENT AND NATURAL RESOURCES
10th St. and Constitution Ave., NW
Washington, DC 20530 United States
Phone: 202-514-2701   Fax: 202-514-0557
Website: www.usdoj.gov/enrd/

Founded: 1909

Membership: 101–1,000

Scope: International

Description: The Environment and Natural Resources Division of the Department of Justice handles litigation involving American's pollution control, land use, wildlife, resource management and Indian laws. Nearly one-half of the Division's lawyers bring cases against those who violate the nation's civil and criminal pollution control laws. Others defend legal challenges to government programs and activities and represent the U.S. in matters concerning stewardship of natural resources and public lands.

Contact(s):
Thomas Sansonetti, Assistant Attorney General; 202-514-2701
Kelly Johnson, Principal Deputy Assistant Attorney General; 202-514-2701
Craig Alexander, Indian Resources Section Chief; 202-514-9080
Robert Bruffy, Executive Officer; 202-616-3100
Virginia Butler, Land Acquisition Section Chief; 202-305-0316
Jeffrey Clark, Deputy Assistant Attorney General; 202-514-2701
John Cruden, Deputy Assistant Attorney General; 202-514-2718
Bruce Gilber, Environmental Enforcement Section Chief; 202-514-4624
Letitia Grishaw, Environmental Defense Section Chief; 202-514-2219
Jack Haugrud, General Litigation Section Chief; 202-305-0438
James Kilbourne, Appellate Section Chief; 202-514-2748
Pauline Milius, Policy of Legislation and Special Litigation Section Chief; 202-514-2586
Eileen Sobeck, Deputy Assistant Attorney General; 202-514-0943
Jean Williams, Wildlife and Marine Resources Section Chief; 202-305-0228

UNITED STATES DEPARTMENT OF LABOR
200 Constitution Ave., NW
Washington, DC 20210 United States
Phone: 202-219-5000   Fax: 202-693-4055
Website: www.dol.gov

Contact(s):
Alexis Herman, Secretary; 202-693-6000
J. McAteer, Mine Safety and Health Administrator; 703-235-1385
Edward Montgomery, Deputy Secretary, Acting; 202-693-6002

UNITED STATES DEPARTMENT OF LABOR
JOB CORPS
Department of Labor, Employment and Training Administration, Office of Job Corps
Frances Perkins Bldg.
200 Constitution Ave., NW
Washington, DC 20210 United States
Phone: 202-693-3000   Fax: 202-693-2767
Website: http://jobcorps.doleta.gov

Founded: 1964

Scope: National

Description: Authorized by the Workforce Investment Act, the program includes conservation centers known as Civilian Conservation Centers, located primarily in rural areas and operated for the Department of Labor by the Departments of Agriculture and Interior. Job Corps is a residential, vocational and educational training program for economically disadvantaged youth ages 16-24.

UNITED STATES DEPARTMENT OF LABOR
MINE SAFETY AND HEALTH ADMINISTRATION
Department of Labor
Mine Safety and Health Administration
4015 Wilson Boulevard
Arlington, VA 22203 United States
Phone: 703-235-2600   Fax: 703-235-4369
E-mail: asmsha@msha.gov
Website: www.msha.gov

Scope: National

Description: Objectives are to administer the Federal Mine Safety and Health Act, thereby promoting safety and health in the mining industry, preventing disasters, and protecting the health and safety of the nation's miners.

Contact(s):
Gordon Burke, Director of Administration and Management; 703-235-1383; Fax: 703-235-1634; Burke-Gordon@msha.gov
Jeffrey Duncan, Director of Educational Policy and Development; 703-235-1515; Fax: 703-235-1634; Duncan-Jeffrey@msha.gov
Katharine Snyder, Director, Office of Information and Public Affairs; 703-235-1452; Fax: 703-235-4323; Snyder-Katharine@msha.gov
Carol Jones, Chief, Metal and Nonmetal Safety and Health; 703-235-8307; Fax: 703-235-9173; Jones-Carol@msha.gov
Dave Lauriski, Assistant Secretary, Mine Safety and Health Administration; 703-235-2600; Fax: 703-235-4369; ASMSHA@msha.gov

UNITED STATES DEPARTMENT OF STATE
Harry S. Truman Bldg., 2201 C St., NW
Washington, DC 20520 United States
Phone: 202-647-4000   Fax: 202-736-7720
E-mail: secretary@state.gov
Website: www.state.gov

Membership: 1,001–10,000

Scope: State

Contact(s):
Colin Powell, U.S. Secretary of State; 202-647-6575; secretary@state.gov

UNITED STATES DEPARTMENT OF STATE
BUREAU OF OCEANS AND INTERNATIONAL
ENVIRONMENTAL AND SCIENTIFIC AFFAIRS
Department of State, 2201 C St., NW
Washington, DC 20520 United States
Phone: 202-647-3004　　　　Fax: 202-647-0217
Website: www.state.gov/g/oes/

Scope: Local, State, Regional, National, International

Description: OES has the principal responsibility for formulating and implementing U.S. policies for oceans, environmental, scientific, and technological aspects of U.S. relations with other governmental and multilateral institutions. The Bureau's activities cover a broad range of foreign policy issues relating to environment, pollution, tropical forests, biological diversity, wildlife, oceans policy, fisheries, global climate change, atmospheric ozone-depletion, space, and advanced technologies.

Contact(s):
 David Balton, Office of Marine Conservation, Director; 202-647-2335
 Ralph Braibanti, Office of Space and Advanced Technology, Director; 202-647-2433
 Nancy Foster, Office of Emerging Infectious Diseases, Director; 202-647-2435
 Leslie Gerson, Office of Science and Environmental Initiative, Director; 202-647-3625
 Stephanie Kinney, Executive Assistant/Executive Director of Administration; 202-647-3622
 Mary McLead, Office of Ecology and Terrestrial Conservation, Director; 202-647-2418
 Michael Mtelits, Office of Environment Policy, Director; 202-647-9266
 Daniel Reifsnyder, Office of Global Change, Director; 202-647-4069
 R. Scully, Office of Oceans Affairs, Director; 202-647-3262
 Roger Soles, U.S. Man and the Biosphere Program, Director; 703-235-2948
 Kenneth Brill, Acting Assistant Secretary; 202-647-1554
 Mark Hambley, Special Negotiator
 Melinda Kimble, Principal Department Assisting Secretary
 Rafe Pomerance, Deputy Assistant Secretary of Environment and Development; 202-647-2232
 Mary West, Deputy Assistant Secretary of Oceans, Fisheries and Space; 202-647-2396

UNITED STATES DEPARTMENT OF STATE
UNITED STATES MAN AND THE BIOSPHERE
PROGRAM (U.S. MAB)
USDA - FOREST SERVICE - R&D
Yates Federal Building (1-NW)
P.O. Box 96090
Washington, DC 20090 United States
Phone: 202-205-0908　　　　Fax: 202-205-1530
E-mail: usmab@state.gov
Website: www.mabnet.org

Description: The mission of the United States Man and the Biosphere Program (U.S. MAB) is to explore, demonstrate, promote, and encourage harmonious relationships between people and their environments, building on the MAB network of Biosphere Reserves and interdisciplinary research. The long-term goal of the U.S. MAB Program is to contribute to achieving a sustainable society early in the 21st century.

Publication(s): Conferences, proceedings of symposia, research reports from U.S. MAB, U.S. MAB Bulletin

Contact(s):
 Roger Soles, Executive Director of U.S. MAB; 202-776-8318
 David Hales, Chairman of U.S. MAB National Committee

UNITED STATES DEPARTMENT OF THE INTERIOR
Interior Bldg., 1849 C St., NW
Washington, DC 20240 United States
Phone: 202-208-3100
Website: www.doi.gov

Description: The mission of the Department of the Interior is to protect and provide access to our Nation's natural and cultural heritage and honor our trust responsibilities to tribes.

UNITED STATES DEPARTMENT OF THE INTERIOR
BUREAU OF INDIAN AFFAIRS
1849 C St., NW
Washington, DC 20240 United States
Phone: 202-208-5116　　　　Fax: 202-208-6334
E-mail: jamesmcdivitt@bia.gov
Website: www.doi.gov

Founded: 1824
Membership: 1–100
Scope: National

Description: An agency charged with carrying out the major portion of the trust responsibility of the United States to Indian tribes. This trust includes the protection and enhancement of Indian lands and the conservation and development of natural resources, including fish, wildlife, and outdoor recreation resources.

Contact(s):
 Terry Virden, Director of Office of Trust Responsibilities; 202-208-5831
 Daphne Berwald, Administrative Assistant; 202-208-7163
 Sharon Blackwell, Deputy Commissioner; 202-208-5116
 Gary Rankel, Chief of Branch of Fish, Wildlife and Recreation; 202-208-4088

UNITED STATES DEPARTMENT OF THE INTERIOR
BUREAU OF LAND MANAGEMENT
ALBUQUERQUE FIELD OFFICE
435 Montano Rd., NE
Albuquerque, NM 87107 United States
Phone: 505-761-8700　　　　Fax: 505-761-8911
Scope: Local

Description: Manages the Public Domain lands in the North Central part of New Mexico

Contact(s):
 Andy Iskra, Manager; BLM, Albuquerque Field Office, 435 Montano NE, Albuquerque, NM 87107; 505-761-8789; Fax: 505-761-8911; aiskra@blm.gov

UNITED STATES DEPARTMENT OF THE INTERIOR
BUREAU OF LAND MANAGEMENT
ALTURAS FIELD OFFICE
708 West 12th Street
Alturas, CA 96101 United States
Phone: 530-233-4666　　　　Fax: 530-233-5696
Scope: Regional

UNITED STATES DEPARTMENT OF THE INTERIOR
BUREAU OF LAND MANAGEMENT
AMARILLO FIELD OFFICE
801 S. Fillmore St., Suite 500
Amarillo, TX 79101-3545 United States
Phone: 806-356-1008　　　　Fax: 806-356-1040
Scope: Regional

Description: An agency within the U.S. Department of the Interior whose area of jurisdiction includes all of Kansas, the panhandle of Oklahoma and those counties in Texas that are west of the 100th Meridian.

Keyword(s): Public Lands/Greenspace
Contact(s):
  Paul Tanner, Natural Resource Specialist; 806-356-1008; Paul_Tanner@Blm.gov

UNITED STATES DEPARTMENT OF THE INTERIOR
BUREAU OF LAND MANAGEMENT
ANASAZI HERITAGE CENTER
27501 Highway 184
Dolores, CO 81323 United States
Phone: 970-882-5600   Fax: 970-882-7035
Founded: 1997
Scope: Regional
Description: A museum for interpreting the history and culture of the Canyons of the Ancients National Monument, Trails of the Ancients, and the Four Corners region.

UNITED STATES DEPARTMENT OF THE INTERIOR
BUREAU OF LAND MANAGEMENT
ANCHORAGE DISTRICT
6881 Abbott Loop Road
Anchorage, AK 99507-2599 United States
Phone: 907-267-1251   Fax: 907-267-1126
Website: www.blm.gov/education/feature/feature1.html
Scope: Regional

UNITED STATES DEPARTMENT OF THE INTERIOR
BUREAU OF LAND MANAGEMENT
ARCATA FIELD OFFICE
1695 Heindon Road
Arcata, CA 95521 United States
Phone: 707-825-2300   Fax: 707-825-2301
Website: www.ca.blm.gov/arcata/
Scope: Regional

UNITED STATES DEPARTMENT OF THE INTERIOR
BUREAU OF LAND MANAGEMENT
ARIZONA STATE OFFICE
222 North Central Avenue
Phoenix, AZ 85004-2203 United States
Phone: 602-417-9200   Fax: 602-417-9556
Membership: 101–1,000
Scope: Regional
Contact(s):
  Lucy Ontiveros, Manager; 602-417-9500; Fax: 602-417-9556; lucy_ontiveros@blm.gov

UNITED STATES DEPARTMENT OF THE INTERIOR
BUREAU OF LAND MANAGEMENT
ARIZONA STRIP FIELD OFFICE
345 East Riverside Drive
St. George, UT 84790-9000 United States
Phone: 801-688-3301   Fax: 435-688-3258
Scope: Regional

UNITED STATES DEPARTMENT OF THE INTERIOR
BUREAU OF LAND MANAGEMENT
BAKERSFIELD FIELD OFFICE
3801 Pegasus Drive
Bakersfield, CA 93308-6837 United States
Phone: 661-391-6000   Fax: 661-391-6040
E-mail: caweb010@ca.blm.gov
Website: www.ca.blm.gov/bakersfield/

Scope: Local
Description: Manages public lands in central California (Ventura, Santa Barbara, San Luis Obispo, Kings, Tulare, Madera, and parts of Kern & Fresno Counties), including the Carrizo Plain National Monument and select portals to the California Coastal National Monument. Areas of emphasis include partnerships with local communities & organizations, managing for ecosystem health and the recovery of threatened & endangered species, oil & gas production, livestock grazing, fire protection, and recreation.
Keyword(s): Ecosystems (precious), Energy, Forests/Forestry, Land Issues, Oceans/Coasts/Beaches, Public Lands/Greenspace, Recreation/Ecotourism, Water Habitats & Quality, Wildlife & Species

UNITED STATES DEPARTMENT OF THE INTERIOR
BUREAU OF LAND MANAGEMENT
BARSTOW FIELD OFFICE
2601 Barstow Road
Barstow, CA 92311 United States
Phone: 760-252-6000   Fax: 760-252-6099
Scope: Regional

UNITED STATES DEPARTMENT OF THE INTERIOR
BUREAU OF LAND MANAGEMENT
BATTLE MOUNTAIN FIELD OFFICE
50 Bastian Rd.
Battle Mountain, NV 89820 United States
Phone: 775-635-4000   Fax: 775-635-4034
Website: www.nv.blm.gov/bmountain
Founded: 1934
Scope: Regional
Description: Public land management

UNITED STATES DEPARTMENT OF THE INTERIOR
BUREAU OF LAND MANAGEMENT
BILLINGS FIELD OFFICE
5001 Southgate Dr.
Billings, MT 59101 United States
Phone: 406-896-5013   Fax: 406-896-5281
Scope: Regional

UNITED STATES DEPARTMENT OF THE INTERIOR
BUREAU OF LAND MANAGEMENT
BISHOP FIELD OFFICE
351 Pacu Lane
Suite 100
Bishop, CA 93514 United States
Phone: 760-872-5000   Fax: 760-872-2894
Website: www.ca.blm.gov/bishop/
Scope: Regional

UNITED STATES DEPARTMENT OF THE INTERIOR
BUREAU OF LAND MANAGEMENT
BRUNEAU FIELD OFFICE
3948 Development Ave.
Boise, ID 83705-5389 United States
Phone: 208-384-3300   Fax: 208-384-3326
Scope: Regional

UNITED STATES DEPARTMENT OF THE INTERIOR
BUREAU OF LAND MANAGEMENT
BUFFALO FIELD OFFICE
1425 Fort St.
Buffalo, WY 82834-2436 United States
Phone: 307-684-1100   Fax: 307-684-1122
Scope: Regional

UNITED STATES DEPARTMENT OF THE INTERIOR
BUREAU OF LAND MANAGEMENT
BURLEY FIELD OFFICE
15 E. 200 South
Burley, ID 83318 United States
Phone: 208-677-6641   Fax: 208-677-6699
Website: id.blm.gov/burley
Scope: Regional

UNITED STATES DEPARTMENT OF THE INTERIOR
BUREAU OF LAND MANAGEMENT
BURNS DISTRICT
28910 Hwy. 20 West
Hines, OR 97738 United States
Phone: 541-573-4400   Fax: 541-573-4411
E-mail: or020mb@or.blm.gov
Website: www.or.blm.gov/Burns/
Scope: Regional

UNITED STATES DEPARTMENT OF THE INTERIOR
BUREAU OF LAND MANAGEMENT
BUTTE FIELD OFFICE
106 N. Parkmont St
Butte, MT 59701 United States
Phone: 406-494-5059   Fax: 406-533-7660
Scope: Regional

UNITED STATES DEPARTMENT OF THE INTERIOR
BUREAU OF LAND MANAGEMENT
CARLSBAD FIELD OFFICE
620 E. Greene St.
Carlsbad, NM 88220-6292 United States
Phone: 505-887-6544   Fax: 505-885-9264
Website: www.nm.blm.gov
Scope: Regional

UNITED STATES DEPARTMENT OF THE INTERIOR
BUREAU OF LAND MANAGEMENT
CARSON CITY FIELD OFFICE
5665 Morgan Mill Rd.
Carson City, NV 89701 United States
Phone: 775-885-6000   Fax: 775-885-6147
Website: nv.blm.gov/carson
Scope: Regional

UNITED STATES DEPARTMENT OF THE INTERIOR
BUREAU OF LAND MANAGEMENT
CASPER DISTRICT
1701 East E St.
Casper, WY 82601 United States
Phone: 307-261-7600   Fax: 307-234-1525
Scope: Regional

UNITED STATES DEPARTMENT OF THE INTERIOR
BUREAU OF LAND MANAGEMENT
CEDAR CITY DISTRICT FIELD OFFICE
176 East D.L. Sargent Dr.
Cedar City, UT 84720 United States
Phone: 435-586-2401   Fax: 435-865-3058
Website: www.ut.blm.gov/cedarcity_fo
Scope: Regional

UNITED STATES DEPARTMENT OF THE INTERIOR
BUREAU OF LAND MANAGEMENT
CHALLIS FIELD OFFICE
50 Highway 93 South
Salmon, ID 83467 United States
Phone: 208-756-5400   Fax: 208-756-5436
Scope: Regional

UNITED STATES DEPARTMENT OF THE INTERIOR
BUREAU OF LAND MANAGEMENT
CODY FIELD OFFICE
1002 Blackburn
P.O. Box 518
Cody, WY 82414-0518 United States
Phone: 307-578-5900   Fax: 307-578-5939
Website: www.wy.blm.gov
Scope: Regional

UNITED STATES DEPARTMENT OF THE INTERIOR
BUREAU OF LAND MANAGEMENT
COEUR D'ALENE FIELD OFFICE
1808 North Third Street
Coeur d'Alene, ID 83814-3407 United States
Phone: 208-769-5030   Fax: 208-769-5050
Website: www.id.blm.gov/offices/coeurd'alene/
Scope: Regional

UNITED STATES DEPARTMENT OF THE INTERIOR
BUREAU OF LAND MANAGEMENT
COLORADO STATE OFFICE
2850 Youngfield Street
Lakewood, CO 80215 United States
Phone: 303-239-3600   Fax: 303-239-3933
Scope: Regional

UNITED STATES DEPARTMENT OF THE INTERIOR
BUREAU OF LAND MANAGEMENT
COOS BAY FIELD OFFICE
1300 Airport Lane
North Bend, OR 97459 United States
Phone: 541-756-0100   Fax: 541-751-4303
Scope: Regional

UNITED STATES DEPARTMENT OF THE INTERIOR
BUREAU OF LAND MANAGEMENT
COTTONWOOD FIELD OFFICE
Route 3
Box 181
Cottonwood, ID 83522-9498 United States
Phone: 208-962-3245   Fax: 208-962-3275
Scope: Regional
Description: Federal Office responsible for Bureau of Land Management Mission accomplishments in north central Idaho

UNITED STATES DEPARTMENT OF THE INTERIOR
BUREAU OF LAND MANAGEMENT
DILLON FIELD OFFICE
1005 Selway Dr.
Dillon, MT 59725-9431 United States
Phone: 406-683-2337 Fax: 406-683-8066
Scope: Regional

UNITED STATES DEPARTMENT OF THE INTERIOR
BUREAU OF LAND MANAGEMENT
EAGLE LAKE FIELD OFFICE
2950 Riverside Drive
Susanville, CA 96130 United States
Phone: 530-257-0456 Fax: 530-257-4831
E-mail: CA350@blm.gov
Website: www.ca.blm.gov/eaglelake/index.html
Scope: Regional

UNITED STATES DEPARTMENT OF THE INTERIOR
BUREAU OF LAND MANAGEMENT
EASTERN STATES OFFICE
7450 Boston Blvd.
Springfield, VA 22153 United States
Phone: 703-440-1713 Fax: 703-440-1722
E-mail: terry_lewis@es.blm.gov
Website: www.es.blm.gov/index.html
Scope: Regional
Description: The U.S. Department of Interior, Bureau of Land Management (BLM), Eastern States is responsible for the stewardship of the public lands and resources under the jurisdiction of the BLM in the 31 states east of and bordering the Mississippi River.

UNITED STATES DEPARTMENT OF THE INTERIOR
BUREAU OF LAND MANAGEMENT
EL CENTRO FIELD OFFICE
1661 South Fourth Street
El Centro, CA 92243 United States
Phone: 760-337-4400 Fax: 760-337-4490
Scope: Regional

UNITED STATES DEPARTMENT OF THE INTERIOR
BUREAU OF LAND MANAGEMENT
ELKO FIELD OFFICE
3900 E. Idaho St.
Elko, NV 89801 United States
Phone: 775-753-0200 Fax: 775-753-0255
Website: www.nv.blm.gov
Scope: Regional

UNITED STATES DEPARTMENT OF THE INTERIOR
BUREAU OF LAND MANAGEMENT
ELY FIELD OFFICE
702 N. Industrial Way
HC 33, Box 33500
Ely, NV 89301 United States
Phone: 775-289-1800 Fax: 775-289-1910
Website: www.nv.blm.gov/ely
Scope: Regional

UNITED STATES DEPARTMENT OF THE INTERIOR
BUREAU OF LAND MANAGEMENT
EUGENE DISTRICT OFFICE
WILDLIFE WORKING GROUP
2890 Chad Drive
P.O. Box 10226
Eugene, OR 97440-2226 United States
Phone: 541-683-6114 Fax: 541-683-6981
E-mail: eric_greenquist@or.blm.gov
Scope: Regional
Description: Comprised of professional staff biologists and technicians, the Wildlife Working Group guides the District wildlife habitat and endangered species programs. In addition to wildlife management activities, the Working Group advises the District supervisory and professional staffs on wildlife resources, laws, policies and methods, coordinates program work, handles special issues, and provides information and educational materials to schools, private organizations and members of the public.
Keyword(s): Development/Developing Countries, Forests/Forestry, Land Issues, Recreation/Ecotourism, Water Habitats & Quality, Wildlife & Species

UNITED STATES DEPARTMENT OF THE INTERIOR
BUREAU OF LAND MANAGEMENT
EUGENE FIELD OFFICE
P.O. Box 10226
Eugene, OR 97440 United States
Phone: 541-683-6600 Fax: 541-683-6981
Website: www.edo.or.blm.gov
Scope: Regional

UNITED STATES DEPARTMENT OF THE INTERIOR
BUREAU OF LAND MANAGEMENT
FILLMORE FIELD OFFICE
35 E. 500 North
Fillmore, UT 84631 United States
Phone: 435-743-6811
Scope: Regional
Contact(s):
Rex Rowley, Manager; 435-743-3100; rex_rowley@blm.gov

UNITED STATES DEPARTMENT OF THE INTERIOR
BUREAU OF LAND MANAGEMENT
FOLSOM FIELD OFFICE
63 Natoma Street
Folsom, CA 95630 United States
Phone: 916-985-4474 Fax: 916-985-3259
Scope: Regional

UNITED STATES DEPARTMENT OF THE INTERIOR
BUREAU OF LAND MANAGEMENT
FOUR RIVERS FIELD OFFICE
3948 Development Ave.
Boise, ID 83705-5389 United States
Phone: 208-384-3300 Fax: 208-384-3493
Scope: Regional

UNITED STATES DEPARTMENT OF THE INTERIOR
BUREAU OF LAND MANAGEMENT
GLENNALLEN DISTRICT
P.O. Box 147
Glennallen, AK 99588 United States
Phone: 907-822-3217   Fax: 907-822-3120
Scope: Regional

UNITED STATES DEPARTMENT OF THE INTERIOR
BUREAU OF LAND MANAGEMENT
GLENWOOD SPRINGS FIELD OFFICE
50629 Hwys. 6 & 24; P.O. Box 1009
Glenwood Springs, CO 81602 United States
Phone: 970-947-2800   Fax: 970-947-2829
Scope: Regional
Contact(s):
  Tom Fresques, Wildlife Biologist; 970-947-2814; thomas_fresques@blm.gov

UNITED STATES DEPARTMENT OF THE INTERIOR
BUREAU OF LAND MANAGEMENT
GRAND JUNCTION FIELD OFFICE/WESTERN SLOPE CENTER
2815 H Rd.
Grand Junction, CO 81506 United States
Phone: 970-244-3000   Fax: 970-244-3083
Website: www.co.blm.gov/gjra/gjra.html
Scope: Regional

UNITED STATES DEPARTMENT OF THE INTERIOR
BUREAU OF LAND MANAGEMENT
GUNNISON FIELD OFFICE
216 N. Colorado St
Gunnison, CO 81230 United States
Phone: 970-641-0471   Fax: 970-642-4425
Scope: Regional

UNITED STATES DEPARTMENT OF THE INTERIOR
BUREAU OF LAND MANAGEMENT
HOLLISTER FIELD OFFICE
20 Hamilton Court
Hollister, CA 95023 United States
Phone: 831-630-5000   Fax: 831-630-5055
Scope: Regional

UNITED STATES DEPARTMENT OF THE INTERIOR
BUREAU OF LAND MANAGEMENT
IDAHO FALLS FIELD OFFICE
1405 Hollypark Dr.
Idaho Falls, ID 83401 United States
Phone: 208-524-7500   Fax: 208-524-7505
Scope: Regional

UNITED STATES DEPARTMENT OF THE INTERIOR
BUREAU OF LAND MANAGEMENT
JACKSON FIELD OFFICE
411 Briarwood Dr., Suite 404
Jackson, MS 39206 United States
Phone: 601-977-5400   Fax: 601-977-5440
Scope: Regional

UNITED STATES DEPARTMENT OF THE INTERIOR
BUREAU OF LAND MANAGEMENT
JARBRIDGE FIELD OFFICE
2620 Kimberly Road
Twin Falls, ID 83301 United States
Phone: 208-736-2350   Fax: 208-736-2375
Scope: Regional

UNITED STATES DEPARTMENT OF THE INTERIOR
BUREAU OF LAND MANAGEMENT
KANAB
318 N. First East
Kanab, UT 84741 United States
Phone: 435-644-2672
Website: www.ut.blm.gov/kanab_fo/information.htm
Scope: Regional

UNITED STATES DEPARTMENT OF THE INTERIOR
BUREAU OF LAND MANAGEMENT
KEMMERER FIELD OFFICE
312 Highway 189 N.
Kemmerer, WY 83101-9710 United States
Phone: 307-828-4500   Fax: 307-828-4539
Scope: Regional

UNITED STATES DEPARTMENT OF THE INTERIOR
BUREAU OF LAND MANAGEMENT
KINGMAN FIELD OFFICE
2475 Beverly Avenue
Kingman, AZ 86401-3629 United States
Phone: 928-692-4400   Fax: 928-692-4414
Scope: Regional

UNITED STATES DEPARTMENT OF THE INTERIOR
BUREAU OF LAND MANAGEMENT
KREMMLING FIELD OFFICE
2103 East Park Avenue
P.O. Box 68
Kremmling, CO 80459 United States
Phone: 970-724-3437   Fax: 970-724-9590
Scope: Regional

UNITED STATES DEPARTMENT OF THE INTERIOR
BUREAU OF LAND MANAGEMENT
LA JARA FIELD OFFICE
15571 County Rd. T-5
La Jara, CO 81140 United States
Phone: 719-274-8971   Fax: 719-274-6301
Scope: Regional

UNITED STATES DEPARTMENT OF THE INTERIOR
BUREAU OF LAND MANAGEMENT
LAKE HAVASU FIELD OFFICE
2610 Sweetwater Avenue
Lake Havasu City, AZ 86406-9071 United States
Phone: 928-505-1200   Fax: 928-505-1208
Scope: Regional

U.S. FEDERAL AND INTERNATIONAL GOVERNMENT AGENCIES – U

UNITED STATES DEPARTMENT OF THE INTERIOR
BUREAU OF LAND MANAGEMENT
LAKEVIEW DISTRICT
1301 S. G St
Lakeview, OR 97630 United States
Phone: 541-947-2177   Fax: 541-947-6399
Website: www.or.blm.gov/Lakeview
Scope: Regional

UNITED STATES DEPARTMENT OF THE INTERIOR
BUREAU OF LAND MANAGEMENT
LAKEVIEW RESOURCE AREA
1301 South G Street
Lakeview, OR 97630 United States
Phone: 541-947-6102
Scope: Regional
Contact(s):
   Thomas Rasmussen, Manager; 435-636-3600; tom_rasmussen@blm.gov

UNITED STATES DEPARTMENT OF THE INTERIOR
BUREAU OF LAND MANAGEMENT
LANDER FIELD OFFICE
1335 Main; P.O. Box 589
Lander, WY 82520-0589 United States
Phone: 307-332-8400   Fax: 307-332-8447
Scope: Regional

UNITED STATES DEPARTMENT OF THE INTERIOR
BUREAU OF LAND MANAGEMENT
LAS CRUCES DISTRICT
1800 Marquess
Las Cruces, NM 88005-3371 United States
Phone: 505-525-4300   Fax: 505-525-4412
Website: www.nm.blm.gov
Scope: Regional

UNITED STATES DEPARTMENT OF THE INTERIOR
BUREAU OF LAND MANAGEMENT
LAS VEGAS FIELD OFFICE
4701 No. Torrey Pines Drive
Las Vegas, NV 89130 United States
Phone: 702-515-5000   Fax: 702-515-5023
Website: www.nv.blm.gov
Scope: Regional

UNITED STATES DEPARTMENT OF THE INTERIOR
BUREAU OF LAND MANAGEMENT
LEWISTOWN FIELD OFFICE
P.O. Box 1160
Lewistown, MT 59457-1160 United States
Phone: 406-538-7461   Fax: 406-538-1904
Scope: Regional

UNITED STATES DEPARTMENT OF THE INTERIOR
BUREAU OF LAND MANAGEMENT
LITTLE SNAKE FIELD OFFICE
455 Emerson St.
Craig, CO 81625 United States
Phone: 970-826-5000   Fax: 970-826-5002
Scope: Regional

UNITED STATES DEPARTMENT OF THE INTERIOR
BUREAU OF LAND MANAGEMENT
MALAD FIELD OFFICE
195 S. 300 E., P.O. Box 146
Malad City, ID 83252-1346 United States
Phone: 208-766-4766   Fax: 208-766-5914
Scope: Regional

UNITED STATES DEPARTMENT OF THE INTERIOR
BUREAU OF LAND MANAGEMENT
MALTA FIELD OFFICE
501 S. 2nd St. E.
HC 65 Box 5000
Malta, MT 59538 United States
Phone: 406-654-5100   Fax: 406-654-5150
Scope: Regional
Description: Our mission is to sustain the health, diversity, and productivity of the public lands for the use and enjoyment of future generations.
Keyword(s): Agriculture/Farming, Ecosystems (precious), Energy, Forests/Forestry, Land Issues, Public Lands/Greenspace, Recreation/Ecotourism, Transportation, Water Habitats & Quality, Wildlife & Species
Contact(s):
   Richard Adams, Asst. Manager; 406-654-5100; Fax: 406-654-5150
   John Fahlgren, Asst. Manager; Glasgow Field Station, Glasgow, MT 59230; 406-228-3750; Fax: 406-228-4121

UNITED STATES DEPARTMENT OF THE INTERIOR
BUREAU OF LAND MANAGEMENT
MEDFORD DISTRICT OFFICE
3040 Biddle Rd.
Medford, OR 97504 United States
Phone: 541-618-2200   Fax: 541-618-2400
Website: or.blm.gov/medford
Scope: Regional
Contact(s):
   Ron Wenker, District Manager

UNITED STATES DEPARTMENT OF THE INTERIOR
BUREAU OF LAND MANAGEMENT
MILES CITY FIELD OFFICE
111 Garryowen Rd.
Miles City, MT 59301 United States
Phone: 406-233-2800   Fax: 406-233-2921
Scope: Regional
Contact(s):
   Dave McIlnay, Field Manager; 406-233-2800

UNITED STATES DEPARTMENT OF THE INTERIOR
BUREAU OF LAND MANAGEMENT
MILWAUKEE FIELD OFFICE
310 W. Wisconsin Ave., Suite 450
Milwaukee, WI 53203 United States
Phone: 414-297-4400   Fax: 414-297-4409
Scope: Regional

UNITED STATES DEPARTMENT OF THE INTERIOR
BUREAU OF LAND MANAGEMENT
MISSOULA FIELD OFFICE
3255 Ft. Missoula Rd.
Missoula, MT 59804-7293 United States
Phone: 406-329-3914   Fax: 406-329-3721
Scope: Regional

UNITED STATES DEPARTMENT OF THE INTERIOR
BUREAU OF LAND MANAGEMENT
MOAB DISTRICT FIELD OFFICE
82 E. Dogwood
Moab, UT 84532 United States
Phone: 435-259-2100
Scope: Regional
Contact(s):
  Maggie Wyatt, Manager; 435-259-2100; maggie_wyatt@blm.gov

UNITED STATES DEPARTMENT OF THE INTERIOR
BUREAU OF LAND MANAGEMENT
MONTICELLO FIELD OFFICE
435 N. Main, P.O. Box 7
Monticello, UT 84535 United States
Phone: 435-587-1502
Scope: Regional

UNITED STATES DEPARTMENT OF THE INTERIOR
BUREAU OF LAND MANAGEMENT
NATIONAL APPLIED RESOURCE CENTER
BLM
1849 C Street
Room 406-LS
Washington, DC 20240 United States
Phone: 202-452-5125   Fax: 202-452-5124
Website: www.blm.gov
Scope: National
Contact(s):
  Robert Abbey, NV State Director; 1340 Financial Blvd., Reno, NV 89502-7147; 702-861-6590
  Lee Barkow, Director of National Science & Tech Center; P.O. Box 25047, Building 50, Dever Federal Center, Denver, CO 80225-0047; lee_barkow@blm.gov
  Henri Bisson, AK State Director; 222 W. 7th Ave., #13, Anchorage, AK 99513; 907-271-5080
  Elaine Marquis-Borng, OR State Director; 1515 SW 5th Ave., Portland, OR 97208; 503-952-6024
  Mike Nedd, Eastern States Director; 7450 Boston Blvd., Springfield, VA 22153; 703-440-1700; Fax: 703-440-1599
  Michael Pool, CA State Director; 28 Cottage Way, Rm. W-1834, Sacramento, CA 95825; 916-978-4600; Fax: 916-978-4699
  Position Vacant, WY State Director; 5353 Yellowstone Rd., Cheyenne, WY 82003
  Position Vacant, NM State Director; 1474 Rodeo Rd., Santa Fe, NM 87505
  Position Vacant, MT State Director; 5001 Southgate Dr, Billings, MT 59107
  Position Vacant, ID State Director; 1387 S. Vinnell Way, Boise, ID 83709-1657
  Position Vacant, CO State Director; 2850 Youngfield St., Lakewood, CO 80215
  Sally Wisely, UT State Director; 324 S. State St., Ste. 301, Salt Lake City, UT 84145; 801-539-4010
  Elaine Zielinski, AZ State Director; 222 North Central Avenue, Phoenix, AZ 85004; 602-417-9500

UNITED STATES DEPARTMENT OF THE INTERIOR
BUREAU OF LAND MANAGEMENT
NATIONAL INTERAGENCY FIRE CENTER
NATIONAL OFFICE OF FIRE AND AVIATION
3833 S. Development Ave.
Boise, ID 83705 United States
Phone: 208-387-5512   Fax: 208-387-5376
Website: www.nifc.gov
Membership: 101–1,000
Scope: National
Publication(s): Burning Issues-newsletter bi-quarterly
Contact(s):
  Larry Hamilton, Director; 208-387-5446

UNITED STATES DEPARTMENT OF THE INTERIOR
BUREAU OF LAND MANAGEMENT
NATIONAL TRAINING CENTER
9828 North 31st Avenue
Phoenix, AZ 85051-2517 United States
Phone: 602-906-5500   Fax: 602-906-5555
Scope: Regional

UNITED STATES DEPARTMENT OF THE INTERIOR
BUREAU OF LAND MANAGEMENT
NEEDLES FIELD OFFICE
101 Spikes Road
Needles, CA 92363 United States
Phone: 760-326-7000   Fax: 760-326-7099
Scope: Regional

UNITED STATES DEPARTMENT OF THE INTERIOR
BUREAU OF LAND MANAGEMENT
NEWCASTLE FIELD OFFICE
1101 Washington Blvd.
Newcastle, WY 82701-2972 United States
Phone: 307-746-6600   Fax: 307-746-6639
Website: www.wy.blm.gov/index.html
Scope: Regional

UNITED STATES DEPARTMENT OF THE INTERIOR
BUREAU OF LAND MANAGEMENT
NORTH DAKOTA FIELD OFFICE
2933 Third Ave., W.
West Dickinson, ND 58601-2619 United States
Phone: 701-227-7700   Fax: 701-227-8510
E-mail: FO@blm.gov
Website: www.mt.blm.gov/ndfo/index.html
Scope: Regional

UNITED STATES DEPARTMENT OF THE INTERIOR
BUREAU OF LAND MANAGEMENT
NORTHERN FIELD OFFICE
1150 University Avenue
Fairbanks, AK 99709 United States
Phone: 907-474-2200   Fax: 907-474-2238
Website: aurora.ak.blm.gov
Scope: Regional
Description: BLM's Northern Field Office administers 55 million acres of public lands in northern Alaska. These lands include eight nationally designated areas, among them historic sites, national wild and scenic rivers, and conservation areas. The office also administers the 23-million-acre National Petroleum Reserve - Alaska, located on the North Slope.

Keyword(s): Air Quality/Atmosphere, Ecosystems (precious), Energy, Ethics/Environmental Justice, Forests/Forestry, Land Issues, Oceans/Coasts/Beaches, Pollution (general), Public Lands/Greenspace, Recreation/Ecotourism, Transportation, Water Habitats & Quality

UNITED STATES DEPARTMENT OF THE INTERIOR
BUREAU OF LAND MANAGEMENT
OKLAHOMA FIELD OFFICE-TULSA #101
7906 East 33rd St.
Tulsa, OK 74145-1352 United States
Phone: 918-621-4100   Fax: 918-621-4130
Website: www.blm.gov
Scope: Regional
Contact(s):
  Phil Keasling; 405-790-1016

UNITED STATES DEPARTMENT OF THE INTERIOR
BUREAU OF LAND MANAGEMENT
OWYHEE FIELD OFFICE
3948 Development Ave.
Boise, ID 83705-5389 United States
Phone: 208-384-3300   Fax: 208-384-3493
Scope: Regional

UNITED STATES DEPARTMENT OF THE INTERIOR
BUREAU OF LAND MANAGEMENT
PALM SPRINGS / SOUTH COAST FIELD OFFICE
690 West Garnet Avenue
P.O. Box 581260
North Palm Springs, CA 92258-1260 United States
Phone: 760-251-4800   Fax: 760-251-4899
Scope: Regional

UNITED STATES DEPARTMENT OF THE INTERIOR
BUREAU OF LAND MANAGEMENT
PHOENIX FIELD OFFICE
21605 North 7th Street
Phoenix, AZ 85027 United States
Phone: 623-580-5500   Fax: 623-580-5580
Scope: Regional

UNITED STATES DEPARTMENT OF THE INTERIOR
BUREAU OF LAND MANAGEMENT
PINEDALE FIELD OFFICE
432 E. Mill Street; P.O. Box 768
Pinedale, WY 82941-0768 United States
Phone: 307-367-5300   Fax: 307-367-5329
Scope: Regional

UNITED STATES DEPARTMENT OF THE INTERIOR
BUREAU OF LAND MANAGEMENT
POCATELLO FIELD OFFICE
1111 N. 8th Ave.
Pocatello, ID 83201 United States
Phone: 208-236-6860   Fax: 208-234-0246
Scope: Regional

UNITED STATES DEPARTMENT OF THE INTERIOR
BUREAU OF LAND MANAGEMENT
PRINEVILLE DISTRICT FIELD OFFICE
3050 NE 3rd St
Prineville, OR 97754 United States
Phone: 541-416-6700   Fax: 541-416-6798
Scope: Regional

UNITED STATES DEPARTMENT OF THE INTERIOR
BUREAU OF LAND MANAGEMENT
PUBLIC AFFAIRS
1849 C St., NW, 406-LS
Washington, DC 20240 United States
Phone: 202-208-3801   Fax: 202-208-5242
Website: www.blm.gov
Founded: 1946
Membership: 101–1,000
Scope: National
Description: Administers the public lands which are located primarily in the Western states and which amount to about 48 percent over 272 million acres of all federally owned lands. These lands and resources are managed under multiple-use principles, including outdoor recreation, fish and wildlife production, livestock grazing, timber, industrial development, watershed protection, and onshore mineral production.
Contact(s):
  Nina Hatfield, Director, Acting
  Henri Bisson, Assistant Director of Renewable Resources & Planning; 202-208-4896
  Carson Culp, Assistant Director of Minerals, Realty, & Resource Protection; 202-208-4201
  Bob Doyle, Assistant Director of Business and Fiscal Services; 202-208-4864
  Larry Finfer, Assistant Director of Communications; 202-208-6913
  Gayle Gordon, Assistant Director of Information Resources Management
  Warren Johnson, Assistant Director of Human Resources; 202-501-6724
  Carol Macdonald, Environmental, NEPA Issues; 202-452-5111
  W. Tipton, Information Resource

UNITED STATES DEPARTMENT OF THE INTERIOR
BUREAU OF LAND MANAGEMENT
RAWLINS FIELD OFFICE
1300 North Third St.; P.O. Box 2407
Rawlins, WY 82301-2407 United States
Phone: 307-328-4200   Fax: 307-328-4224
E-mail: rawlins_wymail@blm.gov
Website: www.wy.blm.gov/rfo/
Founded: 1946
Scope: Local, State, Regional
Description: One of ten BLM field offices in Wyoming
Keyword(s): Agriculture/Farming, Air Quality/Atmosphere, Energy, Forests/Forestry, Land Issues, Public Lands/Greenspace, Recreation/Ecotourism, Water Habitats & Quality, Wildlife & Species

UNITED STATES DEPARTMENT OF THE INTERIOR
BUREAU OF LAND MANAGEMENT
REDDING FIELD OFFICE
355 Hemsted Drive
Redding, CA 96002 United States
Phone: 530-224-2100   Fax: 530-224-2172
Scope: Regional

UNITED STATES DEPARTMENT OF THE INTERIOR
BUREAU OF LAND MANAGEMENT
RENEWABLE ENERGY
1235 La Plata Hwy., Suite A
Farmington, NM 87401 United States
Phone: 505-599-8911   Fax: 505-599-6377
E-mail: www.lotteni@blm.gov
Founded: 2001
Scope: Regional
Description: Renewable Energy Resource Development on Public Land
Keyword(s): Energy

UNITED STATES DEPARTMENT OF THE INTERIOR
BUREAU OF LAND MANAGEMENT
RICHFIELD DISTRICT FIELD OFFICE
150 E. 900, N
Richfield, UT 84701 United States
Phone: 435-896-1523
Website: www.ut.blm.gov/richfield/index.html
Scope: Regional

UNITED STATES DEPARTMENT OF THE INTERIOR
BUREAU OF LAND MANAGEMENT
RIDGECREST FIELD OFFICE
300 South Richmond Road
Ridgecrest, CA 93555 United States
Phone: 760-384-5400   Fax: 760-384-5499
Scope: Regional

UNITED STATES DEPARTMENT OF THE INTERIOR
BUREAU OF LAND MANAGEMENT
ROCK SPRINGS FIELD OFFICE
280 Highway 191 N.
Rock Springs, WY 82901-3448 United States
Phone: 307-352-0256   Fax: 307-352-0329
Scope: Regional

UNITED STATES DEPARTMENT OF THE INTERIOR
BUREAU OF LAND MANAGEMENT
ROSEBURG DISTRICT
777 NW Garden Valley Blvd.
Roseburg, OR 97470 United States
Phone: 541-440-4930   Fax: 541-440-4948
Scope: Regional

UNITED STATES DEPARTMENT OF THE INTERIOR
BUREAU OF LAND MANAGEMENT
ROSWELL DISTRICT
2909 West Second Street
Roswell, NM 88201-2019 United States
Phone: 505-627-0272   Fax: 505-627-0276
Website: www.nm.blm.gov/rfo
Scope: Regional
Description: Field office location serving seven-county area in southeastern NM
Contact(s):
Tim Kreager, Manager; 505-627-0272; Fax: 505-627-0276; tim_kreager@blm.gov

UNITED STATES DEPARTMENT OF THE INTERIOR
BUREAU OF LAND MANAGEMENT
ROYAL GORGE FIELD OFFICE/FRONT RANGE CENTER
3170 E. Main St.
Canon City, CO 81212 United States
Phone: 719-269-8500   Fax: 719-269-8599
Scope: Local
Description: The Bureau of Land Management sustains the health, diversity and productivity of the public lands for the use and enjoyment of present and future generations.

UNITED STATES DEPARTMENT OF THE INTERIOR
BUREAU OF LAND MANAGEMENT
SAFFORD FIELD OFFICE
711 South 14th Avenue
Safford, AZ 85546-3321 United States
Phone: 928-348-4400   Fax: 928-348-4450
E-mail: SFOweb@blm.gov
Website: www.safford.az.blm.gov
Scope: Regional
Description: The Safford Field Office manages 1.5 million acres of public lands in eastern Arizona. These include 20 recreation sites and six wilderness areas. The Gila Box Riparian National Conservation Area includes four perennial waterways. The office boasts 130 miles of perennial streams and abundant riparian habitat. Volunteers can assist with wildlife inventories and projects. Wildlife viewing, hunting, birding are popular; a bird checklist is at www.visitgrahamcounty.com/bird.asp.
Keyword(s): Agriculture/Farming, Air Quality/Atmosphere, Ecosystems (precious), Energy, Land Issues, Pollution (general), Public Lands/Greenspace, Recreation/Ecotourism, Transportation, Water Habitats & Quality, Wildlife & Species

UNITED STATES DEPARTMENT OF THE INTERIOR
BUREAU OF LAND MANAGEMENT
SAGUACHE FIELD OFFICE
46525 Hwy. 114, P.O. Box 67
Saguache, CO 81149 United States
Phone: 719-655-2547   Fax: 719-655-2502
Scope: Regional

UNITED STATES DEPARTMENT OF THE INTERIOR
BUREAU OF LAND MANAGEMENT
SALEM DISTRICT OFFICE
1717 Fabry Rd., SE
Salem, OR 97306 United States
Phone: 503-375-5646   Fax: 503-375-5622
Website: www.or.blm.gov/salem
Scope: Regional

UNITED STATES DEPARTMENT OF THE INTERIOR
BUREAU OF LAND MANAGEMENT
SALMON FIELD OFFICE
50 Hwy. 93, South / Route 2, Box 610
Salmon, ID 83467 United States
Phone: 208-756-5400   Fax: 208-756-5436
Scope: Regional

UNITED STATES DEPARTMENT OF THE INTERIOR
BUREAU OF LAND MANAGEMENT
SALT LAKE FIELD OFFICE
2370 S. 2300 W.
Salt Lake City, UT 84119 United States
Phone: 801-977-4310   Fax: 801-997-4397

Membership: 101–1,000
Scope: Local, Regional
Description: We are responsible for nearly 3.5 million acres of public land in 11 counties in northern Utah. We have a workforce of multiple disciplines to manage a broad spectrum of resources.
Contact(s):
Glenn Carpenter, Field Office Manager
Todd Christensen, Associate Field Office Manager

UNITED STATES DEPARTMENT OF THE INTERIOR
BUREAU OF LAND MANAGEMENT
SAN JUAN FIELD OFFICE
15 Burnett Ct.
Durango, CO 81301 United States
Phone: 970-247-4874   Fax: 970-375-2338
Scope: Regional

UNITED STATES DEPARTMENT OF THE INTERIOR
BUREAU OF LAND MANAGEMENT
SAN PEDRO PROJECT OFFICE
1763 Paseo San Luis
Sierra Vista, AZ 85635-2240 United States
Phone: 520-439-6400   Fax: 520-439-6422
Scope: Regional

UNITED STATES DEPARTMENT OF THE INTERIOR
BUREAU OF LAND MANAGEMENT
SHOSHONE FIELD OFFICE
400 W. F St., P.O. Box 2-B
Shoshone, ID 83352 United States
Phone: 208-732-7200   Fax: 208-732-7213
Scope: Regional

UNITED STATES DEPARTMENT OF THE INTERIOR
BUREAU OF LAND MANAGEMENT
SOCORRO FIELD OFFICE
198 Neel Ave., NW
Socorro, NM 87801 United States
Phone: 505-835-0412   Fax: 505-835-0223
Website: www.nm.blm.gov
Scope: Regional
Description: Federal Land Management Agency
Contact(s):
David Heft, Manager; 505-838-1267; Fax: 505-835-0223; dheft@nm.blm.gov

UNITED STATES DEPARTMENT OF THE INTERIOR
BUREAU OF LAND MANAGEMENT
SOUTH DAKOTA FIELD OFFICE
310 Roundup St.
Belle Fourche, SD 57717-1698 United States
Phone: 605-892-7000   Fax: 605-892-7015
Scope: Regional

UNITED STATES DEPARTMENT OF THE INTERIOR
BUREAU OF LAND MANAGEMENT
SPOKANE DISTRICT
1103 N. Fancher Rd
Spokane, WA 99212 United States
Phone: 509-536-1200   Fax: 509-536-1275
Website: www.or.blm.gov/spokane
Scope: Regional

UNITED STATES DEPARTMENT OF THE INTERIOR
BUREAU OF LAND MANAGEMENT
ST. GEORGE FIELD OFFICE
345 East Riverside Dr.
St. George, UT 84720 United States
Phone: 435-688-3200
Scope: Regional
Contact(s):
James Crisp, Manager; 435-688-3201; james_crisp@blm.gov

UNITED STATES DEPARTMENT OF THE INTERIOR
BUREAU OF LAND MANAGEMENT
STATE OFFICE FOR CA
1800 Cottage Way, Rm. W-1834
Sacramento, CA 95825 United States
Phone: 916-978-4400   Fax: 916-978-4305
Scope: Regional

UNITED STATES DEPARTMENT OF THE INTERIOR
BUREAU OF LAND MANAGEMENT
STATE OFFICE FOR ID
1387 S. Vinnell Way
Boise, ID 83709-1657 United States
Phone: 208-373-4000   Fax: 208-373-4005
Scope: Regional
Description: The BLM is responsible for the stewardship of almost 12 million acres of public land in Idaho. It is committed to manage these lands to serve the needs of the American people for all times. The BLM bases its management on the principles of multiple use and sustained yield.

UNITED STATES DEPARTMENT OF THE INTERIOR
BUREAU OF LAND MANAGEMENT
STATE OFFICE FOR MT, ND AND SD
P.O. Box 36800
Billings, MT 59107-6800 United States
Phone: 406-896-5012   Fax: 406-896-5299
Scope: Regional

UNITED STATES DEPARTMENT OF THE INTERIOR
BUREAU OF LAND MANAGEMENT
STATE OFFICE FOR NM, TX, OK AND KS
P.O. Box 27115
1474 Rodeo Rd
Santa Fe, NM 87502-0115 United States
Phone: 505-438-7501   Fax: 505-438-7452
Scope: Regional

UNITED STATES DEPARTMENT OF THE INTERIOR
BUREAU OF LAND MANAGEMENT
STATE OFFICE FOR NV
P.O. Box 12000
Reno, NV 89520-0006 United States
Phone: 775-861-6586   Fax: 775-861-6602
E-mail: webmaster@nv.blm.gov
Website: www.nv.blm.gov
Membership: 101–1,000
Scope: Regional
Description: The Bureau of Land Management in Nevada manages 48 million acres of the Nation's public lands in Nevada.

UNITED STATES DEPARTMENT OF THE INTERIOR
BUREAU OF LAND MANAGEMENT
STATE OFFICE FOR OR AND WA
P.O. Box 2965
Portland, OR 97208 United States
Phone: 503-808-6003   Fax: 503-808-6333
E-mail: or912mb@or.blm.gov
Website: www.or.blm.gov
Scope: Regional
Description: Communications/Public Affairs Office

UNITED STATES DEPARTMENT OF THE INTERIOR
BUREAU OF LAND MANAGEMENT
STATE OFFICE FOR UT
324 S. State St.
Salt Lake City, UT 84145-0155 United States
Phone: 801-539-4001
Scope: Regional
Contact(s):
   Sally Wisely, Manager; 801-539-4010; sally_wisely@blm.gov

UNITED STATES DEPARTMENT OF THE INTERIOR
BUREAU OF LAND MANAGEMENT
STATE OFFICE FOR WY AND NE
5353 Yellowstone; P.O. Box 1828
Cheyenne, WY 82003 United States
Phone: 307-775-6256
Scope: Regional

UNITED STATES DEPARTMENT OF THE INTERIOR
BUREAU OF LAND MANAGEMENT
SURPRISE FIELD OFFICE
602 Cressler Street
P.O. Box 460
Cedarville, CA 96104 United States
Phone: 530-279-6101   Fax: 530-279-2171
Scope: Regional

UNITED STATES DEPARTMENT OF THE INTERIOR
BUREAU OF LAND MANAGEMENT
TAOS FIELD OFFICE
226 Cruz Alta Rd.
Taos, NM 87571-5983 United States
Phone: 505-758-8852   Fax: 505-758-1620
Website: www.nm.blm.gov
Founded: 1946
Scope: Local, State, Regional, National
Description: The Bureau of Land Management (BLM) is responsible for managing the nation's public lands and natural resources in a combination of ways that best serve the needs of the American people. Management is based on the principles of multiple use and sustained yield. The BLM balances recreation, commercial, scientific, and cultural interests as it strives for long-term protection of renewable and nonrenewable resources.

UNITED STATES DEPARTMENT OF THE INTERIOR
BUREAU OF LAND MANAGEMENT
TUCSON FIELD OFFICE
12661 East Broadway
Tucson, AZ 85748-7208 United States
Phone: 520-258-7200   Fax: 520-258-7238
Website: www.az.blm.gov
Scope: Local, State, Regional, National
Description: The Tucson Field Office manages nearly one million acres across Pima, Pinal, Santa Cruz, Cochise and Graham counties, and encompasses Tucson, the second largest metropolitan area in Arizona.
Keyword(s): Land Issues, Water Habitats & Quality, Wildlife & Species

UNITED STATES DEPARTMENT OF THE INTERIOR
BUREAU OF LAND MANAGEMENT
UKIAH FIELD OFFICE
2550 North State Street
Ukiah, CA 95482 United States
Phone: 707-468-4000   Fax: 707-468-4027
E-mail: ca340@ca.blm.gov
Website: www.ca.blm.gov
Scope: Regional
Description: Management of BLM administered lands in Northwestern California from the Pacific Ocean to the Central Valley and from the Golden Gate Bridge north to include central Mendocino, Lake, and Glenn Counties. Significant landscapes include the California Coastal National Monument, Cow Mountain, Cache Creek, Blue Ridge Berryessa Natural Area, Payne Ranch, and Indian Valley.

UNITED STATES DEPARTMENT OF THE INTERIOR
BUREAU OF LAND MANAGEMENT
UNCOMPAHGRE FIELD OFFICE/SOUTHWEST CENTER
2505 S. Townsend Ave.
Montrose, CO 81401 United States
Phone: 970-240-5300   Fax: 970-240-5367
Scope: Regional

UNITED STATES DEPARTMENT OF THE INTERIOR
BUREAU OF LAND MANAGEMENT
VALE DISTRICT
100 Oregon St.
Vale, OR 97918 United States
Phone: 541-473-3144   Fax: 541-473-6213
E-mail: Vale_Mail@or.blm.gov
Website: www.or.blm.gov/Vale
Scope: Regional
Description: The Vale District of the Bureau of Land Management (BLM) manages 5.1 million acres of public land in eastern Oregon. The mission of the BLM is to sustain the health, diversity, and productivity of the public lands for the use and enjoyment of present and future generations.

UNITED STATES DEPARTMENT OF THE INTERIOR
BUREAU OF LAND MANAGEMENT
VERNAL DISTRICT
170 S. 500 St., East
Vernal, UT 84078 United States
Phone: 801-781-4400   Fax: 801-781-4410
Scope: Regional

UNITED STATES DEPARTMENT OF THE INTERIOR
BUREAU OF LAND MANAGEMENT
WHITE RIVER FIELD OFFICE
73544 Hwy. 64
Meeker, CO 81641 United States
Phone: 970-878-3800   Fax: 970-878-3805
E-mail: wrfo_mail@CO.BLM.GOV
Website: www.co.blm.gov/wrra/index.htm
Scope: Regional

U.S. FEDERAL AND INTERNATIONAL GOVERNMENT AGENCIES – U

UNITED STATES DEPARTMENT OF THE INTERIOR
BUREAU OF LAND MANAGEMENT
WINNEMUCCA FIELD OFFICE
5100 E. Winnemucca Blvd.
Winnemucca, NV 89445 United States
Phone: 775-623-1500   Fax: 775-623-1503
Website: www.nv.blm.gov/winnemucca
Scope: Regional

UNITED STATES DEPARTMENT OF THE INTERIOR
BUREAU OF LAND MANAGEMENT
WORLAND FIELD OFFICE
S. 23rd St., P.O. Box 119
Worland, WY 82401-0119 United States
Phone: 307-347-5100   Fax: 307-347-6195
Scope: Regional

UNITED STATES DEPARTMENT OF THE INTERIOR
BUREAU OF LAND MANAGEMENT
YUMA FIELD OFFICE
2555 East Gila Ridge Road
Yuma, AZ 85365-2240 United States
Phone: 928-317-3200   Fax: 928-317-3250
Scope: Regional

UNITED STATES DEPARTMENT OF THE INTERIOR
BUREAU OF RECLAMATION
1849 C St., NW
Washington, DC 20240 United States
Website: www.usbr.gov/main/index.html
Description: The Bureau of Reclamation was created by the Reclamation Act of 1902 to reclaim arid lands in the 17 Western states. This has been accomplished by the development of a system of works for the storage, diversion, and development of water. Reclamation's future role entails a shift in emphasis from development to total resource management and more effective use of existing facilities. Nonstructural means of meeting future water and power needs is now being emphasized.
Contact(s):
  Stephen Magnussen, Director of Operations; 202-208-4082
  Steven Richardson, Chief of Staff; 202-208-4292
  Paul Bledsoe, Chief of Public Affairs Division; 202-208-4662
  Fluid Martinez, Commissioner; 202-208-4157

UNITED STATES DEPARTMENT OF THE INTERIOR
BUREAU OF RECLAMATION
DENVER OFFICE
Bldg. 67, Denver Federal Center, P.O. Box 25007
Denver, CO 80225 United States
Phone: 303-445-2670
Contact(s):
  Kathy Gordon, Director of Management Services; 303-445-3002
  David Montoya, Director of Human Resources; 303-445-2670
  Neal Stessman, Director of Reclamation Service Center; 303-445-2692
  Wayne Deason, Deputy Director of Office of Policy; 303-445-2781

UNITED STATES DEPARTMENT OF THE INTERIOR
BUREAU OF RECLAMATION
LOWER COLORADO REGION
P.O. Box 61470
Boulder City, NV 89006-1470 United States
Phone: 702-293-8411   Fax: 702-293-8614
E-mail: rwalsh@oc.usbr.gov
Website: www.lc.usbr.gov
Membership: 101–1,000
Scope: Regional
Contact(s):
  Bob Johnson, Director
  Bob Walsh, External Affairs Officer

UNITED STATES DEPARTMENT OF THE INTERIOR
BUREAU OF RECLAMATION
MID PACIFIC REGION
Federal Office Bldg., 2800 Cottage Way
Sacramento, CA 95825 United States
Phone: 916-978-5100   Fax: 916-978-5114
Website: www.usbr.gov/mp
Membership: 101–1,000
Scope: Regional
Contact(s):
  Kirk Rodgers, Director, Acting

UNITED STATES DEPARTMENT OF THE INTERIOR
BUREAU OF RECLAMATION
PACIFIC NORTHWEST REGION
1150 N. Curtis Rd., Suite 100
Boise, ID 83706-1234 United States
Phone: 208-378-5036   Fax: 208-378-5102
E-mail: mmcclendon@pn.usbr.gov
Website: www.usbr.gov/pn
Founded: 1902
Membership: 101–1,000
Scope: Regional
Description: The Bureau of Reclamation is a federal water management agency. Water projects managed by the agency are authorized for irrigation, flood control, hydro-electric power, fish & wildlife, and recreation.
Keyword(s): Agriculture/Farming, Energy, Land Issues, Recreation/Ecotourism, Wildlife & Species
Contact(s):
  Bill Macdonald, Regional Director; 208-378-5012

UNITED STATES DEPARTMENT OF THE INTERIOR
BUREAU OF RECLAMATION
UPPER COLORADO REGION
125 South State St., Rm. 6107
Salt Lake City, UT 84138 United States
Phone: 801-524-3600   Fax: 801-524-5499
Website: www.uc.usbr.gov
Membership: 101–1,000
Scope: Regional
Description: Environmental Resources Division, Adaptive Management Group, Environmental Compliance Group
Keyword(s): Ecosystems (precious), Wildlife & Species
Contact(s):
  Rick Gold, Regional Director
  Randall Peterson, Mgr., Environmental Resources Division; 801-524-3758; Fax: 801-524-3858; rpeterson@uc.usbr.gov
  Nancy Coulam, Chief, Environmental Compliance Group; 801-524-3684; Fax: 801-524-3858; ncoulam@uc.usbr.gov
  Dennis Kubly, Chief, Adaptive Management Group; 801-524-3715; Fax: 801-524-3858; dkubly@uc.usbr.gov
  Barry Wirth, Public Affairs Officer; 801-524-3774

UNITED STATES DEPARTMENT OF THE INTERIOR
DESERT NATIONAL WILDLIFE RANGE
Box 700
HCR 38
Las Vegas, NV 89124 United States
Phone: 702-879-6110　　　　　Fax: 702-879-6115
E-mail: amy_sprunger-allworth@fws.gov
Website: http://desertcomplex.fws.gov

Founded: 1936
Scope: Local, State, Regional, National, International
Description: Desert National Wildlife Range

UNITED STATES DEPARTMENT OF THE INTERIOR
FISH AND WILDLIFE SERVICE
Department of Interior, 1849 C St., NW
Washington, DC 20240 United States
Phone: 202-208-5634　　　　　Fax: 202-208-7407
E-mail: contact@fws.gov
Website: www.fws.gov

Founded: 1871
Scope: National
Description: Effective July 1, 1974, an act of Congress (Public Law 93-271, April 22, 1974), renamed the Bureau of Sport Fisheries and Wildlife, the United States Fish and Wildlife Service, under the Assistant Secretary for Fish and Wildlife and Parks. The Service is the lead federal agency in the conservation of the nation's migratory birds, threatened and endangered species, certain marine mammals, and sport fishing. The Service administers fish and wildlife restoration grant programs to state governments,
Keyword(s): Ecosystems (precious), Land Issues, Oceans/Coasts/Beaches, Public Lands/Greenspace, Recreation/Ecotourism, Water Habitats & Quality, Wildlife & Species
Contact(s):
  Steve Williams, Director; 202-208-4717
  Vaughn Collins, Program Manager of Federal Duck Stamp Program; 703-358-2000; Fax: 703-358-2009; vaughn_collins@fws.gov
  Kevin Adams, Chief of Division of Law Enforcement; 703-358-1949
  Eric Alvarez, Chief of Division of Realty; 703-358-1713
  Robert Ashworth, Chief of Division of Contracting and General Services; 703-358-2181
  Bob Batky, Chief of Division of National Fish Hatcheries; 703-358-1715
  Kent Baum, Chief of Division of Personnel Management; 703-358-1776
  Hannibal Bolton, Chief of Division of Fish and Wildlife Management Assistance; 703-358-1718
  Paul Camp, Chief of Division of Engineering; 303-984-6861
  Shane Compton, Chief of Division of Information Resources Management; 703-358-1787
  Jeff Flemming, Chief of Office of Public Affairs; 202-208-4131
  Arthur Ford, Chief of FWS Finance Center; Denver Federal Center, P.O. Box 25207, Denver, CO 80225-0207
  Gary Frazer, Assistant Director for Endangered Species; 202-208-4646
  William Hartwig, Chief of Division of Refuge; 202-208-5333
  Paul Henne, Assistant Director of Administration; 202-208-4888
  Christopher Jensen, Chief of Division of Fiscal Management; 703-358-2047
  Marshall Jones, Deputy Director; 202-208-4545
  Kris LaMontagne, Chief of Office of Federal Aid; 703-358-2206
  Thomas Melius, Assistant Director of External Affairs; 202-208-6541
  Brian Millsap, Chief of Office of Migratory Bird Management; 703-358-1714
  Mamie Parker, Assistant Director of Fisheries; 202-208-6394
  Alexandra Pitts, Chief of Office of Congressional and Legislative Services; 202-208-5403
  Herbert Raffaele, Chief of Office of International Conservation; 703-358-1754
  Ken Stansell, Assistant Director of International Affairs; 202-208-6393
  Benjamin Tuggle, Chief of Division of Habitat Conservation; 703-358-2161
  Everett Wilson, Chief of Division of Environmental Quality; 703-358-2148

UNITED STATES DEPARTMENT OF THE INTERIOR
FISH AND WILDLIFE SERVICE
ACE BASIN NATIONAL WILDLIFE REFUGE
P.O. Box 848
Hollywood, SC 29449 United States
Phone: 843-889-3084　　　　　Fax: 843-889-3282
E-mail: acebasin@fws.gov
Website: http://acebasin.fws.gov

Scope: Local
Description: National Wildlife Refuge
Keyword(s): Ecosystems (precious)

UNITED STATES DEPARTMENT OF THE INTERIOR
FISH AND WILDLIFE SERVICE
AGASSIZ NATIONAL WILDLIFE REFUGE
22996 290th Street NE
Middle River, MN 56737 United States
Phone: 218-449-4115　　　　　Fax: 218-449-3241

Scope: National

UNITED STATES DEPARTMENT OF THE INTERIOR
FISH AND WILDLIFE SERVICE
ALAMOSA/MONTE VISTA NATIONAL WILDLIFE REFUGE
9383 El Rancho Ln.
Alamosa, CO 81101-9003 United States
Phone: 719-589-4021, ext. 103　　Fax: 719-587-0595

Scope: Regional
Description: Alamosa, Monte Vista and Baca National Wildlife Refuges provide habitat for migratory birds. Habitat management activitites primarily focus on wetlands and riparian habitat in Colorado's San Luis Valley.

UNITED STATES DEPARTMENT OF THE INTERIOR
FISH AND WILDLIFE SERVICE
ALASKA MARITIME NATIONAL WILDLIFE REFUGE
2355 Kachemak Bay Dr., Ste. 101
Homer, AK 99603-8021 United States
Phone: 907-235-6546　　　　　Fax: 907-235-7783

Scope: Regional

UNITED STATES DEPARTMENT OF THE INTERIOR
FISH AND WILDLIFE SERVICE
ALASKA PENINSULA/BECHAROF NATIONAL WILDLIFE REFUGE
P.O. Box 277
King Salmon, AK 99613 United States
Phone: 907-246-3339　　　　　Fax: 907-246-6696

Scope: Regional

UNITED STATES DEPARTMENT OF THE INTERIOR
FISH AND WILDLIFE SERVICE
ALLIGATOR RIVER/PEA ISLAND NATIONAL WILDLIFE REFUGE
P.O. Box 1969
Manteo, NC 27954 United States
Phone: 252-473-1131, ext. 230   Fax: 252-473-1668
E-mail: alligatorriver@fws.gov
Website: http://alligatorriver.fws.gov/

Founded: 1937
Scope: Regional, National
Description: Two National Wildlife Refuges on the coast of NE NC
Keyword(s): Agriculture/Farming, Ecosystems (precious), Forests/Forestry, Oceans/Coasts/Beaches, Recreation/Ecotourism, Wildlife & Species

UNITED STATES DEPARTMENT OF THE INTERIOR
FISH AND WILDLIFE SERVICE
ANAHUAC NATIONAL WILDLIFE REFUGE
P.O. Box 278
Anahuac, TX 77514 United States
Phone: 409-267-3337   Fax: 409-267-4314

Scope: Regional

UNITED STATES DEPARTMENT OF THE INTERIOR
FISH AND WILDLIFE SERVICE
ANKENY NATIONAL WILDLIFE REFUGE
2301 Wintel Road
Jefferson, OR 97352 United States
Phone: 503-588-2701

Scope: Regional

UNITED STATES DEPARTMENT OF THE INTERIOR
FISH AND WILDLIFE SERVICE
ANTIOCH DUNES NATIONAL WILDLIFE REFUGE
c/o Don Edwards
San Francisco Bay NWR Complex
P.O. Box 524
Newark, CA 94560-0524 United States

Scope: Regional
Contact(s):
Anne Badgley, Regional Director; 510-792-0222

UNITED STATES DEPARTMENT OF THE INTERIOR
FISH AND WILDLIFE SERVICE
ARAPAHO NATIONAL WILDLIFE REFUGE
P.O. Box 457
Walden, CO 80480 United States
Phone: 970-723-8202   Fax: 970-723-0520

Scope: Regional

UNITED STATES DEPARTMENT OF THE INTERIOR
FISH AND WILDLIFE SERVICE
ARCHIE CARR NATIONAL WILDLIFE REFUGE
1339 20th Street
Vero Beach, FL 32960-3559 United States
Phone: 772-562-3909   Fax: 772-299-3101
E-mail: archiecarr@fws.gov
Website: http://archiecarr.fws.gov

Founded: 1991
Scope: National
Description: The Carr refuge stretches 20 miles along Florida's central Atlantic coast. The Carr refuge is the Nation's only refuge designated to protect sea turtles. The Carr refuge provides nesting habitat for approximately one-fourth of all sea turtle nesting in the United States. The Carr refuge provides habitat for several other threatened or endangered species.
Keyword(s): Ecosystems (precious), Land Issues, Oceans/Coasts/Beaches, Public Lands/Greenspace, Recreation/Ecotourism, Wildlife & Species
Contact(s):
Paul Tritaik, Refuge Manager; 772-562-3909; ext. 244; Fax: 772-299-3101; paul_tritaik@fws.gov

UNITED STATES DEPARTMENT OF THE INTERIOR
FISH AND WILDLIFE SERVICE
ARCTIC NATIONAL WILDLIFE REFUGE
101 12th Ave., Box 20
Fairbanks, AK 99701 United States
Phone: 907-456-0250   Fax: 907-456-0428
E-mail: richard_voss@fws.gov
Website: http://arctic.fws.gov

Scope: Regional

UNITED STATES DEPARTMENT OF THE INTERIOR
FISH AND WILDLIFE SERVICE
ARKANSAS NATIONAL WILDLIFE REFUGE
P.O. Box 100
Austwell, TX 77950 United States
Phone: 361-286-3559   Fax: 361-286-3722

Scope: Regional

UNITED STATES DEPARTMENT OF THE INTERIOR
FISH AND WILDLIFE SERVICE
ARROWWOOD NATIONAL WILDLIFE REFUGE COMPLEX
7745 11th St. SE
Pingree, ND 58476 United States
Phone: 701-285-3341   Fax: 701-285-3350
E-mail: R6RW_ARR@fws.gov
Website: www.fws.gov

Founded: 1935
Scope: Local, State, Regional, National
Keyword(s): Agriculture/Farming, Recreation/Ecotourism, Reduce/Reuse/Recycle, Water Habitats & Quality, Wildlife & Species
Contact(s):
Kim Hanson, Project Leader; 701-285-3341; kim_hanson@fws.gov
Stacy Adolf-Whipp, Refuge Operations Specialist; 701-285-3341; Fax: 701-285-3350; stacy_whipp@fws.gov
Mark Vaniman, Deputy Project Leader; 701-285-3341; Fax: 701-285-3350; mark_vaniman@fws.gov
Paulette Scherr, Wildlife Biologist; 701-285-3341; Fax: 701-285-3350; paulette_scherr@fws.gov

UNITED STATES DEPARTMENT OF THE INTERIOR
FISH AND WILDLIFE SERVICE
ARTHUR R. MARSHALL LOXAHATCHEE/HOPE SOUND NATIONAL WILDLIFE REFUGE
10216 Lee Rd.
Boynton Beach, FL 33437-4796 United States
Phone: 561-732-3684   Fax: 561-369-7190
E-mail: Loxahatchee@fws.gov
Website: http://Loxahatchee.fws.gov

Founded: 1951
Scope: Local, State, Regional, National
Description: National Wildlife Refuge
Publication(s): Refuge Newsletter

Keyword(s): Air Quality/Atmosphere, Ecosystems (precious), Land Issues, Pollution (general), Public Lands/Greenspace, Recreation/Ecotourism, Water Habitats & Quality, Wildlife & Species

UNITED STATES DEPARTMENT OF THE INTERIOR
FISH AND WILDLIFE SERVICE
ASH MEADOWS NATIONAL WILDLIFE REFUGE
HCR 70, Box 610-Z
Amargosa Valley, NV 89020 United States
Phone: 775-372-5435　　　　Fax: 775-372-5436
E-mail: eric_hopson@fws.gov
Website: http://desertcomplex.fws.gov/

Founded: 1984
Scope: Regional
Description: Ash Meadows NWR encompasses over 22,000 acres of spring-fed wetlands and desert uplands which are managed by the U.S. Fish & Wildlife Service primarily for the benefit of 13 threatened and endangered species. The refuge also provides habitat for at least 24 plants and animals found nowhere else in the world.
Keyword(s): Land Issues, Public Health, Recreation/Ecotourism, Wildlife & Species

UNITED STATES DEPARTMENT OF THE INTERIOR
FISH AND WILDLIFE SERVICE
ATTWATER PRAIRIE CHICKEN NATIONAL WILDLIFE REFUGE
P.O. Box 519
Eagle Lake, TX 77434-0519 United States
Phone: 979-234-3021　　　　Fax: 979-234-3278
Scope: Regional

UNITED STATES DEPARTMENT OF THE INTERIOR
FISH AND WILDLIFE SERVICE
AUDUBON NATIONAL WILDLIFE REFUGE
3275 11th St. NW
Coleharbor, ND 58531 United States
Phone: 701-442-5474　　　　Fax: 701-442-5546
E-mail: audubon@fws.gov
Website: http://audubon.fws.gov
Scope: Regional

UNITED STATES DEPARTMENT OF THE INTERIOR
FISH AND WILDLIFE SERVICE
BACK BAY/PLUM TREE ISLAND NATIONAL WILDLIFE REFUGE
4005 Sandpiper Rd.
Virginia Beach, VA 23456 United States
Phone: 757-721-2412　　　　Fax: 757-721-6141
Scope: Regional

UNITED STATES DEPARTMENT OF THE INTERIOR
FISH AND WILDLIFE SERVICE
BALCONES CANYONLANDS NATIONAL WILDLIFE REFUGE
10711 Burnet Rd., Ste. 201
Austin, TX 78758 United States
Phone: 512-339-9432　　　　Fax: 512-339-9453
E-mail: FW2_RW_Balcones@fws.gov

Founded: 1992
Scope: Regional
Description: Balcones is a National Wildlife Refuge established to protect the nesting habitat of the Golden-cheeked Warbler and Black-capped Vireo, 2 endangered neotropical migrants, as well as endangered cave invertebrates. The Refuge has 3 areas open to the public that provide hiking and wildlife observation. The Refuge also hosts a dove hunt and several deer hunts. The Friends of Balcones Canyonlands NWR is a grass roots organization dedicated to helping the Refuge achieve its objectives.
Keyword(s): Public Lands/Greenspace, Wildlife & Species
Contact(s):
　　Deborah Holle, Refuge Manager; 512-339-9432; fw2_rw_balcones@fws.gov

UNITED STATES DEPARTMENT OF THE INTERIOR
FISH AND WILDLIFE SERVICE
BALD KNOB NATIONAL WILDLIFE REFUGE
Rt. 2, Box 126-T
Augusta, AR 72006 United States
Phone: 870-347-2614　　　　Fax: 870-347-2908
E-mail: baldknob@fws.gov
Website: http://southeast.fws.gov/BaldKnob
Scope: Regional

UNITED STATES DEPARTMENT OF THE INTERIOR
FISH AND WILDLIFE SERVICE
BAYOU COCODRIE NATIONAL WILDLIFE REFUGE
P.O. Box 1772
Ferriday, LA 71334 United States
Phone: 318-336-7119　　　　Fax: 318-336-5610
Founded: 1990
Scope: Local, State, Regional, National
Description: A place where wildlife comes first.

UNITED STATES DEPARTMENT OF THE INTERIOR
FISH AND WILDLIFE SERVICE
BEAR LAKE NATIONAL WILDLIFE REFUGE
P.O. Box 9
Montpelier, ID 83254-1019 United States
Phone: 208-847-1757　　　　Fax: 208-847-1319
Scope: Regional

UNITED STATES DEPARTMENT OF THE INTERIOR
FISH AND WILDLIFE SERVICE
BEAR RIVER MIGRATORY BIRD NATIONAL WILDLIFE REFUGE
58 South 950 West
Brigham City, UT 84302 United States
Phone: 435-723-5887　　　　Fax: 435-723-8873
E-mail: 6DE-RWBRR@fws.gov
Website: http://mountain-prairie.fws.gov/bearriver/
Scope: Regional

UNITED STATES DEPARTMENT OF THE INTERIOR
FISH AND WILDLIFE SERVICE
BENTON LAKE NATIONAL WILDLIFE REFUGE
922 Bootlegger Trail
Great Falls, MT 59404 United States
Phone: 406-727-7400　　　　Fax: 406-727-7432
E-mail: fw6_rw_benton_lake_nwr@fws.gov
Founded: 1929
Description: National Wildlife Refuge and Wetland Management District. Important Bird Area.
Keyword(s): Land Issues, Pollution (general), Recreation/Ecotourism, Water Habitats & Quality

U.S. FEDERAL AND INTERNATIONAL GOVERNMENT AGENCIES – U

UNITED STATES DEPARTMENT OF THE INTERIOR
FISH AND WILDLIFE SERVICE
BIG LAKE NATIONAL WILDLIFE REFUGE
P.O. Box 67
Manila, AR 72442 United States
Phone: 870-564-2429   Fax: 870-564-2573
Scope: Regional
Contact(s):
  Brian Braudis

UNITED STATES DEPARTMENT OF THE INTERIOR
FISH AND WILDLIFE SERVICE
BIG MUDDY NATIONAL FISH & WILDLIFE REFUGE
4200 New Haven Rd.
Columbia, MO 65201 United States
Phone: 573-876-1826   Fax: 573-876-1839
Founded: 1994
Scope: Regional
Description: National Fish & Wildlife Refuge established to benefit floodplain dependent species in the Missouri River valley between the mouth of the Missouri on the Mississippi River at St. Louis to the mouth of the Kansas River in Kansas City. The Big Muddy NFWR currently consists of 10,400 acres. The Big Muddy is authorized to acquire land up to a total of 60,000 acres. Permitted activities include fishing, hunting, nature interpretation, wildlife observation, environmental education and photography.
Contact(s):
  Thomas Bell, Refuge Manager; 573-876-1826; ext. 2; tom_bell@fws.gov

UNITED STATES DEPARTMENT OF THE INTERIOR
FISH AND WILDLIFE SERVICE
BIG STONE NATIONAL WILDLIFE REFUGE
Rt. 1 Box 25
44843 County Rd. 19
Odessa, MN 56276 United States
Phone: 320-273-2191   Fax: 320-273-2231
Scope: National
Contact(s):
  Carole Gerber, Manager

UNITED STATES DEPARTMENT OF THE INTERIOR
FISH AND WILDLIFE SERVICE
BITTER CREEK NATIONAL WILDLIFE REFUGE
c/o Hopper Mountain Complex, P.O. Box 5839
Ventura, CA 93005-0839 United States
Phone: 805-644-5185   Fax: 805-644-1732
Website: http://hoppermountain@fws.gov
Founded: 1985
Scope: National
Description: Bitter Creek NWR was established to protect foraging and roosting habitat for the endangered California condor.

UNITED STATES DEPARTMENT OF THE INTERIOR
FISH AND WILDLIFE SERVICE
BITTER LAKE NATIONAL WILDLIFE REFUGE
4065 Bitter Lakes Road
Roswell, NM 88201-0007 United States
Phone: 505-622-6755, ext. 19   Fax: 505-622-9039
E-mail: fw2_rw_bitterlake@fws.gov
Website: http://southwest.fws.gov/refuges/newmex/bitter.html

Founded: 1937
Scope: Local, State, Regional
Description: A 25,000-acre refuge w/unique wetlands, waterfowl, shorebirds, dragonflies, scenery. Public use facilities include 8-mi. auto tour, hiking trails, bike trail, overlooks, observation platforms, and limited public hunting (call for details).

UNITED STATES DEPARTMENT OF THE INTERIOR
FISH AND WILDLIFE SERVICE
BLACKWATER NATIONAL WILDLIFE REFUGE
2145 Key Wallace Dr.
Cambridge, MD 21613 United States
Phone: 410-228-2692   Fax: 410-228-3261
Scope: National

UNITED STATES DEPARTMENT OF THE INTERIOR
FISH AND WILDLIFE SERVICE
BLUE RIDGE NATIONAL WILDLIFE REFUGE
P.O. Box 670
Delano, CA 93216 United States
Phone: 805-725-2767
Website: http://pacific.fws.gov/hoppermtn/blue.htm
Scope: National

UNITED STATES DEPARTMENT OF THE INTERIOR
FISH AND WILDLIFE SERVICE
BOMBAY HOOK NATIONAL WILDLIFE REFUGE
2591 Whitehall Neck Rd.
Smyrna, DE 19977 United States
Phone: 302-653-9345   Fax: 302-653-0684
E-mail: FW5RW_BHNWR@FWS.GOV
Website: http://bombayhook.fws.gov
Founded: 1937
Scope: National
Description: Bombay Hook NWR was established in 1937 to provide habitat for migratory birds. The refuge includes 15,978 acres with tidal marsh, freshwater impoundments, cropland fields, forestland, and grasslands. The refuge provides habitat for thousands of migrating shorebirds in the Spring and waterfowl in the Fall and Winter. The Refuge hosts 170,000 visitors annually for wildlife-dependent recreation including wildlife observation, interpretation and environmental education, photography, and hunting.
Keyword(s): Public Lands/Greenspace, Recreation/Ecotourism, Wildlife & Species
Contact(s):
  L. Villanueva, Refuge Manager; 302-653-9345; Fax: 302-653-0684

UNITED STATES DEPARTMENT OF THE INTERIOR
FISH AND WILDLIFE SERVICE
BON SECOUR NATIONAL WILDLIFE REFUGE
12295 State Highway 180
Gulf Shores, AL 36542 United States
Phone: 251-540-7720   Fax: 251-540-7301
Scope: Regional

UNITED STATES DEPARTMENT OF THE INTERIOR
FISH AND WILDLIFE SERVICE
BOSQUE DE APACHE NATIONAL WILDLIFE REFUGE
P.O. Box 1246
Socorro, NM 87801 United States
Phone: 505-835-1828   Fax: 505-835-0314
Website: http://southwest.fws.gov
Scope: Regional

UNITED STATES DEPARTMENT OF THE INTERIOR
FISH AND WILDLIFE SERVICE
BOWDOIN NATIONAL WILDLIFE REFUGE
HC 65, Box 5700
Malta, MT 59538 United States
Phone: 406-654-2863   Fax: 406-654-2866
Scope: National

UNITED STATES DEPARTMENT OF THE INTERIOR
FISH AND WILDLIFE SERVICE
BRAZORIA NATIONAL WILDLIFE REFUGE
1212 N. Velasco, Ste. 200
Angleton, TX 77515-1088 United States
Phone: 979-849-7771   Fax: 979-849-5118
Scope: Regional

UNITED STATES DEPARTMENT OF THE INTERIOR
FISH AND WILDLIFE SERVICE
BROWNS PARK NATIONAL WILDLIFE REFUGE
1318 Highway 318
Maybell, CO 81640 United States
Phone: 970-365-3613   Fax: 970-365-3614
E-mail: brownspark@fws.gov
Scope: Regional
Description: National Wildlife Refuge charged with managing for a diversity of habitat and animals along the Green River. Wetland, riparian, grassland, and upland shrub habitats.
Keyword(s): Recreation/Ecotourism, Wildlife & Species

UNITED STATES DEPARTMENT OF THE INTERIOR
FISH AND WILDLIFE SERVICE
BUENOS AIRES NATIONAL WILDLIFE REFUGE
P.O. Box 109
Sasabe, AZ 85633 United States
Phone: 520-823-4251   Fax: 520-823-4247
E-mail: r2rw_bw@fws.gov
Website: http://southwest.fws.gov/refuges/arizona/buenos.html
Scope: Regional

UNITED STATES DEPARTMENT OF THE INTERIOR
FISH AND WILDLIFE SERVICE
BUFFALO LAKE NATIONAL WILDLIFE REFUGE
P.O. Box 179
Umbarger, TX 79091 United States
Phone: 806-499-3382
Scope: Regional

UNITED STATES DEPARTMENT OF THE INTERIOR
FISH AND WILDLIFE SERVICE
CABEZA PRIETA NATIONAL WILDLIFE REFUGE
1611 N. Second Ave.
Ajo, AZ 85321 United States
Phone: 520-387-6483   Fax: 520-387-5359
Scope: Regional

UNITED STATES DEPARTMENT OF THE INTERIOR
FISH AND WILDLIFE SERVICE
CACHE RIVER NATIONAL WILDLIFE REFUGE
26320 Hwy. 33 South
Augusta, AR 72006 United States
Phone: 870-347-2614   Fax: 870-347-2908
E-mail: cacheriver@fws.gov
Website: http://cacheriver.fws.gov
Scope: Regional

UNITED STATES DEPARTMENT OF THE INTERIOR
FISH AND WILDLIFE SERVICE
CALIFORNIA-NEVADA OPERATIONS
2800 Cottage Way, Rm. W-2606
Sacramento, CA 95825 United States
Phone: 916-414-6464   Fax: 916-414-6486
Website: www.fws.gov
Contact(s):
  Steve Thompson, Manager

UNITED STATES DEPARTMENT OF THE INTERIOR
FISH AND WILDLIFE SERVICE
CAMAS NATIONAL WILDLIFE REFUGE
2150 E. 2350 N.
Hamer, ID 83425 United States
Phone: 208-662-5423   Fax: 208-662-5525
Scope: Regional

UNITED STATES DEPARTMENT OF THE INTERIOR
FISH AND WILDLIFE SERVICE
CAMERON PRAIRIE NATIONAL WILDLIFE REFUGE
1428 Highway 27
Bell City, LA 70630 United States
Phone: 318-598-2216   Fax: 318-598-2492
Scope: Regional

UNITED STATES DEPARTMENT OF THE INTERIOR
FISH AND WILDLIFE SERVICE
CANAAN VALLEY NATIONAL WILDLIFE REFUGE
HC 70, Box 200
Davis, WV 26260 United States
Phone: 304-866-3858   Fax: 304-866-3852
E-mail: fw5rw_cvnwr@fws.gov
Website: http://northeast.fws.gov/wv/can.htm
Founded: 1994
Membership: 1–100
Scope: Regional
Description: Tucked in the mountains of West Virginia is the largest high elevation valley east of the Rockies. Northern plants and animals have found a niche here far south of their normal range. The valley also holds the largest wetland complex in West Virginia. The refuge works to conserve these wetlands and adjacent upland habitats for the fish, wildlife and plants that depend on them.
Keyword(s): Ecosystems (precious), Public Lands/Greenspace, Water Habitats & Quality, Wildlife & Species

UNITED STATES DEPARTMENT OF THE INTERIOR
FISH AND WILDLIFE SERVICE
CAPE MAY NATIONAL WILDLIFE REFUGE
24 Kimbles Beach Rd.
Cape May Courthouse, NJ 08210-4207 United States
Phone: 609-463-0994   Fax: 609-463-1667
Scope: Regional

U.S. FEDERAL AND INTERNATIONAL GOVERNMENT AGENCIES – U

UNITED STATES DEPARTMENT OF THE INTERIOR
FISH AND WILDLIFE SERVICE
CAPE ROMAIN/SANTEE NATIONAL WILDLIFE REFUGE
5821 Hwy. 17 N.
Awendaw, SC 29429 United States
Phone: 843-928-3368   Fax: 843-928-3828
E-mail: caperomain@fws.gov
Website: http://seweecenter.fws.gov
Scope: Regional

UNITED STATES DEPARTMENT OF THE INTERIOR
FISH AND WILDLIFE SERVICE
CARIBBEAN ISLANDS NATIONAL WILDLIFE REFUGE
P.O. Box 510
Boqueron, PR 00622 United States
Phone: 787-851-7258   Fax: 787-851-7440
E-mail: caribbeanisland@fws.gov
Website: http://caribbean.fws.gov/index.html
Scope: Regional

UNITED STATES DEPARTMENT OF THE INTERIOR
FISH AND WILDLIFE SERVICE
CAROLINA SANDHILLS NATIONAL WILDLIFE REFUGE
23734 Hwy. 1
McBee, SC 29101 United States
Phone: 803-335-8401   Fax: 803-335-8406
E-mail: fw4rwcarolinasandhills@fws.gov
Website: http://carolinasandhills.fws.gov/
Founded: 1939
Scope: Regional
Description: Endangered species: Red cockaded woodpecker, Habitat Mgmt: Prescribed burning
Keyword(s): Agriculture/Farming, Ecosystems (precious), Forests/Forestry, Recreation/Ecotourism, Water Habitats & Quality, Wildlife & Species

UNITED STATES DEPARTMENT OF THE INTERIOR
FISH AND WILDLIFE SERVICE
CATAHOULA NATIONAL WILDLIFE REFUGE
P.O. Drawer Z
Rhinehart, LA 71363-0201 United States
Phone: 318-992-5261   Fax: 318-992-6023
Scope: Regional

UNITED STATES DEPARTMENT OF THE INTERIOR
FISH AND WILDLIFE SERVICE
CHARLES M. RUSSELL NATIONAL WILDLIFE REFUGE
P.O. Box 110
Lewistown, MT 59457 United States
Phone: 406-538-8706   Fax: 406-538-7521
Scope: National

UNITED STATES DEPARTMENT OF THE INTERIOR
FISH AND WILDLIFE SERVICE
CHASE LAKE NATIONAL WILDLIFE REFUGE
5924 19th St. SE
Woodworth, ND 58496 United States
Phone: 701-752-4218   Fax: 701-752-4216
E-mail: chaselake@fws.gov
Website: http://chaselake.fws.gov/refuge.htm
Scope: Regional
Contact(s):
Mick Erickson; 701-752-4218; Fax: 701-752-4216; michael_erickson@fws.gov

UNITED STATES DEPARTMENT OF THE INTERIOR
FISH AND WILDLIFE SERVICE
CHASSAHOWITZKA NATIONAL WILDLIFE REFUGE
1502 S.E. Kings Bay Dr.
Crystal River, FL 34429 United States
Phone: 352-563-2088   Fax: 352-795-7961
E-mail: fcnwr@atlantic.net
Website: www.fcnwr.org
Scope: Regional

UNITED STATES DEPARTMENT OF THE INTERIOR
FISH AND WILDLIFE SERVICE
CHICKASAW NATIONAL WILDLIFE REFUGE
1505 Sand Bluff Rd.
Ripley, TN 38063 United States
Phone: 731-635-7621   Fax: 731-635-0178
E-mail: chickasaw@fws.gov
Website: http://chickasaw.fws.gov
Founded: 1985
Scope: National
Keyword(s): Forests/Forestry, Land Issues, Recreation/Ecotourism, Water Habitats & Quality, Wildlife & Species

UNITED STATES DEPARTMENT OF THE INTERIOR
FISH AND WILDLIFE SERVICE
CHINCOTEAGUE/WALLOPS ISLAND NATIONAL WILDLIFE REFUGE
P.O. Box 62
8231 Beach Road
Chincoteague Island, VA 23336 United States
Phone: 757-336-6122   Fax: 757-336-5273
Website: http://chinco.fws.gov
Founded: 1943
Scope: Regional
Description: Chincoteague and Wallops Island National Wildlife Refuges are located along the mid Atlantic Coast. Mostly in Virginia with small holdings in Maryland. These refuges are located strategically along the Atlantic flyway and host over 325 species of migratory birds, including several threatened species. Mammals found on Chincoteague Refuge include the endangered Delmarva Peninsula fox squirrel. Chincoteague is one of the most visited refuges in the nation.
Keyword(s): Recreation/Ecotourism, Wildlife & Species

UNITED STATES DEPARTMENT OF THE INTERIOR
FISH AND WILDLIFE SERVICE
CHOCTAW NATIONAL WILDLIFE REFUGE
P.O. Box 808
Jackson, AL 36545 United States
Phone: 251-246-3583   Fax: 251-246-5414
Scope: Regional

UNITED STATES DEPARTMENT OF THE INTERIOR
FISH AND WILDLIFE SERVICE
CLARKS RIVER NATIONAL WILDLIFE REFUGE
91 U.S. Hwy. 641N
Benton, KY 42025 United States
Phone: 270-527-5770   Fax: 270-527-5770
E-mail: fw4_rw_clarks_river@fws.gov
Scope: Regional

UNITED STATES DEPARTMENT OF THE INTERIOR
FISH AND WILDLIFE SERVICE
COLUMBIA NATIONAL WILDLIFE REFUGE
P.O. Drawer F, 735 E. Main St.
Othello, WA 99344 United States
Phone: 509-488-2668   Fax: 509-488-0705
E-mail: bob_flores@fws.gov
Website: www.fws.gov
Scope: Regional, National
Description: National Wildlife Refuge
Keyword(s): Recreation/Ecotourism, Water Habitats & Quality, Wildlife & Species

UNITED STATES DEPARTMENT OF THE INTERIOR
FISH AND WILDLIFE SERVICE
CONBOY LAKE NATIONAL WILDLIFE REFUGE
Box 5
Glenwood, WA 98619-0005 United States
Phone: 509-364-3410   Fax: 509-364-3667
Scope: Regional

UNITED STATES DEPARTMENT OF THE INTERIOR
FISH AND WILDLIFE SERVICE
CRAB ORCHARD NATIONAL WILDLIFE REFUGE
8588 Rt. 148
Marion, IL 62959 United States
Phone: 618-997-3344   Fax: 618-997-8961
Scope: Regional

UNITED STATES DEPARTMENT OF THE INTERIOR
FISH AND WILDLIFE SERVICE
CRESCENT LAKE NATIONAL WILDLIFE REFUGE
10630 Road 181
Elsworth, NE 69340 United States
Phone: 308-762-4893   Fax: 308-762-7606
E-mail: steve_whitson@fws.gov
Scope: Regional

UNITED STATES DEPARTMENT OF THE INTERIOR
FISH AND WILDLIFE SERVICE
CRESCENT LAKE/NORTH PLATTE COMPLEX NATIONAL WILDLIFE REFUGE
115 Railway Street
Scottsbluff, NE 69361-3190 United States
Phone: 308-635-7851   Fax: 308-635-7841
Scope: Regional

UNITED STATES DEPARTMENT OF THE INTERIOR
FISH AND WILDLIFE SERVICE
CROCODILE LAKE NATIONAL WILDLIFE REFUGE
P.O. Box 370
Key Largo, FL 33037 United States
Phone: 305-451-4223   Fax: 305-451-1508
Website: http://southeast.fws.gov/CrocodileLake/index.html
Scope: National

UNITED STATES DEPARTMENT OF THE INTERIOR
FISH AND WILDLIFE SERVICE
CROSBY WMD/LAKE ZAHL NATIONAL WILDLIFE REFUGE
P.O. Box 148
Crosby, ND 58730-0148 United States
Phone: 701-965-6488   Fax: 701-965-6487
Scope: Regional

UNITED STATES DEPARTMENT OF THE INTERIOR
FISH AND WILDLIFE SERVICE
CROSS CREEKS NATIONAL WILDLIFE REFUGE
643 Wildlife Rd.
Dover, TN 37058 United States
Phone: 931-232-7477   Fax: 931-232-5958
Scope: Regional
Description: Cross Creeks is 8862 acres located in the riverbottom lands on both sides of the Cumberland River. The land is primarily managed for migratory birds.

UNITED STATES DEPARTMENT OF THE INTERIOR
FISH AND WILDLIFE SERVICE
CULEBRA NATIONAL WILDLIFE REFUGE
P.O. Box 190
Culebra, PR 00622 United States
Phone: 787-742-0115
E-mail: caribbeanisland@fws.gov
Website: http://southeast.fws.gov/Culebra/index.html
Scope: Regional

UNITED STATES DEPARTMENT OF THE INTERIOR
FISH AND WILDLIFE SERVICE
CYPRESS CREEK NATIONAL WILDLIFE REFUGE
137 Rustic Campus Dr
Ullin, IL 62992 United States
Phone: 618-634-2231   Fax: 618-634-9656
Website: http://midwest.fws.gov/cypresscreek
Scope: Regional
Description: Cypress Creek National Wildlife Refuge is nestled between the Ohio and Mississippi Rivers, a biologically unique area within the Cache River basin. This area has been designated a "Wetlands of International Importance" because of its importance to migratory birds. The refuge will eventually encompass 35,000 acres of the Cache River Wetlands. Refuge emphasizes acquiring land, restoring habitat and providing opportunities for the public to experience and learn about the Cache River Wetlands.

UNITED STATES DEPARTMENT OF THE INTERIOR
FISH AND WILDLIFE SERVICE
DE SOTO (BOYER CHUTE NATIONAL WILDLIFE REFUGE)
1434 316th Ln.
Missouri Valley, IA 51555 United States
Phone: 712-642-4121   Fax: 712-642-2877
Scope: Regional
Contact(s):
Larry Klimek, Manager; larry.klimek@fws.gov

UNITED STATES DEPARTMENT OF THE INTERIOR
FISH AND WILDLIFE SERVICE
DEEP FORK NATIONAL WILDLIFE REFUGE
P.O. Box 816
Okmulgee, OK 74447 United States
Phone: 918-756-0815   Fax: 918-756-0275
Scope: Regional
Contact(s):
Mike Oldham, Refuge Manager; 918-756-0815; Mike_Oldham@fws.gov

UNITED STATES DEPARTMENT OF THE INTERIOR
FISH AND WILDLIFE SERVICE
DEER FLAT NATIONAL WILDLIFE REFUGE
13751 Upper Embankment Rd.
Nampa, ID 83686 United States
Phone: 208-467-9278 Fax: 208-467-1019

Scope: Regional

Description: Deer Flat National Wildlife Refuge is located outside of Nampa, ID. The refuge is a prime nesting area and wintering spot for Canada Geese and migratory waterfowl of various species. Bird watching, nature trails and educational presentations are available on the refuge and at the visitor center.

UNITED STATES DEPARTMENT OF THE INTERIOR
FISH AND WILDLIFE SERVICE
DELAWARE BAY ESTUARY PROJECT
2610 Whitehall Neck Rd.
Smyrna, DE 19977 United States
Phone: 302-653-9152 Fax: 302-653-9421

Founded: 1990

Scope: National

Description: The Delaware Estuary Project was established to coordinate, complement, and support existing U.S. Fish and Wildlife Service programs, focusing on important natural resource issues in the Delaware River watershed. The office provides technical assistance to the EPA's National Estuary Program for the Delaware Bay and Delaware's Inland Bays Estuary programs (started in 1988).

UNITED STATES DEPARTMENT OF THE INTERIOR
FISH AND WILDLIFE SERVICE
DES LACS NATIONAL WILDLIFE REFUGE
P.O. Box 578
Kenmare, ND 58746-0578 United States
Phone: 701-385-4046 Fax: 701-385-3214

Scope: Regional

UNITED STATES DEPARTMENT OF THE INTERIOR
FISH AND WILDLIFE SERVICE
DETROIT LAKES WMD
26624 N. Tower Rd.
Detroit Lakes, MN 56501-7959 United States
Phone: 218-847-4431 Fax: 218-847-4156

Scope: Local, State, Regional, National

Description: Detroit Lakes Wetland Management District is one of more than 540 units of the National Wildlife Refuge System. The purpose of the WMD is to acquire and restore habitat primarily for the purpose of waterfowl production. Major management activities of the District include wetland restoration, and prairie restoration and maintenance. Prescribed fire and invasive species management are important actions in accomplishing the District mission.

UNITED STATES DEPARTMENT OF THE INTERIOR
FISH AND WILDLIFE SERVICE
DEVILS LAKE WMD NATIONAL WILDLIFE REFUGE
P.O. Box 908
Devil's Lake, ND 58301 United States
Phone: 701-662-8611 Fax: 701-662-8612

Scope: Regional

UNITED STATES DEPARTMENT OF THE INTERIOR
FISH AND WILDLIFE SERVICE
EASTERN MASSACHUSETTS NATIONAL WILDLIFE REFUGE COMPLEX
GREAT MEADOWS NATIONAL WILDLIFE REFUGE
73 Weir Hill Rd.
Sudbury, MA 01776 United States
Phone: 508-443-4661 Fax: 508-443-2898
Website: http://greatmeadows.fws.gov

Founded: 1944

Scope: Local, State, Regional, National

Description: Just twenty miles west of Boston lies an oasis for wildlife-Great Meadows NWR. Roughly 85 percent of the refuge's more than 3,600 acres is composed of valuable freshwater wetlands stretching along 12 miles of the Concord and Sudbury Rivers. The refuge also houses an environmental education center, visitor center, and auditorium which are available for groups upon request.

Keyword(s): Agriculture/Farming, Ecosystems (precious), Ethics/Environmental Justice, Land Issues, Public Lands/Greenspace, Recreation/Ecotourism, Water Habitats & Quality, Wildlife & Species

UNITED STATES DEPARTMENT OF THE INTERIOR
FISH AND WILDLIFE SERVICE
EASTERN NECK NATIONAL WILDLIFE REFUGE
1730 Eastern Neck Rd.
Rock Hall, MD 21661 United States
Phone: 410-639-7056 Fax: 410-639-2516

Scope: Regional

UNITED STATES DEPARTMENT OF THE INTERIOR
FISH AND WILDLIFE SERVICE
EASTERN SHORE OF VA/FISHERMAN ISLAND NATIONAL WILDLIFE REFUGE
5003 Hallett Circle
Cape Charles, VA 23310 United States
Phone: 757-331-2760 Fax: 757-331-3424

Scope: Regional

UNITED STATES DEPARTMENT OF THE INTERIOR
FISH AND WILDLIFE SERVICE
EDWIN B. FORSYTHE NATIONAL WILDLIFE REFUGE
P.O. Box 72, Great Creek Rd.
Oceanville, NJ 08231-0072 United States
Phone: 609-652-1665 Fax: 609-652-1474
E-mail: forsythe@fws.gov
Website: http://forsythe.fws.gov/

Founded: 1939

Scope: National, Regional

Description: The Edwin B. Forsythe National Wildlife Refuge is one of over 540 units in the National Wildlife Refuge System. It encompasses about 46,000 acres along the coast of New Jersey and is an important link in the Atlantic Flyway. The refuge is a Wetland of International Importance, a unit of the Western Hemisphere Shorebird Reserve Network, and an internationally recognized birding venue. About 6,000 acres of the refuge are within the National Wilderness Preservation System.

Keyword(s): Recreation/Ecotourism, Wildlife & Species

UNITED STATES DEPARTMENT OF THE INTERIOR
FISH AND WILDLIFE SERVICE
ERIE NATIONAL WILDLIFE REFUGE
11296 Wood Duck Ln.
Guys Mills, PA 16327 United States
Phone: 814-789-3585   Fax: 814-789-2909
E-mail: fw5rw_ernwr@fws.gov
Website: http://erie.fws.gov/
Scope: Regional

UNITED STATES DEPARTMENT OF THE INTERIOR
FISH AND WILDLIFE SERVICE
EUFAULA NATIONAL WILDLIFE REFUGE
509 Old Highway 165
Eufaula, AL 36027 United States
Phone: 334-687-4065   Fax: 334-687-5906
Scope: Regional

UNITED STATES DEPARTMENT OF THE INTERIOR
FISH AND WILDLIFE SERVICE
FELSENTHAL NATIONAL WILDLIFE REFUGE
P.O. Box 1157
Crossett, AR 71635 United States
Phone: 870-364-3167   Fax: 870-364-3757
Website: www.fws.gov
Scope: Regional

UNITED STATES DEPARTMENT OF THE INTERIOR
FISH AND WILDLIFE SERVICE
FERGUS FALLS WMD NATIONAL WILDLIFE REFUGE
21932 State Highway 210 E
Fergus Falls, MN 56537 United States
Phone: 218-739-2291   Fax: 218-739-9534
Scope: National

UNITED STATES DEPARTMENT OF THE INTERIOR
FISH AND WILDLIFE SERVICE
FISH SPRINGS NATIONAL WILDLIFE REFUGE
P.O. Box 568
Dugway, UT 84022 United States
Phone: 435-831-5353   Fax: 435-831-5354
Website: http://fishsprings.fws.gov
Scope: Local, State, Regional

UNITED STATES DEPARTMENT OF THE INTERIOR
FISH AND WILDLIFE SERVICE
FLINT HILLS (MARAIS DES CYGNES) NATIONAL WILDLIFE REFUGE
P.O. Box 128, 530 W. Maple
Hartford, KS 66854 United States
Phone: 620-392-5553
E-mail: http://FlintHills@fws.gov
Scope: Regional

UNITED STATES DEPARTMENT OF THE INTERIOR
FISH AND WILDLIFE SERVICE
FLORIDA PANTHER/TEN THOUSAND ISLAND NATIONAL WILDLIFE REFUGE
3860 Tollgate Blvd., Ste. 300
Naples, FL 34114 United States
Phone: 239-353-8442   Fax: 239-353-8640
E-mail: floridapanther@fws.gov
Website: http://floridapanther.fws.gov
Scope: Regional

UNITED STATES DEPARTMENT OF THE INTERIOR
FISH AND WILDLIFE SERVICE
FORT NIOBRARA/VALENTINE NATIONAL WILDLIFE REFUGE
HC 14, Box 67
Valentine, NE 69201 United States
Phone: 402-376-3789   Fax: 402-376-3217
Scope: Regional
Description: National Wildlife Refuge Complex in north-central Nebraska.

UNITED STATES DEPARTMENT OF THE INTERIOR
FISH AND WILDLIFE SERVICE
GRAYS LAKE NATIONAL WILDLIFE REFUGE
74 Grays Lake Rd.
Wayan, ID 83285 United States
Phone: 208-574-2755   Fax: 208-574-2756
Scope: Regional

UNITED STATES DEPARTMENT OF THE INTERIOR
FISH AND WILDLIFE SERVICE
GREAT DISMAL SWAMP/NANSEMOND NATIONAL WILDLIFE REFUGE
P.O. Box 349
Suffolk, VA 23434 United States
Phone: 757-986-3705   Fax: 757-986-2353
Website: http://greatdismalswamp.fws.gov
Founded: 1974
Scope: Local, State, Regional, National
Description: The refuge incorporates over 111,000 acres in Virginia and North Carolina for the primary purpose of restoring and protecting a unique ecosystem. Restoration and management of the rare Atlantic white cedar forests and pine/pocosin habitat are emphasized. Refuge is known for neotropical migratory birds, wintering snow geese and tundra swans, and large black bear population.
Keyword(s): Ecosystems (precious), Forests/Forestry, Land Issues, Recreation/Ecotourism, Wildlife & Species

UNITED STATES DEPARTMENT OF THE INTERIOR
FISH AND WILDLIFE SERVICE
GREAT RIVER NATIONAL WILDIFE REFUGE
CLARENCE CANNON NATIONAL WILDLIFE REFUGE
P.O. Box 88
Annada, MO 63330 United States
Phone: 573-847-2333   Fax: 573-847-2269
Scope: Regional
Description: These refuges are scattered along 100 miles of the Mississippi River. Managed wetlands, forests and fields provide habitat for over 230 species of birds.

UNITED STATES DEPARTMENT OF THE INTERIOR
FISH AND WILDLIFE SERVICE
GREAT SWAMP NATIONAL WILDLIFE REFUGE
152 Pleasant Plains Rd.
Basking Ridge, NJ 07920 United States
Phone: 973-425-1222   Fax: 973-425-7309
E-mail: FW5RW_GSNWR@fws.gov
Website: http://northeast.fws.gov/nj/grs.htm
Scope: Local, State, Regional, National
Description: National Wildlife Refuge

U.S. FEDERAL AND INTERNATIONAL GOVERNMENT AGENCIES – U

UNITED STATES DEPARTMENT OF THE INTERIOR
FISH & WILDLIFE SERVICE
GUADALUPE-NIPOMO DUNES NATIONAL WILDLIFE REFUGE
P.O. Box 9
Guadalupe, CA 93434 United States
Phone: 805-343-9151   Fax: 805-343-9141
E-mail: guadalupe-nipomo@fws.gov
Website: http://hoppermountain.fws.gov/Guadalupe/index.html

Founded: 2000
Scope: National
Description: Guadalupe-Nipomo Dunes National Wildlife Refuge was established in August 2000, to protect breeding habitat for the endangered California least tern, California red-legged frog, and threatened Western snowy plover. Migratory birds traveling along the Pacific Flyway stop over at the Refuge including the endangered California brown pelican. The Refuge provides protected habitat for more than 16 species of rare or endangered, or sparsely distributed plants.
Keyword(s): Ecosystems (precious), Oceans/Coasts/Beaches, Recreation/Ecotourism, Wildlife & Species

UNITED STATES DEPARTMENT OF THE INTERIOR
FISH AND WILDLIFE SERVICE
GUAM NATIONAL WILDLIFE REFUGE
P.O. Box 8134, MOU-3
Dededo, GU 96912 United States
Phone: 671-355-5096   Fax: 671-355-5098
E-mail: art_webster@fws.gov
Website: http://pacificislands.fws.gov/wnwr/guamnwrindex.html
Scope: Regional

UNITED STATES DEPARTMENT OF THE INTERIOR
FISH AND WILDLIFE SERVICE
HAGERMAN NATIONAL WILDLIFE REFUGE
6465 Refuge Rd.
Sherman, TX 75092 United States
Phone: 903-786-2826   Fax: 903-786-3327
Scope: Regional

UNITED STATES DEPARTMENT OF THE INTERIOR
FISH AND WILDLIFE SERVICE
HAKALAU FOREST NATIONAL WILDLIFE REFUGE
32 Kinoole St., Suite 101
Hilo, HI 96720 United States
Phone: 808-933-6915   Fax: 808-933-6917
Scope: Regional

UNITED STATES DEPARTMENT OF THE INTERIOR
FISH AND WILDLIFE SERVICE
HANFORD COMPLEX/SADDLE MOUNTAIN NATIONAL WILDLIFE REFUGE
3520 Port of Benton Blvd.
Richland, WA 99352 United States
Phone: 509-371-1801   Fax: 509-371-0196
Scope: National

UNITED STATES DEPARTMENT OF THE INTERIOR
FISH AND WILDLIFE SERVICE
HART MOUNTAIN NATIONAL ANTELOPE REFUGE NATIONAL WILDLIFE REFUGE
P.O. Box 111
Lakeview, OR 97630 United States
Phone: 541-947-3315   Fax: 541-947-4414
Scope: Regional

UNITED STATES DEPARTMENT OF THE INTERIOR
FISH AND WILDLIFE SERVICE
HATCHIE NATIONAL WILDLIFE REFUGE
P.O. Box 1031
Brownsville, TN 38012 United States
Phone: 731-772-0501, ext. 25   Fax: 731-772-7839
Website: http://hatchie.fws.gov

Founded: 1964
Membership: 1–100
Scope: Regional
Description: Acres: 11,556. Location: 1 mile S of Brownsville, TN on the S bank of 23.5 miles of the state-designated Hatchie Scenic River; 50 miles E of Memphis and 130 miles W of Nashville, TN. Calendar of Events—March: refuge birthday. April: disabled fishing tourney, spring turkey hunting. June: Jr. / Sr. Fishing Rodeo. September-October: archery/gun deer hunting, Wildlife Refuge Week Celebration. September-February: small game hunting. September and December-January: waterfowl hunting.

Contact(s):
Marvin Nichols; 731-772-0501, ext. 25; Fax: 731-772-7839; Marvin_Nichols@fws.gov

UNITED STATES DEPARTMENT OF THE INTERIOR
FISH AND WILDLIFE SERVICE
HAWAIIAN AND PACIFIC ISLANDS NATIONAL WILDLIFE REFUGE COMPLEX
P.O. Box 50167
Honolulu, HI 96850 United States
Phone: 808-541-1201   Fax: 808-541-1216
Scope: Regional

UNITED STATES DEPARTMENT OF THE INTERIOR
FISH AND WILDLIFE SERVICE
HILLSIDE NATIONAL WILDLIFE REFUGE
1562 Providence Rd.
Cruger, MS 35924 United States
Phone: 662-235-4989   Fax: 662-235-5303
Scope: Regional

UNITED STATES DEPARTMENT OF THE INTERIOR
FISH AND WILDLIFE SERVICE
HOBE SOUND NATIONAL WILDLIFE REFUGE
P.O. Box 645
Hobe Sound, FL 33475-0645 United States
Phone: 772-546-6141   Fax: 772-545-7572
E-mail: margo_stahl@fws.gov

Founded: 1969
Membership: 10,001–100,000
Scope: Regional
Description: Hobe Sound NWR is a coastal refuge consisting of two separate tracts of land located in Martin County, Florida. Over 1000 acres of coastal sand dune, mangrove swamps and sand pine-oak scrub forest can be explored. The refuge was established through the generosity of conservation minded Jupiter Island residents. As a result a unique remnant of South Florida's ecology is being preserved from the encroachment of civilization that is rapidly expanding northward along the South Florida coast.

Publication(s): Mangrove News

Keyword(s): Ecosystems (precious), Forests/Forestry, Oceans/ Coasts/Beaches, Recreation/Ecotourism, Water Habitats & Quality, Wildlife & Species

Contact(s):
Hobe Sound Nature Center, Educator; 772-546-2067; hsnature@aol.com

UNITED STATES DEPARTMENT OF THE INTERIOR
FISH AND WILDLIFE SERVICE
HOLLA BEND/LOGAN CAVE NATIONAL WILDLIFE REFUGE
Rt. 1, Box 59
Dardanelle, AR 72834-9704 United States
Phone: 479-229-4300   Fax: 479-229-4302
E-mail: holla_bend@fws.gov
Website: www.fws.gov
Founded: 1957
Scope: Local, State

UNITED STATES DEPARTMENT OF THE INTERIOR
FISH AND WILDLIFE SERVICE
HOPPER MOUNTAIN COMPLEX NATIONAL WILDLIFE REFUGE
P.O. Box 5839
Ventura, CA 93005 United States
Phone: 805-644-5158   Fax: 805-644-1732
Scope: Regional

UNITED STATES DEPARTMENT OF THE INTERIOR
FISH AND WILDLIFE SERVICE
HORICON COMPLEX NATIONAL WILDLIFE REFUGE
W 4279 Headquarters Rd.
Mayville, WI 53050 United States
Phone: 920-387-2658   Fax: 920-387-2973
E-mail: patti_meyers@fws.gov
Scope: Regional

UNITED STATES DEPARTMENT OF THE INTERIOR
FISH AND WILDLIFE SERVICE
HUMBOLDT BAY NATIONAL WILDLIFE REFUGE
1020 Ranch Rd.
Loleta, CA 95551 United States
Phone: 707-733-5406   Fax: 707-733-1946
Scope: Regional

UNITED STATES DEPARTMENT OF THE INTERIOR
FISH AND WILDLIFE SERVICE
HURON WMD NATIONAL WILDLIFE REFUGE
200 4th St., SW, Rm. 309 Federal Bldg.
Huron, SD 57350-2470 United States
Phone: 605-352-5894   Fax: 605-352-6709
Founded: 1992
Membership: 1–100
Scope: Regional
Keyword(s): Public Lands/Greenspace, Wildlife & Species
Contact(s):
Harris Hoistad, Project Leader; 605-352-5894; ext. 11; harris_hoistad@fws.gov

UNITED STATES DEPARTMENT OF THE INTERIOR
FISH AND WILDLIFE SERVICE
ILLINOIS RIVER NATIONAL WILDLIFE AND FISH REFUGE (CHAUTAUQUA, EMIQUON, MEREDOSIA)
19031 E. County Rd. 2110 N
Havana, IL 62644 United States
Phone: 309-535-2290   Fax: 309-535-3023
E-mail: ross_adams@fws.gov
Website: http://midwest.fws.gov/illinoisriver
Founded: 1936
Scope: Regional
Description: The Illinois River National Wildlife and Fish Refuge contains 12,000 acres of foodplain habitat managed for migratory birds and other wildlife. Refuge staff are committed to working with partners in an effort to restore the Illinois River watershed to sustain migratory bird populations, threatened and endangered species, other native fish and wildlife species for the benefit of Americans.

UNITED STATES DEPARTMENT OF THE INTERIOR
FISH AND WILDLIFE SERVICE
IMPERIAL NATIONAL WILDLIFE REFUGE
P.O. Box 72217
Yuma, AZ 85365 United States
Phone: 928-783-3371   Fax: 928-783-0652
Website: www.fws.gov
Scope: Regional

UNITED STATES DEPARTMENT OF THE INTERIOR
FISH AND WILDLIFE SERVICE
INNOKO NATIONAL WILDLIFE REFUGE
P.O. Box 69
McGrath, AK 99627 United States
Phone: 907-524-3251   Fax: 907-524-3141
E-mail: billschaff/r7/fws/doi@fws.org
Scope: Regional

UNITED STATES DEPARTMENT OF THE INTERIOR
FISH AND WILDLIFE SERVICE
IROQUOIS NATIONAL WILDLIFE REFUGE
1101 Casey Rd.
Basom, NY 14013 United States
Phone: 585-948-5445   Fax: 585-948-9538
Scope: Regional

UNITED STATES DEPARTMENT OF THE INTERIOR
FISH AND WILDLIFE SERVICE
IZEMBEK NATIONAL WILDLIFE REFUGE
P.O. Box 127, #1 Izembek Dr.
Cold Bay, AK 99571 United States
Phone: 907-532-2445   Fax: 907-532-2549
Scope: Regional

UNITED STATES DEPARTMENT OF THE INTERIOR
FISH AND WILDLIFE SERVICE
J. CLARK SALYER NATIONAL WILDLIFE REFUGE
681 Salyer Road
Upham, ND 58789 United States
Phone: 701-768-2548   Fax: 701-768-2834
E-mail: jclarksalyer@fws.gov
Scope: Regional

Contact(s):
Robert Howard, Refuge Manager; 701-768-2548; rgrw_jcs@fws.gov

UNITED STATES DEPARTMENT OF THE INTERIOR
FISH AND WILDLIFE SERVICE
J.N. "DING" DARLING NATIONAL WILDLIFE REFUGE
One Wildlife Dr.
Sanibel, FL 33957 United States
Phone: 941-472-1100 Fax: 941-472-4061
E-mail: dingdarling@fws.gov
Website: http://dingdarling.fws.gov/
Scope: Regional

UNITED STATES DEPARTMENT OF THE INTERIOR
FISH AND WILDLIFE SERVICE
JOHN HEINZ NATIONAL WILDLIFE REFUGE AT TINICUM
8601 Lindbergh Blvd.
Philadelphia, PA 19153 United States
Phone: 215-365-3118 Fax: 215-365-2846
E-mail: FW5RW_JHTNWR@FWS.GOV
Website: http://heinz.fws.gov/
Scope: Regional
Description: This 1,200 acre National Wildlife Refuge is managed by the U.S. Fish & Wildlife Service to include the largest freshwater tidal marsh in Pennsylvania, miles of nature trails, the Cusano National Environmental Education Center, canoe launch, fishing pier, photo blinds and wildlife habitat for more than 300 species of birds, as well as many mammals, reptiles, amphibians, fish, butterflies and plants. Public nature programs are offered every weekend as well as special events throughout the year.
Contact(s):
Gary Stolz, Refuge Manager; 215-365-3118; Fax: 215-365-2846; gary_stolz@fws.gov

UNITED STATES DEPARTMENT OF THE INTERIOR
FISH AND WILDLIFE SERVICE
JOHNSTON ISLAND NATIONAL WILDLIFE REFUGE
Box 396
APO, AP, HI 96558-0396 United States
Phone: 808-421-0011 Fax: 808-422-6905
Scope: Regional

UNITED STATES DEPARTMENT OF THE INTERIOR
FISH AND WILDLIFE SERVICE
JULIA BUTLER HANSEN REFUGE FOR THE COLUMBIA WHITE-TAILED DEER NATIONAL WILDLIFE REFUGE
P.O. Box 566
Cathlamet, WA 98612-0566 United States
Phone: 509-795-3915 Fax: 360-795-0803
Website: http://pacific.fws.gov/refuges/field/WA_julia.htm
Scope: Regional

UNITED STATES DEPARTMENT OF THE INTERIOR
FISH AND WILDLIFE SERVICE
KANUTI NATIONAL WILDLIFE REFUGE
101 12th Ave., Box 11; Rm. 262
Fairbanks, AK 99701 United States
Phone: 907-456-0329 Fax: 907-456-0506
Scope: Regional

UNITED STATES DEPARTMENT OF THE INTERIOR
FISH AND WILDLIFE SERVICE
KEALIA POND NATIONAL WILDLIFE REFUGE
P.O. Box 1042
Kihei, HI 96753-1042 United States
Phone: 808-875-1582 Fax: 808-875-2945
Scope: Regional

UNITED STATES DEPARTMENT OF THE INTERIOR
FISH AND WILDLIFE SERVICE
KENAI NATIONAL WILDLIFE REFUGE
P.O. Box 2139
Soldotna, AK 99669-2139 United States
Phone: 907-262-7021 Fax: 907-262-3599
Scope: Regional

UNITED STATES DEPARTMENT OF THE INTERIOR
FISH AND WILDLIFE SERVICE
KERN/PIXLEY NATIONAL WILDLIFE REFUGE
P.O. Box 670
Delano, CA 93216-0670 United States
Phone: 661-725-2767 Fax: 661-725-6041
Website: www.natureali.com/KNWR.htm
Founded: 1961
Scope: Local, State, Regional, National
Description: Kern National Wildlife Refuge is located between Lost Hills and Delano in northern Kern County, California. Open year round, dawn to dusk.
Keyword(s): Ecosystems (precious), Recreation/Ecotourism, Wildlife & Species
Contact(s):
David Hardt, Refuge Manager; 661-725-2767; dave_hardt@r1.fws.gov

UNITED STATES DEPARTMENT OF THE INTERIOR
FISH AND WILDLIFE SERVICE
KETERSON NATIONAL WILDLIFE REFUGE
P.O. Box 2176
Los Banos, CA 93635-2176 United States
Phone: 209-826-3508 Fax: 209-826-1445
Scope: Regional

UNITED STATES DEPARTMENT OF THE INTERIOR
FISH AND WILDLIFE SERVICE
KILAUEA POINT (HANALEI, HULEIA) NATIONAL WILDLIFE REFUGE
P.O. Box 1128
Kilauea, Kauai, HI 96754-1128 United States
Phone: 808-828-1413 Fax: 808-828-6634
Scope: Regional

UNITED STATES DEPARTMENT OF THE INTERIOR
FISH AND WILDLIFE SERVICE
KIRWIN NATIONAL WILDLIFE REFUGE
702 E. Xavier Road
Kirwin, KS 67644 United States
Phone: 785-543-6673 Fax: 785-543-5464
Founded: 1954
Scope: Regional

UNITED STATES DEPARTMENT OF THE INTERIOR
FISH AND WILDLIFE SERVICE
KLAMATH BASIN COMPLEX NATIONAL WILDLIFE REFUGE
4009 Hill Road
Tule Lake, CA 96134-9750 United States
Phone: 530-667-2231　　　　Fax: 530-667-3299
Scope: Regional

UNITED STATES DEPARTMENT OF THE INTERIOR
FISH AND WILDLIFE SERVICE
KODIAK NATIONAL WILDLIFE REFUGE
1390 Buskin River Rd.
Kodiak, AK 99615 United States
Phone: 907-487-2600　　　　Fax: 907-487-2144
Scope: Regional

UNITED STATES DEPARTMENT OF THE INTERIOR
FISH AND WILDLIFE SERVICE
KOFA NATIONAL WILDLIFE REFUGE
356 W. 1st St.
Yuma, AZ 85364 United States
Phone: 928-783-7861　　　　Fax: 928-783-8611
E-mail: FW2_RW_kofa@fws.gov
Website: http://southwest.fws.gov/refuges/arizona/kofa.html
Founded: 1939
Membership: 1–100
Scope: Local, State, Regional, National
Description: Kofa NWR contains 665,400-acres of pristine Sonoran Desert. Its primary objective is to preserve habitat for desert bighorn sheep. Approximately 80% of the refuge is designated wilderness.
Keyword(s): Ecosystems (precious), Public Lands/Greenspace, Recreation/Ecotourism, Reduce/Reuse/Recycle, Water Habitats & Quality, Wildlife & Species
Contact(s):
   Susanna Henry, Asst. Manager; 928-783-7861; ext. 15; Fax: 928-783-8611
   Ron Kearns, Biologist; 928-783-7861; ext. 11; Fax: 928-783-8611
   Brian Krukoski, Park Ranger; 928-783-7861; ext. 18; Fax: 928-783-8611
   Michelle Willcox, Admin. Tech.; 928-783-7861; ext. 10; Fax: 928-783-8611

UNITED STATES DEPARTMENT OF THE INTERIOR
FISH AND WILDLIFE SERVICE
KOOTENAI NATIONAL WILDLIFE REFUGE
HCR 60, Box 283
Bonners Ferry, ID 83805 United States
Phone: 208-267-3888　　　　Fax: 208-267-5570
Scope: Regional

UNITED STATES DEPARTMENT OF THE INTERIOR
FISH AND WILDLIFE SERVICE
KULM WMD NATIONAL WILDLIFE REFUGE
P.O. Box E
Kulm, ND 58456-0170 United States
Phone: 701-647-2866　　　　Fax: 701-647-2221
Membership: 1–100
Scope: Regional

UNITED STATES DEPARTMENT OF THE INTERIOR
FISH AND WILDLIFE SERVICE
LACASSINE NATIONAL WILDLIFE REFUGE
209 Nature Road
Lake Arthur, LA 70549 United States
Phone: 337-774-5923　　　　Fax: 337-774-9913
E-mail: FW4RWLacassine@fws.gov
Website: http://lacassine.fws.gov
Founded: 1937
Scope: Local, State, Regional, National
Description: Lacassine National Wildlife Refuge is 35,000 acres of freshwater marsh that preserves one of the major wintering grounds for waterfowl in the U.S. and is critically important for pintail. Several nesting colonies of wading birds, a large population of alligators, and furbearers such as otter, nutria and raccoon as well as other marsh species may be seen. Hunting, fishing and bird watching are the most popular refuge activities and a nature drive and observation towers are open year-round.
Keyword(s): Agriculture/Farming, Ecosystems (precious), Land Issues, Public Lands/Greenspace, Recreation/Ecotourism, Reduce/Reuse/Recycle, Water Habitats & Quality, Wildlife & Species
Contact(s):
   Vicki Grafe, Project Leader; 337-774-5923; Fax: 337-774-9913; vicki_grafe@fws.gov

UNITED STATES DEPARTMENT OF THE INTERIOR
FISH AND WILDLIFE SERVICE
LACREEK/BEAR BUTTE NATIONAL WILDLIFE REFUGE
HC 5, Box 114
Martin, SD 57551 United States
Phone: 605-685-6508　　　　Fax: 605-685-1173
E-mail: lacreek@fws.gov
Website: http://lacreek.fws.gov
Scope: Regional

UNITED STATES DEPARTMENT OF THE INTERIOR
FISH AND WILDLIFE SERVICE
LAGUNA ATASCOSA NATIONAL WILDLIFE REFUGE
P.O. Box 450
Rio Hondo, TX 78583 United States
Phone: 956-748-3607　　　　Fax: 956-748-3609
Scope: Regional

UNITED STATES DEPARTMENT OF THE INTERIOR
FISH AND WILDLIFE SERVICE
LAKE ANDES/KARL E. MUNDT NATIONAL WILDLIFE REFUGE
38672 291st St.
Lake Andes, SD 57356 United States
Phone: 605-487-7603　　　　Fax: 605-487-7604
Scope: Regional
Keyword(s): Ecosystems (precious), Land Issues, Public Lands/Greenspace, Wildlife & Species
Contact(s):
   Gene Williams, Project Leader; 605-487-7603; Gene_Williams@fws.gov

UNITED STATES DEPARTMENT OF THE INTERIOR
FISH AND WILDLIFE SERVICE
LAKE UMBAGOG NATIONAL WILDLIFE REFUGE
Box 240
Errol, NH 03579 United States
Phone: 603-482-3415　　　　Fax: 603-482-3308
Scope: Regional

UNITED STATES DEPARTMENT OF THE INTERIOR
FISH AND WILDLIFE SERVICE
LAKE WOODRUFF NATIONAL WILDLIFE REFUGE
P.O. Box 488
DeLeon Springs, FL 32130-0488 United States
Phone: 386-985-4673　　　Fax: 386-985-0926
Website: http://lakewoodruff.fws.gov

Founded: 1964

Scope: Local, State, Regional, National

Description: Lake Woodruff National Wildlife Refuge, located in Central Florida, is situated along the St. John's River, and provides nesting, overwintering and stopover habitat during migration for neotropical songbirds, migratory waterfowl, shorebirds, wading birds and raptors.

UNITED STATES DEPARTMENT OF THE INTERIOR
FISH AND WILDLIFE SERVICE
LAS VEGAS NATIONAL WILDLIFE REFUGE
Rt. 1 Box 399
Las Vegas, NM 87701 United States
Phone: 505-425-3581　　　Fax: 505-454-8510
E-mail: fw2_rw_lasvegas@fws.gov
Website: southwest.fws.gov/refuges/nowmex/lasvegas/index.html

Scope: Regional

UNITED STATES DEPARTMENT OF THE INTERIOR
FISH AND WILDLIFE SERVICE
LEE METCALF NATIONAL WILDLIFE REFUGE
P.O. Box 247
Stevensville, MT 59870 United States
Phone: 406-777-5552　　　Fax: 406-777-4344

Scope: National

UNITED STATES DEPARTMENT OF THE INTERIOR
FISH AND WILDLIFE SERVICE
LEOPOLD NATIONAL WILDLIFE REFUGE
Phone: 920-387-0336　　　Fax: 920-387-2973

Scope: National

UNITED STATES DEPARTMENT OF THE INTERIOR
FISH AND WILDLIFE SERVICE
LITCHFIELD WMD
22274 615th Avenue
Litchfield, MN 55355 United States
Phone: 320-693-2849　　　Fax: 320-693-7207

Founded: 1979

Scope: National

Description: Litchfield Wetland Management District manages Waterfowl Production Areas in seven counties in central Minnesota.

UNITED STATES DEPARTMENT OF THE INTERIOR
FISH AND WILDLIFE SERVICE
LITTLE PEND OREILLE NATIONAL WILDLIFE REFUGE
1310 Bear Creek Rd.
Colville, WA 99114-9713 United States
Phone: 509-684-8384　　　Fax: 509-684-8381

Scope: Regional

UNITED STATES DEPARTMENT OF THE INTERIOR
FISH AND WILDLIFE SERVICE
LITTLE RIVER/LITTLE SANDY NATIONAL WILDLIFE REFUGE
P.O. Box 340
Broken Bow, OK 74728 United States
Phone: 580-584-6211　　　Fax: 580-584-2034

Scope: Regional

UNITED STATES DEPARTMENT OF THE INTERIOR
FISH AND WILDLIFE SERVICE
LONG ISLAND NATIONAL WILDLIFE REFUGE COMPLEX
P.O. Box 21
Shirley, NY 11967 United States
Phone: 631-286-0485　　　Fax: 631-286-4003
Website: http://northeast.fws.gov/ny/lirc.htm

Founded: 1947

Scope: Local, State, Regional, National, International

Description: The Long Island NWR Complex is comprised of nine units, totalling almost 6,500 acres. The purpose for each is to protect & benefit wildlife. These nine units protect many of Long Island's habitat types which are critical to migratory birds, endangered species and other wildlife. Long Island's strategic location along the Atlantic Flyway and within the Long Island Pine Barrens provides important nesting, wintering & migratory stop-over areas for hundreds of bird species.

Keyword(s): Ecosystems (precious), Recreation/Ecotourism, Water Habitats & Quality, Wildlife & Species

Contact(s):
　Mark Maghini, Biologist; 631-286-0485; Fax: 631-286-4003
　Andrea Stewart, Outdoor Recreation Planner; 631-286-0485; Fax: 631-286-4003

UNITED STATES DEPARTMENT OF THE INTERIOR
FISH AND WILDLIFE SERVICE
LONG LAKE NATIONAL WILDLIFE REFUGE
1200 353rd St. SE
Moffit, ND 58560-9740 United States
Phone: 701-387-4397　　　Fax: 701-387-4767

Founded: 1932

Scope: Regional

Description: Long Lake is a 22,310 acre National Wildlife Refuge established in 1932, as a refuge and breeding ground for birds and wild animals.

Keyword(s): Ecosystems (precious), Land Issues, Recreation/Ecotourism, Water Habitats & Quality, Wildlife & Species

Contact(s):
　Paul Van Ningen; 701-387-4397; ext. 14; Paul_vanningen@fws.gov

UNITED STATES DEPARTMENT OF THE INTERIOR
FISH AND WILDLIFE SERVICE
LOUISIANA WMD/HANDY BRAKE NATIONAL WILDLIFE REFUGE
11372 Hwy. 143
Farmerville, LA 71241 United States
Phone: 318-726-4400　　　Fax: 318-726-4667

Scope: Regional

UNITED STATES DEPARTMENT OF THE INTERIOR
FISH AND WILDLIFE SERVICE
LOWER COLORADO RIVER COMPLEX NATIONAL WILDLIFE REFUGE
c/o Bureau of Reclamation
P.O. Box D
Yuma, AZ 85364 United States
Phone: 928-343-8112   Fax: 928-343-8320
Scope: Regional

UNITED STATES DEPARTMENT OF THE INTERIOR
FISH AND WILDLIFE SERVICE
LOWER HATCHIE NATIONAL WILDLIFE REFUGE
1505 Sandy Bluff Rd.
Ripley, TN 38063 United States
Phone: 731-635-7621   Fax: 731-635-0178
Scope: Regional

UNITED STATES DEPARTMENT OF THE INTERIOR
FISH AND WILDLIFE SERVICE
LOWER RIO GRANDE/SANTA ANNA COMPLEX NATIONAL WILDLIFE REFUGE
Rt. 2, Box 202A
Alamo, TX 78516 United States
Phone: 210-787-3079   Fax: 210-787-8338
Website: http://southwest.fws.gov/refuges/texas/lrgv.html
Scope: Regional

UNITED STATES DEPARTMENT OF THE INTERIOR
FISH AND WILDLIFE SERVICE
LOWER SUWANNEE/CEDAR KEYS NATIONAL WILDLIFE REFUGE
16450 NW 31st Pl.
Chiefland, FL 32626 United States
Phone: 352-493-0238   Fax: 352-493-1935
E-mail: lowersuwannee@fws.gov
Website: http://lowersuwannee.fws.gov/
Scope: Regional

UNITED STATES DEPARTMENT OF THE INTERIOR
FISH AND WILDLIFE SERVICE
MACKAY ISLAND/CURRITUCK NATIONAL WILDLIFE REFUGE
P.O. Box 39
Knotts Island, NC 27950 United States
Phone: 252-429-3100   Fax: 252-429-3185
E-mail: fw4rwmackayisland@fws.gov
Website: http://alligatorriver.fws.gov/mackayisland/
Founded: 1960
Scope: Regional
Description: Mackay Island NWR established in 1960 for wintering migratory birds, Currituck NWR established in 1983 for wintering migratory birds and to preserve the fragile barrier island habitat.

UNITED STATES DEPARTMENT OF THE INTERIOR
FISH AND WILDLIFE SERVICE
MADISON WMD NATIONAL WILDLIFE REFUGE
P.O. Box 48
Madison, SD 57042 United States
Phone: 605-256-2974   Fax: 605-256-9432
E-mail: madisonwetlands@fws.gov
Founded: 1969
Scope: Regional
Description: The Madison Wetland Management District is located in nine counties in east central South Dakota. Situated in the heart of the prairie pothole region with a mission to protect wetlands and native grasslands.

UNITED STATES DEPARTMENT OF THE INTERIOR
FISH AND WILDLIFE SERVICE
MALHEUR NATIONAL WILDLIFE REFUGE
36391 Sodhouse Lane
Princeton, OR 97721-9505 United States
Phone: 541-493-2612   Fax: 541-493-2405
Scope: Regional

UNITED STATES DEPARTMENT OF THE INTERIOR
FISH AND WILDLIFE SERVICE
MARK TWAIN NATIONAL WILDLIFE REFUGE
1704 N. 24th St.
Quincy, IL 62301 United States
Phone: 217-224-8580   Fax: 217-224-8583
E-mail: donna_zanger@fws.gov
Website: http://midwest.fws.gov/marktwain
Scope: Regional

UNITED STATES DEPARTMENT OF THE INTERIOR
FISH AND WILDLIFE SERVICE
MARK TWAIN/BRUSSELS DISTRICT NATIONAL WILDLIFE REFUGE
HCR 82, Box 107
Brussels, IL 62013-9711 United States
Phone: 618-883-2524   Fax: 618-883-2201
Scope: Regional

UNITED STATES DEPARTMENT OF THE INTERIOR
FISH AND WILDLIFE SERVICE
MATTAMUSKEET NATIONAL WILDLIFE REFUGE
38 Mattamuskeet Road
Swan Quarter, NC 27885 United States
Phone: 919-926-4021   Fax: 919-926-1743
Website: http://mattamuskeet.fws.gov/index.html
Founded: 1934
Scope: Regional
Description: 50,180 acre national wildlife refuge in northeastern North Carolina serving as a major wintering and migration area for waterfowl in the Atlantic Flyway. Main feature is the 40,000 acre Lake Mattamuskeet.
Keyword(s): Agriculture/Farming, Air Quality/Atmosphere, Public Lands/Greenspace, Recreation/Ecotourism, Water Habitats & Quality, Wildlife & Species

UNITED STATES DEPARTMENT OF THE INTERIOR
FISH AND WILDLIFE SERVICE
MAXWELL NATIONAL WILDLIFE REFUGE
P.O. Box 276
Maxwell, NM 87728 United States
Phone: 505-375-2331   Fax: 505-375-2332
E-mail: fw2_rw_maxwell@fws.gov
Website: http://southwest.fws.gov/refuges/newmex/maxwell.html
Scope: Regional

UNITED STATES DEPARTMENT OF THE INTERIOR
FISH AND WILDLIFE SERVICE
MEDICINE LAKE NATIONAL WILDLIFE REFUGE COMPLEX
MEDICINE LAKE/LAMESTEER NWR, NE MONTANA WETLAND MANAGEMENT DISTRICT
223 Northshore Rd.
Medicine Lake, MT 59247-9600 United States
Phone: 406-789-2305   Fax: 406-789-2350
E-mail: medicinelake@fws.gov

Founded: 1935
Scope: Local, State, Regional, National, International
Description: The complex includes the 31,660 acre Medicine Lake NWR, the 800 acre Lamesteer easement NWR, and the 3-county NE Montana WMD with 45 Waterfowl Production Areas encompassing 12,000 acres.

UNITED STATES DEPARTMENT OF THE INTERIOR
FISH AND WILDLIFE SERVICE
MERRITT ISLAND NATIONAL WILDLIFE REFUGE
P.O. Box 6504
Titusville, FL 32782 United States
Phone: 321-861-0667   Fax: 321-861-1276
E-mail: merrittisland@fws.gov
Website: http://merrittisland.fws.gov

Founded: 1963
Scope: Regional
Description: Merritt Island National Wildlife Refuge is an overlay of NASA's John F,. Kennedy Space Center. The refuge contains over 500 species of wildlife and 1000 species of plants. It is a key resting stop for many migrating bird species. The Refuge Visitor Center is open form 8:00 to 4:30 pm Monday-Friday and from 9:00 am to 5:00 pm on weekends. The center is closed on Sundays from April-October and on all federal holidays. The refuge is closed to the public four days prior to a shuttle launch.

UNITED STATES DEPARTMENT OF THE INTERIOR
FISH AND WILDLIFE SERVICE
MICHIGAN WMD NATIONAL WILDLIFE REFUGE
2651 Coolidgo Rd. Suite 101
East Lansing, MI 48823 United States
Phone: 517-351-4230

Scope: National

UNITED STATES DEPARTMENT OF THE INTERIOR
FISH AND WILDLIFE SERVICE
MID-COLUMBIA RIVER NATIONAL WILDLIFE REFUGE COMPLEX
P.O. Box 2527
2805 St. Andrews Loop
Pasco, WA 99302 United States
Phone: 509-545-8588   Fax: 509-545-8670

Scope: Regional

UNITED STATES DEPARTMENT OF THE INTERIOR
FISH AND WILDLIFE SERVICE
MIDWAY ATOLL NATIONAL WILDLIFE REFUGE
P.O. Box 29460, Midway Island Station #4
Honolulu, HI 96820-1860 United States
Phone: 808-674-8237, ext. 100
E-mail: tim_bodeen@fws.gov
Website: http://midway.fws.gov/contact.html

Scope: Regional

UNITED STATES DEPARTMENT OF THE INTERIOR
FISH AND WILDLIFE SERVICE
MILLE LACS NATIONAL WILDLIFE REFUGE
36289 State Hwy. 65
McGregor, MN 55760 United States
Phone: 218-768-2402   Fax: 218-768-3040
E-mail: Mary_Stefanski@fws.gov
Website: http://midwest.fws.gov/millelacs/

Founded: 1915
Scope: National
Description: One of over 540 National Wildlife Refuges in the country. Mille Lacs is the smallest refuge in the country at less than 0.5 acre. It is the site of a colony of common terns.
Contact(s):
   Mary Stefanski, Refuge Manager; 218-768-2402; Fax: 218-768-3040; Mary_Stefanski@fws.gov

UNITED STATES DEPARTMENT OF THE INTERIOR
FISH AND WILDLIFE SERVICE
MINGO NATIONAL WILDLIFE REFUGE
24279 State Highway 51
Puxico, MO 63960 United States
Phone: 573-222-3589   Fax: 573-222-6343
Website: www.fws.gov/r3pao/ming_nwr

Founded: 1945
Scope: National
Description: Hardwood Swamp National Wildlife Refuge. Fantastic overlooks and boardwalk.
Keyword(s): Water Habitats & Quality, Wildlife & Species
Contact(s):
   Kathleen Maycroft, Refuge Manager

UNITED STATES DEPARTMENT OF THE INTERIOR
FISH AND WILDLIFE SERVICE
MINIDOKA NATIONAL WILDLIFE REFUGE
961 E. Minidoka Dam
Rupert, ID 83350 United States
Phone: 208-436-3589   Fax: 208-436-1570

Founded: 1909
Scope: Regional

UNITED STATES DEPARTMENT OF THE INTERIOR
FISH AND WILDLIFE SERVICE
MINNESOTA VALLEY NATIONAL WILDLIFE REFUGE
3815 E. 80th St.
Bloomington, MN 55425-1600 United States
Phone: 952-854-5900   Fax: 612-725-3279
Website: http://midwest.fws.gov/minnesotavalley.com

Founded: 1976
Scope: National
Description: Minnesota Valley National Wildlife Refuge is part of the National Wildlife Refuge System located in the urban areas of Minneapolis and St. Paul. The Refuge comprises 14,000 acres along a 34-mile portion of the Minnesota River. The Refuge provides high quality production and migration habitat for bald eagles, waterfowl, water birds, song birds, and several species of resident wildlife. The Refuge also provides environmental education and interpretive programs to Twin Cities residents.
Keyword(s): Public Lands/Greenspace, Recreation/Ecotourism, Wildlife & Species

UNITED STATES DEPARTMENT OF THE INTERIOR
FISH AND WILDLIFE SERVICE
MISSISQUOI NATIONAL WILDLIFE REFUGE
371 North River Street
Swanton, VT 05488 United States
Phone: 802-868-4781   Fax: 802-868-2379
E-mail: FW5RW_MSQNWR@fws.gov
Website: refuges.fws.gov/profiles/index.cfm?id=53520
Founded: 1943
Scope: Local, State, Regional, National
Description: Missisquoi National Wildlife Refuge is located on the eastern shore of Lake Champlain near the Canadian border in Franklin County, VT. The 6,592-acre refuge includes most of the Missisquoi River delta where it flows into Missisquoi Bay. The refuge consists of quiet waters and wetlands which attract large flocks of migratory birds. Recreational and educational activities consistent with the primary goals of protecting and managing wildlife habitat are available at the refuge.

UNITED STATES DEPARTMENT OF THE INTERIOR
FISH AND WILDLIFE SERVICE
MISSISSIPPI SANDHILL CRANE/GRAND BAY NATIONAL WILDLIFE REFUGE
7200 Crane Ln.
Gautier, MS 39553 United States
Phone: 601-497-6322   Fax: 601-497-5407
Scope: Regional

UNITED STATES DEPARTMENT OF THE INTERIOR
FISH AND WILDLIFE SERVICE
MISSISSIPPI WMD NATIONAL WILDLIFE REFUGE
P.O. Box 1070, 16736 Hwy. 8 West
Grenada, MS 38902 United States
Phone: 601-226-8286   Fax: 601-226-8488
Scope: Regional

UNITED STATES DEPARTMENT OF THE INTERIOR
FISH AND WILDLIFE SERVICE
MOAPA VALLEY NATIONAL WILDLIFE REFUGE
HCR 38, Box 700
Las Vegas, NV 89124 United States
Phone: 702-879-6110   Fax: 702-879-6115
E-mail: amy_sprunger-allworth@fws.gov
Website: http://desertcomplex.fws.gov
Scope: Local, State, Regional, National
Description: Moapa Valley National Wildlife Refuge, part of the Desert National Wildlife Refuge Complex.
Keyword(s): Wildlife & Species
Contact(s):
  Amy Sprunger-Allworth, Refuge Manager; 702-879-6110; Fax: 702-879-6115; amy_sprunger-allworth@fws.gov

UNITED STATES DEPARTMENT OF THE INTERIOR
FISH AND WILDLIFE SERVICE
MODOC NATIONAL WILDLIFE REFUGE
P.O. Box 1610
Alturas, CA 96101 United States
Phone: 530-233-3572   Fax: 530-233-4143
Website: modoc.fws.gov
Scope: Regional
Description: The 7,000 acre Modoc National Wildlife Refuge was established in 1961 to manage and protect migratory birds.

UNITED STATES DEPARTMENT OF THE INTERIOR
FISH AND WILDLIFE SERVICE
MONOMOY NATIONAL WILDLIFE REFUGE
Wikis Way, Morris Island
Chatham, MA 02633 United States
Phone: 508-945-0594   Fax: 508-945-9559
Scope: National

UNITED STATES DEPARTMENT OF THE INTERIOR
FISH AND WILDLIFE SERVICE
MONTEZUMA NATIONAL WILDLIFE REFUGE
3395 Rt. 5/20 East
Seneca Falls, NY 13148 United States
Phone: 315-568-5987   Fax: 315-568-8835
Scope: Regional

UNITED STATES DEPARTMENT OF THE INTERIOR
FISH AND WILDLIFE SERVICE
MOOSEHORN NATIONAL WILDLIFE REFUGE
R.R. 1, Box 202, Suite 1
Baring, ME 04694 United States
Phone: 207-454-7161   Fax: 207-454-2550
Scope: National

UNITED STATES DEPARTMENT OF THE INTERIOR
FISH AND WILDLIFE SERVICE
MORRIS WETLAND MANAGEMENT DISTRICT
43875 230th St.
Morris, MN 56267 United States
Phone: 320-589-1001   Fax: 320-589-2624
Website: http://midwest.fws.gov/Morris/
Scope: National
Description: A part of the Fish and Wildlife Service's Refuge division devoted to migratory bird and habitat conservation.
Keyword(s): Agriculture/Farming, Ecosystems (precious), Land Issues, Public Lands/Greenspace, Recreation/Ecotourism, Water Habitats & Quality, Wildlife & Species
Contact(s):
  Steve Delehanty, Manager; 320-589-4961; Fax: 320-589-2624; steve_delehanty@fws.gov
  Rodney Ahrndt, Maintenance; 320-589-4967; Fax: 320-589-2624; rodney_ahrndt@fws.gov
  Victor Gades, Maintenance; 320-589-4966; Fax: 320-589-2624; victor_gades@fws.gov
  Deb Gaunitz, Assistant Manager; 320-589-4962; Fax: 320-589-2624; debbie_gaunitz@fws.gov
  Darrell Haugen, Wildlife Biologist; 320-589-4963; Fax: 320-589-2624; darrell_haugen@fws.gov
  Wayne Henderson, Wildlife Biologist; 320-589-4964; Fax: 320-589-2624; wayne_henderson@fws.gov
  Katie Kramer, Refuge Operations Specialist; 320-589-4971; Fax: 320-589-2624; katie_kramer@fws.gov
  Don Lantz, Prescribe Fire Specialist; 320-589-4972; Fax: 320-589-2624; donald_lantz@fws.gov
  Kenton Moos, Refuge Operations Specialist; 320-589-4970; Fax: 320-589-2624; kenton_moos@fws.gov
  Donna Oglesby, Biological Technician; 320-589-4965; Fax: 320-589-2624; donna_oglesby@fws.gov
  Karen Stettner, Administrative Technician; 320-589-1001; Fax: 320-589-2624; karen_stetner@fws.gov
  Sara Vacek, Wildlife Biologist; 320-589-4973; Fax: 320-589-2624; sara_vacek@fws.gov
  Michelle Zastrow, Biological Technician; 320-589-4976; Fax: 320-589-2624; michelle_zastrow@fws.gov

U.S. FEDERAL AND INTERNATIONAL GOVERNMENT AGENCIES – U

UNITED STATES DEPARTMENT OF THE INTERIOR
FISH AND WILDLIFE SERVICE
MULESHOE/GRULLA NATIONAL WILDLIFE REFUGE
P.O. Box 549
Muleshoe, TX 79347 United States
Phone: 806-946-3341   Fax: 806-946-3317
Scope: Regional

UNITED STATES DEPARTMENT OF THE INTERIOR
FISH AND WILDLIFE SERVICE
MUSCATATUCK NATIONAL WILDLIFE REFUGE
12985 E. U.S. Hwy. 50
Seymour, IN 47274 United States
Phone: 812-522-4352   Fax: 812-522-6826
E-mail: Muscatatuck@fws.gov
Website: http://midwest.fws.gov/muscatatuck
Founded: 1966
Scope: Regional
Description: National Wildlife Refuge in south central Indiana. Open 7 days/week, sunrise to sunset. Visitor center, self-guided auto tour, hiking trails, wildlife viewing areas, fishing, limited hunting. Exceptionally fine birding area.

UNITED STATES DEPARTMENT OF THE INTERIOR
FISH AND WILDLIFE SERVICE
NATIONAL BISON RANGE NATIONAL WILDLIFE REFUGE
132 Bison Range Rd.
Moiese, MT 59824 United States
Phone: 406-644-2211   Fax: 406-644-2661
Scope: Regional

UNITED STATES DEPARTMENT OF THE INTERIOR
FISH AND WILDLIFE SERVICE
NATIONAL CONSERVATION TRAINING CENTER
Rt. 1 Box 166
Shepherdstown, WV 25443 United States
Phone: 304-876-1600   Fax: 304-876-7227
Website: www.fws.gov
Membership: 1–100
Scope: National
Description: The mission of the Center is to advance conservation of fish, wildlife, and their habitats through leadership in conservation education for the public, training for the conservation and resource management community, and fostering alliances among diverse interests.
Contact(s):
John Lemon, Director; 304-876-7263
Todd Jones, Chief, Division of Training; 304-876-7431
Mona Womack, Deputy Director; 304-876-7263

UNITED STATES DEPARTMENT OF THE INTERIOR
FISH AND WILDLIFE SERVICE
NATIONAL ELK REFUGE
675 E. Broadway, P.O. Box 510
Jackson, WY 83001 United States
Phone: 307-733-9212   Fax: 307-733-9729
Website: http://nationalelkrefuge.fws.gov
Founded: 1912
Scope: Regional
Description: Provide habitat for elk winter range.
Contact(s):
Barry Reiswig, Refuge Manager

UNITED STATES DEPARTMENT OF THE INTERIOR
FISH AND WILDLIFE SERVICE
NATIONAL FISH AND WILDLIFE FORENSICS LABORATORY
1490 East Main St.
Ashland, OR 97520 United States
Phone: 541-482-4191   Fax: 541-482-4989
Website: www.lab.fws.gov
Description: The mission of the Laboratory is to provide forensic crime lab support for wildlife law enforcement investigations at the federal, state, and international levels.
Contact(s):
Ken Goddard, Director

UNITED STATES DEPARTMENT OF THE INTERIOR
FISH AND WILDLIFE SERVICE
NATIONAL KEY DEER WILDLIFE REFUGE
P.O. Box 43510
Big Pine Key, FL 33043-0510 United States
Phone: 305-872-0774   Fax: 305-872-2154
E-mail: fw4rwkeydeer@fws.gov
Website: http://nationalkeydeer.fws.gov/index.html
Founded: 1957
Scope: Local, State, Regional
Description: National Wildlife Refuge established to protect the endangered key deer in the Florida Keys

UNITED STATES DEPARTMENT OF THE INTERIOR
FISH AND WILDLIFE SERVICE
NEAL SMITH NATIONAL WILDLIFE REFUGE
P.O. Box 399
Prairie City, IA 50228 United States
Phone: 515-994-3400   Fax: 515-994-3459
Website: www.tallgrass.org
Founded: 1990
Scope: Local, State, Regional, National
Description: Neal Smith National Wildlife Refuge/Prairie Learning Center involved in tallgrass prairie reconstruction and restoration; environmental education facility; interpretation; research and monitoring; private lands assistance.
Keyword(s): Ecosystems (precious)
Contact(s):
Pauline Drobney, biologist; 515-994-3400; Fax: 515-994-3459; pauline_drobney@fws.gov

UNITED STATES DEPARTMENT OF THE INTERIOR
FISH AND WILDLIFE SERVICE
NECEDAH NATIONAL WILDLIFE REFUGE
W7996 20th Street West
Necedah, WI 54646-7531 United States
Phone: 608-565-2551   Fax: 608-565-3160
E-mail: necedah@fws.gov
Website: http://midwest.fws.gov/Necedah/
Founded: 1937
Scope: Regional
Description: Necedah National Wildlife Refuge consists of nearly 44,000 acres in central Wisconsin. The Refuge provides habitat for more than 220 bird species, the southernmost pack of gray/timber wolves, the endangered Karner Blue butterfly, and many more animals. The Refuge also is home for whooping crane chicks as part of the Whooping Crane Reintroduction Project.
Keyword(s): Ecosystems (precious), Forests/Forestry, Land Issues, Public Lands/Greenspace, Recreation/Ecotourism, Water Habitats & Quality, Wildlife & Species

Contact(s):
 Molly Mehl, Public Use Specialist

UNITED STATES DEPARTMENT OF THE INTERIOR
FISH AND WILDLIFE SERVICE
NISQUALLY/GRAYS HARBOR NATIONAL WILDLIFE REFUGE
100 Brown Farm Rd.
Olympia, WA 98516-2302 United States
Phone: 360-753-9467   Fax: 360-534-9302
Website: http://nisqually.fws.gov
Scope: Regional

UNITED STATES DEPARTMENT OF THE INTERIOR
FISH AND WILDLIFE SERVICE
NORTH LOUISIANA COMPLEX NATIONAL WILDLIFE REFUGE
11372 Hwy 143
Farmerville, LA 71241 United States
Phone: 318-726-4222   Fax: 318-726-4667
Scope: National
Description: The North Louisiana Refuges Complex is part of the 500 plus unit National Wildlife Refuge System administered by the U.S. Fish and Wildlife Service. The mission of the National Wildlife Refuge System is to administer a network of lands and waters for the conservation, management, and where appropriate, restoration of fish, wildlife, and plant resources and their habitats within the United States for the benefit of present and future generations of Americans.

UNITED STATES DEPARTMENT OF THE INTERIOR
FISH AND WILDLIFE SERVICE
NOWITNA/KOYUKUK NATIONAL WILDLIFE REFUGE
P.O. Box 287
Galena, AK 99741 United States
Phone: 907-656-1231   Fax: 907-656-1708
E-mail: koyukuk@fws.gov
Website: www.r7.fws.gov/nwr/koyukuk/index.html
Scope: Regional

UNITED STATES DEPARTMENT OF THE INTERIOR
FISH AND WILDLIFE SERVICE
NOXUBEE NATIONAL WILDLIFE REFUGE
224 Office Road
Brooksville, MS 39739 United States
Phone: 662-323-5548   Fax: 662-323-5806
E-mail: Noxubee@fws.gov
Website: http://noxubee.fws.gov/
Founded: 1940
Membership: 1–100
Scope: Regional
Keyword(s): Agriculture/Farming, Forests/Forestry, Public Lands/Greenspace, Recreation/Ecotourism, Water Habitats & Quality, Wildlife & Species

UNITED STATES DEPARTMENT OF THE INTERIOR
FISH AND WILDLIFE SERVICE
OAHU NATIONAL WILDLIFE REFUGE COMPLEX
66-590 Kamehameha Hwy., Rm. 2C/D
Haleiwa, HI 96712 United States
Phone: 808-637-6330   Fax: 808-637-3578
Scope: Regional

UNITED STATES DEPARTMENT OF THE INTERIOR
FISH AND WILDLIFE SERVICE
OHIO RIVER ISLANDS NATIONAL WILDLIFE REFUGE
P.O. Box 1811
Parkersburg, WV 26102-1811 United States
Phone: 304-422-0752   Fax: 304-422-0754
Website: www.fws.gov
Scope: Regional

UNITED STATES DEPARTMENT OF THE INTERIOR
FISH AND WILDLIFE SERVICE
OKEFENOKEE (BANKS LAKE) NATIONAL WILDLIFE REFUGE
Rt. 2, Box 3330
Folkston, GA 31537 United States
Phone: 912-496-7366   Fax: 912-496-3332
E-mail: okefenokee@fws.gov
Website: http://okefenokee.fws.gov
Founded: 1937
Scope: Regional
Description: Located in SE Georgia, Okefenokee National Wildlife Refuge encompasses about 396,000 acres. Almost 90 percent of the refuge has increased protection as a National Wilderness Area. From the open, wet "prairies" of the east side to the forested cypress swamps on the west, Okefenokee is a mosaic of habitats, plants, and wildlife. Visitors are welcome to observe and photograph wildlife, take a guided tour, fish, join in special events and programs, and learn more about this diverse ecosystem.
Keyword(s): Ecosystems (precious), Forests/Forestry, Recreation/Ecotourism, Water Habitats & Quality, Wildlife & Species

UNITED STATES DEPARTMENT OF THE INTERIOR
FISH AND WILDLIFE SERVICE
OREGON COAST NATIONAL WILDLIFE REFUGE COMPLEX
2127 SE OSU Dr.
Newport, OR 97365-5258 United States
Phone: 541-867-4550   Fax: 541-867-4551
E-mail: oregoncoast@r1.fws.gov
Website: http://oregoncoast.fws.gov
Founded: 1985
Scope: Regional
Description: Manages six National Wildlife Refuges along the Oregon Coast including Bandon Marsh, Cape Meares, Nestucca Bay, Oregon Islands, Siletz Bay and Three Arch Rocks.

UNITED STATES DEPARTMENT OF THE INTERIOR
FISH AND WILDLIFE SERVICE
OTTAWA NATIONAL WILDLIFE REFUGE
14000 W. State, Rt. 2
Oak Harbor, OH 43449 United States
Phone: 419-898-0014   Fax: 419-898-7895
Scope: Regional
Description: National Wildlife Refuge Complex includes Ottawa NWR, Cedar Point NWR, West Sister Island NWR

UNITED STATES DEPARTMENT OF THE INTERIOR
FISH AND WILDLIFE SERVICE
OURAY NATIONAL WILDLIFE REFUGE
HC 69 Box 232
Randlett, UT 84063 United States
Phone: 435-545-2522   Fax: 435-545-2369

E-mail: r6rw_ory@fws.gov
Website: http://mountain-prairie.fws.gov/ouray/
Scope: Regional

UNITED STATES DEPARTMENT OF THE INTERIOR
FISH AND WILDLIFE SERVICE
OVERFLOW NATIONAL WILDLIFE REFUGE
c/o Felsenthal NWR, P.O. Box 1157
Crossett, AR 71635 United States
Phone: 870-364-3167   Fax: 870-364-3757
E-mail: felsenthal@fws.gov
Website: southeast.fws.gov/Overflow/
Scope: Regional

UNITED STATES DEPARTMENT OF THE INTERIOR
FISH AND WILDLIFE SERVICE
OXFORD SLOUGH WPA NATIONAL WILDLIFE REFUGE COMPLEX
4428 Burley Drive
Chussack, ID 83202 United States
Phone: 208-237-6616   Fax: 208-237-6617
Scope: Regional

UNITED STATES DEPARTMENT OF THE INTERIOR
FISH AND WILDLIFE SERVICE
PACIFIC/REMOTE ISLANDS COMPLEX (HAWAIIAN ISLANDS, BAKER ISLAND, HOWLAND ISLAND, JARVIS ISLAND, ROSE ATOLL) NATIONAL WILDLIFE REFUGE
P.O. Box 50167
Honolulu, HI 96850-5167 United States
Phone: 808-541-1201   Fax: 808-541-1216
Scope: Regional

UNITED STATES DEPARTMENT OF THE INTERIOR
FISH AND WILDLIFE SERVICE
PAHRANAGAT NATIONAL WILDLIFE REFUGE
Box 510
Alamo, NV 89001 United States
Phone: 775-725-3417   Fax: 775-725-3389
E-mail: eddy_pausch@fws.gov
Scope: Regional

UNITED STATES DEPARTMENT OF THE INTERIOR
FISH AND WILDLIFE SERVICE
PANTHER SWAMP NATIONAL WILDLIFE REFUGE
13695 River Rd.
Yazoo City, MS 39194 United States
Phone: 662-746-5060   Fax: 662-746-5065
Scope: National

UNITED STATES DEPARTMENT OF THE INTERIOR
FISH AND WILDLIFE SERVICE
PARKER RIVER/THATCHER ISLAND NATIONAL WILDLIFE REFUGE
261 Northern Blvd., Plum Island
Newburyport, MA 01950 United States
Phone: 978-465-5753   Fax: 978-465-2807
Scope: National

UNITED STATES DEPARTMENT OF THE INTERIOR
FISH AND WILDLIFE SERVICE
PATOKA RIVER NATIONAL WETLANDS PROJECT NATIONAL WILDLIFE REFUGE
P.O. Box 217
510 1/2 West Morton Street
Oakland City, IN 47660 United States
Phone: 812-749-3199   Fax: 812-749-3059
E-mail: bill_mccoy@fws.gov
Founded: 1994
Scope: Local, State, Regional
Description: National Wildlife Refuge - 5131 acres purchased out of 22,089 authorized. River bottom project.
Keyword(s): Forests/Forestry, Land Issues, Pollution (general), Public Lands/Greenspace, Recreation/Ecotourism, Water Habitats & Quality, Wildlife & Species

UNITED STATES DEPARTMENT OF THE INTERIOR
FISH AND WILDLIFE SERVICE
PATUXENT RESEARCH REFUGE
NATIONAL WILDLIFE VISITOR CENTER
10901 Scarlet Tanager Loop
Laurel, MD 20708-4027 United States
Phone: 301-497-5760   Fax: 301-497-5765
Website: http://patuxent.fws.gov
Founded: 1936
Scope: Local, State, Regional, National, International
Description: National Wildlife Visitor Center has interactive exhibits featuring natural areas and endangered species found throughout the United States. Seasonal tram tours are available for a nominal fee.
Keyword(s): Recreation/Ecotourism, Wildlife & Species
Contact(s):
  Brad Knudsen, Refuge Manager

UNITED STATES DEPARTMENT OF THE INTERIOR
FISH AND WILDLIFE SERVICE
PEE DEE NATIONAL WILDLIFE REFUGE
Rt.1, Box 92
Wadesboro, NC 28170 United States
Phone: 704-694-4424   Fax: 704-694-6570
Website: http://peedee.fws.gov/index.html
Scope: Regional

UNITED STATES DEPARTMENT OF THE INTERIOR
FISH AND WILDLIFE SERVICE
PELICAN ISLAND NATIONAL WILDLIFE REFUGE
1339 20th Street
Vero Beach, FL 32960 United States
Phone: 772-562-3909   Fax: 772-299-3101
E-mail: pelicanisland@fws.gov
Website: http://pelicanisland.fws.gov
Founded: 1903
Scope: National
Description: America's first National Wildlife Refuge. A 5.5 acre mangrove island in Florida's Indian River Lagoon, established as a preserve and breeding ground for native birds in 1903 by President Theodore Roosevelt. This was the birth of the National Wildlife Refuge System, which today encompasses 540 refuges on over 95 million acres.
Keyword(s): Ecosystems (precious), Public Lands/Greenspace, Recreation/Ecotourism, Wildlife & Species
Contact(s):
  Paul Tritaik, Refuge Manager; 772-562-3909; ext. 244; Fax: 772-299-3101; paul_tritaik@fws.gov

UNITED STATES DEPARTMENT OF THE INTERIOR
FISH AND WILDLIFE SERVICE
PETIT MANAN NATIONAL WILDLIFE REFUGE
P.O. Box 279
Millbridge, ME 04658 United States
Phone: 207-546-2124   Fax: 207-546-7805
Scope: National
Description: Restore colonial nesting seabirds to historical levels on islands along the coast of Maine.

UNITED STATES DEPARTMENT OF THE INTERIOR
FISH AND WILDLIFE SERVICE
PIEDMONT NATIONAL WILDLIFE REFUGE
718 Juliette Rd.
Round Oak, GA 31038 United States
Phone: 478-986-5441   Fax: 478-986-9646
E-mail: piedmont@fws.gov
Website: http://piedmont.fws.gov
Founded: 1939
Scope: Local, State, Regional
Description: Piedmont National Wildlife Refuge consists of 35,000 acres of beautiful forest. It boasts loblolly pine ridges and hardwoods situated along creek bottoms. Clear streams and green fields are abundant.
Publication(s): Piedmont Bird List
Keyword(s): Recreation/Ecotourism, Wildlife & Species
Contact(s):
   Ronnie Shell, Refuge Manager; Ronnie_Shell@fws.gov
   Jane Whaley, Refuge Ranger; Jane_Whaley@fws.gov

UNITED STATES DEPARTMENT OF THE INTERIOR
FISH AND WILDLIFE SERVICE
PIERCE NATIONAL WILDLIFE REFUGE
Columbia River Gorge Refuges
35510 S.E. Evergreen Highway
Washougal, WA 98671 United States
Phone: 360-835-8767   Fax: 369-835-9780
E-mail: jim_clapp@fws.gov
Website: http://ridgefieldrefuges.fws.gov
Founded: 1983
Scope: Regional
Description: This office manages three refuges located along the Columbia River Gorge - Pierce, Franz Lake, and Steigerwald Lake NWR. Please contact the refuge manager for public use opportunities.

UNITED STATES DEPARTMENT OF THE INTERIOR
FISH AND WILDLIFE SERVICE
POCOSIN LAKES NATIONAL WILDLIFE REFUGE
205 South Ludington Drive
P.O. Box 329
Columbia, NC 27925 United States
Phone: 252-796-3004   Fax: 252-796-3010
E-mail: fw4_rw_pocosin_lakes@fws.gov
Website: http://pocosinlakes.fws.gov/
Founded: 1990
Scope: Local
Keyword(s): Agriculture/Farming, Climate Change, Ecosystems (precious), Land Issues, Public Lands/Greenspace, Recreation/Ecotourism, Wildlife & Species
Contact(s):
   Howard Phillips, Refuge Manager; 252-796-3004; ext. 226; Fax: 252-796-3010
   David Kitts, Deputy Refuge Manager; 252-796-3004; ext. 225; Fax: 252-796-3010
   Stanton Wendy, Wildlife Biologist; 252-796-3004; ext. 224; Fax: 252-796-3010

UNITED STATES DEPARTMENT OF THE INTERIOR
FISH AND WILDLIFE SERVICE
POND CREEK NATIONAL WILDLIFE REFUGE
c/o Felsenthal NWR, P.O. Box 1157
Crossett, AR 71635 United States
Phone: 870-364-3167   Fax: 870-364-3757
E-mail: felsenthal@fws.gov
Website: http://southeast.fws.gov/PondCreek
Scope: Regional

UNITED STATES DEPARTMENT OF THE INTERIOR
FISH AND WILDLIFE SERVICE
PORT LOUISA NATIONAL WILDLIFE REFUGE
10728 County Rd. X-61
Wapello, IA 52653-9477 United States
Phone: 319-523-6982   Fax: 319-523-6960
E-mail: tom_cox@fws.gov
Website: http://midwest.fws.gov/portlouisa
Scope: State, Regional
Description: Port Louisa National Wildlife Refuge was established to manage for migratory waterfowl. Various public use activities are available during the open periods of the refuge.

UNITED STATES DEPARTMENT OF THE INTERIOR
FISH AND WILDLIFE SERVICE
POTOMAC RIVER COMPLEX NATIONAL WILDLIFE REFUGE
14344 Jefferson Davis Hwy.
Woodbridge, VA 22191 United States
Phone: 703-490-4979   Fax: 703-490-5631
Scope: Regional

UNITED STATES DEPARTMENT OF THE INTERIOR
FISH AND WILDLIFE SERVICE
PRIME HOOK NATIONAL WILDLIFE REFUGE
11978 Turkle Pond Road
Milton, DE 19968 United States
Phone: 302-684-8419   Fax: 302-684-8504
E-mail: kelly_hudson@fws.gov
Website: http://primehook.fws.gov
Founded: 1963
Scope: Regional
Description: Prime Hook National Wildlife Refuge spans 10,000 acres along the western Delaware Bay. The marshes of the refuge are ideal habitat for thousands of migrating ducks, geese, and shorebirds. The refuge is also home to woodland and grassland birds, reptiles, amphibians, and mammals, including the endangered Delmarva Peninsula Fox Squirrel. for refuge visitors, there are opportunities in wildlife observation, photography, fishing, hunting, environmental education and environmental interpretation.

UNITED STATES DEPARTMENT OF THE INTERIOR
FISH AND WILDLIFE SERVICE
QUIVIRA NATIONAL WILDLIFE REFUGE
R.R. 3, Box 48A
Stafford, KS 67530 United States
Phone: 316-486-2393   Fax: 316-486-2394
Scope: Regional

U.S. FEDERAL AND INTERNATIONAL GOVERNMENT AGENCIES – U

UNITED STATES DEPARTMENT OF THE INTERIOR
FISH AND WILDLIFE SERVICE
RACHEL CARSON NATIONAL WILDLIFE REFUGE
321 Port Road
Wells, ME 04090 United States
Phone: 207-646-9226   Fax: 207-646-6554
Scope: National

UNITED STATES DEPARTMENT OF THE INTERIOR
FISH AND WILDLIFE SERVICE
RAINWATER BASIN WMD NATIONAL WILDLIFE REFUGE
P.O. Box 1686
Kearney, NE 68848 United States
Phone: 308-236-5015, ext. 27   Fax: 308-237-3899
E-mail: rainwater@fws.gov
Website: http://rainwater.fws.gov
Scope: Regional
Description: Rainwater Basin Wetland Management District is responsible for the management of 24,000 acres scattered over 62 tracts of land. Each tract contains a large wetland used for staging waterfowl and shorebirds. Each spring over 10 million birds use these areas.
Keyword(s): Water Habitats & Quality, Wildlife & Species
Contact(s):
  Gene Mack, Project Leader; 308-236-5015; ext. 27; Fax: 308-236-3899; gene_mack@fws.gov

UNITED STATES DEPARTMENT OF THE INTERIOR
FISH AND WILDLIFE SERVICE
RAPPAHANNOCK RIVER VALLEY NATIONAL WILDLIFE REFUGE
P.O. Box 189
Prince George, VA 23875 United States
Phone: 804-733-8042
Scope: Regional

UNITED STATES DEPARTMENT OF THE INTERIOR
FISH AND WILDLIFE SERVICE
RED ROCK LAKES NATIONAL WILDLIFE REFUGE
27820 Southside Centennial Road
Lima, MT 59739 United States
Phone: 406-276-3536   Fax: 406-276-3538
E-mail: redrocks@fws.gov
Scope: Regional
Description: The 45,000 acre Red Rock Lakes National Wildlife Refuge was established in 1935 to protect the trumpeter swan. The refuge lies in the eastern end of the Centennial Valley near the headwaters of the Missouri River in southwestern Montana. The refuge is one of more than 540 refuges in the National Wildlife Refuge System set aside specifically for wildlife.
Keyword(s): Ecosystems (precious), Wildlife & Species

UNITED STATES DEPARTMENT OF THE INTERIOR
FISH AND WILDLIFE SERVICE
REGION 1
PACIFIC REGIONAL OFFICE
911 North East 11th Avenue
Portland, OR 97232-4181 United States
Phone: 503-231-6828   Fax: 503-231-2364
Website: http://pacific.fws.gov
Scope: Regional
Description: The Pacific Region of USFWS includes the states of California, Hawaii, Idaho, Nevada, Oregon, Washington and the U.S. Trust Territories in the Pacific Ocean, and spans 9 time zones. Approximately half the country's threatened and endangered species are found in the Pacific Region. The Region employs approximately 2,100 people at 105 field stations (as of April, 2002).
Publication(s): Endangered Species Information, Brochures and Fact Sheets
Keyword(s): Ecosystems (precious), Land Issues, Oceans/Coasts/Beaches, Public Lands/Greenspace, Recreation/Ecotourism, Water Habitats & Quality, Wildlife & Species
Contact(s):
  Anne Badgley, Regional Director; 503-231-6118; Fax: 503-231-2716
  Cynthia Barry, Assistant Regional Director - Ecological; 503-231-6151; Fax: 503-231-2240
  Carolyn Bohan, Regional Chief, National Wildlife Refuge System; 503-231-6214; Fax: 503-231-6837
  Daniel Diggs, Assistant Regional Director - Fisheries; 503-872-2763; Fax: 503-231-2062
  Rowan Gould, Deputy Regional Director; 503-231-6122; Fax: 503-231-2716
  David Patte/ Joan Jewett, Acting Assistant Regional Director - External Affairs; 503-231-6120; Fax: 503-231-2122
  Benito Perez, Assistant Regional Director - Law Enforcement; 503-231-6125; Fax: 503-231-6197
  Steve Thompson, California/Nevada Operations Manager; 2800 Cottage Way, Room W-2606, Sacramento, CA 95825; 916-414-6464; Fax: 916-414-6486
  Don Weathers, Assistant Regional Director - Budget & Administration; 503-231-6115; Fax: 503-231-2811
  David Wesley, Assistant Regional Director- Migratory Birds, State Programs; 503-231-6159; Fax: 503-231-2019
  Paul Henson, Pacific Islands Field Supervisor; 300 Ala Moana Blvd., Box 50088, Honolulu, HI 96850; 808-541-3441; Fax: 808-541-3470

UNITED STATES DEPARTMENT OF THE INTERIOR
FISH AND WILDLIFE SERVICE
REGION 2
SOUTHWEST REGIONAL OFFICE
P.O. Box 1306
500 Gold Ave. SW, Room 8526
Albuquerque, NM 87102 United States
Phone: 505-248-6911   Fax: 505-248-6915
Website: http://southwest.fws.gov
Membership: 101–1,000
Scope: Regional
Description: Principal Federal agency responsible for conserving, protecting, and enhancing fish, wildlife and plants and their habitats for the benefit of the American people. The Service manages the 95-million acre National Wildlife Refuge System which includes 540 refuges, operates 69 national fish hatcheries, 64 fishery resource offices, and 78 ecological services field offices.
Keyword(s): Ecosystems (precious), Wildlife & Species
Contact(s):
  Dale Hall, Regional Director; 505-248-6282; Fax: 505-248-6845
  Tom Bauer, Assistant Director of External Affairs; 505-248-6911; Fax: 505-248-6915

UNITED STATES DEPARTMENT OF THE INTERIOR
FISH AND WILDLIFE SERVICE
REGION 3
GREAT LAKES-BIG RIVERS REGIONAL OFFICE
1 Federal Drive
Ft. Snelling, MN 55111 United States
Phone: 612-713-5301   Fax: 612-713-5284
Website: http://midwest.fws.gov

Scope: Local, State, Regional, National, International
Description: Provide the public with opportunities to enjoy their native fish and wildlife now and in the future.
Contact(s):
William Hartwig, Regional Director; 612-713-5301; Fax: 612-713-5284; William_Hartwig@fws.gov

UNITED STATES DEPARTMENT OF THE INTERIOR
FISH AND WILDLIFE SERVICE
REGION 4
SOUTHEAST REGIONAL OFFICE
1875 Century Blvd., Suite 400
Atlanta, GA 30345 United States
Phone: 404-679-4000 Fax: 404-679-4006
E-mail: fw4_dir@fws.gov
Website: http://southeast.fws.gov

Founded: 1903
Membership: 1,001–10,000
Scope: Regional, National
Keyword(s): Ecosystems (precious), Land Issues, Oceans/Coasts/Beaches, Pollution (general), Public Lands/Greenspace, Recreation/Ecotourism, Water Habitats & Quality, Wildlife & Species
Contact(s):
Sam Hamilton, Regional Director; 404-679-4000; Fax: 404-679-4006; fw4_dir@fws.gov

UNITED STATES DEPARTMENT OF THE INTERIOR
FISH AND WILDLIFE SERVICE
REGION 5
NORTHEAST REGIONAL OFFICE
300 Westgate Center Drive
Hadley, MA 01035-9589 United States
Phone: 413-253-8200 Fax: 413-253-8308
Website: http://northeast.fws.gov

Scope: Local, State, Regional, National, International
Description: Our mission is working with others to conserve, protect, and enhance fish, wildlife, and plants and their habitats for the continuing benefit of the American people.
Keyword(s): Ecosystems (precious), Land Issues, Water Habitats & Quality, Wildlife & Species
Contact(s):
Richard Bennett, Acting Regional Director

UNITED STATES DEPARTMENT OF THE INTERIOR
FISH AND WILDLIFE SERVICE
REGION 6
MOUNTAIN-PRAIRIE REGIONAL OFFICE
134 Union Blvd., P.O. Box 25486
Denver, CO 80225 United States
Phone: 303-236-7920 Fax: 303-236-8295
Website: http://mountain-prairie.fws.gov

Scope: Regional
Contact(s):
Ralph Morgenweck, Regional Director; 303-236-7920; Fax: 303-236-8295

UNITED STATES DEPARTMENT OF THE INTERIOR
FISH AND WILDLIFE SERVICE
REGION 7
ALASKA REGIONAL OFFICE
1011 E. Tudor Rd.
Anchorage, AK 99503 United States
Phone: 907-786-3542 Fax: 907-786-3306
Website: http://alaska.fws.gov

Scope: National
Publication(s): See publications on website
Keyword(s): Land Issues, Water Habitats & Quality, Wildlife & Species
Contact(s):
Rowan Gould, Regional Director; 907-786-3542

UNITED STATES DEPARTMENT OF THE INTERIOR
FISH AND WILDLIFE SERVICE
RHODE ISLAND NATIONAL WILDLIFE REFUGE COMPLEX
3769 Old Post Road
P.O. Box 307
Charlestown, RI 02813 United States
Phone: 401-364-9124 Fax: 401-364-0170
E-mail: fw5rw_rinwr@fws.gov

Founded: 1970
Membership: 1–100
Scope: Regional, National
Description: Includes Sachuest Point NWR and non-staffed refuges: Ninigret NWR, Trustom Pond NWR, John H. Chafee NWR at Pettaquamscutt Cove, and Block Island NWR.

UNITED STATES DEPARTMENT OF THE INTERIOR
FISH AND WILDLIFE SERVICE
RICE LAKE NATIONAL WILDLIFE REFUGE
36289 State Hwy. 65
McGregor, MN 55760 United States
Phone: 218-768-2402 Fax: 218-768-3040
E-mail: Mary_Stefanski@fws.gov
Website: http://midwest.fws.gov/ricelake/

Founded: 1935
Scope: National
Description: One of over 540 National Wildlife Refuges in the country, Rice Lake has over 18,000 acres of bog, forest and grassland open to the public.
Contact(s):
Mary Stefanski, Refuge Manager; 218-768-2402; Fax: 218-768-3040; Mary_Stefanski@fws.gov
John Francis, Refuge Operations Specialist; 218-768-2402; Fax: 218-768-3040; John_Francis@fws.gov
Dean Huhta, Maintenance Mechanic; 218-768-7028; Fax: 218-768-3040; Dean_Huhta@fws.gov
Duane King, Biological Technician - Fire; 218-768-2402; Fax: 218-768-3040; Duane_King@fws.gov
Sharon Young, Administrative Technician; 218-768-2402; Fax: 218-768-3040; Sharon_Young@fws.gov

UNITED STATES DEPARTMENT OF THE INTERIOR
FISH AND WILDLIFE SERVICE
RIDGEFIELD NATIONAL WILDLIFE REFUGE
P.O. Box 1022
Ridgefield, WA 98642-0457 United States
Phone: 360-887-9495 Fax: 360-887-4109

Scope: Regional
Contact(s):
Liza Halpenny, EE Coordinator

UNITED STATES DEPARTMENT OF THE INTERIOR
FISH AND WILDLIFE SERVICE
ROANOKE RIVER NATIONAL WILDLIFE REFUGE
P.O. Box 430
Windsor, NC 27983 United States
Phone: 252-794-3808 Fax: 252-794-5755
E-mail: sherrie_jager@fws.gov
Website: roanokeriver.fws.gov/index.html

Founded: 1989

Scope: Local, State

Keyword(s): Ecosystems (precious), Forests/Forestry, Land Issues, Public Lands/Greenspace, Reduce/Reuse/Recycle, Wildlife & Species

Contact(s):
 Harvey Hill, Refuge Manager; 252-794-3808; ext. 26; harvey_hill@fws.gov
 Mike Canada, Assistant Refuge Manager; 252-794-3808; ext. 24; mike_canada@fws.gov
 Michelle Chappell, Biological Science Technician; 252-794-3808; ext. 27; michelle_chappell@fws.gov
 Sherrie Jager, Office Assistant; 252-794-3808; ext. 21; sherrie_jager@fws.gov
 Jean Richter, Fish & Wildlife Biologist; 252-794-3808; ext. 22; jean_richter@fws.gov
 Doak Wilkins, Engineering Equipment Operator; 252-794-5755; doak_wilkins@fws.gov

UNITED STATES DEPARTMENT OF THE INTERIOR
FISH AND WILDLIFE SERVICE
RUBY LAKE NATIONAL WILDLIFE REFUGE
HC 60, Box 860
Ruby Valley, NV 89833 United States
Phone: 775-779-2237 Fax: 775-779-2370
E-mail: marti_collins@fws.gov

Founded: 1938

Scope: Regional

Description: Ruby Lake NWR was established in 1938 as "a refuge and breeding ground for migratory birds and other wildlife". It hosts the largest nesting population of canvasback ducks west of the Mississippi River outside Alaska. In addition, it is one of the most remote refuges in the lower 48 states.

Contact(s):
 Martha Collins, Office Manager; 775-779-2237; marti_collins@fws.gov

UNITED STATES DEPARTMENT OF THE INTERIOR
FISH AND WILDLIFE SERVICE
SABINE NATIONAL WILDLIFE REFUGE
3000 Holly Beach Hwy.
Hackberry, LA 70645 United States
Phone: 337-762-3816 Fax: 337-762-3780

Scope: National

UNITED STATES DEPARTMENT OF THE INTERIOR
FISH AND WILDLIFE SERVICE
SACRAMENTO NATIONAL WILDLIFE REFUGE
752 County Rd. 99W
Willows, CA 95988 United States
Phone: 530-934-2801 Fax: 530-934-7814
Website: http://sacramentovalleyrefuges.fws.gov

Scope: Regional

Description: Administered by the U.S. Fish and Wildlife Service, the Sacramento National Wildlife Refuge is located in the Sacramento Valley of north central California

UNITED STATES DEPARTMENT OF THE INTERIOR
FISH AND WILDLIFE SERVICE
SALT PLAINS NATIONAL WILDLIFE REFUGE
Rt. 1, Box 76
Jet, OK 73749 United States
Phone: 580-626-4794 Fax: 580-626-4793

Scope: Regional

UNITED STATES DEPARTMENT OF THE INTERIOR
FISH AND WILDLIFE SERVICE
SAN ANDRES NATIONAL WILDLIFE REFUGE
P.O. Box 756
Las Cruces, NM 88004 United States
Phone: 505-382-5047 Fax: 505-382-5454
E-mail: fw2_rw_sanandres@fws.gov
Website: http://southwest.fws.gov/refuges/newmex/sanand.html

Scope: Regional

UNITED STATES DEPARTMENT OF THE INTERIOR
FISH AND WILDLIFE SERVICE
SAN BERNARDINO/LESLIE CANYON NATIONAL WILDLIFE REFUGE
P.O. Box 3509
Douglas, AZ 85607 United States
Phone: 520-364-2104 Fax: 520-364-2130
Website: http://southwest.fws.gov/refuges/arizona/sanb.html

Scope: Regional

UNITED STATES DEPARTMENT OF THE INTERIOR
FISH AND WILDLIFE SERVICE
SAN FRANCISCO BAY NATIONAL WILDLIFE REFUGE COMPLEX
P.O. Box 524
Newark, CA 94560 United States
Phone: 510-792-0222 Fax: 510-792-5828
E-mail: info@sfbws.com
Website: http://desfbay.fws.gov/AboutSF.htm

Scope: Regional

UNITED STATES DEPARTMENT OF THE INTERIOR
FISH AND WILDLIFE SERVICE
SAN LUIS NATIONAL WILDLIFE REFUGE COMPLEX
P.O. Box 2176
Los Banos, CA 93635-2176 United States
Phone: 209-826-3508 Fax: 209-826-1445
Website: http://sanluis.fws.gov/

Founded: 1951

Scope: Local, State, Regional

Description: The Refuge System administers a national network of lands and waters for the conservation, management, and where apropriate, restoration of the fish, wildlife, and plant resources and their habitats within the United States for the benefit of present and future Americans.

Keyword(s): Agriculture/Farming, Ecosystems (precious), Land Issues, Public Lands/Greenspace, Recreation/Ecotourism, Sprawl/Urban Planning, Water Habitats & Quality, Wildlife & Species

UNITED STATES DEPARTMENT OF THE INTERIOR
FISH AND WILDLIFE SERVICE
SAND LAKE NATIONAL WILDLIFE REFUGE
39650 Sand Lake Dr.
Columbia, SD 57433 United States
Phone: 605-885-6320 Fax: 605-885-6401
E-mail: sandlake@fws.gov
Website: http://sandlake.fws.gov

Founded: 1935

Scope: Regional, National, International

Description: National Wildlife Refuge totalling 21,500 acres located in northeastern South Dakota.

UNITED STATES DEPARTMENT OF THE INTERIOR
FISH AND WILDLIFE SERVICE
SANDY POINT NATIONAL WILDLIFE REFUGE
3013 Estate Golden Rock, Ste. 167
Christiansted, VI 00820-4355 United States
Phone: 340-773-4554
Website: http://southeast.fws.gov/SandyPoint/index.html
Scope: Regional

UNITED STATES DEPARTMENT OF THE INTERIOR
FISH AND WILDLIFE SERVICE
SAVANNAH COASTAL REFUGES
1000 Business Center Dr., Ste. 10
Savannah, GA 31405 United States
Phone: 912-652-4415   Fax: 912-652-4385
Scope: Regional
Description: Seven National Wildlife Refuges are managed from this office: Savannah, Pinckney Island, Tybee, Wassaw, Harris Neck, Blackbeard Island, and Wolf Island National Wildlife Refuges
Keyword(s): Ecosystems (precious), Forests/Forestry, Land Issues, Public Lands/Greenspace, Water Habitats & Quality, Wildlife & Species
Contact(s):
James Browning, Project Leader; 912-652-4415; Fax: 912-652-4385

UNITED STATES DEPARTMENT OF THE INTERIOR
FISH AND WILDLIFE SERVICE
SEEDSKADEE/COKEVILLE MEADOWS NATIONAL WILDLIFE REFUGE
P.O. Box 700
Green River, WY 82935 United States
Phone: 307-875-2187   Fax: 307-875-4425
Scope: Regional

UNITED STATES DEPARTMENT OF THE INTERIOR
FISH AND WILDLIFE SERVICE
SELAWIK NATIONAL WILDLIFE REFUGE
P.O. Box 270
Kotzebue, AK 99752 United States
Phone: 907-442-3799   Fax: 907-442-3124
Scope: Regional

UNITED STATES DEPARTMENT OF THE INTERIOR
FISH AND WILDLIFE SERVICE
SENEY NATIONAL WILDLIFE REFUGE
1674 Refuge Entrance Road
Seney, MI 49883 United States
Phone: 906-586-9851, ext. 11   Fax: 906-586-3800
E-mail: seney@fws.gov
Website: http://midwest.fws.gov/seney
Founded: 1935
Scope: Local, State, Regional, National
Description: National Wildlife Refuge encompassing over 95,000 acres of wetland and upland wildlife habitat.
Keyword(s): Air Quality/Atmosphere, Ecosystems (precious), Forests/Forestry, Recreation/Ecotourism, Wildlife & Species
Contact(s):
Tracy Casselman, Refuge Manager; 906-586-9851; ext. 11

UNITED STATES DEPARTMENT OF THE INTERIOR
FISH AND WILDLIFE SERVICE
SEQUOYAH/OZARK PLATEAU NATIONAL WILDLIFE REFUGE
Rt. 1, Box 18A
Vian, OK 74962 United States
Phone: 918-773-5251   Fax: 918-773-5598
Scope: Regional
Description: Waterfowl
Contact(s):
Craig Heflebower, Biologist; 918-773-5251; Fax: 918-773-5598

UNITED STATES DEPARTMENT OF THE INTERIOR
FISH AND WILDLIFE SERVICE
SEVILLETA NATIONAL WILDLIFE REFUGE
P.O. Box 1248
Socorro, NM 87801 United States
Phone: 505-864-4021   Fax: 505-864-7761
E-mail: fw2_rw_sevilleta@fws.gov
Scope: Regional

UNITED STATES DEPARTMENT OF THE INTERIOR
FISH AND WILDLIFE SERVICE
SHELDON/HART MOUNTAIN NATIONAL WILDLIFE REFUGE
P.O. Box 111
Room 301, U.S. Post Office Building
Lakeveiw, OR 97630-0107 United States
Phone: 541-947-3315
Scope: Regional

UNITED STATES DEPARTMENT OF THE INTERIOR
FISH AND WILDLIFE SERVICE
SHERBURNE/CRANE MEADOWS NATIONAL WILDLIFE REFUGE
17076 293rd Ave.
Zimmerman, MN 55398 United States
Phone: 763-389-3323   Fax: 763-389-3493
Website: http://midwest.fws.gov/sherburne
Scope: National
Contact(s):
Charles Blair, Refuge Manager; 763-398-3323

UNITED STATES DEPARTMENT OF THE INTERIOR
FISH AND WILDLIFE SERVICE
SHIAWASSEE NATIONAL WILDLIFE REFUGE
6975 Mower Rd.
Saginaw, MI 48601 United States
Phone: 517-777-5930   Fax: 517-777-9200
Scope: National

UNITED STATES DEPARTMENT OF THE INTERIOR
FISH AND WILDLIFE SERVICE
SILVIO O. CONTE NATIONAL WILDLIFE AND FISH REFUGE
52 Ave. A
Turners Falls, MA 01376 United States
Phone: 413-863-0209   Fax: 413-863-3070
E-mail: andrew_french@fws.gov
Website: www.fws.gov/r5soc
Founded: 1997
Scope: National

Description: This national wildlife refuge works with partners to protect the abundance and diversity of native species within the Connecticut River watershed in Vermont, New Hampshire, Massachusetts and Connecticut.

Contact(s):
Beth Goettel, Refuge Manager
Keith Weaver, Refuge Manager; Nulhegan Basin Division, P.O. Box 427, Island Pond, VT 05846

UNITED STATES DEPARTMENT OF THE INTERIOR
FISH AND WILDLIFE SERVICE
SONNY BONO SALTON SEA NATIONAL WILDLIFE REFUGE
906 W. Sinclair
Calipatria, CA 92233 United States
Phone: 760-348-5278   Fax: 760-348-7245

Founded: 1930

Scope: Regional

Description: Established in 1930, this 37,600 acre refuge is home to over 400 avian species. It is of great importance to birds of the Pacific Flyway with 95% of California's inland wetlands gone. 90% of the North American population of eared grebes; 30% of the North American breeding population of American white pelicans; 40% of the U.S. population of endangered Yuma clapper rails; 25% of the endangered California brown pelican population reside on the Sea.

UNITED STATES DEPARTMENT OF THE INTERIOR
FISH AND WILDLIFE SERVICE
SOUTHEAST LOUISIANA COMPLEX NATIONAL WILDLIFE REFUGE
61389 Highway 434
Lacombe, LA 70445 United States
Phone: 985-882-2000   Fax: 985-882-9133
E-mail: elizabeth_souheaver@fws.gov

Scope: National

Description: Complex of 7 National Wildlife Refuges: Atchafalaya, Bayou Sauvage, Big Branch Marsh, Bogue Chitto, Breton, Delta, & Shell Keys.

UNITED STATES DEPARTMENT OF THE INTERIOR
FISH AND WILDLIFE SERVICE
SQUAW CREEK NATIONAL WILDLIFE REFUGE
P.O. Box 158
Mound City, MO 64470 United States
Phone: 660-442-3187   Fax: 660-442-5248
Website: www.squawcreek.org

Founded: 1935

Scope: National

Keyword(s): Ecosystems (precious)

Contact(s):
Ronald Bell, Refuge Manager

UNITED STATES DEPARTMENT OF THE INTERIOR
FISH AND WILDLIFE SERVICE
ST. CATHERINE CREEK NATIONAL WILDLIFE REFUGE
P.O. Box 117
Sibley, MS 39165 United States
Phone: 601-442-6696   Fax: 601-446-8990
Website: http://saintcatherinecreek.fws.gov

Founded: 1990

Scope: Regional

Description: 24,442 acre National Wildlife Refuge

Keyword(s): Ecosystems (precious), Public Lands/Greenspace, Wildlife & Species

UNITED STATES DEPARTMENT OF THE INTERIOR
FISH AND WILDLIFE SERVICE
ST. CROIX WETLAND MANAGEMENT DISTRICT
1764 95th St.
New Richmond, WI 54017 United States
Phone: 715-246-7784   Fax: 715-246-4670
E-mail: chet_mccarty@fws.gov

Founded: 1903

Scope: National

Description: The St. Croix WMD manages wetlands and grasslands for the Service's trust wildlife species (waterfowl, other migratory birds, endangered species and indigenous wildlife). Because tallgrass prairie is the most endangered ecosystem in North America we are committed to reestablishing native prairie throughout the District on public and private land for the benefit of trust wildlife species and the Americans who enjoy them.

UNITED STATES DEPARTMENT OF THE INTERIOR
FISH AND WILDLIFE SERVICE
ST. LAWRENCE NATIONAL WILDLIFE REFUGE
127 N. Water St., c/o U.S. Customs House
Ogdensburg, NY 13669 United States
Phone: 315-393-9002   Fax: 315-393-8570

Scope: Regional

UNITED STATES DEPARTMENT OF THE INTERIOR
FISH AND WILDLIFE SERVICE
ST. MARKS NATIONAL WILDLIFE REFUGE
P.O. Box 68
St. Marks, FL 32355 United States
Phone: 850-925-6121   Fax: 850-925-6930

Scope: Local, State, Regional, National

Description: The refuge system provides habitat and manages for endangered/protected species. Wildlife viewing and limited consumtive uses are allowed in conjunction with management objectives. St. Marks NWR is widely known for Longleaf Wiregrass Ecosystem management and restoration of the Red-cockaded Woodpecker.

Keyword(s): Ecosystems (precious), Forests/Forestry, Land Issues, Oceans/Coasts/Beaches, Public Lands/Greenspace, Recreation/Ecotourism, Wildlife & Species

UNITED STATES DEPARTMENT OF THE INTERIOR
FISH AND WILDLIFE SERVICE
ST. VINCENT NATIONAL WILDLIFE REFUGE
P.O. Box 447
Apalachicola, FL 32329-0447 United States
Phone: 850-653-8808   Fax: 850-653-9893
E-mail: fw4_rw_st._vincent@fws.gov
Website: http://southeast.fws.gov/StVincent/

Scope: Regional

UNITED STATES DEPARTMENT OF THE INTERIOR
FISH AND WILDLIFE SERVICE
STILLWATER NATIONAL WILDLIFE REFUGE COMPLEX
1000 Auction Road
Fallon, NV 89406 United States
Phone: 775-428-6452   Fax: 775-423-5158
E-mail: stillwater@r1.fws.gov
Website: http://stillwater.fws.gov/

Scope: Regional

Description: Stillwater National Wildlife Refuge Complex is comprised of three refuges located within an 80 mile radius of Reno, Nevada.

UNITED STATES DEPARTMENT OF THE INTERIOR
FISH AND WILDLIFE SERVICE
STONE LAKES NATIONAL WILDLIFE REFUGE
1624 Hood-Franklin Rd.
Elk Grove, CA 95758-9774 United States
Phone: 916-775-4418   Fax: 916-775-4407
Website: www.stonelakes.org
Scope: Regional

UNITED STATES DEPARTMENT OF THE INTERIOR
FISH AND WILDLIFE SERVICE
SUNKHAZE MEADOWS NATIONAL WILDLIFE REFUGE/CARLTON POND WATERFOWL PRODUCTION AREA
1168 Main St.
Old Town, ME 04468 United States
Phone: 207-827-6138, ext. 17   Fax: 207-827-6099
E-mail: Tom_Comish@fws.gov
Website: www.Sunkhaze.org
Founded: 1966
Membership: 1–100
Scope: National
Description: Two units of the National Wildlife Refuge System
Publication(s): "Tales of Sunkhaze"
Keyword(s): Recreation/Ecotourism, Wildlife & Species

UNITED STATES DEPARTMENT OF THE INTERIOR
FISH AND WILDLIFE SERVICE
SUPAWNA MEADOWS NATIONAL WILDLIFE REFUGE
197 Lighthouse Rd.
Pennsville, NJ 08070 United States
Phone: 856-935-1487   Fax: 856-935-1198
E-mail: FW5RW_SMNWR@fws.gov
Website: http://northeast.fws.gov/nj/spm.htm
Scope: Regional

UNITED STATES DEPARTMENT OF THE INTERIOR
FISH AND WILDLIFE SERVICE
SWAN LAKE NATIONAL WILDLIFE REFUGE
Rt. 1, Box 29 A
Sumner, MO 64681 United States
Phone: 660-856-3323   Fax: 660-856-3687
Scope: National

UNITED STATES DEPARTMENT OF THE INTERIOR
FISH AND WILDLIFE SERVICE
TAMARAC NATIONAL WILDLIFE REFUGE
35704 County Hwy. 26
Rochert, MN 56578 United States
Phone: 218-847-2641   Fax: 218-847-9141
Scope: National
Contact(s):
   Jay Johnson, Refuge Manager; 218-847-2641

UNITED STATES DEPARTMENT OF THE INTERIOR
FISH AND WILDLIFE SERVICE
TENNESSEE NATIONAL WILDLIFE REFUGE
3006 Dinkins Ln.
Paris, TN 38242 United States
Phone: 731-642-2091   Fax: 731-644-3351
Scope: Regional

UNITED STATES DEPARTMENT OF THE INTERIOR
FISH AND WILDLIFE SERVICE
TENSAS RIVER NATIONAL WILDLIFE REFUGE
Rt. 2, Box 295
Tallulah, LA 71282 United States
Phone: 318-574-2664   Fax: 318-574-1624
Scope: National

UNITED STATES DEPARTMENT OF THE INTERIOR
FISH AND WILDLIFE SERVICE
TETLIN NATIONAL WILDLIFE REFUGE
P.O. Box 779
Tok, AK 99780 United States
Phone: 907-883-5312   Fax: 907-883-5747
E-mail: tetlin@fws.gov
Founded: 1980
Scope: Regional
Description: Tetlin National Wildlife Refuge, located in east-central Alaska, was established to conserve waterfowl, raptors and other migratory birds, furbearers, moose, and caribou populations and their habitats.

UNITED STATES DEPARTMENT OF THE INTERIOR
FISH AND WILDLIFE SERVICE
TEWAUKON NATIONAL WILDLIFE REFUGE
9754 143 1/2 Ave. SE
Cayuga, ND 58013 United States
Phone: 701-724-3598   Fax: 701-724-3683
Scope: Regional

UNITED STATES DEPARTMENT OF THE INTERIOR
FISH AND WILDLIFE SERVICE
TISHOMINGO NATIONAL WILDLIFE REFUGE
12000 S. Refuge Rd.
Tishomingo, OK 73460 United States
Phone: 580-371-2402   Fax: 580-371-9312
Scope: Regional

UNITED STATES DEPARTMENT OF THE INTERIOR
FISH AND WILDLIFE SERVICE
TOGIAK NATIONAL WILDLIFE REFUGE
P.O. Box 270
Dillingham, AK 99576 United States
Phone: 907-842-1063   Fax: 907-842-5402
Scope: Regional

UNITED STATES DEPARTMENT OF THE INTERIOR
FISH AND WILDLIFE SERVICE
TREMPEALEAU NATIONAL WILDLIFE REFUGE
W28488 Refuge Rd.
Trempealeau, WI 54661 United States
Phone: 608-539-2311   Fax: 608-539-2703
E-mail: bob_drieslein@fws.gov
Scope: Regional

UNITED STATES DEPARTMENT OF THE INTERIOR
FISH AND WILDLIFE SERVICE
TRINITY RIVER NATIONAL WILDLIFE REFUGE
P.O. Box 10015
Liberty, TX 77575 United States
Phone: 409-336-9786   Fax: 409-336-9847

E-mail: fw2_rw_trinityriver@fws.gov
Website: http://southwest.fws.gov/refuges/texas/trinityriver
Scope: Regional

UNITED STATES DEPARTMENT OF THE INTERIOR
FISH AND WILDLIFE SERVICE
TUALATIN RIVER NATIONAL WILDLIFE REFUGE
16507 Roy Rogers Rd.
Sherwood, OR 97140 United States
Phone: 503-590-5811 Fax: 503-590-6702
Website: http://pacific.fws.gov/refuges/field/OR_Tualatinriv.htm
Scope: Regional

UNITED STATES DEPARTMENT OF THE INTERIOR
FISH AND WILDLIFE SERVICE
TURNBULL NATIONAL WILDLIFE REFUGE
26010 S. Smith Rd.
Cheney, WA 99004-9326 United States
Phone: 509-235-4723 Fax: 509-235-4703
Scope: Regional

UNITED STATES DEPARTMENT OF THE INTERIOR
FISH AND WILDLIFE SERVICE
TWO PONDS, C/O ROCKY MOUNTAIN ARSENAL NATIONAL WILDLIFE REFUGE
USFWS, Bldg. 111
Commerce City, CO 80022-1748 United States
Phone: 303-280-0232 Fax: 303-289-0579
Scope: Regional

UNITED STATES DEPARTMENT OF THE INTERIOR
FISH AND WILDLIFE SERVICE
UNION SLOUGH (IOWA WMD) NATIONAL WILDLIFE REFUGE
1710 360th St.
Titonka, IA 50480 United States
Phone: 515-928-2523 Fax: 515-928-2230
Scope: Regional

UNITED STATES DEPARTMENT OF THE INTERIOR
FISH AND WILDLIFE SERVICE
UPPER MISSISSIPPI RIVER NATIONAL WILDLIFE AND FISH REFUGE
WINONA DISTRICT
51 E. 4th St., Rm. 203
Winona, MN 55987 United States
Phone: 507-454-7351 Fax: 507-452-0851
Scope: National
Keyword(s): Oceans/Coasts/Beaches, Water Habitats & Quality

UNITED STATES DEPARTMENT OF THE INTERIOR
FISH AND WILDLIFE SERVICE
UPPER SOURIS NATIONAL WILDLIFE REFUGE
17705 212th Ave., NW
Berthold, ND 58718-9666 United States
Phone: 701-468-5467 Fax: 701-468-5600
E-mail: usr@fws.gov
Website: http://uppersouris.fws.gov
Founded: 1935
Scope: Regional
Description: Upper Souris National Wildlife Refuge lies in the picturesque Souris River Valley of north central North Dakota. The 35 mile long corridor is comprised of steep native prairie-covered hills, brush-covered coulees, and wooded river bottomlands. This 32,084-acre Refuge is managed by the U.S. Fish and Wildlife Service. The Refuge was established by Executive Order on August 27, 1935, "... as a refuge and breeding ground for migratory birds and other wildlife...".
Keyword(s): Wildlife & Species

UNITED STATES DEPARTMENT OF THE INTERIOR
FISH AND WILDLIFE SERVICE
VALLEY CITY WETLAND MANAGEMENT DISTRICT
11515 River Road
Valley City, ND 58072-9619 United States
Phone: 701-845-3466 Fax: 701-845-3482
E-mail: valleycitywetlands@fws.gov
Website: www.fws.gov
Scope: Local, State, Regional
Description: The Valley City WMD manages Waterfowl Production Areas, National Wildlife Refuges and Wetland Easements in Barnes, Cass, Griggs, Steele and Traill Counties in Southeast North Dakota.
Contact(s):
Kory Richardson, Staff; 701-845-3466;
kory_richardson@fws.gov

UNITED STATES DEPARTMENT OF THE INTERIOR
FISH AND WILDLIFE SERVICE
WALLKILL RIVER NATIONAL WILDLIFE REFUGE
1547 County Rt. 565
Sussex, NJ 07461 United States
Phone: 973-702-7266 Fax: 973-702-7286
E-mail: wallkillriver@fws.gov
Website: http://wallkillriver.fws.gov
Founded: 1990
Scope: Regional
Description: National Wildlife Refuge in Sussex County, New Jersey and Orange County, New York focused on migratory bird protection and management.
Keyword(s): Public Lands/Greenspace, Recreation/Ecotourism, Wildlife & Species

UNITED STATES DEPARTMENT OF THE INTERIOR
FISH AND WILDLIFE SERVICE
WAPANOCCA NATIONAL WILDLIFE REFUGE
P.O. Box 279
178 Hammond Ave
Turrell, AR 72384 United States
Phone: 870-343-2595 Fax: 870-343-2416
Founded: 1961
Membership: 1–100
Scope: Local
Description: The 5484 acre refuge is open to the public year round during daylight hours. The refuge is managed for wintering migratory waterfowl and other birds. Since it is relatively close to the Mississippi River, it has an abundance of bird species passing through during the fall and spring migration.
Keyword(s): Ecosystems (precious), Recreation/Ecotourism, Wildlife & Species
Contact(s):
Glen Miller, Refuge Manager; 870-343-2595;
Glen_Miller@fws.gov

UNITED STATES DEPARTMENT OF THE INTERIOR
FISH AND WILDLIFE SERVICE
WASHINGTON MARITIME NATIONAL WILDLIFE REFUGE COMPLEX
33 S. Barr Rd.
Port Angeles, WA 98362-9202 United States
Phone: 360-457-8451   Fax: 360-457-9778
Scope: National
Description: Washington Maritime NWRC includes: Flattery Rocks NWR, Quillayute Needles NWR, Copalis NWR, Dungeness NWR, and San Juan Islands NWR.
Keyword(s): Oceans/Coasts/Beaches, Pollution (general), Wildlife & Species

UNITED STATES DEPARTMENT OF THE INTERIOR
FISH AND WILDLIFE SERVICE
WASHINGTON OFFICE
NATIONAL WILDLIFE REFUGE SYSTEM
1849 C Street NW
Washington, DC 20240 United States
Phone: 202-208-5333   Fax: 202-208-3082
E-mail: william_hartwig@fws.gov
Scope: National
Description: Chief, National Wildlife Refuge System

UNITED STATES DEPARTMENT OF THE INTERIOR
FISH AND WILDLIFE SERVICE
WASHITA/OPTIMA NATIONAL WILDLIFE REFUGE
Rt. 1, Box 68
Butler, OK 73625 United States
Phone: 405-664-2205   Fax: 405-664-2206
Scope: Regional

UNITED STATES DEPARTMENT OF THE INTERIOR
FISH AND WILDLIFE SERVICE
WAUBAY NATIONAL WILDLIFE REFUGE
44401-134A
Waubay, SD 57273 United States
Phone: 605-947-4521   Fax: 605-947-4524
E-mail: http://wauby@fws.gov
Scope: Regional

UNITED STATES DEPARTMENT OF THE INTERIOR
FISH AND WILDLIFE SERVICE
WEST TENNESSEE REFUGES
Fed. Bldg. Rm. 201, 309 N. Church St.
Dyersburg, TN 38024 United States
Phone: 731-287-0650   Fax: 731-286-0468
E-mail: westtnrefuges@fws.gov
Website: http://westtnrefuges.fws.gov
Scope: Regional
Description: Complex office for Reelfoot, Lake Isom, Chickasaw, and Lower Hatchie NWR's.

UNITED STATES DEPARTMENT OF THE INTERIOR
FISH AND WILDLIFE SERVICE
WESTERN OREGON NATIONAL WILDLIFE REFUGE COMPLEX
26208 Finley Refuge Rd.
Corvallis, OR 97333-9533 United States
Phone: 541-757-7236   Fax: 541-757-4450
Scope: Regional

UNITED STATES DEPARTMENT OF THE INTERIOR
FISH AND WILDLIFE SERVICE
WHEELER NATIONAL WILDLIFE REFUGE
2700 Refuge Hq. Rd.
Decatur, AL 35603 United States
Phone: 256-353-7243   Fax: 256-340-9728
E-mail: wheeler@fws.gov
Website: http://wheeler.fws.gov
Scope: Regional

UNITED STATES DEPARTMENT OF THE INTERIOR
FISH AND WILDLIFE SERVICE
WHITE RIVER NATIONAL WILDLIFE REFUGE
P.O. 205
St. Charles, AR 72140 United States
Phone: 870-946-1468   Fax: 870-946-2591
E-mail: larry_mallard@fws.gov
Website: http://southeast.fws.gov
Founded: 1935
Scope: Regional
Description: White River National Wildlife Refuge, established in 1935, lies in the floodplain of the White River near where it meets the mighty Mississippi River. It is one of the largest remaining bottomland hardwood forests in the Mississippi River Valley. The refuge's fertile forests and three hundred lakes are interlaced with streams, sloughs, and bayous. The result is a haven for a myriad of native wildlife and migratory birds.
Keyword(s): Agriculture/Farming, Ecosystems (precious), Forests/Forestry, Recreation/Ecotourism, Water Habitats & Quality, Wildlife & Species

UNITED STATES DEPARTMENT OF THE INTERIOR
FISH AND WILDLIFE SERVICE
WICHITA MOUNTAINS NATIONAL WILDLIFE REFUGE
RR 1, Box 448
Indiahoma, OK 73552 United States
Phone: 580-429-3222   Fax: 580-429-9323
E-mail: chip_kimball@fws.gov
Website: http://wichitamountains.fws.gov
Founded: 1901
Scope: Regional, International
Description: The Wichita Mountains Wildlife Refuge encompasses 60,000 acres of grasslands and forests, and provides home to American bison, Texas longhorn cattle, elk and deer, as well as a host of other animals.
Keyword(s): Forests/Forestry, Land Issues, Wildlife & Species

UNITED STATES DEPARTMENT OF THE INTERIOR
FISH AND WILDLIFE SERVICE
WILLAPA/LEWIS AND CLARK NATIONAL WILDLIFE REFUGE
JULIA BUTLER HANSEN REFUGE
3888 SR 101
Ilwaco, WA 98624-9707 United States
Phone: 360-484-3482   Fax: 360-484-3109
E-mail: kristine_massin@fws.gov
Scope: Regional
Keyword(s): Agriculture/Farming, Forests/Forestry, Land Issues, Oceans/Coasts/Beaches, Recreation/Ecotourism, Water Habitats & Quality, Wildlife & Species

U.S. FEDERAL AND INTERNATIONAL GOVERNMENT AGENCIES – U

UNITED STATES DEPARTMENT OF THE INTERIOR
FISH AND WILDLIFE SERVICE
WINDOM WMD NATIONAL WILDLIFE REFUGE
49663 County Rd. 17
Windom, MN 56101-3026 United States
Phone: 507-831-2220   Fax: 507-831-5524
Founded: 1990
Scope: Local
Description: The Windom Wetland Management District is part of the National Wildlife Refuge System.
Keyword(s): Public Lands/Greenspace, Wildlife & Species

UNITED STATES DEPARTMENT OF THE INTERIOR
FISH AND WILDLIFE SERVICE
YAZOO NATIONAL WILDLIFE REFUGE
728 Yazoo Refuge Road
Hollandale, MS 38748 United States
Phone: 662-839-2638   Fax: 662-839-2619
E-mail: yazoo@fws.gov
Website: www.fws.gov
Scope: Regional

UNITED STATES DEPARTMENT OF THE INTERIOR
FISH AND WILDLIFE SERVICE
YUKON DELTA NATIONAL WILDLIFE REFUGE
P.O. Box 346
Bethel, AK 99559-0346 United States
Phone: 907-543-3151   Fax: 907-543-4413
Scope: Regional

UNITED STATES DEPARTMENT OF THE INTERIOR
FISH AND WILDLIFE SERVICE
YUKON FLATS NATIONAL WILDLIFE REFUGE
101 12th Ave., Rm. 264
Fairbanks, AK 99701 United States
Phone: 907-456-0440   Fax: 907-456-0447
Website: www.fws.gov
Scope: Regional

UNITED STATES DEPARTMENT OF THE INTERIOR
GREAT PLAINS REGION
P.O. Box 36900
Billings, MT 59107-6900 United States
Phone: 406-247-7610   Fax: 406-247-7793
Website: www.usbr.gov/gp/
Scope: Regional
Description: Federal water agency.
Contact(s):
  Maryanne Bach, Regional Director
  Mark Andersen, Public Affairs Officer

UNITED STATES DEPARTMENT OF THE INTERIOR
KANSAS STATE COOPERATIVE FISH AND WILDLIFE RESEARCH UNIT
205 Leasure Hall
Manhattan, KS 66506-3501 United States
Phone: 785-532-6070   Fax: 785-532-7159
E-mail: kscfwru@ksu.edu
Website: www.ksu.edu/kscfwru
Founded: 1991
Membership: 1–100
Scope: Local, State, Regional
Description: Provides graduate training and research in fisheries and wildlife biology, research, management, ecology, population dynamics, genetics, and related areas. Supported cooperatively by Kansas State University, The Kansas Department of Wildlife and Parks, the National Biological Service and the Wildlife Management Institute.
Publication(s): Annual Report of Activities
Contact(s):
  Jack Cully, Assistant Leader of Wildlife
  Philip Gipson, Leader

UNITED STATES DEPARTMENT OF THE INTERIOR
MISSOURI COOPERATIVE FISH AND WILDLIFE RESEARCH UNIT
302 Anheuser Busch Natural Resources Building
Fisheries and Wildlife
University of Missouri
Columbia, MO 65211-7240 United States
Phone: 573-882-3634   Fax: 573-884-5070
Founded: 1985
Membership: 1–100
Scope: Local, State, Regional, National, International
Description: Established by cooperative agreement among the U.S. Geological Survey, Missouri Department of Conservation, University of Missouri, and Wildlife Management Institute. Primary purpose is research and graduate student education in wildlife conservation, aquatic ecology, and fisheries management areas.
Keyword(s): Water Habitats & Quality, Wildlife & Species
Contact(s):
  Sandy Clark, Administrative Officer; 573-882-3634
  Ronald Drobney, Assistant Leader: Wildlife; 573-882-9420
  David Galat, Assistant Leader: Fisheries; 573-882-9426
  Charles Rabeni, Leader; 573-882-3524

UNITED STATES DEPARTMENT OF THE INTERIOR
MONTANA COOPERATIVE FISHERY RESEARCH UNIT
Dept. Ecology, Montana State University
Bozeman, MT 59717-3460 United States
Phone: 406-994-4549   Fax: 406-994-7479
Website: www.montana/ecology/facility
Scope: National
Description: Applied Fisheries Research

UNITED STATES DEPARTMENT OF THE INTERIOR
MONTANA STATE EXTENSION SERVICES
219 Linfield Hall
Montana State University
Bozeman, MT 59717-2230 United States
Phone: 406-994-5579   Fax: 406-994-5589
E-mail: jknight@montana.edu
Website: www.extn.msu.montana.edu/
Scope: State
Publication(s): MontGuides - Newsletter
Contact(s):
  David Bryant, Vice Provost Director; dbryant@montana.edu
  Jim Johannes, Statewide Director of Programming
  Jim Knight, Extension Wildlife Specialist; Dept. of Animal and Range Science, Montana State University, Bozeman, MT 59717; 406-994-5579; Fax: 406-944-5589

UNITED STATES DEPARTMENT OF THE INTERIOR
NATIONAL PARK SERVICE
U.S. Department of the Interior, 1849 C St., NW
Washington, DC 20240 United States
Phone: 202-208-6843 Fax: 202-219-0910
E-mail: waso-public-affairs@nps.gov
Website: www.nps.gov

Scope: National

Description: Administers 1,378 parks, monuments, and other administrative classifications of national significance for their recreational, historical, and natural values. Manages landmarks programs for natural and historic properties; coordinates Wild and Scenic Rivers System and National Trail System; administers study and grants programs.

Contact(s):
- Rob Arnberger, Alaska Regional Director
- Jerry Belson, Southeast Regional Director; 100 Alabama St., SW, Atlanta Federal Center, Atlanta, GA 30303; 404-562-3100
- Terry Carlstrom, National Capital Regional Director; 1100 Ohio Dr., SW, Washington, DC 20242; 202-619-7256
- Fran Mainella, Director of the National Park Service
- John Reynolds, Pacific West Regional Director; 600 Harrison St., Suite 600, San Francisco, CA 94107; 415-427-1300
- Marie Rust, Northeast Regional Director; U.S. Customs House, 5th Fl., 200 Chestnut St., Philadelphia, PA 19106; 215-597-7013
- William Schenk, Midwest Regional Director; 1709 Jackson St., Omaha, NE 68102; 402-221-3471
- Karen Wade, Intermountain Regional Director
- David Barna, Chief of Office of Public Affairs; 202-208-6843
- Terrell Emmons, Associate Director of Professional Services
- Denis Galvin, Deputy Director; 202-208-3818
- Sue Masica, Associate Director of Budget and Administration; 202-208-6953
- Dick Ring, Associate Director of Park Operations
- Bill Shaddox, Associate Director of Professional Services; 202-208-3264
- C. Sheaffer, Comptroller; 202-208-4566
- Michael Soukup, Associate Director of Natural Resources; 202-208-3884
- Kate Stevenson, Associate Director of Cultural Resources; 202-208-7625

UNITED STATES DEPARTMENT OF THE INTERIOR
NATIONAL PARK SERVICE
ACADIA NATIONAL PARK
P.O. Box 177
Eagle Lake Road
Bar Harbor, ME 04609-0177 United States
Phone: 207-288-0374 Fax: 207-288-8813
E-mail: Acadia_Information@nps.gov
Website: www.nps.gov/acad

Scope: National

UNITED STATES DEPARTMENT OF THE INTERIOR
NATIONAL PARK SERVICE
ARCHES NATIONAL PARK
P.O. Box 907
Moab, UT 84532-0907 United States
Phone: 435-719-2299 Fax: 435-719-2305
E-mail: archinfo@nps.gov
Website: www.nps.gov/arch/

Founded: 1928

Scope: National

UNITED STATES DEPARTMENT OF THE INTERIOR
NATIONAL PARK SERVICE
ASSATEAGUE ISLAND NATIONAL SEASHORE
7206 National Seashore Ln.
Berlin, MD 21811 United States
Phone: 410-641-1441
Website: www.nps.gov/asis/

Scope: National

UNITED STATES DEPARTMENT OF THE INTERIOR
NATIONAL PARK SERVICE
BADLANDS NATIONAL PARK
P.O. Box 6, Rt. 240
Interior, SD 57750 United States
Phone: 605-433-5361 Fax: 605-433-5248

Scope: National

UNITED STATES DEPARTMENT OF THE INTERIOR
NATIONAL PARK SERVICE
BIG BEND NATIONAL PARK
P.O. Box 129
Big Bend National Park, TX 79834 United States
Phone: 915-477-2251 Fax: 915-477-1175
E-mail: BIBEInformation@nps.gov
Website: www.nps.gov/bibe

Founded: 1944

Membership: 1–100

Scope: National, International

Description: National Park Service site National Park

UNITED STATES DEPARTMENT OF THE INTERIOR
NATIONAL PARK SERVICE
BISCAYNE NATIONAL PARK
9700 SW 328th St.
Homestead, FL 33033-5634 United States
Phone: 305-230-1144 Fax: 305-230-1190
E-mail: BISC_information@nps.gov
Website: www.nps.gov/bisc

Founded: 1968

Scope: Local, State, Regional, National, International

Description: Turquoise waters, emerald islands and fish-bejeweled reefs make Biscayne National Park a paradise for wildlife-watching, snorkeling, diving, boating, fishing and other activities. The Park protects a 20 mile stretch of mangrove forest, the clear shallow waters of Biscayne Bay, the northernmost Florida Keys, and a spectacular living coral reef. Superimposed on all of this natural beauty is 10,000 years of human history, including stories of native peoples, shipwrecks, pirates, and pioneers.

UNITED STATES DEPARTMENT OF THE INTERIOR
NATIONAL PARK SERVICE
BRYCE CANYON NATIONAL PARK
P.O. Box 170001
Bryce Canyon, UT 84717-0001 United States
Phone: 435-834-5322 Fax: 435-834-4102
E-mail: brca_reception_area@nps.gov
Website: www.nps.gov/brca/index.htm

Scope: National

Description: National Park Service "to conserve the scenery and the natural and historic objects and the wildlife therein, and to provide for their enjoyment in such manner as will leave them unimpaired for the enjoyment of future generations" NPS Organic Act of 1916.

U.S. FEDERAL AND INTERNATIONAL GOVERNMENT AGENCIES – U

UNITED STATES DEPARTMENT OF THE INTERIOR
NATIONAL PARK SERVICE
CANAVERAL NATIONAL SEASHORE
308 Julia St.
Titusville, FL 32796-3521 United States
Phone: 321-267-1110　　　　Fax: 321-264-2906
Scope: National

UNITED STATES DEPARTMENT OF THE INTERIOR
NATIONAL PARK SERVICE
CANYONLANDS NATIONAL PARK
2282 SW Resource Blvd.
Moab, UT 84532-3298 United States
Phone: 435-719-2313　　　　Fax: 435-719-2300
E-mail: canyinfo@nps.gov
Website: www.nps.gov/cany/index.htm
Founded: 1964
Scope: National
Description: Supervises National Park areas in southeast Utah.

UNITED STATES DEPARTMENT OF THE INTERIOR
NATIONAL PARK SERVICE
CAPE COD NATIONAL SEASHORE
99 Marconi Site Rd.
Wellfleet, MA 02667 United States
Phone: 508-349-3785　　　　Fax: 508-349-9052
Scope: National

UNITED STATES DEPARTMENT OF THE INTERIOR
NATIONAL PARK SERVICE
CAPE HATTERAS NATIONAL SEASHORE
1401 National Park Dr.
Manteo, NC 27954 United States
Phone: 252-473-2111　　　　Fax: 252-473-2595
Website: www.nps.gov/caha
Scope: National
Description: Cape Hatteras National Seashore was authorized in 1937 and includes 74 miles of the barrier islands in northeastern North Carolina.

UNITED STATES DEPARTMENT OF THE INTERIOR
NATIONAL PARK SERVICE
CAPE LOOKOUT NATIONAL SEASHORE
131 Charles St.
Harkers Island, NC 28531 United States
Phone: 252-728-2250　　　　Fax: 252-728-2160
E-mail: CALO_Information@nps.gov
Website: www.nps.gov/calo/
Scope: National
Description: A unit of the National Park Service; the seashore encompasses 56 miles of undeveloped beach on three barrier islands along the North Carolina Outer Banks coastline. Protected within the boundaries are nesting grounds for endangered species such as plovers and sea turtles as well as two historic districts.

UNITED STATES DEPARTMENT OF THE INTERIOR
NATIONAL PARK SERVICE
CAPITOL REEF NATIONAL PARK
HC 70, Box 15
Torrey, UT 84775-9602 United States
Phone: 435-425-3791
Website: www.mps.gov/care
Scope: National

UNITED STATES DEPARTMENT OF THE INTERIOR
NATIONAL PARK SERVICE
CARLSBAD CAVERNS NATIONAL PARK
3225 National Park Hwy.
Carlsbad, NM 88220 United States
Phone: 505-785-2232　　　　Fax: 505-785-2302
E-mail: cave_interpretation@nps.gov
Website: www.nps.gov/cave/home.htm
Founded: 1930
Scope: National

UNITED STATES DEPARTMENT OF THE INTERIOR
NATIONAL PARK SERVICE
CHANNEL ISLANDS NATIONAL PARK
1901 Spinnaker Dr.
Ventura, CA 93001 United States
Phone: 805-658-5730　　　　Fax: 805-658-5799
E-mail: chis_interpretation@nps.gov
Website: www.nps.gov/chis/
Scope: National

UNITED STATES DEPARTMENT OF THE INTERIOR
NATIONAL PARK SERVICE
CHIHUAHUAN DESERT NETWORK
c/o William Reid, Coordinator
HC 60 Box 400
Salt Flat, TX 79847 United States
Phone: 915-828-3251, ext. 250　　　Fax: 915-828-3269
E-mail: bill_reid@nps.gov
Membership: 1–100
Scope: Local, State, Regional
Description: A network of six Chihuahuan Desert national park units coordinating inventory and monitoring work initially to produce a common database.
Keyword(s): Air Quality/Atmosphere, Climate Change, Development/Developing Countries, Ecosystems (precious), Forests/Forestry, Pollution (general), Recreation/Ecotourism, Wildlife & Species

UNITED STATES DEPARTMENT OF THE INTERIOR
NATIONAL PARK SERVICE
CONSERVATION STUDY INSTITUTE
54 Elm St.
Woodstock, VT 05091 United States
Phone: 802-457-3368
E-mail: stewardship@nps.gov
Website: www.nps.gov/csi
Founded: 1990
Scope: Regional, National, International
Description: The Conservation Study Institute was established by the National Park Service in 1998 to enhance leadership in the field of conservation. A partnership with academic, government, and nonprofit organizations, the Institute provides a forum for the National Park Service, the conservation community, and the public to discuss conservation history, contemporary issues and practices, and future directions for the field.
Contact(s):
Nora Mitchell, Director

UNITED STATES DEPARTMENT OF THE INTERIOR
NATIONAL PARK SERVICE
CRATER LAKE NATIONAL PARK
P.O. Box 7
Crater Lake, OR 97604 United States
Phone: 541-594-3100   Fax: 541-594-3010
E-mail: CRLA_Information_Requests@nps.gov
Website: www.nps.gov/crla/
Founded: 1902
Scope: National

UNITED STATES DEPARTMENT OF THE INTERIOR
NATIONAL PARK SERVICE
CUMBERLAND ISLAND NATIONAL SEASHORE
P.O. Box 806
Saint Marys, GA 31558 United States
Phone: 912-882-4336   Fax: 912-673-7747
Scope: National
Description: Cumberland Island National Seashore is one of the best preserved barrier islands on the U. S. Atlantic coast.

UNITED STATES DEPARTMENT OF THE INTERIOR
NATIONAL PARK SERVICE
DEATH VALLEY NATIONAL PARK
P.O. Box 579
Death Valley, CA 92328 United States
Phone: 760-786-2331   Fax: 760-786-3283
Website: www.nps.gov/deva
Scope: National

UNITED STATES DEPARTMENT OF THE INTERIOR
NATIONAL PARK SERVICE
DENALI NATIONAL PARK
P.O. Box 9
Denali Park, AK 99676 United States
Phone: 907-683-9581   Fax: 907-683-9617
E-mail: denali_info@nps.gov
Website: www.nps.gov/dena/
Scope: National

UNITED STATES DEPARTMENT OF THE INTERIOR
NATIONAL PARK SERVICE
DRY TORTUGAS NATIONAL PARK
P.O. Box 6208
Key West, FL 33041 United States
Phone: 305-242-7700   Fax: 305-242-7711
E-mail: DRTO_Information@nps.gov
Website: www.nps.gov/drto/index.htm
Scope: National

UNITED STATES DEPARTMENT OF THE INTERIOR
NATIONAL PARK SERVICE
EVERGLADES NATIONAL PARK
40001 State Rd. 9336
Homestead, FL 33034-6733 United States
Phone: 305-242-7700   Fax: 305-242-7728
E-mail: EVER_Information@nps.gov
Website: www.nps.gov/ever/
Scope: National

UNITED STATES DEPARTMENT OF THE INTERIOR
NATIONAL PARK SERVICE
FIRE ISLAND NATIONAL SEASHORE
120 Laurel St
Patchogue, NY 11772 United States
Phone: 631-289-4810   Fax: 631-289-4898
Website: www.nps.gov/fiis/
Scope: National

UNITED STATES DEPARTMENT OF THE INTERIOR
NATIONAL PARK SERVICE
GATES OF THE ARCTIC NATIONAL PARK
National Park Service (Fairbanks Hqs.)
Fairbanks, AK 99701 United States
Phone: 907-692-5494   Fax: 907-692-5400
E-mail: GAAR_Visitor_Information@nps.gov
Website: www.nps.gov/gaar/index.htm
Scope: National

UNITED STATES DEPARTMENT OF THE INTERIOR
NATIONAL PARK SERVICE
GLACIER BAY NATIONAL PARK
One Park Rd.
Gustavus, AK 99826-0140 United States
Phone: 907-697-2230   Fax: 907-697-2654
E-mail: GLBA_Administration@nps.gov
Website: www.nps.gov/glba/
Scope: National

UNITED STATES DEPARTMENT OF THE INTERIOR
NATIONAL PARK SERVICE
GLACIER NATIONAL PARK
P.O. Box 128
West Glacier, MT 59936 United States
Phone: 406-888-7901
Scope: National

UNITED STATES DEPARTMENT OF THE INTERIOR
NATIONAL PARK SERVICE
GRAND CANYON NATIONAL PARK
P.O. Box 129
Grand Canyon, AZ 86023 United States
Phone: 928-638-7945; 928-638-7888   Fax: 928-638-7797
Website: www.nps.gov/grca/
Scope: National

UNITED STATES DEPARTMENT OF THE INTERIOR
NATIONAL PARK SERVICE
GRAND TETON NATIONAL PARK
MOOSE VISITOR CENTER & PARK HEADQUARTERS
P.O. Drawer 170
Moose, WY 83012-0170 United States
Phone: 307-739-3300   Fax: 307-739-3438
Website: www.nps.gov/grte
Founded: 1929
Scope: Local, State, Regional, National, International
Description: Grand Teton N.P. features the rugged, awe-inspiring Teton Range. Numerous piedmont lakes nestle along the base of the Teton peaks, and the Snake River bisects the broad sagebrush-covered valley of Jackson Hole. Established in 1929 and enlarged in 1950, present-day Grand Teton is 310,000 acres in size. A variety of wildlife - moose, elk, bison, pronghorn, grizzly and black bears, wolves, coyotes, bald

U.S. FEDERAL AND INTERNATIONAL GOVERNMENT AGENCIES – U

eagles, pelicans, trumpeter swans, and sandhill cranes enhance the park's rich ecosystems.

Keyword(s): Ecosystems (precious), Public Lands/Greenspace, Recreation/Ecotourism, Transportation, Water Habitats & Quality, Wildlife & Species

Contact(s):
Stephen Martin, Superintendent; 307-739-3300; Fax: 307-739-3438

UNITED STATES DEPARTMENT OF THE INTERIOR
NATIONAL PARK SERVICE
GREAT BASIN NATIONAL PARK
100 Great Basin National Park
Baker, NV 89311 United States
Phone: 775-234-7331   Fax: 775-234-7269
E-mail: grba_interpretation@nps.gov
Website: www.nps.gov/grba/
Scope: National

UNITED STATES DEPARTMENT OF THE INTERIOR
NATIONAL PARK SERVICE
GREAT SMOKY MOUNTAINS NATIONAL PARK
107 Park Headquarters Rd.
Gatlinburg, TN 37738 United States
Phone: 865-436-1200   Fax: 865-436-1220
E-mail: grsm_smokies_information@nps.gov
Website: www.nps.gov/grsm/pphtml/contacts.html
Scope: National

UNITED STATES DEPARTMENT OF THE INTERIOR
NATIONAL PARK SERVICE
GUADALUPE MOUNTAINS NATIONAL PARK
HC 60, Box 400
Salt Flat, TX 79847-9400 United States
Phone: 915-828-3251   Fax: 915-828-3269
E-mail: GUMO_Superintendent@nps.gov
Scope: National

UNITED STATES DEPARTMENT OF THE INTERIOR
NATIONAL PARK SERVICE
GULF ISLANDS NATIONAL SEASHORE
1801 Gulf Breeze Pkwy.
Gulf Breeze, FL 32563-5000 United States
Phone: 850-934-2600   Fax: 850-932-9654
Website: www.nps.gov/guis
Founded: 1971
Scope: National
Description: One of ten National Seashores in the National Park System

UNITED STATES DEPARTMENT OF THE INTERIOR
NATIONAL PARK SERVICE
HALEAKALA NATIONAL PARK
P.O. Box 369, Makawao
Maui, HI 96768 United States
Phone: 808-572-4400
E-mail: HALE_Interpretation@nps.gov
Website: www.nps.gov/hale/
Scope: National

UNITED STATES DEPARTMENT OF THE INTERIOR
NATIONAL PARK SERVICE
HAWAII VOLCANOES NATIONAL PARK
P.O. Box 52
Hawaii National Park, HI, 96718-0052 United States
Phone: 808-985-6000   Fax: 808-985-6004
E-mail: HAVO_Interpretation@nps.gov
Scope: National

UNITED STATES DEPARTMENT OF THE INTERIOR
NATIONAL PARK SERVICE
HOT SPRINGS NATIONAL PARK
P.O. Box 1860
Hot Springs, AR 71902 United States
Phone: 501-624-3383 501-624-2701 Fax: 501-624-3458
E-mail: HOSP_Interpretation@nps.gov
Website: www.nps.gov/hosp/
Scope: National

UNITED STATES DEPARTMENT OF THE INTERIOR
NATIONAL PARK SERVICE
ISLE ROYALE NATIONAL PARK
800 E. Lakeshore Dr.
Houghton, MI 49931-1895 United States
Phone: 906-482-0984   Fax: 906-487-7170
E-mail: ISRO_ParksInfo@nps.gov
Website: www.nps.gov/isro
Scope: National

UNITED STATES DEPARTMENT OF THE INTERIOR
NATIONAL PARK SERVICE
JOSHUA TREE NATIONAL PARK
74485 National Park Dr.
Twenty-nine Palms, CA 92277 United States
Phone: 760-367-5502   Fax: 760-367-6392
Website: www.nps.gov/jotr
Scope: National

UNITED STATES DEPARTMENT OF THE INTERIOR
NATIONAL PARK SERVICE
KATMAI NATIONAL PARK
Katmai NP&P Field Headquarters
P.O. Box 7, #1 King Salmon Mall
King Salmon, AK 99613 United States
Phone: 907-246-3305   Fax: 907-246-2116
E-mail: KATM_Visitor_Information@nps.gov
Website: www.nps.gov/katm/index.htm
Scope: National

UNITED STATES DEPARTMENT OF THE INTERIOR
NATIONAL PARK SERVICE
KENAI FJORDS NATIONAL PARK
P.O. Box 1727
Seward, AK 99664 United States
Phone: 907-224-2132   Fax: 907-224-2144
E-mail: KEFJ_Superintendent@nps.gov
Scope: National

UNITED STATES DEPARTMENT OF THE INTERIOR
NATIONAL PARK SERVICE
KOBUK VALLEY NATIONAL PARK
P.O. Box 1029
Kotzebue, AK 99752 United States
Phone: 907-442-3890   Fax: 907-442-8316
E-mail: WEAR_Webmail@nps.gov
Website: www.nps.gov/kova/index.htm
Scope: National

UNITED STATES DEPARTMENT OF THE INTERIOR
NATIONAL PARK SERVICE
LAKE CLARK NATIONAL PARK
Field Headquarters
Port Alsworth, AK 99653 United States
Phone: 907-271-3751   Fax: 907-781-2119
E-mail: LACL_Visitor_Information@nps.gov
Website: www.nps.gov/lacl/
Scope: National

UNITED STATES DEPARTMENT OF THE INTERIOR
NATIONAL PARK SERVICE
LASSEN VOLCANIC NATIONAL PARK
P.O. Box 100, 38050 Hwy. 36E
Mineral, CA 96063 United States
Phone: 530-595-4444   Fax: 530-595-3262
E-mail: LAVO_information@nps.gov
Website: www.nps.gov/lavo/
Founded: 1916
Scope: National

UNITED STATES DEPARTMENT OF THE INTERIOR
NATIONAL PARK SERVICE
MAMMOTH CAVE NATIONAL PARK
P.O. Box 7
Mammoth Cave, KY 42259 United States
Phone: 270-758-2251   Fax: 270-758-2349
E-mail: maca_park_information@nps.gov
Website: www.nps.gov/maca/home.htm
Founded: 1941
Scope: National, International
Description: Mammoth Cave National Park was established to preserve the cave system, including Mammoth Cave (the world's longest cave), scenic river valleys of Green and Nolin Rivers, and a section of the hilly country of south central Kentucky. Designated a World Heritage Site in 1981, and an International Biosphere Reserve in 1990.
Keyword(s): Air Quality/Atmosphere, Ecosystems (precious), Forests/Forestry, Public Lands/Greenspace, Recreation/Ecotourism, Reduce/Reuse/Recycle, Water Habitats & Quality, Wildlife & Species

UNITED STATES DEPARTMENT OF THE INTERIOR
NATIONAL PARK SERVICE
MESA VERDE NATIONAL PARK
Natural Resource Office
P.O. Box 8
Mesa Verde, CO 81330-0008 United States
Phone: 970-529-5069   Fax: 970-529-5071
E-mail: george_san_miguel@nps.gov
Website: www.nps.gov/meve
Founded: 1906
Scope: National
Description: The park's branch of natural resource management is responsible for ensuring that Mesa Verde's native plant and animal life, waters, air, soil, mineral, paleontological resources, and the natural processes that sustain them are left unimpaired for this and future generations.
Keyword(s): Air Quality/Atmosphere, Ecosystems (precious), Forests/Forestry, Recreation/Ecotourism, Water Habitats & Quality, Wildlife & Species

UNITED STATES DEPARTMENT OF THE INTERIOR
NATIONAL PARK SERVICE
MOUNT RAINIER NATIONAL PARK
Tahoma Woods, Star Route
Ashford, WA 98304-9751 United States
Phone: 360-569-2211   Fax: 360-569-2170
E-mail: MORAInfo@nps.gov
Website: www.nps.gov/mora/index.htm
Founded: 1899
Scope: Local, State, Regional, National
Description: Unit of the National Park System, icon of the Pacific Northwest
Keyword(s): Air Quality/Atmosphere, Ecosystems (precious), Forests/Forestry, Land Issues, Public Lands/Greenspace, Recreation/Ecotourism, Reduce/Reuse/Recycle, Water Habitats & Quality, Wildlife & Species

UNITED STATES DEPARTMENT OF THE INTERIOR
NATIONAL PARK SERVICE
NATIONAL PARK OF AMERICAN SAMOA
Superintendent
National Park of American Samoa
Pago Pago, AS 96799 United States
Phone: 011-684-633-7082   Fax: 011-684-633-7085
E-mail: NPSA_Administration@nps.gov
Website: www.nps.gov/npsa/home.htm
Scope: National

UNITED STATES DEPARTMENT OF THE INTERIOR
NATIONAL PARK SERVICE
NORTH CASCADES NATIONAL PARK
810 State Rte. 20
Sedro Woolley, WA 98284-9314 United States
Phone: 360-856-5700
Scope: National

UNITED STATES DEPARTMENT OF THE INTERIOR
NATIONAL PARK SERVICE
OLYMPIC NATIONAL PARK
600 E. Park Ave.
Port Angeles, WA 98362-6798 United States
Phone: 360-565-3130   Fax: 360-565-3147
Website: www.olympic.national-park.com/htm
Scope: National

UNITED STATES DEPARTMENT OF THE INTERIOR
NATIONAL PARK SERVICE
PADRE ISLAND NATIONAL SEASHORE
P.O. Box 181300
Corpus Christi, TX 78480-1300 United States
Phone: 361-949-8173   Fax: 361-949-8023
Website: www.nps.gov/pais/
Scope: National
Contact(s):
Jack Whitworth, Superintendent; 361-949-8173; pais_superintendent@nps.gov

UNITED STATES DEPARTMENT OF THE INTERIOR
NATIONAL PARK SERVICE
PETRIFIED FOREST NATIONAL PARK
P.O. Box 2217
Petrified Forest National Park, AZ 86028 United States
Phone: 928-524-6228   Fax: 928-524-3567
E-mail: PEFO_Superintendent@nps.gov
Website: www.nps.gov/pefo/

Founded: 1962
Scope: National

UNITED STATES DEPARTMENT OF THE INTERIOR
NATIONAL PARK SERVICE
POINT REYES NATIONAL SEASHORE
Point Reyes, CA 94956 United States
Phone: 415-464-5100   Fax: 415-663-8132
Website: www.nps.gov/pore

Founded: 1962
Scope: National
Publication(s): Visitors Guide
Contact(s):
  Don Neubacher, Superintendent

UNITED STATES DEPARTMENT OF THE INTERIOR
NATIONAL PARK SERVICE
REDWOOD NATIONAL PARK
1111 Second St.
Crescent City, CA 95531 United States
Phone: 707-464-6101, ext. 5001   Fax: 707-464-1812
E-mail: REDW_Information@nps.gov
Website: www.nps.gov/redw/

Scope: National

UNITED STATES DEPARTMENT OF THE INTERIOR
NATIONAL PARK SERVICE
ROCKY MOUNTAIN NATIONAL PARK
1000 U.S. Hwy. 36
Estes Park, CO 80517-8397 United States
Phone: 970-586-1206   Fax: 970-586-1256
E-mail: ROMO_Superintendent@nps.gov
Website: www.nps.gov/romo

Founded: 1915
Scope: National
Description: Rocky Mt. Nat'l Park, located in Colorado, preserves one of the most scenic stretches of the southern Rocky Mountains.

UNITED STATES DEPARTMENT OF THE INTERIOR
NATIONAL PARK SERVICE
SEQUOIA AND KINGS CANYON NATIONAL PARK
47050 Generals Hwy.
Three Rivers, CA 93271-9651 United States
Phone: 559-565-3341   Fax: 559-565-3730
E-mail: SEKI_Interpretation@nps.gov
Website: www.nps.gov/seki/

Scope: National

UNITED STATES DEPARTMENT OF THE INTERIOR
NATIONAL PARK SERVICE
SHENANDOAH NATIONAL PARK
3655 U.S. Hwy. 211-E
Luray, VA 22835-9036 United States
Phone: 540-999-3400

Scope: National

UNITED STATES DEPARTMENT OF THE INTERIOR
NATIONAL PARK SERVICE
SONORAN DESERT NETWORK
125 Biological Sciences East
University of Arizona
Tucson, AZ 85719 United States
Phone: 520-670-5834   Fax: 520-670-5612
E-mail: Andy_Hubbard@nps.gov

Founded: 2001
Scope: Regional
Description: The Sonoran Desert Network conducts long-term monitoring of ecological resources on 11 national parks in southern Arizona and New Mexico: Casa Grande Ruins National Monument, Chiricahua National Monument, Coronado National Memorial, Fort Bowie National Historic Site, Gila Cliff Dwellings National Monument, Montezuma Castle National Monument, Organ Pipe Cactus National Monument, Saguaro National Park, Tonto National Monument, Tumacacori National Historic Park, and Tuzigoot National Monument.
Keyword(s): Air Quality/Atmosphere, Ecosystems (precious), Public Lands/Greenspace, Water Habitats & Quality, Wildlife & Species
Contact(s):
  Andy Hubbard, Ecologist; Andy_Hubbard@nps.gov
  Debbie Angell, Data Manager; Deborah_Angell@nps.gov

UNITED STATES DEPARTMENT OF THE INTERIOR
NATIONAL PARK SERVICE
THEODORE ROOSEVELT NATIONAL PARK
P.O. Box 7, 315 2nd Ave.
Medora, ND 58645-0007 United States
Phone: 701-623-4466   Fax: 701-623-4840
E-mail: Thro_Information@nps.gov
Website: www.nps.gov

Founded: 1947
Scope: National
Description: The colorful North Dakota Badlands provides the scenic backdrop to Theodore Roosevelt National Park, which memorializes the 26th president for his outstanding contributions to conservation and environmental efforts. The Little Missouri River has shaped this land which is home to variety of plants and animals.
Keyword(s): Air Quality/Atmosphere, Land Issues, Recreation/Ecotourism, Wildlife & Species

UNITED STATES DEPARTMENT OF THE INTERIOR
NATIONAL PARK SERVICE
VIRGIN ISLANDS NATIONAL PARK
P.O. Box 710, Cruz Bay
Saint John, VI 00830 United States
Phone: 340-775-6201   Fax: 340-693-9301
E-mail: viis_superintendent@nps.gov
Website: www.virgin.islands.national-park.com/

Scope: National

UNITED STATES DEPARTMENT OF THE INTERIOR
NATIONAL PARK SERVICE
VOYAGEURS NATIONAL PARK
3131 Hwy. 53 South
International Falls, MN 56649-8904 United States
Phone: 218-283-9821   Fax: 218-285-7407
E-mail: VOYA_Superintendent@nps.gov
Website: www.nps.gov/voya/

Scope: National

UNITED STATES DEPARTMENT OF THE INTERIOR
NATIONAL PARK SERVICE
WIND CAVE NATIONAL PARK
RR 1, Box 190
Hot Springs, SD 57747-9430 United States
Phone: 605-745-4600　　　Fax: 605-745-4207
E-mail: phyllis_cremonini@nps.gov
Website: www.nps.gov/wica/index.htm
Scope: National

UNITED STATES DEPARTMENT OF THE INTERIOR
NATIONAL PARK SERVICE
WRANGELL-ST. ELIAS NATIONAL PARK
106.8 Richardson Hwy.
P.O. Box 439
Copper Center, AK 99573-0439 United States
Phone: 907-822-5234　　　Fax: 907-822-7216
E-mail: wrst_interpretation@nps.gov
Website: www.nps.gov/wrst/
Founded: 1980
Scope: Local, State, Regional, National, International

UNITED STATES DEPARTMENT OF THE INTERIOR
NATIONAL PARK SERVICE
YELLOWSTONE NATIONAL PARK
Suzanne Lewis
P.O. Box 168
Yellowstone, WY 82190 United States
Phone: 307-344-7381　　　Fax: 307-344-2005
E-mail: yell_superintendent@nps.gov
Website: www.nps.gov/yell
Scope: National
Keyword(s): Air Quality/Atmosphere, Ecosystems (precious), Forests/Forestry, Land Issues, Pollution (general), Recreation/Ecotourism, Reduce/Reuse/Recycle, Transportation, Water Habitats & Quality, Wildlife & Species
Contact(s):
　Suzanne Lewis, Superintendant; 307-344-7381; yell_superintendent@nps.gov

UNITED STATES DEPARTMENT OF THE INTERIOR
NATIONAL PARK SERVICE
YOSEMITE NATIONAL PARK
P.O. Box 577, Administration Bldg.
Yosemite National Park, CA 95389 United States
Phone: 209-372-0200　　　Fax: 209-372-0220
E-mail: yose_web_manager@nps.gov
Website: www.nps.gov/yose/
Scope: National

UNITED STATES DEPARTMENT OF THE INTERIOR
NATIONAL PARK SERVICE
ZION NATIONAL PARK
SR 9
Springdale, UT 84767 United States
Phone: 435-772-3256　　　Fax: 435-772-3426
E-mail: ZION_park_information@nps.gov
Website: www.nps.gov/zion/index.htm
Scope: National
Contact(s):
　Marty Ott, Manager; 435-772-0142; marty_ott@nps.gov

UNITED STATES DEPARTMENT OF THE INTERIOR
NORTH DAKOTA STATE UNIVERSITY EXTENSION SERVICE
North Dakota State University
Fargo, ND 58105-5437 United States
Phone: 701-231-7171　　　Fax: 701-231-8378
Website: www.ag.ndsu.nodak.edu
Scope: State
Contact(s):
　Sharon Anderson, Director, Extension Service; ext-dir@ndsuext.nodak.edu
　Cole Gustafson, Director, North Dakota Agricultural Experiment Station; NDSU, Box 5655, Fargo, ND 58105-5655; 701-231-7655; Fax: 701-231-8520; exp-dir@ndsuext.nodak.edu
　Kevin Sedivec, Natural Resource Information; NDSU, P.O. Box 5053, Fargo, ND 58105

UNITED STATES DEPARTMENT OF THE INTERIOR
OFFICE OF SURFACE MINING RECLAMATION AND ENFORCEMENT
Department of Interior, Interior South Bldg., 1951 Constitution Ave., NW
Washington, DC 20240 United States
Phone: 202-208-2719
E-mail: getinfo@osmre.gov
Website: www.osmre.gov/
Description: Established by the Surface Mining Control and Reclamation Act of 1977 to administer the nationwide program to protect society and the environment from adverse effects of coal mining operations, to establish national standards for regulating the surface environmental effects of coal mining, to support state implementation of such regulatory programs, and to promote reclamation of abandoned mine lands.

UNITED STATES DEPARTMENT OF THE INTERIOR
OREGON COOPERATIVE FISH AND WILDLIFE RESEARCH UNIT
104 Nash Hall
Oregon State University
Corvallis, OR 97331-3803 United States
Phone: 541-737-4531　　　Fax: 541-737-3590
E-mail: or_sfwru@orst.edu
Website: www.orst.edu/dept/fish_wild/
Membership: 1–100
Scope: State, Regional, National
Description: Research focus on physiological, ecological, and genetic factors affecting production and performance of freshwater fishes. The staff consists of two permanent and two-three other Ph.D. level scientists, as well as graduate students and technicians.
Keyword(s): Water Habitats & Quality, Wildlife & Species
Contact(s):
　Carl Schreck, Leader
　Hiram Li, Assistant Leader
　Robert Anthony, Wildlife Leader
　Daniel Roby, Wildlife Assistant Leader

UNITED STATES DEPARTMENT OF THE INTERIOR
UNITED STATES GEOLOGICAL SURVEY
12201 Sunrise Valley Drive National Center
Reston, VA 20192 United States
Phone: 703-648-4000
Website: www.usgs.gov
Founded: 1879
Scope: National

Description: The Geological Survey works in cooperation with more than 2,000 organizations across the country to provide reliable, impartial, scientific information to resource managers, planners, and other customers.

Contact(s):
John Buffington, Western Regional Director; 909 First Ave., 8th Flr., Seattle, WA 98104; 206-220-4600
Thomas Casadevall, Central Regional Director; Denver Federal Center, Mail Stop 150, Denver, CO 80225; 303-202-4740
Charles Groat, Director; 703-648-7411
Bonnie McGregor, Eastern Regional Director; 1700 Leetown Rd., Kearneysville, WV 25430; 304-724-4521
S. Cook, Chief, Office of Equal Opportunity; 703-648-7770
James Devine, Senior Advisor, Science Applications; 703-648-4423
Dennis Fenn, Associate Director for Biology; 703-648-4050
Trudy Harlow, Public Affairs Officer; 703-648-4483
Robert Hirsch, Associate Director for Water; 703-648-5215
Amy Holley, Senior Advisor to the Director; 703-648-4411
Robert Hosenfeld, Chief, Office of Personnel; 703-648-7442
P. Leahy, Associate Director for Geology; 703-648-6600
Barbara Ryan, Associate Director of Operations; 703-648-7413
Carl Shapiro, Strategic Chief Planning, Analysis
Barbara Wainman, Chief, Office of Communications; 703-648-5750
Timothy West, Congressional Liaison Officer; 703-648-4300

UNITED STATES DEPARTMENT OF THE INTERIOR
UNITED STATES GEOLOGICAL SURVEY
BIOLOGICAL RESOURCES DIVISION
12201 Sunrise Valley Dr., MS-300
Reston, VA 20192 United States
Phone: 703-648-4050   Fax: 703-648-4042
Website: biology.usgs.gov/

Description: The Biological Resources Division works with others to provide the scientific understanding and technologies needed to manage the Nation's biological resources.

Contact(s):
Dennis Fenn, Chief Biologist; 703-648-4050
William Gregg, Chief of International Affairs; 703-648-4067
Susan Haseltine, Deputy Chief Biologist for Science; 703-648-4060
Suzzette Kimball, Regional Biologist; Eastern Regional Office, 1700 Leetown Rd., Kearneysville, WV 25430; 304-724-4500
J. Ludke, Regional Biologist; Central Regional Office, Denver Federal Center, P.O. Box 25046, Bldg. 20, Mailstop 300, Denver, CO 80225-0046; 303-236-2730

UNITED STATES DEPARTMENT OF THE INTERIOR
UNITED STATES GEOLOGICAL SURVEY
FOREST AND RANGELAND ECOSYSTEM SCIENCE CENTER
777 NW 9th Street
Suite 400
Corvallis, OR 97330 United States
Phone: 541-750-1047
Website: http://fresc.usgs.gov

Founded: 1994

Scope: Regional, International

Description: The Forest and Rangeland Ecosystem Science Center provides scientific understanding and the technology needed to support sound management and conservation of our nation's natural resources, with emphasis on western ecosystems.

Contact(s):
Ruth Jacobs, Technical Information Specialist; ruth_jacobs@usgs.gov

UNITED STATES DEPARTMENT OF THE INTERIOR
UNITED STATES GEOLOGICAL SURVEY
IOWA COOPERATIVE FISH AND WILDLIFE RESEARCH UNIT
11 Science Hall II
Department of Animal Ecology
Iowa State University
Ames, IA 50011-3221 United States
Phone: 515-294-3056   Fax: 515-294-5468
E-mail: coopunit@iastate.edu
Website: www.cfwru.iastate.edu

Founded: 1932

Membership: 1–100

Scope: Local, State, Regional, National

Description: The Iowa Cooperative Fish and Wildlife Research Unit is a joint venture of the U.S. Geological Survey, the Iowa Department of Natural Resources, Iowa State University, and the Wildlife Management Institute. The Unit was established to research and to provide education for fisheries and wildlife professionals.

Publication(s): Annual Report

Keyword(s): Water Habitats & Quality, Wildlife & Species

Contact(s):
David Otis, Unit Leader
Rolf Koford, Assistant Unit Leader - Wildlife
Clay Pierce, Assistant Unit Leader - Fisheries

UNITED STATES DEPARTMENT OF THE INTERIOR
UNITED STATES GEOLOGICAL SURVEY
NEW MEXICO COOPERATIVE FISH AND WILDLIFE RESEARCH UNIT
P.O. Box 30003, MSC 4901
New Mexico State University
Las Cruces, NM 88003-0003 United States
Phone: 505-646-6053   Fax: 505-646-1281
E-mail: coopunit@nmsu.edu
Website: leopold.nmsu.edu/fwscoop

Founded: 1988

Scope: National

Description: Supported cooperatively by U.S.G.S. Biological Resources, New Mexico State University, New Mexico Department of Game and Fish, the Wildlife Management Institute, and U.S. Fish and Wildlife Service, the New Mexico Research Unit's primary purpose is research on management and conservation of fish and wildlife species and graduate research training in fisheries and wildlife resources.

Keyword(s): Land Issues, Pollution (general), Water Habitats & Quality, Wildlife & Species

Contact(s):
Louis Bender, Assistant Leader - Wildlife; lbender@nmsu.edu
Colleen Caldwell, Assistant Leader - Fisheries; ccaldwel@nmsu.edu
Bruce Thompson, Unit Leader; bthompso@nmsu.edu

UNITED STATES DEPARTMENT OF THE INTERIOR
UNITED STATES GEOLOGICAL SURVEY
WESTERN REGION
909 First Avenue
Suite 704
Seattle, WA 98104 United States
Phone: 206-220-4578   Fax: 206-220-4570
Website: www.usgs.gov/

Founded: 1879

Membership: 1,001–10,000

Scope: State, Regional, National, International

Description: The Western Region includes 9 Western states: CA, OR, WA, ID, UT, NV, AZ, Alaska, Hawaii and U.S. Pacific

Territories. Science includes Geological, Hazards, Water Resources, Biological and Geographic disciplines.

Keyword(s): Agriculture/Farming, Air Quality/Atmosphere, Climate Change, Ecosystems (precious), Energy, Forests/Forestry, Land Issues, Oceans/Coasts/Beaches, Population, Public Lands/Greenspace, Recreation/Ecotourism, Water Habitats & Quality, Wildlife & Species, Oth

Contact(s):
John Buffington, Regional Director
Stephanie Hanna, Communications; 206-220-4573; Fax: 206-220-4570; shanna@usgs.gov
William Lukas, Outreach; 206-220-4576; Fax: 206-220-4570; wlukas@usgs.gov

UNITED STATES DEPARTMENT OF THE INTERIOR
UTAH COOPERATIVE FISH AND WILDLIFE RESEARCH UNIT
College of Natural Resources, Utah State University
Logan, UT 84322-5210 United States
Phone: 435-797-2509   Fax: 435-797-4025
E-mail: utcoop@cc.usu.edu
Website: www.ella.nr.usu.edu/utcop/index.html

Founded: 1935
Membership: 1–100
Scope: National
Description: The unit conducts research and training in all aspects of fishery and wildlife biology and management.
Keyword(s): Land Issues, Recreation/Ecotourism, Reduce/Reuse/Recycle, Water Habitats & Quality, Wildlife & Species

Contact(s):
Esther Biesinger, Financial Assistant; 435-797-2467
John Bissonette, Leader; 435-797-2511; johnbissonette@cnor.usu.edu
Thomas Edwards,, Assistant Leader of Wildlife; 435-797-2529

UNITED STATES DEPARTMENT OF THE INTERIOR
WASHINGTON COOPERATIVE FISH AND WILDLIFE RESEARCH UNIT
SCHOOL OF AQUATIC AND FISHERY SCIENCES
University of Washington
Box 355020
Seattle, WA 98195-5020 United States
Phone: 206-543-6475   Fax: 206-616-9012
E-mail: washcoop@u.washington.edu
Website: www.fish.washington.edu/wacfwru/

Founded: 1988
Scope: Local, State, Regional, National, International
Description: The goals of the WACFWRU are: (1) conduct research in support of the Department of the Interior and Washington State; (2) train graduate students in fisheries and wildlife science by facilitating research support and by teaching; and (3) disseminate research results to the scientific community, management agencies, and the general public.
Keyword(s): Pollution (general), Water Habitats & Quality, Wildlife & Species

Contact(s):
David Beauchamp, Assistant Unit Leader of Fishery
Christian Grue, Leader
Glenn Vanblaricom, Assistant Leader of Wildlife

UNITED STATES DEPARTMENT OF TRANSPORTATION
Office of Public Affairs, Nassif Bldg., 400 7th St., SW
Washington, DC 20590 United States
Phone: 202-366-4000
Website: www.dot.gov
Founded: 1967
Membership: 10,001–100,000
Scope: National
Description: Composed of these main elements: The United States Coast Guard, Federal Aviation Administration, Federal Highway Administration, Federal Railroad Administration, Maritime Administration, St. Lawrence Seaway Development Corporation, National Highway Traffic Safety Administration, Federal Transit Administration, and Research and Special Programs Administration. Major objectives are to develop and improve a coordinated national transportation system consistent with other national objectives.
Publication(s): Merchant Vessels of the United States (United States Coast Guard), Public Roads (Federal Highway Administration)

Contact(s):
Norm Mineta, Assistant to the Secretary and Director of Public Affairs
Mortimer Downey, Deputy Secretary; 202-366-2222

UNITED STATES DEPARTMENT OF TRANSPORTATION
COAST GUARD
2100 2nd St., SW
Washington, DC 20593-0001 United States
Phone: 202-267-2229   Fax: 202-267-4696

Scope: State
Contact(s):
Timothy Josiah, Chief of Staff; 202-267-1642

UNITED STATES DEPARTMENT OF TRANSPORTATION
FEDERAL AVIATION ADMINISTRATION
FOB 10A 800 Independence Ave., SW
Washington, DC 20591 United States
Phone: 202-267-3484
Website: www.faa.gov

Description: Charged with regulating air commerce to foster aviation safety; promoting civil aviation and a national system of airports; achieving efficient use of navigable airspace; and developing and operating a common system of air traffic control and air navigation for both civilian and military aircraft.

Contact(s):
Jane Garvey, Administrator; 202-267-3111

UNITED STATES DEPARTMENT OF TRANSPORTATION
FEDERAL HIGHWAY ADMINISTRATION
OFFICE OF NATURAL AND HUMAN ENVIRONMENT
400 7th St., SW, Rm. 3240
Washington, DC 20590 United States
Phone: 202-366-9173
Website: fhwa.dot.gov/environment/index.htm

Scope: National
Description: We serve as FHWA's advocate and national leader for natural and human environmental protection and enhancement. We focus on programs associated with the natural environment and the built environment, including transportation enhancements, bicycle/pedestrian, recreational trails, and scenic byway programs.
Keyword(s): Air Quality/Atmosphere, Climate Change, Ecosystems (precious), Land Issues, Oceans/Coasts/Beaches, Pollution (general), Recreation/Ecotourism, Reduce/Reuse/Recycle, Transportation, Water Habitats & Quality, Wildlife & Species

Contact(s):
James Shrouds, Director, Office of Natural and Human Environment

UNITED STATES DEPARTMENT OF TRANSPORTATION
FEDERAL RAILROAD ADMINISTRATION
1120 Vermont Ave, NW
Washington, DC 20590 United States
Phone: 202-366-4000   Fax: 202-493-6169
Website: www.fra.dot.gov

Founded: 1967

Scope: National

Description: The FRA promulgates and enforces rail safety regulations, administers financial assistance programs for designated railroads, conducts research and development in support of improved railroad safety and national rail transportation policy, as well as monitors rail passenger service nationwide, and consolidates government support of rail transportation activities.

Contact(s):
S. Lindsey, Chief Counsel
Allan Rutter, Administrator of Federal RR Administration

UNITED STATES DEPARTMENT OF TRANSPORTATION
FEDERAL TRANSIT ADMINISTRATION
400 7th St., SW
Washington, DC 20590 United States
Phone: 202-366-0785
Website: www.fta.dot.gov/

Description: Seeks to improve the environmental standards of American cities through grant programs which extend and modernize existing urban mass transit equipment and facilities and which study, develop, and test new equipment and concepts in urban mass transit applications and operations.

Keyword(s): Transportation

Contact(s):
Bruce Frame, Director, Office of Public Affairs; 202-366-4319
Arthur Lopez, Director, Office of Civil Rights; 202-366-4018
Charlotte Adams, Associate Administrator for Planning; 202-366-4033
Dorrie Aldrich, Associate Administrator for Administration; 202-366-4007
Nuria Fernandez, Deputy Administrator of Office of Administration; 202-366-4325
Mary Knapp, Executive Information, Office of Public Affairs; 202-366-9788
Gordon Linton, Administrator of Office of the Administrator; 202-366-4040
Gregory McBride, Deputy Chief Counsel; 202-366-4063
Patrick Reilly, Chief Counsel; 202-366-4063
Janet Sahaj, Deputy Associate Administrator; 202-366-4020
John Spencer, Deputy Associate Administrator; 202-366-1691
Edward Thomas, Associate Administrator for Research Demonstration and Innovation; 202-366-4052
Hiram Walker, Associate Administrator for Program Management; 202-366-4020
Michael Winter, Associate Administrator for Budget and Policy; 202-366-4050
Timothy Wolgast, Deputy Associate Administrator; 202-366-4007
A. Yen, Deputy Associate Administrator; 202-366-4991

UNITED STATES DEPARTMENT OF TRANSPORTATION
NATIONAL HIGHWAY TRAFFIC SAFETY ADMINISTRATION
Nassif Bldg., 400 7th St., SW
Washington, DC 20590 United States
Phone: 202-366-9550   Fax: 202-366-7402
Website: www.nhtsa.dot.gov/

Scope: State

Contact(s):
Donald Bischoff, Executive Director; 202-366-2111
Ricardo Martinez, Administrator; 202-366-1836
James Nichols, Associate Administrator for Traffic Safety Programs, Acting; 202-366-1755
Raymond Owings, Associate Administrator for Research and Development; 202-366-1537
Philip Recht, Deputy Director; 202-366-2775
Frank Seales, Chief Counsel; 202-366-9511
L. Shelton, Associate Administrator for Safety Performance Standards; 202-366-1810
Herman Simms, Associate Administrator for Administration, Acting; 202-366-1788
William Walsh, Associate Administrator for Plans and Policy; 202-366-2550
Kenneth Weinstein, Associate Administrator for Safety Assurance; 202-366-9700

UNITED STATES DEPARTMENT OF TRANSPORTATION
SAINT LAWRENCE SEAWAY DEVELOPMENT CORPORATION
400 7th St. SW, Suite 5424
Washington, DC 20590 United States
Phone: 202-366-0091   Fax: 202-366-7147
Website: www.greatlakes-seaway.com

Membership: 1-100

Scope: State

Publication(s): Seaway Compass

Contact(s):
Tim Downey, Deputy Director of Office of Congressional and Public Affairs; P.O. Box 44090, Washington, DC 20026-4090; 202-366-0110
Albert Jacquez, Administrator; 202-366-0091

UNITED STATES DEPARTMENT OF TREASURY
1500 Pennsylvania Ave., NW
Washington, DC 20220 United States
Phone: 202-622-2000   Fax: 202-622-1999
Website: www.ustreas.gov

Scope: National

Description: The basic functions of the Department of the Treasury include: economic and fiscal policy; government accounting, cash, and debt management; international economic policy; and enforcement of customs and trade laws.

UNITED STATES ENVIRONMENTAL PROTECTION AGENCY
ADMINISTRATION AND RESOURCES MANAGEMENT
1200 Pennsylvania Avenue NW
Washington, DC 20460 United States
Phone: 202-564-4700
Website: www.epa.gov/oarm

Contact(s):
Mark Day, Director of Information Resources Management; 202-260-4465
William Henderson, Director of Administration, Cincinnati, OH; 513-569-7910
William Laxton, Director of Administration & Resources Management, Research; 919-541-2258
David O'Connor, Human Resources & Organizational Services Director; 202-260-4467

UNITED STATES ENVIRONMENTAL PROTECTION AGENCY
ENFORCEMENT AND COMPLIANCE
1200 Pennsylvania Avenue NW
Washington, DC 20460 United States
Phone: 202-564-4700
Website: www.epa.gov/oeca/

Scope: National

Description: Enforcement and compliance policy issues.

Contact(s):
Barry Breen, Site Remediation Enforcement Director; 202-564-5110
Barry Hill, Environmental Justice Director, Acting; 202-564-2515; Fax: 202-501-0740
Richard Sanderson, Federal Activities Director; 202-564-2400
Eric Schaffer, Regulatory Enforcement Director; 202-564-2220
Gregory Snyder, Compliance Director; 202-564-2461

UNITED STATES ENVIRONMENTAL PROTECTION AGENCY
OFFICE OF RESEARCH AND DEVELOPMENT
1200 Pennsylvania Avenue, N.W.
Ariel Rios Building (8101R)
Washington, DC 20460 United States
Phone: 202-564-6620   Fax: 202-565-2430
Website: www.epa.gov/ord

Founded: 1970
Membership: 1,001–10,000
Scope: National
Description: U.S. EPA's Office of Research and Development (ORD) conducts research on ways to prevent pollution, protect human health, and reduce risk. ORD laboratories, research centers and offices across the country help to improve the quality of the air, water and soil and the way in which we use our resources.
Keyword(s): Air Quality/Atmosphere, Climate Change, Ecosystems (precious), Ethics/Environmental Justice, Forests/Forestry, Oceans/Coasts/Beaches, Pollution (general), Public Health, Reduce/Reuse/Recycle, Water Habitats & Quality

Contact(s):
Mike Moore, External Relations; 202-564-6722; Fax: 202-565-2431; moore.mike@epa.gov
William Farland, Acting Deputy Assistant Administrator

UNITED STATES ENVIRONMENTAL PROTECTION AGENCY
PREVENTION, PESTICIDES, AND TOXIC SUBSTANCES
1200 Pennsylvania Avenue NW
Ariel Rios Bldg.
Washington, DC 20460 United States
E-mail: oppt.homepage@epa.gov
Website: www.epa.gov/opptsfrs

Contact(s):
Marcia Mulkey, Pesticide Programs Director; 703-305-7090
William Sanders, Pollution Prevention and Toxics Director; 202-260-3810
Stephen Johnson, Assistant Administrator; 202-260-2902

UNITED STATES ENVIRONMENTAL PROTECTION AGENCY
SCIENCE POLICY
1200 Pennsylvania Avenue NW
Washington, DC 20460 United States
Phone: 202-564-4700
Website: www.epa.gov/osp/spc

Contact(s):
Leonard Fleckenstein, Sustainable Ecosystems and Communities Director, Acting; 202-260-4002
Thomas Kelly, Regulatory Management and Information Director; 202-260-4335
Albert McGarland, Economy and Environment Director; 202-260-3354
Pamela Sterling, Program Support and Resource Management Director; 202-260-4335

UNITED STATES ENVIRONMENTAL PROTECTION AGENCY
WATER, UNITED STATES
Website: www.epa.gov/ow

Contact(s):
Jeff Besougloff, American Indian Environmental Directory; 202-260-7939
Michael Cook, Wastewater Management Director; 202-260-5850
Cynthia Dougherty, Ground Water and Drinking Water Director; 202-260-5543
Geoffery Grubbs, Science and Technology Director; 202-260-5400
Robert Wayland, Wetlands, Oceans, and Watersheds Director; 202-260-7166
Tracy Mehan, Assistant Administrator; 202-260-5700

UNITED STATES INSTITUTE FOR ENVIRONMENTAL CONFLICT RESOLUTION
130 S. Scott Ave.
Tucson, AZ 85701 United States
Phone: 520-670-5299   Fax: 520-670-5530
E-mail: usiecr@ecr.gov
Website: www.ecr.gov

Founded: 1998
Scope: Local, State, Regional, National, International
Description: The U.S. Institute for Environmental Conflict Resolution is a federal program established by the U.S. Congress to assist parties in resolving environmental, natural resource, and public lands conflicts. The Institute is part of the Morris K. Udall Foundation, an independent federal agency of the executive branch overseen by a board of trustees appointed by the President. The Institute serves as an impartial, non-partisan institution providing professional expertise, services, and resources.
Publication(s): Roster of ECR Professionals
Keyword(s): Agriculture/Farming, Air Quality/Atmosphere, Ecosystems (precious), Energy, Ethics/Environmental Justice, Executive/Legislative/Judicial Reform, Forests/Forestry, Land Issues, Oceans/Coasts/Beaches, Pollution (general), Public Lands/Greenspace, Recreation

Contact(s):
Joan Calcagno, Roster Manager, National Roster of ECR Professionals; 520-670-5299; roster@ecr.gov
Michael Eng, Senior Program Manager, Protected Areas & Resources; 520-670-5299; eng@ecr.gov
Larry Fisher, Senior Program Manager, Public Lands & Natural Resource Mgmt.; 520-670-5299; fisher@ecr.gov
Dale Keyes, Senior Program Manager, Transportation, Energy & Env. Quality; 520-670-5299; keyes@ecr.gov
Sarah Palmer, Program Manager, Native American & Alaskan Native Program; 520-670-5299; palmer@ecr.gov
Cherie Shanteau, Program Manager/Senior Mediator, Litigation Program; 520-670-5299; shanteau@ecr.gov
Melanie Emerson, Program Associate, Public Education & Outreach; 520-670-5659; memerson@ecr.gov
Patricia Orr, Program Associate—Program Evaluation; 520-670-5299; Fax: 520-670-5530; orr@ecr.gov

UPPER COLORADO RIVER COMMISSION
355 S. 400 East
Salt Lake City, UT 84111 United States
Phone: 801-531-1150   Fax: 801-531-9705

Founded: 1949
Scope: Regional
Description: An administrative agency composed of commissioners appointed by the states of the Upper Division of the Colorado River - Colorado, New Mexico, Utah, and Wyoming, and by the President of the U.S.

U.S. FEDERAL AND INTERNATIONAL GOVERNMENT AGENCIES – W

Contact(s):
Wayne Cook, Executive Director and Secretary
Frank Maynes, Chairman; P.O. Drawer 2717, Durango, CO 81501

USAID/TANZANIA
So Mirambo
Dar-Es-Salaam, Tanzania
Phone: 255-511-1753 Fax: 255-111-6559
Description: International Development
Contact(s):
Z. Kristos Minja, Training Officer; 255-511-1753; Fax: 255-111-6559

USDA FOREST PRODUCTS LABORATORY
UNITED STATES FOREST SERVICE
FOREST PRODUCTS LABORATORY
One Gifford Pinchot Dr.
Madison, WI 53705-2398 United States
Phone: 608-231-9200 Fax: 608-231-9592
E-mail: mailroom_forest_products_laboratory@fs.fed.us
Website: www.fpl.fs.fed.us./
Founded: 1910
Membership: 101–1,000
Scope: National, International
Description: Uses science and technology to conserve and extend our Nation's forest resources. We promote healthy forest and forest-based economies through the sustainable use of our wood resources.
Publication(s): Dividends, NewsLine
Keyword(s): Climate Change, Development/Developing Countries, Energy, Forests/Forestry, Pollution (general), Public Health, Reduce/Reuse/Recycle, Water Habitats & Quality
Contact(s):
Chris Risbrudt, Director; 608-231-9318
Gordie Blum, Public Affairs Director; 608-231-9325; gblum@fs.fed.us

W

WESTERN PACIFIC REGIONAL FISHERY MANAGEMENT COUNCIL
1164 Bishop St., Suite 1400
Honolulu, HI 96813 United States
Phone: 808-522-8220 Fax: 808-522-8226
E-mail: info.wpcouncil@noaa.gov
Website: www.wpcouncil.org
Founded: 1977
Membership: 1–100
Scope: Regional, National, International
Description: The Council is the policy-making organization for the management of fisheries in and around the EEZs of American Samoa, Guam, Hawaii, and the Northern Mariana Islands, and U.S. possessions in the Pacific Ocean. Council members and members of its advisory bodies: Scientific and Statistical Committee, Plan Teams, and Advisory Panels represent the fishing community, government agencies, national international fishery management organizations and non-governmental organizations throughout the region.
Publication(s): Pacific Islands Fishery News
Keyword(s): Ecosystems (precious), Oceans/Coasts/Beaches, Recreation/Ecotourism, Wildlife & Species
Contact(s):
Kitty Simonds, Executive Director; 808-522-8220; Fax: 808-522-8226; kitty.simonds@noaa.gov
Judith Guthertz, Chairman

WESTERN SNOWY PLOVER WORKING TEAM
OREGON/WASHINGTON SUBGROUP
Coos Bay BLM
1300 Airport Lane
North Bend, OR 97459 United States
Phone: 541-756-0100 Fax: 541-751-4303
E-mail: kerrie_palermo@or.blm.gov
Website: www.or.blm.gov
Founded: 1992
Membership: 1–100
Scope: State
Description: Group of agency biologists working in a coordinated effort to recover western snowy plovers on the coast of Oregon and Washington through habitat restoration, education, recreation management and predator control.
Publication(s): Plover brochure
Keyword(s): Ecosystems (precious), Oceans/Coasts/Beaches, Wildlife & Species

STATE AND PROVINCIAL GOVERNMENT AGENCIES

A

ADIRONDACK PARK AGENCY
P.O. Box 99
Route 86
Ray Brook, NY 12977 United States
Phone: 518-891-4050, ext. 173   Fax: 518-891-3938
E-mail: vxhristo@gw.dec.state.ny.us
Website: www.northnet.org/adirondackparkagency/

Founded: 1971
Scope: International
Description: Created by state law and charged with developing a state Land Master Plan for the 40% of the park that is public land and a Private Land Use and Development Plan for the private lands within the six-million-acre Adirondack Park. The agency also administers the state's Wild, Scenic, and Recreational Rivers System Act for private lands within the park and the state's Freshwater Wetlands Act for both state and private lands within the park.
Publication(s): State Land Master Plan, Adirondack Park, Land Use Planning, publications list available upon request
Keyword(s): Land Issues, Water Habitats & Quality
Contact(s):
Daniel Fitts, Executive Director
Richard Lefebvre, Chairman
John Banta, Director of Planning
William Curran, Deputy Director, Regulatory Programs
Victoria Hristovski, Director, Public Information
Andy Flynn, Senior Information Specialist, Interpretive Centers

ALABAMA COOPERATIVE EXTENSION SYSTEM
109 Duncan Hall
Auburn University, AL 36849-5612 United States
Phone: 334-844-4444
Website: www.aces.edu

Founded: 1914
Scope: Local, State, Regional, National, International
Description: The Alabama Cooperative Extension System (Alabama A&M and Auburn Universities), through its statewide network of County Extension Offices, conducts informal education programs using research-based knowledge and techniques. Programs are offered in agriculture and forestry profitability; developing, conserving, and managing natural resources; enhancing family and individual well-being; developing human resources; community economic development; youth education through 4-H; and urban affairs.
Publication(s): Contact Extension Communications
Keyword(s): Agriculture/Farming, Air Quality/Atmosphere, Forests/Forestry, Oceans/Coasts/Beaches, Public Health, Public Lands/Greenspace, Recreation/Ecotourism, Water Habitats & Quality, Wildlife & Species
Contact(s):
James Armstrong, Extension Wildlife Specialist; Dept. of Forestry & Wildlife Science, 331 Funchess Hall, Auburn University, AL 36849; 334-844-9233; Fax: 334-844-0234
Carolyn Whatley, Co-Leader Communications; ACES, 122 Duncan Hall Annex, Auburn University, AL 36849; 334-844-5690; cwhatley@acesag.auburn.edu

ALABAMA COOPERATIVE FISH AND WILDLIFE RESEARCH UNIT (USDI)
108 White Smith Hall, Auburn University
Auburn, AL 36849 United States
Phone: 334-844-4796   Fax: 334-887-4509
Website: www.ag.auburn.edu/alcfwru

Founded: 1935
Membership: 1–100
Scope: National
Description: The unit is sponsored by the Biological Resources Division, U.S. Geological Survey; Alabama Department of Conservation and Natural Resources, Division of Game and Fish; Auburn University; and the Wildlife Management Institute. Fish and wildlife research, graduate education, and technical assistance are the unit's primary purposes.
Keyword(s): Wildlife & Species
Contact(s):
James Grand, Leader
Elise Irwin, Assistant Leader of Fisheries
Michael Mitchell, Assistant Leader of Wildlife

ALABAMA DEPARTMENT OF AGRICULTURE AND INDUSTRIES
The Richard Beard Bldg
P.O. Box 3336
Montgomery, AL 36109-0336 United States
Phone: 334-240-7100   Fax: 334-240-7190
E-mail: commtwo@agi.state.al.us
Website: www.agi.state.al.us

Membership: 101–1,000
Scope: State
Description: The Alabama Department of Agriculture and Industries is responsible for enforcing the laws of Alabama relating to agriculture. It also works to provide agribusiness assistance such as marketing, loan mediation, and trade information. The department strives to ensure consumer safety and to promote all of Alabama agriculture.
Publication(s): Alabama Farmers Bulletin, Livestock Mkt. News
Contact(s):
Charles Bishop, Commissioner; commone@agi.state.al.us

ALABAMA DEPARTMENT OF CONSERVATION AND NATURAL RESOURCES
64 North Union Street, Suite 567, P.O. Box 301456
Montgomery, AL 36130 United States
Phone: 334-242-3486   Fax: 334-242-3489
E-mail: commissioner@dcnr.state.al.us
Website: www.dcnr.state.al.us

Founded: 1905
Scope: State
Description: The program goal of the Alabama Department of Conservation and Natural Resources is to protect and, where possible, enhance or restore Alabama's natural resources for this and succeeding generations.
Publication(s): Outdoor Alabama
Keyword(s): Land Issues, Oceans/Coasts/Beaches, Recreation/Ecotourism, Water Habitats & Quality, Wildlife & Species
Contact(s):
Mark Easterwood, Division Director of State Parks; 334-242-3334
William Garner, Division Director of Marine Police; 334-353-2628
James Griggs, Division Director of State Lands; 334-242-3484
R. Vernon Minton, Division Director of Marine Resources; P.O. Box 458, Gulf Shores, AL 36542; 251-968-7576
Corky Pugh, Division Director of Wildlife and Freshwater Fisheries; 334-242-3848
Phillip Hinesley, Program Manager; ADCNR State Lands Division, Coastal Section Office, Suite B-1, 23210 U.S. Highway 98, Fairhope, AL 36532; 251-929-0900; Fax: 251-990-9293
M. Lawley, Commissioner; 334-242-3486; Fax: 334-242-3489
Richard Liles, Operations Director; 334-242-3486; Fax: 334-242-3489

ALABAMA DEPARTMENT OF ENVIRONMENTAL MANAGEMENT
P.O. Box 301463
Montgomery, AL 36130-1463 United States
Phone: 334-271-7700   Fax: 334-271-7950
E-mail: Cab@adem.state.al.us
Website: www.adem.state.al.us/

Founded: 1982

Description: To respond in an efficient, comprehensive, and coordinated manner to environmental problems, thereby assuring a safe, healthful, and productive environment. Encompasses water quality, public water supply, underground injection control, solid waste, hazardous waste, air pollution control, well water standards, operator certification, and coastal area functions.

Publication(s): Environmental Update

Keyword(s): Air Quality/Atmosphere, Oceans/Coasts/Beaches, Reduce/Reuse/Recycle, Water Habitats & Quality

Contact(s):
James Warr, Director
Clark Bruner, Staff of Public Affairs
Gerald Hardy, Staff of Land Division
Charles Horn, Staff of Water Division
Steve Jenkins, Staff of Field Operations
Jim Moore, Staff of Office of Education and Outreach
John Poole, Staff of Permits and Services
Marilyn Elliott, Deputy Director
Ron Gore, Staff of Air Division
Olivia Jenkins, Office of General Counsel

ALABAMA FORESTRY COMMISSION
P.O. Box 302550
Montgomery, AL 36130-2550 United States
Phone: 334-240-9300   Fax: 334-240-9390
Website: www.forestry.state.al.us

Scope: Local, State, Regional

Description: The FC was created by the 1969 regular session of the Alabama Legislature and is charged by law to protect, conserve, and increase the timber and forest resources of this state. A seven-member board is the policymaking body of the Commission. The State Forester is Chief Administrative Officer. Fire prevention and suppression, educational programs and materials, and free forest management assistance are some of the services which the Commission offers to the general public.

Publication(s): Alabama's Treasured Forests

Keyword(s): Development/Developing Countries, Forests/Forestry, Reduce/Reuse/Recycle

Contact(s):
Gary Cole, Director of Administration Division; 334-240-9333
David Frederick, Fire Division Director; 334-240-9335
Timothy Boyce, State Forester; 334-240-9304
Richard Cumbie, Assistant State Forester; 334-240-9367
David Long, Commissioner
Coleen Vansant, Editor; 334-240-9355

ALABAMA SOIL AND WATER CONSERVATION COMMITTEE
Executive Director
100 North Union St. - Suite 334
P.O. Box 304800
Montgomery, AL 36130 United States
Phone: 334-242-2620   Fax: 334-242-0551

Membership: 1–100
Scope: State

Description: The State Committee's main mission is primarily to carry out administrative functions for operation of 67 Soil & Water Conservation Districts and district programs, providing assistance to districts and their 335 supervisors statewide in carrying out their powers and duties.

Contact(s):
Stephen Cauthen, Executive Director; P.O. Box 304800, Montgomery, AL 36130-4800; 334-242-2620; Fax: 334-242-0551; scauthen@swcc.state.al.us
Beverly Riker, Executive Assistant; P.O. Box 304800, Montgomery, AL 36130-4800; 334-242-2620; Fax: 334-242-0551; briker@swcc.state.al.us
George Robertson, Chair; 2181 County Rd. 22, Waverly, AL 36879; 334-887-6070

ALASKA COOPERATIVE FISH AND WILDLIFE RESEARCH UNIT
209 Irving I Bldg., P.O. Box 757020, University of Alaska
Fairbanks, AK 99775-7020 United States
Phone: 907-474-7661   Fax: 907-474-7872
E-mail: fyunit@uaf.edu
Website: mercury.bio.uaf.edu

Founded: 1950
Membership: 1–100
Scope: State

Description: Sponsored jointly by the U.S. Geological Service, Alaska Department of Fish and Game, University of Alaska Fairbanks, U.S. Fish and Wildlife Service and Wildlife Management Institute, the Unit conducts graduate education and research programs on the ecology and management of Alaskan fish and wildlife, and their habitats.

Keyword(s): Water Habitats & Quality, Wildlife & Species

Contact(s):
Brad Griffith, Assistant Leader of Wildlife
F. Margraf, Leader
A. Mcguire, Assistant Leader of Ecology
Abby Powell, Assistant Leader of Wildlife

ALASKA DEPARTMENT OF ENVIRONMENTAL CONSERVATION
410 Willoughby Ave.
Juneau, AK 99801-1795 United States
Phone: 907-465-5010   Fax: 907-465-5770
Website: www.state.ak.us/dec

Founded: 1971
Scope: State

Description: Created by the Seventh Alaska Legislature to protect the quality of the state's natural resources and the health and quality of life of its people. The department has broad regulatory authority in the areas of water quality, drinking water, air quality, solid waste disposal, oil spills, subsurface pollution, pesticides, food safety, seafood wholesomeness, sanitation, and radiation. The department also has programs for construction of water, sewer, and solid waste facilities in Alaskan cities and

Keyword(s): Air Quality/Atmosphere, Public Health, Reduce/Reuse/Recycle, Water Habitats & Quality

Contact(s):
Janice Adair, Director of Division of Environmental Health; 907-269-7644
Tom Chapplo, Director of Division of Air and Water Quality; 907-269-7686
Mike Conway, Director of Statewide Public Service; 907-465-5337
Larry Dietrick, Director of Spill Prevention and Response; 907-465-5250
Dan Easton, Director of Division of Facilities Construction and Operations; 907-465-5180
Barbara Frank, Director of Division of Administrative Services; 907-465-5256
Michele Brown, Commissioner; 907-465-5065
Charles Fedullo, Public Information; 907-269-3784
Kurt Fredriksson, Deputy Commissioner, Acting; 907-465-5065

ALASKA DEPARTMENT OF FISH AND GAME
P.O. Box 25526
Juneau, AK 99802-5526 United States
Phone: 907-465-4100　　　　Fax: 907-465-2332
E-mail: commissioner_fishgame@fishgame.state.ak.us
Website: www.state.ak.us/local/akpages/fish.game/

Scope: State

Description: A research and management agency whose mission is to develop and organize its technical, human, and fiscal assets to maintain, rehabilitate, and enhance the fish and wildlife resources of the state, and to provide for their sustained optimum use consistent with the social, cultural, environmental, and economic needs of the public.

Keyword(s): Recreation/Ecotourism, Reduce/Reuse/Recycle, Wildlife & Species

Contact(s):
- Kevin Brooks, Director of Division of Administration; 907-465-5999
- Diana Cote, Executive Director of Board of Game and Board of Fish; 907-465-6095
- Kelly Hepler, Director of Division of Sport Fish; 907-465-4180
- Doug Mecom, Director of Commercial Fisheries Management and Development; 907-465-4210
- Mary Pete, Director of Division of Subsistence; 907-465-4147
- Wayne Regelin, Director of Division of Wildlife Conservation; 907-465-4190
- Ken Taylor, Director of Habitat and Restoration Division; 907-465-4105
- Robert Bosworth, Deputy Commissioner
- Dan Coffey, Board of Fisheries Vice Chair; 207 E. Northern Lights Blvd., Suite 200, Anchorage, AK 99503
- Kevin Duffy, Deputy Commissioner
- Nancy Long, Public Communications Section; 907-465-6167
- Lori Quakenbush, Board of Game Chair; P.O. Box 82391, Fairbanks, AK 99708
- Greg Roczicka, Board of Game Vice Chairman; P.O. Box 513, Bethel, AK 99559
- Frank Rue, Commissioner
- John White, Board of Fisheries Chairman; Bering Sea Dental Center, P.O. Box 190, Bethel, AK 99559
- Gordy Williams, Special Assistant for Legislative Liaison; 907-465-6143

ALASKA DEPARTMENT OF NATURAL RESOURCES
400 Willoughby
Juneau, AK 99801 United States
Phone: 907-465-2400　　　　Fax: 907-465-3886
Website: www.dnr.state.ak.us

Scope: State

Keyword(s): Agriculture/Farming, Forests/Forestry, Land Issues, Public Lands/Greenspace, Reduce/Reuse/Recycle

Contact(s):
- Bob Loeffler, Director of Division of Mining and Water Management; 3601 C St., Anchorage, AK 99503-5935; 907-269-8600
- Mark Myers, Director of Division of Oil and Gas; 3601 C St. Suite 1380, Anchorage, AK 99503-5948; 907-269-8800
- Jim Stratton, Director of Division of Parks and Outdoor Recreation; 3601 C St. Suite 1200, Anchorage, AK 99503-5921; 907-269-8700
- Rob Wells, Director of Division of Agriculture; 1800 Glenn Hwy. Suite 12, P.O. Box 949, Palmer, AK 99645-0949; 907-745-7200
- Milton Wiltse, Director of Division of Geological and Geophysical Surveys; 794 University Ave. Suite 200, Fairbanks, AK 99709-3654; 907-451-5000
- Jeff Jahnke, State Forester of Division of Forestry; 3601 C St. Suite 1030, Anchorage, AK 99503; 907-269-8463
- Pat Pourchot, Commissioner

ALASKA DEPARTMENT OF PUBLIC SAFETY
P.O. Box 111200
Juneau, AK 99811 United States
Phone: 907-465-4322　　　　Fax: 907-465-4362
E-mail: kathryn_crenshaw@dps.state.ak.us
Website: www.dps.state.ak.us

Membership: 1–100

Scope: State

Description: Responsible for enforcing all of the fish and game laws and regulations of the state.

Publication(s): The Quarterly

Keyword(s): Recreation/Ecotourism

Contact(s):
- Joel Hard, Director of Fish and Wildlife Protection
- Al Cain, Operations Commander
- James Cockrell, Deputy Director
- Del Smith, Commissioner; 907-465-4322; Fax: 907-465-4362

ALASKA DEPARTMENT OF PUBLIC SAFETY
ALASKA STATE TROOPERS
DIVISION OF FISH AND WILDLIFE PROTECTION
5700 E. Tudor Rd.
Anchorage, AK 99507 United States
Phone: 907-269-5509　　　　Fax: 907-269-5616
Website: www.dps.state.ak.us/fwp

Membership: 1–100

Scope: State

Description: Our primary mission is the protection of Alaska's fish and wildlife resources through enforcement of laws and regulations governing use of natural resources within Alaska and its adjacent waters, as well as through increasing the knowledge of, and respect for, fish and wildlife laws and regulations.

Contact(s):
- James Cockrell, Acting Director
- Howard Starbard, Captain

ALASKA HEALTH PROJECT
218 East 4th Avenue
Anchorage, AK 99501 United States
Phone: 907-276-2864　　　　Fax: 907-279-3089

Founded: 1980

Description: To provide information and advocacy on occupational and environmental health issues in Alaska, the Pacific Northwest, and Canada.

Publication(s): Involve waste management and worker health, and are inclusive of a 22 edition list.

Keyword(s): Reduce/Reuse/Recycle

Contact(s):
- Daniel Middaugh, Executive Director
- R. Gryder, Instructor

ALBERTA DEPARTMENT OF ENVIRONMENTAL PROTECTION
COMMUNICATIONS DIVISION
9th Floor, Petroleum Plaza, S. Tower, 9945-108 St.
Edmonton, T5K 2C6 Alberta Canada

Contact(s):
- Bob Scott, Director; 403-427-8636

ALBERTA DEPARTMENT OF ENVIRONMENTAL PROTECTION
ENVIRONMENTAL SERVICE
Information Centre
9920-108 Street
Edmonton, T5K 2G8 Alberta Canada
Phone: 780-427-6247　　　　Fax: 780-427-6247
E-mail: doug.tupper@gov.abc.ca
Website: www.gov.ab.ca/env/

Contact(s):
Doug Tupper, Assistant Deputy Minister; 403-427-6247

ALBERTA DEPARTMENT OF ENVIRONMENTAL PROTECTION
LAND AND FOREST SERVICE
Information Centre
9920-108 Street
Edmonton, T5K 2G8 Alberta Canada
Phone: 780-944-0313   Fax: 780-427-4407
E-mail: cliff.henderson@gov.ab.ca
Website: www.gov.ab.ca/env/

Contact(s):
Cliff Henderson, Assistant Deputy Minister

ALBERTA DEPARTMENT OF ENVIRONMENTAL PROTECTION
NATURAL RESOURCES SERVICE
Information Centre, Main Floor
9920-108 Street
Edmonton, T5K 2G8 Alberta Canada
Website: www.gov.ab.ca/env/

Contact(s):
Morley Barret, Deputy Minister; 780-427-6749; Fax: 780-427-8884; morley.barrett@gov.ab.ca

ALBERTA DEPARTMENT OF SUSTAINABLE RESOURCE DEVELOPMENT
FISH AND WILDLIFE DIVISION
Main Fl., South Tower
9915 - 108 Street
Edmonton, T5K 2G8 Alberta Canada
Phone: 780-944-0313   Fax: 780-422-9557
E-mail: env.infocent@gov.ab.ca
Website: www3.gov.ab.ca/srd/fishwl.html

Founded: 1964
Membership: 101–1,000
Scope: Province
Description: The Fish and Wildlife Division of Alberta Sustainable Resource Development is committed to the wise use and conservation of fish and wildlife resources. The Division seeks to preserve the intrinsic value these resources add to the environment as well as the enjoyment of Albertans now and in the future.
Publication(s): Guide to Trapping Regulations, Guide to Hunting Regulations, Guide to Sportfishing Regulations, Species at Risk series, State of Alberta's Wildlife Report
Keyword(s): Ecosystems (precious), Executive/Legislative/Judicial Reform, Land Issues, Recreation/Ecotourism, Water Habitats & Quality, Wildlife & Species

Contact(s):
Mike Cardinal, Minister

AMERICAN SAMOA DEPARTMENT OF AGRICULTURE
American Samoa Government
Pago Pago, AS 96799 United States
                          Fax: 684-699-4031
E-mail: josephmatua@samoa.as

Contact(s):
Philo Maluia, Director

ARIZONA COOPERATIVE FISH AND WILDLIFE RESEARCH UNIT (USDI)
Rm. 104, Biological Sciences East, University of Arizona
Tucson, AZ 85721 United States
Phone: 520-621-1959   Fax: 520-621-8801

Membership: 1–100
Scope: State
Description: The Unit is a cooperative effort by the U.S. Department of Interior, the Arizona Game and Fish Department, the University of Arizona, and the Wildlife Management Institute. The Unit conducts research on fish and wildlife questions for client agencies.

Contact(s):
Scott Bonar, Leader

ARIZONA COOPERATIVE STATE EXTENSION SERVICES
University of Arizona, P.O. Box 210036
Tucson, AZ 85721-0036 United States
Phone: 520-621-7205   Fax: 520-621-1314
Website: www.ag.arizona.edu/extension/

Membership: 1–100
Scope: State
Publication(s): See publication website

Contact(s):
James Christenson, Associate Dean and Director of Cooperative Extension; 520-621-7209; jimc@ag.arizona.edu
Kevin Fitzsimmons, Aquaculture Specialist; Soil, Water, and Environmental Science, P.O. Box 210038, University of Arizona, Tucson, AZ 85721; 520-626-3324; kevfitz@ag.arizona.edu
Richard Hawkins, Watershed Management Specialist; School of Renewable Natural Resources: College of Agriculture, P.O. Box 210043, University of Arizona, Tucson, AZ 85721; 520-621-7273; rhawkins@ag.arizona.edu
Bill Peterson, Assistant Director, 4-H; 520-621-3623; bpeters@ag.arizona.edu
George Ruyle, Range Management and Forest Resources Program Chair; School of Renewable Natural Resources: College of Agriculture, P.O. Box 210043, University of Arizona, Tucson, AZ 85721; 520-621-1384; gruyle@ag.arizona.edu
Larry Sullivan, Natural Resources Specialist, Wildlife; School of Renewable Natural Resources: College of Agriculture, P.O. Box 210043, University of Arizona, Tucson, AZ 85721; 520-621-7998; Fax: 520-621-8801; sullivan@ag.arizona.edu
Deborah Young, Associate Director, Programs; 520-621-5308; djyoung@ag.arizona.edu

ARIZONA DEPARTMENT OF AGRICULTURE
1688 W. Adams
Phoenix, AZ 85007 United States
Phone: 602-542-4373   Fax: 602-542-5420
Website: agriculture.state.az.us

Scope: International
Description: The ADA regulates and supports Arizona agriculture in a manner that encourages farming, ranching, and agribusiness while protecting consumers and natural resources. The ADA provides a number of services to its regulated industry, as well as the general public.

Contact(s):
Sheldon Jones, Director; 602-542-0998

ARIZONA DEPARTMENT OF AGRICULTURE
ANIMAL SERVICES DIVISION
1688 W. Adams
Phoenix, AZ 85007 United States
Phone: 602-542-6309   Fax: 602-542-3244
E-mail: helen.nasios@agric.state.az.us
Website: www.agriculture.state.az.us/ASD/asd.htm

Scope: State
Description: The Animal Services Division is responsible for the protection of livestock from theft and disease and for the regulation of the state's aquaculture, dairy, egg, and slaughtering and meat-processing industries.

Contact(s):
Sheldon Jones, Director
Al Davis, Associate Director

ARIZONA DEPARTMENT OF AGRICULTURE
ENVIRONMENTAL SERVICES DIVISION
1688 W. Adams
Phoenix, AZ 85007 United States
Phone: 602-542-3579   Fax: 602-542-0466
Website: www.agriculture.state.az.us

Membership: 1–100
Scope: State
Description: The Environmental Services Division is responsible for regulating the agricultural industry to ensure the safe use of pesticides, and to ensure the quality of feed, fertilizer, and pesticide formulations.
Contact(s):
Jack Peterson, Associate Director

ARIZONA DEPARTMENT OF AGRICULTURE
PLANT SERVICES DIVISION
1688 W. Adams St.
Phoenix, AZ 85007 United States
Phone: 602-542-0998   Fax: 602-542-0999
Website: www.agriculture.state.ac.us

Membership: 1–100
Scope: State
Description: The Plant Services Division is responsible for enforcement of state plant regulatory statutes, state agricultural industry plants, and plant health service programs.
Contact(s):
John Caravetta, Associate Director; 602-542-0994

ARIZONA DEPARTMENT OF ENVIRONMENTAL QUALITY
1110 W. Washington Street
Phoenix, AZ 85007-2926 United States
Phone: 602-771-2300   Fax: 602-771-2218
Website: www.adeq.state.az.us

Founded: 1987
Membership: 101–1,000
Scope: Regional
Description: The Arizona Department of Environmental Quality shall preserve, protect, and enhance the environment and the public health, and shall be a leader in the development of public policy to maintain and improve the quality of Arizona's air, land, and water resources.
Keyword(s): Air Quality/Atmosphere, Oceans/Coasts/Beaches, Pollution (general), Reduce/Reuse/Recycle, Water Habitats & Quality
Contact(s):
David Esposito, Southern Regional Office; 400 W. Congress Suite 433, Tucson, AZ; 520-628-6883
Robert Rocha, Director of Administration Services Division; 602-771-4867
Karen Smith, Director of Water Quality Division; 602-771-2306
Nancy Wrona, Director of Air Quality Division; 602-771-2308
Shannon Davis, Director of Waste Programs Division; 602-771-4209

ARIZONA GAME AND FISH DEPARTMENT
2221 W. Greenway Rd.
Phoenix, AZ 85023-4312 United States
Phone: 602-942-3000   Fax: 602-789-3924
Website: www.azgfd.com

Founded: 1929
Membership: 101–1,000
Scope: Local, State
Description: The mission of the Arizona Game and Fish Department is to conserve, enhance, and restore Arizona's diverse wildlife resources and habitats through aggressive protection and management programs, and to provide wildlife resources and safe watercraft and off-highway vehicle recreation for the enjoyment, appreciation, and use by present and future generations.
Publication(s): Arizona Wildlife Views
Keyword(s): Recreation/Ecotourism, Wildlife & Species
Contact(s):
Duane Shroufe, Director
Dick Maze, Heritage Program Coordinator
Diana Shaffer, Personnel Manager
Steve Ferrell, Deputy Director
Marty Macurak, Assistant Director of Information and Education Div.; 942-3000; Fax: 602-789-3924
Bob Miles, Publications Editor
Richard Rico, Assistant Director of Special Services Division
Mike Senn, Assistant Director of Field Operations Division
Alan Silverberg, Funds and Contracts
Bruce Taubert, Assistant Director of Wildlife Management Division

ARIZONA GEOLOGICAL SURVEY
416 W. Congress St.
Tucson, AZ 85701 United States
Phone: 520-770-3500   Fax: 520-770-3505
E-mail: azgs@azgs.az.gov
Website: www.azgs.az.gov

Founded: 1881
Membership: 1–100
Scope: State
Description: Develops, maintains, and disseminates information related to the geologic framework, geological hazards and limitations, and mineral and energy resources. Provides staff support for the Arizona Oil and Gas Conservation Commission, which regulates the drilling and production of oil, gas, geothermal, carbon dioxide and helium resources.
Publication(s): Down-To-Earth, digital information, contributed maps and reports, miscellaneous maps, open-file reports, maps, bulletins, special papers, circulars, Arizona Geology
Keyword(s): Energy, Land Issues
Contact(s):
Larry Fellows, Director and State Geologist; 520-770-3500; fellows_larry@pop.state.az.us

ARIZONA STATE LAND DEPARTMENT
1616 W. Adams St.
Phoenix, AZ 85007 United States
Phone: 602-542-4621   Fax: 602-542-2590
Website: www.land.state.az.us

Founded: 1915
Membership: 101–1,000
Scope: Regional
Description: The purpose of the Arizona State Land Department is to manage 9.4 million acres of Trust lands, through leasing and sale, in order to generate revenue for 14 state institutions. Resource protection and preservation is an integral part of trust land management.
Keyword(s): Development/Developing Countries, Land Issues, Public Lands/Greenspace, Reduce/Reuse/Recycle
Contact(s):
Bill Dowdle, Director of Natural Resources Division; 602-542-4625; Fax: 602-542-3507
T. Hart, Director of Forestry Division; 602-542-4627; Fax: 602-542-2590
Lynn Larson, Director of Administration and Resource Analysis Division; 602-542-4621
Richard Oxford, Director of Operations Division; 602-542-4602; Fax: 602-542-5223
Kirk Rowdabaugh, Director of Fire Management Division; 602-255-4059; Fax: 602-255-1781

Ron Ruzifka, Director of Planning and Land Disposition Division; 602-542-1704
Michael Anable, Deputy Commissioner of State Land
Jody Latimer, NRCD Administrator; 602-542-2699; Fax: 602-542-3507

ARIZONA STATE PARKS BOARD
1300 W. Washington Ave.
Phoenix, AZ 85007 United States
Phone: 602-542-4174　　　　Fax: 602-542-4188
Website: www.azstateparks.com

Founded: 1957
Scope: State
Description: The purposes and objectives of the Arizona State Parks Board are to select, acquire, preserve, establish, and maintain areas of natural features, scenic beauty, historical and scientific interest, zoos, and botanical gardens, for the education, pleasure, recreation, and health of the people.
Publication(s): Access Arizona (disabled/seniors), Arizona Wildlife Viewing Guides, Arizona State Trails Guides, Arizona Rivers and Streams Guide
Keyword(s): Ethics/Environmental Justice, Recreation/Ecotourism, Wildlife & Species
Contact(s):
　　Kenneth Travous, Executive Director
　　Walter Armer, Chairperson
　　Ellen Bilbrey, Public Information Officer; 602-542-1996

ARKANSAS COOPERATIVE RESEARCH UNIT
Department of Interior, U.S. Geological Survey
Biological Sciences
University of Arkansas
Fayetteville, AR 72701 United States
Phone: 479-575-6709　　　　Fax: 479-575-3330
E-mail: coopunit@uark.edu
Website: biology.uakr.edu/coop

Founded: 1988
Membership: 1–100
Scope: Local, State, Regional, National
Description: Primary purpose is field research, graduate research training in fisheries and wildlife resources, technical assistance, and extension activities. Areas of research include habitat selection, life history and demographics, ecology, animal behavior, and fisheries and wildlife biology.
Publication(s): Peer reviewed journals
Keyword(s): Agriculture/Farming, Population, Wildlife & Species
Contact(s):
　　David Krementz, Unit Leader; 479-575-7560; Fax: 479-575-3330; krementz@uark.edu
　　Dan Magoulick, Assistant Unit Leader - Fisheries; 479-575-5449; Fax: 479-575-3330; danmag@uark.edu
　　William Thompson, Assistant Unit Leader - Wildlife; 479-575-4266; Fax: 479-575-3330; thompson@uark.edu

ARKANSAS DEPARTMENT OF ENVIRONMENTAL QUALITY
8001 National Dr., P.O. Box 8913
Little Rock, AR 72219-8913 United States
Phone: 501-682-0744　　　　Fax: 501-682-0798
E-mail: help-cuspsvs@adeq.state.ar.us
Website: www.adeq.state.ar.us

Founded: 1949
Membership: 101–1,000
Scope: State
Description: To prevent, abate, and control all types of pollution and maintain the state's natural environment.
Publication(s): Arkansas Waste Line
Keyword(s): Air Quality/Atmosphere, Oceans/Coasts/Beaches, Reduce/Reuse/Recycle

Contact(s):
　　Richard Weiss, Director
　　Mike Bates, Chief of Hazardous Waste Division
　　Chuck Bennett, Chief of Water Division
　　Dennis Burks, Chief of Solid Waste Division
　　Richard Cassat, Chief of Technical Services Division
　　Leigh Ann Chrouch, Chief of Fiscal Division
　　Al Eckert, Chief of Legal Division
　　Sandy Formica, Chief of Environmental Preservation Division
　　Robert Gage, Chief of Computer Services Division
　　James Gilson, Chief of Customer Service Division
　　Becky Keogh, Deputy Director
　　Mary Leath, Chief Deputy Director; 501-682-0959
　　Keith Michaels, Chief of Air Division
　　Ed Morris, Administrator of Management Services
　　Jim Shell, Chief of Regulated Storage Tank Division

ARKANSAS DEPARTMENT OF PARKS AND TOURISM
One Capitol Mall
Little Rock, AR 72201 United States
Phone: 501-682-7777　　　　Fax: 501-682-1364
E-mail: info@arkansas.com
Website: www.arkansas.com

Membership: 101–1,000
Scope: State
Description: Develop, maintain and operate 50 state parks and four museums; advertise and promote all the state's recreation and travel potentials; provide information to attract retirees and others wanting to relocate; and assist communities in establishing local litter prevention and recycling projects.
Publication(s): The Arkansas Tour Guide, The Arkansas Adventure Guide, Arkansas State Parks Guide, The Arkansas Calendar of Events
Keyword(s): Ethics/Environmental Justice, Land Issues, Recreation/Ecotourism
Contact(s):
　　Greg Butts, Director of Parks Division; 501-682-7743; greg.butts@mail.state.ar.us
　　R. Cargile, Director of Administration; 501-682-2039; rl.cargile@mail.state.ar.us
　　Nancy Clark, Director of Great River Road Division; 501-682-1120; nancy.clark@mail.state.ar.us
　　Richard Davies, Executive Director; 501-682-2535; richardw.davies@mail.state.ar.us
　　John Ferguson, Director of History Commission; 501-682-6900; johnl.ferguson@mail.state.ar.us
　　Patricia Murphy, Director of Historical Resources and Museum Services Section; 501-682-3603; patriciam.murphy@mail.state.ar.us
　　Joe Rice, Director of Tourism Division; 501-682-1088; joedavid.rice@mail.state.ar.us
　　Bryan Kellar, Outdoor Recreation Grants; 501-682-1301; bryan.kellar@mail.stste.ar.us
　　Robert Phelps, Keep Arkansas Beautiful; 501-682-3507; robert.phelps@mail.state.ar.us

ARKANSAS GAME AND FISH COMMISSION
2 Natural Resources Drive
Little Rock, AR 72205 United States
Phone: 501-223-6300　　　　Fax: 501-223-6447
Website: www.agfc.com

Founded: 1915
Membership: 101–1,000
Scope: State
Description: The mission of the Arkansas Game and Fish Commission is to wisely manage the fish and wildlife resources of Arkansas while providing maximum enjoyment for the people.
Publication(s): Arkansas Wildlife Magazine, Arkansas Outdoors Newsletter

Keyword(s): Ecosystems (precious), Forests/Forestry, Recreation/Ecotourism, Wildlife & Species

Contact(s):
R. Henderson, Director; 501-223-6305; Fax: 501-226-6448; shenderson@agfc.state.ar.us
Lester Sitzes, Chairman; 1819 S. Main Street, Hope, AR 71801; 870-777-4466; Fax: 870-777-0718; Lsitzes@ezclick.net
David Goad, Deputy Director; 501-223-6308; Fax: 501-223-6448; dgoad@agfc.state.ar.us
Loren Hitchcock, Deputy Director Enforcement; 501-223-6384; Fax: 501-223-6459; lmhitchcock@agfc.state.ar.us
Jim Goodhart, Legal Counsel; 501-223-6327; Fax: 501-223-6463; jfgoodhart@agfc.state.ar.us
Nancy Ledbetter, Director of Communications; 501-223-6318; Fax: 501-223-6448; nsledbetter@agfc.state.ar.us
Stephen Wilson, Public Affairs Coordinator; 501-223-6408; Fax: 501-223-6447; srwilson@agfc.state.ar.us
Darla Bryant, Chief, Network Services; 501-223-6410; Fax: 501-223-6455; dbryant@agfc.state.ar.us
Neil Curry, Chief of Education & Outreach; 501-223-6402; Fax: 501-223-6310; jncurry@agfc.state.ar.us
Mike Gibson, Chief of Fisheries; 501-223-6371; Fax: 501-223-6461; mgibson@agfc.state.ar.us
Arlene Green, Chief of IT Customer Service; 501-223-6404; Fax: 501-223-6455; algreen@agfc.state.ar.us
Dale Gunter, Chief of Construction/Engineering/Real Estate; 501-223-7309; Fax: 501-978-7395; jdgunter@agfc.state.ar.us
Donny Harris, Chief of Wildlife; 501-223-6359; Fax: 501-223-6452; dmharris@agfc.state.ar.us
Tracy Moy, Chief of Information Services; 501-223-6338; Fax: 501-223-6455; tford@agfc.state.ar.us
Ray Sebren, Chief of Fiscal Services; 501-223-6439; Fax: 501-223-6425; rdsebren@agfc.state.ar.us
Mary Grace Smith, Chief of Human Resources; 501-223-6317; Fax: 501-223-6444; mgsmith@agfc.state.ar.us
Craig Uyeda, Chief of River Basins & Governmental Relations; 501-978-7303; Fax: 501-978-7395; ckuyeda@agfc.state.ar.us
Mike Wilson, Chief of Operational Services; 501-223-6312; Fax: 501-223-6407; jmwilson@agfc.state.ar.us
Keith Stephens, Editor, Arkansas Outdoors Newsletter; 501-223-6342; Fax: 501-223-6447; kastephens@agfc.state.ar.us
Keith Sutton, Editor, Arkansas Wildlife Magazine; 501-223-6406; Fax: 501-223-6447; kbsutton@agfc.state.ar.us

ARKANSAS NATURAL HERITAGE COMMISSION
1500 Tower Building
323 Center Street
Little Rock, AR 72201 United States
Phone: 501-324-9619   Fax: 501-324-9618
E-mail: arkansas@naturalheritage.org
Website: www.naturalheritage.com

Founded: 1973
Membership: 1–100
Scope: Local, State, Regional
Description: The Arkansas Natural Heritage Commission (ANHC) is responsible for maintaining the most up-to-date and comprehensive source of information concerning the rare plant and animal species, and high-quality natural communities of Arkansas. To protect rare species and habitats, the ANHC maintains a System of Natural Areas. Along with comprising remnants of the original natural landscape, lands within the System of Natural Areas provide vital habitat for imperiled plant and animal species.
Publication(s): Natural Area Brochures, Natural Diversity in Arkansas
Keyword(s): Ecosystems (precious), Wildlife & Species
Contact(s):
Karen Smith, Director; 501-324-9614; Fax: 501-324-9618; karen@arkansasheritage.org
Chris Colclasure, Chief of Acquisitions and Stewardship; 501-324-9760; Fax: 501-324-9618; chrisc@arkansasheritage.org
Douglas Fletcher, Chief of Stewardship; 501-324-9612; Fax: 501-324-9618; douglas@arkansasheritage.org
Tom Foti, Chief of Research; 501-324-9761; Fax: 501-324-9618; tom@arkansasheritage.org
Jane Jones-Schulz, Information and Education Coordinator; 501-324-9159; Fax: 501-324-9618; jane@arkansasheritage.org
Cindy Osborne, Data Manager; 501-324-9762; Fax: 501-324-9618; cindy@arkansasheritage.org
Bill Holimon, Zoologist/Grants Coordinator; 501-324-9636; Fax: 501-324-9618; billh@arkansasheritage.org
Jasa Holt, Assistant Data Manager; 501-324-9617; Fax: 501-324-9618; jasa@arkansasheritage.org
John O'Dell, Stewardship Field Ecologist; 501-324-9581; Fax: 501-324-9618; johno@arkansasheritage.org
Amy Thiele, Assistant Data Manager; 501-324-9763; Fax: 501-324-9618; amyt@arkansasheritage.org
Michael Warriner, Invertebrate Zoologist/Information Officer; 501-324-9634; Fax: 501-324-9618; michaelw@arkansasheritage.org
Samuel Wilkes, Stewardship Field Ecologist; 501-324-9581; Fax: 501-324-9618; samuel@arkansasheritage.org
Theo Witsell, Botanist; 501-324-9615; Fax: 501-324-9618; theo@arkansasheritage.org

ARKANSAS STATE EXTENSION SERVICES
FOUR H CENTER
1 4-H Way
Little Rock, AR 72223 United States
Phone: 501-821-4444   Fax: 501-821-2545
Website: www.arkansas4hcenter.org

Membership: 1–100
Scope: State
Description: An off-campus education organization with faculty and offices in each county with the basic mission to disseminate and encourage the application of research-generated knowledge and leadership techniques to individuals, families, and communities. The county faculty is backed by subject matter specialists and their research counterparts.
Publication(s): Brochures
Keyword(s): Agriculture/Farming, Forests/Forestry, Reduce/Reuse/Recycle, Water Habitats & Quality, Wildlife & Species
Contact(s):
Leslie Gall, 4-H Environmental Education Coordinator; 501-821-6884; Fax: 501-821-1170; lgall@uaex.edu
Kevin Jones, Program Specialist for Outdoor Recreation; 501-821-6884; Fax: 501-821-1170; kjones@uaex.edu
Burnett Kessner, 4-H Center Programs Director; #1 Four-H Way, Little Rock, AR 72223; 501-821-6884; Fax: 501-821-1170; bkessner@uaex.edu
J.J. Pitman, 4-H Outdoor Education Coordinator; 501-821-6884; Fax: 501-821-1170; jpitman@uaex.edu

ARKANSAS STATE PLANT BOARD
1 Natural Resources Dr., P.O. Box 72203
Little Rock, AR 72205 United States
Phone: 501-225-1598   Fax: 501-225-3590
Website: www.naturallyarkansas.org

Membership: 101–1,000
Scope: State
Publication(s): Plant Board News
Keyword(s): Wildlife & Species
Contact(s):
Don Alexander, Director
Darryl Little, Assistant Director

STATE AND PROVINCIAL GOVERNMENT AGENCIES – B

ATLANTIC STATES MARINE FISHERIES COMMISSION
1444 Eye St., NW, 6th Fl.
Washington, DC 20005 United States
Phone: 202-289-6400   Fax: 202-289-6051
E-mail: info@asmfc.org
Website: www.asmfc.org

Founded: 1942
Membership: 1–100
Scope: Regional
Description: The Commission was established in 1942 through a Compact of the 15 Atlantic coastal states (Maine to Florida) to promote the better utilization of the fisheries — marine, shell and anadromous — of the Atlantic seaboard through the development of a joint program for the promotion and protection of such fisheries, and by the prevention of physical waste of the fisheries from any cause.
Publication(s): Annual Report, Habitat Hotline Atlantic, Fisheries Focus
Keyword(s): Ecosystems (precious), Oceans/Coasts/Beaches, Water Habitats & Quality
Contact(s):
John O'Shea, Executive Director; 202-289-6400; voshea@asmfc.org
John Nelson, Chairman; New Hampshire Fish & Game, 225 Main Street, Durham, NH 03824; 603-868-1096; jinelson@starband.net
Preston Pate, Vice-Chairman; NC Divison of Marine Fisheries, 3441 Arendell Street, P.O. Box 769, Morehead City, NC 28557; 252-726-7021; Preston.Pate@ncmail.net
Susan Shipman, Past-Chairman

AUSTRALIA DEPARTMENT FOR ENVIRONMENT AND HERITAGE
Level 9 Chesser House
91 97 Grenfell Street
Adelaide, 5000 Australia
Phone: 8204-1910, ext. 8
E-mail: environmentshop@saugov.sa.gov.au
Website: www.environment.sa.gov.au

Founded: 1990
Scope: Local, State, Regional, National
Description: State Government body representing Land, Water, Biodiversity, Conservation, National Parks and Wildlife SA and environmental policy
Keyword(s): Air Quality/Atmosphere, Ecosystems (precious), Land Issues, Oceans/Coasts/Beaches, Pollution (general), Recreation/Ecotourism, Reduce/Reuse/Recycle, Water Habitats & Quality, Wildlife & Species
Contact(s):
Alan Holmes, Chief Executive

AUSTRIALIA DEPARTMENT FOR ENVIRONMENT AND HERITAGE
ENVIRONMENT SHOP, THE
77 Grenfell St.
Adelaide, South Australia, 5000 Australia
Phone: 8204-1910, ext. 618   Fax: 8204-1919
E-mail: environmentshop@saugov.sa.gov.au
Website: www.environment.sa.gov.au

Founded: 1999
Scope: Local, State, Regional, National
Description: The Environment Shop is the Department of Environment and Heritage's one stop shop offering products and services that relate to the activites of the department. Products include: park passes, fauna and hunting license renewal, mapping and spatial information, environmental management and retail products. The shop is the key interface with South Australia National Park visitors and offers information relating to parks, bush-walking trails.
Publication(s): Environmental publications, EPA reports, products for sale, mapping and spatial information
Keyword(s): Air Quality/Atmosphere, Climate Change, Ecosystems (precious), Energy, Land Issues, Oceans/Coasts/Beaches, Pollution (general), Recreation/Ecotourism, Reduce/Reuse/Recycle, Water Habitats & Quality, Wildlife & Species
Contact(s):
Allan Holmes, Chief Executive

B

BOARD OF MINERALS AND ENVIRONMENT
523 E. Capitol Avenue
Pierre, SD 57501 United States
Phone: 605-773-3153   Fax: 605-773-6035
Website: www.state.sd.us/denr

Founded: 1981
Scope: State
Description: The Board of Minerals and Environment promulgates rules and issues permits in the areas of air quality, solid waste, hazardous waste, mineral exploration and mining, and oil and gas exploration and production.
Keyword(s): Air Quality/Atmosphere, Land Issues, Pollution (general)
Contact(s):
Steven Pirner, Secretary of the Department; 605-773-5559; Fax: 605-773-6035

BRITISH COLUMBIA CONSERVATION DATA CENTRE
MINISTRY OF SUSTAINABLE RESOURCE MANAGEMENT
P.O. Box 9993 Station Provincial Gov.
Victoria, V8W 9R7 British Columbia Canada
Phone: 250-356-0928   Fax: 250-387-2733
E-mail: cdcdata@victoria1.gov.bc.ca
Website: srmwww.gov.bc.ca/cdc

Scope: International
Description: Providing information on rare organisms and ecosystems.
Publication(s): See publications on website
Contact(s):
Andrew Harcombe, Coordinator; andrewharcombe@gems2.gov.bc.ca

BRITISH COLUMBIA MINISTRY OF AGRICULTURE FOOD AND FISHERIES
BRITISH COLUMBIA FISHERIES
780 Blanshard St., 3rd. Fl.
Victoria, V8V 1X4 British Columbia Canada
Phone: 250-387-3190   Fax: 307-954-3291
Website: www.gov.bc.ca/fish

Membership: 1–100
Scope: Province
Contact(s):
Jamie Alley, Director of Fisheries Management; 250-387-9711
Joyce Murray, Minister of Water, Land, Air Protection

BRITISH COLUMBIA MINISTRY OF COMMUNITY ABORIGINAL AND WOMEN SERVICES
P.O. Box 9805, Stn. Prov. Govt.
Victoria, V8W 9W1 British Columbia Canada
Phone: 250-356-6305   Fax: 250-387-3798
Website: www.gov.bc.ca/mcaws

Membership: 1–100
Scope: Regional
Contact(s):
George Abbott, Minister; 250-356-3089

BRITISH COLUMBIA MINISTRY OF WATER, LAND AND AIR PROTECTION
P.O . Box 9360
Victoria, V8W 9M2 British Columbia Canada
Phone: 250-387-9422   Fax: 250-356-6464
E-mail: wlapmail@gems5.gov.bc.ca
Website: www.giv.bc.ca/wlap
Membership: 1–100
Scope: Regional
Description: The Ministry of Environment's mission is to provide leadership in building environmental principles into day-to-day decisions of governments, corporations, and private individuals; to monitor and report on the state of the environment, and to ensure that defensible environmental standards are set and complied with; and to manage natural habitats, fish, wildlife, and water resources for ecological diversity and the economic and recreational opportunities they provide.
Contact(s):
   Rod Davis, Director of Resource Stewardship Branch; 250-356-7725
   Doug Dryden, Director of Wildlife; 250-387-9731
   Jim Mattison, Director of Resources Inventory Branch; 250-387-1112
   Margaret Eckenfelder, Assistant Deputy Minister, Environment & Land Headquarters
   Dana Hayden, Assistant Deputy Minister, Corporate Services
   Joyce Murray, Minister
   Denis O'Gorman, Assistant Deputy Minister, Parks Division; 250-387-9997
   Dick Roberts, Assistant Deputy Minister, Region Division
   Derek Thompson, Deputy Minister; 250-387-5429
   Jim Walker, Assistant Deputy Minister for Wildlife, Habitat, and Enforcement; 250-356-0139

BUREAU OF ECONOMIC GEOLOGY
University of Texas at Austin
University Station, Box X
Austin, TX 78713-7508 United States
Phone: 512-471-1534   Fax: 512-471-0140
E-mail: begmail@beg.utexas.edu
Website: www.beg.utexas.edu
Founded: 1909
Membership: 101–1,000
Scope: State, International
Description: Functions as a state geological survey. Program includes basic research; application of geology to resources, conservation, and engineering problems; and publication of varied reports and maps. Maintains an extensive environmental mapping program.
Publication(s): University of Texas Report of Investigations, mineral resource circular, annual reports, handbooks, guidebooks, Geological Quadrangle Maps, Geological Atlas of Texas, Environmental Geologic Atlases, Special Publications, Geological Circulars
Keyword(s): Energy
Contact(s):
   Scott Tinker, Director; 512-471-1534; Fax: 512-471-0140
   Eric Potter, Associate Director for Energy; 512-471-1534; Fax: 512-471-0140
   Jay Raney, Associate Director for Environment; 512-471-1534; Fax: 512-471-0140
   Doug Ratcliff, Associate Director for Administration; 512-471-1534; Fax: 512-471-0140

BYRON FOREST PRESERVE
P.O. Box 1075
Byron, IL 61010 United States
Phone: 8152348535
Website: www.byronillinois.org
Founded: 1980
Scope: Local
Description: Preservation, Education, Recreation in local natural areas.
Keyword(s): Ecosystems (precious), Land Issues, Public Lands/Greenspace, Recreation/Ecotourism, Reduce/Reuse/Recycle, Wildlife & Species
Contact(s):
   Edward Clift, CEO
   Richie Wolf, Superintendent of Education

C

CALIFORNIA COASTAL COMMISSION
RESOURCES AGENCY, THE
45 Fremont St.,
Suite 2000
San Francisco, CA 94105-2219 United States
Phone: 415-904-5200   Fax: 415-904-5400
Website: www.coastal.ca.gov
Scope: State
Description: A coastal management agency which carries out mandated policies on coastal conservation and development through regulation and planning programs. These policies deal with public access to the coast, coastal recreation, the California marine environment, coastal land resources, and coastal development of various types, including power plant and other energy installation.
Contact(s):
   Peter Douglas, Executive Director
   Ralph Faust, Chief Counsel
   Susan Hansch, Chief Deputy Director
   Jaime Kooser, Deputy Director for Energy, Ocean Resources and Water Quality
   Chris Parry, Public Education and Activities Coordinator
   Steve Scholl, Deputy Director for North Coast District
   Lane Yee, Chief of Administrative Services Division

CALIFORNIA COASTAL CONSERVANCY
RESOURCES AGENCY, THE
1330 Broadway, 11th Floor
Oakland, CA 94612-2530 United States
Phone: 510-286-1015   Fax: 510-286-0470
E-mail: dwayman@scc.ca.gov
Website: www.coastalconservancy.ca.gov
Founded: 1976
Membership: 1–100
Scope: State
Description: A state agency using planning, land-use conflict resolution, acquisition, and development techniques in the restoration, enhancement, and preservation of coastal resources. Program areas include agricultural preservation, lot consolidation, urban waterfront restoration, coastal resource enhancement, the reservation of significant resource sites, provision of public access, and assistance to nonprofit organizations.
Publication(s): Coast and Ocean
Keyword(s): Agriculture/Farming, Ecosystems (precious), Land Issues, Oceans/Coasts/Beaches, Public Lands/Greenspace, Recreation/Ecotourism, Water Habitats & Quality, Wildlife & Species
Contact(s):
   Sam Schuchat, Executive Officer

CALIFORNIA CONSERVATION CORPS
RESOURCES AGENCY, THE
1719 24th St.
Sacramento, CA 95816 United States
Phone: 916-341-3177   Fax: 916-324-3347
Website: www.ccc.ca.gov
Founded: 1976

Description: The CCC was created with a dual mission: the employment and development of the state's youth, and the protection and enhancement of California's natural resources. Some 42 million hours of public service conservation work and emergency assistance have been provided by the Corps in its twenty years of existence.

Contact(s):
H. Pratt, Director
Buzz Breedlove, Deputy Director of External Affairs
Patti Keating, Chief Deputy Director
Marie Mijares, Special Assistant to the Director

CALIFORNIA DEPARTMENT OF BOATING AND WATERWAYS
RESOURCES AGENCY, THE
2000 Evergreen, Suite 100
Sacramento, CA 95815-3888 United States
Phone: 888-326-2822 Fax: 916-263-0648
E-mail: pubinfo@dbw.ca.gov
Website: www.dbw.ca.gov/

Founded: 1958
Scope: Local, State, Regional
Description: Makes loans to public agencies and small businesses for small craft harbor development and grants to public agencies for boat launching facilities; licenses yacht and ship brokers and for-hire vessel operators; conducts programs of boating safety, education, and regulation; and grants funds to local entities for boating law enforcement activities. Participates with the Corps of Engineers and local agencies in the construction of beach erosion control projects.
Publication(s): Boating safety pamphlets
Keyword(s): Executive/Legislative/Judicial Reform, Finance/Banking/Trade, Oceans/Coasts/Beaches, Recreation/Ecotourism, Transportation, Water Habitats & Quality
Contact(s):
Raynor Tsuneyoshi, Director; 916-263-4326; Fax: 916-263-0648; pubinfo@dbw.ca.gov
David Johnson, Acting Deputy Director; 916-263-0780; Fax: 916-263-0648; pubinfo@dbw.ca.gov
Dolores Farrell, Chief of Boating Operations Division; 916-262-8181; Fax: 916-263-0357; dfarrell@dbw.ca.gov
Steve Watanabe, Acting Boating Facilities Chief; 916-263-8147; Fax: 916-263-0648; pubinfo@dbw.ca.gov

CALIFORNIA DEPARTMENT OF CONSERVATION
RESOURCES AGENCY, THE
801 K St., MS 24-01
Sacramento, CA 95814 United States
Phone: 916-322-1080 Fax: 916-445-0732
Website: www.consrv.ca.gov

Membership: 101–1,000
Scope: State
Description: The mission of the department is to protect health and safety, ensure environmental quality, and support the state's long-term economic viability in the use of California's land and mineral resources.
Contact(s):
Darryl Young, Director
Pat Meehan, Deputy Director

CALIFORNIA DEPARTMENT OF EDUCATION
OFFICE OF ENVIRONMENTAL EDUCATION
1430 N Street, Suite 4401
Sacramento, CA 95814 United States
Phone: 916-322-9503 Fax: 916-322-9360
Website: www.cde.ca.gov/cilbranch/oee

Founded: 1970
Scope: State, Regional
Description: The California Department of Education, Office of Environmental Education (OEE) provides technical assistance and curriculum leadership in environmental education for K-12 educators in schools and non-formal settings throughout California. The OEE coordinates a statewide CA Regional Environmental Education Community (CREEC) Network which provides high quality resources through a searchable database and Resource Directory located at www.creec.org.
Publication(s): State Plan for Environmental Education, Environmental Education Compendia, Endangered Species Resource Guide
Keyword(s): Air Quality/Atmosphere, Energy, Pollution (general), Reduce/Reuse/Recycle, Water Habitats & Quality, Wildlife & Species
Contact(s):
Kristen Burger, Student Assistant; 916-445-4841; Fax: 916-322-9360; kburger@cde.ca.gov
Bill Andrews, Environmental Education Consultant; 916-322-9503; Fax: 916-322-9360; bandrews@cde.ca.gov
Orysia Moscariello, Student Assistant; 916-319-0258; Fax: 916-322-9360; omoscari@cde.ca.gov

CALIFORNIA DEPARTMENT OF FISH AND GAME
NATIONAL OCEANIC AND ATMOSPHERIC ADMINISTRATION
ELKHORN SLOUGH NATIONAL ESTUARINE RESEARCH RESERVE
1700 Elkhorn Rd.
Watsonville, CA 95076 United States
Phone: 831-728-2822 Fax: 831-728-1056
Website: www.elkhornslough.org

Founded: 1979
Scope: Regional
Description: Located near the Monterey Bay, ESNERR is 1400 acres of salt marsh, mudflat, grassland, coastal scrub, and woodland. It is owned and operated by the State in partnership with NOAA. The local non-profit partner is the Elkhorn Slough Foundation. Strong emphasis on research and monitoring, education, and stewardship. Hiking trails, visitor center, docent-led walks. Open Wed.-Sun. 9:00-5:00
Keyword(s): Ecosystems (precious), Land Issues, Oceans/Coasts/Beaches, Recreation/Ecotourism, Water Habitats & Quality, Wildlife & Species

CALIFORNIA DEPARTMENT OF FISH AND GAME
OFFICE OF SPILL PREVENTION AND RESPONSE
P.O. Box 944209
Sacramento, CA 94244-2090 United States
Phone: 916-445-9338
Website: www.dfg.ca.gov/ospr

Founded: 1990
Scope: State, Regional
Description: State of California trustee agency for wildlife and habitat. OSPR is division that prevents, prepares for & responds to pollution such as oil spills; prosecutes polluters, and ensures restoration of natural resources damaged by spills.
Publication(s): The OSPR News
Keyword(s): Ecosystems (precious), Oceans/Coasts/Beaches, Pollution (general), Transportation, Water Habitats & Quality, Wildlife & Species
Contact(s):
Robert Hughes, Information Officer; 916-323-6286; rhughes@ospr.dfg.ca.gov

CALIFORNIA DEPARTMENT OF FISH AND GAME
RESOURCES AGENCY, THE
1416 9th St. 12th Floor
Sacramento, CA 95814 United States
Phone: 916-653-7667 Fax: 916-653-1856
Website: www.dfg.ca.gov

Membership: 1,001–10,000
Scope: State

Description: Responsible for the protection and management of fish and wildlife and threatened native plants in California. Enforces the laws pertaining to fish and game and threatened native plants enacted by the legislature and the regulations of the Fish and Game Commission.

Publication(s): Track Mangazine, Outdoor California Magazine

Contact(s):
Robert Hight, Director; 916-653-7667
L. Boydstun, Intergovernmental Affairs Representative; 916-653-3136
Gene Fleming, Chief, Fisheries Programs; 916-653-4280
Michael Harris, Deputy Director of Administration; 916-653-4633
Perry Herrgesell, Chief, Central Valley Bay-Delta; 209-948-7800
Greg Laret, Chief of Conservation & Education & Enforcement Branch
Sonke Mastrup, Deputy Director of Wildlife & Inland Fisheries Division
Sandra Morey, Chief Habitat Conservation Planning
Julie Oltmann, Legislative Representative; 916-653-5581
Ron Rempel, Deputy Director of Habitat Conservation Division; 916-653-1070
Jim Steele, Native Anadromous Fish & Watershed Branch,Technical Asst Tea; 916-653-2459
Michael Valentine, General Counsel, Acting; 916-654-3821
Larry Week, Native Anadromouf Fish & Watershed Branch; 916-327-8847

CALIFORNIA DEPARTMENT OF FISH AND GAME
RESOURCES AGENCY, THE
WILDLIFE CONSERVATION BOARD
1807 13th St., Suite 103
Sacramento, CA 95814-7117 United States
Phone: 916-445-8448   Fax: 916-323-0280
Website: www.dfg.ca.gov

Founded: 1947
Membership: 1–100
Scope: State

Description: In concert with the Department of Fish and Game, the board authorizes the acquisition, restoration, and enhancement of land and water for wildlife conservation and related recreational purposes. The board also administers the Inland Wetlands Conservation Program and the California Riparian Habitat Conservation Program to protect, restore, and enhance wetland and riparian habitats.

Contact(s):
Georgia Lipphardt, Assistant Executive Director of Development Program
James Sarro, Assistant Executive Director of Land Acquisition
Al Wright, Executive Director

CALIFORNIA DEPARTMENT OF FOOD AND AGRICULTURE
1220 N St.
Sacramento, CA 95814 United States
Phone: 916-654-0462   Fax: 916-657-4240
E-mail: officeofpublicaffairs@bdfa.ca.gov
Website: www.cdfa.ca.gov

Membership: 1,001–10,000
Scope: National

Description: To assure public health, safety, and welfare; protects agriculture by administering, directing and enforcing the state's agricultural laws and regulations.

Publication(s): See publications on website

Contact(s):
Richard Breitmeyer, Director of Animal Industry; 916-654-0881
Mike Cleary, Director of Measurement Standards; 916-229-3000
John Donahue, Director of Inspection Services; 916-654-0792
Don Henry, Director of Plant Industry; 916-654-0317
Elizabeth Houser, Director of Fairs and Expositions; 916-263-2952
Kelly Krug, Director of Marketing Services; 916-654-1240
Les Lombardo, Planning Information Technology Director; 916-653-7643
Steve Lyle, Director of Public Affairs; 916-654-0462
Janice Strong, Legislative Director; 916-654-0326
Francine Kammeyer, Chief Counsel; 916-654-1393
William Lyons, Secretary; 916-654-0433
Dan Webb, Deputy Secretary; 916-654-0321

CALIFORNIA DEPARTMENT OF FORESTRY AND FIRE PROTECTION
RESOURCES AGENCY, THE
1416 9th St., P.O. Box 944246
Sacramento, CA 94244-2460 United States
Phone: 916-653-5121   Fax: 916-653-4171
Website: www.fire.ca.gov

Scope: State

Description: The department protects the people of California from fires, responds to emergencies, and protects and enhances forest, range, and watershed values providing social, economic, and environmental benefits to rural and urban citizens.

Contact(s):
Andrea Tuttle, Director; 916-653-7772; andrea_tuttle@fire.ca.gov
Ross Johnson, Deputy Director, Resource Management; 916-653-4298; ross_johnson@fire.ca.gov

CALIFORNIA DEPARTMENT OF PARKS AND RECREATION
1416 9th Street
Room 1413-9
Sacramento, CA 95814 United States
Phone: 916-653-1427   Fax: 916-654-7774
Website: www.cal-parks.ca.gov

Scope: Local, State

Description: Responsible for the acquisition, preservation, development, interpretation, and operation of the state park system; also responsible for the administration of grants for recreation to local government and for development of the California Outdoor Recreation Resources Plan.

Keyword(s): Recreation/Ecotourism

Contact(s):
Ruth Coleman, Director; 916-653-8380
John McMahon, Deputy Director of Marketing and Revenue Generation; 916-653-5841; jmcma@parks.ca.gov
Dave Widell, Deputy Director of Off Highway Motor Vehicle Recreation; 916-324-5801
Denzil Verardo, Chief Deputy Director of Administration; 916-653-0528
Bill Berry, Chief Deputy Director of Park Stewardship; 916-653-8288
Dr. Knox Mellon, Deputy Director of Historic Preservation Office; 916-653-6624
Pilar Onate, Deputy Director of Legislation; 916-653-6887
Richard G. Rayburn, Natural Heritage Division; 916-653-6745
Mark Schrader, Acquisition and Development; 916-653-7475; mschrader@parks.ca.gov
Ron Brean, Chief of Northern Division; 916-657-4042
Steven Treanor, Chief of Southern Division; 916-657-4042; strea@parks.ca.gov
George Cook, Central Field Division Chief; 916-653-2021
Tim Lafranchi, Legal Office; 916-653-6884
Ray Ann Watson, Human Rights; 916-653-9990

CALIFORNIA DEPARTMENT OF PESTICIDE REGULATION
1001 I Street
P.O. Box 4015
Sacramento, CA 95812-4015 United States
Phone: 916-445-4300 Fax: 916-324-1452
Website: www.cdpr.ca.gov

Founded: 1991
Scope: State
Description: Mission: To protect human health and the environment by regulating pesticide sales and use, and by fostering reduced-risk pest management.
Keyword(s): Agriculture/Farming, Air Quality/Atmosphere, Pollution (general)

Contact(s):
Paul Helliker, Director; 916-445-4000; Fax: 916-324-1452

CALIFORNIA DEPARTMENT OF WATER RESOURCES
RESOURCE AGENCY, THE
P.O. Box 942836
Sacramento, CA 95814 United States
Phone: 916-653-5791 Fax: 916-653-5028
Website: www.dwr.water.ca.gov

Scope: Regional
Description: To manage the water resources of California in cooperation with other agencies, to benefit the state's people, and to protect, restore, and enhance the natural and human environments.

Contact(s):
Thomas Hannigan, Director; 916-653-7007
Naser Bateni, Division of Planning and Local Assistance; 1020 9th St., Sacramento, CA 95814; 916-327-1646
Randall Brown, Environmental Services Office; 3252 S St., Sacramento, CA 95816; 916-227-7531
L. Chipponeri, Assistant Director of Legislation; 916-653-0488
Frank Conti, Division of Land and Right of Way; 916-653-7891
Les Harder, Division of Engineering; 916-653-3927
Kathy Kelly, State Water Project Planning Office; 916-653-1099
Paula Landis, District Chief of San Joaquin; 559-230-3310
James Libonati, Division of Management Services; 916-653-6743
Steve Macaulay, Chief Deputy Director; 916-653-6055
Jonas Minton, Deputy Director; 916-653-7092
George Qualley, Division of Flood Management; 916-653-7572
Steve Verigin, Division of Safety of Dams; 916-445-7606
Susan Weber, Chief Counsel; 916-653-6186
Pete Weisser, Office of Water Education
Charles White, District Chief of Southern; 818-543-4610
Karl Winkler, District Chief of Central; 916-227-7566
Chester Winn, Division of Fiscal Services; 916-653-4413

CALIFORNIA ENERGY COMMISSION
ENVIRONMENTAL DEPARTMENT
1516 9th St.
Sacramento, CA 95814 United States
Phone: 916-654-4287 Fax: 916-654-4420
Website: www.energy.ca.gov

Founded: 1975
Membership: 101–1,000
Scope: State
Description: To ensure continuation of a reliable and affordable supply of energy for California at a level consistent with the state's needs.

Contact(s):
Steve Larson, Executive Director; 916-654-4996
Nancy Deller, Deputy Director of Energy Technology Division; 916-654-4628; Fax: 916-654-4676
William Keese, Chairman; 916-654-5000
Scott Matthews, Deputy Director of Energy Efficiency Division; 916-654-5013; Fax: 916-654-4304
Robert Pernell, Commissioner; 530-654-5036
Art Rosenfeld, Vice Chair; 916-654-4930
Robert Therkelsen, Deputy Director of Energy Facilities Siting; 916-654-3924; Fax: 916-654-3882

CALIFORNIA ENVIRONMENTAL PROTECTION AGENCY
CALIFORNIA AIR RESOURCES BOARD
OFFICE OF COMMUNICATIONS
P.O. Box 2815
Sacramento, CA 95812 United States
Phone: 916-322-2990 Fax: 916-445-5025
E-mail: helpline@arb.ca.gov
Website: www.arb.ca.gov

Founded: 1968
Scope: Local, State, Regional, National, International
Description: The California Air Resources Board is responsible for the adoption and enforcement of the state's ambient air quality standards and regulations for the control of vehicular, stationary and areawide sources of air pollution and toxic air contaminants throughout the state. Oversees the efforts of 35 air pollution control districts that regulate local facilities. Conducts studies of the causes of air pollution. The Board is comprised of 11 members.
Keyword(s): Air Quality/Atmosphere, Climate Change, Energy, Ethics/Environmental Justice, Pollution (general), Public Health, Sprawl/Urban Planning, Transportation

Contact(s):
Jerry Martin, Communications Director; 916-322-2990; Fax: 916-445-5025
Tom Cackette, Chief Deputy Executive Officer; 916-322-2892
Bart Croes, Research Division Chief; 916-445-0753
Robert Fletcher, Technical Support Division Chief; 916-322-5350
Marie LaVergne, Administrative Services Division Chief; 916-322-8198
Alan Lloyd, Chairman
William Loscutoff, Monitoring and Laboratory Division Chief; 916-445-3742
Rob Oglesby, Legislative Office Chief; 916-322-2896
Michael Scheible, Deputy Executive Officer; 916-322-2890
Lynn Terry, Assistant Executive Officer; 916-322-2739
Kathleen Tschogl, Office of Ombudsman Chief; 916-323-6791
Peter Venturini, Stationary Division Chief; 916-445-0650
Kathleen Walsh, Office of Legal Affairs General Counsel; 916-322-2884
Catherine Witherspoon, Executive Officer; 916-445-4383

CALIFORNIA ENVIRONMENTAL PROTECTION AGENCY
DEPARTMENT OF TOXIC SUBSTANCES CONTROL
P.O. Box 806
Sacramento, CA 95812-0806 United States
Phone: 916-327-6097 Fax: 916-445-9549
Website: www.dtsc.ca.gov

Membership: 101–1,000
Scope: State
Description: Responsible for overseeing the cleanup of hazardous waste sites; monitoring and regulatory management of hazardous waste transportation, treatment, storage and disposal; and promotion of hazardous waste reduction in California.

Contact(s):
Edwin Lowry, Director; 916-322-0504; elowry@dtsc.ca.gov
Bob Borzeueri, Chief Deputy Director; 916-322-0449; bborzeuri@dtsc.ca.gov

CALIFORNIA ENVIRONMENTAL PROTECTION AGENCY
INTEGRATED WASTE MANAGEMENT BOARD, IWMB
1001 I Street
Sacramento, CA 95814 United States
Phone: 916-341-6000
Website: www.calepa.ca.gov

Founded: 1990

Description: The CIWMB is comprised of six members; four appointed by the governor and two by the legislature. CIWMB's goal is to protect the public's health and safety and the environment through waste prevention, waste diversion, and safe waste processing and disposal.

Contact(s):
Linda Moulton-Patterson, Chairman; 916-341-6024; lmoulton@ciwmb.ca.gov

CALIFORNIA ENVIRONMENTAL PROTECTION AGENCY
OFFICE OF ENVIRONMENTAL HEALTH HAZARD ASSESSMENT
P.O. Box 4010
Sacramento, CA 95812-4010 United States
Phone: 916-324-7572   Fax: 916-327-1097
Website: www.oehha.ca.gov

Membership: 1–100
Scope: State

Description: The Office of Environmental Health Hazard Assessment is charged with assessing human health risks posed by chemicals in the environment. The office is also the lead agency for implementation of the Safe Drinking Water and Toxic Enforcement Act of 1986 (Proposition 65).

Contact(s):
Joan Denton, Director

CALIFORNIA ENVIRONMENTAL PROTECTION AGENCY
OFFICE OF THE SECRETARY
P.O. Box 2815
Sacramento, CA 95812 United States
Phone: 916-323-2514   Fax: 916-324-0908
Website: www.calepa.ca.gov

Founded: 1991
Scope: State

Description: The Secretary for Environmental Protection, a member of the Governor's Cabinet, serves as the Governor's principal advisor on environmental protection issues and oversees the activities of the Air Resources Board, Water Resources Control Board, and Integrated Waste Management Board, the Department of Toxic Substances Control, the Office of Environmental Health Hazard Assessment, and the Department of Pesticide Regulation.

Contact(s):
William Rukeyser, Director of Communications; 916-324-9670
Patty Zwarts, Director of Legislative Affairs, Acting; 916-322-7315
Deborah Barnes, Deputy Secretary of Law Enforcement and Counsel; 916-327-2064
C. Haddix, Under Secretary
Winston Hickox, Secretary; 916-445-3846

CALIFORNIA ENVIRONMENTAL PROTECTION AGENCY
STATE WATER RESOURCES CONTROL BOARD
1001 I St.
Sacramento, CA 95814 United States
Phone: 916-341-5250   Fax: 916-341-5252
E-mail: info@exec.swrcb.ca.gov
Website: www.swrcb.ca.gov

Scope: State

Description: To protect water quality and allocate water rights. These objectives are achieved through two action programs: water quality and water rights.

Contact(s):
Celeste Cantu, Executive Director, Acting
Arthur Baggett, Chairman, Acting
Loretta Barsamian, Regional Executive Officer of the San Francisco Bay Region; San Francisco Bay Region, 1515 Clay Street, Suite 1400, Oakland, CA 94612; 510-622-2300; Fax: 510-622-2460
Roger Briggs, Regional Executive Officer of the Central Coast Region; Central Coast Region, 81 Higuera St., Ste. 200, San Luis Obispo, CA 93401; 805-549-3147; Fax: 805-543-0397
Gary Carlton, Regional Executive Officer of the Central Valley Region; Central Valley Region, 3443 Routier Road, Suite A, Sacramento, CA 95827; 916-255-3000; Fax: 916-255-3015
Dennis Dickerson, Regional Executive Officer of the Los Angeles Region; Los Angeles Region, 320 West 4th Street, Ste. 200, Los Angeles, CA 90013; 213-266-7500; Fax: 213-576-6640
Phil Gruenberg, Regional Executive Officer of the Colorado River Basin Region; Colorado River Basin Region, 73-720 Fred Waring Dr., Suite 100, Palm Desert, CA 92260; 760-241-6583; Fax: 760-241-7308
Richard Katz, Board Member
John Robertus, Regional Executive Officer of the San Diego Region; San Diego Region, 9174 Sky Park Court, Suite 100, San Diego, CA 92123; 858-467-2952; Fax: 858-571-6972
Harry Schueller, Deputy Director
Peter Silva, Board Member
Harold Singer, Regional Executive Officer of the Lahontan Region; Lahontan Region, 2501 Lake Tahoe Blvd., South Lake Tahoe, CA 96150; 916-542-5400; Fax: 530-544-2271
Gerald Thibeault, Regional Executive Officer of the Santa Ana Region; Santa Ana Region, 3737 Main Street, Suite 500, Riverside, CA 92501; 909-782-4130; Fax: 909-781-6288
Susan Warner, Regional Executive Officer of the North Coast Region; North Coast Region, 5550 Skylane Blvd., Ste. A, Santa Rosa, CA 95403; 707-576-2220; Fax: 707-523-0135

CALIFORNIA FISH AND GAME COMMISSION
FISH AND GAME COMMISSION
1416 9th St., Rm. 1320,
P.O. Box 944209
Sacramento, CA 94244 United States
Phone: 916-653-4899   Fax: 916-653-5040
E-mail: fgc@dfg.ca.gov
Website: www.dfg.ca.gov/fg_comm/

Founded: 1870
Membership: 1–100
Scope: State

Description: Adopts fish, game, and plant regulations as authorized by the Fish and Game Code and sets policies for the Department of Fish and Game.

Contact(s):
Michael Flores, President
Mike Chrisman, Vice President
Robert Treanor, Executive Director; fgc@dfg.ca.gov

CALIFORNIA GOVERNORS OFFICE OF PLANNING AND RESEARCH
STATE CLEARINGHOUSE
P.O. Box 3044
Sacramento, CA 95812-3044 United States
Phone: 916-445-0613   Fax: 916-323-3018
E-mail: state.clearinghouse@opr.ca.gov
Website: www.opr.ca.gov

Founded: 1970
Scope: Local, State, Regional

Description: Primary areas of concentration are the implementation of the California Environmental Quality Act (CEQA), technical assistance to cities and counties for the development of local general plans; state and local land use planning; evaluation of state plans and programs; and preparation of statewide environmental goals and policies.
Publication(s): Land Use Planning Publications
Keyword(s): Land Issues, Sprawl/Urban Planning
Contact(s):
Tal Finney, Interim Director
Terry Roberts, State Clearinghouse Director; 916-445-0613

CALIFORNIA RECLAMATION BOARD
RESOURCES AGENCY, THE
3310 El Camino Avenue, LL40
Sacramento, CA 95833 United States
Phone: 916-574-0609   Fax: 916-574-0682
E-mail: lorib@water.ca.gov
Website: www.rccbd.ca.gov
Founded: 1911
Membership: 1–100
Scope: State
Description: Agency provides flood protection along the Sacramento and San Joaquin Rivers and their tributaries by planning, constructing, operating, and maintaining flood control projects in cooperation with local, state, and federal agencies, and by implementing nonstructural flood control measures.
Contact(s):
Betsy Marchand, President; 916-574-0609
Anthony Cusenza, Vice President; 916-574-0609
Peter Rabbon, General Manager; 916-574-0609
Lori Buford, Staff Assistant; 916-574-0609
William Edgar, Secretary; 916-574-0609

CALIFORNIA RESOURCES AGENCY, THE
1416 9th St., Rm. 1311
Sacramento, CA 95814 United States
Phone: 916-653-5656   Fax: 916-653-8102
Website: www.resources.ca.gov
Scope: State
Description: Responsible for ensuring an adequate and properly balanced management of government functions related to California's natural environment.
Contact(s):
Jennifer Galehause, Deputy Secretary for Legislative Affairs
Margaret Kim, General Counsel
Mary Nicholas, Secretary of Resources
Michael Sweeney, Under Secretary of Resources
Don Wallace, Assistant Secretary of Administration and Finance
Stanley Young, Communication Director Public Information

CALIFORNIA STATE LANDS COMMISSION
100 Howe Avenue
Suite 100-South
Sacramento, CA 95825-8202 United States
Phone: 916-574-1800   Fax: 916-574-1810
Website: www.slc.ca.gov
Founded: 1938
Membership: 101–1,000
Scope: Local, State
Description: Jurisdiction over state-owned sovereign and legislatively granted lands. Negotiates related land leases, exchanges, and settlements. Conducts oil, gas, geothermal, and leasing of other minerals on state-owned lands. Determine boundaries, ownership, administer granted lands, and maintain land information systems. Conducts inspections of marine oil transfers to and from oil tankers and barges. Responsible for implementing California's ballast water management program.
Keyword(s): Energy, Land Issues, Oceans/Coasts/Beaches, Public Lands/Greenspace
Contact(s):
Cruz Bustamante, Commissioner & Lieutenant Governor (Chair); 916-445-8994
Steve Peace, Commissioner & State Director of Finance; 916-445-4141
Steve Westly, Commissioner & State Controller; 916-445-2636
Paul Thayer, Executive Officer; 916-574-1800; Fax: 916-574-1810; thayerp@slc.ca.gov
William Morrison, Chief, Government and External Affairs; 916-574-1800; Fax: 916-574-1810; morrisb@slc.ca.gov
Jack Rump, Chief Counsel; 916-574-1850; Fax: 916-574-1855; rumpj@slc.ca.gov
Dwight Sanders, Chief, Environmental Planning and Management Division; 916-574-1890; Fax: 916-574-1885; sanderd@slc.ca.gov
Robert Lynch, Chief, Land Management Division; 916-574-1940; Fax: 916-574-1945; lynchr@slc.ca.gov
Gary Gregory, Chief, Marine Facilities Division; 200 Oceangate, Suite 900, Long Beach, CA 90802; 562-499-6312; Fax: 562-499-6317; gregorg@slc.ca.gov
Paul Mount, Chief, Mineral Resources Management Division; 200 Oceangate, Suite 1200, Long Beach, CA 90802; 562-590-5205; Fax: 562-590-5210; mountp@slc.ca.gov

CALIFORNIA WATER COMMISSION
RESOURCES AGENCY, THE
1416 Ninth Street, Suite 1311
Sacramento, CA 95814 United States
Phone: 916-653-5656   Fax: 916-653-9745
Website: ceres.ca.gov/cra/
Founded: 1913
Scope: State
Description: Serves as a policy advisory body to the Director of Water Resources on matters within the Department's jurisdiction and coordinates state and local views on federal appropriations for water projects in California. The commission also conducts public hearings and investigations statewide for the department and provides an open forum for interested citizens to voice their opinion on water development issues.
Keyword(s): Water Habitats & Quality, Wildlife & Species

CITY OF BELDING
COMMUNITY DEVELOPMENT DEPARTMENT
PLANNING DEPARTMENT
120 South Pleasant Street
Belding, MI 48809-1644 United States
Phone: 616-794-1900, ext. 205   Fax: 616-794-4812
E-mail: dreed@ci.belding.mi.us
Website: www.ci.belding.mi.us
Scope: Local
Description: The Belding Community Development Department works to create an environmentaly sensitive community where quality design of the built environment and quality design of the natural environment meet.
Keyword(s): Energy, Land Issues, Public Lands/Greenspace, Recreation/Ecotourism, Sprawl/Urban Planning, Transportation, Water Habitats & Quality
Contact(s):
Mike Wood, City Manager; mwood@ci.belding.mi.us

CLEMSON UNIVERSITY EXTENSION SERVICE
Clemson University, Rm. 103 Barre Hall
Clemson, SC 29634-0101 United States
Phone: 864-656-3382   Fax: 864-656-5819
Website: www.clemson.edu/extension/
Scope: State
Contact(s):
Allen Dunn, Director of School of Natural Resources; 130 Lehotsky Hall, Clemson University, Clemson, SC 29634; 864-656-3215; adunn@clemson.edu

Daniel Smith, Director of Extension Service; 103 Barre Hall, Clemson University, Clemson, SC 29634-0310; 864-656-3382; dbsmith@clemson.edu

P. Horton, Extension Entomologist; 103 Barre Hall, Clemson University, Clemson, SC 29634; 864-656-3382; mhorton@clemson.edu

Larry Nelson, Extension Forester; 272-E Lehotsky Hall, Clemson University, Clemson, SC 29634-1003; 864-656-4866; lnelson@clemson.edu

John Sweeney, Extension Fish Specialist; Department Head of Aquaculture, Fisheries, and Wildlife, Lehotsky Hall, Clemson University, Clemson, SC 29634-0362; 864-656-3117; jswny@clemson.edu

Greg Yarrow, Extension Wildlife Specialist; 864-656-7370; gyarrow@clemson.edu

COASTAL RESOURCE MANAGEMENT PROJECT
5th Floor, CIFC Towers, North Reclamation Area
Cebu City, Cebu, 6000 Philippines
Phone: 63322321822   Fax: 63322321825
E-mail: crmhot@mozcom.com
Website: www.oneocean.org
Founded: 1996
Scope: Local, State, Regional, National
Description: Technical assistance project of the Department of Environment and Natural Resources in the Philippines supported by USAID
Publication(s): Sustainable Coastal Tourism Handbook
Keyword(s): Development/Developing Countries, Ecosystems (precious), Ethics/Environmental Justice, Executive/Legislative/Judicial Reform, Land Issues, Oceans/Coasts/Beaches, Recreation/Ecotourism, Water Habitats & Quality, Wildlife & Species
Contact(s):
Marco Carreon, Deputy Chief of Party; 6332-232-1822; Fax: 6334-232-1825; mcarreon@mozcom.com
Alan White, Chief of Party; 6332-232-1822; Fax: 6332-232-1825; awhite@mozcom.com

COLORADO DEPARTMENT OF AGRICULTURE
700 Kipling St., Suite 4000
Lakewood, CO 80215 United States
Phone: 303-239-4100   Fax: 303-239-4125
Website: www.ag.state.co.us
Founded: 1949
Scope: State
Description: Strives to meet the increasingly complex needs of agriculture through work on marketing problems, technological changes in pest and insect control, and rapidly changing patterns in crop and livestock operations.
Keyword(s): Agriculture/Farming, Pollution (general), Public Lands/Greenspace
Contact(s):
Wayne Cunningham, Director of Animal Industry Division; 303-239-4161
Jim Rubingh, Director of Markets Development Division
Ronald Turner, Director of Plant Industry Division; 303-239-4140
Ronald Turner, Director of Division of Inspection and Consumer Services; 303-477-0076
Don Ament, Commissioner
Robert McLavey, Deputy Commissioner
Gary Shoun, Brand Commissioner of Board of Stock Inspection Division

COLORADO DEPARTMENT OF EDUCATION
STATE OFFICE
201 E. Colfax Ave.
Denver, CO 80203 United States
Phone: 303-866-6600   Fax: 303-830-0793
Website: www.cde.state.co.us
Scope: State
Description: Conservation Education Services, jointly with the Colorado Division of Wildlife.
Keyword(s): Ethics/Environmental Justice, Pollution (general), Reduce/Reuse/Recycle
Contact(s):
Don Hollums, Environmental Education Consultant; 303-866-6787; hollums_d@cde.state.co.us

COLORADO DEPARTMENT OF NATURAL RESOURCES
1313 Sherman St.
Denver, CO 80203 United States
Phone: 303-866-3311   Fax: 303-866-2115
Website: www.dnr.state.co.us
Founded: 1968
Membership: 1,001–10,000
Scope: State
Description: Responsible for mineral and energy, land, water, wildlife, and park resources management for the state. Also responsible for major environmental conservation and management programs.
Publication(s): See publication website
Keyword(s): Ecosystems (precious), Energy, Executive/Legislative/Judicial Reform, Forests/Forestry, Land Issues, Pollution (general), Public Lands/Greenspace, Recreation/Ecotourism, Water Habitats & Quality, Wildlife & Species
Contact(s):
Cindy Horiuchi, Human Resources Director
Greg Walcher, Executive Director
Ronald Cattany, Deputy Director
Bill Daley, Deputy Director

COLORADO DEPARTMENT OF NATURAL RESOURCES
COLORADO GEOLOGIC SURVEY
1313 Sherman St., Rm. 715
Denver, CO 80203 United States
Phone: 303-866-2611   Fax: 303-866-2461
E-mail: cgspubs@state.co.us
Website: geosurvey.state.co.us
Membership: 1–100
Scope: State
Description: State Geological Survey.
Publication(s): Rock Talk - quarterly newsletters

COLORADO DEPARTMENT OF NATURAL RESOURCES
DIVISION OF MINERALS AND GEOLOGY
1313 Sherman St., Rm. 215
Denver, CO 80203 United States
Phone: 303-866-3567   Fax: 303-832-8106
E-mail: dmg_pio@state.co.us
Website: www.mining.state.co.us
Membership: 1–100
Scope: State
Contact(s):
Ronald Cattany, Director; ron.cattany@state.co.us

COLORADO DEPARTMENT OF NATURAL RESOURCES
DIVISION OF PARKS AND OUTDOOR RECREATION
1313 Sherman St., Rm. 618
Denver, CO 80203 United States
Phone: 303-866-3437   Fax: 303-866-3206
Website: www.parks.state.co.us
Membership: 101–1,000
Scope: State

Description: Colorado State Parks operates 40 state parks offering camping, fishing, hiking etc. Staffed with 250+ permanent FTEs.
Keyword(s): Recreation/Ecotourism, Water Habitats & Quality, Wildlife & Species
Contact(s):
  Lyle Laverty, Director; 303-866-3437; Fax: 303-866-3206; lyle.laverty@state.co.us
  Joe Maurier, Deputy Director; 303-866-3437; Fax: 303-866-3206; joe.maurier@state.co.us

COLORADO DEPARTMENT OF NATURAL RESOURCES
DIVISION OF WATER RESOURCES
STATE ENGINEER'S OFFICE
1313 Sherman St., Room 818
Denver, CO 80203 United States
Phone: 303-866-3581   Fax: 303-866-3589
Website: www.water.state.co.us

Membership: 1–100
Scope: State
Description: The Colorado Division of Water Resources issues water well permits, administers water rights, monitors streamflow and water use, inspects dams for safety, maintains databases of Colorado water information and represents Colorado in interstate water compact proceedings. Designated ground water basins are regulated by the 12-member Colorado Ground Water Commission. The safe and proper construction of water wells and pump installation activities are regulated by the 5-member Board of Examiners.
Publication(s): StreamLines - Newsletter
Contact(s):
  Hal Simpson, State Engineer; 303-866-3581
  Will Burt, Deputy State Engineer; 303-866-3581

COLORADO DEPARTMENT OF NATURAL RESOURCES
DIVISION OF WILDLIFE
6060 Broadway
Denver, CO 80216 United States
Phone: 303-297-1192   Fax: 303-294-0894
E-mail: AskDOW@state.co.us
Website: www.wildlife.state.co.us

Scope: State
Contact(s):
  Russell George, Director

COLORADO DEPARTMENT OF NATURAL RESOURCES
OIL AND GAS CONSERVATION COMMISSION
1120 Lincoln St., Suite 801
Denver, CO 80203 United States
Phone: 303-894-2100   Fax: 303-894-2109
E-mail: dnr.ogcc@state.co.us
Website: www.oil-gas.state.co.us

Scope: State
Description: Promotes the responsible development of Colorado's oil and gas natural resources.
Keyword(s): Energy
Contact(s):
  Brian Macke, Deputy Director; 303-894-2100; Fax: 303-894-2109; brian.macke@state.co.us
  Richard Griebling, Director; 303-894-2100; Fax: 303-894-2109; richard.griebling@state.co.us
  Morris Bell, Operations Manager; 303-894-2100; Fax: 303-894-2109; morris.bell@state.co.us

COLORADO DEPARTMENT OF NATURAL RESOURCES
STATE BOARD OF LAND COMMISSIONERS
1313 Sherman St., Rm. 621
Denver, CO 80203 United States
Phone: 303-866-3454   Fax: 303-866-3152
Website: www.trustlands.state.co.us

Membership: 1–100
Scope: State
Publication(s): Available on web
Contact(s):
  Chris Castilian, Acting Director; 303-866-3454

COLORADO DEPARTMENT OF PUBLIC HEALTH AND ENVIRONMENT
4300 Cherry Creek Dr., S.
Denver, CO 80246-1530 United States
Phone: 303-692-2035   Fax: 303-691-7702
E-mail: cdphe.information@state.co.us
Website: www.cdphe.state.co.us/

Scope: State
Description: The Colorado Department of Public Health and Environment has the responsibility for improving and protecting the health and environment for Colorado's citizens by: assuring a healthy working and living environment, protecting people against exposure to diseases, establishing preventive health services, and providing a quality environment through air, waste, water, radiation, and other environmental protection activities.
Contact(s):
  Jane Norton, Executive Director

COLORADO GOVERNOR'S OFFICE OF ENERGY MANAGEMENT AND CONSERVATION
OEMC
225 East 16th Avenue
Suite 650
Denver, CO 80203 United States
Phone: 303-894-2383   Fax: 303-894-2388
E-mail: oemc@state.co.us
Website: www.state.co.us/oemc/

Founded: 1977
Scope: State
Description: OEC's mission includes leading the citizens of Colorado by promoting the efficient use of energy and resources. OEC develops, implements, and monitors energy conservation programs and offers services for individuals, community organizations, institutions, businesses, and government. Those services are designed to reduce energy consumption and increase awareness of the environmental, economic, and personal benefit to efficient energy use.
Publication(s): Recycle Colorado Bulletin
Keyword(s): Energy, Reduce/Reuse/Recycle, Water Habitats & Quality
Contact(s):
  Rick Grice, Director; 303-894-2383; Fax: 303-894-2388; rick.grice@state.co.us
  Ed Lewis, Deputy Director of Programs; 303-894-2383; ext. 1204; Fax: 303-894-2388; ed.lewis@state.co.us
  Megan Castle, Public Information Officer; 303-894-2383; ext. 1211; Fax: 303-894-2388; megan.castle@state.co.us

COLORADO RIVER BOARD OF CALIFORNIA
RESOURCES AGENCY, THE
770 Falrmont Ave., Suite 100
Glendale, CA 91203-1035 United States
Phone: 818-543-4676   Fax: 818-543-4685
E-mail: crb@crb.ca.gov
Website: www.crb.ca.gov

Founded: 1937

Membership: 1–100
Scope: State
Description: The board was established to represent California, its agencies, and citizens in matters concerning the water and power resources provided by the Colorado River and its tributaries. Working with federal and state agencies, Congress, courts, and other Colorado River Basin states, the board analyzes engineering, legal, and economic matters concerning the use of Colorado River resources within the United States.
Publication(s): Western Water, Callifornia Journal
Contact(s):
Gerald Zimmerman, Executive Director

COLORADO STATE CONSERVATION BOARD
COLORADO DEPARTMENT OF AGRICULTURE
700 Kipling Street Suite 4000
Lakewood, CO 80215-8000 United States
Phone: 303-239-4112   Fax: 303-239-4176
Website: www.ag.state.co.us
Founded: 1938
Scope: Local, State
Description: Provide administrative and financial assistance to the 77 conservation districts in Colorado for the protection of the natural resources on private lands.
Keyword(s): Agriculture/Farming, Land Issues, Pollution (general), Wildlife & Species
Contact(s):
Robert Zebroski, Director; robert.zebroski@ag.state.co.us

COLORADO STATE FOREST SERVICE
203 Forestry Building
Ft. Collins, CO 80523-5060 United States
Phone: 970-491-6303   Fax: 970-491-7736
Website: www.colostate.edu/Depts/CSFS
Founded: 1885
Membership: 101–1,000
Scope: State
Description: The mission of the State Forest Service is to achieve stewardship of Colorado's environment through forestry outreach and service.
Keyword(s): Forests/Forestry, Land Issues
Contact(s):
James Hubbard, Director
Phil Hoefer, Community Forestry
Rich Homann, Wildfire Protection
Phil Schwolert, Forest Management
Bob Sturtevant, Conservation Education

COLORADO STATE UNIVERSITY COOPERATIVE EXTENSION
1 Administration Bldg., Colorado State University
Ft. Collins, CO 80523 United States
Phone: 970-491-6281   Fax: 970-491-6208
Website: www.colostate.edu/Depts/CoopExt/
Founded: 1914
Membership: 101–1,000
Scope: State
Description: A branch of Colorado State University. Conducts statewide noncredit educational programs off campus.
Publication(s): Publications listed on website
Keyword(s): Agriculture/Farming, Development/Developing Countries, Pollution (general), Public Health, Recreation/Ecotourism, Reduce/Reuse/Recycle, Sprawl/Urban Planning
Contact(s):
Milan Rewerts, Director of Cooperative Extension; mrewerts@coop.ext.colostate.edu
William Andelt, Extension Wildlife Specialist: Animal Damage Control; Dept. of Fishery and Wildlife Biology, 109 Wagar, Colorado State University, Ft. Collins, CO 80523; 970-491-7093
Delwin Benson, Extension Wildlife Specialist: Wildlife Management; Dept. of Fishery and Wildlife Biology, 109 Wagar, Colorado State University, Ft. Collins, CO 80523; 970-491-6411; Fax: 970-491-5091
Mary Gray, Associate Director of Programs; gray@coop.ext.colostate.edu
Shelley Stanley, Extension Agent-Natural Resources; 15200 W. Sixth Ave., Golden, CO 80401; 303-271-6620

COLORADO WATER CONSERVATION BOARD
WATER CONSERVATION BOARD
1313 Sherman St.
Denver, CO 80203 United States
Phone: 303-866-3441   Fax: 303-866-4474
Website: www.dnr.state.co.us
Scope: State
Keyword(s): Public Lands/Greenspace, Recreation/Ecotourism
Contact(s):
Rod Kuharich, Director

COLUMBIA RIVER GORGE COMMISSION
P.O. Box 730
White Salmon, WA 98672 United States
Phone: 509-493-3323   Fax: 509-493-2229
E-mail: crgc@gorge.net
Website: www.gorgecommission.org
Membership: 1–100
Scope: Regional
Description: Established by the states of Oregon and Washington to implement the Columbia River Gorge National Scenic Area Act by developing a regional management plan, in cooperation with the U.S. Forest Service. The commission is composed of three members from Oregon, three from Washington, and one from each of the six local Gorge counties. A Secretary of Agriculture appointee is a thirteenth nonvoting member.
Keyword(s): Land Issues, Recreation/Ecotourism
Contact(s):
Maratha Bennett, Executive Director; bennett@gorgecommission.org
Anne Squier, Chairman
Wayne Wooster, Vice Chairman; 509-493-3724; wooster@gorge.net

COMITE DESPERTAR CIDRENO
P.O. Box 1714
Cidra, PR 739 United States
Phone: 787-739-5492
Founded: 1987
Description: Primarily devoted to educate and organize communities in the east-central part of the island to deal with water pollution and wildlife habitat. Also deals with toxic waste problems.
Publication(s): Despertar Cidreno
Keyword(s): Air Quality/Atmosphere, Reduce/Reuse/Recycle, Water Habitats & Quality, Wildlife & Species
Contact(s):
Olga Rodriguez Berrios, President
Juanita Garcia, Treasurer
Vivian Santiago, Secretary

CONNECTICUT COUNCIL ON ENVIRONMENTAL QUALITY
79 Elm Street
Hartford, CT 06106 United States
Phone: 860-424-4000   Fax: 860-424-4070
E-mail: karl.wagener@po.state.ct.us
Website: www.ct.gov/ceq
Founded: 1971
Scope: State

Description: Prepares annual reports to the Governor on the status of Connecticut's environment; receives and investigates citizen complaints pertaining to the environment; and reviews environmental assessments of construction activities of state agencies. The council is composed of nine appointed members who serve without compensation.
Publication(s): Environmental Quality in Connecticut
Annual Report
Contact(s):
    Karl Wagener, Executive Director
    Donal O'Brien, Chairman

CONNECTICUT DEPARTMENT OF AGRICULTURE
765 Asylum Ave.
Hartford, CT 06105 United States
Phone: 860-713-2500   Fax: 860-713-2514
E-mail: ctdeptag@po.state.ct.us
Website: www.state.ct.us/doag

Founded: 1971
Membership: 1–100
Scope: State
Description: State Department of Agriculture
Publication(s): Connecticut Weekly
Contact(s):
    Emilie Andrews, Director: Personnel; 860-713-2501; Fax: 860-713-2585; emilie.andrews@po.state.ct.us
    David Carey, Executive Director: Connecticut Marketing Authority; 101 Reserve Rd., Hartford, CT 06114; 860-566-3699; Fax: 860-566-2944; ct.mktg.authority@snet.net
    Dawn Cassada, Director: Administration; 860-713-2502; Fax: 860-713-2585; dawn.cassada@po.state.ct.us
    Joseph Dippel, Director: Farmland Preservation; 860-713-2511; Fax: 860-713-2514; joseph.dippel@po.state.ct.us
    Robert Pellegrino, Director: Marketing and Technology; 860-713-2503; Fax: 860-713-2516; robert.pellegrino@po.state.ct.us
    Bruce Sherman, Director: Regulation and Inspection; 860-713-2504; Fax: 860-713-2515; bruce.sherman@po.state.ct.us
    John Volk, Director: Aquaculture Division; P.O. Box 97, Milford, CT 06460; 203-874-2855; Fax: 203-783-9976; dept.agric@snet.net
    Shirley Ferris, Commissioner; 860-713-2500; Fax: 860-713-2514; commissioner.ctdeptag@po.state.ct.us
    Bruce Gresczyk, Deputy Commissioner; 860-713-2526; Fax: 860-713-2514; commissioner.ctdeptag@po.state.ct.us
    Frank Intino, Deputy Director: Marketing and Technology; 860-713-2503; Fax: 860-713-2516; frank.intino@po.state.ct.us
    Mary Lis, State Veterinarian; 860-713-2505; Fax: 860-713-2515; mary.lis@po.state.ct.us
    Gabriel Moquin, Deputy Director: Regulation and Inspection; 860-713-2508; Fax: 860-713-2515; gabriel.moquin@po.state.ct.us

CONNECTICUT DEPARTMENT OF ENVIRONMENTAL PROTECTION
79 Elm St.
Hartford, CT 06106-5127 United States
Phone: 860-424-3000   Fax: 860-424-4078
Website: www.dep.state.ct.us

Membership: 1–100
Scope: State
Description: Created by the Connecticut General Assembly to conserve, protect, and improve the state's environment and to manage the basic resources of air, water, and land for the benefit of present and future generations.
Publication(s): Connecticut Wildlife Magazine
Contact(s):
    Pamela Adams, Director, Parks Division; 860-424-3200
    Matthew Fritz, Acting Director, Communications, Education and Publications; 860-424-4100
    William Hyatt, Director, Inland Fisheries Division; 860-424-3475
    Dale May, Director, Wildlife Division; 860-424-3011; Fax: 860-424-4078; dale.may@po.state.ct.us
    Eric Nelson, Acting Director, Law Enforcement Division; 860-424-3012; eric.nelson@po.state.ct.us
    Charles Reed, Director, Land Acquisition and Management; 860-424-3016
    Eric Smith, Acting Director, Marine Fisheries Division; 860-424-6043; eric.smith@po.state.ct.us
    Donald Smith, Director, Forestry Division; 860-424-3630
    Yvonne Bolton, Acting Chief, Bureau of Water Management; 860-424-3704
    Ann Gobin, Acting Chief, Bureau of Air Management; 860-424-3026
    Michael Harder, Acting Chief, Bureau of Waste Management; 860-424-3021
    David Leff, Deputy Commissioner Environmental Conservations; 860-424-3005
    Tom Morrissey, Acting Chief, Bureau of Outdoor Recreation; 860-424-3200
    Edward Parker, Chief, Bureau of Natural Resources; 860-424-3010
    Arthur Rocque, Commissioner; 860-424-3001
    Jane Stahl, Assistant Commissioner, Air, Water and Waste; 860-424-3000

COOPERATIVE EXTENSION SERVICE
UNIVERSITY OF ALASKA FAIRBANKS
COLLEGE OF RURAL ALASKA
CES Bldg., University of Alaska
P.O. Box 756180
Fairbanks, AK 99775-6180 United States
Phone: 907-474-7246   Fax: 907-474-6971
E-mail: fyace@uaf.edu
Website: www.uaf.edu/coop-ext

Membership: 1–100
Scope: State
Contact(s):
    Anthony Nakazawa, Director; anatn@uaa.alaska.edu
    Robert Gorman, Land Resources Program Chair; 907-786-6323; ffrfg@uaf.edu
    Michele Hebert, Land Resources Agent; 907-474-1530; ffmah@uaf.edu
    Peter Stortz, Fish and NR Specialist; CES/Palmer Research Center, 533 E. Fireweed Ln., Palmer, AK 99645; 907-746-9459; Fax: 907-746-2677; ffpjs@ufa.edu

COUNTY OF SAN DIEGO
DEPARTMENT OF PLANNING AND LAND USE
MULTIPLE SPECIES CONSERVATION PROGRAM
5201 Ruffin Road
Suite B
San Diego, CA 92123 United States
Phone: 858-694-3075   Fax: 858-694-2555
E-mail: mscp@sdcounty.ca.gov
Website: www.mscp.sandiego.org

Scope: Local, Regional
Description: Working with the Federal, State, local and regional governments to protect the region's biodiversity and 85 sensitive species by linking together large blocks of habitat with County, State and Federal parks, open space and watershsed protection areas to preserve biological core areas and connecting corridors.
Keyword(s): Ecosystems (precious), Land Issues, Public Lands/Greenspace, Wildlife & Species
Contact(s):
    Trish Boaz, Environmental Resource Manager; 858-694-3075; Fax: 858-694-2555; trish.boaz@sdcounty.ca.gov

CRANSTON CONSERVATION COMMISSION
Cranston City Hall
869 Park Avenue
Cranston, RI 02910 United States
Phone: 401-944-1070   Fax: 401-944-1070
E-mail: loupneige@aol.com

Founded: 1973
Scope: Local
Description: Appointed by the mayor, with the consent of the council, this seven member commission recommends and advises the city officials on future planning projects and preservation concerns.
Keyword(s): Development/Developing Countries, Land Issues, Public Lands/Greenspace, Water Habitats & Quality, Wildlife & Species

D

DELAWARE COOPERATIVE EXTENSION SERVICES
Delaware Cooperative Extension, Townsend Hall,
University of Delaware
Newark, DE 19717-1303 United States
Phone: 302-831-2504   Fax: 302-831-6758
E-mail: pbarber@udel.edu
Website: http://bluehen.ags.udel.edu/deces/

Scope: State
Keyword(s): Agriculture/Farming, Energy, Forests/Forestry, Land Issues, Pollution (general), Public Health, Wildlife & Species
Contact(s):
  Robin Morgan, Dean, College of Agricultural Sciences and Director, Agriculture
  Patricia Barber, Associate Dean for Extension and Outreach; pbarber@udel.edu
  John Ewart, Aquaculture Specialist; University of Delaware Aquatic Research Center, 700 Pilottown Rd., Lewes, DE 19958; 302-645-4060; Fax: 302-645-4007

DELAWARE DEPARTMENT OF AGRICULTURE
FOREST SERVICE
2320 S. DuPont Hwy.
Dover, DE 19901 United States
Phone: 302-698-4500   Fax: 302-697-6287
E-mail: kay@dda.state.de.us
Website: www.state.de.us/deptagri/

Founded: 1982
Scope: State
Description: A statewide organization affiliated with the National Woodland Owners Association, dedicated to promote good forest practices and multiple use of private forest lands in Delaware.
Publication(s): DFA Newsletter
Keyword(s): Forests/Forestry
Contact(s):
  W. Jones, President and Editor; 410-742-3163
  Jim Bennett, Vice President

DELAWARE DEPARTMENT OF NATURAL RESOURCES AND ENVIRONMENTAL CONTROL
DIVISION OF AIR & WASTE MANAGEMENT
89 Kings Hwy.
Dover, DE 19901 United States
Phone: 302-739-4764   Fax: 302-739-5060
Website: www.dnrec.state.de.us/dnrec2000/Divisions/AWM/AWM.htm

Scope: State
Description: Environmental regulatory agency.
Contact(s):
  John Blevins, Director; 302-739-4764; Fax: 302-739-5060
  Kathleen Banning, Manager, Tanks Management Branch; 302-395-2500; Fax: 302-395-2555
  Nancy Marker, Manager, Solid & Hazardous Waste; 302-739-3689; Fax: 302-739-5060
  Ali Mirzakhalili, Program Administrator, Air Quality Management; 302-739-4791; Fax: 302-739-3106
  Christina Wirtz, Manager, Site Investigation and Remediation; 302-395-2600; Fax: 302-395-2601
  William Hill, Chief Enforcement Officer; 302-739-5072; Fax: 302-739-5060

DELAWARE DEPARTMENT OF NATURAL RESOURCES AND ENVIRONMENTAL CONTROL
DIVISION OF FISH AND WILDLIFE
89 Kings Hwy.
Dover, DE 19901 United States
Phone: 302-739-5295   Fax: 302-739-6157
Website: www.dnrec.state.de.us/DNREC2000/Divisions/FW/FW.htm

Founded: 1911
Membership: 101–1,000
Scope: State
Description: This is a State Agency having responsibility to conserve wildlife and fisheries natural resources, and enforces laws concerning wildlife, fisheries and boating.
Publication(s): The Observer
Keyword(s): Forests/Forestry, Public Health, Public Lands/Greenspace, Recreation/Ecotourism, Water Habitats & Quality, Wildlife & Species
Contact(s):
  H. Lloyd Alexander, Jr., Acting Director; 302-739-5295
  Phil Carpenter, Manager, Acquisitions; 302-739-3441
  Roy Miller, Administrator, Fisheries; 302-739-3441
  Lacy Nichols, Manager, Construction; 302-739-3441
  H. Alexander, Administrator, Wildlife; 302-739-5297
  James Graybeal, Administrator, Enforcement; 302-739-3440
  Lynn Herman, Federal Aid Coordinator and Senior Planner; 302-739-5296
  William Meredith, Administrator of Mosquito Control; 302-739-3493

DELAWARE DEPARTMENT OF NATURAL RESOURCES AND ENVIRONMENTAL CONTROL
DIVISION OF PARKS AND RECREATION
89 Kings Hwy.
Dover, DE 19901 United States
Phone: 302-739-4401   Fax: 302-739-3817
Website: www.destateparks.com

Founded: 1951
Scope: State
Description: State park agency.
Contact(s):
  Charles Salkin, Director; 302-739-4401
  Mark Chura, Manager, Planning, Preservation and Development; 302-739-5285
  James O'Neill, Manager, Cultural & Recreation Services; 302-739-4413
  Clyde Shipman, Manager, Park Operations; 302-739-4406

DELAWARE DEPARTMENT OF NATURAL RESOURCES AND ENVIRONMENTAL CONTROL
DIVISION OF SOIL AND WATER CONSERVATION
89 Kings Highway
Dover, DE 19901 United States
Phone: 302-739-4403   Fax: 302-739-6242
Website: www.dnrec.state.de.us

Scope: State
Keyword(s): Air Quality/Atmosphere, Land Issues, Water Habitats & Quality

STATE AND PROVINCIAL GOVERNMENT AGENCIES – D

Contact(s):
John Hughes, Director; jhughes@dnrec.state.de.us
Sarah Cooksey, Administrator: Delaware Coastal
   Management Program; 302-739-3451
Robert Henry, Administrator: Shoreline and Waterway
   Management

DELAWARE DEPARTMENT OF NATURAL RESOURCES AND ENVIRONMENTAL CONTROL
DIVISION OF WATER RESOURCES
89 Kings Hwy.
Dover, DE 19901 United States
Phone: 302-739-4860   Fax: 302-739-7864
Website: www.dnrc.state.de.us

Membership: 101–1,000
Scope: State
Description: The Division of Water Resources serves Delaware by monitoring, managing, and protecting Delaware's ground and surface waters, tidal wetlands, and underwater lands.

Contact(s):
Kevin Donnelly, Director; 302-739-4860
Peder Hansen, Manager, Surface Water Discharges; 302-739-5731
Stewart Lovell, Manager, Water Supply; 302-739-4793
William Moyer, Manager, Wetlands and Subaqueous Lands; 302-739-4691
John Schneider, Manager, Watershed Assessment; 302-739-4590
Rodney Wyatt, Manager, Ground Water Discharges; 302-739-4761
Sergio Huerta, Administrator, Environmental Services; 302-739-4771

DELAWARE FOREST SERVICE
2320 S. DuPont Highway
Dover, DE 19901-5515 United States
Phone: 302-698-4500   Fax: 302-697-6245
E-mail: austin.short@state.de.us
Website: www.state.de.us/deptagri/

Founded: 1927
Scope: State
Description: The Delaware Forest Service provides technical forestry assistance to landowners and homeowners and manages Delaware's three State Forests (Blackbird, Redden, and Taber).
Keyword(s): Agriculture/Farming, Forests/Forestry, Land Issues, Pollution (general)

Contact(s):
Teresa Crenshaw, Agriculture Compliance Laboratory; teresa@dda.state.de.us
Anne Fitzgerald, Community Relations Officer; anne.dda.state.de.us
Michael Scuse, Secretary
Bruce Walton, Executive Assistant; brucew@dda.state.de.us

DELAWARE GEOLOGICAL SURVEY
DGS Bldg., University of Delaware
Newark, DE 19716 United States
Phone: 302-831-2833   Fax: 302-831-3579
E-mail: delgeosurvey@udel.edu
Website: www.udel.edu/dgs

Founded: 1951
Membership: 1–100
Scope: State
Description: The survey was formed to study the geology, water, and other earth resources of Delaware; also to prepare reports, maps, and otherwise disseminate its findings, and to provide assistance in its area to other agencies and individuals.

Contact(s):
Robert Jordan, State Geologist and Director
John Talley, Associate Director; waterman@udel.edu
Dorothy Windish, Librarian

DELAWARE SOLID WASTE AUTHORITY
1128 S. Bradford St., P.O. Box 455
Dover, DE 19903 United States
Phone: 302-739-5361   Fax: 302-739-4287
E-mail: dra@dswa.com
Website: www.dswa.com

Founded: 1975
Membership: 101–1,000
Scope: Local
Description: To define, develop, and implement cost-effective plans and programs for solid waste management which best serve Delaware and protect our public health and environment.
Publication(s): Statewide Solid Waste Management Plan and Executive Summary, Marketing Research Findings and Executive Summary, Trash Tracks (DSWA Newsletter), Great Waste Mystery Curriculum
Keyword(s): Public Health, Reduce/Reuse/Recycle

Contact(s):
Pasquale Canzano, Chief Operating Officer; psc@dswa.com
Thomas Houska, Chief of Administrative/ Services Officer; teh@dswa.com
N. Vasuki, Chief Executive Officer; ncv@dswa.com

DEPARTAMENTO DE RECURSOS NATURALES Y AMBIENTALES
AREA DE PLANIFICACION INTEGRAL
DIVISION DE PATRIMONIO NATURAL
P.O. Box 9066600
Puerta de Tierra Station
San Juan 00906-6600 Puerto Rico
Phone: 787-724-8774, ext. 4037   Fax: 787-725-9526
E-mail: dpn@caribe.net
Website: www.natureserve.org/nhp/lacarb/pr/

Founded: 1988
Scope: State
Description: Identify and protect priority conservation areas.
Keyword(s): Ecosystems (precious), Wildlife & Species

Contact(s):
Aida Martinez, Division Director
Daniel Davila-Casanova, Zoologist/Data Manager; 787-724-8774; ext. 2230; dpn@caribe.net

DEPARTMENT OF LAND AND NATURAL RESOURCES (HAWAII)
DIVISION OF AQUATIC RESOURCES
1151 Punchbowl St.
Honolulu, HI 96813 United States
Phone: 808-587-0100   Fax: 808-587-0115
Website: www.state.hi.us/dlnr/dnr

Scope: State

Contact(s):
Michael Fugimoto, Program Manager: Commercial Fisheries Aquaculture Branch; 808-587-0085
William Devick, Administrator, Acting; 808-587-0110

DEPARTMENT OF PARKS AND RECREATION
DEPARTMENT OF PARKS AND RECREATION
1416 9th Street
Room 1413-9
Sacramento, CA 95814 United States
Phone: 916-653-1427   Fax: 916-654-7774
Website: www.cal-parks.ca.gov

Scope: Local, State
Description: Responsible for the acquisition, preservation, development, interpretation, and operation of the state park system; also responsible for the administration of grants for recreation to local government and for development of the California Outdoor Recreation Resources Plan.
Keyword(s): Recreation/Ecotourism

Contact(s):
- Ruth Coleman, Director; 916-653-8380
- Bill Berry, Chief Deputy Director of Park Stewardship; 916-653-8288
- Ron Brean, Chief of Northern Division; 916-657-4042
- George Cook, Central Field Division Chief; 916-653-2021
- Tim Lafranchi, Legal Office; 916-653-6884
- John McMahon, Deputy Director of Marketing and Revenue Generation; 916-653-5841; jmcma@parks.ca.gov
- Knox Mellon, Deputy Director of Historic Preservation Office; 916-653-6624
- Pilar Onate, Deputy Director of Legislation; 916-653-6887
- Richard Rayburn, Natural Heritage Division; 916-653-6745
- Mark Schrader, Acquisition and Development; 916-653-7475; mschrader@parks.ca.gov
- Steven Treanor, Chief of Southern Division; 916-657-4042; strea@parks.ca.gov
- Denzil Verardo, Chief Deputy Director of Administration; 916-653-0528
- Ray Watson, Human Rights; 916-653-9990
- Dave Widell, Deputy Director of Off Highway Motor Vehicle Recreation; 916-324-5801

DEPARTMENT OF TOURISM, CULTURE AND RECREATION
Commerce Court
Cornerbrook, A2H 6J8 Newfoundland Canada
Phone: 709-729-2817   Fax: 709-637-2004
Website: www.gov.nf.ca/tcr

Membership: 1–100
Scope: Province

Contact(s):
- Kevin Aylward, Minister; 709-729-4715
- Clyde Granter, Deputy Minister
- Keith Healey, Associate Deputy Minister

DISTRICT OF COLUMBIA DEPARTMENT OF HEALTH
ENVIRONMENTAL HEALTH ADMINISTRATION, WATERSHED PROTECTION DIVISION
51 N Street NE 5th Floor
Washington, DC 20002 United States
Phone: 202-535-2240   Fax: 202-535-1364
Website: www.dchealth.com/eha/watersheds/welcome.htm

DISTRICT OF COLUMBIA DEPARTMENT OF PUBLIC WORKS
2000 14th St., NW
Washington, DC 20009 United States
Phone: 202-727-1000
Website: http://dpw.dc.gov/main.shtml

Scope: Local
Description: District of Columbia's Department of Public Works.
Keyword(s): Pollution (general), Reduce/Reuse/Recycle, Transportation

Contact(s):
- Leslie Hotaling, Director

DIVISION OF FORESTRY AND SOIL RESOURCES OF GUAM
192 Dairy Road
Mangilao, GU 96923 United States
Phone: 671-735-3949   Fax: 671-734-0111

Founded: 1953
Description: The DFSR was formed for the management, protection, and enhancement of the territory's forest and land resources to produce ample amounts of water, wood, fiber, and recreation to benefit the most number of people.
Keyword(s): Forests/Forestry

Contact(s):
- Joseph Acfalle, Urban and Community Forester; jacfalle@ns.gu
- Rodolfo Ando, Management Forester; rlando@ns.gu
- Louann Guzman, Forester I; lcguzman@ns.gu
- David Limtiaco, Chief; dlimti@ns.gu
- Belmina Soliva, Forester I; bsoliva@ns.gu

E

ENVIRONMENTAL PROTECTION MASSACHUSETTS
DEPARTMENT OF ENVIRONMENTAL PROTECTION
One Winter St.
Dept. of Environmental Affairs
Boston, MA 02108 United States
Phone: 617-292-5500   Fax: 617-556-1049
Website: www.state.ma.us/dep

Membership: 1,001–10,000
Scope: State
Publication(s): Publications on line

Contact(s):
- Barbara Kwetz, Director of Planning and Evaluation; 617-292-5593
- James Coleman, Assistant Commissioner: Waste Prevention; 617-292-5570
- Lauren Liss, Commissioner

F

FLORIDA COOPERATIVE FISH AND WILDLIFE RESEARCH UNIT (USDI)
P.O. Box 110485, Building 810
University of Florida
Gainesville, FL 32611-0485 United States
Phone: 352-392-1861   Fax: 352-846-0841
E-mail: rayc@zoo.ufl.edu
Website: www.wec.ufl.edu/coop/

Founded: 1979
Scope: Local, State, Regional, National
Description: Established by cooperative agreement among the National Biological Survey, Florida Game and Fresh Water Fish Commission, and the University of Florida. Primary purpose is research, graduate education, and extension activities integrating fish and wildlife ecology and management in Florida's unique ecosystems, particularly wetlands.
Keyword(s): Water Habitats & Quality, Wildlife & Species

Contact(s):
- Raymond Carthy, Assistant Unit Leader: Wildlife; 352-392-1861; Fax: 352-846-0841; rayc@zoo.ufl.edu
- Wiley Kitchens, Research Ecologist; 352-392-1861; Fax: 352-846-0841; kitchensw@wec.ufl.edu
- H. Percival, Unit Leader; 352-392-1861; Fax: 352-846-0841; percivalf@wec.ufl.edu

FLORIDA DEPARTMENT OF AGRICULTURE AND CONSUMER SERVICES
The Capitol, PL 10
Tallahassee, FL 32399-0800 United States
Phone: 850-488-3022   Fax: 850-488-7585
Website: www.doacs.state.fl.us

Membership: 1–100
Scope: State

Contact(s):
- Charles Bronson, Commissioner; 850-488-3022

FLORIDA DEPARTMENT OF AGRICULTURE AND CONSUMER SERVICES
DIVISION OF FORESTRY
3125 Conner Blvd.
Tallahassee, FL 32399-1650 United States
Phone: 850-488-4274   Fax: 850-488-0863
Website: www.fl-dof.com

Founded: 1927
Membership: 1,001–10,000
Scope: Regional
Description: To protect and manage Florida's forest resources through a stewardship ethic to assure these resources will be available for future generations. Current number of employees: 1,100.
Contact(s):
  Mike Long, Director
  John Core, Chief of Forest Management; 850-488-9927
  Raymond Geiger, Chief, Field Operations; 850-414-9969
  James Karels, Assistant Director; 850-488-4274
  Charles Maynard, Chief of Planning and Support Services; 850-414-0843

FLORIDA DEPARTMENT OF AGRICULTURE AND CONSUMER SERVICES
OFFICE OF AGRICULTURAL WATER POLICY
1203 Governor Square Blvd.
Tallahassee, FL 32301 United States
Phone: 850-488-6249   Fax: 850-921-2153
Website: www.floridaagwaterpolicy.com

Membership: 1,001–10,000
Scope: State
Description: Provides administrative, legislative, and promotional assistance to 63 Soil and Water Conservation Districts in Florida.
Contact(s):
  Chuck Aller, Director
  John Folks, Environmental Administrator; 850-488-6249

FLORIDA DEPARTMENT OF AGRICULTURE AND CONSUMER SERVICES
SOIL AND WATER CONSERVATION COUNCIL
3125 Conner Blvd., Suite C, Mail Stop C28
Tallahassee, FL 32399 United States
Phone: 850-488-5321   Fax: 850-921-2153

Scope: State
Contact(s):
  Clegg Hooks, SWC Administrator; 3125 Conner Blvd., Suite C, Conner Bldg., Tallahassee, FL 32399; 850-488-6249; Fax: 850-921-2153
  Richard Machek, Chair; 17 NW 16th St., Delray Beach, FL 33444

FLORIDA DEPARTMENT OF ENVIRONMENTAL PROTECTION
3900 Commonwealth Blvd.
M.S. 49
Tallahassee, FL 32399-3000 United States
Phone: 850-245-2118   Fax: 850-245-2128
E-mail: krista.callen@dep.state.fl.us
Website: www.DEP.STATE.FL.US

Membership: 1,001–10,000
Scope: State
Description: More Protection, Less Process. Lead agency in Florida state government for environmental management and stewardship. Administers regulatory programs and issues permits for air, water and waste management. It oversees the State's land and water conservation program, Florida Forever, and manages the Florida Park Service.
Keyword(s): Air Quality/Atmosphere, Ecosystems (precious), Land Issues, Oceans/Coasts/Beaches, Pollution (general), Public Lands/Greenspace, Recreation/Ecotourism, Reduce/Reuse/Recycle, Water Habitats & Quality
Contact(s):
  Denver Stutler, Chief of Staff; 850-488-7131
  Teri Donalson, General Counsel; 850-488-9314
  Pinky Hall, Inspector General; 850-488-2287
  David Struhs, Secretary; 850-488-1154

FLORIDA DEPARTMENT OF ENVIRONMENTAL PROTECTION
AIR RESOURCES MANAGEMENT DIVISION
2600 Blair Stone Rd. MS 5500
Tallahassee, FL 32399-2400 United States
Phone: 850-488-0114   Fax: 850-922-6979
Website: www.dep.state.fl.us

FLORIDA DEPARTMENT OF ENVIRONMENTAL PROTECTION
BUREAU OF BEACHES AND WETLAND RESOURCES
3900 Commonwealth Blvd.
Mail Station 300
Tallahassee, FL 32399-3000 United States
Phone: 850-488-3181   Fax: 850-488-5257
Website: www.floridadep.org/beaches

Scope: State
Description: State agency.
Contact(s):
  Michael Sole, Bureau Chief; 850-488-3181
  Gene Chelecki, P.E. Administrator; 850-488-3181; ext. 111
  Marty Seeling, Environmental Administrator; 850-487-4471
  Jim Stoutamire, Environmental Administrator; 850-245-8490
  Mark Leadon, Coastal Data and Analysis; 850-487-4469
  Paden Woodruff, Environmental Administrator; 850-487-1262

FLORIDA DEPARTMENT OF ENVIRONMENTAL PROTECTION
COASTAL AND AQUATIC MANAGED AREAS
3900 Commonwealth Blvd.
Mail Station 235
Tallahassee, FL 32399 United States
Phone: 850-245-2094   Fax: 850-245-2110
E-mail: larry.nall@dep.state.fl.us
Website: www.dep.state.fl.us/coastal

Founded: 1994
Membership: 101–1,000
Scope: State
Description: Manages Florida's Aquatic Preserves, State Buffer Preserves, National Estuarine Research Reserves and partners with NOAA on management of the Florida Keys National Marine Sanctuary
Contact(s):
  Katherine Andrews, Director; 850-245-2094; ext. 4101; Fax: 850-245-2110; katherine.andrews@dep.state.fl.us
  Dennis Riley, Program Administrator; 850-245-2094; ext. 4102; Fax: 850-245-2110; danny.riley@dep.state.fl.us

FLORIDA DEPARTMENT OF ENVIRONMENTAL PROTECTION
DIVISION OF LAW ENFORCEMENT
3900 Commonwealth Blvd.
Mail Stop 600
Tallahassee, FL 32399-3000 United States
Phone: 850-245-2852   Fax: 850-245-2858
Website: www.dep.state.fl.us/law

Scope: State
Description: The Division of Law Enforcement?s mission is to "protect the people, the environment, the cultural and natural resources, through enforcement, education and public service". The Law Enforcement Program is responsible for statewide environmental resource law enforcement and providing basic

law enforcement services to the state parks, greenways and trails.

Contact(s):
Thomas Tramell, Division Director; 850-245-2852; Fax: 850-245-2858; tom.tramel@dep.state.fl.us

FLORIDA DEPARTMENT OF ENVIRONMENTAL PROTECTION
DIVISION OF RESOURCE ASSESSMENT AND MANAGEMENT
3900 Commonwealth Blvd
Mail Station 200
Tallahassee, FL 32399 United States
Phone: 850-245-3140   Fax: 850-245-3147
Website: www.dep.state.fl.us/resource

Scope: Local, State, Regional, National

Description: Resource Assessment and Management - Geology; Environmental Laboratory; Information Technology; Mercury and Applied Sciences.

Keyword(s): Air Quality/Atmosphere

Contact(s):
Edwin Conklin, Director; 850-245-3140; Fax: 850-245-3147; Edwin.Conklin@dep.state.fl.us

FLORIDA DEPARTMENT OF ENVIRONMENTAL PROTECTION
DIVISION OF STATE LANDS
3900 Commonwealth Blvd.
Mail Station 100
Tallahassee, FL 32399 United States
Phone: 850-245-2555
E-mail: eva.armstrong@dep.state.fl.us
Website: www.dep.state.fl.us/lands

Founded: 1979

Membership: 101–1,000

Scope: Local, State, Regional

Description: Responsible for managing Florida's public lands

Keyword(s): Agriculture/Farming, Ecosystems (precious), Forests/Forestry, Land Issues, Public Lands/Greenspace, Sprawl/Urban Planning, Wildlife & Species

Contact(s):
Eva Armstrong, Director
Rob Lovern, Assistant Director

FLORIDA DEPARTMENT OF ENVIRONMENTAL PROTECTION
DIVISION OF WATER RESOURCE MANAGEMENT
2600 Blair Stone Road
MS 3500
Tallahassee, FL 32399-2400 United States
Phone: 850-245-8335   Fax: 850-245-8356
Website: www.dep.state.fl.us/water

Scope: Local, State, Regional

Description: Protect and enhance Florida's water resources and public health by implementing surface water, ground water and wetlands protection programs; regulating drinking water systems and wastewater facilities; overseeing water supply development in conjunction with Florida's water management districts; and carrying out programs to conserve and restore Florida's beaches and coastal systems and mined lands.

Contact(s):
Mimi Drew, Director; 850-487-1855
Jerry Brooks, Deputy Director; 850-487-1855

FLORIDA DEPARTMENT OF ENVIRONMENTAL PROTECTION
FLORIDA STATE PARKS AMERICORPS
3900 Commonwealth Boulevard
Mail Stop 535
Tallahassee, FL 32399 United States
Phone: 850-245-3098
E-mail: deborah.burr@dep.state.fl.us
Website: www.floridastateparks.org/americorps

Founded: 1997

Membership: 1–100

Scope: Local, State

Description: To serve and strengthen Florida State Parks' natural and cultural resources by addressing critical environmental and human needs.

Keyword(s): Ecosystems (precious), Forests/Forestry, Oceans/Coasts/Beaches, Public Lands/Greenspace, Recreation/Ecotourism, Water Habitats & Quality, Wildlife & Species

Contact(s):
Phillip Werndli, Coordinator of Volunteer Programs; 850-245-3098

FLORIDA DEPARTMENT OF ENVIRONMENTAL PROTECTION
RECREATION AND PARKS DIVISION
3900 Commonwealth Blvd.
Tallahassee, FL 32399 United States
Phone: 850-488-9872
Website: www.dep.state.fl.us/parks

Contact(s):
Joe Bakker, Staff of Mine Reclamation; 904-488-8217
Tom Brown, Staff of Aquatic Plant Management; 904-488-5631
Walter Schmidt, Staff of Geology; 904-488-4191

FLORIDA DEPARTMENT OF ENVIRONMENTAL PROTECTION
WASTE MANAGEMENT DIVISION
2600 Blair Stone Rd., MS 4500
Tallahassee, FL 32399 United States
Phone: 850-245-8705   Fax: 850-245-8803
Website: www.dep.state.fl.us/waste/

Contact(s):
Bill Hinkley, Bureau Chief-Solid and Hazardous Waste; 850-245-8707
Doug Jones, Bureau Chief-Waste Cleanup; 850-245-8927
John Ruddell, Director-Waste Management Division; 850-245-8705

FLORIDA FISH AND WILDLIFE CONSERVATION COMMISSION
OFFICE OF THE EXECUTIVE DIRECTOR
620 S. Meridian St.
Tallahassee, FL 32399-1600 United States
Phone: 850-487-3796   Fax: 850-921-5786
E-mail: commissioners@fwc.state.fl.us
Website: www.state.fl.us/fwc

Scope: State

Description: Agency Mission: Managing fish and wildlife resources for their long-term well-being and for the benefit of the people.

Publication(s): Florida Wildlife

Keyword(s): Recreation/Ecotourism, Water Habitats & Quality, Wildlife & Species

Contact(s):
Robert Edwards, Director: Division of Law Enforcement; 850-488-6251
Allan Egbert, Executive Director; 850-487-3796
Brad Hartman, Director: Office of Environmental Services; 850-488-6661
Victor Heller, Assistant Executive Director; 850-488-3084
Frank Montalbano, Director: Division of Wildlife; 850-488-3831
Edwin Moyer, Director: Division of Freshwater Fisheries; 850-488-0331
Sandra Porter, Director: Division of Administrative Services; 850-488-6551

STATE AND PROVINCIAL GOVERNMENT AGENCIES – G

James Antista, General Counsel; 850-487-1764
Dick Sublette, Editor; 850-488-5564
Susan Weaver, Bureau of Licensing and Permitting

FLORIDA STATE DEPARTMENT OF HEALTH
4052 Bald Cypress Way BIN # AOO
Tallahassee, FL 32399-1701 United States
Phone: 850-245-4321   Fax: 850-922-9453
Website: www.doh.state.fl.us/
Keyword(s): Pollution (general), Public Health
Contact(s):
　Sharon Heber, Division Director of Environmental Health; 850-488-6811
　Bart Bibler, Environmental Programs; 850-488-4070
　Eric Grimm, Environmental Programs; 850-487-0004
　Richard Hunter, Deputy State Health Officer for Prevention and Control Programs; 850-487-2945
　Roger Inman, Environmental Hazards; 850-488-3385
　Russell Mardon, Epidemiology Programs, Acting Chief; 850-488-3370

FORESTRY COMMISSION (ARKANSAS)
3821 W. Roosevelt Rd.
Little Rock, AR 72204-6369 United States
Phone: 501-296-1940   Fax: 501-296-1949
Website: www.forestry.state.ar.us
Membership: 1–100
Scope: Regional
Description: To prevent and suppress forest fires; control forest insects and diseases; grow and distribute forest planting stock; and collect and disseminate information concerning growth, utilization, and renewal of forests.
Keyword(s): Forests/Forestry
Contact(s):
　Robert Araiza, Fiscal Department; 501-296-1931
　James Grant, Conservation Education; 501-296-1937
　Don McBride, Fire Control; 501-296-1870
　Alan Murray, Baucum Nursery; 501-907-2485
　Larry Nance, Deputy State Forester; 501-296-1942
　George Rheinhardt, Forest Management; 501-296-1861
　John Shannon, State Forester; 501-296-1941

FORESTRY COMMISSION (SOUTH CAROLINA)
5500 Broad River Road
Columbia, SC 29221-1707 United States
Phone: 803-896-8800   Fax: 803-798-8097
E-mail: scsc@forestry.state.sc.us
Website: www.state.sc.us/forest
Founded: 1927
Scope: State
Description: Provides basic forest fire protection on all state and private forest lands in South Carolina; assists landowners in proper management and utilization of forest lands; promotes forest fire prevention and other forestry practices through an information and education program; and operates forest tree nursery, seed orchards, and state forests.
Keyword(s): Forests/Forestry, Sprawl/Urban Planning, Water Habitats & Quality
Contact(s):
　Tim Adams, Director of Field Operations Support; 803-896-8802
　Joe Richbourg, Director of Administration Division; 803-896-8858
　Bill Boykin, Deputy State Forester; 803-896-8832
　Cecil Campbell, Coastal Regional Forester; 843-538-3708
　C. Carson, Technical Assistant to the State Forester; 803-896-8822
　Ken Hill, Commission Vice Chairman; 308 Fuller St., Manning, SC 29102; 803-435-8133
　Ed Muckenfuss, Commission Chairman; P.O. Box 1950, Summerville, SC 29484; 843-871-5000
　Charles Ramsey, Piedmont Regional Forester; 803-276-0205
　Steve Scott, Pee Dee Regional Forester; 843-662-5571
　Robert Showalter, State Forester
　Judy Weston, Executive Assistant to State Forester; 803-896-8875

G

GEORGIA DEPARTMENT OF AGRICULTURE
19 Martin Luther King Dr., Capitol Sq.
Atlanta, GA 30334 United States
Phone: 404-656-3608   Fax: 404-656-3683
Website: www.agr.state.ga.us
Founded: 1874
Membership: 101–1,000
Scope: State
Description: The department serves farmers and consumers in the state by verifying and enforcing the accuracy and quality of both products and services in many areas including food products, seed, fertilizers, pesticides, fuel, weights and measures, and bedding, and by overseeing the health and well-being of Georgia's livestock, poultry, and commercial pet industry.
Publication(s): Farmers and Consumers Market Bulletin, Georgia Poultry Facts, Georgia Agricultural Facts
Keyword(s): Agriculture/Farming, Pollution (general), Public Health
Contact(s):
　Bobby Harris, Assistant Commissioner of Marketing; 404-656-3368
　Tommy Irvin, Commissioner of Agriculture
　Brenda James-Griffin, Assistant Commissioner for Public Affairs; 404-656-3689
　Phil Kea, Assistant Commissioner of Finance; 404-656-3608
　Lee Meyers, Assistant Commissioner of Animal Industry; 404-656-3671
　Cameron Smoak, Assistant Commissioner for Consumer Protection Field Forces; 404-656-3627
　Ron Weaver, Assistant Commissioner of Administration; 404-656-3608

GEORGIA DEPARTMENT OF AGRICULTURE
CONSUMER SERVICES LIBRARY
Agriculture Bldg., Capitol Square
Atlanta, GA 30334 United States
Phone: 404-656-3645   Fax: 404-651-7957
Website: www.agr.state.ga.us
Founded: 1874
Scope: State
Description: The Georgia Department of Agriculture has the distinction of being the nation's oldest such agency. The Department operates as a regulatory and enforcement agency, with the major goal of protecting the consuming public and promoting the farming sector. Under the office of Public Affairs, we respond to consumer inquiries on the department's areas of jurisdiction or student requests for project information. The Farmers and Consumers Market Bulletin has been serving Georgia citizens since 1917.
Publication(s): Farmers and Consumers Market Bulletin
Keyword(s): Agriculture/Farming
Contact(s):
　Arty Schronce, Director, Public Affairs; 1-800-282-5852; Fax: 404-651-7957; aschronce@agr.state.ga.us
　Teresa Jenkins, Manager, Consumer Services; 1-800-282-5852; tjenkins@agr.state.ga.us
　Brenda Griffin, Assistant Commissioner; 1-800-282-5852; bgriffin@agr.state.ga.us
　Tommy Irvin, Commissioner; 1-800-282-5852; bgriffin@agr.state.ga.us

GEORGIA DEPARTMENT OF EDUCATION
1766 Twin Towers, East
Atlanta, GA 30334-5040 United States
Phone: 404-656-0913   Fax: 404-651-8582
E-mail: bmoore@doe.k12.ga.us
Website: www.doe.k.ga.us

Membership: 1,001–10,000
Scope: State
Publication(s): Observation - newsletter, Georgia Science Teacher
Contact(s):
    Bob Moore, Science Program Specialist

GEORGIA DEPARTMENT OF NATURAL RESOURCES
2 Martin Luther King, Jr. Dr., SE
Suite 1252 East
Atlanta, GA 30334 United States
Phone: 404-656-3500   Fax: 404-656-0770
Website: www.dnr.state.ga.us

Founded: 1972
Scope: State
Description: Natural Resources
Keyword(s): Air Quality/Atmosphere, Ethics/Environmental Justice, Land Issues, Oceans/Coasts/Beaches, Pollution (general), Public Lands/Greenspace, Recreation/Ecotourism, Reduce/Reuse/Recycle, Water Habitats & Quality, Wildlife & Species
Contact(s):
    Lonice Barrett, Commissioner

GEORGIA DEPARTMENT OF NATURAL RESOURCES
COASTAL RESOURCES DIVISION
One Conservation Way
Brunswick, GA 31520 United States
Phone: 912-264-7218   Fax: 912-262-3143
Website: www.dnr.state.ga.us

Membership: 1–100
Scope: State
Description: The Coastal Resource Division administers many different programs to ensure wise management of Georgia's marshlands, barrier islands and marine commercial and sport species.
Keyword(s): Oceans/Coasts/Beaches
Contact(s):
    Susan Shipman, Director; 912-264-7218

GEORGIA DEPARTMENT OF NATURAL RESOURCES
ENVIRONMENTAL PROTECTION DIVISION
2 Martin Luther King, Jr. Drive, SE, Suite 1152 - East Tower
Atlanta, GA 30334 United States
Phone: 404-656-4713   Fax: 404-651-5778
Website: www.ganet.org/dnr/environ

Scope: Local, State
Description: EPD is responsible for enforcing 23 state laws. In addition, EPD is delegated to carry out the Congressionally mandated permitting and compliance programs for four Federal laws: the Clean Air Act, the Clean Water Act, the Safe Drinking Water Act, and the Resource Conservation and Recovery Act.
Contact(s):
    Harold Reheis, Director; 404-656-4713

GEORGIA DEPARTMENT OF NATURAL RESOURCES
ENVIRONMENTAL PROTECTION DIVISION
COASTAL DIVISION
1 Conservation Way
Brunswick, GA 31520 United States
Phone: 912-264-7284   Fax: 912-262-3160
Website: www.dnr.state.ga.us/dnr/environ

Contact(s):
    Harold Reheis, Director; 404-656-4713
    Alan Hallum, Chief: Water Protection Branch
    Nolton Johnson, Chief: Water Resources Branch
    Jennifer Kaduck, Chief: Hazardous Waste Branch
    Ron Methier, Chief: Air Protection Branch
    Jim Setser, Chief: Program Coordination Branch
    Mark Smith, Chief: Land Protection Branch
    David Word, Assistant Director

GEORGIA DEPARTMENT OF NATURAL RESOURCES
HISTORIC PRESERVATION DIVISION
156 Trinity Ave., SW, Suite 101
Atlanta, GA 30303 United States
Phone: 404-656-2840   Fax: 404-651-8739
Website: www.gashpo.org

Membership: 1–100
Scope: State
Description: Georgia's State Historic Preservation Office.
Publication(s): Publications on line
Contact(s):
    Ray Luce, Director; 404-656-2840

GEORGIA DEPARTMENT OF NATURAL RESOURCES
PARKS, RECREATION AND HISTORIC SITES DIVISION
205 Butler, SE, Suite 1352
Atlanta, GA 30334 United States
Phone: 404-656-2770   Fax: 404-651-5871

Scope: State
Contact(s):
    Burt Weerts, Director; 404-656-2770
    Wayne Escoe, Chief, Parks Operation Section
    David Freedman, Chief, Maintenance and Engineering Section

GEORGIA DEPARTMENT OF NATURAL RESOURCES
POLLUTION PREVENTION ASSISTANCE DIVISION
7 Martin Luther King Jr. Dr., SW, Suite 450
Atlanta, GA 30334-9004 United States
Phone: 404-651-5120   Fax: 404-651-5130
E-mail: info@p2ad.org
Website: www.dnr.state.ga.us/dnr/p2ad/

Founded: 1993
Scope: State
Description: P2AD is a non-regulatory division of DNR. We provide free, confidential technical assistance on cost-effective ways to prevent, reduce, reuse or recycle wastes, and conserve natural resources. Services are available to all Georgia businesses, industries, governmental agencies, institutions, and individual citizens.
Contact(s):
    Robert Kerr, Director; 404-651-5120

GEORGIA DEPARTMENT OF NATURAL RESOURCES
WILDLIFE RESOURCES DIVISION
2070 U.S. Highway 278, SE
Social Circle, GA 30025 United States
Phone: 770-918-6400　　　　Fax: 706-557-3030
Website: www.georgiawildlife.com

Scope: State

Description: The Georgia Department of Natural Resources (DNR) was established in 1972 to manage and protect the state's natural resources. The DNR Wildlife Resources Division is charged with managing, protecting and encouraging the conservation of all wildlife, including game and nongame animals, fish and protected plants.

Publication(s): WRD Website

Contact(s):
  David Waller, Director; 770-918-6401
  Noel Holcomb, Assistant Director; 770-918-6401
  Ron Bailey, Chief: Law Enforcement; 770-918-6408
  Chuck Coomer, Chief: Fisheries Management; 770-918-6406
  Mike Harris, Chief: Nongame Wildlife/Natural Heritage; 770-761-3035
  Todd Holbrook, Chief: Game Management; 770-918-6404

GEORGIA FORESTRY COMMISSION
P.O. Box 819
Macon, GA 31202-0819 United States
Phone: 478-751-3500　　　　Fax: 478-751-3465
E-mail: slong@gfc.state.ga.us
Website: www.gfc.state.ga.us

Founded: 1925

Scope: State

Description: To foster, improve, and encourage reforestation; to engage in research and other projects for better forestry practices; to inform the public of the values and benefits of forestry; and to detect, prevent, and combat forest fires.

Publication(s): Georgia Forestry, Wood Using Industries

Contact(s):
  J. Allen, Director; 478-751-3480
  Sharon Dolliver, Chief of Information and Education; 478-751-3530
  Alan Dozier, Chief of Forest Protection; 478-751-3488
  Robert Farris, Field Supervisor
  Jim Gillis, Board of Commissioner Chairman
  William Lazenby, Deputy Director; 478-751-3400
  Garland Nelson, Chief of Forest Administration; 478-751-3464
  Randall Perry, Personnel Officer; 404-298-4949
  Russ Pohl, Chief of Reforestation; 478-751-3530
  Larry Thompson, Chief of Forest Management; 470-751-3458
  Lynn Walton, Editor; 478-751-3530

GEORGIA STATE EXTENSION SERVICE
College of Agricultural and Environmental Sciences
101 Conner Hall
The University of Georgia
Athens, GA 30602-7501 United States
Phone: 706-542-3924　　　　Fax: 706-542-0803
E-mail: caesdean@uga.edu
Website: http://ugacescn.ces.uga.edu/caeshome

Membership: 1–100
Scope: International

Contact(s):
  Gale Buchanan, Dean and Director; 706-542-3924; caesdean@uga.edu
  Jeffery Jackson, Wildlife Specialist; University of Georgia, Warnell School of Forest Resources, Athens, GA 30602-2152; 706-542-9054; Fax: 706-542-3342
  George Lewis, Aquaculture and Fisheries Specialist; 706-542-9038
  Tony Tyson, Interim Associate Dean for Extension; 111 Conner Hall, Athens, GA 30602; 706-542-3824; Fax: 706-542-8815; caesext@uga.edu

GEORGIA STATE SOIL AND WATER CONSERVATION COMMISSION
P.O. Box 8024
Athens, GA 30603 United States
Phone: 706-542-3065　　　　Fax: 706-542-4242
Website: www.gaswcc.org

Founded: 1937
Membership: 1–100
Scope: Local, Regional

Description: Established under the Soil Conservation Districts Act to work with and assist the 40 Soil and Water Conservation Districts and their 370 District Supervisors throughout Georgia.

Publication(s): Conservation Commission, Conservation Contact

Keyword(s): Agriculture/Farming, Land Issues, Reduce/Reuse/Recycle, Water Habitats & Quality

Contact(s):
  F. Liles, Executive Director; 706-542-3065; Fax: 706-542-4242
  David Bennett, Deputy Director
  Garland Thompson, Chairman

GUADALUPE-BLANCO RIVER AUTHORITY
933 East Court Street
Seguin, TX 78155 United States
Phone: 800-413-4130　　　　Fax: 830-379-9718
Website: www.gbra.org

Founded: 1933
Membership: 101–1,000
Scope: Local, State, Regional

Description: State river authority created by the Texas Legislature in 1933 to develop, conserve, and protect the water and natural resources in a ten county statutory district and to help prevent soil erosion and flooding. GBRA is actively engaged in water supply, irrigation, hydroelectric power generation, water and wastewater treatment, outdoor recreation, engineering and technical assistance, economic and business development, project development, and community and school education programs.

Publication(s): Water Resources Report—Quarterly

Keyword(s): Agriculture/Farming, Ecosystems (precious), Energy, Land Issues, Public Lands/Greenspace, Recreation/Ecotourism, Water Habitats & Quality

Contact(s):
  W. West, General Manager; 830-379-5822; Fax: 830-397-1766; bwest@gbra.org
  Fred Blumberg, Deputy General Manager and Chief Operations Officer; 830-379-5822; Fax: 830-379-9718; fblumberg@gbra.org
  Alvin Schuerg, Exec. Mgr. of Finance and Administration; 830-379-5822; Fax: 830-379-9718; aschuerg@gbra.org
  Randy Worden, Ex. Dir. Bus. Development and Resource Mgmt.; 830-379-5822; Fax: 830-379-9718; rworden@gbra.org
  Todd Votteler, Director of Natural Resource Policy/Special Asst. to G.M.; 830-379-5822; tvotteler@gbra.org
  Judy Gardner, Manager of Communications and Education; 830-379-5822; Fax: 830-379-9718; jgardner@gbra.org
  Thomas Hill, Chief Engineer; 830-379-5822; Fax: 830-379-9718; thill@gbra.org
  Debbie Magin, Director of Water Quality; 830-379-5822; dmagin@gbra.org
  Bryan Serold, Operations Manager-Lower Basin; 365 Coleto Park Road, Victoria, TX 77905; 361-575-6366; Fax: 361-575-2267; bserold@gbra.org
  John Smith, Operations Manager-Upper Basin; 830-379-5822; Fax: 830-379-9718; jsmith@gbra.org
  David Welsch, Director of Project Development; 830-379-5822; Fax: 830-379-9718; dwelsch@gbra.org

GUAM COASTAL MANAGEMENT PROGRAM
Bureau of Planning
P.O. Box 2950
Agana, GU 96932 United States
Phone: 671-472-4201　　　Fax: 671-477-1812
Website: www.ocrm.nos.noaa.gov/czm/czmguam.html
Founded: 1979
Publication(s): Public Television Show: Man, Land, and Sea (Guam only), list of publications, posters, and fliers available upon request.
Keyword(s): Development/Developing Countries, Oceans/Coasts/Beaches
Contact(s):
  Vincent Arriola, Director: Bureau of Planning
  Susan Ham, Library Services: Bureau of Planning: Supervisor
  Michael Ham, Administrator: Guam Coastal Management Program

GUAM COOPERATIVE EXTENSION SERVICE
College of Agriculture and Life Sciences (CALS) Bldg.
Rm. 206, University of Guam
303 University Dr., University of Guam Station
Mangilao, GU 96923 United States
Phone: 671-735-2000　　　Fax: 671-734-6842
Website: www.uog.edu/cals
Contact(s):
  Jeff Barcinas, Dean of CALS and Director of Extension Service and Agriculture; 671-735-2002; jbarcina@uog9.uog.edu
  Victor Artero, Associate Dean, Cooperative Extension, Acting; 671-735-2004; vartero@uog9.uog.edu
  John Brown, Associate Director of the Agricultural Experiment Station; 671-735-2140; Fax: 671-734-4600; gwall@uog9.uog.edu
  David Chrisotomo, Aquaculturist; 303 University Dr., UOG Station, Mangilao, GU 96923; 671-735-2080; Fax: 706-734-5600
  Clarissa San Nicholas, Extension Assistant; cdsannic@uog9.uog.edu

GUAM DEPARTMENT OF AGRICULTURE
192 Dairy Rd.
Mangilao, GU 96923 United States
Phone: 671-734-3942　　　Fax: 671-734-6569
Founded: 1950
Description: Charged with responsibility for the conservation and management of Guam's fish, wildlife, soil, and forestry resources, together with development of agricultural and fishery production for food purposes.
Contact(s):
  Michael Kuhlmann, Director; 192 Dairy Rd., Mangilao, GU 96923; 671-734-3942; Fax: 671-734-6569
  Joseph Sablan, Deputy Director

GUAM DEPARTMENT OF AGRICULTURE
DIVISION OF AQUATIC AND WILDLIFE RESOURCES
192 Dairy Rd.
Mangilao, GU 96923 United States
Phone: 671-734-3944　　　Fax: 671-734-6570
Contact(s):
  Robert Anderson, Chief
  Alan Van Aken, Administrative Officer

GUAM DEPARTMENT OF PARKS AND RECREATION
Building 13-8
Tiyan, GU 96913 United States
Phone: 671-475-9620　　　Fax: 671-472-9626
Keyword(s): Public Lands/Greenspace, Recreation/Ecotourism

Contact(s):
  A. Shelton, Director
  Franklin Gutierrez, Deputy Director

GUAM ENVIRONMENTAL PROTECTION AGENCY
P.O. Box 22439
Guam Main Facility
Barrigada, GU 96921 United States
Phone: 671-477-9402
Founded: 1973
Description: Activities include: land-use planning; review of environmental impact assessments and environmental protection plans; supervision, planning, and regulation of all new or modified wastewater sources; and the development and protection of potable water supplies; solid and hazardous waste management, pesticides importation, distribution, and use; and air pollution sources. Provide field and laboratory support for the agency's water, air, and land regulatory programs.
Publication(s): Annual Report, list available on request.
Contact(s):
  Ben Machol, Guam Program Manager; 415-972-3770
  Grace Garces, Public Information Officer; 671-477-9402

GULF COAST RESEARCH LABORATORY
703 East Beach Drive
Ocean Springs, MS 39566-7000 United States
Phone: 228-872-4200　　　Fax: 228-872-4204
Website: www.cms.usm.edu/gindex.htm
Founded: 1947
Description: Conducts research in marine biology, fisheries, geology, chemistry, and oceanography, and conducts an academic program in the marine sciences.
Publication(s): Marine Briefs Newsletter, Gulf Research Reports-Scientific Journal
Contact(s):
  Robert Vanaller, Interim Director
  Robert Vanaller, Editor
  William Walker, Assistant Director: Research

H

HAWAII COOPERATIVE FISHERY RESEARCH UNIT (USDI)
2538 The Mall, University of Hawaii
Honolulu, HI 96822 United States
Phone: 808-956-8350　　　Fax: 808-956-4238
Scope: State, National, International
Description: Activities include research, graduate program teaching, and public service regarding inshore marine and inland waters with emphasis on native fishes and invertebrates.
Publication(s): Scientic Reports (irregular)
Keyword(s): Oceans/Coasts/Beaches, Water Habitats & Quality, Wildlife & Species
Contact(s):
  Dr. Charles Birkeland, Assistant Leader
  James Parrish, Leader

HAWAII DEPARTMENT OF AGRICULTURE
1428 S. King ST
Honolulu, HI 96814 United States
Phone: 808-973-9560　　　Fax: 808-973-9613
E-mail: hdoa.info@hawaii.gov
Website: www.hawaiiag.org/hdoa
Description: Promotes the best use of Hawaii's agricultural resources. Concerned with the protection of agricultural lands and water and diversification of the state's agricultural economy. Functions include agricultural planning, agricultural credit, product promotion and market development, plant and animal quarantine, plant and animal disease and pest control, milk control, livestock and market reporting service,

commodities grading, pesticide use enforcement, and enforcement of weights and measures standards.

Contact(s):
Elaine Abe, Chief: Administrative Services; 808-973-9606
Samuel Camp, Head: Quality Assurance Division; 808-586-0870
Samuel Camp, Head: Agriculture Development Division; 808-973-9566
Brian Kau, Head: Agricultural Resource Management Division
Sandra Kunimoto, Chairperson
Diane Ley, Deputy to the Chairperson
Kevin Yokoyama, Acting Head: Agricultural Loan Division

HAWAII DEPARTMENT OF HEALTH
OFFICE OF ENVIRONMENTAL QUALITY CONTROL
235 S. Beretania St.
Suite 702
Honolulu, HI 96813 United States
Phone: 808-586-4185   Fax: 808-586-4186
E-mail: OEQC@HEALTH.STATE.HI.US
Website: www.state.hi.us/health/oeqc/index.html

Founded: 1974
Membership: 1–100
Scope: Local, State
Description: OEQC advises the Governor on environmental quality control matters; implements Hawaii's EIS law; reviews all documents required by Hawaii's EIS process; and informs the public of proposed actions through The Environmental Notice (OEQC Bulletin). The director of OEQC is also responsible for environmental education projects, and proposing and encouraging legislation supporting the preservation of environmental resources.
Publication(s): A Guidebook for the Hawaii State Environmental Review Process, Annual Report—Environmental Indicators and Report Card
Contact(s):
Genevieve Salmonson, Director

HAWAII DEPARTMENT OF LAND AND NATURAL RESOURCES
601 Kamokila Blvd.
Kapolei, HI 96707 United States
Phone: 808-692-8015   Fax: 808-692-8020
Website: www.hawaii.gov/dlnr/hpd/hpgreeting

Membership: 1–100
Scope: Local
Contact(s):
Don Hibbard, Administrator; 808-587-0045

HAWAII DEPARTMENT OF LAND AND NATURAL RESOURCES
P.O. Box 621
Honolulu, HI 96809 United States
Phone: 808-587-0400   Fax: 808-587-0390
E-mail: dlnr@pixie.com

Scope: State
Contact(s):
Gilbert Coloma-Agaran, Chairman, Commission on Water Resources Management; 808-587-0401
Janet Kawelo, Deputy to Chairperson; 805-870-0403
Linnel Nishioka, Deputy Director Commission on Water Resouce Management; 808-587-0214

HAWAII DEPARTMENT OF LAND AND NATURAL RESOURCES
DIVISION OF BOATING AND OCEAN RECREATION
333 Queen Street
Ste. 300
Honolulu, HI 96813 United States
Phone: 808-587-1963   Fax: 808-587-1977
Website: www.hawaii.gov/dlnr/ddor

Scope: State
Contact(s):
Mason Young, Administrator, Acting

HAWAII DEPARTMENT OF LAND AND NATURAL RESOURCES
DIVISION OF CONSERVATION AND RESOURCES ENFORCEMENT
1151 Punchbowl St., Rm. 311
Honolulu, HI 96813 United States
Phone: 808-587-0077   Fax: 808-587-0080
Website: www.state.hi.us/dlnr

Scope: State
Publication(s): Hunter Education
Contact(s):
Wendell Kam, Manager: Hunter Education Program; 808-587-0200
Gary Moniz, Administrator, Acting

HAWAII DEPARTMENT OF LAND AND NATURAL RESOURCES
DIVISION OF FORESTRY AND WILDLIFE
1151 Punchbowl St.
Room 325
Honolulu, HI 96813 United States
Phone: 808-587-0166   Fax: 808-587-0160

Membership: 1–100
Scope: State
Contact(s):
Carl Masaki, Manager, Forestry Program
Michael Buck, Administrator

HAWAII DEPARTMENT OF LAND AND NATURAL RESOURCES
DIVISION OF STATE PARKS
P.O. Box 621
Honolulu, HI 96809 United States
Phone: 808-587-0300   Fax: 808-587-0311
Website: www.hawaii.gov/dlnr/dsp/dsp.htm

Contact(s):
Dan Quinn, Administrator: State Parks

HAWAII DEPARTMENT OF LAND AND NATURAL RESOURCES
DIVISION OF WATER RESOURCE MANAGEMENT
P.O. Box 621
Honolulu, HI 96809 United States
Phone: 808-587-0214   Fax: 808-587-0219
Website: www.state.hi.us/dlnr/cwrm

Scope: State
Description: Protect and enhance the water resources of the state of Hawaii through wise and responsible management.
Keyword(s): Land Issues, Wildlife & Species
Contact(s):
Linnel Nishioka, Deputy

HAWAII DEPARTMENT OF LAND AND NATURAL RESOURCES
LAND DIVISION
P. O. Box 621
Honolulu, HI 96809 United States
Phone: 808-587-0446   Fax: 808-587-0455
Website: www.state.hi.us

Membership: 1–100
Scope: State
Contact(s):
  Harry Yada, Administrator

HAWAII INSTITUTE OF MARINE BIOLOGY
University of Hawaii
Kaneohe, HI 96744-1346 United States
Phone: 808-236-7401   Fax: 808-236-7443
Website: www.hawaii.edu/HIMB

Scope: State
Description: Concerned with research in tropical marine biology and oceanography with emphasis on coral reef biology, aquaculture, fish endocrinology, and behavior of reef organisms. Provides research facilities for investigations in tropical marine biology. Offers annual summer program in selected topics for graduate students.
Contact(s):
  Joann Leong, Director

IDAHO DEPARTMENT OF ENVIRONMENTAL QUALITY
1410 N. Hilton St.
Boise, ID 83706-1255 United States
Phone: 208-373-0502   Fax: 208-373-0417
Website: www2.state.id.us/deq

Founded: 1920
Membership: 101–1,000
Scope: State
Description: Administers and directs programs designed to protect and enhance the environment and public health. Emphasis is placed on monitoring, technical assistance, and environmental education at the community level. The agency is additionally responsible for all permitting and permit review functions.
Publication(s): Hazardous Waste Report, Performance Partnership Agreement, State of the Environment Report, Strategic Plan, Groundwater Report, Drinking Water Report
Keyword(s): Air Quality/Atmosphere, Ecosystems (precious), Ethics/Environmental Justice, Land Issues, Pollution (general), Public Health, Reduce/Reuse/Recycle, Water Habitats & Quality
Contact(s):
  C. Allred, Director of Environmental Quality; 208-373-0240; Fax: 208-373-0417; sallred@deq.state.id.us
  J. Sandoval, Chief of Staff; 208-373-0240; Fax: 208-3730417; jsandova@deq.state.id.us
  Orville Green, State Waste Mgmt. & Remediation Administrator; 208-373-0418; Fax: 208-373-0154; ogreen@deq.state.id.us
  David Mabe, State Water Quality Administrator; 208-373-0413; Fax: 208-373-0576; dmabe@deq.state.id.us
  Vacant, State Air Quality Administrator; 208-373-0440; Fax: 208-373-0154

IDAHO DEPARTMENT OF FISH AND GAME
600 S. Walnut
P.O. Box 25
Boise, ID 83707 United States
Phone: 208-334-3700   Fax: 208-334-2114
E-mail: idfginfo@idfg.state.id.us
Website: www2.state.id.us/fishgame

Founded: 1938
Scope: State
Description: To preserve, protect, perpetuate, and manage all wildlife within the state of Idaho; to make and declare such rules and regulations, and to employ personnel necessary to administer and enforce the harvest of wildlife.
Publication(s): Idaho Fish & Game News
Keyword(s): Land Issues, Recreation/Ecotourism, Water Habitats & Quality, Wildlife & Species
Contact(s):
  Steve Huffaker, Director; 208-334-3771
  Terry Mansfield, Deputy Director; 208-334-5159
  Roger Fuhrman, Chief, Communications Bureau; 208-334-3746; Fax: 208-334-2148
  Stephen Barton, Bureau Chief of Administration; 208-334-3782
  Phil Jeppson, Chief of Engineering; 208-334-3730
  Virgil Moore, Chief of Fisheries; 208-334-3791
  Al Nicholson, Chief of Enforcement; 208-334-3736
  Bob Royce, Chief of DP Management; 208-334-3700
  Tracey Trent, Chief of Natural Resources Policy; 208-334-2595
  Jack Trueblood, Editor; 208-334-3746; jtrueblood@idfg.state.id.us

IDAHO DEPARTMENT OF LANDS
P.O. Box 83720
Boise, ID 83720-0050 United States
Phone: 208-334-0200   Fax: 208-334-2339
E-mail: boise@idl.state.id.us
Website: www.state.id.us.lands

Membership: 101–1,000
Scope: State
Description: The State Board of Land Commissioners is a constitutional board charged with administering the trust under which endowment lands are held. These lands were granted to the state at the time of statehood for the financial support of nine beneficiaries, the largest being the common schools.
Publication(s): Sentinel Newsletter Quarterly, Public Involvement Brochure
Contact(s):
  Dirk Kempthorne, State Board of Land Commissioner President; 208-334-2100
  Winston Wiggins, Secretary of Board & Director of the Idaho Dept. of Lands
  Pete Cenarrusa, Secretary of State; 208-334-2300
  Marilyn Howard, Superintendent of Public Instruction; 208-332-6800
  Alan Lance, Attorney General; 208-334-2400
  J. Williams, State Controller; 208-334-3100

IDAHO DEPARTMENT OF PARKS AND RECREATION
P.O. Box 83720
Boise, ID 83720-0065 United States
Phone: 208-334-4199   Fax: 208-334-3741
Website: www.idahoparks.org

Founded: 1965
Scope: State, Regional
Description: To formulate and put into execution a long-range program for the acquisition, planning, protection, operation, maintenance, development, and wise use of parks; and to provide state leadership in recreation.
Publication(s): Idaho State Parks Guide
Keyword(s): Ethics/Environmental Justice, Land Issues, Public Lands/Greenspace, Recreation/Ecotourism, Water Habitats & Quality
Contact(s):
  Rick Cummins, Division Administrator, Management Services; 208-334-4180; ext. 253; rcummins@idpr.state.id.us
  Rick Collignon, Director
  Ernest Lombard, Chairman of the Board; 208-939-3311

IDAHO DEPARTMENT OF WATER RESOURCES
1301 North Orchard
Boise, ID 83706-2237 United States
Phone: 208-327-7900 Fax: 208-327-7866
Website: www.idwr.state.id.us

Membership: 101–1,000
Scope: State
Description: Administration of State Water Plan and Energy Plan; allocation and planning of water resources and energy programs and projects; permit and license procedures for water rights, dams, and mine tailing impoundment structures, well construction, injection wells, and stream channel alterations.
Publication(s): Water and Energy Information Bulletins, State Water Plan, and Newsletter
Contact(s):
  Karl Dreher, Director; 208-327-7910
  Hal Anderson, Administrator of Planning and Technical Services Division; 208-327-7910
  Robert Hoppie, Administrator of Energy Division; 208-327-7910
  Jerry Rigby, Chairman of the Board; 208-356-3633
  L. Saxton, Administrator of Water Management Division; 208-327-7910

IDAHO DEPARTMENT OF WATER RESOURCES
WATER AWARENESS WEEK
c/o Catherine Chertudi
Boise Public Works
P.O. Box 500
Boise, ID 83701-0500 United States
Phone: 208-384-3901 Fax: 208-433-5650
E-mail: cchertudi@cityofboise.org
Website: www.cityofboise.org

Founded: 1994
Membership: 1–100
Scope: Local, State
Description: Water Awareness Week is a statewide program to educate sixth grade students of the importance of water in our lives and that of the businesses, industries and recreation of the state.
Publication(s): Idaho Water Education Flyer
Keyword(s): Agriculture/Farming, Ecosystems (precious), Energy, Ethics/Environmental Justice, Forests/Forestry, Land Issues, Pollution (general), Public Health, Recreation/Ecotourism, Sprawl/Urban Planning, Water Habitats & Quality

IDAHO FISH AND WILDLIFE FOUNDATION
P.O. Box 2254
Boise, ID 83701 United States
Phone: 208-334-2648 Fax: 208-334-2148
E-mail: lcompton@idfg.state.id.us
Website: www.ifwf.org

Founded: 1990
Membership: 1–100
Scope: State
Description: To facilitate the organization and funding of natural resource projects: fish, wildlife, habitat, and education. Work with Idaho Department of Fish and Game and other entities to build public and private partnerships for wildlife projects.
Publication(s): Steelhead Fishing Economic Survey (1996), Salmon Fishing Economic Survey (1998), Steelhead Fishing Economic Values brochure
Keyword(s): Wildlife & Species
Contact(s):
  Gayle Valentine, Executive Director; P.O. Box 2254, Boise, ID 83701; 208-334-2648; gvalenti@idfg.state.id.us

IDAHO GEOLOGICAL SURVEY
Morrill Hall, Third Floor, University of Idaho
Moscow, ID 83844-3014 United States
Phone: 208-885-7991 Fax: 208-885-5826
E-mail: igf@uidaho.edu
Website: www.idahogeology.org

Founded: 1919
Membership: 1–100
Scope: State
Description: The Survey is the lead state agency for the collection, interpretation, and dissemination of all geologic and mineral data for Idaho. Conducts field investigations and laboratory studies; assists in preparation of geologic maps, derivative land-use planning, and geologic hazards maps; provides expertise to individuals and governmental and private groups in planning land use.
Contact(s):
  Earl Bennett, Director; 208-885-7991
  Roy Breckenridge, Associate Director; 208-885-7991
  Kurt Othberg, Associate Director

IDAHO STATE DEPARTMENT OF AGRICULTURE
P.O. Box 790
Boise, ID 83701 United States
Phone: 208-332-8500
Website: www.agri.state.id.us

Keyword(s): Agriculture/Farming, Land Issues, Oceans/Coasts/Beaches, Pollution (general), Public Health, Reduce/Reuse/Recycle, Water Habitats & Quality, Wildlife & Species
Contact(s):
  Patrick Takasugi, Director
  Bob Hillman, Division of Animal Industries Administrator; 208-332-8541
  Laura Johnson, Div. of Agr. Res., Mar., & Dev. Bureau Chief; 208-332-8531

IDAHO STATE SOIL CONSERVATION COMMISSION
P.O. Box 790
Boise, ID 83701-0790 United States
Phone: 208-332-8650 Fax: 208-334-2386
E-mail: bthomass@agri.state.id.us
Website: www.scc.state.id.us

Founded: 1939
Membership: 1–100
Scope: State
Description: Coordinates programs and activities of Soil Conservation Districts in Idaho. Concerned with overall leadership and administration of districts in development, wise use, and conservation of soil and water and other closely related resources. Participates in the National Cooperative Soil Survey Program through employment of soil scientists and has been designated the state water quality management agency for private and state agricultural lands.
Keyword(s): Agriculture/Farming, Land Issues, Reduce/Reuse/Recycle
Contact(s):
  Tom Johnston, Chairman; 22410 Ten Davis Rd., Parma, ID 83660; 208-722-6224; Fax: 208-722-6090; tj@widaho.net
  Jerry Nicolescu, Administrator; 208-332-8649; Fax: 208-334-2386; jnicoles@agri.state.id.us
  Tony Bennett, Technical Program Manager; 208-332-8651; Fax: 208-334-2386; abennett@agri.state.id.us
  David Coburn, RCRDP Program Manager; 208-332-8653; Fax: 208-334-2386; dcoburn@agri.state.id.us
  Brenda Thomasson, Management Assistant; 208-332-8646; Fax: 208-334-2386; bthomass@agri.state.id.us
  Kathy Weaver, District Operations Manager; 3563 Ririe Highway, Idaho Falls, ID 83401; 208-525-7269; Fax: 208-525-7178; kweaver@agri.state.id.us

David Ferguson, Agricultural Program Specialist; 208-332-8654; Fax: 208-334-2386; dferguso@agri.state.id.us
Kathie Shea, Program Coordinator; 208-332-8647; Fax: 208-334-2386; khassels@agri.state.id.us

ILLINOIS DEPARTMENT OF AGRICULTURE
State Fairgrounds, P.O. Box 19281
Springfield, IL 62794-9281 United States
Phone: 217-782-2172
Website: www.agr.state.il.us/

Founded: 1917

Description: The Illinois Department of Agriculture protects and promotes the state's agricultural and natural resources. The agency provides services that benefit consumers, farmers, and agribusinesses.

Publication(s): Illinois Agricultural Guide, Illinois Food Products, Illinois Grain and Livestock Market News, Illinois Agricultural Organizations Directory

Keyword(s): Agriculture/Farming, Land Issues, Pollution (general), Reduce/Reuse/Recycle

Contact(s):
Becky Doyle, Director
Dave Bender, Executive Office: Assistant Director
Chet Boruff, Deputy Director for Natural Resource and Agri-Industry Regulations
Jim Reynolds, Superintendent for Fairs and Promotions

ILLINOIS DEPARTMENT OF AGRICULTURE
BUREAU OF LAND AND WATER RESOURCES
P.O. Box 19281
State Fairgrounds
Springfield, IL 62794-9281 United States
Phone: 217-782-6297   Fax: 217-557-0993
Website: www.agr.state.il.us

Scope: State

Description: Responsible for administering the laws and programs relating to the conservation of Illinois' agricultural, land and water resources.

Keyword(s): Agriculture/Farming, Land Issues, Public Health, Sprawl/Urban Planning, Water Habitats & Quality

Contact(s):
Steve Frank, Bureau Chief; Fax: 217-557-0993

ILLINOIS DEPARTMENT OF NATURAL RESOURCES
One Natural Resources Way
Springfield, IL 62702-1271 United States
Phone: 217-782-6302   Fax: 217-785-9236
Website: www.dnr.state.il.us

Founded: 1913
Membership: 1,001–10,000
Scope: State

Description: The mission of the Illinois Department of Natural Resources is to promote an understanding and appreciation of the state's natural resources and work with the people of Illinois to protect and manage those resources to ensure a high quality of life for present and future generations.

Publication(s): Digest of Hunting and Trapping Regulations, Outdoor Illinois Magazine, State Park Magazine, Illinois Fishing Information Book

Keyword(s): Ecosystems (precious), Energy, Forests/Forestry, Land Issues, Pollution (general), Recreation/Ecotourism, Reduce/Reuse/Recycle, Sprawl/Urban Planning, Water Habitats & Quality, Wildlife & Species

Contact(s):
Russ Breckenridge, Legislative Liaison; 217-785-0073
Anderson Brian, Director of Resource Conservation Office; 217-785-8547
Joal Brunsvold, Director of IDNR; 217-782-6302; Fax: 217-785-9236
Gary Clark, Acting Director of Water Resources Office; 217-782-2152
Tom Flattery, Director of Realty and Environmental Planning Office; 217-782-7940
Jess Hansen, Conservation Foundation Executive Director; 1 Natural Resources Way, Springfield, IL 62702; 217-558-7113
Tim Hickman, Director of Office of Land Management and Education; 217-241-2800
Jerry Jones, Director of Office Mines and Minerals; 217-782-0031
Carol Knowles, Director of Public Affairs Office; 217-785-0970
Andrea Moore, Assistant Director; 217-782-6302
John Pohlman, Director, Office of Administration; 217-782-0179
Sal Raymond, Director of Public Services Office; 217-785-0064
Bob Roads, Director of Office of Capital Development; 217-782-1807
Vacant, Director, Office of Scientific Research & Analysis; 217-524-9506
Brad Hammond, Division Manager of Internal Audit Office; 217-785-0853
Eddy Fisher, Interim Office Director; 217-558-4481
Roger Frazier, Deputy Director; 217-785-0075
Jonathon Furr, Chief Legal Counsel; 217-782-1809
Jenny Henry, Acting Chief of Law Enforcement Office; 217-782-6431
Ed Hoover, Assistant to the Director; 217-785-3224
Jim Riemer, Deputy Director; 217-782-1824
Leslie Sgro, Deputy Director; 217-785-0073
Vacant, Equal Employment Opportunity Officer; 217-785-0067
Roy Williams, Legislative Liaison; 217-785-0073

ILLINOIS DEPARTMENT OF TRANSPORTATION
2300 S. Dirksen Pkwy.
Springfield, IL 62764 United States
Phone: 217-782-7820
Website: www.dot.state.il.us

Scope: State

Keyword(s): Transportation

Contact(s):
James Easterly, Director: Division of Highways; 217-782-2151; Fax: 217-524-2972
Kirk Brown, Secretary; 217-782-6828
Mike Hines, Chief: Bureau of Design and Environment; 217-782-7526; Fax: 217-524-0989

ILLINOIS ENVIRONMENTAL PROTECTION AGENCY
1021 N. Grand Ave E
Springfield, IL 62702 United States
Phone: 217-782-3397   Fax: 217-782-9039
Website: www.epa.state.il.us

Founded: 1970
Membership: 1,001–10,000
Scope: State

Description: Responsible for implementing the environmental program for the state of Illinois. Administers a variety of programs to protect the air, land, and water.

Publication(s): Digester/Over the Spillway, Environmental Progress

Keyword(s): Air Quality/Atmosphere, Land Issues, Oceans/Coasts/Beaches, Pollution (general)

Contact(s):
Renee Cipriano, Director
Dennis McMurray, Manager: Public Information
William Child, Chief: Bureau of Land; 217-785-9407
Dave Kolaz, Chief: Bureau of Air; 217-785-4140
Joan Muraro, Editor; 217-785-7209
James Park, Chief: Bureau of Water; 217-782-1654
William Seith, Deputy Director

Nancy Simpson, Head Librarian; 1021 N. Grand Ave. E., P.O. Box 19276, Springfield, IL 62794-9276; 217-782-9691
Marcia Willhite, Bureau Chief

ILLINOIS NATURE PRESERVES COMMISSION (INPC)
One Natural Resources Way
Springfield, IL 62702-1271 United States
Phone: 217-785-8686   Fax: 217-785-2438
Website: www.dnr.state.il.us/inpc/index.htm
Founded: 1963
Scope: Local, State, Regional
Description: The mission of the Illinois Nature Preserves Commission (INPC) is to assist private and public landowners in protecting high quality natural areas and habitats of endangered and threatened species in perpetuity, through voluntary dedication or registration of such lands into the Illinois Nature Preserves System. The Commission promotes the preservation of these significant lands and provides leadership in their stewardship, management, and protection.
Publication(s): Directory of Illinois Nature Preserves Volume 1 & 2
Keyword(s): Ecosystems (precious), Land Issues, Wildlife & Species
Contact(s):
  Carolyn Grosboll, Director
  Jill Allread, Chairperson
  Harry Drucker, Vice-Chair
  Randy Heidorn, Deputy Director for Stewardship
  Don McFall, Deputy Director for Protection
  John Schwegman, Secretary

INDIANA DEPARTMENT OF ENVIRONMENTAL MANAGEMENT
Indianapolis, IN 46206 United States
Phone: 317-232-8557   Fax: 317-233-6647
Website: www.in.gov/idem
Membership: 101–1,000
Scope: State
Description: The Indiana Department of Environmental Management is dedicated to conserving, protecting, enhancing, restoring, and managing Indiana's environment. We strive to fairly but vigorously enforce laws and standards; promulgate regulations consistent with the law and public policy; and promote conservation, pollution prevention, and a healthy and sustainable ecosystem. We are committed to making Indiana a cleaner, healthier place to live.
Contact(s):
  Terry Coleman, Director of Northern Regional Office; 219-245-4870
  Dan Hottle, Director of Media & Communication Services; 317-232-8557; dhottle@dem.state.in.us
  Paula Smith, Director of Planning & Assessment; 317-233-1210
  Karen Terrell, Director of Community Relations; 317-233-6648; kterrell@dem.state.in.us
  Judy Thomann, Director of Southwest Regional Office; 812-436-2570
  Dana Reed-Wise, Chief of Staff; 317-233-2773
  Lori Kaplan, Commissioner; 317-232-8611
  Jim Mahern, Assistant Commissioner for Office of Pollution Prevention; 317-233-6658
  Janet McCabe, Assistant Commissioner of Air Management; 317-233-6861
  Timothy Method, Deputy Commissioner for Environmental and Regulatory Affairs; 317-233-3706
  Bruce Palin, Deputy Commissioner, Office of Land Quality; 317-233-6591
  Felicia Robinson, Deputy Commissioner of Legal Affairs; 317-233-3706; frobinso@dem.state.in.us

INDIANA DEPARTMENT OF NATURAL RESOURCES
402 W. Washington St., Rm. W255B
Indianapolis, IN 46204-2748 United States
Phone: 317-232-4200
Website: www.state.in.us/dnr
Scope: State
Description: The DNR administers more than 100 properties throughout Indiana, comprising more than 400,000 acres. The DNR provides recreational opportunities for millions of Hoosiers and out-of-state visitors annually at its state parks, forests, reservoirs, and fish and wildlife areas. The DNR also has wide-ranging responsibilities for various programs such as maintaining the Indiana State Museum and more than a dozen historic sites throughout the state.
Publication(s): Outdoor Indiana
Keyword(s): Forests/Forestry, Recreation/Ecotourism
Contact(s):
  John Bacone, Director: Division of Nature Preserves; 317-232-4052
  Thomas Barton, Director: Division of Accounting; 317-232-4041
  John Davis, Director: Division of Land Acquisition; 317-232-4050
  Gary Doxtater, Director: Division of Fish and Wildlife; 317-232-4080
  Daniel Fogerty, Director: Division of Historic Preservation and Archaeology; 317-232-1646
  Richard Gantz, Director: Division of State Museum and Historical Sites; 317-232-1637
  Emily Kress, Director: Division of Outdoor Recreation; 317-232-4070
  James Livorott, Director: Division of Internal Audit; 317-232-8092
  Gerald Pagac, Director: Division of State Parks; 317-232-4124
  Mike Quigley, Director: Management Information Systems; 317-232-4007
  Patrick Ralston, Director; 317-232-4020
  Stephen Sellers, Director: Division of Public Information and Education; 317-232-4200
  John Simpson, Director: Division of Water; 317-232-4160
  Jim Slutz, Director: Division of Oil and Gas; 317-232-4055
  Mike Sponsler, Director: Division of Reclamation; 812-665-2207
  J. Taylor, Director: Division of Reservoir Management; 317-232-4060
  Philip Wagner, Director: Division of Safety and Training; 317-232-4145
  Charles Walker, Director: Division of Law Enforcement; 317-232-4010
  Robert Waltz, State Entomologist Director: Division of Entomology and Planning; 317-232-4120
  John Costello, Deputy Director: Bureau of Lands and Cultural Resources; 317-232-4020
  Paul Ehret, Deputy Director: Bureau of Mine Reclamation; 317-232-4020
  Burnell Fischer, State Forester, Head: Division of Forestry; 317-232-4105
  David Herbst, Deputy Director: Bureau of Water and Resource Regulation; 317-232-4020
  Tom Hohman, Head Chief Engineer: Division of Engineering; 317-232-4150
  Lori Kaplan, Chief Counsel; 317-232-4020
  Michael Kiley, Chairman: Natural Resources Commission; 317-232-4020
  Steven Lucas, Chief Hearings Officer; 317-232-0156
  Jerry Miller, Chairman: Lands and Cultural Resources Advisory Council; 317-232-4020
  Stephen Sellers, Editor; 317-232-4200
  Joseph Siener, Chairman: Water and Resource Regulation Advisory Council; 317-232-4020

David Vice, Deputy Director: Law Enforcement and Administration; 317-232-4020

INDIANA DEPARTMENT OF NATURAL RESOURCES
DIVISION OF SOIL CONSERVATION
402 W. Washington St., Rm. W265
Indianapolis, IN 46204-2782 United States
Phone: 317-233-3870   Fax: 317-233-3882
Website: www.state.in.us/dnr

Membership: 1–100
Scope: Regional
Description: The Division's mission is to facilitate the protection, wise use, and enhancement of Indiana's soil and water resources by: coordinating implementation of the state's T-by-2000 soil conservation/water quality protection program and providing assistance to local soil and water conservation districts.
Publication(s): Indiana Handbook for Erosion Control in Developing Areas, Erosion Control for the Home Builder, Urban Conservation Program, Lake and River Enhancement Program.
Keyword(s): Agriculture/Farming, Land Issues, Water Habitats & Quality
Contact(s):
Harry Nikides, Director
David Avery, Vice Chairman
Peter Hippensteel, Chairman of the Board

INDIANA GEOLOGICAL SURVEY
Institute of Indiana University, 611 N. Walnut Grove
Bloomington, IN 47405 United States
Phone: 812-855-5067   Fax: 812-855-2862
E-mail: igsinfo@indiana.edu
Website: http://igs.indiana.edu

Founded: 1869
Membership: 1–100
Scope: State
Description: Conducts basic and applied research in geology and disseminates geologic information as published reports and maps; consults with industry, academia, and the public on the geologic makeup, mineral and energy resources, and geologic hazards of the state.
Publication(s): Geologic Publications
Keyword(s): Land Issues
Contact(s):
John Stenmetz, Director and State Geologist; 812-855-5067
John Hill, Assistant Director; 812-855-6067

INDIANA STATE DEPARTMENT OF HEALTH
2 North Meridian St.
Indianapolis, IN 46204 United States
Phone: 317-233-1325
E-mail: gwilson@isdh.state.in.us
Website: www.state.in.us/isdh

Scope: State
Keyword(s): Energy, Pollution (general), Public Health
Contact(s):
Gregory Wilson MD, State Health Commissioner

INDUSTRIAL COMMISSION OF NORTH DAKOTA
NORTH DAKOTA GEOLOGICAL SURVEY
600 East Boulevard Avenue
Bismarck, ND 58505-0840 United States
Phone: 701-328-8000   Fax: 701-328-8010
Website: www.state.nd.us/ndgs

Founded: 1895
Membership: 1–100
Scope: State
Description: Responsible for collecting and disseminating geologic information.
Publication(s): NDGS Newsletter
Keyword(s): Energy, Land Issues, Oceans/Coasts/Beaches
Contact(s):
John Bluemle, State Geologist

INSTITUTE FOR ECOLOGICAL STUDIES UNIVERSITY OF NORTH DAKOTA
P.O. Box 7110,
Grand Forks, ND 58202 United States
Phone: 701-777-2851   Fax: 701-777-2623

Founded: 1965
Membership: 1–100
Scope: Local
Description: A nonprofit university research center devoted to ecology, policy analysis, and environmental biology. An interdisciplinary staff composed of university faculty, biologists, and associates conducts basic and applied research centering in the upper Midwest, and provides technical services for government and corporate agencies, and the public.
Publication(s): Contributions, Research Reports
Keyword(s): Water Habitats & Quality, Wildlife & Species
Contact(s):
Richard Crawford, Director

INTERAGENCY COMMITTEE FOR OUTDOOR RECREATION (IAC)
1111 Washington St., SE, P.O. Box 40917
Olympia, WA 98504-0917 United States
Phone: 360-902-3000   Fax: 360-902-3026
E-mail: info@iac.wa.gov
Website: www.iac.wa.gov

Founded: 1965
Scope: State
Description: IAC administers grants and technical assistance programs for public recreation, open space, and conservation projects in Washington state. The agency assists local, state, federal, and nonprofit organizations in planning, acquiring, and developing recreation resources. IAC also writes the state's outdoor recreation and open space plan, as well as plans on trails and nonhighway off-road vehicle recreation.
Publication(s): Refer to Website for publication listings.
Keyword(s): Land Issues, Public Lands/Greenspace, Recreation/Ecotourism, Wildlife & Species
Contact(s):
Laura Johnson, Director; 360-902-3000
Gregory Lovelady, Manager of Applied Planning; 360-902-3008
Jim Fox, Special Assistant to the Director; 360-902-3021
Debra Wilhelmi, Deputy Director of Management Services; 360-902-3005

IOWA ASSOCIATION OF COUNTY CONSERVATION BOARDS
405 SW 3rd, Suite 1
Ankeny, IA 50021 United States
Phone: 515-963-9582   Fax: 515-963-9582
E-mail: iaccb@ecity.net
Website: www.ecity.net/iaccb

Description: Promotes the objectives of Iowa's County Conservation Boards, board member education, information exchange, legislation, and public awareness.
Publication(s): Iowa Board Member, Board Member Handbook, Outdoor Adventure Guide (Area Directory), IACCB Legislative Update, IACCB Newsletter
Contact(s):
Don Brazelton, Executive Secretary; 515-963-9582
Julie Moss, Office Manager; 515-963-9582

IOWA DEPARTMENT OF AGRICULTURE AND LAND STEWARDSHIP
BUREAU OF FIELD SERVICES
502 E. 9th Street, Wallace Bldg.
Des Moines, IA 50319 United States
Phone: 515-281-5321
Website: www.agriculture.state.ia.us

Contact(s):
James Gillespie; 515-281-5258

IOWA DEPARTMENT OF AGRICULTURE AND LAND STEWARDSHIP
BUREAU OF FINANCIAL INCENTIVE PROGRAM
E. 9th and Grand Ave., Wallace Bldg.
Des Moines, IA 50319-0034 United States
Phone: 515-281-5851   Fax: 515-281-6170
Website: www.agriculture.state.ia.us/financialincentives

Scope: State

Contact(s):
William McGill, Bureau Chief; 515-281-5851

IOWA DEPARTMENT OF AGRICULTURE AND LAND STEWARDSHIP
BUREAU OF WATER RESOURCES
E. 9th and Grand Ave., Wallace Bldg.
Des Moines, IA 50319-0050 United States
Phone: 515-281-5851   Fax: 515-281-6170
Website: www.agriculture.state.ia.us/waterresource

Membership: 1–100
Scope: State

Contact(s):
Dean Lemke, Chief Water Resource Bureau; 515-281-3963

IOWA DEPARTMENT OF AGRICULTURE AND LAND STEWARDSHIP
DIVISION OF SOIL CONSERVATION
502 E. 9th
Wallace State Office Bldg.
Des Moines, IA 50319-0034 United States
Phone: 515-281-5851   Fax: 515-281-6170
Website: www.agriculture.state.ia.us/soilconservation

Founded: 1939
Scope: State

Description: The Division of Soil Conservation is responsible for state leadership in the protection and management of soil, water and mineral resources; assisting soil and water conservation districts and private landowners to achieve their agricultural and environmental objectives.

Keyword(s): Agriculture/Farming, Ethics/Environmental Justice, Land Issues, Pollution (general), Water Habitats & Quality

Contact(s):
William Ehm, Director; 515-281-6146; Fax: 515-281-6170; william.ehm@idals.state.ia.us
Jim Gillespie, Bureau Chief, Field Services Bureau; 515-281-5258; Fax: 515-281-6170; jim.gillespie@idals.state.ia.us
Dean Lemke, Bureau Chief, Water Resource Bureau; 515-281-6146; Fax: 515-281-6170; dean.lemke@idals.state.ia.us
Bill McGill, Bureau Chief, Financial Incentives Bureau; 515-281-5851; Fax: 515-281-6170; bill.mcgill@idals.state.ia.us
Kenneth Tow, Bureau Chief, Mines and Minerals Bureau; 515-281-4246; Fax: 515-281-6170; ken.tow@idals.state.ia.us

IOWA DEPARTMENT OF NATURAL RESOURCES
E. 9th and Grand Ave., Wallace Bldg.
Des Moines, IA 50319-0034 United States
Phone: 515-281-5185   Fax: 515-281-8895
E-mail: webmaster@dnr.state.ia.us
Website: www.state.ia.us/government/dnr

Founded: 1986
Scope: State

Description: Established with the merging of the following state agencies: Iowa Conservation Commission, Department of Water, Air and Waste Management; Iowa Geological Survey; and the resources/conservation functions of the Energy Policy Council. The seven-member Natural Resources Commission is a policy and rule-setting authority over the Fish and Wildlife Division, Parks, Recreation, and Preserves Division, and the Forestry Division.

Keyword(s): Air Quality/Atmosphere, Energy, Pollution (general), Recreation/Ecotourism, Reduce/Reuse/Recycle, Water Habitats & Quality, Wildlife & Species

Contact(s):
Jeffrey Vonk, Director
Liz Christiansen, Deputy Director
William Ehm, Environmental Protection Commission Chair
Ross Harrison, Chief of Information-Education Bureau
Joan Schneider, Natural Resource Commission Chair
Julie Sparks, Editor of Iowa Conservationist

IOWA DEPARTMENT OF NATURAL RESOURCES
COOPERATIVE NORTH AMERICAN SHOTGUNNING EDUCATION PROGRAM
Wallace State Office Bldg.
Des Moines, IA 50319 United States
Phone: 515-281-5918   Fax: 515-281-6794
Website: www.state.ia.us/dnr

Founded: 1982
Scope: Regional

Description: The Cooperative North American Shotgunning Program is a research, information, and education program designed to assist wildlife professionals, hunters, and sportsmen in making a successful transition from lead shot to nontoxic shot, as well as educating sportsmen on improving shooting skills and harvest efficiency, thereby reducing wounding losses.

Publication(s): CONSEP Newsletter, Periodic Ballistics Reports
Keyword(s): Recreation/Ecotourism, Wildlife & Species

Contact(s):
Jeffrey Zonk, Director; 515-281-5918; jeff.zonk@dnr.state.ia.us
Lloyd Alexander, Contact for Atlantic Flyway; 89 Kings Highway, P.O. Box 1401, Dover, DE; 302-739-5287
Richard Bishop, Wildlife Bureau Chief; Wallace State Bldg., Des Moines, IA 50319; 515-281-6156
Don Childress, Contact for Pacific Flyway; 1420 E. 6th, Box 20071, Helena, MT 59601; 406-444-2612
Bob McLean, Contact for Canadian Wildlife Service; 17th Fl., Place Vincent Massey, Ottawa, Ontario K1A 0H3; 819-997-2957
Tom Roster, Consultant; 1190 Lynnewood Blvd., Klamath Falls, OR 97601; 503-884-2974
John Smith, Contact for Mississippi Flyway; P.O. Box 180, Jefferson City, MO 65102-0180; 573-751-4115
George Vandel, Contact for Central Flyway; 445 E. Capitol, Pierre, SD; 605-773-3381

IOWA DEPARTMENT OF NATURAL RESOURCES
ENERGY AND WASTE MANAGEMENT BUREAU
Wallace State Office Building
502 E 9th St
Des Moines, IA 50319 United States
Phone: 515-281-8878   Fax: 515-281-8895
Website: www.iowadnr.com

Scope: Local, State

Description: The Energy & Waste Management Bureau is responsible for recommending and carrying out state policies that improve management of energy resources through energy efficiency and the development of renewable energy. The bureau also helps Iowans establish sustainable waste management practices by offering pollution prevention and responsible waste management programs.

Keyword(s): Energy, Reduce/Reuse/Recycle

Contact(s):
Liz Christiansen, Deputy Director
Jeffrey Vonk, Director
Wayne Gieselman, Administrator, Environmental Services Division
Brian Tormey, Chief, Energy and Waste Management Bureau

IOWA DEPARTMENT OF NATURAL RESOURCES
ENVIRONMENTAL PROTECTION DIVISION
Wallace State Office Building
East 9th & Grand Avenue
Des Moines, IA 50319 United States
Phone: 515-281-5918
E-mail: webmaster@dnr.state.ia.us
Website: www.state.ia.us/epd

Contact(s):
Mike Brandup, Division Administrator, Conservation Resources
Richard Bishop, Chief of Wildlife Bureau
Marion Conover, Chief of Fisheries Bureau
Lowell Joslin, Chief of Law Enforcement Bureau
Steve Pennington, Chief of Parks Bureau
John Walkowiak, Chief of Forestry Bureau

IOWA DEPARTMENT OF NATURAL RESOURCES
FISH AND WILDLIFE DIVISION
Wallace State Office Building
East 9th & Grand Avenue
Des Moines, IA 50319 United States
Phone: 515-281-4687   Fax: 515-281-6794
E-mail: webmaster@dnr.state.ia.us

Contact(s):
Mike Brandup, Division Administrator, Conservation Resources
Richard Bishop, Chief of Wildlife Bureau
Marion Conover, Chief of Fisheries Bureau
Allen Farris, Administrator
Lowell Joslin, Chief of Law Enforcement Bureau

IOWA DEPARTMENT OF NATURAL RESOURCES
FORESTS AND PRAIRIES DIVISION
Wallace State Office Building
East 9th & Grand Avenue
Des Moines, IA 50319 United States
Phone: 515-281-8657
E-mail: mike.brandrup@dnr.state.ia.us

Contact(s):
Mike Brandup, Administrator
Jim Bulman, Chief of State Forests Management Bureau
John Walkowiak, Chief of Forestry Services Bureau

IOWA DEPARTMENT OF NATURAL RESOURCES
MANAGEMENT SERVICES DIVISION
502 E. 9th St.
Wallace State Office Building
Des Moines, IA 50319-0034 United States
Phone: 515-281-5918   Fax: 515-281-6794
E-mail: webmaster@dnr.state.ia.us
Website: www.iowadnr.com

Scope: State

Description: The Administrative Services Division (ASD) is comprised of four bureaus: Administrative Services, Acquisition and Construction, Budget and Finance, and Information Technology. The Volunteer Program is also a part of the ASD. The common goal of these areas is to enable and support the Department of Natural Resources in its efforts to provide the highest level of customer service through the most efficient and cost-effective methods.

Contact(s):
Linda Hanson, Administrator
Sally Jagnandan, Chief of Administrative Support Bureau
Basil Nimry, Chief of Construction Services Bureau
Mark Slatterly, Chief of Budget and Finance Bureau

IOWA DEPARTMENT OF NATURAL RESOURCES
PARKS
Wallace State Office Building
502 E. 9th St.
Des Moines, IA 50319 United States
Phone: 515-281-5207   Fax: 515-281-6794
E-mail: mike.brandrup@dnr.state.ia.us
Website: www.exploreiowaparks.com

Scope: State

Description: Parks, Recreation and Preserves management

Contact(s):
Mike Brandrup, Division Administrator; 515-281-8657
Stephen Pennington, Bureau Chief; 515-281-5207

IOWA DEPARTMENT OF NATURAL RESOURCES
WASTE MANAGEMENT DIVISION
Wallace State Office Building
East 9th & Grand Avenue
Des Moines, IA 50319 United States
Phone: 515-281-4367   Fax: 515-281-8895
E-mail: teresa.barrie@dnr.state.ia.us

Contact(s):
Brent Laning, Executive Officer
Roya Stanley, Administrator

IOWA STATE EXTENSION SERVICES
EXTENSION WILDLIFE PROGRAMS
124 Science II
Iowa State University
Ames, IA 50011-3221 United States
Phone: 515-294-7429   Fax: 515-294-7874
E-mail: xiowa@iastate.edu
Website: www.extension.iastate.edu

Scope: State

Description: ISU Extension is a client-centered organization that provides research-based, unbiased information and education to help people make better decisions in their personal, community, and professional lives.

Contact(s):
James Pease, Extension Wildlife Conservationist; 103 Science II, Iowa State University, Ames, IA 50011; 515-294-7429; Fax: 515-294-7874
Paul Wray, Extension Forester; 251 Bessey Hall, Iowa State University, Ames, IA 50011; 515-294-1168

K

KANSAS BIOLOGICAL SURVEY
2021 Constant Ave.
Hugichi Hall
Lawrence, KS 66047-3759 United States
Phone: 785-864-1500   Fax: 785-864-1534
Website: www.kbs.ku.edu

Founded: 1959
Membership: 1–100
Scope: State

Description: A research and development branch of the University of Kansas whose purpose is to survey and inventory the native plants and animals of Kansas, report on its findings, and develop and administer lands for the study and preservation of native animal and plant resources.

Publication(s): Publications on website

Keyword(s): Land Issues, Water Habitats & Quality, Wildlife & Species

Contact(s):
Edward Martinko, Director and State Biologist
Frank Denoyelles, Associate Director
Paul Liechti, Assistant Director

KANSAS COOPERATIVE FISH AND WILDLIFE RESEARCH UNIT

205 Leasure Hall, Kansas State University
Manhattan, KS 66506-3501 United States
Phone: 785-532-6070   Fax: 785-532-7159
E-mail: kscfwru@ksu.edu
Website: www.ksu.edu/kscfwru/

Founded: 1991
Scope: National
Contact(s):
Jack Cully, Assistant Leader of Wildlife
Philip Gipson, Leader
Christopher Guy, Assistant Leader of Fisheries

KANSAS DEPARTMENT OF AGRICULTURE

109 SW 9th St., 2nd Fl.
Topeka, KS 66612-1280 United States
Phone: 785-296-3717   Fax: 785-296-1176
Website: www.accesskansas.org/kda

Membership: 1–100
Scope: State
Keyword(s): Agriculture/Farming, Reduce/Reuse/Recycle, Water Habitats & Quality
Contact(s):
Tom Huntzinger, Water Appropriations Program Manager
Steve Stankiewicz, Operations Manager for Water Resources Division
Jamie Adams, Secretary of Agriculture; 785-296-3902; Fax: 785-296-8389
David Pope, Chief Engineer; 785-296-3717

KANSAS DEPARTMENT OF HEALTH AND ENVIRONMENT

1000 SW Jackson Street, Suite 400
Topeka, KS 66612-1367 United States
Phone: 785-296-1535   Fax: 785-296-8464
E-mail: rhammers@kdhe.state.ks.us
Website: www.kdhe.state.ks.us

Membership: 101–1,000
Scope: State
Description: The Kansas Department of Health and Environment is responsible for administering a diverse collection of programs that enhance public health and state wildlife protection efforts. The path of the department is defined by strengthening programs and developing initatives on pollutant releases, spill cleanup, air and water quality, water resources, pollution prevention, waste management, and general health and environmental protection.
Keyword(s): Air Quality/Atmosphere, Pollution (general), Public Health, Reduce/Reuse/Recycle, Water Habitats & Quality
Contact(s):
Bill Bider, Director: Bureau of Waste Management
Gary Blackburn, Director: Bureau of Environmental Remediation; 785-296-1660
Ron Hammerschmidt, Director: Division of Environment; 785-296-1535
Mike Heideman, Director: Office of Public Information; 785-296-5795
Theresa Hodges, Director: Bureau of Environmental Field Services; 785-296-5572
Michael Moser, Director: Bureau of Environmental Health Services; 785-296-1086
Karl Mueldener, Director: Bureau of Water; 785-296-5500
Clyde Graber, Secretary; 785-296-0461

KANSAS DEPARTMENT OF WILDLIFE AND PARKS

OFFICE OF THE SECRETARY
1020 S. Kansas Ave, Suite 200
Topeka, KS 66612-1237 United States
Phone: 785-296-2281   Fax: 785-296-6953
Website: www.kdwp.state.ks.us

Membership: 101–1,000
Scope: State
Description: Charged with the conservation of state wildlife and fishery resources, provision of environmental services and habitat protection, and park development and management. Administers state boating law, hunter education programs, Land and Water Conservation Funds, and other related functions.
Publication(s): Kansas Wildlife & Parks Magazine
Keyword(s): Agriculture/Farming, Public Lands/Greenspace, Recreation/Ecotourism, Reduce/Reuse/Recycle, Water Habitats & Quality, Wildlife & Species
Contact(s):
Terry Denker, Federal Aid Coordinator
John Dykes, Commissioner Members Chairman; 913-831-3058
J. Michael Hayden, Secretary
Richard Koerth, Assistant Secretary for Administration
Cheryl Swayne, Boating Education, Topeka Office

KANSAS DEPARTMENT OF WILDLIFE AND PARKS

OPERATIONS OFFICE
512 SE 25th Ave.
Pratt, KS 67124-8174 United States
Phone: 620-672-5911   Fax: 620-672-2972
E-mail: feedback@wp.state.ks.us
Website: www.kdwp.state.ks.us

Membership: 101–1,000
Scope: State
Description: State agency responsible for management and protection of fish and wildlife resources.
Publication(s): Kansas Wildlife and Parks Magazine
Keyword(s): Agriculture/Farming, Public Lands/Greenspace, Recreation/Ecotourism, Reduce/Reuse/Recycle, Water Habitats & Quality, Wildlife & Species
Contact(s):
Jerold Hover, Parks Division Director
Kevin Jones, Law Enforcement Division Director
Joe Kramer, Fisheries and Wildlife Division Director
Wayne Doyle, Coordinator, Hunter Education/Fur Harvester Education Service
Cindy Livingston, Administrative Services Division
Bob Mathews, Information and Education
Mike Miller, Editor
Keith Sexson, Assistant Secretary for Operations
Roland Stein, Coordinator, Wildlife Education Service

KANSAS DEPARTMENT OF WILDLIFE AND PARKS

REGION 1
1426 Hwy. 183 Alt.
P.O. Box 338
Hays, KS 67601 United States
Phone: 785-628-8614   Fax: 785-623-2945
Website: www.kdwp.state.ks.us

Membership: 101–1,000
Scope: State
Description: Northwest Regional Office of state agency responsible for management and protection of fish and wildlife resources.

Keyword(s): Agriculture/Farming, Public Lands/Greenspace, Recreation/Ecotourism, Reduce/Reuse/Recycle, Water Habitats & Quality, Wildlife & Species

Contact(s):
Jerry Bump, Law Enforcement Regional Supervisor
Melody Burkholder, Parks Division Regional Supervisor
Steve Price, F&W Division Regional Supervisor
Bruce Taggart, Public Lands Regional Supervisor

KANSAS DEPARTMENT OF WILDLIFE AND PARKS
REGION 2
3300 SW 29th St.
Topeka, KS 66614 United States
Phone: 785-273-6740   Fax: 785-273-6757
Website: www.kdwp.state.ks.us

Membership: 101–1,000
Scope: State
Description: Northeast Regional Office of state agency responsible for management and protection of fish and wildlife resources.
Keyword(s): Agriculture/Farming, Public Lands/Greenspace, Recreation/Ecotourism, Reduce/Reuse/Recycle, Water Habitats & Quality, Wildlife & Species

Contact(s):
Rob Ladner, Law Enforcement Regional Supervisor
Ron Little, Public Lands Regional Supervisor
Bill Porter, Parks Division Regional Supervisor
Roger Wolfe, F&W Division Regional Supervisor

KANSAS DEPARTMENT OF WILDLIFE AND PARKS
REGION 3
1001 W. McArtor
Dodge City, KS 67801 United States
Phone: 620-227-8609   Fax: 620-227-8600
Website: www.kdwp.state.ks.us

Membership: 101–1,000
Scope: State
Description: Southwest Regional Office of state agency responsible for management and protection of fish and wildlife resources.
Keyword(s): Agriculture/Farming, Public Lands/Greenspace, Recreation/Ecotourism, Reduce/Reuse/Recycle, Water Habitats & Quality, Wildlife & Species

Contact(s):
Scotty Baugh, F&W Division Regional Supervisor
Marvin Jensen, Law Enforcement Regional Supervisor
Mark Sexson, Public Lands Regional Supervisor

KANSAS DEPARTMENT OF WILDLIFE AND PARKS
REGION 4
6232 E. 29th St., N
Wichita, KS 67220 United States
Phone: 316-683-8069   Fax: 316-683-4664
Website: www.kdwp.state.ks.us

Membership: 101–1,000
Scope: State
Description: South Central Regional Office of state agency responsible for management and protection of fish and wildlife resources.
Keyword(s): Agriculture/Farming, Public Lands/Greenspace, Recreation/Ecotourism, Reduce/Reuse/Recycle, Wildlife & Species

Contact(s):
Randy Clark, Public Lands Regional Supervisor
Val Jansen, Law Enforcement Regional Supervisor
J. Alan Stark, Parks Division Regional Supervisor
Tom Swan, F&W Division Regional Supervisor

KANSAS DEPARTMENT OF WILDLIFE AND PARKS
REGION 5
1500 W. 7th
P.O. Box 777
Chanute, KS 66720-0777 United States
Phone: 620-431-0380   Fax: 620-431-0381
Website: www.kdwp.state.ks.us

Membership: 101–1,000
Scope: State
Description: Southeast Regional Office of state agency responsible for management and protection of fish and wildlife resources.
Keyword(s): Agriculture/Farming, Public Lands/Greenspace, Recreation/Ecotourism, Reduce/Reuse/Recycle, Water Habitats & Quality, Wildlife & Species

Contact(s):
C. Doug Blex, Public Lands Regional Supervisor
Larry Tiemann, F&W Division Regional Supervisor
Charles Ward, Law Enforcement Regional Supervisor

KANSAS FOREST SERVICE
2610 Claflin Rd.
Manhattan, KS 66502-2798 United States
Phone: 785-532-3300   Fax: 785-532-3305
E-mail: kfs@lists.oznet.ksu.edu
Website: www.kansasforests.org

Scope: State
Description: Provides technical forestry assistance to landowners, wood industries, and communities; conducts a tree distribution program, and a rural fire protection program.
Keyword(s): Forests/Forestry, Reduce/Reuse/Recycle, Water Habitats & Quality

Contact(s):
Eric Berg, Community Forestry Coordinator
Ross Hauck, Fire Protection Specialist
Casey McCoy, Rural Fire Coordinator
Raymond Aslin, State Forester
Robert Atchison, Rural Forestry Coordinator
Joshua Pease, Conservation Forester

KANSAS GEOLOGICAL SURVEY
1930 Constant Ave., Campus West, University of Kansas
Lawrence, KS 66047-3726 United States
Phone: 785-864-3965   Fax: 785-864-5317
Website: www.kgs.ku.edu

Founded: 1889
Membership: 101–1,000
Scope: State
Description: Purpose is to research and develop information about minerals, water resources, and geologic hazards of Kansas, and to publish reports on those subjects.
Publication(s): Bulletin, public information circulars, educational series, technical series, maps, journals
Keyword(s): Energy, Oceans/Coasts/Beaches

Contact(s):
M. Allison, Director and State Geologist; 785-864-2108; Fax: 785-864-5317; lallison@kgs.ku.edu
Timothy Carr, Chief: Petroleum Research; 785-864-2135; Fax: 785-864-5317; tcarr@kgs.ku.edu
William Harrison, Deputy Director; 785-864-2070; Fax: 785-864-5317; harrison@kgs.ku.edu
Don Whittemore, Chief: Geohydrology; 785-864-2182; Fax: 785-864-5317; donwhitt@kgs.ku.edu

KANSAS STATE CONSERVATION COMMISSION
109 SW Ninth St.
Topeka, KS 66612-1215 United States
Phone: 785-296-3600   Fax: 785-296-6172
E-mail: tstreeter@scc.state.ks.us
Website: www.accesskansas.org/kscc

Founded: 1937
Membership: 1–100
Scope: State
Description: The SCC administrative responsibility is to provide leadership, direction, and support to the conservation districts, watershed districts, and other special purpose districts for the protection and enhancement of Kansas' natural resources. It administers a total of ten programs: seven are financial assistance programs funded by appropriations from the Special Revenue Fund of the State Water Plan.
Keyword(s): Land Issues, Oceans/Coasts/Beaches, Water Habitats & Quality
Contact(s):
Tracy Streeter, Executive Director; 913-296-3600; Fax: 913-296-6172

KANSAS STATE EXTENSION SERVICES
Wildlife Damage Control, Dept. of Animal Sciences and Industry
131 Call Hall
Kansas State University
Manhattan, KS 66506-1600 United States
Phone: 785-532-5734   Fax: 785-532-5681
Website: www.oznet.ksu.edu

Founded: 1914
Scope: Local, State, Regional
Keyword(s): Recreation/Ecotourism, Water Habitats & Quality, Wildlife & Species
Contact(s):
Charles Lee, Extension Specialist; 785-532-5734; clee@oznet.ksu.edu

KANSAS WATER OFFICE
901 S. Kansas Ave.
Topeka, KS 66612-1249 United States
Phone: 785-296-3185   Fax: 785-296-0878
Website: www.kwo.org/

Description: State water planning, policy, and coordination agency. Prepares state plan of water resources management; conservation; fish and wildlife, and recreation and development; reviews water laws, and recommends new or amendatory legislation. Administers the state water monitoring program.
Keyword(s): Development/Developing Countries, Water Habitats & Quality
Contact(s):
Joe Harkins, Director
Ken Grotewiel, Assistant Director

KENTUCKY DEPARTMENT OF AGRICULTURE
7th Fl., 500 Mero St.
Frankfort, KY 40601 United States
Phone: 502-564-4696   Fax: 502-564-2133
Website: www.kyagr.com

Founded: 1876
Scope: State
Description: The service, regulatory, and promotional agency for Kentucky's agriculture industry.
Publication(s): Kentucky Agricultural News, Kentucky Agricultural Statistics (Yearly), see publications on website
Keyword(s): Agriculture/Farming, Land Issues, Pollution (general), Water Habitats & Quality
Contact(s):
Doug Thomas, Director: Division of Communications; 502-564-4696; ext. 248
Ted Sloan, Editor; 502-564-4696; ext. 247
Billy Smith, Commissioner

KENTUCKY DEPARTMENT OF FISH AND WILDLIFE RESOURCES
#1 Game Farm Rd.
Frankfort, KY 40601 United States
Phone: 800-858-1549   Fax: 502-564-6508
E-mail: info.center@mail.state.ky.us
Website: www.kyafield.com/

Founded: 1944
Membership: 101–1,000
Scope: State
Description: We are stewards of Kentucky's fish and wildlife resources and their habitats. We manage for the perpetuation of these resources and their use by present and future generations. Through partnerships, we will enhance wildlife diversity and promote sustainable use, including hunting, fishing, boating, and other nature-related recreation.
Publication(s): Kentucky Wildlife Viewing Guide, Hunting and Fishing Regulation Guides, Kentucky Fish, Kentucky Afield Magazine
Keyword(s): Wildlife & Species
Contact(s):
Robert Bates, Director of Administrative Services Division
Charles Bush, Director of Engineering Division
Lee Carolan, Director of Division of Information and Education
Lynn Garrison, Director of Public Affairs Division
Roy Grimes, Director of Division of Wildlife
David Loveless, Director of Division of Law Enforcement
Peter Pfeiffer, Director of Division of Fisheries
John Akers, Superintendent of State Game Farm
Gerald Alexander, Regional Law Enforcement Supervisor; 6575 Beech Grove Rd., Farmington, KY 42040
James Axon, Coordinator of Sport Fish Restoration Section
Tom Baker, District 2 Commissioner; 661 A U.S. 31 W. By-Pass, Bowling Green, KY 42101
Charles Bale, District 4 Commissioner; 855 Parkers Grove Rd., Hodgenville, KY 42748
C. Bennett, Commissioner
Mike Boatwright, District 1 Commissioner; 2601 N. 10th St., Paducah, KY 42001
Frank Brown, District 6 Commissioner; 124 Lancaster Ave., Richmond, KY 40475; Fax: 606-624-0820
Allen Gailor, District 3 Commissioner; 730 W. Market, Louisville, KY 40202
David Godby, District 9 Commissioner; P.O. Box 1277, Somerset, KY 42502; Fax: 606-677-0115
K. Henderson, Regional Boating Supervisor; P.O. Box 131, Clarkson, KY 42726
Doug Hensley, District 7 Commissioner; P.O. Box 480, Hazard, KY 41701; Fax: 606-436-5180
Steve Owens, Regional Boating Supervisor; 338 Candlelite Drive, Almo, KY 42020
James Rich, District 5 Commissioner; 5975 Taylor Mill Rd., Covington, KY 41015
Reed Sanders, Regional Boating Supervisor; 185 Gwinn Island Circle, Danville, KY 40422
Don Walker, Coordinator of Pittman-Robertson Section
Dennis Watson, Regional Boating Supervisor; Route 1 Sand Knob, Falls of Rough, KY 40119
Robert Webb, District 8 Commissioner; 45 Webb Circle, Grayson, KY 41143
Thomas Young, Deputy Commissioner

KENTUCKY DEPARTMENT OF PARKS
10th Fl., Capital Plaza Tower
Frankfort, KY 40601 United States
Phone: 502-564-2172   Fax: 502-564-9096
Website: www.kystateparks.com

Membership: 1,001–10,000
Scope: Regional
Publication(s): Kentucky Hiking Trails, Kentucky State Parks Booklet

Keyword(s): Land Issues, Public Lands/Greenspace, Recreation/Ecotourism

Contact(s):
Jim Goodman, Director of Resort Parks
Danny Reed, Director: Rangers
Bob Bender, Deputy Commissioner
Kenny Rapier, Commissioner
Carey Tichenor, State Naturalist

KENTUCKY GEOLOGICAL SURVEY
228 Mining and Mineral Resources Bldg., University of Kentucky
Lexington, KY 40506-0107 United States
Phone: 859-257-5500   Fax: 859-257-1147
Website: www.uky.edu/kgs

Founded: 1854
Membership: 1–100
Scope: State

Description: Investigates the geology and mineral and water resources of Kentucky and makes this information available to the public. It is a research and service organization.

Publication(s): See publication website

Contact(s):
James Cobb, Director and State Geologist; cobb@kgs.mm.uky.edu
Steven Cordiviola, Head: Computer and Laboratory Services Section; cordiviola@kgs.mm.uky.edu
James Dinger, Head: Water Resources Section; dinger@kgs.mm.uky.edu
James Drahovzal, Head: Energy & Mineral Section; drahovzal@kgs.mm.uky.edu
John Kiefer, Assistant State Geologist for Administration; kiefer@kgs.mm.uky.edu

KENTUCKY NATURAL RESOURCES AND ENVIRONMENTAL PROTECTION CABINET
#2 Hudson Hollow
Frankfort, KY 40601 United States
Phone: 502-564-2320   Fax: 502-564-6764
E-mail: blaine.fennell@mail.state.ky.us

Membership: 1–100
Scope: State

Contact(s):
Larry Adams, Director: Division of Permits; 502-564-2320; Fax: 502-564-6764; larry.adams@mail.state.ky.us
Stephen Hohmann, Director: Division of Abandoned Lands; 502-564-2141; Fax: 502-564-6544; stevehohmann@mail.state.ky.us
Mark Thompson, Director: Division of Field Services; 502-564-2340; Fax: 502-564-5848; markw.thompson@mail.state.ky.us
Carl Campbell, Commissioner
Allen Luttrell, Deputy Commissioner

KENTUCKY NATURAL RESOURCES AND ENVIRONMENTAL PROTECTION CABINET
Capital Plaza Tower
Frankfort, KY 40601 United States
Phone: 502-564-3350   Fax: 502-564-3354
Website: www.kyenvironment.org

Scope: State

Contact(s):
James Bickford, Secretary
Barbara Foster, General Counsel: Office of Legal Services; 502-564-5576; Fax: 502-564-6131
Hank List, Deputy Secretary

KENTUCKY NATURAL RESOURCES AND ENVIRONMENTAL PROTECTION CABINET
14 Reilly Rd.
Frankfort, KY 40601 United States
Phone: 502-564-2150   Fax: 502-564-4245
Website: www.nr.state.ky.us

Membership: 1,001–10,000
Scope: State

Description: Natural Resources and Environmental Protection Cabinet

Contact(s):
Robert Daniell, Director: Division of Waste Management; 502-564-6716; Fax: 502-564-4049
William Davis, Director: Division of Environmental Services; 502-564-6120; Fax: 502-564-8930
John Hornback, Director: Division for Air Quality; 502-573-3382; Fax: 502-573-3787
Jeff Pratt, Director: Division of Water; 502-564-3410; Fax: 502-564-4245
Ralph Collins, Deputy Commissioner
Robert Logan, Commissioner

KENTUCKY NATURAL RESOURCES AND ENVIRONMENTAL PROTECTION CABINET
DEPARTMENT FOR ENVIRONMENTAL PROTECTION
14 Reilly Road
Frankfort, KY 40601 United States
Phone: 502-564-2150   Fax: 502-564-4245
Website: www.kyenvironment.org

Scope: State

Description: The mission of the Kentucky Natural Resources and Environmental Protection Cabinet is to protect and preserve Kentucky's land, air, and water resources.

Contact(s):
Ralph Collins, Deputy Commissioner
Rob Daniell, Division of Waste Management; 502-564-6716
William Davis, Environmental Services; 502-564-6120
Robert Logan, Commissioner
John Lyons, Division for Air Quality; 502-573-3382
Jeff Pratt, Division of Water; 502-564-3410

KENTUCKY NATURAL RESOURCES AND ENVIRONMENTAL PROTECTION CABINET
DEPARTMENT FOR NATURAL RESOURCES
663 Teton Trail
Frankfort, KY 40601 United States
Phone: 502-564-2184   Fax: 502-564-9195
E-mail: steve.coleman@mail.state.ky.us
Website: www.naturalresources.ky.gov

Membership: 1–100
Scope: Regional
Publication(s): Publications on website

Contact(s):
Steve Coleman, Director: Division of Conservation; 502-564-3080; Fax: 502-564-9195
John Davies, Director: Division of Energy; 502-564-7192; Fax: 502-564-7484
Leah MacSwords, Director: Division of Forestry; 502-564-4496; Fax: 502-564-6553
Hugh Archer, Commissioner

KENTUCKY NATURAL RESOURCES AND ENVIRONMENTAL PROTECTION CABINET
ENVIRONMENTAL QUALITY COMMISSION
14 Reilly Rd.
Frankfort, KY 40601 United States
Phone: 502-564-2150   Fax: 502-564-4245
Website: www.kyeqc.net

Founded: 1972
Scope: State

Description: A seven-member citizen board that advises the governor and other state officials on environmental matters

Publication(s): Kentucky's Environment - bimonthly newsletter, State of Kentucky's Environment - biyearly book

Keyword(s): Agriculture/Farming, Air Quality/Atmosphere, Ecosystems (precious), Energy, Ethics/Environmental Justice, Forests/Forestry, Land Issues, Pollution (general), Public Health, Public Lands/Greenspace, Recreation/Ecotourism, Reduce/Reuse/Recycle, Sprawl/Urban

Contact(s):
Leslie Cole, Executive Director
Aloma Dew, Chair

KENTUCKY NATURAL RESOURCES AND ENVIRONMENTAL PROTECTION CABINET
KENTUCKY STATE NATURE PRESERVES COMMISSION
801 Schenkel Ln.
Frankfort, KY 40601 United States
Phone: 502-573-2886 Fax: 502-573-2355
E-mail: nrepc.ksnpcemail@mail.state.ky.us
Website: www.kynaturepreserves.org

Founded: 1976
Scope: State
Description: KSNP's mission is to protect Kentucky's natural heritage by (1) identifying, acquiring, and managing natural areas that represent the best known occurrences of rare native species, natural communitites, and significant natural features in a statewide nature preserve system; (2) working with others to protect biological diveristy; and (3) educating Kentuckians as to the value and purpose of nature preserves and biodiversity conservation..

Publication(s): Naturally Kentucky

Keyword(s): Ecosystems (precious), Forests/Forestry, Land Issues, Public Lands/Greenspace, Recreation/Ecotourism, Water Habitats & Quality, Wildlife & Species

Contact(s):
Don Dott, Director; 502-573-2886; Fax: 502-573-2355; don.dott@mail.state.ky.us
Clara Wheatley, Chairman, KSNPC Citizen Commission

KENTUCKY SOIL AND WATER CONSERVATION COMMISSION
663 Teton Trail
Frankfort, KY 40601 United States
Phone: 502-564-3080 Fax: 502-564-9195
E-mail: steve.coleman@mail.state.ky.us
Website: www.kyenvironment.org/nrepc/dnr/Conserve/doc2.htm

Founded: 1946
Scope: Local, State, Regional
Description: Set policy for state soil and water conservation programs and assist 121 local conservation districts.
Keyword(s): Agriculture/Farming, Land Issues, Pollution (general), Sprawl/Urban Planning

Contact(s):
Stephen Coleman, Director of Division of Conservation; 502-564-3080; Fax: 502-564-9195
David Gerrein, Chair; 606-623-3960

KENTUCKY STATE COOPERATIVE EXTENSION SERVICES
S-107 Agricultural Science Center North
Lexington, KY 40546 United States
Phone: 859-257-4302 Fax: 859-323-1991
Website: www.uky.edu

Membership: 101–1,000
Scope: Local, State
Description: The Kentucky Cooperative Extension Service serves as a link between the counties of the Commonwealth and the state's land grant universities to help people improve their lives through an educational process focusing on their issues and needs.

Publication(s): Extension Today

Contact(s):
Jimmy Henning, Assistant Extension Director of Agriculture; N-122, Agricultural Science Center North, University of Kentucky, Lexington, KY 40546; 606-257-1846; jhenning@uky.edu
Larry Turner, Assistant Dean for Extension; 859-257-4302; Fax: 859-323-1991; lturner@uky.edu
Thomas Barnes, Wildlife Specialist; Univ. of Kentucky, Dept. of Forestry, Lexington, KY 40546-0073; 606-257-8633; Fax: 606-323-1031; tbarnes@uky.edu
Rick Maurer, Assistant Director, Rural and Economic Development; 500 Garrigus Bldg., University of Kentucky, Lexington, KY 40546-0215; 606-257-7585; rmaurer@ca.uky.edu

KENTUCKY STATE NATURE PRESERVES COMMISSION
801 Schenkel Ln.
Frankfort, KY 40601 United States
Phone: 502-573-2886 Fax: 502-573-2355
E-mail: nrepc.ksnpcemail@mail.state.ky.us
Website: www.kynaturepreserves.org

Founded: 1976
Membership: 1–100
Scope: State
Description: KSNP's mission is to protect Kentucky's natural heritage by (1) identifying, acquiring, and managing natural areas that represent the best known occurrences of rare native species, natural communitites, and significant natural features in a statewide nature preserve system; (2) working with others to protect biological diveristy; and (3) educating Kentuckians as to the value and purpose of nature preserves and biodiversity conservation.

Publication(s): Naturally Kentucky

Keyword(s): Ecosystems (precious), Forests/Forestry, Land Issues, Public Lands/Greenspace, Recreation/Ecotourism, Water Habitats & Quality, Wildlife & Species

Contact(s):
Donald Dott, Director; 502-573-2886; Fax: 502-573-2355; don.dott@mail.state.ky.us
Ken Jackson, Secretary of Commission; 606-734-4436
Clara Wheatley, Chair of Commission; 502-358-8643

L

LEE COUNTY PARKS AND RECREATION
E.E. Program Coordinator
3410 Palm Beach Blvd
Fort Myers, FL 33916 United States
Phone: 239-461-7472 Fax: 239-461-7460
E-mail: kisedajb@leegov.com
Website: www.lee-county.com/parksandrec/

Founded: 1990
Scope: Local, State, Regional
Description: To promote and develop environmental awareness in Southwest Florida by conducting educational programs which teach ecological concepts and outdoor skills, and by coordinating informational events which alert citizens and community leaders of environmental concerns.

Publication(s): Florida Native Plant Habitat Guide, Elements Newsletter

Keyword(s): Ecosystems (precious), Land Issues, Oceans/Coasts/Beaches, Public Lands/Greenspace, Recreation/Ecotourism, Reduce/Reuse/Recycle, Water Habitats & Quality, Wildlife & Species

Contact(s):
John Kiseda, Program Coordinator - Environmental Education; kisedajb@leegov.com

LOUISIANA COOPERATIVE FISH AND WILDLIFE RESEARCH UNIT (USDI)
U.S. Geological Survey, School of Forestry, Wildlife and Fisheries
FWF Building, Rm. 124
Louisiana State University
Baton Rouge, LA 70803-6202 United States
Phone: 225-578-4179   Fax: 225-578-4144

Membership: 1–100
Scope: National
Contact(s):
  Alan Afton, Assistant Leader; 225-578-4212; aafton@lsu.edu
  Charles Bryan, Leader; 225-578-4184; Fax: 225-578-4144; cbryan@lsu.edu
  Megan Lapeyre, Assistant Leader Fisheries; 225-578-4180

LOUISIANA DEPARTMENT OF AGRICULTURE AND FORESTRY
P.O. Box 631
Baton Rouge, LA 70821-0631 United States
Phone: 225-922-1234   Fax: 225-922-1253
E-mail: info@ldaf.state.la.us
Website: www.ldaf.state.la.us/

Contact(s):
  Bud Courson, Deputy Commissioner; 504-922-1238; Fax: 504-922-1253
  Bob Odom, Commissioner
  Skip Rhorer, Assistant Commissioner: Office of Management and Finance

LOUISIANA DEPARTMENT OF AGRICULTURE AND FORESTRY
OFFICE OF FORESTRY
Louisiana Department of Agriculture and Forestry
P.O. Box 1628
Baton Rouge, LA 70821-1628 United States
Phone: 225-925-4500   Fax: 225-922-1356
Website: www.ldaf.state.la.us

Founded: 1944
Membership: 101–1,000
Scope: State
Description: Charged with: Detection and suppression of wildfire on forest lands; providing technical management assistance to forest landowners; and dissemination of materials and information for education of the public. Produces approximately 50 million seedlings annually (pine and hardwood) for Louisiana landowners, operates a 400-acre seed orchard that produces improved slash and loblolly pine seed that are genetically improved. Actively engaged in promoting urban forestry activities.
Publication(s): Publications on website
Keyword(s): Forests/Forestry, Recreation/Ecotourism, Reduce/Reuse/Recycle
Contact(s):
  Paul Frey, State Forester; 225-925-4500; Fax: 225-922-1356; paul_f@ldaf.state.la.us
  Louis Heaton, Chief: Forest Management; 225-925-4500; louis_h@ldaf.state.la.us
  Cyril Lejeune, Associate State Forester; 225-952-8002; cyril_l@ldaf.state.la.us
  Charles Matherne, Chief: Reforestation; 225-925-4515
  Burton Weaver, Chairman

LOUISIANA DEPARTMENT OF AGRICULTURE AND FORESTRY
OFFICE OF SOIL AND WATER CONSERVATION, STATE SOIL AND WATER CONSERVATION COMMITTEE
P.O. Box 3554
Baton Rouge, LA 70821-3554 United States
Phone: 225-922-1269   Fax: 225-922-2577
Website: www.ldaf.state.la.us/divisions/swc

Founded: 1938
Description: To assist soil and water conservation districts in carrying out their conservation programs, to coordinate activities among districts, and to secure the cooperation and assistance of state and federal agencies in the work of such districts.
Contact(s):
  Bradley Spicer, Executive Director; 504-922-1269; Fax: 504-922-2577
  A. Allee, Secretary and Treasurer
  Pedro Angelle, Chairman; 4879 Main Hwy., St. Martinville, LA 70582; 318-332-2910; Fax: 318-332-6563
  Thad Spurlock, Vice Chairman

LOUISIANA DEPARTMENT OF NATURAL RESOURCES
617 North Third Street
P. O. Box 94396
Baton Rouge, LA 70802 United States
Phone: 225-342-8955   Fax: 224-342-3442
Website: www.dnr.state.la.us

Scope: State
Contact(s):
  Jack Caldwell, Secretary; 225-342-4503; Fax: 225-342-5861
  Robert Harper, Under Secretary
  Katherine Vaughan, Deputy Secretary; 225-342-1375

LOUISIANA DEPARTMENT OF NATURAL RESOURCES
P.O. Box 94396
Baton Rouge, LA 70804-9396 United States
Phone: 225-342-4500   Fax: 225-342-5861
E-mail: webmaster@dnr.state.la.us
Website: www.dnr.state.la.us

Founded: 1975
Membership: 101–1,000
Scope: State
Description: This is a cabinet-level organization within the State of Louisiana charged with responsibilities related to coastal restoration, mineral conservation, and energy conservation.
Keyword(s): Energy, Oceans/Coasts/Beaches
Contact(s):
  Katherine Vaughan, Assistant Secretary; 225-342-1375; Fax: 225-342-5861

LOUISIANA DEPARTMENT OF NATURAL RESOURCES
OFFICE OF CONSERVATION
P.O. Box 94275
Baton Rouge, LA 70804-9275 United States
Phone: 225-342-5500   Fax: 225-342-3705
E-mail: info@dnr.state.la.us
Website: www.dnr.state.la.us/cons/conserv.ssi

Founded: 1910
Membership: 101–1,000
Scope: Local, State, Regional
Description: State regulatory agency for oil and gas matters.
Keyword(s): Energy, Pollution (general), Transportation, Water Habitats & Quality
Contact(s):
  James Welsh, Commissioner of Conservation; 225-342-5500; Fax: 225-342-3705; jimw@dnr.state.la.us

LOUISIANA DEPARTMENT OF NATURAL RESOURCES
OFFICE OF MINERAL RESOURCES
617 North Third Street, P.O. Box 2827
Baton Rouge, LA 70802 United States
Phone: 225-342-4615   Fax: 225-342-4527
E-mail: omr@dnr.state.la.us
Website: www.dnr.state.la.us

Contact(s):
Gus Rodemacher, Assistant Secretary

LOUISIANA DEPARTMENT OF WILDLIFE AND FISHERIES
P.O. Box 98000
Baton Rouge, LA 70898-9000 United States
Phone: 225-765-2800
Website: www.wlf.state.la.us

Founded: 1872
Scope: State
Description: Established as a part of state government to protect, conserve, and replenish the natural resources of the state, including wild game and nongame quadrupeds or animals, oysters, fish, and other aquatic life.
Publication(s): Louisiana Conservationist
Keyword(s): Wildlife & Species
Contact(s):
Phil Bowman, Assistant Secretary: Office of Wildlife; 225-765-2806
Bill Busbice, Chairman
Bennie Fontenot, Administrator: Inland Fisheries Division; 225-765-2330
Karen Foote, Administrator: Marine Fisheries Division; 225-765-2384
James Jenkins, Secretary; 225-765-2623
James Patton, Under Secretary: Office of Management and Finance; 225-765-2860
Tommy Prickett, Administrator: Wildlife Division; 225-765-2346
John Roussel, Assistant Secretary: Office of Fisheries; 225-765-2801
Brandt Savoie, Administrator: Fur & Refuge Division; 225-765-2811
Winton Vidrine, Administrator: Colonel, Law Enforcement Division; 225-765-2989

LOUISIANA GEOLOGICAL SURVEY
2105 Energy, Coast and Environment Building
Louisiana State University
Baton Rouge, LA 70803 United States
Phone: 225-578-5320   Fax: 225-578-9257
E-mail: hammer@lsu.edu
Website: www.lgs.lsu.edu

Founded: 1934
Description: The Survey is charged with conducting geologic investigations and preparing technical reports that assist in finding and developing new reserves of natural resources in the state and in protecting the state's environment.
Keyword(s): Energy, Oceans/Coasts/Beaches, Water Habitats & Quality
Contact(s):
Chacko John, Director

LOUISIANA OFFICE OF STATE PARKS, DEPARTMENT OF CULTURE, RECREATION, AND TOURISM
P.O. Box 44426
Baton Rouge, LA 70804 United States
Phone: 225-342-8111   Fax: 225-342-8107
E-mail: parks@crt.state.la.us
Website: www.lastateparks.com

Founded: 1934
Scope: State
Description: Created to plan, design, construct, operate, and maintain the state's parks, natural areas, recreational facilities, and commemorative sites. Office has 18 parks or recreational areas, 16 historic sites, and one preservation area open to the public. The Office is assisted by the Parks and Recreation Commission, an advisory board appointed by the Governor.

Keyword(s): Ecosystems (precious), Ethics/Environmental Justice, Land Issues, Public Lands/Greenspace, Recreation/Ecotourism, Wildlife & Species
Contact(s):
Bo Boehringer, Public Information Director; 225-342-2443; Fax: 225-219-9429; bboehringer@crt.state.la.us
Dwight Landreneau, Assistant Secretary; dlandreneau@crt.state.la.us

LSU AGCENTER - LOUISIANA COOPERATIVE EXTENSION SERVICE
P.O. Box 25100
Baton Rouge, LA 70894-5100 United States
Phone: 225-578-6083   Fax: 504-578-2478
Website: www.lsu.edu.center.edu

Scope: State
Publication(s): See publications on website
Contact(s):
Paul Coriel, Director of Extension Service; jlngent@agctr.lsu.edu
Rex Caffey, Assistant Specialist for Wetland and Coastal Resources; 225-388-2266; Fax: 225-388-2478; rcaffey@agctr.lsu.edu
Michael Dunn, Specialist: Forestry; 225-578-4087; Fax: 225-388-2478; mdunn@agctr.lsu.edu
Charles Lutz, Associate Specialist of Aquaculture; 225-388-2152; Fax: 225-388-2478; glutz@agctr.lsu.edu
Michael Moody, Specialist for Seafood Technology; 225-388-2152; Fax: 225-388-2478; mmoody@agctr.lsu.edu
Donald Reed, Assistant Specialist for Forestry and Wildlife; 225-388-4087; Fax: 225-388-2478; dreed@agctr.lsu.edu
Kenneth Roberts, Project Leader of Aquaculture: Fisheries, Wetland & Coastal; 225-388-2145, Fax. 225-388-2478; kroberts@agctr.lsu.edu
Todd Shupe, Assistant Specialist for Forestry; 225-388-4087; Fax: 225-388-2478; tshupe@agctr.lsu.edu

M

MADISON COUNTY SOIL & WATER CONSERVATION DISTRICT
SOIL & WATER CONSERVATION DISTRICT
175-A Commercial Parkway
Canton, MS 39046 United States
Phone: 601-859-4272, ext. 3   Fax: 601-859-7091
E-mail: madison@ms.nrcs.usda.gov
Website: www.madisoncountyswcd.org

Founded: 1939
Membership: 101–1,000
Scope: Local, State, Regional, National
Description: Madison County Soil & Water Conservation District (SWCD) was formed in 1939 to protect and preserve our natural resources. This is accomplished through various programs including: conservation education through field days and classroom demonstrations, cost share incentive programs, conservation equipment rental, poster and essay contests, quarterly newsletter, and annual tree give-away. The District works closely with USDA/NRCS to ensure the conservation goals are met.

MAINE ATLANTIC SALMON COMMISSION
650 State St.
Bangor, ME 04401-5654 United States
Phone: 207-941-4449   Fax: 207-941-4443
Website: www.state.me.us/asa

Founded: 1948
Membership: 1–100
Scope: State
Description: (formerly Maine Atlantic Salmon Authority) The Atlantic Salmon Commission was established for the purposes of undertaking research, planning, management, restoration,

and propagation of the Atlantic sea run salmon in the state. The Commission has authority to adopt and amend regulations to promote the conservation and propagation of Atlantic salmon in all Maine waters.

Keyword(s): Recreation/Ecotourism, Water Habitats & Quality, Wildlife & Species

Contact(s):
   Frederick Kircheis, Executive Director
   Paul Frinsko, Member At Large
   George Lapointe, Commissioner of Marine Resources
   Henry Nichols, Policy Development Specialist
   Lee Perry, Commissioner of Inland Fisheries and Wildlife

MAINE COOPERATIVE FISH AND WILDLIFE RESEARCH UNIT (USDI)
USGS Biological Resources Division, 5755 Nutting Hall, University of Maine
Orono, ME 04469-5755 United States
Phone: 207-581-2870   Fax: 207-581-2858
Website: www.wle.umaine.edu/temp_unit/unitpage.html

Founded: 1935
Membership: 1–100
Scope: Regional
Description: Provide graduate training and research experience in wildlife and fish ecology and management. Supported cooperatively by the University of Maine in Orono, ME, Maine Department of Inland Fisheries and Wildlife, U.S. Geological Survey, and the Wildlife Management Institute.

Keyword(s): Water Habitats & Quality, Wildlife & Species

Contact(s):
   William Krohn, Leader; 258 Nutting Hall, University of Maine, Orono, ME 04469; 207-581-2870; Fax: 207-581-2858
   Cynthia Loftin, Assistant Leader: Wildlife; 230 Nutting Hall, University of Maine, Orono, ME 04469; 207-581-2843; Fax: 207-581-2858
   John Moring, Assistant Leader: Fisheries; 310 Murray Hall, University of Maine, Orono, ME 04469; 207-581-2582

MAINE DEPARTMENT OF AGRICULTURE, FOOD, AND RURAL RESOURCES
DEPARTMENT OF AGRICULTURE, FOOD AND RURAL RESOURCES
Office of Agricultural, Natural and Rural Resources
28 State House Station
Augusta, ME 04333-0028 United States
Phone: 207-287-1132   Fax: 207-287-7548
Website: www.state.me.us/agriculture

Membership: 101–1,000
Scope: State
Description: The Department was established to improve Maine agriculture through: the conservation and improvements of the soil and cropland of the State; the development, compilation and dissemination of scientific and practical knowledge; the marketing and promotion of agricultural products; the detection, prevention and eradication of plant and animal diseases; the protection of the consuming public against harmful and unsanitary products and practices; and the sound development of the natural resources.

Keyword(s): Agriculture/Farming, Water Habitats & Quality

Contact(s):
   Peter Mosher, Director; 207-287-1132; Fax: 207-287-7548; peter.mosher@state.me.us
   Robert Spear, Commissioner; 207-287-3419

MAINE DEPARTMENT OF CONSERVATION
22 State House Station
Augusta, ME 04333-0022 United States
Phone: 207-287-2211   Fax: 208-287-2216
Website: www.doc.maine.gov

Founded: 1973
Membership: 101–1,000
Scope: State
Description: To preserve, protect, and enhance the land resources of the State of Maine; to encourage the wise use of the scenic, mineral, and forest resources; to ensure that coordinated planning for the future allocation of lands for recreational, forest production, mining, and other public and private uses is effectively accomplished; and to provide for the effective management of public lands.

Contact(s):
   Susan Benson, Director of Public Information
   Will Harris, Director of General Services
   Dawn Gallagher, Deputy Commissioner
   Ronald Lovaglio, Commissioner
   Gale Ross, Administrative Assistant

MAINE DEPARTMENT OF CONSERVATION
BUREAU OF GEOLOGY AND NATURAL AREAS
22 State House Station
Augusta, ME 04333 United States
Phone: 207-287-2801   Fax: 207-287-2353
E-mail: mgs@state.me.us
Website: www.state.me.us/doc/nrimc/nrimc.htm

Membership: 1–100
Scope: State
Publication(s): See publications on website

Contact(s):
   Molly Docherty, Director, Maine Natural Areas Program; 207-287-8045
   Robert Marvinney, State Geologist and Director; 207-287-2804; Fax: 207-287-2353; robert.g.marvinney@state,me.us
   Robert Tucker, Director, Earth Resources Information
   Tom Weddle, Hydrogeologist & Divison Director

MAINE DEPARTMENT OF CONSERVATION
BUREAU OF PARKS AND LANDS
Key Bank Plaza
286 Water ST
Augusta, ME 04333 United States
Phone: 207-287-3821   Fax: 207-287-8111
Website: www.state.me.us/doc/parks

Scope: State
Publication(s): Outdoors & Maine - brochure

Contact(s):
   David Soucy, Director; 207-287-3821; dave.soucy@state.me.us
   Marlene Bowman, Resource Administrator; 207-287-4912; marlene.bowman@state.me.us
   Herb Hartman, Deputy Director; 207-287-4961; herb.hartman@state.me.us
   Ralph Knoll, Planning & Land Use Acquisition; 207-287-4911; ralph.knoll@state.me.us
   Scott Ramsay, Off-Road Vehicle Program; 207-287-4956; scott.ramsay@state.me.us
   Richard Skinner, Boating Facilities; 207-287-4953; richard.skinner@state.me.us
   Marilyn Tourtelotte, Allagash Wilderness Waterway; 207-941-4014; marilyn.tourtelotte@state.me.us

MAINE DEPARTMENT OF CONSERVATION
FOREST SERVICE
22 State House Station
Augusta, ME 04333 United States
Phone: 207-287-2791   Fax: 207-287-8422
Website: www.state.me.us/doc/mfs

Membership: 101–1,000
Scope: State

Contact(s):
   Tom Doak, Director
   Peter Beringer, Resource Administrator
   Don Mansius, Forest Policy and Management

Tom Parent, Forest Protection
Dave Struble, State Entomologist

MAINE DEPARTMENT OF CONSERVATION
LAND USE REGULATION COMMISSION
State House Station #22
Augusta, ME 04333-0022 United States
Phone: 207-287-2631 Fax: 207-287-7439
Website: www.state.me.us/doc/lurc/lurchome.htm

Founded: 1971
Membership: 1–100
Scope: State
Description: Maine's planning and zoning authority for the state's plantations and unorganized townships.
Publication(s): Available on Web
Contact(s):
John Williams, Director
Peggy Dwyer, Resource Administrator; 207-287-4924

MAINE DEPARTMENT OF ENVIRONMENTAL PROTECTION
State House Station 17
Augusta, ME 04333 United States
Phone: 207-287-7688 Fax: 207-287-7826
Website: www.state.me.us/dep

Founded: 1972
Membership: 101–1,000
Scope: State
Description: DEP is charged with the protection and improvement of Maine's natural environment and acting in the best interests of the citizens' health and quality of life.
Publication(s): A Citizen's Guide to Lake Watershed Surveys, Planning Guides for Municipalities (series), Watershed: An Action Guide to Improving Maine Waters, The Quality of Maine Waters—A Condensed Version of the 1996 Maine Water Quality Assessment
Keyword(s): Air Quality/Atmosphere, Pollution (general), Reduce/Reuse/Recycle, Water Habitats & Quality
Contact(s):
James Brooks, Director: Bureau of Air Quality
David Lenette, Director: Bureau of Remediation and Waste Management
David Van Wie, Director: Bureau of Land and Water Quality
Brooke Barnes, Deputy Commissioner
Martha Kirkpatrick, Commissioner

MAINE DEPARTMENT OF INLAND FISHERIES AND WILDLIFE
284 State St.
Augusta, ME 04333-0041 United States
Phone: 207-287-8000 Fax: 207-287-6395
E-mail: webmaster_ifw@state.me.us
Website: www.mefishwildlife.com

Founded: 1880
Membership: 1–100
Scope: State
Publication(s): Maine Fish and Wildlife
Keyword(s): Public Lands/Greenspace, Recreation/Ecotourism, Wildlife & Species
Contact(s):
Vesta Billing, Director: Licensing and Registration Division; 207-287-5225
Peter Bourque, Director of Fisheries and Hatcheries Division; 207-287-5261
Kenneth Elowe, Director: Bureau of Resource Management; 207-287-5252
Donald Kleiner, Director: Bureau of Information and Education; 207-287-5244
Richard Record, Director: Bureau of Administrative Service; 207-287-5210
Andrea Erskine, Rules and Regulations Officer; 207-287-5201
Frederick Hurley, Deputy Commissioner; 207-287-5202
Timothy Peabody, Colonel, Bureau of Warden Service; 207-287-2766
Lee Perry, Commissioner; 207-287-5202
G. Stadler, Chief: Wildlife Research and Management Division; 207-287-5252
Ron Taylor, Chief, Engineering & Realty Division

MAINE DEPARTMENT OF MARINE RESOURCES
21 State House Station
Augusta, ME 04333-0021 United States
Phone: 207-624-6550 Fax: 207-624-6024
Website: www.maine.gov/dmr

Founded: 1867
Membership: 101–1,000
Scope: State
Description: Responsible for research, development, promotion, planning, and enforcement of laws relating to conservation of Maine's marine resources. The department was established to conserve and develop marine and estuarine resources of the State of Maine by conducting and sponsoring scientific research, promoting and developing the Maine commercial fishing industry, and by advising agencies of government concerned with development or activity in coastal waters.
Keyword(s): Public Health, Water Habitats & Quality, Wildlife & Species
Contact(s):
Gilbert Bilodeau, Director of Division of Administrative Services; gilbert.m.bilodeau@state.me.us
Dr. Linda Mercer, Director of Bureau of Resource Management; 207-633-9500; Fax: 207-633-9579; linda.mercer@state.me.us
E. Estabrook, Deputy Commissioner
Joseph Fessenden, Chief of Bureau of Marine Patrol; Fax: 207-624-6024
George Lapointe, Commissioner

MANITOBA CONSERVATION
Rm. 333, Legislative Bldg.
Winnipeg, R3C 0V8 Manitoba Canada
Phone: 204-945-3730 Fax: 204-945-3586
E-mail: conmin@leg.gov.mb.ca

Scope: Province
Description: The purpose of Manitoba Natural Resources is to encourage wise use of Manitoba's natural resources and preserve them for future generations.
Contact(s):
Wayne Fisher, Director of Headquarters Operations; Box 44, 200 Saulteaux Cres., Winnipeg, Manitoba R3J 3W3; 204-945-6647
Brian Gillespie, Director of Wildlife; Box 24, 200 Saulteaux Cres., Winnipeg, Manitoba R3J 3W3; 204-945-7761
Harley Jonasson, Director of Lands Branch; 123 Main St., W., Box 20000, Neepawa, Manitoba R0J 1H0; 204-476-3441
Gord Jones, Director of Forestry; Box 70, 200, Saulteaux Cres., Winnipeg, Manitoba R3J 3W3; 204-945-7998
Wayne Leeman, Director of Surveys and Mapping; 1007 Century St., Winnipeg, Manitoba R3H 0W4; 204-945-0011
Peter Lockett, Director of Financial Services; Box 85, 200 Saulteaux, Winnipeg, Manitoba R3J 3W3; 204-945-4187
Blair Mctavish, Director of Policy Coordination; Box 38, 200 Saulteaux Cres., Winnipeg, Manitoba R3J 3W3; 204-945-6658
Lorraine Metz, Director of Human Resources; 500-326 Broadway, Winnipeg, Manitoba MB, R3C 0S5; 204-945-2810
Joe O'Connor, Director of Fisheries Branch; Box 20, 200 Saulteaux Cres., Winnipeg, Manitoba R3J 3W3; 204-945-7814
W. Podolsky, Executive Director of Management Services; Box 85, 200 Saulteaux Cres., Winnipeg, Manitoba R3J 3W3; 204-945-4056

Kerry Poole, Director of Resource Information Systems; Box 90, 200 Saulteaux Cres., Winnipeg, Manitoba R3J 3W3; 204-945-2929
C. Prouse, Director of Parks and Natural Areas; Box 50, 200 Saulteaux Cres., Winnipeg, Manitoba R3J 3W3; 204-945-4362
Jack Schreuder, Executive Director of Land Information Centre; 1007 Century St., Winnipeg, Manitoba R3H 0W4; 204-945-6613
Steven Topping, Director of Water Resources Branch; Box 11, 200 Saulteaux, Winnipeg, Manitoba R3E 3J5; 204-945-7488
Harvey Boyle, Assistant Deputy Minister; Box 80, 200 Saulteaux Cres., Winnipeg, Manitoba R3J 3W3; 204-945-4842
Norm Brandson, Deputy Minister; Rm. 327, Legislative Bldg., Winnipeg, Manitoba R3C 0V8; 204-945-3785
Glen Holmes, Special Assistant to the Minister
Oscar Lathlin, Minister
Merlin Shoesmith, Assistant Deputy Minister; Box 80, 200 Saulteaux Cres., Winnipeg, Manitoba R3J 3W3; 204-945-6829

MANITOBA CONSERVATION
CENTRAL REGION
Box 6000
Gimli, R0C 1B0 Manitoba Canada
Phone: 204-642-6096   Fax: 204-642-6108
Scope: National
Contact(s):
Brian Gillespie, Regional Director

MANITOBA CONSERVATION
EASTERN REGION
Box 4000
Lac du Bonnet, R0E 1A0 Manitoba Canada
Phone: 204-345-1444   Fax: 204-345-1440
Website: www.gov.mb.ca
Scope: National
Contact(s):
Bob Cameron, Assistant Regional Superintendent

MANITOBA CONSERVATION
NORTHEASTERN REGION
Box 28, 59 Elizabeth Rd.
Thompson, R8N 1X4 Manitoba Canada
Phone: 204-677-6628   Fax: 204-677-6359
Scope: Regional
Contact(s):
Steve Kearney, Regional Director; 204-677-6628
Pierce Roberts, Assistant Regional Superintendent; 204-677-6629

MANITOBA CONSERVATION
NORTHWESTERN REGION
Box 2550, 3rd St. and Ross Ave.
The Pas, R9A 1M4 Manitoba Canada
Phone: 204-627-8261   Fax: 204-623-5733
Scope: Regional
Contact(s):
Albert King, Regional Director
Craig Asseltine, Assistant Regional Superintendent; 204-627-8353

MANITOBA CONSERVATION
WESTERN REGION
1129 Queens Ave., Box 13
Brandon, R7A 1L9 Manitoba Canada
Phone: 204-726-6296   Fax: 204-726-6301
Scope: Regional

Contact(s):
Bruce Wright, Acting Regional Director
Jack Dean, Assistant Regional Director

MANITOBA CONSERVATION DATA CENTRE
WILDLIFE AND ECOSYSTEM PROTECTION BRANCH
Box 24, 200 Saulteaux Crescent
Winnipeg, R3J 3W3 Manitoba Canada
Phone: 204-945-7743   Fax: 204-945-3077
E-mail: cdc_wildlife@gov.mb.ca
Website: http://web2.gov.mb.ca/conservation/cdc
Founded: 1994
Membership: 101–1,000
Scope: Local, Province, Regional, National, International
Description: The Manitoba Conservation Data Centre is part of an international network of data centres throughout North America and parts of Latin America.

MANITOBA DEPARTMENT OF CULTURE, HERITAGE, AND TOURISM
Travel Manitoba, Department RHO, 7th Fl., 155 Carlton St.
Winnipeg, R3C 3H8 Manitoba Canada
Phone: 1-800-665-0040   Fax: 204-945-2302
Website: www.travelmanitoba.com
Scope: Province
Description: Coordinates visits to Manitoba by travel and outdoor editors; produces and distributes travel and outdoor literature and films.
Contact(s):
Statia Elliot, Director of Marketing; 204-945-6777
Colette Fontaine, Marketing Consultant; 204-945-4045
Hubert Messman, Assistant Deputy Minister of Tourism and Business Development; 204-945-4204

MARINE LABORATORY (FLORIDA)
Florida State University, Rt. 1, Box 219A
Sopchoppy, FL 32358 United States
Phone: 904-697-4095   Fax: 904-697-4098
Website: www.marinelab.fsu.edu/
Description: Includes studies on the biology, chemistry, and geology of coastal communities, physical oceanography of near-shore waters, aquatic and terrestrial ecosystems, and aquaculture.
Keyword(s): Oceans/Coasts/Beaches, Water Habitats & Quality, Wildlife & Species
Contact(s):
Nancy Marcus, Director

MARYLAND DEPARTMENT OF AGRICULTURE
50 Harry S. Truman Pkwy.
Annapolis, MD 21401 United States
Phone: 410-841-5700   Fax: 410-841-5914
Website: www.mda.state.md.us
Founded: 1972
Membership: 101–1,000
Scope: State
Description: Created as a cabinet-level state agency, the department is charged with assisting soil conservation districts to protect state waters from agricultural nonpoint source pollution, overseeing numerous inspection, testing, grading, and marketing programs, mosquito control and gypsy moth control, and forest pest management under various laws. The department also has responsibility for regulatory functions, such as pesticide applicators, weights and measures, nursery inspection, seed and turf regulations.
Publication(s): MDA Annual Report, Agriculture in Maryland Brochure, MDA News
Contact(s):
Don Vandrey, Director of Communications

Robert Halman, Assistant Secretary: Marketing, Animal Industries
Hagner Mister, Secretary
Craig Nielsen, Counsel; 410-841-5883
Roger Olson, State Veterinarian; 410-841-5810
Royden Powell, Assistant Secretary: Office of Resource Conservation; 410-841-5865
Bradley Powers, Deputy Secretary
Charles Puffinberger, Assistant Secretary: Office of Plant Industries; 410-841-5870

MARYLAND DEPARTMENT OF AGRICULTURE
STATE SOIL CONSERVATION COMMITTEE
50 Harry S. Truman Pkwy.
Annapolis, MD 21401 United States
Phone: 410-841-5700   Fax: 410-841-5736
E-mail: dupontsk@mda.state.md.us
Website: www.mda.state.md.us

Founded: 1937
Membership: 1–100
Scope: State
Description: Established to organize soil conservation districts and to establish policy, resolve problems to give guidance and assistance to districts. The SSCC membership includes representatives from the Maryland Departments of Natural Resources, Agriculture, and Environment, Maryland Agricultural Commission, University of Maryland, Maryland Association of Soil Conservation Districts, and five soil conservation district supervisors. The committee is a unit of the Maryland Dept. of Agriculture.
Publication(s): SSCC Reporter Newsletter
Keyword(s): Agriculture/Farming, Ecosystems (precious), Land Issues, Pollution (general), Water Habitats & Quality, Wildlife & Species
Contact(s):
Robert Fitzgerald, Chairman; 410-841-5863
Louise Lawrence, Executive Secretary; 410-841-5863; Fax: 410-841-5914; lawrenl@mda.state.md.us
Royden Powell, Assistant Secretary; 410-841-5865; Fax: 410-841-5914

MARYLAND DEPARTMENT OF NATURAL RESOURCES
580 Taylor Avenue
Annapolis, MD 21401 United States
Phone: 410-260-8021   Fax: 410-260-8024
E-mail: customerservice@dnr.state.md.us
Website: www.dnr.state.md.us

Membership: 1,001–10,000
Scope: Regional
Description: for today and tomorrow the Department of Natural Resources inspires people to enjoy and live in harmony with their environment, and to protect what makes Maryland unique — our treasured Chesapeake Bay, our diverse landscapes and our living and natural resources.
Publication(s): Natural Resource Magazine, Streams, Trib Team Monitor
Keyword(s): Forests/Forestry, Land Issues, Oceans/Coasts/Beaches, Public Lands/Greenspace, Recreation/Ecotourism, Sprawl/Urban Planning, Water Habitats & Quality, Wildlife & Species
Contact(s):
J. Charles Fox, Secretary; 410-260-8105; Fax: 410-260-8111; customerservice@dnr.state.md.us
Sumita Chaudhuri, Assistant Secretary for Management Service; 410-260-8107; Fax: 410-260-8111; customerservice@dnr.state.md.us
James W. Dunmyer, Assistant Secretary for Public Lands; 410-260-8108; Fax: 410-260-8111; customerservice@dnr.state.md.us
Verna E. Harrison, Assistant Secretary for Chesapeake Bay & Watershed Programs; 410-260-8116; Fax: 410-260-8111; customerservice@dnr.state.md.us
Michael J. Nelson, Assistant Secretary for Capital Grants and Loans; 410-260-8446; Fax: 410-260-8111; customerservice@dnr.state.md.us
Wilson H. Parran, Chief of Information Technology; 410-260-8369; Fax: 410-260-8111; customerservice@dnr.state.md.us
Carolyn V. Watson, Assistant Secretary for Resource Management Service; 410-260-8113; Fax: 410-260-8111; customerservice@dnr.state.md.us
Karen M. White, Deputy Secretary; 410-260-8105; Fax: 410-260-8111; customerservice@dnr.state.md.us

MARYLAND DEPARTMENT OF THE ENVIRONMENT
1800 Washington Blvd
Baltimore, MD 21230 United States
Phone: 410-537-3000   Fax: 410-537-3888
Website: www.mde.state.md.us

Founded: 1987
Scope: State
Description: The Department of the Environment is charged with protection of the state's land, air, and water resources, to ensure the long-term protection of public health and quality of life.
Publication(s): Regulatory Calendar, List of Potential Hazardous Waste Sites, Biennial Water Report, Annual Air Quality Data Report
Keyword(s): Air Quality/Atmosphere, Oceans/Coasts/Beaches, Pollution (general), Reduce/Reuse/Recycle
Contact(s):
Richard Collins, Director of Waste Management Administration; 410-631-3304
Ann Marie Debiase, Director of Air and Radiation Management Administration
Allan Jensen, Director of Administrative and Employee Services; 410-631-3116
Robert Summers, Director of Water Management Administration
Denise Ferguson-Southard, Assistant Secretary
Etta Lyles, Librarian; 410-631-3818
Jane Nishida, Secretary; 410-631-3084
Merrylin Zaw-Mon, Deputy Director

MARYLAND-NATIONAL CAPITAL PARK AND PLANNING COMMISSION
6611 Kenilworth Ave.
Ste. 402
Riverdale, MD 20737 United States
Phone: 301-454-1740   Fax: 301-454-1750
Website: www.mncppc.org

Founded: 1927
Membership: 101–1,000
Scope: National
Description: Established by the General Assembly of the State of Maryland to provide for the orderly development of Montgomery and Prince George's counties; to provide a system of parks to serve the residents of this bi-county region; and to provide recreation programs and services in Prince George's County.
Contact(s):
Donald Cochran, Montgomery County Director: Parks; 301-495-2500
Trudye Johnson, Executive Director; 301-454-1740
Charles Loehr, Director of Montgomery County Department of Parks and Planning; 301-495-4500
Fern Piret, Director: Prince George's County Planning; 301-952-3595

Mary Wells-Harley, Acting Director of Prince George's County Parks and Recreation; 301-699-2582
Patricia Barney, Secretary of Treasurer
Elizabeth Hewlett, Vice Chairman; 14741 Governor Oden Bowie Dr., Upper Marlboro, MD 20772; 301-952-3560
William Hussmann, Vice Chairman; 8787 Georgia Ave., Silver Spring, MD 20910; 301-495-4605
Richard Romine, General Counsel, Legal Department; 301-454-1670

MASSACHUSETTS COOPERATIVE FISH AND WILDLIFE RESEARCH UNIT (USDI)
Box 34220, Holdsworth Natural Resources Ctr., University of Massachusetts
Amherst, MA 01003-4220 United States
Phone: 413-545-0398   Fax: 413-545-4358
Website: www.umass.edu/forwild

Founded: 1948
Scope: National
Description: Provides graduate training and research experience in fisheries and wildlife research management, ecology, habitat, population dynamics, and management. Supported cooperatively by the University of Massachusetts, Massachusetts Division of Fisheries and Wildlife, Massachusetts Division of Marine Fisheries, the U.S. Department of Interior, U.S.G.S.-BRD, and the Wildlife Management Institute.
Keyword(s): Wildlife & Species
Contact(s):
Steve Destefano, Leader
Martha Mather, Assistant Leader: Fisheries
Paul Sievert, Assistant Leader: Wildlife

MASSACHUSETTS DIVISION OF FISHERIES AND WILDLIFE
MASSWILDLIFE
251 Causeway Street
4th Floor
Boston, MA 02114 United States
Phone: 617-626-1590   Fax: 617-626-1517
E-mail: mass.wildlife@state.ma.us
Website: www.masswildlife.org

Founded: 1863
Scope: State
Description: State wildlife agency with a mandate to conserve wildlife and natural resources for the benefit and enjoyment of the citizens.
Publication(s): Guidelines for Vernal Pool Certification, Massachusetts Natural Heritage Atlas, BioMap, Field Guide to Animals in Vernal Pools, Critters of Massachusetts, Fishing & Hunting Abstracts, Massachusetts Wildlife
Keyword(s): Ecosystems (precious), Forests/Forestry, Land Issues, Public Lands/Greenspace, Recreation/Ecotourism, Water Habitats & Quality, Wildlife & Species
Contact(s):
Wayne MacCallum, Director; 617-626-1590; Fax: 617-626-1517; wayne.maccallum@state.ma.us

MASSACHUSETTS EXECUTIVE OFFICE OF ENVIRONMENTAL AFFAIRS
251 Causeway St., 9th Floor
Boston, MA 02114 United States
Phone: 617-626-1000   Fax: 617-626-1181
E-mail: env.internet@state.ma.us
Website: www.state.ma.us/envir/

Description: The cabinet-level environmental agency in the state and includes within the secretariat all state environmental agencies.
Contact(s):
Joel Lerner, Director: Conservation Services; 617-727-1552
Tom Skinner, Director: Coastal Zone Management; 617-727-9530
Jay Wickersham, Director: Impact Review Unit, MEPA; 617-727-5830
Steve Bernard, Under Secretary: Administration & Finance
Bob Durand, Secretary

MASSACHUSETTS EXECUTIVE OFFICE OF ENVIRONMENTAL AFFAIRS
251 Causeway St., 9th Floor
Boston, MA 02114 United States
Phone: 617-626-1000   Fax: 617-626-1181
E-mail: env.internet@state.ma.us
Website: www.mass.gov/envir

Scope: State
Description: Commonwealth of Massachusetts' cabinet department on environmental issues
Keyword(s): Agriculture/Farming, Air Quality/Atmosphere, Climate Change, Development/Developing Countries, Ecosystems (precious), Energy, Ethics/Environmental Justice, Executive/Legislative/Judicial Reform, Forests/Forestry, Land Issues, Oceans/Coasts/Beaches
Contact(s):
Ellen Roy Herzfelder, Secretary; 617-626-1000; Fax: 617-626-1181

MASSACHUSETTS EXECUTIVE OFFICE OF ENVIRONMENTAL AFFAIRS
BUREAU OF PESTICIDES
251 Causeway St., 9th Floor
Boston, MA 02114 United States
Phone: 617-626-1000   Fax: 617-262-1181
E-mail: env.internet@state.ma.us
Website: www.state.ma.us/envir

Scope: State
Description: State Agency
Publication(s): State of Our Environment
Contact(s):
Brad Mitchell, Chief; 617-727-7712

MASSACHUSETTS EXECUTIVE OFFICE OF ENVIRONMENTAL AFFAIRS
DEPARTMENT OF AGRICULTURAL RESOURCES
251 Causeway St., Suite 500
Boston, MA 02114 United States
Phone: 617-626-1700   Fax: 617-626-1850
E-mail: Doug.Gillespie@State.MA.US
Website: www.mass.gov/dfa

Founded: 1852
Scope: State
Description: State agency responsible for farmland preservation, animal health and dairy services, pesticide regulation, feed and fertilizer registration, farm viability, business training and related programs.
Keyword(s): Agriculture/Farming, Ecosystems (precious), Energy, Forests/Forestry, Land Issues, Oceans/Coasts/Beaches, Pollution (general), Public Health, Public Lands/Greenspace, Recreation/Ecotourism, Sprawl/Urban Planning, Water Habitats & Quality, Wildlife & Species

MASSACHUSETTS EXECUTIVE OFFICE OF ENVIRONMENTAL AFFAIRS
DEPARTMENT OF CONSERVATION AND RECREATION
DIVISION OF STATE PARKS AND RECREATION
251 Causeway St. Suite 700
Boston, MA 02114 United States
Phone: 617-626-1250   Fax: 617-626-1449
E-mail: mass.parks@state.ma.us
Website: www.mass.gov/eoea

STATE AND PROVINCIAL GOVERNMENT AGENCIES – M

Contact(s):
Todd Fredericks, Director: Division of Forests and Parks; 617-626-1000
Ralph Silva, Director of Engineering
Richard Thibedeau, Deputy Commissioner, Resource Conservation, Acting; 617-727-3267
Peter Webber, Commissioner

MASSACHUSETTS EXECUTIVE OFFICE OF ENVIRONMENTAL AFFAIRS
DIVISION OF CONSERVATION SERVICES
251 Causeway St., 9th Floor
Boston, MA 02114 United States
Website: www.state.ma.us/envir/dcs

MASSACHUSETTS EXECUTIVE OFFICE OF ENVIRONMENTAL AFFAIRS
GEOGRAPHIC INFORMATION SYSTEM
251 Causeway St., 9th Floor
Boston, MA 02114 United States
Website: www.state.ma.us/mgis

Contact(s):
Christian Jacqz, Director; 617-626-1056

MASSACHUSETTS EXECUTIVE OFFICE OF ENVIRONMENTAL AFFAIRS
MASSACHUSETTS COASTAL ZONE MANAGEMENT
251 Causeway St. Suite 900
Boston, MA 02114 United States
Phone: 617-626-1200   Fax: 617-626-1240
Website: www.state.ma.us/czm

Contact(s):
Tom Skinner, Director; 617-626-1201

MASSACHUSETTS EXECUTIVE OFFICE OF ENVIRONMENTAL AFFAIRS
MASSACHUSETTS ENVIRONMENTAL POLICY ACT.
251 Causeway St. Suite 900
Boston, MA 02114 United States
Phone: 617-626-1020   Fax: 617-626-1181
Website: www.state.ma.us/envir/mepa

Contact(s):
Jay Wickersham, Director; 617-626-1022

MASSACHUSETTS EXECUTIVE OFFICE OF ENVIRONMENTAL AFFAIRS
MASSACHUSETTS ENVIRONMENTAL TRUST
33 Union Street, 4th Floor
Boston, MA 02108 United States
Phone: 617-727-0249   Fax: 617-727-0251
E-mail: env.trust@state.ma.us
Website: www.MassEnvironmentalTrust.org

Founded: 1988
Scope: State
Description: The Trust is a quasi-public environmental philanthropy established by the state legislature in 1988 with proceeds from the Boston Harbor pollution settlement. The Trust gives grants to a variety of entities working on issues dealing with the Commonwealth's water and related resources.
Keyword(s): Ecosystems (precious), Ethics/Environmental Justice, Oceans/Coasts/Beaches, Pollution (general), Water Habitats & Quality, Wildlife & Species

MASSACHUSETTS EXECUTIVE OFFICE OF ENVIRONMENTAL AFFAIRS
OFFICE OF TECHNICAL ASSISTANCE FOR TOXIC USE REDUCTION
251 Causeway St., 9th Floor
Boston, MA 02114 United States
Phone: 617-626-1060   Fax: 617-626-1095
Website: www.mass.gov/ota

Founded: 1998
Membership: 1–100
Scope: State
Description: The Massachusetts Office of Technical Assistance is a non-regulatory agency that promotes toxics use reduction and pollution prevention by providing free and confidential technical and compliance assistance to toxics users in the Commonwealth.
Keyword(s): Reduce/Reuse/Recycle
Contact(s):
Paul Richard, Director; 617-626-1042

MASSACHUSETTS EXECUTIVE OFFICE OF ENVIRONMENTAL AFFAIRS
WETLANDS AND WATERWAYS PROGRAM
1 Winter St.
Boston, MA 02108 United States
Phone: 617-292-5500   Fax: 617-292-5696
Website: www.state.ma.us/dep

Scope: State
Contact(s):
Glenn Haas, Director
Michael Stroman, Acting Director of Wetlands

MASSACHUSETTS HIGHWAY DEPARTMENT
10 Park Plaza
Boston, MA 02116 United States
Phone: 617-973-7800   Fax: 617-973-8040
Website: www.state.ma.us/mhd

Scope: State
Description: The mission of the Massachusetts Highway Department is to provide a safe, efficient, quality highway system in a cost-effective and environmentally sensitive manner that continuously meets the diverse needs of its users.
Keyword(s): Air Quality/Atmosphere, Ethics/Environmental Justice, Pollution (general), Reduce/Reuse/Recycle, Transportation, Water Habitats & Quality

Contact(s):
David Anderson, Deputy Chief Engineer: Construction; 817-973-7491; david.anderson@state.ma.us
Henry Barbaro, Supervisor: Wetlands and Water Resources; 617-973-7419; henry.barbaro@state.ma.us
John Blundo, Deputy Chief Engineer: Highway Engineering; 617-973-7521; john.blundo@state.ma.us
Thomas Broderick, Chief Engineer; 617-973-7830; thomas.broderick@state.ma.us
Gordon Broz, Deputy Chief Engineer: Operations; 617-973-7741; gordon.broz@state.ma.us
John Cogliano, Commissioner; 617-973-7800; john.cogliano@state.ma.us
James Elliott, Supervisor: Cultural Resources Unit; 617-973-7494; james.elliott@state.ma.us
Steven Miller, Supervisor: Permitting and Regulatory Compliance; 617-973-7582; steven.miller@state.ma.us
Gregory Prendergast, Deputy Chief Engineer: Environmental Division; 617-973-7484; gregory.prendergast@state.ma.us
Kevin Walsh, Project Development; 617-973-7529; kevin.walsh@state.ma.us

MECKLENBURG COUNTY PARK AND RECREATION DEPARTMENT
DIVISION OF NATURAL RESOURCES
5841 Brookshire Boulevard
Charlotte, NC 28216 United States
Phone: 704-336-8798
Website: www.parkandrec.com/nature

Founded: 1993
Membership: 1,001–10,000
Scope: Local
Description: The Division of Natural Resources is the principal government agency responsible for the protection, conserva-

tion, and management of Mecklenburg County's natural areas. The Division operates three nature centers - Reedy Creek, McDowell, and Latta Plantation - and offers environmental education programs to students of all ages, manages over 7,500 acres of nature preserves & greenways, monitors wildlife populations, restores habitats for endangered plant species, and conserves natural communities.

Publication(s): Natural Connections

Keyword(s): Public Lands/Greenspace, Recreation/Ecotourism, Water Habitats & Quality, Wildlife & Species

Contact(s):
Steve Law, Division Manager; 704-336-8798; Fax: 704-336-5472; lawsh@co.mecklenburg.nc.us
Bridget Hanifin, Greenways and Trails Planner; 704-336-8466; Fax: 704-336-5472; hanifbe@co.mecklenburg.nc.us
Don Seriff, Conservation Section Supervisor; 2900 Rocky River Road, Charlotte, NC 28215; 704-432-1391; Fax: 704-432-1420; serifdw@co.mecklenburg.nc.us
Marek Smith, Environmental Education Supervisor; 2900 Rocky River Road, Charlotte, NC 28215; 704-598-8857; Fax: 704-599-1770; smithmk@co.mecklenburg.nc.us
Sarah Kiser, Environmental Education Specialist; Reedy Creek Nature Center, 2900 Rocky River Road, Charlotte, NC 28215; 704-598-8857; Fax: 704-599-1770; kisersm@co.mecklenburg.nc.us
Karen McKenzie, Environmental Education Specialist; McDowell Nature Center, 15222 York Road, Charlotte, NC 28278; 704-588-5224; Fax: 704-588-5226; mckenak@co.mecklenburg.nc.us
Charles Yelton, Environmental Education Specialist; Latta Plantation Nature Center, 6211 Sample Road, Huntersville, NC 28078; 704-875-1391; Fax: 704-875-1394; yeltocw@co.mecklenburg.nc.us

METROPOLITAN DISTRICT COMMISSION
20 Somerset St.
Boston, MA 02108 United States
Phone: 617-727-5114   Fax: 617-727-0891
Website: www.state.ma.us

Founded: 1919
Membership: 101–1,000
Scope: State

Description: Operates and maintains 19 swimming pools, 17 salt water beaches, 3 fresh water beaches, 23 skating rinks, and various other recreational facilities; also maintains a network of parkways and main traffic roadways and a police force for protection of its property and people using its facilities.

Contact(s):
Brian Broderick, Director: Reservations and Historic Sites Unit; 617-727-2744
Gary Doak, Director: Division of Recreation; 617-727-9547
David Balfour, Commissioner

MICHIGAN DEPARTMENT OF AGRICULTURE
P.O. Box 30017
Lansing, MI 48909 United States
Phone: 517-373-1104   Fax: 517-373-9146
Website: www.michigan.gov/mda

Scope: Regional

Keyword(s): Agriculture/Farming, Land Issues, Pollution (general), Wildlife & Species

Contact(s):
Ken Rauscher, Director of Pesticide & Plant Pest Management Division; 517-373-1087
Dan Wyant, Director

MICHIGAN DEPARTMENT OF ENVIRONMENTAL QUALITY
525 West Allegan St.
Constitution Hall 6th Fl., South
P.O. Box 30473
Lansing, MI 48909-7973 United States
Phone: 517-373-7917   Fax: 517-241-7401
Website: www.michigan.gov/deq

Founded: 1995
Scope: State

Description: Our mission is to drive improvements in environmental quality for the protection of public health and natural resources to benefit current and future generations. This will be accomplished through effective administration of agency programs, and providing for the use of innovative strategies, while helping to foster a strong and sustainable economy.

Publication(s): See publications on website

Keyword(s): Air Quality/Atmosphere, Land Issues, Oceans/Coasts/Beaches, Pollution (general), Reduce/Reuse/Recycle, Water Habitats & Quality

Contact(s):
Russell Harding, Director; 517-373-7917
David K. Ladd, Director of Office of the Great Lakes; 517-335-4056; Fax: 517-335-4053
Dennis Fedewa, Chief of Financial and Business Services Division; 517-241-7427; Fax: 517-241-7428
Gary Hughes, Deputy Director for Operations; 517-241-7394; Fax: 517-241-7401
Arthur Nash, Deputy Director for Programs and Regulations; 517-241-7392; Fax: 517-241-7401

MICHIGAN DEPARTMENT OF NATURAL RESOURCES
P.O. Box 30028
Lansing, MI 48909 United States
Phone: 517-373-2329   Fax: 517-335-4242
E-mail: dnr-wld-webpages@state.mi.us
Website: www.michigan.gov/dnr

Founded: 1921
Scope: State

Description: State agency for administration, including enforcement of laws and regulations, regarding the state's natural resources; and for enhancing recreational opportunities and quality. Derived from the Department of Conservation.

Keyword(s): Forests/Forestry, Public Lands/Greenspace, Recreation/Ecotourism, Wildlife & Species

Contact(s):
K. Cool, Director; P.O. Box 30028, Lansing, MI 48909; 517-373-2329; Fax: 517-335-4242
Guy Gordon, Chief of Staff; P.O. Box 30028, Lansing, MI 48909; 517-373-2329; Fax: 517-335-4242
Bradley Wurfel, Press Secretary; P.O. Box 30028, Lansing, MI 48909; 517-335-3014; Fax: 517-335-4242
Rob Abent, Chief of Finance and Operations Service Bureau; P.O. Box 30028, Lansing, MI 48909; 517-373-1750; Fax: 517-335-6807
Rick Asher, Chief of Law Enforcement; P.O. Box 30031, Lansing, MI 48909; 517-373-1230; Fax: 517-373-6816
Carol Bambery, Legislative Liaison; P.O. Box 30028, Lansing, MI 48909; 517-373-0023; Fax: 517-335-4242
Thomas Benson, Chief of Office of Internal Audit; P.O. Box 30028, Lansing, MI 48909; 517-373-0755; Fax: 517-241-2986
George Burgoyne, Deputy for Resource Management; P.O. Box 30028, Lansing, MI 48909; 517-373-0046; Fax: 517-335-4242
James Ekdahl, Upper Peninsula Field Deputy; 1990 US-41 South, Marquette, MI 49855; 906-228-6561; Fax: 906-228-9441

Teresa Gloden, Executive Assistant to the Natural Resources Commission; P.O. Box 30028, Lansing, MI 48909; 517-373-2352; Fax: 517-335-4242

Gerald Harris, Chief of Human Resources; P.O. Box 30028, Lansing, MI 48909; 517-373-1207; Fax: 517-373-8063

Rebecca Humphries, Chief of Wildlife; P.O. Box 30444, Lansing, MI 48909; 517-373-1263; Fax: 517-373-6705

Mindy Koch, Forest, Mineral and Fire Management; P.O. Box 30452, Lansing, MI 48909; 517-373-1275; Fax: 517-373-2443

Lowen Schuett, Chief of Property Management Division; P.O. Box 30448, Lansing, MI 48909; 517-241-2438; Fax: 517-241-4278

Kelley Smith, Chief of Fisheries; P.O. Box 30446, Lansing, MI 48909; 517-373-1280; Fax: 517-373-0381

Kelli Sobel, Deputy for Administrative Services; P.O. Box 30028, Lansing, MI 48909; 517-373-2425; Fax: 517-335-4242

Rodney Stokes, Chief of Parks and Recreation; P.O. Box 30257, Lansing, MI 48909; 517-373-9900; Fax: 517-373-4625

MICHIGAN STATE UNIVERSITY EXTENSION
108 Agriculture Hall
East Lansing, MI 48824 United States
Phone: 5173552308
E-mail: msue@msue.msu.edu
Website: www.msue.msu.edu/msue/
Membership: 101–1,000
Scope: State
Description: Helps people improve their lives through an educational process that applies knowledge to critical issues, needs, and opportunities. Publications, instructional videos, and microcomputer software are listed in a catalogue which is available by writing to the Bulletin Office.
Keyword(s): Agriculture/Farming, Forests/Forestry, Land Issues, Oceans/Coasts/Beaches, Pollution (general), Public Health, Public Lands/Greenspace, Recreation/Ecotourism, Sprawl/Urban Planning, Wildlife & Species
Contact(s):
Margaret Bethel, Director; 517-355-2308; Fax: 517-355-6473; msue@msue.msu.edu

MIDLAND CONSERVATION DISTRICT
1031 E. Saginaw Road
Sanford, MI 48657 United States
Phone: 989-687-9760   Fax: 989-687-9678
E-mail: midlandcd@notcoapc.net
Website: www.midlandcd.org
Founded: 1951
Scope: Local
Description: A local unit of government that provides voluntary environmental assistance with the purpose of finding environmentally cooperative means for land usage and sustainability by providing a gateway for information, resources and partnership.
Keyword(s): Agriculture/Farming, Forests/Forestry, Public Lands/Greenspace, Water Habitats & Quality, Wildlife & Species
Contact(s):
Deborah Anderson, Watershed Manager; 989-687-9760; Fax: 989-687-9678; debbie-anderson@mi.nacdnet.org
Patrick Huber, Forester; 989-687-9760; Fax: 989-687-9678; pat-huber@mi.nacdnet.org
Lisa Husted, Administrative Assistant; 989-687-9760; Fax: 989-687-9768; lisa-husted@mi.nacdnet.org
Scott Marsh, Wildlife Biologist; 989-687-9760; Fax: 989-687-9678; scott-marsh@mi.nacdnet.org
Dennis Varner, CREP Technician; 954 E. Isabella Rd., Midland, MI 48640; 989-832-3781; ext. 3; Fax: 989-832-4089; dvarner@mimidland.fsc.usda.gov

MINNESOTA BOARD OF WATER AND SOIL RESOURCES
One W. Water St., Suite 200
St. Paul, MN 55107 United States
Phone: 651-296-3767   Fax: 651-297-5615
Website: www.bwsr.state.mn.us
Founded: 1987
Membership: 1–100
Scope: State
Description: Formed under M.S. chapter 103B to develop the capabilities of local governments in resource management. Works most often with soil and water conservation districts, watershed districts, watershed management organizations, and counties. Provides these local governments with financial and technical assistance. Administers programs focusing on erosion control and water quality.
Publication(s): Water BillBoard, The, various brochures, reports, and fact sheets, Directory of local governments
Keyword(s): Land Issues, Water Habitats & Quality
Contact(s):
Ronald Harnack, Director; Fax: 651-297-5615; ron.harnack@bwsr.state.mn.us
Lee Coc, Chairman

MINNESOTA COOPERATIVE FISH AND WILDLIFE RESEARCH UNIT
U.S. Geological Survey, Biological Resources Division
University of Minnesota, Department of Fisheries and Wildlife
200 Hodson Hall, 1980 Folwell Ave.
St. Paul, MN 55108 United States
Phone: 612-624-3421   Fax: 612-625-5299
E-mail: curtn004@umn.edu
Website: www.fw.umn.edu/co-op/co-op.html
Founded: 1987
Scope: Regional
Description: The research mission of the Minnesota Cooperative Fish and Wildlife Research Unit (MNCFWRU) is to address the biological, social, and economic aspects of both game and nongame wildlife and fisheries management in the context of conservation of biological diversity, and integrity and sustainability of ecosystems.
Keyword(s): Pollution (general), Water Habitats & Quality, Wildlife & Species
Contact(s):
David Andersen, Unit Leader
David Fulton, Assistant Leader: Wildlife
Loralee Kerr, Librarian; 375 Hodson Hall, 1980 Folwell Ave., St. Paul, MN 55108; 612-624-9288
Bruce Vondracek, Assistant Leader: Fisheries

MINNESOTA DEPARTMENT OF AGRICULTURE
90 W. Plato Blvd.
St. Paul, MN 55107 United States
Phone: 651-297-2200   Fax: 651-297-5522
Website: www.mda.state.mn.us
Founded: 1919
Scope: State
Description: Enforces laws to protect the public health, promote family farming and marketing of Minnesota farm products, conserve soil and water, and prevent fraud and deception in the manufacture and distribution of foods, animal feeds, fertilizers, pesticides, seeds, and other items.
Keyword(s): Agriculture/Farming, Development/Developing Countries, Oceans/Coasts/Beaches, Pollution (general), Wildlife & Species
Contact(s):
Shirley Bohm, Director of Dairy and Food Inspection; 651-296-1590

Greg Buzicky, Director: Agronomy and Plant Protection; 651-297-7121
James Gryniewski, Director: Agriculture Certification; 651-297-2230
Gerald Heil, Director: Agriculture Marketing and Development; 651-296-1486
Dale Heimermann, Director of Grain and Produce Inspection; 612-341-7190
Mike Hunst, Director: Agricultural Statistics; 651-296-3896
William Krueger, Director: Laboratory Services; 651-296-3273
Becky Leschner, Director of Accounting Division; 651-215-5770
Larry Palmer, Director: Information Services; 651-296-4659
Curtis Pietz, Director: Agriculture Finance; 651-297-3557
Perry Aasness, Assistant Commissioner
Sharon Clark, Deputy Commissioner
Gene Hugoson, Commissioner
Tom Masso, Assistant Commissioner

MINNESOTA DEPARTMENT OF NATURAL RESOURCES
500 Lafayette Rd.
St. Paul, MN 55155-4001 United States
Phone: 651-296-6157
E-mail: info@dnr.state.mn.us
Website: www.dnr.state.mn.us/

Founded: 1931

Scope: Local, State, Regional

Description: The Department of Conservation was renamed the Department of Natural Resources (DNR) in 1971. The DNR's goal is to achieve optimum natural resources planning, protection, and development responsive to public need, consistent with resource potentials, and for the social and economic well-being of both present and future generations.

Publication(s): Minnesota Conservation Volunteer

Contact(s):
Dennis Asmussen, Director: Trails and Waterways Division; 651-297-1151; Fax: 651-297-5475; dennis.asmussen@dnr.state.mn.us
Karen Beckman, Administrator: License Bureau; 651-297-4941; karen.beckman@dnr.state.mn.us
Tim Bremicker, Director: Division of Wildlife; 651-297-4960; Fax: 651-297-4961; tim.bremicker@dnr.state.mn.us
William Brice, Director: Division of Lands and Minerals; 651-296-4807; Fax: 651-296-5939; william.brice@dnr.state.mn.us
Mike Carroll, Director: Division of Forestry; 651-296-4491; Fax: 651-296-5954; mike.carroll@dnr.state.mn.us
Wayne Edgerton, Director: Agricultural Policy; 651-297-8341; Fax: 651-296-4799; wayne.edgerton@dnr.state.mn.us
Mike Hamm, Director: Division of Enforcement; 651-296-4828; Fax: 651-297-3727; mike.hamm@dnr.state.mn.us
Kent Lokkesmoe, Director: Division of Waters; 651-296-4800; Fax: 651-296-0445; kent.lokkesmoe@dnr.state.mn.us
Colleen Miecoch, Chief Information Officer; 651-297-3906; Fax: 651-297-4946; colleen.miecoch@dnr.state.mn.us
Bill Morrissey, Director: Division of Parks and Recreation; 651-296-9223; Fax: 651-297-2257; bill.morrissey@dnr.state.mn.us
Ron Payer, Director: Division of Fisheries; 651-296-3325; Fax: 651-297-4916; ron.payer@dnr.state.mn.us
Lee Pfannmuller, Director: Ecological Services Division; 651-296-2835; Fax: 651-296-2835; lee.pfannmuller@dnr.state.mn.us
Jo Ann Musumeci, Librarian; 651-297-4929; Fax: 651-297-4946; joann.musumeci@dnr.state.mn.us
John Guenther, Regional Administrator; 1201 E. Highway 2, Grand Rapids, MN 55744; 218-327-4455; Fax: 218-327-4263; john.guenther@dnr.state.mn.us
Cheryl Heide, Regional Administrator; 261 Highway 15 S, New Ulm, MN 56073; 507-359-6000; Fax: 507-359-60018; cheryl.heide@dnr.state.mn.us
Elaine Johnson, Administrator:Facilities & Operations Support Bureau; 651-297-3758; Fax: 651-297-1542; elaine.johnson@dnr.state.mn.us
Joe Kurcinka, Administrator: Management & Budget Services; 651-296-4789; Fax: 651-296-6047; joe.kurcinka@dnr.state.mn.us
Gene Merriam, Commissioner; 651-296-2549; Fax: 651-296-4799; gene.merriam@dnr.state.mn.us
Brad Moore, Assistant Commissioner; 651-296-5229; Fax: 651-296-4799; brad.moore@dnr.state.mn.us
Steve Morse, Deputy Commissioner; 651-296-2540; Fax: 651-296-4799; steve.morse@dnr.state.mn.us
Mary O'Neill, Administrator: Bureau of Human Resources; 651-296-6493; Fax: 651-296-6494; mary.o'neill@dnr.state.mn.us
Adele Smith, Administrator: Information & Education Bureau; 651-297-1899; adele.smith@dnr.state.mn.us
Paul Swenson, Regional Administrator; 2115 Birchmont Beach Rd. NE, Bemidji, MN 56601; 218-755-3955; Fax: 218-755-4024; paul.swenson@dnr.state.mn.us
Kathleen Wallace, Regional Administrator; 1200 Warner Road, St. Paul, MN 55106; 651-772-7900; Fax: 651-772-7977; kathleen.wallace@dnr.state.mn.us

MINNESOTA ENVIRONMENTAL QUALITY BOARD
658 Cedar Street
St. Paul, MN 55155 United States
Phone: 651-296-3985   Fax: 651-296-3698
Website: www.eqb.state.mn.us/

Founded: 1973

Scope: State

Description: The EQB is Minnesota's principal forum for discussing environmental issues.

Publication(s): EQB Monitor

Keyword(s): Development/Developing Countries, Energy

Contact(s):
Michael Sullivan, Executive Director; 651-296-9027

MINNESOTA GEOLOGICAL SURVEY
University of Minnesota
2642 University Ave.
St. Paul, MN 55114-1057 United States
Phone: 612-627-4780, ext. 0   Fax: 612-627-4778
E-mail: mgs@umn.edu
Website: www.geo.umn.edu/mgs

Founded: 1872

Membership: 1–100

Scope: State

Description: Established as a Geological and Natural History Survey, reconstituted in 1911 as the Minnesota Geological Survey to investigate the geology of the state; describe, classify and map the geological formations and mineral and water resources; and investigate all aspects of the geology affecting the environment.

Publication(s): List available on request.

Contact(s):
Val Chandler, Acting Director; 612-627-4780; ext. 0; Fax: 612-627-4778; mgs@umn.edu

MINNESOTA POLLUTION CONTROL AGENCY
BAXTER, MN
1800 College Road South
Baxter, MN 56425 United States
Phone: 218-828-2492   Fax: 218-828-2594
Website: www.pca.state.mn.us

Scope: State

Publication(s): See publications on website

Contact(s):
Reed Larson, Regional Manager

MINNESOTA POLLUTION CONTROL AGENCY
DETROIT LAKES, MN
520 Lafayette Road
St. Paul, MN 55155-4194 United States
Phone: 651-296-6300　　　Fax: 218-846-0719
E-mail: webmaster@pca.state.mn.us
Website: www.pca.state.mn.us

Membership: 1–100
Scope: State
Contact(s):
　Jeff Lewis, Director; 218-846-0730;
　　jeff.lewis@pca.state.mn.us

MINNESOTA POLLUTION CONTROL AGENCY
DULUTH, MN
525 S. Lake Ave., Suite 400
Duluth, MN 55802 United States
Phone: 218-723-4660　　　Fax: 218-723-4727
Website: www.pca.state.mn.us

Membership: 1–100
Scope: Local, State, Regional
Contact(s):
　Suzanne Hanson, Director

MINNESOTA POLLUTION CONTROL AGENCY
MARSHALL, MN
1420 East College
Suite 900
Marshall, MN 56258 United States
Phone: 507-537-7146　　　Fax: 507-537-6001
Website: www.pca.state.mn.us

Membership: 1–100
Scope: Regional
Contact(s):
　Mark Jacobs, Supervisor

MINNESOTA POLLUTION CONTROL AGENCY
ROCHESTER, MN
18 Wood Lake Dr., SE
Rochester, MN 55904 United States
Phone: 507-285-7343　　　Fax: 507-280-5513
Website: www.pca.state.mn.us

Membership: 1–100
Scope: Regional
Description: Helping Minnesotans protect the environment.
Contact(s):
　Larry Landherr, Director

MINNESOTA POLLUTION CONTROL AGENCY
ST. PAUL, MN
520 Lafayette Rd.
St. Paul, MN 55155 United States
Phone: 612-296-6300　　　Fax: 651-297-8687
E-mail: barb.hannegan@tca.state.mn
Website: www.pca.ctato.mn.us

Founded: 1967
Membership: 101–1,000
Scope: State
Description: Administers the state statutes covering water pollution, air pollution, and solid and hazardous waste control.
Contact(s):
　James Warner, Director: Division of Groundwater and Solid Waste; 612-296-7777
　Karen Studders, Chairman of the Board and Commissioner; 612-296-7301
　Lisa Thorvig, Deputy Commissioner; 612-296-7331
　Gordon Wegwart, Assistant Commissioner; 612-296-7319

MINNESOTA STATE EXTENSION SERVICES
University of Minnesota, 475 Coffey Hall
1420 Eckles Ave.
St. Paul, MN 55108-6068 United States
Phone: 612-625-1915　　　Fax: 612-625-2207
Website: www.extension.umn.edu

Membership: 1–100
Scope: State
Contact(s):
　Charles Casey, Dean and Director Extension Service; 612-624-2703; casey002@umn.edu
　Melvin Baughman, Forest Resources Specialist; 612-624-0734
　Stephan Carlson, Youth Specialist; 612-626-1259
　James Cooper, Wildlife Specialist; 104 Hodson, University of Minnesota, St. Paul, MN 55108; 612-624-1223; Fax: 612-625-5299; jac@umn.edu
　Steven Daley Laursen, Associate Dean and Collegiate Program Leader; 612-624-9298
　Jeffrey Gunderson, Sea Grant Extension and Fisheries Educator
　Cynthia Hagley, Water Quality Educator Specialist
　Patrick Huelman, Housing Specialist; 612-624-1286
　Steven Taff, Public Policy Specialist; 612-625-3103

MISSISSIPPI COOPERATIVE FISH AND WILDLIFE RESEARCH UNIT
MISSISSIPPI STATE UNIVERSITY
Mailstop 9691
Mississippi State, MS 39762 United States
Phone: 662-325-2643　　　Fax: 662-325-8276

Founded: 1978
Membership: 1–100
Scope: State
Description: The Unit is sponsored by the U.S.G.S. Biological Resources Division; Mississippi Department of Wildlife, Fisheries, and Parks; Mississippi State University; and the Wildlife Management Institute. Fisheries and wildlife research, graduate education, technical assistance, and extension are the Unit's main missions.
Keyword(s): Recreation/Ecotourism, Water Habitats & Quality, Wildlife & Species
Contact(s):
　L. Miranda, Assistant Leader: Fisheries
　Harold Schramm, Leader; hschramm@cfr.msstate.edu
　Francisco Vilella, Assistant Leader: Wildlife

MISSISSIPPI DEPARTMENT OF AGRICULTURE AND COMMERCE
P.O. Box 1609
Jackson, MS 39215-1609 United States
Phone: 601-359-1100　　　Fax: 601-354-6290
Website: www.mdac.state.ms.us

Founded: 1906
Membership: 101–1,000
Scope: State
Description: The department was created to foster and promote the business of agriculture. Duties include: Regulatory, consumer protection, marketing, and a wide range of service activities.
Publication(s): Mississippi Market Bulletin
Contact(s):
　Roger Barlow, Director of Market Development; 601-359-1158
　Billy Carter, Director of Farmers Market; 601-354-6818
　Billy Carter, Director of Market News; 601-354-6818
　Tommy Gregory, Director of National Agricultural Statistics; 601-965-4575
　Robert Louys, Director of Petroleum; 601-359-1101
　Julia Mclemore, Director of Regulatory Services; 601-359-1144
　Jim Meadows, Director of Meat Inspection

Keith Pouncy, Director of Grain Inspection
Russell Robbins, Director of Weights and Measures; 601-359-1117
Donnis Roberson, Director of Fruit & Vegetable Inspections; 601-354-6573
Rodney Sanders, Director of Administration and Finance; 601-359-1132
Umesh Sanjanwala, Director of Information Systems; 601-359-1151
John Tillson, Director of Consumer Protection; 601-359-1148
Jim Watson, Director of Board of Animal Health; 601-359-1170
Stella Cessna, Personnel Officer; 601-359-1152
Claude Nash, Editor; 601-359-1123
Chris Sparkman, Deputy Commissioner; 601-359-1138
Lester Spell, Commissioner

MISSISSIPPI DEPARTMENT OF ENVIRONMENTAL QUALITY
OFFICE OF LAND AND WATER RESOURCES
Southport Mall, P.O. Box 10631
Jackson, MS 39289 United States
Phone: 601-961-5200   Fax: 601-354-6938
Website: www.deq.state.ms.us

Founded: 1956

Scope: State

Description: Administers Water Use Permitting Act of 1985, licensing of water well drillers, and the 1978 Dam Safety Act; inventories water resources; coordinates water and land resources planning; and conducts reviews of proposed water resources development.

Contact(s):
Jamie Crawford, Head
Patricia Phillips, Chief: Division of Hydrologic Investigation and Reporting; 601-961-5213

MISSISSIPPI DEPARTMENT OF ENVIRONMENTAL QUALITY
OFFICE OF POLLUTION CONTROL
P.O. Box 10385
Jackson, MS 39289-0385 United States
Phone: 601-961-5171   Fax: 601-354-6612
Website: www.deq.state.ms.us

Scope: State

Contact(s):
P. Harkins, Head; 601-961-5002

MISSISSIPPI DEPARTMENT OF WILDLIFE, FISHERIES, AND PARKS
1505 Eastover Drive
Jackson, MS 39211 United States
Phone: 601-432-2400
Website: www.mdwfp.com

Description: The purpose of the MDWFP is to manage, conserve, develop, and protect Mississippi's outdoors, state parks, wildlife and marine resources, and their habitats; and to provide continuing recreational, economic, educational, ecological, aesthetic, social and scientific benefits for present and future generations.

Publication(s): Mississippi Outdoors, Mississippi Soundings

Keyword(s): Recreation/Ecotourism, Water Habitats & Quality, Wildlife & Species

Contact(s):
Robert Cook, Director: Administrative Services; 601-364-2006
Libby Hartfield, Director: Museum of Natural Science; 601-354-7303
Ellen Morgan, Director of Marketing; 601-364-2152
Sam Polles, Executive Director; 601-364-2000
Al Tuck, Director: Support Services Division; 601-364-2046
Jim Walker, Director: Public Information; 601-364-2124
Steve Adcock, Hunter Education; 601-364-2192
Ron Garavelli, Chief: Fisheries; 601-364-2202
Jimmy Laird, Boating Enforcement; 601-364-2182
Randall Miller, Chief: Law Enforcement; 601-364-2232
Bill Quisenberry, Executive Assistant; 601-364-2005
Tommy Shropshire, Coordinator: Planning and Policy; 601-364-2107
Mary Stevens, Head Librarian; Museum of Natural Science, 111 N. Jefferson, Jackson, MS 39202-2897; 601-354-7303
Mitiz Stubbs, Outdoor Recreation Grants; 601-364-2156
Bill Thomason, Chief: Game; 601-364-2212
Bob Tyler, Deputy Administrator; 601-364-2004
David Watts, Editor; 601-364-2129

MISSISSIPPI FORESTRY COMMISSION
301 N. Lamar St., Suite 300
Jackson, MS 39201 United States
Phone: 601-359-1386   Fax: 601-359-1349
Website: www.mfc.state.ms.us

Founded: 1926

Scope: State

Description: Basic duties are forest protection against wildfire, insects, and disease; operation of tree-seedlings nurseries for reforestation; provision of forest resource management assistance to private landowners; and creation of interest in forestry.

Publication(s): Forestry Forum Magazine, various forest management brochures

Keyword(s): Forests/Forestry, Public Lands/Greenspace, Reduce/Reuse/Recycle

Contact(s):
Harold Anderson, Editor and Education Director
Kent Grizzard, Information Director
Lezlin Proctor, Director of Finance & Administration
Everard Baker, Deputy State Forester: Management Chief
William Lambert, Deputy State Forester: Protection Chief
James Mordica, Deputy State Forester Services
James Sledge, State Forester

MISSISSIPPI SOIL AND WATER CONSERVATION COMMISSION
Attn: Public Relations Director
P.O. Box 23005
Jackson, MS 39225 United States
Phone: 601-354-7645   Fax: 601-354-6628
E-mail: asmith@mswcc.state.ms.us
Website: www.mswcc.state.ms.us

Founded: 1938

Scope: Local, State

Description: Originally established as the state agency for the control of soil erosion. Current statutory responsibilities include assistance to local soil and water conservation districts in the areas of water and soil quality projects, qualifications and elections of Commissioners, and administration of programs. Other responsibilities include reviewing and commenting on surface mining reclamation efforts. Serves as the state resource agency for agricultural nonpoint source pollution issues and projects.

Keyword(s): Agriculture/Farming, Ecosystems (precious), Forests/Forestry, Land Issues, Oceans/Coasts/Beaches, Pollution (general), Public Lands/Greenspace, Reduce/Reuse/Recycle, Sprawl/Urban Planning, Water Habitats & Quality

Contact(s):
April Smith, Public Relations Director; P.O. Box 23005, Jackson, MS 39225-3005
Don Underwood, Executive Director; P.O. Box 23005, Jackson, MS 39225-3005; 601-354-7645; Fax: 601-354-6628
Paul Myrick, Chairman

MISSISSIPPI STATE DEPARTMENT OF HEALTH
P.O. Box 1700
Jackson, MS 39215-1700 United States
Phone: 601-576-7634   Fax: 601-576-7931
Website: www.msdh.state.ms.us
Scope: State
Contact(s):
   Mary Currier, Director: Division of Epidemiology / State Epidemiologist; 601-576-7725
   Tim Darnell, Director: General Environmental Services; 601-576-7680
   Brian Amy, State Health Officer; 601-576-7633

MISSOURI DEPARTMENT OF AGRICULTURE
1616 Missouri Blvd.
Jefferson City, MO 65102 United States
Phone: 573-751-4211   Fax: 573-751-1784
Website: www.mda.state.mo.us
Membership: 101–1,000
Scope: State
Contact(s):
   Peter Hofherr, Director; peter_hofherr@mail.mda.state.mo.us
   Dave Dillon, Deputy Director
   Sally Oxenhandler, Public Information Officer; 573-751-4645

MISSOURI DEPARTMENT OF CONSERVATION
P.O. Box 180
Jefferson City, MO 65102-0180 United States
Phone: 573-751-4115   Fax: 573-751-4467
Website: www.conservation.state.mo.us/
Founded: 1937
Scope: State
Description: The department is responsible for the control, management, restoration, conservation and regulation of the bird, fish, game, forestry, and all wildlife resources of the state. These responsibilities are met through a wide variety of programs encompassing fish, wildlife, and forest management, regulations and enforcement, conservation education and interpretation, endangered species, and policy development.
Publication(s): Missouri Conservationist
Keyword(s): Agriculture/Farming, Ecosystems (precious), Forests/Forestry, Recreation/Ecotourism, Water Habitats & Quality, Wildlife & Species
Contact(s):
   John Hoskins, Director; ext. 3212; hoskij@mdc.state.mo.us
   John Smith, Deputy Director; ext. 3217; smithjw@mdc.state.mo.us
   Stephen Wilson, Deputy Director; ext. 3223; wilsos@mdc.state.mo.us
   Carter Campbell, Administrative Services Division Administrator; ext. 3606; campbc@mdc.state.mo.us
   Lorna Domke, Outreach and Education Division Administrator; ext. 3235; domkel@mdc.state.mo.us
   Denise Garnier, Assistant to Director; ext. 3216; garnid@mdc.state.mo.us
   Debbie Goff, Human Resources Division Administrator; ext. 3225; goffd@mdc.state.mo.us
   Dale Humburg, Resource Science Division Administrator; ext. 3191; humbud@mdc.state.mo.us
   Bob Krepps, Forestry Division Administrator; ext. 3300; kreppr@mdc.state.mo.us
   George Seek, Private Land Services Division Administrator; ext. 3873
   Dennis Steward, Protection Division Administrator; ext. 3258; steward@mdc.state.mo.us
   Norm Stucky, Fisheries Division Administrator; ext. 3159
   Robert Ziehmer, Assistant to Director; ext. 3601; ziehmr@mdc.state.mo.us
   Robbie Briscoe, Internal Auditor; ext. 3356; briscr@mdc.state.mo.us
   Dave Erickson, Wildlife Division Administrator; ext. 3142; erickd@mdc.state.mo.us
   Jane Smith, General Counsel; ext. 3210

MISSOURI DEPARTMENT OF CONSERVATION
DESIGN AND DEVELOPMENT DIVISION
2901 W. Truman Blvd.
Jefferson City, MO 65109 United States
Phone: 573-522-2323   Fax: 573-522-2324
Contact(s):
   William Lueckenhoff, Administrator

MISSOURI DEPARTMENT OF CONSERVATION
FISHERIES DIVISION
P.O. Box 180
Jefferson City, MO 65102-0180 United States
Phone: 573-751-4115   Fax: 573-526-4047
Website: www.conservation.state.mo.us/
Contact(s):
   Norman Stucky, Administrator

MISSOURI DEPARTMENT OF CONSERVATION
FORESTRY DIVISION
P.O. Box 180
Jefferson City, MO 65102-0180 United States
Phone: 573-751-4115   Fax: 573-526-6670
Website: www.mdc.state.mo.us
Contact(s):
   Bob Krepps, Administrator

MISSOURI DEPARTMENT OF CONSERVATION
HUMAN RESOURCES SECTION
P.O. Box 180
Jefferson City, MO 65102-0180 United States
Phone: 573-751-4115   Fax: 573-751-9099
Website: www.conservation.state.mo.us/
Contact(s):
   Deborah Goff, Chief

MISSOURI DEPARTMENT OF CONSERVATION
OUTREACH AND EDUCATION DIVISION
P.O. Box 180
Jefferson City, MO 65102-0180 United States
Phone: 573-751-4115   Fax: 573-751-2200
Website: www.mdc.state.mo.us
Contact(s):
   Lorna Domke, Administrator

MISSOURI DEPARTMENT OF CONSERVATION
PROTECTION DIVISION
P.O. Box 180
Jefferson City, MO 65102-0180 United States
Phone: 573-751-4115   Fax: 573-751-8971
Website: www.conservation.state.mo.us/
Contact(s):
   Dennis Steward, Administrator

MISSOURI DEPARTMENT OF CONSERVATION
WILDLIFE DIVISION
2901 W. Truman Blvd.
P.O. Box 180
Jefferson City, MO 65102 United States
Phone: 573-751-4115   Fax: 573-751-4467
Website: www.conservation.state.mo.us
Scope: State
Description: State Conservation Agency
Contact(s):
   David Erickson, Administrator

MISSOURI DEPARTMENT OF NATURAL RESOURCES

P.O. Box 176
Jefferson City, MO 65102 United States
Phone: 573-751-4422   Fax: 573-526-3878
Website: www.dnr.state.mo.us

Scope: State

Description: The Missouri Department of Natural Resources is the state resource management agency responsible for addressing environmental and natural resource-related issues. Areas of responsibility include: protecting Missouri's air, land and water resources, enforcing related laws where applicable; managing and maintaining the state's 80 state parks and state historic sites while protecting and promoting Missouri's cultural heritage and recreational opportunities.

Publication(s): Missouri Resources

Keyword(s): Energy, Land Issues, Public Lands/Greenspace, Recreation/Ecotourism

Contact(s):
Douglas Eiken, Director of Division of State Parks; 573-751-9392
Mimi Garstang, Director of Geological Survey and Resource Assessment; 573-368-2101; garsm@mail.dnr.state.mo.us
Gary Heimericks, Director of Division of Administrative Support; 573-751-7961
Connie Patterson, Communications Director; 573-751-1010; nrpattc@mail.dnr.state.mo.us
Thomas Welch, Director of Environmental Improvement and Energy Resources; P.O. Box 744, Jefferson City, MO 65102-0176; 573-751-4919
John Young, Director of Division of Air and Land Resources; 573-751-0763; younj@mail.dnr.state.mo.us
Sara Parker, Outreach and Assistance; 573-522-8796; parks@mail.dnr.state.mo.us
Scott Totten, Division of Water Quality/Soil Conservation; totts@mail.dnr.state.mo.us

MISSOURI STATE EXTENSION SERVICES

University of Missouri, 309 University Hall
Columbia, MO 65211 United States
Phone: 573-882-7754   Fax: 573-884-4204
Website: http://outreach.missouri.edu

Membership: 1–100
Scope: State

Contact(s):
Ronald Turner, Director: Extension Service
John Slusher, Extension Forester; 203 Natural Resources Bldg., Columbia, MO 65211; 573-882-4444; Fax: 573-882-1977

MONTANA BUREAU OF MINES AND GEOLOGY

GEOLOGY SURVEY
Montana Tech of the University of Montana
Butte, MT 59701-8997 United States
Phone: 406-496-4167   Fax: 406-496-4451
E-mail: pubsales@mtech.edu
Website: www.mbmg.mtech.edu

Founded: 1919
Membership: 1–100
Scope: State

Description: Established by law to aid the development and wise use of the state's mineral, energy, and groundwater resources by geologic and hydrogeologic studies of their occurrence and potential. Publishes formal reports and maps on Montana geology and groundwater.

Keyword(s): Energy

Contact(s):
Edmond Deal, Director and State Geologist; 406-496-4180; edeal@mbmgsun.mtech.edu

MONTANA COOPERATIVE WILDLIFE RESEARCH UNIT (USGS/BRD)

University of Montana
Missoula, MT 59812 United States
Phone: 406-243-5372   Fax: 406-243-6064
E-mail: mtcwru@selway.umt.edu
Website: www.pica.wru.umt.edu/mtcwru

Founded: 1950
Membership: 1–100
Scope: International

Description: Conducts basic and applied research, trains graduate students in wildlife biology and management, and disseminates information. Research specialties include breeding productivity, nest predation, and habitat use by birds (particularly nongame and waterfowl species) in relation to land use practices, predator populations, and natural variation in the environment.

Keyword(s): Forests/Forestry, Land Issues, Water Habitats & Quality, Wildlife & Species

Contact(s):
I. Ball, Leader; ball1@selway.umt.edu
Thomas Martin, Assistant Leader; tmartin@selway.umt.edu

MONTANA DEPARTMENT OF AGRICULTURE

P.O. Box 200201
Helena, MT 59620-0201 United States
Phone: 406-444-3144   Fax: 406-444-5409
E-mail: agr@state.mt.us
Website: www.agr.state.mt.us

Membership: 1–100
Scope: State

Description: To enhance, develop and promote agriculture and allied industries, while protecting producers, consumers and the general public

Keyword(s): Agriculture/Farming, Executive/Legislative/Judicial Reform, Pollution (general), Water Habitats & Quality, Wildlife & Species

Contact(s):
W. Peck, Director; 406-444-3144
Ron Zellar, Information Specialist; 406-444-3144
Gregory Ames, Administrator, Agricultural Sciences Division
Will Kissinger, Administrator: Agricultural Development Division; 406-444-2402

MONTANA DEPARTMENT OF FISH, WILDLIFE, AND PARKS

1420 East Sixth Ave
P.O. Box 200701
Helena, MT 59620-0701 United States
Phone: 406-444-3186   Fax: 406-444-4952
E-mail: fwpgen@state.mt.us
Website: www.fwp.state.mt.us

Founded: 1901
Membership: 101–1,000
Scope: State

Description: Montana state government agency provides for the willdife stewardship of the fish, parks and recreational resources of Montana.

Publication(s): Montana Outdoors

Keyword(s): Recreation/Ecotourism, Water Habitats & Quality, Wildlife & Species

Contact(s):
Jeff Hagener, Director; 406-444-3186; Fax: 406-444-4952; jhagener@state.mt.us
Larry Peterman, Chief of Field Operations; 406-444-3186; Fax: 406-444-4952; lpeterman@state.mt.us
Christian Smith, Chief of Staff; 406-444-3186; Fax: 406-444-4952; crsmith@state.mt.us
Ron Aasheim, Administrator: Conservation Education; 406-444-4038; Fax: 406-444-4952; raasheim@state.mt.us

Don Childress, Administrator: Wildlife; 406-444-2612; Fax: 406-444-4952; dchildress@state.mt.us

Tom Dickson, Editor; Montana Outdoors, 930 Custer Ave W, Helena, MT 59620; 406-495-3255; Fax: 406-495-3259; tdickson@state.mt.us

Dan Ellison, Administrator: Administration and Finance; 406-444-3109; Fax: 406-444-9733; dellison@state.mt.us

Glenn Erickson, Field Service Administrator; 406-444-3196; Fax: 406-444-3023; gerickson@state.mt.us

Spence Hegstad, Foundation Liaison; 406-444-6759; Fax: 406-444-4952; shegstad@state.mt.us

Chris Hunter, Administrator: Fisheries; 406-444-2449; Fax: 406-444-4952; chunter@state.mt.us

Jim Kropp, Administrator: Enforcement; 406-444-5657; Fax: 406-444-7894; jkropp@state.mt.us

Doug Monger, Administrator: Parks; 406-444-3750; Fax: 406-444-4952; dmonger@state.mt.us

MONTANA DEPARTMENT OF NATURAL RESOURCES AND CONSERVATION
1625 11th Ave., P.O. Box 201601
Helena, MT 59620-1601 United States
Phone: 406-444-2074   Fax: 406-444-2684
Website: www.dnrc.state.mt.us

Founded: 1971
Membership: 101–1,000
Scope: State

Description: Administers state-owned water projects; plans, regulates, and coordinates the development and use of 5.2 million acres of state school trust, land, and forest resources; wildland fire suppression and protection; service forestry; water-right adjudication; floodplain management; supervision, assistance, and coordination for local conservation and grazing districts; and regulation of oil and gas production.

Keyword(s): Agriculture/Farming, Energy, Forests/Forestry, Land Issues

Contact(s):
Bud Clinch, Director; 406-444-2074
Don Artley, Administrator: Forestry Division; 2705 Spurgin Rd., Missoula, MT 59801; 406-542-4300
Ann Bauchman, Administrator for Central Services Division; 406-444-6734
Ray Beck, Administrator: Conservation and Resource Development Division; 1520 E. 6th Ave., Helena, MT 59620; 406-444-6667; Fax: 406-444-6721; rbeck@mt.gov
Susan Cottingham, Administrator; Reserved Water Rights Compact Commission; 406-444-6841
Donald MacIntyre, Chief Legal Counsel; 406-444-6713
Carole Massman, Supervisor and Editor for Information Services; 406-444-6737
Mike Mikota, Personnel and EEO Officer
Terri Perrigo, Administrator: Oil and Gas Conservation Division
Tom Schultz, Administration Trust Land Management Division
Jack Stults, Administrator: Water Resources Division; 1520 E. 6th Ave., Helena, MT 59620; 406-444-6605

MONTANA ENVIRONMENTAL QUALITY COUNCIL
State Capitol
P.O. Box 201704
Room 171
Helena, MT 59620-1704 United States
Phone: 406-444-3122   Fax: 406-444-9784
E-mail: teverts@state.mt.us
Website: www.leg.state.mt.us

Founded: 1971
Scope: State

Description: The Environmental Quality Council is a state legislative committee created by the 1971 Montana Environmental Policy Act.

Keyword(s): Air Quality/Atmosphere, Land Issues, Water Habitats & Quality

Contact(s):
Todd Everts, Legislative Environmental Analyst
Bea McCarthy, Chair
Doug Mood, Vice-Chair

MONTANA NATURAL HERITAGE PROGRAM
1515 E 6th Ave.
Helena, MT 59620-1800 United States
Phone: 406-444-5354   Fax: 406-444-0581
E-mail: mtnhp@state.mt.us
Website: http://nhp.nris.state.mt.us/

Founded: 1985
Scope: Local, State

Description: The Montana Natural Heritage Program serves as the state's clearinghouse for information on Montana's native species and habitats, emphasizing those of conservation concern. We collect, validate, and distribute this information, and assist natural resource managers and others in applying it effectively. Established by the Montana State Legislature in 1983, the program is located in the Montana State Library, where it is part of the Natural Resource Information System.

Keyword(s): Public Lands/Greenspace, Water Habitats & Quality, Wildlife & Species

Contact(s):
Susan Crispin, Director

N

NATIVE AMERICAN HERITAGE COMMISSION
915 Capitol Mall, Rm. 364
Sacramento, CA 95814 United States
Phone: 916-653-4082   Fax: 916-657-5390
E-mail: nahc@pacbell.net
Website: www.nahc.ca.gov

Membership: 1–100
Scope: State

Description: The preservation and protection of Native American human remains and associated grave goods.

Publication(s): A Professional Guide

Contact(s):
Larry Myers, Executive Secretary; 916-653-4082; Fax: 916-657-5390; nahc@pacbell.net

NATURAL RESOURCES CANADA
ONTARIO
Toronto, M7A 1W3 Ontario Canada
Phone: 613-995-0947   Fax: 416-314-2102
Website: www.nrcan-rncan.gc.ca/inter/index.html

Scope: Province

Description: The ministry's business plan establishes the following as MNR's core businesses: natural resource management; Crown land management; public safety and enforcement; parks and protected areas; and geographic information. In pursuing these core businesses, the ministry contributes to the environmental, social, and economic well-being of Ontario through the biological features of provincial interest, and protects human life, the resource base, and physical property from the threats of forest fires.

Contact(s):
Jeff Krantzberg, Director of Communications Services Branch; 416-314-2119
John McHugh, Director of Communications Services; 416-314-2119
Gail Beggs, Assistant Deputy Minister for Field Services
John Burke, Deputy Minister
Ted Chudleigh, Parliamentary Assistant; 416-314-2193
Ann-Marie Guttier, Assistant Deputy Minister for Corporate Services
Linda Kemerman, Commissioner of Mining and Land

Patricia Malcolmson, Assistant Deputy Minister for Science and Information Resource
John Snobelen, Minister

NAVAJO NATION DEPARTMENT OF FISH AND WILDLIFE
NAVAJO NATURAL HERITAGE PROGRAM
P.O. Box 1480
Window Rock, AZ 86515 United States
Phone: 520-871-7068   Fax: 520-871-7069
E-mail: jcole@navajofishandwildlife.org
Website: www.navajofishandwildlife.org

Founded: 1984
Membership: 1–100
Scope: Regional
Description: The Navajo Nation Department of Fish and Wildlife is responsible for conserving, protecting, enhancing and restoring the Navajo Nation's fish, wildlife and plants for the spiritual, cultural and material benefit of present and future generations of the Navajo Nation.
Publication(s): Newsletter- Proclamation (Annually)
Keyword(s): Development/Developing Countries, Ecosystems (precious), Ethics/Environmental Justice, Recreation/Ecotourism, Water Habitats & Quality, Wildlife & Species
Contact(s):
Jeff Cole, Coordinator

NEBRASKA CONSERVATION AND SURVEY DIVISION
University of Nebraska-Lincoln, 113 Nebraska Hall
901 N. 17th St.
Lincoln, NE 68588 United States
Phone: 402-472-3471   Fax: 402-472-4608
Website: www.csd.unl.edu

Scope: State
Description: CSD, the state geological, water, soil and land cover survey, has state-mandated responsibilities to inventory and investigate geologically related natural resources of the state; to record the results of these investigations; to assist non-profit, private and governmental agencies working to conserve the state's natural resources; to study the geologic history and geography of the state to aid sustainable economic development; and to publish maps, reports and electronic information.
Publication(s): See publication website
Contact(s):
Mark Kuzila, Director; 402-472-7537

NEBRASKA DEPARTMENT OF AGRICULTURE
301 Centennial Mall S., P.O. Box 94947
Lincoln, NE 68509-4947 United States
Phone: 402-471-2341   Fax: 402-471-6876
E-mail: joannelk@agr.state.ne.us
Website: www.agr.state.ne.us

Membership: 1–100
Scope: State
Contact(s):
Merlyn Carlson, Director
Greg Ibach, Assistant Director; Fax: 402-471-6876

NEBRASKA DEPARTMENT OF ENVIRONMENTAL QUALITY
1200 N Street, Suite 400
Lincoln, NE 68509 United States
Phone: 402-471-2186   Fax: 402-471-2909
Website: www.deq.state.ne.us

Founded: 1971
Scope: State
Description: Created by the Nebraska Environmental Protection Act. Administers and enforces rules and regulations, and monitors the quality of the environment in Nebraska.
Publication(s): Environmental Update
Contact(s):
Michael Linder, Director
Tom Lamberson, Deputy Director, Administration and Hearing Officer
Brian McManus, Public Information Officer and Publications Editor
Jay Ringenberg, Deputy Director, Programs

NEBRASKA DEPARTMENT OF NATURAL RESOURCES
301 Centennial Mall South
Lincoln, NE 68509-4676 United States
Phone: 402-471-2363   Fax: 402-471-2900
E-mail: dnr@dnr.state.ne.us
Website: www.dnr.state.ne.us

Founded: 1937
Membership: 1–100
Scope: State
Description: The state agency responsible for comprehensive water resources planning, flood plain management, administration of state financial assistance for water resources, flood control, and soil and water conservation. It also has advisory and administrative responsibility for Natural Resources Districts throughout the state.
Publication(s): Nebraska Resources - quarterly newsletter
Keyword(s): Land Issues, Water Habitats & Quality
Contact(s):
Richard Jiskra, Chairperson; 2342 County Rd. 1600, Swanton, NE 68445; 402-448-5305

NEBRASKA GAME AND PARKS COMMISSION
2200 N. 33rd St., P.O. Box 30370
Lincoln, NE 68503-0370 United States
Phone: 402-471-0641   Fax: 402-471-5528
E-mail: ngpc@state.ne.us
Website: www.ngpc.state.ne.us

Founded: 1929
Membership: 101–1,000
Scope: State
Description: The commission has sole charge of state parks, game and fish, and all things pertaining thereto; boating; and administration of the Land and Water Conservation Fund. Complete information on Game and Parks Commission facilities is available on the WWW at: www.ngpc.state.ne.us.
Publication(s): Nebraskaland Magazine
Keyword(s): Ecosystems (precious), Executive/Legislative/Judicial Reform, Forests/Forestry, Land Issues, Public Lands/Greenspace, Recreation/Ecotourism, Water Habitats & Quality, Wildlife & Species
Contact(s):
Rex Amack, Director; 402-471-5539
Ted Blume, Administrator: Law Enforcement; 402-471-4010; tblume@ngpc.state.ne.us
Ken Bouc, Administrator: Information and Education; 402-471-5481; kbouc@ngpc.state.ne.us
Mark Brohman, Administrator: Administration; 402-471-5539; mbrohman@ngpc.state.ne.us
James Carney, Central Region Parks Manager; 402-471-5547; jcarney@ngpc.state.ne.us
Patrick Cole, Administrator: Budget and Fiscal; 402-471-5523; pcole@ngpc.state.ne.us
James Douglas, Administrator: Wildlife; 402-471-5411; jdouglas@ngpc.state.ne.us
James Fuller, Administrator: Parks; 402-471-5550; jfuller@ngpc.state.ne.us
Don Gabelhouse, Administrator: Fisheries; 402-471-5515; dgabel@ngpc.state.ne.us

Noelyn Isom, Assistant Director; 402-471-5539; nisom@ngpc.state.ne.us
Earl Johnson, Administrator: Operations and Construction; 402-471-5525
Roger Kuhn, Assistant Director; 402-471-5512; rkuhn@ngpc.state.ne.us
Kirk Nelson, Assistant Director; 402-471-5539; knelson@ngpc.state.ne.us
Bruce Sackett, Administrator: Realty; 402-471-5536; bsackett@ngpc.state.ne.us
Jim Sheffield, Administrator: Engineering; 402-471-5557; jsheff@ngpc.state.ne.us
Jim Swenson, Eastern Region Parks Manager; 402-471-5499; jswenson@ngpc.state.ne.us
Larry Voecks, Western Region Parks Manager; 308-665-2900; lvoecks@ngpc.state.ne.us
Barbara Voeltz, Librarian; 2200 N 33rd St., P.O. Box 30370, Lincoln, NE 68503; 402-471-5587; Fax: 402-471-5528; bvoeltz@ngpc.state.ne.us
Duane Westerholt, Administrator: Planning and Development; 402-471-5511; dwester@ngpc.state.ne.us
Tom White, Editor; 402-471-5471; twhite@ngpc.state.ne.us

NEBRASKA GAME AND PARKS COMMISSION
OMAHA OFFICE
1212 Bob Gibson Blvd.
Omaha, NE 68108 United States
Phone: 402-595-2144   Fax: 402-595-2569
Website: www.outdoornebraska.org
Scope: Local

NEVADA BUREAU OF MINES AND GEOLOGY
Mail Stop 178, University of Nevada, Reno
Reno, NV 89557-0088 United States
Phone: 775-784-6691, ext. 3   Fax: 775-784-1709
E-mail: nbmginfo@unr.edu
Website: www.nbmg.unr.edu
Membership: 1–100
Scope: State
Description: Conducts research on Nevada geology and mineral resources. Collects and disseminates information (including published maps and reports) on Nevada geology, mineral resources, base maps, and airphotos.
Publication(s): Nevada Mineral Industry, Major Mines of Nevada, Living with Earthquakes in Nevada
Keyword(s): Land Issues, Public Lands/Greenspace
Contact(s):
Jonathan Price, Director and State Geologist; jprice@unr.edu
David Davis, Geologic Information Specialist; ext. 133

NEVADA DEPARTMENT OF AGRICULTURE
350 Capitol Hill Ave.
Reno, NV 89502-2923 United States
Phone: 775-688-1180   Fax: 775-688-1178
Website: www.agri.state.nv.us
Membership: 1–100
Scope: State
Publication(s): Test Alert
Contact(s):
Paul Iverson, Director; ext. 222
Robert Gronowski, Administrator, Division of Plant Industry
Edward Hoganson, Administrator Division of Measurement Standards; 775-688-1166; Fax: 775-688-2533
David Thain, Administrator and State Veterinarian

NEVADA DEPARTMENT OF CONSERVATION AND NATURAL RESOURCES
Office of the Director
123 West Nye Lane, Room 230
Carson City, NV 89706-0818 United States
Phone: 775-687-4360   Fax: 775-687-6122
Website: www.dcnr.nv.gov
Membership: 1,001–10,000
Scope: State
Description: State of Nevada Department of Conservation & Natural Resources
Contact(s):
R. Michael Turnipseed, P.E., Director
Glenn Clemmer, Program Manager: Nevada Natural Heritage Program; 775-687-4245
Allen Biaggi, Administrator: Division of Environmental Protection; 775-687-4670
Terry Crawforth, Administrator: Division of Wildlife; 775-688-1500
Wayne Perock, Administrator: Division of State Parks; 775-687-4384
Hugh Ricci, State Engineer: Division of Water Resources; 775-687-4278
Steve Robinson, Administrator: Division of Forestry; 775-684-2500
Pamela Wilcox, Administrator: Division of State Lands; 775-687-4363

NEVADA DEPARTMENT OF WILDLIFE
1100 Valley Rd.
Reno, NV 89512 United States
Phone: 775-688-1500   Fax: 775-688-1595
E-mail: ndowinfo@ndow.org
Website: www.ndow.org
Scope: State
Description: A regulatory and policymaking body, administering laws, regulations, and policies. Mission is the protection, propagation, restoring, introduction, transplanting, and management of wildlife throughout the state.
Contact(s):
Thomas Atkinson, Chief, Enforcement
Steve Bremer, Administrative
Terry Crawforth, Administrator
David Rice, Chief, Conservation Education
Boyd Spratling, Board of Wildlife Commissioner Vice Chairman
Gregg Tanner, Chief, Game
Gene Weller, Chief, Fisheries

NEVADA NATURAL HERITAGE PROGRAM
1550 E. College Parkway, Suite 137
Carson City, NV 89706-7921 United States
Phone: 775-687-4245   Fax: 775-687-1288
Website: www.state.nv.us/nvnhp/
Founded: 1986
Scope: State, National
Description: The program represents an ongoing effort to collect and standardize data on Nevada's sensitive biodiversity and share this information with developers, researchers, and decision-makers for environmentally wise planning.
Keyword(s): Wildlife & Species
Contact(s):
Glenn Clemmer, Program Manager

NEW BRUNSWICK DEPARTMENT OF NATURAL RESOURCES
P.O. Box 6000
Fredericton, E3B 5H1 New Brunswick Canada
Phone: 506-453-3826   Fax: 506-457-4881
Website: www.gnb.ca
Scope: Province
Contact(s):
Michael Sullivan, Executive Director of Fish and Wildlife
David Ferguson, Deputy Minister; 506-453-2501
Jeannot Volp, Minister; 506-453-2510

NEW HAMPSHIRE COUNCIL ON RESOURCES AND DEVELOPMENT

c/o Office of State Planning and Energy Programs
57 Regional Drive
Concord, NH 03301 United States
Phone: 603-271-2155   Fax: 603-271-2615
E-mail: benjamin.frost@nh.gov
Website: www.state.nh.us/osp

Founded: 1963
Scope: State
Description: The thirteen members on the council represent the state's development and resource agencies. The council conducts studies and presents recommendations concerning environmental protection, natural resources, and growth management; consults with, negotiates with, and obtains information from other state and federal agencies; offers guidance and recommendations to the Governor and Executive Council or to the Legislature; recommends sale or lease of state-owned surplus real property.

Contact(s):
Jeffrey Taylor, Chairman

NEW HAMPSHIRE DEPARTMENT OF AGRICULTURE, MARKETS, AND FOOD

P.O. Box 2042
Concord, NH 03302-2042 United States
Phone: 603-271-3551   Fax: 603-271-1109
E-mail: staylor@agr.state.nh.us

Founded: 1913
Scope: State
Description: The department is responsible for a broad range of activities, including protecting the environment, food safety, market integrity, animal and plant health, and the economic security of the New Hampshire agricultural industry.
Publication(s): Weekly Market Bulletin
Keyword(s): Agriculture/Farming, Development/Developing Countries, Ethics/Environmental Justice, Land Issues, Sprawl/Urban Planning

Contact(s):
Stephen Taylor, Commissioner; 603-271-3551; Fax: 603-271-1109; staylor@agr.state.nh.us

NEW HAMPSHIRE DEPARTMENT OF AGRICULTURE, MARKETS, AND FOOD
STATE CONSERVATION COMMITTEE

P.O. Box 2042
Concord, NH 03302-2042 United States
Phone: 603-271-3551
Website: www.agriculture.nh.gov

Founded: 1945
Scope: State
Description: The SCC consists of twelve members. Six members represent state agencies, five are appointed, and one represents the NH Association of Conservation Commissions. Duties are to offer assistance to supervisors of the ten conservation districts, keep supervisors of each district informed of other district activities, and coordinate the conservation of New Hampshire activities.
Keyword(s): Agriculture/Farming, Land Issues, Water Habitats & Quality

Contact(s):
Samuel Doyle, Chair; P.O. Box 4, North Sutton, NH 03260; 603-927-4163; Fax: 603-224-8260
Joanna Pellerin, Coordinator; 118 North Rd., Brentwood, NH 03833-6614; 603-679-2790; Fax: 603-679-2860

NEW HAMPSHIRE DEPARTMENT OF ENVIRONMENTAL SERVICES

6 Hazen Dr.
P. O. Box 95
Concord, NH 03302-0095 United States
Phone: 603-271-2975   Fax: 603-271-8013
E-mail: pip@des.state.nh.us
Website: www.des.state.nh.us

Founded: 1987
Membership: 101–1,000
Scope: Local, State, Regional, National, International
Description: The protection and wise management of the State of New Hampshire's environment are the important goals of the NH Department of Environmental Services. The agency consists of three environmental areas: Air Division, Water Division, and Waste Management Division.
Publication(s): DES Publications Book
Keyword(s): Agriculture/Farming, Air Quality/Atmosphere, Climate Change, Ecosystems (precious), Energy, Ethics/Environmental Justice, Land Issues, Oceans/Coasts/Beaches, Pollution (general), Public Health, Reduce/Reuse/Recycle, Sprawl/Urban Planning, Transportation

Contact(s):
Timothy Drew, Administrator, Public Information and Permitting Unit; 603-271-3306; Fax: 603-271-8013; tdrew@des.state.nh.us
Philip O'Brien, Director of Waste Management Division; 603-271-2905; Fax: 603-271-2456
Harry Stewart, Director of Water Division; 603-271-3308; Fax: 603-271-2982
Michael Nolin, Commissioner; 603-271-2958; Fax: 603-271-2867
Robert Scott, Acting Director of Air Resources Division; 603-271-1088; Fax: 603-271-1381; rscott@des.state.nh.us

NEW HAMPSHIRE DEPARTMENT OF RESOURCES AND ECONOMIC DEVELOPMENT

172 Pembroke Rd.
Concord, NH 03302-1856 United States
Phone: 603-271-2411   Fax: 603-271-2629
E-mail: gbald@dred.state.nh.us
Website: www.dred.state.nh.us

Scope: State

Contact(s):
Stuart Arnett, Director of Division of Economic Development; 603-271-2341
Philip Bryce, Director of Division of Forests and Lands; 603-271-2214
Lauri Klefos, Director of Division of Travel and Tourism Development
Richard McLeod, Director of Division of Parks; 603-271-3556
George Bald, Commissioner; 603-271-2411
J. Cullen, Urban Forester of Urban Forestry Center; 603-431-6774
Paul Gray, Chief of Bureau of Off-Highway Recreational Vehicles; 603-271-3254

NEW HAMPSHIRE FISH AND GAME DEPARTMENT

2 Hazen Dr.
Concord, NH 03301-6500 United States
Phone: 603-271-3422   Fax: 603-271-1438
E-mail: info@wildlife.state.nh.us
Website: www.wildlife.state.nh.us

Founded: 1865
Scope: State
Description: Fish and wildlife management.
Publication(s): New Hampshire Wildlife Journal
Keyword(s): Recreation/Ecotourism, Wildlife & Species

Contact(s):
- William Bartlett, Jr., Acting Executive Director; 603-271-3511; Fax: 603-271-1438; director@wildlife.state.nh.us
- Jeffrey Gray, Colonel, Chief of Law Enforcement Division; 603-271-3128; law@wildlife.state.nh.us
- Ellis Hatch, Commission Chairman; 31 Harding Street, Rochester, NH 03867; 603-332-3500
- Jim Jones, Commissioner, Vice Chairman; 501 Beanhill Rd., Norfield, NH 03276; 603-283-9965
- Daniel Lynch, Assistant Director; dlynch@wildlife.state.nh.us
- Charles Miner, Chief of Access and Engineering; cminer@wildlife.state.nh.us
- John Nelson, Chief: Marine Fisheries Division; 603-868-1095
- Stephen Perry, Chief: Inland Fisheries; sperry@wildlife.state.nh.us
- Judy Stokes, Chief: Public Affairs Division; 603-271-3211; jstokes@wildlife.state.nh.us
- Steven Weber, Chief: Wildlife Division; 603-271-2461; sweber@wildlife.state.nh.us

NEW HAMPSHIRE NATURAL HERITAGE BUREAU
NHB/DRED
172 Pembroke Rd.
P.O. Box 1856
Concord, NH 03302-1856 United States
Phone: 603-271-3623   Fax: 603-271-2629
Website: www.nhdfl.org/formgt/nhiweb

Founded: 1987
Scope: Local, State, Regional
Description: The New Hampshire Natural Heritage Bureau is responsible for finding, tracking, and providing information about the state's rare species and exemplary ecosystems.
Publication(s): Checklist of New Hampshire's Vascular Plants, List of New Hampshire's Rare Animal Species, List of New Hampshire's Rare Plant Species
Keyword(s): Ecosystems (precious), Forests/Forestry, Land Issues, Wildlife & Species
Contact(s):
- Lionel Chute, Coordinator

NEW JERSEY DEPARTMENT OF AGRICULTURE
P.O. Box 330
Trenton, NJ 08625 United States
Phone: 609-292-5530   Fax: 609-292-3978
Website: www.state.nj.us/agriculture/Index.html

Membership: 101–1,000
Scope: Local
Keyword(s): Agriculture/Farming
Contact(s):
- Robert Balaam, Director of Division of Plant Industry; 609-292-5441
- John Gallagher, Director of Division of Administration; 609-292-6931
- George Horzepa, Director of Division of Rural Resources; 609-292-5532
- P. Mullon, Director of Division of Dairy and Commodity Regulation, Act; 609-292-5575
- A. Murray, Director of Division of Markets, Acting; 609-292-5536
- Gregory Romano, Executive Director of State Agriculture Development Committee; 609-984-2504
- Ernest Zirkle, Director of Division of Animal Health; 609-292-3965
- Carol Shipp, Chief of Staff; 609-633-7794
- Samuel Garrison, Assistant Secretary; 609-292-5530

NEW JERSEY DEPARTMENT OF AGRICULTURE
DIVISION OF RURAL RESOURCES
STATE SOIL CONSERVATION COMMITTEE
P.O. Box 330
Trenton, NJ 08625 United States
Phone: 609-292-5540   Fax: 609-633-7229
E-mail: james.sadley@ag.state.nj.us
Website: www.state.nj.us

Founded: 1937
Membership: 1–100
Scope: State
Description: A unit of state government administered by the state Dept. of Agriculture. Responsible for conservation of soil resources and control and prevention of soil erosion and nonpoint source pollution, prevention of damage by floodwater or sediment, and conservation of water for agricultural purposes. Provides direction, leadership, standards, rules, funding, and administrative assistance; coordinates local district conservation programs; and is interagency with 12 members.
Publication(s): Standards for Soil Erosion and Sediment
Keyword(s): Agriculture/Farming, Land Issues, Oceans/Coasts/Beaches, Pollution (general), Reduce/Reuse/Recycle, Water Habitats & Quality
Contact(s):
- Charles Kuperus, Chairman; 609-292-3976; charles.kuperus@ag.state.nj.us
- Jim Sadley, Executive Secretary; 609-292-5540; Fax: 609-633-7229; james.sadley@ag.state.nj.us

NEW JERSEY DEPARTMENT OF ENVIRONMENTAL PROTECTION
401 E. State St.
Trenton, NJ 08625-0402 United States
Phone: 609-292-2885   Fax: 609-292-7695
E-mail: askdep@dep.state.nj.us
Website: www.state.nj.us/dep

Membership: 101–1,000
Scope: State
Description: To assist the residents of New Jersey in preserving, sustaining, protecting and enhancing the environment to ensure the integration of high environmental quality, public health and economic vitality.
Publication(s): New Jersey Outdoors
Contact(s):
- Leslie McGeorge, Director, Div. of Science & Research/Assistant Commissioner; 609-984-6070
- Peter Page, Director; Communications; 609-777-1344; Fax: 609-292-1410
- Gary Sondermeyer, Chief of Staff; 609-292-2795; Fax: 609-292-7695
- Sue Boyle, Assistant Commissioner: Site Remediation; 609-292-1250; Fax: 609-777-1914
- Ray Cantor, Assistant Commissioner: Land Use Management; 609-292-2178
- Marlen Dooley, Assistant Commissioner: Enforcement, 609-984-3285
- Denise Mikics, Editor; 609-777-4182
- Robert Shinn, Commissioner
- Cari Wild, Assistant Commissioner: Natural and Historic Resources; 609-292-3541

NEW JERSEY DEPARTMENT OF ENVIRONMENTAL PROTECTION
DIVISION OF FISH AND WILDLIFE
N.J. Division of Fish and Wildlife
P.O. Box 400
Trenton, NJ 08625-0400 United States
Phone: 609-292-2965   Fax: 609-984-1414
E-mail: njwildlife@nac.net
Website: www.njfishandwildlife.com

Scope: State

Description: The mission of the New Jersey Division of Fish and Wildlife is to protect and manage the State's fish and wildlife to maximize their long-term biological, recreational and economic values for all New Jerseyans.

Keyword(s): Oceans/Coasts/Beaches, Water Habitats & Quality

Contact(s):
Robert McDowell, Director; 609-292-9410
David Chanda, Assistant Director; 609-292-0891
Lawrence Herrighty, Chief: Rural Wildlife Management; 609-292-6685
Jim Joseph, Chief: Shellfisheries; 609-984-5546
Tom McCloy, Chief: Marine Fisheries; 609-984-5546
Martin McHugh, Assistant Director; 609-292-0891
Larry Niles, Chief: Endangered and Nongame Species Program; 609-292-9101
Tony Petrongolo, Chief: Lands Management; 609-292-1599
Jim Sciascia, Chief: Wildlife Information/Education; 609-292-9450; jsciasci@dep.state.nj.us
Robert Soldwedel, Chief: Freshwater Fisheries; 609-292-8642
Rob Winkel, Chief: Law Enforcement; 609-292-9430

NEW JERSEY DEPARTMENT OF ENVIRONMENTAL PROTECTION
DIVISION OF PARKS AND FORESTRY
P.O. Box 404
Trenton, NJ 08625-0404 United States
Phone: 609-292-2733   Fax: 609-984-0503
Website: www.state.nj.us/dep/forestry/parknj/divhome.htm

Scope: Regional

Contact(s):
Gregory Marshall, Director
Richard Barker, Assistant Director: State Park Service; 609-292-2772
James Barresi, Assistant Director: State Park Service; 609-292-2530
Maris Gabliks, Chief: Bureau of Forest Fire Management and State Firewarden; 609-292-2977
Frank Gallagher, Administrator, Office of Interpretive & Educational Services; 609-292-8190
Dorothy Guzzo, Administrator: Office of Historic Preservation; 609-984-0176
Edward Lempicki, Chief: Bureau of Forest Management: State Forester; 609-292-2531
Carl Nordstrom, Deputy Director; 609-292-5990

NEW JERSEY DEPARTMENT OF ENVIRONMENTAL PROTECTION
DIVISION OF PUBLICLY FUNDED SITE REMEDIATION
P.O. Box 402
Trenton, NJ 08625-0402 United States
Phone: 609-984-3081   Fax: 609-777-0756
Website: www.state.nj.us/dep/index.html

Scope: State

Description: To assist the residents of New Jersey in preserving, sustaining, protecting and enhancing the environment to ensure the integration of high environmental quality, public health and economic vitality.

Keyword(s): Development/Developing Countries, Public Lands/Greenspace

Contact(s):
Anthony Farro, Director

NEW JERSEY DEPARTMENT OF ENVIRONMENTAL PROTECTION
DIVISION OF SOLID AND HAZARDOUS WASTE
P.O. Box 414
Trenton, NJ 08625-0414 United States
Phone: 609-984-6880   Fax: 609-984-6874
E-mail: dshweb@dep.state.nj.us
Website: www.state.nj.us/dep

Scope: State

Description: The Division of Solid and Hazardous Waste is dedicated to the environmentally sound and cost effective management of solid and hazardous wastes and recyclable materials, to protect the public health, preserve the environment, and enhance the quality of life for the citizens of the State of New Jersey.

Contact(s):
John Castler, Director

NEW JERSEY DEPARTMENT OF ENVIRONMENTAL PROTECTION
GEOLOGICAL SURVEY
P.O. Box 427
Trenton, NJ 08625-0427 United States
Phone: 609-292-1185   Fax: 609-633-1004
Website: www.state.nj.us/dep/njgs/

Founded: 1835
Membership: 1–100
Scope: State, Regional

Description: Formed to study, evaluate, and prepare maps and reports on New Jersey's resources. In addition to a geologic map and information on the mineral industry and water resources, the survey provides geologic and ground water reports, geologic and topographic maps, ground water monitoring, and other resource information.

Publication(s): Geologic Survey Reports & Maps

Keyword(s): Climate Change, Land Issues, Oceans/Coasts/Beaches, Pollution (general), Public Lands/Greenspace, Sprawl/Urban Planning, Water Habitats & Quality

Contact(s):
Richard Dalton, Chief of Bureau of Geology and Topography; 609-292-2576
Karl Muessig, State Geologist; 609-292-1185
David Pasicznyk, Chief, Ground Water Resource Evaluations; 609-984-6587
Thomas Seckler, Editor; 609-292-1185

NEW JERSEY DEPARTMENT OF ENVIRONMENTAL PROTECTION
GREEN ACRES PROGRAM
501 East State Street
Station Plaza Building 5, Ground Floor
Trenton, NJ 08625-0412 United States
Phone: 609-984-0500   Fax: 609-984-0608
Website: www.state.nj.us/dep/greenacres

Founded: 1961
Scope: State

Description: Green Acres protects open space to enhance New Jersey's natural environment and its historic, scenic, and recreational resources. As the land acquisition agent for NJDEP, Green Acres acquires land, which becomes part of the system of state parks, forests, natural areas and wildlife management areas. Green Acres also provides low interest (2%) loans and partial grants to municipal and county governments to acquire open space and develop outdoor recreation facilities.

Keyword(s): Public Lands/Greenspace, Recreation/Ecotourism

Contact(s):
Dennis Davidson, Deputy Administrator; 609-984-0555; Fax: 609-984-0608; ddavidso@dep.state.nj.us
Thomas Wells, Administrator; 609-984-0508; Fax: 609-984-0608; twells@dep.state.nj.us
Gary Rice, Chief, Local Assistance Program; 609-984-0570; Fax: 609-984-0608; grice@dep.state.nj.us
Robert Stokes, Chief, Planning and Information Management; 609-984-0495; Fax: 609-984-0608; rstokes@dep.state.nj.us
John Watson, Chief, State Land Acquisition; 609-984-0609; Fax: 609-984-0608; jwatson@dep.state.nj.us
Judith Yeany, Chief, Legal Services and Stewardship; 609-984-0631; Fax: 609-984-0608; jyeany@dep.state.nj.us

NEW JERSEY PINELANDS COMMISSION
P.O. Box 7
New Lisbon, NJ 08064 United States
Phone: 609-894-7300   Fax: 609-894-7330
E-mail: info@njpines.state.nj.us
Website: www.nj.gov/pinelands/

Founded: 1979
Membership: 1-100
Scope: State, Regional
Description: State planning and regulatory agency with jurisdiction over land use and development in the million-acre Pinelands national reserve; 53 municipalities in the state Pinelands area have and revise local master plans and zoning ordinances to incorporate standards of regional conservation plan.
Publication(s): Pinelander, The Newsletter, a list of reports and studies is available upon request.
Keyword(s): Land Issues
Contact(s):
   Annette Barbaccia, Executive Director
   Elizabeth Carpenter, Educational Coordinator
   William Harrison, Assistant Director of Development Review and Enforcement
   Jerrold Jacobs, Chairman
   John Stokes, Assistant Director of Planning and Management

NEW MEXICO BUREAU OF GEOLOGY AND MINERAL RESOURCES
GEOLOGICAL INFORMATION CENTER LIBRARY
801 Leroy Place
Socorro, NM 87801 United States
Phone: 505-835-5145   Fax: 505-835-6333
E-mail: bureau@gis.nmt.edu
Website: www.geoinfo.nmt.edu/

Membership: 1-100
Scope: State
Publication(s): New Mexico Geology-quarterly newsletter
Contact(s):
   Peter Scholle, Contact

NEW MEXICO BUREAU OF GEOLOGY AND MINERAL RESOURCES
801 Leroy Pl.
Socorro, NM 87801 United States
Phone: 505-835-5420   Fax: 505-835-6333
E-mail: pubsosc@gis.nmt.edu
Website: www.geoinfo.nmt.edu

Founded: 1927
Membership: 1-100
Scope: Local
Description: Charged with investigating and reporting on all types of mineral resources and the geology of the state, including environmental geology, water resources, and geological hazards; responsible for conducting applied research on all aspects of geology and mineral resources.
Publication(s): Bulletins, Databases on CD-ROM and home page, Scenic Trips to the Geologic Past, Lite Geology, New Mexico Geology, Geologic Maps, Ground Water Reports, Memoirs, Circulars, Topo Maps, Open File Report
Keyword(s): Energy
Contact(s):
   Peter Scholle, Director and State Geologist; 505-835-5302; pscholle@gis.nmt.edu
   Susan Welch, Manager of Geological Extension Service; 505-835-5112; susie@gis.nmt.edu
   Bruce Allen, Environmental Geologist; 505-255-0317; allenb@gis.nmt.edu
   Jane Love, Editor; jane@gis.nmt.edu
   David Love, Environmental Geologist; 505-835-5146; dave@gis.nmt.edu

NEW MEXICO DEPARTMENT OF AGRICULTURE
MSC 3189, P.O. Box 30005
Las Cruces, NM 88003-8005 United States
Phone: 505-646-3007   Fax: 505-646-1540
Website: http://nmdaweb.nmsu.edu

Founded: 1955
Membership: 101-1,000
Scope: State
Description: Organized to protect state agriculture from importation of plant diseases and insects and help control those that gain entrance; to ensure products offered for sale meet quality standards as advertised and labeled; maintain inspection of agricultural products for interstate shipping; laboratory analyses of animal diseases and deaths on fee basis; promote state agricultural commodities; provide market news; and conduct consumer and producer service activities designated by law.
Publication(s): Biennial Report, New Mexico Agricultural Statistics
Contact(s):
   Edward Avalos, Director of Marketing and Development Division; 505-646-4929
   Larry Dominguez, Director of Agricultural and Environmental Services Division; 505-646-3208
   Frank Dubois, Director and Secretary; 505-646-3007
   Richard Larock, Director of Veterinary Diagnostic Services, 505-841-2576
   Gary West, Director of Standards and Consumer Services Division; 505-646-1616
   Ronald White, Director of Agricultural Programs and Resources Division; 505-646-2642
   Rick Janecka, State Chemist of Laboratory; 505-646-3318
   Richard Kochevar, State Seed Analyst of Laboratory; 505-646-3407
   Jeff Witte, Assistant Director; 505-646-3007

NEW MEXICO DEPARTMENT OF GAME AND FISH
P.O. Box 25112
Santa Fe, NM 87504 United States
Phone: 505-476-8000   Fax: 505-476-8124
E-mail: iispa@state.nm.us
Website: www.gmfsh.state.nm.us

Membership: 101-1,000
Scope: State
Description: The State Game Commission and the Game and Fish Department are administratively attached to the Energy, Minerals, and Natural Resources Department. The responsibility of the State Game Commission is to develop policy for the Game and Fish Department.
Publication(s): Publications on line
Contact(s):
   Larry Bell, Director; P.O. Box 25112, Santa Fe, NM 87504; 505-827-6333; lbell@state.nm.us
   Dan Brook, Chief of Law Enforcement; 505-827-7934; dbrook@state.nm.us
   Scott Brown, Assistant Director of Resource Divisions; 505-827-6333; sbrown@state.nm.us
   Lydia Duran, Chief of Administrative Services, Acting; 505-827-7920; lduran@state.nm.us
   Steven Emery, Chairman of State Game Commission; 505-856-0963; semery@state.nm.us
   Barry Hale, Chief of Wildlife Division; 505-827-7885; bhale@state.nm.us
   Jack Kelly, Chief of Fish Management; 505-827-7905; jkelly@state.nm.us
   Don MacCarter, Chief of Public Affairs
   Roberta Salazar-Henry, Assistant Director of Administrative Services and Information; 505-827-6333; rhenry@state.nm.us
   Jennifer Salisbury, Cabinet Secretary of Energy, Minerals, and Natural Resources; 505-827-5950; jsalisbury@state.nm.us

Tod Stevenson, Chief of Conservation Services; 505-827-7882; tstevenson@state.nm.us

NEW MEXICO DEPARTMENT OF GAME AND FISH
ALBUQUERQUE NM OFFICE
3841 Midway Pl., NE
Albuquerque, NM 87109 United States
Phone: 505-841-8881   Fax: 505-841-8885
Website: www.gmfsh.state.nm.us

Membership: 1–100
Scope: State
Contact(s):
Chris Chadwick, Public Affairs Specialist
Luke Shelby, Chief of Operations NW Area

NEW MEXICO DEPARTMENT OF GAME AND FISH
RATON NM OFFICE
P.O. Box 1145, 215 York Canyon Rd.
Raton, NM 87740 United States
Phone: 505-445-2311   Fax: 505-445-5651
E-mail: gmfsh@state.nm.us
Website: www.gmfsh.state.nm.us

Scope: State
Keyword(s): Water Habitats & Quality, Wildlife & Species
Contact(s):
Lief Ahlm, Assistant Chief; 505-445-2311; Fax: 505-445-5651; lahlm@state.nm.us
Bill Hays, Chief; 505-445-2311; Fax: 505-445-5651; bchays@state.nm.us

NEW MEXICO DEPARTMENT OF GAME AND FISH
ROSWELL NM OFFICE
1912 West 2nd St.
Roswell, NM 88201 United States
Phone: 505-624-6135   Fax: 505-624-6136
Website: www.gmfsh.state.nm.us

Scope: State
Contact(s):
Roy Hayes, Chief

NEW MEXICO DEPARTMENT OF GAME AND FISH
SW AREA OPERATIONS
566 N. Telshor Blvd.
Las Cruces, NM 88011 United States
Phone: 505-522-9796   Fax: 505-522-8382
E-mail: jveo@state.nm.us
Website: www.gmfsh.state.nm.us

Membership: 1–100
Scope: Regional
Description: State agency responsible for managing New Mexico's wildlife.
Contact(s):
Steve Henry, Chief

NEW MEXICO ENERGY, MINERALS, AND NATURAL RESOURCES DEPARTMENT
Pinon Building
1220 South St. Francis Drive
Santa Fe, NM 87505 United States
Phone: 505-476-3200   Fax: 505-476-3220
Website: www.emnrd.state.nm.us/default.htm

Scope: State
Description: As the steward for New Mexico's natural resources, the department seeks to preserve the unique natural beauty of New Mexico and to facilitate the beneficial development and use of its resources in an environmentally responsible manner.

Contact(s):
Betty Rivera, Cabinet Secretary

NEW MEXICO ENERGY, MINERALS, AND NATURAL RESOURCES DEPARTMENT
ADMINISTRATIVE SERVICES DIVISION
1220 South St. Francis Drive
Santa Fe, NM 87505 United States
Phone: 505-476-3230   Fax: 505-476-3234
Website: www.emnrd.state.nm.us/default.htm

Scope: State
Description: Provides clerical, recordkeeping, and administrative support to the department in the areas of personnel, budget, procurement and contracting, and administration of federal and state grants.
Keyword(s): Energy, Land Issues, Recreation/Ecotourism, Reduce/Reuse/Recycle
Contact(s):
Dale Lucero, Director

NEW MEXICO ENERGY, MINERALS, AND NATURAL RESOURCES DEPARTMENT
ENERGY CONSERVATION AND MANAGEMENT DIVISION
1220 S. St. Francis Drive
P.O. Box 6429
Santa Fe, NM 87505 United States
Phone: 505-476-3310   Fax: 505-476-3322
Website: www.emnrd.state.nm.us/ecmd

Founded: 1978
Membership: 1–100
Scope: Local, State, Regional, National, International
Description: Administers state and federally funded energy efficiency, renewable energy, and alternative transportation programs to state agencies, political subdivisions, regional organizations, nonprofit community service agencies, and New Mexico energy consumers, by providing engineering and technical assistance, and informational, financial, and programmatic support.
Keyword(s): Agriculture/Farming, Air Quality/Atmosphere, Climate Change, Energy, Forests/Forestry, Pollution (general), Reduce/Reuse/Recycle, Transportation, Water Habitats & Quality
Contact(s):
Chris Wentz, Divisional Director; 505-476-3312; cwentz@state.nm.us

NEW MEXICO ENERGY, MINERALS, AND NATURAL RESOURCES DEPARTMENT
FORESTRY DIVISION
1220 St. Francis Dr., Rm 112
Santa Fe, NM 87505 United States
Phone: 505-476-3325   Fax: 505-476-3330
Website: www.emnrd.state.nm.us/forestry/

Scope: State
Description: Provides management and protection of New Mexico's renewable forest, rangeland, soil, and water resources through professional forest, pest, fire, and land management; provides law enforcement and administration, public education in conservation; and supports to enhance the environment and quality of resources to protect jobs and maintain social and economic benefits.
Publication(s): See publication website
Contact(s):
Toby Martinez, State Forester

NEW MEXICO ENERGY, MINERALS, AND NATURAL RESOURCES DEPARTMENT
MINING AND MINERALS DIVISION
1220 S. St. Francis Drive
Santa Fe, NM 87505 United States
Phone: 505-476-3405
Website: www.emnrd.state.nm.us/mining/

Scope: State

Description: Provides for the study, development, and optimum production of the mineral and energy resources within the state; the reduction of hazards associated with these processes consistent with the conservation of these resources; the protection of public health, safety, and the environment, and the economic well-being of the citizens.

Contact(s):
Douglas Bland, Director

NEW MEXICO ENERGY, MINERALS, AND NATURAL RESOURCES DEPARTMENT
OIL CONSERVATION DIVISION
1220 Saint Francis Drive
Santa Fe, NM 87505 United States
Phone: 505-476-3440   Fax: 505-476-3462
Website: www.emnrd.state.nm.us

Scope: State

Description: Regulates and sets standards for operations related to the drilling and production of crude oil, natural gas, and geothermal resources and promotes the development and conservation of these resources while ensuring the prevention of waste and protection. Cares for the prevention of loss and contamination of freshwater supplies.

Contact(s):
Lori Wrotenberry, Director

NEW MEXICO ENERGY, MINERALS, AND NATURAL RESOURCES DEPARTMENT
STATE PARKS AND RECREATION DIVISION
1220 St. Francis, P.O. Box 1147
Santa Fe, NM 87505 United States
Phone: 505-476-3355   Fax: 505-476-3361
E-mail: nmparks@state.nm.us
Website: www.emnrd.state.nm.us/nmparks/

Scope: State

Description: Provides and cares for the recreational resources, facilities, and opportunities, and promotes user safety on recreational land and water to benefit and enrich the lives of New Mexico residents and visitors alike.

Contact(s):
Tom Trujillo, Director

NEW MEXICO ENVIRONMENT DEPARTMENT
1190 Saint Francis Dr., P.O. Box 26110
Santa Fe, NM 87502 United States
Phone: 505-827-2855   Fax: 505-827-2836
Website: www.nmenv.state.nm.us

Membership: 101–1,000
Scope: State

Description: To preserve, protect, and perpetuate New Mexico's environment for present and future generations.

Contact(s):
Ralph Gruebel, Director of Environmental Protection Division
Robert Horwitz, Director of Administrative Services Division; 505-827-2773; robert_horwitz@nmenv.state.nm.us
Mike Koranda, Director of Field Operations Division; 505-827-1080; mike_koranda@nmenv.state.nm.us
Greg Lewis, Director of Water and Waste Management Division; 505-827-2886; greg_lewis@nmenv.state.nm.us
Darwin Pattengale, Manager of District IV; 505-624-6046; darwin_pattengale@nmenv.state.nm.us
Ken Smith, Manager of District III; 505-524-6300; ken_smith@nmenv.state.nm.us
Courte Vohres, Manager of District II; 505-827-1840; courte_vohres@nmenv.state.nm.us
James Bearzi, Chief of Hazardous & Radioactive Materials Bureau; 505-827-1557; james_bearzi@nmenv.state.nm.us
Sandra Eli, Chief of Air Quality Bureau; 505-827-1494; sandra_eli@nmenv.state.nm.us
Cliff Hawley, Chief of Program Support Bureau; 505-827-2844; cliff_hawley@nmenv.state.nm.us
Marcy Leavitt, Chief of Ground Water Protection and Remediation Bureau; 505-827-2919; marcy_leavitt@nmenv.state.nm.us
Pete Maggiore, Secretary; 505-827-2855; pete_maggiore@nmenv.state.nm.us
John Parker, Chief of Department of Energy Oversight Bureau; 505-827-4252; john_parker@nmenv.state.nm.us
Sam Rogers, Chief of Occupational Health and Safety Bureau; 505-827-2877; sam_rogers@nmenv.state.nm.us
Jerry Scheppner, Chief of Underground Storage Tank Bureau, 505-827-0188; jerry_sheppner@nmenv.state.nm.us
Butch Tongate, Chief of Solid Waste Bureau; 505-827-2775; butch_tongate@nmenv.state.nm.us

NEW MEXICO SOIL AND WATER CONSERVATION COMMISSION
MSC APR P.O. Box 30005
Las Cruces, NM 88003-8005 United States
Phone: 505-646-2642   Fax: 505-646-1540
E-mail: acoleman@nmda.nmsu.edu

Membership: 1–100
Scope: State

Description: Policy making organization for soil and water conservation districts

Keyword(s): Agriculture/Farming, Ecosystems (precious), Ethics/Environmental Justice, Forests/Forestry, Land Issues, Public Lands/Greenspace, Sprawl/Urban Planning, Water Habitats & Quality, Wildlife & Species

Contact(s):
Julie Maitland, Division Director; P.O. Box 30005 MSC APR, Mexico Department of Agriculture, Las Cruces, NM 88003-8005; 505-646-2642; Fax: 505-646-1540

NEW MEXICO STATE UNIVERSITY
COOPERATIVE EXTENSION SERVICES
COLLEGE OF AG AND HOME ECONOMICS
Box 30003, Campus Box 3AG
Las Cruces, NM 88003 United States
Phone: 505-646-3748   Fax: 505-646-5975
E-mail: agdean@nmsu.edu
Website: www.cahe.nmsu.edu/ces/

Scope: State

Contact(s):
Billy Dictson, Associate Dean and Director CES; NM State University, Box 3AE, Las Cruces, NM 88003; 505-646-3015
Chris Allison, Extension Range Management Specialist; Box 3AE, NM State University, Las Cruces, NM 88003; 505-646-1944
Jon Boren, Extension Wildlife Specialist; Box 3AE, NM State University, Las Cruces, NM 88003; 505-646-1164; Fax: 505-646-1281
Ron Byford, Extension Department Head of Plant Sciences; Box 3AE, NM State University, Las Cruces, NM 88003; 505-646-2458
Ron Parker, Extension Department Head of Animal Resources; Box 3AE, NM State University, Las Cruces, NM 88003; 505-646-1709
Jerry Schickedanz, Dean and Chief Administrative Officer

NEW YORK COOPERATIVE FISH AND WILDLIFE RESEARCH UNIT
Department of Natural Resources, Fernow Hall, Cornell University
Ithaca, NY 14853 United States
Phone: 607-255-2839　　　Fax: 607-255-1895
E-mail: dnrcru-mailbox@cornell.edu
Website: www.dnr.cornell.edu

Founded: 1961

Scope: Local, State, Regional, National

Description: Primary purpose is field and laboratory research on management and conservation of a variety of fish and wildlife species, and graduate research training in fisheries and wildlife resources. Supported cooperatively by U.S. Geological Survey, Cornell University, New York State Department of Environmental Conservation, and the Wildlife Management Institute.

Publication(s): See publication website

Contact(s):
Richard Malecki, Assistant Leader of Wildlife; 607-255-2836; ram26@cornell.edu
Milo Richmond, Leader; 607-255-2151; mer6@cornell.edu

NEW YORK DEPARTMENT OF AGRICULTURE AND MARKETS
STATE SOIL AND WATER CONSERVATION COMMITTEE
1 Winners Circle
Albany, NY 12235 United States
Phone: 1-800-554-4501　　　Fax: 518-457-3412
E-mail: info@agmkt.state.ny.us
Website: www.agmkt.state.ny.us

Membership: 1–100
Scope: State
Publication(s): Newsletter - Down to Earth (once a month)
Contact(s):
John Wildeman, Director; 518-457-3738; Fax: 518-457-1204
Philip Griffen, Chair; 28 Spook Hollow Rd., Stillwater, NY 12170; 518-664-5038

NEW YORK DEPARTMENT OF ENVIRONMENTAL CONSERVATION
625 Broadway 12th Fl.
Albany, NY 12233 United States
Phone: 518-474-2121　　　Fax: 518-402-9392
Website: www.dec.state.ny.us

Founded: 1970
Scope: State
Description: The mission of the New York State Department of Environmental Conservation is to conserve, improve, and protect its natural resources and environment, and control water, land and air pollution, in order to enhance the health, safety and welfare of the people of the state and their overall economic and social well-being.

Publication(s): Environmental Notice Bulletin

Contact(s):
Jim Austin, Special Projects; 518-485-8437
Frank Bifera, Deputy Commissioner and Counsel; 518-457-4415
Gordon Colvin, Marine Resources; 631-444-0430
Erin Crotty, Commissioner; 518-402-8540
Peter Duncan, Deputy Commissioner for Natural Resources; 518-457-0975
Fran Dunwell, Hudson River; 914-256-3017
James Ferreira, Assistant Commissioner of Office of Hearings and Mediation Services
Linda Frick, Special Assistant to the Commissioner; 518-457-0904
Carl Johnson, Deputy Commissioner Air and Waste Management
Thomas Kelly, Environmental Facilities Corporation; 518-402-6951
John Kelly, Adirondacks; 518-623-3671
Tom Kunkel, Special Projects; 718-482-4949
John McKeon, Assistant Commissioner for Office of Bond Act; 518-402-9401
Francis Sheehan, Natural Resources Planning; 518-457-4208
Susan Taluto, Assistant Commissioner for Administrative Services; 518-457-6533
James Tuftey, Assistant Commissioner for the Office of Public Protection
Fran Verdoliva, Salmon River; 315-298-7605

NEW YORK DEPARTMENT OF ENVIRONMENTAL CONSERVATION
DIVISION OF PUBLIC AFFAIRS AND EDUCATION
625 Broadway
Second Floor
Albany, NY 12233 United States
Phone: 518-402-8013
Website: www.dec.state.ny.us

Scope: State
Description: Public Affairs unit representing the New York State government department responsible for environmental quality and natural resource management programs.
Publication(s): Environmental Notice Bulletin, The New York State Conservationist

Contact(s):
Laurel Remus, Director; 518-457-0840

NEW YORK DEPARTMENT OF ENVIRONMENTAL CONSERVATION
DIVISION OF SOLID AND HAZARDOUS MATERIALS
625 Broadway
Albany, NY 12232 United States
Phone: 518-402-8540
Website: www.dec.state.ny.us/website/dshm

Scope: State
Description: We regulate and monitor solid and hazardous waste facilities and generators of hazardous waste; control disposal of radioactive materials and use of pesticides; and promote sound management of wastes by communities, businesses and industries.

Contact(s):
Stephen Hammond, Director, Division of Solid & Hazardous Materials; 518-402-8651
Erin Crotty, Commissioner; 518-402-8540

NEW YORK DEPARTMENT OF ENVIRONMENTAL CONSERVATION
DIVISION OF WATER
625 Broadway
4th floor
Albany, NY 12233 United States
Phone: 518-402-8233　　　Fax: 518-402-8230
Website: www.dec.state.ny.us

Membership: 101–1,000
Scope: State
Keyword(s): Population, Public Health, Water Habitats & Quality
Contact(s):
N. Kaul, Director; 518-457-6674

NEW YORK DEPARTMENT OF ENVIRONMENTAL CONSERVATION
REGIONAL DIRECTORS, UNITED STATES

Contact(s):
Raymond Cowen, Region 1; Bldg. 40, State University of New York, Stony Brook, NY 11794; 516-444-0354
Mary Kris, Region 2; Hunters Point Plaza, Long Island City, NY 11101; 718-482-4900

Marc Moran, Region 3; 21 S. Putt Corners Rd., New Paltz, NY 12561; 845-256-3000
Steve Schassler, Region 4; 11 North Westcott Road, Schenectady, NY 12306; 518-357-2234
Stuart Buchanan, Region 5; Route 86, P.O. Box 296, Ray Brook, NY 12977; 518-897-1200
Sandy Lebarron, Region 6; 317 Washington Street, Watertown, NY 13204; 315-785-2239
Kenneth Lynch, Region 7; 615 Erie Blvd., W, Syracuse, NY 13204; 315-426-7400
John Hicks, Region 8; 6274 E. Avon-Lima Road, Avon, NY 14414; 716-226-2466
Gerald Mikol, Region 9; 270 Michigan Avenue, Buffalo, NY 14203; 716-851-7000

NEW YORK DEPARTMENT OF HEALTH
Tower Bldg., Empire State Plaza
Albany, NY 12237 United States
Phone: 800-458-1158   Fax: 518-473-7071
Website: www.health.state.ny.us/home.html
Contact(s):
Ronald Trammontano, Director of Center for Environmental Health; 518-458-1158

NEW YORK GEOLOGICAL SURVEY AND STATE MUSEUM
Cultural Education Center
Albany, NY 12230 United States
Phone: 518-474-5816   Fax: 518-486-2034
Website: www.nysm.nysed.gov
Founded: 1836
Scope: State
Description: The Geological Survey and State Museum serves as a clearinghouse for information concerning bedrock and surficial geology within the state. The survey conducts regular mapping projects and investigations in basic, environmental, and applied geology and publishes maps and reports of investigations.
Publication(s): New York State Geogram, publications list of the New York State Geological Survey
Keyword(s): Energy, Land Issues, Oceans/Coasts/Beaches
Contact(s):
Richard Nyahay, Oil and Gas Office Director; 518-486-2161
Robert Fakundiny, State Geologist and Chief Scientist; 518-474-5816; rnyahay@mail.nysed.gov
Robert Fickies, Engineering and Environmental Geology, Geologic Information; 518-474-5810

NEW YORK OFFICE OF ENERGY EFFICIENCY AND ENVIRONMENT
New York State Dept. of Public Service, 3 Empire State Plaza
Albany, NY 12223 United States
Phone: 518-473-7248   Fax: 518-473-2420
Founded: 1970
Description: The Office of Energy Efficiency and Environment provides staff support in developing and administering policies that assure appropriate consideration of energy efficiency and environmental protection in utility regulation, management, and restructuring. The office also plays a major role in the development of systems and procedures necessary to introduce retail competition in the state.
Keyword(s): Air Quality/Atmosphere, Energy, Land Issues, Reduce/Reuse/Recycle
Contact(s):
Paul Powers, Director

NEW YORK STATE COOPERATIVE EXTENSION
College of Agriculture and Life Sciences, and Human Ecology
365 Roberts Hall, Cornell University
Ithaca, NY 14853-4203 United States
Phone: 607-255-2237   Fax: 607-255-0788
E-mail: cce@cornell.edu
Website: www.cce.cornell.edu/
Membership: 1–100
Scope: State
Keyword(s): Agriculture/Farming, Forests/Forestry, Reduce/Reuse/Recycle, Water Habitats & Quality, Wildlife & Species
Contact(s):
D. Ewert, Director of Cooperative Extension
Steve Brown, Sportfishing and Aquatic Resources Education; Director, Extension Associate, Dept. of Natural Resources, 120 Fernow Hall, Cornell University, Ithaca, NY 14853-3001; 607-255-9370
Tommy Brown, Human Dimensions Research Unit; Sr. Res. Assoc., Dept. of Natural Resources, 122B Fernow Hall, Cornell University, Ithaca, NY 14853-3001; 607-255-7695
Paul Curtis, Wildlife Management; Sr. Extension Associate, Dept. of Natural Resources, 114 Fernow Hall, Cornell University, Ithaca, NY 14853-3001; 607-255-2835; Fax: 607-255-2815
Gary Goff, Forestry/Wildlife; Extension Associate/Director Master Forest Owners/COVERTS Volunteer Program, Dept. of Natural Resources, 104 Fernow Hall, Cornell University, Ithaca, NY 14853-3001; 607-255-2824
David Gross, Protected Area Planning and Management; Sr. Extension Associate & Environmental Program Leader, Department of Natural Resources, 112 Fernow Hall, Cornell University, Ithaca, NY 14853-3001; 607-255-2825
Marianne Krasny, Environmental/Conservation Youth Education; Associate Professor, Dept. of Natural Resources, 16 Fernow Hall, Cornell University, Ithaca, NY 14853-3001; 607-255-2827
Rebecca Schneider, Wetlands; Assistant Professor, Dept. of Natural Resources, 122C Fernow Hall, Cornell University, Ithaca, NY 14853-3001; 607-255-2110
Peter Smallidge, Forestry Resource Management; Sr. Extension Associate, Dept. of Natural Resources, 118 Fernow Hall, Cornell University, Ithaca, NY 14853-3001; 607-255-4696
R. Smith, Agriculture

NEW YORK STATE DEPARTMENT OF AGRICULTURE AND MARKETS
1 Winners Cir.
Albany, NY 12235 United States
Phone: 518-457-3880   Fax: 518-457-3087
E-mail: info@agmkt.state.ny.us
Website: www.agmkt.state.ny.us
Founded: 1884
Membership: 101–1,000
Scope: State
Description: Promotes and regulates production, manufacturing, marketing, storing, and distribution of food. Supervises quality of plant materials, health of animals, and regulates dogs. Also, represents agricultural interests before NY Public Service Commission on siting of transmission lines and power plants.
Publication(s): Available on website
Keyword(s): Agriculture/Farming, Land Issues, Pollution (general), Public Health, Wildlife & Species
Contact(s):
Kim Blot, Director of Division of Agricultural Protection and Support
Robert Mungari, Director of Division of Plant Industry
Jessica Chittenden, Public Information Officer
Nathan Rudgers, Commissioner

NEW YORK STATE FISH AND WILDLIFE MANAGEMENT BOARD
625 Broadway
Albany, NY 12233 United States
Phone: 518-402-8924   Fax: 518-402-9027
E-mail: fwinfo@gw.dec.state.ny.us
Website: www.dec.state.ny.us

Founded: 1957
Scope: State
Description: Membership composed of sportsmen, landowners, and local government representatives. State and regional boards advise the Department of Environmental Conservation in programs designed to improve resource management by landowners and increase public access to private lands.
Keyword(s): Public Lands/Greenspace, Recreation/Ecotourism
Contact(s):
Emory Green, Chairman; 519 Rte. 247, Rushville, NY 14544; 716-554-3362
Lewis Nagy, Vice Chairman; Rte. 1, Box 271-A1, Glenfield, NY 13343; 315-376-3389
Clark Pell, Secretary; 50 Wolf Rd., Albany, NY 12233; 518-457-5420

NEW YORK STATE FISH AND WILDLIFE MANAGEMENT BOARD
REGION 3
2 Ridgeway
Goshen, NY 10924 United States
Phone: 914-294-9360

Contact(s):
Rudy Vallet, Board Chairman

NEW YORK STATE FISH AND WILDLIFE MANAGEMENT BOARD
REGION 4
1150 Westcott Rd.
Schenectady, NY 12306 United States
Phone: 518-357-2234   Fax: 607-547-8814

Scope: State
Contact(s):
Dean Winsor, Board Chaiman

NEW YORK STATE FISH AND WILDLIFE MANAGEMENT BOARD
REGION 5
P.O. Box 123
Paradox, NY 12858 United States
Phone: 518-585-7250   Fax: 518-585-9799

Scope: State, Regional
Contact(s):
Don Sage, Board Chairman

NEW YORK STATE FISH AND WILDLIFE MANAGEMENT BOARD
REGION 6
Harrisville, NY 13648 United States
Phone: 315-543-2781   Fax: 315-543-2781
Membership: 1–100
Scope: State
Contact(s):
Kelley Dickinson, Board Chairman

NEW YORK STATE FISH AND WILDLIFE MANAGEMENT BOARD
REGION 7
NYSDEC
1285 Fisher Avenue
Cortland, NY 13045-1090 United States
Phone: 607-753-3095, ext. 298   Fax: 607-753-8532
E-mail: taphelps@gw.dec.state.ny.us

Membership: 1–100
Scope: Regional
Description: This board is an independent, grass-roots organization, consisting of representatives of landowners, sportsmen, and county legislatures from each county and appointed by each county in the state. Board members identify problems related to access, habitat management, and good landowner-sportsman relations in their local areas. They discuss and consider possible solutions to these problems at board meetings, and then seek to resolve them through meaningful action.
Keyword(s): Land Issues
Contact(s):
Craig Tryon, Board Chairman

NEW YORK STATE FISH AND WILDLIFE MANAGEMENT BOARD
REGION 8
6274 E. Avon-Lima Rd
Avon, NY 14414 United States
Phone: 585-226-2466   Fax: 585-226-3905
Website: www.dec.state.ny.us

Membership: 1–100
Scope: Regional
Description: Deals with access and habitat related issues involving private lands.
Contact(s):
James Runyan, Board Chairman; 22 Woodland Park, Pine City, NY 14871-9006; 607-732-6397; jjrunyan@aol.com
Ron Schroder, Secretary; 6274 E. Avon-Lima Rd., Avon, NY 14414; 585-226-5333; Fax: 585-226-3905; rlschrod@gw.dec.state.ny.us

NEW YORK STATE OFFICE OF PARKS, RECREATION AND HISTORIC PRESERVATION
Empire State Plaza Agency Bldg. 1
Albany, NY 12238 United States
Phone: 518-474-0456   Fax: 518-486-2924
Website: www.nysparks.state.ny.us

Membership: 1,001–10,000
Scope: Regional
Description: Administers and operates 151 parks, park preserves, and recreational facilities, three arboretums, and 35 historic sites throughout the state; administers 15 heritage areas in partnership with local communities. Acquires and protects public lands and open space; coordinates athletic programs; develops environmental interpretive programs; maintains a field services bureau which oversees historic resources and National Historic Register entries; administers boating and snowmobiling laws.
Publication(s): New York State Operated Parks, New York State Boat Launching Sites, New York State Boater's Guide, Exploring New York's Past, Historic Sites and Their Programs
Keyword(s): Ethics/Environmental Justice, Land Issues, Recreation/Ecotourism
Contact(s):
Anthony Ellis, Director of Law Enforcement; 518-474-0456
Wendy Gibson, Director of Public Affairs; 518-486-1868
Dominic Jacangelo, Director of Marine, Coastal, and Legislative Program Development; 518-474-7336
Margaret Reilly, Regional Director Long Island Region; 631-669-1000
Winthrop Aldrich, Deputy Commissioner for Historic Preservation; 518-473-5385
Albert Caccese, Deputy Commissioner for Land Management; 518-474-0402
Bernadette Castro, Commissioner; 518-474-0443
Nancy Palumbo, Deputy Commissioner for Administration; 518-474-0430
Julia Stokes, Deputy Commissioner for Operations, Saratoga/Taconic/Palisade; 518-584-2000

NEW YORK STATE TUG HILL COMMISSION
317 Washington St.
Suite 606
Watertown, NY 13601 United States
Phone: 315-785-2380   Fax: 315-785-2574
E-mail: tughill@tughill.org
Website: www.tughill.org
Founded: 1972
Membership: 1–100
Scope: Local
Description: The Tug Hill Commission is a nonregulatory state agency charged with helping local governments, organizations, and citizens shape the future of this rural, 2,100-square-mile region in northern New York State, especially its environment and economy.
Publication(s): Headwaters, Issue Paper Series, Cooperative Rural Planning, Tug Hill Program, The
Keyword(s): Agriculture/Farming, Energy, Forests/Forestry, Land Issues, Recreation/Ecotourism, Sprawl/Urban Planning, Water Habitats & Quality
Contact(s):
  Robert Quinn, Executive Director

NEWFOUNDLAND DEPARTMENT OF FOREST RESOURCES AND AGRIFOODS
ECOSYSTEM HEALTH DIVISION
P.O. Box 8700
St. John's, A1B 4J6 Newfoundland Canada
Phone: 709-729-4715   Fax: 709-729-2076
E-mail: info@gov.nf.ca
Website: www.gov.nf.ca/fra
Contact(s):
  D. Fong, Director; 709-729-1804
  J. Brazil, Senior Biologist, Endangered Species; 709-729-3773
  C. Butler, Senior Biologist, Environmental/Land Use; 709-729-2543

NEWFOUNDLAND DEPARTMENT OF FOREST RESOURCES AND AGRIFOODS
INLAND FISH AND WILDLIFE DIVISION
Bldg. 810, Pleasantville, P.O. Box 8700
St. John's, A1B 4J6 Newfoundland Canada
Description: Objective is to maintain diverse and abundant wildlife populations and wildlife habitat; provide for the safe and sustainable use of wildlife, both consumptive and nonconsumptive; and help create a social environment conducive to effective wildlife conservation.
Publication(s): Newfoundland and Labrador Hunting and Trapping Guide, Endangered Species Poster and brochure series, Newfoundland and Labrador Hunter Education Manual (student and instructor editions)
Contact(s):
  J. Hancock, Director; 709-729-2817
  J. Blake, Manager of Conservation Services; 709-729-3509
  R. Jarvis, Manager of Salmonier Nature Park and Environmental Education; 709-729-6974
  M. Cahill, Chief of Wildlife Management Planning; 709-729-2548
  L. Croke, Supervisor of Administration; 709-729-2636
  K. Curnew, Chief of Inland Fish; 709-729-2540
  R. Gulliver, Supervisor of Licencing; 709-729-2630
  S. Mahoney, Chief of Research and Inventory; 709-729-3593
  M. Mcgrath, Senior Biologist, Small Game/Fur; 709-729-0748
  M. Vanzyll de Jong, Senior Biologist, Inland Fish; 709-729-4306

NEWFOUNDLAND DEPARTMENT OF FOREST RESOURCES AND AGRIFOODS
LEGISLATION AND COMPLIANCE DIVISION
P.O. Box 8700
St. Johns, A1B 4J6 Newfoundland Canada
Phone: 709-729-2647   Fax: 709-729-6108
Scope: Province
Contact(s):
  R. Whitten, Director; 709-729-2647

NEWFOUNDLAND DEPARTMENT OF FOREST RESOURCES AND AGRIFOODS
REGIONAL OFFICES
P.O. Box 2222
Gander, A1V 2N9 Newfoundland Canada
Phone: 709-256-1450   Fax: 709-256-1459
Membership: 1–100
Scope: Province
Contact(s):
  K. Colbert, Labrador Director, Goose Bay; 709-896-3405
  David Fong, Eastern Director, Gander; 709-256-1451
  A. Masters, Western Director, Corner Brook; 709-637-2370
  D. Leboubon, Regional Compliance Manager; 709-896-2541
  R. Trask, Regional Compliance Manager; 709-256-1461

NIAGARA ESCARPMENT COMMISSION
232 Guelph St.
3rd Floor
Georgetown, L7G 4B1 Ontario Canada
Phone: 905-877-5191   Fax: 905-873-7452
E-mail: nec@escarpment.org
Website: www.escarpment.org
Founded: 1973
Scope: State
Description: Maintains the Niagara Escarpment and land in its vicinity substantially as a continuous natural environment, and ensures that only such development occurs as is compatible with that natural environment. The commission was established under the Niagara Escarpment Planning and Development Act. In 1990, the Niagara Escarpment was designated a World Biosphere Reserve.
Publication(s): Explorer Brochures, Ontario Niagara Escarpment, Annual Reports
Contact(s):
  Mark Frawley, Director; ext. 224
  Richard Murzin, Manager of Commission
  Shannon Cassidy, Public Affairs Officer;
    webmaster@escarpment.org
  Don Scott, Chair; ext. 222

NORTH CAROLINA COOPERATIVE EXTENSION SERVICE
North Carolina State University,
Box 7602 NCSU
Raleigh, NC 27695 United States
Phone: 919-515-2811   Fax: 919-515-3135
Website: www.ces.ncsu.edu
Scope: State
Description: Cooperative Extension Service
Keyword(s): Agriculture/Farming, Forests/Forestry, Land Issues, Oceans/Coasts/Beaches, Public Health, Public Lands/Greenspace, Recreation/Ecotourism, Reduce/Reuse/Recycle, Sprawl/Urban Planning, Water Habitats & Quality, Wildlife & Species
Contact(s):
  Ronald Hodson, Director of Sea Grant Program; Sea Grant, Box 8605, North Carolina State University, Raleigh, NC 27695; 919-515-2455; Fax: 919-515-7095; ronald_hodson@ncsu.edu
  Edwin Jones, Asst. Director

Jon Ort, Director of Extension Service; jon_ort@ncsu.edu
Peter Bromley, Wildlife Specialist; Zoology Dept., Box 7646, North Carolina State University, Raleigh, NC 27695; 919-515-7587; Fax: 919-515-5110; pete_bromley@ncsu.edu
Roger Crickenberger, Assistant Director and State Program Leader; NCSU, Box 7602, Raleigh, NC 27695-7602; 919-515-3252; Fax: 919-515-5950; roger_crickenberger@ncsu.edu
Harry Daniels, Aquaculture Specialist; Vernon James Research and Extension Center, 207 Research Station Rd., Plymouth, NC 27962; 252-793-4428; Fax: 252-793-5142; harry_daniels@ncsu.edu
Jeffrey Hinshaw, Extension Trout Specialist; Research and Extension Center, Box 9628, 2016 Fanning Bridge Rd., Fletcher, NC 28732-9216; 828-684-3562; Fax: 828-684-8715; jeff_hinshaw@ncsu.edu
Thomas Losordo, Aquaculture Specialist; Box 7646, North Carolina State University, Raleigh, NC 29695; 919-515-7587; Fax: 919-515-5110; tlosordo@unity.ncsu.edu
Chris Moorman, Extension Wildlife Specialist; North Carolina State University, Box 8003, Raleigh, NC 27695; 919-515-5578; Fax: 919-515-6883; chris_moorman@ncsu.edu
James Rice, Extension Fisheries Specialist; Box 7617, North Carolina State University, Raleigh, NC 27695; 919-515-4592; Fax: 919-515-5327; jim_rice@ncsu.edu

NORTH CAROLINA COOPERATIVE FISH AND WILDLIFE RESEARCH UNIT (USDI)
201 David Clark Lab
Raleigh, NC 27695 United States
Phone: 919-515-2631   Fax: 919-515-4454
Website: www2.ncsu.edu/nccoopunit

Membership: 1–100
Scope: State
Contact(s):
Tom Kwak, Unit Leader
Wendy Moore, Administrative Assistant

NORTH CAROLINA DEPARTMENT OF AGRICULTURE AND CONSUMER SERVICES
2 W. Edenton ST
Raleigh, NC 27601 United States
Phone: 919-733-7125   Fax: 919-733-1141
Website: www.agr.state.nc.us

Membership: 1,001–10,000
Scope: State
Keyword(s): Agriculture/Farming, Land Issues, Pollution (general), Public Health
Contact(s):
Mike Blanton, Director; 919-733-4216
Jim Burnette, Pesticide Section Staff; 919-733-3556
Bill Dickerson, Plant Industry Division Staff; 919-733-3933
Tom Ellis, Aquaculture & Natural Resources Staff; 919-733-7125
Carl Falco, Structural Pest Staff; 919-733-6100
Cecil Frost, Plant Conservation Program Staff; 919-733-3610
David Marshall, Veterinary Services Staff; 919-733-7601
William McClelland, Pesticide Disposal Staff; 919-733-7366
David McLeod, Legal Staff; 919-733-7125
Richard Reich, Agronomic Services Staff; 919-733-2655
Carl Tart, Research Stations Staff; 919-733-3236
Bruce Williams, Food and Drug Protection Staff; 919-733-7366
Britt Cobb, Interim Commissioner; 919-733-7125

NORTH CAROLINA DEPARTMENT OF ENVIRONMENT AND NATURAL RESOURCES
1601 Mail Services Center
Raleigh, NC 27699-1601 United States
Phone: 919-733-4984   Fax: 919-715-3060
E-mail: denr.csc@ncmail.net
Website: www.enr.state.nc.us

Scope: State
Description: The N.C. Department of Environment and Natural Resources (DENR) is the lead stewardship agency for the preservation and protection of North Carolina's natural resources. The organization administers regulatory and technical assistance programs designed to protect air quality, water quality, and the public's health. Through its natural resource divisions, DENR works to protect fish, wildlife and wilderness areas.
Keyword(s): Executive/Legislative/Judicial Reform
Contact(s):
Stanford Adams, Director of Forest Resources; 919-733-2162
Betsy Bennett, Director of Museum of Natural Sciences; 919-733-7450
Laura DeVivo, Director Legislative Affairs; 715-4189
Charles Fullwood,, Executive Director of Wildlife Resources Commission; 919-733-3391
Charles Gardner, Director of Land Resources; 919-733-3833
Beverley Hall, Acting Director of Division of Radiation Protection; 919-571-4141
Gary Hunt, Director of Office of Pollution Prevention; 919-715-4100
David Jones, Director of Zoological Park; 910-879-7102
Dexter Matthews, Director of Division of Waste Management; 919-733-4996
Phil McKnelly, Director of State Parks and Recreation; 919-733-4181
Donna Moffitt, Director of Coastal Management; 919-733-2293
John Morris, Director of Division of Water Resources; 919-733-4064
Preston Pate, Director of Division of Marine Fisheries; 919-726-7021
Don Reuter, Director of Public Affairs; 919-715-4112
Richard Rogers, Director of Open Spaces; 715-4152
Anne Taylor, Director of Office of Environmental Education; 919-733-0711
Greg Thorpe, Acting Director of Environmental Water Quality; 919-733-7015
David Vogel, Director of Soil and Water Conservation; 919-733-2302
Rhett White, Director of North Carolina Aquariums; 919-733-2290
Dempsey Benton, Chief Deputy Secretary; 919-733-4984
Melanie Buckingham, Librarian
Jimmy Carter, Assistant Secretary, Operations and Development; 919-733-4908
Dan Oakley, General Counsel; 919-715-4142
Bill Ross, Secretary; 919-715-4101
Robin Smith, Assistant Secretary for Planning/Policy; 919-715-4141

NORTH CAROLINA DIVISION OF SOIL AND WATER
STATE SOIL AND WATER CONSERVATION COMMISSION
1614 Mail Service Center
Raleigh, NC 27699-1614 United States
Phone: 919-733-2302   Fax: 919-715-3559
Website: www.ehnr.state.nc.us/DSWC/

Founded: 1937
Membership: 1–100
Scope: State
Description: A unit of state government administered by the Division of Soil and Water Conservation in the Department of Environment and Natural Resources. To organize soil and water conservation districts; grant funds for operations, technical assistance, and the NC Agriculture Cost-Share Program for Nonpoint Source Pollution Control—a water quality program; provide for control of soil erosion and improvement of water quality; accept PL566 Small Watershed applications.

STATE AND PROVINCIAL GOVERNMENT AGENCIES – N

Contact(s):
David Vogel, Director; 919-715-6097; Fax: 919-715-3559; david.vogel@ncmail.net
James Ferguson, Chairman; 11571 Betsy Gap Rd., Clyde, NC 28721; 704-627-6458

NORTH CAROLINA WILDLIFE RESOURCES COMMISSION
1701 Mail Service Center
Raleigh, NC 27699-1701 United States
Phone: 919-733-3391   Fax: 919-733-7083
Website: www.ncwildlife.org

Founded: 1947
Membership: 101–1,000
Scope: State
Description: The commission has the function, purpose, and duty to manage, restore, develop, cultivate, conserve, protect, and regulate the wildlife resources of the state, and to administer the laws relating to boating, hunting, fishing, and other wildlife resources, including nongame.
Publication(s): Wildlife in North Carolina
Keyword(s): Agriculture/Farming, Ecosystems (precious), Forests/Forestry, Land Issues, Oceans/Coasts/Beaches, Public Lands/Greenspace, Recreation/Ecotourism, Water Habitats & Quality, Wildlife & Species
Contact(s):
Charles Fullwood, Executive Director
Carol Batker, Personnel Officer; 919-733-2241
David Cobb, Chief of Division of Wildlife Management; 919-733-7291
Cecilia Edgar, Deputy Director; 1702 Mail Service Center, Raleigh, NC 27699-1702; 919-733-3391; ext. 235; Fax: 919-715-2532; edgarct@mail.wildlife.state.nc.us
Rodney Foushee, Editor, Wildlife in North Carolina; 919-733-7123; ext. 268; Fax: 919-715-2381; foushee.rodney@coned.wildlife.state.nc.us
Richard Hamilton, Chief Deputy Director; 919-733-3391; ext. 222; Fax: 919-733-7083; hamiltrb@mail.wildlife.state.nc.us
Fred Harris, Chief of Division of Inland Fisheries; 919-733-3633; ext. 275; Fax: 919-715-7643; harrisfa@mail.wildlife.state.nc.us
Roger Lequire, Chief of Division of Enforcement, 919-733-7191
Gordon Myers, Division of Engineering Services; 919-715-3156
John Pechmann, Commission Chairman; 910-483-0107
Wes Seegars, Commission Vice Chairman; 919-735-8211
Ginger Williams, Chief of Division of Conservation Education; 1712 Mail Service Center, Raleigh, NC 27699-1712; 919-733-7123; ext. 258; Fax: 919-715-2381; williams.ginger@coned.wildlife.state.nc.us

NORTH DAKOTA DEPARTMENT OF AGRICULTURE
600 E. Blvd. Ave., Department 602
Bismarck, ND 58505-0020 United States
Phone: 701-328-2231   Fax: 701-328-4567
Website: www.agdepartment.com

Membership: 1–100
Scope: State
Description: The North Dakota Department of Agriculture is the regulating and licensing agency for the agricultural industry in North Dakota.
Contact(s):
Roger Johnson, Commissioner; 701-328-2231; Fax: 701-328-4567; rojohnso@state.nd.us

NORTH DAKOTA DEPARTMENT OF HEALTH
600 E. Blvd. Ave.
Bismarck, ND 58506-5520 United States
Phone: 701-328-2372   Fax: 701-328-4727
Website: www.health.state.nd.us

Membership: 101–1,000
Scope: State
Description: State pollution control programs.
Keyword(s): Air Quality/Atmosphere, Ethics/Environmental Justice, Pollution (general), Public Health, Reduce/Reuse/Recycle, Water Habitats & Quality
Contact(s):
Dennis Fewless, Director of Division of Water Quality; P.O. Box 5520, Bismarck, ND 58506-5520; 701-328-5210; Fax: 701-328-5200
Wayne Kern, Director of Division of Waste Management; P.O. Box 5520, Bismarck, ND 58506-5520; 701-328-5166; Fax: 701-328-5200
Jack Long, Director of Division of Municipal Facilities; P.O. Box 5520, Bismarck, ND 58506-5520; 701-328-5211; Fax: 701-328-5200
Terry O'Clair, Director of Divison of Air Quality; P.O. Box 5520, Bismarck, ND 58506-5520; 701-328-5188; Fax: 701-328-5200
L. David Glatt, Chief Environmental Health Section; P.O. Box 5520, Bismarck, ND 58506-5520; 701-328-5150; Fax: 701-328-5200

NORTH DAKOTA FOREST SERVICE
307 First St. E.
Bottineau, ND 58318-1100 United States
Phone: 701-228-5422   Fax: 701-228-5448
E-mail: forest@state.nd.us
Website: www.state.nd.us/forest

Founded: 1891
Membership: 1–100
Scope: State
Description: Mission Statement: Caring for, protecting, and improving forest resources for future generations.
Publication(s): Prairie Forester, The
Keyword(s): Forests/Forestry, Public Lands/Greenspace, Wildlife & Species
Contact(s):
Roy Laframboise, Towner Nursery Manager; 878 Nursery Rd., Towner, ND 58788, 701-537-5636; Fax: 701 537 5680
Thomas Berg, Staff Forester; 701-228-5483
Thomas Claeys, Sustainable Forestry Coordinator, 701-228-5486; Fax: 701-228-5448
Glenda Fauske, Information and Education Coordinator; 701 228-5446
W. Jackson Bird, Community Forestry Coordinator; 1511 E. Interstate Ave., Bismarck, ND 58501; 701-328-9945; Fax: 701-250-4454
Thomas Karch, State Forest Coordinator
Larry Kotchman, State Forester; 701-228-5422
Michael Santucci, Fire Management Coordinator; 1511 E. Interstate Ave., Bismarck, ND 58501; 701-328-9946

NORTH DAKOTA GAME AND FISH DEPARTMENT
100 N. Bismarck Expressway
Bismarck, ND 58501 United States
Phone: 701-328-6300   Fax: 701-328-6352
Website: www.discovernd.com/gnf

Membership: 101–1,000
Scope: State
Description: To protect, conserve and enhance fish and wildlife populations and their habitats for sustained public consumptive and nonconsumptive use.
Keyword(s): Oceans/Coasts/Beaches, Water Habitats & Quality

Contact(s):
  Dean Hildebrand, Director
  Ray Goetz, Chief of Enforcement
  Randy Kreil, Chief of Wildlife
  Mike McKenna, Chief of Conservation & Communication
  Roger Rostvet, Deputy Director
  Paul Schadewald, Chief of Administrative Services
  Terry Steinwand, Chief of Fisheries
  Ron Wilson, Editor

NORTH DAKOTA PARKS AND RECREATION DEPARTMENT
1600 E. Century Ave
Suite 3
Bismarck, ND 58503 United States
Phone: 701-328-5357   Fax: 701-328-5363
E-mail: parkrec@state.nd.us
Website: www.ndparks.com
Founded: 1993
Membership: 1–100
Scope: State
Description: Plan and coordinate government programs encouraging the full development and preservation of existing and future parks, outdoor recreation areas, nature preserves, rare plant and animal species, and unique natural communities.
Publication(s): Discover Newspaper
Keyword(s): Land Issues, Public Lands/Greenspace, Wildlife & Species
Contact(s):
  Douglass Prchal, Director
  Kathy Duttenhefner, Coordinator of Nature Preserve/Natural Heritage Programs
  Jesse Hanson, Coordinator of Planning and Natural Resources

NORTH DAKOTA STATE SOIL CONSERVATION COMMITTEE
2718 Gateway Ave., Unit 104
Bismarck, ND 58503 United States
Phone: 701-328-9715   Fax: 701-328-9721
Website: www.ag.ndsu.nodak.edu/ndsscc/sscc
Founded: 1937
Scope: State
Description: To organize soil conservation districts and provide for control and prevention of soil erosion; represent the state in soil conservation matters; accept P.L. 566 Small Watershed applications and assign planning priority; and administer the Surface Mining Reports Law; and soil conservation technician grants program.
Keyword(s): Agriculture/Farming, Land Issues, Pollution (general), Water Habitats & Quality
Contact(s):
  Thomas Christensen, Vice Chair; 7114 110th Ave. SE, Verona, ND 58490; 701-432-5685; ctomrun@yahoo.com
  Keith Bartholomay, Member; 14618 57th St. SE, Sheldon, ND 58068; 701-882-3460; kbarth@mlgc.com
  Lowell Disrud, Member; 1106 14th St. N, Fargo, ND 58102; 701-293-1505; lowell.disrud@ndsu.nodak.edu
  Russell Fauske, Member; RR1, Box 143, Dunseith, ND 58329; 701-263-4742; rfranch@ndak.net
  Dennis Reich, Member; 4181 82nd Ave. SW, Richardton, ND 58652; 701-878-4397; dreich@westriv.com
  Carol Zuther, Member; 2921 19th Ave. SE, Martin, ND 58758; 701-693-2341; zuther@martin.ndak.net
  Scott Hochhalter, Soil Conservation Specialist; 701-328-5125; Fax: 701-328-5123; shochhal@ndsuext.nodak.edu
  Curtiss Klein, Chairperson; 6025 4th St. SE, Carrington, ND 58421; 701-984-2669; cklein@daktel.com

NORTH DAKOTA WATER COMMISSION
900 E. Blvd. Ave.
Bismarck, ND 58505-0850 United States
Phone: 701-328-2750   Fax: 701-328-3696
Website: www.swc.state.nd.us
Founded: 1905
Membership: 1–100
Scope: State
Description: State Agency: water rights, water development, floodplain management, dam safety.
Keyword(s): Air Quality/Atmosphere, Pollution (general), Recreation/Ecotourism, Wildlife & Species
Contact(s):
  Dale Frink, State Engineeer

NORTHERN VIRGINIA REGIONAL PARK AUTHORITY
5400 Ox Rd.
Fairfax Station, VA 22039 United States
Phone: 703-352-5900   Fax: 703-273-0905
E-mail: info@nvrpa.org
Website: www.nvrpa.org
Founded: 1959
Scope: Regional
Description: To preserve open and wooded areas and provide outdoor recreation to meet the needs of a growing population.
Publication(s): Discover Your Regional Parks, Washington and Old Dominion Railroad Regional Park Trail Guide, Policy Plan, Calendar of Events
Keyword(s): Land Issues, Recreation/Ecotourism, Wildlife & Species
Contact(s):
  Gary Fenton, Executive Director; 703-359-4605; gfenton@nvrpa.org
  Walter Mess, Chairman

NORTHWEST TERRITORIES DEPARTMENT OF RESOURCES, WILDLIFE AND ECONOMIC DEVELOPMENT
P.O. Box 1320
Yellowknife, X1A 2L9 Northwest Territories Canada
Phone: 867-873-7379   Fax: 867-873-0114
Website: www.rwed-hq.gov.nt.ca
Scope: Regional
Description: Has broad responsibility for wildlife, environmental protection, forest management, parks and tourism, trade and investment, and minerals, oil, and gas in the Northwest Territories, and provides assistance to people dependent on these resources to harvest wildlife in a manner which will ensure continued availability of the resource.
Publication(s): Safety in Bear Country, Sport Fishing Guide, NWT Wildlife Sketches, NWT Explorers Guide, Summary of Hunting Regulations
Keyword(s): Agriculture/Farming, Air Quality/Atmosphere, Climate Change, Ecosystems (precious), Energy, Executive/Legislative/Judicial Reform, Forests/Forestry, Land Issues, Pollution (general), Public Lands/Greenspace, Recreation/Ecotourism, Reduce/Reuse/Recycle, Wi
Contact(s):
  Susan Corey, Director of Forest Management; Box 7, Fort Smith, Northwest Territories X0E 0P0; 867-872-7700; Fax: 867-872-2077
  Doris Eggers, Director of Policy and Legislation/Communications; 867-920-8046; Fax: 867-873-0114
  Martin Irving, Director of Diamond Projects; 867-920-3125; Fax: 867-873-0224
  Jim Kennedy, Director of Corporate Service; 867-873-7532; Fax: 867-920-2756
  Gerry LePrieur, Director of Parks and Tourism; 867-873-7902; Fax: 867-873-0163

STATE AND PROVINCIAL GOVERNMENT AGENCIES – O

Doug Matthews, Director of Minerals, Oil and Gas; 867-920-3222; Fax: 867-873-0254

Otto Olah, Director of Investment and Economic Analysis; 867-873-7361; Fax: 867-873-0101

Emery Paquin, Director of Environmental Protection; 867-873-7654; Fax: 867-873-0221

Doug Stewart, Director of Wildlife and Fisheries; 867-920-8064; Fax: 867-873-0293

Jim Antoine, Minister; 867-669-2388; Fax: 867-873-0306; jim_antoine@gov.nt.ca

Robert Bailey, Assistant Deputy Minister, Operations; 867-920-6389; Fax: 867-873-0638

Doug Doan, Assistant Deputy Minister of Resources and Economic Development; 867-873-7115; Fax: 867-873-0114

Lloyd Jones, Regional Superintendent for South Slave; Box 390, Fort Smith, Northwest Territories X0E 0P0; 867-872-6400; Fax: 879-872-4250

Paul Kraft, Regional Superintendent for Deh Cho; Box 240, Fort Simpson, Northwest Territories X0E 0N0; 879-695-2231; Fax: 807-695-2442

Robert McLeod, Deputy Minister; 867-920-8048; Fax: 867-873-0563; bob-mcleod@gov.mt.ca

Ron Morrison, Regional Superintendent for Inuvik; Bag 1, Inuvik, Northwest Territories X0E 0T0; 879-777-7286; Fax: 879-777-7321

Robert Murphy, Regional Superintendent for North Slave, Acting; Box 2668, Yellowknife, Northwest Territories X1A 2P9; 879-920-6134; Fax: 879-873-6230

Celina Stroeder, Regional Superintendent for Sahtu; Box 130, Normal Wells, Northwest Territories X0E 0V0; 879-587-3501; Fax: 879-587-2204

Alison Welch, Librarian; NWT Resources, Wildlife and Economic Development Library, P.O. Box 1320, Yellowknife, Northwest Territories X1A 2L9; 867-920-8606; Fax: 867-873-0293

NORTHWEST TERRITORIES ENVIRONMENTAL PROTECTION SERVICE
AIR POLLUTION PREVENTION
P.O. Box 1320
Yellowknife, X1A 2L9 Northwest Territories Canada
Phone: 867-873-7654   Fax: 867-873-0221
E-mail: llsette_selt@gov.nt.ca
Website: www.gov.nt.ca/RWED/eps/index.htm

Scope: National

Description: Our goal is to protect and enhance the environmental quality in the North.

Contact(s):
D. Egar, Director General; Place Vincent Massey, 10e et., 351 Blvd., St. Joseph, Hull, Quebec K1A 0H3; 819-997-1298; Fax: 819-953-9547

NOVA SCOTIA AGRICULTURE & FISHERIES
P.O. Box 2223
Halifax, B3J 3C4 Nova Scotia Canada
Phone: 902-424-4560   Fax: 902-424-4671
Website: www.gov.ns.ca/nsaf/home.htm

Scope: International

Description: The Department is involved in almost all aspects of the province's fishing industry. It has significant input into some of the policies and programs legislated and administered by the federal government, which has jurisdiction over much of the fishery. The department has jurisdictional responsibility for developing and regulating aquaculture and freshwater recreational fisheries. It is also responsible for the licensing and inspection of fish processing plants. The department provides training,

Publication(s): See publication website

Contact(s):
Jim Sarty, CEO/Fisheries & Aquaculture Loan Board; 902-424-0312

Dave Hansen, Executive Director; 902-424-0337
Murray Hill, Director of Inland Fisheries; 902-485-7021
Leo Muise, Director of Aquaculture; 902-424-3664
Janis Raymond, Acting Director of Marketing Services; 902-424-0330
Greg Roach, Executive Director, Fisheries & Aquaculture Services; 902-424-0348
Ernest Fage, Minister; 902-424-8953
Peter Underwood, Deputy Minister; 902-424-0300

NOVA SCOTIA DEPARTMENT OF NATURAL RESOURCES
P.O. Box 698
Halifax, B3J 2T9 Nova Scotia Canada
Phone: 902-424-5935   Fax: 902-424-7735
E-mail: dnrweb@gov.ns.ca
Website: www.gov.ns.ca/natr

Scope: Local, Province

Description: The Department of Natural Resources has broad responsibilities relative to the development, management, conservation and protection of provincial forest, mineral, parks and wildlife resources and the administration of the province's Crown land.

Publication(s): Nature's Resources

Keyword(s): Ecosystems (precious), Finance/Banking/Trade, Forests/Forestry, Land Issues, Oceans/Coasts/Beaches, Public Lands/Greenspace, Recreation/Ecotourism, Water Habitats & Quality, Wildlife & Species

Contact(s):
Harold Carroll, Director of Parks and Recreation; RR#1, Belmont, Nova Scotia B0M 1C0; 902-662-3030; Fax: 902-662-2160; carrolhe@gov.ns.ca

Brian Gilbort, Executive Director, Regional Services; 902-424-3949; gilbergs@gov.ns.ca

Ed Macaulay, Executive Director, Renewable Resources; 902-424-4103; emmacaul@gov.ns.ca

Nancy McInnis-Leek, Director of Forestry; P.O. Box 68, Truro, Nova Scotia B2N 5B8; 902-893-5749; Fax: 902-893-5662; nrmcinni@gov.ns.ca

Rosalind Penfound, Executive Director, Land Services; 902-424-4267; rcpenfou@gov.ns.ca

Barry Sabean, Director of Wildlife; 136 Exhibition St., Kentville, Nova Scotia B4N 4E5; 902-679-6139; Fax: 902-679-6176; sabeanbc@gov.ns.ca

O

OHIO DEPARTMENT OF AGRICULTURE
8995 E. Main Street
Reynoldsburg, OH 43068 United States
Phone: 614-728-6200   Fax: 614-466-6124
E-mail: agri@odant.agri.state.oh.us
Website: www.state.oh.us/agr

Membership: 101–1,000
Scope: Regional

Contact(s):
Mark Anthony, Communication Director; 614-752-4505
Fred Dailey, Director

OHIO DEPARTMENT OF DEVELOPMENT
OFFICE OF ENERGY EFFICIENCY
77 S. High St.
Columbus, OH 43215 United States
Phone: 614-466-6797   Fax: 614-466-1864
Website: www.odod.state.oh.us

Founded: 1979
Membership: 1–100
Scope: Regional

Description: The Office of Energy Efficiency, Ohio's state energy office, develops policies and programs that use energy efficiency and renewable energy to enhance economic benefits and better Ohio's environment.

Publication(s): 1999 Energy Efficiency Bookmark Contest Winners, Ohio's Home Weatherization Assistance Program (brochure), Ohio's Home Weatherization Assistance Program: An Independent Evaluation

Keyword(s): Air Quality/Atmosphere, Energy, Public Health, Reduce/Reuse/Recycle, Sprawl/Urban Planning, Transportation

Contact(s):
Tim Lenahan, Residential Programs; 614-466-8434; tlenahan@odod.state.oh.us
Bill Manz, Commercial/Industrial Programs; 614-466-7429; wmanz@odod.state.oh.us
Dawn Smith, Assistant Chief; 614-466-1835; dsmith@odod.state.oh.us
Stjepan Vlahovich, Education Programs; 614-466-0545; svlahovich@odod.state.oh.us
Sara Ward, Chief; 614-466-8396; sward@odod.state.oh.us

OHIO DEPARTMENT OF NATURAL RESOURCES

1930 Belcher Dr. Fountain Square
Bldg. D
Columbus, OH 43224-1387 United States
Phone: 614-265-6565   Fax: 614-261-9601
E-mail: dnrmail@dnr.state.oh.us
Website: www.ohiodnr.com

Founded: 1949
Scope: State
Description: The mission of the Ohio Department of Natural Resources is to ensure a balance between the wise use and protection of Ohio's natural resources for the benefit of all.
Publication(s): Wild Ohio
Keyword(s): Ecosystems (precious), Energy, Forests/Forestry, Land Issues, Oceans/Coasts/Beaches, Pollution (general), Public Lands/Greenspace, Recreation/Ecotourism, Reduce/Reuse/Recycle, Water Habitats & Quality, Wildlife & Species

Contact(s):
Samuel Speck, Director; 614-265-6875; Fax: 614-261-9601
J. Moody, Assistant Director; 614-265-6877
Lori Houpe, Deputy Director; 614-265-6845
David Pagnard, Chief of Office of Communications; 614-265-6787; Fax: 614-267-9165
Scott Zody, Deputy Director; 614-265-6845
Jim Lynch, Media Relations Mgr.; 614-265-6886; Fax: 614-268-1943
Ken Alvey, Chief of Division of Watercraft; 614-265-6480
Paul Baldridge, Chief of Division of Real Estate and Land Management; 614-265-6395
Dick Bartz, Chief of Division of Water; 614-265-6717; dick.bartz@dnr.state.oh.us
Thomas Berg, Chief of Division of Geological Survey; 614-265-6576
John Dorka, Chief of Division of Forestry; 614-265-6694
Steve Gray, Chief of Division of Wildlife; 614-265-6300
David Hanselmann, Chief of Division of Soil and Water Conservation; 614-265-6618
Ron Kolbash, Chief of Division of Recycling and Litter Prevention; 614-265-6333
David Mackey, Chief of Office of Coastal Management; 105 W. Shoreline Drive, Sandusky, OH 44870; 419-626-4670; Fax: 419-626-7983
Steve Manilla, Chief of Division of Engineering; 614-265-6948
Mike Sponsler, Chief of Division of Mineral Resources Management; 614-265-6633
Nancy Strayer, Acting Chief of Division of Natural Areas and Preserves; 614-265-6453
Dan West, Chief of Division of Parks and Recreation; 614-265-6561
Michele Willis, Asst. to Director for Water and Great Lakes Issues; 614-265-6894

OHIO ENVIRONMENTAL PROTECTION AGENCY

122 South Front Street
Columbus, OH 43215 United States
Phone: 614-644-3020   Fax: 614-644-3184
Website: www.epa.state.oh.us

Founded: 1972
Scope: State
Description: The mission of the Ohio Environmental Protection Agency is to protect the environment and public health by ensuring compliance with environmental laws and demonstrating leadership in environmental stewardship. This state agency implements laws and regulations regarding air and water quality; solid, hazardous and infectious waste disposal; water quality planning; sewage treatment and public drinking water supplies; and cleanup of unregulated hazardous waste sites.
Keyword(s): Agriculture/Farming, Air Quality/Atmosphere, Land Issues, Oceans/Coasts/Beaches, Pollution (general), Reduce/Reuse/Recycle, Water Habitats & Quality

Contact(s):
Christopher Jones, Director; 614-644-2782
John Albrecht, Chief of Information Technology Services; 614-644-2990
Michael Baker, Chief of Division of Drinking and Ground Waters; 614-644-2752
Bruce Coleman, Chief of Central District Office; 614-728-3778
Bonnie Crockett, Chief of Operations and Facilities; 614-644-2089
Al Franks, Chief of Strategic Management; 614-644-2782
Linda Friedman, Chief of Division of Environmental Services; 614-644-4247
Chris Geyer, Chief of Office of Fiscal Administration; 614-644-2339
Cindy Hafner, Chief of Division of Emergency and Remedial Response; 614-644-2924
Karen Haight, Chief of Office of Employee Services; 614-644-2100
Edwin Hammett, Chief of Northwest District Office; 419-352-8461
Daniel Harris, Chief of Division of Solid and Infectious Waste; 614-644-2621
Carol Hester, Chief of Public Interest Center; 614-644-2160
Robert Hodanbosi, Chief of Division of Air Pollution Control; 614-644-2270
Jacqueline Hymes, Chief of Equal Employment Opportunity; 614-644-3553
Mike Kelley, Chief of Office of Pollution Prevention; 614-644-3469
Joseph Koncelik, Assistant Director; 614-644-2782
Patricia Madigan, Deputy Director of Communication; 614-644-2782
Lisa Morris, Chief of Division of Surface Water; 614-644-2001
Laura Powell, Deputy Director of Policy; 614-644-2782
Michael Savage, Chief of Division of Hazardous Waste Management; 614-644-2917
Steve Skinner, Chief of Southeast District Office; 740-385-8501
Bill Skowronski, Chief of Northeast District Office; 330-963-1200
Greg Smith, Chief of Division of Environmental and Financial Assistance; 614-644-2798
Christine Snider, Executive Assistant to the Director; 614-644-2782
Edmund Tormey, Chief of Legal Affairs; 614-644-3037
Carolyn Watkins, Chief of Office of Environmental Education; 614-644-2873
Tom Winston, Chief of Southwest District Office; 937-285-6357

OHIO ENVIRONMENTAL REVIEW APPEALS COMMISSION
309 S. Fourth St., Room 222
Columbus, OH 43215 United States
Phone: 614-466-8950 Fax: 614-466-8362
Founded: 1972
Scope: Local, State
Description: The Environmental Review Appeals Commission is an administrative commission designed to review the actions of the Ohio EPA, State Fire Marshal, and the various county boards of health charged with environmental jurisdiction in order to determine that the agencies' actions have been reasonable and lawful.

OHIO STATE UNIVERSITY EXTENSION
2120 Fyffe Rd.
Columbus, OH 43210 United States
Phone: 614-292-6181 Fax: 614-688-3807
Website: www.ag.ohio-state.edu/
Membership: 101–1,000
Scope: State
Description: To help people improve their lives through an educational process using scientific knowledge focused on identified issues and needs.
Keyword(s): Agriculture/Farming, Air Quality/Atmosphere, Climate Change, Development/Developing Countries, Ecosystems (precious), Energy, Forests/Forestry, Land Issues, Oceans/Coasts/Beaches, Pollution (general), Public Health, Public Lands/Greenspace, Recreation/Eco
Contact(s):
Gary Mullins, Director of School of Natural Resources; Ohio State University, 210 Kottman Hall, 2021 Coffey Rd., Columbus, OH 43210; 614-292-2265; Fax: 614-292-7432; mullins.2@osu.edu
Keith Smith, Director of Extensions; smith.150@osu.edu
Donald Eckert, Associate Director of School of Natural Resources; School of Natural Resources, the Ohio State University, 2021 Coffey Rd., Columbus, OH 43210-1085; 614-292-9048; Fax: 614-292-7432; eckert.1@osu.edu

OKLAHOMA DEPARTMENT OF AGRICULTURE
P.O. Box 528004
Oklahoma City, OK 73152-8804 United States
Phone: 405-521-3864 Fax: 405-522-0909
Website: www.oda.state.ok.us
Membership: 101–1,000
Scope: State
Description: The Oklahoma Department of Agriculture is principally a service agency, but it is also a promotional and cooperative agency for segments of agriculture and forestry. Major divisions of the department are forestry, animal industry, legal, plant industry, marketing, water quality, agriculture laboratory, and the federal-state cooperative programs of wildlife services and agricultural statistics.
Keyword(s): Agriculture/Farming, Forests/Forestry, Pollution (general), Reduce/Reuse/Recycle
Contact(s):
Barry Bloyd, Director of Agricultural Statistics; 405-525-9226
Roger Davis, Director of Forestry Services; 405-521-3864
Burke Healey, Director of Animal Industry Services; 405-521-3864
Rick Maloney, Director of Market Development 414 Services
John Steuber, Director of Wildlife Services; 405-521-4039
Janet Stewart, Director of Legal Services
Mike Talkington, Director of Agricultural Laboratory
David Ligon, Administration Staff; 405-521-3864; ext. 220
Jack Carson, Information Officer; 405-521-3864; ext. 220
Lynn Davis, Assistant Director; 405-522-5486
Charles Freeman, Deputy Commissioner; 405-521-3864
Dennis Howard, Secretary of Agriculture

OKLAHOMA BIOLOGICAL SURVEY
OKLAHOMA NATURAL HERITAGE INVENTORY
SUTTON AVIAN RESEARCH CENTER
ROBERT BEBB HERBARIUM
111 E. Chesapeake St., University of Oklahoma
Norman, OK 73019 United States
Phone: 405-325-4034 Fax: 405-325-7702
Website: www.biosurvey.ou.edu
Founded: 1927
Scope: State
Description: State office and organized research unit of university. Acquires information on biological resources and natural areas, conducts research on natural biota, jointly maintains Bebb Herbarium, has responsibility for Oklahoma Natural Heritage Inventory, and provides training for students. Jointly operates Oklahoma Fishery Research Laboratory with Oklahoma Department of Wildlife Conservation.
Keyword(s): Reduce/Reuse/Recycle, Wildlife & Species
Contact(s):
Steve Sherrod, Executive Director of Sutton Avian Research Center; G.M. Sutton Avian Research Center, P.O. Box 2007, Bartlesville, OK 74005-2007; 918-336-7778; Fax: 918-336-7783; gmsarc@aol.com
Caryn Vaughn, Director; 405-325-4034; Fax: 405-325-7702; cvaughn@ou.edu
Bruce Hoagland, Coordinator of Oklahoma Natural Heritage Inventory; 405-325-1985; Fax: 405-325-7702; bhoagland@ou.edu
Wayne Elisens, Interim Curator, Robert Bebb Herbarium; Dept. of Botany/Microbiology, 770 Van Vleet Oval, University of Oklahoma, Norman, OK 73019; 405-325-5923; Fax: 405-325-7619; elisens@ou.edu

OKLAHOMA CONSERVATION COMMISSION
STATE OF OKLAHOMA
CONSERVATION COMMISSION
STATE CONSERVATION AGENCY
2800 N. Lincoln Blvd., Suite 160
Oklahoma City, OK 73105 United States
Phone: 405-521-2384 Fax: 405-521-6686
E-mail: markh@okcc.state.ok.us
Website: www.okcc.state.ok.us
Founded: 1937
Membership: 1–100
Scope: Local, State
Description: To assist and supervise the state's 88 local conservation districts in carrying out conservation practices of all renewable natural resources.
Publication(s): Conservation Conversation Newsletter, Geographic Information Systems Newsletter
Keyword(s): Agriculture/Farming, Land Issues, Pollution (general), Water Habitats & Quality
Contact(s):
Mike Thralls, Executive Director; 405-521-2384; Fax: 405-521-6686; miket@okcc.state.ok.us
Ben Pollard, Assistant Director; benp@okcc.state.ok.us
Lawrence Edmison, Director of Water Quality Division; larrye@okcc.state.ok.us
Mike Kastl, Director of Abandoned Mine Land Reclamation Program Division; mikek@okcc.state.ok.us
Lisa Knauf, Director of District Services Division; lisak@okcc.state.ok.us
Dan Sebert, Director of Conservation Programs Division; dans@okcc.state.ok.us
Mike Sharp, Director of Information Technology Division; mikes@okcc.state.ok.us
Mark Harrison, Information Officer; markh@okcc.state.ok.us
Virginia Kidd, Commission Board Chair

OKLAHOMA COOPERATIVE FISH AND WILDLIFE RESEARCH UNIT (USDI)
404 Life Sciences West Bldg., Oklahoma State University
Department of Zoology
Stillwater, OK 74078-3051 United States
Phone: 405-744-6342 Fax: 405-744-5006

Founded: 1948
Membership: 1–100
Scope: State, Regional, National, International
Description: Involved in graduate education in resource conservation.
Keyword(s): Wildlife & Species
Contact(s):
William Fisher, Assistant Leader, Ecology
David Leslie, Leader
Dana Winkleman, Assistant Leader, Fisheries

OKLAHOMA DEPARTMENT OF ENVIRONMENTAL QUALITY
1000 NE 10th St.
Oklahoma City, OK 73117-1212 United States
Phone: 405-271-8056
Website: www.deq.state.ok.us

Description: The Department of Environmental Quality is dedicated to providing quality service to the people of Oklahoma through comprehensive environmental protection and management programs. Those programs are designed to assist the people of the state in sustaining a clean sound environment and in preserving and enhancing our natural surroundings.
Publication(s): Clear View, Air Quality Annual Report, Superfund Program Sites Status Report, Certified Operator News Letter (Waterworks and Wastewater)
Keyword(s): Air Quality/Atmosphere, Pollution (general), Reduce/Reuse/Recycle, Water Habitats & Quality
Contact(s):
Ellen Bussert, Director of Public Information and Education; 405-271-8056
Larry Byrum, Director of Air Quality; 405-271-5220
H.A. Caves, Director of Waste Management; 405-271-5338
Mark Coleman, Executive Director; 405-271-8056
Jon Craig, Director of Water Quality; 405-271-5205
Judy Duncan, Director of Customer Services; 405-271-1400
Lawrence Gales, Director of Support Services; 405-271-8062
Larry McKee, Director of Complaints and Local Services; 405-271-7363
Steven Thompson, Deputy Executive Director; 405-271-8056
Bob Kellogg, General Counsel; 405-271-8056

OKLAHOMA DEPARTMENT OF WILDLIFE CONSERVATION
1801 N. Lincoln, P.O. Box 53465
Oklahoma City, OK 73152 United States
Phone: 405-521-3851 Fax: 405-521-6535
E-mail: pmoore@odwc.state.ok.us
Website: www.wildlifedepartment.com

Founded: 1909
Membership: 101–1,000
Scope: Regional
Publication(s): Outdoor Oklahoma
Keyword(s): Recreation/Ecotourism, Water Habitats & Quality, Wildlife & Species
Contact(s):
Greg Duffy, Director; 405-521-4660
Ed Abel, Commission Secretary
Kyle Eastham, Human Resrources Administrator; 405-521-4640
Kim Erickson, Chief of Fisheries; 405-521-3721
Richard Hatcher, Assistant Director; 405-522-6279
Vyrl Keeter, Vice Chairman
Alan Peoples, Chief Wildlife Division; 405-521-2739
Nels Rodefeld, Editor; 405-521-4635
Harlan Stonecipher, Commissioner Chairman
John Streich, Chief of Law Enforcement; 405-521-3719
Melinda Sturgess-Streich, Chief of Administation; 405-521-4640
Ron Suttles, Natural Resources Coordinator; 405-521-4616
David Warren, Chief of Information-Education; 405-521-3855

OKLAHOMA GEOLOGICAL SURVEY
University of Oklahoma, Sarkeys Energy Center
100 E. Boyd, Rm. N-131
Norman, OK 73019-0628 United States
Phone: 405-325-3031 Fax: 405-325-7689
Website: www.ou.edu/special/ogs-pttc/

Founded: 1908
Membership: 1–100
Scope: State
Description: To investigate and disseminate information on the geology of the state, with special reference to mineral resources and environmental issues. Investigations include: geologic mapping, evaluation of metallic and nonmetallic mineral deposits, and studies of earthquakes, groundwater, and fossil fuels, plus basic research and environmental studies.
Publication(s): Oklahoma Geology Notes, bulletins, circulars, guidebooks, geologic map series, educational publications series, hydrologic atlases
Keyword(s): Energy, Land Issues
Contact(s):
Charles Mankin, Director
Claren Kidd, Librarian; 100 E. Boyd, Rm. 220, Norman, OK 73019-0628
Connie Smith, Promotion and Information Specialist
Joyce Stiehler, Chief Publications Clerk; 405-360-2886; ogssales@ou.edu

OKLAHOMA STATE EXTENSION SERVICES
DIVISION OF AGRICULTURE
Oklahoma State University, Rm. 139, Agricultural Hall
Stillwater, OK 74078 United States
Phone: 405-744-5398 Fax: 405-744-5339
E-mail: securl@okstate.edu
Website: www.dasnr.okstate.edu

Founded: 1946
Scope: International
Description: Extension Forestry and Wildlife are a unit of the Oklahoma Cooperative Extension Service and the Department of Forestry, Division of Agricultural Sciences and Natural Resources, Oklahoma State University. The Department of Forestry provides accredited education in forest resources management, conducts forestry research through the Oklahoma Agricultural Experiment Station, and brings forest resources education to the citizens of Oklahoma through its extension efforts.
Publication(s): OSU Extension Fact Sheets, Oklahoma Renewable Resources newsletter
Keyword(s): Forests/Forestry, Water Habitats & Quality, Wildlife & Species
Contact(s):
Sam Curl, Director of Cooperative Extension Service; Oklahoma State University, DASNR, 139 Agricultural Hall, Stillwater 74078; 405-744-5398
David Foster, Assoc. Director for Oklahoma Cooperative Extension Services; Oklahoma State University, DASNR, 139 Agricultural Hall, Stillwater, OK 74078; 405-744-5398
Marley Beem, Asst. Extension Specialist; 405-744-9636; Fax: 405-744-3530; beem@okstate.edu
Kenneth Hitch, Assistant Extension Forester and Wildlife Specialist; Oklahoma State University, Rm. 008C, Agricultural Hall, Stillwater, OK 74078; 405-744-5442
Craig McKinley, Department Head of Forestry; Oklahoma State University, Rm. 011, Agricultural Hall, Stillwater, OK 74078; 405-744-5438

William Ross, Forestry Extension Specialist; Oklahoma State University, Rm. 008C, Agricultural Hall, Stillwater, OK 74078; 405-744-3854; Fax: 405-744-3530; rossw@okstate.edu

OKLAHOMA TOURISM AND RECREATION DEPARTMENT
15 N. Robinson
Oklahoma City, OK 73102 United States
Phone: 405-521-2409   Fax: 405-521-3992
Website: www.travelok.com

Founded: 1972
Membership: 1–100
Scope: State
Description: To encourage residents and travelers to visit Oklahoma as a vacation destination; and to develop human and natural resources for the purpose of promoting tourism, recreation, wildlife preservation, and environmental conservation. An annual industry conference is held each fall.
Publication(s): Oklahoma State Parks & Resorts Guide, Guide to RV Parks, Lakes & Campgrounds, Oklahoma Today, Oklahoma Travel Guide
Keyword(s): Public Lands/Greenspace, Recreation/Ecotourism, Wildlife & Species
Contact(s):
Jeff Erwin, Parks, Resorts & Golf Division; 405-521-3790
Kris Marek, Division of Planning and Development; 405-521-6891
Hardy Watkins, Division of Travel and Tourism; 405-521-3932

OKLAHOMA WATER RESOURCES BOARD
3800 N. Classen Blvd.
Oklahoma City, OK 73118 United States
Phone: 405-530-8800   Fax: 405-530-8900
Website: www.owrb.state.ok.us

Founded: 1957
Membership: 1–100
Scope: State
Description: Promulgates water quality standards for state; lead agency in Clean Lakes Program; investigates pollution complaints; assesses water quality, quantity of groundwater, and stream water; issues permits for water use; administers dam safety, floodplain management programs, and plans for adequate supplies of good quality water for all beneficial uses; updates plans; administers financial assistance programs for water and wastewater systems.
Publication(s): The Well Drillers Log Newsletter, Oklahoma Water News
Keyword(s): Agriculture/Farming, Land Issues, Pollution (general), Water Habitats & Quality
Contact(s):
Duane Smith, Executive Director
Michael Melton, Assistant to the Director

ONTARIO MINISTRY OF NATURAL RESOURCES
300 Water St., 2nd Fl., North Tower
Peterborough, K9J 8M5 Ontario Canada
Phone: 705-755-2363   Fax: 705-755-1640
E-mail: nric@mnr.gov.on.ca
Website: www.mnr.gov.on.ca

Scope: Province
Description: Provides the ministry with leadership in the development and application of scientific knowledge, information management, and information technology. The division also plays a lead role in the provision of land-related information.
Contact(s):
Jim Hamilton, Director; 705-755-2139
Des McKee, Administrator of Science of Information Division; 705-755-1401

ONTARIO MINISTRY OF NATURAL RESOURCES
ALGONQUIN FORESTRY AUTHORITY
222 Main St. W
Huntsville, P1H 1Y1 Andorra
Phone: 705-789-9647   Fax: 705-789-3353
E-mail: huntsville.office@algonquinforestry.on.ca
Website: www.algonquinforestry.on.ca

Scope: Regional
Contact(s):
Carl Corbett, General Manager

ONTARIO MINISTRY OF NATURAL RESOURCES
CORPORATE SERVICES DIVISION
P.O. Box 7000, 300 Water Street
Peterborough, K9J 8M5 Ontario Canada
Phone: 705-755-2505   Fax: 705-755-2508

Scope: Regional
Description: This division facilitates the delivery of ministry programs by providing leadership, strategic advice, and responsive results-oriented services to ministry clients. These services include business planning, audit and evaluation, financial, administrative, legal, and human resources. The division also develops corporate and administrative policies and gives advice on standards, guidelines, planning, and management. It is the primary liaison with the central agencies of government for corporate
Contact(s):
Anne Marie Gutierrez, Director of Legal Services Branch; 416-314-2025
John Kenrick, Director of Finance and Business Branch; 705-755-2505
Dave Lynch, Director of Human Resources Branch; 705-755-3131
Fadia Mishrigi, Communications Services Branch; 416-314-2119

ONTARIO MINISTRY OF NATURAL RESOURCES
FIELD SERVICES DIVISION
435 S. James St., Ste. 221
Ontario, P7E 6S8 Canada

Description: Delivering resource management programs for Ontario's fisheries, wildlife, forests and provincial lands is the responsibility of this division. It is also responsible for the Aviation, Flood, and Fire Management Branch and the Provincial Enforcement Section. The division's structure is highly decentralized with three regional offices, 25 district offices, and 17 area offices located across the province.
Contact(s):
Charlie Lauer, Director of Northwest Region; 807-475-1264
Jack McFadden, Director of Aviation, Flood, and Fire Management; 705-945-5937
Gregg Sons, Director of Enforcement Branch, Acting; 705-755-1750

ONTARIO MINISTRY OF NATURAL RESOURCES
FISH AND WILDLIFE BRANCH
300 Water St.
Peterborough, K9J 8M5 Ontario Canada
Phone: 705-755-1909   Fax: 705-755-1900

Membership: 1–100
Scope: Regional
Contact(s):
Cameron Mack, Director; 705-755-1909; cameron.mack@mnr.gov.on.ca
Dave Maraldo, Manager of Fisheries; dave.maraldo@mnr.gov.on.ca
Deborah Stetson, Manager of Wildlife; 705-755-1925; deb.stetson@mnr.gov.on.ca

ONTARIO MINISTRY OF NATURAL RESOURCES
NATURAL RESOURCE MANAGEMENT DIVISION
99 Wellesley St. W
Toronto, M7A 1W3 Ontario Canada
Phone: 416-314-2624   Fax: 416-314-1994
E-mail: mnr.nric@mnr.gov.on.ca
Website: www.mnr.gov.on.ca/MNR/

Scope: Local, Regional, International

Description: The division is responsible for ensuring that natural resource programs are responsive to the needs of Ontarians and consistent with the ministry's vision of sustainable development and its mission of ecological sustainability. Its mandate covers lands, waters, forests, fish, wildlife, and parks, and includes fish hatcheries, tree nurseries, and the management of the Great Lakes.

Publication(s): Annual Parks Guide, Fishing Regulations Summary, Hunting Regulations Summary, Fish Ontario, Hunt Ontario

Contact(s):
David de Launay, Director of Lands and Waters Branch; Lands and Waters Branch, 300 Water Street, 5th Fl. South Tower, Peterborough, Ontario K9J 8M5; 705-755-1620; Fax: 705-755-1201; david.delaunay@mnr.gov.on.ca
Adair Ireland-Smith, Managing Director of Ontario Parks; Ontario Parks, 300 Water Street, 6th Fl. South Tower, P.O. Box 7000, Peterborough, Ontario K9J 8M5; 705-755-1702; Fax: 705-755-1701; adair.ireland-smith@mnr.gov.on.ca
Cameron Mack, Director of Fish and Wildlife Branch; Fish and Wildlife Branch, 300 Water Street, 5th Floor North Tower, P.O. Box 7000, Peterborough, Ontario K9J 8M5; 705-755-1909; Fax: 705-755-1845; cameron.mack@mnr.gov.on.ca
Peter Wallace, Assistant Deputy Minister; 99 Wellesley St. W., Toronto, Ontario M7A 1W3; 416-314-6131; Fax: 416-314-1994; peter.wallace@mnr.gov.on.ca

ONTARIO MINISTRY OF NATURAL RESOURCES
NORTHEAST REGION
Ontario Government Complex, Highway 101 East
P.O. Bag 3020
South Porcupine, P0N 1H0 Ontario Canada
Phone: 705-235-1154   Fax: 705-235-1226

Scope: International

Publication(s): North Science & Technology Newsletter

Contact(s):
Rob Galloway, Regional Director
Mary Ellen Stoll, Manager of Science & Technology

ONTARIO MINISTRY OF NATURAL RESOURCES
NORTHWEST REGION
435 James St.,S
Thunder Bay, P7E 6S8 Ontario Canada
Phone: 807-475-1261   Fax: 807-473-3023
Website: www.mnr.gov.on.ca

Membership: 1–100
Scope: Regional

Contact(s):
Charlie Lauer, Regional Director

ONTARIO MINISTRY OF NATURAL RESOURCES
SOUTH CENTRAL REGION
P.O. Box 7000 4th Floor, South Tower, 300 Water Street
Huntsville, K9J 8M5 Ontario Canada
Phone: 705-755-2500

Contact(s):
Allan Stewart, Regional Director

OREGON DEPARTMENT OF AGRICULTURE
NATURAL RESOURCES DIVISION
635 Capitol St., NE
Salem, OR 97310-2532 United States
Phone: 503-986-4700

Founded: 1939
Scope: Local, State

Description: The Natural Resources Division's mission is to conserve, protect, and develop natural resources on public and private land so agriculture will continue to be productive and economically viable. Primary program areas include Water Quality, Confined Animal Feeding Operations, Smoke Mangement, Land Use, Soil and Water Conservation Districtts, Plant Conservation Biology and Shellfish.

Contact(s):
John Byers, Public Information/Outreach Specialist; 503-986-4700
Debbie Gorham, Administrator; 503-986-4700
Bob Graham, Advisory Member; Natural Resource Conservation Service, 101 SW Main St. Suite 1300, Portland, OR 97204-3221; 503-326-2751
Ray Jaindl, Assistant Administrator; 503-986-4700

OREGON DEPARTMENT OF ENVIRONMENTAL QUALITY (DEQ)
811 S.W. 6th Ave.
Portland, OR 97204 United States
Phone: 503-229-5696   Fax: 503-229-6124
Website: www.deq.state.or.us

Founded: 1969
Scope: State

Description: Our mission is to be an active leader in restoring, maintaining, and enhancing the quality of Oregon's air, water, and land.

Publication(s): Recycling Newsletter, Tankline, Beyond Waste
Keyword(s): Air Quality/Atmosphere, Pollution (general), Reduce/Reuse/Recycle, Water Habitats & Quality

Contact(s):
Langdon Marsh, Director; 503-229-5300
Rick Gates, Laboratory Administrator; 503-229-5983
Steve Greenwood, Western Region Administrator; 541-686-7838
Stephanie Hallock, Eastern Region Administrator; 541-338-6146
Michael Llewelyn, Water Quality Administrator; 503-229-5324
Neil Mullane, Northwest Region Administrator; 503-229-5372
Sally Puent, Intern

OREGON DEPARTMENT OF FISH AND WILDLIFE (ODFW)
2501 SW 1st Ave.
Portland, OR 97201 United States
Phone: 503-872-5310   Fax: 503-872-5302
E-mail: odfwinfo@state.or.us
Website: www.dfw.state.or.us

Founded: 1975
Scope: State

Description: Responsibilities include management of fish and wildlife resources and regulation of commercial and recreational harvest.

Publication(s): Oregon Wildlife

Contact(s):
Brian Alula, Director of Information Services; 503-872-5267
Lindsay Ball, Director
Carol Brown, Human Resources Division Director; 503-872-5262
Chip Dale, High Desert Region Director; 61374 Parrell Rd., Bend, OR 97702; 541-388-6363; Fax: 541-388-6281
Steve Denney, SW Regional Director, Acting
Craig Ely, NE Region Director; 107 20th St., LaGrande, OR 97850; 541-963-2138; Fax: 541-963-6670
Dave McAllister, Habitat Division Director; 503-872-5255
Chris Wheaton, NW Region Director; 17330 SE Evelyn St., Clackamas, OR 97015; 503-657-2000; Fax: 503-657-2050
Wayne Rawlins, Manager of Business Services/Realty; 503-872-5310

Susan Adams Gunn, Information and Education
Ron Anglin, Deputy Director
Pat Wray, Editor; 7118 NE Vandenberg Ave., Corvallis, OR 97330; 541-757-4186; Fax: 541-757-4252

OREGON DEPARTMENT OF FORESTRY
2600 State St.
Salem, OR 97310 United States
Phone: 503-945-7200   Fax: 503-945-7212
Website: www.odf.state.or.us
Founded: 1911
Membership: 101–1,000
Scope: State
Description: The department is responsible for fire protection of 15.8 million acres of private and public forests; directs insect and disease management on 11 million acres of state and private forests; manages 789,000 acres of state-owned forests; provides forestry assistance to private forest landowners; enforces other Oregon forest laws; provides forestry information to schools, organizations, and individuals; and advises Governor and State Legislature on forestry matters.
Publication(s): Forest Log, The, The Oregon Forests Report (Annual), CommuniTree News (Quarterly)
Keyword(s): Forests/Forestry, Wildlife & Species
Contact(s):
Rick Gibson, Director of Fire Prevention; 503-945-7440
Cary Greenwood, Director of Public Affairs; 503-945-7420
Lanny Quackenbush, Director of Fire Protection; 503-945-7435
Wallace Rutledge, Director of Forestry Assistance; 503-945-7392
Gayle Birch, Board of Forestry
James Brown, Secretary; 503-945-7211
Dave Gilbert, Chairman
Ted Lorensen, Assistant State Foresters
Charlie Stone, Assistant State Forester of Forest Protection; 503-945-7205
Steve Thomas, Assistant State Foresters
Roy Woo, Deputy State Forrester; 801 Gales Creek Rd., Forest Grove, OR 97117-1199; 503-357-2191; Fax: 503-357-4548

OREGON DEPARTMENT OF GEOLOGY AND MINERAL INDUSTRIES
800 NE Oregon St., Suite 965, #28
Portland, OR 97232-2162 United States
Phone: 503-731-4100   Fax: 503-731-4066
Website: www.oregongeology.com
Membership: 1–100
Scope: State
Publication(s): Oregon Geology - quarterly
Contact(s):
John Beaulieu, State Geologist; john.beaulieu@state.or.us
Klaus Nevendorf, Librarian; 800 NE Oregon St., Suite 965, #28, Portland, OR 97232-2162

OREGON DEPARTMENT OF TRANSPORTATION
Oregon Department of Transportation
1158 Chemeketa NE
Salem, OR 97301-2528 United States
Phone: 503-986-3477   Fax: 503-986-3524
Membership: 1–100
Scope: State
Description: ODOT avoids, minimizes and mitigates the environmental impacts of its highway construction and maintenance activities.
Keyword(s): Ethics/Environmental Justice, Forests/Forestry, Sprawl/Urban Planning, Transportation, Water Habitats & Quality, Wildlife & Species

Contact(s):
Lori Sundstrom, Environmental Services Section Manager; Oregon Department of Transportation, 1158 Chemeketa St., NE, Salem, OR 97310; 503-986-3477

OREGON FISH AND WILDLIFE DIVISION/DEPARTMENT OF STATE POLICE
400 Public Service Bldg.
Salem, OR 97310 United States
Phone: 503-378-3720   Fax: 503-363-5475
E-mail: osp.fwd@state.or.us
Website: www.osp.state.or.us
Scope: State
Description: The Fish and Wildlife Division is charged with the enforcement of fish and game, commercial fish, shellfish, environmental protection laws, and all endangered species laws, rules, and regulations. Also provides general law enforcement services in rural areas. Provides law enforcement services on contract with the Oregon Department of Fish and Wildlife, the Department of Environmental Quality, and the Department of Forestry.
Publication(s): See publication website
Keyword(s): Recreation/Ecotourism, Wildlife & Species
Contact(s):
Lindsay Ball, C & D Director, Captain; 503-378-3720
D. Cleary, Staff of Commercial Fisheries, 503-378-3720
C. Kok, Staff of Wildlife; 503-378-3720
K. Allison, District I Supervisor of Portland, OR; 503-731-3027
J. Hunsaker, Aircraft Supervisor; 503-378-3720
S. Lane, District II Supervisor of Salem, OR; 503-378-2110
W. Markee, Special Investigations Unit Supervisor; 503-378-3387
S. Ross, District III Supervisor of Medford, OR; 503-776-6114
R. Scorby, District IV Supervisor of Baker City, OR; 503-523-5848

OREGON PARKS AND RECREATION DEPARTMENT
1115 Commercial St., NE, Suite 1
Salem, OR 97301-1002 United States
Phone: 503-378-6305   Fax: 503-378-6447
Website: www.oregonparks.org
Founded: 1921
Membership: 101–1,000
Scope: State
Description: To provide and protect outstanding natural, scenic, cultural, historic, and recreational sites for the enjoyment and education of present and future generations.
Keyword(s): Oceans/Coasts/Beaches, Recreation/Ecotourism, Water Habitats & Quality
Contact(s):
Michael Carrier, Director; 503-378-5019

OREGON STATE EXTENSION SERVICES
Oregon State University
101 Ballard Extension Hall
Corvallis, OR 97331-3606 United States
Phone: 541-737-2713   Fax: 541-737-4423
Website: www.osu.orst.edu/extension/
Scope: State
Contact(s):
Lyla Houglum, Dean and Director
Deborah Maddy, Regional Director; 541-737-2711; deborah.maddy@orst.edu
Michael Stoltz, Regional Director; 541-737-2711; michael.stoltz@orst.edu
Peter Bloome, Associate Director; peter.bloome@orst.edu
William Braunworth, Extension Program Coordinator, Agriculture; Stag Hall, Room 138, Oregon State University, Corvallis, OR 97331; 541-737-4251; Fax: 541-737-3178; Bill.Braunworth@orst.edu

W. Edge, Natural Resources Information; 104 Nash Hall, Oregon State University, Corvallis, OR 97331-3803; 541-737-1953; Fax: 541-737-3590

A. Reed, Program Leader, Forestry; 119 Peavy Hall, Oregon State University, Corvallis, OR 97331; 541-737-3700; Fax: 541-737-3008

OREGON STATE MARINE BOARD
P.O. Box 14145
Salem, OR 97309-5065 United States
Phone: 503-378-8587   Fax: 503-378-4597
Website: www.boatoregon.com

Scope: State
Keyword(s): Recreation/Ecotourism, Water Habitats & Quality
Contact(s):
Paul Donheffner, Director

OREGON WATER RESOURCES DEPARTMENT
158 12th St., NE
Salem, OR 97301-4172 United States
Phone: 503-378-8455   Fax: 503-378-2496
Website: www.wrd.state.or.us

Founded: 1909
Membership: 101–1,000
Scope: State
Description: The Water Resources Department is the steward of the state's water resources. The agency enforces state water laws and policies; promotes actions that restore and protect streamflows and watersheds in order to ensure the long-term sustainability of Oregon's ecosystems, economy, and quality of life; addresses water supply needs; and increases the understanding of the resource and the demands on it.
Keyword(s): Agriculture/Farming, Climate Change, Water Habitats & Quality
Contact(s):
Paul Cleary, Director; 503-378-2982
Dick Bailey, Administrator of Water Rights and Adjudications; 503-378-8455
Bruce Moyer, Administrator of Administrative Services Division; 503-378-8455
Barry Norris, Administrator of Technical Services Division; 503-378-8455
Tom Paul, Administrator of Field Services Division; 503-378-8455
Adam Sussman, Senior Policy Coordinator; 503-378-8455

P

PENNSYLVANIA COOPERATIVE FISH AND WILDLIFE RESEARCH UNIT
UNITED STATES GEOLOGICAL SURVEY
Merkle Bldg., Pennsylvania State University
University Park, PA 16802 United States
Phone: 814-865-4511   Fax: 814-863-4710
E-mail: klc2@psu.edu
Website: http://pacfwru.cas.psu.edu

Founded: 1938
Membership: 1–100
Scope: National
Description: Established as a cooperative activity among Pennsylvania State University, Pennsylvania Fish and Boat Commission, Wildlife Management Institute, Pennsylvania Game Commission, and the Department of the Interior. Areas of research are: The effects of natural and manmade forces on aquatic and terrestrial ecosystems, animal-habitat interactions, acid precipitation effects, fish and wildlife management, and health profiles of game animals. Graduate training is also provided.
Publication(s): Annual Report available on request.

Contact(s):
Robert Carline, Leader; f7u@psu.edu
Duane Diefenbach, Assistant Leader for Wildlife; drd11@psu.edu
Erin Snyder, Assistant Unit Leader for Fisheries; ems19@psu.edu

PENNSYLVANIA DEPARTMENT OF AGRICULTURE
REGION I
13410 Dunham Rd.
Meadville, PA 16335 United States
Phone: 814-332-6890   Fax: 814-333-1431
Website: www.tda.state.pa.us

Membership: 1–100
Scope: State
Contact(s):
George Gregg, Director

PENNSYLVANIA DEPARTMENT OF AGRICULTURE
REGION II
542 County Farm Rd., Suite 102
Montoursville, PA 17754-9685 United States
Phone: 570-433-2640   Fax: 570-433-4770
Website: www.pda.state.pa.us

Scope: State
Contact(s):
Dean Ely, Director

PENNSYLVANIA DEPARTMENT OF AGRICULTURE
REGION III
Rt. 92 South, P.O. Box C
Tunkhannock, PA 18657 United States
Phone: 570-836-2181   Fax: 570-836-6266

Membership: 1–100
Scope: State
Contact(s):
Russell Gunton, Director

PENNSYLVANIA DEPARTMENT OF AGRICULTURE
REGION IV
5349 William Flynn Hwy.
Gibsonia, PA 15044 United States
Phone: 724-443-1585   Fax: 724-443-8150

Membership: 1–100
Scope: Local
Contact(s):
R. Nehrig, Director

PENNSYLVANIA DEPARTMENT OF AGRICULTURE
REGION V
1307 7th St.
Cricket Field Plaza
Altoona, PA 16601-4701 United States
Phone: 814-946-7315   Fax: 814-946-7354
Website: www.agriculture.state.pa.us/

Scope: Regional
Contact(s):
Kenneth Mowry, Director

PENNSYLVANIA DEPARTMENT OF AGRICULTURE
REGION VI
P.O. Box 419
Summerdale, PA 17093 United States
Phone: 717-728-2570
Website: www.pda.state.pa.us/

Contact(s):
Sam Hayes, Secretary

PENNSYLVANIA DEPARTMENT OF AGRICULTURE
REGION VII
P.O. Box 300
Creamery, PA 19430 United States
Phone: 610-489-1003   Fax: 610-489-6119
E-mail: pstarr@state.pa.us
Website: www.pda.state.pa.us

Membership: 1–100
Scope: Regional
Description: State regulatory agency

Contact(s):
William Zollers, Director; 610-489-1003; Fax: 610-489-6119

PENNSYLVANIA DEPARTMENT OF AGRICULTURE
STATE CONSERVATION COMMISSION
2301 N. Cameron St.
Agriculture Building, Room 407
Harrisburg, PA 17110-9408 United States
Phone: 717-787-8821   Fax: 717-705-3778
E-mail: ag-ssc@state.pa.us
Website: www.pascc.org

Founded: 1945
Membership: 1–100
Scope: State
Description: To establish policy for Pennsylvania's 66 local conservation districts. Programs administered by the commission include: a $2,850,000 annual grant program, which provides funds to conservation districts for the employment of managerial and technical staff; a $5.2 million annual Chesapeake Bay Program, which provides technical and financial assistance to farmers to install soil conservation and nutrient management practices, and more.
Publication(s): Highlights Newsletter
Keyword(s): Agriculture/Farming, Land Issues

Contact(s):
Karl Brown, Executive Secretary; Fax: 717-705-3778, kbrown@agric.state.us

PENNSYLVANIA DEPARTMENT OF CONSERVATION AND NATURAL RESOURCES
7th Floor
Rachel Carson State Office Bldg.
P.O. Box 8767
Harrisburg, PA 17105-8767 United States
Phone: 717-787-2869   Fax: 717-772-9106
Website: www.dcnr.state.pa.us

Founded: 1995
Scope: State
Description: To maintain and preserve state parks; to manage state forest lands to assure their long-term health, sustainability and economic use; to provide information on Pennsylvania's ecological and geologic resources; and to administer grant and technical assistance programs that will benefit river conservation, trails and greenways, local recreation, regional heritage conservation and environmental education programs across Pennsylvania.
Publication(s): Resource, Become a Conservation Volunteer, Discover DCNR, Penn's Woods, PA State Park Recreation Guide
Keyword(s): Forests/Forestry, Land Issues, Public Lands/Greenspace, Recreation/Ecotourism, Reduce/Reuse/Recycle, Wildlife & Species

Contact(s):
Damon Anderson, Director of Information Technology; 717-783-9732
Frederick Carlson, Director of Policy
Eugene Comoss, Director, Bureau of Facility Design and Construction; 717-787-7398
Dana Datres, Director, Bureau of Administrative Services; 717-787-2362
Joan Dlippinger, Director of Environmental Education; 717-705-2862
Dennis Farley, Director, Bureau of Personnel; 717-787-5496
Roger Fickes, Director, Bureau of State Parks; 717-787-6640
James Grace, Director, Bureau of Forestry; 717-787-2703
Kurt Leitholf, Executive Director, Conservation and Natural Resources; 8th Fl., Rachel Carson State Office Bldg., P.O. Box 8773, Harrisburg, PA 17105-8773; 717-705-0031
Jay Parrish, Director of Dept. of Topographic & Geological Survey
Geralyn Umstead, Director of Community Relations; 717-772-9087
Larry Williamson, Director, Bureau of Recreation and Conservation; 717-783-2658
Karen Deklinski, Deputy Secretary for Administration; 717-772-9100
Joseph Graci, Legislative Liaison; 717-772-9101
Sally Just, Senior Advisor to Secretary; 717-787-2869
Gretchen Leslie, Press Secretary; 717-772-9101
John Oliver, Secretary; 717-787-2869
John Plonski, Executive Deputy Secretary for Parks and Forestry; 717-772-9104
William Shakely, Chief Counsel; 717-772-4171
Richard Sprenkle, Deputy Secretary for Conservation and Engineering Services; 717-787-9306

PENNSYLVANIA DEPARTMENT OF ENVIRONMENTAL PROTECTION
P.O. Box 2063
Harrisburg, PA 17105-2063 United States
Phone: 717-787-2815   Fax: 717-772-3278
E-mail: lisamiller@state.pa.us
Website: www.dep.state.pa.us

Founded: 1995
Scope: State
Description: The Department of Environmental Protection's mission is to protect Pennsylvania's air, land, and water from pollution and to provide for the health and safety of its citizens through a cleaner environment. We will work as partners with individuals, organizations, governments, and businesses to prevent pollution and restore our natural resources.
Keyword(s): Air Quality/Atmosphere, Land Issues, Pollution (general), Public Health

Contact(s):
Larry Brown, Director, Bureau of Network Operations; 717-772-5909
Michael Conway, Director, Bureau of Waterways Engineering; 717-787-3411
James Erb, Director, Bureau of Oil and Gas Management; 717-772-2199
Roderick Fletcher, Director, Bureau of Abandoned Mine Reclamation; 717-783-2267
Stuart Gansell, Director, Bureau of Watershed Conservation; 717-787-5267
Jeffrey Jarrett, Director, District Mining Operations; 724-942-7204
Richard Mather, Director, Bureau of Regulatory Counsel; 717-787-7060
Gary Niland, Director, Bureau of Investigations; 717-787-0453
Richard Stickler, Director, Bureau of Deep Mine Safety; 724-439-7469
Karen Bassett, Deputy Secretary for Management and Technical Services; 717-787-7116
Michael Bedrin, Chief Counsel; 717-787-4449
Eric Conrad, Deputy Secretary for Field Operations; 717-787-5028
Cathy Curren, Deputy Secretary for Water Management; 717-787-4686
Kathleen McGinty, Secretary; 717-787-2814
Jay Roberts, Office of Mining and Reclamation; 717-787-5103

PENNSYLVANIA FISH AND BOAT COMMISSION
P.O. Box 67000
Harrisburg, PA 17106-7000 United States
Phone: 717-705-7800　　　Fax: 717-705-7802
Website: www.fish.state.pa.us

Founded: 1866
Scope: State
Description: To conduct and support public education and information efforts related to aquatic resource protection, improvement, and management programs, and enhance public understanding of the wise and safe use of our fishing and boating resources.
Publication(s): Pennsylvania Angler and Boater
Keyword(s): Recreation/Ecotourism, Water Habitats & Quality, Wildlife & Species
Contact(s):
　William Sabatose, President
　Paul Mahon, Vice President
　Dennis Guise, Deputy Executive Director/Chief Counsel; 717-705-7810
　Rickalon Hoopes, Director of Bureau of Fisheries; 814-359-5169
　Thomas Kamerzel, Director of Bureau of Law Enforcement; 717-705-7861
　Wasyl Polischuk, Director of Bureau of Administration Services; 717-705-7900
　John Simmons, Director of Bureau of Boating and Education; 717-705-7830
　Position Vacant, Executive Director; 717-705-7801
　Ted Walke, Art Director; 717-705-7845
　James Young, Director of Bureau of Engineering and Development; 814-359-5152
　Thomas Ford, Policy & Planning Manager; 717-705-7807
　Arthur Michaels, Editor; 717-705-7844
　Gary Moore, Legislative Liaison; 717-705-7816

PENNSYLVANIA FISH AND BOAT COMMISSION
BUREAU OF LAW ENFORCEMENT
NORTHCENTRAL REGION
466 Robinson Lane
P.O. Box 5306
Bellefonte, PA 16823 United States
Phone: 814-359-5250　　　Fax: 814-359-5254
E-mail: lgarlicki@state.pa.us
Website: www.fish.state.pa.us

Founded: 1866
Membership: 1–100
Scope: Regional
Description: Regional headquarters for agency's law enforcement staff and field operations in a 14 county area of NC Pennsylvania - Cameron, Centre, Clearfield, Clinton, Elk, Jefferson, Lycoming, McKean, Montour, Northumberland, Potter, Snyder, Tioga & Union.
Keyword(s): Water Habitats & Quality
Contact(s):
　Gerald Barton, Assistant Manager; 814-359-5250; Fax: 814-359-5254; ra-ncregion@state.pa.us
　Brian Burger, Region Manager; 814-359-5250; Fax: 814-359-5254; ra-ncregion@state.pa.us
　Barbara Walker, Office Administrator; 814-359-5250; Fax: 814-359-5254; ra-ncregion@state.pa.us

PENNSYLVANIA FISH AND BOAT COMMISSION
BUREAU OF LAW ENFORCEMENT
NORTHEAST REGION
P.O. Box 88
Sweet Valley, PA 18656-0008 United States
Phone: 570-477-5717　　　Fax: 570-477-3221
E-mail: pfbcne1@ptd.net
Website: www.pda.state.pa.us

Contact(s):
　Kerry Messerle, Law Enforcement Supervisor

PENNSYLVANIA FISH AND BOAT COMMISSION
BUREAU OF LAW ENFORCEMENT
NORTHWEST REGION
11528 State Highway 98
Meadville, PA 16335 United States
Phone: 814-337-0444　　　Fax: 814-337-0579
Website: www.fish.state.pa.us

Membership: 1–100
Scope: State
Contact(s):
　Frank Parise, Asistant Regional Manager
　Gary Deiger, Law Enforcement Supervisor
　Robert Nestor, Assistant Regional Manager

PENNSYLVANIA FISH AND BOAT COMMISSION
BUREAU OF LAW ENFORCEMENT
SOUTHCENTRAL REGION
1704 Pine Rd.
Newville, PA 17241-9544 United States
Phone: 717-486-7087　　　Fax: 717-486-8227
E-mail: psbcsc1@epix.net
Website: www.fish.state.pa.us

Scope: State
Publication(s): Pennsylvania Angler & Boater Magazine
Contact(s):
　George Geisler, Regional Manager South Central; 1704 Pine Rd., Newville, PA 17241

PENNSYLVANIA FISH AND BOAT COMMISSION
BUREAU OF LAW ENFORCEMENT
SOUTHEAST REGION
Box 9
Brubaker Valley Road & Lakeview Drive
Elm, PA 17521-0009 United States
Phone: 717-626-0228　　　Fax: 717-626-0486
Website: www.fish.state.pa.us

Membership: 1–100
Scope: State
Description: Region Law Enforcement Office

PENNSYLVANIA FISH AND BOAT COMMISSION
BUREAU OF LAW ENFORCEMENT
SOUTHWEST REGION
236 Lake Rd.
Somerset, PA 15501-1644 United States
Phone: 814-445-8974　　　Fax: 814-445-3497
E-mail: pfbcsw1@twd.net
Website: www.fish.state.pa.us

Membership: 1–100
Scope: Regional
Contact(s):
　Rick Lorson, Area Fisheries Biologist
　Emil Svetahor, Law Enforcement Supervisor; 814-445-3554
　Dennis Tubbs, Aquatic Resource Program Specialist; 814-443-9841

PENNSYLVANIA FOREST STEWARDSHIP PROGRAM
DCNR-BUREAU OF FORESTRY
P.O. Box 8552
400 Market Street
Harrisburg, PA 17105-8552 United States
Phone: 717-787-2106　　　Fax: 717-783-5109
E-mail: godato@state.pa.us
Website: www.dcnr.state.pa.us

Founded: 1990
Membership: 1,001–10,000

Scope: State, Regional

Description: To educate Pennsylvania forest landowners and citizens about the importance of sound forest management and the need to conserve our forest resources for future generations through wise use today. Works in conjunction with the Stewardship Incentive Program, which provides cost-share assistance to landowner's forest management practices.

Publication(s): Forest Stewardship Bulletin Series

Keyword(s): Ethics/Environmental Justice, Forests/Forestry, Land Issues, Public Lands/Greenspace, Recreation/Ecotourism, Sprawl/Urban Planning, Water Habitats & Quality, Wildlife & Species

Contact(s):
James Grace, Director
Gene Odato, Chief of Stewardship & Education Program

PINE BLUFF COOPERATIVE FISHERY RESEARCH PROJECT

USGS-BRG-University of Arkansas
Ag. Exp. Station, 1200 N. University
P.O. Box 4005
Pine Bluff, AR 71611-2799 United States
Phone: 501-543-8165

Description: The Pine Bluff Cooperative Fishery Research Project is a cooperative educational effort between the U.S. Geological Survey-Biological Resources Division, Cooperative Research Units Division, and the University of Arkansas - Pine Bluff. The project provides undergraduate training in fisheries science and biology and conducts research on environmental problems, fisheries, and related topics.

Keyword(s): Water Habitats & Quality, Wildlife & Species

Contact(s):
Steve Lochmann, Project Leader

PRINCE EDWARD ISLAND DEPARTMENT OF FISHERIES, AQUACULTURE AND ENVIRONMENT

P.O. Box 2000
Charlottetown, C1A 7N8 Prince Edward Island Canada
Phone: 888-734-7529   Fax: 902-368-5830
Website: www.gov.pe.ca

Scope: Province

Description: To work with individuals, businesses, groups and communities to protect, enhance and enjoy in a sustainable way the province's environment and natural resources.

Publication(s): Tracks in the Snow, Our Land and Water, The Bald Eagle in Prince Edward Island, Wildlife Policy, Patterns of the Pond

Contact(s):
Arthur Smith, Director of Fish and Wildlife Division; 902-368-6083
Clare Birch, Firearm Safety Coordinator; 902-368-4686
Lewie Creed, Deputy Minister; 902-368-5340
Rosemary Curley, Habitat and Natural Areas Biologist; 902-368-4807
Randall Dibblee, Waterfowl and Furbearer Biologist; 902-368-4666
Chester Gillan, Minister; 902-368-4863
Gerald MacDougall, Head of Investigations and Enforcement; 902-368-4808
Alan McLennan, Eastern Habitat Joint Venture Coordinator

PUERTO RICO DEPARTMENT OF AGRICULTURE

Box 10163
Santurce, PR 00908-1163 United States
Phone: 787-721-2120   Fax: 787-722-0291
Website: www.nass.usda.gov/pr/de_ag_PR.htm

Contact(s):
Brenda Marrero, Executive Secretary

PUERTO RICO DEPARTMENT OF NATURAL AND ENVIRONMENTAL RESOURCES

P.O. Box 5887, Puerta de Tierra Sta.
San Juan, PR 00906 United States
Phone: 787-724-8774   Fax: 787-723-3090
E-mail: reglamentos@drna.gobierno.pr
Website: www.drna.gobierno.pr

Founded: 1973

Description: To develop, protect, manage, evaluate, and administer the natural resources of Puerto Rico; and to derive maximum public benefits.

Keyword(s): Forests/Forestry, Wildlife & Species

Contact(s):
Salvador Salas, Secretary; 787-723-3090; ssalas@drna.gobierno.pr

PUERTO RICO DIVISION DE PATRIMONIO NATURAL

DEPARTMENTO DE RECURSOS NATURALES Y AMBIENTALES DE PUERTO RICO
P.O. Box 9066600
Puerta de Tierra Station
San Juan, Puerto Rico 00906-6600 United States
Phone: 787-724-8774, ext. 4037   Fax: 787 725-9526
E-mail: dpn@caribe.net
Website: www.natureserve.org/nhp/lacarb/pr/

Scope: State

Description: Puerto Rico Natural Heritage Program and Conservation Data Center

Contact(s):
Aida Martinez-Medina, Division Director
Carmen Hernandez-Serrano, Chief, Planning and Acquisitions
Vicente Quevedo-Bonilla, Chief, Research and Data Analysis
Luis Beltran-Burgos, Biologist and Environmental Planner
Amparo Chavez-Quiroga, Environmental Planner
Daniel Davila-Casanova, Biologist and Data Manager
Eliu Rivera-Lucena, Environmental Planner

PUERTO RICO SOIL CONSERVATION COMMITTEE

P.O. Box 10163
Santurce, PR 908 United States
Phone: 787-725-3040   Fax: 787-721-7350

Scope: State

Contact(s):
Ivan Lockward, Executive Secretary; 787-725-3040; Fax: 787-721-7350
Miguel Munoz, Secretary of Agriculture; 787-721-2120; Fax: 787-722-0812

PURDUE UNIVERSITY EXTENSION SERVICES

615 W. State Street
Purdue University
West Lafayette, IN 47907-2053 United States
Phone: 888-398-4636   Fax: 765-494-5876
E-mail: extension@agad.purdue.edu
Website: www.ces.purdue.edu/

Contact(s):
David Petritz, Director, Cooperative Extension Service; david.petritz@ces.purdue.edu
Janet Ayres, Program Leader, Leadership and Community Development; 765-494-4215; ayres@agecon.purdue.edu
Linda Chezem, Program Leader, 4-H/Youth; 765-494-8422; lchezem@.four-h.purdue.edu
Brian Miller, Wildife Specialist and Sea Grant Coordinator; Purdue Univ., 1159 Forestry Building, West Lafayette, IN 47907-1159; 765-494-3586; Fax: 765-496-2422

Q

QUEBEC DEPARTMENT OF ENVIRONMENT AND WILDLIFE
Edifice Marie-Guyart, 675, Blvd. Rene-Levesque East
Quebec City, G1R 5V7 Quebec Canada
Phone: 418-521-3830   Fax: 418-646-5974
E-mail: info@menv.gouv.qc.ca
Website: www.menv.gouv.qc.ca

Contact(s):
George Arsenault, Vice-President of Society of Faune and Parks of Quebec; 418-521-3851
Claudette Blais, Vice-President of Parks for Quebec; 418-521-3850
Luc Berthiaume, Director of Internal Affairs; 418-521-3828
Andre Martel, Director of Wildlife Protection In Outaouais; 418-622-0313
Andre Taillon, Director General of Wildlife Protetection; 819-623-1981
Paul Begin, Minister; 418-521-3911
Herve Bolduc, General Secretary; 418-521-3850
Diane Gian, Deputy Minister; 418-521-3860

R

RHODE ISLAND COOPERATIVE EXTENSION SERVICE
3 East Alumni Avenue
Kingston, RI 02881 United States
Phone: 401-874-2900   Fax: 401-874-2259
E-mail: ceec@etal.uri.edu
Website: www.uri.edu/ce/ceec

Scope: Local, State, National
Publication(s): Publication on website
Keyword(s): Agriculture/Farming, Pollution (general), Water Habitats & Quality

Contact(s):
Jeffrey Seemann, Director
Joseph Dealteris, Aquaculture and Fisheries Leader; 401-874-5333; Fax: 401-789-8930; jdealteris@uri.edu
Art Gold, Natural Resources Leader; 401-874-2903; Fax: 401-874-4561; agold@uri.edu
Patrick Logan, Community Economic Development Leader; 401-874-2970; Fax: 401-874-4017; mayfly@uri.edu

RHODE ISLAND DEPARTMENT OF ENVIRONMENTAL MANAGEMENT
235 Promenade St.
Providence, RI 02908 United States
Phone: 401-222-4700, ext. 2409   Fax: 401-222-6802
E-mail: rsantoro@dem.state.ri.us
Website: www.state.ri.us/dem

Founded: 1977
Membership: 101–1,000
Scope: Local, State, Regional, National, International
Description: The Department of Environmental Management's top priorities include the preservation and protection of the environmental quality of Rhode Island. Air pollution, water pollution, and waste disposal problems are handled by the DEM. The DEM develops, administers, and enforces programs designed to preserve and manage Rhode Island's forests, parks, farms, wildlife, fisheries, and coastline. DEM is also responsible for providing, on the average, 750 full-time jobs for the people of Rhode Island.

Contact(s):
Jan Reitsma, Director; 235 Promenade St., Providence, RI 02908; 401-222-2771
Dean Albro, Compliance and Inspection; 235 Promenade St., Providence, RI 02908; 401-277-6820
Kenneth Ayers, Chief of Agriculture; 83 Park St., Providence, RI 02903; 401-222-2781
Susan Bundy, Chief of Watershed and Standards; 235 Promenade St., Providence, RI 02908
Russell Chateauneuf, Chief of Permitting; 235 Promenade St., Providence, RI 02908; 401-222-2306
Thomas Dupree, Chief of Forest Environment; R.F.D. #2 Box 851, North Scituate, RI 02859; 401-222-1414
Ronald Gagnon, Chief of Technical and Customer Assistance; 291 Promenade St., Providence, RI 02908; 401-277-2797
Alicia Good, Assistant Director of Water Resources; 235 Promenade St., Providence, RI 02908; 401-222-3961
Malcolm Grant, Associate Director for Natural Resource Management; 235 Promenade St., Providence, RI 02908; 401-222-6605
Terrence Gray, Asst. Director for Air, Waste & Compliance; 235 Promenade St., Providence, RI 02908; 401-222-6677
Steven Hall, Chief of Enforcement; 83 Park St., Providence, RI 02903; 401-222-2284
Leo Hellested, Chief of Waste Management; 235 Promenade St., Providence, RI 02908; 401-277-2797
Janet Keller, Chief of Strategic Planning and Policy; 235 Promenade St., Providence, RI 02908; 401-277-3434
Kathleen Lanphear, Chief Hearing Officer of Administrative Adjudication; 235 Promenade, Providence, RI 02908; 401-222-1357
Stephen Majkut, Chief of Air Resources; 235 Promenade St., Providence, RI 02908; 401-222-2808
Melanie Marcaccio, Chief of Office of Human Resources; 235 Promenade St., Providence, RI 02908; 401-222-2774
Donald Mcgovern, Chief of Coastal Resources; 83 Park St., Providence, RI 02903; 401-222-3429
Glenn Miller, Chief of Management Services; 235 Promenade St., Providence, RI 02908; 401-222-6825
Larry Mouradjian, Chief of Parks and Recreation; 2321 Hartford Ave., Johnston, RI 02919; 401-222-2632
Kurt Schatz, Chief of Criminal Investigation Office; 235 Promenade St., Providence, RI 02908; 401-222-6768
John Stolgitis, Chief of Fish and Wildlife; Stedman Government Center, Wakefield, RI 02879; 401-222-3075
Robert Sutton, Chief of Planning and Development; 235 Promenade St., Providence, RI 02908; 401-222-2776
Frederick Vincent, Associate Director for Planning and Administration; 235 Promenade St., Providence, RI 02908; 401-222-2776

RHODE ISLAND DEPARTMENT OF TRANSPORTATION
Two Capitol Hill
Providence, RI 02903 United States
Phone: 401-222-1362

Description: To provide a safe, efficient, effective, and environmentally responsible intermodal transportation system that supports economic development and improves our quality of life.
Keyword(s): Transportation

Contact(s):
William Ankner, Director

RHODE ISLAND STATE WATER RESOURCES BOARD
100 North Main Street, 5th Floor
Providence, RI 02903 United States
Phone: 401-222-2217   Fax: 401-222-4707

Founded: 1967
Description: The Water Resources Board is the key agency in water-supply planning, financing, regulation, and development. The Board also plans for the future water needs of cities and towns.
Publication(s): RI Public Water Supply, RI Legal and Legislative Aspects of Water Supply, RI Industrial Water, RI Fish and Wildlife
Keyword(s): Land Issues, Public Health, Reduce/Reuse/Recycle, Water Habitats & Quality

STATE AND PROVINCIAL GOVERNMENT AGENCIES – S

Contact(s):
 M. Sams, General Manager and Secretary and Treasurer
 Daniel Schatz, Chairman
 Maurice Trudeau, Vice Chairman

RIVERSIDE COUNTY CONSERVATION AGENCY
4080 Lemon Street
Riverside, CA 92501 United States
Phone: 909-955-6625   Fax: 909-955-1817
Scope: Local
Description: The Riverside County Habitat Conservation Agency (RCHCA) was established in 1990 for the purpose of planning, acquiring and managing habitat for the SKR, a federal and state listed species. The RCHCA is a Joint Powers Agency comprised of 8 cities and the County of Riverside.
Keyword(s): Wildlife & Species

RUTGERS COOPERATIVE EXTENSION
Rutgers Cooperative Extension, 88 Lipman Dr.
New Brunswick, NJ 08901 United States
Phone: 732-932-5000   Fax: 732-932-6633
Website: www.rce.rutgers.edu
Membership: 1–100
Scope: State
Keyword(s): Agriculture/Farming, Pollution (general), Reduce/Reuse/Recycle
Contact(s):
 Karyn Malinowski, Senior Assoc. Director; 732-932-5000; ext. 591; malinowski@aesop.rutgers.edu
 David Drake, Extension Specialist in Wildlife; Rutgers Cooperative Extension, 80 Nichol Ave., New Brunswick, NJ 08901-2828; 732-932-1509; ext. 12; Fax: 732-932-3222
 Mark Vodak, Specialist In Forest Resources; Rutgers Cooperative Extension, 80 Nichol Ave., New Brunswick, NJ 08901-2828; 732-932-8993; ext. 10

S

SALTON SEA AUTHORITY
78-401 Highway 111
Suite T
La Quinta, CA 92253-2066 United States
Phone: 760-564-4888   Fax: 760-564-5288
Website: www.saltonsea.ca.gov
Membership: 1–100
Scope: Regional
Description: The Authority is a joint powers agency comprised of the Counties of Imperial and Riverside, the Coachella Valley Water District and the Imperial Irrigation District. The Authority is working with the U.S. Bureau of Reclamation and other agencies to restore the Salton Sea.
Keyword(s): Water Habitats & Quality

SAN FRANCISCO BAY CONSERVATION AND DEVELOPMENT COMMISSION
RESOURCES AGENCY, THE
50 California St., Ste. 2600
San Francisco, CA 94111 United States
Phone: 415-352-3600   Fax: 415-352-3606
E-mail: info@bcdc.ca.gov
Website: www.bcdc.ca.gov/
Founded: 1965
Description: To implement a planning and regulatory program designed to conserve and use beneficially the environmental, economic, social, and aesthetic values of San Francisco Bay through carefully considered and democratically determined policies. Composed of 27 commissioners, representing the public and state, federal, and local governmental agencies.

Contact(s):
 Will Travis, Executive Director; 415-352-3653; travis@bcdc.ca.gov
 Barbara Kaufman, Chairman; 415-352-3663; barbarakaufman01@aol.com

SAN DIEGUITO RIVER PARK JOINT POWERS AUTHORITY
18372 Sycamore Creek Road
Escondido, CA 92025 United States
Phone: 858-674-2275, ext. 15   Fax: 858-674-2280
E-mail: dbobertz@sdrp.org
Website: www.sdrp.org
Founded: 1989
Scope: Local, State, Regional
Description: Five cities and a county cooperating to establish a 55-mile long natural open space park that will preserve an entire river corridor
Keyword(s): Agriculture/Farming, Ecosystems (precious), Executive/Legislative/Judicial Reform, Land Issues, Oceans/Coasts/Beaches, Pollution (general), Public Health, Public Lands/Greenspace, Recreation/Ecotourism, Transportation, Water Habitats & Quality, Wildlife &
Contact(s):
 Dick Bobertz, Executive Director; 858-674-2275; ext. 15; Fax: 858-674-2280; dbobertz@sdrp.org

SAND CREEK WATERSHED PROJECT, THE
DECATUR COUNTY SWCD
108 Smith Road
Greensburg, IN 47240 United States
Phone: 812-663-8685, ext. 3   Fax: 812-663-9261
E-mail: annette-geis@iaswcd.org
Website: www.sandcreekwatershed.com
Founded: 1997
Membership: 1–100
Scope: Local, State
Description: Our mission is to lead the community in ways to improve the Sand Creek Watershed.
Keyword(s): Agriculture/Farming, Forests/Forestry, Land Issues, Pollution (general), Population, Public Health, Public Lands/Greenspace, Recreation/Ecotourism, Reduce/Reuse/Recycle, Sprawl/Urban Planning, Water Habitats & Quality, Wildlife & Species
Contact(s):
 Robert Dawson, Tech Advisor; 812-663-8685; ext. 3; Fax: 812-663-9261; bob-dawson@iaswcd.org

SASKATCHEWAN ENVIRONMENT AND RESOURCE MANAGEMENT
3211 Albert St.
Regina, S4S5W6 Saskatchewan Canada
Phone: 306-787-2700
Website: www.se.gov.sk.ca/
Founded: 1930
Description: To manage, enhance, and protect Saskatchewan's natural and environmental resources - fish, forests, parks, lands, wildlife, air and water for conservation, recreation, social, and economic purposes, all to be sustained for future generations.
Publication(s): State of the Environment Report, Annual Reports
Contact(s):
 Rick Bates, Director of Communication Services; 306-787-0114
 Stuart Kramer, Deputy Minister; 306-787-2930
 Lorne Scott, Minister; 361 Legislative Bldg., Regina, Saskatchewan S4S 0B3; 306-787-0393

SASKATCHEWAN ENVIRONMENT AND RESOURCE MANAGEMENT
CORPORATE SERVICES
3211 Albert St.
Regina, S4S 5W6 Saskatchewan Canada
Phone: 306-787-2933 Fax: 306-787-9374
Website: www.se.gov.sk.ca

Publication(s): State of the Environment Report, Annual Report

Contact(s):
Mike Dumelie, Director of Information Mangement; 306-787-3194
Donna Kellsey, Director of Service Bureau; 306-787-6121
Lynn Tulloch, Executive Director of Corporate Services; 306-787-1176
Sue Mitten, Corporate Development; 306-787-2336
Al Parenteau, Corporate Development; 306-787-8449
Dave Tulloch, Corporate Development; 306-787-1095

SASKATCHEWAN ENVIRONMENT AND RESOURCE MANAGEMENT
EAST BOREAL ECOREGION
Box 3003
800 Central Ave
Prince Albert, S6V 6G1 Saskatchewan Canada
Phone: 306-953-2896 Fax: 306-953-2502
E-mail: hyggen@derm.gov.sk.ca
Website: www.se.gov.sk.ca/corporate/regions/EASTBOR/index.htm

Scope: Regional

Contact(s):
Ron Erickson, Regional Director; erickson@derm.gov.sk.ca

SASKATCHEWAN ENVIRONMENT AND RESOURCE MANAGEMENT
ENFORCEMENT AND COMPLIANCE BRANCH
Box 3003
Prince Albert, S6V 6G1 Saskatchewan Canada
Phone: 306-953-2991 Fax: 306-953-2999
Website: www.serm.gov.sk.ca

Founded: 1991
Membership: 1–100
Scope: International

Description: Enforcement and compliance policy development direction, dispatch services, training, special investigations, aboriginal initiatives and activities related to resource and environmental law enforcement within the Province of Saskatchewan.

Keyword(s): Air Quality/Atmosphere, Ecosystems (precious), Ethics/Environmental Justice, Forests/Forestry, Pollution (general), Water Habitats & Quality, Wildlife & Species

Contact(s):
Dave Harvey, Regional Director; Box 3003, Prince Albert, Saskatchewan S6V 6G1; 306-953-2993
Bill Zimmer, Operations Manager; 306-953-2945; Fax: 306-953-2999; bzimmer@serm.gov.sk.ca

SASKATCHEWAN ENVIRONMENT AND RESOURCE MANAGEMENT
FIRE MANAGEMENT AND FOREST PROTECTION BRANCH
P.O. Box 3003
c/o 800 Central Avenue
Prince Albert, S6V 6G1 Saskatchewan Canada
Phone: 306-953-3459 Fax: 306-953-2530
E-mail: utcoop@cc.usu.edu
Website: www.nr.usu.edu/UTCFWRU/index.html

Membership: 1–100
Scope: International

Contact(s):
Murdoch Carrierre, Regional Director; Box 3003, Prince Albert, Saskatchewan S6V 6G1; 306-953-2206

SASKATCHEWAN ENVIRONMENT AND RESOURCE MANAGEMENT
FISH AND WILDLIFE BRANCH
DIRECTOR
436-3211 Albert Street
Regina, S4S 5W6 Saskatchewan Canada
Phone: 306-787-2309 Fax: 306-787-9544
E-mail: dsherratt@serm.gov.sk.ca
Website: www.se.gov.sk.ca

Founded: 1930
Scope: Province

Description: To manage, enhance, and protect Saskatchewan's natural and environmental resources - fish, forests, parks, lands, wildlife, air and water for conservation, recreation, social and economic purposes, all to be sustained for future generations.

Keyword(s): Wildlife & Species

SASKATCHEWAN ENVIRONMENT AND RESOURCE MANAGEMENT
FISH AND WILDLIFE BRANCH
SASKATCHEWAN CONSERVATION DATA CENTRE (SKCDC)
436-3211 Albert St
Regina, S4S 5W6 Saskatchewan Canada
Phone: 306-787-1288 Fax: 306-787-9544
E-mail: sporter@serm.gov.sk.ca
Website: www.biodiversity.sk.ca

Scope: Local, Regional

Description: SKCDC serves the Saskatchewan public by gathering, interpreting and distributing standardized information on the ecological status of provincial wild species and communities.

Contact(s):
Jeff Keith, Information Manager

SASKATCHEWAN ENVIRONMENT AND RESOURCE MANAGEMENT
GRASSLAND ECOREGION
350 Cheadle St. W.
Box 5000
Swift Current, S9H 4G3 Saskatchewan Canada
Phone: 306-778-8442 Fax: 306-778-8212
Website: www.se.gov.sk.ca/corporate/regions/GRASSLND/index.htm

Scope: Regional

Contact(s):
Syd Barber, Regional Director

SASKATCHEWAN ENVIRONMENT AND RESOURCE MANAGEMENT
OPERATIONS
Rm. 524, 3211 Albert St.
Regina, S4S 5W6 Saskatchewan Canada
Phone: 306-787-9075 Fax: 306-787-0219
Website: www.serm.gov.sk.ca

Scope: Regional

Contact(s):
Hugh Hunt, Director of Regional Services; 306-787-9117
Dave Phillips, Assistant Deputy Minister; 306-787-9079

SASKATCHEWAN ENVIRONMENT AND RESOURCE MANAGEMENT
PARKLAND ECOREGION
112 Research Dr.
Saskatoon, S7K 2H6 Saskatchewan Canada
Phone: 306-933-7950   Fax: 306-933-8442
Website: www.se.gov.sk.ca/corporate/regions/PARKLND/index.htm

Scope: Regional

Contact(s):
   Merv Swanson, Regional Director

SASKATCHEWAN ENVIRONMENT AND RESOURCE MANAGEMENT
POLICY AND ASSESSMENT
3211 Albert St.
Regina, S4S 5W6 Saskatchewan Canada
Phone: 306-787-4931   Fax: 306-787-2947

Scope: State

Contact(s):
   Larry Lechner, Director of Environmental Assessment Branch; 306-787-5786; larry.lechner.erm@govmail.gov.sk.ca
   Seonaid Macpherson, Director of Public Involvement and Aboriginal Affairs; 306-787-8103; seonaid.macpherson.erm@govmail.gov.sk.ca
   Ron Zukowsky, Executive Director; 306-787-6285; ron.zukowsky.erm@govmail.gov.sk.ca
   Lynda Langford, Senior Manager of Policy and Legislation; 306-787-6868; lynda.langford.erm@govmail.gov.sk.ca

SASKATCHEWAN ENVIRONMENT AND RESOURCE MANAGEMENT
SHIELD ECOREGION
Box 5000
1328 La Ronge Avenue
La Ronge, S0J 1L0 Saskatchewan Canada
Phone: 306-425-4234   Fax: 306-425-2580

Scope: Region

Contact(s):
   John Schisler, Regional Director; 306-425-4231
   Tim Trottier, Wildlife Biologist; 306-425-4237

SASKATCHEWAN ENVIRONMENT AND RESOURCE MANAGEMENT
WEST BOREAL ECOREGION
Unit 1, 101 Railway Place
Meadow Lake, S9X 1X6 Saskatchewan Canada
Phone: 306-236-7540   Fax: 306-236-7677
Website: www.se.gov.sk.ca/corporate/regions/WESTBOR/index.htm

Scope: International

Contact(s):
   Tom Harrison, Regional Director

SOUTH CAROLINA COOPERATIVE FISH AND WILDLIFE RESEARCH UNIT
G27 Lehotsky Hall, Clemson University
Clemson, SC 29634 United States
Phone: 864-656-0168   Fax: 864-656-1034
E-mail: sccoop_l@clemson.edu
Website: www.clemson.edu

Founded: 1988

Scope: National

Description: The Unit conducts ecological research of importance to its cooperators, i.e., the Department of Interior, Clemson University, and the State of South Carolina. Its mission also involves training of graduate students in fish and wildlife biology and related fields.

Keyword(s): Land Issues, Recreation/Ecotourism, Water Habitats & Quality, Wildlife & Species

Contact(s):
   Craig Allen, Assistant Leader of Wildlife
   J. Isely, Assistant Leader of Fisheries

SOUTH CAROLINA DEPARTMENT OF AGRICULTURE
Wade Hampton Office Bldg., P.O. Box 11280
Columbia, SC 29211 United States
Phone: 803-734-2210   Fax: 803-734-2192
Website: www.scda.state.sc.us

Founded: 1904

Scope: State

Description: Administers more than 30 state laws relating to agriculture and the consumer. Represents the farmer in national, regional, and state policy matters and is involved in local and international programs of commodity promotion. Enforces regulatory programs affecting the consumer on a statewide basis.

Publication(s): South Carolina Market Bulletin, The

Keyword(s): Agriculture/Farming, Water Habitats & Quality

Contact(s):
   Larry Boylston, Director of Agribusiness Development
   William Brooks, Director of Laboratory Services
   Carol Fulmer, Director of Consumer Services
   Wayne Mack, Director of Marketing
   Becky Walton, Director of Public Information
   Daniel Breazeale, Administrative Manager
   Kay Rike, Executive Assistant to the Commissioner
   D. Tindal, Commissioner
   David Tompkins, Farmers Markets Administrator
   Sidney Whalen, Assistant Editor

SOUTH CAROLINA DEPARTMENT OF HEALTH AND ENVIRONMENTAL CONTROL
2600 Bull Street
Columbia, SC 29201 United States
Phone: 803-896-8940   Fax: 803-896-8941
Website: www.scdhec.net/eqc/

Membership: 1,001–10,000

Publication(s): A General Guide to Environmental Permitting in South Carolina

Keyword(s): Air Quality/Atmosphere, Pollution (general), Public Health, Reduce/Reuse/Recycle

Contact(s):
   Douglas Bryant, Commissioner; 803-734-4880
   James Joy, Bureau of Air Quality; 803-734-4750
   R. Shaw, Deputy Commissioner of Environmental Quality Control Office; 803-734-5360

SOUTH CAROLINA DEPARTMENT OF HEALTH AND ENVIRONMENTAL CONTROL
OFFICE OF OCEAN AND COASTAL RESOURCE MANAGEMENT (OCRM)
Suite 400, 1362 McMillan Avenue
Charleston, SC 29405 United States
Phone: 803-744-5838   Fax: 803-744-5847
Website: www.scdhec.net/eqc/ocrm

Founded: 1975

Scope: Local, State

Description: OCRM is a division of South Carolina's Department of Health and Environmental Control. OCRM has the dual responsibility of protecting the coastal environment while promoting responsible development within the eight coastal counties.

Publication(s): Carolina Currents, Legislature Update

Keyword(s): Land Issues, Oceans/Coasts/Beaches, Water Habitats & Quality

Contact(s):
- Steve Moore, Director of Permitting
- Steve Snyder, Director of Planning
- Christopher Brooks, Bureau Chief

SOUTH CAROLINA DEPARTMENT OF NATURAL RESOURCES
Rembert C. Dennis Bldg.
1000 Assembly Street
P.O. Box 167
Columbia, SC 29202 United States
Phone: 803-734-4007   Fax: 803-734-6310
Website: www.dnr.state.sc.us

Founded: 1994
Membership: 101–1,000
Scope: State
Description: SCDNR was created by Act 181 of 1993 for the conservation, management, utilization, and protection of SC's natural resources. It also administers SC's Heritage Trust Program for significant natural areas and historical sites. On July 1, 1994, the former Wildlife & Marine Resources Dept.; SC Geological Survey; Migratory Waterfowl Committee; and non-regulatory portions of Water Resources and Land Resources Commissions combined to form SCDNR.
Publication(s): South Carolina Wildlife, South Carolina Weekly Climate Summary, South Carolina Geology
Keyword(s): Climate Change, Land Issues, Oceans/Coasts/Beaches, Recreation/Ecotourism, Water Habitats & Quality, Wildlife & Species
Contact(s):
- John Frampton, Director; 803-734-4007; Fax: 803-734-6310
- James Timmerman, Director Emeritus; 803-798-2858
- Cary Chamblee, Associate Director; 803-734-9102
- Carole Collins, Deputy Director Conservation Education & Communication; 803-734-3957
- Joab Lesesne, Board Chairman; 864-597-4010
- William McTeer, Deputy Director of Wildlife and Freshwater Fisheries Division; 803-734-3889
- John Miglarese, Deputy Director of Marine Resources Division; P.O. Box 12559, Charleston, SC 29422-2559; 843-953-9300
- Alfred Vang, Deputy Director of Land, Water and Conservation Division; 2221 Devine St., Suite 222, Columbia, SC 29205; 803-734-9101
- Alvin Wright, Deputy Director of Law Enforcement Division; 803-734-4021

SOUTH CAROLINA DEPARTMENT OF PARKS, RECREATION AND TOURISM
1205 Pendleton St.
Columbia, SC 29201 United States
Phone: 803-734-1700   Fax: 803-734-0138
E-mail: fulfillment@scprt.com
Website: www.discoversouthcarolina.com

Scope: State
Contact(s):
- Curt Cottle, Director of Heritage Tourism Development Office
- Terri Cowling, Director of Marketing Office
- Roger Deaton, Director of Internal Operations
- John Durst, Director
- David Elwart, Director of Information Technology
- Charles Harrison, Director of Division of Parks and Recreation
- Isabel Hill, Director of Division of Tourism Development
- Robert Liming, Director of New Market Development
- Beth McClure, Director of Office of Recreation, Planning, and Engineering
- R. McGowan, Director of Tourism
- Toni Nance, Director of Business Development Office
- Beverly Shelley, Director of Sales Office
- Yvette Sistare, Director of Finance Office
- Van Stickles, Director of State Park Service
- Ronald Carter, Deputy Director
- Amy Duffy, Deputy Director
- Marion Edmonds, Agency Spokesperson

SOUTH CAROLINA ENERGY OFFICE
1201 Main St., Suite 1010
Columbia, SC 29201 United States
Phone: 803-737-8030   Fax: 803-737-9846
E-mail: energy@ogs.state.sc.us
Website: www.state.sc.us/energy/

Scope: State
Description: The SC Energy Office is responsible for the statewide promotion of energy conservation and cost effective use of new energy sources.
Publication(s): Your Mobile Home, Energy Connection Newsletter, The, The Energy Factbook, How to Reduce Your Energy Costs—A Guide for Business, Industry, Government, and Institutions, Passive Solar Home Designs for South Carolina
Keyword(s): Energy, Reduce/Reuse/Recycle, Transportation
Contact(s):
- John Clark, Director; 803-737-8030; Fax: 803-737-9846; jclark@ogs.state.sc.us
- Renee Daggerhart, Public Information Coordinator; 803-737-8030; Fax: 803-737-9846; rdaggerhart@ogs.state.sc.us

SOUTH DAKOTA COOPERATIVE EXTENSION SERVICE
South Dakota State University
826 32nd Ave
Brookings, SD 57006-4715 United States
Phone: 605-688-4792   Fax: 605-688-6347
E-mail: brookings@ces.sdstate.edu
Website: http://sdces.sdstate.edu/

Membership: 101–1,000
Scope: Regional
Publication(s): See publication website
Keyword(s): Agriculture/Farming, Pollution (general), Reduce/Reuse/Recycle
Contact(s):
- Larry Tidemann, Director of Cooperative Extension Service
- Barry Bunn, Range Livestock Production Specialist; 605-688-5455
- Patricia Johnson, Range Management Specialist; West River Ag Center, South Dakota State University, 1905 Plaza Blvd., Rapid City, SD 57702-9302

SOUTH DAKOTA DEPARTMENT OF AGRICULTURE
523 E. Capitol, Foss Bldg.
Pierre, SD 57501-3182 United States
Phone: 605-773-3375   Fax: 605-773-3481
E-mail: agmail@state.sd.us
Website: www.state.sd.us/doa/doa.html

Scope: State
Publication(s): See publication website
Contact(s):
- Larry Gabriel, Secretary
- Raymond Sowers, State Forester; 605-773-3623; raymond.sowers@state.sd.us

SOUTH DAKOTA DEPARTMENT OF AGRICULTURE
DIVISION OF RESOURCE CONSERVATION AND FORESTRY
523 E. Capitol Ave.
Pierre, SD 57501-3182 United States
Phone: 605-773-3623   Fax: 605-773-4003
E-mail: ray.sowers@state.sd.us
Website: www.state.sd.us/doa/forestry/index2.htm

Founded: 1945

Membership: 1–100
Scope: State
Description: State agency responsible for forestry and conservation programs on state and private lands in South Dakota.
Keyword(s): Agriculture/Farming, Forests/Forestry, Land Issues, Public Lands/Greenspace, Reduce/Reuse/Recycle, Sprawl/Urban Planning, Water Habitats & Quality
Contact(s):
Raymond Sowers, Director; 605-773-3623; Fax: 605-773-4003; ray.sowers@state.sd.us

SOUTH DAKOTA DEPARTMENT OF AGRICULTURE
STATE CONSERVATION COMMISSION
523 E. Capitol Ave.
Pierre, SD 57501-3182 United States
Phone: 605-773-3623   Fax: 605-773-4003
Website: www.state.sd.us/doa/forestry/index2.htm
Founded: 1935
Membership: 1–100
Scope: State
Description: Nine member commission appointed by the Governor
Keyword(s): Agriculture/Farming, Executive/Legislative/Judicial Reform, Forests/Forestry, Land Issues, Public Lands/Greenspace, Reduce/Reuse/Recycle, Sprawl/Urban Planning, Water Habitats & Quality, Wildlife & Species
Contact(s):
Raymond Sowers, Director; 605-773-3623; Fax: 605-773-4003; ray.sowers@state.sd.us
Robert Gab, Chairman; 523 E. Capitol, Pierre, SD 57501

SOUTH DAKOTA DEPARTMENT OF ENVIRONMENT AND NATURAL RESOURCES
523 East Capitol Ave.
Joe Foss Building
Pierre, SD 57501 United States
Phone: 605-773-3151   Fax: 605-773-6035
E-mail: DENRINTERNET@state.sd.us
Website: www.state.sd.us/denr
Founded: 1979
Membership: 101–1,000
Scope: State
Description: Our mission is to provide environmental and natural resources assessment, financial assistance, and regulation in a customer service manner that protects the public health, conserves natural resources, preserves the environment, and promotes economic development.
Keyword(s): Air Quality/Atmosphere, Land Issues, Pollution (general), Public Health, Reduce/Reuse/Recycle, Water Habitats & Quality
Contact(s):
Steven Pirner, Secretary; 605-773-5559; Fax: 605-773-6035; denrInternet@state.sd.us
David Templeton, Director of Division of Financial and Technical Assistance; 605-773-4216; Fax: 605-773-4068; dave.templeton@state.sd.us
Tim Tollefsrud, Director of Division of Environmental Services; 605-773-3153; Fax: 605-773-6035; tim.tollefsrud@state.sd.us

SOUTH DAKOTA DEPARTMENT OF GAME, FISH, AND PARKS
523 East Capitol
Joe Foss Office Bldg.
Pierre, SD 57501-3182 United States
Phone: 605-773-3485   Fax: 605-773-6245
E-mail: wildinfo@state.sd.us
Website: www.state.sd.us/gfp
Membership: 1–100

Scope: State
Description: To provide environmental and natural resources assessment, financial assistance, and regulation in a customer service orientated manner which provides protection of public health, conservation of natural resources, preservation of the environment, and promotes economic development.
Publication(s): South Dakota Conservation Digest
Keyword(s): Land Issues, Public Lands/Greenspace, Recreation/Ecotourism, Water Habitats & Quality, Wildlife & Species
Contact(s):
Ken Anderson, Director of Administration Division; 605-773-3396
Doug Hansen, Director of Wildlife Division; 605-773-3381
Doug Hofer, Director of Parks and Recreation Division; 605-773-3391
Rollie Noem, Director of Custer State Park Division; 605-255-4515
Paul Coughlin, Habitat Program Administrator; 605-773-4194; Fax: 605-773-6245; paul.coughlin@state.sd.us
Ron Fowler, Game Program Administrator; 605-773-4193
Dave McCrea, Law Enforcement Program Administrator; 605-773-4243
Chuck Schlueter, Communications Program Administrator; 605-773-3485; Fax: 605-773-6245; chuck.schlueter@state.sd.us
Dennis Unkenholz, Fisheries Program Administrator; 605-773-4508; Fax: 605-773-6245; dennis.unkenholz@state.sd.us
Wayne Winter, Federal Aid Manager; 605-773-6228
Amy Brady, Editor; Game, Fish & Parks, 412 West Missouri Ave., Pierrre, SD 57501; 605-773-3486; Fax: 605-773-6921; amy.brady@state.sd.us
John Cooper, Secretary; 605-773-3387
Emmett Keyser, Operations Assistant Director of Wildlife Division; 605-773-4607
John Kirk, Specialist of Environmental Review; 605-773-4501
Robert Schuurmans, Turn In Poachers, Training Coordinator; Game, Fish & Parks, 412 West Missouri Ave, Pierre, SD 57501; 605-773-5906; Fax: 605-773-6921
William Shattuck, Boating and Hunting Safety; 412 West Missouri Ave, Pierre, SD 57501; 605-773-4506; Fax: 605-773-6921; bill.shattuck@state.sd.us
George Vandel, Technical Services Assistant Director of Wildlife Division; 605-773-4192

SOUTH FLORIDA WATER MANAGEMENT DISTRICT
3301 Gun Club Rd., P.O. Box 24680
West Palm Beach, FL 33416-4680 United States
Phone: 561-686-8800   Fax: 561-602-0200
Website: www.sfwmd.gov
Founded: 1949
Membership: 1,001–10,000
Scope: State
Description: Responsible for local cooperation in the Federal-State Central and Southern Florida Flood Control Project. Goals include: flood control, water supply, water quality, and environmental protection for sixteen counties in south Florida. Additional benefits are preservation of natural conditions in the Everglades, land purchases under Save Our Rivers program and enhancement of wetlands, fish, wildlife, waterfowl and public recreation.
Keyword(s): Ecosystems (precious), Water Habitats & Quality
Contact(s):
Henry Dean, Executive Director; ext. 6136; lhummel@sfwmd.gov
Alvin Jackson, Deputy Executive Director - Corporate Resources; ext. 2805; rsandhau@sfwmd.gov
Pamela Mac'Kie, Deputy Executive Director - Land and West Coast Resources; ext. 7779; cberger@sfwmd.gov
Chip Merriam, Deputy Executive Director - Water Resource Management; ext. 6597; lelias@sfwmd.gov

Carol Wehle, Assistant Executive Director; ext. 2893; cberger@sfwmd.gov

SOUTHWEST FLORIDA WATER MANAGEMENT DISTRICT (SWFWMD)
2379 Broad St., U.S. 41 South
Brooksville, FL 34604-6899 United States
Phone: 352-796-7211   Fax: 352-754-6883
Website: www.watermatters.org

Founded: 1961
Membership: 101–1,000
Scope: State
Description: A governmental agency dedicated to resource protection conservation programs, which are supported through regulatory and nonregulatory initiatives and cooperative funding projects.
Publication(s): 12 Simple Ways to Save Water, various residential and commercial water conservation education resources, list of vendors and manufacturers of water conservation devices and services, Plant Guide and associated technical bulletins
Keyword(s): Reduce/Reuse/Recycle, Water Habitats & Quality
Contact(s):
David Moore, Executive Director; 352-796-7211
Kathy Scott, Conservation Project Manager; 352-796-7211; ext. 4247; kathy.scott@swfwmd.state.fl.us
Kathy Scott, Water Resource Analyst Staff and Secretary of the Florida Water Wise Council; 352-796-7211; ext. 4247; kathy.scott@swfwmd.state.fl.us

STATE ENGINEER OFFICE/INTERSTATE STREAM COMMISSION
Bataan Memorial Bldg
Interstate Stream Commission
P.O. Box 25102
Santa Fe, NM 87504 United States
Phone: 505-827-6160   Fax: 505-827-6188
Website: www.seo.state.nm.us

Membership: 1–100
Scope: State, Regional
Description: Administration, development, protection, and conservation of the water resources of the state of New Mexico.
Publication(s): Water Line
Contact(s):
Norman Gaume, Director of Interstate Stream Commission; 505-827-6160
Elaine Pacheco, Acting Chief of Technical Division
Hoyt Pattison, Vice Chairman
Paul Saavedra, Chief of Water Rights Division
Thomas Turney, State Engineer and Secretary; 505-827-6160

T

TAHOE REGIONAL PLANNING AGENCY
128 Market St
P.O. Box 5310
Stateline, NV 89449-5310 United States
Phone: 775-588-4547   Fax: 775-588-4527
E-mail: trpa@trpa.org
Website: www.trpa.org

Founded: 1969
Membership: 1–100
Scope: Regional
Description: To establish and implement land use and environmental plans and regulations in the Lake Tahoe Region. Established by Public Law No. 91-148, December 1969, amended by Public Law No. 96-551, December 1980.
Keyword(s): Air Quality/Atmosphere, Forests/Forestry, Land Issues, Transportation, Water Habitats & Quality, Wildlife & Species

Contact(s):
Juan Palma, Executive Director
Jordan Kahn, Legal Counsel
John Marshall, Legal Counsel

TENNEESSEE DEPARTMENT OF ENVIRONMENT & CONSERVATION
401 Church Street
21st Floor
L & C Tower
Nashville, TN 37243 United States
Phone: 1-888-891-8332   Fax: 1-615-532-0120
E-mail: ask.tdec@state.tn.us
Website: www.state.tn.us/environment/

Scope: Local, State, Regional
Description: TDEC's responsibility is to ensure that Tennessee has the cleanest and safest environment, the greatest recreation opportunities, and the most valued natural and cultural resources of any state. Our parks, natural areas and communities will be models of environmental stewardship and prosperity.
Contact(s):
Betsy Child, Commissioner; 1-888-891-8332; Fax: 1-615-532-0120; ask.tdec@state.tn.us

TENNESSEE AGRICULTURAL EXTENSION SERVICE
UNIVERSITY OF TENNESSEE, THE
2621 Morgan Circle
121 Morgan Hall
Knoxville, TN 37996-4530 United States
Phone: 865-974-7114   Fax: 865-974-1068
E-mail: clnorman@utk.edu
Website: www.utextension.utk.edu

Membership: 101–1,000
Scope: State
Description: The Tennessee Agricultural Extension Service is an off-campus division of The University of Tennessee Institute of Agriculture. It is a statewide educational organization, funded by federal, state and local governments, that brings research-based information about agriculture, family and consumer sciences, and resource development to the people of Tennessee where they live and work.
Keyword(s): Agriculture/Farming, Air Quality/Atmosphere, Forests/Forestry, Land Issues, Recreation/Ecotourism, Reduce/Reuse/Recycle, Water Habitats & Quality, Wildlife & Species
Contact(s):
Craig Harper, General Wildlife Specialist; 865-974-7346; Fax: 865-974-4714; charper@utk.edu
Thomas Hill, General Fish and Wildlife Specialist; 865-974-7164; Fax: 865-974-4714; tkhill@utk.edu
George Hopper, Head, Forestry, Wildlife & Fisheries; 865-974-7126; Fax: 865-974-0957
Charles Norman, Dean of Extension Service; 865-974-7114; Fax: 865-974-1068; clnorman@utk.edu

TENNESSEE COOPERATIVE FISHERY RESEARCH UNIT (USDI)
Tennessee Technological University, Box 5114
Cookeville, TN 38505 United States
Phone: 931-372-3094   Fax: 931-382-6257

Keyword(s): Wildlife & Species
Contact(s):
James Layzer, Leader

TENNESSEE DEPARTMENT OF AGRICULTURE
Ellington Agricultural Center
Box 40627, Melrose Station
Nashville, TN 37204 United States
Phone: 615-837-5103   Fax: 615-837-5333
E-mail: TN.Agriculture@state.tn.us
Website: www.state.tn.us/agriculture

Scope: State
Contact(s):
Dan Wheeler, Commissioner

TENNESSEE DEPARTMENT OF AGRICULTURE
STATE SOIL CONSERVATION COMMITTEE
Ellington Agriculture Center
P.O. Box 40627
Nashville, TN 37204 United States
Phone: 615-837-5225   Fax: 615-837-5025
E-mail: non.point@state.tn.us
Website: www.state.tn.us/agriculture/mps

Keyword(s): Agriculture/Farming, Land Issues, Pollution (general), Water Habitats & Quality
Contact(s):
Barry Lako, Chair; P.O. Box 107, Hickory Valley, TN 38042; 901-764-2909
Jim Nance, Executive Secretary; 615-360-0108

TENNESSEE DEPARTMENT OF ENVIRONMENT AND CONSERVATION
401 Church St., 21st Fl.
Nashville, TN 37243 United States
Phone: 615-532-0109   Fax: 615-532-0120
E-mail: ask.tdec@state.tn.us
Website: www.tdec.org

Membership: 1,001–10,000
Scope: State
Description: To plan, promote, protect, and conserve this state's natural, cultural, recreational, and historical resources, and to enforce environmental laws and regulations which protect the state's land and water.
Contact(s):
Mike Apple, Director of Solid Waste Management; 615-532-0780; Fax: 615-532-0886
Charles Brewton, Director of Resort Operations; 615-532-0263; Fax: 615-532-0740
Paul Davis, Director of Water Pollution Control; 615-532-0625; Fax: 615-532-0046
David Draughon, Director of Water Supply; 615-532-0191; Fax: 615-532-0503
Tim Eagle, Director of Land Reclamation; 865-594-5609
Wayne Gregory, Director of Underground Storage Tanks; 615-532-0945; Fax: 615-532-0938
Herbert Harper, Director of Historical Commission; 615-532-1550; Fax: 615-532-1549
Jim Haynes, Director of Superfund; 615-532-0900; Fax: 615-532-0938
Toye Heape, Director of Indian Affairs; 615-532-0745; Fax: 615-532-0732
Joyce Hoyle, Director of Recreation Resources; 615-742-0748; Fax: 615-532-0778
Eddie Nanney, Director of Radiological Health; 615-532-0364
Reggie Reeves, Director of Natural Heritage Division; 615-532-0431; Fax: 615-532-0231
Barry Stephens, Director of Air Pollution Control; 615-532-0554; Fax: 615-532-0614
Kent Taylor, Director of Groundwater Protection; 615-532-0762; Fax: 615-532-0778
Ron Zurawski, Director of Geology; 615-532-1500; Fax: 615-532-1517
Tom Callery, Asst. Commissioner for Conservation; 615-532-4511; Fax: 615-532-0231
Nick Fielder, State Archaeologist of Archaeology Division; 615-741-1588; Fax: 615-741-7329
Dodd Galbreagh, Environmental Policy Office; 615-532-8545; Fax: 615-532-0120
Milton Hamilton, Commissioner; 615-532-0109; Fax: 615-532-0120
John Leonard, Asst. Commissioner for Environment; 615-532-0225; Fax: 615-532-0120
Kim Olson, Public Information Officer; 615-532-0288; Fax: 615-532-0740
Joe Sanders, General Counsel; 615-532-0131; Fax: 615-532-0145
Mark Williams, Asst. Commissioner for State Parks; 615-532-0022; Fax: 615-532-0732

TENNESSEE WILDLIFE RESOURCES AGENCY
P.O. Box 40747
Nashville, TN 37204 United States
Phone: 615-781-6500   Fax: 615-741-4606
Website: www.tnwildlife.org

Founded: 1949
Scope: Local, State, Regional, National, International
Description: Created to have full and exclusive jurisdiction of the duties and functions relating to wildlife and boating and to the management, protection, propagation, and conservation of wildlife, including hunting and fishing.
Publication(s): Tennessee Wildlife
Keyword(s): Recreation/Ecotourism, Wildlife & Species
Contact(s):
George Akans, Commission Chairman; 865-546-3173; Fax: 865-546-9744
Hugh Simonton, Commission Vice-Chairman; 901-476-8156; Fax: 731-738-1061
Gary Myers, Executive Director; 615-781-6552; Fax: 615-781-6551; gary.myers@state.tn.us
Clarence Coffey, Regional Manager of Cumberland Plateau, Region III; 464 Industrial Blvd., Crossville, TN 38555; 931-484-9571; Fax: 931-456-1025; clarence.coffey@state.tn.us
Gary Cook, Regional Manager of West Tennessee, Region I; 200 Lowell Thomas Dr., Jackson, TN 38301; 731-423-5725; Fax: 731-423-6483; gary.cook@state.tn.us
Richard Kirk, Manager of Nongame/Endangered Species; 615-781-6619; Fax: 615-781-6654; richard.kirk@state.tn.us
Steve Patrick, Regional Manager of Middle Tennessee, Region II, P. O. Box 41489, Nashville, TN 37204; 615-781-6622; Fax: 615-831-9995; steve.patrick@state.tn.us
Bob Ripley, Regional Manager of East Tennessee, Region IV; 3030 Wildlife Way, Morristown, TN 37814; 423-587-7037; Fax: 423-587-7057; bob.ripley@state.tn.us
Ed Carter, Chief of Boating Division; 615-781-6682; Fax: 615-781-5268; ed.carter@state.tn.us
Don Crawford, Education Supervisor; 615-781-6538; Fax: 514-781-6543; don.crawford@state.tn.us
Jim Dillard, Chief of Personnel; 615-781-6594; Fax: 615-781-6559; jim.dillard@state.tn.us
Ron Fox, Assistant Director of Field Operations; 615-781-6557; Fax: 615-781-6551; ron.fox@state.tn.us
Carol Freeman, Chief of Management Systems; 615-781-6528; Fax: 716-741-4606; carol.freeman@state.tn.us
L. Garland, General Counsel; 615-781-6606; Fax: 615-781-5264; brooks.garland@state.tn.us
Allen Gebhardt, Assistant Director of Staff Operations; 615-781-6555; Fax: 615-781-6551; allen.gebhardt@state.tn.us
John Gregory, Chief of Real Estate and Forestry Division; 615-781-6560; Fax: 615-781-5266; john.c.gregory@state.tn.us
Les Haun, Chief of Engineering Division; 615-781-6545; Fax: 615-781-5274; les.haun@state.tn.us
Larry Marcum, Chief of Wildlife Management Division; 615-781-6610; Fax: 615-781-6654; larry.marcum@state.tn.us
David McKinney, Chief of Environmental Division; 615-781-6643; Fax: 615-781-6667; dave.mckinney@state.tn.us

Bill Reeves, Chief of Fish Management Division; 615-781-6575; Fax: 615-781-6667; bill.reeves@state.tn.us

Sonny Richardson, Chief of Law Enforcement Division; 615-781-6580; Fax: 615-781-6680; sonny.richardson@state.tn.us

Barry Sumners, Chief of Planning and Federal Aid; 615-781-6599; Fax: 615-741-6683; barry.sumners@state.tn.us

Ken Tarkington, Chief of Administrative Services Division; 615-781-6512; Fax: 615-781-5263; ken.tarkington@state.tn.us

Dave Woodward, Chief of Information & Education; 615-781-6502; Fax: 615-781-4252; dave.woodward@state.tn.us

Dave Woodward, Editor; 615-781-6502; Fax: 615-781-4252; dave.woodward@state.tn.us

TEXAS DEPARTMENT OF AGRICULTURE

P.O. Box 12847
Austin, TX 78711 United States
Phone: 512-463-7476   Fax: 512-463-1104
E-mail: contact@agr.state.tx.us
Website: www.agr.state.tx.us

Founded: 1904

Scope: State

Description: Our mission is to make Texas the nation's leader in agriculture while providing efficient and extraordinary service.

Contact(s):
Robert Wood, Assistant Commissioner, Rural Economic Development

Delane Caeser, Assistant Commissioner, Marketing and Promotion; Fax: 512-463-7843

Susan Combs, Commissioner

Raette Hearne, Assistant Commissioner, Administrative Services; Fax: 512-463-7582

Martin Hubert, Deputy Commissioner

David Kostroun, Assistant Commissioner, Regulatory Division; Fax: 512-463-8225

Brian Murray, Special Assistant of Producer Relations; 512-463-7553; brian.murray@agr.state.tx.us

Allen Spelce, Assistant Commissioner, Communications

Phil Tham, Assistant Commissioner, Pesticide Division; Fax: 512-475-1618

TEXAS DEPARTMENT OF HEALTH

1100 W. 49th St.
Austin, TX 78756-3199 United States
Phone: 512-458-7111
E-mail: Webmaster@tdh.state.tx.us
Website: www.tdh.state.tx.us

Founded: 1879

Scope: State

Description: The Department of Health was created to protect and promote the health of the people of Texas.

Keyword(s): Energy, Pollution (general), Public Health

Contact(s):
Kirk Wiles, Director of Seafood Safety Division; 512-719-0215

Joseph Fuller, Associate Commissioner of Environmental and Consumer Health; 512-458-7541

Debra Stabeno, Deputy Commissioner of Public Health Sciences and Quality; 512-458-7437

TEXAS FOREST SERVICE

301 Tarrow, Suite 364
College Station, TX 77840-7896 United States
Phone: 979-458-6600   Fax: 979-458-6610
E-mail: joverhouse@tfs.tamu.edu
Website: http://texasforestservice.tamu.edu

Founded: 1915

Membership: 1–100

Scope: State

Description: To encourage and aid private landowners to practice multiple-use forestry; to protect private forest land against wildfire, insects, and diseases; and to inform the public of the contribution that forests make.

Keyword(s): Forests/Forestry, Public Lands/Greenspace, Reduce/Reuse/Recycle, Water Habitats & Quality, Wildlife & Species

Contact(s):
James Hull, Director; 979-458-6600; Fax: 979-458-6610; jhull@tfs.tamu.edu

Edwin Barron, Associate Director of Forest Resource Development; 979-458-6650; Fax: 979-458-6655; ebarron@tfs.tamu.edu

Tom Boggus, Associate Director for Administration; 979-458-6600; Fax: 979-458-6610; tboggus@tfs.tamu.edu

Robert Fewin, Regional Forester of West Texas; Rt. 3 Box 216, Lubbock, TX 79403; 806-746-5801; Fax: 806-746-6610; rfewin@tfs.tamu.edu

William Oates, Regional Forester of Southern Region; 155 Texas Forest Service Loop, Lufkin, TX 75904; 936-875-4400; Fax: 936-875-4419; boates@tfs.tamu.edu

Ernest Smith, Regional Forester of Northern Region; P.O. Box 3527, Longview, TX 75606-3527; 903-234-2829; Fax: 903-234-2839; esmith@tfs.tamu.edu

Bobby Young, Associate Director of Forest Resources Protection; P.O. Box 310, Lufkin, TX 75902; 936-639-8100; Fax: 936-634-8239; bobby@tfs.tamu.edu

TEXAS GENERAL LAND OFFICE

Stephen F. Austin State Office Bldg.
1700 N. Congress Ave.
Suite 840
Austin, TX 78701-1495 United States
Phone: 512-463-5001   Fax: 512-475-1415
E-mail: webmaster@glo.state.tx.us
Website: www.glo.state.tx.us

Scope: State

Description: Serves as the custodian of approximately 20.5 million acres of state-owned land including 4.25 million acres of submerged coastal land. Responsibilities include: protecting state land from unlawful use; managing special projects which protects the state's natural resources; and providing the public with information pertaining to the state's land resources.

Publication(s): Public Information Office

Keyword(s): Oceans/Coasts/Beaches, Public Lands/Greenspace

Contact(s):
David Dewhurst, Commissioner; 512-463-5256; david.dewhurst@glo.state.tx.us

Ashley Wadick, Deputy Commissioner, Resource Management; 512-305-9121; ashley.wadick@glo.state.tx.us

TEXAS PARKS AND WILDLIFE DEPARTMENT

4200 Smith School Road
Austin, TX 78744 United States
Phone: 512-389-4800
Website: www.tpwd.state.tx.us

Founded: 1963

Membership: 101–1,000

Scope: State

Description: An organization that has approximately 3,000 employees including Law Enforcement for Game Laws. To manage and conserve the natural and cultural resources of Texas and to provide hunting, fishing and outdoor recreation opportunities for the use and enjoyment of present and future generations.

Publication(s): Texas Parks & Wildlife Magazine

Contact(s):
Robert Cook, Executive Director; 512-389-4802; robert.cook@tpwd.state.tx.us

Scott Boruff, Deputy Executive Director, Operations & Acting Director, Wildlife; 512-389-8575; scott.boruff@tpwd.state.tx.us

STATE AND PROVINCIAL GOVERNMENT AGENCIES – U

Ann Bright, General Counsel; 512-389-8558;
ann.bright@tpwd.state.tx.us
Gene McCarty, Chief of Staff; 512-389-4651;
gene.mccarty@tpwd.state.tx.us
Drew Thigpen, Deputy Executive Director, Administration;
512-389-8448; drew.thigpen@tpwd.state.tx.us
Alfred Bingham, Director, Human Resources Division; 512-389-4809; al.bingham@tpwd.state.tx.us
Walt Dabney, Director, State Parks Division; 512-389-8545;
walt.dabney@tpwd.state.tx.us
Phil Durocher, Director, Inland Fisheries Division; 512-389-4643; phil.durocher@tpwd.state.tx.us
Mary Fields, Chief Financial Officer & Director, Admin. Resources Div.; 512-389-4803;
mary.fields@tpwd.state.tx.us
Larry McKinney, Senior Director, Resource Protection Division; 512-389-4636; larry.mckinney@tpwd.state.tx.us
Hal Osburn, Director, Coastal Fisheries Division; 512-389-4648; hal.osburn@tpwd.state.tx.us
Joey Park, Director of Intergovernmental Affairs; 512-389-4530; joseph.park@tpwd.state.tx.us
Lydia Saldana, Director, Communications Division; 512-389-4557; lydia.saldana@tpwd.state.tx.us
Jim Stinebaugh, Director, Law Enforcement Division; 512-389-4409; james.stinebaugh@tpwd.state.tx.us
Steve Whiston, Director, Infrastructure Division; 512-389-4741; stephen.whiston@tpwd.state.tx.us

TEXAS STATE SOIL AND WATER CONSERVATION BOARD
P.O. Box 658
Temple, TX 76503-0658 United States
Phone: 254-773-2250   Fax: 254-773-3311
Website: www.tsswcb.state.tx.us

Scope: Regional

Description: The Texas State Soil and Water Conservation Board is a state agency established to administer and carry out Texas' soil and water conservation law. The Board is charged with the responsibility of administering and coordinating Texas' soil and water conservation program with the state's 216 local soil and water conservation districts. The Board is also the agency responsible for planning, implementing, and managing programs and practices for abating agricultural and silvicultural nonpoint source

Keyword(s): Agriculture/Farming, Land Issues, Reduce/Reuse/Recycle

Contact(s):
Robert Buckley, Executive Director; 311 N. 5th St., Temple, TX 76501-3107; Fax: 254-773-3311

TEXAS WATER DEVELOPMENT BOARD
P.O. Box 13231, Capitol Station
1700 N. Congress Ave.
Austin, TX 78711-3231 United States
Phone: 512-463-7847   Fax: 512-475-2053
E-mail: info@twdb.state.tx.us
Website: www.twdb.state.tx.us

Founded: 1957
Membership: 1–100
Scope: State

Description: Texas Water Development Board provides loans to local governments for water supply projects; water quality projects, including wastewater treatment, municipal solid waste management, and nonpoint source pollution control; agricultural water conservation projects; and flood control projects. Provides water related research and planning and agricultural water conservation funding.

Publication(s): Water for Texas - Today and Tomorrow, bay and estuary reports since 1967, ground water reports since 1957, Texas Water Facts, Rainwater Harvesting - brochure

Keyword(s): Water Habitats & Quality

Contact(s):
Wales Madden, Chairman
Jack Hunt, Vice Chairman
Hugh Bender, Director of Texas Natural Resources Information System; 512-463-8051;
hugh.bender@twdb.state.tx.us
Bill Mullican, Director of Water Resources Information; 512-936-0813; bill.mullican@twdb.state.tx.us
George Green, Northern Project Management Division; 512-463-7853; george.green@twdb.state.tx.us
Tommy Knowles, Deputy Executive Administrator for Planning; 512-463-8043; tommy.knowles@twdb.state.tx.us
Ignacio Madera, Border Project Management Division; 512-463-7509; ignacio.madera@twdb.state.tx.us
Leonard Olson, Special Assistant for Intergovernmental and External Customers; 512-463-7931;
leonard.olson@twdb.state.tx.us
Suzanne Schwartz, General Counsel; 512-463-7981;
suzanne.schwartz@twdb.state.tx.us
J. Ward, Deputy Executive Administrator for Office of Project Finance; 512-463-0991; kevin.ward@twdb.state.tx.us

U

UNITED STATES ENVIRONMENTAL PROTECTION BUREAU
DEPARTMENT OF LAW
120 Broadway
New York City, NY 10271 United States
Phone: 212-416-8446   Fax: 212-416-6007
Website: www.oag.state.ny.us

Scope: State, Regional, National

Description: Institutes legal actions on behalf of the people of New York State in cases involving air and water pollution, protection of wildlife, waste site remediation, and protection of scenic and natural resources. Has responsibility for enforcement of laws protecting endangered species of wildlife, as well as public nuisance actions to restrain pollution and other environmental damage. Defends environmental decisions of state agencies.

Contact(s):
Peter Lehner, Bureau Chief
Peter Skinner, Environmental Scientist; 518-474-2432

UNITED STATES VIRGIN ISLANDS DEPARTMENT OF PLANNING AND NATURAL RESOURCES
DIVISION OF ENVIRONMENTAL PROTECTION
Cyril E. King Airport, 2nd Floor
St. Thomas, VI 00802 United States
Phone: 340-774-3320   Fax: 340-714-9549
E-mail: stt-office@vidpnr-dep.org
Website: www.dpnr.gov.vi/dep/home.htm

Founded: 1970

Description: Responsible for: Fish and wildlife; trees, vegetation and water resources; air and water pollution control; flood control; sewers and sewage disposal; culture and the arts; libraries and museums; minerals and other natural resources; historical preservation; submerged lands; earth change permits; and oil spill prevention and control.

Publication(s): Annual Report, Species Technical Bulletin, Natural History Atlas to the Cays of the Virgin Islands, Proceedings - Fisheries in Crisis Conference (Division of Fish and Wildlife)

Keyword(s): Water Habitats & Quality, Wildlife & Species

Contact(s):
Hollis Griffin, Director, Division of Environmental Protection
Dean Plaskett, Esq., Commissioner, Department of Planning & Natural Resources
Leonard Reed, Esq., Assistant Director, Division of Environmental Protection

UNITED STATES VIRGIN ISLANDS DEPARTMENT OF PLANNING AND NATURAL RESOURCES
DIVISION OF FISH AND WILDLIFE
6291 Estate Nazareth, 101
St. Thomas, VI 00802 United States
Phone: 340-775-6762 Fax: 340-775-3972

Membership: 1–100
Scope: Regional
Publication(s): Wildlife Viewing Guide
Contact(s):
  Barbara Kojis, Director; bkojis@telecom.net
  Judy Pierce, Chief of Wildlife; sula@vitelcom.net

UNIVERSITY OF MARYLAND COOPERATIVE EXTENSION
1296 Symons Hall
College Park, MD 20742 United States
Phone: 301-405-2072 Fax: 301-405-2963
E-mail: jw241@umail.umd.edu
Website: www.agnr.umc.edu

Membership: 101–1,000
Scope: National
Publication(s): Located on website
Contact(s):
  Thomas Fretz, Dean and Director of Agricultural Experiment; 301-405-2072; Fax: 301-314-9146; tf43@umail.umd.edu
  James Hanson, Program Leader and Assistant Director of Agriculture; University of Maryland, Cooperative Extension, 1200 Symons Hall, College Park, MD 20742-5565; 301-405-7992; Fax: 301-405-2963
  Jonathan Kays, Regional Natural Resource Specialist; University of Maryland, Cooperative Extension, Western Maryland Research and Education Center, 18330 Keedysville Road, Keedysville, MD 21756; 301-432-2735; ext. 323; Fax: 301-432-4089
  Doug Lipton, Coordinator: Sea Grant Extension Program; University of Maryland, Cooperative Extension, 2218B Symons Hall, College Park, MD 20742; 301-405-1280
  Bob Tjaden, Regional Natural Resource Specialist; University of Maryland, Cooperative Extension, Wye Research and Education Center, P.O. Box 169, Queenstown, MD 21658; 410-827-8056; Fax: 410-827-9039
  James Wade, Associate Dean & Associate Director Maryland Cooperative Extension; University of Maryland, Cooperative Extension, 1200 Symons Hall, College Park, MD 20742-5565; 301-405-2907; Fax: 301-405-2963

UNIVERSITY OF HAWAII
ENVIRONMENTAL CENTER
WATER RESOURCES RESEARCH CENTER
Krauss Annex 19
2500 Dole St.
Honolulu, HI 96822 United States
Phone: 808-956-7361 Fax: 808-956-3980
E-mail: envctr@hawaii.edu
Website: www2.hawaii.edu/~envctr/

Founded: 1970
Membership: 1–100
Scope: State
Description: To stimulate, expand, and coordinate education, research, and service efforts of the university related to ecological relationships, natural resources, and environmental quality, with special relation to human needs and social institutions, particularly with regard to the state. for information on Liberal Studies BA Degree in Environmental Studies, check the University of Hawaii website: www.hawaii.edu/catalog/special-pgms-files/inter-progs.html#es
Keyword(s): Water Habitats & Quality
Contact(s):
  James Moncur, Director
  John Harrison, Environmental Coordinator; jth@hawaii.edu
  Jacquelin Miller, Associate Environmental Coordinator; jackiem@hawaii.edu

UNIVERSITY OF HAWAII COOPERATIVE EXTENSION PROGRAM
COLLEGE OF TROPICAL AGRICULTURE AND HUMAN RESOURCES
Gilmore Hall 203, 3050 Maile Way
Univ. of Hawaii at Manoa
Honolulu, HI 96822 United States
Phone: 808-956-8397 Fax: 808-956-9105
E-mail: extension@ctahr.hawaii.edu
Website: www.ctahr.hawaii.edu/extout/extout.asp

Founded: 1907
Membership: 101–1,000
Scope: State
Description: The University of Hawaii (UH) Cooperative Extension Service (CES) covers areas of agriculture, natural resources and environment, home economics, community resource development and 4-H and youth development.
Contact(s):
  Barry Brennan, Dean and Director of Cooperative Extension; 808-956-8397; Fax: 808-956-9105; barryb@hawaii.edu
  Richard Brock, Researcher/Fisheries Specialist; Univ. of Hawaii Sea Grant Program, 1000 Pope Rd./MSB 204, Honolulu, HI 96822; 808-956-2859; Fax: 808-956-2858

UNIVERSITY OF MASSACHUSETTS EXTENSION
Stockbridge Hall, Box 30099, University of Massachusetts
Amherst, MA 01003 United States
Phone: 413-545-4800 Fax: 413-545-6555
E-mail: umextadm@umext.umass.edu
Website: www.umassextension.org

Keyword(s): Forests/Forestry, Reduce/Reuse/Recycle, Wildlife & Species
Contact(s):
  John Gerber, Director; jgerber@umext.umass.edu
  Anna Hicks, Natural Resources and Environmental Conservation Program; Holdsworth Hall, University of Massachusetts, Amherst, MA 01003; 413-545-4743; Fax: 413-545-4358; ahicks@umext.umass.edu
  Scott Jackson, Conservation Specialist; University of Massachusetts, Department of Forestry and Wildlife Management, Holdsworth Natural Resources Center, Amherst, MA 01003; 413-545-2665

UNIVERSITY OF NEBRASKA COOPERATIVE EXTENSION
211 Agricultural Hall, University of Nebraska
Lincoln, NE 68583-0703 United States
Phone: 402-472-2966 Fax: 402-472-5557
Website: www.extension.unl.edu

Scope: State, Regional
Description: University of Nebraska Cooperative Extension provides nonformal research-based education to help Nebraskans make sound decisions to improve their social, economic, and evironmental well-being. Faculty are located in 83 county offices, at four Research and Extension Centers, and on the University of Nebraska-Lincoln campus.
Keyword(s): Agriculture/Farming, Air Quality/Atmosphere, Climate Change, Ecosystems (precious), Forests/Forestry, Land Issues, Public Health, Recreation/Ecotourism, Reduce/Reuse/Recycle, Sprawl/Urban Planning, Water Habitats & Quality, Wildlife & Species
Contact(s):
  John Allen, Director, Center for Rural Community Revitalization and Development; 58C H.C. Filley Hall, University of Nebraska, Lincoln, NE 68583-0947; 402-472-8012; Fax: 402-472-3460; jallen1@unl.edu
  Elbert Dickey, Dean and Director of Cooperative Extension; edickey1@unl.edu

Susan Fritz, Dept. Head of Agricultural Leadership, Education and Communication; 300 Agricultural Hall, University of Nebraska, Lincoln, NE 68583-0709; 402-472-9559; Fax: 402-472-5863

Scott Hygnstrom, Vertebrate Pest Specialist; 202 Natural Resources Hall, University of Nebraska, Lincoln, NE 68583-0819; 402-472-6822; Fax: 402-472-2946

Ron Johnson, Wildlife Specialist; 202 Natural Resources Hall, University of Nebraska-Lincoln, P.O. Box 830844, Lincoln, NE 68583-0844; 402-472-6823; Fax: 402-472-2946; rjohnson4@unl.edu

UNIVERSITY OF VERMONT EXTENSION
PUBLICATIONS OFFICE
Communications Technology Resources
Agr. Eng. Bldg
63 Carrigan Drive
Burlington, VT 05405-0004 United States
Phone: 802-656-0319   Fax: 802-656-5878
E-mail: cathy.yandow@uvm.edu
Website: www.uvm.edu/extension/publications/

Membership: 1–100
Scope: Local, Regional

UTAH DEPARTMENT OF AGRICULTURE
P.O. BOX 146500
Salt Lake City, UT 84114-6500 United States
Phone: 801-538-7100   Fax: 801-538-7126
Website: www.ag.state.ut.us

Membership: 101–1,000
Scope: State

Contact(s):
  Renee Matsuura, Director of Administrative Services
  Randy Parker, Director of Marketing
  G. Wilson, Director of Plant Industry
  James Christensen, Staff of Agricultural Development and Conservation
  Bob Smoot, Staff of Weights and Measures
  Kyle Stephens, Staff of Food and Dairy
  Van Burgess, Deputy Commissioner
  Miles Ferry, Commissioner
  Michael Marshall, State Veterinarian
  Ahmad Salari, State Chemist
  El Shaffer, Information Officer

UTAH DEPARTMENT OF HEALTH
P.O. Box 1010
Salt Lake City, UT 84114-1010 United States
Phone: 801-538-6101   Fax: 801-538-6306
Website: http://health.utah.gov/

Scope: State
Publication(s): Health Data Programs, Baby Your Baby
Keyword(s): Pollution (general), Public Health
Contact(s):
  Rod Betit, Executive Director
  Jana Kettering, Department of Health Public Information Officer; 801-538-6339

UTAH DEPARTMENT OF NATURAL RESOURCES
DIVISION OF UTAH STATE PARKS AND RECREATION
1594 W. North Temple, Suite 116
P.O. Box 146001
Salt Lake City, UT 84114-6001 United States
Phone: 801-538-7220   Fax: 801-538-7378
E-mail: parkcomment@utah.gov
Website: www.stateparks.utah.gov

Membership: 101–1,000
Scope: State
Description: Utah State Parks and Recreation is steward of many of Utah's natural and cultural resources.
Publication(s): Utah State Field Guide
Keyword(s): Public Lands/Greenspace, Recreation/Ecotourism
Contact(s):
  Courtland Nelson, Director
  Terry Green, Park Planning Manager; 801-538-7346
  Jim Harland, Regional Manager of Northwest; 1084 North Redwood Road, Salt Lake City, UT 84116; 801-533-5127; Fax: 801-533-4229
  Tim Smith, Regional Manager of Southeast; 435-259-3750
  Gordon Topham, Regional Manager of Southwest; 585 North Main, Cedar City, UT 84720; 435-586-4497; Fax: 435-586-2789
  Dennis Weaver, Regional Manager of Northeast; 435-649-9109
  Jay Christianson, Chief of Law Enforcement; 801-538-7326
  Dave Morrow, Deputy Director
  Mary Tullius, Deputy Director
  Ted Woolley, Boating Coordinator

UTAH DEPARTMENT OF NATURAL RESOURCES
DIVISION OF WILDLIFE RESOURCES
1594 W. North Temple, Suite 2110, P.O. Box 146301
Salt Lake City, UT 84114-6301 United States
Phone: 801-538-4700   Fax: 801-538-4709
Website: www.wildlife.utah.gov

Scope: State
Description: State wildlife management agency.
Publication(s): Wildlife News (Weekly), Wildlife Review (Quarterly)
Contact(s):
  Kevin Conway, Director of Division of Wildlife Resources

UTAH FORESTRY, FIRE AND STATE LANDS
1594 W. North Temple, Suite 3520
P.O. Box 145703
Salt Lake City, UT 84114-5703 United States
Phone: 801-538-5555   Fax: 801-533-4111
Website: www.ffsl.utah.gov/

Scope: State
Description: The Utah Division of Forestry, Fire and State Lands manages all state-owned non-trust lands, and manages state forestry and fire control programs.
Contact(s):
  Arthur Dufault, State Forester and Director
  Karl Kappe, Strategic Planner

UTAH GEOLOGICAL SURVEY
1594 W. North Temple, Suite 3410, P.O. Box 146100
Salt Lake City, UT 84114-6100 United States
Phone: 801-537-3300   Fax: 801-537-3400
Website: www.geology.utah.gov

Scope: State
Publication(s): Geologic
Contact(s):
  Richard Allis, Director

UTAH STATE DEPARTMENT OF NATURAL RESOURCES
1594 W. North Temple, Suite 3710, P.O. Box 145610
Salt Lake City, UT 84114-5610 United States
Phone: 801-538-7200   Fax: 801-538-7315
Website: www.nr.utah.gov

Founded: 1967
Membership: 100,001–500,000
Scope: State
Description: Sustain and enhance the quality of life for people today and tomorrow through the coordinated and balanced stewardship of our natural resources.
Keyword(s): Energy, Forests/Forestry, Land Issues, Public Lands/Greenspace, Recreation/Ecotourism, Water Habitats & Quality, Wildlife & Species

Contact(s):
Robert Morgan, Executive Director; 801-538-7200; Fax: 801-538-7315; nradm.bbarela@state.ut.us
Darin Bird, Assistant Director
Sherm Hoskins, Deputy Director
Hugh Thompson, Deputy Director

UTAH STATE DEPARTMENT OF NATURAL RESOURCES
DIVISION OF WATER RESOURCES
1594 W. North Temple, Suite 310
P.O. Box 146201
Salt Lake City, UT 84114-6201 United States
Phone: 801-538-7230   Fax: 801-538-7279
E-mail: mollywaters@utah.gov
Website: www.nr.uta.gov.

Membership: 1-100
Scope: State
Description: State Agency
Contact(s):
D. Anderson, Director

UTAH STATE DEPARTMENT OF NATURAL RESOURCES
DIVISION OF WILDLIFE RESOURCES
1594 W. North Temple, Suite 2110, P.O. Box 146301
Salt Lake City, UT 84114-6301 United States
Phone: 801-538-4700   Fax: 801-538-4745
E-mail: wcomment.nrdwr@state.ut.us
Website: www.wildlife.utah.gov

Scope: State
Contact(s):
John Kimball, Director
J. Allan, Board Member
Connie Brooks, Board Member
Kevin Conway, Assistant Director
Rick Danvir, Board Member
B. Dastrup, Board Member
Walt Donaldson, Supervisor of Northeast Region; 152 E. 100 N., Vernal, UT 84078; 435-789-3103; Fax: 435-789-8343
Brenda Freeman, Board Member
Jim Guymon, Supervisor of Southern Region; P.O. Box 606, Cedar City, UT 84721; 435-865-6100; Fax: 435-586-2457
Robert Hasenyager, Supervisor of Northern Region; 515 E. 5300 S., Ogden, UT 84405; 435-476-2740; Fax: 435-479-4010
Raymond Heaton, Board Member
Miles Moretti, Supervisor of Southeastern Region; 475 W. Price River Dr., Suite C, Price, UT 84501; 435-636-0260; Fax: 435-637-7361
Max Morgan, Chair Person
Jordan Pedersen, Supervisor of Central Region; 115 N. Main St., Springfield, UT 84663; 435-489-5678; Fax: 435-489-7000

UTAH STATE DEPARTMENT OF NATURAL RESOURCES
UTAH ENERGY OFFICE
1594 W. North Temple, Suite 3610, P.O. Box 146480
Salt Lake City, UT 84114-6480 United States
Phone: 801-538-5428   Fax: 801-538-4795
E-mail: gfleisch.ueo@state.ut.us
Website: www.nr.utah.gov/energy/home.htm

Scope: State
Description: The Utah Energy Office is a state government office that works to promote energy efficiency and conservation.
Keyword(s): Energy
Contact(s):
Michael Glenn, Manager; 801538787; Fax: 801538795; mglenn.ueo@state.ut.us

UTAH STATE SOIL CONSERVATION COMMISSION
350 N. Redwood Rd.
Salt Lake City, UT 84116 United States
Phone: 801-538-7120   Fax: 801-538-4949
E-mail: sadginton@state.ut.us
Website: www.ag.state.ut.us

Founded: 1938
Scope: State
Description: Assists Utah's 39 soil conservation districts (SCD) in encouraging land operators to implement measures and practices; to prevent soil deterioration; restore depleted soil; prevent flood damage; improve irrigation water efficiency; and to encourage nonpoint water pollution control programs. The commission has 12 members; 5 ex-officio, and 7 governor-appointed SCD members with their alternates.
Keyword(s): Agriculture/Farming, Development/Developing Countries, Land Issues, Reduce/Reuse/Recycle
Contact(s):
Miles Ferry, Chairman
K. Jacobson, Executive

V

VERMONT AGENCY OF AGRICULTURE, FOOD, AND MARKETS
NATURAL RESOURCES CONSERVATION COUNCIL
116 State St.
Montpelier, VT 05620-2901 United States
Phone: 802-828-2416   Fax: 802-828-2361
E-mail: jwa@agr.state.vt.us

Membership: 1-100
Scope: Local
Description: The Conservation Council is the administrative body for the 14 conservation districts in Vermont. The goal of conservation districts is to ensure the wise use, protection and enhancement of Vermont soil, water, and related natural resources; to foster public awareness and appreciation of the need for conservation; and to advance the concept that we are all stewards of the living earth.
Keyword(s): Agriculture/Farming, Land Issues, Oceans/Coasts/Beaches

VERMONT AGENCY OF NATURAL RESOURCES
103 S. Main St.
Waterbury, VT 05671 United States
Phone: 802-241-3600   Fax: 802-241-1102
Website: www.anr.state.vt.us

Founded: 1970
Scope: State
Description: The Agency's mission is to act as a steward of Vermont's natural resources. We work to manage Vermont's natural systems and to foster public understanding so that the integrity, vitality, and diversity of these natural systems are sustained or restored.
Contact(s):
James Bressor, Director of Media and Public Relations; 802-241-3600
Stephen Sease, Director of Planning; 802-241-3620
Scott Johnstone, Secretary; 802-241-3600
Salvatore Spinosa, Enforcement; 802-241-3820

VERMONT AGENCY OF NATURAL RESOURCES
DEPARTMENT OF ENVIRONMENTAL CONSERVATION
Waterbury Complex, 103 S. Main St.
Waterbury, VT 05671 United States
Phone: 802-241-3800   Fax: 802-241-3287
Website: www.decweb.anr.state.vt.us
Scope: State
Description: State Environmental Conservation Department

Keyword(s): Water Habitats & Quality
Contact(s):
Larry Fitch, Director of Facilities; 802-241-3742
P. Flanders, Director of Waste Management; 802-241-3888
Wallace McLean, Director of Water Quality; 802-241-3770
Richard Phillips, Director of Environmental Assistance; 802-241-3470
Jay Rutherford, Director of Water Supply; 802-241-3434
Vacant, Director of Wastewater; 802-241-3822
Richard Valentinetti, Director of Air Quality; 802-241-3860
Jeffrey Wennberg, Commissioner; 802-241-3800

VERMONT AGENCY OF NATURAL RESOURCES
DEPARTMENT OF FISH AND WILDLIFE
103 S. Main St.
Waterbury, VT 05671-0501 United States
Phone: 802-241-3700 Fax: 802-241-3295
Website: www.vt.fishandwildlife.com

Scope: National
Keyword(s): Air Quality/Atmosphere, Reduce/Reuse/Recycle, Wildlife & Species
Contact(s):
Angelo Incerpi, Director of Operations
Eric Palmer, Director of Fisheries
Linda Eldredge, Business Manager
John Hall, Information and Education
Dave Mallory, Chair of Fish and Wildlife Board
Ron Regan, Commissioner
Lisa Wright, Hunter Education

VERMONT AGENCY OF NATURAL RESOURCES
DEPARTMENT OF FORESTS, PARKS, AND RECREATION
Commissioners Office, 103 South Main St.
Waterbury, VT 05671-0605 United States
Phone: 802-241-3670 Fax: 802-244-1481
Website: www.state.vt.us/anr/fpr

Membership: 101–1,000
Scope: Local, State, Regional, National, International
Description: The Department monitors and maintains the health, integrity, and diversity of important species, natural communities, and ecological processes; manages forests for sustainable use; provides and promotes opportunities for compatible outdoor recreation; and furnishes related information, education and services.
Contact(s):
Michael Fraysier, Agency Lands Director; 802-241-3682; Fax: 802-244-1481
Larry Simino, Director of State Parks; 802-241-3664; Fax: 802-244-1481
Steven Sinclair, Director of Forests; 802-241-3680; Fax: 802-244-1481
Ed Leary, Chief of Operations; 802-241-3683; Fax: 802-244-1481
M. Stone, Chief of Forest Resource Management; 802-241-3675
H. Teillon, Chief of Forest Resource Protection; 802-241-3676
Craig Whipple, Chief of Park Operations; 802-241-3663
Jonathan Wood, Commissioner; 802-241-3670; Fax: 802-244-1481

VERMONT AGENCY OF NATURAL RESOURCES
VERMONT GEOLOGICAL SURVEY
103 S. Main St., Old Laundry Bldg.
Waterbury, VT 05671-0301 United States
Phone: 802-241-3496 Fax: 802-241-3273
E-mail: laurence.becker@anrmail.anr.state.vt.us
Website: www.anr.state.vt.us/geologyvgshmpg.htm

Founded: 1844
Membership: 1–100
Scope: State
Description: The Vermont Geological Survey encompasses two divisions. The State Geologist provides surveys of the geology, mineral resources, topography and geological information services to citizens, industry, and state and federal agencies. The Radioactive Waste Management Program manages the disposal of low-level radioactive waste generated in Vermont.
Publication(s): Price list sent upon request or visit the website.
Keyword(s): Energy, Land Issues, Pollution (general)
Contact(s):
Laurence Becker, State Geologist; laurencebecker@anrmail.anr.state.vt.us
Marjorie Gale, Geologist; marjieg@dec.anr.state.vt.us

VERMONT DEPARTMENT OF AGRICULTURE, FOOD, AND MARKETS
116 State Street, Drawer 20
Montpelier, VT 05620-2901 United States
Phone: 802-828-2416 Fax: 802-828-3831
E-mail: webmaster@agr.state.vt.us
Website: www.vermontagriculture.com/

Founded: 1908
Membership: 1–100
Scope: State
Publication(s): Agriview, list available on request.
Contact(s):
Philip Benedict, Director of Plant Industry; 802-828-2431
Rudolph Polli, Business Manager of Administrative Services; 802-828-3567
Louise Calderwood, Deputy Commissioner of Administration
Leon Graves, Commissioner; 802-828-2430
Todd Johnson, State Veterinarian; 802-828-2421

VERMONT DEPARTMENT OF AGRICULTURE, FOOD, AND MARKETS
STATE CONSERVATION COMMISSION
48 Bushey Dr.
Shelburne, VT 5482 United States
Phone: 802-985-2048

Scope: State
Contact(s):
Jon Anderson, Executive Secretary, 802-828-3529; Fax: 802-828-2361; jwa@agr.state.vt.us
Thomas Bushey, Chair; 802-985-2048; Fax: 802-951-6327

VERMONT DEPARTMENT OF HEALTH
108 Cherry St.
P.O. Box 70
Burlington, VT 05402-0070 United States
Phone: 802-863-7200 Fax: 802-863-7754
E-mail: webkeeper@vdh.state.vt.us
Website: www.state.vt.us/health

Membership: 101–1,000
Scope: State
Keyword(s): Air Quality/Atmosphere, Pollution (general), Public Health
Contact(s):
Larry Crist, Director of Health Protection; 802-863-7223
Jan Carney, Commissioner; 802-863-7280

VERMONT ENVIRONMENTAL BOARD
WATER RESOURCE BOARD
National Life Records Center Building, Drawer 20
Montpelier, VT 05620 United States
Phone: 802-828-3309
E-mail: bbartlett@envboard.state.vt.us
Website: www.state.vt.us/envboard/

Scope: State
Contact(s):
Marcy Harding, Chairman of the Board; 802-828-5440

VIRGIN ISLANDS COOPERATIVE EXTENSION SERVICE
University of Virgin Islands, R.R. 2,
Box 10,000, Kingshill
St. Croix, VI 00850-9781 United States
Phone: 340-776-9200 Fax: 340-778-1620
E-mail: pr@uvi.edu
Website: http://rps.uvi.edu/?CES/index.html

Scope: National

Contact(s):
Kwame Garcia, Director of CES
James Rakocy, Director of Agricultural Experiment Station; Univeristy of VI, RR2, Box 10,000, Kingshill, VI 00850; 340-692-4031; Fax: 340-692-4035
Clinton George, Program Leader of Agriculture and Natural Resources
Jozef Keularts, Coordinator, Integrated Pest Management of Pesticide Impact

VIRGIN ISLANDS SOIL AND WATER CONSERVATION DIVISION

Contact(s):
Henry Schuster, Commissioner; 809-778-0997

VIRGINIA COOPERATIVE EXTENSION
VIRGINIA POLYTECHNIC INSTITUTE AND STATE UNIVERSITY
101 Hutcheson Hall
Blacksburg, VA 24061-0402 United States
Phone: 540-231-5299 Fax: 540-231-4370
Website: www.ext.vt.edu/

Membership: 101–1,000
Scope: National

Contact(s):
J. Barrett, Director of Cooperative Extension; davebarr@vt.edu
Gerald Cross, Extension Wildlife Specialist; Department of Fisheries and Wildlife Sciences, Virginia Polytechnic Institute and State University, Blacksburg, VA 24061-0321; 540-231-8844; gecross@vt.edu
George Flick, Sea Grant Extension Seafood Technologist; Dept. of Food Science and Technology, Virginia Polytechnic Institute and State University, Blacksburg, VA 24061-0418; 540-231-6965; flickg@vt.edu
Louis Helfrich, Extension Fisheries Specialist; Department of Fisheries and Wildlife Sciences, Virginia Polytechnic Institute and State University, Blacksburg, VA 24061-0321; 540-231-5059; lhelfric@vt.edu
James Johnson, Project Leader of Forestry and Wildlife Extension; College of Natural Resources, Virginia Polytechnic Institute and State University, Blacksburg, VA 24061-0324; 540-231-7679; jej@vt.edu
Brian Nerrie, Extension Aquaculture Specialist; Virginia State University, P.O. Box 9081, Petersburg, VA 23806; 804-524-5903; bnerrie@vsu.edu
James Parkhurst, Extension Wildlife Specialist; Department of Fisheries & Wildlife Sciences, Virginia Polytechnic Institute and State University, Blacksburg, VA 24061-0321; 540-231-9283; Fax: 540-231-7265; jparkhur@vt.edu

VIRGINIA COOPERATIVE FISH AND WILDLIFE RESEARCH UNIT (USDI)
100 Cheatham Hall, Virginia Polytechnic Institute and State University
Blacksburg, VA 24061-0321 United States
Phone: 540-231-5573 Fax: 540-231-7580
E-mail: vsutherl@vt.edu
Website: www.cnr.vt.edu/fisheries/

Founded: 1935
Scope: State

Description: Founded for training graduate students in fisheries and wildlife; with teaching and extension in fisheries and wildlife biology. Cooperatively supported by the Biological Resources Division of U.S.G.S., Department of Game and Inland Fisheries, and Virginia Polytechnic Institute and State University.

Publication(s): Annual reports, research publications, journal articles
Keyword(s): Water Habitats & Quality, Wildlife & Species

VIRGINIA DEPARTMENT OF AGRICULTURE AND CONSUMER SERVICES
1100 Bank Street
Suite 203
Richmond, VA 23219 United States
Phone: 804-786-2373 Fax: 804-371-7679
E-mail: webmaster@vdacs.state.va.us
Website: www.vdacs.state.va.us

Founded: 1877
Membership: 101–1,000
Scope: State

Description: To promote the economic growth and development of Virginia agriculture, encourage environmental stewardship, and provide consumer protection. Thirteen-member board appointed by Governor.

Publication(s): Bulletin
Keyword(s): Agriculture/Farming, Pollution (general), Wildlife & Species

Contact(s):
Elaine Lidholm, Director of Communication; 804-786-7686
Roy Seward, Director of Policy Planning and Research; 804-786-3535
Marvin Lawson, Manager of Pesticides Services; 804-371-6558
J. Courter, Department Commissioner; 804-786-3501
Elaine Lidholm, Editor

VIRGINIA DEPARTMENT OF CONSERVATION AND RECREATION
203 Governor St., Suite 302
Richmond, VA 23219 United States
Phone: 804-786-6124 Fax: 804-786-6141
E-mail: dcr@state.va.us
Website: www.dcr.state.va.us

Membership: 101–1,000
Scope: Local, State, Regional

Description: Mission Statement: "To conserve, protect, enhance, and advocate the wise use of the Commonwealth's unique natural, historic, recreational, scenic and cultural resources."

Contact(s):
Joseph Maroon, Director; 804-786-2123; Fax: 804-786-6141; jmaroon@dcr.state.va.us

VIRGINIA DEPARTMENT OF CONSERVATION AND RECREATION
203 Governor St., Suite 302
Richmond, VA 23219 United States
Phone: 804-786-1712 Fax: 804-786-6141
E-mail: pco@dcr.state.va.us
Website: www.dcr.state.va.us

Scope: State

Description: The Department's mission is to conserve, protect, enhance, and advocate wise use of Virginia's natural, recreational, and scenic resources in order to maintain and improve the quality of life for present and future generations. The Department is responsible for administrative support of various state collegial bodies including: The Board of Conservation and Recreation, the Virginia Cave Board, the Virginia Soil and Water Conservation Board, and the Breaks Interstate Park Commission.

Contact(s):
David Brickley, Director; 804-786-2123;
dgbrickley@dcr.state.va.us
Linda Cox, Administrative Staff Specialist; 804-786-2123;
ljcox@dcr.state va.us
Leon App, Chief Deputy, Acting; 804-786-4570;
leonapp@dcr.state.va.us
David Dowling, Conservation & Development Programs
Supervisor; 804-786-2291; Fax: 804-786-2291;
ddowling@dcr.state.va.us

VIRGINIA DEPARTMENT OF CONSERVATION AND RECREATION
BOARD OF CONSERVATION AND RECREATION
203 Governor St., Suite 302
Richmond, VA 23219 United States

Contact(s):
W. Wingo, Chairman; 203 Governor St., Suite 302, Richmond, VA 23219

VIRGINIA DEPARTMENT OF CONSERVATION AND RECREATION
BREAKS INTERSTATE PARK COMMISSION
203 Governor St., Suite 302
Richmond, VA 23219 United States

Contact(s):
Joseph Elton, Advisor
Jack Sykes, Chairman; 101 Summitt Drive, Pikesville, KY 41501; 606-432-1447

VIRGINIA DEPARTMENT OF CONSERVATION AND RECREATION
CHIPPOKES PLANTATION FARM FOUNDATION
101 North 14th Street
Monroe Building, 11th Floor
Richmond, VA 23219 United States
Phone: 804-786-7950   Fax: 804-371-8500
E-mail: cffmuseum@dcr.state.va.us
Website: www.dcr.state.va.us

Founded: 1977
Scope: Local, State, Regional
Description: Chippokes Plantation Farm Foundation mission is to provide the public with educational experiences that focus on agriculture, forestry and conservation. The Chippokes Farm & Forestry Museum tells the story of life on a farm in rural Virginia through its extensive collection of tools, farm equipment, household items and other artifacts. Other educational offerings include demonstration gardens, a Forestry Interpretive Trail and an authentic 1930's Sawmill.

Contact(s):
Frederick Quayle, Chairman; Member, Senate of Virginia, 3808 Poplar Hill Road, Chesapeake, VA 23321
Katherine Wright, Advisor

VIRGINIA DEPARTMENT OF CONSERVATION AND RECREATION
CONSERVATION AND DEVELOPMENT OF PUBLIC BEACHES BOARD
203 Governor St., Suite 302
Richmond, VA 23209 United States

Contact(s):
Donald Campen, Chairman; 7603 Hillside Avenue, Richmond, VA 23229
Carlton Hill, Advisor

VIRGINIA DEPARTMENT OF CONSERVATION AND RECREATION
DIVISION OF ADMINISTRATION
203 Governor St., Suite 302
Richmond, VA 23219 United States
Phone: 804-786-6124   Fax: 804-786-6141
Website: www.dcr.state.va.us

Membership: 101–1,000
Scope: State
Contact(s):
Timothy Bishton, Director of Finance
Donald Bryne, Director of ADP
Karen Carey, Director of Human Resources
William Price, Director of Adminstration; 203 Governor St, Suite 204, Richmond, VA 23219; 804-786-0001
Gary Waugh, Public Relations Manager; 804-786-5045

VIRGINIA DEPARTMENT OF CONSERVATION AND RECREATION
DIVISION OF DAM SAFETY
203 Governor St., Suite 213
Richmond, VA 23219-2094 United States
Phone: 804-786-1369   Fax: 804-786-0536
E-mail: shawks@dcr.state.va.us
Website: www.dcr.state.va.us/

Membership: 1–100
Scope: State
Keyword(s): Water Habitats & Quality

VIRGINIA DEPARTMENT OF CONSERVATION AND RECREATION
DIVISION OF NATURAL HERITAGE
217 Governor St.
Richmond, VA 23219 United States
Phone: 804-786-7951   Fax: 804-371-2674
E-mail: mgrollins@dcr.state.va.us
Website: www.dcr.state.va.us/dnh

Founded: 1986
Scope: State
Description: The Division of Natural Heritage works to conserve VA's biodiversity through inventory, protection, and stewardship. Scientists collect field data on the location and status of natural communities and rare plant and animal species. Staff manage an information system to facilitate land management and conservation decisions, protect natural areas and manage the State Natural Area Preserve System.
Keyword(s): Ecosystems (precious), Land Issues, Public Lands/Greenspace, Wildlife & Species

Contact(s):
Thomas Smith, Director; 217 Governor St., Richmond, VA 23219; 804-786-7951
Rene Hypes, Project Review Coordinator; 804-371-2708; Fax: 804-371-2674; srhypes@dcr.state.va.us

VIRGINIA DEPARTMENT OF CONSERVATION AND RECREATION
DIVISION OF SOIL AND WATER CONSERVATION
203 Governor St., Suite 213
Richmond, VA 23219 United States
Phone: 804-786-1712
E-mail: pco@dcr.state.va.us
Website: www.dcr.state.va.us

Scope: State
Contact(s):
David Brickley, Director; dordswc@erols.com

VIRGINIA DEPARTMENT OF CONSERVATION AND RECREATION
DIVISION OF STATE PARKS
203 Governor St., Suite 306
Richmond, VA 23219 United States
Phone: 804-692-0403   Fax: 804-786-9294
Website: www.dcr.state.va.us

Scope: State
Publication(s): Virginia State Parks
Contact(s):
Joseph Elton, Director; 203 Governor St., Suite 306, Richmond, VA 23219; 804-786-4377

VIRGINIA DEPARTMENT OF CONSERVATION AND RECREATION
VIRGINIA CAVE BOARD
217 Governor Street, 3rd Floor
Richmond, VA 23219 United States
Phone: 804-786-7951   Fax: 804-371-2674
Contact(s):
Bill Keith, Chairman; Rt. 1 Box 17, Cleveland, VA 24225
Lawrence Smith, Advisor

VIRGINIA DEPARTMENT OF ENVIRONMENTAL QUALITY
629 E. Main St.
Richmond, VA 23219 United States
Phone: 804-698-4000   Fax: 804-698-4500
E-mail: vanaturally@deq.state.va.us
Website: www.deq.state.va.us
Founded: 1993
Scope: State
Description: The Department of Environmental Quality strives to provide efficient, cost-effective services that promote a proper balance between environmental improvement and economic vitality.
Keyword(s): Air Quality/Atmosphere, Reduce/Reuse/Recycle
Contact(s):
Robert Burnley, Director; 804-698-4020; rgburnley@deq.state.va.us
Ann Regan, Environmental Education Coordinator

VIRGINIA DEPARTMENT OF FORESTRY
900 Natural Resources Dr., Suite 800
Charlottesville, VA 22903 United States
Phone: 434-977-6555   Fax: 434-296-2369
Website: www.vdof.org
Founded: 1914
Scope: State
Description: The mission of the Department of Forestry is to protect and develop healthy, sustainable forest resources for Virginians. The Department assists private landowners with the management and protection of forest resources. We also provide at-cost seedlings for reforestation of the state's forestlands, and management of public state forests and other state public forest lands.
Contact(s):
Faye Difazio, Fiscal Director
Ellie Whinnery, Human Resources Director
Edwina Blalock, Team Leader for Information Technology
James Garner, State Forester
Ronald Jenkins, Team Leader for General Services
Bettina Ring, Deputy State Forester
Lou Southard, Forest Protection
James Starr, Team Leader for Forest Management
Timothy Tigner, Team Leader for Resource Information

VIRGINIA DEPARTMENT OF GAME AND INLAND FISHERIES
4010 West Broad Street
P.O. Box 11104
Richmond, VA 23230 United States
Phone: 804-367-1000   Fax: 804-367-9147
E-mail: dgifweb@dgif.state.va.us
Website: www.dgif.state.va.us
Founded: 1916
Membership: 101–1,000
Scope: State
Description: To provide for the management, conservation, restoration, and enhancement of the Commonwealth's fish and wildlife resources. The Department also provides boat registration and titling services and boating law administration and enforcement, as well as providing public informational and educational services related to wildlife resources and recreational boating. Our major publication is Virginia Wildlife magazine, published monthly.
Publication(s): Virginia Wildlife Magazine
Keyword(s): Forests/Forestry, Public Lands/Greenspace, Recreation/Ecotourism, Water Habitats & Quality, Wildlife & Species
Contact(s):
Bill Woodfin, Department Director; 804-367-9231; Fax: 804-367-0405; bwoodfin@dgif.state.va.us
Ray Davis, Director of Administration; 804-367-2387; Fax: 804-367-0405; rdavis@dgif.state.va.us
Bob Duncan, Wildlife Division Director; 804-367-6878; Fax: 804-367-0262; bduncan@dgif.state.va.us
Herb Foster, Law Enforcement Operations; 804-367-0957; Fax: 804-367-2430; hfoster@dgif.state.va.us
Gary Martel, Fisheries Division Director; 804-367-1004; Fax: 804-367-2628; gmartel@dgif.state.va.us
Charles Sledd, Program Development Director; 804-367-6481; Fax: 804-367-0405; csledd@dgif.state.va.us
Jeff Uerz, Law Enforcement Administration; 804-367-1005; Fax: 804-367-2430; juerz@dgif.state.va.us
David Whitehurst, Wildlife Diversity Division Director; 804-367-0940; Fax: 804-367-2427; dwhitehurst@dgif.state.va.us
James Adams, Capital Programs Director; 804-367-0183; Fax: 804-367-2311; jadams@dgif.state.va.us
Larry Harizanoff, Human Resources Director; 804-367-0849; Fax: 804-367-0256; lharizanoff@dgif.state.va.us
Larry Hart, Boating Section Manager; 804-367-1295; Fax: 804-367-1064; lhart@dgif.state.va.us
Virgil Kopf, IMS Director; 804-367-0639; Fax: 804-367-0336; vkopf@dgif.state.va.us
Bobby Mawyer, Outdoor Education Program Manager; 804-367-9274; Fax: 804-367-2430; bmawyer@dgif.state.va.us
Rick Busch, Wildlife Federal Aid Coordinator; 804-367-1215; Fax: 804-367-0262; rbusch@dgif.state.va.us
Jeff Decker, Boating Education Coordinator; 804-367-8693; Fax: 804-367-2311; jdecker@dgif.state.va.us
Fred Leckie, Fisheries Federal Aid Coordinator; 804-367-8994; Fax: 804-367-2628; fleckie@dgif.state.va.us
Julia Smith, Media Relations Coordinator; 804-367-0991; Fax: 804-367-4391; jsmith@dgif.state.va.us
Lee Walker, Virginia Wildlife Magazine Editor; 804-367-0486; Fax: 804-367-0488; lwalker@dgif.state.va.us

VIRGINIA DEPARTMENT OF GAME AND INLAND FISHERIES
REGION II (LYNCHBURG)
1132 Thomas Jefferson Road
Forest, VA 24551-9223 United States
Phone: 434-525-7522   Fax: 434-525-7720
Website: www.dgif.state.va.us
Scope: State
Description: To provide for the management, conservation, restoration, and enhancement of the Commonwealth's fish and wildlife resources. The department also provides boat registration and titling services and boating law administration and enforcement; as well as providing public informational and educational services related to wildlife resources and recreational boating.
Publication(s): Virginia Wildlife
Keyword(s): Recreation/Ecotourism, Water Habitats & Quality, Wildlife & Species
Contact(s):
James Adams, Capital Programs Director
Raymond Davis, Director of Administration; 804-367-2387; rdavis@dgif.state.va.us
Robert Duncan, Director of Wildlife Division; 804-367-9588; rduncan@dgif.state.va.us
Larry Harizanoff, Director of Human Resources; 804-367-8195; lharizanoff@dgif.state.va.us

Virgil Kopf, Director of Information Management Systems; 804-367-0787; vkopf@dgif.state.va.us
Gary Martel, Director of Fisheries Division; 804-367-0509; gmartel@dgif.state.va.us
Charles Sledd, Director of Program Development; 804-367-6481; csledd@dgif.state.va.us
Jeffrey Uerz, Director of Law Enforcement Division; 804-367-0776; juerz@dgif.state.va.us
David Whitehurst, Director of Wildlife Diversity Division; 804-367-4335; dwhitehurst@dgif.state.va.us
Terry Bradberry, Outdoor Education
Rick Busch, Federal Aid Coordinator of Wildlife; 804-367-1215; rbusch@dgif.state.va.us
Larry Hart, Boat Registration Section,Title; 804-367-1295; lhart@dgif.state.va.us
Fred Leckie, Federal Aid Coordinator of Fisheries; 804-367-8629; fleckie@dgif.state.va.us
Charles Sledd, Boating Law Administrator; 804-367-6481; csledd@dgif.state.va.us
Julia Smith, Media Relations Coordinator; 804-367-0991; jsmith@dgif.state.va.us
Lee Walker, Editor; 804-367-0486; Fax: 804-367-0488; lwalker@dgif.state.va.us

VIRGINIA DEPARTMENT OF GAME AND INLAND FISHERIES
REGION III
1796 Highway Sixteen
Marion, VA 24354 United States
Phone: 276-783-4860   Fax: 276-783-6115
E-mail: vjessee@dgif.state.va.us
Website: www.dgif.state.va.us

Founded: 1917
Scope: State
Description: Coordination of wildlife management, fisheries management, and wildlife law enforcement in region.

VIRGINIA DEPARTMENT OF GAME AND INLAND FISHERIES
REGION IV (STAUNTON)
P.O. Box 996
Verona, VA 24482 United States
Phone: 540-248-9360   Fax: 540-248-9399
Website: www.dgif.state.va.us

Membership: 1–100
Scope: Regional

VIRGINIA DEPARTMENT OF HEALTH
Commissioners Office, Suite 214, Main St. Station
Richmond, VA 23219 United States
Phone: 804-786-3561   Fax: 804-786-4616
E-mail: lcheek@vdh.st.va.us
Website: www.vdh.state.va.us

Founded: 1872
Scope: State
Description: The Department carries out protective and preventive public health services for all citizens of the Commonwealth and provides public health care services to the indigent.
Publication(s): Virginia's Health
Contact(s):
Anne Peterson, Commissioner
Helen Tarantino, Deputy Commissioner of Administration

VIRGINIA DEPARTMENT OF MINES, MINERALS AND ENERGY
Ninth St. Office Bldg., 8th Fl., 202 N. Ninth St.
Richmond, VA 23219 United States
Phone: 804-692-3200   Fax: 804-692-3237
E-mail: DmmeInfo@mme.state.va.us
Website: www.mme@state.va.us

Founded: 1985
Membership: 101–1,000
Scope: State
Description: The department is committed to enhancing the development and conservation of energy and mineral resources in a safe and environmentally sound manner in order to support a more productive economy in Virginia.
Contact(s):
O. Dishner, Director

VIRGINIA DEPARTMENT OF MINES, MINERALS AND ENERGY
DIVISION OF ENERGY

Description: The Division of Energy promotes the efficient use and conservation of energy and the use of alternative energy sources.
Contact(s):
Stephen Walz, Director; Ninth St. Office Bldg., 8th Fl., 202 N. Ninth St., Richmond, VA 23219; 540-692-3211

VIRGINIA DEPARTMENT OF MINES, MINERALS AND ENERGY
DIVISION OF GAS AND OIL
P.O. Box 1416
Abingdon, VA 24212 United States
Phone: 276-676-5423   Fax: 276-676-5459
E-mail: DgoInfo@mme.state.va.us
Website: www.mme.state.va.us

Membership: 1–100
Scope: State
Description: The Division of Gas and Oil's responsibilities include regulating the effects of gas and oil operations both on and below the surface, issuing permits, client assistance programs, inspection of well sites and gathering pipelines, reclamation of abandoned well sites, protection of correlative rights, and promotion of resource conservation practices.
Contact(s):
Bob Wilson, Director

VIRGINIA DEPARTMENT OF MINES, MINERALS AND ENERGY
DIVISION OF MINED LAND RECLAMATION
P.O. Drawer 900
Big Stone Gap, VA 24219 United States
Phone: 276-523-8100   Fax: 276-523-8163
E-mail: DmlrInfo@mme.state.va.us
Website: www.mme.state.va.us

Scope: State
Description: The Division of Mined Land Reclamation is responsible for ensuring the reclamation of land affected by surface and underground coal mining activity. Major functions include regulating surface effects of coal mining, reclaiming abandoned mine lands, issuing permits, performing inspections, assisting small operators and responding to citizen concerns.

VIRGINIA DEPARTMENT OF MINES, MINERALS AND ENERGY
DIVISION OF MINERAL MINING
P.O. Box 3727
Charlottesville, VA 22903 United States
Phone: 434-951-6310   Fax: 434-951-6325
E-mail: DmmInfo@mme.state.va.us
Website: www.mme.state.va.us

Scope: State
Description: The Division of Mineral Mining administers both health and safety and surface mining reclamation regulatory programs for all non-coal mineral mining operations. Regulating the surface effects and insuring the reclamation of mineral mining operations, enforcing health and safety

standards in the mines, issuing permits and licenses, providing industry training, reclaiming orphaned lands, and performing regular inspections are the major functions of this division.

Contact(s):
Conrad Spangler, Director; P.O. Box 3727, Charlottesville, VA 22903; 804-951-6310

VIRGINIA MARINE RESOURCES COMMISSION
2600 Washington Avenue, 3rd Floor
Newport News, VA 23607 United States
Phone: 757-247-2200   Fax: 757-247-2020
Website: www.state.va.us/vmrc

Founded: 1875
Membership: 101–1,000
Scope: State
Description: This state agency holds regulatory jurisdiction over all commercial and sports fishing, marine fish, marine shellfish, and marine organisms in the tidal waters of Virginia. Holds permit jurisdiction on all projects involving use of state-owned submerged lands and authority over use or development in vegetated and nonvegetated tidal wetlands and coastal primary sand dunes.
Publication(s): Virginia Landings Bulletin
Contact(s):
Erik Barth, Chief of Management Information Systems
Steven Bowman, Chief of Law Enforcement
Robert Craft, Chief of Administration and Finance
Robert Grabb, Chief, Habitat Management
William Pruitt, Commissioner
Jack Travelstead, Chief of Fisheries Management
Jim Wesson, Chief of Conservation and Replenishment

VIRGINIA MUSEUM OF NATURAL HISTORY
1001 Douglas Ave.
Martinsville, VA 24112 United States
Phone: 276-666-8600   Fax: 276-632-6487
Website: www.vmnh.org

Founded: 1988
Membership: 1–100
Scope: State
Description: Preserves, studies, and interprets Virginia's natural and cultural heritage. Statewide system of museum facilities, research sites, and educational programs. The museum has more than eleven million specimens in collections.
Publication(s): Virginia Explorer, The, Children's Activity Books, Scientific Publication Series, Books, Virginia Naturally
Keyword(s): Wildlife & Species
Contact(s):
Stephen Pike, Executive Director; spike@ngocomm.net
Judy Winston, Research Director; 540-666-8609; jwinston@vmnh.org

VIRGINIA OUTDOORS FOUNDATION
NORTHERN VIRGINIA OFFICE- ALDIE
CHARLOTTESVILLE OFFICE
SOUTHWESTERN VIRGINIA OFFICE- BLACKSBURG
203 Governor St., Suite 316
Richmond, VA 23219 United States
Phone: 804-225-2147   Fax: 804-371-4810
E-mail: achisholm@virginiaoutdoorsfoundation.org
Website: www.virginiaoutdoorsfoundation.org

Founded: 1966
Scope: State
Description: To preserve Virginia's natural, scenic, historic, scientific, open space, and recreational areas. The Foundation accepts gifts of cash, stock, real property, or open space easements to achieve its purpose.
Keyword(s): Agriculture/Farming, Ecosystems (precious), Land Issues, Public Lands/Greenspace, Reduce/Reuse/Recycle

Contact(s):
Sherry Buttrick, Charlottesville Office Director; 1010 Harris St, Suite 4, Charlottesville, VA 22903; 434-293-3423; Fax: 434-293-3859; vofsherryb@aol.com
Faye Cooper, Staunton Office Director; 11 E. Beverly Street, Staunton, VA 24401; 540-886-2460; Fax: 540-886-2464; fcooper@virginiaoutdoorsfoundation.org
Leslie Grayson, Northern Virginia Office Director; P.O. Box 322, Aldie, VA 20105; 703-327-6118; Fax: 703-327-6444; voflgray@aol.com
Leslie Trew, Richmond Office Director; 203 Governor St, Richmond, VA 22319; 804-225-2147; Fax: 804-371-4810; ldt@dcr.state.va.us
Tamara Vance, Executive Director; 302 Royal Lane, Blacksburg, VA 24060; 540-951-2822; Fax: 540-951-2695; voftvance@aol.com

VIRGINIA SOIL AND CONSERVATION BOARD
7293 Hanover Green Dr., Suite B-101
Mechanicsville, VA 23111 United States
Phone: 804-559-0324   Fax: 804-559-0325
E-mail: vaswcd@erols.com
Website: www.vaswcd.erols.com

Scope: Regional
Contact(s):
Stephanie Martin, Executive Director; 804-786-3914; Fax: 804-786-1798
Jack Frye, Advisor
Charles Horn, Chairman; 203 Governor St., Suite 206, Richmond, VA 23219; 804-786-2064

W

WABASH RIVER HERITAGE CORRIDOR COMMISSION
102 North Third Street, Suite 302
Lafayette, IN 47901 United States
Phone: 765-427-1505
E-mail: sbenner@wrhcc.state.in.us
Website: www.in.gov/wrhcc

Founded: 1991
Scope: State
Description: Our vision is to help local communities preserve, enhance, and interpret for educational and inspirational benefit the unique and significant natural, cultural, historical, and recreational resources of the Wabash River Heritage Corridor; promote public/private partnerships; create a corridor identity; expand a variety of opportunities and linkages; encourage a broad range of economic development improving the quality of life for present and future generations.
Keyword(s): Development/Developing Countries, Recreation/Ecotourism, Water Habitats & Quality

WASHINGTON DEPARTMENT OF AGRICULTURE
Olympia, WA 98504-2560 United States
Phone: 360-902-1800
Website: www.wa.gov/agr

Scope: State
Keyword(s): Agriculture/Farming, Pollution (general)
Contact(s):
Jim Jesernig, Director; 360-902-1801
Bob Arrington, Assistant Director of Pesticide Management Division; 360-902-2011
Bill Brookerson, Deputy Director; 360-902-1810
John Daley, Assistant Director of Food Saftey and Animal Health Division
Bob Gore, Assistant Director of Commodity Inspection; 360-902-1827
Robert Mead, State Veterinarian; 360-902-1881
Mary Toohey, Assistant Director of Laboratory Services; 360-902-1907
Linda Waring, Information Officer; 360-902-1815

STATE AND PROVINCIAL GOVERNMENT AGENCIES – W

WASHINGTON DEPARTMENT OF ECOLOGY
CENTRAL REGIONAL OFFICE
15 West Yakima Ave., Suite 200
Yakima, WA 98902 United States
Phone: 509-575-2490   Fax: 509-575-2809
Website: www.ecy.wa.gov

Scope: State
Contact(s):
Polly Zehm

WASHINGTON DEPARTMENT OF ECOLOGY
EASTERN REGIONAL OFFICE
4601 North Monroe
Spokane, WA 99205 United States
Phone: 509-329-3400   Fax: 509-456-6175
Website: www.ecy.wa.gov

Scope: State
Contact(s):
Tony Grover; 509-456-6149; agro461@ecy.wa.gov

WASHINGTON DEPARTMENT OF ECOLOGY
NORTHWEST REGIONAL OFFICE
3190 160th Ave., SE
Bellevue, WA 98008 United States
Phone: 425-649-7000   Fax: 425-649-7098
Website: www.ecy.wa.gov

Membership: 101–1,000
Scope: Regional
Description: Environmental Agency
Contact(s):
Ray Hellwig, Regional Director; 425-649-7010

WASHINGTON DEPARTMENT OF ECOLOGY
SOUTHWEST REGIONAL OFFICE
P.O. Box 47775
Olympia, WA 98504-7775 United States
Phone: 360-407-6300   Fax: 360-407-6305
Website: www.ecy.wa.gov

Membership: 101–1,000
Scope: Regional
Contact(s):
Sue Mauermann, Regional Director; 360-407-6307; smau461@ecy.wa.gov

WASHINGTON DEPARTMENT OF FISH AND WILDLIFE
WASHINGTON FISH AND WILDLIFE COMMISSION
600 Capitol Way N.
Olympia, WA 98501-1091 United States
Phone: 360-902-2200   Fax: 360-902-2947
E-mail: webmaster@dfw.wa.gov
Website: www.wa.gov/wdfw

Founded: 1933
Membership: 1,001–10,000
Scope: State
Description: Mission: "Sound Stewardship of Fish and Wildlife". The Department is responsible for preservation, protection, and perpetuation of wildlife, fish, shellfish, and fish and wildlife habitat; maximizing fishing, hunting, and recreational opportunities compatible with healthy and diverse fish and wildlife populations; maintaining the economic well-being and stability of the fishing industry; promoting orderly fisheries; and enhancing recreational and commercial fishing.
Keyword(s): Ecosystems (precious), Land Issues, Oceans/Coasts/Beaches, Pollution (general), Population, Recreation/Ecotourism, Water Habitats & Quality, Wildlife & Species

Contact(s):
Russ Cahill, Chair, Fish and Wildlife Commission; 360-902-2267; Fax: 360-902-2448; commission@dfw.wa.gov
Jeff Koenings, Ph.D., Director; 360-902-2225; Fax: 360-902-2947; koenijpk@dfw.wa.gov
Larry Peck, Deputy Director; 360-902-2650; Fax: 360-902-2224; peckrlp@dfw.wa.gov
Phil Anderson, Staff Director of Intergovernmental Policy Group; 360-902-2720; Fax: 360-902-2158; anderpma@dfw.wa.gov
John Andrews, Regional Director, Region 1; 8702 N.Division St., Spokane, WA 99218-1199; 509-456-4082; Fax: 509-456-4071; anderjga@dfw.wa.gov
Lew Atkins, Assistant Director of Fish Program; 360-902-2651; Fax: 360-902-2183; atkinlja@dfw.wa.gov
Dennis Beich, Regional Director, Region 2; 1550 Alder St. NW, Ephrata, WA 98823-9699; 509-754-4624; Fax: 509-754-5257; beichdvb@dfw.wa.gov
Bruce Bjork, Assistant Director of Enforcement Program; 360-902-2373; Fax: 360-902-2942; bjorkbb@dfw.wa.gov
Dave Brittell, Assistant Director of Wildlife Program; 360-902-2515; Fax: 360-902-2162; brittjdb@dfw.wa.gov
Penny Cusick, Personnel Manager; 360-902-2276; Fax: 360-902-2392; cusicprc@dfw.wa.gov
Bob Everitt, Regional Director, Region 4; 16018 Mill Creek Blvd., Mill Creek, WA 98012 1296; 425 775 1311; Fax: 425-338-1066; everide@dfw.wa.gov
Greg Hueckel, Assistant Director of Habitat Program; 360-902-2416; Fax: 360-902-2946; hueckgjh@dfw.wa.gov
Jim Lux, Assisant Director of Business Services Program; 360-902-2200; Fax: 360-902-2230; luxjjl@dfw.wa.gov
Sue Patnude, Regional Director, Region 6; 48 Devonshire Rd., Montesano, WA 98563-9618; 360-249-4628; Fax: 360-664-0689; patnusm@dfw.wa.gov
Jeff Tayer, Regional Director, Region 3; 1701 S. 24th Ave., Yakima, WA 98902-5720; 509-575-2740; Fax: 509-575-2474; tayerjjt@dfw.wa.gov
Lee Van Tussenbrook, Regional Director, Region 5; 2108 Grand Blvd., Vancouver, WA 98661-4624; 360-696-6211; Fax: 360-906-6776; vantulv@dfw.wa.gov
Sara LaBorde, Special Assistant of Quality Initiatives; 360-902-2224; Fax: 360-902-2947; laborsgl@dfw.wa.gov
Tim Smith, Special Asst., Nearshore Project & Salmon Recovery Grants Pg; 360-902-2223; Fax: 360-902-2947; smithtrs@dfw.wa.gov
Tim Waters, Special Assistant of Public Affairs; 360-902-2250; Fax: 360-902-2171; watortrw@dfw.wa.gov
Josh Weiss, Special Assistant of Legislative Affairs; 360-902-2220; Fax: 360-902-2157; weissjw@dfw.wa.gov

WASHINGTON NATURAL HERITAGE PROGRAM
P.O. Box 47014
Olympia, WA 98504-7014 United States
Phone: 360-902-1600   Fax: 360-902-1789
Website: www.wa.gov/dnr/

Founded: 1978
Scope: State
Description: Identify and evaluate native ecosystems and species, set conservation priorities, provide information to protect these irreplaceable resources for the benefit of current and future generations.
Publication(s): Endangered, Threatened, and Sensitive Vascular Plants of Washington with working list of Rare Non-vascular Species, State of Washington Natural Heritage Plan
Keyword(s): Wildlife & Species
Contact(s):
John Gamon, Program Manager and Botanist; 360-902-1661

WASHINGTON STATE
DEPARTMENT OF NATURAL RESOURCES
OLYMPIC REGION
411 Tillicum Lane
Forks, WA 98331 United States
Phone: 360-374-6131   Fax: 360-374-5446
Website: www.wa.gov/redirDNR/splash.html

Membership: 1,001–10,000
Scope: State, Regional
Description: On Washington's Olympic Peninsula: administer State Forest Practices Rules for non-federal landowners; manage 376,000 acres of State Forests for environmental and social values as well as for income to public beneficiaries; manage 13 Natural Areas (15,000 acres).
Keyword(s): Ecosystems (precious), Forests/Forestry, Oceans/Coasts/Beaches, Public Lands/Greenspace, Recreation/Ecotourism, Water Habitats & Quality, Wildlife & Species
Contact(s):
  Charlie Cortelyou, Regional Manager; 360-374-6131
  Scott Horton, Wildlife Biologist; 360-374-6131

WASHINGTON STATE CONSERVATION COMMISSION
P.O. Box 47721
300 Desmond Drive
Olympia, WA 98504-7721 United States
Phone: 206-407-6200   Fax: 206-407-6215
Website: www.scc.wa.gov

Founded: 1939
Scope: Local, State
Description: The mission of the Washington State Conservation Commission is to protect, conserve and enhance the natural resources of the state. The Commission provides leadership, partnerships and resources to support 48 locally governed conservation districts in promoting conservation stewardship by all. The Commission encourages the cooperation and collaboration of the federal, state, regional, interstate, and local public agencies which assist them.
Keyword(s): Agriculture/Farming, Land Issues, Pollution (general), Water Habitats & Quality
Contact(s):
  Steven Meyer, Executive Director; 206-407-6201; Fax: 360-407-6215; smey461@ecy.wa.gov
  Kristin Bettridge, Adminstrative Manager; 360-407-6209; Fax: 360-407-6215; kbet461@ecy.wa.gov
  Lynn Brown, Commission Chair; P.O. Box 775, Ellensburg, WA 98926

WASHINGTON STATE DEPARTMENT OF ECOLOGY
WASHINGTON CONSERVATION CORPS
P.O. Box 47600
Olympia, WA 98599-7600 United States
Phone: 360-407-7038   Fax: 360-407-6902
E-mail: lbam461@ecy.wa.gov
Website: www.ecy.wa.gov/programs/sea/wcc/index.html

Founded: 1983
Membership: 101–1,000
Scope: Local, State, Regional
Description: We are an AmeriCorps Program affiliated with Washington State Government. We conduct environmental restoration and recreational trails construction projects in National Parks, Wilderness Areas, and other federal, state, and local lands. Our philosophy is hard work, beautiful locations, and the time of your life. We hire 150 members each year. Call or e-mail for applications.
Keyword(s): Ecosystems (precious), Forests/Forestry, Recreation/Ecotourism, Wildlife & Species

WASHINGTON STATE EXTENSION
Ed Adams, ANR Director
Washington State University Extension
P.O. Box 1495
Spokane, WA 99210-1495 United States
Phone: 509-358-7960   Fax: 509-358-7900
E-mail: loosl@wsu.edu
Website: www.ext.wsu.edu/

Scope: State
Description: Washington State University Extension engages people, organizations and communities to advance knowledge, economic well-being and quality of life by fostering inquiry, learning, and the application of research.
Keyword(s): Agriculture/Farming, Air Quality/Atmosphere, Forests/Forestry, Reduce/Reuse/Recycle
Contact(s):
  Edward Adams, Program Director; Washington State University Extension, 668 N. Riverpoint Blvd., P.O. Box 1495, Spokane, WA 99210-1495; 509-358-7960; Fax: 509-358-7900; adamse@wsu.edu
  David Baumgartner, Extension Forester; Department of Natural Resource Sciences, P.O. Box 646410, Washington State University, Pullman, WA 99164-6410; 509-335-2964
  Donald Hanley, Extension Forester; College of Forest Resources, University of Washington, Box 352100, Seattle, WA 98195-2100; 206-685-4960
  Rod Tinnemore, Extension Master Gardener Coordinator; Washington State University, 207 4th Ave. N., 7612 East Pioneer Way, Puyallup, WA 98371-4998; 253-445-4614; Fax: 253-445-4569; rodt@wsu.edu

WASHINGTON STATE OFFICE OF ENVIRONMENTAL EDUCATION
Office of Superintendent of Public Instruction, 2800 NE 200th St.
Seattle, WA 98155-1418 United States
Phone: 206-365-3893   Fax: 206-367-4540
E-mail: wsoee@earthlink.net
Website: www.k.wa.us/envedu

Membership: 1–100
Scope: Regional
Description: To provide curriculum resources and training for teachers in environmental education, and to evaluate these programs pursuant to improving content and effectiveness. The office is responsible for E.E. program coordination and cooperation as it applies to K-12 public school programs and to state mandate requiring E.E. integrated into the K-12 curriculum.
Publication(s): Clean Water, Streams and Fish: A Holistic View of Watersheds, Closing the Achievement Gap: Using the Environment as an Integrating Context for Learning, Puget Sound Habitats Teachers Guide and Charts, Environmental Education Guidelines for Washington Schools
Keyword(s): Reduce/Reuse/Recycle, Water Habitats & Quality
Contact(s):
  Tony Angell, State Supervisor of Environmental Education
  Michele Halfhill, Administrative Assistant

WASHINGTON STATE PARKS AND RECREATION COMMISSION
7150 Cleanwater Ln., P.O. Box 42650
Olympia, WA 98504-2650 United States
Phone: 360-902-8500
Website: www.parks.wa.gov

Founded: 1912
Scope: State
Description: To acquire, develop, improve, and maintain state parks and recreation areas. Involvement includes but is not limited to state parks, seashore conservation, water and boating safety, snowmobile safety, and natural and historic heritage interpretation.

STATE AND PROVINCIAL GOVERNMENT AGENCIES – W

Keyword(s): Ethics/Environmental Justice, Public Lands/ Greenspace, Recreation/Ecotourism

Contact(s):
- Cleve Pinnix, Director; 360-902-8501
- Frank Boteler, Deputy Director; 360-902-8502
- Tom Boyer, Chief Engineer; 360-902-8616
- Art Brown, Chief of Information Processing; 360-902-8585
- Rita Cooper, Assistant Director of Administrative Services; 360-902-8525
- Rex Derr, Legislative Liaison; 306-902-8504
- Larry Fairleigh, Assistant Director of Resources Development; 360-902-8642
- Jim French, Chief of Boating Programs; 360-902-8515
- Bill Gansberg, Chief of Visitor Protection and Law Enforcement; 360-902-8598
- Paul George, Chief of Parks Maintenance; 360-902-8540
- Ann Hersley, Administrator of Public Affairs; 360-902-8562
- James Horan, Chief of Programs Management; 360-902-8580
- Dan Ingman, Chief of Natural Resource Management; 360-902-8592
- Judy Johnson, Chief of Employee Services; 360-902-8568
- Bill Jolly, Chief of Environmental Coordination; 360-902-8636
- William Jolly, Chief of Research and Long Range Planning; 360-902-8641
- Bill Koss, Chief of Site Planning; 360-902-8629
- Pam McConkey, Chief of Visitor Services; 360-902-8595
- Wayne McLaughlin, Contracts Specialist, 360-902-8599
- Sandy Rees, Chief of Fiscal Services; 360-902-8575
- Marsh Taylor, Chief of Budget Services; 360-902-8532

WASHINGTON STATE PARKS AND RECREATION COMMISSION
EASTERN REGION HEADQUARTERS
2201 N. Duncan Dr.
Wenatchee, WA 98801–1007 United States
Phone: 509-662-0420   Fax: 509-663-9754
Website: www.parks.wa.gov

Founded: 1935
Membership: 101–1,000
Scope: State, Regional
Description: Regional Office for Eastern State Parks
Publication(s): Call information # 1-360-902-8844
Contact(s):
- Jim Harris, Regional Manager; 2201 N. Duncan Dr., Wenatchee, WA 98801; 509-662-0420

WASHINGTON STATE PARKS AND RECREATION COMMISSION
NORTHWEST REGION
220 N. Walnut St.
Burlington, WA 98233 United States
Phone: 360-755-9231   Fax: 360-428-1094
Website: www.parks.wa.gov

Membership: 1–100
Scope: State
Contact(s):
- Terry Doran, Region Mngr.; P.O. Box 487, Burlington, WA 98801–1007; 360-755-9231

WASHINGTON STATE PARKS AND RECREATION COMMISSION
SOUTHWEST REGION
11838 Tilley Rd. S
Olympia, WA 98512 United States
Phone: 360-753-7143   Fax: 360-586-4272
Website: www.parks.wa.gov/

Scope: State
Contact(s):
- Paul Malmberg; 11838 Tilley Rd., S., Olympia, WA 98512-9167; 360-753-7143

WEST VIRGINIA COOPERATIVE FISH AND WILDLIFE RESEARCH UNIT
DIVISION OF FORESTRY
Division of Forestry, West Virginia University
Morgantown, WV 26506-6125 United States
Phone: 304-293-3794, ext. 2430   Fax: 304-293-4826
E-mail: wvcoop@wvu.edu
Website: www.forestry.caf.wvu.edu

Scope: State, National
Description: A cooperative research and graduate education organization sponsored by the Biological Resources Division of USGS, West Virginia Division of Natural Resources, West Virginia University, and Wildlife Management Institute. The role of the unit is to conduct natural resources research of state, regional, or national scope, and to train graduate-level researchers in natural resources.
Keyword(s): Pollution (general), Water Habitats & Quality, Wildlife & Species
Contact(s):
- Joseph McNeel, Director Division of Forestry; jmcneel@wvu.edu
- Patricia Mazik, Unit Leader: Fisheries
- Stuart Welsh, Assistant Leader: Fisheries
- Petra Wood, Assistant Leader: Wildlife

WEST VIRGINIA DEPARTMENT OF AGRICULTURE
1900 Kanawha Blvd. E
Charleston, WV 25305 United States
Phone: 304-558-2201   Fax: 304-558-2203
E-mail: douglass@ag.state.wv.us
Website: www.state.wv.us/agriculture

Scope: State
Keyword(s): Agriculture/Farming, Land Issues, Pollution (general), Public Health
Contact(s):
- Charles Coffman, Director of Plant Industries Division
- Gus Douglass, Commissioner
- Janet Fisher, Deputy Commissioner
- Richard Hannah, Deputy Commissioner

WEST VIRGINIA DEPARTMENT OF ENVIRONMENTAL PROTECTION
Division of Environmental Protection
#10 McJunkin Rd.
Nitro, WV 25143-2546 United States
Phone: 304-759-0515   Fax: 304-759-0562
Website: www.dep.state.wv.us

Founded: 1991
Membership: 101–1,000
Scope: State
Description: The Division of Environmental Protection is charged with the protection of West Virginia's environment through the regulation and administration of the state's abandoned mine lands, air quality, mining & reclamation, oil & gas, waste management, and water resources programs.
Contact(s):
- Michael Callaghan, Director; ext. 301; mcallaghan@mail.dep.state.wv.us
- Matthew Crum, Chief of Mining & Reclamation; 304-759-0510; mcrum@mail.dep.state.wv.us
- Ken Ellison, Chief of Waste Management; 304-558-2508; kellison@mail.dep.state.wv.us
- Andy Gallagher, Chief Communications Officer; 304-558-4253; agallagher@mail.dep.state.wv.us
- Randy Huffman, Chief of Administration; 304-558-5529; rhuffman@mail.dep.state.wv.us
- Perry McDaniel, Chief of Legal Services; 304-558-9160; pmcdaniel@mail.dep.state.wv.us
- Alan Turner, Chief of Water Resources; 304-558-2107; aturner@mail.dep.state.wv.us

WEST VIRGINIA DIVISION OF NATURAL RESOURCES
1900 Kanawha Blvd., East Building 3
Charleston, WV 25305 United States
Phone: 304-558-2754   Fax: 304-558-3147
Website: www.dnr.state.wv.us

Founded: 1933
Scope: State
Description: The Division's objective is to provide a comprehensive program for the exploration, conservation, development, protection, enjoyment, and use of the natural resources of the State of West Virginia. The commission was the forerunner of the Department of Natural Resources, created by the legislature in 1961 and modified to the Division of Natural Resources in 1993.
Publication(s): Wonderful West Virginia, West Virginia Wildlife
Keyword(s): Recreation/Ecotourism, Water Habitats & Quality, Wildlife & Species
Contact(s):
Ed Hamrick, Director; 1900 Kanawha Boulevard, East, Charleston, WV 25305; 304-558-2754; Fax: 304-558-2768; ehamrick@dnr.state.wv.us
Jeffrey Bowers, District I Commissioner; HC 70 Box 40 A, Sugar Grove, WV 26815; 304-358-3333; Fax: 304-358-3334
Charles Capito, District I Commissioner; Suite #3, 2619 Pennsylvania Ave., Weirton, WV 26062; 304-723-3355; Fax: 304-723-5638
William Daniel, Deputy Chief, Law Enforcement; 1900 Kanawha Boulevard, East, Charleston, WV 25305; 304-558-2784; Fax: 304-558-1170; wdaniel@dnr.state.wv.us
Dr. Thomas Dotson, District III Commissioner; the Greenbrier Clinic, 320 West Main Street, White Sulphur Springs, WV 24986; 304-536-4870; Fax: 304-536-1664
Bernard Dowler, Deputy Director; 1900 Kanawha Boulevard, East, Charleston, WV 25305; 304-558-2754; Fax: 304-558-2768; bdowler@dnr.state.wv.us
James Fields, Chief of Law Enforcement; 1900 Kanawha Boulevard, East, Charleston, WV 25305; 304-558-2784; Fax: 304-558-1170; jfields@dnr.state.wv.us
Emily Fleming, Chief of Environmental Resources; 1900 Kanawha Boulevard, East, Charleston, WV 25305; 304-558-3370; Fax: 304-558-6207; efleming@dnr.state.wv.us
Carl Gainer, District II Commissioner; P.O. Box 670, Richwood, WV 26261; 304-846-6247; Fax: 304-846-6145
Charles Hooten, District II Commissioner; 1570 Summit Drive, Charleston, WV 25302; 304-346-0521; Fax: 304-346-3421
Arnout Hyde, Editor; 1900 Kanawha Boulevard, East, Charleston, WV 25305; 304-558-9152; Fax: 304-558-2768
Paul Johansen, Assistant Chief in Charge of Game Management; 1900 Kanawha Boulevard, East, Charleston, WV 25305; 304-558-2771; Fax: 304-558-3147; pjohansen@dnr.state.wv.us
Walt Kordek, Assistant Chief in Charge of Tech. Support & Wildlife Diversity; P.O. Box 67, Elkins, WV 26241; 304-637-0245; Fax: 304-637-0250; wkordek@dnr.state.wv.us
Twila Metheney, District II Commission; 848 Pleasant Hill Road, Morgantown, WV 26508; 304-267-2389
David Milne, District I Commissioner; Route 5, Box 16, Bruceton Mills, WV 26525; 304-292-3339; Fax: 304-292-0093
Hoy Murphy, Public Information Officer; 1900 Kanawha Boulevard, East, Charleston, WV 25305; 304-558-3380; Fax: 304-558-2768; hmurphy@dnr.state.wv.us
J. R. Pope, Chief, Parks and Recreation; 1900 Kanawha Boulevard, East, Charleston, WV 25305; 304-558-2764; Fax: 304-558-0077; jpope@dnr.state.wv.us
Bret Preston, Assistant Chief In Charge of Warmwater Fisheries; 1900 Kanawha Boulevard, East, Charleston, WV 25305; 304-558-2771; Fax: 304-558-3147; bpreston@dnr.state.wv.us
Harry Price, Executive Secretary; 1900 Kanawha Boulevard, East, Charleston, WV 25305; 304-558-3315; Fax: 304-558-2768; hprice@dnr.state.wv.us
Michael Shingleton, Assistant Chief In Charge of Coldwater Fisheries; P.O. Box 67, Elkins, WV 26241; 304-637-0245; Fax: 304-637-0250; mshingleton@dnr.state.wv.us
Curtis Taylor, Chief of Wildlife; 1900 Kanawha Boulevard, East, Charleston, WV 25305; 304-558-2771; Fax: 304-558-3147; ctaylor@dnr.state.wv.us
Mike Withers, Chief of Real Estate Management; 1900 Kanawha Boulevard, East, Charleston, WV 25305; 304-558-3225; Fax: 304-558-3680; mwithers@dnr.state.wv.us

WEST VIRGINIA GEOLOGICAL AND ECONOMIC SURVEY
P.O. Box 879
Morgantown, WV 26507-0879 United States
Phone: 304-594-2331   Fax: 304-594-2575
E-mail: info@geosrv.wvnet.edu
Website: www.wvgs.wvnet.edu

Founded: 1897
Membership: 1–100
Scope: State, International
Description: Charged with the responsibility of examining all geological formations and physical features of the state with particular emphasis on their economic importance, utilization, and conservation and preparing reports and maps of the geology and natural resources of West Virginia.
Publication(s): Field trip guide, state park bulletins, educational series, county geologic reports, basic data reports, river basin bulletins, mineral resources series, environmental geology bulletins, coal-geology bulletins, reports of investigations.
Contact(s):
Larry Woodfork, Director and State Geologist; 304-594-2331; woodfork@geosrv.wvnet.edu
Katherine Avary, Program Manager for Oil and Gas
Mary Behling, Program Manager for Geologic Data
Nick Fedorko, Program Manager for Coal
Charles Gover, Program Manager for Publications and Graphics Section
Steven McClelland, Program Manager for Service
Gloria Rowan, Program Manager for Administration
Chuck Gover, Editor; 304-594-2331
John May, Deputy Director of Finance and Administration
Carl Smith, Associate State Geologist and Deputy Director; 304-594-2331

WEST VIRGINIA SOIL CONSERVATION AGENCY
1900 Kanawha Blvd. East
Charleston, WV 25305-0193 United States
Phone: 304-558-2204   Fax: 304-340-4839
Website: www.wvca.us

Membership: 1–100
Scope: State
Description: This organization is dedicated in assisting landowners in implementing BMP's (Best Management Practices) and works hard with other state and federal agencies along with organized groups of citizens forming Watershed Associations in restoring and cleaning up West Virginia's watersheds.
Contact(s):
Lance Tabor, Executive Director; 304-558-2204; Fax: 304-340-4839; ltabor@wvsca.org

WEST VIRGINIA UNIVERSITY
EXTENSION SERVICE
West Virginia University
817 Knapp Hall
P.O. Box 6031
Morgantown, WV 26506 United States
Phone: 304-293-5691   Fax: 304-293-7163

E-mail: Larry.Cote@mail.wvu.edu
Website: www.wvu.edu/~exten/
Membership: 101–1,000
Scope: State
Description: Extension Service
Keyword(s): Agriculture/Farming, Forests/Forestry, Pollution (general), Reduce/Reuse/Recycle
Contact(s):
  Ken Martin, Director, Center for Agricultural/Natural Resources Dev.; West Virginia University, 2080 Agricultural Sciences Bldg., P.O. Box 6108, Morgantown, WV 26506-6108; 304-293-6131; ext. 4206; Fax: 304-293-6954; Ken.Martin@mail.wvu.edu
  Thomas Basden, Extension Specialist, Nutrient Management; West Virginia University, 1060 Agricultural Sciences Bldg., P.O. Box 6108, Morgantown, WV 26506-6108; 304-293-6131; ext. 4210; Fax: 304-293-6954; Tom.Basden@mail.wvu.edu
  D. Bhumbla, Extension Specialist, Soil and Water Resources; West Virginia University, 1072 Agricultural Sciences Bldg., P.O. Box 6108, Morgantown, WV 26506-6108; 304-293-6131; ext. 4212; Devinder.Bhumbla@mail.wvu.edu
  Lawrence Cote, Associate Provost for Extension and Public Service, West Virginia University, 817 Knapp Hall, P.O. Box 6031, Morgantown, WV 26506-6125, 304-293-5691; Larry.Cote@mail.wvu.edu
  William Grafton, Extension Specialist, Wildlife; West Virginia University, 311-B Percival Hall, P.O Box 6125, Morgantown, WV 26506-6125; 304-293-4797; ext. 2493; Fax: 304-293-7553; Bill.Grafton@mail.wvu.edu
  Jeffrey Skousen, Extension Specialist, Land Reclamation; West Virginia University, 1106 Agricultural Sciences Bldg., P.O. Box 6108, Morgantown, WV 26506-6108; 304-293-6131; Jeff.Skousen@mail.wvu.edu
  Richard Zimmerman, Extension Specialist, Horticulture; West Virginia University, Tree Fruit Research & Ed. Ctr., P.O. Box 609, Kearneysville, WV 25430-0609; 304-876-6353; RKZimmerman@mail.wvu.edu

WISCONSIN COOPERATIVE FISHERY RESEARCH UNIT USGS
College of Natural Resources, University of Wisconsin
Stevens Point, WI 54481 United States
Phone: 715-346-2178   Fax: 715-346-3624
E-mail: coopfish@uwsp.edu
Website: www.uwsp.edu/cnr/wicfru
Membership: 1–100
Scope: International
Description: Interagency organization on the federal, state, and university levels. It carries out research, training, and extension in biology and management of freshwater fishery resources.
Keyword(s): Recreation/Ecotourism, Water Habitats & Quality, Wildlife & Species
Contact(s):
  Michael Bozek, Leader

WISCONSIN COOPERATIVE WILDLIFE RESEARCH UNIT (USDI)
USGS, Department of Wildlife Ecology
Room 204 Russell Laboratories, UW-Madison
1630 Linden Drive
Madison, WI 53706-1598 United States
Phone: 608-263-4519   Fax: 608-263-4519
E-mail: dlziebar@facstaff.wisc.edu
Website: www.wisc.edu/wildlife
Founded: 1972
Membership: 1–100
Scope: International
Description: Wildlife Research Unit
Keyword(s): Wildlife & Species

Contact(s):
  Christine Ribic, Leader; caribic@facstaff.wisc.edu

WISCONSIN DEPARTMENT OF AGRICULTURE TRADE AND CONSUMER PROTECTION
LAND AND WATER RESOURCES BUREAU
2811 Agriculture Dr., P.O. Box 8911
Madison, WI 53708-8911 United States
Phone: 608-224-4622   Fax: 608-224-4615
Website: www.datcp.state.wi.us
Membership: 1–100
Scope: State
Description: Responsible for administering state soil and water conservation and farmland preservation programs.
Keyword(s): Land Issues, Sprawl/Urban Planning, Water Habitats & Quality
Contact(s):
  David Jelinski, Bureau Director; 608-224-4621; Fax: 608-224-4615
  James Harsdorf, Secretary

WISCONSIN DEPARTMENT OF NATURAL RESOURCES
101 South Webster St.
Madison, WI 53702 United States
Phone: 608-266-2121   Fax: 608-266-6983
E-mail: scott.hassett@dnr.wi.us
Website: www.dnr.state.wi.us
Scope: State
Description: Responsibilities include: Fisheries, wildlife, forest, parks management, endangered resources protection, forest fire control, air and water pollution control, solid and hazardous waste management, mining regulation, enforcement of conservation and environmental laws, flood plain and shoreland zoning, water management and regulation, lake rehabilitation, and long-range planning in the broad fields of outdoor recreation and natural resources.
Publication(s): WI Natural Resources Magazine
Keyword(s): Air Quality/Atmosphere, Forests/Forestry, Land Issues, Recreation/Ecotourism, Reduce/Reuse/Recycle
Contact(s):
  James Addis, Director of Bureau of Intergrated Science Services; 608-266-0837
  Ruthe Badger, South Central Regional Director; 3911 Fish Hatchery Road, Madison, WI 53711; 608-275-3260
  Suzanne Bangert, Director of Bureau of Waste Management; 608-266-0014
  Susan Black, Director of Parks and Recreation; 608-266-2185
  Kathryn Curtner, Director of Bureau of Community Financial Assistance; 608-266-0860
  Paul Delong, Director of Bureau of Endangered Resources; 608-264-9224
  Lloyd Eagan, Director of Bureau of Air Management; 608-266-0603
  Gene Francisco, Director of Bureau of Forestry; 608-266-0842
  Mark Giesfeldt, Director of Bureau of Remediation and Redevelopment; 608-267-7562
  Thomas Harelson, Director of Bureau of Law Enforcement; 608-266-1115
  Thomas Hauge, Director of Bureau of Wildlife Management; 608-266-2193
  Scott Humrickhouse, West Central Regional Director; P.O. Box 4001, Eau Claire, WI 54702; 715-839-3711
  Jill Jonas, Director of Bureau of Drinking Water and Ground Water; 608-267-7651
  Ron Kazmierczak, Northeast Regional Director; P.O. Box 10448, Green Bay, WI 54307; 920-492-5815
  Gloria McCutcheon, Southeast Regional Director; P.O. Box 12436, Milwaukee, WI 53212; 414-263-8510

Robert Roden, Director of Bureau of Facilities and Lands; 608-266-2197

William Smith, Northern Regional Director; 810 W. Maple Street, Spooner, WI 54801; 715-635-4010

Michael Staggs, Director of Bureau of Management and Habitat Protection; 608-267-0796

Laurel Steffes, Director of Bureau of Communication and Education; 608-266-8109

Bruce Baker, Deputy Administrator of Bureau of Water; 608-266-1902

Darrell Bazzell, Deputy Secretary; 608-266-2252

Jay Hochmuth, Administrator of Air and Waste Division; 608-267-9521

Mary Kopecky, Deputy Administrator of Air and Waste Division; 608-261-8448

Mark McDermid, Contact

David Meier, Administrator of Enforcement and Science Division; 608-266-0015

George Meyer, Secretary; 608-266-2121

Steven Miller, Administrator of Land Division; 608-266-5782

Allen Shea, Bureau of Watershed Management; 608-267-2759

Trygve Solberg, Natural Resources Board Chairman; 715-356-7711

Susan Sylvester, Administrator of Water Division; 608-266-1099

WISCONSIN DEPARTMENT OF PUBLIC INSTRUCTION

125 S. Webster St.
P. O. Box 7841
Madison, WI 53707-7841 United States
Phone: 800-441-4563   Fax: 608-267-1052
E-mail: barbara.ballweg@dpi.state.wi.us
Website: www.dpi.state.wi.us/

Scope: Local, State

Description: A state government agency that promotes environmental education in public schools and supervises teacher preparation programs. Conducts workshops, and provides consultant services to elementary and secondary schools, colleges and universities. Produces publications to aid in program development.

Publication(s): A Guide to Curriculum Planning in Environmental Education, "Wisconsin's Model Academic Standards for Environmental Education"

Contact(s):
Sue Grady, Environmental Education Consultant; 608-266-2364
Shelley Lee, Environmental Education Consultant; 608-266-3319; shelley.lee@dpi.state.wi.us

WISCONSIN ENVIRONMENTAL EDUCATION BOARD (WEEB)

110B College of Natural Resources UW Stevens Point
Stevens Point, WI 54481 United States
Phone: 715-346-3805   Fax: 715-346-3025
E-mail: weeb@uwsp.edu
Website: www.uwsp.edu/cnr/weeb

Founded: 1990
Scope: State

Description: Grants board providing $50,000 annually to environmental education (EE) initiatives, $190,00 annually to forestry education initiatives, $190,000 annually to school forest initiatives and $180,000 annually to energy education initiatives to projects within the State of Wisconsin, with a maximum grant of $20,000 per project.

Publication(s): Annual Grant Recipients, Annual Report
Keyword(s): Energy, Forests/Forestry

Contact(s):
Ginny Carlton, Program Specialist
Rick Koziel, Chairperson

WISCONSIN GEOLOGICAL AND NATURAL HISTORY SURVEY

University of Wisconsin Extension, 3817 Mineral Point Rd.
Madison, WI 53705 United States
Phone: 608-262-1705   Fax: 608-262-8086
Website: www.uwex.edu/wgnhs

Founded: 1897
Scope: State

Description: Created by the legislature, with the responsibility to survey the state's geology, mineral, water, soil, plant, animal, and climate resources, and to coordinate topographic mapping.

Keyword(s): Land Issues

Contact(s):
James Robertson, State Geologist and Director; 608-263-7384
Ronald Hennings, Assistant Director; 608-263-7395

WISCONSIN STATE EXTENSION SERVICES

COMMUNITY NATURAL RESOURCE AND ECONOMIC DEVELOPMENT
University of Wisconsin Extension, 432 N. Lake St.
Madison, WI 53706 United States
Phone: 608-262-1748   Fax: 608-262-9166
Website: www.uwex.edu/ces/

Scope: State

Contact(s):
Carl O'Connor, Dean and Director of Cooperative Extension
Scott Craven, Wildlife Specialist; 8233 Russel Labs, 1630 Linden Dr., Madison, WI 53706; 608-263-6325; Fax: 608-262-6099; srcraven@facstaff.wisc.edu
Mark Rickenbach, Forest Ecology & Management Specialist; 608-262-0134; mrickenbach@cals.wisc.edu
Patrick Walsh, Statewide Program Leader; Community, Natural Resource and Economic Development, University of Wisconsin Extension, Rm. 625, 432 N. Lake St., Madison, WI 53706; 608-262-1748; patrick.walsh@ces.uwex.edu

WYOMING COOPERATIVE EXTENSION SERVICES

University Station, Box 3354
Laramie, WY 82071 United States
Phone: 307-766-5124   Fax: 307-766-3998
E-mail: glen@uwyo.edu
Website: www.uwyo.edu/ces/ceshome.htm

Membership: 1–100
Scope: State

Publication(s): Journal Articles, Regional Publications, 4-H Publications, Bulletins, Research Journals, Science Monographs, Scientific Abstracts

Keyword(s): Agriculture/Farming, Development/Developing Countries

Contact(s):
Glen Whipple, Director and Associate Dean; glen@uwyo.edu
Barb Farmer, Manager of Communications & Technologies; 307-766-3702; barbaraa@uwyo.edu
Ruth Wilson, Associate Director; drruth@uwyo.edu

WYOMING COOPERATIVE FISH AND WILDLIFE RESEARCH UNIT (USDI)

University of Wyoming, Box 3166, Biological Sciences Bldg., Rm. 419
Box 3166,University Station
Laramie, WY 82071 United States
Phone: 307-766-5415   Fax: 307-766-5400

Founded: 1980
Membership: 1–100
Scope: National

Description: Conducts research under auspices of the USGS Biological Resources Division and Wyoming Game and Fish Department in the northern Rocky Mountain region.
Keyword(s): Wildlife & Species
Contact(s):
Stanley Anderson, Leader; anderson@uwyo.edu
Wayne Hubert, Assistant Leader of Fisheries; drhubert@uwyo.edu
Fred Lindzey, Assistant Leader of Wildlife; flindzey@uwyo.edu

WYOMING DEPARTMENT OF AGRICULTURE
2219 Carey Ave.
Cheyenne, WY 82002 United States
Phone: 307-777-7321   Fax: 307-777-6593
Website: www.wyagric.state.wy.us
Scope: State
Contact(s):
Ron Micheli, Director; 307-777-6569; Fax: 307-777-6593; rmiche@missc.state.wy.us
Grant Stumbough, Natural Resource and Policy Manager; 307-777-6579
Jim Schwartz, Deputy Director; 307-777-6591

WYOMING DEPARTMENT OF ENVIRONMENTAL QUALITY
122 W. 25th St., Herschler Bldg.
Cheyenne, WY 82002 United States
Phone: 307-777-7937   Fax: 307-777-7682
E-mail: deqwyo@state.wy.us
Website: http://.deq.state.wy.us
Founded: 1973
Membership: 101–1,000
Scope: State
Description: Established to plan the development, use, reclamation, preservation, and enhancement of the air, land, and water resources of the state.
Publication(s): Outreach
Contact(s):
Dennis Hemmer, Director; 307-777-7938
David Finley, Manager of Solid Waste Program; 307-777-7752
Gary Beach, Administrator of Water Quality; 307-777-7781
Richard Chancellor, Administrator of Land Quality; 307-777-7756
Evon Green, Administrator of Abandoned Mine Land; 307-777-6145
Dan Olson, Administrator of Air Quality; 307-777-7391
James Uzzell, Administrator of Management Services, 307-777-7937

WYOMING DEPARTMENT OF ENVIRONMENTAL QUALITY
INDUSTRIAL SITING DIVISION
Herschler Bldg. 4-West
122 West 25th Street
Cheyenne, WY 82002 United States
Phone: 307-777-7369   Fax: 307-777-6937
E-mail: tschro@state.wy.us
Website: http://deq.state.wy.us
Founded: 1975
Description: Administers the Wyoming Industrial Development Information and Siting Act, which deals with the social, economic, and environmental impacts of large-scale industrial development. Responsibilities consist of investigating, reviewing, processing, and serving notice of permit applications.
Contact(s):
Gary Beach, Administrator; 307-777-7369

WYOMING GAME AND FISH DEPARTMENT
5400 Bishop Blvd.
Cheyenne, WY 82006 United States
Phone: 307-777-4632   Fax: 307-777-4610
E-mail: connie.coleman@wgf.state.wy.us
Website: http://gf.state.wy.us
Founded: 1939
Membership: 101–1,000
Scope: State
Description: To provide an adequate and flexible system for the control, propagation, management, protection, and regulation of Wyoming wildlife for the public interest.
Publication(s): Wyoming Wildlife News (2 months), Wyoming Wildlife (800-548-9453)
Keyword(s): Recreation/Ecotourism, Wildlife & Species
Contact(s):
Tom Thorne, Acting Director; 307-777-4501; Fax: 307-777-4699; Tom.Thorne@wgf.state.wy.us
Brent Knotts, Acting Services Division Chief; 307-777-4591; Fax: 307-777-4602
Green River Regional Office; 351 Astle, Green River, WY 82935; 307-857-3223; Fax: 307-875-3242
Jackson Regional Office; P.O. Box 67, 360 N. Cache, Jackson, WY 83001; 307-733-2321; Fax: 307-733-2276
Pinedale Regional Office; P.O. Box 850, 117 S. Sublette Avenue, Pinedale, WY 82941; 307-367-4353; Fax: 307-367-4403
Sheridan Regional Office; P.O. Box 6249, 700 Valley View, Sheridan, WY 82801; 307-672-7418; Fax: 307-672-0594
Laramie Regional Office; 528 S. Adams, Laramie, WY 82070; 307-745-4046; Fax: 307-745-8720
Lander Regional Office; 260 Buena Vista, Lander, WY 82520; 307-332-2688; Fax: 307-332-6669
Casper Regional Office; 3030 Energy Ln., Suite 100, Casper, WY 82604; 307-473-3400; Fax: 307-473-3433
Laramie Lab; Room 323, Biological Sciences Bldg., P.O. Box 3312 University Station, Laramie, WY 82071; 307-766-6313
Sybille Wildlife Research and Conservation Unit; 2362 Highway 34, Wheatland, WY 82201; 307-322-2571
Cody Regional Office; 2820 State Highway 120, Cody, WY 82414, 307-527-7125; Fax: 307-587-5430
Gregg Arthur, Deputy Director, Internal Programs
Lynda Cook, Assistant Attorney General; 307-777-4687
Larry Gabriele, Fiscal Division Chief; 307-777-4510; Fax: 307-777-4679; Larry.Gabriele@wgf.state.wy.us
Larry Kruckenberg, Special Assistant for Policy; 307-777-4539
Jay Lawson, Wildife Division Chief; 307-777-4579; Fax: 307-777-4650
Mike Stone, Fish Division Chief; 307-777-4559; Fax: 307-777-4611
Bill Wichers, Deputy Director, External Programs

WYOMING STATE BOARD OF LAND COMMISSIONERS
Herschler Building 3 West
122 West 25th Street
Cheyenne, WY 82002 United States
Phone: 307-777-7331   Fax: 307-777-5400
E-mail: lboomg@state.wy.us
Website: www.state.wy.us
Scope: State
Keyword(s): Land Issues, Public Lands/Greenspace, Reduce/Reuse/Recycle
Contact(s):
Ron Arnold, Secretary
Jim Geringer, Chairman

WYOMING STATE FORESTRY DIVISION
1100 W. 22nd St.
Cheyenne, WY 82002 United States
Phone: 307-777-7586   Fax: 307-777-5986
E-mail: Forestry@state.wy.us

Founded: 1952
Membership: 1–100
Scope: National
Description: Has direction of all forestry matters within the jurisdiction of the State of Wyoming; manages of state-owned forest land; coordinates fire protection on twenty-nine million acres of state and private rural lands; assists landowners and communities in proper management of woody vegetation and forested lands; and provides forestry information to schools, organizations, and individuals.
Publication(s): Wyoming State Forest Resource Program (Executive Summary)
Keyword(s): Forests/Forestry, Public Health, Reduce/Reuse/Recycle, Wildlife & Species
Contact(s):
Thomas Ostermann, State Forester
Daniel Perko, Deputy State Forester
Howard Pickerd, Assistant State Forester of Forest Management
Ray Weidenhaft, Assistant State Forester of Fire Management

WYOMING STATE GEOLOGICAL SURVEY
Box 3008
Laramie, WY 82071 United States
Phone: 307-766-2286   Fax: 307-766-2605
E-mail: wsgs@wsgs.uwyo.edu
Website: www.wsgsweb.uwyo.edu

Founded: 1933
Membership: 1–100
Scope: State
Description: Activities include surface and subsurface geologic mapping; mineral, rock, and fossil investigations; natural resource and natural hazards investigations; and assistance in resources development.
Publication(s): Maps, memoirs, list of publications sent on request., quarterly newsletter (Wyoming Geo-notes), public information circulars, reports of investigations, bulletins
Keyword(s): Energy, Land Issues
Contact(s):
James Case, Geologic Hazards Geologist; 307-766-2286; ext. 225; jcase@wsgs.uwyo.edu
Lance Cook, State Geologist; lcook@wsgs.uwyo.edu
Rodney Debruin, Petroleum Geologist; 307-766-2286; ext. 226; rdebru@wsgs.uwyo.edu
Ray Harris, Industrial Minerals Geologist; 307-766-2286; ext. 228; rharri@wsgs.uwyo.edu
W. Hausel, Senior Economic Geologist of Metals and Precious Stones; 307-766-2286; ext. 229; dhause@wsgs.uwyo.edu
Joe Huss, Head of GIS; 307-766-2286; ext. 234; jhuss@wsgs.uwyo.edu
Richard Jones, Editor; 307-766-2286; ext. 238; rjones@wsgs.uwyo.edu
Robert Lyman, Coal Geologist; 307-766-2286; ext. 233; blyman@wsgs.uwyo.edu
Alan Verploeg, Geologic Mapping Geologist; 307-766-2286; ext. 230; averpl@wsgs.uwyo.edu

WYOMING STATE PARKS AND CULTURAL RESOURCES
DIVISION OF STATE PARKS AND HISTORIC SITES
1st Fl., Herschler Bldg. 1E
Cheyenne, WY 82002 United States
Phone: 307-777-6323   Fax: 307-777-6472
E-mail: sphs@state.wy.us
Website: www.wyobest.org

Founded: 1967
Membership: 1–100
Scope: Regional
Description: Responsible for administering the state parks, state recreation areas, historic sites, petroglyph site, archaeological site, markers and monuments, snowmobile program, and state trails program.
Keyword(s): Land Issues, Public Lands/Greenspace, Recreation/Ecotourism
Contact(s):
Bill Gentle, Director of Division of State Parks and Historic Sites

Y

YUKON DEPARTMENT OF RENEWABLE RESOURCES
Box 2703
Whitehorse, Y1A 2C6 Yukon Canada
Phone: 867-667-5652   Fax: 867-393-6213
Website: www.renres.gov.yk.ca

Contact(s):
Karyn Armour, Acting Director of Policy and Planning; 403-667-5634
Joe Ballantyne, Director of Environmental Protection and Assessment; 403-667-8177
Dave Beckman, Director of Agriculture; 403-667-5838
Stan Marinoske, Director of Finance and Administration; 403-667-5197
Jim McIntyre, Director of Parks and Outdoor Recreation; 403-667-5261
Don Toews, Acting Director of Fish and Wildlife; 403-667-5715
Jim Connell, Acting Assistant Deputy Minister; 402-667-8955
Ed Hubert, Deputy Minister; 867-667-5460; ed.hubert@gov.yk.ca

NON-GOVERNMENTAL NON-PROFIT ORGANIZATIONS

20/20 VISION
1828 Jefferson Pl., NW
Washington, DC 20036 United States
Phone: 202-833-2020　　　　　Fax: 202-833-5307
E-mail: vision@2020vision.org
Website: www.vision.org

Founded: 1986
Membership: 1,001–10,000
Scope: National

Description: 20/20 Vision is a nonprofit grassroots organization dedicated to protecting the environment and promoting peace through lobbying and citizen education and activism. 20/20 Vision empowers citizens to speak out for a clean environment and a world free of weapons of mass destruction. Each month we pick one issue that is critically important to the future of the planet, where your voice will make the most difference. Letters written in just 20 minutes a month can move political mountains.

Publication(s): Tools for Activists Fact Sheets, Action Alert Postcards, Viewpoint

Contact(s):
James Wyerman, Executive Director;
　jwyerman@2020vision.org
Chris Demers, Public Outreach Coordinator;
　chris@2020vision.org
Erik Olsen, Campaigns Coordinator; erik@2020vision.org

A

A CRITICAL DECISION
Please Use EMail
Dayton, OH 45342 United States
E-mail: director@acriticaldecision.org
Website: www.acriticaldecision.org

Founded: 2001
Scope: International

Description: Please enjoy our nature gallery and thought-provoking prose. We encourage citizens to question the dangerous influences large corporations have over democracy, population, and the environment (our life-support system).

Keyword(s): Ecosystems (precious), Population, Reduce/Reuse/Recycle, Wildlife & Species

A.E. HOWELL WILDLIFE CONSERVATION CENTER INC.
HC#61 Box 6
Lycette Rd.
No. Amity, ME 04471-9601 United States
Phone: 207-532-6880, ext 8357　　Fax: 207-532-0910
E-mail: eagleman@mfx.net
Website: spruceacresrefuge.tripod.com

Founded: 1981
Membership: 101–1,000
Scope: Local, State, Regional, National

Description: The A.E.H.W.C.C., Inc. and Spruce Acres Refuge have combined to provide a 65+ acre Wildlife Rehabilitation Center for people from all over the world to enjoy. The center is a non-profit organization established for the purpose of preserving our natural resources and providing educational programs & tours to all people to encourage proper wildlife and natural resource management.

Keyword(s): Recreation/Ecotourism, Water Habitats & Quality, Wildlife & Species

Contact(s):
Penny Kern, VP; 207-764-7945; Fax: 207-769-6680;
　pkern@mfx.net
A. Eric Howell, Manager; 207-532-7981

ABUNDANT LIFE SEED FOUNDATION
P.O. Box 772
Port Townsend, WA 98368 United States
Phone: 360-385-5660　　　　　Fax: 360-385-7455
E-mail: abundant@olypen.com
Website: www.abundantlifeseed.org/

Founded: 1975
Membership: 1,001–10,000
Scope: National

Description: Abundant Life Seed Foundation is a nonprofit, tax-exempt organization that propagates and preserves seeds of Northwest native plants and heritage (non-hybrid) vegetables, herbs, and flowers. The Foundation conducts the distribution of seeds (and related books) via a mail-order catalog. Also operates the World Seed Fund, donating seed internationally to those in need, both in the United States and internationally.

Publication(s): Seed Midden, Seed and Book Catalog

Keyword(s): Agriculture/Farming, Wildlife & Species

Contact(s):
Ken Beal, President
Kirsten Fzykitka, Outreach Coordinator
Gus Rassam, Executive Director; 301-897-8616

ACADEMY FOR EDUCATIONAL DEVELOPMENT
1825 Connecticut Ave., Suite 800
Washington, DC 20009-8721 United States
Phone: 719-556-8318　　　　　Fax: 202-884-8997
E-mail: greencom@aed.org
Website: www.usaid.gov/environment/greencom

Founded: 1961
Scope: International

Description: A domestic and international development organization with a multi-million dollar environmental education, communication and environmental health population agenda working in over 25 countries.

Publication(s): Publication on website

Keyword(s): Agriculture/Farming, Air Quality/Atmosphere, Ethics/Environmental Justice, Recreation/Ecotourism, Reduce/Reuse/Recycle, Water Habitats & Quality, Wildlife & Species

Contact(s):
William Smith, Executive Vice President; 202-884-8750; Fax:
　202-884-8752; bsmith@aed.org
Richard Bassi, Latin America Director; 202-884-8898;
　rbassi@aed.org
Brian Day, Director; 202-884-8897; bday@aed.org
Gregory Niblett, Senior Vice Presdent; niblett@aed.org

ACRES LAND TRUST
2000 N. Wells St.
Fort Wayne, IN 46808-2474 United States
Phone: 260-422-1004　　　　　Fax: 260-422-1004
E-mail: acreslt@fwi.com
Website: www.acres-land-trust.org

Founded: 1960
Membership: 1,001–10,000
Scope: Regional

Description: A nonprofit organization dedicated to the acquisition and permanent preservation of natural areas in northeastern Indiana. Conducts a guided field-trip program for children and adults. Organizes canoe trips, concerts and festivals for the membership and the public. Administers 48 nature preserves totaling more than 3,250 acres.

Publication(s): Acres Quarterly, Field Guide, Acres Brochure

Keyword(s): Land Issues, Water Habitats & Quality, Wildlife & Species

Contact(s):
David Van Gilder, President
Theodore Heemstra, Vice President
Janel Rogers, Vice President
Sam Schwartz, Vice President

Carolyn McNagny, Executive Director
Richard Walker, Treasurer

ACTION FOR NATURE, INC.
2269 Chestnut St., Suite 263
San Francisco, CA 94123 United States
Phone: 415-421-2640   Fax: 415-922-5717
E-mail: action@dnai.com
Website: www.actionfornature.org

Founded: 1983

Scope: National, International

Description: Action for Nature was organized to foster respect and affection for nature through personal action. AFN is a clearing-house and catalyst for personal environmental action projects and publicizes young peoples' successful environmental initiatives through a newsletter, website bulletin board and publication of a book of young people's environmental success stories from around the world. AFN has recently established a Nature Action Program for classrooms and children's groups.

Publication(s): Acting for Nature (book)

Contact(s):
Albert Baez, Science Educator, President, Vivamos Mejor
Evelyn De Ghetaldi, President
Huey Johnson, Founder, President, Renewal Resources Institute
Jean Barish, Attorney
Jerome Dodson, President, Parnassus Fund
Beryl Kay, Director Human Resources, California Academy. of Science
B. Shimon Schwarzschild, Secretary; P.O. Box 1959, Sutter Creek, CA 95685; shimons@earthlink.net
Adrienne Scroggie, Retired Educator
Alan Scroggie, Retired Educator
Maria Cohen, Nature Council
Ruth Gottstein, Publisher, Volcano Press
Mary Griffin-Jones, Retired Physician
Sidney Holt, Biologist, Marine Conservationist, Animal Protector
William Whalen, Consultant

ADIRONDACK COUNCIL, THE
P.O. Box D-2
103 Hand Ave. #3
Elizabethtown, NY 12932 United States
Phone: 877-873-2240   Fax: 518-873-6675
E-mail: info@adirondakcouncil.org
Website: www.adirondakcouncil.org

Founded: 1975

Membership: 10,001–100,000

Scope: Local, State, Regional, National

Description: A nonprofit environmental organization working for protection and preservation of the six million acre Adirondack Park in upstate New York. Programs include monitoring and influencing state programs in the Park, helping to promote understanding of the Park and the need to protect its very special character, and supporting and advancing positive programs to enhance the Park and benefit its people.

Publication(s): Adirondack Council Newsletter, State of the Park, Adirondack Wildguide: A Natural History, Acid Rain: A Continuing National Tragedy

Keyword(s): Air Quality/Atmosphere, Development/Developing Countries, Land Issues, Public Lands/Greenspace

Contact(s):
Bernard Melewski, Executive Director
David Bronston, Vice Chairman
Edward Fowler, Treasurer
Barbara Glaser, Secretary
David Skovron, Chairman
Patricia Winterer, Vice Chairman

ADIRONDACK MOUNTAIN CLUB, INC., THE (ADK)
814 Goggins Rd.
Lake George, NY 12845-4117 United States
Phone: 518-668-4447   Fax: 518-668-3746
E-mail: adkinfo@adk.org
Website: www.adk.org

Founded: 1922

Membership: 10,001–100,000

Scope: State

Description: The Adirondack Mountain Club is dedicated to the protection and responsible recreational use of the New York State Forest Preserve, parks and other wild lands and waters. The Club is a member-directed organization committed to public service and stewardship. ADK employs a balanced approach to outdoor recreation, advocacy, environmental education and natural resource conservation. ADK has 26 chapters in NY and NJ.

Publication(s): Kids on the Trail!, Guidebook & Map to High Peaks Region, Views from on High: Fire Tower Trails, Adirondack Magazine, Annual Calendar, Adirondack Cultural and Literary History, Adirondack Canoe Waters, Guides and Maps to Adirondack and Catskill Trails

Keyword(s): Air Quality/Atmosphere, Forests/Forestry, Land Issues, Public Lands/Greenspace, Recreation/Ecotourism, Reduce/Reuse/Recycle, Transportation, Wildlife & Species

Contact(s):
Terry Sexton, President
Jo Benton, Executive Director; 518-668-4447
Jen Kretzer, Education Director
Greg Macdonald, Director of North Country Operations; P. O. Box 867, Lake Placid, NY 12946
Tim Tierney, Director of Field Programs; P. O. Box 867, Lake Placid, NY 12946
Neil Woodworth, Deputy Executive Director for Public and Legal Affairs; 518-449-3870; nwoodworth@nycap,rr,com
Neal Burdick, Editor; 35 Woods Dr., Canton, NY 13617

ADKINS ARBORETUM
P.O. Box 100
Ridgely, MD 21660 United States
Phone: 410-634-2847   Fax: 410-634-2878
E-mail: adkinsar@intercom.net
Website: www.adkinsarboretum.org

Founded: 1979

Membership: 101–1,000

Scope: Regional

Description: Adkins Arboretum is dedicated to the appreciation, understanding and stewardship of the indigenous, nontidal plant communities of the Central Delmarva Peninsula. It strives to maintain a divers and dynamic living collection that is authentic, engaging and a model for land management. As a significant cultural, education, scientific and recreational resource, the Arboretum fosters civic pride, encourages public dialogue and contributes to the economic vitality of the region.

Publication(s): Native Seed

Keyword(s): Land Issues, Reduce/Reuse/Recycle, Water Habitats & Quality, Wildlife & Species

Contact(s):
Lorie Staber, President of the Board
Kathy Carnean, Vice President
Ellie Altman, Executive Director; 410-634-2847; Fax: 410-634-2878; ealtman@intercom.net
Louise Barton, Secretary
Graham Donaldson, Treasurer

ADOPT-A-STREAM FOUNDATION, THE
600-128th St., SE
Everett, WA 98208-6353 United States
Phone: 425-316-8592   Fax: 425-338-1423
E-mail: aasf@streamkeeper.org
Website: www.streamkeeper.org

Founded: 1985
Membership: 101–1,000
Scope: Local, National

Description: Adopt-A-Stream Foundation's mission is to empower people to become stewards of watersheds, wetlands and streams. The Foundation's long term goal is to ensure that all streams are adopted by watershed residents. The current focus is in the Pacific Northwest. The Foundation conducts "Streamkeeper" workshops that train volunteers and students of all ages how to conduct watershed inventories, monitor small streams and other educational programming.

Publication(s): Video: The Streamkeeper, The Streamkeeper (newsletter), Adopting a Wetland: A Northwest Guide, Adopting a Stream: A Northwest Handbook

Keyword(s): Land Issues, Public Lands/Greenspace, Reduce/Reuse/Recycle, Water Habitats & Quality, Wildlife & Species

Contact(s):
Darryl Williams, Board President
Tom Murdoch, Executive Director
Mike Chamblin, Treasurer
Scott Haeger, Secretary

ADVOCATES OF THE COMMON WEALTH, INC.
ACW, INC.
4651 South Wallace Lane
Salt Lake City, UT 84117 United States
Phone: 801-998-8149   Fax: 801-998-8149
E-mail: JohnSchoppe@aol.com
Website: www.harborvillagerealty.com

Founded: 2001
Scope: Local, State, Regional, National, International

Description: ACW is a Utah nonprofit [IRC 501(c)(3)] company that focuses on Education, Technology, and Financial Services in providing a "Systems approach to optimum lifestyle" through the Paragon Proposal of its CEO, John H. Schoppe. Strategic Environmental Management is one of the many areas of focus.

Keyword(s): Ethics/Environmental Justice, Executive/Legislative/Judicial Reform, Finance/Banking/Trade, Land Issues, Oceans/Coasts/Beaches, Pollution (general), Public Health, Reduce/Reuse/Recycle, Water Habitats & Quality

AFRICA VISION TRUST
P.B. 23389
Dar Es Salaam, Tanzania
Phone: 255-51-601497
E-mail: afrovisn@intafrica.com
Website: www.africavision.org

Founded: 1998
Scope: National

Description: Africa Vision Trust produces media and communications materials for/and in support of environmental and conservation programs. We also offer educational and professional training in these areas.

Publication(s): New Kingo

Keyword(s): Development/Developing Countries, Land Issues, Oceans/Coasts/Beaches, Population, Public Lands/Greenspace, Recreation/Ecotourism, Water Habitats & Quality, Wildlife & Species

Contact(s):
Vincent Shauri, Chairman; 255-51-121315; afrovisn@intafrica.com
S. Granger, Production Manager; 255-51-601497; afrovisn@intafrica.com
M. Macoun, Secretary; 255-51-601497; afrovisn@intafrica.com
D. Mmari, Treasurer/Administrator; 255-51-601497; afrovisn@intafrica.com

AFRICAN AMERICAN ENVIRONMENTALIST ASSOCIATION
CENTER FOR ENVIRONMENT, COMMERCE & ENERGY
ENVIRONMENTAL JUSTICE COALITION
NUCLEAR FUELS REPROCESSING COALITION
9903 Caltor Lane
Ft. Washington, MD 20744-3728 United States
Phone: 301-265-8185
E-mail: AfricanAmericanEnvironmentalist@msn.com
Website: groups.msn.com/AAEA

Founded: 1985
Membership: 1,001–10,000
Scope: Local, State, Regional, National, International

Description: Organization dedicated to protecting the environment, promoting the efficient use of natural resources, enhancing human, animal and plant ecologies and increasing African American participation in the environmental movement.

Keyword(s): Agriculture/Farming, Air Quality/Atmosphere, Climate Change, Development/Developing Countries, Ecosystems (precious), Energy, Ethics/Environmental Justice, Executive/Legislative/Judicial Reform, Finance/Banking/Trade, Forests/Forestry, Land Issues, Pollut

Contact(s):
Norris McDonald, President; 301-265-8185; NorrisMcDonald@msn.com
Kathleen Logan, Director, St. Louis Office; http://groups.msn.com/AAEAStLouis, 4119 Metaxa Lane, Suite D, St. Louis, MO 63129; 314-892-6120; AAEAStLouis@groups.msn.com
Darshoel Willis, Director, Texas; http://groups.msn.com/AAEATexas, Pflugerville, TX 78660; 512-990-9468; AAEATexas@groups.msn.com

AFRICAN CONSERVATION FOUNDATION, THE
ACF
P.O. Box 36
Bingley, W. Yorks, BD16 1LQ United Kingdom
Phone: 0044-1535-274160   Fax: 0044-1535-271631
E-mail: terry@africanconservation.org
Website: www.africanconservation.org

Founded: 2001
Scope: International

Description: The African Conservation Foundation (ACF) is a UK-Registered Not for Profit organisation, primarily concerned with education in Africa in the areas of environment and conservation. Its mission is to support and link African conservation initiatives, groups and NGOs, with the aim of strengthening their capacity, building partnerships and promoting effective communication and co-ordination of conservation efforts.

Keyword(s): Development/Developing Countries, Ecosystems (precious), Forests/Forestry, Land Issues, Oceans/Coasts/Beaches, Public Lands/Greenspace, Recreation/Ecotourism, Water Habitats & Quality, Wildlife & Species

AFRICAN WILDLIFE FOUNDATION
1400 16th St., NW
Washington, DC 20036 United States
Phone: 202-939-3333   Fax: 202-939-3332
E-mail: africanwildlife@awf.org
Website: www.awf.org
Membership: 101–1,000
Scope: International

Description: The African Wildlife Foundation recognizes that the wildlife and wild lands of Africa have no equal. We work with people—our supporters worldwide and our partners in Africa—to craft and deliver creative solutions for the long-term well-being of Africa's remarkable species, habitats, and the people who depend upon them.

Publication(s): African Wildlife News

Keyword(s): Development/Developing Countries, Reduce/Reuse/Recycle, Wildlife & Species

Contact(s):
Patrick Bergin, President of Africa Operations
R. Wright, President
Henry McIntosh, Treasurer
William Richards, Vice Chair of the Board
Stuart Saunders, Chairman of the Board

AIR & WASTE MANAGEMENT ASSOCIATION
One Gateway Center, 3rd Floor
420 Fort Duquesne Blvd.
Pittsburgh, PA 15222 United States
Phone: 412-232-3444   Fax: 412-232-3450
E-mail: info@awma.org
Website: www.awma.org

Founded: 1907
Membership: 1,001–10,000
Scope: Local, State, Regional, National, International
Description: The Air & Waste Management Association is a nonprofit, technical, and environmental association that provides a neutral forum for discussing all sides of environmental issues. The Association's membership includes engineers, scientists, researchers, health professionals and others from government, industry, academia, consulting, and other fields.
Publication(s): EM, other publications include proceedings, Journal of the Air & Waste Management Assocation
Keyword(s): Air Quality/Atmosphere, Climate Change, Reduce/Reuse/Recycle

Contact(s):
Robert Hall, 1st Vice President
Douglas Bisset, Treasure

AIZA BIBY
P.O. Box 701
East Setauket, NY 11733 United States
Phone: 516-658-6871
E-mail: biby@biby.org
Website: www.biby.org

Founded: 1999
Scope: Local, State, Regional, National, International
Description: The purpose of the Aiza Biby charitable trust is to assist children, ages 3-18, in defining the future of conservation biology and to provide these youth with entertaining lessons in conservation education and hands-on experience in land stewardship across the world.
Keyword(s): Agriculture/Farming, Ecosystems (precious), Forests/Forestry, Recreation/Ecotourism, Wildlife & Species

Contact(s):
Rebecca Grella, President; 516-658-6871; becky@biby.org
Robert Meyer, CEO; 631-897-0442
Sarah Karpanty, Executive Director; 631-632-8600

ALABAMA ASSOCIATION OF SOIL AND WATER CONSERVATION DISTRICTS
Attn: Executive Director
P.O. Box 304800
Montgomery, AL 36130-4800 United States
Phone: 334-242-2620   Fax: 334-242-0551
Website: swcc.st.al.us.

Scope: State

Contact(s):
George Robertson, President; 2181 County Rd. 22, Waverly, AL 36879; 334-887-6070; Fax: 334-826-8219
Jake Harper, 1st Vice President; Rt. 1 Box 468, Camden, AL 36726; 334-682-4463
Terry Poague, 2nd Vice President; 3716 Clause Fleahop Rd., Tallahassee, AL 36078; 334-567-6183
Charles Holmes, Board Member; Rt. 1 Box 212, Marion, AL 36756; 334-683-6869; Fax: 334-583-6869
Charles Rittenour, Secretary/Treasurer; 1144 Meriwether Rd., Pike Road, AL 36064; 334-284-5320

ALABAMA BASS FEDERATION
Alabama B.A.S.S. Chapter Federation, Inc
P.O. Box 190
Notasulga, AL 36866 United States
Phone: 334-257-1177   Fax: 334-257-4665
Website: www.albassfed.org

Founded: 1972
Membership: 1,001–10,000
Scope: Local, State, Regional, National
Description: An organization of Bassmaster chapters, affiliated with the Bass Anglers Sportsman Society, organized to fight pollution, assist state and national conservation agencies in their efforts, and teach the young people of our country good conservation practices. Dedicated to the realistic conservation of our water resources.

Contact(s):
Al Redding, President; P.O. Box 190, 209 Tallapoosa St. (shipping), Notasulga, AL 36866; 334-257-1177; Fax: 334-257-4665; alhred@prodigy.net
Jim Howard, Conservation Director; 501 Five Mile Rd., Eufaula, AL 36027; 334-616-6956; Fax: 334-616-7194; bassnbuddy@aol.com

ALABAMA ENVIRONMENTAL COUNCIL
2717 7th Ave., S., Suite 207
Birmingham, AL 35233 United States
Phone: 205-322-3126   Fax: 205-324-3784
E-mail: stateoffice@aeconline.ws
Website: www.aeconline.ws

Founded: 1967
Membership: 101–1,000
Scope: Local, State, Regional
Description: Dedicated to the preservation of Alabama's environment on all fronts: air, water, land and wildlife.
Publication(s): State News
Keyword(s): Agriculture/Farming, Air Quality/Atmosphere, Ecosystems (precious), Energy, Ethics/Environmental Justice, Forests/Forestry, Land Issues, Oceans/Coasts/Beaches, Pollution (general), Public Health, Public Lands/Greenspace, Recreation/Ecotourism, Reduce/Reus

Contact(s):
Thomas Carruthers, President
Rachel Reinhart, Executive Director; 2717 7th Ave. S Suite 207, Birmingham, AL 35233; 205-322-3126; Fax: 205-324-3784; director@aeconline.ws
Jessica Robertson, Administrator; 205-322-3126; Fax: 205-324-3784; stateoffice@aeconline.ws

ALABAMA WATERFOWL ASSOCIATION (AWA)
1346 County Road 11
Scottsboro, AL 35768 United States
Phone: 256-259-2509
E-mail: awa@alabamawaterfowl.org
Website: www.alabamawaterfowl.org

Founded: 1987
Membership: 101–1,000
Scope: State
Description: Conserving Alabama's watersheds, wetlands and coastal regions. Enhancing waterfowl and protecting Alabama's hunting heritage
Keyword(s): Ecosystems (precious)

Contact(s):
Jerry Davis, CEO; 256-259-2509; Fax: 256-259-2509; jd@alabamawaterfowl.org

NON-GOVERNMENTAL NON-PROFIT ORGANIZATIONS – A

ALABAMA WATERFOWL ASSOCIATION, INC. (AWA)
1346 County Road # 11
Scottsboro, AL 35768 United States
Phone: 256-259-2509   Fax: 256-259-2509
E-mail: awa@alabamawaterfowl.org
Website: www.alabamawaterfowl.org

Founded: 1987
Scope: State
Description: To protect, enhance and create wetlands habitat for all wildlife species and other human values; and to enhance waterfowl population and protect our hunting heritage in Alabama.
Publication(s): Wetlands and Waterfowl News
Keyword(s): Recreation/Ecotourism, Water Habitats & Quality, Wildlife & Species
Contact(s):
Gary Benefield, Executive Director; P.O. Box 67, Guntersville, AL 35976; 205-593-7712
Roger Crouch, Executive Treasurer; P.O. Box 67, Guntersville, AL 35976
Jerry Davis, Chief Executive Officer; 1346 County Rd. 11, Scottsboro, AL 35768; 205-259-2509

ALABAMA WILDFLOWER SOCIETY, THE
606 India Rd.
Opelika, AL 36801 United States
Phone: 334-745-2494   Fax: 334-704-0455
E-mail: deancar@auburn.edu
Website: www.auburn.edu/~deancar

Founded: 1971
Membership: 101–1,000
Scope: State
Description: The society promotes knowledge, appreciation, use of native plants, preserves and propagates rare native plants, preserves areas of significant native flora and provides scholarships.
Publication(s): Wildflower Brochure, Newsletter of the Alabama Wildflower Society
Keyword(s): Reduce/Reuse/Recycle, Wildlife & Species
Contact(s):
George Wood, President/Editor; 205-339-2541
Shirley Fifield, Past President; 334-277-2070; rgfifi@aol.com
Caroline Dean, Board Member
Virginia Lusk, Past President; 205-988-0299; ginny1@bellsouth.net

ALABAMA WILDLIFE FEDERATION
3050 Lanark Road
Millbrook, AL 36054 United States
Phone: 334-285-4550 Fax: 334-285-4959
E-mail: awf@alabamawildlife.org
Website: www.alabamawildlife.org

Founded: 1935
Membership: 1,001–10,000
Scope: State
Description: A representative statewide organization affiliated with the National Wildlife Federation, dedicated to the protection and enhancement of wildlife and its habitat through public education and government interaction.
Publication(s): Managing Wildlife, Alabama Wildlife
Contact(s):
Robert Thornton, President
Tim Gothard, Executive Director, Alternate Representative and Editor
Clinton Berry, Treasurer
April Lupardus, Conservation Programs Specialist
Jeff McCollum, Education Programs Contact
Rebecca Prichett, Representative

ALASKA ASSOCIATION OF SOIL AND WATER CONSERVATION DISTRICTS
1700 East Bogard Rd. #203
Wasilla, AK 99654 United States
Phone: 907-271-2424   Fax: 907-373-7192
E-mail: aacd@mtaonline.net

Scope: State
Description: A representative statewide organization affiliated with the National Wildlife Federation, dedicated to the protection and enhancement of wildlife and its habitat through public education and government interaction.
Contact(s):
Omar Stratman, President, Board Member; P.O. Box 2376, Kodiak, AK 99615; 907-486-5578; Fax: 907-486-5578
Meribeth Crick, 2nd Vice President; P.O. Box 56505, North Pole, AK 56505; 907-488-2215
Shirley Schollenberg, 1st Vice President; HC 67 Box 250, Anchor Point, AK 99556; 907-567-3467
Meg Burgett, Secretary-Treasurer; P.O. Box 874554, Wasilla, AK 99687; 907-373-0885
Mike Carlson, Alternate Board Member; P.O. Box 953, Delta Junction, AK 99737; 907-895-4819
Doug Witte, Project Coordinator; 351 W. Parks Hwy. #101, Wasilla, AK 99645; 907-373-7923; Fax: 907-373-7192

ALASKA CENTER FOR THE ENVIRONMENT
807 G Street, Suite 100
Anchorage, AK 99501 United States
Phone: 907-274-3621   Fax: 907-274-8733
E-mail: ace@akcenter.org
Website: www.akcenter.org

Founded: 1971
Membership: 1,001–10,000
Scope: State
Description: Nonprofit organization which functions as an advocacy and citizen organizing facility for Alaskan environmental activities. With a professional staff of twelve and a corps of volunteers, the center conducts policy analysis and encourages grassroots activism to conserve and protect Alaska's natural resources, particularly its wildlands.
Keyword(s): Ecosystems (precious), Forests/Forestry, Land Issues, Oceans/Coasts/Beaches, Pollution (general), Public Lands/Greenspace, Reduce/Reuse/Recycle, Sprawl/Urban Planning, Wildlife & Species
Contact(s):
Tom Burek, Director of Trailside Discovery Camp; trailside@akcenter.org
Dwayne Lee, Financial Director and Officer Manager; dwayno@akcenter.org
Randy Virgin, Executive Director; randy@akcenter.org
Andre Camara, Campaigner, Anchorage Quality of Life; andre@akcenter.org
Cliff Eames, Public Lands Director; cliff@akcenter.org
Theo Saner, Membership Assistant; theo@akcenter.org

ALASKA CONSERVATION ALLIANCE
750 West 2nd Ave., Suite 109
Anchorage, AK 99501 United States
Phone: 907-258-6171   Fax: 907-258-6177
E-mail: unite@akvoice.org
Website: www.akvoice.org

Founded: 1997
Scope: National
Description: An alliance dedicated to strengthening environmental organizations and empowering individuals to protect Alaska's environment through public education, training, advocacy, communication and strategy development, all with respect for communities and human dignity.
Publication(s): GIS
Keyword(s): Air Quality/Atmosphere, Development/Developing Countries, Ecosystems (precious), Forests/Forestry, Land

Issues, Pollution (general), Water Habitats & Quality, Wildlife & Species

Contact(s):
Tom Atkinson, Executive Director; tom@akvoice.org
Christy Garrett, Office Coordinator; christy@akvoice.org
Jason Geck, GIS Analyst; 907-258-6148; jason@akvoice.org
Sue Schrader, Conservation Advocate; sue@akvoice.org
Marlo Shedlock, Program Organizer; marlo@akvoice.org
Sandra Wright, Financial Officer; sandie@akvoice.org

ALASKA CONSERVATION ALLIANCE
810 N Street #203
Anchorage, AK 99501 United States
Phone: 907-258-6171   Fax: 907-258-6177
E-mail: unite@akvoice.org
Website: www.akvoice.org

Founded: 1997
Membership: 1,001–10,000
Scope: State

Description: An organization dedicated to protecting Alaska's environment through public education and advocacy in the Alaska state legislature, Congress and other forums.

Publication(s): The Score Card, newsletter (end of year report) - United Voices

Keyword(s): Air Quality/Atmosphere, Development/Developing Countries, Ecosystems (precious), Energy, Executive/Legislative/Judicial Reform, Forests/Forestry, Land Issues, Pollution (general), Water Habitats & Quality, Wildlife & Species

Contact(s):
Tom Atkinson, Director; 907-258-6174; tom@akvoice.org
Christy Garrett, Office Coordinator; christy@akvoice.org
Andres Porter, Development Director; 907-258-6191; andrew@akvoice.org
Sandra Wright, Financial Officer; sandie@akvoice.org
Matt Davidson, Lobbyist; 907-463-3366; matt@akvoice.org
Marlo Shedlock, Program Coordinator; 906-258-6181; marlo@akvoice.org

ALASKA CONSERVATION FOUNDATION
441 West Fifth Avenue
Suite 402
Anchorage, AK 99501-2340 United States
Phone: 907-276-1917   Fax: 907-274-4145
E-mail: acfinfo@akcf.org
Website: www.akcf.org

Founded: 1980
Membership: 10,001–100,000
Scope: State

Description: A public foundation providing grants for environmental conservation in Alaska. It is not a membership organization. It lists its donors as "Circle of Friends."

Publication(s): Guide to Alaska's Cultures, Dispatch, Alaska Conservation Directory, Grant Guidelines, Annual Report

Keyword(s): Climate Change, Ecosystems (precious), Energy, Forests/Forestry, Oceans/Coasts/Beaches, Public Lands/Greenspace, Transportation, Water Habitats & Quality, Wildlife & Species

Contact(s):
Deborah Williams, Executive Director; 907-276-1917; Fax: 907-274-4145; dwilliams@akcf.org
Kevin Harun, Interim Program Officer; 907-276-1917; Fax: 907-274-4145; kharun@akcf.org
Julie Jessen, Associate Program Officer; 907-276-1917; Fax: 907-274-4145; jjessen@akcf.org
Jimmy Carter, Honorary Chair
Ken Leghorn, Vice Chair of Alaska Trustees
Eric Myers, Chair
David Rockefeller, Advisor
Stacy Studebaker, Secretary

ALASKA NATURAL HISTORY ASSOCIATION
750 West Second Ave., Suite 100
Anchorage, AK 99501-2167 United States
Phone: 907-274-8440   Fax: 907-274-8343
E-mail: info@alaskanha.org
Website: www.alaskanha.org

Founded: 1959
Membership: 1,001–10,000
Scope: State

Description: The Association connects people to Alaska's natural and cultural heritage and public lands. The Association operates educational bookstores across Alaska and offers hands-on learning courses through the Denali Institute. Members receive discounts, newsletters, & other Alaska information. Support to Alaska's public land educational programs is about 1.2 million annually, generated mostly through sales of educational materials in the bookstores. Learn more at www.alaskanha.org

Publication(s): Northern Migrations, Alaska Books Catalog, Online Catalog

Keyword(s): Public Lands/Greenspace, Recreation/Ecotourism

Contact(s):
Charles Money, Executive Director; charles-money@alaskanha.org

ALASKA NATURAL RESOURCE AND OUTDOOR EDUCATION ASSOCIATION
P.O. Box 871528
Wasilla, AK 99654 United States
Phone: 907-456-0558   Fax: 907-376-0970
E-mail: admin@anroe.org
Website: www.anroe.org

Founded: 1983
Membership: 101–1,000
Scope: State

Description: ANROE is a statewide network of K-12 school teachers, state and federal agency staff, university faculty and staff, students and other concerned citizens united to promote the development, delivery and implementation of educational efforts that help people of all ages learn about and appreciate Alaska's natural resources.

Publication(s): Discovering Alaska's Salmon, Children's Activity Guide, Flyways, Pathways, and Waterways (newsletter), Targeting Excellence, ANROE Guide to Natural Resource Education Materials

Contact(s):
Janet Warburton, President

ALASKA RAINFOREST CAMPAIGN
201 Lincoln St., Suite 1
Sitka, AK 99835 United States
Phone: 907-747-8292   Fax: 907-747-8873
E-mail: info@akrain.org
Website: www.akrain.org

Founded: 1992
Scope: State, National

Description: Alaska Rainforest Campaign is a coalition of Alaska-based and national environmental organizations working to protect the coastal old-growth rainforests of Alaska, especially the Tongass and Chugach National Forests.

Keyword(s): Forests/Forestry

Contact(s):
Corrie Bosman, National Field Director
Brian McNitt, Campaign Manager

ALASKA WILDLIFE ALLIANCE, THE
P.O. Box 202022
Anchorage, AK 99520 United States
Phone: 907-277-0897   Fax: 907-277-7423
E-mail: awa@alaska.net
Website: www.akwildlife.org

Founded: 1983
Scope: State
Description: The Alaska Wildlife Alliance is a non-profit organization based in Anchorage, Alaska. Our mission is the protection of Alaska's natural wildlife for its intrinsic value as well as for the benefit of present and future generations. The Alliance advocates an ecosystem approach that represents the non-consumptive values of wildlife.
Publication(s): The Spirit
Keyword(s): Wildlife & Species
Contact(s):
Paul Joslin, Executive Director
Karen Deatherage, Associate Director

ALBERTA FISH AND GAME ASSOCIATION
6924-104 St.
Edmonton, T6H 2L7 Alberta Canada
Phone: 780-437-2342　　　Fax: 780-438-6872
E-mail: office@afga.org
Website: www.afga.org
Founded: 1908
Membership: 10,001–100,000
Scope: Regional
Description: To promote through education, lobbying and programs the conservation and utilization of fish and wildlife and to protect and enhance the habitat they depend upon.
Publication(s): Outdoor Edge, The, Alberta Outdoorsman
Keyword(s): Wildlife & Species
Contact(s):
Rod Dyck, President

ALBERTA TRAPPERS ASSOCIATION
#2 9919 106th St.
Westlock, T7P 2K1 Alberta Canada
Phone: 780-349-6626　　　Fax: 780-427-6247
E-mail: info@albertatrappers.com
Website: www.albertatrappers.com
Founded: 1974
Membership: 1,001–10,000
Scope: Province
Description: Cooperates with all trappers associations and government agencies for a sensible conservation program.
Publication(s): Alberta Trapper, The
Contact(s):
Reed Gauthier, President; 780-826-5026
Gus Deisting, 1st Vice President
Ed Graham, 2nd Vice President
Bob Scott, Director; 780-427-6247

ALBERTA WILDERNESS ASSOCIATION
Box 6398, Station D
Calgary, T2P 2E1 Alberta Canada
Phone: 403-283-2025　　　Fax: 403-270-2743
E-mail: awa@shaw.ca
Website: www.albertawilderness.ca
Founded: 1968
Membership: 1,001–10,000
Scope: Regional
Description: A province-wide, non-profit, charitable organization with a mission to be an advocate for wild Alberta through awareness and action and functioning on the values of eco-centredness, integrity, respectfulness, participation, tenacity and passion. The AWA promotes sound ideas and policies for wilderness conservation, fosters appreciation and enjoyment of wilderness, and works with government, industry, organizations and individuals to encourage careful management of Alberta's natural lands & water
Publication(s): Wild Lands Advocate, Landscapes of Southern Alberta, Eastern Slopes Wildlands: Our Living Heritage

Keyword(s): Forests/Forestry, Land Issues, Public Lands/Greenspace, Reduce/Reuse/Recycle, Water Habitats & Quality, Wildlife & Species
Contact(s):
Cliff Wallis, President
A. Morasch, Finance & Operations Manager; 283-2025; Fax: 270-2743
Shirley Bray, Director, Wilderness Resource Centre; 270-2736; Fax: 270-2743; awa.wrc@shaw.ca
Christyann Olson, Executive Director; 283-2025; Fax: 270-2743

ALDO LEOPOLD FOUNDATION
P.O. Box 77
Baraboo, WI 53913-0077 United States
Phone: 608-355-0279　　　Fax: 608-356-7309
E-mail: mail@aldoleopold.org
Website: www.aldoleopold.org
Founded: 1982
Membership: 101–1,000
Scope: Local, Regional, National
Description: The Aldo Leopold Foundation, founded by the children of Aldo Leopold, keeps his legacy alive by promoting the "Land Ethic" he so eloquently defined. The Foundation actively integrates programs in Land Stewardship, Environmental Education, and Ecological Research to promote care of natural resources and foster an ethical relationship between people and land.
Publication(s): Leopold Outlook, The
Keyword(s): Ethics/Environmental Justice, Land Issues, Wildlife & Species
Contact(s):
Buddy Huffaker, Executive Director; buddy@aldoleopold.org
Sarah Lloyd, Membership Coordinator; sarah@aldoleopold.org
Sarah Hultine, Outreach Coordinator; tours@aldoleopold.org
Estella Leopold, Chairman
Teresa Searock, Administrative Assistant; teresa@aldoleopold.org
Steve Swenson, Ecologist; steve@aldoleopold.org

ALLIANCE FOR THE CHESAPEAKE BAY
6600 York Road #100
Baltimore, MD 21212 United States
Phone: 410-377-6270　　　Fax: 410-377-7144
E-mail: mail@acb-online.org
Website: www.alliancechesbay.org
Founded: 1971
Membership: 101–1,000
Scope: Local, State, Regional
Description: To build, maintain and serve the partnership among the general public, the private sector and the government that is essential for establishing and sustaining policy, programs and the political will to preserve and restore the resources of the Chesapeake Bay.
Publication(s): Bay Journal, Watershed Watch
Keyword(s): Development/Developing Countries, Oceans/Coasts/Beaches, Pollution (general), Population, Water Habitats & Quality, Wildlife & Species
Contact(s):
Torry Harwood, Chairman; 410-377-6270
Charles Conklin, Vice Chairman, MD; 410-377-6270
David Cottingham, Vice Chairman, DC; 410-377-6270
Joseph Gartlan, Vice Chairman, VA; 410-377-6270
Marshall Kaiser, Vice Chairman, PA; 410-377-6270
David Bancroft, Executive Director; 6600 York Rd. Suite 100, Baltimore, MD 21212; 410-377-6270
Brigid Kenney, Secretary; 410-377-6270
Michael Marino, Treasurer; 410-377-6270

ALLIANCE FOR THE CHESAPEAKE BAY
HARRISBURG OFFICE
3310 Market St. #A
Camp Hill, PA 17001 United States
Phone: 717-737-8622   Fax: 717-737-8650
E-mail: acbpa@acb-online.org
Website: www.alliancechesbay.org

Founded: 1971
Scope: Local, State, Regional
Description: The Alliance for the Chesapeake Bay is a regional, non-profit organization that builds consensus and fosters partnerships for the restoration of the Chesapeake Bay and its rivers.
Publication(s): Publications on website
Contact(s):
   David Bancroft, Executive Director; dbancroft@acb-online.org

ALLIANCE FOR THE CHESAPEAKE BAY
RICHMOND, VA OFFICE
P.O. Box 1981
Richmond, VA 23218 United States
Phone: 804-775-0951   Fax: 804-775-0954
E-mail: ACBVA@yahoo.com
Website: www.alliancechesbay.org

Founded: 1971
Membership: 1,001–10,000
Scope: Regional
Description: The Alliance is a coalition of educators, scientists, farmers, recreationists that builds and fosters partnerships to restore the Bay and its rivers. The Alliance has been a leader in facilitating these groups to come to consensus on positions and programs that help to protect the Chesapeake Bay. In addition, the Alliance provides both the general public and decision-makers with information and opportunities to become involved in activities that help to restore the Bay watershed.

AMANAKAA AMAZON NETWORK
60 E. 13th St., 5th Fl.
New York, NY 10003 United States
Phone: 212-253-9502   Fax: 212-253-9507
E-mail: amanakaa@amanakaa.org
Website: www.amanakaa.org

Founded: 1990
Scope: National
Description: The Amanakaa's Amazon Network is a nonprofit environmental and social justice organization. Amanakaa serves as a liaison between the peoples of the Amazon and their allies in the U.S. We work to educate the American public about the Amazon Rainforest and its peoples and support grassroots organizations in the Amazon.
Publication(s): Amanakaa Update, series of booklets by people of the Amazon, Letters from the Amazon
Keyword(s): Development/Developing Countries, Ethics/Environmental Justice, Forests/Forestry
Contact(s):
   Zeze Weiss, President
   John Friede, Vice President
   Christine Halvorson, Executive Director, Acting
   Christine Halvorson, Secretary

AMERICA THE BEAUTIFUL FUND
725 15th Street NW, Suite 605
Washington, DC 20005 United States
Phone: 202-638-1649   Fax: 202-204-0028
E-mail: info@america-the-beautiful.org
Website: www.freeseeds.org

Founded: 1965
Membership: 1,001–10,000
Scope: National
Description: America the Beautiful Fund gives recognition, technical support, small seed grants, gifts of free seeds and national recognition awards to volunteers and community groups to initiate new local action projects improving the quality of the environment, including design, land preservation, local food production, arts, historical and cultural preservation and horticultural therapy.
Publication(s): The Green Earth Guide, Better Times, Old Glory
Keyword(s): Agriculture/Farming, Ethics/Environmental Justice, Public Health, Reduce/Reuse/Recycle, Wildlife & Species
Contact(s):
   Nanine Bilski, President; 1730 K St. Suite 1002, Washington, DC 20006
   Jean Douglas, Vice President; 4733 Woodway Ln., NW, Washington, DC 20016
   Kay Lautman, Vice President; 1730 Rhode Island Ave., NW, Suite 700, Washington, DC 20036
   Susan Anderson, Treasurer; 235 Mason Dr., Manhasset, NY 11030
   Thomas Farrell, Chairman of the Board; First Chicago, 153 W 51 St., New York, NY 10019
   Daniel Schneider, Secretary; 31 Mill Hills Rd., Woodstock, NY 12498; 914-679-9868

AMERICAN ALLIANCE FOR HEALTH, PHYSICAL EDUCATION AND RECREATION AND DANCE
1900 Association Dr.
Reston, VA 20191-1502 United States
Phone: 703-476-3400   Fax: 703-476-9527
Website: www.aahperd.org

Membership: 1,001–10,000
Scope: State
Description: A voluntary professional organization for educators in the fields of physical education, sports and athletics, dance, health and safety, recreation and outdoor and environmental education. Its purpose is the improvement of education through such professional services as consultation, periodicals and special publications, conferences and workshops, leadership development, determination of standards and research.
Publication(s): Strategies, AAHPERD Update, Health Education, Research Quarterly for Exercise and Sports, Journal of Physical Education, Recreation and Dance
Contact(s):
   Lucinda Adams, President of Board of Governors; Westfield State College, Westfield, MA 01086
   Glenn Roswal, President Elect of Board of Governors

AMERICAN ASSOCIATION FOR LEISURE AND RECREATION - AALR
1900 Association Drive
Reston, VA 20191 United States
Phone: 703-476-3472   Fax: 703-476-9527
E-mail: aalr@aahperd.org
Website: www.aahperd.org/aalr

Membership: 1,001–10,000
Scope: National
Description: Mission - The mission of the American Association for Leisure and Recreation (AALR) is to promote and support education, leisure, and recreation by: developing quality programming and professional training, providing leadership opportunities, disseminating guidelines and standards and enhancing public understanding of the importance of leisure and recreation in maintaining a creative and healthy lifestyle.
Publication(s): AAL Reporter, Leisure Today
Keyword(s): Recreation/Ecotourism
Contact(s):
   Marcia Carter, Past President; University of Northern Colorado, Greeley, CO
   Charles Killingsworth, President; Pittsburg State University, Pittsburg, KS
   Randy Swedburg, Representative to the Board of Governors; Concordia University, Montreal, Quebec
   Christine Tipps, President Elect; University Wisconsin - Oshkosh, Oshkosh, WI

AMERICAN ASSOCIATION FOR THE ADVANCEMENT OF SCIENCE
1200 New York Ave., NW
Washington, DC 20005 United States
Phone: 202-326-6400
E-mail: webmaster@aaas.org
Website: www.aaas.org
Founded: 1848
Scope: National
Description: Objectives are to further the work of scientists, to facilitate cooperation among them, to foster scientific freedom and responsibility, to improve the effectiveness of science in the promotion of human welfare and to increase public understanding and appreciation of the importance and promise of the methods of science in human progress.
Publication(s): Science Books and Films, Science's Next Wave
Keyword(s): Climate Change, Population, Wildlife & Species
Contact(s):
   Mary Good, President
   William Golden, Treasurer; 212-425-0333
   Stephen Gould, Chairman of the Board
   Donald Kennedy, Editor In Chief
   Richard Nicholson, Executive Officer; 202-326-6639

AMERICAN ASSOCIATION OF BOTANICAL GARDENS AND ARBORETA
100 West 10th St. Ste. 614
Wilmington, DE 19801 United States
Phone: 302-655-7100   Fax: 302-655-8100
E-mail: aabga@aabga.org
Website: www.aabga.org
Founded: 1940
Membership: 1,001–10,000
Scope: National, International
Description: AABGA is a nonprofit, membership organization serving botanical gardens, arboreta and their professional staff.
Publication(s): Directory of Public Garden Internships, Reaching Out to the Garden Visitor, AABGA Newsletter, The Public Garden
Keyword(s): Public Lands/Greenspace, Recreation/Ecotourism, Wildlife & Species
Contact(s):
   Daniel Stark, Executive Director; 302-655-7100; ext. 16; Fax: 302-655-8100; dstark@aabga.org
   Richard Piacentini, President, Board of Directors; Phipps Conservatory and Botanical Gardens, Pittsburgh, PA

AMERICAN ASSOCIATION OF FIELD BOTANISTS
AAFB
4201 Gann Store Road
Hixson, TN 37343 United States
Phone: 423-875-9625
Founded: 1983
Membership: 101–1,000
Scope: National
Description: Dedicated to protection of rare plants and their habitats. Members share information among each other for planning excursions to observe rare plant species in the wild.
Keyword(s): Ecosystems (precious), Forests/Forestry, Land Issues, Public Lands/Greenspace, Wildlife & Species

AMERICAN ASSOCIATION OF ZOO KEEPERS, INC.
ADMINISTRATIVE OFFICES
3609 SW 29th St.
Topeka, KS 66614 United States
Phone: 785-273-9149   Fax: 785-273-1980
E-mail: akfeditor@kscable.com
Website: www.aazk.org
Founded: 1967
Membership: 1,001–10,000
Scope: National
Description: An international nonprofit organization of animal keepers and other persons interested in quality animal care and in promoting animal keeping as a profession. Chapters are active at zoos throughout North America. Promotes continuing education for keepers, national and international conservation projects, keeper-initiated zoo research, and educational publications.
Publication(s): Crisis Management Resource Notebook, Handbook of Zoonotic Diseases, Enrichment Notebook, second edition, Animal Keepers' Forum
Keyword(s): Reduce/Reuse/Recycle, Wildlife & Species
Contact(s):
   Kevin Shelton, President; kshelton@flaquarium.org
   Ed Hansen, Executive Director of the Board; 3601 SW 29th, Suite 133, Topeka, KS 66614; 785-273-9149
   Jacque Blessington, Board of Directors; Kansas City Zoological Gardens, 6700 Zoo Dr., Kansas City, MO; 816-513-5700
   Susan Chan, Editor
   Bruce Elkins, Board of Directors; belkins@indyzoo.com
   Bob Hayes, Board of Directors; bulletbobhayes@hotmail.com
   Linda King, Board of Directors; lmking83@aol.com
   Barbara Manspeaker, Administrative Secretary of Administrative Offices
   Jan Reed-Smith, Board of Directors; John Ball Zoo, 1300 W. Fulton St., Grand Rapids, MI 49504; 616-336-4301
   Denise Wagner, Board of Directors; dwagner@sandiegoz..org

AMERICAN B.A.S.S. ASSOCIATION OF EASTERN PENNSYLVANIA/ NEW JERSEY, THE
Attn: President, 7 Logan Dr
Summerville, NJ 08876 United States
Phone: 908-526-7721   Fax: 908-685-0970
Website: www.emterco.com
Scope: State
Contact(s):
   Paul Rinaldo, President

AMERICAN BIRD CONSERVANCY
P.O. Box 249
The Plains, VA 20198 United States
Phone: 540-253-5780   Fax: 540-253-5782
E-mail: abc@abcbirds.org
Website: www.abcbirds.org
Founded: 1994
Membership: 1,001–10,000
Scope: International
Description: American Bird Conservancy (ABC) is a U.S. based, nonprofit, membership organization dedicated to the conservation of wild birds and their habitats throughout the Americas. The fundamental role of ABC is to build coalitions of conservation groups, scientists, and members of the public, to tackle key bird priorities using the best resources available. ABC produces the magazine Bird Conservation and the newsletter Bird Calls for its members.
Publication(s): Recovering Paradise, All the Birds of North America, Bird Conservation Directory 2001, Annual Report, Seabird Report, Tower Report, Bird Calls, Bird Conservation, Communication Towers: A Deadly Hazard to Birds, Conservation of Land Birds of The U.S.
Keyword(s): Agriculture/Farming, Climate Change, Development/Developing Countries, Ecosystems (precious), Executive/Legislative/Judicial Reform, Land Issues, Oceans/Coasts/Beaches, Recreation/Ecotourism, Reduce/Reuse/Recycle, Wildlife & Species
Contact(s):
   George Fenwick, President; gfenwick@abcbirds.org
   Merrie Morrison, Vice President for Operations; mmorr@abcbirds.org

Mike Parr, Vice President for Program Development; mparr@abcbirds.org
David Pashley, Vice President of Conservation; dpashley@abcbirds.org
Gerald Winegrad, Vice President for Policy; gww@abcbirds.org
Patricia Bright, Director of Pesticides and Birds Campaign; pbright@abcbirds.org
Robert Chipley, Director of Important Bird Areas; rchipley@abcbirds.org
Elizabeth Ennis, Director for Membership; eennis@abcbirds.org
Gavin Shire, Director of Communications Technology; gshire@abcbirds.org
Linda Winter, Director of Cats Indoors Campaign; lwinter@abcbirds.org
Howard Brokaw, Chairman

AMERICAN BIRDING ASSOCIATION (ABA)
P.O. Box 6599
Colorado Springs, CO 80934 United States
Phone: 719-578-9703   Fax: 719-578-1480
E-mail: member@aba.org
Website: www.americanbirding.org

Founded: 1969
Membership: 10,001–100,000
Scope: National
Description: The American Birding Association provides leadership to field birders by increasing their knowledge, skills and enjoyment of birding. The ABA supports the interests of birders of all ages and experience and actively encourages the conservation of birds and their habitats.
Publication(s): Membership Directory, Volunteer Directory, ABA/Lane Series of Birdfinding Guides, ABA Checklist, North American Birds, Winging It, A Birds Eye View
Keyword(s): Recreation/Ecotourism, Wildlife & Species
Contact(s):
Paul Baicich, Director of Conservation and Public Policy; Baicich@aba.org
Paul Green, Executive Director
Ted Floyd, Editor of the Magazine; tedfloyd@aba.org
Dennis Lacoss, Treasurer; dlacoss@mindspring.com
Richard Payne, Chairman of the Board; rhp@shsu.edu
Matt Pelikan, Editor of Newsletter; winging@aba.org
Ann Stone, Secretary; 104673.1143@compuserve.com

AMERICAN CAMPING ASSOCIATION, INC.
5000 State Rd. 67N
Martinsville, IN 46151 United States
Phone: 765-342-8456   Fax: 765-342-2065
E-mail: aca@acacamps.org
Website: www.acacamps.org

Founded: 1910
Scope: National
Description: The American Camping Association is a national community of camp professionals dedicated to enriching the lives of children and adults through camp experience. ACA recognizes the camp experience as a significant contributor to positive child and youth development. It is the only organization that accredits all types of camps based on 300 standards for health, safety and program quality.
Publication(s): Various camp-related publications, Guide to Accredited Camps, Camping Magazine
Keyword(s): Public Health, Recreation/Ecotourism
Contact(s):
Rodger Popkin, President
Terri Nicodemus, Director of Public Relations
Peg Smith, Executive Director

AMERICAN CANAL SOCIETY, INC.
840 Rinks Ln.
Savannah, TN 38372-6774 United States
Website: www.canals.com/ACS/acs.html

Founded: 1972
Scope: National
Description: A nonprofit organization dedicated to historic canal research, preservation and canal parks.
Publication(s): Best From American Canals #1, #2, #3, #4, American Canals (Quarterly Bulletin)
Keyword(s): Ethics/Environmental Justice
Contact(s):
Terry Woods, President; 6939 Eastham Circle, Canton, OH 44708
Charles Derr, Secretary and Treasurer; 117 Main St., Freemansburg, PA 18017; 610-691-0956
David Ross, Editor

AMERICAN CAVE CONSERVATION ASSOCIATION
P.O. Box 409, 119 East Main Street
Horse Cave, KY 42749 United States
Phone: 270-786-1466   Fax: 270-786-1467
E-mail: debraheavers@cavern.org
Website: www.cavern.org

Founded: 1977
Membership: 101–1,000
Scope: National
Description: The ACCA is a national organization formed to conserve caves and karstlands and other resources associated with them. Primary objectives are to provide information, technical assistance, and public education and management training programs; and operation of the American Cave and Karst Center, a national environmental education center and museum.
Publication(s): American Caves Magazine
Keyword(s): Land Issues, Recreation/Ecotourism, Wildlife & Species
Contact(s):
David Foster, Executive Director; 270-786-1466; Fax: 270-786-1467
Debra Heavers, Associate Director; 270-786-1466; Fax: 270-786-1467; debraheavers@cavern.org

AMERICAN CETACEAN SOCIETY
P.O. Box 1391
San Pedro, CA 90733-0391 United States
Phone: 310-548-6279   Fax: 310-548-6950
E-mail: acs@pobox.com
Website: www.acsonline.org

Founded: 1967
Scope: National
Description: A nonprofit organization that works in the areas of conservation, education and research to protect marine mammals, especially whales, dolphins and porpoises and the oceans they live in.
Publication(s): Whalewatcher: Journal of the American Cetacean Society
Keyword(s): Water Habitats & Quality, Wildlife & Species

AMERICAN CHESTNUT FOUNDATION, THE
P.O. Box 4044
Bennington, VT 05201-4044 United States
Phone: 802-447-0110   Fax: 802-442-6855
E-mail: chestnut@acf.org
Website: www.acf.org

Founded: 1983
Membership: 1,001–10,000
Scope: National

Description: Funded by private contributions, the purpose of The American Chestnut Foundation is to promote the preservation and restoration of the American chestnut, an important wildlife and timber tree killed by a blight early in the Twentieth Century; to operate three research breeding farms in Meadowview, VA; to provide grants for cutting edge research; and to identify surviving trees and establish satellite research plantings.
Publication(s): The Journal, Bark, The
Keyword(s): Forests/Forestry, Wildlife & Species
Contact(s):
  Marshal Case, Executive Director
  Elizabeth Daniels, Membership Director
  Dale Kolenberg, Communications Director
  Sara Fitzsimmons, Tree Breeding Coordinator; TACF Pennsylvania Partnership Office, PSU-School of Forest Resources, 210 Forest Resources Lab, University Park, PA 16802; 814-865-7228; sara@acf.org
  Phil Pritchard, Development Director; Southern Appalachian Regional Office, Asheville, NC 28801; 828-281-0047; Fax: 828-253-5373; asheville@acf.org

AMERICAN CONSERVATION ASSOCIATION, INC.
1200 New York Ave., NW, Suite 400
Washington, DC 20005 United States
Phone: 202-289-2431   Fax: 202-280-1306
E-mail: cclusen@nrdc.org
Founded: 1958
Scope: National
Description: A nonmembership nonprofit, educational and scientific organization formed to advance knowledge and understanding of conservation and to preserve and develop natural resources for public use.
Keyword(s): Air Quality/Atmosphere, Oceans/Coasts/Beaches, Recreation/Ecotourism, Reduce/Reuse/Recycle
Contact(s):
  Laurance Rockefeller, President
  Charles Clusen, Executive Director
  R. Greathead, Secretary
  Carmen Reyes, Treasurer
  Laurance Rockefeller, Founder, Honorary Trustee

AMERICAN CONSERVATION ASSOCIATION, INC.
NEW YORK OFFICE
30 Rockefeller Plaza, Rm. 5402
New York, NY 10112 United States
Phone: 212-649-5822
Website: www.synergos.org/globalphilanthropy/organizations/aca.htm
Scope: National
Contact(s):
  Carmen Meyers, Main Contact

AMERICAN COUNCIL FOR AN ENERGY-EFFICIENT ECONOMY
1001 Connecticut Ave., NW, #801
Washington, DC 20036-5525 United States
Phone: 202-429-8873   Fax: 202-429-2248
E-mail: info@aceee.org
Website: www.aceee.org
Founded: 1980
Scope: National
Description: Advancing energy efficiency as a means of promoting both economic prosperity and environmental protection. ACEEE conducts technical and policy assessments; advises governments and utilities; publishes books, conference proceedings and reports; organizes conferences and workshops; and informs consumers.
Publication(s): Energy Innovations: A Prosperous Path, Using Consensus Building to Improve Utility Regulation, Transportation and Energy: Strategies for a Sustainable Transportation System, Consumer Guide to Home Energy Savings
Keyword(s): Energy, Pollution (general), Transportation
Contact(s):
  Carl Blumstein, President; 202-429-8873; Fax: 202-429-2248
  Steve Nadel, Director; 202-429-8873; Fax: 202-429-2248

AMERICAN COUNCIL FOR THE UNITED NATIONS UNIVERSITY (ACUNU)
MILLENNIUM PROJECT
4421 Garrison Street, NW
Washington, DC 20016 United States
Phone: 202-0686-5179   Fax: 202-686-5179
E-mail: acunu@igc.org
Website: www.acunu.org
Founded: 1996
Membership: 101–1,000
Scope: Local, State, Regional, National, International
Description: The Millennium Project is a participatory think tank for global futures research with 1,200 futurists, scholars, business planners, policymakers who work for the United Nations, governments, corporations, NGOs, universities in 50 countries and produces the annual "State of the Future" reports. There are 18 Nodes (groups of institutions and individuals) around the world.
Publication(s): 2003 State of the Future
Keyword(s): Air Quality/Atmosphere, Climate Change, Development/Developing Countries, Energy, Ethics/Environmental Justice, Finance/Banking/Trade, Water Habitats & Quality

AMERICAN EAGLE FOUNDATION
P.O. Box 333
Pigeon Forge, TN 37868 United States
Phone: 865-429-0157   Fax: 865-429-4743
E-mail: eaglemail@eagles.org
Website: eagles.org
Founded: 1985
Scope: National
Description: Dedicated to saving, restoring, and protecting America's endangered national symbol, the Bald Eagle, and preserving America's wildlife, waterways, forests, natural resources, ecosystems, and environment.
Publication(s): Eagle Extra, American Eagle News
Keyword(s): Ecosystems (precious), Wildlife & Species
Contact(s):
  Al Cecere, President, CEO & Board Member; P.O. Box 333, Pigeon Forge, TN 37868; 865-429-0157; Fax: 865-429-4743; eaglemail@eagles.org
  Bobby Halliburton, Vice President & Board Member
  Steven Compton, Secretary & Board Member
  Joseph Spivey, Treasurer & Board Member

AMERICAN FARMLAND TRUST
1200 18th St., NW
Washington, DC 20036 United States
Phone: 202-331-7300   Fax: 202-659-8339
E-mail: info@farmland.org
Website: www.farmland.org
Founded: 1980
Membership: 10,001–100,000
Scope: State, Regional, National
Description: American Farmland Trust is the only national organization dedicated exclusively to saving farm and ranch land and keeping it productive and healthy. AFT's experts work with communities and individuals to protect the best land, plan for growth with agriculture in mind and keep the land healthy.
Publication(s): Saving American Farmland: What Works, Sharing the Responsibility, Living on the Edge, Farming on the Edge II, Your Land Is Your Legacy

Keyword(s): Agriculture/Farming, Land Issues, Sprawl/Urban Planning, Water Habitats & Quality

Contact(s):
Ralph Grossi, President; rgrossi@farmland.org
Jimmy Daukas, Vice President for Marketing; jdaukas@farmland.org
Edward Thompson, Senior Vice President for Public Policy
Robert Wagner, Assistant Vice President of Field Programs
Tim Warman, Vice President for Programs; twarman@farmland.org
Dennis Bidwell, Director of Land Protection; dbidwell@farmland.org
Julia Freedgood, Director for Farmland Advisory Services; jfreedgood@farmland.org
Bryan Petrucci, Director of Farms
Bernadine Prince, Director of Public Education; bprince@farmland.org
Ann Sorensen, Director of Center for Agriculture in the Environment
Edward Harte, Vice Chairman of the Board
Sharon Phenneger, Controller
William Reilly, Chairman of the Board

AMERICAN FEDERATION OF MINERALOGICAL SOCIETIES (AFMS)
AFMS Central Office
2699 Lascassas Pike
Murfreesboro, TN 37130-1540 United States
Phone: 615-893-8270
E-mail: central_office@amfed.org
Website: www.amfed.org/

Founded: 1945
Membership: 10,001–100,000
Scope: National

Description: To promote popular interest and education in the various earth sciences, in particular, the subjects of geology, mineralogy, paleontology, lapidary and other related subjects, and to sponsor and provide means of coordinating the work and efforts of all persons and groups interested therein; to sponsor and encourage the formation and international development of societies and regional federations, and by and through such means to strive toward greater international goodwill and fellowship.

Publication(s): AFMS Safety Manual, AFMS Uniform Rules booklets, American Federation Newsletter

Keyword(s): Land Issues, Public Lands/Greenspace

Contact(s):
Lewis F. Elrod, CFE, Administrator; 2699 Lascassas Pike, Murfreesboro, TN 37130
Dan McLennan, Secretary; P.O. Box 26523, Oklahoma City, OK 73126-0523
Mel Albright, Editor; Rt. 3 Box 8500, Bartlesville, OK 74003
Toby Cozens, Treasurer; 4401 SW Hill St., Seattle, WA 98116-1924

AMERICAN FISHERIES SOCIETY
5410 Grosvenor Lane
Suite 110
Bethesda, MD 20814 United States
Phone: 301-897-8616   Fax: 301-897-8096
E-mail: main@fisheries.org
Website: www.fisheries.org

Founded: 1870
Membership: 1,001–10,000
Scope: International

Description: Scientific society founded in 1870 dedicated to the conservation of fisheries resources and the professional growth of its members.

Publication(s): The Journal of Aquatic Animal Health (JAAH), North American Journal of Aquaculture (NAJA), North American Journal of Fisheries Management (NAJFM), Transactions of the AFS (TAFS)

Contact(s):
Ira Adelman, President; Dept. Fish & Wildlife, Univ. of Minnesota, 1980 Folwell Ave., St. Paul, MN 55108; 612-624-4228; Fax: 612-625-5299; ira@finsandfur.fw.umn.edu
Fred Harris, Past-President; North Carolina Wildlife Resources Commission, 1721 Mail Service Center, Raleigh, NC 27699; 919-733-3633; ext. 275; Fax: 919-715-7643; fred.harris@ncwildlife.org
Gus Rassam, Executive Director; 5410 Grosvenor Lane, Ste. 110, Bethesda, MD 20814; 301-897-8616; ext. 209; Fax: 301-897-8096; grassam@fisheries.org
Barbara Knuth, President-Elect; DNR, 122A Fernow Hall, Cornell University, Ithaca, NY 14853; 607-255-2822; Fax: 607-255-0349; bak3@cornell.edu
Chris Kohler, 1st Vice President; Fisheries, IL Aquacultural Center, Southern Illinois Univ., Carbondale, IL 62901-6511; 618-453-2890; Fax: 618-453-6095; ckohler@siu.edu

AMERICAN FISHERIES SOCIETY
AGRICULTURE ECONOMICS SECTION
University of Florida
Gainesville, FL 32611 United States
Phone: 352-392-4991   Fax: 352-392-3646
Website: www.fred.ifas.ufl.edu

Membership: 1–100
Scope: Regional

Contact(s):
Charles Adams, President; adams@fred.ifas.ufl.edu
Chris Andrew, Assistant Chairman
John Gordon, Chairman
Burl Long, Assistant Chairman

AMERICAN FISHERIES SOCIETY
ALABAMA CHAPTER
Alabama Chapter, 3355 Audubon Rd.
Montgomery, AL 36106-2404 United States
Phone: 334-353-7998

Founded: 1991
Scope: State

Contact(s):
Gregory Lein, President; 334-844-9318; glein@acesag.auburn.edu

AMERICAN FISHERIES SOCIETY
ALASKA CHAPTER
ASGS/Alaska Science Center
1011 East Tudor Road
Anchorage, AK 99703 United States
Phone: 907-786-3314
Website: www.fisheries.org/afs-ak/

Founded: 1973
Scope: State

Description: The American Fisheries Society is dedicated to the preservation and conservation of aquatic resources, and facilitating the information exchange between students, professionals, and the public regarding our knowledge of aquatic resources.

Contact(s):
Carol Ann Woody, President; 907-786-3314; Fax: 907-786-3636; carol_woody@usgs.gov

AMERICAN FISHERIES SOCIETY
ARIZONA-NEW MEXICO CHAPTER
2221 W. Greenway Rd.
Phoenix, AZ 85023 United States
Phone: 602-789-3258
Website: www.fisheries.org

Founded: 1967

Scope: International
Publication(s): AFS journals, online fisheries magazine
Contact(s):
Larry Riley, President; 602-789-3258

AMERICAN FISHERIES SOCIETY
ARKANSAS CHAPTER
Aquaculture & Fisheries Center UAPB
P.O. Box 4912
Pine Bluff, AR 71611 United States
Founded: 1986
Scope: State
Description: The American Fisheries Society is dedicated to the preservation and conservation of aquatic resources, and facilitating the information exchange between students, professionals, and the public regarding our knowledge of aquatic resources.
Contact(s):
Steve Lochmann, Member; 870-543-8165; slochmann@auex.edu

AMERICAN FISHERIES SOCIETY
ATLANTIC INTERNATIONAL CHAPTER
689 Farmington Rd
Strong, ME 04983 United States
Phone: 207-778-3322   Fax: 207-778-3323
Website: www.state.me.us/ifw
Founded: 1975
Membership: 101–1,000
Scope: International
Publication(s): Atlantic International Chapter Newsletter
Contact(s):
Forrest Bonney, President; forrest.bonney@state.me.us

AMERICAN FISHERIES SOCIETY
AUBURN UNIVERSITY CHAPTER
Attn.: President
203 Swingle Hall
Auburn University, AL 36849 United States
Phone: 334-844-4786   Fax: 334-844-9208
E-mail: herrisj@auburn.edu
Website: www.ag.auburn.edu/faa/amerfishsoc/
Founded: 1973
Membership: 1–100
Scope: State
Description: Our membership draws from a diverse group, including students (undergraduate and graduate), fisheries professionals and university professors. Members encompass a wide variety of fisheries specializations including fisheries management, aquaculture, fish ecology, fish genetics, fish nutrition and fish diseases and seeks to influence and improve fisheries and aquaculture in Alabama through research and communication.
Contact(s):
Jeffrey Jolley; 334-844-9318; Fax: 334-844-9208; jollejc@acesag.auburn.edu

AMERICAN FISHERIES SOCIETY
BIOENGINEERING SECTION
1646 Jeannette Pl.
Bainbridge Island, WA 98110 United States
Phone: 508-829-6000   Fax: 206-842-8195
E-mail: dailydesign@bainbridge.net
Scope: National
Contact(s):
Ned Taft, President; 508-829-6000; ntaft@aldenlab.com
Wayne Daley, Past-President; wjd1163@aol.com

AMERICAN FISHERIES SOCIETY
BONNEVILLE CHAPTER
Attn.: President, P.O. Box 305
Dutch John, UT 84023 United States
Phone: 801-789-3103
Founded: 1963
Scope: State
Publication(s): Quarterly newsletter, bulletins
Contact(s):
Scott Tollentino, President; 801-789-3103; nrdwr.stollent@state.ut.us

AMERICAN FISHERIES SOCIETY
CALIFORNIA-NEVADA CHAPTER
Trust for Public Land
116 New Montgomery Street, Suite 300
San Francisco, CA 94105 United States
Website: www.afs-calneva.org
Founded: 1963
Scope: Regional
Description: The American Fisheries Society is dedicated to the preservation and conservation of aquatic resources, and facilitating the information exchange between students, professionals, and the public regarding our knowledge of aquatic resources.
Contact(s):
Elise Holland, President; 415-495-5660; Fax: 415-495-0541; elise.holland@tpl.org

AMERICAN FISHERIES SOCIETY
CANADIAN AQUATIC RESOURCES SECTION
2204 Main Mall, Univ. BC
Vancouver, V6T 1Z4 British Columbia Canada
Phone: 604-222-6753   Fax: 604-660-1849
Website: www.fisheries.org/cars/index/htm
Scope: National
Contact(s):
Bruce Ward, President; bruce.ward@gems8.gov.bc.ca
Martin Castongue, President-Elect

AMERICAN FISHERIES SOCIETY
College of Environmental Science and Forestry Chapter
Syracuse, NY United States
Website: www.esf.edu/org/afs/
Founded: 1975
Scope: State
Description: The American Fisheries Society is dedicated to the preservation and conservation of aquatic resources, and facilitating the information exchange between students, professionals, and the public regarding our knowledge of aquatic resources.
Contact(s):
Stephen Coghlan, President; 315-472-0488; clapton18@hotmail.com

AMERICAN FISHERIES SOCIETY
COLORADO-WYOMING CHAPTER
CO/WY AFS
Wyoming Game and Fish Department
528 S. Adams St.
Laramie, WY 82070 United States
Phone: 307-745-5180, ext. 235   Fax: 307-745-8720
Website: www.fisheries.org/co-wy/
Founded: 1966
Scope: State, Regional
Description: The American Fisheries Society is dedicated to the preservation and conservation of aquatic resources, and facili-

tating the information exchange between students, professionals, and the public regarding our knowledge of aquatic resources.

Contact(s):
Rob Gipson, President; 307-733-2321; Fax: 307-733-2276; rgipso@state.wy.us

AMERICAN FISHERIES SOCIETY
COMPUTER USER SECTION
Dept. of Natural Sciences, MS Valley State Univ.
Itta Bena, MS 38941 United States
Phone: 601-254-3383   Fax: 601-254-3668
E-mail: cusfisheries@cus.org
Website: www.fisheries.org/cus

Scope: National

Contact(s):
Michael Porter, President; mdporter@cypress.mcsr.olemiss.edu

AMERICAN FISHERIES SOCIETY
DAKOTA CHAPTER
1200 Mossourri Ave. P.O. Box 5520
Bismarck, ND 58506 United States
Phone: 701-328-5210   Fax: 701-328-5200
Website: www.health.state.nd.us/ndhd/default.asp

Founded: 1964
Membership: 1–100
Scope: State
Publication(s): ARI News Bulletin

Contact(s):
Wade King, President
Scott Elstad, Environmental Scientist

AMERICAN FISHERIES SOCIETY
EARLY LIFE HISTORY
NOAA - National Marine Fisheries Service
The Beaufort Laboratory
101 Pivers Island Rd.
Beaufort, NC 28526 United States
Phone: 206-526-4108   Fax: 252-728-8747

Scope: National

Publication(s): Stages Newsletter

Contact(s):
Art Kendal, President; art.kendal@noaa.org

AMERICAN FISHERIES SOCIETY
EQUAL OPPORTUNITIES SECTION
Department of Fisheries and Wildlife-Michigan State University
13 Natural Resources
East Lansing, MI 48824-1222 United States
Phone: 517-432-8086   Fax: 517-432-1699
E-mail: habrong@msu.edu
Website: www.fisheries.org

Scope: National

Description: The Equal Opportunities Section works to encourage the exchange of information pertinent to the promotion of employment, education, scholarships, participation, professionalism, and recruitment for all individuals in the fisheries profession. Our goal is to increase the representation and involvement of diverse ethnic/racial groups and females in the American Fisheries Society.

Contact(s):
Gwen White, President; gwhite@dnr.state.in.us

AMERICAN FISHERIES SOCIETY
FISH CULTURE SECTION
Dept. Wild. & Fish.
P.O. Box 9690
Mississippi State, MS 39762-9690 United States
Phone: 662-325-3220   Fax: 662-325-8726
E-mail: akelly@cfr.msstate.edu

Founded: 1974
Membership: 101–1,000
Scope: National

Description: Government and private fish culturists and fish culture educators and researchers organized to disseminate information

Publication(s): Quarterly Journal-North American Journal of Aquaculture, Quarterly Newsletter

Contact(s):
Steve Flickinger, President; 970-484-4167; flick@worldnet.att.net

AMERICAN FISHERIES SOCIETY
FISH HEALTH SECTION
CA State Univ., Dept. of Biological Sciences
Hayward, CA 94542 United States
Phone: 541-737-1856   Fax: 541-737-0496
Website: www.fisheries.org/fhs/

Scope: National

Publication(s): Publications on website

Contact(s):
Jerri Bartholomew, President; bartholj@bcc.arst.edu

AMERICAN FISHERIES SOCIETY
FISHERIES ADMINISTRATORS SECTION
5410 Grosvenor Lane
Bethesda, MD 20814 United States
Phone: 301-897-8616   Fax: 301-897-8096
E-mail: main@fisheries.org
Website: www.fisheries.org

Scope: National

Contact(s):
Michael Staggs, President; 608-267-0796; Fax: 608-266-2244; staggm@dnr.state.wi.us

AMERICAN FISHERIES SOCIETY
FISHERIES HISTORY SECTION
1900 Franklin
Stevens Point, WI 54481 United States
Phone: 715-346-2178   Fax: 715-346-3624
Website: www.fisheries.org

Membership: 101–1,000
Scope: International
Publication(s): Fisheries History Section Newsletter

Contact(s):
Daniel Coble, President

AMERICAN FISHERIES SOCIETY
FISHERIES MANAGEMENT SECTION
OK Fish Lab, 500 E. Constellation
Norman, OK 73072 United States
Phone: 405-325-7288   Fax: 405-325-7631

Scope: National

Contact(s):
Jeff Boxrucker, President; jboxrucker@aol.com

AMERICAN FISHERIES SOCIETY
FLORIDA CHAPTER
Website: nerps.nerdc.ufl.edu/~fafs/

Founded: 1981
Scope: State

Description: The American Fisheries Society is dedicated to the preservation and conservation of aquatic resources, and facilitating the information exchange between students, professionals, and the public regarding our knowledge of aquatic resources.

Contact(s):
Peter Hood, President; peter.hood@gulfcouncil.org

AMERICAN FISHERIES SOCIETY
GENETICS SECTION
4302 Underwood St.
University Park, MD 20782 United States
Phone: 301-864-2553
Website: www.fisheries.org
Scope: National
Contact(s):
John Epifanio, President; jepifan@atlas.vcu.edu

AMERICAN FISHERIES SOCIETY
GEORGIA CHAPTER
Attn.: President, GA DNR Albany Fisheries
2024 Newton Rd.
Albany, GA 31701-3576 United States
Phone: 229-430-4256   Fax: 229-430-5110
Founded: 1985
Membership: 1 100
Scope: State
Contact(s):
Matthew Thomas, Senior Biologist; 912-430-4256; Fax: 912-430-5110; matt_thomas@mail.dnr.state.ga.us

AMERICAN FISHERIES SOCIETY
GREATER PORTLAND, OR CHAPTER
Science Division, Mt. Hood Community College
26000 SE Stark Street
Gresham, OR 97030 United States
Founded: 1962
Scope: State
Publication(s): Audubon Warbler, Protecting a Vanishing Ecosystem, Familiar Birds of the Northwest, Urban Naturalist
Contact(s):
Todd Hanna, President; 503-491-7163; Fax: 503-491-7481; hannat@mhcc.cc.or.us

AMERICAN FISHERIES SOCIETY
HAWAII CHAPTER
41-202 Kalanianaole Hwy.
P.O. Box 22085
Waimanalo, HI 96795 United States
Website: home.hawaii.rr.com/ikehara/afshi/index.html
Founded: 1982
Scope: State
Description: The American Fisheries Society is dedicated to the preservation and conservation of aquatic resources, and facilitating the information exchange between students, professionals, and the public regarding our knowledge of aquatic resources.
Contact(s):
Walter Ikehara, President; 808-587-0096; Fax: 808-587-0115; walter_n_ikehara@exec.state.hi.us

AMERICAN FISHERIES SOCIETY
HUMBOLDT CHAPTER
Arcata, CA 95521 United States
Founded: 1973
Scope: Local, Regional

Description: The American Fisheries Society is dedicated to the preservation and conservation of aquatic resources, and facilitating the information exchange between students, professionals, and the public regarding our knowledge of aquatic resources.

Contact(s):
Mary Knapp, President; mary_m_knapp@fws.gov

AMERICAN FISHERIES SOCIETY
IDAHO CHAPTER
Eagle, ID 83616 United States
Website: www.fisheries.org/idaho/
Founded: 1963
Scope: State
Description: The American Fisheries Society is dedicated to the preservation and conservation of aquatic resources, and facilitating the information exchange between students, professionals, and the public regarding our knowledge of aquatic resources.
Contact(s):
Steve Elle, President-Elect; selle@idfg.state.id.us

AMERICAN FISHERIES SOCIETY
ILLINOIS CHAPTER
IL Chapter of the Am. Fisheries Society
c/o IL Dept. of Natural Resource Division of Fisheries
One Natural Resources Way
Springfield, IL 62702-1271 United States
Phone: 217-784-4730   Fax: 217-784-8116
E-mail: bschanzle@dnrmail.state.il.us
Website: fisheries.org
Founded: 1963
Scope: Regional
Description: Professional organization
Contact(s):
R. Sallee, President; 309-582-5611

AMERICAN FISHERIES SOCIETY
INDIANA CHAPTER
Attn: President, Scott 5013 S. County Rd. 250 W
Vallonia, IN 47281 United States
Phone: 812-497-2410
Website: www.bsu.edu/csh/bio/inafs/
Founded: 1970
Scope: State
Contact(s):
Scott Shuler, President

AMERICAN FISHERIES SOCIETY
INTRODUCED FISH SECTION
1415 Green Road
Ann Arbor, MI 48105 United States
E-mail: jacqueline_savino@usgs.gov
Scope: National
Contact(s):
John Cassani, President; jcassani@peganet.com

AMERICAN FISHERIES SOCIETY
IOWA CHAPTER
110 Lake Darling Rd.
Brighton, IA 52540 United States
Founded: 1969
Scope: State
Contact(s):
Don Kline, President

AMERICAN FISHERIES SOCIETY
KANSAS CHAPTER
5800 A River Pond Rd.
Tuttle Creek State Park
Manhattan, KS 66502 United States
Phone: 785-539-7941   Fax: 785-539-3183
Website: www.kdwp.state.ks.us
Founded: 1975
Membership: 1–100
Scope: State
Contact(s):
  Chuck Bever, President

AMERICAN FISHERIES SOCIETY
KENTUCKY CHAPTER
Kentucky Department of Fish & Wildlife Resources
1 Game Farm Road
Frankfort, KY 40601 United States
Website: www.kfwis.state.ky.us/AFS/kyafs.htm
Founded: 1990
Scope: State
Description: The American Fisheries Society is dedicated to the preservation and conservation of aquatic resources, and facilitating the information exchange between students, professionals, and the public regarding our knowledge of aquatic resources.
Contact(s):
  Kerry Prather, President; 502-564-5448; Fax: 502-564-4519; kprather@mail.state.ky.us

AMERICAN FISHERIES SOCIETY
LOUISIANA CHAPTER
Terrence R. Tiersch
LSU Aquaculture Research Station
2410 Ben Hur Road
Baton Rouge, LA 70820 United States
Phone: 225-765-2848
E-mail: Holloway_ha@wlf.state.la.us
Website: www.sdafs.org/laafs/
Founded: 1979
Membership: 1–100
Scope: State
Description: The AFS is the oldest and largest organization dealing with conservation and management of our precious fisheries resources. The Louisiana Chapter of the American Fisheries Society strives to influence and improve fisheries and aquaculture in Louisiana through research and communication. Our membership draws from a diverse group, including students (undergraduate and graduate), fisheries professionals, and university professors, and we encourage all concerned individuals to join us!
Publication(s): Abstracts of Annual Technical Session
Contact(s):
  Terry Tiersch, President

AMERICAN FISHERIES SOCIETY
MARINE FISHERIES SECTION
c/o Anne Richards
National Marine Fisheries Service
166 Water St.
Woods Hole, MA 97365 United States
Phone: 508-495-2305   Fax: 508-495-2393
Website: www.fisheries.org
Membership: 101–1,000
Scope: Regional, National, International
Description: The intent of the Marine Fisheries Section is to further the American Fisheries Society's objectives within marine fisheries science and practice. MFS members wish to attain further knowledge about marine fisheries, and to identify and publicize issues and problems related to development and management of marine fisheries. MFS also addresses research and education needs associated with biological, economic, social, and other aspects of marine fisheries.
Publication(s): www.fisheries.org/publications.html
Contact(s):
  Anne Richards, President; Fax: 508-495-2393

AMERICAN FISHERIES SOCIETY
MICHIGAN CHAPTER
Attn: President, 484 Cherry Creek Rd.
Marquette, MI 49855 United States
Phone: 906-249-1611   Fax: 906-249-3190
Website: www.fw.msu.edu/orgf/mi_afs/afs.hdm
Founded: 1973
Scope: State
Contact(s):
  Edgar Baker, President; 906-249-1611

AMERICAN FISHERIES SOCIETY
MID-ATLANTIC CHAPTER
P.O. Box 330
Little Creek, DE 19961 United States
Founded: 1983
Scope: State
Description: The American Fisheries Society is dedicated to the preservation and conservation of aquatic resources, and facilitating the information exchange between students, professionals, and the public regarding our knowledge of aquatic resources.
Contact(s):
  Van Atkins, President; 2040 Church Creek Dr., Charleston, SC 29414; President@carolinabirdclub.org
  Donna Bailey, SC Vice-President; 176 Ravens Place, Winnsboro, SC 29180; dsbailey@conterra.com
  John Wright, NC Vice-President; 1953-A Quail Ridge Rd. Greenville, NC 27858; Jwright@skantech.net
  Patricia Earnhardt Tyndall, Treasurer; 400 Kilmarnock Ct., Wake Forest, NC 27587; ptearn@aol.com
  Sue Pulsipher, Secretary; 2441 Ramey Dr., Linden, NC 28356—9771; puls@infi.net

AMERICAN FISHERIES SOCIETY
MID-CANADA CHAPTER
Attn: President, 19 Acadia Bay
Winnipeg, R3T 3J1 Manitoba Canada
Phone: 204-945-7794
Founded: 1986
Scope: National
Contact(s):
  Arthur Derksen, President; 204-945-7791; Fax: 204-948-2308; aderksen@nr.gov.mb.ca

AMERICAN FISHERIES SOCIETY
MINNESOTA CHAPTER
Attn: President, 5504 Hay Creek Rd.
Fort Ripley, MN 56449 United States
Phone: 218-828-2246   Fax: 218-828-6022
Website: www.fw.umn.edu/mnafs
Founded: 1967
Membership: 101–1,000
Scope: State
Description: The Minnesota Chapter of the American Fisheries Society is a professional organization of individuals interested in maintaining high standards for the fisheries profession and insuring conservation of Minnesota's fisheries.
Publication(s): Ryba (quarterly newsletter)
Keyword(s): Ecosystems (precious), Water Habitats & Quality
Contact(s):
  Paul Radomski, President; 218-828-2246; Fax: 218-828-6022; paul.radomski@dnr.state.mn.us

AMERICAN FISHERIES SOCIETY
MISSISSIPPI CHAPTER
University MS United States
Website: www.cfr.msstate.edu/msafs/msafs.htm

Founded: 1975

Scope: State

Description: The American Fisheries Society is dedicated to the preservation and conservation of aquatic resources, and facilitating the information exchange between students, professionals, and the public regarding our knowledge of aquatic resources.

Contact(s):
Jim Franks, President; jim.franks@usm.edu

AMERICAN FISHERIES SOCIETY
MISSOURI CHAPTER
P.O. Box 10267
Columbia, MO 65205 United States
E-mail: moafs@tranquility.net
Website: www.moafs.org/

Founded: 1963

Scope: State

Description: The American Fisheries Society is dedicated to the preservation and conservation of aquatic resources, and facilitating the information exchange between students, professionals, and the public regarding our knowledge of aquatic resources.

Contact(s):
Bob DiStefano, President
Harold Kearns, President Elect

AMERICAN FISHERIES SOCIETY
MONTANA CHAPTER
President, MT Chapter AFS
4600 Giant Springs Road
Great Falls, MT 59405 United States
Phone: 406-682-7807
E-mail: pcensfwp@3rivers.net
Website: www.fisheries.org/afsmontana

Founded: 1967

Membership: 101–1,000

Scope: State

Description: The American Fisheries Society is dedicated to the preservation and conservation of aquatic resources, and facilitating the information exchange between students, professionals, and the public regarding our knowledge of aquatic resources.

Contact(s):
Michael Enk, President; 406-791-7729; Fax: 406-761-1972; menk@fs.fed.us

AMERICAN FISHERIES SOCIETY
NATIVE PEOPLE FISHERIES SECTION
USFWS, 4401 N. Fairfax Dr., Suite 840
Arlington, VA 22203 United States
Phone: 703-358-1718   Fax: 703-358-2044

Scope: National

Contact(s):
Hannibal Bolton, President; hannibal_bolton@fws.gov

AMERICAN FISHERIES SOCIETY
NEBRASKA CHAPTER
Nebraska Game & Parks
2200 North 33rd Street
Lincoln, NE 68503 United States
Phone: 402-471-7651
Website: nebraskaafs.org/

Founded: 1969

Membership: 1–100

Scope: State

Description: The American Fisheries Society is dedicated to the preservation and conservation of aquatic resources, and facilitating the information exchange between students, professionals, and the public regarding our knowledge of aquatic resources.

Contact(s):
Mark Porath, President; 402-471-7651; Fax: 402-471-7649; mporath@ngpc.state.ne.us

AMERICAN FISHERIES SOCIETY
NEW MEXICO STATE UNIVERSITY STUDENT CHAPTER
1410 Durazno Drive
Las Cruces, NM 88001-4216 United States
Phone: 505-646-1707

Founded: 1972

Scope: State

Description: The American Fisheries Society is dedicated to the preservation and conservation of aquatic resources, and facilitating the information exchange between students, professionals, and the public regarding our knowledge of aquatic resources.

Contact(s):
Richard Saurez, President, 505-527-0172; rsaurez@nmsu.edu
Paul Turner, Research Biologist; 505-646-1707; paturner@nmsu.edu

AMERICAN FISHERIES SOCIETY
NEW YORK CHAPTER
Owego, NY United States

Founded: 1968

Scope: State

Description: The American Fisheries Society is dedicated to the preservation and conservation of aquatic resources, and facilitating the information exchange between students, professionals, and the public regarding our knowledge of aquatic resources.

Contact(s):
John Farrell, President; jmfarrel@mailbox.syr.edu

AMERICAN FISHERIES SOCIETY
NORTH CAROLINA CHAPTER
NC Cooperative Fish and Wildlife Research Unit
NC State Univ., Dept. of Zoology
Campus Box 7617
Raleigh, NC 27695-7617 United States
Phone: 919-513-2696   Fax: 919-515-4454
E-mail: tkwak@ncsu.edu
Website: www.sdafs.org/ncafs

Founded: 1990

Membership: 101–1,000

Scope: State

Description: The American Fisheries Society is dedicated to the preservation and conservation of aquatic resources, and facilitating the information exchange between students, professionals, and the public regarding our knowledge of aquatic resources.

Publication(s): Quarterly Newsletter, Annual Meeting

Contact(s):
Shari Bryant, President; bryants5@earthlink.net
Tom Kwak, President Elect
Bob Curry, Past President

AMERICAN FISHERIES SOCIETY
NORTH PACIFIC INTERNATIONAL CHAPTER
Attn: President
King Cnty. Water & Land Resources, Div. 201
S. Jackson St., Suite 600
Seattle, WA 98104 United States
Phone: 360-902-2756

Founded: 1978

Scope: National

Contact(s):
Kurt Fresh, President; 360-902-2756; Fax: 360-902-2980; freshklf@dfw.wa.gov

AMERICAN FISHERIES SOCIETY
NORTHEASTERN DIVISION
U.S. Fish and Wildlife Service
300 Westgate Center Drive
Hadley, MA 01035-9589 United States
Phone: 413-253-8504   Fax: 413-253-8487
E-mail: ron_essig@fws.gov
Website: www.fisheries.org

Founded: 1951

Membership: 101–1,000

Scope: Regional, International

Description: The Northeastern Division (the Division or NED) is one of four geographic subdivisions of the American Fisheries Society (the Society or AFS) within North America. The mission of the Division is to (a) advance the conservation, development and wise use of fishery resources for optimum use and enjoyment by all, (b) gather and disseminate information on fisheries science and management, and (c) promote and evaluate the educational, scientific and technical aspects of the fisheries profession.

Contact(s):
Douglas Stang, President; 1156 Meadowdale Rd., Altamont, NY; 518-457-9435; Fax: 518-485-5827; dxstang@gw.bec.state.ny.us

AMERICAN FISHERIES SOCIETY
NORTHWESTERN ONTARIO CHAPTER
THUNDER BAY, ONTARIO CANADA

Founded: 1979

Scope: National

Description: The American Fisheries Society is dedicated to the preservation and conservation of aquatic resources, and facilitating the information exchange between students, professionals, and the public regarding our knowledge of aquatic resources.

Contact(s):
Rob Mackereth, President; rob.mackereth@mnr.gov.on.ca

AMERICAN FISHERIES SOCIETY
OHIO CHAPTER
1840 Belcher Dr., G-3
Columbus, OH 43224 United States
Phone: 614-265-6347   Fax: 614-262-1143
Website: www.community.cleveland.com/cc/ocafs

Founded: 1974

Scope: State

Publication(s): A Guide to Ohio Streams

Contact(s):
Debra Walters, President

AMERICAN FISHERIES SOCIETY
OREGON CHAPTER
Attn: President, 2910 NW Miller Ln.
Albany, OR 97321 United States
Phone: 54-175-3044

Founded: 1964

Scope: State

Contact(s):
Timothy Hardin, President; 541-926-2262; Fax: 541-926-1230; hardint@peak.org

AMERICAN FISHERIES SOCIETY
PENNSYLVANIA CHAPTER
1259 Edward St.
State College, PA 16801 United States
Phone: 814-353-2226

Founded: 1969

Scope: State

Contact(s):
Doug Nieman, President; 610-948-4700; dnieman@normandeau.com

AMERICAN FISHERIES SOCIETY
PHYSIOLOGY SECTION
Chris Kennedy, President
Dept. of Biological Sciences
Simon Fraser University
Burnaby, V5A 1S6· British Columbia Canada
Phone: 604-291-5640   Fax: 604-291-3496
E-mail: ckennedy@sfu.ca
Website: www.fisheries.org/phs/

Founded: 1990

Membership: 101–1,000

Scope: International

Description: Although affiliated with the American Fisheries Society, this is a truly international organization for all individuals that work on, or are interested in, how fish work.

Contact(s):
George Iwama, President; giwama@unixg.ubc.ca

AMERICAN FISHERIES SOCIETY
POTOMAC CHAPTER
Attn: President
Dept. of Commerce NOAA, Rm. 6117
14 & Constitution Ave.
Washington, DC 20230 United States
Phone: 202-482-3260   Fax: 202-501-3024
Website: www.potomac-afs.org

Founded: 1976

Membership: 101–1,000

Scope: Regional

Contact(s):
Lee Beneka, President

AMERICAN FISHERIES SOCIETY
SOUTH CAROLINA CHAPTER
South Carolina American Fisheries Society, P.O. Box 1040
West Columbia, SC 29170 United States
Phone: 803-822-3177   Fax: 803-822-3183
E-mail: secretary@scafs.org
Website: www.scafs.org

Founded: 1982

Membership: 1–100

Scope: State

Description: Objectives of our organization include conservation, development and wise utilization of the fisheries, promotion of the educational, scientific, and technological development and advancement of all branches of fisheries science and practice, and exchange and dissemination of knowledge about fish, fisheries and related subjects.

Contact(s):
Wade Bales, President; 864-223-2008; Fax: 864-223-0649
Chris Thomason, President Elect; 803-259-5474

AMERICAN FISHERIES SOCIETY
SOUTH NEW ENGLAND CHAPTER
Southern New England Chapter, AFS
c/o Graduate School of Oceanography
University of Rhode Island
Narragansett, RI 02882 United States
Phone: 401-874-6175 Fax: 401-874-6853
Website: www.nefsc.nmfs.gov/snecafs/index.html

Founded: 1967
Membership: 101–1,000
Scope: Regional
Description: The SNEC was established in 1968 and to provide regional support in the States of Connecticut, Massachusetts, and Rhode Island for the American Fisheries Society.
Contact(s):
Russ Brown, President

AMERICAN FISHERIES SOCIETY
SOUTHERN ONTARIO CHAPTER
Beak International, 14 Abacus Rd
Brampton, L6T 5B7 Ontario Canada
Phone: 905-794-2325 Fax: 905-794-2338
E-mail: bhendley@beak.com
Website: www.beak.com

Founded: 1988
Scope: National
Contact(s):
Cynthia Mitton-Walker, President; 416-235-5230; Fax: 416-235-4940; mitton@mto.gov.on.ca

AMERICAN FISHERIES SOCIETY
TEXAS A AND M CHAPTER
2258 TAMU
College Station, TX 77843-2258 United States
Phone: 979-845-5777 Fax: 979-845-3786
Website: www.wfscnet.tamu.edu

Founded: 1969
Membership: 1–100
Scope: State
Description: This is a chapter of AFS at Texas A&M University for student participation.
Publication(s): Former Student Newsletter

AMERICAN FISHERIES SOCIETY
TIDEWATER CHAPTER
Attn: President James A. Morris
CCFHR, National Ocean Service, NOAA
101 Pivers Island Rd.
Beaufort, NC 28516 United States
Phone: 252-728-8782 Fax: 252-728-8784
E-mail: james.morris@noaa.gov
Website: www.sdafs.org/tidewater

Founded: 1986
Membership: 101–1,000
Scope: State, Regional
Description: The mission of the American Fisheries Society is to improve the conservation and sustainability of fishery resources and aquatic ecosystems by advancing fisheries and aquatic science and promoting the development of fisheries professionals. The Tidewater Chapter is composed of members of the fisheries community from Maryland, Virginia and North Carolina. The Tidewater Chapter membership is quite diverse with expertise ranging from inland to offshore fisheries.
Contact(s):
James Morris, President; 252-728-8782; james.morris@noaa.gov

AMERICAN FISHERIES SOCIETY
UNIVERSITY OF WYOMING STUDENT CHAPTER
Attn: President, P.O. Box 3166
Laramie, WY 82071-3166 United States
Phone: 307-766-2426
Website: www.fisheries.org/co-wy/uwl

Scope: State
Contact(s):
Seth Wite, President; oclark@uwyo.edu
Mark Smith, Vice President; masmith@uwyo.edu
Jason Burckhardt, Treasurer; jburck@uwyo.edu
Leisa Tooker, Secretary; leisatooker@hotmail.com

AMERICAN FISHERIES SOCIETY
VIRGINIA CHAPTER
4010 W. Broad St.
Richmond, VA 23230 United States
Phone: 804-367-8351
Website: fwie.fw.vt.edu/va-afs/index.htm

Founded: 1990
Membership: 101–1,000
Scope: State
Contact(s):
Becky Wajda, President
Charles Gowan, Past President

AMERICAN FISHERIES SOCIETY
VIRGINIA TECH CHAPTER
Attn: President, 101 Cheatham Hall
Blacksburg, VA 24061 United States
Phone: 540-231-3329 Fax: 540-231-7580
Website: filebox.vt.edu/org/vtafs

Founded: 1972
Scope: Regional
Publication(s): Lab Notes
Contact(s):
Anne Holloway, President
Jamie Roberts, Vice President
John Harris, Secretary
Louis Helfrich, Faculty Advisor; lhelfric@vt.edu
Ginnie Linthecum, Treasurer

AMERICAN FISHERIES SOCIETY
WATER QUALITY SECTION
5083 Veranda Terrace
Davis, CA 695616 United States
Phone: 541-754-4516 Fax: 916-278-3071
Membership: 1,001–10,000
Scope: National
Publication(s): Water Quality Matters
Contact(s):
Larry Brown, President
Robert Hughes, Past President
John Meldrum, Secretary-Treasurer

AMERICAN FISHERIES SOCIETY
WEST VIRGINIA
Elkins, WV 26241 United States
Phone: 304-637-0215 Fax: 304-637-0250

Founded: 1989
Scope: State
Contact(s):
Michael Shingleton, President; 304-637-0245; ext. 15; Fax: 304-637-0250; mshingleton@dnr.state.wv.us

AMERICAN FISHERIES SOCIETY
WESTERN DIVISION
Alaska Biological Science Center
1101 East Tubar Road
Anchorage, AK 99503 United States
Phone: 907-786-3842   Fax: 907-786-3636
Website: www.fisheries.org/wd/

Scope: National

Contact(s):
Eric Knudsen, President; 907-786-3842; Fax: 907-786-3636; Eric_Knudsen@usga.gov

AMERICAN FISHERIES SOCIETY
WISCONSIN CHAPTER
University of Wisconsin, Eau Claire Biology Dept.
Eau Claire, WI United States
Phone: 715-836-3260
E-mail: lonzard@uwec.edu

Founded: 1972

Scope: State

Publication(s): Wisconsin Chapter American Fisheries Society Newsletter

Contact(s):
Dr. David Lonzarich, President

AMERICAN FOREST FOUNDATION
AMERICAN TREE FARM SYSTEM
PROJECT LEARNING TREE
1111 19th St., NW, Suite 780
Washington, DC 20036 United States
Phone: 202-463-2462   Fax: 202-463-2461
E-mail: info@forestfoundation.org
Website: www.forestfoundation.org

Founded: 1981

Membership: 10,001–100,000

Scope: Local, State, Regional, National

Description: American Forest Foundation conducts charitable education and research programs. AFF supports American Tree Farm System — 60,000 private landowners managing 26 million acres of forests — and Project Learning Tree (PLT), award-winning pre K-12 environmental education curriculum and training program, active in U.S. and abroad.

Publication(s): PLT Branch, Tree Farmer Magazine

Keyword(s): Forests/Forestry, Reduce/Reuse/Recycle

Contact(s):
Laurence Wiseman, President
Kathy Mcglauflin, Vice President of Project Learning Tree
Robert Simpson, Vice President of American Tree Farm System

AMERICAN FORESTS
P. O. Box 2000
Washington, DC 20013 United States
Phone: 202-955-4500   Fax: 202-955-4588
E-mail: member@amfor.org
Website: www.americanforests.org

Founded: 1875

Membership: 10,001–100,000

Scope: National

Description: (formerly American Forestry Association) Building on its rich history as the oldest national citizens' conservation organization in the U.S. and conservation movement pioneer, American Forests has several programs to address today's environmental challenges: Global ReLeaf, the Urban Forest Center and the Forest Policy Center.

Publication(s): American Forests (quarterly magazine)

Keyword(s): Climate Change, Forests/Forestry, Public Lands/Greenspace, Recreation/Ecotourism, Wildlife & Species

Contact(s):
Karen Fedor, VP, Global ReLeaf Center; 202-955-4500; ext. 224; Fax: 202-955-4588; kfedor@amfor.org
Gerald Gray, Vice President of Forest Policy Center; ext. 217; ggray@amfor.org
Gary Moll, Vice President of Urban Forest Center; ext. 220; gmoll@amfor.org
Lu Rose, VP, Administration; 202-955-4500; ext. 213; Fax: 202-955-4588; lrose@amfor.org
Deborah Gangloff, Executive Director
Doug Cowan, Board Chair
Doug Hall, Treasurer
Jeff Meyer, Famous & Historic Tree Nursery; 904-765-0727; Fax: 904-768-4630; jmeyer@historictrees.org
Michelle Robbins, Editor; ext. 203; Fax: 202-887-1075; mrobbins@amfor.org
Zane Smith, Field Representative; 1243 Delrose Dr., Springfield, OR 97477

AMERICAN GEOGRAPHICAL SOCIETY
120 Wall St.
New York, NY 10005-3904 United States
Phone: 212-422-5456   Fax: 212-422-5480
E-mail: ags@amergeog.org
Website: www.amergeog.org

Founded: 1851

Membership: 101–1,000

Scope: National, International

Description: The AGS has sponsored research projects field work, and educational travel, held symposia and lectures, and published scientific and popular books, periodicals, and maps. Its publications bring accurate, up-to-date information on man and the land to more than 8,000 fellows and subscribers in over 100 countries.

Publication(s): Focus, Geographical Review, Ubique, Around the World Program

Keyword(s): Climate Change, Development/Developing Countries, Land Issues, Reduce/Reuse/Recycle

Contact(s):
William Doyle, President
Hilary Hopper, Editor, Focus and Around the World; Dept. of Geography, University of Kentucky, Lexington, KY 40506
Peter Lewis, Editor, Ubique
John McCabe, Treasurer
Richard Nolte, Chair Emeritus
Paul Starrs, Editor; Geographical Review, Dept. Geography, University of Nevada-Reno, Reno, NV 89557
John Wilford, Secretary

AMERICAN GEOLOGICAL INSTITUTE
4220 King St.
Alexandria, VA 22302-1502 United States
Phone: 703-379-2480   Fax: 703-379-7563
E-mail: agi@agiweb.org
Website: www.agiweb.org

Founded: 1948

Membership: 1–100

Scope: National

Description: AGI provides information services for earth scientists; works to be an advocate for the interests of the earth-science community; plays a major role in strengthening earth-science education; and increases public awareness of the role that earth sciences play in mankind's use of resources and interaction with the environment.

Publication(s): Bibliography and Index of Geology, Geotimes, Directory of Geoscience Departments, Glossary of Geology

Keyword(s): Land Issues

Contact(s):
David Applegate, Director of Government Affairs
Christopher Keane, Director of Program Development and Communications

Marcus Milling, Executive Director
Michael Smith, Director of Education and Outreach
Sharon Tahirkheli, Director of Information Systems

AMERICAN GROUND WATER TRUST
P.O. Box 1796, 16 Centre St.
Concord, NH 03301 United States
Phone: 603-228-5444 Fax: 603-228-6557
E-mail: trustInfo@agwt.org
Website: www.agwt.org
Founded: 1987
Membership: 101–1,000
Scope: National, International
Description: The American Ground Water Trust is an independent nonprofit, membership organization which promotes public awareness of the environmental and economic importance of ground water through public education programs. The Trust promotes opportunity, cooperation and action among individuals, groups and organizations to foster the protection and sustainable use of our ground water resources.
Publication(s): BMPs to Reduce NPS Pollution, Ground Water and Wetlands in the USA, Ground Water information pamphlets, pamphlets on various water topics
Keyword(s): Water Habitats & Quality
Contact(s):
Andrew Stone, Executive Director
Scott Slater, Chairman

AMERICAN HIKING SOCIETY
1422 Fenwick Ln.
Silver Spring, MD 20910 United States
Phone: 301-565-6704 Fax: 301-565-6714
E-mail: info@americanhiking.org
Website: www.americanhiking.org
Founded: 1976
Membership: 1,001–10,000
Scope: National
Description: American Hiking Society (AHS) is a recreation-based conservation organization dedicated to establishing, protecting and maintaining foot trails in America. AHS is comprised of over 120 member trail clubs and 10,000 individual members, represents half a million outdoors people and serves as the voice of the American hiker. AHS effectively lobbies to encourage funding for trails and promotes volunteerism in trail building and maintenance.
Publication(s): Pathways Across America, American Hiker, Helping Out in the Outdoors, Volunteer Vacation
Keyword(s): Forests/Forestry, Land Issues, Public Lands/Greenspace, Recreation/Ecotourism
Contact(s):
Mary Margaret Sloan, President
Susan Crosby, Vice President and Development
Michael Hechter, Membership Coordinator

AMERICAN HORSE PROTECTION ASSOCIATION
1000 29th St., NW Suite T-100
Washington, DC 20007 United States
Phone: 202-965-0500 Fax: 202-965-9621
Website: www.ahpa.us
Founded: 1966
Scope: National
Description: A national nonprofit, tax-exempt organization dedicated entirely to the welfare of horses, both wild and domestic. Works for the enforcement of all humane legislation for both wild and domestic horses.
Publication(s): Special Bulletins, Newsletter
Keyword(s): Land Issues, Public Lands/Greenspace, Wildlife & Species

Contact(s):
Nancy Hargrave, President and Chairman of the Board of Directors
Robin Lohnes, Executive Director

AMERICAN HUMANE
63 Inverness Drive East
Englewood, CO 80112 United States
Phone: 303-792-9900 Fax: 303-792-5333
E-mail: info@americanhumane.org
Website: www.americanhumane.org
Founded: 1877
Membership: 1,001–10,000
Scope: National
Description: AHA provides training and resources to 6,500 animal care and control agencies in the U.S. and Canada; ensures the humane treatment of animals in movies and TV productions; serves as a national coordinator of emergency animal relief during natural disasters and works on legislation to protect animals.
Publication(s): Protecting Animals
Contact(s):
Tim O'Brien, President
Connie Howard, Director of Shelter Programs
Jack Sparks, Director of Communications
Lynn Anderson, Veterinarian; animal@americanhumane.org

AMERICAN INSTITUTE OF BIOLOGICAL SCIENCES
AIBS
1444 I St., NW
Suite 200
Washington, DC 20005 United States
Phone: 202-628-1500 Fax: 202-628-1509
E-mail: admin@aibs.org
Website: www.aibs.org
Founded: 1947
Membership: 1,001–10,000
Scope: State, Regional, National, International
Description: AIBS promotes the biological sciences through coalition activities with its members and others in research, education, and public policy; publishing the peer-reviewed journal, BioScience; providing scientific peer review and advisory services to government agencies and other clients; convening meetings; and performing support services.
Publication(s): BioScience, Scientific Peer Review Services
Contact(s):
Gary Hartshorn, 2003 President; Organization for Tropical Studies, Duke University, P.O. Box 90030, Durham, NC 27708; 919-684-5774; Fax: 919-684-5661; ghartsho@duke.edu
Adrienne Froelich, Director of Public Policy; AIBS, 1444 I Street NW, Suite 200, Washington, DC 20005; 202-628-1500, ext. 232; Fax: 202-628-1509; afroelich@aibs.org
Scott Glisson, Director of Scientific Peer Review Services; AIBS, 107 Carpenter Drive, Suite 100, Sterling, VA 20164; 703-834-0812; ext. 202; Fax: 703-834-1160; sglisson@aibs.org
Richard O'Grady, Executive Director; AIBS, 1444 I Street NW, Suite 200, Washington, DC 20005; 202-628-1500; ext. 258; Fax: 202-628-1509; rogrady@aibs.org
Joel Wagener, Director of IT Operations; 107 Carpenter Drive, Suite 100, Sterling, VA 20164; 703-834-0812; ext. 107; Fax: 703-834-1160; jwagener@aibs.org
Jeffrey Goldman, IBRCS Program Manager; AIBS, 1444 I Street NW, Suite 200, Washington, DC 20005; 202-628-1500; ext. 225; Fax: 202-628-1509; jgoldman@aibs.org
Timothy Beardsley, Editor-in-Chief, BioScience; AIBS, 1444 I Street NW, Suite 200, Washington, DC 20005; 202-628-1500; ext. 226; Fax: 202-628-1509; tbeardsley@aibs.org

AMERICAN INSTITUTE OF FISHERY RESEARCH BIOLOGISTS
c/o National Marine Fisheries Science Center
8604 La Jolla Shores Drive
La Jolla, CA 92037-1508 United States
Phone: 858-546-7100   Fax: 858-546-7133
E-mail: webmaster@iattc.org
Website: www.iattc.org/HomeENG.htm

Founded: 1957

Scope: National

Description: The Institute was founded to advance the science of fishery biology and to promote conservation and proper use of fishery resources. It serves that goal primarily by being concerned with the professional development and performance of its members and recognition of their competence and achievement.

Publication(s): Briefs

Keyword(s): Reduce/Reuse/Recycle, Water Habitats & Quality, Wildlife & Species

Contact(s):
Richard Schaefer, President; dickschaef@aol.com
Gene Huntsman, Editor; 205 Blades Rd., Havelock, NC 28523; 704-274-7773
Alan Shimada, Treasurer; 7909 Sleaford Place, Bethesda, MD 20814
Barbara Warkentine, Secretary; SUNY-Maritime College, Science Dept., 6 Pennyfield Ave., Ft. Schuyler, Bronx, NY 10465-4198; 206-543-1101

AMERICAN LAND CONSERVANCY
1388 Sutter St.
San Francisco, CA 94109 United States
Phone: 415-749-3010   Fax: 415-749-3011
E-mail: mail@alcnet.org
Website: www.alcnet.org

Founded: 1990

Membership: 1–100

Scope: National

Description: To preserve land for this and future generations; in particular, to preserve its scientific, historic, educational, ecological, geological, recreational, agricultural and scenic features, and its native plant and animal life or biotic community.

Publication(s): Statement of Opportunity Brochure, American Land Conservancy Newsletter, Fifty Wildflowers of Bear Valley

Keyword(s): Forests/Forestry, Land Issues, Oceans/Coasts/Beaches, Public Lands/Greenspace, Wildlife & Species

Contact(s):
Harriet Burgess, President; mail@alcnet.org

AMERICAN LANDS
726 7th St., SE
Washington, DC 20003 United States
Phone: 202-547-9400   Fax: 202-547-9213
E-mail: ldix@americanlands.org
Website: www.americanlands.org

Founded: 1991

Scope: National

Description: (formerly Western Ancient Forest Campaign) The mission of American Lands is the protection and recovery of North American native forest, grassland, and aquatic ecosystems; the preservation of biological diversity; the restoration of watershed integrity; and the promotion of environmental justice in connection with these goals. This mission is accomplished by strengthening grassroots conservation networks; providing advocacy services and other assistance to local conservation groups.

Publication(s): Report from Washington

Keyword(s): Forests/Forestry, Public Lands/Greenspace, Water Habitats & Quality

Contact(s):
Randi Spivak, President; 310-458-8869
Jim Jontz, Executive Director; 202-547-9095
Steve Holmer, Campaign Coordinator; 202-547-9105
Christopher Peters, Treasurer; P.O. Box 4569, Arcata, CA 95518; 707-825-7640

AMERICAN LEAGUE OF ANGLERS AND BOATERS
1225 New York Ave., NW
Washington, DC 20005 United States
Phone: 202-682-9530   Fax: 202-682-9529
Website: www.funoutdoors.com

Founded: 1985

Membership: 1–100

Scope: National

Description: ALAB was formed to be a vigilant patron of the Sport Fishing and Boating Enhancement Act (PL 98-369) and the Aquatic Resources Trust Fund created by the Act. Composed of more than 30 organizations, ALAB is dedicated to this pioneering user-pays legislation which provides some $330 million annually in funding for U.S. Coast Guard recreational boating programs and in matching grants to the states for sportfish research and enhancement, as well as wetlands conservation and boating safety.

Keyword(s): Recreation/Ecotourism

Contact(s):
Derrick Crandall, Co-Chair; 301-897-8616
Veronica Floyd, Co-Chair; 703-960-2223
George Stewart, Treasurer; 302-678-9143

AMERICAN LITTORAL SOCIETY
Headquarters, Sandy Hook
Highlands, NJ 07732 United States
Phone: 732-291-0055   Fax: 732-291-3551
E-mail: tim@littoralsociety.org
Website: www.americanlittoralsociety.org

Founded: 1961

Scope: National

Description: A national organization of professionals and amateurs interested in the study and conservation of coastal habitat, barrier beaches, wetlands, estuaries, and near-shore waters, and their fish, shellfish, bird, and mammal resources. Publishes scientific and popular material. Conducts field trips, dive and study expeditions, and a fish tag-and-release program. Special activities for scuba divers.

Publication(s): Coastal Reporter, Underwater Naturalist

Keyword(s): Oceans/Coasts/Beaches, Water Habitats & Quality, Wildlife & Species

Contact(s):
Michael Huber, President
Frank Steimle, Vice President
D. Bennett, Executive Director
Sheldon Abrams, Treasurer
Angela Cristini, Secretary

AMERICAN LITTORAL SOCIETY
NORTHEAST REGION
28 West 9th Rd.
Broad Channel, NY 11693 United States
Phone: 718-318-9344   Fax: 718-318-9345
E-mail: alsbeach@aol.com
Website: www.alsnyc.org

Founded: 1980

Membership: 1,001–10,000

Scope: Local, State, Regional, National

Description: The society is dedicated to the conservation and education of marine resources, wetland protection and habitat restoration.

Publication(s): Littorally Speaking (newsletter)
Keyword(s): Oceans/Coasts/Beaches, Pollution (general), Water Habitats & Quality
Contact(s):
Don Riepe, Director, Northeast Chapter; 718-634-6467; Fax: 718-318-9345; donriepe@aol.com
Barbara Cohen, New York State Beach Cleanup Coordinator; 718-471-2166; alsbeach@aol.com
Barbara Toborg, Editor; 718-474-1127; tobytoborg@aol.com

AMERICAN LIVESTOCK BREEDS CONSERVANCY
P.O. Box 477
15 Hillsboro Street
Pittsboro, NC 27312 United States
Phone: 919-542-5704   Fax: 919-545-0022
E-mail: cbassett@albc-usa.org
Website: www.albc-usa.org
Founded: 1977
Membership: 1,001–10,000
Scope: National
Description: ALBC is a nonprofit membership organization working to protect genetic diversity in domestic animals through the conservation and promotion of nearly 200 rare breeds of livestock and poultry in America. ALBC researchs breed status and characteristics, operates a gene bank to preserve genetic materials for the future and provides technical support on conservation breeding and animal use in sustainable, diversified agriculture.
Publication(s): Taking Stock: The North American Livestock Census, Birds of a Feather: Saving Rare Turkeys from Extinction, A Rare Breeds Album of American Livestock, A Conservation Breeding Handbook, Taking Stock of Water Fowl, ALBC News
Keyword(s): Agriculture/Farming, Development/Developing Countries, Wildlife & Species
Contact(s):
Donald Bixby, Executive Director
Marjorie Bender, Program Coordinator
Phillip Sponenberg, Technical Coordinator

AMERICAN LUNG ASSOCIATION
61 Broadway
New York, NY 10019-4374 United States
Phone: 212-315-8700   Fax: 212-265-5642
E-mail: info@lungusa.org
Website: www.lungusa.org
Founded: 1904
Membership: 1–100
Scope: National
Description: Formerly known as the National Tuberculosis and Respiratory Disease Association. The American Lung Association is a voluntary agency concerned with the conquest of lung disease and the promotion of lung health, which includes preventing and controlling air pollution. National Air Conservation Commission and local and state air conservation committees work with citizenry and other groups for effective air pollution control. Informational material available from national, state and local lung associations.
Publication(s): American Journal of Respiratory Cell and Molecular Biology, American Journal of Respiratory and Critical Care Medicine
Keyword(s): Air Quality/Atmosphere
Contact(s):
John Kirkwood, Chief Operating Officer

AMERICAN MUSEUM OF NATURAL HISTORY
COMMUNICATIONS
Central Park West at 79th St.
New York, NY 10024 United States
Phone: 212-769-5100   Fax: 212-769-5199
Website: www.amnh.org
Founded: 1869
Scope: National, International
Description: The American Museum of Natural History is one of the world's preeminent scientific, educational, and cultural institutions, housing 45 permanent exhibition halls, state-of-the-art laboratories, one of the largest natural history libraries in the Western Hemisphere, and a collection of 32 million specimens and artifacts. With a scientific staff of more than 200 the Museum supports research divisions in Anthropology, Paleontology, Invertebrate and Vertebrate Zoology, and the Physical Sciences.
Publication(s): Bulletin of the American Museum of Natural History, Anthropological Papers of the American Museum of Natural History, Curator, Micropaleontology Press
Keyword(s): Wildlife & Species
Contact(s):
Ellen Futter, President

AMERICAN NATURE STUDY SOCIETY
c/o PEEC, RR2 Box 1010
Dingmans Ferry, PA 18328 United States
Phone: 607-749-3655
Website: hometown.aol.com/anssonlne/
Founded: 1908
Membership: 101–1,000
Scope: National
Description: Promotes environmental education and avocation by conducting meetings, workshops and field excursions, producing and distributing publications, and contributing to publications of other agencies; cooperates with organizations with allied interests, and, through membership in Alliance for Environmental Education, encourages members to contribute consultant services; assists in training nature lay leaders.
Publication(s): Nature Study, A Journal of Environmental Education and Interpretation, ANSS Newsletter
Keyword(s): Recreation/Ecotourism, Reduce/Reuse/Recycle
Contact(s):
Steve Melcher, President; 103 Kreag Rd., Fairport, NY 14450-363; 716-425-1059
Janet Hawkes, Editor; 1420 Tanghannock Blvd., Ithaca, NY 14850; 607-273-6260
Florence Mauro, Editor; PEEC, R.D. 2 Box 1010, Dingmans Ferry, PA 18328; 717-828-2319
Flo Mauro, Recording Secretary; PEEC, R.D. 2 Box 1010, Dingmans Ferry, PA 18328; 717-828-2319
Betty McKnight, Secretary; R.D. 3, Trumansburg, NY 14880
Paul Spector, Treasurer; Holden Arboretum, 9500 Sperry Rd., Mentor, OH 44094; 216-256-1110

AMERICAN ORNITHOLOGISTS UNION
National Museum of Natural History
MRC-116
Smithsonian Institution
Washington, DC 20560-0116 United States
Phone: 202-357-2051   Fax: 202-633-8084
E-mail: aou@nmnh.si.edu
Founded: 1883
Scope: National
Description: Aims to advance ornithological science through its publications, annual meetings, committees and membership.
Publication(s): Ornithological Monographs, Ornithological Newsletter
Keyword(s): Wildlife & Species
Contact(s):
John Fitzpatrick, President; Laboratory of Ornithology at Cornell University, 159 Sap Sucker Woods Rd., Ithaca, NY 14850; 607-254-2410; Fax: 607-254-2415; jwf7@cornell.edu

Mary McDonald, Vice President; Lewis Science Center 129, University of Central Arkansas, Conway, AR 72035; 501-450-5924

Steven Beissinger, Chairman of the Conservation Committee; Director of Ecosystem Science, 151 Hilgard Hall, Suite 3110, University of California, Berkeley, CA 94720-3110; 313-763-5945

Jeff Brawn, Treasurer; Illinois Natural History Survey, 607 E. Peabody Drive, Champaign, IL 61820; 217-244-5937; Fax: 217-333-4949; j-brawn@uiuc.edu

M. Lein, Secretary; Dept. of Biology, University of Calgary, 2500 University Dr., NW, Calgary, Alberta T2N 1N4

Kimberly Smith, Editor; Department of Biological Sciences, University of Arkansas, Fayetteville, AR 72701; 501-575-3251; Fax: 501-575-4010; auk@comp.uark.edu

Cheryl Trine, Newsletter Editor; 3889 E. Valley View, Berrien Springs, MI 49103; 508-224-6521; ctrine@andrews.edu

David Wiedenfeld, Monographs Editor; Sutton Avian Research Center, P.O. Box 2007, Bartlesville, OK 74005

AMERICAN PIE (PUBLIC INFORMATION ON THE ENVIRONMENT)

P.O. Box 676
Northfield, MN 55057 United States
Phone: 800-320-2743   Fax: 507-645-5724
E-mail: info@americanpie.org
Website: www.americanpie.org

Founded: 1993
Membership: 101–1,000
Scope: National

Description: American PIE is a 501(c)3 nonprofit group serving the nation with an 800 Environmental Information Line. The organization offers action programs and uniquely accessible assistance to people who have environmental questions and concerns in a wide variety of subject areas ranging from drinking water safety to wetlands preservation. Trained staff answer the information line Monday-Friday, 8:30 - 5:00 central time.

Publication(s): American PIE

Keyword(s): Ethics/Environmental Justice, Pollution (general)

Contact(s):
Brad Easterson, President and Treasurer
Toni Easterson, Vice President and Secretary
Lawrence Bacon, Director; 36 Carriage Dr., Farmington, CT 06032; 860-674-8442

AMERICAN PLANNING ASSOCIATION

1776 Massachusetts Ave., NW, Ste. 400
Washington, DC 20036 United States
Phone: 202-872-0611   Fax: 202-872-0643
Website: www.planning.org

Founded: 1909
Membership: 10,001–100,000
Scope: National, International

Description: APA is a nonprofit public interest and research organization representing 33,000 practicing planners, officials, and citizens involved with urban and rural planning issues. The American Institute of Certified Planners is APA's professional institute, certifying planners who have met specific educational and work criteria and passed the certification exam. APA's 46 chapters cover all of the states and its 18 divisions address planning specialties, such as environmental planning.

Publication(s): Land Use Law & Zoning Digest, Zoning News, Journal of American Planning Association, Planning Magazine

Keyword(s): Agriculture/Farming, Development/Developing Countries, Energy, Land Issues, Public Health, Public Lands/Greenspace, Sprawl/Urban Planning, Transportation

Contact(s):
W. Paul Farmer, Executive Director
Jeff Soule, Policy Director
David Carrier, Outreach Associate; dcarrier@planning.org
Dennis Johnson, Public Affairs Coordinator; djohnson@planning.org
Jason Jordan, Government Affairs Coordinator; jjordan@planning.org

AMERICAN RECREATION COALITION

1225 New York Ave., NW, Suite 450
Washington, DC 20005 United States
Phone: 202-682-9530   Fax: 202-682-9529
E-mail: arc@funoutdoors.com
Website: www.funoutdoors.com

Founded: 1979
Membership: 1–100
Scope: National

Description: ARC is a national nonprofit, tax-exempt federation of more than 125 recreation-related trade associations, corporations and enthusiasts' organizations that provides a unified voice for American recreation interests to ensure their full participation in government policy-making on such issues as energy and public lands and waters management. ARC also initiates and supports partnerships between public and private recreation providers and conducts meetings, seminars and activities.

Contact(s):
Derrick Crandall, President
Catherine Ahern, Vice President of Member Services
David Humphreys, Chairman; RVIA, 1896 Preston White Dr., Reston, VA 22090; 703-620-6003

AMERICAN RESOURCES GROUP

374 Maple Ave. E., Suite 310
Vienna, VA 22180 United States
Phone: 703-255-2700   Fax: 703-281-9200
Website: www.nationalforestry.net

Founded: 1981
Membership: 1–100
Scope: National

Description: A conservation service organization engaged in education, monitoring, research, and related activities to promote the wise use of America's forest resources. Provides forestry, environmental inventory, conservation support services and land acquisition assistance to conservation organizations, public agencies and landowners. Programs include: Land Conservation Fund of America (land acquisition), National Forestry Network (referrals), National Historic Lookout Register, American Woodlands.

Publication(s): Conservation News Digest, Woodland Report, National Woodlands Magazine

Keyword(s): Forests/Forestry, Public Lands/Greenspace, Reduce/Reuse/Recycle, Wildlife & Species

Contact(s):
Keith Argow, President/Editor
Loren Larson, Vice President of Forestry
David Edson, Green Tag Forestry Certification; 202-827-4456
Ray Kresek, Northwest Representative of National Historic Lookout Register; 509-466-9171
Bob Spear, Northeast Representative of National Historic Lookout Register; 973-209-7897

AMERICAN RIVERS

1025 Vermont Ave. NW 720
Washington, DC 20005 United States
Phone: 202-347-7550   Fax: 202-347-9240
E-mail: americanrivers@americanrivers.org
Website: www.americanrivers.org
Membership: 10,001–100,000
Scope: National

Description: (formerly American Rivers Conservation Council)
Publication(s): Available on website
Contact(s):
Rebecca Wodder, President; 202-347-7550

AMERICAN RIVERS
MONTANA FIELD OFFICE
215 Woodland Estates
Great Falls, MT 59404 United States
Phone: 406-454-2076 Fax: 406-454-2530
E-mail: malbers@amrivers.org
Website: www.americanrivers.org
Membership: 10,001–100,000
Scope: Regional
Description: (formerly American Rivers Conservation Council)
Publication(s): Available on website
Contact(s):
Mark Albers, Office Director

AMERICAN RIVERS
NEBRASKA FIELD OFFICE
650 J St.
Suite 400
Lincoln, NE 68508 United States
Phone: 402-477-7910 Fax: 402-477-2565
E-mail: csmith@amrivers.org
Website: www.SaveTheMissouri.org
Founded: 1998
Scope: Regional
Description: The focus of American Rivers' Nebraska Field Office is the organization's Voyage of Recovery campaign for the rivers of Lewis and Clark.
Keyword(s): Ecosystems (precious), Executive/Legislative/Judicial Reform, Recreation/Ecotourism, Water Habitats & Quality, Wildlife & Species
Contact(s):
Chad Smith, Director; 402-477-7910; Fax: 402-477-2565; csmith@amrivers.org

AMERICAN RIVERS
NORTHWEST REGIONAL OFFICE
150 Nickerson St., Suite 311
Seattle, WA 98109 United States
Phone: 206-213-0330 Fax: 206-213-0334
E-mail: arnw@amrivers.org
Website: www.americanrivers.org
Founded: 1992
Scope: Regional
Description: American Rivers' Northwest Regional Office was founded in 1992 in order to restore the rivers of the Northwest and the region's once-magnificent Pacific salmon runs. Today, we're leading river restoration efforts throughout Idaho, Oregon, and Washington.
Keyword(s): Water Habitats & Quality, Wildlife & Species
Contact(s):
Rob Masonis, Regional Director; rmasonis@amrivers.org

AMERICAN RIVERS
VOYAGE OF RECOVERY
1025 Vermont Ave., NW
Suite 720
Washington, DC 20005 United States
Phone: 202-347-7550 Fax: 202-347-9240
E-mail: amrivers@americanrivers.org
Website: www.americanrivers.org
Founded: 1973
Membership: 10,001–100,000
Scope: National
Description: American Rivers is the leader of America's river conservation movement and is dedicated to preserving and restoring America's river systems and fostering a river stewardship ethic. Conservation goals include protecting wild rivers; restoring hometown rivers; repairing big rivers; removing dams that no longer make sense; reforming the operation of hydroelectric dams; and restoring portions of the rivers of Lewis & Clark to benefit people and wildlife.
Publication(s): River Monitor, America's Most Endangered Rivers, Voyage of Recovery, American Rivers Newsletter
Keyword(s): Ecosystems (precious), Energy, Recreation/Ecotourism, Reduce/Reuse/Recycle, Sprawl/Urban Planning, Transportation, Water Habitats & Quality, Wildlife & Species
Contact(s):
Rebecca Wodder, President
Pat Appel Cornell, Vice-President for Resource Development; ext. 3017; pappel@americanrivers.org
Peter Kelley, Vice President for Strategic Communications; ext. 3057; pkelley@americanrivers.org
Ann Mills, Vice-President for Conservation; ext. 3013; amills@americanrivers.org
Margaret Bowman, Deputy Vice President for Conservation; mbowman@americanrivers.org
Eric Eckl, Director of Media Affairs; 202-347-7550; ext. 3023; eeckl@americanrivers.org
Andrew Fahlund, Policy Director of Hydropower Programs; afahlund@americanrivers.org
Betsy Otto, Community Rivers Director; botto@americanrivers.org
Amy Souers, Managing Editor, American Rivers Online; asouers@americanrivers.org
Bea Keller, Manager, Membership Services; bkeller@americanrivers.org
Chad Smith, Missouri River Regional Representative; 402-477-7910; csmith@americanrivers.org

AMERICAN SOCIETY FOR ENVIRONMENTAL HISTORY
701 Vickers Ave.
Durham, NC 27701 United States
Phone: 919-682-9319 Fax: 919-682-2349
Website: www.h-net.msu.edu/~aseh
Founded: 1976
Scope: National
Description: A nonprofit international society that seeks understanding of human ecology through the perspectives of history and the humanities.
Publication(s): Newsletter, Environmental History
Keyword(s): Public Lands/Greenspace
Contact(s):
Carolyn Merchant, President
Lisa Mighetto, Secretary; Historical Research Associates, 119 Pine St., Suite 207, Seattle, WA 98101
Hal Rothman, Editor; Department of History, University of Nevada-Las Vegas, Las Vegas, NV 89154; 702-739-3349
Ed Russell, Book Review Editor
Jeffrey Stine, Past President; National Museum of American History, Smithsonian Institute, Washington, DC 20560; 202-357-2058

AMERICAN SOCIETY OF ICHTHYOLOGISTS AND HERPETOLOGISTS
Attn: Secretary College of Arts & Science
Florida International University
Maureen Donnelly
Dept. of Biological Sciences
North Miami, FL 33181 United States
Phone: 305-919-5651 Fax: 305-919-5964
E-mail: donnelly@fiu.edu
Founded: 1913
Scope: International
Description: To advance the scientific study of fishes, amphibians and reptiles.
Publication(s): ASIH Special Publications, Copeia
Keyword(s): Water Habitats & Quality, Wildlife & Species

Contact(s):
Harry Greene, President
Brooks Burr, President-Elect
Maureen Donnelly, Secretary
Larry Page, Treasurer
Margaret Stewart, Historian

AMERICAN SOCIETY OF INTERNATIONAL LAW/WILDLIFE INTEREST GROUP

1702 Arlington Boulevard
El Cerrito, CA 94530 United States
Phone: 650-703-3280   Fax: 801-838-4710
E-mail: jiwlp@internationalwildlifelaw.org
Website: www.internationalwildlifelaw.org

Founded: 1984
Membership: 101–1,000
Scope: International

Description: The ASIL and WIG works to improve the effectiveness of international wildlife treaty regimes and national legislation that implements such regimes.

Publication(s): Journal of International Wildlife Law and Policy
Keyword(s): Finance/Banking/Trade, Wildlife & Species
Contact(s):
William Burns, Co-Chairman; jiwlt@internationalwildlifelaw.org

AMERICAN SOCIETY OF LANDSCAPE ARCHITECTS

636 Eye Street, NW
Washington, DC 20001-3736 United States
Phone: 202-898-2444   Fax: 202-898-1185
Website: www.asla.org

Founded: 1899
Membership: 10,001–100,000
Scope: National

Description: Founded in 1899, the American Society of Landscape Architects is the professional association representing landscape architects nationwide. Beginning with 11 original members, ASLA has grown to more than 13,500 members and 48 chapters, in all 50 states, the U.S. territories and 42 countries around the world. ASLA promotes the landscape architecture profession and advances the practice through advocacy, education, communication and networking.

Publication(s): Landscape Architecture
Keyword(s): Land Issues, Public Lands/Greenspace, Reduce/Reuse/Recycle, Sprawl/Urban Planning
Contact(s):
Nancy Somerville, Executive Vice President; nsomerville@asla.org
Marcia Argust, Director, Public and Government Affairs; margust@asla.org
Susan Cahill-Aylward, Managing Director, Information and Professional Practice; scahill@asla.org

AMERICAN SOCIETY OF LIMNOLOGY AND OCEANOGRAPHY

5400 Bosque Blvd., Suite 680
Waco, TX 76710-4446 United States
Phone: 254-399-9635   Fax: 254-776-3767
E-mail: business@aslo.org
Website: www.aslo.org/

Founded: 1936
Membership: 1,001–10,000
Scope: International

Description: To promote the advancement of the various aquatic science disciplines through scientific and technical symposia, colloquia and meetings; promotion of scientific research; discussion, publication and education; and conducting special programs in response to community interest.

Publication(s): Bulletin, Limnology and Oceanography
Keyword(s): Oceans/Coasts/Beaches, Water Habitats & Quality

Contact(s):
William Lewis, President
Jonathan Phinney, Executive Director; 1444 I St. NW Ste. 200, Washington, DC 20005; jpinney@aslo.org
Denise Breitburg, Secretary
Everett Fee, Editor-In-Chief; 343 Lady MacDonald Crescent, Canmore, Alberta T1W 1H5; 403-609-2456; Fax: 403-609-2400; efee@telusplanet.net

AMERICAN SOCIETY OF MAMMALOGISTS

Humboldt State University
Arcata, CA 95521 United States
Phone: 805-892-2504   Fax: 707-826-3201
E-mail: asm@aibs.org
Website: www.mammalsociety.org

Founded: 1919
Scope: National

Description: Encourages research and learning in all phases of mammalogy and by holding annual meetings for presentation and discussion of the results of research dealing with mammals, through issuing periodicals and other publications and by giving advice on matters pertaining to mammals, particularly conservation issues.

Publication(s): Mammalian Species, Special Publications of American Society of Mammalogists, Journal of Mammalogy
Keyword(s): Wildlife & Species

Contact(s):
Tom Kunz, President; Dept. of Biology, Boston University, 2 Cummington St., Boston, MA 02215
Sarah George, 2nd Vice President; Utah Museum of Natural History, University of Utah, Salt Lake City, UT 84112; 801-581-4889
Troy Best, Managing Editor; Department of Zoology, 331 Funchess Hall, Auburn University, AL 36849; 205-844-9260
John Hayning, Chairman of Committee on Marine Mammals; Natural History Museum of Los Angeles, 900 Exposition Blvd., Los Angeles, CA 90007; 213-746-2999
Gordon Kirkland, Chairman of Committee on Conservation of Land Mammals; the Vertebrate Museum, Shippensburg University, Shippensburg, PA 17257
Winston Smith, Chairman of Committee on Legislation and Regulations; Southern Forest Experimental Station, S. Hardwoods Laboratory, P.O. Box 227, Stoneville, MS 38776
H. Smith, Secretary and Treasurer; Department of Zoology, Brigham Young University, Provo, UT 84602; 801-378-2492

AMERICAN SPORTFISHING ASSOCIATION

225 Reinekers Lane
Suite 420
Alexandria, VA 22314 United States
Phone: 703-519-9691   Fax: 703-519-1872
E-mail: info@asafishing.org
Website: www.asafishing.org

Founded: 1994
Scope: National

Description: ASA is a nonprofit industry association working to ensure healthy and sustainable fisheries resources and increase sportfishing participation through education, conservation, promotion and marketing.

Publication(s): American Sportfishing

Contact(s):
Mike Hayden, President and CEO
Michael Nussman, Vice President
Norville Prosser, Vice President
Burt Steinberg, Chairman

AMERICAN SPORTFISHING ASSOCIATION
FISHAMERICA FOUNDATION
FUTURE FISHERMAN FOUNDATION
225 Reinekers Ln.
Suite 420
Alexandria, VA 22314 United States
Phone: 703-519-9691   Fax: 703-519-1872
E-mail: info@asafishing.org
Website: www.asafishing.org
Membership: 101–1,000
Scope: National
Description: The American Sportfishing Association is the leading recreational fishing trade association, uniting 500 members of the sportfishing and boating industries, state and federal natural resource agencies, conservation groups, angler advocacy groups and outdoor journalists. The ASA safeguards and promotes the enduring social, economic and conservation values of sportfishing.
Publication(s): Future Fisherman Foundation
Keyword(s): Land Issues, Oceans/Coasts/Beaches, Pollution (general), Public Lands/Greenspace, Recreation/Ecotourism, Water Habitats & Quality
Contact(s):
Mike Nussman, President/CEO; info@asafishing.org
Gordon Robertson, Vice President
Johanna DeGroff, Managing Director (Acting); 7035199691; ext. 245; Fax: 703-519-1872; jdegroff@asafishing.org
Anne Glick, Executive Director; 703-519-9691; ext. 238; Fax: 703-519-1872; aglick@asafishing.org
Janet Tennyson, Director of Communications; 703-519-9691; ext. 227; Fax: 703-519-1872; info@asafishing.org

AMERICAN WATER RESOURCES ASSOCIATION
4 West Federal St., P.O. Box 1626
Middleburg, VA 20118-1626 United States
Phone: 540-687-8390   Fax: 540-687-8395
E-mail: info@awra.org
Website: www.awra.org
Founded: 1964
Membership: 1,001–10,000
Scope: International
Description: A nonprofit scientific organization which advances water resources research, planning, development and management; establishes a common meeting ground for engineers and physical, biological, and social scientists concerned with water resources; disseminates information in the field of water resources policy, science and technology through the publication of a scientific journal, newsletter and symposium proceedings. Two specialty conferences/symposia and one Annual Conference on Water Resources
Publication(s): Conference Proceedings, Water Resources IMPACT, Journal of the American Water Resources Association
Keyword(s): Reduce/Reuse/Recycle, Water Habitats & Quality
Contact(s):
Robert Moresi, President Elect
Jane Valentine, President
Kenneth Reid, Executive Vice President
D. Adams, Secretary and Treasurer
N. Spangenberg, Editor of Water Resources Impact
John Warwick, Editor of the Journal

AMERICAN WATER WORKS ASSOCIATION (AWWA)
6666 W. Quincy Ave.
Denver, CO 80235 United States
Phone: 303-794-7711   Fax: 303-795-1440
Website: www.awwa.org
Founded: 1881
Membership: 10,001–100,000
Scope: International
Description: The AWWA advances the science, technology, consumer awareness management, government policies and water use efficiencies related to public drinking water.
Publication(s): AWWA Journal, WaterWiser, Opflow, Water Week, Mainstream
Keyword(s): Pollution (general), Public Health, Water Habitats & Quality
Contact(s):
Tom Curtis, Deputy Executive Director of Government Affairs Division; 202-628-8803
Jack Hoffbuhr, Executive Director
Robert Renner, Deputy Executive Director

AMERICAN WHITEWATER
AMERICAN WHITEWATER AFFILIATION, INC.
1424 Fenwick Ln.
Silver Spring, MD 20910 United States
Phone: 301-589-9453   Fax: 301-565-6714
E-mail: nick@amwhitewater.org
Website: www.americanwhitewater.org
Founded: 1957
Membership: 1,001–10,000
Scope: National
Description: American Whitewater's mission is to conserve and restore America's whitewater resources and enhance opportunities to enjoy them safely. This is achieved by means of conservation, river access, education, safety and event programs.
Publication(s): American Whitewater Journal, Safety Code of American Whitewater - Pamphlet
Keyword(s): Energy, Land Issues, Recreation/Ecotourism, Water Habitats & Quality
Contact(s):
Scott Collins, Technology Director; Scott@amwhitewater.org
John Gangemi, Conservation Director; jgangemi@digisys.net
A.J. McIntyre, Corporate Relations Director; aj@amwhitewater.org
Michael Phelan, Events Director; Michael@amwhitewater.org
Jason Robertson, Access Policy Director; jason@amwhitewater.org
Risa Shimoda, Executive Director; risa@amwhitewater.org
Nick Lipkowski, Office Manager; nick@amwhitewater.org

AMERICAN WILDERNESS COALITION
122 C Street NW
Suite 240
Washington, DC 20000-2109 United States
Phone: 202-266-0455   Fax: 202-544-5197
E-mail: info@americanwilderness.org
Website: www.americanwilderness.org
Founded: 2000
Membership: 1–100
Scope: Local, State, Regional, National
Description: The American Wilderness Coalition seeks to expand and protect our National Wilderness Preservation System by providing additive resources and advocacy assistance to the many individuals and organizations involved in campaigns to protect additional Wilderness Areas today.
Keyword(s): Land Issues
Contact(s):
Melyssa Watson, Chair of the Board; P.O. Box 1620, Durango, CO 81302; 970-247-8788; Fax: 970-247-9020; mwatson@tws.org
Sara Shipley, Administrative Assistant; 202-266-0456; Fax: 202-544-5197; sara@americanwilderness.org

AMERICAN WILDLANDS
P.O. Box 6669
Bozeman, MT 59771 United States
Phone: 406-586-8175   Fax: 406-586-8242
E-mail: info@wildlands.org
Website: www.wildlands.org/
Founded: 1977

Scope: Regional

Description: A nonprofit conservation organization dedicated to ecologically sustainable use and protection of America's wildland resources in the Rocky Mountains West, including wilderness, wetlands, rangelands, free-flowing rivers, wildlife and fisheries and forests.

Publication(s): Forest Activist Green Papers, Policy Reports, On The Wild Side

Keyword(s): Forests/Forestry, Land Issues, Public Lands/Greenspace, Wildlife & Species

Contact(s):
Sally Ranney, President
Jeff Larmer, Executive Director
William Cunningham, Vice Chairman
Clifton Merritt, Executive Editor
Clifton Merritt, Secretary and Treasurer

AMERICAN WILDLIFE RESEARCH FOUNDATION, INC.
50 West High St.
Balton Spa, NY 12020 United States
E-mail: wms4@cornell.edu

Founded: 1911
Membership: 1–100
Scope: International

Description: AWRF uses the interest income of its funds to support research of wildlife and its habitats. Its mission is to enhance fish and wildlife resources and their habitats through research, education and conservation, ensuring that present and future generations can continue to use and enjoy them.

Publication(s): Newsletter

Contact(s):
Stuart Free, President; 518-861-5357; Fax: 518-452-6392
William Schwerd, Secretary; 518-885-8995; Fax: 518-885-9078

AMERICAN ZOO AND AQUARIUM ASSOCIATION (AZA)
8403 Colesville Rd., Suite 710
Silver Spring, MD 20910 United States
Phone: 301-562-0777   Fax: 301-562-0888
Website: www.aza.org

Founded: 1924
Membership: 101–1,000
Scope: National

Description: Dedicated to the improvement of modern, professionally-managed zoological parks and aquariums through conservation, public education, scientific research and membership services. Administers scientifically-managed captive breeding and field conservation programs for 134 threatened and endangered species through its Species Survival Plan Program.

Publication(s): AZA Membership Directory, Annual and Regional Conference Proceedings, Annual Report on Conservation and Science, COMMUNIQUE

Keyword(s): Oceans/Coasts/Beaches, Wildlife & Species

Contact(s):
Ted Beattie, President
Jane Ballentine, Director of Public Affairs; ext. 252
Laura Benson, Director of Finance and Administration; ext. 233
Sydney Butler, Executive Director
Bruce Carr, Director of Conservation Education; ext. 251
Michael Hutchins, Director of Conservation and Science
Linda Martin-MCormic, Director of Development and Marketing; ext. 243
Kristin Vehrs, Deputy Director and Director of Government Affairs

ANACOSTIA WATERSHED SOCIETY
4302 Baltimore Ave.
Bladensburg, MD 20710 United States
Phone: 301-699-6204   Fax: 301-699-3317
Website: www.anacostiaws.org

Founded: 1989
Membership: 101–1,000
Scope: Regional

Description: The Anacostia Watershed Society provides opportunities for volunteers to take part in local environmental restoration projects and provides advocacy for environmental equity issues in the Anacostia-Washington region.

Publication(s): Voice of the River

Keyword(s): Ecosystems (precious), Ethics/Environmental Justice, Pollution (general), Public Lands/Greenspace, Reduce/Reuse/Recycle, Sprawl/Urban Planning, Water Habitats & Quality

Contact(s):
Robert Boone, President; robert@anacostiaws.org
James Connolly, Executive Director; jim@anacostiaws.org

ANCIENT FOREST INTERNATIONAL
P.O. Box 1850
Redway, CA 95560 United States
Phone: 707-923-3015   Fax: 707-923-4486
E-mail: afi@ancientforest.org
Website: www.ancientforest.org

Founded: 1989
Scope: International

Description: An alliance of conservationists dedicated to helping preserve, study and increase awareness of the Earth's few still-intact forest ecosystems, while providing habitat continuity through the creation of corridors. Old-growth forests of southern Chile, highland Mexico, Ecuador and the north Pacific coast are current projects. Work is also underway to document the distribution of ancient rainforests worldwide and to promote their preservation.

Publication(s): Chile's Native Forest: An Overview, News of Old Growth

Keyword(s): Forests/Forestry, Wildlife & Species

Contact(s):
Rick Klein, President
Suzelle Hunt, Secretary
Tim Metz, Treasurer

ANGLERS FOR CLEAN WATER
P.O. Box 17900
Montgomery, AL 36141-0900 United States
Phone: 334-272-9530   Fax: 334-396-8230

Founded: 1970
Scope: National

Description: A nonprofit organization dedicated to educating the American public on the status of America's natural resources, to provide education and information on conservation of aquatic resources and to serve as a strong advocate for sportfishing.

Publication(s): Living Waters

Keyword(s): Pollution (general), Recreation/Ecotourism, Water Habitats & Quality, Wildlife & Species

Contact(s):
Bruce Shupp, Conservation Director
Matt Vincent, Editor

ANIMAL PROTECTION INSTITUTE
P.O. Box 22505
Sacramento, CA 95822 United States
Phone: 916-447-3085   Fax: 916-447-3070
E-mail: info@api4animals.org
Website: www.apianimals.org

Founded: 1968

Membership: 1,001–10,000
Scope: National
Description: The Animal Protection Institute is a national animal advocacy nonprofit organization dedicated to protecting animals against abuse through enforcement and legislative actions, investigations, advocacy campaigns, crisis intervention, public awareness and education. Specific areas of concern are wildlife protection and habitat conservation, companion animals, marine mammals, domestic and farm animals, animals used in research and humane education.
Publication(s): Animal Issues
Keyword(s): Public Lands/Greenspace, Recreation/Ecotourism, Wildlife & Species
Contact(s):
Alan Berger, Executive Director
Gil Lamont, Editor
Barbara Lawrie, Creative Services
Gary Pike, Chairman of the Board

ANIMAL WELFARE INSTITUTE
P.O. Box 3650
Washington, DC 20027 United States
Phone: 703-836-4300   Fax: 703-836-0400
E-mail: awi@awionline.org
Website: www.awionline.org
Founded: 1951
Membership: 10,001–100,000
Scope: National
Description: Active in improvement of conditions for laboratory animals and reducing the numbers used in research, protection of endangered species, Save the Whales campaign, ending use of steel jaw traps, stopping imports of wild birds for the pet trade and humane education. Albert Schweitzer award is presented for outstanding contributions to animal welfare.
Publication(s): Animals and Their Legal Rights, Alternative Traps, Endangered Species Handbook, Animal Welfare Institute Quarterly
Keyword(s): Wildlife & Species
Contact(s):
Christine Stevens, President; 202-337-2332
Cynthia Wilson, Vice President
Cathy Liss, Executive Director; 202-337-2332
Ava Armandarez, Publications Coordinator; 202-337-2332
Diane Halverson, Farm Animal Consultant
Lynne Hutchison, Executive Secretary
Fred Hutchison, Treasurer
Nell Naughton, Mail Order Secretary
Viktor Reinhardt, Laboratory Animal Consultant
Adam Roberts, Research Associate; 202-337-2332
Ben White, International Coordinator

ANIMALS ASIA FOUNDATION
P.O. Box 82
Sai Kung Post Office
Sai Kung
Kowloon, Hong Kong
Phone: 852-2791-2225   Fax: 852-2791-2320
E-mail: info@animalsasia.org
Website: www.animalsasia.org
Scope: Regional
Description: The Animals Asia Foundation is devoted to the needs of wild, domesticated and endangered species throughout the Asian continent. Our mission is to end cruelty and promote an inherent respect for animals Asia wide. Animals Asia is currently undertaking the rescue of 500 farmed Moon Bears in China
Publication(s): Campaigns of Animals Asia
Keyword(s): Executive/Legislative/Judicial Reform, Wildlife & Species

Contact(s):
Jill Robinson, Founder & CEO; 852-2791-2225; Fax: 852-2791-2320; jrobinson@animalsasia.org
Gail Cochrane, Veterinary Director; 852-2791-2225; Fax: 852-2791-2320; gcochrane@animalsasia.org
Annie Mather, Media Director; 852-2791-2225; Fax: 852-2791-2320; amather@animalsasia.org
Hanni Bevand, German Representative; Postfach 82 01 73, 81801, Munich; 894-277-5301; Fax: 894-277-5302; hbevand@animalsasia.org
David Neale, UK Representative; P.O. Box 5713, Clacton on Sea, Essex CO15 6QT; 0870-241-3723; Fax: 0870-225-6062; dneale@animalsasia.org
Ingrid Seymour, New Zealand Representative; P.O. Box 12440, Hamilton 2001; 07-829-4905; Fax: 07-829-4904; iseymour@animalsasia.org
Lyn White, Australia Representative; P.O. Box 1, Woodside, SA5244; 1800-666-004; Fax: 6188-389-7367; lwhite@animalsasia.org

ANTARCTICA PROJECT, THE
1630 Connecticut Ave., NW
3rd Floor
Washington, DC 20009 United States
Phone: 202-234-2480   Fax: 202-387-4823
E-mail: info@asoc.org
Website: www.asoc.org
Founded: 1982
Membership: 1,001–10,000
Scope: International
Description: Works to preserve Antarctica by monitoring all activities to ensure minimal environmental impact and consulting with key users of Antarctica, including scientists, tourists, governments. Conducts legal and policy research and analysis; produces educational materials; focuses international scientific community on globally-significant research. Secretariat to Antarctic and Southern Ocean Coalition (ASOC), composed of 240 conservation groups in 50 nations.
Publication(s): Antarctica Project (Quarterly Newsletter)
Keyword(s): Climate Change, Ecosystems (precious), Land Issues, Recreation/Ecotourism, Reduce/Reuse/Recycle, Wildlife & Species
Contact(s):
Beth Clark, Director
Jim Barnes, Counsel
Karen Sack, Coordinator Fisheries Campaign; 202-238-8052; karen.antarctica@igc.org
Josh Stevens, North America Campaigner; josh.antarctica@igc.org

APPALACHIAN MOUNTAIN CLUB
5 Joy St.
Boston, MA 02108 United States
Phone: 617-523-0636   Fax: 617-523-6617
E-mail: information@amcinfo.org
Website: www.outdoors.org
Founded: 1876
Membership: 10,001–100,000
Scope: Regional
Description: The AMC pursues a far-reaching conservation agenda while encouraging responsible recreation, based on the philosophy that successful, long-term conservation depends on firsthand experience and enjoyment of the natural environment. Areas of focus: Northern Forest, Sterling Forest, White Mountain N.F., NY and NJ Highlands, Berkshire and Taconics Region, Delaware Water Gap National Recreation Area, and Acadia National Park. Expertise: Conservation policy, advocacy; land, trail, river and greenways.
Publication(s): AMC Outdoors, AMC guidebooks and maps, Appalachia Journal
Keyword(s): Air Quality/Atmosphere, Public Lands/Greenspace, Recreation/Ecotourism, Water Habitats & Quality

Contact(s):
Laurie Burt, President
Susan Arnold, Director of Conservation; 617-523-0655; ext. 353
Andrew Falender, Executive Director
Kenneth Kimball, Research Director; 603-466-2721
Walter Graff, Deputy Director; 603-466-2721

APPALACHIAN TRAIL CONFERENCE
P.O. Box 807
Harpers Ferry, WV 25425-0807 United States
Phone: 304-535-6331   Fax: 304-535-2667
E-mail: general@appalachiantrail.org
Website: www.appalachiantrail.org
Founded: 1925
Membership: 10,001–100,000
Scope: Regional
Description: Coordinates preservation and management of the Appalachian Trail, a 2,173-mile footpath and protective corridor generally following the crest of the Appalachian Mountains from Maine to Georgia. Publishes and distributes trail guidebooks and other user information.
Publication(s): Ultimate A.T. Store, Register, The, Appalachian Trailway News
Keyword(s): Agriculture/Farming, Air Quality/Atmosphere, Ecosystems (precious), Forests/Forestry, Land Issues, Public Lands/Greenspace, Recreation/Ecotourism, Wildlife & Species
Contact(s):
Brian King, Director of Public Affairs; bking@atconf.org
David Startzell, Executive Director
Robert Proudman, Director of Trail Management; bproudman@appalachiantrail.org
Robert Rubin, Editor; rrubin@appalachiantrail.org

APROVECHO RESEARCH CENTER
80574 Hazelton Road
Cottage Grove, OR 97424 United States
Phone: 541-942-8198
E-mail: apro@efn.org
Website: www.efn.org/~apro
Founded: 1976
Membership: 101–1,000
Scope: International
Description: Aprovecho Research Center does research and development of appropriate technology specifically designed to be made and used in Third World countries. We have been helping folks in more than 60 countries to build fuel efficient, low emission wood burning cooking stoves, for example. Aprovecho also runs a school for college aged students teaching organic agriculture, sustainable forestry, appropriate technology, permaculture. Semester courses are offered every spring, summer and fall.
Publication(s): Books on vernacular stoves
Keyword(s): Agriculture/Farming, Air Quality/Atmosphere, Climate Change, Development/Developing Countries, Energy, Forests/Forestry, Pollution (general), Public Health

ARCHAEOLOGICAL CONSERVANCY
5301 Central Ave., NE, Suite 902
Albuquerque, NM 87108 United States
Phone: 505-266-1540   Fax: 505-266-0311
E-mail: tacstaff@nm.net
Website: www.americanarchaeology.org
Founded: 1979
Membership: 10,001–100,000
Scope: National
Description: National nonprofit membership organization dedicated to the permanent preservation of the most significant archaeological sites in the United States, usually through acquisition. Cooperates with government, universities, museums, and private conservation organizations to acquire lands for permanent archaeological preserves.
Publication(s): American Archaeology
Keyword(s): Ethics/Environmental Justice, Wildlife & Species
Contact(s):
Mark Michel, President
Rob Crisell, Eastern Regional Director; 1307 S. Glebe Rd., Arlington, VA 22204; 703-979-4410
Lynn Dunbar, Western Regional Office Director; 1217 23rd St., Sacramento, CA 95816-4917; 916-448-1892
Paul Gardner, Midwest Regional Office Director; 295 Acton Rd., Columbus, OH 43214; 614-267-1100
Alan Gruber, Southeastern Regional Office Director; 5997 Cedar Crest Rd., Acworth, GA 30101; 770-975-4344
James Walker, Southwest Regional Office Director; 5301 Central Ave. NE, Suite 1218, Albuquerque, NM 87108; 505-266-1540
Earl Gadbery, Chairman of the Board

ARCHBOLD BIOLOGICAL STATION
P.O. Box 2057
Lake Placid, FL 33862-2057 United States
Phone: 863-465-2571   Fax: 863-699-1927
E-mail: archbold@archbold-station.org
Website: www.archbold-station.org
Founded: 1941
Scope: State
Description: The Station is an independent, nonprofit facility devoted to long-term ecological research and conservation. Primary focus is on organisms, including many endangered species, and environments of the unique Lake Wales Ridge and adjacent Florida.
Publication(s): Biennial Report
Keyword(s): Agriculture/Farming, Land Issues, Wildlife & Species
Contact(s):
Hilary Swain, Executive Director; 863-465-2571; ext. 251
Patrick Bolen, Assistant Director for Agro-Ecology; 863-699-0242
Nancy Deyrup, Education Coordinator; 863-465-2571; ext. 233
Cheryl Henderson, Internship Coordinator; 863-465-2571; ext. 251
Fred Lohrer, Librarian; 863-465-2571; ext. 236

ARCHERY TRADE ASSOCIATION (ATA)
ARROWSPORT
BOWHUNTING PRESERVATION ALLIANCE
304 Brown St. East
P.O. Box 258
Comfrey, MN 56019 United States
Phone: 507-877-5300   Fax: 507-877-2149
E-mail: kellykelly@archerytrade.org
Website: www.archerytrade.org
Founded: 1953
Membership: 101–1,000
Scope: International
Description: Since 1953, ATA has been the small business trade association for manufacturers, retailers, distributors, sales representatives, and others working in the archery and bowhunting industry. ATA is dedicated to making the archery and bowhunting industry profitable by decreasing business overhead, reducing taxes and government regulation and by increasing participation in archery and bowhunting. ATA owns and manages the Archery and Bowhunting Trade Show.
Keyword(s): Recreation/Ecotourism
Contact(s):
Jay McAninch, President and CEO
Kelly Kelly, Director of Operations and Membership Services; kelly@amoarchery.com

ARCTIC INSTITUTE OF NORTH AMERICA
University of Calgary
2500 University Drive NW
Calgary, T2N 1N4 Alberta Canada
Phone: 403-220-7515   Fax: 403-282-4609
Website: www.ucalgary.ca/aina
Founded: 1945
Membership: 1,001–10,000
Scope: Local, Regional, National, International
Description: A nonprofit research organization dedicated to acquisition, interpretation, and dissemination of knowledge of the polar regions. Sponsors research by its forty research associates.
Publication(s): Arctic, AINA Library
Keyword(s): Ecosystems (precious)
Contact(s):
Karla Jessen Williamson, Executive Director; 403-220-7515; wkjessen@ucalgary.ca
Ross Goodwin, Manager, ASTIS Database; 403-220-4036; rgoodwin@ucalgary.ca
Sonja Hogg, Business Manager; 403-220-7517; hogg@ucalgary.ca
Carl Benson, Chair of the U.S. Board of Governors
Karen McCullough, Editor; 403-220-4049; kmccullo@ucalgary.ca
Murray Todd, Chair of the Canadian Board of Directors

ARIZONA ASSOCIATION OF CONSERVATION DISTRICTS
Attn: Executive Director, 3003 N. Central Ave., Suite 800
Phoenix, AZ 85012 United States
Phone: 602-280-8803   Fax: 602-280-8779
E-mail: aacd@az.nrcs.usda.gov
Website: www.aacdonline.com
Scope: State
Contact(s):
Sharon Reid, President and Board Member; Rt. 1 Box 49-C, St. David, AZ 85630; 520-586-3347
Robert Ahkeah, Vice President; P.O. Box 550, Shiprock, NM 87420; 505-368-5430
Frank Martinez, 1st Vice President; Box 1152, Parker, AZ 85344; 520-669-8459
Marcareo Herrera, Executive Director; 602-280-8803; Fax: 602-280-8779
Johnny Lavin, Secretary/Treasurer; HC 1 Box 760, Benson, AZ 83602; 520-212-3211; Fax: 520-384-2735

ARIZONA BASS FEDERATION
P.O. Box 577
Kearny, AZ 85237 United States
Phone: 520-363-5912
Membership: 101–1,000
Scope: State
Description: An organization of Bassmaster chapters, affiliated with the Bass Anglers Sportsman Society, organized to fight pollution, assist state and national conservation agencies in their efforts, and teach the young people of our country good conservation practices. Dedicated to the realistic conservation of our water resources.
Contact(s):
Mike Johnson, President
Dave Cohen, Conservation Director; 839 S. Westwood #266, Mesa, AZ 85210; 602-962-9009

ARIZONA STATE ENVIROTHON, INC.
P.O. Box 1248
Phoenix, AZ 85001 United States
Phone: 602-771-4162
E-mail: ls3@ev.state.az.us
Website: www.azenvirothon.org
Founded: 1997
Scope: Local, State
Description: Natural resource competition for high school students (grades 9-12). Core study areas are: aquatics, forestry, soils, wildlife and a fifth issue on a current environmental issue that changes each year. Our mission is to promote an awareness and understanding of ecological and natural resource management concepts among Arizona High School students via an annual statewide competition.
Keyword(s): Agriculture/Farming, Ecosystems (precious), Forests/Forestry, Land Issues, Water Habitats & Quality, Wildlife & Species
Contact(s):
Lisa Schmoetzer, Coordinator; P.O. Box 1248, Phoenix, AZ 85001; 602-771-4162; ls3@ev.state.az.us
Rodney Held, Chair; 500 N. 3rd St, Phoenix, AZ 85004; 602-417-2400; ext. 7012; Fax: 602-417-2423; rjheld@adwr.state.az.us

 ARIZONA WILDLIFE FEDERATION
644 N. Country Club Dr. - Suite E
Mesa, AZ 85201-4983 United States
Phone: 480-644-0077   Fax: 480-644-0078
E-mail: awf@azwildlife.org
Website: www.azwildlife.org
Founded: 1923
Membership: 1,001–10,000
Scope: State
Description: A representative statewide organization, affiliated with the National Wildlife Federation, dedicated to the protection and enhancement of wildlife and its habitat through public education and government interaction.
Publication(s): Arizona Wildlife News
Keyword(s): Wildlife & Species
Contact(s):
Jerry Thorson, President & Acting Treasurer
Randy Lamb, Vice-President
Mike Perkinson, Vice-President
Dave Gowdey, Executive Director; 644 N Country Club Dr.; Suite E, Mesa, AZ 85201; 480-644-0077; dgowdey@azwildlife.org
Ken Haefner, Publications / Volunteers Director; 644 N Country Club Dr., Suite E, Mesa, AZ 85201; 480-644-0077; Fax: 480-644-0078; haefner@azwildlife.org
Web Parton, Education / Outreach Coodinator
Don Farmer, Alternate Representative
Jack Simon, Representative

ARIZONA-SONORA DESERT MUSEUM
2021 North Kinney Road
Tucson, AZ 85743 United States
Phone: 520-883-1380   Fax: 520-883-2500
E-mail: mdimmitt@desertmuseum.org
Website: www.desertmuseum.org
Founded: 1952
Membership: 100,001–500,000
Scope: International
Description: The mission of the Arizona-Sonora Desert Museum is to inspire people to live in harmony with the natural world by fostering love, appreciation, and understanding of the Sonoran Desert.
Publication(s): Invasive Exotic Species in the Sonora Region, Cactficeas de Sonora, Mexico, A Guide to Southern Arizona Bird Nests, The Secret Lives of Hummingbirds, Desert Dogs: Coyotes, Foxes & Wolves, ASDM Book of Answers, A Field Guide to Desert Holes
Keyword(s): Development/Developing Countries, Ecosystems (precious), Forests/Forestry, Land Issues, Oceans/Coasts/Beaches, Public Lands/Greenspace, Recreation/Ecotourism, Sprawl/Urban Planning, Water Habitats & Quality, Wildlife & Species

Contact(s):
Richard Brusca, Director, Programs; 520-883-1380; Fax: 520-883-2500; rbrusca@desertmuseum.org
Robert Edison, Director, Administration; 520-883-1380; Fax: 520-883-2500; redison@desertmuseum.org
Mark Dimmitt, Director of Natural History; 520-883-1380; Fax: 520-883-2500; mdimmitt@desertmuseum.org

ARKANSAS ASSOCIATION OF CONSERVATION DISTRICTS
Attn: Exec. Vice President
101 E. Capital
Suite 350
Little Rock, AR 72201 United States
Phone: 479-643-3385

Scope: State

Contact(s):
Bill Rainwater, President; P.O. Box 2245, Jonesboro, AR 72401; 870-935-1624
Paul Mayfield, 1st Vice President; 783 Rio Vista Rd., Bald Knob, AR 72010; 501-724-5932; mayfield@IPA.Net
Debbie Moreland, Executive Vice President; 20311 Lake Vista, Roland, AR 72135; 501-868-5294
Roy Mahler, Secretary/Treasurer; Rt. 2 Box 130, Elkins, AR 72727; 501-643-3385

ARKANSAS BASS FEDERATION
500 Coles Chapel Circle
Branch, AR 72928 United States
Phone: 479-635-5951
E-mail: scarson@mailcity.com
Website: www.arkansasbass.com
Membership: 101–1,000
Scope: National

Description: An organization of Bassmaster chapters, affiliated with the Bass Anglers Sportsman Society, organized to fight pollution, assist state and national conservation agencies in their efforts, and teach the young people of our country good conservation practices. Dedicated to the realistic conservation of our water resources.

Publication(s): Arkansas Bass Newsletter, available on website

Contact(s):
Gene Carson, President
Bobby Davenport, Conservation Director; 870-673-1799

ARKANSAS ENVIRONMENTAL EDUCATION ASSOCIATION
P.O. Box 488
Hackett, AR 72937 United States
Phone: 479-638-7151   Fax: 479-638-7151
E-mail: arkenved@aol.com

Founded: 1995
Membership: 1–100
Scope: Local, State, Regional, National

Description: The Association promotes environmental education and supports the work of environmental educators in Arkansas.

Publication(s): Membership Directory, EE Resource Directory

Contact(s):
Frank Chandler, President-Elect
Michelle Viney, President; 479-444-1860; Fax: 479-444-1880; mviney@tcswd.com
Robert McAfee, Executive Director; 479-638-7151; Fax: 479-638-7151; arkenved@aol.com
Suzanne Hirrel, President; 501-671-2288; Fax: 501-671-2110; shirrel@uaex.edu

ARKANSAS WATERSHED ADVISORY GROUP (AWAG)
Environmental Preservation Division
8001 National Drive
P.O. Box 8913
Little Rock, AR 72219-8193 United States
Phone: 501-682-0022   Fax: 501-682-0010
E-mail: awag@adeq.state.ar.us
Website: www.awag.org

Founded: 2000
Membership: 101–1,000
Scope: Local, State

Description: The Arkansas Watershed Advisory Group assists interested citizens and organizations by promoting local voluntary approaches to watershed management and conservation

Keyword(s): Agriculture/Farming, Ecosystems (precious), Forests/Forestry, Land Issues, Pollution (general), Population, Public Health, Public Lands/Greenspace, Recreation/Ecotourism, Sprawl/Urban Planning, Water Habitats & Quality

Contact(s):
Sandi Formica, Chair; 501-682-0020; Fax: 501-682-0010; formica@adeq.state.ar.us

 ## ARKANSAS WILDLIFE FEDERATION
9700 Rodney Parham Road, Suite I-2
Little Rock, AR 72227-6212 United States
Phone: 501-224-9200   Fax: 501-224-9214
E-mail: arkwildlifefed@aristotle.net
Website: www.arkansaswildlifefederation.org

Founded: 1936
Membership: 1,001–10,000
Scope: State

Description: A representative statewide organization, affiliated with the National Wildlife Federation, dedicated to the protection and enhancement of wildlife and its habitat through public education and government interaction.

Publication(s): Arkansas Fish and Wildlife

Contact(s):
Ducote Haynes, President
Terry Horton, Executive Director & Education Programs Contact
Bob Apple, Editor
Steve Duzan, Alternate Representative
Jim Wood, Representative & Treasurer

ARLINGTON OUTDOOR EDUCATION ASSOCIATION, INC. (AOEA)
PHOEBE HALL KNIPLING OUTDOOR LABORATORY
P.O. Box 5646
Arlington, VA 22205 United States
Phone: 540-347-2258
Website: CharityAdvantage.com/AOEA

Founded: 1967
Membership: 1,001–10,000
Scope: Local, Regional

Description: AOEA's Outdoor Lab annually provides approximately 9,000 northern Virginia school children, in grades kindergarten through twelve, with enriching environmental and educational opportunities in a natural setting. In addition to daily classes during the school year, the lab conducts camps during the summer and astronomical observatory sessions throughout the year.

Keyword(s): Land Issues, Water Habitats & Quality, Wildlife & Species

Contact(s):
Terry Rusnak, President; 703-228-7650
Lori Lowe, Vice President
Neil Heinekamp, Lab Director

Maureen McManus, Treasurer
Anita Scott, Secretary

ASSOCIATION FOR CONSERVATION INFORMATION, INC.
Attn: President
New Hampshire Fish and Game Department
2 Hazen Dr.
Concord, NH 33301 United States
Website: www.aci-net.org

Founded: 1938

Scope: National

Description: Facilitates free exchange of ideas, materials, techniques, experiences, and procedures bearing on conservation information and education and establishes media furthering such exchange; promotes public understanding of basic conservation principles; informs states, territories, and provinces that do not have conservation education programs of their desirability and assists them in setting up conservation education, information and public relations programs.

Publication(s): Balance Wheel, The

Contact(s):
Judy Stokes, President; New Hampshire Fish & Game Department, 2 Hazen Drive, Concord, NH 03301; 603-271-3211

ASSOCIATION FOR NATURAL RESOURCES ENFORCEMENT TRAINING
Missouri Department of Conservation Box 180
Jefferson City, MO 65102 United States
Phone: 573-751-4115
E-mail: yamnil@mail.conservation.state.mo.us
Website: www.dirdid.com\anret

Scope: National

Description: The goal of the association is to promote and enhance professional standards of training in fish and wildlife enforcement. The objectives are: to promote officer safety and a safer working environment; exchange training information; promote law enforcement research and development; to encourage cost-effective training programs; to act as a repository for catalogue agency training personnel and materials; and to host annual workshop to facilitate the exchange of training information.

Keyword(s): Ethics/Environmental Justice

Contact(s):
Dave Windsor, Vice President; Indiana Department of Natural Resources, Law Enforcement Division 402 W. Washington Street, Indianapolis, IN 46204; 317-232-4014; dwindsor@dnr.state.in.us
Fred Campbell, Treasurer; Natural Resources Conservation Authority, 10 Caledonia Ave., Kingston; 876-754-7567; fcampbell@nrca.org
Scottey Roxburgh, Secretary; Department of Fisheries and Oceans, 400-555 West Hasting St., Vancouver, British Columbia V6B 5G3; 604-666-0123; roxburgh@dfo/moo.ga.ca

ASSOCIATION FOR THE PROTECTION OF THE ADIRONDACKS, THE
P.O. Box 951
Schenectady, NY 12301 United States
Phone: 518-377-1452   Fax: 518-377-1452
Website: www.protectadks.org

Founded: 1901

Membership: 1,001–10,000

Scope: International

Description: To protect the natural character of the state forest preserve lands in the Adirondacks and Catskills as water-holding and regulating forests which serve as a home for wildlife and as wilderness recreation areas, and to protect and enhance the natural resources of the Adirondack Park.

Publication(s): The Forest Preserve Magazine, The Association News Quarterly Newsletter

Keyword(s): Development/Developing Countries, Land Issues, Public Lands/Greenspace, Water Habitats & Quality, Wildlife & Species

Contact(s):
Abbey Verner, President
David Gibson, Executive Director

ASSOCIATION OF AMERICAN GEOGRAPHERS
AAG
1710 16th St., NW
Washington, DC 20009-3198 United States
Phone: 202-234-1450   Fax: 202-234-2744
E-mail: gaia@aag.org
Website: www.aag.org

Founded: 1904

Membership: 1,001–10,000

Scope: National, International

Description: To further professional investigations in geography and encourage the application of geographic findings in education, government, and business.

Publication(s): Professional Geographer, The, The Annals, AAG Newsletter

Keyword(s): Climate Change, Development/Developing Countries, Ecosystems (precious), Energy, Ethics/Environmental Justice, Land Issues, Oceans/Coasts/Beaches, Population, Public Health, Public Lands/Greenspace, Recreation/Ecotourism, Sprawl/Urban Planning, Transportation

Contact(s):
Jan Monk, President
Duane Neelis, Vice President
Douglas Richardson, Executive Director; 202-234-1450; Fax: 202-234-2744; gaia@aag.org
Megan Nortrup, Editor; 202-234-1450; Fax: 202-234-2744; gaia@aag.org
Heather Baker, Editor of Newsletter
Susan Cutter, Past President
Robert Kent, Treasurer
Jennifer Wolch, Secretary
Amy Jo Woodruff, Managing Editor

ASSOCIATION OF AVIAN VETERINARIANS
P.O. Box 811720
Boca Raton, FL 33481 United States
Phone: 561-393-8901   Fax: 561-393-8902
E-mail: aavctrlofc@aol.com
Website: www.aav.org/aav

Founded: 1980

Membership: 1,001–10,000

Scope: International

Description: The Association of Avian Veterinarians is a nonprofit international organization dedicated to advancing and promoting avian medicine and stewardship.

Publication(s): Journal of Avian Medicine and Surgery, The Proceedings of the Assoc. of Avian Veterinarians

Keyword(s): Wildlife & Species

Contact(s):
Robert Groskin, Conservation Committee

ASSOCIATION OF CONSULTING FORESTERS OF AMERICA
ACF
732 North Washington St.
Suite 4-A
Alexandria, VA 22314-1921 United States
Phone: 703-548-0990   Fax: 703-548-6395
E-mail: director@acf-foresters.com
Website: www.acf-foresters.com

Founded: 1948

Membership: 100,001–500,000
Scope: National
Description: The Association of Consulting Foresters of America, Inc. represents the interests of private consulting foresters. Administers a continuing education program, enforces a code of ethics, and promotes use of private consulting foresters.
Publication(s): Membership Specialization Directory
Keyword(s): Forests/Forestry, Reduce/Reuse/Recycle
Contact(s):
Lynn Wilson, Executive Director

ASSOCIATION OF FIELD ORNITHOLOGISTS
AMERICAN FIELD ORINTHOLOGISTS
Attn: President, Inst. for Field Ornithology
Cornell
159 Sapsucker
Ithaca, NY 14850 United States
Website: www.afonet.org/

Founded: 1922
Scope: National
Description: To promote the study of birds in their natural habitats throughout the new world and dissemination of the information obtained from this study.
Publication(s): Journal of Field Ornithology
Keyword(s): Wildlife & Species
Contact(s):
Jerome Jackson, President; Whitaker Center, College of Arts & Sciences, Florida Gulf Coast University, 10501 FGCU Blvd. South, Fort Myers, FL 33965; jjackson@fgcu.edu
C. Chandler, Editor; Dept. of Bio., GA Southern Univ., Statesboro, GA 30460-8042; 912-681-5657; chandler@gasou.edu
Russ McClain, Secretary; Department of Biology, University of Memphis, Memphis, TN 38152; 901-678-2581; wrmcclain@msuvxi.memphis.edu
George Mock, Treasurer; P.O. Box 393, Mattapoisett, MA 02739; 508-758-4408; gmock@nyclubricants.com

ASSOCIATION OF GREAT LAKES OUTDOOR WRITERS (AGLOW)
P.O. Box 35
Benld, IL 62009 United States
Phone: 217-839-2490   Fax: 217-839-2490
E-mail: curthicken@aol.com
Website: www.greatlakeswriters.org

Founded: 1957
Membership: 101–1,000
Scope: Regional
Description: A nonprofit professional association of outdoor communicators dedicated to perpetuate the great outdoors through the judicious use of the written and spoken word.
Publication(s): AGLOW Horizons
Contact(s):
David Mull, President; pondermull@aol.com
Curt Hicken, Executive Director; 217-839-2490; Fax: 217-839-2490; curthicken@aol.com
Clayton Diskerud, Secretary
Dan Donarski, Vice President; 404 Golf Court, Sault Ste. Marie, MI 49783
P.J. Perea, Treasurer; 224 N. Shore Dr., Petersburg, IL 62675
Bob Schmidt, Editor; 5016 Argyle, Chicago, IL 60630; 773-283-7871
Mike Seeling, Chairman of the Board; 13608 Rt. 176, Woodstock, IL 60098

ASSOCIATION OF NEW JERSEY ENVIRONMENTAL COMMISSIONS (ANJEC)
P.O. Box 157
Mendham, NJ 07945 United States
Phone: 973-539-7547   Fax: 973-539-7713
E-mail: anjec@aol.com
Website: www.anjec.org

Founded: 1969
Membership: 1,001–10,000
Scope: State
Description: Private, nonprofit environmental organization serving the state's municipal environmental commissions, environmental organizations, and individual members by providing training programs, publications, research, reference, and liaison services.
Publication(s): ANJEC Report, Environmental Commission Handbook, Keeping Our Garden State Green, Freshwater Wetlands Protection in New Jersey, Environmental Manual for Municipal Officials
Keyword(s): Development/Developing Countries, Land Issues, Pollution (general), Public Lands/Greenspace, Sprawl/Urban Planning, Water Habitats & Quality
Contact(s):
Gary Szelc, President
Sandy Batty, Executive Director
Michelle Gaynor, Resource Center Director

ASSOCIATION OF PARTNERS FOR PUBLIC LANDS
2401 Blueridge Avenue, Suite 303
Wheaton, MD 20902 United States
Phone: 301-946-9475   Fax: 301-946-9478
E-mail: appl@appl.org
Website: www.appl.org

Founded: 1977
Membership: 1–100
Scope: National
Description: The Association of Partners for Public Lands (APPL) is a membership organization of not-for-profit partners who support the interpretive mission of our nation's parks, forests, open spaces and historic places. APPL's membership of 75 interpretive associations and friends groups serve nearly 600 public lands sites throughout the nation. Through education, information, and representation, APPL promotes the vitality of its members and their programs of service and support.
Publication(s): Newswire, Cooperating Association Directory
Keyword(s): Public Lands/Greenspace, Recreation/Ecotourism
Contact(s):
Donna Asbury, Executive Director; 2401 Blueridge Avenue, Suite 303, Wheaton, MD 20902; 301-946-9475; Fax: 301-946-9478; dasbury@appl.org
Nancy Kotz, Member Services Coordinator; 301-946-9475; Fax: 301-946-9478; nkotz@appl.org
Amy Matthews, Program Associate; 301-946-9475; Fax: 301-946-9478; amatthews@appl.org
Krista Muddle, Administration and Education Services Coordinator; 301-946-9475; Fax: 301-946-9478; kmuddle@appl.org

ASSOCIATION OF STATE AND TERRITORIAL HEALTH OFFICIALS
1275 K St., NW, Suite 800
Washington, DC 20005 United States
Phone: 202-371-9090   Fax: 202-371-9797
E-mail: enviornmentalhealth@astho.org
Website: www.astho.org

Founded: 1941
Scope: National
Description: ASTHO represents the directors of public health in each of the 50 states, the District of Columbia, and the U.S.

Territories. Its purpose is to formulate and influence through collective action the establishment of sound national public health policy. ASTHO also assists and serves state health agencies in the development and implementation of state programs and policies in advancing the public health and prevention of disease.

Publication(s): Tobacco-Free Press, ASTHO Report, Environmental Health News

Keyword(s): Public Health

Contact(s):
George Hardy, Executive Director; 202-371-9090; Fax: 202-371-9797

ATLANTIC CENTER FOR THE ENVIRONMENT
NEW ENGLAND OFFICE
P.O. Box 217
Montpelier, VT 5602 United States
Phone: 802-229-0707   Fax: 802-223-3593
Website: www.qlf.org
Membership: 1–100
Scope: Regional
Publication(s): Compass

Contact(s):
Thomas Horn, Vice President

ATLANTIC CENTER FOR THE ENVIRONMENT
QUEBEC-LABRADOR FOUNDATION
CANADA
1253 McGill College Ave., Suite 680
Montreal, H3B 2Y5 Quebec Canada
Phone: 514-395-6020   Fax: 514-395-4505
E-mail: montreal@qlf.org
Website: www.qlf.org
Scope: Local, Regional, National, International
Description: The mission of QLF Atlantic Center for the Environment is to: Support the rural communities and environment of eastern Canada and New England with special emphasis on encouraging education and leadership in young people. Create models for stewardship of natural resources and cultural heritage that can be applied worldwide.
Publication(s): Compass

Contact(s):
Christine Diguer, Staff; 514-395-6020; Fax: 514-395-4505; montreal@qlf.org

ATLANTIC CENTER FOR THE ENVIRONMENT
QUEBEC-LABRADOR FOUNDATION
QLF
55 S. Main St.
Ipswich, MA 01938-2396 United States
Phone: 978-356-0038   Fax: 978-356-7322
E-mail: atlantic@qlf.org
Website: www.qlf.org
Membership: 1–100
Scope: Local, Regional, International
Description: A regional community based conservation organization promoting public involvement in resource management. The mission of QLF Atlantic Center for the Environment is to: 1) Support the rural communities and environment of eastern Canada and New England with special emphasis on encouraging education and leadership in young people, and 2) Create models for stewardship of natural resources and cultural heritage that can be applied worldwide.
Publication(s): Compass
Keyword(s): Agriculture/Farming, Development/Developing Countries, Ecosystems (precious), Energy, Forests/Forestry, Land Issues, Oceans/Coasts/Beaches, Pollution (general), Public Lands/Greenspace, Recreation/Ecotourism, Reduce/Reuse/Recycle, Sprawl/Urban Planning

Contact(s):
Lawrence Morris, President
Jessica Brown, Vice President for International Programs
Thomas Horn, Senior Vice President; P.O. Box 217, Montpelier, VT 05602; 802-229-0707; Fax: 802-223-3593
Brent Mitchell, Director, Stewardship; 978-356-0038; ext. 408; Fax: 978-356-7322; brentmitchell@qlf.org
Linda Mitton, Administrative Assistant

ATLANTIC SALMON FEDERATION
ASF
International Headquarters, P.O. Box 5200
P. O. Box 5200
St. Andrews, E5B 3S8 New Brunswick Canada
Phone: 506-529-4581   Fax: 506-529-4438
E-mail: asf@nbnet.nb.ca
Website: www.asf.ca
Founded: 1982
Membership: 1,001–10,000
Scope: Local, State, Regional, National, International
Description: ASF, the largest international, nonprofit organization dedicated to conserving and managing the wild Atlantic salmon and its habitat, was established when two leading salmon groups, The Atlantic Salmon Association and The International Atlantic Salmon Foundation, consolidated. ASF programs are directed toward research, conservation, education, and international cooperation. ASF supports a network of 7 regional councils and 150 affiliates throughout the Atlantic salmon's North American range.
Publication(s): Atlantic Salmon Journal, The
Keyword(s): Agriculture/Farming, Climate Change, Ecosystems (precious), Energy, Forests/Forestry, Land Issues, Oceans/Coasts/Beaches, Pollution (general), Recreation/Ecotourism, Reduce/Reuse/Recycle, Water Habitats & Quality, Wildlife & Species

Contact(s):
Bill Taylor, President
Robert Beatty, Vice President of Development; 506-529-1031; rbeatty@nbnet.nb.ca
Sue Scott, Vice President, Communications; 506-529-1027; policy@nbnet.nb.ca
Frederick Whoriskey, Vice President, Research and Environment; 506-529-1039; asfres@nbnet.nb.ca
Charles Cusson, Director of Quebec Programs; Atlantic Salmon Federation, 1253 McGill College Ave., Bureau 680, Montreal, Quebec H3B 2Y5; 514-871-9660; fsa-asf-quebec@globetrotter.net
Andrew Goode, Director, U.S. Programs; 207-725-2833; goodeasf@blazenetme.net
Bill Mallory, Controller; 506-529-1075; wmallory@nbnet.nb.ca
Donald O'Brien, Chairman of New York Office; Milbank, Tweed, Hadley, and McCloy, One Chase Manhattan Plaza, 54th Floor, New York, NY 10005-1413; 212-530-5818
Martin Silverstone, Editor; P.O. Box 5200, St. Andrews, New Brunswick E5B 3S8; 506-529-4581; silverstone@nb.aibn.com

ATLANTIC STATES LEGAL FOUNDATION
658 W. Onondaga St.
Syracuse, NY 13204-3757 United States
Phone: 315-475-1170   Fax: 315-475-6719
E-mail: atlantic.states@aslf.org
Website: www.aslf.org
Founded: 1982
Membership: 101–1,000
Scope: Local, State, Regional, National, International
Description: Atlantic States Legal Foundation, Inc., enforces environmental laws, engages in public education, conducts research and promotes environmental justice for the economically disadvantaged and people of color.
Publication(s): Superfund Review, Onondaga Lake Review, quarterly newsletter

Keyword(s): Agriculture/Farming, Development/Developing Countries, Ecosystems (precious), Ethics/Environmental Justice, Land Issues, Oceans/Coasts/Beaches, Pollution (general), Public Health, Recreation/Ecotourism, Reduce/Reuse/Recycle, Water Habitats & Quality

Contact(s):
Samuel Sage, Senior Scientist

AUDUBON INTERNATIONAL
Headquarters, 46 Rarick Rd.
Selkirk, NY 12158 United States
Phone: 518-767-9051   Fax: 518-767-9076
E-mail: acss@audubonintl.org
Website: www.audubonintl.org

Founded: 1987
Membership: 1,001–10,000
Scope: International
Description: Audubon International is an environmental organization dedicated to improving the quality of the environment for the benefit of people, wildlife, and the natural systems that support life where people live, work, and play.
Publication(s): Guides to Environmental Stewardship, Landscape Restoration Handbook, Managing Wildlife Habitat on Golf Courses, Stewardship News, Audubon Cooperative Sanctuary System
Keyword(s): Agriculture/Farming, Development/Developing Countries, Ecosystems (precious), Energy, Land Issues, Pollution (general), Public Lands/Greenspace, Recreation/Ecotourism, Reduce/Reuse/Recycle, Sprawl/Urban Planning, Water Habitats & Quality, Wildlife & Species

Contact(s):
Kevin Fletcher, Director of Programs and Administration; 518-767-9051; ext. 26; Fax: 518-767-9076; kfletcher@audubonintl.org
Jean Mackay, Director of Educational Services; 518-767-9051; ext. 13; Fax: 518-767-9076; jmackay@audubonintl.org
Nancy Richardson, Director of Audubon Signature Program; Audubon Signature Program, 230 Second Street, Henderson, KY 42420; 270-869-9419; Fax: 270-869-9956; nrichardson@audubonintl.org
Miles Smart, Director of Environmental Planning; Environmental Planning Department, P.O. Box 1226, Cary, NC 27515; 919-380-9640; bsmart@audubonintl.org
Lawrence Woolbright, Director of Research; Research Department, P.O. Box 170, Ballston Spa, NY 12020; 518-885-7819; lwoolbright@audubonintl.org
Joellen Zeh, Program Manager; 518-767-9051; ext. 14; Fax: 518-767-9076; jzeh@audubonintl.org
Peter Bronski, Staff Ecologist; 518-767-9051; ext. 24; Fax: 518-767-9076; pbronski@audubonintl.org

AUDUBON NATURALIST SOCIETY OF THE CENTRAL ATLANTIC STATES
8940 Jones Mill Rd.
Chevy Chase, MD 20815 United States
Phone: 301-652-9188   Fax: 301-951-7179
E-mail: hq@audubonnaturalist.org
Website: www.audubonnaturalist.org

Founded: 1897
Scope: Regional
Description: One of the original independent Audubon societies active in environmental education, conservation issues, sanctuaries, and natural science studies in the greater Washington metropolitan area for 100 years. The ANS is headquartered at Woodend, a 40-acre Nature Preserve in suburban Maryland.
Publication(s): Audubon Naturalist News, Environmental Education and Conservation Brochure
Keyword(s): Development/Developing Countries, Public Lands/Greenspace, Water Habitats & Quality, Wildlife & Species

Contact(s):
Neal Fitzpatrick, Director of Conservation
Mike Nelson, Executive Director
Muriel Robinson, Manager of Accounting
Leslie Cronin, Editor
Tara Fuad, Volunteer Coordinator
Regina Sakaria, Volunteer Coordinator

Description: The focus of The Audubon Society of New State, Inc. (ASNY) is on the protection of water and watersheds, the protection of wildlife and wildlife habitat, and the education of people throughout the state.
Eugenia Marks, Research, Advocacy & Publications Director; 401-949-5454; emarks@asri.org
Lee Schisler, Executive Director; 401-949-5454
Lawrence Taft, Director of Properties and Acquistions; 401-949-5454; Fax: 401-949-5788; ltaft@asri.org
Sharon Cresci, Development Assistant
Joseph Dimase, Secretary
Frank Sciuto, Treasurer
Doris Thorpe, Membership Secretary
Ken Weber, Editor

B

BACK COUNTRY LAND TRUST
338 West Lexington
Suite 204
El Cajon, CA 92020 United States
Phone: 619-590-2258   Fax: 619-590-2248
E-mail: noelle@bclt.org
Website: www.bclt.org

Founded: 1990
Membership: 101–1,000
Scope: Regional
Description: Conserving and managing rare habitat in eastern San Diego County.

Contact(s):
Don Hohimer, President; 619-590-2258; Fax: 619-590-2248; don@bclt.org
Noelle Collins, Executive Director; 619-590-2258; Fax: 619-590-2248; noelle@bclt.org

BAMA BACKPADDLERS ASSOCIATION
307 Madison Pl.
Trussville, AL 35173 United States
Phone: 205-592-2117
E-mail: backpaddlers@aol.com
Website: members.aol.com/backpaddlers/

Founded: 1978
Scope: State
Description: Dedicated to promoting recreation, conservation, education and safety on Alabama's waterways.
Publication(s): As the Eddy Turns
Keyword(s): Development/Developing Countries, Oceans/Coasts/Beaches, Recreation/Ecotourism, Reduce/Reuse/Recycle, Water Habitats & Quality

Contact(s):
Renee Clark, President
Nancy Cate, Treasurer
Betty Harrison, Newsletter; kayakbba@aol.com
Bob Shepard, Trip Coordinator
Jennifer Taylor, Conservation; 205-951-0320; cahabasierra@aol.com

BARRIER ISLAND TRUST, INC.
P.O. Box 37310
Tallahassee, FL 32315 United States
Phone: 850-697-4721   Fax: 203-629-2453
Website: www.bit.org

Founded: 1989
Scope: State

Description: To preserve the natural resources of Florida's barrier islands, initially focusing on Dog Island and Apalachicola Bay, hold and manage barrier island property to preserve it in its natural state, promote research on barrier island ecology and translate research into educational programs and effective policies for protection of barrier islands.
Keyword(s): Land Issues, Oceans/Coasts/Beaches
Contact(s):
  Leroy Collins, Board of Trustee President; 16 Davis Blvd. Suite 12, Tampa, FL 33606; 813-259-9484
  Dianne Mellon, Board of Trustee Vice President; 1515 Country Club, Tallahassee, FL 32301; 850-877-3942
  Guy Smith, Board of Trustee Chair; 352 North St., Greenwich, CT 06830; 203-629-1264
  Mitchell Smith, Board of Trustee Treasurer; P.O. Box 1912, Albany, GA 31702

BAT CONSERVATION INTERNATIONAL
P.O. Box 162603
Austin, TX 78716 United States
Phone: 512-327-9721   Fax: 512-327-9724
E-mail: batinfo@batcon.org
Website: www.batcon.org
Founded: 1982
Membership: 10,001–100,000
Scope: Local, State, Regional, National, International
Description: A nonprofit organization with 14,000 members in 72 countries. BCI's purpose is to document and publicize the values and conservation needs of bats, to promote bat conservation projects, and to assist with management initiatives worldwide.
Publication(s): Catalog of educational products, BATS Magazine
Keyword(s): Agriculture/Farming, Ecosystems (precious), Forests/Forestry, Public Health, Recreation/Ecotourism, Wildlife & Species
Contact(s):
  Merlin Tuttle, Founder and President
  Bob Benson, Public Information Manager and Bracken Campaign Manager; bbenson@batcon.org

BEAR SPRINGS BLOSSOM NATURE CONSERVATION GROUP INC.
BSBNCG
P.O. Box 63295
949 West Bear Springs Road
Pipe Creek, TX 78063 United States
Phone: 830-510-4084
E-mail: bearspringsblossom@yahoo.com
Website: geocities.com/bearspringsblossom/
Founded: 2002
Membership: 101–1,000
Scope: International
Description: We are dedicated to education about the environment and the restoration of nature habitats.
Publication(s): Newsletter
Keyword(s): Agriculture/Farming, Air Quality/Atmosphere, Climate Change, Ecosystems (precious), Energy, Pollution (general), Recreation/Ecotourism, Reduce/Reuse/Recycle
Contact(s):
  Peter Bonenberger, President; 830-510-4084; bearsprings-blossom@yahoo.com

BERKSHIRE-LITCHFIELD ENVIRONMENTAL COUNCIL, INC.
P.O. Box 552
Lakeville, CT 6039 United States
Phone: 203-435-2004
Founded: 1970
Scope: State
Description: Primarily concerned with energy, invasive transportation, and land use issues in the southern Berkshires and Litchfield Hills. Offers public programs and environmental education for all ages.
Publication(s): BLEC News
Keyword(s): Agriculture/Farming, Land Issues, Wildlife & Species
Contact(s):
  Starling Childs, President; 203-542-5569
  Nic Osborn, Vice President
  Judy Thomas, Executive Director
  Peter Dolan, Treasurer
  William Morrill, Counsel; datibbetts@annapolis.net
  Ellery Sinclair, Secretary

BEYOND PESTICIDES
NATIONAL COALITION AGAINST THE MISUSE OF PESTICIDES (NCAMP)
701 E St., SE, Suite 200
Washington, DC 20003 United States
Phone: 202-543-5450   Fax: 202-543-4791
E-mail: info@beyondpesticides.org
Website: www.beyondpesticides.org
Founded: 1981
Membership: 1,001–10,000
Scope: National
Description: Nonprofit membership organization committed to assisting individuals, organizations, and communities with useful information on pesticides and their alternatives. NCAMP's information clearinghouse provides material on a wide range of both agricultural and urban issues concerning protection of children, workers' safety, food safety, lawn care safety, groundwater problems, and alternatives to pesticides, as well as legislation.
Publication(s): Bi-monthly newsletter, Pesticides and You Newsletter (Quarterly), Safety at Home: A Guide to the Hazards of Lawn and Garden Pesticides and Safer Ways to Manage Pests, Poison Poles: Their Toxic Trial and the Safer Alternatives, Beyond Pesticides, NCAMP's Technical Report (Monthly)
Keyword(s): Agriculture/Farming, Air Quality/Atmosphere, Executive/Legislative/Judicial Reform, Pollution (general), Public Health, Wildlife & Species
Contact(s):
  Jay Feldman, Executive Director; 202-453-5450; info@beyondpesticides.org
  Becky Crouse, Information Coordinator; bcrouse@beyondpesticides.org
  John Kepner, Program Associate; jkepner@beyondpesticides.org
  Toni Nunes, Special Projects Director; tnunes@beyondpesticides.org
  Kagan Owens, Program Director; 202-545-5450; Fax: 202-543-4791; kowens@beyondpesticides.org
  Meghan Taylor, Public Education Associate; mtaylor@beyondpesticides.org

BIG BEND NATURAL HISTORY ASSOCIATION
P.O. Box 196
Big Bend National Park, TX 79834 United States
Phone: 432-477-2236   Fax: 432-477-2234
E-mail: bbnha@nps.gov
Website: www.bigbendbookstore.org
Founded: 1956
Membership: 101–1,000
Scope: National
Description: A private nonprofit organization whose main objectives are to facilitate popular interpretation of the scenic, scientific and historical values of Big Bend, and to encourage research related to those values. To accomplish these goals, the association is authorized by the National Park Service to publish, print, or otherwise provide books, maps, and illustra-

tive material on the Big Bend region and to sponsor a Big Bend seminar program.

Publication(s): Big Bend Paisano

Keyword(s): Agriculture/Farming, Public Lands/Greenspace, Wildlife & Species

Contact(s):
Mike Boren, Executive Director
Rob Dunagan, Chairman; 915-336-5274
Thomas Vandenberg, Editor

BILLFISH FOUNDATION, THE
2161 E Commercial Blvd. 2nd Fl.
Ft. Lauderdale, FL 33308 United States
Phone: 954-938-0150   Fax: 954-938-5311
E-mail: tbf@billfish.org
Website: www.billfish.org
Membership: 10,001–100,000
Scope: International
Description: The Billfish Foundation is a nonprofit organization dedicated to the conservation of billfish worldwide through scientific research, education, and advocacy. Through scientific, economic and conservation decisions provided through research, TBF strives for sound and constructive measures to recover overfished stocks.

Publication(s): Billfish, Spearfish, TBF News, Tag & Brag - Quarterly Newsletter

Keyword(s): Recreation/Ecotourism, Wildlife & Species

Contact(s):
Ellen Peel, President
Paxson Offield, Treasurer of Trustees
Hal Prewitt, Vice Chairman
Winthrop Rockefeller, Chairman of Trustees
Ralph Vicente, Vice Chairman of Trustees

BIODIVERSITY CONSERVATION ALLIANCE
P.O. Box 1512
Laramie, WY 82073 United States
Phone: 307-742-7978   Fax: 307-742-7989
E-mail: ebonds@voiceforthewild.org
Website: www.voiceforthewild.org
Founded: 1989
Membership: 101–1,000
Scope: Local, State, Regional
Description: BCA is a nonprofit group working to protect and restore wild places, wildlife, and habitats in Wyoming and surrounding states. We concentrate our efforts on the Red Desert, Medicine Bow National Forest, Thunder Basin National Grassland, and other public lands of Wyoming as well as the Black Hills of South Dakota. We started in 1989 as Friends of the Bow, a local group working to protect the natural values of the Medicine Bow National Forest in southeastern Wyoming.

Keyword(s): Ecosystems (precious), Energy, Executive/Legislative/Judicial Reform, Forests/Forestry, Land Issues, Public Lands/Greenspace, Water Habitats & Quality, Wildlife & Species

BIODIVERSITY NORTHWEST
4649 Sunnyside Avenue North #321
Seattle, WA 98103 United States
Phone: 206-545-3734
E-mail: info@biodiversitynw.org
Website: www.biodiversitynw.org
Founded: 1993
Scope: Local, State, Regional
Description: Our mission is to protect and restore the ecological integrity of forests in the Pacific Northwest.

BIO-INTEGRAL RESOURCE CENTER
P.O. Box 7414
Berkeley, CA 94707 United States
Phone: 510-524-2567   Fax: 510-524-1758
E-mail: birc@igc.org
Website: www.birc.org
Founded: 1979
Membership: 1,001–10,000
Scope: International
Description: A nonprofit educational organization dedicated to providing information on least-toxic pest control.

Publication(s): Common Sense Pest Control Quarterly, Least-toxic Pest Management

Keyword(s): Agriculture/Farming, Pollution (general), Reduce/Reuse/Recycle, Wildlife & Species

Contact(s):
William Quarles, Executive Director, Managing Editor of Publications
Jennifer Bates, Business Manager

BIOSIS
2001 Market Street
Suite 700
Philadelphia, PA 19103 United States
Phone: 800-523-4806   Fax: 215-587-2016
E-mail: info@biosis.org
Website: www.biosis.org
Scope: Local, State, Regional, National, International
Description: Established in 1926, BIOSIS' mission is to facilitate understanding of the living world by helping researchers, educators, students and others to access information relevant to the life sciences. As the world's largest life sciences indexing and abstracting service, BIOSIS produces the BIOSIS Previews family of products, including Biological Abstracts, and jointly publishes Zoological Record with the Zoological Society of London.

Publication(s): Biosis Previews, Toxline

Keyword(s): Agriculture/Farming, Climate Change, Development/Developing Countries, Ecosystems (precious), Forests/Forestry, Oceans/Coasts/Beaches, Pollution (general), Population, Public Health, Water Habitats & Quality, Wildlife & Species

Contact(s):
Marisa Westcott, Director of Marketing; mwestcott@biosis.org

BIOSPHERE EXPEDITIONS
Sprat's Water
nr Carlton Colville
The Broads National Park
Suffolk, NR33 8BP United Kingdom
Phone: 0044-1502-583085   Fax: 0044-1502-587414
E-mail: info@biosphere-expeditions.org
Website: www.biosphere-expeditions.org
Founded: 1999
Scope: International
Description: Award-winning, non-profit wildlife conservation organisation with world-wide expeditions open to all. No special skills (biological or otherwise) required to join and no age limits whatsoever. You can join for anything from two weeks to several months and at least two-thirds of your expedition contribution will go directly into the conservation project. We always work with local scientists and people from the host country, teams are small and an expedition leader will be by your side.

Publication(s): Expedition reports

Keyword(s): Recreation/Ecotourism, Wildlife & Species

Contact(s):
Matthias Hammer, Dr.; 0044-1502-583085; Fax: 0044-1502-587414; info@biosphere-expeditions.org

BIRDLIFE INTERNATIONAL
Canada Nature Federation
1 Nicholas St., Ste. 606
Ottawa, KIN 7B7 Ontario Canada
Phone: 613-562-3947 Fax: 613-562-3371
E-mail: cnf@cnf.ca
Website: www.cnf.ca
Membership: 10,001–100,000
Scope: National
Description: Protection of birds and their habitats in Canada, in their winter quarters in North and South America, and off Canada's coasts are among major concerns.
Publication(s): Nature Matters-Newsletter, Nature Canada
Keyword(s): Land Issues, Public Lands/Greenspace, Reduce/Reuse/Recycle, Wildlife & Species
Contact(s):
  Michael Bradstreet, Contact; Bird Studies Canada, Box 160, Port Rowan, Ontario N0E 1M0; 519-586-3531; Fax: 519-586-3532
  Caroline Schultz, Contact

BIRDS PROTECTION AND STUDY SOCIETY OF VOJVODINA
Drustvo za zastitu i proucavanje ptica Vojvodina
Radnicka 20, 21000 Novi Sad, Yugoslavia
Phone: 381-21-616344 Fax: 381-21-616252
E-mail: zzpsns@EUnet.yu
Founded: 1988
Membership: 1–100
Scope: Regional, National
Description: Birds Protection and Study Society of Vojvodina aims to conserve and protect birds and their habitats. With about 100 members, the society has conducted many research projects, one of the most recent being the survey of Serbian heronries in 1998 (when there were about 7,500 breeding pairs of herons and cormorants dispersed in about 60 heronries). Membership fee includes a free copy of annual journal Ciconia with papers and notes on birds and reports of rarities and interesting sightings.
Publication(s): Ciconia
Keyword(s): Wildlife & Species

BLUE GOOSE ALLIANCE
2988 St. Johns Blvd.
Jacksonville Beach, FL 32250 United States
Phone: 904-241-1007
E-mail: DGAstuff@aol.com
Website: www.bluegoosealliance.org
Founded: 2001
Scope: National
Description: The mission of the Blue Goose Alliance is to promote the establishment of the National Wildlife Refuge System as a separate agency within the Department of the Interior.
Keyword(s): Public Lands/Greenspace
Contact(s):
  Noreen Clough, President; 4007 Wood Acres Ct., Duluth, GA 30096

BOONE AND CROCKETT CLUB
250 Station Dr.
Missoula, MT 59801 United States
Phone: 406-542-1888 Fax: 406-542-0784
E-mail: bcclub@boone-crockett.org
Website: www.boone-crockett.org
Founded: 1887
Membership: 1,001–10,000
Scope: National, International
Description: A 501 (c) (3) organization. Established by Theodore Roosevelt and other concerned sportsmen to promote hunting ethics, foster the concept of Fair Chase, and help establish wildlife conservation practices which led to the recovery of big game animals in North America. The Club documents the records of North American big game and exhibits its National Collection of Heads and Horns in Cody, WY.
Publication(s): Records of North American Big Game, Return of Royalty, Records of North American Whitetail Deer, An American Crusade for Wildlife, World's Record Calendar, Fair Chase
Keyword(s): Land Issues, Recreation/Ecotourism, Wildlife & Species
Contact(s):
  Robert Model, President
  F.R. Daily, First Vice President
  Thomas Price, Vice President
  George Bettas, Executive Director; 406-542-1888
  Julie Houk, Director of Publications; 406-542-1888
  Jack Reneau, Director of North American Big Game Records; 406-542-1888
  Eldon "Buck" Buckner, Records of North American Big Game Committee
  Robert Hanson, Secretary
  Joseph Ostervich, Treasurer

BOONE AND CROCKETT FOUNDATION
250 Station Dr.
Missoula, MT 59801 United States
Phone: 406-542-1888 Fax: 406-542-0784
E-mail: bcclub@boone-crockett.org
Website: www.boone-crockett.org
Founded: 1986
Scope: National
Description: The BCF owns and operates the 6,000 acre Theodore Roosevelt Memorial Ranch near Dupuyer, MT, as a working cattle ranch for research, education and demonstration. BCF supports natural resource conservation research, education, and demonstration primarily through the Boone and Crockett wildlife conservation program in conjunction with the University of Montana.
Publication(s): Grizzly Bears of Montana, Fair Chase Magazine
Keyword(s): Agriculture/Farming, Development/Developing Countries, Land Issues, Public Lands/Greenspace, Recreation/Ecotourism, Reduce/Reuse/Recycle
Contact(s):
  Robert Model, President
  Lisa Flowers, Conservation Education Program Manager; 406-472-3311
  John Rappold, TRMR Manager; 406-472-3380
  George Bettas, Executive Director; 406-542-1888; bcclub@boone-crockett.org
  Robert Hanson, Secretary
  Jack Thomas, Professor of Wildlife Conservation; 406-243-5566

BORDER ECOLOGY PROJECT (BEP)
Drawer CP
Bisbee, AZ 85603 United States
Phone: 520-432-7456 Fax: 520-432-7473
E-mail: bep@primenet.com
Website: www.borderep.org
Founded: 1983
Scope: National
Description: BEP advocates for solutions to environmental problems along the U.S. and Mexico border. Areas of focus include Right-to-Know, environmental pollution, international trade, mining, hazardous materials trucking, and bi-national environmental health issues including lupus.
Publication(s): Environmental Protection within the Mexican Mining Sector, Environmental and Health Conditions in the Interior of Mexico
Keyword(s): Air Quality/Atmosphere, Pollution (general), Reduce/Reuse/Recycle, Water Habitats & Quality

Contact(s):
  Dick Kamp, Director
  A. Hotaling, Coordinator

BORN FREE FOUNDATION
3 Grove House
Foundry Lane
Horsham, RG13 5PL United Kingdom
Phone: 0044-1403-240170   Fax: 0044-1403-327838
E-mail: wildlife@bornfree.org.uk
Website: www.bornfree.org.uk

Founded: 1984
Membership: 1,001–10,000
Scope: International
Description: The Born Free Foundation campaigns for the protection and conservation of animals in their natural habitat and against the keeping of animals in zoos and circuses and as exotic pets. Born Free, inspired by the true story of Elsa the lioness, believes that individuals matter. Born Free stands for compassion and a commitment to encourage a more caring world.
Keyword(s): Oceans/Coasts/Beaches, Recreation/Ecotourism, Wildlife & Species
Contact(s):
  Will Travers, CEO

BOTANICAL CLUB OF WISCONSIN
c/o Wisconsin Academy of Science, Arts, and Letters,
1922 University Ave.
Madison, WI 53705 United States
Phone: 608-262-5489   Fax: 608-265-2993

Founded: 1969
Membership: 101–1,000
Scope: State, Regional
Description: Botanical Club of Wisconsin promotes preservation of Wisconsin's native plants and educates the public as to the value of plants. The Club also fosters research on plant biology and provides a means for fellowship and information exchange.
Publication(s): The Bulletin of the Botanical Club of Wisconsin, Wisconsin Flora
Keyword(s): Public Lands/Greenspace, Wildlife & Species
Contact(s):
  Emmet Judziewicz, President; 715-346-4248; Emmet.Judziewicz@uwsp.edu
  James Bennett, Vice President; 608-262-5489; Fax: 608-265-2993; jpbennet@facstaff.wisc.edu
  Edward Glover, Treasurer; 608-437-4578; glover@oncology.wisc.edu

BOTANICAL SOCIETY OF WESTERN PENNSYLVANIA
279 Orr Rd
West Newton, PA 15089 United States
Phone: 724-872-5232
E-mail: yoree@sgi.net
Website: home.kiski.net/~speedy/b.html

Founded: 1886
Membership: 101–1,000
Scope: Local
Description: Botanical Society of Western Pennsylvania brings together those who are interested in botany and encourages the study of botany and knowledge of plants.
Publication(s): Wildflowers of Pennsylvania
Keyword(s): Agriculture/Farming, Reduce/Reuse/Recycle, Wildlife & Species
Contact(s):
  Mary Haywood, President; 412-578-6175
  Walter Gardill, Treasurer; 412-364-5308
  Loree Speedy, Secretary

BOUNTY INFORMATION SERVICE
WILDLIFE BOUNTY INFORMATION SERVICE
4849 E. St. Charles Rd.
Columbia, MO 65201 United States
Phone: 573-474-6967
E-mail: Claun01@aol.com

Founded: 1966
Membership: 101–1,000
Scope: National, International
Description: Promotes the removal of bounties in North America by publishing Bounty News and studies of the bounty system and by coordinating activities and legal aspects.
Publication(s): A Guide to the Removal of Bounties, Bounty News, A History of Wildlife Bounties
Keyword(s): Wildlife & Species
Contact(s):
  H. Laun, Director and Editor

BOY SCOUTS OF AMERICA
National Office, P.O. Box 152079
1325 West Walnut Hill Ln.
Irving, TX 75015-2079 United States
Phone: 972-580-2000   Fax: 972-580-2399
Website: www.scouting.org

Founded: 1910
Membership: 1,000,001 +
Scope: National
Description: Boy Scouts of America (BSA) was chartered by Congress in 1916 to provide an educational program for boys and young adults that builds character and develops responsibility, citizenship, and personal fitness. Community groups with goals compatible with BSA receive national charters to use the Scouting program as part of their own youth work.
Keyword(s): Recreation/Ecotourism
Contact(s):
  Milton Ward, President
  David Bates, Conservation Director
  Raymond Blackwell, Regional Executive; P.O. Box 3085, Naperville, IL 60566-7085; 630-983-6730
  Kenneth Connelly, Regional Executive of Northeast Region; P.O. Box 268, Jamesburg, NJ 08831-0268; 609-655-9600
  John Cushman, Treasurer
  Erik Nystrom, Regional Executive; P. O. Box 22019, Tempe, AZ 85285-2019
  Francis Olmstead, Assistant Treasurer
  Roy Williams, Chief Scout Executive

BRANDYWINE CONSERVANCY INC.
U.S. 1 and Creek Rd
P.O. Box 141
Chadds Ford, PA 19317 United States
Phone: 610-388-2700   Fax: 610-388-1575
E-mail: emc@brandywine.org
Website: www.brandywineconservancy.org

Founded: 1967
Scope: Regional
Description: A nonprofit organization providing model land use and environmental regulations for Pennsylvania municipalities. Brandywine Conservancy provides land, water resources and historic site conservation and management assistance to landowners and conservation organizations, primarily in southeastern Pennsylvania and northern Delaware.
Publication(s): Catalyst, Environmental Management Handbook, Environmental Currents
Keyword(s): Land Issues, Pollution (general), Water Habitats & Quality
Contact(s):
  James Duff, Executive Director
  Kathryn Saterson, Director of Environmental Management Center

Wesley Horner, Associate Director of Municipal Assistance, Environmental Management Center
David Shields, Associate Director of Land Stewardship, Environmental Management Center
John Snook, Associate Director of Design, Environmental Management Center
Halsey Spruance, Public Relations
George Weymouth, Chairman

BRITISH COLUMBIA FIELD ORNITHOLOGISTS
P.O. Box 8059
Victoria, V8W 3R7 British Columbia Canada
Website: birding.bc.ca/bcfo/
Founded: 1991
Scope: Province
Description: To promote the study and enjoyment of birds in British Columbia; to disseminate knowledge and appreciation of birds by means of publications; to foster cooperation between amateur and professional ornithologists; and to promote conservation of birds and their habitats.
Publication(s): British Columbia Birds (journal), BC Birding (newsletter)
Keyword(s): Wildlife & Species
Contact(s):
Tony Greenfield, President; P.O. Box 319, Sechelt, British Columbia V0N 3A0; 250-885-5539
Bryan Gates, Vice President; 3085 Uplands Rd., Victoria, British Columbia V8R 6B3; 250-598-7789
Marilyn Buhler, Editor; 1132 Loenholm Rd., Victoria, British Columbia V8Z 2Z6; 250-744-2521
Andy Buhler, Editor; 1132 Loenholm Rd., Victoria, British Columbia V8Z 2Z6; 250-744-2521
Jim Fliczuck, Treasurer; 3614-1507 Queensbury Ave., Victoria, British Columbia V8P 5M5; 250-656-8066
Martin McNicholl, Editor; 4735 Canada Way, Burnaby, British Columbia V5G 1L3; 250-294-9333

BRITISH COLUMBIA WATERFOWL SOCIETY, THE
5191 Robertson Rd.
Delta, V4K 3N2 British Columbia Canada
Phone: 604-946-6980   Fax: 604-946-6980
Membership: 1,001–10,000
Scope: International
Description: The organization was set in 1963 on federal land leased for 30 years to be opened to the public as a bird viewing area at the mouth of the Fraser River, which supports one of the largest wintering populations of waterfowl in Canada. The organization attempts to promote awareness of all parts of the environment.
Publication(s): Marsh Notes, BirdCheck List
Contact(s):
Jack Bates, President
John Ireland, Manager
James Morrison, Treasurer

BROOKS BIRD CLUB INC., THE
P.O. Box 4077
Wheeling, WV 26003 United States
Phone: 304-233-3174
Website: www.brooksbirdclub.org
Founded: 1932
Scope: National
Description: A nonprofit organization formed to encourage the study and conservation of birds and other phases of natural history. Members in thirty-eight states, Canada, and eight foreign countries. Named in honor of A.B. Brooks, naturalist.
Publication(s): Mail Bag, The, Redstart, The
Keyword(s): Public Lands/Greenspace, Wildlife & Species
Contact(s):
Fred McCullough, President; P.O. Box 4077, Wheeling, WV 26003
Scott Emrick, Treasurer; P.O. Box 4077, Wheeling, WV 26003
Carl Slater, Administrator; P.O. Box 4077, Wheeling, WV 26003

BROTHERHOOD OF THE JUNGLE COCK, INC., THE
P.O. Box 576
Glen Burnie, MD 21061 United States
Phone: 410-761-7727   Fax: 410-553-0575
Membership: 1,001–10,000
Scope: National
Description: Seeks to teach youth the true meaning of conservation. Primary interest is the preservation of American game fishes, placing great emphasis on adult responsibility of personal instruction along those lines.
Keyword(s): Oceans/Coasts/Beaches, Wildlife & Species
Contact(s):
William Simms, President
Bosley Wright, Executive Vice President
M. Day, Treasurer; 706 Orchard Way, Silver Spring, MD 20904
Edward Little, Secretary; 6623 Kenwood Ave., Baltimore, MD 21237; 401-682-4631

BUN-CA
BIOMASS USERS NETWORK - CENTROAMERICA
CENTRAL AMERICA
573-2050
San Pedro Montes de Oca
San Jose, - Costa Rica
Phone: 506-283-8835   Fax: 506-283-8845
E-mail: bun-ca@bun-ca.org
Website: www.bun-ca.org
Founded: 1985
Scope: International
Description: To advance rural economic development in Third World countries in an environmentally sound manner, through the innovative production and efficient use of natural resources. Work areas on Renewable Energy, Energy Efficiency and Sustainable Agriculture.
Publication(s): Various on Sustainable Agriculture, Various on Energy Efficiency, Off-grid Manual, Carbon Reduction Guide, Renewable Energy Technical Publications
Keyword(s): Agriculture/Farming, Climate Change, Development/Developing Countries, Energy, Land Issues, Wildlife & Species
Contact(s):
José Ma. Blanco, Regional Director; 506-283-8835; ext. 102; Fax: 506-283-8045; jblanco@bun-ca.org
Kathya Fajardo, Sustainable Agriculture Director; 506-283-8835; ext. 105; Fax: 506-283-8845; kfajardo@bun-ca.org
Kattia Quirós, Energy Efficiency Director; 506-283-8835; ext. 107; Fax: 506-283-8845; kquiros@bun-ca.org
Leonel Umaña, Renewable Energy Director; 506-283-8835; ext. 111; Fax: 506-283-8845; lumana@bun-ca.org

C

C.A.S.T. FOR KIDS FOUNDATION
296 Southwest 43rd Street
Renton, WA 98055 United States
Phone: 425-251-3214   Fax: 425-251-3272
E-mail: castforkids@msn.com
Website: castforkids.org
Founded: 1991
Scope: National
Description: A national, non-profit organization that provides outdoor recreation opportunities and education to disabled and disadvantaged children through the sport of fishing.
Publication(s): Catch A Special Thrill
Keyword(s): Recreation/Ecotourism

Contact(s):
Patrick McBride, President; 1804 136th Place, N.E., #1, Redmond, WA 98005; 425-644-1446; Fax: 425-644-1921; office@gmsarch.com
Wayne Deason, Vice President; 786 Chimney Creek Road, Golden, CO 80401; 303-445-2781; Fax: 303-445-6464; wdeason@do.usbr.gov
Jim Owens, Executive Director; 425-251-3214; Fax: 425-251-3272; jowens@castforkids.org
Karen Megorden, Secretary/Treasurer; 4470 E. Columbia Road, Meridian, ID 83642; 208-378-5053; Fax: 208-378-5056; kmegorden@pn.usbr.gov

CADDO LAKE INSTITUTE, INC.
P.O. Box 2710
Aspen, CO 81612 United States
Phone: 970-925-2710   Fax: 970-923-4245
E-mail: dks@sopris.net
Website: www.caddolakeinstitute.org

Founded: 1993
Scope: Local
Description: A non-profit organization whose purpose is environmental awareness. The program director is based near Caddo Lake, Texas. The director will coordinate college programs. Students are paid a stipend to collect samples and return to the student's laboratory for analysis; will also give seminars at secondary schools, all to promote environmental awareness.
Publication(s): See publication web site
Keyword(s): Water Habitats & Quality
Contact(s):
Dwight Shellman, President; dks@sopris.net
Sara Kneipp, Education Director; sjkneipp@aol.com

CALCASIEU PARISH ANIMAL CONTROL AND PROTECTION DEPARTMENT
5500A Swift Plant Rd.
Lake Charles, LA 70615 United States
Phone: 337-439-8879   Fax: 337-437-3343
Website: cpac.cppj.net

Scope: State
Description: Regional branch of Elsa Wild Animal Appeal; concerned with wildlife matters, educational programs, liaison with other wildlife and governmental groups for the betterment of natural environment and wildlife protection; establishes local volunteer corps to implement programs in conjunction with the Calcasieu Parish Animal Control and Protection Department; and participates in Wildlife Rehabilitation Programs with Heck Haven and Westlake Bird Sanctuary.
Keyword(s): Reduce/Reuse/Recycle, Wildlife & Species
Contact(s):
David Marcantel, Operations Supervisor

CALIFORNIA ACADEMY OF SCIENCES
55 Concourse Dr.
Golden Gate Park
San Francisco, CA 94118 United States
Phone: 415-221-5100   Fax: 415-750-7346
Website: www.calacademy.org

Founded: 1853
Scope: State
Description: The Academy of Sciences' goal is the exploration and interpretation of natural history. Maintains research collections and operates a museum-aquarium-planetarium complex to which one and one-half million visitors come each year.
Publication(s): Academy Newsletter, Occasional Papers, Proceedings, California Wild
Keyword(s): Oceans/Coasts/Beaches, Public Lands/Greenspace, Wildlife & Species

Contact(s):
John Pearse, President
Patrick Kociolek, Director
W. Bingham, Board of Trustees Chairman
Lewis Coleman, Vice Chairman
John Larson, Vice Chairman
Sandra Linder, Secretary

CALIFORNIA ACADEMY OF SCIENCES LIBRARY
Golden Gate Park
San Francisco, CA 94118 United States
Phone: 415-750-7102   Fax: 415-750-7106
E-mail: biodiversity@calacademy.org
Website: www.calacademy.org/research/library/

Founded: 1853
Scope: International
Description: Non-circulating, closed-stack collection open to the public. Reference requests accepted by mail, phone, fax or e-mail. Interlibrary loan requests accepted. Library holdings included in OCLC, University of CA MELVYL on-line catalog and CA Union List of Periodicals.
Contact(s):
Diane T. Sands, Reference Librarian

CALIFORNIA ASSOCIATION OF RESOURCE CONSERVATION DISTRICTS
3823 V Street
Suite 3
Sacramento, CA 95817 United States
Phone: 916-457-7904   Fax: 916-457-7934
E-mail: staff@carcd.org
Website: www.carcd.org

Founded: 1945
Membership: 101–1,000
Scope: State
Description: CARCD's mission is to enhance Resource Conservation Districts' effectiveness.
Publication(s): CARCD Newsline, Conservation Express, CCP News
Contact(s):
John Schramel, President; 681 Main St., Greenville, CA 95947; 530-284-7954; Fax: 530-284-6211
Nadine Scott, Vice President; 550 Hoover Street, Oceanside, CA 92054; 760-757-6685
Tom Wehri, Executive Director; 801 K St. Suite 1318, Sacramento, CA 95814; 916-447-7237; Fax: 916-447-2532; carcd@ns.net
Robert Beegle, Secretary-Treasurer; 3911 Yellowstone Ln., El Dorado, CA 95762; 916-852-6691; Fax: 916-852-6693
Donna Thomas, Past President; 760-377-4525; Fax: 760-377-4525

CALIFORNIA BASS FEDERATION
President
21517 Appaloosa Court
Canyon Lake, CA 92587 United States
Phone: 909-244-6320
E-mail: fsh4bss@dellepro.com
Website: www.californiabass.org

Founded: 1989
Membership: 1,001–10,000
Scope: State
Description: An organization of Bassmaster chapters, affiliated with the Bass Anglers Sportsman Society, organized to fight pollution, assist state and national conservation agencies in their efforts, and teach the young people of our country good conservation practice. Dedicated to the realistic conservation of our water resources.
Contact(s):
Gary Bradford, President; 909-244-6320; fsh4bss@dellepro.com

CALIFORNIA INSTITUTE OF PUBLIC AFFAIRS
INTERENVIRONMENT
P.O. Box 189040
Sacramento, CA 95818 United States
Phone: 916-442-2472 Fax: 916-442-2478
E-mail: info@interenvironment.org
Website: www.interenvironment.org

Founded: 1969
Scope: State, National, International
Description: Works to improve policy-making on complex environmental issues in California and internationally through convening, research, publishing, and advice. Current major activities are the World Directory of Environmental Organizations, now online at www.InterEnvironment.org; and an international project on major cities and protected areas, both in cooperation with IUCN - The World Conservation Union.
Publication(s): California Environmental Directory, World Directory of Environmental Organizations
Contact(s):
  Ted Trzyna, President
  Michael Eaton, Senior Associate
  Monty Hempel, Senior Associate
  Daniel Mazmanian, Senior Associate
  John Zierold, Senior Associate
  Julie Didion, Program Coordinator

CALIFORNIA NATIVE PLANT SOCIETY, THE
2707 K Street, Suite 1
Sacramento, CA 95816-5113 United States
Phone: 916-447-2677 Fax: 916-447-2727
E-mail: cnps@cnps.org
Website: www.cnps.org

Founded: 1965
Membership: 1,001–10,000
Scope: State
Description: A statewide nonprofit organization of amateurs and professionals with a common interest in California's native plants. The society, working through its local chapters, seeks to increase understanding of California's native flora and to preserve the rich resource for future generations. Membership is open to all.
Publication(s): Fremontia, Plant Communities, Flora of San Bruno Mountain, Inventory of Rare and Endangered Vascula, California's Changing Landscape, Terrestrial Vegetation of California, Conservation & Management of Rare and Endangered Plants
Keyword(s): Land Issues, Water Habitats & Quality, Wildlife & Species
Contact(s):
  Sue Britting, President; 530-333-2679; Fax: 530-333-9178; britting@innercite.com
  Jim Bishop, Vice President for Administration; 530-538-6761; cjbishop@cnc.net
  Lorrae Fuentes, Vice President for Education; 909-625-8767; Fax: 909-626-7670; lorrae.fuentes@cgu.edu

CALIFORNIA TRAPPERS ASSOCIATION
Attn: Executive Secretary, 99 Poinsettia Gardens Dr.
Ventura, CA 93004 United States
Phone: 805-647-8903 Fax: 805-647-9970

Founded: 1969
Membership: 1,001–10,000
Scope: State
Description: Dedicated to the encouragement of conservation, enhancement, and scientific management of all our natural resources, especially furbearing mammals. Promotes state and federal wildlife projects through volunteer skilled labor and financial contributions. Gives $500 to $1,000 grants each year to college students studying furbearing mammals.
Publication(s): Fur Facts, Legislative Alerts

Keyword(s): Ethics/Environmental Justice, Land Issues, Reduce/Reuse/Recycle, Water Habitats & Quality, Wildlife & Species
Contact(s):
  Keith Carly, President; P.O. Box 73, Elk Creek, CA 95939; 916-968-5038
  John Clark, Vice President; 907 Holmes Flat Rd., Red Crest, CA 95569; 707-722-4259
  Tom Laustalot, Treasurer; 18907 Indian Creek Rd., Fort Jones, CA 96032; 916-468-2228
  Kathy Lynch, Lobbyist; 916-537-7169
  Donald Stehsel, Executive Secretary

CALIFORNIA TROUT, INC.
870 Market St., Suite 1185
San Francisco, CA 94102 United States
Phone: 415-392-8887 Fax: 415-392-8895
E-mail: info@caltrout.org
Website: www.caltrout.org

Founded: 1970
Membership: 1,001–10,000
Scope: State
Description: Statewide organization of anglers dedicated to protection and restoration of wild trout, native steelhead, and their waters in California, and to the creation of high-quality angling adventures for the public to enjoy. Motto: "Keeper of the Streams."
Publication(s): Streamkeepers Log
Keyword(s): Energy, Forests/Forestry, Recreation/Ecotourism, Water Habitats & Quality, Wildlife & Species
Contact(s):
  Gary Seput, Executive Director; bergstrom@caltrout.org
  Katrina Kuznick, Office Manager
  Jeff Eshbaugh, Streamkeeper Coordinator

CALIFORNIA WATERFOWL ASSOCIATION
4630 Northgate Blvd., Suite 150
Sacramento, CA 95834 United States
Phone: 916-648-1406 Fax: 916-648-1665
E-mail: cwa_hq@calwaterfowl.org
Website: www.calwaterfowl.org

Founded: 1945
Membership: 10,001–100,000
Scope: State
Description: A statewide nonprofit, public benefit corporation, whose principal objectives are the conservation, protection, and enhancement of California's waterfowl resources and the waterfowling opportunities which they provide. The association directly represents the interests of over 13,000 sportsmen and conservationists throughout the state and indirectly represents the interests of other Californians who are concerned with and benefit from these unique resources.
Publication(s): California Waterfowl Magazine, Sprig Tales Newsletter
Keyword(s): Recreation/Ecotourism, Water Habitats & Quality, Wildlife & Species
Contact(s):
  Robert McLandress, President; 916-648-1406; Fax: 916-648-1665; cwa@calwaterfowl.org
  Mark Bergstrom, Director of Development; 916-648-1406; Fax: 916-648-1665; fund_aa@calwaterfowl.org
  Becky Easter, Director of Communications/Education; 916-648-1406; Fax: 916-648-1665; cwacomm@calwaterfowl.org
  Bill Gaines, Director of Government Affairs; 916-648-1406; Fax: 916-648-1665; cwa_gov@calwaterfowl.org
  Dennis Orthmeyer, Director of Waterfowl and Wetland Programs; 916-648-1406; Fax: 916-648-1665; cwawwp@calwaterfowl.org
  Rob Plath, Chairman of the Board; 916-648-1406; Fax: 916-648-1665; cwa@calwaterfowl.org

CALIFORNIA WILD HERITAGE CAMPAIGN
915 20th Street
Sacramento, CA 95814 United States
Phone: 916-442-3155　　　Fax: 916-442-3396
E-mail: info@californiawild.org
Website: www.californiawild.org

Founded: 1997
Membership: 1,001–10,000
Scope: State
Description: The California Wild Heritage Campaign works to save California's last wild places.
Publication(s): Headwaters
Keyword(s): Ecosystems (precious), Forests/Forestry, Land Issues, Public Lands/Greenspace, Reduce/Reuse/Recycle, Water Habitats & Quality, Wildlife & Species
Contact(s):
　Pamela Flick, Administrative Director; ext. 207
　Jean Munoz, Communications Director; ext. 216
　Traci Van Thull, Outreach Director; ext. 222
　Craig Thomas, Forest Defense Coordinator; cthomas@innercite.com

CALIFORNIA WILDERNESS COALITION
2655 Portage Bay East #5
Davis, CA 95616 United States
Phone: 530-758-0380　　　Fax: 530-758-0382
E-mail: info@calwild.org
Website: www.calwild.org

Founded: 1976
Membership: 1,001–10,000
Scope: Local, State, Regional
Description: Our mission is to defend the landscapes that make California unique, provide a home to our wildlife, and preserve a place for spiritual renewal. We protect wilderness for its own sake, for ourselves, and for generations yet to come. We identify and protect the habitat necessary for the long-term survival of California's plants and animals. Since 1976, through advocacy and public education, we have enlisted the support of citizens and policy-makers in our efforts to preserve wildlands.
Publication(s): Wild Harvest: Farming for Wildlife, Restoring California's Forests, 10 Most Threatened Wild Places, California's Last Wild Places, Missing Linkages, Off-Road to Ruin, Wilderness Record
Keyword(s): Ecosystems (precious), Forests/Forestry, Land Issues, Public Lands/Greenspace, Sprawl/Urban Planning, Wildlife & Species

CALIFORNIA WILDLIFE DEFENDERS
P.O. Box 2025
Hollywood, CA 90078 United States
Phone: 323-663-1856

Founded: 1967
Scope: State
Description: A non-profit association working to eradicate the prejudice towards predatory animals, especially coyotes. Responsible for the discontinuation of the removal and destruction of wildlife policies in the city of Los Angeles, halting the use of leghold traps, and author of an ordinance enacted in several California cities banning the feeding of coyotes in order to limit exacerbation of urban coyote problems.
Publication(s): How to Co-exist with Urban Wildlife
Keyword(s): Sprawl/Urban Planning, Wildlife & Species
Contact(s):
　Lila Brooks, Director
　Alberta Burke, Associate
　Jessica Gates, Associate
　Suzanne Ulman, Associate

CALIFORNIA WILDLIFE FEDERATION
P.O. Box 1527
Sacramento, CA 95812-1527 United States
Phone: 916-441-7563　　　Fax: 916-441-6490

Founded: 1952
Membership: 1,001–10,000
Scope: State
Description: A nonprofit statewide organization of councils, clubs, and individual members dedicated to promote the conservation, enhancement, scientific management, and wise use of all our natural resources.
Publication(s): California Wildlife
Keyword(s): Recreation/Ecotourism, Wildlife & Species
Contact(s):
　Randy Walker, President; 4908 Sunset Dr,, Fresno, CA 93704; 559-225-9003
　Tim Leblanc, Vice President; P.O. Box 1343, Lake Arrowhead, CA 92352; 909-336-1048
　Cheri Fuller, Editor; 916-441-7563; cheri_fuller@hotmail.com
　C. Starr, Treasurer; 2105 Westhaven Ave., Bakersfield, CA 93304; 661-835-8337

CALIFORNIANS FOR POPULATION STABILIZATION (CAPS)
1129 State Street
Suite 3-D
Santa Barbara, CA 93101 United States
Phone: 805-564-6626　　　Fax: 805-564-6636
E-mail: info@capsweb.org
Website: www.capsweb.org

Founded: 1986
Membership: 1,001–10,000
Scope: State, National
Description: CAPS is a nonprofit membership organization dedicated to stabilizing population in California to protect and preserve the state's environment, ecology, and resources. CAPS believes overpopulation is the ultimate environmental threat. Activities include: public education, media campaigns, public policy research and advocacy, and grassroots organizing.
Publication(s): CAPS Data Reports, brochures and fact sheets, action alerts, CAPS Newsletters
Keyword(s): Air Quality/Atmosphere, Energy, Executive/Legislative/Judicial Reform, Land Issues, Population, Public Lands/Greenspace, Sprawl/Urban Planning
Contact(s):
　Diana Hull, President of the Board
　Jo Wideman, Director of Operations & Development; 805-564-6626; Fax: 805-564-6636; caps@cap-s.org

CAM VALLEY WILDLIFE GROUP
Bronwen
Farrington Road
Paulton
Bristol, BS39 7LP United Kingdom
Phone: 01761410731
E-mail: jim-helena@supanet.com
Website: www.camvalleywildlifegroup.org.uk

Founded: 1994
Membership: 101–1,000
Scope: Local
Description: A volunteer-run biodiversity organisation based around Midsomer Norton and Radstock, Somerset, England
Keyword(s): Wildlife & Species

CAMP FIRE CLUB OF AMERICA
230 Campfire Rd.
Chappaqua, NY 10514 United States
Phone: 914-941-0199　　　Fax: 914-923-0977
E-mail: campfireclub@aol.com

Founded: 1897
Scope: National
Description: Works to preserve forests and woodland; to protect and conserve the wildlife of our country; and to sponsor and support all reasonable measures to the end that present and future generations may continue to enjoy advantages and benefits of life outdoors.
Publication(s): Backlog, The
Keyword(s): Forests/Forestry, Recreation/Ecotourism
Contact(s):
Lewis Jordan, President
David Petzal, Publications Chairman
Thomas Quirk, Secretary of Committee on Conservation of Forests and Wildlife
Leonard Vallender, Chairman of Committee on Conservation of Forests and Wildlife

CAMP FIRE CONSERVATION FUND
230 Campfire Rd.
Chappaqua, NY 10514 United States
Phone: 914-941-9861
Founded: 1977
Scope: National
Description: A tax-exempt membership organization, dedicated to the preservation of wildlife and its habitat to coordinate the efforts of sportsmen's and conservation organizations; to inform the general public and governmental agencies with regard to intelligent use of our natural resources; and to support and promote conservation research.
Keyword(s): Wildlife & Species
Contact(s):
George Lamb, President
Henry Ayres, Secretary
Mottell Peek, Treasurer

CAMP FIRE USA
4601 Madison Ave.
Kansas City, MO 64112-1278 United States
Phone: 816-756-1950   Fax: 816-756-0258
E-mail: info@campfire.usa.org
Website: www.campfireusa.org
Founded: 1910
Membership: 500,001–1,000,000
Scope: National
Description: Open to preschoolers to teens, without regard to race, creed, ethnic origin, sex, or income level. Provides a program of informal education that focuses on developing skills in interpersonal relationships, decision-making, leadership, creativity, citizenship, community service, and individual growth.
Keyword(s): Air Quality/Atmosphere, Public Health, Recreation/Ecotourism, Wildlife & Species
Contact(s):
Judy O'Connor, National President
Stewart Smith, National Executive Director and CEO

CAMPAIGN FOR AMERICA'S WILDERNESS
Administrative Office
850 1/2 Main Avenue
Durango, CO 81301 United States
Phone: 970-247-2888   Fax: 970-247-2774
E-mail: info@leaveitwild.org
Website: www.leaveitwild.org
Founded: 2002
Scope: Local, State, Regional, National
Description: The Campaign for America's Wilderness works with you to add public land to the National Wilderness Preservation System for the benefit of future generations.
Publication(s): America's Western Arctic Is In Danger, A Mandate to Protect America's Wilderness
Keyword(s): Land Issues
Contact(s):
John Gilroy, Associate Director; 585-249-0978; Fax: 585-249-0979; jgilroy@leaveitwild.org
Mike Matz, Executive Director; 850 1/2 Main Avenue, Durango, CO 81301; 970-247-2888; Fax: 970-247-2774
Sherry Lynn McLaughlin, Administrative Director; Administrative Office:, 850 1/2 Main Avenue, Durango, CO 81301; 970-247-2888; Fax: 970-247-2774; slynn@leaveitwild.org
Ken Rait, Policy Director; 4035 NE Sandy Boulevard, #242, Portland, OR 97212; 503-460-9453; Fax: 503-493-0744; krait@leaveitwild.org
Jen Schmidt, Field Director; 307 7th Avenue, Ste. 1201, New York, NY 10001; 212-645-9880; ext. 17; Fax: 212-645-9881; jschmidt@leaveitwild.org
Doug Scott, Policy Director; 705 2nd Avenue, Ste. 203, Seattle, WA 98104-1711; 206-342-9212; Fax: 206-343-1526; dscott@leaveitwild.org
Kathryn Seck, Deputy Communications Director; 122 C Street, NW, Ste. 240, Washington, DC 20001; 202-266-0436; Fax: 202-544-5197; kseck@leaveitwild.org
Susan Whitmore, Communications Director; 122 C Street, NW, Ste. 240, Washington, DC 20001; 202-266-0435; Fax: 202-544-5197; swhitmore@leaveitwild.org
Marcia Argust, Washington Representative; 122 C Street, NW, Ste. 240, Washington, DC 20001; 202-266-0434; Fax: 202-544-5197; margust@leaveitwild.org
Jonathan Greenberg, Internet Organizer; 307 7th Avenue, Ste. 1201, New York, NY 10001; 212-645-9880; ext. 14; Fax: 212-645-9881; jgreenberg@leaveitwild.org
Maureen Rose, Washington Representative; 122 C Street, NW, Ste. 240, Washington, DC 20001; 202-266-0432; Fax: 202-544-5197; mrose@leaveitwild.org
Erica Stanley, Communications Specialist; 122 C Street, NW, Ste. 240, Washington, DC 20001; 202-266-0437; Fax: 202-544-5197; estanley@leaveitwild.org

CANADA GOOSE PROJECT
11576 Morrison Street
Valley Village, CA 91601 United States
Phone: 818-769-1521, ext. 1
E-mail: canadagooseproj@aol.com
Website: canadagooseproject.org
Founded: 1989
Membership: 101–1,000
Scope: Local, State, Regional, National, International
Description: The Mission of the Canada Goose Project is to protect and conserve the Canada Geese and other migratory waterfowl using the Pacific Flyway, through habitat preservation, data collection, public education and through collaboration with other interested agencies and organizations.
Keyword(s): Ecosystems (precious), Land Issues, Public Lands/Greenspace, Sprawl/Urban Planning, Water Habitats & Quality, Wildlife & Species

CANADIAN ARCTIC RESOURCE COMMITTEE, INC.
7 Hinton Ave. N., Suite 200
Ottawa, K1Y 4P1 Ontario Canada
Phone: 613-759-4284   Fax: 613-722-3318
E-mail: info@carc.org
Website: www.carc.org
Founded: 1971
Membership: 1,001–10,000
Scope: International
Description: To ensure that important social, environmental, and economic ramifications of northern development are studied and analyzed before major decisions relating to northern Canada are made; to exchange information and viewpoints among the public, government, and industry; to develop better perspectives on options available; and to inform the public.

Publication(s): List of books on request, Northern Perspectives Member's Update, see publications on website
Keyword(s): Air Quality/Atmosphere, Ecosystems (precious), Reduce/Reuse/Recycle, Wildlife & Species
Contact(s):
Karen Wristen, Executive Director; kwristen@carc.org
Melissa Douglas, Information Officer; 613-759-4284; ext. 247; mdouglas@carc.org

CANADIAN COOPERATIVE WILDLIFE HEALTH CENTRE
Dept. of Veterinary Pathology, WCVM
Univ. of Saskatchewan
52 Campus Dr.
Saskatoon, S7N 5B4 Saskatchewan Canada
Phone: 306-966-5099   Fax: 306-966-7439
E-mail: ccwhc@sask.usask.ca
Website: wildlife.usask.ca
Founded: 1992
Scope: Regional, National
Description: The Canadian Cooperative Wildlife Health Centre is a university-based, inter-agency partnership among Canada's four colleges of veterinary medicine, Federal, Provincial and Territorial government agencies and non-government organizations. It is a national science centre for wild animal diseases. The core activities of the CCWHC are a national wildlife disease surveillance program, educational programs including chemical immobilization of wildlife, information services and research.
Publication(s): Bulletin du Centre de la Sante de la Faune, Directory of Wildlife Health Expertise, Wildlife Disease Investigation Manual, Wildlife Health Centre Newsletter
Keyword(s): Wildlife & Species
Contact(s):
F. Leighton, Co-Director; 306-966-7281
G. Wobeser, Co-Director; 306-966-7310
I. Barker, Contact for Ontario Region; 519-823-8800
Trent Bollinger, Contact for West and North Region; 306-966-5099
Pierre Yves Daoust, Contact for Atlantic Region; 902-566-0667
Daniel Martineau, Contact for Quebec Region; 514-773-8521

CANADIAN ENVIRONMENTAL LAW ASSOCIATION
130 Spadina Avenue
Suite 301
Toronto, M5V 2L4 Ontario Canada
Phone: 416-960-2284   Fax: 416-960-9392
E-mail: intake@cela.ca
Website: www.cela.ca
Founded: 1970
Scope: National
Description: Nonprofit, independent, public-interest legal group formed to use current environmental laws to protect the environment, and to promote better environmental legislation throughout Canada.
Publication(s): Intervenor, The, Newsletter
Contact(s):
Paul Muldoon, Executive Director; mschanel@lao.on.ca
Michelle Swenarchuk, Director of International Programs; muldoonp@loa.on.ca
Kathy Cooper, Researcher; cela@web.ca
Richard Lindgren, Counsel; r.lindgren@sympatico.ca
Theresa Mclenaghan, Counsel; cela@web.ca
Lisa McShane, Librarian; r.lindgren@sympatico.ca
Sarah Miller, Coordinator; mcclenat@lao.on.ca
Ramani Nadarajah, Counsel; millers@lao.on.ca

CANADIAN FEDERATION OF HUMANE SOCIETIES
30 Concourse Gate, Suite 102
Nepean, K2E 7V7 Ontario Canada
Phone: 613-224-8072   Fax: 613-723-0252
E-mail: info@cfhs.ca
Website: www.cfhs.ca
Founded: 1957
Membership: 101–1,000
Scope: National
Description: CFHS is a national body comprised of animal welfare organizations and individuals whose purpose is to promote compassion and humane treatment for all animals.
Publication(s): Animal Welfare in Focus, The Humane Educator, publications available on website
Keyword(s): Agriculture/Farming, Wildlife & Species
Contact(s):
J. Ripley, President
Robert Van Tongerloo, Executive Director
Shelagh MacDonald, Program Director; 613-224-8072; Fax: 613-723-0252; shelaghm@cfhs.ca

CANADIAN FORESTRY ASSOCIATION
185 Somerset St., W., Suite 203
Ottawa, K2P 0J2 Ontario Canada
Phone: 613-232-1815   Fax: 613-232-4210
E-mail: cfa@canadianforestry.com
Website: www.canadianforestry.com
Founded: 1900
Scope: National
Description: The Canadian Forestry Association is Canada's oldest conservation organization. It is nongovernmental and nonindustrial. Its purpose is to develop public understanding and cooperation in the wise use, conservation, and sustainable development of Canada's forests and related resources of land, water, and wildlife.
Publication(s): Smokey Bear Products Catalogue, Proceedings of National Forest Congress, Forest Forum, National Forest Week Teaching Guide, Proceedings: Canadian Urban Forests Conference, National Forest Education Resources Catalogue
Keyword(s): Forests/Forestry
Contact(s):
Barry Waito, President
David Lemkay, General Manager; 613-232-1815; Fax: 613-232-4210; lemkayd@canadianforestry.com
Sheila Rust, Office Administrator; 613-232-1815; Fax: 613-232-4210; rusts@canadianforestry.com
Susan Gesner, Immediate Past President

CANADIAN INSTITUTE FOR ENVIRONMENTAL LAW AND POLICY (CIELAP)
130 Spadina Ave. Suite 305
Toronto, M5V 2L4 Ontario Canada
Phone: 416-923-3529   Fax: 416-923-5949
E-mail: cielap@cielap.org
Website: www.cielap.org
Founded: 1970
Scope: National
Description: CIELAP is an independent, not-for-profit research and education institute providing environmental law and policy analysis. CIELAP provides leadership in the development of environmental law and policy which promotes the public interest and the principles of sustainability, including the protection of the health and well-being of present and future generations, and of the natural environment.
Publication(s): Ontario's Environment and the "Common Sense Revolution", A Carbon Dioxide Strategy for Ontario: A Discussion Paper, Environment on Trial: A Guide to Ontario Environmental Law and Policy, Hazardous Waste Management in Ontario: A Report and Recommendation

Contact(s):
David Powell, President
Anne Mitchell, Executive Director
Murray Klippenstein, Secretary and Treasurer

CANADIAN INSTITUTE OF FORESTRY/ INSTITUTE FORESTIER DU CANADA
151 Slater St., Suite 606
Ottawa, K1P 5H3 Ontario Canada
Phone: 613-234-2242   Fax: 613-234-6181
E-mail: cif@cif-ifc.org
Website: www.cif-ifc.org

Founded: 1908
Membership: 1,001–10,000
Scope: Local, Regional, National
Description: Our mission is to advance the stewardship of Canada's forest resources through leadership, professional competence and public awareness. Our membership includes foresters, forest technicians, academics, scientists and others with a professional interest in Forestry. CIF/IFC represents the largest professional voice for forestry in Canada.
Publication(s): The Forestry Chronicle
Keyword(s): Forests/Forestry
Contact(s):
Roxanne Comeau, Executive Director; 151 Slater St., Suite 606, Ottawa, Ontario K1P 5H3; 613-234-2242; Fax: 613 234-6181; cif@cif-ifc.org

CANADIAN NATIONAL SPORTSMENS SHOWS
703 Evans Ave., Suite 202
Toronto, M9C 5E9 Ontario Canada
Phone: 416-695-0311   Fax: 416-695-0381
E-mail: info@sportshows.ca
Website: www.sportshows.ca

Founded: 1948
Membership: 1–100
Scope: National
Description: A national corporation presenting outdoor shows and events. Products relate to fishing, hiking, camping, boating, skiing, and the consumer shows are produced from Vancouver to Quebec City. All net proceeds are distributed to projects which encourage Canadians to appreciate, enjoy, and protect Canada's outdoor heritage.
Keyword(s): Recreation/Ecotourism
Contact(s):
Walter Oster, President; ext. 208
B. Meadows, Executive Assistant

CANADIAN NATURE FEDERATION
1 Nicholas St., Suite 606
Ottawa, K1N 7B7 Ontario Canada
Phone: 613-562-3447   Fax: 613-562-3371
Website: www.cnf.ca

Founded: 1971
Membership: 1–100
Scope: National
Description: Canada's national naturalists' organization promotes protection of nature, its diversity and the processes that sustain it. The Federation was formed from the Canadian Audubon Society, the CNF represents over 150 affiliated conservation groups and 40,000 individual supporters across the country.
Publication(s): Nature Canada Magazine, Nature Matters
Contact(s):
Jackie Krindle, President
Julie Gelfand, Executive Director; 613-562-3447
Caroline Schultz, Director of Conservation & Affiliate Development
Barbara Stevenson, Editor

CANADIAN PARKS AND WILDERNESS SOCIETY
880 Wellington St., Suite 506
Ottawa, K1R 6K7 Ontario Canada
Phone: 613-569-7226   Fax: 613-569-7098
E-mail: info@cpaws.org
Website: www.cpaws.org

Founded: 1963
Membership: 10,001–100,000
Scope: National
Description: A national, nonprofit advocacy organization dedicated to the protection of wilderness areas and the preservation and proper stewardship of Canada's national and provincial parks.
Publication(s): Wilderness Activist, The
Keyword(s): Land Issues, Public Lands/Greenspace
Contact(s):
David Thomson, President
Stephen Hazell, Executive Director; shazell@cpaws.org
Clayton Forrest, Manager of Membership Services

CANADIAN SOCIETY OF ENVIRONMENTAL BIOLOGISTS
P.O. Box 962, Station F
Toronto, M4Y 2N9 Ontario Canada
E-mail: cseb@freenet.edmonton.ab.ca
Website: www.freenet.edmonton.ab.ca./cseb/

Founded: 1959
Scope: National
Description: A Canada-wide society of environmental biologists whose primary goals are: the conservation of the natural resources of Canada; the prudent management of these resources so as to minimize adverse environmental effects; the interchange of ideas among environmental biologists; and maintaining high professional standards in education, research, and management related to natural resources and the environment.
Publication(s): Canadian Society of Environmental Biologists
Keyword(s): Wildlife & Species
Contact(s):
Patrick Stewart, President; 902-798-4022; Fax: 902-798-4022; enviroco@ns.sympatico.ca

CANADIAN WILDLIFE FEDERATION
350 Michael Cowpland Dr.
Kanata, K2M 2W1 Ontario Canada
Phone: 613-599-9594   Fax: 613-599-4428
E-mail: info@cwf-fcf.org
Website: www.cwf-fcf.org

Founded: 1961
Membership: 100,001–500,000
Scope: National
Description: To foster understanding of natural processes so that people may live in harmony with the land and its resources for the long-term benefit and enrichment of society; to maintain a substantial program of information and education based on ecological principles; and to conduct or sponsor research and scientific investigation.
Publication(s): Canadian Wildlife, Wildlife Update, You Can Do It, Biosphere, Your Big Backyard, Wild Magazine
Contact(s):
Derrek Stanley, President
Bob Barton, 1st Vice President
Pat Doyle, 3rd Vice President
Nicholas Laurin, 2nd Vice President
Colin Maxwell, Executive Vice President
Nestor Romaniuk, Past President

CANON ENVIROTHON
P.O. Box 855
408 E. Main
League City, TX 77574-0855 United States
Phone: 800-825-5547, ext. 16 Fax: 281-332-5259
E-mail: kay-asher@nacdnet.org
Website: www.envirothon.org

Founded: 1989
Membership: 1–100
Scope: Local, State, Regional, National, International
Description: Natural resource competition for high school students (grades 9-12). Core study areas are: aqautics, forestry, soils, wildlife and a fifth issue that comprises a current environmental issue that changes each year. Scholarship awards for 1st, 2nd and 3rd place winners at the international level.
Keyword(s): Agriculture/Farming, Forests/Forestry, Land Issues, Public Lands/Greenspace, Water Habitats & Quality, Wildlife & Species
Contact(s):
Clay Burns, Exec. Director; P.O. Box 23005, Jackson, MS 39225; 866-854-2898; Fax: 601-354-6628; clay-burns@nacdnet.org
Ellen Hutto, Manager; P.O. Box 855, 408 E. Main, League City, TX 77574; 800-825-5547; ext. 27; Fax: 281-332-5259; ellen-hutto@nacdnet.org
Kay Asher, Program Coordinator; P.O. Box 855, 408 E. Main, League City, TX 77574; 800-825-5547; ext. 16; Fax: 281-332-5259; kay-asher@nacdnet.org

CANVASBACK SOCIETY
P.O. Box 101
Gates Mills, OH 44040 United States

Founded: 1975
Scope: National
Description: A nonprofit, tax-exempt organization established to conserve, restore, and promote the increase of the canvasback species of duck on the North American continent.
Keyword(s): Reduce/Reuse/Recycle, Water Habitats & Quality, Wildlife & Species
Contact(s):
Oakley Andrews, President and Treasurer; 216-621-0200
Keith Russell, Chairman of the Board

CARIBBEAN CONSERVATION CORPORATION
4424 NW 13th St. Suite 8A1
Gainesville, FL 32609 United States
Phone: 352-373-6441 Fax: 352-375-2449
E-mail: ccc@cccturtle.org
Website: www.cccturtle.org

Founded: 1959
Membership: 1,001–10,000
Scope: International
Description: A nonprofit international membership organization founded in 1959 to support research and conservation of marine turtles in the Caribbean and throughout the world. In addition to conservation and education activities, CCC operates research programs in Tortuguero, Costa Rica—the site of the largest green turtle nesting colony in the Caribbean Sea.
Publication(s): Sea Turtle Educator's Guide
Keyword(s): Ecosystems (precious), Oceans/Coasts/Beaches, Pollution (general), Wildlife & Species
Contact(s):
Peggy Cavanaugh, President
David Godfrey, Executive Director
L. Clay, Chairman of the Board of Directors
Roger Stone, Secretary

CARIBBEAN NATURAL RESOURCES INSTITUTE
CANARI
Fernandes Industrial Centre, Administration Building
Eastern Main Road
Laventille, W.I. Trinidad and Tobago
Phone: 868-626-6062 Fax: 868-626-1788
E-mail: canari@tstt.net.tt
Website: www.canari.org

Founded: 1986
Scope: Regional
Description: To create avenues for the equitable participation and effective collaboration of Caribbean communities and institutions in managing the use of natural resources critical to development.
Keyword(s): Development/Developing Countries, Forests/Forestry, Sprawl/Urban Planning, Water Habitats & Quality
Contact(s):
Vijay Krishnarayan, Managing Partner
Patricia Charles, Partnership Chairperson

CAROLINA BIRD CLUB, INC.
11 W. Jones St.
Raleigh, NC 27601-1029 United States
Phone: 919-733-7450, ext. 605 Fax: 919-733-1573
Website: www.naturalsciences.org

Founded: 1937
Scope: State
Description: A nonprofit, educational ornithological organization to promote bird study and conservation. Affiliated local chapters.
Publication(s): Chat, The, CBC Newsletter
Keyword(s): Wildlife & Species
Contact(s):
Len Pardue, President; 16th Circle, Asheville, NC 28801
Tullie Johnson, Headquarters Secretary; 919-733-7450
Judy Walker, Editor; 7639 Farm Gate Dr., Charlotte, NC 28215; jwalker@email.uncc.edu
Bob Wood, Editor; 2421 Owl Circle, West Columbia, NC 29169

CARRYING CAPACITY NETWORK
2000 P St., NW, Suite 310
Washington, DC 20036-5915 United States
Phone: 202-296-4548 Fax: 202-296-4609
E-mail: carryingcapacity@covad.net
Website: www.carryingcapacity.org

Founded: 1989
Scope: National
Description: CCN is a nonprofit network which mobilizes many diverse individuals and groups to meet the critical challenges facing our nation with solid information and analysis, effective advocacy tools, and targeted solutions. CCN's action-oriented initiatives focus on achieving national revitalization, population stabilization, immigration limitation, resource conservation, and economic sustainability.
Publication(s): FOCUS, Network Bulletin
Keyword(s): Agriculture/Farming, Development/Developing Countries, Land Issues, Population, Reduce/Reuse/Recycle, Sprawl/Urban Planning
Contact(s):
David Durham, President of the Board
Virginia Abernethy, Vice President

CASCADIA RESEARCH
218 1/2 W. 4th Ave.
Olympia, WA 98501 United States
Website: www.cascadiaresearch.org

Founded: 1979
Scope: National

Description: A nonprofit, tax-exempt organization established to conduct scientific research and education related to marine mammals and birds. Primary funding for research projects comes from federal and state agencies and environmental groups.
Keyword(s): Oceans/Coasts/Beaches, Wildlife & Species
Contact(s):
  Gretchen Steiger, President
  James Cubbage, Vice President
  John Calambokidis, Secretary and Treasurer

CATSKILL CENTER FOR CONSERVATION AND DEVELOPMENT, INC., THE
P. O. Box 504 Route 28
Arkville, NY 12406-0504 United States
Phone: 845-586-2611   Fax: 845-586-3044
E-mail: cccd@catskillcenter.org
Website: www.catskillcenter.org
Founded: 1969
Membership: 1,001–10,000
Scope: Regional
Description: The Catskill Center is a not for profit membership organization concerned with increasing public awareness of and involvement with issues affecting human communities and the natural environment of the Catskill Mountain Region. Its activities emphasize public education and regional planning advocacy, as well as development and support of programs relating to historic preservation, sustainable economic development and regional arts and culture in the Catskill Mountain Region of New York State.
Publication(s): Catskill Center News, Summary Guide to the Terms of the Watershed Agreement, Successful Catskill Communities
Keyword(s): Agriculture/Farming, Development/Developing Countries, Land Issues, Recreation/Ecotourism, Sprawl/Urban Planning
Contact(s):
  Geddy Sveikauskas, President
  Philip Weinberg, Vice President
  Helen Chase, Treasurer
  H. Shostal, Secretary

CATSKILL FOREST ASSOCIATION
P.O. Box 336
Arkville, NY 12406 United States
Phone: 845-586-3054   Fax: 845-586-4071
E-mail: cfa@catskill.net
Website: www.catskillforest.org
Founded: 1982
Membership: 101–1,000
Scope: Local
Description: Advocates of quality forest management practices to improve the health of the forest and prevent threats to the forest ecosystem. The Catskill Forest Association is an independent nonprofit regional organization that supports forest conservation efforts in New York's Catskill Mountains through the promotion of forest stewardship by landowners, foresters, timber harvesters, and the general public.
Publication(s): Tree Tubes & Forest Books, CFA News
Keyword(s): Development/Developing Countries, Energy, Forests/Forestry, Land Issues, Recreation/Ecotourism, Water Habitats & Quality, Wildlife & Species
Contact(s):
  Joe Kraus, President
  Robert Bishop, Vice President
  Jim Waters, Executive Director
  Jude Zicot, Secretary
  Tom Foulkrod, Natural Resource Specialist
  Dave Elmore, Treasurer

CAVE RESEARCH FOUNDATION
Rick Toomey, President
Kartchner Caverns State Park
P.O. Box 1849
Benson, AZ 85602-1849 United States
Phone: 520-586-4138   Fax: 520-586-4113
E-mail: rtoomey@pr.state.az.us
Website: www.cave-research.org
Founded: 1957
Membership: 101–1,000
Scope: International
Description: The Foundation is a nonprofit organization that supports and promotes research, interpretation, and conservation activities in caves and karst areas. Permanent field operations are maintained within Mammoth Cave National Park, Carlsbad Caverns National Park, Sequoia and Kings Canyon National Parks, and Lava Beds National Monument. Approximately 800 joint-venturers participate in program.
Publication(s): CRF Newsletter, Annual Report, Cave Books
Keyword(s): Ecosystems (precious), Land Issues, Public Lands/Greenspace
Contact(s):
  Pat Kambesis, President; P.O. Box 343, Winona, IL 61377-0343; 815-863-5184; kembesis@jun
  Peter Bosted, Secretary; 2301 Sharon Rd., Menlo Park, CA 94025-680; 650-926-2319; bosted@slac.spanford.edu
  Paul Cannaley, Treasurer; 317-862-5618
  Paul Nelson, Editor; 2644 S. Quarry Lane #D, Walnut, CA 91789-4067

CENTER FOR A NEW AMERICAN DREAM, THE
6930 Carroll Ave. #900
Takoma Park, MD 20912 United States
Phone: 301-891-3683   Fax: 301-891-3684
E-mail: newdream@newdream.org
Website: www.newdream.org
Founded: 1996
Membership: 1,001–10,000
Scope: National
Description: The Center for a New American Dream helps Americans consume responsibly to protect the environment, enhance quality of life, and promote social justice. We work with individuals, institutions, communities, and businesses to conserve natural resources, counter the commercialization of our culture, and promote positive changes in the way goods are produced and consumed.
Publication(s): Enough!, Simply the Holidays, and Tips for Parenting in a Commercial Culture.
Keyword(s): Climate Change, Energy, Forests/Forestry, Oceans/Coasts/Beaches, Population, Reduce/Reuse/Recycle, Transportation, Wildlife & Species
Contact(s):
  Eric Brown, Communications Director; Eric@newdream.org
  Nancy Smith, Director of Administration
  Betsy Taylor, Executive Director; Betsy@newdream.org
  Monique Tilford, Development Director; Monique@newdream.org
  Sean Sheehan, National Outreach Manager; Sean@newdream.org

CENTER FOR A SUSTAINABLE COAST
221B Mallory St.
Saint Simons Island, GA 31522 United States
Phone: 912-638-3612   Fax: 912-638-3615
E-mail: susdev@gate.net
Website: www.sustainablecoast.com
Founded: 1997
Scope: Regional
Description: To promote sustainable use, protection, enhancement, and understanding of coastal Georgia's natural,

economic, historic, and cultural resources through education, advocacy, technical assistance, and research.

Publication(s): Fisheries and Water Resource Permit Issues in the Lower Altamaha and Other Coastal Georgia Rivers, Surface Water Withdrawal and Coastal Economic Issues

Keyword(s): Water Habitats & Quality

Contact(s):
David Kyler, Executive Director

CENTER FOR BIOLOGICAL DIVERSITY
P.O. Box 710
Tucson, AZ 85702-0710 United States
Phone: 520-623-5252   Fax: 520-623-9797
E-mail: center@biologicaldiversity.org
Website: www.biologicaldiversity.org

Founded: 1989
Membership: 1,001–10,000
Scope: National

Description: The Center for Biological Diversity uses research, public education, and strategic litigation to defend the forests, rivers and deserts of western North America.

Publication(s): White Papers, Biodiversity Activist

Keyword(s): Ecosystems (precious), Energy, Forests/Forestry, Land Issues, Oceans/Coasts/Beaches, Pollution (general), Public Health, Public Lands/Greenspace, Sprawl/Urban Planning, Transportation, Water Habitats & Quality, Wildlife & Species

Contact(s):
Peter Galvin, Biologist; 510-663-0616; pgalvin@biological-diversity.org
Todd Schulke, Ecosystem Restoration; P.O. Box 53166, Pinos Altos, NM 88053; 505-388-8799; tschulke@biologicaldiversity.org
Kieran Suckling, Executive Director; 520-623-5252; ext. 304; ksuckling@biologicaldiversity.org
Shane Jimerfield, IT; 520-623-5252; ext. 302
Kim Beck, Grant Writer; 520-623-5252; ext. 309
Monica Bond, Biologist; P.O. Box 493, Idyllwild, CA 92549; 909-659-6053; ext. 304
Corrie Bosman, Lawyer; P.O. Box 6157, Sitka, AK 99835; 907-747-1463
Curt Bradley, GIS; 520-623-5252; ext. 310
Brendan Cummings, Lawyer; P.O. Box 493, Idyllwild, CA 92549; 909-659-6053; ext. 301
Sonya Diehn, Office Manager; 520-623-5252; ext. 300
Keri Dixon, Membership Associate; 520-623-5252; ext. 312
Noah Greenwald, Conservation Biologist
Chelsea Gwyther, Associate Director; 520-623-5252; ext. 301
Michelle Harrington, Ecologist; P.O. Box 39629, Phoenix, AZ 85069; 602-246-6498
Meredith Hartwell, Administrative Assistant; 520-623-5252; ext. 304
David Hogan, Ecologist; P.O. Box 7745, San Diego, CA 92167; 619-574-6800
Julie Miller, Membership Director; 520-623-5252; ext. 303
Jeff Miller, Watersheds; 510-663-0616
Brian Nowicki, Policy; 520-623-5252; ext. 311
Daniel Patterson, Ecologist; 909-659-6053; ext. 306
Brent Plater, Lawyer; 510-663-0616
Michael Robinson, Carnivore Conservation Campaign; P.O. Box 53166, Pinos Altos, NM 88053; 505-534-0360
Susie Roe, Office Administrator; P.O. Box 493, Idyllwild, CA 92549; 909-659-6053; ext. 307
Brian Segee, Southwest Public Lands Director; 520-623-5252; ext. 308
Kassie Siegel, Lawyer; P.O. Box 493, Idyllwild, CA 92549; 909-659-6053; ext. 302
Martin Taylor, Grazing Reform Coordinator; 520-623-5252; ext. 307
Julie Teel, Lawyer; P.O. Box 493, Idyllwild, CA 92549; 909-659-6053; ext. 308
Jay Tutchton, Lawyer
Robin Silver, Conservation Chair; P.O. Box 39629, Phoenix, AZ 85069; 602-246-4170; Fax: 602-249-2576; rsilver@biologicaldiversity.org

CENTER FOR CHESAPEAKE COMMUNITIES
229 Hanover St. Suite 101
Annapolis, MD 21401 United States
Phone: 410-267-8595   Fax: 410-267-8597
E-mail: gallen@chesapeakecommunities.org
Website: www.chesapeakecommunities.org

Founded: 1997
Scope: Regional

Description: A nonprofit, independent organization dedicated to assisting local governments in the Chesapeake Bay watershed in their environmental restoration and protection initiatives.

Keyword(s): Air Quality/Atmosphere, Energy, Forests/Forestry, Land Issues, Pollution (general), Public Lands/Greenspace, Wildlife & Species

Contact(s):
Gary Allen, Executive Director

CENTER FOR ENVIRONMENT AND POPULATION (CEP)
100 Market Street, Suite 204
Portsmouth, NH 03801 United States
Phone: 603-431-4066   Fax: 603-431-4063
E-mail: vmarkham@cepnet.org
Website: www.cepnet.org

Founded: 1999
Scope: Local, State, Regional, National, International

Description: The Center for Environment and Population (CEP) is a non-profit organization that works to strengthen the scientific basis of policies and public outreach on human population's environmental impacts in the United States and internationally.

Publication(s): U.S. Reports on Population & Environment, AAAS Atlas of Population and Environment, Water and Population, Yale Bulletin #107, Issues on Population and Environment

Keyword(s): Agriculture/Farming, Air Quality/Atmosphere, Climate Change, Development/Developing Countries, Ecosystems (precious), Energy, Forests/Forestry, Land Issues, Oceans/Coasts/Beaches, Pollution (general), Population, Public Health, Public Lands/Greenspace

CENTER FOR ENVIRONMENT, COMMERCE & ENERGY
AFRICAN AMERICAN ENVIRONMENTALIST ASSOCIATION
ENVIRONMENTAL JUSTICE COALITION
NUCLEAR FUELS REPROCESSING COALITION
9903 Caltor Lane
Ft. Washington, MD 20744-3728 United States
Phone: 301-265-8185   Fax: 301-265-2952
E-mail: CfECE@msn.com
Website: groups.msn.com/centerforenvironmentcommerceenergy

Founded: 1985
Scope: Local, State, Regional, National, International

Description: A nonprofit public interest organization dedicated to protecting the environment, enhancing the human, animal and plant ecologies, and working to ensure the efficient use of natural resources. The major areas of concern are: Air quality and pollution, water resources and pollution, energy, renewable resources, toxic substances, Africa and Third World environment, land use, internships, and pro-nuclear power.

Keyword(s): Agriculture/Farming, Air Quality/Atmosphere, Climate Change, Development/Developing Countries, Ecosystems (precious), Energy, Ethics/Environmental Justice, Executive/Legislative/Judicial Reform, Finance/Banking/Trade, Forests/Forestry, Land Issues

Contact(s):
  Norris McDonald, President; 301-265-8185;
    NorrisMcDonald@msn.com
  Kathleen Logan, Director, St. Louis Office; 314-892-6120;
    CKlogan@sbcglobal.net
  Darshoel Willis, Texas Office Director; 512-990-9468

CENTER FOR ENVIRONMENTAL EDUCATION
ANTIOCH
c/o Antioch New England Institute
40 Avon St.
Keene, NH 03431 United States
Phone: 603-355-3251   Fax: 603-357-0718
E-mail: cee@antiochne.edu
Website: www.schoolsgogreen.org

Founded: 1989
Membership: 1,001–10,000
Scope: National
Description: A nonprofit environmental education resource center housing one of the nation's most comprehensive collections of environmental education materials. The library has over 10,000 materials—books, videos, curricula and resources that can be accessed in person, by phone, fax, or through the website.
Publication(s): Grapevine Newsletter, Natures Course, Blueprint for a Green School
Contact(s):
  David Sobel, Co-Executive Director
  Cindy Thomashow, Co-Executive Director
  Jayni Chase, Founder

CENTER FOR ENVIRONMENTAL HEALTH (CEH)
528 61st Street
Suite A
Oakland, CA 94609 United States
Phone: 510-594-9864   Fax: 510-594-9863
E-mail: ceh@cehca.org
Website: www.cehca.org

Founded: 1996
Scope: National
Description: CEH protects the public from environmental and consumer health hazards. We are committed to environmental justice, reducing the use of toxic chemicals, supporting communities in their quest for a safer environment and corporate accountability. We change corporate behavior through education, litigation, and advocacy.
Keyword(s): Air Quality/Atmosphere, Ethics/Environmental Justice, Pollution (general), Public Health
Contact(s):
  Michael Green, Executive Director; 510-594-9864; ext. 101; Fax: 510-594-9863; ceh@cehca.org
  Alise Cappel, Research Director; 510-594-9864; ext. 102; Fax: 510-594-9863; ceh@cehca.org
  Ignacio Gonzalez, Office Manager; 510-594-9864; ext. 103; Fax: 510-594-9863; ceh@cehca.org
  Mamta Khanna, Health Care Without Harm Coordinator; 510-594-9864; ext. 109; Fax: 510-594-9863; ceh@cehca.org
  Katherine Silberman, Public Policy Advocate; 510-594-9864; ext. 106; Fax: 510-594-9864; ceh@cehca.org

CENTER FOR ENVIRONMENTAL INFORMATION
55 St. Paul St.
Rochester, NY 14604-1314 United States
Phone: 585-262-2870   Fax: 585-262-4156
E-mail: ceiroch@frontiernet.net
Website: www.ceinfo.org

Founded: 1974
Membership: 101–1,000
Scope: National
Description: Provides on-call reference and referral and current awareness and educational services to scientists, educators, government agency staff, policymakers, business and industry managers and interested citizens. Sponsors conferences and seminars.
Publication(s): Proceedings of Annual Conferences
Keyword(s): Air Quality/Atmosphere, Climate Change, Energy

CENTER FOR ENVIRONMENTAL PHILOSOPHY
University of North Texas,
P.O. Box 310980
Denton, TX 76203-0980 United States
Phone: 940-565-2727   Fax: 940-565-4439
E-mail: ee@unt.edu
Website: www.cep.unt.edu

Founded: 1980
Scope: International
Description: A nonprofit, tax-deductible organization. The Center promotes research and instruction in environmental ethics and its application in environmental policy and decision-making. The Center works with governmental and environmental organizations on conferences, workshops, and other educational projects.
Publication(s): Environmental Ethics
Keyword(s): Ethics/Environmental Justice, Land Issues
Contact(s):
  Eugene Hargrove, President, Editor and Publisher; Center for Environmental Philosophy, Univ. of North TX, P.O. Box 310980, Denton, TX 76203-0980; 940-565-2727; Fax: 940-565-4439; hargrove@unt.edu
  J. Callicott, Vice President; Dept. of Philosophy, Univ. of North TX, P.O. Box 310920, Denton, TX 76203-0920; 940-565-2255; Fax: 940-565-4448; callicott@unt.edu
  Jan Dickson, Executive Director; Center for Environmental Philosophy, Univ. of North TX, P.O. Box 310980, Denton, TX 76203-0980; 940-565-2727; Fax: 940-565-4439; jdickson@unt.edu
  Max Oelschlaeger, Secretary and Treasurer; Dept. Humanities, Arts & Religion, Northern Arizona, P.O. Box 6031, Flagstaff, AZ 86011-6031; 520-523-0389; max.oelschlaeger@nau.edu

CENTER FOR ENVIRONMENTAL STUDY
528 Bridge St. NW, 1-C
Grand Rapids, MI 49504 United States
Phone: 616-988-2854   Fax: 616-988-2857
E-mail: ces1@cesmi.org
Website: www.cesmi.org

Founded: 1969
Membership: 101–1,000
Scope: Local, State, Regional
Description: The Center for Environmental Study, a 501C (3) organization, has served its community as an independent, science-based environmental education and awareness provider. It provides awareness programs on a variety of subjects ranging from water and air quality to Great Lakes issues.
Publication(s): Landscaping for Water Quality, Mahogany, The Great Lakes - An Interactive CD-ROM
Keyword(s): Air Quality/Atmosphere, Water Habitats & Quality
Contact(s):
  Jane Secord, Director of Program Administration; 616-988-2854; Fax: 616-988-2857; jsecord@cesmi.org
  Peter Wege, Founder

CENTER FOR HEALTH, ENVIRONMENT, AND JUSTICE
ALLIANCE FOR SAFE ALTERNATIVES
CHILD PROOFING OUR COMMUNITIES
ENVIRONMENTAL HEALTH ALLIANCE - BE SAFE
P.O. Box 6806
Falls Church, VA 22040-6806 United States
Phone: 703-237-2249   Fax: 703-237-8389
E-mail: chej@chej.org
Website: www.chej.org

Founded: 1981
Membership: 10,001–100,000
Scope: National, International

Description: CHEJ believes in the principle that people have the right to a clean and healthy environment regardless of their race or economic standing. The Center believes the most effective way to win environmental justice is from the bottom up through community organizing and empowerment. CHEJ seeks to help local citizens and organizations come together and take an organized, unified stand in order to hold industry and government accountable and work toward a healthy, environmentally sustainable future.

Publication(s): Love Canal, The Story Continues, Dying from Dioxin, Everyone's Backyard, CHEJ's Catalog

Keyword(s): Ethics/Environmental Justice, Executive/Legislative/Judicial Reform, Pollution (general), Public Health, Water Habitats & Quality

Contact(s):
  Lois Gibbs, Executive Director; 703-237-2249; Fax: 703-237-8389; chej@chej.org
  Stephen Lester, Science Director; 703-237-2249; ext. 16; Fax: 703-237-8389; slester@chej.org
  Michele Roberts, National Organizing Director; 703-237-2249; ext. 18; Fax: 703-237-8389; mroberts@chej.org
  Monica Buckhorn, Alliance for Safe Alternatives Coordinator; 703-237-2249; ext. 19; Fax: 703-237-8389; monica@chej.org
  Paul Ruther, Child Proofing Our Communities Coordinator; 703-237-2249; ext. 21; Fax: 703-237-8389; childproofing@chej.org

CENTER FOR INDEPENDENT SOCIAL RESEARCH
Department of Environmental Sociology, 14 Vine
St. Petersburg, 197002 Russia
Phone: 812-234-50-18
E-mail: centre@indepsocres.org

Founded: 1994
Membership: 1–100
Scope: International

Description: Environmental nongovernmental management and accountability research collection of best sustainability practices in St. Petersburg region.

Contact(s):
  Victor Voronkov, Director

CENTER FOR INTERNATIONAL ENVIRONMENTAL LAW (CIEL)
1367 Connecticut Ave., NW, Suite 300
Washington, DC 20036-1860 United States
Phone: 202-785-8700   Fax: 202-785-8701
E-mail: info@ciel.org
Website: www.ciel.org

Founded: 1989
Membership: 1–100
Scope: International

Description: The CIEL is a public interest environmental law organization founded to focus the energy and experience of the public interest environmental law movement on reforming international environmental law and institutions, and on forging stronger and more meaningful connection between the top down diplomatic approach of international law, and the bottom up participatory approach that has been the hallmark of the public interest environmental law movement.

Publication(s): International Environmental Law and Policy, Trade and the Environment: Law, Economics, and Policy, A Citizen's Guide to the World Bank Inspection Panel, Biodiversity in the Seas: Implementing the Convention on Biological Diversity in Marine and Coastal Habitats

Keyword(s): Climate Change, Finance/Banking/Trade, Wildlife & Species

Contact(s):
  Durwood Zaelke, President
  David Hunter, Executive Director
  Jeffrey Wanha, Director for Finance & Administration

CENTER FOR NATIVE ECOSYSTEMS
FRONT RANGE OFFICE
4990 Pearl East Circle, Suite 301
Boulder, CO 80301 United States
Phone: 303-546-0214   Fax: 303-447-8612
E-mail: cne@nativeecosystems.org
Website: www.nativeecosystems.org

Founded: 1999
Membership: 101–1,000
Scope: Regional

Description: Center for Native Ecosystems is a non-profit advocacy organization dedicated to recovering the native ecosystems of the Greater Southern Rockies. We passionately believe that all species and their natural communities have the right to exist and thrive. CNE uses the best available science to forward its mission through participation in policy, administrative processes, legal action, public outreach and organizing, and education.

Keyword(s): Ecosystems (precious), Energy, Executive/Legislative/Judicial Reform, Forests/Forestry, Land Issues, Public Lands/Greenspace, Sprawl/Urban Planning, Wildlife & Species

CENTER FOR NATIVE ECOSYSTEMS
WEST SLOPE OFFICE
P.O. Box 1365
Paonia, CO 81428 United States
Phone: 970-527-8993   Fax: 970-527-5308
E-mail: cne@nativeecosystems.org
Website: nativeecosystems.org

Founded: 1999
Membership: 101–1,000
Scope: Regional

Description: Center for Native Ecosystems is a non-profit advocacy organization dedicated to recovering the native ecosystems of the Greater Southern Rockies. We passionately believe that all species and their natural communities have the right to exist and thrive. CNE uses the best available science to forward its mission through participation in policy, administrative processes, legal action, public outreach and organizing, and education.

Keyword(s): Ecosystems (precious), Energy, Executive/Legislative/Judicial Reform, Forests/Forestry, Land Issues, Public Lands/Greenspace, Sprawl/Urban Planning, Wildlife & Species

CENTER FOR PLANT CONSERVATION
P.O. Box 299
St. Louis, MO 63166 United States
Phone: 314-577-9450   Fax: 314-577-9465
E-mail: cpc@mobot.org
Website: www.centerforplantconservation.org

Founded: 1984
Membership: 1–100
Scope: National

Description: A national network of over 30 botanical gardens and arboreta dedicated to the conservation and study of rare and endangered U.S. plants. The Center establishes conservation collections of endangered species in regional gardens and seed banks as a resource for conservation and research efforts: The National Collection of Endangered Plants.

Publication(s): Plant Conservation (newsletter), Guidelines for the Management of Orthodox Seeds, Plants in Peril, America's Vanishing Flora

Keyword(s): Land Issues, Wildlife & Species

Contact(s):
  Kathryn Kennedy, Executive Director

CENTER FOR RESOURCE ECONOMICS/ISLAND PRESS
Island Press, 1718 Connecticut Ave., NW, Suite 300
Washington, DC 20009 United States
Phone: 202-232-7933   Fax: 202-234-1328
E-mail: info@islandpress.org
Website: www.islandpress.org

Founded: 1978
Scope: International
Description: The Center for Resource Economics, known as Island Press, is a nonprofit organization that develops, publishes, markets and disseminates books and other information products essential for solving local and global environmental problems.
Publication(s): Contact Island Press Book Distribution Center 800-828-1302
Keyword(s): Agriculture/Farming, Air Quality/Atmosphere, Climate Change, Development/Developing Countries, Ecosystems (precious), Energy, Ethics/Environmental Justice, Forests/Forestry, Land Issues, Oceans/Coasts/Beaches, Pollution (general), Public Lands/Greenspace,
Contact(s):
  Charles Savitt, President; 202-232-7933; csavitt@islandpress.org
  Jan Curtis, VP for Development; 202-232-7933; jcurtis@islandpress.org
  Kristy Manning, VP for Programs; 919-545-0286; kmanning@islandpress.org
  Dan Sayre, VP and Publisher; 202-232-7933; dsayre@islandpress.org
  Amelia Durand, Director of Communications; 202-232-7933; ext. 18; Fax: 202-234-1328, adurand@islandpress.org
  Joanne Gibbs, Director of Operations; 800-828-1302; jgibbs@islandpress.org
  Alphonse MacDonald, Director of New Media and IT; 202-232-7933; amacdonald@islandpress.org
  Lani Hinman, Copyrights & Permissions Manager; 800-828-1302; lhinman@islandpress.org
  Jonathon Cobb, Editor, Shearwater Books; 914-631-7088; jcobb@islandpress.org
  Kenneth Hartzell, VP Finance and Administration, CFO; 202-232-7933; khartzell@islandpress.org

CENTER FOR SCIENCE IN THE PUBLIC INTEREST
1875 Connecticut Ave., NW, Suite 300
Washington, DC 20009 United States
Phone: 202-332-9110   Fax: 202-265-4954
E-mail: cspi@cspinet.org
Website: www.cspinet.org

Founded: 1971
Scope: National
Description: National consumer advocacy organization that focuses on health, nutrition, and alcohol issues. CSPI informs the public of its findings through a variety of publications, press releases, speeches, media appearances, and initiates legal actions. The Center has an intern program throughout the year.
Publication(s): Nutrition Action Healthletter, reports, posters, books, and video
Keyword(s): Agriculture/Farming, Pollution (general), Public Health
Contact(s):
  Michael Jacobson, Executive Director

CENTER FOR SIERRA NEVADA CONSERVATION
P.O. Box 603
Georgetown, CA 95634 United States
Phone: 530-333-1113   Fax: 530-333-1113
E-mail: csnc@innercite.com
Website: sierraconservation.org

Founded: 1986
Membership: 101–1,000
Scope: Local, State, Regional, National
Description: Grassroots group dedicated to preserving the wildlife and ecosystem values of the Sierra Nevada.
Keyword(s): Forests/Forestry, Recreation/Ecotourism

CENTER FOR THE STUDY OF TROPICAL BIRDS, INC.
ADMINISTRATIVE OFFICE
218 Conway Drive
San Antonio, TX 78209-1716 United States
Phone: 210-828-5306   Fax: 210-828-9732
E-mail: office@cstbinc.org
Website: www.cstbinc.org

Founded: 1987
Scope: International
Description: Non-profit organization devoted to tropical bird conservation issues. Current activities include research on Altamira Yellowthroat and Fuertes Oriole in N.E. Mexico, operation of a field station on the Rio Grande of Texas (Muscovy Duck nestbox project, research on Red-billed Pigeons, population dynamics of White-tipped Doves, status of Brown Jays) and publication of the proceedings of the Neotropical Quail workshop held at the NOC in Monterrey, Mexico in 1999.
Publication(s): Publications available on website
Keyword(s): Water Habitats & Quality, Wildlife & Species
Contact(s):
  Jack Eitniear, Director
  Michael Gartside, Treasurer
  Alvaro Tapia, Mexico Program Coordinator

CENTER FOR THE STUDY OF TROPICAL BIRDS, INC.
FIELD OFFICE
22 Cesar Lopez de Lara y Carranza No. 553
Fovissste, Ciudad Victoria, C.P. 87020 Mexico
Phone: 5213160952

Scope: International

CENTER FOR WATERSHED PROTECTION
8390 Main St.
2nd Floor
Ellicott City, MD 21043 United States
Phone: 410-461-8323   Fax: 410-461-8324
E-mail: center@cwp.org
Website: www.cwp.org

Founded: 1992
Membership: 1–100
Scope: National
Description: Founded in 1992, the Center for Watershed Protection is a non-profit 501(c)3 organization dedicated to protecting & restoring watershed through effective land & water management. Joining forces with local watershed groups, federal & local governments, & nationally respected experts, the Center has developed a multi-disciplinary strategy to watershed protection.
Publication(s): The Practice of Watershed Protection
Keyword(s): Land Issues, Reduce/Reuse/Recycle, Water Habitats & Quality
Contact(s):
  Hye Kwon, Administrative Director; hyk@cwp.org
  Thomas Schueler, Executive Director

CENTER FOR WILDLIFE LAW
Institute of Public Law at
MSC 11 6060
1 University of New Mexico
Albuquerque, NM 87131-0001 United States
Phone: 505-277-5006   Fax: 505-277-5483
Website: ipl.unm.edu/cwl

Founded: 1990
Scope: National
Description: Through projects, publications, conferences, and training programs, the Center provides wildlife law and policy analysis and other educational information to legal and nonlegal communities. The Center also conducts a unique law-related wildlife education program. Staff have expertise in wildlife and environmental law and policy, biology, education, geographic information systems, publishing.
Publication(s): Wildlife Law News Quarterly, Wild News, The Status of Poaching in the U.S., Wild Friends: Kids Bringing People Together on Wildife Issues, Federal Wildlife Laws Handbook with Related Laws
Contact(s):
Ruth Musgrave, Director

CENTRAL OHIO ANGLERS AND HUNTERS CLUB
P.O. Box 28224
Columbus, OH 43228 United States
Phone: 614-879-7757
Scope: Local
Description: Promotion of conservation and conservation education in all their phases, with a particular reference to land, air, and water; to promote good fellowship and good citizenship; to inculcate regard for the rights of others and respect for the obedience to law; to support a safe and effective conservation program for and by the state and nation.
Keyword(s): Recreation/Ecotourism, Reduce/Reuse/Recycle
Contact(s):
Doug Eakins, President; 767 Larri Ct., W. Jefferson, OH 43162; 614-879-7757
Kevin Burke, Secretary
Eric Obrein, Treasurer

CENTRO DE INFORMACION, INVESTIGACION Y EDUCACION SOCIAL (CIIES)
RR-9, Buzon 1722
San Juan, PR 00926-9736 United States
Phone: 787-292-0620   Fax: 787-760-0496
E-mail: sctinc@coqui.net
Founded: 1989
Scope: State
Description: CIIES was founded as a part of Servicios Cientificos y Tecnicos, a nonprofit organization dealing with natural resources, environmental health, and safety issues. It provides services in the form of seminars, workshops, and a resource center to students, teachers, journalists, communities, and workers.
Keyword(s): Ethics/Environmental Justice, Pollution (general), Wildlife & Species
Contact(s):
Neftali Martinez, Director
Jose Sepulveda, Secretary
Maria Vilches, Treasurer

CETACEAN SOCIETY INTERNATIONAL
P.O. Box 953
Georgetown, CT 06829 United States
Phone: 203-431-1606   Fax: 203-431-1606
E-mail: rossiter@csiwhalesalive.org
Website: www.csiwhalesalive.org
Founded: 1974
Membership: 101–1,000
Scope: State, Regional, National, International
Description: CSI is dedicated to the preservation and protection of all cetaceans (whales, dolphins, and porpoises) and the marine environment on a global basis. CSI is an all-volunteer, nonprofit conservation education and research organization with representatives in over 21 countries.
Publication(s): Whales Alive (newsletter), several education packages, Meet the Great Ones
Keyword(s): Climate Change, Development/Developing Countries, Ecosystems (precious), Oceans/Coasts/Beaches, Recreation/Ecotourism, Wildlife & Species
Contact(s):
William Rossiter, President; 16 Mountain Laurel Lane, Redding, CT 06896; 203-431-1606; Fax: 203-431-1606; rossiter@csiwhalesalive.org
Barbara Kilpatrick, Vice President; 15 Wood Pond Rd., West Hartford, CT 06107; 860-561-0187
Robbins Barstow, Director Emeritus; 190 Stillwold Dr., Wethersfield, CT 06109; 860-563-2565; robbinsb@aol.com
Martha Fitzgerald, Secretary; 120 Retreat Ave. C-3, Hartford, CT 06106; 860-246-3143
Robert Victor, Treasurer; 57 Crossroads Ln., Glastonbury, CT 06033; rfvictor@juno.com

CHARLES A. AND ANNE MORROW LINDBERGH FOUNDATION, THE
2150 Third Ave. N., Suite 310
Anoka, MN 55303-2200 United States
Phone: 763-576-1596   Fax: 763-576-1664
E-mail: info@lindberghfoundation.org
Website: www.lindberghfoundation.org
Founded: 1977
Membership: 1,001–10,000
Scope: International
Description: The Charles A. and Anne Morrow Lindbergh Foundation is a nonprofit organization, advancing Charles and Anne Morrow Lindbergh's vision of a balance between technological progress and environmental preservation by offering Lindbergh Grants to individuals for research and educational projects which will further this balance, presenting the Lindbergh Award for extraordinary contributions to the nature/technology balance, and sponsoring other projects and programs.
Publication(s): Newsletter
Keyword(s): Agriculture/Farming, Population, Public Health, Reduce/Reuse/Recycle
Contact(s):
Reeve Lindbergh, President
Clare Hallward, Vice President
Kristina Lindbergh, Vice President
Gene Bratsch, Secretary/Treasurer
Marlene White, Executive Director

CHAUTAUQUA WATERSHED CONSERVANCY
413 North Main Street
Jamestown, NY 14701 United States
Phone: 716-664-2166   Fax: 716-483-3524
E-mail: chautwsh@netsync.net
Website: chautauquawatershed.org
Founded: 1990
Membership: 101–1,000
Scope: Local
Description: The Chautauqua Watershed Conservancy is a county-wide organization with the mission to preserve and enhance the water quality, scenic beauty and ecological health of the lakes, streams and watersheds of the Chautauqua region.
Publication(s): The Shed Sheet
Contact(s):
John Jablonski, Executive Director; 413 N. Main Street, Jamestown, NY 14701; 716-664-2166; Fax: 716-483-3524; chautwsh@netsync.net
Lori Scott, Administrative Assistant; 413 N. Main Street, Jamestown, NY 14701; 716-664-2166; Fax: 716-483-3524; chautwsh2@netsync.net
Tracy Wilkin, Outreach Coordinator; 413 N. Main Street, Jamestown, NY 14701; 716-664-2166; Fax: 716-483-3524; chautwsh2@netsync.net

CHELONIA INSTITUTE
402 South Ventura Avenue
Oviedo, FL 32765 United States
Phone: 703-516-2600   Fax: 703-522-1427
Website: www.truland.com
Founded: 1977
Membership: 101–1,000
Scope: National
Description: A private operating foundation with ecological concerns focused primarily on the conservation of marine turtles. The Institute undertakes a broad range of programs including technical publications, land acquisition, and so on, and works cooperatively with other organizations.
Contact(s):
Robert Truland, President
Mary Truland, Assistant Director

CHESAPEAKE BAY FOUNDATION, INC.
Philip Merrill Environmental Center
6 Herndon Avenue
Annapolis, MD 21403 United States
Phone: 410-268-8816   Fax: 410-268-6687
E-mail: chesapeake@cbf.org
Website: www.savethebay.cbf.org
Founded: 1966
Membership: 100,001–500,000
Scope: National
Description: A nonprofit membership organization established to promote the environmental protection and restoration of Chesapeake Bay and its full watershed. CBF operates programs in environmental education and environmental protection and restoration.
Publication(s): Save the Bay, Grassroots Bulletin, Megalops
Keyword(s): Water Habitats & Quality
Contact(s):
William Baker, President
Donald Baugh, Vice President for Education
Michael Shultz, Vice President for Public Affairs
Wayne Mills, Chairman

CHESAPEAKE BAY FOUNDATION, INC.
MARYLAND OFFICE
Philip Merrill Environmental Center
6 Herndon Avenue
Annapolis, MD 21403 United States
Phone: 410-268-8833   Fax: 410-280-3513
E-mail: chesapeake@cbf.org
Website: www.cbf.org
Founded: 1967
Membership: 100,001–500,000
Scope: Local, State, Regional
Description: The Chesapeake Bay Foundation's Maryland office conducts activities of the foundation specific to the state of Maryland and operates a field office on the Eastern Shore of Maryland as well as a farm (Clagett Farm) in Southern Maryland.
Publication(s): Save the Bay, Bay Savers Bulletin
Keyword(s): Agriculture/Farming, Air Quality/Atmosphere, Energy, Ethics/Environmental Justice, Executive/Legislative/Judicial Reform, Forests/Forestry, Land Issues, Pollution (general), Public Lands/Greenspace, Reduce/Reuse/Recycle, Sprawl/Urban Planning, Transportation
Contact(s):
Kim Coble, Executive Director; 410-268-8833; Fax: 410-280-3513; kcoble@cbf.org

CHESAPEAKE BAY FOUNDATION, INC.
PENNSYLVANIA OFFICE
The Old Waterworks Bldg.
614 N. Front St., Suite G
Harrisburg, PA 17101 United States
Phone: 717-234-5550   Fax: 717-234-9632
E-mail: chesapeake@cbf.org
Website: www.cbf.org
Founded: 1966
Membership: 10,001–100,000
Scope: State
Description: The Foundation conducts activities and programs specific to the Commonwealth of Pennsylvania.
Publication(s): Bay Beginnings - newsletter
Keyword(s): Air Quality/Atmosphere, Energy, Reduce/Reuse/Recycle, Transportation
Contact(s):
Jolene Chinchilli, Pennsylvania Executive Director

CHESAPEAKE BAY FOUNDATION, INC.
VIRGINIA OFFICE
1108 East Main St., Suite 1600
Richmond, VA 23219 United States
Phone: 804-780-1392   Fax: 804-648-4011
Website: www.cbf.org
Founded: 1967
Scope: State
Description: The Chesapeake Bay Foundation conducts activities of the foundation in the Commonwealth of Virginia and operates field offices in Norfolk and Tappahannock, Virginia.
Keyword(s): Public Lands/Greenspace, Water Habitats & Quality, Wildlife & Species
Contact(s):
Joseph Maroon, Executive Director
Roy Hoagland, Assistant Director

CHESAPEAKE WILDLIFE HERITAGE (CWH)
P.O. Box 1745
Easton, MD 21601 United States
Phone: 410-822-5100   Fax: 410-822-4016
E-mail: info@cheswildlife.org
Website: www.cheswildlife.org
Founded: 1980
Membership: 101–1,000
Scope: State, Regional
Description: A private, nonprofit conservation group working with private and public landowners to restore and protect wildlife habitat in the Chesapeake Bay watershed. CWH constructs and manages wetlands, warm season grass and wildflower meadows, nesting structures, marshes, and woodlands. CWH advises on and carries out sustainable farming techniques in order to benefit the Chesapeake Bay and its wildlife. CWH also conducts ecological research on plants and migratory birds.
Publication(s): Annual Report, Habitat Works
Keyword(s): Agriculture/Farming, Ecosystems (precious), Water Habitats & Quality, Wildlife & Species
Contact(s):
Larry Albright, Board of Directors President
Susanna Engvall, Webmaster/PR
John Gerber, Habitat Ecologist
Michael Haggie, Habitat Ecologist
Chris Pupke, Development Director
Andi Pupke, Education Director

CHICAGO HERPETOLOGICAL SOCIETY
2060 N. Clark St.
Chicago, IL 60614 United States
Phone: 219-464-8514
E-mail: chris@graptemys.com
Website: www.chicagoherp.org
Founded: 1966
Membership: 1,001–10,000
Scope: State

Description: The Chicago Herpetological Society is a group of reptile and amphibian enthusiasts. Its goals are education, conservation, and the advancement of herpetology.
Publication(s): Bulletin of the Chicago Herpetological Society
Keyword(s): Wildlife & Species
Contact(s):
Jack Schoenfelder, President; c/o Ivy Tech College, 2401 Valley Dr., Valparaiso, IN 46383; 219-929-1525
Lori King, Vice President; 773-447-3645; loriguanid@aol.com
Greg Brim, Treasurer; 603-834-4446; gregbrim@mediaone.net

CHICAGO PARK DISTRICT
JUNIOR EARTH TEAM
541 North Fairbanks
4th Floor
Chicago, IL 60611 United States
Phone: 312-742-4967   Fax: 312-742-5346
E-mail: dayna.decker@chicagoparkdistrict.com
Website: www.chicagoparkdistrict.org
Founded: 1995
Membership: 1–100
Scope: Local
Description: The Junior Earth Team (JET) employs 100 teens from across Chicago each year. JET provides hands-on stewardship projects, conservation science curricula, and career exposure through field trips and guest speakers.
Keyword(s): Ecosystems (precious), Energy, Ethics/Environmental Justice, Forests/Forestry, Oceans/Coasts/Beaches, Pollution (general), Population, Public Health, Public Lands/Greenspace, Recreation/Ecotourism, Water Habitats & Quality, Wildlife & Species

CHICAGO REGION BIODIVERSITY COUNCIL
CHICAGO WILDERNESS
8 S. Michigan Ave.
Suite 900
Chicago, IL 60603 United States
Phone: 312-580-2156   Fax: 312-346-5606
Website: www.chicagowilderness.org
Founded: 1996
Scope: Local, Regional
Description: The Chicago Wilderness coalition is an unprecedented partnership of more than 160 public and private organizations that have joined forces to protect, restore and manage the Chicago region's natural lands and the plants and animals that inhabit them. The consortium's mission is to restore the region's natural communities to long-term viability, enrich local residents' quality of life, and contribute to the preservation of global biodiversity.
Publication(s): CW Atlas of Biodiversity, CW Biodiversity Recovery Plan, Teacher Toolkit on Biodiversity
Keyword(s): Ecosystems (precious), Land Issues, Public Lands/Greenspace, Sprawl/Urban Planning, Water Habitats & Quality, Wildlife & Species
Contact(s):
Lucy Hutcherson, Director of Communications; 3300 Golf Rd., Brookfield, IL 60513; 708-485-0263; ext. 253; Fax: 708-485-6048; luhutche@brookfieldzoo.org
Elizabeth McCance, Program Director; 312-580-2138; Fax: 312-346-5606; emccance@tnc.org
Debra Shore, Director of Development; 5225 Old Orchard Rd., Suite 37, Skokie, IL 60077; 847-965-9275; ext. 14; Fax: 847-965-9282; dshore@chicagowilderness.org

CHIHUAHUAN DESERT RESEARCH INSTITUTE
P.O. Box 905
Ft. Davis, TX 79734 United States
Phone: 432-364-2499   Fax: 432-364-2509
E-mail: manager@cdri.org
Website: www.cdri.org
Founded: 1974
Membership: 101–1,000
Scope: National
Description: Nonprofit organization formed to promote public awareness, appreciation, and concern for the natural diversity of the Chihuahuan Desert region through research and education programs. Current studies include life history related studies, systematic zoology, systematic botany, desert ecology, anthropology, archeology, geology, and theoretical ecology.
Publication(s): Chihuahuan Desert Discovery
Keyword(s): Agriculture/Farming, Climate Change, Land Issues, Wildlife & Species
Contact(s):
Cathryn Hoyt, Executive Director; 915-364-2499; Fax: 915-364-2504; manager@cdri.org
Jennifer Bauer, Education Coordinator; 915-364-2499; education_cdri@overland.net
Martha Latta, Business Manager; 432-364-2499

CHINA REGION LAKES ALLIANCE
571 Lakeview Drive
China, ME 04358 United States
Phone: 207-445-5021   Fax: 207-445-3208
E-mail: lakesalliance@yahoo.com
Founded: 1994
Membership: 1–100
Scope: Local
Description: To protect and improve water quality in 4 culturally eutrophic Maine lakes, (China Lake, Threecornered Pond, Threemile Pond and Webber Pond) and to benefit our local economy through integrated watershed management.
Publication(s): Walk for a Rainy Day: What You Can Do for Your Camp Road, Starting a Local Youth Conservation Corps, Vegetative Buffer Strips
Keyword(s): Oceans/Coasts/Beaches, Pollution (general), Water Habitats & Quality
Contact(s):
Daniel Dubord, President; 207-872-2743; Fax: 207-872-2962
Rebecca Manthey, Executive Director

CHISHOLM WOLF FOUNDATION, INC.
P.O. Box 190
Dale, TX 78616 United States
Phone: 512-601-1314
E-mail: cwfiwolves@juno.com
Founded: 1989
Membership: 101–1,000
Scope: Local, State
Description: The Chisholm Wolf Foundation, Inc. is dedicated to saving the North American Timber Wolf from extinction. CWFI is the only corporation in Texas with Federal and State permits for education, research, and preservation. Our goal is to preserve the natural existance of the wolf through our educational seminars and observational research.
Keyword(s): Wildlife & Species
Contact(s):
Vivian Chisholm, Chief Executive Officer; P.O. Box 190, Dale, TX 78616; 512-601-1314; cwfiwolves@juno.com
John Baccus, Wildlife Biologist; P.O. Box 190, Dale, TX 78616; 512-601-1314; cwfiwolves@juno.com
Chris Berdoll, Eco Biologist; P.O. Box 190, Dale, TX 78616; 512-601-1314; cwfiwolves@juno.com
Paul Brandt, Exotic Veterinarian; P.O. Box 190, Dale, TX 78616; 512-601-1314; cwiwolves@juno.com
Sherri Brewer, Educational Coordinator; P.O. Box 190, Dale, TX 78616; 512-601-1314; cwfiwolves@juno.com
Dan Castro, Attorney at Law; P.O. Box 190, Dale, TX 78616; 512-601-1314; cwfiwolves@juno.com
Joan Crossley, Sec./Treas.; P.O. Box 190, Dale, TX 78616; 512-601-1314; cwfiwolves@juno.com
Trudy Dixon, Grant Writer; P.O. Box 190, Dale, TX 78616; 512-601-1314; cwfiwolves@juno.com

Rita Hersey, Fund Raising; P.O. Box 190, Dale, TX 78616; 512-601-1314; cwfiwolves@juno.com
Daniel Hurst, Wolf Rescue; P.O. Box 190, Dale, TX 78616; 512-601-1314; cwfiwolves@juno.com

CHLORINE-FREE PAPER CONSORTIUM
1411 Ellis Ave.
Northland College
Ashland, WI 54806 United States
Phone: 715-682-1847   Fax: 715-682-1308
E-mail: mail@clfree.org
Website: www.clfree.org
Scope: National
Description: The CPC aims to reduce the use of chlorinated substances in the paper-making process by informing people about the effects of chlorine by-products and facilitating communication between buyers and sellers of chlorine-free paper products. A project of Northland College and the National Wildlife Federation.
Publication(s): Brochure
Keyword(s): Finance/Banking/Trade, Pollution (general), Public Health, Water Habitats & Quality
Contact(s):
Jeffery Huxmann, Executive Coordinator; huxmann@clfree.org

CHRISTINA CONSERVANCY, INC.
P.O. Box 1680
Wilmington, DE 19899-1680 United States
Phone: 302-984-3801   Fax: 302-652-5379
Founded: 1981
Scope: Local
Description: The purpose of the Christina Conservancy, Inc. is to preserve, protect, and urge the wise use of the Christina River.
Keyword(s): Water Habitats & Quality
Contact(s):
Edward Cooch Jr., President; 302-984-3801; Fax: 302-652-5379

CINCINNATI NATURE CENTER
ROWE WOODS, LONG BRANCH FARM & TRAILS
4949 Tealtown Road
Milford, OH 45150-9752 United States
Phone: 513-831-1711   Fax: 513-831-8052
E-mail: cnc@cincynature.org
Website: www.cincynature.org
Founded: 1965
Membership: 1,001–10,000
Scope: Local, State
Description: A private, non-profit organization consisting of a nature preserve and a working farm. The mission of CNC is to inspire passion for nature through experience and education.
Publication(s): Newsleaf (newsletter)
Keyword(s): Agriculture/Farming, Ecosystems (precious), Recreation/Ecotourism, Reduce/Reuse/Recycle, Wildlife & Species
Contact(s):
William Hopple, President/Executive Director; 513-965-4246; Fax: 513-831-8052; bhopple@cincynature.org
Connie Brockman, Education Director; 513-965-4891; Fax: 513-831-8052; cbrockman@cincynature.org
Ted Grannan, Operations Director; 513-965-4890; Fax: 513-831-8052; tgrannan@cincynature.org

CIRCUMPOLAR CONSERVATION UNION
1612 K Street, NW
Suite 401
Washington, DC 20006 United States
Phone: 202-675-8370   Fax: 202-675-8373
E-mail: circumpolar@igc.org
Website: www.circumpolar.org
Founded: 1993
Scope: State, Regional, National, International
Description: The Circumpolar Conservation Union is dedicated to protecting the ecological and cultural integrity of the Arctic for present and future generations. CCU works nationally and internationally through policy advocacy, public education, and by building links among diverse constituencies, to achieve comprehensive legal protection for the Arctic.
Publication(s): Persistent Organic Pollutants in Alaska
Keyword(s): Agriculture/Farming, Air Quality/Atmosphere, Climate Change, Development/Developing Countries, Ecosystems (precious), Ethics/Environmental Justice, Oceans/Coasts/Beaches, Pollution (general), Public Health, Wildlife & Species
Contact(s):
Evelyn Hurwich, President

CITIZENS ALLIANCE FOR SAVING THE ATMOSPHERE AND THE EARTH (CASA)
1-3-17-711 Tanimachi
Chuo-ku, Osaka, 540-0012 Japan
Phone: 8169413745   Fax: 8169415699
E-mail: casa@netplus.ne.jp
Website: www.netplus.ne.jp/~casa/
Founded: 1988
Scope: International
Description: CASA is committed to preserving both the local and global environment through solidarity with both Japanese and international environmental NGO's. CASA is composed of 50 NGO's and about 500 individuals, such as scientists, teachers, lawyers, farmers, grassroots activists, artists, consumer group leaders, and others.
Contact(s):
Mitsutoshi Hayakawa, Managing Director
Yuji Nishi, Executive Director
Tsunetoshi Yamamura, Representative Director

CITIZENS FOR A SCENIC FLORIDA, INC.
4401 Emerson St., Suite 10
Jacksonville, FL 32207 United States
Phone: 904-396-0037   Fax: 904-398-4647
E-mail: scenicfl@scenicflorida.org
Website: www.scenicflorida.org
Founded: 1998
Scope: Regional
Description: Citizens for a Scenic Florida: Preserving Florida's Scenic Heritage.
Publication(s): Scenic Watch, Florida View Points
Keyword(s): Forests/Forestry, Land Issues, Sprawl/Urban Planning
Contact(s):
Lane Welch, Director

CITIZENS NATURAL RESOURCES ASSOCIATION OF WISCONSIN, INC.
Attn: President, 3805 Paunack St.
Madison, WI 53711 United States
Phone: 608-231-9721   Fax: 608-218-1647
E-mail: ekolink@aol.com
Founded: 1951
Scope: State
Description: To protect Wisconsin's natural resources through education, legislation, and the courts. The CNRA initiated and sponsored the action which resulted in the banning of DDT in Wisconsin and two years later in the United States. Recently, the CNRA has been concentrating on protecting and restoring native vegetation along Wisconsin's roads.
Publication(s): CNRA Report, The, Wisconsin Roadsides

Contact(s):
- Kira Henschel, President
- Jan Calpone, Vice President/ Editor; 2 Meminiee Dr., Oskosh, WI 54901
- Louise Coumbe, Membership Chair; 1028 Elmwood Ave., Oshkosh, WI 54901
- Zaiga Maassen, Secretary; 913 Honey Creek, Oshkosh, WI 54904
- Charles Sturm, Treasurer; J-1233 Mayfair Rd. Suite 125, Milwaukee, WI 53226

CITIZENS' NUCLEAR INFORMATION CENTER
1-58-15-3F Higashi-Nakano
Nakano-ku, Tokyo, 164-0003 Japan
Phone: 81353309520   Fax: 81353309530
Founded: 1975
Scope: International
Description: A nonprofit organization to collect and provide the public a broad range of information on nuclear power issues, and cooperate with individuals and other organizations concerned with nuclear proliferation in Japan and around the world. Information includes the Japanese government policy of plutonium utilization, effects of radioactive contamination, nuclear power plant accidents, economics, and other impacts on the local communities caused by construction of nuclear power plants.
Keyword(s): Energy
Contact(s):
- Hideyuki Ban, Co-Director
- Gaia Hoerner, International Relations Officer

CLEAN OCEAN ACTION
MAIN OFFICE
P.O. Box 505
Sandy Hook, NJ 07732 United States
Phone: 732-872-0111   Fax: 732-872-8041
E-mail: sandyhook@cleanoceanaction.org
Website: www.cleanoceanaction.org
Founded: 1984
Scope: Local, State, Regional, National
Description: A broad-based coalition of 175 conservation, fishing, diving, boating, real estate, student, and civic groups; over 300 businesses; and thousands of citizens concerned with the degraded waters off the New York and New Jersey coasts. COA uses education, research, and citizen action to pressure public officials to enact and enforce protective laws for our marine resources. Programs include: storm drain stenciling; regulatory reviews; contaminated sediments; and non-point source pollution.
Publication(s): The Ocean is a Flush Away, Ocean Advocate, Annual Statewide Beach Sweep Report, Wasting Our Waters Away, Citizen Guide for Dredged Material Management
Keyword(s): Oceans/Coasts/Beaches, Pollution (general)
Contact(s):
- Dery Bennett, President
- William Decamp, Vice President
- Cindy Zipf, Executive Director
- Ben Forest, Treasurer
- Pat Schneider, Secretary

CLEAN OCEAN ACTION
MID-COAST OFFICE
P.O. Box 1303
Wildwood, NJ 08087 United States
Phone: 732-729-9262
E-mail: Tuckerton@cleanoceanaction.org
Website: www.cleanoceanaction.org
Scope: Local, State, Regional, National
Description: See COA Main Office.
Keyword(s): Oceans/Coasts/Beaches, Pollution (general)

CLEAN OCEAN ACTION
SOUTH JERSEY OFFICE
P.O. Box 1098
Wildwood, NJ 08260 United States
Phone: 609-729-7262   Fax: 609-729-1091
E-mail: Wildwood@cleanoceanaction.org
Website: www.cleanoceanaction.org
Scope: Local, State, Regional, National
Description: See Main Office
Keyword(s): Oceans/Coasts/Beaches, Pollution (general)
Contact(s):
- Anthony Totah, South Jersey Coordinator/ICE Coordinator; P.O. Box 1098, 3419 Pacific Avenue, Wildwood, NJ 08260; 609-729-9262; Fax: 609-729-1091; Wildwood@cleanoceanaction.org

CLEAN WATER ACTION
4455 Connecticut Ave., NW, Suite A300
Washington, DC 20008-2328 United States
Phone: 202-895-0420   Fax: 202-895-0438
E-mail: cwa@cleanwater.org
Website: www.cleanwateraction.org
Scope: National
Description: The national citizen's organization working full-time for clean safe water at an affordable cost, control of toxic chemicals, and protection of our natural resources.
Contact(s):
- Jim Pierce, Development Associate

CLEAN WATER FUND
4455 Connecticut Ave. NW Suite A300-16
Washington, DC 20008-2328 United States
Phone: 202-895-0432   Fax: 202-895-0438
E-mail: cwf@cleanwater.org
Website: www.cleanwaterfund.org
Scope: National
Description: Clean Water Fund is a 501 (3) research, training and educational organization that advances environmental and consumer protection with a special focus on water pollution, toxic hazards, solid waste management, and natural resources.
Publication(s): WATER: Riches for Clean Up, Pennies for Prevention; TOXICS: Toxic Metals in Batteries, If It's Broke, Fix It; SOLID WASTE: Expanding Rhode Island's Market with RI War on Waste
Contact(s):
- Peter Van Lockwood, Board of Directors, President
- David Zwick, Board of Directors, Executive Vice President; ext. 103; dzwick@cleanwater.org
- Kathleen Aterno, Board of Directors, Treasurer; ext. 106; katerno@cleanwater.org
- Jim Pierce, Development Associate; ext. 110; jpierce@cleanwater.org

CLEAN WATER NETWORK, THE
1200 New York Avenue, NW, Suite 400
Washington, DC 20005 United States
Phone: 202-289-2395   Fax: 202-289-1060
E-mail: cleanwaternt@igc.org
Website: www.cwn.org
Founded: 1992
Membership: 101–1,000
Scope: National
Description: The Clean Water Network is a national alliance of more than 900 organizations representing environmentalists, commercial fishers, anglers, surfers, family farmers, justice advocates, faith communities, and labor unions working together to strengthen federal laws that protect our water quality.
Publication(s): Prescription for Clean Water, Wetlands for Clean Water, America's Animal Factories, Spilling Swills, Spills and Kills

Keyword(s): Water Habitats & Quality
Contact(s):
Ami Grace, Grass Roots Director; 202-289-2421; agrace@nrdc.org
Merritt Frey, Policy Analyst/Idaho; 208-345-7776
Linda Young, Southeast Field Coordinator/Florida; 850-222-9188

CLEAR CREEK ENVIRONMENTAL FOUNDATION
507 Houston Avenue
League City, TX 77573 United States
Phone: 281-332-5822   Fax: 281-557-1302
E-mail: jol111@aol.com
Website: clearcreekcleanup.org
Founded: 2000
Scope: Local
Description: Caretaker of Clear Creek, Texas. Cleanup and trash pickup. Habitat restoration—Cordgrass planting.
Keyword(s): Ecosystems (precious)

CLEVELAND MUSEUM OF NATURAL HISTORY, THE
1 Wade Oval Drive
University Circle
Cleveland, OH 44106 United States
Phone: 216-231-4600, ext. 219   Fax: 216-231-5919
E-mail: botany@cmnh.org
Website: www.cmnh.org
Founded: 1920
Membership: 1,001–10,000
Scope: Regional
Description: To instill an understanding of and appreciation for nature and inspire responsibility for conservation and stewardship of natural diversity. The Museum program areas include exhibits, publications, education, collections, research, and natural areas. The Museum owns a system of 25 sanctuaries.
Publication(s): Explorer, Kirtlandia
Contact(s):
James Bissell, Coordinator of Natural Areas

CLIMATE INSTITUTE
333 1/2 Pennsylvania Ave., SE
Washington, DC 20003-1148 United States
Phone: 202-547-0104   Fax: 202-547-0111
E-mail: info@climate.org
Website: www.climate.org
Founded: 1986
Scope: International
Description: Designed to serve as a catalyst for international response and cooperation to address the threats posed by climate change and depletion of the stratospheric ozone layer. The Climate Institute operates as a bridge between scientists and policymakers with the intent of expediting policy responses to the challenges posed by human-induced climate change.
Publication(s): Climate Alert, Environmental Exodus, Climate Change in Asia, Forests in a Changing Climate, Coping with Climate Change
Keyword(s): Development/Developing Countries, Energy, Forests/Forestry, Oceans/Coasts/Beaches
Contact(s):
John Topping, President; 202-547-0104; ext. 14; jtopping@climate.org

CLINTON RIVER WATERSHED COUNCIL (CRWC)
101 Main Street, Suite 100
Rochester, MI 48307 United States
Phone: 248-601-0606   Fax: 248-601-1280
E-mail: contact@crwc.org
Website: www.crwc.org
Founded: 1972
Membership: 101–1,000
Scope: Local, State
Description: CRWC is a non-profit coalition of individuals, businesses, local governments, and other community groups dedicated to protecting, enhancing, and celebrating the Clinton River, its watershed, and Lake St. Clair.
Publication(s): Clinton River Resource Center
Keyword(s): Ecosystems (precious), Land Issues, Pollution (general), Public Lands/Greenspace, Recreation/Ecotourism, Water Habitats & Quality, Wildlife & Species

COALITION FOR CLEAN AIR
10780 Santa Monica Blvd., # 210
Los Angeles, CA 90025 United States
Phone: 310-441-1544   Fax: 310-446-4362
Website: www.coalitionforcleanair.org
Founded: 1970
Membership: 1,001–10,000
Scope: State
Description: A nonprofit, tax-exempt organization dedicated to restoring clean, healthful air to Southern California residents through a combination of efforts including outreach and education, litigation, research, and policy advocacy.
Publication(s): Clearing the Air, publications available on website
Keyword(s): Air Quality/Atmosphere, Pollution (general)
Contact(s):
David Allgood, President
Wendy James, Vice President
Todd Campbell, Policy Director
Tim Carmichael, Executive Director
Abby Arnold, Treasurer

COALITION FOR EDUCATION IN THE OUTDOORS
E331 Park Center, S.U.N.Y. at Cortland, Box 2000
Cortland, NY 13045 United States
Phone: 607-753-4968   Fax: 607-753-5982
E-mail: taproot@cortland.edu
Website: www.outdooredcoalition.org
Founded: 1986
Membership: 101–1,000
Scope: National, International
Description: The Coalition is composed of more than 100 businesses, institutions, organizations, associations, centers, agencies, and individuals affiliated in support of communicating and networking concerning education in, for and about the outdoors. The Coalition's magazine is a critically acclaimed education resource. The Coalition also conducts a biennial Outdoor Education Research Symposium.
Publication(s): Taproot, Outdoor Education Research Symposium Proceedings
Keyword(s): Ethics/Environmental Justice, Land Issues, Public Lands/Greenspace, Recreation/Ecotourism
Contact(s):
Charles Yaple, Executive Coordinator

COALITION FOR NATURAL STREAM VALLEYS, INC.
430 Orchard Rd.
Newark, DE 19711-5137 United States
Phone: 302-366-8059
Scope: Regional
Description: The purpose of the Coalition for Natural Stream Valleys, Inc. is to promote the wise use of, and the preservation of natural stream valleys.
Contact(s):
Dorothy Miller, Corresponding Secretary
Roland Roth, Chairman; 302-831-1300

COAST ALLIANCE
600 Pennsylvania Ave., SE
Suite 340
Washington, DC 20003 United States
Phone: 202-546-9554 Fax: 202-546-9609
E-mail: coast@coastalliance.org
Website: www.coastalliance.org

Founded: 1979
Membership: 101–1,000
Scope: Local, State, Regional, National
Description: The Coast Alliance is a nonprofit public interest group dedicated to raising public awareness about our priceless coastal resources. Composed of concerned activists across the United States, the Coast Alliance provides information on activities affecting the nation's four coasts: the Atlantic, Pacific, Gulf of Mexico, and Great Lakes.
Publication(s): And Two If By Sea: Fighting The Attack on America's Coasts, Using Common Sense to Protect The Coasts, Mission Possible, Muddy Waters, Pointless Pollution, Storm on The Horizon: The National Flood Insurance Program and America's Coasts
Keyword(s): Development/Developing Countries, Executive/Legislative/Judicial Reform, Land Issues, Oceans/Coasts/Beaches, Pollution (general), Water Habitats & Quality
Contact(s):
Dawn Hamilton, Executive Director; 202-546-9554; Fax: 202-546-9609; jsavitz@coastalliance.org
Jaime Matera, Outreach Coordinator; 202-546-9554; Fax: 202-546-9609; jmatera@coastalliance.org
Dery Bennett, Chairperson of the Board; American Littoral Society, Bldg. 18 Hartshorne Drive, Sandy Hook Highlands, NJ 07732; 732-872-8041
Todd Miller, Treasurer and Secretary; North Carolina Coastal Federation, 3609 Hwy. 24, Newport, NC 28570; 252-393-8185

COASTAL AMERICA FOUNDATION
100 Muron Avenue
Bellingham, MA 02019 United States
Phone: 508-292-0251
E-mail: cmail@coastalamericafoundation.org
Website: www.coastalamericafoundation.org

Founded: 1998
Scope: National, International
Description: The Coastal America Foundation is dedicated to supporting the restoration of our nation's wetlands and aquatic habitats.
Keyword(s): Ecosystems (precious), Energy, Ethics/Environmental Justice, Land Issues, Oceans/Coasts/Beaches, Pollution (general), Public Lands/Greenspace, Recreation/Ecotourism, Reduce/Reuse/Recycle, Sprawl/Urban Planning, Transportation, Water Habitats & Quality

COASTAL CONSERVATION ASSOCIATION
6919 Port West Drive Suite 100
Houston, TX 77024 United States
Phone: 713-626-4234 Fax: 713-626-5852
E-mail: ntl@joincca.org
Website: www.joincca.org

Founded: 1977
Membership: 10,001–100,000
Scope: National
Description: A national nonprofit corporation organized exclusively for the purpose of promoting and advancing the conservation, and protection of the marine, animal, and plant life both onshore and offshore along the coastal areas of the United States for the benefit and enjoyment of the general public.
Publication(s): Tide
Keyword(s): Oceans/Coasts/Beaches, Recreation/Ecotourism, Water Habitats & Quality, Wildlife & Species
Contact(s):
David Cummins, President
Gus Schram, Vice President
Jeff Angers, Executive Director of Louisiana Regional Office; P.O. Box 373, Baton Rouge, LA 70821; 225-952-9200; Fax: 225-952-9204
Kevin Daniels, Executive Director of Texas Regional Office; 4801 Woodway, Suite 220W, Houston, TX 77056; 713-626-4222; Fax: 713-961-3801
David Dexter, Executive Director of Alabama Regional Office; 144 Florence Place, Mobile, AL 36607; 334-478-3474; Fax: 334-476-5214
Ted Forsgren, Executive Director of Florida Regional Office; 905 East Park Ave., Tallahassee, FL 32301-2646; 850-224-3474; Fax: 850-224-5199
Pat Keliher, Executive Director of Maine Regional Office; 40 Lafayette St., Yarmouth, ME 04096; 207-846-1015; Fax: 207-846-1168
Austin Ragsdale, Executive Director of North Carolina Regional Office; 3701 National Drive Suite 217, Raleigh, NC 27612; 919-781-3474; Fax: 919-781-3475
Richard Welton, Executive Director of Virginia Regional Office; 2100 Marina Shores Dr., Suite 108, Virginia Beach, VA 23451; 757-481-1226; Fax: 757-481-6910
Scott Whitaker, Executive Director of South Carolina Regional Office; P.O. Box 290640, Columbia, SC 29229; 803-865-4164; Fax: 803-865-5104
Walter Fondren, Chairman of the Board
Alex Jernigan, Vice Chairman
Will Ohmstede, Vice Chairman
Doug Pike, Editor

COASTAL CONSERVATION ASSOCIATION GEORGIA
515 Denmark St. Suite 300
Statesboro, GA 30458 United States
Phone: 912-764-6222 Fax: 912-764-6497
E-mail: info@ccaga.org
Website: www.ccaga.org

Founded: 1987
Membership: 1,001–10,000
Scope: State
Description: The CCAG promotes conservation through education—promoting, protecting and enhancing the availability of marine, animal, plant life and other coastal resources for the benefit and enjoyment of the general public.
Publication(s): Tide Magazine, Tidelines (newsletter)
Keyword(s): Oceans/Coasts/Beaches, Reduce/Reuse/Recycle, Water Habitats & Quality, Wildlife & Species
Contact(s):
Martin Nesmith, Chairman; 912-739-1744; Fax: 912-739-4889
William Phillips, Vice-Chairman; 912-764-6567; Fax: 912-764-6568; ringo@bulloch.com

COASTAL GEORGIA LAND TRUST INC.
428 Bull St., Suite 210
Savannah, GA 31401 United States
Phone: 912-231-0507 Fax: 912-231-1143
E-mail: bill@cglt.org
Website: www.cglt.org

Founded: 1993
Membership: 101–1,000
Scope: Regional
Description: The mission of the Coastal Georgia Land Trust, Inc., a nonprofit organization, is to promote the responsible stewardship and preservation of land in coastal Georgia.
Publication(s): Coastal Georgia Land Trust Newsletter, Coastal Georgia Land Trust Brochure
Keyword(s): Development/Developing Countries, Forests/Forestry, Land Issues, Public Lands/Greenspace, Water Habitats & Quality, Wildlife & Species

NON-GOVERNMENTAL NON-PROFIT ORGANIZATIONS – C

Contact(s):
Rhett Mouchet, President of the Board of Directors
Alan Bailey, Vice President, Board of Directors; 912-925-3159; Fax: 912-927-9766; acbailey@worldnet.atf.net
Mary Elfner, Executive Director

COASTAL SOCIETY, THE
P.O. Box 25408
Alexandria, VA 22313-5408 United States
Phone: 703-768-1599   Fax: 703-768-1598
E-mail: coastalsoc@aol.com
Website: www.coastalsociety.org

Founded: 1975
Membership: 101–1,000
Scope: International
Description: The Coastal Society is an organization of private sector, academic and governmental professionals and students dedicated to actively addressing emerging coastal issues, fostering dialog, forging partnerships and promoting communication and education.
Publication(s): Coastal Society, The Bulletin, conference proceedings
Keyword(s): Development/Developing Countries, Oceans/Coasts/Beaches, Water Habitats & Quality

Contact(s):
John Duff, President; University of Washington, Box 355060, Seattle, WA 98105-5060; 207-228-8290
Judy Tucker, Executive Director
Robert Boyles, Secretary; University of Rhode Island, Kingston, RI; 301-713-3155
Walter Clark, Past President; 919-515-1895
Mo Lynch, Treasurer; 3635 Fremont Ave. North, #307, Seattle, WA 98103; 804-684-7151

COEREBA SOCIETY
7336 16th Ave. SW
Seattle, WA 98106 United States
Phone: 206-768-8827
E-mail: info@coereba.org
Website: www.coereba.org

Founded: 1999
Membership: 1–100
Scope: State, Regional, National, International
Description: Seattle-based 501-c-3 environmental nonprofit educating about nature and its conservation in Puerto Rico and the Virgin Islands through mass media channels, including a nature magazine for the islands and mainland American audiences currently (April 2003) being developed.

Contact(s):
José Placer, Executive Director; jplacer@coereba.org

COLORADO ASSOCIATION OF SOIL CONSERVATION DISTRICTS
3000 Youngfield, #163
Lakewood, CO 80215 United States
Phone: 303-232-232-6242   Fax: 303-232-1624
E-mail: info@cascd.com
Website: www.cascd.com

Scope: National

Contact(s):
Robert Cordova, President, Alternate Board Member; 18105 Enoch Rd., Colorado Springs, CO 80930; 719-683-2126
Jim Rossi, Vice President; P.O. Box 247, Oak Creek, CO 80467; 970-638-4459
John Freziers, Board Member/Exec. Director; 1858 M Rd., Fruita, CO 81521; 970-858-7165
Lee Campbell, Secretary and Treasurer; 1603 Eastlawn Ave., Durango, CO 81301; 970-247-1496; Fax: 970-385-7910

COLORADO BASS FEDERATION
Attn: President, 4485 Enchanted Circle N.
Colorado Springs, CO 80917 United States
Phone: 719-597-2304
Website: www.coloradobassfederation.org
Membership: 101–1,000
Scope: State
Description: An organization of Bassmaster chapters, affiliated with the Bass Anglers Sportsman Society, organized to fight pollution, assist state and national conservation agencies in their efforts, and teach the young people of our country good conservation practices. Dedicated to the realistic conservation of our water resources.

Contact(s):
John Bentz, President; 719-597-2304
Bernie Stein, Conservation Director; 1218 N 3rd St., Johnstown, CO 80534; 970-587-9163

COLORADO ENVIRONMENTAL COALITION
1536 Wynkoop #5C
Denver, CO 80202 United States
Phone: 303-534-7066   Fax: 303-534-7063
E-mail: info@cecenviro.org
Website: www.ourcolorado.org

Founded: 1965
Membership: 1,001–10,000
Scope: State
Description: The Colorado Environmental Coalition is the grass roots action arm of Colorado's environmental movement. The Coalition coordinates the conservation community and mobilizes citizen constituencies behind environmental campaigns to preserve wilderness, wildlife, and a sustainable way of life.
Publication(s): Colorado Environmental Report, Conservationist's Wilderness Proposal for BLM Lands, Colorado Environmental Handbook-State of the State
Keyword(s): Land Issues, Public Lands/Greenspace

Contact(s):
John Powers, President
Elise Jones, Executive Director; ext. 204; sjtix@cecenviro.org
Monica Piergrossi, Front Range Field Director; ext. 207; monica@cecenviro.org
Carter Johnson, Circuit Rider; ext. 303; trey@cecenviro.org
Pete Kolbenschlag, West Slope Field Organizer; 1000 N. 9th St., #29, Grand Junction, CO 81501; 970-243-0002; pete@cecenviro.org
Jeff Widen, Associate; 970-385-8500; widen@cecenviro.org

COLORADO FORESTRY ASSOCIATION
P.O. Box 270132
Ft. Collins, CO 80527 United States
Phone: 970-223-3255

Founded: 1982
Membership: 101–1,000
Scope: State
Description: A statewide organization affiliated with the National Woodland Owners Association, concerned with forest ecology and advocating a forest-perpetuating balance between preservation and harvest of Colorado forests.
Publication(s): Colorado Forestry
Keyword(s): Forests/Forestry

Contact(s):
Chris Crowley, President; 10961 Stuart Ct., Westminister, CO 80031; 720-887-3052
Phil Hoefer, Vice President; 38 Dartmouth Ave., Pueblo, CO 81005; 719-566-1648; pjhoefer@aol.com
Ken Ashley, Secretary; 5227 South County Rd. #7, Fort Collins, CO 80528; 970-223-3255
Edwin Olmsted, Treasurer; 1065 West 112th Ave. #B, Northglenn, CO 80234; 303-452-8643
John Oram, Editor; 303-477-0552;

COLORADO MOUNTAIN CLUB
710 10th Street
Suite 200
Golden, CO 80401 United States
Phone: 303-996-2746   Fax: 303-279-9690
E-mail: conservation@cmc.org
Website: www.cmc.org

Founded: 1912
Membership: 1,001–10,000
Scope: Local, State, Regional
Description: Outdoor organization founded in 1912 that brings those who care about the Rocky Mountains together, perserves Rocky Mountain habitats and species, preserves and restores non-motorized recreation opportunities, and collects information on and educate about alpine environments.
Keyword(s): Forests/Forestry, Land Issues, Public Lands/Greenspace, Recreation/Ecotourism
Contact(s):
   Clare Bastable, West Slope Conservation Coordinator; 1000 N. 9th St. #29, Grand Junction, CO 81501; 970-618-1341; bastac@cmc.org

COLORADO NATURAL HERITAGE PROGRAM
Colorado Natural Heritage Program
8002 Campus Delivery
Fort Collins, CO 80523-8002 United States
Phone: 970-491-1309   Fax: 970-491-3349
E-mail: heritage@lamar.colostate.edu
Website: www.cnhp.colostate.edu

Founded: 1979
Scope: State
Description: The mission of the Colorado Natural Heritage Program is to preserve the natural diversity of life by contributing the scientific foundation that leads to lasting conservation of Colorado's biological wealth.
Publication(s): Rare and Imperiled Animals, Plants, and Plant Communities of Colorado, Colorado Conservation Status Handbook, Colorado Rare Plant Guide
Keyword(s): Land Issues, Wildlife & Species
Contact(s):
   Boyce Drummond, Director; 970-491-1309; Fax: 970-491-3349; heritage@lamar.colostate.edu

COLORADO TRAPPERS ASSOCIATION
0250 County Rd. 127
Glenwood Springs, CO 81601 United States
Phone: 970-945-7193   Fax: 970-945-0449

Founded: 1975
Membership: 101–1,000
Scope: Regional
Description: Associate of Fur Takers of America and National Trappers Association. Dedicated to the wise conservation and management of furbearing animals, the education of fur harvesters and public about furbearer management and the preservation of America's rich heritage in the harvest of wild furs.
Publication(s): Managing Rocky Mountain Furbearers, Fur Marketing and Trappers Supply Handbook
Keyword(s): Agriculture/Farming, Recreation/Ecotourism, Wildlife & Species
Contact(s):
   Al Davidson, President; P.O. Box 625, Saguache, CO 81149; 719-655-2777
   Marvin Miller, Vice President; 29156 Summit Ranch Dr., Golden, CO 80401; 303-526-9207
   Maj. Boddicker, Director of Publications
   Eddie Montoya, Metro Director
   Maj. Boddicker, Editor
   Kandy Herrman, Secretary; 0250 County Rd. 127, #19, Glenwood Springs, CO 81601; 970-945-7193; Fax: 970-945-0449
   Darla Jackson, Treasurer; 719-643-5263

COLORADO WATER CONGRESS
1580 Logan St., Suite 400
Denver, CO 80203 United States
Phone: 303-837-0812   Fax: 303-837-1607
E-mail: macravey@cowatercongress.org
Website: www.cowatercongress.org

Founded: 1958
Scope: State
Description: To institute and advance programs for the conservation, development, protection, and efficient utilization of the water resources of Colorado.
Publication(s): Colorado Water Rights, Colorado Laws Enacted of Interest to Water Users, Water Quality News, Water Special Report, Water Research News, Water Legislative Report, Water Legal News, Water Intelligence Report, Colorado Water Almanac & Directory
Contact(s):
   Rod Kuharich, President
   Daniel Birch, Vice President
   Richard Macravey, Executive Director

COLORADO WILDLIFE FEDERATION
445 Union Blvd., Suite 302
P.O. Box 280967
Lakewood, CO 80228-1243 United States
Phone: 303-987-0400   Fax: 303-987-0200
E-mail: cfw@coloradowildlife.org
Website: www.coloradowildlife.org

Founded: 1953
Membership: 1,001–10,000
Scope: State
Description: A representative statewide organization, affiliated with the National Wildlife Federation, dedicated to the protection and enhancement of wildlife and its habitat through public education and government interaction.
Publication(s): Colorado Wildlife
Contact(s):
   Wayne East, Executive Director
   Mike Brogan, Education Programs Contact
   Dennis Buechler, Chair and Alternate Representative
   Colleen Gadd, Representative
   Jim Goddard, Treasurer
   Suzanne O'Neill, Board Chair
   Barbara Young, Editor

COLORADO WILDLIFE HERITAGE FOUNDATION
6060 Broadway
Denver, CO 80216 United States
Phone: 303-291-7212   Fax: 303-291-7416
E-mail: karin.ballard@state.co.us
Website: www.coloradowildlifefoundation.org

Founded: 1989
Membership: 101–1,000
Scope: State
Description: Ensuring a Wildlife Legacy for Colorado today and tomorrow by securing and managing funds for wildlife projects.
Publication(s): Colorado Catch Cookbook, Colorado Biggest Bucks & Bulls, Colorado Breeding Bird Atlas, The Colorado Wildlife Viewing Guide
Keyword(s): Finance/Banking/Trade, Water Habitats & Quality, Wildlife & Species
Contact(s):
   Terry Combs, President; American Cargo Handling, P.O. Box 17594, Denver, CO 80217; 303-398-2416; Fax: 303-322-6142
   Karin Ballard, Executive Director; Colorado Wildlife Heritage Foundation, 6060 Broadway, Denver, CO 80216; 303-291-7212; Fax: 303-291-7416; karin.ballard@state.co.us
   Charles Warren, Nominating Chair; 333 Logan St., Denver, CO 80203; 303-778-7797; Fax: 303-698-5091

Bill Daley, Treasurer; Hutchison Western, P.O. Box 1158, Adams City, CO 80022; 303-287-2826; Fax: 303-289-3286
Ed Erickson, Secretary; 100 Dexter St., Denver, CO 80220; 303-388-8176
Linda Hamlin, Chairman; 378 S. Pontiac Way, Denver, CO 80224; 303-355-3957

COLUMBIA BASIN FISH AND WILDLIFE AUTHORITY
2501 SW 1st Ave. Suite 200
Portland, OR 97201 United States
Phone: 503-229-0191   Fax: 503-229-0443
Website: www.cbfwa.org
Founded: 1982
Scope: Regional
Description: A regional association of all the fish and wildlife agencies (two federal, five state) and Indian tribes (13) in the Columbia River Basin (Idaho, Montana, Oregon, and Washington). Established to coordinate planning and implementation of the fish and wildlife provisions of the Pacific Northwest Electric Power Planning and Conservation Act and for oversight of fish and wildlife resource management under the Fish and Wildlife Coordination Act and other authorities. Current charter: 1987.
Keyword(s): Wildlife & Species
Contact(s):
Jan Eckman, Staff

COLUMBIA ENVIRONMENTAL RESEARCH CENTER
USGS-BRD-ECRC, 4200 New Haven Rd.
Columbia, MO 65201-9634 United States
Phone: 573-875-5399   Fax: 573-876-1896
Membership: 101–1,000
Scope: National
Contact(s):
Pam Haverland, Past-President; pamela_haverland@usgs.gov

COMMITTEE FOR NATIONAL ARBOR DAY
National Chairman
63 Fitzrandolph Rd.
West Orange, NJ 07052 United States
Founded: 1936
Scope: National
Description: To establish a unified national observance date on the last Friday in April.
Keyword(s): Wildlife & Species
Contact(s):
Harry Banker, National Chairman; 63 Fitzrandolph Rd., West Orange, NJ 07052; 973-731-3736

COMMUNITIES FOR A BETTER ENVIRONMENT
1611 Telegraph Ave. Suite 450
Oakland, CA 94612 United States
Phone: 510-302-0430   Fax: 510-302-0437
Website: www.cbecal.org
Founded: 1971
Membership: 10,001–100,000
Scope: State
Description: The CBE is a nonprofit, multiracial environmental health organization working to prevent public exposure to toxic chemical pollutants. CBE has over 19 years experience in the California environmental arena. CBE uses science-based research, legal tactics, and organizing strategies to prevent air and water pollution, to eliminate toxic hazards, and to improve the health of the people of California.
Publication(s): Environmental Review, Oil Rag
Keyword(s): Air Quality/Atmosphere, Ethics/Environmental Justice, Oceans/Coasts/Beaches
Contact(s):
Stephanie Pincetl, Board President
Richard Drury, Executive Director
Everett Delano, Secretary

COMMUNITY CONSERVATION /HOWLERS FOREVER, INC.
50542 One Quiet Lane
Gays Mills, WI 54631 United States
Phone: 608-735-4717   Fax: 608-735-4765
E-mail: communityconservation@mwt.net
Website: www.communityconservation.org
Founded: 1989
Membership: 101–1,000
Scope: International
Description: Specializing in catalyzing community-based conservation initiatives and designing for their sustainability. Active in Wisconsin, Belize, El Salvador, Nicaragua, Papua New Guinea and India.
Publication(s): Books, Newsletter
Keyword(s): Development/Developing Countries, Ecosystems (precious), Land Issues, Oceans/Coasts/Beaches, Public Lands/Greenspace, Recreation/Ecotourism, Wildlife & Species
Contact(s):
Rob Horwich, Director; 608-735-4717; Fax: 608-735-4765; ccc@mwt.net
Lamar Janes, Projects Coordinator; 608-735-4717; Fax: 608-735-4765; communityconservation@mwt.net

COMMUNITY ENVIRONMENTAL COUNCIL (CEC)
930 Miramonte Dr.
Santa Barbara, CA 93109 United States
Phone: 805-963-0583   Fax: 805-962-9080
E-mail: cecadmin@cecmail.org
Website: www.communityenvironmentalcouncil.org
Founded: 1970
Membership: 1,001–10,000
Scope: Local
Description: Operating 6 centers and 10 programs, CEC's primary goal is to serve as a connecting institution linking government agencies, business and industry, universities and regulatory bodies, environmental organizations, and the community. Using Santa Barbara as its urban laboratory, CEC conducts research and develops local programs in recycling, hazardous waste, sustainable agriculture, and environmental education.
Publication(s): Gildea Review, A Question of Responsibility: Recycling Market Development, Manufacturing with Recyclables
Keyword(s): Agriculture/Farming, Development/Developing Countries, Land Issues, Pollution (general), Reduce/Reuse/Recycle
Contact(s):
Kim Kimbell, President
Sarita Vasquez, Vice President
Laurence Laurent, Executive Director

COMMUNITY RIGHTS COUNSEL
1726 M St., NW, Suite 703
Washington, DC 20036-4524 United States
Phone: 202-296-6889   Fax: 202-296-6895
E-mail: crc@communityrights.org
Website: www.communityrights.org
Founded: 1997
Membership: 1–100
Scope: National
Description: CRC is a public interest law firm defending laws that make our communities healthier, more livable, and socially just.
Publication(s): The Takings Project: Using Federal Courts to Attack Community and Environmental Protections, Hostile Environment: How Activist Federal Judges Threaten our Air,

Water, Land, Nothing for Free: How Private Judicial Seminars are Undermining Environmental Protection and Breaking the Public's Trust

Keyword(s): Development/Developing Countries, Land Issues, Public Lands/Greenspace, Reduce/Reuse/Recycle, Water Habitats & Quality, Wildlife & Species

Contact(s):
Douglas Kendall, Executive Director; 202-296-6889; Fax: 202-296-6895; crc@communityrights.org
Leah Doney Neel, Research Associate; 202-296-6889; Fax: 202-296-6895; crc@communityrights.org
Timothy Dowling, Chief Counsel; 202-296-6889; Fax: 202-296-6895; crc@communityrights.org
Jason Rylander, Litigation and Policy Counsel; 202-296-6889; Fax: 202-296-6895; crc@communityrights.org

CONCERN, INC.
1794 Columbia Rd., NW
Washington, DC 20009 United States
Phone: 202-328-8160   Fax: 202-387-3378
E-mail: concern@igc.org
Website: www.sustainable.org

Founded: 1970
Scope: National
Description: A national nonprofit environmental education organization with a focus on sustainable communities. Its Sustainable Communities Program features initiatives that are environmentally sound, economically vital, and socially just. CONCERN offers resources and action steps. It facilitates the exchange of information on sustainability and smart growth through the Sustainable Communities Network website (www.sustainable.org) and the management of the Smart Growth Network website (www.smartgrowth.org).
Publication(s): Community Action Guides on Pesticides, Drinking Water, Farmland Waste, Household Waste, and Global Warming, Building Sustainable Communities, Sustainability In Action
Keyword(s): Development/Developing Countries, Pollution (general), Reduce/Reuse/Recycle
Contact(s):
Susan Boyd, Executive Director
Burks Lapham, Chair

CONFEDERATED SALISH AND KOOTENAI TRIBES
P.O. Box 278
Highway 93 N
Pablo, MT 59855 United States
Phone: 406-675-2700   Fax: 406-675-2806
E-mail: csktcouncil@cskt.org
Website: www.cskt.org
Membership: 1,001–10,000
Scope: National
Description: The 1.25 million acre Flathead Indian Reservation was created in 1855 by the Treaty of the Hellgate as a homeland for the Salish, Kootenai, and Pend d'Oreille Tribes. The constitutional government of the Confederated Salish and Kootenai Tribes was formed in 1934 and approved by the Secretary of the Interior in 1935 to establish a more responsible organization, promote our general welfare, conserve and develop our land and resources.
Publication(s): Char-Koosta News
Keyword(s): Ethics/Environmental Justice, Land Issues, Reduce/Reuse/Recycle
Contact(s):
Fred Matt, Tribal Chairman
Sandra Morigeau, Executive Secretary; ext. 1312
Gary Orr, Forestry Department Head; ext. 6028
Rhonda Swaney, Natural Resources Department Head; ext. 1263; rhondas@cskt.org

CONNECTICUT ASSOCIATION OF CONSERVATION DISTRICTS, INC.
900 Northrop Rd. Suite A
Wallingford, CT 06492 United States
Phone: 203-269-7509   Fax: 203-294-9741
Scope: State
Contact(s):
Ann Hadley, President
John Breakell, Vice President; 860-491-2243
Tony Inch, Secretary/Treasurer; 134 Heather Lane, Wilton, CT 06897; 203-762-9994

CONNECTICUT BASS FEDERATION
Attn: President, 119 Straitsville Rd.
Prospect, CT 06712 United States
Phone: 203-758-0069
Website: www.geocities.com/Yosemite/Rapids/8723/
Scope: State
Description: An organization of Bassmaster chapters, affiliated with the Bass Anglers Sportsman Society, organized to fight pollution, assist state and national conservation agencies in their efforts, and teach the young people of our country good conservation practices. Dedicated to the realistic conservation of our water resources.
Contact(s):
Tom Reynolds, President; 309 Hamburg Road, Lyme, CT 06371; 863-434-7677
Ken Bell, Vice President; 21 Cloud Street, Enfield, CT 06082; 860-749-2044; gretafudge@earthlink.net
Lee Johnson, Conservation Director; 155 Candlewood Lake Rd. North, New Milford, CT 06776; 860-350-1368
Ron Murack, Tournament Director; P.O. Box 416, Granby, CT 06035; 860-653-6397
Jon Puhalski, Environmental Director; 53 Overlook Road, Winstead, CT 06098; 860-379-9387
Jim Marenzana, Secretary; 40 South Street Unit 17C, Bristol, CT 06010; J.Haren@snet.net
Joe Rackiewicz, Treasurer; 21 Birch Place, Milford, CT 06460; 203-878-8909

CONNECTICUT BOTANICAL SOCIETY
CBS
P.O. Box 9004
New Haven, CT 06532 United States
Phone: 860-633-7557
Website: www.ct-botanical-society.org
Founded: 1903
Membership: 101–1,000
Scope: State
Description: The Society increases knowledge of the state's flora accumulate and maintains specimens and records for a permanent botanical record. The Society also recommends botanically significant areas for protection and supports scholarly botanical research.
Publication(s): The Vascular Flora of Southeastern Connecticut, Yearbook, Newsletter
Keyword(s): Public Lands/Greenspace, Reduce/Reuse/Recycle, Water Habitats & Quality, Wildlife & Species
Contact(s):
Casper Ultee, President; 860-633-7557; casperu@aol.com
Carol Lemmon, Vice President; 203-488-7813
Karen Sexton, Secretary; 860-228-4647
Paul Stetson, Treasurer

CONNECTICUT FOREST AND PARK ASSOCIATION
16 Meriden Rd.
Rockfall, CT 06481-2961 United States
Phone: 860-346-2372   Fax: 860-347-7463
E-mail: info@ctwoodlands.org
Website: www.ctwoodlands.org

Founded: 1895
Membership: 1,001–10,000
Scope: State
Description: A representative statewide organization, affiliated with the National Wildlife Federation and the National Woodland Owners Association, dedicated to the protection and enhancement of wildlife and its habitat through public education and government interaction.
Contact(s):
Richard Whitehouse, President
Adam Moore, Executive Director
Ruth Cutler, Representative
Ron Manzi, Treasurer

CONNECTICUT FUND FOR THE ENVIRONMENT
205 Whitney Ave. 1st floor
New Haven, CT 06511 United States
Phone: 203-787-0646   Fax: 203-787-0246
E-mail: protect@cfenv.org
Website: www.cfenv.org
Founded: 1978
Membership: 1,001–10,000
Scope: State
Description: CFE is a nonprofit group dedicated to protecting Connecticut's natural resources through legal action, education and scientific investigation.
Publication(s): Newsletter, Annual Reports, Fact Sheets
Keyword(s): Air Quality/Atmosphere, Energy, Ethics/Environmental Justice, Land Issues, Oceans/Coasts/Beaches, Pollution (general), Public Lands/Greenspace, Sprawl/Urban Planning, Transportation, Water Habitats & Quality
Contact(s):
Michael Kashgarian, Vice-President
Donald Strait, Executive Director
Nancy Faesy, Secretary
Thomas Holloway, Treasurer

CONNECTICUT PUBLIC INTEREST RESEARCH GROUP (CONN PIRG)
198 Park Rd. 2nd floor
W. Hartford, CT 06119 United States
Phone: 860-233-7554   Fax: 860-233-7574
Website: www.connpirg.org
Founded: 1972
Membership: 10,001–100,000
Scope: State
Description: Works for concrete solutions to improve and protect our environment. Engaged in public education, study, and legislative action in many areas of the environment, including water and air pollution and solid waste.
Publication(s): ConnPIRG Reports
Keyword(s): Air Quality/Atmosphere, Pollution (general), Reduce/Reuse/Recycle, Water Habitats & Quality, Wildlife & Species

CONNECTICUT RIVER WATERSHED COUNCIL INC.
15 Bank Row
Greenfield, MA 01301-3511 United States
Phone: 413-772-2020   Fax: 413-772-2090
E-mail: crwc@crocker.com
Website: www.ctriver.org
Founded: 1952
Membership: 1,001–10,000
Scope: Regional
Description: A member-supported nonprofit organization, CRWC is a regional voice for improvement and protection of the Connecticut River and water resources throughout the 11,260 square-mile, four-state river basin of Vermont, New Hampshire, Massachusetts, and Connecticut. CRWC participates in relevant environmental and resource allocation issues through its land conservancy, water quality improvement, and watershed stewardship programs. Land conservancy revolving loan fund. Conservation education and research.
Publication(s): Tidewaters of the Connecticut River, Complete Boating Guide to the Connecticut River, Currents and Eddies
Keyword(s): Ecosystems (precious), Forests/Forestry, Land Issues, Oceans/Coasts/Beaches, Pollution (general), Water Habitats & Quality
Contact(s):
Tom Miner, Executive Director
Michael Newbold, Treasurer
Neil Sheridan, Chairman
Van Wood, Secretary

CONNECTICUT WATERFOWL ASSOCIATION, INC.
P.O. Box 74
Bozrah, CT 06334-0074 United States
Phone: 860-848-1879   Fax: 860-642-7964
E-mail: pcapotosto@snet.net
Website: www.geocities.com/ctwaterfowlersassociation
Founded: 1967
Membership: 101–1,000
Scope: State
Description: To preserve, reclaim, and enhance wetland and wildlife habitat in the State of Connecticut in a manner that promotes the wise use of our natural resources and the progress of our society.
Publication(s): Connecticut Waterfowl and Wetlands
Keyword(s): Water Habitats & Quality, Wildlife & Species
Contact(s):
Jack Harder, President; 203-227-9505; ext. 25; Jack.H@snet.net
Michael Ward, Vice President; 203-254-2600; WardMT@aol.com
Paul Capotosto, Treasurer
Chris Samor, Secretary; 203-888-0352; csamor16@aol.com

CONSERVAMERICA
REP ENVIRONMENTAL EDUCATIONAL FOUNDATION
3200 Carlisle Blvd. NE, Suite 228
Albuquerque, NM 87110 United States
Phone: 505-889-4576
E-mail: repenviro@thuntek.net
Website: www.ConservAmerica.org
Founded: 2000
Scope: National
Description: ConservAmerica is a non-partisan 501(c)(3) organization dedicated to building a broader constituency for conservation and environmental protection.
Publication(s): Conservation IS Conservative
Keyword(s): Air Quality/Atmosphere, Climate Change, Energy, Forests/Forestry, Land Issues, Oceans/Coasts/Beaches, Pollution (general), Public Lands/Greenspace, Water Habitats & Quality, Wildlife & Species
Contact(s):
Anthony Cobb, Executive Director; 505-889-4576; REPbalto@aol.com
Ruth Fish, Executive Assistant; 505-889-4576; ruthrep@thuntek.net
Oscar Simpson, Four Corners States Field Representative; 505-259-5766; oscarsimpson3@yahoo.com

CONSERVANCY OF SOUTHWEST FLORIDA, THE
1450 Merrihue Dr.
Naples, FL 34102-3449 United States
Phone: 941-262-0304   Fax: 941-262-0672
E-mail: info@conservancy.org
Website: www.conservancy.org
Founded: 1964

Membership: 1,001–10,000
Scope: Local, Regional
Description: Leading the challenge to protect and sustain Southwest Florida's natural environment through environmental policy, science and education. The Conservancy manages two nature centers, offers learning adventures, rehabilitates injured wildlife, monitors sea turtles and acquires land.
Publication(s): Update, Learning Adventures, Yearbook, Eye on the Issues
Keyword(s): Land Issues, Wildlife & Species
Contact(s):
Kathy Prosser, President and CEO; kathyp@conservancy.org
Steve Bortone, Director, Environmental Science; steveb@conservancy.org
Tracy Zanpaglione, Director of Communications Marketing; tracyz@conservancy.org
E. Louise Taylor, School Programs Manager; 941-403-4239; Fax: 941-263-3019
Michael Simonik, VP, Environmental Policy michaels@conservancy.org

CONSERVATION ALLIANCE OF ST. LUCIE CO.
P.O. Box 12515
Fort Pierce, FL 34979 United States
Phone: 772-465-0196   Fax: 772-465-8624
E-mail: bangert@digital.net
Founded: 1972
Membership: 101–1,000
Scope: Local
Description: Our mission is a pledge to protect the water, soil, air, native flora and fauna upon which all of earth's creatures depend for survival
Keyword(s): Ecosystems (precious), Executive/Legislative/Judicial Reform, Forests/Forestry, Land Issues, Oceans/Coasts/Beaches, Pollution (general), Public Lands/Greenspace, Reduce/Reuse/Recycle, Sprawl/Urban Planning, Water Habitats & Quality, Wildlife & Species

CONSERVATION BIOLOGY INSTITUTE
260 Southwest Madison Avenue
Suite 106
Corvallis, OR 97333 United States
Phone: 541-757-0687   Fax: 541-757-0518
E-mail: stritt@consbio.org
Website: www.consbio.org
Founded: 1997
Scope: Local, State, Regional, National, International
Description: CBI is a non-profit research and planning institute. We work collaboratively to help conserve biodiversity through research, education, planning, and community service.

CONSERVATION COUNCIL FOR HAWAII
250 Ward Avenue
Suite 217
Honolulu, HI 96802 United States
Phone: 808-593-0255   Fax: 808-968-0896
E-mail: cch@conservation-hawaii.org
Website: www.conservation-hawaii.org
Scope: State
Description: A representative statewide organization, affiliated with the National Wildlife Federation, dedicated to the protection and enhancement of wildlife and its habitat through public education and government interaction.
Publication(s): The Hawaii Conserver
Contact(s):
Steven Montgomery, President
Karen Blue, Executive Director and Editor
Janet Dellaria, Alternate Representative
Kate Schuerch, Representative & Treasurer

CONSERVATION COUNCIL OF NORTH CAROLINA
P.O. Box 12671
Raleigh, NC 27605 United States
Phone: 919-839-0006   Fax: 919-839-0767
E-mail: info@conservationcouncilnc.org
Website: www.conservationcouncilnc.org
Founded: 1968
Membership: 101–1,000
Scope: State
Description: A statewide lobbying and electoral group dedicated to protecting, preserving, and enhancing NC's natural environment through lobbying, educating and mobilizing citizens, making the environment a priority for legislators and the public, holding legislators accountable for their environmental decisions, and electing pro-environmental candidates to the state legislature.
Publication(s): Carolina Conservationist Newsletter, Legislative Scorecard
Keyword(s): Air Quality/Atmosphere, Energy, Forests/Forestry, Land Issues, Oceans/Coasts/Beaches, Pollution (general), Reduce/Reuse/Recycle, Sprawl/Urban Planning, Transportation, Water Habitats & Quality
Contact(s):
Nina Szlosberg, President
Laura Lauffer, Vice President
Dan Besse, Political Director
Carrie Oren, Executive Director; 919-839-0006
Steve Wall, Director of Governmental Relations; 919-839-0020; steve@conservationcouncilnc.org

CONSERVATION EDUCATION CENTER, THE
2473 160th Rd.
Guthrie Center, IA 50115 United States
Phone: 641-747-8383   Fax: 641-747-3951
Founded: 1958
Scope: State
Description: To encourage and lead the development and practice of a widespread and effective conservation education program in Iowa.
Contact(s):
Don Sievers, Training Officer; dsievers@pionet.net
A. Jay Winter, Training Officer; ajwinter@pionet.net

CONSERVATION FEDERATION OF MARYLAND/ F.A.R.M.
P.O. Box 455
Poolesville, MD 20837 United States
Phone: 301-916-3510   Fax: 301-349-5941
E-mail: f.a.r.m@erols.com
Website: www.zarnet.com
Membership: 1,001–10,000
Scope: Regional
Description: The Conservation Federation of Maryland is devoted to the wise use, conservation, aesthetic appreciation, and restoration of wildlife and other natural resources. The Conservation Federation of Maryland was recently merged with for A Rural Maryland to help safeguard the dwindling supply of farmland and open space in the State of Maryland.
Publication(s): This Place We Call Home, Keep It Country (Newsletter)
Keyword(s): Agriculture/Farming, Development/Developing Countries, Ethics/Environmental Justice, Land Issues, Reduce/Reuse/Recycle
Contact(s):
Dolores Milmoe, President; 18801 River Rd., Poolesville, MD 20837
Caroline Taylor, Executive Director; 15711 Hughes Rd., Poolesville, MD 20837; 301-972-7866

NON-GOVERNMENTAL NON-PROFIT ORGANIZATIONS – C

Rudy Gole, Treasurer; 17105 Oxley Farm Rd, Poolesville, MD 20837
Cathy Hall, Secretary; 17826 Walling Rd., Poolesville, MD 20837

CONSERVATION FEDERATION OF MISSOURI
728 West Main Street
Jefferson City, MO 65101-1159 United States
Phone: 573-634-2322   Fax: 573-634-8205
E-mail: confedmo@socket.net
Website: www.confedmo.com
Founded: 1935
Membership: 10,001–100,000
Scope: State
Description: A representative statewide organization, affiliated with the National Wildlife Federation, dedicated to the protection and enhancement of wildlife and its habitat through public education and government interaction.
Publication(s): Missouri Wildlife
Contact(s):
   Ike Lovan, President and Alternate Representative
   Denny Ballard, Executive Director; 573-634-2322; Fax: 573-634-5290; moted@socket.net
   Charles Davidson, Editor; cdfed@socket.net
   Arnold Meysenburg, Secretary
   Jennifer Mills, Education Programs Contact; 573-634-2322; Fax: 573-634-5290; confedmo@socket.net
   Abe Phillips, Representative
   Randy Washburn, Treasurer

CONSERVATION FORCE
3900 N. Causeway Blvd., Suite 1045
Metairie, LA 70002 United States
Phone: 504-837-1233   Fax: 504-837-1145
Website: www.conservationforce.org
Founded: 1997
Scope: International
Description: The force was formed to unify sportsmen's organizations, improve the profile of hunters and further the role and value of hunting in wildlife conservation as a force.
Publication(s): Conservation Force Supplement to Hunting Report
Keyword(s): Ethics/Environmental Justice, Recreation/Ecotourism, Reduce/Reuse/Recycle, Wildlife & Species
Contact(s):
   John Jackson, President; One Lakeway Center, 3900 N. Causeway Blvd., Suite 1045, Metairie, LA 70002; 504-837-1233; Fax: 504-837-1145; jjw no@att.net
   Bertrand Des Clers, International Vice President; 15 Rue de Teheran, 75008, Paris; 33-156-597755; Fax: 33-142-607763; igf@foundation-igf.fr
   James Teer, Vice President; Texas A&M University, Department of Wildlife & Fisheries, College Station, TX 77845; 409-458-1359; Fax: 409-845-3786; jteer@tamu.edu
   Bert Klineburger, CF Board Member; International Hunting Consultant, Inc., Box 3F, San Antonio, TX 78217; 2108228535; Fax: 2108264765; klineburgr@aol.com
   Don Lindsay, CF Board Member; 707-448-1902; Fax: 011-271-18843743; railwood@iafrica.com

CONSERVATION FUND, THE
1800 North Kent St., Suite 1120
Arlington, VA 22209-2156 United States
Phone: 703-525-6300   Fax: 703-525-4610
E-mail: postmaster@conservationfund.org
Website: www.conservationfund.org
Founded: 1985
Scope: National
Description: The Conservation Fund forges partnerships to protect America's legacy of land and water resources. Through land acquisition, community initiatives, and leadership training, the Fund and its partners demonstrate sustainable conservation solutions emphasizing the integration of economic and environmental goals.
Publication(s): Common Ground
Keyword(s): Forests/Forestry, Land Issues, Public Lands/Greenspace, Sprawl/Urban Planning, Water Habitats & Quality, Wildlife & Species
Contact(s):
   Patrick Noonan, Chairman
   Lawrence Selzer, President & CEO
   Richard Erdmann, Executive Vice President, General Counsel
   Sydney Macy, Senior Vice President, Western Regional Office; 303-444-4369; Fax: 303-938-3763
   David Sutherland, Senior Vice President, Real Estate
   Rex Boner, Vice President, Georgia Office; 770-414-0211; Fax: 770-938-0585
   Elizabeth Dowdle, Vice President, Florida Office; 561-832-7665; Fax: 561-832-8102
   Pamela Gray, Vice President, Administration
   Elizabeth Madison, Vice President, Development
   Edward McMahon, Vice President, Director of Center for Conservation & Development
   Jodi O'Day, Vice President, Regional General Counsel; 410-757-0370; Fax: 410-757-3791
   David Phillips, Vice President & Chief Financial Officer
   Mike McQueen, Editor, Common Ground; 804-973-7324

CONSERVATION INTERNATIONAL
1919 M St., NW, Suite 600
Washington, DC 20036 United States
Phone: 202-912-1000   Fax: 202-912-1045
Website: www.conservation.org
Founded: 1987
Scope: International
Description: Conservation International is a global, field-based environmental organization that works to protect biological diversity. CI focuses on the biodiversity hotspots, tropical wilderness areas and key marine ecosystems. The majority of CI staff work on the front lines where unique plant and animal species are most threatened. CI builds alliances with other NGOs, foreign governments, indigenous communities and industry, and works with communities living in biodiversity-rich areas.
Keyword(s): Forests/Forestry, Wildlife & Species
Contact(s):
   Russell Mittermeier, President; 202-973-2212; Fax: 202-887-0192
   Peter Seligmann, CEO and Chairman of the Board; 202-973-2275; p.seligmann.org

CONSERVATION LAW FOUNDATION, INC. (CLF)
120 Tillson Ave.
Rockland, ME 04841 United States
Phone: 207-594-8107   Fax: 207-596-7706
E-mail: pshelley@clf.org
Website: www.clf.org
Founded: 1966
Membership: 1,001–10,000
Scope: Local, State, Regional
Description: CLF is a regional environmental advocacy organization with offices in Rhode Island, Massachusetts, Vermont, New Hampshire, and Maine.
Publication(s): Conservation Matters, The Wild Sea, City Routes City Rights, Effects of Fishing Gear on the Sea Floor of New England
Keyword(s): Agriculture/Farming, Climate Change, Ecosystems (precious), Forests/Forestry, Land Issues, Oceans/Coasts/Beaches, Public Health, Public Lands/Greenspace, Sprawl/Urban Planning, Transportation, Water Habitats &

Quality, Wildlife & Species

Contact(s):
Peter Shelley, Center Director
Chris DeScherer, Staff Advocate; cdescherer@clf.org
Roger Fleming, Staff Advocate; rfleming@clf.org

CONSERVATION LAW FOUNDATION, INC. (CLF)
NEW ENGLAND REGION
62 Summer St.
Boston, MA 02110 United States
Phone: 617-350-0990   Fax: 617-350-4030
Website: www.clf.org

Founded: 1966
Membership: 1–100
Scope: Regional
Description: CLF is a nonprofit, member-supported environmental law organization dedicated to improving resource management, environmental protection, and public health in New England. Work includes: Energy and water conservation, environmental health, transportation planning, water resources protection, land preservation, and marine resources protection.
Publication(s): Take Back Your Streets, Troubled Waters, A Silent and Costly Epidemic, Power to Spare I&II
Keyword(s): Air Quality/Atmosphere, Energy, Forests/Forestry, Land Issues, Oceans/Coasts/Beaches, Pollution (general), Public Health, Public Lands/Greenspace, Sprawl/Urban Planning, Transportation, Water Habitats & Quality

Contact(s):
Douglas Foy, President
Charles Cabot, Chairman of the Board
Eugene Clapp, Treasurer
Paula Gold, Vice Chairman of the Board
John Teal, Vice Chairman of the Board

CONSERVATION TECHNOLOGY INFORMATION CENTER
1220 Potter Dr.
West Lafayette, IN 47906-1383 United States
Phone: 765-494-9555   Fax: 765-494-5969
E-mail: ctic@ctic.purdue.edu
Website: www.ctic.purdue.edu

Founded: 1982
Membership: 1–100
Scope: National
Description: Conservation Technology Information Center (CTIC) is a nonprofit information and data transfer center. The national Center promotes environmentally and economically beneficial agricultural decision-making by: producing and circulating information, data, and contacts, coordinating national initiatives, and sponsoring interactive meetings and conferences. The Center is supported by members and participating governmental agencies.
Publication(s): CTIC Partners Newsletter, Watershed Management, Conservation Tillage: A Checklist for U.S. Farmers
Keyword(s): Agriculture/Farming, Water Habitats & Quality

Contact(s):
John Hassell, Executive Director; hassell@ctic.purdue.edu
Ed Frye, Project Manager
Bruno Alesii, Chair, Board of Directors; 106 Pebble Creek, Boerne, TX 78006
Dan Towery, Natural Resources Specialist; towery@ctic.purdue.edu

CONSERVATION TREATY SUPPORT FUND
3705 Cardiff Rd.
Chevy Chase, MD 20815 United States
Phone: 301-654-3150   Fax: 301-652-6390
E-mail: ctsf@conservationtreaty.org
Website: www.conservationtreaty.org

Founded: 1986
Scope: International
Description: CTSF provides direct support to major inter-governmental treaties, including CITES (the endangered species treaty), the wetlands and the migratory species treaty, through fund-raising and education.
Publication(s): Conservation & Educational Brochure, CITES Jigsaw Puzzles, "Another Point of View" print, Bateman prints and posters, "Treasures of Wetlands" poster, Caribbean Buyer Beware poster "Wild Treasures of the Caribbean", CITES Video (also Wetlands Video), CITES Endangered Species Book
Keyword(s): Water Habitats & Quality, Wildlife & Species

Contact(s):
George Furness, President; 301-654-3150; Fax: 301-652-6390; ctsf@conservationtreaty.org
Frederick Morris, Vice President; 703-683-8512; Fax: 703-683-4622
Faith Campbell, Secretary; 202-547-9120; Fax: 202-547-9213
Lawrence Mason, Treasurer; 703-241-8896; Fax: 703-241-8896; lnmason@compuserve.com

CONSERVATION TRUST OF PUERTO RICO
P.O. Box 9023554
San Juan, 00902-3554 Puerto Rico
Phone: 787-722-5834   Fax: 787-722-5872
E-mail: fideicomiso@fideicomiso.org
Website: www.fideicomiso.org

Founded: 1970
Scope: State
Description: A private nonprofit institution created by the Governor of Puerto Rico and the U.S. Secretary of the Interior to preserve and enhance Puerto Rico's natural beauty and resources, primarily through land acquisition. Owns or manages over 17,000 acres representative of the island's major endangered habitats. It educates the public about environmental issues; manages a vast reforestation program; and finances conservation in Caribbean countries via debt-for-nature swaps.
Keyword(s): Land Issues

Contact(s):
Thomas Lovejoy, Chairman
Kate Romero, Trustee
Fernando Lloveras, Executive Director
Blanca Santos, Administration Director

COOK INLET KEEPER
P.O. Box 3269 / 3734 Ben Walters Lane
Homer, AK 99603 United States
Phone: 907-235-4068   Fax: 907-235-4069
E-mail: keeper@inletkeeper.org
Website: www.inletkeeper.org

Founded: 1995
Scope: Regional
Description: The mission of Cook Inlet Keeper is to protect the Cook Inlet Watershed and the life it sustains. Keeper relies on environmental monitoring, research, education, and advocacy to give citizens the tools they need to protect water quality.
Publication(s): Cook Inlet GIS Atlas on CD-ROM, Cook Inlet Watershed Directory, State of the Inlet Report
Keyword(s): Pollution (general), Water Habitats & Quality

Contact(s):
Bob Shavelson, Executive Director

COOPER ORNITHOLOGICAL SOCIETY
ORNITHOLOGICAL SOCIETIES OF NORTH AMERICA
P.O. Box 1897
Lawrence, KS 66044 United States
Phone: 800-627-0629, ext. 217   Fax: 208-378-5347
Website: www.cooper.org

Founded: 1893
Membership: 1,001–10,000

Scope: National, International

Description: Observation and cooperative study of birds; the spread of interest in bird study; the conservation of birds and wildlife in general; the publication of ornithological knowledge.

Publication(s): Condor, The, Studies in Avian Biology

Contact(s):
  Bonnie Bowen, President; Department of Animal Ecology; 124 Science Hall II Iowa State Univ., Ames, IA 50011; 515-294-6391; bsbowen@iastate.edu
  David Dobkin, Editor, the Condor; High Desert Ecological Research Institute, Suite 300, 15 S.W. Colorado Avenue, Bend, OR 97702; 541-382-1117; Fax: 541-382-1117; dobkin@hderi.org
  Eileen Kirsch, Secretary; BRD/USGS, Upper Mississippi Science Center, P.O. Box 818, LaCrosse, WI 54602; 608-783-6451; ext. 226; eileen_kirsch@usgs.gov
  John Rotenberry, Editor, Studies in Avian Biology; Department of Biology, University of California, Riverside, CA 92521; 909-787-3953; rote@citrus.ucr.edu

COOSA RIVER BASIN INITIATIVE
408 Broad St.
Rome, GA 30161 United States
Phone: 706-232-2724   Fax: 706-235-9066
E-mail: info@coosa.org
Website: www.coosa.org

Founded: 1992
Membership: 101–1,000
Scope: Regional

Description: CRBI works to inform and empower citizens so they may become involved with the process of creating a cleaner, healthier, economically viable Coosa River Basin.

Publication(s): Main Stream, The
Keyword(s): Pollution (general), Water Habitats & Quality

Contact(s):
  Ben Harrison, President; 706-295-0858; benhar@bellsouth.net
  Joe Cook, Vice President; 706-235-117-; jmc@artfamily.com
  Monica Cook, Publication Chair; 706-235-1170; jmc@artfamily.com
  Bill Davin, Education Chair
  Mitch Lawson, Coordinator; 700-232-2724

CORAL REEF ALLIANCE, THE (CORAL)
417 Montgomery St., Suite 205
San Francisco, CA 94104 United States
Phone: 415-834-0900   Fax: 415-834-0999
E-mail: info@coral.org
Website: www.coralreefalliance.org/

Founded: 1994
Scope: International

Description: The Coral Reef Alliance is a nonprofit organization that works with divers, government conservation organizations, and others to promote coral reef conservation around the world. CORAL focuses primarily on helping local communities to establish their own marine protected area. CORAL also sponsors a number of educational programs and publications.

Publication(s): Coral News, Coral Reefs - The Vanishing Rainbow
Keyword(s): Oceans/Coasts/Beaches, Reduce/Reuse/Recycle

Contact(s):
  Kalli De Meyer, Director Coral Parks Program; CORAL Bonaire Office, Kaya Madrid 3A, Sabana Bonaire; 599-717-3465; Fax: 599-717-3476; kdemeyer@coral.org
  Ellen Horne, Director of Development; 510-848-0110; Fax: 510-848-3720; ehorne@coral.org
  Brian Huse, Executive Director; 510-848-0110; Fax: 510-848-3720
  Janine Kraus, Managing Director; 510-848-0110; Fax: 510-848-3720; jkraus@coral.org
  Anita Daley, ICRIN Manager; 510-848-0110; ext. 313; Fax: 510-848-3720; adaley@coral.org

CORLANDS
25 E. Washington St.
Suite 1650
Chicago, IL 60602 United States
Phone: 312-427-4256   Fax: 312-427-6251
E-mail: jgreenspan@corlands.org
Website: corlands.org

Scope: Local

Description: CorLands is a nonprofit organization that works with park and forest preserve districts, and other local governments and concerned citizens to save open space for public enjoyment.

CORNELL LAB OF ORNITHOLOGY
159 Sapsucker Woods Rd.
Ithaca, NY 14850 United States
Phone: 800-843-2473   Fax: 607-254-2415
E-mail: cornellbirds@cornell.edu
Website: www.birds.cornell.edu

Founded: 1917
Membership: 10,001–100,000
Scope: International

Description: The Lab is a membership institution interpreting and conserving the earth's biological diversity through research, education, and citizen science focused on birds.

Publication(s): Birdscope, Living Bird
Keyword(s): Wildlife & Species

Contact(s):
  Rick Bonney, Director of Education Program; 607-254-2440; birdeducation@cornell.edu
  Christopher Clark, Director of Bioacoustics Research Program; 607-254-2405
  John Fitzpatrick, Louis Agassiz Fuertes Director; 607-254-2410
  Jennifer Smith, Communications Assistant; 607-254-2497
  Gregory Budney, Curator of Library of Natural Sounds; 607-254-2406
  Tim Gallagher, Living Bird Editor; 607-254-2443

COTTONWOOD FOUNDATION
P.O. Box 10803
White Bear Lake, MN 55110 United States
Phone: 651-426-8797   Fax: 651-426-0320
E-mail: cottonwood@igc.org
Website: www.cottonwoodfdn.org

Founded: 1992
Scope: International

Description: Cottonwood Foundation provides small grants to grassroots nonprofit organizations worldwide that are working for a sustainable future by combining all of the following: protecting the environment, promoting cultural diversity, empowering people to meet their basic needs, and relying on volunteer efforts.

Keyword(s): Agriculture/Farming, Development/Developing Countries, Ecosystems (precious), Energy, Ethics/Environmental Justice, Forests/Forestry, Land Issues, Oceans/Coasts/Beaches, Pollution (general), Public Health, Public Lands/Greenspace, Recreation/Ecotourism, Reduce/Reuse/Recycle

COUNCIL FOR ENVIRONMENTAL EDUCATION
Executive Director c/o Josetta Hawthorne
5555 Morningside Dr.
Suite 212
Houston, TX 77005 United States
Phone: 713-520-1936   Fax: 713-520-8008
E-mail: info@c-e-e.org
Website: www.c-e-e.org

Founded: 1970
Scope: National

Description: The Council for Environmental Education is a nonprofit education organization creating a partnership and network between education and natural resource professionals. CEE co-sponsors balanced, non-biased environmental education programs such as Project WILD, Project WILD Aquatic, and WET in the City. In an effort to encourage more environmental education outreach to urban youth, CEE has launched WET in the City, a community-based water education initiative.

Publication(s): WET in The City Curriculum & Activity Guide, Project WILD Aquatic K-12 Curriculum & Activity Guide, Project WILD K-12 Curriculum & Activity Guide

Keyword(s): Reduce/Reuse/Recycle

Contact(s):
  Bill Andrews, President; 916-657-5374
  Josetta Hawthorne, Executive Director and Director, Wet In the City
  Kathy Mcglauflin, Project Learning Tree Director; 1111 19TH St., NW, Suite 780, Washington, DC 20036; 202-436-2468

COUNCIL FOR PLANNING AND CONSERVATION
Box 228
Beverly Hills, CA 90213 United States
Phone: 310-276-2685
E-mail: esharris@earthlink.net
Website: www.beverlyhillscitizen.org

Founded: 1970
Scope: Local, State, Regional
Description: Serves as a clearinghouse for information and gives inexperienced groups ready access to advice and assistance. Provides a center through which opportunities for southern California's environmental protection and enhancement may be communicated. Concerns include: air and water quality, water supply, energy options, waste management, land use, transportation, coastal conservation, urban planning and housing.

Keyword(s): Air Quality/Atmosphere, Energy, Forests/Forestry, Oceans/Coasts/Beaches, Public Health, Public Lands/Greenspace, Reduce/Reuse/Recycle, Transportation, Water Habitats & Quality

Contact(s):
  Ellen Harris, President and Executive Director
  Betty Harris, Vice President

COUSTEAU SOCIETY, INC., THE
710 Settlers Landing Road
Hampton, VA 23669 United States
Phone: 757-722-9300   Fax: 727-722-8185
E-mail: cousteau@cousteausociety.org
Website: www.cousteau.org

Founded: 1973
Membership: 10,001–100,000
Scope: International
Description: A nonprofit, membership-supported environmental education organization dedicated to the protection and improvement of the quality of life for present and future generations. Believing that an informed and alerted public can best make the choices that will sustain the water planet, it produces television films, research, books and other publications, exploring relationships between humans and ecosystems.

Publication(s): Calypso Log, Dolphin Log
Keyword(s): Oceans/Coasts/Beaches, Wildlife & Species
Contact(s):
  Francine Cousteau, President; 757-722-9300; Fax: 757-722-8185; f.cousteau@cousteau.org
  Robert Steele, Vice President Finance; 757-722-9300; Fax: 757-722-8185; rsteele@cousteausociety.org
  John Huncke, Chief Operating Officer; 757-722-9300; Fax: 757-722-8185; jhuncke@msn.com

COUSTEAU SOCIETY, INC., THE
FRANCE OFFICE
92 Avenue Kleber
Paris, 75116 France
Phone: 44340606

Scope: International

CRAIGHEAD ENVIRONMENTAL RESEARCH INSTITUTE
201 S. Wallace Ave. Apt. B2
Bozeman, MT 59715 United States
Phone: 406-585-8705   Fax: 406-585-8220
E-mail: ceri@avicom.net
Website: www.grizzlybear.org

Founded: 1955
Membership: 1–100
Scope: Regional, International
Description: A nonprofit professional organization of scientists, dedicated to exploring the cause-and-effect relationships of man and his environment. Activity includes research, education, and conservation, with emphasis on ecological studies and interdisciplinary approach. Originally the Outdoor Recreation Institute. Staff Members: 6.

Keyword(s): Water Habitats & Quality, Wildlife & Species
Contact(s):
  Frank Craighead, President, Program Director
  Charles Craighead, Media Director
  April Craighead, Secretary

CRAIGHEAD WILDLIFE-WILDLANDS INSTITUTE
5200 Upper Miller Creek Rd.
Missoula, MT 59803 United States
Phone: 406-251-3867

Founded: 1977
Scope: National
Description: A nonprofit, multidisciplinary research center in the Northern Rockies devoted to field-based ecological discovery and scientific activism. The Institute's mission is to generate new ecological information and concepts, widely communicate these insights, and influence public policy and individual behavior in directions that preserve regional biodiversity.

Publication(s): The Grizzly Bears of Yellowstone: Their Ecology in the Yellowstone Ecosystem 1959-1992 (1995), Mapping Arctic Vegetation in Northwest Alaska Using Landsat MSS Imagery (1988), An Integrated Satellite Technique to Evaluate Grizzly Bear Habitat Use (1997)

Keyword(s): Wildlife & Species
Contact(s):
  John Craighead, Chairman of the Board; 5125 Orchard Ln., Missoula, MT 59803; 406-251-3944

CRESTON VALLEY WILDLIFE MANAGEMENT AREA
Box 640
Creston, V0B 1G0 British Columbia Canada
Phone: 250-402-6900   Fax: 250-402-6910
E-mail: info@crestonwildlife.ca
Website: www.crestonwildlife.ca

Founded: 1968
Membership: 101–1,000
Scope: International
Description: Established in 1968, the Creston Valley Wildlife Management Area was the first and largest Management Area in the Province of British Columbia. Our mission is to manage the 17,000-acre (7,000-ha) wetland and upland area for conservation and natural species diversity. We do this through active habitat and wildlife management, research, education and public support.

Publication(s): Creston Valley Wildlife Management Area Annual

Contact(s):
   Brian Stushnoff, Area Manager; 250-428-3260
   Steve Bullock, Chairman of the Management Authority; 250-428-2214

CRITICAL ECOSYSTEM PARTNERSHIP FUND
CEPF
Conservation International
1919 M Street NW
Suite 600
Washington, DC 20036 United States
Phone: 202-912-1808   Fax: 202-912-1045
E-mail: cepf@conservation.org
Website: www.cepf.net

Founded: 2000
Scope: International
Description: CEPF aims to dramatically advance conservation of biodiversity hotspots in developing countries. CEPF provides funding and technical assistance to community groups, non-governmental organizations and others working to conserve hotspots in developing countries. It is a joint initiative of Conservation International, the Global Environment Facility, the Government of Japan, the MacArthur Foundation and the World Bank.
Publication(s): Ecosystem profiles, E-newsletter
Keyword(s): Ecosystems (precious)

CROSBY ARBORETUM, THE
MISSISSIPPI STATE UNIVERSITY
370 Ridge Rd.
Picayune, MS 39466 United States
Phone: 601-799-2311   Fax: 601-799-2372
E-mail: crosbyar@datastar.net
Website: www.msstate.edu/dept/crec/camain.html

Founded: 1980
Membership: 101–1,000
Scope: State
Description: The main activity of the Arboretum is to preserve, protect and display plants native to the Pearl River drainage basin. Additionally, we provide environmental and horticultural research opportunities and offer educational, scientific, and recreational programs.
Publication(s): Native Trees for Urban Landscapes
Keyword(s): Reduce/Reuse/Recycle, Wildlife & Species
Contact(s):
   Stewart Gammill, President
   Richard Clark, Vice President
   Bob Brzuszek, Senior Curator; 601-799-2311; Fax: 601-799-2372; crosbyar@datastar.net
   Jennifer McKay, Secretary
   Norman Stevens, Treasurer

D

D ACRES
Josh Trought
P.O. Box 98
Rumney, NH 03266 United States
Phone: 603-786-2366
E-mail: info@dacres.org
Website: www.dacres.org

Founded: 1997
Membership: 1–100
Scope: Local, State, Regional, National, International
Description: D Acres is an experimental center that researches, applies and teaches skills of subsistence living and small-scale organic farming within a communal living situation in which people come to respect and share values of interdependence, and love of nature. In addition, the organization will support educational activities directed toward "improving the quality of life".

Keyword(s): Agriculture/Farming, Energy, Forests/Forestry, Recreation/Ecotourism

DAWES ARBORETUM, THE
7770 Jacksontown Rd., SE
Newark, OH 43056-9380 United States
Phone: 740-323-2355   Fax: 740-323-4058
Website: www.dawesarb.org

Founded: 1929
Membership: 1,001–10,000
Scope: State
Description: A not-for-profit organization that promotes the planting of forest and ornamental trees, and promotes increased love and knowledge of trees, shrubs, and related subjects. The 1,341-acre grounds are open daily from dawn to dusk, free of charge.
Publication(s): Dawes Arboretum Newsletter, The
Keyword(s): Wildlife & Species
Contact(s):
   Luke Messinger, Director; lemessinger@ee.net
   Michael Ecker, Horticulturist; meecker@ee.net
   Laura Kaparoff, Public Relations Editor; lakaparoff@ee.net
   Timothy Mason, Natural Resource Specialist; tamason@ee.net
   Lori Totman, Naturalist and Educator; latotman@ee.net

DEEP-PORTAGE CONSERVATION RESERVE
2197 Nature Center Dr., NW
Hackensack, MN 56452-2431 United States
Phone: 218-682-2325   Fax: 218-682-3121
E-mail: portage@uslink.net
Website: www.deep-portage.org

Founded: 1975
Membership: 1–100
Scope: State
Description: Deep-Portage is a 6,100-acre demonstration working forest with a primary purpose of environmental education. The campus includes dormitories, classrooms, laboratory, theater, interpretive center, natural history museum, and thirty-seven miles of recreational trails. It is owned by Cass County and operated by the Deep-Portage Conservation Foundation, a nonprofit corporation.
Publication(s): Camp Brochures, Deep-Portage Log
Keyword(s): Forests/Forestry
Contact(s):
   Bruce Steiner, President
   Dale Yerger, Executive Director

DEFENDERS OF WILDLIFE
1130 17th Street, NW
Washington, DC 20036-4604 United States
Phone: 202-682-9400   Fax: 202-682-1331
E-mail: information@defenders.org
Website: www.defenders.org

Founded: 1947
Membership: 100,001–500,000
Scope: National
Description: Since 1947, Defenders of Wildlife has been one of the nation's most effective advocates for wildlife, endangered species, and habitat. Defenders works to protect and restore native species, habitats, ecosystems, and overall biological diversity. Defenders is a nonprofit, tax-exempt organization, supported by 430,000 members.
Publication(s): Defenders
Keyword(s): Land Issues, Oceans/Coasts/Beaches, Public Lands/Greenspace, Transportation, Wildlife & Species
Contact(s):
   Rodger Schlickeisen, President
   Robert Dewey, Vice President for Government Relations
   Kate Mathews, Vice President of Membership
   Charles Orasin, Senior Vice President for Operations

Philip Rabin, Vice President for Communications
Martha Schumacher, Vice President of Development
Mark Shaffer, Senior Vice President for Program
William Snape, Vice President for Law and Litigation
Sajjad Ahrabi, Director of Information Systems
Mary Beth Beetham, Director of Legistative Affairs
Maria Cecil, Director of Publications and Executive Editor
Kimberley Delfino, Director of California Programs; 926 J St., Ste. 522, Sacramento, CA 95814
Nina Fascione, Director of Carnivore Conservation
Robert Jones, Director of Finance and Administration
Caroline Kennedy, Director of Special Projects, Species Conservation
Laurie MacDonald, Director of Florida Programs
Craig Miller, Southern Rockies Director; 302 S. Convent Ave., Tucson, AZ 85701
Michael Senatore, Director of Legal Department
Sara Vickerman, Director of West Coast; 1637 Laurel St., Lake Oswego, OR 97034; 503-697-3222
Laura Watchman, Director of Habitat Conservation Planning
Edward Asner, Secretary
Caroline Gabel, Vice Chairman
Winsome McIntosh, Chairman of the Board
Alan Steinberg, Treasurer

DELAWARE ASSOCIATION OF CONSERVATION DISTRICTS
President, P.O. Box 242
Dover, DE 19903-0242 United States
Phone: 302-739-4411   Fax: 302-739-6724
Founded: 1953
Membership: 1–100
Scope: Regional
Description: DACD is a voluntary nonprofit alliance that provides a forum for discussion and coordination among the Delaware Conservation Districts as they work to ensure the wise use and treatment of renewable resources.
Keyword(s): Agriculture/Farming, Land Issues, Reduce/Reuse/Recycle, Water Habitats & Quality
Contact(s):
Terry Pepper, President; 104 Captain Davis Dr., Campden-Wyoming, DE 19934; 302-697-6176; Fax: 303-736-2040; kentcol@aol.com
Ron Breeding, Vice President; Rt. 1, Box 345-B, Seaford, DE 19973; 302-629-3964; Fax: 302-739-6724
Martha Pileggi, Staff Assistant; P.O. Box 242, Dover, DE 19903-0242; 302-739-4411; Fax: 302-739-6724; mpilegg@state.de.us
Dariel Rakestraw, Past President, Board Member; 2138 Graves Rd., Hockessin, DE 19707; 302-239-2969

DELAWARE BASS FEDERATION
Attn: President, 3700 South State St.
Camden, DE 19934 United States
Phone: 302-698-9257   Fax: 302-698-9257
Website: www.ezy.net/~delbass/
Membership: 101–1,000
Scope: State
Description: An organization of Bassmaster chapters, affiliated with the Bass Anglers Sportsman Society, organized to fight pollution, assist state and national conservation agencies in their efforts, and teach the young people of our country good conservation practices. Dedicated to the realistic conservation of our water resources.
Publication(s): Bassing on Delmarva
Contact(s):
Jim Fields, President; 302-698-9257
Roger Richardson, Conservation Director; 632 Fencepost Ln., Viola, DE 19979; 302-284-8383

DELAWARE GREENWAYS, INC.
P.O. Box 2095
Wilmington, DE 19899 United States
Phone: 302-655-7275   Fax: 302-655-7274
E-mail: greenwalks@dca.net
Website: www.delawaregreenways.org
Founded: 1989
Membership: 101–1,000
Scope: State
Description: Preserve, enhance, and connect the ecological, scenic, historical, cultural, and recreational resources in Delaware.
Publication(s): See publications on website
Keyword(s): Development/Developing Countries, Ethics/Environmental Justice, Land Issues, Transportation
Contact(s):
Tim Plemmons, Assistant Executive Director
Gail Van Gilder, Executive Director

DELAWARE MUSEUM OF NATURAL HISTORY
P.O. Box 3937
Wilmington, DE 19807 United States
Phone: 302-658-9111   Fax: 302-658-2610
Website: www.delmnh.org
Founded: 1957
Membership: 1,001–10,000
Scope: Regional
Description: The Delaware Museum of Natural History exists to excite and inform people about the natural world. The Museum's core purpose is to help develop a caring society which respects and values our planet. The major focus of the Museum is continued leadership in research and collections in malacology and ornithology and the ecology of the Delmarva Peninsula.
Publication(s): Nemouria, Musenews
Keyword(s): Ecosystems (precious), Wildlife & Species
Contact(s):
Geoff Halfpenny, Executive Director
Gene Hess, Collection Manager, Ornithology
Stephen Reynolds, Editor and Public Relations
Jean Woods, Curator of Birds

DELAWARE NATURE SOCIETY
ASHLAND NATURE CENTER
ABBOTTS MILL NATURE CENTER
P.O. Box 700
Hockessin, DE 19707-0700 United States
Phone: 302-239-2334   Fax: 302-239-2473
E-mail: webpage@dnsashland.org
Website: www.delawarenaturesociety.org
Founded: 1964
Membership: 1,001–10,000
Scope: Local, State, Regional, National, International
Description: A representative statewide organization, affiliated with the National Wildlife Federation, dedicated to the protection and enhancement of wildlife and its habitat through public education and government interaction. Operates two nature centers and manages four nature preserves.
Publication(s): Butterflies of Delmarva, Eastern Shore, Amphibians & Reptiles of Delmarva, Delaware Nature Society Voice
Keyword(s): Agriculture/Farming, Air Quality/Atmosphere, Development/Developing Countries, Ecosystems (precious), Executive/Legislative/Judicial Reform, Forests/Forestry, Land Issues, Oceans/Coasts/Beaches, Pollution (general), Public Lands/Greenspace, Recreation/Ecotourism
Contact(s):
Peter Flint, President
Mike Riska, Executive Director
Lori Spagnolo, Assoc. Dir., Natural Resources Conservation

Eileen Butler, Advocacy Coordinator
Linda Young, Communications/Website Coordinator; 302-239-2334; ext. 110; Fax: 302-239-2473; webpage@dnsashland.org
Bernard Dempsey, Alternate Representative
Helen Fischel, Education Programs Contact
George Fisher, Treasurer
Richard Fleming, Representative
Janice Taylor, Editor, Delaware Nature Society VOICE

DELAWARE RIVERKEEPER NETWORK
P.O. Box 326
Washington Crossing, PA 18977 United States
Phone: 215-369-1188   Fax: 215-369-1181
E-mail: drn@delawareriverkeeper.org
Website: www.delawareriverkeeper.org
Founded: 1988
Membership: 1,001–10,000
Scope: Regional
Description: The Delaware Riverkeeper Network works to protect and restore the Delaware River, its tributaries and habitats through advocacy, enforcement and citizen action.
Publication(s): In Defense of Watersheds, Stream Restoration In Pennsylvania, Stormwater Runoff: Lost Resource or Asset
Keyword(s): Ecosystems (precious), Ethics/Environmental Justice, Land Issues, Pollution (general), Public Lands/Greenspace, Recreation/Ecotourism, Sprawl/Urban Planning, Water Habitats & Quality, Wildlife & Species
Contact(s):
Maya van Rossum, Delaware Riverkeeper

DELAWARE WILD LANDS, INC.
P.O. Box 505
Odessa, DE 19730-0505 United States
Phone: 302-378-2736   Fax: 302-378-3629
E-mail: dwl@delanet.com
Website: dwl@delanet.com
Founded: 1961
Scope: Local
Description: A nonprofit charitable land conservancy actively engaged in acquiring areas on the Delmarva Peninsula for their natural resource values and for educational purposes; presently owns and manages approximately 20,000 acres. Produced two films, "The Endangered Shore" and "Swamp," available on loan or for purchase.
Keyword(s): Land Issues, Oceans/Coasts/Beaches, Water Habitats & Quality, Wildlife & Species
Contact(s):
Holger Harvey, Executive Director
Susan Crawford, Administrative Assistant

DELMARVA ORNITHOLOGICAL SOCIETY
P.O. Box 4247
Greenville, DE 19807 United States
Founded: 1963
Scope: State
Description: The purpose of this society shall be the promotion of the study of birds, the advancement and diffusion of ornithological knowledge, and the conservation of birds and their environment.
Publication(s): Delmarva Ornithologist, DOS Flyer
Contact(s):
Jim White, President; 3507 Barley Mill Rd., Hockessin, DE 19707; 302-239-7065
Mike Smith, Vice President; msmith10@student.vill.edu
Irene Goverts; bbcdel@ezd.com

DELTA WATERFOWL FOUNDATION
R.R. 1 Box 1
Portage la Prairie, R1N 3A1 Manitoba Canada
Phone: 204-239-1900   Fax: 203-239-5950
E-mail: canada@deltawaterfowl.org
Website: www.deltawaterfowl.org
Scope: International
Description: Delta Waterfowl's primary mission is to support graduate student training and research on all aspects of waterfowl and wetlands ecology and management. Since 1938, Delta students have produced over 200 graduate theses and 600 scientific publications. In addition to graduate research, Delta is currently involved in several demonstration projects incuding Adopt-A-Pothole, a habitat easement program; Hen Houses, predator-resistant nesting structures, Voluntary Restraint, a hunter ethics program
Publication(s): Publications on website
Keyword(s): Water Habitats & Quality, Wildlife & Species
Contact(s):
Jonathan Scarth, President
Lloyd Jones, Vice President
Donald Douglas, Vice Chair
Daniel Hughes, Chair
Thomas Hutchens, Treasurer
George Nolte, Secretary

DELTA WILDLIFE INC.
P.O. Box 276
433 Stoneville Road
Stoneville, MS 38776 United States
Phone: 662-686-3370   Fax: 662-686-3382
E-mail: info@deltawildlife.org
Website: deltawildlife.org
Founded: 1990
Membership: 1,001–10,000
Scope: Regional
Description: Delta Wildlife is committed to wildlife habitat enhancement, habitat restoration and conservation education in northwest Mississippi.
Publication(s): Delta Wildlife Magazine
Keyword(s): Agriculture/Farming, Ecosystems (precious), Forests/Forestry, Pollution (general), Public Lands/Greenspace, Water Habitats & Quality, Wildlife & Species
Contact(s):
Trey Cooke, Executive Director; 662-686-3370; trey@deltawildlife.org
Mary Helen Blossom, Marketing Director; 662-686-3370; maryhelen@deltawildlife.org
Junior Cobb, Field Biologist; 662-686-3370; junior@deltawildlife.org
Gayden Pollan, Senior Field Biologist; 662-686-3370; gayden@deltawildlife.org

DESCHUTES BASIN LAND TRUST
760 NW Harriman
Suite 100
Bend, OR 97701 United States
Phone: 541-330-0017   Fax: 541-330-0013
E-mail: info@deschuteslandtrust.org
Website: www.deschuteslandtrust.org
Founded: 1995
Membership: 101–1,000
Scope: Regional
Description: A regional land trust, based in Bend, Oregon, committed to conserving the special lands of the 6.8 million acre Deschutes Basin for present and future generations by working cooperatively with private landowners and local communities. Two primary programs are "Community Preserves" which engages local communities with the landscape and "Back to Home Waters" which lays the

groundwork to restore the legendary salmon and steelhead fisheries of the Deschutes Basin.

Keyword(s): Agriculture/Farming, Ecosystems (precious), Forests/Forestry, Land Issues, Public Lands/Greenspace, Water Habitats & Quality, Wildlife & Species

DESERT FISHES COUNCIL
Attn.: Dean Hendrickson
Texas Natural History Collection
University of Texas, R4000
Austin, TX 78712 United States
Phone: 760-872-8751   Fax: 760-872-8751
E-mail: phildesfish@telis.org
Website: www.desertfishes.org

Founded: 1969
Membership: 101–1,000
Scope: International

Description: A nationwide and international representation of state, federal, and university scientists and resource specialists and private conservation groups to provide for the exchange and transmittal of information on the status, protection, and management of the endemic fauna and flora of North American desert ecosystems.

Publication(s): Proceedings of the Desert Fishes Council

Keyword(s): Development/Developing Countries, Ecosystems (precious), Ethics/Environmental Justice, Land Issues, Reduce/Reuse/Recycle, Water Habitats & Quality, Wildlife & Species

Contact(s):
Paul Marsh, President; Box 871501, Tempe, AZ 85287; 480-965-2977; Fax: 480-965-2519; fish.dr@asu.edu
Dean Hendrickson, Editor of the Proceedings; 512-471-9774; Fax: 512-471-9775
Edwin Pister, Executive Secretary; Desert Fishes Council, P.O. Box 337, Bishop, CA 93515; 760-872-8751; phildesfish@telis.org

DESERT PROTECTIVE COUNCIL
P.O. Box 3635
San Diego, CA 92163 United States
Phone: 619-543-0757   Fax: 619-543-0757
E-mail: jtdesert@ixpres.com
Website: www.dpcinc.org

Founded: 1954
Membership: 101–1,000
Scope: Regional

Description: National desert oriented membership organization dedicated to educating the public about desert ecosystems and promoting wise and reverent enjoyment of desert lands.

DESERT RESEARCH FOUNDATION OF NAMIBIA, THE
7 Rossini Street
Windhoek, 9000 Namibia
Phone: 26461229855   Fax: 26461230172
E-mail: drfn@drfn.org.na
Website: www.drfn.org

Founded: 1963
Scope: Local, Regional, National, International

Description: The DRFN is a centre for arid land studies that conducts and facilitates appropriate, participatory and applied short- and long-term research on the environment. It is an independent, non governmental organisation dedicated to sustainable use of Namibia's environment.

Keyword(s): Development/Developing Countries, Energy, Land Issues, Water Habitats & Quality, Wildlife & Species

Contact(s):
Mary Seely, Contact

DESERT TORTOISE COUNCIL
P.O. Box 3141
Wrightwood, CA 92397 United States
Phone: 619-431-8449
E-mail: info@deserttortoise.org
Website: www.deserttortoise.org

Founded: 1975
Scope: National

Description: Formed to assure the continued survival of viable populations of the desert tortoise, Gopherus agassizi, which is endemic to Arizona, California, Nevada, and Utah.

Keyword(s): Land Issues, Public Health, Public Lands/Greenspace, Reduce/Reuse/Recycle, Wildlife & Species

Contact(s):
Mike Coffeen, Treasurer
Tim Duck, Co-Chairman
Tracy Goodlett, Co-Chairman
Ed Larue, Secretary
Ed Larue, Recording Secretary

DESERT TORTOISE PRESERVE COMMITTEE, INC.
4067 Mission Inn Ave.
Riverside, CA 92501 United States
Phone: 909-683-3872   Fax: 909-683-6949
E-mail: dtpc@pacbell.net
Website: www.tortoise-tracks.org

Founded: 1974
Scope: Regional

Description: A nonprofit organization formed to promote the welfare of the desert tortoise in the southwestern United States and to manage and establish preserves in the Western Mojave Desert.

Publication(s): Tortoise Tracks

Keyword(s): Ecosystems (precious), Land Issues, Public Lands/Greenspace, Wildlife & Species

Contact(s):
Michael Connor, Executive Director; 909-683-3872; Fax: 909-638-6949; dtpc@pacbell.net

DISTRICT OF COLUMBIA SOIL AND WATER CONSERVATION - DISTRICT
825 North Capitol St. NE
Washington, DC 20002 United States
Phone: 202-442-8982   Fax: 202-442-4808
Website: www.obc.dc.gov

Scope: State

Contact(s):
Theodore Gordon, Chair; 202-442-8989

DRAGONFLY SOCIETY OF THE AMERICAS, THE
2091 Partridge Ln.
Binghamton, NY 13903 United States
Phone: 607-722-4939
E-mail: tdonelly@binghamton.edu

Founded: 1989
Membership: 101–1,000
Scope: International

Description: The organization is concerned with all factors relevant to the world species assemblage of odonata (Insecta: Dragonflies). We study their systematics, biology, and taxonomy. The organization is also concerned with maintaining and improving the environmental conditions for Odonata through better water quality management, wetlands conservation, and aquatic habitat preservation.

Publication(s): ARGIA, Bulletin of American Odonatology

Keyword(s): Land Issues, Water Habitats & Quality, Wildlife & Species

Contact(s):
Roy Beckemeyer, President; 957 Perry, Wichita, KS 67203; royb@southwind.net
J.J. Daigle, Treasurer
T.W. Donnelly, Editor; 2091 Partridge Lane, Binghamton, NY 13903
S.W. Dunkle, Secretary; Biology Department, Collin County Community College, Plano, TX 75074

DUCKS UNLIMITED CANADA
ALBERTA OFFICE
#200, 10720 - 178 St.
Edmonton, T5S 1J3 Alberta Canada
Phone: 780-489-2002   Fax: 780-489-1856
E-mail: du_edmonton@ducks.ca
Website: www.ducks.ca

Scope: Regional

Description: Ducks Unlimited Canada is a private, nonprofit charitable organization dedicated to conserving wetlands for the benefit of North America's waterfowl, other wildlife and people.

Publication(s): Conservator

Keyword(s): Land Issues, Recreation/Ecotourism, Water Habitats & Quality, Wildlife & Species

Contact(s):
Gordon Edwards, Director of Regional Operations, Prairie Regions
Brett Calverley, Alberta NAWMP Coordinator
Gary Stewart, Conservation Programs Biologist, WBFI
Jim Wohl, Engineer

DUCKS UNLIMITED CANADA
MANITOBA OFFICE
1 Mallard Bay at Hwy. 220, P.O. Box 11660
Stonewall, R0C 2Z0 Manitoba Canada
Phone: 204-467-3000   Fax: 204-467-9028
E-mail: webfoot@ducks.ca
Website: www.ducks.ca

Founded: 1938
Membership: 101–1,000
Scope: National

Description: Ducks Unlimited Canada's mission is to conserve wetlands and associated habitats for the benefit of North America's waterfowl, which in turn provide healthy environments for wildlife and people.

Keyword(s): Water Habitats & Quality, Wildlife & Species

Contact(s):
Rod Fowler, Executive Vice President
Brian Gray, Director of Conservation Programs; 204-467-3349; Fax: 204-467-9028
Richard Walker, Director of Corporate Development and Major Gifts; 100-279 Midpark Way S.E., Calgary AB T2X IM2; 403-201-5577; Fax: 403-201-5580
Gary Goodwin, Human Resources Manager/Corporate Counsel
Robert Kindrachuk, Communications Manager
Rick Wishart, Manager of Education Program
L. Warren, Chief Financial Officer

DUCKS UNLIMITED CANADA
NOVA SCOTIA OFFICE
P.O. Box 430, 64 Highway 6
Amherst, B4H 3Z5 Nova Scotia Canada
Phone: 902-667-8726   Fax: 902-667-0916
E-mail: m_gloutney@ducks.ca
Website: www.ducks.ca

Founded: 1938

Scope: Local, Regional, National, International

Description: Ducks Unlimited Canada is a private, nonprofit charitable organization dedicated to conserving wetlands for the benefit of North America's waterfowl, other wildlife and people

Contact(s):
Mark Gloutney, Manager of Conservation Programs-Atlantic Canada; m_gloutney@ducks.ca
Brian McCullough, Atlantic Engineer; b_mccullough@ducks.ca

DUCKS UNLIMITED CANADA
ONTARIO OFFICE
566 Welham Rd.
Barrie, L4N 8Z7 Ontario Canada
Phone: 705-721-4444   Fax: 705-721-4999
E-mail: du_barrie@ducks.ca
Website: www.ducks.ca

Membership: 10,001–100,000
Scope: Regional

Contact(s):
Bob Clay, Manager Western Ontario Field Office
Ron Maher, Manager Eastern Ontario Field Office

DUCKS UNLIMITED CANADA
QUEBEC OFFICE
Suite 260, 710 Bouvier St.
Quebec, G2J 1C2 Quebec Canada
Phone: 418-623-1650   Fax: 418-623-0420
E-mail: du_quebec@ducks.ca
Website: www.ducks.ca

Founded: 1938
Membership: 100,001–500,000
Scope: International

Description: Ducks Unlimited Canada is an international, private, non-profit organization dedicated to the conservation of wetlands and associated habitats for the perpetuation of North America's waterfowl, which in turn provide healthy environments for wildlife and people.

Publication(s): Conservator, Conservationniste

Contact(s):
Patrick Plante, Director of Regional Operations
Paul St. George, Director of Fund Raising
Bernard Filion, Manager of Field Operations

DUCKS UNLIMITED CANADA
SASKATCHEWAN OFFICE
P.O. Box 4465, 1030 Winnipeg St.
Regina, S4P 3W7 Saskatchewan Canada
Phone: 306-569-0424   Fax: 306-565-3699
E-mail: du_regina@ducks.ca
Website: www.ducks.ca

Founded: 1938
Scope: International

Description: A private, nonprofit, conservation organization dedicated to preserving waterfowl by creating and restoring breeding habitat in Canada. This organization is funded by sportsmen of United States and Canada.

Publication(s): Newsletter

Contact(s):
D. Chekay, Director of Public Policy
Tim Thiele, Manager of Field Operations
L. Moats, Agricultural Program Specialist

DUCKS UNLIMITED, INC.
One Waterfowl Way
Memphis, TN 38120 United States
Phone: 901-758-3825   Fax: 901-758-3850
E-mail: nhq@ducks.org
Website: www.ducks.org

Founded: 1937
Membership: 500,001–1,000,000
Scope: National, International

Description: Ducks Unlimited conserves, restores, and manages wetlands and associated habitats for North America's waterfowl. These habitats also benefit other wildlife and people.

Publication(s): Ducks Unlimited Magazine, Puddler Magazine

Contact(s):
- L. Mayeux, Chairman of the Board; P.O. Box 1529, 1444 South Main, Marksville, LA 71351; 318-253-9643
- John Tomke, President; Dow AgroSciences, LLP, 9330 Zionsville Road, Indianapolis, IN 46268; 317-337-4442; Fax: 317-337-4455
- Jim Boyd, Group Manager Management Information Systems
- James Ware, Group Manager Fundraising/Membership & Marketing
- W. Wentz, Group Manager Conservation Programs
- D. Young, Executive Vice-President
- Bruce Batt, Chief Biologist/Director, IWWR
- Montserrat Carbonell, Director of Latin American Programs
- Wayne Dierks, Director of Human Resources and Staff Development
- Gary Goodpaster, Director of National Events
- Eric Keszler, Director of Communications
- Keith McKnight, Director of Conservation Programs
- Linda Schoenrock, National Director of Marketing & Communications
- Dan Thiel, National Director Development
- James Flood, General Counsel
- Tom Fulgham, Magazine Editor-in-Chief
- Randy Graves, Chief Financial Officer
- W. Lewis, Treasurer; P.O. Box 1344, Natchez, MS 39120; 601-446-6621
- Robert Mims, Controller
- Stephen Reynolds, Secretary; 899 Madison Avenue, Memphis, TN 38146; 901-227-5117
- Bill Willsey, Executive Secretary

DUCKS UNLIMITED, INC.
WETLANDS AMERICA TRUST, INC. OFFICE
One Waterfowl Way
Memphis, TN 38120 United States
Phone: 901-758-3825   Fax: 901-758-3850
Website: www.ducks.org

Scope: Regional

Description: A nonprofit trust organized to operate exclusively for charitable, educational, scientific and conservation purposes. The Trust seeks to protect the natural balance of our continent's wetland ecosystems, ensuring the future viability of waterfowl and other wetland wildlife.

Keyword(s): Water Habitats & Quality, Wildlife & Species

Contact(s):
- L. J. Mayeux, President
- Bill Willsey, Assistant Secretary
- D. Young, Chief Operating Officer

E

EAGLE NATURE FOUNDATION, LTD.
300 East Hickory Street
Apple River, IL 61001 United States
Phone: 815-594-2306   Fax: 815-594-2305
E-mail: eaglenature.tni@juno.com
Website: www.eaglenature.org

Founded: 1995

Membership: 101–1,000

Scope: Local, State, Regional, National, International

Description: ENF is a nonprofit international organization, which develops and implements habitat preservation strategies, conducts a wide variety of nature education and awareness programs, and engages in and supports bald eagle research.

Publication(s): Bald Eagle Bus Tours, Nature News, Bald Eagle News

Keyword(s): Agriculture/Farming, Air Quality/Atmosphere, Development/Developing Countries, Ecosystems (precious), Ethics/Environmental Justice, Forests/Forestry, Land Issues, Pollution (general), Population, Public Lands/Greenspace, Recreation/Ecotourism, Reduce/Reuse/Recycle

Contact(s):
- Terrence Ingram, President and Executive Director
- Wayne Fox, Second Vice President; 847-573-0601
- Eugene Small, First Vice President; 773-434-8328
- Joseph Lukascyk, Director; 708-430-0779
- James Ronnerud, Director; 608-776-2755
- Marvin Thill, Director; 815-947-3197
- Mark Werner, Director; 309-347-4543
- Sally Beyer, Secretary; 815-594-2362
- Susan Ertmer, Treasurer; 815-845-2253

EARTH DAY NETWORK
1616 P St. NW
Suite 200
Washington, DC 20036 United States
Phone: 202-518-0044   Fax: 202-518-8794
E-mail: earthday@earthday.net
Website: www.earthday.net

Scope: International

Description: Founded by the organizers of Earth Day 1970, Earth Day Network's mission is to promote environmental awareness and stewardship by engaging grassroots organizations worldwide in environmental education, citizen action and organizing, capacity building, coordinated global campaigns, and annual Earth Day celebrations.

Contact(s):
- Kathleen Rogers, President

EARTH DAY NEW YORK
201 E. 42nd St.
Suite 3200
New York, NY 10017 United States
Phone: 212-922-0048   Fax: 212-922-1936
E-mail: education@earthdayny.org
Website: www.earthdayny.org

Founded: 1989

Scope: Local, State, Regional, National

Description: Earth Day New York is a low-overhead, broadly educational nonprofit 501c(3) organization that promotes environmental awareness and solutions through a three-pronged program: 1) involving schools, teachers, and students through the Earth Day Education Program; 2) educating public and private policymakers through conferences; and 3) involving the general public in annual Earth Day events.

Publication(s): Lessons Learned, High Performance Buildings, Building the Sustainable Economy Conference

Keyword(s): Climate Change, Energy, Pollution (general), Sprawl/Urban Planning

Contact(s):
- Fred Kent, President; 212-620-5660; Fax: 212-620-3821
- Pamela Lippe, Executive Director and Vice President; 212-922-0048; Fax: 212-922-1936; plippe@aol.com
- Laura Gunlogson, Deputy Director; 212-922-0048; Fax: 212-922-1936; laura@earthdayny.org
- Douglas Durst, Chairman; 212-789-1155; Fax: 212-789-1199
- Timon Malloy, Treasurer; 203-535-5326; Fax: 203-353-5329
- Jim Tripp, Secretary; 212-505-2100; Fax: 212-505-2375

EARTH FORCE
1908 Mount Vernon Ave.
Alexandria, VA 22301 United States
Phone: 703-299-9400   Fax: 703-299-9485
E-mail: earthforce@earthforce.org
Website: www.earthforce.org

Founded: 1993

Membership: 1–100

Scope: National

Description: Earth Force is a national nonprofit environmental organization. Earth Force is dedicated to young people changing their communities and caring for our environment

now, while developing life-long habits of active citizenship and environmental stewardship.
Publication(s): Free Campaign Materials for Kids and Educators
Keyword(s): Water Habitats & Quality
Contact(s):
Thomas Martin, President and Director; 703-519-6867; Fax: 703-299-9485
Vince Meldrum, Vice President for National Programs
Donna Power, Vice President for Local Programs
Christine Bates, Board of Directors
F. Hagele, Secretary; 9th Flr., 1515 Market St., Philadelphia, PA 19102; 212-851-8640

EARTH FORCE
GREEN (GLOBAL RIVERS ENVIRONMENTAL EDUCATION NETWORK)
1908 Mt. Vernon Ave., Second Fl.
Alexandria, VA 22301 United States
Phone: 703-299-9400   Fax: 703-299-9485
E-mail: green@earthforce.org
Website: www.earthforce.org
Founded: 1984
Scope: Local, National, International
Description: Earth Force is youth for a change! Earth Force gives youth the skills and knowledge to create lasting solutions to local environmental problems. GREEN is program of Earth Force that offers watershed education resources.
Publication(s): Protecting Our Watersheds, Field Manual for Water Quality Monitoring, Sourcebook for Watershed Education, Investigating Streams and Rivers
Keyword(s): Land Issues, Oceans/Coasts/Beaches, Pollution (general), Reduce/Reuse/Recycle, Water Habitats & Quality, Wildlife & Species
Contact(s):
Thomas Martin, President; 703-519-6867
Vince Meldrum, COO; 703-519-6864

EARTH FOUNDATION
5401 Mitchelldale, Suite B4
Houston, TX 77092 United States
Phone: 713-686-9453
E-mail: sales@earthfound.com
Website: www.earthfound.com
Founded: 1990
Membership: 1–100
Scope: National
Description: The purpose of Earth Foundation is to empower educators and students to work towards a sustainable economy, just society, and healthy environment. Our focus is on education, fundraising for conservation, and cooperative programs with conservation groups and indigenous organizations working in the race to save the planet.
Publication(s): Rainforest Rescue Campaign Teacher Update
Keyword(s): Forests/Forestry, Land Issues, Wildlife & Species
Contact(s):
Cynthia Everage, President and Director; 5151 Mitchelldale B11, Houston, TX 77092

EARTH FRIENDS WILDLIFE FOUNDATION
P.O. Box 11217
Jackson, WY 83002-1217 United States
Phone: 307-734-5333   Fax: 307-739-0133
E-mail: lee@earthfriends.com
Website: www.earthfriends.com
Founded: 1995
Scope: Regional, National
Description: Earth Friends Wildlife Foundation is a charitable support organization committed to using its resources to support the work of conservation and wildlife protection groups. Our gifts are given as matching grants to make resources do more. We recognize the need for partnership among the concerns of business, wildlife interests and of those who will inherit the quality of life we create on this earth.
Publication(s): Yearly Annual Report
Keyword(s): Ecosystems (precious), Reduce/Reuse/Recycle, Wildlife & Species

EARTH ISLAND INSTITUTE
300 Broadway, Suite 28
San Francisco, CA 94133 United States
Phone: 415-788-3666   Fax: 415-788-7324
E-mail: earthisland@earthisland.org
Website: www.earthisland.org
Founded: 1982
Scope: National, International
Description: Through education and activism, Earth Island Institute counteracts threats to the biological and cultural diversity that sustains and enriches the global environment. The Institute develops and supports projects that promote the conservation, preservation, and restoration of the Earth. The Institute was founded by David Brower, veteran environmental leader.
Publication(s): Earth Island Journal, Ocean Alert, Paper Locator
Keyword(s): Development/Developing Countries, Reduce/Reuse/Recycle, Wildlife & Species
Contact(s):
Bob Wilkinson, President
John Knox, Executive Director
David Phillips, Executive Director
Maria Moyer-Angus, Secretary
Tim Rands, Treasurer

EARTH POLICY INSTITUTE
1350 Connecticut Ave., NW
Suite 403
Washington, DC 20036 United States
Phone: 2924969290   Fax: 2024969325
E-mail: epi@earth-policy.org
Website: earth-policy.org
Founded: 2001
Scope: International
Description: Earth Policy Institute, an independent environmental research organization founded by Lester R. Brown, is dedicated to providing a vision of what an environmentally sustainable economy—"an eco-economy"—is and a plan on how to get from here to there. EPI is disseminating its vision of an eco-economy via its books, including Eco-Economy: Building an Economy for the Earth, and through brief Eco-Economy Updates, that are designed for the media, policy-makers, and easy Internet distribution.
Publication(s): The Earth Policy Reader, Eco-Economy: Building an Economy for Earth, Plan B: Rescuing a Planet under Stress, Eco-Economy Indicators, Eco-Economy Updates
Keyword(s): Agriculture/Farming, Air Quality/Atmosphere, Climate Change, Development/Developing Countries, Ecosystems (precious), Energy, Finance/Banking/Trade, Forests/Forestry, Land Issues, Oceans/Coasts/Beaches, Population, Reduce/Reuse/Recycle, Transportation
Contact(s):
Lester Brown, President & Senior Researcher; 2024969290; ext. 11; Fax: 2024969325; lesterbrown@earth-policy.org
Reah Janise Kauffman, Vice President; 2024969290; ext. 12; Fax: 2024969325; rjkauffman@earth-policy.org

EARTH SHARE
7735 Old Georgetown Road
Suite 900
Bethesda, MD 20814 United States
Phone: 240-333-0300   Fax: 240-333-0301
E-mail: info@earthshare.org
Website: www.earthshare.org
Founded: 1988

Membership: 101–1,000
Scope: Local, State, Regional, National, International
Description: Earth Share is a nonprofit, federated fund-raising organization that represents nonprofit environmental and conservation organizations in workplace payroll deduction campaigns nationwide. Funds raised support these organizations' environmental and conservation programs and services. Earth Share also provides educational public service announcements about the environment.
Publication(s): Tips, Annual Newsletter
Contact(s):
  Kalman Stein, President
  Robin Perkins, Communications and Development Manager; 240-333-0300; Fax: 240-333-0301; info@earthshare.org
  Paul Lambert, Chairman

EARTH SHARE OF GEORGIA
ENVIRONMENTAL FUND FOR GEORGIA
1447 Peachtree St
Suite 214
Atlanta, GA 30309 United States
Phone: 404-873-3173   Fax: 404-873-3135
E-mail: info@earthsharega.org
Website: www.earthsharega.org
Founded: 1992
Scope: Local, State, Regional, National, International
Description: Earth Share of Georgia offers citizens one smart and simple way to care for our air, land and water. As Georgia's only environmental fund, Earth Share partners with businesses and employees to support 60 leading environmental groups through workplace campaigns and other activities.
Contact(s):
  Alice Rolls, Executive Director; 404-873-3173; Fax: 404-873-3135; alice@earthsharega.org
  Elicia Fritsch, Campaign Director; 404-873-3173; Fax: 404-873-3135; elicia@earthsharega.org
  Polly Sattler, Director of Corporate Partnerships; 404-873-3173; Fax: 404-873-3135; polly@earthsharega.org
  Annie Nixon, Administrative Assistant; 404-873-3173; Fax: 404-873-3135; annie@earthsharega.org

EARTHJUSTICE
HEADQUARTERS
426 Seventeenth Street
Sixth Floor
Oakland, CA 94612 United States
Phone: 510-550-6700   Fax: 510-550-6740
E-mail: eajus@earthjustice.org
Website: www.earthjustice.org
Founded: 1971
Scope: National, International
Description: Non-profit public interest law firm dedicated to protecting the magnificent places, natural resources, and wildlife of this earth and to defending the right of all people to a healthy environment. We bring about far-reaching change by enforcing and strengthening environmental laws on behalf of hundreds of organizations and communities.
Publication(s): In Brief
Keyword(s): Air Quality/Atmosphere, Development/Developing Countries, Ecosystems (precious), Energy, Ethics/Environmental Justice, Executive/Legislative/Judicial Reform, Finance/Banking/Trade, Forests/Forestry, Land Issues, Oceans/Coasts/Beaches, Pollution (general)
Contact(s):
  Buck Parker, Executive Director
  Barbara Bosma, Vice President of Human Resources & Administration
  Bill Curtiss, Vice President of Programs
  Bruce Neighbor, Vice President of Finance and Administration
  Cara Pike, Vice President of Communications
  Kathryn Knight, Vice President for Development

EARTHJUSTICE
BOZEMAN OFFICE
209 South Willson Avenue
Bozeman, MT 59715 United States
Phone: 406-586-9699   Fax: 406-586-9695
E-mail: eajusmt@earthjustice.org
Website: www.earthjustice.org
Scope: Regional
Description: Protects the rivers, streams, and wildlands of the Northern Rockies, the only place in the lower-48 states where grizzly bears, gray wolves, and bison still roam freely. Uses the power of the law to secure Endangered Species Act listings for imperiled species, challenge oil and gas development and mining operation on sensitive public lands, compel government agencies to restore Montana's water quality, and halt destructive logging and road building in national forests.
Contact(s):
  Douglas Honnold, Managing Attorney
  Abigail Dillen, Associate Attorney
  Tim Preso, Staff Attorney

EARTHJUSTICE
DENVER OFFICE
1631 Glenarm Place
Suite 300
Denver, CO 80202 United States
Phone: 303-623-9466   Fax: 303-623-8083
E-mail: eajusco@earthjustice.org
Website: www.earthjustice.org
Scope: Regional
Description: Protects the raging rivers, inspiring land formations, and wide open spaces of the Four Corners states. Uses the power of the law to limit overgrazing on public lands, restore critical rivers and streams, prevent motor vehicle use and logging in roadless areas, and secure critical habitat for threatened and endangered species. Our office also works in conjunction with the Environmental Law Clinic at the University of Denver College of Law.
Keyword(s): Ecosystems (precious), Energy, Land Issues, Public Lands/Greenspace
Contact(s):
  Jim Angell, Staff Attorney
  Keith Bauerle, Associate Attorney
  Susan Daggett, Managing Attorney
  Ted Zukoski, Project Attorney

EARTHJUSTICE
ENVIRONMENTAL LAW CLINIC AT STANFORD UNIVERSITY
Owen House
553 Salvatierra Walk
Stanford, CA 94305 United States
Phone: 650-725-8571   Fax: 650-725-8509
E-mail: info@earthjustice.org
Website: www.earthjustice.org
Scope: Regional
Description: Environmental law clinic and regional litigation office.
Contact(s):
  Debbie Sivas, Managing Attorney
  Michael Lozeau, Staff Attorney

EARTHJUSTICE
ENVIRONMENTAL LAW CLINIC AT THE UNIVERSITY OF DENVER
University of Denver
Forbes House
1714 Poplar Street
Denver, CO 80220 United States
Phone: 303-871-6996   Fax: 303-871-6991
E-mail: info@earthjustice.org
Website: www.earthjustice.org

Scope: Regional
Description: Regional law clinic and litigation office of Earthjustice.
Publication(s): Publications on website
Keyword(s): Air Quality/Atmosphere, Ecosystems (precious), Energy, Forests/Forestry, Land Issues, Public Lands/Greenspace, Water Habitats & Quality, Wildlife & Species
Contact(s):
Neil Levine, Staff Attorney
Jay Tutchton, Staff Attorney

EARTHJUSTICE
HONOLULU OFFICE
223 S. King Street #400
Honolulu, HI 96813-4501 United States
Phone: 808-599-2436   Fax: 808-521-6841
E-mail: eajushi@earthjustice.org
Website: www.earthjustice.org
Founded: 1971
Scope: Local, State, Regional
Description: Protects island and ocean ecosystems, native cultures, and endangered species in the mid-Pacific. Uses the power of the law to compel federal agencies to address the harmful effects of commercial fishing on marine ecosystems, restore contaminated inland waterways, secure endangered species, and support the islands' indigenous people and culture by safeguarding fragile ecosystems and water rights for local communities.
Publication(s): Brochure
Contact(s):
Paul Achitoff, Managing Attorney
David Henkin, Staff Attorney
Kapua Sproat, Associate Attorney
Isaac Moriwake, Associate Attorney

EARTHJUSTICE
INTERNATIONAL PROGRAM
426 Seventeenth Street
Seventh Floor
Oakland, CA 94612 United States
Phone: 510-550-6700   Fax: 510-550-6740
E-mail: eajusintl@earthjustice.org
Website: www.earthjustice.org
Scope: International
Description: Uses the power of the law to protect the environment and human health worldwide. Represents public interest and community groups in international tribunals and domestic courts to hold corporations and governments responsible for environmental harm, prevent trade rules from undermining public health and environmental protections, and create strong tools for citizens to defend the right to a healthy environment.
Keyword(s): Agriculture/Farming, Air Quality/Atmosphere, Development/Developing Countries, Energy, Ethics/Environmental Justice, Pollution (general)
Contact(s):
Martin Wagner, Director
Anna Cederstav, Staff Scientist
Marcello Mollo, Associate Attorney

EARTHJUSTICE
JUNEAU OFFICE
325 4th Street
Juneau, AK 99801 United States
Phone: 907-586-2751   Fax: 907-463-5891
E-mail: eajusak@earthjustice.org
Website: www.earthjustice.org
Scope: Regional
Description: Protects Alaska's pristine wilderness, marine ecosystems, and wildlife. Uses the power of the law to safeguard Alaska's public lands and watersheds from the destructive effects of logging, road building, mining, and oil and gas drilling, and protect the sensitive North Pacific ecosystem from industrial trawl fishing.
Keyword(s): Energy, Forests/Forestry, Land Issues, Oceans/Coasts/Beaches, Wildlife & Species
Contact(s):
Dierdre McDonnell, Project Attorney
Thomas Waldo, Staff Attorney
Layla Hughes, Associate Attorney
Eric Jorgensen, Managing Attorney
Michael LeVine, Associate Attorney
Demian Schane, Project Attorney

EARTHJUSTICE
OAKLAND OFFICE
426 Seventeenth Street
Fifth Floor
Oakland, CA 94612 United States
Phone: 510-550-6725   Fax: 510-550-6749
E-mail: eajusca@earthjustice.org
Website: www.earthjustice.org
Scope: Regional
Description: Protects ecosystems and communities, from the rolling hills of the San Francisco Bay Area through the rich agricultural lands of the Central Valley to the ancient forests and high peaks of the Sierra. The campaign "Healthy Cities, Healthy Wildlands" uses the power of the law to promote smart growth, and limit destructive activities that threaten wildlands and endangered species.
Keyword(s): Agriculture/Farming, Air Quality/Atmosphere, Forests/Forestry, Land Issues, Pollution (general), Public Health, Transportation, Wildlife & Species
Contact(s):
Greg Loarie, Associate Attorney
Deborah Reames, Managing Attorney
Susan Britton, Staff Attorney
Anne Harper, Staff Attorney
Mike Sherwood, Staff Attorney
Laura Robb, Associate Attorney

EARTHJUSTICE
POLICY AND LEGISLATION
1625 Massachussets Avenue, NW
Suite 702
Washington, DC 20036 United States
Phone: 202-667-4500   Fax: 202-667-2356
E-mail: eajusdc@earthjustice.org
Website: www.earthjustice.org
Scope: National
Description: Works to defend and strengthen the environmental laws that Earthjustice attorneys enforce in the courts and to block congressional attempts to override Earthjustice's legal victories.
Keyword(s): Energy, Executive/Legislative/Judicial Reform, Forests/Forestry, Land Issues, Public Lands/Greenspace, Wildlife & Species
Contact(s):
Joan Mulhern, Senior Legislative Counsel
Glenn Sugameli, Senior Legislative Counsel
Marty Hayden, Vice President of Policy and Legislation
Susan Holmes, Legislative Representative
Randall Moorman, Legislative Research Assistant
Sarah Wilhoite, Policy Associate

EARTHJUSTICE
SEATTLE OFFICE
705 Second Avenue
Suite 203
Seattle, WA 98104 United States
Phone: 206-343-7340   Fax: 206-343-1526
E-mail: eajuswa@earthjustice.org
Website: www.earthjustice.org
Scope: Regional
Description: Protects the cathedral forests, pristine waters, and wild salmon that are the heart and soul of the Pacific Northwest. A strategic campaign "Fish-Trees-Water" uses the power of the law to save endangered species from extinction, halt deforestation and road building on public lands, and restore streams and rivers impacted by hydroelectric dams, agriculture, mining, and other activities.
Keyword(s): Ecosystems (precious), Forests/Forestry, Land Issues, Pollution (general), Public Health, Public Lands/Greenspace, Wildlife & Species
Contact(s):
Patti Goldman, Managing Attorney
Kristen Boyles, Staff Attorney
Steve Mashuda, Project Attorney
Mike Mayer, Associate Attorney
Todd True, Staff Attorney
Grant Cope, Associate Attorney
Amy Derry, Associate Attorney

EARTHJUSTICE
TALLAHASSEE OFFICE
111 S. Martin Luther King Jr. Blvd.
Tallahassee, FL 32301 United States
Phone: 850-681-0031   Fax: 850-681-0020
E-mail: eajusfl@earthjustice.org
Website: www.earthjustice.org
Scope: Regional
Description: Protects Florida's subtropical forests, wetlands, waterways, coastal ecosystems, and communities. Uses the power of the law to restore and maintain the state's surface and ground waters, defend public lakes and rivers against exploitation by mining, logging, and cattle interests, and safeguard marine species and ecosystems from environmentally unsound development, oil and gas drilling, and destructive industrial fishing practices.
Keyword(s): Agriculture/Farming, Land Issues, Oceans/Coasts/Beaches, Pollution (general), Public Health, Water Habitats & Quality, Wildlife & Species
Contact(s):
Aliki Moncrief, Project Attorney
Monica Reimer, Staff Attorney
Eric Giroux, Associate Attorney
David Guest, Managing Attorney

EARTHJUSTICE
WASHINGTON, DC, OFFICE
1625 Massachusetts Avenue, NW
Suite 702
Washington, DC 20036 United States
Phone: 202-667-4500   Fax: 202-667-2356
E-mail: eajusdc@earthjustice.org
Website: www.earthjustice.org
Scope: Regional, National
Description: Protects water quality, public health, and ecosystems in Washington, DC, the mid-Atlantic region, and nationwide. Uses the power of the law to defend and strengthen federal Clean Air Act and Clean Water Act standards, ensure that federal, state, and municipal governments adopt and enforce these standards, and safeguard poor communities and communities of color from the harmful effects of toxic pollution and sewage discharges.
Keyword(s): Air Quality/Atmosphere, Land Issues, Oceans/Coasts/Beaches, Pollution (general), Public Health, Water Habitats & Quality, Wildlife & Species
Contact(s):
Howard Fox, Managing Attorney
David Baron, Staff Attorney
Jim Pew, Project Attorney
Steve Roady, Staff Attorney
Jennifer Kefer, Associate Attorney
Keri Powell, Associate Attorney

EARTHSCAN
120 Pentonville Rd.
London, N1 9JN United Kingdom
Phone: 2072780433   Fax: 2072781142
E-mail: earthinfo@earthscan.co.uk
Website: www.earthscan.co.uk
Scope: International
Description: A publishing house for books addressing environment and development issues in both industrialized countries and the developing world, taking as a starting point the inescapable link between poverty and environmental degradation. All aspects of sustainable development are covered, including international relations, environmental law and institutions, global environmental change, population growth, and the management of resources and economics, as well as social and cultural questions.
Keyword(s): Agriculture/Farming, Air Quality/Atmosphere, Climate Change, Development/Developing Countries, Ethics/Environmental Justice, Finance/Banking/Trade, Forests/Forestry, Land Issues, Oceans/Coasts/Beaches, Pollution (general), Population, Recreation/Ecotourism
Contact(s):
Jonathan Wilson, Publishing Director
Victoria Burrows, Desk Editor
Alan Leander, Editor
Frances MacDermott, Editor
Helen Rose, Marketing Executive

EARTHSTEWARDS NETWORK
P.O. Box 10697
Bainbridge Island, WA 98110 United States
Phone: 206-842-7986   Fax: 206-842-8918
E-mail: outreach@earthstewards.org
Website: www.earthstewards.org
Founded: 1980
Membership: 101–1,000
Scope: International
Description: Earthstewards is an international, multicultural network dedicated to inspiring and empowering ordinary people to take bold action for conflict transformation and the creation of positive relationships bridging boundaries of gender, race, culture, nations, age and beliefs. Our projects include: PeaceTrees Vietnam and other projects involving people to people diplomacy, global networking and conflict resolution.
Publication(s): Essene Book of Meditations and Blessings, Essene Book of Days, Earthstewards Newsletter, Warriors of the Heart
Contact(s):
Chuck Meadows, Executive Director; 206-842-7986; chuckm@peacetreesvietnam.org

EARTHTRUST
1118 Maunawili Road
Kailua, HI 96734 United States
Phone: 808-261-5339   Fax: 808-333-1158
E-mail: sue@flipperfun.com
Website: www.earthtrust.org
Founded: 1976
Scope: International
Description: Earthtrust is an international nonprofit wildlife conservation organization. It involves small groups of highly

capable people, involved with innovative investigations and projects, in partnership with private industry, governments and other environmental groups. Earthtrust is aimed at resolving wildlife crisis situations. Earthtrust's focus is to expose the poaching of endangered species and the sale of endangered whale meat in Asian markets through the use of DNA analysis.

Keyword(s): Wildlife & Species

Contact(s):
Donald White, President

EARTHWATCH INSTITUTE
3 Clocktower Place, Suite 100
Box 75
Maynard, MA 01754-0075 United States
Phone: 978-461-0081   Fax: 978-461-2332
E-mail: info@earthwatch.org
Website: www.earthwatch.org

Founded: 1971
Membership: 10,001–100,000
Scope: National, International

Description: The mission of Earthwatch Institute is to engage people worldwide in scientific field research and education to promote the understanding and action necessary for a sustainable environment. Earthwatch recruits volunteers of all ages and abilities to assist noted scientists with their field research.

Publication(s): Earthwatch Expedition Guide, Earthwatch Journal

Keyword(s): Climate Change, Development/Developing Countries, Ecosystems (precious), Ethics/Environmental Justice, Forests/Forestry, Land Issues, Oceans/Coasts/Beaches, Public Health, Recreation/Ecotourism, Water Habitats & Quality, Wildlife & Species

Contact(s):
Roger Bergen, President; rbergen@earthwatch.org
Edward Wilson, Vice President; ewilson@earthwatch.org
Marie Studer, Chief Scientific Officer; mstuder@earthwatch.org
John Walker, Chief Financial Officer; jwalker@earthwatch.org

EAST CENTRAL ILLINOIS FUR TAKERS
853 E. 1000 N. Rd
Onarga, IL 60955 United States
Phone: 217-394-2577

Founded: 1974
Membership: 1–100
Scope: Local

Description: State chapter of Fur Takers of America. Helps monitor furbearing wildlife populations in the state and helps conserve this renewable resource.

Contact(s):
Louis Krumwiede, President; 217-394-2577

EASTERN SHORE LAND CONSERVANCY (ESLC)
P.O. Box 109
Queenstown, MD 21658 United States
Phone: 410-827-9756   Fax: 410-827-5765
E-mail: INFO@ESLC.ORG
Website: www.eslc.org

Founded: 1990
Membership: 101–1,000
Scope: Regional

Description: The Eastern Shore Land Conservancy preserves farms, forests and natural areas for future generations, utilizing a variety of voluntary land protection tools that are available to landowners.

Publication(s): Eastern Shore 2010: A Regional Vision, How to Hold on to the Family Farm, The Future Eastern Shore - Your Choice, Panorama, Fact Sheets, Preserving Land for Our Future

Keyword(s): Land Issues, Public Lands/Greenspace, Sprawl/Urban Planning

Contact(s):
Robert Etgen, Executive Director; 410-827-9756; ext. 166; Fax: 410-827-5765; retgen@eslc.org
Jennifer Nutt, Director of Development; 410-827-9756; ext. 155; Fax: 410-827-5765; jnutt@eslc.org
Amy Owsley, Director of Community Planning; 410-827-9756; ext. 168; Fax: 410-827-5765; aowsley@eslc.org
Nina White, Director of Administration; 410-827-9756; ext. 164; Fax: 410-827-5765; nwhite@eslc.org
Sandra Edwards, Land Protection Specialist; 410-827-9756; ext. 163; Fax: 410-827-5765; sedwards@eslc.org
Rex Linville, Land Protection Specialist; 410-827-9756; ext. 157; Fax: 410-827-5765; rlinville@eslc.org
Laurie Wilson, Administrative Assistant; 410-827-9756; ext. 162; Fax: 410-827-5765; lwilson@eslc.org

ECODEFENSE
Moskowsky pr. 120-34
Kaliningrad, 236006 Russia
Phone: 70112437286   Fax: 70112437286
E-mail: ecodefense@ecodef.koenig.su

Scope: Regional, International

Description: Ecodefense is a nongovernmental, nonprofit environmental organization that works to inform and involve more ordinary citizens to envirnment and social activity through organizing environmental events and spread of the information.

Keyword(s): Agriculture/Farming, Energy, Oceans/Coasts/Beaches, Public Lands/Greenspace, Recreation/Ecotourism

Contact(s):
Alexandra Korolera, Director of the Centre for Coordination of Education Project
Galina Ragouzina, Editor

ECOLOGICAL SOCIETY OF AMERICA, THE
1707 H St., NW, Suite 400
Washington, DC 20006 United States
Phone: 202-833-8773   Fax: 202-833-8775
E-mail: esahq@esa.org
Website: www.esa.org

Founded: 1915
Membership: 1,001–10,000
Scope: National

Description: The Ecological Society of America is the nation's premier professional society of ecologists. ESA promotes the responsible application of ecological principles to the solution of environmental problems through ESA reports, journals, and expert testimony to Congress. Each summer, ESA convenes a conference featuring the latest findings in ecological research.

Publication(s): Frontiers in Ecology and the Environment, Ecology, Issues in Ecology, Bulletin of the Ecological Society of America, Ecological Monographs, Ecological Applications

Keyword(s): Air Quality/Atmosphere, Climate Change, Ecosystems (precious), Ethics/Environmental Justice, Forests/Forestry, Land Issues, Oceans/Coasts/Beaches, Pollution (general), Public Lands/Greenspace, Water Habitats & Quality, Wildlife & Species

Contact(s):
Nadine Lymn, Director for Public Affairs
Katherine McCarter, Executive Director

ECOLOGY CENTER
2530 San Pablo Ave.
Berkeley, CA 94702 United States
Phone: 510-548-2220   Fax: 510-548-2240
E-mail: info@ecologycenter.org
Website: www.ecologycenter.org

Founded: 1969
Membership: 1,001–10,000
Scope: Local, State, Regional

Description: A nonprofit organization working to develop a more responsible society by identifying environmentally destructive practices and demonstrating sound alternatives. Programs include an environmental information clearinghouse, library, classes, book and ecoproducts store, sponsorship of three weekly farmers' markets, and weekly residential curbside recycling service in the city of Berkeley, CA. Primary service area: Greater San Francisco Bay region.

Publication(s): Terrain

Keyword(s): Agriculture/Farming, Ethics/Environmental Justice, Forests/Forestry, Land Issues, Pollution (general), Public Lands/Greenspace, Reduce/Reuse/Recycle, Wildlife & Species

Contact(s):
Laird Townsend, Editor

ECO-SEA
52 Stevens St., Suite 1100
White Plains, NY 10606 United States
Phone: 914-684-6539   Fax: 914-684-9607
E-mail: anderson@eco-sea.org
Website: www.eco-sea.org

Founded: 1995
Membership: 1–100
Scope: Local, National, International

Description: Global problems need a global response: ECO-SEA is a truly global program which will be based on a large sailing ship. Our goal is to increase global awareness for global issues. This program is unusual because we offer contributors a unique manner in which to earn enough money to more then compensate them for their donations. This is particularly true for multinational corporations

Publication(s): Information available upon request

Keyword(s): Climate Change, Development/Developing Countries, Ecosystems (precious), Energy, Population

Contact(s):
D. Anderson, Executive Director

EDUCATIONAL COMMUNICATIONS
P.O. Box 351419
Los Angeles, CA 90035 United States
Phone: 310-559-9160   Fax: 310-559-9160
E-mail: ecnp@aol.com
Website: www.ecoprojects.org

Founded: 1958
Scope: International

Description: EC creates and promotes educational and scientific projects and programs for the public, focusing on environmental concerns. It founded The Ecology Center of Southern California in 1972; since 1977 has sponsored the award-winning Environmental Directions, a weekly national and international radio series heard in 8 states and on shortwave and internet; and since 1984 has produced three-time Emmy-nominated ECONEWS, a weekly television series broadcast on over 100 cable and PBS outlets nationally.

Publication(s): The Compendium Newsletter: A Guide to Ecological Activism, Directory of Environmental Organizations, Econews TV and Environmental Directions Radio

Keyword(s): Population, Recreation/Ecotourism

Contact(s):
Nancy Pearlman, Executive Producer and Director
Anna Harlowe, Associate Director
Leslie Lewis, Administrative Coordinator

ELM RESEARCH INSTITUTE
11 Kit Street
Keene, NH 03431 United States
Phone: 603-358-6198   Fax: 603-358-6305
E-mail: libertyelm@webryders.com
Website: www.libertyelm.com

Founded: 1967
Membership: 1,001–10,000
Scope: National

Description: A nonprofit organization which has funded over $1,000,000 in research for the treatment of Dutch elm disease and development of the disease-resistant American Liberty Elm, supplies equipment and information pertaining to elm care and treatment of Dutch elm disease, propagates the American Liberty Elm and distributes it under the auspices of the Johnny Elmseed Project with the assistance of local Boy Scouts and other nonprofit groups. Over 750 nurseries have been established since 1984.

Publication(s): Specialized Elm Care Information, Data on Elm Injections, Elm Leaves

Keyword(s): Forests/Forestry, Wildlife & Species

Contact(s):
John Hansel, Executive Director
Yvonne Spalthoff, Assistant Director

ENDANGERED HABITATS LEAGUE
8424-A Santa Monica Boulevard, #592
Los Angeles, CA 90069-4267 United States
Phone: 213-804-2750   Fax: 323-654-1931
E-mail: dsilverla@earthlink.net
Website: ehleague.org

Founded: 1991
Membership: 101–1,000
Scope: State, Regional

Description: The Endangered Habitats League is a Southern California organization dedicated to ecosystem protection, improved land use planning, and collaborative conflict resolution.

ENDANGERED SPECIES COALITION
1101 14th St., NW, Suite 1400
Washington, DC 20005 United States
Phone: 202-682-9400   Fax: 202-756-2804
E-mail: esc@stopextinction.org
Website: www.stopextinction.org

Founded: 1982
Scope: Local, State, Regional, National

Description: The goal of the Coalition is to broaden and mobilize public support for protecting endangered species.

Publication(s): Activist Tools, Newsletter

Keyword(s): Wildlife & Species

Contact(s):
Brock Evans, Executive Director

ENGENDERHEALTH
440 9th Ave.
New York, NY 10001 United States
Phone: 212-561-8000   Fax: 212-561-8067
E-mail: info@engenderhealth.org
Website: www.engenderhealth.org

Founded: 1943
Scope: International

Description: EngenderHealth is an international nonprofit agency that works worldwide to support and strengthen reproductive health services for women and men; providing technical assistance, training and information in the areas of family planning, maternity care, STIs/HIV/AIDS, quality improvement and reproductive health programs for men.

Publication(s): EngenderHealth News, see publications on website

Keyword(s): Population, Public Health

Contact(s):
Amy Pollack, M.D., M.P.H., President
Lynn Bakamjian, M.P.H., Senior Vice President of Programs
Jeanne Haws, M.P.A., Vice President for Operations
Terrence Jezowski, M.S., Vice President for Development
Maurice Middleberg, Executive Vice President
Rachael Pine, J.D., Vice President for Public Affairs
Lyman Brainerd, Board Chair

ENTOMOLOGICAL SOCIETY OF AMERICA
9301 Annapolis Rd.
Lanham, MD 20706-3115 United States
Phone: 301-731-4535　　　　Fax: 301-731-4538
E-mail: esa@entsoc.org
Website: www.entsoc.org

Founded: 1889
Membership: 1,001–10,000
Scope: International
Description: To promote the scientific study of insects and related arthropods. Specialty sections include systematic behavior, toxicology, biogenetics, plant protection, medical and veterinary, regulatory and extension, and related scientific disciplines.
Publication(s): Annals of the Entomological Society of America, ESA Newsletter, American Entomologist, Journal of Medical Entomology, Environmental Entomology, Journal of Economic Entomology
Keyword(s): Agriculture/Farming, Forests/Forestry, Public Health, Sprawl/Urban Planning, Wildlife & Species
Contact(s):
　Kevin Steffey, President; ksteffey@uiuc.edu
　Paula Lettice, Executive Director; 301-731-4535; ext. 0; esa@entsoc.org

ENVIRONMENT COUNCIL OF RHODE ISLAND
ECRI
P.O. Box 9061
Providence, RI 02940 United States
Phone: 401-621-8048　　　　Fax: 401-331-5266
E-mail: environmentcouncil@earthlink.net
Website: www.environmentcouncilri.org

Founded: 1972
Membership: 101–1,000
Scope: Local, State, National
Description: A representative statewide organization, affiliated with the National Wildlife Federation, dedicated to the protection and enhancement of wildlife and its habitat through public education and government interaction.
Keyword(s): Agriculture/Farming, Air Quality/Atmosphere, Climate Change, Ecosystems (precious), Energy, Ethics/Environmental Justice, Executive/Legislative/Judicial Reform, Forests/Forestry, Land Issues, Oceans/Coasts/Beaches, Pollution (general), Population
Contact(s):
　Sheila Dormody, President
　Paul Beaudette, Representative

ENVIRONMENTAL ACTION FUND (EAF)
P.O. Box 22421
Nashville, TN 37202 United States
Phone: 615-385-4389
Website: www.civictrust.org.uk/eaf

Founded: 1976
Scope: State
Description: A nonprofit, nonpartisan union of citizen groups joined to preserve and protect Tennessee's natural resources and environmental health. EAF works for strong environmental legislative programs and policies.
Contact(s):
　Mark Manner, President; 2424 Golf Club Ln., Nashville, TN 37215
　Sandy Bivens, Secretary; 3504 General Bates Dr., Nashville, TN 37204
　Paul Davis, Treasurer; 5462 Vanderbilt Rd., Old Hickory, TN 37138

ENVIRONMENTAL ADVOCATES OF NEW YORK
353 Hamilton St.
Albany, NY 12210 United States
Phone: 518-462-5526　　　　Fax: 518-427-0381
E-mail: info@eany.org
Website: www.eany.org

Founded: 1969
Membership: 1,001–10,000
Scope: State
Description: A representative statewide organization, affiliated with the National Wildlife Federation, dedicated to the protection and enhancement of wildlife and its habitat through public education and government interaction.
Publication(s): Voters Guide, The Greensheet, Albany Report
Contact(s):
　Oakes Ames, President
　Val Washington, Executive Director & Education Programs Contact; ext. 220; vwash@eany.org
　Steve Allinger, Representative
　Jeff Jones, Editor; ext. 233; jjones@eany.org
　Charles Kruzansky, Alternate Representative & Treasurer

ENVIRONMENTAL ALLIANCE FOR SENIOR INVOLVEMENT (EASI)
P.O. Box 250, 9292 Old Dumfries Rd
Catlett, VA 20119 United States
Phone: 540-788-3274　　　　Fax: 540-788-9301
E-mail: easi@easi.org
Website: www.easi.org

Founded: 1990
Scope: Local, State, Regional, National, International
Description: EASI is the primary organization encouraging senior volunteers to use their expertise and leadership in restoring and sustaining communities while promoting intergenerational environmental stewardship, through an international network of Senior Environment Corps, wherever older citizens want to participate. EASI is the largest senior environmental action network in the world.
Contact(s):
　Thomas (Tom) Benjamin, President; P.O. Box 250, 9292 Old Dumfries Road, Catlett, VA 20119-0250; 540-788-3274; Fax: 540-788-9301; tom@easi.org
　Roy Geiger, VP-Administration; P.O. Box 250, 9292 Old Dumfries Road, Catlett, VA 20119-0250; 540-788-3274; Fax: 540-788-9301; rgeiger@swimmail.com
　Peggy Knight, V.P. - Programs; 5616 North 26th St., Arlington, VA 22207-1407; 703-241-0019; Fax: 703-538-5504; mknighteco@aol.com
　Karen Caron, Asst. to President; P.O. Box 250, 9292 Old Dumfries Road, Catlett, VA 20119-0250; 540-788-3274; Fax: 540-788-9301; karen@easi.org

ENVIRONMENTAL AND ENERGY STUDY INSTITUTE (EESI)
122 C St., NW, Suite 630
Washington, DC 20001 United States
Phone: 202-628-1400　　　　Fax: 202-628-1825
E-mail: mail@eesi.org
Website: www.eesi.org

Founded: 1985
Membership: 1–100
Scope: National
Description: The EESI is dedicated to promoting environmentally sustainable societies. EESI produces credible, timely information, and innovative public policy initiatives that lead to transitions to social and economic patterns that sustain people, the environment, and the natural resources upon which present and future generations depend.
Publication(s): Briefing Summaries, The ECO Newsletter
Keyword(s): Climate Change, Energy, Transportation

Contact(s):
  Carol Werner, Director of Energy and Climate Change Program
  Richard Ottinger, Chair

ENVIRONMENTAL CAREERS ORGANIZATION, INC., THE
179 South St., 3rd Fl.
Boston, MA 02111 United States
Phone: 617-426-4375   Fax: 617-423-0998
Website: www.eco.org

Founded: 1972
Scope: National
Description: ECO protects and enhances the environment through the development of professionals, the promotion of careers and the inspiration of individual action. This is accomplished through placement, career advisement, career products and research and consulting. ECO has three regional offices and an alumni network of over 6,500 individuals.
Publication(s): Complete Guide to Environmental Careers, Beyond the Green
Keyword(s): Ethics/Environmental Justice
Contact(s):
  John Cook, President; ext. 125; jcook@eco.org

ENVIRONMENTAL CONCERN INC.
201 Boundary Lane
P.O. Box P
St. Michaels, MD 21663 United States
Phone: 410-745-9620   Fax: 410-745-3517
E-mail: order@wetland.org
Website: www.wetland.org

Founded: 1972
Scope: National
Description: Environmental Concern Inc., founded in 1972 as a not-for-profit corporation, is dedicated to promoting public understanding and stewardship of wetlands, through experiential learning, native species horticulture, and creation and restoration initiatives. Environmental Concern Inc. focuses on wetland creation and restoration, a wholesale native species nursery, and educator and professional trainings.
Publication(s): Do's and Don'ts of Wetland Construction, POW!: The Planning of Wetlands, A Comprehensive Review of Wetlands, Evaluation for Planned Wetlands, Wetland Planting Guide for the Northeast, WOW! The Wonders of Wetlands
Keyword(s): Agriculture/Farming, Oceans/Coasts/Beaches, Water Habitats & Quality, Wildlife & Species
Contact(s):
  Suzanne Pittenger-Slear, President
  Edgar Garbisch, Vice President

ENVIRONMENTAL DEFENSE
ALLIANCE FOR ENVIRONMENTAL INNOVATION
18 Vermont Street, 8th floor
Boston, MA 02108 United States
Phone: 617-723-2996   Fax: 617-723-2999
Website: www.envirnomentaldefense.org/alliance

Founded: 1967
Scope: Regional
Description: The Alliance for Environmental Innovation is a joint project of EDF and The Pew Charitable Trusts.
Contact(s):
  Gwen Ruta, Director

ENVIRONMENTAL DEFENSE
CAPITAL OFFICE
1875 Connecticut Ave., NW Ste. 600
Washington, DC 20009 United States
Phone: 202-387-3500   Fax: 202-234-6049
E-mail: members@enviromentaldefense.org
Website: www.enviromentaldefense.org

Membership: 101–1,000
Scope: National
Contact(s):
  Fred Krupp, Executive Director; 257 Park Ave. S., New York, NY 10010; 212-505-2100; fkrupp@enviromentaldefense.org

ENVIRONMENTAL DEFENSE
HEADQUARTERS
257 Park Ave. South
New York, NY 10010 United States
Phone: 212-505-2100   Fax: 212-505-2375
Website: www.enviromentaldefense.org

Founded: 1967
Membership: 100,001–500,000
Scope: Local, State, Regional, National, International
Description: Environmental Defense is an advocacy and research organization made up of scientists, economists, engineers, and attorneys who seek practical solutions to a broad range of environmental and human health problems. The organization represents more than 300,000 members, and since 1967 has linked science, economics, law and innovative private-sector partnerships to create breakthrough solutions to the most serious environmental problems.
Publication(s): EDF Letter
Keyword(s): Agriculture/Farming, Air Quality/Atmosphere, Climate Change, Development/Developing Countries, Ecosystems (precious), Energy, Ethics/Environmental Justice, Finance/Banking/Trade, Forests/Forestry, Oceans/Coasts/Beaches, Pollution (general), Public Health
Contact(s):
  Fred Krupp, President; 212-505-2100
  Steve Cochran, Strategic Communications Director; 202-387-3500
  Allan Margolin, Media Director; 212-505-2100
  Elizabeth Thompson, Legislative Director; 202-387-3500
  Marcia Aronoff, Vice President for Programs; 212-505-2100
  Peter Klebnikov, Editor; 212-505-2100
  Debbie McGinn, Vice President for Finance and Administration; 212-505-2100
  Nick Nicholas, Chairman of the Board of Trustees
  Annie Petsonk, International Counsel; 212-505-2100
  James Tripp, General Counsel

ENVIRONMENTAL DEFENSE
NORTH CAROLINA OFFICE
2500 Blue Ridge Rd., Suite 330
Raleigh, NC 27607 United States
Phone: 919-881-2601   Fax: 919-881-2607
Website: www.environmentaldefense.org

Membership: 101–1,000
Scope: Regional

ENVIRONMENTAL DEFENSE
ROCKY MOUNTAIN OFFICE
2334 N. Broadway
Boulder, CO 80304 United States
Phone: 303-440-4901   Fax: 303-440-8052
Website: www.environmentaldefense.org

Founded: 1967
Membership: 100,001–500,000
Scope: International
Description: Environmental Defense is a leading national nonprofit organization representing more than 300,000 members. Since 1967, we have linked science, economics and law to create innovative, equitable and cost-effective solutions to society's most urgent environmental problems.
Keyword(s): Ethics/Environmental Justice, Executive/Legislative/Judicial Reform

Contact(s):
Fred Krupp, Regional Director; 257 Park Ave. S., 17th Floor, New York, NY 10010; 212-505-2100

ENVIRONMENTAL DEFENSE
TEXAS OFFICE
44 East Ave., Suite 304
Austin, TX 78701 United States
Phone: 512-478-5161   Fax: 512-478-8140
Website: www.enviromentaldefense.org
Membership: 100,001–500,000
Scope: Regional
Keyword(s): Ethics/Environmental Justice, Executive/Legislative/Judicial Reform

ENVIRONMENTAL DEFENSE
WEST COAST OFFICE
5655 College Ave. Suite 304
Oakland, CA 94618 United States
Phone: 510-658-8008   Fax: 510 658-0630
Website: www.environmentaldefense.org
Membership: 1,000,001+
Scope: International

ENVIRONMENTAL DEFENSE CENTER
906 Garden St.
Santa Barbara, CA 93101 United States
Phone: 805-963-1622   Fax: 805-962-3152
E-mail: edc@edcnet.org
Website: www.edcnet.org
Founded: 1977
Membership: 1,001–10,000
Scope: Regional
Description: A nonprofit, public-interest environmental law firm providing legal services to citizens' groups and environmental organizations on environmental issues facing California's central coast region since 1977. The Center focuses on a wide range of issues, including oil development, toxic wastes, air and water pollution, species and habitat protection, open space preservation, land use, and coastal access.
Keyword(s): Agriculture/Farming, Air Quality/Atmosphere, Ecosystems (precious), Energy, Ethics/Environmental Justice, Forests/Forestry, Land Issues, Oceans/Coasts/Beaches, Pollution (general), Public Health, Public Lands/Greenspace, Recreation/Ecotourism, Reduce/Reuse/Recycle

ENVIRONMENTAL EDUCATION ASSOCIATES
2929 Main Street
Buffalo, NY 14214 United States
Phone: 716-833-2929   Fax: 716-833-9292
E-mail: training@EnvironmentalEducation.com
Website: www.environmentaleducation.com/
Founded: 1994
Scope: State, National
Description: A non-profit organization working in public high schools to provide students with coursework in environmental law and policy with a focus on endangered species, environmental justice and water quality.
Publication(s): Environmental Justice: A Planning Commission Hearing to Approve/Deny a Household Hazardous Waste Facility Plan, Endangered Species Act: The Case of the Yellow-backed Rat Skunk
Keyword(s): Air Quality/Atmosphere, Ethics/Environmental Justice, Reduce/Reuse/Recycle, Water Habitats & Quality, Wildlife & Species

ENVIRONMENTAL EDUCATION ASSOCIATION OF ILLINOIS
Attn: Judy Miller, Anita Purves Nature Center
1505 N. Broadway
Urbana, IL 61801 United States
Phone: 217-384-4062   Fax: 217-384-1052
E-mail: kmiller@urbanaparks.org
Website: www.eeai.net
Founded: 1970
Scope: State
Description: Environmental Education Association of Illinois is the only organization in Illinois that makes environmental literacy its primary goal as it strives to instill a sense of community between the native ecosystems and people.
Publication(s): Illinois Environmental Education Update
Keyword(s): Reduce/Reuse/Recycle, Water Habitats & Quality, Wildlife & Species
Contact(s):
Deb Chapman, President
Curt Carter, Membership; S.I.U.E. Mail Code 6888, Carbondale, IL 62901; 618-453-1121
Dave Guritz, Treasurer; 847-428-2240
Kim Petzing, Secretary; 217-384-4062
Karen Zuckerman, President-Elect; 309-697-1325

ENVIRONMENTAL EDUCATION ASSOCIATION OF INDIANA
Attn: Paul McAfee, President
6530 W. Wallen Rd.
Fort Wayne, IN 46818 United States
Phone: 260-489-5032
E-mail: pmcafee@onemain.com
Website: www.eeai.org
Founded: 1969
Scope: State
Description: A statewide, nonprofit organization dedicated to the wise use and management of natural resources through environmental conservation education. Activities include an annual meeting, workshops, teaching materials, exhibits, and youth environmental summit.
Publication(s): CREED Newsletter
Contact(s):
Paul Steury, President Elect; P.O. Box 263, Wolf Lake, IN 46796; 219-779-5869; paulds@goshen.edu
Deborah Messenger, Vice President; 402 W. Washington St. W-265, Indianapolis, IN 46204-2739; 317-233-3872; deborahmessenger@netzero.net
Doug Waldman, Treasurer; 11832 Kress Rd., Roanoke, IN 46783; 317 672-3042

ENVIRONMENTAL EDUCATION ASSOCIATION OF WASHINGTON
2142 Cispus Rd
Randle, WA 98377 United States
Phone: 360-497-7131   Fax: 360-497-7132
E-mail: eeaw@eeaw.org
Website: www.eeaw.org
Founded: 1991
Membership: 101–1,000
Scope: State
Description: The EEAW promotes and stimulates the development of effective environmental education in our state's schools and communities. The organization successfully creates an environmentally literate citizenry who practice care and respect for our state's natural environments. EEAW is a strong and vital organization that has successfully positioned environmental education as a resource to improve student learning and achievement, enhance business practices and support sustainable communities.
Publication(s): EEAW Newsletter
Keyword(s): Agriculture/Farming, Air Quality/Atmosphere, Climate Change, Development/Developing Countries, Ecosystems (precious), Energy, Ethics/Environmental Justice, Forests/Forestry, Land Issues, Oceans/Coasts/Beaches, Pollution (general), Population, Public Health

Contact(s):
Heather Moss, President; 206-615-1554; heather.moss@ci.seattle.wa.us
Robert Olson, Past-President; 509-624-4884; robert@arrowroot.net

ENVIRONMENTAL EDUCATION COUNCIL OF OHIO
P.O. Box 2911
Akron, OH 44309-2911 United States
Phone: 330-322-3953   Fax: 330-761-0856
E-mail: director@eeco-online.org
Website: www.eeco-online.org

Founded: 1967
Membership: 101–1,000
Scope: State

Description: EECO is a statewide organization whose purpose is to promote environmental education which nurtures knowledge, attitudes, and behaviors that foster global stewardship. EECO brings together educators from many settings to provide opportunities to share ideas, materials, and techniques. Members include classroom teachers, naturalists, camp staff, teacher educators, youth leaders, and agency personnel.

Publication(s): EECO Newsletter, Integrating Environmental Education and Science, Directory of Ohio Environmental Education Sites and Resources, Ohio Sampler: Outdoor and Environmental Education

Contact(s):
Chuck McClaugherty, President; 330-823-3655; mcclauca@muc.edu
Jeanne Russell, Secretary; 614-265-6682; jeanne.russell@dnr.state.oh.us

ENVIRONMENTAL EDUCATORS OF NORTH CAROLINA (EENC)
P.O. Box 4904
Chapel Hill, NC 27515-4904 United States
Phone: 919-250-1050
E-mail: eenc@rtpnet.org
Website: www.eenc.org

Founded: 1990
Membership: 101–1,000
Scope: State

Description: EENC advocates and supports the development and implementation of quality education which promotes responsible environmental decision-making and actions. Sponsors workshops and an annual conference.

Publication(s): EENC Networking Directory, EENC Newsletter, EENC Brochure

Contact(s):
Aaryn Kay, President; 910-251-0191
Deborah Miller, Advisor; 919-541-5552

ENVIRONMENTAL ENTERPRISES ASSISTANCE FUND, INC.
1655 N. Fort Meyer Dr., Fifth Fl.
Arlington, VA 22209 United States
Phone: 703-522-5928   Fax: 703-522-6450
E-mail: eeaf@igc.org
Website: www.eeaf.org

Founded: 1990
Membership: 1–100
Scope: International

Description: EEAF is a non-profit organization that operates as a venture capital fund; it provides long term risk capital and management asistance to environmentally beneficial businesses in developing countries, where such capital is otherwise unavailable.

Keyword(s): Agriculture/Farming, Development/Developing Countries, Energy, Oceans/Coasts/Beaches, Pollution (general), Reduce/Reuse/Recycle, Wildlife & Species

Contact(s):
Brooks Browne, President
J. Doliner, Vice President
Marion Heckclay, Chief Financial Officer

ENVIRONMENTAL FRONTLINES
P.O. Box 43
Menlo Park, CA 94026 United States
Phone: 650-323-8452
E-mail: info@envirofront.org
Website: www.envirofront.org

Founded: 2002
Scope: State, National, International

Description: An independent non-profit organization that tracks and reports on what is happening on the "environmental frontlines" in California, the U.S. and internationally. Overall, seeks to serve as a reliable guidepost to all parties interested/involved in environmentally-relevant issues/ activities. Offers "The Environmental Guidebook," a critically-acclaimed "Who's Who"-type reference guide to 500 key orgs/entities. Also operates in several specific program areas and provides various non-profit support services.

Publication(s): The California Environmental Guide, The Environmental Guidebook

Contact(s):
Jeff Staudinger, President/Director of Operations; 6503238452; jstaudinger@envirofront.org

ENVIRONMENTAL JUSTICE COALITION
9903 Caltor Lane
Ft. Washington, MD 20744 United States
Phone: 301-265-8185   Fax: 301-265-2952
E-mail: EJCoalition@msn.com
Website: groups.msn.com/EnvironmentalJusticeCoalition

Founded: 2003
Membership: 1–100
Scope: National

Description: The Environmental Justice Coalition was formed to pass an Environmental Justice Act in the U.S. Congress.

Contact(s):
Norris McDonald, Chairman; 301-265-8185; Fax: 301-265-2952; NorrisMcDonald@msn.com
Marsha Adebayo, Member

ENVIRONMENTAL LAW ALLIANCE WORLDWIDE, U.S. (E-LAW U.S.)
1877 Garden Avenue
Eugene, OR 97403 United States
Phone: 541-687-8454   Fax: 541-687-0535
E-mail: elawus@elaw.org
Website: www.elaw.org

Founded: 1989
Scope: International

Description: E-LAW U.S. gives public interest lawyers and scientists the skills and resources they need to protect the environment through law. These advocates, working in their home countries, know best how to protect the environment. By giving grassroots advocates the tools and resources they need, E-LAW U.S. helps these advocates challenge environmental abuses and builds a worldwide corps of skilled, committed advocates working to protect ecosystems and public health for generations to come.

Publication(s): E-LAW Advocate

Contact(s):
Bern Johnson, Executive Director

ENVIRONMENTAL LAW AND POLICY CENTER OF THE MIDWEST
35 East Wacker Dr., Suite 1300
Chicago, IL 60601-2208 United States
Phone: 312-673-6500 Fax: 312-795-3730
E-mail: elpc@elpc.org
Website: www.elpc.org
Founded: 1993
Membership: 1–100
Scope: Regional
Description: A nonprofit public interest environmental advocacy organization working to implement sustainable energy strategies, promote innovative transportation approaches, expand and develop green markets and develop sound environmental management practices in Illinois, Indiana, Michigan, Minnesota, Ohio and Wisconsin.
Publication(s): Repowering of the Midwest, Lake County at the Crossroads No. 2, Visions, Choosing a Future for Growing Communities
Keyword(s): Energy, Transportation
Contact(s):
  Kevin Brubaker, Director of Operations; kbrubaker@elpc.org
  Howard Learner, Executive Director; hlearner@elpc.org

ENVIRONMENTAL LAW INSTITUTE, THE
1616 P St., NW
Suite 200
Washington, DC 20036 United States
Phone: 202-939-3800 Fax: 202-939-3868
Website: www.eli.org
Founded: 1969
Membership: 1,001–10,000
Scope: State, National, International
Description: The Environmental Law Institute advances environmental protection by improving law, policy and management. ELI researches pressing problems, educates professionals and citizens about the nature of these issues, and convenes all sectors in forging effective solutions.
Publication(s): Deskbooks & Monographs, ELR - Environmental Law Reporter, The, Environmental Forum, The, National Wetlands Newsletter
Keyword(s): Agriculture/Farming, Air Quality/Atmosphere, Development/Developing Countries, Ecosystems (precious), Ethics/Environmental Justice, Land Issues, Pollution (general), Reduce/Reuse/Recycle, Sprawl/Urban Planning, Water Habitats & Quality, Wildlife & Species
Contact(s):
  Leslie Carothers, President
  John Thompson, Director of Marketing, 202-939-3833; thompson@eli.org
  Kenneth Berlin, Chairman of the Board

ENVIRONMENTAL LEAGUE OF MASSACHUSETTS
14 Beacon St.
Boston, MA 02108 United States
Phone: 617-742-2553 Fax: 617-742-9656
E-mail: elm@environmentalleague.org
Website: www.environmentalleague.org
Founded: 1898
Scope: State
Description: Advocates for responsible environmental policy on the state level and the effective implementation of state programs dealing with issues such as land use, toxics use reduction, recycling, water resources protection and funding for environmental programs, in addition to educating the public about the environment and environmental issues.
Publication(s): ELM Bulletin, ELM Action Alerts
Keyword(s): Air Quality/Atmosphere, Development/Developing Countries, Land Issues, Oceans/Coasts/Beaches, Pollution (general), Public Lands/Greenspace, Water Habitats & Quality

Contact(s):
  James Gomes, President
  Pamela Dibona, Legislative Director
  Nancy Goodman, Researcher Director
  Jeremy Marin, Communications/ Mktg. Director
  Jessica Champness, Business Manager
  John Cronin, Treasurer
  Lauren Stiller-Rikleen, Chairman

ENVIRONMENTAL MEDIA ASSOCIATION
EMA
10780 Santa Monica Blvd., Suite 210
Los Angeles, CA 90025 United States
Phone: 310-446-6244 Fax: 310-446-6255
E-mail: ema@ema-online.org
Website: www.ema-online.org
Founded: 1989
Scope: National
Description: EMA works to mobilize the entertainment community in a global effort to educate people about environmental issues and inspire them to act on those issues.
Publication(s): Green Light
Contact(s):
  Debbie Levin, Executive Director
  Patie Maloney, Director of Public Relations
  Jennifer DePeralta, Director of Programs

ENVIRONMENTAL POLICY CENTER, THE
2962 Fillmore St.
San Francisco, CA 94123 United States
Phone: 415-775-0791 Fax: 415-775-4159
E-mail: info@epolicycenter.org
Website: www.policyscan.net/frontpage/whoweare.html
Founded: 1989
Scope: National
Description: Environmental Policy Center provides the most comprehensive environmental program and policy information available to decision-makers and opinion leaders engaged in building sustainable communities, by offering proven environmental options to meet their specific goals; promotes the replication of innovative, effective and efficient local sustainable policies and programs; and provides a forum for the exchange of information between decision-makers in the development of environmental policies.
Publication(s): Building Sustainable Communities: A Guide for Local Government
Keyword(s): Air Quality/Atmosphere, Development/Developing Countries, Energy, Forests/Forestry, Land Issues, Pollution (general), Public Lands/Greenspace, Reduce/Reuse/Recycle, Transportation, Water Habitats & Quality
Contact(s):
  Walter McGuire, President
  Colleen McCarty, Chief Financial Officer; 2962 Fillmore St., San Francisco, CA 94123; 415-775-0791

ENVIRONMENTAL PROTECTION ASSOCIATION OF GHANA
P.O. Box AS 32
Asawasi-Kumasi, Ghana
Phone: 23305129950 Fax: 2335122537
Founded: 1987
Membership: 101–1,000
Scope: International
Description: The Association was established with the major objective of promoting an environmentally clean society and ecologically sustainable development. Association activities have been concentrated on the following: tree planting, afforestation, education, awareness, seminars and workshops, health, women and development, income generation, and rural development.

Contact(s):
F. Jantuah, Director
John Owusu, Project Manager
Kwabena Antwi, First Deputy Director
F. Owusu, Second Deputy Director

ENVIRONMENTAL RESOURCE CENTER (ERC)
P.O. Box 819
411 East Sixth Street
Ketchum, ID 83340 United States
Phone: 208-726-4333   Fax: 208-726-1531
E-mail: erc@ercsv.org
Website: www.ercsv.org

Founded: 1989
Membership: 101–1,000
Scope: Local, State
Description: The ERC is a nonprofit organization that provides resources and educational programs to the public about local, regional, and global environmental issues.
Publication(s): Local Dirt
Keyword(s): Agriculture/Farming, Energy, Reduce/Reuse/Recycle, Water Habitats & Quality
Contact(s):
Craig Barry, Executive Director

ENVIROSOUTH, INC.
P.O. Box 11468
Montgomery, AL 36111 United States
Phone: 334-277-7050   Fax: 205-277-7080
E-mail: scrc@mindspring.com

Founded: 1975
Scope: Regional
Description: A private nonprofit organization specializing in recycling information and related services for the Southeast Recycling Market Council, and the annual Southeast Recycling Conference and Trade Show.
Keyword(s): Reduce/Reuse/Recycle
Contact(s):
Martha McInnis, President

E-P EDUCATION SERVICES, INC.
15 Brittany Ct.
Cheshire, CT 99999 United States
Phone: 203-271-2756   Fax: 203-271-2756

Founded: 1972
Scope: State
Description: A nonprofit group formed to promote environmental and population education in Connecticut and committed to assisting educators in the task of providing quality environmental education for the citizens of our state.
Keyword(s): Land Issues, Pollution (general), Water Habitats & Quality
Contact(s):
Larry Schaefer, President and Executive Director
Michael Schaefer, Vice President
J. Bouchard, Treasurer
Lina Lawall, Secretary

EQUESTRIAN LAND CONSERVATION RESOURCE
ELCR
P.O. Box 423
Elizabeth, IL 61028 United States
Phone: 815-858-3501   Fax: 815-858-3508
E-mail: info@elcr.org
Website: www.elcr.org

Founded: 1997
Membership: 101–1,000
Scope: National
Description: National nonprofit organization dedicated to the preservation of access to and conservation of land for equestrian use. "Resource" is the operative word in our name as we assist individuals and groups to become effective land issue advocates.
Publication(s): Equestrian Economic Impact, Getting Organized, Equestrian Land Protection Guide
Keyword(s): Agriculture/Farming, Land Issues, Public Lands/Greenspace, Recreation/Ecotourism, Sprawl/Urban Planning
Contact(s):
Kandee Haertel, Executive Director

EUROPARC FEDERATION
Kroellstrasse 5
D - 94481 Grafenau, 94481 Germany
Phone: 49855296100   Fax: 4.9855296102e+011
E-mail: office@europarc.org
Website: www.europarc.org

Founded: 1973
Membership: 101–1,000
Scope: International
Description: The EUROPARC Federation (formally known as the Federation of Nature and National Parks of Europe) is a pan-European, not-for-profit, non-governmental organisation, which promotes and supports the full range of protected areas in Europe. EUROPARC aims to facilitate the exchange of technical and scientific expertise, information and personnel between parks and reserves. It organizes training and exchange programmes, and provides professional advice on the establishment and development of protected areas.
Keyword(s): Reduce/Reuse/Recycle
Contact(s):
Patrizia Rossi, President
Eva Pongratz, Director
Rachel Gray, Deputy Director

EUROPEAN ASSOCIATION FOR AQUATIC MAMMALS
P.O. Box 58, 3910AB
Rhenen, Netherlands
Phone: 31317612294

Founded: 1973
Membership: 101–1,000
Scope: National
Description: To promote the free exchange of knowledge and to further scientific progress pertaining to the treatment, management, and conservation of aquatic mammals; to provide an organization for the above individuals, to improve practical husbandry; and to advance, by continued study, the basis for maintaining aquatic mammals in captivity.
Keyword(s): Water Habitats & Quality, Wildlife & Species
Contact(s):
John Baker, President
Geraldine Lacave, President Elect
Frans Engelsma, Secretary and Treasurer

EUROPEAN CETACEAN SOCIETY
UNIVERSITT DE LIEGE
Laboratoire d'Océanologie
BGt B-6 Sart Tilman
B-4000 Liège, Belgium
Phone: 4-9383126502-011   Fax: 4-9383126506-011
E-mail: cristinabeans@yahoo.com
Website: http://web.inter.NL.net/users/J.W.Broekema/ecs

Founded: 1987
Membership: 101–1,000
Scope: International
Description: The European Cetacean Society's main focus is to promote and coordinate scientific study and conservation of cetaceans and to gather and disseminate information to members and to the public.

Keyword(s): Land Issues, Wildlife & Species

Contact(s):
Peter Evans, Editor
Beatrice Jann, Secretary
Roland Lick, Treasurer; Rlick2059@aol.com
Christina Lockyer, Chairman

EVERGLADES COORDINATING COUNCIL (ECC)
22951 Southwest 190 Ave.
Miami, FL 33170 United States
Phone: 305-248-9924   Fax: 305-248-9924
E-mail: evcoord@aol.com

Founded: 1970

Scope: Local, State, Regional, National

Description: ECC is an umbrella organization of South Florida sportsmen's conservation organizations united in a desire to protect wildlife habitat, assure sound wildlife management practices, and preserve traditional outdoor recreational opportunities.

Publication(s): Newsletter

Keyword(s): Ecosystems (precious), Recreation/Ecotourism, Water Habitats & Quality

Contact(s):
Bishop Wright, President
Ralph Johnson, Director; 7901 W. 25th Ct., Hialeah, FL 33016; 305-825-4667; Fax: 305-362-7584; rj005@aol.com
Dave Charland, Treasurer; 3559 NW 52nd St., Ft. Lauderdale, FL 33309; 305-484-7777; Fax: 954-484-7834
Barbara Powell, Secretary; 22951 SW 190th Ave., Miami, FL 33170; barjnpwll@aol.com

F

FEDERAL CARTRIDGE COMPANY
900 Ehlen Dr.
Anoka, MN 55303 United States
Phone: 612-323-3827   Fax: 612-323-2506
Website: www.federalcartridge.com

Scope: National

Keyword(s): Recreation/Ecotourism

Contact(s):
William Stevens, Conservation Manager

FEDERAL WILDLIFE OFFICERS ASSOCIATION
P.O. Box 646
Harrisburg, PA 17108 United States
Phone: 717-221-4425
E-mail: president@fwoa.org
Website: www.fwoa.org

Founded: 1987

Membership: 101–1,000

Scope: National

Description: The Federal Wildlife Officers Association is an organization dedicated to the protection of wildlife and plants, the enforcement of federal wildlife law, the fostering of cooperation and communication among federal wildlife officers and the perpetuation, enhancement and defense of the wildlife officer profession.

Publication(s): The Federal Wildlife Officer Newsletter

Keyword(s): Ethics/Environmental Justice, Pollution (general), Recreation/Ecotourism, Wildlife & Species

Contact(s):
Mark Webb, President; 402-476-3747; Fax: 402-476-3836
Doug Goessman, Vice President; 406-582-0336; Fax: 406-582-0343
William Anderson, Secretary and Treasurer; 717-221-4425; Fax: 717-221-4419

FEDERATION OF ALBERTA NATURALISTS
11759 Groat Road
Edmonton, T5M 3K6 Canada
Phone: 708-427-8124   Fax: 780-422-2663
E-mail: info@fanweb.ca
Website: www.fanweb.ca

Founded: 1970

Scope: Province

Description: To increase Albertans' knowledge of natural history; foster creation of new natural history groups; promote natural areas; and provide a forum for discussion and means of taking action on environmental problems of concern to naturalists.

Publication(s): Alberta Naturalist

Keyword(s): Public Lands/Greenspace, Wildlife & Species

Contact(s):
Derek Johnson, President
Glen Semenchuk, Executive Director
Pat Clayton, Treasurer
Brian Parker, Editor

FEDERATION OF ENVIRONMENTAL EDUCATION IN ST. PETERSBURG
Lomonosov St., 11
St. Petersburg, 191002 Russia
Phone: 8121106849   Fax: 8121106849
E-mail: fee@mail.spb.org
Website: spb.org.ru/fee

Founded: 1994

Scope: International

Description: The basic direction of the Federation is culture, education, enlightenment, public health, science, economics, business, and enterprise.

Keyword(s): Agriculture/Farming, Air Quality/Atmosphere, Development/Developing Countries, Recreation/Ecotourism

Contact(s):
Sergei Alexeev, President

FEDERATION OF FLY FISHERS
502 S. 19th, Suite 101
Bozeman, MT 59718 United States
Phone: 406-585-7592   Fax: 406-585-7596
E-mail: execdirector@fedflyfishers.org
Website: www.fedflyfishers.org

Founded: 1965

Membership: 10,001–100,000

Scope: Local, Regional, National, International

Description: Founded in 1865, FFF promotes the sport of fly fishing through education and conservation activities. FFF operates the International Fly Fishing Center in Livingston, MT, and has 14 regional councils and over 250 clubs throughout the U.S. and other nations.

Publication(s): Flyfisher, The, Clubwire, The, Osprey, The

Keyword(s): Land Issues, Recreation/Ecotourism, Water Habitats & Quality, Wildlife & Species

Contact(s):
Bob Wiltshire, Director, International Fly Fishing Center; International Fly Fishing Center, 215 East Lewis, Livingston, MT 59047; 406-222-9369; iffc@fedflyfishers.org

FEDERATION OF FLY FISHERS (NCCFFF)
NORTHERN CALIFORNIA COUNCIL
115 Wellfleet Court
Folsom, CA 95630 United States
Phone: 9163565913
E-mail: president@nccfff.org
Website: www.nccfff.org

Founded: 1965

Membership: 1,001–10,000

Scope: Local, State, Regional, National, International

Description: The NCCFFF, made up of Clubs and individual members, is dedicated to enhancing Fly Fishing through Education, Conservation, and Restoration in Northern California and Northern Nevada.

Publication(s): Flyfisher, The River Mouth

Keyword(s): Forests/Forestry, Land Issues, Oceans/Coasts/Beaches, Pollution (general), Public Lands/Greenspace, Recreation/Ecotourism, Reduce/Reuse/Recycle, Water Habitats & Quality, Wildlife & Species

FEDERATION OF NEW YORK STATE BIRD CLUBS, INC.
P.O. Box 95
Durhamsville, NY 13054 United States
Phone: 716-945-2539
Website: www.fnysbc.org

Founded: 1947
Membership: 101–1,000
Scope: State

Description: To further the study of birdlife in New York state and to disseminate knowlege thereof, to educate the public on the need for conserving natural resources and to document the ornithology of the state.

Publication(s): Kingbird, The, Checklist of the Birds of New York State, New York Birders

Keyword(s): Wildlife & Species

Contact(s):
Timothy Baird, President; 242 East State Street, Salamanca, NY 14779; 716-945-2539; tbaird@salamancany.org

FEDERATION OF ONTARIO NATURALISTS
355 Lesmill Rd.
Don Mills, M3B 2W8 Ontario Canada
Phone: 416-444-8419   Fax: 416-444-9866
E-mail: info@ontarionature.org
Website: www.ontarionature.org

Founded: 1931
Scope: Province

Description: Committed to protecting and increasing awareness of Ontario's natural areas and wildlife, and exerts influence to protect our natural environment. Eighty-three federated clubs across Ontario.

Publication(s): Seasons

Contact(s):
Mark Dorfman, President
Gregory Beck, Director of Conservation
Ric Stymmes, Executive Director
Nancy Clarke, Editor
Jean Labrecque, Chief Administrative Officer

FEDERATION OF WESTERN OUTDOOR CLUBS
512 Boylston Ave. E., #106
Seattle, WA 98102 United States
Phone: 206-322-3041

Founded: 1932
Scope: Regional

Description: Established for mutual service and for the promotion of the proper use, enjoyment and protection of America's scenic, wilderness, and outdoor recreation resources. Forty-three affiliated clubs in Alaska, British Columbia, and the western states.

Publication(s): Outdoors West

Keyword(s): Forests/Forestry, Land Issues, Recreation/Ecotourism

Contact(s):
Brock Evans, President; 5449 33rd Ave., NW, Washington, DC 20015
Winchell Hayward, Vice President; 208 Willard N., San Francisco, CA 94118
Martin Huebner, Treasurer; 1995 McKinzie Dr., Idaho Falls, ID 83404
Nancy Kroening, Secretary; 5615 40th Ave., W, Seattle, WA 98199
Hazel Wolf, Editor; 512 Boylston Ave., E, #106, Seattle, WA 98102

FISH FOREVER
1271 Quaker Hill Dr.
Alexandria, VA 22314 United States
Phone: 703-461-9201   Fax: 703-461-9290
Membership: 1,001–10,000
Scope: National

Contact(s):
David Allison, President; dallison@msn.com

FISHAMERICA FOUNDATION
225 Reinekers Lane
Suite 420
Alexandria, VA 22314 United States
Phone: 703-519-9691, ext. 245   Fax: 703-519-1872
E-mail: fishamerica@asafishing.org
Website: www.fishamerica.org

Founded: 1983
Scope: Local, State, Regional, National

Description: FishAmerica Foundation is a non-profit conservation organization focused on a healthy and productive fresh and saltwater environment conducive to successful sportfishing. We provide funding for hands on-projects at the local level to enhance fish populations, improve water quality, and advance applied fisheries research in North America to increase sportfishing success. Since 1983, FishAmerica has funded more than 620 projects in all 50 states and Canada valued at nearly $6 million.

Keyword(s): Oceans/Coasts/Beaches, Pollution (general), Recreation/Ecotourism, Water Habitats & Quality

Contact(s):
Johanna DeGroff, Acting Director; 703-519-9691; ext. 245; Fax: 703-519-1872; jdegroff@asafishing.org
Wendy Cook, Program Assistant; 703-519-9691; ext. 247; Fax: 703-519-1872; wcook@asafishing.org

FLAGSTAFF DARK SKIES COALITION (FDSC)
P.O. Box 1892
Flagstaff, AZ 86002 United States
Phone: 928-525-6280
E-mail: darkskies@flagstaff.az.us
Website: infomagic.net/fdsc

Founded: 1997
Membership: 1–100
Scope: Local, Regional

Description: A community coaltion to celebrate, promote and protect the glorious dark skies of Flagstaff and northern Arizona.

Keyword(s): Air Quality/Atmosphere

FLINTSTEEL RESTORATION ASSOCIATION, INC.
E6298 West U.S. 2
Bessemer, MI 49911 United States
Phone: 906-932-5554   Fax: 906-932-5563
E-mail: flintsteel@skyenet.net
Website: flintsteel.org

Founded: 1995
Scope: Regional

Description: Natural resource conservation organization.

Keyword(s): Ethics/Environmental Justice, Land Issues, Oceans/Coasts/Beaches, Public Lands/Greenspace, Water Habitats & Quality

NON-GOVERNMENTAL NON-PROFIT ORGANIZATIONS – F

FLORIDA ASSOCIATION OF SOIL AND WATER CONSERVATION DISTRICTS
Attn: President, 16806 NW 40th Pl.
Newberry, FL 32669 United States
Phone: 352-472-5462   Fax: 352-472-4473
Scope: State
Contact(s):
  Tim Ford, President; 352-472-5462; Fax: 352-472-5435

FLORIDA BASS CHAPTER FEDERATION
Attn: President
585 Roberts Rd.
Jacksonville, FL 32259 United States
Phone: 904-230-0628
E-mail: ppierce201@msn.com
Website: www.floridabassfederation.com
Membership: 1,001–10,000
Scope: State
Description: An organization of Bassmaster chapters, affiliated with the Bass Anglers Sportsman Society, organized to fight pollution, assist state and national conservation agencies in their efforts, and teach young people of our good conservation practices. Dedicated to the realistic conservation of our water resources.
Publication(s): See website for publications listings
Contact(s):
  Harvey Ford, President; 863-763-9265
  Carroll Head, Conservation Director; 2252 SW 22nd Circle, Okeechobee, FL 34974; 863-763-3568

FLORIDA DEFENDERS OF THE ENVIRONMENT, INC.
HOME OFFICE
4424 NW 13 St., Suite C-8
Gainesville, FL 32609 United States
Phone: 352-378-8465   Fax: 352-377-0869
E-mail: fde@fladefenders.org
Website: www.fladefenders.org
Founded: 1969
Scope: State
Description: FDE promotes conservation, restoration, and sustainable use of Florida's natural resources by providing the public and private sector with objective information and analysis developed through a statewide network of volunteer specialists. Guided by the motto "FDE gets the facts," the organization achieves realistic goals by targeting a limited number of complex environmental issues and providing expert scientific analysis, sustained tracking, advocacy, and litigation when necessary.
Publication(s): Monitor, The
Keyword(s): Climate Change, Energy, Land Issues, Water Habitats & Quality, Wildlife & Species
Contact(s):
  Richard Hamann, President; 352-392-2237; Fax: 352-392-1457
  Joe Little, Vice President
  Nick Williams, Interim Executive Director; 352-378-8465; Nick@fladefenders.org
  David Bruderly, Secretary
  Kristina Jackson, Ocklawaha Project Consultant; 352-378-8465; jackson@fladefenders.org
  Steve Leitman, Coordinator of Apalachicola River
  Frank Nordlie, Treasurer
  Bob Simons, Coordinator of Suwannee River & Public Lands Committee

FLORIDA EXOTIC PEST PLANT COUNCIL
40001 SR 9336
Homestead, FL 33034 United States
Phone: 305-242-7846
E-mail: tony_pernas@nps.gov
Website: www.fleppc.org
Founded: 1984
Membership: 101–1,000
Scope: State
Description: FLEPPC goals are directed toward building public awareness about the serious threat invasive plants pose to native ecosystems, secure funding, and support for control and management of exotic plants, and developing integrated management and control methods.
Publication(s): Florida Exotic Pest Plant Council Newsletter, Wildland Weeds
Keyword(s): Land Issues, Reduce/Reuse/Recycle, Wildlife & Species
Contact(s):
  Amy Ferriter, Editor; 561-682-6097; aferriter@sfwmd.gov
  Ken Langeland, Chairperson; 305-242-7846; tony_pernas@nps.gov
  Jackie Smith, Secretary; 561-791-4720
  Dan Thayer, Treasurer; 561-682-6129; Fax: 561-681-6232

FLORIDA FEDERATION OF GARDEN CLUBS, INC.
1400 South Denning Drive
Winter Park, FL 32789-5662 United States
Phone: 407-647-1160   Fax: 407-647-5479
Website: www.ffgc.org
Founded: 1924
Membership: 10,001–100,000
Scope: Local, State, Regional, National
Description: Organized to further the education of the members and the public in the fields of gardening, horticulture, botany, environmental awareness through the conservation of natural resources, civic beautification, and nature studies. FFGC has an extensive youth activity program; provides for a six-week summer nature and environmental youth camp; college level scholarships; and an extensive youth activity program.
Publication(s): The Florida Gardener
Keyword(s): Air Quality/Atmosphere, Ecosystems (precious), Energy, Forests/Forestry, Land Issues, Oceans/Coasts/Beaches, Pollution (general), Public Lands/Greenspace, Reduce/Reuse/Recycle, Water Habitats & Quality, Wildlife & Species
Contact(s):
  Gloria Blake, President; 3616 N. Indian River Drive, Cocoa, FL 32926-8704; 321-636-1299; Fax: 321-633-6500
  Joan Ochs, Second Vice President; 2013 Summerfield Road, Winter Park, FL 32792-5113; 407-671-4597; Fax: 407-678-9157; jnhochs@aol.com
  Joan Pryor, First Vice President; P.O. Box 1465, Dade City, FL 33526-1465; 352-567-2109; Fax: 352-542-2211; pryor3498@aol.com
  Marion Hilliard, Government/Agency Liaison; 2902 Greenridge Road, Orange Park, FL 32073-6412; 904-264-0019; Fax: 904-264-2440; marionh@bellsouth.net

FLORIDA FORESTRY ASSOCIATION
P.O. Box 1696
Tallahassee, FL 32302 United States
Phone: 850-222-5646   Fax: 850-222-6179
E-mail: info@forestfla.org
Website: www.floridaforest.org
Founded: 1923
Membership: 1,001–10,000
Scope: State
Description: Nonprofit, trade-supported organization of industries, businesses, and individuals who encourage the promotion, development and protection of forestry in Florida.
Publication(s): Pines and Needles, Florida Forests Magazine
Keyword(s): Forests/Forestry

Contact(s):
  Doyle Majors, President
  Jeff Doran, Executive Vice President and Editor
  Charles Thompson, Secretary & Treasurer

FLORIDA NATIVE PLANT SOCIETY
P.O. Box 278
Melbourne, FL 32902-0278 United States
Phone: 772-462-0000   Fax: 772-462-0000
E-mail: info@fnps.org
Website: www.fnps.org
Founded: 1980
Membership: 1,001–10,000
Scope: State
Description: Promotes preservation, conservation, and restoration of native plants and native plant communities of Florida, and provides information through publications, conferences, workshops and a statewide membership organized by local chapters.
Publication(s): Palmetto, The, Big Trees: The Florida Register, Common Grasses of Florida and the Southeast, Butterfly Gardening with Florida's Native Plants, Planning and Planting Your Native Plant Yard, Florida's Incredible Wild Edibles
Keyword(s): Ecosystems (precious), Forests/Forestry, Land Issues, Public Lands/Greenspace, Recreation/Ecotourism, Sprawl/Urban Planning, Wildlife & Species
Contact(s):
  Candace Weller, President; 1515 Country Club Rd. N., St. Petersburg, FL 33710; 727-345-4619
  Kim Zarillo, President; 5575 Willoughby Dr., Melbourne, FL 32935; 321-255-5074; kearthwalkz@aol.com
  Don Spence, Vice President; P.O. Box 321, Roseland, FL 32957; 407-589-0319
  Robert Bareiss, Treasurer; 10301 Bellwood Ave., New Port Richey, FL 34654; 727-842-3133

FLORIDA NATURAL AREAS INVENTORY
1018 Thomasville Rd., Suite 200-C
Tallahassee, FL 32303 United States
Phone: 850-224-8207   Fax: 850-681-9364
E-mail: joetting@fnai.org
Website: www.fnai.org
Founded: 1981
Scope: State
Description: Information is collected on the status and distribution of natural communities, rare and endangered species of plants and animals and other natural features, then analyzed through an integrated data management system.
Publication(s): Florida Conservation Lands 2001, Field Guides
Keyword(s): Ecosystems (precious), Land Issues, Public Lands/Greenspace, Wildlife & Species

FLORIDA ORNITHOLOGICAL SOCIETY
Frances C. James
Department of Biological Science
Florida State University
Tallahassee, FL 32306-1100 United States
Phone: 850-644-2217
E-mail: james@bio.fsu.edu
Website: www.fosbirds.org
Founded: 1972
Membership: 101–1,000
Scope: Regional
Description: To engage in pursuits that advance ornithology in Florida; to facilitate education about birds in the wild; to unite amateurs and professionals on the study of birds in the wild; and to publish a scientific journal and other publications relevant to the members' common interests.
Publication(s): Florida Field Naturalist, Florida Ornithological Society Newsletter
Keyword(s): Wildlife & Species

Contact(s):
  Frances James, President; Department of Biological Science, Florida State University, Tallahassee, FL 32306-1100; james@bio.fsu.edu
  Joyce King, Vice President; 11645 69th Way N, Largo, FL 33773; sjking@mindspring.com
  Peter Merritt, Past President; 8558 SE Sharon Street, Hobe Sound, FL 33455; merritt@gate.net
  Pamela Bowen, Secretary; 309 Moonstone Drive, East Palatka, FL 32131; PJBowen@aol.com
  Jerome Jackson, Editor; Whitaker Center, 10501 Fl. Coast University Blvd., Fort Myers, FL 33965-6565; 941-590-7193; Fax: 941-590-7200; picus@fgcu.edu
  Dean Jue, Treasurer; 3455 Dorchester Court, Tallahassee, FL 32312-1300; dsjue@earthlink.net

FLORIDA PANTHER PROJECT, INC., THE
Rt. 1, Box 1895
White Springs, FL 32096 United States
Phone: 386-397-2945
Website: www.atlantic.net/~oldfla/panther/panther.html
Founded: 1993
Scope: State
Description: To assist in the sensible and responsible recovery of the Florida Panther in Florida, by raising funds to purchase environmentally sensitive panther habitat across Florida. Guest Speakers Available
Keyword(s): Wildlife & Species
Contact(s):
  William Samuels, President; P.O. Box 19866, Sarasota, FL 34276; 941-379-2221
  Bob Mills, Executive Director; Gifts and Fundraising, 4269 Hearthstone Pl., Sarasota, FL 34238; 941-966-7765
  Judy Conda, Board of Directors; 6551 Gulfgate Pl., Sarasota, FL 34321; 941-921-7300
  Tim Mallon, Advisory Board; 3715 Felda St., Cocoa, FL 32926; 407-633-4799

FLORIDA PANTHER SOCIETY, INC., THE
377 NW Stephen Foster Drive
White Springs, FL 32096 United States
Phone: 386-397-2945   Fax: 386-397-2945
E-mail: info@panthersociety.org
Website: www.panthersociety.org
Founded: 1994
Membership: 101–1,000
Scope: Local, State, Regional
Description: We are an environmental education and support organization. Our purpose is to provide a means of protection and support of Puma concolor coryi, the endangered Florida Panther.
Publication(s): Cat Track, Quarterly Newsletter
Keyword(s): Land Issues, Wildlife & Species
Contact(s):
  Stephen Williams, President; 377 NW Stephen Foster Dr., White Springs, FL 32096; 386-397-2945; info@panthersociety.org
  Karen Hill, Vice President; 25 NW 5th Street, High Springs, FL 32643; 386-454-3570; info@panthersociety.org

FLORIDA PUBLIC INTEREST RESEARCH GROUP (FLORIDA PIRG)
FLORIDA PIRG EDUCATION FUND
PIRG
704 West Madison St.
Tallahassee, FL 32304 United States
Phone: 850-224-3321   Fax: 850-224-1310
E-mail: info@floridapirg.org
Website: www.floridapirg.org
Founded: 1981
Scope: State, National

Description: Florida PIRG is a nonprofit organization committed to researching, educating, organizing, and advocating programs to protect Florida's environment. These programs include preventing offshore drilling, stopping water pollution, promoting energy efficiency, and other vital issues.
Publication(s): Citizen Agenda, Florida PIRG reports
Contact(s):
Mark Ferrulo, Executive Director

FLORIDA SPORTSMEN'S CONSERVATION ASSOCIATION
P.O. Box 20051
West Palm Beach, FL 33416-0051 United States
Phone: 561-478-5965
Founded: 1994
Scope: State
Description: The Florida Sportsmen's Conservation Association promotes conservation, preservation, and propagation of all forms of game wildlife species, nongame wildlife species, and marine life. The Association stimulates a greater interest in any and all legitimate outdoor recreational activities, assures sportsmen that they may continue to use areas for legitimate outdoor recreational activities, works towards the opening of all lands and waters for legitimate outdoor recreational activities.
Keyword(s): Land Issues, Public Lands/Greenspace, Recreation/Ecotourism
Contact(s):
Bishop Wright, President; 15439-94th St. N., West Palm Beach, FL 33412; 561-795-1375
Mark Dombroski, 2nd Vice President; 1842 Lynton Cir., Wellington, FL 33414; 561-793-7200
Robert Stossel, 1st Vice President; 14241-77th Pl. N., Loxahatchee, FL 33470; 561-753-7880
Bruce Britt, Publication Director; 7407 Southern Blvd., West Palm Beach, FL 33413; 561-688-2553
Richard Andrea, Treasurer; 12334-77th Pl. N., West Palm Beach, FL 33412; 561-795-1136
Kevin Smith, Secretary; 15856-93rd St. N., West Palm Beach, FL 33412; 561-795-4112

FLORIDA TRAIL ASSOCIATION, INC.
5415 SW 13th St.
Gainesville, FL 32608 United States
Phone: 877-445-3352   Fax: 352-378-4550
E-mail: fta@florida-trail.org
Website: www.florida-trail.org
Founded: 1964
Membership: 1,001–10,000
Scope: State
Description: This association was formed to instill in Floridians and in visitors to Florida an appreciation and a desire to conserve the natural beauty of Florida by all lawful means; to promote the creation of a hiking trail, to be called the Florida Trail, to run the length of the state; and to provide an opportunity for hiking and camping.
Publication(s): Footprint
Keyword(s): Recreation/Ecotourism, Transportation
Contact(s):
Deborah Stewart-Kent, Executive Director
Eileen Wyland, President
Sylvia Dunnam, 4th Vice President for Public Relations
Peter Durnell, 1st Vice President for Administration
Joan Hobson, 3rd Vice President for Trails
Leslie Wheeler, 2nd Vice President for Membership
Mary Anne Freyer, Secretary
Pam Hale, Treasurer

FLORIDA WILDLIFE FEDERATION
P.O. Box 6870
Tallahassee, FL 32314-6870 United States
Phone: 850-656-7113   Fax: 850-942-4431
E-mail: wildfed@aol.com
Website: www.flawildlife.org
Founded: 1937
Membership: 10,001–100,000
Scope: State
Description: A representative statewide organization, affiliated with the National Wildlife Federation, dedicated to the protection and enhancement of wildlife and its habitat through public education and government interaction.
Publication(s): Florida Fish and Wildlife News
Contact(s):
Jenny Brock, Chair
Manley Fuller, Executive Director/President
Jenny Brock, NWF Representative
Manley Fuller, Editor
Diane Hines, Education Programs Contact
Patricia Pearson, Backyard Wildlife Habitats Contact
Bob Reid, NWF Alternate Representative
Mike Webster, Treasurer & Vice Chair of Records

FOOD AND AGRICULTURE ORGANIZATION OF THE UNITED NATIONS
PLANT PRODUCTION AND PROTECTION DIVISION
Viale di Termi di Caracalla
Rome, 00 100 Italy
Phone: 39-06-57053643   Fax: 39-06-57056347
Website: www.fao.org
Founded: 1945
Membership: 101–1,000
Scope: International
Description: To raise levels of nutrition and standards of living, to improve the production and distribution of agricultural products, and to better the conditions of rural populations. FAO has adopted an overriding strategy of integrated sustainable development. All operations are geared to meet basic human needs without compromising those of future generations.
Keyword(s): Agriculture/Farming, Forests/Forestry, Public Health, Sprawl/Urban Planning, Wildlife & Species
Contact(s):
Jacques Diouf, Director-General
Christina Engfeldt, Director of Information Division
H. Carsalade, Contact for the Sustainable Development Department
D. Harcharik, Deputy Director-General
P. Wilson, Inspector-General

FOOD SUPPLY / HUMAN POPULATION EXPLOSION CONNECTION
1834 North Lakeshore Drive
Chapel Hill, NC 27514-6733 United States
Phone: 919-967-5764   Fax: 919-968-3331
E-mail: SESALMONY@aol.com
Founded: 2002
Membership: 1–100
Scope: International
Description: Develop viable strategies that protect Earth and all of its inhabitants. Promote consideration and discussion of unforeseen scientific facts of human overpopulation presumably in their correct relations. Thank those who discover ways to protect Earth and its inhabitants.
Publication(s): Human Population Numbers/Function/Food
Keyword(s): Agriculture/Farming, Air Quality/Atmosphere, Climate Change, Development/Developing Countries, Ecosystems (precious), Energy, Ethics/Environmental Justice, Executive/Legislative/Judicial Reform, Finance/Banking/Trade, Forests/Forestry, Land Issues, Oceans

Contact(s):
Steven Salmony, President; 919-967-5764; Fax: 919-968-3331; SESALMONY@aol.com

FOREST FIRE LOOKOUT ASSOCIATION
374 Maple Ave., E., Suite 210
Vienna, VA 22180 United States
Phone: 703-255-2700   Fax: 703-281-9200
Website: www.firelookout.org

Founded: 1990

Scope: National

Description: A national organization devoted to forest protection through the inventory, maintenance and volunteer staffing of forest fire lookouts and fire towers in the 49 states that have them and throughout the world. Maintains a data base of designs and available lookout parts and salvage. Organized into 21 states and regional chapters.

Publication(s): Lookout Network (quarterly)

Keyword(s): Forests/Forestry, Land Issues

Contact(s):
Keith Argow, Chairman of the Board; 703-255-2700
Nancy Gabriel, National Historic Lookout Register; 703-255-2700
Shirley Goodrich, Treasurer; 207-324-6537
Ray Grimes Jr., Secretary; 973-835-4487
Mark Haughwout, Eastern Deputy Chair; 802-476-8341
Joseph Higgins, Legal Counsel; 201-391-1091
Henry Isenberg, Restorations; 508-883-0834
Michael Pfeiffer, Historian; 501-967-4167
Gary Weber, Western Deputy Chair; 207-443-2465

FOREST HISTORY SOCIETY, INC.
701 William Vickers Ave.
Durham, NC 27701 United States
Phone: 919-682-9319   Fax: 919-682-2349
Website: www.foresthistory.org

Founded: 1946
Membership: 1,001–10,000
Scope: National

Description: A nonprofit educational institution, the Forest History Society is dedicated to the advancement of historical understanding of human interaction with the forest environment—forest industries, forestry, conservation, and other forms of use and appreciation. A membership organization, it sponsors programs in research, publication, archives-library, and professional service.

Publication(s): Forest History Today, Environmental History, Forest Time Line Newsletter

Keyword(s): Forests/Forestry, Land Issues, Public Lands/Greenspace, Reduce/Reuse/Recycle

Contact(s):
Steve Anderson, President
William Bauthman, Chairman; 843-851-4653
Cheryl Oakes, Librarian
Adam Rome, Editor; Pennsylvania State University, University Park, PA; 814-863-0184; axr26@psu.edu

FOREST LANDOWNERS ASSOCIATION, INC.
3776 Lavista Rd. Suite 250
Tucker, GA 30084 United States
Phone: 404-325-2954   Fax: 404-325-2955
E-mail: snswton@forestland.org
Website: www.forestlandowners.com

Founded: 1941
Membership: 10,001–100,000
Scope: National

Description: Nonprofit forestry organization of timberland owners large and small in 17 southern states seeking to give private timberland owners and related interests a greater voice in matters affecting their business.

Publication(s): Forest Landowner Magazine, Forest Landowner Manual

Keyword(s): Forests/Forestry, Reduce/Reuse/Recycle

Contact(s):
John Bowen, Regional Vice President; Box 159, Louisville, TN 37777
C. Bush, Regional Vice President; 6701 Carmel Road, Suite 404, Charlotte, NC 28226
Carroll Cochran, Regional Vice President
Guerry Doolittle, Regional Vice President; Champion International, 9485 Regency Sq. Blvd., Jacksonville, FL 32225-8155
L. Larson, Regional Vice President; P.O. Box 2143, Mobile, AL 36652
Steve Newton, Executive Vice President
Kirk Rodgers, Regional Vice President
Charles Tomlinson, Regional Vice President
Paige Cash, Editor
Otis Ingram, Government Affairs Chairman

FOREST LANDOWNERS OF CALIFORNIA
980 9th St., Suite 1600
Sacramento, CA 95814 United States
Phone: 916-972-0273   Fax: 916-979-7892
Website: www.forestlandowners.org

Founded: 1974

Scope: Regional

Description: A statewide organization affiliated with the National Woodland Owners Association that provides educational programs, information services, and legislative representation to families who own forest land for long-term investment, recreational, and conservation reasons.

Publication(s): Forest Landowner

Keyword(s): Forests/Forestry

Contact(s):
Jim Little, President; 707-964-0690
Jim Chapin, 1st Vice President
John Williams, 2nd Vice President
Daniel Weldon, Executive Director and Editor
Ron Adams, Secretary

FOREST MANAGEMENT TRUST
P.O. Box 110760
Gainesville, FL 32611-0760 United States
Phone: 352-846-2240   Fax: 352-846-1332
E-mail: info@foresttrust.org
Website: www.foresttrust.org

Founded: 1997

Scope: Local, State, Regional, National, International

Description: Dedicated to maintaining forest cover and biological diversity through ecologically, economically, and socially sustainable management for timber and non-timber forest products and services.

Publication(s): Model forest workshops

Keyword(s): Development/Developing Countries, Ecosystems (precious), Forests/Forestry, Land Issues, Wildlife & Species

Contact(s):
Steve Taranto, Project Manager; 352-846-2240; staranto@foresttrust.org

FOREST SERVICE EMPLOYEES FOR ENVIRONMENTAL ETHICS (FSEEE)
P.O. Box 11615
Eugene, OR 97440 United States
Phone: 541-484-2692   Fax: 541-484-3004
E-mail: fseee@fseee.org
Website: www.fseee.org

Founded: 1989
Membership: 10,001–100,000
Scope: National, International

Description: A national nonprofit organization of Forest Service employees, retirees, other resource professionals, and concerned citizens working to change from within the Forest Service's basic management philosophy to a land ethic that ensures ecologically and economically sustainable management.
Publication(s): Forest Magazine, see publications on website
Keyword(s): Ecosystems (precious), Ethics/Environmental Justice, Executive/Legislative/Judicial Reform, Forests/Forestry, Land Issues, Public Lands/Greenspace, Wildlife & Species
Contact(s):
  Dave Iverson, President
  Andy Stahl, Executive Director; 541-484-2692; Fax: 541-484-3004; andy@fseee.org
  Mark Blaine, Editor, Forest Magazine; 541-484-3170; Fax: 541-484-3004; mark@fseee.org
  Stephanie Detwiler, Dir. of Administration; 541-484-2692; Fax: 541-484-3004; stephanie@fseee.org
  Martha Carlisle, Art Director; 541-484-3170; Fax: 541-484-3004; marthacarlisle@attbi.com
  Kay Crider, Director of Development; 541-484-2692; Fax: 541-484-3004; kay@fseee.org
  Bob Dale, Field Director; 541-484-2692; Fax: 541-484-3004; bobdale@fseee.org
  Patricia Marshall, Asst. Editor, Forest Magazine; 541-484-3170; Fax: 541-484-3004; patricia@fseee.org
  Chuck Roth, Office Manager; 541-484-2692; Fax: 541-484-3004; chuck@fseee.org

FOREST SOCIETY OF MAINE
P.O. Box 775
115 Franklin Street
Bangor, ME 04402 United States
Phone: 207-945-9200   Fax: 207-945-9229
E-mail: info@fsmaine.org
Website: www.fsmaine.org
Founded: 1984
Scope: State
Description: A statewide land trust working with landowners on forest land conservation projects that maintain the environmental, recreational and economic values of Maine's forests, primarily through conservation easements.
Keyword(s): Ecosystems (precious), Forests/Forestry, Land Issues, Reduce/Reuse/Recycle, Wildlife & Species
Contact(s):
  Alan Hutchinson, Executive Director

FOREST STEWARDS GUILD
P.O. Box 8309
Santa Fe, NM 87504 United States
Phone: 505-983-3887   Fax: 505-986-0798
E-mail: info@foreststewardsguild.org
Website: www.foreststewardsguild.org
Founded: 1997
Membership: 101–1,000
Scope: Local, State, Regional, National, International
Description: The mission of the Guild is to promote ecologically and economically responsible resource management that sustains the entire forest across the landscape. The Guild provides a forum and support system for practicing foresters and other resource management professionals working to advance this vision.
Publication(s): Resource Manager Certification Handbook, Distant Thunder
Keyword(s): Ethics/Environmental Justice, Forests/Forestry, Land Issues
Contact(s):
  Mary Chapman, Director; 505-983-3887; ext. 37; Fax: 505-986-0798; mary@foreststewardsguild.org
  Angela Caro, Administrative Assistant; 505-983-3887; ext. 10; Fax: 505-986-0798; angela@foreststewardsguild.org

FOREST STEWARDS GUILD
NORTHWEST REGIONAL CHAPTER (GUILDNW)
8400 Rocky Lane SE
Olympia, WA 98513 United States
Phone: 360-459-0946
E-mail: jeanforest@cco.net
Website: www.foreststewardsguild.org
Founded: 2000
Membership: 101–1,000
Scope: Local, State, Regional, National, International
Description: The Guild is a group of foresters and others committed to ecologically sustaining the entire forest across the landscape. The forum the NW Chapter provides to support this is hosting forest field trips, talks, producing a newsletter and running a moderated email list serve. Anyone can join the list serve by emailing jeanforest@cco.net, to talk, shop, teach, learn and network.
Publication(s): GuildNW Newsletter, Email list serve
Keyword(s): Forests/Forestry, Wildlife & Species
Contact(s):
  Mary Chapman, Director; 505-983-8992; ext. 37; Fax: 509-986-0798; mary@foreststewardsguild.org
  Steve Harrington, Coordinator; 505-983-8992; ext. 16; Fax: 505-986-0798; steve@foreststewardsguild.org

FOREST TRUST
P.O. Box 519
Santa Fe, NM 87504-0519 United States
Phone: 505-983-8992   Fax: 505-986-0798
E-mail: forest@theforesttrust.org
Website: www.theforesttrust.org
Founded: 1984
Scope: Regional, National
Description: A nonprofit organization dedicated to protecting the integrity of the forest ecosystem and improving the lives of people in rural communities. The Trust challenges conventional forest management philosophies and provides protection strategies to grassroots environmental organizations, rural communities, and public agencies. The Trust also provides land management services to owners of private lands with significant conservation values and serves as the institutional home for the Forest Stewards
Publication(s): Forest Trust Quarterly Report, Distant Thunder, Annual Report
Keyword(s): Development/Developing Countries, Forests/Forestry, Land Issues
Contact(s):
  Henry Carey, Director
  Ron Dryden, Accountant
  Steven Harrington, Forest Stewards Guild
  Shirl Harrington, National Forest Program
  Laura McCarthy, Assistant Director

FOREST WATCH
10 Langdon St., Suite 1
Montpelier, VT 05602 United States
Phone: 802-223-3216   Fax: 802-223-1363
E-mail: forestwatch@forestwatch.org
Website: www.forestwatch.org
Founded: 1994
Membership: 1,001–10,000
Scope: Regional
Description: Forest Watch saves and recreates wild forests, reforms public land management, advocates ecological forestry and watches over the forests with a network of citizen volunteers.
Publication(s): State of the Forest Report, Visions, Quarterly

Keyword(s): Forests/Forestry, Public Lands/Greenspace, Wildlife & Species

Contact(s):
Jim Northup, Executive Director; jnorthup@forestwatch.org
Andrew Vota, Advocacy Director; avota@forestwatch.org
Sue Higby, Deputy Director; shigby@forestwatch.org

FOSSIL RIM WILDLIFE CENTER
P.O. Box 2189
Glen Rose, TX 76043 United States
Phone: 254-897-2960   Fax: 254-897-3785
E-mail: visitor-services@fossilrim.org
Website: www.fossilrim.org

Founded: 1987

Scope: National

Description: A 2,100-acre wildlife preserve dedicated to the preservation of endangered and rare species with the ultimate goal of returning these species to the wild. Sixty animal species are represented, and Fossil Rim participates in 12 Species Survival Plan programs. Programs include public education, research into the management and propagation of endangered species, training of conservation professionals, and support for the creation of similar efforts around the world.

Keyword(s): Wildlife & Species

Contact(s):
Bruce Williams, Vice President of Conservation; 254-897-2960; ext. 304
Yola Carlough, Director of Communications; 254-897-2960; ext. 206
M. Jurzykowski, Chairman of the Board
Jerry Millhon, Chief Operating Officer; 254-897-2960; ext. 202

FOUNDATION FOR NORTH AMERICAN BIG GAME
P.O. Box 2710
Woodbridge, VA 22193 United States
Phone: 703-878-2119   Fax: 703-878-2119

Founded: 1992
Membership: 101–1,000
Scope: National

Description: A nonprofit membership organization with major objectives of protection and encouragement of sport hunting in North America; education of the general public to the values of sport hunting, both direct and indirect; and the conservation and welfare of the big-game species of the continent.

Publication(s): North American Big Game (quarterly magazine)
Keyword(s): Recreation/Ecotourism, Wildlife & Species

Contact(s):
Don Kirn, President; 816-761-4351; Fax: 816-761-8737
Warren Parker, Vice President; 816-229-8899; Fax: 816-229-5933
William Nesbitt, Executive Director; 703-590-4449; Fax: 703-878-2119
Don Morgan, Secretary; 352-473-2662; Fax: 352-473-2166
Edward Nannini, Board Member; 916-485-8111; Fax: 916-485-1709
E. Pocius, Treasurer; 215-536-9616; Fax: 215-536-5815

FOUNDATION FOR NORTH AMERICAN WILD SHEEP
720 Allen Ave.
Cody, WY 82414 United States
Phone: 307-527-6261   Fax: 307-527-7117
E-mail: fnaws@fnaws.org
Website: www.fnaws.org

Founded: 1977
Membership: 1,001–10,000
Scope: International

Description: A nonprofit organization whose purposes are to: promote the management of and safeguard against the extinction of all species of wild sheep native to the continent of North America; promote the protection of the remaining wild sheep populations and their habitat; and promote the re-establishment of wild sheep populations in suitable habitat. The Foundation funds wild sheep research, wildlife studies, improves habitat, finances sheep transplants, and supports hunting and game management policies

Publication(s): Wild Sheep
Keyword(s): Wildlife & Species

Contact(s):
Raymond Lee, President/CEO; 307-527-6261; Fax: 307-527-7117; rlee@fnaws.org

FOUR CORNERS INSTITUTE, THE
1477 1/2 Canyon Road
Santa Fe, NM 87501 United States
Phone: 505-983-8515
E-mail: forests@ucla.edu
Website: fourcornersinstitute.org

Founded: 2000
Scope: Regional

Description: The Institute partners with local communities in the Southwest to conserve natural places and ensure that use of the environment is socially equitable and ecologically sustainable. The current focus of the Institute's work is restoration of natural ecosystems in the Southwest. The Institute aims to bring together the diverse voices of the Southwest and endeavors to bring scientific knowledge to assist partners in making resource choices that restore and revive our natural places.

Keyword(s): Ecosystems (precious), Forests/Forestry

FRANKFURT ZOOLOGICAL SOCIETY—HELP FOR THREATENED WILDLIFE
Alfred-Brehm-Platz 16
Frankfurt, D-60316 Germany
Phone: 6994344644   Fax: 69439348
E-mail: info@zgf.de
Website: www.zgf.de

Founded: 1858
Membership: 1,001–10,000
Scope: International

Description: A private organization that supports wildlife/nature conservation and environmental/conservation education with international, national, and regional projects.

Contact(s):
Richard Faust, President
Ingrid Koberstein, Projects Officer and Executive Assistant to the President
Markus Borner, Regional Representative for Eastern Africa

FRIENDS OF ACADIA
43 Cottage Street
P.O. Box 45
Bar Harbor, ME 04609 United States
Phone: 207-288-3340   Fax: 207-288-8938
E-mail: info@friendsofacadia.org
Website: www.friendsofacadia.org

Founded: 1986
Membership: 1,001–10,000
Scope: National

Description: Friends of Acadia is a nonprofit organization providing citizen support in partnership with the National Park Service to preserve and protect Acadia National Park and the communities that surround it.

Publication(s): Friends of Acadia Journal
Keyword(s): Air Quality/Atmosphere, Public Lands/Greenspace, Recreation/Ecotourism, Transportation

Contact(s):
W. Olson, President
Stephanie Clement, Conservation Director

Kelly Dickson, Director of Development
Marla Major, Stewardship Director
Diana McDowell, Director of Operations
Dianna Emory, Chair, Board of Directors

FRIENDS OF ANIMALS INC.
777 Post Rd., Suite 205
Darien, CT 06820 United States
Phone: 203-656-1522   Fax: 203-656-0267
E-mail: info@friendsofanimals.org
Website: www.friendsofanimals.org
Founded: 1957
Membership: 100,001–500,000
Scope: Local, State, Regional, National, International
Description: An international animal protection organization that works to protect animals from cruelty, abuse, and institutionalized exploitation. FOA's efforts protect and preserve animals and their habitats around the world.
Publication(s): ActionLine
Keyword(s): Agriculture/Farming, Development/Developing Countries, Recreation/Ecotourism, Wildlife & Species
Contact(s):
   Priscilla Feral, President; 203-656-1522; Fax: 203-656-0267

FRIENDS OF DISCOVERY PARK
P.O. Box 99662
Seattle, WA 98139 United States
Phone: 206-283-8643
E-mail: info@discoveryparkfriends.org
Website: www.discoveryparkfirends.org
Founded: 1974
Membership: 101–1,000
Soopc: Regional
Description: To create and protect an open space of quiet and tranquility where the works of man are minimized. A place which emphasizes its natural environment and to promote the development of Discovery Park according to a master plan responsive to these goals.
Publication(s): Explorer - Quarterly Newsletter
Keyword(s): Land Issues, Public Lands/Greenspace, Water Habitats & Quality, Wildlife & Species
Contact(s):
   Valerie Cholvin, President
   Terry Mueller, Treasurer
   John Wooten, Secretary

FRIENDS OF FAMOSA SLOUGH
FFS
P.O. Box 87280
San Diego, CA 92138-7280 United States
Phone: 619-224-4591
E-mail: famosa-slough@home.com
Website: groups.sdinsider.com/ffs
Founded: 1984
Membership: 101–1,000
Scope: Local
Description: Works to protect and restore Famosa Slough, an urban tidal wetland with lots of birdlife.
Keyword(s): Water Habitats & Quality, Wildlife & Species

FRIENDS OF MISSISQUOI NATIONAL WILDLIFE REFUGE, INC.
371 North River St.
Swanton, VT 05488 United States
Phone: 802-868-4781
Website: northeast.fws.gov
Founded: 2001
Membership: 1–100
Scope: Local, National
Description: This non profit group is dedicated to the conservation and preservation of Missisquoi National Wildlife Refuge and to promoting public awareness and appreciation of the natural and cultural history of the refuge.

FRIENDS OF SUNKHAZE MEADOWS NATIONAL WILDLIFE REFUGE
1168 Main Street
Old Town, ME 04468 United States
Phone: 207-827-6138   Fax: 207-827-6099
E-mail: info@sunkhaze.org
Website: www.sunkhaze.org
Founded: 1997
Membership: 1–100
Scope: Local
Description: Non profit organization formed to support the U.S. Department of the Interior, Fish and Wildlife Service, to protect Sunkhaze Meadows National Wildlife Refuge. Group sponsors community activities as well as engages in trail maintenance, fund raising, and community education.
Keyword(s): Ecosystems (precious), Land Issues, Recreation/ Ecotourism, Water Habitats & Quality, Wildlife & Species

FRIENDS OF THE BOUNDARY WATERS WILDERNESS
401 North 3rd St., Suite 290
Minneapolis, MN 55401 United States
Phone: 612-332-9630   Fax: 612-332-9624
E-mail: info@friends-bwca.org
Website: www.friends-bwca.org
Founded: 1976
Membership: 1,001–10,000
Scope: International
Description: Established to protect, preserve, and restore the wilderness character of the Boundary Waters Canoe Area Wilderness (BWCAW) and the surrounding Quetico-Superior Ecosystem.
Publication(s): Quarterly newsletter
Keyword(s): Air Quality/Atmosphere, Forests/Forestry, Land Issues, Water Habitats & Quality, Wildlife & Species
Contact(s):
   Melissa Lindsay, Executive Director
   Donna McNamara, Finance and Administration Director
   Sarah Strommen, Policy Director
   Sean Wherley, Policy and Education Coordinator
   Amy Wilkenloh, Membership and Outreach Coordinator

FRIENDS OF THE CARR REFUGE
P.O. Box 510988
Melbourne Beach, FL 32951 United States
Phone: 321-676-1701
E-mail: gheyes@aol.com
Website: www.nbbd.com/npr/fcr
Founded: 1998
Membership: 1–100
Scope: Local
Description: Support organization for the Archie Carr National Wildlife Refuge
Publication(s): Befriending a Refuge
Keyword(s): Ecosystems (precious), Oceans/Coasts/Beaches, Public Lands/Greenspace, Wildlife & Species

FRIENDS OF THE EARTH
The Global Bldg., 1025 Vermont Ave., NW, Suite 300
Washington, DC 20005 United States
Phone: 202-783-7400   Fax: 202-783-0444
E-mail: foe@foe.org
Website: www.foe.org
Founded: 1969
Scope: Local, State, Regional, National, International
Description: A global environmental advocacy organization based

in Washington, DC, with 70 international affiliates. Merged with Environmental Policy Institute and the Oceanic Society in 1990. Dedicated to protecting the planet from environmental disaster and preserving biological, cultural, and ethnic diversity. With strong ties to the grassroots in the U.S. and around the world, Friends of the Earth believes individuals and communities must have a voice in environmental policymaking that affects their lives.

Publication(s): Friends of the Earth Newsmagazine, Green Scissors Annual Report

Keyword(s): Air Quality/Atmosphere, Climate Change, Energy, Ethics/Environmental Justice, Executive/Legislative/Judicial Reform, Land Issues, Pollution (general), Public Lands/Greenspace, Reduce/Reuse/Recycle, Sprawl/Urban Planning, Transportation, Water Habitats & Quality

Contact(s):
Brent Blackwelder, President; 202-783-7400; ext. 284
Norman Dean, Executive Director; 202-783-7400; ext. 193

FRIENDS OF THE LITTLE PEND OREILLE NATIONAL WILDLIFE REFUGE, THE

P.O.Box 215
Colville, WA 99114 United States
Phone: 509-684-8384
E-mail: editor@refugefriends.com
Website: www.refugefriends.com

Founded: 2001
Membership: 1–100
Scope: Local, State, Regional

Description: The Friends of the Little Pend Oreille NWR is an independent, nonprofit organization dedicated to promoting the conservation of native fish, wildlife, plants and their habitats on the Refuge, providing educational opportunities, and fostering understanding and appreciation of the Refuge.

Keyword(s): Wildlife & Species

FRIENDS OF THE REEDY RIVER

P.O. Box 9351
Greenville, SC 29604 United States
E-mail: reedyriver@aol.com
Website: www.reedyriver.org

Founded: 1993
Scope: Regional

Description: FORR is a nonprofit river advocacy group committed to watershed protection and restoration of the Reedy River in upstate South Carolina.

Publication(s): Paddling Guide, NPS Brochure, Membership Brochure and Newsletter

Keyword(s): Forests/Forestry, Pollution (general), Public Lands/Greenspace, Water Habitats & Quality

Contact(s):
Dave Hargett, Executive Director; 864-297-3566; hargett@prodigy.net

FRIENDS OF THE RIVER

915 20th Street
Sacramento, CA 95814 United States
Phone: 916-442-3155   Fax: 916-442-3396
E-mail: info@friendsoftheriver.org
Website: www.friendsoftheriver.org

Founded: 1973

Description: Friends of the River was founded in 1973 during the struggle to save the Stanislaus River from New Melones Dam. Following that campaign, the organization grew to become California's statewide river conservation group. Friends of the River is dedicated to preserving, protecting, and restoring California's rivers, streams, and their watersheds.

Contact(s):
Meg Johnson
Julie Mitchell

FRIENDS OF THE SAN JUANS

P.O. Box 1344
Friday Harbor, WA 98250 United States
Phone: 360-378-2319   Fax: 360-378-2324
E-mail: friends@sanjuans.org
Website: www.sanjuans.org

Founded: 1979
Membership: 1,001–10,000
Scope: Local, State, Regional, National, International

Description: We are an environmental advocacy group committed to protecting the land, water, and shorelines through education, science, policy, citizen involvement, and environmental laws

FRIENDS OF THE SEA OTTER

125 Ocean View Blvd. #204
Pacific Grove, CA 93950 United States
Phone: 831-373-2747   Fax: 831-373-2749
E-mail: info@seaotters.org
Website: www.seaotters.org

Founded: 1968
Membership: 1,001–10,000
Scope: Local, State, Regional, National

Description: A nonprofit organization dedicated to the protection and maintenance of a healthy population of southern sea otters, a threatened species, as well as sea otters throughout their North Pacific range, and all sea otter habitat. Encourages research and public education to develop a sound conservation program.

Publication(s): Otter Raft, The

Keyword(s): Ecosystems (precious), Ethics/Environmental Justice, Executive/Legislative/Judicial Reform, Oceans/Coasts/Beaches, Pollution (general), Recreation/Ecotourism, Water Habitats & Quality, Wildlife & Species

Contact(s):
Tom Kieckhefer, Education Director; 831 373-2747; Fax: 831 373-2749; education@seaotters.org
Matt Rutishauser, Science Director; 831 373-2747; Fax: 831 373-2749; science@seaotters.org
Esther Trosow, Center Director; 381 Cannery Row, Suite Q, Monterey, CA; 831 642-9057; Fax: 831 642-9057; center-director@seaotters.org

FUND FOR ANIMALS

8121 Georgia Avenue
Suite 301
Silver Spring, MD 20910 United States
Phone: 301-585-2591   Fax: 301-585-2595
E-mail: fundinfo@fund.org
Website: www.fund.org

Founded: 1967
Membership: 100,001–500,000
Scope: National, International

Description: National nonprofit animal-protection organization founded by author Cleveland Amory, whose purpose is to preserve wildlife and promote humane treatment for all animals. Primarily serves as an advocacy group and information and education agency to help domestic and wild animals. The Fund operates four hands-on animal care facilities including the world-famous Black Beauty Ranch in Texas.

Keyword(s): Executive/Legislative/Judicial Reform, Land Issues, Wildlife & Species

Contact(s):
Michael Markarian, President; 301-585-2591; ext. 216; Fax: 301-585-2595; mmarkarian@fund.org
Heidi Prescott, National Director; 301-585-2591; ext. 213; Fax: 301-585-2591; hprescott@fund.org

FUNDACION NATURA COLOMBIA
Calle 61 No. 4-26
Santa Fe De Bogota, Colombia
Phone: 571-345-6188   Fax: 571-249-6250
E-mail: enatura@impsar.net.co
Website: www.natura.org.co

Founded: 1983

Description: Fundacion Natura is a Colombian nonprofit, non-governmental organization. It works with other national governmental and non-governmental organizations as well as international partners to attain the required knowledge to design viable conservation strategies which encompass biological, social, political, and economic variables.

Keyword(s): Reduce/Reuse/Recycle, Wildlife & Species

Contact(s):
Elsa Escobar, Executive Director

FUTURE FISHERMAN FOUNDATION
225 Reinekers Lane Ste. 420
Alexandria, VA 22314 United States
Phone: 703-519-9691   Fax: 703-519-1872
E-mail: info@asafishing.org
Website: www.asafishing.org

Founded: 1985
Membership: 1–100
Scope: National, International

Description: The educational arm of the American Sportfishing Association, the Foundation is a nonprofit organization dedicated to promoting participation and education in fishing as well as enhancement and protection of aquatic resources. Develops and coordinates the national program "Hooked On Fishing - Not on Drugs". The Foundation is a national leader in recreational fishing and aquatic resource education and offers student and instructor educational materials.

Keyword(s): Recreation/Ecotourism, Water Habitats & Quality

Contact(s):
Anne Glick, Executive Director; 703-519-9691; Fax: 703-519-1872; aglick@asafishing.org
Laura Jerome, National Coordinator - Hooked on Fishing - Not on Drugs; 703-519-9691; Fax: 703-519-1872; ljerome@asafishing.org
Portia Moore, National Coordinator - National PE Grants Coordinator; 703-519-9691; Fax: 703-519-1872; pmoore@asafishing.org
Wendy Cook, Program Assistant; 703-519-9601; Fax: 703-519-1872; wcook@asafishing.org
Bob Southwick, Tackle Sales Marketing; 904-277-9705; Fax: 904-261-1145; rob@southwickassociates.com

FUTURE GENERATIONS
HC 73 Box 100
North Mountain
Franklin, WV 26807 United States
Phone: 304-358-2000   Fax: 304-358-3008
E-mail: info@future.org
Website: www.future.org

Founded: 1992
Scope: International

Description: Future Generations offers an inexpensive and systematic process for community-based change to realize the dual objectives of insuring sustainability on our planet and reducing the equity gap between rich and poor.

Publication(s): Just and Lasting Change

Keyword(s): Development/Developing Countries, Ecosystems (precious), Forests/Forestry, Public Health, Wildlife & Species

Contact(s):
Daniel Taylor-Ide, President

G

GALIANO CONSERVANCY ASSOCIATION
R.R. 1, Sturdies Bay Rd.
Galiano Island, V0N 1P0 British Columbia Canada
Phone: 250-539-2424   Fax: 250-539-2424
E-mail: galiano_conservancy@gulfislands.com

Founded: 1989
Scope: Local

Description: The Galiano Conservancy Association is a community-based, regionally-oriented conservation organization and land trust. Its purposes are to preserve, protect, and enhance the quality of the human and natural environment of the area through public education; management, and ownership of conservatrion land; and research and restoration projects.

Publication(s): Archipelago, Bulletin, Newsletter

Keyword(s): Forests/Forestry, Land Issues, Oceans/Coasts/Beaches, Pollution (general), Reduce/Reuse/Recycle, Water Habitats & Quality, Wildlife & Species

Contact(s):
Rose Longini, Secretary; 250-539-2424; Fax: 250-539-2424
Ken Millard, Coordinator; 250-539-2424; Fax: 250-539-2424
John Pritchard, Co-Coordinator; 250-539-2424

GAME AND PARKS COMMISSION-NEBRASKA
AK-SAR-BEN AQUARIUM
21502 W Hwy. 31
Gretna, NE 68028 United States
Phone: 402-332-3901   Fax: 402-332-5853
Website: www.outdoornebraska.org

Membership: 1–100
Scope: State

Contact(s):
Darrell Feit, Director; dfeit@ngpc.state.nd.us

GAME CONSERVANCY U.S.A.
340 West Putnam Ave.
Greenwich, CT 06830 United States
Phone: 203-661-7900   Fax: 203-661-7997
E-mail: info@gcusa.org
Website: www.gcusa.org

Founded: 1985
Membership: 101–1,000
Scope: National, International

Description: (formerly American Friends of the Game Conservancy) Game Conservancy USA's primary function is to raise funds to support the scientific research and educational activities of The Game Conservancy Trust in the U.K.

Publication(s): American Friends of the Game Conservancy Newsletter

Keyword(s): Ecosystems (precious), Land Issues, Water Habitats & Quality, Wildlife & Species

Contact(s):
Edward Shugrue, III, President; 212-949-1710; Fax: 212-867-8723; eshugrue@imowitz.com
Guy Bignell, Executive Director; 203-661-7900; Fax: 203-661-7997; gbignell@gcusa.org
Claudine Cavalier, Assistant to Executive Director; 203-661-7900; Fax: 203-661-7997; ccavalier@gcusa.org

GAME CONSERVATION INTERNATIONAL (GAME COIN)
4600 Broad Ave.
Ft. Worth, TX 76107 United States
Phone: 817-738-5438   Fax: 817-737-2911

Founded: 1967
Scope: International

Description: A nonprofit organization dedicated to responsible sustainable use of fish and wildlife and preserving the hunting and fishing heritage for future generations. Supports strong educational programs for classrooms and sponsors the state and province Outstanding Hunter Education awards from Mexico to Canada. Its National Junior Wildlife Artist competition encourages high school youngsters to compete for thousands of dollars in prizes under the theme: Our Wildlife Heritage: Pass It On!

Keyword(s): Wildlife & Species

Contact(s):
Harry Tennison, President; 817-738-5438

GARDEN CLUB OF AMERICA, THE
14 East 60th St.
New York, NY 10022 United States
Phone: 212-753-8287   Fax: 212-753-0134
E-mail: hq@gcamerica.org
Website: www.gcamerica.org

Founded: 1913
Membership: 10,001–100,000
Scope: National

Description: A national nonprofit organization with member clubs from coast to coast and in Hawaii. Its purpose is to stimulate the knowledge and love of gardening, to share the advantages of association by means of educational meetings, conferences, correspondence and publications, and to restore, improve, and protect the quality of the environment through educational programs and action in the fields of conservation and civic improvement.

Keyword(s): Agriculture/Farming, Wildlife & Species

Contact(s):
Joseph Frierson, President
Peter Goedecke, Conservation Chairman
A. Gregg, Horticulture Chairman
John Murphy Jr., National Chairman
Daniel Will III, Corresponding Secretary

GECKO PRODUCTIONS, INC.
Attn: Director Dr. Nathalie Ward
P.O. Box 573
Woods Hole, MA 02543 United States
Phone: 508-548-3313   Fax: 508-548-1393
E-mail: nward@mbl.edu

Founded: 1995
Scope: National, International

Description: Designs conservation education materials and workshops about marine endangered species and marine protected areas, with emphasis on bringing environmental awareness and cultural understanding to the Caribbean, United States and beyond.

Contact(s):
Nathalie Ward, Director; 508-548-3313; Fax: 508-548-1393; nward@mbl.edu

GENERAL FEDERATION OF WOMEN'S CLUBS
1734 N St., NW
Washington, DC 20036 United States
Phone: 202-347-3168   Fax: 202-835-0246
E-mail: gfwc@gfwc.org
Website: www.gfwc.org

Founded: 1890
Scope: National

Description: The General Foundation of Women's Clubs (GFWC) is an international organization of community-based volunteer women's clubs dedicated to community service since 1890. GFWC programs and projects encompass the major issues of our time including literacy, health, preservation of natural resources, abuse prevention, and solid waste management.

Publication(s): GFWC Clubwoman

Keyword(s): Energy, Land Issues, Public Lands/Greenspace, Reduce/Reuse/Recycle

Contact(s):
Shelby Hamlett, President
Judy Lutz, 1st Vice President
Ernie Shriner, 2nd Vice President
Pat Nolan, Program Director
Maryanne Potter, Director of Junior Clubs
Kelly Buckheit, Editor
Norma Chesney, Water Quality Program Chair; 1331 Jill Terrace, Homewood, IL 60430
Rose Ditto, Treasurer
Judy Lutz, President-Elect
Barbara Nunnari, Resource Conservation Program Chair; 13200 Ridge Dr., Rockville, MD 20850
Jacquelyn Pierce, Recording Secretary
Joyce Schaefer, Beautification Program Chair; Rt. #4 Box 32, Seaford, DE 19973
Terri Wogan, Conservation Department Coordinator; 5401 E. Marilyn Rd., Scottsdale, AZ 85254

GEORGE MIKSCH SUTTON AVIAN RESEARCH CENTER INC.
P.O. Box 2007
Bartlesville, OK 74005-2007 United States
Phone: 918-336-7778   Fax: 918-336-7783
E-mail: gmsarc@aol.com
Website: www.suttoncenter.org

Founded: 1983
Membership: 101–1,000
Scope: Local, State, Regional, National, International

Description: The Sutton Research Center is a non-profit, tax-exempt organization conducting scientific studies, conservation projects and educational programs regarding avian species worldwide. Topics of particular interest include raptor population surveys and studies, bald eagle population monitoring, avian captive breeding and reintroductions, ecological studies of grassland birds including songbirds and gamebirds, public education projects and cooperative wildlife conservation efforts with landowners.

Publication(s): The Sutton Newsletter

Keyword(s): Agriculture/Farming, Ecosystems (precious), Land Issues, Wildlife & Species

Contact(s):
Steve Sherrod, Executive Director; 918-336-7778; sksherrod@ou.edu
Michael Patten, Director of Research; 918-336-7778; Fax: 918-336-7783; mpatten@ou.edu

GEORGE WASHINGTON CARVER OUTDOOR SCHOOL, INC., THE
P.O. Box 60579
Washington, DC 20039 United States
Phone: 202-723-5437   Fax: 202-723-0411
E-mail: outdoorsch@aol.com
Website: www.gwcods.org

Founded: 1990
Scope: Local, State, Regional

Description: The GWC Outdoor School, Inc. is a year round, non-profit, 501(c)(3), tax-exempt, community based, health promotion and environmental awareness enrichment program for boys and girls, ages 7–17. Cultural adaptations and historical re-enactments are used in addition to nationally recognized curriculums to make learning more relevant for our youth. Our programs are safe, educational and fun. We provide cultural camping at its best.

Publication(s): Facilitators

Contact(s):
Jawara Kasimu-Graham, Founder & Director; 5702 Fourth Street, NW, Washington, DC 20011; 202-427-5437; Fax: 202-723-0411; outdoorsch@aol.com

GEORGE WRIGHT SOCIETY, THE
P.O. Box 65
Hancock, MI 49930 United States
Phone: 906-487-9722　　　　Fax: 906-487-9405
E-mail: info@georgewright.org
Website: www.georgewright.org
Founded: 1980
Membership: 101–1,000
Scope: International
Description: The George Wright Society, a professional association of researchers and resource managers, advances the scientific and heritage values of parks, other protected natural areas, and cultural sites. The GWS promotes professional research and resource stewardship across disciplines, provides avenues of communication, and encourages public policies that embrace these values.
Publication(s): George Wright Forum, The
Keyword(s): Land Issues, Wildlife & Species
Contact(s):
　David Harmon, Executive Director; Hancock Office,
　Emily Dekker-Fiala, Conference Coordinator; 906-487-9722; Fax: 906-487-9405; efiala@georgewright.org
　Robert Linn, Membership Coordinator; 906-487-9722; Fax: 906-487-9405; rmlinn@georgewright.org

GEORGIA ASSOCIATION OF CONSERVATION DISTRICT SUPERVISORS
P.O. Box 8024
Athens, GA 30603 United States
Phone: 706-542-3065　　　　Fax: 706-542-4242
E-mail: info@gacds.org
Website: www.gacds.org
Scope: State

GEORGIA BASS FEDERATION
Attn: President, 11575 Northgate Trail
Roswell, GA 30075 United States
Phone: 770-993-6597
Website: www.gabassfed.org
Scope: State
Description: An organization of Bassmaster chapters, affiliated with the Bass Anglers Sportsman Society, organized to fight pollution, assist state and national conservation agencies in their efforts, and teach young people of our country's good conservation practices. Dedicated to the realistic conservation of our water resources.
Publication(s): Georgia Federation Newsletter, Georgia Outdoor News
Contact(s):
　Larry Lewis, President; 770-993-6597
　Scott Hendricks, Conservation Director; 5131 Maner Rd., Smyrna, GA 30080; 404-799-2159

GEORGIA CONSERVANCY, INC., THE
1776 Peachtree St. NW, Suite 400, S.
Atlanta, GA 30309 United States
Phone: 404-876-2900　　　　Fax: 404-872-9229
E-mail: mail@gaconservancy.org
Website: www.gaconservancy.org
Founded: 1967
Membership: 1,001–10,000
Scope: State
Description: The Georgia Conservancy works to protect Georgia's air, water and natural areas. Through environmental education and community outreach, the Conservancy teaches present and future leaders about responsible stewardship of Georgia's natural resources and works at the state level in support of thoughtful environmental policies. Serving as a resource to business and political leaders, planners and individual citizens, the Conservancy seeks to make Georgia a better place to live.
Publication(s): Teaching Conservation, Panorama, Wetlands: Georgia's Vanishing Treasure, The Hiking Trails of North Georgia, Highroad Guide to the Georgia Coast and Okefenokee
Keyword(s): Air Quality/Atmosphere, Forests/Forestry, Land Issues, Oceans/Coasts/Beaches, Pollution (general), Public Lands/Greenspace, Sprawl/Urban Planning, Transportation, Water Habitats & Quality
Contact(s):
　John Sibley, President
　Susan Kidd, Vice President for Education and Advocacy
　Robert Smulian, Vice President for Planning and Development
　Patricia McIntosh, Coastal Programs Director; 428 Bull St., Savannah, GA 31410; 912-447-5910; Fax: 912-447-0740
　James Bostic, Treasurer
　Joe Montgomery, Chairman of the Board

GEORGIA ENVIRONMENTAL COUNCIL, INC.
GEC
P.O. Box 997
Suwanee, GA 30024 United States
Phone: 706-546-7507　　　　Fax: 770-614-0593
Website: www.gecweb.org
Founded: 1973
Membership: 1–100
Scope: State
Description: A statewide umbrella for organizations interested in environmental protection that increases the effectiveness of member groups to protect and enhance Georgia's environment. GEC facilitates information exchange among member organizations, provides a forum for discussion of environmental issues of Interest to the members, and monitors state government legislative and regulatory activities relating to the environment.
Publication(s): Issues Forums, Legislative Monitor, Directory of Environmental Groups in Georgia
Contact(s):
　Carol Hassell, Executive Director

GEORGIA ENVIRONMENTAL ORGANIZATION, INC. (GEO)
3185 Center St.
Smyrna, GA 30080-7039 United States
Phone: 404-605-0000　　　　Fax: 404-350-9997
E-mail: info@gaenv.org
Website: www.gaenv.org
Founded: 1991
Membership: 101–1,000
Scope: State
Description: GEO is a non-profit, citizen-oriented organization established to preserve and protect Georgia's environment through education, collaboration, research, planning, legislation, and grassroots organizing. The mission of GEO is to create an ecologically sound, sustainable society by developing and implementing cooperative, long-range policies, plans and programs and by carrying out hands-on projects within local communities.
Publication(s): Georgians on Sustainability
Keyword(s): Development/Developing Countries, Forests/Forestry, Land Issues, Pollution (general), Public Lands/Greenspace, Recreation/Ecotourism, Sprawl/Urban Planning, Water Habitats & Quality, Wildlife & Species
Contact(s):
　Trey Gibbs, Executive Director; 404-605-0000; Fax: 404-350-9997; tgibbs@gaenv.org
　Brandon Moody, Director of Education; 404-605-0000; Fax: 404-350-9997; bmoody@gaenv.org
　Brooke Brandenburg, Public Relations Coordinator; 404-605-0000; Fax: 404-350-9997; bbrandenburg@gaenv.org
　Mitchell Catoe, Land Steward; 404-605-0000; Fax: 404-350-9997; mcatoe@gaenv.org

GEORGIA ENVIRONMENTAL POLICY INSTITUTE
GEORGIA LAND TRUST SERVICE CENTER
380 Meigs St.
Athens, GA 30601 United States
Phone: 706-546-7507   Fax: 706-613-7775
E-mail: gepi@ix.netcom.com
Website: www.gepinstitute.com

Founded: 1993
Scope: Local, State, Regional, National, International
Description: GEPI helps communities develop proactive strategies for a healthy environment through technical and legal services. The organization's primary focus is on land conservation.
Publication(s): Right Whale News, A Summary of Takings Law, A Landowner's Guide - Conservation Easements for Natural Resources Protection, see publications on website
Keyword(s): Agriculture/Farming, Ecosystems (precious), Ethics/Environmental Justice, Forests/Forestry, Land Issues, Oceans/Coasts/Beaches, Public Lands/Greenspace, Reduce/Reuse/Recycle, Water Habitats & Quality, Wildlife & Species
Contact(s):
Hans Neuhauser, Executive Director; 706-546-7507; Fax: 706-613-7775; gepi@ix.netcom.com
Edwin Speir, Chair; 455 Riverview Road, Athens, GA 30606; 706-548-7943; Fax: 706-613-7775

GEORGIA FEDERATION OF FOREST OWNERS
2402 Manchester Drive
Waycross, GA 31501-7554 United States
Phone: 912-283-0871   Fax: 912-283-9141
E-mail: aemceuen@wayxcable.com

Founded: 1974
Scope: State
Description: A statewide organization affiliated with the National Woodland Owners Association to perpetuate good forest practices on private woodlands in Georgia including soil and water conservation, wildlife management, reforestation, and utilization of forest products.
Keyword(s): Forests/Forestry
Contact(s):
Patricia McCarthy, V P; 6043 Telmore-Dixie Union Rd., Millwood, GA 31552; 912-283-0075; mccarthy5@aol.com
Archie McEuen, Secretary; 2402 Manchester Dr., Waycross, GA 31501-7554; 912-283-0871; Fax: 912-283-0871; aemceuen@wayxcable.com

GEORGIA FORESTRY ASSOCIATION, INC.
551 North Frontage Rd
Forsyth, GA 31029 United States
Phone: 1-800-947-6942   Fax: 770-840-8961
E-mail: info@gfagrow.org
Website: www.gfagrow.org

Founded: 1907
Membership: 1,001–10,000
Scope: Regional
Publication(s): Tops, Legislative Bulletin, GFA News
Keyword(s): Forests/Forestry, Transportation
Contact(s):
Blake Sullivan, President
Paul Mott, Vice President
Dale Greene, Treasurer

GEORGIA TRAPPERS ASSOCIATION
P.O. Box 335
Doerun, GA 31744 United States
Phone: 912-782-5417
E-mail: tbehle@indy.tds.net
Website: www.geocities.com/yosemite/trails//GA-app.html

Founded: 1979
Scope: State
Description: An organization of Georgia trappers and friends of trappers, affiliated with Georgia Wildlife Federation and National Trappers Association, organized to protect the rights of trappers to trap, to coordinate a trappers education program with the Georgia Department of Natural Resources and to conserve and protect the natural resources of Georgia.
Contact(s):
Tom Ethridge, President; P.O. Box 335, Doerun, GA 31744
Ralph Goodson, NTA Director; P.O. Box 4398, Albany, GA 31706
Grace Conder, Secretary and Treasurer; P.O. Box 474, Brooklet, GA 30415
Tommy Key, General Organizer; Rt. 2, Newnan, GA 30623

GEORGIA TRUST FOR HISTORIC PRESERVATION
1516 Peachtree St., NW
Atlanta, GA 30309-2916 United States
Phone: 404-881-9980   Fax: 404-875-2205
E-mail: info@georgiatrust.org
Website: www.georgiatrust.org

Founded: 1973
Membership: 1,001–10,000
Scope: Local, State
Description: The Georgia Trust for Historic Preservation promotes an appreciation of Georgia's diverse historic resources and provides for their protection and use to preserve, enhance and revitalize Georgia's communities.
Publication(s): The Rambler (bi-monthly newsletter)
Keyword(s): Ethics/Environmental Justice, Land Issues, Public Lands/Greenspace, Recreation/Ecotourism, Reduce/Reuse/Recycle, Sprawl/Urban Planning, Transportation
Contact(s):
Gregory Paxton, President and CEO; 404-885-7801; gpaxton@georgiatrust.org

GEORGIA WILDLIFE FEDERATION
11600 Hazelbrand Road
Covington, GA 30014 United States
Phone: 770-787-7887   Fax: 770-787-9229
E-mail: gwf@gwf.org
Website: www.gwf.org

Founded: 1936
Scope: State
Description: A representative statewide organization, affiliated with the National Wildlife Federation, dedicated to the protection and enhancement of wildlife and its habitat through public education and government interaction.
Publication(s): Georgia Wildlife Magazine
Contact(s):
Jerry McCollum, President and CEO and Alternate Representative
Laura Bryant, Education Programs Contact
David Haire, Representative
James Hayes, Treasurer
Charles Rabolli, Chair
James Wilson, Editor

GEORGIANS FOR CLEAN ENERGY
427 Moreland Ave., Suite 100
Atlanta, GA 30307 United States
Phone: 404-659-5675   Fax: 770-234-3909
E-mail: georgia@cleanenergy.ws
Website: www.cleanenergy.ws

Founded: 1983
Membership: 101–1,000
Scope: State
Description: Georgians for Clean Energy is a nonprofit statewide organization, protects the environment and improves the

economy by changing the way energy is produced and consumed in Georgia through public education and advocacy.
Publication(s): Plugging In, Technical Reports
Keyword(s): Air Quality/Atmosphere, Development/Developing Countries, Energy
Contact(s):
Amy Macklin, President
Na`taki Osborne, Vice President
C. Copeland, Secretary
Miki Davis, Treasurer
Amy Macklin, Board Chair

GET AMERICA WORKING!
1700 North Moore Street
Arlington, VA 22209 United States
Phone: 703-527-8300, ext. 224   Fax: 703-527-8383
E-mail: info@getamericaworking.org
Website: www.getamericaworking.org
Founded: 1998
Membership: 1–100
Scope: National
Description: Get America Working! believes that a sustainable economy must reduce pollution and resource waste, while greatly expanding employment opportunities and improving the use of human capital. To this end, GAW! advocates a tax shift — reducing payroll taxes to encourage job creation, and instead taxing pollution, energy inefficiency, and resource waste. GAW! works with diverse constituencies including seniors, minorities, environmentalists, labor, women, and the disabled.
Publication(s): Key Questions & Answers, A Fresh Point of View: When Americans Get to Work, America Works!, Job Creation Tax Options: A Background Paper from Get America Working!
Contact(s):
Susan Davis, Associate Chair
William Drayton, Chairman

GIRL SCOUTS OF THE USA
420 Fifth Ave.
New York, NY 10018-2798 United States
Phone: 212-852-8000   Fax: 212-852-6509
E-mail: wildlife@girlscouts.org
Website: www.girlscouts.org
Founded: 1912
Membership: 1,000,001+
Scope: National
Description: The national organization offers an informal education and recreation program designed to help each girl develop her own values and sense of worth. It provides opportunities for girls to experience, to discover, and to share planned activities that meet their interests. These activities encourage personal development through a wide variety of projects in social action, environmental action, wildlife values education, youth leadership, career exploration and community service.
Publication(s): Outdoor Education in Girl Scouting, Fun & Easy Nature & Science Investigations, Fun and Easy Activities-Nature & Science, Investigaciones divertidas y faciles de la naturaleza y ciencia, Earth Matters
Keyword(s): Ethics/Environmental Justice, Recreation/Ecotourism, Reduce/Reuse/Recycle
Contact(s):
Connie Matsui, President; 212-852-5001; Fax: 212-852-6517; cmatsui@girlscouts.org
Jackie Barnes, Interim National Executive Director; 212-852-8624; Jbarnes@girlscouts.org
Sharon Woods-Hussey, Senior VP of Program, Membership and Research; 212-852-8150; Fax: 212-852-6515; shussey@girlscouts.org
Laurie Westley, Vice President, Government Relations and Advocacy; 1025 Connecticut Ave. NW, Suite 309, Washington, DC 20036-5405; 202-659-3780; Fax: 202-331-8065; lwestley@girlscouts.org

GLACIER INSTITUTE, THE
P.O. Box 7457
Kalispell, MT 59904 United States
Phone: 406-755-1211   Fax: 406-755-7154
E-mail: register@glacierinstitute.org
Website: www.glacierinstitute.org
Founded: 1983
Membership: 101–1,000
Scope: International
Description: The Glacier Institute serves students of all ages as an educational leader in the Crown of the Continent Ecosystem, emphasizing hands-on, field-based experiences promoting a balanced understanding of the science of ecology and human interaction with the environment.
Publication(s): Annual Course Catalog
Keyword(s): Reduce/Reuse/Recycle, Water Habitats & Quality
Contact(s):
Bruce Hird, President
Doug Morehouse, Vice President
Jami Belt, Program Director
R. Devitt, Program Director
Alice Hutchison, Secretary

GLEN CANYON INSTITUTE
450 S. 900 E.
Ste. 160
Salt Lake City, UT 84102 United States
Phone: 801-363-4450   Fax: 801-363-4451
E-mail: info@glencanyon.org
Website: www.glencanyon.org
Founded: 1996
Membership: 1,001–10,000
Scope: Regional, National
Description: Dedicated to restoration of a free flowing Colorado River through Glen Canyon and Grand Canyon through decommissioning Glen Canyon Dam.
Publication(s): Report on Initial Studies, Hidden Passage
Keyword(s): Ecosystems (precious), Energy, Ethics/Environmental Justice, Pollution (general), Public Health, Public Lands/Greenspace, Recreation/Ecotourism, Water Habitats & Quality, Wildlife & Species
Contact(s):
Andrea Jaussi, Outreach Director; andrea@glencanyon.org
Jeri Ledbetter, Executive Director; jeri@glencanyon.org

GLOBAL ENVIRONMENTAL MANAGEMENT INITIATIVE (GEMI)
One Thomas Circle NW, 10th Fl.
Washington, DC 20005 United States
Phone: 202-296-7449   Fax: 202-296-7442
E-mail: info@gemi.org
Website: www.gemi.org
Founded: 1990
Membership: 1–100
Scope: International
Description: The Global Environmental Management Initiative (GEMI), an industry-initiated coalition of domestic and multinational Fortune 500 companies, is dedicated to helping businesses achieve environmental, health, and safety excellence and corporate citizenship. Through the activities of its workgroups, it has generated and distributed concrete tools for industry use in a number of environmental management fields.
Publication(s): Fostering Environmental Prosperity Multinationals, Information Systems for Health, Safety & Environmental Management, New Paths to Business Value, Strategic Sourcing - Environment, Health & Safety
Keyword(s): Development/Developing Countries

Contact(s):
Steven Hellem, Executive Director
Amy Goldman, Contact
Richard Guimond, Chairman

GLOBAL INDUSTRIAL AND SOCIAL PROGRESS RESEARCH INSTITUTE (GISPRI)
3rd Fl., Skousenmitsui Bldg., 2-1-1 Toranomon
Minato-ku, Tokyo, 105-0001 Japan
Phone: 81355638800   Fax: 81355638810
E-mail: info@gispri.or.jp
Website: www.gispri.or.jp
Founded: 1988
Scope: International
Description: A nonprofit foundation established to conduct research and submit policy proposals in such areas as resource conservation, global environmental problems, and relationship between industry and economy.
Contact(s):
Gaishi Hiraiwa, President
Kotaro Kimura, Executive Director
Syozaburo Honne, Secretary General

GLOBAL INFORMATION NETWORK
146 West 29th St., # 7E
New York, NY 10001 United States
Phone: 212-244-3123   Fax: 212-244-3522
E-mail: ipsgin@igc.org
Website: www.globalinfo.org
Founded: 1984
Membership: 101–1,000
Scope: International
Description: GIN is the distributor of Inter Press Service and other news wires from developing countries with unique coverage on the environment in those regions.
Contact(s):
Katherine Stapp

GOPHER TORTOISE COUNCIL
Florida Museum of Natural History
University of Florida
P.O. Box 117800
Gainesville, FL 32611 United States
Phone: 229-246-7374
Website: www.gophertortoisecouncil.org
Founded: 1978
Membership: 101–1,000
Scope: Regional
Description: A nonprofit organization formed to assure the continued survival of viable populations of the gopher tortoise, Gopherus polyphemus, and its associated upland habitat in the southeastern United States.
Publication(s): Tortoise Burrow, The Bulletin
Keyword(s): Wildlife & Species
Contact(s):
Mark Bailey, Editor/Web Manager
Matt Dinkins, Treasurer
Colleen Heise, Secretary
Sharon Hermann, Co-Chair
Lora L. Smith, Co-Chair

GRAND CANYON TRUST
2601 N. Fort Valley Rd
Flagstaff, AZ 86001 United States
Phone: 928-774-7488   Fax: 928-774-7570
E-mail: steele@grandcanyontrust.org
Website: www.grandcanyontrust.org
Founded: 1985
Membership: 1,001–10,000
Scope: Regional, National
Description: Regional Conservation Group working on the Colorado Plateau in Arizona and Utah.
Publication(s): Colorado Plateau Advocate
Keyword(s): Air Quality/Atmosphere, Climate Change, Ecosystems (precious), Energy, Forests/Forestry, Land Issues, Public Lands/Greenspace, Sprawl/Urban Planning, Water Habitats & Quality, Wildlife & Species
Contact(s):
Bill Hedden, Executive Director; 928-774-7488; ext. 202; Fax: 928-774-7570

GRASSLAND HERITAGE FOUNDATION
P.O. Box 394
Shawnee Mission, KS 66201 United States
Phone: 913-262-3506
E-mail: grasslandheritage@grapevine.net
Website: www.grasslandheritage.org
Founded: 1976
Membership: 101–1,000
Scope: Local, Regional
Description: A tax-exempt, nonprofit organization dedicated to prairie preservation and education. We encourage the preservation of all remaining prairies and work to increase public awareness of our prairie heritage.
Publication(s): GHF News
Keyword(s): Public Lands/Greenspace
Contact(s):
Sue Holcomb, Office Manager; 913-829-0037

GREAT BEAR FOUNDATION
P.O. Box 9383
Missoula, MT 59807 United States
Phone: 406-829-9378   Fax: 406-829-9379
E-mail: gbf@greatbear.org
Website: www.greatbear.org
Founded: 1982
Membership: 1,001–10,000
Scope: International
Description: A membership-based organization dedicated to protecting all eight species of bears and their habitat. Programs range from supporting scientific research to educational outreach in schools and through field courses.
Publication(s): Bear News, Biological Consulting
Keyword(s): Public Lands/Greenspace, Wildlife & Species
Contact(s):
Charles Jonkel, President
Patti Sowka, Assistant Director
Pam Uihlein, Education Outreach; 406-829-9638; pam@greatbear.org

GREAT LAKES SPORT FISHING COUNCIL
P.O. Box 297
Elmhurst, IL 60126 United States
Phone: 630-941-1351   Fax: 630-941-1196
E-mail: info@great-lakes.org
Website: www.great-lakes.org
Founded: 1973
Membership: 100,001–500,000
Scope: Regional, National
Description: A nonprofit confederation of organizations and individuals throughout the Great Lakes states and provinces whose members are concerned with the present and future of sport fishing in the Great Lakes and adjoining waters. The Council, which acts as a clearinghouse for the exchange of information among members, also seeks to protect the Great Lakes against pollution and exploitation by commercial, individual, or other interests.
Publication(s): Great Lakes Basin Report, Regional Government Reference Guide
Keyword(s): Recreation/Ecotourism, Water Habitats & Quality, Wildlife & Species

Contact(s):
- Dan Thomas, President; P.O. Box 297, Elmhurst, IL 60126; 630-941-1351; Fax: 630-941-1196; dan@great-lakes.org
- Robert Mitchell, Vice President; 6466 Parkview, Troy, MI 48098; 810-558-6547; Fax: 810-575-9713; bmitchel@cecom.com
- Mel Both, Secretary; 4633 Ridgecrest Dr., Racine, WI 53403; 262-598-8802; rodnreel@wi.net
- Tom Couston, Treasurer; 12 W. Schaumburg Rd., Schaumburg, IL 60194; 847-519-1711; tomdds@megsinet.net
- R. James, Webmaster; webmaster@great-lakes.org
- Bob Schmidt, Editor; 5016 West Argyle St., Chicago, IL 60630; 773-283-7871; editor@great-lakes.org

GREAT LAKES UNITED
Headquarters, Buffalo State College, Cassety Hall,
1300 Elmwood Ave.
Buffalo, NY 14222 United States
Phone: 716-886-0142   Fax: 716-886-0303
E-mail: glu@glu.org
Website: www.glu.org

Founded: 1982
Membership: 101–1,000
Scope: International
Description: An international coalition of environmental, conservation, sports, labor, business, and community organizations, and individuals throughout the eight Great Lakes states, two Canadian provinces. GLU is dedicated to the protection and restoration of the Great Lakes-St. Lawrence River Basin ecosystem.
Publication(s): Great Lakes News, occasional reports, Great Lakes: Habitat Watch, Sustainable Waters Watch, and Toxic Watch
Keyword(s): Ethics/Environmental Justice, Oceans/Coasts/Beaches, Pollution (general), Reduce/Reuse/Recycle, Water Habitats & Quality, Wildlife & Species
Contact(s):
- Ed Michael, President, Trout Unlimited; 223 Barberry Rd., Highland Park, IL 60035; 847-831-4159; Fax: 847-831-1035; e1michael@cs.com
- Lynda Lukasik, Vice President, Friends of Red Hill Valley; 148 Oakland Dr., Hamilton, Ontario L8E 1B6; 905-560-1177; lynda.lukasik@sympatico.ca
- Margaret Wooster, Executive Director
- Reg Gilbert, Senior Coordinator; reg@glu.org
- Stephane Gingras, Coordinator, Quebec; 514-396-3333; Fax: 514-396-0297; sgingras@glu.org
- John Jackson, Past President
- Jim Mahon, Canadian Treasurer, Canadian Auto Workers, Local 1520; 120 Tufton Pl., London, Ontario N6C 4W9; 519-681-3680; Fax: 519-652-0586; jimahon@home.com
- Robin McClellan, United States Treasurer, NYS Citizens Environmental Coalition; 2877 Gaines Basin Rd., Albion, NY 14411; 716-589-4695; robinm@eznet.net
- Alexandra McPherson, Clean Production Coordinator; alex@glu.org
- Jennifer Nalbone, Habitat and Biodiversity Coordinator; jen@glu.org
- Patty O'Donnell, Secretary, Grand Traverse Band of Ottawa and Chippewa; 2605 NW Bay Shore Dr., Suttons Bay, MI 49682; 231-271-7368; Fax: 231-271-3576; patty@freeway.net

GREAT LAKES UNITED
CANADA OFFICE
C.P. 56557
Plaza Ontario
Montreal, H1W 3Z3 Quebec Canada
Phone: 514-396-3333   Fax: 514-396-0297
E-mail: genevieve@glu.org
Website: www.glu.org

Scope: National
Publication(s): Newsletter-Great Lakes
Contact(s):
- Ed Michael, President
- Liliane Cotnoir, Director; Front Common Quebecois pour une Gestion Ecologique des Dechets, 2025 A Masson #001, Montreal, Quebec H2H 2P7; 514-396-2286; Fax: 514-396-9041; cotnoirl@mlink.net
- Daniel Green, Director; Societe pour Vaincre la Pollution; C.P. 65 Place D'Armes, Montreal, Quebec H2Y 3E9; 514-844-5477; Fax: 514-844-1446; greentox@total.net
- Julian Holenstein, Director; Environment North; 427 Queen St., Thunder Bay, Ontario P7B 2K3; 807-345-7784; julian@tbaytel.net
- Jim Mahon, Director; Canadian Auto Workers Local 1520; 120 Tufton Pl., London, Ontario N6C 4W9; 519-681-3680; Fax: 519-652-0586; jimahon@home.com
- Jane Wilkins, Director; Sierra Club of Eastern Canada; 699 Bush St., Bel Fountain, Ontario L0N 1B0; 519-927-5924; Fax: 519-927-9828
- Margaret Wooster, Executive Director

GREAT OUTDOORS CONSERVANCY, THE
4311 Manatee Avenue West, Suite 210
Bradenton, FL 34209-3948 United States
Phone: 941-708-3456   Fax: 941-708-3535
E-mail: conserve@TheGreatOutdoors.org
Website: www.thegreatoutdoors.org

Founded: 1998
Membership: 1,001–10,000
Scope: National
Description: The conservancy is a nonprofit national marketing, fundraising, and educational organization for land conservation and expands wild, natural, scenic and recreational areas in the United States by the acquisition of land for the benefit of wildlife and the public's enjoyment for generations to come.
Publication(s): Partnerships in Preservation
Keyword(s): Forests/Forestry, Land Issues, Public Lands/Greenspace, Recreation/Ecotourism, Water Habitats & Quality, Wildlife & Species
Contact(s):
- Bill LaMee, President; 941-708-3456; Fax: 941-708-3535; BLaMee@TheGreatOutdoors.org

GREAT PLAINS NATIVE PLANT SOCIETY
P.O. Box 461
Hot Springs, SD 57747 United States
Phone: 605-745-3397   Fax: 605-745-3397
E-mail: cascade@gwtc.net

Founded: 1984
Membership: 101–1,000
Scope: Regional
Description: Promotes the protection and study of native plants of the Great Plains through the formation of a Botanic Garden, an annual seed exchange, field trips and newsletter.
Publication(s): Plains Plants
Keyword(s): Agriculture/Farming, Land Issues, Wildlife & Species
Contact(s):
- Cynthia Reed, President
- Ronald Weedon, Vice-President
- Joe Lux, Secretary, Treasurer

GREAT SMOKY MOUNTAINS INSTITUTE AT TREMONT
9275 Tremont Rd.
Townsend, TN 37882 United States
Phone: 865-448-6709   Fax: 865-448-9250
E-mail: mail@gsmit.org
Website: www.gsmit.org

Founded: 1969
Membership: 1–100

Scope: State, National

Description: A residential environmental education center in the Great Smoky Mountains National Park. Programs promote awareness, appreciation, and stewardship of national parks and are offered for children and adults.

Publication(s): Connecting People and Nature, Walker Valley Reflections (Newsletter)

Keyword(s): Public Lands/Greenspace

Contact(s):
Bill Cobble, President; 800-721-6064; Fax: 423-982-6583
Bill Oliphant, Vice President
Ken Voorhis, Executive Director; 423-448-6709; Fax: 423-448-9250; ken@smokiesnha.org
Herb Handly, Treasurer; 423-974-1755; Fax: 423-974-4631
Norma Ogle, Secretary; 803-635-3561; Fax: 803-635-3561

GREATER YELLOWSTONE COALITION
P.O. Box 1874, 13 S. Willson, Suite 2
Bozeman, MT 59771 United States
Phone: 406-586-1593   Fax: 406-586-0851
E-mail: gyc@greateryellowstone.org
Website: www.greateryellowstone.org

Founded: 1983
Membership: 10,001–100,000
Scope: Local, State, Regional, National

Description: A nonprofit, tax-exempt organization to preserve and protect the Greater Yellowstone Ecosystem and its unique quality of life by enhancing the ecosystem concept, raising the national public consciousness about the Greater Yellowstone Ecosystem, and combining the political effectiveness of the coalition's 14,000 individual members and more than 85 national and regional member organizations.

Publication(s): Greater Yellowstone Report, EcoAction Alerts, Annual Report

Keyword(s): Ecosystems (precious), Forests/Forestry, Land Issues, Public Lands/Greenspace, Water Habitats & Quality, Wildlife & Species

Contact(s):
Stephen Unfried, President
Dotty Ballantyne, Vice President
Michael Scott, Executive Director
Al Jaeger, Communications Director
D. Curtis Starr, Secretary and Treasurer

GREEN BALKANS FEDERATION OF NATURE CONSERVATION NGOS
160 Shesti Septemvri Boulevard
Plovdiv, 4000 Bulgaria
Phone: 359-32-626977   Fax: 359-32-635921
E-mail: greenbal@mbox.digsys.bg
Website: www.greenbalkans.org

Founded: 1988
Membership: 1,001–10,000
Scope: Local, State, Regional, National, International

Description: Green Balkans exists to preserve, study, and restore biodiversity throughout Bulgaria and the Balkan Peninsula as a whole. Our goals are to raise environmental and nature conservation awareness among a diverse range of community members, to involve citizens in volunteer activities for biodiversity conservation and sustainable development, and to create an effective system of citizen control for compliance with Bulgarian and International Nature Protection Legislation.

Publication(s): Strategy for Conservation & Restoration, Bulgarian Danube Islands, Far From the Commotion of the West, The Pygmy Cormorant in Bulgaria

Keyword(s): Agriculture/Farming, Development/Developing Countries, Ecosystems (precious), Ethics/Environmental Justice, Executive/Legislative/Judicial Reform, Forests/Forestry, Land Issues, Oceans/Coasts/Beaches, Pollution (general), Population, Public Lands/Greenspace

GREEN GUIDES
SUSTAINABLE LANDSCAPES
P.O. Box 1543
Bend, OR 97708 United States
Phone: 541-948-0661   Fax: 541-318-1756
E-mail: sustainablelands@aol.com

Founded: 2002
Scope: Local, State

Description: A nonprofit organization working toward sustainable landscaping and land management practices throughout Oregon. Emphasis on conservation of native floral species ecotypes; water conservation practices in Oregon's High Desert; sustainable development; and creation of economic incentive for commercial and residential developers.

Keyword(s): Ecosystems (precious), Land Issues, Water Habitats & Quality

Contact(s):
Richard Martinson, President
Brandon Reese, Vice President
Karen Theodore, Secretary/Treasurer

GREEN MEDIA TOOLSHED
1200 New York Ave., NW
Suite 300
Washington, DC 20005 United States
Phone: 202-326-6200   Fax: 202-682-2154
E-mail: info@greenmediatoolshed.org
Website: www.greenmediatoolshed.org

Founded: 2000
Scope: Local, State, Regional, National

Description: Effective communications takes people training and tools. Green Media Toolshed provides the tools. Green Media Toolshed offers: * A media contact database * An image management system * A polling library * Training content * Online Press Rooms * Campaign coordination tools * Secure online campaign coordination area. * Enhancements to member web sites for managing calendars, press releases and images in real time by program staff.

Keyword(s): Agriculture/Farming, Air Quality/Atmosphere, Climate Change, Energy, Ethics/Environmental Justice, Executive/Legislative/Judicial Reform, Forests/Forestry, Land Issues, Oceans/Coasts/Beaches, Pollution (general), Population, Public Health, Public Lands/Greenspace

Contact(s):
Martin Kearns, Executive Director; 202-326-8728; Fax: 202-682-2154; kearns@greenmediatoolshed.org
Bobbi Russell, Director of Media Services and Marketing; 202-326-8709; Fax: 202-682-2154; bobbi@greenmediatoolshed.org

GREEN MOUNTAIN CLUB INC., THE
4711 Waterbury-Stowe Rd.
Waterbury Center, VT 05677 United States
Phone: 802-244-7037   Fax: 802-244-5867
E-mail: gmc@greenmountainclub.org
Website: www.greenmountainclub.org

Founded: 1910
Membership: 1,001–10,000
Scope: National

Description: The mission of the GMC is to make Vermont mountains play a larger part in the life of the people by protecting and maintaining the Long Trail System and fostering, through education, the stewardship of Vermont's hiking trails and mountains. The Club operates field programs and publishes guidebooks, maps, and educational materials in its efforts to maintain and protect the 440-mile Long Trail system. It is the advocate group for hiking in Vermont.

Publication(s): Long Trail News, The Long Trail Guide, Long Trail End-to-Ender's Guide, Day Hiker's Guide to Vermont

Keyword(s): Ecosystems (precious), Executive/Legislative/Judicial Reform, Land Issues, Recreation/Ecotourism

NON-GOVERNMENTAL NON-PROFIT ORGANIZATIONS – G

Contact(s):
Andrew Nuquist, President; 29 Bailey Ave., Montpelier, VT 05602; 802-223-3550; nuquist@together.net
Ben Rose, Executive Director
Michael Chernick, Secretary; 75 Cityside Dr., Montpelier, VT 05602; 802-223-0918; chernick@together.net
Walter Pomroy, Treasurer; Box 280, Johnson, VT 05606

GREEN PARTNERS
P.O. Box 1551
Lakeland, FL 33802-1551 United States
Phone: 863-679-3932
E-mail: bfenton@greenpartners.org
Website: greenpartners.org

Founded: 1999
Scope: Local, State
Description: Green Partners is a partnership of businesses dedicated to protecting our environment.
Publication(s): Environmental Checklist
Keyword(s): Ethics/Environmental Justice, Pollution (general), Reduce/Reuse/Recycle

GREEN SEAL
1001 Connecticut Ave., NW, Suite 827
Washington, DC 20036 United States
Phone: 202-872-6400   Fax: 202-872-4324
E-mail: greenseal@greenseal.org
Website: www.greeenseal.org

Founded: 1989
Membership: 1–100
Scope: National
Description: Green Seal helps organizations and individuals make environmentally responsible choices in their purchases. It develops environmental standards and tests products against these standards, identifying those products that are environmentally responsible through the award of an environmental "seal of approval.". The Environmental Partners Program helps businesses develop green procurement plans through buying guides and monthly reports on green products.
Publication(s): Environmental Criteria and Standards, Greening Your Property, Monthly Choose Green Reports, Office Green Buying Guide, Campus Green Buying Guide, Catalog of Green Seal-Certified Products
Keyword(s): Air Quality/Atmosphere, Development/Developing Countries, Energy, Reduce/Reuse/Recycle

Contact(s):
Arthur Weissman, President
Bryan Thomlison, Chair of the Board; 609-737-8841

GREEN SPHERE INC.
86-02 Park Lane South, Suite 6B5
Woodhaven, NY 11421 United States
Phone: 718-846-6243   Fax: 718-846-6243
E-mail: info@greensphere.org
Website: greensphere.org

Founded: 1987
Scope: Local, State, Regional, National, International
Description: Nonprofit grassroots media organization. Defending the rights of the people and the planet.
Keyword(s): Agriculture/Farming, Air Quality/Atmosphere, Climate Change, Development/Developing Countries, Ecosystems (precious), Energy, Ethics/Environmental Justice, Forests/Forestry, Land Issues, Oceans/Coasts/Beaches, Pollution (general), Population, Public Health

Contact(s):
Alvin Jones, President; 718-846-6243; Fax: 718-846-6243; info@greensphere.org
Betty Quick, Vice President
Frank Melli, Executive Director; 718-846-6243; Fax: 718-846-6243; info@greensphere.org

Glyn Emmerson, Secretary
Teresa Cristina Silva, Treasurer

GREEN TV
1125 Hayes St.
San Francisco, CA 94117 United States
Phone: 415-255-4797   Fax: 415-255-4664
E-mail: fgreen@greentv.org
Website: www.greentv.org

Founded: 1992
Scope: National
Description: A non-profit video production company specializing in television programming on subjects about human interaction with the natural world. Offers catalog of stock footage of California wildlife, endangered species habitats and the timber industry.

Contact(s):
Frank Green, Owner/President
Jeanne Jesse, Office Manager; 415-255-4797; jeanne@greentv.org

GREENPEACE, INC.
702 H St., NW, Suite 300
Washington, DC 20001 United States
Phone: 202-462-1177   Fax: 202-462-4507
E-mail: gp1@sharewest.com
Website: www.greenpeaceusa.org

Founded: 1971
Scope: National
Description: A nonprofit organization dedicated to preserving the earth and the life it supports through nonviolent direct action, lobbying, public education, and research. Greenpeace seeks to protect biodiversity in all its forms; prevent pollution and abuse of the earth's ocean, land, air, and fresh water; end all nuclear threats; and promote peace, global disarmament, and nonviolence.
Publication(s): Greenpeace Quarterly (magazine)
Keyword(s): Climate Change, Energy, Pollution (general), Wildlife & Species

Contact(s):
David Barre, Director of Communications
Julie Crudele, Director of Development
Lynn Thorp, National Campaigns Director
David Barre, Editor-In-Chief
Susan Sabella, Biodiversity and Ocean Ecology Campaign Coordinator

GROUNDWATER FOUNDATION, THE
P.O. Box 22558
Lincoln, NE 68542-2558 United States
Phone: 402-434-2740   Fax: 402-434-2742
E-mail: info@groundwater.org
Website: www.groundwater.org

Founded: 1985
Membership: 101–1,000
Scope: National
Description: The Groundwater Foundation is a nonprofit foundation dedicated to educating the public about conservation and management of groundwater. The Foundation is a clearinghouse for general groundwater information, sponsors the Nebraska Children's Groundwater Festival, and coordinates "Groundwater Guardian", a national community recognition program.
Publication(s): The Aquifer, The Groundwater Catalog
Keyword(s): Pollution (general), Water Habitats & Quality

Contact(s):
Susan Seacrest, President
Rachael Herpel, Groundwater Guardian Program Director

GROWLING
GRASSFROG PROJECT
P.O. Box 76
Creswick, Victoria, 3363 Australia
Phone: 0353452826   Fax: 0353372911
E-mail: calcan@netconnect.com.au
Website: www.goldlinksweb.com/growlinggrassfrog/

Founded: 1998
Membership: 101–1,000
Scope: Local, State, Regional
Description: Study of endangered amphibians in Victoria, Australia plus conducting a census of frogs in Western Victoria
Keyword(s): Climate Change, Ecosystems (precious), Ethics/Environmental Justice, Land Issues, Pollution (general), Population, Public Lands/Greenspace, Recreation/Ecotourism, Reduce/Reuse/Recycle, Sprawl/Urban Planning, Transportation, Water Habitats & Quality, Wildlife & Species

Contact(s):
Ray Draper, Coordinator; Growling Grassfrog Project, P.O. Box 76, Creswick, Victoria 3363; 0353452826; Fax: 0353372911; calcan@netconnect.com.au

GULF COAST ENVIRONMENTAL DEFENSE
P.O. Box 732
Gulf Breeze, FL 32562 United States
Phone: 850-432-3001
E-mail: GCED@mchsi.com

Founded: 1992
Membership: 1–100
Scope: Regional
Description: GCED was formed to prevent offshore drilling off the coast of Florida. We are active now in other issues, including stopping water pollution, and promoting energy conservation and use of alternative sources of energy in the Florida Panhandle.
Keyword(s): Energy, Water Habitats & Quality

GULF OF MEXICO FISHERY MANAGEMENT COUNCIL
The Commons at Rivergate
3018 N. U.S. Highway 301, Suite 1000
Tampa, FL 33619-2272 United States
Phone: 813-228-2815   Fax: 813-225-7015
E-mail: gulfcouncil@gulfcouncil.org
Website: www.gulfcouncil.org

Founded: 1976
Membership: 1–100
Scope: Regional
Description: The Gulf Council is responsible for developing and monitoring fishery management plans to provide for the best use of the fishery resources in the federal waters of Gulf of Mexico.
Keyword(s): Wildlife & Species

Contact(s):
Wayne Swingle, Executive Director

GWINNETT OPEN LAND TRUST, INC.
3280 Westbrook Road
Suwanee, GA 30024 United States
Phone: 770-945-3111   Fax: 770-614-0593
E-mail: chassell@mindspring.com
Website: www.gwinnettlandtrust.org

Founded: 1998
Membership: 101–1,000
Scope: Local
Description: Land conservation membership organization committed to the preservation of open and greenspace in Gwinnett County and northern Georgia, and to education about the value of environmental conservation and protection.
Keyword(s): Land Issues

Contact(s):
Carol Hassell, President; 770-945-3111; Fax: 770-614-0593; chassell@mindspring.com
Joyce Nuszbaum, Vice President; 678-428-7849; Fax: 770-806-8111; joyce.nuszbaum@omnexus.com

H

H. JOHN HEINZ III CENTER FOR SCIENCE, ECONOMICS, AND THE ENVIRONMENT
1001 Pennsylvania Ave., NW, Suite 735, South
Washington, DC 20004 United States
Phone: 202-737-6307   Fax: 202-737-6410
E-mail: info@heinzctr.org
Website: www.heinzctr.org

Founded: 1995
Membership: 1–100
Scope: National
Description: The H. John Heinz III Center is a nonprofit institution dedicated to improving the scientific and economic foundation of environmental policy. The Center's mission is to collaboratively identify emerging environmental issues, conduct related scientific research and economic analyses, and create and disseminate nonpartisan policy options for solving environmental problems.
Keyword(s): Oceans/Coasts/Beaches, Wildlife & Species

Contact(s):
William Merrell, Senior Fellow and President
Robert Friedman, Senior Fellow and Vice President for Research
Mary Katsouros, Senior Fellow and Senior Vice President
G. William Miller, Board of Trustees Chair

HARBOR BRANCH OCEANOGRAPHIC INSTITUTION
5600 North U.S. 1
Fort Pierce, FL 34946 United States
Phone: 772-465-2400   Fax: 772-465-5957
E-mail: webmaster@hboi.edu
Website: www.hboi.edu

Founded: 1971
Membership: 1,001–10,000
Scope: Local, State, Regional, National, International
Description: Harbor Branch Oceanographic Institution is dedicated to exploring the world's oceans, integrating the science and technology of the sea with the needs of humankind. We are involved in a wide variety of research programs: to understand the life histories of marine species; to improve the health of threatened marine mammals; to establish environmentally responsible aquaculture techniques; and to discover novel marine compounds that may hold the cure to human diseases like cancer.
Keyword(s): Agriculture/Farming, Ecosystems (precious), Oceans/Coasts/Beaches, Water Habitats & Quality, Wildlife & Species

HARDWOOD FOREST FOUNDATION
P.O. Box 34518
Memphis, TN 38184-0518 United States
Phone: 901-377-1818   Fax: 901-382-6419
E-mail: info@natlhardwood.org
Website: www.natlhardwood.org

Founded: 1989
Membership: 1,001–10,000
Scope: National, International
Description: The Hardwood Forest Foundation is a nonprofit public foundation with the mission to give the public a new pair of eyes to see and understand the forest and the trees. The Foundation carries out its mission by supporting conservation, research, and educational programs designed to educate and reach the largest number of concerned citizens possible.

Keyword(s): Forests/Forestry, Land Issues, Reduce/Reuse/Recycle

Contact(s):
Christopher Allen, Director; 901-377-1818; ext. 106; Fax: 901-382-6419; c.allen@natlhardwood.org

HAWAII NATURE CENTER
INTERACTIVE NATURE MUSEUM, IAO VALLEY
MAKIKI FOREST RECREATION LEARNING CENTER
2131 Makiki Heights Dr.
Honolulu, HI 96822 United States
Phone: 808-955-0100   Fax: 808-955-0116
E-mail: hawaiinaturecenter@hawaii.rr.com
Website: hawaiinaturecenter.org

Founded: 1981
Membership: 1,001–10,000
Scope: Local, State
Description: The Hawaii Nature Center promotes stewardship through environmental education for school children and the public. School programs are full-day, hands-on field adventures; community programs include adult interpretive hikes, family nature adventures and custom excursions for Scouts, senior citizens and other special groups. The Iao Valley Interactive Nature Museum on Maui includes hands-on exhibits of native flora, fauna and streamlife for residents and visitors.
Publication(s): The Steward (Newsletter Quarterly)
Keyword(s): Forests/Forestry, Land Issues, Oceans/Coasts/Beaches, Pollution (general), Reduce/Reuse/Recycle, Water Habitats & Quality, Wildlife & Species

Contact(s):
Gregory Dunn, Executive Director, 808-955-0100; ext. 29; Fax: 808-955-0116; hnced@hawaii.rr.com
Alfred Herrera, Director of Development and Communications; 808-955-0100; ext. 26; Fax: 808-955-0116; hncmktg@hawaii.rr.com
Atilano Jeffers-Fabro, Director of Programs; 808-955-0100; ext. 29; Fax: 808-955-0116; edudirector@hawaii.rr.com
James Wyatt, Director of Maui Operations; 875 Iao Valley Road, Wailuku, HI; 808-244-6500; ext. 12; jd@hawaiinaturecenter.org

HAWAIIAN BOTANICAL SOCIETY
3190 Maile Way
Honolulu, HI 96822 United States
Phone: 808-956-8072   Fax: 808-956-3923

Founded: 1924
Membership: 101–1,000
Scope: State
Description: Objectives of society are: to advance the science of botany in all of its applications; to encourage research in botany in all of its phases; to promote the botanical welfare of its members; and to develop the spirit of good fellowship and cooperation in botanical matters. The Society is particularly interested in the preservation of the Hawaiian flora.
Publication(s): Newsletter of the Hawaiian Botanical Society
Keyword(s): Ecosystems (precious), Forests/Forestry, Public Lands/Greenspace

Contact(s):
Jeff Preble, President
Alvin Yoshinaga, Vice President; 808-988-0469; Fax: 808-988-0462
Ron Fenstemacher, Treasurer
Christina McGuire, Secretary; 808-956-9305; Fax: 808-956-3923
Clifford Morden, Editor

HAWK AND OWL TRUST, THE
c/o Zoological Society of London
Regent's Park, London, NW1 4RY United Kingdom
Phone: 1814500662   Fax: 1814500662
Founded: 1969

Scope: National
Description: The Hawk and Owl Trust works for the conservation and appreciation of wild birds of prey and their habitats through projects which involve practical research, creative conservation, and imaginative education. Current projects include: Barn Owl Conservation Network; Operation Raptor Link; Farmland, Riverside and Forestry Link Scheme; Habitat Link. Its National Conservation and Education Centre is situated in Buckinghamshire
Keyword(s): Wildlife & Species

Contact(s):
Colin Shawyer, Director of Conservation and Research
Barbara Hall, Press and Public Relations
Barbara Handley, Chairman
Robin Rees-Webbe, Vice Chairman

HAWK MIGRATION ASSOCIATION OF NORTH AMERICA
Attn: Treasurer, 16 Thomas St.
High Bridge, NJ 8829 United States
Phone: 908-638-5616
E-mail: eagletotem@nac.net
Website: hmana.org

Founded: 1974
Membership: 101–1,000
Scope: National
Description: A nonprofit organization whose purpose is to advance the knowledge of bird-of-prey migration across the continent, to monitor raptor populations as an indicator of environmental health, to study further the behavior of raptors, and to contribute to greater public understanding of birds of prey.
Publication(s): Hawk Migration Studies
Keyword(s): Wildlife & Species

Contact(s):
Kirk Moulton, Chair; kirk.moulton@unisys.com
Will Weber, Vice-Chair; will@journeys-intl.com
Mark Blauer, Membership Secretary; 6595@email.msn.com
Eileen Halko, Treasurer; eagletotem@nac.net

HAWK MOUNTAIN SANCTUARY ASSOCIATION, VISITOR CENTER
1700 Hawk Mountain Rd.
Kempton, PA 19529 United States
Phone: 610-756-6961   Fax: 610-756-4468
Website: www.hawkmountain.org

Founded: 1934
Membership: 1,001–10,000
Scope: International
Description: The Association is a nonprofit organization devoted to the conservation of birds of prey worldwide and a greater understanding of the central Appalachian environment. A full-time staff assisted by interns and volunteers carries out coordinated programs in education, research, monitoring, and sanctuary management. A visitor center is open year-round, and the 2,400-acre Sanctuary is maintained as a high-quality natural area with trails open to the public.
Publication(s): Hawk Mountain News, Raptor Watch, A Global Directory in Raptor Migration Sites, Hawks Aloft, Mountain and the Migration
Keyword(s): Land Issues, Wildlife & Species

Contact(s):
Keith Bildstein, Research Director
Cynthia Lenhart, Executive Director
Harry Cerino, Treasurer
Jeffrey Weil, Chairman

HAWKWATCH INTERNATIONAL
HawkWatch
1800 South West Temple
Suite 226
Salt Lake City, UT 84115 United States
Phone: 801-484-6808   Fax: 801-484-6810
E-mail: hwi@hawkwatch.org
Website: www.hawkwatch.org

Founded: 1986
Membership: 1,001–10,000
Scope: Local, State, Regional, National, International
Description: HawkWatch International is a nonprofit organization that monitors and protects hawks, eagles, owls, falcons, and other birds of prey and our environment through research, education and conservation.
Publication(s): Raptorwatch
Keyword(s): Land Issues, Pollution (general), Public Lands/Greenspace, Wildlife & Species
Contact(s):
   Howard Gross, Executive Director; 801-484-6502; hgross@hawkwatch.org
   Jeff Smith, Science Director; 801-484-6758; jsmith@hawkwatch.org
   Benita Pulins, Treasurer; C/O Pricewaterhouse Coopers LLP, 36 S. State St., Suite 1700, Salt Lake City, UT 84111; 801-537-5227; benita.r.pulins@us.pwcglobal.com
   Dawn Sebesta, Chair; 2466 Meadows Dr., Park City, UT 84060-7032; 435-649-3024; stoney@pcfastnet.com

HEADLANDS INSTITUTE
Golden Gate National Recreation Area, Bldg. 1033
Sausalito, CA 94965 United States
Phone: 415-332-5771   Fax: 415-332-5784
E-mail: hi@yni.org
Website: www.yni.org

Founded: 1977
Membership: 1–100
Scope: State
Description: Headlands Institute is a campus of Yosemite National Institutes, a private, nonprofit organization dedicated to providing educational adventures in nature's classroom to inspire a personal connection to the natural world and responsible actions to sustain it.
Keyword(s): Ecosystems (precious), Forests/Forestry, Land Issues, Oceans/Coasts/Beaches, Pollution (general), Population, Reduce/Reuse/Recycle, Water Habitats & Quality, Wildlife & Species
Contact(s):
   Mike Lee, Executive Director

HEAL THE BAY
3220 Nebraska Avenue
Santa Monica, CA 90404 United States
Phone: 310-453-0395   Fax: 310-453-7927
E-mail: info@healthebay.org
Website: www.healthebay.org

Founded: 1985
Membership: 1,001–10,000
Scope: Local, State, Regional
Description: Heal the Bay is a non-profit environmental group dedicated to making Santa Monica Bay and Southern California coastal waters safe and healthy for people and marine life.
Contact(s):
   Mark Gold, Executive Director

HELPING OUR PENINSULA'S ENVIRONMENT
P.O. Box 1495
Carmel, CA 93921 United States
Phone: 831-624-6500
E-mail: HOPEinfo@MNCmail.com
Website: www.1hope.org

Founded: 1998
Membership: 1,001–10,000
Scope: Local
Description: Protecting our environment and democracy using science and law.
Keyword(s): Agriculture/Farming, Air Quality/Atmosphere, Development/Developing Countries, Ecosystems (precious), Forests/Forestry, Land Issues, Oceans/Coasts/Beaches, Pollution (general), Population, Public Health, Public Lands/Greenspace, Recreation/Ecotourism, Sprawl/Urban Planning

HENRY A. WALLACE INSTITUTE FOR ALTERNATIVE AGRICULTURE (HAWIAA)
9200 Edmonston Rd., Suite 117
Greenbelt, MD 20770-1551 United States
Phone: 301-441-8777   Fax: 301-220-0164
E-mail: hawiaa@access.digex.net
Website: igc.apc.org

Founded: 1983
Scope: National
Description: HAWIAA is a nonprofit, membership research and education organization established to encourage and facilitate adoption of resource-conserving, low-cost, environmentally sound, and economically viable farming systems.
Keyword(s): Agriculture/Farming
Contact(s):
   David Ervin, Policy Studies Program Director
   Garth Youngberg, Executive Director

HENRY STIFEL SCHRADER ENVIRONMENTAL EDUCATION CENTER
Oglebay Institute, Burton Center
Wheeling, WV 26003 United States
Phone: 304-242-6855   Fax: 304-242-5197
E-mail: schradercustomerservice@oionline.com
Website: www.oionline.com

Scope: State
Description: Oglebay Institute operates a variety of programs: Resident nature summer camps for adults and children; Ecotourism Club; resident environmental education programs; children's day camping; special workshops and weekends; exhibits; school programs; and also the A.B. Brooks Environmental Education Center and Speidel Observatory.
Keyword(s): Reduce/Reuse/Recycle, Water Habitats & Quality, Wildlife & Species
Contact(s):
   Steve Gerkin, Director of Environmental Education; 304-242-6855; Fax: 304-242-5197; sgerkin@oionline.com
   Cathy Gielty, Associate Director of Environmental Education
   Lisa Mustico, Assistant Director; 304-242-6855; Fax: 304-242-5197; lmustico@oionline.com
   Greg Park, Associate Director of Environmental Education

HERPDIGEST
67-87 Booth Street
Forest Hills, NY 11375 United States
Phone: 718-275-2190   Fax: 718-275-3307
E-mail: asalzberg@herpdigest.org
Website: www.herpdigest.org

Founded: 2000
Membership: 1,001–10,000
Scope: International
Description: The first and only free weekly newsletter to deliver the latest conservation and science news on reptiles and amphibians.
Publication(s): HerpDigest
Keyword(s): Wildlife & Species

Contact(s):
Allen Salzberg, Publisher/Editor; 718-275-2190; Fax: 718-275-3307; asalzberg@herpdigest.org

HIGH DESERT MUSEUM, THE
59800 S. Highway 97
Bend, OR 97702-7963 United States
Phone: 541-382-4754   Fax: 541-382-5256
E-mail: info@highdesertmuseum.org
Website: www.highdesertmuseum.org

Founded: 1974
Membership: 1,001–10,000
Scope: National
Description: Created to broaden the knowledge and understanding of the natural and cultural history and resources of the high desert country for the purpose of promoting thoughtful decision-making that will sustain the region's natural and cultural heritage. It is a "living," participation-oriented museum which focuses on the Intermountain West — portions of eight Western states and the Canadian province of British Columbia. Opened to the public in 1982.
Publication(s): High Desert Quarterly, Sagebrush Legacy
Keyword(s): Ethics/Environmental Justice, Land Issues
Contact(s):
Forrest Rodgers, President; Frodgers@highdesert.org
Kevin Britz, Vice President for Programs; Kbritz@highdesert.org
Becky Anderson, Zoological Manager; BAnderson@highdesert.org
Kristi Jacobs, Volunteer Program Manager; Kjacobs@highdesert.org
Sue McWilliams, Education Manager; SMcWilliams@highdesert.org
Sheila Timony, Exhibits Manager; Stimony@highdesert.org

HIGHLANDS CENTER FOR NATURAL HISTORY
P.O. Box 12828
Prescott, AZ 86304 United States
Phone: 928-776-9550   Fax: 928-776-9530
E-mail: highlands@cableone.net
Website: highlandscenter.org

Founded: 1973
Membership: 101–1,000
Scope: Local, Regional
Description: Provides: environmental-science programs to school children in Central Arizona, programs to prevent at-risk behavior, and adult programs.

HILTON POND CENTER FOR PIEDMONT NATURAL HISTORY
1432 DeVinney Road
York, SC 29745 United States
Phone: 803-684-5852
E-mail: education@hiltonpond.org
Website: www.hiltonpond.org

Founded: 1982
Scope: Local, State, Regional, National, International
Description: Mission is "to conserve animals, plants, habitats, and other natural components of the Piedmont Region of the eastern United States through observation, scientific study, and education for students of all ages." The Center is the most active bird banding site in the Carolinas. Its website includes text and photos of flora and fauna found in most habitats in the eastern U.S. There are descriptions of long-term bird banding research (including hummingbirds) and "This Week at Hilton Pond."
Keyword(s): Development/Developing Countries, Ecosystems (precious), Wildlife & Species
Contact(s):
Bill Hilton, Executive Director; 803-684-5852; education@hiltonpond.org

HIMALAYAN WILDLIFE FOUNDATION
Centre One, House 1, Street 15
Islamabad, F 7/2 Pakistan
Phone: 9251276113   Fax: 9251824484
E-mail: vzakaria@hbp.sdnpk.undp.org

Founded: 1993
Scope: International
Description: HWF is a nonprofit, nongovernmental organization dedicated to safeguarding the biodiversity of Pakistan's northern areas. The efforts of HWF have included: involving local communities in the conservation process, coordinating protection and park management activities with the local administration and wildlife department.
Keyword(s): Ecosystems (precious), Public Lands/Greenspace, Wildlife & Species
Contact(s):
Mujahid Ahmad, Coordinator
Anis Rahman, Contact

HOLDEN ARBORETUM, THE
9500 Sperry Rd.
Kirtland, OH 44094-5172 United States
Phone: 440-946-4400   Fax: 440-602-3857
E-mail: holden@holdenarb.org
Website: www.holdenarb.org

Founded: 1931
Membership: 1,001–10,000
Scope: Local, State, Regional, National
Description: The Holden Arboretum connects people with nature for inspiration and enjoyment, fosters learning and promotes conservation.
Publication(s): Arboretum Leaves, The, The Arboretum Class Schedule
Keyword(s): Agriculture/Farming, Ecosystems (precious), Forests/Forestry, Land Issues, Public Lands/Greenspace, Reduce/Reuse/Recycle, Sprawl/Urban Planning, Water Habitats & Quality, Wildlife & Species
Contact(s):
Brian Parsons, Director of Conservation; 440-602-3841; Fax: 440-602-3857; bparsons@holdenarb.org

HOLLOW OAK LAND TRUST
400 Mill Street
P.O. Box 741
Coraopolis, PA 15108 United States
Phone: 412-264-5354   Fax: 412-264-5354
E-mail: info@hollowoak.org
Website: www.hollowoak.org

Founded: 1991
Membership: 101–1,000
Scope: Local, Regional
Description: The Hollow Oak Land Trust is a grassroots organization that acquires undeveloped properties to be preserved as conservation areas; promotes sustainable communities; and educates the public about important environmental issues affecting western Allegheny County, PA. The Land Trust works with schools and communities in this region and particularly the area surrounding the Pittsburgh International Airport.
Publication(s): Roots
Keyword(s): Ecosystems (precious), Forests/Forestry, Land Issues, Pollution (general), Public Lands/Greenspace, Reduce/Reuse/Recycle, Sprawl/Urban Planning, Water Habitats & Quality, Wildlife & Species
Contact(s):
Janet Thorne, Executive Director; 412-264-5354; Fax: 412-264-5354; jthorne@hollowoak.org

HOLLY SOCIETY OF AMERICA, INC.
4738 Hale Haven Dr.
Ellicott City, MD 21043-6669 United States
Phone: 410-730-0243
E-mail: SECRETARY@HOLLYSOCAM.ORG
Website: www.hollysocam.org

Founded: 1947
Membership: 101–1,000
Scope: National
Description: National nonprofit organization dedicated to bringing together persons interested in any phase of holly culture. Collects and disseminates information about holly; studies methods of conservatively cutting and marketing holly; promotes research and hybridization; publishes research papers; and popularizes the use of holly as a landscape material.
Publication(s): Holly Society Journal
Contact(s):
  Daniel Turner, President
  Michael Pontti, Executive Vice President; ponttim@gunet.georgetown.edu
  Ronald Solt, Administrative Vice President; esolt79087@aol.com
  Ruth Bradley, Treasurer
  Rondalyn Reeser, Secretary
  Nancy Smith, Editor

HOOSIER ENVIRONMENTAL COUNCIL
1915 W 18th St
Indianapolis, IN 46202 United States
Phone: 317-685-8800   Fax: 317-686-4794
E-mail: hec@hecweb.org
Website: www.hecweb.org

Founded: 1983
Membership: 10,001–100,000
Scope: State
Description: To encourage and promote more aggressive environmental regulation and enforcement in the state of Indiana. The Council objectives are as follows: Facilitation of communication between environmental groups and individuals; coordination of action on current environmental issues, educational programs and publications; and representation of the concerns of the membership before administrative officials and regulatory boards/agencies of the state and federal government.
Publication(s): Monitor, LDF Report, Boardwatch
Keyword(s): Air Quality/Atmosphere, Reduce/Reuse/Recycle, Water Habitats & Quality, Wildlife & Species
Contact(s):
  Jack Miller, President; 520 E. 12th St., Suite 14, Indianapolis, IN 46202; 317-872-3516; Fax: 317-297-9271
  Tim Maloney, Executive Director; 520 E 12th St. Ste. 14, Indianapolis, IN 46202; 317-685-8800; Fax: 317-686-4794
  Denise Baker, Editor
  Alice Schloss, Treasurer; 4525 N. Park Ave., Indianapolis, IN 46205
  Dona Young, Secretary

HUDSONIA LIMITED
Bard College Field Station P.O Box 5000
Annandale, NY 12504-0500 United States
Phone: 845-758-7053   Fax: 914-758-7033
Website: www.hudsonia.org

Founded: 1981
Scope: Regional
Description: Hudsonia Limited is a nonprofit, nonadvocacy institute for research, education, and technical assistance in the environmental sciences, focusing on the Hudson River Valley. There are over 25 research associates and other technical personnel. Hudsonia conducts pure and applied research on natural and social-sciences aspects of the environment, produces educational publications, and offers programs for environmental decision makers and natural history courses for a broader audience.
Publication(s): News From Hudsonia (quarterly), Guide to Biodiversity in the Hudson River Valley
Keyword(s): Water Habitats & Quality, Wildlife & Species
Contact(s):
  Erik Kiviat, Science Director; kiviat@bard.edu
  Gretchen Stevens, Staff Botanist

HUMAN ECOLOGY ACTION LEAGUE, INC., THE (HEAL)
P.O. Box 29629
Atlanta, GA 30359-0629 United States
Phone: 404-248-1898   Fax: 404-248-0162
E-mail: healnatnl@aol.com
Website: www.members.aol.com/healNatnl/index.html

Founded: 1977
Scope: International
Description: A nonprofit volunteer organization of people affected by or concerned about environmental conditions that are hazardous to human health. It serves as an information clearinghouse on exposure-related illness; alerts the general public about the potential dangers of chemicals; and encourages healthy lifestyles that minimize potentially hazardous environmental exposures.
Publication(s): Resource List, Human Ecologist, The, Fragrance and Health, Environmental Consultant Directory, Travel Directory, Bibliographies
Keyword(s): Air Quality/Atmosphere, Pollution (general), Public Health, Reduce/Reuse/Recycle
Contact(s):
  Muriel Dando, President
  Donald Jones, Treasurer and Business Manager
  Kenneth King, Secretary
  Diane Thomas, Editor

HUMANE SOCIETY OF THE UNITED STATES, THE
2100 L St., NW
Washington, DC 20037 United States
Phone: 202-452-1100   Fax: 301-258-3077
Website: www.hsus.org

Founded: 1954
Membership: 1,000,001 +
Scope: Local, State, Regional, National, International
Description: A nonprofit organization dedicated to the protection of animals, both domestic and wild. Professional staff experienced in animal control, cruelty investigation, humane and environmental education, farm animals, federal and state legislative activities, wildlife and habitat protection, and laboratory animal welfare; offer resources to local organizations, government, media, and the general public.
Publication(s): All Animals, Animal Sheltering, Kind News, Kind Teacher
Keyword(s): Agriculture/Farming, Development/Developing Countries, Ecosystems (precious), Executive/Legislative/Judicial Reform, Finance/Banking/Trade, Oceans/Coasts/Beaches, Public Lands/Greenspace, Sprawl/Urban Planning, Water Habitats & Quality, Wildlife & Species
Contact(s):
  Paul Irwin, President, Humane Society International
  Paul Irwin, President, CEO
  Paul Irwin, President of Earthvoice
  Patricia Forkan, Executive Vice President
  John Grandy, Senior Vice President of Wildlife
  Roger Kindler, Vice President and General Counsel
  Wayne Pacelle, Senior VP, Govt. Affairs & Communications; 202-452-1100
  Richard Clugston, Director of the Center for Respect of Life and Environment

Sharon Geiger, Library Assistant; the Joyce Mertz Gilmore Library, HSUS Offices, 700 Professional Dr., Gaithersburg, MD 20879; 202-452-1100
Amy Lee, Secretary
G. Waite, CFO
David Wiebers, Vice Chairman
David Wiebers, Chairman of the Board

HUMBOLT FIELD RESEARCH INSTITUTE
P.O. Box 9
Steuben, ME 04680-0009 United States
Phone: 207-546-2821   Fax: 207-546-3042
E-mail: humboldt@nemaine.com
Website: www.maine.maine.edu/~taglehill

Founded: 1981

Scope: International

Description: A nonprofit educational and research organization providing advanced and professional training programs in all aspects of natural history (terrestrial, freshwater and marine) and encouraging similar pursuits. Classical natural history training programs are held in Maine and the American Tropics. Ecological restoration seminars are held in a number of cities across the United States and Canada.

Publication(s): Northeastern Naturalist

Keyword(s): Water Habitats & Quality, Wildlife & Species

Contact(s):
Joerg-Henner Lotze, Director

HUMMINGBIRD SOCIETY, THE
P.O. Box 394
Newark, DE 19715 United States
Phone: 302-369-3699   Fax: 302-369-1816
E-mail: info@hummingbird.org
Website: www.hummingbird.org

Founded: 1996
Membership: 1,001–10,000
Scope: National, International

Description: The Hummingbird Society is a nonprofit corporation dedicated solely to hummingbirds, through disseminating information, education, support of scientific research, and protection of habitat.

Publication(s): The Hummingbird Connection

Keyword(s): Wildlife & Species

Contact(s):
H. Hawkins, President; 302-369-3699; Fax: 302-369-1816; hummerman@hummingbird.org
Gary Griffith, Vice President; 410-392-4491; garygriffith@mris.com
Douglas Everett, Director; 610-469-0535
Robert Gell, Director; 410-287-2988
William Barry, Treasurer; 302-239-1797; billb@wserve.com

HUNTSMAN MARINE SCIENCE CENTRE
1 Lower Campus Rd.
St. Andrews, E5B 2L7 New Brunswick Canada
Phone: 506-529-1200   Fax: 506-529-1212
E-mail: huntsman@huntsmanmarine.ca
Website: www.huntsmanmarine.ca

Founded: 1969
Membership: 1–100
Scope: State, Regional, National, International

Description: The HMSC is a nonprofit organization with a reputation for excellence in coastal and marine science research and education. It is supported by universities, corporations, federal and provincial government agencies, and the public. Located on one of the most biologically active bodies of water in the world, it provides information, research, education, and training opportunities for students, investigators, industry, government and the public.

Publication(s): Huntsman Marine Science News, Atlantic Reference Centre Species Identification Series, Sea Trek Bulletin, Seawords

Keyword(s): Agriculture/Farming, Air Quality/Atmosphere, Climate Change, Ecosystems (precious), Oceans/Coasts/Beaches, Pollution (general), Recreation/Ecotourism, Reduce/Reuse/Recycle, Water Habitats & Quality, Wildlife & Species

Contact(s):
Mark Costello, Executive Director; 506-529-1200; Fax: 506-529-1212; costello@huntsmanmarine.ca
Gerhard Pohle, Associate Director; Fax: 506-5291212; huntsman@huntsmanmarine.ca
Tracey Dean, Director of Education; Fax: 506-5291212; huntsman@huntsmanmarine.ca

HYDE CREEK WATERSHED SOCIETY
c/o 1515 Eastern Drive
Port Coquitlam, V3C 2S5 British Columbia Canada
Phone: 604-468-1515
E-mail: marianne-wotherspoon@shaw.ca
Website: www.hydecreek.org

Founded: 1997
Membership: 1–100
Scope: Local

Description: The Hyde Creek Watershed Society's goal is to ensure that watershed health within the Hyde Creek Watershed is sustained through environmental stewardship and education. The Hyde Creek Watershed is located within north Port Coquitlam and the northeast sector of Coquitlam in BC and is approximately 1,118 hectares in area. This watershed supports populations of Coho and Chum Salmon, Cutthroat Trout, Steelhead and provides valuable habitat for wildlife.

Keyword(s): Water Habitats & Quality, Wildlife & Species

Contact(s):
Ted Wingrove, President; 1091 Spruce Avenue, Port Coquitlam, British Columbia V3B 5T9; 604-941-2176
Linda Dore, Treasurer; 3864 Robin Place, Port Coquitlam, British Columbia V3B 4Y7; 604-944-6464; ledore@telus.net

IDAHO ASSOCIATION OF SOIL CONSERVATION DISTRICTS
P.O. Box 2637
Boise, ID 83701 United States
Phone: 208-338-5900   Fax: 208-338-9537
E-mail: kfoster@agri.state.id.us
Website: www.iascd.state.id.us

Scope: State

Contact(s):
Alice Wallace, President; 921 N. 5th Ave., Sandpoint, ID 83864; 208-263-0895; Fax: 208-265-8486
Kyle Hawley, Vice President; 1180 Lewis Rd., Moscow, ID 83843; 208-882-1290; Fax: 208-883-4239
Kent Foster, Executive Director; P.O. Box 2637, Boise, ID 83701; 208-338-5900; Fax: 208-338-9537
Kevin Koester, Director; 208-776-5382; Fax: 208-776-5043
Art Beal, Treasurer
David Ellsworth, Board Member
Roger Stutzman, Secretary; 1037 B E. 4100 N, Buhl, ID 83316; 208-543-6824; Fax: 208-543-6824

IDAHO BASS FEDERATION
3650 Rugby Dr.
Boise, ID 83704 United States
Phone: 208-376-7289
E-mail: stevejburk@yahoo.com
Website: www.bassclubs.net/clubpages/idahofed

Scope: State

Description: An organization of Bassmaster chapters, affiliated with the Bass Anglers Sportsman Society, organized to fight pollution, assist state and national conservation agencies in their efforts, and teach the young people of our country good conservation practices. Dedicated to the realistic conservation of our water resources.

Contact(s):
Allan Chandler, President; 208-286-7138
James Raitter, Vice President, Communication
Steve Spicklemier, Conservation Director; 3766 S. Rush Creek Place, Boise, ID 83706; 208-342-5006
J. Worthen, Tournament Director
Steve Day, Secretary, Treasurer
Larry Raganit, Youth

IDAHO CONSERVATION LEAGUE
P.O. Box 844
Boise, ID 83701 United States
Phone: 208-345-6933   Fax: 208-344-0344
E-mail: icl@wildidaho.org
Website: www.wildidaho.org

Founded: 1973
Membership: 1,001–10,000
Scope: State
Description: The Idaho Conservation League is Idaho's largest statewide conservation organization. for people who cherish Idaho's clean water, wildlands and wildlife, the Idaho Conservation League protects Wild Idaho for future generations.

Publication(s): Idaho Conservationist
Keyword(s): Forests/Forestry, Land Issues, Public Lands/Greenspace, Water Habitats & Quality, Wildlife & Species

Contact(s):
Justin Hayes, Program Director
Rick Johnson, Executive Director
John McCarthy, Policy Director
Suki Molina, Deputy Director
Mary Abbott, Office Manager
Andrea Bogle, Membership Assistant
Liz Edrich, Development Coordinator
Mary Beth Whitaker, Editor/Designer
Rachel Winer, Outreach Coordinator
Linn Kincannon, Central Idaho Director

IDAHO ENVIRONMENTAL COUNCIL
1568 Lola St.
Idaho Falls, ID 83402 United States
Phone: 208-523-6692

Scope: State
Description: Founded to coordinate and stimulate the creative ideas, manpower, and financial resources of conservation-minded individuals and organizations; and to provide an increased understanding of modern man's impact upon his environment. Action, the objective, is based on information and research.

Publication(s): IEC Newsletter

Contact(s):
Alan Hausrath, President; 208-336-4930
Dennis Baird, Vice President for Northern Idaho; 208-882-8289
Ralph Maughan, Vice President for Southeastern Idaho; 208-233-7091
Jerry Jayne, Editor; 208-523-6692

IDAHO TROUT LIMITED
P.O. Box 72
Buhl, ID 83316-0072 United States
Phone: 208-543-6444   Fax: 208-543-8476
E-mail: info@idahotrout.com
Website: www.idahotrout.com

Membership: 1,001–10,000
Scope: State
Description: A statewide council with eight active chapters dedicated to the protection and enhancement of the coldwater fishery resource.

Contact(s):
Robert Dunnagan, President; 57 Maxie Ln., Sandpoint, ID 83864; 208-263-4433; Fax: 815-346-1400; rdunnagan@nidlink.com

IDAHO WILDLIFE FEDERATION
P.O. Box 6426
Boise, ID 83707-6426 United States
Phone: 208-342-7055   Fax: 208-342-7097
E-mail: iwfboise@micron.net

Scope: Regional
Description: A representative statewide organization, affiliated with the National Wildlife Federation, dedicated to the protection and enhancement of wildlife and its habitat through public education and government interaction.

Publication(s): Idaho Wildlife News

Contact(s):
Jack Fisher, President and Representative
Corrine Fisher, Alternate Representative
Bill Goodnight, Editor

ILLINOIS ASSOCIATION OF CONSERVATION DISTRICTS
9313 Bull Valley Rd.
Woodstock, IL 60098 United States
Phone: 815-338-7664   Fax: 815-338-2773
E-mail: conserveone@aol.com

Founded: 1972
Membership: 1–100
Scope: State
Description: To promote the objectives and activities of the Conservation District of Illinois as set forth in the Illinois Conservation District Act and to cooperate with county, state, federal, and private agencies in resource management.

Keyword(s): Ethics/Environmental Justice, Land Issues, Wildlife & Species

Contact(s):
Kathy Merner, President; 3939 Nearing Lane, Decatur, IL 62521; 217-423-7708; Fax: 217-423-2837; MCCD@fgi.net
Ken Konsis, Vice President; 217-442-1691; Fax: 217-442-1695; vccd@soltec.net
Ken Fiske, Assistant Secretary and Treasurer; 815-338-7664; Fax: 815-338-2773; ohanas@aol.com
Dan Kane, Secretary/Treasurer; 603 Appleton Road, Belvidere, IL 61008; 815-547-7935; Fax: 815-547-7939; CONSDIST1@AOL.COM

ILLINOIS ASSOCIATION OF SOIL AND WATER CONSERVATION DISTRICTS
2520 Main St. State Fairgrounds, Emerson Bldg.
Springfield, IL 62702 United States
Phone: 217-744-3414   Fax: 217-744-3420
E-mail: aiswctd@aol.com
Website: www.ilconservation.com

Membership: 1–100
Scope: State

Contact(s):
Mark Besse, President; 7341 Sand Rd., Erie, IL 61250; 309-659-7716; Fax: 309-659-7716
Jerry Snodgrass, Vice President; 13501 N.1700th Ave., Geneseo, IL 61254; 309-944-2869; Fax: 309-937-2171; jerrypam@netexpress.net
Chris Stone, Executive Director; 217-744-3414; Fax: 217-744-3420
Terry Bogner, Board Member; Rte. 1 Box 186, Henry, IL 61537; 309-364-3478; Fax: 309-364-3802

Virginia Hayter, Treasurer; 2020 Hassell Rd. Apt. 101, Hoffman, IL 60195; 847-882-9100; Fax: 847-882-2621; virginia.hayter@hoffmanestate.org
Kim Pate, Administrative Coordinator

ILLINOIS BASS FEDERATION
Attn: President, 2425 Huntington Rd.
Springfield, IL 62703 United States
Phone: 217-529-8341
Website: www.ilbassfed.com

Scope: State

Description: An organization of Bassmaster chapters, affiliated with the Bass Anglers Sportsman Society, organized to fight pollution, assist state and national conservation agencies in their efforts, and to teach the young people of our country good conservation practices. Dedicated to the realistic conservation of our water resources.

Publication(s): Illinois B.A.S.S. Federation Newsletter

Contact(s):
Stan Leigh, President; Sleach183@aol.com

ILLINOIS ENVIRONMENTAL COUNCIL
107 W. Cook St., Suite E
Springfield, IL 62704 United States
Phone: 217-544-5954   Fax: 217-544-5958
E-mail: iec@ilenviro.org
Website: www.ilenviro.org

Founded: 1975

Scope: State

Description: Statewide coalition committed to advocating for Illinois laws and policies that promote a healthful environment and conservation of resources. The Illinois Environmental Council Education Fund administers programs of education and outreach for the coalition.

Publication(s): IEC Bulletin, Environmental Voting Record, Action Alerts

Keyword(s): Agriculture/Farming, Air Quality/Atmosphere, Energy, Land Issues, Pollution (general), Public Health, Public Lands/Greenspace, Sprawl/Urban Planning, Transportation, Water Habitats & Quality

Contact(s):
Jonathan Goldman, Executive Director

ILLINOIS NATIVE PLANT SOCIETY
Forest Glen Preserve, 20301 E. 900 N. Rd.
Westville, IL 61883 United States
Phone: 217-662-2142   Fax: 217-662-2142
E-mail: ilnps@aol.com
Website: www.vccd.org

Founded: 1982
Membership: 101–1,000
Scope: State

Description: Dedicated to the preservation, conservation, and study of the native plants and vegetation of Illinois.

Publication(s): Erigenia, Harbinger

Keyword(s): Land Issues, Reduce/Reuse/Recycle, Water Habitats & Quality, Wildlife & Species

Contact(s):
Ken Konsis, Executive Board

ILLINOIS PRAIRIE PATH
P.O. Box 1086
Wheaton, IL 60189 United States
Phone: 630-752-0120
Website: www.ipp.org

Founded: 1963
Scope: State

Description: To preserve natural areas and establish footpaths and other protected areas to be used for scientific, educational, and recreational purposes by the public. Adds trail amenities and promotes development of a 61-mile trail for bicyclists, hikers, and joggers on a former railroad right-of-way spanning DuPage County, extended Jan. 1972 into Kane County to the Fox River, and extended Dec. 1979 4 1/2 miles into Cook County. Incorporated 1965, in 1971 designated part of National Trails System.

Publication(s): Newsletter, Trail Map, Illinois Prairie Path, The

Keyword(s): Land Issues, Public Lands/Greenspace, Recreation/Ecotourism, Transportation

Contact(s):
David Tate, President
Nancy Becker, Secretary
Jean Mooring, Editor; 295 Abbotsford Ct., Glen Ellyn, IL 60137; 630-469-4289
Paul Mooring, Treasurer

ILLINOIS RAPTOR CENTER
5695 W. Hill Road
Decatur, IL 62522 United States
Phone: 963-6909, ext. 217
E-mail: barnowl@illinoisraptorcenter.org
Website: www.illinoisraptorcenter.org

Founded: 1991
Membership: 101–1,000
Scope: State

Description: The Illinois Raptor Center provides wildlife and environmental education to Illinois through its "Education on the Wing" Presentations.

Keyword(s): Wildlife & Species

Contact(s):
Jacques Nuzzo, Program Director; 963-6909; ext. 217; nuzzoraptorequipment@juno.com
Jane Seltz, Executive Director; 963-6909; ext. 217; barnowl@illinoisraptorcenter.org

ILLINOIS STUDENT ENVIRONMENTAL NETWORK
ISEN
110 S. Race St., Suite 202
Urbana, IL 61801 United States
Phone: 217-384-0830   Fax: 217-278-2105
E-mail: isen@isenonline.org
Website: www.isenonline.org

Founded: 1996
Membership: 101–1,000
Scope: State

Description: Through educational programs such as email alerts, conferences, trainings, capacity building workshops, and how-to manuals, ISEN keeps 3,500 students in 126 student groups on 90 Illinois college campuses updated on critical environmental issues.

Publication(s): Greening Your Campus Cafeteria, Tips for the Environmental Job Search, Leaving a Legacy, Recycling on Your Campus, Resource Library and Action Center

Keyword(s): Agriculture/Farming, Air Quality/Atmosphere, Climate Change, Energy, Forests/Forestry, Land Issues, Public Lands/Greenspace, Reduce/Reuse/Recycle, Sprawl/Urban Planning, Transportation, Water Habitats & Quality, Wildlife & Species

Contact(s):
Laura Huth, Executive Director; 217-384-0830; Fax: 217-278-2105; isen@isenonline.org
Andy Borbely, Campus Energy Efficiency Program Coordinator; 217-384-0830; Fax: 217-278-2105; andy@isenonline.org
Chris Lempa, Member Services Coordinator; 217-384-0830; Fax: 217-278-2105; chris@isenonline.org

ILLINOIS WALNUT COUNCIL
Forest Glen Preserve, 20301 E. 900 N. Rd.
Westville, IL 61883 United States
Phone: 217-442-1691   Fax: 217-442-1695
E-mail: vccd@vccd.org
Website: www.vccd.org

Scope: Regional

Description: To promote the growth and use of the black walnut (Juglans nigra), and the education of good forestry practices with concerns toward wildlife and soil erosion.

Publication(s): Walnut Council Bulletin, Juglans

Keyword(s): Development/Developing Countries, Forests/Forestry, Land Issues, Pollution (general), Reduce/Reuse/Recycle, Water Habitats & Quality, Wildlife & Species

Contact(s):
Doug Bleichner, President; 2290 Knox Road 1000 N, Yates City, IL 61572
John Katzke, Vice President; 2619 North Woodhaven, Peoria, IL 61604
Steve Felt, Secretary; 522 Roberts Ln., Sherrard, IL 61281

INDIAN CREEK NATURE CENTER
6665 Otis Rd., SE
Cedar Rapids, IA 52403 United States
Phone: 319-362-0664   Fax: 319-362-2876
E-mail: naturecenter@aol.com
Website: www.indiancreeknaturecenter.org

Founded: 1973
Membership: 101–1,000
Scope: State

Description: The Indian Creek Nature Center is dedicated to fostering an appreciation of nature through environmental education and providing a natural facility for education and non-obtrusive recreation.

Publication(s): Indian Creek Currents

Contact(s):
Leslie Smith, President; lsmith@berthel.com
Rich Patterson, Director
Dennis Redmond, Past President; 319-366-2163; Fax: 319-366-7710; dredmond@rbjcpas.com

INDIANA ASSOCIATION OF SOIL AND WATER CONSERVATION DISTRICTS, INC.
225 S. East St., Suite 740
Indianapolis, IN 46202 United States
Phone: 317-692-7325   Fax: 317-423-0756
E-mail: iaswcd@iaswcd.org
Website: www.iaswcd.org

Founded: 1968
Scope: State

Description: We represent Indiana's 92 soil and water conservation districts. We support the districts in their efforts to combat non-point source pollution.

Contact(s):
Steve Graber, President; 3850 Greenhurst Court, Auburn, IN 46706; 219-925-0676
Sherman Bryant, Vice-President; 7343 N 650 E., N. Webster, IN 46555-9332; 219-834-2496

INDIANA AUDUBON SOCIETY, INC.
Mary Gray Bird Sanctuary, R.R. 6 Box 163
Connersville, IN 47331 United States
Phone: 765-825-9788
Website: www.indianaaudubon.org

Founded: 1898
Scope: State

Description: Works for the conservation of wildlife, especially birds.

Keyword(s): Reduce/Reuse/Recycle, Wildlife & Species

Contact(s):
Jane Miller, President; 4020 S. Rural, Independence, IN 46227-3865
Larry Carter, Vice President; 7496 N. County. Rd. 2005, Ridgeville, IN 47380-9546
Deanna Barricklow, Resident Agent and Manager of Sanctuary Management; 3499 S. Bird Sanctuary Rd., Connersville, IN 47331-8721; 317-825-9788
Mary Gough, Editor; 901 Maplewood Dr., New Castle, IN 47362; 317-529-5225
Charles Keller, Editor; 2505 E. Maynard Dr., Indianapolis, IN 46226; 317-786-5822
Dan Leach, Secretary; 2313 S. 30th St., Bedford, IN 47421-5415
Clare Oskay, Treasurer; 551 Teton Trail, Indianapolis, IN 46217-3927

INDIANA BASS FEDERATION
Attn: President, 1415 Cherokee Rd.
Ft. Wayne, IN 46808 United States
Phone: 219-483-0525
Website: www.indianabass.com/ibf/index.html

Scope: State

Description: An organization of Bassmaster chapters, affiliated with the Bass Anglers Sportsman Society, organized to fight pollution, assist state and national conservation agencies in their efforts, and teach the young people of our country good conservation practices. Dedicated to the realistic conservation of our water resources.

Contact(s):
Paul Hollabaugh, President; 1415 Cherokee Rd., Ft. Wayne, IN 46808; 219-483-0525
Dan Pardue, Conservation Director; 7244 Holmestead Rd., Morgantown, IN 46160; 812-988-8763

INDIANA FORESTRY AND WOODLAND OWNERS ASSOCIATION
5578 South 500 W.
Atlanta, IN 46031-9363 United States
Phone: 317-758-4735

Founded: 1977
Scope: State

Description: A statewide organization affiliated with the National Woodland Owners Association, providing leadership and programs to advance forestry in Indiana.

Publication(s): Leaves and Limbs

Keyword(s): Forests/Forestry

Contact(s):
Robert Koenig, President
Alan Bolenbaugh, 2nd Vice President
Thomas Moehl, 1st Vice President
Warren Baird, Treasurer
Pete Halstead, Forestry Educational Foundation
Jan Myers, Editor; 317-583-2422
William Sigman, Secretary

INDIANA NATIVE PLANT AND WILDFLOWER SOCIETY
6106 Kingsley Dr.
Indianapolis, IN 46220 United States
Phone: 317-253-3863
E-mail: rai38@aol.com
Website: www.inpaws.org

Founded: 1993
Scope: State

Description: To promote the appreciation, preservation, conservation, utilization and scientific study of the flora native to Indiana; and to educate the public about the values, beauty, diversity, and environmental importance of indigenous vegetation.

Publication(s): Indiana Native Plant and Wildflower Society News

Keyword(s): Land Issues, Public Lands/Greenspace, Wildlife & Species

Contact(s):
Carolyn Bryson, President; quinnell@iquest.net
Ken Collins, Vice President; 317-891-9804

INDIANA STATE TRAPPERS ASSOCIATION, INC.
20941 Fir Road
Tippecanoe, IN 46570 United States
Phone: 219-498-6354
Website: www.krause.com/outdoors/tr/associations

Founded: 1961
Scope: State
Description: A statewide organization dedicated to the conservation, restoration, and wise use of wildlife and other renewable natural resources. Provides public education concerning the role of trapping in the management of wildlife.

Contact(s):
Doyle Flory, President; 219-498-6354
Richard McOlvanine, Vice President; 812-834-5514

INDIANA WILDLIFE FEDERATION
950 N. Rangeline Rd., Suite A
Carmel, IN 46032-1315 United States
Phone: 317-571-1220 Fax: 317-571-1223
E-mail: iwf@indy.net
Website: www.indianawildlife.org

Founded: 1939
Membership: 1,001–10,000
Scope: State, Regional, National
Description: A representative statewide organization, affiliated with the National Wildlife Federation, dedicated to the protection and enhancement of wildlife and its habitat through public education and government interaction.

Publication(s): Hoosier Conservation

Contact(s):
Dale Back, President; back@indianawildlife.org
Paula Yeager, Executive Director; 317-571-1220; yeager@indianawildlife.org
Jack Dold, Editor and Alternate Representative; dold@indianawildlife.org
Becky Scheibelhut, Education Programs Contact
George Vargo, Treasurer

INDO-PACIFIC CONSERVATION ALLIANCE
1620-D Belmont St., NW
Washington, DC 20009 United States
Phone: 202-939-9773 Fax: 202-265-1169
E-mail: info@indopacific.org
Website: www.indopacific.org

Founded: 1998
Scope: International
Description: IPCA is a science-oriented conservation organization dedicated to the study and conservation of the native ecosystems of the tropical Indo-Pacific and support for traditional peoples in their stewardship of these globally significant natural resources. Current activities are in Papua, Indonesia, incl. Asmat (Lorentz National Park & World Heritage Site). Activities: environmental education, community forest/marine mapping & monitoring, NGO capacity-building, ecotourism, & ecological surveys.

Publication(s): Biodiversity Report, Tangguh Project
Keyword(s): Development/Developing Countries, Ecosystems (precious), Forests/Forestry, Oceans/Coasts/Beaches, Recreation/Ecotourism, Wildlife & Species

Contact(s):
Neville Kemp, Programme Manager; kemp@indopacific.org

INFORM, INC.
120 Wall St., 16th Fl.
New York, NY 10005 United States
Phone: 212-361-2400 Fax: 212-361-2412
E-mail: brown@informinc.org
Website: www.informinc.org

Founded: 1973
Scope: National
Description: A nonprofit tax-exempt environmental research and education organization that identifies and reports on practical solutions for problems in municipal solid waste, chemical hazards, air quality, and alternative vehicle fuels, with an emphasis on pollution prevention and waste reduction.

Publication(s): INFORM Reports (Newsletter), Rethinking Resources, Tracking Toxic Chemicals, Building for the Future, Gearing up for Hydrogen, China at the Crossroads
Keyword(s): Air Quality/Atmosphere, Energy, Pollution (general), Reduce/Reuse/Recycle, Transportation

Contact(s):
Joanna Underwood, President; ext. 222; underwood@informinc.org
Samuel Arnoff, Director of Operation; ext. 238; arnoff@informinc.org
Joanna Underwood, Director of Research
Stephen Land, Chairman of the Board; 212-424-9018; sbland@linklaters.com

INITIATIVE FOR SOCIAL ACTION AND RENEWAL IN EURASIA
ISAR
1601 Connecticut Ave., NW, Suite 301
Washington, DC 20009 United States
Phone: 202-387-3034 Fax: 202-667-3291
E-mail: postmaster@isar.org
Website: www.isar.org

Founded: 1983
Membership: 101–1,000
Scope: International
Description: ISAR promotes citizens' participation and the development of the NGO sector in the former Soviet Union by supporting community activists and grassroots groups.

Publication(s): ISAR in Focus, Give and Take
Keyword(s): Energy, Ethics/Environmental Justice, Oceans/Coasts/Beaches, Public Health, Water Habitats & Quality

Contact(s):
Eliza Klose, Executive Director; eliza@isar.org
Kathleen Watters, Deputy Director; kwatters@isar.org

INLAND BIRD BANDING ASSOCIATION
P.O. Box 832
Tiffin, OH 44883 United States
E-mail: MCGREEN@AOL.COM
Website: www.aves.net/inlandbba/ibbamain.htm

Founded: 1922
Scope: National
Description: Promotes cooperation among its members and other organizations, with state, federal, or other officials or individuals engaged in bird banding or other scientific work with birds; informs the public of the purposes and results secured by banding.

Publication(s): North American Bird Bander, Inland Bird Banding Newsletter

Contact(s):
Ruth Green, President
Dan Kramer, Editor; 3451 County Rd. 256, Victory, OH 43464
Wiletta Lueshen, Editor; R. 2 Box 26, Wisner, NE 68791
Carol Rudy, Secretary; W. 3866 Hwy. H, Chilton, WI 53084
C. Smith, Treasurer; 6305 Cumberland Rd. SW, Sherrodsville, OH 44675
Al Valentine, Membership Secretary; 17403 Oakington Ct., Dallas, TX 75252

INSTITUTE FOR AGRICULTURE AND TRADE POLICY
COMMUNITY FORESTRY RESOURCE CENTER
2105 First Avenue South
Minneapolis, MN 55404 United States
Phone: 612-870-3415 Fax: 612-813-5612
E-mail: forestrycenter@iatp.org
Website: www.forestrycenter.org

Founded: 1986
Scope: Local, State, Regional, National, International
Description: The Community Forestry Resource Center established by the Institute for Agriculture and Trade Policy promotes responsible forest management by encouraging the long-term health and prosperity of small, privately owned woodlots, their owners, and their communities.
Keyword(s): Agriculture/Farming, Forests/Forestry

INSTITUTE FOR CIVIC INITIATIVES SUPPORT
Chayanova St., 4-13
Moscow, Russia
Phone: 70952517617 Fax: 70952517617
E-mail: clearh@glasnet.ru

Founded: 1993
Scope: International
Description: The Institute supports civic initiatives through information, publications, training, grant-making programs, and environmental education projects.
Contact(s):
Bogdan Mila, Director

INSTITUTE FOR CONSERVATION LEADERSHIP
EASTERN OFFICE
6930 Carroll Ave. Suite 420
Takoma Park, MD 20912 United States
Phone: 301-270-2900 Fax: 301-270-0610
E-mail: icl@icl.org
Website: www.icl.org

Founded: 1990
Scope: National, International
Description: The mission of the Institute is to train and empower volunteer leaders and to build volunteer institutions that protect and conserve the earth's environment. Services offered include training and technical assistance for nonprofit organizations and leaders in organizational development, fundraising, board development, volunteer recruitment, strategic planning, and related topics. Services also include meeting facilitation, coalition development, and network building.
Publication(s): Benchmarking Workbook, The Network
Contact(s):
Dianne Russell, Executive Director; dianne@icl.org
Baird Straughan, Associate Director; baird@icl.org
Chiquita Edwards, Office Manager; chiquita@icl.org
Peter Lane, Program Associate; peter@icl.org
Grant LaRouche, Development & Outreach Associate; grant@icl.org
Brian Lewis, Administrative Assistant; 13 South Willson Ave., Suite 9, Bozeman, MT 59715; 406-582-1838; Fax: 406-582-0323; brian@icl.org
Barbara Rusmore, Senior Program Associate; 13 South Willson Ave., Suite 9, Bozeman, MT 59715; 406-582-1838; Fax: 406-582-0323; barbara@icl.org
Brad Webb, Program Associate; 13 South Willson Ave., Suite 9, Bozeman, MT 59715; 406-582-1838; Fax: 406-582-0323; brad@icl.org

INSTITUTE FOR EARTH EDUCATION, THE
Cedar Cove
P.O. Box 115
Greenville, WV 24945 United States
Phone: 304-832-6404 Fax: 304-832-6077
E-mail: iee1@aol.com
Website: www.eartheducation.org

Founded: 1974
Membership: 101–1,000
Scope: International
Description: The Institute for Earth Education develops and disseminates focused educational programs to promote an understanding of, appreciation for, and harmony with the earth's natural systems and communities. The Institute conducts workshops, provides a seasonal journal, hosts an international conference, supports local and international branches, and publishes numerous books and program materials.
Publication(s): Talking Leaves Journal, Sunship III, Earth Speaks, The, Earthkeepers, Earth Education: A New Beginning, Earth Education Sourcebook, Sunship Earth
Contact(s):
Bill Weiler, Executive Staff Chair
Fran Bires, International Internship Coordinator
Laurie Farber, International Membership Services Coordinator
Bruce Johnson, International Program Coordinator
Mike Mayer, International Training Coordinator
Steve Van Matre, Chair

INSTITUTE FOR TROPICAL ECOLOGY AND CONSERVATION (ITEC)
1023 SW 2nd Avenue
Gainesville, FL 32601 United States
Phone: 352-337-0223
E-mail: ITEC@ITEC-edu.org
Website: itec-edu.org

Founded: 1997
Scope: International
Description: Dedicated to conservation and education in the neotropics. Offers college level field courses, marine turtle research, forest restoration, local education and conservation programs, internships, volunteering opportunities. Scientific research projects are on-going, and more are welcome.
Keyword(s): Agriculture/Farming, Climate Change, Development/Developing Countries, Ecosystems (precious), Forests/Forestry, Land Issues, Oceans/Coasts/Beaches, Recreation/Ecotourism, Reduce/Reuse/Recycle, Water Habitats & Quality, Wildlife & Species

INSTITUTE OF ECOSYSTEM STUDIES
Millbrook, NY 12545-0129 United States
Phone: 845-677-5343 Fax: 845-677-5976
Website: www.ecostudies.org

Scope: International
Description: Devoted to the understanding of ecosystem structure and function. The program focus is on disturbance and recovery of northern temperate ecosystems. Education and research interests include wildlife management, biogeochemistry, landscape ecology, aquatic ecology, plant-animal interactions, microbial ecology, forest ecology, chemical ecology, and air and water quality.
Publication(s): Newsletter, occasional publications, scientific journals
Keyword(s): Air Quality/Atmosphere
Contact(s):
Gene Likens, Director
Alan Berkowitz, Head of Education; 845-677-5359
Charles Canham, Forest Ecologist
Nina Caraco, Biogeochemist
Jonathan Cole, Aquatic Microbiologist
Stuart Findlay, Aquatic Ecologist
Peter Groffman, Microbial Ecologist
Clive Jones, Ecologist
Chloe Keefer, Librarian
Gary Lovett, Plant Ecologist
Richard Ostfeld, Animal Ecologist

Michael Pace, Aquatic Ecologist
Steward Pickett, Plant Ecologist
David Strayer, Freshwater Ecologist
Joseph Warner, Administrator
Kathleen Weathers, Forest Ecologist
Raymond Winchcombe, Wildlife Biologist and Field Research Facilities; 845-677-9818

INSTITUTO BRASIL DE EDUCACAO AMBIENTAL
Rua Visconde De Piraja 547 Sala 710
Ipanema CEP, Rio De Janeiro, 22410-003 Brazil
Phone: 55-21-294-1231   Fax: 55-21-294-1231
E-mail: instbrasil@openlink.com.br

Description: Instituto Brasil is an environmental institution throughout Brazil among education NGOs that works with teachers and community leaders in their capacity. Its network is currently 60 partner city councils, universities, other NGOs and 2000 teachers and members. Implementation of local projects building through courses.

Contact(s):
Vera Rodrigues, Executive Director

INTER-AMERICAN TROPICAL TUNA COMMISSION
COMISION INTERAMERICANA DEL ATUN TROPICAL
8604 La Jolla Shores Drive
La Jolla, CA 92037-1508 United States
Phone: 858-546-7100   Fax: 858-546-7133
E-mail: wbayliff@iattc.org
Website: www.iattc.org

Founded: 1949
Membership: 1–100
Scope: International

Description: Charged with the investigation and conservation of the tuna and dolphin resources of the eastern Pacific Ocean. Member nations: U.S., Costa Rica, El Salvador, Ecuador, France, Guatemala, Japan, Mexico, Nicaragua, Panama, Peru, Vanuatu, and Venezuela. Established by convention between the U.S. and Costa Rica.

Publication(s): Stock Assessment Report of the IATTC, Special Report of the IATTC, Annual Report of the IATTC, Bulletin of the IATTC

Contact(s):
Robin Allen, Director; 858-546-7019
William Bayliff, Editor; 858-546-7025

INTERFAITH COUNCIL FOR THE PROTECTION OF ANIMALS AND NATURE INC. (ICPAN)
3691 Tuxedo Rd., NW
Atlanta, GA 30305 United States
Phone: 404-814-1371   Fax: 404-814-0440

Founded: 1980
Membership: 1,001–10,000
Scope: National

Description: Composed of people of all faiths, ICPAN works to promote conservation and environmental and humane education, mainly within the religious community. We try to make religious leaders, institutions, and the general public aware of our moral spiritual obligations, as emphasized in the Bible, to protect animals and the natural environment.

Publication(s): Replenish the Earth: The Teachings of the World's Religions on Protecting Animals and Nature, Losing Paradise: The Growing Threat to Our Animals, Our Environment and Ourself, Cleaning up America the Poisoned: How to Survive our Polluted Society, Replenish the Earth: A Booklet on The Bible's Message of Conservation and Kindness to Animals

Keyword(s): Development/Developing Countries, Wildlife & Species

Contact(s):
Lewis Regenstein, President; 3691 Tuxedo Rd. NW, Atlanta, GA 30327; 404-814-1371
Paul Irwin, Director; 2100 L St. NW, Washington, DC 20037; 202-452-1100
John Hoyt, Chairman; 2100 L St. NW, Washington, DC 20037; 202-452-1100

INTERNATIONAL ASSOCIATION FOR BEAR RESEARCH AND MANAGEMENT
University of Tennessee
274 Ellington Hall
Knoxville, TN 37996 United States
Phone: 865-974-4790   Fax: 865-974-3555
E-mail: jclark1@utk.edu
Website: www.bearbiology.com

Founded: 1968
Membership: 101–1,000
Scope: International

Description: A professional organization of biologists, animal or land managers, and private citizens with an interest or involvement in bear research and management. The Association encourages and reports research and management by various agencies or university research groups, sponsors the triannual International Conference on Bear Research and Management, publishes the proceedings of the conference, and sponsors or aids a world network of regional bear workshops, groups, and committees, and the IUCN Bear

Publication(s): International Bear News (Quarterly Newsletter), Ursus, formerly Bears: Their Biology and Management (Conference Proceedings)

Keyword(s): Land Issues, Public Lands/Greenspace, Wildlife & Species

Contact(s):
Harry Reynolds, President; 1300 College Rd., Fairbanks, AK 99701; 907-459-7238
Sterling Miller, Vice President; 240 N. Higgins Ste. 2, Missoula, MT 59802; 406-721-6705
Joe Clark, Secretary; 274 Ellington PSB, University of Tennessee, Knoxville, TN 37996; 865-974-4790
Frank van Manen, Treasurer, 274 Ellington PSB, Knoxville, TN 37996; 865-974-0200

INTERNATIONAL ASSOCIATION FOR ENVIRONMENTAL HYDROLOGY (IAEH)
P.O. Box 35324
San Antonio, TX 78235 United States
Phone: 210-344-5418   Fax: 210-344-9941
E-mail: hydroweb@mail.org
Website: www.hydroweb.com

Founded: 1991
Scope: International

Description: IAEH works to foster a global interchange of ideas, approaches, and technologies for environmental cleanup and protection of fresh water resources and pollution prevention; to place special focus on approaches to cleanup, prevention, and protection that are practical in less affluent countries; to further the development of environmentally sound solutions that are realistic from the economic standpoint; to seek solutions to cleanup, pollution prevention, and environmental protection.

Publication(s): Journal of Environmental Hydrology, Environmental Hydrology Report

Keyword(s): Development/Developing Countries, Oceans/Coasts/Beaches, Pollution (general)

Contact(s):
Roger Peebles, President; 308 Montfort Dr., San Antonio, TX 78216; 210-344-5418

INTERNATIONAL ASSOCIATION OF FISH AND WILDLIFE AGENCIES
444 North Capitol St., NW Suite 544
Washington, DC 20001 United States
Phone: 202-624-7890   Fax: 202-624-7891
E-mail: iafwa@sso.org
Website: www.iafwa.org

Founded: 1902
Membership: 101–1,000
Scope: International

Description: Association of states or territories of the United States, provinces of Canada, the Commonwealth of Puerto Rico, the United States Government, the Dominion Government of Canada, and governments of countries located in the western hemisphere, as well as individual associate members whose principal objective is conservation, protection, and management of wildlife and related natural resources.

Publication(s): Managing American Wildlife, Annual Proceedings, Newsletter

Keyword(s): Agriculture/Farming, Air Quality/Atmosphere, Forests/Forestry, Land Issues, Public Lands/Greenspace, Recreation/Ecotourism, Water Habitats & Quality, Wildlife & Species

Contact(s):
   Brent Manning, President; Wyoming Game & Fish Department, 5400 Bishop Boulevard, Cheyenne, WY 82006; 307-777-4501; Fax: 307-777-4699
   John Baughman, Executive Vice President; 202-624-7890; Fax: 202-624-7891; baughman@sso.org
   Thomas Bennett, Vice President; Kentucky Department of Fish and Wildlife Resources, One Game Farm Road, Frankfort, KY 40601; 502-564-7109; Fax: 502-564-0506
   Rex Amack, Executive Committee Member; Nebraska Game & Parks Commission, 2200 North 33rd, Box 30370, Lincoln, NE 68510; 402-471-5539; Fax: 402-471-5528
   Gerry Barnhart, Executive Committee Member; New York Department of Environmental Conservation, Division of Fish, Wildlife and Marine Resources, 625 Broadway, 5th Floor, Albany, NY 12233-4750; 518-402-8924; Fax: 518-402-8925
   John Cooper, Vice Chair, Executive Committee; 605-773-3387; Fax: 605-773-6245
   Terry Crawforth, Chair, Executive Committee; Nevada Division of Wildlife, 1100 Valley Road, Reno, NV 89512; 775-688-1599; Fax: 775-688-1595
   Kenneth Haddad, Executive Committee Member; Florida Fish & Wildlife Conservation Commission, 620 S. Meridian Street, Tallahassee, FL 32399-1600; 850-488-2975; Fax: 850-921-5786
   Jeff Koenings, Executive Committee Member; Washington Department of Fish and Wildlife, 600 Capitol Way North, Olympia, WA 98501-1091; 360-902-2225; Fax: 360-902-2947
   Cameron Mack, Executive Committee; Director, Fish and Wildlife Branch, Ontario Ministry of Natural Resources, 300 Water Street, 5th Floor, P.O. Box 7000, Peterborough, Ontario K9J 8M5; 705-755-1909
   Ira Palmer, Executive Committee Member; Fisheries and Wildlife Division, Environmental Health Administration, 51 N Street, NE, 5th Floor, Washington, DC 20002-3323; 202-535-2266; Fax: 202-535-1373
   Edward Parker, Executive Committee Member; 860-424-3010; Fax: 860-424-4078
   M.N. "Corky" Pugh, Secretary/Treasurer; Alabama Division of Freshwater Fisheres, 64 N. Union Street, Montgomery, AL 36130; 334-242-3849; Fax: 334-242-3032
   Curtis Taylor, Ex Officio Member; West Virginia Division of Natural Resources, 1900 Kanawha Boulevard, East, Charleston, WV 25305; 304-558-2771; Fax: 304-558-3147
   Naomi Edelson, Wildlife Diversity Director
   Donald MacLauchlan, International Resource Director
   Bob Miles, Resource Director
   Gary Taylor, Legislative Director
   Samara Trusso, Project Manager
   Len Ugarenko, NAWMP Coordinator
   David Walker, Agriculture Conservation Policy Analyst
   Paul Lenzini, Legal Counsel; 703-684-4450; Fax: 703-684-4428
   Wm. Nesbitt, Annual Proceedings Editor; 703-590-4449; Fax: 703-878-2119

INTERNATIONAL ASSOCIATION OF FISH AND WILDLIFE AGENCIES
NORTHEAST ASSOCIATION OF FISH AND WILDLIFE RESOURCE AGENCIES
c/o Maine Department of Inland Fisheries and Wildlife
Attention: Roland D. Martin
41 State House Station
Augusta, ME 04333 United States
Phone: 207-287-5202   Fax: 207-287-6395
E-mail: r.dan.martin@maine.gov

Membership: 1–100
Scope: State, Regional, National, International

Description: State and Canadian provincial agencies protecting fish and wildlife resources in the northeast U.S. and eastern Canada.

Publication(s): Northeast Fish and Wildlife Conference

Contact(s):
   Gerry Barnhart, President; 518-402-8924; Fax: 518-402-8925
   Lee Perry, Secretary/Treasurer; 207-287-5202; Fax: 207-287-6395; lee.perry@state.me.us

INTERNATIONAL ASSOCIATION OF NATURAL RESOURCE PILOTS
IANRP
9740 Briarwood Drive
Plain City, OH 43064 United States
Phone: 614-873-4163   Fax: 614-873-4860
E-mail: info@ianrp.org
Website: ianrp.org

Founded: 1972
Membership: 101–1,000
Scope: State, National, International

Description: Performs aviation and aircrew conservation-related responsibilities for federal and state environmental, forestry, parks, game and fish divisions and departments of natural resources throughout the U.S. and for their counterparts in the Canadian provinces. Additional membership includes a variety of aviation-oriented corporations and advanced technological suppliers of equipment used in the performance of the aviation missions.

Publication(s): Conservation Aviation

Keyword(s): Air Quality/Atmosphere, Forests/Forestry, Land Issues, Pollution (general), Recreation/Ecotourism, Reduce/Reuse/Recycle, Transportation, Water Habitats & Quality, Wildlife & Species

Contact(s):
   Greg Stacey, President; 3911 Fish Hatchery Road, Fitchburg, WI 53711; 608-245-2303; staceg@dnr.state.wi.us
   Al Buchert, Vice President; 28497 Alicia Place, Grand Rapids, MN 55744; 218-326-9465; Fax: 218-327-4507; al.buchert@dnr.state.mn.us
   John Clem, Librarian; 9740 Briarwood Drive, Plain City, OH 43064; 614-873-4163; Fax: 614-873-4860; john@clem.ws
   Fred Kruger, Treasurer; 27102 County Highway A, Spooner, WI 54801; 715-635-7788; kruger8@juno.com
   Michael Jeffries, Secretary; Technical Representative OAS, 2741 Airport Hwy., Boise, ID 83705; 208-334-9310; Fax: 208-334-9303; michael_jefferies@oas.gov

INTERNATIONAL ASSOCIATION OF WILDLAND FIRE
E. 8109 Bratt Rd.
Fairfield, WA 99012 United States
Phone: 509-523-4003   Fax: 509-523-5001
E-mail: greenlee@cet.com
Website: www.wildfiremagazine.com

Founded: 1991
Membership: 1,001–10,000
Scope: International
Description: (formerly Fire Research Institute) The International Association of Wildland Fire was organized to promote a fuller understanding of wildland fire. The Association is built on the belief that an understanding of this dynamic natural force is vital for natural resource management, firefighter safety, and harmonious interactions between people and their environment.
Publication(s): International Directory of Wildland Fire, Current Titles in Wildland Fire, Wildfire Magazine, International Journal of Wildland Fire, International Bibliography of Wildland Fire
Keyword(s): Forests/Forestry, Land Issues, Wildlife & Species
Contact(s):
   Mike Degrosky, President; 307-543-0949
   Jason Greenlee, Executive Director; 509-283-2397
   Mike Weber, Editor; 403-435-7210

INTERNATIONAL BICYCLE FUND
4887 Columbia Dr. S.
Seattle, WA 98108-1919 United States
Phone: 206-767-0848
E-mail: ibike@ibike.org
Website: www.ibike.org

Founded: 1983
Scope: International
Description: The International Bicycle Fund's programs fall into the areas of transportation planning, sustainable economic development, safety education and promoting international understanding. Within these programs we address issues of the environment, energy policy, public health, appropriate technology, land use patterns, sustainable systems, resource conservation and employment generation. IBF coordinates and cooperates with organizations and individuals worldwide. IBF is a nonprofit organization.
Publication(s): See publications on website, IBF News
Keyword(s): Development/Developing Countries, Land Issues, Transportation
Contact(s):
   David Mozer, President; ibike@ibike.org

INTERNATIONAL CENTER FOR EARTH CONCERNS
2162 Baldwin Rd.
Ojai, CA 93023 United States
Phone: 805-649-3535   Fax: 805-649-1757
E-mail: information@earthconcerns.org
Website: www.earthconcerns.org

Founded: 1994
Membership: 101–1,000
Scope: Local
Description: The ICEC involves people with nature by fostering their appreciation of the natural world through environmental education and training.
Publication(s): Brochure, Annual Newsletters
Contact(s):
   Paul Irwin, President
   Melody Taft, Executive Director
   John Taft, Chairman

INTERNATIONAL CENTER FOR GIBBON STUDIES
P.O. Box 800249
Santa Clarita, CA 91380 United States
Phone: 661-296-2737   Fax: 661-296-1237
E-mail: gibboncntr@aol.com
Website: www.gibboncenter.org

Founded: 1977
Scope: International
Description: The International Center for Gibbon Studies ensures the preservation and propagation and a safe haven for all gibbon species living in the wild and in captivity; supports ongoing field conservation projects; and educates the public about the importance of this species and saving their natural habitat.
Publication(s): Brochures, The Gibbon's Voice - yearly newletters
Contact(s):
   Alan Mootnick, Board of Directors President, Facility Director, and Chairman; P.O. Box 800249, Santa Clarita, CA 91380; 661-296-2737
   Geri-Ann Galanti, Board of Directors Vice President; 2906 Ocean Ave., Venice, CA 90291; 310-827-0937
   Bjorn Merker, Acting Director of Research; Institute for Biomusicology, Mid Sweden, Ostersund S-83125
   Lori Sheeran, Director of Education and Conservation; California State University at Fullerton; 714-773-2765
   Elaine Baker, Assistant Director of Research; Department of Psychology, Marshall University, Huntington, WV 25755

INTERNATIONAL CENTER FOR TROPICAL ECOLOGY
The University of Missouri at St. Louis
R233 Research Bldg.
8001 Natural Bridge Rd.
St. Louis, MO 63121-4499 United States
Phone: 314-516-5219   Fax: 314-516-6233
E-mail: icte@umsl.edu
Website: icte.umsl.edu

Founded: 1990
Scope: International
Description: The ICTE is one of the premier institutes in the United States for the study of tropical biology and conservation. The Center's three primary missions include the training of graduate students in the vital areas of tropical ecology and conservation, the education of undergraduates about the importance of these areas, and involvement of the community in educational actvities with respect to issues related to conservation and biodiversity.
Keyword(s): Development/Developing Countries, Ecosystems (precious), Wildlife & Species
Contact(s):
   Bette Loiselle, Director; 314-516-6224; Fax: 314-516-6233; loiselle@umsl.edu
   Patrick Osborne, Executive Director; 314-516-5219; Fax: 314-516-6233; posborne@jinx.umsl.edu

INTERNATIONAL CENTRE FOR CONSERVATION EDUCATION
Greenfield House
Guiting Power, Cheltenham, GL54 5TZ United Kingdom
Phone: 1.4412426748e+012   Fax: 1.4412426748e+012
E-mail: maikcec@aol.com

Founded: 1984
Scope: International
Description: ICCE works to promote a greater understanding of global environmental issues and sustainable development.
Keyword(s): Development/Developing Countries, Wildlife & Species
Contact(s):
   Mark Boulton, Director; Greenfield House Guiting Power, Cheltenham GL54 5TZ; 1441242674

INTERNATIONAL CHILDREN'S CONFERENCE ON THE ENVIRONMENT
17 Britton Drive
Bloomfield, CT 06002 United States
Phone: 860-286-0708, ext. 707   Fax: 860-293-1414
E-mail: nptyler@aol.com

Founded: 2002
Scope: Local, State, Regional, National, International
Description: A United Nations Environment Programme event being held in the United States for the first time, the International Children's Conference on the Environment invites children ages 10 to 13 to join together for a four day conference to brainstorm about environmental challenges. From July 19 - 23, 2004, 800 international children will attend workshops and fieldtrips to learn about issues and solutions. The conference takes place at Connecticut College in the New England harbor city of New London.
Keyword(s): Climate Change, Development/Developing Countries, Ecosystems (precious), Energy, Forests/Forestry, Land Issues, Oceans/Coasts/Beaches, Pollution (general), Population, Public Lands/Greenspace, Reduce/Reuse/Recycle, Water Habitats & Quality, Wildlife & Species

INTERNATIONAL COUNCIL OF ENVIRONMENTAL LAW
COUNSEIL INTERNATIONAL DU DROIT DE L'ENVIRONNMENT
ICEL/CIDE
Godesberger Allee 108-112
Bonn, D-53175 Germany
Phone: 4-9228269224-011   Fax: 4-9228269225-011
E-mail: icel@intlawpol.org
Website: www.i-c-e-l.org

Founded: 1969
Membership: 101–1,000
Scope: Regional, International
Description: A nonprofit, nongovernmental international organization with elected membership, structured in ten regions worldwide, for the purpose of exchange of information on international environmental law, policy, and administration and mutual assistance among members.
Publication(s): Conservation in Sustainable Development, International Environmental Soft Law, International Environmental Law, Environmental Policy and Law
Contact(s):
Wolfgang Burhenne, Executive Governor
Amado Tolentino, Executive Governor; Embassy of the Philippines, Doha

INTERNATIONAL CRANE FOUNDATION
E-11376 Shady Ln. Rd., P.O. Box 447
Baraboo, WI 53913-0447 United States
Phone: 608-356-9462   Fax: 608-356-9465
E-mail: cranes@savingcranes.org
Website: www.savingcranes.org

Founded: 1973
Membership: 1,001–10,000
Scope: International
Description: Preservation of cranes through research, conservation, captive propagation, restocking, field ecology, and public education.
Publication(s): ICF Bugle, The (Quarterly Magazine), Reflections: The Story of Cranes, Proceedings of the 7th N. American Crane Workshop, 1997
Keyword(s): Water Habitats & Quality, Wildlife & Species
Contact(s):
James Harris, President; 608-356-9462; ext. 129; Fax: 608-356-9465; harris@savingcranes.org
Kate Fitzwilliams, Director of Public Relations and Marketing; 608-356-9462; ext. 147; kate@savingcranes.org
David Chesky, Site Manager; 608-356-9462; ext. 120; dchesky@savingcranes.org
Susan Finn, Office Administrator; 608-356-9462; ext. 118; sfinn@savingcranes.org
George Archibald, Co-Founder; george@savingcranes.org
Jeb Barzen, Field Ecologist; 608-356-9462; ext. 125; jeb@savingcranes.org
Betsy Didrickson, Librarian; the Ron Sauey Memorial Library for Bird Conservation, Baraboo, WI 53913-0447; 608-356-9462; ext. 124; betsy@savingcranes.org
Bob Lange, Development; 608-356-9462; ext. 140; blange@savingcranes.org
Claire Mirande, Conservation Coordinator; 608-356-9462; ext. 122; mirande@savingcranes.com
Mike Putnam, Curator of Birds; 608-356-9462; ext. 159; putnam@savingcranes.org

INTERNATIONAL ECOLOGY SOCIETY (IES)
1471 Barclay St.
St. Paul, MN 55106-1405 United States
Phone: 612-579-7008

Founded: 1975
Scope: International
Description: Volunteer-staffed, nonprofit organization dedicated to the protection of the environment and the encouragement of better understanding of all life forms.
Publication(s): Eco-Humane Letter, Action Alerts, Sunrise (neighborhood news)
Keyword(s): Wildlife & Species
Contact(s):
R. Kramer, President and Publisher
George Johnson, Vice President
Bina Robinson, North East Representative; Box 26, Swain, NY 14884-0026

INTERNATIONAL ECOTOURISM SOCIETY, THE
733 15 Street NW Suite 1000
Washington, DC 20005 United States
Phone: 202-347-9203   Fax: 202-387-7915
E-mail: ecomail@ecotourism.org
Website: www.ecotourism.org

Founded: 1990
Membership: 1,001–10,000
Scope: Local, State, Regional, National, International
Description: The Ecotourism Society is an international nonprofit membership organization dedicated to finding the resources and building the expertise to make tourism a viable tool for conservation and sustainable development.
Publication(s): Flagship Species: Case Studies in Wildlife Tourism Management, The Business of Ecolodges, Ecotourism: Principles, Practices and Policies for Sustainability, Ecotourism: A Guide for Planners and Managers Volume I&II, Ecolodge Sourcebook for Planners and Developers, Ecotourism Guidelines for Nature Tour Operators
Keyword(s): Development/Developing Countries, Ecosystems (precious), Land Issues, Oceans/Coasts/Beaches, Population, Recreation/Ecotourism, Wildlife & Species
Contact(s):
Megan Wood, President; P.O. Box 668, Burlington, VT 05402; 802-651-9818; Fax: 802-651-9819; ecomail@ecotourism.org
Jeremy Garrett, Membership and Publications Director; 802-651-9818; Fax: 802-651-9819; jeremy@ecotuorism.org
Fergus Maclaren, Director, International Year of Ecotourism; 802-651-9818; Fax: 802-651-9819; fergus@ecotourism.org
Patricia Carrington, Media Relations Manager; 802-651-9818; Fax: 8002-651-9819; patricia@ecotourism.org
Anjanette DeCarlo, Information and Education Specialist; 802-651-9818; Fax: 802-651-9819; anjanette@ecotourism.org
Jessica Staats, Assistant to the President; 802-651-9818; Fax: 802-651-9819; jessica@ecotourism.org

INTERNATIONAL EROSION CONTROL ASSOCIATION (IECA)
P.O. Box 774904
Steamboat Springs, CO 80477 United States
Phone: 970-879-3010 Fax: 970-879-8563
E-mail: ecinfo@ieca.org
Website: www.ieca.org

Founded: 1972
Membership: 1,001–10,000
Scope: International
Description: To provide opportunities for the worldwide exchange of information and economic methods of erosion control.
Publication(s): News To Use, Erosion Control Journal, Proceedings of Annual Conference, Products and Services Directory, Membership Directory
Keyword(s): Agriculture/Farming, Air Quality/Atmosphere, Development/Developing Countries, Forests/Forestry, Land Issues, Oceans/Coasts/Beaches, Water Habitats & Quality
Contact(s):
  Ben Northcutt, Executive Director; ben@ieca.org
  Sheryl Shipley, Member Service Manager; 970-879-3010; ext. 21; Fax: 970-879-8563; sheryl@ieca.org

INTERNATIONAL FUND FOR ANIMAL WELFARE
411 Main St.
Yarmouth Port, MA 02675 United States
Phone: 508-362-4944 Fax: 508-744-2009
E-mail: info@ifaw.org
Website: www.ifaw.org

Founded: 1969
Membership: 100,001–500,000
Scope: International
Description: An International nonprofit, tax-exempt organization in the U.S. dedicated to the protection of wild and domestic animals and their habitats. IFAW's goals are pursued through a strategic plan consisting of three distinct program areas: Commercial Expoitation and Trade of Wild Animals, Animals in Crisis and Distress, and Habitat for Animals.
Contact(s):
  Aczedine Downes, Contact
  Fred O'Regan, Chief Executive Officer

INTERNATIONAL FUND FOR ANIMAL WELFARE
ASIA/PACIFIC
8 Belmore Street
Surry Hills NSW 2010
Sydney, NSW 2010 Australia
Phone: 61-2-9288-4900 Fax: 61-2-9288-4901
E-mail: info-au@ifaw.org
Website: www.ifaw.org

Scope: International
Contact(s):
  Sally Wilson, Contact

INTERNATIONAL FUND FOR ANIMAL WELFARE
EUROPEAN UNION
13 Rue Boduognat B-1000
Brussels, Belgium
Phone: 322-230-9717 Fax: 322-231-0402
Website: www.ifaw.org

Scope: International
Contact(s):
  Stanley Johnson, Contact

INTERNATIONAL FUND FOR ANIMAL WELFARE
FRENCH OFFICE
BP 78 51170
Fismes, France
Phone: 33-326-480-548 Fax: 33-326-481-435
Website: www.ifaw.org

Scope: International
Contact(s):
  Chantal Derty, Contact

INTERNATIONAL FUND FOR ANIMAL WELFARE
GERMAN OFFICE
Postfach 10 46 23 20032
Hamburg, Germany
Phone: 040-866-5000 Fax: 040-866-500-22

Scope: International
Contact(s):
  Tom Martens, Contact

INTERNATIONAL FUND FOR ANIMAL WELFARE
HOLLAND OFFICE
Bezuidenhoutseweg 225
Den Haag
Nederland 2594 AL
Holland, Netherlands
Phone: 31-070-3355011 Fax: 31-070-3850940
E-mail: info-nl@ifaw.org
Website: www.ifaw.org/

Scope: International
Contact(s):
  Jetty Tak, Office Manager

INTERNATIONAL FUND FOR ANIMAL WELFARE
HONG KONG OFFICE
P.O. Box 82 Sai Kung P.O.
Kowloon, Hong Kong

Scope: International
Contact(s):
  Jill Robinson, Contact

INTERNATIONAL FUND FOR ANIMAL WELFARE
ITALIAN OFFICE
Via Bocca di Leone 36-Int 4
Rome, 187 Italy

Scope: International
Contact(s):
  Walter Caporale, Contact

INTERNATIONAL FUND FOR ANIMAL WELFARE
PHILIPPINES OFFICE
14 East Maya
Phil-Am Homes, Quezon City, 1100 Philippines

Soopc: International
Contact(s):
  Mel Alipio, Contact

INTERNATIONAL FUND FOR ANIMAL WELFARE
RUSSIAN OFFICE
19-B Khlebny Pereulok
Moscow, 21099 Russia
Phone: 7-502-933-34-11 Fax: 7-502-933-34-14
Website: www.ifaw.org

Scope: International
Contact(s):
  Masha Vorontsova, Contact

INTERNATIONAL FUND FOR ANIMAL WELFARE
SOUTH AFRICAN OFFICE
P.O. Box 16497
Vlaeberg, 8018, 2128 South Africa
Phone: 27-21-424-2086 Fax: 27-21-424-2727
E-mail: info-za@ifaw.org
Website: www.ifaw.org

Scope: International
Contact(s):
  David Barritt, Contact

INTERNATIONAL FUND FOR ANIMAL WELFARE
UNITED KINGDOM
87-90 Albert Embankment
London, SE1 7UD United Kingdom
Phone: 4-020-7587-6720 Fax: 4-020-7587-6700
E-mail: info-uk@ifaw.org
Website: www.ifaw.org

Scope: International

Contact(s):
Cindy Milburn, Director

INTERNATIONAL GAME FISH ASSOCIATION
300 Gulf Stream Way
Dania Beach, FL 33004 United States
Phone: 954-927-2628 Fax: 954-924-4299
E-mail: igfahq@aol.com
Website: www.igfa.org

Founded: 1939

Scope: International

Description: Nonprofit, tax-deductible organization which maintains and promotes ethical international angling regulations and compiles world game fish records for saltwater, freshwater, and fly fishing. Also represents and informs recreational fishermen regarding research, conservation, and legislative developments related to the sport. Encourages and supports game fish tagging programs and other scientific data collection efforts. More than 250 IGFA international representatives worldwide.

Publication(s): World Record Game Fishes, Rule Book for Freshwater, Saltwater and Fly Fishing, International Angler, The

Keyword(s): Recreation/Ecotourism, Wildlife & Species

Contact(s):
Michael Leech, President
John Anderson, Vice Chairman
Pamela Basco, Treasurer
Michael Levitt, Chairman
Roy Naftzger, Secretary

INTERNATIONAL HUNTER EDUCATION ASSOCIATION
P.O. Box 490
Wellington, CO 80549 United States
Phone: 970-568-7954 Fax: 970-568-7955
E-mail: info@ihea.com
Website: www.ihea.com

Scope: International

Description: To provide leadership and establish standards in the development of hunters to be safe, responsible, knowledgeable, and involved.

Publication(s): Hunter Education Journal, Hunter Education Student Guide

Keyword(s): Recreation/Ecotourism

Contact(s):
Mac Lang, President-Elect
Tim Lawhern, President
David Knotts, IHEA Executive Vice President
Helen McCracken, Vice President of Zone 2
Robert Paddon, Vice President of Zone 1
Keith Snyder, Vice President of Zone 3
Mark Birkhauser, Secretary
Bill Blackwell, Instructor Board Representative
Joe Huggins, Treasurer
Jan Morris, Instructor Board Representative of Zone 3
John Panio, Instructor Board Member
Albert Ross, IHEA Legal Councel
Christopher Tymeson, Instructor Board Representative of Zone 2

INTERNATIONAL INSTITUTE FOR ENERGY CONSERVATION
CERF/IIEC
2131 K Street, NW, Suite 700
Washington, DC 20037 United States
Phone: 202-785-6420 Fax: 202-785-2604
Website: www.cerf.org

Founded: 1984

Scope: International

Description: A nonprofit organization established to accelerate the global adoption of energy-efficiency policies, technologies, and practices to enable economically and ecologically sustainable development.

Publication(s): E-Notes, Global Energy Efficiency Initiative Sustainable Energy Guide, Integrated Transport Management and Development, Opportunities for the U.S. Energy Efficiency Industry in Chile

Keyword(s): Climate Change, Development/Developing Countries, Energy, Transportation

Contact(s):
Russell Sturm, Executive Director and President
Stewart Boyle, Director
Steve Hall, Director
Terry Oliver, Director
John Fox, Chairman of the Board

INTERNATIONAL MARINE MAMMAL PROJECT, THE
EARTH ISLAND INSTITUTE
300 Broadway
Suite 28
San Francisco, CA 94133 United States
Phone: 415-788-3666 Fax: 415-788-7324
Website: www.earthisland.org

Founded: 1982

Scope: International

Description: IMMP is a nonprofit research, education, and monitoring project of Earth Island Institute. IMMP is committed to ending dolphin mortality caused by the U.S. and international tuna industries, stopping the use of driftnets, and promoting sustainable fishing practices. In addition, IMMP aims to halt commercial whaling worldwide and ban live capture and display of marine mammals.

Publication(s): Earth Island Journal, Ocean Alert

Keyword(s): Oceans/Coasts/Beaches, Public Lands/Greenspace, Water Habitats & Quality, Wildlife & Species

Contact(s):
David Phillips, Executive Director

INTERNATIONAL MARITIME ORGANIZATION
4 Albert Embankment
London, SE1 7SR United Kingdom
Phone: 1717357611 Fax: 7178573210
E-mail: info@imo.org
Website: www.imo.org

Founded: 1959

Membership: 101–1,000

Scope: International

Description: To improve maritime safety and to prevent marine pollution from ships, through the adoption of international conventions, protocols, codes, and recommendations.

Keyword(s): Climate Change, Development/Developing Countries, Transportation, Water Habitats & Quality

Contact(s):
William O'Neil, Secretary-General

INTERNATIONAL MIRE CONSERVATION GROUP
Grimmer Strasse 88
Greifswald, D-17487 Germany
Phone: 49-3834-864128   Fax: 49-3834-864114
E-mail: info@imcg.net
Website: www.imcg.net

Founded: 1984
Membership: 101–1,000
Scope: International

Description: The International Mire Conservation Group (IMCG) is an international network of specialists who a. internationally promote, encourage, and co-ordinate the conservation of mires and related ecosystems; and b. internationally enhance the exchange of information and experience relating to mires and factors affecting them. The network encompasses a wide spectrum of expertise and interests, from research scientists to consultants, government agency specialists to peatland site managers.

Publication(s): CA Weber and the Raised Bog of Augstumal, The Wise Use of Mires and Peatlands, IMCG Newsletter

Keyword(s): Climate Change, Development/Developing Countries, Ecosystems (precious), Energy, Ethics/Environmental Justice, Forests/Forestry, Land Issues, Wildlife & Species

Contact(s):
Jan Sliva, Chairman; Technische Universitaet Muenchen, Chair of Vegetation Ecology, Am Hochanger 6, Freising-Weihenstephan, D-85350; 49-8161-713715; Fax: 49-8161-714143; sliva@wzw.tum.de
Hans Joosten, Secretary-General; 49-3834-864128; Fax: 49-3834-864114; joosten@uni-greifswald.de
Philippe Julve, Treasurer; Hermine Recherches sur les Milieux Naturels, 159 rue Sadi Carnot, Armentieres 59280; 33-3-20-358697; Fax: 33-3-20-358697
Stuart Brooks, Executive Committee Member; Scottish Wildlife Trust, Cramond House, Kirk Cramond, Cramond Glebe Road, Edinburgh EH4 6NS; 44-131-3124743; Fax: 44-131-3128705; sbrooks@swt.org.uk
Tatiana Minaeva, Executive Committee Member; Wetlands International Russia Programme, Nikoloyamskaya Ulitsa, 19, strn. 3, Moscow 109240; 7-095-7270939; Fax: 7-095-7270938; tminaeva@wwf.ru

INTERNATIONAL OCEANOGRAPHIC FOUNDATION
University of Miami
Rosenstiel School of Marine & Atmosphere Science
4600 Rickenbacker Causeway, Virginia Key
Miami, FL 33149 United States
Phone: 305-301-4001   Fax: 305-361-4931
Website: www.rsmas.miami.edu/iof/

Founded: 1953
Scope: International

Description: Nonprofit foundation organized to encourage the extension of human knowledge by scientific study and exploration of the oceans in all their aspects and to acquaint and educate the general public concerning the vital role of the oceans to all life on this planet.

Keyword(s): Oceans/Coasts/Beaches, Recreation/Ecotourism, Wildlife & Species

Contact(s):
Edward Foote, President
Otis Brown, Vice President
Luis Glaser, Vice President
David Lieberman, Vice President
Diane Cook, Treasurer
Lourdes Lapaz, Secretary; 400 SE 2nd Ave., 4th Fl., Miami, FL 33131; 305-375-8498; Fax: 305-375-9188

INTERNATIONAL OSPREY FOUNDATION INC., THE
P.O. Box 250
Sanibel, FL 33957 United States
Phone: 941-472-1862

Founded: 1981
Scope: International

Description: A nonprofit organization dedicated to studying the problem of restoring osprey numbers to a stable population, making recommendations to enhance the continued survival of the osprey and initiating educational programs. Yearly grant of up to $1000.00 given for graduate work. Work relating to all raptors is acceptable, but osprey study is given priority.

Publication(s): TIOF Newsletter
Keyword(s): Wildlife & Species

Contact(s):
Tim Gardner, President
Anne Mitchell, Vice President
Inge Glissman, Secretary and Treasurer

INTERNATIONAL PLANT PROPAGATORS SOCIETY, INC.
Washington Park Arboretum, 2300 Arboretum Dr.
Seattle, WA 98112 United States
Phone: 206-543-8602   Fax: 206-325-8893
E-mail: ippsint@aol.com
Website: www.ipps.org

Founded: 1950
Membership: 1,001–10,000
Scope: International

Description: The Society was founded to seek and share information on plant propagation. The Society has nine regional chapters, three in USA and Canada, Australia, New Zealand, Great Britain and Ireland, Scandinavia, Japan and Southern Africa and holds area meetings in Latin America.

Publication(s): Annual Proceedings of all regional meetings, regional newsletters of meetings for members

Keyword(s): Agriculture/Farming, Forests/Forestry, Reduce/Reuse/Recycle, Wildlife & Species

Contact(s):
John Wott, Executive Secretary and Treasurer

INTERNATIONAL PRIMATE PROTECTION LEAGUE
P.O. Box 766
Summerville, SC 29484 United States
Phone: 843-871-2280   Fax: 843-871-7988
E-mail: info@ippl.org
Website: www.ippl.org/

Founded: 1973
Membership: 10,001–100,000
Scope: International

Description: A nonprofit international organization devoted to the conservation and protection of nonhuman primates. There are branches in the United States and United Kingdom, and field representatives in 32 countries.

Publication(s): International Primate Protection League News
Keyword(s): Forests/Forestry, Wildlife & Species

Contact(s):
Shirley McGreal, Chairwoman
Marjorie Doggett, Secretary
Diane Walters, Treasurer

INTERNATIONAL PROFESSIONAL HUNTERS' ASSOCIATION
P. O. Box 702
Irene, 0062 South Africa
Phone: 27-12-663-7226   Fax: 27-12-663-7228
E-mail: ipha@yebo.co.za

Founded: 1969
Membership: 101–1,000
Scope: International
Description: It is the mission of the International Professional Hunters' Association (IPHA) and its worldwide members to advise, educate and facilitate public enjoyment of the natural world. IPHA embraces sound conservation practices, sustained utilization of renewable resources and ethical hunting practices. IPHA is pledged by its bylaws to insure the highest level of professionalism and integrity to the benefit of recreational sports hunters and outdoor enthusiasts around the world

INTERNATIONAL RIVERS NETWORK (IRN)
1847 Berkeley Way
Berkeley, CA 94703 United States
Phone: 510-848-1155 Fax: 510-848-1008
E-mail: irn@irn.org
Website: www.irn.org

Founded: 1986
Scope: International
Description: IRN supports local communities working to protect their rivers and watersheds. We work to halt destructive river development projects and encourage equitable and sustainable methods of meeting needs for water, energy and flood management. Members include environmentalists, engineers, hydrologists, human rights activists, and academics who are committed to the study and defense of rivers and riverine communities.
Publication(s): World Rivers Review, working papers, action alerts, special briefings
Keyword(s): Development/Developing Countries, Water Habitats & Quality
Contact(s):
Annie Ducmanis, Assistant to Executive Director; ext. 329; annie@irn.org
Juliette Majot, Executive Director; ext. 305; juliette@irn.org
Patrick McCully, Campaign Director; ext. 309; patrick@irn.org
Yvonne Cuellar, Library Coordinator
Lori Pottinger, Africa Campaigns & Editor; ext. 306; lori@irn.org
Glenn Switkes, South America Campaigns; glenn@altanet.com.br

INTERNATIONAL SNOW LEOPARD TRUST
4649 Sunnyside Ave., N., Suite 325
Seattle, WA 98103 United States
Phone: 206-632-2421 Fax: 206-632-3967
E-mail: info@snowleopard.org
Website: www.snowleopard.org

Founded: 1981
Membership: 1,001–10,000
Scope: International
Description: A nonprofit organization dedicated to the conservation of the endangered snow leopard and its mountain habitat through a balanced approach that considers the needs of the local people and the environment; and provides workshops, field training, equipment, publications, conservation education programs, and a centralized database for organizing and disseminating information.
Publication(s): Snow Leopard News
Keyword(s): Wildlife & Species
Contact(s):
Charlie Morse, President
Lewis Macfarlane, Vice President
Tom McCarthy, Conservation Director; tmccarthy@snowleopard.org
Brad Rutherford, Executive Director; brad@snowleopard.org
Peter Graham, Intern; 206-632-2421; peter@snowleopard.org
Owen Rogers, Program Assistant; 206-632-2421; owen@snowleopard.org
Priscilla Allen, Conservation Program Officer; 206-632-2421; priscilla@snowleopard.org
Helen Freeman, Founder
Steven Kearsley, Treasurer

INTERNATIONAL SOCIETY FOR ECOLOGICAL ECONOMICS (ISEE)
1313 Dolley Madison Blvd., Suite 402
McLean, VA 22101 United States
Phone: 703-790-1745 Fax: 703-790-2672
E-mail: isee@igc.com
Website: www.ecologicaleconomics.org

Founded: 1988
Scope: International
Description: ISEE actively encourages the integration of the study and the management of ecology and economics in order to achieve an ecologically and economically sustainable world.
Publication(s): Ecological Economics
Keyword(s): Development/Developing Countries, Wildlife & Species
Contact(s):
Richard Norgarrd, President of Board of Directors

INTERNATIONAL SOCIETY FOR ENDANGERED CATS
ISEC CANADA
124 Lynnbrook Road SE
Calgary, T2C 1S6 Alberta Canada
Phone: 800-465-6384 Fax: 403-279-3304
E-mail: isec@wildcatconservation.org
Website: www.wildcatconservation.org

Founded: 1989
Membership: 101–1,000
Scope: International
Description: Working to conserve the small wild cats of the world and their habitat.
Publication(s): Feline Fans, Cat Times, Resource Library
Keyword(s): Development/Developing Countries, Wildlife & Species

INTERNATIONAL SOCIETY FOR ENDANGERED CATS (ISEC)
3070 Riverside Dr., Suite 160
Columbus, OH 43221 United States
Phone: 614-487-8760 Fax: 614-487-8769
E-mail: education@isec.org
Website: www.isec.org

Founded: 1988
Scope: International
Description: ISEC's purpose is to raise awareness of the plight of endangered wild cats, and thereby prevent their extinction. ISEC offers conservation education programs, collects and disseminates information about wild cats, and supports specific conservation projects around the world.
Publication(s): Cat Tales
Keyword(s): Wildlife & Species
Contact(s):
Bill Simpson, President; 3070 Riverside Dr., Suite 160, Columbus, OH 43221
Patricia Currie, Executive Director; 196 W. Central, Delaware, OH 43015; 740-369-9794

INTERNATIONAL SOCIETY FOR ENVIRONMENTAL ETHICS
Department of Philosophy, University of Windsor
Windsor, N9B 3P4 Ontario Canada
Phone: 519-253-3000 Fax: 519-971-3610
E-mail: philos@uwindsor.ca
Website: www.cep.unt.edu/isEE.html

Founded: 1990
Scope: International
Description: The International Society for Environmental Ethics' main purpose is to promote the critical analysis of ethical issues related to the natural environment, to further and support philosophical and scientific meetings and conferences nationally and internationally, and to provide material and media aids suitable for teaching environmental philosophy and environmental ethics.
Publication(s): International Society for Environmental Ethics Newsletter
Contact(s):
  Mark Sagoff, President; Director of Institute for Philosophy and Public Policy, University of Maryland, Baltimore, MD 20742
  J. Callicott, Vice President; Philosophy Department, University of Wisconsin at Stevens Point, Stevens Point, WI 54481
  Edward Hettinger, Treasurer; College of Charleston, Charleston, SC 29424
  Laura Westra, Secretary; University of Windsor, Windsor, Ontario N9B 3P4; 519-253-4232

INTERNATIONAL SOCIETY FOR THE PRESERVATION OF THE TROPICAL RAINFOREST, THE
3931 Camino De La Cumbre
Sherman Oaks, CA 91423 United States
Phone: 818-788-2002   Fax: 818-990-3333
E-mail: rain.forest@earthlink.net
Founded: 1984
Membership: 1,001–10,000
Scope: International
Description: The International Society for the Preservation of the Tropical Rainforest is dedicated to the global conservation of tropical forest resources through the promotion of park implementation, sustainable agriculture, and timber harvesting.
Publication(s): Tropical Rainforest Our Most Valuable and Endangered Habitat with a Blueprint for Its Survival Into The Third Millennium
Keyword(s): Climate Change, Ethics/Environmental Justice, Land Issues, Wildlife & Species
Contact(s):
  Edward Asner, Co-Director; 3931 Camino De La Cumbre, Sherman Oaks, CA 91423; 818-788-2002
  Roxanne Kremer, Co-Director; 3931 Camino De La Cumbre, Sherman Oaks, CA 91423; 626-572-0233; Fax: 6265729521
  Arnold Newman, Co-Director; 3931 Camino De La Cumbre, Sherman Oaks, CA 91423; 818-788-2002

INTERNATIONAL SOCIETY OF ARBORICULTURE
P.O. Box 3129
Champaign, IL 61826-3129 United States
Phone: 217-355-9411   Fax: 217-355-9516
E-mail: isa@isa-arbor.com
Website: www.isa-arbor.com
Founded: 1924
Membership: 10,001–100,000
Scope: International
Description: Through research, technology, and education promote the professional practice of arboriculture and foster a greater public awareness of the benefits of trees.
Publication(s): Journal of Arboriculture, "Arborist Certificate Guide", publication listings to include "A Photographic Guide for Evaluation of Hazard Trees in Urban Areas", Valuation of Landscape Trees, Shrubs, and Other Plants, Arborist News
Contact(s):
  Kim Coder, President
  Michael Neal, President-Elect
  Harvey Holt, Vice President
  Melinda Jones, Vice President
  Lauren Lanphear, Vice President
  Paul Harter, Executive Director
  Peggy Currid, Managing Editor
  Bailey Hudson, President-Elect
  Robert Miller, Editor

INTERNATIONAL SOCIETY OF TROPICAL FORESTERS, INC.
5400 Grosvenor Ln.
Bethesda, MD 20814 United States
Phone: 301-897-8720   Fax: 301-897-3690
E-mail: istf.bethesda@verizon.net
Website: www.istf-bethesda.org
Founded: 1950
Membership: 1,001–10,000
Scope: International
Description: A nonprofit organization founded with the objective of providing an information exchange for members involved in the management, protection, and wise use of tropical forests.
Publication(s): ISTF News, ISTF Notices (Spanish)
Keyword(s): Forests/Forestry, Reduce/Reuse/Recycle, Wildlife & Species
Contact(s):
  Warren Doolittle, President; USA,
  Napoleon Vergara, Vice President & Director of Asia & Philippines
  Jeffery Burley, Director At Large; United Kingdom
  John Fox, Director At Large; Australia
  Chun K. Lai, Director At Large; Philippines
  Rodolfo Salazar, Director of Latin America; Costa Rica
  B. Taal, Director of Africa; Gambia
  Napoleon Vergara, Director of Asia; Philippines
  Patricia Heaton Holmgren, Office Manager
  Frank Wadsworth, Editor

INTERNATIONAL SONORAN DESERT ALLIANCE
201 Esperanza Ave.
P.O.Box 687
Ajo, AZ 85321 United States
Phone: 520-387-6823   Fax: 520-387-5626
E-mail: alianza@tabletoptelephone.com
Website: www.isdanet.org
Founded: 1992
Membership: 1,001–10,000
Scope: International
Description: The purpose of the International Sonoran Desert Alliance is to promote environmentally sustainable and culturally sound economic development while protecting the natural and tri cultural heritage of the western Sonoran Desert.
Keyword(s): Development/Developing Countries, Ethics/Environmental Justice, Land Issues
Contact(s):
  Carlos Nagel, President; closfree@aol.com
  Manuel Gonzalez, Vice President
  Reynaldo Cantu, Executive Director
  Isabel Granillo, Secretary; isabel@laruta.org
  Sue Tout, Treasurer

INTERNATIONAL UNION FOR CONSERVATION OF NATURE AND NATURAL RESOURCES (IUCN) THE WORLD CONSERVATION UNION
HEADQUARTERS
Rue Mauverney 28, CH-1196
Gland, Switzerland
Phone: 41 22 999 001
Website: www.iucn.org
Founded: 1948
Scope: International
Description: An independent body to promote scientifically-based action for the conservation of nature and to ensure that

development is sustainable and provides a lasting improvement in the quality of life for people all over the world. Eight hundred eighty voting members in 138 countries; 73 states, 107 government agencies, and 623 non-governmental organizations. Also 35 non-voting affiliate members. Maintains a global network of more than 6,000 scientists and professionals organized into six commissions

Keyword(s): Development/Developing Countries, Reduce/Reuse/Recycle

Contact(s):
Yolanda Kakabadse, President
Patrick Dugan, Director of Global Programme, Switzerland
Maria Iuri, Director of Finance
Marietta Koch-Weser, Director General, Germany
Jeffrey McNeely, Director of Biodiversity Policy Coordination Division
David Brackett, Chairman for Species Survival Commission
Tariq Bunuri, Chairman of Commission on Environmental Economic and Social Justice
Claes De Dardel, Treasurer
Fritz Hesselink, Chairman of Commission on Education and Communication
Yolanda Kakabadse, Chairman of the Bureau, Ecuador
Edward Maltby, Chairman of Commission on Ecosystem Management, United Kingdom
Adrian Phillips, Chairman of Commission on Protected Areas
Nicholas Robinson, Chairman of Commission on Environmental Law

INTERNATIONAL UNION FOR CONSERVATION OF NATURE AND NATURAL RESOURCES (IUCN) THE WORLD CONSERVATION UNION
BANGLADESH COUNTRY OFFICE
House #3 A, Road 15, Dhanmondi, RIA 1205
Dhaka, 1207 Bangladesh
Phone: 880 2 8122577   Fax: 880 2 8126209
E-mail: iucnbd@citechco.net

Scope: International

Contact(s):
Anwarul Islam, Head

INTERNATIONAL UNION FOR CONSERVATION OF NATURE AND NATURAL RESOURCES (IUCN) THE WORLD CONSERVATION UNION
BOTSWANA COUNTRY OFFICE
Plot 2403 Hospital Way, Extension 9, Private Bag 00300
Gaborone, Botswana
Phone: 267 371 584   Fax: 267 371 584
E-mail: iucn@iucnbot.bw

Scope: International

Contact(s):
Ruud Jansen, Country Representative

INTERNATIONAL UNION FOR CONSERVATION OF NATURE AND NATURAL RESOURCES (IUCN) THE WORLD CONSERVATION UNION
BURKINA COUNTRY FASO OFFICE
01 BP 3133
Ouagadougou, 01 Burkina Faso
Phone: 226-307-047   Fax: 226-308-580
E-mail: uicnbrao@fasonet.bf

Scope: International

Contact(s):
Michel Kouda, Country Representative

INTERNATIONAL UNION FOR CONSERVATION OF NATURE AND NATURAL RESOURCES (IUCN) THE WORLD CONSERVATION UNION
CANADA OFFICE
555 René-Lévesque Blvd. W., Office 500
Montréal, Québec, H2Y 3X7, H2Z 1B1 Quebec Canada
Phone: 514-287-9704, ext. 357   Fax: 514-287-9687
E-mail: poste@iucn.ca
Website: www.iucn.ca

Founded: 1948
Membership: 101–1,000
Scope: International

Description: Canada Office of IUCN - The World Conservation Union

Keyword(s): Agriculture/Farming, Climate Change, Development/Developing Countries, Ecosystems (precious), Forests/Forestry, Land Issues, Oceans/Coasts/Beaches, Water Habitats & Quality

Contact(s):
Andrew Deutz, Head; 287-9704; ext. 355; Fax: 287-9687; adeutz@iucn.ca
Micheline Legault-Alaurent, Office Manager; 287-9704; ext. 353; Fax: 287-9687; mil@iucn.ca
Thérèse Beaudet, Programme Officer; 287-9704; ext. 354; Fax: 287-9687; beaudet@iucn.ca
Danielle Cantin, Project Officer; 287-9704; ext. 358; Fax: 287-9687; dcantin@iucn.ca
Chris Morry, Programme Officer; 287-9704; ext. 357; Fax: 287-9687; cmorry@iucn.ca
Elizabeth Pelletier, Project Assistant; 287-9704; ext. 356; Fax: 287-9687; epelletier@iucn.ca

INTERNATIONAL UNION FOR CONSERVATION OF NATURE AND NATURAL RESOURCES (IUCN) THE WORLD CONSERVATION UNION
ENVIRONMENTAL LAW CENTRE
Godesbergerallee 108-112
Bonn, 53175 Germany
Phone: 49-228-2692-231   Fax: 49-228-2692-250
E-mail: secretariat@elc.iucn.org
Website: www.iucn.org/themes/law

Founded: 1970
Scope: International

Description: The IUCN Environmental Law Centre serves as secretariat to the IUCN Commission on Environmental Law dealing with emerging issues in international and national environmental law. The Centre houses a large library on environmental law and policy literature.

Keyword(s): Air Quality/Atmosphere, Climate Change, Development/Developing Countries, Ecosystems (precious), Energy, Ethics/Environmental Justice, Forests/Forestry, Land Issues, Oceans/Coasts/Beaches, Wildlife & Species

Contact(s):
John Scanlon, Head

INTERNATIONAL UNION FOR CONSERVATION OF NATURE AND NATURAL RESOURCES (IUCN) THE WORLD CONSERVATION UNION
GUINEA-BISSAU COUNTRY OFFICE
Apartado 23, 1031
Bissau, Guinea Bissau
Phone: 245 201 230/245 203 264   Fax: 245 201 168
E-mail: uicn.bi@sol.gtelecom.gw

Scope: International

Contact(s):
Nelson Dias, Chef de Mission

INTERNATIONAL UNION FOR CONSERVATION OF NATURE AND NATURAL RESOURCES (IUCN) THE WORLD CONSERVATION UNION
IUCN BEIRA PROJECT OFFICE
MOZAMBIQUE COUNTRY OFFICE
635 Eduardo Mondlane Ave.
P.O. Box 4770 - Maputo
Beira, Mozambique
Phone: 258 3323 807   Fax: 258 3322 957
E-mail: uicn@sortmoz.com
Scope: International
Contact(s):
  Ebenizario Chonguica, Country Representative

INTERNATIONAL UNION FOR CONSERVATION OF NATURE AND NATURAL RESOURCES (IUCN) THE WORLD CONSERVATION UNION
LAO PEOPLE'S DEMOCRATIC REPUBLIC COUNTRY OFFICE
P.O. Box 4340, 15 Fa Ngum Rd.
Vientiane, Laos
Phone: 856 21 216 401   Fax: 856 21 216 127
E-mail: iucnlao@loxlnfo.co.th
Scope: International
Contact(s):
  Stuart Chape, Country Representative

INTERNATIONAL UNION FOR CONSERVATION OF NATURE AND NATURAL RESOURCES (IUCN) THE WORLD CONSERVATION UNION
MALI COUNTRY OFFICE
BP 1567
Bamako, Mali
Phone: 223 227 572   Fax: 223 230 092
E-mail: uicn@spider.toolnet.org
Scope: International
Contact(s):
  Moctar Traore, Chef de Mission

INTERNATIONAL UNION FOR CONSERVATION OF NATURE AND NATURAL RESOURCES (IUCN) THE WORLD CONSERVATION UNION
NEPAL COUNTRY OFFICE
P.O. Box 3923, Lalitpur
Kathmandu, Nepal
Phone: 977-1 52876   Fax: 977- 536786
E-mail: info@iucn.org.np
Website: www.iucn.org/places/Nepal
Founded: 1948
Scope: International
Description: The main purpose for IUCN's activities in Nepal is to strengthen Institutional capacity for conservation and sustainable use of natural resources in Nepal. IUCN will use its comparative advantage to transfer to Nepalese organizations relevant information, management tools, and essential skills to strengthen their capacity to manage natural resources. This is in line with IUCN's overall mission.
Contact(s):
  Ambika Adhikari, Country Representative

INTERNATIONAL UNION FOR CONSERVATION OF NATURE AND NATURAL RESOURCES (IUCN) THE WORLD CONSERVATION UNION
NIGER COUNTRY OFFICE
BP 10933
Niamey, Niger
Phone: 227 724 028   Fax: 227 724 005
E-mail: iucn@intnet.ne
Scope: International
Contact(s):
  M. Mamane, Country Representative

INTERNATIONAL UNION FOR CONSERVATION OF NATURE AND NATURAL RESOURCES (IUCN) THE WORLD CONSERVATION UNION
PAKISTAN COUNTRY OFFICE
1 Bath Island Rd.
Karachi, 75530 Pakistan
Phone: 92 21 586 1543   Fax: 92 21 587 0287
E-mail: amk@iucn.khi.sdnpk.undp.org
Scope: International
Contact(s):
  Aban Kabraji, Country Representative

INTERNATIONAL UNION FOR CONSERVATION OF NATURE AND NATURAL RESOURCES (IUCN) THE WORLD CONSERVATION UNION
REGIONAL OFFICE FOR CENTRAL AFRICA
B.P. 5506, c/o IUCN Project Office DHA
Yaounde, Cameroon
Phone: 237-221-6496   Fax: 237-221-6497
E-mail: pwl@iccnct.com
Scope: International
Contact(s):
  Assitou Ndinga, Coordinator for Central Africa

INTERNATIONAL UNION FOR CONSERVATION OF NATURE AND NATURAL RESOURCES (IUCN) THE WORLD CONSERVATION UNION
REGIONAL OFFICE FOR EASTERN AFRICA
P.O. Box 68200, Mukoma Rd.
Langata, Nairobi, Kenya
Phone: 254 2890 605   Fax: 254 2890 615
E-mail: emt@iucrearo.org
Scope: International
Contact(s):
  Eldad Tukahirwa, Regional Representative

INTERNATIONAL UNION FOR CONSERVATION OF NATURE AND NATURAL RESOURCES (IUCN) THE WORLD CONSERVATION UNION
REGIONAL OFFICE FOR EUROPE
Rue Vergot, 15
Brussels, 1030 Belgium
Phone: 0032-2-7328299   Fax: 0032-2-7320400
E-mail: europe@iucn.org
Website: www.iucn-ero.nl
Membership: 101–1,000
Scope: International
Description: To contribute to a sustainable Europe by influencing policy development and implementation for biodiversity and landscape conservation, restoration and sustainable use inside and outside Europe.
Keyword(s): Agriculture/Farming, Ecosystems (precious), Forests/Forestry, Wildlife & Species
Contact(s):
  Tamas Marghescu, Regional Director
  Edina Biro, Project Operations Officer
  Pien Zalen, Office Manager
  Jean-Claude Jacques, Senior Officer

INTERNATIONAL UNION FOR CONSERVATION OF NATURE AND NATURAL RESOURCES (IUCN) THE WORLD CONSERVATION UNION
REGIONAL OFFICE FOR MESOAMERICA
Apartado 0146-2150
Moravia, San Jose, 2150 Costa Rica
Phone: 001 506 241 0101   Fax: 001 506 240 9934
E-mail: correo@orma.iucn.org
Website: www.iucn.org//places/orma

Founded: 1989
Membership: 1–100
Scope: International
Description: Conservation and Sustainable Development
Contact(s):
    Enrique Lahmann, Regional Director

INTERNATIONAL UNION FOR CONSERVATION OF NATURE AND NATURAL RESOURCES (IUCN) THE WORLD CONSERVATION UNION
REGIONAL OFFICE FOR SOUTH AMERICA
Casilla Postal 17-17-626
Avenida Atahualpa 955
y Republica Edificio Digicom Piso 4
Quito, Ecuador
Phone: 593 2466 622/623   Fax: 593 2466 624
E-mail: samerica@iucnsur.satnet.net

Scope: International
Contact(s):
    Roberto Franco, Regional Representative

INTERNATIONAL UNION FOR CONSERVATION OF NATURE AND NATURAL RESOURCES (IUCN) THE WORLD CONSERVATION UNION
REGIONAL OFFICE FOR SOUTHERN AFRICA (ROSA)
P.O. Box 745
Harare, Zimbabwe
Phone: 263 4728 266   Fax: 263 4720 738
E-mail: postmaster@iucnrosa.org.zw

Scope: International
Contact(s):
    Yemi Katerere, Regional Representative

INTERNATIONAL UNION FOR CONSERVATION OF NATURE AND NATURAL RESOURCES (IUCN) THE WORLD CONSERVATION UNION
REGIONAL OFFICE FOR WEST AFRICA
BP 1618
Ouagadougou, 1 Burkina Faso
Phone: 226 307 047   Fax: 226 307 561

Scope: International
Contact(s):
    Ibrahim Thiaw, Regional Representative

INTERNATIONAL UNION FOR CONSERVATION OF NATURE AND NATURAL RESOURCES (IUCN) THE WORLD CONSERVATION UNION
REGIONAL OFFICE OF SOUTH AND SOUTHEAST ASIA
P.O. Box 4, 302 Outreach Bldg., AIT
Klong Luang, Pathumthani, 12120 Thailand
Phone: 662-524-6745   Fax: 662-524-5392

Scope: International
Contact(s):
    Mohammed Hussain, Head

INTERNATIONAL UNION FOR CONSERVATION OF NATURE AND NATURAL RESOURCES (IUCN) THE WORLD CONSERVATION UNION
SENEGAL COUNTRY OFFICE
BP 3215 Ave. Bourguiba x rue 3
Castors, Dakar, Senegal
Phone: 221 824 0545   Fax: 221 824 9246

Scope: International
Contact(s):
    Abdoulaye Kane, Chef de Mission

INTERNATIONAL UNION FOR CONSERVATION OF NATURE AND NATURAL RESOURCES (IUCN) THE WORLD CONSERVATION UNION
SOUTH AFRICA COUNTRY OFFICE
P.O. Box 11536
Hatfield, Pretoria, 28 South Africa
Phone: 27 12 420 4116   Fax: 27 12 420 3917

Scope: International
Contact(s):
    Saliem Fakir

INTERNATIONAL UNION FOR CONSERVATION OF NATURE AND NATURAL RESOURCES (IUCN) THE WORLD CONSERVATION UNION
SRI LANKA COUNTRY OFFICE
48 Vajira Ln.
Colombo, 5 Sri Lanka
Phone: 941 580 202   Fax: 941 580 202
E-mail: twcus@sri.lanka.net

Scope: International
Contact(s):
    Shiranee Yasaratne, Country Representative

INTERNATIONAL UNION FOR CONSERVATION OF NATURE AND NATURAL RESOURCES (IUCN) THE WORLD CONSERVATION UNION
SUBREGIONAL OFFICE FOR CENTRAL EUROPE
U1 Narbutta 40/21
Warsaw, 02-541 Poland
Phone: 48 22 881 0552 (53)   Fax: 48 22 881 0554
E-mail: iucr@iucr-ce.org.pl

Scope: International
Contact(s):
    Zenon Tederko, Head

INTERNATIONAL UNION FOR CONSERVATION OF NATURE AND NATURAL RESOURCES (IUCN) THE WORLD CONSERVATION UNION
SUBREGIONAL OFFICE FOR THE COMMONWEALTH OF INDEPENDENT STATES
P.O. Box 265
Moscow, 1254755 Russia
Phone: 7095 190 7077   Fax: 7095 490 5878

Scope: International
Contact(s):
    Vladimir Moshkalo, Head

INTERNATIONAL UNION FOR CONSERVATION OF NATURE AND NATURAL RESOURCES (IUCN) THE WORLD CONSERVATION UNION
UGANDA COUNTRY OFFICE
P.O. Box 10950, Plot 39 Acacia Ave.
Kampala, Uganda
Phone: 256 41 344 508   Fax: 256 41 342 298

Contact(s):
    Alex Muhweezi, Country Representative

INTERNATIONAL UNION FOR CONSERVATION OF NATURE AND NATURAL RESOURCES (IUCN) THE WORLD CONSERVATION UNION
UNITED STATES OFFICE, WASHINGTON, DC
1630 Connecticut Ave., NW
Washington, DC 20009 United States
Phone: 202-387-4826   Fax: 202-387-4823
E-mail: postmaster@iucnus.org
Website: www.iucn.org
Membership: 1–100
Scope: International
Publication(s): Amman 2000, Life At The Edge, Tooth & Law-newsletter

INTERNATIONAL UNION FOR CONSERVATION OF NATURE AND NATURAL RESOURCES (IUCN) THE WORLD CONSERVATION UNION
VIETNAM COUNTRY OFFICE
P.O. Box 60, International Post Office, 13, Tran Hung Dao
8 Chuong Duong Do
Hanoi, Vietnam
Phone: 844 9320 970   Fax: 844 9320 996
E-mail: ntfp.project@hn.vnn.vn
Scope: International
Contact(s):
Nguyen Thong, Country Representative

INTERNATIONAL UNION FOR CONSERVATION OF NATURE AND NATURAL RESOURCES (IUCN) THE WORLD CONSERVATION UNION
ZAMBIA COUNTRY OFFICE
Asco Bldg., Private Bag W, 356 Luanshya Rd., Plot No 5116
Lusaka, Zambia
Phone: 260 1231 866   Fax: 260 1231 867
Scope: International
Contact(s):
Sally Mulala, Country Representative

INTERNATIONAL WILD WATERFOWL ASSOCIATION
10114 54th Place N.E.
Everett WA 98205
Website: www.wildwaterfowl.org
Founded: 1958
Scope: International
Description: Works toward protection, conservation, and reproduction of any species of wild waterfowl considered in danger of eventual extinction; encourages breeding of well known and rare species in captivity. Established Avicultural Hall of Fame. Sponsors annual conference and gives grants in field.
Publication(s): IWWA Newsletter
Keyword(s): Wildlife & Species
Contact(s):
Walter Sturgeon, President; 7 James Farm, Durham, NH 03824; 603-659-5442
Edward Asper, 1st Vice President; Vice President of Sea World, 7007 Sea World Dr., Orlando, FL 32821; 407-351-3600
Paul Dye, 2nd Vice President; 10114 54th Pl. NE, Everett, WA 98205; 425-334-8223; Fax: 425-397-8136; dye@greatnorthern.net
Nancy Collins, Secretary; 5614 River Styx Rd., Medina, OH 44256; 330-725-8782
William Lowe, Treasurer; 3010 Shady Ln., Billings, MT 59102; 406-245-6119

INTERNATIONAL WILDLIFE COALITION (IWC) AND THE WHALE ADOPTION PROJECT
70 E. Falmouth Highway
E. Falmouth, MA 2536 United States
Phone: 508-548-8328   Fax: 508-548-8542
Website: www.iwc.org
Founded: 1984
Scope: International
Description: IWC is a nonprofit, tax-exempt organization dedicated to preserving wildlife and their habitats. As an internationally recognized non-governmental organization, IWC's achievements have been accomplished through grassroots advocacy, activism, research, and education efforts. IWC's Whale Adoption Project protects and researches marine mammals.
Publication(s): WhaleWatch, Wildlife and You and What You Can Do To Help, Whales of the World Teacher's Kit, Wildlife Watch
Keyword(s): Wildlife & Species
Contact(s):
Daniel Morast, President; 70 E. Falmouth Highway, E. Falmouth, MA 02536; 508-548-8328; Fax: 508-548-8542; dmorast@iwc.org
Ronald Orenstein, Canada Project Director; 130 Adelaide St. West, Suite 1940, Toronto, Ontario M5H 3P5; 905-820-7886; Fax: 905-569-0116; ornstn@inforamp.net
Charles Wartenberg, United Kingdom Director; 141A, High St., Edenbridge, Kent TN8 5AX
Jose Palazzo, Brazil Project Coordinator; P.O. Box 5087, Florianopolis, SC 88040; brazilian_wildlife@zaz.com.br

INTERNATIONAL WILDLIFE REHABILITATION COUNCIL
IWRC
829 Bancroft Way
Berkeley, CA 94710 United States
Phone: 707-864-1761   Fax: 707-864-3106
E-mail: info@iwrc-online.org
Website: www.iwrc-online.org
Founded: 1972
Membership: 1,001–10,000
Scope: International
Description: An organization dedicated to conserving and protecting wildlife and habitat through wildlife rehabilitation
Publication(s): Journal of Wildlife Rehabilitation, IWRC Literature Catalog, other publications and catalog available.
Keyword(s): Wildlife & Species
Contact(s):
Edward Clark, President
Penny Elliston, Vice President
Lee Theisen-Watt, Secretary
Dody Wyman, Treasurer

INTERNATIONAL WOLF CENTER
1396 Highway 169
Ely, MN 55731 United States
Phone: 218-365-4695   Fax: 218-365-3318
E-mail: wolfinfo@wolf.org
Website: www.wolf.org
Founded: 1985
Membership: 1,001–10,000
Scope: International
Description: The International Wolf Center advances the survival of wolf populations by teaching about wolves, their relationship to wild lands and the human role in their future.
Publication(s): International Wolf Magazine, various educational pamphlets, Guidelines for Gray Wolf Management
Keyword(s): Wildlife & Species

Contact(s):
    Walter Medwid, Executive Director; 3300 Bass Lake Road, Suite 202, Minneapolis, MN 55429; 763-560-7374; Fax: 763-560-7368; wmedwid@wolf.org
    Gretchen Diessner, Assistant Director; 218-365-4695; ext. 23; Fax: 218-365-3318; asstdir@wolf.org
    Nancy Schwartz, Museum Retail Manager; 218-365-4695; Fax: 218-365-3318; wolfden@wolf.org

INTERNATIONAL WOLF CENTER
ADMINISTRATIVE OFFICES
OUTREACH EDUCATION
3300 Bass Lake Road
Suite 202
Minneapolis, MN 55429 United States
Phone: 763-560-7374   Fax: 763-560-7368
E-mail: wolfinfo@wolf.org
Website: www.wolf.org

Founded: 1985
Membership: 1,001–10,000
Scope: International
Description: The International Wolf Center advances the survival of wolf populations by teaching about wolves, their relationship to wild lands and the human role in their future.
Publication(s): International Wolf
Contact(s):
    George Knotek, Development Director; 3300 Bass Lake Rd., Suite 202, Minneapolis, MN 55429; 763-560-7374; Fax: 763-560-7368; develop@wolf.org
    Walter Medwid, Executive Director; 3300 Bass Lake Rd., Suite 202, Minneapolis, MN 55429; 763-560-7374; Fax: 763-560-7368
    Mary Ortiz, Marketing & Communications Director; 3300 Bass Lake Road, Suite 202, Minneapolis, MN 55429; 763-560-7374; Fax: 763-560-7368; comdir@wolf.org
    Anne Koenke, Outreach Educator; 763-560-7374; ext. 224; Fax: 763-560-7368; outreach@wolf.org

INTERPRETATION CANADA
c/o Kerry Wood Nature Centre, 6300-45 Ave.
Red Deer, T4N 3M4 Alberta Canada
Phone: 604-737-7008   Fax: 604-648-8757
E-mail: membership@interpcan.ca
Website: www.interpcan.ca

Founded: 1973
Membership: 101–1,000
Scope: National
Description: Interpretation Canada is dedicated to raising public awareness, understanding, and appreciation for Canada's natural and cultural heritage, provides training, networking, and advocacy for interpretors, and promotes the role of interpretation in fields such as conservation, education, recreation, and tourism.
Publication(s): Interpscan - national journal, annual membership directory, regional newsletters from Northwest Territories, British Columbia, Alberta, Ontario, and Atlantic region

INTERTRIBAL BISON COOPERATIVE (ITBC)
1560 Concourse Drive
Rapid City, SD 57703 United States
Phone: 605-394-9730   Fax: 605-394-7742
E-mail: itbc@enetis.net
Website: www.intertribalbison.org

Founded: 1992
Membership: 1–100
Scope: National
Description: Native American Cooperative made up of federally recognized tribes, whose mission is to restore bison to Native lands.
Publication(s): Buffalo Tracks
Keyword(s): Development/Developing Countries, Ecosystems (precious), Wildlife & Species

IOWA ACADEMY OF SCIENCE
University of Northern Iowa
175 Baker Hall
Cedar Falls, IA 50614-0508 United States
Phone: 319-273-2021   Fax: 319-273-2807
Website: www.iacad.org

Founded: 1875
Membership: 101–1,000
Scope: State
Description: The Iowa Academy of Science is established to further scientific research and its dissemination, education in the sciences, public understanding of science, and recognition of excellence in these endeavors.
Publication(s): IAS Bulletin, Journal of the Iowa Academy of Science, Iowa Science Teachers Newsletter

IOWA ASSOCIATION OF NATURALISTS
CONSERVATION EDUCATION CENTER
2473 160th Rd.
Guthrie Center, IA 50115 United States
Phone: 641-747-8383   Fax: 641-747-3951
E-mail: ajay.winter@dnr.state.ia.us
Website: www.ianpage.20m.com

Founded: 1978
Membership: 101–1,000
Scope: State
Description: Organization of persons interested in promoting the development of skills and education within the art of interpreting the natural and cultural environment. Members representing county, state, federal, and private conservation education agencies, organizations, and facilities.

IOWA BASS FEDERATION
Attn: President, 3282 Midway
Marion, IA 52302 United States
Phone: 319-393-1481
E-mail: tbowler1@go.com

Scope: State
Description: An organization of Bassmaster chapters, affiliated with the Bass Anglers Sportsman Society, organized to fight pollution, assist state and national conservation agencies in their efforts, and teach the young people of our country good conservation practices. Dedicated to the realistic conservation of our water resources.
Contact(s):
    Tom Bowler, President; 319-393-1481
    Russell Engelbart, Conservation Director; 12565 Amber Rd., Highway X44, Anamosa, IA 52205; engelbartbass101@uswest.net

IOWA ENVIRONMENTAL COUNCIL
711 E. Locust St.
Des Moines, IA 50309 United States
Phone: 515-244-1194   Fax: 515-244-7856
E-mail: iecmail@earthweshare.org
Website: www.earthweshare.org

Founded: 1994
Membership: 101–1,000
Scope: State
Description: The Iowa Environmental Council is an alliance of diverse organizations and individuals working with all Iowans to protect our natural environment. We seek a sustainable future through shaping public policy, research and education, coalition-building, and advocacy.
Publication(s): Legislative Action, News Bulletin, Iowa Environmental Quarterly
Keyword(s): Agriculture/Farming, Pollution (general), Public Health, Water Habitats & Quality, Wildlife & Species
Contact(s):
    David Hurd, President

Debbie Neustadt, Vice President
Elizabeth Plasket, Executive Director; 515-244-1194; ext. 11; Fax: 515-244-7856; plasket@earthweshare.org
Mark Ackelson, Treasurer
Ray Heinicke, Secretary

IOWA NATIVE PLANT SOCIETY
EEOB Department
341A Bessey Hall
Iowa State University
Ames, IA 50011-1020 United States
Phone: 515-294-9499   Fax: 515-294-1337
E-mail: dlewis@iastate.edu
Website: www.public.iastate.edu/~herbarium/inps/inpshome.htm

Founded: 1995
Membership: 101–1,000
Scope: Local, State
Description: Iowa Native Plant Society is an organization of amateurs and professionals who are interested in the scientific, educational, cultural aspects, preservation, and conservation of Iowa's native plants.
Publication(s): Iowa Native Plant Society Newsletter
Keyword(s): Land Issues, Reduce/Reuse/Recycle, Water Habitats & Quality, Wildlife & Species
Contact(s):
Sibylla Brown, President; Rt. 1 Box 240A, Leon, IA 50144; 641-446-7358; timbrhll@grm.net
Connie Mutel, Vice President; 2345 Sugar Bottom Road, Solon, IA 52333
Diana Horton, Treasurer; 720 Sandusky Drive, Iowa City, IA 52240; 319-337-5430; diana-horton@uiowa.edu
Linda Scarth, Secretary; 1630 Wildwood Drive NE, Cedar Rapids, IA 52402

IOWA NATURAL HERITAGE FOUNDATION
Attn: Director of Communications
Insurance Exchange Bldg.
Suite 444, 505 Fifth Ave.
Des Moines, IA 50309 United States
Phone: 515-288-1846   Fax: 515-288-0137
E-mail: info@inhf.org
Website: www.inhf.org

Founded: 1979
Membership: 1,001–10,000
Scope: State
Description: An independent, statewide, nonprofit organization that protects Iowa's land, water and wildlife "for those who follow." Program emphasis on land protection, landowner education, resource planning, wetland restoration and rail-trail development in Iowa.
Publication(s): A Bird's Eye View, Iowa by Trail Guidebook, Iowa Natural Heritage, The Landowner's Options
Keyword(s): Development/Developing Countries, Ecosystems (precious), Land Issues, Public Lands/Greenspace, Recreation/Ecotourism, Reduce/Reuse/Recycle, Sprawl/Urban Planning, Water Habitats & Quality, Wildlife & Species
Contact(s):
Mark Ackelson, President
Anita O'Gara, VP, Director of Development; aogara@inhf.org
Judy Frazier, Director of Administration; jfrazier@inhf.org
Lisa Hein, Program & Planning Director; lhein@inhf.org
Joe McGovern, Director of Land Stewardship; jmcgovern@inhf.org
Bruce Mountain, Director of Land Projects; bmountain@inhf.org
Laura McVay, Finance Manager; lmcvay@inhf.org
Chris Clingan, Land Stewardship Program Specialist; cclingan@inhf.org
Marlene Ehresman, Program & Planning Associate; mehresman@inhf.org
Michelle Fehring, Development Database Manager; mfehring@inhf.org
Diane Graves, Administrative Assistant/Receptionist; dgraves@inhf.org
Mimi Habhab, Development & Communications Associate; mhabhab@inhf.org
Heather Jobst, Program & Development Assistant; hjobst@inhf.org
Darrel Mills, Blufflands Conservation Coordinator; dmills@omnitelcom.com
David Zahrt, Loess Hills Conservation Specialist; dlzahrt@pionet.net
Cathy Engstrom, Communications Coordinator; cengstrom@inhf.org
Cheri Grauer, Gift Planner; cgrauer@inhf.org
Mike Lamair, Board Chairman

IOWA PRAIRIE NETWORK
IPN
P.O. Box 572
Nevada, IA 50201 United States
Phone: 515-963-7681
E-mail: webmaster@iowaprairienetwork.org
Website: www.IowaPrairieNetwork.org

Founded: 1990
Scope: State
Description: The Iowa Prairie Network is dedicated to protecting Iowa prairie heritage.
Publication(s): A Prairie Bioliography, Native Prairie Management Guide, IPN News
Keyword(s): Land Issues
Contact(s):
Glenn Pollock, President
Cindy Hildebrand, Vice President
David Hansen, Director; 515-357-3665
Carole Kern, Treasurer; 319-273-2813

IOWA TRAILS COUNCIL
P.O. Box 131
Center Point, IA 52213-0131 United States
Phone: 319-849-1844   Fax: 319-849-1044

Founded: 1983
Membership: 1,001–10,000
Scope: National
Description: A membership nonprofit organization primarily active in the Midwest, but with membership in over one-half the states and in several foreign countries. Primary purpose is to acquire and convert former railroad rights-of-way into recreational trails.
Publication(s): Trails Advocate, Bicycle Trails of Iowa
Keyword(s): Land Issues, Public Lands/Greenspace, Recreation/Ecotourism, Transportation
Contact(s):
Tom Neenan, Secretary/Treasurer and Executive Director; P.O. Box 131, Center Point, IA 52213-0131; 319-849-1844; tomneenan1@aol.com
Eldon Colton, Chairman; 1008 Bowler St., Hiawatha, IA 52233; 319-378-8971; Fax: 319-294-1914
David Lyon, Vice Chairman; 116 10th Ave., S., Mt. Vernon, IA 52314; 319-895-8240

IOWA TRAPPERS ASSOCIATION, INC.
c/o Anna Marie Scalf, 123 N. Madison Ave.
Ottumwa, IA 52501 United States
Phone: 641-682-3937   Fax: 641-682-9092
E-mail: iantadtr@lisco.com

Founded: 1950
Scope: State
Description: A nonprofit organization that works to continue the wise use and harvest of Iowa's renewable resource of furbearing animals. Cooperates with all recognized conserva-

tion agencies, law enforcement agencies, and legislative committees, and provides input on the benefits and necessity of trapping.
Publication(s): Trapper and Predator Caller, The
Keyword(s): Recreation/Ecotourism
Contact(s):
  Spencer Hill, President; P. O. Box 94, Kanawha, IA 50447; 641-762-3454; spjohill@comm1net.net
  Jeff Kempf, Vice-President; 3371 130th Street, Jamaica, IA 50128; 641-429-3401; longpond@iowatelecom.net
  Chris Grillot, Secretary; 2769 110th Ave., Wheatland, IA 52777; 319-374-1074
  Anna Scalf, Treasurer; 123 N. Madison Ave., Ottumwa, IA 52501; 515-682-3937
  Paul Wait, Editor; 700 E. State St., Iola, WI 54990; 715-445-2214

IOWA WILDLIFE FEDERATION
P.O. Box 3332
Des Moines, IA 50316-0332 United States
Phone: 319-624-3107   Fax: 319-644-3213

Scope: State
Description: A representative statewide organization, affiliated with the National Wildlife Federation, dedicated to the protection and enhancement of wildlife and its habitat through public education and government interaction.
Contact(s):
  Joe Wilkinson, President and Education Program Contact
  Mike Hodges, Editor
  Kevin Thomasson, Treasurer
  Doug Thompson, Representative
  John Zietlow, Alternate Representative

IOWA WILDLIFE REHABILITATORS ASSOCIATION
1005 Harken Hill Dr., P.O. Box 217
Osceola, IA 50213 United States
Phone: 641-342-2783

Founded: 1986
Membership: 1–100
Scope: State
Description: A nonprofit organization established to disseminate information pertaining to wildlife rehabilitation and medicine to veterinarians, rehabilitators, naturalists and others; to communicate and cooperate with environmental/conservation organizations; and to encourage the public to become more aware of the earth and its wild creatures. This is done through newsletters, educational material, state and regional conferences, and presentations.
Publication(s): Newsletters, educational materials
Contact(s):
  Marlene Ehresman, President; 515-296-2995
  Heather Blevins, Vice President; 641-277-7745
  Beth Brown, Treasurer; 641-342-2783
  Wendy Dewalle, Secretary; 641-964-9592

IOWA WOMEN IN NATURAL RESOURCES
P.O. Box 20083
Des Moines, IA 50320-0083 United States
Phone: 515-795-2354
E-mail: KShannon@aol.com
Website: www.hometown.aol.com

Founded: 1988
Membership: 1–100
Scope: State
Description: A nonprofit organization dedicated to providing professional development to individuals interested in all natural resource careers by promoting communication among professionals, encouraging girls and women to consider natural resource careers, conducting outdoor skills workshops, providing networking and support systems for women working in natural resources and providing career enhancement training.
Publication(s): IWINR News, IWINR Membership Directory
Keyword(s): Ethics/Environmental Justice
Contact(s):
  Kathy Shannon, President; 515-795-2354; KShannon@aol.com
  Theresa Blackburn, Education Chair; 563-872-5495; Fax: 563-872-5659; theresa_blackburn@usgs.gov
  Theresa Minaya, Treasurer; 712-258-0838

IOWA WOODLAND OWNERS ASSOCIATION
2735 14th Ave.
Marion, IA 52302-1848 United States
Phone: 319-665-2489

Founded: 1987
Scope: State
Description: A statewide organization affiliated with the National Woodland Owners Association, organized to advance good forestry on the 1.5 million acres of timberland owned by 28,000 nonindustrial private landowners in Iowa.
Publication(s): Timber Talk
Keyword(s): Forests/Forestry
Contact(s):
  Al Manning, President
  Tom Woodruff, Vice President
  E. Frye, Secretary and Editor; 319-377-2540
  Joanne Mensinger, Treasurer; 319-259-1160

ISLAND CONSERVATION EFFORT
15500 NW 180th Avenue
Alachua, FL 32615 United States
Phone: 386-418-0628
E-mail: tropbird@unspoiledqueen.com

Founded: 1988
Scope: International
Description: Island Conservation Effort is dedicated to the preservation of island natural resources, fauna, and habitats on which their preservation depends. We promote conservation, education, and research to obtain necessary data to support conservation measures.
Keyword(s): Oceans/Coasts/Beaches, Wildlife & Species
Contact(s):
  Martha Walsh-McGehee, President; 386-418-0628; tropbird@unspoiledqueen.com
  Michelle Pugh, Vice President; P.O. Box 4254, Christiansted, St. Croix, VI 00820; 340-773-7030; divexp@viaccess.net
  Rosemarie Gnam, Secretary and Treasurer; 1872 Stanhope St., Ridgewood, NY 11385

ISLAND INSTITUTE, THE
P.O. Box 648
Rockland, ME 04841 United States
Phone: 207-594-9209   Fax: 207-594-9314
E-mail: inquiry@islandinstitute.org
Website: www.islandinstitute.org

Founded: 1983
Membership: 10,001–100,000
Scope: Local, State, Regional, National
Description: Private, nonprofit organization dedicated to sustaining Maine island and coastal communities through community initiatives, publications, resource management, science and marine research.
Publication(s): Lobsters Great and Small, Islands in Time, Gulf of Maine Environmental Atlas, Island Journal, Working Waterfront
Keyword(s): Development/Developing Countries, Ecosystems (precious), Oceans/Coasts/Beaches, Sprawl/Urban Planning, Water Habitats & Quality
Contact(s):
  Philip Conkling, President; 207-594-9209

Peter Ralston, Vice President for Development; 207-594-9209
Sandra Thomas, Vice President for Programs; 207-594-9209
Michael Felton, Education Outreach Officer; 207-594-9209
Nathan Michaud, Community Planning Officer; 207-594-9209
Bart Morrison, Chief Operating Officer; 207-594-9209
Benjamin Neal, Marine Resources Coordinator; 207-594-9209
David Platt, Publications Director; 207-594-9209

ISLAND RESOURCES FOUNDATION
6292 Estate Nazareth, #100
St. Thomas, VI 00802 United States
Phone: 340-775-6225   Fax: 340-779-2022
E-mail: irf@irf.org
Website: www.irf.org
Founded: 1972
Membership: 101–1,000
Scope: State, Regional, National, International
Description: A 30-year old international NGO devoted to solving the problems of sustainable development in small tropical islands
Publication(s): E-mail groups, publications on website
Keyword(s): Climate Change, Development/Developing Countries, Ecosystems (precious), Ethics/Environmental Justice, Land Issues, Oceans/Coasts/Beaches, Pollution (general), Recreation/Ecotourism, Water Habitats & Quality, Wildlife & Species
Contact(s):
Bruce Potter, President; bpotter@irf.org
Jean Pierre Bacle, Cartographer; 1718 P Street NW, Suite T-4, Washington, DC 20036; 202-265-9712; Fax: 202-232-0748; jpbacle@irf.org
Charles Consolvo, Secretary
Edward Towle, Chairman; etowle@irf.org
Judith Towle, Treasurer; jtowle@irf.org
Henry Wheatley, Vice Chairman

ISLAND RESOURCES FOUNDATION
EASTERN CARIBBEAN BIODIVERSITY PROGRAM OFFICE
P.O. Box 2103
St. Johns, Antigua Barbuda
Phone: 2684637740   Fax: 2684637740
E-mail: klindsay@irf.org
Scope: Regional

ISLESBORO ISLANDS TRUST
376 West Bay Road
P.O. Box 182
Islesboro, ME 04848 United States
Phone: 207-734-6907   Fax: 207-734-6747
E-mail: iitsmill@midcoast.com
Founded: 1985
Membership: 101–1,000
Scope: Local
Description: Preservation of open space, education about the value of natural ecosystems and environmental advocacy on behalf of Islesboro and the surrounding Penobscot Bay region.
Keyword(s): Agriculture/Farming, Ecosystems (precious), Ethics/Environmental Justice, Finance/Banking/Trade, Forests/Forestry, Land Issues, Oceans/Coasts/Beaches, Pollution (general), Public Health, Public Lands/Greenspace, Recreation/Ecotourism, Sprawl/Urban Planning
Contact(s):
Devens Hamlen, President
Stephen Miller, Executive Director; 207-734-6907; Fax: 207-734-6747; iitsmill@midcoast.com
Arch Gillies, Development Director; 207-734-6907; Fax: 207-734-6747
Sue Hatch, Trails and Preserves Chair; 207-734-6907; Fax: 207-734-6747

ISSAQUAH ALPS TRAILS CLUB (I.A.T.C.)
P.O. Box 351
Issaquah, WA 98027 United States
Phone: 425-392-4432
E-mail: IATCDrew@aol.com
Website: www.issaquahalps.org
Founded: 1979
Scope: Local
Description: A nonprofit membership organization established to preserve and promote trails and open space in the area east of Seattle along the I-90 highway corridor from Lake Washington to the Cascades, primarily in the area known as the "Issaquah Alps."
Publication(s): Washington State Public Port Districts, Speaking of Ground Water, Targeting Tomorrow
Keyword(s): Air Quality/Atmosphere, Energy, Reduce/Reuse/Recycle, Water Habitats & Quality
Contact(s):
Steve Drew, President
Barbara Johnson, Vice President of Operations
Steve Drew, Treasurer-Acting
Kitty Gross, Secretary
Harvey Manning, Founder

IZAAK WALTON LEAGUE OF AMERICA ENDOWMENT
3185 Dubuque St., NE
Iowa City, IA 52240 United States
Phone: 319-351-7037   Fax: 319-351-7037
Website: www.iwla.org
Founded: 1943
Scope: National
Description: Organized to help rebuild Outdoor America by the acquisition by governmental agencies of unique natural areas for the use of future generations. Members of the Izaak Walton League of America.
Keyword(s): Air Quality/Atmosphere, Recreation/Ecotourism, Wildlife & Species
Contact(s):
Wendell Haley, President; 1840 NE 92nd Ave., Portland, OR 97220; 503-253-9749
Larry Smith, Vice President; 1611 Alderman Dr., Greensboro, NC 27408; 336-834-0018
Charles Eldridge, Secretary; 2008 74th St., Des Moines, IA 50322; 515-244-0932
Robert Russell, Executive Secretary
William Weber, Treasurer; 6357 W. Encantado Ct., Rockford, MI 49341; 616-456-8601; Fax: 616-450-1915
Howard White, Honorary President; P.O. Box 527, Havana, IL 62644; 309-543-4391

IZAAK WALTON LEAGUE OF AMERICA, INC., THE
Headquarters, 707 Conservation Ln.
Gaithersburg, MD 20878-2983 United States
Phone: 301-548-0150, ext. 222   Fax: 301-548-0146
Website: www.iwla.org
Founded: 1922
Membership: 10,001–100,000
Scope: National
Description: Promotes means and opportunities for educating the public to conserve, maintain, protect, and restore the soil, forest, water, air, and other natural resources of the U.S. and promotes the enjoyment and wholesome utilization of those resources.
Publication(s): Outdoor America
Keyword(s): Air Quality/Atmosphere, Ethics/Environmental Justice, Public Lands/Greenspace, Recreation/Ecotourism, Water Habitats & Quality

Contact(s):
  Stan Adams, National President
  Chuck Clayton, National Vice President
  Paul Hansen, Executive Director
  Jason McGarvey, Editor
  Jim Mosher, Conservation Director
  Georgia Townsend, Secretary
  William West, Treasurer

IZAAK WALTON LEAGUE OF AMERICA, INC., THE
ALASKA DIVISION
P.O. Box 670650
Chugiak, AK 99567 United States
Phone: 907-333-0243

Scope: State

Contact(s):
  Thomas Carter, President; 907-333-0243

IZAAK WALTON LEAGUE OF AMERICA, INC., THE
CALIFORNIA DIVISION
504 E. Oakmont Avenue
Orange, CA 92867 United States
Phone: 714-516-9483

Founded: 1938

Scope: State

Contact(s):
  Peter Hillebrecht, President; 310-791-0793

IZAAK WALTON LEAGUE OF AMERICA, INC., THE
CALIFORNIA STATE IWLA
3601 S. Gaffey Street #625
San Pedro, CA 90731 United States
Phone: 310-832-1907
E-mail: general@iwla.org
Website: www.iwla.org

Founded: 1946
Membership: 1–100
Scope: Local, State, National

Description: Grassroots conservation organization dedicated to the wise use of our natural resources and educate the public on their wise use.

Keyword(s): Forests/Forestry, Land Issues, Oceans/Coasts/Beaches, Water Habitats & Quality, Wildlife & Species

IZAAK WALTON LEAGUE OF AMERICA, INC., THE
COLORADO DIVISION
12175 West Ohio Place
Lakewood, CO 80228-3319 United States
Phone: 303-986-1747
Website: www.iwla.org

Membership: 101–1,000
Scope: State
Publication(s): Outdoor America-Magazine

Contact(s):
  Leah Whellan, President
  Nelson Burton, National Director; 719-473-0700
  Amy Miller, Secretary and National Director; 513 Strachan Dr., Fort Collins, CO 80525-2130; 970-223-5379

IZAAK WALTON LEAGUE OF AMERICA, INC., THE
FLORIDA DIVISION
P.O. Box 97
Estero, FL 33928 United States
Phone: 239-992-2184   Fax: 239-495-0201
E-mail: koreshanfound@mindspring.com
Website: www.iwla.org
Membership: 1–100
Scope: Regional

Contact(s):
  Charles Dauray, President
  Michael Chenoweth, National Director; P. O. Box 236, Homestead, FL 33090-0236; 305-451-0993; Fax: 305-451-3627; michael.chenoweth@mail.com
  Sarah Bergquist, Secretary

IZAAK WALTON LEAGUE OF AMERICA, INC., THE
ILLINOIS DIVISION
1514 45th St.
Moline, IL 61548 United States
Phone: 309-797-8255

Scope: State

Publication(s): Illini Ike (Newsletter)

Contact(s):
  Jim Tyas, President; 309-383-4203
  Marsha Johnson, Secretary; 1512 45th St., Moline, IL 61265-3544; 309-797-8255

IZAAK WALTON LEAGUE OF AMERICA, INC., THE
INDIANA DIVISION
Attn: President, 2173 Pennsylvania St.
Portage, IN 46368-2444 United States
Phone: 219-762-4876
Website: www.in-iwla.org

Founded: 1922
Membership: 1,001–10,000
Scope: Local, State, National

Description: Grassroots organization mission: To conserve, maintain, protect and restore the soil, forest, water and other natural resources of the United States and other lands; to promote means and opportunities for the education of the public with respect to such resources and their enjoyment and wholesome utilization.

Publication(s): Hoosier Waltonian, The

Contact(s):
  Charles Siar, President; 219-762-4876
  Ed Bohle, Secretary; 206 Greenwood Ave., Michigan City, IN 46360; 219-879-8020
  James Daniels, Editor/Vice Pres.; 1808 Ravenswood Dr., Evansville, IN 47717; 812-477-7250; jimdaniels3@juno.com
  Emil Garcia, Treasurer; 3420 W. 40th Pl., Gary, IN 46408; 219-980-2612; elgarcia@earthlink.net

IZAAK WALTON LEAGUE OF AMERICA, INC., THE
IOWA DIVISION
321 East Walnut Street
Suite 130
Des Moines, IA 50309-2048 United States
Phone: 515-883-2358   Fax: 515-883-2362
E-mail: iowaikes@mcleodusa.net
Website: www.iowaikes.net

Founded: 1922
Scope: State
Description: Non-Profit Conservation Organization

Contact(s):
  Tom Holm, President; 3607 Crocker Street, Des Moines, IA 50312; 515-255-5164

IZAAK WALTON LEAGUE OF AMERICA, INC., THE
MARYLAND DIVISION
703 Conservation Lane
Gaithersburg, MD 20871 United States
Phone: 301-972-1627
Membership: 1,001–10,000
Scope: Local, State, Regional
Description: To conserve, maintain, protect and restore the soil, forest, water and other natural resources of the United States and other lands; to promote means and opportunities for the education of the public with respect to such resources and their enjoyment and wholesome utilization.
Contact(s):
  Georgia Townsend, President; 406 Leighton Ave., Silver Spring, MD 20901; 301-588-8335
  Bill Gorman, Executive Sécretary

IZAAK WALTON LEAGUE OF AMERICA, INC., THE
MICHIGAN DIVISION
c/o President, 6260 Blythefield NE
Rockford, MI 49341 United States
Phone: 616-866-8475
E-mail: jtrimber@earthlink.net
Website: www.mich-iwla.org
Founded: 1927
Membership: 101–1,000
Scope: State, National
Description: Conservation organization with a mission to conserve, maintain, protect and restore our natural resources and educate the public on their wise use.
Keyword(s): Agriculture/Farming, Air Quality/Atmosphere, Development/Developing Countries, Ecosystems (precious), Energy, Ethics/Environmental Justice, Executive/Legislative/Judicial Reform, Forests/Forestry, Land Issues, Oceans/Coasts/Beaches, Pollution (general)
Contact(s):
  E. John Trimberger, President; 6260 Blythefield NE, Rockford, MI 49341; 616-866-8475; jtrimber@earthlink.net
  Robert Stegmier, Secretary; 5285 Windmill Dr. NE, Rockford, MI 49341-9311; 616-866-4769

IZAAK WALTON LEAGUE OF AMERICA, INC., THE
MINNESOTA DIVISION
555 Park St., Suite 140
St. Paul, MN 55103 United States
Phone: 651-221-0215   Fax: 651-221-0215
E-mail: mn-ikes@mtn.org
Website: www.mtn.org/mn-ikes
Founded: 1923
Membership: 1,001–10,000
Scope: State
Description: Works to conserve, maintain and restore the soil, forest, water and other natural resources of Minnesota; to promote means and opportunities for the education of the public with respect to such resources and their enjoyment and wholesome utilization.
Publication(s): Citizen Leadership in Conservation, Waltonian
Contact(s):
  Steve McNaughton, President

IZAAK WALTON LEAGUE OF AMERICA, INC., THE
NEBRASKA DIVISION
Attn: President, 3017 Midway Rd.
Grand Island, NE 68803-2436 United States
Phone: 308-384-0656
Scope: State
Contact(s):
  Roger Mettenbrink, President; 308-384-0656
  Lurlie Campbell, Secretary; 17125 Sodtown Rd., Ravenna, NE 68869; 308-452-3800

IZAAK WALTON LEAGUE OF AMERICA, INC., THE
NEW YORK STATE DIVISION
c/o President, 3826 Lane Rd.
Cazenovia, NY 13035 United States
Phone: 315-655-3375
E-mail: cheneyweb@aol.com
Membership: 101–1,000
Scope: Regional
Description: New York State Division of IWLA
Publication(s): Periodical Outdoor America
Contact(s):
  Matt Webber, President; 315-655-3375
  Les Monostory, Secretary; 315-435-6600; hllmomo@health.ongov.net

IZAAK WALTON LEAGUE OF AMERICA, INC., THE
OHIO DIVISION
Attn: Secretary, 953 Greenwood Ave.
Hamilton, OH 45011 1817 United States
Phone: 513-697-6100
E-mail: kflowers@fuse.net
Website: www.iwla.org
Founded: 1922
Membership: 1,001–10,000
Scope: State
Publication(s): Quarterly magazine - Outdoor America, Tri-annual newsletter - Buckeye Ike Line
Contact(s):
  Bill Ashbaugh, President
  Kevin Flowers, Environmental Director; 6793 Midnight Sun Dr., Mainville, OH 45039; 513-697-6100
  Yvonne Hayes, Secretary; 513-863-8018

IZAAK WALTON LEAGUE OF AMERICA, INC., THE
OREGON DIVISON
15056 Quall Rd.
Silverton, OR 97381 United States
Phone: 503-873-2681
E-mail: olsondaw@juno.com
Founded: 1930
Scope: State
Description: To protect, perpetuate, and strive for renewal of Oregon's natural resources, including the air, soil, woods, waters, and wildlife; to promote means and opportunities for education of the public in respect to such resources and the enjoyment and utilization thereof.
Contact(s):
  Jeanne Norton, President; 503-235-7634
  Coral Torley, Secretary; 1820 NW Woodland Dr., Corvallis, OR 97330-1019; 541-752-0114

IZAAK WALTON LEAGUE OF AMERICA, INC., THE
OWATONNA MINNESOTA CHAPTER
IKES
WALTONIANS
c/o Cherry Schwartz, President
100 Shady Avenue
Owatonna, MN 55060 United States
Phone: 507-451-6676   Fax: 507-444-8999
E-mail: ikepres@hotmail.com
Founded: 1926

Membership: 101–1,000
Scope: Local
Description: This 100+ member environmental organization advocates for land, water, air and wildlife. Major projects include the Game and Fish Building at the Steele County Free Fair (mid-August) and the restoration of an Oak Savanna on a 23 acre parcel south of Owatonna, MN. The Ikes chapterhouse is in these woods and can be rented by members of the public. It seats 100, has a full kitchen, gas grills and is completely handicapped accessible.
Publication(s): Izaak Walton League, Owatonna Chapter
Keyword(s): Agriculture/Farming, Ecosystems (precious), Ethics/Environmental Justice, Executive/Legislative/Judicial Reform, Forests/Forestry, Land Issues, Oceans/Coasts/Beaches, Pollution (general), Public Lands/Greenspace, Recreation/Ecotourism, Reduce/Reuse/Recycling

IZAAK WALTON LEAGUE OF AMERICA, INC., THE
PENNSYLVANIA DIVISION
701 Locust Grove Rd
York, PA 17402 United States
Phone: 717-757-2193
E-mail: wfrey34112@aol.com
Website: www.iwla.org

Founded: 1926
Membership: 1,001–10,000
Scope: State
Description: Conservation organization. Defenders of air, soil, woods, waters, and wildlife.
Keyword(s): Land Issues, Water Habitats & Quality, Wildlife & Species
Contact(s):
Raymond Kossler, President; 460 New Salem Rd., Uniontown, PA 15401-9013; 724-437-5356
Martha Shaffer, Secretary; P.O. Box 35, Loganville, PA 17342-0035; 717-428-2883

IZAAK WALTON LEAGUE OF AMERICA, INC., THE
SOUTH DAKOTA DIVISION
Attn: President, 798 11th St., SW
Watertown, SD 57350-3060 United States
Phone: 605-352-2598
E-mail: clayton@santel.net
Website: itc-web.com/sdikes#

Scope: State
Contact(s):
Charles Clayton, President; 605-352-2598

IZAAK WALTON LEAGUE OF AMERICA, INC., THE
VIRGINIA DIVISION
Attn: President, 5235 Richardson Dr.
Fairfax, VA 22032-3930 United States
Phone: 703-361-5729

Scope: State
Publication(s): PEC Newsreporter, periodic books and special reports.
Contact(s):
Birtrun Kidwell, President; 703-232-6563
Jeanne Kling, Secretary; 6110 Occoquan Forest Drive, Manassas, VA 20112-3018

IZAAK WALTON LEAGUE OF AMERICA, INC., THE
WASHINGTON DIVISION
Attn: Bruce McGlenn, 2031 Franklin Ave. E, # 304
Seattle, WA 98102 United States
Phone: 425-455-1986   Fax: 425-453-9629
Website: www.seattleikes.org

Scope: State
Contact(s):
Ronni McGlenn, President, Washington State Division; ronnimc@juno.com

IZAAK WALTON LEAGUE OF AMERICA, INC., THE
WEST VIRGINIA DIVISION
P.O. Box 921
Shepherdstown, WV 25443-0921 United States
Phone: 304-876-2457
Website: www.izaakwaltonleague.com

Scope: State
Contact(s):
Don McClung, President; 304-876-2457

IZAAK WALTON LEAGUE OF AMERICA, INC., THE
WISCONSIN DIVISION
Attn: President, 5316 Forest Cir., N
Stevens Point, WI 54481-5605 United States
Phone: 715-344-1803
E-mail: bob_elliker@usa.net
Website: www.iwla.org

Founded: 1922
Membership: 1,001–10,000
Scope: State
Description: Wisconsin Division of the Izaak Walton League of America, a national conservation organization whose goal is to protect, manage, and use America's natural resources in such a way as to assure long term quality of life.
Publication(s): Wisconsin Waltonian Newsletter
Keyword(s): Water Habitats & Quality
Contact(s):
Robert Elliker, President; 715-344-1803; bob_elliker@usa.net
Gerald Ernst, Secretary; 811 4th St., Plover, WI 54467-2253; 715-344-4668

IZAAK WALTON LEAGUE OF AMERICA, INC., THE
WYOMING DIVISION
Attn: President, 1072 Empinado
Laramie, WY 82070 United States
Phone: 307-742-2785
E-mail: quot@uwyo.edu

Scope: State
Keyword(s): Agriculture/Farming, Energy, Reduce/Reuse/Recycle
Contact(s):
Raymond Jacquot, President; 307-742-2785

IZAAK WALTON LEAGUE OF AMERICA, INC., THE
YORK CHAPTER #57
Attn: William Shaffer, P.O. Box 35
Loganville, PA 17342 United States
Phone: 717-428-2883
E-mail: reg6govike@aol.com
Website: www.iwla.org

Founded: 1926
Description: To strive for the purity of water, the clarity of air, the wise stewardship of the land and its resources; to know the beauty and understanding of nature and the value of wildlife, woodlands, and open space; to the preservation of this heritage and to man's sharing in it. Mission Statement: We're a diverse group of 50,000 men and women dedicated to protecting our nation's soil, air, woods, waters and wildlife.
Publication(s): Outdoor America, Waltonian News Monthly

Contact(s):
William Shaffer, Corresponding Secretary; P.O. Box 35, Loganville, PA 17342

J

J.N. (DING) DARLING FOUNDATION
785 Crandon Blvd., Suite 1206
Key Biscayne, FL 33149 United States
Phone: 305-361-9788   Fax: 305-361-9789
E-mail: kipkoss@hotmail.com
Website: www.dingdarling.org
Founded: 1962
Membership: 1–100
Scope: National
Description: A nonprofit organization formed to continue the ideals and work of pioneer conservationist "Ding" Darling, with an emphasis on conservation education. The Foundation has no paid staff. With all services, including legal and accounting, provided by its trustees, the Foundation is able to funnel 100% of contributed funds into selected projects.
Publication(s): "Ding", The Life of Jay N. Darling, "Ding" Darling's Conservation Cartoons
Keyword(s): Agriculture/Farming, Climate Change, Ecosystems (precious), Energy, Ethics/Environmental Justice, Finance/Banking/Trade, Forests/Forestry, Land Issues, Pollution (general), Population, Public Health, Public Lands/Greenspace, Transportation, Water Habitats
Contact(s):
Christopher Koss, President of Board of Trustees and Chairman of Executive Committee; 305-361-9788; Fax: 305-361-9789; kipkoss@hotmail.com
Kristie Anders, Executive Director; P.O. Box 978, Sanibel, FL 33957; 239-472-2329; Fax: 239-472-6421; kanders@sccf.org

JACK H. BERRYMAN INSTITUTE FOR WILDLIFE DAMAGE MANAGEMENT
DEPT. OF FISHERIES AND WILDLIFE
Utah State University
Logan, UT 84322-5210 United States
Phone: 435-797-2436   Fax: 435-797-1871
Website: www.berrymaninstitute.org
Membership: 1–100
Scope: National
Description: The Jack H. Berryman Institute is a national nonprofit organization which is centered at Utah State University. It engages in research, education, and extension activities aimed at resolving human and wildlife conflicts, enhancing the positive aspects of wildlife, and increasing human tolerance of wildlife problems.

JACK MINER MIGRATORY BIRD FOUNDATION, INC.
P.O. Box 39
Kingsville, N9Y 2E8 Ontario Canada
Phone: 519-733-4034
E-mail: info@jackminer.com
Website: www.jackminer.com
Founded: 1904
Scope: International
Description: A nonprofit (501(c)3) foundation in both the U.S. and Canada. This sanctuary and its founder, Jack Miner, have become internationally known as one of the earliest efforts in waterfowl conservation. Often referred to as "The Father of Conservation", Jack Miner pioneered the tagging of waterfowl in 1909. The sanctuary is open year round to the public with no admission fee.
Keyword(s): Wildlife & Species
Contact(s):
Kirk Miner, President and Treasurer
Edna Miner, Vice President
Marilyn Hageniers, Secretary

JACKSON HOLE CONSERVATION ALLIANCE
P.O. Box 2728
Jackson, WY 83001 United States
Phone: 307-733-9417   Fax: 307-733-9008
E-mail: info@jhalliance.org
Website: www.jhalliance.org
Founded: 1979
Membership: 1,001–10,000
Scope: Local, Regional
Description: The Alliance is a nonprofit organization dedicated to responsible land stewardship in Jackson Hole, Wyoming, to ensure that human activities are in harmony with the area's irreplaceable wildlife, scenic and other natural resources.
Publication(s): Welcome to the Neighborhood, Mosquito Abatement Program in Teton County, Fiscal Impacts of Growth in Teton County, Alliance News
Keyword(s): Forests/Forestry, Land Issues, Public Lands/Greenspace, Reduce/Reuse/Recycle, Wildlife & Species
Contact(s):
Marcia Kunstel, President
Julius Muschaweck, Co-Vice President
Becky Woods-Bloom, Co-Vice President
Franz Camenzind, Executive Director; franz@jhalliance.com
Pamela Lichtman, Program Director; pam@jhalliance.com
Jean Barash, Secretary; 307-739-8669; Fax: 307-739-9691; jbarash@wyoming.com
John Carney, Treasurer

JACKSON HOLE LAND TRUST
P.O. Box 2897
555 East Broadway #228
Jackson, WY 83001 United States
Phone: 307-733-4707   Fax: 307-733-4144
E-mail: info@jhlandtrust.org
Website: www.jhlandtrust.org
Founded: 1980
Scope: Local
Description: A private, nonprofit land conservation organization which works to preserve open space and the scenic, ranching, and wildlife values of Jackson Hole by assisting landowners who wish to protect their land in perpetuity. Not a membership organization.
Publication(s): Land Trust Newsletter
Keyword(s): Agriculture/Farming, Land Issues, Public Lands/Greenspace, Wildlife & Species
Contact(s):
Scott Pierson, President
Michael Caruso, Second Vice President
Leslie Mattson, Executive Director
Mia Jensen, Treasurer
Richard Vangyeek, Secretary

JACKSON HOLE PRESERVE, INC.
30 Rockefeller Plaza, Rm. 5600
New York, NY 10112 United States
Phone: 212-649-5819   Fax: 212-649-5729
Founded: 1940
Scope: National
Description: Nonprofit, charitable, and educational organization, established to conserve areas of outstanding primitive grandeur and natural beauty and to provide facilities for their use and enjoyment by the public.
Contact(s):
C.W. Frye, Chairman of the Board
Antonia Grumbach, Secretary
Carmen Reyes, Treasurer

JANE GOODALL INSTITUTE, THE
8700 Georgia Ave. Suite 500
Silver Spring, MD 20910-3605 United States
Phone: 301-565-0086   Fax: 301-565-3188
E-mail: jgiinformation@janegoodall.org
Website: www.janegoodall.org

Founded: 1977
Membership: 1–100
Scope: International
Description: The Jane Goodall Institute is an international organization dedicated to the conservation and understanding of wildlife, particularly chimpanzees, and to promoting environmental education, reforestation, and humanitarianism worldwide.
Publication(s): ChimpanZOO Newsletter, Semi-annual Roots and Shoots Network, Annual JGI World Report
Keyword(s): Forests/Forestry, Wildlife & Species
Contact(s):
  Jeanne McCarty, Director of Roots and Shoots;
    j.mccarty@janegoodall.org
  Gary North, Deputy Director of Merchandise;
    gwnjhu@aol.com

JAPAN WILDLIFE RESEARCH CENTER (JWRC)
Shitaya 3-10-10
Taito-ku, Tokyo, 110-8676 Japan
Phone: 81-3-5824-0953   Fax: 81-3-5824-0956
E-mail: mkomoda@jwrc.or.jp
Website: www.jwrc.or.jp/

Founded: 1978
Scope: Local, Regional, National, International
Description: JWRC has carried out research works and has accumulated data on nature of Japan and developed techniques for research and management of wildlife and its habitat. JWRC is also trying to contribute to the conservation of nature through fact finding and accumulation of basic data.
Keyword(s): Ecosystems (precious), Recreation/Ecotourism, Wildlife & Species
Contact(s):
  Yasuhiko Taki, Professor; 81-3-5824-0960
  Kazuhiro Yamase, Executive Director; 81-3-5824-0960

JOHN INSKEEP ENVIRONMENTAL LEARNING CENTER
19600 S. Molalla Ave.
Oregon City, OR 97045 United States
Phone: 503-657-6958, ext. 2351   Fax: 503-650-6669
E-mail: elc@clackamas.cc.or.us
Website: www.clackamas.cc.or.us

Founded: 1972
Scope: State
Description: A source of teacher training and community education on environmental education topics, focusing on urban watershed issues. Located on a restored industrial site featuring buildings made from salvaged and recycled materials.
Keyword(s): Reduce/Reuse/Recycle, Water Habitats & Quality
Contact(s):
  John Lecavalier, Director

JOURNALISM TO RAISE ENVIRONMENTAL AWARENESS
San Francisco de los Viveros 701, E2-104
Fracc. Ojocaliente
Aguascalientes, 20190 Mexico
Phone: 449-970-1593   Fax: 449-970-1593
E-mail: jaguar@infosel.net.mx

Founded: 1994
Scope: Local, State, Regional, National, International
Description: Improve environmental education in the mass media.

K

KANSAS ACADEMY OF SCIENCE
c/o Brenda Oppert
USDA ARS GMPRC
1515 College Ave.
Manhattan, KS 66502 United States
Phone: 785-776-2780   Fax: 785-537-5584
E-mail: bso@ksu.edu
Website: www.washburn.edu/kas

Founded: 1868
Membership: 101–1,000
Scope: State
Description: The purposes of the Academy are to encourage education in the sciences and dissemination of scientific information through the facilities of the Academy, and to achieve closer cooperation and understanding between scientists and nonscientists, so that they may work together in a common cause of furthering science.
Publication(s): Transactions of the Kansas Academy of Science
Keyword(s): Agriculture/Farming, Ecosystems (precious), Water Habitats & Quality, Wildlife & Species
Contact(s):
  James Aber, Editor; Earth Science Department, Emporia, KS 66801; aberjame@emporia.edu
  Pieter Berendsen, Secretary; Kansas Geological Survey University of Kansas, Lawrence, KS 66047; 785-864-4991
  Brenda Oppert, Treasurer; USDA ARS GMPRC, 1515 College Ave., Manhattan,, KS 66502; 785-776-2780; Fax: 785-537-5584; bso@ksu.edu

KANSAS ASSOCIATION FOR CONSERVATION AND ENVIRONMENTAL EDUCATION, KACEE
2610 Claflin Rd.
Manhattan, KS 66502-2743 United States
Phone: 785-532-3322   Fax: 785-532-3305
E-mail: ldowney@oznet.ksu.edu
Website: www.kacee.org

Founded: 1969
Membership: 101–1,000
Scope: Local, State, Regional
Description: Kansas Association for Conservation and Environmenal Education was organized to promote and support effective conservation and environmental education in Kansas. The Association is made up of over 200 public and private organizations and 300+ individuals.
Publication(s): Strategic Plan, Workshop Brochure, Annual Report, KACEE news
Keyword(s): Air Quality/Atmosphere, Energy, Forests/Forestry, Land Issues, Pollution (general), Public Health, Reduce/Reuse/Recycle, Sprawl/Urban Planning, Water Habitats & Quality, Wildlife & Species
Contact(s):
  Brad Loveless, President; 785-575-8115; Fax: 785-575-8039; brad_loveless@wstnres.com
  Kate Grover, Vice President; 785-368-3801; Fax: 785-368-3806; kgover@topeka.org
  Laura Downey, Executive Director; 785-532-3322; Fax: 785-532-3305; ldowney@oznet.ksu.edu
  John Strickler, Treasurer; 785-565-9721; Fax: 785-532-3305; jstrickl@oznet.ksu.edu

KANSAS ASSOCIATION OF CONSERVATION DISTRICTS
Attn: President, Rt. 1 Box 110
Glen Elder, KS 67446 United States
Phone: 785-475-2342   Fax: 785-475-3886

Scope: State
Contact(s):
  Carl Jordan, President, Alternate Board Member; 785-545-3361; Fax: 785-545-3659

Sandra Jones, Vice President; 5160 E Rd. 17, Johnson, KS 67855; 316-492-6495; Fax: 316-492-2772
Richard Jones, Executive Director; 522 Winn Rd., Salina, KS 67401-3668; 785-827-5847; Fax: 785-827-7784
Don Paxson, Board Member; P.O. Box 487, Penokee, KS 67659; 785-421-2480; Fax: 785-421-5662
Don Rezac, Secretary-Treasurer; 12350 Ranch Rd., Emmett, KS 66422; 785-535-2961; Fax: 785-457-2868

KANSAS BASS FEDERATION
Attn: President, P.O. Box 330
Alba, MO 64830 United States
Phone: 417-525-4940
E-mail: onemorefish@ckt.net
Website: www.kbcf.com

Scope: State

Description: An organization of Bassmaster chapters, affiliated with the Bass Anglers Sportsman Society, organized to fight pollution, assist state and national conservation agencies in their efforts, and teach the young people of our country good conservation practices. Dedicated to the realistic conservation of our water resources.

Publication(s): KBCF News and Views

Contact(s):
Jon Stewart, President; 417-525-4940
Greg Clark, Conservation Director; 9320 E. Osie, Apt. #2104, Wichita, KS 67207; 316-681-1887

KANSAS DEPTARTMENT OF WILDLIFE AND PARKS
MIDWEST ASSOCIATION OF FISH AND WILDLIFE AGENCIES
512 Southeast 25th Avenue
Pratt, KS 67124 United States
Phone: 620-672-5911   Fax: 620-672-2972
E-mail: joek@wp.state.ks.us

Founded: 1934

Scope: State, Regional, National

Description: State agencies/Canadian provinces protecting wildlife resources on public and private lands; scrutinize state and federal wildlife legislation; clearinghouse for the exchange of ideas concerning wildlife management, research techniques, wildlife law enforcement, hunting and outdoor safety, and information and education; assist sportsmen's and conservationists' organizations in the protection, preservation, restoration and management of our fish and wildlife resources.

Publication(s): Proceedings of the MAFWA

Keyword(s): Agriculture/Farming, Ecosystems (precious), Executive/Legislative/Judicial Reform, Forests/Forestry, Land Issues, Pollution (general), Public Lands/Greenspace, Recreation/Ecotourism, Water Habitats & Quality, Wildlife & Species

Contact(s):
Dean Hildebrand, President, North Dakota Game and Fish Dept., 100 N. Bismarck Expressway, Bismarck, ND 58501; 701-328-6300; Fax: 701-328-6352; cdhildebrand@state.nd.us
Joe Kramer, Secretary/Treasurer; Kansas Department of Wildlife & Parks, 512 SE 25th Ave., Pratt, KS 67124; 620-672-5911; ext. 190; Fax: 620-672-2972; joek@wp.state.ks.us
Ollie Torgerson, Coordinator; Missouri Dept. of Conservation, P.O. Box 180, Jefferson City, MO 65102-0180; 573-751-4115; ext. 3149; Fax: 573-526-3976; torgeo@mdc.state.mo.us

KANSAS HERPETOLOGICAL SOCIETY
University of Kansas Natural History Museum, Dyche Hall
Lawrence, KS 66045 United States

Founded: 1974

Scope: State

Description: The Kansas Herpetological Society is a nonprofit organization designed to encourage education and dissemination of scientific information through the facilities of the Society; and to encourage conservation of wildlife in general and of amphibians and reptiles in Kansas in particular.

Publication(s): Kansas Herpetological Society Newsletter

Keyword(s): Wildlife & Species

Contact(s):
Eric Rundquist, Editor; Animal Care Unit, B054 Malott, University of Kansas, Lawrence, KS 66045
Karen Toepfer, Treasurer; 303 W. 39th St., Hays, KS 67601; 785-628-1437

KANSAS NATURAL RESOURCE COUNCIL
P.O. Box 2635
Topeka, KS 66601 United States
Phone: 785-746-8885
E-mail: robert.c.haughawout@boeing.com
Website: www.knrc.ws

Founded: 1981

Membership: 101–1,000

Scope: State

Description: Environmental advocacy including public education, lobbying, and litigation.

Publication(s): KNRC Journal, Weekly Legislative Updates

Keyword(s): Agriculture/Farming, Energy, Land Issues, Water Habitats & Quality

Contact(s):
Joan Vibert, President; 1981 Indiana, Ottawa, KS 66067; 785-746-8885; joan@windwalker-farm.com
John Barnes, Executive Director

KANSAS ORNITHOLOGICAL SOCIETY
14207 Robin Rd.
Leavenworth, KS 66048 United States
Phone: 913-651-2565
Website: ksbirds.org/kos

Founded: 1949

Scope: State

Description: Formed to promote the study of ornithology, to advance the members in ornithological science, to promote conservation, and the appreciation of birds by the general public.

Publication(s): K.O.S. Bulletin, Horned Lark, The

Keyword(s): Wildlife & Species

Contact(s):
John Schukman, President; schuksaya@aol.com
Gene Young, Vice President; P.O. Box 1147 Natural Science Dept., Cowley County Community College, Arkansas City, KS 67005; youngg@cowley.cc.ks.us

KANSAS WILDFLOWER SOCIETY
R.L. McGregor Herbarium, 2045 Constant Ave.
Lawrence, KS 66047-3729 United States
Phone: 785-864-3453   Fax: 785-864-5093

Founded: 1978

Scope: State

Description: The Society provides educational materials and sponsors activities to promote the conservation and cultivation of the native plants of Kansas.

Publication(s): KWS Newsletter

Keyword(s): Land Issues, Reduce/Reuse/Recycle, Wildlife & Species

Contact(s):
Dwight Platt, President; 316-283-2500; Fax: 316-284-5286
Cynthia Ford, Secretary; 316-235-4726
Craig Freeman, Agent
Patricia Stanley, Treasurer; 316-689-4070; wichitacsj@feist.com

KANSAS WILDLIFE FEDERATION

P.O. Box 8237
Wichita, KS 67208-0237 United States
Phone: 785-526-7466   Fax: 785-658-2466

Scope: State

Description: A representative statewide organization, affiliated with the National Wildlife Federation, dedicated to the protection and enhancement of wildlife and its habitat through public education and government interaction.

Publication(s): Kansas Wildlife Federation: The Voice of Outdoor Kansas (Newsletter)

Contact(s):
Tommie Berger, President & Representative; 785-658-2465
Roger Brooner, Treasurer; 316-768-3827
Velma Miller, Alternate Representative & Editor
Steve Montgomery, Education Programs Contact

KANSAS WILDSCAPE FOUNDATION

1 Riverfront Plaza
Suite 123
Lawrence, KS 66044 United States
Phone: 785-843-9453   Fax: 785-843-6379
E-mail: wildscape@sunflower.com
Website: kansaswildscape.com

Founded: 1991
Membership: 1,001–10,000
Scope: State

Description: The Kansas Wildscape Foundation is dedicated to conserving and perpetuating the land, wild species, and the rich beauty of Kansas for the use and enjoyment of all. Wildscape is dedicated to providing outdoor opportunities to all people in Kansas and to teach the children of Kansas a good outdoor ethic that they can pass along to future generations.

Keyword(s): Ethics/Environmental Justice, Land Issues, Public Health, Recreation/Ecotourism, Reduce/Reuse/Recycle, Water Habitats & Quality, Wildlife & Species

Contact(s):
Gene Argo, Chairman
Hank Booth, Executive Director; 785-843-9453; Fax: 785-843-6379; hankbooth@sunflower.com
Rachael Humphrey, Director of Member Services & Administration; 1 Riverfront Plaza, Suite 123, Lawrence, KS 66044; 785-843-9453; Fax: 785-843-6379; rachael@sunflower.com
Megan Krier, Events Coordinator; 785-843-9453; Fax: 785-843-6379; megankrier@sunflower.com
Charlie Becker, Treasurer

KEEP AMERICA BEAUTIFUL, INC.

1010 Washington Blvd., 7th Fl.
Stamford, CT 06901 United States
Phone: 203-323-8987   Fax: 203-325-9199
E-mail: info@kab.org
Website: www.kab.org

Founded: 1953
Scope: National

Description: A national nonprofit public education organization dedicated to developing community improvement programs in litter prevention, beautification and recycling.

Publication(s): Network News

Keyword(s): Land Issues, Public Lands/Greenspace, Reduce/Reuse/Recycle

Contact(s):
G. Empson, President
Susanne Woods, Senior Vice President of Development and Environmental Programs
John Bard, Vice Chairman of the Board
Thomas Tomoney, Chairman of the Board

KEEP FLORIDA BEAUTIFUL, INC.

201 East Park Avenue
Tallahassee, FL 32301 United States
Phone: 850-385-1528   Fax: 850-385-4020
Website: www.keepfloridabeautiful.org

Founded: 1991
Membership: 1–100
Scope: State

Description: KFB's mission is to empower individuals to take greater responsibility for their community environment.

Keyword(s): Land Issues, Reduce/Reuse/Recycle, Water Habitats & Quality

Contact(s):
Shane McIntosh, Chairman, Board of Directors

KEEPING TRACK, INC

P.O. Box 444
Huntington, VT 05462 United States
Phone: 802-434-7000   Fax: 802-434-5383
E-mail: info@keepingtrackinc.org
Website: www.keepingtrackinc.org

Founded: 1994
Membership: 1,001–10,000
Scope: Local, State, Regional, National

Description: Keeping Track teaches adults and children to observe, interpret, record, and monitor evidence of wildlife, especially wide-ranging carnivores, in their communities, and support citizens' use of monitoring data in local and regional conservation planning. The Keeping Track Youth Program focuses on educating youth in grades K - 12 about tracking as a monitoring tool, wildlife ecology, and habitat conservation.

Publication(s): The Woods Scientist, Guide to Photographing Tracks & Signs, Project and Data Management Protocol, Keeping Track quarterly newsletter

Keyword(s): Sprawl/Urban Planning, Wildlife & Species

Contact(s):
Lars Botzojorns, Executive Director; lars@keepingtrackinc.org
Susan Morse, Program and Research Director
Sean Lawson, Youth Program Coordinator; sean@keepingtrackinc.org
Monica Mac, Office Manager; monica@keepingtrackinc.org

KENTUCKY ACADEMY OF SCIENCE

Robert J. Barney, President
Land Grant Program
Kentucky State University
Frankfort, KY 40601 United States
Phone: 502-597-6178   Fax: 502-597-6381
E-mail: rbarney@gwmail.kysu.edu
Website: kas.wku.edu/kas/

Founded: 1914
Membership: 101–1,000
Scope: Regional

Description: To encourage scientific research, promote the diffusion of scientific knowledge, and unify the scientific interests of Kentucky.

Publication(s): Newsletter of Kentucky Academy of Science, Journal of the Kentucky Academy of Science

Contact(s):
Jerry Warner, President; Department of Biological Sciences, Northern Kentucky University, Nunn Drive, Highland Heights, KY 41099; 859-572-5277; Fax: 859-572-5639; warner@nku.edu
Robert Kingsolver, Vice President; Department of Biology, Kentucky Wesleyan College, Owensboro, KY 42302; 270-852-3161; Fax: 270-926-3196; kingsol@kwc.edu
Robert Barney, President Elect; Atwood Research Facility, Kentucky State University, Frankfort, KY 40601; 502-597-6178; rbarney@gwmail.kysu.edu

Kenneth Crawford, Treasurer; Dept. of Biology, Western Kentucky University, Bowling Green, KY 42101; 270-745-6005; Fax: 270-745-6856; kenneth.crawford@wku.edu

Stephanie Dew, Secretary; Dept. of Biology, Centre College, 600 West Walnut Street, Danville, KY 40422; 859-238-5316; dews@centre.edu

Claire Rinehart, Webpage Editor; Department of Biology, Western Kentucky University, Bowling Green, KY 42101; 270-745-6006; Fax: 270-745-6856; claire.rinehart@wku.edu

Ron Rosen, Past President; Dept. of Biology, Berea College, Berea, KY 40404; 859-985-3345; Fax: 859-985-3303; ron_rosen@berea.edu

Raymond Sicard, Editor; School of Osteopathic Medicine, Pikeville College, 147 Sycamore Street, Pikeville, KY 41501; 606-218-5426; Fax: 606-218-5442; rsicard@pc.edu

Elizabeth Sutton, Director, Jr. Academy of Science; Department of Chemistry, Campbellsville University, 1 University Drive, Campbellsville, KY 42718; 270-789-5327; oksutton@campbellsvil.edu

Susan Templeton, Newsletter Editor; 130 Atwood Research Faciltiy, Kentucky State University, Frankfort, KY 40601; 502-597-6030; Fax: 502-597-6381; stempleton@gwmail.kysu.edu

KENTUCKY ASSOCIATION FOR ENVIRONMENTAL EDUCATION (KAEE)
P.O Box 7
Mammoth Cave National Park
Mammoth Cave, KY 42259 United States
Phone: 270-758-2354   Fax: 270-758-2613
Website: www.kaee.org
Scope: State
Description: Organized to promote and support formal and nonformal environmental education programs throughout the state. Promotes information sharing, research, and development of EE programs and activities. Annually sponsors a three-day conference.
Publication(s): Newsletter, Earth Day Handbook, E.E. Resource Guide
Contact(s):
Joe Baust, President; Center for Environmental Education, Murray State University, Murray, KY 42071; 270-762-2595; joe.baust@coe.murraystate.edu
Karen Reagor, Executive Director; P.O. Box 176055, Covington, KY 41017; 606-578-0312; KPReagor@aol.com

KENTUCKY ASSOCIATION OF CONSERVATION DISTRICTS
663 Teton Trail
Frankfort, KY 40601 United States
Phone: 502-564-3080   Fax: 502-564-9195
Scope: State
Contact(s):
John Chism, President, Alternate Board Member; 606-744-8909; Fax: 502-564-0105
Patrick Henderson, Vice President; Rt. 1 Box 146, Irvington, KY 40146; 502-547-6206; Fax: 502-564-9195
Kevin Jeffries, Secretary-Treasurer; 1503 E. Hwy. 22, Crestwood, KY 40014; 502-222-9877; Fax: 502-222-0046
James Lacy, Board Member; 300 Sanfield Rd., Campton, KY 41301; 606-662-4161; Fax: 606-668-7033

KENTUCKY BASS FEDERATION
P.O. Box 71
4058 U.S. 42 W
Warsaw, KY 41095 United States
Phone: 859-567-2885
E-mail: donkee311@earthlink.net
Website: www.kybassfed.com
Scope: State
Description: An organization of Bassmaster chapters, affiliated with the Bass Anglers Sportsman Society, organized to fight pollution, assist state and national conservation agencies in their efforts, and teach the young people of our country good conservation practices. Dedicated to the realistic conservation of our water resources.
Contact(s):
Donnie Keeton, President; P.O. Box 71, 4058 US 42 West, Warsaw, KY; 859-567-2885; donkee311@earthlink.net
John Romans, Conservation Director; 209 Park Ave., Carrollton, KY 41008; john.romans@dowcorning.com

KENTUCKY NATURAL LANDS TRUST
433 Chestnut Street
Berea, KY 40403 United States
Phone: 1-877-367-5658   Fax: 1-859-986-1299
E-mail: info@blantonforest.org
Website: www.blantonforest.org
Founded: 1995
Scope: State
Description: Kentucky Natural Lands Trust is a statewide land trust working with the Kentucky State Nature Preserves Commission and other organizations to secure funds for the protection of natural land and its long-term stewardship and to serve as a resource and partner to other land trusts and conservation groups.
Publication(s): Blanton Forest Journal
Keyword(s): Forests/Forestry, Land Issues, Public Lands/Greenspace, Wildlife & Species
Contact(s):
Donna Alexander, Development Assistant; 1-877-367-5658; ext. 228; dalexander@blantonforest.org

KENTUCKY RESOURCES COUNCIL
P.O. Box 1070
Frankfort, KY 40602-1070 United States
Phone: 502-875-2428   Fax: 502-875-2845
E-mail: fitzkrc@aol.com
Website: www.kyrc.org
Scope: State
Description: The KRC is a nonprofit, membership-based statewide organization dedicated to the conservation and prudent use of Kentucky's natural resources. The membership shares a common concern with the impact of mineral extraction, natural resource development, and economic development on our homes, health, and quality of life. The Council provides legal assistance to individuals and groups, without charge, on air, waste, water and mining issues in the state.
Keyword(s): Pollution (general), Water Habitats & Quality
Contact(s):
Tom FitzGerald, Director

KENTUCKY WOODLAND OWNERS ASSOCIATION
1483 Big Run Rd.
Wallingford, KY 41093 United States
Phone: 859-986-2373   Fax: 859-986-1299
E-mail: herbloyd@aol.com
Website: www.kentuckywoodlandownersassociation.com
Founded: 1991
Membership: 1–100
Scope: State
Description: A statewide nonprofit organization, affiliated with the National Woodland Owners Association, organized to promote good forest stewardship, circulate information on timber marketing, and encourage private property responsibility among woodland owners throughout the Commonwealth of Kentucky.
Publication(s): Kentucky Woodlands
Keyword(s): Forests/Forestry

Contact(s):
Joe Ball, President
Herb Loyd, Vice-President
Bill Green, Secretary
Pete McNeill, Treasurer

KEYSTONE CENTER, THE
1628 Saints John Rd.
Keystone, CO 80435 United States
Phone: 970-513-5800   Fax: 970-262-0152
E-mail: tkcspp@keystone.org
Website: www.keystone.org

Founded: 1975
Membership: 1–100
Scope: National
Description: A nonprofit center for environmental dispute resolution, mediation, and facilitation. Conducts national policy dialogues on environmental, energy, natural resources, health, and science/technology issues; assists in environmental decisionmaking and regulatory negotiations; provides environmental mediation services; provides training and organizational development services in environmental conflict resolution.
Publication(s): Consensus, Discovery
Keyword(s): Energy, Public Health
Contact(s):
Tom Grumbly, President

KIDS FOR A BETTER ENVIRONMENT
K.F.A.B.E.
HEADQUARTERS
17 Otter Drive
Ft. Mitchell, KY 41017 United States
Phone: 859-322-3901   Fax: 859-363-8536
E-mail: ccblum1@msn.com
Website: groups.msn.com/KidsForABetterEnvironment K-F-A-B-E/homepagewelcome.msnw

Founded: 2003
Membership: 1–100
Scope: International
Description: K.F.A.B.E. Is an organization of kids and adults working together to educate the public, inform, campaign, help out making parks and yards more friendly for nature and raise funds for environmental and animal organizations.
Contact(s):
Cristine Blum, Founder; 859-322-3901; Fax: 859-363-8536; ccblum1@msn.com

KIDS FOR SAVING EARTH WORLDWIDE
P.O. Box 421118
Minneapolis, MN 55442 United States
Phone: 763-559-1234   Fax: 763-559-6980
E-mail: kseww@aol.com
Website: www.kidsforsavingearth.org/

Founded: 1989
Membership: 1,001–10,000
Scope: National
Description: KSEW's mission is to educate and empower children to help to protect the Earth's environment by providing free educational materials to kids, schools, and organizations through the KSE Network. Curriculum guides are also available.
Publication(s): The Earth is a Gift Poster, So What's a Toxic Waste Site, Travel the Earth Book, A Trip to a Forest, Toxic Waste Site Poster, KSE News, Rock the World Concert Kit, KSE Action Guide
Keyword(s): Air Quality/Atmosphere, Energy, Land Issues, Pollution (general), Public Lands/Greenspace, Reduce/Reuse/Recycle, Water Habitats & Quality, Wildlife & Species
Contact(s):
Tessa Hill, President and Director

Steve Henningsgaard, Webmaster
Jacob Taintor, Educational Support Services

KIDS ON THE BAYOU
P.O. Box 440490
Houston, TX 77219-1563 United States
Phone: 281-759-8343   Fax: 281-759-8313
E-mail: lawrence_spence@yahoo.com
Website: bayoupreservation.org

Founded: 2000
Scope: Local, State
Description: Supplemental environmental education programs in an after-school setting. Kids on the Bayou (KOB) assists lower income schools in the Greater Houston, Texas area with field trips, activities, curriculum, educational presentations, teaching-assistants, school-yard habitats and service-learning projects. KOB emphasizes the importance of water, watersheds and bayous. KOB is a resource for educators, activists and students.
Keyword(s): Ecosystems (precious), Pollution (general), Recreation/Ecotourism, Sprawl/Urban Planning, Water Habitats & Quality
Contact(s):
Duncan Ragsdale, Program Coordinator; P.O. Box 440490, Houston, TX 77244-0490; 281-759-8343; duncanrags@ev1.net
Lawrence Spence, After-School Coordinator; 281-684-0288; lawrence_spence@yahoo.com

KODIAK BROWN BEAR TRUST
11930 Circle Dr.
Anchorage, AK 99516 United States
Phone: 907-345-2939   Fax: 907-348-0450

Founded: 1981
Scope: National
Description: The Kodiak Brown Bear Trust is an Alaska-based nonprofit wildlife conservation trust whose mission is to support conservation of the majestic Kodiak brown bear through funding of habitat protection, research and public education.
Publication(s): Exxon Valdez conservation saga in Alaska.
Keyword(s): Wildlife & Species
Contact(s):
Tim Richardson, Executive Director; 6707 Old Stage Rd., North Bethesda, MD 20852-4329; 301-770-6496
Dave Cline, Chairman

L

LA JOLLA FRIENDS OF THE SEALS (LJFS)
P.O. Box 2016
La Jolla, CA 92038 United States
Phone: 619-687-3588
E-mail: phoca@lajollaseals.org
Website: www.lajollaseals.org

Founded: 1999
Membership: 101–1,000
Scope: Local
Description: La Jolla Friends of the Seals is an independent non-profit organization that was established in 1999 to protect the La Jolla Harbor seal colony and promote safe viewing of the seals by way of education and respect through its naturalist-docent program. In addition to educating the public, docents gather valuable data about the seals.
Keyword(s): Ecosystems (precious), Oceans/Coasts/Beaches, Recreation/Ecotourism, Water Habitats & Quality, Wildlife & Species
Contact(s):
Patrick Hord, Executive Director; patrick@lajollaseals.org

LADY BIRD JOHNSON WILDFLOWER CENTER
4801 La Crosse Ave.
Austin, TX 78739 United States
Phone: 512-292-4100   Fax: 512-292-4627
Website: www.wildflower.org

Founded: 1982
Scope: National
Description: The Lady Bird Johnson Wildflower Center's purpose is to educate people about the environmental necessity, economic value, and natural beauty of native plants. The Wildflower Center, a nonprofit organization, serves North America by promoting the preservation and use of native plants through education programs, information dissemination, and by example.
Publication(s): Native Plants magazine, Wild Ideas, The Store Catalog
Keyword(s): Land Issues, Wildlife & Species
Contact(s):
Robert Breunig, Executive Director
Denise Delaney, Director of Horticulture
Flo Oxley, Acting Director of Education/Senior Botanist
Karen Stevenson, Communications Director
Helen Hayes, Co-Founder
Lady Bird Johnson, Co-Founder
Leslie Lewis, Contact

LAKE ERIE CLEAN-UP COMMITTEE, INC.
Attn: President, 29789 Fort Rd.
Rockwood, MI 48173 United States
Phone: 313-379-3891

Founded: 1959
Scope: National
Description: The LECC's mission is to stop pollution of Lake Erie and of all freshwater lakes and streams; to inform the public of the need for greater pollution controls; to prevent the return to the methods of the past; and to encourage industry to do more research. Our Great Lakes are a fragile part of our ecosystem and we must continue to protect them. Membership includes representatives of Michigan and Ohio citizen groups.
Keyword(s): Oceans/Coasts/Beaches, Water Habitats & Quality, Wildlife & Species
Contact(s):
Leonard Mannausa, President; 29789 Fort Rd., Rockwood, MI 48173; 313-370-3801
Jerome Falwell, Treasurer; 30251 Worth, Gibraltar, MI 48173
Richard Micka, Secretary; 47 E. Elm, Monroe, MI 48162; 313-242-0909

LAKE HOPATCONG PROTECTIVE ASSOCIATION
P.O. Box 443
Lake Hopatcong, NJ 7849 United States
Phone: 973-398-2511   Fax: 973-398-2511
E-mail: lakehse8@yahoo.com

Founded: 1955
Membership: 101–1,000
Scope: Regional
Description: Preserve and protect Lake Hopatcong
Contact(s):
Clifford Lundin, President; 973-398-2511; Fax: 973-398-2511; lakehse8@yahoo.com

LAKE MICHIGAN FEDERATION
220 S. State St., Suite 1900
Chicago, IL 60604 United States
Phone: 312-939-0838   Fax: 312-939-2708
E-mail: Info@lakemichigan.org
Website: www.lakemichigan.org

Founded: 1970
Membership: 101–1,000
Scope: Regional
Description: A coalition of citizens and citizen organizations in Wisconsin, Illinois, Indiana, and Michigan dedicated to protecting Lake Michigan through community action and research. Supported by foundation and corporate grants, membership and contributions.
Publication(s): Lake Michigan Monitor, Wetlands and Water Quality: A Citizen's Guide to Cleaning Up Contaminated Sediments, A Citizen's Action Guide
Keyword(s): Oceans/Coasts/Beaches, Pollution (general), Water Habitats & Quality
Contact(s):
Cameron Owens, Executive Director
Sophia Twichell, Board of Directors

LAKE SUPERIOR GREENS
P.O. Box 1144
Superior, WI 54880 United States
Phone: 715-392-5782

Founded: 1991
Membership: 1–100
Scope: National
Description: Lake Superior Greens is a grassroots group joined to other Green groups in our dedication to a more sustainable lifestyle and a healthy planet. We are active locally as well as on a state, national, and international basis, recognizing that all issues are interrelated.
Publication(s): Monthly newsletter
Keyword(s): Pollution (general), Water Habitats & Quality
Contact(s):
Bob Browne, Contact; 422 Fisher Ogden, Superior, WI 54880; 715-394-6235
Jan Conley, Steering Committee; 2406 Hughitt, Superior, WI 54880; 715-392-5782
John Schraufnagel, Contact; 1506 N. 19th, Superior, WI 54880; 715-394-6660
Rosie Seymour, Contact; 1606 N. 18th St., Superior, WI 54880; 715-395-0494

LAKENET
300 State St.
Annapolis, MD 21403 United States
Phone: 410-268-5155   Fax: 410-268-8788
E-mail: info@worldlakes.org
Website: www.worldlakes.org

Founded: 1978
Membership: 1,001–10,000
Scope: National, International
Description: LakeNet is a global network of people and organizations in 90+ countries working for the conservation and sustainable development of lakes. The LakeNet Secretariat is a U.S.-based nonprofit organization dedicated to bringing together people and solutions to protect and restore the health of the world's lakes.
Publication(s): LakeNet Report Series, Success Stories, Sustainable Development
Keyword(s): Development/Developing Countries, Ecosystems (precious), Land Issues, Oceans/Coasts/Beaches, Pollution (general), Public Health, Recreation/Ecotourism, Water Habitats & Quality, Wildlife & Species
Contact(s):
David Barker, President; 410-268-5155; Fax: 410-268-8788; drbarker@monitorinternational.org
Lisa Borre, Vice President; 410-268-5155; Fax: 410-268-8788; lborre@monitorinternational.org
Laurie Duker, LakeNet Conservation Director; 410-268-5155; Fax: 410-268-8788; lduker@worldlakes.org
John Dolan, Secretary
Jan Hartke, Board of Trustees Chairman
Richard Tobin, Treasurer

LAND AND WATER FUND OF THE ROCKIES
2260 Baseline Rd., Suite 200
Boulder, CO 80302 United States
Phone: 303-444-1188 Fax: 303-786-8054
E-mail: landwater@lawfund.org
Website: www.lawfund.org

Founded: 1991

Scope: Regional

Description: Founded in 1991, the Land and Water Fund of the Rockies (LAW Fund) is an environmental law and policy center serving the Interior West. The LAW Fund uses law, economics, and policy analysis to protect land and water resources, protect essential habitats for plants and animals, and assure that energy demands are met in environmentally sound and sustainable ways.

Keyword(s): Air Quality/Atmosphere, Ecosystems (precious), Energy, Forests/Forestry, Water Habitats & Quality, Wildlife & Species

LAND BETWEEN THE LAKES ASSOCIATION
345 Maintenance Road
Golden Pond, KY 42211-9001 United States
Phone: 270-924-2000 Fax: 270-924-2119
Website: www.lbl.org

Founded: 1983

Membership: 1,001–10,000

Scope: National

Description: A private nonprofit membership organization supporting and promoting USDA Forest Service's Land Between The Lakes National Recreation Area, a 170,000-acre national demonstration in natural resource management, environmental education, and recreation.

Keyword(s): Ethics/Environmental Justice, Land Issues, Public Lands/Greenspace, Water Habitats & Quality

Contact(s):
Windel Wooton, President
Gaye Luber, Director
Jim Wallace, Chairman

LAND CONSERVANCY OF WEST MICHIGAN
1345 Monroe Avenue NW
Suite 324
Grand Rapids, MI 49505 United States
Phone: 616-451-9476
E-mail: lcwm@naturenearby.org
Website: www.naturenearby.org

Founded: 1976

Scope: Local

Description: Local land conservancy that works to protect lands that contribute to the scenic and natural heritage of central west Michigan, including Oceana, Muskegon, Newaygo, Ottawa, Kent, northern Allegan, and southern Lake counties.

Keyword(s): Agriculture/Farming, Ecosystems (precious), Land Issues, Oceans/Coasts/Beaches, Public Lands/Greenspace, Recreation/Ecotourism, Water Habitats & Quality, Wildlife & Species

Contact(s):
Nora Callow, Membership and Business Coordinator; 616-451-9476; lcwm@naturenearby.org
Rhoda deJonge, Land Protection Specialist; 616-451-9476; lcwm@naturenearby.org
Danielle Fogel, Outreach & Communications Coordinator; 616-451-9476; lcwm@naturenearby.org
Douglas Powless, Science and Stewardship Coordinator; 616-451-9476; ext. 6; doug@naturenearby.org
April Scholtz, Land Protection Director; 616-451-9476; lcwm@naturenearby.org
Julie Stoneman, Executive Director; 616-451-9476; lcwm@naturenearby.org

LAND TRUST ALLIANCE, THE
1331 H St., NW, 4th Fl.
Washington, DC 20005 United States
Phone: 202-638-4725 Fax: 202-638-4730
E-mail: lta@lta.org
Website: www.lta.org

Founded: 1982

Membership: 101–1,000

Scope: National

Description: Provides training, technical assistance and publications for local and regional land trusts to increase their skills and strengthen the land trust movement; fosters public policies that further land trusts' goals; sponsors the National Land Trust Rally; and builds awareness among a broad constituency of the consequences of diminishing land resources and the role of land trusts in saving land.

Publication(s): Exchange, Conservation Easement Stewardship Guide, National Directory of Conservation Land Trusts, Starting a Land Trust, Federal Tax Law of Conservation Easements, Appraising Easements, Conservation Easement Handbook.

Keyword(s): Forests/Forestry, Land Issues, Wildlife & Species

Contact(s):
Rand Wentworth, President
Phil Jones, Vice President of Operations
Mary Pope Hutson, Vice President of Development
Andrew Zepp, Vice President for Programs
Robert Bowers, Chairman
David Hartwell, Treasurer
Will Shafroth, Secretary
Anthony Wood, Vice Chair

LANDOWNER PLANNING CENTER
P.O. Box 2242
Boston, MA 2101 United States

Publication(s): Preserving Family Lands, Book 2, Preserving Family Lands, Book 1

Contact(s):
Connie Small

LANDWATCH MONTEREY COUNTY
Box 1876
Salinas, CA 93902 United States
Phone: 831-422-9390 Fax: 831-422-9391
E-mail: landwatch@mclw.org
Website: www.landwatch.org

Founded: 1997

Membership: 1,001–10,000

Scope: Regional

Description: LandWatch is committed to fundamental land use reform and works to build public support for better land use policies at the local, regional, and state level.

Publication(s): Update, State of Monterey County

Keyword(s): Agriculture/Farming, Ethics/Environmental Justice, Land Issues, Public Lands/Greenspace, Sprawl/Urban Planning, Transportation, Wildlife & Species

Contact(s):
Gary Patton, Executive Director; 831-422-9390; ext. 10; Fax: 831-422-9391; gapatton@mclw.org
Lupe Garcia, Community Action Advocate; 831-422-9390; ext. 13; Fax: 831-422-9391; lygarcia@mclw.org
Arianne Tucker, Administrative Director; 831-422-9390; ext. 11; Fax: 831-422-9391; atucker@mclw.org
Chris Fitz, Deputy Director; 831-422-9390; ext. 12; Fax: 831-422-9391; cfitz@mclw.org

LAUDHOLM TRUST
P.O. Box 1007
Wells, ME 04090 United States
Phone: 207-646-4521
E-mail: trust@laudholm.org
Website: www.laudholm.org

Founded: 1982
Membership: 1,001–10,000
Scope: Regional
Description: Promoting stewardship of coastal environments around the Gulf of Maine. We provide financial and logistical support to the Wells National Estuarine Research Reserve.

LEAGUE OF CONSERVATION VOTERS
1920 L St., NW, Suite 800
Washington, DC 20036 United States
Phone: 202-785-8683   Fax: 202-835-0491
E-mail: lcv@lcv.org
Website: www.lcv.org
Founded: 1970
Membership: 1–100
Scope: National
Description: The LCV is the national, bipartisan political action arm of the environmental movement. LCV works to elect pro-environment candidates to Congress; publishes the National Environmental Scorecard, which rates members of Congress on key environmental votes; raises funds for campaigns through its Political Action Committee and Earthlist; and is governed by a Board of Directors made up of leaders from major national environmental organizations.
Publication(s): National Environmental Scorecard, LCV Insider Newsletter., Presidential Scorecard
Keyword(s): Reduce/Reuse/Recycle
Contact(s):
  Deb Callahan, President
  Beth Sullivan, Executive Director, Educational Fund
  Wade Greene, Secretary
  Winsome McIntosh, Treasurer
  Theodore Roosevelt, Chair
  Anne Saer, Chief Financial Officer

LEAGUE OF ENVIRONMENTAL JOURNALISTS
P.O. Box 2062
Accra, na Ghana
Phone: 233-21-236806   Fax: 233-21-310028
E-mail: lejcec@ghana.com
Founded: 1992
Membership: 1–100
Scope: National, International
Description: To mobilize journalists and the mass media for the effective and meaningful coverage of the environment and development issues.
Keyword(s): Development/Developing Countries, Energy, Finance/Banking/Trade, Reduce/Reuse/Recycle, Water Habitats & Quality, Wildlife & Species
Contact(s):
  Mike Anane, President; 233-21-236806; Fax: 233-21-310028; lejcec@ghana.com
  Isabella Gyan, Vice President
  Elliot Ansah, Treasurer

LEAGUE OF KENTUCKY SPORTSMEN, INC.
Jim Thompson/Robert Smith
P.O. Box 8527
Lexington, KY 40533 United States
Phone: 859-276-3518   Fax: 859-276-3518
E-mail: office@kentuckysportsmen.com
Website: kentuckysportsmen.com
Founded: 1935
Membership: 1,001–10,000
Scope: State
Description: A representative statewide organization, affiliated with the National Wildlife Federation, dedicated to the protection and enhancement of wildlife and its habitat through public education and government interaction.
Publication(s): Kentucky Sportsman, The
Keyword(s): Air Quality/Atmosphere, Ecosystems (precious), Ethics/Environmental Justice, Forests/Forestry, Land Issues, Pollution (general), Recreation/Ecotourism, Reduce/Reuse/Recycle, Water Habitats & Quality, Wildlife & Species
Contact(s):
  Jim Thompson, President and Education Programs Contact
  Robert Fraley, Alternate
  Ben Hall, Editor
  Robert Smith, Representative
  Don York, Treasurer

LEAGUE OF OHIO SPORTSMEN
642 West Broad Street
Columbus, OH 43215 United States
Phone: 614-224-8970   Fax: 614-224-8971
E-mail: info@leagueofohiosportsmen.org
Website: www.leagueofohiosportsmen.org
Scope: State
Description: A representative statewide organization, affiliated with the National Wildlife Federation, dedicated to the protection and enhancement of wildlife and its habitat through public education and government interaction.
Publication(s): Ohio Out Of Doors Magazine
Contact(s):
  Larry Mitchell, President & Representative
  Larry Mitchell, Editor & Executive Director
  Pat Agner, Secretary
  Marilyn Lieb, Alternate Representative, Treasurer & Education Programs
  George Lynch, Alternate Representative

LEAGUE OF WOMEN VOTERS OF IOWA
P.O. Box 93775
Des Moines, IA 50393-3775 United States
Phone: 641-777-9739
E-mail: vote@lwvia.org
Website: www.lwvia.org/
Founded: 1920
Membership: 101–1,000
Scope: State
Description: A nonpartisan organization of local chapters and members-at-large, affiliated with the League of Women Voters of the U.S., whose purpose is to promote political responsibility through informed and active participation of citizens in government and to act on selected governmental issues. We promote and support management, preservation, and conservation of our natural resources.
Publication(s): Iowa Voter, Legislative Newsletter
Keyword(s): Air Quality/Atmosphere, Energy, Land Issues, Pollution (general), Reduce/Reuse/Recycle, Water Habitats & Quality
Contact(s):
  Jan McNelly, President
  Cheryl Kieffer, Vice President
  Judie Hoffman, Environmental Coordinator; 515-292-2660

LEAGUE OF WOMEN VOTERS OF THE U.S.
1730 M St., NW #1000
Washington, DC 20036 United States
Phone: 202-429-1965   Fax: 202-429-0854
E-mail: lwv@lwv.org
Website: www.lwv.org
Founded: 1920
Scope: National
Description: Nonpartisan organization of 100,000 members located in all 50 states, the District of Columbia, Hong Kong, and the Virgin Islands, working to promote political responsibility through informed and active participation of citizens in government. Takes political action on water and air quality, solid and hazardous waste management, land use, and energy.

The League of Women Voters Education Fund carries out educational projects, publishes materials, and arranges conferences on water and energy issue

Publication(s): National Voter, The

Keyword(s): Energy

Contact(s):
Carolyn Jenkins, President
Nancy Tate, Executive Director
Bob Adams, Editor

LEAGUE OF WOMEN VOTERS OF WASHINGTON

4710 University Way NE
#214
Seattle, WA 98105 United States
Phone: 206-622-8961   Fax: 206-622-4908
E-mail: lwvwa@lwvwa.org
Website: www.lwvwa.org

Founded: 1920
Membership: 1,001–10,000
Scope: State

Description: The League of Women Voters is a nonpartisan political organization that encourages the informed and active participation of citizens in government and influences public policy through education and advocacy. Any citizen over 18 may become a voting member.

Publication(s): The State We're In: Washington, Gun Control in Washington, Washington State Public Port Districts, Speaking of Ground Water, Washington's Dynamic Forest 1&2, Evaluation of Major Election Methods & Selected laws

Keyword(s): Climate Change, Energy, Forests/Forestry, Land Issues, Public Lands/Greenspace, Transportation, Water Habitats & Quality

LEAGUE TO SAVE LAKE TAHOE

955 Emerald Bay Rd.
South Lake Tahoe, CA 96150 United States
Phone: 530-541-5388   Fax: 530-541-5454
E-mail: info@keeptahoeblue.org
Website: www.keeptahoeblue.org

Founded: 1957
Membership: 1,001–10,000
Scope: Regional

Description: A private, nonprofit corporation dedicated to preserving the environmental balance, scenic beauty, and recreational opportunities of the Lake Tahoe Basin.

Publication(s): Keep Tahoe Blue

Keyword(s): Ecosystems (precious), Forests/Forestry, Land Issues, Public Lands/Greenspace, Recreation/Ecotourism, Sprawl/Urban Planning, Transportation, Water Habitats & Quality, Wildlife & Species

Contact(s):
Rochelle Nason, Executive Director

LEARNING FOR ENVIRONMENTAL ACTION PROGRAMME (LEAP)

University of Victoria, Faculty of Educaton
MacLaurin Building
Victoria, V8W 3N4 British Columbia Canada
Phone: 250-721-7784   Fax: 250-721-6190
E-mail: clover@uvic.ca

Founded: 1990
Scope: International

Description: Book by LEAP: The Nature of Transformation: Environmental Adult Education. The book contains theory but also more than 50 hands-on activities that stimulate critical and creative thinking, teach about "place", weave environmental, cultural, economic, political and social issues, and examine a diversity of local and global issues. To purchase a copy make cheque or money order payable to Darlene E. Clover and post to her at the University of Victoria.

Publication(s): Convergence on Environmental Adult Education, The Nature of Transformation: Environmental Adult Education

Keyword(s): Ethics/Environmental Justice, Reduce/Reuse/Recycle

Contact(s):
Darlene Clover, International Coordinator; 250-721-7785; Fax: 250-721-6190; clover@uvic.ca

LEGACY INTERNATIONAL

GLOBAL YOUTH VILLAGE
1020 Legacy Drive
Bedford, VA 24523 United States
Phone: 540-297-5982   Fax: 540-297-1860
E-mail: mail@legacyintl.org
Website: www.legacyintl.org

Founded: 1979
Membership: 1,001–10,000
Scope: Local, National, International

Description: Mission: Creating environments to address community & global needs while developing effective responses to change. The Global Youth Village challenges teens to turn cross-cultural theory into action while living with others from 20+ cultures. Workshops address issues concerning youth: prejudice, conflict, & more. Cooperative living helps participants respect differences & discover similarities that transcend cultural, religious & political barriers. (Summer staff openings - visit website.)

Publication(s): Organization Brochure, Global Youth Village

Keyword(s): Development/Developing Countries

Contact(s):
Leila Baz, GYV Staff Director; 540-298-5982; Fax: 540-297-1860; staff@legacyintl.org
Mary Helmig, GYV Director; 540-297-5982; youthvillage@legacyintl.org

LEGACY LAND TRUST

214 S. College Ave.
#200
Fort Collins, CO 80524 United States
Phone: 970-266-1711   Fax: 970-482-4858
E-mail: llt@frii.com
Website: www.legacylandtrust.org

Founded: 1993
Membership: 101–1,000
Scope: Regional

Description: We are a regional land trust serving northern Colorado. Working with private landowners and local governments, we have helped protect over 11,000 acres of natural areas, agricultural lands, and open space.

Keyword(s): Agriculture/Farming, Ecosystems (precious), Forests/Forestry, Land Issues, Sprawl/Urban Planning, Wildlife & Species

LEGAL ENVIRONMENTAL ASSISTANCE FOUNDATION INC. (LEAF)

1114 Thomasville Rd., Suite E
Tallahassee, FL 32303-6290 United States
Phone: 850-681-2591   Fax: 850-224-1275
E-mail: leaf@leaflaw.org
Website: www.leaflaw.org

Founded: 1979
Membership: 101–1,000
Scope: Regional

Description: LEAF is a charitable public-interest environmental law firm that protects people's health and natural resources primarily in Alabama, Florida and Georgia.

Publication(s): LEAF Newsletter, various educational documents.

Keyword(s): Air Quality/Atmosphere, Ethics/Environmental Justice, Pollution (general), Public Health, Water Habitats & Quality

Contact(s):
- Robert Martin, President; 850-681-2591; Fax: 850-224-1275; rmartin@leaflaw.org
- David Ludder, General Counsel; 850-681-2591; Fax: 850-224-1275; dludder@leaflaw.org
- Cynthia Valencic, Vice President; 850-681-2591; Fax: 850-224-1275; cvalencic@leaflaw.org
- Scott Randolph, Attorney; 850-681-2591; Fax: 850-224-1275; srandolph@leaflaw.org
- Jeanne Zokovitch, Attorney; 850-681-2591; Fax: 850-224-1275; jzokovitch@leaflaw.org

LIFE OF THE LAND
76 North King St., Suite 203
Honolulu, HI 96817 United States
Phone: 808-533-3454   Fax: 808-533-0993
E-mail: life_of_the_land@hotmail.com
Website: www.lifeoftheland.orf

Founded: 1970
Membership: 101–1,000
Scope: Local, State
Description: To preserve and protect the life of the land through sustainable land use and energy policies and to promote open government through research, education, advocacy and, when necessary, litigation.
Publication(s): Ka Uila News, Life of the Land Newsletter
Keyword(s): Agriculture/Farming, Air Quality/Atmosphere, Climate Change, Ecosystems (precious), Energy, Ethics/Environmental Justice, Executive/Legislative/Judicial Reform, Forests/Forestry, Land Issues, Oceans/Coasts/Beaches, Pollution (general), Recreation/Ecotourism

Contact(s):
- Kapua Sproat, President
- Kat Brady, Asst. Executive Director; 808-533-3454; katbrady@hotmail.com
- Henry Curtis, Executive Director; 808-533-3454; life_of_the_land@hotmail.com

LIGHTHAWK
P.O. Box 653
Lander, WY 82520 United States
Phone: 307-332-3242   Fax: 307-332-1641
E-mail: info@lighthawk.org
Website: www.lighthawk.org

Founded: 1979
Scope: International
Description: LightHawk's Mission is to champion environmental protection utilizing the unique perspective of flight. LightHawk's all-volunteer pilot corps conducts aerial missions with key decision-makers, media representatives, community leaders and conservation groups, illuminating critical environmental concerns by flying over and into lands otherwise inaccessible. LightHawk operates regional programs in the Pacific Northwest, British Columbia, California, the Rocky Mountains, and Mesoamerica
Publication(s): LightHawk Newsletter
Keyword(s): Forests/Forestry, Land Issues, Oceans/Coasts/Beaches, Reduce/Reuse/Recycle, Water Habitats & Quality, Wildlife & Species

Contact(s):
- Michael Azeez, President
- Marty Fujita, Executive Director
- Patricia Farrar, Treasurer
- Blaine Townsend, Secretary

LIGHTHAWK
NEW ENGLAND REGION
NORTHERN WINGS
2040 Route 4A East
Castletown, VT 05735 United States
Phone: 802-468-2121   Fax: 802-468-2121
E-mail: info@lighthawk.org
Website: www.lighthawk.org

Founded: 1989
Scope: International
Description: A nonprofit membership organization dedicated to providing free aviation services to environmental and conservation groups worldwide. These services are provided through a network of member pilots and include aerial surveys and photography, flying essential observers, etc.
Publication(s): Despatches
Keyword(s): Land Issues

Contact(s):
- Alan Brecher, Executive Director

LIGHTHAWK
NORTHERN ROCKY MOUNTAIN FIELD OFFICE
31845 Frontage Rd.
Bozeman, MT 59715 United States
Phone: 307-332-1642
E-mail: sarahd@lighthawk.org

Scope: Regional
Contact(s):
- Sarah Deopscine, Program Coordinator

LIGHTHAWK
NORTHWEST FIELD OFFICE
2915 E. Madison St., Suite 306
Seattle, WA 98112 United States
Phone: 360-344-3550   Fax: 360-301-4253
E-mail: susen@lighthawk.org
Website: www.lighthawk.org

Scope: Regional
Contact(s):
- Susen Seth, Program Manager; susen@lighthawk.org

LITERACY FOR ENVIRONMENTAL JUSTICE
HERON'S HEAD PARK PROGRAMS
LIVING CLASSROOM PROGRAMS
6220 Third Street
San Francisco, CA 94124 United States
Phone: 415-508-0575   Fax: 415-508-0576
E-mail: info@lejyouth.org
Website: www.lejyouth.org

Founded: 1998
Membership: 101–1,000
Scope: Local
Description: Literacy for Environmental Justice (LEJ) is an urban environmental education and youth empowerment organization created specifically to address the unique ecological and social concerns of Southeast San Francisco. Our mission is to foster an understanding of the principles of environmental justice and urban sustainability in our young people in order to promote the long-term health of their communities.
Keyword(s): Agriculture/Farming, Air Quality/Atmosphere, Ecosystems (precious), Energy, Ethics/Environmental Justice, Oceans/Coasts/Beaches, Reduce/Reuse/Recycle, Water Habitats & Quality

Contact(s):
- Dana Lanza, Executive Director; 415-508-0575; Fax: 415-508-0576; dana@lejyouth.org
- CeCe Carpio, Youth Envision Coordinator; 415-508-0575; Fax: 415-508-0576; youthenvision@lejyouth.org
- Brenda Salgado, Environmental Justice Coordinator; 415-508-0575; Fax: 415-508-0576; info@lejyouth.org
- Jenn Sramek, Living Classroom Coordinator; 415-508-0575; Fax: 415-508-0576; livingclassroom@lejyouth.org
- Cleo Woelfle-Erskine, Heron's Head Park Coordinator; 415-508-0575; Fax: 415-508-0576; heronshead@lejyouth.org

LITTLE JUNIATA RIVER CHAPTER
(LJRC)
RD5 Box 210B
Tyrone, PA 16686 United States
Phone: 814-684-4274
E-mail: webmaster@littlejuniata.org
Website: www.littlejuniata.org

Founded: 2002
Membership: 1–100
Scope: Local
Description: Working to promote fly fishing, watershed restoration and conservation in Central Pennsylvania through educational programs and volunteer activities.

LIVING RIVERS
UTAH OFFICE
ARIZONA OFFICE
GLEN CANYON ACTION NETWORK
P.O. Box 466
21 North Main Street
Moab, UT 84532 United States
Phone: 435-259-1063   Fax: 435-259-7612
E-mail: info@livingrivers.net
Website: www.livingrivers.net

Founded: 2000
Scope: Local, State, Regional, National, International
Description: Living Rivers promotes large-scale river restoration through broad-based mobilization. People putting rivers first, reviving their natural habitat and spirit by undoing the extensive damage brought on by dams, diversions, and unmitigated pollution. Whether investigation, litigation or demonstration, Living Rivers is on the front lines articulating the conservation and alternative management strategies necessary to bring rivers back to life.
Publication(s): Living Rivers Currents
Keyword(s): Agriculture/Farming, Ecosystems (precious), Energy, Ethics/Environmental Justice, Executive/Legislative/Judicial Reform, Forests/Forestry, Land Issues, Oceans/Coasts/Beaches, Public Health, Public Lands/Greenspace, Recreation/Ecotourism, Water Habitats & Quality
Contact(s):
- Lisa Force, Program Director; P.O. Box 1589, Scottsdale, AZ 85252; 480-990-7839; Fax: 480-990-2662; lforce@livingrivers.net
- Owen Lammers, Executive Director; 435-259-1063; Fax: 435-259-7612; owen@livingrivers.net
- David Orr, Director of Field Programs; 435-259-1063; Fax: 435-259-7612; david@livingrivers.net
- John Weisheit, Conservation Director; 435-259-1063; Fax: 435-259-7612; john@livingrivers.net

LONG LIVE THE KINGS
1305 4th Ave.Suite 810
Seattle, WA 98101 United States
Phone: 206-382-9555
E-mail: lltk@lltk.org
Website: www.longlivethekings.org

Founded: 1986
Scope: Regional
Description: To rebuild wild salmon populations in the Pacific Northwest. We are supported by individuals, foundations, corporations, government agencies, Indian tribes, and fishing and environmental organizations.
Publication(s): Long Live the Kings Newsletter
Keyword(s): Wildlife & Species
Contact(s):
- Barbara Cairns, Executive Director
- Jim Youngren, Chairman of the Board

LOS ANGELES AND SAN GABRIEL RIVERS WATERSHED COUNCIL, THE
700 N. Alameda St.
Los Angeles, CA 90012 United States
Phone: 213-229-9945   Fax: 213-229-9952
E-mail: infolasg@lasgrwc.org
Website: www.lasgrwc.org

Founded: 1996
Membership: 1,001–10,000
Scope: Local, Regional
Description: The Watershed Council is an organization of community groups, government agencies, business and academia working cooperatively to solve problems in the watershed.
Publication(s): Beneficial Uses of the LA & San Gabriel, Stormwater: Asset Not Liability, WatershedWise

LOUISIANA ASSOCIATION OF CONSERVATION DISTRICTS
Attn: President, 663 Holmes Rd.
Keatchie, LA 71046 United States
Phone: 318-933-5375

Scope: State
Contact(s):
- Jerry Holmes, President; 663 Holmes Rd., Keatchie, LA 71046; 318-933-5375; Fax: 318-872-3178
- John Woodward, Vice President, Board Member; 1902 Savanne Rd., Houma, LA 70360; 504-879-3528; Fax: 504-876-5267
- John Compton, Board Member; 6267 Moss Side Ln., Baton Rouge, LA 70808; 225-766-7979
- Charles Dupuy, Secretary/Treasurer and Board Member; 313 N. Monroe St., Ste #4, Marksville, LA 71351; 318-253-7603; Fax: 318-253-8890

LOUISIANA BASS FEDERATION
Attn: President, 4548 Chelsea Dr.
Baton Rouge, LA 70809 United States
Phone: 225-923-1908
E-mail: mwcourtney1@cox.net
Website: www.louisianabass.org

Scope: State
Description: An organization of Bassmaster chapters, affiliated with the Bass Anglers Sportsman Society, organized to fight pollution, assist state and national conservation agencies in their efforts, and teach the young people of our country good conservation practices. Dedicated to the realistic conservation of our water resources.
Contact(s):
- Kevin Gaubert, President; 504-785-9069
- Will Courtney, Conservation Director; 4548 Chelsea Dr., Baton Rouge, LA 70809; 225-923-1908

LOUISIANA FORESTRY ASSOCIATION
P.O. Drawer 5067
Alexandria, LA 71307-5067 United States
Phone: 318-443-2558   Fax: 318-443-1713
E-mail: lfa@laforestry.com
Website: www.laforestry.com

Founded: 1947
Membership: 1,001–10,000
Scope: State
Description: Non-profit trade association whose mission is to promote the health and productivity of Louisiana's forests for present and future generations through the practice of sustainable forestry.
Publication(s): Forests and People, Louisana Logger
Keyword(s): Forests/Forestry
Contact(s):
- Charles Vandersteen, Executive Director
- Clyde Todd, Staff Forester

LOUISIANA WILDLIFE FEDERATION, INC.

P.O. Box 65239
337 South Acadian Thruway
Baton Rouge, LA 70896-5239 United States
Phone: 225-344-6762   Fax: 225-344-6707
E-mail: lawildfed@aol.com

Founded: 1940
Membership: 10,001–100,000
Scope: State
Description: A representative statewide organization, affiliated with the National Wildlife Federation, dedicated to the protection and enhancement of wildlife and its habitat through public education and government interaction.
Publication(s): Louisiana Wildlife Federation magazine
Keyword(s): Oceans/Coasts/Beaches, Recreation/Ecotourism, Water Habitats & Quality, Wildlife & Species
Contact(s):
  Randy Lanctot, Executive Director and Editor; 225-344-6762; Fax: 225-344-6707; lawildfed@aol.com
  Jodie Singer, Office Manager; 225-344-6762; Fax: 225-344-6707

LOUISIANA WILDLIFE REHABILITATORS ASSOCIATION
LAWRA
P. O. Box 90201
Lafayette, LA 70509 United States
Phone: 985-796-9679   Fax: 985-796-8426
E-mail: bgast@lawraonline.com
Website: www.lawraonline.com

Scope: Local, State, Regional
Description: State organization of licensed wildlife rehabilitators, who take in injured/orphaned/displaced wildlife and release them after adequate care is given.
Publication(s): Wildlife Rehabilitation Textbook, The Wildlife Connection
Keyword(s): Ethics/Environmental Justice, Wildlife & Species
Contact(s):
  Gina Stanton, President
  Leslie Lattimore, Vice-President
  Beau Gast, Director of Communications, Public Relations

LOWER MERION CONSERVANCY
1301 Rose Glen Road
Gladwyne, PA 19035 United States
Phone: 610-645-9030
E-mail: dbetz@dragonfly.org
Website: www.lmconservancy.org

Founded: 1995
Membership: 1,001–10,000
Scope: Local
Description: The Lower Merion Conservancy is a local conservation organization in Pennsylvania that acts to protect our area's natural and historic resources, open space and watersheds for area residents and future generations. Through education, advocacy and research, the Conservancy promotes collective responsibility for these resources.
Keyword(s): Forests/Forestry, Land Issues, Pollution (general), Public Lands/Greenspace, Recreation/Ecotourism, Reduce/Reuse/Recycle, Sprawl/Urban Planning, Water Habitats & Quality, Wildlife & Species
Contact(s):
  Mike Weilbacher, Executive Director

LOWER MISSISSIPPI RIVER CONSERVATION COMMITTEE
2524 S. Frontage Rd., Suite C
Vicksburg, MS 39180-5269 United States
Phone: 601-629-6602   Fax: 601-636-9541
Website: www.lmrcc.org

Scope: Regional
Description: The Committee provides an organizational structure and forum for coordinating and facilitating cooperative activities involving the natural resources of the Lower Mississippi River. Also encourages sustainable use of Lower Mississippi River natural resources for long-term environmental, social, and economic benefits.
Publication(s): LMRCC Newsletter, The
Keyword(s): Land Issues, Water Habitats & Quality, Wildlife & Species
Contact(s):
  Ron Nassar, Coordinator; 2524 S. Frontage Rd., Ste. C, Vicksburg, MS 39180-5269; 601-629-6602
  Dugan Sabins, Chairman; P.O. Box 82178, Baton Rouge, LA 70884; 225-765-0246; Fax: 225-765-0617; dugans@deq.state.la.us

LVIV REGIONAL INSTITUTE OF EDUCATION
18A Ohiyenko St.
Lviv, 79007 Ukraine
Phone: 3.8032272475e+011   Fax: 3.8032272807e+011
E-mail: lonmio@lonmio.lviv.ua

Founded: 1992
Scope: Regional
Description: Provides updated scientific and methodological information on different disciplines to the schools of Lviv region as well as postgraduate training for school teachers.
Keyword(s): Ethics/Environmental Justice, Water Habitats & Quality
Contact(s):
  Oleh Harasewych, Senior Researcher; oharasew@lonmio.lviv.ua

M

MACBRIDE RAPTOR PROJECT
W.H., KCC, 6301 Kirkwood Blvd., SW
Cedar Rapids, IA 52406 United States
Phone: 319-398-5495   Fax: 319-398-5611
E-mail: iaraptor@avalon.net
Website: www.macbrideraptorproject.org

Founded: 1985
Membership: 101–1,000
Scope: State
Description: The Macbride Raptor Project is devoted to the preservation of Iowa's birds of prey and their natural habitats through rehabilitation of sick or injured raptors, education of the public to the role of raptors in our environment, and research on various aspects of raptor biology.
Publication(s): Raptor Review
Keyword(s): Wildlife & Species
Contact(s):
  Jodeane Cancilla, Director
  Eric Burrough, Veterinarian; 319-398-4979
  Mary Ebert, Veternarian; 319-398-5495

MACOMB LAND CONSERVANCY
P.O. Box 332
Romeo, MI 48065 United States
Phone: 5867845848   Fax: 5867845848
E-mail: info@savingplaces.org
Website: www.savingplaces.org

Founded: 2000
Membership: 101–1,000
Scope: Local, Regional
Description: A public land trust dedicated to the preservation of forests, wetlands, wildlife habitats, farmland, rivers and streams of Macomb County

Keyword(s): Agriculture/Farming, Ecosystems (precious), Forests/Forestry, Land Issues, Oceans/Coasts/Beaches, Public Health, Public Lands/Greenspace, Sprawl/Urban Planning, Water Habitats & Quality, Wildlife & Species

MAGIC
P.O. Box 15894
Stanford, CA 94309 United States
Phone: 650-323-7333 Fax: 650-323-4232
E-mail: magic@ecomagic.org
Website: www.ecomagic.org

Founded: 1979

Scope: Local, State, Regional, National, International

Description: Magic's programs apply methods and principles of ecology to clarify values, improve health, increase cooperation, and steward the environment. Activities include lectures and seminars about the nature of value; life-planning workshops, swim, run, and hatha yoga instruction; mentoring, community organizing, habitat enhancement, water and land, resource planning; neighborhood design and publishing.

Publication(s): Human Ecology, A Science for Living Well, Oak Regeneration on Stanford Lands, Liveable City

Keyword(s): Agriculture/Farming, Forests/Forestry, Public Health, Sprawl/Urban Planning, Transportation, Water Habitats & Quality

Contact(s):
Robin Bayer, President; robin@ecomagic.org
David Schrom, Treasurer; david@ecomagic.org

MAINE ASSOCIATION OF CONSERVATION COMMISSIONS (MACC)
P.O. Box 702
Bath, ME 04530 United States
Phone: 207-443-2925
E-mail: macc@clinic.net

Founded: 1969
Membership: 1–100
Scope: State

Description: A membership organization whose objectives are twofold: to assist Maine municipalities in establishing conservation commissions; to assist the existing 200+ conservation commissions through technical assistance and educational programs.

Publication(s): Grass Roots

Keyword(s): Land Issues, Oceans/Coasts/Beaches, Pollution (general), Public Lands/Greenspace, Recreation/Ecotourism, Reduce/Reuse/Recycle, Sprawl/Urban Planning, Water Habitats & Quality, Wildlife & Species

Contact(s):
Mike Cline, President
Bob Cummings, Executive Director; 616 Main Road, Phippsburg, ME 04562; 2074432925; macc@clinic.net

MAINE ASSOCIATION OF CONSERVATION DISTRICTS
Attn: President, 2467 Exeter Rd.
Exeter, ME 04435-3107 United States
Phone: 207-622-7589

Scope: State

Contact(s):
Neil Crane, President, Alternate Board Member; 207-379-2641; Fax: 207-379-2644
John Hemond, President; 46 N. Verreill Rd., Minot, ME 04258; 207-345-5333
Bruce Roope, Vice President
William Bell, Executive Director; P.O. Box 228, Augusta, ME 04330; 207-622-4443; Fax: 207-623-3748; newengag@mint.net
Fred Hardy, Treasurer; 879 Weeks Mill Rd., New Sharon, ME 04955; 207-778-4320
Raymond Harris, Board Member; Rt. 1 Box 8396, Washburn, ME 04786; 207-764-3217
Larry Macdonald, Secretary; Box 1187, Greenville, ME 04441; 207-695-2639

MAINE BASS FEDERATION
Heath Morris
15 Blue Rock Road Lot 12
Monmouth, ME 04259 United States
Phone: 207-933-5978

Membership: 101–1,000
Scope: State

Description: An organization of Bassmaster chapters, affiliated with the Bass Anglers Sportsman Society, organized to fight pollution, assist state and national conservation agencies in their efforts, and teach young people of our country good conservation practices. Dedicated to the realistic conservation of our water resources.

Publication(s): Federation Guide

Contact(s):
Norm Moulton, President; 207-266-6914

MAINE COAST HERITAGE TRUST
1 Main St.
Topsham, ME 04086 United States
Phone: 207-729-7366 Fax: 207-729-6863
E-mail: info@mcht.org
Website: www.mcht.org

Founded: 1970
Membership: 1–100
Scope: State

Description: To protect land that is essential to the character of Maine, in particular its coastline and islands. Provides free advisory services on open-space protection to landowners, town officials, state and federal agencies, land trusts, and other private conservation organizations.

Publication(s): Technical Bulletins, Maine Heritage, Annual Report, Conservation Options, A Guide for Maine Landowners, Directory of Maine Land Conservation Trusts

Keyword(s): Land Issues, Oceans/Coasts/Beaches, Public Lands/Greenspace

Contact(s):
James Espy, President; jespy.mcht.org
Chris Hamilton, Editor; chamiltin@mcht.org
John Robinson, Treasurer
Harold Woodsum, Chairman

MAINE ENVIRONMENTAL EDUCATION ASSOCIATION
485 Chewonki Neck Rd.
Wiscasset, ME 4578 United States
Phone: 207-882-7323 Fax: 207-882-4074

Founded: 1981
Membership: 101–1,000
Scope: State

Description: The Maine Environmental Education Association (MEEA) facilitates and promotes environmental education in Maine through the sharing of ideas, resources, information and cooperative programs among educators, organizations and concerned individuals. MEEA offers a newsletter, annual conference, Environmental Educator of the Year award and Teacher Mine Grants.

Publication(s): New England Journal of Environmental Education, Connections

Contact(s):
Dot Lamson, President; 207-882-7323; dlamson@chewonki.org

MANASOTA-88
P.O. Box 1728
Nokomis, FL 34274 United States
Phone: 941-966-6256   Fax: 941-966-0659
E-mail: info@manasota-88.org
Website: www.manasota-88.org

Founded: 1968
Membership: 101–1,000
Scope: Local, State, Regional, National
Description: ManaSota-88 is a non-profit public health and environmental organization. Volunteers are unpaid. We receive no contributions from the government or special interest groups, nor does ManaSota-88 accept contributions from any polluting industries. We have been active since 1968.
Keyword(s): Energy, Pollution (general), Wildlife & Species
Contact(s):
  Rebecca Eger, Director; 941-366-1765
  Laurence Quy, Director; 1619 Palma Sola Blvd., Bradenton, FL 34209; 941-792-5509
  Glenn Compton, Editor
  Glenn Compton, Chairman; 419 Reubens Drive, Nokomis, FL 34275; 941-966-6256

MANITOBA NATURALISTS SOCIETY
401-63 Albert St.
Winnipeg, R3B 1G4 Manitoba Canada
Phone: 204-943-9029   Fax: 204-943-9029
E-mail: mns@escape.ca
Website: www.manitobanature.ca

Founded: 1920
Membership: 1,001–10,000
Scope: Regional
Description: Fosters an awareness and appreciation of the natural environment and an understanding of humanity's place therein; and sponsors lectures, workshops, field trips on natural history topics, and recreational outings that are environmentally friendly.
Publication(s): The Wild Plants of the Great Plains, The Wild Plants of Birds Hill Park, Wings Along Winnipeg, The Birds of Southeastern Manitoba, Bulletin, Manitoba's Tall Grass Prairie
Keyword(s): Recreation/Ecotourism
Contact(s):
  Ward Christianson, President; 204-943-9029
  Gordon Fardoe, Executive Director; 204-943-9029

MANITOBA WILDLIFE FEDERATION
70 Stevenson Rd.
Winnipeg, R3H 0W7 Manitoba Canada
Phone: 204-633-5967   Fax: 204-632-5200
E-mail: mwf@mb.sympatico.ca
Website: www.mwf.mb.ca

Founded: 1944
Membership: 10,001–100,000
Scope: State
Description: Promotes conservation and education with respect to our natural resources, provides outdoor skills training, administers the hunter education program for Manitoba, manages the Habitat Trust Fund which secures critical land to ensure habitat for wildlife, protects the interests of anglers and hunters.
Publication(s): Wildlife Crusader/Outdoor Edge
Keyword(s): Land Issues, Wildlife & Species
Contact(s):
  Lloyd Lintott, President
  Darlene Garnham, Administrative Assistant; 633-5967; Fax: 632-5200; mwf@mb.sympatico.ca
  Randy Walker, Past President

MANOMET CENTER FOR CONSERVATION SCIENCES
P.O. Box 1770
Manomet, MA 02345-1770 United States
Phone: 508-224-6521   Fax: 508-224-9220
E-mail: info@manomet.org
Website: www.manomet.org

Founded: 1969
Membership: 1,001–10,000
Scope: Local, State, Regional, National, International
Description: Manomet is a non-profit conservation research institute dedicated to promoting informed conservation policy and natural resource management through applied research. At study sites throughout the Americas, Manomet scientists and volunteers are working to conserve migratory songbird and shorebird populations, design sustainable fisheries conservation and management strategies, and develop the scientific basis for sustainable forestry in temperate forest ecosystems.
Publication(s): Various articles and books, Conservation Sciences
Keyword(s): Agriculture/Farming, Ecosystems (precious), Forests/Forestry, Land Issues, Oceans/Coasts/Beaches, Pollution (general), Wildlife & Species
Contact(s):
  Linda Leddy, President and Director; lleddy@manomet.org
  John Nordgren, Conservation Sciences Program Manager; jnordgren@manomet.org
  Jeptha Wade, Chair

MANTA MEXICO
105 Rose Ave
Venice, CA 90291 United States
Phone: 310-314-6875
E-mail: paul@mantamexico.org
Website: www.mantamexico.org

Founded: 2001
Scope: International
Description: Research, public education leading to greater understanding and conservation of the Giant Manta Ray in the Sea of Cortez, Mexico
Publication(s): Manta Mexico Photo Catalog
Keyword(s): Ecosystems (precious), Oceans/Coasts/Beaches, Pollution (general), Recreation/Ecotourism, Wildlife & Species

MARIE SELBY BOTANICAL GARDENS, THE
811 South Palm Ave.
Sarasota, FL 34236-7726 United States
Phone: 941-366-5731   Fax: 941-366-9807
E-mail: contactus@selby.org
Website: www.selby.org

Founded: 1975
Membership: 1,001–10,000
Scope: International
Description: A 13-acre bayfront botanical garden whose mission is to passionately pursue knowledge about tropical plants and their habitats and apply that expertise to advance their conservation and display.
Publication(s): Selbyana Bulletin-Newsletter, Selbyana-Journal
Contact(s):
  Margaret Lowman, President & CEO; mlowman@selby.org
  Wesley Higgins, Director, Systematics; whiggins@selby.org
  Bruce Holst, Director, Plant Collections; bholst@selby.org
  Harry Luther, Director, Bromeliad Identification Center; hluther@selby.org
  H. Bruce Rinker, Director of Canopy Ecology; brinker@selby.org
  John Beckner, Curator, Orchid Identification Center; jbeckner@selby.org
  Barry Walsh, Staff Editor; 941-955-7553; ext. 10; bwalsh@selby.org

MARIN CONSERVATION LEAGUE
1623A Fifth Avenue
San Rafael, CA 94901 United States
Phone: 415-485-6257   Fax: 415-485-6259
E-mail: mcl@marinconservationleague.org
Website: www.marinconservationleague.org

Founded: 1934

Scope: State

Description: The Marin Conservation League has worked to preserve and protect the natural assets of Marin County. The league works on all issues affecting the county environment, seeking partnerships with diverse groups to influence public policy and educate citizens and decisionmakers in understanding critical issues and options.

Publication(s): MCL News

Keyword(s): Agriculture/Farming, Land Issues, Public Lands/Greenspace

Contact(s):
Kathy Lowrey, President
Jana Haehl, 1st Vice President
Charles McGlashan, 2nd Vice President
Kenneth Drexler, Treasurer
Tim Duane, Secretary

MARINE CONSERVATION BIOLOGY INSTITUTE
15805 NE 47th Ct.
Redmond, WA 98052-5208 United States
Phone: 425-883-8914   Fax: 425-883-3017
Website: www.mcbi.org

Founded: 1996

Scope: National

Description: MCBI is a nonprofit, non-partisan, tax-exampt organization dedicated to advancing the multidisciplinary science of marine conservation biology. MCBI helps scientists to generate information that arms people with knowledge crucial for informed decision-making.

Keyword(s): Oceans/Coasts/Beaches, Wildlife & Species

Contact(s):
Elliott Norse, President; 425-883-8914; elliott@mcbi.org
William Chandler, Vice President; 702-465-5959; bill@mcbi.org

MARINE ENVIRONMENTAL RESEARCH INSTITUTE (MERI)
772 W. End Ave.
New York, NY 10025 United States
Phone: 212-864-6285   Fax: 212-864-1470
E-mail: meri@downeast.net
Website: www.merireserch.org

Founded: 1990

Membership: 101–1,000

Scope: National

Description: MERI is a nonprofit organization dedicated to protecting the health and biodiversity of the marine environment. MERI's programs are international in scope and include direct field research, environmental and conservation education, training, and collaboration with the world's scientific community. MERI strives to address the problems of global marine pollution, endangered species and habitat degradation, and environmental emergencies affecting marine life.

Publication(s): MERI News, research publications, MERI Resource Center News

Keyword(s): Wildlife & Species

Contact(s):
Susan Shaw, President; P.O. Box 179, Brooklin, ME 04616
Suzanne Hopkins, Vice President; 15200 Old York Road, Monkton, MD 21111
Elizabeth Petterson, Resource Center Director; MERI Resource Center, Main St., P.O. Box 300, Brooklin, ME 04616; 207-359-8078; Fax: 207-359-8079; meri@downeast.net
Lemuel Evans, Chairman; 3536 Paintwater Pl., Las Vegas, NV 89129-7338
Joan Koven, Secretary; Astrolabe Inc., 4812 V St. NW, Washington, DC 20007
Pamela Stacey, Treasurer

MARINE FISH CONSERVATION NETWORK
600 Pennsylvania Avenue, Suite 210
Washington, DC 20003-4344 United States
Phone: 202-543-5509   Fax: 202-543-5774
E-mail: network@conservefish.org
Website: www.conservefish.org

Membership: 101–1,000

Scope: National

Description: The Marine Fish Conservation Network is a coalition of national and regional environmental organizations, commerical and recreational fishing associations, aquariums, and marine science groups dedicated to promoting the long-term sustainability of marine fisheries.

Publication(s): Network News

Keyword(s): Ecosystems (precious), Oceans/Coasts/Beaches, Water Habitats & Quality, Wildlife & Species

Contact(s):
Lee Crockett, Executive Director

MARINE MAMMAL CENTER, THE
Marin Headlands
1065 Fort Cronkhite
Sausalito, CA 94965 United States
Phone: 415-289-7325   Fax: 415-289-7333
E-mail: com@tmmc.org
Website: www.marinemammalcenter.org

Founded: 1975

Membership: 10,001–100,000

Scope: Local, State, National, International

Description: The Marine Mammal Center is a nonprofit organization dedicated to the rescue and rehabilitation of sick, injured, and orphaned marine mammals that strand along 600 miles of northern and central California coast. Information derived from routine medical treatment is shared with scientists worldwide. Through education and communication programs, the Center promotes public awareness of the ocean environment among over 100,000 visitors annually.

Publication(s): Release, various scientific papers., Annual Report

Keyword(s): Oceans/Coasts/Beaches

Contact(s):
B.J. Griffin, Executive Director
Dennis Di Domenico, Chairman of the Board
Sheldon Wolfe, Treasurer

MARINE SCIENCE INSTITUTE
500 Discovery Parkway
Redwood City, CA 94063 United States
Phone: 650-364-2760   Fax: 650-364-0416
E-mail: info@sfbaymsi.org
Website: www.sfbaymsi.org

Founded: 1970

Membership: 101–1,000

Scope: Local, State, Regional

Description: The Marine Science Institute is a non-profit organization that provides interdisciplinary science programs, using a marine biology theme, to help students develop a responsibility for the natural environment and our human communities.

Keyword(s): Oceans/Coasts/Beaches, Recreation/Ecotourism, Water Habitats & Quality, Wildlife & Species

Contact(s):
Jeff Rutherford, President; 650-364-2760; ext. 13; Fax: 650-364-0416; Jeff@sfbaymsi.org

MARINE TECHNOLOGY SOCIETY
5565 Sterrett Place
Suite 108
Columbia, MD 21044 United States
Phone: 410-884-5330   Fax: 410-884-9060
E-mail: mtspubs@aol.com
Website: www.mtsociety.org
Founded: 1963
Scope: International
Description: An ocean-oriented, multidisciplinary, international professional society, formed to encourage the development of the technology, education, operational expertise, and public awareness needed to advance man's capability to work effectively in all ocean areas and depths.
Publication(s): Marine Technology Society Journal, various proceedings, MTS Newsletter Currents
Keyword(s): Oceans/Coasts/Beaches
Contact(s):
  Judith Krauthamer, Executive Director

MARYLAND ASSOCIATION OF CONSERVATION DISTRICTS
53 Slama Rd
Edgewater, MD 21037 United States
Phone: 410-956-5771   Fax: 410-956-0161
E-mail: lynnehoot@al.com
Founded: 1946
Membership: 1–100
Scope: Local
Description: The mission of MASCD is to promote practical and effective soil, water, and related natural resource programs to all citizens through individual conservation districts on a voluntary basis through leadership, education, cooperation, and local direction.
Keyword(s): Agriculture/Farming
Contact(s):
  Robert Wilson, President and Alternative Board Member
  Robert Fitzgerald, Vice President; 27570 Fitzgerald Rd., Princess Anne, MD 21853; 410-651-3701
  Lynne Hoot, Executive Director; 53 Slama Rd., Edgewater, MD 21037; 410-956-5771; Fax: 410-956-0161
  Sharon Mariaca, Secretary
  Donald Spickler, Treasurer and Council Member; 14854 Hicksville Rd., Clear Spring, MD 21722; 301-842-2534; Fax: 301-842-2534; dspick@erols.com

MARYLAND BASS FEDERATION
Attn: President, 1106 West Washington St.
Hagerstown, MD 21740 United States
Phone: 301-791-3724
Website: www.mdbass.com
Scope: State
Description: An organization of Bassmaster chapters, affiliated with the Bass Anglers Sportsman Society, organized to fight pollution, assist state and national conservation agencies in their efforts, and teach the young people of our country good conservation practices. Dedicated to the realistic conservation of our water resources.
Publication(s): Maryland State Federation Update
Contact(s):
  Jim Kline, Conservation Rep. - Western; 301-791-3724
  Ken Penrod, Conservation Director; 4708 Sellman Rd, Beltsville, MD 20705; 301-937-0010

MARYLAND FORESTS ASSOCIATION
P.O. Box 599
Grantsville, MD 21536 United States
Phone: 301-895-5369   Fax: 301-895-5369
E-mail: mfa@hereintown.net
Website: www.mdforests.org
Membership: 101–1,000
Scope: State
Description: A nonprofit 501c (3) citizens organization for people interested in trees, forests, related natural resources, and forestry. To promote the maintenance of a healthy and productive forestland base to enhance the economic, environmental, and social well-being of all who live in the state.
Publication(s): Crosscut, The, MFA Legislative Update
Keyword(s): Forests/Forestry, Reduce/Reuse/Recycle
Contact(s):
  Peter Alexander, President
  Tony Dipaolo, Vice President
  Kevin Simpson, Vice President
  Karin Miller, Executive Director
  Richard Stanfield, Secretary and Treasurer

MARYLAND NATIVE PLANT SOCIETY
P.O. Box 4877
Silver Spring, MD 20914 United States
Phone: 410-286-2928
E-mail: mnps@toad.net
Website: www.mdflora.org/index.html
Founded: 1992
Membership: 101–1,000
Scope: Local, State, Regional
Description: MNPS is a nonprofit organization that uses education, research, and community service to foster awareness and appreciation for Maryland's native flora and habitats, leading to their conservation.
Publication(s): Native News, Marilandica (Journal/Newsletter)
Keyword(s): Ecosystems (precious), Forests/Forestry, Public Lands/Greenspace, Wildlife & Species
Contact(s):
  Karyn Molines, President
  Marc Imlay, Vice President; 301-283-0808
  John Parrish, Vice President
  Roderick Simmons, Vice President
  Jean Cantwell, Treasurer
  Jane Osburn, Secretary

MARYLAND ORNITHOLOGICAL SOCIETY, INC.
Cylburn Mansion, 4915 Greenspring Ave.
Baltimore, MD 21209 United States
Phone: 800-823-0050
Website: www.mdbirds.org
Founded: 1945
Membership: 1,001–10,000
Scope: State
Description: Nonprofit statewide organization of 16 chapters. Aims to promote the knowledge, protection, and conservation of wildlife and natural resources; to foster appreciation of the natural environment; to establish educational and scientific projects to inform and enrich the public; and to record, evaluate, and publish observations of birdlife in Maryland.
Publication(s): Maryland Birdlife, Maryland Yellowthroat, The
Keyword(s): Wildlife & Species
Contact(s):
  Robert Rineer, President; 8326 Philadelphia Rd., Baltimore, MD 21237; 410-391-8499
  Norm Saunders, Vice President; 1261 Cavendish Rd., Colesville, MD 20905; 301-989-9035
  Jeff Metter, Treasurer; 1301 N. Rolling Rd., Catonsville, MD 21228; 410-788-4877
  Chandler Robbins, Editor; Patuxent Wildlife Research Center, Laurel, MD 20811; 301-498-0281
  Sybil Williams, Secretary; 2000 Baltimore Rd. #A24, Rockville, MD 20851; 301-762-0560

MASSACHUSETTS ASSOCIATION OF CONSERVATION COMMISSIONS (MACC)
10 Juniper Rd.
Belmont, MA 02478 United States
Phone: 617-489-3930 Fax: 617-489-3935
E-mail: staff@maccweb.org
Website: www.maccweb.org

Founded: 1961
Membership: 1,001–10,000
Scope: Local, State
Description: Protects wetlands and open space through education and advocacy.
Publication(s): Newsletter of the Association, Environmental Handbook for Massachusetts
Keyword(s): Land Issues, Public Lands/Greenspace, Water Habitats & Quality, Wildlife & Species
Contact(s):
George Hall, President
Patrick Garner, V.P. for Advocacy
Ingeborg Hegemann, President Elect; ingeborg@maccweb.org
Kenneth Pruitt, Executive Director; kenneth.pruitt@maccweb.org
Helen Bethell, Treasurer; helen@maccweb.org

MASSACHUSETTS ASSOCIATION OF CONSERVATION DISTRICTS
Attn: President, 25 Shore Rd.
Bourne, MA 2532 United States
Phone: 508-759-4363 Fax: 508-759-4363

Scope: State
Contact(s):
Peggy Pacheco, President, Alternate Board Member; 25 Shore Rd., Bourne, MA 02532; 508-759-4363; Fax: 508-759-4363
Ed Himlan, Vice President; P.O. Box 577, Leominster, MA 01453; 978-534-0379; Fax: 978-534-1329
Donald Lambert, Treasurer; 178 Moulton Hill Rd., Monson, MA 01057; 413-267-4837
Anne Merriam, Secretary; 157 State Rd. E, Westminster, MA 01473; 978-874-2432
Thomas Quink, Board Member; 67 Church St., Gilbertville, MA 01031-9864; 413-477-8870; Fax: 413-477-8870

MASSACHUSETTS BASS FEDERATION
Attn: President, 15A Bolton St.
Waltham, MA 02453 United States
Phone: 781-647-5288
Website: www.massbass.com

Scope: State
Description: An organization of Bassmaster chapters, affiliated with the Bass Anglers Sportsman Society, organized to fight pollution, assist state and national conservation agencies in their efforts, and teach young people of our country good conservation practices. Dedicated to the realistic conservation of our water resources.
Contact(s):
Joe Mckinnon, President; 781-647-5288
Dean Percival, Conservation Director; 396 Green St., Northboro, MA 01532; 508-366-2030; mail@whiznet.com

MASSACHUSETTS FORESTRY ASSOCIATION
MASSACHUSETTS TREE FARM PROGRAM
MASSACHUSETTS PROJECT LEARNING TREE
P.O. Box 1096
Belchertown, MA 01007-1096 United States
Phone: 413-323-7326 Fax: 413-339-5526
E-mail: gcox@crocker.com
Website: massforests.org

Founded: 1970
Membership: 1,001–10,000
Scope: State
Description: A voluntary nonprofit association, affiliated with the National Woodland Owners Association; dedicated to conservation, stewardship, and advocacy of the forests and trees of Massachusetts. An educational organization offering information, workshops, conferences, publications, and professional assistance. Begun in 1970 as the Massachusetts Land League, changed to present name in 1986.
Publication(s): Woodland Steward, The
Keyword(s): Forests/Forestry, Land Issues
Contact(s):
Ron Cloutier, President; 978-544-7500
William Hull, Vice President; 101 Hampton Road, Pomfret Center, CT 06259; 860-974-0127; hull@hullforest.com
Gregory Cox, Executive Director, Editor
Tim Fowler, Secretary and Treasurer

MASSACHUSETTS TRAPPERS ASSOCIATION, INC.
741 Pulaski Blvd.
Bellingham, MA 02019 United States
Phone: 508-883-4214

Founded: 1950
Scope: State
Description: Objectives are to develop leadership for the advancement of the interests of the trapper and the fur industry, and to promote sound management for the conservation of furbearing animals.
Publication(s): Fur Ever
Keyword(s): Water Habitats & Quality, Wildlife & Species
Contact(s):
David Black, President; 741 Pulaski Blvd., Bellingham, MA 02019; 508-883-4214
Frederick Frazier, Vice President East; 111 Newport Rd., Hull, MA 02045; 781-925-5841
Debra Benedetto, Treasurer; P.O. Box 60, Wakefield, MA 01880; 781-246-2136
Irene Hayes, Secretary; 155 Williams Rd., Concord, MA 01742; 978-369-5065
Tom Hayes, Public Relations; 155 Williams Rd., Concord, MA 01742; 508-369-5065

MATTS (MID-ATLANTIC TURTLE AND TORTOISE SOCIETY, INC.)
2914 E. Joppa Rd.
Baltimore, MD 21234-3031 United States
Phone: 410-882-2769 Fax: 410-882-0839
Website: matts.herptiles.com/

Founded: 1997
Scope: National
Description: A nonprofit organization dedicated to promoting the study of Mid-Atlantic chelonian natural history, responsible herpetoculture, and conservation of habitat.
Publication(s): Terrapin Tales, The
Keyword(s): Reduce/Reuse/Recycle, Wildlife & Species
Contact(s):
Gregory Pokrywka, President
Brian McLaren, Vice President; 301-384-7444; briancrcc@aol.com
Donald Keefer, Secretary; 410-561-1668; keefercham@aol.com

MAX MCGRAW WILDLIFE FOUNDATION
P.O. Box 9
Dundee, IL 60118 United States
Phone: 847-741-8000 Fax: 847-741-8157
E-mail: info@mcgrawwildlife.org
Website: www.mgrawwildlife.org

Founded: 1962

Scope: National

Description: Conducts wildlife and fisheries research and management and conservation education projects; cooperates with other conservation agencies and institutions.

Publication(s): Descriptive Brochure, Annual Research Report, Wildlife Management Notes Series

Keyword(s): Land Issues, Public Lands/Greenspace, Recreation/Ecotourism, Wildlife & Species

Contact(s):
John Thompson, Director of Research

MERCK FOREST AND FARMLAND CENTER
P.O. Box 86
Rte. 315
Rupert, VT 05768 United States
Phone: 802-394-7836   Fax: 802-394-2519
E-mail: merck@vermontel.net
Website: www.merckforest.org

Founded: 1950
Membership: 101–1,000
Scope: Local, State

Description: Over 3,100 acres of field, farm, and forest open year-round to the public in the heart of the Taconic range in southwestern Vermont. Outdoor and environmental education experiences for individuals, families, and organized groups. Over 28 miles of trails, 65-acre organic demonstration farm, camping cabins and sites, a solar-powered visitor center and sustainable forestry information.

Publication(s): Ridgeline-newsletter

Keyword(s): Agriculture/Farming, Energy, Forests/Forestry

Contact(s):
Alan Calfee, President
Ken Smith, Director

MICHIGAN ASSOCIATION OF CONSERVATION DISTRICTS
Attn: President, 14302, OP Ave. E.
Climax, MI 49034 United States
Phone: 231-876-0348   Fax: 231-871-0372

Scope: State

Contact(s):
Larry Leach, President and Board Member; 616-746-4648; Fax: 616-746-4393
Joe Slater, Vice President; 6780 Brunswick Rd., Holton, MI 49425; 616-821-2843
Marilyn Shy, Executive Director; 101 S. Main, P.O. Box 539, Lake City, MI 49651; 616-839-3360; Fax: 616-839-3361; mdistricts@aol.com
Carol Bogard, Administrative Assistant; 101 S. Main, P.O. Box 539, Lake City, MI 49651; 616-839-3360; Fax: 616-839-3361
Rodney Dragicevich, Secretary and Treasurer, Alternate Board Member; 29396 Heritage Lane, Paw Paw, MI 49079; 616-375-3005

MICHIGAN BASS FEDERATION
Attn: President, 2710 Browning Dr.
Lake Orion, MI 48360 United States
Phone: 248-391-4393
E-mail: rspitler@michiganbass.org
Website: www.michiganbass.org

Founded: 1974
Membership: 101–1,000
Scope: State

Description: An organization of Bassmaster chapters, affiliated with the Bass Anglers Sportsman Society, organized to fight pollution, assist state and national conservation agencies in their efforts, and teach the young people of our country good conservation practice. Dedicated to the realistic conservation of our water resources.

Publication(s): Bass Lines

Contact(s):
Dennis Beltz, President; 810-286-3523
Ron Spitler, Conservation Director; 2710 Browning Dr., Lake Orion, MI 48360; 248-391-4393

MICHIGAN ENVIRONMENTAL COUNCIL
119 Pere Marquette
Ste. 2A
Lansing, MI 48912 United States
Phone: 517-487-9539   Fax: 917-487-9541
E-mail: mec@voyager.net
Website: www.mecprotects.org

Founded: 1980
Scope: State

Description: A statewide coalition of more than 50 environmental, public health and faith-based organizations with a collective membership of over 175,000 residents. In addition to serving as a clearinghouse of environmental information, MEC develops public policy, educates state officials and the public, and provides technical assistance and support to member organizations.

Publication(s): Michigan Environmental Report, Groundwater at Risk: A Citizen's Guide, Land: Michigan's Promise, Michigan's Future

Keyword(s): Energy, Land Issues, Pollution (general), Reduce/Reuse/Recycle

Contact(s):
Lana Pollack, President; 517-487-9539
Carol Misseldine, Executive Director
Alice Austin, Vice Chair; 517-663-2400
Elizabeth Harris, Chairman; E. Michigan Environmental Action Council, 21220 W. 14 Mile Rd., Bloomfield Township, MI 48301-4000; 313-258-5188
Alison Horton, Vice Chair
Brian Imus, Secretary; 734-662-6597

MICHIGAN FORESTS ASSOCIATION
1558 Barrington Pl.
Ann Arbor, MI 48103-5603 United States
Phone: 734-665-8279   Fax: 734-913-9167
E-mail: mfa@i-star.com
Website: www.michiganforests.com

Founded: 1951
Membership: 101–1,000
Scope: State

Description: A statewide organization affiliated with the National Woodland Owners Association, with concern for the full spectrum of forest activity, enterprise, development, and conservation in Michigan.

Publication(s): Green Gold: Michigan Forest History, Leaves - Newsletter, Michigan Forests

Keyword(s): Forests/Forestry

Contact(s):
Gordon Terry, President
Collin Burnett, Vice President
McClain Smith, Executive Director
Don Ingle, Editor; P.O. Box 78, Baldwin, MI 49304-0078
Allan Kerton, Treasurer

MICHIGAN LAND USE INSTITUTE
P.O. Box 228
Benzonia, MI 49016 United States
Phone: 231-882-4723   Fax: 213-882-7350
Website: www.mlui.org

Founded: 1995
Membership: 1,001–10,000
Scope: State

Description: Michigan Land Use Institute is a nonprofit environmental economic policy research organization focused on reforming land use policy and curbing sprawl.

Publication(s): Benzie County Wetlands - A Resource Worth Protecting, Rivers at Risk, Great Lakes Bulletin

Contact(s):
Keith Schneider, Program Director
Hans Voss, Executive Director
Richard Hitchingham, Treasurer

MICHIGAN NATURAL AREAS COUNCIL
University of Michigan
Botanical Gardens
1800 N. Dixboro Rd.
Ann Arbor, MI 48105 United States
Phone: 313-461-9390
E-mail: mnac@cyberspace.org
Website: www.cyberspace.org/~mnac

Founded: 1947
Scope: State
Description: The Michigan Natural Areas Council promotes the preservation of outstanding natural areas, prepares reports based on field investigations, and serves as an informed-citizens advisory on such matters.
Publication(s): Michigan Natural Areas News and Views
Keyword(s): Land Issues, Public Lands/Greenspace, Wildlife & Species

Contact(s):
Christopher Graham, Treasurer; 725 Peninsula Ct., Ann Arbor, MI 48105; kfdh64@prodigy.com
Robert Grese, Vice Chair; 1512 Carlton, Ann Arbor, MI 48103; bgrese@umich.edu
Phyllis Higman, Chair; P.O. Box 30444, Mason Bldg., Lansing, MI 48909; 517-373-6983; higmanp@michigan.gov
Sylvia Taylor, Past Chair; 10353 Judd Rd., Willis, MI 48191; 313-461-9390; smtaylor@umich.edu

MICHIGAN NATURE ASSOCIATION
326 E. Grand River Ave.
Williamston, MI 48895 United States
Phone: 517-655-5655   Fax: 517-655-5506
E-mail: michignnature@michignnature.org
Website: www.michignnature.org

Founded: 1952
Membership: 101–1,000
Scope: State
Description: Purpose is to acquire and maintain nature sanctuaries that contain examples of Michigan's original flora and fauna. Has 160 nature sanctuaries and preserves totaling over 8,000 acres in 54 counties of Michigan. MNA lands contain 206 of Michigan's endangered, threatened, and of special concern species. Available to public for nature education and appreciation.
Publication(s): Members' Newsletter, In Our Trust, Walking Paths in Keweenaw, MNA—In Retrospect: A Celebration of 28 Years of Preserving Michigan's Wild and Rare Natural Lands, MNA Nature Sanctuary Guidebook
Keyword(s): Ecosystems (precious), Ethics/Environmental Justice, Forests/Forestry, Land Issues, Oceans/Coasts/Beaches, Public Lands/Greenspace, Sprawl/Urban Planning, Water Habitats & Quality, Wildlife & Species

Contact(s):
Karen Weingarden, President; 248-546-5429
Jeremy Emmi, Executive Director; 326 E. Grand River Ave., Williamston, MI 48895; 517-655-5655
Bertha Daubendiek, Founder and Trustee; 810-324-2626

MICHIGAN UNITED CONSERVATION CLUBS, INC.
2101 Wood St.
Lansing, MI 48912-3728 United States
Phone: 517-371-1041   Fax: 517-371-1505
E-mail: mucc@mucc.org
Website: www.mucc.org

Founded: 1937
Membership: 10,001–100,000
Scope: State
Description: A representative statewide organization, affiliated with the National Wildlife Federation, dedicated to the protection and enhancement of wildlife and its habitat through public education and government interaction.
Publication(s): Michigan Out-of-Doors Magazine

Contact(s):
Dan Delisle, President
Jim Goodheart, Executive Director
James Campbell, Representative
Kevin Frailey, Education Programs Contact
Dennis Knickerbocker, Editor
Michael Leach, Treasurer
William Whippen, Alternate Representative

MICHIGAN WILDLIFE CONSERVANCY
6380 Drumheller Road, P.O. Box 393
Bath, MI 48808 United States
Phone: 517-641-7677   Fax: 517-641-7877
E-mail: wildlife@miwildlife.org
Website: www.miwildlife.org

Founded: 1982
Membership: 101–1,000
Scope: State
Description: The Michigan Wildlife Conservancy is a nonprofit membership organization, which restores and improves wildlife habitat through cost-effective projects. We want future generations to enjoy the same world of natural experiences we do today.
Publication(s): Wildlife Volunteer, The
Keyword(s): Land Issues, Reduce/Reuse/Recycle, Water Habitats & Quality

Contact(s):
Keith Groty, President
Dennis Fijalkowski, Executive Director
Michael Depolo, Chairman

MID-ATLANTIC COUNCIL OF WATERSHED ASSOCIATIONS
12 Morris Rd.
Ambler, PA 19002 United States
Phone: 215-372-3916

Scope: National
Description: Promotes exchange of ideas on citizen watershed association activities and advises any group wishing to start a new watershed association.
Keyword(s): Land Issues, Oceans/Coasts/Beaches, Water Habitats & Quality

MID-ATLANTIC FISHERY MANAGEMENT COUNCIL
300 S. New St., Rm. 2115
Dover, DE 19904 United States
Phone: 302-674-2331   Fax: 302-674-5399
Website: www.mafmc.org

Founded: 1976
Membership: 1–100
Scope: National
Description: Mid-Atlantic Fishery Management Council is one of eight regional fishery management councils established to carry out provisions of Magnuson-Stevens Fishery Conservation and Management Act. The Council is charged with responsibility to prepare fishery management plans and amendments to such plans for implementation by the Secretary of Commerce.
Publication(s): Newsletter

Keyword(s): Oceans/Coasts/Beaches, Water Habitats & Quality, Wildlife & Species

Contact(s):
Daniel Furlong, Executive Director; dfurlong@mafmc.org
Marla Trollan, Public Affairs; mtrollan@mafmc.org

MINERAL POLICY CENTER
1612 K St., NW, Suite 808
Washington, DC 20006 United States
Phone: 202-887-1872   Fax: 202-887-1875
E-mail: mpc@mineralpolicy.org
Website: www.mineralpolicy.org

Founded: 1988
Membership: 1,001–10,000
Scope: International

Description: MPC is a national environmental membership organization. The Center is a research, education, and advocacy organization dedicated to cleaning up and preventing pollution from mining. The Center works for common sense environmental reform of mineral policy. The Center produces educational materials on mining impact, offers training for and works closely with citizens groups affected by mining damage.

Publication(s): MPC News, Golden Dreams, Poison Streams, Mine Wire, Canary Calls

Keyword(s): Land Issues, Oceans/Coasts/Beaches, Pollution (general), Public Lands/Greenspace, Reduce/Reuse/Recycle

Contact(s):
Alan Septoff, Research Director; ext. 205

MINNESOTA ASSOCIATION OF SOIL AND WATER CONSERVATION DISTRICTS
790 Cleveland Ave. S.
Ste. 201
St. Paul, MN 55116 United States
Phone: 651-690-9028   Fax: 651-690-9065
E-mail: maswcd@maswcd.org
Website: www.maswcd.org

Founded: 1952
Scope: State

Description: MASWCD is a nonprofit organization which exists to provide a common voice for Minnesota soil and water conservation districts and to maintain a positive, results-oriented relationship with rule making agencies, partners and legislators; expanding education opportunities to the districts so they may carry out effective conservation programs.

Contact(s):
Scott Hoese, President; 5520 Polk Ave., Mayer, MN 55360; 952-657-2223; sthoese@aol.com
LeAnn Buck, Executive Director; 790 Cleveland Ave. S., Ste. 201, St. Paul, MN 55116; 651-690-9028; Fax: 651-690-9065; leann.buck@maswcd.org

MINNESOTA BASS FEDERATION
Attn: President, P.O. Box 551
Howard Lake, MN 55349 United States
Phone: 612-770-8626
Website: www.mnbf.org

Founded: 1974
Membership: 101–1,000
Scope: State

Description: An organization of Bassmaster chapters, affiliated with the Bass Anglers Sportsman Society, organized to fight pollution, assist state and national conservation agencies in their efforts, and teach the young people of our country good conservation practices. Dedicated to the realistic conservation of our water resources.

Contact(s):
Jay Green, President; 612-770-8626; jgreen@mnbf.org

MINNESOTA CENTER FOR ENVIRONMENTAL ADVOCACY (MCEA)
26 E. Exchange St., Suite 206
St. Paul, MN 55101-2264 United States
Phone: 651-223-5969   Fax: 651-223-5967
E-mail: mcea@mncenter.org
Website: www.mncenter.org

Founded: 1974
Membership: 1,001–10,000
Scope: State

Description: The Minnesota Center for Environmental Advocacy is a nonprofit organization that uses law, science, and research to protect Minnesota's natural resources, wildlife, and the health of its people.

Publication(s): Advocacy Update

Keyword(s): Air Quality/Atmosphere, Pollution (general), Water Habitats & Quality

Contact(s):
Peter Bachman, Executive Director
Steven Thorne, Chair

MINNESOTA CONSERVATION FEDERATION
551 S. Snelling Avenue South, Suite B
St. Paul, MN 55116-1525 United States
Phone: 651-690-3077
E-mail: mncf@mtn.org
Website: www.mncf.org

Founded: 1935
Membership: 1,001–10,000
Scope: State

Description: A representative statewide organization, affiliated with the National Wildlife Federation, dedicated to the protection and enhancement of wildlife and its habitat through public education and government interaction.

Publication(s): Walk-on-the-Wildside, Minnesota-Out-of-Doors

Keyword(s): Public Lands/Greenspace, Water Habitats & Quality

Contact(s):
Kenneth Hiemenz, President; kenny406@juno.com
Gordy Meyer, Past President; gmeyer9330@aol.com
Leigh Currie, Editor and Office Manager; 651-690-3077; Fax: 651-690-3077; mncf@mtn.org
Joan Moore, Treasurer
Barb Prindle, Education Programs Contact; bprindle@msn.com
Chris Vokaty, Secretary; chrisvokaty@cmgate.com

MINNESOTA FORESTRY ASSOCIATION
P.O. Box 496
Grand Rapids, MN 55744 United States
Phone: 800-821-8733   Fax: 218-326-3224
E-mail: john@b-green.us
Website: www.mnforest.com

Founded: 1876
Membership: 101–1,000
Scope: State

Description: A nonprofit organization, affiliated with the National Woodland Owners Association, dedicated to promoting the high potential advantages of intensive scientific management of forests, woodlots, and other renewable resources.

Publication(s): Minnesota Better Forests, Minnesota Forest newsletter

Keyword(s): Forests/Forestry

Contact(s):
James Lemmerman, President; 6316 Nashua St., Duluth, MN 55807; 218-624-3847
Culver Adams, Vice President; 612-823-2618
John Bathke, Executive Director; 651-688-0587; john@b-green.us
Richard Holter, Treasurer; 218-328-5173

MINNESOTA GROUND WATER ASSOCIATION
4779 126th St., N.
White Bear Lake, MN 55110-5910 United States
Phone: 651-296-7822   Fax: 651-297-8676

Founded: 1981
Membership: 101–1,000
Scope: State
Description: MGWA's mission is to advocate the wise use and protection of ground water, and to provide education to the users of Minnesota's ground water.
Publication(s): Minnesota Ground Water Association Newsletter, Minnesota Ground Water Association Directory
Keyword(s): Land Issues, Water Habitats & Quality
Contact(s):
  James Lundy, President; 651-296-7822; Fax: 651-297-8676; jm.lundy@pca.state.mn.us
  Leigh Harrod, Advertising Manager; 651-474-8678; mn_homebase@worldnet.att.net
  Jeanette Leete, Business Manager; 651-426-6122; Fax: 651-426-5449
  Tom Clark, Editor; 651-296-8580; Fax: 651-297-7709; tom.p.clark@pca.state.mn.us
  Jan Falteisek, Secretary and Membership; 651-296-3877; Fax: 651-296-0445; jan.falteisek@dnr.state.mn.us
  James Piegat, Past President; 612-470-6075
  Lee Trotta, Treasurer; 651-638-3160; Fax: 651-638-3226; trottaLC@usfilter.com

MINNESOTA HERPETOLOGICAL SOCIETY
JAMES FORD BELL MUSEUM OF NATURAL HISTORY
10 Church St., SE, University of Minnesota
Minneapolis, MN 55455-0104 United States
Phone: 612-624-7065

Founded: 1981
Scope: State
Description: A nonprofit organization chartered for the conservation and preservation of reptiles and amphibians, through the education of members and the public.
Publication(s): MHS Newsletter
Keyword(s): Public Lands/Greenspace, Wildlife & Species
Contact(s):
  Bill Moss, President; mngatorguy@qwest.net

MINNESOTA LAND TRUST
2356 University Ave. West
Suite 240
Saint Paul, MN 55114 United States
Phone: 651-647-9590   Fax: 651-647-9769
E-mail: mnland@mnland.org
Website: www.mnland.org

Founded: 1991
Membership: 101–1,000
Scope: State
Description: The Minnesota Land Trust works with landowners and communities to permanently protect Minnesota's lands and waters with conservation easements.
Publication(s): Landowner Options Book
Keyword(s): Land Issues, Water Habitats & Quality

MINNESOTA NATIVE PLANT SOCIETY
220 Biological Sciences Center
1445 Gortner Ave.
University of Minnesota
St. Paul, MN 55108 United States
Phone: 507-867-4692
E-mail: mnps@HotPOP.com
Website: www.stolaf.edu/depts/biology/mnps

Founded: 1982
Membership: 101–1,000
Scope: State
Description: A nonprofit organization dedicated to education about native Minnesota flora and to its preservation and conservation. Activities include monthly meetings, summer field trips, sponsorship of symposia and publication of a regular newsletter.
Publication(s): Minnesota Plant Press
Keyword(s): Land Issues, Wildlife & Species

MINNESOTA ORNITHOLOGISTS' UNION
James Ford Bell Museum of Natural History
10 Church St. SE
University of Minnesota
Minneapolis, MN 55455 United States
Phone: 763-780-8890
E-mail: mou@biosci.umn.edu

Founded: 1937
Membership: 1,001–10,000
Scope: State
Description: Statewide organization contributing to scientific knowledge through bird observations; stimulating public interest in birds; and working to preserve bird life and bird habitat.
Publication(s): Loon, The, Minnesota Birder
Keyword(s): Wildlife & Species
Contact(s):
  Ann Kessen, President; 31145 Genesis Ave., Stacy, MN 55079
  Al Batt, Recording Secretary; RR 1, Box 56A, Hartland, MN 56042
  Elizabeth Bell, Membership Secretary; 5868 Pioneer Rd., St. Paul Park, MN 55071
  Mark Citsay, Treasurer; 210 Mariner Way, Bayport, MN 55003
  Anthony Hertzel, Editor; 8461 Pleasant View Dr., Mounds View, MN 55112
  Jim Williams, Editor; 5239 Cranberry Lane, Webster, WI 54893

MINNESOTA WILDLIFE HERITAGE FOUNDATION, INC.
5701 Normandale Rd., Suite 325
Minneapolis, MN 55424 United States
Phone: 952-925-1923   Fax: 952-925-3487
Membership: 101–1,000
Scope: State
Description: Formed to promote the idea of charitable giving for conservation purposes and to assist people in making charitable donations of property for wildlife habitat.
Contact(s):
  James Mady, President; 7338 Frontier Trail, Chanhassen, MN 55317
  Hugh Price, Vice President and Director; 5707 Knox Ave. S., Minneapolis, MN 55419; 612-925-2486
  Laurence Koll, Secretary and Legal Counsel; 633 Sunset Ln., Mendota Heights, MN 55118; 612-291-9155

MINNESOTA WINGS SOCIETY, INC.
P.O. Box 11323
Minneapolis, MN 55411 United States
Phone: 612-588-2966

Founded: 1978
Scope: State
Description: To present a program to high school students called "Sight and Save Wildlife Management." This program helps students and enables them to improve wildlife habitat around some of the species they see every day.
Publication(s): Wings (newsletter)
Keyword(s): Land Issues, Wildlife & Species
Contact(s):
  Thurman Tucker, President; 1321 N. Irving Ave., Minneapolis, MN 55411; 612-588-2466

David Donna, Vice President; 4200 IDS Center, 80 S. 8th St., Minneapolis, MN 55402; 612-371-3211
Martin Hanson, Secretary; 1530 Quinlan Ave., So., St. Croix Beach, MN 55043; 612-436-8242
Jim McLellan, Treasurer; 10273 Yellow Cir. Dr., Minnetonka, MN 55343; 612-933-2263

MISSISSIPPI ASSOCIATION OF CONSERVATION DISTRICTS, INC.
P.O. Box 23005
Jackson, MS 39225-3005 United States
Phone: 601-354-7645   Fax: 601-354-6628
Website: www.mswcc.state.ms.us
Scope: State
Contact(s):
Benny Goff, President; 228-769-3070; Fax: 228-769-3005
Marc Curtis, 1st Vice President; P.O. Box 958, Leland, MS 38756; 601-686-2321
Jack Winstead, 2nd Vice President; 5337 Lawrence Rd., Lawrence, MS 39336
Daryl Burney, Board Member; P.O. Box 603, Coffeeville, MS 38922; 601-675-2703; Fax: 601-675-2786
Gale Martin, Secretary and Treasurer; P.O. Box 23005, Jackson, MS 39225-3005; 601-354-7645; Fax: 601-354-6628

MISSISSIPPI BASS FEDERATION
P.O. Box 13
Hattiesburg, MS 39403 United States
Phone: 601-544-8703
Website: www.msbass.org
Scope: State
Description: An organization of Bassmaster chapters, affiliated with the Bass Anglers Sportsman Society, organized to fight pollution, assist state and national conservation agencies in their efforts, and teach the young people of our country good conservation practices. Dedicated to the realistic conservation of our water resources.
Contact(s):
John Hamilton, Conservation Director; 404 Meadow Lane, Aberdeen, MS 39730; 662-369-8290

MISSISSIPPI INTERSTATE COOPERATIVE RESOURCE ASSOCIATION
P.O. Box 774
Bettendorf, IA 52722-0774 United States
Phone: 309-793-5811
Website: wwwaux.cerc.cr.usgs.gov/MICRA/
Founded: 1989
Membership: 101–1,000
Scope: Regional
Description: An interstate organization of 28 state departments of conservation and natural resources working in collaboration with federal agencies, Native American tribes, and other interests to improve the conservation, development, management, and utilization of interjurisdictional fishery resources in the Mississippi River basin through improved coordination and communication among the responsible management entities.
Publication(s): River Crossings, other periodic reports
Keyword(s): Recreation/Ecotourism, Water Habitats & Quality, Wildlife & Species
Contact(s):
Norm Stucky, Chairman; 573-781-4115; Fax: 573-526-4047; stuckyn@mail.conservation.state.mo.us
Bill Reeves, Past Chairman; 615-781-6575; Fax: 615-781-6667; breeves@mail.state.tn.us

MISSISSIPPI NATIVE PLANT SOCIETY
Millsaps College
Box 150307
1701 North State Street
Jackson, MS 39210 United States
Phone: 662-325-3012   Fax: 662-325-7893
Website: groups.msn.com/MississippiNativePlantSociety
Founded: 1981
Membership: 101–1,000
Scope: Local, State
Description: The Mississippi Native Plant Society promotes the appreciation of native plants of Mississippi, their use in landscaping, and the conservation of natural ecological communities of the state.
Publication(s): Mississippi Native Plants
Keyword(s): Land Issues, Wildlife & Species
Contact(s):
Bob Brzuszek, President; Department of Landscape Architecture, Box 9725, Mississippi State, MS 39762-9725; 662-325-3012; Fax: 662-325-7893
Debora Mann, Secretary and Treasurer; Millsaps College 1701 North State St., Jackson, MS 39210; 601-974-1415; Fax: 601-974-1401; manndl@millsap.edu

MISSISSIPPI RIVER BASIN ALLIANCE
708 N. First St. Ste. 238
Minneapolis, MN 55401 United States
Phone: 612-334-9460   Fax: 612-340-1632
E-mail: ininfo@mrba.org
Website: www.mrba.org
Founded: 1992
Membership: 101–1,000
Scope: Regional
Description: To protect and restore the ecological, economic, cultural, historical, and recreational resources in the Basin, and to eliminate barriers of race, class, and economic status which divide us in the quest to achieve these purposes.
Publication(s): Alliance Newsletter, Mississippi River Basin Directory
Keyword(s): Ethics/Environmental Justice, Public Lands/Greenspace, Water Habitats & Quality
Contact(s):
James Falvey, Assistant Director
Tim Sullivan, Executive Director; ext. 111

MISSISSIPPI WILDLIFE FEDERATION
855 South Pear Orchard Road, Suite 500
Ridgeland, MS 39157-5138 United States
Phone: 601-206-5703 Fax: 601-206-5705
E-mail: cshropshire@mswf.org
Website: www.mswildlife.org
Founded: 1946
Membership: 1,001–10,000
Scope: State
Description: A representative statewide organization, affiliated with the National Wildlife Federation, dedicated to the protection and enhancement of wildlife and its habitat through public education and government interaction.
Publication(s): Mississippi Wildlife Magazine
Contact(s):
Bob Fairbank, President
Cathy Shropshire, Executive Director
Melanie Starnes, Office Manager
Jimmy Bullock, Representative
Bob Fairbank, Alternate Representative
Johnny McArthur, Treasurer
Deborah Pearson, Member/Affiliate Coordinator
Cathy Shropshire, Education Programs Contact

MISSOURI ASSOCIATION OF SOIL AND WATER CONSERVATION DISTRICTS
19050 State Hwy. O
Tarkio, MO 64491 United States
Phone: 660-736-4368

Scope: State

Contact(s):
Steve Hopper, President and Board Member; 660-639-2575
David Dix, Treasurer; P.O. Box 756, Eminence, MO 65466; 573-226-3787
Peggy Lemons, Executive Secretary; 1209 Biscayne Dr., Jefferson City, MO 65109; 573-893-5188; Fax: 573-893-7328; peggy@mojefferso.fsc.usda.gov

MISSOURI BASS FEDERATION
Attn: President, 220 W. 6th Street
Sedalia, MO 65301 United States
Phone: 660-826-5251
Website: www.mobass.com

Scope: State

Description: An organization of Bassmaster chapters, affiliated with the Bass Anglers Sportsman Society, organized to fight pollution, assist state and national conservation agencies in their efforts, and teach the young people of our country good conservation practices. Dedicated to the realistic conservation of our water resources.

MISSOURI FOREST PRODUCTS ASSOCIATION
MFPA
611 E. Capitol Ave., Suite One
Jefferson City, MO 65101 United States
Phone: 573-634-3252   Fax: 573-636-2591
E-mail: moforest@moforest.org
Website: www.moforest.org

Founded: 1970
Membership: 101–1,000
Scope: State

Description: The Missouri Forest Products Association is a nonprofit organization committed to promoting closer working relationships among the wood products industry and the conservation and wise use of natural resources.

Publication(s): Professional Timber Harvester, MFPA News

Keyword(s): Agriculture/Farming, Air Quality/Atmosphere, Ethics/Environmental Justice, Executive/Legislative/Judicial Reform, Forests/Forestry, Reduce/Reuse/Recycle, Water Habitats & Quality, Wildlife & Species

Contact(s):
Cory Ridenhour, Executive Director; 573-634-3252; Fax: 573-636-2591; cory@moforest.org
Glenda Fry, Education Manager; 573-634-3252; Fax: 573-636-2591; glenda@moforest.org
Becky Crowley, Administrative Assistant; 573-634-3252; Fax: 573-636-2591; becky@moforest.org
Lisa Griggs, Communications Coordinator; 573-634-3252; Fax: 573-636-2591; lisa@moforest.org

MISSOURI NATIVE PLANT SOCIETY
P.O. Box 20073
St. Louis, MO 63144-0073 United States
Phone: 314-894-9021
Website: www.missouri.edu/~umo_herb/monps

Founded: 1979
Scope: State

Description: To promote the enjoyment, preservation, conservation, restoration, and study of the flora native to Missouri; to educate the public about the values of the beauty, diversity and environmental importance of indigenous vegetation; and to publish related information.

Publication(s): Missouriensis, Petal Pusher

Keyword(s): Agriculture/Farming, Forests/Forestry, Land Issues, Public Lands/Greenspace, Wildlife & Species

Contact(s):
Jack Harris, President
Sue Hollis, Vice President; 816-561-9419; serngro@worldnet.att.net
Pat Harris, Editor; 314-894-9021; pharris@stlnet.com
Donna Kennedy, Treasurer; 636-256-7578; fishn2@primary.net
George Yatskievych, Editor; 314-577-9522; gyatskievych@rschctr.mobot.org

MISSOURI PRAIRIE FOUNDATION
P.O. Box 200
Columbia, MO 65205 United States
Phone: 888-843-6739   Fax: 573-442-0260
E-mail: gfreeman@coin.org
Website: www.moprairie.org

Founded: 1966
Membership: 1,001–10,000
Scope: State

Description: A nonprofit citizens' group organized to ensure the preservation of native prairie along with associated plant and animal life by acquisition, management protection, control, and perpetuation of the prairie; to carry on educational programs; and to provide scientific research relative to native prairie.

Publication(s): Missouri Prairie Journal

Keyword(s): Ecosystems (precious), Land Issues, Public Lands/Greenspace, Recreation/Ecotourism, Reduce/Reuse/Recycle, Wildlife & Species

Contact(s):
Robert Elworth, President; 417-742-2775; bobelworth@aol.com
Wayne Morton, Vice President; 417-646-2450; wayne2946@yahoo.com
Carol Davit, Editor; 573-751-4115; ext. 874; davitleahy@earthlink.net
Gary Freeman, Membership Coordinator; 888-843-6739; Fax: 573-442-0260; gfreeman@coin.org
Warren Lammert, Treasurer; 314-961-8768; wlamm01@earthlink.net
W. Washburn, Secretary; 573-636-2765; wrwashburn@socket.net

MONO LAKE COMMITTEE
P.O. Box 29
Lee Vining, CA 93541 United States
Phone: 760-647-6595   Fax: 760-647-6377
E-mail: info@monolake.org
Website: www.monolake.org

Founded: 1978
Membership: 10,001–100,000
Scope: Local, State, Regional, International

Description: The Mono Lake Committee is a nonprofit citizens' group dedicated to protecting and restoring the Mono Basin ecosystem; educating the public about Mono Lake and the impacts on the environment of excessive water use; and promoting cooperative solutions that protect Mono Lake and meet real water needs without transferring environmental problems to other areas.

Publication(s): Geology of the Mono Basin, Plants of the Mono Basin, Mono Lake Guidebook, South Tufa: A Self-guided Walking Tour, Mono Lake Newsletter

Keyword(s): Air Quality/Atmosphere, Climate Change, Development/Developing Countries, Ecosystems (precious), Energy, Land Issues, Pollution (general), Recreation/Ecotourism, Reduce/Reuse/Recycle, Transportation, Water Habitats & Quality, Wildlife & Species

Contact(s):
Geoffrey McQuilkin, Executive Director-Operations
Francis Spivy-Weber, Executive Director-Policy; 310-316-0041

Lisa Cutting, Acting E.S. Policy Director
Arya Degenhardt, Communications Director
Bartshe Miller, Education Director

MONTANA ASSOCIATION OF CONSERVATION DISTRICTS
501 N. Sanders, Suite 2
Helena, MT 59601 United States
Phone: 406-443-5711   Fax: 406-443-0174
E-mail: mail@macdnet.org
Website: www.macdnet.org
Membership: 1–100
Scope: State
Publication(s): Conservation Conversation - Monthly Newsletter
Contact(s):
  Mike Wendland, President
  Bob Fossum, Vice President
  Jan Fontaine, Administrative Assistant; 501 N. Sanders, Suite 2, Helena, MT 59601; 406-443-5711; Fax: 406-443-0174
  Dale Marxer, Treasurer

MONTANA BASS FEDERATION
Attention: President, P.O. Box 4952
Missoula, MT 59808 United States
Phone: 406-549-1303
E-mail: riska@montana.com
Scope: State, Regional
Description: An organization of Bassmaster chapters, affiliated with the Bass Anglers Sportsman Society, organized to fight pollution, assist state and national conservation agencies in their efforts, and teach the young people of our country good conservation practice. Dedicated to the realistic conservation of our water resources.
Contact(s):
  Mike Riska, President; 406-549-1303
  Tony Quinnell, Conservation Director; 1535 Trumbel Creek Rd., Kallispell, MT 59901; 406-755-7867

MONTANA ENVIRONMENTAL INFORMATION CENTER
P.O. Box 1184
Helena, MT 59624 United States
Phone: 406-443-2520   Fax: 406-443-2507
E-mail: meic@meic.org
Website: www.meic.org
Founded: 1973
Membership: 1,001–10,000
Scope: State
Description: Overall purpose is to protect and restore Montana's natural environment. Educates and mobilizes citizens on Montana environmental issues to press for wise decisions at local, state, and federal levels. Priority issues include: energy policy and energy conservation, hardrock mining, water quality, land use and growth management, air quality, hazardous waste, environmental policy, and toxic chemicals..
Publication(s): Down to Earth, Capitol Monitor, Montana Environment
Keyword(s): Air Quality/Atmosphere, Climate Change, Energy, Forests/Forestry, Land Issues, Sprawl/Urban Planning, Transportation, Water Habitats & Quality
Contact(s):
  Jim Jensen, Executive Director; jjensen@meic.org
  Anne Hedges, Program Director; ahedges@meic.org
  Adam McLane, Business Manager; mclane@meic.org

MONTANA FOREST OWNERS ASSOCIATION
17975 Ryan's Ln.
Evaro, MT 59808 United States
Phone: 406-726-3787   Fax: 406-549-2287
E-mail: info@forestsmontana.com
Website: www.forestsmontana.com
Scope: State
Description: A statewide organization affiliated with the National Woodland Owners Association, dedicated to the careful use and active enjoyment of private forest lands in Montana. Goals are achieved through active forestry education programs, public communications, networking, and political advocacy.
Publication(s): Big Sky NIPF-TY Notes
Keyword(s): Forests/Forestry
Contact(s):
  Thorn Liechty, President
  Tom Castles, Vice President
  Peter Kolb, Vice President
  Jim Haviland, Treasurer
  Karen Liechty, Secretary

MONTANA LAND RELIANCE
P.O. Box 355
Helena, MT 59624-0355 United States
Phone: 406-443-7027   Fax: 406-443-7061
E-mail: info@mtlandreliance.org
Website: www.mtlandreliance.org
Founded: 1978
Scope: State
Description: A private nonprofit land trust protecting and conserving ecologically and agriculturally significant land in Montana, as well as sharing knowledge of voluntary, private-sector land conservation techniques. Pioneering ways to assure a legacy of responsibly managed private land.
Publication(s): A Guide to Planned Giving: Creation of a Conservation Legacy, Tax Implications of Donated Conservation Easements: An Introduction to Conservation Easements, The Montana Land Reliance - spring & fall newsletter, Better Trout Habitat, The Montana Land Reliance, Annual Report, Montana Spaces
Keyword(s): Agriculture/Farming, Forests/Forestry, Land Issues, Public Lands/Greenspace, Water Habitats & Quality, Wildlife & Species
Contact(s):
  Roy O'Connor, President; 5015 Larch Ave., Missoula, MT 59802; rsocmt@bigsky.net
  Jerry Townsend, Vice President; Elk Run Ranch, Highwood, MT; elkrun@3rivers.net
  Christopher Montague, Eastern Manager; P.O. Box 171, Billings, MT 59103-0171; 406-259-1382; mlr@mcn.net
  Amy Eaton, Glacier/Flathead Regional Office; P.O. Box 460, Bigfork, MT 59911-0460; 406-837-2178; mlrnw@digisys.net
  George Olsen, Secretary and Treasurer; Galusha, Higgens & Galusha, Box 1699, Helena, MT 59624-1699

MONTANA WILDERNESS ASSOCIATION
P.O. Box 635
Helena, MT 59624 United States
Phone: 406-443-7350   Fax: 406-443-0750
E-mail: mwa@wildmontana.org
Website: www.wildmontana.org
Founded: 1958
Membership: 1,001–10,000
Scope: Local, State, Regional
Description: A nonprofit membership organization dedicated to the preservation and proper management of Montana's wild lands, including designated and de facto wilderness areas, national parks, national forests, wildlife refuges, and BLM lands in Montana. The Montana Wilderness Association has five chapter affiliates and four field offices.
Publication(s): Wild Montana, Wilderness Walks Program
Keyword(s): Air Quality/Atmosphere, Ecosystems (precious), Forests/Forestry, Land Issues, Public Lands/Greenspace, Water Habitats & Quality, Wildlife & Species
Contact(s):
  Ross Rogers, President
  Gerry Jennings, Vice President

Bob Decker, Executive Director
John Gatchell, Conservation Director; 406-443-7350; Fax: 406-443-0750; jgatchell@wildmontana.org
Karole Lee, Administrative Director; 406-443-7350; Fax: 406-443-0750; klee@wildmontana.org
Susan Miles, Director of Membership Services

MONTANA WILDLIFE FEDERATION

P.O. Box 1175
Helena, MT 59624-1175 United States
Phone: 406-458-0227   Fax: 406-458-0373
E-mail: mwf@mtwf.org
Website: www.montanawildlife.com

Founded: 1935

Scope: State

Description: A representative statewide organization, affiliated with the National Wildlife Federation, dedicated to the protection and enhancement of wildlife and its habitat through public education and government interaction.

Publication(s): Montana Wildlife

Contact(s):
John Gibson, President; jcgibson@imt.net
Craig Sharpe, Editor & Executive Director
Stan Frasier, Alternate Representative
Kathy Hadley, Representative; khadley@ncat.org
Brian Logan, Education Programs Contact
Bill Orsello, Treasurer

MORONGO BASIN WILDLIFE REHAB STATION
P.O. Box 597
Morongo Valley, CA 92256 United States
Phone: 760-363-1966   Fax: 760-363-1966
E-mail: byrdman@telis.org
Website: morongowildliferehab.com

Founded: 1985
Membership: 1–100
Scope: Local

Description: Non-profit, licensed wildlife rehabilitation organization. Will rescue, rehabilitate, release or relocate wildlife in Southern California including mammals, raptors and reptiles.

Keyword(s): Wildlife & Species

Contact(s):
Jim Byrd, Founder; 760-363-1966; Fax: 760-363-1966; byrdman@telis.org
Jeanne Cosby, Biologist; 760-363-1966
Michele Pinney, Facility Manager; 760-363-1966

MOTE MARINE LABORATORY
MOTE ENVIRONMENTAL SERVICES, INC.
1600 Ken Thompson Parkway
Sarasota, FL 34236 United States
Phone: 941-388-4441   Fax: 941-388-4312
E-mail: info@mote.org
Website: www.mote.org

Founded: 1955
Membership: 1,001–10,000
Scope: Local, State, Regional, National, International

Description: MML is an independent, nonprofit research organization dedicated to excellence in marine and environmental sciences. Since its inception, the laboratory's primary mission has been the pursuit of excellence in scientific research and the dissemination of information to the scientific community as well as to the general public. MML specializes in fifteen research programs, the Arthur Vining Davis Library, marine science education and distance learning programs, and operates the public Mote Aquarium.

Publication(s): Mote Technical Reports, 2000 Annual Report, Mote Marine Laboratory Collected Papers, Mote News

Keyword(s): Agriculture/Farming, Ecosystems (precious), Oceans/Coasts/Beaches, Public Health, Wildlife & Species

Contact(s):
Kumar Mahadevan, Executive Director; 941-388-4441; Fax: 941-388-4007; info@mote.org
Daniel Bebak, Director, Aquarium and Special Projects Division; 941-388-4441; Fax: 941-388-4312; danbebak@mote.org
Howard Crowell, Vice-President, Development Division; 941-388-4441; Fax: 941-388-4312; howard@mote.org
Ernest Estevez, Director, Center for Coastal Ecology; 941-388-4441; Fax: 941-388-4312; estevez@mote.org
Don Hayward, Director, Information Systems Division; 941-388-4441; Fax: 941-388-4312; don@mote.org
Robert Hueter, Director, Center for Shark Research; 941-388-4441; Fax: 941-388-4007; rhueter@mote.org
Peter Hull, Director, Marine Operations Division; 941-388-4441; Fax: 941-388-4312; pete@mote.org
Kenneth Leber, Director, Center for Fisheries Enhancement; 941-388-4441; Fax: 941-388-6461; kleber@mote.org
Steve LeGore, President, Mote Environmental Services, Inc.; 941-388-4441; Fax: 941-388-4312; slegore@mote.org
Kevan Main, Director, Center for Aquaculture Research and Development; 941-388-4441; Fax: 941-388-4312; kmain@mote.org
Erich Mueller, Director, Center for Tropical Research; 305-745-2729; Fax: 305-745-2730; emueller@mote.org
Richard Pierce, Director, Center for Eco-Toxicology; 941-388-4441; Fax: 941-388-4312; rich@mote.org
Dena Smith, Director, Administration Division; 941-388-4441; Fax: 941-388-4312; dena@mote.org
Derek Templeton, Director, Facilities Division; 941-388-4441; Fax: 941-388-4007; temple@mote.org
Randall Wells, Director, Center for Marine Mammal and Sea Turtle Research; 941-388-4441; Fax: 941-388-4317; rwells@mote.org
Nelio Barros, Manager, Marine Mammal Stranding Program; 941-388-4441; Fax: 941-388-4317; nbarros@mote.org
John Buck, Manager, Marine Microbiology Program; 941-388-4441; Fax: 941-388-4312; jbuck@mote.org
Karen Burns, Manager, Fisheries Biology Program; 941-388-4441; Fax: 941-388-4312; kburns@mote.org
James Culter, Manager, Benthic Ecology Program; 941-388-4441; Fax: 941-388-4312; jculter@mote.org
L. Dixon, Manager, Chemical Ecology Program; 941-388-4441; Fax: 941-388-4312; lkdixon@mote.org
Jerris Foote, Manager, Sea Turtle Research Program; 941-388-4441; Fax: 941-388-4317; jerris@mote.org
Jay Gorzelany, Manager, Waterways Management Program; 941-388-4441; Fax: 941-388-4317
Robert Griffin, Manager, Offshore Cetacean Ecology Program; 941-388-4441; Fax: 941-388-4312; bgriffin@mote.org
Michael Henry, Manager, Chemical Fate and Effects Program; 941-388-4441; Fax: 941-388-4312; mhenry@mote.org
Barbara Kirkpatrick, Manager, Environmental Health Program; 941-388-4441; Fax: 941-388-4312; bkirkpat@mote.org
Gary Kirkpatrick, Manager, Phytoplankton Ecology Program; 941-388-4441; Fax: 941-388-4312; gkirkpat@mote.org
Carl Luer, Manager, Biomedical Research Program; 941-388-4441; Fax: 941-388-4312; caluer@mote.org
John Miller, Manager, Fisheries Habitat Program; 941-388-4441; Fax: 941-388-6461; jmiller@mote.org
John Reynolds, Manager, Manatee Research Program; 941-388-4441; Fax: 941-388-4317; reynolds@mote.org
Brad Robbins, Manager, Landscape Ecology Program; 941-388-4441; Fax: 941-388-4312; robbins@mote.org
William Tavolga, Manager, Sensory Biology and Behavior Program; 941-388-4441; Fax: 941-388-4312; tavolga@mote.org
Dana Wetzel, Manager, Aquatic Toxicology Program; 941-388-4441; Fax: 941-388-4312; dana@mote.org
Eugenie Clark, Mote Eminent Scientist; 941-388-4441; Fax: 941-388-4312; yoppe@mote.org

MOUNT GRACE LAND CONSERVATION TRUST
1461 Old Keene Road
Athol, MA 01331 United States
Phone: 978-248-2043   Fax: 978-248-2053
E-mail: landtrust@mountgrace.org
Website: www.mountgrace.org
Founded: 1986
Membership: 101–1,000
Scope: Regional
Description: Mount Grace Land Conservation Trust is dedicated to the protection of forests, agricultural land, and other open space in North Central Massachusetts. In 16 years, Mount Grace Land Conservation Trust has permanently protected 17,500 acres in 195 separate projects.
Publication(s): Views From Mount Grace Quarterly
Keyword(s): Agriculture/Farming, Ecosystems (precious), Forests/Forestry, Land Issues
Contact(s):
Leigh Youngblood, Executive Director
Pam Kimball-Smith, Development Administrator
Chuck Levin, Land Protection Specialist
Alain Peteroy, Stewardship Coordinator

MOUNTAIN CONSERVATION TRUST OF GEORGIA, INC.
104 N. Main St., Suite B3
Jasper, GA 30143 United States
Phone: 706-253-4077   Fax: 706-253-4078
E-mail: bdecker@mctga.org
Website: www.mctga.org
Founded: 1994
Membership: 101–1,000
Scope: Local, Regional
Description: Dedicated to the permanent conservation of the natural resources and scenic beauty of the mountains and foothills of north Georgia through land protection, partnerships and education.
Keyword(s): Land Issues, Water Habitats & Quality
Contact(s):
Gary Reece, President; 706-692-2424
Barbara Decker, Executive Director

MOUNTAIN DEFENSE LEAGUE
434 Creelman Lane
Ramona, CA 92065 United States
Phone: 760-789-8134   Fax: 760-789-8134
E-mail: PandoraRose_farm@hotmail.com
Website: mountaindefenseleague.org
Founded: 1973
Membership: 101–1,000
Scope: Local, Regional
Description: Mountain Defense League is a grassroots organization dedicated to the protection of the local and regional mountains, wildlands, and rural communities through wise land-use planning.
Contact(s):
Pandora Rose, Executive Director; 760-789-8134; PandoraRose_farm@hotmail.com

MOUNTAIN LION FOUNDATION
P.O. Box 1896
Sacramento, CA 95812 United States
Phone: 916-442-2666   Fax: 916-442-2871
E-mail: mlf@mountainlion.org
Website: www.mountainlion.org
Founded: 1986
Membership: 10,001–100,000
Scope: National
Description: The Mountain Lion Foundation is a nonprofit conservation and education organization dedicated to Saving America's Lion.
Publication(s): Crimes Against the Wild: Poaching in California, Preserving Cougar Country, Mountain Lion Update, Cougar: The American Lion
Keyword(s): Agriculture/Farming, Ecosystems (precious), Executive/Legislative/Judicial Reform, Land Issues, Public Lands/Greenspace, Recreation/Ecotourism, Sprawl/Urban Planning, Water Habitats & Quality, Wildlife & Species
Contact(s):
Lynn Sadler, Executive Director; 916-442-2666
Tim Dunbar, Associate Director
Michelle Cullens, Director of Conservation Pograms
Marla Stallworth, Office Manager
Christopher Papouchis, Conservation Biologist

MOUNTAINEERS, THE
CONSERVATION DIVISION
300 3rd Ave., W.
Seattle, WA 98119 United States
Phone: 206-284-6310   Fax: 206-284-4977
E-mail: clubmail@mountaineers.org
Website: www.mountaineers.org
Founded: 1906
Membership: 10,001–100,000
Scope: Regional
Description: The Mountaineers provides opportunities for outdoor recreation and training to its members and strives to protect the environment through community outreach, education, and political action.
Publication(s): Numerous titles published by Mountaineers Books, see publications on website
Keyword(s): Climate Change, Forests/Forestry, Land Issues, Oceans/Coasts/Beaches, Public Lands/Greenspace, Recreation/Ecotourism, Water Habitats & Quality, Wildlife & Species
Contact(s):
Glenn Eades, President
Steve Costie, Executive Director
Fatima Oswald, Public Policy Assistant

MRFC FISH CONSERVATION
PITTSBURGH OFFICE
1058 Larchdale Drive
Pittsburgh, PA 15243 United States
Phone: 412-279-0793   Fax: 412-279-4753
E-mail: serval05@aol.com
Founded: 1997
Membership: 1–100
Scope: Local, State
Description: A volunteer service born out of Pittsburgh, Pennsylvania in 1997. The group focuses on preventing housing/building development on state park lands and sport fishing lakes, streams, etc. Ensuring the survival and welfare of all species of gamefish has been the top priority since the introduction of the MRFC. Everyone who loves the outdoors knows it worth conserving for future generations.
Keyword(s): Water Habitats & Quality, Wildlife & Species
Contact(s):
Matt Kiswardy, President; 1058 Larchdale Drive, Pittsburgh, PA 15243; 412-279-0793; Fax: 412-279-4753; serval05@aol.com
Robert Truesdell, Vice President; 412-302-8749; rjtrues@aol.com

MULE DEER FOUNDATION
1005 Terminal Way, Suite 170
Reno, NV 89502 United States
Phone: 775-322-6558   Fax: 775-322-3421
E-mail: muledeer@muledeer.org
Website: www.muledeer.org
Founded: 1988
Membership: 10,001–100,000

Scope: National

Description: The Mule Deer Foundation's mission is to ensure the conservation of mule and blacktail deer and their habitats.

Publication(s): Mule Deer Magazine, Mule Deer Chronicle Newsletter

Keyword(s): Recreation/Ecotourism, Wildlife & Species

Contact(s):
Terry Cloutier, President/CEO; 775-322-6558; Fax: 775-322-3421; twc@muledeer.org

Steve Cranney, Regional Director for WY, ID and UT; 2425 East 3500 South, Vernal, UT 84078; 435-789-5357; scranney@muledeer.org

Rich Day, Regional Director for CA and NV; 775-322-6558; Fax: 775-322-3421; rday@muledeer.org

Ron Knapp, Regional Director for WA, OR, ID; 706 F and S Grade Road, Sedro-Wooley, WA 98284; 360-856-2188; Fax: 360-856-4047; rknapp@muledeer.org

Ken Kortan, Merchandise Director; 21362 Twin Peaks Lane, Morrison, CO 80467; 303-697-3829; Fax: 303-697-2691; mdfmerchandise@muledeer.org

Bob Meulengracht, Regional Director for CO, KS, NE, MO and all states East; P.O. Box 16728, Golden, CO 80402; 303-384-0103; Fax: 303-374-8858; meulengracht@muledeer.org

Todd Rathner, Regional Director for AZ, NM, TX & OK; 1173 N. Thunder Ridge, Tucson, AZ 85745; 520-903-1666; Fax: 520-388-9857; trathner@muledeer.org

Shawna Huckabey, Membership Manager; 775-322-6558; Fax: 775-322-3421; shuckabey@muledeer.org

Crystal Parrish, Convention Manager; 775-322-6558; Fax: 775-322-3421; cparrish@muledeer.org

Mark Smith, Accountant; 775-322-6558; Fax: 775-322-3421; msmith@muledeer.org

Wayne van Zwoll, Editor; 2610 Highland Drive, Bridgeport, WA 98813; 509-686-9051; Fax: 509-686-5191; publications@muledeer.org

MUNDO AZUL
BLUE WORLD
Las Acacias 185-A
Lima, 18 Peru
Phone: 511-4460414
E-mail: mundoazul@terra.com.pe
Website: www.peru.com/mundoazul

Founded: 1999
Membership: 1–100
Scope: Local, National

Description: Peruvian NGO working for the conservation and sustainable development of marine, coastal and aquatic ecosystems and species in Peru. (scientific research, environmental education, sustainable development projects, ecotourism, media work, lobbying, etc)

Keyword(s): Climate Change, Development/Developing Countries, Ecosystems (precious), Oceans/Coasts/Beaches, Pollution (general), Recreation/Ecotourism, Reduce/Reuse/Recycle, Sprawl/Urban Planning, Water Habitats & Quality, Wildlife & Species

Contact(s):
Nina Pardo, President; 551-9755571; ninapardo@terra.com.pe

Stefan Austermuhle, Executive Director; 511-975-5591; mundoazul@terra.com.pe

MUSKIES, INC.
P.O. Box 120870
New Brighton, MN 58112 United States
Phone: 1-888-710-8286
E-mail: info@muskiesinc.org
Website: www.muskiesinc.org

Founded: 1966
Membership: 1,001–10,000
Scope: National

Description: A nonprofit organization dedicated to establishing hatcheries and introducing the Muskellunge into suitable waters, abating water pollution, promoting a high quality muskellunge sport fishery, supporting selected conservation practices, promoting muskellunge research, disseminating muskellunge information, maintaining records of habits, growth, and range, and promoting good fellowship and sportsmanship.

Publication(s): Muskie

Keyword(s): Recreation/Ecotourism, Water Habitats & Quality

N

NATIONAL 4-H COUNCIL
7100 Connecticut Ave.
Chevy Chase, MD 20815-4999 United States
Phone: 301-961-2800   Fax: 301-961-2894
Website: www.fourhcouncil.edu

Founded: 1976
Scope: Local, State, Regional, National

Description: The mission statement of National 4-H Council is "To advance the 4-H youth development movement, building a world in which youth and adults learn, grow and work together as catalysts for positive change." The Environmental Stewardship program engages youth and adults to work as partners in developing creative, community-based solutions to environmental challenges. We also provide science-based educational materials that promote critical thinking skills and youth action grants.

Publication(s): Monthly e-mail update, environmental education materials on biotechnology, energy, transportation, food issues, endangered species and water quality

Keyword(s): Development/Developing Countries, Energy, Pollution (general), Public Health, Reduce/Reuse/Recycle, Transportation

Contact(s):
Kashyap Choksi, Project Director; Fax: 301-961-2894; choksi@fourhcouncil.edu

David Carrier, Project Coordinator; Fax: 301-961-2894; carrier@fourhcouncil.edu

NATIONAL ANTI-VIVISECTION SOCIETY
53 W. Jackson Boulevard
Suite 1552
Chicago, IL 60604 United States
Phone: 1-800-888-6287   Fax: 312-427-6524
E-mail: navs@navs.org
Website: www.navs.org

Founded: 1929
Scope: State, National, International

Description: The National Anti-Vivisection Society is a national, not-for-profit educational organization incorporated in the State of Illinois. NAVS promotes greater compassion, respect and justice for animals through educational programs based on respected ethical and scientific theory and supported by extensive documentation of the cruelty and waste of vivisection.

Contact(s):
Peggy Cunniff, Executive Director

NATIONAL ARBOR DAY FOUNDATION
100 Arbor Avenue
Nebraska City, NE 68410 United States
Phone: 402-474-5655   Fax: 402-474-0820
E-mail: info@arborday.org
Website: www.arborday.org

Founded: 1971
Membership: 1,000,001 +
Scope: National

Description: A nonprofit, membership organization, sponsors Trees for America, Arbor Day, Tree City USA, Conservation

Trees and Rain Forest Rescue educational programs. The Foundation publishes "Arbor Day National Poster Contest" and other instructional units for grade schools.

Publication(s): Arbor Day, all publications on website, Library of Trees, Celebrate Arbor Day (booklet), Conservation Trees (booklet), Tree City USA Bulletin

Keyword(s): Forests/Forestry, Land Issues, Wildlife & Species

Contact(s):
Bill Kruidenier, Chairman
John Rosenow, President
Dick Beahrs, Vice Chairman
Gary Brienzo, Information Director
Mary Yager, Program Director
James Fazio, Editor

NATIONAL ASSOCIATION FOR INTERPRETATION
P.O. Box 2246
Fort Collins, CO 80522 United States
Phone: 970-484-8283   Fax: 970-484-8179
E-mail: membership@interpnet.com
Website: www.interpnet.com

Founded: 1954
Membership: 1,001–10,000
Scope: National, International

Description: A nonprofit professional organization, employed by agencies and organizations concerned with natural and cultural resources, conservation, management and with the interpretation of the natural and historical environment.

Publication(s): Legacy, Journal of Interpretation Research, Interpretunities, Interp News, Centers Directory

Contact(s):
Sarah Blodgett, President; 978-369-5655; Fax: 978-369-6241; sdblodge@earthlink.net
Lisa Brochu, Associate Director; 2668 FM 1704, Elgin, TX 78621; 866-326-4642; Fax: 512-285-4105; naiprograms@aol.com
Tim Merriman, Executive Director; P.O. Box 2246, Fort Collins, CO 80522; 970-484-8283; Fax: 970-484-8179; naiexec@aol.com
Heather Manier, Membership Manager
Paul Caputo, Editor; Publications Diector of NAI, P.O. Box 2246, Fort Collins, CO 80522; 888-900-8383; Fax: 970-484-8179; naicom@aol.com

NATIONAL ASSOCIATION OF BIOLOGY TEACHERS
12030 Sunrise Valley Drive
Suite 110
Reston, VA 20190-5202 United States
Phone: 703-264-9696   Fax: 703-264-7778
E-mail: office@nabt.org
Website: www.nabt.org

Founded: 1938
Membership: 1,001–10,000
Scope: National

Description: The only national association specifically organized to assist teachers in the improvement of biology/life science teaching. NABT offers teachers an opportunity to develop professionally through its journal, annual convention, summer workshops, and other publication programs.

Publication(s): American Biology Teacher, The, The Monograph Series, News and Views

Keyword(s): Public Health, Wildlife & Species

Contact(s):
Richard Storey, President; Chair, Dept. of Biology, the Colorado College, Colorado Springs, CO 80903; 719-389-6406; rstorey@coloradocollege.edu
Wayne Carley, Executive Director; NABT, 11250 Roger Bacon Drive, #19, Reston, VA 20190-5202; 703-471-1134; nabt31@bellatlantic.net
Christine Chantry, Managing Editor; NABT, 11250 Roger Bacon Drive, #19, Reston, VA 20190-5202; 703-471-1134
Randy Moore, Editor; College of Arts & Sciences, University of Louisville, Louisville, KY 40292; 502-852-6490; r0moor01@homer.louisville.edu
Vivian Ward, Past President; Access Excellence-Genentech, Inc., Mail Stop 16B, 460 Point San Bruno Blvd., South San Francisco, CA 94080; 650-225-8750; vlward@gene.com
Catherine Wilcoxson, Secretary and Treasurer; 2833 Douglas Dr., Fremont, NE 68025; catherine.wilcoxson@nau.edu

NATIONAL ASSOCIATION OF CONSERVATION DISTRICTS
509 Capitol Ct., NE
Washington, DC 20002 United States
Phone: 202-547-6223   Fax: 202-547-6450
E-mail: info@nacdnet.org
Website: www.nacdnet.org

Founded: 1946
Membership: 1,001–10,000
Scope: National

Description: A nonprofit organization serving as the national instrument of its membership - 3,000 local districts and 54 state and territorial associations. Conservation districts, local subdivisions of state government work to promote the conservation, wise use and orderly development of land, water, forests, wildlife, and related natural resources.

Publication(s): Buffer Notes, Forestry Notes, Environmental Film Service Catalogue, Guide to Conservation Careers, America's Conservation Districts, District Leader, The, Tuesday Letter

Keyword(s): Agriculture/Farming, Land Issues, Oceans/Coasts/Beaches, Reduce/Reuse/Recycle

Contact(s):
J. Smith, President; 11751 Lancaster Rd., St. John, WA 99171-9723; 509-648-3922; Fax: 509-648-3293; readsmith@nacdnet.org
Gary Mast, 2nd Vice President; 6055 CR 203 Rte. 4, Millersburg, OH 44654; 330-674-6278; Fax: 330-674-3690
Billy Wilson, Second Vice President; 918-768-3542; bwilson@cwis.net
Debra Bogar, Director of Leadership Services, North; 9150 W. Jewell Ave. Ste. 111, Lakewood, CO 80232-6469; 303-988-1893; Fax: 303-988-1896
Robert Doucette, Director of Operations; bobdoucctto@nacdnet.org
Ron Francis, Director of Public Affairs; 408 East Main Street, League City, TX 77574; 281-332-3402; ext. 28; Fax: 281-332-5259; ron-francis@nacdnet.org
David Gagner, Director of Government Affairs; davidgagner@nacdnet.org
Bill Horvath, Director of North Central Program Office; 1052 Main St. Ste. 204, Stevens Point, WI 54481-2895; 715-341-1022; Fax: 715-341-1023
Eugene Lamb, Director of Programs; eugenelamb@nacdnet.org
Ray Ledgerwood, Director of Leadership Services, West; NE 1615 Eastgate Blvd., Suite B, Pullman, WA 99163; 509-334-1823; Fax: 509-334-3453
Robert Toole, Director of Leadership Services, South; 4617 Cahaan Creek Rd., Edmond, OK 73034; 405-359-9011; Fax: 405-359-9047
Linda Neel, Meeting Services Manager; 9150 W. Jewell Ave. Suite 102, Lakewood, CO 80232-6469; 303-988-1810; Fax: 303-988-1896
Laura McNichol, Government Affairs/Communications Specialist; laura-mcnichol@nacdnet.org
Tim Reich, Secretary/Treasurer; 1007 Kingsbury St., Belle Fourche, SD 57717; 605-892-4366
Ernest Shea, Chief Executive Officer; 202-547-6223; Fax: 202-547-6450; ernie-shea@nacdnet.org
Donna Smith, Administrative Assistant; donnasmith@nacdnet.org

NATIONAL ASSOCIATION OF CONSERVATION DISTRICTS
LEAGUE CITY OFFICE
P.O. Box 855
League City, TX 77574 United States
Phone: 281-332-3402 Fax: 281-332-5259
Website: www.nacdnet.org
Membership: 1,001–10,000
Scope: National
Description: tf
Publication(s): NACD News & Views - newsletter
Contact(s):
 Ronald Francis, Office of Public Affairs Director; ext. 27; ronfrancis@nacdnet.org
 Maxine Mathis, Service Center Production Manager; ext. 32; maxine-mathis@nacdnet.org

NATIONAL ASSOCIATION OF ENVIRONMENTAL PROFESSIONALS, THE
NATIONAL OFFICE
P.O. Box 2086
Bowie, MD 20718 United States
Phone: 888-251-9902 Fax: 301-860-1141
E-mail: office@naep.org
Website: www.naep.org
Founded: 1975
Membership: 1,001–10,000
Scope: National
Description: NAEP is the professional association of the environmental professions, dedicated to the promotion of ethical practice, technical competency, and professional standards in the environmental field and recognition of the environmental profession since 1975.
Keyword(s): Air Quality/Atmosphere, Energy, Reduce/Reuse/Recycle

NATIONAL ASSOCIATION OF RECREATION RESOURCE PLANNERS
c/o Tim Hogsett
Treasurer, Texas Parks & Wildlife Dept.
4200 Smith School Rd.
Austin, TX 78744-3291 United States
Phone: 512-912-7109 Fax: 512-707-2742
E-mail: rec.grants@tpwd.state.tx.us
Website: www.tpwd.state.tx.us/park/grants
Membership: 1–100
Scope: State
Description: A nonprofit organization involved in the exchange of recreation resource planning information among fedreal, state and regional agencies. Participates in national recreation concerns, promotes improvements in the state-of-the-art of recreation planning and professionalism among its members and acts as an advocate for conservation and recreation opportunities for the future.
Publication(s): NARRP Newsletter
Keyword(s): Land Issues, Public Lands/Greenspace, Recreation/Ecotourism
Contact(s):
 Gordon Kimball, President; Minnesota,
 Robert Sammon, Vice President; New Hampshire,

NATIONAL ASSOCIATION OF SERVICE AND CONSERVATION CORPS (NASCC)
666 11th St., NW, Suite 1000
Washington, DC 20001 United States
Phone: 202-737-6272 Fax: 202-737-6277
E-mail: nascc@nascc.org
Website: www.nascc.org
Founded: 1985
Membership: 101–1,000
Scope: Local, State, National
Description: NASCC unites and supports youth corps as a preminent strategy for achieving the nation's youth development, community service, and environmental restoration goals. NASCC serves as an advocate, central reference point, and source of assistance for the growing number of state and local youth corps around the country.
Publication(s): Youth Corps Profiles, Urban Waterways Restoration Training Manual, Corpsmember Wellness Guide, Youth Corps Resource Book
Keyword(s): Agriculture/Farming, Air Quality/Atmosphere, Climate Change, Development/Developing Countries, Energy, Ethics/Environmental Justice, Forests/Forestry, Oceans/Coasts/Beaches, Public Lands/Greenspace, Recreation/Ecotourism, Reduce/Reuse/Recycle, Transportatation
Contact(s):
 Harry Bruell, Vice President, Field Services; ext. 103; hbruell@nascc.org
 Andrew Moore, Vice President, Government Relations and Public Affairs; ext. 107; amoore@nascc.org
 Leslie Wilkoff, Director for Member Services; ext. 101; lwilkoff@nascc.org

NATIONAL ASSOCIATION OF STATE DEPARTMENTS OF AGRICULTURE
1156 15th St., NW, Suite 1020
Washington, DC 20005 United States
Phone: 202-296-9680 Fax: 202-296-9686
E-mail: nasda@patriot.net
Website: www.nasda.org
Scope: National
Description: The National Association of State Departments of Agriculture (NASDA) is a nonprofit, nonpartisan association of public officials comprised of the executive heads of the fifty State Departments of Agriculture and those from territories of Puerto Rico, Guam, American Samoa, and the Virgin Islands. NASDA's mission is to support and promote the American agriculture industry, while protecting consumers and the environment, through the development, implementation, and communication of sound policy.
Publication(s): NASDA News (weekly), Ag In Perspective (quarterly)
Keyword(s): Agriculture/Farming, Oceans/Coasts/Beaches, Pollution (general), Public Health, Public Lands/Greenspace, Reduce/Reuse/Recycle, Sprawl/Urban Planning, Water Habitats & Quality
Contact(s):
 Richard Kirchhoff, Chief Executive Officer; ext. 209; rick@nasda-hq.org

NATIONAL ASSOCIATION OF STATE FORESTERS
NASF
444 N. Capitol St., NW, Suite 540
Washington, DC 20001 United States
Phone: 202-624-5415 Fax: 202-624-5407
E-mail: nasf@sso.org
Website: www.stateforesters.org
Founded: 1920
Membership: 1–100
Scope: National
Description: Members are state foresters or equivalent officials whose agencies are the legally-constituted authorities for public forestry work within the states. In cooperation with federal agencies, private organizations, and individuals, NASF promotes sound forest management on public and private lands.
Keyword(s): Forests/Forestry
Contact(s):
 Anne Heissenbuttel, Executive Director; Hall of States, 444 North Capitol Street, NW, Suite 540, Washington, DC 20001; 202-624-5415; Fax: 202-624-5407; nasf@sso.org

NATIONAL ASSOCIATION OF STATE PARK DIRECTORS
9894 E. Holden Pl.
Tucson, AZ 85748 United States
Phone: 520-298-4924   Fax: 520-298-6515
Website: www.naspd.org
Founded: 1962
Membership: 1–100
Scope: National
Description: Works to unite the states on a common ground for the development of park systems to meet the intensive public demand for out-of-doors recreational opportunities; to promote the exchange of ideas regarding the development of state park systems; to encourage and develop professional leadership; and to expand and improve park policies and practices.
Publication(s): NASPD, The Directory, NASPD Annual Information Exchange
Keyword(s): Land Issues, Public Lands/Greenspace, Recreation/Ecotourism, Wildlife & Species
Contact(s):
   Phil Mcknelly, President
   Glen Alexander, Executive Director; 9894 E. Holden Pl., Tucson, AZ 85748

NATIONAL ASSOCIATION OF UNIVERSITY FISHERIES AND WILDLIFE PROGRAMS
President
Department of Animal Ecology
124 Science, Iowa State University
Ames, IA 50011-3221 United States
Phone: 515-294-6148   Fax: 515-294-7874
Website: www.naufwp.iastate.edu
Founded: 1991
Membership: 1–100
Scope: National
Description: Meets annually at the North American Wildlife and Natural Resources Conference. The purpose is to foster improved communications among members and between other agencies, organizations, and the general public in order to provide a unified voice for academic fisheries and wildlife programs.
Keyword(s): Wildlife & Species
Contact(s):
   Bruce Menzel, President and Chair; Department of Animal Ecology, Iowa State University, Ames, IA 50011-3221; 515-294-7419
   Erik Fritzell, Secretary and Treasurer; Department of Fisheries and Wildlife, Oregon State University, Corvallis, OR 97331; 541-737-5906
   Daniel Pletscher, President-Elect; Wildlife Biology Program, School of Forestry at the University of Montana, Missoula, MT 59812; 406-243-6364

NATIONAL AUDUBON SOCIETY
Headquarters, 700 Broadway
New York, NY 10003-9501 United States
Phone: 212-979-3000   Fax: 212-979-3188
Website: www.audubon.org
Founded: 1905
Membership: 500,001–1,000,000
Scope: National
Description: Solid science, policy research, lobbying, citizen science and action, and education — these are the tools used by the Audubon Society to protect the land and habitat that are critical to our health and the health of the planet. With the support of 550,000 members (in addition to the 500,000 elementary school students in the Audubon Adventures Program) and an extensive chapter network in the United States and Latin America, Audubon draws on the enthusiasm and power of the grassroots to save our planet.
Publication(s): Audubon Magazine, Audubon Adventures, Audubon Field Notes
Keyword(s): Wildlife & Species
Contact(s):
   John Flicker, President and CEO
   Alan Bayersdorfer, Vice President of Membership
   James Cunningham, Senior Vice President of Operations
   Patrick Downes, Vice President of Publishing
   Frank Gill, Senior Vice President of Science
   Carol May, Senior Vice President of Development
   Carole McNamara, Vice President/Controller
   Glenn Olson, Senior Vice President of Field Operations and Sanctuaries
   Daniel Beard, Chief Operating Officer
   Donal O'Brien, Chairman of the Board; Fax: 212-353-0377
   David Seideman, Editor-In-Chief Audubon Magazine

NATIONAL AUDUBON SOCIETY
ATLANTA AUDUBON SOCIETY
Box 29189
Atlanta, GA 30359 United States
Phone: 770-913-0511
Website: www.atlantaaudubon.org
Founded: 1975
Membership: 1,001–10,000
Scope: Local
Description: Atlanta Chapter of the National Audubon Society. Mission is to promote the enjoyment and understanding of birds and to protect and restore the ecosystems that support them.
Publication(s): Wingbars
Keyword(s): Ecosystems (precious), Forests/Forestry, Land Issues, Oceans/Coasts/Beaches, Pollution (general), Population, Public Lands/Greenspace, Reduce/Reuse/Recycle, Sprawl/Urban Planning, Water Habitats & Quality, Wildlife & Species
Contact(s):
   Jim Wilson, IBA Coordinator

NATIONAL AUDUBON SOCIETY
AUDUBON ALASKA
308 G St., Suite 217
Anchorage, AK 99501 United States
Phone: 907-276-7034   Fax: 907-276-5069
Website: www.audubon.org/chapter/ak/ak
Founded: 1977
Membership: 1,001–10,000
Scope: State, National, International
Description: Audubon Alaska applies sound science and common sense to protect birds, other wildlife and their habitats in Alaska. The staff works in cooperation with six local chapters to foster an environmental ethic that supports a healthy, sustainable economy and a quality of life in harmony with Alaska's natural environment.
Publication(s): Alaska Audubon News
Keyword(s): Ecosystems (precious), Forests/Forestry, Public Lands/Greenspace, Wildlife & Species
Contact(s):
   Stanley Senner, Executive Director
   Catherine Dennerlein, Education Specialist
   Rebecca Downey, Office Manager
   John Schoen, Senior Scientist

NATIONAL AUDUBON SOCIETY
AUDUBON COUNCIL OF CONNECTICUT
c/o Audubon Center in Greenwich, 613 Riversville Rd.
Greenwich, CT 6831 United States
Phone: 203-629-1248
Founded: 1967
Scope: State
Description: The Audubon Council of Connecticut is a coalition of 16 chapters and affiliates of the National Audubon Society in Connecticut, representing close to 10,000 residents. The

Council recognize humankind's dependence on the natural environment and appreciates the beauty and wondrous diversity of the natural world. The mission of the Council is, therefore, to protect and restore biodiversity in our state and on our planet.
Keyword(s): Wildlife & Species

NATIONAL AUDUBON SOCIETY
AUDUBON COUNCIL OF ILLINOIS
434 N Charlotte
Palatine, IL 60067 United States
Phone: 847-797-7820

Founded: 1973
Membership: 10,001–100,000
Scope: State
Description: Composed of representatives of 13 National Audubon Society chapters in Illinois, the Council's purpose is to coordinate efforts of the chapters on statewide environmental issues.
Keyword(s): Land Issues, Water Habitats & Quality, Wildlife & Species
Contact(s):
Brian Herner, President; 434 N Charlotte, Palatine, IL 60067; 630-891-4879; brian_herner@premierinc.com
Marianne Hahn, Vice President; 18429 Gottschalk Ave., Homewood, IL 60430; 708-799-0249
Mary Blackmore, Treasurer; 9024 W. Grove Rd., Forreston, IL 61030; 815-938-3204
Bonnie John, Secretary; 824 S. Dunton, Arlington Heights, IL 60005; 847-259-5168; hayspella@aol.com

NATIONAL AUDUBON SOCIETY
AUDUBON MARYLAND-DC
11450 Audubon Lane
Easton, MD 21601 United States
Phone: 410-822-4903   Fax: 410-822-5041
E-mail: pcec@pickeringcreek.org
Website: www.pickeringcreek.org

Founded: 1980
Scope: Local, State, Regional
Description: Pickering Creek is a 400 acre Audubon Center which provides science education to over 16,000 students a year. Located on a tributary of the Chesapeake the center has forest, meadow, and fresh and brackish water wetland habitats. The center is staffed M-F 9-5 and Saturday 10-4. Visitors are welcome to explore on their own seven days a week. Groups must call ahead.
Publication(s): Views
Keyword(s): Agriculture/Farming, Forests/Forestry, Recreation/Ecotourism, Reduce/Reuse/Recycle, Water Habitats & Quality, Wildlife & Species
Contact(s):
Mark Scallion, Center Director; 410-822-4903; mscallion@pickeringcreek.org
Justin Benz, Director of Education; 410-822-4903; jbenz@audubon.org

NATIONAL AUDUBON SOCIETY
AUDUBON MISSOURI
1001 E. Walnut Ste. 200
Columbia, MO 65201 United States
Phone: 573-442-2139   Fax: 573-443-4378
Website: www.audubon.org/chapter/mo/

Founded: 1999
Membership: 1,001–10,000
Scope: State
Description: A statewide council composed of delegates from 14 National Audubon chapters and the Audubon Society of Missouri. Formed to coordinate efforts on various conservation and environmental issues in Missouri. Advised and assisted by the National Audubon Society.
Keyword(s): Water Habitats & Quality, Wildlife & Species
Contact(s):
Karen Uhlenhuth, Chairperson; 3714 E. Roanoke Dr., Kansas City, MO 64111; 816-561-1371

NATIONAL AUDUBON SOCIETY
AUDUBON OF FLORIDA
444 Brickell Ave.
Suite 850
Miami, FL 33131 United States
Phone: 305-371-6399   Fax: 305-371-6398
E-mail: info@audubonofflorida.org
Website: www.audubonofflorida.org

Founded: 1900
Membership: 10,001–100,000
Scope: Local, State, Regional, National
Description: Florida division of National Audubon Society formed to promote public interest, understanding, and protection of Florida wildlife, and of the environment and habitats that support it.
Publication(s): Florida Naturalist, The
Keyword(s): Climate Change, Ecosystems (precious), Forests/Forestry, Land Issues, Oceans/Coasts/Beaches, Population, Public Lands/Greenspace, Reduce/Reuse/Recycle, Sprawl/Urban Planning, Water Habitats & Quality, Wildlife & Species
Contact(s):
Stuart Strahl, President; 305-371-6399; Fax: 305-371-6398; sstrahl@audubon.org
Mark Kraus, Conservation Science Director; 305-371-6399; Fax: 305-371-6398; mkraus@audubon.org

NATIONAL AUDUBON SOCIETY
AUDUBON OF KANSAS
206 Southwind Pl.
Manhattan, KS 66503 United States
Phone: 785-537-4385   Fax: 785-537-4395
E-mail: aok@audubonofkansas.org
Website: www.audubonofkansas.org

Founded: 1974
Membership: 1,001–10,000
Scope: State
Description: (formerly Kansas Audubon Council) A statewide nonprofit organization working in partnership with eleven local Audubon chapters, a Board of Trustees and other members. Established in 1974, leadership was expanded in 1999 to establish Audubon of Kansas as a broad-based alliance to promote appreciation and stewardship of the natural ecosystems of Kansas, with special emphasis on conservation of prairies, grassland birds and other wildlife.
Publication(s): Prairie Wings
Keyword(s): Land Issues, Reduce/Reuse/Recycle, Wildlife & Species
Contact(s):
Ron Klataske, Executive Director
Carol Cumberland, Treasurer; 1106 Gretchen, Wichita, KS 67206
Patricia Marlett, Secretary; 4406 W. 11th, Wichita, KS 67212
Robert McElroy, Vice Chairman
Dick Seaton, Chairman of Board

NATIONAL AUDUBON SOCIETY
AUDUBON OHIO
692 N. High St. Ste. 208
Columbus, OH 43215-1585 United States
Phone: 614-224-3303   Fax: 614-224-3305
E-mail: ohio@audubon.org
Website: http://oh.audubon.org

Scope: State
Description: The mission of Audubon Ohio is to conserve and restore ecosystems, focusing on birds and other wildlife

through advocacy, education, stewardship and chapter support for the benefit of Ohio citizens of today and tomorrow.

NATIONAL AUDUBON SOCIETY
AUDUBON PENNSYLVANIA
100 Wildwood Way
Harrisburg, PA 17110 United States
Phone: 717-213-6880   Fax: 717-213-6883
Website: www.audubon.org
Founded: 1987
Membership: 10,001–100,000
Scope: State
Description: The Pennsylvania Audubon Society promotes and encourages the conservation and protection of our natural resources through public education, communication with public officials, and sponsorship of programs to help children and adults become aware of their relationship to the environment.
Publication(s): Quarterly Newsletter, Wetlands Action Guide, Project Mayfly, Audubon Protecting Animals Through Habitat, Important Bird Areas of Pennsylvania Report, Pennsylvania Songbirds, Population & Habitat Newsletter
Keyword(s): Recreation/Ecotourism, Water Habitats & Quality, Wildlife & Species
Contact(s):
  Carmen Santasania, President; 1410 Charles St., State College, PA 16801; 814-359-5760
  Cindy Dunn, Executive Director
  Leigh Altadonna, Treasurer; 161 Greenwood Ave., Wyncote, PA 15834; 215-886-0656
  Marian Crossman, Secretary; 6 Tussey Circle, Pittsburgh, PA 15237; 412-366-3339

NATIONAL AUDUBON SOCIETY
AUDUBON SOCIETY OF MISSOURI
Attn: Jerry Wade, President
2101 W. Broadway #122
Columbia, MO 65203-1261 United States
Phone: 573-445-6697
E-mail: wadej@missouri.edu
Website: www.mobirds.org
Founded: 1901
Membership: 101–1,000
Scope: State
Description: A nonprofit statewide ornithological society dedicated to the preservation and protection of birds and all wildlife forms and habitat; to educate citizenry toward appreciation of the natural world; and to work for wise conservation practices related to people and wildlife.
Publication(s): Bluebird, The, Guide to the Birding Areas of Missouri, Annotated Checklist of the Birds of Missouri
Keyword(s): Wildlife & Species
Contact(s):
  Susan Hazelwood, President; 3005 Chapel Hill Rd., Columbia, MO 65203; 573-445-4925; shazelwood@socket.net
  Jerry Wade, Vice President; 1221 Bradshaw Ave., Columbia, MO 65203; 573-445-6697; wadej@missouri.edu
  Susan Dornfeld, Secretary; 700 S. Weller, Springfield, MO 65802; 417-831-9702; dornfelds@hotmail.com
  Jean Graebner, Treasurer; 1800 S. Roby Farm Rd., Rocheport, MO 65279; 314-698-2855
  Bonnie Heidy, Membership Chair; 501 Parkade, Columbia, MO 65202; 573-442-2191; bheidy@socket.net
  Edge Wade, Bird Alert Compiler; 1221 Bradshaw Ave., Columbia, MO 65203-0807; 573-445-6697; edgew@socket.net

NATIONAL AUDUBON SOCIETY
AUDUBON SOCIETY OF NEW HAMPSHIRE
3 Silk Farm Rd.
Concord, NH 03301-8200 United States
Phone: 603-224-9909   Fax: 603-226-0902
Website: www.nhaudubon.org
Founded: 1914
Membership: 1,001–10,000
Scope: State
Description: Independent statewide nonprofit organization dedicated to the preservation, understanding, and appreciation of New Hampshire's wildlife and other natural resources.
Publication(s): Newsletter, Bi-Monthly
Contact(s):
  Richard Moore, President
  Cynthia Belowski, Vice President for Conservation
  Scott Fitzpatrick, Director of Education
  Kent Taylor, Director for Membership
  Harry Vogel, Director of Loon Preservation Committee
  Julian Zelazny, Director of Environmental Affairs
  Sylvia Bates, Vice Chairperson; Rt. 1, Box 313, Ashland, NH 03217
  Tupper Kinder, Chair of the Board of Trustees; Sheehan Phinney, Bas and Green, 1000 Elm St., Manchester, NH 03105-3701
  Anita Maclean, Treasurer
  Larry Sunderland, Secretary; RFD 1 Box 179, Hillsboro, NH 03244

NATIONAL AUDUBON SOCIETY
AUDUBON SOCIETY OF NEW YORK
200 Trillium Lane
Albany, NY 12203 United States
Phone: 518-869-9731   Fax: 518-869-0737
E-mail: nasnys@audubon.org
Website: http://ny.audubon.org/
Scope: Local

NATIONAL AUDUBON SOCIETY
AUDUBON SOCIETY OF OMAHA
11809 Old Maple Road
Omaha, NE 68164 United States
Phone: 402-493-0373   Fax: 402-493-0373
Founded: 1985
Membership: 1,001–10,000
Scope: Local
Description: A statewide council of representatives of the eight National Audubon Society chapters in Nebraska. The Council's purpose is to coordinate efforts of the chapters on statewide environmental issues and advocate protection, preservation, and wise use of our soil, water, plants, and wildlife.
Contact(s):
  Ione Werthen, Contact

NATIONAL AUDUBON SOCIETY
AUDUBON SOCIETY OF PORTLAND
5151 NW Cornell Rd.
Portland, OR 97210 United States
Phone: 503-292-6855   Fax: 503-292-1021
E-mail: general@audubonportland.org
Website: www.audubonportland.org
Founded: 1902
Membership: 1,001–10,000
Scope: Local, State, Regional, National
Description: The Audubon Society of Portland promotes the enjoyment, understanding and protection of native birds, other wildlife and their habitats, focusing on the local community and the Pacific Northwest.
Publication(s): Audubon Warbler
Keyword(s): Development/Developing Countries, Ecosystems (precious), Forests/Forestry, Land Issues, Oceans/Coasts/Beaches, Public Lands/Greenspace, Recreation/Ecotourism, Reduce/Reuse/Recycle, Sprawl/Urban Planning, Water Habitats & Quality, Wildlife & Species
Contact(s):
  Jim Rapp, Board President

Sybil Ackerman, Director of Conservation
Mitch Luckett, Sanctuary Director
Steve Robertson, Education Director
Bob Wilson, Nature Store Director
Scott Lukens, Secretary

NATIONAL AUDUBON SOCIETY
AUDUBON SOCIETY OF RHODE ISLAND
12 Sanderson Rd.
Smithfield, RI 02917-2600 United States
Phone: 401-949-5454   Fax: 401-949-5788
Website: www.asri.org

Founded: 1897
Membership: 1,001–10,000
Scope: State
Description: To focus attention on critical natural resource problems, provide leadership when conservation action is necessary, carry out a broad program of public conservation education, and preserve examples of unique natural areas and native wildlife habitat.
Publication(s): Audubon Society of Rhode Island Report, Fields Notes of Rhode Island Birds, Checklist of Rhode Island Birds
Keyword(s): Air Quality/Atmosphere, Land Issues, Oceans/Coasts/Beaches, Public Lands/Greenspace, Reduce/Reuse/Recycle, Wildlife & Species

Contact(s):
Dickson Boenning, 2nd Vice President
A. Kohlenberg, 1st Vice President
Jeff Hall, Environmental Education Center Director; 401-245-7500; EEC@asri.org
Eugenia Marks, Research, Advocacy & Publications Director; emarks@asri.org
Lee Schisler, Executive Director
Lawrence Taft, Director of Properties and Acquistions; ltaft@asri.org
Sharon Cresci, Development Assistant
Joseph Dimase, Secretary
Frank Sciuto, Treasurer
Doris Thorpe, Membership Secretary
Ken Weber, Editor

NATIONAL AUDUBON SOCIETY
AUDUBON SOCIETY OF WESTERN PENNSYLVANIA
BEECHWOOD FARMS NATURE RESERVE
TODD SANCTUARY
Beechwood Farms Nature Reserve
614 Dorseyville Road
Pittsburgh, PA 15238-1618 United States
Phone: 412-963-6100   Fax: 412-963-6761
E-mail: aswp@aswp.org
Website: www.aswp.org

Founded: 1916
Membership: 1,001–10,000
Scope: Local
Description: The mission of the Audubon Society of Western Pennsylvania is to inspire and educate the people of southwestern Pennsylvania to be respectful and responsible stewards of the natural world.
Publication(s): Bulletin, Teacher Guide, Seasoning
Keyword(s): Ecosystems (precious), Wildlife & Species

Contact(s):
Richard Adams, Executive Director
Roy Lenhardt, Director of Development
Trisha Harger, Director of Education

NATIONAL AUDUBON SOCIETY
AUDUBON VERMONT
255 Sherman Hollow Rd.
Huntington, VT 05462 United States
Phone: 802-434-3068   Fax: 802-434-4686
E-mail: vermont@audubon.org
Website: www.vt.audubon.org

Founded: 1962
Membership: 1,001–10,000
Scope: Local, State
Description: Audubon Vermont is a program of the National Audubon Society. We protect birds, other wildlife and their habitat by creating a culture of conservation through education, research and advocacy. We educate focusing on site-based learning at the Green Mountain Audubon Center and the High Pond camps. Our conservation programs focus on citizen science initiatives that identify and protect Important Bird Areas. Audubon advocates for ecosystem management of our state's natural communities.

Contact(s):
Shirley Johnson, Board President

NATIONAL AUDUBON SOCIETY
CONNECTICUT AUDUBON SOCIETY
2325 Burr Street
Fairfield, CT 06824 United States
Phone: 203-259-6305, ext. 103   Fax: 203-254-7673
E-mail: Kayhankes@ctaudubon.org
Website: www.ctaudubon.org

Founded: 1898
Membership: 10,001–100,000
Scope: State
Description: Connecticut Audubon is a statewide, non-profit membership organization dedicated to providing excellence in environmental education, encouraging the conservation of the state's natural resources and advocating for enlightened leadership on ecological matters.
Publication(s): The Connecticut Audubon News - quarterly
Keyword(s): Air Quality/Atmosphere, Ecosystems (precious), Executive/Legislative/Judicial Reform, Land Issues, Oceans/Coasts/Beaches, Pollution (general), Public Lands/Greenspace, Recreation/Ecotourism, Reduce/Reuse/Recycle, Water Habitats & Quality, Wildlife & Species

Contact(s):
Robert Martinez, Executive Director; 2325 Burr St., Fairfield, CT 06430; 203-259-6305; ext. 101; Fax: 203-254-7673
Peter Kunkel, Vice President
W. Morehouse, Vice President of Legal
Judith Richardson, Vice President
Duffy Schade, Vice President
Milan Bull, Director; CT Audubon Coastal Center, 1 Milford Point Rd., Milford, CT 06460; 203-878-7440; Fax: 203-876-2813
Andrew Griswold, Director Eco Travel; 67 Main St., Essex, CT 06426; 860-767-0660; Fax: 860-767-9988
Ann Guion, Director of Pomfret Center; 189 Pomfret St., Pomfret Center, CT 06259; 860-928-4948
Judy Harper, Director of Glastonbury Center; 1361 Main St., Glastonbury, CT 06033; 860-633-8402; Fax: 860-659-9467
Patricia Kriss, Director of Development; 203-259-6305; ext. 102
Betty McLaughlan, Director of Environmental Affairs; 860-527-6750
Christopher Nevins, Director of Fairfield Region; 2325 Burr St., Fairfield, CT 06430; 203-259-6305; ext. 113
Christopher Nevins, Director of Birdcraft Museum; 314 Unquowa Rd., Fairfield, CT 06430; 203-259-0416; Fax: 203-259-1344
Kasha Breau, Teacher/Naturalist; 1361 Main St., Glastonbury, CT 06033; 860-633-8402
Debbie Dubitsky, Coordinator, Rolling Nature Center; 118 Oak St., Hartford, CT 06106; 860-246-6285
Ken Elkins, Coordinator, School Nature Area Program; 118 Oak St., Hartford, CT 06106; 860-246-6285
David Engelman, Chairman of the Board
Richard Julian, Teacher/Naturalist; 1 Milford Point Rd., Milford, CT 06460; 203-878-7440
Chris Krumperman, Teacher/Naturalist; 1361 Main St., Glastonbury, CT 06033

Cathy O'Donnell, Director Marketing Communications; 203-259-6305; ext. 103
Todd Russo, Teacher/Naturalist; 1361 Main St., Glastonbury, CT 06033; 860-633-8402; Fax: 860-659-9467
Jeff Weiler, Teacher/Naturalist; 189 Pomfret St., Pomfret Center, CT 06259; 860-928-4948

NATIONAL AUDUBON SOCIETY
DAVIESS COUNTY AUDUBON SOCIETY
11201 Fields Road South
Utica, KY 42376 United States
Phone: 270-275-4250
E-mail: rerphoto@bellsouth.net
Website: http://audubon.wku.edu/daviess/

Founded: 1967
Membership: 101–1,000
Scope: Local
Description: A local chapter of the National Audubon Society dedicated to nature conservation and education based in Daviess County, KY.
Publication(s): The Goldfinch
Contact(s):
   Robert Rold, President; 270-684-3209; rerphoto@bellsouth.net

NATIONAL AUDUBON SOCIETY
DELAWARE AUDUBON SOCIETY
P.O. Box 1713
Wilmington, DE 19899 United States
Phone: 302-428-3959
E-mail: mail@delawareaudubon.org
Website: www.delawareaudubon.org

Founded: 1976
Membership: 10,001–100,000
Scope: State
Description: The Delaware Audubon Society promotes an appreciation and understanding of nature to preserve and protect our natural environment and to affirm the necessity for clean air and water and the stewardship of our natural resources.
Publication(s): Delaware Audubon Journal
Keyword(s): Ecosystems (precious), Energy, Oceans/Coasts/Beaches, Pollution (general), Water Habitats & Quality, Wildlife & Species
Contact(s):
   Matthew Delpizzo, Vice-President; mail@delawareaudubon.org
   Leslie Savago, Vice President; mail@delawareaudubon.org

NATIONAL AUDUBON SOCIETY
FAIRFAX AUDUBON SOCIETY
4022 Hummer Rd.
Annandale, VA 22003-0128 United States
Phone: 703-256-6895   Fax: 703-256-2060
E-mail: fas@fairfaxaudubon.org
Website: www.fairfaxaudubon.org

Founded: 1980
Membership: 1,001–10,000
Scope: Local, State, Regional, National, International
Description: The Fairfax Audubon Society—a chapter of the National Audubon Society, is committed to the Audubon mission which is to conserve and restore natural ecosystems, focusing on birds and other wildlife, and their habitats.
Publication(s): Potomac Flier, Species Checklists
Keyword(s): Development/Developing Countries, Ecosystems (precious), Land Issues, Public Lands/Greenspace, Recreation/Ecotourism, Sprawl/Urban Planning, Water Habitats & Quality, Wildlife & Species
Contact(s):
   Deblyn Flack, Executive Director
   Christine Winslow, President

NATIONAL AUDUBON SOCIETY
HAWAII AUDUBON SOCIETY
850 Richards Street, #505
Honolulu, HI 96813-4709 United States
Phone: 212-979-3000   Fax: 808-537-5294
E-mail: hiaudsoc@pixi.com
Website: www.audubon.org#www.audubon.org#

Founded: 1939
Membership: 1,001–10,000
Scope: State
Description: for better understanding, appreciation, and conservation of Hawaii's native wildlife resources, especially its unique and endangered bird species and their associated ecosystems.
Publication(s): Elepaio (Journal), Map-Treasures of Oahu, field card checklist, checklists, Voice of Hawaii's Birds (cassette tapes), Hawaii's Birds
Keyword(s): Land Issues, Public Lands/Greenspace, Reduce/Reuse/Recycle, Water Habitats & Quality, Wildlife & Species
Contact(s):
   Wendy Johnson, President
   Sharon Reilly, Recording Secretary

NATIONAL AUDUBON SOCIETY
ILLINOIS AUDUBON SOCIETY
425 B N. Gilbert St., P.O. Box 2418
Danville, IL 61834 United States
Phone: 217-446-5085   Fax: 217-446-6375
Website: www.illinoisaudubon.org

Founded: 1897
Membership: 1,001–10,000
Scope: State
Description: The Society is dedicated to the preservation and enjoyment of wildlife and their habitats.
Publication(s): Illinois Audubon, Cardinal News, The
Keyword(s): Land Issues, Wildlife & Species
Contact(s):
   David Miller, President; 813 N. Center, McHenry, IL 60050
   Mary Hoeffliger, Vice President; 6752 E 2000th Ave., Shumway, IL 62461
   Marilyn Campbell, Executive Director and Editor, Cardinal News
   Susan Shaw, Sanctuary Director; Adams Wildlife Sanctuary, P.O. Box 20106, Springfield, IL 62708; 217-544-5781
   Tracy Cade, Editor; 225 W. 7th St., Spring Valley, IL 61362; 815-343-5400; pipntc@ivnet.com

NATIONAL AUDUBON SOCIETY
IOWA AUDUBON
P.O. Box 71174
Grinnell, IA 50325 United States
Phone: 515-727-4271
E-mail: p2eph@audubon.org

Scope: State
Description: The state office of the National Audubon Society supporting the 12 Audubon groups in Iowa. Iowa Audubon's mission is to promote the enjoyment, protection and restoration of Iowa's natural ecosystems with a focus on birds, other wildlife and their habitats.
Keyword(s): Wildlife & Species
Contact(s):
   Paul Zeph, Executive Director

NATIONAL AUDUBON SOCIETY
KENTUCKY AUDUBON COUNCIL
Attn: President, 306 Hoover Hill Rd.
Hartford, KY 42347 United States
Phone: 270-298-4237
E-mail: xlavian@starband.net
Website: www.kentuckyaudubon.org

Founded: 1971
Membership: 1,001–10,000
Scope: Regional
Description: A statewide Audubon Council for the seven key chapters of the National Audubon Society. Works to promote, foster, and encourage the conservation and preservation of all wildlife, plants, soils, water, air, and other natural resources for the benefit of all people.
Publication(s): Kentucky's Cause
Contact(s):
George W. (Bill) Little, President; 270-298-4237
Jeff Frank, Past-President; 16509 Bradbe Rd., Fisherville, KY 40023; 502-266-7181
Maggie Selvidge, Secretary; 904 North Dr., Hopkinsville, KY 42240; 502-886-8078
Bertha Timmel, Treasurer; 3604 Graham Rd., Louisville, KY 40207; 502-893-5601

NATIONAL AUDUBON SOCIETY
LIVING OCEANS PROGRAM
550 South Bay Ave.
Islip, NY 11751 United States
E-mail: livingoceans@audubon.org
Website: www.audubon.org/campaign/lo

Founded: 1993
Scope: National
Description: Living Oceans is the marine conservation program of National Audubon Society. The program is dedicated to reversing the mismanagement of marine fisheries which has led to the depletion of marine wildlife, and to restore the health of our marine environment and coastal habitats.
Publication(s): Audubon Guide to Seafood, Living Oceans News
Keyword(s): Oceans/Coasts/Beaches
Contact(s):
Carl Safina, Director
Merry Camhi, Staff Scientist; 516-581-2927
Mercedes Lee, Assistant Director; 516-224-3669

NATIONAL AUDUBON SOCIETY
LOUISIANA AUDUBON COUNCIL
355 Napoleon St.
Baton Rouge, LA 70802-5955 United States
Phone: 225-346-8761   Fax: 225-338-9806

Founded: 1989
Membership: 1–100
Scope: State
Description: To implement the Audubon cause in Louisiana on issues of statewide concern; coordinate activities among the Audubon chapters in Louisiana; and advocate on behalf of birds, wildlife and their habitat.
Keyword(s): Water Habitats & Quality, Wildlife & Species
Contact(s):
Doris Falkenheiner, President
Donna Lafleur, Vice President
Esther Boykin, Secretary
Clyde Mattison, Treasurer

NATIONAL AUDUBON SOCIETY
MAINE AUDUBON
20 Gilsland Farm Rd.
Falmouth, ME 04105 United States
Phone: 207-781-2330   Fax: 207-781-0974
E-mail: info@maineaudubon.org
Website: www.maineaudubon.org

Founded: 1843
Scope: State
Description: Dedicated to the protection, conservation, and enhancement of Maine's ecosystems through the promotion of individual understanding and actions. Programs focusing on forest conservation, endangered and threatened species protection, wildlife and wildlife habitats, grassroots activism, environmental education, and school curriculum enhancement. Nature day camp, field trip and world tour program, store, and 13 sanctuaries.
Publication(s): Habitat: Journal of the Maine Audubon Society
Keyword(s): Forests/Forestry, Oceans/Coasts/Beaches, Wildlife & Species
Contact(s):
Carol Hammond, Editor; chammond@maineaudubon.org

NATIONAL AUDUBON SOCIETY
MARICOPA AUDUBON SOCIETY
Maricopa Audubon Society
P.O.Box 15451
Phoenix, AZ 85060-5451 United States
Phone: 480-829-8209
E-mail: laurienessel@hotmail.com
Website: maricopaaudubon.org

Founded: 1953
Membership: 1,001–10,000
Scope: Local, State, National
Description: Maricopa Audubon Society is an organization of volunteers dedicated to the enjoyment of birds and other wildlife with a primary focus on the protection and restoration of the habitat of the Southwest through fellowship, education and community involvement.
Keyword(s): Ecosystems (precious), Energy, Forests/Forestry, Public Lands/Greenspace, Sprawl/Urban Planning, Water Habitats & Quality, Wildlife & Species
Contact(s):
Laurie Nessel, President; laurienessel@hotmail.com

NATIONAL AUDUBON SOCIETY
MASSACHUSETTS AUDUBON SOCIETY
208 South Great Road
Lincoln, MA 01773 United States
Phone: 781-259-9500   Fax: 781-259-8899
E-mail: info@massaudubon.org
Website: www.massaudubon.org

Founded: 1896
Membership: 10,001–100,000
Scope: State
Description: A nonprofit organization committed to the protection of the environment for people and wildlife. One of the oldest conservation organizations in the world and the largest in New England. Owns and protects more than 29,000 acres with 42 wildlife sanctuaries across Massachusetts. Programming priorities: conservation, education and advocacy.
Publication(s): Connections, Sanctuary
Keyword(s): Air Quality/Atmosphere, Ecosystems (precious), Land Issues, Wildlife & Species
Contact(s):
Laura Johnson, President; 781-259-9500; ext. 2222; Fax: 781-259-8899; ljohnson@massaudubon.org
Gary Clayton, VP-Programs; 781-259-2160; Fax: 781-259-2360; gclayton@massaudubon.org
Bancroft Poor, CFO; 781-259-2110; Fax: 781-259-2310; bpoor@massaudubon.org
Steve Solomon, VP- Resources; 781-259-2120; Fax: 781-259-2320; ssolomon@massaudubon.org
John Mitchell, Editor; 781-259-2169; Fax: 781-259-2369; jmitchell@massaudubon.org

NATIONAL AUDUBON SOCIETY
MICHIGAN AUDUBON SOCIETY
6011 W. St. Joseph, Suite 403, P.O. Box 80527
Lansing, MI 48908-0527 United States
Phone: 517-886-9144   Fax: 517-886-9466
E-mail: mas@michiganaudubon.org
Website: www.mas.mi.audubon.org

Founded: 1904

Membership: 1,001–10,000
Scope: State
Description: The Michigan Audubon Society works to protect the Great Lakes ecosystem for people and wildlife. The society conducts scientific research, educates, and advocates for the protection of species and habitats through five major centers, three affiliate organizations, forty-six chapters, and sanctuaries totalling over 5,000 acres of land.
Publication(s): Jack-Pine Warbler, Michigan Birds & Natural History
Keyword(s): Land Issues, Wildlife & Species
Contact(s):
  Gary Siegrist, President; 11772 Trist Rd., Grass Lake, MI 49240
  Loretta Gold, 1st Vice President; 143 Lillie Ave., Battle Creek, MI 49015
  Harold Prowse, 2nd Vice President; P.O. Box 336, Metamora, MI 48455
  Eileen Scamehorn, Business Manager
  Julie Craves, Editor-in-Chief
  Charles Macdonald, Treasurer; 945 Tihart, Okemos, MI 48864
  Larry Uhrie, Secretary; 19057 12 Mile Rd., Battle Creek, MI 49014
  David Worthington, Editor-In-Chief

NATIONAL AUDUBON SOCIETY
MONTANA AUDUBON
P.O. Box 595
Helena, MT 59624 United States
Phone: 406-443-3949   Fax: 406-443-7144
E-mail: mtaudubon@montana.com
Website: www.mtaudubon.org

Founded: 1976
Membership: 1,001–10,000
Scope: State
Description: Montana Audubon works with people to identify and conserve vital ecological systems for birds and other wildlife. We use the best available science to identify the threats to systems such as riparian zones, grasslands and forests. Our programs are designed to be applicable to diverse audiences, local interests, concerns and needs. It is a focused, community-based program to assist people in attaining the inspiration, knowledge and desire to take action to conserve these vital systems.
Publication(s): Montana Bird Distribution
Keyword(s): Agriculture/Farming, Ecosystems (precious), Energy, Forests/Forestry, Land Issues, Recreation/Ecotourism, Water Habitats & Quality, Wildlife & Species
Contact(s):
  Dorothy Poulsen, President; 406-727-7516
  Ray Johnson, Executive Director
  Bill Ballard, Treasurer; 5120 Larch Ave., Missoula, MT 59802; 406-549-5097
  Chuck Carlson, Secretary; P.O. Box 227, Ft. Peck, MT 59223; 406-526-3245

NATIONAL AUDUBON SOCIETY
NEW JERSEY CHAPTER
P.O. Box 126
9 Hardscrabble Road
Bernardsville, NJ 07924 United States
Phone: 908-204-8998   Fax: 908-204-8960
E-mail: hq@njaudubon.org
Website: www.njaudubon.org

Founded: 1897
Membership: 10,001–100,000
Scope: State
Description: Fosters environmental awareness and a conservation ethic among New Jersey citizens; protects New Jersey's birds, mammals, other animals, and plants, especially endangered and threatened species; and promotes preservation of New Jersey's valuable natural habitats.
Publication(s): Bridges to the Natural World, Birds of New Jersey, Records of New Jersey Birds, New Jersey Audubon
Keyword(s): Land Issues
Contact(s):
  Thomas Gilmore, President and CEO; 908-204-8998; Fax: 908-204-8960
  John Carno, Vice President for Development; 908-204-8998; jcarno@njaudubon.org
  Peter Dunne, Vice President of Natural History Information; Cape May Bird Observatory, Center for Research and Education, 600 Rt. 47 N., Cape May Court House, NJ 08210; 609-861-0700
  Dale Rosselet, Vice President for Education; Cape May Bird Observatory, Center for Research & Education, 600 Route 47 North, Cape May, NJ 08210; 609-861-0700
  Eric Stiles, Vice President for Conservation; Scherman–Hoffman Sanctuaries P.O. Box 693, Bernardsville, NJ 07924; 908-766-5787
  Karl Anderson, Director of Rancocas Nature Center; 794 Rancocas Rd., Mt. Holly, NJ 08060; 609-261-2495
  Pete Bacinski, Director of Sandy Hook Bird Observatory; Sandy Hook Bird Observatory, 2 Hart Shoren Drive, P.O. Box 446, Fort Hancock, NJ 07732; 732-780-7007
  Gretchen Ferrante, Director of Nature Center of Cape May; 1600 Delaware Ave., Cape May, NJ 08204; 609-898-8848
  Karla Risdon, Director of Weis Ecology Center; 150 Snake Den Rd., Ringwood, NJ 07456; 973-835-2160
  Gordon Schultze, Director of Lorrimer Sanctuary; P.O. Box 125, 790 Ewing Ave., Franklin Lakes, NJ 07417; 201-891-2185
  Brian Vernachio, Director of Plainsboro Preserve; Plainsboro Preserve, P.O. Box 446, Plainsboro, NJ 08536; 609-897-9400
  Jean Clark, Board Chairperson

NATIONAL AUDUBON SOCIETY
OKLAHOMA AUDUBON COUNCIL
P.O. Box 2476
Tulsa, OK 74101 United States
Phone: 918-592-1614
E-mail: info@tulsaaudubon.org

Founded: 1987
Membership: 1,001–10,000
Scope: State
Description: A statewide council of representatives of the eight National Audubon Society chapters in Oklahoma. The council coordinates the efforts of the chapters on statewide environmental issues, and advocates protection, preservation, and wise use of soil, water, plants, and wildlife.

NATIONAL AUDUBON SOCIETY
PROJECT PUFFIN
159 Sapsucker Woods Rd.
Ithaca, NY 14850 United States
Phone: 212-979-3000   Fax: 212-979-3188

Scope: Regional
Contact(s):
  Stephen Kress, Director

NATIONAL AUDUBON SOCIETY
PUBLIC POLICY OFFICE
GRASSROOTS DEPARTMENT
P.O. Box 15726
Washington, DC 20003 United States
Phone: 202-547-2355   Fax: 202-861-4290
E-mail: audubonaction@audubon.org
Website: www.audubon.org

Scope: National
Description: Enhance & expand Audubon's grassroots constituency and capabilities to promote effective conservation

policies that will conserve and restore natural ecosytems for birds and other wildlife that will benefit humanity and the earth's biological diversity.

Keyword(s): Agriculture/Farming, Ecosystems (precious), Forests/Forestry, Land Issues, Oceans/Coasts/Beaches, Population, Public Lands/Greenspace, Water Habitats & Quality, Wildlife & Species

Contact(s):
Kristen Berry, Grassroots Coordinator - IN, MT, WA, OR, ID, WY, IL; 202-861-2242; Fax: 202-861-4290; kberry@audubon.org
Emily Byram, Grassroots Coordinator - AL, AR, LA, MS, KY, TN, OK, TX; 202-861-2242; Fax: 202-861-4290; ebyram@audubon.org
Janine Clifford, Grassroots Coordinator - NJ, PA, AZ, CO, NV, NM, UT; 202-861-2242; Fax: 202-861-4290; jclifford@audubon.org
Judd Klement, Grassroots Coordinator - CA, AK, HI; 415-222-9246; Fax: 415-947-0332; jklement@audubon.org
Jason Kneeland, Grassroots Coordinator - ME, VT, NH, MA, CT, RI, NY, DE; 202-861-2242; Fax: 202-861-4290; jkneeland@audubon.org
Desiree Sorenson Groves, Grassroots Coordinator - IA, KS, MN, MO, NE, WI, SD, ND; 202-861-2242; Fax: 202-861-4290; dgroves@audubon.org
Corry Westbrook, Grassroots Coordinator - OH, MD, WV, VA, SC, NC, GA, FL; 202-861-2242; Fax: 202-861-4290; cwestbrook@audubon.org

NATIONAL AUDUBON SOCIETY
SAN DIEGO CHAPTER
2321 Morena Boulevard, Suite D
San Diego, CA 92110 United States
Phone: 619-275-0557
E-mail: sdaudubon@aol.com

Founded: 1916
Membership: 101–1,000
Scope: Local, State, Regional, National
Description: The mission of the San Diego Audubon Society is to foster the protection and appreciation of birds, other wildlife and their habitats through study and education and advocate for a cleaner, healthier environment.
Keyword(s): Ecosystems (precious), Land Issues, Oceans/Coasts/Beaches, Public Lands/Greenspace, Recreation/Ecotourism, Sprawl/Urban Planning, Transportation, Water Habitats & Quality, Wildlife & Species

NATIONAL AUDUBON SOCIETY
SCULLY SCIENCE CENTER
700 Broadway
New York, NY 10003 United States
Phone: 212-979-3000   Fax: 212-979-3188
E-mail: education@audubon.org
Website: www.audubon.org

Scope: Regional
Contact(s):
Carl Safina, Director

NATIONAL AUDUBON SOCIETY
SEATTLE AUDUBON SOCIETY
8050 35th Avenue NE
Seattle, WA 98115 United States
Phone: 206-523-4483   Fax: 206-528-7779
E-mail: info@seattleaudubon.org
Website: www.seattleaudubon.org

Founded: 1916
Membership: 1,001–10,000
Scope: Local, Regional
Description: Seattle Audubon cultivates and leads a community that values and protects birds and the natural environment.
Publication(s): Nature publications

Keyword(s): Agriculture/Farming, Ecosystems (precious), Forests/Forestry, Land Issues, Oceans/Coasts/Beaches, Public Lands/Greenspace, Recreation/Ecotourism, Sprawl/Urban Planning, Water Habitats & Quality, Wildlife & Species

Contact(s):
Christina Peterson, Executive Director; 206-523-8243; Fax: 206-528-7779; info@seattleaudubon.org

NATIONAL AUDUBON SOCIETY
TAVERNIER SCIENCE CENTER
115 Indian Mound Tr.
Tavernier, FL 33070 United States
Phone: 305-852-5318   Fax: 305-852-8012
Membership: 1–100
Scope: Regional
Contact(s):
Jerry Lorenz, Director of Reserch

NATIONAL AUDUBON SOCIETY
TUCSON AUDUBON SOCIETY
300 E. University Blvd. #120
Tucson, AZ 85705 United States
Phone: 520-622-5622   Fax: 520-623-3476
E-mail: tucsonaudubonso1@qwest.net
Website: www.tucsonaudubon.org

Founded: 1946
Membership: 1,001–10,000
Scope: Local
Description: Tucson Audubon Society is dedicated to improving the quality of the environment by providing education, conservation, and recreation programs, as well as environmental leadership and information.
Publication(s): Vermilion Flycatcher
Keyword(s): Ecosystems (precious), Land Issues, Recreation/Ecotourism, Sprawl/Urban Planning, Wildlife & Species

NATIONAL AUDUBON SOCIETY
WASHINGTON, D.C. OFFICE
P.O. Box 15726
Suite 1100
Washington, DC 20003 United States
Phone: 202-547-2355   Fax: 202-861-4290
E-mail: judyschaefer@attglobal.net
Website: www.dcaudubon.org

Scope: National
Publication(s): Audubon Magazine
Contact(s):
Dan Beard, Senior Vice President; dbeard@audubon.org

NATIONAL BIRD-FEEDING SOCIETY
P.O. Box 23
Northbrook, IL 60065-0023 United States
Phone: 847-272-0135   Fax: 773-404-0923
E-mail: questions@birdfeeding.org
Website: www.birdfeeding.org

Founded: 1989
Membership: 10,001–100,000
Scope: National
Description: Every bird-friendly backyard is one more link in the emerald necklace circling urban development. Helping people create good bird habitat, one backyard at a time, is the Society's goal. Society resources help people learn ways to attract and care for birds, to experience the environment where it's close and easy to do—right outside their doors. For many people, bird feeding is their only connection with nature. Sponsors support research to further enhance positive backyard experiences.
Publication(s): The Bird-Eye reView
Keyword(s): Reduce/Reuse/Recycle, Wildlife & Species

Contact(s):
  Sue Wells, Executive Director
  Donald Stokes, Chairman Emeritus

NATIONAL BISON ASSOCIATION
4701 Marion St., Suite 100
Denver, CO 80216 United States
Phone: 303-292-2833   Fax: 303-292-2564
E-mail: info@bisoncentral.com
Website: www.bisoncentral.com
Membership: 1,001–10,000
Scope: National
Description: The National Bison Association represents public and private bison herds through educational programs, public education and scholarships.
Publication(s): Bison World (quarterly)

NATIONAL BOATING FEDERATION
P.O. Box 4111
Annapolis, MD 21403 United States
Founded: 1966
Scope: National
Description: National, all-volunteer, non-profit boating organization consisting principally of regional or special interest boating organizations and yacht clubs. Activities include monitoring federal legislation and rule-making as they affect recreational boating. The NBF promotes the interests of those who use boats for cruising, water skiing, fishing, and other water sports.
Publication(s): The LOOKOUT, Recreational Boating News and Legislative Issues
Keyword(s): Oceans/Coasts/Beaches, Recreation/Ecotourism, Water Habitats & Quality
Contact(s):
  Robert David, President; 70 Garfield Lane, West Dennis, MA 02670-2321; 508-394-5670; Fax: 508-394-7236
  Roger Brown, Vice-President; 111 S. View Court, Shore Acres, NJ 08723-7520; 732-236-3516; Fax: 732-477-0071
  Jill Andrick, Public Relations and Editor; P.O. Box 211, Salem, OR 97308-0211; 503-580-0769
  William Heider, Secretary and Treasurer; 1114 Appletree Lane, Erie, PA 16509-3917; 814-825-3011; Fax: 814-825-5284
  William Mitchelson, Past President; 9483 N. Fairway Cr., Milwaukee, WI 53217-1316; 414-352-0967

NATIONAL BOWHUNTER EDUCATION FOUNDATION (NBEF)
P.O. Box 180757
Ft. Smith, AR 72918 United States
Phone: 479-649-9036   Fax: 479-649-3098
E-mail: mbentz@nbef.org
Website: www.nbef.org
Founded: 1979
Scope: International
Description: To promote responsible bowhunting through education.
Publication(s): Bowhunter Education Materials
Keyword(s): Agriculture/Farming, Forests/Forestry, Land Issues, Wildlife & Species

NATIONAL CAUCUS OF ENVIRONMENTAL LEGISLATORS (NCEL)
1625 K Street, NW
Suite 790
Washington, DC 20006 United States
Phone: 202-293-7800   Fax: 202-293-7808
E-mail: adam@ncel.net
Website: www.ncel.net
Founded: 1996
Membership: 101–1,000
Scope: State, Regional, National
Description: The National Caucus of Environmental Legislators (NCEL) was organized for the purpose of providing environmentally progressive legislators with an opportunity to coordinate their activities with respect to national legislative organizations, and to share ideas both on affirmative and negative environmental issues.
Keyword(s): Agriculture/Farming, Air Quality/Atmosphere, Climate Change, Energy, Ethics/Environmental Justice, Land Issues, Pollution (general), Public Health, Reduce/Reuse/Recycle, Sprawl/Urban Planning, Transportation, Water Habitats & Quality
Contact(s):
  Leon Billings, Chair Emeritus; 202-293-7800; Fax: 202-293-7808

NATIONAL CENTER FOR APPROPRIATE TECHNOLOGY
P.O. Box 3838
Butte, MT 59702 United States
Phone: 406-494-4572   Fax: 406-494-2905
E-mail: info@ncat.org
Website: www.ncat.org
Founded: 1976
Scope: Local, State, Regional, National
Description: Provide technical assistance to people in sustainable energy, housing and agriculture areas, with a special emphasis on assisting low income people
Publication(s): ATTRA Publications
Keyword(s): Agriculture/Farming, Climate Change, Energy, Land Issues
Contact(s):
  Kathleen Hadley, Executive Director; 406-494-4572; Fax: 406-494-2905; kathyh@ncat.org

NATIONAL CENTER FOR APPROPRIATE TECHNOLOGY
CENTER FOR RESOURCEFUL BUILDING TECHNOLOGY
P.O. Box 100
Missoula, MT 59806 United States
Phone: 406-549-7678   Fax: 406-549-4100
E-mail: crbt@ncat.org
Website: www.crbt.ncat.org
Founded: 1991
Scope: National
Description: NCAT's Center for Resourceful Building Technology (CRBT) is dedicated to promoting environmentally responsible practices in construction. It serves as both catalyst and facilitator in encouraging building technologies which realize a sustainable and efficient use of resources.
Publication(s): Building Our Children's Future, ReCraft 90 Handbook
Keyword(s): Energy, Reduce/Reuse/Recycle
Contact(s):
  Tracy Mumma, Program Specialist

NATIONAL COALITION FOR MARINE CONSERVATION
3 N. King St.
Leesburg, VA 20176 United States
Phone: 703-777-0037   Fax: 703-777-1107
E-mail: christine@savethefish.org
Website: www.savethefish.org
Founded: 1973
Membership: 1,001–10,000
Scope: National
Description: A nonprofit, privately-supported organization devoted exclusively to the conservation of ocean fish and the protection of their environment. Promotes public awareness of marine

conservation issues and stimulates the formulation of responsible public policy.
Publication(s): Marine Bulletin
Keyword(s): Oceans/Coasts/Beaches, Recreation/Ecotourism, Water Habitats & Quality, Wildlife & Species
Contact(s):
Ken Hinman, President and Editor
Tim Hobbs, Fisheries Project Director
Christine Snovell, Director of Communications and Development

NATIONAL COUNCIL FOR GEOGRAPHIC EDUCATION
16A Leonard Hall, Indiana University of Pennsylvania
Indiana, PA 15705-1807 United States
Phone: 724-357-6290   Fax: 724-357-7708
E-mail: ncge-org@grove.iup.edu
Website: www.ncge.org
Founded: 1915
Membership: 1,001–10,000
Scope: National
Description: To promote and advance geographic and environmental education in the public schools and colleges of the U.S. and Canada.
Publication(s): Journal of Geography, list of other publications available upon request, Water In the Global Environment
Contact(s):
James Peterson, President
Robert Bednarz, Vice President of Curriculum and Instruction
Gary Elbow, Vice President of Publications and Products
Celeste Fraser, Vice President of Finance
Ruth Shirey, Executive Director
Jonathan Leib, Editor; Department of Geography, Florida State University, Tallahassee, FL 32306-4016
Sandra Mather, Secretary

NATIONAL COUNCIL FOR SCIENCE AND THE ENVIRONMENT, THE
1707 H Street NW
Suite 200
Washington, DC 20006 United States
Phone: 202-530-5810   Fax: 202-628-4311
E-mail: rob@NCSEonline.org
Website: www.NCSEonline.org
Founded: 1990
Scope: National, International
Description: NCSE works to improve the scientific basis for environmental decisionmaking. With the support by nearly 500 academic, scientific, environmental, business and governmental organizations, NCSE promotes a new crosscutting approach to environmental science that integrates interdisciplinary research; scientific assessment; communication of science-based information to decisionmakers and the general public; and environmental education.
Publication(s): Over 800 Congressional Service Reports and many other resources available through on-line library, Federal Environmental Research and Development Programs
Keyword(s): Development/Developing Countries
Contact(s):
Richard Benedick, President
Peter Saundry, Executive Director
A. Ahmed, Secretary and Treasurer; President, Global Children's Health and Environmental Fund; 202-789-1201; Fax: 202-789-1206
Stephen Hubbell, Chair; Professor of Botany, University of Georgia, Dept. of Botany, Athens, GA 30602; 706-583-0393; Fax: 706-542-1805

NATIONAL EDUCATION ASSOCIATION
1201 16th St., NW
Washington, DC 20036 United States
Phone: 202-833-4000
Website: www.nea.org
Founded: 1857
Membership: 1,000,001 +
Scope: National
Description: Works to elevate the character and advance the interests of the teaching profession and to promote the cause of education in the U.S.
Publication(s): Newsletter- NEA Today, newletter- NEA Now
Contact(s):
Robert Chase, President
Reg Weaver, Vice President
John Wilson, Executive Director
Dennis Roekel, Secretary and Treasurer

NATIONAL ENVIRONMENTAL EDUCATION AND TRAINING FOUNDATION
ENVIRONMENTORS PROJECT, THE
NATIONAL PUBLIC LANDS DAY
GREEN BUSINESS NETWORK
1707 H Street, NW
Suite 900
Washington, DC 20006 United States
Phone: 202-833-2933   Fax: 202-261-6464
E-mail: info@neetf.org
Website: neetf.org
Founded: 1990
Scope: National
Description: A 501(c)(3) non-profit organization established by Congress, NEETF strives to help America meet critical challenges by connecting environmental learning to subjects of national concern including education, health care, and economic growth.
Publication(s): The National Report Card
Keyword(s): Energy, Pollution (general), Public Lands/Greenspace, Sprawl/Urban Planning, Water Habitats & Quality
Contact(s):
Kevin Coyle, President; coyle@neetf.org
Deborah Sliter, Vice President for Programs; sliter@neetf.org

NATIONAL ENVIRONMENTAL HEALTH ASSOCIATION
720 S. Colorado Blvd., S. Tower, Suite 970
Denver, CO 80246-1925 United States
Phone: 303-756-9090   Fax: 303-691-9490
E-mail: staff@neha.org
Website: www.neha.org
Founded: 1937
Membership: 1,001–10,000
Scope: National
Description: NEHA is a member nonprofit organization that offers a wide variety of educational credentialing and advancement opportunities for people involved or interested in environmental health issues. It is the largest society of environmental health practitioners in the nation today, numbering almost 5,000 members and growing.
Publication(s): Journal of Environmental Health, various books, manuals, etc., Self Paced Learning Modules
Keyword(s): Air Quality/Atmosphere, Oceans/Coasts/Beaches, Pollution (general), Public Health, Reduce/Reuse/Recycle
Contact(s):
Nelson Fabian, Executive Director; ext. 300

NATIONAL FARMERS UNION
11900 E. Cornell Ave.
Aurora, CO 80014-3194 United States
Phone: 303-337-5500 Fax: 303-368-1390
Website: www.nfu.org

Founded: 1902

Scope: National

Description: Believes that the soil, water, forest and other natural resources of the nation should be used and conserved in a manner to pass these resources on undiminished to future generations and that publicly and privately owned land and resources should be administered in the interest of all the public.

Publication(s): National Farmers Union News

Keyword(s): Agriculture/Farming, Land Issues, Public Health, Reduce/Reuse/Recycle

Contact(s):
David Frederickson, President
Tom Buis, Vice President of Legislative Services; 400 Virginia Ave. SW, Suite 710, Washington, DC 20024
Clay Pederson, Vice President
David Carter, Treasurer/Secretary
Rae Price, Editor; 11900 E. Cornell Ave., Aurora, CO 80014-3194; 303-337-5500

NATIONAL FFA ORGANIZATION
P.O. Box 68960, 6060 FFA Drive
Indianapolis, IN 46268-0960 United States
Phone: 317-802-6060 Fax: 317-802-6061
E-mail: info@ffa.org
Website: www.ffa.org

Founded: 1928

Membership: 100,001–500,000

Scope: National

Description: The FFA is a national organization of high school agriculture students in public secondary schools. Congress granted the organization a federal charter in 1950, making it an integral part of the high school agriculture program. Major aims are to provide activities that will stimulate students to higher achievement in the study of production agriculture, agriscience, agribusiness, and agrimarketing, and give them opportunities through student-planned programs for leadership and self-development.

Publication(s): FFA New Horizons Magazine, The, Update Newsletter, FFA Advisor Publication

Keyword(s): Agriculture/Farming, Public Health, Reduce/Reuse/Recycle

Contact(s):
Larry Case, National FFA Advisor and CEO; 1410 King Street, Ste. 400, Alexandria, VA 22314; 703-838-5889; Fax: 703-838-5888; lcase@ffa.org
C. Harris, Executive Secretary; 1410 King Street, Ste. 400, Alexandria, VA 22314; 703-838-5889; Fax: 703-838-5888; charris@ffa.org

NATIONAL FIELD ARCHERY ASSOCIATION
31407 Outer I-10
Redlands, CA 92373 United States
Phone: 909-794-2133 Fax: 909-794-8512
E-mail: nfaarchery@aol.com
Website: www.nfaaarchery.com

Founded: 1939

Membership: 10,001–100,000

Scope: National

Description: A nonprofit national membership headquarters for all archers.

Publication(s): Archery Magazine

Keyword(s): Recreation/Ecotourism

Contact(s):
Walter Rueger, President; 122 Stanton Ave., Ripon, WI 54971
Tim Atwood, Bowhunting Committee Chairman; 3175 Racine, Riverside, CA 92503
Marihelen Rogers, Executive Secretary and Editor

NATIONAL FISH AND WILDLIFE FOUNDATION
1120 Connecticut Ave., NW, Suite 900
Washington, DC 20036 United States
Phone: 202-857-0166 Fax: 202-857-0162
E-mail: info@nfwf.org
Website: www.nfwf.org

Founded: 1984

Scope: National

Description: A national nonprofit grant-making and grant-seeking organization dedicated to the conservation of natural resources—fish, wildlife, and plants. NFWF was established by Congress to leverage federally appropriated funds by forging public and private partnerships which result in conservation activities that pinpoint and solve root causes of environmental problems.

Keyword(s): Wildlife & Species

Contact(s):
John Berry, Executive Director, berry@nfwf.org
Gary Guinn, Director of Development and Marketing, guinn@nfwf.org
Lorraine Howerton, Director of Conservation Policy
Cary Kania, Director of Wildlife and Habitat Initiative
Tom Kelsch, Director of Conservation Education Initiative
Peter Stangel, Regional Director of Southeast; stangel@nfwf.org
Whitney Tilt, Director of Conservation Programs
Jerry Clark, Deputy Director Regional Programs; clark@nfwf.org
Alex Echols, Special Assistant
Steve Peet, Chairman of the Board
Ginette Ring, Chief Financial Officer

NATIONAL FLYWAY COUNCIL
CENTRAL FLYWAY OFFICE
WY Game & Fish Dept.
5400 Bishop Blvd.
Cheyenne, WY 82006 United States
Phone: 307-777-4501
E-mail: bwiche@missc.state.wy.us

Scope: National

Contact(s):
William Wichers, Chairman

NATIONAL FLYWAY COUNCIL
MISSISSIPPI FLYWAY OFFICE
IA DEPARTMENT OF NATURAL RESOURCES
Wallace State Office Bldg. 502 E. 9th St.
Des Moines, IA 50036 United States
E-mail: rbishop@max.state.ia.us

Scope: National

Contact(s):
Richard Bishop, Chairman

NATIONAL FLYWAY COUNCIL
NORTH DAKOTA GAME AND FISH DEPARTMENT
100 North Bismarck Expressway
Bismarck, ND 58501-5086 United States
Phone: 701-328-6330 Fax: 701-328-6352
E-mail: rkreil@state.nd.us

Founded: 1952

Scope: National

Description: Composed of a representative from each of the four Flyway Councils. Purpose is to facilitate actions neccessary to manage waterfowl and other migratory game birds from a national perspective.

Contact(s):
Gerald Barnhart, Chairman

NATIONAL FLYWAY COUNCIL
SOUTH DAKOTA GAME, FISH AND PARKS
523 E. Capitol
Pierre, SD 57501 United States
Phone: 605-773-4192 Fax: 605-773-6245
E-mail: george.vandel@state.sd.us
Website: www.st.sd.us/gfp
Scope: National
Description: The National Flyway Council contains one appointed representative from each of the four Flyway Councils, Atlantic, Mississippi, Central and Pacific. The purpose of the NFC is to coordinate and facilitate resolving migratory game bird regulatory issues that cross flyway boundaries. Meetings are held in conjunction with the North American Fish and Wildlife Conference and the Service Regulations Committee meetings.
Contact(s):
George Vandel, Chairman; South Dakota Game, Fish, and Parks Department, 523 E. Capitol, Pierre, SD 57501

NATIONAL FOREST FOUNDATION
Building 27, Suite #3
Fort Missoula Road
Missoula, MT 59803 United States
Phone: 406-542-2805 Fax: 406-542-2810
Website: www.natlforests.org
Founded: 1993
Membership: 1,001–10,000
Scope: National
Description: As the independent, not-for-profit partner organization of the U.S. Forest Service, the NFF seeks to build relationships that result in measurable improvements in the health, productivity, and diversity of our National Forests and Grasslands for present and future generations.
Publication(s): Mosaic
Keyword(s): Forests/Forestry, Public Lands/Greenspace, Recreation/Ecotourism, Water Habitats & Quality, Wildlife & Species
Contact(s):
William Possiel, President
Doug Crandall, Vice President
Mary Mitsos, V.P. of Conservation Programs
Alexandra Kenny, Director, Grants Programs Officer
Jennifer McConnell, Director, Foundation Giving
Cindy Pandini, Director of Marketing and Communications
Maria Ferrio, Office Services Coordinator

NATIONAL FORESTRY ASSOCIATION
374 Maple Ave. E.
Vienna, VA 22180 United States
Phone: 703-255-2300 Fax: 703-281-9200
E-mail: info@nationalforestry.org
Website: www.nationalforestry.org
Founded: 1981
Membership: 1,001–10,000
Scope: National
Description: Organized in 1981 as the National Forestry Network, the National Forestry Association assumed its present name in 1996 and expanded its mission to include Green Tag Forestry Certification and Professional Forester Referrals to associations and landowners nationwide. The association also convenes the Forestry Advisory Board, a national panel of expert foresters to evaluate important forestry issues.
Publication(s): The Forestry Advantage
Keyword(s): Forests/Forestry
Contact(s):
Keith Argow, President
Nels Hanson, Vice President

NATIONAL GARDEN CLUBS, INC.
4401 Magnolia Ave.
St. Louis, MO 63110-3492 United States
Phone: 314-776-7574 Fax: 314-776-5108
E-mail: headquarters@gardenclub.org
Website: www.gardenclub.org
Founded: 1929
Membership: 100,001–500,000
Scope: International
Description: Coordinates and furthers the interests and activities of the State Federations of Garden Clubs and aids in the protection and conservation of natural resources; protects civic beauty and encourages the improvement of roadsides and parks; encourages and assists in establishing and maintaining botanical gardens and horticultural centers; and advances the arts of gardening and landscape design, and study of horticulture.
Publication(s): National Gardener, The
Keyword(s): Agriculture/Farming
Contact(s):
June Wood, President; 7000 Seminole Rd., NE, Albuquerque, NM 87110-2739
Fran Mantler, Executive Director
Jan Blair, Conservation/Natural Resources Wildlife/Endangered Species; Louis Rd., Irvington, NY; 914-591-6959; envirojb@aol.com
Susan Davidson, Editor; 102 S. Elm St., St. Louis, MO 63119; Fax: 314-968-1664; susand4@juno.com
Susan Slivken, Treasurer; 4613 37th Ave., Rock Island, IL 61201-7108
Katrina Vollmer, Corresponding Secretary; 3134 N. Greenbriar, Nashville, IN 47448; 812-988-0063; katrina@bigfoot.com

NATIONAL GARDENING ASSOCIATION
KIDSGARDENING.COM
GARDEN.ORG
GARDENRESEARCH.COM
1100 Dorset St.
South Burlington, VT 05403 United States
Phone: 800-538-7476 Fax: 802-864-6889
Website: www.kidsgardening.com
Founded: 1972
Membership: 1,001–10,000
Scope: National
Description: The mission of the National Gardening Association is to sustain the essential values of life and community, renewing the fundamental links between people, plants, and the earth. Through gardening, we promote environmental responsibility, advance multidisciplinary learning and scientific literacy, and create partnerships that restore and enhance communities.
Publication(s): Growlab Activities, National Gardening Survey, Schoolyard Mosaics, Garden Market Research, Guide to Design of Gardens/Habitats, GrowLab: A Complete Guide to Gardening in the Classroom
Keyword(s): Agriculture/Farming, Wildlife & Species
Contact(s):
Valerie Kelsey, President; valeriek@kidsgardening.com
Larry Sommers, VP, Business Development; 802-863-5251; ext. 128; Fax: 802-864-6889; larrys@garden.org
Bruce Butterfield, Market Research; 802-863-5251; ext. 113; bruceb@gardenresearch.com
Amy Gifford, Education Associate; amyg@garden.org
Charlie Nardozzi, Senior Horticulturist; 802-863-5251; ext. 105; Fax: 802-864-6889; charlien@garden.org
Eve Pranis, Director of Educational Media; 802-863-5251; ext. 114; evep@kidsgardening.com
Anthony Vargo, CFO; 802-863-5251; ext. 112; tonyv@kidsgardening.com

NATIONAL GEOGRAPHIC SOCIETY
1145 17th St., NW
Washington, DC 20036 United States
Phone: 800-647-5463		Fax: 202-775-6141
E-mail: askngs@nationalgeographic.com
Website: www.nationalgeographic.com

Founded: 1888

Scope: International

Description: for the increase and diffusion of geographic knowledge.

Publication(s): National Geographic, National Geographic Channel, National Geographic Adventure Magazine, Classroom Materials, Documentary Films, Filmstrips, Globes, Books/Maps/Atlases, National Geographic Traveler, National Geographic World Magazine (for children)

Keyword(s): Oceans/Coasts/Beaches, Public Lands/Greenspace

NATIONAL GRANGE, THE
1616 H St., NW
Washington, DC 20006-4999 United States
Phone: 202-628-3507		Fax: 202-347-1091
Website: www.nationalgrange.org

Founded: 1867

Scope: National

Description: Rural family service organization with special interests in community service and agriculture.

Publication(s): View from the Hill, New Grange

Keyword(s): Agriculture/Farming, Air Quality/Atmosphere, Energy, Land Issues, Transportation

Contact(s):
Leroy Watson, Legislative Director; Washington, D.C. Office; ext. 114
Bob Clouse, Executive Committee Chairman; 9267 Greenback Lane #B-6, Orangevale, CA 95662; 916-988-3457
Bruce Croucher, Executive Committee Secretary; 100 Grange Pl., Cortland, NY 13045-1330; 607-756-7553
Henrietta Keller, Secretary; 955 Keller Ln., O'Fallon, IL 62269-4218; 618-632-4322
Kermit Richardson, Master; Washington, DC Office; 202-628-3507

NATIONAL GROUND WATER ASSOCIATION, THE
601 Dempsey Rd.
Westerville, OH 43081 United States
Phone: 614-898-7791		Fax: 614-898-7786
E-mail: ngwa@ngwa.org
Website: www.ngwa.org

Founded: 1948

Membership: 10,001–100,000

Scope: International

Description: The NGWA is the world's leading organization committed to the study of the occurrence, development, and protection of ground water. The Association annually sponsors educational programs dealing with a wide variety of water issues, including toxic substances, solid waste, and water pollution. Operates on-line data bases at Website.

Publication(s): Water Well Journal, Journal of Ground Water, Ground Water Monitoring and Remediation

Keyword(s): Oceans/Coasts/Beaches

Contact(s):
Kevin McCray, Executive Director; ext. 503
Sandy Masters, Information; National Ground Water Information Center, 601 Dempsey Dr., Westerville, OH 43081; ext. 502

NATIONAL HUNTERS ASSOCIATION, INC.
P.O. Box 820
Knightdale, NC 27545 United States
Phone: 919-365-7157		Fax: 919-366-2142
E-mail: nhadvs@worldnet.att.net
Website: www.nationalhunters.com

Founded: 1976

Scope: National

Description: The National Hunters Association, Inc. was incorporated under the laws of NC to protect your hunting rights in the U.S. and around the world. Dedicated to hunter safety, the preservation of the rights of the individual sportsman to pursue the sport of hunting and the preservation of an adequate supply of game for the sportsman to hunt — now and in the future.

Publication(s): NHA Newsletter

Keyword(s): Recreation/Ecotourism

NATIONAL MARINE FISHERIES SERVICE
OFFICE OF PROTECTIVE RESOURCES
NOAA/NMFS F/HP4 Off., Hab. Prot., 1315 East-West Highway
Silver Spring, MD 20910-3282 United States
Phone: 301-713-2319		Fax: 301-713-0376
Website: www.noaa.gov

Membership: 1–100

Scope: National

Contact(s):
Don Knowles, Director; don.knowles@noaa.org

NATIONAL MILITARY FISH AND WILDLIFE ASSOCIATION
12428 Pinecrest Ln.
Newburg, MD 20664 United States
Phone: 845-691-6878		Fax: 619-545-5225
E-mail: nmfwa@nmfwa.org
Website: www.nmfwa.org

Founded: 1983

Membership: 101–1,000

Scope: National

Description: A nonprofit organization established to promote professional natural resources management on over 25.5 million acres of United States Department of Defense lands worldwide. Membership is comprised primarily of professional Department of Defense natural resources personnel.

Publication(s): Fish and Wildlife News (FAWN)

Keyword(s): Ecosystems (precious), Forests/Forestry, Land Issues, Public Lands/Greenspace, Water Habitats & Quality, Wildlife & Species

Contact(s):
James Beemer, President; 20 Roxanne Boulevard, Highland, NY 12528; 845-691-6878; Fax: 845-938-2324; ravenwindrider@earthlink.net
Chester Martin, President-Elect; 113 Estelle Drive, Vicksburg, MS 39180; martinc@wes.army.mil
Jim Bailey, Vice President; 93 Windmill Road, Conowingo, MD 21918; jim.bailey@usag.apg.army.mil
Coralie Cobb, Regional Director-West; 10054 Creekbridge Place, San Diego, CA 92131; 858-748-1719; CobbCH@efdsw.navfac.navy.mil
Jim Copeland, At-Large Director; Jim.Copeland@cnet.navy.mil
Rhys Evans, At-Large Director; 760-; ext. 234; Fax: 760-; evansrm@29palms.usmc.mil
Hildy Reiser, Regional Director - West; Hildy.Reiser@holloman.af.mil
Scott Smith, Regional Director-East; Dare County AF Range, P.O. Box 2480, Mantelo, NC 27954; 919-722-1011; Fax: 919-722-0494; scott.smith@seymourjohnson.af.mil
Tammy Conkle, Treasurer; Natural Resources Office, P.O. Box 357088 (Code N4515TC), NAS North Island (Bldg.3), San Diego, CA 92135-7088; 619-545-3703; Fax: 619-545-3489; conkle.tamara@ni.cnrsw.navy.mil
Julie Eliason, Secretary; julie.eliason@ca.ngb.army.mil

Mike Passmore, Newsletter Editor; Environmental Laboratory, U.S. Army Engineer Research & Development Center, 3909 Halls Ferry Rd., Attn: CEERD-EN-S, Vicksburg, MS 39180-6199; 601-634-4862; Fax: 601-634-3726; passmom@wes.army.mil

Carl Petrick, Regional Director-East; carl.petrick@eglin.af.mil

Don Pitts, Immediate Past President; Attn:CEERD-CD-N, P.O. Box 9005, Champaign, IL 61825-9005; Fax: 217-373-7266; donald.pitts@erdc.usace.army.mil

NATIONAL NETWORK OF FOREST PRACTITIONERS
305 S. Main St.
Providence, RI 02903 United States
Phone: 401-273-6507   Fax: 401-273-6508
E-mail: info@nnfp.org
Website: www.nnfp.org

Founded: 1990
Membership: 101–1,000
Scope: National

Description: The National Network of Forest Practitioners is a grassroots alliance of rural people, organizations and businesses finding practical ways to integrate economic development, environmental protection and social justice.

Publication(s): Engaging Communities in the Research Process, Directory, Practitioner (newsletter)

Keyword(s): Development/Developing Countries, Ethics/Environmental Justice, Forests/Forestry, Sprawl/Urban Planning

Contact(s):
Thomas Bendler, Executive Director; 401-273-6507; Fax: 401-273-6508; thomas@nnfp.org
Wendy Gerlitz, Director of Projects; 503-449-0009; wgerlitz@nnfp.org
Ajit Krishnaswamy, Director, NCFC; 401-273-6507; Fax: 401-273-6508; ajit@nnfp.org
Nanda Shewmangal, Coordinator, Cultural Diversity Program; 401-273-6507; Fax: 401-273-6508; nanda@nnfp.org
Kim Kiegelmayer, Research Assistant; 401-273-6507; Fax: 401-273-6508; kim@nnfp.org

NATIONAL ORGANIZATION FOR RIVERS (NORS)
212 W. Cheyenne Mountain Blvd.
Colorado Springs, CO 80906 United States
Phone: 719-579-8759   Fax: 719-576-6238
E-mail: nationalrivers@msm.com
Website: www.nationalrivers.org

Founded: 1979
Scope: National

Description: A nonprofit organization dedicated to education about whitewater river sports, including kayaking, rafting, and canoeing; to preserving rivers; and to protecting river access rights of the general public.

Publication(s): Currents

Contact(s):
Gary Lacy, President
Ben Harding, Vice President
Eric Leaper, Secretary, Treasurer and Executive Director
Fletcher Anderson, Board Member
Earl Perry, Board Member

NATIONAL PARK FOUNDATION
NPF
11 Dupont Circle, N.W.
6th Floor
Washington, DC 20036 United States
Phone: 202-238-4200   Fax: 202-234-3103
Website: www.nationalparks.org

Founded: 1967
Scope: National

Description: The National Park Foundation, chartered by Congress, strengthens the enduring connection between the American people and their National Parks by raising private funds, making strategic grants, creating innovative partnerships and increasing public awareness.

Publication(s): Complete Guide to America's National Parks

Keyword(s): Ethics/Environmental Justice, Public Lands/Greenspace, Recreation/Ecotourism

Contact(s):
James Maddy, President
Jill Nicoll, Executive Vice President
Claudia Schechter, Treasurer
Robert Stanton, Secretary
B. West, Vice Chairman

NATIONAL PARK TRUST
415 2nd St., NE, Suite 210
Washington, DC 20002 United States
Phone: 202-548-0500   Fax: 202-548-0595
E-mail: npt@parktrust.org
Website: www.parktrust.org

Founded: 1983
Membership: 10,001–100,000
Scope: National

Description: The private nonprofit land conservancy dedicated exclusively to protecting resources within and around parklands and other natural and historic properties. The Trust is the only private citizen group recognized by Congress to own and manage, in cooperation with the National Park Service, a unit of the National Park System, the Tallgrass Prairie National Preserve. Established in 1996. The Trust has acquired land in over 40 other parks units and finished 4 parks.

Publication(s): Park Education Resource Center, Parkland News, NPT Legacy News, Legacy Report

Keyword(s): Land Issues, Public Lands/Greenspace, Wildlife & Species

Contact(s):
Paul Pritchard, President; paul@parktrust.org
Davinder Khanna, Senior Vice President; 202-548-0500; ext. 15; Fax: 202-548-0595; davinder@parktrust.org
William Brownell, Secretary
Paul Duffendack, Vice Chairman of the Board of Trustees
Stephan Miller, Chairman of the Board of Trustees
Barry Schimel, Treasurer

NATIONAL PARKS CONSERVATION ASSOCIATION (NPCA)
1300 19th St. NW
Suite 300
Washington, DC 20036 United States
Phone: 800-628-7275
E-mail: npca@npca.org
Website: www.npca.org

Founded: 1919
Scope: National

Description: The nation's only private nonprofit citizen organization, dedicated solely to preserving, protecting, and enhancing the U.S. National Park System. As a watchdog group, NPCA has been an advocate as well as a constructive critic of the National Park Service. NPCA concerns itself with the health of the entire system and specific sites, programs, the processes of planning, management, and evaluation.

Publication(s): National Parks, Park Lines

Keyword(s): Air Quality/Atmosphere, Ecosystems (precious), Ethics/Environmental Justice, Land Issues, Public Lands/Greenspace, Transportation, Water Habitats & Quality, Wildlife & Species

NATIONAL PARKS CONSERVATION ASSOCIATION (NPCA)
ALASKA REGIONAL OFFICE
750 West 2nd Ave.
Suite 205
Anchorage, AK 99501 United States
Phone: 907-277-6722   Fax: 907-277-6723
E-mail: akro@npca.org
Website: www.eparks.org
Membership: 100,001–500,000
Scope: Regional, National
Description: The mission of The National Parks Conservation Association (NPCA) is to protect and enhance America's National Park System for present and future generations. Founded in 1919, NPCA has over 300,000 members of which 1,000 reside in Alaska.
Publication(s): National Parks Magazine

NATIONAL PARKS CONSERVATION ASSOCIATION (NPCA)
PACIFIC REGIONAL OFFICE
1904 Franklin St
Suite 705
Oakland, CA 94612 United States
Phone: 510-839-9922   Fax: 510-839-9926
E-mail: pacific@npca.org
Website: www.npca.org
Founded: 1919
Membership: 100,001–500,000
Scope: Regional
Description: Regional office that serves as a watchdog of units of the National Park System in California, Hawaii, American Samoa and Guam.
Contact(s):
Courtney Cuff, Regional Director
Michelle Jesperson, Associate Regional Director
Elizabeth North, Regional Director of Development
Alan Baker, Office Coordinator

NATIONAL PARKS CONSERVATION ASSOCIATION (NPCA)
SOUTHEAST REGIONAL OFFICE
706 Walnut St. #200
Knoxville, TN 37902 United States
Phone: 865-457-7775   Fax: 865-329-2422
E-mail: sero@npca.org
Website: www.npca.org/
Scope: Regional
Contact(s):
Don Barger, Director

NATIONAL PARKS CONSERVATION ASSOCIATION (NPCA)
STATE OF THE PARKS PROGRAM OFFICE
P.O. Box 737
Fort Collins, CO 80522 United States
Phone: 970-493-2545   Fax: 970-493-9164
E-mail: stateoftheparks@npca.org
Website: www.npca.org
Founded: 1919
Membership: 100,001–500,000
Scope: National
Description: Since 1919, the National Parks Conservation Association has been the sole voice of the American people in the fight to safeguard the scenic beauty, wildlife, and historical and cultural treasures of the largest and most diverse park system in the world.
Contact(s):
Mark Peterson, Director for State of the Parks Program

NATIONAL PARKS CONSERVATION ASSOCIATION (NPCA)
SUN COAST REGIONAL OFFICE
1909 Harrison Street
Suite 208
Hollywood, FL 33020-5071 United States
Phone: 954-926-6327
E-mail: npca@npca.org
Scope: Regional
Description: A regional office of the National Parks Conservation Association, the nation's only private, nonprofit advocacy organization dedicated solely to protecting, preserving, and enhancing the National Park System. NPCA's Sun Coast Regional Office is focused on the national parks of Florida, Puerto Rico, and the Gulf Coasts of Alabama, Mississippi, and Louisiana
Keyword(s): Air Quality/Atmosphere, Development/Developing Countries, Ecosystems (precious), Oceans/Coasts/Beaches, Public Lands/Greenspace, Recreation/Ecotourism, Water Habitats & Quality, Wildlife & Species
Contact(s):
Mary Munson, Director
John Adornato, Program Representative

NATIONAL RECREATION AND PARK ASSOCIATION
22377 Belmont Ridge Rd.
Ashburn, VA 20148 United States
Phone: 703-858-0784   Fax: 703-858-0794
E-mail: info@nrpa.org
Website: www.nrpa.org
Membership: 10,001–100,000
Scope: National
Description: A national nonprofit service, education, and research organization dedicated to the improvement of park and recreation leadership, programs, and facilities. The Association attempts to build public understanding that leisure programs and environments are indispensable to the well-being of a nation and its citizens.
Publication(s): Parks and Recreation Magazine, Dateline, Recreation and Parks Law Reporter, Therapeutic Recreation Journal, Journal of Leisure Research
Contact(s):
Alice Conkey, President; aconkey@nrpa.org
Pamela Earle, Pacific Regional Director; 350 S. 333rd St., #103, Federal Way, WA 98003; 206-661-2265; pearle@nrpa.org
Kathy Spangler, National Programs Director; Recreation and Park Assoc., 22377 Belmont Ridge Road, Ashburn, VA 20148; 703-858-0784; kspangler@nrpa.org
Maria Stamats, Western Regional Director; 719-632-7031; mstamats@nrpa.org
Barry Tindall, Director of Public Policy; btindall@nrpa.org
Larry Zehnder, Southeast Regional Director; 1285 Parker Rd., Conyers, GA 30207; 404-760-1668; lzehnder@nrpa.org
T. Jarvis, Contact; tjarvis@nrpa.org
Suzanne Mathis, Trustee Liaison & Coordinator of Friends of Parks and Recreation; smathis@nrpa.org
Rip Wilkenson, Chairman; rwilkenson@nrpa.org

NATIONAL RESEARCH COUNCIL
2101 Constitution Ave., NW
Washington, DC 20418 United States
Phone: 202-334-2000
Website: www.nas.edu
Founded: 1916
Scope: National
Description: An independent advisor to the federal government on scientific and technical questions of national importance. Jointly administered by the National Academies of Sciences and Engineering and the Institute of Medicine.

Publication(s): Catalogue available upon request.

Contact(s):
- Susan Vines, Director of Office of News and Public Information
- Bruce Alberts, Chairman
- Suzanne Woolsey, Chief Operating Officer

NATIONAL RIFLE ASSOCIATION OF AMERICA
11250 Waples Mill Rd.
Fairfax, VA 22030 United States
Phone: 703-267-1000 Fax: 703-267-3909
E-mail: nra.contact@nra.org
Website: www.nra.org

Founded: 1871
Membership: 1,000,001 +
Scope: National

Description: A nonprofit organization dedicated to protect and defend the Constitution of the United States, especially the right to possess and use firearms for recreation and personal protection; to promote public safety, law and order, and the national defense; and to train members of law enforcement agencies, the military, and private citizens of good repute in marksmanship and the safe handling and efficient use of small arms.

Publication(s): American Rifleman, America's First Freedom, Insights, American Hunter

Keyword(s): Recreation/Ecotourism

Contact(s):
- Charlton Heston, President
- Sandra Froman, 2nd Vice President
- Wayne Lapierre, Executive Vice President
- Kayne Robinson, 1st Vice President
- Susan Lamson, Director of Conservation, Wildlife and Natural Resources Division; 703-267-1541
- William Poole, Director of Education and Training Division; 703-267-1414
- Craig Sandler, Executive Director of General Operations
- Robert Davis, Manager of Hunter Services; 703-267-1522
- Charles Mitchell, Manager for Training; 703-267-1431
- Matthew Szramoski, Manager for Youth Programs; 703-267-1596
- Montey Embrey, Program Assistant of Hunter Services; 703-267-1503
- Britt Ford, Program Coordinator of Hunter Services; 703-267-1516
- Edward Land, Secretary
- Howard Moody, Instructor and Coach/Trainer for Training; 703-267-1401
- Wilson Phillips, Treasurer
- Janice Taylor, Assistant Manager of Hunter Services; 703-267-1523
- Billy Templeton, Wildlife Management Specialist of Hunter Services, ECHO; 703-267-1501

NATIONAL RIFLE ASSOCIATION WEST VIRGINIA
WHITE HORSE FIREARMS AND OUTDOOR EDUCATION CENTER, INC.
P.O. Box 4538
Bridgeport, WV 26330 United States
Phone: 304-472-1449 Fax: 304-472-9489
E-mail: nrdc@westvirginia.net
Website: www.wvsrpa.org/news/education.htm

Founded: 1983
Scope: Local, State, Regional
Description: Outdoor Education
Keyword(s): Recreation/Ecotourism, Wildlife & Species

NATIONAL SCIENCE TEACHERS ASSOCIATION
1840 Wilson Blvd.
Arlington, VA 22201 United States
Phone: 703-243-7100 Fax: 703-243-7177
E-mail: carla.daniels@nsta.org
Website: www.nsta.org

Founded: 1944
Membership: 10,001–100,000
Scope: National

Description: NSTA is the world's largest organization committed to improving science education at all levels - preschool through college. NSTA's membership includes science teachers, science supervisors, administrators, scientists, business and industry representatives, and others involved in science education.

Publication(s): Science and Children, Quantum, NSTA Reports!, Journal of College Science Teaching, The Science Teacher, Science Scope

Contact(s):
- Gerald Wheeler, Executive Director; 703-312-9254; gwheeler@nsta.org
- Shelley Carey, Editor; 703-312-9238; scarey@nsta.org

NATIONAL SHOOTING SPORTS FOUNDATION, INC.
Flintlock Ridge Office Center, 11 Mile Hill Rd.
Newtown, CT 06470-2359 United States
Phone: 203-426-1320 Fax: 203-426-1087
E-mail: info@nssf.org
Website: www.nssf.org

Founded: 1960
Membership: 1,001–10,000
Scope: National

Description: Nonprofit educational, trade-supported association sponsors a wide variety of programs to create a better understanding of and a more active participation in the shooting sports and in practical conservation.

Keyword(s): Recreation/Ecotourism, Reduce/Reuse/Recycle

Contact(s):
- Doug Painter, President; 203-426-1320; Fax: 203-426-1245; dpainter@nssf.org
- Nancy Coburn, VP of Operations; 203-426-1320; Fax: 203-426-1087; ncoburn@nssf.org
- Bill Brassard, Managing Director Communications; 203-426-1320; Fax: 203-426-1245; bbrassard@nssf.org
- Chris Dolnack, Managing Director of Program Development; 203-426-1320; Fax: 203-426-1087; cdolnack@nssf.org
- Jodi Valenta, Director Recruitment & Retention; 203-426-1320; Fax: 203-426-1087; jvalenta@nssf.org
- Cindy Dalena, Step Outside National Coordinator; 203-426-1320; Fax: 203-426-1087; cdalena@nssf.org

NATIONAL SPELEOLOGICAL SOCIETY, INC.
NSS
2813 Cave Ave.
Huntsville, AL 35810-4431 United States
Phone: 256-852-1300 Fax: 256-851-9241
E-mail: nss@caves.org
Website: www.caves.org

Founded: 1941
Membership: 10,001–100,000
Scope: National

Description: A nonprofit membership organization dedicated to the exploration, study, and conservation of America's caves and caverns, related features, and the ecology of caves.

Publication(s): NSS News, publishers of speleological books, Journal of Cave and Karst Studies

Keyword(s): Land Issues, Wildlife & Species

Contact(s):
- Scott Fee, President; P.O. Box 7036, Greenwood, IN 46142; 317-706-9386; scottfee@caves.org
- David Jagnow, Conservation Chairman; 1300 Iris St., Apt. 103, Los Alamos, NM 87544-3140; 505-662-0553; djagnow@roadrunner.com
- John Moses, International Secretary; 15807 River Roads Dr., Houston, TX 77079-5041; 281-597-1494

NATIONAL TRAPPERS ASSOCIATION, INC.
P.O. Box 632018
Nacogdoches, TX 75963-2018 United States
Phone: 304-455-2656   Fax: 309-829-7615
E-mail: NTAheadquarters@nationaltrappers.com
Website: www.nationaltrappers.com

Founded: 1959

Scope: National, International

Description: A national trappers organization dedicated to promoting sound conservation legislation; to conserving the nation's natural resources; to helping implement environmental education programs; and to promoting a continued annual furbearer harvest as a necessary wildlife management tool.

Publication(s): American Trapper

Keyword(s): Development/Developing Countries, Reduce/Reuse/Recycle

Contact(s):
Dave Sollman, President; RR 1, Box 391-1, Heltonsville, IN 47436; 812-834-5334; Fax: 812-834-5334
Steve Fitzwater, Vice President; P.O. Box 106, Dubois, ID 83423-0106; 208-374-5479; dubois5@yahoo.com
Robert Colona, Conservation Director; 5539 Sharptown Rd., Rhodesdale, MD 21659; 410-883-2607; Fax: 410-376-3916
Scott Hartman, Director of National and International Affairs; 304-455-4065; Fax: 304-455-5735
Tom Krause, Editor and Advertising Manager; P.O. Box 513, Riverton, WY 82501; 307-856-3830; Fax: 307-857-2993; tkrause@wyoming.com
Royl Schoonover, General Organizer; P.O. Box 308, Westminster, VT 05158-0308; 802-722-9062; Fax: 802-722-9062

NATIONAL TREE TRUST
1120 G St., NW, Suite 770
Washington, DC 20005 United States
Phone: 202-628-8733   Fax: 202-628-8735
E-mail: info@nationaltreetrust.org
Website: www.nationaltreetrust.org

Founded: 1990

Scope: National

Description: The National Tree Trust promotes healthy communities by providing resources that educate and empower people to grow and care for urban and community forests. Our current grant program focuses on seven areas of concentration: Education, Minority Involvement, Canopy Restoration, Community Building, Community Nursery, Service Learning, and Civil/Civic Partnership. Each year, hundreds of communities around the country turn to the National Tree Trust to support their local efforts.

Keyword(s): Forests/Forestry, Public Lands/Greenspace

NATIONAL TRUST FOR HISTORIC PRESERVATION
1785 Massachusetts Ave., NW
Washington, DC 20036 United States
Phone: 202-588-6000   Fax: 202-588-6038
E-mail: feedback@nthp.org
Website: www.nthp.org

Founded: 1949

Membership: 100,001–500,000

Scope: National

Description: Private nonprofit membership organization chartered by Congress to encourage the public to participate in the preservation of America's historic and cultural heritage through advocacy, education, technical assistance, financial aid to nonprofit groups, and demonstration programs.

Publication(s): Historic Preservation Forum, Preservation Law Reporter, Preservation Magazine

Keyword(s): Land Issues, Reduce/Reuse/Recycle

Contact(s):
Richard Moe, President; 202-588-6000

NATIONAL TRUST FOR HISTORIC PRESERVATION
MID ATLANTIC
One Penn Center at Suburban Station
Suite 1520
1617 John F. Kennedy Blvd.
Philadelphia, PA 19144 United States
Phone: 215-568-8162

Scope: Regional

Contact(s):
Patricia Wilson, Director

NATIONAL TRUST FOR HISTORIC PRESERVATION
MIDWEST OFFICE
53 W. Jackson Blvd., Suite 350
Chicago, IL 60604 United States
Phone: 312-939-5547   Fax: 312-939-5651

Scope: Regional

Publication(s): Preservation Magazine

Contact(s):
James Mann, Director

NATIONAL TRUST FOR HISTORIC PRESERVATION
MOUNTAINS - PLAINS OFFICE
535 16th St., Ste. 750
Denver, CO 80202 United States
Phone: 303-623-1504   Fax: 303-623-1508
E-mail: mpro@nthp.org
Website: www.nthp.org

Scope: Regional

Description: The National Trust for Historic Preservation is a private, nonprofit membership organization dedicated to protecting the irreplaceable. Recipient of the National Humanities Medal, the Trust provides leadership, education and advocacy to save America's diverse historic places and revitalize communities. Its Washington, DC headquarters staff, six regional offices and 21 historic sites work with the Trust's quarter-million members and thousands of local community groups in all 50 states.

Contact(s):
Barbara Pahl, Director

NATIONAL TRUST FOR HISTORIC PRESERVATION
NORTHEAST OFFICE
7 Faneuil Hall Marketplace, 4th Fl.
Boston, MA 02109 United States
Phone: 617-523-0885   Fax: 617-523-1199
E-mail: nero@nthp.org
Website: www.nationaltrust.org

Membership: 100,001–500,000

Scope: National

Contact(s):
Wendy Nicholas, Director
Tina White, Admistrative Assistant; 7 Faneuil Hall Marketplace, Boston, MA 02109

NATIONAL TRUST FOR HISTORIC PRESERVATION
SOUTHERN OFFICE
456 King St.
Charleston, SC 29403 United States
Phone: 803-722-8552   Fax: 843-722-8652
E-mail: soro@nthp.org
Website: www.nationaltrust.org

Founded: 1949
Scope: Regional
Contact(s):
  John Hildreth, Director

NATIONAL TRUST FOR HISTORIC PRESERVATION
SOUTHWEST OFFICE
500 Main St., Suite 1030
Fort Worth, TX 76102 United States
Phone: 817-332-4398   Fax: 817-332-4512
E-mail: swo@nthp.org
Website: www.nthp.org
Scope: Regional
Contact(s):
  Daniel Carey, Director

NATIONAL TRUST FOR HISTORIC PRESERVATION
WESTERN
8 California Street
Suite 400
San Francisco, CA 94111-4828 United States
Phone: 415-956-0610   Fax: 415-956-0837
E-mail: wro@nthp.org
Scope: Regional
Description: The National Trust for Historic Preservation, the country's largest private nonprofit preservation organization, is dedicated to protecting the irreplaceable. With more than a quarter million members nationwide, it provides leadership, education and advocacy to save America's diverse historic places and revitalize communities. It has six regional offices and 20 historic sites and works with thousands of local community groups in all 50 states.
Contact(s):
  Holly Fiala, Director

NATIONAL WATER RESOURCES ASSOCIATION
3800 N. Fairfax Dr., Suite 4
Arlington, VA 22203 United States
Phone: 703-524-1544   Fax: 703-524-1548
E-mail: nwra@nwra.org
Website: www.nwra.org
Membership: 1,001–10,000
Scope: National
Description: Promotes development, conservation and management of the water resources of 17 western state associations, including cities, counties, conservation districts, and individual members.
Publication(s): National Waterline, Water Report
Keyword(s): Agriculture/Farming, Oceans/Coasts/Beaches, Pollution (general), Water Habitats & Quality, Wildlife & Species
Contact(s):
  David Sprynczynatyk, President
  Thomas Donnelly, Executive Vice President

NATIONAL WATERSHED COALITION
9304 Lundy Ct.
Burke, VA 22015-3431 United States
Phone: 703-455-6886   Fax: 703-455-6888
E-mail: jwpeterson@erols.com
Website: www.watershedcoalition.org
Founded: 1989
Membership: 1,001–10,000
Scope: National
Description: The NWC is a nonprofit coalition made up of national, regional, state, and local organizations, associations, and individuals, that advocate dealing with natural resources problems and issues using the watershed as the planning and implementation unit.
Publication(s): Congressional Testimony, Watershed News, Watershed Newsletter & Conference Proceedings
Keyword(s): Agriculture/Farming, Development/Developing Countries, Ecosystems (precious), Forests/Forestry, Land Issues, Oceans/Coasts/Beaches, Pollution (general), Public Lands/Greenspace, Recreation/Ecotourism, Water Habitats & Quality, Wildlife & Species
Contact(s):
  John Peterson, Executive Director; 703-455-4387; Fax: 703-455-6888; jwpeterson@erols.com
  Tammy Sawatzky, Accountant
  Dan Lowrance, Vice Chair
  Dan Sebert, Secretary, Treasurer
  Larry Smith, Chair

NATIONAL WATERWAYS CONFERENCE INC.
1130 17th St., NW, #200
Washington, DC 20036-4676 United States
Phone: 202-296-4415   Fax: 202-835-3861
E-mail: info@waterways.org
Website: www.waterways.org
Founded: 1960
Scope: National
Description: To promote a better understanding of the public value of water resources and water transportation programs and to show their importance to the environment and economy.
Publication(s): Washington Watch
Keyword(s): Air Quality/Atmosphere, Energy, Oceans/Coasts/Beaches, Transportation, Water Habitats & Quality, Wildlife & Species
Contact(s):
  Worth Hager, Executive Director
  Alison Heath, Director of Environmental Research
  Andrew Riester, Director of Communications

NATIONAL WHISTLEBLOWER LEGAL DEFENSE & EDUCATION FUND
NWLDEF
P.O. Box 3768
Washington, DC 20027 United States
Phone: 202-342-1902   Fax: 202-342-1904
E-mail: whistle@whistleblowers.org
Website: www.whistleblowers.org
Founded: 1988
Scope: National
Description: The Fund is the only public interest law firm dedicated to enforcing and enhancing the legal protections of employees who blow the whistle on significant violations of law, environmental protection, nuclear safety, and first amendment rights. The Fund provides legal advice, resources, and referrals for counsel to whistleblowers nationwide and conducts seminars and other outreach activities.
Publication(s): Concepts and Procedures, Comprehensive Whistleblower Law Text
Keyword(s): Ethics/Environmental Justice
Contact(s):
  Kris Kolesnik, Executive Director; 202-342-1902; Fax: 202-342-1904; whistle@whistleblowers.org

NATIONAL WILD TURKEY FEDERATION, CANADA, INC., THE
c/o Kevin Townsend, Regional Director
75 Mill Street
Wroxeter, N0G 2X0 Ontario Canada
Phone: 519-335-6893   Fax: 519-335-6050
E-mail: ontrdkt@wcl.on.ca
Founded: 1998
Scope: International
Description: A nonprofit organization dedicated to the conservation and management of the North American wild turkey and

the preservation of the hunting tradition. The organization supports an annual research grants program.

Keyword(s): Recreation/Ecotourism, Wildlife & Species

Contact(s):
Russ Davies, President
Rob Keck, CEO
James Kennamer, Vice President of Conservation Programs
Randy Roloson, Vice President
Jack Playne, Secretary-Treasurer

NATIONAL WILD TURKEY FEDERATION, INC., THE

770 Augusta Rd., P.O. Box 530
Edgefield, SC 29824-0530 United States
Phone: 803-637-3106   Fax: 803-637-0034
E-mail: nwtf@nwtf.net
Website: www.nwtf.org

Founded: 1973
Membership: 500,001–1,000,000
Scope: International

Description: A nonprofit organization dedicated to the conservation of the wild turkey and the preservation of the hunting tradition. Comprised of 2,050 state and local chapters. The organization supports an annual research grants program.

Publication(s): Wheelin' Sportsmen magazine, Turkey Call magazine, Women in the Outdoors magazine, JAKES magazine, The Caller

Keyword(s): Forests/Forestry, Public Lands/Greenspace, Recreation/Ecotourism, Wildlife & Species

Contact(s):
Rob Keck, Chief Executive Officer
Tammy Bristow Sapp, Vice President of Communications
Carl Brown, Chief Operating Officer
James Kennamer, Sr., Vice President for Conservation Programs
Dick Rosenlieb, Vice President of Sales & Marketing
James Sparks, Chief Financial Officer
Donna Leggett, Director of Development

NATIONAL WILDLIFE FEDERATION
HEADQUARTERS
11100 Wildlife Center Drive
Reston, VA 20190-5362 United States
Phone: 703-438-6000   Fax: 703-442-7332
E-mail: info@nwf.org
Website: www.nwf.org/

Founded: 1936
Membership: 1,000,001+
Scope: Local, State, Regional, National, International

Description: A non-profit organization whose mission is to educate, inspire, and assist individuals and organizations of diverse cultures to conserve wildlife and other natural resources and to protect the Earth's environment in order to achieve a peaceful, equitable, and sustainable future. NOTE. Any correspondence for a member of the Board of Directors of the National Wildlife Federation should be directed to the National Wildlife Federation mailing address or fax number.

Publication(s): NatureScope, Conservation Directory, National Wildlife, Wild Animal Baby, EarthSavers, EnviroAction, Your Big Backyard, Ranger Rick, National Wildlife Week

Keyword(s): Agriculture/Farming, Climate Change, Development/Developing Countries, Ecosystems (precious), Executive/Legislative/Judicial Reform, Finance/Banking/Trade, Forests/Forestry, Land Issues, Population, Public Lands/Greenspace, Recreation/Ecotourism, Sprawl/Urban Planning

Contact(s):
Lawrence J. Amon, Acting President and Chief Executive Officer
Rebecca Scheibelhut, Board of Directors, Chair
Jerome Ringo, Board of Directors, Vice Chair
Christopher Palmer, President and CEO of National Wildlife Productions
Eileen Morgan Johnson, General Counsel
Dan Chu, Senior Vice President Affiliate and Field Programs
Jaime Berman Matyas, Senior Vice President for Marketing
Jessie A. Brinkley, Vice President of Development
Robert S. Ertter, Vice President of Human Resources and Administration
Carole Fox, Vice President of Operations, Winchester Facility
Patty Key, Acting Vice President for Education Programs
Thomas F. McGuire, Vice President of Membership Programs
Gaby Chavarria, Policy Director
R. Montgomery Fischer, Policy Director; 802-229-0650; fischer@nwf.org
Susan Rieff, Policy Director; 512-476-9805; rieff@nwf.org
Doug Inkley, Senior Advisor
Wayne Schmidt, Senior Director for Program Communications
Bill Street, Senior Director of Education, Editor of Conservation Directory

NATIONAL WILDLIFE FEDERATION
ALASKA NATURAL RESOURCE CENTER
750 W. Second Ave.
Anchorage, AK 99501 United States
Phone: 907-258-8480   Fax: 907-258-4811
Website: www.nwf.org

Scope: Regional

Description: National Wildlife Federation's Alaska office was established in 1988 and specializes in wetlands issues. Our work ranges from educational programs in public schools to federal court lawsuits designed to influence national wetlands policy. Increasingly, the office builds and leads conservation coalitions. NWF currently coordinates the Cooper River Delta Coalition and Prince William Sound Alliance. We also manage Alaska Women's Environmental Network and Alaska Youth for Environmental Action, and

Contact(s):
Tony Turrini, Director; Turrini@nwf.org

NATIONAL WILDLIFE FEDERATION
GREAT LAKES NATURAL RESOURCE CENTER
213 W. Liberty, Suite 200
Ann Arbor, MI 48104-1398 United States
Phone: 734-769-3351   Fax: 734-769-1449
E-mail: greatlakes@nwf.org
Website: www.nwf.org

Founded: 1982
Scope: State, Regional, National

Description: The National Wildlife Federation's Great Lakes Natural Resource Center unites people throughout the eight-state Great Lakes region, the U.S. and Canada to protect the world's greatest freshwater seas and the surrounding ecosystem. The Center's staff of scientists, educators, lawyers, and organizers work with citizens and activists to end the toxic pollution and habitat destruction that threaten the health of wildlife, fish, and people in the Great Lakes region.

Publication(s): "Mercury Product Guide", "Getting Serious About Mercury", "A Woman's Guide to Eating Fish Safely"

Keyword(s): Air Quality/Atmosphere, Ecosystems (precious), Ethics/Environmental Justice, Executive/Legislative/Judicial Reform, Forests/Forestry, Land Issues, Oceans/

Coasts/Beaches, Public Health, Water Habitats & Quality, Wildlife & Species

Contact(s):
Andrew Buchsbaum, Center Director; 734-769-3351; Fax: 734-769-1449; buchsbaum@nwf.org
Noah Hall, Water Resources Program Manager; hall@nwf.org
Zoe Lipman, Clean the Rain Program Manager; lipman@nwf.org
Michelle Halley, Lake Superior Attorney; halley@nwf.org
Neil Kagan, Water Quality Team Leader, Senior Counsel; kagan@nwf.org

NATIONAL WILDLIFE FEDERATION
GULF STATES NATURAL RESOURCE CENTER
44 East Ave., Suite 200
Austin, TX 78701 United States
Phone: 512-476-9805   Fax: 512-476-9810
Website: www.nwf.org
Scope: Regional
Description: The Gulf States Natural Resource Center is working to protect threatened rivers and bays and important wetlands in the region and to restore polluted watersheds. The Center also promotes NWF's education programs by working with schools and other organizations.
Publication(s): Publications on website
Keyword(s): Water Habitats & Quality
Contact(s):
Susan Kaderka, Director; 512-476-9805; ext. 14; Fax: 512-476-9810; kaderka@nwf.org
Myron Hess, Water Program Manager; 512-476-9805; ext. 13; Fax: 512-476-9810; hess@nwf.org

NATIONAL WILDLIFE FEDERATION
INTERNATIONAL AFFAIRS
1400 16th St., NW, Suite 501
Washington, DC 20036 United States
Phone: 202-797-6800
Website: www.nwf.org
Scope: Regional
Description: The international affairs team, also based in Washington, D.C. office, works to advance the conservation agenda, recognizing the borderless reality of ecosystems and migratory species in North America and beyond. Staff members work with state affiliates and field offices to educate and to build a constituency for U.S. leadership on key international conservation issues and with other stakeholders and like-minded organizations, domestic and foreign, to address international conservation priorities.
Contact(s):
Paul Joffe, Senior Director, International Affairs; Joffe@nwf.org

NATIONAL WILDLIFE FEDERATION
NORTHEAST NATURAL RESOURCE CENTER
58 State St., Suite 1
Montpelier, VT 5602 United States
Phone: 802-229-0650   Fax: 802-229-4532
Website: www.nwf.org
Scope: Regional
Description: The Northeast Natural Resource Center of the National Wildlife Federation works on a range of conservation and natural resource issues across the six-state New England region and often in close coordination with our state-based affiliate conservation groups. We also collaborate with a variety of other like-minded organizations to focus on the protection and restoration of our unique "woods, water, and wildlife" across the region.
Contact(s):
Eric Palola, Director; palola@nwf.org

NATIONAL WILDLIFE FEDERATION
NORTHERN ROCKIES NATURAL RESOURCE CENTER
240 N. Higgins, Suite 2
Missoula, MT 59802 United States
Phone: 406-721-6705   Fax: 406-721-6714
Website: www.nwf.org
Scope: Regional
Description: The Northern Rockies Project Office focuses on endangered species recovery as a key to protecting not only the species themselves, but many other fish and wildlife populations as well. Projects include work on wolf, grizzly bear, sage grouse, and black-tailed prairie dog recovery. The Northern Rockies office works at a landscape level to ensure the conservation of these species across millions of acres of important wildlife habitat.
Keyword(s): Ethics/Environmental Justice, Executive/Legislative/Judicial Reform, Land Issues, Wildlife & Species
Contact(s):
Thomas France, Director & Legal Counsel; 406-721-6705; Fax: 406-721-6714; france@nwf.org
Ben Deeble, Sage Grouse Project Coordinator
Hank Fischer, Wildlife Conflict Resolution Coordinator
Sterling Miller, Senior Wildlife Biologist
Susan Scaggs, Staff Assistant

NATIONAL WILDLIFE FEDERATION
NORTHWESTERN NATURAL RESOURCE CENTER
418 First Ave. West
Seattle, WA 98119 United States
Phone: 206-285-8707   Fax: 206-285-8698
E-mail: salmon@nwf.org
Website: www.nwf.org
Scope: Regional
Description: Located in Seattle, Washington, the Northwestern Natural Resource Center focuses on the issues critical to this region, such as wild salmon, water quality, smart growth, and wolf recovery. NWF provides the tools, the expertise, and the grassroots clout to make a difference for wildlife and wild places in the Northwest, the nation, and the world.
Contact(s):
Paula Del Giudice, Director; 206-285-8707; delgiudice@nwf.org

NATIONAL WILDLIFE FEDERATION
OFFICE OF CONGRESSIONAL AND FEDERAL AFFAIRS
1400 16th St., NW, Suite 501
Washington, DC 20036 United States
Phone: 202-797-6800   Fax: 202-797-6646
Website: www.nwf.org
Scope: Regional, National
Description: Advocates NWF's position on conservation issues of national importance. It provides technical, scientific, and legal support to state affiliates and field offices on selected issues. Advocates NWF's position before all three branches of government and works cooperatively with the private sector to achieve mutually desired goals.
Contact(s):
Jim Lyon, Senior Director for Congressional and Federal Affairs; Lyon@nwf.org

NATIONAL WILDLIFE FEDERATION
ROCKY MOUNTAIN NATURAL RESOURCE CENTER
2260 Baseline Rd., Suite 100
Boulder, CO 80302 United States
Phone: 303-786-8001   Fax: 303-786-8911
Website: www.nwf.org/rockymountain
Scope: Regional

Description: The Rocky Mountain Natural Resource Center is dedicated to the conservation of wildlife and natural resources on public, private, and tribal lands throughout the interior west and Great Plains. Center staff are working to restore biological diversity on millions of acres of native grasslands, to promote the restoration of water quality in our streams and rivers, and to promote the restoration of bison populations residing in Yellowstone National Park to lands throughout their historic range.

Keyword(s): Land Issues, Public Lands/Greenspace, Water Habitats & Quality, Wildlife & Species

Contact(s):
Stephen Torbit, Director; torbit@nwf.org

NATIONAL WILDLIFE FEDERATION
SOUTHEASTERN NATIONAL RESOURCE CENTER
1330 West Peachtree St., Suite 475
Atlanta, GA 30309 United States
Phone: 404-876-8733   Fax: 404-892-1744
Website: www.nwf.org

Scope: Regional

Description: The Southeastern Natural Resource Center in Atlanta forges links between people and the environment, promoting sustainable practices to enhance the quality of life in our communities for people and wildlife. The SE Natural Resource Center was established in 1986 to address the water issues that affect both people and animals in the southeastern United States. In fact, the southeastern states are home to some of the highest levels of freshwater and upland diversity in the world.

Contact(s):
Andrew Schock, Director; schock@nwf.org

NATIONAL WILDLIFE FEDERATION
WESTERN NATURAL RESOURCE CENTER
3500 5th Avenue
Suite 101
San Diego, CA 92103 United States
Phone: 619-296-8353   Fax: 619-296-8355
E-mail: wnrc@nwf.org
Website: www.nwf.org/western

Founded: 2000
Scope: State, Regional, National

Description: The mission of the Western Natural Resource Center of the National Wildlife Federation is to educate, inspire and empower people from all walks of life to conserve wildlife and other natural resources throughout California, Nevada, Arizona and within the Mexico/U.S. border region.

Keyword(s): Land Issues, Public Lands/Greenspace, Wildlife & Species

Contact(s):
Robert Opliger, Sr. Education Coordinator; 619-296-8353; ext. 204; Fax: 619-296-8355; opliger@nwf.org
Melody College, Office Manager; 619-296-8353; ext. 200; Fax: 619-296-8355; college@nwf.org
Myra Wilensky, Regional Organizer; 619-296-8353; ext. 207; Fax: 619-296-8355; wilensky@nwf.org

NATIONAL WILDLIFE FEDERATION ENDOWMENT, INC.
11100 Wildlife Center Drive
Reston, VA 20190-5362 United States
Phone: 703-438-6000   Fax: 703-438-6060

Scope: Regional

Description: Established to support the conservation education and resource management programs of the National Wildlife Federation. Gifts and bequests are invested, and income is transferred to the National Wildlife Federation.

Contact(s):
Lawrence Amon, Treasurer

Raymond Golden, Board of Trustee
Allen Guisinger, Board of Trustee Vice Chair
Mary Harris, Board of Trustee
Eileen Johnson, Secretary
John Rainey, Chairman and Trustee

NATIONAL WILDLIFE PRODUCTIONS, INC.
11100 Wildlife Center Drive
Reston, VA 20190-5362 United States
Phone: 703-438-6077   Fax: 703-438-6076
E-mail: palmer@nwf.org
Website: www.nwf.org

Founded: 1994
Scope: National, International

Description: National Wildlife Productions is the television, film, and multimedia arm of the National Wildlife Federation (NWF). The goal of NWP is to fulfill NWF's conservation mission by creating and producing television and mass-media projects, including children's television programs, documentaries, large format films for IMAX theaters, feature films, TV movies, and interactive multimedia programs.

Publication(s): India - Kingdom of the Tiger (Poster), Bears Educator's Guide, Dolphins, Wolves, Bears

Keyword(s): Climate Change, Ecosystems (precious), Energy, Ethics/Environmental Justice, Forests/Forestry, Land Issues, Oceans/Coasts/Beaches, Pollution (general), Population, Public Lands/Greenspace, Recreation/Ecotourism, Reduce/Reuse/Recycle, Sprawl/Urban Planning

Contact(s):
Christopher Palmer, President and Chief Executive Officer; 703-438-6077; palmer@nwf.org

NATIONAL WILDLIFE REFUGE ASSOCIATION
1010 Wisconsin Avenue NW, Suite 200
Washington, DC 20007 United States
Phone: 202-333-9075   Fax: 202-333-9077
E-mail: nwra@refugenet.org
Website: www.refugenet.org

Founded: 1975
Scope: Local, Regional, National

Description: The mission of the NWRA is to protect, enhance and expand the National Wildlife Refuge System, lands set aside by the American people to protect our country's diverse wildlife heritage. NWRA is the only national membership organization dedicated solely to protecting the Refuge System.

Publication(s): Shortchanging America's Wildlife, Building Your Nest Egg, Taking Flight, Blue Goose Flyer

Keyword(s): Land Issues, Public Lands/Greenspace, Water Habitats & Quality, Wildlife & Species

Contact(s):
Evan Hirsche, President; 202-333-9075; Fax: 202-333-9077; ehirsche@refugenet.org
Debbie Harwood, Office Manager; dharwood@refugenet.org
Gretchen Muller, Project Manager; gmuller@refugenet.org

NATIONAL WILDLIFE REHABILITATORS ASSOCIATION
NWRA
14 N. 7th Ave.
St. Cloud, MN 56303 United States
Phone: 320-259-4086
E-mail: nwra@nwrawildlife.org
Website: www.nwrawildlife.org

Founded: 1982
Membership: 1,001–10,000
Scope: International

Description: A nonprofit membership organization committed to promoting and improving the integrity and professionalism of wildlife rehabilitation and contributing to the preservation of natural ecosystems. The organization disseminates information, provides training, and encourages networking through a quarterly journal, an annual membership directory, reviewed publications, annual symposia, and active committees for standards, wildlife medicine, education, awards, and grants.

Publication(s): Wildlife Rehabilitation annual volumes, Minimum Standards for Wildlife Rehabilitation, Training Opportunities in Wildlife Rehabilitation, NWRA Quick Reference Guide, Principles of Wildlife Rehabilitation, Wildlife Rehabilitation Bulletin

Keyword(s): Wildlife & Species

Contact(s):
 Erica Miller, President
 Curtiss Clumpner, President Elect
 Lessie Davis, Vice President
 Diane Nickerson, Vice President
 Florina Tseng, Vice President
 Barbara Suto, Treasurer
 Elaine Thrune, Past President
 Sandy Woltman, Secretary

NATIONAL WOODLAND OWNERS ASSOCIATION
374 Maple Ave., E., Suite 310
Vienna, VA 22180 United States
Phone: 703-255-2700   Fax: 703-281-9200
E-mail: info@woodlandowners.org
Website: www.woodlandowners.org

Founded: 1983
Membership: 10,001–100,000
Scope: National, International

Description: A nationwide organization made up of non-industrial private woodland owners. Membership includes landowners in all 50 states and Canada and also includes affiliations with 32 state and 287 county woodland owner associations throughout the United States. Programs and benefits include the National Woodlands Magazine, Woodland Report Newsletter, representation in Washington, DC, professional forester referrals, and the Green Tag Forest Certification Program.

Publication(s): Woodland Report, National Woodlands Magazine, Green Tag Certification Program, Professional Forester Referrals

Keyword(s): Agriculture/Farming, Ecosystems (precious), Ethics/Environmental Justice, Executive/Legislative/Judicial Reform, Forests/Forestry, Land Issues, Public Lands/Greenspace, Reduce/Reuse/Recycle, Sprawl/Urban Planning, Water Habitats & Quality, Wildlife & Species

Contact(s):
 Donald Girton, Southern Vice President; kwoa@fuse.net
 Nels Hanson, Western Vice President; nelswh@attbi.com
 Jerry Rose, Midwest Vice President; jerryrose@uplogon.com
 Keith Argow, President; 703-255-2700; Fax: 703-281-9200; argow@nwoa.net
 Virginia Tillotson, Member Services/Webmaster; 703-255-2700; Fax: 703-281-9200; tillotson@nwoa.net
 Eric Johnson, Editor National Woodlands Magazine; 41 Fountain St., Clinton, NY 13323; 315-369-3078; nela@telenet.net
 Bert Udell, Chairman of the Board; budell@oregonisonline.com

NATIVE AMERICAN FISH AND WILDLIFE SOCIETY (NAFWS)
750 Burbank St.
Broomfield, CO 80020 United States
Phone: 303-466-1725   Fax: 303-466-5414
Website: www.nafws.org

Founded: 1982
Membership: 1,001–10,000
Scope: National

Description: The Native American Fish and Wildlife Society is a nonprofit organization serving the needs of fish, wildlife, and natural resources on Tribal lands across the United States, including Alaska. The Society membership is comprised of approximately 1,500 professional and technical personnel associated with Native American natural resource programs. Two hundred sixteen federally-recognized tribes represent the Society, and many federal agencies rely on the Society's expertise and established network

Publication(s): From the Eagles Nest

Keyword(s): Ethics/Environmental Justice, Forests/Forestry, Wildlife & Species

Contact(s):
 Matthew Vanderhoop, President; 508-645-9265; natres@vineyard.net
 Teresa Harris, Vice President; 803-366-4792; harristeresa@yahoo.com
 Mike Fox, Technical Services Director
 Ira New Breast, Director; 303-466-1725
 Ken Poynter, Executive Director; 303-466-1725
 Faith McGruther, Secretary and Treasurer; 906-632-0043; cotfma@up.net

NATIVE PLANT SOCIETY OF NORTHEASTERN OHIO
640 Cherry Park Oval
Aurora, OH 44202 United States
Phone: 330-562-4053
E-mail: npsohio@hotmail.com

Founded: 1982
Membership: 101–1,000
Scope: Local, State, Regional

Description: The Native Plant Society of Northeastern Ohio promotes education about and conservation of native plants, encourages research, publication of the information and cooperation with other programs and organizations concerned with conservation of natural resources.

Publication(s): On the Fringe

Keyword(s): Forests/Forestry, Land Issues, Public Lands/Greenspace, Reduce/Reuse/Recycle, Water Habitats & Quality, Wildlife & Species

Contact(s):
 Jean Roche, President; 640 Cherry Park Oval, Aurora, OH 44202; 330-562-4053; bjroche@aol.com
 George Wilder, Vice President; 216-932-3351
 Judy Bradt-Barnhart, Treasurer; 440-548-2414
 Brian Gilbert, Secretary; 216-486-8765
 Tom Sampliner, Board Member; 216-371-4454

NATIVE PLANT SOCIETY OF OREGON
P.O. Box 902
Eugene, OR 97440 United States
Phone: 541-343-2364   Fax: 541-341-1752
Website: www.npsoregon.org/

Founded: 1961
Scope: State

Description: The Native Plant Society of Oregon is a nonprofit statewide organization. The Society is dedicated to the enjoyment, conservation, and study of Oregon's native vegetation.

Publication(s): Bulletin of the Native Plant Society of Oregon, KALMIOPSIS: Journal of the Native Plant Society of Oregon, Proceedings from a Conference of the Native Plant Society of Oregon, Conservation and Management of Native Plants and Fungi, Biography of Louis F. Henderson

Keyword(s): Reduce/Reuse/Recycle, Wildlife & Species

Contact(s):
 Bruce Newhouse, President; 541-343-2364
 Michael McKeag, Vice-President; 503-642-3965; vice_president@npsoregon.org
 Candice Guth, Treasurer
 Kelli Van Norman, Secretary

NATIVE PLANT SOCIETY OF TEXAS
P.O. Box 891
Georgetown, TX 78627 United States
Phone: 512-868-8799 Fax: 512-931-1166
E-mail: dtucker@io.com
Website: www.npsot.org

Founded: 1980
Membership: 1,001–10,000
Scope: State
Description: A nonprofit organization dedicated to the education and promotion of conservation, preservation, and utilization of the native plants and the plant habitats of Texas.
Publication(s): Native Plant Society of Texas News
Keyword(s): Wildlife & Species

NATIVE PRAIRIES ASSOCIATION OF TEXAS
P.O. Box 210
Georgetown, TX 78627-0210 United States
Phone: 512-339-0618
E-mail: prairie65@aol.com
Website: www.texasprairie.org

Founded: 1986
Membership: 101–1,000
Scope: State
Description: Native Prairies Association of Texas is dedicated to conservation and restoration of native prairies, through education, research, public awareness, agency cooperation, management, restoration, and acquisitions.
Publication(s): Prairie Dog, The
Keyword(s): Forests/Forestry, Land Issues
Contact(s):
  Gene Heinemann, President
  Clint Josey, Vice President
  Lee Stone; 512-581-9822

NATURAL AREAS ASSOCIATION
Bend, OR 97709 United States
Phone: 541-317-0199 Fax: 541-317-0140
E-mail: naa@natareas.org
Website: www.naturalarea.org

Founded: 1980
Membership: 1,001–10,000
Scope: International
Description: A nonprofit organization of professional and active volunteers in natural area identification, preservation, protection, management, and research. Provides a medium of exchange and coordination to advance the understanding and appreciation of natural areas and natural diversity.
Publication(s): Natural Areas Journal, Natural Area News
Keyword(s): Land Issues, Public Lands/Greenspace, Reduce/Reuse/Recycle, Wildlife & Species
Contact(s):
  Kim Herman, Vice President; Michigan Dept. of Natural Resources, Escanaba Field Office, 6833 US 2, 41, & M-05, Gladstone, MI 49007; 1-906-786-2000, ext. 00; Fax: 1-906-786-2384; hermank@michigan.gov
  J. Ralph Jordan, President; Resource Stewardship, Tennessee Valley Authority, P.O. Box 1589, Norris 37828-1589; 1-865-632-1604; Fax: 1-865-632-1795; jrjordan@tva.gov
  Reid Schuller, Executive Director; P.O. Box 1504, Bend, OR 97709; 541-317-0199; Fax: 541-317-0140; naa@natareas.org
  Vickie Larson, Secretary; Dynamac Corporation, 100 Spaceport Way, Cape Canaveral, FL 32920; 1-321-730-0770; vlarson@dynamac.com
  Lydia Macauley, Treasurer; P.O. Box 665, Highlands, NC 28741-0665; 1-828-526-4887; Fax: 1-828-526-5339; Lydward@aol.com
  Gerry Wright, Journal Editor; Dept. of Fish & Wildlife Resources, P.O. Box 44-1136, University of Idaho, Moscow, ID 83844-1136; 1-208-885-7990; Fax: 1-208-885-9080; cwilliams@mail.clarion.edu

NATURAL HISTORY SOCIETY OF MARYLAND, INC., THE
2643 N. Charles St.
Baltimore, MD 21218-4590 United States
Phone: 410-235-6116
E-mail: membership@naturalhistory.org
Website: www.naturalhistory.org

Founded: 1929
Membership: 101–1,000
Scope: Local, State
Description: A nonprofit membership organization formed to promote the appreciation of natural history through education, research, and publication—thereby fostering stewardship of natural and cultural resources. The Society bestows the Edmund B. Fladung Award to recognize persons exemplifying the society's goals.
Publication(s): Bulletin of the Maryland Herpetological Society, News and Views, The Maryland Naturalist
Keyword(s): Wildlife & Species
Contact(s):
  Joe McSharry, President, jmcsharry@naturalhistory.org
  Charles Davis, Chairman of the Board

NATURAL LAND INSTITUTE
320 S. 3rd St.
Rockford, IL 61104 United States
Phone: 815-964-6666 Fax: 815-964-6661
E-mail: nli@aol.com
Website: www.naturalland.org

Founded: 1958
Membership: 101–1,000
Scope: Regional
Description: A nonprofit organization to protect Illinois's native flora and fauna, and to encourage wise stewardship of the natural resources that affect them.
Publication(s): Pecatonica River Water Shed, Flora of Winnebago County, Land and Nature (Quarterly Newsletter)
Keyword(s): Land Issues, Wildlife & Species
Contact(s):
  Randall Vincent, President
  Gary McIntyre, Vice President
  Jerry Paulson, Executive Director
  Jill Kennay, Assistant Director
  Rebecca Olson, Land Preservation Specialist

NATURAL LANDS TRUST
Hildacy Farm, 1031 Palmers Mill Rd.
Media, PA 19063 United States
Phone: 610-353-5587 Fax: 610-353-0517
E-mail: info@natlands.org
Website: www.natlands.org

Founded: 1953
Membership: 1,001–10,000
Scope: Regional
Description: Natural Lands Trust is a regional land trust working to protect the most critical remaining open lands in the extended Philadelphia area. Primary programs include: permanently protecting land through acquisition and easements; providing conservation planning services to communities, institutions and landowners; and, managing the group's 45 nature preserves in southeastern Pennsylvania and southern New Jersey.
Publication(s): Native Trees and Plants, Controlling Invasive Plants, Environmentally Friendly Lawn, Growing Greener

Keyword(s): Forests/Forestry, Land Issues, Public Lands/Greenspace, Sprawl/Urban Planning, Water Habitats & Quality, Wildlife & Species

NATURAL RESOURCES COUNCIL OF AMERICA
1025 Thomas Jefferson St., NW, Suite 109
Washington, DC 20007-5291 United States
Phone: 202-333-0411   Fax: 202-333-0412
E-mail: nrca@naturalresourcescouncil.org
Website: www.naturalresourcescouncil.org
Founded: 1946
Membership: 1–100
Scope: National
Description: An association of nonprofit environmental and conservation organizations dedicated to the protection, conservation, and responsible management of the nation's natural resources. The Council coordinates cooperative efforts between its members, government agencies, private citizens, and businesses. The Council also administers the Conservation Round Table Luncheon series, an annual Conservation Community Banquet and Awards program, and publishes a bimonthly newsletter.
Publication(s): NEP, The Conservation Voice
Contact(s):
  Andrea Yank, Executive Director; andrea@nationalresourcescouncil.org
  Melissa Bondi, Assistant Director; melissa@nationalresourcescouncil.org

NATURAL RESOURCES COUNCIL OF MAINE
3 Wade St.
Augusta, ME 04330-6351 United States
Phone: 207-622-3101   Fax: 207-622-4343
E-mail: nrcm@nrcm.org
Website: maineenvironment.org
Membership: 1–100
Scope: State
Description: A representative statewide organization, affiliated with the National Wildlife Federation, dedicated to the protection and enhancement of wildlife and its habitat through public education and government interaction.
Publication(s): Maine Environment, others available on website
Contact(s):
  Ellen Baum, President
  Brownie Carson, Executive Director and Alternate Representative
  Mac Deford, Treasurer
  Paul Liebow, Representative
  Patty Renaud, Editor & Education Programs Contact

NATURAL RESOURCES DEFENSE COUNCIL, INC.
NRDC
Headquarters, 40 W. 20th St.
New York, NY 10011 United States
Phone: 212-727-2700   Fax: 212-727-1773
E-mail: nrdcinfo@nrdc.org
Website: www.nrdc.org
Founded: 1970
Membership: 500,001–1,000,000
Scope: National
Description: Nonprofit membership organization dedicated to protecting America's endangered natural resources and to improving the quality of the human environment. Combines interdisciplinary legal and scientific approach in crafting innovative solutions, monitoring government agencies, bringing legal action, and disseminating citizen information. Areas of concentration: air and water pollution, global warming, nuclear safety, land use, urban environment, pollution prevention, ecosystem management.
Publication(s): On Earth Magazine
Contact(s):
  John Adams, President; 212-727-2700
  Frances Beinecke, Executive Director
  Douglas Barasch, Editor-in-Chief, on Earth; 212-727-2700

NATURAL RESOURCES FOUNDATION OF WISCONSIN
P.O. Box 2317
Madison, WI 53701 United States
Phone: 608-266-3138
E-mail: conservation@nrfwis.org
Website: www.nrfwis.org
Founded: 1986
Membership: 1,001–10,000
Scope: Local, State
Description: Our organization is an independent, nonprofit organization devoted to protecting, conserving, and restoring Wisconsin's natural heritage. We accomplish our mission through financial support of local conservation efforts and selected DNR stewardship programs, education outreach, and facilitation of 60 field trips each year to Wisconsin's wild places. Recent restoration efforts include partnering in the Whooping Crane Reintroduction Project and raising funds to protect Wisconsin's State Natural Areas.
Publication(s): Quarterly newsletter

NATURAL RESOURCES INFORMATION COUNCIL
Lenora Oftedahl
Streamnet Library, Columbia River Inter-Tribal Fish Commission
Ste. 190, 729 NE Oregon St.
Portland, OR 97232 United States
Phone: 503-736-3581   Fax: 503-731-1260
E-mail: oftl@critfc.org
Website: www.quinneylibrary.usu.edu/nric
Founded: 1991
Scope: International
Description: Federal, state, provincial, academic, and special research librarians and information specialists from U.S. and Canada who facilitate the exchange of information on sustainable natural resources. Goals are to build a network of resource people to collect and disseminate information on sustainable natural resources and to provide continuing education.
Publication(s): Annual Newsletter (Yearly), Fish and Game Natural Resource Library Survey
Keyword(s): Reduce/Reuse/Recycle
Contact(s):
  Anne Hedrich, Membership; 435-797-2165; Fax: 435-797-7475; annhed@cc.usu.edu
  Barbara Voeltz, Treasurer; bvoeltz@ngpc.state.ne.us

NATURAL SCIENCE FOR YOUTH FOUNDATION
130 Azalea Dr.
Roswell, GA 30075 United States
Phone: 770-594-9367
E-mail: info@slpt.org
Website: www.slpt.org
Founded: 1952
Scope: National
Description: Provides counseling to community groups in the planning and development of environmental and natural science centers, museums, and native animal parks which are designed particularly to meet the needs and interests of children and young people. Conducts an annual conference as part of its widespread effort to promote professional excellence in environmental and natural science centers and museums.
Publication(s): Directory of Natural Science Centers

Keyword(s): Recreation/Ecotourism
Contact(s):
    John Forbes, Founder and President Emeritus
    Joe Witley, President
    Owen Winters, Publications Director
    John Hammaker, Treasurer
    Georgine Pindar, Secretary

NATURE AND NATURAL RESOURCES (IUCN)
PISO 4
Quito, Ecuador
Phone: 593-2-466-622   Fax: 593-2-466-624
E-mail: SAMERICA@SUR.IUCN.ORG
Website: www.iucn.org

Contact(s):
    Roberto Franco, Regional Representative

NATURE CONSERVANCY, THE
4245 North Fairfax Dr.
Arlington, VA 22208 United States
Phone: 703-841-5300   Fax: 703-841-1283
Website: www.nature.org

Founded: 1951
Membership: 1,000,001 +
Scope: International
Description: International nonprofit organization committed to preserving the plants, animals and natural communities that represent the diversity of life on Earth by protecting the lands and waters they need to survive. TNC works closely with communities, businesses and individuals. By practicing sound science that achieves tangible results the Conservancy has protected more than 116 million acres of valuable lands and waters worldwide.
Publication(s): The Nature Conservancy Magazine
Keyword(s): Wildlife & Species
Contact(s):
    Steve McCormick, President; 703-841-5300
    Donna Cherel, Membership; 703-841-5300
    Maggie Coon, Government Relations; 703-841-5300; mcoon@tnc.org
    Ray Culter, Administration; 703-841-5300
    Mike Dennis, General Counsel; 703-841-5300
    Joy Gaddy, Human Resources Field Services; 703-841-5300
    Ron Geatz, Editor-In-Chief; 703-841-5300
    Diane Gosting, Human Resources Business Services; 703-841-5300
    Steve Howell, Chief Operations Officer; 703-841-5300
    Deborah Jensen, Conservation Science; 703-841-5300
    Bob Reynolds, Chairman of the Board; 703-841-5300
    Greg How, Domestic Conservation; 703-841-5300
    Grace Vance, Development and Marketing; 703-841-5300
    Alexander Watson, International Conservation; 703-841-5300
    Bill Weeks, Chief Conservation Officer; 703-841-5300
    David Williamson, Communications; 703-841-5300

NATURE CONSERVANCY, THE
ADIRONDACK CHAPTER
ADIRONDACK LAND TRUST
P.O. Box 65
Keene Valley, NY 12943 United States
Phone: 518-576-2082
E-mail: cprickett@tnc.org
Website: www.nature.org/adirondacks

Founded: 1971
Membership: 1,001–10,000
Scope: Local
Description: The Adirondack Nature Conservancy and Adirondack Land Trust are separate land conservation organizations that have acted in partnership since 1988, coordinating programs and staff. The Adirondack Nature Conservancy protects the plants, animals, and natural communities that represent the diversity of life in the Adirondacks by protecting the lands and waters they need to survive.
Publication(s): Developing a Land Conservation Strategy: A Handbook for Land Trusts (1987)
Keyword(s): Agriculture/Farming, Development/Developing Countries, Ecosystems (precious), Forests/Forestry, Land Issues, Public Lands/Greenspace
Contact(s):
    Timothy Barnett, Vice President; 518-576-2082; Fax: 518-576-4203; tbarnett@tnc.org
    Dirk Bryant, Director of Conservation Programs; 518-576-2082; ext. 114; Fax: 518-576-4203; dbryant@tnc.org
    Michael Carr, Executive Director; 518-576-2082; Fax: 518-576-4203; mcarr@tnc.org
    Todd Dunham, Director of Land Protection; 518-576-2082; Fax: 518-576-4203; tdunham@tnc.org

NATURE CONSERVANCY, THE
ALABAMA CHAPTER
ALABAMA NATURAL HERITAGE PROGRAM
Huntingdon College
1500 E. Fairview Ave.
Montgomery, AL 36106 United States
Phone: 334-834-4519   Fax: 334-834-5439
E-mail: bhastings@alnhp.org
Website: alnhp.org

Founded: 1989
Membership: 1–100
Scope: State, Regional
Description: The mission of the Alabama Natural Heritage program is to provide the best available scientific information on the biological diversity of Alabama, guide conservation action and promote sound stewardship practices within the state and throughout the Southeast.
Publication(s): Inventory List of Rare Threatened and Endangered Plants, Animals, and Natural Communities of Alabama, Natural Heritage News
Keyword(s): Land Issues, Public Lands/Greenspace, Reduce/Reuse/Recycle, Wildlife & Species
Contact(s):
    Robert Hastings, Director, Heritage Program; 334-834-4519; ext. 21; bhastings@alnhp.org

NATURE CONSERVANCY, THE
ALABAMA OPERATING UNIT
2821 2nd Avenue S., Suite C
Birmingham, AL 35233 United States
Phone: 205-251-1155   Fax: 205-251-4444
E-mail: cwilborn@tnc.org
Website: www.nature.org

Founded: 1989
Membership: 1,001–10,000
Scope: State
Description: The mission of The Nature Conservancy is to preserve the plants, animals, and natural communities that represent the diversity of life on Earth by protecting the lands and waters they need to survive.
Keyword(s): Agriculture/Farming, Executive/Legislative/Judicial Reform, Forests/Forestry, Land Issues, Oceans/Coasts/Beaches, Public Lands/Greenspace, Recreation/Ecotourism, Water Habitats & Quality, Wildlife & Species
Contact(s):
    Kathy Stiles Freeland, State Director

NATURE CONSERVANCY, THE
ALASKA CHAPTER
421 W. First Ave., Suite 200
Anchorage, AK 99501 United States
Phone: 907-276-3133   Fax: 907-276-2584
E-mail: alaska@tnc.org
Website: www.nature.org

Founded: 1988
Membership: 1,001–10,000
Scope: State
Description: The mission of The Nature Conservancy is to preserve the plants, animals, and natural communities that represent the diversity of life on Earth by protecting the lands and waters they need to survive.
Publication(s): Nature Conservancy of Alaska
Keyword(s): Ecosystems (precious), Land Issues
Contact(s):
　David Banks, State Director; 907-276-3133; ext. 110; alaska@tnc.org
　Rob Bosworth, Southeast Alaska Program Director; 119 Seward Street, Suite #2, Juneau, AK 99801; 907-586-8621; Fax: 907-586-8622; alaska@tnc.org
　Erin Dovichin, Director of Communications; 907-276-3133; ext. 114; alaska@tnc.org
　Randy Hagenstein, Director of Conservation; 907-276-3133; ext. 119; alaska@tnc.org
　Paul Jackson, Director of Native Partnerships and Freshwater Ecology; 907-276-3133; ext. 115; alaska@tnc.org
　Cheryl McGrew, Director of Philanthropy; 907-276-3133; ext. 104; alaska@tnc.org

NATURE CONSERVANCY, THE
ARKANSAS FIELD OFFICE
601 N. University Ave.
Little Rock, AR 72205 United States
Phone: 501-663-6699   Fax: 501-663-8332
Website: www.nature.org

Scope: State
Contact(s):
　Nancy Delamar, State Director; cbornemeier@tnc.org

NATURE CONSERVANCY, THE
ASIA/PACIFIC PROGRAM
1116 Smith St., #201
Honolulu, HI 96817 United States
Phone: 808-537-4508

Scope: International

NATURE CONSERVANCY, THE
CALIFORNIA CHAPTER
201 Mission St., 4th Fl.
San Francisco, CA 94105 United States
Phone: 415-777-0487   Fax: 415-777-0244
Website: www.tnccalifornia.org

Founded: 1951
Membership: 500,001–1,000,000
Scope: State, Regional, International
Description: The mission of The Nature Conservancy is to preserve plants, animals, and natural communities that represent the diversity of life on Earth by protecting the lands and waters they need to survive.
Contact(s):
　Williams Jody, Program Manager

NATURE CONSERVANCY, THE
CANADA CHAPTER
110 Eglinton Ave. W., Suite 400
Toronto, M4R 1A3 Ontario Canada
Phone: 416-932-3202   Fax: 416-932-3208
E-mail: nature@natureconservancy.ca
Website: www.natureconservancy.ca

Founded: 1962
Scope: National
Description: The Nature Conservancy of Canada is the only national charity dedicated to preserving ecologically significant areas, places of special beauty and education interest through outright purchase, donations and conservation agreements.
Publication(s): Annual Report, The Ark
Keyword(s): Land Issues, Wildlife & Species
Contact(s):
　Lynn Gran, Director of Development; lynn.gran@natureconservancy.ca
　John Lounds, President
　Ted Boswell, Past Chair

NATURE CONSERVANCY, THE
COLORADO CHAPTER
2424 Spruce Street
Boulder, CO 80302 United States
Phone: 303-444-2950   Fax: 303-444-2986
E-mail: gbailey@tnc.org
Website: www.nature.org /colorado

Membership: 1,000,001 +
Scope: State
Description: The Nature Conservancy is a private, international, non-profit organization that preserves plants, animals and natural communities representing the diversity of life on Earth by protecting the lands and waters they need to survive. To date, the Conservancy and its more than one million members have been responsible for the protection of more than 12 million acres in the U.S. and have helped preserve more than 80 million acres in Latin America, the Caribbean, Asia and the Pacific.
Publication(s): Land Mark, The
Keyword(s): Ecosystems (precious), Ethics/Environmental Justice, Forests/Forestry, Land Issues, Pollution (general), Public Lands/Greenspace, Recreation/Ecotourism, Water Habitats & Quality, Wildlife & Species
Contact(s):
　Mark Burget, State Director; 303-444-2950; ext. 1010; Fax: 303-444-2986; mburget@tnc.org
　Geneva Bailey, Office Co-ordinator; 303-444-2950
　Charles Bedford, Associate Director; 303-444-2950; ext. 1232; Fax: 303-444-2968; cbedford@tnc.org

NATURE CONSERVANCY, THE
CONNECTICUT CHAPTER
55 High Street
Middletown, CT 06457 United States
Phone: 860-344-0716
E-mail: ct@tnc.org
Website: nature.org/connecticut

Founded: 1960
Scope: International
Description: The mission of The Nature Conservancy is to preserve the plants, animals and natural communities that represent the diversity of life on Earth by protecting the lands and waters they need to survive.
Contact(s):
　Dennis McGrath, State Director

NATURE CONSERVANCY, THE
DELAWARE CHAPTER
100 W. 10th Street
Suite 1107
Wilmington, DE 19801 United States
Phone: 302-654-4707   Fax: 302-654-4708
E-mail: delaware@tnc.org
Website: www.nature.org

Founded: 1989
Membership: 1,001–10,000
Scope: State, Regional

Description: The mission of The Nature Conservancy is to preserve the plants, animals and natural communities that represent the diversity of life on Earth by protecting the lands and waters they need to survive.
Keyword(s): Land Issues, Public Lands/Greenspace, Water Habitats & Quality, Wildlife & Species
Contact(s):
Jennifer Burns, Director of Development & Communications; 302-654-4707; ext. 125; jburns@tnc.org
Roger Jones, State Director

NATURE CONSERVANCY, THE
EASTERN NEW YORK CHAPTER
19 North Moger Avenue
Mount Kisco, NY 10549 United States
Phone: 914-244-3271   Fax: 914-244-3275
Website: www.nature.org
Founded: 1951
Membership: 10,001–100,000
Scope: Local, State, Regional, National, International
Description: The mission of The Nature Conservancy is to protect the plants, animals, & natural communities that represent the diversity of life on Earth by protecting the lands and waters they need to survive.
Publication(s): Preserve Guide, available on website
Keyword(s): Ecosystems (precious), Forests/Forestry, Land Issues, Recreation/Ecotourism, Water Habitats & Quality, Wildlife & Species
Contact(s):
Kathy Moser, Executive Director

NATURE CONSERVANCY, THE
FLORIDA CHAPTER
222 S. Westmonte Dr. Suite 300
Altamonte Springs, FL 32714 United States
Phone: 407-682-3664   Fax: 407-682-3077
E-mail: mcantillo@tnc.org
Website: nature.org/
Scope: State

NATURE CONSERVANCY, THE
GEORGIA CHAPTER
1330 W. Peachtree St., Ste. 410
Atlanta, GA 30309-2904 United States
Phone: 404-873-6946   Fax: 404-873-6984
Website: www.nature.org
Founded: 1987
Membership: 10,001–100,000
Scope: State
Publication(s): Quarterly newsletter
Contact(s):
Tavia McCuean, Vice President and State Director

NATURE CONSERVANCY, THE
GREAT PLAINS DIVISION
1101 West River Parkway
Suite 200
Minneapolis, MN 55415 United States
Phone: 612-331-0750   Fax: 612-331-0770
Website: www.nature.org
Founded: 1951
Membership: 10,001–100,000
Scope: Local, State, Regional, International
Description: The mission of The Nature Conservancy is to protect plants, animals and natural communities that represent the diversity of life on Earth by protecting the land and water they need to survive. The Great Plains Division includes the programs in 7 states: Iowa, Kansas, Minnesota, Missouri, Nebraska, North Dakota and South Dakota and concentrates on the protection of Great Plains ecoregions including Tallgrass Prairie.
Publication(s): National Magazine, Newsletter, Annual Report
Contact(s):
Robert McKim, Division Director; 1101 West River Parkway, Suite 200, Minneapolis, MN 55415

NATURE CONSERVANCY, THE
HAWAII CHAPTER
923 Nu'uanu Avenue
Honolulu, HI 96817 United States
Phone: 808-537-4508   Fax: 808-545-2019
E-mail: mwaits@tnc.org
Website: nature.org
Scope: State

NATURE CONSERVANCY, THE
IDAHO CHAPTER
Sun Valley, ID 83353 United States
Phone: 208-726-3007   Fax: 208-726-1258
Website: www.nature.org
Scope: State
Contact(s):
Geoff Pampush, State Director

NATURE CONSERVANCY, THE
ILLINOIS CHAPTER
8 S. Michigan Ave.
Suite 900
Chicago, IL 60603 United States
Phone: 312-580-2100   Fax: 312-346-5600
Scope: State
Contact(s):
Bruce Boyd, State Director

NATURE CONSERVANCY, THE
INDIANA CHAPTER
1505 N. Delaware St.
Suite 200
Indianapolis, IN 46202 United States
Phone: 317-951-8818   Fax: 317-917-2478
E-mail: csutton@tnc.org
Website: www.nature.org/indiana
Founded: 1959
Membership: 10,001–100,000
Scope: Regional
Description: Not-for-profit land conservation organization.
Publication(s): Preserve Guide, Chapter Newsletter (twice yearly)
Keyword(s): Ecosystems (precious), Forests/Forestry, Water Habitats & Quality, Wildlife & Species
Contact(s):
Mary McConnell, State Director; 317-951-8818; Fax: 317-917-2478; mmcconnell@tnc.org

NATURE CONSERVANCY, THE
IOWA CHAPTER
303 Locust Street Suite 402
Des Moines, IA 50309-4758 United States
Phone: 515-244-5044   Fax: 515-244-8890
E-mail: iowa@tnc.org
Website: nature.org/iowa
Membership: 1,001–10,000
Scope: State
Description: The mission of The Nature Conservancy is to preserve the plants, animals and natural communities that represent the diversity of life on Earth by protecting the lands and waters they need to survive
Publication(s): Nature Conservancy, Iowa Field Notes
Contact(s):
Leslee Spraggins, State Director; 515-244-5044

NATURE CONSERVANCY, THE
KANSAS CHAPTER
700 SW Jackson Street
Suite 804
Topeka, KS 66603 United States
Phone: 785-233-4400   Fax: 785-233-2022
E-mail: rpalmer@tnc.org
Website: nature.org/kansas

Founded: 1989
Membership: 1,001–10,000
Scope: State
Description: The mission of The Nature Conservancy is to preserve plants, animals, and natural communities that represent the diversity of life on Earth by protecting the lands and waters they need to survive.
Contact(s):
Alan Pollom, Vice President
Ruth Palmer, Development & Communications Coordinator; 785-233-4400; Fax: 785-233-2022; rpalmer@tnc.org

NATURE CONSERVANCY, THE
KENTUCKY CHAPTER
642 W. Main St.
Lexington, KY 40508 United States
Phone: 859-259-9655   Fax: 859-259-9678
E-mail: nature@mis.net
Website: www.nature.org
Membership: 10,001–100,000
Scope: Regional
Contact(s):
James Aldrich, State Director

NATURE CONSERVANCY, THE
LOUISIANA CHAPTER
P.O. Box 4125
Baton Rouge, LA 70821 United States
Phone: 225-338-1040   Fax: 225-338-0103
E-mail: lafo@tnc.org
Website: www.louisiananature.org
Membership: 1,001–10,000
Scope: State
Contact(s):
Keith Ouchley, State Director

NATURE CONSERVANCY, THE
MAINE CHAPTER
14 Maine St., #401
Brunswick, ME 40111 United States
Phone: 207-729-5181
E-mail: naturemaine@tnc.org
Website: nature.org
Scope: Local, State, Regional, National, International
Description: The Maine Chapter is an operating unit, located in Maine, of The Nature Conservancy nationwide.

NATURE CONSERVANCY, THE
MARYLAND/DISTRICT OF COLUMBIA CHAPTER
5410 Grosvenor Lane
Suite 100
Bethesda, MD 20814 United States
Phone: 301-897-8570   Fax: 301-897-0858
E-mail: ndeane@tnc.org
Website: nature.org/marylanddc
Scope: Local, State, Regional, National, International
Description: The Nature Conservancy's mission is to preserve the plants, animals and natural communities that represent the diversity of life on Earth by protecting the lands and waters they need to survive.
Contact(s):
Nat Williams, State Director & Vice President

NATURE CONSERVANCY, THE
MASSACHUSETTS CHAPTER
205 Portland Street
Suite 400
Boston, MA 02114 United States
Phone: 617-227-7017   Fax: 617-227-7688
E-mail: mmail@tnc.org
Website: nature.org/massachusetts
Scope: Local, State, Regional, National, International
Description: Environmental non-profit organization.
Keyword(s): Ecosystems (precious), Forests/Forestry, Land Issues, Public Lands/Greenspace, Sprawl/Urban Planning, Water Habitats & Quality, Wildlife & Species

NATURE CONSERVANCY, THE
MICHIGAN CHAPTER
2840 E. Grand River Ave., Suite 5
East Lansing, MI 48823 United States
Phone: 517-332-1741   Fax: 517-332-8382
Scope: State
Contact(s):
Helen Taylor, State Director

NATURE CONSERVANCY, THE
MID-ATLANTIC DIVISION OFFICE
4705 University Dr., Suite 290
Durham, NC 27707 United States
Phone: 919-403-8558   Fax: 919-403-0379
Scope: Regional
Contact(s):
Katherine Skinner, Vice President

NATURE CONSERVANCY, THE
MINNESOTA CHAPTER
1101 West River Parkway Suite 200
Minneapolis, MN 55415-1291 United States
Phone: 612-331-0750   Fax: 612-331-0770
Website: www.nature.org
Scope: State
Contact(s):
Rob McKim, State Director

NATURE CONSERVANCY, THE
MISSISSIPPI CHAPTER
6400 Lakeover Rd., Suite C
Jackson, MS 39213 United States
Phone: 601-713-3355   Fax: 601-982-9499
Website: www.nature.org/Mississippi
Scope: National, International
Description: Private non-profit organization whose mission is to preserve plants, animals and natural communities by protecting the lands and water they need to survive.
Contact(s):
Robbie Fisher, State Director

NATURE CONSERVANCY, THE
MISSOURI CHAPTER
2800 S. Brentwood Blvd.
St. Louis, MO 63144 United States
Phone: 314-968-1105   Fax: 314-968-3659
E-mail: missouri@tnc.org
Website: nature.org
Membership: 1–100
Scope: State

NATURE CONSERVANCY, THE
MONTANA CHAPTER
32 South Ewing Street
Suite 215
Helena, MT 59601 United States
Phone: 406-443-0303   Fax: 406-443-8311
E-mail: ktrepanier@tnc.org
Website: nature.org

Founded: 1950
Membership: 1,001–10,000
Scope: State
Description: The mission of The Nature Conservancy is to preserve the plants, animals, and natural communities that represent the diversity of life on Earth by protecting the lands and waters they need to survive.
Contact(s):
  Jamie Williams, State Director

NATURE CONSERVANCY, THE
NATURE CONSERVANCY OF NEW YORK, THE
NEW YORK CITY OFFICE
570 Seventh Avenue
Suite 601
New York, NY 10018 United States
Phone: 212-997-1880   Fax: 212-997-8451
E-mail: pyurgosky@tnc.org
Website: nature.org/newyork

Founded: 1951
Membership: 1,000,001+
Scope: Local, State, Regional, National, International
Description: The Nature Conservancy works to preserve the plants, animals and natural communities that represent the diversity of life on Earth, by protecting the lands and waters they need to survive.
Keyword(s): Air Quality/Atmosphere, Climate Change, Development/Developing Countries, Ecosystems (precious), Forests/Forestry, Land Issues, Oceans/Coasts/Beaches, Recreation/Ecotourism, Water Habitats & Quality, Wildlife & Species
Contact(s):
  Steve Dennin, Director, NYC Office, 212-997-1880; ext. 2181; Fax: 212-997-8451; sdennin@tnc.org
  Sandy Owen, Director of Major Gifts; 212-997-1880; ext. 2182; Fax: 212-997-8451; sowen@tnc.org
  Rose Alovera, Office Manager; 212-997-1880; ext. 2184; Fax: 212-997-8451; ralovera@tnc.org
  Molly Northrup, Events & Outreach Manager; 212-997-1880; ext. 2187; Fax: 212-997-8451; mnorthrup@tnc.org
  Anne Marie Ventola, Events Coordinator; 212-997-1880; ext. 2186; Fax: 212-997-8451; aventola@tnc.org
  Patrick Yurgosky, Philanthropy Assistant; 212-997-1880; ext. 2192; Fax: 212-997-8451; pyurgosky@tnc.org

NATURE CONSERVANCY, THE
NEBRASKA CHAPTER
1019 Leavenworth St.
Omaha, NE 68102 United States
Phone: 402-342-0282   Fax: 402-342-0474
E-mail: nebraska@tnc.org
Website: www.nature.org

Founded: 1951
Membership: 1,001–10,000
Scope: International
Description: Private, non-profit conservation organization.
Contact(s):
  Vince Shay, State Director

NATURE CONSERVANCY, THE
NEVADA CHAPTER
One East First St.
Suite 500
Reno, NV 89501 United States
Phone: 775-322-4990
E-mail: nevada@tnc.org
Website: www.nature.org

Membership: 1,001–10,000
Scope: State
Description: The Nature Conservancy, Nevada State Chapter
Contact(s):
  Ame Hellman, State Director

NATURE CONSERVANCY, THE
NEW HAMPSHIRE CHAPTER
22 Bridge 4th floor
Concord, NH 03301 United States
Phone: 603-224-5853   Fax: 603-228-2459
Website: nature.org/newhampshire

Founded: 1951
Membership: 1,000,001+
Scope: Local, State, Regional, National, International
Description: The Nature Conservancy is a private, non-profit organization whose mission is to preserve the plants, animals and natural communities that represent the diversity of life on Earth by protecting the lands and waters they need to survive.
Contact(s):
  Daryl Burtnett, State Director; 603-224-5853; dburtnett@tnc.org

NATURE CONSERVANCY, THE
NEW JERSEY CHAPTER
200 Pottersville Rd.
Chester, NJ 7930 United States
Phone: 908-879-7262   Fax: 908-879-2172
Website: www.nature.org

Founded: 1988
Membership: 10,001–100,000
Scope: Local
Description: The Nature Conservancy (est. 1951) is an international, non-profit organization dedicated to preserving the plants, animals and natural communities that represent the diversity of life on Earth by protecting the lands and waters they need to survive. Active in the Garden State since 1955, the New Jersey Chapter was established in 1988. Through more than 300 conservation transactions with the help of corporate sponsors, foundations and 33,000 members we have protected more than 54,000 acres.
Publication(s): Oak Leaf Quarterly Newsletter
Contact(s):
  Michael Catania, State Director

NATURE CONSERVANCY, THE
NEW MEXICO CHAPTER
212 E. Marcy, #200
Santa Fe, NM 87501 United States
Phone: 505-988-3867
E-mail: nm@tnc.org
Website: nature.org/newmexico

Founded: 1951
Membership: 1,001–10,000
Scope: State
Description: The Nature Conservancy is a leading international, nonprofit organization that preserves plants, animals and natural communities representing the diversity of life on Earth by protecting the lands and waters they need to survive. To date, the Conservancy has helped to protect more than 15 million acres in the United States and more than 83 million

acres worldwide. Active in New Mexico since 1973, The Nature Conservancy has preserved more than 1.2 million acres throughout the state.

Contact(s):
Bill Waldman, State Director

NATURE CONSERVANCY, THE
NEW YORK ADIRONDACK CHAPTER
P.O. Box 65
8 Nature Way
Keene Valley, NY 12943 United States
Phone: 518-576-2082   Fax: 518-576-4203
Membership: 1–100
Scope: Local, Regional
Description: Non-profit organization dedicated to the protection of land, plants and animals.

Contact(s):
Michael Carr, Director

NATURE CONSERVANCY, THE
NEW YORK CENTRAL/WESTERN CHAPTER
339 East Ave.
Rochester, NY 14604 United States
Phone: 716-546-8030   Fax: 706-546-7825
Website: www.nature.org
Membership: 1–100
Scope: Local, Regional
Publication(s): Quarterly newsletter

NATURE CONSERVANCY, THE
NEW YORK CITY CHAPTER
570 Seventh Ave.,
New York, NY 10018 United States
Phone: 212-997-1880   Fax: 212-997-8451
Website: www.nature.org
Scope: International
Publication(s): Nature Conservancy of New York

NATURE CONSERVANCY, THE
NEW YORK LONG ISLAND CHAPTER
250 Lawrence Hill Rd.
Cold Spring Harbor, NY 11724 United States
Phone: 631-367-3225   Fax: 631-367-4715
E-mail: cgordon@tnc.org
Website: nature.org
Founded: 1951
Scope: Local, State, Regional, National, International
Description: Works cooperatively with other conservation groups, businesses and many levels of government. Two conservancy chapters on Long Island have protected 40,000 acres and own approximately 5,000 acres in preserves.
Keyword(s): Ecosystems (precious), Forests/Forestry, Land Issues, Oceans/Coasts/Beaches, Public Lands/Greenspace, Water Habitats & Quality, Wildlife & Species

Contact(s):
Paul Rabinovitch, Executive Director
John Turner, Director of Conservation

NATURE CONSERVANCY, THE
NEW YORK SOUTH FORK/ SHELTER ISLAND CHAPTER
P.O. Box 5125
E. Hampton, NY 11937 United States
Phone: 631-329-7689   Fax: 631-329-0215
Scope: Local, Regional

Contact(s):
Nancy Kelley, Director

NATURE CONSERVANCY, THE
NORTH CAROLINA CHAPTER
4705 Univeristy Dr., #290
Durham, NC 27707 United States
Phone: 919-403-8558   Fax: 919-403-0379
Website: nature.org/northcarolina
Scope: State
Description: Celebrating 25 years of conservation in the Tar Heel State, the North Carolina Chapter of The Nature Conservancy has protected more than 560,000 acres of our state's natural heritage. With the help of 26,000 members, the Conservancy works with communities, businesses, donors and foundations to protect our state's special places. Our mission is to protect the biodiversity of life on earth by protecting plant, animals and natural communities and the lands and waters they need to survive.

Contact(s):
Katherine Skinner, Executive Director

NATURE CONSERVANCY, THE
NORTH DAKOTA CHAPTER
1256 N. Parkview Dr.
Bismarck, ND 58501 United States
Phone: 701-222-8464   Fax: 701-222-8061
Website: www.nature.org
Membership: 1,001–10,000
Scope: State
Description: The mission of The Nature Conservancy is to preserve the plants, animals, and natural communities that represent the diversity of life on Earth by protecting the lands and waters they need to survive.

Contact(s):
Gerald Reichert, Field Representative; 1256 North Parkview Dr., Bismarck, ND 58501; 701-222-8464; Fax: 701-222-8061; greichert@tnc.org
Eric Rosenquist, Preserve Manager; 1401 River Road, Center, ND 58530-9445; 701-794-8741; Fax: 701-794-3544; erosenquist@tnc.org

NATURE CONSERVANCY, THE
NORTHEAST/ CARIBBEAN DIVISION OFFICE
159 Waterman St.
Providence, RI 2906 United States
Phone: 401-751-2521   Fax: 401-751-7596
Website: www.tnc.org
Scope: International
Description: Mission is to preserve the plants, animals and natural communities that represent the diversity of life on Earth by protecting the lands and waters they need to survive.
Publication(s): Nature Conservancy - bi-monthly magazine

Contact(s):
John Cook, Vice President
Jennifer Bristol, Sr. Exec. Assistant; 401-751-2521

NATURE CONSERVANCY, THE
NORTHWEST AND HAWAII DIVISION OFFICE
217 Pine St., Suite 1100
Seattle, WA 98101 United States
Phone: 206-343-4344   Fax: 206-343-5608
Website: www.nature.org
Scope: Regional

Contact(s):
Elliot Marks, Vice President

NATURE CONSERVANCY, THE
OHIO CHAPTER
6375 Riverside Dr.
Dublin, OH 43017 United States
Phone: 614-717-2770   Fax: 614-717-2777
Website: www.nature.org

Founded: 1951
Membership: 10,001–100,000
Scope: State, National
Description: The mission of The Nature Conservancy is to preserve the plants, animals and natural communities that represent the diversity of life on Earth by protecting the lands and waters they need to survive.
Keyword(s): Agriculture/Farming, Development/Developing Countries, Ecosystems (precious), Forests/Forestry, Land Issues, Public Lands/Greenspace, Sprawl/Urban Planning, Water Habitats & Quality, Wildlife & Species
Contact(s):
Rich Shank, State Director

NATURE CONSERVANCY, THE
OKLAHOMA CHAPTER
2727 East 21st
Tulsa, OK 74114 United States
Phone: 918-585-1117   Fax: 918-585-2383
Website: www.nature.org
Scope: State
Contact(s):
Mary Collins, State Director

NATURE CONSERVANCY, THE
OREGON CHAPTER
821 SE 14th Ave.
Portland, OR 97214 United States
Phone: 503-230-1221   Fax: 503-230-9639
Website: www.nature.org
Founded: 1961
Membership: 10,001–100,000
Scope: Local, State, Regional, National, International
Description: The Nature Conservancy's mission is to preserve the plants, animals and natural communities representing the diversity of life on Earth by protecting the lands and waters they need to survive. The Conservancy has projects in every state and 29 countries.
Publication(s): Newsletter, Annual Report
Keyword(s): Ecosystems (precious), Forests/Forestry, Land Issues, Oceans/Coasts/Beaches, Public Lands/Greenspace, Water Habitats & Quality, Wildlife & Species
Contact(s):
Russell Hoeflich, State Director

NATURE CONSERVANCY, THE
PENNSYLVANIA CHAPTER
1100 E. Hector St.
Suite 470
Conshohocken, PA 19428 United States
Phone: 610-834-1323   Fax: 610-834-6533
Website: www.nature.org
Founded: 1981
Membership: 10,001–100,000
Scope: State
Description: Biodiversity Conservation
Publication(s): Penns Woods–bi-annually
Keyword(s): Development/Developing Countries, Ecosystems (precious), Forests/Forestry, Land Issues, Water Habitats & Quality, Wildlife & Species
Contact(s):
P. Gray, State Director
Scott Anderson, Director of Development & Communications; 610-834-1323; ext. 119
Nels Johnson, Director of Conservation Programs; 717-232-6001; ext. 108
Ron Ramsey, Director of Government Relations; 717-232-6001; ext. 106

NATURE CONSERVANCY, THE
RHODE ISLAND CHAPTER
159 Waterman Street
Providence, RI 02906 United States
Phone: 401-331-7110   Fax: 401-273-4902
Website: www.nature.org
Scope: Local, State, Regional, National, International
Description: Saving biodiversity
Keyword(s): Climate Change, Development/Developing Countries, Ecosystems (precious), Forests/Forestry, Land Issues, Oceans/Coasts/Beaches, Water Habitats & Quality, Wildlife & Species
Contact(s):
Terry Sullivan, State Director

NATURE CONSERVANCY, THE
ROCKY MOUNTAIN DIVISION OFFICE
117 E. Mountain Ave.
Fort Collins, CO 80524 United States
Phone: 970-484-2886   Fax: 970-498-0225
Website: www.nature.org
Scope: National
Description: Conservation
Contact(s):
Bruce Runnels, Vice President

NATURE CONSERVANCY, THE
SOUTH CAROLINA CHAPTER
P.O. Box 5475
Columbia, SC 29250 United States
Phone: 803-254-9049   Fax: 803-252-7134
Website: www.tnc.org/southcarolina
Scope: State
Contact(s):
Mark Robertson, State Director

NATURE CONSERVANCY, THE
SOUTHEAST DIVISION OFFICE
222 S. Westmonte Dr., Suite 300
Altamonte Springs, FL 32714 United States
Phone: 407-682-3664   Fax: 407-682-3077
Scope: Regional
Contact(s):
Robert Benedick, Vice-President

NATURE CONSERVANCY, THE
TENNESSEE CHAPTER
2021 21st. Ave. S.
Nashville, TN 37212 United States
Phone: 615-383-9909   Fax: 615-383-9717
Website: www.nature.org/tennessee
Membership: 10,001–100,000
Scope: State
Publication(s): Newsletter–bi-annual
Contact(s):
Scott Davis, State Director

NATURE CONSERVANCY, THE
TEXAS CHAPTER
P.O. Box 1440
San Antonio, TX 78295-1440 United States
Phone: 210-224-8774   Fax: 210-228-9805
Website: nature.org/texas
Scope: State
Contact(s):
Robert Potts, State Director

NATURE CONSERVANCY, THE
UTAH CHAPTER
559 E. South Temple
Salt Lake City, UT 84102 United States
Phone: 801-531-0999 Fax: 801-531-1003
Website: www.nature.org

Founded: 1995
Membership: 1,001–10,000
Scope: Local, State, Regional, National, International
Description: Our mission is to preserve the plants, animals and natural communities in Utah by protecting the lands & waters they need to survive.
Keyword(s): Agriculture/Farming, Development/Developing Countries, Ecosystems (precious), Executive/Legislative/Judicial Reform, Land Issues, Population, Public Lands/Greenspace, Recreation/Ecotourism, Sprawl/Urban Planning, Transportation, Water Habitats & Quality,

Contact(s):
David Livermore, State Director; 801-531-0999; Fax: 801-531-1003; dlivermore@tnc.org
Larisa Barry, Communications Manager; 801-531-0999; ext. 21; Fax: 801-531-1003; lbarry@tnc.org
Libby Ellis, Director of Development; 801-531-0999; ext. 17; Fax: 801-531-1003; lellis@tnc.org
Jill Lehmann, Executive Assistant; 801-531-0999; Fax: 801-531-1003; jlehmann@tnc.org
Chris Montague, Director of Conservation Programs; 801-531-0999; ext. 13; Fax: 801-531-1003; cmontague@tnc.org
Elaine York, Director of Volunteer & Education Programs; 801-531-0999; ext. 20; Fax: 801-531-1003; eyork@tnc.org

NATURE CONSERVANCY, THE
VERMONT CHAPTER
27 State. St., Suite 4
Montpelier, VT 05602 United States
Phone: 802-229-4425 Fax: 802-229-1347
Website: nature.org

Scope: State
Description: The mission of The Nature Conservancy is to preserve the plants, animals and natural communities that represent the diversity of life on Earth by protecting the lands and waters they need to survive.

Contact(s):
Robert Klein, State Director

NATURE CONSERVANCY, THE
VIRGIN ISLANDS CHAPTER
14B Norre Gade, 2nd Fl.
Charlotte Amalie, VI 802 United States
Phone: 340-774-7633 Fax: 340-774-7736
E-mail: c.philyaw@att.net
Website: www.nature.org

Scope: State
Publication(s): Available on web

Contact(s):
Robert Weary, Director

NATURE CONSERVANCY, THE
VIRGINIA PROGRAM
490 Westfield Rd.
Charlottesville, VA 22901 United States
Phone: 434-295-6106 Fax: 434-979-0370
E-mail: dwhite@tnc.org
Website: nature.org/virginia

Founded: 1960
Membership: 10,001–100,000
Scope: Local, State, Regional
Description: The Nature Conservancy seeks to protect the diversity of life on Earth by protecting land and water habitats.
Publication(s): Virginia News

Contact(s):
Michael Lipford, Executive Director

NATURE CONSERVANCY, THE
WASHINGTON CHAPTER
217 Pine St., #1100
Seattle, WA 98101 United States
Phone: 206-343-4344 Fax: 206-343-5608
E-mail: washington@tnc.org
Website: nature.org/washington

Membership: 10,001–100,000
Scope: State, Regional
Description: The Nature Conservancy is a private, international, non-profit organization that preserves plants, animals and natural communities representing the diversity of life on Earth by protecting the lands and waters they need to survive. In Washington State, the Conservancy has helped to protect nearly 400,000 acres.

Contact(s):
David Weekes, State Director

NATURE CONSERVANCY, THE
WEST VIRGINIA CHAPTER
723 Kanawha Blvd. East, #500
Charleston, WV 25301 United States
Phone: 304-345-4350 Fax: 304-345-4351
Website: www.nature.org

Membership: 1,001–10,000
Scope: State

Contact(s):
Paul Trianosky, State Director

NATURE CONSERVANCY, THE
WISCONSIN CHAPTER
633 W. Main St.
Madison, WI 53703 United States
Phone: 608-251-8140 Fax: 608-251-8535
E-mail: wmail@tnc.org
Website: nature.org/wisconsin

Founded: 1960
Membership: 10,001–100,000
Scope: State
Description: Preserves habitat for native plants and animals.
Publication(s): The Places We Save
Keyword(s): Ecosystems (precious), Water Habitats & Quality, Wildlife & Species

Contact(s):
Cate Harrington, Director of Communications/Media; 608-251-8140

NATURE CONSERVANCY, THE
WYOMING CHAPTER
258 Main St., #200
Lander, WY 82520 United States
Phone: 307-332-2971 Fax: 307-332-2974
E-mail: wyoming@tnc.org
Website: tncwyoming.org

Scope: State
Description: The Nature Conservancy is a private, non-profit, 501(c)(3) international membership organization whose mission is to preserve the plants, animals and natural communities that represent the diversity of life on earth by protecting the lands and waters they need to survive.

NATURE CONSERVATION SOCIETY OF JAPAN, THE (NACS-J)
Yamaji Sanbancho Bldg. 3F,
5-24 Sanbancho
Chiyoda-Ku, Tokyo, 102-0075 Japan
Phone: 81332650521 Fax: 81332650527
E-mail: nature@nacsj.or.jp

Website: www.nacsj.or.jp
Founded: 1951
Membership: 10,001–100,000
Scope: National
Description: A nonprofit, membership conservation organization devoted to promoting conservation, research, and education concerning the natural areas and wildlife in Japan, and also a recently launched international project to support biodiversity in developing countries.
Contact(s):
Masahito Yoshida, Executive Director; 81332650523; Fax: 81332650527; myoshida@nacsj.or.jp

NATURE SASKATCHEWAN
1860 Lorne St.
Room 206
Regina, S4P 2L7 Saskatchewan Canada
Phone: 306-780-9273   Fax: 306-780-9263
E-mail: info@naturesask.com
Website: www.naturesask.com
Founded: 1947
Membership: 1,001–10,000
Scope: Regional
Description: Nature Saskatchewan is the largest non-profit nature organization in the province, committed to preserving our natural environment. We own nature sanctuaries, and support conservation and research activities and nature education.
Publication(s): Blue Jay, special publication, Nature Views
Keyword(s): Land Issues, Reduce/Reuse/Recycle, Water Habitats & Quality, Wildlife & Species

NATURESAVERS
407 West Stevens Drive
Kershaw, SC 29067 United States
Phone: 803-475-9320
E-mail: naturesavers@lycos.com
Founded: 2002
Membership: 1–100
Scope: State
Description: We are in our initial startup phase. We strongly feel the need to clean and maintain our natural areas, not just talk about or legislate over. We will focus mainly on historic sites, rivers, and public land. We do everything on a volunteer basis. We will offer nature classes such as kayaking, backpacking, and minimalist camping procedures such as "leave no trace".
Keyword(s): Recreation/Ecotourism, Reduce/Reuse/Recycle

NATURESERVE
1101 Wilson Blvd.
15th floor
Arlington, VA 22209 United States
Phone: 703-908-1800   Fax: 703-908-1917
E-mail: laura_jarrell@natureserve.org
Website: www.natureserve.org
Founded: 1994
Scope: Regional
Description: NatureServe is a non-profit organization dedicated to providing knowledge to protect natural heritage programs and conservation data centers, NatureServe is a leading source for scientific information on rare and endangered species and threatened ecosystems. NatureServe and its member programs operate in the United States, Canada, Latin America, and the Caribbean providing essential information for conservation action.
Contact(s):
Mark Schaefer, President and CEO
Joy Gaddy, Vice President for Operations
Dennis Grossman, Vice President for Science
Mary Klein, Vice President for Natural Heritage Network Operations
Bruce Stein, Vice President for Programs
Larry Sugarbaker, Chief Information Officer

NAVARINO NATURE CENTER
W5646 Lindsten Road
Shiocton, WI 54170 United States
Phone: 715-758-6999   Fax: 715-758-2730
E-mail: nnc1@tds.net
Website: navarino.org
Founded: 1986
Membership: 101–1,000
Scope: Local, State
Description: Non-profit nature center located on the Navarino Wildlife Area (WDNR) in NE Wisconsin. Providing environmental education programs to the general public and schools in our region of NE Wisconsin.
Contact(s):
Dave Prey, President

NEBRASKA ASSOCIATION OF RESOURCE DISTRICTS
601 South 12th St.
Suite 201
Lincoln, NE 68508 United States
Phone: 402-471-7670   Fax: 402-471-7677
E-mail: nard@nrd.net.org
Website: www.nrd.net.org
Founded: 1972
Membership: 1–100
Scope: Local, State, Regional, National
Description: Advocacy organization for Nebraska's Natural resource Districts (NRDs)
Keyword(s): Agriculture/Farming, Executive/Legislative/Judicial Reform, Forests/Forestry, Land Issues, Pollution (general), Public Health, Recreation/Ecotourism, Reduce/Reuse/Recycle, Sprawl/Urban Planning, Water Habitats & Quality, Wildlife & Species
Contact(s):
Orval Gigstad, President; Rt. 1, Box 54, Syracuse, NE 68446; 402-269-3267
Dave Nelson, Vice President; 402-756-0724
Dean Edson, Executive Director; 601 S. 12th St., Suite 201, Lincoln, NE 68508; 402-471-7674; Fax: 402-471-7677; dedson@nrdnet.org
Justin Apel, Information/Education Director; 402-471-7673; Fax: 402-471-7677; japel@nrdnet.org
Jeanne Dryburgh, Office Manager; 402-471-7670; Fax: 402-471-7677; jdryburgh@nrdnet.org

NEBRASKA BASS FEDERATION
Attn: President, 1518 Kozy Dr.
Columbus, NE 68601 United States
Phone: 402-563-2297
E-mail: jlcitta@nppd.com
Scope: State
Description: An organization of Bassmaster chapters, affiliated with the Bass Anglers Sportsman Society, organized to fight pollution, assist state and national conservation agencies in their efforts, and teach the young people of our country good conservation practices. Dedicated to the realistic conservation of our water resources.
Contact(s):
Joe Citta, President; 402-563-2297
Tom Boyd, Conservation Director; 1610 S. Blaine, Grand Island, NE 68803; 308-382-8357

NEBRASKA ORNITHOLOGISTS UNION, INC.
W. 436 Nebraska Hall
Lincoln, NE 68588-0514 United States
Phone: 402-472-8366
Website: rip.physics.unk.edu/nou/

Founded: 1899
Scope: State
Description: To promote the study of ornithology in Nebraska by both professionals and amateurs; to publish the results of independent studies; and to promote the passage and enforcement of judicious laws for bird protection.
Publication(s): Nebraska Bird Review, The
Keyword(s): Wildlife & Species
Contact(s):
  Clem Klaphake, President
  Janice Paseka, Vice President
  Mark Brogie, Director; 508 Seeley, Box 316, Creighton, NE 68729; 402-358-5675
  Mitzi Fox, Secretary
  Mary Pritchard, Librarian; 6325 O St. #515, Lincoln, NE 68510-2246
  Jan Uttecht, Board of Directors

NEBRASKA WILDLIFE FEDERATION, INC.
P.O. Box 81437
Lincoln, NE 68501-1437 United States
Phone: 402-994-2001   Fax: 402-994-2021
E-mail: nebraskawildlife@alltel.net
Website: www.omaha.org/newf

Founded: 1970
Membership: 101–1,000
Scope: State
Description: A representative statewide organization, affiliated with the National Wildlife Federation, dedicated to the conservation of wildlife and its habitat through environmental education, fish and wildlife conservation, and common sense public policy.
Publication(s): Prairie Blade, Stream Conservation - quarterly newsletter
Keyword(s): Agriculture/Farming, Ecosystems (precious), Energy, Executive/Legislative/Judicial Reform, Finance/Banking/Trade, Land Issues, Population, Public Lands/Greenspace, Sprawl/Urban Planning, Water Habitats & Quality, Wildlife & Species
Contact(s):
  Gene Oglesby, President
  Duane Hovorka, Editor & Executive Director
  Mike Coe, Education Programs Contact
  David Koukol, Representative
  Galen Wray, Alternate Representative & Treasurer

NEGATIVE POPULATION GROWTH (NPG)
2861 Duke St. #36
Alexandria, VA 22314 United States
Phone: 703-370-9510   Fax: 703-370-9514
E-mail: npg@npg.org
Website: www.npg.org

Founded: 1972
Membership: 10,001–100,000
Scope: Local, State, Regional, National, International
Description: NPG is a national nonprofit organization founded in 1972 to educate the American public and political leaders about the detrimental effects of overpopulation on our environment, resources, and quality of life.
Publication(s): Forum Series, state population reports, Population and Resource Outlook
Keyword(s): Air Quality/Atmosphere, Ecosystems (precious), Forests/Forestry, Land Issues, Oceans/Coasts/Beaches, Pollution (general), Population, Public Lands/Greenspace, Sprawl/Urban Planning, Water Habitats & Quality, Wildlife & Species

NEVADA ASSOCIATION OF CONSERVATION DISTRICTS
Attn: President
2002 Idaho St.
Elko, NV 89810 United States
Phone: 775-738-8431, ext. 11   Fax: 775-738-7229
Membership: 101–1,000
Scope: Local
Contact(s):
  Patsy Tomera, President, Alternative Board Member; Attn: President, HC 65 Box 11, Carlin, NV 89822-9701; 775-754-2333
  Eleanor O'Donnell, Executive Director; 775-738-8431; Fax: 775-738-7229
  Joe Sicking, Board Member; 1550 Cushman Rd., Fallon, NV 89406; 775-423-5216; Fax: 775-738-7229

NEVADA WILDLIFE FEDERATION, INC.
P.O. Box 71238
Reno, NV 89570 United States
Phone: 702-253-0104   Fax: 775-677-0927
E-mail: nvwf@nvwf.org
Website: www.nvwf.org

Scope: State
Description: A representative statewide organization, affiliated with the National Wildlife Federation, dedicated to the protection and enhancement of wildlife and its habitat through public education and government interaction.
Publication(s): Nevada Wildlife

NEVIS HISTORICAL AND CONSERVATION SOCIETY
P.O. Box 563
Charlestown, 99999 St. Kitts and Nevis
Phone: 8694695786   Fax: 8694690274
E-mail: nhcs@caribsurf.com
Website: www.nevis-nhcs.org

Founded: 1980
Membership: 101–1,000
Scope: National
Description: To foster the conservation of the natural, historic, and cultural aspects of Nevis and its surrounding waters by educational programs, publishing projects, and other awareness endeavors.
Keyword(s): Development/Developing Countries, Ethics/Environmental Justice, Oceans/Coasts/Beaches, Public Lands/Greenspace, Recreation/Ecotourism, Reduce/Reuse/Recycle
Contact(s):
  David Robinson, President; 869-469-2117; Fax: 469-0274; drobinson@nevis-nhcs.org
  Clara Walters, Vice President; 869-469-2289
  Suzanne Gordon, Secretary; 869-469-1093; limehill@caribsurf.com
  Kay Loomis, Treasurer; 869-469-5752

NEW BRUNSWICK WILDLIFE FEDERATION
P.O. Box 20211
Fredericton, E3B 7A2 New Brunswick Canada
Phone: 888-272-6411   Fax: 506-458-9941
E-mail: nbwf1@nbnet.nb.ca
Website: www.wildlife.nb.ca/

Founded: 1924
Membership: 1,001–10,000
Scope: Province
Description: Promotes the wise use of renewable natural resources, with prime emphasis on education of the young. Affiliated with the Canadian Wildlife Federation.
Keyword(s): Forests/Forestry, Wildlife & Species
Contact(s):
  Sharon Kingston Eldridge, President; 1-88-272-6411; nbwf1@nbnet.nb.ca

NEW ENGLAND ASSOCIATION OF ENVIRONMENTAL BIOLOGISTS (NEAEB)
60 Westview St.
Lexington, MA 2173 United States
Phone: 617-860-4300

Founded: 1976

Scope: Regional

Description: A professional society of environmental scientists, engineers and planners from industry and state and federal agencies in the northeast, working to coordinate and enhance environmental programs in each state. The organization advances technical information on environmental research, planning and management and evaluates the effectiveness of environmental regulations for protection of water quality.

Contact(s):
David McDonald, Information Officer; EPA 60 Westview St., Lexington, MA 02421; 781-860-4609
Ernest Pizzuto, Executive Committee

NEW ENGLAND COALITION FOR SUSTAINABLE POPULATION (NECSP)
P.O. Box 903
Williamsburg, MA 01096 United States
Phone: 603-847-9798
E-mail: d9cat@cheshire.net
Website: cheshire.net/~dcat/necsp.html

Founded: 1996

Scope: Regional

Description: NECSP is a network of organizations and individuals committed to achieving a sustainable human population at the local, state, regional, national and global levels.

Publication(s): NECSP News (quarterly newsletter)

Keyword(s): Population, Reduce/Reuse/Recycle

Contact(s):
Annie Faulkner, Coordinator

NEW ENGLAND INTERSTATE WATER POLLUTION CONTROL COMMISSION
Boott Mills South, 100 Foot of John St.
Lowell, MA 01852-1124 United States
Phone: 978-323-7929   Fax: 978-323-7919
E-mail: mail@neiwpcc.org
Website: www.neiwpcc.org

Founded: 1947

Scope: Regional

Description: The Commission provides a forum for interstate communication on high priority water-related environmental issues; provides training opportunities for state environmental staff and wastewater treatment plant operators; and provides the public with outreach and training materials on a wide range of environmental issues.

Publication(s): NEIWPCC Resource Catalog, Annual Report, NEIWPCC Training Catalog, LUSTLine, Interstate Water Report

Keyword(s): Oceans/Coasts/Beaches, Pollution (general), Water Habitats & Quality

Contact(s):
Ronald Poltak, Executive Director; 978-323-7929; Fax: 978-323-7919; rpoltak@neiwpcc.org
Susan Sullivan, Deputy Director; 978-323-7929; Fax: 978-323-7919; ssullivan@neiwpcc.org
Beth Card, Director of Water Quality Programs; 978-323-7929; Fax: 978-323-7919; bcard@neiwpcc.org
Tom Groves, Director of Wastewater and on-site Programs; 978-323-7929; Fax: 978-323-7919; tgroves@neiwpcc.org
Denise Springborg, Director of Drinking Water Programs; 978-323-7929; Fax: 978-323-7919; dspringborg@neiwpcc.org

NEW ENGLAND NATURAL RESOURCES CENTER
Box 44
Wayland, MA 01778 United States
Phone: 508-358-2261   Fax: 508-358-2261
E-mail: hagenstein@aol.com

Founded: 1970

Membership: 1–100

Scope: Regional

Description: A nonprofit trust organized to provide a focal point for discussion and resolution of regional natural resource and environmental issues.

Keyword(s): Reduce/Reuse/Recycle

Contact(s):
Russell Brenneman, Vice Chairman; Murtha, Cullina, Richter & Pinney, 101 Pearl St., Hartford, CT 06102
Robert Eisenmenger, Treasurer
Perry Hagenstein, Chairman; Box 44, Wayland, MA 01778

NEW ENGLAND WILD FLOWER SOCIETY, INC.
NEWFS
180 Hemenway Rd.
Framingham, MA 01701-2699 United States
Phone: 508-877-7630   Fax: 508-877-3658
E-mail: newfs@newfs.org
Website: www.newfs.org

Founded: 1900

Membership: 1,001–10,000

Scope: Regional

Description: The New England Wild Flower Society is a nonprofit organization that promotes the conservation of temperate North American plants through education, research, horticulture, habitat preservation, and advocacy.

Publication(s): Online bookstore, New England Wild Flower - Conservation Notes, Journal and Program Events Catalog

Keyword(s): Agriculture/Farming, Land Issues, Public Lands/Greenspace, Wildlife & Species

NEW HAMPSHIRE ASSOCIATION OF CONSERVATION COMMISSIONS
54 Portsmouth St.
Concord, NH 03301 United States
Phone: 603-224-7867   Fax: 603-228-0423
E-mail: info@nhacc.org
Website: www.nhacc.org

Founded: 1970

Scope: State

Description: A nonprofit organization of municipal conservation commissions whose purpose is to foster conservation and appropriate use of New Hampshire's natural resources by providing assistance to conservation commissions, facilitating communication and cooperation among commissions, and helping to create a climate in which commissions can be successful.

Publication(s): Handbook for New Hampshire Conservation Commission, New Hampshire Commission News, Conservation News Bulletin

Keyword(s): Forests/Forestry, Land Issues, Public Lands/Greenspace, Sprawl/Urban Planning, Water Habitats & Quality, Wildlife & Species

Contact(s):
Marjory Swope, Executive Director; 603-224-7867; Fax: 603-228-0423; info@nhacc.org

NEW HAMPSHIRE ASSOCIATION OF CONSERVATION DISTRICTS
NHACD
P.O. Box 2311
Concord, NH 03302-2311 United States
Phone: 603-796-2615   Fax: 603-796-2600
E-mail: mtrembla@tds.net
Website: www.nhacd.org

Founded: 1946

Scope: Local, State, National

Description: Since 1946, the New Hampshire Association of Conservation Districts has provided statewide coordination, representation, and leadership for Conservation Districts to conserve, protect, and promote responsible use of New Hampshire's natural resources.

Keyword(s): Agriculture/Farming, Forests/Forestry, Land Issues, Oceans/Coasts/Beaches, Pollution (general), Public Lands/Greenspace, Recreation/Ecotourism, Sprawl/Urban Planning, Water Habitats & Quality, Wildlife & Species

Contact(s):
Calvin Perkins, President; 68 Isaac Perkins Rd., Lyme, NH 03768
Robert Goodrich, 1st Vice President; 321 Portsmouth Av, Stratham, NH 03885
Stanley Grimes, 2nd Vice President; 529 Buck St., Pembroke, NH 03275
Michele Tremblay, Executive Director; P.O. Box 3019, Boscawen, NH 03303; 603-796-2615; Fax: 603-796-2600
Stanely Grimes, Secretary and Treasurer; 529 Buck St., Pembroke, NH 03275; 603-485-9326; Fax: 603-233-6030
John Hodsdon, Board Member; 85 Daniel Webster Hwy, Meredith, NH 03253; 603-279-6126; Fax: 603-528-8783
Joan Richardson, Administrator; 73 Main St., P.O. Box 533, Conway, NH 03818-0533; 603-447-2771; Fax: 603-447-8945

NEW HAMPSHIRE BASS FEDERATION
Attn: President, P.O. Box 282
Wolfeboro, NH 03894 United States
Phone: 603-569-6035
Website: www.nhbassfederation.com

Scope: State

Description: An organization of Bassmaster chapters, affiliated with the Bass Anglers Sportsman Society, organized to fight pollution, assist state and national conservation agencies in their efforts, and teach the young people of our country good conservation practices. Dedicated to the realistic conservation of our water resources.

Contact(s):
Doug Plasencia, President; 603-569-6035
A. Disilva, Conservation Director; P.O. Box 923, North Conway, NH 03860; 603-356-2220

NEW HAMPSHIRE LAKES ASSOCIATION
5 South State St.
Concord, NH 03301 United States
Phone: 603-226-0299   Fax: 603-224-9442
E-mail: info@nhlakes.org
Website: www.nhlakes.org

Founded: 1992

Membership: 101–1,000

Scope: State

Description: The New Hampshire Lakes Association is a nonprofit, state-wide, member-supported education and advocacy organization dedicated to protecting New Hampshire's lakes and ponds. NHLA addresses lake issues such as appropriate public access, balanced use, improved water quality, prevention of exotic aquatic species, boater safety education, and wildlife habitat protection.

Contact(s):
Nancy Christie, President; 603-226-0299; Fax: 603-224-9442; nchristie@nhlakes.org

NEW HAMPSHIRE TIMBERLAND OWNERS ASSOCIATION
54 Portsmouth St.
Concord, NH 03301 United States
Phone: 603-224-9699   Fax: 603-225-5898
E-mail: info@nhtoa.org
Website: www.nhtoa.org

Founded: 1911

Membership: 1,001–10,000

Scope: Local, National

Description: A statewide organization dedicated to the promotion of wise forest management and the protection of forestry interests in New Hampshire.

Publication(s): The Forest Bulletin, The Forest Fax, The Timber Crier

Keyword(s): Forests/Forestry

Contact(s):
Bruce Jacobs, President
Hunter Carbee, Program Director; hcarbee@nhtoa.org
Jasen Stock, Executive Director; 603-224-9699; Fax: 603-225-5898; jstock@nhtoa.org
Eric Darbe, Communications Director; edarbe@nhtoa.org
Tim Frizzell, Treasurer
Don Winsor, Secretary

NEW HAMPSHIRE WILDLIFE FEDERATION
54 Portsmouth St.
Concord, NH 03301 United States
Phone: 603-224-5953
E-mail: nhwf@aol.com
Website: www.nhwf.org

Membership: 1,001–10,000

Scope: State

Description: A representative statewide organization, affiliated with the National Wildlife Federation, dedicated to the protection and enhancement of wildlife and its habitat through public education and government interaction.

Publication(s): New Hampshire Wildlife

Contact(s):
Sharon Guaraldi, President
Mary Brown, Executive Director
Russ Kott, Alternate Representative
Margaret Lane, Editor
John Monson, Representative

NEW JERSEY AGRICULTURAL SOCIETY
P.O. Box 331
Trenton, NJ 08625 United States
Phone: 609-394-7766   Fax: 609-292-3978
Website: www.state.nj.us/agriculture/agsociety

Founded: 1781

Membership: 101–1,000

Scope: Regional

Description: The Society has continually worked to educate the public and promote agriculture in New Jersey. The Society is charitable, nonprofit, and conducts numerous educational programs about agriculture's vital role in the economy of New Jersey.

Publication(s): Harbinger, Garden View

Keyword(s): Agriculture/Farming

Contact(s):
Pam Mount, President
Richard Nieuwenhuis, Vice President
Arthur Brown, Secretary and Treasurer
Joni Elliott, Editor
Terry Haaf, Assistant Secretary and Treasurer

NEW JERSEY ASSOCIATION OF CONSERVATION DISTRICTS
P.O. Box 330
Trenton, NJ 8625 United States
Phone: 973-398-2511 Fax: 973-398-2511
E-mail: clifford-lundin@nj.nacdnet.org

Founded: 1955
Membership: 1–100
Scope: State

Description: Represents New Jersey's 16 Soil Conservation Districts and 80 soil conservation supervisors

Keyword(s): Agriculture/Farming, Development/Developing Countries, Executive/Legislative/Judicial Reform, Forests/Forestry, Land Issues

Contact(s):
Clifford Lundin, President; 8 Skytop Rd., Andover, NJ 07821; 973-398-2511
Kenneth Marsh, 1st Vice President; 534 Hanford Place, Westfield, NJ 07909; 908-233-4528
Allen Carter, Treasurer; P.O. Box 403, Tuckahoe, NJ 08250; 609-628-2466
Edward Dipolvere, Secretary, Alternative Board Member; 53 Cubberly Rd., Trenton, NJ 08690; 609-586-2684
Jay Kandle, Past President; 609-589-7916
Kenneth Roehrich, Board Member; 451 Schooley's Mountain Rd., Hackettstown, NJ 07840; 908-852-5787

NEW JERSEY BASS FEDERATION
Attn: President, 77 Kenvil Ave.
Succasunna, NJ 07876 United States
Phone: 973-584-9387
E-mail: amgoing@bellatlantic.net
Website: www.njbassfed.org
Membership: 101–1,000
Scope: International

Description: An organization of Bassmaster chapters, affiliated with the Bass Anglers Sportsman Society, organized to fight pollution, assist state and national conservation agencies in their efforts, and teach the young people of our country good conservation practices. Dedicated to the realistic conservation of our water resources.

Publication(s): Reel to Reel, Fishing Line

Contact(s):
Tony Going, President; 973-584-9387
John Carlone, Conservation Director; 402 Ames Rd., Highland Lakes, NJ 07422; 973-764-9723

NEW JERSEY CONSERVATION FOUNDATION
170 Longview Rd.
Far Hills, NJ 07931 United States
Phone: 908-234-1225 Fax: 908-234-1189
E-mail: info@njconservation.org
Website: www.njconservation.org

Founded: 1900
Membership: 1,001–10,000
Scope: Local, State, Regional

Description: A nonprofit organization founded in 1960, the mission of New Jersey Conservation Foundation is to preserve New Jersey's land and natural resources for the benefit of all. As a leading innovator and catalyst for saving land, New Jersey Conservation Foundation: protects strategic lands through acquisition and stewardship; promotes strong land use policies; and forges partnerships to achieve conservation goals.

Publication(s): Charting a Course for the Delaware Bay Watershed, Greenways to the Arthurkill, New Jersey Conservation, New Jersey Highlands, The: Treasures at risk

Keyword(s): Agriculture/Farming, Development/Developing Countries, Forests/Forestry, Land Issues, Public Lands/Greenspace, Sprawl/Urban Planning, Water Habitats & Quality, Wildlife & Species

NEW JERSEY ENVIRONMENTAL LOBBY
204 W. State St.
Trenton, NJ 08608 United States
Phone: 609-396-3774 Fax: 609-396-4521
Website: www.njenvironment.org

Founded: 1969
Scope: State

Description: To advocate for legislation and regulation that is protective and preservative of both the natural and the built environment with a view, always, of protecting human health for all citizens and future generations. Conversely, we oppose those laws and regulations that are detrimental to the above.

Publication(s): NJ Environmental Lobby News, periodic special reports

Keyword(s): Air Quality/Atmosphere, Development/Developing Countries, Energy, Land Issues, Transportation

Contact(s):
Anne Poole, President; 43 Four Mile Rd., Pemberton, NJ 08068, 609-894-4113; newpoole@bellatlantic.net
Eileen Hogan, Vice President; 96 Briarcliff Rd., Mountain Lakes, NJ 07046; 973-267-6100
Mark Herzberg, Treasurer; 24 Clinton Pl., Metuchen, NJ 08840; 908-494-4883, mherzb8468@aol.com

NEW JERSEY FORESTRY ASSOCIATION
P.O. Box 130
Milmay, NJ 08340 United States
Phone: 856-696-5300 Fax: 856-205-0009
Website: www.njforestry.org

Founded: 1975
Scope: State

Description: A statewide organization affiliated with the National Woodland Owners Association. Formed to encourage the scientific management and perpetuation of woodlands in New Jersey.

Publication(s): New Jersey Woodlands
Keyword(s): Forests/Forestry

Contact(s):
Thomas Bullock, President; 609-696-5300
Tracy Cate, Vice President; 609-737-0489
Richard Conley, Executive Secretary and Editor
Thomas Niederer, Treasurer
Richard West, Editor

NEW MEXICO ASSOCIATION OF CONSERVATION DISTRICTS
163 Trail Canyon Rd.
Carlsbad, NM 88220 United States
Phone: 505-981-2400 Fax: 505-981-2422
E-mail: nmacd@dellcity.com
Website: www.nm.nacdnet.org
Membership: 1–100
Scope: State

Contact(s):
Brian Greene, President; Rt. 1 Box 22, Mountainair, NM 87036; 505-849-1080; Fax: 505-847-0615
Leedrue Hyatt, Vice President; 8410 Flying U Rd., NE, Deming, NM 88030; 505-546-9694; Fax: 505-546-3265
Debbie Hughes, Executive Director; 163 Trail Canyon Rd., Carlsbad, NM 88220; 505-981-2400; Fax. 505-981-2422
Eddie Vigil, Secretary Treasurer

NEW MEXICO ENVIRONMENTAL LAW CENTER
1405 Luisa St., Suite 5
Santa Fe, NM 87505 United States
Phone: 505-989-9022 Fax: 505-989-3769
E-mail: nmelc@nmelc.org
Website: nmenvirolaw.org

Founded: 1987
Membership: 101–1,000

Scope: State

Description: The New Mexico Environmental Law Center is a nonprofit, public interest law firm. The Law Center is the only New Mexico organization that provides free and at-cost legal services for the preservation of the state's natural resources and protection of citizens against environmental hazards. The Law Center represents grassroots organizations, individuals, and environmental groups in site-specific efforts; participates in statewide and federal legislative advocacy; and provides public education.

Publication(s): The Green Fire Report

Keyword(s): Air Quality/Atmosphere, Energy, Ethics/Environmental Justice, Land Issues, Public Health, Public Lands/Greenspace

Contact(s):
Douglas Meiklejohn, Executive Director

NEW YORK ASSOCIATION OF CONSERVATION DISTRICTS, INC.
Attn: President, 104 Edwards Ave.
Calberton, NY 11933 United States
Phone: 631-727-3777   Fax: 631-727-3721
Website: www.agmkt.state.ny.us/soilwater/intro.asp#www.agmkt.stats.ny.us/soilwater/intro.asp

Scope: State

Contact(s):
Joe Gerdela, President; P.O. Box 341, Center Moriches, NY 11934; 631-727-3777
Anita Cartin, Executive Vice President; 1 Winners Cir., Albany, NY 12235; 518-457-7229; Fax: 518-457-2716
William Chamberlain, Treasurer; Box 487, Henderson Harbor, NY 13651; 315-938-7106
Carl Seymour, Secretary; 242 Grange Hall Rd., Schuylerville, NY 12871; 518-695-9249

NEW YORK BASS FEDERATION
Attn: President, 177 Barmore Rd.
LaGrangeville, NY 12540 United States
Phone: 845-902-1204
E-mail: wayne@nybassfed.com
Website: www.nybassfed.com

Scope: State

Description: An organization of Bassmaster chapters, affiliated with the Bass Anglers Sportsman Society, organized to fight pollution, assist state and national conservation agencies in their efforts, and teach the young people of our country good conservation practices. Dedicated to the realistic conservation of our water resources.

Publication(s): Fishlines

Contact(s):
Wayne Tomassi, President; wayne@nybassfed.com
Bernie Haney, Conservation Director; 826 C Tamarack Dr., West Carthage, NY 13619; 315-493-2356; bernie@nybassfed.com

NEW YORK FOREST OWNERS ASSOCIATION, INC.
P.O. Box 1055
Penfield, NY 14526 United States
Phone: 585-377-6060   Fax: 585-388-7592
E-mail: nyfoainc@hotmail.com
Website: www.nyfoa.org

Founded: 1963
Membership: 1,001–10,000
Scope: State

Description: A statewide organization organized to unite the 500,000 owners of 11 million acres of forest land in New York in encouraging the wise management of private woodland resources in New York State by promoting, protecting, representing, and serving the interests of woodland owners.

Publication(s): Forest Owner

Keyword(s): Forests/Forestry

Contact(s):
Ronald Pederson, President; 518-785-6061
Deborah Gill, Administrator; 716-377-6060
Mary Malmsheimer, Editor; Desktop Solutions, 34 Lincklaen St., Cazenovia, NY 13035; 315-655-4110; Fax: 315-655-9694
Jerry Michael, Treasurer; 315-733-7391

NEW YORK PUBLIC INTEREST RESEARCH GROUP (NYPIRG)
NYPIRG
Main Office, 9 Murray St.,
3rd Fl.
New York, NY 10007 United States
Phone: 212-349-6460   Fax: 212-349-7474
E-mail: nypirg@nypirg.org
Website: www.nypirg.org

Founded: 1973
Membership: 10,001–100,000
Scope: Local, State

Description: The NYPIRG is a nonprofit, nonpartisan research group established and directed by New York state college students. Staff lawyers, researchers, and advocates work with students and other citizens developing citizenship skills and shaping public policy on environmental preservation, good government, and consumer issues.

Publication(s): Get the Lead Out, NYC CouncilWatch, NYPIRG Agenda

Keyword(s): Ethics/Environmental Justice, Pollution (general), Reduce/Reuse/Recycle, Transportation

NEW YORK TURTLE AND TORTOISE SOCIETY
P.O. Box 878
Orange, NJ 07051-0878 United States
Phone: 212-459-4803
E-mail: info@nytts.org
Website: www.nytts.org/

Founded: 1970
Scope: National

Description: The Society is dedicated to the conservation and preservation of habitat, and the promotion of proper husbandry and captive propagation of turtles. Education of members and the public is a key goal. Events held in the NYC area include a seminar, field trips, and show.

Publication(s): Plastron Papers, NewsNotes, NYTTS, Journal of the New York Turtle and Tortoise Society

Keyword(s): Wildlife & Species

Contact(s):
Suzanne Dohm, President
Allen Foust, Vice President
Lori Craner, Treasurer of Wildlife Rehabilitation
Rita Devine, Secretary
Joan Frumkies, Membership
Jim Van Abbemg, Editor of Proceedings

NEW YORK-NEW JERSEY TRAIL CONFERENCE INC.
NY-NJ Trail Conference
156 Ramapo Valley Road Route 202
Mahwah, NJ 07430 United States
Phone: 201-512-9348   Fax: 212-779-8102
E-mail: info@nynjtc.org
Website: www.nynjtc.org

Founded: 1920
Scope: Regional

Description: A nonprofit organization which coordinates the efforts of hiking and outdoor groups in New York and New Jersey to build and maintain over 1,300 miles of foot trails and whose purpose is to protect and conserve open space, wildlife, and places of natural beauty and interest.

Publication(s): Trail Walker, Delaware Water Gap National Recreation Area Hiking, Iron Mine Trails, Hiking the Catskills, Catskill Trails Map Set, Guide to the Long Path, Guide to the Appalachian Trail in New York and New Jersey, New Jersey Walk Book, New York Walk Book

Keyword(s): Land Issues, Public Lands/Greenspace, Recreation/Ecotourism

Contact(s):
Gary Haugland, President
Jane Daniels, Vice President
Daniel Chazin, Secretary
Gary Haughland, Chairman of Trails Council

NEWFOUNDLAND LABRADOR WILDLIFE FEDERATION
15 Conran Street
St. Johns, A1E 5L8 Newfoundland Canada
Phone: 709-364-8415   Fax: 709-753-4709
Membership: 10,001–100,000
Scope: International
Keyword(s): Air Quality/Atmosphere, Ethics/Environmental Justice, Forests/Forestry, Reduce/Reuse/Recycle, Water Habitats & Quality, Wildlife & Species

Contact(s):
Gordon Cooper, Vice President; 67 Commonwealth Ave., Mount Pearl, Newfoundland A1N 1W7; 709-368-6180
Clifford Head, Secretary; 49 Harnum Crescent, Mt. Pearl, Newfoundland A1N 1W7; 709-335-2226

NIPPON ECOLOGY NETWORK
Ecology Center Bldg., 3 Fukuromachi
Shinjukku-ku, Tokyo, 162 Japan
Phone: 81352283344   Fax: 81352286040
Website: www.venture-web.or.jp/ecoland
Scope: International
Description: NEN is currently involved in many aspects of environment, agriculture, and food safety issues. Among NEN operations are: Radish boya, an organic and natural food home delivery system servicing over 55,000 homes; the Japan Ecology Center, an information center; Atopikko Chikyu no ko, a network of medical advisors and the allergy afflicted; and the Tree Free Club, an organization that promotes the use of alternatives to tree-based papers and manages the Tree Free Fund.

Contact(s):
Michiaki Tokue, Chairman

NORTH AMERICAN ASSOCIATION FOR ENVIRONMENTAL EDUCATION
410 Tarvin Rd.
Rock Spring, GA 30739 United States
Phone: 706-764-2708   Fax: 706-764-2094
E-mail: email@naaee.org
Website: www.naaee.org
Founded: 1971
Scope: National
Description: NAAEE is dedicated to promoting environmental education and supporting the work of environmental educators in North America and around the world. NAAEE is made up of students and professionals who have thought seriously about how individuals become literate concerning environmental issues and about how to prepare people to work together towards resolving environmental problems.

Publication(s): NAAEE Directory of Environmental Educators, Annual Conference Proceedings, Environmental Communicator

Keyword(s): Reduce/Reuse/Recycle

Contact(s):
Judy Braus, President
Bonnie Shelton, Executive Director
James Elder, Treasurer

NORTH AMERICAN ASSOCIATION FOR ENVIRONMENTAL EDUCATION
CONFERENCE, PUBLICATIONS AND MEMBERSHIP OFFICE
410 Tarvin Rd.
Rock Spring, GA 30739 United States
Phone: 706-764-2926   Fax: 706-764-2094
Website: www.naaee.org
Membership: 1,001–10,000
Scope: International
Description: NAAEE is a network of people who practice and support environmental education. Our mission is to provide environmental educators with quality resources, training, publications, and networking opportunities to enable them to spread environmental knowledge.

Contact(s):
Barbara Eager, Acting Deputy Director
Connie Smith, Membership Development Services Manager
Sarah Gray, Conference & Publications Administrative Assistant

NORTH AMERICAN BEAR FEDERATION
3503 Hwy 89
South Livingston, MT 59047 United States
Phone: 406-333-4414   Fax: 406-333-9733
E-mail: nabear@nabear.org
Website: www.nabear.org
Membership: 1,001–10,000
Scope: National
Publication(s): Bear Bulletin - every other month, The Bear Facts

Contact(s):
Carl Brooke, President, Co-Founder; 406-333-4414

NORTH AMERICAN BENTHOLOGICAL SOCIETY
c/o Allen Marketing and Management, P.O. Box 1897
Lawrence, KS 66044-8897 United States
Website: www.benthos.org
Founded: 1953
Scope: National
Description: The Society is an international scientific organization whose purpose is to promote better understanding of the biotic communities of lake and stream bottoms and their role in aquatic ecosystems. The Society provides media for disseminating results of scientific investigations and other information to aquatic biologists and to the scientific community at large.

Publication(s): Current and Selected Bibliography of Benthic Biology, Bulletin of the North American Benthological Society, Journal of the North American Benthological Society

Keyword(s): Water Habitats & Quality, Wildlife & Species

Contact(s):
Nancy Grimm, President; 602-965-4735
Steve Canton, Editor; Chadwick and Associates Inc., 5575 S. Sycamore St., Suite 101, Littleton, CO 80120
Donna Giberson, Secretary; 902-566-0797
Kim Haag, Treasurer; 813-243-5800
David Rosenberg, Editor; Freshwater Institute, 501 University Crescent, Winnipeg, Manitoba R3T 2N6
Donald Webb, Editor; Illinois Natural History Survey, 607 E. Peabody St., Champaign, IL 61820

NORTH AMERICAN BLUEBIRD SOCIETY
The Wilderness Center
P.O. Box 244
Wilmot, OH 44689-0244 United States
Phone: 330-359-5511   Fax: 330-359-5455
E-mail: info@nabluebirdsociety.org
Website: www.nabluebirdsociety.org

Founded: 1978
Membership: 1,001–10,000
Scope: Local, State, Regional, National, International
Description: The North American Bluebird Society, a non-profit conservation, education and research organization, promotes the recovery of bluebirds and other native, cavity-nesting species. On-going research, educational material development, outreach initiatives through the NABS Speakers Bureau and a comprehensive website on bluebirding, address issues related to bluebirds and other native cavity-nesting bird species.
Publication(s): Transcontinental Bluebird Trail Program, Bluebird Educators Packet, Educational Bluebird Posters and Educational Slide Program, Stokes Bluebird Basics "10 Minute Introductory Video", Bluebird Magazine (formerly Sialia)
Keyword(s): Wildlife & Species
Contact(s):
Doug LeVasseur, President; emdlev@clover.net
Joan Harmet, Vice President; joandick@aeroinc.net
Arlene Ripley, Webmaster; webmaster@nabluebirdsociety.org
Bob Martin, Treasurer
Darlene Sillick, Secretary; azuretrails@columbus.rr.com
Jim Williams, Editor

NORTH AMERICAN BUTTERFLY ASSOCIATION
4 Delaware Rd.
Morristown, NJ 07960 United States
Phone: 973-285-0907   Fax: 973-285-0936
E-mail: naba@naba.org
Website: www.naba.org
Founded: 1993
Membership: 1,001–10,000
Scope: International
Description: NABA promotes public enjoyment and conservation of butterflies, encouraging non-consumption activities such as butterfly watching, gardening and photography.
Publication(s): NABA 4th of July Butterfly Count Report, Butterfly Gardener, American Butterflies, NABA Checklist and English Names of Butterflies
Keyword(s): Agriculture/Farming, Recreation/Ecotourism, Reduce/Reuse/Recycle, Wildlife & Species
Contact(s):
Jeffrey Glassberg, President
Ann Swengel, Vice-President
Jim Springer, Webmaster; springer@naba.org

NORTH AMERICAN COALITION ON RELIGION AND ECOLOGY (NACRE)
5 Thomas Cir., NW
Washington, DC 20005 United States
Phone: 202-462-2591   Fax: 202-462-6534
E-mail: nacre@earthlink.net
Website: www.caringforcreation.net
Founded: 1989
Membership: 1,001–10,000
Scope: National
Description: NACRE is an ecumenical and interfaith environmental organization designed to help the North American religious community enter into the environmental movement and to help environmental organizations and the wider society become aware and act upon these same ethical values.
Publication(s): ECO-Letter
Keyword(s): Reduce/Reuse/Recycle, Wildlife & Species
Contact(s):
Donald Conroy, President and CEO
Bruce Anderson, Chairman of the Board
Carolyn Gutowski, Secretary and Treasurer

NORTH AMERICAN CRANE WORKING GROUP
NACWG
341 W. Olympic Pl. Suite 300
Seattle, WA 98119-3719 United States
Phone: 206-286-8607
E-mail: thoffmann@hoffmanns.com
Website: www.nacwg.org
Founded: 1988
Membership: 101–1,000
Scope: International
Description: An organization of professional biologists, aviculturists, land managers, and other interested individuals dedicated to the conservation of cranes and their habitats in North America.
Publication(s): Workshop Proceedings, Unison Call, The
Keyword(s): Water Habitats & Quality, Wildlife & Species
Contact(s):
Thomas Hoffmann, Treasurer; 206-286-8607; thoffmann@hoffmanns.com

NORTH AMERICAN FALCONERS ASSOCIATION
559 Fuller Road
Chicopee, MA 01020 United States
Phone: 4135925696
Website: www.n-a-f-a.org
Founded: 1962
Scope: International
Description: A nonprofit fraternal organization with the following purposes: improve and encourage competency in the practice of falconry; urge recognition of falconry as a legal field sport; and promote scientific study, conservation, and welfare of birds of prey with an appreciation of their value in nature.
Publication(s): Journal (annual), Hawk Chalk (quarterly)
Keyword(s): Recreation/Ecotourism, Reduce/Reuse/Recycle, Wildlife & Species

NORTH AMERICAN GAMEBIRD ASSOCIATION, INC.
1214 Brooks Ave.
Raleigh, NC 27607 United States
Phone: 919-782-6758   Fax: 919-515-7070
E-mail: gamebird@naga.org
Website: www.naga.org
Founded: 1932
Scope: National
Description: To promote educational work and develop interest in game bird breeding and hunting preserves (nonprofit); to afford a means of cooperation with the federal and state governments in all matters of concern to the industry; and to encourage study of the sciences connected with the live production, preparation for markets, and marketing of game bird eggs and game birds.
Publication(s): Membership Directory, Wildlife Harvest Magazine, List of Hunting Resort Members, Game Bird Propagation Book
Keyword(s): Recreation/Ecotourism, Wildlife & Species
Contact(s):
Royd Hatt, President; Box 134, Green River, UT 84525; 801-564-3224
Gary Davis, Executive Director; 1214 Brooks Ave., Raleigh, NC 27607; 919-782-6758

NORTH AMERICAN LOON FUND
6 Lily Pond Rd.
Gilford, NH 32460 United States
Phone: 989-772-9611
Website: facstaff.uww.edu/wentzl/nalf/aNALFhomepage.html
Founded: 1979
Scope: National

Description: A nonprofit organization established to sponsor loon conservation, public education, and scientific research projects across the U.S. and Canada. Sponsors annual grant program, and organizes annual research conference.
Publication(s): Annotated Bibliography of the Loons, Gaviidae, educational poster and resource directory, educational poster and resource directory, Loon Call Newsletter
Keyword(s): Water Habitats & Quality, Wildlife & Species
Contact(s):
Linda Obara, Executive Director
Ellen Barth, Treasurer
Jordan Prouty, Chairman
Guy Swenson, Clerk

NORTH AMERICAN MEMBERSHIP GROUP
NORTH AMERICAN FISHING CLUB
12301 Whitewater Dr.
Minnetonka, MN 55343 United States
Phone: 952-936-9333   Fax: 952-936-9755
E-mail: mail@namginc.com
Website: www.namginc.com
Founded: 1978
Membership: 1,000,001 +
Scope: International
Description: The North American Fishing Club is a membership organization dedicated to enhancing the fishing skills and enjoyment of anglers. The NAFC is the largest association of multi-species anglers in North America.
Publication(s): North American Fisherman
Keyword(s): Recreation/Ecotourism, Water Habitats & Quality, Wildlife & Species
Contact(s):
Nancy Evensen, President
Steve Pennaz, Executive Director

NORTH AMERICAN NATIVE FISHES ASSOCIATION
1107 Argonne Dr
Baltimore, MD 21218 United States
Phone: 410-243-9050
E-mail: nanfa@att.net
Website: www.nanfa.org
Founded: 1972
Membership: 101–1,000
Scope: State, Regional, National
Description: Membership includes ichthyologists, students, sportsmen, amateur naturalists, and aquarists who seek to promote the study, research, and conservation of North American native fishes. Goals are to promote the restoration and protection of habitat and to distribute information about native fishes.
Publication(s): American Currents Magazine
Keyword(s): Water Habitats & Quality, Wildlife & Species
Contact(s):
Bruce Stallsmith, President; 8200 Hickory Hill Lane, Huntsville, AL 35802; 256-882-9919; fundulus@hotmail.com
Rob Denkhaus, Vice President; Forth Worth Nature Center and Reserve, 9601 Fossil Ridge Rd, Fort Worth, TX 76135; 817-237-1111; Robert.Denkhaus@fortworthgov.org
D. Martin Moore, Secretary; 155 David Henderson Rd., Penahatchie, MS 39145; 601-546-2320; archimed@netdoor.com
Stephanie Scharpf, Treasurer; 1107 Argonne Dr., Baltimore, MD 21218; 410-243-9050; ichthos@charm.net

NORTH AMERICAN WILDLIFE PARK FOUNDATION, INC.
WOLF PARK
4004 E 800 N.
Battle Ground, IN 47920 United States
Phone: 765-567-2265   Fax: 765-567-4299
E-mail: wolfpark@wolfpark.org
Website: www.wolfpark.org
Founded: 1972
Membership: 1,001–10,000
Scope: International
Description: A nonprofit organization which features socialized wolves, coyote, foxes and bison; provides continuous behavior research programs; offers lectures and a teaching program, as well as four Wolf Behavior seminars per year; monitors legislation on predators; and provides research opportunities for scientists and students.
Publication(s): Wolf ! Magazine, Wolf Park News
Keyword(s): Wildlife & Species
Contact(s):
Erich Klinghammer, Director

NORTH AMERICAN WOLF ASSOCIATION
23214 Tree Bright Lane
Spring, TX 77373 United States
Phone: 281-821-4439   Fax: 281-821-4417
E-mail: nawa@nawa.org
Website: www.nawa.org
Founded: 1993
Membership: 10,001–100,000
Scope: Local, State, Regional, National, International
Description: NAWA is a nonprofit organization dedicated to natural wolf recovery, rescue, preservation and education. Produces educational materials/programs (all age levels), an electronic newsletter (includes news of wolves and wolf-related issues internationally), lectures in universities, colleges & schools in addition to comprehensive workshops, wolf ambassador programs and an Adopt-A-Wolf program. NAWA is highly focused on the plight of captive wolves and the epidemic of wolfdog breeding.
Publication(s): Yearly summaries, publications on web, NAWA News (newsletter)
Keyword(s): Ecosystems (precious), Ethics/Environmental Justice, Wildlife & Species
Contact(s):
Rae Evening Earth Ott, Director; 281-821-4439; Fax: 281-821-4417; nawa@nawa.org
Tina Hart, Assistant Director; 281-821-4439; Fax: 281-821-4417; tina@nawa.org
Eric Schweig, International Celebrity Spokesperson

NORTH ATLANTIC SALMON CONSERVATION ORGANIZATION
11 Rutland Square
Edinburgh, EH1 2AS United Kingdom
Phone: 1312282551   Fax: 1312284384
E-mail: hq@nasco.int
Website: www.nasco.int
Founded: 1984
Scope: International
Description: NASCO is an intergovernmental treaty organization established to contribute to the conservation, restoration, enhancement, and rational management of salmon stocks in the North Atlantic Ocean through international cooperation. The member parties are: Canada, Denmark (in respect to the Faroe Islands and Greenland), the European Union, Iceland, Norway, the Russian Federation, and the USA.
Keyword(s): Air Quality/Atmosphere, Climate Change, Wildlife & Species
Contact(s):
M.I. Windsor, Secretary

NORTH CAROLINA ASSOCIATION OF SOIL AND WATER CONSERVATION DISTRICTS
512 N. Salisbury St.
1614 Mail Service Center, Raleigh, NC 27699
Raleigh, NC 27604 United States
Phone: 919-733-2302   Fax: 919-715-3559
Website: www.enr.state.nc.us

Scope: State
Contact(s):
  David Vogel, Director; 919-715-6097; david.vogel@ncmail.net

NORTH CAROLINA BASS FEDERATION
Attn: President, 403 Red Wood Ct.
Lenoir, NC 28645 United States
Phone: 828-728-8550   Fax: 828-728-8549
Website: www.ncbass.com

Membership: 1,001–10,000
Scope: State
Description: An organization of Bassmaster chapters, affiliated with the Bass Anglers Sportsman Society, organized to fight pollution, assist state and national conservation agencies in their efforts and teach the young people of our country good conservation practices. Dedicated to the realistic conservation of our water resources.

Contact(s):
  Ed Cannon, President; 828-728-8550
  Randy Lee, Conservation Director; 1730 Allens Crossroads Road, Four Oaks, NC 27524; SmTrp19@aol.com

NORTH CAROLINA BEACH BUGGY ASSOCIATION, INC.
Box 940
Manteo, NC 27954 United States
Phone: 252-473-4880
E-mail: ncbba@simflex.com
Website: www.ncbba.org

Founded: 1964
Membership: 1,001–10,000
Scope: National
Description: NCBBA is an organization dedicated to preserving natural resources and coastal areas of North Carolina. Its purpose is to unite in an organization all persons interested in the natural beach resources of the Outer Banks of North Carolina and elsewhere, and establish a Code of Ethics of beach behavior to which each member must subscribe to uphold.

Publication(s): NCBBA News, The
Keyword(s): Oceans/Coasts/Beaches, Recreation/Ecotourism, Wildlife & Species

Contact(s):
  W. Keene, President; 23134 Homestead Lane, Franklin, VA 23851; 757-562-2554
  David Flanigan, Vice President; 1337 Whisper Drive, Virginia Beach, VA 23454; 757-481-1250; jflaniga@hampton-roads.com
  John Newbold, Editor; 2515 S. Pilot Lane, Nags Head, NC 27949; 252-480-2453; fishnfools@beachlink.com
  Sharon Newbold, Secretary; 2515 S. Pilot Lane, Nags Head, NC 27949; 252-480-2453; fishnfools@beachlink.com
  Brenda Outlaw, Treasurer; P.O. Box 940, Manteo, NC 27954; 252-473-4880; brendaoutlaw@hotmail.com

NORTH CAROLINA COASTAL FEDERATION, INC.
Attn: Sheila Broadnick, 3609 Highway 24 (Ocean)
Newport, NC 28570 United States
Phone: 252-393-8185   Fax: 252-393-7508
E-mail: nccf@nccoast.org
Website: www.nccoast.org

Founded: 1982
Membership: 1,001–10,000
Scope: Local, State, Regional
Description: The Coastal Federation focuses on the twenty coastal counties in North Carolina, with citizens working together for a healthy coast..
Publication(s): State of Coast Report, Coastal Review, Annual Report, Newsletter, Alternative to Shoreline Erosion Control magazine
Keyword(s): Ecosystems (precious), Land Issues, Oceans/Coasts/Beaches, Water Habitats & Quality

Contact(s):
  Kathleen McEvoy, Director of Education; 252-393-8185; ext. 38; Fax: 252-393-7508; kmcevoy@nccoast.org
  Todd Miller, Executive Director; 252-393-8185; ext. 25; Fax: 252-393-7508; toddm@nccoast.org
  Sally Steele, Director of Development; ext. 28; sallys@nccoast.org

NORTH CAROLINA CONSERVATION NETWORK
112 South Blunt Street
Raleigh, NC 27601 United States
Phone: 919-857-4699
E-mail: info@ncconnet.org
Website: www.ncconnet.org

Founded: 1999
Membership: 101–1,000
Scope: State
Description: NC ConNet is an environmental nonprofit organization that deals primarily with strengthening and uniting other grassroots organizations within the state through a variety of services and tools.
Keyword(s): Air Quality/Atmosphere, Energy, Ethics/Environmental Justice, Forests/Forestry, Land Issues, Oceans/Coasts/Beaches, Pollution (general), Public Health, Public Lands/Greenspace, Sprawl/Urban Planning, Transportation, Water Habitats & Quality, Wildlife & Species

Contact(s):
  Brian Buzby, Executive Director
  Mindy Hiteshue, Administrative Associate
  Robert Matthews, Director of Development
  Grady McCallie, Environmental Liaison
  Heather Yandow, Outreach Coordinator

NORTH CAROLINA FORESTRY ASSOCIATION (NCFA)
1600 Glenwood Ave
Suite I
Raleigh, NC 27608 United States
Phone: 919-834-3943   Fax: 919-832-6188
E-mail: cbrown@ncforestry.org
Website: www.ncforestry.org

Founded: 1911
Membership: 1,001–10,000
Scope: State
Description: The NCFA is North Carolina's oldest forest conservation group. The NCFA is a private, non-profit organization comprised of over 2,700 forest managers, landowners, mill operators, loggers, furniture manufacturers and educators.
Keyword(s): Forests/Forestry

Contact(s):
  Chris Brown, Director of Communications; 919-834-3943; Fax: 919-832-6188; cbrown@ncforestry.org
  Bob Slocum, Executive Vice President; 919-834-3943; Fax: 919-832-6188; rwslocum@ncforestry.org

NORTH CAROLINA MUSEUM OF NATURAL SCIENCES
11 W. Jones
Raleigh, NC United States
Phone: 877-462-8724
Website: www.naturalsciences.org

Founded: 1978

Scope: State

Description: A nonprofit group formed to promote an interest in and to educate members and the general public concerning the ecological importance and conservation of reptiles and amphibians.

Publication(s): NC HERPS

Keyword(s): Wildlife & Species

Contact(s):
　Tom Thorp, President; 804-261-8230; tt-threelakes@juno.com
　Dan Lockwood, Vice President; 112 E. Skyhawk Dr., Cary, NC 27513; 919-460-3504; ddlockwood@email.msn.com
　Jeff Beane, Editor; 4433 Graham Newton Rd., Raleigh, NC 27606; 919-733-7450; ext. 754; jeff_beane@mail.enr.state.nc.us
　Alvin Braswell, Advisor; 1208 Buffaloe Rd., Garner, NC 27529; 919-733-7450; ext. 751; alvin_braswell@mail.enr.state.nc.us
　Dan Dombrowski, Treasurer; NC State Museum of Natural Sciences, P.O. Box 29555, Raleigh, NC 27626-0555; 919-733-7450; ext. 504; dan_dombrowski@mail.enr.state.nc.us
　Joe Zawadowski, Secretary; 503 Valley Dr., Durham, NC 27704; 919-684-6062; Joe_Zawadowski@bba.mc.duke.edu

NORTH CAROLINA RECREATION AND PARK SOCIETY, INC.
883 Washington St.
Raleigh, NC 27605 United States
Phone: 919-832-5868　　　Fax: 919-832-3323
E-mail: ncrps@bellsouth.net
Website: www.ncrps.org

Founded: 1944

Scope: State

Description: A nonprofit organization formed to promote the wise use of leisure and intelligent development of the state's recreation resources. An affiliate of The National Recreation and Park Association.

Publication(s): North Carolina Recreation and Park Review, NCRPS News

Keyword(s): Land Issues, Public Lands/Greenspace, Recreation/Ecotourism

Contact(s):
　Phil Rea, President; NC State University, P.O. Box 8004, Raleigh, NC 27695; 919-515-3675; Fax: 919-515-3687; phil_rea@ncsu.edu
　Mike Waters, Executive Director; 883 Washington St., Raleigh, NC 27605
　Paul Herbert, Editor; Cornelius Park Recreation, P.O. Box 399, Cornelius, NC 28031; 704-892-6031; Fax: 704-892-2462; pherbert@cornelius.org

NORTH CAROLINA WATERSHED COALITION, INC.
P.O. Box 337
Colfax, NC 27235 United States
Phone: 336-992-8734
E-mail: ncwcom@vnet.net
Website: www.ncwatershedcoalition.org

Founded: 1998

Scope: State

Description: The coalition promotes conservation, protection and enhancement of watersheds and rivers; encourages founding and growth of local organizations devoted to those ends through information sharing and cooperation.

Keyword(s): Air Quality/Atmosphere, Oceans/Coasts/Beaches, Pollution (general), Reduce/Reuse/Recycle, Water Habitats & Quality

NORTH CAROLINA WILD FLOWER PRESERVATION SOCIETY
NC NATIVE PLANT SOCIETY
c/o NC Botanical Garden, CB #3375, Totten Center, UNC-CH
Chapel Hill, NC 27599-3375 United States
Phone: 919-834-4172　　　Fax: 336-370-8172
E-mail: alice@ncwildflower.org
Website: www.ncwildflower.org

Founded: 1951

Membership: 101–1,000

Scope: State

Description: A non-profit organization dedicated to the enjoyment and conservation of native plants and their habitats through education, protection and propagation.

Publication(s): NC Native Plant Propagation Handbook, NC Wild Flower Preservation Society Newsletter

Keyword(s): Agriculture/Farming, Wildlife & Species

Contact(s):
　Ken Bridle, President; 336-591-5882; Fax: 336-591-5882; bridle@netunlimited.net
　Alice Zawadzki, Vice-President; 919-834-4172; alice@ncwildflower.org
　Ginny Bacik, Treasurer; ginny@ncwildflower.org
　Marlene Kinney, Corresponding Secretary; marlenek@ncwildflower.org
　Zack Murrell, Recording Secretary; murrellze@appstate.edu
　Ed Tokas, Editor; eteditor@ncwildflower.org

NORTH CAROLINA WILDLIFE FEDERATION

P.O. Box 10626
Raleigh, NC 27605 United States
Phone: 919-833-1923　　　Fax: 919-829-1192
E-mail: ncwf_lisa@mindspring.com
Website: www.ncwf.org

Founded: 1945

Membership: 1,001–10,000

Scope: State

Description: A representative statewide organization, affiliated with the National Wildlife Federation, dedicated to the protection and enhancement of wildlife and its habitat through public education and government interaction.

Publication(s): Friend Of Wildlife Magazine

Contact(s):
　Gary Shull, President and Alternate Representative
　Chuck Rice, Executive Director
　Richard Mode, Representative
　Eddie Nickens, Editor
　Stan Warlen, Treasurer
　Lisa West, Education Programs Contact

NORTH CASCADES CONSERVATION COUNCIL
P.O. Box 95980
Seattle, WA 98145-2980 United States
Phone: 206-282-1644　　　Fax: 206-684-1379
Website: www.northcascade.org

Founded: 1957

Membership: 101–1,000

Scope: Regional

Description: The Council seeks to protect and perserve the North Cascades' scenic, scientific, recreational, educational, wildlife, and wilderness values from the Columbia River to the U.S.-Canadian border in the State of Washington.

Publication(s): Wild Cascades, The

Keyword(s): Forests/Forestry, Land Issues, Public Lands/Greenspace, Recreation/Ecotourism, Reduce/Reuse/Recycle, Water Habitats & Quality, Wildlife & Species

Contact(s):
- Marc Bardsley, President; steveb@premier1.net
- Charles Ehlert, Vice President
- Thomas Brucker, Treasurer
- Patrick Goldsworthy, Chairman; 206-282-1644
- Phil Zalesky, Secretary

NORTH DAKOTA ASSOCIATION OF SOIL CONSERVATION DISTRICTS
3310 University Drive
P.O. Box 1601
Bismarck, ND 58502-1601 United States
Phone: 701-223-8575 Fax: 701-223-1291
E-mail: lincolnoakes@tic.bisman.com
Website: www.lincolnoakes.com
Membership: 101–1,000
Scope: State
Contact(s):
- Rodney Hickle, President; 1631 28th Ave., SW, Center, ND 58530; 701-794-3342
- Gary Puppe, Executive Vice President; P.O. Box 1601, 3310 University Dr., Bismarck, ND 58502-1601; 701-223-8518; Fax: 701-223-1291
- Dale Tinjum, Vice President

NORTH DAKOTA NATURAL SCIENCE SOCIETY
Dept. of Biological Sciences
600 Park Street
Fort Hays State University
Hays, KS 67601-4099 United States
Phone: 785-628-4214 Fax: 785-628-4153
E-mail: efinck@fhsu.edu
Website: www.npwrc.usgs.gov/ndnss/
Founded: 1967
Membership: 101–1,000
Scope: Regional
Description: Dedicated to the observation, recording, study, and preservation of all aspects of the natural history of the Great Plains.
Publication(s): Prairie Naturalist, The
Keyword(s): Land Issues, Wildlife & Species
Contact(s):
- Johnathan Jenks, President; Department of Wildlife and Fisheries Sciences, South Dakota State University, Brookings, SD 57007; 605-688-4783; jenksj@mg.sdstate.edu
- Elmer Finck, Editor; Department of Biological Sciences, Box 4050, Fort Hays State University, Hays, KS 66801

 NORTH DAKOTA WILDLIFE FEDERATION
1605 E. Capitol Ave.
Bismarck, ND 58501 United States
Phone: 701-222-2557 Fax: 701-222-0334
E-mail: ndwf@ndwf.org
Website: www.ndwf.org
Founded: 1935
Membership: 1,001–10,000
Scope: State
Description: A representative statewide organization, affiliated with the National Wildlife Federation, dedicated to the protection and enhancement of wildlife and its habitat through public education and government interaction.
Publication(s): Flickertales
Keyword(s): Recreation/Ecotourism
Contact(s):
- John Kopp, President
- Dick McCabe, Vice-President and NWF Representative
- Conrad Carlson, Treasurer
- Paula Mielke, Education Programs
- Cameo Skager, Office Manager

NORTHCOAST ENVIRONMENTAL CENTER
575 H Street
Arcata, CA 95521 United States
Phone: 707-822-6918 Fax: 707-822-0827
E-mail: info@necandeconews.to
Website: www.necandeconews.to
Founded: 1971
Membership: 1,001–10,000
Scope: Regional
Description: A tax-exempt educational organization dedicated to illuminating the relationships between humankind and the biosphere. The Center provides environmental information and referral services for northwestern California and southwestern Oregon and operates a library open to the public.
Publication(s): Econews
Keyword(s): Forests/Forestry, Land Issues, Public Lands/Greenspace, Water Habitats & Quality, Wildlife & Species
Contact(s):
- Tim McKay, Director
- Connie Stewart, Office Manager
- Sid Dominitz, Editor
- Gail Sellstrom, Librarian

NORTHEAST CONSERVATION LAW ENFORCEMENT CHIEFS' ASSOCIATION (CLECA)
Attn: Secretary
RI Dept. of Environmental Management
83 Park St.
Providence, RI 2908 United States
Phone: 401-277-2284
Scope: Regional
Contact(s):
- Ronald Alie, President; Chief, New Hampshire Fish and Game Dept., Law Enforcement Division, 2 Hazen Dr., Concord, NH 033301; 603-271-3127; Fax: 603-271-1438
- Thomas Kamerzel, Vice President; Director, Bureau of Law Enforcement, Pennsylvania Fish and Boat Commission, P.O. Box 67000, Harrisburg, PA 17106-7000; 717-567-4542; Fax: 717-657-4033
- Thomas Greene, Secretary and Treasurer

NORTHEAST SUSTAINABLE ENERGY ASSOCIATION
50 Miles St.
Greenfield, MA 01301 United States
Phone: 413-774-6051 Fax: 413-774-6053
E-mail: nesea@nesea.org
Website: www.nesea.org
Founded: 1974
Membership: 1,001–10,000
Scope: Regional
Description: The Northeast Sustainable Energy Association (NESEA) aims to strengthen the economy and lessen our impact on the environment by bringing sustainable energy into everyday use. Through its programs and activities, NESEA offers an alternative vision of responsible energy use and works with policymakers, industry, educators, students, and the general public to make this vision a reality.
Publication(s): Northeast Sun, Totally Tree-mendous Activities, Getting Around Without Gasoline
Keyword(s): Energy, Sprawl/Urban Planning, Transportation
Contact(s):
- Nancy Hazard, Director of Transportation Programs; nhazard@nesea.org
- Warren Leon, Executive Director; wleon@nesea.org
- Chris Mason, Director of Education; cmason@nesea.org
- Sandy Thomas, Director of Energy Park; sthomas@nesea.org
- Jonathon Tauer, Manager of Building Program; jtauer@nesea.org

Nancy Hazard, Associate Director; nhazard@nesea.org
Peter Taggert, Board of Directors Chair
Michael Tennis, Secretary

NORTHERN ALASKA ENVIRONMENTAL CENTER
830 College Rd
Fairbanks, AK 99701-1535 United States
Phone: 907-452-5021   Fax: 907-452-3100
E-mail: info@northern.org
Website: www.northern.org

Founded: 1970
Membership: 1,001–10,000
Scope: Local, State, Regional, National, International
Description: The Northern Alaska Environmental Center promotes conservation of the environment in Interior and Arctic Alaska through advocacy, education, and sustainable resource stewardship.
Publication(s): Local Alert, Mining Memos - email list, Northern Line, The, Conservation Abstracts, Boreal Briefs, Arctic Action, Camp Habitat-email list
Keyword(s): Air Quality/Atmosphere, Ecosystems (precious), Forests/Forestry, Land Issues, Pollution (general), Public Lands/Greenspace, Reduce/Reuse/Recycle, Water Habitats & Quality
Contact(s):
  Arthur Hussey, Executive Director; arthur@northern.org
  Mara Bacsujlaky, Assistant Director and Mining Coordinator; mara@northern.org
  Sara Elzey, Bookkeeper; sara@northern.org
  Jessica Groshek, Membership and Communications Director; jessica@northern.org
  Linda Paganelli, Denali Watch Coordinator; lindapag@mtaonline.net
  Ruth Prokopowich, Camp Habitat Director; ruth@northern.org
  Nancy Fresco, Boreal Forest Campaign Coordinator; nancy@northern.org
  Kelly Scanlon, Arctic Coordinator; kelly@northern.org

NORTHERN PLAINS RESOURCE COUNCIL
2401 Montana Ave., Suite 200
Billings, MT 59101-2336 United States
Phone: 406-248-1154   Fax: 406-248-2110
E-mail: info@northernplains.org
Website: www.northernplains.org

Founded: 1972
Membership: 1,001–10,000
Scope: State
Description: NPRC is a grassroots citizens' organization of farmers, ranchers, townspeople, and other conservationists. NPRC works on natural resource and agricultural issues to promote sustainable economic development, and to maintain Montana's unique rural quality of life. NPRC is dedicated to family agriculture and to stewardship of air, land, and water.
Publication(s): Plains Truth, The, Legislative Bulletin, Reclaiming the Wealth (A Citizens' Guide to Hard Rock Mining in Montana)
Keyword(s): Agriculture/Farming, Air Quality/Atmosphere, Energy, Land Issues, Reduce/Reuse/Recycle, Water Habitats & Quality
Contact(s):
  Teresa Erickson, Staff Director
  Jeanie Alderson, Secretary
  Mary Fitzpatrick, Vice Chair
  Amy Frykman, Research Coordinator
  Denna Hoff, Chair
  Dan Teigen, Treasurer

NORTHWEST ATLANTIC FISHERIES ORGANIZATION (NAFO)
P.O. Box 638
Dartmouth, B2Y 3Y9 Nova Scotia Canada
Phone: 902-468-5590   Fax: 902-468-5538
E-mail: info@nafo.int
Website: www.nafo.int

Founded: 1979
Membership: 1–100
Scope: International
Description: Works for the optimum utilization, rational management, and conservation of the fishery resources of the convention area in the Northwest Atlantic. Contracting Parties: Bulgaria, Canada, Cuba, Denmark for the Faroes and Greenland, Estonia, European Union, France (for St. Pierre and Miquelon), Iceland, Japan, Korea, Latvia, Lithuania, Norway, Poland, Romania, Russia and the USA.
Publication(s): Annual Report, Index of Meeting Documents, Sampling Yearbook, Scientific Council Studies, Statistical Bulletin, Journal of Northwest Atlantic Fishery Science, all publications available on web
Keyword(s): Oceans/Coasts/Beaches, Wildlife & Species
Contact(s):
  E. Otuski, President of NAFO and Chairman of General Council
  T. Amaratunga, Assistant Executive Secretary
  W. Brodie, Scientific Council Chairman
  P. Chamut, General Council, Vice Chairman
  Leonard Chepel, Executive Secretary
  P. Gullestad, Fisheries Commission Chairman
  R. Mayo, Scientific Council Vice Chairman
  D. Swanson, Fisheries Commission Vice Chairman

NORTHWEST COALITION FOR ALTERNATIVES TO PESTICIDES
P.O. Box 1393
Eugene, OR 97440 United States
Phone: 541-344-5044, ext. 20   Fax: 541-344-6923
E-mail: info@pesticide.org
Website: www.pesticide.org

Founded: 1977
Membership: 1,001–10,000
Scope: Regional
Description: The Northwest Coalition for Alternatives to Pesticides works to protect people and the environment by advancing healthy solutions to pest problems.
Publication(s): Farmer Exchange, The, Journal of Pesticide Reform
Keyword(s): Agriculture/Farming, Pollution (general), Public Health, Water Habitats & Quality
Contact(s):
  Norma Grier, Executive Director
  Becky Long, Development Director
  Caroline Cox, Editor/Staff Scientist
  Jennifer Miller, Sustainable Agriculture Program Coordinator; 210 N Straughan Ave, Boise, ID 03712
  Aimee Code, Right-to-Know Coordinator
  Megan Kemple, Public Education Coordinator; info@pesticide.org
  Pollyanna Lind, Salmon and Water Quality
  Kay Rumsey, Librarian
  Edward Winter, Office Coordinator/ Financial Coordinator

NORTHWEST ECOSYSTEM ALLIANCE
CASCADES CONSERVATION PARTNERSHIP, THE
1208 Bay St., Suite 201
Bellingham, WA 98225 United States
Phone: 360-671-9950   Fax: 360-671-8429
E-mail: nwea@ecosystem.org
Website: www.ecosystem.org

Founded: 1989
Membership: 10,001–100,000
Scope: Regional
Description: Northwest Ecosystem Alliance protects and restores wildlands in the Pacific Northwest and supports such efforts in British Columbia. The Alliance bridges science and advocacy, working with activists, policymakers, and the public to conserve our natural heritage.
Publication(s): Cascadia Wild, Northwest Conservation

Keyword(s): Ecosystems (precious), Forests/Forestry, Public Lands/Greenspace, Wildlife & Species

Contact(s):
Mitch Friedman, Executive Director; mf@ecosystem.org
Jodi Broughton, Business Manager and Development Director; jbroughton@ecosystem.org
Lisa McShane, Community Outreach Director; lmcshane@ecosystem.org
Fred Munson, Deputy Director; 206-675-9747; ext. 202; fmunson@ecosystem.org
Hudson Dodd, Volunteer Coordinator; 360-671-9950; ext. 26; hdodd@ecosystem.org

NORTHWEST ENVIRONMENT WATCH
NEW
1402 3rd Ave., Suite 500
Seattle, WA 98101 United States
Phone: 206-447-1880   Fax: 206-447-2270
E-mail: new@northwestwatch.org
Website: www.northwestwatch.org

Founded: 1993
Membership: 1,001–10,000
Scope: Regional

Description: Northwest Environment Watch (NEW) promotes an environmentally sound economy and way of life in the Pacific Northwest. Since 1994, NEW has published books and reports on topics ranging from transportation to taxes to ecological health. NEW is currently developing an index of social and environmental well-being for the Northwest's regional index that monitors key trends affecting people, place, and the future of both.

Publication(s): This Place on Earth, Green Collar Jobs, State of the Northwest, Stuff, Misplaced Blame, The Car and The City, Tax Shift

Keyword(s): Air Quality/Atmosphere, Climate Change, Ecosystems (precious), Energy, Forests/Forestry, Land Issues, Pollution (general), Population, Public Health, Sprawl/Urban Planning, Transportation

Contact(s):
Alan Durning, Executive Director; ext. 120
Clark Williams Derry, Research Director; 447-1880; ext. 106

NORTHWEST INTERPRETIVE ASSOCIATION
909 1st Ave., Suite 630
Seattle, WA 98104-3627 United States
Phone: 206-220-4140   Fax: 206-220-4143
Website: www.nwpubliclands.com

Founded: 1974
Scope: Regional

Description: The Association supports interpretation and education on public lands administered by the National Park Service, U.S. Forest Service, and other agencies in the Pacific Northwest. Proceeds from the sale of interpretive publications are donated to these agencies to educate visitors in the area's natural and cultural history.

Keyword(s): Ethics/Environmental Justice, Land Issues, Recreation/Ecotourism

Contact(s):
Mary Quackenbush, Executive Director
Tom Scribner, Vice Chairman
Jim Torrence, Chairman of the Board

NORTHWEST RESOURCE INFORMATION CENTER
P.O. Box 427
Eagle, ID 83616 United States
Phone: 208-939-0714   Fax: 208-939-0714
E-mail: edchaney@nwric.org
Website: www.nwric.org

Founded: 1976
Scope: Local, State, Regional, National, International

Description: NRIC promotes through research, public education, technology transfer, and litigation the concept that ecological diversity and environmental quality are synonymous with long-term economic productivity and quality of life.

Publication(s): Miscellaneous

Keyword(s): Agriculture/Farming, Ecosystems (precious), Energy, Ethics/Environmental Justice, Executive/Legislative/Judicial Reform, Land Issues, Oceans/Coasts/Beaches, Public Lands/Greenspace, Water Habitats & Quality, Wildlife & Species

Contact(s):
Ed Chaney, Executive Director; P.O. Box 427, Eagle, ID 83616; 208-939-0714; Fax: 208-939-0714; edchaney@nwric.org

NOVA SCOTIA FEDERATION OF ANGLERS AND HUNTERS
NOVA SCOTIA WILDLIFE FEDERATION
P.O. Box 654
Halifax, B3J 2T3 Nova Scotia Canada
Phone: 902-477-8898   Fax: 902-477-8898
E-mail: tony.rodgers@3web.net

Founded: 1930
Membership: 1,001–10,000
Scope: Province, National

Description: Affiliated with the Canadian Wildlife Federation and the National Coalition of Provincial and Territorial Wildlife Federations. Aims to unite all conservation organizations in Nova Scotia, fosters appreciation of wildlife and habitat, promotes fish and game management, seeks enactment and enforcement of laws necessary for environmental controls as well as conservation of wildlife resources.

Publication(s): Nova Outdoors

Keyword(s): Ecosystems (precious), Ethics/Environmental Justice, Executive/Legislative/Judicial Reform, Forests/Forestry, Land Issues, Oceans/Coasts/Beaches, Pollution (general), Recreation/Ecotourism, Water Habitats & Quality, Wildlife & Species

Contact(s):
Gary Penney, President
A.J. (Tony) Rodgers, Executive Director; tony.rodgers@3web.net

NOVA SCOTIA FORESTRY ASSOCIATION
P.O. Box 6901
Port Hawkesbury, B9A 2W2 Nova Scotia Canada
Phone: 902-625-2935   Fax: 902-625-2388
Website: www.nsfa.ca

Founded: 1959
Scope: International

Description: The Nova Scotia Forestry Association is a nonprofit, charitable organization dedicated to promoting the wise use and management of our forest resources through education programs for youth. Programs emphasize the importance of being good stewards of our natural resources.

Publication(s): Annual Teachers Guide for National Forest Week

Keyword(s): Forests/Forestry, Pollution (general)

Contact(s):
Russ Waycott, President
Debbie Totten, Executive Director

NW ENERGY COALITION
219 First Ave., S.
#100
Seattle, WA 98104 United States
Phone: 206-621-0094   Fax: 206-621-0097
E-mail: nwec@nwenergy.org
Website: www.nwenergy.org

Founded: 1981
Membership: 101–1,000
Scope: State, Regional, National

Description: The NW Energy Coalition is a regionwide alliance of progressive utilities, consumer advocates, and green businesses. The Coalition advocates cost-effective energy conservation, renewable energy resources, low-income/consumer protection and the restoration of fish and wildlife.
Publication(s): NW Energy Coalition Report, Plugging People into Power, Energy Activist
Keyword(s): Energy, Reduce/Reuse/Recycle, Wildlife & Species
Contact(s):
  Rob Gala, Outreach Director
  Mark Glyde, Communications Director
  Nancy Hirsh, Policy Director
  Sara Patton, Director

O

OCEAN CONSERVANCY, THE
1725 DeSales St., NW, Suite 600
Washington, DC 20036 United States
Phone: 202-429-5609   Fax: 202-872-0619
Website: www.oceanconservancy.org
Founded: 1972
Membership: 100,001–500,000
Scope: National
Description: A nonprofit, scientific organization dedicated to protecting marine wildlife and its habitats, and to conserving coastal and ocean resources. The center's programs are conducted in five major areas: Fisheries and Wildlife Conservation, Ecosystem Protection, Biodiversity Conservation, International Initiatives, Citizen Monitoring, and Outreach. Program efforts focus on research, policy analysis, education, and public information and involvement.
Publication(s): International Coastal Cleanup Report, Coastal Connection, Blue Planet Quarterly, list of additional publications on request
Keyword(s): Oceans/Coasts/Beaches, Pollution (general), Reduce/Reuse/Recycle, Water Habitats & Quality, Wildlife & Species
Contact(s):
  Roger Rufe, President; 202-429-5609
  Warner Chabot, Vice President for Regions; 580 Market St., Suite 550, San Francisco, CA 94104, 415-391-6204
  Stephanie Drea, Vice President for Communications and Marketing; 202-429-5609
  Elliot Gruber, Vice President for Development and Membership; 202-429-5609
  David Guggenheim, Vice President for Conservation Policy; 202-429-5609
  David Hoskins, Vice President for Government Affairs and General Counsel; 202-429-5609
  Peter Jones, Vice President for Finance and Administration
  Kris Balliet, Director of the Alaska Region; 425 G. St., Anchorage, AK; 907-258-9922
  David Dixon, Director of Constituency Development; 202-429-5609
  Linda Sheehan, Director of the Pacific Coast Region; 580 Market St., Suite 550, San Francisco, CA 94104, 415-391-6204
  Jack Sobel, Director of Ecosystem Programs; 202-429-5609
  David White, Director of the Southeast Atlantic & Gulf of Mexico Region; One Beach Dr. SE, #304, St. Petersburg, FL 33701; 727-895-2188
  Nina Young, Director of Marine Conservation Wildlife; 202-429-5609; Fax: 202-872-0619
  Nicole Sandberg, International Coastal Cleanup Manager; 202-429-5609; Fax: 202-872-0619
  John Bierwirth, Chairman of the Board

OCEAN PROJECT, THE
102 Waterman Street
Suite 16
Providence, RI 02906 United States
Phone: 401-272-8822   Fax: 401-272-8877
E-mail: info@theoceanproject.org
Website: www.theoceanproject.org
Founded: 1998
Scope: Local, State, Regional, National, International
Description: The Ocean Project is an unprecedented collaboration of over 450 aquariums, zoos, museums, conservation organizations and others. TOP helps its partners become more effective at communicating conservation to their visitors and members and empowering them to take responsibility for conserving our ocean planet by integrating conservation into their lives through changed behaviors, and personal involvement with conservation efforts and activities.
Keyword(s): Oceans/Coasts/Beaches, Water Habitats & Quality, Wildlife & Species
Contact(s):
  Bill Mott, Director; 401-272-8822; Fax: 401-272-8877; bmott@theoceanproject.org

OCEAN VOICE INTERNATIONAL
3332 McCarthy Rd.
Ottawa, K1V 0W0 Ontario Canada
Phone: 613-721-4541   Fax: 613-721-4562
E-mail: oceans@superaje.com
Website: www.ovi.ca
Founded: 1987
Membership: 101–1,000
Scope: National
Description: To conserve the diversity of marine life, protect and restore marine ecosystems and ecological services, enhance the quality of life and equity of benefits for coastal peoples, and promote ecologically sustainable harvest of marine resources.
Publication(s): Sea Wind, Striving for the Integrity of Freshwater Ecosystems, Global Freshwater Biodiversity, Green School Biodiversity Booklet, The Status of the World Ocean and its Biodiversity, How Green is Your School?, Save Our Coral Reefs
Keyword(s): Development/Developing Countries, Water Habitats & Quality, Wildlife & Species
Contact(s):
  Jaime Baquero, President; 819-243-1334

OCEANIA
AMERICAN OCEANS CAMPAIGN
2501 M Street NW
Washington, DC 20007 United States
Phone: 202-833-3900   Fax: 202-544-5625
E-mail: info@americanoceans.org
Website: www.americanoceans.org
Founded: 1987
Scope: National
Description: The well-being and sustainability of the Earth is dependent upon healthy oceans. The mission of American Oceans Campaign is to safeguard the vitality of the oceans and our coastal waters. AOC is committed to scientific information in advocating for sound public policy. We are equally committed to developing partnerships with all entities interested in protecting the environment. AOC seeks to ensure healthy sources of food and coastal recreation as well as to protect the ocean's grandeur.
Publication(s): Estuaries on the Edge: The Vital Link Between Land and Sea, Drainage to the Oceans: The Effects of Stormwater Pollution on Coastal Waters, Chemical Contaminant Release Into the Santa Monica Bay: A Pilot Study, Fish Briefs, Splash

Keyword(s): Oceans/Coasts/Beaches, Pollution (general), Public Health, Water Habitats & Quality, Wildlife & Species

Contact(s):
Ted Danson, Founding President
Annett Wolf, Vice President
Barbara Polo, Executive Director; bjpolo@americanoceans.org
Warner Chabot, Board Chair
Barbara Kohn, Treasurer

OCEANIC SOCIETY
Fort Fort Mason Center, Building E
San Francisco, CA 94123 United States
Phone: 415-441-1106   Fax: 415-474-3395
E-mail: office@oceanic-society.org
Website: www.oceanic-society.org

Founded: 1969
Membership: 101–1,000
Scope: International

Description: Founded in 1969, The Oceanic Society is a non-profit marine conservation organization whose mission is to protect marine wildlife through an integrated program of scientific research, environmental education, and volunteerism.

Keyword(s): Ecosystems (precious), Ethics/Environmental Justice, Oceans/Coasts/Beaches, Recreation/Ecotourism, Wildlife & Species

OHIO ACADEMY OF SCIENCE, THE
1500 W. Third Ave. Ste. 223
Columbus, OH 43212-2817 United States
Phone: 614-488-2228   Fax: 614-488-7629
E-mail: oas@iwaynet.net
Website: www.ohiosci.org

Founded: 1891
Membership: 1,001–10,000
Scope: Local, State, Regional

Description: A nonprofit organization designed to stimulate interest in the sciences, to promote research, to improve instruction in the sciences, to disseminate scientific knowledge, and to recognize high achievement in attaining these objectives.

Publication(s): Ohio Journal of Science, The

Contact(s):
Lynn Elfner, Executive Officer; 614-488-2228; Fax: 614-488-7629; oas@iwaynet.net

OHIO ALLIANCE FOR THE ENVIRONMENT
Suite 30
1500 West Third Ave.
Columbus, OH 43212 United States
Phone: 614-487-9957   Fax: 614-487-9957
E-mail: smith@ohioalliance.org
Website: www.ohioalliance.org

Founded: 1977
Membership: 101–1,000
Scope: State

Description: The Ohio Alliance for the Environment is a statewide nonprofit organization which promotes education, communication and interaction on environmental issues among diverse groups including representatives from government, education, business and environmental organizations. We accomplish this through conferences, seminars, publications, and roundtable discussions.

Publication(s): Focus on the Issue, OAE Newsletter

Contact(s):
Lisa Novosat-Gradert, President; Environmental Attorney, Brouse McDowell, 500 First National Tower, Akron, OH 44308-1471; 330-535-5711; ext. 316; Fax: 330-253-8601; lngradert@brouse.com
Mike Parkes, President Elect; Community Relations Manager, Waste Technologies Industries, 1250 St. George Street, East Liverpool, OH 43920; 330-385-7337; Fax: 330-650-1853; mparkes@vonrollwti.com
Irene Probasco, Executive Director; 1500 West Third Ave., Suite 30, Columbus, OH 43212; 614-487-9957; Fax: 614-487-9957; probasco@ohioalliance.org
Jane Haynes, Newsletter Editor; 614-885-3735; Fax: 614-885-3735; sjhaynes@juno.com

OHIO BASS FEDERATION
Attn: President, 2572 Renwick Way
Troy, OH 45373 United States
Phone: 937-335-2078
E-mail: dbecker@erinet.com
Website: www.ohiobass.org

Scope: State

Description: An organization of Bassmaster chapters, affiliated with the Bass Anglers Sportsman Society, organized to fight pollution, assist state and national conservation agencies in their efforts, and teach the young people of our country good conservation practices. Dedicated to the realistic conservation of our water resources.

Keyword(s): Water Habitats & Quality, Wildlife & Species

Contact(s):
Dennis Becker, President; 2572 Renwick Way, Troy, OH 45373; 937-335-2078; dbecker@erinet.com
Jim Doss, Conservation Director; 43 Portsmouth Rd., Gallipolis, OH 45631; 740-446-9810; JSDoss@zoomnet.net

OHIO BIOLOGICAL SURVEY
P.O. Box 21370
Columbus, OH 43221-0370 United States
Phone: 614-899-7417   Fax: 614-899-7610
E-mail: ohiobiosurvinc@aol.com
Website: www.msj.edu/cicada/obs/

Founded: 1912
Membership: 101–1,000
Scope: Regional

Description: An inter-institutional organization of 106 colleges, universities, museums and other organizations in Ohio, ten other states and the province of Ontario. Produces and disseminates scientific and technical information concerning the flora and fauna of the Ohio environment, and larger areas of which Ohio is an integral part.

Publication(s): Bulletins, In Ohio's Backyard Series, Informative Publications, Notes, Miscellaneous Publications, publications available on website

Keyword(s): Public Lands/Greenspace, Wildlife & Species

Contact(s):
Brian Armitage, Executive Director; armitage.7@osu.edu
Terry Keiser, Chairman of the Advisory Board; Ohio Northern University

OHIO ENERGY PROJECT
OHIO NEED PROJECT
640 Enterprise Dr.
Suite A
Lewis Center, OH 43035-9440 United States
Phone: 614-785-1717   Fax: 614-785-1731
E-mail: oep@ohioenergy.org
Website: www.ohioenergy.org

Founded: 1984
Membership: 10,001–100,000
Scope: State

Description: A nonprofit organization promoting energy education, efficiency and conservation and youth leadership development, using a fun hands-on, Inter-disciplinary approach and the "kids teaching kids" philosophy.

Publication(s): Curriculum Materials

Keyword(s): Energy

Contact(s):
Shauni Nix, Executive Director
Rich Smith, Director
Annie Rasor, Programs Manager
Melissa Fu, Education Coordinator
Mary McCarron, Statewide Coordinator
Mike Stranges, Education Coordinator

OHIO ENVIRONMENTAL COUNCIL, INC.
1207 Grandview Ave.
Suite 201
Columbus, OH 43212 United States
Phone: 614-487-7506   Fax: 614-487-7510
E-mail: oec@theoec.org
Website: www.theoec.org

Founded: 1969
Membership: 1,001–10,000
Scope: State

Description: The Ohio Environmental Council is a statewide organization providing resources for local environmental organizations across Ohio. The OEC promotes improved environmental quality in the state through advocacy, research, education and collaborative efforts.

Publication(s): Ohio Environmental Report Newsletter, variety of other publications on critical environmental issues for Ohio, Green Pages (listing of Ohio environmental groups and resources), publications available on web.

Keyword(s): Agriculture/Farming, Air Quality/Atmosphere, Development/Developing Countries, Energy, Ethics/Environmental Justice, Pollution (general), Water Habitats & Quality

Contact(s):
Daniel Binder, Board President; 817 S. Remmington Rd., Bexle, OH
Vicki Deisner, Executive Director
Keith Dimoff, Water Program Manager
Sarah Hovanec, Development and Program Coordinator
Peter Johnsen, Business and Technology Manager
Jack Shaner, Public Affairs Manager
Susan Studer King, Community Outreach and Development Manger
Kurt Waltzer, Clean Air Program Manager
Lindy Black, Membership and Administrative Assistant
Heidi Ehret, Power Plant Campaign Coordinator
Alice Woerner, Outreach Coordinator

OHIO FEDERATION OF SOIL AND WATER CONSERVATION DISTRICTS
4383 Fountain Sq. Ct. Building B-3
Columbus, OH 43224 United States
Phone: 614-265-6610   Fax: 614-262-2064
Website: www.dnr.state.oh.us/odnr/soil+water

Scope: State

Description: To provide leadership and services that enable Ohioans to conserve, protect and enhance soil, water and land resources

Contact(s):
Brad Ross, Administrator; 614-265-6616

OHIO FEDERATION OF SOIL AND WATER CONSERVATION DISTRICTS
OFSWCD
P.O. Box 24518
Columbus, OH 43224 United States
Phone: 6147841900   Fax: 6147849181
E-mail: alicia-connelly@oh.nacdnet.org

Founded: 1943
Membership: 101–1,000
Scope: Local, State

Description: Statewide federation representing 88 Soil & Water Conservation Districts and their 440 publicly elected board members. SWCDs assist local land users with information and technical assistance in making land use decisions on private working lands.

Keyword(s): Agriculture/Farming, Forests/Forestry, Pollution (general), Sprawl/Urban Planning, Water Habitats & Quality

OHIO FORESTRY ASSOCIATION, INC.
4080 South High St.
Columbus, OH 43207 United States
Phone: 614-497-9580   Fax: 614-497-9581
E-mail: bobr@ohioforest.org
Website: www.ohioforest.org

Founded: 1903
Membership: 101–1,000
Scope: Regional

Description: A statewide organization, affiliated with the National Woodland Owners Association, organized to promote the welfare of the people and private enterprise of Ohio by improving, through education, the wise management of Ohio's forest resource. Sponsors annual forestry camp for youths 14-19; assists schools' conservation activities and education; and coordinates American Tree Farm Program in Ohio.

Publication(s): Ohio Woodlands, Bark and Bunk

Keyword(s): Forests/Forestry, Recreation/Ecotourism

Contact(s):
Melvin Yoder, President
Jim Doll, 2nd Vice President
C. Wayne Lashbrook, 1st Vice President
Roy Palmer, 3rd Vice President
Robert B. Redett, Treasurer
Karl Gebhardt, Legislative Consultant

OHIO NATIVE PLANT SOCIETY
6 Louise Dr.
Chagrin Falls, OH 44022 United States
Phone: 440-338-6622
Website: dir.gardenweb.com/directory/onps#

Founded: 1982
Membership: 101–1,000
Scope: Local, State, Regional

Description: The Ohio Native Plant Society is dedicated to preservation, conservation and education concerning all native plants of Ohio.

Keyword(s): Ecosystems (precious), Ethics/Environmental Justice, Land Issues, Wildlife & Species

Contact(s):
A. Malmquist, Executive Secretary

OHIO STREAM PRESERVATION
P.O. Box 23835
Chagrin Falls, OH 44023-0835 United States
Phone: 440-439-2920   Fax: 440-439-2920
E-mail: info@ohiostream.org

Founded: 1999
Scope: State

Description: Ohio Stream Preservation, Inc. is a non-profit 501(c)(3) organization whose mission is to provide effective methods for the long-term preservation of rivers, wetlands, and streams within the State of Ohio.

Keyword(s): Land Issues, Water Habitats & Quality, Wildlife & Species

Contact(s):
Jeff Markley, Executive Director; 8535 Lucerne Drive, Bainbridge Township, OH 44023-4605; 440-543-7038; Fax: 440-543-7037; landesign@msn.com

OKLAHOMA ASSOCIATION OF CONSERVATION DISTRICTS
Attn: President, P.O. Box 107
Chelsea, OK 74016-0107 United States
Phone: 918-696-7612
Scope: State
Keyword(s): Reduce/Reuse/Recycle
Contact(s):
 Carol Gaunt, President, Alternate Board Member; Rt. 5 Box 244, Weatherford, OK 73096-8815; 405-772-5107
 Matt Gard, Vice President; Rt. 1, Box 16, Fairview, OK 73737-9621; 580-438-2320
 Rick Jeans, Vice President; Rt. 1 Box 184, Tonkawa, OK 74653; 405-628-2223
 Mark Moehle, Vice President; 1601 Shadow Court, Edmond, OK 73013-2683; 405-340-8884; Fax: 405-842-8744
 George Fraley, Past President; P.O. Box 107, Chelsea, OK 74016-0107; 918-789-2511; Fax: 918-789-2835
 Christy Kimble, Secretary; Oklahoma County CD, 1120 NW 63rd Ste. G101, Oklahoma City, OK 73116; 405-848-1933; Fax: 405-842-8744
 Wayne Smith, Treasurer; 506 N. Pennsylvania, Mangum, OK 73554-3036; 405-782-3575; Fax: 405-782-3581
 Billy Wilson, Board Member; P.O. Box 208, Kinta, OK 74552-0208; 918-768-3542; bwilson@cwis.net

OKLAHOMA BASS FEDERATION
Attn: President, 2300 E. Coleman Rd.
Ponca City, OK 74604 United States
Phone: 580-765-0165
E-mail: bigc@ponca.net
Website: www.okbass.org
Scope: State
Description: An organization of Bassmaster chapters, affiliated the with Bass Anglers Sportsman Society, organized to fight pollution, assist state and national conservation agencies in their efforts, and teach the young people of our country good conservation practices. Dedicated to the realistic conservation of our water resources.
Publication(s): Scissortail, The, Oklahoma B.A.S.S. Federation Newsletter, Bulletin of the Oklahoma Ornithological Society, The
Contact(s):
 Robert Cartlidge, President; 2300 E. Coleman Road, Ponca City, OK 74604; 580-765-0165
 Don Linder, Conservation Director; 2409 Cardinal, Ponca City, OK 74604; 580- 76-3301; dlinder@horizon.hit.net
 James Hardage, Treasurer; 1352 Bridle Path Lane, Lindale, TX 75771; 903-882-8652
 R. Kitterman, Secretary, Editor; 411 W. 6th, Dewey, OK 74029; 918-534-1720

OKLAHOMA DEPARTMENT OF WILDLIFE CONSERVATION
2021 Caddo Hwghy
Caddo, OK 74729-3807 United States
Phone: 580-924-4087   Fax: 580-924-9132
E-mail: ser@texomaonline.com
Website: www.wildlifedepartment.com
Founded: 1968
Membership: 1–100
Scope: State
Contact(s):
 Paul Balkenbush, Regional Supervisor

OKLAHOMA NATIVE PLANT SOCIETY
c/o Tulsa Garden Center, 2435 S. Peoria
Tulsa, OK 74114 United States
Phone: 405-872-9652   Fax: 405-872-8361
E-mail: cox.chadwick@worldnet.att.net
Website: www.usao.edu/~onps/
Founded: 1986
Membership: 101–1,000
Scope: State
Description: Oklahoma Native Plant Society encourages the study, protection, propagation, appreciation, and use of Oklahoma's native plants.
Publication(s): Gaillardia, The, Native Plant Selection Guide for Oklahoma Woody Plants
Keyword(s): Land Issues, Public Lands/Greenspace, Reduce/Reuse/Recycle, Sprawl/Urban Planning, Water Habitats & Quality, Wildlife & Species
Contact(s):
 Jim Elder, President; 918-747-0735; jfeok@aol.com
 Connie Murray, Vice President; 405-598-6742; cmurray@tulsa.cc.ok.us
 Chad Cox, Conservation Chair/Newsletter Editor; cox.chadwick@worldnet.att.net

OKLAHOMA ORNITHOLOGICAL SOCIETY
Attn: Business Manager, 1701 W. Will Rogers
Claremore, OK 74017 United States
Phone: 918-343-7706   Fax: 918-343-7563
E-mail: kwmartin@rsu.edu
Founded: 1950
Membership: 101–1,000
Scope: State
Description: Affiliated with National Audubon Society and the Oklahoma Wildlife Federation. Dedicated to the observation, study, and conservation of birds in Oklahoma.
Publication(s): Bulletin of the Oklahoma Ornithological Society
Contact(s):
 Keith Martin, President
 Jo Loyd, Business Manager; 6736 E. 28th St., Tulsa, OK 74129; 918-835-2946
 Michael Bay, Secretary; Dept. Biology, East Central State Univ., Ada, OK 74820
 Charles Brown, Editor; Biology Dept. University of Tulsa, Tulsa, OK 74104; 918-631-3943
 Marty Kamp, Treasurer; 6422 S. Indianapolis Pl., Tulsa, OK 74136
 Richard Stewart, Editor; birdbander@aol.com

 ## OKLAHOMA WILDLIFE FEDERATION
P.O. Box 60126
Oklahoma City, OK 73146-0126 United States
Phone: 580-584-2130   Fax: 405-521-9270
E-mail: owf@nstar.net
Website: www.okwildlife.org
Founded: 1963
Scope: State
Description: A representative statewide organization, affiliated with the National Wildlife Federation, dedicated to the protection and enhancement of wildlife and its habitat through public education and government interaction.
Publication(s): Outdoor News, Urban Landscaping
Contact(s):
 Royce Meek, President and Representative
 Margaret Ruff, Education Programs Contact & Executive Director
 Mich Entz, Alternate Representative
 Dick Gunn, Secretary
 Lance Meek, Editor
 James Menzer, Treasurer

OKLAHOMA WOODLAND OWNERS ASSOCIATION (OWOA)
2657 S. Trenton
Tulsa, OK 74114-2727 United States
Phone: 918-569-4287   Fax: 918-743-6941
Founded: 1994

NON-GOVERNMENTAL NON-PROFIT ORGANIZATIONS – O

Scope: State
Description: A statewide organization affiliated with the National Woodland Owners Association to advance forest management skills of Oklahoma woodland owners. Other objectives are to promote education and networking, provide timber marketing, and to monitor and act upon legislation.
Publication(s): OWOA Bulletin
Keyword(s): Forests/Forestry
Contact(s):
Patt Nelson, President and Editor
John Ahern, 1st Vice President
Rick Hutchinson, Board Member
Tom Kee, Secretary
Sue Paschall, Treasurer and Board Member
Miles Schulze, Board Member

OLYMPIC PARK ASSOCIATES
168 Lost Mountain Lane
Sequim, WA 98362-9292 United States
Phone: 360-681-2480   Fax: 360-681-2480
E-mail: mcmorgan@olypen.com
Website: www.drizzle.com/~rdpayne/opa.htmo

Founded: 1948
Membership: 101–1,000
Scope: Local, State, Regional, National
Description: Dedicated to preserving the wilderness and integrity of Olympic National Park and the surrounding Olympic ecosystem, as well as supporting wild land and wildlife habitat protection elsewhere in the nation. Currently working on restoration of the Elwha River ecosystem, reintroduction of extirpated species like the wolf, and elimination of exotic species from Olympic National Park. We also promote restoration and protection of native salmon stocks in Olympic Peninsula waters.
Publication(s): Voice of the Wild Olympics
Keyword(s): Ecosystems (precious), Forests/Forestry, Land Issues, Public Lands/Greenspace, Wildlife & Species
Contact(s):
Polly Dyer, President; 206-364-3933
Tim McNulty, Vice President; 360-681-2480
John Anderson, Treasurer; 206-523-5043
Sally Soest, Editor; 206-860-2865
Philip Zalesky, Secretary; 425-337-2479

OLYMPIC PARK INSTITUTE
111 Barnes Point Rd.
Port Angeles, WA 98363 United States
Phone: 800-775-3720   Fax: 360-928-3046
E-mail: opi@yni.org
Website: www.yni.org/opi

Founded: 1987
Scope: Local, Regional, National
Description: Mission is to inspire personal connection to the natural world and responsible actions to sustain it. OPI provides residential field science programs in Olympic National Park for adults, families and K-12 classrooms. Elderhostel and field seminar programs are also available. Programs introduce themes of ecology, sustainability and stewardship.
Publication(s): Publications on website
Keyword(s): Energy, Ethics/Environmental Justice, Forests/Forestry, Oceans/Coasts/Beaches, Public Lands/Greenspace, Reduce/Reuse/Recycle, Wildlife & Species

ONEWILDWORLD
WE HAVE ONLY ONEWILDWORLD
3161 SW McMullen Street
Port St. Lucie, FL 34953 United States
Phone: 772-336-9252   Fax: 336-9063
E-mail: onewildworld@aol.com
Website: www.onewildworld.org

Founded: 1999
Membership: 1–100
Scope: Local, State
Description: Volunteers Helping to Save Paradise Florida and our ONLY OneWildWorld (Oceans, Nature, Environment, Wildlife, IRL, Dolphins & Whales, Oceans, Resources, Links, Directory), One Ocean, One Nature, One Day at a Time Everyday Because EXTINCTION Is FOREVER!
Keyword(s): Ecosystems (precious), Oceans/Coasts/Beaches, Pollution (general), Recreation/Ecotourism, Water Habitats & Quality, Wildlife & Species
Contact(s):
Lee Hedrick, Director; onewildworld@aol.com

ONTARIO FEDERATION OF ANGLERS AND HUNTERS
Box 2800
Peterborough, K9J 8L5 Ontario Canada
Phone: 705-748-6324   Fax: 705-748-9577
E-mail: ofah@ofah.org
Website: www.ofah.org

Founded: 1928
Membership: 10,001–100,000
Scope: Local, Province, Regional, National
Description: Canada's largest Provincial conservation organization with over 83,000 members and 645 affiliated Member Clubs. Nonprofit, nongovernment agency respresenting hunting and angling interests related to natural resources managment in the Province of Ontario.
Publication(s): Call of the Loon, Angler & Hunter Hotline
Keyword(s): Agriculture/Farming, Air Quality/Atmosphere, Climate Change, Ecosystems (precious), Energy, Executive/Legislative/Judicial Reform, Forests/Forestry, Land Issues, Pollution (general), Public Health, Public Lands/Greenspace, Recreation/Ecotourism, Reduce/Reuse/Recycle
Contact(s):
Michael Reader, Executive Director; 705-748-6324; Fax: 705-748-9577; mike_reader@ofah.org
Greg Farrant, Government Relations & Communications Manager; 705-748-6324; Fax: 705-748-9577; greg_farrant@ofah.org
Terry Quinney, Provincial Manager of Fish & Wildlife; 705-748-6324; Fax: 705-755-1757; terry_quinney@ofah.org

ONTARIO FORESTRY ASSOCIATION
107—200 Consumers Rd.
Toronto, M2J 4R4 Ontario Canada
Phone: 416-493-4565   Fax: 416-493-4608
E-mail: forestry@oforest.on.ca
Website: www.oforest.on.ca

Founded: 1949
Membership: 101–1,000
Scope: Province
Description: Ontario Forestry Association works to raise awareness and understanding of all aspects of Ontario's forests and to develop commitment to stewardship of forest ecosystems. Programs include: Envirothon, Focus on Forests, Community Woodland Steward Initiative, Consultant Registry, land use and forest management, forestry publicity and historical data.
Publication(s): Ontario Forest Products Marketing Bulletin, Re:View
Keyword(s): Forests/Forestry
Contact(s):
Blair Peberdy, President; Toronto Hydro, 14 Carlton Street, Toronto, Ontario M58 1K5
James Farrell, 1st Vice President
Rob Keen, 2nd Vice President
Anne Koven, Executive Director; 416-493-4565; annek@oforest.on.ca

OPENLANDS PROJECT
25 E. Washington St., Suite 1650
Chicago, IL 60602 United States
Phone: 312-427-4256   Fax: 312-427-6251
E-mail: info@openlands.org
Website: www.openlands.org

Founded: 1963
Membership: 101–1,000
Scope: Local, State, Regional
Description: A private, nonprofit organization, Openlands Project was founded in 1963 to provide a healthy environment and a more livable place for all people of the region. Openlands preserves, protects, enhances, and expands open space through land acquisition, greenways, watershed planning and restoration, urban greening initiatives, advocacy and technical assistance.
Publication(s): Openlander, Under Pressure: Land Consumption in the Chicago Region, Annual Report
Keyword(s): Forests/Forestry, Land Issues, Public Lands/Greenspace, Recreation/Ecotourism, Reduce/Reuse/Recycle, Sprawl/Urban Planning, Water Habitats & Quality, Wildlife & Species
Contact(s):
Susan Bell, President
Gerald Adelmann, Executive Director
Ders Anderson, Greenways Director
Glenda Daniel, Urban Greening Director
Kirsten Powers, Development Director
J. Ritchie, Treasurer
Charles Saltzman, Secretary

OPERATION MIGRATION
174 Mary St.
Suite 101
Port Perry, L9L 1B7 Ontario Canada
Phone: 800-675-2618   Fax: 905-982-1097
E-mail: opmig@durham.net
Website: www.operationmigration.org

Founded: 1994
Membership: 101–1,000
Scope: International
Description: Dedicated to the restoration of migration routes for endangered or threatened species of birds through the use of ultralight aircraft
Keyword(s): Wildlife & Species

ORANGUTAN FOUNDATION INTERNATIONAL
4201 Wilshire Boulevard
Suite 407
Los Angeles, CA 90010 United States
Phone: 323-938-6046   Fax: 323-938-6047
E-mail: webmaster@orangutan.org
Website: www.orangutan.org

Founded: 1986
Membership: 1,001–10,000
Scope: National, International
Description: Orangutan Foundation International's mission is to support the conservation of the orangutan and its habitat. Probably no more than 15,000 orangutans survive in the wild. Illegal mining and logging and the conversion of land into palm oil plantations pose the most serious threats. Some conservationists estimate that if illegal logging continues at its current rate, the rain forests in Indonesia could be gone in five to ten years, leading to the extinction of the orangutan in the wild.
Publication(s): Reflections of Eden, Orangutan Odyssey
Keyword(s): Development/Developing Countries, Ecosystems (precious), Forests/Forestry, Land Issues, Recreation/Ecotourism, Water Habitats & Quality, Wildlife & Species

OREGON BASS FEDERATION
Attn: President, 1601 S. Dogwood St.
Cornelius, OR 97113 United States
Phone: 503-357-4798
Website: orbass.oregonbass.net

Scope: State
Description: An organization of Bassmaster chapters, affiliated with Bass Anglers Sportsman Society, organized to fight pollution, assist state and national conservation agencies in their efforts, and teach the young people of our country good conservation practices. Dedicated to the realistic conservation of our water resources.
Publication(s): EarthWatch Oregon
Keyword(s): Air Quality/Atmosphere, Land Issues, Transportation, Water Habitats & Quality
Contact(s):
Orville Alleman, President
Chuck Lang, Conservation Director; 4775 Gardner Rd., SE, Salem, OR 97302; 503-588-1920; charleslang@home.com

OREGON ENVIRONMENTAL COUNCIL
520 SW 6th Ave
Suite 940
Portland, OR 97204-1535 United States
Phone: 503-222-1963   Fax: 503-222-1405
E-mail: oec@orcouncil.org
Website: www.orcouncil.org

Founded: 1968
Membership: 1,001–10,000
Scope: State
Description: Oregon Environmental Council is a nonprofit organization whose mission is to bring Oregonians together for a healthy environment.
Publication(s): One Oregon, One Environment
Keyword(s): Air Quality/Atmosphere, Climate Change, Ethics/Environmental Justice, Pollution (general), Public Health, Transportation, Water Habitats & Quality
Contact(s):
Jeff Allen, Executive Director
Matt Blevins, Media Contact
Cheryl Bristah, Office Manager; 503-222-1963; ext. 100; cheryl@orcouncil.org
Kevin Kasowski, Development Director

OREGON NATURAL RESOURCES COUNCIL
5825 N. Greeley Avenue
Portland, OR 97217 United States
Phone: 503-283-6343   Fax: 503-283-0756
E-mail: sr@onrc.org
Website: www.onrc.org

Founded: 1972
Membership: 1,001–10,000
Scope: Local, State, Regional, National
Description: A nonprofit, state-wide organization working to aggressively protect and restore Oregon's wildlands, wildlife, and waters as an enduring legacy.
Publication(s): Wild Oregon
Keyword(s): Ecosystems (precious), Forests/Forestry, Land Issues, Public Lands/Greenspace, Reduce/Reuse/Recycle, Water Habitats & Quality, Wildlife & Species
Contact(s):
Regna Merritt, Executive Director; 503-283-6343; ext. 214; rm@onrc.org
Jay Ward, Conservation Director; 503-283-6343; ext. 210; jw@onrc.org
David Wilkins, Director of Development; 503-283-6343; ext. 223; dw@onrc.org
Jacki Richey, Director of Finance; jr@onrc.org
Doug Heiken, Western Oregon Field Rep.; P.O. Box 11648, Eugene, OR 97440; 541-344-0675; Fax: 541-343-0996; dh@onrc.org

Wendell Wood, Southern Oregon Field Rep.; ww@onrc.org
Erik Fernandez, GIS/Adopt-A-Wilderness; ef@onrc.org
Jeremy Hall, NW Field Representative; 541-344-0675; jh@onrc.org
Tim Lillebo, Eastern Oregon and Advocacy D.C.; 16 NW Kansas, Bend, OR 97701; 541-382-2616; Fax: 503-385-3370; tl@onrc.org
Sumner Robinson, Information Systems Manager; sr@onrc.org
Leeanne Siart, Conservatiopn Associate; ls@onrc.org
Alex Brown, Grassroots Coordinator; 503-283-6343; ext. 224; ab@onrc.org
Erin Fagely, Volunteer Coordinator; efa@onrc.org
Joellen Pail, Membership Coordinator; jp@onrc.org

OREGON SMALL WOODLANDS ASSOCIATION
1775 32nd Place, NE, Suite C
Salem, OR 97303 United States
Phone: 503-588-1813   Fax: 503-588-1970
E-mail: oswa@oswa.org
Website: www.oswa.org

Founded: 1967
Membership: 1,001–10,000
Scope: State
Description: A statewide organization affiliated with the National Woodland Owners Association, dedicated to the protection, management, use and enhancement of Oregon's forest resources.
Publication(s): Northwest Woodlands, The Update
Keyword(s): Forests/Forestry, Reduce/Reuse/Recycle
Contact(s):
John Poppino, President; 541-447-1342
Bill Arsenault, 1st Vice-President; 541-584-2272
Ken Faulk, 2nd Vice-President; 541-447-6762
Denny Miles, Executive Director
Lori Rasor, Editor; 503-228-3624

OREGON SOCIETY OF AMERICAN FORESTERS
NORTHWEST OFFICE
4033 SW Canyon Rd.
Portland, OR 97221 United States
Phone: 503-224-8046   Fax: 503-226-2515
Website: www.forestry.org

Founded: 1900
Membership: 1,001–10,000
Scope: Regional
Description: The mission of the society is to advance the science, education, technology, and practice of forestry; enhance its members' competency and professionalism; and use the knowledge and skills of the profession to benefit society.
Publication(s): Western Forester
Contact(s):
Lori Rasor, Manager and Editor; 4033 SW Canyon Rd., Portland, OR 97221; 503-224-0046

OREGON TROUT
117 SW Naito Parkway
Portland, OR 97204-3595 United States
Phone: 503-222-9091   Fax: 503-222-9187
E-mail: info@ortrout.org
Website: www.ortrout.org
Membership: 1,001–10,000
Scope: Regional
Description: An Oregon-based organization focused on the protection and restoration of native fish and their ecosystems.
Publication(s): Riverkeeper
Contact(s):
Jim Myron, Conservation Director
Joe Whitworth, Executive Director

OREGON WILDLIFE HERITAGE FOUNDATION
P.O. Box 30406
Portland, OR 97294-3406 United States
Phone: 503-255-6059   Fax: 503-255-6467
E-mail: owhf@aol.com
Website: www.owhf.org

Founded: 1981
Membership: 101–1,000
Scope: State
Description: The Oregon Wildlife Heritage Foundation is a nonprofit, tax-exempt foundation incorporated under the laws of the State of Oregon. It has a 501(c)3 determination under the I.R.S. code. It receives grants and contributions to be used to fund selected projects beneficial to the fish and wildlife resources of Oregon and the people who enjoy them.
Contact(s):
E. Kimbark MacColl, President
Charles Lilley, Vice President
Rod Brobeck, Executive Director
Kenneth Klarquist, Jr, Secretary
Nelson Rutherford, Treasurer

ORGANIZATION FOR BAT CONSERVATION
39221 Woodward Avenue
P.O. Box 801
Bloomfield Hills, MI 48303 United States
Phone: 248-645-3232   Fax: 248-645-3242
E-mail: obcbats@aol.com
Website: www.batroost.com

Founded: 1990
Membership: 1,001–10,000
Scope: Local, State, Regional, National, International
Description: One of the only international non-profit organizations dedicated to bat conservation. This mission is fulfilled through education and habitat preservation. Find great info. on bat houses, bat habitat, West Nile and more!
Publication(s): Stokes Guide to Bat Identification, Simple Guide to Bat House Designs, Understanding Bats
Keyword(s): Agriculture/Farming, Development/Developing Countries, Public Health, Recreation/Ecotourism, Reduce/Reuse/Recycle, Sprawl/Urban Planning, Water Habitats & Quality, Wildlife & Species
Contact(s):
Rob Mies, Director; 517-339-5200; ext. 9; Fax: 517-339-5619; obcbats@aol.com
Kim Williams, Executive Director; 517-339-5200; ext. 9; Fax: 517-339-5618; obcbats@aol.com

ORGANIZATION OF WILDLIFE PLANNERS
1900 Kanawha Blvd., East
Charleston, WV 25305 United States
Phone: 304-558-2771   Fax: 304-558-3147
E-mail: wildlife@dnr.state.wv.us
Website: www.dnr.state.wv.us

Founded: 1978
Membership: 1–100
Scope: State
Description: A nonprofit, tax-exempt organization comprised of professional state and federal fish and wildlife resource planners, natural resources educators, professional conservationists, and associated interests dedicated to improving, through education and training, the quality of state-level resources management and planning. The focus of the organization is on developing the necessary tools and skills to conduct effective planned management systems.
Publication(s): Tomorrow's Management, Newsletter
Contact(s):
Paul Johansen, Assistant Chief, Game Management

ORION SOCIETY, THE
187 Main St
Great Barrington, MA 01230 United States
Phone: 413-528-4422   Fax: 413-528-0676
E-mail: orion@orionsociety.org
Website: www.oriononline.org
Membership: 1,001–10,000
Scope: National, International
Description: The Orion Society is an award-winning publisher, an environmental education organization, and a communication support network for grassroots environmental and community organizations across North America. It is a nonprofit member organization with 8000 members, individual and organization, representing all fifty states and thirty-one countries.
Publication(s): Orion Afield magazine, Orion magazine, The Orion Grassroots Network

ORNITHOLOGICAL COUNCIL
1707 H St., N.W., Suite 200
Washington, DC 20006 United States
Phone: 301-986-8568   Fax: 301-986-5205
Website: nmnh.si.edu/BIRDNET
Founded: 1992
Membership: 1,001–10,000
Scope: International
Description: The Council provides impartial scientific information about birds for sound decisions, policies, or management actions; links the scientific community with public and private decision-makers; informs ornithologists of actions that affect birds or the study of birds; and speaks for scientific ornithology when the study of birds might be affected. Website contains links to ornithological scientific societies.
Keyword(s): Wildlife & Species
Contact(s):
David Blockstein, Chairman; 1707 H St., N.W., Suite 200, Washington, DC 20006; 202-530-5810; Fax: 202-628-4311
Ellen Paul, Executive Director; 301-986-8568; Fax: 301-986-5205; epaul@concentric.net

OTTER PROJECT, THE
3098 Stewart Court
Marina, CA 93933 United States
Phone: 831-883-4159   Fax: 831-883-4159
E-mail: exec@otterproject.org
Website: www.otterproject.org
Founded: 1998
Membership: 1,001–10,000
Scope: Local, State, Regional, National
Description: The Otter Project supports critical research and recovery efforts for the California sea otter and the nearshore marine environment. The Otter Project communicates scientific information to policy makers.
Keyword(s): Ecosystems (precious), Oceans/Coasts/Beaches, Pollution (general), Water Habitats & Quality, Wildlife & Species
Contact(s):
Steve Shimek, Executive Director

OUTDOOR CIRCLE, THE
1314 S. King, Suite 306
Honolulu, HI 96814 United States
Phone: 808-593-0300   Fax: 808-593-0525
E-mail: mail@outdoorcircle.org
Website: www.outdoorcircle.org
Founded: 1912
Membership: 1,001–10,000
Scope: Local, State
Description: A nonprofit organization whose purpose is to work for and develop a more beautiful state, freeing it from disfigurement, conserving and developing its natural beauty, and cooperating in educational and other efforts towards preservation of open spaces, parklands, recycling, and antilitter.
Publication(s): Our Familiar Island Trees, Trees and Flowers of the Hawaiian Islands, Majesty II, Majesty: Exceptional Trees of Hawaii, Pua Nani: Hawaii is a Garden, The Greenleaf Newsletter, Keep Hawaii Green, Exceptional Trees of Hawaii, The
Keyword(s): Forests/Forestry, Land Issues, Public Lands/Greenspace, Wildlife & Species
Contact(s):
Mary Steiner, Chief Executive Officer; 808-593-0300; ext. 13; Fax: 808-593-0525; mary@outdoorcircle.org
Kimberly Hillebrand, Landscape & Planting Project Manager; 808-593-0300; ext. 14; Fax: 808-593-0525; kimberly@outdoorcircle.org
Leona Loo, Administrative Assistant; leona@outdoorcircle.org
Aldrina Ventura, Membership Manager; aldrina@outdoorcircle.org

OUTDOOR RECREATION COUNCIL OF BRITISH COLUMBIA
1367 W. Broadway
Suite 334
Vancouver, V6H 4A9 British Columbia Canada
Phone: 604-737-3058   Fax: 604-737-3666
E-mail: orc@intergate.ca
Website: www.orcbc.ca
Founded: 1976
Scope: Province
Description: The Outdoor Recreation Council of BC works to maintain wild spaces and free-flowing rivers, and access for outdoor recreation. The ORC of BC is a nonprofit society formed to serve as a mechanism independent from government, through which the interests and activities of groups organized on a provincial basis concerned with outdoor recreation, education, and conservation can be coordinated and represented to government, industry, and the public.
Publication(s): Reference library on outdoor recreation, Outdoor Report
Keyword(s): Land Issues, Public Lands/Greenspace, Recreation/Ecotourism, Reduce/Reuse/Recycle, Water Habitats & Quality

OUTDOOR WRITERS ASSOCIATION OF AMERICA, INC.
121 Hickory St., Suite 1
Missoula, MT 59801 United States
Phone: 406-728-7434   Fax: 406-728-7445
E-mail: owaa@montana.com
Website: www.owaa.org
Founded: 1927
Membership: 1,001–10,000
Scope: National
Description: We strive to improve ourselves in the art and media of our craft and to increase our knowledge and understanding in supporting the conservation of our natural resources. To this end we pledge ourselves to maintain the highest ethical standards in the exercise of our craft.
Publication(s): Printed OWAA Directory, Outdoors Unlimited
Keyword(s): Ethics/Environmental Justice, Recreation/Ecotourism
Contact(s):
William Geer, Executive Director; 406-728-7434; Fax: 406-728-7445; owaa@montana.com
Katie McKalip, Assistant Editor; 406-728-7434; Fax: 406-728-7445; editorassist@montana.com
Lisa Carter, Membership Services Manager; 406-728-7434; Fax: 406-728-7445; members@montana.com
Kevin Rhoades, Editor; 406-728-7434; Fax: 406-728-7445; oueditor@montana.com

OZARK SOCIETY, THE
P.O. Box 2914
Little Rock, AR 72203 United States
Phone: 501-666-2989 Fax: 501-666-2989
E-mail: steward810@aol.com
Website: www.ozarksociety.net

Founded: 1962
Membership: 101–1,000
Scope: State
Description: To promote the knowledge and enjoyment of the scenic and scientific resources, particularly free-flowing streams, wilderness areas, and unique natural areas of the Ozark-Ouachita mountain region, and to help protect those resources for present and future generations.
Publication(s): Pack and Paddle, The
Keyword(s): Land Issues
Contact(s):
Alice Andrews, President; 5524 Southwood, Little Rock, AR 72205; 501-666-5070; alice2090k@yahoo.com

OZARKS RESOURCE CENTER
P.O. Box 3
Brixey, MO 65618 United States
Phone: 417-679-4773
E-mail: jlorrain@goin.missouri.org

Founded: 1978
Membership: 1,001–10,000
Scope: National
Description: The Center provides research, education, technical assistance, and dissemination of information on renewable resources-based technology, sustainable agriculture, environmentally responsible practices, sustainable community economic development, and self-reliance for the family, farm, community, Ozarks, and other bio-regions.
Publication(s): Broadcaster, The (newsletter), Talking Oak Leaves (newsletter)
Keyword(s): Development/Developing Countries, Ethics/Environmental Justice, Land Issues, Sprawl/Urban Planning
Contact(s):
Donna Jones, President; RR 1 Box 68A-1, Dora, MO 65637; 417-201-2518
Corliss Schaffer, Vice President; HCR 64 Box 221, West Plains, MO 65775; 417-257-0670
Janice Lorrain, Executive Director; Rt. 1 Box 303, Ava, MO 65608; 417-683-5049
Kathi Trantham, Secretary; 7969 County Rd. 3010, West Plains, MO 65775; 417-256-6518
Denise Vaughn, Treasurer; Rt. 3 Box 200, Mtn. View, MO 65548; 417-256-6518

OZONE ACTION
1700 Connecticut Ave., NW, 3rd Fl.
Washington, DC 20009 United States
Phone: 202-265-6738 Fax: 202-986-6041
E-mail: ozone_action@ozone.org

Founded: 1992
Scope: National
Description: Ozone Action educates the public about threats from ozone depletion and human-induced climate change. Ozone Action investigates and publicizes attempts to weaken our global environmental protections and exposes attempts by industry to distort public debate.
Publication(s): Ozone Action News, Climate Change Current Effects Summaries, Black Market CFC Reports, Ties That Blind
Keyword(s): Air Quality/Atmosphere, Climate Change
Contact(s):
Kevin Sweeney, Board Chair

P

PA CLEANWAYS
VENANGO COUNTY
105 W. Fourth St.
Greensburg, PA 15601 United States
Phone: 724-836-4121 Fax: 724-836-1980
E-mail: info@pacleanways.org
Website: www.pacleanways.org

Founded: 1999
Membership: 1–100
Scope: Local
Description: PA CleanWays has helped people and their communities clean up mountains of trash from PA lands and waters. If you're offended by litter and trash in your community, PA CleanWays, a nonprofit environmental organization, can help you.

PACIFIC BASIN ASSOCIATION OF SOIL AND WATER CONSERVATION DISTRICTS
Attn: President, P.O. Box 12596
Tamuning, GU 96931 United States

Scope: State
Contact(s):
Felix Quan, President; 671-632-7114; Fax: 671-632-7114
Patrick Calvo, Vice President; P.O. Box 2795, Saipan MP, GU 96950; 670-234-6120; Fax: 670-235-6122
Estanislao Hocog, Secretary-Treasurer; P.O. Box 12, Tinian MP, GU 96952; 670-433-0690; Fax: 670-433-3152

PACIFIC FISHERY MANAGEMENT COUNCIL
7700 Northeast Ambassador Pl.
Suite 200
Portland, OR 97220 United States
Phone: 503-820-2280 Fax: 503-820-2299
Website: www.pcouncil.org

Scope: National
Description: Nonprofit organization established by the Magnuson-Stevens Fishery Conservation and Management Act of 1976. Develops management plans for fisheries off the coasts of Washington, Oregon, and California. Fourteen voting and five nonvoting members, of which nine are appointed by the Secretary of Commerce. Members include state and federal fishery agency managers, knowledgeable citizens, and a tribal representative.
Keyword(s): Recreation/Ecotourism, Reduce/Reuse/Recycle, Water Habitats & Quality, Wildlife & Species
Contact(s):
Donald McIsaac, Executive Director
John Coon, Fishery Management Coordinator, Salmon
James Glock, Fishery Management Coordinator, Marine
James Seger, Economic Analysis Coordinator

PACIFIC INSTITUTE FOR STUDIES IN DEVELOPMENT, ENVIRONMENT, AND SECURITY
654 13th St.
Oakland, CA 94612 United States
Phone: 510-251-1600 Fax: 510-251-2203
E-mail: pistaff@pacinst.org
Website: www.pacinst.org

Founded: 1987
Scope: Local, State, Regional, National, International
Description: The institute is a policy research organization that focuses on the interface of security, development, and environmental protection issues. Areas of focus include climate change and water.
Publication(s): Global Change, Pacific Institute Reports

Keyword(s): Air Quality/Atmosphere, Climate Change, Development/Developing Countries, Reduce/Reuse/Recycle, Water Habitats & Quality

Contact(s):
Nick Cain, Director of Communications; ncain@pacinst.org
Peter Gleick, Executive Director; pgleick@pipeline.com

PACIFIC MARINE CONSERVATION COUNCIL
PMCC
P.O. Box 59
Astoria, OR 97103 United States
Phone: 503-325-8188   Fax: 503-325-9681
E-mail: info@pmcc.org
Website: PMCC.org

Founded: 1999
Scope: Local, State, Regional, National
Description: We represent fishing communities and concerned citizens including fishermen, scientists, conservationists and others dedicated to the health and diversity of our marine ecosytems on the west coast
Keyword(s): Ecosystems (precious), Ethics/Environmental Justice, Executive/Legislative/Judicial Reform, Oceans/Coasts/Beaches, Water Habitats & Quality, Wildlife & Species

PACIFIC NORTHWEST TRAIL ASSOCIATION
P. O. Box 1817
Mount Vernon, WA 98273 United States
Phone: 306-854-9415   Fax: 360-854-7665
E-mail: PNT@PNT.org
Website: www.pnt.org

Founded: 1977
Membership: 101–1,000
Scope: Local, State, Regional, National
Description: The PNTA was formed to promote the development of a continuous foot and horse trail from the Continental Divide at Glacier National Park to the Pacific Ocean at Olympic National Park. The PNTA encourages land use and conservation education through exposure to the historic and natural diversity of the Pacific Northwest. Check our website for information about our education programs for youth.
Publication(s): Nor'wester, Blanchard Hill and Chuckanut Mountain Map, Pacific Northwest Trail, The
Keyword(s): Public Lands/Greenspace, Recreation/Ecotourism, Transportation

Contact(s):
Duane Melcher, Chair; 306-424-0407

PACIFIC RIVERS COUNCIL
P.O. Box 10798
Eugene, OR 97440 United States
Phone: 541-345-0119   Fax: 541-345-0710
E-mail: info@pacrivers.org
Website: www.pacrivers.org

Founded: 1987
Membership: 1,001–10,000
Scope: National
Description: The Pacific Rivers Council's mission is to protect and restore rivers, their watersheds and the native aquatic species that depend on them.
Publication(s): Entering the Watershed, various briefing books and reports, Freeflow
Keyword(s): Agriculture/Farming, Ecosystems (precious), Executive/Legislative/Judicial Reform, Forests/Forestry, Land Issues, Pollution (general), Public Lands/Greenspace, Water Habitats & Quality, Wildlife & Species

Contact(s):
David Bayles, Executive Director (Acting)

PACIFIC SEABIRD GROUP
University of Victoria Biology Department
Box 179, 4505 University Way, NE
Seattle, WA 98105 United States
Website: www.pacificseabirdgroup.org

Founded: 1972
Scope: International
Description: An international organization to promote the knowledge, study and conservation of Pacific seabirds.
Publication(s): Pacific Seabird Group Bulletin
Keyword(s): Wildlife & Species

Contact(s):
David Irons, Chair; USFWS, 1011 E. Tudor Road, Anchorage, AK 99503; david_irons@fws.gov
Breck Tyler, Treasurer; Long Marine Laboratory, 100 Shaffer Rd., Santa Cruz, CA 95060; 831-426-5740; ospr@cats.ucsc.edu
Dan Roby, Chair Elect; Oregon Cooperative Fish & Wildlife Research Unit, Department of Fisheries and Wildlife, 104 Nash Hall, Oregon State University, Corvallis, Oregon 97331-3803; 541-737-1955; Fax: 541-737-3590; Daniel.Roby@orst.edu
Ron LeValley, Treasurer; Mad River Biologists, 1497 Central Avenue, McKinleyville, CA 95519; 707-839-0900; Fax 839-0867; ron@madriverbio.com
Lora Leschner, Secretary; Washington Dept. of Fish & Wildlife, 16018 Mill Creek Blvd., Mill Creek, WA 98012; 425-776-1311, ext. 421; Fax: 425-338-1066; leschlll@dfw.wa.gov
Vivian Mendenhall, Editor; 4600 Rabbit Creek Rd., Anchorage, AK 99516; 907-345-7124; Fax: 907-345-0686; fasgadair@worldnet.att.net

PACIFIC WHALE FOUNDATION
OCEAN SCIENCE DISCOVERY CENTER
PACIFIC WHALE FOUNDATION ECO-ADVENTURES
The Harbor Shops at Maalaea
300 Maalaea Rd. Suite 211
Wailukuk, HI 96793 United States
Phone: 808-879-8860   Fax: 808-879-2615
E-mail: info@pacificwhale.org
Website: www.pacificwhale.org

Founded: 1980
Membership: 10,001–100,000
Scope: Local, Regional, National
Description: A nonprofit tax-exempt 501(c)(3) organization dedicated to saving whales, dolphins and the ocean through marine research, public education and marine conservation. Pacific Whale Foundation's Eco-Adventures promote eco-friendly interactions with the marine environment with the goal of promoting ocean stewardship. The new Ocean Science Discovery Center builds on Pacific Whale Foundation's award-winning marine education programs and offers interactive, hands-on learning about the sea.
Publication(s): Fin and Fluke, Maui Outdoor Adventure, Whalewatch News, Soundings
Keyword(s): Water Habitats & Quality, Wildlife & Species

Contact(s):
Gregory Kaufman, President
Paul Forestell, Vice President
Dixie Bongolan, Secretary and Treasurer
Anne Rillero, Editor

PANOS INSTITUTE, THE
1701 K St., NW, 11th Fl.
Washington, DC 20006 United States
Phone: 202-223-7949   Fax: 202-223-7947
E-mail: panos@cais.com
Website: www.panosinst.org

Founded: 1986
Scope: International

Description: The Panos Institute consists of three autonomous nonprofit, nongovernmental organizations located in London, Paris, and Washington, DC, working to raise public understanding of sustainable development issues. The Washington, DC institute focuses its work on Latin America, the Caribbean, and the United States.
Publication(s): We Speak for Ourselves, From Information to Education, Eco-Reports, SIDAmerica
Keyword(s): Development/Developing Countries, Population
Contact(s):
Gretchen Maynes, Executive Director/ Secretary
John Kramer, Acting Chairman
Michael McDowell, Vice Chairman
George Woodring, Treasurer

PARKS AND TRAILS COUNCIL OF MINNESOTA
275 E. 4th St. #642
St. Paul, MN 55101 United States
Phone: 651-726-2457 Fax: 651-726-2458
E-mail: info@parksandtrails.org
Website: www.parksandtrails.org
Founded: 1954
Membership: 1,001–10,000
Scope: State
Description: The mission of the Council is to further the establishment, development, and enhancement of parks and trails within the state of Minnesota, and to encourage their prudent use and protection.
Publication(s): Newsletter
Keyword(s): Land Issues, Public Lands/Greenspace, Recreation/Ecotourism, Transportation, Wildlife & Species
Contact(s):
Jeffrey Olson, President
Barbara Burgum, Vice President
David Hartwell, Vice President
Greg Murray, Vice President
Dorian Grilley, Executive Director
Howard Olson, Secretary
Michael Prichard, Treasurer

PARTNERS IN AMPHIBIAN AND REPTILE CONSERVATION (PARC)
P.O. Drawer E
Aiken, SC 29802 United States
Phone: 803-725-2473 Fax: 803-725-3309
E-mail: forrest@srel.edu
Website: www.parcplace.org
Founded: 1998
Scope: National, International
Description: PARC is an international organization and a multi-sector partnership dedicated to the conservation of the herepetofauna (amphibians and reptiles) and their habitats.
Keyword(s): Ecosystems (precious), Land Issues, Water Habitats & Quality, Wildlife & Species

PARTNERS IN PARKS
P.O. Box 130
205 E 3rd St.
Paonia, CO 81428 United States
Phone: 970-527-6691 Fax: 970-527-7297
E-mail: partpark@mindspring.com
Website: www.partnersinparks.org
Founded: 1988
Scope: National
Description: A nonprofit organization that encourages, promotes, and establishes professional level partnerships and educational opportunities between national park and other public land managers and those who would contribute their time and skills to studying, protecting, and interpreting natural and cultural features.
Keyword(s): Ecosystems (precious), Land Issues, Public Lands/Greenspace, Water Habitats & Quality, Wildlife & Species
Contact(s):
Sarah Bishop, President
Kate Zachmann, Executive Officer; partpark2@mindspring.com

PARTNERSHIP FOR SUSTAINABLE FORESTRY
229 Hanover Street
Suite 101
Annapolis, MD 21401 United States
Phone: 410-267-8595 Fax: 410-267-8597
E-mail: gallenbay@aol.com
Website: psf.biz
Founded: 2001
Scope: State
Description: An alliance of business and civic organizations dedicated to sustainable forestry practices in rural and urban Maryland.
Keyword(s): Forests/Forestry, Public Lands/Greenspace
Contact(s):
Gary Allen, Co-Director

PENNSYLVANIA ASSOCIATION OF CONSERVATION DISTRICTS, INC.
25 North Front Street
Harrisburg, PA 17101 United States
Phone: 717-238-7223 Fax: 717-238-7201
E-mail: pacd@pacd.org
Website: www.pacd.org
Membership: 101–1,000
Scope: State
Description: The Pennsylvania Association of Conservation Districts, Inc. (PACD) was organized in 1950 to serve as a collective voice of Pennsylvania's conservation districts. PACD provides districts with education and information to help them in their work in land and water conservation. Over the years, the Association has been an integral part of the shaping of the modern conservation district.
Contact(s):
Ron Rohall, President; P.O. Box 27, Rector, PA 15677; 724-238-4973; Fax: 724-238-4973; rjrohall@westol.com
Susan Fox Marquart, Executive Director; 25 North Front Street, Harrisburg, PA 17101; 717-238-7223; Fax: 717-238-7201; susan-marquart@pacd.org

PENNSYLVANIA CENTER FOR ENVIRONMENTAL EDUCATION (PCEE)
010 Eisenberg
Slippery Rock University
Slippery Rock, PA 16057 United States
Phone: 724-738-4555 Fax: 724-738-4502
E-mail: pcee@sru.edu
Website: www.pcee.org
Founded: 1997
Scope: State
Description: The PCEE is a cooperative partnership of 13 Pennsylvania organizations formed to maximize statewide environmental education resources and efforts and to ensure continued access to high quality environmental education for all commonwealth citizens.
Contact(s):
Paulette Johnson, Executive Director; 724-738-4555; Fax: 724-738-4502; paulette.johnson@sru.edu
Richard Knight, Project Manager; 724-738-4528; Fax: 724-738-4502; richard.knight@sru.edu
Elissa Totin, Project Manager; 724-738-4527; Fax: 724-738-4502; elissa.totin@sru.edu
Lisa Theodorson, Secretary; 724-738-4555; Fax: 724-738-4502; lisa.theodorson@sru.edu

PENNSYLVANIA CITIZENS ADVISORY COUNCIL TO DEPARTMENT OF ENVIRONMENTAL PROTECTION
Rachel Carson State Office Building, Floor 13
P.O. Box 8459
Harrisburg, PA 17105-8459 United States
Phone: 717-787-4527   Fax: 717-787-2878
E-mail: suswilson@state.pa.us
Website: www.cacdep.state.pa.us
Membership: 1–100
Scope: Regional
Description: Created by Act 275 of the PA General Assembly, 1971.
Publication(s): Advisory, Regional Report, Annual Report
Keyword(s): Air Quality/Atmosphere, Reduce/Reuse/Recycle
Contact(s):
 Susan Wilson, Executive Director
 Stephanie Mioff, Administrative Assistant
 Dave Strong, Chairperson

PENNSYLVANIA ENVIRONMENTAL COUNCIL, INC. (PEC)
130 Locust Street
Suite 200
Harrisburg, PA 17101 United States
Phone: 717-230-8044   Fax: 215-563-0528
Website: www.pecpa.org
Founded: 1969
Scope: State
Description: Private nonprofit statewide membership organization devoted to the protection and improvement of Pennsylvania's environment through education, advocacy and consensus-building. PEC brings together nonprofits, government agencies, businesses and citizens to develop environmental policy, take action on environmental issues and work for effective environmental legislation, regulation and enforcement.
Publication(s): Environmental Forum Newsletter, Urban Vacant Land Handbook, Transit-Oriented Development Handbook, Environmental Advisory Council Handbook, Building Better Communities and Preserving our Countryside, Guiding Growth, Pennsylvania Legislative Updates
Keyword(s): Development/Developing Countries, Public Lands/Greenspace, Water Habitats & Quality
Contact(s):
 Andrew McElwaine, President and CEO
 Brian Hill, Vice President and Director of French Creek Project
 Ellen Alaimo, Regional Director of Northeastern PA Office
 Anna Brienich, Regional Director of Community Planning Western PA Office
 Patrick Starr, Regional Director of Southeastern Office
 Davitt Woodwell, Regional Director of Western PA Office

PENNSYLVANIA FEDERATION OF SPORTSMENS CLUBS
2426 N. Second St.
Harrisburg, PA 17110 United States
Phone: 717-232-3480   Fax: 717-231-3524
E-mail: info@pfsc.org
Website: www.pfsc.org
Founded: 1932
Membership: 10,001–100,000
Scope: State
Description: A representative statewide organization, affiliated with the National Wildlife Federation, dedicated to the protection and enhancement of wildlife and its habitat, and preserving, promoting, and protecting our Outdoor Heritage through public education and government interaction.
Publication(s): On Target
Contact(s):
 Lowell Graybill, President
 Melody Zullinger, Executive Director
 Ray Martin, Treasurer
 Lester McNutt, Alt. Rep. to NWF
 Linda Steiner, Editor
 Ed Zygmut, Rep. to NWF

PENNSYLVANIA FORESTRY ASSOCIATION, THE
56 E. Main St.
Mechanicsburg, PA 17055 United States
Phone: 717-766-5371
E-mail: thepfa@juno.com
Website: www.pfa.cas.psu.edu
Founded: 1886
Membership: 1,001–10,000
Scope: State
Description: An independent nonprofit conservation organization, affiliated with the National Woodland Owners Association dedicated to environmental improvement and wise use of natural resources in Pennsylvania. Membership includes a cross section of all groups and individuals interested in true conservation.
Publication(s): Pennsylvania Forest Magazine - Quarterly
Keyword(s): Forests/Forestry, Public Lands/Greenspace, Recreation/Ecotourism
Contact(s):
 Lloyd Casey, President; 717-225-4711
 William Cook, Treasurer; 717-787-2039
 William Corlett, Secretary; 717-737-7118
 Jan Zinn, Editor; 717-632-1648

PENNSYLVANIA ORGANIZATION FOR WATERSHEDS AND RIVERS (POWR)
P. O. Box 765
Harrisburg, PA 17101 United States
Phone: 717-234-7910   Fax: 717-234-7929
E-mail: info@pawatersheds.org
Website: www.pawatersheds.org
Founded: 1993
Membership: 101–1,000
Scope: Local, State
Description: POWR is dedicated to the protection, sound management and enhancement of Pennsylvania's rivers and watersheds and to the empowerment of local organizations with the same commitment. This is done through advocacy, publications, educational activities, public and open conferences/workshops, leadership training and through direct assistance.
Publication(s): Pennsylvania's Watersheds Map, River Sojourn Organizers Manual, Fact Packs, Main Stream newsletter, Monitoring Matters newsletter, Watershed Weekly newsletter
Keyword(s): Ecosystems (precious), Executive/Legislative/Judicial Reform, Forests/Forestry, Land Issues, Pollution (general), Public Lands/Greenspace, Recreation/Ecotourism, Water Habitats & Quality
Contact(s):
 Walt Pomeroy, Executive Director; wpomeroy@pawatersheds.org
 Sue Brockman, Environmental Monitoring Project Coordinator; sbrockman@pawatersheds.org
 Lisa Daly, Office Manager; sdaly@pawatersheds.org
 Susan Parry, Watershed Programs Coordinator; sparry@pawatersheds.org
 John Coutts, Director of Information Technology; jcoutts@pawatersheds.org
 Bonnie Swinehart, Editor/Writer; bswinehart@pawatersheds.org

PENNSYLVANIA RECREATION AND PARK SOCIETY, INC.
1315 W. College Ave., Suite 200
State College, PA 16801-2776 United States
Phone: 814-234-4272 Fax: 814-234-5276
E-mail: prps@vicon.net
Website: www.prps.org
Founded: 1935
Membership: 1,001–10,000
Scope: State
Description: To promote quality recreation and park opportunities for all the citizens of the Commonwealth of Pennsylvania by actively involving professionals and citizens in recreation, park, and conservation programs, by fostering and maintaining high standards of professional qualifications and ethics, and by providing quality educational opportunities.
Publication(s): The PRPS Update (Monthly), Pennsylvania Recreation and Parks
Keyword(s): Forests/Forestry, Land Issues, Pollution (general), Public Health, Public Lands/Greenspace, Recreation/Ecotourism
Contact(s):
Robert Griffith, Executive Director
Steven Landes, Secretary
R. Mcfate, President; Park Manager, Caledonia State Park, 40 Rocky Mtn. Rd., Fayetteville, PA 17222-9610; 717-352-2161
William Rosevear, Treasurer; Park Manager, PA Bureau of State Parks, 1100 Pine Grove Rd., Gardners, PA 17324-7174; 717-486-7174; Fax: 717-486-4961
Vanyla Tierney, Editor; Recreation Planner, DCNR-Bureau of State Parks, P.O. Box 1519, Mechanicsburg, PA 17055-9019; 717-783-2654

PENNSYLVANIA RESOURCES COUNCIL, INC.,
3606 Providence Rd.
Newtown Square, PA 19073 United States
Phone: 610-353-1555 Fax: 610-353-6257
Website: www.prc.org
Founded: 1939
Scope: Regional
Description: (formerly PA Roadside Council) The Pennsylvania Resources Council (PRC) is recognized nationally for its expertise in recycling, waste reduction, and litter control. PRC produces educational materials, as well as seminars and conferences for citizens, municipalities, civic groups and corporations. PRC also sponsors the nation's only environmental shopping hotline (1-800-Go-To-PRC). Open to the public, PRC's environmental living center has exhibits and workshops.
Publication(s): Environmental Living Magazine, Recyclers Roundup
Keyword(s): Pollution (general), Public Health, Recreation/Ecotourism, Reduce/Reuse/Recycle
Contact(s):
Howard Wein, President
David Mazza, Regional Director Pittsburgh Area; 412-488-7490
Marcia Weller, Regional Director Philadelphia Area

PEOPLE FOR PUGET SOUND
911 Western Ave.
Suite 580
Seattle, WA 98104 United States
Phone: 206-382-7007 Fax: 206-382-7006
E-mail: people@pugetsound.org
Website: www.pugetsound.org
Founded: 1991
Membership: 1,001–10,000
Scope: Regional
Description: People for Puget Sound works to protect and restore the imperiled marine and estuarine ecosystems of Puget Sound and the Northwest Straits.
Publication(s): Toxics in the Puget Sound Food Web, KidSound, Sound & Straits
Keyword(s): Oceans/Coasts/Beaches, Pollution (general), Water Habitats & Quality, Wildlife & Species
Contact(s):
Christopher Townsend, President of the Board of Directors
Kathy Fletcher, Executive Director; 206-382-7007; Fax: 206-382-7006; kfletcher@pugetsound.org
Pam Johnson, Field Director; 206-382-7007; Fax: 206-382-7006; pjohnson@pugetsound.org
Jacques White, Habitat Director; 206-382-7007; Fax: 206-382-7006; jwhite@pugetsound.org
Stephanie Raymond, Education Coordinator; 206-382-7007; Fax: 206-382-7006; sraymond@pugetsound.org

PEOPLE FOR PUGET SOUND
NORTH SOUND OFFICE
911 Western Avenue, Suite 580
Seattle, WA 98104 United States
Phone: 206-382-7007 Fax: 206-382-7006
E-mail: northsound@pugetsound.org
Website: www.pugetsound.org
Scope: Local, Regional
Contact(s):
Mike Sato, Director

PEOPLE FOR PUGET SOUND
SOUTH SOUND OFFICE
1063 Capitol Way S., Suite 206
Olympia, WA 98501 United States
Phone: 360-754-9177 Fax: 360-534-9371
E-mail: southsound@pugetsound.org
Website: www.pugetsound.org
Founded: 1991
Membership: 1,001–10,000
Scope: Regional
Description: People for Puget Sound works to protect and restore the imperiled marine and estuarine ecosystems of Puget Sound and the Northwest Straits.
Publication(s): Sound and Straits
Keyword(s): Oceans/Coasts/Beaches, Pollution (general), Water Habitats & Quality, Wildlife & Species
Contact(s):
Bruce Wishart, Director; bwishart@pugetsound.org
Lisa Noble, Outreach Coordinator; lnoble@pugetsound.org

PEOPLE'S FORUM 2001, JAPAN
Maruko Bldg. 3F, 1-20-6 Higashiueno
Taitou-ku, Tokyo, 110-0015 Japan
Phone: 81338342436 Fax: 81338342406
E-mail: pf2001jp@jca.ax.apc.org
Scope: International
Description: People's Forum 2001, Japan is an NGO network of national environmental NGO's, CBO's, and individuals being active to bring about sustainable society. The Forum's task is to serve as a clearinghouse as well as to provide a framework of activities for the members. The Forum's activities include research, education, publication, and policy dialogues with different sectors to alter current economic and political systems to be ecologically and socially sustainable.
Contact(s):
Tomoko Sakuma, Director

PEREGRINE FUND, THE
5668 W. Flying Hawk Ln.
Boise, ID 83709 United States
Phone: 208-362-3716 Fax: 208-362-2376
E-mail: tpf@peregrinefund.org
Website: www.peregrinefund.org
Founded: 1970
Membership: 1,001–10,000

Scope: National, International

Description: The Peregrine Fund works nationally and internationally to conserve biological diversity and enhance environmental health by working with birds of prey through management and conservation of species and their habitat, and through education and scientific investigation. Although best known nationally for species restoration, they have assisted on conservation projects in over 40 countries.

Publication(s): The Peregrine Fund Newsletter, progress reports, Operation Report, Annual Report

Keyword(s): Wildlife & Species

Contact(s):
William Burnham, President and CEO
Jeffrey Cilek, Vice President
J. Jenny, Vice President
Karen Hixon, Treasurer
D. Nelson, Chairman of Board
Paxson Offield, Vice Chairman of the Board
Ronald Yanke, Secretary

PHEASANTS FOREVER, INC.
1783 Buerkle Circle
St. Paul, MN 55110 United States
Phone: 651-773-2000   Fax: 651-773-5500
E-mail: pf@pheasantsforever.org
Website: www.pheasantsforever.org

Founded: 1982

Membership: 1,000,001 +

Scope: Local, State, Regional, National

Description: Pheasants Forever, Inc. is a nonprofit conservation organization formed in response to the continued decline of ring-necked pheasants. The mission of Pheasants Forever is to protect and to enhance pheasant and other wildlife populations throughout North America through public awareness and education, habitat restoration, development and maintenance, and improvements in land and water management policies.

Publication(s): Pheasants Forever

Keyword(s): Agriculture/Farming, Recreation/Ecotourism, Wildlife & Species

Contact(s):
Paul Hanson, Chairman of the Board; paul.hanson.jdwm@statefarm.com
Howard Vincent, President and Chief Executive Officer; 651-773-2000; hvincent@pheasantsforever.org
Joseph Duggan, Vice President of Development and Public Affairs; 651-773-2000; jduggan@pheasantsforever.org
David Nomsen, Vice President of Governmental Affairs; 2101 Ridgewood Dr., Alexandria, MN 56308; 320-763-6103; pfnomsen@rea-alp.com
Rick Young, Vice President of Field Operations; 651-773-2000; ryoung@pheasantsforever.org
Peter Berthelsen, Director of Conservation-Nebraska; 1101 Alexander Ave., Elba, NE 68835; 308-754-5339; phasianus@aol.com
Matthew Holland, Director of Conservation, MN; 679 W. River Dr., New London, MN 56273; 320-354-4377; ringneck@tds.net
James Wooley, Senior Regional Wildlife Biologist; 1205 Ilion Ave., Chariton, IA 50049; 641-774-2238; jwooley@lisco.com
Bob St. Pierre, Manager of Public Relations; 651-773-2000; Fax: 651-773-5500; stpete@pheasantsforever.org
Jim Inglis, Regional Wildlife Biologist; 11821 Township Hwy. 49 Rear, Upper Sandusky, OH 43351; 419-209-0851; jinglis@pheasantsforever.org
Aaron Kuehl, Regional Wildlife Biologist; 401 E. 1st Street, Janesville, MN 56048; 507-231-4752; akuehl@pheasantsforever.org
David Van Waus, Regional Wildlife Biologist; 72408 270th St., Colo, IA 50056; 641-377-3480; davwpf@netins.net
Walt Bodie, Regional Representative; 2909 Navajo Drive, Nampa, ID 83686; 208-461-7350; wbodie@pheasantsforever.org
Keith Brus, Regional Representative; 1858 Cody Road, St. Paul, NE 68873; 308-754-4815; keithbrus@cccusa.net
Barth Crouch, Regional Representative; 205 S, Santa Fe, Salina, KS 67401; 785-823-0240; vcrouch@juno.com
Andy Edwards, Regional Wildlife Biologist; 1212 Jackson Blvd., Rochester, IN 46975; 574-224-4868; inpf@rtcol.com
Jeff Gaska, Regional Represenative; W. 9947 Ghost Hill Rd., Beaver Dam, WI 53916; 920-927-3579; jgaska@pheasantsforever.org
Dan Hare, Regional Representative; 315 Tucson Ave, Bismarck, ND 58504; 701-250-9921; danhare@bis.midco.net
Mark Heckenlaible, Regional Representative; 2103 County Rd. 23, Lyons, NE 68038; 402-687-2004; colchicus@alltel.net
Eric Henning, Regional Representative; 29570 Camp Adair Rd., Monmouth, OR 97361; 541-745-5363; henning_erk@hotmail.com
Mark Herwig, Editor; 651-773-2000; herwig@pheasantsforever.org
Brandon Hoffner, Regional Representative; P.O. Box 228, 19551 Marigold Dr., Sterling, CO 80751; 970-522-3822; hoffnerbm@yahoo.com
Thomas Kirschenmann, Regional Representative; 600 W. Beck St., Worthing, SD 57077; 605-372-2037; tkirschenmann@pheasantsforever.org
Matthew O'Connor, Regional Field Representative; 2880 Thunder Rd., Hopkinton, IA 52237; 319-926-2357; niapfmatt@n-connect.net
Mike Parker, Regional Reptresentative; 117 Wilson St., De Witt, MI 48820; 517-668-1033; mparkerpf@aol.com
Mike Pruss, Regional Representative; 105 Jennie Lane, Lewistown, PA 17044; 717-242-4157; mpruss@pheasantsforever.org
Tom Schwartz, Regional Representative; 40 Crater Lake Dr., Springfield, IL 62707; 214-498-7558; tschwartz@pheasantsforever.org

PHILIPPINES ENVIRONMENT AND NATURAL RESOURCES MANAGEMENT DIVISION
Capital Area
Prov. of Negros Oriental, Philippines, 2600
Phone: 352251601

Description: A Division of the Provincial Governor's Office of Negros Oriental in Central Philippines engaged in community-based resource management: near shore fisheries development; upland and agro forestry development.

Contact(s):
Josie Columna, Information Officer; 0352251691; Fax: 0352254835; jrcolumna@speed.com.ph
Mercy Teven, Division Chief; 0352251601; Fax: 0352254835

PHYSICIANS FOR SOCIAL RESPONSIBILITY
1875 Connecticut Avenue NW, Suite 1012
Washington, DC 20009 United States
Phone: 202-667-4260   Fax: 202-667-4201
E-mail: psrnatl@psr.org
Website: www.psr.org

Founded: 1961

Scope: National

Description: Promotes arms reduction, international cooperation to protect the environment, and education and programs aimed at reducing violence.

Publication(s): Monitor, PSR Reports

Keyword(s): Energy, Pollution (general)

Contact(s):
Peter Wilk, President
Robert Musil, Executive Director

PIEDMONT ENVIRONMENTAL COUNCIL
PEC
P.O. Box 460
Warrenton, VA 20188 United States
Phone: 540-347-2334   Fax: 540-349-9003
E-mail: pec@pecva.org
Website: pec@pecva.org

Founded: 1972
Membership: 1,001–10,000
Scope: Local, State, Regional
Description: Established in 1972 to promote and protect the rural economy, natural resources, history and beauty of the Piedmont
Keyword(s): Air Quality/Atmosphere, Energy, Land Issues, Sprawl/Urban Planning, Transportation, Water Habitats & Quality

Contact(s):
Christopher Miller, President; 540-347-2334; ext. 13; Fax: 540-349-9003; cmiller@pecva.org
Douglas Larson, Vice President; 540-347-2334; ext. 21; Fax: 540-349-9003; dlarson@pecva.org

PINCHOT INSTITUTE FOR CONSERVATION
1616 P St., NW
Suite 100
Washington, DC 20036 United States
Phone: 202-797-6580   Fax: 202-797-6583
E-mail: pinchot@pinchot.org
Website: www.pinchot.org

Founded: 1963
Scope: National, International
Description: The Pinchot Institute for Conservation is an independent nonprofit organization established in 1963 by President John F. Kennedy, Jr. to advance forest conservation thought, policy, and action. The Institute serves as a bridge between the scientific and policymaking communities, providing timely, objective policy research, facilitation, leadership training, and environmental education on issues relating to the protection and sustainable management of forests and other natural resources.
Publication(s): The Pinchot Letter, numerous policy reports, discussion papers and lecture series, Grey Towers Press books
Keyword(s): Forests/Forestry, Public Lands/Greenspace

Contact(s):
V. Sample, President; 202-797-6580; Fax: 202-797-6583; alsample@pinchot.org
Nancy Pinchot, Conservation & the Arts; 570-296-9669; Fax: 570-296-9675; nancepin@aol.com
Peter Pinchot, Milford Experimental Forest; 570-296-9313; Fax: 570-296-7940; peterpin@aol.com
Andrea Bedell Loucks, Community-based Forest Stewardship; 202-939-3455; Fax: 202-797-6583; andreabedell@pinchot.org
Stephanie Kavanaugh, International Forest Policy & Planning; 202-797-0585; Fax: 202-797-6583; skavanaugh@pinchot.org
Will Price, Conservation Policy & Organizational Change; 202-797-6578; Fax: 202-797-6583; willprice@pinchot.org
Naureen Rana, Community-based Forest Stewardship; 202-797-6584; Fax: 202-797-6583; nrana@pinchot.org

PLANNED PARENTHOOD FEDERATION OF AMERICA, INC.
434 West 33rd St.
New York, NY 10001 United States
Phone: 212-541-7800   Fax: 212-245-1845
E-mail: communications@ppfa.org
Website: www.plannedparenthood.org

Founded: 1916
Membership: 101–1,000
Scope: National
Description: Planned Parenthood Federation of America (PPFA) is a federation of 132 not-for-profit affiliates operating nearly 900 medically-supervised health centers nationwide. Planned Parenthood centers provide a wide range of services—including family planning counseling, contraception, prenatal care, adoption referrals, abortion services, cancer screening, testing and treatment for HIV/AIDS, and other sexually transmitted infections, and sexuality education—to nearly 5 million men and women each year.
Keyword(s): Population, Public Health

Contact(s):
Gloria Feldt, President
Susan Pichler, Librarian; Katherine Dexter McCormick Library, 810 Seventh Ave., New York, NY 10019; 212-261-4637
Alfred Poindexter, Secretary
John Romo, Chief Operating Officer
Mary Shallenberger, Chairperson
Barbara Singhaus, Treasurer
Alfredo Vigil, Vice Chairperson

 PLANNING AND CONSERVATION LEAGUE
926 J St., Suite 612
Sacramento, CA 95814 United States
Phone: 916-444-8726   Fax: 916-448-1789
E-mail: pclmail@pcl.org
Website: www.pcl.org

Founded: 1965
Membership: 10,001–100,000
Scope: Local, State, Regional
Description: A representative statewide organization, affiliated with the National Wildlife Federation, dedicated to the protection and enhancement of wildlife and its habitat through public education and government interaction.
Publication(s): Central Valley Grassroots Guide, Merging Currents, Cost Saving Solutions to Save Energy, Community Guide to Urban Parks, Citizens Guide to the General Plan, Community Guide to CEQA, Guide to Local Growth Control Initiative, California Today
Keyword(s): Agriculture/Farming, Air Quality/Atmosphere, Climate Change, Energy, Ethics/Environmental Justice, Forests/Forestry, Land Issues, Oceans/Coasts/Beaches, Public Health, Public Lands/Greenspace, Sprawl/Urban Planning, Transportation, Water Habitats & Quality

Contact(s):
Sage Sweetwood, President
Karen Douglas, Natural Resources Director; 916-313-4512; Fax: 916-448-1789; kdouglas@pcl.org
Gerald Meral, Executive Director, Editor and Alternate Representative; 916-313-4514; Fax: 916-448-1789; jmeral@pcl.org
Sandra Spelliscy, General Counsel; 916-313-4513; Fax: 916-448-1789; sas@pcl.org
Dan Frost, Representative
William Yeates, Treasurer

PLAYA LAKES JOINT VENTURE
103 E. Simpson
Suite 200
Lafayette, CO 80026 United States
Phone: 303-926-0777   Fax: 303-926-8102
E-mail: info@pljv.org
Website: www.pljv.org

Founded: 1989
Scope: Regional
Description: Playa Lakes Joint Venture is a public-private partnership whose mission is to conserve Playa Lakes, other wetlands and associated landscapes for the benefit of birds, other wildlife, water and people. The Joint Venture works in portions of six states: Colorado, Kansas, Nebraska, New Mexico, Oklahoma and Texas.

Keyword(s): Agriculture/Farming, Ecosystems (precious), Land Issues, Recreation/Ecotourism, Sprawl/Urban Planning, Water Habitats & Quality, Wildlife & Species

Contact(s):
Michael Carter, Coordinator; mike.carter@pljv.org
Christopher Rustay, Shortgrass BCR Coordinator; chrustay@aol.com
Debbie Slobe, Communications Team Leader; debbie.slobe@pljv.org
Brian Sullivan, Biological Team Leader; brian.sullivan@pljv.org

POCONO ENVIRONMENTAL EDUCATION CENTER

R.R. 2 Box 1010
Dingmans Ferry, PA 18328 United States
Phone: 570-828-2319 Fax: 570-828-9695
E-mail: peec@ptd.net
Website: www.peec.org

Founded: 1986
Scope: State, National, International
Description: The Pocono Environmental Education Center (PEEC) enhances environmental awareness, knowledge and appreciation through hands-on experience in a natural outdoor classroom.
Publication(s): PEEC Seasons

Contact(s):
James Rienhardt, Executive Director/CEO; jimpeec@aol.com
Florence Mauro, Director of Education; fmauro@peec.org
Richard Porvaznik, Director of Marketing & Development; 570-828-9693; rporvaz@peec.org
Thomas Shimalla, Director of Operations; shimalla@peec.org
Sharon Wary, Director of Business Management; 570-828-2319; Fax: 570-828-9695; swary@peec.org

POCONO WILDLIFE REHABILITATION CENTER

361 Cherry Drive
Stroudsburg, PA 18360 United States
Phone: 570-402-0223
E-mail: pocowild@ptd.net
Website: poconowildlife.org

Founded: 1985
Membership: 101–1,000
Scope: Local, Regional
Description: The Pocono Wildlife Rehabilitation Center is a place where injured and orphaned wild animals are cared for until they can fend for themselves, when they are released back to the wild. The center treats more than 1000 animals per year and offers educational programs to the public year round.
Keyword(s): Wildlife & Species

POLLUTION PROBE

625 Church St., Suite 402
Toronto, M4Y 2G1 Ontario Canada
Phone: 416-926-1907 Fax: 416-926-1601
E-mail: pprobe@pollutionprobe.org
Website: www.pollutionprobe.org

Founded: 1969
Scope: National
Description: Pollution Probe is a Canadian nonprofit organization that exists to define environmental problems through research; to promote understanding through education; and to press for practical solutions through advocacy.
Publication(s): See publications on website
Keyword(s): Air Quality/Atmosphere, Climate Change, Energy, Ethics/Environmental Justice, Pollution (general), Water Habitats & Quality

Contact(s):
Ken Ogilvie, Executive Director; 416-926-1907; ext. 231; kogilvie@pollutionprobe.org

POPE AND YOUNG CLUB

273 Mill Creek Rd.
P.O. Box 548
Chatfield, MN 55923 United States
Phone: 507-867-4144 Fax: 507-867-4144
E-mail: pyclub@isl.net
Website: www.pope-young.org

Founded: 1961
Membership: 1,001–10,000
Scope: National
Description: A North American bowhunting and wildlife conservation organization dedicated to the promotion and protection of our bowhunting heritage and North America's wildlife.
Publication(s): Bow Hunting Record Book—"Bow Hunting Big Game Records of North America"

Contact(s):
G. Asbell, President
C. Randall Byers, First Vice President
Kevin Hisey, Executive Secretary
Donald Morgan, Treasurer

POPULATION ACTION INTERNATIONAL

1300 19th St., NW, 2nd Fl.
Washington, DC 20036 United States
Phone: 202-557-3400 Fax: 202-728-4177
E-mail: pai@popact.org
Website: www.populationaction.org

Founded: 1965
Scope: International
Description: Develops worldwide support for international population and voluntary family planning programs through public education, policy analysis, and liaison with international leaders and organizations.
Publication(s): Population & reproductive health, studies of population-environment linkages, annual report of activities, legislative and policy updates, population funding by country
Keyword(s): Development/Developing Countries, Population, Public Health, Reduce/Reuse/Recycle

Contact(s):
Amy Coen, President
Terri Bartlett, Vice President, Public Policy
Robert Engelman, Vice President, Research
Sally Ethelston, Vice President, Communications
Phyllis Piotrow, Secretary
Scott Spangler, Treasurer

POPULATION COMMUNICATIONS INTERNATIONAL

777 United Nations Plaza 5th Fl.
New York, NY 10017 United States
Phone: 212-687-3366 Fax: 212-661-4188
E-mail: pciny@population.org
Website: www.population.org

Founded: 1985
Scope: International
Description: PCI works through mass media and nongovernmental organizations to promote elevation of women's status, use of family planning, and small family norms. PCI's social-content soap operas in developing countries are locally researched and produced and weave social themes into long-term script development for radio and television dramas. In the United States PCI also works with broadcasters and NGOs. Currently PCI is collaborating with NWF to develop an environmental/human sexuality soap opera.
Publication(s): On Air (quarterly newsletter), Global Intersections (Monthly Electronic Newsletter), see publications on website
Keyword(s): Population, Public Health

Contact(s):
David Andrews, President

POPULATION CONNECTION
1400 16th St., NW. #320
Washington, DC 20036 United States
Phone: 202-332-2200 Fax: 202-332-2302
E-mail: info@popconnect.org
Website: www.popconnect.org

Founded: 1968
Membership: 10,001–100,000
Scope: National
Description: ZPG is a national nonprofit membership organization that works to educate and motivate Americans to help meet the global population challenge. ZPG mobilizes grassroots support for the adoption of policies and programs necessary to stabilize global population growth.
Publication(s): ZPG Reporter, Action Alerts, Factsheets, Backgrounders, Media Targets, reports, and promotional brochures, Teachers' PET Term Paper
Keyword(s): Development/Developing Countries, Population, Public Health, Reduce/Reuse/Recycle
Contact(s):
Elizabeth Borg, Director of Membership and Development; liz@zpg.org
Tim Cline, Director of Communications; tim@zpg.org
Brian Dixon, Director of Government Relations; brian@zpg.org
Jay Keller, Field Director; jay@zpg.org
John Seager, Executive Director; john@zpg.org
Pamela Wasserman, Director of Population Education; pam@zpg.org
Peter Kostmayer, Policy Counselor; peter@zpg.org

POPULATION INSTITUTE, THE
107 Second St., NE
Washington, DC 20002 United States
Phone: 202-544-3300 Fax: 202-544-0068
E-mail: web@populationinstitute.org
Website: www.populationinstitute.org

Founded: 1969
Membership: 10,001–100,000
Scope: International
Description: To enlist and motivate key leadership groups to participate in the effort to bring population growth into balance with resources by means consistent with human dignity and freedom. Works in communications and with mass membership organizations, educational leaders, and policy leaders.
Publication(s): POPLINE World Population News Service, Towards The 21st Century (Monograph Series), Annual Report
Keyword(s): Development/Developing Countries, Population
Contact(s):
Werner Fornos, President; 202-544-3300; ext. 104

POPULATION REFERENCE BUREAU, INC.
1875 Connecticut Ave., NW, Suite 520
Washington, DC 20009 United States
Phone: 202-483-1100 Fax: 202-328-3937
E-mail: popref@prb.org
Website: www.prb.org

Founded: 1929
Scope: National
Description: PRB is a nonprofit educational organization which provides timely and objective information on U.S. and international population trends and their implications.
Publication(s): Population Bulletin, list available on request, World and U.S. Population Data Sheets, teaching kits on population topics, Population Today, PRB Reports on America
Keyword(s): Development/Developing Countries, Population
Contact(s):
Peter Donaldson, President
Ellen Carnevale, Director of Communications
Michael Bentzmen, Chair of the Board
Carl Haub, Senior Demographer
Zuali Malsawma, Librarian

POPULATION-ENVIRONMENT BALANCE, INC.
2000 P St., NW, Suite 600
Washington, DC 20036-5915 United States
Phone: 202-955-5700 Fax: 202-955-6161
E-mail: uspop@us.net
Website: www.balance.org

Founded: 1973
Membership: 10,001–100,000
Scope: National
Description: Population-Environment Balance is a grassroots membership organization dedicated to public education regarding the adverse effects of population growth on the environment. "BALANCE" advocates measures that would encourage population stabilization in the U.S.; encourages a responsible immigration policy for the U.S.; and promotes increased funding for contraceptive research and availability. Activities include public education, advocacy, media campaigns, and publications.
Publication(s): Balance Activist, Action Alerts, Balance Data
Keyword(s): Air Quality/Atmosphere, Energy, Forests/Forestry, Land Issues, Pollution (general), Population, Reduce/Reuse/Recycle, Sprawl/Urban Planning, Transportation, Water Habitats & Quality
Contact(s):
Virginia Abernethy, Chairman of the Board

POTOMAC APPALACHIAN TRAIL CLUB
118 Park St., SE
Vienna, VA 22180 United States
Phone: 703-242-0693 Fax: 703-242-0968
Website: www.patc.net

Founded: 1927
Membership: 1,001–10,000
Scope: Regional
Description: Maintains 240 miles of the Appalachian Trail from Rock Fish Gap in Virginia to Pine Grove Furnace State Park in Pennsylvania. Also maintains an additional 750 miles of trails. Activities include publication of maps and guidebooks, outdoor recreation leadership, construction and maintenance of shelters and cabins and conservation of trail lands through purchase or easements.
Publication(s): Newsletter Monthly- The Potomac Appalachian
Keyword(s): Recreation/Ecotourism
Contact(s):
Walter Smith, President
Wilson Riley, Director of Administration
Gerhard Salinger, Treasurer
Linda Shannon-Beaver, Chief Editor; PA@patc.net
Warren Sharp, General Secretary
Kerry Snow, Supervisor of Trails

POULSBO MARINE SCIENCE CENTER
18743 Front St., NE, P.O. Box 2079
Poulsbo, WA 98370 United States
Phone: 360-779-5549 Fax: 360-779-8960
E-mail: info@poulsbomsc.org
Website: www.poulsbomsc.org

Founded: 1968
Scope: Regional
Description: The Marine Science Center works to meet the science education needs of public citizens and of students and teachers nationally, regionally, and locally. Hands-on environmental education is at the heart of its mission and is reflected in direct instruction from its facility on Washington State's Liberty Bay, part of the Puget Sound.
Keyword(s): Oceans/Coasts/Beaches
Contact(s):
Cindy Rathbone, Marine Society of the Pacific Northwest, President
Michelle Benedict, Director

POWDER RIVER BASIN RESOURCE COUNCIL
P.O. Box 1178
Douglas, WY 82633 United States
Phone: 307-358-5002   Fax: 307-358-6771
E-mail: doprbrc@coffey.com
Website: powderriverbasin.org/prbrc

Founded: 1973
Membership: 101–1,000
Scope: State
Description: Nonprofit grassroots organization whose major purpose is to help Wyoming people work to prevent and alleviate environmental and rural problems. Major issues include: Coal mining, water development, toxics, wastes, energy conservation, agriculture, and accountable government.
Publication(s): The Powder River Breaks - quarterly newsletter
Keyword(s): Agriculture/Farming, Air Quality/Atmosphere, Energy, Land Issues, Pollution (general), Reduce/Reuse/Recycle
Contact(s):
Kevin Lind, Director; 23 N. Scott, Sheridan, WY 82801; 307-672-5809; Fax: 307-672-5800; klind@powderriverbasin.org
Vickie Goodwin, Organizer; P.O. Box 1178, Douglas, WY 82633; 307-358-5002; Fax: 307-358-6771; doprbrc@coffey.com
Jill Morrison, Organizer; 307-672-5809; jillm@powderriverbasin.org
Cheyrl Phinney, Organizer; 307-672-5809; cheyrlp@powderriverbasin.org

PRAIRIE CLUB, THE
533 W. North Ave. Suite 10
Elmhurst, IL 60126 United States
Phone: 630-516-1277   Fax: 630-516-1278
E-mail: prairieclb@aol.com
Website: www.prairieclub.org

Founded: 1911
Membership: 101–1,000
Scope: National
Description: Organized for the promotion of outdoor recreation in the form of walks, outings, camping, and canoeing; the establishment and maintenance of permanent and temporary camps; and the encouragement of the love of nature.
Publication(s): The Bulletin
Keyword(s): Land Issues, Recreation/Ecotourism, Wildlife & Species
Contact(s):
Lloyd Anderson, President
Linda Mullikin, 2nd Vice President
Leo Nelson, 1st Vice President
Loretta Davies, Executive Director
Milt Davies, Chairman of Conservation Committee
Glenn Krus, Secretary
Susan Messer, Editor
Tom Meyers, Treasurer

PRAIRIE GROUSE TECHNICAL COUNCIL
WILDLIFE AND FISHERIES SCIENCES DEPT.
Wildlife and Fisheries Sciences Department 2258 TAMU
College Station, TX 77843-2258 United States
Phone: 979-845-5777   Fax: 979-845-3786
Website: wfscnet.tamu.edu

Scope: National
Description: Comprises federal, state, and private agency biologists or administrators concerned with the status, research, and management of the prairie-chicken and sharp-tailed grouse in North America.
Publication(s): Newsletter and Proceedings
Keyword(s): Land Issues, Wildlife & Species
Contact(s):
Kenneth Giesen, Executive Committee; 317 W. Prospect, Ft. Collins, CO 80526

PRAIRIE RIVERS NETWORK
809 S. Fifth St.
Champaign, IL 61820 United States
Phone: 217-344-2371   Fax: 217-344-2381
E-mail: info@prairierivers.org
Website: www.prairierivers.org

Founded: 1968
Membership: 101–1,000
Scope: State
Description: (Formerly Central States Education Center) A statewide river conservation organization working to protect the rivers and streams of illinois. Organizational and technical assistance is provided to persons and organizations in related activities.
Publication(s): Dirty Water, Dirty Business, NPDES Permit Handbook, Rivers Directory
Keyword(s): Water Habitats & Quality
Contact(s):
Bruce Hannon, President; 217-352-3646
Robert Moore, Executive Director; robmoore@prairierivers.org
John McNussen, Treasurer; 217-398-8531
Marc Miller, Watershed Organizer; 217-344-2371; mmiller@prairierivers.org

PRAIRIE WILDLIFE RESEARCH
P.O. Box 515
Wall, SD 57790 United States
Phone: 605-279-2380   Fax: 605-279-2725
E-mail: tlivieri@prairiewildlife.org
Website: www.prairiewildlife.org

Founded: 2001
Scope: Regional
Description: Prairie Wildlife Research is dedicated to the conservation, restoration and research of wildlife inhabiting prairie habitats. We are primarily involved with black-footed ferrets, prairie dogs, and other species of concern.
Keyword(s): Ecosystems (precious), Wildlife & Species

PREDATOR CONSERVATION ALLIANCE
PREVIOUSLY KNOWN AS PREDATOR PROJECT
P.O. Box 6733
Bozeman, MT 59771-6733 United States
Phone: 406-587-3389   Fax: 406-587-3178
E-mail: pca@predatorconservation.org
Website: www.predatorconservation.org

Founded: 1991
Membership: 1,001–10,000
Scope: National
Description: Predator Conservation Alliance (PCA) is dedicated to conserving, protecting and restoring native predators and their habitats in the Northern Rockies and Northern Plains. In short, we are saving a place for America's predators. This place is on the ground where we work to protect predators and the places they live. This place is also within the human heart and mind where we strive to increase public awareness about the important ecological role predators play.
Publication(s): The Wolf and its Place in the N. Rockies, Roaded Lands, Eroded Habitat, The Wild Bunch, Restoring the Prairie Dog Ecosystem, The Home Range (quarterly newsletter)
Keyword(s): Ecosystems (precious), Land Issues, Public Lands/Greenspace, Transportation, Wildlife & Species
Contact(s):
David Engel, Board President; dengel@san.rr.com
Thomas Skeele, Executive Director; 406-587-3389; Fax: 406-587-3178; tom@predatorconservation.org
Sara Folger, Conservation Director; 406-587-3389; Fax: 406-587-3178; sara@predatorconservation.org

PRESERVATION SOCIETY FOR SPRING CREEK FOREST
Preservation Society for Spring Creek Forest
P.O. Box 450176
Garland, TX 75045-0176 United States
Phone: 972-272-2094
E-mail: jfdanahy@juno.com
Website: springcreekforest.virtualave.net

Founded: 1985
Membership: 1–100
Scope: Local
Description: To promote preservation and protection and educational and scientific pursuits at Spring Creek Forest and Preserve.
Contact(s):
Jack Hill, Board of Directors; 1511 Baltimore Drive, Richardson, TX 75081; 214-665-6497; hill.jack@epa.gov

PRIORITIES INSTITUTE, THE
1565 California St. #607
Denver, CO 80202 United States
Phone: 303-777-5511   Fax: 303-777-5511
E-mail: mail@priorities.org
Website: www.priorities.org

Founded: 1996
Scope: State, Regional, National, International
Description: Non-partisan, non-profit research organization focusing on sustainable land use planning, designing car-free eco-cities, international communities, holistic indexing and moral evolution.
Publication(s): Perspectives and Priorities, Livable Cities
Keyword(s): Development/Developing Countries, Land Issues, Reduce/Reuse/Recycle, Transportation
Contact(s):
Logan Perkins, Director/Founder; logan@priorities.org
Melissa Moon, Assistant

PRO PENINSULA
P.O. Box 7175
San Diego, CA 92167 United States
Phone: 619-723-0700   Fax: 619-374-7162
E-mail: kama@propeninsula.org
Website: www.propeninsula.org

Founded: 2001
Membership: 101–1,000
Scope: Local, Regional, International
Description: Pro Peninsula is a U.S.-based organization dedicated to strengthening the environmental movement in Baja California. We envision the creation of a network of effective environmental organizations backed by an educated and active public working towards the common goal of environmental preservation. Pro Peninsula is led by a dedicated board, employs two full-time staff members, and is supported by an active and dedicated membership.
Publication(s): Pro Peninsula News/Noticias de Pro Peninsula
Contact(s):
Kama Dean, Co-Executive Director; 619-226-4277; ksdean@ucsd.edu
Chris Pesenti, Co-Executive Director; 858-551-4231; cpesenti@ucsd.edu

PROFESSIONAL BOWHUNTERS SOCIETY
P.O. Box 246
Terrell, NC 28682 United States
Phone: 704-664-2534   Fax: 704-664-7471
E-mail: bowhunters@worldnet.att.net
Website: www.bowsite.com/pbs

Founded: 1963
Membership: 1,001–10,000
Scope: National
Description: Created as an organization of dedicated bowhunters interested in promoting a high level of ethics in the taking of wild game with bow and arrow. To provide training for others in safety, shooting skill, and hunting techniques. To practice and promote the wise use of our natural resources and conservation of wildlife.
Publication(s): Professional Bowhunter Magazine, The
Contact(s):
Wayne Capp, President
Larry Fischer, Vice President
Louie Adams, Senior Councilman
Brenda Kisner, PBS Office; 704-664-2534; Fax: 704-664-7471
Jack Smith, Secretary and Treasurer; P.O. Box 246, Terrell, NC 28682; 704-664-2534; Fax: 704-664-7471
Jack Smith, Editor

PROGRESSIVE ANIMAL WELFARE SOCIETY
PAWS WILDLIFE DEPARTMENT
LYNNWOOD WILDLIFE CENTER
15305 44th Ave. West
Lynnwood, WA 98037 United States
Phone: 425-787-2500, ext. 817   Fax: 425-742-5711
E-mail: info@paws.org
Website: www.paws.org

Founded: 1901
Scope: Local, State, Regional, National, International
Description: PAWS is a nonprofit, tax-exempt organization that advocates for animals through education, legislation, and direct care. We operate a wildlife rehabilitation center dedicated to the care of sick, injured, and orphaned wildlife in Lynnwood, north of Seattle, Washington.
Publication(s): PAWS News, Habitat Conservation Program, PAWS Lynnwood Wildlife Center
Keyword(s): Ethics/Environmental Justice, Land Issues, Pollution (general), Public Health, Recreation/Ecotourism, Reduce/Reuse/Recycle, Sprawl/Urban Planning, Wildlife & Species
Contact(s):
Kip Parker, Wildlife Director; 425-787-2500; ext. 815; Fax: 425-742-5711; kparker@paws.org
Kevin Mack, Naturalist; 425-787-2500; ext. 854; Fax: 425-742-5711; kmack@paws.org

PROJECT SEAHORSE
Fisheries Centre
University of British Columbia
2204 Main Mall
Vancouver, V6T1Z4 British Columbia Canada
Phone: 604-827-5139
E-mail: info@projectseahorse.org
Website: www.projectseahorse.org

Founded: 1996
Scope: International
Description: Project Seahorse is an international marine conservation organisation. In securing the future for the threatened and charismatic seahorses, Project Seahorse is addressing many of the most pressing issues affecting marine life. The team undertakes biological and socio-economic research, facilitates community-based management, shapes sustainable trade, and catalyses international policy.
Keyword(s): Development/Developing Countries, Ecosystems (precious), Oceans/Coasts/Beaches, Wildlife & Species
Contact(s):
Heather Hall, Associate Director
Amanda Vincent, Director

PROTECTED AREAS ASSOCIATION OF NEWFOUNDLAND AND LABRADOR
Box 1027 Station C
St. John's, A1C 5M5 Newfoundland Canada
Phone: 709-726-2603   Fax: 709-726-2764
E-mail: paa@nf.aibn.com
Website: www.nfld.net/paa

Founded: 1989
Membership: 101–1,000
Scope: Local
Description: The Protected Areas Association of Newfoundland and Labrador is a non-governmental, not-for-profit organization working for wildernes conservation goals in this province.
Publication(s): Fresh Tracks
Keyword(s): Air Quality/Atmosphere, Climate Change, Ecosystems (precious), Forests/Forestry, Land Issues, Oceans/Coasts/Beaches, Public Health, Public Lands/Greenspace, Water Habitats & Quality, Wildlife & Species

PROVINCE OF QUEBEC SOCIETY FOR THE PROTECTION OF BIRDS, INC.
Station B
P.O. Box 43
Montreal, H3B 3J5 Quebec Canada
Phone: 514-637-2141
Website: www.pqspb.org

Founded: 1917
Membership: 101–1,000
Scope: Regional
Publication(s): Tchebec (Annual Review), The Song Sparrow (monthly newsletter), Birdfinding in the Montreal Area, Field Check List of Birds in the Montreal Area
Keyword(s): Wildlife & Species
Contact(s):
 Betsy McFarlane, President; 4807 Jeanne Mance, Montreal, Quebec H2V 4J6; 514-274-3810
 Eve Marshall, Vice President
 Rodger Titmann, Vice President
 Kyra Emo, Hon. Secretary; 140 Irvine Ave., Westmount, Quebec H3Z 2K2; 514-939-9666
 Kenneth Thorpe, Hon. Treasurer; 5615 Eldridge, Cote St-Luc, Quebec H4W 2C9; 514-483-5031

PTARMIGANS, THE
P.O. Box 1821
Vancouver, WA 98668 United States
Phone: 360-834-4520
Website: www.ptarmigans.org

Founded: 1960
Membership: 1–100
Scope: State
Description: The Ptarmigans were established for the purpose of conducting mountaineering activities in the northwest and in promoting the preservation of the northwest forests, wilderness lands, and mountain scenery. The only membership requirement is a love of the outdoors. Offer a variety of outdoor activities led in an ecologically-minded manner. Help maintain several local trail systems and conduct an annual Basic Climbing School. Visit and observe changes proposed in our northwest forests and mountains
Keyword(s): Land Issues, Wildlife & Species
Contact(s):
 Ruth Rowland, President
 Jon Bell, 1st Vice President
 Linda Lebard, Treasurer
 Don Spencer, Secretary

PUBLIC EMPLOYEES FOR ENVIRONMENTAL RESPONSIBILITY (PEER)
PEER
2001 S St., NW, Suite 570
Washington, DC 20009 United States
Phone: 202-265-7337   Fax: 202-265-4192
E-mail: info@peer.org
Website: www.peer.org

Founded: 1993
Membership: 1,001–10,000
Scope: Local, State, National
Description: PEER is an alliance of land managers, scientists, biologists, law enforcement officials, and other government professionals dedicated to the protection of the nation's environment. PEER advocates the responsible management of natural resources and promotes environmental ethics, professional integrity and accountability within local, state and federal agencies.
Publication(s): PEEReview, various employee-authored white papers
Keyword(s): Air Quality/Atmosphere, Ecosystems (precious), Ethics/Environmental Justice, Forests/Forestry, Land Issues, Oceans/Coasts/Beaches, Public Lands/Greenspace, Recreation/Ecotourism, Water Habitats & Quality, Wildlife & Species
Contact(s):
 Amanda Carufel, Communications Director
 Danielle Lawson, Administrative Director
 Dennis McKinney, Development Director
 Jeffrey Ruch, Executive Director
 Eric Wingerter, National Field Director
 Mark Davis, Outreach Membership Coordinator
 Dan Meyer, General Counsel
 Howard Wilshire, Board Chair

PUBLIC LANDS FOUNDATION
P.O. Box 7226
Arlington, VA 22207 United States
Phone: 703-790-1988   Fax: 703-821-3490
E-mail: leaplf@erols.com
Website: www.publicland.org

Founded: 1987
Membership: 1,001–10,000
Scope: National
Description: A national, nonprofit, independent advocate to keep the public lands public and for the proper use and protection of the public lands administered by the Bureau of Land Management; implementation of the Federal Land Policy and Management Act (FLPMA); and for professional land management by professional employees.
Publication(s): Public Lands Monitor
Keyword(s): Land Issues, Public Lands/Greenspace, Reduce/Reuse/Recycle
Contact(s):
 George Lea, President/ Editor; 703-790-1988
 Ed Spang, Vice President; 541-889-2556

PUERTO RICO ASSOCIATION OF SOIL AND WATER CONSERVATION DISTRICTS
Attn: President, P.O. Box 91
Orocovis, PR 720 United States

Scope: State
Publication(s): Puerto Rican Parrot Teacher's Kit, Pablo y Marisol van a la Playa, Puerto Rico Conservation Directory, Verde Luz Newsletter, Puerto Rico Environmental Laws
Keyword(s): Oceans/Coasts/Beaches, Water Habitats & Quality, Wildlife & Species
Contact(s):
 Pedro Fuentes, President; P.O. Box 91, Orocovis, PR 00720; 787-867-4707

Carlos Mantras, Vice President, Board Member; 1722 Pastemark St., Urb Purple Tree, San Juan, PR 00926; 787-761-6247
Hilda Bonilla, Secretary; HC 1 Box 8162, Luquillo, PR 00773; 787-860-0045
Norberto Colon, Treasurer; P.O. Box 175, Barranquitas, PR 00794; 787-857-7965
Migdalia Rodriguez, Administrative Secretary; P.O. Box 1225, Casguas, PR 00726; 787-258-0490; Fax: 787-258-0490

PUERTO RICO CONSERVATION FOUNDATION, THE (PRCF)
Urb Sagrado Corazon
382 Ave. San Claudio PMB 97
San Juan, PR 00926-4107 United States
Phone: 787-760-2115   Fax: 787-761-3889
E-mail: fconserv@tld.net
Website: www.fundacionpr.org
Founded: 1987
Membership: 1-100
Scope: Local
Description: The PRCF is a private nonprofit tax-exempt 501(c)3 organization, dedicated to protect Puerto Rico's biological biodiversity, focusing on the conservation of threatened and endangered species and other keystone and lesser known species.
Publication(s): Sea Turtle Kit and various brochures, Pablo y Marisol van a la Playa, Puerto Rican Parrot Teacher's Kit, Puerto Rico NGOs Directory, Verde Luz Newsletter
Keyword(s): Reduce/Reuse/Recycle, Wildlife & Species
Contact(s):
Roberto Biaggi, President
Miguel Iturregui, Director
Esther Rojas, Executive Director
Juan Ricart, Secretary

PUGET SOUNDKEEPER ALLIANCE
4401 Leary Way NW
Seattle, WA 98107 United States
Phone: 206-297-7002   Fax: 206-297-0409
E-mail: psa@pugetsoundkeeper.org
Website: www.pugetsoundkeeper.org
Founded: 1984
Membership: 101-1,000
Scope: Regional
Description: A nonprofit organization whose mission is to protect and preserve Puget Sound by stopping the discharge of pollution into the waters of the Sound.
Publication(s): Sounder
Keyword(s): Pollution (general), Recreation/Ecotourism, Water Habitats & Quality
Contact(s):
Sue Joerger, Executive Director / Soundkeeper
Tom Diller, Board of Directors - President

PURPLE MARTIN CONSERVATION ASSOCIATION
Edinboro University of Pennsylvania
Edinboro, PA 16444 United States
Phone: 814-734-4420   Fax: 814-734-5803
E-mail: pmca@edinboro.edu
Website: www.purplemartin.org
Founded: 1987
Membership: 1,001-10,000
Scope: Local, State, Regional, National, International
Description: An international tax-exempt, nonprofit organization dedicated to the conservation of the Purple Martin (Progne subis) species of bird through scientific research, state-of-the-art wildlife management techniques, and public education. The PMCA's scientific staff conducts research on all aspects of martin biology throughout the bird's North, South, and Middle American breeding, wintering, and migratory ranges. The organization functions as a centralized data-gathering/information source on martins.
Publication(s): Purple Martin Update
Keyword(s): Agriculture/Farming, Air Quality/Atmosphere, Climate Change, Ecosystems (precious), Ethics/Environmental Justice, Land Issues, Pollution (general), Population, Public Lands/Greenspace, Recreation/Ecotourism, Sprawl/Urban Planning, Water Habitats & Quality
Contact(s):
James Hill, Director and Editor; 814-734-4420; Fax: 814-734-5803; jhill@edinboro.edu

Q

QUAIL UNLIMITED, INC.
31 Quail Run, P.O. Box 610
Edgefield, SC 29824-0610 United States
Phone: 803-637-5731   Fax: 803-637-0037
E-mail: national@qu.org
Website: www.qu.org
Founded: 1981
Scope: National
Description: A national nonprofit conservation organization dedicated to improving quail and upland game bird populations through habitat management and research. Organized to re-establish and manage suitable upland game habitat, both public and private lands across the country, and to educate the public to the needs for wildlife habitat management.
Publication(s): Quail Unlimited Magazine Bi-Monthly
Keyword(s): Wildlife & Species
Contact(s):
Steve Mcghee, President; 100 Patterson Circle, Oliver Springs, TN 37840; 423-574-3685
Jerry Allen, Administrative Vice President; 1884 Highway 23 West, Edgefield, SC 29824; 803-637-5877; national@qu.org
Joseph Evans, Executive Vice President; 3012 Sussex Rd., Augusta, GA 30909; 706-738-0692; national@qu.org
Harvey Bray, Rocky Mountain Regional Director; 13 Archway Lane, Pueblo, CO 81005; 719-561-3825; Fax: 719-561-8977
Tommy Dean, Director of Chapter Development; 815 Shawnee Dr., N. Augusta, SC 29841; 803-637-5731; chapterdev@qu.org
Randy Guthrie, South Central Regional Director; 2061 Crow Mt. Rd., Russellville, AR 72801; 501-967-2200; Fax: 501 767-2716; rguthrie@cswnet.com
Dick Haldeman, Western Regional Director; 39455 Black Oak Rd., Temecula, CA 92592; 909-767-3435; Fax: 909-767-2716; quwest@pe.net
Jeff Hodges, Great Plains Regional Director; 382 NW Hwy. 18, Clinton, MO 64735; 660-885-7057; Fax: 660-885-7152
David Howell, Director of Agricultural Wildlife Services; 10364 S. 950 E., Stendal, IN 47585; 812-536-2272; dhowell@psci.net
Yale Leiden, Southeast Regional Director
Chip Martin, Southwest Regional Director; 3320 FM 3326, Anson, TX 79501; 915-823-3347; Fax: 915-823-3340
Mike Newell, Oklahoma Regional Director; 2607 NW Columbia, Lawton, OK 73505; Fax: 580-357-0619; mnewell@qu.org
Wade Teague, Mid-Atlantic Regional Director; 271 Stevens Church Rd., Goldsboro, NC 27530; 919-689-3884; Fax: 919-689-2726; wadequ@earthlink.net
Chris Wolkonowski, Midwest Regional Director; HCR 76 Box 645 Hwy. 108, Gruetli-Laager, TN 37339; 931-779-4868; Fax: 812-536-2272; cwolk@qu.org
D. Kogon, Editor; qumag@qu.org
Roger Wells, National Habitat Coordinator; 868 Road 290, Americus, KS; 316-443-5834; rwells@americusks.net

QUALITY DEER MANAGEMENT ASSOCIATION
QDMA
P.O. Box 227
Watkinsville, GA 30677 United States
Phone: 800-209-3337 Fax: 706-769-3464
E-mail: qdma@charter.net
Website: www.qdma.com

Founded: 1988
Membership: 10,001–100,000
Scope: State, National, International
Description: National nonprofit wildlife conservation organization dedicated to promoting sustainable, high-quality white-tailed deer populations, wildlife habitats and ethical hunting experiences through education, research and management in partnership with hunters, landowners, natural resource professionals and the public.
Publication(s): Educational Resources, Quality Whitetails journal
Keyword(s): Ethics/Environmental Justice, Forests/Forestry, Wildlife & Species
Contact(s):
Brian Murphy, Executive Director; 800-209-3337; Fax: 706-769-3464; bmurphy-qdma@charter.net
Jared Bailey, Promotions Director; 800-209-3337; Fax: 706-769-3464; jbailey-qdma@charter.net
James Guthrie, Publications Director; 800-209-3337; Fax: 706-769-3464; jguthrie-qdma@charter.net

QUEBEC WILDLIFE FEDERATION
6780 1st Ave., Bureau 109
Charlesbourg, G1H 2W8 Quebec Canada
Phone: 888-523-2863 Fax: 418-622-6168
E-mail: fede@fqf.qc.ca
Website: www.fqf.qc.ca

Founded: 1945
Scope: Regional
Description: Its mission is to regroup, represent and defend hunters and anglers rights and interests and to contribute to the management, development and perpetuation of hunting and angling as traditional and sporting activities while preserving habitats and wildlife.
Publication(s): INFO-FQF
Keyword(s): Development/Developing Countries, Public Lands/Greenspace, Recreation/Ecotourism, Reduce/Reuse/Recycle, Wildlife & Species
Contact(s):
Aurele Blais, President
Alain Bisson, Vice President and Secretary
Alain Gagnon, Vice President
Rodolphe Lasalle, Vice President
Michel Savard, Vice President
Alain Cossette, General Director
Stephanie Boucher, Biologist
Annie Guertin, Communication Coordinator
Guy Vezina, Treasurer

R

RACHEL CARSON COUNCIL, INC.
P.O. Box 10779
Silver Spring, MD 20914 United States
Phone: 301-593-7507 Fax: 301-5936251
E-mail: rccouncil@aol.com
Website: members.aol.com/rccouncil/ourpage

Founded: 1965
Scope: National
Description: (Formerly: Rachel Carson Trust for the Living Environment Inc.) An international clearinghouse for information on toxic substances, particularly pesticides, for both scientists and laymen. Information is distributed by means of publications, workshops, conferences, and responses to specific questions. Rachel Carson Council is devoted to fostering a sense of wonder and respect toward nature and to helping society realize Rachel Carson's vision of a healthy and diverse environment.
Publication(s): Basic Guide to Pesticides, list of current publications available on request, books, pamphlets and sheets on specific alternative pest control methods and on pesticides effects, Rachel Carson Council News
Keyword(s): Agriculture/Farming, Land Issues, Pollution (general), Public Health, Water Habitats & Quality, Wildlife & Species
Contact(s):
Martha Talbot, Vice President
Diana Post, Executive Director and Secretary
Aaron Blair, Liaison to the Board
David McGarth, Treasurer

RAINBOW PUSH COALITION
1131 8th St. NE
Washington, DC 20002 United States
Phone: 202-547-3235 Fax: 202-547-7397
E-mail: info@rainbowpush.org
Website: www.rainbowpush.org

Founded: 1984
Scope: International
Description: RPC is a national progressive membership organization committed to public education, empowerment, economic and social justice, and gender and racial equality. The Rainbow Push Coalition has state chapters and a national membership base. The Rainbow Push Coalition addresses such issues as education, voter registration, economic justice, civil rights, environment, labor, and working people's rights.
Publication(s): Rainbow Newsletter, Rainbow Push Magazine or The Rainbow JaxFax, various issue papers, speeches, and briefings
Keyword(s): Development/Developing Countries, Pollution (general), Reduce/Reuse/Recycle
Contact(s):
Jesse Jackson, President and Founder
Willie Barrow, Co-Chairman of the Board
Dennis Rivera, Co-Chairman of the Board

RAINFOREST ACTION NETWORK
221 Pine St.,
Suite 500
San Francisco, CA 94104 United States
Phone: 415-398-4404 Fax: 415-398-2732
E-mail: rainforest@ran.org
Website: www.ran.org

Founded: 1985
Scope: National
Description: RAN works nationally and internationally on major campaigns to protect rainforests and defend the rights of indigenous people, using non-violent direct action such as: letter-writing campaigns, boycotts, and demonstrations against corporations and lending agencies contributing to rainforest destruction. RAN also produces educational materials, a teachers' packet, and fact sheets for community organizers.
Publication(s): World Rainforest Week Organizers Manual, Action Alert
Keyword(s): Forests/Forestry, Wildlife & Species
Contact(s):
Randall Hayes, Board Secretary, President
Christopher Hatch, Executive Director
Sara Riggs, Communications Director
Laura Fauth, Publications Editor
Jim Gollin, Board Chair
Scott Price, Board Treasurer

RAINFOREST ALLIANCE
665 Broadway St. #500
New York, NY 10012 United States
Phone: 212-677-1900   Fax: 212-677-2187
E-mail: canopy@ra.org
Founded: 1986
Scope: International
Description: The Rainforest Alliance is an international nonprofit organization dedicated to the conservation of tropical forests for the benefit of the global community. Its primary mission is to develop and promote economically viable and socially desirable alternatives to the destruction of tropical forests.
Publication(s): CANOPY, The, Catfish Connection, The, So Fruitful a Fish, Tales from the Jungle, Floods of Fortune
Keyword(s): Development/Developing Countries, Forests/Forestry, Wildlife & Species
Contact(s):
   Tensie Whealan, President
   Daniel Katz, Executive Director
   Karin Kreider, Associate Director

RAINFOREST RELIEF
P.O. Box 150566
Brooklyn, NY 11215 United States
Phone: 718-398-3760   Fax: 212-741-4563
E-mail: relief@igc.org
Website: www.enviroweb.org/rainrelief
Founded: 1989
Membership: 101–1,000
Scope: Local, State, Regional, National, International
Description: Rainforest Relief, a nonprofit 501(c)(3) organization, works through research, education and non-violent direct action to end the loss of tropical and temperate rainforests by reducing the demand for products and materials for which rainforests are destroyed. These materials include tropical hardwoods, paper, petroleum, metals and agricultural products such as bananas, beef, coffee and chocolate. The organization has prevented more tropical hardwood use in the U.S. than any group in history.
Publication(s): Roots, Rainforest Relief Reports, Raindrops
Keyword(s): Agriculture/Farming, Climate Change, Ecosystems (precious), Ethics/Environmental Justice, Forests/Forestry, Pollution (general), Reduce/Reuse/Recycle, Wildlife & Species
Contact(s):
   Tim Keating, President and Director; 718-398-3760; Fax: 212-741-4563; t.keating@rainforestrelief.org
   Jeffrey Lockwood, Vice President and Portland Oregon Chapter Director; P.O. Box 14232, Portland, OR 97293; 503-236-3031; j.lockwood@rainforestrelief.org
   Carrie McCracken, Forest Banana Project Coordinator; carrielmccracken@yahoo.com
   Brian Hires, Outreach Coordinator; b.hires@rainforestrelief.org

RAINFOREST TRUST
SAVE THE JAGUAR
6001 SW 63rd Avenue
Miami, FL 33143 United States
Phone: 305-669-2115   Fax: 305-665-0691
E-mail: rft@rainforesttrust.com
Website: www.rainforesttrust.com
Founded: 1995
Membership: 1–100
Scope: International
Description: The Rainforest Trust supports and maintains a jaguar sanctuary and rainforest preserve in Belize. It also promotes eco-tourism and sustainable agriculture as economically viable alternatives to deforestation, and actively promotes educational programmes to teach farmers and school children about conservation, fragile eco-systems, organic agriculture, and wildlife preservation. The Trust has also recently established a second wildlife sanctuary and rainforest preserve in Jamaica.
Keyword(s): Agriculture/Farming, Ecosystems (precious), Forests/Forestry, Recreation/Ecotourism, Reduce/Reuse/Recycle, Wildlife & Species
Contact(s):
   Brett Ashmeade-Hawkins, President; 305-669-2115; Fax: 305-665-0691; rft@rainforesttrust.com
   Mark Ashmeade-Hawkins, Secretary and Treasurer; 305-669-2115; Fax: 305-665-0691; rft@rainforesttrust.com
   T. Hawkins, Chairman; 305-666-2158

RAPTOR EDUCATION FOUNDATION, INC.
P.O. Box 200400
Denver, CO 80220 United States
Phone: 303-680-8500   Fax: 303-680-8502
E-mail: raptor2@usaref.org
Website: www.usaref.org
Founded: 1980
Membership: 1,001–10,000
Scope: National
Description: A nonprofit, charitable educational organization utilizing nonreleasable raptors to promote environmental literacy. Lecturers travel nationwide.
Publication(s): Talon, Castings (volunteer newsletter), Talon Supplement
Keyword(s): Ecosystems (precious), Ethics/Environmental Justice, Land Issues, Wildlife & Species
Contact(s):
   Peter Reshetniak, President and Editor
   Patrick Duran, Executive Director
   Shellie Sage, Mews Manager
   Anne Price, Secretary and Curator of Raptors

RAPTOR RESEARCH FOUNDATION, INC.
USGS Forest and Rangeland
Ecosystem Science Center
Snake River Field Station, 970 Lusk St.
Boise, ID 83706 United States
Phone: 208-426-5201
Website: biology.boisestate.edu/raptor
Founded: 1966
Scope: National
Description: A nonprofit corporation formed to stimulate and coordinate the dissemination of information on the biology and management of birds of prey and their habitats. Areas of particular interest include: raptor banding, behavior, captive breeding, conservation, ecology, research techniques, management, migration, population monitoring, pathology, and rehabilitation.
Publication(s): Journal of Raptor Research, Wingspan
Keyword(s): Wildlife & Species
Contact(s):
   Michael Kochert, President; 208-426-5201; Fax: 208-426-5210; mkochert@eagle.idbsu.edu
   Keith Bildstein, Vice President; Hawk Mountain Sanctuary, Route 2, Box 191, Kempton, PA 19529; 910-756-6961; bildstein@hawkmountain.org
   James Bednarz, Editor-in-Chief; Department of Biology, Boise State University,
   Jim Fitzpatrick, Treasurer and Membership Information; Carpenter, St. Croix Valley Nature Center, 12805 St. Croix Tr., Hastings, MN 55033; 651-437-4359; jim@cncstcroix.com
   Patricia Hall, Secretary; 436 David Dr. E, Flagstaff, AZ 86001; 520-526-6222; pah@alpine.for.nau.edu

RARE CENTER FOR TROPICAL CONSERVATION
1840 Wilson Blvd., Ste. 204
Arlington, VA 22201 United States
Phone: 703-522-5070   Fax: 703-522-5027
E-mail: rare@rarecenter.org
Website: www.rarecenter.org

Founded: 1973
Membership: 1,001–10,000
Scope: International
Description: RARE Center's mission is to protect wildlands of globally significant biological diversity by enabling local people to benefit from their protection. Focusing on education and economic opportunities, we pursue this mission by working in partnership with local communities, non-governmental organizations (NGOs) and other stakeholders to develop and replicate locally managed conservation strategies.
Publication(s): Nature Guide Training, Nature Trails, Conservation Education, Radio Dramas
Keyword(s): Ecosystems (precious), Population, Public Lands/Greenspace, Recreation/Ecotourism, Wildlife & Species
Contact(s):
Brett Jenks, President/CEO

REEF RELIEF
P.O. Box 430
201 William Street
Key West, FL 33041 United States
Phone: 305-294-3100   Fax: 305-293-9515
E-mail: reef@bellsouth.net
Website: www.reefrelief.org

Founded: 1989
Membership: 1,001–10,000
Scope: Local, Regional, International
Description: Reef Relief is a nonprofit membership organization dedicated to preserve and protect Living Coral Reef Ecosystems through local, regional, and global efforts.
Publication(s): Reef Line Newsletter, Coral Reefs brochure
Keyword(s): Ecosystems (precious), Oceans/Coasts/Beaches, Pollution (general), Recreation/Ecotourism, Water Habitats & Quality, Wildlife & Species
Contact(s):
Paul Johnson, Special Projects
DeeVon Quirolo, Executive Director
Craig Quirolo, Founder and Director of Marine Projects
Joel Biddle, Educational Director
Michael Blades, Project Director

REEFGUARDIAN INTERNATIONAL
2829 Bird Avenue - Suite 5, PMB 162
Miami, FL 33133-4668 United States
Phone: 301-358-4600   Fax: 301-371-6188
E-mail: info@ReefGuardian.org
Website: www.reefguardian.org/

Scope: International
Publication(s): Reef Monitor Update, Reef Dispatch, Reef Alert, ReefKeeper Report
Contact(s):
Alexander Stone, Director

RENEW THE EARTH
1200 18th St., NW, Suite 1100
Washington, DC 20036 United States
Phone: 202-262-1630   Fax: 202-467-5780
E-mail: renew@renewtheearth.org
Website: www.renewtheearth.org

Founded: 1978
Scope: International
Description: Renew the Earth, formerly Renew America, identifies, links and awards sustainable environmental programs from civil society, all levels of government and the private sector worldwide. We have created an internet-based international Success Index to list and disseminate information about verified, solution-orientd programs; a global network of practitioners and an annual awards program to recognize environmental achievement.
Publication(s): Environmental Ambassador Index
Contact(s):
Katy Moran, Executive Director; 202-721-1545; katymoran@renewtheearth.org

RENEWABLE ENERGY POLICY PROJECT (REPP)
1612 K St., NW, Suite 202
Washington, DC 20006 United States
Phone: 202-293-2898   Fax: 202-293-5857
Website: www.repp.org

Founded: 1995
Scope: International
Description: The Renewable Energy Policy Project (REPP) investigates the emerging relationships among policies, markets and public demand for renewable energy technologies. REPP's mission is to accelerate growth of the renewable energy industry and maximize deployment of renewable energy technology, by providing credible information, insightful analysis and innovative strategies.
Publication(s): Wind Clusters: Expanding the Market Appeal of Wind Energy Systems (Nov. 1996), Natural Gas: Bridge to a Renewable Energy Future (May 1997), Clean Government: Options for Governments to Buy Renewable Energy (May 1999), Renewable Energy Policy Outside the United States (Oct. 1999), Federal Energy Subsidiaries: Not all Technologies are Created Equal (July 2000), Rural Electrification with Solar Energy as a Climate Protection Strategy (Jan. 2000)
Keyword(s): Energy, Reduce/Reuse/Recycle
Contact(s):
Fred Beck, Research Manager
Kelly Ross, Internet and Research Associate; 202-293-2898; ext. 208; kross@repp.org

RENEWABLE NATURAL RESOURCES FOUNDATION
RNRF
5430 Grosvenor Ln.
Bethesda, MD 20814-2193 United States
Phone: 301-493-9101   Fax: 301-493-6148
E-mail: info@rnrf.org
Website: www.rnrf.org

Founded: 1972
Membership: 1–100
Scope: National
Description: A public, nonprofit, operating foundation. Members are 16 professional, scientific and educational organizations. Conducts meetings on public policy issues. Publisher of Renewable Resources Journal. Developer of the 35-acre Renewable Natural Resources Center, an office complex for natural resource organizations.
Publication(s): Renewable Resources Journal
Keyword(s): Agriculture/Farming, Air Quality/Atmosphere, Climate Change, Ecosystems (precious), Forests/Forestry, Land Issues, Oceans/Coasts/Beaches, Pollution (general), Population, Public Lands/Greenspace, Recreation/Ecotourism, Reduce/Reuse/Recycle, Sprawl/Urban Planning
Contact(s):
Robert Day, Executive Director
Albert Grant, Chairman
Barry Starke, Vice-Chairman
Ryan Colker, Director, Programs
Chandru Krishna, Director, Administration and Finance

REP AMERICA
REPUBLICANS FOR ENVIRONMENTAL PROTECTION
3200 Carlisle Blvd. NE, #228
Albuquerque, NM 87110 United States
Phone: 505-889-4544
E-mail: info@repamerica.org
Website: www.repamerica.org

Founded: 1995
Membership: 1,001–10,000
Scope: State, National

Description: The mission of REP America, the national grassroots organization of Republicans for environmental protection, is to resurrect the GOP's great conservation tradition and to restore natural resource conservation and sound environmental protection as fundamental elements of the Republican Party's vision for America.

Publication(s): The Green Elephant

Keyword(s): Air Quality/Atmosphere, Climate Change, Energy, Forests/Forestry, Land Issues, Pollution (general), Public Health, Public Lands/Greenspace, Sprawl/Urban Planning, Water Habitats & Quality, Wildlife & Species

Contact(s):
Martha Marks,, President/Managing Director; 505-690-9601; martha@repamerica.org
Jim DiPeso, Policy Director; 325 Washington Ave. S, #206, Kent, WA 98032; 253-740-2066; dipeso@repamerica.org
Ruth Fish, Executive Assistant; 505-889-4544; ruth@repamerica.org
Bridgett Thompson, Development Director; 3053 Fillmore Street, #291, San Francisco, CA 94123; 415-385-3399; bridgett@repamerica.org

RESIDENTS FOR A MORE BEAUTIFUL PORT WASHINGTON
P.O. Box 864
Port Washington, NY 11050 United States
Phone: 516-767-9151   Fax: 516-883-2066
E-mail: rfmbpw@optonline.net
Website: pwresidents.org

Founded: 1968
Membership: 10,001–100,000
Scope: Local

Description: The organizaiton is dedicated to protecting and improving the environment and the quality life in Port Washington, Manhasset, and Roslyn Peninsula of Nassau County, New York.

Keyword(s): Development/Developing Countries, Energy, Land Issues, Oceans/Coasts/Beaches, Pollution (general), Public Lands/Greenspace, Reduce/Reuse/Recycle, Sprawl/Urban Planning, Transportation

Contact(s):
Myron Blumenfeld, Chairman; myronblu@msn.com
Jennifer Rimmer, Executive Director; 516-767-9151; Fax: 516-883-2066; rfmbpw@optonline.net

RESOURCE CENTER FOR ENVIRONMENTAL EDUCATION, THE
Okeanskill Prospect
Vladivostok, 690106 Russia
Phone: 4.2322505662e+015   Fax: 4232225763
E-mail: liliko@mail.primorye.ru

Founded: 1997
Scope: International

Description: The RCEE is the only center in the Russian Far East, dedicated to promoting experiential learning in the fields of environmental education, science, and art for students and teachers.

Keyword(s): Oceans/Coasts/Beaches, Recreation/Ecotourism

Contact(s):
Lilia Kondrashova, Director; 742-324-2801; Fax: 423-222-5763; liliko@mail.primorye.ru

RESOURCE RENEWAL INSTITUTE, THE
Fort Mason Center Building D #290
San Francisco, CA 94123 United States
Phone: 415-928-3774   Fax: 415-928-4050
E-mail: info@rri.org
Website: www.rri.org

Founded: 1983
Scope: National, International

Description: The RRI is a national, nonprofit organization advocating state and national comprehensive, integrated environmental strategies (known as Green Plans), modeled on those of the Netherlands and New Zealand. RRI has set up a Global Green Plan Center to act as a clearinghouse for information on Green Plans. for more information, use RRI's e-mail address.

Publication(s): Saving Cities, Saving Money, Green Plans: Greenprint for Sustainability, The International Green Planner

Keyword(s): Development/Developing Countries, Executive/Legislative/Judicial Reform

Contact(s):
Huey Johnson, President
Allison Lengauer, Acting Executive Director; 415-928-3774

RESOURCES FOR THE FUTURE
1616 P St., NW
Washington, DC 20036 United States
Phone: 202-328-5000   Fax: 202-939-3460
Website: www.rff.org

Founded: 1952
Scope: National

Description: An independent nonprofit organization that works to advance research and education in the development, conservation, and use of environmental and natural resources. Staff is comprised primarily of economists and policy analysts who research a variety of environmental and natural resource issues.

Publication(s): Resources

Keyword(s): Air Quality/Atmosphere, Development/Developing Countries, Energy, Forests/Forestry, Land Issues, Reduce/Reuse/Recycle, Transportation, Wildlife & Species

Contact(s):
Paul Portney, President; 202-328-5000; portney@rff.org.com
Edward Hand, Vice President of Finance and Administration; 202-328-5029; hand@rff.org.com
Lesli Creedon, Director of Development; creedon@rff.org.com
J. Davies, Center for Risk Managomont Dircotor; 202-328-5093; davies@rff.org.com
Alan Krupnick, Quality of the Environment Division Director; 202-328-5059; krupnick@rff.org.com
Michael Toman, Energy and Natural Resources Division Director; 202-328-5091; toman@rff.org.com
Dan Quinn, Manager of Public Affairs; 202-328-5019; quinn@rff.org.com
Christopher Clotworthy, Librarian; 202-328-5089; clotworthy@rff.org.com

RESTORE HETCH HETCHY
P.O. Box 3591
Walnut Creek, CA 94598 United States
Phone: 209-372-8660
E-mail: info@hetchhetchy.org
Website: www.hetchhetchy.org

Founded: 1999
Membership: 10,001–100,000
Scope: National

Description: The mission of Restore Hetch Hetchy is to restore the Hetch Hetchy Valley in Yosemite Valley, currently inundated by the O'Shaughnessy Dam. Our goal is to accomplish a "win-win" outcome for Hetch Hetchy Valley, and for the cities of the Bay Area and the Turlock and Modesto Irrigation Districts that rely on Hetch Hetchy water and power — drop for drop, kilowatt for kilowatt, and dollar for dollar — to the extent that is technically feasible.

Keyword(s): Finance/Banking/Trade, Public Lands/Greenspace, Water Habitats & Quality

Contact(s):
Ron Good, Executive Director; 209-372-8660; info@hetchhetchy.org

RETURNED PEACE CORPS VOLUNTEERS FOR ENVIRONMENT AND DEVELOPMENT (RPCVS-ED)
P.O. Box 102
Iowa City, IA 52244-0102 United States
Phone: 319-351-3375
E-mail: kwhansen@ia.net
Website: www.cboss.com/rpcv-eandd/

Founded: 1991
Membership: 101–1,000
Scope: National

Description: The RPCVs-E&D was formed to serve as a focal point for action on environment and development issues by Peace Corps alumni and friends.

Publication(s): Under the Village Tree

Keyword(s): Climate Change, Development/Developing Countries, Energy

Contact(s):
Katy Hansen, Chair; kwhansen@ia.net
Susan Singh, Editor; 918-749-7004; sukising@aol.com

RHODE ISLAND BASS FEDERATION
156 Ridgeway Rd.
Middletown, RI 02842 United States
Phone: 401-846-0512
E-mail: ribassfed@aol.com
Website: hometown.aol.com/bassbks/index10.html

Scope: State

Description: An organization of Bassmaster chapters, affiliated with the Bass Anglers Sportsman Society, organized to fight pollution, assist state and national conservation agencies in their efforts, and teach the young people of our country good conservation practices. Dedicated to the realistic conservation of our water resources.

Publication(s): Forest Conservationist, The

Keyword(s): Forests/Forestry

Contact(s):
Roger Pray, President
Bill Weikert, Conservation Director; 156 Ridgewood Rd., Middletown, RI 02842; 401-846-0512; riscnrdbil@aol.com

RHODE ISLAND FOREST CONSERVATOR'S ORGANIZATION, INC.
P.O. Box 53
No. Scituate, RI 02857 United States
Phone: 401-568-3421
E-mail: info@rifco.org
Website: www.rifco.org/resources.htm

Founded: 1989
Membership: 1–100
Scope: State

Description: A statewide organization affiliated with the National Woodland Owners Association organized to promote stewardship of Rhode Island's wooded lands and watersheds and protect their heritage for future generations.

Publication(s): Newsletter

Keyword(s): Agriculture/Farming, Forests/Forestry, Land Issues

Contact(s):
Milton Schumacher, President
John Macera, Vice President
Marc Tremblay, Outreach Coordinator. & Editor
Donald Hayden, Secretary
Virginia Warrender, Treasurer

RHODE ISLAND STATE CONSERVATION COMMITTEE
Chair, Sosnowski Farm, P.O. Box 722
W. Kingston, RI 2892 United States

Contact(s):
Susan Sosnowski, Chair; Sosnowski Farm, P.O. Box 722, W. Kingston, RI 02892; 401-783-7704; senmike@uriacc.uri.edu

RHODE ISLAND WILD PLANT SOCIETY
Box 114
Peace Dale, RI 02883-0114 United States
Phone: 410-783-5895
Website: www.riwps.org/

Founded: 1987
Membership: 101–1,000
Scope: State

Description: The Rhode Island Wild Plant Society is a nonprofit conservation organization dedicated to the preservation and protection of Rhode Island's native plants and their habitats. Activities include talks, inventories of local flora, native plant restoration projects and a spring flower show and garden exhibit.

Publication(s): RIWPS Newsletter (biannual newsletter)

Keyword(s): Land Issues, Wildlife & Species

Contact(s):
Jules Cohen, President; 85 Scrabbletown Rd., N. Kingston, RI 02852
Deborah Poor, Executive Director

RIVER ALLIANCE OF WISCONSIN
306 East Wilson, Suite 2W
Madison, WI 53703 United States
Phone: 608-257-2424   Fax: 608-260-9799
E-mail: wisrivers@wisconsinrivers.org
Website: www.wisconsinrivers.org

Founded: 1993
Membership: 1,001–10,000
Scope: State

Description: The River Alliance is a nonprofit, nonpartisan citizen advocacy organization for rivers. Our mission is to lead the growing statewide effort to protect, enhance and restore Wisconsin's rivers and watersheds for their ecological, recreational, aesthetic, and cultural values. Recent program work includes education and information about the impacts of dams on river system health, minimizing ecosystem damage through federal relicensing of hydro dams, and advocacy for selective removal of uneconomic dams.

Publication(s): Small Groups Building Tool Kit, Local Groups Directory for Wisconsin, Dam Removal, Canoe (e-mail newsletter), News Bulletins and Fact Sheets, Wisconsin Rivers (Quarterly), Periodic Action Alerts

Keyword(s): Energy, Oceans/Coasts/Beaches, Water Habitats & Quality, Wildlife & Species

Contact(s):
Todd Ambs, Executive Director

RIVER NETWORK
520 SW 6th Ave., Suite 1130
Portland, OR 97204-1511 United States
Phone: 503-241-3506   Fax: 503-241-9256
E-mail: info@rivernetwork.org
Website: www.rivernetwork.org

Founded: 1988

Scope: Local, State, Regional, National

Description: River Network supports river advocates at the grassroots, state and regional levels; helps them build effective organizations; and links them together in a national movement to protect and restore America's rivers and watersheds.

Publication(s): Testing the Waters, Permitting an End to Pollution, Tracking TMDLs: Field Guide, River Talk!Communicate

Watershed Message, Clean Water Act: An Owner's Manual, Starting Up: A Handbook for New Organizations, Living Waters, How to Save a River, River Fundraising Alert

Keyword(s): Water Habitats & Quality

Contact(s):
Don Elder, CEO; 503-241-3506; ext. 43
Geoff Dates, River Watch Program Director; 802-436-2544
Gayle Killam, Director, River Protection and Restoration; 503-241-3506; ext. 46
Katherine Luscher, Partnership Program Director; 503-241-3506; ext. 16
Lisa Mattes, Director of Development; 503-241-3506; ext. 49
Susan Schwartz, Director of Finance & Administration; 503-241-3506; ext. 23
Wendy Wilson, Director of Organizational Development; 208-345-3689
David Borden, Chairman of Board of Directors

RIVER NETWORK
EASTERN OFFICE
3814 Albemarle St., NW
Washington, DC 20016 United States
Phone: 202-364-2550   Fax: 202-364-2520
E-mail: pmunoz@rivernetwork.org
Website: www.rivernetwork.org

Founded: 1988
Membership: 101–1,000
Scope: National

Description: River Network is a national non-profit organization dedicated to helping people understand, protect and restore rivers and their watersheds.

Publication(s): Fundraising Alert, River Voices, How to Save a River, The Clean Water Act Owners Manual

Keyword(s): Water Habitats & Quality

Contact(s):
Don Elder, President; 520 SW 6th Ave., #1130, Portland, OR; 503-241-3506; delder@rivernetwork.org

RIVER OTTER ALLIANCE, THE
6733 S. Locust Ct.
Englewood, CO 80112 United States
Phone: 303-773-2749
Website: www.otternet.com/ROA

Founded: 1990
Membership: 101–1,000
Scope: National

Description: The River Otter Alliance promotes the survival of the North American River Otter through education, research, and habitat protection. We support current research and reintroduction programs, monitor abundance and distribution in the United States, and educate through our newsletter on the need to restore and sustain river otter populations.

Publication(s): River Otter Journal, The
Keyword(s): Water Habitats & Quality, Wildlife & Species

Contact(s):
Tracy Johnston, President
Carol Peterson, Vice President
John Mulvihill, Treasurer; 6733 S. Locust Ct., Englewood, CO 80112-1007

RIVER PROJECT, THE
11950 Ventura Boulevard, #7
Studio City, CA 91604 United States
Phone: 818-980-9660   Fax: 818-980-0700
E-mail: winter@theriverproject.org
Website: www.theriverproject.org

Founded: 2001
Scope: Local, Regional

Description: A 501(c)(3) non-profit organization engaged in outreach, advocacy, education, scientific study, habitat restoration and multi-use open space projects along the rivers and streams of Los Angeles County watersheds.

Keyword(s): Ecosystems (precious), Ethics/Environmental Justice, Land Issues, Oceans/Coasts/Beaches, Pollution (general), Public Health, Public Lands/Greenspace, Recreation/Ecotourism, Reduce/Reuse/Recycle, Sprawl/Urban Planning, Water Habitats & Quality, Wildlife & Species

RIVERS COUNCIL OF WASHINGTON
509 10th Ave., East, Suite 200
Seattle, WA 98102 United States
Phone: 206-568-1380   Fax: 206-568-1381
E-mail: riverswa@brigadoon.com
Website: www.riverscouncilofwa.org

Founded: 1984
Scope: State

Description: (formerly Northwest Rivers Council) The mission of the Rivers Council of Washington is to lead an expanding grassroots effort to preserve, enhance, and restore rivers and their watersheds in Washington state for their natural, recreational, and cultural values, and support compatible efforts of other organizations in the Pacific Northwest.

Publication(s): Washington Rivers
Keyword(s): Recreation/Ecotourism, Water Habitats & Quality

Contact(s):
Doug North, President and Chair of Trustees
Kate Sullivan, Vice President
Scott Andrews, Executive Director
Andy Held, Secretary
Matt Scobel, Treasurer

ROBERT ROADS ILLINOIS DEPARTMENT OF NATURAL RESOURCES
524 S. Second St
Springfield, IL 62701 United States
Phone: 217-782-1329   Fax: 217-782-9599
E-mail: BROADS@DNRMAIL.IL.STATE.US
Website: www.conservation.state.mo.us/engineering/ace/

Founded: 1961
Scope: National

Description: To encourage and broaden the educational, social, and economic interests of conservation engineering practices; to promote recognition of the importance of sound engineering practices in fish, wildlife, and recreation development; to enable each member to take advantage of the experience of other states.

Publication(s): Membership Directory, A.C.E. Newsletter, Informational Brochure, Conference Proceedings, Handbook

Keyword(s): Recreation/Ecotourism

Contact(s):
Robert Roads, President; 217-782-2605
Norval Olson, Secretary and Treasurer

ROCK RIVER HEADWATERS, INC.
(RRHI)
P.O. Box 151
Horicon, WI 53032 United States
Phone: 920-485-3019
E-mail: lynn_hanson@lycos.com

Founded: 2000
Membership: 101–1,000
Scope: Regional

Description: Builds collaboration between citizens, organizations and governments in the Upper Rock River Basin of Wisconsin

Publication(s): Finding the Common Ground
Keyword(s): Land Issues, Water Habitats & Quality

Contact(s):
Lynn Hanson, Director; P.O. Box 75, Horicon, WI 53032; 920-485-3019; Fax: 920-485-3028; lynn_hanson@lycos.com

ROCKY MOUNTAIN BIGHORN SOCIETY
P.O. Box 8320
Denver, CO 80201 United States
Phone: 303-697-4896   Fax: 303-697-2921
Website: www.bighornsheep.org

Founded: 1975
Membership: 1,001–10,000
Scope: National
Description: The purpose of the Society is to support the sound management of the Rocky Mountain bighorn sheep and its habitat and to promote the advancement and knowledge of the bighorn.
Publication(s): The Bighorn
Keyword(s): Recreation/Ecotourism
Contact(s):
  Dennis Gardner, President; 19114 Silver Ranch Rd., Conifer, CO 80433; 303-697-4896
  Victor Lauer, Vice President; P. O. Box 1811, Woodland, CO 80866
  Todd Brickell, Secretary; 8181 Cooper River Dr., Colorado Springs, CO 80920
  Kevin Wilson, Treasurer; P.O. Box 485, Conifer, CO 80433

ROCKY MOUNTAIN BIOLOGICAL LABORATORY, THE
P.O. Box 519
Crested Butte, CO 81224 United States
Phone: 970-349-7231
E-mail: info@rmbl.org
Website: www.rmbl.org

Founded: 1928
Membership: 10,001–100,000
Scope: International
Description: We are a private, non-profit corporation providing facilities for research and education in the biological sciences in the Rocky Mountains.
Keyword(s): Climate Change, Wildlife & Species
Contact(s):
  Ian Billick, Director; ibillick@rmbl.org

ROCKY MOUNTAIN BIRD OBSERVATORY
14500 Lark Bunting Lane
Brighton, CO 80603-8311 United States
Phone: 303-659-4348   Fax: 303-654-0791
E-mail: william.palmer@rmbo.org
Website: www.rmbo.org

Founded: 1988
Membership: 101–1,000
Scope: Local, State, Regional, National, International
Description: A non-profit NGO dedicated to the conservation of Rocky Mountains and Great Plains birds and their habitats through research, monitoring, education, and outreach.
Keyword(s): Agriculture/Farming, Ecosystems (precious), Forests/Forestry, Land Issues, Wildlife & Species
Contact(s):
  William Palmer, Executive Director; 303-659-4348; Fax: 303-654-0791; william.palmer@rmbo.org
  Alison Banks, Wetlands Program Coordinator; 1510 South College Avenue, Fort Collins, CO 80524; 970-482-1707; Fax: 970-407-9996; alison.banks@rmbo.org
  Scott Gillihan, Forested Ecosystems Program Coordinator; 1510 South College Ave., Fort Collins, CO 80524; 970-482-1707; Fax: 970-407-9996; scott.gillihan@rmbo.org
  Tony Leukering, Monitoring Program Coordinator; 303-659-4348; Fax: 303-654-0791; tony.leukering@rmbo.org
  Shelly Morrell, Education Program Coordinator; 1510 S. College Ave., Fort Collins, CO 80524; 970-482-1707; Fax: 970-407-9996; shelly.morrell@rmbo.org
  Ted Toombs, Prairie Partners Program Coordinator; 1510 South College Avenue, Fort Collins, CO 80524; 970-482-1707; Fax: 970-407-9996; ted.toombs@rmbo.org

ROCKY MOUNTAIN ELK FOUNDATION
P.O. Box 8249
Missoula, MT 59807 United States
Phone: 406-523-4500   Fax: 406-523-4581
E-mail: info@elkfoundation.org
Website: www.elkfoundation.org

Founded: 1984
Membership: 100,001–500,000
Scope: Regional, National, International
Description: The Foundation's mission is to ensure the future of elk, other wildlife and their habitat. Projects funded by RMEF include: land protection, habitat enhancement, management, research, conservation education, and hunting heritage.
Publication(s): Bugle
Keyword(s): Ecosystems (precious), Forests/Forestry, Land Issues, Public Lands/Greenspace, Recreation/Ecotourism, Wildlife & Species
Contact(s):
  Rance Block, Regional VP - Northwest Region; 9407 N. Oakland Court, Newman Lake, WA 99025; 509-226-0388; Fax: 509-226-3722; rblock@rmef.org
  Mike Carter, Regional VP - Southwest Region; 2291 W. Broadway, Missoula, MT 59808; 406-523-3452; Fax: 406-523-4581; mike@rmef.org
  Dave Messics, Regional VP - Northeast Region; 198 Bennett Rd., Julian, PA 16844; 814-353-1667; Fax: 814-353-2963; dmessics@rmef.org
  Ron White, Regional VP - Southeast Region; 1323 Robert E. Lee Lane, Brentwood, TN 37027; 615-370-0370; Fax: 615-373-2383; rwhite@rmef.org

ROGER TORY PETERSON INSTITUTE OF NATURAL HISTORY
311 Curtis St.
Jamestown, NY 14701 United States
Phone: 716-665-2473   Fax: 716-665-3794
E-mail: webmaster@rtpi.org
Website: www.rtpi.org

Founded: 1984
Membership: 1,001–10,000
Scope: National
Description: The mission of the Roger Tory Peterson Institute is to create a passion for and knowledge of the natural world in the hearts and minds of children by guiding and inspiring the study of nature in our schools and communities.
Publication(s): Quarterly publication for members
Keyword(s): Reduce/Reuse/Recycle
Contact(s):
  Jim Berry, President; 716-665-2473; Fax: 716-665-3794; jim@rtpi.org
  Mark Baldwin, Director of Education; 716-665-2473; Fax: 716-665-3794; mark@rtpi.org
  Mike Lyons, Director of Development; 716-665-2473; Fax: 716-665-3794; mike@rtpi.org

RUFFED GROUSE SOCIETY, THE
451 McCormick Rd.
Coraopolis, PA 15108 United States
Phone: 412-262-4044   Fax: 412-262-9207
E-mail: rgs@ruffedgrousesociety.org
Website: www.ruffedgrousesociety.org

Founded: 1961
Membership: 10,001–100,000
Scope: National
Description: Nonprofit conservation organization dedicated to improving the environment for ruffed grouse, woodcock, and other forest wildlife through maintenance, improvement, and expansion of their habitat. Assists private, industrial, county, state, and federal landholders in forest wildlife habitat improvement programs.
Publication(s): RGS Magazine

NON-GOVERNMENTAL NON-PROFIT ORGANIZATIONS – S

Keyword(s): Forests/Forestry, Wildlife & Species
Contact(s):
- Edwin Gott, President
- Robert Patterson, Executive Director; 412-262-4044; ext. 11; Fax: 412-262-9207; BobP@ruffedgrousesociety.org
- James Jurries, Secretary
- S. Mellon, Executive Vice President
- Stephen Quill, Vice President
- David Sandstrom, Treasurer
- Ronald Burkert, Group Director, Administration and Information Systems; 412-262-4044; ext. 10; Fax: 412-262-9207; RonB@ruffedgrousesociety.org
- Michelle Benedict, Director - Chapter Operations; 412-262-4044; ext. 21; Fax: 412-262-9207; MichelleB@ruffedgrousesociety.org
- Paul Carson, Group Director, Publications and Communications; 412-262-4044; ext. 16; Fax: 412-262-9207; PaulC@ruffedgrousesociety.org
- Dan Dessecker, Sr. Biologist; P.O. Box 2, Rice Lake, WI 54868; 715-234-8302; Fax: 715-234-5051; rgsdess@chibardun.net
- Louis George, Regional Director/WI, LA, MO, WI States; 964 Milson Ct., LaCrosse, WI 54601; 608-793-1114; Fax: 608-793-1115; GeorgeLou@msn.com
- Roberta Sandell, Manager - Membership Services; 412-262-4044; ext. 14; Fax: 412-262-9207; RobertaS@ruffedgrousesociety.org
- Lisa Turner, Director - HQ Operations; 412-262-4044; ext. 15; Fax: 412-262-9207; LisaT@ruffedgrousesociety.org
- Thomas Word, Financial Development Director; P.O. Box 29672, Richmond, VA 23242; 804-784-8895; Fax: 804-784-8895; rgsdevelopment@comcast.net
- Mark Banker, Regional Biologist, Mid-Atlantic; P.O. Box 1171, Lemont, PA 16851-1171; 814-867-7946; Fax: 814-867-8436; rgsbank@lazerlink.com
- C. Bump, Regional Biologist, Eastern Great Lakes; 300 W. Hibbard Rd, Owosso, MI 48867; 989-729-9378; Fax: 989-729-9369; rgsbump@onemain.com
- Douglas Doherty, Regional Director, LP, MI; 03695 Cobb Rd., Boyne Falls, MI 49713; 231-549-5063; Fax: 231-549-5063; rgsdrd@hotmail.com
- Mark Fouts, Regional Director/MN, ND; 8154 S. Dowling Lake Rd. W, Superior, WI 54880; 715-399-2270; Fax: 715-399-2296; mfouts@lbdata2.net
- Stuart Henderson, Regional Director, UP, MI, NE WI; N3714 Hickory Rd., Fond du Lac, WI 54937; 920-583-4207; Fax: 920-583-4216; swampcollie@core.com
- Rick Horton, Regional Biologist, MN; P.O. Box 657, Grand Rapids, MN 55744; 218-697-2820; Fax: 218-697-2860; rgshort@uslink.net
- Paul Karczmarczyk, Regional Biologist, New England; P.O. Box 2504, West Brattleboro, VT 05303; 802-325-2114; Fax: 802-325-2143; rgskarz@prodigy.net
- William Klein, Regional Director, Mid-Atlantic, Southeast; P.O. Box 243, Roscoe, PA 15477; 724-938-3705; Fax: 724-938-0283; billklein_rgs@yahoo.com
- Brian Parsons, Regional Director, NC and NE PA, NY, New England; 4054 Spruce Creek Rd., Spruce Creek, PA 16683; 814-632-8671; Fax: 814-632-8671; coalrainkennel@msn.com
- Gary Zimmer, Regional Biologist, Western Great Lakes; P.O. Box 116, Laona, WI 54541; 715-674-7505; Fax: 715-674-7540; rgszimm@newnorth.net
- Jim Abbey, RGS-Canada Executive Director; RR 1, 1053 County Road 38, Courtland, Ontario N0J 1E0; 519-842-9286; Fax: 519-842-9286; jimabbey@oxford.net

RUFFNER MOUNTAIN NATURE COALITION, INC.
1214 81st Street South
Birmingham, AL 35206 United States
Phone: 205-833-8264
Website: www.ruffnermountain.org
Founded: 1978
Membership: 1,001–10,000
Scope: Local
Description: Ruffner Mountain is a 1,000-acre nature preserve in eastern Birmingham that provides outdoor education and recreation opportunities to the surrounding communities. The protected forest, ridges and valleys provide a sanctuary for a wide variety of native plants and wildlife in the center of Alabama's largest urban area. With the addition of 416 acres in 2000, Ruffner Mountain is now the second largest urban nature preserve in the country and is larger than New York's Central Park.
Keyword(s): Forests/Forestry, Public Lands/Greenspace, Recreation/Ecotourism, Wildlife & Species

S

SACRED PASSAGE AND THE WAY OF NATURE
Nature Fellowship
P.O. Box CZ
Bisbee, AZ 85603 United States
Phone: 877-818-1881
E-mail: info@sacredpassage.com
Website: www.sacredpassage.com
Founded: 1972
Scope: International
Description: An international center seeking to improve mankind's understanding of and relationship to the environment at five levels: Individual and home, neighborhood, city, bioregion, national, and international. Projects involve environmental research, case studies, planning, education, communication, conferencing, and demonstration activities. Primary focus is on wilderness retreats, vision quests, and awareness training in nature.
Keyword(s): Land Issues
Contact(s):
- John Milton, Spiritual Director; 877-818-1881; officemanager@sacredpassage.com
- Sarah Sher, Visual Arts Director and Media Consultant
- Jennifer Lennon, Editor and Office Manager
- Vasken Kalayjian, Graphic Design Angel
- Bud Wilson, Director of Public Relations and Senior Guide

SAFARI CLUB INTERNATIONAL
INTERNATIONAL HEADQUARTERS
4800 W. Gates Pass Rd.
Tucson, AZ 85745 United States
Phone: 520-620-1220   Fax: 520-622-1205
Website: www.safariclub.org
Founded: 1971
Membership: 10,001–100,000
Scope: International
Description: A world-wide charitable organization of hunter-conservationists dedicated to the conservation of wildlife, education of people, service to people in need and the protection of hunters' rights. Sponsors wildlife management research, field projects and works with national and international agencies and governments to promote conservation programs worldwide. Operates two education facilities: the International Wildlife Museum at headquarters and the American Wilderness Leadership School.
Publication(s): Safari Magazine, Record Book of Trophy Animals, Safari Times
Keyword(s): Recreation/Ecotourism, Wildlife & Species
Contact(s):
- Gary Bogner, President
- James Brown, Public Relations Director
- Donald Brown, Education Director
- Steve Comus, Publications Director
- Richard Parsons, Director of Governmental Affairs and Conservation; 501 2nd Street, NE, Washington, DC 20002; 202-543-8733; Fax: 202-543-1205
- Tom Stevenson, Conventions Director
- Barbara Strawberry, Corporate Secretary

SAFARI CLUB INTERNATIONAL
SOUTH AFRICA OFFICE
P.O. Box 10362
Centurion, 46 South Africa
Phone: 27126638073　　　Fax: 27126638075
Scope: National

SAFARI CLUB INTERNATIONAL
WASHINGTON, DC OFFICE
501 2nd St., NE
Washington, DC 20002 United States
Phone: 202-543-8733　　　Fax: 202-543-1205
Website: www.sci-dc.org
Scope: International
Publication(s): Safari Magazine, Safari Times

SALMON-SAFE
805 SE 32nd Avenue
Portland, OR 97214 United States
Phone: 503-232-3750　　　Fax: 503-232-3791
E-mail: info@salmonsafe.org
Website: salmonsafe.org
Founded: 2001
Scope: Regional
Description: Salmon-Safe works to restore West Coast agricultural and urban watersheds and the species that inhabit them through certification and other market-based incentives.
Contact(s):
　Dan Kent, Managing Director

SAN DIEGO NATURAL HISTORY MUSEUM
P.O. Box 121390
San Diego, CA 92112-1390 United States
Phone: 619-232-3821　　　Fax: 619-232-0248
E-mail: mhager@sdnhm.org
Website: www.sdnhm.org
Founded: 1874
Membership: 1,001–10,000
Scope: Local
Description: Binational natural history museum.
Keyword(s): Ecosystems (precious), Recreation/Ecotourism, Wildlife & Species

SAN ELIJO LAGOON CONSERVANCY
P. O. Box 230634
Encinitas, CA 92023-0634 United States
Phone: 760-436-3944　　　Fax: 760-944-9606
E-mail: info@sanelijo.org
Website: www.sanelijo.org
Founded: 1987
Membership: 1,001–10,000
Scope: Local
Description: A 401 (c) (3) non-profit organization dedicated to the preservation, protection, and enhancement of the 1000-acre San Elijo Lagoon Ecological Reserve, a coastal wetland in northern San Diego County.
Keyword(s): Ecosystems (precious), Land Issues, Oceans/Coasts/Beaches, Pollution (general), Recreation/Ecotourism, Wildlife & Species
Contact(s):
　Andrew Mauro, President
　Doug Gibson, Executive Director
　Maryanne Bache, Administrative Officer

SAN JUAN PRESERVATION TRUST, THE
P.O. Box 327
Lopez Island, WA 98261 United States
Phone: 360-468-3202　　　Fax: 360-468-3509
E-mail: sjpt@sjpt.org
Website: www.sjpt.org
Founded: 1979
Membership: 1,001–10,000
Scope: Local
Description: The trust is supported by voluntary contributions from members who support the preservation of wildlife, scenery, and natural heritage of the San Juan Islands of Washington State.
Publication(s): Mom's Marsh and Other Fine Places (video) Landowner's Guide, Preserve Farmlands, A Place in the Islands
Keyword(s): Ecosystems (precious), Forests/Forestry, Land Issues, Oceans/Coasts/Beaches, Water Habitats & Quality, Wildlife & Species
Contact(s):
　Karin Agosta, President
　David Ashbaugh, Vice President
　Tim Seifert, Executive Director; 360-468-3202; Fax: 360-468-3509
　Mike Cooper, Planned Giving and Outreach; 360-468-3202; Fax: 360-468-3509
　Ruthie Johns, Preservation Lands Manager; 360-468-3202; Fax: 360-468-3509
　Dean Dougherty, Land Steward; 360-468-3202; Fax: 360-468-3509
　Sheri Miklaski, Office Manager; 360-468-3202; Fax: 360-468-3509
　Alan Davidson, Treasurer
　Anne Hay, Secretary

SANIBEL-CAPTIVA CONSERVATION FOUNDATION, INC.
P.O. Box 839, 3333 Sanibel-Captiva Rd.
Sanibel, FL 33957-0839 United States
Phone: 239-472-2329　　　Fax: 239-472-6421
E-mail: sccf@sccf.org
Website: www.sccf.org
Founded: 1967
Membership: 1,001–10,000
Scope: Regional
Description: The Sanibel-Captiva Conservation Foundation is a not-for-profit organization dedicated to the preservation of natural resources and wildlife habitat on and around Sanibel and Captiva Islands. Community programs include: land acquisition, habitat restoration and management, landscaping for wildlife, estuarine research (at Tarpon Bay Laboratory), environmental education, and sea turtle conservation program.
Publication(s): Stewardship Update Newsletter
Keyword(s): Ecosystems (precious), Land Issues, Water Habitats & Quality
Contact(s):
　Steve Bortone, Director, Tarpon Bay Laboratory; sbortone@sccf.org
　Erick Lindblad, Executive Director
　Beth Degrauwe, Native Plant Nursery Manager
　Kristie Anders, Education Director
　Brad Smith, Restoration Ecologist

SASKATCHEWAN WILDLIFE FEDERATION
444 River St., W.
Moose Jaw, S6H 6J6 Saskatchewan Canada
Phone: 306-692-8812　　　Fax: 306-692-4370
E-mail: sask.wildlife@sk.sympatico.ca
Website: www.swf.sk.ca
Founded: 1929
Membership: 10,001–100,000
Scope: State
Description: Affiliated with the Canadian Wildlife Federation. A nonprofit, citizens' conservation group established for the protection and enhancement of fish and wildlife habitat. One hundred and thirty-seven local branches representing 32,000 members. Includes the Habitat Trust Fund holding title to 15,000 purchased and donated acres, and the Wildlife Tomorrow Program with 400,000 acres under free easement.

Publication(s): Outdoor Edge
Contact(s):
Joe Schemenauer, President
Sandra Dewald, Office Manager; 444 River St. W., Moose Jaw, Saskatchewan S6H 6J6; 306-692-8812
James Kroshus, Land Coordinator; 444 River St. W., Moose Jaw, Saskatchewan S6H 6J6; 306-693-9022

SAVE AMERICA'S FORESTS
4 Library Ct., SE
Washington, DC 20003 United States
Phone: 202-544-9219
E-mail: info@saveamericasforests.org
Website: www.saveamericasforests.org
Founded: 1990
Membership: 1,001–10,000
Scope: National
Description: A nationwide coalition of grassroots regional and national environmental groups, public interest groups, responsible businesses, and individuals working together to pass strong forest protection legislation in the U.S. Congress.
Keyword(s): Development/Developing Countries, Forests/Forestry, Public Lands/Greenspace, Wildlife & Species
Contact(s):
Carl Ross, Director

SAVE OUR RIVERS, INC.
P.O. Box 122
Franklin, NC 28744 United States
Phone: 828-369-7877   Fax: 828-369-7877
E-mail: rivers@dnet.net
Founded: 1990
Scope: State
Description: Committed to facilitating active public involvement in decisions concerning our rivers by providing information, initiating programs, encouraging public awareness, promoting coordination of services, activities, resources and opportunities.
Publication(s): The Current
Keyword(s): Ethics/Environmental Justice, Oceans/Coasts/Beaches, Pollution (general), Reduce/Reuse/Recycle, Water Habitats & Quality
Contact(s):
Peg Jones, President

SAVE SAN FRANCISCO BAY ASSOCIATION
SAVE THE BAY
1600 Broadway
Suite 300
Oakland, CA 94612 United States
Phone: 510-452-9261   Fax: 510-452-9266
E-mail: savebay@savesfbay.org
Website: www.savesfbay.org
Founded: 1961
Membership: 10,001–100,000
Scope: Regional
Description: Member-supported, non-profit environmental organization dedicated to restoring and protecting San Francisco Bay. We work for the improvement of water quality, adequate fresh water inflow and protection of the Bay's plant, wildlife, fish and human populations and their habitats. Our efforts are focused on public education, collaboration with other organizations, coalition-building, litigation, the monitoring of regulatory agencies and input into the legislative process.
Publication(s): Protecting Local Wetlands, Volunteer Opportunities, Watershed, information fact sheets
Keyword(s): Ecosystems (precious), Ethics/Environmental Justice, Oceans/Coasts/Beaches, Pollution (general), Public Health, Recreation/Ecotourism, Reduce/Reuse/Recycle, Sprawl/Urban Planning, Transportation, Water Habitats & Quality, Wildlife & Species
Contact(s):
Ralph Benson, President
Joe Engbeck, Vice President
David Lewis, Executive Director
Jen Jackson, Community Organizer; jjackson@savesfbay.org
Jessica Parsons, Outings Coordinator; jparsons@savesfbay.org
Paul Revier, Outreach and Communications Director

SAVE THE BAY - PEOPLE FOR NARRAGANSETT BAY
434 Smith St.
Providence, RI 02908-3770 United States
Phone: 401-272-3540   Fax: 401-273-7153
E-mail: savebay@savebay.org
Website: www.savebay.org
Founded: 1970
Membership: 10,001–100,000
Scope: Local, State, Regional
Description: Save The Bay is dedicated to protecting, restoring and exploring Narragansett Bay—a designated estuary of national significance. As a nonprofit, member-supported environmental organization, Save The Bay works to ensure that the environmental quality of Narragansett Bay and its watershed is restored and protected from the harmful effects of human activity.
Publication(s): Coastal Property and Landscape Management Guidebook, The Uncommon Guide to Common Life of Narragansett Bay, Backyards on the Bay: A Yard Care Guide for the Coastal Home Owner
Keyword(s): Ecosystems (precious), Land Issues, Oceans/Coasts/Beaches, Pollution (general), Public Lands/Greenspace, Recreation/Ecotourism, Sprawl/Urban Planning, Water Habitats & Quality
Contact(s):
H. Spalding, Executive Director

SAVE THE DUNES CONSERVATION FUND
444 Barker Rd.
Michigan City, IN 46360 United States
Phone: 219-879-3564   Fax: 219-872-4875
E-mail: sand@savedunes.org
Website: www.savedunes.org
Founded: 1994
Membership: 101–1,000
Scope: Local, Regional
Description: The Mission of Save the Dunes Conservation Fund is to preserve, protect, and restore the Indiana Dunes and all natural resources in Northwest Indiana's Lake Michigan Watershed for an enhanced quality of life. This Mission is pursued ethically with perserverance, credibility, nonpartisanship, informed positions, and a holistic approach.
Publication(s): Save the Dunes (newsletter)
Keyword(s): Ecosystems (precious), Water Habitats & Quality, Wildlife & Species
Contact(s):
Thomas Anderson, Executive Director
Sandra Wilmore, Fund Director

SAVE THE DUNES COUNCIL
444 Barker Rd.
Michigan City, IN 46360 United States
Phone: 219-879-3937   Fax: 219-872-4875
E-mail: std@savedunes.org
Website: www.savedunes.org
Founded: 1952
Membership: 101–1,000
Scope: National
Description: Dedicated to the preservation of the Indiana Dunes National Lakeshore for public use and enjoyment. Concerned with protecting the ecological values of the dunes region,

preserving Lake Michigan, and combating air, water, and hazardous waste pollution. Established by Dorothy Buell.

Publication(s): Newsletter

Keyword(s): Air Quality/Atmosphere, Land Issues, Oceans/Coasts/Beaches, Public Lands/Greenspace, Recreation/Ecotourism

Contact(s):
Thomas Serynek, President; 1000 N. Warrick, Gary, IN 46403; 219-938-5410
Dorothy Potucek, 1st Vice President; 1608 Parkview Ave., Whiting, IN 46394
Thomas Anderson, Executive Director
Sandra Wilmore, Program Director
Christine Livingston, Administrative Assistant
Mark Mihalo, Treasurer; 8 Diana Road, Ogden Dunes, Portage, IN 46368; 219-763-4871
Charlotte Read, Assistant Director

SAVE THE HARBOR/SAVE THE BAY
59 Temple Pl., Suite 304
Boston, MA 02111 United States
Phone: 617-451-2860   Fax: 617-451-0496
E-mail: info@savetheharbor.org
Website: www.savetheharbor.org

Founded: 1986
Membership: 1,001–10,000
Scope: State
Description: Save the Harbor/Save the Bay is a nonprofit organization whose mission is to foster a positive vision of Boston Harbor and Massachusetts Bay, and to build a broad-based constituency to promote the restoration and protection of these valuable resources. Services include narrated boat tours of Boston Harbor, discussions of harbor pollution, cleanup projects, history, celebratory events, summer youth program, and a Baywatch Program.

Publication(s): Splash (newsletter)

Keyword(s): Oceans/Coasts/Beaches, Water Habitats & Quality

Contact(s):
Bruce Berman, Baywatch & Communications Director
Patricia Foley, Executive Director
Lisa Mantoni, Program Coordinator; ext. 102; mantoni@savetheharbor.org
Beth Nicholson, Chairperson & President
Matt Wolfe, Events Coordinator

SAVE THE MANATEE CLUB
500 N. Maitland Ave.
Maitland, FL 32751 United States
Phone: 407-539-0990   Fax: 407-539-0871
E-mail: education@savethemanatee.org
Website: www.savethemanatee.org

Founded: 1981
Membership: 10,001–100,000
Scope: International
Description: A national nonprofit organization founded by Governor Bob Graham and singer and songwriter Jimmy Buffett. Objectives are public awareness and education; funding research, rescue, rehabilitation and advocacy and appropriate legal action for the endangered West Indian manatee and its habitat. Funded primarily by the club's Adopt-a-Manatee program.

Keyword(s): Wildlife & Species

Contact(s):
Nancy Sadusky, Communications Director
Judith Vallee, Executive Director
Jimmy Buffett, Co-Chairman
Helen Spivey, Co-Chairman

SAVE THE SOUND, INC.
20 Marshall Street
South Norwalk, CT 06854 United States
Phone: 203-354-0036   Fax: 203-354-0041
E-mail: savethesound@savethesound.org
Website: www.savethesound.org

Founded: 1972
Membership: 1,001–10,000
Scope: Local, State, Regional, National
Description: Save the Sound, Inc. is devoted to protecting, restoring, and appreciating Long Island Sound and its watershed. With a staff of nine full-time employees and additional seasonal employees, STS operates year-round programs in education, research, and advocacy, including Sea Camp, Soundshore Ecology, water quality monitoring, habitat restoration, beach cleanups, and an extensive library.

Publication(s): Annual Water Quality Report, SoundBites, Long Island Sound Municipal Report Cards, Water Quality Monitoring: A Guide for Concerned Citizens

Keyword(s): Ecosystems (precious), Executive/Legislative/Judicial Reform, Pollution (general), Public Lands/Greenspace, Sprawl/Urban Planning, Water Habitats & Quality

Contact(s):
John Atkin, President; 203-354-0036; Fax: 203-354-0041; jatkin@savethesound.org
John Brooks, Vice President, Marketing & Development; 203-354-0036; Fax: 203-354-0041; jbrooks@savethesound.org
Bridgett Byrnes, Director of Education; 203-354-0036; Fax: 203-354-0041; bbyrnes@savethesound.org
Leah Lopez, Staff Attorney; 203-354-0036; Fax: 203-354-0041; llopez@savethesound.org
William Shadel, Director of Research and Restoration; 203-354-0036; Fax: 203-354-0041; wshadel@savethesound.org

SAVE THE SOUND, INC.
20 Marshall St.
South Norwalk, CT 06854 United States
Phone: 203-354-0036   Fax: 203-354-0041
E-mail: savethesound@savethesound.org
Website: www.savethesound.org

Founded: 1972
Membership: 1,001–10,000
Scope: Local, State, Regional, National
Description: Save the Sound is dedicated to protecting and restoring Long Island Sound and its watershed through advocacy, education and research.

Publication(s): Long Island Sound Conservation Blueprint, SoundBites

Keyword(s): Ecosystems (precious), Executive/Legislative/Judicial Reform, Pollution (general), Public Lands/Greenspace, Sprawl/Urban Planning, Water Habitats & Quality

Contact(s):
Nina Sankovitch, Executive Director and President; 203-354-0036; Fax: 203-354-0041; nsankovitch@savethesound.org

SAVE WETLANDS AND BAYS
24353 Thorneby Trace
Millsboro, DE 19966 United States
Phone: 302-945-1317   Fax: 302-945-1317

Founded: 1989
Membership: 101–1,000
Scope: Local
Description: To protect Delaware's inland bays and fringing marshes from perceived threats.

Contact(s):
Til Purnell, Executive Director; purnell@ce.net

SAVE-THE-REDWOODS LEAGUE
114 Sansome St., Suite 1200
San Francisco, CA 94104 United States
Phone: 415-362-2352   Fax: 415-362-7017
E-mail: info@savetheredwoods.org
Website: www.savetheredwoods.org
Founded: 1918
Membership: 10,001–100,000
Scope: State
Description: The League purchases redwood forest and associated lands for inclusion in State and Federal parks and reserves. The League also sponsors research and education through a grants program. Please visit www.savetheredwoods.org for more information.
Publication(s): California Redwood Parks and Preserves, Redwoods of the Past, The Redwood Forest, Trees, Shrubs and Flowers of the Redwood, Bulletin
Keyword(s): Ecosystems (precious), Forests/Forestry, Public Lands/Greenspace, Wildlife & Species
Contact(s):
Richard Otter, President of the Board
Kate Anderton, Secretary and Executive Director
Bruce Howard, Chairman of the Board
Frank Westworth, Treasurer; P.O. Box 44614, San Francisco, CA 94144-0001

SCENIC AMERICA
801 Pennsylvania Ave., SE, Suite 300
Washington, DC 20003 United States
Phone: 202-543-6200   Fax: 202-543-9130
E-mail: scenic@scenic.org
Website: www.scenic.org
Founded: 1978
Membership: 1,001–10,000
Scope: National
Description: National membership organization dedicated to preserving and enhancing the scenic character of America's communities and countryside. Provides information and technical assistance on billboard and sign control, scenic byways, tree preservation, highway design, cellular tower siting, and other scenic conservation issues.
Publication(s): Scenic News, Viewpoints, series of videos and technical bulletins, Fighting Billboard Blight: An Action Guide for Citizens and Elected Officials
Keyword(s): Land Issues, Public Lands/Greenspace, Reduce/Reuse/Recycle
Contact(s):
Meg Maguire, President

SCENIC AMERICA
SCENIC CALIFORNIA
2215 Fifth Street
Berkeley, CA 94710 United States
Phone: 510-883-0390   Fax: 510-883-0391
E-mail: sceniccalifornia@earthlink.net
Website: www.sceniccalifornia.org
Founded: 1998
Scope: State
Description: Scenic California is dedicated to protecting natural beauty in the environment, preserving and enhancing landscapes and streetscapes, protecting historical and cultural resources, promoting the enhancement of scenic approaches and settings of cities and towns, improving community appearance and fostering the establishment and preservation of scenic roads and viewsheds.
Contact(s):
Sheila Brady, Manager

SCENIC AMERICA
SCENIC MICHIGAN
445 E. Mitchell St.
Petoskey, MI 49770 United States
Phone: 231-347-1171   Fax: 231-347-1185
E-mail: info@scenicmichigan.org
Website: www.scenicmichigan.org
Scope: State
Description: Scenic Michigan started under the aegis of Michigan United Conservation Clubs, the largest nonprofit conservation organization in the United States, as a billboard control task force in 1989. The mission of Scenic Michigan is to protect and enhance the appearance and scenic character of Michigan's communities and countryside.
Publication(s): Recommended Elements of a Sign Ordinance
Contact(s):
Debbie Rohe, President
Julie Metty, Vice President
Rick Barber, Admin. Asst.; 231-347-1171; Fax: 231-347-1185, rick@scenicmichigan.org
Bethany Goodman, Secretary
Mary Tanton, Treasurer

SCENIC AMERICA
SCENIC MISSOURI
401 Locust, Suite 302
Columbia, MO 65201 United States
Phone: 573-256-2550   Fax: 573-443-8155
E-mail: scenicmo@tranquility.net
Website: www.scenicmissouri.org
Founded: 1993
Membership: 101–1,000
Scope: State
Description: Scenic Missouri was founded because of a growing concern about the loss of Missouri's scenic heritage. Its mission is to preserve and enhance the scenic beauty of Missouri.
Publication(s): Model Ordinance, Scenic Views, Scenic Missouri Website
Keyword(s): Public Lands/Greenspace, Sprawl/Urban Planning, Transportation
Contact(s):
Karl Kruse, Executive Director; 573-256-2550; Fax: 573-443-8155; scenicmo@tranquility.net
Amelia Miner Cottle, Membership Director; 573-256-2550; Fax: 573-443-8155; scenicmo@tranquility.net

SCENIC AMERICA
SCENIC TEXAS
3015 Richmond Suite 220
Houston, TX 77098 United States
Phone: 713-629-0481   Fax: 713-629-0485
E-mail: scenic@scenictexas.org
Website: www.scenictexas.org
Membership: 1,001–10,000
Scope: Local, State
Description: The mission of Scenic Texas is to preserve and enhance the scenic character of the visual environment. Scenic Texas has chapters in Houston, Dallas, Austin, San Antonio, Fort Worth, and an affiliate in Galveston.
Publication(s): Scenic Views
Contact(s):
Susan Teich, Executive Director; 713-533-9149; ext. 14; Fax: 713-629-0485; teich@scenictexas.org

SCENIC HUDSON, INC.
One Civic Center Plaza
Suite 200
Poughkeepsie, NY 12601 United States
Phone: 845-473-4440
E-mail: info@scenichudson.org
Website: www.scenichudson.org

Founded: 1963

Scope: Local, State, Regional

Description: A nonprofit conservation and environmental organization dedicated to protecting and enhancing the scenic, natural, recreational and historic treasures of the Hudson River Valley. Speakers' Bureau available to the public.

Publication(s): Your Valley, Scenic Hudson News, Adventure Guide

Keyword(s): Agriculture/Farming, Air Quality/Atmosphere, Land Issues, Pollution (general), Public Lands/Greenspace, Sprawl/Urban Planning, Water Habitats & Quality

Contact(s):
Ned Sullivan, President
Jay Burgess, Communications & Public Outreach Program Director
Deborah DeWan, Riverfront Communities Program Director
Alix Gerosa, Environmental Quality Program Director
Warren Reiss, General Counsel
Erin Riley-West, Development Director
Steve Rosenberg, Executive Director, the Scenic Hudson Land Trust, Inc.
Theresa Vanyo, Human Resources Director
Marjorie Hart, Chairman
Joseph Kazlauskas, CFO & COO

SCIENTISTS CENTER FOR ANIMAL WELFARE
7833 Walker Drive, Suite 410
Greenbelt, MD 20770 United States
Phone: 301-345-3500   Fax: 301-345-3503
E-mail: info@scaw.com
Website: www.scaw.com

Founded: 1978

Membership: 1,001–10,000

Scope: National, International

Description: A nonprofit educational organization that promotes the belief that high standards of animal welfare complement the quality of scientific results. SCAW publishes educational material about current issues of animal use in research, testing, and teaching.

Publication(s): SCAW (newsletter), see publications on website

Keyword(s): Oceans/Coasts/Beaches, Public Health, Wildlife & Species

Contact(s):
Lee Krulisch, Executive Director

SEA SHEPHERD CONSERVATION SOCIETY
INTERNATIONAL HEADQUARTERS
P.O Box 2670
Malibu, CA 90265 United States
Phone: 360-370-5650   Fax: 360-370-5651
E-mail: seashepherd@seashepherd.org
Website: www.seashepherd.com

Founded: 1977

Scope: International

Description: An international direct action marine mammal conservation organization involved in stopping marine mammal slaughters. SSCS works directly with the Galapagos park rangers intercepting poachers. Other special projects include: campaigns against drift net fishing, whaling, the Faeroese pilot whale slaughter, and sealing. The Society owns and operates two ships, the Farley Mowat and the Sirenian.

Publication(s): Sea Shepherd Log Quarterly

Keyword(s): Wildlife & Species

Contact(s):
Captain Paul Watson, Founder and President; paul@seashepherd.org

SEA SHEPHERD CONSERVATION SOCIETY
AUSTRALIA OFFICE
P.O. Box A2330
Sydney South, NSW 1235 Australia
Phone: 02 9976 5001
E-mail: seashepherd@chilli.net.au

Scope: International

Contact(s):
Sue Marshall
Peter Ward

SEA SHEPHERD CONSERVATION SOCIETY
BRAZIL-INSTITUTO SEA SHEPHERD BRASIL
Caixa Postal 21402
CEP 902220-021 Porto Alegre, RS Brasil
Phone: 51 32.22.08.55
E-mail: fylomena@terra.com.br
Website: www.seashepherd.org.br

Scope: International

Contact(s):
Alex Castro

SEA SHEPHERD CONSERVATION SOCIETY
CANADA OFFICE
P.O. Box 48446
Vancouver, B.C., V7X 1A2 Canada
Phone: 604-688-7325   Fax: 360-370-5651
E-mail: sscscanada@seashepherd.org
Website: www.seashepherd.org

Membership: 10,001–100,000

Scope: International

Publication(s): Ocean Warrior, Annual Report, Captain Log, Earth Force

Contact(s):
Starlet Lum

SEA SHEPHERD CONSERVATION SOCIETY
NETHERLANDS
EUROPEAN COMMUNITY
Postbus 6095, 4000 HB Tiel
The Netherlands
Phone: 0344-604-103
E-mail: info@seashepherd.nl
Website: www.seashepherd.nl

Founded: 1977

Scope: International

Contact(s):
Ivor Verbon

SEA SHEPHERD CONSERVATION SOCIETY
SINGAPORE/ASIA
Block 503 #02-237
Pasir Ris St. 52
Singapore 510503 Republic of Singapore
Phone: 65-583673
E-mail: grant@seashpherd.org
Website: www.seashepherd.org

Scope: International

Contact(s):
Grant Pereira

SEA SHEPHERD CONSERVATION SOCIETY
UNITED KINGDOM
P.O. Box 22
Beauth, IV4 7WG Scotland, United Kingdom
E-mail: Oceanica@sea-shepherd.fsbusiness.co.uk

Website: www.seashepherd.org
Scope: International
Contact(s):
 Patrick O'Brian

SEA SHEPHERD CONSERVATION SOCIETY
USA REGIONAL-SSCS MONTEREY
P.O. Box 729
Monterey, CA 93942-0729 United States
Phone: 831-659-5006   Fax: 831-659-8604
E-mail: evo34988@aol.com
Website: www.seashepherd.org
Scope: National, International
Contact(s):
 Thomas Heinemann

SEA TURTLE PRESERVATION SOCIETY
P. O. Box 510988-0988
Melbourne Beach, FL 32951-0988 United States
Phone: 321-676-1701
E-mail: webmaster@seaturtlespacecoast.org
Website: www.SeaTurtleSpaceCoast.org
Founded: 1982
Membership: 101–1,000
Scope: Local
Description: Nonprofit conservation group located in Brevard County working for preservation of sea turtles along Florida's East Coast. Largest turtle rescue & recovery program in state. Conducting educational presentations and walks to over 5000 visitors each year under Florida Fish & Wildlife Conservation Commission (FFWCC) permits.
Publication(s): STPS Newsletter
Keyword(s): Ecosystems (precious), Oceans/Coasts/Beaches, Water Habitats & Quality, Wildlife & Species
Contact(s):
 Richard Winn, Chairman; 321-984-2960; Fax: 321-951-0701; rjpjotb@Juno.com
 Christin Stewart, Managing Director; 321-676-1701

SEACAMP ASSOCIATION, INC.
1300 Big Pine Ave.
Big Pine Key, FL 33043-3336 United States
Phone: 305-872-2331   Fax: 305-872-2555
E-mail: info@seacamp.org
Website: www.seacamp.org
Founded: 1904
Scope: International
Description: Non-profit organization encompassing two marine education organizations in the Florida Keys, a summer camp and the school program Newfound Harbor Marine Institute (NHMI). Strong international program with Russia. Member NAAEE.
Keyword(s): Oceans/Coasts/Beaches, Recreation/Ecotourism, Water Habitats & Quality
Contact(s):
 Russel Bachert, Director of Special Projects
 John Booker, Program Director
 Chuck Brand, Institute Director, NHMI
 Mary Hensel, Development Director
 Irene Hooper, Executive Director
 Elena Istoma, Director of International Programs
 Grace Upshaw, Camp Director

SEACOAST ANTI-POLLUTION LEAGUE
P.O. Box 1136
Portsmouth, NH 3802 United States
Phone: 603-431-5089
Website: www.sapl.org
Founded: 1969
Scope: State
Description: To promote the wise use of natural resources of the seacoast region, and to alert and educate the community and relevant government agencies of threats to the environment. SAPL works to prevent ecological, economic and public health damage from the Seabrook nuclear reactor, the Portsmouth Naval Shipyard and over-development.
Keyword(s): Development/Developing Countries, Energy
Contact(s):
 Davie Hills, President
 Mary Metcalf, Vice President
 Steve Haberman, Executive Director
 Jim Horrigan, Treasurer
 Johanna Lyons, Secretary
 Peter Vandermark, Tag Coordinator

SEAPLANE PILOTS ASSOCIATION
4315 Highland Park Blvd. Suite C
Lakeland, FL 33813 United States
Phone: 863-701-7979   Fax: 863-701-7588
E-mail: spa@seaplanes.org
Website: www.seaplanes.org
Founded: 1972
Membership: 1,001–10,000
Scope: National
Description: An organization founded to represent and assist seaplane pilots. Provides information and problem-solving assistance to local, state and federal agencies, organizations, and groups.
Publication(s): Seaplane Compatibility Issues Report, Water Flying, Water Landing Directory, Water Flying Annual
Keyword(s): Oceans/Coasts/Beaches, Recreation/Ecotourism, Transportation, Water Habitats & Quality
Contact(s):
 J. Frey, President
 Walter Windus, Vice President
 Michael Volk, Executive Director
 Jerry Potter, Secretary

SEAWEB
1731 Connecticut Ave., NW
4th Floor
Washington, DC 20009 United States
Phone: 202-483-9570   Fax: 202-483-9354
E-mail: seaweb@seaweb.org
Website: www.seaweb.org
Founded: 1996
Scope: National, International
Description: SeaWeb was launched in 1996 to raise awareness of the growing threats to the ocean and its living resources. SeaWeb's goal is to make ocean protection a high environmental priority in the U.S. and around the world. SeaWeb provides science-based information from a variety of sources to a variety of media outlets. With the help of scientists, educators, researchers and communications specialists, SeaWeb has become a respected independent resource for journalists, government officials and concerned citizens.
Keyword(s): Oceans/Coasts/Beaches
Contact(s):
 Vikki Spruill, President
 Will Ferretti, Executive Director
 Tom Johnson, Director of Operations

SHEEPSCOT VALLEY CONSERVATION ASSOCIATION, THE
624 Sheepscot Road
Newcastle, ME 04553 United States
Phone: 207-586-5616   Fax: 207-586-6442
E-mail: svca@sheepscot.org
Website: www.sheepscot.org
Founded: 1970
Membership: 101–1,000

Scope: Local, State, Regional

Description: Our mission is to conserve and restore the natural and historic heritage of the Sheepscot Watershed

Contact(s):
Sam Merrill, Executive Director

SHELBURNE FARMS
1611 Harbor Rd.
Shelburne, VT 05482 United States
Phone: 802-985-8686   Fax: 802-985-8123
Website: www.shelburnefarms.org/
Membership: 1,001–10,000
Scope: Local, State, Regional, National, International

Description: Shelburne Farms is a 1,400 acre working farm, National Historic Landmark and non-profit environmental education center. Our mission is to cultivate a conservation ethic by teaching and demonstrating stewardship of our natural and agricultural resources.

Publication(s): This Lake Alive, Project Seasons

Keyword(s): Agriculture/Farming, Forests/Forestry, Land Issues, Recreation/Ecotourism, Water Habitats & Quality

Contact(s):
Alexander Webb, President; ext. 16; awebb@shelburnefarms.org
Megan Camp, VP and Program Director; ext. 14; mcamp@shelburnefarms.org
Linda Wellings, School Programs Director; ext. 27; jelson@shelburnefarms.org

SIERRA CLUB
ALABAMA CHAPTER
1330 21st Way South, Suite 110
Birmingham, AL 35205 United States
Phone: 205-972-0252
Website: http://alabama.sierraclub.org/
Scope: State

Contact(s):
Jay Hudson, Chair; 205-972-0252; jayhudson@mindspring.com

SIERRA CLUB
ALASKA CHAPTER
P.O Box 103441
Anchorage, AK 99501-3441 United States
Phone: 907-276-4048   Fax: 907-276-4048
E-mail: nw-ak.field@sierraclub.org
Website: www.alaska.sierraclub.org
Scope: State

SIERRA CLUB
ALASKA FIELD OFFICE
201 Barrow St.
Suite 101
Anchorage, AK 99501-2429 United States
Phone: 907-276-4068   Fax: 907-258-6807
E-mail: nw-ak.field@sierraclub.org
Website: www.sierraclubalaska.org
Founded: 1892
Membership: 1,001–10,000
Scope: Regional

Description: Purpose is to explore, enjoy and protect the wild places of the earth; practice and promote responsible use of earth's ecosystems/resources.

Keyword(s): Agriculture/Farming, Air Quality/Atmosphere, Climate Change, Development/Developing Countries, Ecosystems (precious), Energy, Ethics/Environmental Justice, Executive/Legislative/Judicial Reform, Forests/Forestry, Land Issues, Oceans/Coasts/Beaches, Pollution

Contact(s):
Maryellen Oman, Program Assistant; 907-276-4068; Fax: 907-258-6807; maryellen@sierraclubalaska.org
Betsy Goll, Forest Organizer; 907-276-4044; Fax: 907-258-6807; betsy@sierraclubalaska.org
Rebecca Kyle, Volunteer Coordinator; 907-276-4088; Fax: 907-258-6807; rebecca@sierraclubalaska.org
Sara Callaghan-Chapell, Regional Representative; P.O. Box 574, Haines, AK 99827; 907-766-3204; Fax: 907-766-3204; sara@sierraclubalaska.org
Jack Hession, Senior Regional Representative; 907-276-4078; Fax: 907-258-6807; jack@sierraclubalaska.org

SIERRA CLUB
ANGELES CHAPTER
3435 Wilshire Blvd., Suite 320
Los Angeles, CA 90010-1904 United States
Phone: 213-387-4287   Fax: 213-387-5383
E-mail: info@angeleschapter.org
Website: www.angeles.sierraclub.org
Scope: Local, Regional

Publication(s): The Southern Sierran, The Schedule of Activities (quarterly)

Contact(s):
Bill Corcoran, Public Lands Coordinator
Martin Schlageter, Conservation Coordinator

SIERRA CLUB
ATLANTIC CHAPTER
353 Hamilton St.
Albany, NY 12210-1709 United States
Phone: 518-426-0144   Fax: 518-426-3052
E-mail: john.stouffer@sierraclub.org
Website: www.newyork.sierraclub.org
Membership: 10,001–100,000
Scope: State

Description: The New York State division of the National Sierra Club.

Publication(s): Sierra Atlantic

SIERRA CLUB
BAY AREA FIELD OFFICE
827 Broadway, Suite 310
Oakland, CA 94607 United States
Phone: 510-622-0290   Fax: 510-622-0278
E-mail: ca.field@sierraclub.org
Website: www.sierraclub.org/field/ca_nv_hi
Founded: 1892
Scope: Regional

Description: Regional Field Office for National Sierra Club priorities, ranging from Wilderness Preservation to Energy Action Network

SIERRA CLUB
BRITISH COLUMBIA CHAPTER
576 Johnson St.
Victoria, V8W 1M3 British Columbia Canada
Phone: 250-386-5255   Fax: 250-386-4453
E-mail: info@sierraclubbc.org
Website: www.sierraclub.ca/bc/
Scope: Regional

Publication(s): The Sierra Report - magazine

Contact(s):
Bill Warham, Executive Director

SIERRA CLUB
CALIFORNIA/NEVADA/HAWAII OFFICE AND CALIFORNIA LEGISLATIVE OFFICE
1414 K St., Suite 300
Sacramento, CA 95814-3929 United States
Phone: 916-557-1100   Fax: 916-557-9669
E-mail: ca.field@sierraclub.org
Website: www.sierraclub.org
Membership: 101–1,000

Scope: Regional
Contact(s):
  Barbara Boyle, Staff Director
  Bill Craven, State Director

SIERRA CLUB
CASCADE CHAPTER
8511 15th Ave. NE, Rm. 201
Seattle, WA 98115-3101 United States
Phone: 206-523-2147   Fax: 206-378-0034
E-mail: cascade.chapter@sierraclub.org
Website: www.cascade.sierraclub.org/
Membership: 10,001–100,000
Scope: Local, State
Description: Representing more than 25,000 Sierra Club members in Western and Central Washington State.
Publication(s): The Cascade Crest
Contact(s):
  Roy Goodman, Chapter Coordinator

SIERRA CLUB
COLORADO FIELD OFFICE
2260 Baseline Rd. Ste. 105
Boulder, CO 80302-7737 United States
Phone: 303-449-5595   Fax: 303-449-6520
E-mail: sw.field@sierraclub.org
Website: www.rmc.sierraclub.org/sw-co
Membership: 10,001–100,000
Scope: Regional

SIERRA CLUB
COLUMBIA BASIN OFFICE
2703 Klemgaurd Road
Pullman, WA 99163 United States
Phone: 509-332-5173   Fax: 509-332-5173
E-mail: nw-wa.field@sierraclub.org
Website: www.sierraclub.org
Scope: Regional

SIERRA CLUB
CONNECTICUT CHAPTER
118 Oak St.
Hartford, CT 06106-1514 United States
Phone: 860-525-2500
E-mail: connecticut.chapter@sierraclub.org
Website: www.sierraclub.org/ct
Scope: State

SIERRA CLUB
CUMBERLAND CHAPTER
259 W. Short St.
Lexington, KY 40507-1226 United States
Phone: 606-255-7946   Fax: 606-233-4099
E-mail: lanebold@earthlink.net
Website: www.kentucky.sierraclub.org
Founded: 1968
Scope: State

SIERRA CLUB
DACOTAH CHAPTER
311 E. Thayer #113
Bismarck, ND 58501 United States
Phone: 701-530-9288   Fax: 701-530-9290
Website: www.sierraclub.org/nd
Membership: 101–1,000
Scope: Local, State
Description: Grassroots environmental organization
Publication(s): Dakota Prairie, newsletter
Keyword(s): Agriculture/Farming, Air Quality/Atmosphere, Climate Change, Ecosystems (precious), Energy, Ethics/Environmental Justice, Land Issues, Pollution (general), Public Health, Public Lands/Greenspace, Recreation/Ecotourism, Reduce/Reuse/Recycle, Sprawl/Urban Planning
Contact(s):
  Jonathan Bry, Conservation Organizer; 701-530-9288; Fax: 701-530-9290; jonathan.bry@sierraclub.org

SIERRA CLUB
DELAWARE CHAPTER
100 West 10th St.
Suite 1107
Wilmington, DE 19801 United States
Phone: 302-425-4911
E-mail: delaware.chapter@sierraclub.org
Website: www.delaware.sierraclub.org
Scope: State
Publication(s): Chapter Newsletter
Contact(s):
  Matt Urban, Chapter Chair; 302-661-2050; mattsierra@yepatata.com
  Shiray Shipley, Chapter Coordinator; 302-425-4911; shiray.shipley@sierraclub.org

SIERRA CLUB
DELTA CHAPTER
P.O. Box 19469
New Orleans, LA 70179-0469 United States
Phone: 504-836-3062
E-mail: barbara.vincent@sierraclub.org
Website: www.louisiana.sierraclub.org
Scope: State

SIERRA CLUB
EASTERN CANADA CHAPTER
24 Mercer St., Suite 102
Toronto, M5V 1H3 Ontario Canada
Phone: 416-960-9606   Fax: 416-960-0020
E-mail: easterncanadachapter@sierraclub.org
Website: eastern.sierraclub.ca
Membership: 101–1,000
Scope: Regional
Description: The Sierra Club Eastern Canada Chapter is a regional entity of the Sierra Club of Canada, a registered not-for-profit corporation. Our mandate is to protect and restore the health of the natural environment, including human communities in Ontario and Quebec, by empowering the membership through education, advocacy and outdoor adventures.
Publication(s): Newsletters
Contact(s):
  Kim Neill, Chapter Coordinator; 416-960-9606

SIERRA CLUB
FLORIDA CHAPTER
475 Central Ave., Suite M1
St. Petersburg, FL 33701-3817 United States
Phone: 727-824-8813   Fax: 727-824-0936
E-mail: frank.jackalone@sierraclub.org
Website: www.florida.sierraclub.org
Scope: State
Contact(s):
  Geraldine Swormstead, Chair

SIERRA CLUB
FLORIDA REGIONAL FIELD OFFICE
475 Central Ave., Suite M-1
St. Petersburg, FL 33701 United States
Phone: 727-824-8813   Fax: 727-824-0936
E-mail: frank.jackalone@sierraclub.org
Website: www.sierraclub.org

Founded: 1892
Membership: 500,001–1,000,000
Scope: Local, State, Regional, National, International
Description: The Sierra Club's members are more than 700,000 of your friends and neighbors. Inspired by nature, we work together to protect our communities and the planet. The Club is America's oldest, largest and most influential grassroots environmental organization.

SIERRA CLUB
FLORIDA (SOUTH) FIELD OFFICE
2700 SW 3rd Ave., Suite 2F
Miami, FL 33129 United States
Phone: 305-860-9888   Fax: 305-860-9862
E-mail: jonathan.ullman@sierraclub.org
Website: www.sierraclub.org
Membership: 500,001–1,000,000
Scope: Local, Regional, National

SIERRA CLUB
GEORGIA CHAPTER
1401 Peachtree St., NE
Suite 345
Atlanta, GA 30309 United States
Phone: 404-607-1262   Fax: 404-876-5260
E-mail: georgia.chapter@sierraclub.org
Website: www.georgia.sierraclub.org

Founded: 1894
Membership: 10,001–100,000
Scope: State, National
Description: Protection for The Land, Protection for The People, Explore, Enjoy, and Protect the Wild Places on the Earth
Publication(s): Georgia Sierran (newsletter)
Keyword(s): Air Quality/Atmosphere, Ecosystems (precious), Energy, Ethics/Environmental Justice, Executive/Legislative/Judicial Reform, Forests/Forestry, Land Issues, Oceans/Coasts/Beaches, Pollution (general), Public Lands/Greenspace, Reduce/Reuse/Recycle, Sprawl/Urban Planning
Contact(s):
Bryan Hager, Conservation Organizer; ext. 226
Genie Strickland, Chapter Coordinator; ext. 221

SIERRA CLUB
GEORGIA FIELD OFFICE/LOUISIANA AND ALABAMA FIELD OFFICE
1447 Peachtree St., NE, Suite 305
Atlanta, GA 30309-3034 United States
Phone: 404-888-9778   Fax: 404-876-5260
E-mail: ap-ga.field@sierraclub.org
Scope: Regional

SIERRA CLUB
GRAND CANYON CHAPTER
202 East McDowell Road
Suite 277
Phoenix, AZ 85004 United States
Phone: 602-253-8633   Fax: 602-258-6533
E-mail: grand.canyon.chapter@sierraclub.org
Website: www.arizona.sierraclub.org/
Membership: 10,001–100,000
Scope: State
Publication(s): Canyon Echo - monthy newsletter

SIERRA CLUB
HAWAII CHAPTER
P.O. Box 2577
Honolulu, HI 96803-2577 United States
Phone: 808-538-6616   Fax: 808-537-9019
E-mail: hawaii.chapter@sierraclub.org
Website: hi.sierraclub.org/
Scope: State

SIERRA CLUB
HOOSIER CHAPTER
1915 West 18th Street
Suite D
Indianapolis, IN 46202 United States
Phone: 317-822-3750
E-mail: sierra@netdirect.net
Website: hoosier.sierraclub.org/
Scope: State
Description: To explore, enjoy and protect the wildplaces of the Earth; to practice and promote the responsible use of the Earth's ecosystems and resources; to educate and enlist humanity to protect and restore the quality of the natural and human environment; and to use all lawful means to carry out these objectives.
Keyword(s): Agriculture/Farming, Water Habitats & Quality

SIERRA CLUB
ILLINOIS CHAPTER
200 N. Michigan Ave., Suite. 505
Chicago, IL 60601-5908 United States
Phone: 312-251-1680   Fax: 312-251-1780
E-mail: illinois.chapter@sierraclub.org
Website: www.illinois.sierraclub.org
Membership: 10,001–100,000
Scope: Local, State
Description: State chapter of national Sierra Club, focused on protecting Illinois' remaining wild places and cleaning up water, air, and land pollution.
Publication(s): Lake and Prairie
Contact(s):
Jack Darin, Contact

SIERRA CLUB
IOWA CHAPTER
3839 Merle Hay Rd.
Suite 280
Des Moines, IA 50310 United States
Phone: 515-277-8868
E-mail: iowa.chapter@sierraclub.org
Website: iowa.sierraclub.org
Scope: State
Contact(s):
Charlie Winterwood, Chair; 319-588-2783

SIERRA CLUB
JOHN MUIR CHAPTER
222 S. Hamilton St., Suite 1
Madison, WI 53703-3201 United States
Phone: 608-256-0565   Fax: 608-256-4562
E-mail: john.muir.chapter@sierraclub.org
Website: wisconsin.sierraclub.org
Founded: 1965
Membership: 10,001–100,000
Scope: State
Description: Protecting Wisconsin's clean air, land and water for our families and our future, the John Muir Chapter represents over 13,000 Sierra Club members living in Wisconsin. The Sierra Club is the nation's largest grassroots conservation organization. We empower people to influence public policy that protects or improves our environment through grassroots activism, public education, outings, electoral process, lobbying, and when necessary, litigation. We welcome your involvement.
Publication(s): The Muir View
Keyword(s): Agriculture/Farming, Air Quality/Atmosphere, Climate Change, Ecosystems (precious), Energy, Ethics/Environmental Justice, Executive/Legislative/Judicial Reform, Finance/Banking/Trade, Forests/Forestry, Land Issues, Oceans/Coasts/Beaches, Pollution (general)

SIERRA CLUB
KANSAS CHAPTER
9844 Georgia St.
Kansas City, KS 66109-4326 United States
Phone: 913-299-4443
E-mail: seawolf@kssierra.org
Website: www.kssierra.org/

Scope: State

Contact(s):
Scott Smith, Chair; 9844 Georgia Avenue, Kansas City, KS 66109; 785-539-1973; wizard1@kscable.com

SIERRA CLUB
KERN-KAWEAH CHAPTER
P.O. Box 3357
Bakersfield, CA 93385-3357 United States
Phone: 661-323-5569
E-mail: pgipe@igc.apc.org
Website: kernkaweah.sierraclub.org/
Membership: 1,001–10,000
Scope: Local, Regional
Publication(s): The Road Runner

Contact(s):
Lorraine Unger, Executive Officer

SIERRA CLUB
LOMA PRIETA CHAPTER
3921 E. Bayshore Rd., Suite 204
Palo Alto, CA 94303-4303 United States
Phone: 650-390-8411   Fax: 650-390-8497
E-mail: loma.prieta.chapter@sierraclub.org
Website: lomaprieta.sierraclub.org
Membership: 10,001–100,000
Scope: Local, Regional
Publication(s): Loma Prietan

Contact(s):
Dan Kalb, Director; loma.prieta.director@sierraclub.org

SIERRA CLUB
LONE STAR CHAPTER
P.O. Box 1931
Austin, TX 78767 United States
Phone: 512-477-1729   Fax: 512-477-8526
E-mail: lonestar.chapter@sierraclub.org
Website: www.texas.sierraclub.org
Membership: 10,001–100,000
Scope: State
Publication(s): The Lone Star Sierran, State Capitol Report

Contact(s):
Tracy Arambula, Environmental Justice Director; tracy.arambula@sierraclub.org
Neil Carman, Clean Air Program Director
Ken Kramer, Chapter Director
Fred Richardson, Communications Director; fred.richardson@sierraclub.org
Erin Rogers, Grass Roots Coordinator; erin.rogers@sierraclub.org
Brian Sybert, Natural Resources
Jennifer Walker, Adminstrative Assistant

SIERRA CLUB
LOS PADRES CHAPTER
P.O. Box 90924
Santa Barbara, CA 93190-0924 United States
Phone: 805-966-6622
E-mail: los.padres.chapter@sierraclub.org
Website: lospadres.sierraclub.org/

Scope: State

Contact(s):
Rick Skillin, Chapter Chair; 805-735-4190; rick.skillin@sierraclub.org

SIERRA CLUB
MACKINAC CHAPTER
109 E. Grand River
Lansing, MI 48906 United States
Phone: 517-484-2372   Fax: 517-484-3108
E-mail: mackinac.chapter@sierraclub.org
Website: www.michigan.sierraclub.org
Membership: 10,001–100,000
Scope: State
Publication(s): Mackinac, The, Quarterly

Contact(s):
Anne Woiwode, Director

SIERRA CLUB
MAINE CHAPTER
One Pleasant St.
Portland, ME 04101-3936 United States
Phone: 207-761-5616   Fax: 207-773-6690
E-mail: sierraclubmc@sierraclub.org
Website: www.sierraclub.org/me

Founded: 1992
Membership: 1,001–10,000
Scope: State

Description: for over a century the Sierra Club has been devoted to the conservation of our forests, mountains, rivers, coasts and other natural areas. The Maine Chapter, a volunteer-run grassroots organization, is working to restore the natural and human communities of the North Woods, halt global warming, protect Maine's clean water and coastline, and support pro-environmental candidates for public office.

Publication(s): Mainely Sierran Bimonthly Newsletter

Keyword(s): Air Quality/Atmosphere, Climate Change, Ecosystems (precious), Energy, Forests/Forestry, Oceans/Coasts/Beaches, Pollution (general), Population, Public Lands/Greenspace, Recreation/Ecotourism, Sprawl/Urban Planning, Water Habitats & Quality, Wildlife & Species

Contact(s):
Karen Woodsum, Maine Woods Regional; 207-791-2821; maine.woods@prodigy.net

SIERRA CLUB
MARYLAND CHAPTER
7338 Baltimore Ave., Suite 101A
College Park, MD 20740-3211 United States
Phone: 301-277-7111   Fax: 301-277-6699
E-mail: maryland.chapter@sierraclub.org
Website: www.maryland.sierraclub.org
Membership: 10,001–100,000
Scope: Local, State, National

Description: "To explore, enjoy and protect the wild places of the Earth; to practice and promote the responsible use of the Earth's ecosystems and resources; to educate and enlist humanity to protect and restore the quality of the natural and human environment; and to use all lawful means to carry out these objectives."

Publication(s): See publication website

Contact(s):
Jon Robinson, Chapter Chairman

SIERRA CLUB
MASSACHUSETTS CHAPTER
100 Boylston St., Suite 760
Boston, MA 02116-4610 United States
Phone: 617-423-5775   Fax: 617-423-5858
E-mail: office@sierraclubmass.org
Website: www.sierraclubmass.org
Membership: 10,001–100,000
Scope: State
Description: Environmental
Publication(s): Massachusetts Sierran

Keyword(s): Air Quality/Atmosphere, Ecosystems (precious), Forests/Forestry, Land Issues, Oceans/Coasts/Beaches, Pollution (general), Population, Public Lands/Greenspace, Reduce/Reuse/Recycle, Sprawl/Urban Planning, Transportation, Water Habitats & Quality, Wildlife

Contact(s):
James McCaffrey, Director; director@sierraclubmass.org
Lorraine Foster, Office Administrator; 617-423-5775; Fax: 617-423-5885; office@sierraclubmass.org

SIERRA CLUB
MID-ATLANTIC REGIONAL OFFICE
200 N. Glebe Rd., Suite 905
Arlington, VA 22203-3728 United States
Phone: 703-312-0533   Fax: 703-312-0508
Website: www.sierraclub.org

Scope: Regional
Description: DC, DE, GA, MD, NC, SC, TN, VA, WV
Contact(s):
Joy Oakes, Appalachian Field Director

SIERRA CLUB
MIDWEST OFFICE
MADISON OFFICE
214 N. Henry St., Suite 203
Madison, WI 53703 United States
Phone: 608-257-4994   Fax: 608-257-3513
E-mail: mw.field@sierraclub.org
Website: www.sierraclub.org

Founded: 1892
Membership: 500,001–1,000,000
Scope: Regional
Description: IA, IL, IN, KY, MI, MN, MO, OH, WI
Publication(s): Mississippi Times
Contact(s):
Emily Green, Great Lakes Program Director; emily.green@sierraclub.org
Brett Hulsey, Senior Regional Representative; brett.hulsey@sierraclub.org
Jennifer Feyerherm, Great Lakes Toxins Specialist; jennifer.feyerherm@sierraclub.org
Eric Uram, Midwest Regional Representative; eric.uram@sierraclub.org
Bill Redding, Midwest Regional Representative; bill.redding@sierraclub.org

SIERRA CLUB
MIDWEST OFFICE
TRAVERSE CITY OFFICE
229 Lake Avenue, Suite 4
Traverse City, MI 49684 United States
Phone: 231-922-2201   Fax: 231-922-2909
Website: sierraclub.org

Founded: 1892
Membership: 500,001–1,000,000
Scope: Local, State, Regional, National, International
Description: Regional Field Office for National Sierra Club: IA, IL, IN, KY, MI, MN, MO, OH, WI
Contact(s):
Alison Horton, Midwest Regional Staff Director; alison.horton@sierraclub.org

SIERRA CLUB
MISSISSIPPI CHAPTER
P.O. Box 4335
Jackson, MS 39296-4335 United States
Phone: 601-352-1026
Website: mississippi.sierraclub.org/
Scope: State

SIERRA CLUB
MONTANA CHAPTER
P. O. Box 1290
Bozeman, MT 59771 United States
Phone: 406-582-8365   Fax: 406-582-9417
E-mail: accipiter4@juno.com
Website: www.montana.sierraclub.org

Scope: Regional
Publication(s): Big Sky Sierrian
Contact(s):
Kathryn Hohmann, Associate Field Rep.; kathryn.holmann@sierraclub.org
Christine Phillips, Contact; 406-582-1281; magpie@mcn.net

SIERRA CLUB
MONTANA FIELD OFFICE
P.O. Box 1290
Bozeman, MT 59771-1290 United States
Phone: 406-582-8365, ext. 3002   Fax: 406-582-9417
E-mail: np.field@sierraclub.org
Website: www.sierraclub.org

Founded: 1892
Membership: 500,001–1,000,000
Scope: Local, State, Regional, National, International
Description: Largest and oldest grassroots conservation organization in the U.S.
Publication(s): Newsletter
Contact(s):
Kathryn Hohmann, Sr. Regional Representative

SIERRA CLUB
MOTHER LODE CHAPTER
1414 K St., Suite 500
Sacramento, CA 95814-3929 United States
Phone: 916-557-1100, ext. 108   Fax: 916-557-9669
E-mail: motherlode@mcsweb1.com
Website: www.motherlode.sierraclub.org

Scope: Regional
Publication(s): The Bonanza, bimonthly newsletter
Contact(s):
Julie Parker, Administrative Assistant; ext. 119

SIERRA CLUB
NEBRASKA CHAPTER
P.O. Box 4664
Omaha, NE 68104 United States
Phone: 402-556-1830
E-mail: nebraska.chapter@sierraclub.org
Website: www.sierraclub.org/chapters/ne/
Membership: 1–100
Scope: State
Publication(s): The Nebraska Sierran (newsletter)
Contact(s):
Mary Green, Chair.
Pat Knapp, State Coordinator; 1614 N. 31st. St., Lincoln, NE 68503; 402-464-8537; patanap@alltel.net

SIERRA CLUB
NEW HAMPSHIRE CHAPTER
Three Bicentennial Sq.
Concord, NH 03301-4058 United States
Phone: 603-224-8222   Fax: 603-224-4719
Website: www.nhsierraclub.org

Scope: State
Description: This is the New Hampshire chapter of the Sierra Club, the nation's oldest and largest grassroots environmental organization. We have roughly 5500 members in New Hampshire.
Publication(s): The New Hampshire Sierran

Keyword(s): Agriculture/Farming, Air Quality/Atmosphere, Climate Change, Energy, Executive/Legislative/Judicial Reform, Forests/Forestry, Pollution (general), Public Lands/Greenspace, Sprawl/Urban Planning, Transportation

Contact(s):
Cathy Corkery, Legislative Advocate; 603-224-8222; Fax: 603-224-4719; catherine.corkery@sierraclub.org

SIERRA CLUB
NEW JERSEY CHAPTER
57 Mountain Ave.
Princeton, NJ 08540-2611 United States
Phone: 609-924-3141   Fax: 609-924-8799
E-mail: svsomalwar@sierraactivist.org
Website: www.sierraactivist.org
Founded: 1970
Membership: 10,001–100,000
Scope: Local, State
Description: Grassroots Environmental Organization
Publication(s): The Sierran

Contact(s):
Jeff Tittel, Director; 609-924-3141; Jefft1@voicenet.com
Lori Herpen, Chapter Coordinator; 609-924-3141;
    lori.herpen@sierraclub.org
Bill Wolfe, Policy Director; 609-924-3141;
    bill.wolfe@sierraclub.org

SIERRA CLUB
NEW YORK CITY OFFICE
116 John St., 31st Fl.
New York, NY 10038 United States
Phone: 212-791-9707   Fax: 212-791-0839
E-mail: ne-nyc.field@sierraclub.org
Website: www.sierraclub.org
Scope: Regional
Description: This is the New York City office of the Sierra Club, the nation's oldest and largest grassroots conservation organization.
Keyword(s): Ethics/Environmental Justice

Contact(s):
Emma McGregor, Administrative Assistant

SIERRA CLUB
NORTH CAROLINA CHAPTER
112 S. Blount St.
Raleigh, NC 27601 United States
Phone: 919-833-8467   Fax: 919-833-8460
E-mail: info@sierraclub-nc.org
Website: www.sierraclub-nc.org
Membership: 10,001–100,000
Scope: State
Publication(s): Footnotes

Contact(s):
Molly Diggins, State Director
John Hudson, Resources Development Coordinator
David Knight, Lobbyist

SIERRA CLUB
NORTH STAR CHAPTER (MINNESOTA)
2327 E. Franklin Ave., Suite 1
Minneapolis, MN 55406 United States
Phone: 612-659-9124   Fax: 612-659-9129
E-mail: north.star.chapter@sierraclub.org
Website: www.northstar.sierraclub.org/
Membership: 10,001–100,000
Scope: Regional
Publication(s): The North Star Journal - bimonthly newsletter

Contact(s):
Scott Elkins, State Director; selkins@igc.org

SIERRA CLUB
NORTHEAST REGIONAL FIELD OFFICE
85 Washington St.
Saratoga Springs, NY 12866 United States
Phone: 518-587-9166   Fax: 518-583-9062
E-mail: ne-ny.field@sierraclub.org
Website: www.sierraclub.org
Membership: 100,001–500,000
Scope: Regional
Description: CT, MA, ME, NH, NJ, NY, PA, RI, VT
Publication(s): Magazine-Sierra

Contact(s):
Mark Bettinger, Regional Staff Director
Chris Ballantyne, Sr. Regional Representative
Mary Anne Jaffe, Regional Administrative Coordinator

SIERRA CLUB
NORTHERN PLAINS REGION
247 Cotfeen
Sheridan, WY 82801 United States
Phone: 307-672-0425   Fax: 307-674-6187
E-mail: np-wy.field@sierraclub.org
Website: www.sierraclub.org/wy/
Membership: 1,001–10,000
Scope: Regional
Description: KS, MT, NE, ND, SD, WY
Publication(s): National Sierra newsletter

Contact(s):
Steve Thomas, Deputy Field Director;
    larry.mehlhaff@sierra.org
Liz Howell, Conservation Organizer
Kirk Koepsel, Regional Rep.; kirk.koepsel@sierra.org

SIERRA CLUB
NORTHERN ROCKIES CHAPTER
(IDAHO/WASHINGTON)
P.O. Box 552
Boise, ID 83701-0552 United States
Phone: 208-384-1023   Fax: 208-384-0239
E-mail: northern.rockies.chapter@sierraclub.org
Website: idaho.sierraclub.org
Membership: 1,001–10,000
Scope: Regional

Contact(s):
Roger Singer, Chapter Director; roger.singer@sierraclub.org

SIERRA CLUB
NORTHWEST OFFICE
180 Nickerson Ave. Suite 202
Seattle, WA 98109 United States
Phone: 206-378-0114   Fax: 206-378-0034
E-mail: nw-wa.field@sierraclub.org
Website: www.sierraclub.org
Membership: 100,001–500,000
Scope: Regional
Description: AK, ID, OR, WA
Publication(s): Sierra Magazine
Keyword(s): Agriculture/Farming, Air Quality/Atmosphere, Climate Change, Ecosystems (precious), Energy, Ethics/Environmental Justice, Finance/Banking/Trade, Forests/Forestry, Land Issues, Oceans/Coasts/Beaches, Pollution (general), Population, Public Lands/Greenspace

Contact(s):
Bill Arthur, Staff Director
Jim Young, Associate Representative

SIERRA CLUB
OHIO CHAPTER
36 W. Gay St.
Columbus, OH 43215 United States
Phone: 614-461-0734   Fax: 614-461-0730
E-mail: ogeralds@lexkylaw.com
Website: www.sierraclub.org/oh
Scope: State
Publication(s): Ohio Sierran Chapter Newsletter
Contact(s):
   Marc Conte, Legislative Coordinator
   Shannon Harps, Transportation Policy Specialist

SIERRA CLUB
OKLAHOMA CHAPTER
P.O. Box 60644
Oklahoma City, OK 73146-0644 United States
Phone: 415-977-5500   Fax: 415-977-5799
E-mail: oklahoma.chapter@sierraclub.org
Website: oklahoma.sierraclub.org
Founded: 1892
Scope: State

SIERRA CLUB
OREGON CHAPTER
2950 SE Stark St., Suite 110
Portland, OR 97214 United States
Phone: 503-238-0442   Fax: 503-238-6281
E-mail: oregon.chapter@sierraclub.org
Website: www.oregon.sierraclub.org
Founded: 1973
Membership: 10,001–100,000
Scope: Local, State
Description: Explore, enjoy and protect the wild places of the earth.
Publication(s): The Conifer
Keyword(s): Air Quality/Atmosphere, Ecosystems (precious), Energy, Forests/Forestry, Land Issues, Pollution (general), Population, Public Lands/Greenspace, Recreation/Ecotourism, Sprawl/Urban Planning, Transportation, Water Habitats & Quality, Wildlife & Species
Contact(s):
   Paul Shively, Regional Manager; 503-243-6656; Fax: 503-243-2416; paul.shively@sierraclub.org

SIERRA CLUB
OZARK CHAPTER (MISSOURI)
1007 North College Ave., Suite 1
Columbia, MO 65201-4725 United States
Phone: 573-815-9250   Fax: 573-442-7051
E-mail: ozark.chapter@sierraclub.org
Website: missouri.sierraclub.org
Membership: 10,001–100,000
Scope: State
Description: Grassroots advocacy to protect the environment.
Publication(s): Ozark Sierran
Keyword(s): Agriculture/Farming, Air Quality/Atmosphere, Climate Change, Ecosystems (precious), Energy, Ethics/Environmental Justice, Forests/Forestry, Land Issues, Recreation/Ecotourism, Sprawl/Urban Planning, Transportation, Water Habitats & Quality, Wildlife & Species
Contact(s):
   Carla Klein, Director; 573-815-9250; ozark.chapter@sierraclub.org
   Keet Kopecky, Chair; 816-966-9544; kkopecky@kc.rr.com

SIERRA CLUB
PENNSYLVANIA CHAPTER
P.O. Box 663
Harrisburg, PA 17108 United States
Phone: 717-232-0101   Fax: 717-238-6330
E-mail: sierraclub.pa@paonline.com
Website: pennsylvania.sierraclub.org/
Founded: 1892
Membership: 10,001–100,000
Scope: Local, State
Description: Non-profit environmental advocacy organization
Publication(s): Sierra Club Chapter Newsletter, The Sylvanian
Keyword(s): Agriculture/Farming, Air Quality/Atmosphere, Energy, Forests/Forestry, Land Issues, Pollution (general), Public Health, Reduce/Reuse/Recycle, Sprawl/Urban Planning, Transportation, Water Habitats & Quality, Wildlife & Species
Contact(s):
   Jeff Schmidt, Senior Chapter Director; 717-232-0101; Fax: 717-238-6330; jeff.schmidt@sierraclub.org
   Monica Willett, Administrative Assistant; 717-232-0101; Fax: 717-238-6330; monica.willett@sierraclub.org

SIERRA CLUB
PRAIRIE CHAPTER (AB, MB, SK)
10125 97th Ave.
Edmonton, T5K OB3 Alberta Canada
Phone: 780-439-1160   Fax: 780-437-3932
E-mail: prairiechapter@sierraclub.ca
Website: www.prairie.sierraclub.ca
Scope: Regional

SIERRA CLUB
REDWOOD CHAPTER (NORTHERN CALIFORNIA)
P. O. Box 466
Santa Rosa, CA 95402 United States
Phone: 707-544-7651   Fax: 707-544-9861
E-mail: heyneedles@aol.com
Website: redwood.sierraclub.org
Scope: State
Publication(s): Redwood Needles
Contact(s):
   Margaret Pennington, Chapter Chair; penningt@sonic.net

SIERRA CLUB
RHODE ISLAND CHAPTER
21 Meeting St. Garden Entrance
Providence, RI 02903-1000 United States
Phone: 401-521-4734   Fax: 401-521-4001
E-mail: alicia@sierraclubri.org
Website: www.sierraclubri.org
Membership: 1,001–10,000
Scope: State
Publication(s): Transportation Reform Alliance, Coastlines (newsletter), Transit Users Survey 2000, Nasty Nine Sprawl Report

SIERRA CLUB
RIO GRANDE CHAPTER (NEW MEXICO/WEST TEXAS)
207 Ricardo Road
Santa Fe, NM 87501 United States
Phone: 505-988-5760
E-mail: jhanna505@aol.com
Website: riogrande.sierraclub.org/
Scope: Regional
Contact(s):
   Jennifer De Garmo, Staff Member; 202 Central Avenue SE, Albuquerque, NM 87102; 505-243-7767; nmex.field1@prodigy.net

SIERRA CLUB
ROCKY MOUNTAIN CHAPTER (COLORADO)
1536 Wynkoop #4C
Denver, CO 80202 United States
Phone: 303-861-8819   Fax: 303-861-2436
Website: www.rmc.sierraclub.org/
Membership: 10,001–100,000
Scope: Local, State
Description: We are the statewide Sierra Club for Colorado. See our webpage for a more extensive explanation of what we do or give us a call!
Publication(s): The Sierra - bimonthly magazine, The Peak & Prairie - quarterly
Keyword(s): Agriculture/Farming, Air Quality/Atmosphere, Development/Developing Countries, Energy, Ethics/Environmental Justice, Executive/Legislative/Judicial Reform, Finance/Banking/Trade, Forests/Forestry, Land Issues, Pollution (general), Population, Public Health
Contact(s):
  Susan Lefever, Chapter Director; susan.lefever@rmc.sierraclub.org
  Dan Disner, Administrative Assistant/Part-time Graduate Student; dan.disner@rmc.sierraclub.org
  Adriana Raudzens, Transit Organizer; adriana.raudzens@rmc.sierraclub.org
  John Rosapepe, Energy Organizer; john.rosapepe@sierraclub.org
  Libby Tart, Chapter Coordinator; libby.tart@rmc.sierraclub.org

SIERRA CLUB
SAN DIEGO CHAPTER (SOUTHERN CALIFORNIA)
3820 Ray St.
San Diego, CA 92104-3623 United States
Phone: 619-299-1743   Fax: 619-299-1742
E-mail: san-diego.chapter@sierraclub.org
Website: sandiego.sierraclub.org/home/index.asp
Founded: 1948
Scope: Local, Regional
Contact(s):
  Cheryl Reiff, Office Administrator

SIERRA CLUB
SAN FRANCISCO BAY CHAPTER
2530 San Pablo Ave., Suite 1
Berkeley, CA 94702-2000 United States
Phone: 1-510-848-0800   Fax: 1-510-848-3383
E-mail: san-francisco-bay.chapter@sierraclub.org
Website: http://sanfranciscobay.sierraclub.org/
Founded: 1892
Membership: 500,001–1,000,000
Scope: National
Description: To explore, enjoy, and protect the wild places of the earth; to practice and promote the responsible use of the earth's ecosystems and resources; to educate and enlist humanity to protect and restore the quality of the natural and human environment; and to use all lawful means to carry out these objectives. With 65 chapters and 396 groups in North America, the Club's nonprofit program work includes legislation, litigation, public information, publishing, wilderness outings, and conferences.
Publication(s): Sierra, chapter and group newsletters, Planet, The
Keyword(s): Air Quality/Atmosphere, Energy, Pollution (general), Public Lands/Greenspace
Contact(s):
  Jennifer Ferenstein, President; jennifer.ferenstein@sierraclub.org
  Charlie Ogle, Vice President
  Bob Bingaman, Director of Conservation Field Services
  Gene Coan, Senior Advisor to the Executive Director
  Kim Haddow, Communication Director
  Bruce Hamilton, Associate Executive Director of Conservation and Communication
  Carl Pope, Executive Director
  Joan Hamilton, Editor-In-Chief of Sierra
  Helen Sweetland, Publisher of Books

SIERRA CLUB
SAN GORGONIO CHAPTER (SOUTHERN CALIFORNIA)
4079 Mission Inn Ave.
Riverside, CA 92501-3204 United States
Phone: 909-684-6203   Fax: 909-684-6172
E-mail: gorgonio@pe.net
Website: sangorgonio.sierraclub.org/
Founded: 1932
Membership: 1,001–10,000
Scope: Local, State, Regional, National, International
Description: The San Gorgonio Chapter covers Riverside and San Bernardino counties in southern California. It has five groups: Big Bear Lake, Los Serranos, Mojave, Moreno Valley Mountains and Tahquitz. Membership is around 7,000.

SIERRA CLUB
SANTA LUCIA CHAPTER
P.O. Box 15755
San Luis Obispo, CA 93406-5755 United States
Phone: 805-543-8717   Fax: 805-543-8727
E-mail: gfelsman@thegrid.net
Website: santalucia.sierraclub.org/
Membership: 1,001–10,000
Scope: Local, Regional
Description: Sierra Club group working to preserve the resources on the Central Coast.
Keyword(s): Land Issues, Oceans/Coasts/Beaches, Public Lands/Greenspace, Sprawl/Urban Planning
Contact(s):
  Terri Knowlton, Chapter Coordinator; 805-543-8717

SIERRA CLUB
SOUTH CAROLINA CHAPTER
P.O. Box 2388, 1314 Lincoln St., Suite 211
Columbia, SC 29202 United States
Phone: 803-256-8487   Fax: 803-256-8448
E-mail: scsierra@earthlink.net
Website: www.southcarolina.sierraclub.org
Founded: 1978
Membership: 1,001–10,000
Scope: State
Publication(s): The Congaree Chronicle - bi-monthy newsletter
Contact(s):
  Dell Isham, Chapter Director; 803-256-8487; scsierra@conterra.com

SIERRA CLUB
SOUTH DAKOTA CHAPTER
P.O. Box 1624
Rapid City, SD 57709-1624 United States
Phone: 605-348-1345   Fax: 605-348-1344
E-mail: brademey@rapidnet.com
Website: southdakota.sierraclub.org
Membership: 1,000,001 +
Scope: Local, Regional, National
Publication(s): Newsletter Quarterly, Sierra Magazine, Pines & Prairie
Contact(s):
  Sam Clauson, S. D. Chapter Chair
  Heather Morijah, Conservation Organizer; 1101 E. Phildelphia St., Rapid City, SD 57701; 605-342-2244; Fax: 605-342-2255; heather.morijah@sierraclub.org

SIERRA CLUB
SOUTHEAST OFFICE
1330 21st Way South, Suite 100
Birmingham, AL 35205 United States
Phone: 205-933-9111   Fax: 205-939-1020
E-mail: jim.price@sierraclub.org
Website: www.sierraclub.org
Scope: National
Description: AL, AR, FL, LA, MS, TX
Contact(s):
　Jim Price, Senior Regional Staff Director; jimprice@sierraclub.org

SIERRA CLUB
SOUTHERN CALIFORNIA/NEVADA FIELD OFFICE
3435 Wilshire Blvd., Suite #660
Los Angeles, CA 90010 United States
Phone: 213-387-6528   Fax: 213-387-5383
E-mail: ca.field@sierraclub.org
Website: www.sierraclub.org/field/southerncal
Scope: Regional
Publication(s): Publications on website
Contact(s):
　Jim Blomquist, Sr. Regional Representative

SIERRA CLUB
SOUTHERN PLAINS NATIONAL FIELD OFFICE
2906 Medical Arts St.
Austin, TX 78705 United States
Phone: 512-472-9094   Fax: 512-472-8710
E-mail: txar@earthlink.net
Website: www.sierraclub.org/field/southernplains
Founded: 1892
Membership: 500,001–1,000,000
Scope: Local, Regional, National
Description: National representatives of the Sierra Club. Assisting volunteers in the planning and implimentation of grassroots based conservation campaigns.
Contact(s):
　Alejandro Queral, Border Representative
　Larry Freilich, Representative
　Ayelet Hines, End Commercial Logging on Public Land Organizer
　Nicole Holt, Global Warming & Energy Program Organizer

SIERRA CLUB
SOUTHWEST OFFICE
812 N. Third St.
Phoenix, AZ 85004 United States
Phone: 602-254-9330   Fax: 602-258-6533
E-mail: sw.field@sierraclub.org
Website: www.sierraclub.org
Membership: 10,001–100,000
Scope: Regional
Description: AZ, CO, NM, OK, UT
Contact(s):
　Rob Smith, Staff Director
　Philip Church, Administrative Coordinator, Southwest Region

SIERRA CLUB
TEHIPITE CHAPTER (NORTHERN CALIFORNIA)
P.O. Box 5396
Fresno, CA 93755-5396 United States
Phone: 559-271-0652
E-mail: Tehipite.Chapter@sierraclub.org
Website: tehipite.sierraclub.org/
Scope: Local, Regional

SIERRA CLUB
TENNESSEE CHAPTER
2021 21st Ave. S., Suite 436
Nashville, TN 37212 United States
Phone: 615-386-3640
E-mail: tennessee.chapter@sierraclub.org
Website: www.tennessee.sierraclub.org/
Membership: 1,001–10,000
Scope: Local, State, Regional
Description: The Tennessee Chapter of the Sierra Club has local groups Chattanooga, Cookeville, Knoxville, Memphis, Nashville and the Tri-Cities. Our volunteers work on a diverse range of environmental issues.
Keyword(s): Agriculture/Farming, Air Quality/Atmosphere, Climate Change, Energy, Ethics/Environmental Justice, Forests/Forestry, Land Issues, Pollution (general), Population, Public Lands/Greenspace, Reduce/Reuse/Recycle, Sprawl/Urban Planning, Transportation, Water Habitats & Quality

SIERRA CLUB
TOIYABE CHAPTER (NEVADA/EASTERN CALIFORNIA)
P.O. Box 8096
Reno, NV 89507-8096 United States
Phone: 775-323-3162
Website: nevada.sierraclub.org/
Scope: State

SIERRA CLUB
UTAH CHAPTER
2120 South 1300 East, Ste. 204
Salt Lake City, UT 84106-3785 United States
Phone: 801-467-9297
E-mail: utah.chapter@sierraclub.org
Website: http://utah.sierraclub.org/
Founded: 1962
Scope: State
Description: We work within the State of Utah to advance the goals and policies of the National Sierra Club and of Utah volunteers.
Keyword(s): Ecosystems (precious), Land Issues, Sprawl/Urban Planning
Contact(s):
　Nina Dougherty, Chapter Chair
　Tony Guay, Vice-Chair; tpguay@hotmail.com
　Dan Schroeder, Secretary/Treasurer; dschroeder@weber.edu

SIERRA CLUB
UTAH FIELD OFFICE
2120 South 1300 East
Salt Lake City, UT 84106-3785 United States
Phone: 801-467-9294   Fax: 801-467-9296
E-mail: sw.field@sierraclub.org
Website: www.sierraclub.org
Membership: 1,001–10,000
Scope: Regional

SIERRA CLUB
VENTANA CHAPTER (NORTHERN CALIFORNIA)
P.O. Box 5667
Carmel, CA 93921-5667 United States
Phone: 831-624-8032   Fax: 831-624-3371
E-mail: ventana@mbay.net
Website: www.ventana.sierraclub.org/
Scope: Local, Regional

SIERRA CLUB
VERMONT CHAPTER
508 Main Street
Warren, VT 05674 United States
Phone: 802-651-0169   Fax: 802-496-6459
Website: vermont.sierraclub.org/

Membership: 1,001–10,000
Scope: State
Description: Vermont State chapter of the national Sierra Club
Publication(s): Vermont Sierran (quarterly newsletter)
Keyword(s): Agriculture/Farming, Energy

SIERRA CLUB
VIRGINIA CHAPTER
Six N. 6th St., Suite 102
Richmond, VA 23219-2419 United States
Phone: 804-225-9113   Fax: 804-225-9114
Website: www.virginia.sierraclub.org
Membership: 10,001–100,000
Scope: State
Publication(s): Old Dominion Sierran
Contact(s):
Pat Dezern, Conservation Organizer

SIERRA CLUB
WASHINGTON, DC CHAPTER
Sierra Club
408 C Street, N.E.
Washington, DC 20002 United States
Phone: 202-547-3410
E-mail: mwenzler@environet.org
Website: www.dc.sierraclub.org/
Founded: 1892
Membership: 1,001–10,000
Scope: Local, State
Description: Largest and most active local conservation advocacy organization in the District of Columbia.
Contact(s):
Danilo Pelletiere, Conservation Chair; 202-543-7791; dpelleti@gmu.edu
Mark Wenzler, Vice Chair; 202-547-3410

SIERRA CLUB
WASHINGTON, DC OFFICE
408 C St., NE
Washington, DC 20002 United States
Phone: 202-547-1141   Fax: 202-547-6009
Website: www.sierraclub.org
Founded: 1892
Membership: 500,001–1,000,000
Scope: Local, State, Regional, National, International
Description: The Sierra Club is a non-profit, 501(c)(4), member-supported, public interest organization that promotes conservation of the natural environment by influencing public policy decisions: legislative, administrative, legal and electoral.
Publication(s): Sierra Magazine
Keyword(s): Agriculture/Farming, Air Quality/Atmosphere, Climate Change, Energy, Ethics/Environmental Justice, Forests/Forestry, Land Issues, Pollution (general), Population, Public Lands/Greenspace, Sprawl/Urban Planning, Water Habitats & Quality, Wildlife & Species
Contact(s):
Bob Bingaman, Field Director
Debbie Sease, Legislative Director

SIERRA CLUB
WEST VIRGINIA CHAPTER
P.O. Box 4142
Morgantown, WV 26504-4142 United States
Phone: 304-725-4360
E-mail: pjgrunt@lycos.com
Membership: 1,001–10,000
Scope: State
Description: West Virginia chaper contains 1600+ members that work on Mountaintop Removal, coal-fired power plants, wilderness, and other environmental issues
Publication(s): Chapter Newsletter - Mountain State Sierran
Keyword(s): Energy, Ethics/Environmental Justice, Public Lands/Greenspace
Contact(s):
Paul Wilson, Chapter Chair; 304-725-4360; pjgrunt@lycos.com

SIERRA CLUB
WYOMING CHAPTER
247 Coffeen
Sheridan, WY 82801 United States
Phone: 307-672-0425   Fax: 307-674-6187
E-mail: wyoming.chapter@sierraclub.org
Website: www.sierraclub.org/chapters/wy/
Membership: 1,001–10,000
Scope: State
Description: Protecting Wyoming's wild places for our families and for our future
Publication(s): Wyoming Sierran Newsletter
Keyword(s): Air Quality/Atmosphere, Forests/Forestry, Public Lands/Greenspace, Water Habitats & Quality, Wildlife & Species
Contact(s):
Liz Howell, Wyoming Chapter Staff; 307-672-0425; liz.howell@sierraclub.org

SIERRA CLUB CALIFORNIA
1414 K St.
Suite 500
Sacramento, CA 95814 United States
Phone: 916-557-1100
E-mail: batchelder@sierraclub-sac.org
Founded: 1987
Membership: 100,001–500,000
Scope: Local, State
Description: Advocate for environmental protection and natural resource management before the State Legislature, Governor, and agencies.
Keyword(s): Agriculture/Farming, Air Quality/Atmosphere, Climate Change, Ecosystems (precious), Energy, Ethics/Environmental Justice, Executive/Legislative/Judicial Reform, Forests/Forestry, Land Issues, Oceans/Coasts/Beaches, Pollution (general), Population, Public Lands/Greenspace

SIERRA CLUB FOUNDATION, THE
85 Second Street
Suite 750
San Francisco, CA 94105 United States
Phone: 415-995-1780   Fax: 415-995-1791
E-mail: sierraclub.foundation@sierraclub.org
Website: www.tscf.org
Founded: 1960
Scope: National
Description: A nonprofit, tax-deductible, public foundation established to finance the educational, literary, and scientific projects of citizen-based groups working on national and international environmental problems. Manages assets in excess of $70 million and over 600 regional or special interest funds principally for charitable conservation purposes. Also manages charitable remainder unitrusts and a pooled income fund with assets over $7.5 million.
Publication(s): Annual Report
Keyword(s): Agriculture/Farming, Air Quality/Atmosphere, Ecosystems (precious), Energy, Ethics/Environmental Justice, Forests/Forestry, Land Issues, Oceans/Coasts/Beaches, Pollution (general), Population, Public Health, Public Lands/Greenspace, Reduce/Reuse/Recycle,
Contact(s):
Michael Loeb, President; sierraclub.foundation@sierraclub.org
John DeCock, Executive Director; sierraclub.foundation@sierraclub.org

SIERRA CLUB OF CANADA
#1 Nicholas St., Suite 620
Ottawa, K1N 7B7 Ontario Canada
Phone: 613-241-4611 Fax: 613-241-2292
E-mail: sierra.club.canada@sierraclub.org
Website: www.sierraclub.ca

Scope: International

Publication(s): SCAN, Sierra Magazine

Contact(s):
Elizabeth May, Executive Director

SIERRA CLUB OF CANADA
ATLANTIC CANADA CHAPTER
1657 Barrington St.
Suite 502
Halifax, B3J 2A1 Nova Scotia Canada
Phone: 902-444-3113 Fax: 902-444-3116
E-mail: atlanticcanadachapter@sierraclub.ca
Website: www.sierraclub.org

Founded: 2000
Membership: 101–1,000
Scope: Regional

Description: The Sierra Club of Canada is a membership-based, volunteer-governed national environmental organization with chapters across the country. It is dedicated to exploring, enjoying and protecting the wild places of the earth and to practice and promote the responsible use of the earth's ecosystems. The Atlantic Canada Chapter covers all four Atlantic Provinces, and supports communities on issues such as industrial farming, sustainable forestry, sustainable mining, and contaminated lands.

Keyword(s): Agriculture/Farming, Air Quality/Atmosphere, Climate Change, Ecosystems (precious), Energy, Ethics/Environmental Justice, Forests/Forestry, Land Issues, Oceans/Coasts/Beaches, Pollution (general), Public Health, Sprawl/Urban Planning, Wildlife & Species

SIERRA STUDENT COALITION
408 C St. NE
Washington, DC 22030 United States
Phone: 888-548-4593 Fax: 202-675-6277
E-mail: ssc-info@ssc.org
Website: www.ssc.org

Founded: 1991
Membership: 10,001–100,000
Scope: Local, State, Regional, National

Description: The Sierra Student Coalition is the largest, most influential student environmental group in the country. We have 25,000 members and 250 groups around the country. We work on strategic campaigns to protect wilderness, make globalization sustainable and fair, and advocate for clean energy. We also train today's young leaders and lead youth run outings to explore, enjoy and protect our wilderness.

Publication(s): Live From Earth

Keyword(s): Climate Change, Energy, Forests/Forestry, Land Issues, Public Lands/Greenspace, Wildlife & Species

Contact(s):
Meighan Davis, National Director

SILK CITY NATURE ASSOCIATION
120 S. Pleasant Street
Belding, MI 48809-1644 United States
Phone: 616-794-1900, ext. 205 Fax: 616-794-4812
E-mail: dreed@ci.belding.mi.us

Founded: 2003
Membership: 101–1,000
Scope: Local

Description: The mission of the Silk City Nature Association is to enhance human stewardship of the natural world by providing the citizens of the greater Belding area with: quality environmental and natural science education, ecologically sound management of the community's natural resources, preservation and interpretation of the community's natural resources, increased opportunities for personal reflection and enjoyment of the outdoors.

Keyword(s): Land Issues, Public Lands/Greenspace, Sprawl/Urban Planning, Water Habitats & Quality

SINAPU
4990 Pearl East Circle, Suite 301
Boulder, CO 80301 United States
Phone: 303-447-8655 Fax: 303-447-8612
E-mail: sinapu@sinapu.org
Website: www.sinapu.org

Founded: 1991
Membership: 101–1,000
Scope: Regional

Description: We recognize the critical role top predators play in maintaining the health and diversity of the wild systems to which they belong. Only now are scientists beginning to uncover the complex relationships that predators hold together in the wild. Sinapu works tirelessly to undo over a century of Western politics, aiming to restore wolves, grizzly bears, wolverines, lynx, and river otter to their rightful place in the wild

Publication(s): Wild Again

Keyword(s): Forests/Forestry, Land Issues, Public Lands/Greenspace, Wildlife & Species

Contact(s):
Rob Edward, Program Director
Kimberly Riggs, Executive Director; kim@sinapu.org
Wendy Keefover-Ring, Program Staff; wendy@sinapu.org

SISKIYOU PROJECT
9335 Takilma Rd.
Cave Junction, OR 97523 United States
Phone: 541-592-4459

Description: We believe in the power of place and of biological cycles, and in modeling our lives, actions, and community on the ideals of wholeness and being-of-a-place. For us the ultimate model is the wild, and we are reaching for the wild inside ourselves as well as "out there". We see all life forms as interconnected and inseparable, and realizing that we are in a time of crisis, we feel urgency in effecting change in the way human industrial culture deals with wild nature.

Contact(s):
David Johns, President
Dave Willis, Vice President
Romain Cooper, Program Director
Steve Marsden, Executive Director
Jennifer Marsden, SFI Director
Jim McBride, Finance Director
Barbara Ulliam, Conservation Director
Kelpie Wilson, Development Director
Kindi Fahrnkopf, Office Manager
Lori Cooper, Staff Attorney
Tom Dimitre, East Siskiyou Conservation Coordinator
Lou Gold, Storyteller Emeritus
Steven Jessup, Secretary
Erik Jules, Treasurer
Julie Norman, Video Project Coordinator
Marjorie Reynolds, Mail and Data Processor
Vicky Rummel, SFI Admin. Coordinator
Linda Serrano, Network Coordinator
Barry Snitkin, Community Outreach

SISKIYOU REGIONAL EDUCATION PROJECT
9335 Takilma Rd.
Cave Junction, OR 97523 United States
Phone: 541-592-4459 Fax: 541-592-2653
Website: www.siskiyou.org

Founded: 1983
Membership: 1,001–10,000

Scope: Local, State, Regional, National
Description: To educate the public about the environmental Issues of the Siskiyou Bio-region.

SMALL WOODLAND OWNERS ASSOCIATION OF MAINE
153 Hospital St., P.O. Box 836
Augusta, ME 04332 United States
Phone: 207-626-0005   Fax: 207-626-7992
E-mail: info@swoam.com
Website: www.swoam.com
Founded: 1975
Scope: State
Description: A statewide nonprofit organization, affiliated with the National Woodland Owners Association, which pursues better understandings, skills, and directions in small woodland ownership/management under integrated use objectives.
Publication(s): SWOAM News
Keyword(s): Forests/Forestry

SMITHSONIAN INSTITUTION
1000 Jefferson Dr., SW
Washington, DC 20560 United States
Phone: 202-357-2700
Website: www.smithsonian.org
Founded: 1846
Membership: 1,000,001 +
Scope: National
Description: An education, museum, and research complex as well as an independent trust instrumentality of the United States, established for the increase and diffusion of knowledge. Mission accomplished by: field investigations; national collections development in arts, history, and science, and their preservation for study, reference, and exhibition; scientific research and publications; programs of national and international cooperative research, conservation, education, and training; answering inquiries.
Publication(s): Smithsonian Institution Press, The Smithsonian Magazine
Keyword(s): Agriculture/Farming, Ethics/Environmental Justice, Forests/Forestry, Water Habitats & Quality, Wildlife & Species
Contact(s):
Lawrence Small, Secretary

SMITHSONIAN INSTITUTION
NATIONAL MUSEUM OF NATURAL HISTORY
1000 Jefferson Drive, SW
Washington, DC 20560 United States
Phone: 202-357-2700   Fax: 202-357-1729
E-mail: info@infor.si.edu
Website: www.si.edu
Scope: National
Description: A center for the study of humans, plants, animals, fossil organisms, terrestrial and extraterrestrial rocks, and minerals as well as other fields of scientific investigation.
Contact(s):
Robert Fri, Director
David Correll, Chief Scientist of Environmental Research Center; Smithsonian Environmental Research Center, P.O. Box 28, Edgewater, MD 21037; 301-261-4190

SMITHSONIAN INSTITUTION
OFFICE OF FELLOWSHIPS
Victor Bldg., 750 9th St. N. W.
Suite 9300
Washington, DC 20560 United States
Phone: 202-275-0655   Fax: 202-275-0489
E-mail: siofg@si.edu
Website: www.si.edu/research+study
Membership: 1–100
Scope: International
Description: Oversees all Smithsonian fellowships and supports a wide range of research activities. It also provides program and administrative assistance for cooperative teaching arrangements between the Institution and local universities in American history, museum studies, and other areas.
Contact(s):
Catherine Harris, Director; siofg@si.edu
Pamela Hudson, Program Manager; siofg@si.edu

SMITHSONIAN INSTITUTION
OFFICE OF INTERNATIONAL RELATIONS
Smithsonian Institution
1100 Jefferson Dr., SW
Washington, DC 20560 United States
Phone: 202-357-4795   Fax: 202-786-2557
Website: www.si.edu
Membership: 1–100
Scope: National
Description: The Foreign Currency Program supports the research activities of American institutions of higher learning through grants in U.S.-owned local currencies.
Contact(s):
Francine Berkowitz, Director

SMITHSONIAN INSTITUTION
SMITHSONIAN INSTITUTION PRESS
750 9th St. NW
Room 4300
MRC 950
Washington, DC 20560 United States
Phone: 202-275-2300
Website: www.si.edu/sipress/
Founded: 1846
Membership: 1,000,001 +
Scope: National
Description: Information on history, art, and science research is presented in non-technical style in Smithsonian Institution Research Reports issued four times a year by the Office of Public Affairs (202-357-2627). Smithsonian, the official magazine of the Institution, presents general interest feature articles each month in every subject area of the Smithsonian museums: art, culture, history, science, and technology.
Publication(s): Research in various fields is reported in a continuing series of publications by the Smithsonian Institution Press
Contact(s):
Daniel Goodwin, Director
David Umansky, Director of Communications; Arts and Industries Bldg., 900 Jefferson Dr. SW, Rm. 4210, Washington, DC 20560; 202-357-2627
Don Moser, Editor; Smithsonian Magazine, Arts and Industries, Bldg. 900 Jefferson Dr. SW, Rm. 1310C, Washington, DC 20560

SMITHSONIAN INSTITUTION
SMITHSONIAN TROPICAL RESEARCH INSTITUTE
APO AA, FL 34002-0948 United States
Phone: 202-357-2700
Scope: National

SMITHSONIAN INSTITUTION NATIONAL ZOOLOGICAL PARK
3001 Connecticut Ave. NW
Washington, DC 20008 United States
Phone: 202-673-4717
Website: www.nationalzoologicalpark.com
Founded: 1889
Membership: 10,001–100,000
Scope: Local, Regional, National, International

Description: Research concentrates on a better understanding of animal behavior and health, particularly endangered species. Through the operation of the zoo's Conservation and Research Center in Front Royal, VA, the NZP is developing a program of animal propagation which will aid in the survival of threatened and endangered species. Undertakes a number of programs overseas to develop new methodology and increase knowledge of species in the wild. The Migratory Bird Center is located at the zoo.

Contact(s):
Lucy Spelman, Director; 202-673-4721

SMITHSONIAN MARINE STATION AT FORT PIERCE
701 Seaway Dr.
Fort Pierce, FL 34949 United States
Phone: 772-465-6630   Fax: 772-461-8154
Website: www.sms.si.edu

Scope: Local, International

Description: Marine studies aim at understanding the ecological function of inland waterways and their relationship to land use policy.

Contact(s):
Valerie Paul, Head Scientist; 772-465-6630; ext. 140; Fax: 772-461-8154; paul@sms.si.edu

SOCIEDAD AMBIENTE MARINO
Sociedad Ambiente Marino
P.O. Box 22158
San Juan, PR 931 United States
Phone: 787-485-2896
E-mail: sambientemarino@aol.com

Founded: 2001
Membership: 101–1,000
Scope: Regional

Description: Censos de corales y peces, limpiezas de playa, transplante de coral. Educacion en Ambiente Marino.

Keyword(s): Ecosystems (precious), Oceans/Coasts/Beaches, Recreation/Ecotourism, Water Habitats & Quality

Contact(s):
Samuel Suleiman, President; 787-485-2896; buzo@coqui.net

SOCIETY FOR ANIMAL PROTECTIVE LEGISLATION
P.O. Box 3719, Georgetown Station
Washington, DC 20027 United States
Phone: 703-836-4300   Fax: 703-836-0400
E-mail: sapl@saplonline.org
Website: www.saplonline.org

Founded: 1955
Membership: 1,001–10,000
Scope: National

Description: Nonprofit organization which keeps its 7,000 correspondents apprised of current developments in legislation for the protection of animals. Has been instrumental in obtaining enactment of 14 federal laws.

Keyword(s): Wildlife & Species

Contact(s):
John Gleiber, Executive Secretary

SOCIETY FOR CONSERVATION BIOLOGY
4245 North Fairfax Dr.
Suite 400
Arlington, VA 22203-1651 United States
Phone: 703-276-2384   Fax: 703-995-4633
E-mail: information@conbio.org
Website: www.conservationbiology.org

Founded: 1985
Membership: 1,001–10,000
Scope: National, International

Description: A professional society dedicated to providing the scientific information and expertise required to protect the world's biological diversity. Incorporated as a tax-exempt scientific organization, the Society has a board composed of scholars, government personnel, and members of both national and international scientific and conservation organizations.

Publication(s): Conservation Biology, SCB Newsletter, Conservation In Practice

Keyword(s): Development/Developing Countries, Wildlife & Species

Contact(s):
Malcolm Hunter, President; Dept. of Wildlife Ecology, University of Maine, Orono, ME 04469; 207-581-2865; Fax: 207-581-2858
Alan Thornhill, Executive Director; 703-276-2384; ext. 102; Fax: 703-995-4633; athornhill@conbio.org
Autumn-Lynn Harrison, Project Manager; 703-276-2384; ext. 100; aharrison@conbio.org
Stephen Humphrey, Treasurer; 352-392-9230; Fax: 352-392-9748; humphrey@ufl.edu
Kathy Kohm, Editor of Conservation Biology In Practice; 206-685-4724; Fax: 206-221-7839; kkohm@u.washington.edu
Gary Meffe, Editor of Conservation Biology; 352-846-0557; Fax: 352-846-2823; conbio@gnv.ifas.ufl.edu
Elizabeth Parish, Operations Manager; 703-276-2384; Fax: 703-995-4633; membership@conbio.org

SOCIETY FOR ECOLOGICAL RESTORATION
1955 W. Grant Rd. #150
Tucson, AZ 85745 United States
Phone: 520-622-5485
E-mail: info@ser.org
Website: www.ser.org

Founded: 1989
Membership: 1,001–10,000
Scope: International

Description: Created to promote the development of ecological restoration both as a discipline and as a model for a healthy relationship with nature, and to raise awareness of the value and limitations of restoration as a conservation strategy.

Publication(s): Ecological Restoration, Proceedings from the Seventh SER Conference, 1995, Restoration Ecology, SER News

Keyword(s): Reduce/Reuse/Recycle

Contact(s):
Donald Falk, Executive Director; 520-626-7201
George Gann, Vice Chair; 305-245-6547
William Halvorson, Treasurer; 520-670-6885
Eric Higgs, Secretary; 403-492-5469
William Niering, Editor; 203-447-1911
Edith Read, Chair; 714-751-7373

SOCIETY FOR INTEGRATIVE AND COMPARATIVE BIOLOGY
1313 Dolley Madison Blvd. Ste. 402
McLean, VA 22101 United States
Phone: 703-790-1745   Fax: 703-790-2672
E-mail: sicb@burkinc.com
Website: www.sicb.org

Founded: 1890
Membership: 1,001–10,000
Scope: National

Description: (formerly American Society of Zoologists) The Society for Integrative and Comparative Biology (SICB) is one of the largest and most prestigious professional associations of its kind. SICB is dedicated to promoting the pursuit and public dissemination of important information relating to comparative biology.

Publication(s): American Zoologist, The
Keyword(s): Wildlife & Species

Contact(s):
  Albert Bennett, President; School of Biological Sciences, University of California+I365, Irvine, CA 92717; 714-856-6930; Fax: 714-725-2181
  Marquesa Mills, Business Manager; 104 Sirius Cir., Thousand Oaks, CA 91360; 805-492-3585; Fax: 805-492-0370
  Mary Adams-Wiley, Executive Officer; 104 Sirius Cir., Thousand Oaks, CA 91360; 805-492-3585; Fax: 805-492-0370
  Milton Fingerman, Managing Editor; Department of Biology, Tulane University, New Orleans, LA 70118; 504-865-5546
  Mary Ottinger, Secretary; Department of Poultry Science, University of Maryland, College Park, MD 20742; 301-405-5780; Fax: 301-314-9557
  Marjorie Reaka, Treasurer; Department of Zoology, University of Maryland, College Park, MD 20742; 301-454-0259

SOCIETY FOR MARINE MAMMALOGY, THE
BIOLOGICAL SCIENCES AND CENTER FOR MARINE SCIENCE RESEARCH
University of Hawaii
Hawaii Institute of Marine Biology
Kailua, HI 96734 United States
Phone: 808-247-5297   Fax: 808-247-5831
E-mail: dan.odell@seaworld.com
Website: www.marinemammalogy.org/
Founded: 1981
Scope: National
Description: To promote the educational, scientific, and managerial advancement of marine mammal science; gather and disseminate scientific, technical, and management information, through publications and meetings to members of the society, the public, and public and private institutions; and promote the wise conservation and management of marine mammal resources.
Publication(s): Marine Mammal Science
Keyword(s): Wildlife & Species
Contact(s):
  Carol Fairfield, Awards & Scholarship Committee; NOAA/NMFS/SEFSC, 1002 Forest Dr., Arnold, MD 21012; 410-757-7224; carol.fairfield@noaa.gov
  Edward Keith, Education Committee; Oceanographic Center, Nova Southeastern University, 8000 N. Ocean Dr., Dania, FL 33004; 954-262-8322; Fax: 954-921-7764; edwardok@hpd.nova.edu
  Paul Nachtigall, Scientific Program Committee; Marine Mammal Research Program, Hawaii Institute of Marine Science, University of Hawaii, P.O. Box 1106, Kailua, HI 96734; 808-247-5297; Fax: 808-247-5831; nachtiga@hawaii.edu
  Daniel Odell, President-Elect; Sea World, Inc., 7007 Sea World Dr., Orlando, FL 32821-8097
  D. Pabst, Secretary; 910-962-7266; Fax: 910-962-4066; pabsta@uncwil.edu
  William Perrin, Editor; Southwest Fisheries Science Center, NMFS, P.O. Box 271, LaJolla, CA 92109; 619-546-7093; Fax: 619-546-7003; wperrin@ucsd.edu
  Steven Swartz, Committee of Scientific Advisors; National Marine Fisheries Service, 75 Virginia Beach Dr., Miami, FL 33149; 305-361-4487; Fax: 305-361-4478; Steven.Swartz@noaa.gov
  Glenn Vanblaricom, Membership Committee; WA Cooperative Fish & Wildlife Research Unit, Box 357980, University of Washington, Seattle, WA 98195; 206-543-6475; Fax: 206-616-9012

SOCIETY FOR RANGE MANAGEMENT
445 Union Blvd #230
Lakewood, CO 80228 United States
Phone: 303-986-3309   Fax: 303-986-3892
Website: www.rangelands.org
Founded: 1948
Membership: 1,001-10,000
Scope: Local, State, Regional, National, International
Description: The vision of the Society for Range Management is productive, sustainable rangelands. The mission of the Society for Range Management is to promote and enhance the stewardship of rangeland ecosystems and associated renewable resources to meet human needs based upon scientific research and sound policies.
Publication(s): Journal of Range Management, Rangelands
Keyword(s): Agriculture/Farming, Ecosystems (precious), Forests/Forestry, Land Issues, Public Lands/Greenspace, Recreation/Ecotourism, Water Habitats & Quality, Wildlife & Species

SOCIETY FOR THE PRESERVATION OF BIRDS OF PREY
P.O. Box 66070
Mar Vista Station
Los Angeles, CA 90066-0070 United States
Phone: 310-840-2322
Founded: 1966
Scope: National
Description: A private charity, nonmembership, national association advocating the strictest protection for birds of prey; educates about the role of raptors in the ecosystem; opposes lenient harvesting practices & the sale of birds of prey for profit; endorses captive raptor breeding as a conservation technique; & supports the largest collection of literature on birds of prey at any public university. The Society is the oldest organization emphasizing birds of prey occurring naturally in the wild.
Publication(s): Leaflet Series, Raptor Report
Keyword(s): Ecosystems (precious), Wildlife & Species
Contact(s):
  Richard Hilton, President and Editor; 310-319-9417

SOCIETY FOR THE PROTECTION OF NEW HAMPSHIRE FORESTS
FOREST SOCIETY, THE
54 Portsmouth St.
Concord, NH 03301-5400 United States
Phone: 603-224-9945   Fax: 603-228-0423
E-mail: info@spnhf.org
Website: www.spnhf.org
Founded: 1901
Membership: 1,001-10,000
Scope: State
Description: Founded in 1901, the Society for the Protection of New Hampshire Forests is a 10,000-member non-profit organization that has helped protect over one million acres of land across the state.
Publication(s): Forest Notes
Keyword(s): Forests/Forestry, Land Issues, Wildlife & Species
Contact(s):
  Jane Difley, President/ Forester
  Paul Doscher, Senior Director of Land Conservation

SOCIETY OF AMERICAN FORESTERS
5400 Grosvenor Ln.
Bethesda, MD 20814-2198 United States
Phone: 301-897-8720   Fax: 301-897-3690
E-mail: safweb@safnet.org
Website: www.safnet.org
Founded: 1900
Membership: 1,000,001 +
Scope: National
Description: The national organization representing all segments of the forestry profession and the accreditation authority for professional forestry education in the U.S. Objectives are to advance the science, technology, education, and practice of professional forestry and to use the knowledge and skills of the profession to benefit society.

Publication(s): Forestry Source, The, Western Journal of Applied Forestry, Northern Journal of Applied Forestry, Southern Journal of Applied Forestry, Forest Science, Journal of Forestry

Keyword(s): Forests/Forestry, Land Issues, Public Lands/Greenspace, Reduce/Reuse/Recycle, Sprawl/Urban Planning, Wildlife & Species

SOCIETY OF AMERICAN FORESTERS

UNIVERSITY OF KENTUCKY
DEPARTMENT OF FORESTRY
UK Thomas Poe Cooper Bldg.
Lexington, KY 40546-0073 United States
Phone: 859-257-5994   Fax: 859-257-9086
Website: www.uky.edu-agriculture-forestry-forestry.html

Membership: 1–100
Scope: Regional, National
Description: K-T SAF is the Kentucky-Tennessee section of the Society of American Foresters, and carries out the policies and programs of SAF within these two states. See the Society of American Foresters listing for more information.

Keyword(s): Forests/Forestry, Reduce/Reuse/Recycle

Contact(s):
Jim Ringe, Director of Undergraduate Studies; 859-257-7594; jringe@uky.edu
Jeff Stringer, Extension Coordinator; Dept. of Forestry, Universtity of Ky., Lexington, KY 40546-0073; 859-257-5994

SOCIETY OF TYMPANUCHUS CUPIDO PINNATUS LTD.

Stone Ridge II, Suite 280, N 14 W23777 Stone Ridge Dr.
Waukesha, WI 53188-1188 United States
E-mail: mihal@execpc.com

Founded: 1961
Scope: National
Description: Nonprofit organization dedicated to the preservation of the prairie chicken for all future generations in Wisconsin and all threatened and endangered species native to the State of Wisconsin.

Publication(s): Boom
Keyword(s): Land Issues, Wildlife & Species

Contact(s):
Russell Schallert, President
Lawrence Deleers, Jr., Vice President; 4665 Highway Y, Saukville, WI 53080; 773-373-3366
William Emory, Vice President; Klug and Smith Company, 4425 W. Mitchell, Milwaukee, WI 53214
Gregory Septon, Vice President; Milwaukee Public Museum; 800 W. Wells Street, Milwaukee, WI 53233
Glenn Goergen, Treasurer; Deloitte and Touche, 250 E. Wisconsin Ave., Milwaukee, WI 53202
Kurt Remus, Jr., Secretary; 3860 N. Port Washington Rd., Milwaukee, WI 53217

SOCIETY OF WETLAND SCIENTISTS

1313 Dolley Madison Blvd
Suite 402
McLean, VA 22101 United States
Phone: 703-790-1745   Fax: 703-790-2672
E-mail: SWS@BurkInc.com
Website: www.sws.org

Founded: 1979
Membership: 1,001–10,000
Scope: International
Description: International nonprofit education and charitable society of persons interested in wetland science, technology, and related fields. Encourages educational, scientific, and technological development and advancement in all fields of wetland science. Encourages protection, restoration, and stewardship of wetlands. Student memberships and scholarships.

Publication(s): Wetlands, SWS Bulletin

Keyword(s): Water Habitats & Quality

Contact(s):
Barry Warner, President
Virginia Carter, Past President
Glenn Guntenspergen, Secretary; 301-497-5523
Mary Kentula, Treasurer; 541-754-4478; ext. 5682

SOIL AND WATER CONSERVATION SOCIETY

Attn: Deb Happe,
945 SW Ankeny Rd.
Ankeny, IA 50021-9764 United States
Phone: 515-289-2331   Fax: 515-289-1227
E-mail: swcs@swcs.org
Website: www.swcs.org

Founded: 1945
Membership: 1,001–10,000
Scope: National, International
Description: (formerly Soil Conservation Society of America) The Soil and Water Conservation Society is a multidisciplinary membership organization advocating protection, enhancement, and wise use of soil, water, and related natural resources. SWCS programs emphasize the interdependence of natural resources through education, publications, and a network of local chapters throughout the U.S. and Canada. SWCS also manages the World Association of Soil and Water Conservation.

Publication(s): Conservation Implications Climate Change, Journal of Soil and Water Conservation

Keyword(s): Agriculture/Farming, Climate Change, Ecosystems (precious), Ethics/Environmental Justice, Forests/Forestry, Land Issues, Oceans/Coasts/Beaches, Recreation/Ecotourism, Sprawl/Urban Planning, Water Habitats & Quality, Wildlife & Species

Contact(s):
Craig Cox, Executive Director; 945 SW Ankeny Road, Ankeny, IA 50021; 515-289-2331; ext. 13; Fax: 515-289-1227; craigcox@swcs.org
Deborah Cavanaugh-Grant, President; Univ. of Illinois, P.O. Box 410, Greenview, IL 62642; 217-968-5512; Fax: 217-968-5583; cvnghgrn@uiuc.edu
Deb Happe, Communications Director/Editor; 945 SW Ankeny Road, Ankeny, IA 50021; 515-289-2331; ext. 26; Fax: 515-289-1227; deb@swcs.org
Norman Berg, Washington, DC Representative; 202-659-5668; Fax: 202-659-8339; nberg46738@aol.com
James Bruce, Ottawa, Canada Representative; 613-731-5929; Fax: 613-731-3509; jpbruce@sympatico.ca

SONORAN DESERT NATIONAL PARK FRIENDS

P.O. Box 40427
Tucson, AZ 85717-0427 United States
Phone: 520-206-9691
E-mail: SonoranDesertNP@aol.com
Website: SonoranDesertNP.org

Founded: 1998
Membership: 101–1,000
Scope: International
Description: We work to improve management and conservation of the Sonoran Desert in southwestern Arizona and northwestern Sonora, Mexico, through education, service, publication, and advocacy. We are working to create a Sonoran Desert National Park by expanding Organ Pipe National Monument to be a sister park for the Pinacate Biosphere Reserve and the Upper Gulf Biosphere in Sonora. Together they will heighten protection of 5.3 million acres of wild desert and enhance local economies through eco-tourism.

Keyword(s): Land Issues, Public Lands/Greenspace, Recreation/Ecotourism, Wildlife & Species

SONORAN INSTITUTE
7650 E. Broadway Blvd.
Suite 203
Tucson, AZ 85710 United States
Phone: 520-290-0828 Fax: 520-290-0969
E-mail: sonoran@sonoran.org
Website: www.sonoran.org
Founded: 1990
Scope: Local, State, Regional, National, International
Description: The Sonoran Institute works with communities to conserve and restore important natural landscapes in Western North America, including the wildlife and cultural values of these lands. The Sonoran Institute also operates an office in Bozeman, Montana: the Sonoran Institute Northwest Office: 210 S. Wallace Avenue, Bozeman, Montana 59715 Phone: 406-587-7331 Fax: 406-587-2027
Publication(s): Integrating Natural Open Space, Human Dimensions of the Sonoran Desert, El Articulo 27 de la Constitucion, Bringing Conservation Home, Measuring Change in Rural Communities, National Parks and their Neighbors, Beyond the Hundredth Meeting, A Desktop Reference into Land Development, A Summary Report, Politica de los Estados Unidos Mexicanos y sus Efectos en los Cambios, Caring for Land, Economics, and Communities in Western Canada, An Economics Workbook for Western Canada, Lessons Learned for the Field on Building Partnerships with Local Communities, Field Guide to Collaborative Conservation on the West's Public Lands, Collaborative, Community-Based Planning, Business Diversification and Land Stewardship, Demographic, Economic, Fiscal Trends, Community Workbook-Habitat Conservation
Keyword(s): Agriculture/Farming, Development/Developing Countries, Ecosystems (precious), Land Issues, Oceans/Coasts/Beaches, Public Lands/Greenspace, Recreation/Ecotourism, Sprawl/Urban Planning, Water Habitats & Quality, Wildlife & Species
Contact(s):
  Barb Cestero, Director, Northern Rockies Program; Sonoran Institute Northwest Office, 201 S. Wallace Ave., Bozeman, MT 59715; 406-587-7331; ext. 103; Fax: 406-587-2027; barb@sonoran.org
  Steve Cornellus, Director, Sonoran Desert Ecoregion Program; Sonoran Institute, 7650 E. Broadway Blvd., Suite 203, Tucson, AZ 85710; 520-290-0828; ext. 218; Fax: 520-290-0969; steve@sonoran.org
  Dennis Glick, Director, Northwest Office; Sonoran Institute Northwest Office, 201 S. Wallace Avenue, Bozeman, MT 59715; 406-587-7331; ext. 101; Fax: 406-587-2027; dennis@sonoran.org
  Roseann Hanson, Director, Southeast Arizona Program; Sonoran Institute, 7650 E. Broadway Blvd., Suite 203, Tucson, AZ 85710; 520-290-0828; ext. 225; Fax: 520-290-0969; roseann@sonoran.org
  Andy Laurenzi, Director, State Trust Lands Program; Sonoran Institute, 7650 E. Broadway Blvd., Suite 203, Tucson, AZ 85710; 520-290-0828; ext. 213; Fax: 520-290-0969; andy@sonoran.org
  Luther Propst, Executive Director; Sonoran Institute, 7650 E. Broadway Blvd., Suite 203, Tucson, AZ 85710; 520-290-0828; Fax: 520-290-0969; luther@sonoran.org
  Ray Rasker, Director, SocioEconomics Program; Sonoran Institute Northwest Office, 201 S. Wallace Avenue, Bozeman, MT 59715; 406-587-7331; ext. 108; Fax: 406-587-2027; ray@sonoran.org
  John Shepard, Associate Director; Sonoran Institute, 7650 E. Broadway Blvd., Suite 203, Tucson, AZ 85710; 520-290-0828; ext. 208; Fax: 520-290-0969; john@sonoran.org
  Whitney Tilt, Director, Resources for Community Collaboration; Sonoran Institute Northwest Office, 201 S. Wallace Ave., Bozeman, MT 59715; 406-587-7331; ext. 105; Fax: 406-587-2027; whitney@sonoran.org
  Wendy Erica Werden, Director, Strategic Communications; Sonoran Institute, 7650 E. Broadway Blvd., Suite 203, Tucson, AZ 85710; 520-290-0828; ext. 210; Fax: 520-290-0969; wendyerica@sonoran.org

SOUND EXPERIENCE
HISTORIC SCHOONER ADVENTURESS
2310 Washington St.
Port Townsend, WA 98368 United States
Phone: 360-379-0438 Fax: 360-379-0439
E-mail: soundexp@soundexp.org
Website: www.soundexp.org
Founded: 1989
Scope: National
Description: Sound Experience involves participants in exploration of Puget Sound from the decks of a traditional sailing ship (the 101' Schooner Adventuress). Our mission is protecting Puget Sound through education.
Publication(s): Publications available on website
Keyword(s): Recreation/Ecotourism
Contact(s):
  Nick Worden, President
  Jenell DeMatteo, Executive Director; 360-379-0438; Fax: 360-379-0439; soundexp@olypen.com
  Dani Turissini, Communications Manager; 360-379-0438; Fax: 360-379-0439; soundexp@olypen.com
  Kelley Watson, Education Director; 360-379-0438; Fax: 360-379-0439; soundexp@olypen.com

SOUNDWATERS
COMMUNITY CENTER FOR ENVIRONMENTAL EDUCATION
SCHOONER SOUNDWATERS
1281 Cove Road in Cove Island Park
Stamford, CT 06902 United States
Phone: 2033231978 Fax: 2039671123
E-mail: connect@soundwaters.org
Website: www.soundwaters.org
Founded: 1990
Scope: Local, State, Regional
Description: A non-profit educational organization that is dedicated to preserving Long Island Sound through hands-on learning experiences. Come learn something new in our environmental community center, take a sail on our floating classroom - the Schooner SoundWaters, or bring a whole school to learn during an unforgettable, outdoor education experience.
Contact(s):
  Anne Harper, Executive Director; 203-406-3304
  Diane Selditch, Center Co-Director; 203-406-3302
  Jeff Cordulack, Urban Ecology Program Coordinator; 203-406-3308

SOUTH CAROLINA ASSOCIATION OF CONSERVATION DISTRICTS
1835 Assembly St., Rm. 950 Strom Thurmond Federal Building
Columbia, SC 29201 United States
Phone: 803-253-3314 Fax: 803-253-3670
E-mail: ltansill.scacd@sc.usda.gov
Founded: 1939
Membership: 101–1,000
Scope: State
Description: To protect the natural resources of South Carolina through its 46 member Cosnervation Districts by providing the leadership, information, and tools which enable Districts to achieve their goals.
Contact(s):
  Larry Nates, President; 112 Luther Dr., Gaston, SC 29053; 803-755-0319

Ed McAllister, Vice President
Linda Tansill, Executive Director
Amanda Bauknight, Secretary; 1967 Burles Ridge Rd., Easley, SC 23640
Diane Edwins, Treasurer; 4169 State Rd., Ridgeville, SC 29472; 843-688-5461

SOUTH CAROLINA BASS FEDERATION
Attn: President, 1469 Schurlknight Rd.
St. Stephen, SC 29479-3627 United States
Phone: 803-567-4680
E-mail: tonybennett@dycon.com
Website: www.scbass.com

Scope: State

Description: An organization of Bassmaster chapters, affiliated with the Bass Anglers Sportsman Society, organized to fight pollution, assist state and national conservation agencies in their efforts, and teach the young people of our country good conservation practices. Dedicated to the realistic conservation of our water resources.

Publication(s): South Carolina Forestry Journal, South Carolina B.A.S.S. Federation, Inc. Newsletter

Keyword(s): Forests/Forestry, Land Issues, Transportation, Water Habitats & Quality

Contact(s):
Tony Bennett, President; 803-567-4680
Tom Hueble, Conservation Director; 446 Baker Rd., Whitmire, SC 29178; 803-694-3602; hueblefamily@mindsprings.com

SOUTH CAROLINA ENVIRONMENTAL LAW PROJECT
P.O. Box 1380
Pawleys Island, SC 29585 United States
Phone: 843-527-0078   Fax: 843-527-0540
Website: www.scelp.org

Founded: 1987
Scope: Regional

Description: SCELP is a nonprofit organization whose mission is to protect the natural environment of South Carolina by providing legal services and advice to environmental organizations and concerned citizens, and by improving the state's system of environmental regulation.

Publication(s): Mountains and Marshes
Keyword(s): Land Issues, Water Habitats & Quality

Contact(s):
James Chandler, President and General Counsel

SOUTH CAROLINA FORESTRY ASSOCIATION
4901 Broad River Rd., P.O. Box 21303
Columbia, SC 29221 United States
Phone: 803-798-4170   Fax: 803-798-2340
E-mail: scfa@scforestry.org
Website: www.scforestry.org

Founded: 1968
Scope: State

Description: A nonprofit educational organization with a membership of timberland owners, wood dealers, wood-using industries, equipment suppliers, and individuals interested in forest conservation and wise use of natural resources.

Contact(s):
Robert Scott, President
Sam Coker, Chairman of the Board; SC Pole at Piling Company P.O. Box 3309, Leesville, SC 29070; 803-532-5806

SOUTH CAROLINA NATIVE PLANT SOCIETY
P.O. Box 759
Pickens, SC 29671 United States
Phone: 864-898-1221
E-mail: john.brubaker@scnps.org
Website: www.scnps.org

Founded: 1996
Scope: State

Description: Promotes native plants and plant communities through an education-based agenda. The Society sponsors field trips, symposiums, workshops and lectures. The Society also works with government agencies to assist in seed collection and management.

Publication(s): Newsletter, Brochure
Keyword(s): Wildlife & Species

Contact(s):
Rick Huffman, President; 864-868-7798; rhuffman@innova.net
Bill Stringer, Vice-President; 864-656-3527

SOUTH CAROLINA WILDLIFE FEDERATION
2711 Middleburg Dr.
Suite 104
Columbia, SC 29204 United States
Phone: 803-256-0670   Fax: 803-256-0690
E-mail: mail@scwf.org
Website: www.scwf.org

Founded: 1931
Membership: 1,001–10,000
Scope: State

Description: South Carolina Wildlife Federation is a nonprofit citizens' conservation organization that advocates environmental stewardship by promoting wildlife habitat enhancement and natural resources conservation. SCWF is active in promoting sound stewardship of SC's natural treasures through educational and public awareness programs. Drawing strength from a committed membership and unique partnerships, SCWF establishes policies that protect and enhance the natural systems which give life to us all.

Publication(s): Out of Doors
Keyword(s): Ethics/Environmental Justice, Forests/Forestry, Land Issues, Oceans/Coasts/Beaches, Public Lands/Greenspace, Reduce/Reuse/Recycle, Water Habitats & Quality, Wildlife & Species

Contact(s):
Andy Brack, President
Angela Viney, Executive Director
Robert Barber, Lobbyist
Sara Green, Director of Education
Katie Myers, Development Coordinator
Rose Thielke, Membership Administrative Assistant

SOUTH DAKOTA ASSOCIATION OF CONSERVATION DISTRICTS
SDACD
P.O. Box 275
116 N. Euclid
Pierre, SD 57501 United States
Phone: 695-895-4099   Fax: 605-895-9424
E-mail: info@sdconservation.org
Website: sdconservation.org

Founded: 1942
Membership: 1–100
Scope: State

Description: Our mission is to assist, lead, and coordinate conservation districts (local units of government) in their efforts to promote sensible, voluntary, self-governed conservation management and development of South Dakota's natural resources for ourselves and our posterity.

Keyword(s): Agriculture/Farming, Air Quality/Atmosphere, Climate Change, Ecosystems (precious), Forests/Forestry, Land Issues, Pollution (general), Public Lands/Greenspace, Recreation/Ecotourism, Reduce/Reuse/Recycle, Water Habitats & Quality, Wildlife & Species

Contact(s):
Lynn Denke, President; 19580 224th St., Creighton, SD 57729-9747; 605-279-2633; ldenke@gwtc.net

Angela Ehlers, Executive Director; 116 N. Euclid, P.O. Box 275, Pierre, SD 57501-0275; 605-895-4099; Fax: 605-895-9424; info@sdconservation.org

Justin (Judge) Jessop, Grasslands Mgt. Technical Assistance Team; 24690 299th Avenue, Presho, SD 57568; 605-280-0127; Justin-Jessop@sd.nacdnet.org

Duane Murphey, Project Coordinator; 1124 Westwood Drive, Pierre, SD 57501; 605-280-8504; DuaneMurphey@pie.midco.net

SOUTH DAKOTA BASS FEDERATION

Attn: President SD BASS
6212 W. Thatcher Dr.
Sioux Falls, SD 57106 United States
Phone: 605-361-6657   Fax: 605-367-5830
E-mail: kyle.helseth@state.sd.us
Website: www.sdbassfederation.com

Founded: 1979
Membership: 101–1,000
Scope: State
Description: An organization of Bassmaster chapters, affiliated with the Bass Anglers Sportsman Society, organized to fight pollution, assist state and national conservation agencies in their efforts, and teach young people of our country good conservation practices. Dedicated to the realistic conservation of our water resources.
Publication(s): B.A.S.S. Federation Newsletter "Dakota Bassin",
Keyword(s): Wildlife & Species
Contact(s):
  Chuck Doom, President
  Phillip Risnes, Conservation Director; 26643 461st. Ave., Hartford, SD 57033; 605-526-4339; philrisnes@aol.com

SOUTH DAKOTA ORNITHOLOGISTS UNION

Dept. of Biology, University of South Dakota
Vermillion, SD 57069 United States
Phone: 605-677-6175   Fax: 605-677-6557

Founded: 1949
Membership: 101–1,000
Scope: State
Description: To encourage the study of birds in South Dakota and to promote the study of ornithology by more closely uniting the students of this branch of natural science.
Publication(s): South Dakota Bird Notes, South Dakota Breeding Bird Atlas, The (1995), Birds of South Dakota (1991)
Keyword(s): Agriculture/Farming, Air Quality/Atmosphere, Energy, Reduce/Reuse/Recycle
Contact(s):
  Robb Schenck, President, 422 N. Linwood Ct., Sioux Falls, SD 57103
  Nelda Holden, Treasurer; 1620 Elmwood Dr., Brookings, SD 57006; 605-692-8278
  Jeffrey Palmer, Past President; 821 NW Fifth St., Madison, SD 57041; 605-256-9745
  David Swanson, Secretary; Biology Department, University of South Dakota, Vermillion, SD 57069; 605-624-0203
  Dan Tallman, Editor; Box 740, Northern State University, Aberdeen, SD 57401; 605-226-2255

SOUTH DAKOTA RESOURCES COALITION

P.O. Box 66
Brookings, SD 57006 United States
Phone: 605-697-6675   Fax: 605-697-6675
E-mail: sdrc@brookings.net
Website: www.stdrworks.org

Founded: 1972
Membership: 101–1,000
Scope: State
Description: Seeks to promote the survival and integrity of water, energy, land, wildlife, and air resources, along with justice in their allocation.
Publication(s): ECO FORUM
Keyword(s): Agriculture/Farming, Energy, Executive/Legislative/Judicial Reform, Pollution (general), Water Habitats & Quality
Contact(s):
  Luanne Napton, President; 605-693-4893
  Lawrence Novotny, Board Secretary; 605-688-6171
  Sue Grant, Staff Assistant; 605-697-6675; Fax: 605-697-6675; sdrc@brookings.net

SOUTH DAKOTA WILDLIFE FEDERATION

P.O. Box 7075
Pierre, SD 57501-7075 United States
Phone: 605-224-7524   Fax: 605-224-7524
E-mail: sdwf@sbtc.net
Website: www.sdwf.org

Founded: 1945
Membership: 1,001–10,000
Scope: National
Description: A representative statewide organization, affiliated with the National Wildlife Federation, dedicated to the protection and enhancement of wildlife and its habitat through public education and government interaction.
Publication(s): Out of Doors
Keyword(s): Reduce/Reuse/Recycle, Water Habitats & Quality, Wildlife & Species
Contact(s):
  Mike Larsen, President and Representative
  Chris Hesla, Executive Director and Editor. Education Programs Contact
  Chuck Clayton, Alternate Representative
  Robert Jacobson, Treasurer

SOUTH OAHU SOIL AND WATER CONSERVATION DISTRICT

938 Kamiloniu Place,
Honolulu, HI 96825 United States
E-mail: swcd@soswcd.org
Website: sos.wcd.org

Founded: 1939
Membership: 1,001–10,000
Scope: State
Description: for better understanding, appreciation, and conservation of Hawaii's native wildlife resources, especially its unique and endangered bird species and their associated ecosystems.
Contact(s):
  David Norbriga, President; 808-244-7951; Fax: 808-244-4108
  Joloyce Kaia, 1st Vice President; P.O. Box 404, Hana, HI 96713; 808-248-7725
  Mike Tulang, Executive Director; 919 Ala Moana Blvd. Rm. 309, Honolulu, HI 96814; 808-586-4389; Fax: 808-586-4300
  Ted Inouye, Alternate Board Member; P.O. Box 278, Hanamaulu, HI 96715; 808-245-3027
  Valerie Mendes, Alternate Board Member; 1100 Alakea St. #1200, Honolulu, HI 96813; 808-531-8181

SOUTHEAST ALASKA CONSERVATION COUNCIL (SEACC)

419 6th St., Suite 200
Juneau, AK 99801 United States
Phone: 907-586-6942   Fax: 907-463-3312
E-mail: info@seacc.org
Website: www.seacc.org

Founded: 1969
Membership: 1,001–10,000
Scope: Regional

Description: SEACC is a coalition of 18 local conservation groups, dedicated to preserving the integrity of Southeast Alaska's magnificent natural environment. SEACC works to protect the region's pristine coastal rainforest, abundant fish and wildlife, and outstanding scenery. SEACC helps foster a sustainable approach to economic stability, subsistence use areas, recreational opportunities, and Southeast Alaska's unique way of life.

Publication(s): RAVENCALL, Action Alerts

Keyword(s): Development/Developing Countries, Forests/Forestry, Land Issues, Oceans/Coasts/Beaches, Pollution (general), Public Lands/Greenspace, Recreation/Ecotourism, Reduce/Reuse/Recycle, Transportation, Water Habitats & Quality, Wildlife & Species

Contact(s):
  Wayne Weihing, President; P.O. Box 1193, Ward Cove, AK 99928
  John Wisenbaugh, Vice President; P.O. Box 512, Tenakee Springs, AK 99841
  Katya Kirsch, Executive Director
  Buck Lindekugel, Conservation Director and Staff Attorney
  Bart Koehler, Associate Director; 432 Country Rd. 312, Ignacio, CO 81137
  Dana Owen, Treasurer; 949 Goldbelt, Juneau, AK 99801
  Sue Schrader, Secretary; 10780 Mendenhall Loop Rd, Juneau, AK 99801

SOUTHEASTERN ASSOCIATION OF FISH AND WILDLIFE AGENCIES
8005 Freshwater Farms Rd.
Tallahassee, FL 32309 United States
Phone: 850-893-1204   Fax: 850-893-6204
E-mail: seafwa@aol.com
Website: www.seafwa.org

Founded: 1938

Scope: State, Regional, National, International

Description: Members are state agencies with responsibility for management and protection of fish and wildlife resources in 16 states, Puerto Rico, and the U. S. Virgin Islands; reviews state and federal legislation and regulations and consults with and makes suggestions to federal agencies in order that programs are in the best interest of states; serves as clearinghouse for exchange of ideas concerning wildlife and fisheries management, research techniques, law enforcement, and information and education

Publication(s): Proceedings of the SEAFWA

Keyword(s): Agriculture/Farming, Ecosystems (precious), Executive/Legislative/Judicial Reform, Forests/Forestry, Land Issues, Oceans/Coasts/Beaches, Pollution (general), Public Lands/Greenspace, Recreation/Ecotourism, Water Habitats & Quality, Wildlife & Species

Contact(s):
  Robert Brantly, Executive Secretary; 8005 Freshwater Farms Rd., Tallahassee, FL 32309; 850-893-1204; Fax: 850-893-6204; seafwa@aol.com
  James Jenkins, Vice President; Secretary, Department of Wildlife and Fisheries, P. O. Box 98000, Baton Rouge, LA 70898-9000; 225-765-2623
  Paul Sandifer, President; Department of Natural Resources, Rembert C. Dennis Building, P. O. Box 167, Columbia, SC 29202; 803-734-4007

SOUTHEASTERN COOPERATIVE WILDLIFE DISEASE STUDY
College of Veterinary Medicine, University of Georgia
Athens, GA 30602 United States
Phone: 706-542-1741   Fax: 706-542-5865
Website: www.scwds.org

Founded: 1957

Membership: 1–100

Scope: Regional, National

Description: The first regional diagnostic and research service in the U.S. for the specific purpose of investigating wildlife diseases. This joint-state organization currently is sponsored by the Southeastern Association of Fish and Wildlife Agencies; Veterinary Services of APHIS, USDA; and the Biological Resources Division of USDI. Participating states: AL, AR, FL, GA, KY, LA, MD, MO, MS, NC, PR, SC, TN, VA, WV.

Publication(s): SCWDS BRIEFS Newsletter

Keyword(s): Agriculture/Farming, Public Health

Contact(s):
  John Fischer, Director

SOUTHEASTERN FISHES COUNCIL
c/o Stephen T. Ross
Dept. of Biological Studies
University of Southern Mississippi
Hattiesburg, MS 39406-5018 United States
E-mail: STEPHENROSS@USM.EDU
Website: www.flmnh.ufl.edu/fish/organizations/sfc/minutes2001.htm

Scope: National

Description: Objectives are to provide for the pursuit and transmittal of information on the status and protection of southeastern fishes and their habitats, and to promote the perpetuation of rich natural assemblages of fishes and their habitats, as well as the localized unique forms and their habitats.

Publication(s): Proceedings of the Southeastern Fishes Council

Keyword(s): Reduce/Reuse/Recycle, Water Habitats & Quality, Wildlife & Species

Contact(s):
  Gerry Dinkins, Secretary; 3D International Environmental Group, 7039 Maynardville Highway, Knoxville, TN 37830-7976
  Frank Pezold, Editor; Department of Biology, Northeast Louisiana State University, Monroe, LA 71209
  Stephen Ross, Chair
  Peggy Shute, Treasurer; Tennessee Valley Authority, Natural Heritage Program, Norris, TN 37820
  Melvin Warren, Past Chair

SOUTHERN AFRICAN INSTITUTE OF FORESTRY
Postnet, Suite 329, P/Bag X4
Menlo Park, Pretoria, 102 South Africa
Phone: 271-234-81745

Founded: 1967

Membership: 101–1,000

Scope: International

Description: Represents professional forestry science at all levels in silviculture, forestry conservation, and timber processing, and disseminates information about forestry inside and outside of the profession.

Keyword(s): Forests/Forestry

Contact(s):
  W. Olivier, President
  P. Kime, Vice President
  D. Van der Zel, Publicity Officer; P.O. Box 1673, Pretoria 0001, South Africa; 271-254-5926
  C. Viljoen, Secretary

SOUTHERN APPALACHIAN BOTANICAL SOCIETY
Biology Department, 2100 College St., Newberry College
Newberry, SC 29108 United States
Phone: 803-321-5257   Fax: 803-321-5636

Founded: 1936

Membership: 101–1,000

Scope: Regional

Description: A nonprofit organization to disseminate information on the native plants of eastern North America through research, meetings and publications.

Publication(s): Castanea (journal), Chinquapin (newsletter)

Keyword(s): Ecosystems (precious), Forests/Forestry, Public Lands/Greenspace, Wildlife & Species

Contact(s):
Zack Murrell, President; Biology Department, Appalachian State University, Boone, NC 28608; 828-262-2674; murrellze@appstate.edu

Patricia Cox, Membership Secretary; Botany Department, University of Tennessee, Knoxville, TN 37996; 865-974-6225; pcox@utk.edu

Charles Horn, Treasurer; 803-321-5257; Fax: 803-321-5636; chorn@newberry.edu

SOUTHERN ENVIRONMENTAL LAW CENTER
201 W. Main St., Suite 14
Charlottesville, VA 22902-5065 United States
Phone: 434-977-4090   Fax: 434-977-1483
E-mail: selcva@selcva.org
Website: www.SouthernEnvironment.org

Founded: 1986
Membership: 1,001–10,000
Scope: Local, State, Regional, National
Description: A regional nonprofit advocacy organization committed to protecting the natural resources of the Southeast through regulatory reform and the judicial process; through partnerships with more than 100 federal, state and local organizations; and through providing regional leadership on key Southeastern environmental issues. SELC works in Alabama, Georgia, North Carolina, South Carolina, Tennessee and Virignia.
Publication(s): Beyond Asphalt, Power That Pollutes, Where Are We Growing?, Smart Growth in the Southeast, Southern Resources, Phil Reed Writing Award, A Better Transportation Future for Virginia, Land Use and Transportation in Middle Tennessee, New Approaches to Guiding Development, Quarterly Newsletter of SELC
Keyword(s): Agriculture/Farming, Air Quality/Atmosphere, Executive/Legislative/Judicial Reform, Forests/Forestry, Oceans/Coasts/Beaches, Pollution (general), Sprawl/Urban Planning, Transportation, Water Habitats & Quality, Wildlife & Species

Contact(s):
Ciannat Howett, Deep South Office; 127 Peachtree Street, Suite 605, Atlanta, GA 30303-1800; 404-521-9900

Frederick Middleton, Executive Director; 434-977-4090

Trip Van Noppen, Carolinas Office; 200 West Franklin Street, Suite 330, Chapel Hill, NC 27516-2559; 919-967-1450

Cathryn McCue, Media Director; 434-977-4090

Deaderick Montague, Board Chairman

SOUTHERN ENVIRONMENTAL LAW CENTER
NORTH CAROLINA OFFICE
200 W. Franklin St., Suite 330
Chapel Hill, NC 27516-2559 United States
Phone: 919-967-1450   Fax: 919-929-9421
E-mail: selcnc@selcnc.org
Website: www.southernenviroment.org

Scope: Regional
Description: Environmental Law Center
Publication(s): Southern Resources

SOUTHERN NEW ENGLAND FOREST CONSORTIUM, INC. (SNEFCI)
P.O. Box 760
Chepachet, RI 02816 United States
Phone: 401-568-1610   Fax: 401-568-7874
E-mail: sneforest@efortress.com

Founded: 1985
Membership: 1–100
Scope: Regional
Description: SNEFCI promotes wise conservation practices in Southern New England. Our goals are to reduce forest fragmentation, promote stewardship of forest resources, and enhance urban and community forest resources.
Publication(s): Preferential Property Tax Treatment of Open Space Land in New England, Forest Land Conversion, Fragmentation, and Partialization, Threatened and Endangered Species Field Guide in New England, Land Conservation Development and Property Taxes in Rhode Island, Cost of Community Services in Southern New England, Your Family Lands: Legacy or Memory: Commonly Asked Questions
Keyword(s): Forests/Forestry

Contact(s):
Thomas Dupree, President; 1037 Hartford Pike, North Scituate, RI 02857; 401-647-3367; Fax: 401-647-3590; tdupree@dem.state.ri.us

Donald Smith, Vice President; 860-424-3630; Fax: 860-424-4070; don.smith@po.state.ct.us

Christopher Modisette, Executive Director; 401-568-1610; sneforest@efortress.com

Hans Bergey, Treasurer; 401-821-8746; Fax: 401-821-8746; hberg16@aol.com

SOUTHERN RHODE ISLAND STATE ASSOCIATION OF CONSERVATION DISTRICTS
60 Quaker Ln., Suite 46
Warwick, RI 02866-0114 United States
Phone: 401-822-8832   Fax: 401-828-0433
Website: www.sricd.org

Scope: State
Publication(s): Wild Plants!, Bi-Annual Newsletter, Cultivation Notes 1-16, other resources and fact sheets
Keyword(s): Land Issues, Public Lands/Greenspace, Wildlife & Species

Contact(s):
Jesse Carpenter, President, Board Member; 401-762-7346; Fahma1@aol.com

Emerson Wildes, Vice President; Whimshaw Farm, Shaw Rd., Little Compton, RI 02837; 401-635-2935

John Devany, Treasurer

Robert Swanson, Chair; 39 Shannock Hill Rd., Carolina, RI 02812; 401-364-4069

SOUTHERN UTAH WILDERNESS ALLIANCE
Headquarters, 1471 S. 1100 E.
Salt Lake City, UT 84105-2423 United States
Phone: 801-486-3161   Fax: 801-486-4233
E-mail: suwa@suwa.org
Website: www.suwa.org

Founded: 1983
Membership: 10,001–100,000
Scope: International
Description: SUWA advocates wilderness preservation for qualifying federal public lands in Utah's incomparable canyon country. Through the allied efforts of SUWA's staff, Utah activists, and concerned citizens across the United States, SUWA seeks to give its members and the general public a voice in deciding the fate of America's redrock wilderness.
Publication(s): America's Redrock Wilderness-quarterly newsletter, bulletins

Contact(s):
Larry Young, Executive Director
Greg Miner, Secretary
Mark Ristow, Treasurer
Ted Wilson, Vice Chairman
Hansjorg Wyss, Chairman

SOUTHERN UTAH WILDERNESS ALLIANCE
MOAB OFFICE
P.O.Box 968
Moab, UT 84532-0968 United States
Phone: 435-259-5440 Fax: 435-259-9151
E-mail: suwa@suwa.org
Website: www.suwa.org
Scope: State

SOUTHERN UTAH WILDERNESS ALLIANCE
ST. GEORGE OFFICE
P.O. Box 1726
Cedar City, UT 84721 United States
Phone: 801-486-3161
Scope: State

SOUTHERN UTAH WILDERNESS ALLIANCE
WASHINGTON, DC OFFICE
122 C St., NW
Suite 240
Washington, DC 20001 United States
Phone: 202-546-2215 Fax: 202-544-5197
E-mail: sean@suwa.org
Website: www.suwa.org
Scope: State
Publication(s): Redrock Wilderness (quarterly newsletter)
Contact(s):
  Keith Hammond

SOUTHFACE ENERGY INSTITUTE
SOUTHFACE ENERGY AND ENVIRONMENTAL RESOURCE CENTER
241 Pine St.
Atlanta, GA 30308 United States
Phone: 404-872-3549 Fax: 404-872-5009
E-mail: info@southface.org
Website: www.southface.org
Founded: 1978
Membership: 101–1,000
Scope: International
Description: Southface is a nonprofit organization that promotes sustainable homes, workplaces and communities through education, research, advocacy and technical assistance. 2003 is our 25th year of demonstrating responsible solutions for environmental living. Our resource center and demonstration home will be enhanced in the near future by the addition of our Southface ECO Office. Visit www.southface.org for updates.
Publication(s): The Southface Journal of Sustainable Building, A Builder's Guide to Energy Efficient Homes in Georgia, Sustainable Design, Construction & Land Development Guidelines for the Southeast
Keyword(s): Development/Developing Countries, Energy, Pollution (general), Reduce/Reuse/Recycle, Sprawl/Urban Planning, Transportation, Water Habitats & Quality
Contact(s):
  Dennis Creech, Executive Director; ext. 110; dcreech@southface.org
  Aziza Cooper, Outreach Coordinator; aziza@southface.org

SOUTHWEST CONSERVATION DISTRICT
900 Northrop Road
Suite A
Wallingford, CT 06492 United States
Phone: 203-269-7509 Fax: 203-294-9741
E-mail: swcd43@sbcglobal.net
Website: www.conservect.org
Founded: 1940
Membership: 1–100
Scope: Local
Description: Non-profit, local soil and water conservation work with towns and residents
Keyword(s): Agriculture/Farming, Development/Developing Countries, Forests/Forestry, Land Issues, Oceans/Coasts/Beaches, Pollution (general), Public Lands/Greenspace, Water Habitats & Quality, Wildlife & Species

SOUTHWEST RESEARCH AND INFORMATION CENTER
105 Standford SE
P.O Box 4524
Albuquerque, NM 87106 United States
Phone: 505-262-1862 Fax: 505-262-1864
E-mail: sricdon@earthlink.net
Website: www.sric.org
Founded: 1971
Scope: Regional, National
Description: SRIC is a nonprofit organization founded to provide timely, accurate information to the public on a broad range of issues related to the environment, human, and natural resources. SRIC's twin objectives are to promote citizen participation and environmental justice, and to protect natural resources.
Publication(s): Voices from the Earth, Workbook, The
Keyword(s): Ethics/Environmental Justice, Land Issues, Pollution (general), Public Health, Sprawl/Urban Planning
Contact(s):
  Anne Albrink, Vice President
  Lalora Charles, Secretary
  Don Hancock, Administrator
  Wilfred Rael, Treasurer

SOUTHWESTERN HERPETOLOGISTS SOCIETY
P.O. Box 7469
Van Nuys, CA 91409 United States
Phone: 818-503-2052
E-mail: SWHS@SWHS.org
Website: www.swhs.org
Founded: 1954
Membership: 101–1,000
Scope: Local, State, Regional, National, International
Description: A California non profit corporation dedicated to the education of its members and the public concerning the roles of reptiles and amphibians in the natural world, the conservation of all wildlife, in particular reptiles and amphibians, and the cooperation between amateur and professional herpetologists, the hobbyist and the academician, for the promotion of the study of lizards, snakes, turtles, tortoises, geckos, skinks, monitors, frogs, toads, and all other reptiles and amphibians.
Publication(s): Herpetology, SWHS Newsletter
Contact(s):
  Tim Haub, President
  Hanna Strauss, Vice President
  Curt Steindler, Secretary; 310-213-5420; Fax: 310-391-6599; SWHS@Lawrax.com
  John Holmes, Treasurer

SPORTSMAN NETWORK, INC., THE
501 S. Kentucky Ave.,
Corbin, KY 40701 United States
Phone: 606-528-9353 Fax: 606-528-2287
E-mail: sportsman@sportsmansnetwork.org
Website: www.sportsmansnetwork.org
Founded: 1991
Membership: 1,000,001 +
Scope: Regional
Description: An incorporated 501(c)(3) nonprofit organization, the Sportsman's Network, Inc., is dedicated to raising the public awareness of wildlife conservation issues through programs which promote controlled hunting, fishing, trapping and other

related activities. It produces the "Moment in Conservation" radio program and operates and maintains a wildlife refuge and wildlife animal rehabilitation center and conducts research for restoration of endangered wildlife.
Keyword(s): Wildlife & Species
Contact(s):
Peter Samples, State Chairman; 7905 Highway 22 W, Falmouth, KY 41040; 859-824-6526; Fax: 859-824-0556; pos1944@hotmail.com
Elmer Chavies, Jr., Executive Director; 606-528-9353; Fax: 606-528-2287; sportsman@sportsmansnetwork.org
Paul Cookendorfer, 1st Vice President
Kenneth Hale, Treasurer
Dean Russell, Secretary
Stacy Suter, 2nd Vice President

SPORTSMANS ALLIANCE OF MAINE
205 Church Hill Rd.
Augusta, ME 04330-9749 United States
Phone: 207-622-5503   Fax: 207-622-5596
E-mail: members@samcef.org
Website: www.samcef.org
Founded: 1975
Membership: 10,001–100,000
Scope: State
Description: SAM is a statewide nonprofit organization of sportsmen and women dedicated to hunting, fishing, trapping, protection of wildlife habitat, and conservation. Lobbies and works with state agencies on behalf of Maine sportsmen.
Publication(s): SAM News
Contact(s):
Edye Cronk, President
Alfred Ockentels, Vice President
James Hilly, Treasurer
George Smith, Executive Director and Editor
Kelly Cochara, Office Staff; members@samcef.org
Herbert Morse, Secretary and Clerk

SPORTSMEN'S NATIONAL LAND TRUST, THE
NATIONAL HEADQUARTERS
4311 Manatee Avenue West
Suite 210
Bradenton, FL 34209 United States
Phone: 941-708-3456   Fax: 941-708-3535
E-mail: Blamee@thegreatoutdoors.org
Website: www.Sportslandtrust.org
Founded: 1998
Membership: 101–1,000
Scope: National
Description: Dedicated to accumulating land for sportsmen to be owned and managed in perpetuity for wildlife habitat, for public access and for responsible use by anglers and hunters.
Keyword(s): Land Issues, Public Lands/Greenspace, Recreation/Ecotourism, Sprawl/Urban Planning, Wildlife & Species
Contact(s):
Bill LaMee, President; 941-708-3456; Fax: 941-708-3535; BillLaMee@TheSportsmens.org
Terry Steele, Vice President - National Programs Director; 14 Boxelder Court, Homosassa, FL 34446; 941-708-3456; Fax: 941-708-3535; bigt2@mindspring.com

ST. CROIX INTERNATIONAL WATERWAY COMMISSION
P. O. Box 610
Calais, ME 04619 United States
Phone: 506-466-7550   Fax: 506-466-7551
E-mail: staff@stcroix.org
Founded: 1989
Membership: 1–100
Scope: International
Description: A commission of the State of Maine and Province of New Brunswick that assists to implement a cooperative, inter-disciplinary management plan for the St. Croix River corridor, which forms 110 miles of the US/Canada border.
Publication(s): St. Croix Heritage Brochure, Annual Report, Management Plan for the St. Croix International Waterway
Keyword(s): Forests/Forestry, Land Issues, Oceans/Coasts/Beaches, Pollution (general), Public Lands/Greenspace, Recreation/Ecotourism, Transportation, Water Habitats & Quality, Wildlife & Species
Contact(s):
Lee Sochasky, Executive Director
Ken Gordon, Co-Chairman
Tom Moffatt, Co-Chairman

ST. FRANCIS WILDLIFE ASSOCIATION
P.O. Box 38160
Tallahassee, FL 32315 United States
Phone: 850-386-6296
E-mail: ellen@stfranciswildlife.org
Website: www.stfranciswildlife.org
Founded: 1978
Membership: 1,001–10,000
Scope: Regional
Description: Providing humane wildlife care, rehabilitation, and environmental education to promote responsible relationships with our natural wildlife resources.
Keyword(s): Wildlife & Species
Contact(s):
Ellen Eichorn, Development Director; 850-893-7577; Fax: 850-893-7135; ellen@stfranciswildlife.org
Jon Johnson, Executive Director; 850-386-6296; jon@stfranciswildlife.org

ST. REGIS MOHAWK TRIBE
Environment Division 412 State Rt. 37
Akwesasne, NY 13655 United States
Phone: 518-358-5937   Fax: 518-358-6252
E-mail: jim_snyder@srmtenv.org
Website: www.srmtenv.org
Membership: 1–100
Scope: Local, State, Regional, National
Description: To monitor, maintain, and protect the environment of the St. Regis Mohawk Tribe for the prevention of disease and injury to body, mind, and spirit. Participation in hazardous waste remediation, Superfund site cleanups, reservation environmental protection, and air and water quality.
Publication(s): Iroquois Environmental Newsletter
Contact(s):
Ken Jock, Director of Environment Division; ext. 16
Les Benedict, Assistant Director of Environment Division; ext. 18; earth-lbenedic@northnet.org

STANFORD ENVIRONMENTAL LAW SOCIETY
Stanford Law School-559 Nathan Abbott Way
Stanford, CA 94305-8610 United States
Phone: 650-723-4421   Fax: 650-723-0501
Website: www.els.stanford.edu
Founded: 1969
Scope: Local
Description: The Stanford Environmental Law Society is the oldest student organization of its kind in the United States. Its primary function is sponsorship of original research in developing areas of environmental law. The Society relies on contributions, grants, and proceeds from the sale of publications.
Publication(s): Stanford Environmental Law Journal, Who Runs the Rivers', Hazardous Waste Disposal Sites, Endangered Species Act, Handbook, Strategies for Environmental Law Enforcement

Contact(s):
  Janelle Smith, Co-President
  Katherine Wannamaker, Co-President
  Louise Warren, Business Manager

STATE AND TERRITORIAL AIR POLLUTION PROGRAM ADMINISTRATORS AND THE ASSOCIATION OF LOCAL AIR POLLUTION CONTROL OFFICIALS
STAPPA/ALAPCO
444 N. Capitol St., NW, Suite 307
Washington, DC 20001 United States
Phone: 202-624-7864   Fax: 202-624-7863
E-mail: 4clnair@4cleanairworld.org
Website: www.cleanairworld.org

Founded: 1980
Membership: 101–1,000
Scope: National
Description: The national associations of air pollution control agencies in the states, territories, and major metropolitan areas. The associations' members have primary responsibility for ensuring healthy air quality and represent the technical expertise behind the implementation of our nation's air pollution control laws and regulations.
Publication(s): Meeting the 15% Rate of Progress Requirement Under The Clean Air Act: A Menu of Options (1993), Controlling Particulate Matter Under The Clean Air Act: A Menu of Options (1995), Controlling Nitrogen Oxides Under The Clean Air Act: A Menu of Options (1994)
Keyword(s): Air Quality/Atmosphere, Climate Change, Pollution (general)
Contact(s):
  S. Becker, Executive Director; 202-624-7864; Fax: 202-624-7863; bbecker@sso.org

STATE ENVIRONMENTAL RESOURCE CENTER (SERC)
106 East Doty Street, #200
Madison, WI 53703 United States
Phone: 608-252-9800
E-mail: info@serconline.org
Website: www.serconline.org

Membership: 1–100
Scope: State
Description: The State Environmental Resource Center is working state by state to promote positive state legislation, while combating the harmful legislation currently so prevalent at the state level. Working directly with a nationwide network of pro-environmental state legislators, SERC is the first — and only — project of its kind.
Keyword(s): Agriculture/Farming, Air Quality/Atmosphere, Ecosystems (precious), Energy, Ethics/Environmental Justice, Forests/Forestry, Land Issues, Pollution (general), Public Health, Public Lands/Greenspace, Reduce/Reuse/Recycle, Sprawl/Urban Planning, Transportation

STATEWIDE PROGRAM OF ACTION TO CONSERVE OUR ENVIRONMENT (SPACE)
N.H. Current Use Coalition, 54 Portsmouth St.
Concord, NH 03301 United States
Phone: 603-224-3306   Fax: 603-228-0423
E-mail: space@conknet.com
Website: www.nhspace.org

Founded: 1966
Scope: State
Description: A private, not-for-profit advocacy coalition of groups dedicated to conserving open space land. S.P.A.C.E.'s work includes advocacy, education, supporting research and working with the state, towns, and individuals on the administration and monitoring of the current use program.
Publication(s): SPACE Newsletter
Keyword(s): Land Issues

STEAMBOATERS, THE
P.O. Box 176
Idleyld Park, OR 97447 United States
Website: www.steamboaters.org

Founded: 1966
Membership: 101–1,000
Scope: National
Description: Formed to preserve, promote, and restore the natural production of wild fish populations, the habitat which sustains them, and the unique aesthetic values of the North Umpqua River for present and future generations.
Keyword(s): Wildlife & Species
Contact(s):
  Jim Watson, President; 541-496-3512; samnjim@rosenet.net
  Len Janssen, Vice President; 541-440-9375
  Paul Moore, Treasurer
  Charlie Spooner, Secretary

STOP
230-651 Notre Dame West
Montreal, H3C 1H9 Quebec Canada
Phone: 514-393-9559   Fax: 514-393-9588

Founded: 1970
Scope: State
Description: Devoted to preserving and improving the quality of the physical and human environment, and to promoting rational utilization of natural resources.
Publication(s): Stop Press
Keyword(s): Air Quality/Atmosphere, Oceans/Coasts/Beaches, Pollution (general), Reduce/Reuse/Recycle, Transportation

STROUD WATER RESEARCH CENTER
970 Spencer Rd.
Avondale, PA 19311 United States
Phone: 610-268-2153   Fax: 610-268-0490
E-mail: webmaster@stroudcenter.org
Website: www.stroudcenter.org

Founded: 1967
Membership: 101–1,000
Scope: International
Description: The mission of the Stroud Center is to advance the knowledge of river and stream ecosystems through research and education.
Publication(s): Upstream (newsletter)
Keyword(s): Climate Change, Ecosystems (precious), Land Issues, Water Habitats & Quality, Wildlife & Species
Contact(s):
  Claire Birney, Development Director; clairebirney@stroudcenter.org
  James Mcgonigle, Education Director; jmcgonigle@stroudcenter.org
  Bernard Sweeney, Director; sweeney@stroudcenter.org

STUDENT CONSERVATION ASSOCIATION, INC.
689 River Rd.
Charlestown, NH 03603 United States
Phone: 603-543-1700   Fax: 603-543-1828
Website: www.theSCA.org

Founded: 1957
Scope: National
Description: SCA's mission is "To build the next generation of conservation leaders and inspire lifelong stewardship of our environment and communities by engaging young people in hands-on service to the land."
Keyword(s): Ecosystems (precious), Forests/Forestry, Land Issues, Oceans/Coasts/Beaches, Pollution (general), Public Lands/Greenspace, Recreation/Ecotourism, Reduce/Reuse/Recycle, Water Habitats & Quality, Wildlife & Species

Contact(s):
  Dale Penny, President
  Elizabeth Titus, Founding President
  Robert Holley, Vice President of Development
  Scott Weaver, Vice President of Programs
  Edmund Bartlett, Chair of the Board
  Mark Bodin, Chief Financial Officer
  Kevin Hamilton, Communications

STUDENT CONSERVATION ASSOCIATION, INC.
CALIFORNIA SOUTHWEST REGIONAL OFFICE
655 13th St., Suite 100
Oakland, CA 94612 United States
Phone: 510-832-1966   Fax: 510-832-4726
E-mail: arobinson@thesca.org
Website: www.thescaa.org

Scope: Regional, National

Publication(s): The Volunteer - newsletter

Contact(s):
  Bob Coates, Regional Vice President
  Rick Covington, Director of Regional Programs; ext. 306; rick@sca-inc.org

STUDENT CONSERVATION ASSOCIATION, INC.
NORTHWEST OFFICE
1265 S. Main St., Suite 210
Seattle, WA 98144 United States
Phone: 206-324-4649   Fax: 206-324-4998
E-mail: swermus@thesca.org
Website: www.thesca.org

Founded: 1957

Scope: Regional, National, International

Description: SCA's mission statement: To build the next generation of conservation leaders and inspire lifelong stewardship of our environment and communities by engaging young people in hands-on service to the land.

Publication(s): The Volunteer - quarterly newletters

Contact(s):
  Jay Satz, Vice President, National Field Operations NW Regional Officer; ext. 11

STUDENT CONSERVATION ASSOCIATION, INC.
OFFICE OF THE NATIONAL CAPITAL REGION
MID-ATLANTIC/SOUTHEAST REGIONAL OFFICE
1800 N. Kent St.
Suite 102
Arlington, VA 22209 United States
Phone: 703-524-2441   Fax: 703-524-2451
E-mail: info@sca-inc.org
Website: www.thesca.org

Scope: Local, Regional, National

Description: Our mission is to help build the next generation of conservation leaders in the 16 state Mid-Atlantic/ Southeast region which includes Alabama, Arkansas, Delaware, DC, Florida, Georgia, Kentucky, Louisiana, Maryland, Mississippi, North Carolina, Oklahoma, South Carolina, Tennessee, Texas and Virginia.

Contact(s):
  R. Flip Hagood, Vice President; 703-524-2441; ext. 18; Fax: 703-524-2451; flip@sca-inc.org
  Karen Blaney, Director of College Program; 703-524-2441; ext. 22; Fax: 703-524-2451; karen@sca-inc.org
  Gary King, Director of Regional Programs; 703-524-2441; ext. 12; Fax: 703-524-2451; gary@sca-inc.org
  Nadine Morrison, Administrative Coordinator; 703-524-2441; ext. 10; Fax: 703-524-2451; nadine@sca-inc.org
  Nancy Oswald, Regional Program Manager; 703-524-2441; ext. 13; Fax: 703-524-2451; nancyo@sca-inc.org
  Leib Kaminsky, Regional Development Officer; 703-524-2441; ext. 19; Fax: 703-524-2451; leib@sca-inc.org

STUDENT ENVIRONMENTAL ACTION COALITION (SEAC)
P.O. Box 31909
Philadelphia, PA 19104-0609 United States
Phone: 215-222-4711   Fax: 215-222-4788
E-mail: seac@seac.org
Website: www.seac.org

Founded: 1988

Membership: 101–1,000

Scope: Local, State, Regional, National, International

Description: SEAC is a student and youth-run national network of progressive organizations and individuals whose aim is to uproot environmental injustices through action and education. We define the environment to include the physical, economic, political, and cultural conditions in which we live. By challenging the power structure which threatens these environmental conditions, SEAC works to create progressive social change on both the local and global levels.

Publication(s): Resource Materials, Student Environmental Organizing Guide, Threshold, Internships

Keyword(s): Climate Change, Energy, Ethics/Environmental Justice, Forests/Forestry, Pollution (general), Public Health

Contact(s):
  Jason Fults, National Council Coordinator; 215-222-4711; ncc@seac.org

STUDENT PUGWASH USA
2029 P St. NW
Suite 301
Washington, DC 20036 United States
Phone: 202-429-8900   Fax: 202-429-8905
E-mail: spusa@spusa.org
Website: www.spusa.org

Scope: National

Description: The mission of Student Pugwash USA is to promote the socially-responsible application of science and technology in the 21st century. As a student organization, Student Pugwash USA encourages young people to examine the ethical, social, and global implications of science and technology, and to make these concerns a guiding focus of their academic and professional endeavors.

Publication(s): Jobs You Can Live With: Working at the Crossroads of Science, Technology, and Society, Mindfull: A Brainsnack for Future Leaders with Ethical Appetites, Pugwatch

Keyword(s): Energy, Public Health

Contact(s):
  Susan Veres, Executive Director
  Eric Roberts, Executive Committee Chairman

STUDENTS PARTNERSHIP WORLDWIDE
Lazimpat, Near Hotel Radisson, P.O. Box 4892
Kathmandu, Nepal
Phone: 9771435107   Fax: 9771434645
E-mail: spwnepal@mos.com.np
Website: www.spw.org

Founded: 1986

Membership: 1,001–10,000

Scope: International

Description: Youth focus development programme, working in the field of formal and non-formal education and environmental education in rural government, school of Nepal, and form Green Club school student group to conserve environment in their own surroundings.

Keyword(s): Development/Developing Countries, Ecosystems (precious), Ethics/Environmental Justice, Forests/Forestry, Oceans/Coasts/Beaches, Reduce/Reuse/Recycle, Sprawl/Urban Planning

Contact(s):
  Bishnu Bhalta, Extension Coordinator
  Gaurab Rene, Administrative Coordinator

STURGEON FOR TOMORROW
MICHIGAN CHAPTER
1604 N. Black River Road
Cheboygan, MI 49721 United States
Phone: 231-625-2776   Fax: 231-625-2775
E-mail: brenda@sturgeonfortomorrow.org
Website: sturgeonfortomorrow.org

Founded: 1999
Membership: 101–1,000
Scope: Local, State, Regional, National, International
Description: Lake sturgeon conservation, public relations/education, research and funding
Keyword(s): Ecosystems (precious), Recreation/Ecotourism, Water Habitats & Quality, Wildlife & Species

SUDBURY VALLEY TRUSTEES
Two Clock Tower Place
Maynard, MA 01754 United States
Phone: 978-897-5500   Fax: 978-461-0322
E-mail: svt@sudburyvalleytrustees.org
Website: www.sudburyvalleytrustees.org

Founded: 1953
Scope: Local, Regional
Description: Sudbury Valley Trustees was founded in 1953, committed to protecting wildlife habitat and the ecological integrity of the Sudbury, Assabet and Concord Rivers for the benefit of present and future generations. SVT carries out its mission through land acquisition and stewardship, advocacy and education.

SUNCOAST SEABIRD SANCTUARY INC.
18328 Gulf Blvd.
Indian Shores, FL 33785 United States
Phone: 727-391-6211   Fax: 727-399-2923
E-mail: seabird@seabirdsanctuary.org
Website: www.seabirdsanctuary.org

Founded: 1972
Membership: 10,001–100,000
Scope: Local, State, Regional, National, International
Description: A private, nonprofit, membership organization dedicated to the rescue, repair, rehabilitation, and release of healed sick and injured wild birds. Considered the largest wild bird center in the United States, the Sanctuary treats over 10,500 birds each year. It provides a safe home for over 600 permanently injured avian species and sends others to wildlife zoos and parks worldwide. The Sanctuary is open FREE for visitation daily from 9:00 a.m. till dusk. Guided tours available - free admission.
Publication(s): If You Find A Baby Bird Book, Suncoast Seabird Sanctuary Newsletter, Help for Hooked Birds Flyer, S.S.S. Brochure (Blue)
Keyword(s): Oceans/Coasts/Beaches, Wildlife & Species
Contact(s):
  Ralph Heath Jr., Founder and Director; 18323 Sunset Blvd., Redington Shores, FL 33708; 727-391-6211; Fax: 727-399-2923; seabird@seabirdsanctuary.org
  Suzanne Sakal, Marketing/PR Director; 18328 Gulf Blvd., Indian Shores, FL 33785; 727-392-4291; Fax: 727-399-2923; Suzanne@webcoast.com
  Barbara Suto, Hospital Supervisor; 18328 Gulf Blvd., Indian Shores, FL 33785; 727-391-6211; Fax: 727-399-2923; seabird@ij.net

SUSTAIN
ENVIRONMENTAL INFORMATION GROUP, THE
920 N. Franklin St. #301
Chicago, IL 60610 United States
Phone: 312-951-8999, ext. 101   Fax: 312-951-5696
E-mail: info@sustainusa.org
Website: www.sustainusa.org

Founded: 1996
Scope: Local, State, Regional, National, International
Description: Sustain is a full-service non-profit advertising and public relations agency which partners with regional and national organizations to promote a healthy, sustainable environment. Sustain has played a key role in many national and regional environmental victories. The leading graphic arts publication in the country, Communication Arts, recently raved, "In an eye catching, direct style with an emotional appeal, Sustain aims to make people see things in a way that they might not have before."
Publication(s): The Power of Images
Keyword(s): Agriculture/Farming, Air Quality/Atmosphere, Climate Change, Ecosystems (precious), Energy, Ethics/Environmental Justice, Executive/Legislative/Judicial Reform, Finance/Banking/Trade, Forests/Forestry, Land Issues, Oceans/Coasts/Beaches, Pollution (general)
Contact(s):
  John Beske, Creative Director; 312-951-8999; ext. 103; Fax: 312-951-5696; john@sustainusa.org
  Jim Slama, Executive Director; 312-951-8999; ext. 107; Fax: 312-951-5696; jim@sustainusa.org
  Ilsa Flanagan, Associate Director; 312-951-8999; ext. 105; Fax: 312-951-5696; ilsa@sustainusa.org
  James Bell, Program Director; 312-951-8999; ext. 101; Fax: 312-951-5696; jamesbell@sustainusa.org

SUSTAINABLE ENERGY INSTITUTE
CULTURE CHANGE MAGAZINE
P.O. Box 4347
Arcata, CA 95518 United States
Phone: 707-826-7775   Fax: 603-825-2696
E-mail: info@culturechange.org
Website: www.culturechange.org

Founded: 1988
Membership: 1,001–10,000
Scope: Local, State, Regional, National, International
Description: We assist people in defining sustainability, mainly through discussing petroleum dependence and solutions such as human-powered transport and local economics. As reforms and regulations have only fed the status quo, we promote cultural change to deal with the ecological crisis.
Publication(s): Sail Transport Network
Keyword(s): Agriculture/Farming, Air Quality/Atmosphere, Climate Change, Energy, Oceans/Coasts/Beaches, Population, Sprawl/Urban Planning, Transportation
Contact(s):
  Raul Riutor, South American Correspondent

SUSTAINABLE ENERGY INSTITUTE
CULTURE CHANGE
FOOD NOT LAWNS
PEDAL POWER PRODUCE
P.O. Box 4347
Arcata, CA 95518-4347 United States
Phone: 707-826-2565
E-mail: info@culturechange.org
Website: www.culturechange.org

Founded: 1988
Membership: 1,001–10,000
Scope: Local, State, Regional, National, International
Description: SEI is an action-advocacy group grounded in petroleum market expertise. Reducing massively today's oil use is our purpose. A radical critique that shatters illusions and offers solutions to war for oil and accommodating overpopulation is reflected in our e-Letter and programs. We monitor the peak of global oil production, but also understand the immediacy of market response and the world's vulnerability to the collapse of petroleum civilization. SEI founded Alliance for a Paving Moratorium.
Publication(s): Food Not Lawns, Culture Change

Keyword(s): Agriculture/Farming, Air Quality/Atmosphere, Climate Change, Development/Developing Countries, Energy, Finance/Banking/Trade, Land Issues, Population, Reduce/Reuse/Recycle, Transportation, Water Habitats & Quality

Contact(s):
Jan Lundberg, Board of Directors President
Eve Gilmore, Vice President, Board Member and Secretary
Michael Kunz, Development Director
Pincas Jawetz, Board Member
Debbie Lukas, Board of Directors Member
Lonnie Maxfield, Board of Directors Member
Richard Register, Board of Directors Member

T

TALL TIMBERS RESEARCH STATION (TTRS)
13093 Henry Beadel Dr.
Tallahassee, FL 32312-9712 United States
Phone: 850-893-4153, ext. 258   Fax: 850-668-7781
Website: www.talltimbers.org

Founded: 1958
Membership: 101–1,000
Scope: International
Description: A nonprofit, tax-exempt scientific and educational organization with a focus on land management, conservation, ecological research, and fire ecology. Information is exchanged in print and on the Internet. Tall Timbers provides publications, seminars, conferences and training programs for land owners and managers, scholars, research scientists, students and concerned citizens.
Publication(s): Newsletters, annual reports, proceedings, technical reports, and informational bulletins.
Keyword(s): Ecosystems (precious), Forests/Forestry, Land Issues, Sprawl/Urban Planning, Wildlife & Species

Contact(s):
Lane Green, Executive Director; 850-893-4153; ext. 239; Fax: 850-893-6470; lane@ttrs.org
Ronald Masters, Research Director; 850-893-4153; ext. 229; Fax: 850-668-7781; rmasters@ttrs.org
Kevin McGorty, Director, Red Hills Conservation Program; 850-893-4153; ext. 238; Fax: 850-893-7954; kmcgorty@ttrs.org
Tom Barron, Treasurer
Ann Bruce, Librarian, Tall Timbers Library, ; 850-893-4153; ext. 234; Fax: 850-668-7781; brucea@ttrs.org
Kate Ireland, Chairman
Walter Sedgwick, Vice Chairperson

TALLAHASSEE MUSEUM OF HISTORY AND NATURAL SCIENCE
3945 Museum Dr.
Tallahassee, FL 32310 United States
Phone: 850-575-8684   Fax: 850-574-8243
Website: www.tallahasseemuseum.org

Founded: 1957
Membership: 1,001–10,000
Scope: Local, State, Regional
Description: To educate residents of and visitors to Tallahassee and the Big Bend area about the region's natural and cultural history, from the beginning of the 19th-century until the present. for this purpose, the museum collects, preserves, and exhibits artifacts and historic buildings, maintains native animals in natural habitats, and operates a 19th century farmstead.
Publication(s): The Newsletter of The Tallahassee Museum of History and Natural Science
Keyword(s): Recreation/Ecotourism, Wildlife & Species

Contact(s):
Russell Daws, Executive Director/CEO; daws@tallhasseemuseum.org
Jennifer Golden, Director of Education
Paula Moyer, Director of Institutional Advancement
Linda Deaton, Curator of Collections and Exhibits
Mike Jones, Curator of Animals

TEENS FOR RECREATION AND ENVIRONMENTAL CONSERVATION (TREC)
100 Dexter Ave. North
Seattle, WA 98109 United States
Phone: 206-684-7097   Fax: 206-684-7025
Website: www.seattletrec.org

Founded: 1992
Scope: State
Description: TREC is an outdoor expedition-level program designed to expose multi-ethnic teens to environmental education, urban conservation, and stewardship, while creating an environment for community leadership and empowerment.

Contact(s):
Robert Warner, Contact; 360-705-1903; robert.warner@ci.seattle.wa.us

TENNESSEE BASS FEDERATION
P.O. Box 68
Cedar Grove, TN 38321 United States
Phone: 731-987-3061
E-mail: tnxpress@bellsouth.net
Website: www.tnbass.com

Founded: 1973
Membership: 100,001–500,000
Scope: State
Description: An organization of Bassmaster chapters, affiliated with the Bass Anglers Sportsman Society, organized to fight pollution, assist state and national conservation agencies in their efforts, and teach the young people of our country good conservation practices. Dedicated to the realistic conservation of our water resources.
Publication(s): Chapter Newsletter
Keyword(s): Water Habitats & Quality, Wildlife & Species

Contact(s):
Charles Mitchell, President; 931-296-4428
Chuck Harger, Conservation Director; 731 Oakland Dr., New Johnsonville, TN 37134; 931-535-2209

TENNESSEE CITIZENS FOR WILDERNESS PLANNING
130 Tabor Rd.
Oak Ridge, TN 37830 United States
Phone: 865-481-0286
E-mail: tcwp@korrnet.org
Website: www.korrnet.org/tcwp/

Founded: 1966
Membership: 101–1,000
Scope: Local, State, Regional, National
Description: Dedicated to achieving and perpetuating protection of natural lands and waters by means of public ownership, legislation, or cooperation with the private sector. Our first focus is the Cumberland and Appalachian regions of East Tennessee, but efforts may extend to the rest of the state and the nation.
Publication(s): TCWP Newsletter
Keyword(s): Forests/Forestry, Land Issues, Public Lands/Greenspace, Water Habitats & Quality, Wildlife & Species

Contact(s):
Jimmy Groton, President; 87 Outer Dr., Oak Ridge, TN 37830; 423-482-5799
Eric Hirst, Vice President; 106 Capital Cir., Oak Ridge, TN 37830; 423-483-1289
Mary Lynn Dobson, Secretary; 209 Cove Point Road, Rockwood, TN 37854; 423-354-4924

TENNESSEE CONSERVATION LEAGUE

300 Orlando Ave.
Nashville, TN 37209-3257 United States
Phone: 615-353-1133　　Fax: 615-353-0083
E-mail: tcl@conservetn.com
Website: www.conservetn.com

Founded: 1946
Membership: 1,001–10,000
Scope: State

Description: A representative statewide organization, affiliated with the National Wildlife Federation, dedicated to the protection and enhancement of wildlife and its habitat through public education and government interaction.

Publication(s): Tennessee Out-of-Doors

Contact(s):
Monty Halcomb, President
Phil Craig, Vice-President
Marty Marina, Executive Director, Alternate Representative
Rick Murphree, Treasurer
Bruce Newport, Director of Development and Communications

TENNESSEE ENVIRONMENTAL COUNCIL

One Vantage Way, Suite D-105
Nashville, TN 37228 United States
Phone: 615-248-6500　　Fax: 615-248-6545
E-mail: tec@tectn.org
Website: www.tectn.org/tectnhome.html

Founded: 1970
Membership: 1,001–10,000
Scope: State

Description: A nonprofit coalition working to protect and improve Tennessee's public health, quality of life, and natural heritage. TEC is a 28-year-old organization, focused on carrying out the state's environmental policies and regulations on behalf of Tennessee citizens.

Publication(s): ProTECt

Keyword(s): Air Quality/Atmosphere, Development/Developing Countries, Ethics/Environmental Justice, Forests/Forestry, Pollution (general), Public Health, Reduce/Reuse/Recycle

Contact(s):
Robert Diehl, President
Will Callaway, Executive Director; will@tectn.org
Renee Zaremba, Office Director; 615-248-6500; ext. 100
Gwen Griffith, Program Director; 615-248-6500; ext. 101

TENNESSEE FORESTRY ASSOCIATION

P.O. Box 290693
Nashville, TN 37229 United States
Phone: 615-883-3832　　Fax: 615-883-0515
E-mail: info@tnforestry.com
Website: www.tnforestry.com

Founded: 1950
Membership: 1,001–10,000
Scope: State, National, International

Description: TFA is a nonprofit trade association representing over 2,000 woodland owners, public and private foresters, educators, and wood using industries, as well as individual citizens and allied businesses. TFA encourages sustainable forestland management and wise use of Tennessee's forest resources.

Publication(s): Treeline Newsletter, TN Sustainable Forestry Initiative

Keyword(s): Executive/Legislative/Judicial Reform, Forests/Forestry, Land Issues, Pollution (general), Population, Public Lands/Greenspace, Recreation/Ecotourism, Sprawl/Urban Planning, Transportation, Water Habitats & Quality, Wildlife & Species

Contact(s):
Candace Dinwiddie, Executive Director; 615-883-3832; Fax: 615-883-0515; cdinwiddie@tnforestry.com
Tracy O'Neill, Communications & Government Affairs; 615-883-3832; Fax: 615-883-0515; toneill@tnforestry.com

TERRA NATURE FUND

TERRANATURE TRUST
1644 Clay Street
Suite 1
San Francisco, CA 94109 United States
Phone: 415-474-7241　　Fax: 415-409-1610
E-mail: woodhouse@terranature.org
Website: terranature.org

Founded: 2000
Membership: 1–100
Scope: International

Description: Terra Nature Fund is a California nonprofit corporation working with its affiliated New Zealand charitable trust, TerraNature Trust, to conserve open space for the public benefit through land acquisition, restore native habitat, protect endangered indigenous fauna, and help prevent the loss of New Zealand's unique biodiversity. The group promotes the international importance of New Zealand's "edge ecology" that evolved during 80 million years of isolation from the rest of the world.

Keyword(s): Ecosystems (precious), Forests/Forestry, Land Issues, Oceans/Coasts/Beaches, Public Lands/Greenspace, Wildlife & Species

Contact(s):
Graeme Woodhouse, Chairman/President; 415-474-7241; Fax: 415-409-1610; woodhouse@terranature.org

TERRA PENINSULAR

Belgrado 101
Colonia Ampliación Moderna
Ensenada, 22879 Mexico
Phone: 52-646-174-5397　　Fax: 52-646-174-5397
E-mail: info@terrapeninsular.org
Website: www.terrapeninsular.org

Founded: 2000
Scope: Regional

Description: Terra Peninsular is a land conservation organization dedicated to protecting the landscapes of the Baja California peninsula.

Keyword(s): Development/Developing Countries, Land Issues, Public Lands/Greenspace, Recreation/Ecotourism, Sprawl/Urban Planning

Contact(s):
Alberto Carreto, General Director; 52-646-174-5397; Fax: 52-646-174-5397; albertocarreto@hotmail.com
Rosi Bustamante, Institutional Development Director; 3560 24th Street #5, San Francisco, CA 94110; 415-821-2495; Fax: 415-821-2495; rosibustamante@yahoo.com
Oscar Rivera, Community Coordinator; 52-646-174-5397; Fax: 52-646-174-5397

TEXAS ASSOCIATION OF SOIL AND WATER CONSERVATION DISTRICTS

Attn: President P.O. Box 658
Temple, TX 76503 United States
Phone: 254-778-8741　　Fax: 254-773-3311

Scope: State

Publication(s): Big Bend Paisano, The, Big Bend seminars and sales catalog available on request, Official Park Newspaper

Contact(s):
Jose Dodier, President; P.O. Box 13, Zapata, TX 78076; 956-936-2007
Aubrey Russell, Vice President
Dayton Elam, Secretary-Treasurer; 600 SW 21st St., Seminole, TX 79360; 915-758-3504
Beatrice White, Secretary; P.O. Box 658, Temple, TX 76503; 254-778-8741; Fax: 254-773-3311

TEXAS BASS FEDERATION
Attn: President, 2221 Apache Dr.
Harker Heights, TX 76548 United States
Phone: 254-698-2015
Website: www.texas-bass.com
Scope: State
Description: An organization of Bassmaster chapters, affiliated with the Bass Anglers Sportsman Society, organized to fight pollution, assist state and national conservation agencies in their efforts, and teach the young people of our country good conservation practices. Dedicated to the realistic conservation of our water resources.
Publication(s): SCOT Sportsmen Conservation of Texas, Texas Tightline Magazine
Keyword(s): Forests/Forestry, Land Issues, Water Habitats & Quality
Contact(s):
Stacy Twiggs, President
Alan Allen, Conservation Director; 807 Brazos, Suite 311, Austin, TX 78701; 512-472-2267; AlanAllen-SCOT@att.net

TEXAS COMMITTEE ON NATURAL RESOURCES
3532 Bee Caves Road, Suite 110
Austin, TX 78746 United States
Phone: 512 441 1122   Fax: 512-857-0594
E-mail: tconr@texas.net
Website: tconr.org
Founded: 1968
Membership: 1,001–10,000
Scope: State, National
Description: A representative statewide organization, affiliated with the National Wildlife Federation, dedicated to the protection and enhancement of wildlife and its habitat through public education and government interaction.
Publication(s): Conservation Progress
Keyword(s): Ecosystems (precious), Forests/Forestry, Oceans/Coasts/Beaches, Pollution (general), Public Lands/Greenspace, Reduce/Reuse/Recycle, Water Habitats & Quality, Wildlife & Species
Contact(s):
David Gray, Chair/President; 214-342-2019; Dgraytconr@aol.com
Richard Donovan, Vice Chair; 936-637-1228; ddonovan@lcc.net
Susan Petersen, NWF Representative; 512-451-9672; scpetersen@earthlink.net
Janice Bezanson, Executive Director, Alternate Representative, 3532 Bee Caves Road, Suite 110, Austin, TX 78746; 512-327-4119; Fax: 512-857-0594; bezanson@texas.net

TEXAS DISCOVERY GARDENS
LIVE BUTTERFLY EXHIBIT
CERTIFIED BUTTERFLY HABITAT
TEXAS NATIVE PLANT COLLECTION
P.O. Box 152537
Dallas, TX 75315 United States
Phone: 214-428-7476   Fax: 214-428-5338
E-mail: tdg@texasdiscoverygardens.org
Website: www.texasdiscoverygardens.org
Founded: 1936
Membership: 101–1,000
Scope: Local, State, Regional
Description: Year-round urban oasis and showcase garden of native and adapted plants. Exhibits on butterflies, bugs and botany in the historic Art Deco main building. Committed to teaching people effective ways to conserve, restore and preserve the urban environment using native and adapted plants.
Keyword(s): Ecosystems (precious), Public Lands/Greenspace, Recreation/Ecotourism, Reduce/Reuse/Recycle, Sprawl/Urban Planning, Water Habitats & Quality, Wildlife & Species

TEXAS ORGANIZATION FOR ENDANGERED SPECIES
P.O. Box 12773
Austin, TX 78711-2773 United States
Website: www.rice.edu
Founded: 1972
Membership: 101–1,000
Scope: State
Description: A nonprofit statewide organization dedicated to the conservation of endangered, threatened, or rare species and biotic communities of Texas.
Publication(s): TOES News & Notes
Keyword(s): Development/Developing Countries, Recreation/Ecotourism
Contact(s):
Gary Valentine, President; 254-297-1291
Deborah Holle, Secretary; 512-482-5700
Peggy Homer, Chair of Natural Resources; 512-912-7047
David Lemke, Editor; 512-245-2178
Lee Ann Linam, Past-President; 512-847-9480
Bob Murphy, Education Chairman
C. Sherrod, Treasurer; 512 328 2430
Jason Singhurst, Chair of Conservation Committee; 512-912-7011

TEXAS RIPARIAN ASSOCIATION
2210 South FM 973
Austin, TX 78725 United States
Phone: 512-972-1960   Fax: 512-972-1900
E-mail: kevin.anderson@ci.austin.tx.us
Founded: 2002
Membership: 101–1,000
Scope: State
Description: The Texas Riparian Association is an effort to encourage healthy riparian systems in Texas and to educate Texans about their ecological and economic importance.
Keyword(s): Agriculture/Farming, Ecosystems (precious), Forests/Forestry, Land Issues, Public Lands/Greenspace, Recreation/Ecotourism, Sprawl/Urban Planning, Water Habitats & Quality, Wildlife & Species

TEXAS WILDLIFE ASSOCIATION
401 Isom Rd. Ste. 237
San Antonio, TX 78216 United States
Phone: 210-826-2004   Fax: 210-826-4933
E-mail: twa@texas-wildlife.org
Website: www.texas-wildlife.org
Founded: 1985
Scope: State
Description: Texas Wildlife Association is a nonprofit corporation, formed to protect and promote the rights of Texas' wildlife managers, land owners, sportsmen, and the state's wildlife resources—especially on private lands.
Publication(s): Texas Wildlife
Keyword(s): Ethics/Environmental Justice, Land Issues, Recreation/Ecotourism, Water Habitats & Quality, Wildlife & Species
Contact(s):
Kirby Brown, Executive VP; 210-826-2904; ext. 125; Fax: 210-826-4933; k_brown@texas-wildlife.org

THEODORE PAYNE FOUNDATION FOR WILDFLOWERS AND NATIVE PLANTS, INC.
10459 Tuxford Street
Sun Valley, CA 91352-2126 United States
Phone: 818-768-1802 Fax: 818-768-3533
E-mail: info@theodorepayne.org
Website: www.theodorepayne.org

Founded: 1960
Membership: 101–1,000
Scope: Local
Description: Founded and incorporated in 1960, the Theodore Payne Foundation promotes the understanding and preservation of California native flora. Our mission is: to promote and restore California landscapes, and habitats, to propagate and make available California native plants and wildflowers, to educate and acquire knowledge about California flora and natural history.
Publication(s): The Poppy Print
Keyword(s): Ecosystems (precious)
Contact(s):
Margaret Robison, Office Manager/Bookkeeper; 818-768-1802; Fax: 818-768-5215; info@theodorepayne.org
Frances Liau, President, Board of Directors

THEODORE ROOSEVELT CONSERVATION PARTNERSHIP
555 Eleventh St. NW
6th Floor
Washington, DC 20004 United States
Phone: 202-508-3449 Fax: 202-508-3402
E-mail: info@trcp.org
Website: www.trcp.org

Founded: 1999
Membership: 10,001–100,000
Scope: National
Description: Our Mission: To ensure that America's lands, both public and private, will always provide clean water, healthy habitat, bountiful fish and wildlife populations, and opportunities to fish, hunt and enjoy the outdoors.
Publication(s): Square Dealer-quarterly newsletter
Keyword(s): Forests/Forestry, Public Lands/Greenspace
Contact(s):
Kristen Wagner, Office Manager/Executive Assistant; 406-549-0101; Fax: 406-549-7402; kwagner@trca.org

THORNE ECOLOGICAL INSTITUTE
P.O Box 19107
Boulder, CO 80308-2107 United States
Phone: 303-447-1769 Fax: 720-565-3873
E-mail: info@thorne-eco.org
Website: www.thorne-eco.org

Founded: 1954
Scope: State
Description: A nonprofit educational institute creating innovative outdoor learning experiences and other educational opportunities that teach stewardship of the earth to children and adults. The Institute offers a variety of environmental education classes to children from the Boulder, Denver area with science-based activities and exciting hands-on lessons.
Keyword(s): Recreation/Ecotourism, Water Habitats & Quality
Contact(s):
Susan Peterson, Chairman; susankae@aol.com
Oakleigh Thorne, Founder and Honorary President

THREE CIRCLES CENTER FOR MULTICULTURAL ENVIRONMENTAL EDUCATION
P.O. Box 1946
Sausalito, CA 94965 United States
Phone: 415-331-4540
E-mail: circlecenter@igc.apc.org

Founded: 1990
Scope: National
Description: Three Circles Center introduces, encourages, and cultivates multicultural perspectives and values in environmental and outdoor education, recreation, and interpretation.
Publication(s): Journal of Multicultural Environmental Education, Research Papers, Monographs, Perspectives
Keyword(s): Ethics/Environmental Justice
Contact(s):
Running-Grass, Executive Director; P.O. Box 1946, Sausalito, CA 94965; 415-331-4540

TOGETHER FOUNDATION, THE
Room DC2-0943
Two U.N. Plaza
NYC, NY 10017 United States
Phone: 212-963-4200 Fax: 212-963-8721
E-mail: habitatny@un.org
Website: www.sustainabledevelopment.org

Founded: 1989
Scope: Local, State, Regional, National, International
Description: To facilitate positive global change by establishing communications and information systems that inventory and integrate the resources and needs of people, projects, and organizations working on environment, sustainable development, and human rights.
Keyword(s): Development/Developing Countries
Contact(s):
Ella Cisneros, President; 212-879-9334; Fax: 212-879-9440; info@together.org
Martha Vargas, Executive Director; 212-879-9334; Fax: 212-879-9440; info@together.org
Carol Simon, Information Manager; 212-879-9334; Fax: 212-879-9440; info@together.org
Rafael Oliveira, System Administrator; 212-879-9334; Fax: 212-879-9440; info@together.org

TRAFFIC NORTH AMERICA
c/o World Wildlife Fund
1250 24th Street NW
Washington, DC 20037 United States
Phone: 202-293-4800 Fax: 202-775-8287
E-mail: tna@wwfus.org
Website: www.traffic.org

Scope: National, International
Description: TRAFFIC is an information-gathering program that monitors the trade in wild animals and plants and the products made from them. It is a program of World Wildlife Fund and IUCN and is a part of an international network of TRAFFIC offices.
Publication(s): Traffic North America, Special Reports
Keyword(s): Wildlife & Species
Contact(s):
Simon Habel, Director; simon.habel@wwfus.org
Leigh Henry, Program Officer; leigh.henry@wwfus.org
Craig Hoover, Deputy Director; craig.hoover@wwfus.org
Tina Leonard, Program Assistant; tina.leonard@wwfus.org

TREAD LIGHTLY! INC
298 24th St., Suite 325
Ogden, UT 84401 United States
Phone: 801-627-0077 Fax: 801-621-8633
E-mail: tlinc@xmission.com
Website: www.treadlightly.org

Founded: 1990
Membership: 1–100
Scope: National
Description: Tread Lightly!, Inc. is a nonprofit organization that is an ethical and educational force among outdoor enthusiasts and the industries that serve them. Tread Lightly annually

carries out programs designed to instill a proactive, low impact message among enthusiasts, manufacturers, advertising agencies, the media and children of all ages.

Publication(s): Tread Lightly! Trails Newsletter, Guide to Responsible Personal Watercraft Use, Guide to Responsible Mountain Biking, Guide to Responsible ATV Riding, Guide to Responsible Trail Biking, Guide To Responsible Snowmobiling, Guide to Responsible Four-Wheeling

Keyword(s): Land Issues, Recreation/Ecotourism

Contact(s):
Lori Davis, Executive Director; lori@treadlightly.org
Andrew Clurman, Secretary and Treasurer; 929 Pearl St., Suite 200, Boulder, CO 80302; aclurman@skinet.com
Scott Heath, Vice Chairman; 9 Calle Catrina, Rancho Santa Margarita, CA 92688; 949-713-6574; Fax: 949-713-6579; scottheath4@home.com
Philip Milburn, Chairman; 1 Olympic Plaza, Colorado Springs, CO 80909; pmilburn@usacycling.org

TREEPEOPLE
12601 Mulholland Dr.
Beverly Hills, CA 90210 United States
Phone: 818-753-4600   Fax: 818-753-4635
E-mail: info@treepeople.org
Website: www.treepeople.org

Founded: 1973
Scope: Regional
Description: Andy Lipkis and his teenage friends became known as the "TreePeople" when they began planting trees to restore a dying forest. Through innovative education and training programs, TreePeople has involved thousands of students and volunteers in neighborhood renewal and community service throughout southern California. Today, TreePeople is at the forefront of the urban forestry movement, offering sustainable solutions for the urban ecosystem.

Publication(s): Seedling News (member newsletter), Second Nature: Adapting L.A.'s Landscape for Sustainable Living, Healing Your Neighborhood, Your City and Your World, The Simple Act of Planting a Tree

Keyword(s): Forests/Forestry, Reduce/Reuse/Recycle, Wildlife & Species

Contact(s):
Andy Lipkis, President
Jeff Hohensee, Director of Education Programs
Jim Summers, Director of Forestry Programs

TREES ATLANTA
96 Poplar St., NW
Atlanta, GA 30303 United States
Phone: 404-522-4097   Fax: 404-522-6855
E-mail: info@treesatlanta.org
Website: www.treesatlanta.org

Founded: 1984
Membership: 1,001–10,000
Scope: Local, Regional
Description: Trees Atlanta is a citizens group that plants, maintains, and conserves trees in metro Atlanta area and educates the public about the importance of trees.

Publication(s): Tree Walk Brochure, Atlanta Treebune

Keyword(s): Climate Change, Ecosystems (precious), Forests/Forestry, Pollution (general), Public Health, Sprawl/Urban Planning, Wildlife & Species

Contact(s):
Marcia Bansley, Executive Director
Cheryl Bramblett, Director of Communications
Andrew Kramb, NeighborWoods Coordinator; 404-522-4097
Greg Levine, Volunteer Coordinator

TREES FOR THE FUTURE, INC.
9000 16th St., P.O. Box 7027
Silver Spring, MD 20907 United States
Phone: 800-643-0001   Fax: 301-565-5012
E-mail: info@treesftf.org
Website: www.treesftf.org

Founded: 1989
Membership: 1,001–10,000
Scope: International
Description: Trees for the Future offers multi-purpose tree seeds, training materials, and technical assistance for requesting communities, institutions and individuals throughout the developing regions of the world. In addition, Trees for the Future creates awareness of the potential threat of Global Climatic Change and the simple, cost-effective solutions of tree-planting to counter the "Global Warming" effect.

Publication(s): Johnny Appleseed News, Technical Papers

Keyword(s): Agriculture/Farming, Air Quality/Atmosphere, Climate Change, Development/Developing Countries, Energy, Land Issues, Pollution (general), Reduce/Reuse/Recycle, Sprawl/Urban Planning, Wildlife & Species

Contact(s):
Dave Deppner, President Emeritus
Bill Ligon, Executive Director
Julio Navarro-Monzo, Executive Director
Joseph Permetti, Director of Development
Amy Martin Burns, Office Manager
Patricia Aiken, Secretary
Scott Bode, Africa Program Coordinator
Celso Maatac, Treasurer
John Moore, Chairman

TREES FOR TOMORROW, NATURAL RESOURCES EDUCATION CENTER
P.O. Box 609
519 Sheridan St.
Eagle River, WI 54521 United States
Phone: 800-838-9472   Fax: 715-479-2318
E-mail: learning@treesfortomorrow.com
Website: www.treesfortomorrow.com

Founded: 1944
Membership: 101–1,000
Scope: Regional
Description: An accredited specialty school which conducts multi-day workshops with natural resource themes for elementary, middle and high school students and others from WI, MI and IL. Most topics taught outdoors. Also offer teacher graduate courses and adult special interest courses. Call for free brochure. Tree seedlings available for sale.

Publication(s): Tree Tips - biweekly newsletter, Northbound- natural resources journal

Keyword(s): Energy, Forests/Forestry, Land Issues, Public Lands/Greenspace, Recreation/Ecotourism, Reduce/Reuse/ Recycle, Water Habitats & Quality, Wildlife & Species

Contact(s):
Lee Jackson, President; 800-838-9472; Fax: 715-479-2318; trees@nnex.net
Jim Holperin, Director

TREES, WATER, AND PEOPLE
633 S. College Ave.
Fort Collins, CO 80524 United States
Phone: 970-484-3678   Fax: 970-224-0126
E-mail: twp@treeswaterpeople.org
Website: www.treeswaterpeople.org

Founded: 1998
Membership: 1,001–10,000
Scope: Local, Regional, International
Description: Trees, Water, and People is a nonprofit conservation organization established in 1998 with the mission of working collaboratively with communities to establish sustainable

forests and watersheds while improving people's lives. We currently have programs in four countries in Central America, and in Colorado, and Wyoming in the U.S.

Publication(s): Forests Forever, Watershed Currents

Contact(s):
Tempra Board, Director of Development; tempra@treeswaterpeople.org
Stuart Conway, International Director; stuart@treeswaterpeople.org
Richard Fox, National Director; twp@treeswaterpeople.org

TRIANGLE RAILS-TO-TRAILS CONSERVANCY
344 Roberson Creek Rd
Pittsboro, NC 27312-8804 United States
Phone: 919-545-9104   Fax: 320-210-0357
E-mail: billbuss@eathlink.net
Website: www.ncrail-trails.org/trtc/

Founded: 1992
Membership: 101–1,000
Scope: Regional
Description: The mission of the Triangle Rails-to-Trails Conservancy is to work with local and state government officials to preserve local abandoned railroad corridors for future transportation and other interim uses such as recreational trails. TRTC works within the Triangle J Council of Governments Service area of Durham, Orange, Wake, Chatham, Johnston, and Lee counties of North Carolina.

Keyword(s): Land Issues, Recreation/Ecotourism, Sprawl/Urban Planning, Transportation

Contact(s):
Bill Bussey, President; 919-233-8444; Fax: 919-851-0531; billbus@gte.net

TRI-STATE BIRD RESCUE AND RESEARCH, INC.
110 Possum Hollow Rd.
Newark, DE 19711 United States
Phone: 302-737-9543   Fax: 302-737-9562
Website: www.tristatebird.org

Founded: 1976
Membership: 101–1,000
Scope: National, International
Description: To study and promote healthy populations of native wildlife by rehabilitation of oiled birds; rehabilitation of injured, diseased, and orphaned birds for release back into the wild; conducting training and education programs for colleagues, peers, and the general public; and conducting medical and biological research consistent with goals of providing for the general well-being of native wildlife.

Publication(s): Effects of Oil on Wildlife, The, Wildlife and Oil Spills: Rehabilitation, Research, and Contingency Planning, Wildlife and Oil Spills Bulletin, Oiled Bird Rehabilitation, Medical Notes for Rehabilitators

Keyword(s): Pollution (general), Wildlife & Species

Contact(s):
Chris Motoyoshi, Executive Director

TROUT UNLIMITED
NATIONAL HEADQUARTERS
1500 Wilson Blvd., #310
Arlington, VA 22209-2404 United States
Phone: 703-522-0200   Fax: 703-284-9400
E-mail: trout@tu.org
Website: www.tu.org

Founded: 1959
Membership: 100,001–500,000
Scope: National
Description: A nonprofit, tax-deductible international coldwater fisheries organization dedicated to the conservation, protection, and restoration of coldwater fisheries and their watersheds. Affiliates in Canada, New Zealand, and Australia.

Publication(s): Trout Magazine, Lines to Leaders
Keyword(s): Air Quality/Atmosphere, Water Habitats & Quality, Wildlife & Species

Contact(s):
Charles Gauvin, President and Chief Executive Officer
Lorine Albright, Regional Vice President of Northern Rockies; P.O. Box 1525, Great Falls, MT 59403-1525; 406-454-1384; Fax: 406-761-2610; evenson@mch.net
David Bowie, Regional Vice President of New England; 540 Duck Pond Rd., Westbrook, ME 04092-2510; 207-854-9978; Fax: 207-770-1211; usunmz6m@ibmmail.com
Mike Brock, Regional Vice President of Great Lakes; 23410 Beech Rd., Southfield, MI 48034-3482; 248-356-8195; Fax: 810-592-6098; mikebrock@medidone.net
Stan Griffin, Regional Vice President of Southwest; 27 Dorset Ln., Mill Valley, CA 94941-5203; 510-528-5390; Fax: 510-528-7880; tucalif@ziplink.net
K. Johnson, Regional Vice President of Pacific Northwest; 14727 SE 145th Pl., Renton, WA 98059-7336; 425-865-2201; Fax: 425-271-6378; kbob@halcyon.com
Paul Maciejewski, Regional Vice President of Northeast; 47 Flintlock Dr., Long Valley, NJ 07835-0320; 973-765-6673; Fax: 973-705-5974; 72077.1327@compuserve.com
Steven Moyer, Vice President of Conservation Programs
Kirk Otey, Regional Vice President of Southeast; 1308 Lexington Ave., Charlotte, NC 28203-4837; 704-334-3060; Fax: 704-334-0768; kskotey@mindspring.com
Fred Rasmussen, Regional Vice President of Southern Rockies; 225 County Road 516, Ignacio, CO 81137-9728; 790-563-6517; Fax: 970-563-9599; engelbj@compuserve.com
Lou Schmidt, Regional Vice President of Mid-Atlantic; Rt. 1 Box 109-A, Bristol, WV 26332-9801; 304-367-2724; Fax: 304-367-2727; lschmidt@lolina.net
Ray Smith, Regional Vice President of Midwest; 70 N. College Ave., Suite 11, Fayetteville, AR 72701-5337; 501-521-7011; Fax: 501-443-4333; rsmith7011@aol.com
Whit Fosburgh, Director of Development
Sarah Johnson, Director, National Volunteer Operations; 608-250-2757; Fax: 608-255-1326; johnson@tu.org
Joseph Mcgurrin, Director of Resources
David Nickum, Regional Director of Southern Rockies; 1900 13th St., Ste. 101, Boulder, CO 80302; 303-440-2937; Fax: 303-440-7933
Wendy Reed, Manager of Membership Services
Christine Arena, Editor
Stephen Born, Chairman of National Resource Board; 424 Washburn Pl., Madison, WI 53403; 608-257-6625
Kathy Buchner, Wyoming TU Office Administrator; P.O. Box 4069, Jackson, WY 83001; 307-733-6991; Fax: 307-733-9678; kbuchner@wyoming.com
Don Duff, Coordinator of TU and FS
Kenneth Mendez, Chief Operating and Financial Officer
Oakleigh Thorne, Chairman of the Board

TROUT UNLIMITED
ALASKA COUNCIL
P.O. Box 876675, Wasilla, AK 99687-6675
Homer, AK 99603-3324 United States
Phone: 907-376-1666   Fax: 907-376-1666
E-mail: tuakcoun@alaska.net

Founded: 1988
Membership: 101–1,000
Scope: State
Description: A statewide council with ten active chapters dedicated to the protection and enhancement of the cold water fishery resource.

Contact(s):
Jack Willis, Chairman; 907-235-3860

TROUT UNLIMITED
ARIZONA COUNCIL
7830 N. 23rd Avenue
Phoenix, AZ 85021 United States
Phone: 602-995-0551   Fax: 602-995-0551
E-mail: cdl@azjurist.com

Founded: 1989
Membership: 1,001–10,000
Scope: State

Description: A statewide council with four active chapters working for the protection and enhancement of coldwater fishery resources.

Keyword(s): Ecosystems (precious), Forests/Forestry, Recreation/Ecotourism, Water Habitats & Quality, Wildlife & Species

Contact(s):
Craig Hegel, Treasurer; 830 E. Seldon Lane, Phoenix, AZ 85020; 602-437-5030; Fax: 602-944-9193; craig.h@ix.netcom.com
Carm Moehle, Chairman; 602-264-5840; Fax: 602-230-7579; carm.moehle@azbar.org

TROUT UNLIMITED
CALIFORNIA COUNCIL
State Office, 828 San Pablo Ave.
Suite 208
Albany, CA 94706 United States
Phone: 510-528-5390   Fax: 510-528-7880
E-mail: tucalif@earthlink.net
Website: californiatu.org

Founded: 1984
Membership: 1,001–10,000
Scope: State

Description: A statewide council with ten active chapters working for the protection and enhancement of coldwater fishery resources.

Keyword(s): Water Habitats & Quality

Contact(s):
Stan Griffin, Office Director

TROUT UNLIMITED
COLORADO COUNCIL
1320 Pearl St., Suite 320
Boulder, CO 80302 United States
Phone: 303-440-2937   Fax: 303-440-7933
E-mail: dnickum@tu.org
Website: www.cotrout.org

Founded: 1983
Membership: 1,001–10,000
Scope: State

Description: A statewide council with 20 active chapters working for the protection and enhancement of coldwater fishery resources.

Publication(s): Currents, Rocky Mountain Streamside

Contact(s):
Ken McClatchy, State Chairman
David Nickum, Executive Director

TROUT UNLIMITED
CONNECTICUT COUNCIL
654 Cyprus Rd.
Newington, CT 06111-5612 United States
Phone: 860-667-2515
E-mail: fraa@fraa.org

Scope: State

Description: A statewide council with nine active chapters working for the protection and enhancement of coldwater fishery resources.

Contact(s):
Steve Lewis, Chairman

TROUT UNLIMITED
GEORGIA COUNCIL
65 Cumberland Way
Dallas, GA 30132 United States
Phone: 770-443-1467
E-mail: kshaw01@mindspring.com
Website: gatu.org

Founded: 1980
Membership: 1,001–10,000
Scope: State

Description: A statewide council with 14 active chapters working for the protection and enhancement of coldwater fishery resources.

TROUT UNLIMITED
ILLINOIS COUNCIL
Attn: Chairman, P.O. Box 1280
Oak Brook, IL 60522-1280 United States
Phone: 312-751-4730   Fax: 219-756-7735
E-mail: wjbock1@attbi.com
Website: www.tu.org

Membership: 1,001–10,000
Scope: State, Regional

Description: A statewide council with four active chapters working for the protection and enhancement of coldwater fishery resources.

Contact(s):
Walter Bock, Chairman; wjbock1@home.com

TROUT UNLIMITED
MARYLAND COUNCIL, MID-ATLANTIC
Attn: President, 3509 Pleasant Plains Dr.
Reisterstown, MD 21136-4417 United States
Phone: 410-239-8468   Fax: 410-374-5719
E-mail: tedgodfrey@erols.com
Website: www.tu.org

Scope: State

Description: A statewide council with seven active chapters working for the protection and enhancement of coldwater fishery resources.

Contact(s):
Ted Godfrey, Chairman

TROUT UNLIMITED
MICHIGAN COUNCIL
7 Trowbridge NF
Grand Rapids, MI 49503 United States
Phone: 616-460-0477
Website: www.montanatu.org/

Scope: State

Description: A statewide council with 21 active chapters working for the protection and enhancement of coldwater fishery resources.

Contact(s):
Richard Rowman, Executive Director

TROUT UNLIMITED
MINNESOTA COUNCIL
820 Old Crystal Bay Rd.
Wayzata, MN 55391-9365 United States
Phone: 612-341-9360   Fax: 612-341-9363

Scope: State

Description: A statewide council with nine active chapters working for the protection and enhancement of coldwater fishery resources.

Contact(s):
George Hust, Chairman; 952-475-2054

TROUT UNLIMITED
MISSOURI COUNCIL
2010 Daisy Ln.
Jefferson, MO 65109-1810 United States
Phone: 573-751-1039   Fax: 573-634-3096
Website: www.agron.missouri.edu/lyfishing/mmtu.html
Membership: 1,001–10,000
Scope: State
Description: A statewide council with four active chapters working for the protection and enhancement of coldwater fishery resources.
Contact(s):
John Wenzlick, Chairman

TROUT UNLIMITED
MONTANA COUNCIL
P.O. Box 7186
Missoula, MT 59807 United States
Phone: 406-543-0054   Fax: 406-543-0054
E-mail: montrout@montana.com
Website: www.montanatu.org
Membership: 1,001–10,000
Scope: State
Description: A statewide council with 12 chapters working for the protection and enhancement of coldwater fishery resources.
Contact(s):
Bruce Farling, Executive Director

TROUT UNLIMITED
NEVADA COUNCIL
474 South Blakeland Drive
Spring Creek, NV 89815 United States
Phone: 775-778-3159   Fax: 775-778-8199
E-mail: nvtu@rabbitbrush.com
Website: www.rabbitbrush.com/nvtu/
Scope: State
Description: A statewide council with three active chapters, dedicated to the protection and enhancement of coldwater fishing resources.
Contact(s):
Matt Holford, Executive Director

TROUT UNLIMITED
NEW HAMPSHIRE COUNCIL
Attn: Chairman, 9 Sirod Rd.
Windham, NH 03087-1401 United States
Phone: 603-896-2236
Scope: State
Description: A statewide council with six active chapters working for the protection and enhancement of coldwater fishery resources.
Contact(s):
James Norton, Chairman

TROUT UNLIMITED
NEW YORK COUNCIL
Attn: Chairman, 111 High Point Mountain Rd.
West Shokan, NY 12494-5337 United States
Phone: 914-892-8630
E-mail: karwac@ibm.org
Website: nyscounciltu.homestead.com/HOME.html
Scope: State
Description: A statewide council with 37 active chapters working for the protection and enhancement of coldwater fishery resources.
Publication(s): Long Casts
Contact(s):
Chester Karwatowski, Chairman

TROUT UNLIMITED
NORTH CAROLINA COUNCIL
7626 Bedfordshire Dr.
Charlotte, NC 28226 United States
Phone: 704-442-1253
E-mail: twilhelm@carolina.rr.com
Website: www.nctu.org
Membership: 1,001–10,000
Scope: State
Description: Dedicated to the protection and enhancement of coldwater fishing resources.
Contact(s):
David Stewart, Chairman

TROUT UNLIMITED
OHIO COUNCIL
Attn: Chairman, 1487 New Way Dr.
Beaver Creek, OH 45434-6925 United States
Phone: 937-426-5757
E-mail: mark.blauvelt@stdreg.com
Scope: State
Description: Dedicated to the protection and enhancement of the coldwater fishery resource.
Contact(s):
Mark Blauvelt, President

TROUT UNLIMITED
OREGON COUNCIL
22875 N. W. Chestnut
Hillsboro, OR 97024 United States
Phone: 503-640-2123   Fax: 503-844-9929
E-mail: tmilowolf@msn.com
Website: www.teleport.com/~wsc/octu
Scope: State
Description: A statewide council with seven active chapters working for the protection and enhancement of the coldwater fishery resource.
Contact(s):
Jeff Curtis, Western Conservation Director; jcurtis@tu.org
Alan Moore, Western Communications Coordinator; dmoore@tu.org
Scott Yates, Western Legal and Policy Coordinator; syates@tu.org

TROUT UNLIMITED
PENNSYLVANIA COUNCIL
RD #2, Box 520
Greensburg, PA 15601 United States
Phone: 724-423-8428
E-mail: president@patrout.org
Website: www.patrout.org
Membership: 10,001–100,000
Scope: Regional
Description: A statewide council with 56 active chapters working for the protection and enhancement of the coldwater fishery resource.
Publication(s): Pennsylvania Trout
Keyword(s): Land Issues, Water Habitats & Quality
Contact(s):
Ken Undercoffer, Chairman

TROUT UNLIMITED
SOUTH CAROLINA COUNCIL
115 Conrad Cir.
Columbia, SC 29212-2619 United States
Phone: 803-777-7652
E-mail: malcolml@gwm.sc.edu
Website: www.tu.org
Founded: 1983
Membership: 1,001–10,000

Scope: State

Description: A statewide council with four active chapters working for the protection and enhancement of coldwater fishery resources.

Keyword(s): Agriculture/Farming, Ecosystems (precious), Ethics/Environmental Justice, Forests/Forestry, Land Issues, Public Health, Public Lands/Greenspace, Recreation/Ecotourism, Sprawl/Urban Planning, Water Habitats & Quality

Contact(s):
Malcolm Leaphart, Chairman

TROUT UNLIMITED
TENNESSEE COUNCIL
P.O. Box 1125
Brentwood, TN 37024 United States
Phone: 615-371-9211
E-mail: johns@bwood.com

Scope: State

Description: A statewide council with 10 active chapters working for the protection and enhancement of the coldwater fishery resource.

Contact(s):
John Smitherman, Chairman

TROUT UNLIMITED
UTAH COUNCIL
611 East Taylor Lane
#G
Murray, UT 84170 United States
Phone: 801-573-0770
E-mail: ekent@co.slc.ut.us

Scope: State

Description: Dedicated to the protection and enhancement of the coldwater fishery resource.

Contact(s):
Wes Johnson, Chairman

TROUT UNLIMITED
VIRGINIA COUNCIL
Attn: Chairman, 202 Deerfield Ln.
Lynchburg, VA 24502-3122 United States
Phone: 804-239-1017
E-mail: dorffly@aol.com

Scope: State

Description: A statewide organization with 16 active chapters working for the protection and enhancement of the coldwater fishery resource.

Contact(s):
Thomas Reisdorf, Chairman

TROUT UNLIMITED
WASHINGTON COUNCIL
Attn: Chairman, 2701 NE 148th Ave.
Vancouver, WA 98684-7877 United States
Phone: 360-896-6967   Fax: 360-896-1265
E-mail: jjderry@earthlink.net

Scope: State

Description: A statewide council with 31 active chapters working for the protection and enhancement of coldwater fishery resources.

Publication(s): Trout and Salmon Leader

Contact(s):
James Derry, Chairman

TROUT UNLIMITED
WEST VIRGINIA COUNCIL
Attn: Dave Bott, 124 Ohio Ave
Westover, WV 26501 United States
Phone: 304-937-2214
E-mail: dwbott@wstdm1.westco.net

Website: www.tu.org

Membership: 1,001–10,000

Scope: State

Description: A statewide council with 8 active chapters working for the protection and enhancement of coldwater fishery resources.

Contact(s):
Dave Bott, Chairman of West Virginia Council

TROUT UNLIMITED
WYOMING COUNCIL
Attn: Chairman, P.O. Box 1022
Jackson, WY 83001 United States
Phone: 307-733-4944   Fax: 413-383-1125

Scope: State

Description: A statewide council with 16 active chapters dedicated to the protection and enhancement of the coldwater fishery resource.

Contact(s):
Kathy Buchner, Director; kbuchner@wyoming.com
Jay Buchner, Chairman

TRUMPETER SWAN SOCIETY, THE
3800 County Rd. 24
Maple Plain, MN 55359 United States
Phone: 763-476-4663, ext. 113   Fax: 763-476-1514
E-mail: ttss@threeriversparkdistrict.org
Website: www.taiga.net/swans/index.html

Founded: 1968

Membership: 101–1,000

Scope: International

Description: International scientific and educational organization dedicated to assuring the vitality and welfare of wild Trumpeter Swan populations in North America, and to restoring the species to its original range. The Society promotes research into Trumpeter ecology and management, and provides a framework for exchange of knowledge about the species.

Publication(s): North American Swans, Bulletin of the Trumpeter Swan Society, Proceedings and Papers of the 16th Trumpeter Swan Society Conference, Proceedings and Papers of the 15th Trumpeter Swan Society Conference, Proceedings and Papers of the 14th Trumpeter Swan Society Conference

Keyword(s): Water Habitats & Quality, Wildlife & Species

Contact(s):
Harvey Nelson, President and Editor; 10515 Kell Ave., Bloomington, MN 55437
Gary Ivey, Vice President; ivey@oregonvos.net
Ruth Shea, Executive Director; 3346 East 200 N., Rigby, ID 83442
Madeleine Linck, Editor

TRUST FOR PUBLIC LAND, THE
Headquarters, National Office
Attn: Public Affairs Assistant, 4th Fl.
116 New Montgomery St.
San Francisco, CA 94105 United States
Phone: 415-495-4014   Fax: 415-495-4103
E-mail: info@tpl.org
Website: www.tpl.org

Founded: 1972

Scope: Local, State, Regional, National

Description: Since its founding in 1972, TPL has worked with public agencies, landowners and citizen groups to protect more than 1.2 million acres in 45 states nationwide and has recently launched its Greenprint for Growth campaign to help sprawl-threatened communities protect land as a way to guide development and sustain a healthy economy and a high quality of life.

Publication(s): Land and People, regional newsletters

Keyword(s): Land Issues, Public Lands/Greenspace, Recreation/Ecotourism, Reduce/Reuse/Recycle, Sprawl/Urban Planning, Water Habitats & Quality, Wildlife & Species

Contact(s):
- Will Rogers, President
- W. Allen, Senior Vice President & Regional Director; 306 N. Monroe St., Tallahassee, FL 32301-7635; 904-222-7911
- Kathy Blaha, Senior Vice President & Green Cities Initiative Program Director; 666 Pennsylvania Ave. SE, Washington, DC 20003; 202-543-7552
- Bowen Blair, Senior Vice President & National Director of Projects; 1211 SW Sixth Ave., Portland, OR 97204-1001; 503-228-6620
- Laura Brehm, V.P. & Director of Development
- Ernest Cook, Senior Vice President; 33 Union St., 4th Fl., Boston, MA 02108; 617-367-6200
- Tod Dobratz, V.P. & Asst. CFO
- Alan Front, Senior Vice President & Director of Federal Affairs
- Rose Harvey, Senior Vice President & Mid-Atlantic Regional Director; 666 Broadway, New York, NY 10012; 212-677-7171
- Whitney Hatch, Vice President & New England Regional Director; 33 Union St., 4th Fl., Boston, MA 02108; 617-367-6200
- Reed Holderman, V.P. & Western Regional Director; 116 New Montgomery, 3rd Fl., San Francisco, CA 94105; 415-495-5660
- Susan Ives, V.P./Director of Public Affairs and Editor of Land & People
- Lesley Kane-Synal, V.P. & Director Federal Legislative Office; 666 Pennsylvania Ave. SE Suite 401, Washington, DC 20003-4334; 202-543-7552
- Nelson Lee, Senior Vice President and General Counsel
- Felicia Marcus, Executive Vice President
- Robert McIntyre, Senior Vice President and CFO
- Stephen Thompson, Senior Vice President; 418 Montezuma, Santa Fe, NM 87501; 505-988-5922
- Cynthia Whiteford, V.P. & Regional Director
- Becky Mitchell, Director of External Affairs

TRUST FOR WILDLIFE, INC.
127 Ehrich Rd.
Shaftsbury, VT 05262 United States
Phone: 802-447-0746   Fax: 802-442-6855
E-mail: marshalc@acf.org
Website: www.neotropicalbirds.net

Founded: 1983
Membership: 1–100
Scope: Local, State, Regional, International
Description: Dedicated to wildlife conservation and education with a focus on wildlife habitats, international partnerships with a focus on Russia, Central and South America and wildlife rehabilitation with an emphasis on public education.
Keyword(s): Agriculture/Farming, Forests/Forestry, Public Lands/Greenspace, Water Habitats & Quality, Wildlife & Species
Contact(s):
- Marshal Case, President; 802-447-0110; Fax: 802-442-6855; marshalc@acf.org
- Les Line, Director; P.O. Box 323, Amenia, NY 12501; 914-373-9135
- Ed Metcalfe, Director; 6373 Vermont Rt. 100, Whitingham, VT 05361; 802-464-0048
- Gregory Sharp, Secretary; 225 Reeds Gap Rd., East Northford, CT 6472; 203-240-6046

TRUSTEES FOR ALASKA
1026 West 4th Ave., Suite 201
Anchorage, AK 99501-2101 United States
Phone: 907-276-4244   Fax: 907-276-7110
E-mail: ecolaw@trustees.org
Website: www.trustees.org

Founded: 1974
Scope: State
Description: Trustees for Alaska is a public interest law firm whose mission is to provide legal counsel to protect and sustain Alaska's natural environment. We represent local and national environmental groups, Alaska Native villages and nonprofit organizations, community groups, hunters, fishers and others where the outcome of our advocacy could benefit Alaska's environment.
Publication(s): Under the Influence of Oil, The Environmental Advocate, Industrialization of America's Arctic, Quarterly Newsletter
Contact(s):
- Ann Rothe, Executive Director; ext. 111
- Peter van Tuyn, Litigation Director; ext. 110
- Michael Frank, Staff Attorney; ext. 116
- Steve Koteff, Chair
- Mary Mcburney, Secretary
- Chris Rose, Vice Chair
- Paul Wilchorek, Treasurer

TRUSTEES OF RESERVATIONS, THE
572 Essex St.
Beverly, MA 01915-1530 United States
Phone: 978-921-1944   Fax: 978-921-1948
E-mail: information@ttor.org
Website: www.thetrustees.org

Founded: 1891
Membership: 10,001–100,000
Scope: Local, State
Description: The Trustees of Reservations has been conserving the Massachusetts landscape since 1891. Our mission is to preserve, for public use and enjoyment, properties of exceptional scenic, historic and ecological value in Massachusetts.
Publication(s): Conserving our Common Wealth: A Vision for the Massachusetts Landscape, Land Conservation Options: A Guide for Massachusetts Landowners, Annual Report, Land of Commonwealth
Keyword(s): Agriculture/Farming, Ecosystems (precious), Forests/Forestry, Land Issues, Oceans/Coasts/Beaches, Public Lands/Greenspace, Recreation/Ecotourism, Water Habitats & Quality, Wildlife & Species
Contact(s):
- Janice Hunt, President
- John Bradley, Director of Membership
- Sarah Carothers, Director of Planned Giving
- Andy Kendall, Executive Director
- John McCrae, Director of Finance and Administration
- Ann Powell, Director of Development
- Michael Triff, Director of Communications and Marketing
- Wesley Ward, Director of Land Conservation
- Charles Kane, Treasurer
- F. Smithers, Secretary
- Elliot Surkin, Chairman

TUG HILL TOMORROW LAND TRUST
P.O. Box 6063
Watertown, NY 13601 United States
Phone: 315-779-8240   Fax: 315-785-2574
E-mail: thtomorr@northnet.org
Website: www.tughilltomorrowlandtrust.org

Founded: 1990
Membership: 101–1,000
Scope: Regional
Description: Tug Hill Tomorrow is a private nonprofit corporation that works to help retain the forests, farms, recreational, and wild lands of the Tug Hill region through education, research, and voluntary land protection.
Publication(s): Tug Hill Natural History Field Guide, Tug Hill Working Lands, Greenings, quarterly newsletter, Tug Hill Resource Guide to Educational Programs, Tug Hill Recreation Guide: A Guide to Cross-Country Skiing, Hiking, Biking, and Fishing

Keyword(s): Agriculture/Farming, Forests/Forestry, Land Issues, Public Lands/Greenspace, Recreation/Ecotourism

Contact(s):
Linda Garrett, Executive Director; 315-779-8240; thtomorr@northnet.org

TUMAINI ENVIRONMENTAL CONSERVATION GROUP
P.O. Box 1353 Tanga Tanzania
Phone: 0255-2647366   Fax: 0255-2646114
E-mail: victormassawe@hotmail.com
Website: www.nwf.org/conservationdirectory
Founded: 1997
Scope: Local, Regional
Description: Engaged in forestation and sensitization of communties in rationally exploiting natural resources available in the area.
Publication(s): NIL
Contact(s):
N. Kiariro, Secretary; 0272643117
V. Massawe, Executive Chairman; 0811 60826; tccia.tanga@cats-net.com

TURTLE CREEK WATERSHED ASSOCIATION, INC.
325 Commerce Street, Suite 204
Wilmerding, PA 15148 United States
Phone: 412-829-2817
E-mail: good.fish@verizon.net
Website: www.trfn.org/tcwa/
Founded: 1969
Membership: 101–1,000
Scope: Local, Regional
Description: The objective of the Turtle Creek Watershed Association, Inc. is to preserve and protect natural resources; manage AMD remediation projects and stream stabilization projects, educate the community about important environmental issues; monitor and improve water quality; and work with responsible agencies to encourage wise land use planning in the Turtle Creek Watershed.
Publication(s): TCWA Report, Business Associate
Keyword(s): Agriculture/Farming, Ecosystems (precious), Energy, Ethics/Environmental Justice, Executive/Legislative/Judicial Reform, Forests/Forestry, Land Issues, Pollution (general), Public Lands/Greenspace, Recreation/Ecotourism, Reduce/Reuse/Recycle, Water Habitat & Quality
Contact(s):
Steve Wiedemer, President
James Brucker, Vice President; ftma@westol.com
Edward Fischer, Executive Director, Acting; 412-829-2817; Fax: 412-829-2817; goodfish@helicon.net
James Tempero, Director Emeritus
Chris Droste, Secretary
Edward Fischer, Treasurer; 412-824-3376; goodfish@helicon.net

TWO WHITE WOLVES SANCTUARY
SANCTUARY - MAINE
SANCTUARY - CANADA
8561 De Soto Ave
#191
Canoga Park, CA 91304 United States
Phone: 818-464-3585   Fax: 818-727-7992
E-mail: twowhitewolvesretreat@yahoo.com
Founded: 1955
Scope: Local, State, Regional, National, International
Description: Sanctuary in Maine & Canada. Houses & protects fauna & flora. Writer's colony as an example. Short or long term stay. Barter services. Staff needed. Habitat for flora & fauna. Learning centers accepted. Networking invited. Canada location soon. Texas location pending. Maine location available. Send for portfolio/photographs. Web page open soon. Planet protection. No monies, just barter & learning & giving back to the earth.
Publication(s): Two White Wolves Sanctuary Newsletter
Keyword(s): Agriculture/Farming, Air Quality/Atmosphere, Ecosystems (precious), Energy, Ethics/Environmental Justice, Executive/Legislative/Judicial Reform, Forests/Forestry, Land Issues, Pollution (general), Population, Public Health, Public Lands/Greenspace, Reduce

U

UNEP WORLD CONSERVATION MONITORING CENTRE
219 Huntingdon Rd.
Cambridge, CB3 0DL United Kingdom
Phone: 123277314   Fax: 1223277136
E-mail: info@unep-wcmc.org
Website: www.unep-wcmc.org
Founded: 1979
Scope: International
Description: The World Conservation Monitoring Centre is UNEP's resource centre for assessment and sustainable use of the living world. It provides specialised services that include ecosystem assessments, capacity building for implementation of conventions, regional and global biodiversity information support, research on threats to ecosystems and species and development of future scenarios for the living world.
Keyword(s): Development/Developing Countries, Forests/Forestry, Land Issues, Oceans/Coasts/Beaches, Reduce/Reuse/Recycle, Water Habitats & Quality, Wildlife & Species
Contact(s):
Mark Collins, Chief Executive

UNION OF CONCERNED SCIENTISTS
Two Brattle Square
Cambridge, MA 2238 United States
Phone: 617-547-5552   Fax: 617-864-9405
E-mail: ucs@ucsusa.org
Website: www.ucsusa.org
Founded: 1969
Membership: 10,001–100,000
Scope: National
Description: The Union of Concerned Scientists is a national non-profit alliance working for a cleaner environment and a safer world. UCS is working to encourage preservation of life-sustaining resources, promote energy technologies that are renewable, safe, and cost-effective, promote advanced transportation technologies, encourage sustainable agriculture, and curtail weapons proliferation.
Publication(s): Newsletter: NUCLEUS, Now or Never: Serious New Plans to Save a Natural Pest Control, Powerful Solutions: Seven Ways to Switch America to Renewable Electricity, The Consumer's Guide to Effective Environmental Choices, Earthwise
Keyword(s): Agriculture/Farming, Climate Change, Development/Developing Countries, Ecosystems (precious), Energy, Forests/Forestry, Public Health, Reduce/Reuse/Recycle, Transportation, Wildlife & Species
Contact(s):
Howard Ris, President
Kurt Gottfried, Chairman

UNITED NATIONS ENVIRONMENT PROGRAMME
P.O. Box 30552
Nairobi, Kenya
Phone: 2542623089   Fax: 2542623692
E-mail: ipainfo@unep.org
Website: www.unep.org

Founded: 1972
Scope: International
Description: The United Nations Environment Programme (UNEP) was established by the U.N. General Assembly to be the environmental conscience of the U.N. system. It assesses the state of the world's environment; environmental management capacity of developing countries; and raises environmental considerations for the social and economic policies and programmes of UN agencies. UNEP provides a unique forum to bring countries to the table for negotiations, to build consensus and forge international agreements.
Keyword(s): Air Quality/Atmosphere, Ethics/Environmental Justice, Oceans/Coasts/Beaches, Pollution (general), Public Health, Reduce/Reuse/Recycle, Wildlife & Species
Contact(s):
Shafqat Kakakhel, Deputy Executive Director
Klaus Toepfer, Under Secretary General of the United Nations

UNITED NATIONS ENVIRONMENT PROGRAMME
LATIN AMERICA AND CARIBBEAN REGION
UNEP-ROLAC
(United Nations Environment Programme)
Apdo.Postal 10.793
D.F., 11000 Mexico
Phone: 5252024841   Fax: 5252020950
E-mail: rolac@rolac.unep.mx
Website: www.rolac.unep.org
Scope: International

UNITED NATIONS ENVIRONMENT PROGRAMME
LATIN AMERICAN AND CARIBBEAN
Boulevard De Los Virreyes 155 Lomas De Virreyes
Mexico D.F., Mexico
Phone: 52-5-202-6394   Fax: 52-5-202-0950
E-mail: rolac@rolac.unep.mx
Website: www.rolac.unep.org
Contact(s):
Ricardo Sosa, Director
Rody Zuniga, Information

UNITED NATIONS ENVIRONMENT PROGRAMME
NEW YORK OFFICE
2 United Nations Plaza
Room DC-2-803
New York, NY 10017 United States
Phone: 1-212-963-8210   Fax: 1-212-963-7341
E-mail: info@nyo.unep.org
Website: www.nyo.unep.org
Founded: 1972
Membership: 101–1,000
Scope: International
Description: UNEP's mission is to provide leadership and encourage partnerships in caring for the environment by inspiring, informing and enabling nations and peoples to improve their quality of life without compromising that of future generations.
Publication(s): The Global Environment Outlook, Our Planet
Contact(s):
Adnan Amin, Director; 1-212-963-8138; adnan.amin@nyo.unep.org
James Sniffen, Information Officer; 1-212-963-8094; sniffenj@nyo.unep.org

UNITED STATES CHAMBER OF COMMERCE
ENVIRONMENT, TECHNOLOGY AND REGULATORY AFFAIRS
1615 H St., NW
Washington, DC 20062 United States
Phone: 202-463-5533   Fax: 202-887-3445
E-mail: environment@uschamber.com
Website: www.uschamber.com
Founded: 1912
Membership: 1,000,001 +
Scope: Local, State, Regional, National, International
Description: The U.S. Chamber of Commerce is the world's largest business federation, representing more than three million businesses and organizations of every size, sector, and region. Positions on national issues are developed by a cross-section of Chamber members serving on committees, subcommittees, and task forces. Currently, some 1,800 business people participate in this process.
Keyword(s): Agriculture/Farming, Air Quality/Atmosphere, Climate Change, Energy, Ethics/Environmental Justice, Executive/Legislative/Judicial Reform, Finance/Banking/Trade, Forests/Forestry, Land Issues, Oceans/Coasts/Beaches, Pollution (general), Public Lands/Greenspace
Contact(s):
William Kovacs, Vice President

UNITED STATES COMMITTEE FOR THE UNITED NATIONS ENVIRONMENT PROGRAMME, THE (U.S. AND UNEP)
2013 Q St., NW
Washington, DC 20009-1009 United States
Phone: 202-234-3600   Fax: 202-332-3221
E-mail: rahmercl@starpower.net
Scope: National
Description: A nonprofit support group for the U.N. Environment Programme, U.S. and UNEP generates public awareness of global environmental issues, including ozone layer depletion, the greenhouse effect, and the transport of hazardous chemicals, and UNEP's response to these issues. The organization links UNEP to environmental groups across the U.S.
Publication(s): US - UNEP News
Keyword(s): Agriculture/Farming, Climate Change, Wildlife & Species
Contact(s):
Richard Hellman, President

UNITED STATES PUBLIC INTEREST RESEARCH GROUP
U.S. PIRG
218 D St., SE
Washington, DC 20003 United States
Phone: 202-546-9707   Fax: 202-546-2461
E-mail: uspirg@pirg.org
Website: www.uspirg.org
Founded: 1983
Membership: 500,001–1,000,000
Scope: State, National
Description: U.S. PIRG is the national advocacy office for state PIRGs around the country, representing more than one million members. We conduct independent research and lobby for national environmental and consumer protections.
Publication(s): Congressional Scorecard, Citizen Agenda - newsletter, various reports
Keyword(s): Air Quality/Atmosphere, Climate Change, Ecosystems (precious), Energy, Finance/Banking/Trade, Forests/Forestry, Land Issues, Oceans/Coasts/Beaches, Pollution (general), Public Health, Public Lands/Greenspace, Water Habitats & Quality, Wildlife & Species,

UNITED STATES SPORTSMEN'S ALLIANCE AND UNITED STATES SPORTSMEN'S ALLIANCE FOUNDATION
801 Kingsmill Parkway
Columbus, OH 43229-1137 United States
Phone: 614-888-4868   Fax: 614-888-0326
E-mail: info@ussportsmen.org
Website: www.ussportsmen.org
Founded: 1978
Scope: National

Description: Companion nonprofit organizations established to protect America's hunting, trapping and fishing heritage, and the scientific wildlife management practices that support it. The U.S. Sportsmen's Alliance is the legislative arm. The U.S. Sportsmen's Alliance Foundation is the legal defense, public education and research arm.
Publication(s): On Target, Update
Keyword(s): Recreation/Ecotourism
Contact(s):
Walter Pidgeon, President & CEO
Rick Story, Vice President
William Horn, Director of Federal Affairs
Doug Jeanneret, Director of Communcations
William McKinley, Membership Director
Robert Sexton, Manager of Government Affairs
Richard Cabela, Chairman of the Board
Gilbert Humphrey, Treasurer
Mason Lampton, Finance Chairman
C. Wood, Vice Chairman

UNITED STATES TOURIST COUNCIL
Drawer 1875
Washington, DC 20013-1875 United States
Scope: National
Description: A nonprofit association of conservation-concerned individuals, industries, and institutions who travel or cater to the traveler. Emphasis is on historic and scenic preservation, wilderness and roadside development, ecology through sound planning and education, and support of scientific studies of natural wilderness.
Keyword(s): Forests/Forestry, Water Habitats & Quality
Contact(s):
Stanford West, Chairman of Board of Trustees and Executive Director

UPPER CHATTAHOOCHEE RIVERKEEPER
916 Joseph Lowery Blvd
3 Puritan Mill
Atlanta, GA 30318 United States
Phone: 404-352-9828   Fax: 404-352-8676
E-mail: bbolton@ucriverkeeper.org
Website: www.chattahoochee.org
Founded: 1994
Membership: 1,000,001 +
Scope: Regional
Description: To advocate snd secure the protection and stewardship of the Chattahoochee River, its tributaries and watershed using education, research, communication, cooperation, monitoring and legal actions.
Publication(s): Stream Chat, River Chat
Keyword(s): Water Habitats & Quality
Contact(s):
Sally Bethea, Executive Director; ext. 11; sbethea@mindspring.com
Darcie Doden, Director of Headwater Conservation
Matt Kales, Program Manager for River Basin Protection; mkriverkeeper@mindspring.com
Alice Chamipagne, Watershed Protection Specialist
Michelle Fried, General Counsel; mfriverkeeper@mindspring.com

UPPER MISSISSIPPI RIVER CONSERVATION COMMITTEE
4469 - 48th Avenue Ct.
Rock Island, IL 61201 United States
Phone: 309-793-5800, ext. 207   Fax: 309-739-5804
E-mail: umrcc@mississippi-river.com
Website: www.mississippi-river.com/umrcc
Founded: 1943
Membership: 101–1,000
Scope: Regional

Description: Promotes preservation, development, and wise use of the natural and recreational resources of the Upper Mississippi River and formulates policies, plans, and programs for conducting cooperative studies. Members: state conservation departments of Illinois, Iowa, Minnesota, Missouri, and Wisconsin.
Publication(s): Annual Proceedings, and miscellaneous technical reports, Newsletter
Keyword(s): Ecosystems (precious), Forests/Forestry, Water Habitats & Quality, Wildlife & Species
Contact(s):
Jon Duyvejonck, Coordinator; 309-793-5800; ext. 207
Dan Sallee, Chairman; Illinois Department of Natural Resources; 815-625-2968

UPPER SKAGIT BALD EAGLE FESTIVAL
SKAGIT RIVER BALD EAGLE INTERPRETIVE CENTER
P.O. Box 571
Concrete, WA 98237 United States
Phone: 360-853-7283
E-mail: eaglecenter@fidalgo.net
Website: www.skagiteagle.org
Founded: 1907
Scope: Local
Description: The Skagit River Bald Eagle Interpretive Center at Hockport (mid-December through mid-February) and the annual Upper Skagit Bald Eagle Festival (first weekend in February) are opportunities to learn more about one of the largest wintering bald eagle populations in the lower 48 states, and the Skagit River watershed. We contact thousands of visitors on winter weekends, and coordinate with the Forest Service "Eagle Watchers" volunteer host programs and viewing sites.
Keyword(s): Wildlife & Species
Contact(s):
Matthew Jager, Education Coordinator; 360-853-7283; eaglecenter@fidalgo.net

URBAN HABITAT PROGRAM
P.O. Box 29908, Presidio Station
San Francisco, CA 94129 United States
Phone: 415-561-3333   Fax: 415-561-3334
E-mail: contact@urbanhabitatprogram.org
Website: www.urbanhabitatprogram.org
Founded: 1989
Scope: National
Description: The Urban Habitat Program is a project of Tides Center. Its mission is to build multi-cultural urban environmental leadership for socially-just and sustainable communities in the San Francisco Bay area. Our project areas include transportation, regional land use and social justice, land recycling and brown fields, leadership institute for sustainability and justice, and the goal of ecological literacy, all from an ecological and social justice perspective.
Publication(s): Race, Poverty & the Environment
Keyword(s): Ethics/Environmental Justice, Land Issues, Reduce/Reuse/Recycle, Transportation
Contact(s):
Carl Anthony, Director

URBAN WILDLIFE RESOURCES
5130 W. Running Brook Rd.
Columbia, MD 21044 United States
Phone: 410-997-7161   Fax: 410-997-6849
Website: www.erols.com/urbanwildlife
Founded: 1995
Scope: International
Description: Urban Wildlife Resources works to facilitate interaction and cooperation among land managers and planners, biologists, landscape architects, and others in

achieving better management of natural resources in urban and urbanizing areas.
Publication(s): Urban Open Space Manager, The
Keyword(s): Forests/Forestry, Public Lands/Greenspace, Reduce/Reuse/Recycle
Contact(s):
Lowell Adams, President

UTAH ASSOCIATION OF CONSERVATION DISTRICTS
1860 N. 100 East
Logan, UT 84341 United States
Phone: 435-753-6029, ext. 31   Fax: 435-755-2117
E-mail: uacd@ut.nacdnet.org
Website: www.uacd.org
Founded: 1948
Membership: 101–1,000
Scope: Local, State
Description: The UACD was founded in February 1948. We are nongovernmental, nonprofit organization representing 38 local conservation districts created by the state legislature in 1937.
Publication(s): Book-Saving the American Cowboy, Range Magazine, newsletter - The Leader
Keyword(s): Agriculture/Farming
Contact(s):
Randy Greenhalgh, President; 435-623-0845; Fax: 435-623-0845
Larry Johnson, Vice President /Board Member; P.O. Box 177, Randolph, UT 84064; 435-793-5625; Fax: 435-793-5625
Gordon Younker, Executive Vice President; 1860 N. 100 E., North Logan, UT 84341-2215; 435-753-6029; Fax: 435-755-2117; gordon-younker@ut.nacdnet.org
William Rigby, Past President
Richard Saunders, Secretary and Treasurer; 4083 W. 12680 S., Payson, UT 84651; 801-465-2777

UTAH BASS FEDERATION
Attn: President, 3460 Scott Cir.
Salt Lake City, UT 84115 United States
Phone: 801-487-8711
E-mail: gjlables@aol.com
Website: www.utahbassfederation.org
Scope: State
Description: An organization of Bassmaster chapters, affiliated with the Bass Anglers Sportsman Society, organized to fight pollution, assist state and national conservation agencies in their efforts, and teach young people of our country good conservation practices. Dedicated to the realistic conservation of our water resources.
Publication(s): Nature News Notes
Keyword(s): Public Lands/Greenspace, Wildlife & Species
Contact(s):
George Sommer, President; 801-487-8711
Walter Maldonado, Conservation Director; P.O. Box 482, Green River, UT 84525-0482; 435-564-8147; viper@etv.net

UTAH NATIVE PLANT SOCIETY
P.O. Box 520041
Salt Lake City, UT 84152-0041 United States
Phone: 801-272-3275
E-mail: unps@xmission.com
Website: www.unps.org
Founded: 1978
Membership: 101–1,000
Scope: Local
Description: Our organization is charitable and non-profit dedicated to the understanding, preservation, enjoyment, and responsible use of the Utah native plants. We wish to foster public recognition of the diverse flora of the state.
Publication(s): Sego Lily, Heritage Garden Native Plant Propagation Workshop Booklet
Contact(s):
Mindy Wheeler, Salt Lake Chapter President; 801-561-0779; mindywheeler@usa.net
Susan Meyer, Chairman; smeyer@sisna.com
Therese Meyer, Secretary; 801-272-3275; tmeyer@xmission.com
Janett Warner, Central Utah Chapter; janettw@hubwest.com

UTAH NATURE STUDY SOCIETY
Attn: President Utah Nature Study Society, 2853 S. 23rd East
Salt Lake City, UT 84109 United States
Phone: 801-484-2366
Founded: 1954
Scope: State
Description: Promotes conservation and nature education through workshops and field trips for members; publicizes conservation problems and issues through meetings and its newsletter. Member of Utah Associated Garden Clubs.
Publication(s): UWA Review
Keyword(s): Land Issues, Public Lands/Greenspace, Wildlife & Species
Contact(s):
Dorothy Platt, President; 2853 S. 23rd East, Salt Lake City, UT 84109
Maria Dickerson, Secretary; 323 S. 2nd W., Tooele, UT 84074
Catherine Quinn, Editor; 1383 S. 300 East, Salt Lake City, UT 84115
Jean White, Executive Secretary; 377 E. 5300 S., Murray, UT 84107-6019

UTAH WILDERNESS COALITION
P.O. Box 520974
Salt Lake City, UT 84152-0974 United States
Phone: 801-486-2872   Fax: 801-485-5572
E-mail: wildutah@xmission.com
Website: www.uwcoalition.org
Founded: 1985
Scope: National
Description: Promote and coordinate the preservation of U.S. BLM wildlands in southern and western Utah through public education and the passage of America's Redrock Wilderness Act. The goal includes protection of the remaining wilderness quality public lands under the National Wilderness Preservation System.
Keyword(s): Land Issues, Public Lands/Greenspace, Recreation/Ecotourism

UTAH WILDLIFE FEDERATION
P.O. Box 526367
Salt Lake City, UT 84152-6367 United States
Phone: 801-487-1946   Fax: 801-773-0412
E-mail: uwfhal@xmission.com
Scope: State
Description: A representative statewide organization, affiliated with the National Wildlife Federation, dedicated to the protection and enhancement of wildlife and its habitat through public education and government interaction.
Publication(s): Utah Wildlife News

UTAH WOODLAND OWNERS COUNCIL
Utah State Forestry Extension
5215 Old Maine Hill
Logan, UT 84322-5215 United States
Phone: 801-277-1615
E-mail: darrenm@cnr.usu.edu
Founded: 1997
Membership: 1–100

Scope: State

Description: A statewide organization affiliated with the National Woodland Owners Association and associated with Utah Farms Bureau, that is working for good forest management practices on the private forest and ranch land in Utah.

Keyword(s): Forests/Forestry

V

VENICE AREA BEAUTIFICATION, INC
VENETIAN WATERWAY PARK
Venice Area Beautification. Inc
333 South Tamiami Trail, Suite 225
Venice, FL 34285 United States
Phone: 941-486-8756   Fax: 941-486-8795
E-mail: knight.marketing@verizon.net
Website: www.vabi.org

Founded: 1993
Membership: 1-100
Scope: Local, State

Description: Venice Area Beautification, Inc (VABI) is the non-profit organization constructing and maintaining the Venetian Waterway Park (VWP). This linear trail upon completion will run along both sides of the Intracoastal Waterway in Venice, FL. To date, 2.5 of the planned 10-mile trail are complete. The trail is promoting a clean environment, stressing the importance of protecting natural habitats and encouraging daily outdoor exercise.

VERMONT ASSOCIATION OF CONSERVATION DISTRICTS
487 Rowell Hill Rd.
Berlin, VT 5602 United States
Phone: 802-229-9250

Scope: State

Publication(s): Annual Reports

Contact(s):
Claire Ayer, Vice President; 802-545-2142
Rita Visson, Treasurer; 240 Vermont Rt. 100, Orange, VT 05641; 802-479-9538

VERMONT BASS FEDERATION
Attn: President, 19 Pinewood Rd.
Montpelier, VT 05602 United States
Phone: 802-223-7793
E-mail: nsk1@together.net
Website: www.vermontbass.com

Founded: 1991
Membership: 101-1,000
Scope: State

Description: An organization of Bassmaster chapters, affiliated with the Bass Anglers Sportsman Society, organized to fight pollution, assist state and national conservation agencies in their efforts, and teach the young people of our country good conservation practices. Dedicated to the realistic conservation of our water resources.

Keyword(s): Pollution (general), Recreation/Ecotourism, Water Habitats & Quality, Wildlife & Species

Contact(s):
David Derner, Conservation Director; 46 Cooper Rd., Milton, VT 05468-4013; 802-893-1386; docbass@sover.net

VERMONT INSTITUTE OF NATURAL SCIENCE
27023 Church Hill Rd.
Woodstock, VT 05091 United States
Phone: 802-457-2779   Fax: 802-457-1053
E-mail: info@vinsweb.org
Website: www.vinsweb.org

Founded: 1972
Scope: State

Description: The mission of VINS is to protect Vermont's natural heritage through environmental education and research. VINS Raptor Center, Living Museum of birds of prey, on VINS nature preserve.

Publication(s): Hands on Nature, Records of Vermont Birds, Vermont Institute of Natural Science

Keyword(s): Agriculture/Farming, Forests/Forestry, Land Issues

Contact(s):
Deborah Granquist, President Board of Directors
Jenepher Linglebach, Vice President
Sherman Kent, Executive Director
Christopher Rimmer, Research Director
Marsha Whitney, Education Director

VERMONT LAND TRUST
8 Bailey Ave.
Montpelier, VT 05602 United States
Phone: 802-223-5234   Fax: 802-223-4223
E-mail: info@vlt.org
Website: www.vlt.org

Founded: 1977
Membership: 1,001-10,000
Scope: Regional

Description: Conserving the productive, recreational, and scenic lands that help give Vermont and its communities their distinctive rural character.

Publication(s): Tri-annual newsletters, Annual Report

Keyword(s): Land Issues

Contact(s):
Darby Bradley, President; 8 Bailey Ave., Montpelier, VT 05602; 802-223-5234; darby@vlt.org
Gil Livingston, Vice President for Land Concervation; 8 Bailey Ave., Montpelier, VT 05602; 802-223-5234
Barbara Wagner, Vice President of Operations; 8 Bailey Ave., Montpelier, VT 05602; 802-223-5234

VERMONT NATURAL RESOURCES COUNCIL
9 Bailey Ave.
Montpelier, VT 05602 United States
Phone: 802-223-2328, ext. 110   Fax: 802-223-0287
E-mail: info@vnrc.org
Website: www.vnrc.org

Founded: 1963
Membership: 1,001-10,000
Scope: Local, State, Regional, National

Description: The Vermont Natural Resources Council is Vermont's leading environmental education, policy, & advocacy organization since 1963. VNRC maintains strong programs in forests, land use and water quality. VNRC uses a 4 point strategy in its conservation programs: 1) research, 2) policy development, 3) passage, implementation and/or enforcement of the environmental laws, 4) citizen education and grassroots action. VNRC contributes to statewide and national environmental policy development

Publication(s): The Legislative Bulletin, Vermont Environmental Directory, Vermont Environmental Report

Keyword(s): Agriculture/Farming, Air Quality/Atmosphere, Climate Change, Ecosystems (precious), Energy, Executive/Legislative/Judicial Reform, Forests/Forestry, Land Issues, Pollution (general), Public Lands/Greenspace, Reduce/Reuse/Recycle, Sprawl/Urban Planning, Transportation

Contact(s):
Elizabeth Courtney, Executive Director; 802-223-2328; ext. 116; Fax: 802-223-0287; ecourtney@vnrc.org
Kelly Lowry, General Counsel/Water Program Director; 802-223-2328; ext. 119; Fax: 802-223-0287; klowry@vnrc.org
Patrick Berry, Communication Director; 802-223-2328; ext. 111; Fax: 802-223-0287; pberry@vnrc.org
Matteo Burani, Outreach Coordinator; 802-223-2328; ext. 112; Fax: 802-223-0287; mburani@vnrc.org

Jamey Fidel, Forest/Biodiversity Program Director; 802-223-2328; ext. 117; Fax: 802-223-0287; jfidel@vnrc.org

Jimmy Fordham, Office Mgr./Admin. Asst.; 802-223-2328; ext. 110; Fax: 802-223-0287; jfordham@vnrc.org

Kim Kendall, Staff Scientist; 802-223-2328; ext. 118; Fax: 802-223-0287; kkendall@vnrc.org

Lucy Morini, Financial Coordinator; 802-223-2328; ext. 114; Fax: 802-223-0287; lmorini@vnrc.org

Erin Tittel, Membership Coordinator; 802-223-2328; ext. 114; Fax: 802-223-0287; etittel@vnrc.org

Steve Holmes, Sustainable Communities Director; 802-223-2328; ext. 120; Fax: 802-223-0287; sholmes@vnrc.org

Stephanie Mueller, Editor/Development Director; 802-223-2328; ext. 113; Fax: 802-223-0287; smueller@vnrc.org

VERMONT STATE-WIDE ENVIRONMENTAL EDUCATION PROGRAMS (SWEEP)

c/o Vermont Natural Resources Council
9 Bailey Avenue
Montpelier, VT 05602 United States
Phone: 802-985-8686

Founded: 1973
Membership: 1–100
Scope: State

Description: SWEEP is a coalition of individuals and organizations promoting environmental education in Vermont. SWEEP's purpose is to foster environmental appreciation and understanding in order to enable Vermonters to make responsible decisions affecting the environment.

Publication(s): SWEEP Newsletter

Keyword(s): Agriculture/Farming, Ecosystems (precious), Forests/Forestry, Population, Reduce/Reuse/Recycle, Water Habitats & Quality, Wildlife & Species

Contact(s):
Steve Hagenbuch, Co-Chair; Audubon Vermont, 255 Sherman Hollow Rd., Huntington,, VT 05462; 802-434-3068
Linda Wellings, Co-Chair; Shelburne Farms, 1611 Harbor Rd., Shelburne, VT 05482; 802-985-8686

VERMONT WOODLANDS ASSOCIATION

P.O. Box 196
Poultney, VT 05764 United States
Phone: 802-287-4284   Fax: 802-287-4285
E-mail: info@vermontwoodlands.org
Website: www.vermontwoodlands.org

Founded: 1993
Membership: 101–1,000
Scope: State

Description: A statewide organization, affiliated with the National Woodland Owners Association, organized to promote sound forest management throughout Vermont.

Publication(s): Vermont Woodlands

Keyword(s): Forests/Forestry

Contact(s):
Putnam W. Blodgett, President; putblodgett@valley.net
John Hemenway, Vice President; 802-765-4324; jthemenway@aol.com
Stanley James, Vice President; 822 Lemon Fair Rd., Weybridge VT, 05753,
Harry Chandler, Executive Director
Robert Darrow, Immediate Past President; 802-773-7144

VERNAL POOL SOCIETY, THE

P.O. Box 2154
Ramona, CA 92065 United States
Phone: 760-789-4085   Fax: 760-789-4566
E-mail: maryanne@pentis.com
Website: www.pentis.com

Founded: 1999
Scope: Local, State

Description: The Vernal Pool Society is dedicated to the preservation of the few remaining Vernal Pools by maintaining a voice for this precious and unique biome. We are creating an awareness and understanding of the environmental problems facing these isolated wetlands through education and advocacy. We develop and promote effective management and monitoring practices which will ensure survival of the entire Vernal Pool ecosystem.

Publication(s): The Magic of Vernal Pools, Vernal Pool Consulting

Keyword(s): Ecosystems (precious), Ethics/Environmental Justice, Land Issues, Public Lands/Greenspace, Recreation/Ecotourism, Sprawl/Urban Planning, Water Habitats & Quality, Wildlife & Species

Contact(s):
Mary Anne Pentis, President/CEO; 760-789-4085; Fax: 760-789-4566; maryanne@pentis.com
Alisha Leigh, Director; 760-789-4085; Fax: 760-789-40566; moonbeam@adnc.com
Al Pentis, Wetland Biologist; 760-789-4085; Fax: 760-789-40566; al@pentis.com

VINEYARD CONSERVATION SOCIETY

VINEYARD CONSERVATION ALMANAC
P.O. Box 2189
Vineyard Haven, MA 02568 United States
Phone: 508-693-9588   Fax: 508-693-0683
E-mail: almanac@vineyardconservationsociety.org
Website: almanac.vineyardconservationsociety.org

Founded: 1965
Scope: Local

Description: The Vineyard Conservation Society was founded in 1965 on the Island of Martha's Vineyard and is proactively involved in preserving land, protecting the Island from unwise development and educating the public on environmental issues. The Vineyard Conservation Almanac is the Island's most comprehensive online resource for information relating to the Vineyard environment. The Conservation Almanac offers quick and easy access to the Island's government processes and environmental community.

Keyword(s): Agriculture/Farming, Air Quality/Atmosphere, Climate Change, Ecosystems (precious), Energy, Land Issues, Oceans/Coasts/Beaches, Pollution (general), Public Lands/Greenspace, Reduce/Reuse/Recycle, Sprawl/Urban Planning, Transportation, Water Habitats & Quality

VIRGIN ISLANDS CONSERVATION DISTRICT

Attn: President, P.O. Box 1576
Fredericksted, VI 841 United States

Scope: State

Publication(s): Federation Record, The

Contact(s):
Hans Lawaetz, President and Board Member; P.O. Box 1576, Fredericksted, VI 00841; 340-788-2229; Fax: 340-778-0270
Joseph Samuel, Vice President; P.O. Box 241, Fredericksted, St. Croix, VI 00841; 340-772-3168
Enrico Gasperi, Secretary and Treasurer; P.O. Box 895, Christiansted, VI 00824; 340-773-2386
Cedrick Lewis, Alternate Board Member; P.O. Box 303142, St. Thomas, VI 00803; 340-775-7393

VIRGIN ISLANDS CONSERVATION SOCIETY, INC.

Arawak Bldg., Suite 3, Gallows Bay
Christiansted, VI 00820 United States
Phone: 340-773-1989   Fax: 340-773-7545
E-mail: sea@viaccess.net
Website: stxenvironmental.tripod.com

Founded: 1968
Membership: 101–1,000
Scope: Regional

Description: A representative statewide organization, affiliated with the National Wildlife Federation, dedicated to the

protection and enhancement of wildlife and its habitat through public education and government interaction.
Keyword(s): Agriculture/Farming, Land Issues, Pollution (general)
Contact(s):
Carlos Tesitor, President
Carla Joseph, Representative
Tysha Jules, Education Programs Contact
Stevie Ketcham, Treasurer
Emy Thomas, Editor; fhenry@vvi.edu

VIRGINIA ASSOCIATION FOR PARKS
5616 Bloomfield Drive #103
Alexandria, VA 22312 United States
Phone: 703-941-1350   Fax: 202-548-0595
E-mail: info@virginiaparks.org
Website: www.virginiaparks.org
Founded: 1997
Membership: 1–100
Scope: State
Description: Assisting park friends organizations where they exist and helping to organize them in parks without a support group.
Keyword(s): Land Issues, Public Lands/Greenspace, Recreation/Ecotourism, Wildlife & Species
Contact(s):
Johnny Finch, Co-Chairman; 540-895-5061; johnny_finch@yahoo.com
Davinder Khanna, Treasurer; davinder@parksonline.org

VIRGINIA ASSOCIATION OF CONSERVATION DISTRICTS
7293 Hanover Green Dr., Suite B-101
Mechanicsville, VA 23111 United States
Phone: 804-559-0324
Scope: State
Contact(s):
Daphne Jamison, President; 540-721-2361; rjam229@aol.com
Greg Evans, 2nd Vice President; 8400 Oakford Dr., Springfield, VA 22152; 703-644-1227; soilandh2o@aol.com
Jay Gilliam, 1st Vice President; 540-377-0179; strmiwla@cfw.com
Stephanie Martin, Executive Director; 7293 Hanover Green Dr., Suite B101, Mechanicsville, VA 23111; 804-559-0324; Fax: 804-559-0325
James Byrne, Secretary/Treasurer; Rt. 1 Box 351, Reva, VA 22735; 540-547-2932; tohisplace1@juno.com
John Dixon, Past President; 1228 Rendezous Ln., Bedford, VA 24523, 540-586-8969

VIRGINIA BASS FEDERATION
Attn: President, 28447 Cabin Point Rd.
Disputanta, VA 23842 United States
Phone: 757-428-4280   Fax: 804-834-8198
Website: www.vabass.com
Membership: 1,001–10,000
Scope: State
Description: An organization of Bassmaster chapters, affiliated with the Bass Anglers Sportsman Society, organized to fight pollution, assist state and national conservation agencies in their efforts, and teach the young people of our country good conservation practices. Dedicated to the realistic conservation of our water resources.
Publication(s): Virginia B.A.S.S. Federation Newsletter "Tightlines"
Keyword(s): Air Quality/Atmosphere, Land Issues, Water Habitats & Quality
Contact(s):
Roger Fitchett, President
Mitchell Perkins, Acting Conservation Director; 12003 Bourne Road, Glen Allen, VA 23059; 804-264-1124; HUNTNBASS1@aol.com

VIRGINIA CONSERVATION NETWORK
1001 E. Broad St., Suite LL 35-C
Richmond, VA 23219 United States
Phone: 804-644-0283   Fax: 804-644-0286
E-mail: vcngeneral@aol.com
Website: www.vcnva.org
Founded: 1969
Membership: 101–1,000
Scope: State
Description: The Virginia Conservation Network is a network of 100 organizations. VCN's mission is to protect the Commonwealth's air, lands, and waters for the benefit of the people, as guaranteed by the Virginia Constitution.
Publication(s): 1999 Voting Summary
Keyword(s): Agriculture/Farming, Air Quality/Atmosphere, Land Issues, Sprawl/Urban Planning, Transportation, Water Habitats & Quality
Contact(s):
Chris Miller, President; cmiller@pecva.org
Anne Marshall, Vice President; aamvirginia@hotmail.com
Jo Ann Spevacek, Secretary
Martha Wingfield, Treasurer; marlridge@aol.com

VIRGINIA FORESTRY ASSOCIATION
P.O. Box 72080
Richmond, VA 23255 United States
Phone: 804-741-0836
E-mail: vafa@erols.com
Website: www.vaforestry.org
Founded: 1943
Membership: 1,001–10,000
Scope: Local, State, National
Description: An association of landowners and forest industry that promotes stewardship and wise use of forest resources for the economic and environmental benefits of all Virginians.
Publication(s): Fact sheets, News and Notes - newsletter, Virginia Forests Magazine
Keyword(s): Forests/Forestry, Land Issues, Pollution (general), Sprawl/Urban Planning, Water Habitats & Quality, Wildlife & Species
Contact(s):
Paul Howe, Executive Vice President

VIRGINIA NATIVE PLANT SOCIETY
Blandy Experimental Farm, 400 Blandy Farm Lane
Unit 2
Boyce, VA 22620 United States
Phone: 540-837-1600   Fax: 540-837-1523
E-mail: vnpsofc@shentel.net
Website: www.vnps.org
Founded: 1982
Membership: 1,001–10,000
Scope: State
Description: The VNPS and ten chapters throughout Virginia seek further appreciation and conservation of Virginia's wild plants and habitats. Programs emphasize public education, protection of endangered species, habitat preservation, control of invasive alien plants and encouragement of appropriate landscape use of native plants. Includes both amateurs and professionals.
Publication(s): Bulletin, Chapter Newsletters, List of Recommended Native Plants for Landscaping and Restoration, Factsheets on Invasive Alien Plants, List of Invasive Alien Plants for Virginia, Nursery Sources to Native Plants, Virginia Wildflower of the Year
Keyword(s): Forests/Forestry, Land Issues, Public Lands/Greenspace, Reduce/Reuse/Recycle, Water Habitats & Quality, Wildlife & Species
Contact(s):
Carol Gardner, Shenandoah President; 3858 Wayfarers Trail, Bridgewater, VA 22812; w-cgardner@rica.net

Kit Hayden, South Hampton Roads President; 841 Five Point Rd., Virginia Beach, VA 23454
Butch Kelly, Blue Ridge Wildflower Society Chapter President; 8564 Gravel Hill Rd., Catawba, VA 24070; 540-427-0117
Jocelyn Slayden & Mary Anne Gibbons, Piedmont Co-Presidents; P.O. Box 677, the Plains, VA 20198; 540-349-3248; jocelyna@erols.com
Ann Messick, John Clayton Northern Neck Chapter President; 157 Otter Cove Lane, Kilmarnock, VA 22482; 804-435-6673; annm@crosslink.net
Marianne Mooney, Potowmack President; 1112 N. Powhatan St., Arlington, VA 22205; e-mail-moosfy@webtv.net
Charles Smith, Prince William Wildflower Society President; 8407 Sunset Dr., Manassas, VA 20110-3827; chrlssmith@juno.com
Nicky Staunton, President; 8815 Fort Drive, Manassas, VA 20110; 703-368-9803; nstaunton@earthlink.net
Phil Stokes, Jefferson Chapter President; 110 Apple Lane, Charlottesville, VA 22903; 434-293-4217
Anita Tuttle, Fredericksburg Area-President; 7286 Sherwood Forest Dr., King George, VA 22485; 540-775-4188; amtuttle@crosslink.net
Dean Walton, Pocahontas President; 1700 Blakemore Rd, Richmond, VA 23225
Sally Annderson, 2nd Vice President
Michael Swayer, 1st Vice President; P.O. Box 677, Yorktown, VA 23690; 804-262-9887; ext. 333; waterborne@aol.com
Pat Baldwin, Director; 430 Yale Dr., Hampton, VA 23666; 757-874-0892; Fax: 757-874-3037
Allen Bellden, Director; 1202 W. 45th St., Richmond, VA 23225; 804-786-7951; ajb@dcr.state.va.us
Jim Bruce, Director; 20042 Sterling Creek Ln., Rockville, VA 23146; 804-749-4304; jgbruce@erols.com
Cole Burrell, Director; P.O. Box 76, Free Union, VA 22940; 804-975-2859; nldr@aol.com
Faith Campbell, Director; 8208 Dabney Ave., Springfield, VA 22152; phytodoer@aol.com
Boleyn Dale, Director of Registry; P.O. Box 85, Rt. 1006, Moon, VA 23119; bkd@visi.net
Deanne Eversmyer, Director of Horticulture; 1918 Leonard Road, Falls Church, VA 22043; d.eversmeyer@prodigy.net
Carol Gardner, Director of Publicity; 3858 Wayfarers Trail, Bridgewater, VA 22812; w-cgardner@rica.net
Nancy Hugo, Director; 11208 Gwathmey Church Rd., Ashland, VA 23005; nancyhugo@aol.com
Mary Painter, Director of Membership Chair; P.O. Box D, Hume, VA 22639; vanatvs@erols.com
Stanwyn Shetler, Director of Botany; 142 E. Meadowland Lane, Sterling, VA 20164-1144; 202-786-2996; Fax: 202-786-2563; shetler.stanwyn@nmnh.si.edu
Charles Smith, Director of Fund Raising; 8407 Sunset Dr., Manassas, VA 201112; chrissmith@juno.com
Jessica Strother, Director of Conservation; 6004 Windward Dr., Burke, VA 22015; 703-324-1795; sylvantica9@juno.com
Pam Weiringo, Director of Publication; 2740 Derwent Dr., SW, Roanoke, VA 24015; 540-772-3660
Sally Anderson, Co-Recording Secretary; 112 Old Forest Circle, Winchester, VA 22602; 540-722-3072; rccsca@visuallink.com
John Magee, Corresponding Secretary; 2716 West Ox Road, Herndon, VA 20171; euphoria@aol.com
Mary Pockman, Co-Recording Secretary; 7301 Hooking Road, McLean, VA 22101
Roma Sherman, Treasurer; 658 Federal St., Paris, VA 20130; roma@ashbyinn.com

VIRGINIA RESOURCE-USE EDUCATION COUNCIL
P.O. Box 11109
Richmond, VA 23240 United States
Phone: 804-698-4442   Fax: 804-698-4533
E-mail: amregn@deq.state.va.us
Website: www.vanaturally.com
Founded: 1952
Membership: 1–100
Scope: State
Description: A volunteer, nonprofit organization, composed of members of the state and federal government, colleges, and private industry, working to promote the broad principle of environmental education. The Council offers conservation education workshops for educators across Virginia, and is staff to the Commonwealth's EE network and statewide education program.
Publication(s): The Virginia Natural Resources Education Guide
Contact(s):
Dawn Shank, Chairman; Dept. of Conservation & Recreation, 203 Governor Street, Richmond, VA 23219; 804-692-0903; dshank@dcr.state.va.us
Susan Gilley, Secretary; Department of Game and Inland Fisheries, Box 11104, Richmond, VA 23230; 804-367-1000
Ann Regn, Treasurer; Department of Environmental Quality, P.O. Box 10009, Richmond, VA 23240-0009; 804-698-4442; Fax: 804-698-4453; amregn@deq.state.va.us

VIRGINIA SOCIETY OF ORNITHOLOGY
7451 Little River Turnpike, #202
Annandale, VA 22003 United States
Phone: 703-305-7381
Founded: 1929
Scope: State
Description: Dedicated to all aspects of the birds of Virginia, including conservation, field research, education of any interested person or group, and dissemination of all types of information. The VSO coordinates with state agencies and with other private organizations in this mission.
Publication(s): Raven, The, VSO Newsletter
Keyword(s): Wildlife & Species
Contact(s):
Larry Lynch, President; 9430 Tuxford Rd., Richmond, VA 23236; 804-272-8582
Lauren Scott, Secretary
Barbara Thrasher, Treasurer; 120 Woodbine Dr., Lynchburg, VA 24502; 804-239-5850

W

WARREN COUNTY CONSERVATION BOARD
ANNETT NATURE CENTER
15565 118th Avenue
Indianola, IA 50125 United States
Phone: 515-961-6169   Fax: 515-961-7100
E-mail: wccb@mindspring.com
Website: www.warrenccb.org
Membership: 1,001–10,000
Scope: Local, State
Description: Located in central Iowa, the Warren County Conservation Board provides environmental and outdoor education for all ages for nearly all environmental concerns. County parks include points of interest such as biking trails, public hunting, and historical landmarks.
Publication(s): Three Rivers Journal
Keyword(s): Air Quality/Atmosphere, Climate Change, Ecosystems (precious), Energy, Ethics/Environmental Justice, Forests/Forestry, Land Issues, Pollution (general), Public Lands/Greenspace, Recreation/Ecotourism, Reduce/Reuse/Recycle, Sprawl/Urban Planning, Water Habitats & Quality
Contact(s):
Laura Surber, Naturalist
Joel Van Roeckel, Naturalist

WASHINGTON ASSOCIATION OF CONSERVATION DISTRICTS
Attn: Executive Director
16564 Bradley Rd.
Bow, WA 98232 United States
Phone: 360-757-1094   Fax: 360-757-3923
E-mail: wacd@mcia.com
Website: www.wacd.org

Founded: 1942
Membership: 101–1,000
Scope: State
Description: Association of Conservation District supervisors
Contact(s):
- Colin Bennett, President; 185 Beebe Rd., Goldendale, WA 98620; 509-773-5065; Fax: 509-773-5600; cbennett@gorge.net
- Wade Troutman, Vice President; 509-686-2061
- Bob Haberman, National Director; 771 Hungry Junction Rd., Ellensburg, WA 98926; 509-925-1713; Fax: 509-925-7730; bobhaber@eburg.net
- Pat McGregor, Executive Director; 3911 S. K St., Tacoma, WA 98418; 253-473-4999; Fax: 253-473-7246
- Monte Marti, Secretary and Treasurer; 11605 33rd Ct., NE, Lake Stevens, WA 98258; 425-261-6678; Fax: 425-258-4839

WASHINGTON BASS FEDERATION
1721 South Methow St.
Wenatchee, WA 98801 United States
Phone: 425-251-3214
E-mail: joe.arballo@wabass.org
Website: www.wabass.org

Membership: 101–1,000
Scope: State
Description: An organization of Bassmaster chapters, affiliated with the Bass Anglers Sportsman Society, organized to fight pollution, assist state and national conservation agencies in their efforts, and teach the young people of our country good conservation practices. Dedicated to the realistic conservation of our water resources.
Publication(s): The Washington State B.A.S.S (Quarterly Newsletter)
Keyword(s): Energy, Land Issues, Reduce/Reuse/Recycle
Contact(s):
- Joe Arballo, President
- Martin Bixby, Conservation Director; 427 West 18th Ave., Kennewick, WA 99337; 509-582-7239; martin.bixby@wabass.org

WASHINGTON ENVIRONMENTAL COUNCIL
615 2nd Avenue, Suite 380
Seattle, WA 98104 United States
Phone: 206-622-8103   Fax: 206-622-8113
E-mail: wec@wecprotects.org
Website: www.wecprotects.org

Founded: 1967
Membership: 1,001–10,000
Scope: State
Description: The Washington Environmental Council protects Washington's environment & natural heritage for this and future generations by educating key state decision-makers and advocating for the improvement and enforcement of environmental laws.
Publication(s): WEC Voices, State Legislative Agenda
Keyword(s): Development/Developing Countries, Forests/Forestry, Oceans/Coasts/Beaches, Water Habitats & Quality, Wildlife & Species
Contact(s):
- Jay Manning, President
- Josh Baldi, Policy Director
- Joan Crooks, Executive Director
- Tom Geiger, Editor

WASHINGTON FARM FORESTRY ASSOCIATION
P.O. Box 7663
Olympia, WA 98507 United States
Phone: 360-459-0984   Fax: 360-459-0984
E-mail: info@wafarmforestry.com
Website: www.wafarmforestry.com

Founded: 1944
Membership: 1,001–10,000
Scope: State
Description: A statewide organization affiliated with the National Woodland Owners Association, founded to help small woodland owners acquire information on better management of small timber tracts.
Publication(s): Northwest Woodlands, Landowner News
Keyword(s): Forests/Forestry
Contact(s):
- Bob Playfair, President
- Rick Dunning, Executive Director and Editor, Landowner News; 360-943-3875; nelswh@home.com
- Norma Green, Treasurer; nfgreen@reachone.com
- Lori Rasor, Editor, Northwest Woodlands; 4033 SW Canyon Rd., Portland, OR 97221; 502-228-1367
- Bill Woods, Secretary
- Erin Woods, Secretary

WASHINGTON FOUNDATION FOR THE ENVIRONMENT
P.O. Box 2123
Seattle, WA 98111 United States
Phone: 253-838-3466
E-mail: info@wffe.org
Website: www.wffe.org

Founded: 1979
Scope: State
Description: Dedicated to preserving and enhancing the environmental heritage of Washington state by making small grants to support educational and innovative projects in both the public and private sectors. for grant guidelines, send a message to JudyTurpin@aol.com

WASHINGTON NATIVE PLANT SOCIETY
6310 NE 74th Street, Ste. 215E
Seattle, WA 98115 United States
Phone: 206-527-3210
E-mail: wnps@wnps.org
Website: www.wnps.org

Founded: 1976
Membership: 1,001–10,000
Scope: State
Description: To promote the appreciation and conservation of Washington's native plants and their habitats through study, education, and advocacy.
Publication(s): Occasional Papers, Douglasia
Keyword(s): Ecosystems (precious), Forests/Forestry, Public Lands/Greenspace, Recreation/Ecotourism, Water Habitats & Quality, Wildlife & Species
Contact(s):
- Tom Johnson, President; 7742 32nd Ave., Seattle, WA 98115; 206-525-3176
- Catherine Hovanic, Administrator; Washington Native Plant Society, 6310 NE 74th St., Ste. 215E, Seattle, WA 98115; 206-527-3210; wnps@wnps.org

WASHINGTON RECREATION AND PARK ASSOCIATION
350 S. 333rd St., Suite 103
Federal Way, WA 98003 United States
Phone: 253-874-1283   Fax: 253-661-3929
E-mail: wrpa@wrpatoday.org
Website: www.wrpatoday.org

Founded: 1947
Membership: 1,001–10,000
Scope: State
Description: Dedicated to enhancing and promoting parks, recreation, and leisure pursuits in Washington state, and plays a vital role in promoting public support for parks and recreation.
Publication(s): Syllabus
Keyword(s): Recreation/Ecotourism
Contact(s):
   Daryl Faber, President
   Mike Dobb, Vice President
   Brit Kramer, Executive Director

WASHINGTON STATE SOCIETY OF AMERICAN FORESTERS
NORTHWEST OFFICE
4033 SW Canyon Rd.
Portland, OR 97221 United States
Phone: 503-224-8046   Fax: 503-226-2515
Website: www.waforestry.org

Founded: 1900
Scope: State
Description: Represents the forestry profession in advancing the science, technology, education, and practice of forestry for the benefit of forests, forest managers, and the public.
Publication(s): Western Forester
Contact(s):
   Lori Rasor, Manager/Editor; 4033 SW Canyon Rd., Portland, OR 97221

WASHINGTON TOXICS COALITION
4649 Sunnyside Avenue N
Suite 540
Seattle, WA 98103 United States
Phone: 206-632-1545   Fax: 206-632-8661
E-mail: info@watoxics.org
Website: www.watoxics.org

Founded: 1981
Membership: 1,001–10,000
Scope: Local, State, Regional
Description: Works to reduce society's reliance on toxic chemicals through research, education, advocacy, organizing and litigation.
Publication(s): Alternatives, Fact Sheets, Home Safe Home (fact sheets), No Place for Poisons: Reducing Pesticides in School, Trubbling Bubbles: The Case for Replacing Alkylphenol Ethoxylate Surfacants, Grow Smart, Grow Safe: A Consumer Guide to Lawn and Garden Products
Keyword(s): Ethics/Environmental Justice, Pollution (general), Public Lands/Greenspace, Recreation/Ecotourism, Transportation
Contact(s):
   David Stitzhal, President
   Gregg Small, Executive Director
   Don Bollinger, Treasurer
   Dave Coffman, Secretary
   Martha Dale, Secretary

WASHINGTON TRAILS ASSOCIATION
1305 4th Ave., Suite 512
Seattle, WA 98101-2401 United States
Phone: 206-625-1367   Fax: 206-625-9249
Website: www.wta.org

Founded: 1973
Membership: 1,001–10,000
Scope: State
Description: Washington Trails Association works to protect and enhance hiking opportunities in Washington State through education, volunteer trail maintenance, advocacy and cooperation with other trail users.
Publication(s): Washington Trails - Monthly Magazine
Keyword(s): Public Lands/Greenspace, Recreation/Ecotourism
Contact(s):
   Elizabeth Lunney, Executive Director; elunney@wta.org

WASHINGTON WILDERNESS COALITION
4649 Sunnyside Ave., N., Suite 520
Seattle, WA 98103 United States
Phone: 206-633-1992   Fax: 206-633-1996
E-mail: info@wawild.org
Website: www.wawild.org

Founded: 1979
Membership: 10,001–100,000
Scope: State
Description: WWC is a statewide organization of individuals and groups dedicated to preserving wilderness and biodiversity for the benefit of future generations. WWC works to protect and restore wildlands and waters in Washington State through outreach, public education, organizing, and support of grassroots conservation groups.
Publication(s): Washington Wildfire Journal
Keyword(s): Land Issues, Wildlife & Species
Contact(s):
   Martin Loesch, President
   Mike Peterson, Vice President
   John Leary, Executive Director
   Jon Owen, Campaign Director
   Kristen Tremoulet, Canvass Director
   Michelle Kinsch, Treasurer
   Cyndi Lewis, Secretary

WASHINGTON WILDLIFE AND RECREATION COALITION
811 First Avenue, Suite 262
Seattle, WA 98104 United States
Phone: 206-748-0082   Fax: 206-748-0580
E-mail: info@WildlifeRecreation.org
Website: www.WildlifeRecreation.org

Founded: 1989
Scope: State
Description: A diverse group of more than 135+ environmental, business, labor, sporting, and community organizations dedicated to advocating for the permanent protection of parks and habitat in Washington State. The Coalition works to secure funding for the Washington Wildlife and Recreation Program, a competitive state grant program that enables local and state agencies to acquire and develop land for neighborhood parks and wildlife habitat areas.
Publication(s): E-newsletter, Land News
Keyword(s): Public Lands/Greenspace, Recreation/Ecotourism, Wildlife & Species
Contact(s):
   Joanna Grist, Executive Director; 206-748-0082; joanna@WildlifeRecreation.org
   Carrie Powell, Program Assistant; 206-748-0082; carrie@WildlifeRecreation.org
   Kirk Thomson, President

WASHINGTON WILDLIFE FEDERATION
P.O. Box 1966
Olympia, WA 98507-1966 United States
Phone: 360-705-1903
Website: www.washingtonwildlife.org

Scope: State
Description: A representative statewide organization, affiliated with the National Wildlife Federation, dedicated to the protection and enhancement of wildlife and its habitat through public education and government interaction.
Publication(s): Washington Wildlife News

Keyword(s): Land Issues, Water Habitats & Quality, Wildlife & Species

Contact(s):
Ed Forslof, President
Kyle Winton, Executive Director; 360-951-1727

WATER EDUCATION FOUNDATION
717 K Street
Suite 317
Sacramento, CA 95814 United States
Phone: 916-444-6240   Fax: 916-448-7699
E-mail: feedback@watereducation.org
Website: www.watereducation.org

Founded: 1977
Membership: 1–100
Scope: Local, State, Regional, National
Description: for more than 25 years, the Water Education Foundation has provided in-depth, unbiased information about water resource issues through its publications, school programs, conferences, tours, maps and videos. The Foundation's mission is to develop and implement education programs leading to a broader understanding of water issues and to resolution of water problems.

Contact(s):
Christine Schmidt, Development Director; 916-444-6240; Fax: 916-448-7699; cschmidt@watereducation.org

WATER ENVIRONMENT FEDERATION
601 Wythe St.
Alexandria, VA 22314-1994 United States
Phone: 703-684-2400   Fax: 703-684-2492
E-mail: csc@wef.org
Website: www.wef.org

Founded: 1928
Membership: 10,001–100,000
Scope: International
Description: A nonprofit technical and educational organization with the mission to preserve and enhance the global water environment. Federation members are water quality specialists from around the world, including environmental, civil and chemical engineers, biologists, government officials, treatment plant managers and operators, laboratory technicians, college professors, students, and equipment manufacturers and distributors.
Publication(s): Water Environment Research, other titles available on request, Watershed and Wet Weather Technical Bulletin, WEF Industrial Wastewater, Water Environment Regulation Watch, WEF Highlights, Water Environment and Technology
Keyword(s): Pollution (general), Water Habitats & Quality

Contact(s):
James Clark, President
William Bertera, Executive Director

WATER RESOURCES ASSOCIATION OF THE DELAWARE RIVER BASIN
P.O. Box 867
Valley Forge, PA 19482-0867 United States
Phone: 610-917-0090   Fax: 610-917-0091
E-mail: wra@wradrb.org
Website: www.wradrb.org

Founded: 1959
Scope: Regional
Description: Nonprofit federation of businesses, industries, academia, government, environmental, and citizen organizations which serves to advise of and advocate the need for adequate water supplies through the orderly conservation, development, and equitable use and reuse of the water and related land resources of the Delaware River Basin.
Publication(s): Newsletter

Keyword(s): Oceans/Coasts/Beaches, Water Habitats & Quality

Contact(s):
William Palmer, Executive Director
William McElroy, Chair

WATERLOO-WELLINGTON WILDFLOWER SOCIETY
c/o Botany Dept., University of Guelph
Guelph, N1G 2W1 Ontario Canada
Phone: 519-821-7766   Fax: 519-767-1991
E-mail: bph9@cornell.edu
Website: www.uoguelph.ca/~botcal/

Founded: 1990
Membership: 1–100
Scope: Local, Regional
Description: (Formerly the Dogtooth Group) A non-profit organization based in Guelph, Ontario dedicated to the use and protection of native plants in parks, gardens and other open spaces.
Publication(s): Dogtooth
Keyword(s): Agriculture/Farming, Ecosystems (precious), Public Lands/Greenspace, Wildlife & Species

Contact(s):
Barbara Hallett, President; bhallett@jullet.albedo.net

WATERMAN CONSERVATION EDUCATION CENTER
P.O. Box 377
403 Hilton Road
Apalachin, NY 13732 United States
Phone: 607-625-2221   Fax: 607-625-2221
E-mail: info@watermancenter.org
Website: www.watermancenter.org

Founded: 1976
Membership: 101–1,000
Scope: Regional
Description: Waterman Conservation Education Center promotes conservation education and outdoor recreation activities. We serve our members, the citizens of the Twin Tiers of New York State and Pennsylvania, and all visitors to our four wildlife refuge sites.
Keyword(s): Ecosystems (precious), Recreation/Ecotourism, Water Habitats & Quality, Wildlife & Species

Contact(s):
Scott MacDonald, Executive Director; 607-625-2221; Fax: 607-625-2221; director@watermancenter.org

WATERSHED MANAGEMENT COUNCIL
P.O. Box 1090
Mammoth Lakes, CA 93546 United States
E-mail: WMC@watershed.org
Website: www.watershed.org/

Founded: 1986
Scope: Regional
Description: The Watershed Management Council is a nonprofit, educational organization dedicated to advancing the art and science of watershed management, with an emphasis on the Western region.
Publication(s): Proceedings, Networker, The
Keyword(s): Land Issues, Pollution (general), Water Habitats & Quality

WELDER WILDLIFE FOUNDATION
P.O. Box 1400
Sinton, TX 78387 United States
Phone: 361-364-2643   Fax: 361-364-2650
E-mail: welderwf@aol.com
Website: www.hometown.aol.com/welderwf/welderweb.html

Founded: 1954

Scope: National

Description: Established by the will of the late Rob Welder, the Foundation is dedicated to the cause of conservation through research and education in wildlife ecology and management and closely related fields. Operates through a small staff, with research fellowships to graduate students only.

Keyword(s): Wildlife & Species

Contact(s):
D. Drawe, Director
Terry Blankenship, Assistant Director/Wildlife Biologist
Selma Glasscock, Assistant Director/Conservation Educator

WEST MICHIGAN ENVIRONMENTAL ACTION COUNCIL
1514 Wealthy SE, Suite 280
Grand Rapids, MI 49506-2755 United States
Phone: 616-451-3051   Fax: 616-451-3054
Website: www.wmeac.org

Founded: 1968

Scope: Local

Description: Provide leadership in environmental protection and preservation in west Michigan and throughout Michigan on issues such as water quality, land use planning and sustainable business. Through the involvement of concerned volunteers, WMEAC has helped landmark environmental legislation and assured application of existing laws.

Publication(s): Action Issue, see publications on website

Keyword(s): Air Quality/Atmosphere, Land Issues, Reduce/Reuse/Recycle

Contact(s):
Karel Rogers, President
Tom Leonard, Executive Director

WEST VIRGINIA ASSOCIATION OF CONSERVATION DISTRICT SUPERVISORS ASSOCIATION, INC.
Attn: President, P.O. Box 711
Gallipolis Ferry, WV 25515 United States

Scope: State

WEST VIRGINIA BASS FEDERATION
Attn: President
John Burdette
P. O. Box 418
Buckhannon, WV 26201 United States
Phone: 304-472-3600   Fax: 304-472-3601
E-mail: jburdette@wvbass.com
Website: www.wvbass.com

Founded: 1973

Membership: 101–1,000

Scope: State

Description: An organization of Bassmaster chapters, affiliated with the Bass Anglers Sportsman Society, organized to fight pollution, assist state and national conservation agencies in their efforts, and teach the young people of our country good conservation practices. Dedicated to the realistic conservation of our water resources.

Publication(s): Monongahela National Forest Hiking Guide, Highlands Voice, The

Keyword(s): Forests/Forestry, Land Issues, Public Lands/Greenspace, Water Habitats & Quality

Contact(s):
John Burdette, President; 304-472-3600; Fax: 304-472-3601; jburdette@wvbass.com
Jim Summers, Conservation Director; Rte. 1 Box 205, worthington, WV 26591; 304-287-7700; jsummers@wvbass.com

WEST VIRGINIA HIGHLANDS CONSERVANCY
P.O. Box 306
Charleston, WV 25321 United States

Founded: 1967

Membership: 101–1,000

Scope: State

Description: An organization devoted to the conservation and wise management of West Virginia's natural and historic resources. Active in wilderness preservation, river conservation, public lands management, forestry, mining, air and water quality, water resources management and a wide variety of other environmental and conservation issues.

Publication(s): The Highlands Voice, The Monongahela National Forest Hiking Guide

Keyword(s): Forests/Forestry, Land Issues

Contact(s):
Frank Young, President; Rt. 1 Box 108, Ripley, WV 25271; 304-372-9329
Judy Rodd, Senior Vice President; Rt. 1, Box 178, Moatsville, WV 26405; 304-265-0018
Norm Steenstra, Vice President of State Affairs; 1001 Valley Rd., Charleston, WV 25302; 304-346-5891
Jacqueline Hallinan, Treasurer; 1120 Swan Rd., Charleston, WV 25314; 304-345-3718
Andrew Maier, Secretary; Rt. 1 Box 27, Hinton, WV 25952; 304-466-3864
Bill Reed, Editor; 350 Bucks Branch, Beckley, WV 25801; 304-934-5828
Dave Saville, Membership Secretary; P.O. Box 569, Morgantown, WV 26507; 304-284-9548

WEST VIRGINIA RAPTOR REHABILITATION CENTER
P.O. Box 333
Morgantown, WV 26507 United States
Phone: 304-366-2867   Fax: 304-592-1482
E-mail: raptor@wvrrc.org
Website: www.wvrrc.org

Founded: 1983

Membership: 101–1,000

Scope: Regional

Description: The WVRRC, established in 1983, is a non-profit volunteer based organization dedicated to the rehabilitation and ultimate release of injured, sick and orphaned wild birds of prey while providing environmental education to the general public, schools and other organizations.

Publication(s): The Falcon

Keyword(s): Air Quality/Atmosphere, Ecosystems (precious), Pollution (general), Water Habitats & Quality, Wildlife & Species

Contact(s):
Natasha Diamond, Executive Director; 304-366-2867; raptor@wvrrc.org

WEST VIRGINIA WILDLIFE FEDERATION, INC.
P.O. Box 275
Paden City, WV 26159 United States
Phone: 304-782-3685
E-mail: wvwf@wvwf.org
Website: www.wvwf.org

Founded: 1950

Membership: 1,001–10,000

Scope: State

Description: A representative statewide organization, affiliated with the National Wildlife Federation, dedicated to the protection and enhancement of wildlife and its habitat through public education and government interaction.

Publication(s): West Virginia Wildlife Notes

Keyword(s): Water Habitats & Quality, Wildlife & Species

Contact(s):
William Mullins, President and Alternate Representative

WESTERN ASSOCIATION OF FISH AND WILDLIFE AGENCIES
5400 Bishop Blvd.
Cheyenne, WY 82006 United States
Phone: 307-777-4569   Fax: 307-777-4699
Website: www.wafwa.org

Scope: Regional, National
Description: A regional organization including 18 fish and wildlife agencies of 15 states and three Canadian provinces. Meets annually to consider mutual problems and provide a forum for the exchange of information at both administrative and technical levels.
Publication(s): Western Proceedings
Keyword(s): Wildlife & Species
Contact(s):
Jeff Koenings, President
Ken Ambrock, 2nd Vice President
Steven Huffaker, 1st Vice President
Dean Hildebrand, Secretary and Treasurer; 307-777-4569

WESTERN ENVIRONMENTAL LAW CENTER
1216 Lincoln Street
Eugene, OR 97401 United States
Phone: 541-485-2471   Fax: 541-485-2457
E-mail: eugene@westernlaw.org
Website: www.westernlaw.org

Founded: 1993
Membership: 1,001–10,000
Scope: Regional
Description: The Western Environmental Law Center is a nonprofit public interest law firm with offices in Eugene, Oregon; Boise, Idaho; and Taos, New Mexico. The Center represents activists, conservation groups, Indian tribes, and local governments that seek to protect and restore the forests, rivers, deserts, grasslands, wildlife, and human communities in the West.
Publication(s): Biannual Report, Defending the West
Keyword(s): Air Quality/Atmosphere, Ethics/Environmental Justice, Forests/Forestry, Land Issues, Pollution (general), Water Habitats & Quality
Contact(s):
Corrie Yackulic, President, yackulic@schroeter-goldmark.com
Mary Wood, Vice President, Secretary and Treasurer; mwood@law.uoregon.edu
Michael Axline, Litigation Director
Grove Burnett, Director of Taos Office; 505-751-0351; Fax: 505-751-1775; law@welctaos.org
Peter Frost, Executive Director

WESTERN FORESTRY AND CONSERVATION ASSOCIATION
4033 SW Canyon Rd.
Portland, OR 97221 United States
Phone: 503-226-4562   Fax: 503-226-2515
E-mail: richard@westernforestry.org
Website: www.westernforestry.org

Founded: 1909
Membership: 1–100
Scope: Regional
Description: The mission of the WFCA is to promote forest stewardship in western North America. The Association's objectives are to promote the science and practice of forestry, promote the dissemination of forestry research and technical information, and foster cooperation between federal, state, provincial, and private forest agencies.
Keyword(s): Forests/Forestry

Contact(s):
Richard Zabel, President

WESTERN HEMISPHERE SHOREBIRD RESERVE NETWORK (WHSRN)
c/o Manomet Center for Conservation Sciences
81 Stage Point Rd.
P.O. Box 1770
Manomet, MA 02345 United States
Phone: 508-224-6521   Fax: 508-224-9220
E-mail: sbrown@manomet.org
Website: www.manomet.org/WHSRN.htm

Founded: 1985
Membership: 101–1,000
Scope: International
Description: WHSRN is a voluntary nonregulatory network of over 225 partner organizations at 54 critical wetland sites in seven countries of South and North America that have joined together to study, manage, and promote the sustainable conservation of shorebirds and their habitats for the benefit of the ecosystems and people. WHSRN's strategy promotes a multiple species ecosystem approach to protection of over twenty million acres of habitats that are critical staging, nesting, and nonbrooding sites.
Publication(s): Shorebirds Across the Americas, Conservation Sciences Quarterly, Magazine of Manomet Center, Save Our Migratory Shorebirds (curriculum guide), Shorebird Atlas, Important Shorebird Staging Sites Meeting WHSRN Criteria in the U.S., Shorebird Migrations: Fundamentals for Land Managers
Keyword(s): Ecosystems (precious), Oceans/Coasts/Beaches, Public Lands/Greenspace, Recreation/Ecotourism, Water Habitats & Quality, Wildlife & Species
Contact(s):
Jim Corven, Director; 508-224-6521; ext. 227; Fax: 508-224-9220; jmcorven@manomet.org
Brian Harrington, Senior Scientist; 508-224-6521; ext. 241; Fax: 508-224-9220; BHarr@manomet.org
Heidi Luquer, Education/Outreach Coordinator; 802-436-1999; Fax: 802-436-1998; HLuquer@manomet.org

WESTERN PENNSYLVANIA CONSERVANCY
209 4th Ave.
Pittsburgh, PA 15222 United States
Phone: 412-288-2777   Fax: 412-281-1792
E-mail: wpc@paconserve.org
Website: www.paconserve.org/

Founded: 1932
Membership: 10,001–100,000
Scope: Local, State, Regional, National
Description: The Western Pennsylvania Conservancy, working together to save the places we care about, protects natural lands, promotes healthy and attractive communities and preserves Frank Lloyd Wright's masterwork Fallingwater. The Conservancy fosters the integration of ecological protection with economic and social needs while building on the core values of the community and has protected more than 200,000 acres of natural lands in Pennsylvania.
Publication(s): Conserve, Annual Calendar
Keyword(s): Agriculture/Farming, Forests/Forestry, Land Issues, Public Lands/Greenspace, Reduce/Reuse/Recycle, Wildlife & Species
Contact(s):
Larry Schweiger, President and CEO
Jacquelyn Bonomo, Vice President of Conservation Programs
Cynthia Carrow, Executive Vice President and COO
Lynda Waggoner, Vice President and Director of Fallingwater
Mike Boyle, Chairman
Julie Lalo, Vice President of Public Affairs

WESTERN WATERSHEDS PROJECT
P.O. Box 1770
Hailey, ID 83333 United States
Phone: 208-788-2290   Fax: 208-788-2298
E-mail: wwp@westernwatersheds.org
Website: www.westernwatersheds.org

Founded: 1993
Membership: 101–1,000
Scope: Local, State, Regional, National
Description: The mission of Western Watersheds Project is to protect and restore watersheds and wildlife in eight western states. WWP uses monitoring, scientific analysis, education and litigation to restore habitats, improve water quality, increase biodiversity, and protect wilderness and wildlife on public lands.
Publication(s): Welfare Ranching, Watersheds Messenger
Keyword(s): Ecosystems (precious), Ethics/Environmental Justice, Public Lands/Greenspace, Water Habitats & Quality, Wildlife & Species
Contact(s):
Jon Marvel, Executive Director; 208-788-2290; Fax: 208-788-2298; jon@westernwatersheds.org
Miriam Austin, Resources Specialist; Red Willow Research, 780 Falls Ave., #390, Twin Falls, ID 83301-3316; 208-358-0759; red_willow@mindspring.com
John Carter, Utah Director; WWP/Utah, P.O. Box 280, Mendon, UT 84325; 435-881-1232; utah@westernwatersheds.org
Stew Churchwell, Central Idaho Director; East Fork, HC67 Box 2096, Challis, ID 83226; 208-838-2374; Fax: 208-838-2374; stew@westernwatersheds.org
Judy Hall, Director of Fund Development; 208-788-2290; Fax: 208-788-2298; judy@westernwatersheds.org
Keith Raether, Director of Public Information; WWP/Montana, 2220 Landusky Ct., Missoula, MT 59801; 406-543-3030; Fax: 406-543-3769; kraether@westernwatersheds.org
Jonathan Ratner, Wyoming Director; WWP/Wyoming, P.O. Box 1160, Pinedale, WY 82941; 307-537-3111; Fax: 307-597-4058; wyoming@westernwatersheds.org
Teri Stewart, Office Administrator; 208-788-2290; Fax: 208-788-2298; teri@westernwatersheds.org

WETLAND HABITAT ALLIANCE OF TEXAS
118 E. Hospital, Suite 208
Nacogdoches, TX 75961 United States
Phone: 936-569-9428   Fax: 936-569-6349
E-mail: whatduck@txucom.net
Website: www.whatduck.org

Founded: 1984
Membership: 1,001–10,000
Scope: State, Regional
Description: A nonprofit organization of conservationists, dedicated to preserving, reclaiming, and enhancing Texas wetland habitat, that promotes the wise use of our natural resources and the progress of our society. Constructs habitat improvement projects on public and private lands, promotes educational programs, performs priority wetland research, and supports legislative conservation efforts.
Publication(s): Texas Wetlands
Keyword(s): Water Habitats & Quality
Contact(s):
John Gardere, Vice President
John Frasier, Executive Director
Neal Jenkins, Treasurer
Bruce Klingman, Chairman

WETLANDS ACTION NETWORK
P.O. Box 1145
Malibu, CA 90265 United States
Phone: 310-456-5604   Fax: 310-456-5612
E-mail: wetlandact@earthlink.net
Website: www.wetlandsactionnetwork.org

Founded: 1995
Membership: 1,001–10,000
Scope: Local, State, Regional, International
Description: We work to protect and restore wetlands along the Pacific Migratory Pathways, serving as a resource and network for wetlands activists in ten western states, Canada, Mexico and Central America. A primary focus area is Southern California, where more than 95% of historical wetlands have been destroyed in the heart of the Pacific Flyway. Los Angeles' Ballona Wetlands is a prominent campaign to recover wetlands in the Pacific bioregion.
Publication(s): Great Blue Heron Report
Keyword(s): Ecosystems (precious), Ethics/Environmental Justice, Executive/Legislative/Judicial Reform, Land Issues, Oceans/Coasts/Beaches, Water Habitats & Quality, Wildlife & Species
Contact(s):
Robert Roy van de Hoek, Director of Research and Restoration; 310-456-5604; Fax: 310-456-5612; rjvandehoek@yahoo.com

WETLANDS INTERNATIONAL
P.O. Box 471
Wageningen, 6700 AL Netherlands
Phone: 0031317478854   Fax: 0031317478850
E-mail: post@wetlands.org
Website: www.wetlands.org

Founded: 1995
Membership: 1–100
Scope: International
Description: Wetlands International is a leading global non-profit organisation dedicated solely to the crucial work of wetland conservation and sustainable management. Well-established networks of experts and close partnerships with key organisations provide Wetlands International with the essential tools for catalysing conservation activities worldwide. Our activities are based on sound science and have been carried out in over 120 countries.

WHALE AND DOLPHIN CONSERVATION SOCIETY
WDCS
Brookfield House
38 St. Paul Street
Chippenham, SN15 1LY United Kingdom
Phone: 1249449500   Fax: 12494495017
E-mail: campaign@wdcs.org
Website: www.wdcs.org

Founded: 1987
Membership: 10,001–100,000
Scope: International
Description: WDCS, the Whale and Dolphin Conservation Society, is the global voice for the protection of cetaceans (whales, dolphins and porpoises) and their environment.
Keyword(s): Oceans/Coasts/Beaches, Recreation/Ecotourism, Wildlife & Species
Contact(s):
S. Davis-Hilton, Director of Finance
Mark Simmonds, Director of Science
Chris Vick, Marketing & Communications Director
Alison Wood, Director of Conservation
Victoria Reinthal, Communications Officer; vreinthal@wdcs.org
Chris Stroud, Chief Executive

WHITE CLAY WATERSHED ASSOCIATION
P.O. Box 10
Landenberg, PA 19350 United States
Phone: 610-274-8499
E-mail: dhawk@ccil.org
Website: home.ccil.org/~wcwa/

Founded: 1965
Scope: Regional
Description: The White Clay Watershed Association is a nonprofit organization devoted to protection and improvement of the environmental quality of the White Clay Creek and valley. The Association works to improve water quality in local streams, conserve open space, woodlands, wetlands and geological features; aid in the preservation of cultural, historical and archaeological sites; increase outdoor recreation opportunities; and conduct educational programs relating to the environment.
Keyword(s): Ethics/Environmental Justice, Public Lands/Greenspace, Water Habitats & Quality
Contact(s):
John Murray, President
Robert Stark, Vice President
Donna Bush, Treasurer
Carol Catanese, Secretary

WHITETAILS UNLIMITED, INC.
P.O. Box 720, 1715 Rhode Island St.
Sturgeon Bay, WI 54235 United States
Phone: 920-743-6777   Fax: 920-743-4658
E-mail: nh@whitetailsunlimited.com
Website: www.whitetailsunlimited.com
Founded: 1982
Membership: 1–100
Scope: National
Description: Whitetails Unlimited is a national, nonprofit conservation organization. Its purpose is to raise funds in support of education, habitat enhancement, and the preservation of the hunting tradition for the direct benefit of the white-tailed deer and other wildlife species.
Publication(s): Whitetails Unlimited Magazine
Keyword(s): Recreation/Ecotourism
Contact(s):
Jeffrey Schinkten, President
William Gerl, Executive Vice President
David Hawkey, Vice President of Field Operations
Peter Gerl, Executive Director and Production Manager
Eric Carper, Manager of Merchandise and Advertising
Kevin Devault, Manager of Conservation Funding
Janet Gerl, Office Manager
Kim McKinney, Event Program Manager
Denise Dubick, Production/Design
Kevin Naze, Field Editor
Arlene Peterson, Inventory Shipment Coordinator
Peter Schoonmaker, Field Editor
Cheryl Uecker, Membership Services Coordinator

WHOOPING CRANE CONSERVATION ASSOCIATION INC.
1393 Henderson Highway
Breaux Bridge, LA 70517 United States
Phone: 337-228-7563   Fax: 337-228-7424
E-mail: wcca@myexcel.com
Website: www.whoopingcrane.com
Founded: 1961
Membership: 101–1,000
Scope: National, International
Description: A scientific and educational organization, international in scope, working to prevent the extinction of the whooping crane and save wetland habitats.
Publication(s): Grus Americana, The Whooping Crane, North America's Symbol of Conservation by Jerome J. Pratt
Keyword(s): Water Habitats & Quality, Wildlife & Species
Contact(s):
Mary Courville, Secretary and Treasurer
Marie Maltese, Editor
Jerome Pratt, Past Editor & Communication Coordinator

WILD CANID SURVIVAL AND RESEARCH CENTER
P.O. Box 760
Eureka, MO 63025 United States
Phone: 636-938-5900   Fax: 636-938-6490
E-mail: wildcanidcenter@onemain.com
Website: www.wolfsanctuary.org
Founded: 1971
Membership: 101–1,000
Scope: National
Description: A nonprofit, conservation organization dedicated to the preservation of wolves and other wild canids through education, research, and captive breeding.
Publication(s): Wild Canid Center Review, Wolf Pack Press
Keyword(s): Wildlife & Species
Contact(s):
Sue Lindsey, Executive Director
Patricia Biggerstaff, Treasurer
Margaret Ratz, Vice-Chair
William Sadler, Chairman

WILD DOG FOUNDATION, THE
P.O. Box 1603
Mineola, NY 11501-0901 United States
Phone: 516-746-0005   Fax: 516-746-0005
E-mail: info@wilddog.org
Website: www.wilddog.org
Founded: 1996
Membership: 1–100
Scope: International
Description: The foundation is a conservation and educational group. The foundation promotes wolf restoration to the Adirondack State Park in New York and the Northeast, and deals with less popular predators, mostly wild canines and hyenas. Its flagship species are the African wild dog, and coyote.
Publication(s): Wild, The
Keyword(s): Reduce/Reuse/Recycle, Wildlife & Species
Contact(s):
Frank Vincenti, President; 516-746-0005;
    savewilddogs@hotmail.com
Robert Berghaier, Vice President
Hope Ryden, Vice President
Pat Traub, Vice President
Peggy Weinberg, Vice President
Lew Egol, Vice Presdent

WILD FOUNDATION, THE
(INTERNATIONAL WILDERNESS LEADERSHIP FOUNDATION)
P.O. Box 1380
Ojai, CA 93024 United States
Phone: 805-640-0390   Fax: 805-640-0230
E-mail: info@wild.org
Website: www.wild.org
Founded: 1974
Scope: National, International
Description: Working for wilderness, wildife and people. The WILD Foundation protects and promotes the sustainability of wilderness and wildlands worldwide, and provides environmental information, education, experience and training.
Publication(s): Wilderness and Human Communities, Wilderness and Humanity - A Global issue, Wilderness, Arctic Wilderness, Wilderness, the Way Ahead for the Conservation of Earth, Wilderness Management, International Journal of Wilderness, Leaf Newsletter, The
Keyword(s): Development/Developing Countries, Ecosystems (precious), Forests/Forestry, Land Issues, Recreation/Ecotourism, Wildlife & Species

Contact(s):
- Vance Martin, President; 805-640-0390
- John Hendee, Editor in Chief, International Journal of Wilderness; hendeejo@uidaho.edu
- Michael Sweatman, Chairman, Treasurer; michael@gmtcap.com

WILD HORSE ORGANIZED ASSISTANCE, INC. (WHOA)
P.O. Box 555
Reno, NV 89504 United States
Phone: 702-851-4817
Website: www.ipt.com/htmlpub/jpi/whoa.htm

Founded: 1971
Membership: 10,001–100,000
Scope: National
Description: Directs efforts toward the welfare of wild horses and burros; implementation of federal efforts in carrying out terms of the management, protection, and control program for their welfare; student projects pertaining to all phases of our heritage.
Keyword(s): Wildlife & Species

Contact(s):
- Dawn Lappin, Executive Director and Chairman of the Board; 702-851-4817
- Leslie Johnson, Treasurer; 702-851-4817
- Russell Johnson, Vice Chairman; 702-786-7600
- Bert Lappin, Secretary; 702-851-4817

WILD ONES NATURAL LANDSCAPERS, LTD
WILD ONES
Headquarters
P.O. Box 1274
Appleton, WI 54912-1274 United States
Phone: 877-394-9453   Fax: 920-730-8654
E-mail: woresource@aol.com
Website: www.for-wild.org

Founded: 1977
Membership: 1,001–10,000
Scope: Local, National
Description: Wild Ones is a nonprofit organization seeking to educate and inform members and the public at the plants-roots level and to promote biodiversity and environmental sound practices, through natural landscaping using native species in developing plant communities.
Publication(s): Wild Ones Journal, Wild Ones Handbook
Keyword(s): Agriculture/Farming, Ecosystems (precious), Ethics/Environmental Justice, Forests/Forestry, Land Issues, Public Lands/Greenspace, Reduce/Reuse/Recycle, Water Habitats & Quality, Wildlife & Species

Contact(s):
- Joe Powelka, President; President@for-wild.org
- Mariette Nowak, Vice President; VicePresident@for-wild.org
- Steve Maassen, SFE Director; SFEdirector@for-wild.org
- Donna VanBuecken, Executive Director; ExecDirector@for-wild.org
- Portia Brown, Secretary; Secretary@for-wild.org
- Klaus Wisiol, Treasurer; Treasurer@for-wild.org

WILDCOAST
757 Emory Street
P.O. Box 161
Imperial Beach, CA 91932 United States
Phone: 619-423-8665   Fax: 619-423-8488
E-mail: sdedina@wildcoast.net
Website: www.wildcoast.net

Founded: 1999
Scope: Local, State, Regional, National, International
Description: WiLDCOAST is a partnership-based international conservation team preserving the endangered marine species and coastal wildlands of the Calfornias. Our projects include: Sea turtle recovery program of the Eastern Pacific—halting the slaughter of 30,000 sea turtles annually in Baja California, developing three protected areas totalling 1.3 million acres in the Baja California Peninsula.
Keyword(s): Ecosystems (precious), Land Issues, Oceans/Coasts/Beaches

WILDERNESS EDUCATION ASSOCIATION
900 East 7th Street
Bloomington, IN 47405 United States
Phone: 812-855-4095   Fax: 812-855-8697
E-mail: wea@indiana.edu
Website: www.ebl.org/wea/

Founded: 1977
Membership: 1,001–10,000
Scope: National
Description: WEA is a nonprofit membership organization. It promotes national wilderness education and preservation programs by providing for-credit, expedition-based wilderness leadership training programs, developing and publishing state-of-the-art wilderness education publications and training manuals, promoting scholarly research programs, establishing and maintaining national outdoor leadership certification standards, and providing support to wildland management agencies to promote wilderness education.
Publication(s): WEA Legend, Wilderness Educator, New Wilderness Handbook, WEA Affiliate Handbook, The Backcountry Classroom, Trustees and Affiliates Briefing System (TABS)
Keyword(s): Land Issues, Recreation/Ecotourism

Contact(s):
- David Cockrell, President; Department of Human Performance and Leisure Studies, University of Southern Colorado, 2200 Bonforte Blvd., Pueblo, CO 81001-4901; 719-549-2775; Fax: 719-549-2732
- Mitchell Sakofs, Vice President; Outward Bound USA, Rt. 9, R. D. 2, Box 280, Garrison, NY 10524-9757; 914-424-4000
- Darla Deruiter, Executive Director; WEA Department of Natural Resource Recreation and Tourism, Colorado State University, Fort Collins, CO 80523; 970-223-6252; Fax: 970-223-6252
- William Forgey, Treasurer; One Tower Plaza, 109 E. 89th Ave., Merrillville, IN 46410; 219-769-6055; Fax: 219-769-6035
- W. Norton, Publisher
- Jeff Olson, Secretary; Confidence Learning Center, 6260 Mary Fawcett Memorial Dr., Brainerd, MN 56401; 218-828-2344

WILDERNESS LAND TRUST, THE
P.O. Box 1420
Carbondale, OR 81623 United States
Phone: 970-963-1725   Fax: 970-963-1725
Website: www.wildernesstrust.org

Founded: 1992
Scope: Regional
Description: To facilitate public acquisition of private lands (inholdings) within units of the National Wilderness Preservation System to fulfill the promise of Congress made in The Wilderness Act of 1964 that all generations of Americans will enjoy an enduring resource of wilderness.
Publication(s): Wilderness Heritage Newsletter
Keyword(s): Land Issues, Reduce/Reuse/Recycle, Wildlife & Species

Contact(s):
- Jon Mulford, President
- John Fielder, Chairman; P.O. Box 1261, Englewood, CO 80150; 303-935-0900
- Andy Wiessner, Secretary and Treasurer; 811 Potato Patch Dr., Vail, CO 81657; 303-715-3570

WILDERNESS SOCIETY, THE
1615 M Street, NW
Suite 100
Washington, DC 20036 United States
Phone: 202-833-2300   Fax: 202-429-3958
Website: www.wilderness.org

Founded: 1935
Membership: 100,001–500,000
Scope: Regional, National
Description: A membership based organization devoted to protecting America's wilderness and wildlife, and to developing a nationwide network of wildland through public education, scientific analysis, and advocacy. The Society welcomes membership inquiries, contributions and bequests
Publication(s): Annual Report, Quarterly Newsletter, Wilderness Magazine
Keyword(s): Ecosystems (precious), Energy, Forests/Forestry, Land Issues, Public Lands/Greenspace, Wildlife & Species
Contact(s):
   Donald Barry, Executive VP; 202-833-2300; Fax: 202-429-3958
   William Meadows, President; 202-833-2300; Fax: 202-429-3958
   Gaylord Nelson, Counselor; 202-833-2300; Fax: 202-429-3958
   Becky Rom, Chair, 202-833-2300
   Michelle Ackermann, Vice President of Communications; 202-833-2300; Fax: 202-429-8443
   G. Bancroft, Vice President of Ecology and Economic Research; 202-833-2300; Fax: 202-429-3945
   Elizabeth Coit, Vice President of Membership and Development; 202-833-2300; Fax: 202-429-3957
   Jerry Greenberg, Vice President of Regional Conservation; 202-833-2300; Fax: 202-429-3945
   Linda Lance, Vice President of Public Policy; 202-833-2300; Fax: 202-429-3945
   Barrington McFarlane, Vice President of Finance and Administration; 202-833-2300; Fax: 202-429-3959
   Sara Barth, Regional Director, California/Nevada; P.O. Box 29241, Presidio Building 1016, San Francisco, CA 94129; 415-561-6641; Fax: 415-561-6640; ca_office@tws.org
   Pamela Eaton, Regional Director (Four Corners); 7475 Dakin St., Suite 410, Denver, CO 80221; 303-650-5818; Fax: 303-650-5942; co_office@tws.org
   Robert Ekey, Regional Director, Montana; 105 W. Main Street, Suite E, Bozeman, MI 59715; 406-586-1600; Fax: 406-586-4700; mt_office@tws.org
   Robert Freimark, Regional Director, Northwest; 1424 Fourth Avenue, Suite 816, Seattle, WA 98101; 206-624-6430; Fax: 206-624-7101
   Craig Gehrke, Regional Director, Idaho; 2600 Rose Hill, Suite 201, Boise, ID 83705; 208-343-8153; Fax: 208-343-8184; id_office@tws.org
   Eleanor Huffines, Regional Director, Alaska; 430 West 7th Avenue, Suite 210, Anchorage, AK 99501; 907-272-9453; Fax: 907-272-1670; ak_office@tws.org
   Fran Hunt, Deputy VP of Regional Conservation; 202-833-2300; Fax: 202-429-3945
   Bart Koehler, Regional Director (Wilderness Support Center); 835 East 2nd Ave., Suite 440, Durango, CO 81301; 970-247-8788; Fax: 970-247-9020; wsc@tws.org
   Frank Peterman, Regional Director, Southeast; 112 Krog Street, Suite 26, Atlanta, GA 30307; 404-872-9453; Fax: 404-872-8540; ga_office@tws.org
   Julie Wormser, Regional Director, Northeast; 45 Bromfield Street, Suite 1101, Boston, MA 02108; 617-350-8866; Fax: 617-426-3213; ma_office@tws.org
   Dave Alberswerth, Director, BLM Program; 202-833-2300; Fax: 202-429-3945
   Michael Francis, Director, National Forests Program; 202-833-2300; Fax: 202-429-3945
   Bonnie Galvin, Director, Budget & Appropriations Program; 202-833-2300; Fax: 202-429-3945
   Sue Gunn, Director, National Parks Program; 202-833-2300; Fax: 202-429-3945
   Leslie Jones, Staff Attorney; 202-833-2300; Fax: 202-429-3945
   Jim Waltman, Director, National Wildlife Refuge & Alaska Programs; 202-833-2300; Fax: 202-429-3945

WILDERNESS WATCH
P.O. Box 9175
Missoula, MT 59807 United States
Phone: 406-542-2048   Fax: 406-542-7714
E-mail: wild@wildernesswatch.org
Website: www.wildernesswatch.org

Founded: 1989
Membership: 101–1,000
Scope: Local, State, Regional, National
Description: Wilderness Watch is a national, nonprofit, citizen organization dedicated solely to the protection and proper stewardship of lands within the National Wilderness Preservation System and Wild and Scenic Rivers System. We achieve our goals through the efforts of citizen activists, local chapters, wilderness "adopters", and by working with other local organizations concerned about wilderness and wild river issues.
Publication(s): Wilderness Activists' Handbook, 2003 National Wilderness Forum Report, Wilderness Watcher, Wilderness Guardian
Keyword(s): Ecosystems (precious), Land Issues, Oceans/Coasts/Beaches, Public Lands/Greenspace, Water Habitats & Quality, Wildlife & Species
Contact(s):
   George Nickas, Executive Director

WILDFLOWER ASSOCIATION OF MICHIGAN
c/o Marji Fuller
3853 Farrell Road
Hastings, MI 49058 United States
Phone: 269-948-2496   Fax: 269-948-2957
E-mail: wam@iserv.net
Website: www.wildflowersmich.org

Founded: 1986
Membership: 101–1,000
Scope: State
Description: The Wildflower Association of Michigan promotes, coordinates, and participates in education, enjoyment, science, and stewardship of native wildflowers and their habitats.
Publication(s): Wildflowers
Keyword(s): Land Issues, Reduce/Reuse/Recycle, Wildlife & Species
Contact(s):
   Stephan Keto, President; 616-343-1669; Fax: 616-343-0768
   Marilyn Case, Membership Coordinator; 15232 24 Mile Road, Albion, MI 49224; 269-630-8546; mcase15300@aol.com
   Marji Fuller, Managing Editor; 269-948-2496; Fax: 269-948-2957; marjif@iserv.net
   Kathryn Johnson, Editor; 11155 Hastings Pt. Road, Middleville, MI 49333; 269-795-9691; Fax: 269-795-8730; kathyj@voyager.net
   Valerie Reed, Secretary; 269-964-0477; vfrrabbit@aol.com

WILDFOWL TRUST OF NORTH AMERICA, INC., THE
P.O. Box 519, 600 Discovery Ln.
Grasonville, MD 21638 United States
Phone: 410-827-6694   Fax: 410-827-6713
E-mail: cbec@cbec-wtna.org
Website: cbec-wtna.org

Founded: 1979
Membership: 101–1,000
Scope: International

Description: A nonprofit, tax-exempt organization dedicated to the preservation of wildlife and wetlands through education, conservation, and research. The Trust operates The Horsehead Wetlands Center on its 500-acre wetland refuge on the Chesapeake Bay's Eastern Shore. The Center provides environmental education programs, a collection of resident waterfowl and raptors in natural habitat settings, a Visitor's Center, trails, and observation blinds and towers. Canoes are available for rental.
Publication(s): On The Wing-Newsletter
Keyword(s): Water Habitats & Quality, Wildlife & Species
Contact(s):
Torrey Brown, President
Laura Ricciardelli, Volunteer, Trustee, VP Administration
Judy Wink, Exec.Director

WILDFUTURES
353 Wallace Way, NE
Suite 12
Bainbridge Island, WA 98110 United States
Phone: 206-780-9718   Fax: 206-780-1022
E-mail: snegri@igc.org
Website: www.earthisland.org/wildfutures
Founded: 1994
Scope: National
Description: WildFutures provides essential tools and training to groups working to protect wildlife and habitat. WildFutures also works to bridge the gap between science and conservation, finding collaborative ways to develop and implement effective conservation strategies. Produced a PBS wildland/wildlife video and is now for sale.
Keyword(s): Wildlife & Species

WILDLANDS CONSERVANCY
3701 Orchid Pl.
Emmaus, PA 18049-1637 United States
Phone: 610-965-4397   Fax: 610-965-7223
E-mail: info@wildlandspa.org
Website: www.wildlandspa.org
Founded: 1973
Membership: 1,001–10,000
Scope: Local
Description: The mission of Wildlands Conservancy is to preserve, protect, and enhance the land, water, ecological, and recreational resources of the Lehigh River watershed, and beyond.
Publication(s): Wildlands quarterly newsletter
Keyword(s): Agriculture/Farming, Development/Developing Countries, Ecosystems (precious), Forests/Forestry, Land Issues, Pollution (general), Public Lands/Greenspace, Recreation/Ecotourism, Reduce/Reuse/Recycle, Sprawl/Urban Planning, Water Habitats & Quality, Wildlife & Species
Contact(s):
David Kepler, Chairman; 702 Hamilton Mall, Allentown, PA 18101

WILDLANDS PROJECT
WILD EARTH SOCIETY, INC.
P.O. Box 455
Richmond, VT 05477 United States
Phone: 802-434-4077   Fax: 802-434-5980
E-mail: info@wildlandsproject.org
Website: www.wildlandsproject.org
Founded: 1992
Membership: 1,001–10,000
Scope: International
Description: The Wildlands Project is working to restore and protect the natural heritage of North America. Through advocacy, education, scientific consultation, and cooperation with partners, we are designing and helping create systems of interconnected wilderness areas that can sustain the diversity of life.
Publication(s): Wild Earth - special edition, Wildlands Project, The: First Thousand Days of the Next Thousand Years
Keyword(s): Land Issues, Reduce/Reuse/Recycle, Wildlife & Species
Contact(s):
Bob Howard, President
Leanne Klyza Linck, Executive Director
Dave Foreman, Chairman
David Johns, Secretary and Treasurer

WILDLIFE ACTION, INC.
P.O. Box 866
Mullins, SC 29574 United States
Phone: 843-464-8473   Fax: 843-464-8859
E-mail: bunnybee@bellsouth.net
Website: www.wildlifeaction.com
Founded: 1977
Membership: 10,001–100,000
Scope: Local, State, Regional, National
Description: Wildlife Action is a private nonprofit 501(c)3 tax-exempt organization dedicated to the appreciation and enjoyment of our wildlife heritage and to educating the public in the value of protection, restoration, enhancement, and wise use of our natural resources.
Publication(s): Wildlife Pride, Wild Things - Our Resource Education Center
Keyword(s): Air Quality/Atmosphere, Development/Developing Countries, Ecosystems (precious), Energy, Ethics/Environmental Justice, Executive/Legislative/Judicial Reform, Forests/Forestry, Land Issues, Oceans/Coasts/Beaches, Pollution (general), Population, Public Health
Contact(s):
M. Beeson, President and CEO; P.O. Box 866, Mullins, SC 29574; 843-464-8473; Fax: 843-464-8859; info@wildlifeaction.com
Tommy Simpson, Vice President
Sandra Bane, Secretary
Ted Williams, Treasurer

WILDLIFE CENTER OF VIRGINIA, THE
P.O. Box 1557
Waynesboro, VA 22980-1414 United States
Phone: 540-942-9453   Fax: 540-943-9453
E-mail: wildlife@wildlifecenter.org
Website: www.wildlifecenter.org
Founded: 1982
Membership: 1–100
Scope: International
Description: A nonprofit organization that operates the nation's largest professionally-staffed veterinary teaching and research hospital for native wildlife. Study and documentation of environmental factors that cause injuries, especially pesticide poisoning, are used to monitor environmental and wildlife health trends and support public policy positions. The Center also trains students and professionals from the fields of veterinary medicine, wildlife management and wildlife rehabilitation.
Publication(s): Handbook of Wildlife Medicine, Annual and Mid-year reports, The Wildlife Center Teacher's Packet
Keyword(s): Wildlife & Species
Contact(s):
Edward Clark, President; eclark@wildlifecenter.org
Lisa Briskey, Vice President
Lisa Briskey, Director of Environmental Education; briskey@wildlifecenter.org
Jonathan Sleeman, Director of Veterinary Services
Erwin Bohmfalk, Chairman of the Board

NON-GOVERNMENTAL NON-PROFIT ORGANIZATIONS – W

WILDLIFE CONSERVATION ENFORCEMENT FUND, INC.
P.O. Box 302
Oakland, MD 21550-0302 United States
Phone: 888-231-5925   Fax: 301-334-0630
E-mail: jlwilliams@gcnetmail.net
Website: www.mdwildlifeprotection.org

Founded: 1998

Scope: State

Description: WCEF is a 501(c)(3) nonprofit organization, dedicated to wildlife and fisheries protection in Maryland. WCEF enhances the conservation and protection of wildlife and fisheries resources by directly supporting field-level conservation law enforcement. WCEF enhances the effectiveness of conservation law enforcement officers by acquiring and donating equipment which would otherwise be unavailable to them. Memberships are obtained via tax-deductible donations. There are no annual dues.

WILDLIFE CONSERVATION SOCIETY
BRONX ZOO
NEW YORK AQUARIUM
CENTRAL PARK ZOO
2300 Southern Blvd.
Bronx, NY 10460-1099 United States
Phone: 718-220-5100
E-mail: pr@wcs.org
Website: www.wcs.org

Founded: 1895

Membership: 100,001–500,000

Scope: Local, State, Regional, National, International

Description: WCS operates an international conservation program with a full-time staff of wildlife biologists conducting field research and training programs around the world. Headquartered in New York City, the Society operates the Bronx Zoo, New York Aquarium, Central Park Zoo, Queens Zoo, Prospect Park Zoo, and St. Catherines Wildlife Survival Center off the coast of Georgia. Their award-winning education programs are used in all 50 U.S. states.

Publication(s): Wildlife Conservation, Annual Report

Keyword(s): Oceans/Coasts/Beaches, Wildlife & Species

Contact(s):
Steven Sanderson, President and CEO
Annette Berkovits, Senior Vice-President of Education; 718-220-5131; aberkovits@wcs.org
Robert Cook, Vice-President for Wildlife Health Science
Louis Garibaldi, Vice-President, Director of Aquarium Science
John Hoare, Vice-President—Financial Services & Comptroller
Richard Lattis, Senior Vice-President for Zoos and Aquariums
W. McKeown, Vice-President—General Counsel
John Robinson, Senior Vice-President of International Conservation
George Amato, Director of Science Resource Center
Joan Downs, Editor-In-Chief; 718-220-5897; Fax: 718-584-2625; jdowns@wcs.org
Jennifer Herring, Public Affairs and Development
Steve Johnson, Librarian; 718-220-6874
David Schiff, Chairman

WILDLIFE DAMAGE REVIEW (WDR)
P.O. Box 85218
Tucson, AZ 85754 United States
E-mail: wdr@azstarnet.com
Website: www.Azstarnet.com/~WDR

Founded: 1991

Membership: 1,001–10,000

Scope: National

Description: Wildlife Damage Review's mission is to bring much needed public attention to the USDA's Animal Damage Control (ADC) program, renamed Wildlife Services in 1997. This taxpayer supported program traps, snares, poisons, and aerial guns 1-2 million of America's wildlife yearly for private interests. WDR's ultimate goal is to place wildlife management into the hands of those agencies whose vested interest is protection of native diversity and banish management guided by predator prejudice.

Publication(s): Investigating J.F.K. International Airport Gull Hazard Reduction, The War on Wildlife (audio CD), Audit of the USDA Animal Damage Control Program, Wildlife Damage Review, Waste, Fraud, Abuse in the U.S. Animal Damage Control Program

Keyword(s): Agriculture/Farming, Pollution (general), Wildlife & Species

Contact(s):
Nancy Zierenberg, Executive Director

WILDLIFE DISEASE ASSOCIATION
6006 Shroeder Road
Madison, WI 53711 United States
Phone: 785-843-1221   Fax: 785-843-1274
Website: www.wildlifedisease.org

Founded: 1951

Membership: 1,001–10,000

Scope: International

Description: An international nonprofit organization of scientists interested in advancing knowledge of the effects of infectious, parasitic, toxic, genetic, and physiologic diseases and environmental factors upon the health and survival of free-living and captive wild animals, and upon their relationships to humans.

Publication(s): Journal of Wildlife Diseases, Newsletter

Keyword(s): Public Health, Wildlife & Species

Contact(s):
Scott Wright, President
Irwin Polls, Business Manager
Elizabeth Howerth, Secretary
Daniel Pence, Editor
Leslie Uhazy, Treasurer

WILDLIFE EDUCATION PROGRAM AND DESIGN
44781 Bittner Point Rd
Bovey, MN 55709 United States
Phone: 218-245-3049

Membership: 1–100

Scope: International

Description: A non-profit education organization with slide lectures, Wolf Display, education programs and teachers workshops with "Wolves and Humans" curriculum and a Wolf and Wetland Learning Stations box of environmental education materials. Nationwide programs available. No jobs available.

Contact(s):
Karlyn Berg, Director; karlyn@uslink.net

WILDLIFE FEDERATION OF ALASKA
1120 E. Huffman Road, #216
Anchorage, AK 99515-3516 United States
Phone: 907-274-3388   Fax: 907-258-4811
E-mail: wfa@micronet.net
Website: www.micronet/users/~wfa/default.html

Founded: 1985

Scope: State

Description: A representative statewide organization, affiliated with the National Wildlife Federation, dedicated to the protection and enhancement of wildlife ands its habitat through public education and government interaction.

Publication(s): Tracks

Contact(s):
Tracy Shafer, President and Representative
Laurie Fairchild, Editor & Alternate Representative
Rosa Meehan, Education Programs Contact & Treasurer

WILDLIFE FOREVER
2700 Freeway Blvd
Suite 1000
Brooklyn Center, MN 55430 United States
Phone: 763-253-0222 Fax: 763-560-9961
E-mail: info@wildlifeforever.org
Website: www.wildlifeforever.org

Founded: 1987
Membership: 10,001–100,000
Scope: National
Description: Wildlife Forever is a non-profit conservation organization dedicated to preserving America's wildlife heritage through conservation education, the preservation of habitat, and the management of fish and wildlife.
Publication(s): Cry of the Wild, Annual Report, Wildlife Forever Fish, Wildlife Forever Critter Pocket Guide Series, Wildlife Forever CD-ROM Curriculum, Sports Fish Pocket Guide Series
Keyword(s): Public Lands/Greenspace, Recreation/Ecotourism, Water Habitats & Quality, Wildlife & Species
Contact(s):
  Douglas Grann, President, CEO
  Ann McCarthy, Director of Education
  Pete Wuebker, Director of Marketing
  Mark Petersen, Merchandise Manager
  David Fredrick, Grants Coordinator
  James Gallagher, Accountant

WILDLIFE FOUNDATION OF FLORIDA, INC.
Post Office Box 11010
Tallahassee, FL 32302 United States
Phone: 850-487-3796 Fax: 850-488-6988
Website: www.wildlifefoundationofflorida.com

Founded: 1994
Membership: 1–100
Scope: State
Description: The mission of the Wildlife Foundation of Florida, Inc. is to provide assistance, funding, and promotional support for the Florida Game and Wildlife Conservation Commission, and in so doing, contribute to the health and well-being of Florida's fish and wildlife resources and their habitats.
Keyword(s): Recreation/Ecotourism, Wildlife & Species
Contact(s):
  William Blake, Board of Directors
  William Bostick, Board of Directors
  Robert Brantly, Board of Directors
  Linda Bremer, Board of Directors
  Allan Egbert, Board of Directors
  George Matthews, Board of Directors
  C. Rainey, Board of Directors

WILDLIFE HABITAT CANADA
1750 Courtwood Crescent, Suite 310
Ottawa, K2C 2B5 Ontario Canada
Phone: 613-722-2090 Fax: 613-722-3318
E-mail: reception@whc.org
Website: www.whc.org

Founded: 1984
Scope: National, International
Description: Wildlife Habitat Canada is a national non-profit organization dedicated to working with private citizens, governments, non-government organizations, and industry to conserve the great variety of wildlife habitats across Canada. The organization develops and implements its own conservation initiatives, such as the Forest Biodiversity Program, but also provides grants for conservation, research, communication and education projects and has a graduate scholarship program.
Publication(s): Investors in Habitat Report, Stewardship Programs Annual Reports, State of Wildlife Habitat in Canada, Annual Reports
Keyword(s): Agriculture/Farming, Forests/Forestry, Water Habitats & Quality, Wildlife & Species
Contact(s):
  Jean Cinq-Mars, Executive Director
  Doug Wolthausen, Director of Programs

WILDLIFE HABITAT COUNCIL
8737 Colesville Road, Suite 800
Silver Spring, MD 20910 United States
Phone: 301-588-8994 Fax: 301-588-4629
E-mail: Whc@wildlifehc.org
Website: www.wildlifehc.org

Founded: 1988
Membership: 101–1,000
Scope: Local, State, Regional, National, International
Description: The Wildlife Habitat Council is a nonprofit, non-lobbying group of corporations, conservation organizations and individuals dedicated to enhancing and restoring wildlife habitat. Created in 1988, WHC helps large landowners, particularly companies, manage their unused lands in an ecologically sensitive manner for the benefit of wildlife. More than 2 million acres in 48 states, Puerto Rico and 15 other countries are managed for wildlife through WHC-assisted projects.
Publication(s): Habitat Management Leaflets, Registry of Certified Sites, Corporate Homes for Wildlife Calendar, Wildlife Habitat, Nest Monitoring Brochure
Keyword(s): Development/Developing Countries, Ecosystems (precious), Forests/Forestry, Land Issues, Public Lands/Greenspace, Recreation/Ecotourism, Water Habitats & Quality, Wildlife & Species
Contact(s):
  William Howard, President
  Robert Johnson, Executive Vice President
  Laurie Coran, Controller
  Vanessa Kauffman, Director of Marketing & Communications
  Rob Pauline, Director of Field Programs
  Tanya Suphatranand, Manager of Membership & Development
  David Carroll, Board of Directors Secretary/Treasurer
  Stephen A. Elbert, Chairman of the Board
  Robert A. Fenech, Past-Chairman
  Lawrence A. Selzer, Board of Directors Vice Chairman

WILDLIFE HERITAGE FOUNDATION OF WYOMING (WHFW)
P.O. Box 20088
Cheyenne, WY 82003-7002 United States
Phone: 307-777-4529 Fax: 307-777-4699
E-mail: wildlifeheritage@wyoming.com
Website: whfw.org

Founded: 2000
Scope: State
Description: The Wildlife Heritage Foundation of Wyoming was established in April 2000 as an independent, 501(c)(3) nonprofit corporation. The purpose of the foundation is to provide financial support, through philanthropy, to the critical conservation efforts of the Wyoming Game and Fish Department and its many partners. Its mission is to create an enduring natural legacy for future generations through stewardship of all Wyoming's wildlife.
Keyword(s): Wildlife & Species
Contact(s):
  Katie Gray, Grants/Administration; 307-777-4529; Fax: 307-777-4699; wildlifeheritage@wyoming.com
  Marlene Brown, Executive Director; 307-777-4693; Fax: 307-777-4699; wildlifeheritage@wyoming.com

WILDLIFE INFORMATION CENTER, INC.
P.O. Box 198
Slatington, PA 18080 United States
Phone: 610-760-8889　　　　Fax: 610-760-8889
E-mail: wildlife@fast.net
Website: www.wildlifeinfo.org

Founded: 1986
Membership: 101–1,000
Scope: Local, State, Regional, National
Description: A nonprofit, member-supported organization whose mission is to preserve wildlife and habitat through education, research, and conservation for the benefit of the earth and all its inhabitants. The Center owns and operates the Lehigh Gap Wildlife Refuge. Programs include: The Kittatinny Raptor Corridor Project and long-term hawk migration field studies at Bake Oven Knob, PA.; public education; maintaining a wildlife library; and advocating preservation of wildlife habitat and biodiversity.
Publication(s): Wildlife Conservation Reports, American Hawkwatcher, Wildlife Activist
Keyword(s): Ecosystems (precious), Land Issues, Recreation/Ecotourism, Wildlife & Species
Contact(s):
　Ken Medd, President
　Dan Kunkle, Executive Director
　Robert Hoopes, Treasurer; 610-760-8889; Fax: 610-760-8889
　Dan Kunkle, Editor
　Kathie Romano, Secretary

WILDLIFE MANAGEMENT INSTITUTE
1146 19th Street NW
7th Floor
Washington, DC 20036 United States
Phone: 202-371-1808　　　　Fax: 202-478-0090
Website: www.wildlifemanagementinstitute.org

Founded: 1915
Membership: 1–100
Scope: National
Description: International nonprofit scientific and educational private membership organization, supported by industries, groups, and individuals, promoting improved professional management of wildlife and other natural resources for the benefit of those resources and North America, including its people.
Publication(s): Outdoor News Bulletin, books and booklets, Transactions North American Wildlife and Natural Resources
Contact(s):
　Rollin Sparrowe, President
　Richard McCabe, Executive Vice President
　Scot Williamson, Vice President/Northeast Field Representative; R.R. 1, Box 587, Spur Rd., North Stratford, NH 03590; 603-636-9846; Fax: 603-636-9853; wmisw@together.net
　Robert Byrne, Wildlife Program Coordinator
　Ronald Helinski, Conservation Policy Specialist
　Terry Riley, Director of Conservation
　Carol Peddicord, Finance Manager
　Kathryn Reis, Partners Network Coordinator
　James Woehr, Senior Scientist
　Len Carpenter, Southwest Field Representative; 4015 Cheney Dr., Fort Collins, CO 80526; 970-223-1099; Fax: 970-204-9198; lenc@verinet.com
　Robert Davison, Northwestern Field Representative; 20325 Sturgeon Road, Bend, OR 97701; 541-330-9045; Fax: 541-382-9372; wmibd@aol.com
　Katherine Lawson, Secretary/Receptionist
　Rob Manes, Midwest Field Representative; 10201 South Highway 281, Pratt, KS 67124; 620-672-5650; Fax: 620-672-5650; wmimanes@prattusa.com
　Donald McKenzie, Southeast Field Representative; 2388 Cocklebur Road, Ward, AR 72176; 501-941-7994; Fax: 501-941-7995; wmidm@ipa.net
　Bette McKown, Administrative/Conference Secretary
　Jennifer Rahm, Assistant Publications Director

WILDLIFE ORPHANAGE, INC., THE
P.O. Box 4706
Stamford, CT 06907 United States
Phone: 888-727-6774　　　　Fax: 203-968-8280
E-mail: Ahumanesolution@aol.com
Website: wildlifeorphanage.org

Founded: 1999
Membership: 1–100
Scope: Local
Description: Rescue, rehabilitation and release of injured and orphaned wildlife in Fairfield County, CT as well as the education of our communities in ways to peacefully coexist with wildlife.
Keyword(s): Wildlife & Species
Contact(s):
　Cathie Kovacs, President; 888-727-6774; Fax: 203-968-8280; wildlifeorphan@aol.com
　Florence Chiappetta, Vice President; 203-253-7584; Fax: 203-968-8280; wildorphanage@aol.com
　Heather Bernatchez, Board Member; 888-727-6774; Fax: 203-968-8280; hbernatchez@yahoo.com

WILDLIFE PRESERVATION TRUST CANADA
120 King Street
Guelph, N1E 4P8 Ontario Canada
Phone: 519-836-9314　　　　Fax: 519-836-8840
E-mail: wptc@wptc.org
Website: www.wptc.org

Founded: 1985
Membership: 1,001–10,000
Scope: International
Description: The Trust exists to save critically endangered animal species from extinction through focussed species recovery programs; research; professional training; public education and habitat stewardship.
Keyword(s): Wildlife & Species

WILDLIFE SOCIETY
5410 Grosvenor Ln.
Bethesda, MD 20814 United States
Phone: 301-897-9770　　　　Fax: 301-530-2471
E-mail: tws@wildlife.org
Website: www.wildlife.org

Founded: 1937
Membership: 1,001–10,000
Scope: National
Description: International scientific and educational organization of professionals and students engaged in wildlife research, management, education, and administration. Dedicated to sound stewardship of wildlife resources and the environments upon which wildlife and humans depend; undertakes an active role in preventing human-induced environmental degradation; increases awareness and appreciation of wildlife values; and seeks the highest standards in all activities of the wildlife profession.
Publication(s): The Journal of Wildlife Management, The Wildlifer, Wildlife Society Bulletin, Wildlife Monographs
Keyword(s): Reduce/Reuse/Recycle, Wildlife & Species
Contact(s):
　Diana Hallett, Past President; 2901 West Truman Blvd., Jefferson City, MO 65109; 573-751-4115; ext. 3631; halled@mdc.state.mo.us
　Robert Warren, President; Warnell School of Forest Resources, University of Georgia, Athens, GA 30602; 706-542-6474; warren@smokey.forestry.uga.edu
　Richard Lancia, Vice President; Forestry Dept. Box 8002, North Carolina State University, Raleigh, NC 27695; 919-515-7578; lancia@unity.ncsu.edu

Daniel Decker, President Elect; Cornell Univ. Agricultural Experiment Station, 245 Roberts Hall, Ithaca, NY 14853; 607-255-2559; djd6@cornell.edu

Thomas Franklin, Wildlife Policy Director; the Wildlife Society, 5410 Grosvenor Lane, Bethesda, MD 20814; 301-897-9770; tom@wildlife.org

Harry Hodgdon, Executive Director; the Wildlife Society, 5410 Grosvenor Lane, Bethesda, MD 20814; 301-897-9770; harry@wildlife.org

Sandra Staples-Bortner, Program Director; 18214 NE 125th Way, Brush Prairie, WA 98606; 360-253-4611; sstaples-bortner@msn.com

William Baughman, Southeastern Section Representative; Meadwestvaco, 180 Westvaco Road, Summerville, SC 29484; 843-851-4629; wmb3@meadwestvaco.com

Robert Brown, Southwest Section Representative; Dept. of Wildlife & Fisheries Sciences, 210 Nagle Hall, Texas A&M University, College Station, TX 77843; 979-845-1261; rdbrown@tamu.edu

Winifred Kessler, Northwest Section Representative; USDA Forest Service, P.O. Box 21628, Juneau, AK 99802; 907-586-7916; wkessler@fs.fed.us

Marti Kie, Western Section Representative; CALFED Bay-Delta Program, 1416 Ninth St., Suite 630, Sacramento, CA 95814; 916-653-6059; mkie@water.ca.gov

John Organ, Northeast Section Representative; U.S. Fish & Wildlife Service, 300 Westgate Center Drive, Hadley, MA 01035; 413-253-8501; john_organ@fws.gov

Gary Potts, North Central Section Representative; Illinois Dept. of Natural Resources, 129 North Kennedy Blvd., Vandalia, IL 62471; 618-283-3070; gpotts@dnrmail.state.il.us

Thomas Ryder, Central Mountains & Plains Section Representative; Wyoming Game and Fish Department, 260 Buena Vista, Lander, WY 82520; 307-332-2688; Tom.Ryder@wgf.state.wy.us

WILDLIFE SOCIETY
ALABAMA CHAPTER
Attn: President, 331 Funchess Hall, Auburn University
Auburn, AL 36830 United States
Phone: 205-345-3807
E-mail: jmakemso@bellsouth.net

Scope: State

Contact(s):

James Armstrong, President; Auburn University 108 M. White Smith Hall, Auburn, AL 36830; 334-844-9233; Fax: 334-844-9234; jarmstro@acesag.auburn.edu

Tommy Counts, Past-President; P.O. Box 278, Double Springs, AL 35553; 205-489-5111; Fax: 205-489-3427; tom.counts@al.usda.gov

Jeff Makemson, Secretary-Treasurer; 11481 Colonial Dr., Duncanville, AL 35456; 205-345-3807; Fax: 205-333-2900

WILDLIFE SOCIETY
ALASKA CHAPTER
Attn: President, P.O. Box 1413
Homer, AK 99603 United States
Phone: 907-235-8191

Scope: State

Description: Professional Organization

Contact(s):

Gino Del Frate, President; AK Dept. of Fish and Game, 3298 Douglas Place, Homer, AK 99603-8027; 907-235-8191; Fax: 907-235-2448; gino_delfrate@fishgame.state.ak.us

Jackie Kephart, Secretary-Treasurer

Doug Larsen, President-Elect; AK Dept. of Fish and Game, 1910 Glacier Ave., Juneau, AK 99801-7802; 907-465-5277; Fax: 907-465-6142; doug_larsen@fishgame.state.ak.us

Roger Post, Past-President; P.O. Box 72962, Fairbanks, AK 99707; 907-455-6583; Fax: 907-455-6583; rpost@mosquitonet.com

Kevin White, Newsletter Editor

WILDLIFE SOCIETY
ALBERTA CHAPTER
Attn: President, Rural Route 4
Sherwood Park, T8A 3K4 Alberta Canada
Phone: 780-778-7116
E-mail: uasctws@ualberta.ca
Website: www.rr.ualberta.ca/wildlifesociety/

Scope: Province

Contact(s):

Elston Dzus, President; AB Pacific Forest Ind. Inc. P.O. Box 8000, Boyle, Alberta T0A 0M0; 780-525-8393; Fax: 780-525-8097; dzusel@alpac.ca

Michael Dorrance, Past-President; RR4, Sherwood Park, Alberta T8A 3K4; 780-467-4396; Fax: 780-436-9540; mathdorr@telusplanet.net

Ronald Mumme, Secretary-Treasurer; Dept. Bio. Allegheny College, Meadville, PA 16335; 814-332-2382; rmumme@alleg.edu

Troy Sorensen, Newsletter Editor; Suite 203, 111-54 St., Edson, Alberta T7E 1T2; 780-723-8244; Fax: 780-723-8502; troy.sorensen@gov.ab.ca

Arlen Todd, President-Elect; 1263 Berkley Dr. NW, Calgary, Alberta T3K 1T1; 403-297-7349; Fax: 403-297-3362; arlen.todd@gov.ab.ca

WILDLIFE SOCIETY
ARIZONA CHAPTER
Attn: President
P.O. Box 41337
Phoenix, AZ 85080 United States
Phone: 520-670-4860
E-mail: fldhcky@earthlink.net
Website: www.aztws.org

Founded: 1964

Membership: 101–1,000

Scope: State

Description: Professional Wildlife Biologists

Keyword(s): Agriculture/Farming, Ecosystems (precious), Forests/Forestry, Land Issues, Wildlife & Species

Contact(s):

Doug Duncan, President

WILDLIFE SOCIETY
ARKANSAS CHAPTER
Attn: President, P.O. Box 279 - Arkansas Tech University
Altus, AR 72821-0279 United States

Scope: State

Contact(s):

Kendall Moles, President; P.O. Box 599, State University, AR 72467; 870-972-3082

WILDLIFE SOCIETY
CALIFORNIA CENTRAL COAST CHAPTER
Attn: President, USDA Forest Service 6144 Calle Real
Goleta, CA 93117 United States
Phone: 805-961-5764   Fax: 805-961-5729
Website: www.wildlife.org

Membership: 1–100

Scope: State

Description: A professional wildlife society dedicated to wildlife conservation, education, and research.

Contact(s):

Maeton Freel, President; 273 Santa Barbara Shore Dr., Goleta, CA 93117; 805-681-2764

Kevin Cooper, Vice-President; 452 Lawrence Dr., San Luis Obispo, CA 93401; 805-925-9538; Fax: 805-681-2781; lecoop@juno.com

Michael Hanson, Treasurer; 1203 Madonna, San Luis Obispo, CA 93405; 805-541-0272; Fax: 805-756-1419; mthanson@calpoly.edu

Justin Vreeland, Secretary; UCCE, 425 Waupelani Dr. #508, State College, PA 16801; 814-237-8567; jkv104@psu.edu

WILDLIFE SOCIETY
CALIFORNIA NORTH COAST CHAPTER
Attn: President, Simpson Timber Co., P.O. Box 68
Korbel, CA 95550 United States
Website: www.wildlife.org

Scope: State

Contact(s):
Sandra Arb, President; P.O. Box 532, Scotia, CA 95565-0532; 707-764-4488; Fax: 707-764-4118; vonarb@scopac.com

WILDLIFE SOCIETY
COLORADO CHAPTER
CNHP
Colorado State University
254 General Services Building
Fort Collins, CO 80523 United States
E-mail: cws_fmp@cws.cnchost.com
Website: cws.cnchost.com

Scope: State

Contact(s):
Francie Pusateri, President; 317 Prospect Rd., Ft. Collins, CO 82526; 970-472-4336; franciep@concentric.net

WILDLIFE SOCIETY
FLORIDA CHAPTER
Carrie Sekerak, President
40929 SR 19
Umatilla, FL 32784 United States
Phone: 352-669-3153   Fax: 352-669-2385
E-mail: csekerak@fs.fed.us
Website: http://fltws.org

Founded: 1968
Membership: 101–1,000
Scope: State

Description: The Florida Chapter of The Wildlife Society (FCTWS) is an organization of wildlife professionals. Founded in 1968, the Chapter consists of over 200 members who are dedicated to sustainable management of wildlife resources and their habitats in Florida. The Chapter is involved with many of the environmental issues facing Florida, and is recognized as a proactive group that develops its positions based on sound biological data and principles.

Keyword(s): Agriculture/Farming, Ecosystems (precious), Forests/Forestry, Land Issues, Oceans/Coasts/Beaches, Pollution (general), Population, Public Lands/Greenspace, Recreation/Ecotourism, Water Habitats & Quality, Wildlife & Species

Contact(s):
Paul Moler, President; 352-955-2230; Fax: 352-376-5359; molerp@fwc.state.fl.us

WILDLIFE SOCIETY
GEORGIA CHAPTER
Jim Ozier, President TWS-GA
Georgia Dept. Natural Resources
116 Rum Creek Drive
Forsyth, GA 31029 United States
Phone: 478-994-1438   Fax: 478-993-3050
E-mail: Jim_Ozier@dnr.state.ga.us
Membership: 101–1,000
Scope: State

Description: An international, nonprofit, scientific and educational organization comprised of professionals serving the resource management fields, especially wildlife ecology and management. Founded in 1937 and based in Bethesda, Maryland, The Wildlife Society has more than 9,000 members from 40 countries. This chapter serves the needs of the state of Georgia.

Contact(s):
Sara Schweitzer, President; U. of Ga., D.B. Warnell Sch. Forest Res., Athens, GA 30602-2152; 706-542-1150; Fax: 706-542-8356; schweitz@smokey.forest.uga.edu

Douglass Hall, Past-President; 1161 Crooked Creek Rd., Watkinsville, GA 30677; 706-546-2020; Fax: 706-546-2004; douglas.i.hall@usda.gov

Douglas Hoffman, Secretary-Treasurer; 120 Diamond Dr., Athens, GA 30605; 706-546-2020; Fax: 706-546-2004; douglas.m.hoffman@usda.gov

Chuck Waters, Newsletter Editor; 2150 Dawsonville Highway, Gainesville, GA 30501; 770-535-5700; Fax: 770-535-5953; chuck_waters@mail.dnr.state.ga.us

Mark Whitney, President-Elect; 1057 Plantation Way SE, Conyers, GA 30094; 770-761-1697; Fax: 706-557-3042; mark_whitney@mail.dnr.state.ga.us

WILDLIFE SOCIETY
HAWAII CHAPTER
40 Kunihi Ln., #221
Kahului, HI 96732 United States

Scope: State

Contact(s):
Carrie Haurez, President; 40 Kunihi Ln. #221, Kahului, HI 96732; 808-877-1455

Fern Duvall, President-Elect; 211 Ulana St., Makawao, HI 96768-8034; 808-873-3502; Fax: 808-873-3505; mawildl@aloha.net

Cathleen Hodges, Newsletter Editor; 20 Kumano Dr., Pukalani, HI 96768; cathleen_hodges@nps.gov

Cathleen Hodges, Past-President; 20 Kumano Dr., Pukalani, HI 96768; cathleen_hodges@nps.gov

Dan McNulty-Huffman, Treasurer; 85 Haele Place, Makawao, HI 96768-8053; 808-572-4485; dmh@t-link.net

Joy Tamayose, Secretary, c/o Haleakala National Park P.O. Box 369, Makawao, HI 96822; 808-572-4492; Fax: 808-572-4498; ulukitty@aol.com

WILDLIFE SOCIETY
IDAHO CHAPTER
Attn: President
College of Forestry, Wildlife & Range Sciences
University of Idaho
Moscow, ID 83843-1136 United States
E-mail: tws@uidaho.edu
Website: www.ictws.org

Scope: State

Contact(s):
Robyn Januszewski, President; Fax: 208-324-1160; mcommons@idfg.state.id.us

WILDLIFE SOCIETY
ILLINOIS CHAPTER
1701 North Market Street Suite 7
P.O. Box 69
Sparta, IL 62286 United States
Phone: 217-333-6856
Website: www.eiu.edu/~biology/ICTWS/

Scope: State

Contact(s):
Tim Van Deelen, President; 607 E. Peabody, Champaign, IL 61820; 217-333-6856; Fax: 618-453-2806; feldhamer@zoology.siu.edu

WILDLIFE SOCIETY
INDIANA CHAPTER
P.O. Box 318
Brookville, IN 47012 United States
Phone: 765-647-3538   Fax: 765-647-4150
E-mail: bmacgowan@fnr.purdue.edu
Website: www.agriculture.purdue.edu/fnr/html/faculty/Rhodes/ITWSweb/Home%20Page.htm

Founded: 1968
Membership: 101–1,000
Scope: State

Description: The Indiana Chapter of The Wildlife Society is a professional organization of trained wildlife ecologists, biologists, and managers in the state. Our mission is to enhance the ability of wildlife professionals to conserve diversity, sustain productivity, and ensure responsible use of wildlife resources for the benefit of society. The Wildlife Society encourages professional growth through certification, peer-reviewed publications, conferences, and working groups.

Keyword(s): Agriculture/Farming, Ecosystems (precious), Executive/Legislative/Judicial Reform, Forests/Forestry, Land Issues, Pollution (general), Public Lands/Greenspace, Recreation/Ecotourism, Sprawl/Urban Planning, Water Habitats & Quality, Wildlife & Species

Contact(s):
- Olin Rhodes, President; Department of Forestry and Natural Resources, 1159 Forestry, West Lafayette, IN 47907; 765-494-3601; Fax: 765-496-2422; gener@fnr.purdue.edu
- Linda Byer, Newsletter Editor; 6615 S. 875 E., Monterey, IN 46960; 219-896-3522; Fax: 219-896-3038; byer@pwtc.com
- Brian MacGowan, President-Elect; Courthouse Annex Bldg., 115 South Line Street, Columbia City, IN 46725; 219-248-4231; Fax: 219-244-6751; bmacgowan@fnr.purdue.edu
- Patrick Mayer, Secretary-Treasurer; Huntington Reservoir, 517 N. Warren Rd., Huntington, IN 46750; 219-468-2165; pmayer@dnr.state.in.us
- Phil Seng, Past President; 1010 Yeardley Ln., Mishawaka, IN 46544-6766; 219-258-0100; Fax: 219-258-0189; phil@djcase.com
- Jeff Thompson, Member at Large; Sugar Ridge FWA, 2310 E. SR 364, Winslow, IN 47598; 812-789-2724; jthompson@dnr.state.in.us

WILDLIFE SOCIETY
IOWA CHAPTER
631 West Washington Boulevard
Washington, IA 52353 United States
Phone: 319-653-4912
E-mail: dpfeiffer@onlineia.com
Website: www.wildlife.org

Membership: 1–100
Scope: State

Description: Professional biologists and educators in the management of wildlife and their habitats.

Contact(s):
- Donald Pfeiffer, President; 631 West Washington Blvd., Washington, IA 52353; 319-653-4912
- Donald Sievers, Past-President; 109 W. Wilcoxway, Jefferson, IA 50129; 515-747-8383; Fax: 515-747-3951; dsiever@pionet.net
- Chuck Steffen, President-Elect; USDA Service Center, 700 Farm Credit Drive, Ottumwa, IA 52501; 641-682-3552
- Todd Bogenschutz, Secretary-Treasurer; Wildlife Res. Sta. 1436 255 St., Boone, IA 50036; 515-432-2823; Fax: 515-432-2835
- Peter Fritzell, Newsletter Editor; Boone Research Station, 1436 255th St., Boone, IA 50036; 515-432-2823

WILDLIFE SOCIETY
KANSAS CHAPTER
Scope: State
Contact(s):
- Helen Hands, President; 56 NE 40 Road, Great Bend, KS 67530; 620-793-3066; helenh@wp.state.ks.us
- Elmer Finck, Past President; Department of Biological Sciences, Fort Hays State University, 600 Park Street, Hays, KS 67601-4099; 785-628-4214; Fax: 785-628-4153; efinck@fhsu.edu
- Dan Haines, Secretary-Treasurer; 2640 Reaper Road, Waverly, KS 66871; 620-364-8831; ext. 4672; Fax: 785-733-2829; dahaine@wcnoc.com
- Mark Sexson, President-Elect; 1001 W. McArtor, Dodge City, KS 67801; 620-227-8609; marks@wp.state.ks.us
- Matt Smith, Newsletter Editor; P.O. Box 177, Wilson, KS 67490; 785-625-2588; mattas@wp.state.ks.us

WILDLIFE SOCIETY
KENTUCKY CHAPTER
Attn: President, KY Dept. Fish & Wildlife
#1 Game Farm Rd.
Frankfort, KY 40601 United States

Scope: State
Contact(s):
- Roy Grimes, President; #1 Game Farm Road, Frankfort, KY 40601; 502-564-4404; Fax: 502-564-6508; roy.grimes@mail.state.ky.us
- Mark Cramer, Newsletter Editor; KY Dept. F & W Resources #1 Game Farm Road, Frankfort, KY 40601; 502-564-4404; Fax: 502-564-6508; roy.grimes@mail.state.ky.us
- Charles Elliot, President-Elect; Dept. of Biology EKU, 521 Lancaster Ave., Richmond, KY 40475-3102; 606-622-1538; Fax: 606-622-1020; bioelliott@acs.eku.edu
- Dan Figert, Secretary-Treasurer; KY Dept. Fish & Wildlife #1 Game Farm Rd., Frankfort, KY 40601; 800-858-1549; Fax: 502-564-4859; dan.figert@mail.state.ky.us
- Robert Morton, Past-President; 8407 US 41 A, Henderson, KY 42420-9637; 502-827-2673; mmorton@apex.net

WILDLIFE SOCIETY
LOUISIANA CHAPTER
Attn: President, 5492 Grand Chenier Hwy
Grand Chenier, LA 70643 United States

Scope: State
Contact(s):
- Martin Floyd, President; 2044 Bayou Road, Cheneyville, LA 71325; 318-473-7690; Fax: 318-473-7747; marty_floyd@la.usda.gov
- Edmond Mouton, Past-President; LDWF, 2415 Darnall Rd, New Iberia, LA 70560; 318-373-0032; Fax: 318-373-0181; mouton_ec@wlf.state.la.us
- Mike Olinde, President-Elect; 2130 Terrace Ave., Baton Rouge, LA 70806; 225-765-2353; olinde_mw@wlf.state.la.us
- John Pitre, Treasurer; 263 White Oak Blvd., Boyce, LA 71409; 318-473-7809; Fax: 318-473-7616; john.pitre@la.usda.gov
- Virginia Rettig, Secretary; USFWS, 1010 Gause Blvd. Bldg. 936, Slidell, LA 70458; 540-646-7555; Fax: 504-646-7588; virginia_rettig@fws.gov
- Frank Rohwer, Newsletter Editor; Louisiana State U. Forestry, Wildlife, & Fisheries, Baton Rouge, LA 70803; 504-388-4131; Fax: 504-388-4227; frohwer@lsu.edu

WILDLIFE SOCIETY
MAINE CHAPTER
Attn: Secretary, ME Dept. Inland Fish & Wildlife
P.O. Box 416
Ashland, ME 47320 United States
Phone: 207-948-3131   Fax: 207-948-6277
E-mail: jnelson@unity.edu

Scope: State

NON-GOVERNMENTAL NON-PROFIT ORGANIZATIONS – W

Contact(s):
James Ecker, President; 58 Canterbury Rd., Brewer, ME 04412; 207-827-6191; Fax: 207-827-8441; jestump@aol.com
Mitschka Hartley, Past-President; U of ME Natl. Audubon Soc., 230 E. Lake Rd., DeRuyter, NY 13052; 315-662-7900; mhartley@audubon.org
James Nelson, Executive Committee; 34 Cates Rd., Thorndike, ME 04986; 207-948-3131; Fax: 207-948-6277; jnelson@unity.unity.edu
Joseph Wiley, Secretary-Treasurer; Bureau of Parks and Lands, 22 State House Station, Augusta, ME 04333; 207-287-4921; Fax: 207-287-8111; joe.wiley@state.me.us

WILDLIFE SOCIETY
MANITOBA CHAPTER
Attn: President, Dillion Consulting Ltd., 6 Donald St. S.
Winnipeg, R3L 0K6 Manitoba Canada
Website: twsmb.tripod.com

Scope: Province

Contact(s):
Cory Lindgren, President; One Hammock Marsh Box 1160, Stonewall, Manitoba R0C 2Z0; 204-437-3000; c_lindgren@ducks.ca
Rhiannon Christle, Past-President; 3-395 River Ave., Winnipeg, Manitoba R3L 0C5; 204-632-2938; Fax: 204-693-9673; rchristie@mb.sympatico.ca
Neil Mochnacz, Student Representative; 468 Chelsea Avenue, Winnipeg, Manitoba R2K 1A1; 204-984-2425; Fax: 204-983-2403; mochnaczn@dfg-mpo.gc.ca
Marc Schuster, Newsletter Editor; 242 Hartford Ave., Winnipeg, Manitoba R2V 0W1, 204-269-2184; Fax: 204-983-5248; marc.schuster@ec.gc.ca
Tanys Uhmann, Secretary and Treasurer; 1017 Kilkenny Dr., Winnipeg, Manitoba R3T 4K5; 204-261-2184; Fax: 204-261-0038; umuhmann@cc.umanitoba.ca

WILDLIFE SOCIETY
MARYLAND-DELAWARE CHAPTER
Attn: Past President, 7120 Oakland Mills Rd
Columbia, MD 21046 United States
Phone: 410-313-1675   Fax: 410-313-4660
E-mail: pnorman@co.ho.md.us
Website: www.dnrec.state.de.us/fw/mddel

Scope: State

Contact(s):
Philip Norman, President; 723 Holand Ave., Bel Air, MD 21014; 410-313-1675; Fax: 410-313-4660; pnorman@co.ho.md.us
Brenda Belensky, Newsletter Editor; 25 Montrose Manor Ct. #H, Baltimore, MD 21228; 410-313-4724; Fax: 410-313-4660; bbelensky@co.ho.md.us
Carol Bernstein, Past-President; 1053 Hampton Drive, Crownsville, MD 21032-1315; 410-962-3208; Fax: 410-962-4698; carol.l.bernstein@usace.army.mil
Amy Deller-Jacobs, Secretary; P.O. Box 1455, Cambridge, MD 21613-5455; 410-330-3911
Edward Morgereth, President-Elect; Biohabitat, Inc., #602 15 W. Aylesbury Rd., Timonium, MD 21093; 410-337-3659; Fax: 410-583-5678; edward@biohabitat.com
Donald Rohrback, Treasurer; Reg. Wldlf. Manager, Indian Springs WMA, 14038 Blairs Valley Rd., Clear Spring, MD 21722; 301-842-3355

WILDLIFE SOCIETY
MICHIGAN CHAPTER
Attn: President, 5525 Hayes Tower Rd.
Highway 2, 41 & M-35
Gladstone, MI 49837 United States
Phone: 906-786-2351   Fax: 906-786-1300
E-mail: albrighc@state.mi.us

Scope: State

Contact(s):
Craig Albright, President; Hwy. 2, 41, & M-35, Gladstone, MI 49837; 906-786-2351; Fax: 906-786-1300; albrighc@state.mi.us
Craig Albright, Newsletter Editor; Hwy. 2, 41, & M-35, Gladstone, MI 49837; 906-786-2351; Fax: 906-786-1300; albrighc@state.mi.us
Larry Caldwell, Past-President; Central MI Univ. Biology Dept., Mt. Pleasant, MI 48859; 517-774-3387; Fax: 517-774-3462; larry.caldwell@cmich.edu
Henry Campa, President-Elect; MI State University Dept. of Fish & Wildlife, East Lansing, MI 48824; 517-353-2042; Fax: 517-432-1699; campa@pilot.msu.edu
Kelly Millenbah, Secretary-Treasurer; MI State U., 13 Natural Resources Bldg., East Lansing, MI 48824-1222; 517-353-4802; Fax: 517-432-1699; millenba@pilot.msu.edu

WILDLIFE SOCIETY
MINNESOTA CHAPTER
Attn. President
3651 SE 128th Street
Blooming Prairie, MN 55917 United States
Phone: 507-455-5841
Website: www.crk.umn.edu/tws/mn

Founded: 1944
Membership: 101–1,000
Scope: State

Description: Membership is open to all individuals interested in the perpetuation of Minnesota's wildlife resources. Our objectives are to manage wildlife resources on a sound biological basis that benefit ecosystems and people and to encourage the highest possible professional standards in those working with wildlife resources. We share knowledge and ideas through meetings and publications and recognize and commend outstanding work by professional and lay individuals and groups.

Keyword(s): Agriculture/Farming, Energy, Forests/Forestry, Land Issues, Transportation, Water Habitats & Quality, Wildlife & Species

Contact(s):
Jeanine Vorland, President; 3651 SE 128th Street, Blooming Prairie, MN 55917; 507-455-5841; Fax: 507-446-2326; jvorland@citlink.net
Shelly Gorham, Newsletter Editor; 217 East River Street, Lake Bronson, MN 56734; 218-436-2427; rmgorham@wiktel.com
Brian Haroldson, Membership; RR 1 Box 181, Madelia, MN 56062; 507-642-8478; ext. 29; Fax: 507-642-3178; brian.haroldson@dnr.state.mn.us
Doug Wells, Secretary-Treasurer; 20274 250th Street, Fergus Falls, MN 56537; 218-736-0636; bdwells@prtel.com

WILDLIFE SOCIETY
MISSISSIPPI CHAPTER
Attn: President, P.O. Box 451
Jackson, MS 39205 United States
Phone: 662-245-5249   Fax: 662-245-5228
Website: www.cfr.msstate.edu/mstws

Scope: State

Contact(s):
Kristina Godwin, President; 610 Hospital Rd., Starkville, MS 39759; 662-325-3014; Fax: 662-325-3690; kris.godwin@usda.gov
K. Godwin, President-Elect; 610 Hospital Rd., Starkville, MS 39759; 662-325-5119; Fax: 662-325-8726; dgodwin@cfr.msstate.edu
Julie Marcy, Secretary-Treasurer; P.O. Box 820161, Vicksburg, MS 39182; 601-631-5302; Fax: 601-631-7133; julie.b.marcy@usace.army.mil
Darren Miller, Newsletter Editor; Weyerhaeuser Co. Southern Forestry Res., Box 2288, Columbus, MS 39704-2288; 662-245-5249; Fax: 662-245-5228; darren.miller@weyerhaeuser.com

Marcus Spencer, Past-President; 104 Jess Dean Dr., Brandon, MS 39047-9539; 601-364-2229; Fax: 601-364-2209; randys@mdwfp.state.ms.us

WILDLIFE SOCIETY
MISSOURI CHAPTER
Attn: President, 21999 Hwy. B
Maitland, MO 64466 United States

Scope: State

Contact(s):
Dave Murphy, President; 1709 Cliff Drive, Columbia, MO 65201; 573-443-2687; mgallopavo@aol.com
Dennis Browning, Secretary; 1811 Eastview Dr., Trenton, MO 64683; 816-675-2205; Fax: 816-675-2221; brownd@mail.conservation.state.mo.us
Donald Martin, Newsletter Editor; 2207 Oak Cliff Dr., Columbia, MO 65203; 573-751-4115; martind@mail.conservation.state.mo.us
Donald Martin, President-Elect; 5875 Van Horn Tvrn. Rd. W., Columbia, MO 65203; 573-751-4115; martind@mail.conservation.state.mo.us
Phil Rockers, Treasurer; P.O. Box 248, Sullivan, MO 63080; 573-468-3335; Fax: 573-468-5434; rockep@mail.conservation.state.mo.us
Dan Zekor, Past-President; P.O. Box 180, Jefferson City, MO 65102; 573-753-4115

WILDLIFE SOCIETY
MONTANA CHAPTER
Attn: President, 107 Mark Jensen Ln.
Polson, MT 59860 United States
Website: www.montanatws.org/

Scope: State

Contact(s):
Bev Dickerson, President-Elect; 3710 Fallon, Suite C, Bozeman, MT 59718; 406-522-2541; Fax: 406-522-2528; bdixon@fs.fed.us
Marion Cherry, Secretary-Treasurer; 518 Fieldstone Dr., Bozeman, MT 59715; 406-587-6257; mcherry@fs.fed.us
Frank Pickett, President; 45 Basin Creek Road, Butte, MT 59701; 406-533-3445; Fax: 406-533-6000; fjpickett@pplmt.com
Daniel Young, Newsletter Editor; Box 916, Eureka, MT 59917; 406-296-2536; Fax: 406-296-2588; lyoung@fs.fed.us

WILDLIFE SOCIETY
NATIONAL CAPITAL CHAPTER
Attn: President
5807 Blaine Drive
Alexandria, VA 22303 United States

Scope: State

Contact(s):
Douglas Hobbs, President; 5807 Blaine Dr., Alexandria, VA 22303-1914; 703-960-4271; doug_hobbs@fws.gov
Douglas Hobbs, Newsletter Editor; 5807 Blaine Dr., Alexandria, VA 22303-1914; 703-960-4271; doug_hobbs@fws.gov
Stephanie Hussey, Newsletter Editor; 208 N. Trenton St. #4, Arlington, VA 22203; 703-526-0272; saoffice1@pipeline.com
Stephanie Hussey, Secretary-Treasurer; 208 N. Trenton St. #4, Arlington, VA 22203; 703-526-0272; saoffice1@pipeline.com
Kristen La Vine, Past-President; 1912 N. Rhodes Street, Arlington, VA 22201; 703-519-0013; Fax: 703-519-9565; kp_lavine@yahoo.com

WILDLIFE SOCIETY
NEBRASKA CHAPTER
Grand Island, NE 68801 United States
Website: www.wildlifeconsult.com/netws

Scope: State

Contact(s):
Garry Steinauer, President; Nebraska Game and Parks Commission, 1703 L Street, Aurora, NE 68818; 402-694-2498; Fax: 402-684-2816; gstein@hgpc.state.ne.us
Laurel Badura, Secretary; 306 E. 29th, Kearney, NE 68847; 308-865-5332; Fax: 308-865-5309; lbadura@ngpc.state.ne.us
Mark Czaplewski, Past-President; NE Game & Parks Commission, 1617 First Avenue, Kearney, NE 68847; 308-385-6282; Fax: 308-385-6285; czaplews@linux3.nrc.state.ne.us
Mark Humpert, Newsletter Editor; 45090 Elm Island Rd., Gibbon, NE 68840; 308-865-5308; Fax: 308-865-5309; mhumpert@ngpun.ngpc.state.ne.us
Mark Humpert, President-Elect; 45090 Elm Island Rd., Gibbon, NE 68840; 308-865-5308; Fax: 308-865-5309; mhumpert@ngpun.ngpc.state.ne.us
Jeanine Lackey, Treasurer; 18909 N. 84th St., Ceresco, NE 68017-4209; jlackey2@unl.edu

WILDLIFE SOCIETY
NEVADA CHAPTER
Attn: President, 4321 Jody Ave.
Las Vegas, NV 89120 United States

Scope: State

Contact(s):
James Jeffress, President; 2085 Skyland Blvd., Winnemucca, NV 89445; 702-623-4959
Alan Jenne, Secretary and Treasurer; 4080 Bluewing Ln., Carson City, NV 89704; 775-888-7689
David Pulliam, President-Elect; 8003 Moss Creek Dr., Reno, NV 89506; 775-688-1561; dpulliam@govmail.state.nv.us

WILDLIFE SOCIETY
NEW ENGLAND CHAPTER
MA, United States

Scope: National

Contact(s):
John McDonald, President; MA Div. Fish and Wildlife Field HQ, Westborough, MA 01581; 508-792-7270; Fax: 508-792-7275; john.mcdonald@state.ma.us
Jenny Dickson, President-Elect; 391 Jackson St., Thomaston, CT 06787-2016; 860-675-8130; Fax: 860-675-8141; jenny.dickson@po.state.ct.us
Robert Gilmore, Newsletter Editor; P.O. Box 121, West Simsbury, CT 06092; 860-424-3866; Fax: 860-424-4075
Susan Langlois, Secretary-Treasurer; MA Div. Fish and Wildlife Field Headquarters, Westboro, MA 01581; 508-792-7270; Fax: 508-792-7275; sue.langlois@state.ma.us
Paul Rego, Past-President; Sessions Woods WMA P.O. Box 1550, Burlington, CT 06013; 860-675-8130; Fax: 860-675-8141; paul.rego@po.state.ct.us

WILDLIFE SOCIETY
NEW JERSEY CHAPTER
Attn: Secretary
139 George Street
Lambertville, NJ 08530-1611 United States
Phone: 609-633-6755

Membership: 1–100

Scope: State

Description: Wildlife professionals from the government and private sector

Contact(s):
James Sciasca, Treasurer; 4667 McDermott Rd., Bangor, PA 18013; 908-735-8975
Laurance Torok, Secretary; 139 George St., Lambertville, NJ 08530-1611; 609-633-6755

WILDLIFE SOCIETY
NEW MEXICO CHAPTER
NM, United States
Scope: State
Contact(s):
- Eric Rominger, President-; 141 Sereno Dr., Santa Fe, NM 87501; 505-992-8651; e_rominger@gmfsh.state.nm.us
- James Biggs, Past President; M887ESH-20, Albuquerque, NM 87545; 505-665-5714; Fax: 505-667-0731; biggsj@lanl.gov
- Gail Tunberg, Past-President; 331 Camino de la Tierra, Corrales, NM 87048-8554; 505-842-3151; Fax: 505-842-3457; gtunberg@fs.fed.us

WILDLIFE SOCIETY
NEW YORK CHAPTER
Geneva, NY 14456 United States
Phone: 315-787-2408
Website: cobleskill.edu/nychaptws
Scope: State
Description: State chapter of The Wildlife Society, the major professional organization of wildlife biologists
Contact(s):
- George Mattfeld, President Elect
- Michael Matthews, President; NYS DEC 108 Game Farm Road, Delmar, NY 12054; 518-457-3720; mjmatthe@gw.dec.state.ny.us
- Chuck Dente, Vice-President; 14 Marvin Ave., Demar, NY 12054; 518-478-3009; Fax: 518-478-3004; cxdente@gw.dec.state.ny.us
- Richard Chipman, Secretary; USDA/APHIS/WS, 1930 Route 9, Castleton, NY 12033-9653; 518-477-4837; Fax: 518-477-4899; richard.b.chipman@usda.gov
- James Daley, Treasurer; 9 Dunbar Rd., Westerlo, NY 12193-2505; 518-783-5733; jgdaley@gw.dec.state.ny.us
- Nancy Heaslip, Newsletter Editor; 3750 Skyline Dr., Schenectady, NY 12306; 518-357-2156; Fax: 518-357-2460; nxheasli@gw.dec.state.ny.us
- Mark Lowery, Past-President; 325 Randall Road, Ridge, NY 11961; 516-444-0350; Fax: 516-444-0349; mdlowery@gw.dec.state.ny.us

WILDLIFE SOCIETY
NORTH CAROLINA CHAPTER
P.O. Box 37742
Raleigh, NC 27627 United States
Phone: 910-695-3323
Website: main.nc.us/nctws/
Membership: 101–1,000
Scope: State
Description: State chapter of TWS composed of wildlife professionals from many different agencies and the private sector. Agencies represented include: USDA Wildlife Svcs., NCWildlife Resources Commission, USFWS, NRCS, etc.
Keyword(s): Agriculture/Farming, Ecosystems (precious), Forests/Forestry, Land Issues, Public Lands/Greenspace, Reduce/Reuse/Recycle, Sprawl/Urban Planning, Wildlife & Species
Contact(s):
- Peter Campbell, President; 144 Pine Ridge Dr, Whispering Pines, NC; 910-695-3323; pete_campbell@fws.gov
- Mike Carraway, President-Elect; 828-646-9913; carrawmb@brinet.com
- Patrick Farrell, Treasurer; 1793 Old Cullowee Rd., Sylva, NC; 828-293-5231; pjf@dnet.net
- Mark Johns, Secretary; P.O. Box 564, Cary, NC; 919-852-5124; johnsme@mindspring.com
- Gary Marshall, Past President; Latta Plantation Nature Center, 6211 Sample Road, Huntersville, NC 28078; 704-875-1391; Fax: 704-875-1394; marshgd@co.mecklenburg.nc.us
- Chris Moorman, Board Member; Box 8003, NC State University, Raleigh, NC; 919-515-5578; chris_moorman@ncsu.edu
- Donald Seriff, Newsletter Editor; 9401 Plaza Rd. Ext., Charlotte, NC 28215; 704-432-1391; Fax: 704-432-1420; serifdw@co.mecklenburg.nc.us

WILDLIFE SOCIETY
NORTH DAKOTA CHAPTER
Attn: President, USFWS, 1500 E. Capital Ave.
Bismarck, ND 58501 United States
Website: ndctws.homestead.com/ndctws_home.html
Scope: State
Contact(s):
- Greg Hiemenz, Secretary-Treasurer; 830 N. 34th Street, Bismarck, ND 58501; 701-250-4242; Fax: 701-250-4590; ghiemenz@gp.usbr.gov
- Tim Phalen, President-Elect; 701-439-2007; phalen@rrt.net
- John Schulz, President-Past; 7928 45th St. NE, Devil's Lake, ND 58301-8501; 701-662-3617; Fax: 701-662-3618; jwschulz@state.nd.us
- Alicia Waters, Newsletter Editor; 6721 Valley Vista Lane, Bismarck, ND 58501; 701-250-4242; Fax: 701-250-4590

WILDLIFE SOCIETY
OHIO CHAPTER
952 Lima Avenue
Findley, OH 45840 United States
Phone: 419-424-5000
Scope: State
Contact(s):
- Scott Butterworth, President; 952 Lima Ave., Findley, OH 45840; 419-424-5000
- Tim Plageman, Treasurer; 7403 Twp. Rd. 32, Jenera, OH 45841; 419-424-5000; Fax: 419-422-4875; tim.plagman@dnr.state.oh.us
- Edward Smith, Newsletter Editor; OSU Ext. E. District Ofc. 16714 SR 215, Caldwell, OH 43724; 740-732-2381; Fax: 740-732-5992; smith.25@osu.edu
- Kendra Wecker, Secretary; 107 Glenmont Ave., Columbus, OH 43214; 614-265-7043; Fax: 614-262-1143; kendra.wecker@dnr.state.oh.us

WILDLIFE SOCIETY
OKLAHOMA CHAPTER
919 Kerr Research Drive
Ada, OK 74820 United States
Phone: 580-436-8703
E-mail: jorgensen.eric@epamail.epa.gov
Scope: State
Contact(s):
- Michael Porter, President; Noble Foundation, P.O. Box 2180, Ardmore, OK 73402-2180; 580-221-7272; Fax: 580-221-7320; mdporter@noble.org
- Jerry Brabander, Treasurer; U.S. Fish and Wildlife Services, 10960 S. 241st West Ave., Sapulpa, OK 74066; 918-581-7458; Fax: 918-581-7467; jerry_brabander@fws.gov
- Eric Jorgensen, Newsletter Editor; Environmental Protection Agency, Robt. S. Kerr Env. Res. Center, 919 Kerr Research Drive, Ada, OK 74820; 580-436-8545; Fax: 580-436-8703; jorgensen.eric@epamail.epa.gov
- James Shaw, Past-President; OK State U. Dept. of Zoology, Stillwater, OK 74078; 405-744-9668; Fax: 405-744-7824; shawjh@okstate.edu
- John Skeen, President-Elect; OK Dept. Wldlf. Cons. HCR 75, Box 308-12, Broken Bow, OK 74728-9020; 580-241-7875; okwild@pine-net.com
- Jullianne Whitaker-Hoagland, Secretary; OK Dept. of Wildlife. Cons., 1801 N. Lincoln Blvd., P.O. Box 53465, Oklahoma City, OK 73152; 405-522-0189; Fax: 405-521-6235; jhoagland@odwc.state.ok.us

WILDLIFE SOCIETY
OREGON CHAPTER
P.O. Box 2214
Corvallis, OR 97339-2214 United States
Website: www.orst.edu/dept/fish_wild/tws
Scope: State
Publication(s): On Target
Contact(s):
- Jim Thraikill, President; OR Coop. Wldlf. Res. Unit, McKenzie Ecological, 45304 Goodpasture Rd., Vida, OR 97488; 541-687-9076; Fax: 541-687-1065; jimt@pond.net
- Edward Arnett, Treasurer; Weyerhaeuser Co., OR State U., 321 Richardson Hall, Corvallis, OR 97331; 541-737-8469; Fax: 541-737-1393; ed.arnett@orst.edu
- Katherine Beal, Secretary; P.O. Box 429, Lowell, OR 97452; 541-937-2131; Fax: 541-937-3401; kat.beal@usace.army.mil
- Cheryl Friesen, President-Elect; 45304 Goodpasture Road, Vida, OR 97488; 541-822-7232; Fax: 541-822-7254; cafriesen@msh.com
- Laura Todd, Past-President; P.O. Box 50, Rhododendron, OR 97049; 503-231-6179; Fax: 503-231-6195; Laura_Todd@fws.gov

WILDLIFE SOCIETY
PENNSYLVANIA CHAPTER
Attn: President, 415 E. McCormick Ave.
State College, PA 16801 United States
Scope: State
Contact(s):
- Shayne Hoachlander, President; Rd. 2 Box 140 Factory Rd., Corry, PA 16407; 814-664-8867; shoachlander@tbscc.com
- J. Benner, Secretary; Rd. 1 Box 87, Liverpool, PA 17045; 717-787-3706; Fax: 717-783-5109; mbenner@dcnr.state.pa.us
- Michelle Cohen, President-Elect; 3490 North Third Street, Harrisburg, PA 17110; 717-232-0593; Fax: 717-232-0593; mcohen@skellyloy.com
- Michelle Cohen, Past-President; 3490 North Third Street, Harrisburg, PA 17110; 717-232-0593; Fax: 717-232-0593; mcohen@skellyloy.com
- Thomas Hardisky, Treasurer; 2621 E. Winter Rd., Loganton, PA 17747; 570-725-2287; Fax: 570-725-2287; disky@cub.kcnet.org
- Carolyn Mahan, Newsletter Editor; Penn State Altoona Dept. Bio., 205 Force Bldg., Altoona, PA 16601; 814-949-5530; Fax: 814-865-3725; cgm2@psu.edu

WILDLIFE SOCIETY
SACRAMENTO-SHASTA CHAPTER
Attn: President, W.M. Beaty & Associates
P.O. Box 990898
Redding, CA 96099-0898 United States
E-mail: cbailey@wildlandsinc.com
Website: www.tws-west.org/sac-shasta/index.htm
Scope: State
Contact(s):
- Robert Carey, President; W.M. Beaty & Associates, P.O. Box 990898, Redding, CA 96099-0898; 530-243-2783; Fax: 530-243-2900; bobc@sunset.net
- Craig Bailey, President-Elect; 1313 Shadowglen Rd., Sacramento, CA 95864-2723; 916-331-8810; Fax: 916-331-8755; craig_bailey73@hotmail.com
- Thomas Boullion, Secretary-Treasurer; 18005 Willow Dr., Cottonwood, CA 96022; 530-244-8600; Fax: 530-244-7656; boullion@shasta.com
- Michael Bradbury, Past-President; 3251 S Street, Sacramento, CA 95816; 916-227-7527; Fax: 916-227-7554; mbradbur@water.ca.gov
- Debra Hawk, Newsletter Editor; P.O. Box 610, Mammoth Lakes, CA 93546-0610; 760-872-1134; dhawk@dfg.ca.gov

WILDLIFE SOCIETY
SAN FRANCISCO BAY AREA CHAPTER
3003 Magawon
Santa Rosa, CA 95405 United States
Website: www.tws-west.org/bayarea/index.htm
Scope: State
Contact(s):
- David Cook, President; Sonoma County Water Agency, Oakland, CA 94605-0381; 707-547-1944; dcook@scwa.ca.gov
- John Baas, President-Elect; 210 MacCalvey Dr., Martinez, CA 94553; 510-335-9778; Fax: 510-335-9778; karthikl@value.net
- Steven Bobzien, Past-President; 2950 Peralta Oaks Ct. P.O. Box 5381, Oakland, CA 94605-0381; 510-635-0138; Fax: 510-635-3478; sbobzien@ebparks.org
- Jessica Martini-Lamb, Secretary-Treasurer; 2643 Diablo Street, Napa, CA 94558; 707-547-1903; Fax: 707-524-3782; jesmartini@hotmail.com

WILDLIFE SOCIETY
SAN JOAQUIN VALLEY CHAPTER
Attn: President, P.O. Box 2176
947-C West Pachaco Boulevard
Los Manos, CA 93635 United States
Phone: Fax: 209-826-1445
Website: www.sanluis.fws.gov/
Scope: State
Contact(s):
- Scott Frazer, President; 1017 Jefferson Avenue, Los Banos, CA 93635; 209-826-3508; Fax: 209-826-1445; scott_frazer@fws.gov
- Brian Cypher, Past-President; Endangered Species Rec. Prog., P.O. Box 9622, Bakersfield, CA 93389-9622; 661-398-2201; Fax: 661-398-0549; bcypher@tcsn.net
- Brian Cypher, Newsletter Editor; Endangered Species Rec. Prog., P.O. Box 9622, Bakersfield, CA 93389-9622; 661-398-2201; Fax: 661-398-0549; bcypher@tcsn.net
- Christine Horn, Treasurer; 3517 Sedona Way, Bakersfield, CA 93309; 661-834-6781; cvanjob@aol.com
- Michelle Selmon, Secretary; 628 W. Euclid Ave., Clovis, CA 93612; mselmon@esrp.org
- Marcia Wolfe, President-Elect; P.O. Box 10254, Bakersfield, CA 93389; 661-837-1169; Fax: 661-837-8467; yakimapark@aol.com

WILDLIFE SOCIETY
SOUTH CAROLINA CHAPTER
P.O. Box 1950
Summerville, SC 29485 United States
Phone: 843-851-4629   Fax: 843-873-2654
Website: www.tws-west.org/sjvc/
Scope: State
Contact(s):
- Kevin O'Conner, President; koconner@dfg.ca.gov
- William Baughman, President-Elect; P.O. Box 1950, Summerville, SC 29485; 843-851-4629; Fax: 843-873-2654; wmbaugh@westvaco.com
- Karen Dulik, Newsletter Editor; kdulik@water.ca.gov
- Paul Jones, Secretary-Treasurer; 2441 Williston Rd., Aiken, SC 29803; 803-725-5337; Fax: 803-725-3309; jones@srel.edu
- Benjamin Miller, Past-President; Mulberry Plantation 1904 N. Mulberry Dr., Moncks Corner, SC 29461; 843-761-5220; Fax: 843-761-5292

WILDLIFE SOCIETY
SOUTH DAKOTA CHAPTER
200 South Tyler Ave
Pierre, SD 57501 United States
Phone: 605-773-4194
Website: www.wfs.sdstate.edu/sdtws.htm

Membership: 101–1,000
Scope: State
Description: Wildlife science and management
Keyword(s): Agriculture/Farming, Ecosystems (precious), Land Issues, Public Lands/Greenspace, Recreation/Ecotourism, Water Habitats & Quality
Contact(s):
   Paul Coughlin, Past-President; SD Game, Fish & Parks, 523 East Capitol Ave., Pierre, SD 57501; 605-773-4194; Fax: 605-773-6245; paul.coughlin@state.sd.us
   Arthur Smith, President; SD Game, Fish & Parks, 523 E. Capitol Ave., Pierre, SD 57501; 605-773-7595; Fax: 605-773-6245

WILDLIFE SOCIETY
SOUTHERN CALIFORNIA CHAPTER
133 Martin Alley
Pasadena, CA 91105 United States
Phone: 626-683-3547   Fax: 626-683-3548
Website: www.tws-west.org/social/index.html
Scope: State
Contact(s):
   Brad Blood, President, 12702 Cowley Ave., Downey, CA 90242; 626-683-3547; Fax: 626-683-3548; pizonyx@aol.com
   Mari Schroeder, Vice President; 12551 Hinton Way, Santa Ana, CA 92705; 949-261-5414; Fax: 649-261-8950; mschroeder@chambersgroupinc.com
   Kathleen Keane, Secretary; 5546 E. Parkcrest St., Long Beach, CA 90808; 310-425-6842
   Mari Schroeder, President-Past; 12551 Hinton Way, Santa Ana, CA 92705; 949-261-5414; Fax: 649-261-8950; mschroeder@chambersgroupinc.com
   John Stephenson, Treasurer; 199 Via Del Cerrito, Encinitas, CA 92024; 619-436-8340; jstephen/r5_cleveland@fs.fed.us

WILDLIFE SOCIETY
TENNESSEE CHAPTER
TN, United States
Website: www.utm.edu/department/gr/agnatres/tn-tws/tn-tws.html
Scope: State
Contact(s):
   Eric Pelren, President; Dept. Agri. & Nat. Res., 114 Brehm Hall, Martin, TN 38238; 901-587-7263; Fax: 901-587-7968; epelren@utm.edu
   David Buehler, Past-President; U. of Tennessee Dept. for., Wldlf. & Fish, P.O. Box 1071, Knoxville, TN 37901; 423-974-7992; Fax: 423-974-4714; dbuehler@utk.edu
   Lisa Muller, Secretary-Treasurer; Dept. for., Wldlf., & Fish, P.O. Box 1071, Knoxville, TN 37901; 423-974-7981; Fax: 423-974-4714; lmuller@utk.edu
   Edward Warr, Newsletter Editor; Tennessee Wldlf. Res. Agency Wildlife Division, P.O. Box 40747, Nashville, TN 37204; 615-781-6613; Fax: 615-781-6654; ewarr@mail.state.tn

WILDLIFE SOCIETY
TEXAS CHAPTER
TX, United States
Website: www.tctws.org
Scope: State
Contact(s):
   Kirby Brown, President; Texas Wildlife Association, 401 Isom Road #237, San Antonio, TX 78216; 210-826-2904; Fax: 210-826-4933; k_brown@texas-wildlife.org
   Terry Blankenship, President Elect; Welder Wildlife Foundation, P.O. Box 1400, Sinton, TX 78387; 361-364-2643; Fax: 361-364-2650; welderwf@aol.com
   Neal Wilkins, Vice President; Dept. Wildlife and Fisheries Sciences, SFSC 2258, TAMU, College Station, TX 77843; 979-845-7471; Fax: 979-845-7103; nwilkins@tamu.edu
   Donald Davis, Treasurer; TX A&M U. Dept. Vet. Pathology, College Station, TX 77843; 409-845-5174; Fax: 409-862-1088; ddavis@cvm.tamu.edu
   Fidel Hernandez, Secretary; Dept. Wildlife Sciences, 700 University Blvd., MSC 218, TAMUK, Kingsville, TX 78363; 915-828-3926; Fax: 361-593-3924; fidel.hernandez@tamuk.edu

WILDLIFE SOCIETY
UTAH CHAPTER
Attn: President, Bureau of Land Management
318 N. 100 E.
Kanab, UT 84741 United States
Scope: State
Contact(s):
   Kathleen Paulin, President; Vernal Ranger District Ashley National Forest, 355 North Vernal Avenue, Vernal, UT 84078; 435-781-5160; kpaulin@fs.fed.us
   Harry Barber, Past-President; BLM 318 N. 100 E., Kanab, UT 84741; 435-644-4311; Fax: 435-644-2672; hbarber@ut.blm.gov
   Stanley Beckstrom, Newsletter Editor; 4311 S. 4625 W., Salt Lake City, UT 84120-4931; 435-865-6112; nrdwr.sbeckstr@state.ut.us
   Stanley Beckstrom, Secretary; 4311 S. 4625 W., Salt Lake City, UT 84120-4931; 435-865-6112; nrdwr.sbeckstr@state.ut.us
   Lisa Church, President-Elect; 1381 S. Ford, Kanab, UT 84741; 435-644-4600; Fax: 435-644-4620; lchurch@ut.blm.gov
   Randall Thacker, Treasurer; P.O. Box 337, Altamont, UT 84001; 435-454-3081; mrdwr/rtjacler@state.ut.us

WILDLIFE SOCIETY
VIRGINIA CHAPTER
HC 6, Box 46
Farmville, VA 23901 United States
Phone: 434-392-9645
Membership: 101–1,000
Scope: State
Description: Virginia's chapter of the nation's society of wildlife professionals.
Contact(s):
   Bruce Lemmert, President; 21 S. Church St., Lovettsville, VA 22080; 540-822-4219; blemmert@dgif.state.va.us
   Jefferson Waldon, Vice-President; VPI & SU, Fish & Wildlife Info Exchange, 203 W. Roanoke St., Blacksburg, VA 24061; 540-231-7348; Fax: 540-231-7019; fwiexchg@vt.edu
   Jack Gwynn, Newsletter Editor; 2503 Brunswick Rd., Charlottesville, VA 22903; 804-295-4681; Fax: 804-975-1005; jackgwynn@aol.com
   Ralph Keel, Treasurer; 1232 Geranium Crescent, Virginia Beach, VA 23456; 757-986-3706; Fax: 757-986-2353; r5rw_gdsnwr@mail.fws.gov
   Jesse Overcash, Past-President; 110 Southpark Dr., Blacksburg, VA 24060; 540-522-4641; Fax: 540-552-4376; jovercas@vt.edu
   Lisa Sausville, Secretary; 966 Rt. 17 W., Addison, VT 05491

WILDLIFE SOCIETY
WASHINGTON CHAPTER
WA, United States
Phone: 509-663-8121
Website: www.washingtonwildlifesoc.org/ns/default_ns.htm
Founded: 1966
Membership: 101–1,000
Scope: State

Contact(s):
- Paul Fielder, President; 1633 Concord Place, Wenatchee, WA 98801; 509-663-8121; Fax: 509-664-2338; paul@chelanpud.org
- Con Utzinger, President-Elect; 44691 Baker Lake Road, Concrete, WA 98237; 360-853-7806; Fax: 360-853-7806; utzinger@fidalgo.net
- Kenneth Bevis, Newsletter Editor; Yakima Indian Nation Wildlife P.O. Box 151, Toppenish, WA 98948-0151; beviskrb@dfw.wa.gov
- John Lehmkuhl, President-Past; 1133 N. Western Ave., Wenatchee, WA 98801; 509-662-4315; jlehmkhul/r6pnw_wenatchee@fs.fed.us
- Catherine Raley, Treasurer; Forestry Sciences Lab, 3625 93rd Ave. SW, Olympia, WA 98502; 360-753-7686; craley@fs.fed.us
- Ann Sprague, Secretary; Box 188, Twisp, WA 98856; 509-997-2131; Fax: 509-997-9770; sprague@nethow.com

WILDLIFE SOCIETY
WEST VIRGINIA CHAPTER
WV, United States

Scope: State

Contact(s):
- Jim Fregonara, President; 210 Boundary Ave., Elkins, WV 26241; 304-637-0245; Fax: 304-637-0250
- Christopher Ryan, Vice-President; P.O. Box 73, Shirley, WV 26434; 304-758-2681
- James Anderson, Secretary-Treasurer; WV DNR-Wildlife, 2006 Robert C. Byrd Drive, Beckley, WV 25801; 304-293-2941; ext. 2445; Fax: 304-293-2441; jander25@wvu.edu
- Shawn Head, Past-President; WV DNR P.O. Box 67, Elkins, WV 26241; 304-637-0245

WILDLIFE SOCIETY
WISCONSIN CHAPTER
Rt. 3 Box 174D
Ashland, WI 54806 United States

Scope: State

Publication(s): Wisconsin Association for Environmental Education Bulletin

Contact(s):
- Jonathan Gilbert, President; 25350 Fischer Rd., Ashland, WI 54806; 715-682-6619; Fax: 715-682-9294; jgilbert@glifwc.org
- Gerald Bartelt, Past President; 6315 Clovernook Rd., Middletown, WI 53562-3824; 608-221-6344; Fax: 608-221-6353; barteg@dnr.state.wi.us
- Alan Crossley, Newsletter Editor; 459 Sidney St., Madison, WI 53703; 608-275-3242; Fax: 608-275-3338; crossa@dnr.state.wi.us
- Gary Zimmer, Secretary-Treasurer; P.O. Box 116, Laona, WI 54541; 715-674-4481; Fax: 715-276-3594; gzimmer@fs.fed.us

WILDLIFE SOCIETY
WYOMING CHAPTER
Attn: President, 260 Buena Vista
Lander, WY 82520 United States
Phone: 307-766-5415
Website: www.wyotws.org

Scope: State

Description: Professsional society

Contact(s):
- Stan Anderson, President; Wyoming Cooperative Fish and Wildlife Research Unit, Dept. of Zoology & Physiology, Biology Sciences Bldg., Room 419, Laramie, WY 82071; 307-455-2466; anderson@uwyo.edu
- Mark Hinschberger, Past President; U.S. Forest Service, P.O. Box 186, Dubois, WY 82513; 307-455-2466; mhinschb/r2_shashone@fs.fed.us
- Karli Allanson, Secretary; 307-548-6541; kallanson@fs.fed.us
- Frank Bloomquist, Treasurer; 307-328-4207; frank_bloomquist@blm.gov
- Tim Byer, President Elect; 307-358-3670; tbyer@fs.fed.us
- Christina Schmidt, Newsletter Editior; 307-733-2383; ext. 32; christina.schmidt@wgf.state.wy.us

WILDLIFE TRUST
WILDLIFE PRESERVATION TRUST INTERNATIONAL
Lamont-Doherty Earth Observatory
The Nafe House #8
61 Route 9W
Palisades, NY 10964 United States
Phone: 845-365-8337   Fax: 845-365-8177
E-mail: homeoffice@wildlifetrust.org
Website: www.wildlifetrust.org

Founded: 1971

Membership: 1,001–10,000

Scope: Regional, National, International

Description: Wildlife Trust conserves threatened wild species and their habitats in partnership with local scientists and educators around the world.

Publication(s): Annual Report, On the Edge

Keyword(s): Ecosystems (precious), Oceans/Coasts/Beaches, Public Health, Wildlife & Species

Contact(s):
- Mary Pearl, President
- Joanne Gullifer, Director for Board Stewardship & Membership Officer; 610-461-2744
- Fred Koontz, Deputy Director for North American Conservation
- Michael Boss, Treasurer
- Susan Chevalier, Senior Development Officer; 845-365-8390; chevalier@wildlifetrust.org
- Julie Hughes, Foundation Officer; 845-365-8442; hughes@wildlifetrust.org
- Martin Kaplan, Vice President
- Virginia Mars, President and Secretary
- James Powell, Director for Aquatic Conservation; Mote Marine Laboratory, 1600 Ken Thompson Pkwy., Sarasota, FL 34236; 941-388-4441; ext. 253
- Ann Seligman, Director for Finance and Human Resources; 845-365-8466; seligman@wildlifetrust.org
- Cynthia Stebbins, Vice President
- Florence Swanstrom, Director for Communications; 845-365-8455; Fax: 845-365-8177; swanstrom@wildlifetrust.org

WILDLIFE WAYSTATION
14831 Little Tujunga Canyon Rd.
Angeles National Forest, CA 91342-5999 United States
Phone: 818-899-5201   Fax: 818-890-1107
E-mail: info@waystation.org
Website: www.wildlifewaystation.org

Founded: 1969

Membership: 10,001–100,000

Scope: National

Description: A southern California nonprofit refuge providing medical care, refuge, rehabilitation, and placement services for over 4,000 wild and exotic animals annually. Public tours and educational programs available.

Publication(s): Wildlife Waystation (newsletter), Wild Proofing the Human Habitat (brochure)

Keyword(s): Wildlife & Species

Contact(s):
- Martine Colette, Founder and President

WILSON ORNITHOLOGICAL SOCIETY
Wilson Ornithological Society
Museum of Zoology, Univ. of Michigan
1109 Geddes Ave.
Ann Arbor, MI 48109 United States
Phone: 804-828-1562
E-mail: wedavis@bu.edu
Website: www.ummz.lsa.umich.edu/birds/wos.html

Founded: 1888
Membership: 1,001–10,000
Scope: International
Description: To advance the science of ornithology and to secure cooperation in measures tending to this end.
Publication(s): Wilson Bulletin, The
Keyword(s): Wildlife & Species
Contact(s):
- Charles Blem, First Vice President; Dept. of Biology, 816 Park Ave., P.O. Box 842012, Virginia Commonwealth University, Richmond, VA 23284-2012; 804-828-1562; Fax: 804-828-0503; cblem@saturn.vcu.edu
- William Davis, President; College of General Studies, 871 Commonwealth Avenue, Boston University, Boston, MA 02215; 017-353-2886; Fax: 617-353-5868; wedavis@bu.edu
- Doris Watt, Second Vice President; Dept. of Biology, Saint Mary's College, Notre Dame, IN 46556-5001; 219-284-4668; Fax: 219-284-4716; dwatt@jade.saintmarys.edu
- Sara Morris, Secretary; Dept. of Biology, Canisius College, 2001 Main St., Buffalo, NY 14208; 716-888-2567; Fax: 716-888-3157; morriss@canisius.edu
- John Smallwood, Editor; Dept. of Biology, Montclair State University, Upper Montclair, NJ 07043; 973-655-5345; Fax: 973-655-7047; smallwood@saturn.montclair.edu

WINCHESTER NILO FARMS
Olin Corporation, 427 N. Shamrock
E. Alton, IL 62024 United States
Phone: 618-258-3133   Fax: 618-258-2370
Website: NiloFarms.com

Membership: 1–100
Scope: National
Description: Wildlife Hunting Preserve
Contact(s):
- Roger Jones, Manager; 618-466-0613

WINDSTAR FOUNDATION, THE
P.O. Box 656
Snowmass, CO 81654 United States
Phone: 970-927-5435   Fax: 970-963-1463
E-mail: windstar@rof.net
Website: www.wstar.org

Founded: 1976
Scope: National
Description: A nonprofit organization co-founded by John Denver and Tom Crum. Windstar works to inspire individuals to make responsible choices and take direct action to achieve a peaceful and environmentally sustainable future.
Contact(s):
- Cheryl Charles, Chairman of Board of Trustees
- Beth Miller, Secretary and Treasurer
- Jeanie Tomlinson, Liaison; 970-963-5534

WINDSTAR WILDLIFE INSTITUTE
10072 Vista Court
Myersville, MD 21773 United States
Phone: 301-293-3351   Fax: 801-740-7384
E-mail: wildlife@windstar.org
Website: www.windstar.org

Founded: 1986
Membership: 1,001–10,000
Scope: National
Description: WindStar Wildlife Institute is a national 501(c)(3) non-profit, conservation organization whose mission and solution to the loss of native plants and wildlife habitat focuses on effectively teaching wildlife habitat improvement practices through proven methods such as "neighbor helping neighbor" and "education through demonstration". WindStar strives to be the "trainer of choice" for both nature center and wild bird store staff through its education programs.!
Publication(s): Wildlife Habitat Improvement Kit, Tips on Improving Wildlife Habitat, WindStar Wildlife Garden Weekly
Keyword(s): Agriculture/Farming, Forests/Forestry, Public Lands/Greenspace, Water Habitats & Quality, Wildlife & Species
Contact(s):
- Thomas Patrick, President; 301-293-3351; Fax: 801-740-7384; tom@windstar.org

WISCONSIN ASSOCIATION FOR ENVIRONMENTAL EDUCATION, INC. (WAEE)
8 Nelson Hall, UWSP
Stevens Point, WI 54481 United States
Phone: 715-346-2796   Fax: 715-346-3835
E-mail: waee@uwsp.edu
Website: www.uwsp.edu/cnr/waee

Founded: 1974
Membership: 101–1,000
Scope: State, Regional
Description: Promotes environmental education in schools and other institutions and organizations in Wisconsin.
Publication(s): EE News
Keyword(s): Water Habitats & Quality
Contact(s):
- Paul Denowski, Chair; 262-642-7466; pdenowski@yahoo.com
- Jim McGinity, Co-Chair; 414-964-8505; irishmist@rocketmail.com
- Christy Allar, Administrative Assistant; 715-346-2796; Fax: 715-346-3835; callar@uwsp.edu

WISCONSIN ASSOCIATION OF LAKES (WAL)
1 Point Pl.
Suite 101
Madison, WI 53719 United States
Phone: 608-662-0923   Fax: 608-833-7179
E-mail: wal@wisconsinlakes.org
Website: www.wisconsinlakes.org

Founded: 1980
Scope: State
Description: WAL is a coalition of 287 lake management organizations, as well as hundreds of individual members. The organization is dedicated to the protection of lake ecosystems in Wisconsin. WAL works closely with the Wisconsin Department of Natural Resources and University Extension in the Wisconsin Lakes Partnership.
Publication(s): Lake Connection, The
Keyword(s): Land Issues, Pollution (general), Water Habitats & Quality
Contact(s):
- Jim Burgess, President; 608-257-4443; jeburg@aol.com
- Donna Sefton, Executive Director
- Judy Jooss, Secretary; 414-877-9301; jjooss@techheadnet.com
- Hal Krueger, Communications and Development Coordinator
- John Seibel, Treasurer; 715-479-4714; jpsmis@nnex.net
- Debra Sweeney, Membership Coordinator
- Susan Tesarik, Water Classification Outreach Coordinator

WISCONSIN BASS FEDERATION
Attn: President, 6503 Lani Ln.
McFarland, WI 53558 United States
Phone: 608-838-3040   Fax: 608-838-3040
Website: www.swiftsite.com/wsbf

Scope: State

Description: An organization of Bassmaster chapters, affiliated with the Bass Anglers Sportsman Society, organized to fight pollution, assist state and national conservation agencies in their efforts, and teach young people good conservation practices. Dedicated to the realistic conservation of our water resources.

Publication(s): Wisconsin Bass News

Contact(s):
Chuck Rolfsmeyer, President
Kevin Fassbind, Conservation Director; 12 Bel Aire, Madison, WI 53713; 608-224-0029; fassbind@hotmail.com

WISCONSIN DEPARTMENT OF NATURAL RESOURCES
101 S. Webster St. P.O. Box 7921
Madison, WI 53707-7921 United States
Phone: 608-266-2121   Fax: 267-938-9380
Website: www.dnr.state.wi.us

Scope: National

Contact(s):
Darrell Bazzell, Secretary

WISCONSIN LAND AND WATER CONSERVATION ASSOCIATION
One Point Place, Suite 101
Madison, WI 53719 United States
Phone: 608-833-1833   Fax: 608-833-7179
E-mail: wlwca@execpc.com
Website: www.execpc.com/~wlwca

Founded: 1952
Membership: 1–100
Scope: State

Description: Wisconsin Land and Water Conservation Association is a 501(c)(3) non-profit organization representing Wisconsin's 72 county land conservation committees and departments, assisting them with the protection, enhancement and sustainable use of Wisconsin's natural resources, and representing them through education and government interaction.

Publication(s): Thursday Note

Keyword(s): Agriculture/Farming, Pollution (general), Public Health, Public Lands/Greenspace, Reduce/Reuse/Recycle, Water Habitats & Quality, Wildlife & Species

Contact(s):
Marvin Fox, President; N2538 Cty. Road J, Kaukauna, WI 54130; 414-766-3242
Robert Washkuhn, Vice President; W8225 Sand Rd., Shell Lake, WI 54871; 715-468-7657
Rebecca Baumann, Executive Director; One Point Place, Ste. 101, Madison, WI 53719-2809; 608-833-1833; Fax: 608-833-7179; wlwca3@execpc.com
Roger Hahn, Board Member; 705 Pease St., Augusta, WI 54722; 715-286-5343

WISCONSIN PARK AND RECREATION ASSOCIATION
6601-C Northway
Greendale, WI 53129 United States
Phone: 414-423-1210   Fax: 414-423-1296
E-mail: wpra@execpc.com
Website: www.wpraweb.org

Membership: 1,001–10,000
Scope: State

Description: A nonprofit organization, affiliated with the National Recreation and Park Association, working with other groups and organizations to achieve the best in park services and recreational opportunities.

Publication(s): Impact Magazine, P.R. Monthly Newsletter

Contact(s):
Roger Kist, President; Washington County
Steve Thompson, Editor; 7000 Greenway, Suite 201, Greendale, WI 53129; 414-423-1210

WISCONSIN SOCIETY FOR ORNITHOLOGY, INC., THE
5188 Bittersweet Ln.
Oshkosh, WI 54901 United States
Phone: 920-233-1973
Website: www.uwgb.edu/birds/wso

Founded: 1939
Membership: 1,001–10,000
Scope: State

Description: To stimulate interest in and promote the study of birds in Wisconsin for a better understanding of their biology and basis for their preservation.

Publication(s): Passenger Pigeon, Badger Birder

Keyword(s): Agriculture/Farming, Recreation/Ecotourism, Wildlife & Species

Contact(s):
Noel Cutright, President; 3352 Knollwood Road, West Bend, WI 53095-9414; 414-221-2179; Noel.Cutright@we-energies.com
Jeffrey Baughman, Vice President; W4026 Middle Road, Campbellsport, WI 53010; 920-477-2387; jeff@csd.k12.wi.us
Jesse Peterson, Membership Chair; 810 Ganser Drive, Waunakee, WI 53597-1930; 608-849-3108; peterson.jesse@tds.net
Christine Reel, Treasurer; 2022 Sherryl Lane, Waukesha, WI 53188-3142; 262-547-6128; dcreel@execpc.com
Jane Dennis, Secretary; 138 S. Franklin Ave., Madison, WI 53705-5248; 608-231-1741
Bettie Harriman, Publicity Chair; 5188 Bittersweet Ln., Oshkosh, WI 54901; 920-233-1973
R. Highsmith, Editor; 702 Schiller Ct., Madison, WI 53704; 608-242-1168
Mary Uttech, Editor; 262-675-6482; muttech@asq.org

WISCONSIN WATERFOWL ASSOCIATION, INC.
614 W. Capitol Drive
Hartland, WI 53029 United States
Phone: 262-369-6309   Fax: 262-369-7813
E-mail: h2ofowl@powercom.net
Website: www.wisducks.org

Founded: 1983
Membership: 1,001–10,000
Scope: State

Description: A statewide nonprofit environmental/educational organization that establishes, promotes, assists, and contributes to conservation, restoration, and management of Wisconsin wetlands to perpetuate waterfowl and wildlife. Represents waterfowl enthusiasts via a unified statewide voice on Wisconsin migratory bird hunting regulations and conservation legislation benefiting the protection of wetlands. Educational programs and waterfowl hunting seminars.

Publication(s): Wisconsin Waterfowl

Keyword(s): Reduce/Reuse/Recycle, Water Habitats & Quality, Wildlife & Species

Contact(s):
Kelcy Boettcher, Director of Administrative Services; 262-369-6309; ext. 21; Fax: 262-369-7813; h2ofowl@powercom.net
Jeff Nania, Executive Director/Project Director; W11360 Hwy. 127, Portage, WI 53901; 608-742-6699; Fax: 608-742-1669
Tom Seibert, Regional Director; 262-369-6309; ext. 23; Fax: 262-369-7813; h2ofowl@powercom.net

Matt Ruwaldt, Ecologist; W9560 Aldercate Drive, Lodi, WI 53555; 608-516-2441; Fax: 262-369-7813; h2ofowl@powercom.net

WISCONSIN WILDLIFE FEDERATION

720 St. Croix Street
Suite 101
Prescott, WI 54021 United States
Phone: 715-262-9279   Fax: 715-262-5856
E-mail: ruthann@wiwf.org
Website: www.execpc.com/~wiwf

Founded: 1949
Membership: 1,001–10,000
Scope: State
Description: A representative statewide organization, affiliated with the National Wildlife Federation, dedicated to the protection and enhancement of wildlife and its habitat through public education and government interaction.
Publication(s): Wisconservation
Keyword(s): Reduce/Reuse/Recycle, Water Habitats & Quality, Wildlife & Species

Contact(s):
James Weishan, President and Alternate Representative
Daniel Gries, Editor
Russell Hltz, Treasurer
Martha Kilishek, Representative
Ruth Lee, Education Programs Contact

WISCONSIN WOODLAND OWNERS ASSOCIATION
P.O. Box 285
Stevens Point, WI 54481-0285 United States
Phone: 715-346-4798   Fax: 715-346-4821
Website: www.wisconsinwoodlands.org

Founded: 1979
Membership: 1,001–10,000
Scope: Local, State
Description: A statewide, nonprofit, educational association for and by private woodland owners in Wisconsin who want to learn more about good forest stewardship. Publish a quarterly award-winning magazine, co-sponsor conference, workshops, and field days for woodland owners. Thirteen local chapters throughout Wisconsin offer field days for woodland owners. Affiliated with the National Woodland Owners Association.
Publication(s): WWOA Seedlings, Woodland Management
Keyword(s): Ecosystems (precious), Forests/Forestry, Land Issues

Contact(s):
Marvin Meier, President; 715-355-9034
Alvin Barden, Vice President; 715-479-8449
Nancy Bozek, Executive Director; 715-346-4798; Fax: 715-346-4821; nbozek@uwsp.edu
Evelyn Charlson, Secretary; 920-982-4076
Timothy Eisele, Editor; 608-233-2904
Virgil Kopitske, Treasurer; 715-758-8960

WOLF EDUCATION AND RESEARCH CENTER
P. O. Box 217
Winchester, ID 83555 United States
Phone: 208-924-6960   Fax: 208-924-6959
E-mail: werc@camasnet.com
Website: www.wolfcenter.org

Founded: 1992
Membership: 1,001–10,000
Scope: State, Regional
Description: The Wolf Education and Research Center is dedicated to providing public information, education, and research concerning endangered species, with an emphasis on the gray wolf, its habitat and ecosystem in the Northern Rocky Mountain region. Our efforts seek to improve public awareness of endangered and threatened species in the area and to develop, in concert with regional cultures and residents, ways to coexist with these species.
Publication(s): Sawtooth Pack Sponsorship Newsletter, Wolf Education and Research Center Membership Newsletter, Educational Track of Wolf - monthly publication
Keyword(s): Ethics/Environmental Justice, Public Lands/Greenspace, Recreation/Ecotourism, Wildlife & Species

Contact(s):
Douglass Christensen, President; Fax: 208-726-1982; 1dmc@sunvalley.net
Roy Farrar, Vice President; Fax: 208-384-0540; wolfsta@mce.net
Nick Fiore, Membership; 111 Main Street, #150, Lewiston, ID 83501; 208-743-9554; Fax: 208-743-9534; werc@camasnet.com
Sally Farrar, Secretary; 208-336-6562; Fax: 208-384-0540

WOLF GROUP, THE
P.O. Box 303
Cherokee, TX 76832 United States
Phone: 915-622-4810
E-mail: sky@wolf.com
Website: www.wolf.com

Founded: 1996
Membership: 10,001–100,000
Scope: International
Description: Advocates for wolves and other endangered species and habitat
Keyword(s): Agriculture/Farming, Ecosystems (precious), Land Issues, Wildlife & Species

WOLF HAVEN INTERNATIONAL
3111 Offut Lake Rd.
Tenino, WA 98589 United States
Phone: 360-264-4695   Fax: 360-264-4639
E-mail: info@wolfhaven.org
Website: www.wolfhaven.org

Founded: 1982
Membership: 1,001–10,000
Scope: National, International
Description: The organization's mission is "Working for Wolf Conservation" done primarily through providing public education on the value of all wildlife; providing sanctuary for captive-born wolves; promoting wolf reestablishment in historic ranges; and protecting our remaining wild wolves. Wolf Haven is also one of three pre-release breeding facilities for the Mexican Wolf Recovery Program.
Publication(s): Wolf Tracks
Keyword(s): Wildlife & Species

Contact(s):
Rick Schaefer, President
Rick Castellano, Executive Director
Julie Palmquist, Communications Director; julie@wolfhaven.org
Dana Maher, Treasurer

WOMEN'S ENVIRONMENT AND DEVELOPMENT ORGANIZATION (WEDO)
355 Lexington Avenue, 3rd Floor
New York, NY 10017 United States
Phone: 212-973-0325   Fax: 212-973-0335
E-mail: wedo@wedo.org
Website: www.wedo.org

Founded: 1990
Scope: National
Description: On January 27, 1995, Women USA Fund, Inc. changed its name to WEDO. The organization is an international advocacy network actively working to transform society to achieve social, political, economic, and environmental justice for all through the empowerment of women, in all their diversity,

and through their equal participation with men in decision-making from grassroots to global arenas.
Publication(s): News and Views (contact WEDO for a comprehensive list)
Keyword(s): Population, Public Health, Reduce/Reuse/Recycle
Contact(s):
Jocelyn Dow, President; jocelyndow@hotmail.com
Thais Corral, Vice President
Bisi Ogunleye, Vice President
June Zeitlin, Executive Director
Elizabeth Calvin, Secretary
Brownie Ledbetter, Treasurer

WOMEN'S SHOOTING SPORTS FOUNDATION
4620 Edison Ave., Suite C
Colorado Springs, CO 80915 United States
E-mail: wssf@worldnet.att.net
Website: www.wssf.org/
Founded: 1993
Membership: 1,001–10,000
Scope: National
Description: The Women's Shooting Sports Foundation is a national, nonprofit membership organization offering an ongoing series of programs to expand shooting opportunities for women.
Publication(s): Outdoors for Women, Women's Resource List, The
Keyword(s): Ethics/Environmental Justice, Recreation/Ecotourism, Wildlife & Species
Contact(s):
Shari Legate, Executive Director

WOODLAND OWNERS ASSOCIATION OF WEST VIRGINIA
P.O. Box 206
Weston, WV 26452 United States
Phone: 304-594-3648   Fax: 304-594-3648
Website: www.woaofwv.org
Founded: 1991
Scope: State
Description: A statewide organization affiliated with the National Woodland Owners Association that promotes good forestry and sustainable management by non-industrial private owners in West Virginia.
Publication(s): West Virginia Woods
Keyword(s): Forests/Forestry
Contact(s):
Mark Burke, President; dadobourke@aol.com
Russ Richardson, Vice-President; P.O. Box 206, Weston, WV 26452; 304-269-3862; Fax: 304-269-3964; forestruss@aol.com
Mark Metz, Treasurer; 1017 Mt. Vernon Circle, Barboursville, WV 25504; 304-733-1043; themetzs@gateway.net
Edward Murriner, Secretary; Rt. 3. Box 186D, Hurricane, WV 25526; 304-727-5591; Fax: 304-558-0143; emmurin@gwmail.state.wv.us
Clay Smith, Editor; HC 64 Box 50, Parsons, WV 26287-9709; 304-478-2104
Bob Whipkey, Forestry Advisor; 304-558-2788

WORLD ASSOCIATION OF GIRL GUIDES AND GIRL SCOUTS (WAGGGS)
World Bureau Olave Centre; 12c Lyndhurst Rd.
London, NW3-5PQ United Kingdom
Website: www.waggsworld.org
Founded: 1928
Membership: 101–1,000
Scope: International
Description: WAGGGS is a voluntary worldwide movement open to all girls and young women. Based on spiritual values and dedicated to the education of girls and young women, WAGGGS provides them with opportunities of self-training in the development of character, responsible citizenship, and service in their own and world communities. WAGGGS works for peace by promoting increased understanding between individuals through community, environmental, and international projects.
Keyword(s): Development/Developing Countries, Ethics/Environmental Justice, Public Health
Contact(s):
Lesley Bulman, Director
Carol Brown, Treasurer
Larae Orvillian, World Board Vice Chairman
Ginny Radford, World Board Chairman

WORLD BIRD SANCTUARY (WBS)
125 Bald Eagle Ridge Road
Valley Park, MO 63088 United States
Phone: 636-938-6193   Fax: 636-861-3240
E-mail: info@worldbirdsanctuary.org
Website: www.worldbirdsanctuary.org
Founded: 1977
Membership: 1,001–10,000
Scope: International
Description: (formerly The Raptor Rehabilitation and Propagation Project Inc.) The WBS was established by Walter C. Crawford, Jr. near St. Louis, Missouri. It is a nonprofit, tax-exempt organization whose mission is to preserve the earth's biological diversity and to secure the future of threatened bird species in their natural environments. We work to fullfill that mission through education, propagation, and rehabilitation. We also have a hands-on internship program.
Publication(s): Education Department, Mews News, Stress in Captive Birds of Prey, Techniques for Artificial Incubation and Methods of Feather Replacement in Birds
Keyword(s): Wildlife & Species
Contact(s):
Walter Crawford, Jr., Executive Director; 636-861-3225; ext. 13; info@worldbirdsanctuary.org
Simon Davies, Director of Development; 636-861-3225; info@worldbirdsanctuary.org
Roger Holloway, Director of Interpretive Services; 636-225-4390; WBSEducation@aol.com
Jeffery Meshach, Director of Animal Management; 636-938-6175; info@worldbirdsanctuary.org

WORLD CONSERVATION UNION
Rue Mauverney 28
Gland, 1196 Switzerland
Phone: 41-22-999-0001
Website: www.iucn.org
Description: The IUCN mission is to influence, encourage and assist societies throughout the world to conserve the integrity and diversity of nature and to ensure that any use of natural resources is equitable and ecologically sustainable.
Contact(s):
Yolanda Kakabadse-Navarro, President; president@iucn.org
William Jackson, Director of Global Programme; 412-299-0276; Fax: 412-299-0025; bill.jackson@iucn.org
Achim Steiner, Director General; 412-299-0297; Fax: 412-299-0029; achim.steiner@iucn.org

WORLD FORESTRY CENTER
4033 SW Canyon Rd.
Portland, OR 97221 United States
Phone: 503-228-1367   Fax: 503-228-4608
Website: www.worldforestry.org
Founded: 1966
Scope: National
Description: The World Forestry Center is a nonprofit organization promoting a greater appreciation and understanding of the

world's forests and related natural resources. The Center operates a forestry museum adjacent to the Hoyt Arboretum, conference facilities, an international institute, and an 80-acre demonstration forest and outdoor education site. Public tours and classes, school programs, exhibits and special events, conferences, curriculum materials, and publications are available.

Publication(s): Forest Education Program Guide, Branching Out Newsletter

Keyword(s): Forests/Forestry, Reduce/Reuse/Recycle

Contact(s):
Dennis Dykstra, President
Rick Zenn, Education Director

WORLD PARKS ENDOWMENT INC.
1616 P St., NW
Suite #200
Washington, DC 20036 United States
Phone: 202-939-3808   Fax: 202-939-3868
E-mail: worldparks@worldparks.org
Website: www.worldparks.org

Founded: 1988
Scope: International
Description: World Parks Endowment, Inc. is a low-overhead organization that provides funds for the creation of new protected areas in tropical rain forests and other ecosystems of great conservation importance. World Parks is unique in that it works exclusively through local conservation organizations. So far World Parks has developed projects in over 12 countries, including the Sierra de las Minas Biosphere Reserve in Guatemala and the Bilsa Reserve in Ecuador.

Publication(s): Annual Report
Keyword(s): Forests/Forestry, Land Issues, Wildlife & Species
Contact(s):
Daniel Katz, Chairman and Board President
Byron Swift, President and Board Member
Roger Pasquier, Vice President and Treasurer
Cheri Sugal, Executive Director; 202-939-3255; cheri_sugal@yahoo.com

WORLD PHEASANT ASSOCIATION
P.O. Box 5 Lower Basildon
Reading, Berks, RG8 9PF United Kingdom
Phone: 1189845140   Fax: 1189843369
E-mail: wpa@gr.apc.org

Founded: 1975
Scope: National
Description: Aims are to develop, promote, and support conservation of all species of the order galliformes with initial emphasis on the family phasianidae.

Contact(s):
Keith Howman, President
Derek Bingham, Editor; c/o World Pheasant Association, P.O. Box 5, Lower Basildon, Reading, Berks RG8 9PF
Nicola Chalmers-Watson, Administrator
Richard Howard, Chairman

WORLD RESOURCES INSTITUTE
10 G St., NE, Suite 800
Washington, DC 20002 United States
Phone: 202-729-7600   Fax: 202-729-7610
E-mail: front@wri.org
Website: www.wri.org

Founded: 1982
Membership: 101–1,000
Scope: International
Description: A policy research center created with funding from the John D. and Catherine T. MacArthur Foundation and others, to help governments, international organizations, the private sector, and others address vital issues of environmental integrity, natural resource management, economic growth, and international security.

Publication(s): Policy Studies Series, World Resources Report, Research Report Series
Keyword(s): Air Quality/Atmosphere, Climate Change, Development/Developing Countries, Ecosystems (precious), Energy, Forests/Forestry, Oceans/Coasts/Beaches, Reduce/Reuse/Recycle, Transportation

Contact(s):
Jonathan Lash, President; jlash@wri.org
Marjorie Beane, V.P. for Administration and CFO

WORLD SOCIETY FOR THE PROTECTION OF ANIMALS (WSPA)
34 Deloss Street
Framingham, MA 01702 United States
Phone: 508-879-8350   Fax: 508-620-0786
E-mail: wspa@wspausa.com
Website: www.wspa-usa.org

Founded: 1981
Scope: International
Description: The World Society for the Protection of Animals (WSPA) is a unique international organization dedicated to raising the standard of animal welfare throughout the world. We provide direct hands-on help to stop cruelty and relieve animal suffering. WSPA achieves long-term improvements for animals by lobbying for effective animal welfare laws and providing education to change attitudes towards animals.

Publication(s): Animals International, WSPA Campaign News, WSPA World, Annual Report
Keyword(s): Wildlife & Species
Contact(s):
Andrew Dickson, Chief Executive
Laura Salter, USA Director
John Walsh, International Projects Director

WORLD WILDLIFE FUND
1250 24th St., NW
Washington, DC 20037 United States
Phone: 202-243-4800   Fax: 202-293-9211
E-mail: archer@wwfus.org
Website: www.worldwildlife.org

Founded: 1961
Scope: International
Description: WWF is the largest private U.S. organization working worldwide to protect wildlife and wildlands—especially in the tropical forests of Latin America, Asia, and Africa. WWF has helped create and protect more than 450 national parks and nature reserves; supports scientific investigations; monitors international trade in wildlife; promotes ecologically-sound development; assists local groups to take the lead in needed conservation projects; and seeks to influence public opinion and the policies

Publication(s): FOCUS
Keyword(s): Reduce/Reuse/Recycle, Wildlife & Species
Contact(s):
Kathryn Fuller, President
Bruce Bunting, Asia, Conservation Finance and Species Conservation Vice President
William Eichbaum, U.S. Conservation and Global Threats Vice President
David Evanich, Marketing, Membership and Communications Vice President
Deborah Hechinger, Managing Vice President for Operations
Twig Johnson, Latin America and Caribbean Vice President
James Leape, Senior Vice President
Diane Wood, Vice President of Research and Development
Margaret Ackerly, General Counsel
Edward Bass, Chairman of Executive Committee
Lou Ann Dietz, LAC Senior Program Officer; 202-778-9657; dietz@wwfus.org
Roger Sant, Chairman of Board

WORLD WILDLIFE FUND
GULF OF CALIFORNIA REGIONAL OFFICE
A.P. 423
Guaymas, Sonora, Mexico
Phone: 62211902
E-mail: nnwwfmex@campus.zym.itesm.mx

Founded: 1999

Description: Conservation of the Gulf of California ecoregion through land management enforce policy, partnerships, communications, conservation biologies, natural protected areas, etc.

Contact(s):
Juan Barrera, Office Coordinator; gce-wwfmex@campus.gym.itesm.mx
Norma Nvitez, Communications Officer; nnwwfmex@campus.gym.itesm.mx

WORLD WILDLIFE FUND
PERU PROGRAM OFFICE
Av. San Felipe 720
Jesus Maria
Lima, Peru
Phone: 5112615300   Fax: 5114634459
E-mail: fiorella@wwfperu.org.pe

Description: Conservation of biodiversity and ecological processes

Contact(s):
Fiorella Ceruti, Env. Ed. and Communication Officer; 511-261-5300; Fax: 511-463-4459

WORLDWATCH INSTITUTE
1776 Massachusetts Ave., NW
Washington, DC 20036-1904 United States
Phone: 202-452-1999   Fax: 202-296-7365
E-mail: worldwatch@worldwatch.org
Website: www.worldwatch.org

Founded: 1974
Membership: 10,001–100,000
Scope: International

Description: A nonprofit research organization designed to inform policymakers and the public about emerging global problems and trends and the complex links between the world economy and its environmental support systems. Recent studies have covered issues such as global warming, world water shortages, soil erosion, and the decline in food production compared to population growth, renewable energy, deforestation, transportation, oceans, fisheries, carrying capacity and environmental refugees.

Publication(s): Worldwatch papers, Environmental Book series, Vital Signs 2002, State of the World 2002, World Watch Magazine

Keyword(s): Agriculture/Farming, Climate Change, Development/Developing Countries, Ecosystems (precious), Energy, Ethics/Environmental Justice, Finance/Banking/Trade, Forests/Forestry, Oceans/Coasts/Beaches, Pollution (general), Population, Public Health, Recreation/Ecotourism

Contact(s):
Christopher Flavin, President; 202-452-1999; Fax: 202-296-7365; cflavin@worldwatch.org
Adrianne Greenlees, Vice President for Development; 202-452-1999; Fax: 202-296-7365; agreenlees@worldwatch.org
Leanne Mitchell, Director of Communications; 202-452-1999; Fax: 202-296-7365; lmitchell@worldwatch.org
Elizabeth Nolan, Vice President for Business Development; 202-452-1999; Fax: 202-296-7365; enolan@worldwatch.org
Gary Gardner, Director of Research; 202-452-1999; Fax: 202-296-7364; garygardner@worldwatch.org
Ed Ayres, Worldwatch Magazine Editor; 202-452-1999; Fax: 202-296-7365; edayres@worldwatch.org
Dick Bell, Senior Policy Advisor; 202-452-1999; Fax: 202-296-7365; dbell@worldwatch.org
Patrick Settle, Info Tech Manager and Web Master; 202-452-1999; Fax: 202-296-7365; psettle@worldwatch.org
Lori Brown, Research Librarian; 202-452-1999; Fax: 202-296-7365; lorib@worldwatch.org

WWF JAPAN (WORLD WIDE FUND FOR NATURE JAPAN)
Nihonseimei Akabanebashi Bldg., 3-1-14 Shiba
Minato-Ku, Tokyo, 1050-0014 Japan
Phone: 337691711   Fax: 337691717

Founded: 1971
Membership: 10,001–100,000
Scope: International

Description: WWF Japan is a national organization of WWF - World Wide Fund for Nature - which is one of the world's largest private international conservation organizations.

Contact(s):
Makoto Hoshino, Chief Executive Director
Prince Akishino, Honorary President
Hisako Hatakeyama, Chairperson
Mitsugu Kawamura, Vice Chairman
Tomio Yoshida, Vice Chairman

WWW.ACTIONBIOSCIENCE.ORG
1401 Casey Key Road
Nokomis, FL 34275 United States
Phone: 941-423-8636   Fax: 941-423-4486
E-mail: info@actionbioscience.org
Website: www.actionbioscience.org

Founded: 1998
Scope: International

Description: Educational web site promoting bioscience literacy with peer-reviewed articles by respected experts in the fields of environment, biodiversity, genomics, biotechnology, evolution, new frontiers, and bioscience education. Articles are accompanied by educator-written lesson plans for high school and undergraduate levels.

Keyword(s): Agriculture/Farming, Air Quality/Atmosphere, Climate Change, Development/Developing Countries, Ecosystems (precious), Ethics/Environmental Justice, Forests/Forestry, Land Issues, Oceans/Coasts/Beaches, Pollution (general), Population, Public Health, Public Lands/Greenspace

WYOMING ASSOCIATION OF CONSERVATION DISTRICTS
2304 E 13th St.
Cheyenne, WY 82001 United States
Phone: 307-632-5716   Fax: 307-638-4099
E-mail: waocd@trib.com
Website: www.conservewy.com

Membership: 1–100
Scope: State

Contact(s):
Olin Sims, President; 307-632-5716; Fax: 307-632-5716
Veronica Canfield, Vice President; P.O. Box 952, Sundance, WY 82729; 307-283-2062; Fax: 307-283-2170
Bobbie Frank, Director
Tracy Renner, Board Member; P.O. Box 271, Meeteetse, WY 82433; 307-868-2355; Fax: 307-868-2470

WYOMING BASS FEDERATION
Attn: President, 421 Sage Ave
Kemmerer, WY 83101 United States
Phone: 307-877-3629
E-mail: nichols@hamsfork.net

Scope: State

Description: An organization of Bassmaster chapters, affiliated with the Bass Anglers Sportsman Society, organized to fight pollution, assist state and national conservation agencies in

their efforts, and teach the young people of our country good conservation practices. Dedicated to the realistic conservation of our water resources.
Publication(s): Wyoming B.A.S.S. Frederation (Newsletter
Contact(s):
John Weber, President
Leonard Nichols, Conservation Director; 421 Sage Avenue, Kemmer, WY 83101; 307-877-3629; nichols@hamsfork.net

WYOMING NATIVE PLANT SOCIETY
P.O. Box 3452
Laramie, WY 82071 United States
Phone: 307-766-3020
Website: www.uwadmnweb.uwyo.edu/wyndd/wnps/wnps_home.htm
Founded: 1981
Membership: 101–1,000
Scope: State
Description: The Wyoming Native Plant Society promotes the use and appreciation of the state's native flora through education and supporting research.
Publication(s): Landscaping with Wildflowers and Native Plants, Castilleja
Keyword(s): Agriculture/Farming, Land Issues, Wildlife & Species
Contact(s):
Joy Handley, President
Nina Haas, Vice President
Walter Fertig, Secretary and Treasurer and Editor

WYOMING OUTDOOR COUNCIL
262 Lincoln St.
Lander, WY 82520 United States
Phone: 307-332-7031   Fax: 307-332-6899
E-mail: woc@wyomingoutdoorcouncil.org
Website: www.wyomingoutdoorcouncil.org
Founded: 1967
Membership: 1,001–10,000
Scope: Local, State
Description: A statewide membership organization dedicated to the conservation of Wyoming's natural resources. Promotes sound environmental policy and education of the public for wise decisionmaking. Serves as an active citizen lobby for environmental policies, and uses administrative and legal advocacy to monitor state and federal agencies. Current Issues Include Red Desert and Greater Yellowstone ecosystem protection, restoring wild patterns and oil and gas development concerns.
Publication(s): Various reports and alerts, Frontline Report (newsletter), State Legislative Analysis
Keyword(s): Air Quality/Atmosphere, Ecosystems (precious), Energy, Ethics/Environmental Justice, Forests/Forestry, Pollution (general), Public Lands/Greenspace, Reduce/Reuse/Recycle, Water Habitats & Quality
Contact(s):
Joyce Evans, President
Nancy Debevoise, Vice President
Dan Heilig, Executive Director
Barbara Oakleaf, Secretary
Lorna Wilkes, Treasurer

WYOMING WILDLIFE FEDERATION
P.O. Box 106
Cheyenne, WY 82003 United States
Phone: 307-637-5433   Fax: 307-637-6629
E-mail: admin@wyomingwildlife.org
Website: www.wyomingwildlife.org
Founded: 1937
Membership: 1,001–10,000
Scope: State
Description: A representative statewide organization, affiliated with the National Wildlife Federation, dedicated to the protection and enhancement of wildlife and its habitat through public education and government interaction.
Publication(s): The Pronghorn News
Contact(s):
Larry Baesler, Executive Director
Vickie Baker, Editor and Education Programs Contact
Al Weston, Treasurer
Mark Winland, Representative

X

XERCES SOCIETY, THE
4828 SE Hawthorne Blvd.
Portland, OR 97215 United States
Phone: 503-232-6639   Fax: 503-233-6794
E-mail: info@xerces.org
Website: www.xerces.org
Founded: 1971
Membership: 1,001–10,000
Scope: National
Description: An international nonprofit organization dedicated to invertebrates and the preservation of critical biosystems worldwide. The Society is committed to protecting invertebrates as major components of biological diversity. Emphasis: aquatic invertebrate monitoring to assist in conservation of Pacific Northwest watersheds, butterfly farming in NE Costa Rica, enhancing wild pollinator populations in out-of-play areas of selected Columbia Plateau golf courses, and education through publications.
Publication(s): Wings: Essays on Invertebrate Conservation (membership magazine), Common Names of North American Butterflies, The, Butterfly Gardening: Creating Summer Magic in Your Garden
Keyword(s): Wildlife & Species
Contact(s):
Thomas Eisner, President; Cornell University, Neurobiology and Behavior, W347 Mudd Hall, Ithaca, NY 14853-2702; 607-255-4464
Kathy Parker, Vice President
Scott Hoffman Black, Executive Director
Ed Grosswiler, Secretary, Treasurer
Katherine Janeway, Legal Advisor; 1932 First Avenue, Suite 510, Seattle, WA 98101; 206-583-8304
Matthew Shepherd, Editor

Y

YELL COUNTY WILDLIFE FEDERATION
Route 3 Box 223
Dardanelle, AR 72834 United States
Phone: 501-229-4692
Founded: 1946
Membership: 101–1,000
Scope: Local
Description: Local County affiliate of Arkansas Wildlife Federation consisting primarily of sportsmen, rod and gun enthusiasts, conservationists, nature-lovers and others recognizing basic responsibility to fish and wildlife conservation.
Keyword(s): Ecosystems (precious), Executive/Legislative/Judicial Reform, Forests/Forestry, Land Issues, Pollution (general), Public Lands/Greenspace, Recreation/Ecotourism, Water Habitats & Quality, Wildlife & Species
Contact(s):
Keith Blakemore, President; Route 3 Box 380, Dardanelle, AR 72834; 501-229-1133

YMCA NATURE AND COMMUNITY CENTER
1413 Highway 45
McClellanville, SC 29458 United States
Phone: 843-887-4195   Fax: 843-887-4256
E-mail: ymcawoodruff@aol.com
Website: hometown.aol.com/natureymca/go.html
Founded: 1999
Scope: Regional
Description: Provides creative nature education opportunities through various community programs. YMCA programs include a nature based summer camp for 7-12 year olds, Earth Leadership Institute camp for 13-17 year olds, a Teen YMCA Earth Service program, a Tree Ecology and Conservation program utilizing the YMCA's 71 acres and onsite nursery, and our discovery programs.
Keyword(s): Ecosystems (precious), Forests/Forestry, Pollution (general), Recreation/Ecotourism, Reduce/Reuse/Recycle, Water Habitats & Quality, Wildlife & Species
Contact(s):
Diane Moore Woodruff, Assistant Director; 843-887-4195; Fax: 843-887-4256; ymcawoodruff@aol.com
Lori Sheridan, Education Director; 843-887-4195; Fax: 843-887-4256; ymcals@hotmail.com

YOSEMITE RESTORATION TRUST
1212 Broadway, Suite 810
Oakland, CA 94612 United States
Phone: 510-763-1403   Fax: 510-208-4435
Website: www.yosemitetrust.org
Founded: 1990
Scope: National
Description: To ensure protection of the natural, scenic, and historic resources of Yosemite National Park and its ecosystems, and to ensure that visitors have the highest quality experience of the park's natural environment.
Publication(s): Yosemite Viewpoints (Newsletter), special reports on regional transportation, day-use reservations, and housing
Keyword(s): Land Issues, Public Lands/Greenspace, Recreation/Ecotourism, Sprawl/Urban Planning, Transportation
Contact(s):
Janet Cobb, President
Hal Browder, Vice President
Walter Kieser, Vice President
Thomas Gwyn, Treasurer

YOUNG ENTOMOLOGISTS SOCIETY, INC.
6907 W. Grand River Ave.
Lansing, MI 48906-9131 United States
Phone: 517-886-0630   Fax: 517-886-0630
E-mail: yesbugs@aol.com
Website: members.aol.com/yesbugs/bugclub.html
Founded: 1965
Membership: 101–1,000
Scope: National
Description: An international nonprofit organization educates and serves youth and amateur entomologists via publications, programs and the minibeast Zooseum and Education Center; assists in information, talent, scientific literature, and insect specimen exchanges (informational networks); distributes and develops resource materials; and promotes awareness of arthropod importance and the contributions youth and amateur entomologists make to the science of entomology. Founded as Teen International Entomology
Publication(s): Caring for Insect Livestock, Insect Indentification Guide, Project B.U.G.S., Insect World
Keyword(s): Recreation/Ecotourism, Wildlife & Species
Contact(s):
Dianna Dunn, Executive Director; 517-887-0499
Gary Dunn, Director of Education

YUKON FISH AND GAME ASSOCIATION
P.O. Box 4434
Whitehorse, Y1A 3T5 Yukon Canada
Phone: 403-667-2843
Scope: Province
Description: Affiliated with the Canadian Wildlife Federation.

Z

ZERO
158 Fife Ave., Greenwood Park, P.O. Box 5338
Harare, Zimbabwe
Phone: 2634791333   Fax: 2634732858
E-mail: zero@harare.iafrica.com
Founded: 1987
Scope: International
Description: ZERO, a regional environmental organization, is an independent professional, not-for-profit institution dedicated to the development of the rural peoples of southern Africa, especially through the promotion of sustainable management of land resources. ZERO pursues this goal through applied research, policy analysis and influencing national, regional, and international environmental policy making.
Keyword(s): Development/Developing Countries, Land Issues
Contact(s):
Joseph Matowanyika, Director
Yemi Katerere, Chairperson to the Board
Sam Moyo, Secretary to the Board
J. Mutsigwa, Librarian and Information Officer

ZUNGARO COCHA RESEARCH CENTER
EXPLORATION EDUCATIONAL EXPEDITIONS
P.O. Box 696
Raton, NM 87740 United States
Website: www.nvo.com/zungarococha
Founded: 1997
Scope: International
Description: Working to promote both human and wildlife interests in the Peruvian Amazon and provide information to help resolve their conflicts with special attention to acculturation. A permanat facility in collaboration with U.S. and Peruvian institutions for long-term research and training in pure and applied environmental sciences and conservation.
Keyword(s): Forests/Forestry, Wildlife & Species
Contact(s):
Denise Bacca, President; P.O. Box 696, Raton, NM 87740; 505-445-3603; Fax: 505-445-4101; tsi@raton.com
Carlos Acosta, Manager; Prospero 652, Iquitos; 0115194232; Fax: 011-519-423-2131

NON-GOVERNMENTAL FOR-PROFIT ORGANIZATIONS

A

ABSEARCH, INC.
NATURAL RESOURCE DATABASES
ASHA
1150 Alturas Dr.
Suite 103
Moscow, ID 83843 United States
Phone: 800-867-1877 Fax: 208-883-5554
E-mail: custinfo@absearch.com
Website: www.absearch.com

Founded: 1992

Scope: Local, State, Regional, National, International

Description: Produces ABSEARCH databases which include thousands of abstracts and citations from professional research journals in the area of natural resources. The databases are updated as new research becomes available. Format: CD-ROM and online subscription.

Contact(s):
Leah Lipar, Director of Operations; 208-883-5544; Fax: 208-883-5554; sales@absearch.com
Jennifer Bulson, Marketing Manager; 208-883-5594; Fax: 208-883-5554; marketing@absearch.com

ALDEANATURAL.COM
AREAS NATURALES PROTEGIDAS DE VENEZUELA Y EL MUNDO
NATURAL PROTECTED AREAS OF VENEZUELA AND THE WORLD
Apartado 63011
Chacafto
Caracas, 1067-A Venezuela
Phone: 58-416-607-4585
E-mail: carivero@telcel.net.ve
Website: venezuelatuya.com/natura

Founded: 2001

Scope: Local, State, Regional, National, International

Description: Research and publication of information on biodiversity and natural protected areas in Venezuela and the rest of the world. Will soon be aired as a very colorful and informative Website.

Keyword(s): Development/Developing Countries, Ecosystems (precious), Land Issues, Recreation/Ecotourism, Wildlife & Species

Contact(s):
Carlos Rivero-Blanco, Director; 58-416-607-4585; carivero@telcel.net.ve

AMERICAN AQUATICS, INC
273 Midway Lane
Oak Ridge, TN 37830 United States
Phone: 865-483-0600 Fax: 865-483-0674
E-mail: jfredd@aol.com
Website: www.american-aquatics.com

Founded: 1996
Membership: 1–100
Scope: State, Regional

Description: Biological consulting firm that specializes in collecting fish, benthic organisms and wildlife particularly from contaminated sites.

Keyword(s): Water Habitats & Quality, Wildlife & Species

Contact(s):
J. Heitman, President; 865-483-0600; Fax: 865-483-0674; jfredd@aol.com

AMERICAN CHEMICAL SOCIETY
1155 16th St. NW
Washington, DC 20036 United States
Phone: 202-872-4600 Fax: 202-872-4615
E-mail: help@acs.org
Website: www.acs.org

Founded: N/A
Membership: 100,001–500,000
Scope: National
Publication(s): Environmental Science and Technology

Contact(s):
Sally Pecor, Key Contact

ANIMALS AGENDA
3500 Boston St.
Suite 325
Baltimore, MD 21224 United States
Phone: 410-675-4566 Fax: 410-675-0066
E-mail: kim.stallwood@animalsandsociety.org
Website: www.animalsandsociety.org

Scope: International
Publication(s): The Animals' Agenda

Contact(s):
Kim Stallwood, Editor In Chief

ARENA CONSULTORES AMBIENTALES
ADMINISTRACIÓN DE RECURSOS NATURALES, S.A. DE C.V.
ARENA ENVIRONMENTAL CONSULTANTS
ARENA CONSULTORES
Boulevard Costero # 263-5
Zona Centro
Ensenada, 22800 Mexico
Phone: 646-178-3319 Fax: 646-178-3319
E-mail: ecoarena@telnor.net

Founded: 1991
Membership: 1–100
Scope: Local, State, Regional, National

Description: Arena provides services pertaining to environmental assessment, environmental risk, restoration, air quality monitoring and environmental analysis.

Keyword(s): Air Quality/Atmosphere, Energy, Oceans/Coasts/Beaches, Pollution (general)

Contact(s):
Octavio Telles Hirsch, General Director; 646-178-3319; Fax: 646-178-3319; ecoarena@telnor.net
Varinka Aguilar, Coordinadora Tecnica; 646-178-3319; Fax: 646-178-3319; ecoarena@telnor.net
Carlos Peynador Sfinchez, Gerente de Oceanograffa; 646-178-3319; Fax: 646-178-3319; ecoarena@telnor.net
Roberto Quero Santiago, Gerente de Campo; 646-178-3319; Fax: 646-178-3319; ecoarena@telnor.net

AUSTRALIAN MINERAL FOUNDATION
63 Conyngham St.
Glenside, S.A., 5065 Australia
Phone: 61883790444
E-mail: amf@amf.com.au
Website: www.amf.com.au/amf

Description: Produces "Australian Earth Sciences Information System (AESIS)", a bibliographic database covering Australian-generated published and unpublished documented material over the full range of the geosciences. AESIS also covers materials published on continental Australia by non-Australian sources.

B

BASS DIVISION OF ESPN PRODUCTIONS INC
5845 Carmichael Rd.
Montgomery, AL 36117 United States
Phone: 334-272-9530   Fax: 334-396-8230
E-mail: conservation@bassmaster.com
Website: www.bassmaster.com

Founded: 1968
Membership: 500,001–1,000,000
Scope: Local, State, National, International
Description: Organized to fight pollution, assist state and national conservation agencies in their efforts, and teach the young people of our country good conservation practices. Dedicated to the realistic conservation of our water resources.
Publication(s): Television Show: The Bassmasters, Fishing Tackle Retailer, BASS Times, Bassmaster Magazine
Keyword(s): Executive/Legislative/Judicial Reform, Land Issues, Oceans/Coasts/Beaches, Pollution (general), Recreation/Ecotourism, Reduce/Reuse/Recycle, Water Habitats & Quality, Wildlife & Species
Contact(s):
Bruce Shupp, National Conservation Director; 334-272-9530; ext. 422; Fax: 334-396-8230; bruce.shupp@bassmaster.com
Al Smith, National Federation Director; 334-272-9530; ext. 406; Fax: 334-270-8549; al.smith@bassmaster.com
Chris Horton, Conservation Manager; 334-272-9530; ext. 414; Fax: 334-396-8230; christopher.m.horton@bassmaster.com

BERLET FILMS AND VIDEOS
1646 West Kimmel Rd
Jackson, MI 49201 United States
Phone: 517-784-6969   Fax: 517-796-2646
E-mail: mark@berletfilms-video.com
Website: www.berletfilms-video.com

Scope: International
Description: Produces environmental/nature audio-video resources. Free brochures upon request.
Contact(s):
Mark Snedeker, General Manager

BRAUER PRODUCTIONS
530 S. Union St
Traverse City, MI 49684 United States
Phone: 231-941-0850   Fax: 231-941-0947
E-mail: brauer@brauer.com
Website: www.brauer.com

Founded: 1978
Scope: National
Description: Full service film and video production company serving Traverse City and clients throughout Michigan and the N.W. since 1978.
Contact(s):
Richard Brauer, President
Susan McQuaid, Contact

BROOKVIEW PRESS
901 Western Road
Castleton-on-Hudson, NY 12033 United States
Phone: 518-732-7093   Fax: 518-732-7093
E-mail: info@brookviewpress.com
Website: www.brookviewpress.com

Founded: 2001
Scope: Local, State, Regional, National, International
Description: Brookview Press is a small independently owned publisher located in Castleton-on-Hudson, about 2 hours north of New York City. We publish unique, quality paperback books about nature and the environment.
Publication(s): Steep Passages: A World-wide Eco-adventurer Unlocks Nature's Spiritual Truths

BUILDINGGREEN, INC.
122 Birge St.
Suite 30
Brattleboro, VT 05301 United States
Phone: 802-257-7300   Fax: 802-257-7304
E-mail: ebn@buildinggreen.com
Website: www.buildinggreen.com

Founded: 1992
Membership: 1,001–10,000
Scope: International
Description: Publisher of Environmental Building News, the leading newsletter on environmentally responsible design and construction.
Publication(s): Environmental Building News and Green Spec Directory
Keyword(s): Energy, Reduce/Reuse/Recycle, Sprawl/Urban Planning
Contact(s):
Dan Woodbury, Publisher

BULLFROG FILMS
P.O. Box 149
Olney, PA 19547 United States
Phone: 800-543-3764   Fax: 610-370-1978
E-mail: video@bullfrogfilms.com
Website: www.bullfrogfilms.com

Scope: International
Description: Films and videos rented and sold worldwide to educational institutions. Most programs come with study guide, with suggested activities, research topics, debate subjects, and bibliographies. Free catalogues available.
Contact(s):
Sieglinde Abromaitis

BUSINESS PUBLISHERS, INC.
8737 Colesville Rd.
Suite 1100
Silver Spring, MD 20910 United States
Phone: 301-589-5103   Fax: 301-587-4530
E-mail: bpinews@bpinews.com
Website: www.bpinews.com

Contact(s):
Beth Early

C

C.A.R.E (CITIZENS AGAINST RACCOON EXTERMINATION)
27479 Schulte Road
Carmel, CA 93923 United States
Phone: 831-626-7227   Fax: 831-626-7228
E-mail: Lpasten@aol.com
Website: www.drpasten.com

Scope: Local
Description: The goal of C.A.R.E is to save the raccoons on the Central Coast.
Contact(s):
Mari Fuentes-Jones, Administrator

CHESAPEAKE FARMS
7319 Remington Dr.
Chestertown, MD 21620 United States
Phone: 410-778-8400   Fax: 410-778-8405

Founded: 1956
Scope: Local, State, Regional
Description: Operated by DuPont Crop Protection to demonstrate, research, and promote sustainable farming and

wildlife management practices. Provides a forum for exploring agricultural issues and interactions between environmental and economic sustainability. Agricultural project conducted by coalition of Dupont, universities, government and private organizations. Wildlife research conducted through graduate fellows.

Keyword(s): Agriculture/Farming

Contact(s):
Mark Conner, Manager; 410-778-8402; Fax: 410-778-8405; mark.c.conner@usa.dupont.com

CJE ASSOCIATES
237 Gretna Green Ct.
Alexandria, VA 22304 United States
Phone: 703-823-0662   Fax: 703-823-5923
E-mail: eeiserer@netscape.net

Scope: National

Publication(s): Ecology USA

Contact(s):
Elaine Eiserer, Editor

COASTAL CONSERVATION AND EDUCATION FOUNDATION, INC.
SULU FUND FOR MARINE CONSERVATION
Room 302, Third Floor, PDI Condominium
Archbishop Reyes Avenue
Banilad
Cebu City, 6000 Philippines
Phone: 032-233-6947   Fax: 032-233-6891
E-mail: ccef@mozcom.com
Website: www.coast.ph

Founded: 1998

Membership: 1–100

Scope: Local, National, International

Description: The vision of CCE Foundation is the management and sustainable use of Philippine coastal resources through the active leadership and participation of coastal resource users, local governments, non-government organizations, academe and other stakeholders.

Publication(s): Publications, reports, etc.

Keyword(s): Oceans/Coasts/Beaches, Population, Water Habitats & Quality

Contact(s):
Alan White,, President; 032-233-6947; Fax: 032-233-6891; awhite@mozcom.com
Rose-Liza Eisma, Executive Director; 032-233-6947; Fax: 032-233-6891; ccef@mozcom.com

CONGRESSIONAL GREEN SHEETS, INC.
ENVIRONMENT AND ENERGY WEEKLY BULLETIN
GREEN SHEETS EXPRESS
NEWSROOM
406 E St., SE
Washington, DC 20003 United States
Phone: 202-546-2220   Fax: 202-546-7490
E-mail: wb@greensheets.com
Website: www.greensheets.com

Founded: 1975

Membership: 1,001–10,000

Scope: Local, State, Regional, National, International

Description: Newsletter

Publication(s): Environment and Energy Weekly Bulletin, Newsroom, Green Sheets Express

Keyword(s): Agriculture/Farming, Air Quality/Atmosphere, Climate Change, Development/Developing Countries, Ecosystems (precious), Energy, Ethics/Environmental Justice, Executive/Legislative/Judicial Reform, Finance/Banking/Trade, Forests/Forestry, Land Issues, Oceans

Contact(s):
John Dineen, Editor

CONNECTICUT CARIBOU CLAN
P.O. Box 9344
Bolton, CT 6043 United States
Phone: 860-643-2948
E-mail: captundra@aol.com
Website: hometown.aol.com/captundra/index.html

Founded: 1989

Scope: National

Description: Tundra Talk Newsletter focuses on energy, transportation, and the environment, with special emphasis on permanently preserving the Arctic Refuge.

Keyword(s): Ecosystems (precious), Energy, Transportation, Wildlife & Species

Contact(s):
Rodney Parlee, Editor/Publisher

CROWNPOINT INSTITUTE OF TECHNOLOGY
NATURAL RESOURCE DEPARTMENT
P.O. Box 849
Crownpoint, NM 87313 United States
Phone: 505-786-4100
E-mail: mattie@cit.cc.nm.us
Website: www.cit.cc.nm.us

CUTTER INFORMATION CORPORATION
37 Broadway
Suite 1
Arlington, MA 02474 United States
Phone: 781-648-8700   Fax: 781-648-1950
E-mail: cdoucette@cutter.com
Website: www.cutter.com

Membership: 1–100

Scope: International

Publication(s): Business & The Environment ISO 140 Update, Air Quality Global Environmental Change Report, Environmental Design Update

Contact(s):
Christine Doucette

E

EAGLES 4 KIDS
258 Baker Street
Berea, OH 44017 United States
Phone: 440-239-0903
E-mail: dylage@aol.com

Founded: 2001

Scope: Local, State, National

Description: Educational materials and merchandise based on our mascot, Elmer the Eagle. Elmer travels the U.S. educating elementary students about Bald Eagles.

Keyword(s): Reduce/Reuse/Recycle, Wildlife & Species

EARTH SCHOOL
P.O. Box 777
Tryon, NC 28782 United States
Phone: 866-504-3199   Fax: 866-504-3199
E-mail: richard@lovetheearth.com
Website: www.lovetheearth.com/

Scope: Local, State, Regional

Description: Earth School promotes nature awareness & self reliance through a dedication to reconnecting people to the natural world. Programs are available for all ages.

ECONOVA INC.
453 North Main Street
Kaysville, UT 84037 United States
Phone: 801-336-3300, ext. 123   Fax: 801-336-3600
E-mail: Research@econovainc.com
Website: econovainc.com

Founded: 1991
Membership: 1–100
Scope: Local, State, Regional, National, International
Description: Manufacturing and sales of the "Next Generation" water management equipment.
Keyword(s): Agriculture/Farming, Development/Developing Countries, Pollution (general), Reduce/Reuse/Recycle, Water Habitats & Quality

ECOROOMMATES.COM
420 Raymond Ave. Ste. #12
Santa Monica, CA 90405 United States
Phone: 310-399-9355
E-mail: admin@ecoroommates.com
Website: www.ecoroommates.com

Founded: 2003
Membership: 101–1,000
Scope: International
Description: Roommate finder service for vegetarians, vegans, rawfood, macrobiotic and other environmentally oriented / holistically oriented lifestyles.

ELEMENTAL TECHNOLOGY, LLC
301 West Deer Valley Road
Suite 10
Phoenix, AZ 85027 United States
Phone: 623-581-3150   Fax: 623-581-2581
E-mail: info@elementaltech.com
Website: elementaltech.com

Founded: 1979
Scope: Local, State, Regional, National, International
Description: Environmental research software designer - products allow standardization of field data entry using handheld PCs, group information sharing, and report generation on a daily basis help to preserve validity and reliability of data. Customizable to accommodate most taxonomies/species studies.

ENDANGERED SPECIES AND WETLANDS REPORT
P.O. Box 5393
Takoma Park, MD 20913 United States
Phone: 301-891-3791   Fax: 301-891-3507
E-mail: poplar@crosslink.net
Website: www.eswr.com

Founded: 1995
Scope: National
Description: Independent monthly publication covering the ESA, wetlands and "takings" issues.
Publication(s): Endangered Species & Wetlands Report
Keyword(s): Wildlife & Species

ENVIRONMENT AND ENERGY PUBLISHING, LLC
122 C St., NW
Washington, DC 20001 United States
Phone: 202-628-6500   Fax: 202-737-5299
E-mail: pubs@eenews.net
Website: www.eenews.net
Membership: 1–100
Scope: International
Publication(s): Land Letter (The Newsletter for Natural Resource Professionals), Greenwire and Environmental and Energy Daily

Contact(s):
Drew Gagliano, Marketing Director
Kevin Braun, Managing Editor

ENVIRONMENTAL CAREER CENTER
2 Eaton Street
Suite 711
Hampton, VA 23669 United States
Phone: 757-727-7895   Fax: 757-727-7904
E-mail: eccinfo@environmentalcareer.com
Website: www.environmentalcareer.com

Founded: 1980
Membership: 1,001–10,000
Scope: National, International
Description: Helping people work for the environment since 1980 through: paid environmental internships, National Environmental Employment Report - monthly newspaper, EnvironmentalCAREER.com jobs and resume database, careers research, and career seminars/conferences.

Contact(s):
John Esson, President; 757-727-7895; Fax: 757-727-7904; eccinfo@environmentalcareer.com
Chris Sabo, Chief Editor, Nat'l Env. Employment Report; 757-727-7895; Fax: 757-727-7904; eccinfo@environmentalcareer.com

ENVIRONMENTAL MEDIA CORPORATION
1008 Paris Ave.
Port Royal, SC 29935-2418 United States
Phone: 843-986-9034, ext. 10   Fax: 843-986-9093
E-mail: enewton@envmedia.com
Website: www.envmedia.com

Founded: 1989
Scope: National, International
Description: Environmental Media designs, produces, and distributes media to support environmental education. Programs are curriculum-based and most are accompanied by teaching guides. Free catalogue available and other educational material.
Publication(s): See publications on website
Keyword(s): Ecosystems (precious), Oceans/Coasts/Beaches, Pollution (general), Reduce/Reuse/Recycle, Water Habitats & Quality, Wildlife & Species

Contact(s):
Eileen Newton, Reseller Manager
Bill Pendergraft, Owner

ENVIROSCAPE
JT&A, Inc.
14524-F Lee Road
Chantilly, VA 20151 United States
Phone: 703-631-8810   Fax: 703-631-6558
E-mail: info@enviroscapes.com
Website: enviroscapes.com

Founded: 1984
Scope: International
Description: Interactive, hands-on models that make learning about watersheds & the environment fun. Wetlands, nonpoint source, stormwater, landfills, wastes, coastal, air, and more. Models, puzzles, kits, posters and more. Tools that tackle language and learning style barriers while engaging people of all ages. EnviroScape models are patented under No. 5,427,530. EnviroScape is a registered trademark of JT&A, Inc.

G

GOOD NATURE PUBLISHING CO.
1904 Third Ave #415
Seattle, WA 98101 United States
Phone: 800-631-3086   Fax: 206-749-0446
E-mail: tim@goodnaturepublishing.com
Website: www.goodnaturepublishing.com

Founded: 1998
Membership: 1–100

Scope: Local, State, Regional, National, International

Description: Good Nature Publishing Co. is a green business based in Seattle. We design and illustrate poster size field guides of flora and fauna in color pencil and watercolor. We work for natural resource agencies, environmental groups, and individuals who want to paint a story about a species, bioregion, or just make something beautiful for their organization. See Good Nature's website for complete catalog. We print on 100% recycled papers, process chlorine free.

Keyword(s): Agriculture/Farming, Climate Change, Ecosystems (precious), Energy, Forests/Forestry, Oceans/Coasts/Beaches, Public Lands/Greenspace, Recreation/Ecotourism, Reduce/Reuse/Recycle, Sprawl/Urban Planning, Transportation

GRANT TECH CONSULTING AND CONSERVATION SERVICES
9564 Cheyenne Rd.
Meriden, KS 66512 United States
Phone: 785-876-0106   Fax: 785-876-0106
E-mail: kellyhiesberger@hotmail.com
Website: www.granttechconsulting.com

Founded: 1999

Scope: Local, State, Regional, National

Description: At Grant Tech Consulting and Conservation Services our goal is to bring nature and people together one habitat project at a time. We offer a broad range of services to private land owners, schools, community organizations, and non-profit organizations. We offer funding proposal development, trail design and construction services, design for outdoor education and recreation sites, interpretive nature programs, wetland development, teacher in-service training programs, and much more.

Keyword(s): Agriculture/Farming, Ecosystems (precious), Land Issues, Public Lands/Greenspace, Recreation/Ecotourism, Water Habitats & Quality, Wildlife & Species

GREEN MOUNTAIN POST FILMS
P.O. Box 229
Turners Falls, MA 01376 United States
Phone: 413-863-4754   Fax: 413-863-8248
Website: www.gmpfilms.com

Founded: 1975
Membership: 1–100
Scope: International

Description: A film/video production and distribution company that specializes in media concerning environmental issues.

Contact(s):
Charles Light, Business Manager

GREENWIRE
ENVIRONMENT AND ENERGY PUBLISHING, LLC
122 C St., NW Suite 722
Washington, DC 20001 United States
Phone: 202-628-6500   Fax: 202-737-5299
E-mail: pubs@eenews.net
Website: www.eenews.net

Description: An online daily publication providing comprehensive coverage of environmental, energy and natural resources issues, politics, developments and policy action. Greenwire tracks and reports on the White House, federal agencies, states, court decisions and the stories being reported on by the media nationwide.

Publication(s): The Environment and Energy Daily, Greenwire, and Land Letter

Contact(s):
Drew Gagliano, Marketing Director

ILOVEPARKS.COM
913 Totonaca Lane
El Paso, TX 79912 United States
Phone: 915-587-6641
E-mail: info@iloveparks.com
Website: iloveparks.com

Founded: 2000
Membership: 101–1,000
Scope: International

Description: ILoveParks.com is helping people connect with parks around the world through information provision and education for a variety of related issues.

Keyword(s): Development/Developing Countries, Ecosystems (precious), Ethics/Environmental Justice, Executive/Legislative/Judicial Reform, Forests/Forestry, Land Issues, Oceans/Coasts/Beaches, Pollution (general), Population, Public Lands/Greenspace, Recreation/Ecotourism

INSTITUTE FOR GLOBAL COMMUNICATIONS
P.O. Box 29904
San Francisco, CA 94129-0904 United States
Phone: 415-561-6100   Fax: 415-561-6101
E-mail: econet@igc.apc.org
Website: www.igc.org

Founded: 1984
Scope: International

Description: Creates and manages "EcoNet". Through the development of communication and information sharing systems, EcoNet seeks to increase collaboration and cooperation between organizations seeking environmental sustainability.

Contact(s):
Debra Farrell, Executive Director

INTERNATIONAL ACADEMY
ENVIRONMENTAL
Santa Barbara, CA 93140 United States
Phone: 805-964-0790   Fax: 805-564-4634
E-mail: info@iasb.org
Website: www.iasb.org

Scope: International

Description: Produces "Environmental Bibliography", bibliographic database covering more than 400 scientific and popular journals in social, political and philosophical issues, air, energy, land and water resources, nutrition and health. Author Abstracts, 1997 forward.

Publication(s): CD Rom Issued Quarterly Online, Environmental Knowledge Base by Subscription

Contact(s):
Joann St. John, President
Steven Popps, Director of Sales and Customer Service
Eric Boehm, Chairman
Lauren Everett, Editor
Amy Rushing, Editor

INTERNATIONAL RESEARCH AND EVALUATION
21098 IRE Control Center
Eagan, MN 55121 United States
                          Fax: 952-888-9124

Description: Environmental library for the application of knowledge, methods and means.

Publication(s): Waste Management Information Database, World Environment Report, World Environment Directory

Contact(s):
R. Danford

J

JAGRATA JUBA SHANGHA (JJS)
96 South Central Rd.
Khulna, 9100 Bangladesh
Phone: 88041731013　　　Fax: 88041730146
E-mail: jjs@khulnanet.net

Founded: 1985

Description: JJS is working with the people living around the Sundarban (world's largest Mangroves) in Bangladesh for conservation of the resources of the Sundarban environment.

Publication(s): JJS News, Posters on Sundarbans, Jagrata Barta

Contact(s):
Atm Hossain, Executive Director; zakir@khulnanet.net
Khadiza Khatun, Manager Administration
Mesbahul Mokarebin, Manager Education
Saifuddin Ahmed, Finance Officer
Kaniz Fatima, Head of Planning
Khaza Mohiuddin, Head of Program

JERE MOSSIER PRODUCTIONS/ UNDERWATER IMAGES
P.O. Box 1415
Hayden, ID 83835 United States
Phone: 208-683-8112
Website: www.jeremossier.com

Scope: International

Description: Licensing of underwater and wildlife stock footage and professional video production of fisheries, underwater programs, wildlife, and natural history videos.

Publication(s): Videos, Underwater Exploration

Contact(s):
Jere Mossier

JONES AND STOKES
2600 V Street
Sacramento, CA 95818 United States
Phone: 916-737-3000　　　Fax: 916-737-3030
Website: www.jonesandstokes.com

Founded: 1970

Scope: Local, State, Regional, National

Description: Jones and Stokes provide their clients with scientifically accurate, innovative, and practical solutions to their environmental challenges. Their reputation for providing clients with incomparable quality and the broadest diversity of expertise in the industry is unsurpassed. Their unique teams of knowledgeable, experienced professionals embrace a multidisciplinary, problem-solving philosophy and approach that benefits both their clients and the environment.

Contact(s):
John Cowdery, President; 916-737-3000; Fax: 916-737-3030
Michael Stuhr, VP Business Development; 916-737-3000; Fax: 916-737-3030
Julie Jessen; julieb@jsanet.com

L

LAST WIZARDS, THE
3400 W. 111th St. #154
Chicago, IL 60655 United States
Phone: 708-507-4306　　　Fax: 708-974-4356
E-mail: info@lastwizards.com
Website: www.lastwizards.com/

Founded: 2002

Scope: Local, State, Regional, National, International

Description: When visiting The Last Wizards website you will find essays and discussions on the tools, techniques and forces that shift and alter perceptions in our world. The Last Wizards are concerned with philosophy, environmental politics, postmodernism, mass media, scholarly occult theory, culture and the legacies and prophecies of world war, globalization, and technology.

Publication(s): Book of Green Shadows

Keyword(s): Agriculture/Farming, Ecosystems (precious), Finance/Banking/Trade, Forests/Forestry, Pollution (general), Public Health, Wildlife & Species

Contact(s):
James Bell, Editor; 708-507-4306; james@lastwizards.com

LEXIS/NEXIS ACADEMIC AND LIBRARY SOLUTIONS
4520 East-West Hwy., Suite 800
Bethesda, MD 20814-3389 United States
Phone: 301-654-1550　　　Fax: 301-657-3203
E-mail: academicinfo@lexis-nexis.com
Website: www.lexisnexis.com/academic

Scope: International

Description: Publishes indexes, electronic databases and microform collections that provide access to information published by government, private and international sources.

Publication(s): Enviroline, Environment Abstracts

Contact(s):
Henry Stoever, Marketing Director
Marcy Taylor, Contact

LUMMI ISLAND HERITAGE TRUST
P.O. Box 158
Lummi Island, WA 98262-0158 United States
Phone: 360-758-7997　　　Fax: 360-758-7001
E-mail: info@liht.org
Website: www.liht.org

Scope: National

Contact(s):
Dave Kershner

N

NATIONAL AVIARY
Allegheny Commons West
Pittsburgh, PA 15212-5248 United States
Phone: 412-323-7235　　　Fax: 412-321-4364
E-mail: info@aviary.org
Website: www.aviary.org

Founded: 1952

Membership: 1,001–10,000

Scope: National

Description: The National Aviary works to inspire respect for nature through the appreciation of birds. Travel the world at the National Aviary and visit over 600 exotic and endangered birds in natural habitats.

Publication(s): Bird Calls

Keyword(s): Reduce/Reuse/Recycle, Wildlife & Species

Contact(s):
Dayton Baker, Executive Director; ext. 217; dayton.baker@aviary.org

NATIONAL GROUND WATER INFORMATION CENTER
601 Dempsey Rd.
Westerville, OH 43081 United States
Phone: 614-898-7791, ext. 502　　Fax: 614-898-7786
E-mail: ngwa@ngwa.org
Website: www.ngwa.org

Founded: 1960

Membership: 10,001–100,000

Scope: Local, State, Regional, National, International

Description: Produces "Ground Water On Line", a members-only database of nearly 90,000 ground water abstracts. The NGWIC is a fee-based information service conducting literature searches and document delivery. By drawing upon a 30,000+

volume collection of books and over 300 journals, NGWIC staff can aid in the retrieval of information for your ground water projects. The Center has been serving ground water information needs since 1960.

Contact(s):
Sandy Masters, Director of the Information Center

NEAL COMMUNICATIONS
1220 Bald Eagle Rd.
Kingston Springs, TN 37082 United States
Phone: 615-952-5323   Fax: 615-952-5323
E-mail: cindy@nealcommunications.com

Founded: 1985
Membership: 1–100
Scope: International
Description: Produce outreach videos and communications consulting services supporting sustainable ecosystems and development, conservation of natural resources, wildlife, and cultural integrity. Specialists in translating complex issues into compelling, motivating communications.

NISC (NATIONAL INFORMATION SERVICES CORPORATION)
3100 St. Paul St.
Suite 806
Baltimore, MD 21218 United States
Phone: 410-243-0797   Fax: 410-243-0982
E-mail: sales@nisc.com
Website: www.nisc.com

Scope: Local, State, Regional, National, International
Description: National Information Services Corporation (NISC) publishes information products for access through BiblioLine, our web search service, or on CD-ROM. NISC's bibliographic and full-text databases cover a wide range of topics in the natural sciences.
Keyword(s): Agriculture/Farming, Oceans/Coasts/Beaches, Public Health, Water Habitats & Quality, Wildlife & Species

Contact(s):
Debbie Durr, Sales & Marketing Manager

NOAH'S NOTES, INC.
18430 NW 9th Ct.
Pembroke Pines, FL 33029 United States
Phone: 954-438-8147
E-mail: webmaster@noahsnotes.com
Website: noahsnotes.com

Founded: 2000
Scope: Local, State, Regional, National
Description: From home and garden eco-tips to eco-products, Noah's Notes shows how you can make the difference right in your own backyard!

NOLTE ASSOCIATES, INC.
15090 Avenue of Science, Suite 101
San Diego, CA 92128 United States
Phone: 858-385-0500   Fax: 858-385-0400
E-mail: sandiego_info@nolte.com
Website: www.nolte.com

Founded: 1949
Scope: Local, State, Regional
Description: The value of a practice that spans more than a half century is a legacy of experience and knowledge. Nolte is a full-service civil engineering firm with the expertise to successfully complete a wide variety of projects. We are committed to using sustainable development practices whenever possible to reduce potable water consumption, protect storm water quality, create environmentally responsible land use patterns, preserve habitat, provide livable communities, and control development costs.

Keyword(s): Agriculture/Farming, Development/Developing Countries, Ecosystems (precious), Energy, Land Issues, Reduce/Reuse/Recycle, Transportation, Water Habitats & Quality

P

PARQUE NACIONAL SIERRA NEVADA
MUCUBAJF NATURE CENTER
Apartado Postal 63011
Chacaito Caracas, 1067-A Venezuela
Phone: 58-416-607-4585
E-mail: carivero@telcel.net.ve

Founded: 1994
Scope: Local, State, Regional, National, International
Description: A Nature Center in the high Venezuelan Andes, at 11.444 feet elevation. The exhibits feature the Paramo ecosystem, and its inhabitants, the Sierra Nevada National Park and the Venezuelan Park System. Carlos Rivero Blanco, Ph.D., and Machela Rivero designed the exhibits and hold the concession since 1994. The Nature Center is visited yearly by several thousand people. It serves students from the vicinity and tourists from abroad.
Keyword(s): Ecosystems (precious), Land Issues, Recreation/Ecotourism, Wildlife & Species

Contact(s):
Carlos Rivero-Blanco, Director
Machela Rivero, Directora
Carlos Rivero-Fuentes, Asistente

POINT TO POINT COMMUNICATIONS
15 North King Street
Suite 203
Leesburg, VA 20176 United States
Phone: 703-669-9910   Fax: 703-669-9913
E-mail: skenyon@erols.com
Website: www.pt2ptcom.com

Founded: 1997
Scope: Local, State, Regional, National, International
Description: Point to Point Communications specializes in helping the conservation community communicate. We are a full service public relations firm dedicated to conservation issues. We provide media training, strategic planning, writing, editing, congressional education and general public relations services.
Keyword(s): Oceans/Coasts/Beaches, Recreation/Ecotourism, Sprawl/Urban Planning, Water Habitats & Quality, Wildlife & Species

Contact(s):
Stephanie Kenyon, Parnter; skenyon@erols.com
Carol Wynne, Partner; cawynne@attglobal.net

PROPERTY CARETAKING OPPORTUNITIES WORLDWIDE
HOUSESITTING
EMPLOYMENT
NATURE
P.O. Box 540
River Falls, WI 54022 United States
Phone: 715-426-5500
E-mail: caretaker@caretaker.org
Website: www.caretaker.org

Founded: 1983
Membership: 10,001–100,000
Scope: International
Description: Helping landowners and property caretakers find one another since 1983
Publication(s): Caretaker Gazette, The Caretaker bi-monthly newsletter
Keyword(s): Agriculture/Farming, Development/Developing Countries, Ecosystems (precious), Forests/Forestry, Land Issues, Oceans/Coasts/Beaches, Public Lands/Greenspace,

Recreation/Ecotourism, Water Habitats & Quality, Wildlife & Species

Contact(s):
Gary Dunn, Owner; 715-426-5500; caretaker@caretaker.org

PS ENTERPRISES
430 Colorado Avenue
Suite 401
Santa Monica, CA 90401 United States
Phone: 310-393-3305   Fax: 310-260-2553
E-mail: info@psenterprises.com
Website: www.psenterprises.com

Founded: 1989
Scope: Local, State, Regional, National, International
Description: PS Enterprises specializes in media & governmental relations, policy development, marketing, investor relations, public outreach, grass-roots organizing, and crisis communications management — as they relate to improving the environment and quality of life for the health, enjoyment and sustainability of current and future generations.
Keyword(s): Air Quality/Atmosphere, Climate Change, Energy, Ethics/Environmental Justice, Executive/Legislative/Judicial Reform, Land Issues, Oceans/Coasts/Beaches, Pollution (general), Public Health, Public Lands/Greenspace, Reduce/Reuse/Recycle, Sprawl/Urban Planning
Contact(s):
Tom Soto, President/CEO
Rick Ruiz, Vice President
David Barberis, Chief Financial Officer
Kevin Doyle, Sr. Client Executive

PUBLIC LANDS INTERPRETIVE ASSOCIATION
SOUTHWEST NATURAL AND CULTURAL HERITAGE ASSN.
6501 Fourth NW Suite I
Albuquerque, NM 87107 United States
Phone: 505-345-9498   Fax: 505-344-1543
Website: www.publiclandsinfo.org

Founded: 1981
Scope: Regional
Description: Educational and interpretive not for profit organization operating bookstores in federal visitor centers as well as publisher of local interpretive booklets.
Publication(s): Wild & Scenic Rio Grande, Merritt Island National Wildlife Refuge, Pecos Wilderness Trail Guide, Bosque Del Apache Nation
Contact(s):
Lisa Madsen, CEO
Ted Peay, President
Stephen Maurer, Director of Publications

R

RED BUFFALO, LLC
205 Bisonte Rojo Road
Medina, TX 78055 United States
Phone: 830-589-2999
E-mail: redbuff@indian-creek.net
Website: myredbuffalo.com

Founded: 1999
Membership: 1–100
Scope: Local, State, Regional
Description: Provides land management services including prescribed fire, restoration, and training. Products include slip-on pumper units for prescribed burning and bumper stickers supporting prescribed burning.
Keyword(s): Land Issues, Wildlife & Species
Contact(s):
Amy Blair, Owner; 830-589-2999; redbuff@indian-creek.net

RESPONSIVE MANAGEMENT
130 Franklin St.
Harrisonburg, VA 22801 United States
Phone: 540-432-1888   Fax: 540-432-1892
Website: www.responsivemanagement.com

Founded: 1986
Scope: State, Regional, National, International
Description: Developed to help fish and wildlife organizations understand and work with their constituents. Responsive Management conducts focus group research, telephone and mail surveys, public opinion and attitude research, literature reviews, demographic analysis, and workshops in public opinion polling, marketing, change, communications, dispute resolution, and human dimensions of natural resource management.
Publication(s): Responsive Management E-Report
Contact(s):
Mark Duda, Executive Director; 540-432-1888; Fax: 540-432-1892; mdduda@rica.net

S

SHARING NATURE FOUNDATION
14618 Tyler Foote Road
Nevada City, CA 95959 United States
Phone: 530-478-7650   Fax: 530-478-7562
E-mail: info@sharingnature.com
Website: www.sharingnature.com

Founded: 1979
Membership: 1,001–10,000
Scope: International
Description: Established in 1979 by naturalist and author, Joseph Cornell, the Sharing Nature Foundation uses creative nature activities to give people joyful experiences of nature. We believe it's only by uplifting people's consciousness that we change their way of looking at, and relating to the world around them. To do this we use Flow Learning™, a playful and inspirational teaching strategy that works with people where they are and gently brings them to a deeper, more profound experience of nature.
Publication(s): Journey to the Heart of Nature, With Beauty Before Me, John Muir: My Life with Nature, Listening to Nature, Sharing Nature with Children I & II

SPORTSMANS NETWORK, INC., THE
501 S. Kentucky Ave
Corbin, KY 40701 United States
Phone: 606-528-9353   Fax: 606-528-2287
E-mail: sportsmen@sportsmansnetwork.org
Website: www.sportsmansnetwork.org

Founded: 1991
Scope: State
Description: The Sportsman's Network is an incorporated statewide nonprofit conservation organization dedicated to educating the public and raising awareness of wildlife conservation through programs which promote controlled hunting, fishing, and other related activities. Also produces "A Moment in Conservation" radio program.
Keyword(s): Land Issues, Public Lands/Greenspace, Recreation/Ecotourism, Water Habitats & Quality, Wildlife & Species
Contact(s):
Keith Fullwood, Vice President
Elmer Chavies, Jr., Regional Director
Ernie Samples, Executive Director
Paul Cookendorfer, Secretary
Ken Hale, Treasurer
Peter Samples, State Chairman

T

TURNER ENDANGERED SPECIES FUND
1123 Research Dr.
Bozeman, MT 59718 United States
Phone: 406-556-8500 Fax: 406-763-4419
E-mail: tesf@montana.net
Website: www.tesf.org

Contact(s):
Kyran Kunkel

V

VIDEO PROJECT, THE
P.O. Box 411376
San Francisco, CA 94141-1376 United States
Phone: 800-475-2638
E-mail: video@videoproject.net
Website: www.videoproject.net/

Scope: International

Description: Media for a safe and sustainable world. Affordable films and videos on environmental and related issues. The project now offers over 600 programs for sale.

W

WALKABOUT PRODUCTIONS, INC.
45 Old Solomons Island Rd.
Suite 201
Annapolis, MD 21401 United States
Phone: 410-573-1228 Fax: 410-573-9521
E-mail: info@walkaboutInc.com
Website: www.walkaboutinc.com

Founded: 1980
Scope: International

Description: Walkabout Productions, Inc., is an EMMY award winning production team that focuses on environment, wildlife, and science documentaries. Filmography is available.

Contact(s):
Allison Nichols, Producer

WELLSPRING INTERNATIONAL, INC.
830 Bear Tavern Rd
Suite 301
Ewing, NJ 08628 United States
Phone: 609-530-1990 Fax: 609-530-1991
E-mail: mschoen@wellspringwireless.com
Website: www.wellspringwireless.com

Founded: 1995
Scope: Local, State, Regional, National, International

Description: Wellspring is a water conservation and sub-metering company with offices nationwide. Water sub-metering (metering individual apartment units) promotes conservation by giving tenants direct control over their water bills; wasted water (e.g. long showers and leaky toilets) is money down the drain. As a result of this connection between tap and wallet, sub-metered communities generally see a 20% reduction in water usage.

Keyword(s): Energy, Reduce/Reuse/Recycle, Water Habitats & Quality

Contact(s):
Michael Schoen, Environmental Affairs; 609-530-1990; Fax: 609-530-1991; mschoen@wellspringwireless.com

WYOMING NATURAL DIVERSITY DATABASE
P.O. Box 3381
Laramie, WY 82071-3381 United States
Phone: 307-766-3023 Fax: 307-766-3026
E-mail: wndd@uwyo.edu
Website: www.uwyo.edu/wyndd

Membership: 1–100
Scope: Regional

Contact(s):
Gary Beauvais

EDUCATIONAL INSTITUTIONS

A

ACADIA UNIVERSITY
24 University Ave., Patterson Hall
Wolfville, B0P 1X0 Nova Scotia Canada
Phone: 902-542-2201　　　　　Fax: 902-585-1059
E-mail: biology@acadiau.ca
Website: www.acadiau.ca

Founded: 1838
Membership: 1–100
Scope: National, International
Description: Primarily an undergraduate university, emphasizing a liberal education in a balanced blend of arts, science, and professional studies. Masters degrees are offered in biology, chemistry, computer science, education, English, geology, political science, physiology, and sociology.
Publication(s): See publication website
Contact(s):
　Tom Herman, Head of Biology Department; 902-585-1469; tom.herman@acadiau.ca
　Glyn Bissex, Recreation Management; glyn.bissex@acadiau.ca
　Soren Bondrup-Nielsen, Wildlife, Fisheries, Aquatic Biology, Marine Ecology, Mammal; 902-585-1424; Fax: 902-585-1059; soren.bondrup-nielsen@acadiau.ca
　Robert Raeside, Environmental Geology; 902-585-1323; robert.raeside@acadiau.ca
　Don Stewart, Assistant Professor, Biology Department; 902-585-1391; Fax: 902-585-1059; don.stewart@acadiau.ca
　David Stiles, Environmental Chemistry; 902-585-1325; Fax: 902-585-1114; david.stiles@acadiau.ca

ALFRED UNIVERSITY
DIVISION OF ENVIRONMENTAL STUDIES
1 Saxon Dr.
Alfred, NY 14802-1205 United States
Phone: 607-871-2634　　　　　Fax: 607-871-2697
E-mail: ens@alfred.edu
Website: www.alfred.edu

Founded: 1971
Scope: State
Description: The program offers an undergraduate degree in multidisciplinary environmental studies in a liberal arts setting. Students can focus on either natural or social sciences, and many take a second major in biology, geology, political science, economics, etc. The project-oriented program is supervised by fifteen faculty members from different disciplines.
Contact(s):
　Michele Hluchy, Chair of Division of Environmental Studies and Professor of Geology and Environment; 507-871-2634; ens@alfred.edu
　Diana Sinton, Assistant Professor of Geography and Environmental Studies; ens@alfred.edu

ANTIOCH COLLEGE
795 Livermore St.
Yellow Springs, OH 45387 United States
Phone: 937-769-1000　　　　　Fax: 937-767-7331
E-mail: admissions@anitoch-college.edu
Website: www.antioch-college.edu/
Membership: 101–1,000
Scope: National
Publication(s): Colleges that Changes Lives
Contact(s):
　Charles Taylor, Physics and Solar Energy/Alternative Technology; ext. 5355; ctaylor@antioch-college.edu
　Peter Townsend, Geology; ext. 6879; ptownsend@antioch-college.edu
　Jill Yager, Biology; ext. 6878; jyager@antioch-college.edu

ANTIOCH NEW ENGLAND GRADUATE SCHOOL
40 Avon St.
Keene, NH 03431-3552 United States
Phone: 603-357-6265　　　　　Fax: 603-357-0718
E-mail: admissions@antiochne.edu
Website: www.antiochne.edu

Founded: 1964
Scope: Local, State, Regional, National
Description: Antioch New England Graduate School is an innovative, vibrant institution offering practice-based, student-centered graduate programs designed for adult learners. Antioch New England's programs combine internships with academic studies and provide students with the knowledge and practical skills they need to be effective in their careers and communities. Master's programs in education, environmental studies, management, and psychology; doctoral programs in environmental studies and psychology.
Contact(s):
　Peter Temes, President

ANTIOCH NEW ENGLAND GRADUATE SCHOOL, ENVIRONMENTAL STUDIES
40 Avon St.
Keene, NH 03431-3552 United States
Phone: 603-357-3122　　　　　Fax: 603-357-0718
E-mail: admissions@antiochne.edu
Website: www.antiochne.edu

Founded: 1964
Scope: Local, State, Regional, National
Description: Antioch New England Graduate School educates, trains, and develops environmental leaders through its master's and doctoral degree programs in environmental studies. Antioch New England offers master's programs in conservation biology, environmental advocacy and organizing, environmental education, and resource management and administration, as well as a Ph.D. program in environmental studies.

ANTIOCH UNIVERSITY SEATTLE
ENVIRONMENT AND COMMUNITY PROGRAM
2326 Sixth Avenue
Seattle, WA 98121-1814 United States
Phone: 206-441-5352　　　　　Fax: 206-441-3307
E-mail: jjoichi@antiochsea.edu
Website: www.antiochsea.edu/ec

Founded: 1852
Scope: Local, State, Regional, National, International
Description: The E&C program approaches environmental challenges via social science perspectives and natural science literacy for professionals in environmental or community development fields. Students gain a clear understanding of the social, economic, political, and institutional dimensions of environmental issues. The program publishes "Sense of Place", the Environment and Community Newsletter.
Contact(s):
　Jean Joichi, Admission Associate; 206-268-4208; jjoichi@antiochsea.edu
　Jonathan Scherch, Program Chair; 206-268-4710; scherch@antiochsea.edu

APPALACHIAN STATE UNIVERSITY
426 Sanford Hall
Boone, NC 28608 United States
Phone: 828-262-2000　　　　　Fax: 828-262-6472
Website: www.appstate.edu
Membership: 1,001–10,000
Scope: State
Contact(s):
　Jeff Boyer, Sustainable Development Minor, Director; 426 Sanford Hall, Boone, NC 28608; boyerjc@appstate.edu

Kim Siegenthaler, Recreation Management Program, Director; 828-262-2540; siegenthalkl@appstate.edu
Francis Borkowski, Chancellor

ARIZONA STATE UNIVERSITY
CENTER FOR ENVIRONMENTAL STUDIES
CENTRAL ARIZONA - PHOENIX LONG TERM ECOLOGICAL RESEARCH PROJECT
CONSORTIUM FOR THE STUDY OF RAPIDLY URBANIZING REGIONS
Box 873211, Arizona State University
Tempe, AZ 85287-3211 United States
Phone: 480-965-2975   Fax: 480-965-8087
Website: www.asu.edu/ces or http://caplter.asu.edu

Scope: Local, State, Regional, National, International

Description: The Center is involved in the Central Arizona-Phoenix Long Term Ecological Research (CAP LTER) project at Arizona State University, funded by the NSF and is one of the first urban sites in the LTER network. CAP LTER provides a unique addition to LTER research by focusing upon an arid-land ecosystem profoundly influenced, even defined by the presence and activities of humans.

Keyword(s): Air Quality/Atmosphere, Climate Change, Ecosystems (precious), Land Issues, Pollution (general), Population, Public Lands/Greenspace, Sprawl/Urban Planning, Transportation, Water Habitats & Quality, Wildlife & Species

Contact(s):
Nancy Grimm, Co-Project Director
Charles Redman, Co-Project Director
Shirley Stapleton, Administrative Assistant to the Director; 965-2975; Fax: 965-8087; shirley.stapleton@asu.edu

ARKANSAS STATE UNIVERSITY
DEPARTMENT OF BIOLOGICAL SCIENCE
DEPT. OF ENVIRONMENTAL SCIENCES
P. O. Box 847
State University, AR 72467 United States
Phone: 870-972-3082   Fax: 870-972-2008
Website: www.csm.astate.edu/~biology/biology.html

Founded: 1997
Membership: 1–100
Scope: State

Contact(s):
Jerry Farris, Director of Environmental Sciences Program; 870-972-2007; Fax: 870-972-2638; envirsci@navajo.astate.edu

ARKANSAS TECH UNIVERSITY
DEPARTMENT OF PARKS, RECREATION, AND HOSPITALITY ADMINISTRATION
1205 North El Paso Avenue
Russellville, AR 72801 United States
Phone: 479-968-0852   Fax: 479-968-0600
E-mail: info@atu.edu
Website: www.atu.edu

Founded: 1909
Membership: 101–1,000
Scope: State

Description: Recreation and Park Adminstration offers five areas of emphasis: Recreation Administration, Therapeutic Recreation, Park Administration, Turf Management and Interpretive Naturalist

Keyword(s): Development/Developing Countries, Public Lands/Greenspace, Recreation/Ecotourism

Contact(s):
Theresa Herrick, Recreation and Park Administration, Director; Williamson Hall, Room 100, Russellville, AR 72081; 501-968-0378; theresa.herrick@mail.atu.edu
Joseph Stoeckel, Fisheries and Wildlife Biology, Director; 501-964-0852; joe.stoeckel@mail.atu.edu
Charlie Gagen, Head of Biological Sciences; 501-964-0814; charlie.gagen@mail.atu.edu

ARKANSAS TECH UNIVERSITY
FISHERIES AND WILDLIFE BIOLOGY PROGRAM
McEver Science Building
1701 North Boulder Avenue
Russellville, AR 72801 United States
Phone: 479-964-0852   Fax: 479-960-0837
E-mail: joe.stoeckel@mail.atu.edu
Website: pls.atu.edu/biology/fw

Founded: 1904
Scope: State

Description: Tech offers B.S. and M.S. degrees in Fisheries and Wildlife Biology. Our location, in the Arkansas River Valley between the Ouachita and Ozark mountains, is ideally suited to this program, because it encompasses an exceptionally wide range of fish and wildlife habitats. A trademark of our program is a field-oriented approach that provides numerous opportunities for hands-on learning through field laboratories, research projects, and solid working relationships with natural resource agencies.

Keyword(s): Ecosystems (precious), Forests/Forestry, Public Lands/Greenspace, Water Habitats & Quality, Wildlife & Species

ASSOCIATION FOR THE STUDY OF LITERATURE AND ENVIRONMENT (ASLE)
Annie Merrill Ingram, Sec.-Treas.
Davidson College
English Department, Box 7056
Davidson, NC 28035-7056 United States
Phone: 704-894-2487
E-mail: aningram@davidson.edu
Website: www.asle.umn.edu/

Founded: 1992
Membership: 101–1,000
Scope: International

Description: The Association for the Study of Literature and Environment (ASLE) was founded in October 1992 to promote the exchange of ideas and information about literature and other cultural representations that consider human relationships with the natural world. The name of the organization is meant to be as inclusive as possible, encompassing any text that illuminates the ways humans perceive and interact with the nonhuman environment.

AUBURN UNIVERSITY
COLLEGE OF AGRICULTURE
DEPARTMENT OF FISHERIES AND ALLIED AQUACULTURES
203 Swingle Hall
Auburn University, AL 36849 United States
Phone: 334-844-4786   Fax: 334-844-9208
Website: www.ag.auburn.edu/dept/faa/

Membership: 1–100
Scope: State

Description: The department sponsors the Southeastern Cooperative Fish Disease Project, providing a fish-kill diagnostic service, training in fish diseases and research on fish diseases to the cooperating member states.

Publication(s): Publications on website
Keyword(s): Agriculture/Farming

Contact(s):
B. Duncan, Director, International Center for Aquaculture and Aquatic Environments; bduncan@acesag.auburn.edu
John Grizzle, Associate Project Director
John Jensen, Department Head; jjensen@acesag.auburn.edu

AUBURN UNIVERSITY
COLLEGE OF SCIENCES AND MATHEMATICS
DEPARTMENT OF BIOLOGICAL SCIENCES
59 Duggar Dr., Extension Cottage
Auburn University, AL 36849 United States
Phone: 334-844-4830   Fax: 334-844-5748
Website: www.auburn.edu/cosam

Scope: State

Description: Newly formed from merger of Zoology and Botany departments.

Contact(s):
  Alfred Brown, Department Co-Head; 101 Life Science Bldg., Dept. of Biological Sciences, Auburn University, AL 36849; 334-844-1661; Fax: 334-844-1645

AUBURN UNIVERSITY
SCHOOL OF FORESTRY AND WILDLIFE SCIENCES
108 M. White Smith Hall
Auburn University, AL 36849-5418 United States
Phone: 334-844-1007   Fax: 334-844-1084
Website: www.forestry.auburn.edu/

Membership: 1–100
Scope: International
Keyword(s): Forests/Forestry, Wildlife & Species

Contact(s):
  Richard Brinker, Dean

B

BALL STATE UNIVERSITY
DEPARTMENT OF NATURAL RESOURCES AND ENVIRONMENTAL MANAGEMENT
NREM Dept.
Muncie, IN 47306 United States
Phone: 765-285-5780   Fax: 765-285-2606
E-mail: nrem@bsu.edu
Website: www.bsu.edu/nrem

Membership: 1–100
Scope: State
Description: tba

Contact(s):
  Hugh Brown, Dept. Chair; Soil Resources; 765-285-5788; hbrown@bsu.edu
  Paul Chandler, International Resource Management; 765-285-5788; pchandle@bsu.edu
  James Eflin, Energy Resources and Environmental Policy; 765-285-2327; jeflin1@bsu.edu
  Thad Godish, Occupational/Industrial Hygiene; Air Quality; 765-285-5782; 00tjgodish@bsu.edu
  Timothy Lyon, Natural Resource Studies; 765-285-5783; tlyon@bsu.edu
  John Pichtel, Waste Management; 765-285-2182; jpichtel@bsu.edu
  Amy Sheaffer, Environmental Communication; Park and Recreation Mgt.; 765-285-5781; asheaffer@bsu.edu
  Fred Siewert, Water Resources; 765-285-5790; fsiewert@bsu.edu

BARD COLLEGE
BARD CENTER FOR ENVIRONMENTAL POLICY
Hegeman 001
Annandale-on-Hudson, NY 12504-5000 United States
Phone: 845-758-7073   Fax: 845-758-7636
E-mail: cep@bard.edu
Website: www.bard.edu/cep

Founded: 2001
Membership: 1–100
Scope: Local, State, Regional, National, International

Description: Bard College offers an innovative graduate program leading to a Master of Science in Environmental Policy. BCEP's unique modular curriculum integrates a basic knowledge of scientific methods, tools of economic analysis, legal and ethical principles and the politics of policy making. The program stresses communication strategies and leadership skills as well as hands-on internships and a Master's Project.

Publication(s): Open Forum Reports

Contact(s):
  Joanne Fox-Przeworski, Ph.D., Director; 845-758-7067; jfp@bard.edu
  Jennifer Phillips, Ph.D., Professor of Science; 845-758-7845; phillips@bard.edu
  Gautam Sethi, Ph.D., Professor of Economics; 845-758-7386; sethi@bard.edu

BEMIDJI STATE UNIVERSITY
CENTER FOR ENVIRONMENTAL, EARTH AND SPACE STUDIES
P.O. Box 27, 1500 Birchmont Dr., NE
Bemidji, MN 56601 United States
Phone: 218-755-2910   Fax: 218-755-4107
Website: www.bemidji.msus.edu/

Founded: 1968
Membership: 1–100
Scope: International

Description: The Center for Environmental Studies is a research and teaching unit directed towards understanding our physical, biological, and social environment, and preventing its deterioration. The center conducts laboratory and field studies, both internally and externally funded, and offers baccalaureate and master's degree programs.

Contact(s):
  Patrick Welle, Director

BOSTON UNIVERSITY
SCHOOL FOR FIELD STUDIES
10 Federal Street
Salem, MA 01970 United States
Phone: 978-741-3567   Fax: 978-741-3551
E-mail: admissions@fieldstudies.org
Website: www.fieldstudies.org

Founded: 1980

Description: The mission of The School for Field Studies is to provide highly motivated young people from the U.S. and abroad with an excellent practical education in environmental studies, in order that tomorrow's leaders may become more environmentally literate/aware as well as make immediate and future contributions toward the sustainable management of natural resources.

Contact(s):
  Terry Andreas, President

BOWLING GREEN STATE UNIVERSITY
Center for Environmental Programs
153 College Park Office Building
Bowling Green, OH 43403 United States
Phone: 419-372-8207   Fax: 419-372-7243
E-mail: envs@bgnet.bgsu.edu
Website: www.bgsu.edu/department/envp

Founded: 1969
Membership: 101–1,000
Scope: State

Description: Offer undergraduate environmental degree programs in Environmental Policy and Analysis and Environmental Science through the College of Arts & Sciences and a degree in Environmental Health through the College of Health and Human Services.

Contact(s):
  Holly Myers-Jones, Director

BRADLEY UNIVERSITY
ENVIRONMENTAL SCIENCE PROGRAM
1501 W. Bradley Ave.
Peoria, IL 61625 United States
Phone: 309-677-3020　　　　Fax: 309-677-3558
E-mail: kdm@bradley.edu
Website: www.bradley.edu/academics/las/bio/

Founded: 1960
Membership: 1–100
Scope: Local, State, Regional, National, International
Description: Environmental Science program at Bradley University.
Keyword(s): Air Quality/Atmosphere, Ecosystems (precious), Forests/Forestry, Land Issues
Contact(s):
  Barbara Frase, Ethology and Evolution; 309-677-3014
  Sherri Morris, Ecosystem Ecology; 309-677-3016; sjmorris@bradley.edu
  Janet Gehring, Plant Biology; 309-677-3017; jgehring@bradley.edu
  Kelly McConnaughay, Plant Ecology; 309-677-3018; kdm@bradley.edu

BROWN UNIVERSITY
CENTER FOR ENVIRONMENTAL STUDIES
Box 1943
Providence, RI 02912 United States
Phone: 401-863-3449　　　　Fax: 401-863-3503
E-mail: envstu@brown.edu
Website: envstudies.brown.edu/Dept/

Founded: 1978
Membership: 1–100
Scope: Local, State, Regional, National, International
Description: The Center for Environmental Studies offers three interdisciplinary degrees (A.B., Sc.B., and M.A.) in environmental problem-solving; coordinates and facilitates environmental efforts within the university community; and collaborates with both state government agencies and community-based groups on projects to improve environmental quality for all Rhode Island residents. All programs aim to integrate teaching, scholarship, and service.
Keyword(s): Air Quality/Atmosphere, Climate Change, Ethics/Environmental Justice, Forests/Forestry, Land Issues, Oceans/Coasts/Beaches, Public Health, Reduce/Reuse/Recycle, Sprawl/Urban Planning, Water Habitats & Quality
Contact(s):
  Harold Ward, Director; harold_ward@brown.edu
  Patti Caton, Administrative Manager; patti_caton@brown.edu
  Kurt Teichert, Environmental Coordinator, Kurt_Teichert@brown.edu

C

CALIFORNIA POLYTECHNIC STATE UNIVERSITY
COLLEGE OF ARCHITECTURE AND ENVIRONMENTAL DESIGN
One Grand Ave.
San Luis Obispo, CA 93407 United States
Phone: 805-756-1321　　　　Fax: 805-756-5986
E-mail: caed@polymail.calpoly.edu
Website: www.calpoly.edu/~caed/

Scope: State
Publication(s): Publications on website
Contact(s):
  Walter Bremer, Department Head, Landscape Architecture; wbremer@calpoly.edu
  William Siembieda, Department Head, City and Regional Planning; 805-756-1315; wsiembie@calpoly.edu

CALIFORNIA STATE UNIVERSITY AT CHICO
DEPARTMENT OF RECREATION AND PARKS MANAGEMENT
PARKS AND NATURAL RESOURCES MANAGEMENT OPTION
Dept. of Recreation and Parks Management
California State University, Chico
Chico, CA 95929-0560 United States
Phone: 530-898-6408　　　　Fax: 530-898-6557
E-mail: recr@csuchico.edu
Website: www.csuchico.edu/recr

Founded: 1962
Membership: 1–100
Scope: National
Description: "Patterns" of study include Environmental Education/Interpretation, Human Dimensions in Parks Management, Outdoor Leadership, and Parks and Facilities Management
Keyword(s): Recreation/Ecotourism
Contact(s):
  Jon Hooper, Coordinator, Parks and Natural Resources Management Option; 530-898-5811
  Emilyn Sheffield, Department Chair; 530-898-4855; esheffield@csuchico.edu

CALIFORNIA STATE UNIVERSITY AT FULLERTON
SCHOOL OF HUMANITIES AND SOCIAL SCIENCES
ENVIRONMENTAL STUDIES PROGRAM
Humanities H-420A
Fullerton, CA 92834-9480 United States
Phone: 714-278-4373
E-mail: mhogarth@fullerton.edu
Website: hss.fullerton.edu/envstud/index.html

Founded: 1970
Scope: State
Description: Interdisciplinary graduate program leading to master's degree in environmental sciences, environmental policy and planning, or environmental education and communication.
Contact(s):
  Robert Voeks, Program Director; 714-278-3361

CALIFORNIA STATE UNIVERSITY AT SACRAMENTO
ENVIRONMENTAL STUDIES DEPARTMENT
6000 J St.
Sacramento, CA 95819 United States
Phone: 916-278-6338　　　　Fax: 916-278-7584
E-mail: infodesk@csus.edu
Website: www.csus.edu\index.stm

Membership: 1–100
Scope: State
Description: Biology Department offers a concentration in Biological Conservation. Interdisciplinary Environmental Studies program offers a B.A. Recreation and Leisure Studies program offers a B.S. or B.A. in Park and Recreation Resource Management.
Contact(s):
  Cary Goulard, Graduate Coordinator, Recreation and Leisure Studies; goulardc@hhsserver.hhs.csus.edu
  Steven Gray, Chair, Recreation and Leisure Studies; graysw@csus.edu
  Laurel Heffernan, Chair, Dept. of Biological Sciences; 916-278-6535; Fax: 916-278-6993
  Tom Krabacher, Environmental Studies; 916-278-6620; Fax: 916-278-7582; wrighta@csus.edu
  C. Vanicek, Advisor, Conservation Biology; 916-278-6569

CALIFORNIA UNIVERSITY OF PENNSYLVANIA
BIOLOGICAL AND ENVIRONMENTAL SCIENCES DEPARTMENT
250 University Ave.
California, PA 15419-1394 United States
Phone: 724-938-4200   Fax: 724-938-1514
Website: www.cup.edu

Scope: State

Description: University Biology Department

Keyword(s): Ethics/Environmental Justice, Forests/Forestry, Pollution (general), Wildlife & Species

Contact(s):
- David Argent, Wildlife Biology, Option; 724-938-1529; argent@cup.edu
- David Boehm, Biology, Chair; 724-938-4200
- William Kimmel, Environmental Pollution Control, Option; 724-938-4213; kimmel@cup.edu
- Allan Miller, Environmental Studies Program Coordinator; 724-938-4462; miller@cup.edu
- Thomas Moon, Environmental Conservation; 724-938-4204; moon@cup.edu
- Brian Paulson, Professor; 724-938-5978; paulson@cup.edu

CENTRAL MICHIGAN UNIVERSITY
Department of Biology, 184 Brooks Hall
Mt. Pleasant, MI 48859 United States
Phone: Fax: 987-774-4000
Website: www.cmich.edu/

Contact(s):
- Michael Hamas, Conservation Biology, Contact; 517-774-3185
- John Krull, Wildlife, Contact; 517-774-3412
- Scott McNaught, Water Resources, Contact; 517-774-1335
- Douglas Peterson, Fisheries, Contact; 517-774-3377

CENTRE FOR RESEARCH IN EDUCATION AND THE ENVIRONMENT, THE
CREE, Department of Education, University of Bath
Bath, BA2 7AY United Kingdom
Phone: 4.4012258266e+012   Fax: 4.4012258261e+012
E-mail: cree@bath.ac.uk
Website: www.bath.ac.uk/education/cree

Scope: International

Description: The Centre for Research in Education and the Environment (CREE) is part of the Culture and Environment Research Group (CERG). Research focuses on the development of world views, and the implications of these for educational practice. A particular emphasis of the Centre is on environmental sustainability. The Centre incorporates those with interests in environment, language and culture in education.

Contact(s):
- Stephen Gough, Lecturer. Director of Studies for Advanced Courses; S.R.Gough@bath.ac.uk
- Elisabeth Barratt Hacking, Lecturer In Education; 44-122-6768; Fax: 44-122-6113; edsecbh@bath.ac.uk
- Keith Bishop, Lecturer In Education; 01225 826826; ext. 5027; Fax: 01225 826113; K.N.Bishop@bath.ac.uk
- John Fisher, Lecturer; 44-122-6826; ext. 5330; Fax: 44-122-6113; J.A.Fisher@bath.ac.uk
- Alan Reid, Associate Lecturer; 44-122-6294; Fax: 44-122-6113; a.d.reid@bath.ac.uk
- William Scott, Head of Department; 44-122- 648; Fax: 44-122-6113; w.a.h.scott@bath.ac.uk
- Andrew Stables, Senior Lecturer; 44-122-6826; ext. 5186; Fax: 44-122-6113; A.W.G.Stables@bath.ac.uk

CITY UNIVERSITY OF NEW YORK
COLLEGE OF STATEN ISLAND
ENVIRONMENTAL SCIENCE MASTERS PROGRAM
6S-310, 2800 Victory Blvd.
Staten Island, NY 10314 United States
Phone: 718-982-3920   Fax: 718-982-3923
E-mail: gerstle@postbox.csi.cuny.edu
Website: www.library.csi.cuny.edu/dept/as/ces/escpgm.htm

Scope: Local, International

Description: The interdisciplinary masters program in Environmental Science includes ecology, geology, chemistry, environmental engineering, and computer modeling. The objective of the masters program is to expose the students to the scientific principles underlying environmental problems. Research is carried out on wetlands, park planning, air, water and soil pollution, waste disposal, aquatic toxics, environmental epidemiology and risk analysis. Courses are offered in the evenings for full and part time students.

Keyword(s): Air Quality/Atmosphere, Climate Change, Ecosystems (precious), Ethics/Environmental Justice, Executive/Legislative/Judicial Reform, Land Issues, Oceans/Coasts/Beaches, Pollution (general), Population, Public Health, Public Lands/Greenspace, Sprawl/Urban Planning

Contact(s):
- Alfred Levine, Director

CITY UNIVERSITY OF NEW YORK
HUNTER COLLEGE
695 Park Ave.
New York, NY 10021 United States
Phone: 212-772-4490
Website: www.hunter.cuny.edu

Contact(s):
- Charles Heatwole, Department of Geography, Affiliated with City University of N.Y.; 212-772-5265; Fax: 212-772-5268
- Jeffery Osleeb, Energy and Environmental Policy Studies Program; 212-772-5413; Fax: 212-772-5268
- Louise Sherby, Wexler Library Chief Librarian; 212-772-4146; Fax: 212-772-4142

CLARK UNIVERSITY
INTERNATIONAL DEVELOPMENT, COMMUNITY, AND ENVIRONMENT
950 Main St.
Worcester, MA 01610 United States
Phone: 508-793-7201   Fax: 508-793-8820
E-mail: idce@clarku.edu
Website: www.clarku.edu/departments/idce

Founded: 1972

Membership: 101–1,000

Scope: Local, State, Regional, National, International

Description: The International Development Program uses a multidisciplinary approach in research and teaching to analyze issues of underdevelopment in Asia, Africa, and Latin America. It draws on faculty from the fields of geography (including GIS), environmental studies, management, anthropology, economics, politics, and history, and serves both U.S. and international students. (B.A. and M.A. degree offered)

Publication(s): Tools of Gender Analysis, A Manual for Socio-Economic and Gender Analysis, Implementing PRA, PRA Handbook, Introduction to PRA

Keyword(s): Agriculture/Farming, Air Quality/Atmosphere, Development/Developing Countries, Ethics/Environmental Justice, Forests/Forestry, Land Issues, Pollution (general), Population, Public Health, Recreation/Ecotourism, Reduce/Reuse/Recycle, Sprawl/Urban Planning,

Contact(s):
- Richard Ford, Center for Community-Based Development, Director; 508-793-7691; rford@clarku.edu
- William Fisher, International Development Community Planning & Environment; 508-421-3765; wfisher@clarku.edu
- Barbara Thomas-Slayter, International Development Program; 508-793-7454; bslayer@clarku.edu

CLEMSON UNIVERSITY
FORESTRY AND NATURAL RESOURCES
261 Lehotsky Hall
Clemson, SC 29634 United States
Phone: 864-656-3032　　　Fax: 864-656-3034
E-mail: playton@clemson.edu
Website: www.clemson.edu/for
Founded: 1889
Membership: 101–1,000
Scope: State, Regional
Description: The curriculum leading to a B.S. degree provides a solid foundation in basic and applied science, social science, and communication skills. Emphasis areas permit students to broaden their technical knowledge in their chosen career path. Those interested in pursuing a graduate degree program in aquaculture, fisheries, or wildlife management should have sound undergraduate training in the biological or related sciences. Programs of study are designed to emphasize relationships between wild animals
Publication(s): See publication website
Contact(s):
Robert Barkley, Director of Admissions; 864-656-2287; Fax: 864-656-2464
John Sweeney, Chair, 864-656-5333; jrswny@clemson.edu

CLEMSON UNIVERSITY
SCHOOL OF THE ENVIRONMENT
342 Computer Court Rich Lab, Research Park
Anderson, SC 29625 United States
Phone: 864-656-5568　　　Fax: 864-656-0672
Website: www.ces.clemson.edu/ees/
Founded: 1995
Membership: 1–100
Scope: Local, State, Regional, National, International
Description: Made up of the Environmental Engineering and Science Dept., the Environmental Toxicology Dept., and the Geological Sciences Dept. Administers university-wide Environmental Science and Policy Program.
Keyword(s): Air Quality/Atmosphere, Ecosystems (precious), Pollution (general), Reduce/Reuse/Recycle, Water Habitats & Quality, Wildlife & Species
Contact(s):
Alan Elzerman, Geological Science, Chair; 864-656-5568; awlzrmn@clemson.edu
Alan Elzerman, Chair of Env. Engineering and Science; Director; 864-656-5568; awlzrmn@clemson.edu
Pam Fjeld, Student Services Coordinator; 864-656-1010; hpamela@clemson.edu
John Rodgers, Environmental Toxicology, Chair; 864-646-2691

COASTAL RESOURCES CENTER
U.R.I. Narragansett Bay Campus, South Ferry Rd.
Narragansett, RI 02882 United States
Phone: 401-874-6224　　　Fax: 401-789-4670
E-mail: cyoung@gso.uri.edu
Website: www.crc.uri.edu
Founded: 1971
Membership: 1–100
Scope: Local, State, Regional, National, International
Description: CRC is active in the U.S. and world advancing coastal management through field projects, education and training, research and learning and sharing lessons learned throughout the coastal community.
Publication(s): Aquidneck Island: Our Shared Vision, A World of Learning in Coastal Management, Intercoast Network
Keyword(s): Ecosystems (precious), Oceans/Coasts/Beaches
Contact(s):
Chip Young, Communications Liaison; 401-874-6630; Fax: 401-789-4670

COLLEGE OF THE ATLANTIC
HUMAN ECOLOGY
105 Eden St.
Bar Harbor, ME 04609 United States
Phone: 207-288-5015　　　Fax: 207-288-3780
E-mail: inquiry@ecology.coa.edu
Website: www.coa.edu
Membership: 1–100
Scope: National, International
Description: The College of the Atlantic is a fully accredited four-year residential college. Students are attracted to its excellent programs in marine biology, environmental studies and ecology, environmental design, public policy, education, and selected humanities. Over 250 students. Awards a B.A. and M. PH. in human ecology. Summer programs in field studies for teachers.
Contact(s):
Steven Katona, President

COLLEGE OF WILLIAM AND MARY
VIRGINIA INSTITUTE OF MARINE SCIENCE/SCHOOL OF MARINE SCIENCE
P.O. Box 1346
Gloucester Point, VA 23062 United States
Phone: 804-684-7000　　　Fax: 804-684-7097
Website: www.vims.edu/
Founded: 1940
Membership: 101–1,000
Description: A state institution founded for providing research, advisory services, and education for the public and for state and federal agencies responsible for managing marine resources.
Contact(s):
E. Burreson, Director of Research and Advisory Services; 804-684-7108
L. Wright, Dean and Director; 804-684-7103
William Dupaul, Head of Marine Advisory Services; 804-684-7164
J. Graves, Fisheries Sciences, Chair; 804-684-7352
S. Kuehl, Physical Sciences, Chair; 804-684-7118
M. Roberts, Environmental Sciences, Chair, 804-684-7260
Gene Silberhorn, Coastal and Ocean Policy, Chair; 804-684-7382
Richard Wetzel, Biological Sciences, Chair; 804-684-7381

COLORADO MOUNTAIN COLLEGE
NATURAL RESOURCE MANAGEMENT INSTITUTE
TIMBERLINE CAMPUS
901 S. Hwy. 24
Leadville, CO 80461 United States
Phone: 719-486-2015　　　Fax: 719-486-3212
Website: www.coloradomtn.edu
Membership: 1–100
Scope: Local, State, Regional, National
Description: CMC/Timberline offers two-year degrees (AS) in Natural Resource Mgmt., Natural Resource Recreation Mgmt., and Outdoor Recreation Leadership; one-year certificates in International Environmental Studies and Wilderness Studies; one semester certificate-Outdoor Semester in the Rockies. These programs combine on-campus academic classes/activities, as well as hands-on field components and/or work experience. CMC is a public 2-year community college with transfer options to 4-year schools.
Keyword(s): Air Quality/Atmosphere, Climate Change, Development/Developing Countries, Ecosystems (precious), Ethics/Environmental Justice, Land Issues, Oceans/Coasts/Beaches, Pollution (general), Population, Recreation/Ecotourism, Reduce/Reuse/Recycle, Water Habitats
Contact(s):
Virginia Espinoza, Admissions; 719-486-4291; tespinoza@coloradomtn.edu

Jerry Andrew, Associate Professor Outdoor Recreation Leadership; 719-486-4218; jandrew@coloradomtn.edu
Nancy Cain, Associate Professor of Biology; 719-486-4241; ncain@coloradomtn.edu
Jessica Clement, Division Director; 719-486-4209; jclement@coloradomtn.edu
Kent Clement, Professor of Outdoor Recreational Leadership; 719-486-4270; kclement@coloradomtn.edu
Karmen King, Associate Professor of Environmental Technology; 719-486-4230; kking@coloradomtn.edu
Rosemarie Russo, Assistant Campus Dean; 719-486-4215; rrusso@coloradomtn.edu

COLORADO STATE UNIVERSITY
COLLEGE OF NATURAL RESOURCES
101 Metro Resources Bldg.
Fort Collins, CO 80523 United States
Phone: 970-491-6675 Fax: 970-491-0279
E-mail: webadmin@cnr.collstate.edu
Website: www.cnr.colostate.edu
Membership: 1,001–10,000
Scope: State

Contact(s):
David Anderson, Cooperative Fish and Wildlife Research Unit, Leader; 970-491-1414
Joyce Berry, Assistant Dean; 970-491-5405; Fax: 970-491-0279; joyceb@cnr.colostate.edu
Dennis Child, Rangeland Ecosystem Science, Head; 970-491-4994; Fax: 970-491-2339; dennisc@cnr.colostate.edu
A. Dyer, Dean; 970-491-4997
Judith Hannah, Earth Resources, Head; 970-491-5662
Michael Manfredo, Natural Resources Recreation and Tourism, Head; 970-491-0474; Fax: 970-491-2255; manfredo.cnr.colostate.edu
Randall Robinette, Fishery and Wildlife Biology, Head; 970-491-5020
Susan Stafford, Forest Sciences, Head; 970-491-6911; Fax: 970-491-6754; stafford@cnr.colostate.edu
Diana Wall, Natural Resources Ecology Laboratory, Contact; 970-491-2504

COLORADO STATE UNIVERSITY
DEPARTMENT OF FISHERY AND WILDLIFE BIOLOGY
COLORADO COOPERATIVE FISH AND WILDLIFE RESEARCH UNIT
201 Wagar Bldg.
Ft. Collins, CO 80523-1484 United States
Phone: 970-491-5396 Fax: 970-491-1413
Founded: 1947
Membership: 1–100
Scope: Local, State, Regional, National, International
Description: Offers expertise and training facilities in fish and wildlife population ecology, aquatic habitat analysis, sampling and analysis theory, and biostatistics.
Keyword(s): Wildlife & Species

Contact(s):
Eric Bergersen, Acting Unit Leader
Kenneth Burnham, Assistant Leader

COLORADO STATE UNIVERSITY
DEPARTMENT OF POLITICAL SCIENCE
ENVIRONMENTAL POLITICS AND POLICY
Political Science Department
Clark Building C-346
Fort Collins, CO 80523-1782 United States
Phone: 970-491-5157 Fax: 970-491-2490
Website: www.colostate.edu/depts/polisci/grad.html
Founded: 1975
Scope: State

Description: All Ph.D. students in the program choose Environmental Politics and Policy as one of three subfields in political science offered in preparation for their degree. Most write dissertations involving environmental policy. This focus is unique among political science departments in the U.S. The program prepares doctoral students for university positions and a wide variety of private and public sector careers related to environmental politics and policy.

Contact(s):
Robert Duffy, Graduate Coordinator; Robert.Duffy@colostate.edu

CONNECTICUT COLLEGE
DEPARTMENT OF BOTANY
270 Mohegan Ave.
New London, CT 06320 United States
Phone: 860-439-5021 Fax: 860-439-2519
E-mail: etsmi@conncoll.edu
Website: www.conncoll.edu
Founded: 1911
Membership: 1–100
Scope: International

Description: Environmental Studies has a long and successful history at Connecticut College beginning in 1931 with the establishment of the Connecticut College Arboretum. Since then, a common theme in the program has been to understand the structure and functioning of both natural and managed ecosystems.

Contact(s):
Glenn Dreyer, Center for Conservation Biology and Environmental Studies; 860-439-2144; Fax: 860-439-5482; gddre@conncoll.edu
Peter Siver, Director, Environmental Studies Program; 860-439-2160; Fax: 860-439-2519; pasiv@conncoll.edu
Phillip Barnes, Zoology Department, Chair; 860-439-2148; Fax: 860-439-2519; ptbar@conncoll.edu
T. Owen, Botany Department, Chair; 860-439-2147; tpowe@conncoll.edu

CONWAY SCHOOL OF LANDSCAPE DESIGN
P.O. Box 179
332 South Deerfield Road
Conway, MA 01341 United States
Phone: 413-369-4044
E-mail: info@csld.edu
Website: www.csld.edu
Founded: 1972
Scope: Local, State, Regional

Description: CSLD is a ten-month graduate program in environmentally sound site design and land use planning. The degree offered is a M.A. degree in Landscape Design. The curriculum is structured around professional level work for residential clients, municipal agencies, and non-profit organizations. Through these projects, students produce the drawings and reports characteristic of the designer/planner while learning technical skills and developing intellectual abilities.

Publication(s): Con Text (annual newsletter)
Keyword(s): Ecosystems (precious), Land Issues, Public Lands/Greenspace, Recreation/Ecotourism, Sprawl/Urban Planning

Contact(s):
Nancy Braxton, Administrative Director
Donald Walker, Director

CORNELL UNIVERSITY
COLLEGE OF AGRICULTURAL AND LIFE SCIENCES
DEPARTMENT OF NATURAL RESOURCES
118 Fernow Hall
Ithaca, NY 14853 United States
Phone: 607-255-2821 Fax: 607-255-0349
Website: www.dnr.cornell.edu
Membership: 1–100

EDUCATIONAL INSTITUTIONS – D

Scope: International
Contact(s):
    Richard Baer, Environmental Ethics; 607-255-7797; rab12@cornell.edu
    Timothy Fahey, Forest Science; 607-255-5470; tjf5@cornell.edu
    Marian Hovencamp, Undergraduate Program, Assistant; 607-255-2809; mth6@cornell.edu
    Barbara Knuth, Co-Leader, Human Dimensions Research Unit; 607-255-2822; bak3@cornell.edu
    James Lassoie, Chair; jpl4@cornell.edu
    Edward Mills, Cornell Biological Field Station; 900 Shackelton Point Rd., Bridgeport, NY 13030-9750; 315-633-9243; Fax: 315-633-2358; elm5@cornell.edu
    Charles Smith, Plant and Wildlife Inventory; 607-255-3219; crs6@cornell.edu

D

DALHOUSIE UNIVERSITY
SCHOOL FOR RESOURCE AND ENVIRONMENTAL STUDIES (SRES)
1322 Robie St.
Halifax, B3H 3J5 Nova Scotia Canada
Phone: 902-494-3632   Fax: 902-494-3728
E-mail: sres@dal.ca
Website: www.mgmt.dal.ca/sres/
Founded: 1975
Scope: Regional
Description: Graduate school within the Faculty of Management of Dalhousie University, offering a master of environmental studies (M.E.S.) degree, through a two year programme (thesis required). Emphasis of programme is on policy and management aspects.
Contact(s):
    Peter Duinker, Director

DARTMOUTH COLLEGE
ENVIRONMENTAL STUDIES PROGRAM
6182 Steele Hall, Rm. 113
Hanover, NH 03755-3577 United States
Phone: 603-646-2838   Fax: 603-646-1682
Website: www.dartmouth.edu/~envs/
Founded: 1970
Scope: International
Description: Interdisciplinary academic program providing students with the opportunity to assess the seriousness and complexity of environmental problems and to understand how to search for solutions. Faculty research interests include biological conservation, ecosystem ecology, air pollution, economics, and international environmental governance.
Contact(s):
    Andrew Friedland, Chairman

DELTA COLLEGE
SMALL SCALE CHEMISTRY
GREEN CHEMISTRY PROJECT
Green Chemistry Project
C-141 Chemistry Dept.
Delta College
Unversity Center, MI 48710 United States
Phone: 989-686-9272, ext. 9272   Fax: 989-686-8736
E-mail: slime@alpha.delta.edu
Website: www.delta.edu/slime/ssc.html
Founded: 1997
Scope: Local, State, Regional
Description: The Green Chemistry Project is a group of environmentally concerned instructors at Delta College, who promote source reduction, small-scale chemistry, micro-scale chemistry, and training. The goal is to spread the knowledge and use of positive green methods in education and training programs in Michigan.
Publication(s): Case Study-Small Scale Green Chemistry
Keyword(s): Air Quality/Atmosphere, Oceans/Coasts/Beaches, Pollution (general), Reduce/Reuse/Recycle
Contact(s):
    Michael Garlick, Laboratory Manager; 221 Victor Drive, Saginaw, MI 48609; 989-686-9272; ext. 9272; Fax: 989-686-8736; slime@alpha.delta.edu

DEPAUL UNIVERSITY
BIOLOGICAL SCIENCES
McGowan Center - Biology
2325 North Clifton Ave.
Chicago, IL 60614-3207 United States
Phone: 773-325-7595   Fax: 773-325-7596
Website: www.depaul.edu/~biology
Membership: 1–100
Scope: State, Regional
Description: Department of Biological Sciences
Contact(s):
    Stan Cohn, Contact

DEPAUL UNIVERSITY
ENVIRONMENTAL SCIENCE PROGRAM
2325 N. Clifton Ave.
Chicago, IL 60614-3207 United States
Phone: 773-325-7422   Fax: 773-325-7448
E-mail: vhenegha@depaul.edu
Website: http://gis.depaul.edu/envirsci/Administrative/default.htm
Founded: 1986
Scope: Local, State, Regional, National
Description: This is an undergraduate program leading to a B.S. degree. It is science based and many of the majors are involved in research on prairie, wetland and savanna natural areas in the Chicago region.
Keyword(s): Ecosystems (precious), Forests/Forestry, Water Habitats & Quality
Contact(s):
    Thomas Murphy, Chair; tmurphy@depaul.edu

DONALD BREN SCHOOL OF ENVIRONMENTAL SCIENCE AND MANAGEMENT
University of California
2400 Bren Hall
Santa Barbara, CA 93106-5131 United States
Phone: 805-893-7611   Fax: 805-893-7612
E-mail: gradasst@bren.ucsb.edu
Website: www.bren.ucsb.edu
Founded: 1991
Membership: 101–1,000
Scope: Local, State, Regional, National, International
Description: We are an environmental graduate program on the UC Santa Barbara campus where science, management, and law converge to shape the future. The Bren School offers a professional Master's and traditional Ph.D. in environmental science and management.
Contact(s):
    Jill Richardson, Outreach Coordinator; 805-893-7980; jrichardson@bren.ucsb.edu

DREXEL UNIVERSITY
SCHOOL OF ENVIRONMENTAL SCIENCE, ENGINEERING, AND POLICY
32nd and Chestnut St.
Philadelphia, PA 19104 United States
Phone: 215-895-2266   Fax: 215-895-2267
E-mail: sesep@drexel.edu
Website: www.drexel.edu/sesep/
Scope: International

Description: Environmental Engineering and Science undergraduate and graduate study is offered by the School of Environmental Science, Engineering, and Policy at Drexel University. Over 25 faculty participate in SESEP programs. Degrees available with specializations in air pollution, environmental assessment, environmental biotechnology, environmental chemistry, environmental health, hazardous and solid waste, subsurface contaminant hydrology, water and wastewater treatment, water resources and more.

Contact(s):
Claire Welty, Associate Director; 215-895-2281; weltyc@drexel.edu

DUKE UNIVERSITY
NICHOLAS SCHOOL OF THE ENVIRONMENT AND EARTH SCIENCES
Box 90328
Durham, NC 27708-0328 United States
Phone: 919-613-8004   Fax: 919-613-8741
E-mail: envadm@duke.edu
Website: www.nicholas.duke.edu

Founded: 1991
Membership: 1,001–10,000
Scope: Local, State, Regional, National, International
Description: The Nicholas School of the Environment and Earth Sciences is one of the world's premier graduate/professional schools for the interdisciplinary study of the environment, combining resources from the biological, physical and social sciences.

Contact(s):
William Schlesinger, Dean; 919-613-8004; Fax: 919-613-8007; schlesin@duke.edu
Ken Knoerr, Director of Graduate Studies, Environmental Sciences and Policy; gradadm@pinus.env.duke.edu
Michael Orbach, Director, Duke University Marine Laboratory; 252-504-7604; Fax: 252-504-7648; mko@duke.edu
Cindy Peters, Director of Enrollment Services; 919-613-8070; Fax: 919-684-8741; envadm@duke.edu
Lincoln Pratson, Director of Graduate Studies, Earth and Ocean Sciences; 919-681-8077; Fax: 919-684-5833; lincoln.pratson@duke.edu
Dan Rittschof, Director of Graduate Studies, Program in the Ocean Sciences; 252-504-7634; Fax: 252-504-7648; ritt@duke.edu
Norman Christensen, Professor of Ecology and Founding Dean; 919-613-8052; Fax: 919-684-8741; normc@duke.edu
Richard Di Giulio, Enviromental Toxicology and Chemistry; richd@duke.edu
Jeffrey Karson, Earth and Ocean Sciences; 919-684-2731; Fax: 919-684-5833; jkarson@duke.edu
Randall Kramer, Program Chair of Resource Economics and Policy; 919-613-8072; Fax: 919-684-8741
Kenneth Reckhow, Water & Air Resouces; reckhow@duke.edu
Curtis Richardson, Chair, Division of Environmental Sciences and Policy; 919-613-8009; Fax: 919-684-8741
Daniel Richter, Forest Resource Management and Resource Ecology; drichter@duke.edu

DUKE UNIVERSITY - ORGANIZATION FOR TROPICAL STUDIES
LA SELVA BIOLOGICAL STATION
LAS CRUCES BIOLOGICAL STATION AND WILSON BOTANICAL GARDEN
PALO VERDE BIOLOGICAL STATION
Box 90630
Durham, NC 27708-0630 United States
Phone: 919-684-5774   Fax: 919-684-5661
E-mail: nao@duke.edu
Website: www.ots.duke.edu/

Founded: 1963
Membership: 1–100
Scope: International
Description: OTS, a nonprofit consortium of universities and research institutions from the U.S., Costa Rica, Peru, Mexico, South Africa, Canada, and Australia, provides leadership in education, research, and the responsible use of natural resources in the tropics. OTS offers graduate, undergraduate, and professional training; facilitates research; participates in tropical forest conservation; and maintains three biological stations in Costa Rica.

Publication(s): Liana, see website
Keyword(s): Agriculture/Farming, Climate Change, Development/ Developing Countries, Ecosystems (precious), Forests/ Forestry, Oceans/Coasts/Beaches

Contact(s):
Gary Hartshorn, President and CEO; 919-684-5774; Fax: 919-684-5661; ghartsho@duke.edu
Luis Gomez, Director; 506-773-4004; Fax: 506773-3665; ldgomez@hortus.ots.ac.cr
Eugenio Gonzalez, Director; 506-384-6106; Fax: 506-240-6783; egonza@jabiru.ots.ac.cr
Jorge Jimenez, Director in Costa Rica; 506-240-6696; Fax: 506-240-6783; jjimenez@ots.ac.cr
Robert Matlock, Scientific Director; 506-766-6565; Fax: 506-766-6535; rmatlock@sloth.ots.ac.cr

E

EASTERN ILLINOIS UNIVERSITY
Department of Biological Sciences
600 Lincoln Avenue
Charleston, IL 61920 United States
Phone: 217-581-3126   Fax: 217-581-7141
E-mail: cfkck@eiu.edu
Website: www.eiu.edu/~biology/

Founded: 1972
Membership: 101–1,000
Scope: State
Description: Eastern Illinois University offers an undergraduate degree in biology, with three options: Teacher Certification, Environmental Biology and Biological Sciences. Within the Biological Sciences, students choose from among 4 concentrations: Biology, Botanical Sciences, Ecology and Systematics, and Cell and Functional Biology. Emphasis is placed upon a fundamental understanding of biology and environmental concerns.

Contact(s):
Charles Costa, Biological Sciences, Contact; 217-581-2520; cfcjc@eiu.edu
Robert Fischer, Environmental Biology Option Coordinator; 217-581-2817; cfruf@eiu.edu
Kipp Kruse, Biology, Chair; 217-581-3126; cfkck@eiu.edu
James McGaughey, Biology Teacher Certificate Option Coordinator; 217-581-2928; cfjam@eiu.edu

EASTERN KENTUCKY UNIVERSITY
BIOLOGICAL SCIENCES DEPARTMENT
521 Lancaster Ave.
Richmond, KY 40475-3102 United States
Phone: 859-622-1531   Fax: 859-622-1399
E-mail: barbara.ramey@eku.edu
Website: www.biology.eku.edu

Membership: 1–100
Scope: National
Publication(s): Newsletter

Contact(s):
Ross Clark, Biology—Botany Option; bioclark@acs.eku.edu
Charles Elliott, Environmental Studies, Contact; 859-622-1531; bioelliott@acs.eku.edu
Robert Frederick, Wildlife Management, Contact; 859-622-1531; biofred@acs.eku.edu
William Martin, Lillie Woods Research Natural Area;

narmartin@acs.eku.edu
Barbara Ramey, Applied Ecology, Contact; 606-622-1531; bioramey@acs.eku.edu
Guenter Shuster, Biology—Aquatic Option; bioschus@acs.eku.edu

EASTERN MICHIGAN UNIVERSITY
316 Mark Jefferson
Ypsilanti, MI 48197 United States
Phone: 734-487-4242 Fax: 734-487-9235
Website: www.emich.edu

Founded: 1847

Scope: Local, State, Regional, National, International

Description: Regional university with a broad array of environmental programs and faculty expertise in various university departments.

Contact(s):
Ben Czinski, Kresge Environmental Education Center, Director; 2816 Fish Lake Rd., Lapeer, MI 48446; 810-667-2350; bio_czinski@online.emich.edu
Catherine Bach, Conservation Resource Use, Contact; 734-487-0212; cbach@omich.edu
Michael Kasenow, Geography and Geology, Head; 203 Strong Hall, EMU, Ypsilanti, MI 48197; 734-487-0218; geo_kasenow@online.emich.edu
Robert Neely, Biology, Head; 316 Mark Jefferson, EMU, Ypsilanti, MI 48197; 734-487-4242; rneely@emich.edu

EMORY UNIVERSITY
BIOLOGY DEPARTMENT
Rollins Research Center Emory University
Atlanta, GA 30322 United States
Phone: 404-727-6048 Fax: 404-727-2880
Website: www.emory.edu/biology/

Membership: 1–100
Scope: State

Contact(s):
Chris Beck, Ecology and Evolution, Professor
John Lucchesi, Biology Department, Chair

EMPORIA STATE UNIVERSITY
BIOLOGICAL SCIENCES
Department of Biological Sciences
Emporia State University
Campus Box 4050
Emporia, KS 66801-5087 United States
Phone: 620-341-5311 Fax: 620-341-5607
E-mail: sundberm@emporia.edu
Website: www.emporia.edu/biosci/biology

Founded: 1863
Membership: 101–1,000
Scope: State, Regional

Description: The Department of Biological Sciences at Emporia State University offers undergraduate and graduate training in botany, cell and microbiology, conservation and wildlife biology, ecology, genetics, physiology, teacher education, and zoology. The department has 15 fulltime faculty members, approximately 25 graduate students, and approximately 270 undergraduate majors. Field and laboratory work are emphasized. Over 1100 acres of native habitats are managed for teaching, research, and preservation.

Publication(s): Departmental website

Contact(s):
Marshall Sundberg, Dept. of Biological Sciences, Ecology and Wildlife Biology

FAU PINE JOG ENVIROMENTAL EDUCATION CENTER
6301 Summit Blvd.
West Palm Beach, FL 33415 United States
Phone: 561-686-6600 Fax: 561-687-4968
Website: www.pinejog.org

Founded: 1960
Membership: 101–1,000
Scope: Local, State, Regional, National

Description: Pine Jog is an environmental education center within the College of Education of Florida Atlantic University. The purpose of the Center is to provide environmental education programs which foster an awareness and appreciation of the natural world, promote an understanding of ecological concepts, and instill a sense of stewardship towards the earth and all of its inhabitants.

Contact(s):
Patricia Welch, Executive Director; 561-686-6600

FERRIS STATE UNIVERSITY
COLLEGE OF ALLIED HEALTH SCIENCES
200 Ferris Dr.
Big Rapids, MI 49307-2740 United States
Phone: 231-591-2295 Fax: 231-591-2325
Website: www.ferris.edu/htmls/colleges/alliedhe/

Founded: 1964
Membership: 1–100
Scope: State

Description: Educational institution offering B.S. in industrial and environmental health management with options in general environmental health, hazardous materials management, industrial hygiene, and industrial safety.

Contact(s):
Ellen Haneline, Health Management Department, Head; 231-591-2313; ellen_j_haneline@ferris.edu

FERRUM COLLEGE
DEPARTMENT OF FORESTRY AND WILDLIFE
P.O. Box 1000
Ferrum, VA 24088 United States
Phone: 540-365-2121
E-mail: webmaster@ferrum.edu
Website: www.ferrum.edu

Scope: Local, State, Regional, National

Description: An interdisciplinary program in the U.S.'s second oldest Environmental Science major. A living laboratory, including a 700 acre campus, abundant forestland, three ponds, streams, stands of white and loblolly pines, and wildlife, located on the eastern slope of the Blue Ridge Parkway, allows for exceptional field-oriented instruction and learning.

Publication(s): The Chrysalis, Ferrum Magazine, The Iron Blade

Keyword(s): Agriculture/Farming, Climate Change, Ecosystems (precious), Energy, Forests/Forestry, Land Issues, Oceans/Coasts/Beaches, Pollution (general), Public Lands/Greenspace, Recreation/Ecotourism, Reduce/Reuse/Recycle, Water Habitats & Quality, Wildlife & Species

Contact(s):
Rathin Basu, Economics; 540-365-4204, rbasu@ferrum.edu
James Bier, Chemistry; 540-365-4362; jbier@ferrum.edu
George Byrd, Agriculture; 540-365-4378; gbyrd@ferrum.edu
David Johnson, Chemistry; 540-365-4364; djohnson@ferrum.edu
John Leffler, Biology/Zoology; 540-365-4361; jleffler@ferrum.edu
Kathy Mengak, Leisure Services and Recreation; 540-365-4387; kmengak@ferrum.edu
Daryl Nash, Agriculture; 540-365-4363; dnash@ferrum.edu
Bob Pohlad, Biology; 540-365-4367; bpohlad@ferrum.edu

Jason Powell, Chemistry/Physics; 540-365-4374; jpowell@ferrum.edu
Joseph Stogner, Environmental Studies; 540-365-4369; jstogner@ferrum.edu
Carolyn Thomas, Environmental Science/Biology; 540-365-4368; cthomas@ferrum.edu
Linda Williams, Biology/Agriculture; 540-365-4372; lmwilliams@ferrum.edu

FLORIDA COOPERATIVE EXTENSION SERVICE
1038 McCarty Hall, P.O. Box 110210, University of Florida
Gainesville, FL 32611-0210 United States
Phone: 352-392-1761   Fax: 352-846-0458
Website: www.ifas.ufl.edu
Founded: 1914
Scope: State, Regional
Description: Provides researched-based information to the public in partnership with federal and local governments.
Publication(s): See publications on website
Keyword(s): Forests/Forestry, Water Habitats & Quality, Wildlife & Species
Contact(s):
Pierce Jones, Director of Energy Extension Service, Acting; Box 110570, 102 Rogers Hall, University of Florida, Gainesville, FL 32611-0570; 352-392-8074; Fax: 352-392-4092; ez@agen.ufl.edu
Joesph Schaefer, Director of Natural Resources; Univ. of Florida, Wildlife Ecology and Conservation, P.O. Box 110430, Gainesville, FL 32611-0430; 352-846-0568; Fax: 352-392-6984
Nat Frazer, Assistant Extension Scientist, Wildlife; Pinellas County Extension Office, 12175 125th St. North, Largo, FL 33774-3695; 813-582-2100; Fax: 813-582-2149; whk@gnv.ifas.ufl.edu
Christine Waddill, Dean of Extension; 1038 McCarty Hall, P.O. Box 110210, University of Florida, Gainesville, FL 32611-0210

FLORIDA STATE UNIVERSITY
UNIVERSITY RELATIONS
216 Westcott Bldg
Tallahassee, FL 32306 United States
Phone: 850-644-1000   Fax: 850-644-3612
Website: www.fsu.edu
Membership: 1–100
Scope: Regional
Contact(s):
Bruce Grindal, Anthropology, Chairman; Bellamy G-24, Tallahassee, FL 32306-2150; 850-644-8147; Fax: 850-644-4283; bgrindal@mailer.fsu.edu
Patrick O'Sullivan, Geography, Political Geography and Environmental Studies; P.O. Box 2190, Tallahassee, FL 32306-2190; 850-644-7175; Fax: 850-644-5913; kmcclell@mailer.fsu.edu
Thomas Roberts, Biological Science, Chairman; P.O. Box 4340, Tallahassee, FL 32306-4340; 850-644-3700; Fax: 850-644-9829
David Stuart, Meteorology, Chairman; 404 Love Building, Tallahassee, FL 32306-4520; 850-644-6205; Fax: 850-644-9642; stuart@met.fsu.edu
Wilton Sturges, Oceanography, Chairman; 329 OSB, West Call Street, Tallahassee, FL 32306-4320; 850-644-6700; Fax: 850-644-2581; sturges@ocean.fsu.edu
J. Tull, Geology, Chairman; Carraway Bldg., Tallahassee, FL 32306-4100; 904-644-1448; Fax: 904-644-4214; tull@gly.fsu.edu

FROSTBURG STATE UNIVERSITY (UNIVERSITY OF MARYLAND)
DEPARTMENT OF BIOLOGY
101 Braddock Rd.
Frostburg, MD 21532 United States
Phone: 301-687-4166   Fax: 301-687-3034
Website: www.fsu.umd.edu
Scope: State
Description: Wildlife and Fisheries Program (B.A, M.A., Ph.D.), Wildlife/Fisheries Biology (M.S.), Applied Ecology; Conservation Biology (M.S.), Biology (B.S., Ph.D.)
Publication(s): See publications website
Contact(s):
David Morton, Dept. Chair; 301-687-4355; dmorton@frostburg.edu.

G

GEORGE WASHINGTON UNIVERSITY
2121 I Street NW
Washington, DC 20052 United States
Phone: 202-994-4949
Website: www.gwu.edu/
Scope: State
Contact(s):
Henry Merchant, Environmental Studies, Director; 202-994-7118
Henry Merchant, Environmental and Resource Policy, Director; 202-994-7123; Fax: 202-994-6100
Theodore Toridis, Environmental Engineering, Acting Chair; 801 22nd St., Washington, DC 20052; 202-994-6749; Fax: 202-944-0238; toridis@seas.gwu.edu

GEORGE WASHINGTON UNIVERSITY
LAW SCHOOL
2000 H St., NW
Washington, DC 20052 United States
Phone: 202-994-6260
Website: www.law.gwu.edu/
Founded: 1865
Scope: International
Description: Nation's largest graduate and undergraduate environmental law program. Twenty-two environmental courses for J.D. and LL.M. students in addition to land use and other related topics. Emphasizes a practical approach.
Contact(s):
Laurent Hourcle, Co-Director; 202-994-4823; lhourcle@main.nlc.gwu.edu

GEORGETOWN COLLEGE
ENVIRONMENTAL SCIENCE PROGRAM
400 E. College St.
Georgetown, KY 40324 United States
Phone: 502-863-8088   Fax: 502-868-7744
Website: www.georgetowncollege.edu
Scope: State
Description: Environmental Science Degree with tracks in Chemical Science, Biological Science, Chemical-Biological Science and Environmental Policy.
Contact(s):
Rick Kopp, Program Coordinator; Fax: 502-868-7744; rkopp@georgetowncollege.edu

GEORGETOWN ENVIRONMENTAL LAW & POLICY INSTITUTE
600 New Jersey Avenue NW
Washington, DC 20001 United States
Phone: 202-662-9850   Fax: 202-662-9005
E-mail: gelpi@law.georgetown.edu
Website: www.law.georgetown.edu/gelpi
Scope: National
Description: Conducts research and education on legal and policy issues relating to protection of the environment and conservation of natural resources
Contact(s):
Judith Areen, Dean

GEORGIA INSTITUTE OF TECHNOLOGY
GEORGIA WATER INSTITUTE
School of Civil & Environmental Engineering
Georgia Institute of Technology
Atlanta, GA 30332-0335 United States
Phone: 404-894-3776   Fax: 404-894-3828
Website: www.gatech.edu

Scope: State

Contact(s):
Aris Georgakokos, Director, Georgia Water Institute; 404-894-2240

H

HAMLINE UNIVERSITY
CENTER FOR GLOBAL ENVIRONMENTAL EDUCATION
1536 Hewitt Ave.
MS A1760
St. Paul, MN 55104-1284 United States
Phone: 651-523-2480   Fax: 651-523-3041
E-mail: cgee@hamline.edu
Website: cgee.hamline.edu

Founded: 1990

Scope: Local, State, Regional, National, International

Description: CGEE was founded to nurture greater understanding of the interconnectedness of local and global environments among educators, students, scientists, and citizens.

Publication(s): Publications on website

Keyword(s): Ecosystems (precious), Energy, Pollution (general), Reduce/Reuse/Recycle, Water Habitats & Quality

Contact(s):
Tracy Fredin, Director; 651-523-3105; Fax: 651-523-3041; tfredin@gw.hamline.edu
Peggy Knapp, Rivers of Life Program Director; 651-523-2393; Fax: 651-523-3041; pknapp@hamline.edu

HOCKING COLLEGE
SCHOOL OF NATURAL RESOURCES
3301 Hocking Parkway
Nelsonville, OH 45764 United States
Phone: 740-753-3591   Fax: 740-753-2021
E-mail: admissions@hocking.edu
Website: www.hocking.edu

Founded: 1969

Scope: State

Description: The mission of our School of Natural Resources is to prepare individuals for careers as technicians in the natural resources profession. Emphasis is placed on basic theory, developing a sustained positive work ethic and the practical application of the development of the competencies required for entry-level positions in recreation, wildlife, forestry, timber harvesting/tree care and a wide variety of land management technology fields.

Contact(s):
Albert Lecount, Wildlife, Biologist; ext. 2918; lecount_a@hocking.edu
Russell Tippett, Dean; 740-753-3591; ext. 2317; tippet_r@hocking.edu
Lloyd Wright, Fisheries, Biologist; ext. 2919; wright_ll@hocking.edu

HUMBOLDT STATE UNIVERSITY
1 Harpst St.
Arcata, CA 95521-8299 United States
Phone: 707-826-3256   Fax: 707-826-3562
E-mail: cnrs@humboldt.edu
Website: www.humboldt.edu/~cnrs/

Scope: State

Description: College of Natural Resources and Sciences—one of the largest and most highly respected programs in the nation.

Contact(s):
James Howard, Dean, College of Natural Resources and Sciences; 707-826-3256
Russel Boham, Director, Indian Natural Resources, Sciences & Engineering; 707-826-4994
Milton Boyd, Chairman, Biological Sciences; 707-826-3246
Steven Carlson, Chairman, Environmental & Natural Resource Sciences; 707-826-4147
Steven Carlson, Chairman, Rangeland Resources and Wildland Soils; 707-826-4147
Gregory Crawford, Chairman, Oceanography; 707-826-4147
Walter Duffy, Leader, Cooperative Fishery Research Unit; 707-826-3268
Beth Eschenbach, Chairman, Environmental Resources Engineering; 707-826-4348
Luke George, Chairman, Wildlife; 707-826-3430
David Hankin, Chairman, Fisheries Biology; 707-825-5645
John Stuart, Chairman, Forestry and Watershed Management; 707-826-3823
Robert Ziemer, Project Leader, Experiment Station, Pacific Southwest Forest; 707-825-2936

I

IDAHO STATE UNIVERSITY
DEPARTMENT OF BIOLOGICAL SCIENCES
Box 8007
Pocatello, ID 83209-8007 United States
Phone: 208-282-3765   Fax: 208-236-4570
E-mail: bios@isu.edu
Website: www.isu.edu/departments/bios/

Description: The Department of Biological Sciences at Idaho State University has high quality degree programs in ecology. Strong basic coursework and original investigations are emphasized at the undergraduate and graduate levels. Habitats available for study range from cold sagebrush deserts to heavily forested areas and include streams and riparian areas in the Snake River Canyon to its headwaters in Yellowstone National Park.

Contact(s):
Rod Seeley, Ecology; 208- 28-2181; seelrodn@isu.edu
Mary Watwood, Associate Professor; 208- 23-3090; watwmari@isu.edu

ILLINOIS STATE UNIVERSITY
ENVIRONMENTAL HEALTH PROGRAM, DEPARTMENT OF HEALTH SCIENCES
Campus Box 5220
Normal, IL 61790-5220 United States
Phone: 309-438-8329   Fax: 309-438-2450
Website: www.ilstu.edu/

Founded: 1974

Membership: 1–100

Scope: State

Description: Undergraduate education for B.S. in environmental health. Five faculty persons and 165 enrolled students. Four-year undergraduate curriculum accredited by National Environmental Health Science and Protection Accreditation Council. Graduate Education for M.S. in Environmental Health and Safety.

Contact(s):
Marilyn Morrow, Program Director, Acting
Thomas Bierma, Masters Program Coordinator

INDIANA STATE UNIVERSITY
LIFE SCIENCES
Science Bldg., Rm. 283
Terre Haute, IN 47809 United States
Phone: 812-237-2400   Fax: 812-237-4480
Website: www.biology.indstate.edu/dls/

Membership: 101–1,000

Scope: State

Publication(s): See publication website
Contact(s):
  Marion Jackson, Ecology and Wildlife; lsmjack@scifac.indstate.edu

INDIANA UNIVERSITY
SCHOOL OF PUBLIC AND ENVIRONMENTAL AFFAIRS
1315 E. 10th St.
Bloomington, IN 47405 United States
Phone: 812-855-2840 Fax: 812-855-7802
E-mail: speainfo@indiana.edu
Website: www.spea.indiana.edu

Founded: 1972
Membership: 101–1,000
Scope: Local, State, Regional, National, International
Description: The School of Public Environmental Affairs brings an interdisciplinary approach to the study of the environmental sciences. The focus of the academic programs is to teach techniques that will help graduates preserve and protect the quality of natural resources, identify environmental hazards, and significantly contribute to solutions to enhance quality of life in the world's communities.

Contact(s):
  John Mikesell, Director of Graduate Programs; 812-855-9485; mikesell@indiana.edu
  Roger Parks, Director of Ph.D. Programs In Public Policy/Public Affairs; 812-855-0563; parks@indiana.edu
  J. Randolph, Director of Ph.D. Programs In Environmental Science; 812-855-4953; randolph@indiana.edu
  Frank Vilardo, Director of Undergraduate Programs; 812-855-9485; vilardo@indiana.edu
  Astrid Merget, Dean; 812-855-1432; merget@indiana.edu
  Jeffrey White, Associate Dean; 812-855-5058; whitej@indiana.edu

IOWA STATE UNIVERSITY
COLLEGE OF AGRICULTURE
COMMUNICATIONS OFFICE
304 Curtiss Hall
Ames, IA 50011-1050 United States
Phone: 515-294-5616 Fax: 515-294-8662
E-mail: edadcock@iastate.edu
Website: www.ag.iastate.edu/

Founded: 1850
Membership: 1,001–10,000
Scope: Regional
Description: Communications and information in Iowa State University agriculture, natural resources, food and nutrition, and other areas.
Keyword(s): Agriculture/Farming, Air Quality/Atmosphere, Climate Change, Ecosystems (precious), Forests/Forestry, Land Issues, Pollution (general), Public Lands/Greenspace, Recreation/Ecotourism, Reduce/Reuse/Recycle, Water Habitats & Quality, Wildlife & Species

Contact(s):
  Jeff Iles, Horticulture, Head; Rm. 106B Horticulture Hall, Ames, IA 50011-1100; 515-294-3718; Fax: 515-294-0730; iles@iastate.edu
  J. Kelly, Natural Resource Ecology and Management, Chairman; Dept. of Natural Resource Ecology and Management, 251 Bessey, Ames, IA 50011-1021; 515-294-1166; jmkelly@iastate.edu

IOWA STATE UNIVERSITY
COLLEGE OF DESIGN
146 College of Design, Iowa State University
Ames, IA 50011 United States
Phone: 515-294-5676
E-mail: landarch@iastate.edu
Website: www.design.iastate.edu/

Scope: State

Publication(s): Design News
Contact(s):
  J. Keller, Landscape Architecture, Chairman; 515-294-5676; tkeller@iastate.edu
  Riad Mahayni, Community and Regional Planning, Chair; 515-294-8958; Fax: 515-294-4015; rmahayni@iastate.edu

J

JOHN GRAY HIGH SCHOOL, GRAND CAYMAN
JOHN GRAY RECYCLERS
P.O. Box 174 NS
North Side
Grand Cayman
North Side, B W I United Kingdom
Phone: 345-947, ext. 7649
E-mail: johngrayrecyclers@hotmail.com
Website: johngrayrecyclers.org

Founded: 1996
Membership: 1–100
Scope: Local, National, International
Description: We are an environmental/recycling club at the John Gray High School in Grand Cayman, Cayman Islands. Our major aim is to protect coral reefs worldwide. We would like other young people to join us with our conservation work. Our pledge is to increase the public's awareness of the importance of the protection of the ocean and the world's coral reefs. We believe that we must all take action to conserve the ocean to sustain the wonderful web of life on our planet Earth.
Keyword(s): Ecosystems (precious), Oceans/Coasts/Beaches

JOHNS HOPKINS UNIVERSITY
CENTER FOR A LIVABLE FUTURE
BLOOMBERG SCHOOL OF PUBLIC HEALTH
615 N. Wolfe Street, Suite W8503
Baltimore, MD 21205 United States
Phone: 410-502-7578 Fax: 410-502-7579
E-mail: clf@jhsph.edu
Website: www.jhsph.edu/environment/

Founded: 1996
Scope: Local, State, Regional, National, International
Description: The mission of the Center for a Livable Future is to establish a global resource to develop and disseminate information and to promote policies for the protection of health, the global environment, and our ability to sustain life for future generations.
Keyword(s): Agriculture/Farming, Ecosystems (precious), Public Health, Reduce/Reuse/Recycle

Contact(s):
  Robert Lawrence, Director; 410-614-4590; rlawrenc@jhsph.edu
  Shawn McKenzie, Program Director, Spira/Grace Project Industrial Animal Products; 410-502-7575; smckenzi@jhsph.edu
  Pam Rhubart, Program Coordinator; 410-502-7578; prhubart@jhsph.edu
  Kelly Green, Administrative Assistant; 410-502-7578; khoban@jhsph.edu
  Polly Walker, Associate Director; 410-502-7578; pwalker@jhsph.edu

JOHNS HOPKINS UNIVERSITY
DEPARTMENT OF GEOGRAPHY AND
ENVIRONMENTAL ENGINEERING
313 Ames Hall
3400 North Charles St.
Baltimore, MD 21218 United States
Phone: 410-516-7092 Fax: 410-516-8996
E-mail: dogee@jhu.edu
Website: www.jhu.edu/~dogee
Membership: 1–100

EDUCATIONAL INSTITUTIONS – K

Scope: State, Regional, National, International

Description: The Department of Geography and Environmental Engineering is concerned with the improved understanding and description of environmental problems including questions of pollutant fate and transport, water resources engineering, environmental chemistry, geomorphology, drinking water and wastewater treatment, ecosystem dynamics, and technology, society and environmental change. Drawing from a number of disciplines and approaches, elements within these systems are examined.

Contact(s):
Edward Bouwer, Environmental Engineering, Contact; 410-516-7437; bouwer@jhu.edu
Grace Brush, Ecology, Contact; 410-516-7107; gbrush@jhu.edu
Alan Stone, Environmental Chemistry, Contact; 410-516-8476; astone@jhu.edu
M. Wolman, Natural Resources, Contact; 410-516-7090; wolman@jhu.edu

JOHNS HOPKINS UNIVERSITY
SCHOOL OF PUBLIC HEALTH
PEW ENVIRONMENTAL HEALTH COMMISSION
111 Market Pl., Suite 850
Baltimore, MD 21202 United States
Phone: 410-659-2690   Fax: 410-659-2699
E-mail: cllee@jhsph.edu
Website: pewenvirohealth.jhsph.edu/

Scope: National

Description: The Pew Environmental Health Commission works to strengthen the country's public health system to protect against sickness and disease caused by environmental threats.

Publication(s): America's Environmental Health Gap, Attack Asthma, Healthy From the Start

Contact(s):
Shelley Hearn, Executive Director
Paul Locke, Deputy Director

JOHNSON STATE COLLEGE
DEPARTMENT OF ENVIRONMENTAL AND HEALTH SCIENCES
337 College Hill
Johnson, VT 05656-9464 United States
Phone: 800-635-2356   Fax: 802-635-1230
E-mail: jscapply@badger.jsc.vsc.edu
Website: http://ehs.academic.jsc.vsc.edu/

Scope: Local, State, Regional, National

Description: All academic programs (biology, environmental science, health science, and outdoor education) in the Dept. of Env. and Health Sciences aim to foster the development of content-rich curricula for students through active engagement in scientific inquiry and analysis. Across the disciplines in our department, emphasis is placed on development of critical thinking skills; laboratory and field-based problem solving skills; scientific and general writing; library and Internet research; and teamwork.

Keyword(s): Agriculture/Farming, Air Quality/Atmosphere, Climate Change, Ecosystems (precious), Energy, Ethics/Environmental Justice, Forests/Forestry, Land Issues, Oceans/Coasts/Beaches, Pollution (general), Population, Public Health, Public Lands/Greenspace, Recreation

Contact(s):
John Wrazen, Babcock Nature Preserve, Director
Tania Bacchus, Associate Professor
Robert Genter, Biology
Leslie Kanat, Associate Professor of Geology; 802-635-1327; Fax: 802-635-1461; kanatL@jsc.vsc
Brad Moskowitz, Outdoor Education
Karen Uhlendorf, Outdoor Education
John Wrazen, Ecology

K

KANSAS SCHOOL NATURALIST
Kansas School Naturalist
Department of Biological Sciences, Box 4050
Emporia State University
Emporia, KS 66801 United States
Phone: 620-341-5614   Fax: 620-341-5997
E-mail: ksnaturl@emporia.edu
Website: www.emporia.edu/ksn/

Founded: 1954
Membership: 10,001–100,000
Scope: State, International

Description: The Kansas School Naturalist is an accurate, high-interest natural history publication that serves science teachers, naturalists, Scout leaders, and others interested in all aspects of physical and biological sciences. From one to four issues are published each year. It is free upon request. Some issues have been translated into Spanish and Chinese. In-print back issues are available free upon request. Out-of-print issues are photocopied and sent for $1.00 each to cover costs.

Publication(s): Role of Animals in Succession, Making an Insect Collection, Scientific Names, Common Names, Kansas Butterflies, Bone Names, Snow Flies, Springtails, Prairie Fires, Checklist of Kansas Ants, Collecting and Studying Ants, Yucca Plant and Yucca Moth

KANSAS STATE UNIVERSITY
COLLEGE OF AGRICULTURE
117 Waters Hall
Manhattan, KS 66506-5506 United States
Phone: 785-532-6151   Fax: 785-532-6897
E-mail: kstate@k-state.edu
Website: www.ag.ksu.edu/

Founded: 1863
Membership: 1–100
Scope: International
Keyword(s): Agriculture/Farming, Land Issues, Public Lands/Greenspace

Contact(s):
Ted Cable, Natural Resource Management; 785-532-1408; tcable@oznet.ksu.edu
David Mengel, Dept. of Agronomy, Head; 2004 Throckmorton Plant Science Center, Manhattan, KS 66506; 785-532-6101; Fax: 785-532-6094; dmengel@bear.agron.ksu.edu
Michel Ransom, Soil and Water Conservation; mdransom@ksu.edu
Thomas Warner, Horticulture, Forestry and Recreation Resources, Dept. Head; 2021 Throckmorton Plant Science Center, Manhattan, KS 66506; 785-532-6170; twarner@oznet.ksu.edu

KANSAS STATE UNIVERSITY
DEPARTMENT OF LANDSCAPE ARCHITECTURE /
REGIONAL AND COMMUNITY PLANNING
302 Seaton Hall
Manhattan, KS 66506-2909 United States
Phone: 785-532-5961   Fax: 785-532-6722
E-mail: la-rcp@ksu.edu
Website: larcp.arch.ksu.edu/larcp

Founded: 1960
Membership: 1–100
Scope: State, International
Keyword(s): Agriculture/Farming, Ecosystems (precious), Ethics/Environmental Justice, Forests/Forestry, Land Issues, Pollution (general), Population, Public Health, Public Lands/Greenspace, Recreation/Ecotourism, Reduce/Reuse/Recycle, Sprawl/Urban Planning, Transportation

Contact(s):
C. Keithley, Regional and Community Planning, Director; 785-532-2440; cak@ksu.edu
Dan Donelin, Dept. Head; dandon@ksu.edu

EDUCATIONAL INSTITUTIONS– K

KANSAS STATE UNIVERSITY
DIVISION OF BIOLOGY
232 Ackert Hall
Manhattan, KS 66506 United States
Phone: 785-532-6615　　　　Fax: 785-532-6653
Website: www.ksu.edu/biology/
Membership: 101–1,000
Scope: State
Contact(s):
　David Hartnett, Director, Konza Prairie Research Natural Area; 785-532-5925; dchart@ksu.edu
　Brian Spooner, Director of Biology; spoon1@ksu.edu

KEENE STATE COLLEGE
DEPARTMENT OF GEOLOGY AND ENVIRONMENTAL STUDIES
229 Main St.
Keene, NH 03435 United States
Phone: 603-352-1909　　　　Fax: 603-358-2897
Website: www.keene.edu/
Founded: 1909
Scope: State
Description: A multipurpose, predominantly undergraduate college with a central focus in the liberal arts and sciences. B.S. in Environmental Studies with options in Environmental Policy and Environmental Science and specializations in Environmental Biology, Environmental Chemistry and Environmental Geology
Contact(s):
　Tim Allen, Program Coordinator; 603-358-2571; tallen@keene.edu

L

LAKE SUPERIOR STATE UNIVERSITY
COLLEGE OF ARTS & SCIENCES
650 W. Easterday Ave.
Sault Ste. Marie, MI 49783 United States
Phone: 906-635-2267　　　　Fax: 906-635-2266
Website: www.lssu.edu
Scope: Local, State
Description: Degrees offered in biological science, conservation law enforcement, environmental chemistry, environmental science, fisheries/wildlife management and natural resources technology (A.D.).
Keyword(s): Ecosystems (precious), Forests/Forestry, Oceans/Coasts/Beaches, Pollution (general), Public Lands/Greenspace, Reduce/Reuse/Recycle, Water Habitats & Quality, Wildlife & Species
Contact(s):
　Michael Donovan, Associate Provost, College of Arts & Sciences; 906-635-2267; Fax: 906-635-2266; mdonovan@lssu.edu
　Lewis Brown, Chair, School of Environmental & Physical Sciences; 906-635-2155; lbrown@lssu.edu
　Gregory Zimmerman, Chair, School of Biological Sciences; 906-635-2470; Fax: 906-635-2266; gzimmerman@lssu.edu

LAKEHEAD UNIVERSITY
FACULTY OF FORESTRY AND FOREST ENVIRONMENT
955 Oliver Rd.
Thunder Bay, P7B 5E1 Ontario Canada
Phone: 807-343-8507　　　　Fax: 807-343-8116
E-mail: sandy.dunning@lakeheadu.ca
Website: www.lakeheadu.ca/~forwww/forestry.html
Membership: 101–1,000
Scope: Local, State, Regional, National, International
Description: H.B.Sc. in Forestry, Bachelor of Environmental Studies, Honours Bachelor of Environmental Studies, M.Sc.F. and M.F. in Forestry
Keyword(s): Air Quality/Atmosphere, Development/Developing Countries, Ecosystems (precious), Ethics/Environmental Justice, Executive/Legislative/Judicial Reform, Forests/Forestry, Land Issues, Public Lands/Greenspace, Recreation/Ecotourism, Sprawl/Urban Planning, Water Habits & Quality
Contact(s):
　Reino Pulkki, Dean; 807-343-8564; Fax: 807-343-8116; reino.pulkki@lakeheadu.ca
　Sandy Dunning, Administrative Assistant; 807-343-8507; Fax: 807-343-8116; sandy.dunning@lakeheadu.ca
　K. Brown, Chair, Graduate Forestry Programs; 807-343-8114; ken.brown@lakeheadu.ca
　L. Meyer, Chair, Undergraduate Forestry Programs; 807-343-8445; leni.meyer@lakeheadu.ca
　Yves Prevost, Chair, Environmental Studies Program; 807-343-8342; yves.prevost@lakeheadu.ca

LEWIS AND CLARK COLLEGE
COLLEGE OF ARTS AND SCIENCES
ENVIRONMENTAL STUDIES PROGRAM
0615 S.W. Palatine Hill Road
Portland, OR 97219 United States
Phone: 503-768-7699
E-mail: etw@lclark.edu
Website: www.lclark.edu
Founded: 1997
Scope: Local, State, Regional, National, International
Description: Undergraduate major in Environmental Studies. Interdisciplinary with participating faculty drawn from all divisions of the college.
Contact(s):
　Evan Williams, Director of Environmental Studies; 503-768-7699; Fax: 503-768-7369; etw@lclark.edu

LEWIS AND CLARK COLLEGE
LAW SCHOOL
10015 S.W. Terwilliger Blvd .
Portland, OR 97219 United States
Phone: 503-768-6613　　　　Fax: 503-768-6850
E-mail: lawadmss@lclark.edu
Website: law.lclark.edu
Scope: International
Description: Strong environmental law training program (Environmental Law Certificate at J.D. level and specialized LL.M. in Environmental and Natural Resources Law); publish journal of Environmental Law; research program in Natural Resources Law Institute (newsletter: NRLI News); conferences and workshops through continuing education program; internships in natural resources; and environmental clinical opportunities.
Publication(s): Brochures, 2002-2003 Catalog
Keyword(s): Ethics/Environmental Justice

LOUISIANA STATE UNIVERSITY SCHOOL OF FORESTRY, WILDLIFE AND FISHERIES
SCHOOL OF FORESTRY, WILDLIFE AND FISHERIES
Renewable Natural Resources, Rm. 121, 124
Baton Rouge, LA 70803 United States
Phone: 225-578-4179　　　　Fax: 225-578-4144
Website: www.coa.lsu.edu/fores/fores.html
Membership: 1–100
Scope: State, National
Keyword(s): Ecosystems (precious), Land Issues, Public Lands/Greenspace, Water Habitats & Quality, Wildlife & Species
Contact(s):
　Charles Bryan, Cooperative Fish and Wildlife Research Unit, Leader
　Mary Ehrett, Secretary; mehrett@lsu.edu
　Megan Lapayere, Assistant Leader - Fisheries

EDUCATIONAL INSTITUTIONS – M

LOUISIANA TECH UNIVERSITY
SCHOOL OF FORESTRY
WILDLIFE CONSERVATION
FORESTRY
P.O. Box 10138
Ruston, LA 71272 United States
Phone: 318-257-4985 Fax: 318-257-5061
Website: www.ans.latech.edu/forestry-index.html
Membership: 1–100
Scope: Regional
Description: Located in Louisiana's major forest region, the School of Forestry offers Bachelor of Science degrees in Forestry and Wildlife Conservation. Highlights include a practical, field-oriented education, a GIS/Remote Sensing Laboratory, a highly trained and diverse faculty, and a successful placement record.
Publication(s): Wildlife of Southern Forests
Contact(s):
John Adams, Director; 318-257-4985; jadams@latech.edu
James Dickson, Coordinator, Wildlife Program; 318-257-4020; jdickson@rans.latech.edu

M

MANCHESTER COLLEGE
KOINONIA ENVIRONMENTAL AND RETREAT CENTER
604 College Ave.
North Manchester, IN 46962 United States
Phone: 219-982-5010 Fax: 219-982-5043
Website: www.ares.manchester.edu/academic/koin.html
Founded: 1974
Scope: Regional
Description: The 100-acre facility is used extensively to provide hands-on environmental science education for area students in grades, K-12. A two-story building houses the nature center with many educational displays. The retreat facility will accommodate 32 persons.
Contact(s):
Barbara Ehrhardt, Director

MCGILL UNIVERSITY
DEPARTMENT OF NATURAL RESOURCE SCIENCES
AVIAN SCIENCE AND CONSERVATION CENTRE
(ASCC)
21,111 Lakeshore Road
Ste. Anne de Bellevue, H9X 3V9 Quebec Canada
Phone: 514-398-7760 Fax: 514-398-7990
Website: www.nrs.mcgill.ca/ascc
Founded: 1974
Membership: 1–100
Scope: Regional, National, International
Description: To promote the study of birds and their conservation, we conduct pure and applied research in the field and laboratory; breed, release and manage endangered species; and train students and interns from all over the world. The Centre publishes an annual newsletter, The Talon.
Publication(s): The Talon
Keyword(s): Agriculture/Farming, Development/Developing Countries, Ecosystems (precious), Energy, Forests/Forestry, Pollution (general), Public Lands/Greenspace, Recreation/Ecotourism, Water Habitats & Quality, Wildlife & Species
Contact(s):
David Bird, Director
Ian Ritchie, Curator; 514-398-7932; Fax: 514-398-7540; ritchie@nrs.mcgill.ca
Rodger Titman, Associate Director; 514-398-7933; Fax: 514-398-7990; titman@nrs.mcgill.ca

MCNEESE STATE UNIVERSITY
DEPARTMENT OF AGRICULTURE, WILDLIFE
4205 Ryan Street
Lake Charles, LA 70609 United States
Phone: 337-475-5000
E-mail: webmaster@mail.mcneese.edu
Website: www.mcneese.edu/
Scope: State
Contact(s):
Billy Delany, Department of Agriculture, Wildlife Mangement Professor; 318-475-5690

MIAMI UNIVERSITY
INSTITUTE OF ENVIRONMENTAL SCIENCES
102 Boyd Hall
Oxford, OH 45056 United States
Phone: 513-529-5811 Fax: 513-529-5814
E-mail: havener@muohio.edu
Website: www.muohio.edu/ies
Founded: 1969
Membership: 1–100
Scope: Local, State, Regional, National
Description: The Institute of Environmental Sciences has offered a professional Master of Environmental Science degree since 1969. This interdisciplinary program stresses problem solving and community service. The curriculum provides practical experience in an area of concentration, preparing students for a variety of practical careers in public and private sector jobs.
Keyword(s): Air Quality/Atmosphere, Climate Change, Ecosystems (precious), Energy, Ethics/Environmental Justice, Land Issues, Pollution (general), Public Lands/Greenspace, Reduce/Reuse/Recycle, Sprawl/Urban Planning, Water Habitats & Quality, Wildlife & Species
Contact(s):
Gene Willeke, Institute of Environmental Sciences, Director; 513-529-5811; Fax: 513-529-5814; willekge@muohio.edu
William Hegge, Ohio Private Lands Coordinator; 513-529-8398; Fax: 513-529-5814; bill_hegge@fws.gov
Susan Crate, Ph.D.; 513-529-8356; crates@muohio.edu
Vincent Hand, Deputy Director, Research; 513-529-5811; Fax: 513-529-5814; handvc@muohio.edu
Sandra Woy-Hazleton, Deputy Director, Academic Affairs; 513-529-5811; Fax: 513-529-5814; woyhazs@muohio.edu

MICHIGAN STATE UNIVERSITY
DEPARTMENT OF FISHERIES AND WILDLIFE
13 Natural Resources Building
East Lansing, MI 48824-1222 United States
Phone: 517-355-4478 Fax: 517-432-1699
E-mail: webmaster@perm3.sw.msu.edu
Website: www.fw.msu.edu
Founded: 1951
Scope: Local, State, Regional, National, International
Description: The Department of Fisheries and Wildlife focuses on the management of natural resources with particular reference to the management of ecosystems that support wild populations of birds, mammals, fish and other vertebrates. The department's mission is to provide the education, research, and outreach needed by society for the conservation and rehabilitation of fish and wildlife resources and their ecosystems.
Contact(s):
Thomas Coon, Associate Chair; 517-355-4478; Fax: 517-432-1699; coontg@msu.edu
William Taylor, Chair; 517-355-4478; Fax: 517-432-1699; taylorw@msu.edu
Jim Schneider, Academic Specialist - Academic Adviser; 517-353-9091; Fax: 517-432-1699; schne181@msu.edu

EDUCATIONAL INSTITUTIONS– M

MICHIGAN TECHNOLOGICAL UNIVERSITY; SCHOOL OF FORESTRY AND WOOD PRODUCTS
SCHOOL OF FOREST RESOURCES AND ENVIRONMENTAL SCIENCE
1400 Townsend Dr.
Houghton, MI 49931 United States
Phone: 906-487-2454 Fax: 906-487-2915
E-mail: forest@mtu.edu
Website: www.forest.mtu.edu/

Founded: 1885
Scope: Local, State, Regional, National, International
Description: Undergraduate and graduate programs in forestry, conservation biology, wildlife ecology, management science, forest ecology/biology, teacher education, wood science.
Keyword(s): Air Quality/Atmosphere, Climate Change, Development/Developing Countries, Ecosystems (precious), Forests/Forestry, Land Issues, Water Habitats & Quality, Wildlife & Species
Contact(s):
   Margaret Gale, Associate Dean; 906-487-2352; Fax: 906-487-2915; mrgale@mtu.edu
   Glenn Mroz, Dean; 906-487-2454; Fax: 906-487-2915; gdmroz@mtu.edu

MIDDLE TENNESSEE STATE UNIVERSITY
CENTER FOR ENVIRONMENTAL EDUCATION
MTSU BIOLOGY DEPARTMENT
MTSU Box 60
Murfreesboro, TN 37132 United States
Phone: 615-904-8575 Fax: 615-217-7870
E-mail: csmithwa@mtsu.edu
Website: www.mtsu.edu/%7Ecntr4ee/

Founded: 1970
Scope: Local, State, Regional
Description: The Center for EE, an arm of MTSU's Biology Department, offers a variety of environmental programs on topics including but not limited to, waste reduction & recycling. We develop, host, & conduct after school workshops 2x a semester, consult with schools, parks and nature centers, youth leaders, & education organizations on EE, curriculum, teacher training, outdoor classrooms, & hands-on learning. We also conduct research on cooperative and group learning in EE and biology education at all levels.
Keyword(s): Agriculture/Farming, Air Quality/Atmosphere, Ecosystems (precious), Energy, Ethics/Environmental Justice, Forests/Forestry, Land Issues, Oceans/Coasts/Beaches, Pollution (general), Population, Reduce/Reuse/Recycle, Water Habitats & Quality, Wildlife & Species
Contact(s):
   Karen Hargrove, Natural Resources Coordinator; 615-898-2660; Fax: 615-217-7865; khargrov@mtsu.edu
   Padgett Kelly, Professor; 615-898-5615; Fax: 615-217-7870; jpkelly@mtsu.edu
   Cindi Smith-Walters, Biology Professor; 615-898-5449; ext. 1; Fax: 615-217-7870; csmithwa@mtsu.edu
   Pandy English, Outreach Coordinator; 615-904-8574; Fax: 615-217-7865; penglish@mtsu.edu
   Renee Dunn, Executive Secretary; 615-904-8575; Fax: 615-217-7865
   Kim Sadler, Assistant Professor; 615-904-8283; Fax: 615-217-7870; ksadler@mtsu.edu

MISSISSIPPI STATE UNIVERSITY
COLLEGE OF FOREST RESOURCES
Box 9680
Mississippi State, MS 39762 United States
Phone: 662-325-8530 Fax: 662-325-8726
Website: www.cfr.msstate.edu/
Founded: 1954
Membership: 101–1,000
Scope: Local, State, Regional, National, International
Description: The mission of the CFR is to promote the professional and intellectual development of its students, expand through research the fundamental knowledge upon which the natural resource disciplines are based, and help with the development and use of the forest, wildlife, and water resources of the state and nation through appropriate applied research, service, and technology transfer activities.
Keyword(s): Forests/Forestry, Recreation/Ecotourism, Water Habitats & Quality, Wildlife & Species
Contact(s):
   Bob Karr, Interim Dean; 662-325-2696; Fax: 662-325-8726; bkarr@cfr.msstate.edu
   Liam Leightley, Department Head, Forest Products; Forest Products Department, Box 9820, MS State, MS 39762; 662-325-4444; Fax: 662-325-8126; lleightley@cfr.msstate.edu
   Bruce Leopold, Department Head, Wildlife & Fisheries; Wildlife & Fisheries Department, Box 9690, Mississippi State, MS 39762; 662-325-2615; Fax: 662-325-8726; bleopold@cfr.msstate.edu
   Douglas Richards, Department Head, Forestry; Forestry Department, Box 9681, Mississippi State, MS 39762; 662-325-2948; Fax: 662-325-8726; drichards@cfr.msstate.edu
   Warren Thompson, Emeritus; 662-325-2952; wthompson@cfr.msstate.edu

MISSISSIPPI STATE UNIVERSITY
FOREST AND WILDLIFE RESEARCH CENTER
Box 9680
Mississippi State, MS 39762 United States
Phone: 662-325-8530 Fax: 662-325-8726
Website: www.cfr.msstate.edu/fwrc/fwrc.htm

Founded: 1994
Membership: 101–1,000
Scope: Local, State, Regional, National, International
Description: The mission of the FWRC is to conduct research and technical assistance programs relevant to the efficient management and utilization of the forest, wildlife, and fisheries of the state and region, and the protection and enhancement of these resources.
Keyword(s): Forests/Forestry, Recreation/Ecotourism, Sprawl/Urban Planning, Water Habitats & Quality, Wildlife & Species
Contact(s):
   Bob Karr, Interim Director; 662-325-2696; Fax: 662-325-8726; bkarr@cfr.msstate.edu
   Liam Leightley, Forest Products Head; Box 9820, MS State, MS 39762; 662-325-4444; Fax: 662-325-8126; lleightley@cfr.msstate.edu
   Bruce Leopold, Wildlife & Fisheries Head; Box 9690, MS State, MS 39762; 662-325-2615; Fax: 662-325-8726; bleopold@cfr.msstate.edu
   Douglas Richards, Forestry Head; Box 9681, MS State, MS 39762; 662-325-2948; Fax: 662-325-8726; drichards@cfr.msstate.edu

MISSISSIPPI STATE UNIVERSITY
FOREST AND WILDLIFE RESEARCH CENTER
DEPARTMENT OF WILDLIFE FISHERIES
Box 9690
Mississippi State, MS 39762 United States
Phone: 662-325-3133 Fax: 662-325-8750
E-mail: wildlife@ext.msstate.edu
Website: www.cfr.msstate.edu/fwrc/fwrc.htm

Founded: 1878
Membership: 1–100
Scope: Local, State, Regional, National, International
Description: This is a comprehensive department in a Land Grant University responsible for conducting research in wildlife, fisheries and aquaculture, training graduate students, training undergraduate students, and serving the people of Mississippi

and the nation regarding wise use and management of our renewable natural resources.

Keyword(s): Agriculture/Farming, Forests/Forestry, Recreation/Ecotourism, Water Habitats & Quality, Wildlife & Species

MONTANA STATE UNIVERSITY
COLLEGE OF AGRICULTURE
MONTANA AGRICULTURE EXPERIMENT STATION
202 Linfield Hall
P.O. Box 172860
Bozeman, MT 59717-2860 United States
Phone: 406-994-3681   Fax: 406-994-6579
E-mail: agweb@montana.edu
Website: www.montana.edu/agriculture

Scope: State

Description: Land Grant University — Dean and Director's Office for the College of Agriculture and Montana Agricultural Research Centers

Keyword(s): Agriculture/Farming, Land Issues, Public Lands/Greenspace, Water Habitats & Quality, Wildlife & Species

Contact(s):
Allen Harmsen, Veterinary Molecular Biology
Greg Johnson, Entomology
John Sherwood, Plant Sciences and Plant Pathology
Mike Tess, Animal & Range Sciences
Myles Watts, Ag Economics & Economics
Mal Westcott, Agricultural Research Centers
Jon Wraith, Land Resources and Environmental Sciences

MONTANA STATE UNIVERSITY
DEPARTMENT OF ECOLOGY
310 Lewis Hall
Bozeman, MT 59717 United States
Phone: 406-994-4548   Fax: 406-994-3190
E-mail: ecology@montana.edu
Website: www.montana.edu/ecology/

Membership: 1–100
Scope: Local, State, Regional, National, International
Description: Ecology Dept. offers B.S. in Organismal Biology, Biology Teaching, Ecology & Evolution, and Fish and Wildlife Management and M.S. and Ph.D. programs with a concentration in Ecology or Fish & Wildlife Biology.

Contact(s):
Lynn Irby, Fish and Wildlife Management Program, Coordinator; 406-994-3252; ubili@montana.edu
Jay Rotella, Department Head; 406-994-5070; rotella@montana.edu

MONTCLAIR STATE UNIVERSITY
COLLEGE OF SCIENCE AND MATHEMATICS
One Normal Ave.
Upper Montclair, NJ 07043 United States
Phone: 973-655-4448
Website: csam.montclair.edu/

Contact(s):
Bonnie Lustigman, Biology, Chair; lustigman@saturn.montclair.edu
Robert Taylor, Earth and Environmental Science, Professor; taylorr@saturn.montclair.edu

MOREHEAD STATE UNIVERSITY
DEPARTMENT OF BIOLOGICAL AND ENVIRONMENTAL SCIENCES
123 Lappin Hall
Morehead, KY 40351 United States
Phone: 606-783-2944   Fax: 606-783-5002
Website: www.morehead-st.edu

Membership: 1–100
Scope: State
Publication(s): See publication website

Contact(s):
David Magrane, Biology; d.magrane@morehead-st.edu

MOUNT UNION COLLEGE
BRUMBAUGH CENTER FOR ENVIRONMENTAL SCIENCE
HUSTON-BRUMBAUGH NATURE CENTER
1972 Clark Avenue
Alliance, OH 44601 United States
Phone: 330-823-7487   Fax: 330-823-8531
E-mail: mucnature@igc.org

Founded: 1988
Scope: Local, State
Description: The Brumbaugh Center for Environmental Science offers environmental education for college students, children and youth, and adults with an emphasis on outdoor activities.

Keyword(s): Forests/Forestry, Land Issues, Water Habitats & Quality

Contact(s):
Charles McClaugherty, Director; 330-823-3655; Fax: 330-823-8531; mcclauca@muc.edu
Patricia Rickard, Naturalist; 330-823-7487; Fax: 330-823-8531; rickarpa@muc.edu

MURRAY STATE UNIVERSITY
BIOLOGICAL SCIENCE
334 Blackburn Science
Murray, KY 42071-3346 United States
Phone: 270-762-2786   Fax: 270-762-2788
Website: www.murraystate.edu

Membership: 1–100
Scope: State
Description: Offering B.S. and M.S in Biology, and Wildlife and Conservation Biology

Publication(s): See publication website
Keyword(s): Agriculture/Farming, Ecosystems (precious), Water Habitats & Quality, Wildlife & Species

Contact(s):
Tom Timmons, Department of Biological Sciences, Fisheries, Chairman; 270-762-6754; tom.timmons@murraystate.edu
David White, Center for Reservoir Research, Contact; 270-474-2272; david.white@murraystate.edu
Stephen White, Wildlife, Contact; 270-762-6298; steve.white@murraystate.edu
Howard Whiteman, Conservation Amphibian Research; 270-762-6753; Fax: 270-762-2788; howard.whiteman@murraystate.edu

MUSASHI INSTITUTE OF TECHNOLOGY
3-3-1 Ushikubo-nishi, Tsuzuki-ku
Yokohama, 224-0015 Japan
Phone: 81452600   Fax: 81452626

Founded: 1938
Description: The University consists of two departments: Civil Engineering and Environmental and Information Studies. Publishes Conservation Biology and Issues on Environment.

N

NEW MEXICO STATE UNIVERSITY
COLLEGE OF AGRICULTURE AND HOME ECONOMICS
DEPARTMENT OF ANIMAL AND RANGE SCIENCES
Department of Animal and Range Sciences
Box 30003
Las Cruces, NM 88003 United States
Phone: 505-646-2515   Fax: 505-646-5975
Website: www.nmsu.edu/~dars

Scope: State
Description: In the Department of Animal and Range Sciences, students can major in animal or range science. The Department also offers pre-veterinary studies. In addition to

undergraduate degrees, the Department offers graduate degrees at the Master of Science and Doctor of Philosophy levels. The M.S. or Ph.D. in Animal Science can emphasize nutrition or physiology, and the M.S. or Ph.D. in Range Science students have the option to study in areas including, but not exclusive to, range ecology and watershed

Keyword(s): Agriculture/Farming, Ecosystems (precious), Forests/Forestry, Public Lands/Greenspace, Recreation/Ecotourism, Water Habitats & Quality, Wildlife & Species

Contact(s):
Jerry Schickedanz, Dean

NEW MEXICO STATE UNIVERSITY
COLLEGE OF AGRICULTURE AND HOME ECONOMICS
DEPARTMENT OF FISHERY AND WILDLIFE SCIENCES
P.O. Box 30003, Dept. 4901
Las Cruces, NM 88003 United States
Phone: 505-646-7051   Fax: 505-646-1281
E-mail: natres@nmsu.edu
Website: leopold.nmsu.edu

Scope: State

Description: The Department offers training in Fishery & Wildlife Science at the undergraduate and graduate level. The curricula are designed to prepare students for work in the fields of research, teaching, extension and management. With a diversified faculty working in a broad range of terrestrial and aquatic systems, students have excellent opportunities for study in a wide variety of sub-disciplines in the fishery and wildlife sciences.

Keyword(s): Forests/Forestry, Land Issues, Water Habitats & Quality, Wildlife & Species

Contact(s):
Donald Caccamise, Department Head

NORTH CAROLINA STATE UNIVERSITY
COLLEGE OF AGRICULTURE AND LIFE SCIENCES
115 Patterson Hall
Box 7642
Raleigh, NC 27695-7642 United States
Phone: 919-515-2614   Fax: 919-515-5266
Website: www.cals.ncsu.edu/

Membership: 1,001–10,000
Scope: State
Keyword(s): Agriculture/Farming, Air Quality/Atmosphere, Ecosystems (precious), Forests/Forestry, Pollution (general), Water Habitats & Quality, Wildlife & Species

Contact(s):
William Grant, Director of Undergraduate Biology Programs; 919-515-3341
James Gilliam, Zoology, Head; 919-515-5978
John Havlin, Soil Science, Head; 919-515-2655; john_havlin@ncsu.edu
Gerald Leblanc, Environmental and Molecular Toxicology, Head; 919-515-7404; Fax: 919-515-7169; gal@unity.ncsu.edu
Samuel Mozley, Ecology, Environmental Sciences; 919-515-1981
Gerald Van Dyke, Botany, Head; 919-515-2222
James Young, Biological and Agricultural Engineering, Head; 919-515-2694; Fax: 919-515-6772; jim_young@ncsu.edu

NORTH DAKOTA STATE UNIVERSITY
DEPARTMENT OF BIOLOGICAL SCIENCES
Fargo, ND 58105-5517 United States
Phone: 701-231-7087   Fax: 701-231-7149
E-mail: william.bleier@ndsu.nodak.edu
Website: www.ndsu.nodak.edu/zoology/

Founded: 1890
Membership: 1–100
Scope: Local, State, Regional, National, International
Description: Wildlife and Fisheries Biology Option in Zoology Conservation Science
Keyword(s): Agriculture/Farming, Water Habitats & Quality, Wildlife & Species

Contact(s):
Will Bleier, Department Chair; Vertebrate Pest Management; 701-231-8421; Fax: 701-231-7149; william.bleier@ndsu.nodak.edu
Mac Butler, Professor; Aquatic Ecology; 701-231-7398; Fax: 701-231-7149; Malcolm.Butler@ndsu.nodak.edu
Gary Clambey, Associate Professor; Ecology; 701-231-8404; Fax: 701-231-7149; Gary.Clambey@ndsu.nodak.edu
Mark Clark, Assistant Professor; Population Biology; 701-231-8246; Fax: 701-231-7149; M.E.Clark@ndsu.nodak.edu
Gary Nuechterlein, Professor; Behavioral Ecology; 701-231-8436; Fax: 701-231-7149; Gary.Nuechterlein@ndsu.nodak.edu
Wendy Reed, Assistant Professor; Physiological Ecology of Coots; 701-231-7012; Fax: 701-231-7149; Wendy.Reed@ndsu.nodak.edu
Craig Stockwell, Assistant Professor; Conservation Biology; 701-231-8449; Fax: 701-231-7149; craig.stockwell@ndsu.nodak.edu

NORTHEASTERN UNIVERSITY
BIOLOGY DEPARTMENT
360 Huntington Avenue, 134 Mugar Sciences
Boston, MA 02115 United States
Phone: 617-373-2260   Fax: 617-373-3724
E-mail: gradbio@neu.edu
Website: www.biology.neu.edu/

Membership: 1–100
Scope: State
Keyword(s): Ecosystems (precious), Ethics/Environmental Justice, Wildlife & Species

Contact(s):
Joseph Ayers, Marine Science Center/Marine Biology, Director; East Point, Nahant, MA 01908; 617-581-7370; lobster@neu.edu
Gwilym Jones, Vertebrate Systematics and Ecology; 617-373-2851; g.jones@nunet.neu.edu

NORTHERN ARIZONA UNIVERSITY
COLLEGE OF ARTS AND SCIENCES
NAU Box 5640
Flagstaff, AZ 86011-5621 United States
Phone: 520-523-2381   Fax: 520-523-7500
E-mail: biology@nau.edu
Website: www.nau.edu/

Scope: State
Description: Dept. of Biology offers an emphasis in the areas of: Applied Plant Science, Aquatic Biology, Ecology, Cellular and Molecular Biology and Fish and Wildlife Management. Available emphasis areas for Environmental Science are: Biology, Chemistry, Applied Geology, Applied Mathematics, Microbiology, Environmental Administration and Policy, Environmental Communications and Environmental Management.

Contact(s):
Lee Drickamer, Chair, Dept. of Biological Sciences; 520-523-7501; Fax: 520-523-7500; lee.drickamer@nau.edu

NORTHERN ARIZONA UNIVERSITY
COLLEGE OF ECOSYSTEM SCIENCE AND MANAGEMENT
Box 15018
Flagstaff, AZ 86011-5018 United States
Phone: 520-523-3031   Fax: 520-523-1080
E-mail: esm.info@nau.edu
Website: www.cesm.nau.edu

Scope: State

Description: Northern Arizona University is in an ideal location for the study of both forestry and recreation. Near Flagstaff are the largest ponderosa pine forest in America, five life zones within fifty miles, recreation and aesthetic areas, and extensive wildlife, grazing and watershed areas.

Contact(s):
Donald Arganbright, Interim Dean; donald.g.arganbright@nau.edu

NORTHERN ARIZONA UNIVERSITY
DEPARTMENT OF GEOGRAPHY, PLANNING, AND RECREATION
Box 15016
Flagstaff, AZ 86011-5016 United States
Phone: 928-523-2650   Fax: 928-523-2275
E-mail: geog@nau.edu
Website: www.geog.nau.edu/

Founded: 1967

Scope: State

Description: Degrees Offered: B.S. and B.S.Ed. in Geography, B.S. in Applied Geography; B.S. in Public Planning; B.S. in Parks and Recreation Management; M.A. in Rural Geography; Certificate in Parks and Recreation Management; Graduate Certificate in Geographic Information Systems

Keyword(s): Climate Change, Ecosystems (precious), Ethics/Environmental Justice, Land Issues, Public Lands/Greenspace, Recreation/Ecotourism, Reduce/Reuse/Recycle, Sprawl/Urban Planning

Contact(s):
Alan Lew, Chair, Department of Geography, Planning, and Recreation

NORTHERN ARIZONA UNIVERSITY
NORTHERN ARIZONA ENVIRONMENTAL EDUCATION RESOURCES CENTER
CENTER FOR ENVIRONMENTAL SCIENCES AND EDUCATION
S. San Francisco St. 860011
Flagstaff, AZ 86011 United States
Phone: 928-523-9011   Fax: 520-523-5441
E-mail: paul.rowland@nau.edu
Website: www.nau.edu/~envsci/naeerc/index.html

Founded: 1994

Contact(s):
Paul Rowland, Associate Director; 520-523-5853

NORTHERN MICHIGAN UNIVERSITY
COLLEGE OF ARTS AND SCIENCES
BIOLOGY
1401 Presque Isle Ave.
Marquette, MI 49855 United States
Phone: 906-227-2700   Fax: 906-227-2703
E-mail: artssci@nmu.edu
Website: www.nmu.edu

Membership: 1–100

Scope: State

Publication(s): Update (Newsletter)

Contact(s):
Michael Broadway, Department of Geography, Earth Science, Conservation, and Planning; Luther S. West Science Bldg., Rm. 213, Marquette, MI 49855; 906-227-2500; Fax: 906-227-1621; mbroadwa@nmu.edu
Neil Cumberlidge, Department of Biology, Head; Luther S. West Science Bldg., Rm. 277, Marquette, MI 49855; 906-227-2310; Fax: 906-227-1063; ncumberl@nmu.edu

NORTHLAND COLLEGE
SIGURD OLSON ENVIRONMENTAL INSTITUTE
1411 Ellis Ave
Ashland, WI 54806 United States
Phone: 715-682-1223   Fax: 715-682-1218
Website: www.northland.edu/soei

Founded: 1972

Membership: 1,001–10,000

Scope: Regional, National

Description: The Sigurd Olson Environmental Institute was founded at Northland College in 1972 to increase public understanding of the complex relationships between natural and cultural environments in the Lake Superior region and to assist in developing workable solutions to regional environmental problems. The institute seeks to carry out Sigurd Olson's vision by fostering environmental citizenship and educating citizens for a sustainable future.

Keyword(s): Air Quality/Atmosphere, Ecosystems (precious), Forests/Forestry, Land Issues, Water Habitats & Quality, Wildlife & Species

Contact(s):
Kenneth Bro, Executive Director
Carolyn Hanna, Officer Manager; 715-682-1392; Fax: 715-682-1218; channa@northland.edu
Paula Bonk, Assistant/Lake Superior Binational Forum
Mike Gardner, Assistant Director; 715-682-1481; Fax: 715-682-1218; mgardner@northland.edu
Jim Musso, Advisory Board Chair
Jerri Ridlon, Communications Specialist
Pam Troxell, Timber Wolf Alliance Coordinator

NORTHWESTERN STATE UNIVERSITY OF LOUISIANA
WILDLIFE PROGRAM
Biology Dept.
Natchitoches, LA 71497 United States
Phone: 318-357-5323   Fax: 318-357-4518
Website: www.nsula.edu

Membership: 1–100

Scope: Local

Description: To educate students in principles and science of wildlife management; to prepare students for management of natural resources at the professional entry levels; and to provide an emphasis on biodiversity and ecosystems; to orient students toward interpersonal communication

Keyword(s): Forests/Forestry, Wildlife & Species

Contact(s):
Steven Gabrey, Biology/Wildlife Management, Advisor; 318-357-5375; steveng@alpha.nsula.edu
Dick Stalling, Biology Sciences, Head

O

OBERLIN COLLEGE
ADAM JOSEPH LEWIS CENTER
ENVIRONMENTAL STUDIES PROGRAM
122 Elm Street
Oberlin, OH 44074-1095 United States
Phone: 440-775-8747   Fax: 440-775-8946
E-mail: bev.burgess@oberlin.edu
Website: www.oberlin.edu/~envs/

Description: An interdisciplinary program which includes 30+ courses across ten departments. Students are required to do significant academic work that spans the sciences, social sciences, and the humanities. The program offers significant off-campus opportunities for students through a Watershed Education Program, a local initiative in sustainable agriculture, and work with the city on energy and development issues.

Contact(s):
David Orr, Program Chair

OHIO STATE UNIVERSITY
SCHOOL OF NATURAL RESOURCES
2021 Coffey Rd.
210 Kottman Hall
Columbus, OH 43210-1085 United States
Phone: 614-292-2265   Fax: 614-292-7432
Website: http://snr.osu.edu
Scope: Local, State, Regional, National, International
Description: We offer BS, MS and PhD programs in Natural Resources.
Keyword(s): Agriculture/Farming, Ecosystems (precious), Oceans/Coasts/Beaches, Pollution (general), Public Health, Recreation/Ecotourism, Water Habitats & Quality, Wildlife & Species
Contact(s):
  Gary Mullins, Director of the School of Natural Resources; mullins.2@osu.edu

OKLAHOMA STATE UNIVERSITY
COOPERATIVE FISH AND WILDLIFE RESEARCH UNIT
404 Life Sciences
Stillwater, OK 74078 United States
Phone: 405-744-6342   Fax: 405-744-5006
E-mail: coopunit@okstate.edu
Website: www.okstate.edu
Scope: Local, State, Regional, National
Description: Research and education in resource conservation
Keyword(s): Climate Change, Ecosystems (precious), Forests/Forestry, Water Habitats & Quality, Wildlife & Species
Contact(s):
  David Engle, Range Management, Program Coordinator; 477 Ag Hall, Stillwater, OK 74078; 405-744-6410
  Becky Johnson, Department of Botany, Head; 405-744-5559
  Edward Knobbe, Environmental Science, Program Coordinator; 405-744-9229
  David Leslie, Cooperative Fish and Wildlife Research Unit, Leader; 404 Life Sciences West; 405-744-6342
  Craig McKinley, Department of Forestry, Head; 405-744-5437
  James Shaw, Department of Wildlife/Fisheries/Ecology/Zoology, Head; 405-744-5555

OREGON STATE UNIVERSITY DEPT OF FISHERIES AND WILDLIFE
DEPARTMENT OF FISHERIES AND WILDLIFE
104 Nash
Corvallis, OR 97331 United States
Phone: 541-737-4531   Fax: 541-737-3590
Website: fw.oregonstate.edu/
Membership: 101–1,000
Scope: State, Regional
Description: Education in Fisheries & Wildlife topics
Contact(s):
  Robert Anthony, Cooperative Fishery and Wildlife Research Unit, Leader
  Daniel Edge, Fisheries and Wildlife, Head of Wildlife, Interim
  Steven Radosevich, Sustainable Forestry Program, Leader of Forestry
  Harold Salwasser, Forestry and Forest Recreation, Dean
  Carl Schreck, Cooperative Fishery and Wildlife Research Unit, Leader

P

PENNSYLVANIA STATE EXTENSION SERVICES
217 Agricultural Administration Bldg., Pennsylvania State University
University Park, PA 16802-2600 United States
Phone: 814-863-3438   Fax: 814-863-7905
Website: www.extension.psu.edu
Scope: State
Description: The mission of Penn State Cooperative Extension is to extend nonformal outreach educational opportunities to individuals, families, businesses, and communities throughout Pennsylvania. Cooperative Extension education programs enable the Commonwealth to maintain a competitive and environmentally sound food and fiber system and prepare Pennsylvania's youth, adults, and families to enhance the quality of their lives and participate more fully in community decisions.
Contact(s):
  Theodore Alter, Director of Extension; 217 Agricultural Administration Building, Pennsylvania State University, University Park, PA 16802; 814-863-3438; Fax: 814-863-7905
  Mary Jo Depp-Nestlerode, Interim Associate Director of Extension; 217 Agricultural Administration Bldg., Pennsylvania State University, University Park, PA 16802-2600; 814-863-3438; Fax: 814-863-7905; mjdepp@psu.edu
  Jack Watson, Assistant Director of Extension, State Program Leader; 401 Agricultural Administration Bldg., Pennsylvania State University, University Park, PA 16802; 814-863-6114; Fax: 814-863-7776; JackWatson@psu.edu

PENNSYLVANIA STATE UNIVERSITY
SCHOOL OF FOREST RESOURCES
113 Ferguson Bldg. Schl. Forest Resources,
University Park, PA 16802 United States
Phone: 814-863-7093   Fax: 814-865-3725
Website: www.sfr.cas.psu.edu
Membership: 101–1,000
Scope: State
Contact(s):
  Charles Strauss, Director Interim
  M. Brittingham, Wildlife and Fisheries, Contact; 320 Forest Resources Lab, University Park, PA 16802; 814-863-8442; Fax: 814-863-7193; mxb21@psu.edu
  Robert Carline, Fisheries and Wildlife Cooperative Research Unit, Leader; 113A Merkle Bldg., Univeristy Park, PA 16802; 814-865-4511; Fax: 814-863-4710; f7u@psu.edu
  John Janowiak, Wood Products, Professor; 307 Forest Resources Laboratory, University Park, PA 16802; 814-865-5722; Fax: 814-863-7193; jjj2@psu.edu

PINES ROWAN UNIVERSITY
120-13 Whitesbog Rd.
Browns Mills, NJ 8015 United States
Phone: 609-893-1765   Fax: 609-893-8297
Scope: State
Contact(s):
  Gary Patterson, Director
  Maria Peter, Program Coordinator

POLYTECHNIC UNIVERSITY OF NEW YORK
CIVIL AND ENVIRONMENTAL ENGINEERING DEPARTMENT
6 Metro Tech Center
Brookyn, NY 11201 United States
Phone: 718-260-3220   Fax: 718-260-3433
E-mail: cee@poly.edu
Website: www.poly.edu/cee
Membership: 1–100
Scope: International
Description: The Department is engaged in teaching and research in several areas of environmental science and engineering. Masters degrees with environmental focus are offered in civil engineering, environmental engineering, and environmental health science. The Ph.D. is also offered.
Contact(s):
  David Chang, President
  F. (Bud) Grisses, Dept. Chair of Civil Engineering

PORTLAND STATE UNIVERSITY
ENVIRONMENTAL SCIENCES AND RESOURCES
P.O. Box 751
Portland, OR 97207-0751 United States
Phone: 503-725-4980   Fax: 503-725-3888
E-mail: esr@pdx.edu
Website: www.esr.pdx.edu

Scope: State

Description: The focus of the program is research on the problems of the environment and resources. The program offers Ph.D. degrees in cooperation with the departments of biology, chemistry, civil engineering, economics, geography, geology, and physics. Master programs include M.S., M.E.M. (Master of Environmental Management), and M.S.T (Master of Science in Teaching). Bachelor's programs (B.A., B.S.) include tracks in environmental science and environmental policy and management.

Contact(s):
Roy Koch, Director; 503-725-8038; kochr@mall.pdx.edu

PRESCOTT COLLEGE, LIBERAL ARTS AND THE ENVIRONMENTAL STUDIES PROGRAM
ENVIRONMENTAL STUDIES PROGRAM
220 Grove Ave.
Prescott, AZ 86301 United States
Phone: 520-778-2090   Fax: 928-776-5137
Website: www.prescott.edu/rdp/rdp_es.html

Scope: Regional

Description: The Environmental Studies Program is one of four programs within Prescott College. The program emphasizes experiential and interdisciplinary learning, and focuses on the interrelationships between the human and nonhuman worlds and the reciprocal influences each has on the other.

Publication(s): Wolfberry Sun, semi-annual newsletter, Alligator Juniper, poems, stories and photographs, Transitions, brochure

Contact(s):
Lisa Floyd-Hanna, Program Coordinator

PURDUE UNIVERSITY
DEPARTMENT OF FORESTRY AND NATURAL RESOURCES
195 Marsteller Street
West Lafayette, IN 47907-2033 United States
Phone: 765-494-3591   Fax: 765-496-2422
E-mail: fnrweb@fnr.purdue.edu
Website: www.fnr.purdue.edu/

Scope: State

Contact(s):
W. Mills, Undergraduate Programs, Director of Student Services; 765-494-3575; Fax: 765-496-2422
Robert Swihart, Graduate Program, Director of Graduate Studies; 765-494-3621; Fax: 765-496-2422
Dennis Lemaster, Department of Forestry and Natural Resources, Head; 765-494-3590; Fax: 765-496-2422

R

RAPTOR CENTER, THE
University of Minnesota
1920 Fitch Avenue
St. Paul, MN 55108 United States
Phone: 612-624-4745   Fax: 612-624-8740
E-mail: raptor@umn.edu
Website: www.raptor.cvm.umn.edu

Founded: 1974
Membership: 1,001–10,000
Scope: International

Description: The Raptor Center specializes in the medical care, rehabilitation, and conservation of birds of prey (eagles, hawks, owls, and falcons). In addition to treating approximately 800 raptors a year, the internationally known program provides specialized training in raptor medicine and surgery for veterinarians from around the world. The Raptor Center also reaches 250,000 people each year through public education programs and events.

Publication(s): Raptor Release, The, Care and Management of Captive Raptors

Keyword(s): Wildlife & Species

Contact(s):
Patrick Redig, Director; 612-624-4969; Fax: 612-624-8740; redig001@umn.edu
Lori Arent, Rehabilitation Coordinator; 612-624-0762; Fax: 612-624-8740; arent@umn.edu
Sue Kirchoff, Publications Editor; Fax: 612-624-8740; kirch004@umn.edu

RENSSELAER POLYTECHNIC INSTITUTE
DEPARTMENT OF EARTH AND ENVIRONMENTAL SCIENCES
Jonsson-Rowland Science Center, Rm. 1C25
Troy, NY 12180-3590 United States
Phone: 518-276-6474   Fax: 518-276-6680
E-mail: ees@rpi.edu
Website: www.rpi.edu/dept/geo/

Scope: International

Contact(s):
Frank Spear, Chair; spearf@rpi.edu

RENSSELAER POLYTECHNIC INSTITUTE
LALLY SCHOOL OF MANAGEMENT AND TECHNOLOGY
110 8th St., Pittbsurgh Building
Troy, NY 12180-3590 United States
Phone: 518-276-6565   Fax: 518-276-2665
E-mail: mendef@rpi.edu
Website: lallyschool.rpi.edu

Scope: International

Description: Rensselaer's EMP program educates students at the masters of science level to undertake a professional role in companies, governmental agencies, and other organizations dealing with environmental and energy matters from a base of technical and managerial knowledge and understanding.

Publication(s): Corporate Environmental Strategy

Contact(s):
Frank Mendelson, Director, Acting

RHODE ISLAND SCHOOL OF DESIGN
DEPARTMENT OF LANDSCAPE ARCHITECTURE
Two College St.
Providence, RI 02903 United States
Phone: 401-454-6282   Fax: 401-454-6299
E-mail: ldardept@risd.edu
Website: www.risd.edu

Founded: 1945
Membership: 1–100
Scope: State

Description: Graduates depart RISD with the necessary training to work from an informed position, with an environmental ethic, a personal philosophy, their interpretive abilities honed and with creative vision.

Contact(s):
Colgate Searle, Professor; 401-454-6287; Fax: 401-454-6299; csearle@ids.net
Derek Bradford, Professor; 401-454-6292; Fax: 401-454-6299; cercis@compuserve.com
Elizabeth Hermann, Associate Professor; 401-454-6275; Fax: 401-454-6299; hermann.arrowhead@verizon.net
Mikyoung Kim, Associate Professor; 401-454-6285; Fax: 401-454-6299; info@mikyoungkim.com
Leonard Newcomb, Department Head/Associate Professor; 401-454-6286; Fax: 401-454-6299; lnewcomb@jumboprawn.net

RICE UNIVERSITY
6100 Main St.
Houston, TX 77251 United States
Phone: 713-527-8101
Website: www.rice.edu

Founded: 1912

Contact(s):
  Frank Fisher, Director of Wetland Studies, Ecology Dept.; 713-527-5917; fisher@rice.edu
  C. Ward, Energy and Environmental Systems Institute, Director; 6100 Main St., MS 316, Houston, TX 77005; eesi@rice.edu
  Ronald Sass, Ecology and Evolutionary Biology Dept., Chair; 6100 Main St., MS 170, Houston, TX 77005; 713-527-4919; Fax: 713-285-5232; sass@ruf.rice.edu

RICE UNIVERSITY
RICE SCHOOL OF ARCHITECTURE
MS 50, 6100 Main Street
Houston, TX 77005 United States
Phone: 713-348-4864   Fax: 713-348-5277
E-mail: arch@rice.edu
Website: www.arch.rice.edu/

Membership: 1–100
Scope: Regional
Description: Master of Architecture in Urban Design for individuals who already hold a professional degree qualifying them for registration as architects or landscape architects
Publication(s): See publication website

Contact(s):
  Lars Lerup, Dean; lars@rice.edu

RICHARD STOCKTON COLLEGE
DIVISION OF NATURAL SCIENCES AND MATHEMATICS
P.O. Box 195
Pomona, NJ 08240 United States
Phone: 609-652-4546   Fax: 609-748-5515
E-mail: dennis.weiss@stockton.edu
Website: www.stockton.edu/

Founded: 1969
Membership: 1–100
Scope: State, Regional, National, International
Description: 4 year public liberal arts college

Contact(s):
  Weihong Fan, Environmental Science & Geology
  Gordan Grguric, Marine Science
  Tim Haresign, Biology Coordinator
  Edward Paul, Chemistry Coordinator
  Dennis Weiss, Dean

ROGER WILLIAMS UNIVERSITY
DEPARTMENT OF BIOLOGY, MARINE BIOLOGY, CHEMISTRY AND ENVIRONMENTAL SCIENCE
One Old Ferry Rd.
Bristol, RI 02809 United States
Phone: 401-254-3108   Fax: 401-254-3310
Website: www.rwuonline.cc/

Founded: 1957
Membership: 1–100
Scope: International
Description: Waterfront Liberal Arts University with a strong program in marine biology and aquaculture.
Keyword(s): Agriculture/Farming, Oceans/Coasts/Beaches

Contact(s):
  Delia Anderson, Assistant Dean; danderson@rwu.edu

RUTGERS UNIVERSITY, COOK COLLEGE
DEPARTMENT ENVIRONMENTAL SCIENCE
14 College Farm Road
New Brunswick, NJ 08901-8551 United States
Phone: 732-932-9185
Website: www.envsci.rutgers.edu/

Founded: 1920
Membership: 101–1,000
Scope: Local, State, Regional, National, International
Description: We believe we are the oldest Department of Environmental Science in the world (1920). We focus on the science of pollution control, fate and effects of pollutants, atmospheric science, environmental toxicology, and pollution exposure assessment. We offer undergraduate, graduate, and professional programs..
Keyword(s): Air Quality/Atmosphere, Climate Change, Pollution (general), Public Health, Reduce/Reuse/Recycle, Water Habitats & Quality

Contact(s):
  Barbara Turpin, Graduate Program Director; 732-932-8609; env_gradpgm@envsci.rutgers.edu
  Adesoji Adelaja, Executive Dean, Cook College and the New Jersey Agricultural; Cook College, Martin Hall, Lipman Drive, New Brunswick, NJ 08901-8551; 732-932-9155; Fax: 732-932-8887; adelaja@aesop.rutgers.edu
  Peter Strom, Professor; 732-932-8078; Fax: 732-932-8644; strom@envsci.rutgers.edu
  Robert Tate, Undergraduate Program Coordinator; 732-932-9810; tate@envsci.rutgers.edu
  Lily Young, Environmental Sciences Dept., Chair; 14 College Farm Road, New Brunswick, NJ 08901-8551; 732-932-9185; Fax: 732-932-8644; chair@envsci.rutgers.edu

S

SAN JOSE STATE UNIVERSITY
DEPARTMENT OF ENVIRONMENTAL STUDIES
One Washington Sq.
San Jose, CA 95192-0115 United States
Phone: 408-924-5450   Fax: 408-924-5477
E-mail: envstdys@email.sjsu.edu
Website: www.sjsu.edu/depts/EnvStudies/

Founded: 1970
Scope: State
Description: Special interests of the faculty include habitat restoration, environmental impact assessment, energy, water, and forest resource management, human ecology, international development, coastal resource management, solid waste management, and environmental education for teachers. Credit is given for beyond-the-classroom experiences for appropriate Peace Corps Service, Internships programs, Center for Development of Recycling (CDR) and Environmental Resource Center (ERC).

Contact(s):
  Lester Rowntree, Department Chairperson

SANTA CLARA COMMUNITY ACTION PROGRAM
ENVIRONMENTAL AWARENESS
500 El Camino Real
P.O. Box 2946
Santa Clara, CA 95053-2946 United States
Phone: 408-551-4182

Founded: 2001
Membership: 1–100
Scope: Local, State, National, International
Description: Based in Santa Clara University's Community Action Program, the Environmental Awareness network empowers students to plant native vegetation at a local habitat restoration site, reduce campus consumption, collaborate with local conservation groups, educate each other on issues of internation

EDUCATIONAL INSTITUTIONS – S

al importance, and explore overall the ways in which we as students can and do affect the living earth.

Keyword(s): Ecosystems (precious), Energy, Ethics/Environmental Justice, Land Issues, Pollution (general), Public Health, Reduce/Reuse/Recycle, Sprawl/Urban Planning, Transportation

SHAWNEE STATE UNIVERSITY
DEPARTMENT OF NATURAL SCIENCES
940 Second St.
Portsmouth, OH 45662 United States
Phone: 740-351-3205
Website: www.shawnee.edu
Membership: 1–100
Scope: State
Description: B.S. in Natural Science field with minor or certificate in Environmental Studies

Contact(s):
Jeffrey Bauer, Environmental Certificate Advisor; 740-351-3421; Fax: 740-351-3596; jbauer@shawnee.edu

SHEPHERD COLLEGE
INSTITUTE FOR ENVIRONMENTAL STUDIES
P.O. Box 3210, Byrd Science Center
Shepherdstown, WV 25443 United States
Phone: 304-876-5227   Fax: 304-876-5028
Website: www.shepherd.wvnet.edu/iesweb/
Membership: 1–100
Scope: State
Description: B.S. in Environmental Studies with focus in physical and biological sciences or resource management.

Keyword(s): Ecosystems (precious), Oceans/Coasts/Beaches, Public Lands/Greenspace, Recreation/Ecotourism, Sprawl/Urban Planning, Water Habitats & Quality, Wildlife & Species

Contact(s):
Ed Snyder, Director; 304-876-5227; Fax: 304-876-5028; iesweb@shepherd.edu

SILLMAN UNIVERSITY
CENTER OF EXCELLENCE—COASTAL RESOURCE MANAGEMENT
Dumaguete City, 6200 Philippines
Phone: 63 35 225 6711/225 6855   Fax: 63 35 225 4608
E-mail: admsucrm@mozcom.com
Website: http://su.edu.ph
Founded: 1901
Description: Sillman University, with USAID, created an environmental awareness program. Starting with a coastal resource management, it specifically works with the marine laboratory of the university and is currently working on environmental education and environmental communication within the university and in the community through extension programs.

Contact(s):
Hilconida Calumpong, Researcher; 633-522-5250; mlsucrm@mozcom.com
Janet Estacion, Researcher/Professor; 633-522-5250; mlsucrm@mozcom.com
Mikhail Maxino, Dean, College of Law/Researcher; 633-522-5671; admsucrm@mozcom.com
Roy Olsen de Leon, Researcher/Teacher; 633-522-5671; admsucrm@mozcom.com
Betsy Tan, Dean, College of Education; 633-522-5671; admsucrm@mozcom.com

SLIPPERY ROCK UNIVERSITY
101 Eisenberg Bldg. SRU
Slippery Rock, PA 16057 United States
Phone: 724-738-4555   Fax: 724-738-4502
E-mail: pcee@sru.edu
Website: www.pcee.org/

Membership: 1,001–10,000
Scope: State, National, International
Description: Slippery Rock University provides five environmental degree programs. They include three undergraduate: environmental education, studies and science and two graduate programs: environmental education and sustainable systems

Keyword(s): Agriculture/Farming, Ecosystems (precious), Forests/Forestry, Land Issues, Water Habitats & Quality, Wildlife & Species

Contact(s):
Paulette Johnson, Pennsylvania Center for Environmental Education, Director; 724-738-4555
Bruce Boliver, Park and Resource Management, Chairman; 724-738-2068
Beverly Buchert, Environmental Studies, Coordinator; 724-738-2389
Dan Dziubek, Institute for the Environment Executive, Committee Chair; 724-738-2958
Dan Dziubek, Environmental Education, Coordinator; 724-738-2958
Michael Stapleton, Environmental Science, Program Coordinator; 724-738-2495

SONOMA STATE UNIVERSITY
DEPARTMENT OF ENVIRONMENTAL STUDIES AND PLANNING
Rachel Carson Hall 18
1801 E. Cotati Avenue
Rohnert Park, CA 94928 United States
Phone: 707-664-2306   Fax: 707-664-4202
E-mail: ensp@sonoma.edu
Website: www.sonoma.edu/ensp/
Scope: National
Description: Interdisciplinary academic program with B.S. and B.A. degrees. Study tracks in environmental education, energy management and design, city and regional planning, water quality, hazardous materials management, and environmental conservation and restoration

Contact(s):
Steve Orlick, Department Chair; 707-664-2414; steve.orlick@sonoma.edu

SONOMA STATE UNIVERSITY
DEPARTMENT OF ENVIRONMENTAL STUDIES AND PLANNING
ENVIRONMENTAL TECHNOLOGY CENTER
1801 E. Cotati Ave.
Rohnert Park, CA 94928 United States
Phone: 707-664-2577   Fax: 707-664-3920
E-mail: armando.navarro@sonoma.edu
Website: www.sonoma.edu/ensp/etc.html
Founded: 2001
Membership: 1–100
Scope: Local, State
Description: The Environmental Technology Center (ETC) is an on-campus demonstration, education, and research center which serves the campus and surrounding communities through programs in environmental education, professional training, teacher workshops, demonstration projects, and scientific research. The ETC focuses its activities in the fields of renewable energy, energy efficiency, and green building design and construction.

SOUTH DAKOTA STATE UNIVERSITY
DEPARTMENT OF WILDLIFE AND FISHERIES SCIENCES
P.O. Box 2140B
Brookings, SD 57007-1696 United States
Phone: 605-688-6121   Fax: 605-688-4515
E-mail: charles_scalet@sdstate.edu
Website: wfs.sdstate.edu

Founded: 1963

Scope: Local, State, Regional, National

Description: Fish and wildlife research, education, and services with emphasis on fisheries management, wildlife management, fisheries and wildlife ecology, and wetland ecology and management.

Contact(s):
Charles Berry, Cooperative Fish and Wildlife Research Unit, Leader; charles_berry@sdstate.edu
Michael Brown, Professor; michael_brown@sdstate.edu
Steven Chipps, Assistant Professor; steven_chipps@sdstate.edu
Lester Flake, Distinguished Professor; lester_flake@sdstate.edu
Kenneth Higgins, Professor; kenneth_higgins@sdstate.edu
Daniel Hubbard, Professor; daniel_hubbard@sdstate.edu
Jonathan Jenks, Professor; jonathan_jenks@sdstate.edu
Charles Scalet, Head; charles_scalet@sdstate.edu
David Willis, Distinguished Professor; david_willis@sdstate.edu

SOUTHERN CONNECTICUT STATE UNIVERSITY
CENTER FOR THE ENVIRONMENT
501 Crescent St., Jennings Hall, Rm. 342
New Haven, CT 06515 United States
Phone: 203-392-6600   Fax: 203-392-6614
Website: www.scsu.ctstateu.edu

Membership: 1–100

Scope: International

Description: The Center for the Environment is an academic center granting graduate and undergraduate degrees in environmental areas, conducting research, and developing epistemological models. An active field study program includes experiences in Costa Rica, South Africa, Madagascar, Ecuador (including the Galapagos Islands) and various sites in the U.S.

Publication(s): SEED Newsletter

Contact(s):
Vincent Breslin, Professor of Environmental Studies
Susan Hageman, Chair of Science Education and Environmental Studies

SOUTHERN ILLINOIS UNIVERSITY CARBONDALE
DEPARTMENT OF FORESTRY
Southern Illinois University, Carbondale
Department of Foresty
1205 Lincoln Drv., Rm 184
Carbondale, IL 62901-4411 United States
Phone: 618-453-3341   Fax: 618-453-7475
E-mail: plc1@siu.edu
Website: www.siu.edu/~forestry.com

Founded: 1956

Membership: 101–1,000

Scope: Local, State, Regional, National, International

Description: The SIUC forestry program provides a comprehensive foundation in forestry. Our educational program leads to a bachelor of science degree in forestry and is accredited by the Society of American Foresters (SAF). Forestry students may choose to specialize in forest resource management or outdoor recreation resource management. In addition to the bachelor's degree, the department offers a master's degree in forestry and cooperative doctor's degree in geography and plant biology.

Keyword(s): Agriculture/Farming, Ecosystems (precious), Forests/Forestry, Land Issues, Public Lands/Greenspace, Recreation/Ecotourism, Water Habitats & Quality, Wildlife & Species

Contact(s):
John Phelps, Professor and Department Chair; SIUC-Department of Forestry, 1205 Lincoln Dr., Rm. 184, Mailcode 4411, Carbondale, IL 62901-4411; 618-453-3341; Fax: 618-453-7475; jphelps@siu.edu
Sara Baer, Researcher II; 618-453-3708
David Close, Researcher II; 618-453-7467; dclose@siu.edu
Patti Cludray, Office System Spec. I, Student Services - Web Master; 618-453-3341; plc1@siu.edu
Bonnie Middleton, Account Tech. III, Departmental Accountant; 618-453-3341
Cem Basman, Assistant Prof., Forest Recreation, Visitor Behavior, Social Psych.; 618-453-7476; cbasman@siu.edu
John Burde, Professor, Forest Recreation; 618-453-7463; jburde@siu.edu
Andrew Carver, Assistant Professor, Land Use and Resource Planning; 618-453-7461; acarver@siu.edu
John Groninger, Assistant Professor, Ecophysiology and Silviculture; 618-453-7462; jgroninge@siu.edu
Jean Mangun, Associate Professor, Human Dimensions of Natural Res. Mgmnt.; 618-453-3341; mangfor@siu.edu
Paul Roth, Professor, Forest Management and Protection; 618-453-7468
Charles Ruffner, Assistant Professor, Forest Measurements, Historical Ecology; 618-453-7469; ruffner@siu.edu
Karl Williard, Assistant Professor, Forest Hydrology, Watershed Mgmnt.; 618-453-7478; williard@siu.edu
James Zaczek, Assistant Professor, Forest Resources; 618-453-7465; zaczek@siu.edu

SOUTHERN OREGON UNIVERSITY
ENVIRONMENTAL EDUCATION PROGRAM
BIOLOGY DEPARTMENT
1250 Siskiyou Blvd.
Ashland, OR 97520 United States
Phone: 541-552-6876   Fax: 541-552-6415
E-mail: seec@students.sou.edu
Website: www.sou.edu/biology/enved/mainpage.htm

Founded: 1990

Membership: 1–100

Scope: State

Description: This graduate program grants a Master of Science degree, and provides hands-on learning experiences in conservation biology, interpretive practices, field interpretation, and field studies in southwestern Oregon and elsewhere in the state for students committed to careers in environmental education. Studies are also required in biology and related disciplines of choice to complete the program.

Contact(s):
Stewart Janes, Contact

SOUTHWEST CENTER FOR ENVIRONMENTAL RESEARCH AND POLICY (SCERP)
5250 Campanile Drive
San Diego, CA 92182-1913 United States
Phone: 619-594-0568   Fax: 619-594-0752
E-mail: scerp@mail.sdsu.edu
Website: www.scerp.org

Founded: 1989

Scope: Local, State, Regional, National, International

Description: Research and policy for environmental, ecological and human health issues in the U.S.-Mexican border region.

Publication(s): Technical reports, Border Institute reports, Border Monograph

Keyword(s): Agriculture/Farming, Air Quality/Atmosphere, Climate Change, Development/Developing Countries, Ecosystems (precious), Energy, Ethics/Environmental Justice, Executive/Legislative/Judicial Reform, Finance/Banking/Trade, Forests/Forestry, Land Issues, Oceans

Contact(s):
D. Van Schoik, Director; 619-594-0568; Fax: 619-594-0752; scerp@mail.sdsu.edu

EDUCATIONAL INSTITUTIONS – S

ST. CLOUD STATE UNIVERSITY
720 4th Ave., S
St. Cloud, MN 56301-4498 United States
Phone: 320-255-3235   Fax: 320-308-0121
E-mail: ets@condor.stcloudstate.edu
Website: www.stcloudstate.edu

Scope: State

Description: Linking the human and natural world with programs designed to foster environmental and technological literacy and prepare students who can integrate the interconnections of science, technology, society and the environment through research and assessment.

Contact(s):
Charles Rose, Director of Environmental and Technological Studies
Michael Karian, Associate Professor; 320-255-3966

ST. LAWRENCE UNIVERSITY
ENVIRONMENTAL STUDIES PROGRAM
Canton, NY 13617 United States
Phone: 315-229-5814   Fax: 315-229-5802
Website: web.stlawu.edu/envstudies

Founded: 1856

Scope: State

Description: St. Lawrence University is a liberal arts and sciences institution. The institution offers one of the oldest environmental studies programs in the nation. The university is committed to environmentally responsible management practices and comprehensive outdoor education programs.

Keyword(s): Ecosystems (precious)

Contact(s):
Glenn Harris, Director

ST. NORBERT COLLEGE
CENTER FOR INTERNATIONAL EDUCATION
100 Grant St.
De Pere, WI 54115-2099 United States
Phone: 920-337-3181   Fax: 920-403-4010
E-mail: mediarel@mail.snc.edu
Website: www.snc.edu/

Founded: 1990

Scope: State

Description: The Center conducts an Annual Global Ecology Series on themes such as the Great Lakes as an endangered resource of North America, Africa and women, population, and international policy-making. Instructional resources and In-service programs are provided for K-1.

Contact(s):
Joseph Tullbane, Associate Dean for International Studies; 920-403-3378; Fax: 920-403-4083; tulljd@mail.snc.edu

STANFORD UNIVERSITY
DEPARTMENT OF BIOLOGICAL SCIENCES
CENTER FOR CONSERVATION BIOLOGY
Herrin Labs, 385 Sierra Mall
Stanford, CA 94305-5020 United States
Phone: 650-723-5924   Fax: 650-723-5920
E-mail: consbio@bing.stanford.edu
Website: www.stanford.edu/group/CCB/index.htm

Founded: 1984

Scope: National

Description: To develop the science of conservation biology, including its application to solutions for critical conservation problems. The Center conducts scientific and policy research that is building a sound basis for the conservation, management, and restoration of biotic diversity around the world. The overall goal is to develop ways and means for protecting Earth's life support systems and thus enhancing future human well-being.

Publication(s): See publication website

Contact(s):
Paul Ehrlich, President

STANFORD UNIVERSITY
MORRISON INSTITUTE FOR POPULATION AND RESOURCE STUDIES
371 Sierra Mall (Gilbert Bldg.)
Stanford, CA 94305-5020 United States
Phone: 650-723-7518   Fax: 650-725-8244
E-mail: morrinst@stanford.edu
Website: www.stanford.edu/group/morrinst/

Founded: 1986

Scope: National, International

Description: To support research and education in the interconnected global issues of population growth, its effects on the environment, the pressure on natural resources, and the capacity of many nations to achieve sustainable socioeconomic development. Issues are approached through interdisciplinary perspectives of population biology, economics, and social and medical sciences.

Contact(s):
Marcus Feldman, Director; 650-725-1867

STATE UNIVERSITY OF NEW YORK AT CORTLAND
GEOLOGY DEPARTMENT
P.O. Box 2000
Cortland, NY 13045-0900 United States
Phone: 607-753-2011   Fax: 607-753-2927
E-mail: stouts@cortland.edu
Website: www.cortland.edu/

Scope: State

Contact(s):
Christopher Cirmo, Environmental Geology and Environmental Sciences, Coordinator; 607-753-2924; cirmoc@cortland.edu
Jack Sheltmire, Environmental and Outdooor Education, Coordinator; 607-753-5488; sheltmirej@cortland.edu

STATE UNIVERSITY OF NEW YORK AT STONY BROOK
MARINE SCIENCES RESEARCH CENTER
Nickels Road
Stony Brook, NY 11794 United States
Phone: 631-632-8700   Fax: 631-632-8820
Website: www.msrc.sunysb.edu/

Description: University-wide center to develop marine and atmospheric research, instructional programs and facilities for the State University of New York. Ongoing research projects are directed toward coastal oceanographic processes, marine environmental problems and management, atmospheric sciences and resources management. Among the Center's organized units are the Living Marine Resources Institute, the Waste Reduction and Management Institute, and the Coastal Ocean Action Strategies Institute

Keyword(s): Air Quality/Atmosphere, Oceans/Coasts/Beaches, Water Habitats & Quality

Contact(s):
Marvin Geller, Dean and Director; 516-632-8701, mgeller@notes.cc.sunysb.edu
Nicholas Fisher, Associate Dean; 516-632-8649; nfisher@notes.cc.sunysb.edu
Glenn Lopez, Graduate Programs; 516-632-8660; glopez@notes.cc.sunysb.edu
W. Wise, Associate Director; 516-632-8656

STATE UNIVERSITY OF NEW YORK COLLEGE OF ENVIRONMENTAL SCIENCE AND FORESTRY
1 Forestry Dr.
Syracuse, NY 13210-2778 United States
Phone: 315-470-6500   Fax: 315-470-6953
E-mail: esfinfo@esf.edu
Website: www.esf.edu

Founded: 1911

Scope: State

Description: Research has been a hallmark of ESF since its inception. Recent wildlife studies have aimed toward reintroducing lynx and moose to the Adirondack Park; application of molecular biology techniques to identify migrant bird populations; restoration of muskellunge and sturgeon in the St. Lawrence River system; analysis of flamingo population dynamics in Mexico; tailoring black cherry clones for fast growth and straight limbs; and researching willow plantations as a source of biomass energy

Contact(s):
Israel Cabasso, Polymer Research Institute, Director; 315-470-4767
Robert Hanna, N.C. Brown Laboratory for Ultrastructure Studies, Director; 315-470-6880
Hannu Makkonen, Empire State Paper Research Institute, Director; 315-470-6900
William Porter, Adirondack Ecological Center, Director; 315-470-6798
Neil Ringler, Roosevelt Wildlife Station, Director; 315-470-6770
Richard Smardon, Great Lakes Research Consortium, Co-Director; 315-470-6816
Richard Smardon, Environmental Institute, Randolf G. Pack, Director; 315-470-6636
H. Underwood, Cooperative Park Studies Unit, Director; 315-470-6820
Christopher Westbrook, Forest Technician Program, Director; 315-848-2566
William Winter, Cellulose Research Institute, Acting Director; 315-470-6855
Thomas Amidon, Faculty of Paper Science and Engineering, Chair; 315-470-6502
William Bentley, Faculty of Forestry, Chair; 315-470-6536
James Hassett, Faculty of Environmental Resources and Forest Engineering, Chair; 315-470-6633
John Hassett, Faculty of Chemistry, Chair; 315-470-6855
George Kyanka, Faculty of Construction Management and Wood Products Engineering; 315-470-6880
Neil Ringler, Faculty of Environmental and Forest Biology, Chair; 315-470-6743
Richard Smardon, Faculty of Environmental Studies, Chair; 315-470-6636
Wayne Zipperer, U.S. Forest Service Unit, Deputy Project Leader; 315-448-3201

STEPHEN F. AUSTIN STATE UNIVERSITY ARTHUR TEMPLE COLLEGE OF FORESTRY
P.O. Box 6109-SFA
Nacogdoches, TX 75962-6109 United States
Phone: 936-468-3301   Fax: 936-468-2489
Website: www.sfasu.edu

Founded: 1946

Membership: 101–1,000

Scope: State, Regional, National

Description: Our mission is to maintain excellence in teaching, research and outreach to enhance the health and vitality of the environment through sustainable management, conservation, and protection of our forests and natural resources.

Keyword(s): Climate Change, Ecosystems (precious), Energy, Forests/Forestry, Land Issues, Pollution (general), Public Lands/Greenspace, Recreation/Ecotourism, Water Habitats & Quality, Wildlife & Species

Contact(s):
R. Beasley, Water Quality/Forest Hydrology
R. Beasley, Dean; 936-468-2164; sbeasley@sfasu.edu
Mingteh Chang, Forest Hydrology; 936-468-2195; mchang@sfasu.edu
Edward Dougal, Forest Products; 936-468-2006; edougal@sfasu.edu
Jeffery Duguay, Forest Resources/Wildlife Management; 936-468-2196; jduguay@sfasu.edu
Kenneth Farrish, Soil Science; 936-468-2475; kfarrish@sfasu.edu
Michael Fountain, Silviculture/Forest Ecology; 936-468-2313; mfountain@sfasu.edu
James Kroll, Forest Wildlife Management; 936-468-1198; jkroll@sfasu.edu
Gary Kronrad, Forest Economics; 936-468-2473; gdkronrad@sfasu.edu
David Kulhavy, Landscape Ecology
David Kulhavy, Forest Entomology; 936-468-2141; dkulhavy@sfasu.edu
Michael Legg, Forest Recreation Management; 936-468-2246; mlegg@sfasu.edu
Shiyou Li, Medicinal Plants; 936-468-2071; lis@sfasu.edu
Brian Oswald, Fire Management and Silviculture; 936-468-2275; boswald@sfasu.edu
Paul Risk, Interpretation/Conflict Resolution; 936-468-2492; prisk@sfasu.edu
Peter Siska, GIS/Remote Sensing; 936-468-1347; siska@sfasu.edu
Daniel Unger, Remote Sensing/Mensuration; 936-468-2234; unger@sfasu.edu
R. Whiting, Forest Wildlife Management; 936-468-2125; mwhiting@sfasu.edu
Hans Williams, Urban Forestry
Hans Williams, Forest Eco-Physiology; 936-468-2127; hwilliams@sfasu.edu

STERLING COLLEGE
P.O. Box 72
Craftsbury Common, VT 05827-0072 United States
Phone: 802-586-7711   Fax: 802-586-2596
E-mail: admissions@sterlingcollege.edu
Website: www.sterlingcollege.edu

Founded: 1958

Membership: 101–1,000

Scope: Regional

Description: Sterling College offers a Bachelor of Arts degree with concentrations in outdoor education and leadership, sustainable agriculture, and wildlands ecology, and management.

Publication(s): Common Voice

Keyword(s): Agriculture/Farming, Ecosystems (precious), Energy, Forests/Forestry, Oceans/Coasts/Beaches, Water Habitats & Quality, Wildlife & Species

Contact(s):
John Williamson, President
John Zaber, Director of Admissions
Chris Monz, Dean; cmonz@sterlingcollege.edu

T

TANZANIA SCHOOL OF JOURNALISM
Box 4067
Dar-Es-Salaam, 4067 Tanzania
Phone: 255-51-700236   Fax: 255-51-700756
E-mail: info@tsjtz.com
Website: www.tsjtz.com

Scope: International

Description: The Tanzania School of Journalism is charged by law with journalism training. It annually enrollls about ninety university potential students, turning out the same number of journalists.

EDUCATIONAL INSTITUTIONS – T

Keyword(s): Ethics/Environmental Justice
Contact(s):
Wilhelmina Balygatti
Robert Mfugale
Ernest Mrutu
Jerome Ng'itu
Ayub Rioba, Coordinator of Studies
Mwajabu Rossi, Principal Prof.

TEMPLE UNIVERSITY
ENVIRONMENTAL STUDIES PROGRAM
309 Gladfelter Hall
Philadelphia, PA 19122 United States
Phone: 215-204-5918   Fax: 215-204-7833
Website: www.temple.edu/env-stud
Scope: State
Description: Students majoring in Environmental Studies will be equipped with the scholarly background and intellectual skills to understand a wide range of pressing environmental issues, and they will come to appreciate the physical, economic, political, demographic, and ethical factors that define those issues. Among the many environmental problems central to our program are groundwater contamination, suburban sprawl, river basin management, and the greening of abandoned urban spaces.
Contact(s):
Robert Mason, Director

TENNESSEE TECHNOLOGICAL UNIVERSITY
DEPARTMENT OF BIOLOGY
Department of Biology
Box 5063
TTU
Cookeville, TN 38505 United States
Phone: 931-372-3134   Fax: 931-372-6257
E-mail: dlcombs@tntech.edu
Website: www.tntech.edu/www/acad/biol/
Contact(s):
Jeffrey Boles, Environmental Science; P.O. Box 5055, Cookeville, TN 38505; 931-372-3844; jboles@tntech.edu
Daniel Combs, Wildlife and Fisheries Science; dlcombs@tntech.edu

TEXAS A AND M UNIVERSITY AT COLLEGE STATION
COLLEGE OF AGRICULTURE AND LIFE SCIENCES
113 Administration Bldg.
College Station, TX 77843-2142 United States
Phone: 979-845-4747   Fax: 979-845-9938
E-mail: agprogram@tamu.edu
Website: www.agprogram.tamu.edu
Membership: 101–1,000
Scope: State
Contact(s):
Bob Brown, Institute for Renewable Natural Resources, Director; 979-845-5777
Bob Brown, Wildlife and Fisheries Sciences, Head; 979-845-5777
Tat Smith, Forest Science, Head; 979-845-5000
Bob Whitson, Rangeland Ecology and Management, Head; 979-845-5579
Peter Witt, Recreation, Parks, and Tourism Sciences, Head; 979-845-7324

TEXAS A AND M UNIVERSITY AT COMMERCE
DEPARTMENT OF AGRICULTURAL SCIENCES
2600 S. Neal St.
Commerce, TX 75429-3011 United States
Phone: 903-886-5358   Fax: 903-886-5990
Website: www.tamu-commerce.edu
Founded: 1889
Membership: 1–100
Scope: State
Description: Educational institution offering B.S. and M.S. degrees in agricultural fields and pre-wildlife management programs.
Contact(s):
David Crenshaw, Pre-Wildlife Management, Advisor; 903-886-5329; david_crenshaw@tamu-commerce.edu
Robert Williams, Interim, Dept. Head

TEXAS A AND M UNIVERSITY AT KINGSVILLE
CAESAR KLEBERG WILDLIFE RESEARCH INSTITUTE
MSC 218
Kingsville, TX 78363 United States
Phone: 361-593-3922   Fax: 361-593-3924
Website: ckwri.tamuk.edu/
Founded: 1981
Scope: State, Regional, International
Description: A nonprofit institute that emphasizes research on wildlife and range management in Texas. Some work also done in Mexico and Canada. Research specialties include deer, quail, waterfowl, wild oats, wildlife diseases, semi-arid land ecology, animal nutrition, habitat requirements, GIS applications, and nongame wildlife.
Keyword(s): Agriculture/Farming, Ecosystems (precious), Forests/Forestry, Land Issues, Public Lands/Greenspace, Water Habitats & Quality, Wildlife & Species
Contact(s):
Fred Bryant, Director; 361-593-4025; Fax: 361-593-3924

TEXAS A AND M UNIVERSITY SYSTEM
TEXAS COOPERATIVE EXTENSION
DEPARTMENT OF WILDLIFE AND FISHERIES SCIENCES
210 Nagle Hall
TAMUS 2258
Texas A&M
College Station, TX 77843-2258 United States
Phone: 979-845-5777   Fax: 979-845-7103
E-mail: tony@tamu.edu
Website: wildlife.tamu.edu
Scope: Local, State, Regional, National, International
Description: Texas Cooperative Extension — Wildlife & Fisheries develops and delivers outreach, technology transfer and extension education programs to land managers, youth, and the citizens of Texas. We also participate in applied research projects, as well as provide liaison among public and private organizations on natural resource issues.
Keyword(s): Agriculture/Farming, Development/Developing Countries, Ecosystems (precious), Forests/Forestry, Land Issues, Oceans/Coasts/Beaches, Sprawl/Urban Planning, Water Habitats & Quality, Wildlife & Species
Contact(s):
Bob Brown, Director & Department Head; Institute of Renewable Natural Resources,
C. Hanselka, Associate Department Head and Extension Program Leader; Rangeland Ecology and Management, Rt. 2 Box 589, Corpus Christi, TX 78406-9704; 361-265-9203; Fax: 361-265-9434; c-hanselka@tamu.edu
Neal Wilkins, Associate Department Head and Extension Program Leader; Department of Wildlife and Fisheries Sciences, 2258 TAMU, 111 Nagle Hall, Texas A&M University, College Station, TX 77843-2258; 979-845-7471; Fax: 979-845-7103; nwilkins@tamu.edu

TEXAS CHRISTIAN UNIVERSITY
ENVIRONMENTAL SCIENCE PROGRAM
2800 South University Drive
Fort Worth, TX 76109 United States
Phone: 817-257-7271
Website: www.ensc.tcu.edu/
Membership: 1–100

Scope: State
Keyword(s): Air Quality/Atmosphere, Ecosystems (precious), Oceans/Coasts/Beaches, Water Habitats & Quality
Contact(s):
Leo Newland, Director; L.Newland@tcu.edu

TEXAS TECH UNIVERSITY
DEPARTMENT OF RANGE WILDLIFE AND FISHERIES
P.O. Box 42125
Lubbock, TX 79409-2125 United States
Phone: 806-742-2841   Fax: 806-742-2280
Website: www.rw.ttu.edu/dept
Membership: 1–100
Scope: State
Description: University Department
Publication(s): See publication website
Contact(s):
Ernest Fish, Wildlife Science and Fisheries Science, Chairman; fish@water.rw.ttu.edu

TREASURE VALLEY COMMUNITY COLLEGE
DEPARTMENT OF NATURAL RESOURCES
650 College Blvd.
Ontario, OR 97914 United States
Phone: 541-881-8822, ext. 258
E-mail: jtiffany@tvcc.cc
Website: www.tvcc.cc.or.us/NatRes/
Description: Offers Associate of Applied Science focusing on forestry, range management or wildland fire management.
Contact(s):
John Russell, Professor; John_Russell@mailman.tvcc.cc.or.us

TUFTS UNIVERSITY CIVIL ENGINEERING
Anderson Hall
Medford, MA 02155 United States
Phone: 617-627-3211   Fax: 617-627-3994
Website: www.tufts.edu/cee
Membership: 101–1,000
Scope: National, International
Contact(s):
Linfield Brown, Environmental Engineering, Contact; 617-627-2273; lbrown1@tufts.edu
John Durant, Hazardous Material Management, Contact; 617-627-5489; jdurant@emerald.tufts.edu
Christopher Swan, Environmental Geotechnology and Geotechnical Engineering; 617-627-2212; cswan@emerald.tufts.edu
Richard Vogel, Water Resources, Contact; 617-627-4260; rvogel@tufts.edu

TULANE ENVIRONMENTAL LAW CLINIC
ENVIRONMENTAL LAW CLINIC
6329 Freret St.
New Orleans, LA 70118-6231 United States
Phone: 504-865-5789   Fax: 504-862-8721
Website: www.tulane.edu/~telc
Founded: 1989
Membership: 1–100
Scope: State
Description: Provides free legal assistance through its student attorneys to community organizations and indigent persons seeking to protect public health and the environment.
Keyword(s): Agriculture/Farming, Air Quality/Atmosphere, Ethics/Environmental Justice, Land Issues, Oceans/Coasts/Beaches, Pollution (general), Water Habitats & Quality, Wildlife & Species
Contact(s):
Adam Babich, Director
Rebecca Dayries, Community Outreach Director
Karla Raettig, Staff Attorney
John Suttles, Deputy Director

TULANE INSTITUTE FOR ENVIRONMENTAL LAW AND POLICY
TULANE LAW SCHOOL
6329 Freret St.
New Orleans, LA 70118-6231 United States
Phone: 504-862-8829   Fax: 504-862-8857
E-mail: edan@law.tulane.edu
Website: www.law.tulane.edu/prog/specialty/environmental/envirolaw/institute.htm
Scope: Local, State, Regional, National, International
Description: The Institute is designed to enhance the intellectual contributions of the Tulane Law School as a leader in environmental law, to provide a center for discussion of critical issues, and to provide its law students with opportunities for involvement in environmental policy-making. It initiates and facilitates conferences, symposia and workshops that support the development of environmental policy.
Contact(s):
Eric Dannenmaier, Director; 504-862-8829; Fax: 504-862-8857; edan@law.tulane.edu

TULANE UNIVERSITY
DEPARTMENT OF ECOLOGY AND EVOLUTIONARY BIOLOGY
Dinwiddie Hall, Room 310
6823 Saint Charles Avenue
New Orleans, LA 70118 United States
Phone: 504-865-5191   Fax: 504-862-8706
Website: www.tulane.edu/~eeob
Membership: 1–100
Scope: State, Regional
Description: The faculty and students of the Department of Ecology and Evolutionary Biology (EEB) are actively engaged in the study of organisms, populations, communities, ecosystems, and global systems. We endeavor to create, communicate, and apply knowledge of these biological systems.
Keyword(s): Ecosystems (precious), Forests/Forestry, Land Issues, Oceans/Coasts/Beaches, Pollution (general), Population, Public Lands/Greenspace, Water Habitats & Quality, Wildlife & Species
Contact(s):
David Heins, Professor and Chair; 504-865-5563; heins@tulane.edu

TULANE UNIVERSITY
TULANE LAW SCHOOL
ENVIRONMENTAL LAW PROGRAM
Weinmann Hall, Suite 255
6329 Freret Street
New Orleans, LA 70118-6231 United States
Phone: 504-865-5946   Fax: 504-862-8855
E-mail: admissions@law.tulane.edu
Website: www.law.tulane.edu/
Founded: 1981
Scope: Local, State, Regional, National
Description: Environmental law education, research, and advocacy through faculty, staff, JD and graduate student body.
Publication(s): See publication website
Contact(s):
Adam Babich, Director, Environmental Law Clinic
Eric Dannenmaier, Director, Institute of Environmental Law and Policy
Oliver Houck, Director; ohouck@law.tulane.edu
Gunther Handl, Chair, International Environmental Law

EDUCATIONAL INSTITUTIONS – U

U

UNC-CH ENVIRONMENTAL RESOURCE PROGRAM
CB# 1105 Miller Hall
UNC-CH
Chapel Hill, NC 27599 United States
Phone: 919-966-7754   Fax: 919-966-9920
E-mail: erp@sph.unc.edu
Website: www.sph.unc.edu/erp

Founded: 1985

Scope: State

Description: The ERP was established to link the resources of the University with North Carolina communities. Since its inception, the ERP has provided information, technical assistance, and training to citizen groups, local governments and school teachers, and has facilitated collaborative decisionmaking about environmental issues. The ERP's main program areas include environmental education, community outreach and education, and collaborative and policy research.

Publication(s): CEHS Sentinel, The Guide to North Carolina Environmental Groups, Working Together, Community Based Approaches to Prevent Childhood Lead Poisoning, Superfund Research Program activities, The Superfund Scoop, The Link

Keyword(s): Public Health

Contact(s):
Frances Lynn, Director
Kathleen Gray, Associate Director

UNITY COLLEGE
90 Quacker Hill Rd
Unity, ME 04988 United States
Phone: 207-948-3131   Fax: 207-948-6277
Website: www.unity.edu/

Founded: 1966
Membership: 101–1,000
Scope: National

Description: Unity College is a small, liberal arts college in rural Maine with degree programs specializing in natural resource management and wilderness-based recreation.

Keyword(s): Agriculture/Farming, Ecosystems (precious), Executive/Legislative/Judicial Reform, Forests/Forestry, Public Health, Public Lands/Greenspace, Recreation/Ecotourism, Water Habitats & Quality, Wildlife & Species

Contact(s):
Ed Beals, Botany and Ecology
A. Chacko, Aquaculture
Larry Farnsworth, Conservation Law Enforcement
Doug Fox, Arboriculture
Tom Mullins, Park Management,
Jim Nelson, Wildlife
David Oakes, Environmental Education
Dave Potter, Fisheries

UNIVERSIDADE FEDERAL DO PARANA
A.P. 19031 Centro
Politechnico-Curitiba, Parana, 81531-970
Phone: 55-41-366-3144   Fax: 55-41-266-2042
E-mail: nimad@cce.ufpr.br

Contact(s):
Jose Andriguetto, Research Director
Edith Fanta, Adjunct Professor

UNIVERSIDADE FEDERAL DO PARANA
NIMAD-NUCI FOUS INTERDISCIPLINAR DE MELO AMBIENTE E DESENVOLVIMENTO
Centro Politechnico
Curitiba, Brazil
Phone: 5.5041366272e+011   Fax: 5.5041366272e+011
E-mail: nimad@cce.ufpr.br

Founded: 1989

Description: The objective of the NUCLEOUS e NIMAD is interdisciplinary research, teaching and extension directed to natural resource preservation, environmental education and sustainable development promotion.

Contact(s):
Jose Andriguetto, E. Research Coordinator and Research Director; 550-413-6627; nimad@cce.ufpr.br
Ziole Malhadas, E. Coordinator; 550-412-5244; ziolezm@cwb.matrix.com.br

UNIVERSITE LAVAL
Université Laval
Quebec, G1K 7P4 Quebec Canada
Phone: 418-656-3333   Fax: 418-656-2809
E-mail: sg@sg.ulaval.ca
Website: www.ulaval.ca/

Founded: 1852
Membership: 10,001–100,000
Scope: Local, State, Regional, National, International

Description: First francophone university in North America and firmly established as a leader among large research universities in Canada and in the francophone world, the Université Laval has a highly enviable tradition and reputation with respect to teaching, research and creativity.

Keyword(s): Agriculture/Farming, Air Quality/Atmosphere, Climate Change, Development/Developing Countries, Ecosystems (precious), Energy, Ethics/Environmental Justice, Executive/Legislative/Judicial Reform, Finance/Banking/Trade, Forests/Forestry, Land Issues, Oceans

Contact(s):
Michel Pigeon, Rector; Pavillon des Sciences de l'éducation, Bureau 1656, Université Laval, Quebec, Quebec G1K 7P4; 418-656-2272; Fax: 418-656-7917; Michel.Pigeon@rec.ulaval.ca
Lise Darveau-Fournier, Vice-Rector (Human Resources); Pavillon Jean-Charles-Bonenfant, 5e Etage, Université Laval, Quebec, Quebec G1K 7P4; 418-656-3154; Fax: 418-656-2455; vrrh@vrrh.ulaval.ca
Claude Godbout, Vice-Rector (Administration and Finance); Pavillon Jean-Charles-Bonenfant, Bureau 3380, Université Laval, Quebec, Quebec G1K 7P4; 418-656-3988; Fax: 418-656-3300; Claude.Godbout@vrex.ulaval.ca
Gilles Kirouac, Secretary General; Pavillon Jean-Charles-Bonenfant, Bureau 2183, Université Laval, Quebec, Quebec G1K 7P4; 418-656-2732; Fax: 418-656-7394
Diane Lachapelle, Vice-Rector (Development); Pavillon Alphonse-Desjardins, Bureau 3555, Université Laval, Quebec, Quebec G1K 7P4; 418-656-2676; Fax: 418-656-5238; vrd@vrd.ulaval.ca
Raymond Leblanc, Vice-Rector (Research); Pavillon des Sciences de l'éducation, Bureau 1454, Université Laval, Quebec, Quebec G1K 7P4; 418-656-2599; Fax: 418-656-2401
Christiane Piché, Vice-Rector (Academic and Student Affairs); Pavillon des Sciences de l'éducation, Bureau 1534, Université Laval, Quebec, Quebec G1K 7P4; 418-656-2591; Fax: 418-656-3686; vraae@vraae.ulaval.ca
Michel Blackburn, (acting) Dean (Graduate Studies); Pavillon Jean-Charles-Bonenfant, Bureau 3460, Université Laval, Quebec, Quebec G1K 7P4; 418-656-2131; ext. 8383; Fax: 418-656-3691; Michel.Blackburn@fes.ulaval.ca
Serge Talbot, Director General (Undergraduate Studies); Pavillon Félix-Antoine-Savard, Bureau 332B, Université Laval, Quebec, Quebec G1K 7P4; 418-656-2131; ext. 5882; Fax: 418-656-3500; Serge.Talbot@dgpc.ulaval.ca

UNIVERSITE LAVAL
FACULTY OF AGRICULTURAL AND FOOD SCIENCES
Pavillon Paul-Comtois
Bureau 1122
Université Laval
Quebec, G1K 7P4 Quebec Canada
Phone: 418-656-3145   Fax: 418-656-7806
E-mail: fsaa@fsaa.ulaval.ca
Website: www.fsaa.ulaval.ca

Scope: Local, State, Regional, National, International

Description: Environment; Biological Agriculture; Plant Physiology; Plant Biology; Plant Ecology; Fodder Plants; Hydrology; Pollution; International Development; Natural Resources; Nordic Studies; Botany.

Contact(s):
   Guy Allard, Dean; Pavillon Paul-Comtois, Bureau 3219, Université Laval, Quebec, Quebec G1K 7P4; 418-656-2131; ext. 2706; Fax: 418-656-7856; Guy.Allard@plg.ulaval.ca
   Josée Fortin, Professor (expert in environment); Pavillon Paul-Comtois, Bureau 2201, Université Laval, Quebec, Quebec G1K 7P4; 418-656-2131; ext. 5528; Fax: 418-656-3723; Josee.Fortin@sga.ulaval.ca
   Jean-Paul Laforest, Professor (expert in environment); 418-656-2131; ext. 3496; Fax: 418-7806; Jean-Paul.Laforest@san.ulaval.ca
   Alain Olivier, Professor (expert in environment); Pavillon Paul-Comtois, Bureau 3425, Université Laval, Quebec, Quebec G1K 7P4; 418-656-2131; ext. 3601; Fax: 418-656-7856; Alain.Olivier@plg.ulaval.ca
   Line Rochefort, Professor (expert in environment); Pavillon Paul-Comtois, Bureau 3403, Université Laval, Quebec, Quebec G1K 7P4; 418-656-2131; ext. 2583

UNIVERSITE LAVAL
FACULTY OF ARCHITECTURE, PLANNING AND VISUAL ARTS
Edifice du Vieux-Seminaire de Quebec
1, Côte de la Fabrique
Université Laval
Quebec, G1R 3V6 Quebec Canada
Phone: 418-656-2546   Fax: 418-656-3325
E-mail: faaav@faaav.ulaval.ca
Website: www.faaav.ulaval.ca

Scope: Local, State, Regional, National, International

Description: Program in Regional Planning and Development

Contact(s):
   Claude Dubé, Dean; 418-656-2131; ext. 2546; Fax: 418-656-3325; Claude.Dube@faaav.ulaval.ca

UNIVERSITE LAVAL
FACULTY OF FORESTRY AND GEOMATICS
Pavillon Abitibi-Price
Bureau 1151
Université Laval
Quebec, G1K 7P4 Quebec Canada
Phone: 418-656-2131, ext. 3880   Fax: 418-656-3177
E-mail: ffg@ffg.ulaval.ca
Website: www.ffg.ulaval.ca

Scope: Local, State, Regional, National, International

Description: Programs in Agroforestry, Forest Ecosystem Management, Forestry, Geography, Forestry Management, Forest Operation, Wood Sciences, Forestry Sciences.

Contact(s):
   Denis Brière, Dean; 418-656-2131; ext. 7907; Fax: 418-656-5411; Denis.Briere@ffg.ulaval.ca
   Claude Camiré, Professor (expert in environment); Pavillon Abitibi-Price, Bureau 3163, Université Laval, Quebec, Quebec G1K 7P4; 418-656-2131; ext. 7773; Fax: 418-656-5262; Claude.Camire@sbf.ulaval.ca
   Luc Lebel, Professor (expert in environment); 418-656-2131; ext. 8835; Fax: 418-656-5262; Luc.Lebel@sbf.ulaval.ca
   Germain Tremblay, Professor (expert in environment); Pavillon Charles-De Koninck, Bureau 6249, Université Laval, Quebec, Quebec G1K 7P4; 418-656-2131; ext. 2230; Fax: 418-656-3960; Germain.Tremblay@ggr.ulaval.ca

UNIVERSITE LAVAL
FACULTY OF LAW
Pavillon Charles-De Koninck
Bureau 2407
Université Laval
Quebec, G1K 7P4 Quebec Canada
Phone: 418-656-3036   Fax: 418-656-7230
E-mail: fd@fd.ulaval.ca
Website: www.ulaval.ca/fd

Scope: Local, State, Regional, National, International

Description: Program in International and Transnational Law

Contact(s):
   Pierre Lemieux, Dean; 418-656-3511; Fax: 418-656-7714; Pierre.Lemieux@fd.ulaval.ca
   Maurice Arbour, Professor (expert in environment); Pavillon Charles-De Koninck, Bureau 2137, Université Laval, Quebec, Quebec G1K 7P4; 418-656-2131; ext. 5311; Fax: 418-656-7230; Maurice.Arbour@fd.ulaval.ca
   Lorne Giroux, Professor (expert in environment); Pavillon Charles-De Koninck, Bureau 2107, Université Laval, Quebec, Quebec G1K 7P4; 418-656-2131; ext. 3891; Fax: 418-656-7230; Lorne.Giroux@fd.ulaval.ca

UNIVERSITE LAVAL
FACULTY OF MEDICINE
Pavillon Ferdinand-Vandry
Bureau 1236
Université Laval
Quebec, G1K 7P4 Quebec Canada
Phone: 418-656-2331   Fax: 418-656-3442
E-mail: fmed@fmed.ulaval.ca
Website: www.fmed.ulaval.ca

Scope: Local, State, Regional, National, International

Description: Program in Community Health that analyzes environmental influences on social well-being.

Contact(s):
   Pierre Durand, Dean; 418-656-2131; ext. 2301; Fax: 418-656-5062; Pierre.Durand@fmed.ulaval.ca
   Yvon Cormier, Professor (expert in environment); 418-656-8711; Fax: 418-656-4762; Yvon.Cormier@med.ulaval.ca
   Roger Guay, Professor (expert in environment); Pavillon Ferdinand-Vandry, Bureau 2316, Université Laval, Quebec, Quebec G1K 7P4; 418-656-2131; ext. 5795; Fax: 418-656-7666; Roger.Guay@mcb.ulaval.ca

UNIVERSITE LAVAL
FACULTY OF PHILOSOPHY
Pavillon Félix-Antoine-Savard
Bureau 644
Université Laval
Quebec, G1K 7P4 Quebec Canada
Phone: 418-656-2244   Fax: 418-656-7267
E-mail: fp@fp.ulaval.ca
Website: www.fp.ulaval.ca

Scope: Local, State, Regional, National, International

Description: Programs in Philosophy and Thought Critical Dialogue. Courses include discussion of environmental influences.

Contact(s):
   Luc Langlois, Dean; 418-656-2642; Fax: 418-656-7267; doyen.langlois@fp.ulaval.ca

EDUCATIONAL INSTITUTIONS – U

UNIVERSITE LAVAL
FACULTY OF SCIENCES AND ENGINEERING
Pavillon Alexandre-Vachon
Bureau 1033
Université Laval
Quebec, G1K 7P4 Quebec Canada
Phone: 418-656-2163   Fax: 418-656-5902
E-mail: fsg@fsg.ulaval.ca
Website: www.fsg.ulaval.ca

Scope: Local, State, Regional, National, International

Description: Programs in Biochemistry, Biotechnology, Chemistry, Earth Sciences and Oceanography.

Contact(s):
- Jean Serodes, Dean; 418-656-2131; ext. 2354; Fax: 418-656-5902; Jean.Serodes@fsg.ulaval.ca
- Claude Barbeau, Professor (expert in environment); Pavillon Alexandre-Vachon, Bureau 1222C, Université Laval, Quebec, Quebec G1K 7P4; 418-656-2131; ext. 3537; Fax: 418-656-7916; Claude.Barbeau@chm.ulaval.ca
- Marcel Baril, Professor (expert in environment); 418-656-2131; ext. 2577; Fax: 418-656-2040; Marcel.Baril@phy.ulaval.ca
- Louis Bernatchez, Professor (expert in environment); Pavillon Alexandre-Vachon, Bureau 4042A, Université Laval, Quebec, Quebec G1K 7P4; 418-656-2131; ext. 3402; Fax: 418-656-2043; Louis.Bernatchez@bio.ulaval.ca
- Li Cheng, Professor (expert in environment); Pavillon Adrien-Pouliot, Bureau 3316-D, Université Laval, Quebec, Quebec G1K 7P4; 418-656-2131; ext. 7920; Fax: 418-656-7415; Li.Cheng@gmc.ulaval.ca
- Robert Chénevert, Professor (expert in environment); Pavillon Alexandre-Vachon, Bureau 1421, Université Laval, Quebec, Quebec G1K 7P4; 418-656-2131; ext. 3283; Fax: 418-656-7916; Robert.Chenevert@chm.ulaval.ca
- Josée Duchesne, Professor (expert in environment); Pavillon Adrien-Pouliot, Bureau 4501, Université Laval, Quebec, Quebec G1K 7P4; 418-656-2131; ext. 2177; Fax: 418-656-7339; Josee.Duchesne@ggl.ulaval.ca
- Rosa Galvez-Cloutier, Professor (expert in environment); Pavillon Adrien-Pouliot, Bureau 2915, Université Laval, Quebec, Quebec G1K 7P4; 418-656-2131; ext. 2045; Fax: 418-656-2928; Rosa.Cloutier@gci.ulaval.ca
- Marc Lavoie, Professor (expert in environment); Pavillon Alexandre-Vachon, Bureau 3426-B, Université Laval, Quebec, Quebec G1K 7P4; 418-656-2131; ext. 2151; Fax: 418-656-3664; Marc.Lavoie@bcm.ulaval.ca
- Jean-Baptiste Sérodes, Professor (expert in environment); Pavillon Alexandre-Vachon, Bureau 1040B, Université Laval, Quebec, Quebec G1K 7P4; 418-656-2131; ext. 2354; Fax: 418-656-5902; Jean.Serodes@fsg.ulaval.ca
- Jacques Turcotte, Professor (expert in environment); Pavillon Alexandre-Vachon, Bureau 1222A, Université Laval, Quebec, Quebec G1K 7P4; 418-656-2131; ext. 7474; Fax: 418-656-7916; Jacques.Turcotte@chm.ulaval.ca

UNIVERSITE LAVAL
FACULTY OF SOCIAL SCIENCES
Pavillon Charles-De Koninck
Bureau 3456
Université Laval
Quebec, G1K 7P4 Quebec Canada
Phone: 418-656-2615   Fax: 481-656-2114
E-mail: fss@fss.ulaval.ca
Website: www.fss.ulaval.ca

Scope: Local, State, Regional, National, International

Description: Programs in Economics and Politics.

Contact(s):
- Claude Beauchamp, Dean; 418-656-2131; ext. 2744; Fax: 418-656-3697; Claude.Beauchamp@fss.ulaval.ca
- Louis Guay, Professor (expert in environment); Pavillon Charles De Koninck, Bureau 4477, Université Laval, Quebec, Quebec G1K 7P4; 418-656-2131; ext. 6042; Fax: 418-656-7390; Louis.Guay@soc.ulaval.ca
- Louise Quesnel, Professeur (expert in environment); Pavillon Charles-De Koninck, Bureau 4403, Université Laval, Quebec, Quebec G1K 7P4; 418-656-2131; ext. 3989; Fax: 418-656-7861; Louise.Quesnel@pol.ulaval.ca
- Pierre St-Arnaud, Professor (expert in environment); Pavillon Charles-De Koninck, Bureau 6453, Université Laval, Quebec, Quebec G1K 7P4; 418-656-2131; ext. 3773; Fax: 418-656-7390; Pierre.St-Arnaud@soc.ulaval.ca

UNIVERSITE LAVAL
GROUP FOR RESEARCH ON ENERGY, ENVIRONMENT AND NATURAL RESOURCE ECONOMICS (GREEN)
Pavillon J.-A.-DeSeve
Université Laval
Quebec, G1K 7P4 Quebec Canada
Phone: 418-656-2131, ext. 2096   Fax: 418-656-7412
E-mail: green@ecn.ulaval.ca
Website: www.green.ecn.ulaval.ca

Founded: 1973

Scope: Local, State, Regional, National, International

Description: Fields of expertise of the GREEN are: theoretical and applied econometrics; theoretical and applied industrial engineering; renewable and not-renewable natural resources; regulation of the markets of energy; environmental regulation.

Contact(s):
- Philippe Barla, Director; 418-656-7707; Fax: 418-656-7412; philippe.barla@ecn.ulaval.ca

UNIVERSITE LAVAL
NORDIC STUDIES CENTER (CEN)
Pavillon Abitibi-Price
Université Laval
Quebec, G1K 7P4 Quebec Canada
Phone: 418-656-3340   Fax: 418-656-2978
E-mail: cen@cen.ulaval.ca
Website: www.cen.ulaval.ca

Founded: 1961

Scope: Local, State, Regional, National, International

Description: Fields of expertise of the CEN are: climatic changes; ecology of the caribou; balances and stability of the Nordic ecosystems; geophysics of permafrost; Nordic hydrology and limnology; trees line; paleoecology; network of environmental telemetry.

Contact(s):
- Yves Bégin, Director; 418-656-2131; ext. 3340; Fax: 418-656-2978; Yves.Begin@cen.ulaval.ca

UNIVERSITE LAVAL
QUEBEC-OCEAN
Pavillon Alexandre-Vachon
Bureau 2078
Université Laval
Quebec, G1K 7P4 Quebec Canada
Phone: 418-656-5917   Fax: 418-656-2339
E-mail: quebec-ocean@giroq.ulaval.ca
Website: www.quebec-ocean.ulaval.ca

Founded: 1970

Scope: Local, State, Regional, National, International

Description: Fields of the GIROQ are: littoral benthos; marine biochemistry; comportment of the marine invertebrates; marine ecology; carbon flux; genetics of the watery populations; macroalgaes; oceanography; plankton.

Contact(s):
- Louis Fortier, Director; 418-656-5917; Fax: 418-656-2339; quebec-ocean@giroq.ulaval.ca

UNIVERSITE LAVAL
RESEARCH CENTER FOR PLANNING AND REGIONAL DEVELOPMENT (CRAD)
Pavillon Félix-Antoine-Savard
Bureau 1636
Université Laval
Quebec, G1K 7P4 Quebec Canada
Phone: 418-656-2131, ext. 5899   Fax: 418-656-2018
E-mail: crad@crad.ulaval.ca
Website: www.crad.ulaval.ca

Founded: 1972
Scope: Local, State, Regional, National, International
Description: Fields of expertise of the CRAD are: regional planning; regional development; studies of urban dynamics; social space analysis; spatiality of the ratios men and women; transports and behaviors of mobility; land market; economic effects; architecture; town planning; drinking water management; ecology of the disturbed environments; quantitative and qualitative methods; geographical information systems.
Contact(s):
Marius Thériault, Director; 418-656-2131; ext. 5899; Fax: 418-656-2018; marius.theriault@crad.ulaval.ca

UNIVERSITE LAVAL
CENTER FOR RESEARCH IN ECONOMICS OF AGRI-FOOD (CREA)
Pavillon Paul-Comtois
Université Laval
Quebec, G1K 7P4 Quebec Canada
Phone: 418-656-2131, ext. 3254   Fax: 418-656-7821
E-mail: crea@eac.ulaval.ca
Website: www.fsaa.ulaval.ca/crea

Scope: Local, State, Regional, National, International
Description: Fields of expertise of the CREA are: agriculture; analysis of policies; comparative advantages; commerce; behavior of the consumer; durable development; agroalimentary economy; technical and allocative efficacy; world organization of trade (OMC); performance and strategy of enterprises; and food security.
Contact(s):
Robert Romain, Director; crea@eac.ulaval.ca

UNIVERSITE LAVAL
FACULTY OF AGRICULTURAL AND FOOD SCIENCES
1122, Pavillon Paul-Comtois
Université Laval
Quebec, G1K 7P4 Quebec Canada
Phone: 418-656-2131, ext. 3145   Fax: 418-656-7806
E-mail: fsaa@fsaa.ulaval.ca
Website: www.fsaa.ulaval.ca

Scope: Local, State, Regional, National, International
Description: Programs in Agroeconomics, Agrobiology, Agronomy, Plant Biology, Integrated Rural Development, Agri-Food Economics and Management, Agricultural Economics, Environmental Studies, Agri-Food Engineering, Agri-Environmental Engineering, Horticulture and Landscape Management, Agricultural Microbiology, Plant Technology, Dairy and Beef Production, Soil and Environment Science.
Contact(s):
Jean-Claude Dufour, Dean; fsaa@fsaa.ulaval.ca

UNIVERSITE LAVAL
FOREST BIOLOGY RESEARCH CENTER (CRBF)
Pavillon Charles-Eugene-Marchand
Université Laval
Quebec, G1K 7P4 Quebec Canada
Phone: 418-656-2131, ext. 3493   Fax: 418-656-7493
E-mail: crbf@crbf.ulaval.ca
Website: www.crbf.ulaval.ca

Founded: 1985
Scope: Local, State, Regional, National, International
Description: Fields of expertise of the CRBF are: biogeochemistry; in vitro culture; animal ecology; ecophysiology; entomology; genomics; hydrology; microbiology; pedology; pathology; physiology; and sylviculture.
Contact(s):
Louis Bernier, Director; crbf@crbf.ulaval.ca

UNIVERSITY OF AKRON
CENTER FOR ENVIRONMENTAL STUDIES
215 Crouse Hall
Akron, OH 44325-4102 United States
Phone: 330-972-5389   Fax: 330-972-7611
Website: www.uakron.edu/envstudies/

Founded: 1970
Membership: 1–100
Scope: Local, State, Regional
Description: The Center is a cooperative effort of several departments; biology, chemistry, chemical engineering, civil engineering, economics, education, geography, geology, history, library, political science, and sociology. The Center has directed: an undergraduate and graduate certificate program of study; responses to local inquiries regarding environmental problems; workshops and seminars on environmental issues.
Contact(s):
Ira Sasowsky, Director

UNIVERSITY OF ALASKA AT FAIRBANKS
COLLEGE OF SCIENCE, ENGINEERING AND MATHEMATICS
DEPARTMENT OF BIOLOGY AND WILDLIFE
211 Irving
Fairbanks, AK 99775 United States
Phone: 907-474-7671   Fax: 907-474-5101
Website: www.uaf.edu/csem

Scope: State
Contact(s):
Brian Barnes, Institute of Arctic Biology, Interim Director; 907-474-7648
Joe Margraf, Alaska Cooperative Fish and Wildlife Research Unit, Leader; 209 Irving, UAF, Fairbanks, AK 99775-7020; 907-474-7661; Fax: 907-474-6716; ffjfm1@uaf.edu
David Woodall, Dean of College of Science, Engineering & Mathematics

UNIVERSITY OF ALASKA FAIRBANKS
SCHOOL OF FISHERIES AND OCEAN SCIENCES
245 O'Neill Building, P.O. Box 757220
Fairbanks, AK 99775-7220 United States
Phone: 907-474-7824   Fax: 907-474-7204
E-mail: fysfos@uaf.edu
Website: www.sfos.uaf.edu

Membership: 101–1,000
Scope: Regional, International
Publication(s): SFOS Today
Contact(s):
Vera Alexander, Dean

UNIVERSITY OF ALBERTA
FACULTY OF AGRICULTURE, FORESTRY, AND HOME ECONOMICS
2-14 Agriculture Forestry Centre
Edmonton, T6G 2P5 Alberta Canada
Phone: 780-492-7042   Fax: 780-492-0097
Website: www.afhe.ualberta.ca/

Scope: National
Description: Undergraduate Degree Programs: B.Sc. in Agricultural and Food Business Management; Agriculture; Environmental and Conservation Sciences; Forest Business Management; Forestry; Human Ecology; Nutrition and Food

Sciences; and Human Ecology/Bachelor of Education. Graduate Degree Programs: M.Sc., M.Ag., M.Eng., Ph.D. in Agricultural Food and Nutritional Science; M.A., MSc., and Ph.D. in Human Ecology; M.Sc., M. Ag., M.F., Ph. D., MBA/MF in Renewable Resources; MSc., MAg., Ph.D., MBA/MAg in Rural Ecology

Contact(s):
Nancy Gibson, Human Ecology, Chair; 780-492-3883; Fax: 780-492-4821
John Kennelly, Agricultural, Food and Nutritional Science, Chair; 780-492-3239; Fax: 780-492-4265
John Spence, Renewable Resources, Chair
Michele Veeman, Rural Economy, Chair; 780-492-4225; Fax: 780-492-0268

UNIVERSITY OF ARIZONA
DEPARTMENT OF HYDROLOGY AND WATER RESOURCES
P.O. Box 210011
Tucson, AZ 85721-0011 United States
Phone: 520-621-5082   Fax: 520-621-1422
E-mail: programs@hwr.arizona.edu
Website: www.hwr.arizona.edu
Membership: 101–1,000
Scope: State
Description: The mission of the department is to provide education, research, and service in the fields of hydrology and water resources and to engage in basic and applied research. The department offers comprehensive programs in all areas of surface and subsurface hydrology, water quality, and water resources systems (management, administration, engineering).
Publication(s): Publications website www.hwr.arizona.edu/pubs.html, Arizona HWR report
Keyword(s): Ecosystems (precious), Water Habitats & Quality
Contact(s):
Victor Baker, Department Head; Dept. of Hydrology, ; 520-621-7120; Fax: 520-621-1422; baker@hwr.arizona.edu
Carla Stoffle, Main Library; P.O. Box 210055, ; 520-621-7440; Fax: 520-621-9733
Terrie Thompson, Academic Advising Coordinator; 520-621-3131; Fax: 520-621-1422; terrie@hwr.arizona.edu

UNIVERSITY OF ARIZONA
SCHOOL OF RENEWABLE NATURAL RESOURCES
325 Biological Sciences East
P.O. Box 210043
Tucson, AZ 85721-0043 United States
Phone: 520-621-7255   Fax: 520-621-8801
E-mail: llee@ag.arizona.edu
Website: www.cals.arizona.edu/
Membership: 101–1,000
Scope: Local, State, Regional, National, International
Description: The School of Renewable Natural Resources provides instruction, research, and extension in a range of disciplines. The specific academic programs of landscape resources, rangeland and forest resources, watershed resources, and wildlife and fisheries resources provide undergraduate and graduate education. Physical and biological sciences are integrated with socioeconomic and political factors necessary for the conservation, protection, and management of renewable natural resources.
Keyword(s): Development/Developing Countries
Contact(s):
C.P. Reid, Director; 520-621-7257; Fax: 520-621-8801; cppr@ag.arizona.edu
Scott Bonar, Cooperative Fish and Wildlife Research Unit, Leader; 520-626-8535; Fax: 520-621-8801; sbonar@ag.arizona.edu
Carl Edminster, Forest Service Cooperative Research Unit, Leader; 520-556-2177
D. Guertin, Landscape Studies Program Chair; 520-621-1723; Fax: 520-621-8801; phil@srnr.arizona.edu
William Halvorson, Cooperative National Park Resources Studies Unit, Leader; 520-621-1174; Fax: 520-621-8801; halvor@srnr.arizona.edu
Michael Johnson, Cooperative Social Sciences Institute, USDA Natural Resource; 520-626-4685; Fax: 520-621-8801; mdjnrcs@ag.arizona.edu
Mitchel McClaren, RNR Studies Program Chair; 520-621-1673; Fax: 520-621-8801
C. P. Reid, Watershed Resources Acting Program Chair; 520-621-7257; Fax: 520-621-8801; cppr@ag.arizona.edu
George Ruyle, Rangeland and Forest Resources; 520-621-1384; Fax: 520-621-8801; gruyle@ag.arizona.edu
William Shaw, Wildlife and Fisheries Resources Program Chair; 520-621-7265; Fax: 520-621-8801; wshaw@ag.arizona.edu
Malcom Zwolinski, Associate Director; 520-621-1432; Fax: 520-621-8801; mjz@ag.arizona.edu

UNIVERSITY OF ARKANSAS AT LITTLE ROCK
DEPARTMENT OF BIOLOGY
2801 S. University Ave.
Little Rock, AR 72204-1099 United States
Phone: 501-569-3270   Fax: 501-569-3271
E-mail: webmaster@ualr.edu
Website: www.ualr.edu
Scope: Local, State, Regional
Description: The Environmental Health Sciences Program (www.ualr.edu/~ehsp/) curriculum consists of a common core and a choice from four areas of concentrated study: Environmental quality management; occupational safety and health; environmental planning; and environmental/public health sciences. Fish and Wildlife Management Program (www.ualr.edu/~biology/programs/wild/) prepares students for conservation biology research and management positions.
Contact(s):
Gary Heidt, Professor and Chair of Biology Dept.; 501-569-3511; gaheidt@ualr.edu
Carl Stapleton, Director, Environmental Health Sciences Program; 501-569-3501; crstapleton@ualr.edu

UNIVERSITY OF ARKANSAS AT MONTICELLO
SCHOOL OF FOREST RESOURCES/ARKANSAS FOREST RESOURCES CENTER
P.O. Box 3468, Forestry & Wildlife
Monticello, AR 71656 United States
Phone: 870-460-1052   Fax: 870-460-1092
Website: www.afrc.uamont.edu/sfr/index.htm
Membership: 1–100
Scope: State
Contact(s):
Richard Klunder, Dean

UNIVERSITY OF BATH
CENTRE FOR RESEARCH IN EDUCATION AND THE ENVIRONMENT (CREE)
Department of Education
University of Bath
Bath, BA2 7AY United Kingdom
Phone: 1225-386648
E-mail: cree@bath.ac.uk
Website: www.bath.ac.uk/cree
Founded: 1995
Scope: Local, Regional, National, International
Description: The Centre, based at the University of Bath, carries out research and evaluation studies on environmental and sustainable education. The academic journals: Environmental Education Research, and Assessment and Evaluation in Higher Education are edited from the Centre.
Contact(s):
William Scott, Director; cree@bath.ac.uk
Andrew Stables, Reader; a.w.g.stables@bath.ac.uk

Keith Bishop, Lecturer; k.n.bishop@bath.ac.uk
John Fisher, Lecturer; j.a.fisher@bath.ac.uk
Stephen Gough, Lecturer; s.r.gough@bath.ac.uk
Elisabeth Hacking, Lecturer; e.c.b.hacking@bath.ac.uk
Alan Reid, Lecturer; a.d.reid@bath.ac.uk

UNIVERSITY OF BRITISH COLUMBIA
ENVIRONMENTAL PROGRAMS
2075 Wesbrook Mall
Vancouver, V6T 1Z1 British Columbia Canada
Phone: 604-822-2029   Fax: 604-822-1637
Website: www.hse.uvc.ca
Membership: 1–100
Scope: Local
Contact(s):
   M. Healey, Westwater Research Centre, Director; 1933 W. Mall Annex, Rm. 200, Vancouver, British Columbia V6T 1Z2
   L. Lavkulich, Institute for Resources and Environment, Director; Rm. 436E, 2206 E. Mall, Vancouver, British Columbia V6T 1Z3
   J. Berger, Zoology Department, Head; 6270 University Blvd., Vancouver, British Columbia V6T 1Z4
   M. Isaacson, Civil Engineering Department, Head; 2324 Main Mall, Vancouver, British Columbia V6T 1Z4
   A. Lewis, Oceanography Department, Head; 6270 University Blvd., Vancouver, British Columbia V6T 1Z2
   J. McLean, Forestry, Acting Dean; 2424 Main Mall, Vancouver, British Columbia V6T 1Z4
   Moura Quayle, Agricultural Sciences, Dean; 248-2357 Main Mall University Campus, Vancouver, British Columbia V6T 1Z4
   D. Shackleton, Animal Sciences Department, Contact; 248-2357 Main Mall University Campus, Vancouver, British Columbia V6T 1Z4
   G. Wynn, Geography Department, Head; 1984 West Mall, Vancouver, British Columbia V6T 1Z5

UNIVERSITY OF CALIFORNIA AT DAVIS
COLLEGE OF AGRICULTURE AND ENVIRONMENTAL SCIENCE
One Shields Ave.
Davis, CA 95616-8571 United States
Phone: 530-752-6586   Fax: 530-752-4154
Website: www.wscb.ucdavis.edu
Membership: 1–100
Scope: State
Description: Agricultural research programs and 21 departments.
Contact(s):
   Ruth Reck, Director, National Institute for Global Environmental Change; 530-757-3401; Fax: 530-756-6499; rareck@ucdavis.edu
   Arnold Bloom, Chair, Vegetable Crops Program; 530-752-1743; Fax: 530-752-9659; ajbloom@ucdavis.edu
   D. Burger, Chair, Environmental Horticulture; 530-752-0130; Fax: 530-752-1819; dwburger@ucdavis.edu
   Colin Carter, Chair, Agricultural and Resource Economics; 530-752-1517; Fax: 530-752-5614; cacarter@ucdavis.edu
   Deborah Elliot-Fisk, Chair, Wildlife, Fish & Conservation Biology; 530-752-6586; Fax: 530-752-4514; dlelliottfisk@ucdavis.edu
   Larry Harper, Chair, Human and Community Development; 530-752-3624; lharper@ucdavis.edu
   Harry Kaya, Chair, Nematology; 530-752-1051; Fax: 530-752-5809; hkkaya@ucdavis.edu
   Dean MacCannell, Chair, Landscape Architecture; 530-752-6437; edmaccannell@ucdavis.edu
   Jim Macdonald, Chair, Plant Pathology; 530-752-6897; Fax: 530-752-5674; jdmacdonald@ucdavis.edu
   Marion Miller, Chair, Environmental Toxicology; 530-752-4526; mgmiller@ucdavis.edu
   Michael Parrella, Chair, Entomology; 530-752-0492; mpparrella@ucdavis.edu
   Gary Polis, Chair, Environmental Science and Policy; 530-754-8994; Fax: 530-752-3350; gapolis@ucdavis.edu
   Dennis Rolston, Chair, Land, Air and Water Resources; 530-752-2113; Fax: 530-752-1552; derolston@ucdavis.edu
   Roger Shaw, Vice-Chair, Land, Air and Water Resources; 530-752-1822; Fax: 530-752-1552; rhshaw@ucdavis.edu
   Jo Stabb, Chair, Environmental Design; 530-752-6809; jcstabb@ucdavis.edu

UNIVERSITY OF CALIFORNIA AT DAVIS
HERBARIUM
One Shields Ave.
Herbarium Plant Biology, University of California
Davis, CA 95616 United States
Phone: 530-752-1091   Fax: 530-752-5410
Website: herbarium.ucdavis.edu
Founded: 1923
Membership: 1–100
Scope: State
Description: The UC Davis Herbarium is the center for research in plant systematics at the University of California, Davis. The Herbarium, of worldwide scope, includes 200,000 specimens. Holdings from California include documentation for many rare and endangered species.
Contact(s):
   Ellen Dean, Director and Curator

UNIVERSITY OF CALIFORNIA AT DAVIS
SCHOOL OF VETERINARY MEDICINE
WILDLIFE HEALTH CENTER
VM: Wildlife Health Center
TB 128 Old Davis Road
Davis, CA 95616 United States
Phone: 530-752-4167   Fax: 530-752-3318
Website: www.vetmed.ucdavis.edu/whc
Founded: 1990
Membership: 1–100
Scope: Regional
Description: The Wildlife Health Center is dedicated to balancing the needs of people, wildlife, and the environment. We seek to restore and maintain wildlife, human, and environmental health. We use science, technology, and education as our tools.
Publication(s): WildlifeLines
Keyword(s): Ecosystems (precious), Land Issues, Oceans/Coasts/Beaches, Pollution (general), Water Habitats & Quality, Wildlife & Species
Contact(s):
   Walter Boyce, Director; 530-752-4167; Fax: 530-752-3318
   Jonna Mazet, Director; 530-752-4167; Fax: 530-752-3318

UNIVERSITY OF CALIFORNIA AT LOS ANGELES
COLLEGE LETTERS AND SCIENCE
1312 Murphy Hall
Box 951438
Los Angeles, CA 90095-3801 United States
Phone: 310-825-9009   Fax: 310-825-9368
E-mail: webadmin@college.ucla.edu
Website: www.college.ucla.edu/
Membership: 1,001–10,000
Scope: National
Contact(s):
   Roger Wakimoto, Chair, Department of Atmospheric Sciences; 310-825-1751

EDUCATIONAL INSTITUTIONS – U

UNIVERSITY OF CALIFORNIA AT LOS ANGELES
SCHOOL OF ENGINEERING AND APPLIED SCIENCE
CIVIL AND ENVIRONMENTAL ENGINEERING
DEPARTMENT
5731 Boelter Hall, P.O. Box 951593
Los Angeles, CA 90095-1593 United States
Phone: 310-825-1346 Fax: 310-206-2222
E-mail: deeona@ea.ucla.edu
Website: www.cee.ucla.edu/
Membership: 1–100
Scope: Local, International
Contact(s):
    Jiann-Wen Ju Ju, Chair; 310-206-1751; Fax: 310-206-2222; juj@seas.ucla.edu

UNIVERSITY OF CALIFORNIA AT RIVERSIDE
GRADUATE SCHOOL OF ENVIRONMENTAL SCIENCE
AND ENGINEERING
2217 Geology, University of California
Riverside, CA 92521 United States
E-mail: karenh@mail.ucr.edu
Website: ese.ucr.edu/

UNIVERSITY OF CALIFORNIA AT RIVERSIDE ENVIRONMENTAL DEPT
DEPARTMENT OF ENVIRONMENTAL SCIENCE
Riverside, CA 92521 United States
Phone: 909-787-5116 Fax: 909-787-4652
E-mail: mari.ridgeway@ucr.edu
Website: envisci.ucr.edu/
Founded: 1971
Membership: 101 1,000
Scope: State
Description: The Environmental Sciences Program offers four curriculum tracks: Natural Science, Social Science, Environmental Toxicology and Soil Science. Opportunities are available for students to conduct research and to engage in environmental internships. Graduate Degrees available in Soil and Water Science.
Contact(s):
    Walt Farmer, Chair of Environmental Sciences; 909-787-5116; wfarm@citrus.ucr.edu

UNIVERSITY OF CALIFORNIA AT SAN DIEGO
SCRIPPS INSTITUTION OF OCEANOGRAPHY
9500 Gilman Dr.
UCSD Mail Code 0208
La Jolla, CA 92093-0208 United States
Phone: 858-534-3206 Fax: 858-534-7889
E-mail: siodept@sio.ucsd.edu
Website: www.sio.ucsd.edu/
Founded: 1903
Membership. 101–1,000
Scope: International
Description: A part of the University of California, San Diego, the Scripps Institution of Oceanography is one of the oldest, largest, and most important centers for marine science research and graduate training in the world. The Birch Aquarium serves as the public education center for the institution.
Publication(s): Explorations Magazine
Keyword(s): Air Quality/Atmosphere, Climate Change, Ecosystems (precious), Oceans/Coasts/Beaches, Pollution (general), Water Habitats & Quality, Wildlife & Species
Contact(s):
    Charles Kennel, Director and Vice Chancellor for Marine Sciences; ckennel@ucsd.edu
    Myrl Hendershott, Chair of the Graduate Department

UNIVERSITY OF CALIFORNIA AT SANTA BARBARA
ENVIRONMENTAL STUDIES PROGRAM
Environmental Studies Program @ University of California
Santa Barbara, CA 93106-4170 United States
Phone: 805-893-2968 Fax: 805-893-8686
E-mail: es_info@es.ucsb.edu
Website: www.es.ucsb.edu
Scope: State
Description: The Environmental Studies Program at UCSB remains one of the strongest in terms of student demand and national reputation. The Environmental Studies curriculum is designed to provide students with the scholarly background and intellectual skills necessary to understand complex environmental problems and formulate decsions that are environmentally sound. While the E.S. Program offers both a B.S. and B.A. degree.
Publication(s): See publication web site
Contact(s):
    Jo-Ann Shelton, Program Chair; ext. 4505
    Eric Zimmerman, Academic Advisor; ext. 3185

UNIVERSITY OF CALIFORNIA AT SANTA CRUZ
ENVIRONMENTAL STUDIES
1156 High Street
Santa Cruz, CA 95064 United States
Phone: 831-459-3718
E-mail: envstudies@ucsc.edu
Website: www.ucsc.edu
Founded: 1970
Scope: Local, Regional, International
Description: Undergraduate degree program in environmental studies. Doctoral program in environmental studies.
Contact(s):
    David Goodman, Chairperson

UNIVERSITY OF CALIFORNIA, BERKELEY
DEPARTMENT OF ENVIRONMENTAL SCIENCE,
POLICY, AND MANAGEMENT
145 Mulford Hall
Berkeley, CA 94720-3114 United States
Phone: 510-642-4249 Fax: 510-642-4034
E-mail: espmug@nature.berkeley.edu
Website: nature.berkeley.edu/espm/
Founded: 1993
Scope: International
Description: The Department has a strong undergraduate program awarding the B.S. degree in Forestry, Resource Management, Molecular Environmental Biology and Conservation and Resource Studies. The graduate degree program (M.S., Ph.D.) integrates the biological, social and physical sciences to provide advanced education in basic and applied environmental sciences, develops critical analytical abilities and fosters the capacity to conduct research on the structure and function of ecosystems.
Contact(s):
    Sue Baumgartner, Director of Student Services; 510-642-1546; susan@nature.berkeley.edu

UNIVERSITY OF CALIFORNIA, SANTA BARBARA
WILDLANDS STUDIES PROGRAM
3 Mosswood Circle
Cazadero, CA 95421 United States
Phone: 707-632-5665 Fax: 707-632-5665
E-mail: wildlands@sonic.net
Website: wildlandsstudies.com
Founded: 1979
Scope: State, Regional, National, International

Description: Wildlands Studies offers a year-round series of field study programs in North American and international wilderness locations. Participants join backcountry research teams in a search for answers to important environmental problems concerning wildlife populations and/or wildland habitats. Participants can earn 5-15 units of university credit.
Publication(s): Course Catalog
Contact(s):
Crandall Bay, Director; 707-632-5665

UNIVERSITY OF COLORADO
SCHOOL OF LAW
NATURAL RESOURCES LAW CENTER
Campus Box 401
Boulder, CO 80309-0401 United States
Phone: 303-492-1286   Fax: 303-492-1297
E-mail: nrlc@spot.colorado.edu
Website: www.colorado.edu/law/nrlc
Membership: 1–100
Scope: National, International
Description: Conducts research on environmental and natural resources law and policy, including water, public lands, minerals, Indian law, etc. Sponsors conferences and workshops and hosts visiting scholars. Publishes books, research papers, and Resource Law Notes newsletter.
Keyword(s): Ethics/Environmental Justice, Executive/Legislative/Judicial Reform, Forests/Forestry, Land Issues, Public Lands/Greenspace
Contact(s):
Jim Martin, Director

UNIVERSITY OF COLORADO AT BOULDER
ENVIRONMENTAL CENTER
207 UCB
Boulder, CO 80309 United States
Phone: 303-492-8308   Fax: 303-492-1897
E-mail: ecenter@colorado.edu
Website: www.colorado.edu/ecenter
Founded: 1970
Membership: 101–1,000
Scope: Local
Description: The CU Environmental Center is the nation's largest student-run environmental resource center. With over 40 student staff and interns, five permanent staff and 100 volunteers, it is the focal point for efforts to make the Boulder campus more environmentally responsible. Besides giving students applied experience in interdisciplinary environmental problem solving, the center provides direct services to the University community, including award-winning recycling and student bus pass programs.
Publication(s): Blueprint for a Green Campus, Finding a New Way
Contact(s):
Will Toor, Director; 303-492-8309; toor@spot.colorado.edu

UNIVERSITY OF CONNECTICUT
WBY, Room 308, 1376 Storrs Road, Unit 4087
Storrs, CT 06269-4087 United States
Phone: 860-486-2840   Fax: 860-486-5408
Website: www.canr.uconn.edu/nrme/
Scope: State
Description: The department offers degrees in natural resources with emphasis in forestry, fisheries, wildlife, biometeorology, watershed hydrology, remote sensing, soil and water conservation and natural resources engineering.
Contact(s):
David Schroeder, Department Head; dschroed@canr.uconn.edu

UNIVERSITY OF CONNECTICUT COOPERATIVE EXTENSION
COLLEGE OF AGRICULTURE AND NATURAL RESOURCES
Unit 4066 1376 Storrs Rd., University of Connecticut
Storrs, CT 06269-4066 United States
Phone: 860-486-2918   Fax: 860-486-5113
Website: www.canr.uconn.edu
Founded: 1881
Scope: State
Description: Natural resource components include forest management, forest stewardship, urban forestry, water resources, and wildlife management.
Contact(s):
John Barclay, Extension Specialist: Wildlife and Director, Wildlife Conservation; Natural Resources Management and Engineering, Box U-87, University of Connecticut, Storrs, CT 06269-4087; 860-486-0143; Fax: 860-486-5875
Norman Bender, Program Leader: Marine Advisory Program; University of CT-MAS: 1084 Shennecossett Rd., Groton, CT 06340-6097; 860-445-8664
Stephen Broderick, Extension Educator: Forest Management; 139 Wolf Den Rd., Brooklyn, CT 06234; 860-774-9600
Glenn Warner, Extension Specialist: Water Resources; Natural Resources Management and Engineering: Box U-87: University of Connecticut, Storrs, CT 06269-4087; 860-486-2840
Xiusheng Yang, State Climatologist; Natural Resources Management and Engineering, Box U-87, University of Connecticut, Storrs, CT 06269-4087; 860-486-2840

UNIVERSITY OF DAR ES SALAAM
JOINT ENVIRONMENT AND DEVELOPMENT MANAGEMENT ACTION (JEMA)
Main Campus
P.O. Box 35081
Dar Es Salaam, Tanzania
Phone: 255-51-410500-8, ext. 2403 Fax: 255-51-410078
E-mail: jema@ucc.udsm.ac.tz
Website: udsm.ac.tz/jema.html
Description: JEMA aims at facilitating technical community outreach services which are environmentally sound to the rural society for sustainable utilization of available natural resources towards poverty alleviation.
Publication(s): Biodiversity Conservation Study on the Slopes of Mt. Kilimanjaro, Environmental Learning Programme in schools and communities in East and South Africa, Environmental Assessment of institutional transformation programmes in East Africa.
Keyword(s): Agriculture/Farming, Development/Developing Countries, Forests/Forestry, Land Issues, Recreation/Ecotourism, Reduce/Reuse/Recycle, Sprawl/Urban Planning, Wildlife & Species
Contact(s):
Cosmas Bahali, Coordinator; Fax: 255-514-1007; jema ucc.udsm.ac.tz
Theodora Bali, Gender Advocacy; 255- 51- 410
Romuli John, Executive Secretary
Rogasian Massue, Treasurer
Filos Mayayi, Publicity Secretary

UNIVERSITY OF DELAWARE
COLLEGE OF AGRICULTURE AND NATURAL RESOURCES
531 S. College Ave., Townsend Hall
Newark, DE 19717 United States
Phone: 302-831-2501   Fax: 302-831-6758
Website: www.ag.udel.edu
Membership: 1–100
Scope: State, Regional

EDUCATIONAL INSTITUTIONS – U

Description: B.S. in wildlife conservation; M.S. and Ph.D. in entomology and applied ecology

Contact(s):
Judith Hough-Stein, Department of Entomology and Applied Ecology, Chairperson; 302-831-8889; Fax: 302-831-3651; jhough@udel.edu
Roland Roth, Professor Entomology and Applied Ecology; rroth@udel.edu

UNIVERSITY OF FLORIDA
SCHOOL OF FOREST RESOURCES AND CONSERVATION
P.O. Box 110410
Gainesville, FL 32611-0410 United States
Phone: 352-846-0850   Fax: 352-392-1707
E-mail: sfrc@ifas.ufl.edu
Website: www.sfrc.ufl.edu

Founded: 1937

Scope: Local, State, Regional, National, International

Description: The School seeks to advance the understanding and management of natural resources, especially forests, and the interactions between the ecological, social, and economic demands placed on them. This is accomplished through established programs in undergraduate and graduate education, research, and extension.

Publication(s): Extension Information

Keyword(s): Agriculture/Farming, Air Quality/Atmosphere, Climate Change, Development/Developing Countries, Energy, Finance/Banking/Trade, Forests/Forestry, Land Issues, Public Lands/Greenspace, Recreation/Ecotourism, Sprawl/Urban Planning, Water Habitats & Quality, Wildlife & Species

Contact(s):
George Blakeslee, Assoc. Director of Academic Programs; 352-846-0845; Fax: 352-392-1707; gb4stree@ufl.edu
Alan Long, Assoc. Professor of Extension; 352-846-0891; Fax: 352-846-1277; ajl2@ufl.edu
Scott Sager, Student Services Coordinator; 352-846-0847; Fax: 352-392-1707; sasager@ufl.edu

UNIVERSITY OF FLORIDA
SOLAR ENERGY AND ENERGY CONVERSION LABORATORIES
237 MEB, Box 116300
Gainesville, FL 32611 United States
Phone: 352-392-0812   Fax: 352-392-1071
E-mail: solar@cimar.mae.ufl.edu
Website: seecl.mae.ufl.edu/solar

Founded: 1954

Membership: 1,001–10,000

Scope: International

Publication(s): Principles of Solar Engineering (textbook), Advances in Solar Energy (published every other year), Solar Touch Newsletter

Contact(s):
D. Goswami, Director

UNIVERSITY OF FLORIDA INSTITUTE OF FOOD AND AGRICULTURAL SCIENCES
CENTER FOR NATURAL RESOURCES
1051 McCarthy Hall
P.O. Box 110230
University of Florida
Gainesville, FL 32611-0230 United States
Phone: 352-392-7622   Fax: 352-846-2856
E-mail: cnr_mail@mail.ifas.ufl.edu
Website: cnr.ifas.ufl.edu/

Founded: 1973

Scope: Local, State, Regional, National, International

Description: The Center for Natural Resources works to conserve, preserve and restore our nation's natural resources by facilitating interdisciplinary collaborations between University of Florida faculty members and external stakeholders. CNR sponsors and organizes various natural resource-related research, training workshops, conferences and seminars.

Publication(s): Natural Resources Programs and Summaries, Linkages

Keyword(s): Agriculture/Farming, Air Quality/Atmosphere, Climate Change, Ecosystems (precious), Energy, Ethics/Environmental Justice, Forests/Forestry, Land Issues, Oceans/Coasts/Beaches, Pollution (general), Public Lands/Greenspace, Recreation/Ecotourism, Reduce/Reuse/Recycle

Contact(s):
Randall Stocker, Director
Wendy Graham, Associate Director
Nancy Peterson, Program Coordinator
Aziz Shiralipour, Associate Director - Biomass Programs
Margie Owens, Office Manager

UNIVERSITY OF GEORGIA
DANIEL B. WARNELL SCHOOL OF FOREST RESOURCES
Athens, GA 30602-2152 United States
Phone: 706-542-2686   Fax: 706-542-8356
E-mail: fordean@smokey.forestry.uga.edu
Website: www.uga.edu/w3fr/

Founded: 1906

Scope: Local, State, Regional, National, International

Description: The undergraduate degree (B.S.F.R.) offers majors in Forestry, Wildlife, Fisheries and Aquaculture and Forest Environmental Resources. Graduate programs (M.S., M.F.R., Ph.D.) offer a focus in Wildlife Ecology and Management, Fisheries and Aquaculture and a variety of forest biology and management fields.

Keyword(s): Agriculture/Farming, Air Quality/Atmosphere, Climate Change, Ecosystems (precious), Energy, Ethics/Environmental Justice, Forests/Forestry, Land Issues, Pollution (general), Public Lands/Greenspace, Recreation/Ecotourism, Reduce/Reuse/Recycle, Water Habitats & Quality

Contact(s):
James Sweeney, Interim Dean; 706-542-4741; Fax: 706-542-2281; fordean@smokey.forestry.uga.edu

UNIVERSITY OF GEORGIA
MARINE INSTITUTE
UGA Marine Institute
Sapelo Island, GA 31327 United States
Phone: 912-485-2221   Fax: 912-485-2133
Website: www.uga.edu/ugami/

Founded: 1953

Membership: 1–100

Scope: Regional

Description: Concerned with research into the system ecology, biology, chemistry, and geology of the salt marshes, barrier islands, and nearshore zone of the Georgia coast.

Publication(s): University of Georgia Marine Institute Collected Reprints

Contact(s):
Jon Garbisch, Education Program Specialist; jgarbisch@peachnet.campuscwix.net

UNIVERSITY OF GEORGIA
SAVANNAH RIVER ECOLOGY LABORATORY
Savannah River Ecology Laboratory
Drawer E
Aiken, SC 29803 United States
Phone: 803-725-2472   Fax: 803-725-3309
E-mail: forrest@srel.edu
Website: www.uga.edu/srel/

Membership: 101–1,000

Scope: Regional, International

Description: Learning and communicating ecological processes and principles is the mission of the University of Georgia's Savannah River Ecology Laboratory. The Lab accomplishes its mission through research, outreach and education, and service. Research is conducted in wetlands ecology, wildlife ecology and toxicology, and biogeochemical ecology, including radioecology. Outreach and education activities reach more than 120,000 people annually in Georgia and South Carolina.
Publication(s): EcoLines, most publications on website
Contact(s):
  Paul Bertsch, Director
  Whit Gibbons, Outreach and Education Director
  Rosemary Forrest, Public Relations
  Carl Strojan, Associate Director; Savannah River Ecology Lab, Drawer E, Aiken, SC 29802; 803-725-8217; strojan@serl.edu

UNIVERSITY OF GUELPH
ONTARIO AGRICULTURAL COLLEGE
OAC Deans Office
Guelph, N1G 2W1 Ontario Canada
Phone: 519-824-4120　　　Fax: 519-766-1423
E-mail: oacinfo@oac.uoguelph.ca
Website: www.oac.uoguelph.ca
Scope: International
Contact(s):
  John Fitzgibbon, Executive Director, College Faculty of Environmental Design; ext. 6784; jfitzgib@rpd.uoguelph.ca
  Alan Watson, Arboretum Director; 519-824-4120; ext. 2356; awatson@uoguelph.ca
  Stu Hilts, Chair of Land Resource Science
  S. Marshall, University of Guelph Insect Collection, Curator; ext. 2720; smarshal@evbhort.uoguelph.ca
  Nathan Perkins, Undergraduate Program Coordinator; ext. 8758; nperkins@la.uoguelph.ca
  Mark Sears, Environmental Biology, Dept. Chair; ext. 3921; msears@evbhort.uoguelph.ca

UNIVERSITY OF HAWAII
COLLEGE OF TROPICAL AGRICULTURE AND HUMAN RESOURCES
University of Hawaii at Manoa
3050 Maile Way
202-B Gilmore Hall
Honolulu, HI 96822 United States
Phone: 808-956-8131　　　Fax: 808-956-9105
E-mail: research@ctahr.hawaii.edu
Website: www.ctahr.hawaii.edu
Founded: 1901
Membership: 101–1,000
Scope: State
Description: Plan and implement research and extension in agriculture, natural resources, and human resources relevant to Hawaii and the tropics, with emphasis on the Pacific and Asia.
Publication(s): Various research and extension publications
Keyword(s): Agriculture/Farming, Land Issues, Pollution (general), Public Health, Reduce/Reuse/Recycle, Wildlife & Species
Contact(s):
  Catherine Chanhalbrandt, Associate Dean and Associate Director for Research

UNIVERSITY OF HAWAII AT MANOA
WATER RESOURCES RESEARCH CENTER
2540 Dole St.
Room 283
University of Hawaii at Manoa
Honolulu, HI 96822 United States
Phone: 808-956-7847　　　Fax: 808-956-5044
E-mail: jmoncur@hawaii.edu
Website: www.wrcc.hawaii.edu
Founded: 1964
Scope: State, Regional
Description: WRRC's mission is to coordinate and conduct research to identify, characterize and quantify water and environmental concerns of the state, the nation and other Pacific Islands and formulate methods for resolving these concerns. WRRC produces reports, national and international journal articles, books, newsletters and project bulletins and organizes seminars, workshops and conferences.
Publication(s): Technical Report, Project Reports and Special Publications, Publications List, Cooperative Report, Annual Report, Technical Memorandum Report
Keyword(s): Energy, Oceans/Coasts/Beaches, Pollution (general), Public Health, Water Habitats & Quality
Contact(s):
  James Moncur, Director; 808-956-7847; Fax: 808-956-5044; jmoncur@hawaii.edu
  Philip Moravcik, Communications Coordinator

UNIVERSITY OF HOUSTON
DEPARTMENT OF CIVIL AND ENVIRONMENTAL ENGINEERING
4800 Calhoun Rd.
Houston, TX 77204-4003 United States
Phone: 713-743-4250　　　Fax: 713-743-4260
Website: www.egr.uh.edu/cive/
Membership: 1–100
Scope: International
Contact(s):
  Theodore Cleveland, Environmental Engineering Program, Director; 713-743-4250; cleveland@uh.edu

UNIVERSITY OF IDAHO
COLLEGE OF NATURAL RESOURCES
DEPARTMENT OF FISH AND WILDLIFE RESOURCES
P.O. Box 441136
Moscow, ID 83844-1136 United States
Phone: 208-885-4006　　　Fax: 208-885-9080
E-mail: fish_wildlife@uidaho.edu
Website: www.cnr.uidaho.edu/fishwild
Membership: 1–100
Scope: Local, State, Regional, National
Description: Academic department in the College of Natural Resources at the University of Idaho.
Keyword(s): Ecosystems (precious), Forests/Forestry, Land Issues, Pollution (general), Public Lands/Greenspace, Water Habitats & Quality, Wildlife & Species
Contact(s):
  George LaBar, Department Head, Professor of Fisheries; 208-885-4006; Fax: 208-885-9080; glabar@uidaho.edu
  J. Scott, Cooperative Fish and Wildlife Research Unit, Leader; 208-885-6336; Fax: 208-885-9080; mscott@uidaho.edu

UNIVERSITY OF IDAHO
COLLEGE OF NATURAL RESOURCES
IDAHO COOPERATIVE FISH AND WILDLIFE RESEARCH UNIT
P.O. Box 44-1141
6th & Line Sts., Room 103
Moscow, ID 83844-1141 United States
Phone: 208-885-2750　　　Fax: 208-885-9080
E-mail: sarahm@uidaho.edu
Website: www.its.uidaho.edu/coop
Founded: 1963
Membership: 101–1,000
Scope: State, Regional, National, International
Description: An interagency organization which conducts research, graduate level training, and extension in the fields of fish, wildlife, and conservation biology.

EDUCATIONAL INSTITUTIONS – U

Keyword(s): Wildlife & Species

Contact(s):
- James Congleton, Assistant Leader; 208-885-7521; Fax: 208-885-9080; jconglet@uidaho.edu
- Christine Moffitt, Assistant Leader; 208-885-7047; Fax: 208-885-9080; cmoffitt@uidaho.edu
- J. Scott, Leader; 208-885-6960; Fax: 208-885-9080; mscott@uidaho.edu
- R. Wright, Assistant Leader; 208-885-7990; Fax: 208-885-9080; gwright@uidaho.edu

UNIVERSITY OF IDAHO
WOMEN IN NATURAL RESOURCES
P.O. Box 441114
Moscow, ID 83844-1114 United States
Phone: 208-885-6754
Website: www.cnr.uidaho.edu\winr

Founded: 1968
Scope: International
Description: E-journal focused on women working in the environmental sciences and natural resource management. Also, job listings.
Publication(s): Jobs Flyer (Monthly), Women in Natural Resources (Quarterly)
Contact(s):
- Sandra Martin, Editor; winr@uidaho.edu

UNIVERSITY OF IDAHO EXTENSION
P.O. Box 442338
Moscow, ID 83844-2338 United States
Phone: 208-885-5883   Fax: 208-885-6654
E-mail: extdir@uidaho.edu
Website: www.uidaho.edu/extension/

Founded: 1914
Membership: 101–1,000
Scope: State
Description: The University of Idaho Extension (UIExt) is a partnership with the Cooperative Extension System. Cooperating County, State, and Federal governments deliver knowledge and education to the people of the State to improve social, economic, and environmental conditions. UIExt is located across the State, in 11 research and extension centers and 42 county extension offices.
Contact(s):
- Charlotte Eberlein, Interim Extension Director; P.O. Box 1827, 315 Falls Avenue, Evergreen Bldg, Twin Falls, ID 83303; 208-736-3603; Fax: 208-736-0843; extdir@uidaho.edu
- Paul McCawley, Associate Extension Director, Interim, P.O. Box 442338, Moscow, ID 83844; 208-885-5883; Fax: 208-885-6654; pmccawley@uidaho.edu
- Ronald Mahoney, Extension Forester; Univ. of Idaho, College of Natural Resources, Moscow, ID 83844-1140; 208-885-6356; Fax: 208-885-6226
- Lou Riesenberg, Agriculture and Extension Education; P.O. Box 442040, 1134 W 6th Street, Moscow, ID 83844; 208-885-6358; Fax: 208-885-4039; lriesenb@uidaho.edu

UNIVERSITY OF ILLINOIS AT URBANA-CHAMPAIGN
SAFTEY AND COMPLIANCE
205 N. Mathews Ave.
1114 Newmark Civil Engineering Lab
Urbana, IL 61801 United States
Phone: 217-333-1000
E-mail: consult@uiuc.edu
Website: www.uiuc.edu/

Scope: State
Contact(s):
- Vincent Bellafiore, Landscape Architecture, Head
- Patrick Brown, Natural History Survey Professor
- David Daniel, Civil Engineering, Head
- Scott Robinson, Animal Biology, Head
- Gary Rolfe, Natural Resources and Environmental Sciences, Head
- Christopher Silver, Urban and Regional Planning, Head
- Colin Thorn, Geography, Head

UNIVERSITY OF ILLINOIS EXTENSION
214 Mumford Hall (MC-710), 1301 W. Gregory Dr.
Urbana, IL 61801 United States
Phone: 217-333-5900   Fax: 217-244-5403
E-mail: gseeber@uiuc.edu
Website: www.extension.uiuc.edu/welcome.html

Founded: 1914
Scope: Local, State
Description: University of Illinois Extension provides researched based information in four core program areas. The core areas are agriculture and natural resources, 4-H youth development, community & economic development and nutrition, family & consumer sciences. Extension is part of the College of ACES at the University of Illinois.
Keyword(s): Agriculture/Farming, Air Quality/Atmosphere, Energy, Forests/Forestry, Public Health, Public Lands/Greenspace, Recreation/Ecotourism, Reduce/Reuse/Recycle, Sprawl/Urban Planning, Water Habitats & Quality, Wildlife & Species
Contact(s):
- Dennis Campion, Associate Dean; dcampion@uiuc.edu
- Mike Grey, Assistant Dean, Extension Program Coordination; 217-333-5900; Fax: 217-244-5403; megray@staff.uiuc.edu
- Glenn Seeber, Assistant Dean, Extension Operations; 217-333-5900; Fax: 217-244-5403; gseeber@uiuc.edu

UNIVERSITY OF IOWA
E107 General Hospital
Iowa City, IA 52242 United States
Phone: 319-384-8241   Fax: 319-335-9200
Website: www.public-health.uiowa.edu

Scope: State
Contact(s):
- James Merchant, Environmental Health Sciences Research Center, Director; 2707 Steindler Bldg., Iowa City, IA 52242; 319-335-9833; james-merchant@uiowa.edu
- Robert Ettema, Civil and Environmental Engineering Program, Dept. Chair; Dept. Office: 2130 Seamans Center, Iowa City, IA 52242; 319-335-5647; Fax: 319-335-5660; cee@engineering.uiowa.edu

UNIVERSITY OF ITO PUNJAB
INSTITUTE OF EDUCATION AND RESEARCH
New Campus
Lahore, 54590 Pakistan
Phone: 92425864468   Fax: 92425864004
Description: Environmental Education for Masters students
Contact(s):
- Hafiz Qzbal, Contact; hafizm@paknet4.ptc.pk

UNIVERSITY OF KANSAS
DEPARTMENT OF ENVIRONMENTAL STUDIES
517 W. 14th St., Bldg. 138
Lawrence, KS 66044-3401 United States
Phone: 785-842-2059   Fax: 785-842-4041
E-mail: env-studies@ku.edu
Website: www.ku.edu/~kuesp

Membership: 1–100
Scope: State
Description: Environmental Studies Program offers options in ecology and field biology, environmental policy, environmental impact analysis, environmental health, geology and meteorology, water resources, and environmental land-use analysis
Contact(s):
- Stanford Loeb, Director; 785-842-2059
- Deborah Snyder, Secretary

UNIVERSITY OF KANSAS FIELD STATION AND ECOLOGICAL RESERVES
Kansas Biological Survey
2101 Constant Avenue
Lawrence, KS 66047-3759 United States
Phone: 785-864-1500　　　　Fax: 785-864-1534
E-mail: pliechti@ku.edu
Website: www.ksr.ku.edu
Founded: 1947
Membership: 1–100
Scope: Local, State, Regional, National
Description: The University of Kansas Field Station and Ecological Reserves (KSR) is the field station for the University of Kansas. Both terrestrial and aquatic research projects are ongoing at KSR, located 10 miles north of the KU campus.
Contact(s):
　Edward Martinko, Director, Univ. Kansas Field Station and Ecological Reserves; 785-864-7720; Fax: 785-864-5093; martinko@ku.edu
　W. Kettle, Assoc. Dir. Univ. Kansas Field Station & Ecological Reserves; 785-864-3241; Fax: 785-864-5093; kettle@ku.edu

UNIVERSITY OF KENTUCKY
COLLEGE OF AGRICULTURE
Lexington, KY 40546 United States
Phone: 606-257-7596
Website: www.ca.uky.edu
Contact(s):
　Karen Goodlet, Landscape Architecture; 606-257-7295; kgoodlet@ca.uky.edu
　Donald Graves, Forestry, Chairman
　Dewayne Ingram, Horticulture, Chair; 606-257-1758; dingram@ca.uky.edu

UNIVERSITY OF LOUISVILLE
UNIVERSITY OF LOUISVILLE BIOLOGY
Life Sciences Building 139
Belknap Campus
Louisville, KY 40292 United States
Phone: 502-852-6771　　　　Fax: 502-852-0725
Website: www.louisville.edu/a-s/biology.edu
Membership: 1–100
Scope: Local, Regional
Description: The Large River Laboratory was established in 1992 to conduct research on river and freshwater systems in Kentucky and surrounding states. Community and population studies of rivers and smaller streams constitute the primary focus of the laboratory.
Keyword(s): Ecosystems (precious), Forests/Forestry, Land Issues, Pollution (general), Water Habitats & Quality, Wildlife & Species
Contact(s):
　Jeff Jack, Dept. of Biology; 502-852-5940; jdjack01@gwise.louisville.edu
　William Pearson, Professor; 502-852-3727; wdpear01@gwise.louisville.edu

UNIVERSITY OF MAINE
COLLEGE OF NATURAL SCIENCES, FORESTRY AND AGRICULTURE
5782 Winslow Hall, Suite 105
Orono, ME 04469-5782 United States
Phone: 207-581-3202　　　　Fax: 207-581-3207
Website: www.umaine.edu/
Membership: 101–1,000
Scope: State
Keyword(s): Agriculture/Farming, Air Quality/Atmosphere, Ecosystems (precious), Forests/Forestry, Land Issues, Oceans/Coasts/Beaches, Pollution (general), Recreation/Ecotourism, Wildlife & Species
Contact(s):
　Mark Anderson, Program Director
　Dave Townsend, School of Marine Sciences, Director
　Daniel Belknap, Department of Geological Sciences, Chair; 207-581-2152
　Rodney Bushway, Department of Food Science and Human Nutrition; 207-581-1621
　Christopher Campbell, Department of Biological Sciences, Chairman; 207-581-2551
　George Criner, Department of Resource Economics and Policy, Chairman; 207-581-3150
　Ivan Fernandez, Department of Plant, Soil and Environmental Science, Chairman; 207-581-2932
　David Field, Department of Forest Management, Chairman; 207-581-2856
　Dan Harrison, Department of Wildlife Ecology
　William Krohn, Cooperative Fish and Wildlife Research Unit, Leader; 207-581-2870
　William Livingston, Department of Forest Ecosystem Science, Chairman; 207-581-2884
　John Singer, Department of Biochemistry, Microbiology and Molecular Biology; 207-581-2810
　Charles Wallace, Chairman for Animal & Horticultural Sciences; 207-581-2770
　Bruce Wiersma, Dean; 207-581-3202

UNIVERSITY OF MAINE AT FORT KENT
23 University Drive
Fort Kent, ME 04743 United States
Phone: 207-834-7617　　　　Fax: 207-834-7503
E-mail: sselva@maine.edu
Website: www.umfk.maine.edu/
Founded: 1878
Scope: Regional
Description: Located in the heart of Maine's Acadian forest region. Our Bachelor of Science in Environmental Studies degree program provides a solid experiential and academic background to students preparing for careers in education, industry, and public service.
Publication(s): University Catalog and Brochures
Keyword(s): Forests/Forestry
Contact(s):
　Richard Cost, President; 207-834-7504; Fax: 207-834-7503; rcost@maine.edu
　Steven Selva, Professor of Biology and Environmental Studies; 207-834-7617; Fax: 207-834-7503; sselva@maine.edu

UNIVERSITY OF MAINE AT ORONO
SCHOOL OF MARINE SCIENCES
5741 Libby Hall
Orono, ME 4469 United States
Phone: 207-581-4381　　　　Fax: 207-581-4388
E-mail: marine@maine.edu
Website: www.umaine.edu/
Scope: State
Contact(s):
　Bruce Sidell, Chair; 207-581-4381

UNIVERSITY OF MAINE COOPERATIVE EXTENSION
FORESTRY AND WILDLIFE OFFICE
5755 Nutting Hall
Orono, ME 04469-5755 United States
Phone: 207-581-2892　　　　Fax: 207-581-3466
Website: www.umext.maine.edu
Scope: Local, State

EDUCATIONAL INSTITUTIONS – U

Description: University of Maine Cooperative Extension is a major outreach education and applied research arm of the university. Our mission is "To help Maine people improve their lives through an educational process that uses research-based knowledge focused on issues and needs."

Contact(s):
Catherine Elliott, Program Administrator; 207-581-2902; Fax: 207-581-3325; celliott@umext.maine.edu
Les Hyde, Forestry Educator; 5755 Nutting Hall, UMaine, Orono, ME 04469-5755; 207-581-2818; Fax: 207-581-3466; lhyde@umext.maine.edu
James Philip, Forestry Specialist; 5755 Nutting Hall, UMaine, Orono, ME 04469-5755; 207-581-2885; Fax: 207-581-3466; jphilp@umext.maine.edu

UNIVERSITY OF MANITOBA
DEPARTMENT OF ZOOLOGY
320 Duff Roblin
Winnipeg, R3T 2N2 Manitoba Canada
Phone: 204-474-9245   Fax: 204-474-7588
Website: www.umanitoba.ca/faculties/science/
Membership: 1–100
Scope: International
Publication(s): See publication website
Keyword(s): Ecosystems (precious), Wildlife & Species

Contact(s):
Norman Hunter, Environmental Science Program, Director; 231C Machray Hall, Winnipeg, Manitoba R3T 2N2; 204-474-9897; Fax: 204-275-3147; hunter@ms.umanitoba.ca
Richard Baydack, Natural Resources Institute, Associate Director; 307 St. Pauls College, West Wing,
Erwing Huebner, Zoology, Head; Z320 Duff Roblin Bldg., Winnipeg, Manitoba R3T 2N2; 204-474-9245; Fax: 204-474-7588; ehuebner@ccumanitoba.ca
David Punter, Botany Dept., Head; 505 Buller Bldg., Winnipeg, Manitoba R3T 2N2; 204-474-9813; Fax: 204-474-7604; punterd@cc.umanitoba.ca

UNIVERSITY OF MARYLAND - AT COLLEGE PARK
COLLEGE OF AGRICULTURE AND NATURAL RESOURCES
0107 Symons Hall
College Park, MD 20742 United States
Phone: 301-405-7761   Fax: 301-405-8570
Website: www.agnr.umd.edu
Membership: 101–1,000
Scope: State
Keyword(s): Agriculture/Farming, Air Quality/Atmosphere, Development/Developing Countries, Ecosystems (precious), Energy, Ethics/Environmental Justice, Forests/Forestry, Land Issues, Oceans/Coasts/Beaches, Pollution (general), Population, Recreation/Ecotourism, Sprawl/Urban Planning

Contact(s):
Mark Varner, Director of Graduate Program & Avian Sciences; Animal Sciences Center, College Park, MD 20742; 301-405-1396; varner@umd5.umd.edu
John Doerr, Dept. of Animal and Avian Sciences, Undergraduate Coordinator; Animal Sciences Center, College Park, MD 20742; 301-405-1373; Fax: 301-314-9059
Thomas Fretz, Dean
Richard Weismiller, Dept. of Natural Resource Sciences and Landscape Architecture; Room 2104, Plant Sciences Bldg., College Park, MD 20742; 301-405-1306; Fax: 301-314-9308; rw22@umail.umd.edu

UNIVERSITY OF MARYLAND AT EASTERN SHORE
DEPARTMENT OF NATURAL SCIENCES
Carver Hall
Princess Anne, MD 21853 United States
Phone: 301-651-2200
Website: hawk.umes.edu/sciences/index.html
Description: Environmental Sciences (B.S.), Marine Sciences (B.S., M.S.), Marine, Estuarine, and Environmental Sciences (M.S., Ph.D), Environmental Chemistry (B.S., M.S.)

Contact(s):
Gian Gupta, Environmental Science/Marine Science, Contact; 410-651-6030; GGUPTA@UMES_BIRD.UMD.EDU
Charles Hocutt, Coastal Ecology Research Center, Contact
Joseph Okoh, Dept. Chair, Acting
Steve Rebach, Marine, Estuarine, and Environmental Sciences, Contact; 410-651-6013

UNIVERSITY OF MARYLAND BALTIMORE COUNTY
DEPARTMENT OF BIOLOGICAL SCIENCES
1000 Hilltop Cir.
Baltimore, MD 21250 United States
Phone: 410-455-2261   Fax: 410-455-3875
E-mail: sschneid@umbc.edu
Website: www.umbc.edu/biosci
Scope: State
Description: Ecology and Environmental Biology focus with a strong emphasis on research, scientific approach, faculty contact and extensive lab offerings
Keyword(s): Agriculture/Farming, Ethics/Environmental Justice, Population, Public Health, Water Habitats & Quality, Wildlife & Species

Contact(s):
Lasse Lindahl, Professor and Chair; lindahl@umbc.edu

UNIVERSITY OF MARYLAND CENTER FOR ENVIRONMENTAL SCIENCE
P.O. Box 775
Cambridge, MD 21613 United States
Phone: 410-228-9250   Fax: 410-228-3843
E-mail: webmaster@ca.umces.edu
Website: www.umces.edu
Founded: 1925
Scope: International
Description: UMCES is an institution of the University System of Maryland, with a special mission in multidisciplinary environmental research on Chesapeake Bay, the mid-Atlantic region, and coastal systems around the world.

Contact(s):
Donald Boesch, President; P.O. Box 775, Cambridge, MD 21613-0775; 410-228-9250; ext. 601; boesch@ca.umces.edu
Louis Pitelka, Appalachian Laboratory, Director; 301 Braddock Rd., Frostburg, MD 21532; 301-689-7101; Fax: 301-689-7200; pitelka@al.umces.edu
Michael Roman, Horn Point Laboratory, Director and Professor; 410-221-8406; Fax: 410-221-8490; roman@hpl.umces.edu
Kenneth Tenore, Chesapeake Biological Laboratory, Director; P.O. Box 38, Solomons, MD 20688; 410-326-7241; Fax: 410-326-7263; tenore@cbl.umces.edu

UNIVERSITY OF MARYLAND EASTERN SHORE
MARYLAND COOPERATIVE FISH AND WILDLIFE RESEARCH UNIT
1120 Trigg Hall
Princess Anne, MD 21853 United States
Phone: 410-651-7663　　　　Fax: 410-651-7662
Founded: 1994
Membership: 1–100
Scope: National
Description: The unit is sponsored by the Biological Resources Division, U.S. Geological Survey, Maryland Department of Natural Resources, U.S. Fish & Wildlife Service, University of Maryland Eastern Shore and the Wildlife Management Institute. Fish and wildlife research, graduate education, and technical assistance are the unit's primary purposes.
Keyword(s): Forests/Forestry, Oceans/Coasts/Beaches, Water Habitats & Quality, Wildlife & Species
Contact(s):
　Daphne Chatham, Administrative Assistant; 410-651-7663; Fax: 410-651-7662; dfchatham@mail.umes.edu
　Dr. Dixie Bounds, Assistant Unit Leader of Wildlife; 410-651-6913; Fax: 410-651-7662; dlbounds@mail.umes.edu
　Dr. Steven Hughes, Assistant Unit Leader of Fisheries; 410-651-7664; Fax: 410-651-7662; sghughes@mail.umes.edu
　James Wiley, Unit Leader; 410-651-7654; Fax: 410-651-7662; jwwiley@mail.umes.edu

UNIVERSITY OF MARYLAND, COLLEGE PARK
GRADUATE SCHOOL
2123 Lee Bldg.
College Park, MD 20742-5121 United States
Phone: 301-405-4198　　　　Fax: 301-314-9305
E-mail: gradmit@deans.umd.edu
Website: www.inform.umd.edu/grad/
Membership: 1–100
Scope: State
Publication(s): Graduate applications available on website
Contact(s):
　Trudy Lindsey, Director

UNIVERSITY OF MASSACHUSETTS
DEPARTMENT OF NATURAL RESOURCES CONSERVATION
Holdsworth NRC
Amherst, MA 01003-4210 United States
Phone: 413-545-2665　　　　Fax: 413-545-4358
Website: www.umass.edu/forwild/
Membership: 1–100
Scope: State
Description: University of Massachusetts Department of Natural Resources Conservation
Contact(s):
　Kevin Friedland, U.S. National Oceanic and Atmospheric Administration Cooperative; 413-545-2842
　Guy Lanza, Environmental Sciences, Program Director; 413-545-3747
　Richard Degraaf, U.S. Forest Service; 413-545-0357
　Martha Mather, U.S. Geological Survey, Massachusetts Cooperative Fish and Wildlife; 413-545-4895
　William McComb, Department of Natural Resources Conservation, Head

UNIVERSITY OF MASSACHUSETTS
URBAN HARBORS INSTITUTE
100 Morrissey Blvd.
Boston, MA 02125-3393 United States
Phone: 617-287-5570　　　　Fax: 617-287-5575
E-mail: urban.harbors@umb.edu
Website: www.uhi.umb.edu
Founded: 1989
Membership: 1–100
Scope: International
Description: The Urban Harbors Institute was founded as a center for the study of harbor, coastal and ocean issues. It conducts multidisciplinary research on the policy and management issues affecting the coastal area, with emphasis on the urban waterfront. It also promotes linkages between scientists, government, academic, and business communities to improve decision-making. The institute publishes research, sponsors seminars, conferences, and public forums to disseminate and exchange information.
Publication(s): The Coastlines
Contact(s):
　Richard Delaney, Director; rich.delaney@umb.edu

UNIVERSITY OF MIAMI
ROSENSTIEL SCHOOL OF MARINE AND ATMOSPHERIC SCIENCE
4600 Rickenbacker Causeway
Miami, FL 33149 United States
Phone: 305-361-4000　　　　Fax: 305-361-4711
E-mail: libcirc@rsmas.miami.edu
Website: www.rsmas.miami.edu/
Membership: 101–1,000
Scope: State
Contact(s):
　Otis Brown, Dean

UNIVERSITY OF MICHIGAN
SCHOOL OF NATURAL RESOURCES AND ENVIRONMENT
Dana Bldg., 430 East University
Ann Arbor, MI 48109-1115 United States
Phone: 734-764-6453　　　　Fax: 734-615-1277
Website: www.snre.umich.edu/
Membership: 101–1,000
Scope: State
Keyword(s): Agriculture/Farming, Air Quality/Atmosphere, Climate Change, Development/Developing Countries, Ecosystems (precious), Energy, Ethics/Environmental Justice, Executive/Legislative/Judicial Reform, Finance/Banking/Trade, Forests/Forestry, Land Issues, Oceans
Contact(s):
　Bunyan Bryant, Resource Policy and Behavior, Concentration Chair
　James Diana, Resource Ecology and Management, Concentration Chair
　Donna Erickson, Landscape Architecture, Concentration Chair
　Daniel Mazmanian, Dean

UNIVERSITY OF MINNESOTA AT CROOKSTON
NATURAL RESOURCES DEPARTMENT
2900 University Ave.
Crookston, MN 56716 United States
Phone: 218-281-8129　　　　Fax: 218-282-8603
Website: www.crk.umn.edu
Founded: 1968
Membership: 101–1,000
Scope: Regional
Description: Offers a broadly-oriented natural resource program which prepares students for entry-level resource management positions. Practical and field instruction in integrated land management is emphasized leading to a B.S. degree in Natural Resource Management, Wildlife Management, Park Management, Water Resource Management, Natural Resources Aviation, Natural Resources Law Enforcement, and Law Enforcement Aviation.
Contact(s):
　Bill Haase, Department Technician; 218-281-8131; bhaase@mail.crk.umn.edu
　Philip Baird, Park & Recreation Professor; 218-281-8130; pbaird@mail.crk.umn.edu

EDUCATIONAL INSTITUTIONS – U

Thomas Feiro, Environmental Health and Safety Specialist; 218-281-8131

Ross Hier, Wildlife Management Adjunct Professor; Minnesota Department of Natural Resources, 203 West Fletcher, Crookston, MN 56716; 218-281-6063

John Loegering, Wildlife Management Professor; 218-281-8132; jloegeri@mail.crk.umn.edu

Daniel Svedarsky, Program Leader and Wildlife Professor; Natural Resources Department, University of Minnesota, Crookston, MN 56716; 218-281-8129; dsvedars@mail.crk.umn.edu

UNIVERSITY OF MINNESOTA AT ST. PAUL
FISHERIES WILDLIFE CONSERVATION BIOLOGY
COLLEGE OF NATURAL RESOURCES
200 Hodson Hall, 1980 Falwell Ave
St. Paul, MN 55108 United States
Phone: 612-624-3400   Fax: 612-625-5299
E-mail: jperry@umn.edu
Website: www.fw.umn.edu/

Founded: 1903

Scope: Local, State, Regional, National, International

Description: The mission of the College of Natural Resources is to foster a quality environment by contributing to the management, protection, and sustainable use of our natural resources through teaching, research, and outreach.

Keyword(s): Agriculture/Farming, Climate Change, Development/Developing Countries, Ecosystems (precious), Forests/Forestry, Land Issues, Sprawl/Urban Planning, Water Habitats & Quality, Wildlife & Species

Contact(s):
Susan Stafford, Dean of College of Natural Resources
Jim Perry, Department Head Fisheries, Wildlife and Conservation Biology; 6126243600
Shri Ramaswamy, Department of Wood and Paper Science, Interim Head; 612-624-5200
Deb Swackhamer, Water Resources Center, Director; 612-624-9282
Ira Adelman, Department of Fisheries and Wildlife; 612-624-3600
David Andersen, Minnesota Cooperative Fish and Wildlife Research Unit, Leader; 612-624-3421
Dorothy Anderson, Center for Environmental Learning and Leadership; 612-624-2721
Barbara Coffin, Institute for Sustainable Natural Resource Management; 612-624-4986
Francesca Cuthbert, Conservation Biology Program, Director; 612-624-1756
Alan Ek, Department of Forest Resources, Head; 612-624-3400
Bill Ganzlin, Student Services Office, Director; 612-624-6768
Anne Kapuscinski, Institute for Social Economic and Ecological Sustainability; 612-624-7719
Mike Kilgore, Center for Natural Resource Policy and Management; 612-624-3400
David Smith, Professor; 612-624-5369
Robert Sterner, Department of Ecology, Evolution and Behavior, Head; 1987 Upper Buford Cir., St. Paul, MN 55108; 612-625-6790
Bob Stine, Outreach and Extension, Associate Dean; 612-624-9298

UNIVERSITY OF MISSOURI
SCHOOL OF NATURAL RESOURCES
103 Anheuser-Busch Natural Resources Bldg.
Columbia, MO 65211-7220 United States
Phone: 573-882-6446   Fax: 573-884-2636
Website: www.snr.missouri.edu
Membership: 101–1,000
Scope: State

Keyword(s): Air Quality/Atmosphere, Climate Change, Forests/Forestry, Pollution (general), Public Lands/Greenspace, Recreation/Ecotourism, Wildlife & Species

Contact(s):
Albert Vogt, Director
R. Hammer, Soil and Atmospheric Sciences Department, Chair; 302 Anheuser-Busch Natural Resources Bldg.; 573-882-6301
Jack Jones, Fisheries and Wildlife Dept., Chair; 302 Anheuser-Busch Natural Resources Bldg.; 573-882-3436
Charles Rabeni, Cooperative Fish and Wildlife Research Unit, Leader; 302 Anheuser-Busch Natural Resources Bldg.; 573-882-3524
Carl Settergren, Forestry Dept., Chair; B.S., M.S., Ph.D.; 302 Anheuser-Busch Natural Resources Bldg., ; 573-882-2627

UNIVERSITY OF MONTANA
WILDLIFE BIOLOGY
Building 32 Campus Drive
Missoula, MT 59812-0596 United States
Phone: 406-243-5272   Fax: 406-243-4557
E-mail: pletsch@forestry.umt.edu
Website: www.forestry.umt.edu/academics/wildlife/
Scope: International

Description: Wildlife Biology is the study of wild animals and their habitat. We combine a vertebrate and plant ecology focus in the Division of Biological Sciences with conservation and management activities within the School of Forestry.

UNIVERSITY OF MONTANA SCHOOL OF FORESTRY
32 Campus Dr.
Missoula, MT 59812-0576 United States
Phone: 406-243-5521   Fax: 406-243-4845
E-mail: jilyon@forestry.umt.edu
Website: www.forestry.umt.edu
Membership: 1–100
Scope: State

Description: Educators and Researchers

Contact(s):
Perry Brown, Montana Forest and Conservation Experiment Station, Director; 406-243-5522
Daniel Pletscher, Wildlife Biology Program, Director; 406-243-5272
Perry Brown, School of Forestry Dean; 406-243-5522
James Burchfield, Bolle Center for People and Forests; 406-243-6650
Wayne Freimund, Wilderness Institute; 406-243-5184
Kelsey Milner, Inland Northwest Growth and Yield Cooperative; 406-243-6653
Norma Nickerson, Institute for Tourism and Recreation Research; 406-243-5686
Robert Pfister, Mission Oriented Research Program; 406-243-6582
Steven Running, Numerical Terradynamic Simulation Group; 406-243-6311
Jack Thomas, Boone and Crockett Wildlife Conservation Program; 406-243-5566
Hans Zuuring, Quantitative Services Group; 406-243-6465

UNIVERSITY OF NEBRASKA
SCHOOL OF NATURAL RESOURCE SCIENCES
309 Biochemistry Hall, Box 830758
Lincoln, NE 68583-0758 United States
Phone: 402-472-9873   Fax: 402-472-3610
Website: snr.unl.edu
Membership: 1–100
Scope: State

Contact(s):
Marcy Tintera, Graduate Programs; 402-472-6622; fofw031@unlvm.unl.edu

EDUCATIONAL INSTITUTIONS- U

UNIVERSITY OF NEVADA - AT RENO
DEPARTMENT OF ENVIRONMENTAL AND
RESOURCES SCIENCES
1000 Valley Rd.
Reno, NV 89512 United States
Phone: 775-784-6763   Fax: 702-784-4583
Website: www.ag.unr.edu/ers/default.htm
Membership: 1–100
Scope: State, Regional, National, International
Description: The mission of the Department of Environmental and Resource Sciences is to provide and apply scientific knowledge and understanding of inter-relationships among people, living organisms and the environments of the Intermountain West, through outreach in teaching, research and service.
Publication(s): See publication website
Contact(s):
   Michael Collopy, Professor, Chair; 775-784-6763; Fax: 775-784-4583; mcollopy@cabnr.unr.edu
   James Sedinger, Professor; 775-784-5665; Fax: 775-784-4583; JSedinger@cabnr.unr.edu
   Dale Johnson, Natural Resource Management; ext. 4511
   Glenn Miller, Environmental Science; 775-784-4108; Fax: 775-784-1142; gcmiller@scs.unr.edu
   Watkins Miller, Department of Environmental and Resource Sciences, Chairman
   Roger Walker, Natural Resource Management; ext. 4039; walker@unr.edu

UNIVERSITY OF NEVADA AT LAS VEGAS
ENVIRONMENTAL SCIENCE PROGRAM
4505 Maryland Parkway, Box 454030
Las Vegas, NV 89154-4030 United States
Phone: 702-895-4440   Fax: 702-895-4436
E-mail: biology@neveda.edu
Website: www.unlv.edu/Other_Programs/Environmental_Studies/
Membership: 1–100
Scope: Local
Contact(s):
   Carl Reiber, Chairman; reiber@nevada.edu
   Helen Neil, Environmental Studies Dept.; neil@nevada.edu

UNIVERSITY OF NEVADA AT LAS VEGAS
WATER RESOURCES PROGRAM
4505 Maryland Pkwy.
Las Vegas, NV 89154-4029 United States
Phone: 702-895-4006   Fax: 702-895-4064
E-mail: wrmunlv@hotmail.com
Website: www.unlv.depts/wrm
Scope: State
Description: The Water Resources Management Graduate Program at the University of Nevada is an interdisciplinary environmental program. The curriculum includes studies in water quality and quantity; surface water and groundwater; and water law, regulation, and management. Offers environmental programs at graduate level.
Contact(s):
   David Kreamer, Director; kreamerd@nevada.edu

UNIVERSITY OF NEVADA COOPERATIVE EXTENSION
University of Nevada Cooperative Extension
Dean & Director's Office/MS404
Reno, NV 89557 United States
Phone: 775-784-7070   Fax: 775-784-7079
E-mail: burtonj@unce.unr.edu
Website: www.unce.unr.edu
Founded: 1914
Scope: Local, State, Regional
Description: Community-based outreach educational programs and applied research.
Keyword(s): Agriculture/Farming, Forests/Forestry, Land Issues, Public Lands/Greenspace, Water Habitats & Quality
Contact(s):
   Dixie Allsbrook, Area Director; 2345 Red Rock St., Suite 100, Las Vegas, NV 89146; 702-222-3130; Fax: 702-222-3100; allsbrookd@unce.unr.edu
   Karen Hinton, Dean and Director; Dean & Director's Office/MS 404, Reno, NV 89557; 775-784-7070; Fax: 775-784-7079; hintonk@unce.unr.edu
   John Burton, Assistant Director; Dean & Director's Office/MS 404, Reno, NV 89557; 7775-784-7070; burtonj@unce.unr.edu
   John Cobourn, Western Area Water Specialist; P.O. Box 8208, Incline Village, NV 89452; 775-832-4150; cobournj@unce.unr.edu
   Jason Davison, Central Area Agronomy and Range Specialist; 111 Sheckler Rd., Fallon, NV 89406; 775-423-5121; davisonj@unce.unr.edu
   Ed Smith, Western Area Natural Resources Specialist; P.O. Box 338, Minden, NV 89423; 775-782-9960; smithe@unce.unr.edu
   Sherman Swanson, State Range Specialist and Riparian Scientist; 1000 Valley Rd., Reno, NV 89512; 775-784-4057; Fax: 775-784-4583; sswanson@cabnr.unr.edu
   Mark Walker, State Water Specialist; 775-784-1938; mwalker@equinox.unr.edu

UNIVERSITY OF NEW BRUNSWICK
FORESTRY AND ENVIRONMENTAL MANAGEMENT
P. O. Box 44555
Fredericton, E3B 6C2 New Brunswick Canada
Phone: 506-453-4501   Fax: 506-453-3538
E-mail: daug@unb.ca
Website: www.unb.ca/departs/forestry/
Founded: 1908
Scope: State
Description: B.S. in Forest Ecosystem Management or Forest Engineering; Minors include Environmental Science, Wildlife Conservation and Management and Parks and Wilderness.
Keyword(s): Air Quality/Atmosphere, Climate Change, Ecosystems (precious), Forests/Forestry, Land Issues, Public Lands/Greenspace, Recreation/Ecotourism, Water Habitats & Quality, Wildlife & Species
Contact(s):
   David Maclean, Dean; Box 44555, Fredericton, New Brunswick E3A 6C2; 506-453-4501; Fax: 506-453-3538; macleand@unb.ca
   David Daugharty, Assistant Dean and Undergraduate Information; Box 44555, Fredericton, New Brunswick E3A 6C2; 506-453-4501; Fax: 506-453-3538; daug@unb.ca
   John Kershaw, Director of Graduate Studies; Box 44555, Fredericton, New Brunswick E3A 6C2; 506-453-4501; Fax: 506-453-3538; kershaw@unb.ca

UNIVERSITY OF NEW HAMPSHIRE
Natural Resources, 215 James Hall, 56 College Rd.
Durham, NH 03824 United States
Phone: 603-862-1234   Fax: 603-862-1234
Website: www.unh.edu
Scope: State
Description: Department of Natural Resources
Publication(s): New Hampshire, The, Campus Journal
Contact(s):
   John Aber, Natural Resources and Earth System Sci., Program Coordinator
   Mimi Becker, Environmental Conservation, Program Coordinator
   Carl Bolster, Jr., Water Resources Management, Program Coordinator

Russell Congalton, Forestry/Natural Resources Graduate Program Coordinator
Mark Ducey, Forestry, Program Coordinator
Serita Frey, Soil Science, Program Coordinator
Thomas Lee, Environmental Conservation, Program Coordinator
John Litvaitis, Wildlife Ecology, Program Coordinator
William McDowell, Water Resources Mgt., Program Coordinator; Department Chair; Department of Natural Resources
Peter Pekins, Wildlife Management, Program Coordinator

UNIVERSITY OF NEW HAMPSHIRE COOPERATIVE EXTENSION
FORESTRY AND WILDLIFE PROGRAM
214 Nesmith Hall
131 Main Street
Durham, NH 03824-3597 United States
Phone: 603-862-1028   Fax: 603-862-0107
E-mail: debra.anderson@unh.edu
Website: ceinfo.unh.edu

Founded: 1925
Scope: Local, State, Regional
Description: The natural resource components include Wildlife, Forest Stewardship, Community Forestry, Rural Economic Well-Being, Agriculture, and Natural Resource Conservation Education.
Keyword(s): Ecosystems (precious), Forests/Forestry, Land Issues, Public Lands/Greenspace, Water Habitats & Quality, Wildlife & Species

Contact(s):
Robert Edmonds, Program Leader: Forestry/Wildlife; 603-862-2619; bob.edmonds@unh.edu
Karen Bennett, Extension Specialist, Forest Resources; 603-862-4861; karen.bennett@unh.edu
Darrel Covell, Extension Specialist, Wildlife; 603-862-3594; darrel.covell@unh.edu
Frank Mitchell, Extension Specialist: Land and Water Conservation; 603-862-1067; frank.mitchell@unh.edu
Sarah Smith, Extension Specialist, Forest Industry; 603-862-2647; Fax: 603-862-0107; sarah.smith@unh.edu
Ellen Snyder, Extension Specialist, Biodiversity, 603-862-4277; ellen.snyder@unh.edu
Jeffrey Schloss, Extension Specialist: Water Resources; 603-862-3848; jeff.schloss@unh.edu

UNIVERSITY OF NEW HAVEN DEPT. OF BIOLOGY AND ENVIRONMENTAL SCIENCES
GRADUATE AND UNDERGRADUATE PROGRAMS IN ENVIRONMENTAL SCIENCES
300 Orange Ave.
West Haven, CT 06516 United States
Phone: 203-932-7101   Fax: 203-931-6097
Website: www.newhaven.edu/

Membership: 1–100
Scope: National
Description: We offer full and part-time undergraduate and graduate programs leading to a B.S. or M.S. in Environmental Science. Five-year combined program also available. Graduate concentrations include Env. Geoscience, Geographical Information Systems, Env. Ecology, Env. Health and Safety, and a "make-your-own" concentration. We are also implementing a new concentration in Environmental Education. The University of New Haven is affiliated with the Gerace Research Station on San Salvador Island, Bahamas.
Publication(s): Bahamian Field Station Affiliation, Geographical Information System Lab
Keyword(s): Development/Developing Countries, Land Issues, Oceans/Coasts/Beaches, Public Lands/Greenspace, Water Habitats & Quality

Contact(s):
Carmela Cuomo, Coordinator of Program in Marine Biology; 203-932-7101; Fax: 203-931-6097; ccuomo@newhaven.edu
R. Laurence Davis, Coordinator of Programs in Environmental Science; 203-932-7108; Fax: 203-931-6097; rldavis@newhaven.edu
Michael Rossi, Chair of Biology and Environmental Science; 203-932-7101; Fax: 203-931-6097; mrossi@newhaven.edu
Roman Zajac, Professor of Biology and Environmental Science; 203-932-7101; Fax: 203-931-6097; rzajac@newhaven.edu

UNIVERSITY OF NORTH CAROLINA AT ASHEVILLE
ENVIRONMENTAL STUDIES DEPARTMENT
CPO 2330, One University Heights
Asheville, NC 28804-8511 United States
Phone: 828-251-6441   Fax: 828-251-6041
Website: www.unca.edu/envr_studies/

Founded: 1983
Membership: 101–1,000
Scope: State
Description: UNCA offers a Bachelor of Science Degree in Environmental Studies, with degree concentrations in Earth Science, Ecology and Environmental Biology, Natural Resource Management, and Pollution Control, plus individualized courses of study. The Environmental Studies degree is enhanced with a required internship that provides real-world experience and potential employment opportunities from many public and private organizations located in the Asheville area, elsewhere in the U.S., and abroad.
Keyword(s): Air Quality/Atmosphere, Climate Change, Development/Developing Countries, Ecosystems (precious), Energy, Ethics/Environmental Justice, Forests/Forestry, Land Issues, Oceans/Coasts/Beaches, Pollution (general), Population, Public Health, Sprawl/Urban Planning

Contact(s):
Richard Maas, Contact; 828-251-6366; maas@unca.edu

UNIVERSITY OF NORTH CAROLINA AT CHAPEL HILL
Campus Box 7400 Rosenau Hall
Chapel Hill, NC 27599-7431 United States
Phone: 919-966-1171   Fax: 919-966-7911
Website: www.unc.edu

Membership: 1–100
Scope: State

Contact(s):
Louise Ball, Environmental Health Sciences; Environmental Science and Engineering, 4114 E McGavran-Greenberg Hall, Chapel Hill, NC 27599; 919-966-7306; lmball@sph.unc.edu
Russell Christman, Aquatic and Atmospheric Sciences; Environmental Science and Engineering, 164 Rosenau Hall, Chapel Hill, NC 27599; 919-966-1683; russ_christman@unc.edu
William Glaze, Environmental Sciences and Engineering; Environmental Science and Engineering, 105 Miller Hall, Chapel Hill, NC 27599; 919-966-9917; bill_glaze@unc.edu
Richard Kamens, Air, Radiation, and Industrial Hygiene; Environmental Science and Engineering, 115 Rosenau Hall, Chapel Hill, NC 27599; 919-966-5452; kamens@unc.edu
Christopher Martens, Marine Sciences; 12-4A Venable Hall, Chapel Hill, NC 27599; 919-962-0152; martens@marine.unc.edu
Frederic Pfaender, Institute for Environmental Science & Engineering; Environmental Science and Engineering, 157 Rosenau Hall, Chapel Hill, NC 27599; 919-966-3842; fred_pfaender@unc.edu

Seth Reice, Ecology, Chairman; 244 Wilson Hall, Chapel Hill, NC 27599; 919-962-1375; sreice@biomass.bio.unc.edu

Philip Singer, Water Resources Engineering; Environmental Science and Engineering,110 Rosenau Hall, Chapel Hill, NC 27599; 919-962-3865; phil_singer@unc.edu

UNIVERSITY OF NORTH DAKOTA
BIOLOGY DEPARTMENT
Box 9019
Grand Forks, ND 58202-9019 United States
Phone: 701-777-2621 Fax: 701-777-2623
Website: www.und.nodak.edu/

Founded: 1883
Membership: 1–100
Scope: Local, State, Regional, National, International
Description: Wildlife - B.S., M.S., Ph.D. Dr. Richard D. Crawford, Dr. Richard S. Sweitzer; Fisheries - B.S., M.S., Ph.D. Dr. Steven Kelsch; Conservation Biology - Specialization within B.S., M.S., and Ph.D. in Biology Dr. Issac Schlosser, Dr. Robert Newman
Keyword(s): Agriculture/Farming, Climate Change, Ecosystems (precious), Energy, Land Issues, Population, Public Lands/Greenspace, Water Habitats & Quality, Wildlife & Species

Contact(s):
Richard Crawford, Professor; richard.crawford@und.nodak.edu
Robert Newman, Associate Professor; robert.newman@und.nodak.edu
Issac Schlosser, Professor; issac.schlosser@und.nodak.edu
Richard Sweitzer, Assistant Professor; richard.sweitzer@und.nodak.edu
Steven Kelsch, Fishery Research Unit, Leader; steven.kelsch@und.nodak.edu

UNIVERSITY OF NORTH TEXAS
INSTITUTE OF APPLIED SCIENCES
NT Box 310559
Denton, TX 76203 United States
Phone: 940-565-2694 Fax: 940-565-4297
Website: www.ias.unt.edu/

Founded: 1976
Scope: State
Description: An interdisciplinary unit whose primary research activities are oriented towards land and water resources. Research includes aquatic toxicology, surface and groundwater quality, archaeology, remote sensing, geographic information systems and environmental modeling. In 1998, the institute took on an environmental outreach program which includes the Outdoor Environmental Learning Area (ODELA) and the Sky Theater.
Keyword(s): Ecosystems (precious), Water Habitats & Quality, Wildlife & Species

Contact(s):
Miguel Acevedo, Environmental Modeling Laboratory, Director; 940-565-2091
Samuel Atkinson, Center for Remote Sensing, Director; 940-565-2694
Robert Doyle, Wetlands Research, Director; 940-565-2694
Reid Ferring, Center for Environmental Archaeology, Director; 940-565-2694
Eugene Hargrove, Faculty for Environmental Philosophy, Executive Director; 940-565-2266
Bruce Hunter, Environmental Visualization Laboratory, Director; 940-565-2694
James Kennedy, Water Research Field Station, Director; 940-565-2694
Thomas Lapoint, Director; 940-369-7776
Tom Lapoint, Experimental Stream Director; 940-565-2694
Chris Littler, Planetarium Director; 940-565-2694
Mike Nieswiadomy, Center for Environmental Economics, Director; 940-565-2573
Farida Saleh, Environmental Chemistry Laboratory, Director; 940-565-2694
Andy Schoolmaster, Center for Spatial Analysis, Director; 940-565-2901
William Waller, Aquatic Toxicology and Reservoir Limnology, Director; 940-565-2694
Samuel Atkinson, Graduate Program In Environmental Science, Coordinator; 940-565-2694
Kenneth Dickson, Professor
Jan Dickson, Faculty for Environmental Ethics, Coordinator; 940-565-2727
Eugene Hargrove, Graduate Program in Environmental Ethics, Coordinator; 940-565-2266
Steve Spurger, Elm Fork Education Center, Coordinator; 940-565-2694
Sandra Terrell, Interdisciplinary Graduate Studies, Dean
Rudi Thompson, Elm Fork Education Center, Coordinator; 940-565-2694

UNIVERSITY OF NORTHERN BRITISH COLUMBIA
ECOSYSTEM SCIENCE & MANAGEMENT PROGRAM
3333 University Way
Prince George, V2N 4Z9 British Columbia Canada
Phone: 250-960-5555 Fax: 250-960-5539
Website: www.unbc.ca

Founded: 1990
Membership: 1–100
Scope: Regional, National, International
Description: UNBC is a research intensive, small university founded in 1990 as "a university in the north, for the north." The Ecosystem Science & Management Program develops managers and scientists to effectively meet the demands for natural resources products and services while maintaining a quality environment. The Program offers majors in Biology, Wildlife and Fisheries, Forestry (accredited by the Canadian Forestry Accreditation Board) and a BA in Environmental Studies.
Keyword(s): Climate Change, Ecosystems (precious), Ethics/Environmental Justice, Forests/Forestry, Land Issues, Pollution (general), Wildlife & Species

Contact(s):
Keith Egger, Professor; 250-960-5860; Fax: 250-960-5539; egger@unbc.ca

UNIVERSITY OF NORTHERN COLORADO
DEPARTMENT OF BIOLOGICAL SCIENCES
501 20th Street
Greeley, CO 80639 United States
Phone: 970-351-2921 Fax: 970-351-2335
Website: www.unco.edu/biology/

Membership: 1–100
Scope: State
Description: The UNC Dept. of Biological Sciences offers undergraduate and masters degrees in Biology and a Ph.D. in Biology Education, which may emphasize environmental education research.

Contact(s):
Curt Peterson, Dept. Chair, Biological Sciences; 970-351-2923; curt.peterson@unco.edu
Gerry Saunders, Associate Professor, Biological Sciences

UNIVERSITY OF OREGON
INSTITUTE FOR A SUSTAINABLE ENVIRONMENT
5247 University of Oregon
130 Hendricks Hall
Eugene, OR 97403-5247 United States
Phone: 541-346-0675 Fax: 541-346-2040
E-mail: rribe@darkwing.uoregon.edu
Website: gladstone.uoregon.edu~enviro

Founded: 1994

Membership: 1–100
Scope: Regional
Description: Foster research and education at the University of Oregon with regard to environmental issues. The Institute's program encompass environmental themes in the natural sciences, the social sciences, policy studies, humanities and professional fields.
Publication(s): Organization Brochure
Contact(s):
Robert Ribe, Director

UNIVERSITY OF OREGON
SCHOOL OF LAW
1221 UOFO School of Law
Eugene, OR 97403-1221 United States
Phone: 541-346-3852   Fax: 541-346-1564
Website: www.law.uoregon.edu/home.html
Scope: State
Contact(s):
Michael Axline, Western Natural Resource Law Clinic, Director; maxline@law.uoregon.edu
Rennard Strickland, Dean; mholland@law.uoregon.edu

UNIVERSITY OF PENNSYLVANIA
GRADUATE SCHOOL OF FINE ARTS
DEPARTMENT OF LANDSCAPE ARCHITECTURE
119 Meyerson Hall, 210 S. 34th St
Philadelphia, PA 19104-6311 United States
Phone: 215-898-6591   Fax: 215-573-3770
E-mail: larp@pobox.upenn.edu
Website: www.upenn.edu/gsfa/
Membership: 1–100
Scope: National
Keyword(s): Public Lands/Greenspace
Contact(s):
James Corner, Department of Landscape Architecture, Chairman; corner@pobox.upenn.edu

UNIVERSITY OF PITTSBURGH
BIOLOGY DEPARTMENT
Langley Hall
4249 Fifth & Luskin Aves.
Pittsburgh, PA 15260 United States
Phone: 412-624-4266   Fax: 412-624-4759
Website: www.pitt.edu/~biolohome/main.html
Membership: 1–100
Scope: State
Description: The Biology Department offers a major in Ecology and Evolution, designed to provide the student with a selection of courses covering various aspects of these two fields of biology. The Department operates the Pymatuning Laboratory of Ecology with laboratories and teaching facilities in northwestern Pennsylvania, offering year-round research opportunites and summer courses.
Keyword(s): Ecosystems (precious)
Contact(s):
Gail Johnston, Ecology and Pymatuning Laboratory of Ecology, Director
James Pipas, Department of Biological Sciences, Chairman; 412-624-4350; Fax: 412-624-9311
Stephen Tonsor, Associate Professor

UNIVERSITY OF PITTSBURGH
GRADUATE SCHOOL OF PUBLIC HEALTH
DEPARTMENT OF ENVIRONMENTAL AND OCCUPATIONAL HEALTH
260 Kappa Dr.
Pittsburgh, PA 15238 United States
Phone: 412-967-6500   Fax: 412-624-1020
Website: server.ceoh.pitt.edu/

Scope: International
Description: The mission of the Department of Environmental and Occupational Health is to reduce the health risks associated with exposure to chemical, physical, and biological agents found in industry and nature. Three degrees and a specialty certificate in risk assessment are offered.
Contact(s):
Herbert Rosenkranz, Chairperson

UNIVERSITY OF REGINA
DEPARTMENT OF BIOLOGY
3737 Wascana Parkway
Regina, S4S 0A2 Saskatchewan Canada
Phone: 306-585-4145   Fax: 306-585-4894
E-mail: william.chapco@uregina.ca
Website: www.uregina.ca/science/biology/index.htm
Founded: 1973
Membership: 1–100
Scope: Local, Regional, National, International
Description: An academic department in a university with 12 faculty members, 4 of whom currently do conservation oriented research.
Contact(s):
Mark Brigham; m.brigham@uregina.ca
William Chapco, Dept. Head; 306-585-4478; William.Chapco@uregina.ca
Peter Leavitt, Limnology Laboratory; 306-585-4253; Leavitt@uregina.ca
Mary Vetter; mary.vetter@uregina.ca
Rolf Vinebrooke
Scott Wilson, Plant Ecology Laboratory; 306-585-4287; scott.wilson@uregina.ca

UNIVERSITY OF RHODE ISLAND
DEPARTMENT OF NATURAL RESOURCES SCIENCE
105 Coastal Institute
Kingston, RI 02881 United States
Phone: 401-874-2495   Fax: 401-874-4561
E-mail: nrs@etal.uri.edu
Website: nrs.uri.edu/
Founded: 1983
Membership: 1–100
Scope: Local, State, Regional, National, International
Description: The teaching mission of the Department of Natural Resources Science is to help students acquire the technical knowledge and practical skills needed to understand and wisely manage natural and disturbed ecosystems and their basic components: soil, water, air and biota. The research mission of the department is to use hypothesis-based methods of scientific inquiry toward development of applicable solutions to environmental problems.
Keyword(s): Climate Change, Ecosystems (precious), Forests/Forestry, Oceans/Coasts/Beaches, Pollution (general), Public Health, Sprawl/Urban Planning, Water Habitats & Quality, Wildlife & Species
Contact(s):
Thomas Husband, Professor and Chair; 401-874-2912; Fax: 401-874-4561; tom@uri.edu

UNIVERSITY OF RHODE ISLAND
GRADUATE SCHOOL OF OCEANOGRAPHY AND COASTAL RESOURCES CENTER
URI Bay Campus, South Ferry Rd.
Narragansett, RI 02882-1197 United States
Phone: 401-874-6246   Fax: 401-874-6889
E-mail: thedean@gso.uri.edu
Website: www.gso.uri.edu
Founded: 1972
Membership: 101–1,000
Scope: State

Description: Dedicated to advancing coastal ecosystem management, nationally and internationally.
Publication(s): Publications on website
Contact(s):
David Farmer, Director
Scott Nixon, Director, RI Sea Grant College Program
Chip Young, CRC Communications Director; 401-874-6630; cyoung@gso.uri.edu

UNIVERSITY OF SASKATCHEWAN
COLLEGE OF AGRICULTURE
2D30 - 51 Campus Dr.
Saskatoon, S7N 5A8 Saskatchewan Canada
Phone: 306-966-4050 Fax: 306-966-8894
Website: www.ag.usask.ca/
Membership: 1,001–10,000
Scope: Regional
Keyword(s): Agriculture/Farming, Air Quality/Atmosphere, Climate Change, Development/Developing Countries, Ecosystems (precious), Energy, Forests/Forestry, Land Issues, Pollution (general), Public Lands/Greenspace, Water Habitats & Quality, Wildlife & Species
Contact(s):
M. E. Fulton, Head of Agricultural Economics
Jim Germida, Dept. of Soil Science, Head; 5E34.1, Agriculture Building , 51 Campus Dr., Saskatoon, Saskatchewan S7N 5A8; 306-966-6836; Fax: 306-966-6881; germida@sask.usask.ca
B Laarveld, Head, Department of Animal Poultry Science
Graham Scoles, Dept. of Plant Sciences, Head; Rm. 4D36 Agriculture Bldg., 51 Campus Dr., Saskatoon, Saskatchewan S7N 5A8; 306-966-5855; Fax: 306-966-5015; graham.scoles@sask.usask.ca
R. Tyler, Head Dept. Applied Microbiology & Food Science

UNIVERSITY OF SOUTH CAROLINA
BARUCH MARINE FIELD LABORATORY
NORTH INLET- WINYAH BAY NATIONAL ESTUARINE RESEARCH RESERVE
P.O. Box 1630
Georgetown, SC 29442 United States
Phone: 843-546-3623 Fax: 843-546-1632
E-mail: dallen@belle.baruch.sc.edu
Website: www.baruch.sc.edu
Founded: 1969
Membership: 1–100
Scope: State, Regional, National
Description: Coastal and estuarine research and monitoring; long-term ecological research and impacts of watershed development; 75 active projects in 2003; undergraduate and graduate programs; training programs for coastal decision-makers; public education
Keyword(s): Ecosystems (precious), Oceans/Coasts/Beaches, Water Habitats & Quality, Wildlife & Species
Contact(s):
Dennis Allen, Resident Director; 843-546-3623; dallen@belle.baruch.sc.edu

UNIVERSITY OF SOUTH CAROLINA
MARINE SCIENCE PROGRAM
EWS 603, 712 Main Street
Columbia, SC 29208 United States
Phone: 803-777-2692 Fax: 803-777-3935
E-mail: marisci@vm.sc.edu
Website: www.msci.sc.edu/
Scope: State
Description: The Marine Science Program, in the College of Science and Mathematics at the University of South Carolina, is an interdisciplinary educational program offering curricula which lead to the Bachelor of Science, Master of Science, and Doctor of Philosophy degrees.

Contact(s):
Bjorn Kjerfve, Marine Science Program Director; 803-777-2692

UNIVERSITY OF SOUTH CAROLINA BEAUFORT
CENTER FOR COASTAL ECOLOGY & PRITCHARDS ISLAND
467 Tarpon Boulevard
St. Helena, SC 29920 United States
Phone: 843-575-7432
E-mail: pritchards_island@hotmail.com
Website: www.sc.edu/beaufort/pritchar/index.htm
Founded: 1996
Membership: 101–1,000
Scope: Local, State, Regional
Description: The USCB Center for Coastal Ecology & Pritchards Island provides community-based education, conservation, and research programs to increase environmental awareness and stewardship of coastal ecology. Primary project consists of the 21 year old loggerhead sea turtle conservation project that allows citizens to become scientists through hands-on education and research experiences. All field programs are offered on Pritchards Island, a remote, undeveloped barrier island owned by the University.
Keyword(s): Ecosystems (precious), Oceans/Coasts/Beaches

UNIVERSITY OF SOUTHERN CALIFORNIA
DEPARTMENT OF CIVIL AND ENVIRONMENTAL ENGINEERING
Los Angeles, CA 90089-2531 United States
Phone: 213-740-7832
E-mail: civileng@usc.edu
Website: www.usc.edu/dept/engineering/
Contact(s):
Donald Lewis, Environmental Social Sciences Program, Dean of the Division
L. Wellford, Chair, Civil and Environmental Engineering Department

UNIVERSITY OF SOUTHERN CALIFORNIA
ENVIRONMENTAL STUDIES PROGRAM
Allan Hancock Foundation Bldg. Rm. M232
Los Angeles, CA 90089-0373 United States
Phone: 213-740-7770 Fax: 213-740-8566
E-mail: environ@usc.edu
Website: www.usc.edu/dept/LAS/envir
Membership: 1–100
Scope: National
Description: B.A. combines basic science with the study of social aspects of environmental issues. B.S. combines a concentration in Geology, Biology or Chemistry with social science. The graduate program offers a choice of three concentrations: Global Environmental Issues and Development; Law, Policy and Management; and Environmental Planning and Analysis.
Contact(s):
Linda Duguay, Director; duguay@usc.edu

UNIVERSITY OF SOUTHERN MISSISSIPPI
DEPARTMENT OF BIOLOGICAL SCIENCES
USM, P.O. Box 5018
Hattiesburg, MS 39406 United States
Phone: 601-266-4748 Fax: 601-266-5797
Website: www.biology.usm.edu
Membership: 1–100
Scope: State
Publication(s): See publication website
Keyword(s): Agriculture/Farming, Ecosystems (precious), Oceans/Coasts/Beaches
Contact(s):
David Beckett, Aquatic Biology and Aquatic Ecology
Patricia Biesiot, Marine Biology, Contact

Glenn Matlack, Resource Mangement and Environmental Planning, Contact
Stephen Ross, Fisheries Biology and Aquatic Ecology

UNIVERSITY OF TENNESSEE - AT KNOXVILLE
DEPARTMENT OF FORESTRY, WILDLIFE AND FISHERIES
Plant Sciences Bldg
Knoxville, TN 37996 United States
Phone: 865-974-7126 Fax: 865-974-4714
E-mail: fwf@utk.edu
Website: fwf.ag.utk.edu

Founded: 1964
Membership: 101–1,000
Scope: State, Regional, National, International
Description: Offer B.S. degree in forestry, forest management concentration, wildland recreation concentration, M.S. in forestry, Thesis and Non-Thesis Option, and B.S. and M.S. degrees in wildlife and fisheries science. Ph.D. in natural resources.
Keyword(s): Air Quality/Atmosphere, Ecosystems (precious), Forests/Forestry, Land Issues, Public Lands/Greenspace, Recreation/Ecotourism, Water Habitats & Quality, Wildlife & Species
Contact(s):
Richard Evans, Superintendent, Forestry Experiment Station; revans@utk.edu
George Hopper, Professor and Department Head; ghopper@utk.edu
J. Wilson, Associate Dept. Head, Fisheries; jlwilson@utk.edu

UNIVERSITY OF TENNESSEE AT MARTIN
COLLEGE OF AGRICULTURE AND APPLIED SCIENCES
Martin, TN 38238 United States
Phone: 901-587-7250 Fax: 901-587-7968
Website: www.utm.edu/departments/agr/agr.html

Scope: National
Description: Offers a B.S. degree in natural resources management with concentrations in wildlife biology, environmental management, soil and water conservation, and park and recreation administration.
Contact(s):
Jim Byford, Dean

UNIVERSITY OF THE DISTRICT OF COLUMBIA
4200 Connecticut Avenue, NW
Washington, DC 20008 United States
Phone: 202-274-6474
Website: www.udc.edu/welcome.htm

Keyword(s): Agriculture/Farming, Ecosystems (precious), Energy, Oceans/Coasts/Beaches, Pollution (general), Sprawl/Urban Planning, Wildlife & Species
Contact(s):
Freddie Dixon, Department of Biological and Environmental Sciences, Acting; Bldg. 44; 202-274-7401

UNIVERSITY OF THE SOUTH (SEWANEE)
DEPARTMENT OF FORESTRY AND GEOLOGY
735 University Ave.
Sewanee, TN 37383 United States
Website: www.sewanee.edu/Forestry_Geology/ForestryGeology.html

Description: B.S. in Forestry, B.S. or B.A. in Geology or Natural Resources
Contact(s):
Stephen Shaver, Chairman; 931-598-1116; sshaver@seraph1.sewanee.edu

UNIVERSITY OF THE VIRGIN ISLANDS
DIVISION OF SCIENCE AND MATHEMATICS
CENTER FOR MARINE AND ENVIRONMENTAL STUDIES
No. 2 John Brewers Bay
Charlotte Amalie, St. Thomas, VI 00802-9990
United States
Phone: 340-693-1380 Fax: 340-693-1385
Website: www.uvi.edu

Founded: 1962
Scope: State
Description: Historically Black University, with undergraduate degrees in the sciences, including Marine Biology and research activities in Marine Science through the Center for Marine and Environmental Studies
Publication(s): The Effect of Natural Variation in Substrate Architecture on the Survival of Juvenile Bi-color Dansel Fish by R.S. Nemet, Monitoring the Effects of Land Development on Near Shore Reef Environment of St. Thomas, U.S. Virgin Islands written by R.S Nemet
Contact(s):
Richard Nemeth, Maclean Marine Science Center, Center for Marine and Environ; 340-693-1381; Fax: 340-693-1385; rncmcth@uvi.edu
Robert Stolz, Division of Science and Mathematics, Chair

UNIVERSITY OF TORONTO
FORESTRY DEPARTMENT
33 Willcocks St.
Toronto, M5S 3B3 Ontario Canada
Phone: 416-978-6152 Fax: 416-978-3834
E-mail: gradprog@forestry.utoronto.ca
Website: www.forestry.utoronto.ca

Scope: Province
Description: Master of Forest Conservation Program (M.F.C.)
Contact(s):
D. Balsillie, M.F.C. Coordinator; 416-978-4638; david.balsillie@utoronto.ca
Rorke Bryan, Dean; r.bryan@utoronto.ca

UNIVERSITY OF TULSA
PETROLEUM ABSTRACTS
600 S. College
101 Harwell
Tulsa, OK 74104-3189 United States
Phone: 918-631-2295 Fax: 918-599-9361
E-mail: dbrown@utulsa.edu
Website: www.pa.utulsas.edu

Founded: 1961
Membership: 1–100
Scope: State, International
Description: Information on ecology and pollution related to petroleum exploration, production and transportation, plus environmental, health and safety topics. PA's online TULSA database includes more than 50,000 environmentally related entries.
Contact(s):
David Brown, Marketing Manager

UNIVERSITY OF VERMONT EXTENSION
University of Vermont Extension
Adams House/601 Main Street
Burlington, VT 05401-3439 United States
Phone: 802-656-2990 Fax: 802-656-8642
E-mail: doug.lantagne@uvm.edu
Website: www.uvm.edu/extension

Founded: 1914
Membership: 101–1,000
Scope: State

Description: UVM Extension is a system of nonformal education, bringing research information in a practical form to Vermonters. Extension with the specific expertise of our state university meets the needs of agriculture, communities, families, and youth. Programs are specifically focused on natural resource conservation, sustainable agriculture and rural development, health care in rural areas, resource distribution in communities, and the contemporary stresses on the American family.

Keyword(s): Agriculture/Farming, Forests/Forestry, Land Issues, Recreation/Ecotourism

Contact(s):
  Vern Grubinger, Director of Sustainable Agriculture Center; UVM Extension, 157 Old Guilford Rd., #4, Brattleboro, VT 05301; 802-257-7967; ext. 13; Fax: 802-257-0112; vernon.grubinger@uvm.edu
  Douglas Lantagne, Interim Director University of Vermont Extension; UVM Extension State Office, Adams House/601 Main St., Burlington, VT 05401; 802-656-2990; Fax: 802-656-8642; doug.lantagne@uvm.edu
  Linda Berlin, Youth, Family and Strong Communities; UVM Extension, 309A Terrill Hall, Burlington, VT 05405; 802-656-0669; Fax: 802-656-0407; linda.berlin@uvm.edu
  Gary Deziel, Dairy Agriculture; UVM Extension, 278 So. Main Street, Ste. 2, St. Albans, VT 05478; 802-524-6501; ext. 125; Fax: 802-524-6062; gary.deziel@uvm.edu
  Jurij Homziak, Natural Resources and Sustainable Economic Development; School of Natural Resources, 317 Aiken Center, Burlington, VT 05405; 802-656-0682; Fax: 802-656-8683; jurij.homziak@uvm.edu
  Thom McEvoy, Extension Forester; School of Natural Resources, 345 Aiken Center, Burlington, VT 05405; 802-656-2913; Fax: 802-656-8683; thomas.mcevoy@uvm.edu
  Mary Peabody, Diversified Agriculture; UVM Extension, 617 Comstock Rd, Ste. 5, Berlin, VT 05602; 802-223-2389; ext. 13; Fax: 802-223-6500; mary.peabody@uvm.edu

UNIVERSITY OF VERMONT, SCHOOL OF NATURAL RESOURCES
SCHOOL OF NATURAL RESOURCES
George D. Aiken Center
81 Carrigan Dr.
Burlington, VT 05405 United States
Phone: 802-656-4280   Fax: 802-656-8683
Website: www.uvm.edu/snr
Membership: 1–100
Scope: State

Contact(s):
  Alan McIntosh, Water Resources and Lake Studies Center, Director
  Ian Worley, Environmental Studies Program, Interim Director
  Donald Dehayes, Dean
  Donald Dehayes, Natural Resources
  David Hirth, Wildlife and Fisheries Biology Program
  Robert Manning, Recreation Management,
  Alan McIntosh, Environmental Sciences Program, Director of Water
  Carlton Newton, Forestry
  John Shane, Chair of Forestry Program; jshane@nature.fnr.uvn.edu
  Patricia Stokowski, Graduate Program Coordinator; pstokows@nature.fnr.uvm.edu
  Deane Wang, Natural Resources Planning; 802-656-2694; dwang@snr.uvm.edu

UNIVERSITY OF WEST FLORIDA
11000 University Parkway
Pensacola, FL 32514 United States
Phone: 850-474-3000
Website: www.uwf.edu
Membership: 1,001–10,000
Scope: International
Description: Provides guided nature trail tours.

Contact(s):
  Joe Lepo, Institute for Coastal & Estuarine Research, Acting Director; 850-857-6098; jlepo@uwf.edu
  George Stewart, Departmant of Biology, Chair; 850-474-2748

UNIVERSITY OF WISCONSIN
SEA GRANT PROGRAM
1975 Willow Dr.
Madison, WI 53706-1177 United States
Phone: 608-262-0905   Fax: 608-262-0591
E-mail: administrator@seagrant.wisc.edu
Website: www.seagrant.wisc.edu/
Founded: 1968
Scope: National
Description: The University of Wisconsin Sea Grant Institute supports basic and applied research, education, outreach and technology transfer for the conservation, restoration and protection of Great Lakes, coastal and ocean resources.
Keyword(s): Air Quality/Atmosphere, Climate Change, Ecosystems (precious), Land Issues, Oceans/Coasts/Beaches, Pollution (general), Public Health, Recreation/Ecotourism, Sprawl/Urban Planning, Transportation, Water Habitats & Quality, Wildlife & Species

Contact(s):
  Anders Andren, Director; 608-262-0905; Fax: 608-262-0591; awandren@seagrant.wisc.edu
  James Hurley, Assistant Director for Research and Outreach; 608-262-1136; Fax: 608-262-0591; hurley@aqua.wisc.edu
  Mary Reeb, Assistant Director for Administration and Information; 608-263-3296; Fax: 608-262-0591; mlreeb@seagrant.wisc.edu
  Stephen Wittman, Communications Director; 608-263-5371; Fax: 608-262-0591; swittman@seagrant.wisc.edu

UNIVERSITY OF WISCONSIN AT EAU CLAIRE
Eau Claire, WI 54701 United States
Phone: 715-836-4166   Fax: 715-836-5089
Website: www.uwec.edu
Membership: 1–100
Scope: State

Contact(s):
  Brady Foust, Geography, Chairman
  Paula Kleintjes, Environmental Science; Minor
  Michael Weil, Biology, Chairman

UNIVERSITY OF WISCONSIN AT GREEN BAY
NATURAL AND APPLIED SCIENCES DEPARTMENT
2420 Nicolet Dr.
Green Bay, WI 54311-7001 United States
Phone: 920-465-2000   Fax: 920-465-2376
Website: www.uwgb.edu
Membership: 1,001–10,000
Scope: State
Description: Natural and Applied Sciences Dept. offers a Bachelor's degree in Environmental Studies. Areas of emphasis focus on Physical Systems and Ecology and Biological Resources. The Dept. of Public and Environmental Affairs offers a Bachelor's degree in Environmental Studies and Planning with an emphasis in public policy or planning. The graduate school offers a M.S. in Environmental Science and Policy with an emphasis in Ecosystems Studies, Resource Management and Environmental Policy and Administration.

Contact(s):
  Robert Howe, Cofrin Arboretum Center for Biodiversity, Director; 920-465-2272; hower@uwgb.edu
  Hallett Harris, Environmental Science, Chair; 920-465-2369; Fax: 920-465-2376; harrish@uwgb.edu
  Denise Scheberle, Interim Dean of Liberal Arts and Science; Theatre Hall 335; 920-465-2595; scheberd@gbms01.uwgb.edu

EDUCATIONAL INSTITUTIONS – U

Ronald Stieglitz, Environmental Science and Policy Program, Associate Dean; 920-465-2123; Fax: 920-465-2718; gradstu@uwgb.edu.

UNIVERSITY OF WISCONSIN AT LA CROSSE
COLLEGE OF SCIENCE AND ALLIED HEALTH
1725 State St.
La Crosse, WI 54601 United States
Phone: 608-785-8218   Fax: 608-785-8221
Website: www.uwlax.edu/sah/
Membership: 1,001–10,000
Scope: Local
Description: Biology, Chemistry and Geography offer B.S. degrees with a concentration in Environmental Science. Biology also offers a concentration in Aquatic Sciences for B.S. and M.S. degrees.
Keyword(s): Ecosystems (precious), Ethics/Environmental Justice, Pollution (general), Public Lands/Greenspace, Water Habitats & Quality
Contact(s):
Mark Sandheinrich, River Studies Center, Director; 608-785-8261; sandhein@mail.uwlax.edu
Roger Haro, Aquatic Science Advisor; 608-785-6970; haro_rj@mail.uwlax.edu
George Huppert, Geography and Earth Science, Chairman; 608-785-8333; Fax: 608-785-8332; huppert@mail.uwlax.edu
Bruce Osterby, Chemistry Dept., Chair; 608-785-8266; Fax: 608-785-8281; oster_br@mail.uwlax.edu
Robin Tyser, Biology Dept./Environmental Science, Contact; 608-785-8238; Fax: 608-785-6959; tyser@mail.uwlax.edu

UNIVERSITY OF WISCONSIN AT MADISON
COLLEGE OF AGRICULTURAL AND LIFE SCIENCES
1450 Linden Dr.
Madison, WI 53706-1562 United States
Phone: 608-262-4930   Fax: 608-262-4556
Website: www.cals.wisc.edu
Membership: 1,001–10,000
Scope: State
Description: The School of Natural Resources is within the College of Agricultural and Life Sciences. The school offers 13 undergraduate options in natural resources. Graduate instruction is available in many specialized and interdisciplinary areas.
Keyword(s): Agriculture/Farming, Ecosystems (precious), Forests/Forestry, Land Issues, Recreation/Ecotourism, Sprawl/Urban Planning, Wildlife & Species
Contact(s):
Kevin McSweeney, Director, School of Natural Resources; 1450 Linden Dr., Rm. 146, Madison, WI 53706; 608-262-6968
Elton Aberle, College Dean

UNIVERSITY OF WISCONSIN AT STEVENS POINT
COLLEGE OF NATURAL RESOURCES
1900 Franklin Street
Stevens Point, WI 54481 United States
Phone: 715-346-4081   Fax: 715-346-3624
E-mail: smenzel@uwsp.edu
Website: www.uwsp.edu/acad/cnr
Founded: 1946
Scope: Local, State, Regional, National, International
Description: Located in Central Wisconsin, the College of Natural Resources began in 1946 with the nation's first conservation education major. The college now has over 80 faculty and staff, 1,500 undergraduates and 60 graduate students. The college offers 18 majors and 14 minors.
Publication(s): Becoming an Outdoors Woman
Contact(s):
Eric Anderson, Wildlife Degrees
Michael Bozek, Cooperative Fishery Unit, Leader
Randy Champeau, Environmental Education,
Mike Dombeck, Professor of Global Environmental Management; 715-346-3946; Fax: 715-346-4554; mike.dombeck@uwsp.edu
Ronald Hensler, Soil Science
Victor Phillips, Dean
Stan Szczytko, Water Science,
Christine Thomas, Associate Dean; ext. 4185; Fax: 715-346-4554; cthomas@uwsp.edu

UNIVERSITY OF WISCONSIN-MADISON
GAYLORD NELSON INSTITUTE FOR ENVIRONMENTAL STUDIES
550 N. Park St., Science Hall
Madison, WI 53706 United States
Phone: 608-265-5296   Fax: 608-262-0014
Website: www.ies.wisc.edu/
Founded: 1970
Scope: Local, State, Regional, National, International
Description: The Nelson Institute promotes and administers interdisciplinary environmental instruction, research, and outreach at the University of Wisconsin-Madison. It offers graduate degrees in conservation biology and sustainable development, environmental monitoring, land resources, and water resources management; graduate-level certificates in air resources management, energy analysis and policy, and transportation management and policy; and an undergraduate certificate in environmental studies.
Keyword(s): Air Quality/Atmosphere, Climate Change, Development/Developing Countries, Ecosystems (precious), Energy, Ethics/Environmental Justice, Land Issues, Pollution (general), Transportation, Water Habitats & Quality, Wildlife & Species
Contact(s):
Erhard Joeres, Interim Director; 608-265-5296; joeres@engr.wisc.edu

UNIVERSITY OF WYOMING
P.O. Box 3166
University Station
Laramie, WY 82071 United States
Phone: 307-766-5415   Fax: 307-766-5400
Website: www.uwyo.edu/
Scope: Regional
Description: Teaching and research in wildlife and fisheries biology
Publication(s): Newsletter
Contact(s):
Henry Harlow, National Park Service Research Center, Director; 307-766-4227; Fax: 307-766-5625
Joseph Meyer, Red Buttes Environmental Biology Laboratory, Director; 307-766-2017; Fax: 307-766-5625
Merav Ben-David, Asst. Professor; 307-766-5307; bendavid@uwyo.edu
Steve Buskirk, Prof.; 307-766-5626; marten@uwyo.edu
Fred Lindzey, Assoc. Prof.; 307-766-5415; flindzey@uwyo.edu
James Lovvorn, Professor; 307-766-6100; lovvorn@uwyo.edu
David McDonald, Asst. Prof.; 307-766-3012; dbmcd@uwyo.edu
Stanley Anderson, Wyoming Cooperative Fish and Wildlife Research Unit, Leader; 307-766-5415; Fax: 907-766-5400
Nancy Stanton, Department of Zoology and Physiology, Head; 307-766-4207; Fax: 307-766-5625

UNIVERSITY OF WYOMING
WILLIAM D. RUCKELSHAUS INSTITUTE AND THE SCHOOL OF ENVIRONMENT AND NATURAL RESOURCES
P.O. Box 3971
Laramie, WY 82071 United States
Phone: 307-766-5080 Fax: 307-766-5099
E-mail: ienr@uwyo.edu
Website: www.uwyo.edu/enr/

Founded: 1994
Membership: 1–100
Scope: Local, State, Regional, National, International
Description: Current projects include providing research and information on: preserving open space; the Endangered Species Act and private property; and collaborative natural resource management.
Publication(s): Private Property and the ESA, Reclaiming NEPA's Potential, Can Collaborative Processes Improve Environmental Decision Making?
Keyword(s): Land Issues, Public Lands/Greenspace, Sprawl/Urban Planning, Wildlife & Species
Contact(s):
Harold Bergman, Director; 307-766-5150; bergman@uwyo.edu
Diana Hulme, Assistant Director; 307-766-5354

URBAN WASTE MANAGEMENT & RESEARCH CENTER
UNIVERSITY OF NEW ORLEANS
DEPARTMENT OF ENVIRONMENTAL ENGINEERING
Engineering Building
Room 822
New Orleans, LA 70148 United States
Phone: 504-280-6189 Fax: 504-280-5586
E-mail: jsuthe9831@aol.com
Website: www.uwmrc.org

Founded: 1991
Scope: Local, State, Regional, National, International
Description: A university research organization working in the fields of solid waste management, storm water collection, urban air quality, brownfields and wastewater collection and treatment.
Publication(s): Projects Summaries
Keyword(s): Air Quality/Atmosphere, Development/Developing Countries, Ethics/Environmental Justice, Executive/Legislative/Judicial Reform, Public Health, Reduce/Reuse/Recycle, Sprawl/Urban Planning, Water Habitats & Quality
Contact(s):
Kenneth McManis, Director; 504-280-6668; Fax: 280-5586; kmcmanis@uno.edu
Rita Czek, Projects Manager; 504-280-7089; Fax: 280-5586; rlcce@uno.edu
John Sutherlin, Research Associate; 504-280-6189; jsuthe9831@aol.com
Marty Tittlebaum, Associate Director; 504-280-5524; Fax: 280-5586; mtittleb@uno.edu

UTAH STATE UNIVERSITY
BERRYMAN INSTITUTE FOR WILDLIFE DAMAGE MANAGEMENT
Utah State U.
Logan, UT 84322-5270 United States
Phone: 435-797-2436 Fax: 435-797-1871
E-mail: conover@cc.usu.edu
Website: www.berrymaninstitute.org

Founded: 1990
Membership: 1–100
Scope: State
Description: The Jack H. Berryman Institute is a national non-profit organization which is centered at Utah State University. It engages in research, education, and extension activities aimed at resolving human and wildlife conflicts, enhancing the positive aspects of wildlife, and increasing human tolerance of wildlife problems.
Contact(s):
Michael Conover, Director; conover@cc.usu.edu

UTAH STATE UNIVERSITY
COLLEGE OF NATURAL RESOURCES
5200 Old Main Hill
Logan, UT 84322-5200 United States
Phone: 435-797-2445 Fax: 435-797-2443
Website: www.cnr.usu.edu/

Membership: 1–100
Scope: International
Description: The College of Natural Resources at Utah State University promotes, through undergraduate and graduate education, scholarship and creativity in discovery, synthesis and transfer of knowledge for the mutual sustainability of terrestrial and aquatic ecosystems and human communities.
Publication(s): See publication website
Keyword(s): Ecosystems (precious), Pollution (general), Wildlife & Species
Contact(s):
Martyn Caldwell, USU Ecology Center, Director; 435-797-2555; ecol@cc.usu.edu
Joanna Endter-Wada, Natural Resource Policy Institute, Director
Fee Busby, College of Natural Resources, Dean; 435-797-2452; Fax: 435-797-2443; feebusby@cnr.usu.edu
Raymond Dueser, College of Natural Resources, Assoc. Dean; 435-797-2445; Fax: 435-797-2443; dueser@cnr.usu.edu
Chris Luecke, Aquatic, Watershed, and Earth Resources Dept. Head; 435-797-2459; Fax: 435-797-1871; luecke@cc.usu.edu
David Roberts, Forest, Range, and Wildlife Sciences Acting Dept. Head; 435-797-3219; dvrbts@nr.usu.edu
Terry Sharik, Environment and Society Dept. Head; 435-797-1790; Fax: 435-797-4040; tlsharik@cnr.usu.edu
Derrick Thom, Geography Dept. M.S. Program, Contact; 435-797-1292; djthom@cc.usu.edu

UTAH STATE UNIVERSITY
COLLEGE OF NATURAL RESOURCES
DEPARTMENT OF AQUATIC, WATERSHED, & EARTH RESOURCES
5210 Old Main Hill
Natural Resources Room 210
Logan, UT 84322-5210 United States
Phone: 435-797-2459 Fax: 435-797-1871
E-mail: awer_info@cnr.usu.edu
Website: www.cnr.usu.edu/awer

Founded: 2002
Scope: Local, State, Regional, National, International
Description: The Department of Aquatic, Watershed & Earth Resources at Utah State University is focused on educational, research, and outreach activities designed to better understand and communicate the ecosystem processes that link the atmosphere and the land to the earth's water cycle.
Keyword(s): Climate Change, Ecosystems (precious), Land Issues, Oceans/Coasts/Beaches, Sprawl/Urban Planning, Water Habitats & Quality, Wildlife & Species
Contact(s):
Frank (Fee) Busby, Dean; 435-797-2452; Fax: 435-797-2443; feebusby@cnr.usu.edu
Chris Luecke, Interim Department Head; 435-797-2463; Fax: 435-797-1871; luecke@cnr.usu.edu

V

VANDERBILT CENTER FOR ENVIRONMENTAL MANAGEMENT (VCEMS)
1207 18th Avenue South
Nashville, TN 37212 United States
Phone: 615-322-8004 Fax: 615-322-8081
E-mail: vcems@vanderbilt.edu
Website: www.vanderbilt.edu/vcems

Founded: 1995
Scope: Local, State, Regional, National, International
Description: VCEMS is a Vanderbilt University system-wide initiative jointly led by the School of Engineering, the Graduate School, the Owen Graduate School of Management, the Law School, and the Institute for Public Policy Studies. VCEMS offers two different Master's degrees and a Ph.D. in Environmental Management Studies. Center activities are interdisciplinary and focus on environmental business, management and technology.
Publication(s): Annual Newsletter
Keyword(s): Transportation
Contact(s):
Mark Abkowitz, Center Co-Director; 615-343-3436
Mark Cohen, Center Co-Director; 615-322-8004
Tricia Drake, Program Director; 615-322-8004; Fax: 615-322-8081; vcems@vanderbilt.edu

VANDERBILT UNIVERSITY
CIVIL AND ENVIRONMENTAL ENGINEERING
VU Station B 351831
Nashville, TN 37235 United States
Phone: 615-322-2697 Fax: 615-322-3365
Website: www.cee.vanderbilt.edu/

Membership: 1–100
Scope: Local, State, Regional, National, International
Description: We tackle tough problems with a major impact on individuals, communities, the nation, and the world.
Contact(s):
David Kosson, Professor and Chairman

VERMONT LAW SCHOOL
ENVIRONMENTAL LAW CENTER
P.O. Box 96
Chelsea St.
South Royalton, VT 05068 United States
Phone: 800-277-5985, ext. 1201 Fax: 802-763-2940
E-mail: elcinfo@vermontlaw.edu
Website: www.vermontlaw.edu/elc

Founded: 1973
Scope: International
Description: Administers three degrees in environmental law: the Master of Studies in Environmental Law (M.S.E.L.), the J.D./M.S.E.L. (joint degree), and the LL.M. in Environmental Law. The curriculum at VLS includes approx. fifty courses in environmental law, policy, science, and ethics. Its Summer Session offers over thirty courses for law students, attorneys, and non-lawyers interested in environmental policy and management and public interest advocacy.
Contact(s):
Anne Mansfield, Assistant Director; 803-763-8303; Fax: 803-763-2940

VIRGINIA POLYTECHNIC INSTITUTE
FISH AND WILDLIFE INFORMATION EXCHANGE
DEPARTMENT OF FISHERIES AND WILDLIFE
203 W. Roanoke St.
Blacksburg, VA 24060 United States
Phone: 540-231-7348 Fax: 540-231-7019
E-mail: fwiexchg@vt.edu
Website: fwie.fw.vt.edu

Description: Produces "The Master Species File", an archive of species accounts compiled by state and federal fish and wildlife agencies in North America.
Contact(s):
Sheila Ratcliff

VIRGINIA POLYTECHNIC INSTITUTE AND STATE UNIVERSITY
COLLEGE OF NATURAL RESOURCES
Attn: Peggy Quarterman, 324 Cheatham Hall
Blacksburg, VA 24061-0324 United States
Phone: 540-231-5481 Fax: 540-231-7664
E-mail: cfwr@vt.edu
Website: www.cnr.vt.edu

Membership: 101–1,000
Scope: State
Contact(s):
John Cairns, Center for Environmental and Hazardous Materials Studies; 540-231-7075
Gregory Brown, Dean; browngn@vt.edu
Harold Burkhart, Department of Forestry, Head; 540-231-5483; burkhart@vt.edu
C. Dolloff, U.S. Forest Service Coldwater and Trout Research Unit, Leader; 540-231-4864; adoll@vt.edu
Richard Neves, Cooperative Fish and Wildlife Unit, Leader; 540-231-5927, mussel@vt.edu
Donald Orth, Department of Fisheries and Wildlife Sciences, Head; 540-231-5573; dorth@vt.edu
Paul Winistorfer, Wood Science & Forest Product

VIRGINIA TECH
DEPARTMENT OF FISHERIES AND WILDLIFE SCIENCES
100 Cheatham Hall
Virginia Tech
Blacksburg, VA 24061-0321 United States
Phone: 540-231-5573
E-mail: vsutherl@vt.edu
Website: www.fishwild.vt.edu

Founded: 1973
Membership: 101–1,000
Scope: State, Regional, National, International
Description: We are an academic department that shares and celebrates our passions, ideas, and discoveries in the conservation and management of natural resources.
Keyword(s): Agriculture/Farming, Development/Developing Countries, Ecosystems (precious), Forests/Forestry, Land Issues, Oceans/Coasts/Beaches, Recreation/Ecotourism, Sprawl/Urban Planning, Water Habitats & Quality, Wildlife & Species
Contact(s):
Donald Orth, Department Head; 540-231-5573; Fax: 540-231-7580; dorth@vt.edu

VIRGINIA TECH UNIVERSITY
COLLEGE OF NATURAL RESOURCES
CONSERVATION MANAGEMENT INSTITUTE
203 W. Roanoke St.
Blacksburg, VA 24061 United States
Phone: 540-231-7348 Fax: 540-231-7019
E-mail: fwiexchg@vt.edu
Website: www.cmiweb.org

Founded: 2000
Membership: 1–100
Scope: Local, State, Regional, National, International
Description: The Conservation Management Institute was established to address multidisciplinary research questions that affect conservation management effectiveness in Virginia, North America, and the world. Faculty from Virginia Tech and other research institutions work collaboratively to provide support to conservation and management agencies and organ-

izations worldwide in their efforts to assess, monitor, protect, and manage the earth's renewable natural resources.

Keyword(s): Agriculture/Farming, Development/Developing Countries, Ecosystems (precious), Forests/Forestry, Land Issues, Oceans/Coasts/Beaches, Recreation/Ecotourism, Sprawl/Urban Planning, Transportation, Water Habitats & Quality, Wildlife & Species

Contact(s):
Jefferson Waldon, Asst. Director; 540-231-7348; Fax: 540-231-7019; fwiexchg@vt.edu

W

WASHINGTON STATE UNIVERSITY
Attn: William Budd, 305 Troy Hall
Pullman, WA 99164-4430 United States
Phone: 509-335-8536   Fax: 509-335-7636
E-mail: admiss2@wsu.edu
Website: www.wsu.edu

Scope: State

Description: WSU has tripartite goals of providing higher education, research, and outreach/service programs relevant to the needs of Washington's citizens. The Department of Natural Resource Sciences (NRS) (http://coopext.cahe.wsu.edu/~nrs/) and Program in Environmental Science and Regional Planning (ESRP) (www.sci.wsu.edu/envsci/) are the chief academic units at WSU.

Contact(s):
William Budd, Environmental Science and Regional Planning, Chair; Washington State University, P.O. Box 644430, Pullman, WA 99164-4430; 509-335-8536; Fax: 509-335-7636

Edward Depuit, Natural Resource Sciences, Chair; Washington State University, P.O. Box 646410, Pullman, WA 99164-6410; 509-335-6166; Fax: 509-335-7862

Charles Johnson, Horticulture and Landscape Architecture, Chair; Washington State University, P. O. Box 646414, 149 Johnson Hall, Pullman, WA 99164-6414; 509-335-9502; Fax: 509-335-8690

WASHINGTON UNIVERSITY
BIOLOGY DEPARTMENT
1 Brookings Dr., Campus Box 1137
St. Louis, MO 63110 United States
Phone: 314-935-6860   Fax: 314-935-4432
E-mail: webmaster@biology.wustl.edu
Website: www.biology.wustl.edu

Scope: State

Description: The laboratory is active in applying modern genetic techniques to problems in conservation biology such as conservation forensics (e.g., DNA fingerprinting of elephant tusks), systematics (identifying taxa that are significant evolutionary units), inter- and intraspecific hybridizataion, and genetic management of captive, translocated, and natural populations.

Contact(s):
Ralph Quatrano, Department of Biology, Head; 314-935-6868; rsq@wustl.edu

WAYNE STATE UNIVERSITY DEPARTMENT OF BIOLOGICAL SCIENCES
DEPARTMENT OF BIOLOGICAL SCIENCES
5047 Gullen Mall
Detroit, MI 48202-3917 United States
Phone: 313-577-2873   Fax: 313-577-6891
Website: www.biosci.wayne.edu

Scope: National

Description: Courses offered in such subjects as limnology, ornithology, mammalogy, biogeography, natural history of vertebrates, animal behavior, population genetics, population ecology, microbial ecology, aquatic botany, ecology, advanced ecology, and evolutionary ecology.

Contact(s):
Allen Nicholson, Chairman; 313-577-2783

WEST VIRGINIA UNIVERSITY
COLLEGE OF AGRICULTURE, FORESTRY AND CONSUMER SCIENCES
1170 Agriculture Sciences Building
Morgantown, WV 26506-6108 United States
Phone: 304-293-2395   Fax: 304-293-3740
Website: www.caf.wvu.edu/

Scope: International

Contact(s):
Joseph McNeel, Division of Forestry, Director; P.O. Box 6125, Morgantown, WV 26506-6125; 304-293-2941; jmcneel@wvu.edu

James Armstrong, Wood Industries, Program Coordinator; 304-293-2941; ext. 2486; jarmstro@wvu.edu

Donald Armstrong, Landscape Architecture, Chair; 304-293-2142; ext. 4489; Fax: 304-293-3752; darmstro@wvu.edu

Alan Collins, Agricultural and Resource Economics, Undergraduate Coordinator; P.O. Box 6108, Morgantown, WV 26506; 304-293-4832; acollins@wvu.edu

Tim Phipps, Natural Resource Economics, Coordinator; P.O. Box 6108, Morgantown, WV 26506; 304-293-4832; tphipps@wvu.edu

Steve Selin, Recreation and Parks Management, Program Coordinator; 304-293-2941; ext. 2442; sselin@wvu.edu

Robert Whitmore, Wildlife and Fisheries Management, Program Coordinator; 304-293-2941; ext. 2491; u0eae@wvnvm.wvnet.edu

WESTERN ILLINOIS UNIVERSITY
DEPARTMENT OF BIOLOGICAL SCIENCES
372 Waggoner Hall
Macomb, IL 61455 United States
Phone: 309-298-2408   Fax: 309-298-2270
E-mail: mibiol@wiu.edu
Website: www.wiu.edu/users/mibiol/

Membership: 1–100

Scope: Regional

Description: Office of Aquatic Studies offers courses at the Shedd Aquarium in Chicago.

Keyword(s): Ecosystems (precious), Public Lands/Greenspace, Water Habitats & Quality, Wildlife & Species

Contact(s):
Sean Jenkins, Director; 309-298-2045
Thomas Dunstan, Wildlife; 309-298-1752; thomas_dunstan@ccmail.wiu.edu
Larry Jahn, Fisheries; 309-298-1266; la-jahn@wiu.edu

WESTERN MICHIGAN UNIVERSITY
ENVIRONMENTAL STUDIES PROGRAM
3900 Wood Hall
Kalamazoo, MI 49008-5419 United States
Phone: 616-387-2716   Fax: 616-387-2272
Website: www.wmich.edu/environmental-studies

Membership: 101–1,000

Scope: Local, State

Description: This undergraduate interdisciplinary program provides intellectual and practical experience that provokes thought about the complex interrelationships between humans, the social and technological systems they develop, and the natural environment. The program encourages students to develop an appreciation for the many elements of planetary health and to devise creative solutions to environmental problems.

Contact(s):
Kathy Mitchelll, Program Coordinator for Environmental Studies

WESTERN WASHINGTON UNIVERSITY
HUXLEY COLLEGE OF THE ENVIRONMENT
516 High Mail Stop 9079
Bellingham, WA 98225 United States
Phone: 360-650-3520 Fax: 360-650-2842
E-mail: huxley@cc.wwu.edu
Website: www.ac.wwu.edu/~huxley/

Founded: 1968
Membership: 101–1,000
Scope: State, Regional
Description: Principally a two-year, upper division and M.S. program; B.A., B.S. in environmental studies; M.S. in environmental science and geography. Also cooperative program: M.S. in marine and estuarine science.
Publication(s): Available on web
Contact(s):
 Gigi Berardi, Chair, Environmental Studies Department; 360-650-3284; Fax: 360-650-7702; gigi.berardi@wwu.edu
 John Hardy, Chair, Department of Environmental Studies; 360-650-6108; Fax: 360-650-7284; jhardy@cc.wwu.edu
 Wayne Landis, Institute of Environmental Toxicology and Chemistry, Director; 360-650-6136; Fax: 360-650-6556; landis@cc.wwu.edu
 Robin Matthews, Institute for Watershed Studies, Director; 360-650-3510; rmatthews@wwu.edu
 Bradley Smith, Dean; bfs@admsec.wwu.edu

WIDENER UNIVERSITY
DEPARTMENT OF CIVIL ENGINEERING
One University Place
Chester, PA 19013-5792 United States
Phone: 610-499-4042 Fax: 610-499-4059
E-mail: solid.waste@widener.edu
Website: www.widener.edu/solid.waste

Founded: 1821
Scope: International
Description: The Department of Civil Engineering at Widener University offers undergraduate and graduate degrees which include courses in water resources, solid waste management, and environmental engineering. Continuing education seminars are taught in solid waste management and recycling. Research and development is performed in solid waste and recycling and water resources and water quality. The department publishes The Journal of Solid Waste Technology and Management.
Publication(s): Proceedings of International Conference on Solid Waste Technology and Management, The Journal of Solid Waste Technology and Management
Keyword(s): Pollution (general), Reduce/Reuse/Recycle
Contact(s):
 Vicki Brown, Chair of Civil Engineering; 610-499-4607; vicki.l.brown@widener.edu
 Ronald Mersky, Waste Management Programs, Coordinator; 610-499-1146; Fax: 610-499-4059; solid.waste@widener.edu
 Theresea Taborsky, Wolfgram Memorial Library; One University Pl., Chester, PA 19013-5792; 610-499-4087

WILKES UNIVERSITY
GEO-ENVIRONMENTAL SCIENCES/ENGINEERING DEPARTMENT
P.O. Box 111
Wilkes Barre, PA 18766 United States
Phone: 570-408-4610 Fax: 570-408-7865
E-mail: gse@wilkes.edu
Website: www.wilkes.edu
Membership: 1–100
Scope: Local
Description: The department offers two degree programs. The Environmental Engineering curriculum highlights a balance among the basic areas of water and waste-water engineering, water quality measurement, air pollution measurement and control technology, as well as the more recent demands in the areas of hazardous and solid waste management. The Earth and Environmental Science curriculum requires a concentration of departmental electives that can be used to create an area of specialization.
Contact(s):
 Dale Bruns, Co-Chairman; 717-408-4610; Fax: 570-408-7865; dbruns@wilkes.edu
 Sid Halfor, Co-Chairman; 570-408-4611; Fax: 570-408-7865; shalfor@wilkes.edu

WILLIAMS COLLEGE
CENTER FOR ENVIRONMENTAL STUDIES PROGRAM
Box 632
Williamstown, MA 01267 United States
Phone: 413-597-2346 Fax: 413-597-3489
Website: www.williams.edu/

Founded: 1967
Scope: Local, State, Regional, National, International
Description: The Center for Environmental Studies offers an integrated undergraduate program of studies to liberal arts students in combination with their major discipline. The Center also administers the 2,400 acre Hopkins Memorial Forest, a research and educational facility, as well as the Environmental Science Laboratory and the Matt Cole Memorial Library.
Publication(s): Field Notes-Newsletter
Contact(s):
 Kai Lee, Director
 Andrew Jones, Hopkins Memorial Forest Manager
 Rachel Louis, Program Assistant

WILLOW MIXED MEDIA INC.
P.O. Box 194
Glenford, NY 12433-0194 United States
Phone: 845-657-2914
E-mail: willowmx@ulster.net
Website: www.hudsonvalley.com/willow

Founded: 1979
Scope: Local
Description: Willow Mixed Media is a not for profit organization, dealing with documentary video and arts projects on issues of social concern—health, environment, the arts, criminal justice, etc.
Publication(s): Building the Achokan Reservoir, Cancer: Just a Word Not a Sentence, The Hudson River PCB Story: A Toxic Heritage
Contact(s):
 Tobe Carey, President; willowmx@ulster.net

Y

YALE LAW SCHOOL
CAREER DEVELOPMENT OFFICE
127 Wall Street
New Haven, CT 6511 United States
Phone: 203-432-1676 Fax: 203-432-8423
E-mail: cdolaw@yale.edu
Website: www.law.yale.edu/cdo
Scope: National
Contact(s):
 Cathy Woods, Contact

YALE UNIVERSITY
SCHOOL OF FORESTRY AND ENVIRONMENTAL STUDIES
205 Prospect St.
Sage Hall
New Haven, CT 06511 United States
Phone: 203-432-5100 Fax: 203-432-5942
E-mail: fesinfo@yale.edu
Website: www.yale.edu/environment

Founded: 1900

Scope: Local, State, Regional, National, International

Description: Graduates of this interdisciplinary program assume influential roles in government, business, NGOs, public and international affairs, research and education. Master's degrees: Environmental Management (MEM), Environmental Science (MESc), Forestry (MF), Forest Science (MFS). Joint degrees: Yale School's of Management, Law, Public Health, International Relations, Developmental Economics, and Divinity; Pace Law School and Vermont Law School. Doctoral Degrees: Ph.D. or DFES

Publication(s): Bulletin of Yale University, Yale School of Forestry and Environmental Studies Bulletin Series

Contact(s):
Emly McDiarmid, Admissions Director; emly.mcdiarmid@yale.edu
Gordon Geballe, Associate Dean

YORK UNIVERSITY
FACULTY OF ENVIRONMENTAL STUDIES
355 Lumbers Bldg., 4700 Keele St.
Toronto, M3J 1P3 Ontario Canada
Phone: 416-736-5252 Fax: 416-736-5679
E-mail: fesinfo@yorku.ca
Website: www.yorku.ca/faculty/fes

Founded: 1968

Membership: 1–100

Scope: National, International

Description: The Faculty of Environmental Studies offers interdisciplinary, flexible, individualized programs at both the undergraduate and graduate levels. FES is committed to a broad definition of environment, offering the opportunity to study natural, built, organizational, and social environments.

Contact(s):
Mora Campbell, Graduate Program Director
Raymond Rogers, Undergraduate Program Director; rrogers@yorku.ca
Barbara Rahder, Graduate Planning Programs Coordinator; rahder@yorku.ca
Brent Rutherford, MES Program Coordinator; brentr@yorku.ca

ORGANIZATION NAME INDEX

20/20 VISION, 241

A

A CRITICAL DECISION, 241
A.E. HOWELL WILDLIFE CONSERVATION CENTER INC., 241
ABSEARCH, INC., 563
ABUNDANT LIFE SEED FOUNDATION, 241
ACADEMY FOR EDUCATIONAL DEVELOPMENT, 241
ACADIA UNIVERSITY, 572
ACRES LAND TRUST, 241
ACTION FOR NATURE, INC., 242
ADIRONDACK COUNCIL, THE, 242
ADIRONDACK MOUNTAIN CLUB, INC., THE (ADK), 242
ADIRONDACK PARK AGENCY, 132
ADKINS ARBORETUM, 242
ADOPT-A-STREAM FOUNDATION, THE, 242
ADVISORY COUNCIL ON HISTORIC PRESERVATION, 16
ADVOCATES OF THE COMMON WEALTH, INC., 243
AFRICA VISION TRUST, 243
AFRICAN AMERICAN ENVIRONMENTALIST ASSOCIATION, 243
AFRICAN CONSERVATION FOUNDATION, THE, 243
AFRICAN WILDLIFE FOUNDATION, 243
AIR & WASTE MANAGEMENT ASSOCIATION, 244
AIZA BIBY, 244
ALABAMA ASSOCIATION OF SOIL AND WATER CONSERVATION DISTRICTS, 244
ALABAMA BASS FEDERATION, 244
ALABAMA COOPERATIVE EXTENSION SYSTEM, 132
ALABAMA COOPERATIVE FISH AND WILDLIFE RESEARCH UNIT (USDI), 132
ALABAMA DEPARTMENT OF AGRICULTURE AND INDUSTRIES, 132
ALABAMA DEPARTMENT OF CONSERVATION AND NATURAL RESOURCES, 132
ALABAMA DEPARTMENT OF ENVIRONMENTAL MANAGEMENT, 133
ALABAMA ENVIRONMENTAL COUNCIL, 244
ALABAMA FORESTRY COMMISSION, 133
ALABAMA SOIL AND WATER CONSERVATION COMMITTEE, 133
ALABAMA WATERFOWL ASSOCIATION (AWA), 244
ALABAMA WATERFOWL ASSOCIATION, INC. (AWA), 245
ALABAMA WILDFLOWER SOCIETY, THE, 245
ALABAMA WILDLIFE FEDERATION, 245
ALASKA ASSOCIATION OF SOIL AND WATER CONSERVATION DISTRICTS, 245
ALASKA CENTER FOR THE ENVIRONMENT, 245
ALASKA CONSERVATION ALLIANCE, 245, 246
ALASKA CONSERVATION FOUNDATION, 246
ALASKA COOPERATIVE FISH AND WILDLIFE RESEARCH UNIT, 133
ALASKA DEPARTMENT OF ENVIRONMENTAL CONSERVATION, 133
ALASKA DEPARTMENT OF FISH AND GAME, 134
ALASKA DEPARTMENT OF NATURAL RESOURCES, 134
ALASKA DEPARTMENT OF PUBLIC SAFETY, 134
  Alaska State Troopers, 134
ALASKA HEALTH PROJECT, 134
ALASKA NATURAL HISTORY ASSOCIATION, 246
ALASKA NATURAL RESOURCE AND OUTDOOR EDUCATION ASSOCIATION, 246
ALASKA RAINFOREST CAMPAIGN, 246
ALASKA WILDLIFE ALLIANCE, THE, 246
ALBERTA DEPARTMENT OF ENVIRONMENTAL PROTECTION
  Communications Division, 134
  Environmental Service, 134
  Land and Forest Service, 135
  Natural Resources Service, 135
ALBERTA DEPARTMENT OF SUSTAINABLE RESOURCE DEVELOPMENT
  Fish and Wildlife Division, 135
ALBERTA ENVIRONMENTAL CONSERVATION SERVICE, 16
ALBERTA FISH AND GAME ASSOCIATION, 247
ALBERTA TRAPPERS ASSOCIATION, 247
ALBERTA WILDERNESS ASSOCIATION, 247
ALDEANATURAL.COM, 563
ALDO LEOPOLD FOUNDATION, 247
ALFRED UNIVERSITY, 572
ALLIANCE FOR THE CHESAPEAKE BAY, 247
  Harrisburg Office, 248
  Richmond, VA office, 248
AMANAKAA AMAZON NETWORK, 248
AMERICA THE BEAUTIFUL FUND, 248
AMERICAN ALLIANCE FOR HEALTH, PHYSICAL EDUCATION AND RECREATION AND DANCE, 248
AMERICAN AQUATICS, INC, 563
AMERICAN ASSOCIATION FOR LEISURE AND RECREATION - AALR, 248
AMERICAN ASSOCIATION FOR THE ADVANCEMENT OF SCIENCE, 249
AMERICAN ASSOCIATION OF BOTANICAL GARDENS AND ARBORETA, 249
AMERICAN ASSOCIATION OF FIELD BOTANISTS, 249
AMERICAN ASSOCIATION OF ZOO KEEPERS, INC., 249
AMERICAN B.A.S.S. ASSOCIATION OF EASTERN PENNSYLVANIA/ NEW JERSEY, THE, 249
AMERICAN BIRD CONSERVANCY, 249
AMERICAN BIRDING ASSOCIATION (ABA), 250
AMERICAN CAMPING ASSOCIATION, INC., 250
AMERICAN CANAL SOCIETY, INC., 250
AMERICAN CAVE CONSERVATION ASSOCIATION, 250
AMERICAN CETACEAN SOCIETY, 250
AMERICAN CHEMICAL SOCIETY, 563
AMERICAN CHESTNUT FOUNDATION, THE, 250
AMERICAN CONSERVATION ASSOCIATION, INC., 251
  New York Office, 251
AMERICAN COUNCIL FOR AN ENERGY-EFFICIENT ECONOMY, 251
AMERICAN COUNCIL FOR THE UNITED NATIONS UNIVERSITY (ACUNU), 251
AMERICAN EAGLE FOUNDATION, 251
AMERICAN FARMLAND TRUST, 251
AMERICAN FEDERATION OF MINERALOGICAL SOCIETIES (AFMS), 252
AMERICAN FISHERIES SOCIETY, 252
  Agriculture Economics Section, 252
  Alabama Chapter, 252
  Alaska Chapter, 252
  Arizona-New Mexico Chapter, 252
  Arkansas Chapter, 253
  Atlantic International Chapter, 253
  Auburn University Chapter, 253
  Bioengineering Section, 253
  Bonneville Chapter, 253
  California-Nevada Chapter, 253
  Canadian Aquatic Resources Section, 253
  College of Environmental Science and Forestry Chapter, 253
  Colorado-Wyoming Chapter, 253
  Computer User Section, 254
  Dakota Chapter, 254
  Early Life History, 254
  Equal Opportunities Section, 254
  Fish Culture Section, 254
  Fish Health Section, 254
  Fisheries Administrators Section, 254
  Fisheries History Section, 254
  Fisheries Management Section, 254
  Florida Chapter, 254
  Genetics Section, 255
  Georgia Chapter, 255
  Greater Portland, OR Chapter, 255
  Hawaii Chapter, 255
  Humboldt Chapter, 255
  Idaho Chapter, 255
  Illinois Chapter, 255
  Indiana Chapter, 255
  Introduced Fish Section, 255
  Iowa Chapter, 255
  Kansas Chapter, 256
  Kentucky Chapter, 256
  Louisiana Chapter, 256
  Marine Fisheries Section, 256
  Michigan Chapter, 256
  Mid-Atlantic Chapter, 256
  Mid-Canada Chapter, 256
  Minnesota Chapter, 256
  Mississippi Chapter, 257
  Missouri Chapter, 257
  Montana Chapter, 257
  Native People Fisheries Section, 257
  Nebraska Chapter, 257
  New Mexico State University Student Chapter, 257
  New York Chapter, 257
  North Carolina Chapter, 257
  North Pacific International Chapter, 258
  Northeastern Division, 258
  Northwestern Ontario Chapter, 258
  Ohio Chapter, 258
  Oregon Chapter, 258
  Pennsylvania Chapter, 258
  Physiology Section, 258
  Potomac Chapter, 258
  South Carolina Chapter, 258

ORGANIZATION NAME INDEX – A

AMERICAN FISHERIES SOCIETY (continued)
  South New England Chapter, 259
  Southern Ontario Chapter, 259
  Texas A and M Chapter, 259
  Tidewater Chapter, 259
  University of Wyoming Student Chapter, 259
  Virginia Chapter, 259
  Virginia Tech Chapter, 259
  Water Quality Section, 259
  West Virginia, 259
  Western Division, 260
  Wisconsin Chapter, 260
AMERICAN FOREST FOUNDATION, 260
AMERICAN FORESTS, 260
AMERICAN GEOGRAPHICAL SOCIETY, 260
AMERICAN GEOLOGICAL INSTITUTE, 260
AMERICAN GROUND WATER TRUST, 261
AMERICAN HIKING SOCIETY, 261
AMERICAN HORSE PROTECTION ASSOCIATION, 261
AMERICAN HUMANE, 261
AMERICAN INSTITUTE OF BIOLOGICAL SCIENCES, 261
AMERICAN INSTITUTE OF FISHERY RESEARCH BIOLOGISTS, 262
AMERICAN LAND CONSERVANCY, 262
AMERICAN LANDS, 262
AMERICAN LEAGUE OF ANGLERS AND BOATERS, 262
AMERICAN LITTORAL SOCIETY, 262
  Northeast Region, 262
AMERICAN LIVESTOCK BREEDS CONSERVANCY, 263
AMERICAN LUNG ASSOCIATION, 263
AMERICAN MUSEUM OF NATURAL HISTORY, 263
AMERICAN NATURE STUDY SOCIETY, 263
AMERICAN ORNITHOLOGISTS UNION, 263
AMERICAN PIE (PUBLIC INFORMATION ON THE ENVIRONMENT), 264
AMERICAN PLANNING ASSOCIATION, 264
AMERICAN RECREATION COALITION, 264
AMERICAN RESOURCES GROUP, 264
AMERICAN RIVERS, 264
  Montana Field Office, 265
  Nebraska Field Office, 265
  Northwest Regional Office, 265
  Voyage of Recovery, 265
AMERICAN SAMOA DEPARTMENT OF AGRICULTURE, 135
AMERICAN SOCIETY FOR ENVIRONMENTAL HISTORY, 265
AMERICAN SOCIETY OF ICHTHYOLOGISTS AND HERPETOLOGISTS, 265
AMERICAN SOCIETY OF INTERNATIONAL LAW/WILDLIFE INTEREST GROUP, 266
AMERICAN SOCIETY OF LANDSCAPE ARCHITECTS, 266
AMERICAN SOCIETY OF LIMNOLOGY AND OCEANOGRAPHY, 266
AMERICAN SOCIETY OF MAMMALOGISTS, 266
AMERICAN SPORTFISHING ASSOCIATION, 266
AMERICAN WATER RESOURCES ASSOCIATION, 267
AMERICAN WATER WORKS ASSOCIATION (AWWA), 267
AMERICAN WHITEWATER, 267
AMERICAN WILDERNESS COALITION, 267
AMERICAN WILDLANDS, 267
AMERICAN WILDLIFE RESEARCH FOUNDATION, INC., 268
AMERICAN ZOO AND AQUARIUM ASSOCIATION (AZA), 268
ANACOSTIA WATERSHED SOCIETY, 268
ANCIENT FOREST INTERNATIONAL, 268
ANGLERS FOR CLEAN WATER, 268
ANIMAL PROTECTION INSTITUTE, 268
ANIMAL WELFARE INSTITUTE, 269
ANIMALS AGENDA, 563
ANIMALS ASIA FOUNDATION, 269
ANTARCTICA PROJECT, THE, 269
ANTIOCH COLLEGE, 572
ANTIOCH NEW ENGLAND GRADUATE SCHOOL, 572
ANTIOCH NEW ENGLAND GRADUATE SCHOOL, ENVIRONMENTAL STUDIES, 572
ANTIOCH UNIVERSITY SEATTLE, 572
APPALACHIAN MOUNTAIN CLUB, 269
APPALACHIAN REGIONAL COMMISSION, 16
APPALACHIAN STATE UNIVERSITY, 572
APPALACHIAN TRAIL CONFERENCE, 270
APROVECHO RESEARCH CENTER, 270
ARCHAEOLOGICAL CONSERVANCY, 270
ARCHBOLD BIOLOGICAL STATION, 270
ARCHERY TRADE ASSOCIATION (ATA), 270
ARCTIC INSTITUTE OF NORTH AMERICA, 271
ARENA CONSULTORES AMBIENTALES, 563
ARIZONA ASSOCIATION OF CONSERVATION DISTRICTS, 271
ARIZONA BASS FEDERATION, 271

ARIZONA COOPERATIVE FISH AND WILDLIFE RESEARCH UNIT (USDI), 135
ARIZONA COOPERATIVE STATE EXTENSION SERVICES, 135
ARIZONA DEPARTMENT OF AGRICULTURE, 135
  Animal Services Division, 135
  Environmental Services Division, 136
ARIZONA DEPARTMENT OF AGRICULTURE PLANT SERVICES DIVISION, 136
ARIZONA DEPARTMENT OF ENVIRONMENTAL QUALITY, 136
ARIZONA GAME AND FISH DEPARTMENT, 136
ARIZONA GEOLOGICAL SURVEY, 136
ARIZONA STATE ENVIROTHON, INC., 271
ARIZONA STATE LAND DEPARTMENT, 136
ARIZONA STATE PARKS BOARD, 137
ARIZONA STATE UNIVERSITY
  Center for Environmental Studies, 573
ARIZONA WILDLIFE FEDERATION, 271
ARIZONA-SONORA DESERT MUSEUM, 271
ARKANSAS ASSOCIATION OF CONSERVATION DISTRICTS, 272
ARKANSAS BASS FEDERATION, 272
ARKANSAS COOPERATIVE RESEARCH UNIT, 137
ARKANSAS DEPARTMENT OF ENVIRONMENTAL QUALITY, 137
ARKANSAS DEPARTMENT OF PARKS AND TOURISM, 137
ARKANSAS ENVIRONMENTAL EDUCATION ASSOCIATION, 272
ARKANSAS GAME AND FISH COMMISSION, 137
ARKANSAS NATURAL HERITAGE COMMISSION, 138
ARKANSAS STATE EXTENSION SERVICES
  Four H Center, 138
ARKANSAS STATE PLANT BOARD, 138
ARKANSAS STATE UNIVERSITY
  Department of Biological Science, 573
ARKANSAS TECH UNIVERSITY
  Department of Parks, Recreation, and Hospitality Administration, 573
  Fisheries and Wildlife Biology Program, 573
ARKANSAS WATERSHED ADVISORY GROUP (AWAG), 272
ARKANSAS WILDLIFE FEDERATION, 272
ARLINGTON OUTDOOR EDUCATION ASSOCIATION, INC. (AOEA), 272
ASSOCIATION FOR CONSERVATION INFORMATION, INC., 273
ASSOCIATION FOR NATURAL RESOURCES ENFORCEMENT TRAINING, 273
ASSOCIATION FOR THE PROTECTION OF THE ADIRONDACKS, THE, 273
ASSOCIATION FOR THE STUDY OF LITERATURE AND ENVIRONMENT (ASLE), 573
ASSOCIATION OF AMERICAN GEOGRAPHERS, 273
ASSOCIATION OF AVIAN VETERINARIANS, 273
ASSOCIATION OF CONSULTING FORESTERS OF AMERICA, 273
ASSOCIATION OF FIELD ORNITHOLOGISTS, 274
ASSOCIATION OF GREAT LAKES OUTDOOR WRITERS (AGLOW), 274
ASSOCIATION OF NEW JERSEY ENVIRONMENTAL COMMISSIONS (ANJEC), 274
ASSOCIATION OF PARTNERS FOR PUBLIC LANDS, 274
ASSOCIATION OF STATE AND TERRITORIAL HEALTH OFFICIALS, 274
ATLANTIC CENTER FOR THE ENVIRONMENT
  New England Office, 275
  Quebec-Labrador Foundation, 275
ATLANTIC SALMON FEDERATION, 275
ATLANTIC STATES LEGAL FOUNDATION, 275
ATLANTIC STATES MARINE FISHERIES COMMISSION, 139
AUBURN UNIVERSITY
  College of Agriculture, 573
  College of Sciences and Mathematics, 574
  School of Forestry and Wildlife Sciences, 574
AUDUBON INTERNATIONAL, 276
AUDUBON NATURALIST SOCIETY OF THE CENTRAL ATLANTIC STATES, 276
AUSTRALIA DEPARTMENT FOR ENVIRONMENT AND HERITAGE, 139
AUSTRALIAN MINERAL FOUNDATION, 563
AUSTRIALIA DEPARTMENT FOR ENVIRONMENT AND HERITAGE
  Environment Shop, The, 139

B

BACK COUNTRY LAND TRUST, 276
BALL STATE UNIVERSITY, 574
BAMA BACKPADDLERS ASSOCIATION, 276
BARD COLLEGE, 574
BARRIER ISLAND TRUST, INC., 276
BASS DIVISION OF ESPN PRODUCTIONS INC, 564
BAT CONSERVATION INTERNATIONAL, 277
BEAR SPRINGS BLOSSOM NATURE CONSERVATION GROUP INC., 277
BEMIDJI STATE UNIVERSITY, 574
BERKSHIRE-LITCHFIELD ENVIRONMENTAL COUNCIL, INC., 277

ORGANIZATION NAME INDEX – C

BERLET FILMS AND VIDEOS, 564
BEYOND PESTICIDES, 277
BIG BEND NATURAL HISTORY ASSOCIATION, 277
BILLFISH FOUNDATION, THE, 278
BIODIVERSITY CONSERVATION ALLIANCE, 278
BIODIVERSITY NORTHWEST, 278
BIOINTEGRAL RESOURCE CENTER, 278
BIOSIS, 278
BIOSPHERE EXPEDITIONS, 278
BIRDLIFE INTERNATIONAL, 279
BIRDS PROTECTION AND STUDY SOCIETY OF VOJVODINA, 279
BLUE GOOSE ALLIANCE, 279
BOARD OF MINERALS AND ENVIRONMENT, 139
BOONE AND CROCKETT CLUB, 279
BOONE AND CROCKETT FOUNDATION, 279
BORDER ECOLOGY PROJECT (BEP), 279
BORN FREE FOUNDATION, 280
BOSTON UNIVERSITY, 574
BOTANICAL CLUB OF WISCONSIN, 280
BOTANICAL SOCIETY OF WESTERN PENNSYLVANIA, 280
BOUNTY INFORMATION SERVICE, 280
BOWLING GREEN STATE UNIVERSITY, 574
BOY SCOUTS OF AMERICA, 280
BRADLEY UNIVERSITY, 575
BRANDYWINE CONSERVANCY INC., 280
BRAUER PRODUCTIONS, 564
BRITISH COLUMBIA CONSERVATION DATA CENTRE
   Ministry of Sustainable Resource Management, 139
BRITISH COLUMBIA ENVIRONMENTAL CONSERVATION SERVICE, 16
BRITISH COLUMBIA FIELD ORNITHOLOGISTS, 281
BRITISH COLUMBIA MINISTRY OF AGRICULTURE FOOD AND FISHERIES
   British Columbia Fisheries, 139
BRITISH COLUMBIA MINISTRY OF COMMUNITY ABORIGINAL AND WOMEN SERVICES, 139
BRITISH COLUMBIA MINISTRY OF WATER, LAND AND AIR PROTECTION, 140
BRITISH COLUMBIA WATERFOWL SOCIETY, THE, 281
BROOKS BIRD CLUB INC., THE, 281
BROOKVIEW PRESS, 564
BROTHERHOOD OF THE JUNGLE COCK, INC., THE, 281
BROWN UNIVERSITY, 575
BUILDINGGREEN, INC., 564
BULLFROG FILMS, 564
BUN-CA, 281
BUREAU OF ECONOMIC GEOLOGY, 140
BUSINESS PUBLISHERS, INC., 564
BYRON FOREST PRESERVE, 140

C

C AND O CANAL NATIONAL HISTORICAL PARK, 16
C.A.R.E (CITIZENS AGAINST RACCOON EXTERMINATION), 564
C.A.S.T. FOR KIDS FOUNDATION, 281
CADDO LAKE INSTITUTE, INC., 282
CALCASIEU PARISH ANIMAL CONTROL AND PROTECTION DEPARTMENT, 282
CALIFORNIA ACADEMY OF SCIENCES, 282
CALIFORNIA ACADEMY OF SCIENCES LIBRARY, 282
CALIFORNIA ASSOCIATION OF RESOURCE CONSERVATION DISTRICTS, 282
CALIFORNIA BASS FEDERATION, 282
CALIFORNIA COASTAL COMMISSION, 140
CALIFORNIA COASTAL CONSERVANCY, 140
CALIFORNIA CONSERVATION CORPS, 140
CALIFORNIA COOPERATIVE FISHERY RESEARCH UNIT (USGS), 16
CALIFORNIA DEPARTMENT OF BOATING AND WATERWAYS, 141
CALIFORNIA DEPARTMENT OF CONSERVATION, 141
CALIFORNIA DEPARTMENT OF EDUCATION
   Office of Environmental Education, 141
CALIFORNIA DEPARTMENT OF FISH AND GAME
   Elkhorn Slough National Estuarine Research Reserve, 141
   Office of Spill Prevention and Response, 141
   Resources Agency, The, 141
   Wildlife Conservation Board, 142
CALIFORNIA DEPARTMENT OF FOOD AND AGRICULTURE, 142
CALIFORNIA DEPARTMENT OF FORESTRY AND FIRE PROTECTION, 142
CALIFORNIA DEPARTMENT OF PARKS AND RECREATION, 142
CALIFORNIA DEPARTMENT OF PESTICIDE REGULATION, 143
CALIFORNIA DEPARTMENT OF WATER RESOURCES, 143
CALIFORNIA ENERGY COMMISSION
   Environmental Department, 143
CALIFORNIA ENVIRONMENTAL PROTECTION AGENCY
   California Air Resources Board, 143

   Department of Toxic Substances Control, 143
   Integrated Waste Management Board, IWMB, 144
   Office of Environmental Health Hazard Assessment, 144
   Office of the Secretary, 144
   State Water Resources Control Board, 144
CALIFORNIA FISH AND GAME COMMISSION
   Fish and Game Commission, 144
CALIFORNIA GOVERNORS OFFICE OF PLANNING AND RESEARCH
   State Clearinghouse, 144
CALIFORNIA INSTITUTE OF PUBLIC AFFAIRS, 283
CALIFORNIA NATIVE PLANT SOCIETY, THE, 283
CALIFORNIA POLYTECHNIC STATE UNIVERSITY, 575
CALIFORNIA RECLAMATION BOARD, 145
CALIFORNIA RESOURCES AGENCY, THE, 145
CALIFORNIA STATE LANDS COMMISSION, 145
CALIFORNIA STATE UNIVERSITY AT CHICO, 575
CALIFORNIA STATE UNIVERSITY AT FULLERTON, 575
CALIFORNIA STATE UNIVERSITY AT SACRAMENTO, 575
CALIFORNIA TRAPPERS ASSOCIATION, 283
CALIFORNIA TROUT, INC., 283
CALIFORNIA UNIVERSITY OF PENNSYLVANIA, 576
CALIFORNIA WATER COMMISSION, 145
CALIFORNIA WATERFOWL ASSOCIATION, 283
CALIFORNIA WILD HERITAGE CAMPAIGN, 284
CALIFORNIA WILDERNESS COALITION, 284
CALIFORNIA WILDLIFE DEFENDERS, 284
CALIFORNIA WILDLIFE FEDERATION, 284
CALIFORNIANS FOR POPULATION STABILIZATION (CAPS), 284
CAM VALLEY WILDLIFE GROUP, 284
CAMP FIRE CLUB OF AMERICA, 284
CAMP FIRE CONSERVATION FUND, 285
CAMP FIRE USA, 285
CAMPAIGN FOR AMERICA'S WILDERNESS, 285
CANADA GOOSE PROJECT, 285
CANADIAN ARCTIC RESOURCE COMMITTEE, INC., 285
CANADIAN COOPERATIVE WILDLIFE HEALTH CENTRE, 286
CANADIAN ENVIRONMENTAL LAW ASSOCIATION, 286
CANADIAN FEDERATION OF HUMANE SOCIETIES, 286
CANADIAN FOREST SERVICE NATURAL RESOURCES CANADA, 16
CANADIAN FORESTRY ASSOCIATION, 286
CANADIAN INSTITUTE FOR ENVIRONMENTAL LAW AND POLICY (CIELAP), 286
CANADIAN INSTITUTE OF FORESTRY/INSTITUTE FORESTIER DU CANADA, 287
CANADIAN NATIONAL SPORTSMENS SHOWS, 287
CANADIAN NATURE FEDERATION, 287
CANADIAN PARKS AND WILDERNESS SOCIETY, 287
CANADIAN SOCIETY OF ENVIRONMENTAL BIOLOGISTS, 287
CANADIAN WILDLIFE FEDERATION, 287
CANADIAN WILDLIFE SERVICE, 17
CANON ENVIROTHON, 288
CANVASBACK SOCIETY, 288
CARIBBEAN CONSERVATION CORPORATION, 288
CARIBBEAN NATURAL RESOURCES INSTITUTE, 288
CAROLINA BIRD CLUB, INC., 288
CARRYING CAPACITY NETWORK, 288
CASCADIA RESEARCH, 288
CATSKILL CENTER FOR CONSERVATION AND DEVELOPMENT, INC., THE, 289
CATSKILL FOREST ASSOCIATION, 289
CAVE RESEARCH FOUNDATION, 289
CENTER FOR A NEW AMERICAN DREAM, THE, 289
CENTER FOR A SUSTAINABLE COAST, 289
CENTER FOR BIOLOGICAL DIVERSITY, 290
CENTER FOR CHESAPEAKE COMMUNITIES, 290
CENTER FOR ENVIRONMENT AND POPULATION (CEP), 290
CENTER FOR ENVIRONMENT, COMMERCE & ENERGY, 290
CENTER FOR ENVIRONMENTAL EDUCATION, 291
CENTER FOR ENVIRONMENTAL HEALTH (CEH), 291
CENTER FOR ENVIRONMENTAL INFORMATION, 291
CENTER FOR ENVIRONMENTAL PHILOSOPHY, 291
CENTER FOR ENVIRONMENTAL STUDY, 291
CENTER FOR HEALTH, ENVIRONMENT, AND JUSTICE, 291
CENTER FOR INDEPENDENT SOCIAL RESEARCH, 292
CENTER FOR INTERNATIONAL ENVIRONMENTAL LAW (CIEL), 292
CENTER FOR NATIVE ECOSYSTEMS
   Front Range Office, 292
   West Slope Office, 292
CENTER FOR PLANT CONSERVATION, 292
CENTER FOR RESOURCE ECONOMICS/ISLAND PRESS, 293
CENTER FOR SCIENCE IN THE PUBLIC INTEREST, 293
CENTER FOR SIERRA NEVADA CONSERVATION, 293

ORGANIZATION NAME INDEX – C

CENTER FOR THE STUDY OF TROPICAL BIRDS, INC.
   Administrative Office, 293
   Field Office, 293
CENTER FOR WATERSHED PROTECTION, 293
CENTER FOR WILDLIFE LAW, 293
CENTRAL MICHIGAN UNIVERSITY, 576
CENTRAL OHIO ANGLERS AND HUNTERS CLUB, 294
CENTRE FOR RESEARCH IN EDUCATION AND THE ENVIRONMENT, THE, 576
CENTRO DE INFORMACION, INVESTIGACION Y EDUCACION SOCIAL (CIIES), 294
CETACEAN SOCIETY INTERNATIONAL, 294
CHARLES A. AND ANNE MORROW LINDBERGH FOUNDATION, THE, 294
CHAUTAUQUA WATERSHED CONSERVANCY, 294
CHELONIA INSTITUTE, 295
CHESAPEAKE BAY FOUNDATION, INC., 295
   Maryland Office, 295
   Pennsylvania Office, 295
   Virginia Office, 295
CHESAPEAKE FARMS, 564
CHESAPEAKE WILDLIFE HERITAGE (CWH), 295
CHICAGO HERPETOLOGICAL SOCIETY, 295
CHICAGO PARK DISTRICT, 296
CHICAGO REGION BIODIVERSITY COUNCIL, 296
CHIHUAHUAN DESERT RESEARCH INSTITUTE, 296
CHINA REGION LAKES ALLIANCE, 296
CHISHOLM WOLF FOUNDATION, INC., 296
CHLORINE-FREE PAPER CONSORTIUM, 297
CHRISTINA CONSERVANCY, INC., 297
CINCINNATI NATURE CENTER, 297
CIRCUMPOLAR CONSERVATION UNION, 297
CITIZENS ALLIANCE FOR SAVING THE ATMOSPHERE AND THE EARTH (CASA), 297
CITIZENS FOR A SCENIC FLORIDA, INC., 297
CITIZENS NATURAL RESOURCES ASSOCIATION OF WISCONSIN, INC., 297
CITIZENS' NUCLEAR INFORMATION CENTER, 298
CITY OF BELDING, 145
CITY UNIVERSITY OF NEW YORK
   College of Staten Island, 576
   Hunter College, 576
CJE ASSOCIATES, 565
CLARK UNIVERSITY, 576
CLEAN OCEAN ACTION
   Main Office, 298
   Mid-Coast Office, 298
   South Jersey Office, 298
CLEAN WATER ACTION, 298
CLEAN WATER FUND, 298
CLEAN WATER NETWORK, THE, 298
CLEAR CREEK ENVIRONMENTAL FOUNDATION, 299
CLEMSON UNIVERSITY
   Forestry and Natural Resources, 577
   School of the Environment, 577
CLEMSON UNIVERSITY EXTENSION SERVICE, 145
CLEVELAND MUSEUM OF NATURAL HISTORY, THE, 299
CLIMATE INSTITUTE, 299
CLINTON RIVER WATERSHED COUNCIL (CRWC), 299
COALITION FOR CLEAN AIR, 299
COALITION FOR EDUCATION IN THE OUTDOORS, 299
COALITION FOR NATURAL STREAM VALLEYS, INC., 299
COAST ALLIANCE, 300
COASTAL AMERICA FOUNDATION, 300
COASTAL CONSERVATION AND EDUCATION FOUNDATION, INC., 565
COASTAL CONSERVATION ASSOCIATION, 300
COASTAL CONSERVATION ASSOCIATION GEORGIA, 300
COASTAL GEORGIA LAND TRUST INC., 300
COASTAL RESOURCE MANAGEMENT PROJECT, 146
COASTAL RESOURCES CENTER, 577
COASTAL SOCIETY, THE, 301
COEREBA SOCIETY, 301
COLLEGE OF THE ATLANTIC, 577
COLLEGE OF WILLIAM AND MARY, 577
COLORADO ASSOCIATION OF SOIL CONSERVATION DISTRICTS, 301
COLORADO BASS FEDERATION, 301
COLORADO DEPARTMENT OF AGRICULTURE, 146
COLORADO DEPARTMENT OF EDUCATION, 146
COLORADO DEPARTMENT OF NATURAL RESOURCES, 146
   Colorado Geologic Survey, 146
   Division of Minerals and Geology, 146
   Division of Parks and Outdoor Recreation, 146
   Division of Water Resources, 147
   Division of Wildlife, 147
   Oil and Gas Conservation Commission, 147
   State Board of Land Commissioners, 147
COLORADO DEPARTMENT OF PUBLIC HEALTH AND ENVIRONMENT, 147
COLORADO ENVIRONMENTAL COALITION, 301
COLORADO FORESTRY ASSOCIATION, 301
COLORADO GOVERNOR'S OFFICE OF ENERGY MANAGEMENT AND CONSERVATION, 147
COLORADO MOUNTAIN CLUB, 302
COLORADO MOUNTAIN COLLEGE, 577
COLORADO NATURAL HERITAGE PROGRAM, 302
COLORADO RIVER BOARD OF CALIFORNIA, 147
COLORADO STATE CONSERVATION BOARD
   Colorado Department of Agriculture, 148
COLORADO STATE FOREST SERVICE, 148
COLORADO STATE UNIVERSITY
   College of Natural Resources, 578
COLORADO STATE UNIVERSITY
   Department of Fishery and Wildlife Biology, 578
   Department of Political Science, 578
COLORADO STATE UNIVERSITY COOPERATIVE EXTENSION, 148
COLORADO TRAPPERS ASSOCIATION, 302
COLORADO WATER CONGRESS, 302
COLORADO WATER CONSERVATION BOARD
   Water Conservation Board, 148
COLORADO WILDLIFE FEDERATION, 302
COLORADO WILDLIFE HERITAGE FOUNDATION, 302
COLUMBIA BASIN FISH AND WILDLIFE AUTHORITY, 303
COLUMBIA ENVIRONMENTAL RESEARCH CENTER, 303
COLUMBIA RIVER GORGE COMMISSION, 148
COLUMBIA RIVER INTER-TRIBAL FISH COMMISSION, 17
COMITE DESPERTAR CIDRENO, 148
COMMITTEE FOR NATIONAL ARBOR DAY, 303
COMMUNITIES FOR A BETTER ENVIRONMENT, 303
COMMUNITY CONSERVATION /HOWLERS FOREVER, INC., 303
COMMUNITY ENVIRONMENTAL COUNCIL (CEC), 303
COMMUNITY RIGHTS COUNSEL, 303
CONCERN, INC., 304
CONFEDERATED SALISH AND KOOTENAI TRIBES, 304
CONGRESSIONAL GREEN SHEETS, INC., 565
CONNECTICUT ASSOCIATION OF CONSERVATION DISTRICTS, INC., 304
CONNECTICUT BASS FEDERATION, 304
CONNECTICUT BOTANICAL SOCIETY, 304
CONNECTICUT CARIBOU CLAN, 565
CONNECTICUT COLLEGE, 578
CONNECTICUT COUNCIL ON ENVIRONMENTAL QUALITY, 148
CONNECTICUT DEPARTMENT OF AGRICULTURE, 149
CONNECTICUT DEPARTMENT OF ENVIRONMENTAL PROTECTION, 149
CONNECTICUT FOREST AND PARK ASSOCIATION, 304
CONNECTICUT FUND FOR THE ENVIRONMENT, 305
CONNECTICUT PUBLIC INTEREST RESEARCH GROUP (CONN PIRG), 305
CONNECTICUT RIVER WATERSHED COUNCIL INC., 305
CONNECTICUT WATERFOWL ASSOCIATION, INC., 305
CONSERVAMERICA, 305
CONSERVANCY OF SOUTHWEST FLORIDA, THE, 305
CONSERVATION ALLIANCE OF ST. LUCIE CO., 306
CONSERVATION BIOLOGY INSTITUTE, 306
CONSERVATION COUNCIL FOR HAWAII, 306
CONSERVATION COUNCIL OF NORTH CAROLINA, 306
CONSERVATION COUNCIL OF WESTERN AUSTRALIA, INC., 17
CONSERVATION EDUCATION CENTER, THE, 306
CONSERVATION FEDERATION OF MARYLAND/ F.A.R.M., 306
CONSERVATION FEDERATION OF MISSOURI, 307
CONSERVATION FORCE, 307
CONSERVATION FUND, THE, 307
CONSERVATION INTERNATIONAL, 307
CONSERVATION LAW FOUNDATION, INC. (CLF), 307
   New England Region, 308
CONSERVATION TECHNOLOGY INFORMATION CENTER, 308
CONSERVATION TREATY SUPPORT FUND, 308
CONSERVATION TRUST OF PUERTO RICO, 308
CONWAY SCHOOL OF LANDSCAPE DESIGN, 578
COOK INLET KEEPER, 308
COOPER ORNITHOLOGICAL SOCIETY, 308
COOSA RIVER BASIN INITIATIVE, 309
CORAL REEF ALLIANCE, THE (CORAL), 309
CORLANDS, 309
CORNELL LAB OF ORNITHOLOGY, 309
CORNELL UNIVERSITY, 578
COTTONWOOD FOUNDATION, 309

ORGANIZATION NAME INDEX – E

COUNCIL FOR ENVIRONMENTAL EDUCATION, 309
COUNCIL FOR PLANNING AND CONSERVATION, 310
COUNTY OF SAN DIEGO, 149
COUSTEAU SOCIETY, INC., THE, 310
  France Office, 310
CRAIGHEAD ENVIRONMENTAL RESEARCH INSTITUTE, 310
CRAIGHEAD WILDLIFE-WILDLANDS INSTITUTE, 310
CRANSTON CONSERVATION COMMISSION, 150
CRESTON VALLEY WILDLIFE MANAGEMENT AREA, 310
CRITICAL ECOSYSTEM PARTNERSHIP FUND, 311
CROSBY ARBORETUM, THE, 311
CROWNPOINT INSTITUTE OF TECHNOLOGY, 565
CUTTER INFORMATION CORPORATION, 565
CZECH REPUBLIC MINISTRY OF THE ENVIRONMENT, 17

D

D ACRES, 311
DALHOUSIE UNIVERSITY, 579
DARTMOUTH COLLEGE, 579
DAWES ARBORETUM, THE, 311
DEEP-PORTAGE CONSERVATION RESERVE, 311
DEFENDERS OF WILDLIFE, 311
DELAWARE ASSOCIATION OF CONSERVATION DISTRICTS, 312
DELAWARE BASS FEDERATION, 312
DELAWARE COOPERATIVE EXTENSION SERVICES, 150
DELAWARE DEPARTMENT OF AGRICULTURE, 150
DELAWARE DEPARTMENT OF NATURAL RESOURCES AND ENVIRONMENTAL CONTROL
  Division of Air & Waste Management, 150
  Division of Fish and Wildlife, 150
  Division of Parks and Recreation, 150
  Division of Soil and Water Conservation, 150
  Division of Water Resources, 151
DELAWARE FOREST SERVICE, 151
DELAWARE GEOLOGICAL SURVEY, 151
DELAWARE GREENWAYS, INC., 312
DELAWARE MUSEUM OF NATURAL HISTORY, 312
DELAWARE NATURE SOCIETY, 312
DELAWARE RIVER BASIN COMMISSION, 17
DELAWARE RIVERKEEPER NETWORK, 313
DELAWARE SOLID WASTE AUTHORITY, 151
DELAWARE WILD LANDS, INC., 313
DELMARVA ORNITHOLOGICAL SOCIETY, 313
DELTA COLLEGE, 579
DELTA WATERFOWL FOUNDATION, 313
DELTA WILDLIFE INC., 313
DEPARTAMENTO DE RECURSOS NATURALES Y AMBIENTALES, 151
DEPARTMENT OF LAND AND NATURAL RESOURCES (HAWAII), 151
DEPARTMENT OF PARKS AND RECREATION, 151
DEPARTMENT OF TOURISM, CULTURE AND RECREATION, 152
DEPAUL UNIVERSITY
  Biological Sciences, 579
  Environmental Science Program, 579
DESCHUTES BASIN LAND TRUST, 313
DESERT FISHES COUNCIL, 314
DESERT PROTECTIVE COUNCIL, 314
DESERT RESEARCH FOUNDATION OF NAMIBIA, THE, 314
DESERT TORTOISE COUNCIL, 314
DESERT TORTOISE PRESERVE COMMITTEE, INC., 314
DISTRICT OF COLUMBIA DEPARTMENT OF HEALTH
  Environmental Health Administration, Watershed Protection Division, 152
DISTRICT OF COLUMBIA DEPARTMENT OF PUBLIC WORKS, 152
DISTRICT OF COLUMBIA SOIL AND WATER CONSERVATION DISTRICT, 314
DIVISION OF FORESTRY AND SOIL RESOURCES OF GUAM, 152
DONALD BREN SCHOOL OF ENVIRONMENTAL SCIENCE AND MANAGEMENT, 579
DRAGONFLY SOCIETY OF THE AMERICAS, THE, 314
DREXEL UNIVERSITY, 579
DUCKS UNLIMITED CANADA
  Albert Office, 315
  Manitoba Office, 315
  Nova Scotia Office, 315
  Ontario Office, 315
  Quebec Office, 315
  Saskatchewan Office, 315
DUCKS UNLIMITED, INC., 315
  Wetlands America Trust, Inc. Office, 316
DUKE UNIVERSITY, 580
DUKE UNIVERSITY - ORGANIZATION FOR TROPICAL STUDIES, 580

E

EAGLE NATURE FOUNDATION, LTD., 316
EAGLES 4 KIDS, 565
EARTH DAY NETWORK, 316
EARTH DAY NEW YORK, 316
EARTH FORCE, 316
  GREEN (Global Rivers Environmental Education Network), 317
EARTH FOUNDATION, 317
EARTH FRIENDS WILDLIFE FOUNDATION, 317
EARTH ISLAND INSTITUTE, 317
EARTH POLICY INSTITUTE, 317
EARTH SCHOOL, 565
EARTH SHARE, 317
EARTH SHARE OF GEORGIA, 318
EARTHJUSTICE
  Bozeman Office, 318
  Denver Office, 318
  Environmental Law Clinic at Stanford University, 318
  Environmental Law Clinic at the University of Denver, 318
  Headquarters, 318
  Honolulu Office, 319
  International Program, 319
  Juneau Office, 319
  Oakland Office, 319
  Policy and Legislation, 319
  Seattle Office, 320
  Tallahassee Office, 320
  Washington, DC, Office, 320
EARTHSCAN, 320
EARTHSTEWARDS NETWORK, 320
EARTHTRUST, 320
EARTHWATCH INSTITUTE, 321
EAST CENTRAL ILLINOIS FUR TAKERS, 321
EASTERN ILLINOIS UNIVERSITY, 580
EASTERN KENTUCKY UNIVERSITY, 580
EASTERN MICHIGAN UNIVERSITY, 581
EASTERN SHORE LAND CONSERVANCY (ESLC), 321
ECODEFENSE, 321
ECOLOGICAL SOCIETY OF AMERICA, THE, 321
ECOLOGY CENTER, 321
ECONOVA INC., 565
ECOROOMMATES.COM, 566
ECOSEA, 322
EDUCATIONAL COMMUNICATIONS, 322
EGYPTIAN ENVIRONMENTAL AFFAIRS AGENCY, 18
ELEMENTAL TECHNOLOGY, LLC, 566
ELM RESEARCH INSTITUTE, 322
EMORY UNIVERSITY, 581
EMPORIA STATE UNIVERSITY, 581
ENDANGERED HABITATS LEAGUE, 322
ENDANGERED SPECIES AND WETLANDS REPORT, 566
ENDANGERED SPECIES COALITION, 322
ENGENDERHEALTH, 322
ENTOMOLOGICAL SOCIETY OF AMERICA, 323
ENVIRONMENT AND ENERGY PUBLISHING, LLC, 566
ENVIRONMENT CANADA, 18
ENVIRONMENT COUNCIL OF RHODE ISLAND, 323
ENVIRONMENTAL ACTION FUND (EAF), 323
ENVIRONMENTAL ADVOCATES OF NEW YORK, 323
ENVIRONMENTAL ALLIANCE FOR SENIOR INVOLVEMENT (EASI), 323
ENVIRONMENTAL AND ENERGY STUDY INSTITUTE (EESI), 323
ENVIRONMENTAL CAREER CENTER, 566
ENVIRONMENTAL CAREERS ORGANIZATION, INC., THE, 324
ENVIRONMENTAL CONCERN INC., 324
ENVIRONMENTAL CONSERVATION SERVICE, 18
  Atlantic Region Environment Canada, 18
ENVIRONMENTAL DEFENSE
  Alliance for Environmental Innovation, 324
  Capital Office, 324
  Headquarters, 324
  North Carolina Office, 324
  Rocky Mountain Office, 324
  Texas Office, 325
  West Coast Office, 325
ENVIRONMENTAL DEFENSE CENTER, 325
ENVIRONMENTAL EDUCATION ASSOCIATES, 325
ENVIRONMENTAL EDUCATION ASSOCIATION OF ILLINOIS, 325
ENVIRONMENTAL EDUCATION ASSOCIATION OF INDIANA, 325
ENVIRONMENTAL EDUCATION ASSOCIATION OF WASHINGTON, 325
ENVIRONMENTAL EDUCATION COUNCIL OF OHIO, 326
ENVIRONMENTAL EDUCATORS OF NORTH CAROLINA (EENC), 326
ENVIRONMENTAL ENTERPRISES ASSISTANCE FUND, INC., 326
ENVIRONMENTAL FRONTLINES, 326

ENVIRONMENTAL JUSTICE COALITION, 326
ENVIRONMENTAL LAW ALLIANCE WORLDWIDE, U.S. (E-LAW U.S.), 326
ENVIRONMENTAL LAW AND POLICY CENTER OF THE MIDWEST, 327
ENVIRONMENTAL LAW INSTITUTE, THE, 327
ENVIRONMENTAL LEAGUE OF MASSACHUSETTS, 327
ENVIRONMENTAL MEDIA ASSOCIATION, 327
ENVIRONMENTAL MEDIA CORPORATION, 566
ENVIRONMENTAL POLICY CENTER, THE, 327
ENVIRONMENTAL PROTECTION AGENCY, 18
  Air and Radiation, 18
  Region 1 (CT, ME, MA, NH, RI, VT), 18
  Region 2 (NJ, NY, PR, VI), 18
  Region 3 (DE, DC, MD, PA, VA, WV), 19
  Region 4 (AL, FL, GA, KY, MS, NC, SC, TN), 19
  Region 5 (IL, IN, MI, NM, OH, WI), 19
  Region 6 (AR, LA, NM, OK, TX), 19
  Region 7 (KS, MO, NE), 19
  Region 8 (CO, MT, ND, SD, UT, WY), 19
  Region 9 (GU, AS, NV, HI, CA, AZ), 19
  Region 10 (WA, OR, ID, AK), 19
  Solid Waste and Emergency Response, 19
ENVIRONMENTAL PROTECTION ASSOCIATION OF GHANA, 327
ENVIRONMENTAL PROTECTION MASSACHUSETTS, 152
ENVIRONMENTAL RESOURCE CENTER (ERC), 328
ENVIROSCAPE, 566
ENVIROSOUTH, INC., 328
EP EDUCATION SERVICES, INC., 328
EQUESTRIAN LAND CONSERVATION RESOURCE, 328
EUROPARC FEDERATION, 328
EUROPEAN ASSOCIATION FOR AQUATIC MAMMALS, 328
EUROPEAN CETACEAN SOCIETY, 328
EVERGLADES COORDINATING COUNCIL (ECC), 329

F

FAU PINE JOG ENVIROMENTAL EDUCATION CENTER, 581
FEDERAL CARTRIDGE COMPANY, 329
FEDERAL WILDLIFE OFFICERS ASSOCIATION, 329
FEDERATION OF ALBERTA NATURALISTS, 329
FEDERATION OF ENVIRONMENTAL EDUCATION IN ST. PETERSBURG, 329
FEDERATION OF FLY FISHERS, 329
FEDERATION OF FLY FISHERS (NCCFFF), 329
FEDERATION OF NEW YORK STATE BIRD CLUBS, INC., 330
FEDERATION OF ONTARIO NATURALISTS, 330
FEDERATION OF WESTERN OUTDOOR CLUBS, 330
FERRIS STATE UNIVERSITY, 581
FERRUM COLLEGE, 581
FISH AND WILDLIFE REFERENCE SERVICE, 19
FISH FOREVER, 330
FISHAMERICA FOUNDATION, 330
FISHERIES AND OCEANS CANADA
  Communications Directorate, 20
  Fisheries and Management, 20
FLAGSTAFF DARK SKIES COALITION (FDSC), 330
FLINTSTEEL RESTORATION ASSOCIATION, INC., 330
FLORIDA ASSOCIATION OF SOIL AND WATER CONSERVATION DISTRICTS, 331
FLORIDA BASS CHAPTER FEDERATION, 331
FLORIDA COOPERATIVE EXTENSION SERVICE, 582
FLORIDA COOPERATIVE FISH AND WILDLIFE RESEARCH UNIT (USDI), 152
FLORIDA DEFENDERS OF THE ENVIRONMENT, INC., 331
FLORIDA DEPARTMENT OF AGRICULTURE AND CONSUMER SERVICES, 152
  Division of Forestry, 153
  Office of Agricultural Water Policy, 153
  Soil and Water Conservation Council, 153
FLORIDA DEPARTMENT OF ENVIRONMENTAL PROTECTION, 153
  Air Resources Management Division, 153
  Bureau of Beaches and Wetland Resources, 153
  Coastal and Aquatic Managed Areas, 153
  Division of Law Enforcement, 153
  Division of Resource Assessment and Management, 154
  Division of State Lands, 154
  Division of Water Resource Management, 154
  Florida State Parks AmeriCorps, 154
  Recreation and Parks Division, 154
  Waste Management Division, 154
FLORIDA EXOTIC PEST PLANT COUNCIL, 331
FLORIDA FEDERATION OF GARDEN CLUBS, INC., 331
FLORIDA FISH AND WILDLIFE CONSERVATION COMMISSION, 154
FLORIDA FORESTRY ASSOCIATION, 331
FLORIDA NATIVE PLANT SOCIETY, 332
FLORIDA NATURAL AREAS INVENTORY, 332
FLORIDA ORNITHOLOGICAL SOCIETY, 332
FLORIDA PANTHER PROJECT, INC., THE, 332
FLORIDA PANTHER SOCIETY, INC., THE, 332
FLORIDA PUBLIC INTEREST RESEARCH GROUP (FLORIDA PIRG), 332
FLORIDA SPORTSMEN'S CONSERVATION ASSOCIATION, 333
FLORIDA STATE DEPARTMENT OF HEALTH, 155
FLORIDA STATE UNIVERSITY, 582
FLORIDA TRAIL ASSOCIATION, INC., 333
FLORIDA WILDLIFE FEDERATION, 333
FOOD AND AGRICULTURE ORGANIZATION OF THE UNITED NATIONS, 333
FOOD SUPPLY / HUMAN POPULATION EXPLOSION CONNECTION, 333
FOREST FIRE LOOKOUT ASSOCIATION, 334
FOREST HISTORY SOCIETY, INC., 334
FOREST LANDOWNERS ASSOCIATION, INC., 334
FOREST LANDOWNERS OF CALIFORNIA, 334
FOREST MANAGEMENT TRUST, 334
FOREST SERVICE EMPLOYEES FOR ENVIRONMENTAL ETHICS (FSEEE), 334
FOREST SOCIETY OF MAINE, 335
FOREST STEWARDS GUILD, 335
  Northwest Regional Chapter (GuildNW), 335
FOREST TRUST, 335
FOREST WATCH, 335
FORESTRY COMMISSION (ARKANSAS), 155
FORESTRY COMMISSION (SOUTH CAROLINA), 155
FOSSIL RIM WILDLIFE CENTER, 336
FOUNDATION FOR NORTH AMERICAN BIG GAME, 336
FOUNDATION FOR NORTH AMERICAN WILD SHEEP, 336
FOUR CORNERS INSTITUTE, THE, 336
FRANKFURT ZOOLOGICAL SOCIETY-HELP FOR THREATENED WILDLIFE, 336
FRIENDS OF ACADIA, 336
FRIENDS OF ANIMALS INC., 337
FRIENDS OF DISCOVERY PARK, 337
FRIENDS OF FAMOSA SLOUGH, 337
FRIENDS OF MISSISQUOI NATIONAL WILDLIFE REFUGE, INC., 337
FRIENDS OF SUNKHAZE MEADOWS NATIONAL WILDLIFE REFUGE, 337
FRIENDS OF THE BOUNDARY WATERS WILDERNESS, 337
FRIENDS OF THE CARR REFUGE, 337
FRIENDS OF THE EARTH, 337
FRIENDS OF THE LITTLE PEND OREILLE NATIONAL WILDLIFE REFUGE, THE, 338
FRIENDS OF THE REEDY RIVER, 338
FRIENDS OF THE RIVER, 338
FRIENDS OF THE SAN JUANS, 338
FRIENDS OF THE SEA OTTER, 338
FROSTBURG STATE UNIVERSITY (UNIVERSITY OF MARYLAND), 582
FUND FOR ANIMALS, 338
FUNDACION NATURA COLOMBIA, 339
FUTURE FISHERMAN FOUNDATION, 339
FUTURE GENERATIONS, 339

G

GALIANO CONSERVANCY ASSOCIATION, 339
GAME AND PARKS COMMISSION-NEBRASKA, 339
GAME CONSERVANCY U.S.A., 339
GAME CONSERVATION INTERNATIONAL (GAME COIN), 339
GARDEN CLUB OF AMERICA, THE, 340
GECKO PRODUCTIONS, INC., 340
GENERAL FEDERATION OF WOMEN'S CLUBS, 340
GENERAL SERVICES ADMINISTRATION, 20
GEORGE MIKSCH SUTTON AVIAN RESEARCH CENTER INC., 340
GEORGE WASHINGTON CARVER OUTDOOR SCHOOL, INC., THE, 340
GEORGE WASHINGTON UNIVERSITY, 582
  Law School, 582
GEORGE WRIGHT SOCIETY, THE, 341
GEORGETOWN COLLEGE, 582
GEORGETOWN ENVIRONMENTAL LAW & POLICY INSTITUTE, 582
GEORGIA ASSOCIATION OF CONSERVATION DISTRICT SUPERVISORS, 341
GEORGIA BASS FEDERATION, 341
GEORGIA CONSERVANCY, INC., THE, 341
GEORGIA COOPERATIVE FISH AND WILDLIFE RESEARCH UNIT (USDI), 20
GEORGIA DEPARTMENT OF AGRICULTURE, 155

ORGANIZATION NAME INDEX – I

GEORGIA DEPARTMENT OF EDUCATION, 156
GEORGIA DEPARTMENT OF NATURAL RESOURCES, 156
  Coastal Resources Division, 156
  Environmental Protection Division, 156
    Coastal Division, 156
  Historic Preservation Division, 156
  Parks, Recreation and Historic Sites Division, 156
  Pollution Prevention Assistance Division, 156
  Wildlife Resources Division, 157
GEORGIA ENVIRONMENTAL COUNCIL, INC., 341
GEORGIA ENVIRONMENTAL ORGANIZATION, INC. (GEO), 341
GEORGIA ENVIRONMENTAL POLICY INSTITUTE, 342
GEORGIA FEDERATION OF FOREST OWNERS, 342
GEORGIA FORESTRY ASSOCIATION, INC., 342
GEORGIA FORESTRY COMMISSION, 157
GEORGIA INSTITUTE OF TECHNOLOGY, 583
GEORGIA STATE EXTENSION SERVICE, 157
GEORGIA STATE SOIL AND WATER CONSERVATION COMMISSION, 157
GEORGIA TRAPPERS ASSOCIATION, 342
GEORGIA TRUST FOR HISTORIC PRESERVATION, 342
GEORGIA WILDLIFE FEDERATION, 342
GEORGIANS FOR CLEAN ENERGY, 342
GET AMERICA WORKING!, 343
GIRL SCOUTS OF THE USA, 343
GLACIER INSTITUTE, THE, 343
GLEN CANYON INSTITUTE, 343
GLOBAL ENVIRONMENTAL MANAGEMENT INITIATIVE (GEMI), 343
GLOBAL INDUSTRIAL AND SOCIAL PROGRESS RESEARCH INSTITUTE (GISPRI), 344
GLOBAL INFORMATION NETWORK, 344
GOOD NATURE PUBLISHING CO., 566
GOPHER TORTOISE COUNCIL, 344
GRAND CANYON TRUST, 344
GRANT TECH CONSULTING AND CONSERVATION SERVICES, 567
GRASSLAND HERITAGE FOUNDATION, 344
GREAT BEAR FOUNDATION, 344
GREAT LAKES FISHERY COMMISSION, 20
GREAT LAKES INDIAN FISH AND WILDLIFE COMMISSION, 20
GREAT LAKES SPORT FISHING COUNCIL, 344
GREAT LAKES UNITED, 345
  Canada Office, 345
GREAT OUTDOORS CONSERVANCY, THE, 345
GREAT PLAINS NATIVE PLANT SOCIETY, 345
GREAT SMOKY MOUNTAINS INSTITUTE AT TREMONT, 345
GREATER YELLOWSTONE COALITION, 346
GREEN BALKANS FEDERATION OF NATURE CONSERVATION NGOS, 346
GREEN GUIDES, 346
GREEN MEDIA TOOLSHED, 346
GREEN MOUNTAIN CLUB INC., THE, 346
GREEN MOUNTAIN POST FILMS, 567
GREEN PARTNERS, 347
GREEN SEAL, 347
GREEN SPHERE INC., 347
GREEN TV, 347
GREENPEACE, INC., 347
GREENWIRE, 567
GROUNDWATER FOUNDATION, THE, 347
GROWLING, 348
GUADALUPE-BLANCO RIVER AUTHORITY, 157
GUAM COASTAL MANAGEMENT PROGRAM, 158
GUAM COOPERATIVE EXTENSION SERVICE, 158
GUAM DEPARTMENT OF AGRICULTURE, 158
  Division of Aquatic and Wildlife Resources, 158
GUAM DEPARTMENT OF PARKS AND RECREATION, 158
GUAM ENVIRONMENTAL PROTECTION AGENCY, 158
GULF COAST ENVIRONMENTAL DEFENSE, 348
GULF COAST RESEARCH LABORATORY, 158
GULF OF MEXICO FISHERY MANAGEMENT COUNCIL, 348
GULF STATES MARINE FISHERIES COMMISSION, 20
GWINNETT OPEN LAND TRUST, INC., 348

H

H. JOHN HEINZ III CENTER FOR SCIENCE, ECONOMICS, AND THE ENVIRONMENT, 348
HAMLINE UNIVERSITY, 583
HARBOR BRANCH OCEANOGRAPHIC INSTITUTION, 348
HARDWOOD FOREST FOUNDATION, 348
HAWAII COOPERATIVE FISHERY RESEARCH UNIT (USDI), 158
HAWAII DEPARTMENT OF AGRICULTURE, 158
HAWAII DEPARTMENT OF HEALTH
  Office of Environmental Quality Control, 159
HAWAII DEPARTMENT OF LAND AND NATURAL RESOURCES, 159
  Division of Boating and Ocean Recreation, 159
  Division of Conservation and Resources Enforcement, 159
  Division of Forestry and Wildlife, 159
  Division of State Parks, 159
  Division of Water Resource Management, 159
  Land Division, 160
HAWAII INSTITUTE OF MARINE BIOLOGY, 160
HAWAII NATURE CENTER, 349
HAWAIIAN BOTANICAL SOCIETY, 349
HAWK AND OWL TRUST, THE, 349
HAWK MIGRATION ASSOCIATION OF NORTH AMERICA, 349
HAWK MOUNTAIN SANCTUARY ASSOCIATION, VISITOR CENTER, 349
HAWKWATCH INTERNATIONAL, 350
HEADLANDS INSTITUTE, 350
HEAL THE BAY, 350
HELPING OUR PENINSULA'S ENVIRONMENT, 350
HELSINKI COMMISSION/ BALTIC MARINE ENVIRONMENT PROTECTION COMMISSION, 21
HENRY A. WALLACE INSTITUTE FOR ALTERNATIVE AGRICULTURE (HAWIAA), 350
HENRY STIFEL SCHRADER ENVIRONMENTAL EDUCATION CENTER, 350
HERPDIGEST, 350
HIGH DESERT MUSEUM, THE, 351
HIGHLANDS CENTER FOR NATURAL HISTORY, 351
HILTON POND CENTER FOR PIEDMONT NATURAL HISTORY, 351
HIMALAYAN WILDLIFE FOUNDATION, 351
HOCKING COLLEGE, 583
HOLDEN ARBORETUM, THE, 351
HOLLOW OAK LAND TRUST, 351
HOLLY SOCIETY OF AMERICA, INC., 352
HOOSIER ENVIRONMENTAL COUNCIL, 352
HOUSE COMMITTEE ON AGRICULTURE, 21
HOUSE COMMITTEE ON APPROPRIATIONS, 21
HOUSE COMMITTEE ON EDUCATION AND THE WORKFORCE, 21
HOUSE COMMITTEE ON ENERGY AND COMMERCE, 21
HOUSE COMMITTEE ON INTERNATIONAL RELATIONS, 21
HOUSE COMMITTEE ON RESOURCES, 22
HOUSE COMMITTEE ON RULES, 22
HOUSE COMMITTEE ON TRANSPORTATION AND INFRASTRUCTURE, 22
HUDSONIA LIMITED, 352
HUMAN ECOLOGY ACTION LEAGUE, INC., THE (HEAL), 352
HUMANE SOCIETY OF THE UNITED STATES, THE, 352
HUMBOLDT STATE UNIVERSITY, 583
HUMBOLT FIELD RESEARCH INSTITUTE, 353
HUMMINGBIRD SOCIETY, THE, 353
HUNTSMAN MARINE SCIENCE CENTRE, 353
HYDE CREEK WATERSHED SOCIETY, 353

I

IDAHO ASSOCIATION OF SOIL CONSERVATION DISTRICTS, 353
IDAHO BASS FEDERATION, 353
IDAHO CONSERVATION LEAGUE, 354
IDAHO DEPARTMENT OF ENVIRONMENTAL QUALITY, 160
IDAHO DEPARTMENT OF FISH AND GAME, 160
IDAHO DEPARTMENT OF LANDS, 160
IDAHO DEPARTMENT OF PARKS AND RECREATION, 160
IDAHO DEPARTMENT OF WATER RESOURCES, 161
  Water Awareness Week, 161
IDAHO ENVIRONMENTAL COUNCIL, 354
IDAHO FISH AND WILDLIFE FOUNDATION, 161
IDAHO GEOLOGICAL SURVEY, 161
IDAHO STATE DEPARTMENT OF AGRICULTURE, 161
IDAHO STATE SOIL CONSERVATION COMMISSION, 161
IDAHO STATE UNIVERSITY, 583
IDAHO TROUT LIMITED, 354
IDAHO WILDLIFE FEDERATION, 354
ILLINOIS ASSOCIATION OF CONSERVATION DISTRICTS, 354
ILLINOIS ASSOCIATION OF SOIL AND WATER CONSERVATION DISTRICTS, 354
ILLINOIS BASS FEDERATION, 355
ILLINOIS DEPARTMENT OF AGRICULTURE, 162
  Bureau of Land and Water Resources, 162
ILLINOIS DEPARTMENT OF NATURAL RESOURCES, 162
ILLINOIS DEPARTMENT OF TRANSPORTATION, 162
ILLINOIS ENVIRONMENTAL COUNCIL, 355
ILLINOIS ENVIRONMENTAL PROTECTION AGENCY, 162
ILLINOIS NATIVE PLANT SOCIETY, 355
ILLINOIS NATURE PRESERVES COMMISSION (INPC), 163
ILLINOIS PRAIRIE PATH, 355

ILLINOIS RAPTOR CENTER, 355
ILLINOIS STATE UNIVERSITY, 583
ILLINOIS STUDENT ENVIRONMENTAL NETWORK, 355
ILLINOIS WALNUT COUNCIL, 356
ILOVEPARKS.COM, 567
INDIAN CREEK NATURE CENTER, 356
INDIANA ASSOCIATION OF SOIL AND WATER CONSERVATION
    DISTRICTS, INC., 356
INDIANA AUDUBON SOCIETY, INC., 356
INDIANA BASS FEDERATION, 356
INDIANA DEPARTMENT OF ENVIRONMENTAL MANAGEMENT, 163
INDIANA DEPARTMENT OF NATURAL RESOURCES, 163
  Division of Soil Conservation, 164
INDIANA FORESTRY AND WOODLAND OWNERS ASSOCIATION, 356
INDIANA GEOLOGICAL SURVEY, 164
INDIANA NATIVE PLANT AND WILDFLOWER SOCIETY, 356
INDIANA STATE DEPARTMENT OF HEALTH, 164
INDIANA STATE TRAPPERS ASSOCIATION, INC., 357
INDIANA STATE UNIVERSITY, 583
INDIANA UNIVERSITY, 584
INDIANA WILDLIFE FEDERATION, 357
INDO-PACIFIC CONSERVATION ALLIANCE, 357
INDUSTRIAL COMMISSION OF NORTH DAKOTA, 164
INFORM, INC., 357
INITIATIVE FOR SOCIAL ACTION AND RENEWAL IN EURASIA, 357
INLAND BIRD BANDING ASSOCIATION, 357
INSTITUTE FOR AGRICULTURE AND TRADE POLICY, 358
INSTITUTE FOR CIVIC INITIATIVES SUPPORT, 358
INSTITUTE FOR CONSERVATION LEADERSHIP, 358
INSTITUTE FOR EARTH EDUCATION, THE, 358
INSTITUTE FOR ECOLOGICAL STUDIES UNIVERSITY OF NORTH
    DAKOTA, 164
INSTITUTE FOR GLOBAL COMMUNICATIONS, 567
INSTITUTE FOR TROPICAL ECOLOGY AND CONSERVATION (ITEC), 358
INSTITUTE OF ECOSYSTEM STUDIES, 358
INSTITUTO BRASIL DE EDUCACAO AMBIENTAL, 359
INSTITUTO NACIONAL DE BIODIVERSIDAD (INBIO), 22
INTERAGENCY COMMITTEE FOR OUTDOOR RECREATION (IAC), 164
INTERAMERICAN TROPICAL TUNA COMMISSION, 359
INTERFAITH COUNCIL FOR THE PROTECTION OF ANIMALS AND
    NATURE INC. (ICPAN), 359
INTERNATIONAL ACADEMY, 567
INTERNATIONAL ASSOCIATION FOR BEAR RESEARCH AND
    MANAGEMENT, 359
INTERNATIONAL ASSOCIATION FOR ENVIRONMENTAL HYDROLOGY
    (IAEH), 359
INTERNATIONAL ASSOCIATION OF FISH AND WILDLIFE AGENCIES,
    360
INTERNATIONAL ASSOCIATION OF NATURAL RESOURCE PILOTS, 360
INTERNATIONAL ASSOCIATION OF WILDLAND FIRE, 361
INTERNATIONAL BICYCLE FUND, 361
INTERNATIONAL BOUNDARY AND WATER COMMISSION, UNITED
    STATES AND MEXICO, 22
INTERNATIONAL CENTER FOR EARTH CONCERNS, 361
INTERNATIONAL CENTER FOR GIBBON STUDIES, 361
INTERNATIONAL CENTER FOR TROPICAL ECOLOGY, 361
INTERNATIONAL CENTRE FOR CONSERVATION EDUCATION, 361
INTERNATIONAL CHILDREN'S CONFERENCE ON THE
    ENVIRONMENT, 362
INTERNATIONAL COUNCIL OF ENVIRONMENTAL LAW, 362
INTERNATIONAL CRANE FOUNDATION, 362
INTERNATIONAL ECOLOGY SOCIETY (IES), 362
INTERNATIONAL ECOTOURISM SOCIETY, THE, 362
INTERNATIONAL EROSION CONTROL ASSOCIATION (IECA), 363
INTERNATIONAL FUND FOR ANIMAL WELFARE, 363
  Asia/Pacific, 363
  European Union, 363
  French Office, 363
  German Office, 363
  Holland Office, 363
  Hong Kong Office, 363
  Italian Office, 363
  Philippines Office, 363
  Russian Office, 363
  South African Office, 363
  United Kingdom, 364
INTERNATIONAL GAME FISH ASSOCIATION, 364
INTERNATIONAL HUNTER EDUCATION ASSOCIATION, 364
INTERNATIONAL INSTITUTE FOR ENERGY CONSERVATION, 364
INTERNATIONAL JOINT COMMISSION
  Canadian Section, 22
  Great Lakes Regional Office, 22
  United States Section, 23

INTERNATIONAL MARINE MAMMAL PROJECT, THE, 364
INTERNATIONAL MARITIME ORGANIZATION, 364
INTERNATIONAL MIRE CONSERVATION GROUP, 365
INTERNATIONAL OCEANOGRAPHIC FOUNDATION, 365
INTERNATIONAL OSPREY FOUNDATION INC., THE, 365
INTERNATIONAL PACIFIC HALIBUT COMMISSION, 23
INTERNATIONAL PLANT PROPAGATORS SOCIETY, INC., 365
INTERNATIONAL PRIMATE PROTECTION LEAGUE, 365
INTERNATIONAL PROFESSIONAL HUNTERS' ASSOCIATION, 365
INTERNATIONAL RESEARCH AND EVALUATION, 567
INTERNATIONAL RIVERS NETWORK (IRN), 366
INTERNATIONAL SNOW LEOPARD TRUST, 366
INTERNATIONAL SOCIETY FOR ECOLOGICAL ECONOMICS (ISEE), 366
INTERNATIONAL SOCIETY FOR ENDANGERED CATS, 366
INTERNATIONAL SOCIETY FOR ENDANGERED CATS (ISEC), 366
INTERNATIONAL SOCIETY FOR ENVIRONMENTAL ETHICS, 366
INTERNATIONAL SOCIETY FOR THE PRESERVATION OF THE
    TROPICAL RAINFOREST, THE, 367
INTERNATIONAL SOCIETY OF ARBORICULTURE, 367
INTERNATIONAL SOCIETY OF TROPICAL FORESTERS, INC., 367
INTERNATIONAL SONORAN DESERT ALLIANCE, 367
INTERNATIONAL UNION FOR CONSERVATION OF NATURE AND
    NATURAL RESOURCES (IUCN) THE WORLD CONSERVATION
    UNION
  Bangladesh Country Office, 368
  Botswana Country Office, 368
  Burkina Country Faso Office, 368
  Canada Office, 368
  Environmental Law Centre, 368
  Guinea-Bissau Country Office, 368
  Headquarters, 367
  IUCN Beira Project Office, 369
  Lao People's Democratic Republic Country Office, 369
  Mali Country Office, 369
  Nepal Country Office, 369
  Niger Country Office, 369
  Pakistan Country Office, 369
  Regional Office for Central Africa, 369
  Regional Office for Eastern Africa, 369
  Regional Office for Europe, 369
  Regional Office for MesoAmerica, 370
  Regional Office for South America, 370
  Regional Office for Southern Africa (ROSA), 370
  Regional Office for West Africa, 370
  Regional Office of South and Southeast Asia, 370
  Senegal Country Office, 370
  South Africa Country Office, 370
  Sri Lanka Country Office, 370
  Subregional Office for Central Europe, 370
  Subregional Office for the Commonwealth of Independent States, 370
  Uganda Country Office, 370
  United States Office, Washington, DC, 371
  Vietnam Country Office, 371
  Zambia Country Office, 371
INTERNATIONAL WHALING COMMISSION, 23
INTERNATIONAL WILD WATERFOWL ASSOCIATION, 371
INTERNATIONAL WILDLIFE COALITION (IWC) AND THE WHALE
    ADOPTION PROJECT, 371
INTERNATIONAL WILDLIFE REHABILITATION COUNCIL, 371
INTERNATIONAL WOLF CENTER, 371
  Administrative Offices, 372
INTERPRETATION CANADA, 372
INTERSTATE COMMISSION ON THE POTOMAC RIVER BASIN, 23
INTERTRIBAL BISON COOPERATIVE (ITBC), 372
IOWA ACADEMY OF SCIENCE, 372
IOWA ASSOCIATION OF COUNTY CONSERVATION BOARDS, 164
IOWA ASSOCIATION OF NATURALISTS, 372
IOWA BASS FEDERATION, 372
IOWA DEPARTMENT OF AGRICULTURE AND LAND STEWARDSHIP
  Bureau of Field Services, 165
  Bureau of Financial Incentive Program, 165
  Bureau of Water Resources, 165
  Division of Soil Conservation, 165
IOWA DEPARTMENT OF NATURAL RESOURCES, 165
  Cooperative North American Shotgunning Education Program, 165
  Energy and Waste Management Bureau, 165
  Environmental Protection Division, 166
  Fish and Wildlife Division, 166
  Forests and Prairies Division, 166
  Management Services Division, 166
  Parks, 166
  Waste Management Division, 166
IOWA ENVIRONMENTAL COUNCIL, 372

ORGANIZATION NAME INDEX – L

IOWA NATIVE PLANT SOCIETY, 373
IOWA NATURAL HERITAGE FOUNDATION, 373
IOWA PRAIRIE NETWORK, 373
IOWA STATE EXTENSION SERVICES
  Extension Wildlife Programs, 166
IOWA STATE UNIVERSITY
  College of Agriculture, 584
  College of Design, 584
IOWA TRAILS COUNCIL, 373
IOWA TRAPPERS ASSOCIATION, INC., 373
IOWA WILDLIFE FEDERATION, 374
IOWA WILDLIFE REHABILITATORS ASSOCIATION, 374
IOWA WOMEN IN NATURAL RESOURCES, 374
IOWA WOODLAND OWNERS ASSOCIATION, 374
ISLAND CONSERVATION EFFORT, 374
ISLAND INSTITUTE, THE, 374
ISLAND RESOURCES FOUNDATION, 375
  Eastern Caribbean Biodiversity Program Office, 375
ISLESBORO ISLANDS TRUST, 375
ISSAQUAH ALPS TRAILS CLUB (I.A.T.C.), 375
IZAAK WALTON LEAGUE OF AMERICA ENDOWMENT, 375
IZAAK WALTON LEAGUE OF AMERICA, INC., THE, 375
  Alaska Division, 376
  California Division, 376
  California State IWLA, 376
  Colorado Division, 376
  Florida Division, 376
  Illinois Division, 376
  Indiana Division, 376
  Iowa Division, 376
  Maryland Division, 377
  Michigan Division, 377
  Minnesota Division, 377
  Nebraska Division, 377
  New York State Division, 377
  Ohio Division, 377
  Oregon Divison, 377
  Owatonna Minnesota Chapter, 377
  Pennsylvania Division, 378
  South Dakota Division, 378
  Virginia Division, 378
  Washington Division, 378
  West Virginia Division, 378
  Wisconsin Division, 378
  Wyoming Division, 378
  York Chapter #57, 378

J

J.N. (DING) DARLING FOUNDATION, 379
JACK H. BERRYMAN INSTITUTE FOR WILDLIFE DAMAGE
  MANAGEMENT, 379
JACK MINER MIGRATORY BIRD FOUNDATION, INC., 379
JACKSON HOLE CONSERVATION ALLIANCE, 379
JACKSON HOLE LAND TRUST, 379
JACKSON HOLE PRESERVE, INC., 379
JAGRATA JUBA CHANGHA (JJS), 508
JANE GOODALL INSTITUTE, THE, 380
JAPAN WILDLIFE RESEARCH CENTER (JWRC), 380
JERE MOSSIER PRODUCTIONS/ UNDERWATER IMAGES, 568
JOHN GRAY HIGH SCHOOL, GRAND CAYMAN, 584
JOHN INSKEEP ENVIRONMENTAL LEARNING CENTER, 380
JOHNS HOPKINS UNIVERSITY
  Center for a Livable Future, 584
  Department of Geography and Environmental Engineering, 584
  School of Public Health, 585
JOHNSON STATE COLLEGE, 585
JONES AND STOKES, 568
JOURNALISM TO RAISE ENVIRONMENTAL AWARENESS, 380

K

KANSAS ACADEMY OF SCIENCE, 380
KANSAS ASSOCIATION FOR CONSERVATION AND ENVIRONMENTAL
  EDUCATION, KACEE, 380
KANSAS ASSOCIATION OF CONSERVATION DISTRICTS, 380
KANSAS BASS FEDERATION, 381
KANSAS BIOLOGICAL SURVEY, 166
KANSAS COOPERATIVE FISH AND WILDLIFE RESEARCH UNIT, 167
KANSAS DEPARTMENT OF AGRICULTURE, 167
KANSAS DEPARTMENT OF HEALTH AND ENVIRONMENT, 167
KANSAS DEPARTMENT OF WILDLIFE AND PARKS
  Office of the Secretary, 167
  Operations Office, 167
  Region 1, 167
  Region 2, 168
  Region 3, 168
  Region 4, 168
  Region 5, 168
KANSAS FOREST SERVICE, 168
KANSAS GEOLOGICAL SURVEY, 168
KANSAS HERPETOLOGICAL SOCIETY, 381
KANSAS NATURAL RESOURCE COUNCIL, 381
KANSAS ORNITHOLOGICAL SOCIETY, 381
KANSAS SCHOOL NATURALIST, 585
KANSAS STATE CONSERVATION COMMISSION, 168
KANSAS STATE EXTENSION SERVICES, 169
KANSAS STATE UNIVERSITY
  College of Agriculture, 585
  Department of Landscape Architecture / Regional and Community
    Planning, 585
  Division of Biology, 586
KANSAS WATER OFFICE, 169
KANSAS WILDFLOWER SOCIETY, 381
KANSAS WILDLIFE FEDERATION, 382
KANSAS WILDSCAPE FOUNDATION, 382
KEENE STATE COLLEGE, 586
KEEP AMERICA BEAUTIFUL, INC., 382
KEEP FLORIDA BEAUTIFUL, INC., 382
KEEPING TRACK, INC, 382
KENTUCKY ACADEMY OF SCIENCE, 382
KENTUCKY ASSOCIATION FOR ENVIRONMENTAL EDUCATION
  (KAEE), 383
KENTUCKY ASSOCIATION OF CONSERVATION DISTRICTS, 383
KENTUCKY BASS FEDERATION, 383
KENTUCKY DEPARTMENT OF AGRICULTURE, 169
KENTUCKY DEPARTMENT OF FISH AND WILDLIFE RESOURCES, 169
KENTUCKY DEPARTMENT OF PARKS, 169
KENTUCKY GEOLOGICAL SURVEY, 170
KENTUCKY NATURAL LANDS TRUST, 383
KENTUCKY NATURAL RESOURCES AND ENVIRONMENTAL
  PROTECTION CABINET, 170
  Department for Environmental Protection, 170
  Department for Natural Resources, 170
  Environmental Quality Commission, 170
  Kentucky State Nature Preserves Commission, 171
KENTUCKY RESOURCES COUNCIL, 383
KENTUCKY SOIL AND WATER CONSERVATION COMMISSION, 171
KENTUCKY STATE COOPERATIVE EXTENSION SERVICES, 171
KENTUCKY STATE NATURE PRESERVES COMMISSION, 171
KENTUCKY WOODLAND OWNERS ASSOCIATION, 383
KEYSTONE CENTER, THE, 384
KIDS FOR A BETTER ENVIRONMENT, 384
KIDS FOR SAVING EARTH WORLDWIDE, 384
KIDS ON THE BAYOU, 384
KODIAK BROWN BEAR TRUST, 384

L

LA JOLLA FRIENDS OF THE SEALS (LJFS), 384
LADY BIRD JOHNSON WILDFLOWER CENTER, 385
LAKE ERIE CLEAN-UP COMMITTEE, INC., 385
LAKE HOPATCONG PROTECTIVE ASSOCIATION, 385
LAKE MICHIGAN FEDERATION, 385
LAKE SUPERIOR GREENS, 385
LAKE SUPERIOR STATE UNIVERSITY, 586
LAKEHEAD UNIVERSITY, 586
LAKENET, 385
LAND AND WATER FUND OF THE ROCKIES, 386
LAND BETWEEN THE LAKES ASSOCIATION, 386
LAND CONSERVANCY OF WEST MICHIGAN, 386
LAND TRUST ALLIANCE, THE, 386
LANDOWNER PLANNING CENTER, 386
LANDWATCH MONTEREY COUNTY, 386
LAST WIZARDS, THE, 568
LAUDHOLM TRUST, 386
LEAGUE OF CONSERVATION VOTERS, 387
LEAGUE OF ENVIRONMENTAL JOURNALISTS, 387
LEAGUE OF KENTUCKY SPORTSMEN, INC., 387
LEAGUE OF OHIO SPORTSMEN, 387
LEAGUE OF WOMEN VOTERS OF IOWA, 387
LEAGUE OF WOMEN VOTERS OF THE U.S., 387
LEAGUE OF WOMEN VOTERS OF WASHINGTON, 388
LEAGUE TO SAVE LAKE TAHOE, 388
LEARNING FOR ENVIRONMENTAL ACTION PROGRAMME (LEAP), 388
LEE COUNTY PARKS AND RECREATION, 171

ORGANIZATION NAME INDEX – L

LEGACY INTERNATIONAL, 388
LEGACY LAND TRUST, 388
LEGAL ENVIRONMENTAL ASSISTANCE FOUNDATION INC. (LEAF), 388
LEWIS AND CLARK COLLEGE
   College of Arts and Sciences, 586
   Law School, 586
LEXIS/NEXIS ACADEMIC AND LIBRARY SOLUTIONS, 568
LIFE OF THE LAND, 389
LIGHTHAWK, 389
   New England Region, 389
   Northern Rocky Mountain Field Office, 389
   Northwest Field Office, 389
LITERACY FOR ENVIRONMENTAL JUSTICE, 389
LITTLE JUNIATA RIVER CHAPTER, 390
LIVING RIVERS, 390
LONG LIVE THE KINGS, 390
LOS ANGELES AND SAN GABRIEL RIVERS WATERSHED COUNCIL, THE, 390
LOUISIANA ASSOCIATION OF CONSERVATION DISTRICTS, 390
LOUISIANA BASS FEDERATION, 390
LOUISIANA COOPERATIVE FISH AND WILDLIFE RESEARCH UNIT (USDI), 172
LOUISIANA DEPARTMENT OF AGRICULTURE AND FORESTRY, 172
   Office of Forestry, 172
   Office of Soil and Water Conservation, State Soil and Water Conservation Committee, 172
LOUISIANA DEPARTMENT OF NATURAL RESOURCES, 172
   Office of Conservation, 172
   Office of Mineral Resources, 172
LOUISIANA DEPARTMENT OF WILDLIFE AND FISHERIES, 173
LOUISIANA FORESTRY ASSOCIATION, 390
LOUISIANA GEOLOGICAL SURVEY, 173
LOUISIANA OFFICE OF STATE PARKS, DEPARTMENT OF CULTURE, RECREATION, AND TOURISM, 173
LOUISIANA STATE UNIVERSITY SCHOOL OF FORESTRY, WILDLIFE AND FISHERIES, 586
LOUISIANA TECH UNIVERSITY, 587
LOUISIANA WILDLIFE FEDERATION, INC., 391
LOUISIANA WILDLIFE REHABILITATORS ASSOCIATION, 391
LOWER MERION CONSERVANCY, 391
LOWER MISSISSIPPI RIVER CONSERVATION COMMITTEE, 391
LSU AGCENTER - LOUISIANA COOPERATIVE EXTENSION SERVICE, 173
LUMMI ISLAND HERITAGE TRUST, 568
LVIV REGIONAL INSTITUTE OF EDUCATION, 391

M

MACBRIDE RAPTOR PROJECT, 391
MACOMB LAND CONSERVANCY, 391
MADISON COUNTY SOIL & WATER CONSERVATION DISTRICT
   Soil & Water Conservation District, 173
MAGIC, 392
MAINE ASSOCIATION OF CONSERVATION COMMISSIONS (MACC), 392
MAINE ASSOCIATION OF CONSERVATION DISTRICTS, 392
MAINE ATLANTIC SALMON COMMISSION, 173
MAINE BASS FEDERATION, 392
MAINE COAST HERITAGE TRUST, 392
MAINE COOPERATIVE FISH AND WILDLIFE RESEARCH UNIT (USDI), 174
MAINE DEPARTMENT OF AGRICULTURE, FOOD, AND RURAL RESOURCES, 174
MAINE DEPARTMENT OF CONSERVATION, 174
   Bureau of Geology and Natural Areas, 174
   Bureau of Parks and Lands, 174
   Forest Service, 174
   Land Use Regulation Commission, 175
MAINE DEPARTMENT OF ENVIRONMENTAL PROTECTION, 175
MAINE DEPARTMENT OF INLAND FISHERIES AND WILDLIFE, 175
MAINE DEPARTMENT OF MARINE RESOURCES, 175
MAINE ENVIRONMENTAL EDUCATION ASSOCIATION, 392
MANASOTA-88, 393
MANCHESTER COLLEGE, 587
MANITOBA CONSERVATION, 175
   Central Region, 176
   Eastern Region, 176
   Northeastern Region, 176
   Northwestern Region, 176
   Western Region, 176
MANITOBA CONSERVATION DATA CENTRE
   Wildlife And Ecosystem Protection Branch, 176
MANITOBA DEPARTMENT OF CULTURE, HERITAGE, AND TOURISM, 176
MANITOBA NATURALISTS SOCIETY, 393

MANITOBA WILDLIFE FEDERATION, 393
MANOMET CENTER FOR CONSERVATION SCIENCES, 393
MANTA MEXICO, 393
MARIE SELBY BOTANICAL GARDENS, THE, 393
MARIN CONSERVATION LEAGUE, 394
MARINE CONSERVATION BIOLOGY INSTITUTE, 394
MARINE ENVIRONMENTAL RESEARCH INSTITUTE (MERI), 394
MARINE FISH CONSERVATION NETWORK, 394
MARINE LABORATORY (FLORIDA), 176
MARINE MAMMAL CENTER, THE, 394
MARINE MAMMAL COMMISSION, 23
MARINE SCIENCE INSTITUTE, 394
MARINE TECHNOLOGY SOCIETY, 395
MARYLAND ASSOCIATION OF CONSERVATION DISTRICTS, 395
MARYLAND BASS FEDERATION, 395
MARYLAND DEPARTMENT OF AGRICULTURE, 176
   State Soil Conservation Committee, 177
MARYLAND DEPARTMENT OF NATURAL RESOURCES, 177
MARYLAND DEPARTMENT OF THE ENVIRONMENT, 177
MARYLAND FORESTS ASSOCIATION, 395
MARYLAND NATIVE PLANT SOCIETY, 395
MARYLAND ORNITHOLOGICAL SOCIETY, INC., 395
MARYLAND-NATIONAL CAPITAL PARK AND PLANNING COMMISSION, 177
MASSACHUSETTS ASSOCIATION OF CONSERVATION COMMISSIONS (MACC), 396
MASSACHUSETTS ASSOCIATION OF CONSERVATION DISTRICTS, 396
MASSACHUSETTS BASS FEDERATION, 396
MASSACHUSETTS COOPERATIVE FISH AND WILDLIFE RESEARCH UNIT (USDI), 178
MASSACHUSETTS DIVISION OF FISHERIES AND WILDLIFE
   MassWildlife, 178
MASSACHUSETTS EXECUTIVE OFFICE OF ENVIRONMENTAL AFFAIRS, 178
   Bureau of Pesticides, 178
   Department of Agricultural Resources, 178
   Department of Conservation and Recreation, 178
   Division of Conservation Services, 179
   Geographic Information System, 179
   Massachusetts Coastal Zone Management, 179
   Massachusetts Environmental Policy Act., 179
   Massachusetts Environmental Trust, 179
   Office of Technical Assistance for Toxic Use Reduction, 179
   Wetlands and Waterways Program, 179
MASSACHUSETTS FORESTRY ASSOCIATION, 396
MASSACHUSETTS HIGHWAY DEPARTMENT, 179
MASSACHUSETTS TRAPPERS ASSOCIATION, INC., 396
MATTS (MID-ATLANTIC TURTLE AND TORTOISE SOCIETY, INC.), 396
MAX MCGRAW WILDLIFE FOUNDATION, 396
MCGILL UNIVERSITY, 587
MCNEESE STATE UNIVERSITY, 587
MECKLENBURG COUNTY PARK AND RECREATION DEPARTMENT, 179
MERCK FOREST AND FARMLAND CENTER, 397
METROPOLITAN DISTRICT COMMISSION, 180
MIAMI UNIVERSITY, 587
MICHIGAN ASSOCIATION OF CONSERVATION DISTRICTS, 397
MICHIGAN BASS FEDERATION, 397
MICHIGAN DEPARTMENT OF AGRICULTURE, 180
MICHIGAN DEPARTMENT OF ENVIRONMENTAL QUALITY, 180
MICHIGAN DEPARTMENT OF NATURAL RESOURCES, 180
MICHIGAN ENVIRONMENTAL COUNCIL, 397
MICHIGAN FORESTS ASSOCIATION, 397
MICHIGAN LAND USE INSTITUTE, 397
MICHIGAN NATURAL AREAS COUNCIL, 398
MICHIGAN NATURE ASSOCIATION, 398
MICHIGAN STATE UNIVERSITY, 587
MICHIGAN STATE UNIVERSITY EXTENSION, 181
MICHIGAN TECHNOLOGICAL UNIVERSITY; SCHOOL OF FORESTRY AND WOOD PRODUCTS, 588
MICHIGAN UNITED CONSERVATION CLUBS, INC., 398
MICHIGAN WILDLIFE CONSERVANCY, 398
MID-ATLANTIC COUNCIL OF WATERSHED ASSOCIATIONS, 398
MID-ATLANTIC FISHERY MANAGEMENT COUNCIL, 398
MIDDLE TENNESSEE STATE UNIVERSITY, 588
MIDLAND CONSERVATION DISTRICT, 181
MIGRATORY BIRD CONSERVATION COMMISSION, 23
MINERAL POLICY CENTER, 399
MINNESOTA ASSOCIATION OF SOIL AND WATER CONSERVATION DISTRICTS, 399
MINNESOTA BASS FEDERATION, 399
MINNESOTA BOARD OF WATER AND SOIL RESOURCES, 181
MINNESOTA CENTER FOR ENVIRONMENTAL ADVOCACY (MCEA), 399
MINNESOTA CONSERVATION FEDERATION, 399

ORGANIZATION NAME INDEX – N

MINNESOTA COOPERATIVE FISH AND WILDLIFE RESEARCH UNIT, 181
MINNESOTA DEPARTMENT OF AGRICULTURE, 181
MINNESOTA DEPARTMENT OF NATURAL RESOURCES, 182
MINNESOTA ENVIRONMENTAL QUALITY BOARD, 182
MINNESOTA FORESTRY ASSOCIATION, 399
MINNESOTA GEOLOGICAL SURVEY, 182
MINNESOTA GROUND WATER ASSOCIATION, 400
MINNESOTA HERPETOLOGICAL SOCIETY, 400
MINNESOTA LAND TRUST, 400
MINNESOTA NATIVE PLANT SOCIETY, 400
MINNESOTA ORNITHOLOGISTS' UNION, 400
MINNESOTA POLLUTION CONTROL AGENCY
  Baxter, MN, 182
  Detroit Lakes, MN, 183
  Duluth, MN, 183
  Marshall, MN, 183
  Rochester, MN, 183
  St. Paul, MN, 183
MINNESOTA STATE EXTENSION SERVICES, 183
MINNESOTA WILDLIFE HERITAGE FOUNDATION, INC., 400
MINNESOTA WINGS SOCIETY, INC., 400
MINNESOTA-WISCONSIN BOUNDARY AREA COMMISSION, 24
MISSISSIPPI ASSOCIATION OF CONSERVATION DISTRICTS, INC., 401
MISSISSIPPI BASS FEDERATION, 401
MISSISSIPPI COOPERATIVE FISH AND WILDLIFE RESEARCH UNIT, 183
MISSISSIPPI DEPARTMENT OF AGRICULTURE AND COMMERCE, 183
MISSISSIPPI DEPARTMENT OF ENVIRONMENTAL QUALITY
  Office of Land and Water Resources, 184
  Office of Pollution Control, 184
MISSISSIPPI DEPARTMENT OF WILDLIFE, FISHERIES, AND PARKS, 184
MISSISSIPPI FORESTRY COMMISSION, 184
MISSISSIPPI INTERSTATE COOPERATIVE RESOURCE ASSOCIATION, 401
MISSISSIPPI NATIVE PLANT SOCIETY, 401
MISSISSIPPI RIVER BASIN ALLIANCE, 401
MISSISSIPPI SOIL AND WATER CONSERVATION COMMISSION, 184
MISSISSIPPI STATE DEPARTMENT OF HEALTH, 185
MISSISSIPPI STATE UNIVERSITY
  College of Forest Resources, 588
  Forest and Wildlife Research Center, 588
MISSISSIPPI WILDLIFE FEDERATION, 401
MISSOURI ASSOCIATION OF SOIL AND WATER CONSERVATION DISTRICTS, 402
MISSOURI BASS FEDERATION, 402
MISSOURI DEPARTMENT OF AGRICULTURE, 185
MISSOURI DEPARTMENT OF CONSERVATION, 185
  Design and Development Division, 185
  Fisheries Division, 185
  Forestry Division, 185
  Human Resources Section, 185
  Outreach and Education Division, 185
  Protection Division, 185
  Wildlife Division, 185
MISSOURI DEPARTMENT OF NATURAL RESOURCES, 186
MISSOURI FOREST PRODUCTS ASSOCIATION, 402
MISSOURI NATIVE PLANT SOCIETY, 402
MISSOURI PRAIRIE FOUNDATION, 402
MISSOURI STATE EXTENSION SERVICES, 186
MONO LAKE COMMITTEE, 402
MONTANA ASSOCIATION OF CONSERVATION DISTRICTS, 403
MONTANA BASS FEDERATION, 403
MONTANA BUREAU OF MINES AND GEOLOGY, 186
MONTANA COOPERATIVE WILDLIFE RESEARCH UNIT (USGS/BRD), 186
MONTANA DEPARTMENT OF AGRICULTURE, 186
MONTANA DEPARTMENT OF FISH, WILDLIFE, AND PARKS, 186
MONTANA DEPARTMENT OF NATURAL RESOURCES AND CONSERVATION, 187
MONTANA ENVIRONMENTAL INFORMATION CENTER, 403
MONTANA ENVIRONMENTAL QUALITY COUNCIL, 187
MONTANA FOREST OWNERS ASSOCIATION, 403
MONTANA LAND RELIANCE, 403
MONTANA NATURAL HERITAGE PROGRAM, 187
MONTANA STATE UNIVERSITY
  College of Agriculture, 589
  Department of Ecology, 589
MONTANA WILDERNESS ASSOCIATION, 403
MONTANA WILDLIFE FEDERATION, 404
MONTCLAIR STATE UNIVERSITY, 589
MOREHEAD STATE UNIVERSITY, 589
MORONGO BASIN WILDLIFE REHAB STATION, 404
MOTE MARINE LABORATORY, 404
MOUNT GRACE LAND CONSERVATION TRUST, 405
MOUNT UNION COLLEGE, 589
MOUNTAIN CONSERVATION TRUST OF GEORGIA, INC., 405
MOUNTAIN DEFENSE LEAGUE, 405
MOUNTAIN LION FOUNDATION, 405
MOUNTAINEERS, THE, 405
MRFC FISH CONSERVATION, 405
MULE DEER FOUNDATION, 405
MUNDO AZUL, 406
MURRAY STATE UNIVERSITY, 589
MUSASHI INSTITUTE OF TECHNOLOGY, 589
MUSKIES, INC., 406

N

NATIONAL 4-H COUNCIL, 406
NATIONAL AGRICULTURAL LIBRARY, 24
NATIONAL ANTI-VIVISECTION SOCIETY, 406
NATIONAL ARBOR DAY FOUNDATION, 406
NATIONAL ASSOCIATION FOR INTERPRETATION, 407
NATIONAL ASSOCIATION OF BIOLOGY TEACHERS, 407
NATIONAL ASSOCIATION OF CONSERVATION DISTRICTS, 407
  League City Office, 408
NATIONAL ASSOCIATION OF ENVIRONMENTAL PROFESSIONALS, THE, 408
NATIONAL ASSOCIATION OF RECREATION RESOURCE PLANNERS, 408
NATIONAL ASSOCIATION OF SERVICE AND CONSERVATION CORPS (NASCC), 408
NATIONAL ASSOCIATION OF STATE DEPARTMENTS OF AGRICULTURE, 408
NATIONAL ASSOCIATION OF STATE FORESTERS, 408
NATIONAL ASSOCIATION OF STATE PARK DIRECTORS, 409
NATIONAL ASSOCIATION OF UNIVERSITY FISHERIES AND WILDLIFE PROGRAMS, 409
NATIONAL AUDUBON SOCIETY, 409
  Atlanta Audubon Society, 409
  Audubon Alaska, 409
  Audubon Council of Connecticut, 409
  Audubon Council of Illinois, 410
  Audubon Maryland-DC, 410
  Audubon Missouri, 410
  Audubon of Florida, 410
  Audubon of Kansas, 410
  Audubon Ohio, 410
  Audubon Pennsylvania, 411
  Audubon Society of Missouri, 411
  Audubon Society of New Hampshire, 411
  Audubon Society of New York, 411
  Audubon Society of Omaha, 411
  Audubon Society of Portland, 411
  Audubon Society of Rhode Island, 412
  Audubon Society of Western Pennsylvania, 412
  Audubon Vermont, 412
  Connecticut Audubon Society, 412
  Daviess County Audubon Society, 413
  Delaware Audubon Society, 413
  Fairfax Audubon Society, 413
  Hawaii Audubon Society, 413
  Illinois Audubon Society, 413
  Iowa Audubon, 413
  Kentucky Audubon Council, 413
  Living Oceans Program, 414
  Louisiana Audubon Council, 414
  Maine Audubon, 414
  Maricopa Audubon Society, 414
  Massachusetts Audubon Society, 414
  Michigan Audubon Society, 414
  Montana Audubon, 415
  New Jersey Chapter, 415
  Oklahoma Audubon Council, 415
  Project Puffin, 415
  Public Policy Office, 415
  San Diego Chapter, 416
  Scully Science Center, 416
  Seattle Audubon Society, 416
  Tavernier Science Center, 416
  Tucson Audubon Society, 416
  Washington, D.C. Office, 416
NATIONAL AVIARY, 568
NATIONAL BIRD-FEEDING SOCIETY, 416
NATIONAL BISON ASSOCIATION, 417
NATIONAL BOATING FEDERATION, 417

ORGANIZATION NAME INDEX – N

NATIONAL BOWHUNTER EDUCATION FOUNDATION (NBEF), 417
NATIONAL CAUCUS OF ENVIRONMENTAL LEGISLATORS (NCEL), 417
NATIONAL CENTER FOR APPROPRIATE TECHNOLOGY, 417
   Center for Resourceful Building Technology, 417
NATIONAL COALITION FOR MARINE CONSERVATION, 417
NATIONAL COUNCIL FOR GEOGRAPHIC EDUCATION, 418
NATIONAL COUNCIL FOR SCIENCE AND THE ENVIRONMENT, THE, 418
NATIONAL EDUCATION ASSOCIATION, 418
NATIONAL ENVIRONMENTAL EDUCATION AND TRAINING FOUNDATION, 418
NATIONAL ENVIRONMENTAL HEALTH ASSOCIATION, 418
NATIONAL FARMERS UNION, 419
NATIONAL FFA ORGANIZATION, 419
NATIONAL FIELD ARCHERY ASSOCIATION, 419
NATIONAL FISH AND WILDLIFE FOUNDATION, 419
NATIONAL FLYWAY COUNCIL
   Central Flyway Office, 419
   Mississippi Flyway Office, 419
   North Dakota Game and Fish Department, 419
   South Dakota Game, Fish and Parks, 420
NATIONAL FOREST FOUNDATION, 420
NATIONAL FORESTRY ASSOCIATION, 420
NATIONAL GARDEN CLUBS, INC., 420
NATIONAL GARDENING ASSOCIATION, 420
NATIONAL GEOGRAPHIC SOCIETY, 421
NATIONAL GRANGE, THE, 421
NATIONAL GROUND WATER ASSOCIATION, THE, 421
NATIONAL GROUND WATER INFORMATION CENTER, 568
NATIONAL HUNTERS ASSOCIATION, INC., 421
NATIONAL MARINE FISHERIES SERVICE, 421
NATIONAL MILITARY FISH AND WILDLIFE ASSOCIATION, 421
NATIONAL NETWORK OF FOREST PRACTITIONERS, 422
NATIONAL ORGANIZATION FOR RIVERS (NORS), 422
NATIONAL PARK FOUNDATION, 422
NATIONAL PARK TRUST, 422
NATIONAL PARKS CONSERVATION ASSOCIATION (NPCA), 422
   Alaska Regional Office, 423
   Pacific Regional Office, 423
   Southeast Regional Office, 423
   State of the Parks Program Office, 423
   Sun Coast Regional Office, 423
NATIONAL RECREATION AND PARK ASSOCIATION, 423
NATIONAL RESEARCH COUNCIL, 423
NATIONAL RIFLE ASSOCIATION OF AMERICA, 424
NATIONAL RIFLE ASSOCIATION WEST VIRGINIA
   White Horse Firearms and Outdoor Education Center, Inc., 424
NATIONAL SCIENCE FOUNDATION, 24
NATIONAL SCIENCE TEACHERS ASSOCIATION, 424
NATIONAL SHOOTING SPORTS FOUNDATION, INC., 424
NATIONAL SPELEOLOGICAL SOCIETY, INC., 424
NATIONAL TRANSPORTATION SAFETY BOARD, 24
NATIONAL TRAPPERS ASSOCIATION, INC., 425
NATIONAL TREE TRUST, 425
NATIONAL TRUST FOR HISTORIC PRESERVATION, 425
   Mid Atlantic, 425
   Midwest Office, 425
   Mountains - Plains Office, 425
   Northeast Office, 425
   Southern Office, 425
   Southwest Office, 426
   Western, 426
NATIONAL WATER RESOURCES ASSOCIATION, 426
NATIONAL WATERSHED COALITION, 426
NATIONAL WATERWAYS CONFERENCE INC., 426
NATIONAL WHISTLEBLOWER LEGAL DEFENSE & EDUCATION FUND, 426
NATIONAL WILD TURKEY FEDERATION, CANADA, INC., THE, 426
NATIONAL WILD TURKEY FEDERATION, INC., THE, 427
NATIONAL WILDLIFE FEDERATION
   Alaska Natural Resource Center, 427
   Great Lakes Natural Resource Center, 427
   Gulf States Natural Resource Center, 428
   Headquarters, 427
   International Affairs, 428
   Northeast Natural Resource Center, 428
   Northern Rockies Natural Resource Center, 428
   Northwestern Natural Resource Center, 428
   Office of Congressional and Federal Affairs, 428
   Rocky Mountain Natural Resource Center, 428
   Southeastern National Resource Center, 429
   Western Natural Resource Center, 429
NATIONAL WILDLIFE FEDERATION ENDOWMENT, INC., 429
NATIONAL WILDLIFE PRODUCTIONS, INC., 429
NATIONAL WILDLIFE REFUGE ASSOCIATION, 429
NATIONAL WILDLIFE REHABILITATORS ASSOCIATION, 429
NATIONAL WOODLAND OWNERS ASSOCIATION, 430
NATIVE AMERICAN FISH AND WILDLIFE SOCIETY (NAFWS), 430
NATIVE AMERICAN HERITAGE COMMISSION, 187
NATIVE PLANT SOCIETY OF NORTHEASTERN OHIO, 430
NATIVE PLANT SOCIETY OF OREGON, 430
NATIVE PLANT SOCIETY OF TEXAS, 431
NATIVE PRAIRIES ASSOCIATION OF TEXAS, 431
NATURAL AREAS ASSOCIATION, 431
NATURAL HISTORY SOCIETY OF MARYLAND, INC., THE, 431
NATURAL LAND INSTITUTE, 431
NATURAL LANDS TRUST, 431
NATURAL RESOURCES CANADA
   Ontario, 187
NATURAL RESOURCES COUNCIL OF AMERICA, 432
NATURAL RESOURCES COUNCIL OF MAINE, 432
NATURAL RESOURCES DEFENSE COUNCIL, INC., 432
NATURAL RESOURCES FOUNDATION OF WISCONSIN, 432
NATURAL RESOURCES INFORMATION COUNCIL, 432
NATURAL SCIENCE FOR YOUTH FOUNDATION, 432
NATURE AND NATURAL RESOURCES (IUCN), 433
NATURE CONSERVANCY, THE, 433
   Adirondack Chapter, 433
   Alabama Chapter, 433
   Alabama Operating Unit, 433
   Alaska Chapter, 434
   Arkansas Field Office, 434
   Asia/Pacific Program, 434
   California Chapter, 434
   Canada Chapter, 434
   Colorado Chapter, 434
   Connecticut Chapter, 434
   Delaware Chapter, 434
   Eastern New York Chapter, 435
   Florida Chapter, 435
   Georgia Chapter, 435
   Great Plains Division, 435
   Hawaii Chapter, 435
   Idaho Chapter, 435
   Illinois Chapter, 435
   Indiana Chapter, 435
   Iowa Chapter, 435
   Kansas Chapter, 436
   Kentucky Chapter, 436
   Louisiana Chapter, 436
   Maine Chapter, 436
   Maryland/District of Columbia Chapter, 436
   Massachusetts Chapter, 436
   Michigan Chapter, 436
   Mid-Atlantic Division Office, 436
   Minnesota Chapter, 436
   Mississippi Chapter, 436
   Missouri Chapter, 436
   Montana Chapter, 437
   Nebraska Chapter, 437
   Nevada Chapter, 437
   New Hampshire Chapter, 437
   New Jersey Chapter, 437
   New Mexico Chapter, 437
   New York Adirondack Chapter, 438
   New York Central/Western Chapter, 438
   New York City Chapter, 438
   New York City Office, 437
   New York Long Island Chapter, 438
   New York South Fork/ Shelter Island Chapter, 438
   North Carolina Chapter, 438
   North Dakota Chapter, 438
   Northeast/ Caribbean Division Office, 438
   Northwest and Hawaii Division Office, 438
   Ohio Chapter, 438
   Oklahoma Chapter, 439
   Oregon Chapter, 439
   Pennsylvania Chapter, 439
   Rhode Island Chapter, 439
   Rocky Mountain Division Office, 439
   South Carolina Chapter, 439
   Southeast Division Office, 439
   Tennessee Chapter, 439
   Texas Chapter, 439
   Utah Chapter, 440
   Vermont Chapter, 440

ORGANIZATION NAME INDEX – N

Virgin Islands Chapter, 440
Virginia Program, 440
Washington Chapter, 440
West Virginia Chapter, 440
Wisconsin Chapter, 440
Wyoming Chapter, 440
NATURE CONSERVATION SOCIETY OF JAPAN, THE (NACS-J), 440
NATURE SASKATCHEWAN, 441
NATURESAVERS, 441
NATURESERVE, 441
NAVAJO NATION DEPARTMENT OF FISH AND WILDLIFE, 188
NAVARINO NATURE CENTER, 441
NEAL COMMUNICATIONS, 569
NEBRASKA ASSOCIATION OF RESOURCE DISTRICTS, 441
NEBRASKA BASS FEDERATION, 441
NEBRASKA CONSERVATION AND SURVEY DIVISION, 188
NEBRASKA DEPARTMENT OF AGRICULTURE, 188
NEBRASKA DEPARTMENT OF ENVIRONMENTAL QUALITY, 188
NEBRASKA DEPARTMENT OF NATURAL RESOURCES, 188
NEBRASKA GAME AND PARKS COMMISSION, 188
  Omaha Office, 189
NEBRASKA ORNITHOLOGISTS UNION, INC., 441
NEBRASKA WILDLIFE FEDERATION, INC., 442
NEGATIVE POPULATION GROWTH (NPG), 442
NEVADA ASSOCIATION OF CONSERVATION DISTRICTS, 442
NEVADA BUREAU OF MINES AND GEOLOGY, 189
NEVADA DEPARTMENT OF AGRICULTURE, 189
NEVADA DEPARTMENT OF CONSERVATION AND NATURAL RESOURCES, 189
NEVADA DEPARTMENT OF WILDLIFE, 189
NEVADA NATURAL HERITAGE PROGRAM, 189
NEVADA WILDLIFE FEDERATION, INC., 442
NEVIS HISTORICAL AND CONSERVATION SOCIETY, 442
NEW BRUNSWICK DEPARTMENT OF NATURAL RESOURCES, 189
NEW BRUNSWICK WILDLIFE FEDERATION, 442
NEW ENGLAND ASSOCIATION OF ENVIRONMENTAL BIOLOGISTS (NEAEB), 443
NEW ENGLAND COALITION FOR SUSTAINABLE POPULATION (NECSP), 443
NEW ENGLAND INTERSTATE WATER POLLUTION CONTROL COMMISSION, 443
NEW ENGLAND NATURAL RESOURCES CENTER, 443
NEW ENGLAND WILD FLOWER SOCIETY, INC., 443
NEW HAMPSHIRE ASSOCIATION OF CONSERVATION COMMISSIONS, 443
NEW HAMPSHIRE ASSOCIATION OF CONSERVATION DISTRICTS, 444
NEW HAMPSHIRE BASS FEDERATION, 444
NEW HAMPSHIRE COUNCIL ON RESOURCES AND DEVELOPMENT, 190
NEW HAMPSHIRE DEPARTMENT OF AGRICULTURE, MARKETS, AND FOOD, 190
  State Conservation Committee, 190
NEW HAMPSHIRE DEPARTMENT OF ENVIRONMENTAL SERVICES, 190
NEW HAMPSHIRE DEPARTMENT OF RESOURCES AND ECONOMIC DEVELOPMENT, 190
NEW HAMPSHIRE FISH AND GAME DEPARTMENT, 190
NEW HAMPSHIRE LAKES ASSOCIATION, 444
NEW HAMPSHIRE NATURAL HERITAGE BUREAU, 191
NEW HAMPSHIRE TIMBERLAND OWNERS ASSOCIATION, 444
NEW HAMPSHIRE WILDLIFE FEDERATION, 444
NEW JERSEY AGRICULTURAL SOCIETY, 444
NEW JERSEY ASSOCIATION OF CONSERVATION DISTRICTS, 445
NEW JERSEY BASS FEDERATION, 445
NEW JERSEY CONSERVATION FOUNDATION, 445
NEW JERSEY DEPARTMENT OF AGRICULTURE, 191
  Division of Rural Resources, 191
NEW JERSEY DEPARTMENT OF ENVIRONMENTAL PROTECTION, 191
  Division of Fish and Wildlife, 191
  Division of Parks and Forestry, 192
  Division of Publicly Funded Site Remediation, 192
  Division of Solid and Hazardous Waste, 192
  Geological Survey, 192
  Green Acres Program, 192
NEW JERSEY ENVIRONMENTAL LOBBY, 445
NEW JERSEY FORESTRY ASSOCIATION, 445
NEW JERSEY PINELANDS COMMISSION, 193
NEW MEXICO ASSOCIATION OF CONSERVATION DISTRICTS, 445
NEW MEXICO BUREAU OF GEOLOGY AND MINERAL RESOURCES, 193
  Geological Information Center Library, 193
NEW MEXICO DEPARTMENT OF AGRICULTURE, 193
NEW MEXICO DEPARTMENT OF GAME AND FISH, 193
  Albuquerque NM Office, 194
  Raton NM Office, 194

  Roswell NM Office, 194
  SW Area Operations, 194
NEW MEXICO ENERGY, MINERALS, AND NATURAL RESOURCES DEPARTMENT, 194
  Administrative Services Division, 194
  Energy Conservation and Management Division, 194
  Forestry Division, 194
  Mining and Minerals Division, 195
  Oil Conservation Division, 195
  State Parks and Recreation Division, 195
NEW MEXICO ENVIRONMENT DEPARTMENT, 195
NEW MEXICO ENVIRONMENTAL LAW CENTER, 445
NEW MEXICO SOIL AND WATER CONSERVATION COMMISSION, 195
NEW MEXICO STATE UNIVERSITY
  College of Agriculture and Home Economics, 589
    Department of Fishery and Wildlife Sciences, 590
  Cooperative Extension Services, 195
NEW YORK ASSOCIATION OF CONSERVATION DISTRICTS, INC., 446
NEW YORK BASS FEDERATION, 446
NEW YORK COOPERATIVE FISH AND WILDLIFE RESEARCH UNIT, 196
NEW YORK DEPARTMENT OF AGRICULTURE AND MARKETS, 196
NEW YORK DEPARTMENT OF ENVIRONMENTAL CONSERVATION, 196
  Division of Public Affairs and Education, 196
  Division of Solid and Hazardous Materials, 196
  Division of Water, 196
  Regional Directors, United States, 196
NEW YORK DEPARTMENT OF HEALTH, 197
NEW YORK FOREST OWNERS ASSOCIATION, INC., 446
NEW YORK GEOLOGICAL SURVEY AND STATE MUSEUM, 197
NEW YORK OFFICE OF ENERGY EFFICIENCY AND ENVIRONMENT, 197
NEW YORK PUBLIC INTEREST RESEARCH GROUP (NYPIRG), 446
NEW YORK STATE COOPERATIVE EXTENSION, 197
NEW YORK STATE DEPARTMENT OF AGRICULTURE AND MARKETS, 197
NEW YORK STATE FISH AND WILDLIFE MANAGEMENT BOARD, 198
  Region 3, 198
  Region 4, 198
  Region 5, 198
  Region 6, 198
  Region 7, 198
  Region 8, 198
NEW YORK STATE OFFICE OF PARKS, RECREATION AND HISTORIC PRESERVATION, 198
NEW YORK STATE TUG HILL COMMISSION, 199
NEW YORK TURTLE AND TORTOISE SOCIETY, 446
NEW YORK-NEW JERSEY TRAIL CONFERENCE INC., 446
NEWFOUNDLAND DEPARTMENT OF FOREST RESOURCES AND AGRIFOODS
  Ecosystem Health Division, 199
  Inland Fish and Wildlife Division, 199
  Legislation and Compliance Division, 199
  Regional Offices, 199
NEWFOUNDLAND LABRADOR WILDLIFE FEDERATION, 447
NIAGARA ESCARPMENT COMMISSION, 199
NIPPON ECOLOGY NETWORK, 447
NISC (NATIONAL INFORMATION SERVICES CORPORATION), 569
NOAH'S NOTES, INC., 569
NOLTE ASSOCIATES, INC., 569
NORTH AMERICAN ASSOCIATION FOR ENVIRONMENTAL EDUCATION, 447
  Conference, Publications and Membership Office, 447
NORTH AMERICAN BEAR FEDERATION, 447
NORTH AMERICAN BENTHOLOGICAL SOCIETY, 447
NORTH AMERICAN BLUEBIRD SOCIETY, 447
NORTH AMERICAN BUTTERFLY ASSOCIATION, 448
NORTH AMERICAN COALITION ON RELIGION AND ECOLOGY (NACRE), 448
NORTH AMERICAN CRANE WORKING GROUP, 448
NORTH AMERICAN DEVELOPMENT BANK, 24
NORTH AMERICAN FALCONERS ASSOCIATION, 448
NORTH AMERICAN GAMEBIRD ASSOCIATION, INC., 448
NORTH AMERICAN LOON FUND, 448
NORTH AMERICAN MEMBERSHIP GROUP, 449
NORTH AMERICAN NATIVE FISHES ASSOCIATION, 449
NORTH AMERICAN WETLANDS CONSERVATION COUNCIL, 24
NORTH AMERICAN WILDLIFE PARK FOUNDATION, INC., 449
NORTH AMERICAN WOLF ASSOCIATION, 449
NORTH ATLANTIC SALMON CONSERVATION ORGANIZATION, 449
NORTH CAROLINA ASSOCIATION OF SOIL AND WATER CONSERVATION DISTRICTS, 450
NORTH CAROLINA BASS FEDERATION, 450
NORTH CAROLINA BEACH BUGGY ASSOCIATION, INC., 450
NORTH CAROLINA COASTAL FEDERATION, INC., 450

NORTH CAROLINA CONSERVATION NETWORK, 450
NORTH CAROLINA COOPERATIVE EXTENSION SERVICE, 199
NORTH CAROLINA COOPERATIVE FISH AND WILDLIFE RESEARCH UNIT (USDI), 200
NORTH CAROLINA DEPARTMENT OF AGRICULTURE AND CONSUMER SERVICES, 200
NORTH CAROLINA DEPARTMENT OF ENVIRONMENT AND NATURAL RESOURCES, 200
NORTH CAROLINA DIVISION OF SOIL AND WATER, 200
NORTH CAROLINA FORESTRY ASSOCIATION (NCFA), 450
NORTH CAROLINA MUSEUM OF NATURAL SCIENCES, 450
NORTH CAROLINA RECREATION AND PARK SOCIETY, INC., 451
NORTH CAROLINA STATE UNIVERSITY, 590
NORTH CAROLINA WATERSHED COALITION, INC., 451
NORTH CAROLINA WILD FLOWER PRESERVATION SOCIETY, 451
NORTH CAROLINA WILDLIFE FEDERATION, 451
NORTH CAROLINA WILDLIFE RESOURCES COMMISSION, 201
NORTH CASCADES CONSERVATION COUNCIL, 451
NORTH DAKOTA ASSOCIATION OF SOIL CONSERVATION DISTRICTS, 452
NORTH DAKOTA DEPARTMENT OF AGRICULTURE, 201
NORTH DAKOTA DEPARTMENT OF HEALTH, 201
NORTH DAKOTA FOREST SERVICE, 201
NORTH DAKOTA GAME AND FISH DEPARTMENT, 201
NORTH DAKOTA NATURAL SCIENCE SOCIETY, 452
NORTH DAKOTA PARKS AND RECREATION DEPARTMENT, 202
NORTH DAKOTA STATE SOIL CONSERVATION COMMITTEE, 202
NORTH DAKOTA STATE UNIVERSITY, 590
NORTH DAKOTA WATER COMMISSION, 202
NORTH DAKOTA WILDLIFE FEDERATION, 452
NORTH PACIFIC ANADROMOUS FISH COMMISSION, 25
NORTHCOAST ENVIRONMENTAL CENTER, 452
NORTHEAST ATLANTIC FISHERIES COMMISSION, 25
NORTHEAST CONSERVATION LAW ENFORCEMENT CHIEFS' ASSOCIATION (CLECA), 452
NORTHEAST SUSTAINABLE ENERGY ASSOCIATION, 452
NORTHEASTERN FOREST FIRE PROTECTION COMMISSION, 25
NORTHEASTERN UNIVERSITY, 590
NORTHERN ALASKA ENVIRONMENTAL CENTER, 453
NORTHERN ARIZONA UNIVERSITY
  College of Arts and Sciences, 590
  College of Ecosystem Science and Management, 590
  Department of Geography, Planning, and Recreation, 591
  Northern Arizona Environmental Education Resources Center, 591
NORTHERN MICHIGAN UNIVERSITY
  Biology, 591
NORTHERN PLAINS RESOURCE COUNCIL, 453
NORTHERN VIRGINIA REGIONAL PARK AUTHORITY, 202
NORTHLAND COLLEGE, 591
NORTHWEST ATLANTIC FISHERIES ORGANIZATION (NAFO), 453
NORTHWEST COALITION FOR ALTERNATIVES TO PESTICIDES, 453
NORTHWEST ECOSYSTEM ALLIANCE, 453
NORTHWEST ENVIRONMENT WATCH, 454
NORTHWEST INTERPRETIVE ASSOCIATION, 454
NORTHWEST RESOURCE INFORMATION CENTER, 454
NORTHWEST TERRITORIES DEPARTMENT OF RESOURCES, WILDLIFE AND ECONOMIC DEVELOPMENT, 202
NORTHWEST TERRITORIES ENVIRONMENTAL PROTECTION SERVICE, 203
NORTHWESTERN STATE UNIVERSITY OF LOUISIANA, 591
NOVA SCOTIA AGRICULTURE & FISHERIES, 203
NOVA SCOTIA DEPARTMENT OF NATURAL RESOURCES, 203
NOVA SCOTIA FEDERATION OF ANGLERS AND HUNTERS, 454
NOVA SCOTIA FORESTRY ASSOCIATION, 454
NUCLEAR REGULATORY COMMISSION, 25
NW ENERGY COALITION, 454

O

OBERLIN COLLEGE, 591
OCEAN CONSERVANCY, THE, 455
OCEAN PROJECT, THE, 455
OCEAN VOICE INTERNATIONAL, 455
OCEANIA, 455
OCEANIC SOCIETY, 456
OHIO ACADEMY OF SCIENCE, THE, 456
OHIO ALLIANCE FOR THE ENVIRONMENT, 456
OHIO BASS FEDERATION, 456
OHIO BIOLOGICAL SURVEY, 456
OHIO DEPARTMENT OF AGRICULTURE, 203
OHIO DEPARTMENT OF DEVELOPMENT, 203
OHIO DEPARTMENT OF NATURAL RESOURCES, 204
OHIO ENERGY PROJECT, 456
OHIO ENVIRONMENTAL COUNCIL, INC., 457
OHIO ENVIRONMENTAL PROTECTION AGENCY, 204
OHIO ENVIRONMENTAL REVIEW APPEALS COMMISSION, 205
OHIO FEDERATION OF SOIL AND WATER CONSERVATION DISTRICTS, 457
OHIO FORESTRY ASSOCIATION, INC., 457
OHIO NATIVE PLANT SOCIETY, 457
OHIO RIVER VALLEY WATER SANITATION COMMISSION, 26
OHIO STATE UNIVERSITY, 592
OHIO STATE UNIVERSITY EXTENSION, 205
OHIO STREAM PRESERVATION, 457
OKLAHOMA ASSOCIATION OF CONSERVATION DISTRICTS, 458
OKLAHOMA BASS FEDERATION, 458
OKLAHOMA BIOLOGICAL SURVEY, 205
OKLAHOMA CONSERVATION COMMISSION, 205
OKLAHOMA COOPERATIVE FISH AND WILDLIFE RESEARCH UNIT (USDI), 206
OKLAHOMA DEPARTMENT OF AGRICULTURE, 205
OKLAHOMA DEPARTMENT OF ENVIRONMENTAL QUALITY, 206
OKLAHOMA DEPARTMENT OF WILDLIFE CONSERVATION, 206, 458
OKLAHOMA GEOLOGICAL SURVEY, 206
OKLAHOMA NATIVE PLANT SOCIETY, 458
OKLAHOMA ORNITHOLOGICAL SOCIETY, 458
OKLAHOMA STATE EXTENSION SERVICES, 206
OKLAHOMA STATE UNIVERSITY, 592
OKLAHOMA TOURISM AND RECREATION DEPARTMENT, 207
OKLAHOMA WATER RESOURCES BOARD, 207
OKLAHOMA WILDLIFE FEDERATION, 458
OKLAHOMA WOODLAND OWNERS ASSOCIATION (OWOA), 458
OLYMPIC PARK ASSOCIATES, 459
OLYMPIC PARK INSTITUTE, 459
ONEWILDWORLD, 459
ONTARIO DEPARTMENT OF FISHERIES AND OCEANS
  Canada Division, 26
  Canadian Coast Guard, 26
  Corporate Services, 27
  Legal Services, 27
  Oceans, 27
  Policy, 27
  Science, 27
ONTARIO FEDERATION OF ANGLERS AND HUNTERS, 459
ONTARIO FORESTRY ASSOCIATION, 459
ONTARIO MINISTRY OF NATURAL RESOURCES, 207
  Algonquin Forestry Authority, 207
  Corporate Services Division, 207
  Field Services Division, 207
  Fish and Wildlife Branch, 207
  Natural Resource Management Division, 208
  Northeast Region, 208
  Northwest Region, 208
  South Central Region, 208
OPENLANDS PROJECT, 460
OPERATION MIGRATION, 460
ORANGUTAN FOUNDATION INTERNATIONAL, 460
OREGON BASS FEDERATION, 460
OREGON DEPARTMENT OF AGRICULTURE, 208
OREGON DEPARTMENT OF ENVIRONMENTAL QUALITY (DEQ), 208
OREGON DEPARTMENT OF FISH AND WILDLIFE (ODFW), 208
OREGON DEPARTMENT OF FORESTRY, 209
OREGON DEPARTMENT OF GEOLOGY AND MINERAL INDUSTRIES, 209
OREGON DEPARTMENT OF TRANSPORTATION, 209
OREGON ENVIRONMENTAL COUNCIL, 460
OREGON FISH AND WILDLIFE DIVISION/DEPARTMENT OF STATE POLICE, 209
OREGON NATURAL RESOURCES COUNCIL, 460
OREGON PARKS AND RECREATION DEPARTMENT, 209
OREGON SMALL WOODLANDS ASSOCIATION, 461
OREGON SOCIETY OF AMERICAN FORESTERS, 461
OREGON STATE EXTENSION SERVICES, 209
OREGON STATE MARINE BOARD, 210
OREGON STATE UNIVERSITY DEPT OF FISHERIES AND WILDLIFE, 592
OREGON TROUT, 461
OREGON WATER RESOURCES DEPARTMENT, 210
OREGON WILDLIFE HERITAGE FOUNDATION, 461
ORGANIZATION FOR BAT CONSERVATION, 461
ORGANIZATION OF WILDLIFE PLANNERS, 461
ORION SOCIETY, THE, 462
ORNITHOLOGICAL COUNCIL, 462
OTTER PROJECT, THE, 462
OUTDOOR CIRCLE, THE, 462
OUTDOOR RECREATION COUNCIL OF BRITISH COLUMBIA, 462

ORGANIZATION NAME INDEX – R

OUTDOOR WRITERS ASSOCIATION OF AMERICA, INC., 462
OZARK SOCIETY, THE, 463
OZARKS RESOURCE CENTER, 463
OZONE ACTION, 463

P

PA CLEANWAYS, 463
PACIFIC BASIN ASSOCIATION OF SOIL AND WATER CONSERVATION DISTRICTS, 463
PACIFIC FISHERY MANAGEMENT COUNCIL, 463
PACIFIC INSTITUTE FOR STUDIES IN DEVELOPMENT, ENVIRONMENT, AND SECURITY, 463
PACIFIC MARINE CONSERVATION COUNCIL, 464
PACIFIC NORTHWEST TRAIL ASSOCIATION, 464
PACIFIC RIVERS COUNCIL, 464
PACIFIC SALMON COMMISSION, 27
PACIFIC SEABIRD GROUP, 464
PACIFIC STATES MARINE FISHERIES COMMISSION, 27
PACIFIC WHALE FOUNDATION, 464
PANOS INSTITUTE, THE, 464
PARKS AND TRAILS COUNCIL OF MINNESOTA, 465
PARQUE NACIONAL SIERRA NEVADA, 569
PARTNERS IN AMPHIBIAN AND REPTILE CONSERVATION (PARC), 465
PARTNERS IN PARKS, 465
PARTNERSHIP FOR SUSTAINABLE FORESTRY, 465
PEACE CORPS, 27
PEACE CORPS
  Ecuador, 28
PENNSYLVANIA ASSOCIATION OF CONSERVATION DISTRICTS, INC., 465
PENNSYLVANIA CENTER FOR ENVIRONMENTAL EDUCATION (PCEE), 465
PENNSYLVANIA CITIZENS ADVISORY COUNCIL TO DEPARTMENT OF ENVIRONMENTAL PROTECTION, 466
PENNSYLVANIA COOPERATIVE FISH AND WILDLIFE RESEARCH UNIT, 210
PENNSYLVANIA DEPARTMENT OF AGRICULTURE
  Region I, 210
  Region II, 210
  Region III, 210
  Region IV, 210
  Region V, 210
  Region VI, 211
  Region VII, 211
  State Conservation Commission, 211
PENNSYLVANIA DEPARTMENT OF CONSERVATION AND NATURAL RESOURCES, 211
PENNSYLVANIA DEPARTMENT OF ENVIRONMENTAL PROTECTION, 211
PENNSYLVANIA ENVIRONMENTAL COUNCIL, INC. (PEC), 466
PENNSYLVANIA FEDERATION OF SPORTSMENS CLUBS, 466
PENNSYLVANIA FISH AND BOAT COMMISSION, 212
  Bureau of Law Enforcement
    Northcentral Region, 212
    Northeast Region, 212
    Northwest Region, 212
    SouthCentral Region, 212
    Southeast Region, 212
    Southwest Region, 212
PENNSYLVANIA FOREST STEWARDSHIP PROGRAM, 212
PENNSYLVANIA FORESTRY ASSOCIATION, THE, 466
PENNSYLVANIA ORGANIZATION FOR WATERSHEDS AND RIVERS (POWR), 466
PENNSYLVANIA RECREATION AND PARK SOCIETY, INC., 467
PENNSYLVANIA RESOURCES COUNCIL, INC.,, 467
PENNSYLVANIA STATE EXTENSION SERVICES, 592
PENNSYLVANIA STATE UNIVERSITY, 592
PEOPLE FOR PUGET SOUND, 467
  North Sound Office, 467
  South Sound Office, 467
PEOPLE'S FORUM 2001, JAPAN, 467
PEREGRINE FUND, THE, 467
PHEASANTS FOREVER, INC., 468
PHILIPPINES ENVIRONMENT AND NATURAL RESOURCES MANAGEMENT DIVISION, 468
PHYSICIANS FOR SOCIAL RESPONSIBILITY, 468
PIEDMONT ENVIRONMENTAL COUNCIL, 469
PINCHOT INSTITUTE FOR CONSERVATION, 469
PINE BLUFF COOPERATIVE FISHERY RESEARCH PROJECT, 213
PINES ROWAN UNIVERSITY, 592
PLANNED PARENTHOOD FEDERATION OF AMERICA, INC., 469
PLANNING AND CONSERVATION LEAGUE, 469

PLAYA LAKES JOINT VENTURE, 469
POCONO ENVIRONMENTAL EDUCATION CENTER, 470
POCONO WILDLIFE REHABILITATION CENTER, 470
POINT TO POINT COMMUNICATIONS, 569
POLLUTION PROBE, 470
POLYTECHNIC UNIVERSITY OF NEW YORK, 592
POPE AND YOUNG CLUB, 470
POPULATION ACTION INTERNATIONAL, 470
POPULATION COMMUNICATIONS INTERNATIONAL, 470
POPULATION CONNECTION, 471
POPULATION INSTITUTE, THE, 471
POPULATION REFERENCE BUREAU, INC., 471
POPULATION-ENVIRONMENT BALANCE, INC., 471
PORTLAND STATE UNIVERSITY, 593
POTOMAC APPALACHIAN TRAIL CLUB, 471
POULSBO MARINE SCIENCE CENTER, 471
POWDER RIVER BASIN RESOURCE COUNCIL, 472
PRAIRIE CLUB, THE, 472
PRAIRIE GROUSE TECHNICAL COUNCIL, 472
PRAIRIE RIVERS NETWORK, 472
PRAIRIE WILDLIFE RESEARCH, 472
PREDATOR CONSERVATION ALLIANCE, 472
PRESCOTT COLLEGE, LIBERAL ARTS AND THE ENVIRONMENTAL STUDIES PROGRAM, 593
PRESERVATION SOCIETY FOR SPRING CREEK FOREST, 473
PRINCE EDWARD ISLAND DEPARTMENT OF FISHERIES, AQUACULTURE AND ENVIRONMENT, 213
PRIORITIES INSTITUTE, THE, 473
PRO PENINSULA, 473
PROFESSIONAL BOWHUNTERS SOCIETY, 473
PROGRESSIVE ANIMAL WELFARE SOCIETY, 473
PROJECT SEAHORSE, 473
PROPERTY CARETAKING OPPORTUNITIES WORLDWIDE, 569
PROTECTED AREAS ASSOCIATION OF NEWFOUNDLAND AND LABRADOR, 474
PROVINCE OF QUEBEC SOCIETY FOR THE PROTECTION OF BIRDS, INC., 474
PS ENTERPRISES, 570
PTARMIGANS, THE, 474
PUBLIC EMPLOYEES FOR ENVIRONMENTAL RESPONSIBILITY (PEER), 474
PUBLIC LANDS FOUNDATION, 474
PUBLIC LANDS INTERPRETIVE ASSOCIATION, 570
PUERTO RICO ASSOCIATION OF SOIL AND WATER CONSERVATION DISTRICTS, 474
PUERTO RICO CONSERVATION FOUNDATION, THE (PRCF), 475
PUERTO RICO DEPARTMENT OF AGRICULTURE, 213
PUERTO RICO DEPARTMENT OF NATURAL AND ENVIRONMENTAL RESOURCES, 213
PUERTO RICO DIVISION DE PATRIMONIO NATURAL, 213
PUERTO RICO SOIL CONSERVATION COMMITTEE, 213
PUGET SOUNDKEEPER ALLIANCE, 475
PURDUE UNIVERSITY, 593
PURDUE UNIVERSITY EXTENSION SERVICES, 213
PURPLE MARTIN CONSERVATION ASSOCIATION, 475

Q

QUAIL UNLIMITED, INC., 475
QUALITY DEER MANAGEMENT ASSOCIATION, 476
QUEBEC DEPARTMENT OF CANADIAN HERITAGE, 28
QUEBEC DEPARTMENT OF ENVIRONMENT AND WILDLIFE, 214
QUEBEC ENVIRONMENTAL CONSERVATION SERVICE
  Ecosystem and Environmental Resources Directorate, 28
  Quebec Region Environment Canada, 28
QUEBEC WILDLIFE FEDERATION, 476

R

RACHEL CARSON COUNCIL, INC., 476
RAINBOW PUSH COALITION, 476
RAINFOREST ACTION NETWORK, 476
RAINFOREST ALLIANCE, 477
RAINFOREST RELIEF, 477
RAINFOREST TRUST, 477
RAPTOR CENTER, THE, 593
RAPTOR EDUCATION FOUNDATION, INC., 477
RAPTOR RESEARCH FOUNDATION, INC., 477
RARE CENTER FOR TROPICAL CONSERVATION, 478
RED BUFFALO, LLC, 570
REEF RELIEF, 478
REEFGUARDIAN INTERNATIONAL, 478
RENEW THE EARTH, 478

RENEWABLE ENERGY POLICY PROJECT (REPP), 478
RENEWABLE NATURAL RESOURCES FOUNDATION, 478
RENSSELAER POLYTECHNIC INSTITUTE
  Department of Earth and Environmental Sciences, 593
  Lally School of Management and Technology, 593
REP AMERICA, 479
RESIDENTS FOR A MORE BEAUTIFUL PORT WASHINGTON, 479
RESOURCE CENTER FOR ENVIRONMENTAL EDUCATION, THE, 479
RESOURCE RENEWAL INSTITUTE, THE, 479
RESOURCES FOR THE FUTURE, 479
RESPONSIVE MANAGEMENT, 570
RESTORE HETCH HETCHY, 479
RETURNED PEACE CORPS VOLUNTEERS FOR ENVIRONMENT AND DEVELOPMENT (RPCVS-ED), 480
RHODE ISLAND BASS FEDERATION, 480
RHODE ISLAND COOPERATIVE EXTENSION SERVICE, 214
RHODE ISLAND DEPARTMENT OF ENVIRONMENTAL MANAGEMENT, 214
RHODE ISLAND DEPARTMENT OF TRANSPORTATION, 214
RHODE ISLAND FOREST CONSERVATOR'S ORGANIZATION, INC., 480
RHODE ISLAND SCHOOL OF DESIGN, 593
RHODE ISLAND STATE CONSERVATION COMMITTEE, 480
RHODE ISLAND STATE WATER RESOURCES BOARD, 214
RHODE ISLAND WILD PLANT SOCIETY, 480
RICE UNIVERSITY, 594
  Rice School of Architecture, 594
RICHARD STOCKTON COLLEGE, 594
RIVER ALLIANCE OF WISCONSIN, 480
RIVER NETWORK, 480
  Eastern Office, 481
RIVER OTTER ALLIANCE, THE, 481
RIVER PROJECT, THE, 481
RIVERS COUNCIL OF WASHINGTON, 481
RIVERSIDE COUNTY CONSERVATION AGENCY, 215
ROBERT ROADS ILLINOIS DEPARTMENT OF NATURAL RESOURCES, 481
ROCK RIVER HEADWATERS, INC., 481
ROCKY MOUNTAIN BIGHORN SOCIETY, 482
ROCKY MOUNTAIN BIOLOGICAL LABORATORY, THE, 482
ROCKY MOUNTAIN BIRD OBSERVATORY, 482
ROCKY MOUNTAIN ELK FOUNDATION, 482
ROGER TORY PETERSON INSTITUTE OF NATURAL HISTORY, 482
ROGER WILLIAMS UNIVERSITY, 594
RUFFED GROUSE SOCIETY, THE, 482
RUFFNER MOUNTAIN NATURE COALITION, INC., 483
RUTGERS COOPERATIVE EXTENSION, 215
RUTGERS UNIVERSITY, COOK COLLEGE, 594

S

SACRED PASSAGE AND THE WAY OF NATURE, 483
SAFARI CLUB INTERNATIONAL
  International Headquarters, 483
  South Africa Office, 484
  Washington, DC Office, 484
SALMON-SAFE, 484
SALTON SEA AUTHORITY, 215
SAN DIEGO NATURAL HISTORY MUSEUM, 484
SAN DIEGUITO RIVER PARK JOINT POWERS AUTHORITY, 215
SAN ELIJO LAGOON CONSERVANCY, 484
SAN FRANCISCO BAY CONSERVATION AND DEVELOPMENT COMMISSION, 215
SAN JOSE STATE UNIVERSITY, 594
SAN JUAN PRESERVATION TRUST, THE, 484
SAND CREEK WATERSHED PROJECT, THE, 215
SANIBEL-CAPTIVA CONSERVATION FOUNDATION, INC., 484
SANTA CLARA COMMUNITY ACTION PROGRAM, 594
SASKATCHEWAN ENVIRONMENT AND RESOURCE MANAGEMENT, 215
  Corporate Services, 216
  East Boreal EcoRegion, 216
  Enforcement and Compliance Branch, 216
  Fire Management and Forest Protection Branch, 216
  Fish and Wildlife Branch
    Director, 216
    Saskatchewan Conservation Data Centre(SKCDC), 216
  Grassland EcoRegion, 216
  Operations, 216
  Parkland EcoRegion, 217
  Policy and Assessment, 217
  Shield EcoRegion, 217
  West Boreal EcoRegion, 217
SASKATCHEWAN WILDLIFE FEDERATION, 484

SAVE AMERICA'S FORESTS, 485
SAVE OUR RIVERS, INC., 485
SAVE SAN FRANCISCO BAY ASSOCIATION, 485
SAVE THE BAY - PEOPLE FOR NARRAGANSETT BAY, 485
SAVE THE DUNES CONSERVATION FUND, 485
SAVE THE DUNES COUNCIL, 485
SAVE THE HARBOR/SAVE THE BAY, 486
SAVE THE MANATEE CLUB, 486
SAVE THE SOUND, INC., 486
SAVE WETLANDS AND BAYS, 486
SAVE-THE-REDWOODS LEAGUE, 487
SCENIC AMERICA, 487
  Scenic California, 487
  Scenic Michigan, 487
  Scenic Missouri, 487
  Scenic Texas, 487
SCENIC HUDSON, INC., 488
SCIENTISTS CENTER FOR ANIMAL WELFARE, 488
SEA SHEPHERD CONSERVATION SOCIETY
  Australia Office, 488
  Brazil-Instituto Sea Shepherd Brasil, 488
  Canada Office, 488
  International Headquarters, 488
  Netherlands, 488
  Singapore/Asia, 488
  United Kingdom, 488
  USA Regional-SSCS Monterey, 489
SEA TURTLE PRESERVATION SOCIETY, 489
SEACAMP ASSOCIATION, INC., 489
SEACOAST ANTI-POLLUTION LEAGUE, 489
SEAPLANE PILOTS ASSOCIATION, 489
SEAWEB, 489
SENATE COMMITTEE ON AGRICULTURE, NUTRITION, AND FORESTRY, 28
SENATE COMMITTEE ON APPROPRIATIONS, 28
SENATE COMMITTEE ON COMMERCE, SCIENCE, AND TRANSPORTATION, 28
SENATE COMMITTEE ON ENERGY AND NATURAL RESOURCES, 29
SENATE COMMITTEE ON ENVIRONMENT AND PUBLIC WORKS, 29
SENATE COMMITTEE ON FOREIGN RELATIONS, 29
SENATE COMMITTEE ON HEALTH, EDUCATION, LABOR, AND PENSIONS, 29
SHARING NATURE FOUNDATION, 570
SHAWNEE STATE UNIVERSITY, 595
SHEEPSCOT VALLEY CONSERVATION ASSOCIATION, THE, 489
SHELBURNE FARMS, 490
SHEPHERD COLLEGE, 595
SIERRA CLUB
  Alabama Chapter, 490
  Alaska Chapter, 490
  Alaska Field Office, 490
  Angeles Chapter, 490
  Atlantic Chapter, 490
  Bay Area Field Office, 490
  British Columbia Chapter, 490
  California/Nevada/Hawaii Office and California Legislative Office, 490
  Cascade Chapter, 491
  Colorado Field Office, 491
  Columbia Basin Office, 491
  Connecticut Chapter, 491
  Cumberland Chapter, 491
  Dacotah Chapter, 491
  Delaware Chapter, 491
  Delta Chapter, 491
  Eastern Canada Chapter, 491
  Florida (South) Field Office, 492
  Florida Chapter, 491
  Florida Regional Field Office, 491
  Georgia Chapter, 492
  Georgia Field Office/Louisiana and Alabama Field Office, 492
  Grand Canyon Chapter, 492
  Hawaii Chapter, 492
  Hoosier Chapter, 492
  Illinois Chapter, 492
  Iowa Chapter, 492
  John Muir Chapter, 492
  Kansas Chapter, 493
  Kern-Kaweah Chapter, 493
  Loma Prieta Chapter, 493
  Lone Star Chapter, 493
  Los Padres Chapter, 493
  Mackinac Chapter, 493
  Maine Chapter, 493

ORGANIZATION NAME INDEX – S

Maryland Chapter, 493
Massachusetts Chapter, 493
Mid-Atlantic Regional Office, 494
Midwest Office
  Madison Office, 494
  Traverse City Office, 494
Mississippi Chapter, 494
Montana Chapter, 494
Montana Field Office, 494
Mother Lode Chapter, 494
Nebraska Chapter, 494
New Hampshire Chapter, 494
New Jersey Chapter, 495
New York City Office, 495
North Carolina Chapter, 495
North Star Chapter (Minnesota), 495
Northeast Regional Field Office, 495
Northern Plains Region, 495
Northern Rockies Chapter (Idaho/Washington), 495
Northwest Office, 495
Ohio Chapter, 496
Oklahoma Chapter, 496
Oregon Chapter, 496
Ozark Chapter (Missouri), 496
Pennsylvania Chapter, 496
Prairie Chapter (AB, MB, SK), 496
Redwood Chapter (Northern California), 496
Rhode Island Chapter, 496
Rio Grande Chapter (New Mexico/West Texas), 496
Rocky Mountain Chapter (Colorado), 497
San Diego Chapter (Southern California), 497
San Francisco Bay Chapter, 497
San Gorgonio Chapter (Southern California), 497
Santa Lucia Chapter, 497
South Carolina Chapter, 497
South Dakota Chapter, 497
Southeast Office, 498
Southern California/Nevada Field Office, 498
Southern Plains National Field Office, 498
Southwest Office, 498
Tehipite Chapter (Northern California), 498
Tennessee Chapter, 498
Toiyabe Chapter (Nevada/Eastern California), 498
Utah Chapter, 498
Utah Field Office, 498
Ventana Chapter (Northern California), 498
Vermont Chapter, 498
Virginia Chapter, 499
Washington, DC Chapter, 499
Washington, DC Office, 499
West Virginia Chapter, 499
Wyoming Chapter, 499
SIERRA CLUB CALIFORNIA, 499
SIERRA CLUB FOUNDATION, THE, 499
SIERRA CLUB OF CANADA, 500
  Atlantic Canada Chapter, 500
SIERRA STUDENT COALITION, 500
SILK CITY NATURE ASSOCIATION, 500
SILLMAN UNIVERSITY, 595
SINAPU, 500
SISKIYOU PROJECT, 500
SISKIYOU REGIONAL EDUCATION PROJECT, 500
SLIPPERY ROCK UNIVERSITY, 595
SMALL WOODLAND OWNERS ASSOCIATION OF MAINE, 501
SMITHSONIAN INSTITUTION, 501
  National Museum of Natural History, 501
  Office of Fellowships, 501
  Office of International Relations, 501
  Smithsonian Institution Press, 501
  Smithsonian Tropical Research Institute, 501
SMITHSONIAN INSTITUTION NATIONAL ZOOLOGICAL PARK, 501
SMITHSONIAN MARINE STATION AT FORT PIERCE, 502
SOCIEDAD AMBIENTE MARINO, 502
SOCIETY FOR ANIMAL PROTECTIVE LEGISLATION, 502
SOCIETY FOR CONSERVATION BIOLOGY, 502
SOCIETY FOR ECOLOGICAL RESTORATION, 502
SOCIETY FOR INTEGRATIVE AND COMPARATIVE BIOLOGY, 502
SOCIETY FOR MARINE MAMMALOGY, THE, 503
SOCIETY FOR RANGE MANAGEMENT, 503
SOCIETY FOR THE PRESERVATION OF BIRDS OF PREY, 503
SOCIETY FOR THE PROTECTION OF NEW HAMPSHIRE FORESTS, 503
SOCIETY OF AMERICAN FORESTERS, 503
  University of Kentucky, 504

SOCIETY OF TYMPANUCHUS CUPIDO PINNATUS LTD., 504
SOCIETY OF WETLAND SCIENTISTS, 504
SOIL AND WATER CONSERVATION SOCIETY, 504
SONOMA STATE UNIVERSITY
  Department of Environmental Studies and Planning, 595
  Environmental Technology Center, 595
SONORAN DESERT NATIONAL PARK FRIENDS, 504
SONORAN INSTITUTE, 505
SOUND EXPERIENCE, 505
SOUNDWATERS, 505
SOUTH ATLANTIC FISHERY MANAGEMENT COUNCIL, 29
SOUTH CAROLINA ASSOCIATION OF CONSERVATION DISTRICTS, 505
SOUTH CAROLINA BASS FEDERATION, 506
SOUTH CAROLINA COOPERATIVE FISH AND WILDLIFE RESEARCH UNIT, 217
SOUTH CAROLINA DEPARTMENT OF AGRICULTURE, 217
SOUTH CAROLINA DEPARTMENT OF HEALTH AND ENVIRONMENTAL CONTROL, 217
  Office of Ocean and Coastal Resource Management (OCRM), 217
SOUTH CAROLINA DEPARTMENT OF NATURAL RESOURCES, 218
SOUTH CAROLINA DEPARTMENT OF PARKS, RECREATION AND TOURISM, 218
SOUTH CAROLINA ENERGY OFFICE, 218
SOUTH CAROLINA ENVIRONMENTAL LAW PROJECT, 506
SOUTH CAROLINA FORESTRY ASSOCIATION, 506
SOUTH CAROLINA NATIVE PLANT SOCIETY, 506
SOUTH CAROLINA WILDLIFE FEDERATION, 506
SOUTH DAKOTA ASSOCIATION OF CONSERVATION DISTRICTS, 506
SOUTH DAKOTA BASS FEDERATION, 507
SOUTH DAKOTA COOPERATIVE EXTENSION SERVICE, 218
SOUTH DAKOTA COOPERATIVE FISH AND WILDLIFE RESEARCH UNIT (USDI-USGS), 29
SOUTH DAKOTA DEPARTMENT OF AGRICULTURE, 218
  Division of Resource Conservation and Forestry, 218
  State Conservation Commission, 219
SOUTH DAKOTA DEPARTMENT OF ENVIRONMENT AND NATURAL RESOURCES, 219
SOUTH DAKOTA DEPARTMENT OF GAME, FISH, AND PARKS, 219
SOUTH DAKOTA ORNITHOLOGISTS UNION, 507
SOUTH DAKOTA RESOURCES COALITION, 507
SOUTH DAKOTA STATE UNIVERSITY, 595
SOUTH DAKOTA WILDLIFE FEDERATION, 507
SOUTH FLORIDA WATER MANAGEMENT DISTRICT, 219
SOUTH OAHU SOIL AND WATER CONSERVATION DISTRICT, 507
SOUTHEAST ALASKA CONSERVATION COUNCIL (SEACC), 507
SOUTHEASTERN ASSOCIATION OF FISH AND WILDLIFE AGENCIES, 508
SOUTHEASTERN COOPERATIVE WILDLIFE DISEASE STUDY, 508
SOUTHEASTERN FISHES COUNCIL, 508
SOUTHERN AFRICAN INSTITUTE OF FORESTRY, 508
SOUTHERN APPALACHIAN BOTANICAL SOCIETY, 508
SOUTHERN CONNECTICUT STATE UNIVERSITY, 596
SOUTHERN ENVIRONMENTAL LAW CENTER, 509
  North Carolina Office, 509
SOUTHERN ILLINOIS UNIVERSITY CARBONDALE, 596
SOUTHERN NEW ENGLAND FOREST CONSORTIUM, INC. (SNEFCI), 509
SOUTHERN OREGON UNIVERSITY, 596
SOUTHERN RHODE ISLAND STATE ASSOCIATION OF CONSERVATION DISTRICTS, 509
SOUTHERN UTAH WILDERNESS ALLIANCE, 509
  Moab Office, 510
  St. George Office, 510
  Washington, DC Office, 510
SOUTHFACE ENERGY INSTITUTE, 510
SOUTHWEST CENTER FOR ENVIRONMENTAL RESEARCH AND POLICY (SCERP), 596
SOUTHWEST CONSERVATION DISTRICT, 510
SOUTHWEST FLORIDA WATER MANAGEMENT DISTRICT (SWFWMD), 220
SOUTHWEST RESEARCH AND INFORMATION CENTER, 510
SOUTHWESTERN HERPETOLOGISTS SOCIETY, 510
SPORTSMAN NETWORK, INC., THE, 510
SPORTSMANS ALLIANCE OF MAINE, 511
SPORTSMANS NETWORK, INC., THE, 570
SPORTSMEN'S NATIONAL LAND TRUST, THE, 511
ST. CLOUD STATE UNIVERSITY, 597
ST. CROIX INTERNATIONAL WATERWAY COMMISSION, 511
ST. FRANCIS WILDLIFE ASSOCIATION, 511
ST. LAWRENCE UNIVERSITY, 597
ST. NORBERT COLLEGE, 597
ST. REGIS MOHAWK TRIBE, 511

STANFORD ENVIRONMENTAL LAW SOCIETY, 511
STANFORD UNIVERSITY
   Department of Biological Sciences, 597
   Morrison Institute for Population and Resource Studies, 597
STATE AND TERRITORIAL AIR POLLUTION PROGRAM ADMINISTRATORS AND THE ASSOCIATION OF LOCAL AIR POLLUTION CONTROL OFFICIALS, 512
STATE ENGINEER OFFICE/INTERSTATE STREAM COMMISSION, 220
STATE ENVIRONMENTAL RESOURCE CENTER (SERC), 512
STATE UNIVERSITY OF NEW YORK AT CORTLAND, 597
STATE UNIVERSITY OF NEW YORK AT STONY BROOK, 597
STATE UNIVERSITY OF NEW YORK COLLEGE OF ENVIRONMENTAL SCIENCE AND FORESTRY, 598
STATEWIDE PROGRAM OF ACTION TO CONSERVE OUR ENVIRONMENT (SPACE), 512
STEAMBOATERS, THE, 512
STEPHEN F. AUSTIN STATE UNIVERSITY ARTHUR TEMPLE COLLEGE OF FORESTRY, 598
STERLING COLLEGE, 598
STOP, 512
STROUD WATER RESEARCH CENTER, 512
STUDENT CONSERVATION ASSOCIATION, INC., 512
   California Southwest Regional Office, 513
   Northwest Office, 513
   Office of the National Capital Region, 513
   Mid-Atlantic/Southeast Regional Office, 513
STUDENT ENVIRONMENTAL ACTION COALITION (SEAC), 513
STUDENT PUGWASH USA, 513
STUDENTS PARTNERSHIP WORLDWIDE, 513
STURGEON FOR TOMORROW, 514
SUDBURY VALLEY TRUSTEES, 514
SUNCOAST SEABIRD SANCTUARY INC., 514
SUSQUEHANNA RIVER BASIN COMMISSION, 29
SUSTAIN, 514
SUSTAINABLE ENERGY INSTITUTE
   Culture Change, 514
   Culture Change Magazine, 514
   Food Not Lawns, 514
   Pedal Power Produce, 514
SWAZILAND ENVIRONMENT AUTHORITY (SEA), 30

T

TAHOE REGIONAL PLANNING AGENCY, 220
TALL TIMBERS RESEARCH STATION (TTRS), 515
TALLAHASSEE MUSEUM OF HISTORY AND NATURAL SCIENCE, 515
TANZANIA COASTAL MANAGEMENT PARTNERSHIP, 30
TANZANIA SCHOOL OF JOURNALISM, 598
TEENS FOR RECREATION AND ENVIRONMENTAL CONSERVATION (TREC), 515
TEMPLE UNIVERSITY, 599
TENEESSEE DEPARTMENT OF ENVIRONMENT & CONSERVATION, 220
TENNESSEE AGRICULTURAL EXTENSION SERVICE, 220
TENNESSEE BASS FEDERATION, 515
TENNESSEE CITIZENS FOR WILDERNESS PLANNING, 515
TENNESSEE CONSERVATION LEAGUE, 516
TENNESSEE COOPERATIVE FISHERY RESEARCH UNIT (USDI), 220
TENNESSEE DEPARTMENT OF AGRICULTURE, 221
   State Soil Conservation Committee, 221
TENNESSEE DEPARTMENT OF ENVIRONMENT AND CONSERVATION, 221
TENNESSEE ENVIRONMENTAL COUNCIL, 516
TENNESSEE FORESTRY ASSOCIATION, 516
TENNESSEE TECHNOLOGICAL UNIVERSITY, 599
TENNESSEE VALLEY AUTHORITY, 30
   Muscle Shoals Technical Library, 30
   Research Library, Knoxville and Chattanooga, 30
TENNESSEE WILDLIFE RESOURCES AGENCY, 221
TERRA NATURE FUND, 516
TERRA PENINSULAR, 516
TEXAS A AND M UNIVERSITY AT COLLEGE STATION
   College of Agriculture and Life Sciences, 599
TEXAS A AND M UNIVERSITY AT COMMERCE
   Department of Agricultural Sciences, 599
TEXAS A AND M UNIVERSITY AT KINGSVILLE
   Caesar Kleberg Wildlife Research Institute, 599
TEXAS A AND M UNIVERSITY SYSTEM
   Texas Cooperative Extension, 599
TEXAS ASSOCIATION OF SOIL AND WATER CONSERVATION DISTRICTS, 516
TEXAS BASS FEDERATION, 517

TEXAS CHRISTIAN UNIVERSITY, 599
TEXAS COMMITTEE ON NATURAL RESOURCES, 517
TEXAS COOPERATIVE FISH AND WILDLIFE RESEARCH UNIT, 30
TEXAS DEPARTMENT OF AGRICULTURE, 222
TEXAS DEPARTMENT OF HEALTH, 222
TEXAS DISCOVERY GARDENS, 517
TEXAS FOREST SERVICE, 222
TEXAS GENERAL LAND OFFICE, 222
TEXAS ORGANIZATION FOR ENDANGERED SPECIES, 517
TEXAS PARKS AND WILDLIFE DEPARTMENT, 222
TEXAS RIPARIAN ASSOCIATION, 517
TEXAS STATE SOIL AND WATER CONSERVATION BOARD, 223
TEXAS TECH UNIVERSITY, 600
TEXAS WATER DEVELOPMENT BOARD, 223
TEXAS WILDLIFE ASSOCIATION, 517
THEODORE PAYNE FOUNDATION FOR WILDFLOWERS AND NATIVE PLANTS, INC., 518
THEODORE ROOSEVELT CONSERVATION PARTNERSHIP, 518
THORNE ECOLOGICAL INSTITUTE, 518
THREE CIRCLES CENTER FOR MULTICULTURAL ENVIRONMENTAL EDUCATION, 518
TOGETHER FOUNDATION, THE, 518
TRAFFIC NORTH AMERICA, 518
TREAD LIGHTLY! INC, 518
TREASURE VALLEY COMMUNITY COLLEGE, 600
TREEPEOPLE, 519
TREES ATLANTA, 519
TREES FOR THE FUTURE, INC., 519
TREES FOR TOMORROW, NATURAL RESOURCES EDUCATION CENTER, 519
TREES, WATER, AND PEOPLE, 519
TRIANGLE RAILS-TO-TRAILS CONSERVANCY, 520
TRI-STATE BIRD RESCUE AND RESEARCH, INC., 520
TROUT UNLIMITED
   Alaska Council, 520
   Arizona Council, 521
   California Council, 521
   Colorado Council, 521
   Connecticut Council, 521
   Georgia Council, 521
   Illinois Council, 521
   Maryland Council, Mid-Atlantic, 521
   Michigan Council, 521
   Minnesota Council, 521
   Missouri Council, 522
   Montana Council, 522
   National Headquarters, 520
   Nevada Council, 522
   New Hampshire Council, 522
   New York Council, 522
   North Carolina Council, 522
   Ohio Council, 522
   Oregon Council, 522
   Pennsylvania Council, 522
   South Carolina Council, 522
   Tennessee Council, 523
   Utah Council, 523
   Virginia Council, 523
   Washington Council, 523
   West Virginia Council, 523
   Wyoming Council, 523
TRUMPETER SWAN SOCIETY, THE, 523
TRUST FOR PUBLIC LAND, THE, 523
TRUST FOR WILDLIFE, INC., 524
TRUSTEES FOR ALASKA, 524
TRUSTEES OF RESERVATIONS, THE, 524
TUFTS UNIVERSITY CIVIL ENGINEERING, 600
TUG HILL TOMORROW LAND TRUST, 524
TULANE ENVIRONMENTAL LAW CLINIC, 600
TULANE INSTITUTE FOR ENVIRONMENTAL LAW AND POLICY, 600
TULANE UNIVERSITY
   Department of Ecology and Evolutionary Biology, 600
   Tulane Law School, 600
TUMAINI ENVIRONMENTAL CONSERVATION GROUP, 525
TURNER ENDANGERED SPECIES FUND, 571
TURTLE CREEK WATERSHED ASSOCIATION, INC., 525
TWO WHITE WOLVES SANCTUARY, 525

U

UNC-CH ENVIRONMENTAL RESOURCE PROGRAM, 601
UNEP WORLD CONSERVATION MONITORING CENTRE, 525
UNION OF CONCERNED SCIENTISTS, 525

ORGANIZATION NAME INDEX – U

UNITED NATIONS ENVIRONMENT PROGRAMME, 526
  Latin America and Caribbean, 526
  New York Office, 526
UNITED NATIONS RESEARCH INSTITUTE FOR SOCIAL DEVELOPMENT (UNRISD), 30
UNITED STATES CHAMBER OF COMMERCE
  Environment, Technology and Regulatory Affairs, 526
UNITED STATES COMMITTEE FOR THE UNITED NATIONS ENVIRONMENT PROGRAMME, THE (U.S. AND UNEP), 526
UNITED STATES COUNCIL ON ENVIRONMENTAL QUALITY, 31
UNITED STATES DEPARTMENT OF AGRICULTURE, 31
  Agricultural Research Service, 31
  Animal and Plant Health Inspection Service
    Animal Care, 31
    Animal Care Central Regional Office, 31
    Animal Care Eastern Regional Office, 31
    Animal Care Western Regional Office, 32
    International Services Asia and Pacific Office, 32
    International Services Central America, Caribbean and Panama Office, 32
    International Services Europe, Africa, Russia, Near East Office, 32
    International Services Mexico Office, 32
    International Services Screwworm Eradication Program Office, 32
    International Services South America Office: USDA/APHIS, 32
    National Wildlife Research Center, 32
    Plant Protection and Quarantine, 32
    Veterinary Services, 32
  Cooperative State Research, Education, Extension Service (CSREES), 33
  Economic Research Center, 33
  Farm Service Agency (FSA), 33
  Forest Service, 33
    Allegheny National Forest, 34
    Angeles National Forests, 34
    Angelina National Forest, 34
    Angelina, Davy Crockett, Sabine and Sam Houston National Forest, 34
    Apache-Sitgreaves National Forest, 34
    Arapaho and Roosevelt National Forests, 34
    Ashley National Forest, 34
    Beaverhead-Deerlodge National Forest, 34
    Bienville, Delta, Desoto, Holly Springs, Homochitto, and Tombigbee National Forests, 34
    Bighorn National Forest, 34
    Bitterroot National Forest, 34
    Black Hills National Forest, 34
    Boise National Forest, 35
    Bridger-Teton National Forest, 35
    Buffalo Gap National Grassland, 35
    Buffalo Gap National Grassland, Fall River Ranger District, 35
    Butte Valley National Grassland, 35
    Caribbean National Forest, 35
    Caribou-Targhee National Forest, 35
    Carson National Forest, 35
    Cedar River / Grand River National Grassland, 35
    Chattahoochee and Oconee National Forests, 35
    Chequamegon-Nicolet National Forest, 35
    Cherokee National Forest, 35
    Cheyenne National Grassland, 36
    Chippewa National Forest, 36
    Chugach National Forest, 36
    Cibola National Forest, 36
    Cimarron National Grassland, 36
    Clearwater National Forest, 36
    Cleveland National Forest, 36
    Coconino National Forest, 36
    Colville National Forest, 36
    Comanche National Grassland, 36
    Coronado National Forest, 36
    Croatan, Nantahala, Pisgah and Uwharrie National Forests, 36
    Crooked River National Grassland, 37
    Curlew National Grassland, 37
    Custer National Forest, 37
    Daniel Boone National Forest, 37
    Deschutes National Forest, 37
    Dixie National Forest, 37
    Eldorado National Forest, 37
    Finger Lakes National Forest, 37
    Fishlake National Forest, 37
    Flathead National Forest, 37
    Fort Pierre National Grassland, 38
    Francis Marion and Sumter National Forest, 38
    Fremont National Forest, 38
    Gallatin National Forest, 38
    George Washington and Jefferson National Forests, 38
    Gifford Pinchot National Forest, 38
    Gila National Forest, 38
    Grand Mesa, Uncompahgre and Gunnison National Forests, 38
    Green Mountain National Forest, 38
    Helena National Forest, 38
    Hiawatha National Forest, 39
    Hoosier National Forest, 39
    Humboldt-Toiyabe National Forest, 39
    Huron-Manistee National Forest, 39
    Idaho Panhandle National Forests, 39
    Inyo National Forest, 39
    Kaibab National Forest, 39
    Kiow / Rita Blanca National Grassland, 39
    Kisatchie National Forest, 39
    Klamath National Forest, 39
    Kootenai National Forest, 39
    Lake Tahoe Basin Management Unit, 39
    Lewis and Clark National Forest, 39
    Lincoln National Forest, 39
    Little Missouri National Forest, McKenzie Ranger District, 40
    Little Missouri National Grasslands, Medora Ranger District, 40
    Lolo National Forest, 40
    Los Padres National Forest, 40
    Lyndon B. Johnson / Caddo National Forest, 40
    Malheur National Forest, 40
    Manti-LaSal National Forest, 40
    Mark Twain National Forest, 40
    McClellan Creek/Black Kettle National Grassland, 40
    Medicine Bow-Routt National Forest, 40
    Mendocino National Forest, 40
    Modoc National Forest, 41
    Monongahela National Forest, 41
    Mt. Hood National Forest, 41
    National Forests in Alabama, 41
    National Forests in Florida, 41
    Nebraska National Forest, 41
    Nez Perce National Forest, 41
    North Central Research Station, 41
    Northeastern Research Station, 41
    Ochoco National Forest, 41
    Oglala National Grassland, 41
    Okanogan National Forest, 41
    Olympic National Forest, 42
    Ottawa National Forest, 42
    Ouachita National Forest, 42
    Ozark-St. Francis National Forest, 42
    Pacific Northwest Research Station, 42
    Pacific Southwest Research Station, 42
    Pawnee National Grassland, 42
    Payette National Forest, 42
    Pike and San Isabel National Forests, 42
    Plumas National Forest, 42
    Prescott National Forest, 42
    Region 01 (Northern), 43
    Region 02 (Rocky Mountain), 43
    Region 03 (Southwestern), 43
    Region 04 (Intermountain), 43
    Region 05 (Pacific Southwest), 43
    Region 06 (Pacific Northwest), 43
    Region 08 (Southern), 43
    Region 09 (Eastern), 43
    Region 10 (Alaska), 43
    Rio Grande National Forest, 44
    Rocky Mountain Research Station, 44
    Rogue River National Forest, 44
    Routt National Forest, 44
    Salmon-Challis National Forest, 44
    San Bernardino National Forest, 44
    San Juan National Forest, 44
    Santa Fe National Forest, 44
    Sawtooth National Forest, 44
    Sequoia National Forest, 44
    Shasta-Trinity National Forest, 44
    Shawnee National Forest, 44
    Shoshone National Forest, 44
    Sierra National Forest, 45
    Siskiyou National Forest, 45
    Siuslaw National Forest, 45
    Six Rivers National Forest, 45
    Southern Research Station, 45
    Stanislaus National Forest, 45
    Superior National Forest, 45

ORGANIZATION NAME INDEX – U

UNITED STATES DEPARTMENT OF AGRICULTURE (continued)
  Forest Service (continued)
    Tahoe National Forest, 45
    Thunder Basin National Grasslands, 45
    Tongass National Forest, 45
    Tongass-Ketchikan Area National Forest, 45
    Tongass-Petersburg Office National Forest, 45
    Tonto National Forest, 46
    Uinta National Forest, 46
    Umatilla National Forest, 46
    Umpqua National Forest, 46
    Wallowa Whitman National Forests, 46
    Wasatch-Cache National Forest, 46
    Wayne National Forest, 46
    Wenatchee National Forest, 46
    White Mountain National Forest, 46
    White River National Forest, 46
    Willamette National Forest, 46
    Winema National Forest, 46
  Natural Resources Conservation Service, 46
  Research Education and Economics, 48
    ARS Beltsville Area, 48
    ARS Mid South Office, 48
    ARS Midwest Office, 48
    ARS North Atlantic Office, 48
    ARS Northern Plains Area Office, 48
    ARS Pacific West Area, 48
    ARS South Atlantic Office, 48
    ARS Southern Plains Office, 48
    Cooperative State Research, Education, and Extension Service, 49
UNITED STATES DEPARTMENT OF COMMERCE, 49
  Economic Development Administration, 49
  National Oceanic and Atmospheric Administration, 49
    ACE Basin National Estuarine Research Reserve, 49
    Apalachicola National Estuarine Research Reserve, 49
    Channel Islands National Marine Sanctuary, 49
    Chesapeake Bay National Estuarine Research Reserve
      Maryland Office, 49
      Virginia Office, 50
    Cordell Bank National Marine Sanctuary, 50
    Delaware National Estuarine Research Reserve, 50
    Florida Keys National Marine Sanctuary, 50
    Flower Garden Banks National Marine Sanctuary, 50
    Gray's Reef National Marine Sanctuary, 50
    Great Bay National Estuarine Research Reserve, 50
    Gulf of Farallones National Marine Sanctuary, 50
    Hawaiian Islands Humpback Whale National Sanctuary, 51
    Hudson River National Estuarine Research Reserve, 51
    Jacques Cousteau National Estuarine Research Reserve Institute of Marine and Coastal Sciences, 51
    Jobos Bay National Estuarine Research Reserve, 51
    Kachemak Bay National Estuarine Research Reserve, 51
    Monitor National Marine Sanctuary, 51
    Monterey Bay National Marine Sanctuary, 51
    Narragansett Bay National Estuarine Research Reserve, 51
    National Environmental Satellite, Data, and Information Service, 52
    National Marine Fisheries Service, 52
    National Ocean Service, 52
    National Weather Service, 52
    North Carolina National Estuarine Research Reserve, 52
    North Inlet National Estuarine Research Reserve, 52
    Office of Global Program, 53
    Office of Oceanic and Atmospheric Research, 53
    Old Woman Creek National Estuarine Research Reserve, 53
    Olympic Coast National Marine Sanctuary, 53
    Padilla Bay National Estuarine Research Reserve, 53
    Rookery Bay National Estuarine Research Reserve, 53
    Sapelo Island National Estuarine Research Reserve, 53
    Sea Grant Program - Alabama, 53
    Sea Grant Program - Alaska, 53
    Sea Grant Program - California, 54
    Sea Grant Program - Connecticut, 54
    Sea Grant Program - Delaware, 54
    Sea Grant Program - Florida, 55
    Sea Grant Program - Georgia, 55
    Sea Grant Program - Hawaii, 55
    Sea Grant Program - Illinois-Indiana, 55
    Sea Grant Program - Louisiana, 56
    Sea Grant Program - Maine, 56
    Sea Grant Program - Maryland, 56
    Sea Grant Program - Massachusetts, 56
    Sea Grant Program - Massachusetts, 56
    Sea Grant Program - Michigan, 57
    Sea Grant Program - Minnesota, 57
    Sea Grant Program - Mississippi-Alabama Consortium, 57
    Sea Grant Program - New Hampshire, 57
    Sea Grant Program - New Jersey, 57
    Sea Grant Program - New York, 58
    Sea Grant Program - North Carolina, 58
    Sea Grant Program - Ohio, 58
    Sea Grant Program - Oregon, 58
    Sea Grant Program - Puerto Rico, 59
    Sea Grant Program - Rhode Island, 59
    Sea Grant Program - South Carolina, 59
    Sea Grant Program - Texas, 59
    Sea Grant Program - Virginia, 59
    Sea Grant Program - Washington, 59
    South Slough National Estuarine Research Reserve, 60
    Stellwagen Bank National Marine Sanctuary, 60
    Tijuana River National Estuarine Research Reserve, 60
    Waquoit Bay National Estuarine Research Reserve, 60
    Weeks Bay National Estuarine Research Reserve, 60
    Wells National Estuarine Research Reserve, 60
UNITED STATES DEPARTMENT OF DEFENSE, 61
  Air Force
    Center For Environmental Excellence, 61
    Pope AFB, NC, 61
  Air Force Major Air Commands
    AFBCA/EV Headquarters, 61
    AFSOC/EV Headquarters, 61
    Air Mobility Command (AMC), 61
    Andrews AFB, MD, 61
    Bolling AFB, DC, 61
    Germany AFB, 62
    Kirtland AFB, NM, 62
    Langley AFB, VA, 62
    Peterson AFB, CO, 62
    Randolph AFB, TX, 62
    Robins AFB, GA, 62
    Special Operations Command, 62
    USAF Academy, 62
    USAF/ILEV Headquarters, 62
    Wright Patterson AFB, OH, 62
  Air Force Major U.S. Installations
    Altus AFB, OK, 63
    Anderson AFB, Guam, 63
    Andrews AFB, MD, 63
    Arnold AFB, TN, 63
    Avon Park AFB, FL, 63
    Barksdale AFB, LA, 63
    Beale AFB, CA, 63
    Bolling AFB, DC, 63
    Brooks AFB, TX, 63
    Cannon AFB, NM, 63
    Charleston AFB, SC, 63
    Columbus AFB, MS, 63
    Davis-Monthan AFB, AZ, 63
    Dover AFB, DE, 63
    Dyess AFB, TX, 63
    Edwards AFB, CA, 63
    Eglin Air Force Base, 63
    Eielson AFB, AK, 64
    Ellsworth AFB, SD, 64
    Elmendorf AFB, AK, 64
    F.E. Warren AFB, WY, 64
    Fairchild AFB, WA, 64
    Goodfellow AFB, TX, 64
    Grand Forks AFB, ND, 64
    Hanscom AFB, MA, 64
    Hickam AFB, HI, 64
    Hill AFB, UT, 64
    Holloman AFB, NM, 64
    Hurlburt Field, FL, 64
    Keesler AFB, MS, 64
    Kirtland AFB, NM, 64
    Lackland AFB, TX, 64
    Langley AFB, VA, 64
    Laughlin AFB, TX, 64
    Little Rock AFB, AR, 65
    Luke AFB (and the Barry M. Goldwater AFR), AZ, 65
    MacDill AFB, FL, 65
    Malmstrom AFB, MT, 65
    Maxwell AFB, AL, 65
    McChord AFB, WA, 65
    McClellan AFB, CA, 65
    McConnell AFB, KS, 65

ORGANIZATION NAME INDEX – U

McGuire AFB, NJ, 65
Moody AFB, GA, 65
Mountain Home AFB, ID 83648, 65
Nellis AFB, NV, 65
Offutt AFB, NE, 66
Patrick AFB, FL, 66
Peterson AFB, CO, 66
Randolph AFB, TX, 66
Remote Sites (611 Support Group), AK, 66
Scott AFB, IL, 66
Seymour Johnson AFB (and Dare County AFR), NC, 66
Shaw AFB, SC, 66
Sheppard AFB, TX, 66
Shriever AFB, CO, 66
Tinker AFB, OK, 66
Travis AFB, CA, 66
Tyndall AFB, FL, 66
Vance AFB, OK, 66
Vandenberg AFB, CA, 66
Whiteman AFB, MO, 66
Wright-Patterson AFB, OH, 66
Army, 67
Army Corps of Engineers
  Alaska Engineer District, 67
  Albuquerque Engineer District, 67
  Alexandria Engineer District, 67
  Alexandria Engineer District, 67
  Baltimore Engineer District, 67
  Buffalo Engineer District, 67
  Champaign Engineer District, 67
  Charleston Engineer District, 68
  Chicago Engineer District, 68
  Detroit Engineer District, 68
  Fort Worth Engineer District, 68
  Galveston Engineer District, 68
  Great Lakes and Ohio Engineer District, 68
  Hanover Engineer District, 68
  Headquarters, 67
  Honolulu Engineer District, 68
  Huntington Engineer District, 68
  Jacksonville Engineer District, 68
  Kansas City Engineer District, 69
  Little Rock Engineer District, 69
  Los Angeles Engineer District, 69
  Louisville Engineer District, 69
  Memphis Engineer District, 69
  Mississippi Valley Engineer Division, 69
  Mobile Engineer District, 69
  Nashville Engineer District, 69
  New England District, 69
  New Orleans Engineer District, 70
  New York engineer district., 70
  Norfolk Engineer District, 70
  North Atlantic Engineer District, 70
  Northwestern Division, 70
  Omaha Engineer District, 70
  Pacific Ocean Engineer District, 70
  Philadelphia District, 70
  Pittsburgh Engineer District, 71
  Portland Engineer District, 71
  Rock Island Engineer District, 71
  Sacramento Engineer District, 71
  San Francisco Engineer District, 71
  Seattle Engineer District, 71
  South Atlantic Engineer District, 71
  South Pacific Engineer District, 71
  Southwestern Engineer District, 71
  St. Louis Engineer District, 71
  St. Paul Engineer District, 71
  Tulsa Engineer District, 71
  Vicksburg Engineer District, 72
  Vicksburg Engineer District, 72
  Walla Walla Engineer District, 72
  Wilmington Engineer District, 72
Army Engineer Research and Development Center, 72
Army Forces Command, 72
Army Materiel Command, 72
Army Military Academy, 73
Army Training and Doctrine Command, 73, 74
Assistant Chief of Staff for Installation Management, Office of the Director of Environmental Programs, and Conservation Team, 74
HQ PACAF/CEVQ, 74
Marine Corps, 74

Marine Corps Installations, United States, 74
Navy, 74
Office of the Civil Engineer, 74
UNITED STATES DEPARTMENT OF EDUCATION, 75
UNITED STATES DEPARTMENT OF ENERGY, 75
  Carbon Dioxide Information Analysis Center, 75
  Federal Energy Regulatory Commission, 75
UNITED STATES DEPARTMENT OF HEALTH AND HUMAN SERVICES, 75
  Food and Drug Administration, 75
UNITED STATES DEPARTMENT OF HOMELAND SECURITY
  Customs and Border Protection
    East Texas CMC, 76
    Gulf CMC, 76
    Mid-America CMC, 76
    New York CMC, 76
    North Atlantic CMC, 76
    Office of Public Affairs, 76
    South Florida CMC, 76
    South Pacific CMC, 77
UNITED STATES DEPARTMENT OF HOUSING AND URBAN DEVELOPMENT, 77
UNITED STATES DEPARTMENT OF JUSTICE, 77
UNITED STATES DEPARTMENT OF LABOR, 77
  Job Corps, 77
  Mine Safety and Health Administration, 77
UNITED STATES DEPARTMENT OF STATE, 77
  Bureau of Oceans and International Environmental and Scientific Affairs, 78
  United States Man and the Biosphere Program (U.S. MAB), 78
UNITED STATES DEPARTMENT OF THE INTERIOR, 78
  Bureau of Indian Affairs, 78
  Bureau of Land Management
    Albuquerque Field Office, 78
    Alturas Field Office, 78
    Amarillo Field Office, 78
    Anasazi Heritage Center, 79
    Anchorage District, 79
    Arcata Field Office, 79
    Arizona State Office, 79
    Arizona Strip Field Office, 79
    Bakersfield Field Office, 79
    Barstow Field Office, 79
    Battle Mountain Field Office, 79
    Billings Field Office, 79
    Bishop Field Office, 79
    Bruneau Field Office, 79
    Buffalo Field Office, 80
    Burley Field Office, 80
    Burns District, 80
    Butte Field Office, 80
    Carlsbad Field Office, 80
    Carson City Field Office, 80
    Casper District, 80
    Cedar City District Field Office, 80
    Challis Field Office, 80
    Cody Field Office, 80
    Coeur d'Alene Field Office, 80
    Colorado State Office, 80
    Coos Bay Field Office, 80
    Cottonwood Field Office, 80
    Dillon Field Office, 81
    Eagle Lake Field Office, 81
    Eastern States Office, 81
    El Centro Field Office, 81
    Elko Field Office, 81
    Ely Field Office, 81
    Eugene District Office, 81
    Eugene Field Office, 81
    Fillmore Field Office, 81
    Folsom Field Office, 81
    Four Rivers Field Office, 81
    Glennallen District, 82
    Glenwood Springs Field Office, 82
    Grand Junction Field Office/Western Slope Center, 82
    Gunnison Field Office, 82
    Hollister Field Office, 82
    Idaho Falls Field Office, 82
    Jackson Field Office, 82
    Jarbridge Field Office, 82
    Kanab, 82
    Kemmerer Field Office, 82
    Kingman Field Office, 82
    Kremmling Field Office, 82
    La Jara Field Office, 82

ORGANIZATION NAME INDEX – U

UNITED STATES DEPARTMENT OF THE INTERIOR (continued)
  Bureau of Land Management (continued)
    Lake Havasu Field Office, 82
    Lakeview District, 83
    Lakeview Resource Area, 83
    Lander Field Office, 83
    Las Cruces District, 83
    Las Vegas Field Office, 83
    Lewistown Field Office, 83
    Little Snake Field Office, 83
    Malad Field Office, 83
    Malta Field Office, 83
    Medford District Office, 83
    Miles City Field Office, 83
    Milwaukee Field Office, 83
    Missoula Field Office, 84
    Moab District Field Office, 84
    Monticello Field Office, 84
    National Applied Resource Center, 84
    National Interagency Fire Center, 84
    National Training Center, 84
    Needles Field Office, 84
    Newcastle Field Office, 84
    North Dakota Field Office, 84
    Northern Field Office, 84
    Oklahoma Field Office-TuLSa #101, 85
    Owyhee Field Office, 85
    Palm Springs / South Coast Field Office, 85
    Phoenix Field Office, 85
    Pinedale Field Office, 85
    Pocatello Field Office, 85
    Prineville District Field Office, 85
    Public Affairs, 85
    Rawlins Field Office, 85
    Redding Field Office, 85
    Renewable Energy, 86
    Richfield District Field Office, 86
    Ridgecrest Field Office, 86
    Rock Springs Field Office, 86
    Roseburg District, 86
    Roswell District, 86
    Royal Gorge Field Office/Front Range Center, 86
    Safford Field Office, 86
    Saguache Field Office, 86
    Salem District Office, 86
    Salmon Field Office, 86
    Salt Lake Field Office, 86
    San Juan Field Office, 87
    San Pedro Project Office, 87
    Shoshone Field Office, 87
    Socorro Field Office, 87
    South Dakota Field Office, 87
    Spokane District, 87
    St. George Field Office, 87
    State Office for CA, 87
    State Office FOR ID, 87
    State Office for MT, ND and SD, 87
    State Office for NM, TX, OK and KS, 87
    State Office for NV, 87
    State Office for OR and WA, 88
    State Office FOR UT, 88
    State Office for WY and NE, 88
    Surprise Field Office, 88
    Taos Field Office, 88
    Tucson Field Office, 88
    Ukiah Field Office, 88
    Uncompahgre Field Office/Southwest Center, 88
    Vale District, 88
    Vernal District, 88
    White River Field Office, 88
    Winnemucca Field Office, 89
    Worland Field Office, 89
    Yuma Field Office, 89
  Bureau of Reclamation, 89
    Denver Office, 89
    Lower Colorado Region, 89
    Mid Pacific Region, 89
    Pacific Northwest Region, 89
    Upper Colorado Region, 89
  Desert National Wildlife Range, 90
  Fish & Wildlife Service, 90
    ACE Basin National Wildlife Refuge, 90
    Agassiz National Wildlife Refuge, 90
    Alamosa/Monte Vista National Wildlife Refuge, 90
    Alaska Maritime National Wildlife Refuge, 90
    Alaska Peninsula/Becharof National Wildlife Refuge, 90
    Alligator River/Pea Island National Wildlife Refuge, 91
    Anahuac National Wildlife Refuge, 91
    Ankeny National Wildlife Refuge, 91
    Antioch Dunes National Wildlife Refuge, 91
    Arapaho National Wildlife Refuge, 91
    Archie Carr National Wildlife Refuge, 91
    Arctic National Wildlife Refuge, 91
    Arkansas National Wildlife Refuge, 91
    Arrowwood National Wildlife Refuge Complex, 91
    Arthur R. Marshall Loxahatchee/Hope Sound National Wildlife Refuge, 91
    Ash Meadows National Wildlife Refuge, 92
    Attwater Prairie Chicken National Wildlife Refuge, 92
    Audubon National Wildlife Refuge, 92
    Back Bay/Plum Tree Island National Wildlife Refuge, 92
    Balcones Canyonlands National Wildlife Refuge, 92
    Bald Knob National Wildlife Refuge, 92
    Bayou Cocodrie National Wildlife Refuge, 92
    Bear Lake National Wildlife Refuge, 92
    Bear River Migratory Bird National Wildlife Refuge, 92
    Benton Lake National Wildlife Refuge, 92
    Big Lake National Wildlife Refuge, 93
    Big Muddy National Fish & Wildlife Refuge, 93
    Big Stone National Wildlife Refuge, 93
    Bitter Creek National Wildlife Refuge, 93
    Bitter Lake National Wildlife Refuge, 93
    Blackwater National Wildlife Refuge, 93
    Blue Ridge National Wildlife Refuge, 93
    Bombay Hook National Wildlife Refuge, 93
    Bon Secour National Wildlife Refuge, 93
    Bosque de Apache National Wildlife Refuge, 93
    Bowdoin National Wildlife Refuge, 94
    Brazoria National Wildlife Refuge, 94
    Browns Park National Wildlife Refuge, 94
    Buenos Aires National Wildlife Refuge, 94
    Buffalo Lake National Wildlife Refuge, 94
    Cabeza Prieta National Wildlife Refuge, 94
    Cache River National Wildlife Refuge, 94
    California-Nevada Operations, 94
    Camas National Wildlife Refuge, 94
    Cameron Prairie National Wildlife Refuge, 94
    Canaan Valley National Wildlife Refuge, 94
    Cape May National Wildlife Refuge, 94
    Cape Romain/Santee National Wildlife Refuge, 95
    Caribbean Islands National Wildlife Refuge, 95
    Carolina Sandhills National Wildlife Refuge, 95
    Catahoula National Wildlife Refuge, 95
    Charles M. Russell National Wildlife Refuge, 95
    Chase Lake National Wildlife Refuge, 95
    Chassahowitzka National Wildlife Refuge, 95
    Chickasaw National Wildlife Refuge, 95
    Chincoteague/Wallops Island National Wildlife Refuge, 95
    Choctaw National Wildlife Refuge, 95
    Clarks River National Wildlife Refuge, 95
    Columbia National Wildlife Refuge, 96
    Conboy Lake National Wildlife Refuge, 96
    Crab Orchard National Wildlife Refuge, 96
    Crescent Lake National Wildlife Refuge, 96
    Crescent Lake/North Platte Complex National Wildlife Refuge, 96
    Crocodile Lake National Wildlife Refuge, 96
    Crosby WMD/Lake Zahl National Wildlife Refuge, 96
    Cross Creeks National Wildlife Refuge, 96
    Culebra National Wildlife Refuge, 96
    Cypress Creek National Wildlife Refuge, 96
    De Soto (Boyer Chute National Wildlife Refuge), 96
    Deep Fork National Wildlife Refuge, 96
    Deer Flat National Wildlife Refuge, 97
    Delaware Bay Estuary Project, 97
    Des Lacs National Wildlife Refuge, 97
    Detroit Lakes WMD, 97
    Devils Lake WMD National Wildlife Refuge, 97
    Eastern Massachusetts National Wildlife Refuge Complex, 97
    Eastern Neck National Wildlife Refuge, 97
    Eastern Shore of VA/Fisherman Island National Wildlife Refuge, 97
    Edwin B. Forsythe National Wildlife Refuge, 97
    Erie National Wildlife Refuge, 98
    Eufaula National Wildlife Refuge, 98
    Felsenthal National Wildlife Refuge, 98
    Fergus Falls WMD National Wildlife Refuge, 98
    Fish Springs National Wildlife Refuge, 98
    Flint Hills (Marais des Cygnes) National Wildlife Refuge, 98

ORGANIZATION NAME INDEX – U

Florida Panther/Ten Thousand Island National Wildlife Refuge, 98
Fort Niobrara/Valentine National Wildlife Refuge, 98
Grays Lake National Wildlife Refuge, 98
Great Dismal Swamp/Nansemond National Wildlife Refuge, 98
Great River National Wildlfe Refuge, 98
Great Swamp National Wildlife Refuge, 98
Guadalupe-Nipomo Dunes National Wildlife Refuge, 99
Guam National Wildlife Refuge, 99
Hagerman National Wildlife Refuge, 99
Hakalau Forest National Wildlife Refuge, 99
Hanford Complex/Saddle Mountain National Wildlife Refuge, 99
Hart Mountain National Antelope Refuge National Wildlife Refuge, 99
Hatchie National Wildlife Refuge, 99
Hawaiian and Pacific Islands National Wildlife Refuge Complex, 99
Hillside National Wildlife Refuge, 99
Hobe Sound National Wildlife Refuge, 99
Holla Bend/Logan Cave National Wildlife Refuge, 100
Hopper Mountain Complex National Wildlife Refuge, 100
Horicon Complex National Wildlife Refuge, 100
Humboldt Bay National Wildlife Refuge, 100
Huron WMD National Wildlife Refuge, 100
Illinois River National Wildlife and Fish Refuge (Chautauqua, Emiquon, Meredosia), 100
Imperial National Wildlife Refuge, 100
Innoko National Wildlife Refuge, 100
Iroquois National Wildlife Refuge, 100
Izembek National Wildlife Refuge, 100
J. Clark Salyer National Wildlife Refuge, 100
J.N. "Ding" Darling National Wildlife Refuge, 101
John Heinz National Wildlife Refuge at Tinicum, 101
Johnston Island National Wildlife Refuge, 101
Julia Butler Hansen Refuge for the Columbia White-tailed Deer National Wildlife Refuge, 101
Kanuti National Wildlife Refuge, 101
Kealia Pond National Wildlife Refuge, 101
Kenai National Wildlife Refuge, 101
Kern/Pixley National Wildlife Refuge, 101
Keterson National Wildlife Refuge, 101
Kilauea Point (Hanalei, Huleia) National Wildlife Refuge, 101
Kirwin National Wildlife Refuge, 101
Klamath Basin Complex National Wildlife Refuge, 102
Kodiak National Wildlife Refuge, 102
Kofa National Wildlife Refuge, 102
Kootenai National Wildlife Refuge, 102
Kulm WMD National Wildlife Refuge, 102
Lacassine National Wildlife Refuge, 102
Lacreek/Bear Butte National Wildlife Refuge, 102
Laguna Atascosa National Wildlife Refuge, 102
Lake Andes/Karl E. Mundt National Wildlife Refuge, 102
Lake Umbagog National Wildlife Refuge, 102
Lake Woodruff National Wildlife Refuge, 103
Las Vegas National Wildlife Refuge, 103
Lee Metcalf National Wildlife Refuge, 103
Leopold National Wildlife Refuge, 103
Litchfield WMD, 103
Little Pend Oreille National Wildlife Refuge, 103
Little River/Little Sandy National Wildlife Refuge, 103
Long Island National Wildlife Refuge Complex, 103
Long Lake National Wildlife Refuge, 103
Louisiana WMD/Handy Brake National Wildlife Refuge, 103
Lower Colorado River Complex National Wildlife Refuge, 104
Lower Hatchie National Wildlife Refuge, 104
Lower Rio Grande/Santa Anna Complex National Wildlife Refuge, 104
Lower Suwannee/Cedar Keys National Wildlife Refuge, 104
Mackay Island/Currituck National Wildlife Refuge, 104
Madison WMD National Wildlife Refuge, 104
Malheur National Wildlife Refuge, 104
Mark Twain National Wildlife Refuge, 104
Mark Twain/Brussels District National Wildlife Refuge, 104
Mattamuskeet National Wildlife Refuge, 104
Maxwell National Wildlife Refuge, 104
Medicine Lake National Wildlife Refuge Complex, 105
Merritt Island National Wildlife Refuge, 105
Michigan WMD National Wildlife Refuge, 105
Mid-Columbia River National Wildlife Refuge Complex, 105
Midway Atoll National Wildlife Refuge, 105
Mille Lacs National Wildlife Refuge, 105
Mingo National Wildlife Refuge, 105
Minidoka National Wildlife Refuge, 105
Minnesota Valley National Wildlife Refuge, 105
Missisquoi National Wildlife Refuge, 106
Mississippi Sandhill Crane/Grand Bay National Wildlife Refuge, 106
Mississippi WMD National Wildlife Refuge, 106

Moapa Valley National Wildlife Refuge, 106
Modoc National Wildlife Refuge, 106
Monomoy National Wildlife Refuge, 106
Montezuma National Wildlife Refuge, 106
Moosehorn National Wildlife Refuge, 106
Morris Wetland Management District, 106
Muleshoe/Grulla National Wildlife Refuge, 107
Muscatatuck National Wildlife Refuge, 107
National Bison Range National Wildlife Refuge, 107
National Conservation Training Center, 107
National Elk Refuge, 107
National Fish and Wildlife Forensics Laboratory, 107
National Key Deer Wildlife Refuge, 107
Neal Smith National Wildlife Refuge, 107
Necedah National Wildlife Refuge, 107
Nisqually/Grays Harbor National Wildlife Refuge, 108
North Louisiana Complex National Wildlife Refuge, 108
Nowitna/Koyukuk National Wildlife Refuge, 108
Noxubee National Wildlife Refuge, 108
Oahu National Wildlife Refuge Complex, 108
Ohio River Islands National Wildlife Refuge, 108
Okefenokee (Banks Lake) National Wildlife Refuge, 108
Oregon Coast National Wildlife Refuge Complex, 108
Ottawa National Wildlife Refuge, 108
Ouray National Wildlife Refuge, 108
Overflow National Wildlife Refuge, 109
Oxford Slough WPA National Wildlife Refuge Complex, 109
Pacific/Remote Islands Complex (Hawaiian Islands, Baker Island, Howland Island, Jarvis Island, Rose Atoll) National Wildlife Refuge, 109
Pahranagat National Wildlife Refuge, 109
Panther Swamp National Wildlife Refuge, 109
Parker River/Thatcher Island National Wildlife Refuge, 109
Patoka River National Wetlands Project National Wildlife Refuge, 109
Patuxent Research Refuge, 109
Pee Dee National Wildlife Refuge, 109
Pelican Island National Wildlife Refuge, 109
Petit Manan National Wildlife Refuge, 110
Piedmont National Wildlife Refuge, 110
Pierce National Wildlife Refuge, 110
Pocosin Lakes National Wildlife Refuge, 110
Pond Creek National Wildlife Refuge, 110
Port Louisa National Wildlife Refuge, 110
Potomac River Complex National Wildlife Refuge, 110
Prime Hook National Wildlife Refuge, 110
Quivira National Wildlife Refuge, 110
Rachel Carson National Wildlife Refuge, 111
Rainwater Basin WMD National Wildlife Refuge, 111
Rappahannock River Valley National Wildlife Refuge, 111
Red Rock Lakes National Wildlife Refuge, 111
Region 1, Pacific Regional Office, 111
Region 2, Southwest Regional Office, 111
Region 3, Great Lakes-Big Rivers Regional office, 111
Region 4, Southeast Regional office, 112
Region 5, Northeast Regional office, 112
Region 6, Mountain-Prairie Regional Office, 112
Rregion 7, Alaska Regional Office, 112
Rhode Island National Wildlife Refuge Complex, 112
Rice Lake National Wildlife Refuge, 112
Ridgefield National Wildlife Refuge, 112
Roanoke River National Wildlife Refuge, 112
Ruby Lake National Wildlife Refuge, 113
Sabine National Wildlife Refuge, 113
Sacramento National Wildlife Refuge, 113
Salt Plains National Wildlife Refuge, 113
San Andres National Wildlife Refuge, 113
San Bernardino/Leslie Canyon National Wildlife Refuge, 113
San Francisco Bay National Wildlife Refuge Complex, 113
San Luis National Wildlife Refuge Complex, 113
Sand Lake National Wildlife Refuge, 113
Sandy Point National Wildlife Refuge, 114
Savannah Coastal Refuges, 114
Seedskadee/Cokeville Meadows National Wildlife Refuge, 114
Selawik National Wildlife Refuge, 114
Seney National Wildlife Refuge, 114
Sequoyah/Ozark Plateau National Wildlife Refuge, 114
Sevilleta National Wildlife Refuge, 114
Sheldon/Hart Mountain National Wildlife Refuge, 114
Sherburne/Crane Meadows National Wildlife Refuge, 114
Shiawassee National Wildlife Refuge, 114
Silvio O. Conte National Wildlife and Fish Refuge, 114
Sonny Bono Salton Sea National Wildlife Refuge, 115
Southeast Louisiana Complex National Wildlife Refuge, 115

UNITED STATES DEPARTMENT OF THE INTERIOR (continued)
   Fish & Wildlife Service (continued)
      Squaw Creek National Wildlife Refuge, 115
      St. Catherine Creek National Wildlife Refuge, 115
      St. Croix Wetland Management District, 115
      St. Lawrence National Wildlife Refuge, 115
      St. Marks National Wildlife Refuge, 115
      St. Vincent National Wildlife Refuge, 115
      Stillwater National Wildlife Refuge Complex, 115
      Stone Lakes National Wildlife Refuge, 116
      Sunkhaze Meadows National Wildlife Refuge/Carlton Pond Waterfowl Production Area, 116
      Supawna Meadows National Wildlife Refuge, 116
      Swan Lake National Wildlife Refuge, 116
      Tamarac National Wildlife Refuge, 116
      Tennessee National Wildlife Refuge, 116
      Tensas River National Wildlife Refuge, 116
      Tetlin National Wildlife Refuge, 116
      Tewaukon National Wildlife Refuge, 116
      Tishomingo National Wildlife Refuge, 116
      Togiak National Wildlife Refuge, 116
      Trempealeau National Wildlife Refuge, 116
      Trinity River National Wildlife Refuge, 116
      Tualatin River National Wildlife Refuge, 117
      Turnbull National Wildlife Refuge, 117
      Two Ponds, C/O Rocky Mountain Arsenal National Wildlife Refuge, 117
      Union Slough (Iowa WMD) National Wildlife Refuge, 117
      Upper Mississippi River National Wildlife and fish refuge, 117
      Upper Souris National Wildlife Refuge, 117
      Valley City Wetland Management District, 117
      Wallkill River National Wildlife Refuge, 117
      Wapanocca National Wildlife Refuge, 117
      Washington Maritime National Wildlife Refuge Complex, 118
      Washington Office, 118
      Washita/Optima National Wildlife Refuge, 118
      Waubay National Wildlife Refuge, 118
      West Tennessee Refuges, 118
      Western Oregon National Wildlife Refuge Complex, 118
      Wheeler National Wildlife Refuge, 118
      White River National Wildlife Refuge, 118
      Wichita Mountains National Wildlife Refuge, 118
      Willapa/Lewis and Clark National Wildlife Refuge, 118
      Windom WMD National Wildlife Refuge, 119
      Yazoo National Wildlife Refuge, 119
      Yukon Delta National Wildlife Refuge, 119
      Yukon Flats National Wildlife Refuge, 119
   Great Plains Region, 119
   Kansas State Cooperative Fish and Wildlife Research Unit, 119
   Missouri Cooperative Fish and Wildlife Research Unit, 119
   Montana Cooperative Fishery Research Unit, 119
   Montana State Extension Service, 119
   National Park Service, 120
      Acadia National Park, 120
      Arches National Park, 120
      Assateague Island National Seashore, 120
      Badlands National Park, 120
      Big Bend National Park, 120
      Biscayne National Park, 120
      Bryce Canyon National Park, 120
      Canaveral National Seashore, 121
      Canyonlands National Park, 121
      Cape Cod National Seashore, 121
      Cape Hatteras National Seashore, 121
      Cape Lookout National Seashore, 121
      Capitol Reef National Park, 121
      Carlsbad Caverns National Park, 121
      Channel Islands National Park, 121
      Chihuahuan Desert Network, 121
      Conservation Study Institute, 121
      Crater Lake National Park, 122
      Cumberland Island National Seashore, 122
      Death Valley National Park, 122
      Denali National Park, 122
      Dry Tortugas National Park, 122
      Everglades National Park, 122
      Fire Island National Seashore, 122
      Gates of the Arctic National Park, 122
      Glacier Bay National Park, 122
      Glacier National Park, 122
      Grand Canyon National Park, 122
      Grand Teton National Park, 122
      Great Basin National Park, 123
      Great Smoky Mountains National Park, 123
      Guadalupe Mountains National Park, 123
      Gulf Islands National Seashore, 123
      Haleakala National Park, 123
      Hawaii Volcanoes National Park, 123
      Hot Springs National Park, 123
      Isle Royale National Park, 123
      Joshua Tree National Park, 123
      Katmai National Park, 123
      Kenai Fjords National Park, 123
      Kobuk Valley National Park, 124
      Lake Clark National Park, 124
      Lassen Volcanic National Park, 124
      Mammoth Cave National Park, 124
      Mesa Verde National Park, 124
      Mount Rainier National Park, 124
      National Park of AmericaN Samoa, 124
      North Cascades National Park, 124
      Olympic National Park, 124
      Padre Island National Seashore, 124
      Petrified Forest National Park, 125
      Point Reyes National Seashore, 125
      Redwood National Park, 125
      Rocky Mountain National Park, 125
      Sequoia and Kings Canyon National Park, 125
      Shenandoah National Park, 125
      Sonoran Desert Network, 125
      Theodore Roosevelt National Park, 125
      Virgin Islands National Park, 125
      Voyageurs National Park, 125
      Wind Cave National Park, 126
      Wrangell-St. Elias National Park, 126
      Yellowstone National Park, 126
      Yosemite National Park, 126
      Zion National Park, 126
   North Dakota State University Extension Service, 126
   Office of Surface Mining Reclamation and Enforcement, 126
   Oregon Cooperative Fish and Wildlife Research Unit, 126
   United States Geological Survey, 126
      Biological Resources Division, 127
      Forest and Rangeland Ecosystem Research Center, 127
      Iowa Cooperative Fish and Wildlife Research Unit, 127
      New Mexico Cooperative Fish and Wildlife Research Unit, 127
      Western Region, 127
   Utah Cooperative Fish and Wildlife Research Unit, 128
   Washington Cooperative Fish and Wildlife Research Unit School of Aquatic and Fishery Sciences, 128
UNITED STATES DEPARTMENT OF TRANSPORTATION, 128
   Coast Guard, 128
   Federal Aviataion Administration, 128
   Federal Highway Administration, 128
   Federal Railroad Administration, 129
   Federal Transit Administration, 129
   National Highway Traffice Safety Administration, 129
   Saint Lawrence Seaway Development Corporation, 129
UNITED STATES DEPARTMENT OF TREASURY, 129
UNITED STATES ENVIRONMENTAL PROTECTION AGENCY
   Administration and Resources Management, 129
   Enforcement and Compliance, 129
   Office of Research and Development, 130
   Prevention, Pesticides, and Toxic Substances, 130
   Science Policy, 130
   Water, United States, 130
UNITED STATES ENVIRONMENTAL PROTECTION BUREAU, 223
UNITED STATES INSTITUTE FOR ENVIRONMENTAL CONFLICT RESOLUTION, 130
UNITED STATES PUBLIC INTEREST RESEARCH GROUP, 526
UNITED STATES SPORTSMEN'S ALLIANCE AND UNITED STATES SPORTSMEN'S ALLIANCE FOUNDATION, 526
UNITED STATES TOURIST COUNCIL, 527
UNITED STATES VIRGIN ISLANDS DEPARTMENT OF PLANNING AND NATURAL RESOURCES
   Division of Environmental Protection, 223
   Division of Fish and Wildlife, 224
UNITY COLLEGE, 601
UNIVERSIDADE FEDERAL DO PARANA, 601
UNIVERSITE LAVAL, 601
   Center for Research in Economics of Agri-Food (CREA), 604
   Faculty of Agricultural and Food Sciences, 602, 604
   Faculty of Architecture, Planning and Visual Arts, 602
   Faculty of Forestry and Geomatics, 602
   Faculty of Law, 602
   Faculty of Medicine, 602

ORGANIZATION NAME INDEX – U

Faculty of Philosophy, 602
Faculty of Sciences and Engineering, 603
Faculty of Social Sciences, 603
Forest Biology Research Center (CRBF), 604
Group for Research on Energy, Environment and Natural Resource Economics (GREEN), 603
Nordic Studies Center (CEN), 603
Quebec-Ocean, 603
Research Center for Planning and Regional Development (CRAD), 604
UNIVERSITY OF AKRON, 604
UNIVERSITY OF ALASKA AT FAIRBANKS
   College of Science, Engineering and Mathematics, 604
   Cooperative Extension Service College of Rural Alaska, 149
   School of Fisheries and Ocean Sciences, 604
UNIVERSITY OF ALBERTA, 604
UNIVERSITY OF ARIZONA
   Department of Hydrology and Water Resources, 605
   School of Renewable Natural Resources, 605
UNIVERSITY OF ARKANSAS AT LITTLE ROCK, 605
UNIVERSITY OF ARKANSAS AT MONTICELLO, 605
UNIVERSITY OF BATH, 605
UNIVERSITY OF BRITISH COLUMBIA, 606
UNIVERSITY OF CALIFORNIA AT DAVIS
   College of Agriculture and Environmental Science, 606
   Herbarium, 606
   School of Veterinary Medicine, 606
UNIVERSITY OF CALIFORNIA AT LOS ANGELES
   College Letters and Science, 606
   School of Engineering and Applied Science, 607
UNIVERSITY OF CALIFORNIA AT RIVERSIDE
   Department of Environmental Science, 607
   Graduate School of Environmental Science and Engineering, 607
UNIVERSITY OF CALIFORNIA AT SAN DIEGO, 607
UNIVERSITY OF CALIFORNIA AT SANTA BARBARA, 607
UNIVERSITY OF CALIFORNIA AT SANTA CRUZ, 607
UNIVERSITY OF CALIFORNIA, BERKELEY, 607
UNIVERSITY OF CALIFORNIA, SANTA BARBARA, 607
UNIVERSITY OF COLORADO, 608
UNIVERSITY OF COLORADO AT BOULDER, 608
UNIVERSITY OF CONNECTICUT, 608
UNIVERSITY OF CONNECTICUT COOPERATIVE EXTENSION, 608
UNIVERSITY OF DAR ES SALAAM, 608
UNIVERSITY OF DELAWARE, 608
UNIVERSITY OF FLORIDA
   School of Forest Resources and Conservation, 609
   Solar Energy and Energy Conversion Laboratories, 609
UNIVERSITY OF FLORIDA INSTITUTE OF FOOD AND AGRICULTURAL SCIENCES, 609
UNIVERSITY OF GEORGIA
   Daniel B. Warnell School of Forest Resources, 609
   Marine Institute, 609
   Savannah River Ecology Laboratory, 609
UNIVERSITY OF GUELPH, 610
UNIVERSITY OF HAWAII, 610
   Environment Center, 224
UNIVERSITY OF HAWAII AT MANOA, 610
UNIVERSITY OF HAWAII COOPERATIVE EXTENSION PROGRAM, 224
UNIVERSITY OF HOUSTON, 610
UNIVERSITY OF IDAHO
   College of Natural Resources
      Department of Fish and Wildlife Resources, 610
      Idaho Cooperative Fish and Wildlife Research Unit, 610
   Women in Natural Resources, 611
UNIVERSITY OF IDAHO EXTENSION, 611
UNIVERSITY OF ILLINOIS AT URBANA-CHAMPAIGN, 611
UNIVERSITY OF ILLINOIS EXTENSION, 611
UNIVERSITY OF IOWA, 611
UNIVERSITY OF ITO PUNJAB, 611
UNIVERSITY OF KANSAS, 611
UNIVERSITY OF KANSAS FIELD STATION AND ECOLOGICAL RESERVES, 612
UNIVERSITY OF KENTUCKY, 612
UNIVERSITY OF LOUISVILLE, 612
UNIVERSITY OF MAINE, 612
UNIVERSITY OF MAINE AT FORT KENT, 612
UNIVERSITY OF MAINE AT ORONO, 612
UNIVERSITY OF MAINE COOPERATIVE EXTENSION, 612
UNIVERSITY OF MANITOBA, 613
UNIVERSITY OF MARYLAND - AT COLLEGE PARK, 613
UNIVERSITY OF MARYLAND AT EASTERN SHORE, 613
UNIVERSITY OF MARYLAND BALTIMORE COUNTY, 613
UNIVERSITY OF MARYLAND CENTER FOR ENVIRONMENTAL SCIENCE, 613

UNIVERSITY OF MARYLAND COOPERATIVE EXTENSION, 224
UNIVERSITY OF MARYLAND EASTERN SHORE, 614
UNIVERSITY OF MARYLAND, COLLEGE PARK
   Graduate School, 614
UNIVERSITY OF MASSACHUSETTS
   Department of Natural Resources Conservation, 614
   Urban Harbors Institute, 614
UNIVERSITY OF MASSACHUSETTS EXTENSION, 224
UNIVERSITY OF MIAMI, 614
UNIVERSITY OF MICHIGAN, 614
UNIVERSITY OF MINNESOTA AT CROOKSTON, 614
UNIVERSITY OF MINNESOTA AT ST. PAUL, 615
UNIVERSITY OF MISSOURI, 615
UNIVERSITY OF MONTANA, 615
UNIVERSITY OF MONTANA SCHOOL OF FORESTRY, 615
UNIVERSITY OF NEBRASKA, 615
UNIVERSITY OF NEBRASKA COOPERATIVE EXTENSION, 224
UNIVERSITY OF NEVADA - AT RENO, 616
UNIVERSITY OF NEVADA AT LAS VEGAS
   Environmental Science Program, 616
   Water Resources Program, 616
UNIVERSITY OF NEVADA COOPERATIVE EXTENSION, 616
UNIVERSITY OF NEW BRUNSWICK, 616
UNIVERSITY OF NEW HAMPSHIRE, 616
UNIVERSITY OF NEW HAMPSHIRE COOPERATIVE EXTENSION, 617
UNIVERSITY OF NEW HAVEN DEPT. OF BIOLOGY AND ENVIRONMENTAL SCIENCES, 617
UNIVERSITY OF NORTH CAROLINA AT ASHEVILLE, 617
UNIVERSITY OF NORTH CAROLINA AT CHAPEL HILL, 617
UNIVERSITY OF NORTH DAKOTA, 618
UNIVERSITY OF NORTH TEXAS, 618
UNIVERSITY OF NORTHERN BRITISH COLUMBIA, 618
UNIVERSITY OF NORTHERN COLORADO, 618
UNIVERSITY OF OREGON, 619
   Institute for a Sustainable Environment, 619
   School of Law, 618
UNIVERSITY OF PENNSYLVANIA, 619
UNIVERSITY OF PITTSBURGH
   Biology Department, 619
   Graduate School of Public Health
      Department of Environmental and Occupational Health, 619
UNIVERSITY OF REGINA, 619
UNIVERSITY OF RHODE ISLAND
   Department of Natural Resources Science, 619
   Graduate School of Oceanography and Coastal Resources Center, 619
UNIVERSITY OF SASKATCHEWAN, 620
UNIVERSITY OF SOUTH CAROLINA
   Baruch Marine Field Laboratory, 620
   Marine Science Program, 620
UNIVERSITY OF SOUTH CAROLINA BEAUFORT, 620
UNIVERSITY OF SOUTHERN CALIFORNIA
   Department of Civil and Environmental Engineering, 620
   Environmental Studies Program, 620
UNIVERSITY OF SOUTHERN MISSISSIPPI, 620
UNIVERSITY OF TENNESSEE - AT KNOXVILLE, 621
UNIVERSITY OF TENNESSEE AT MARTIN, 621
UNIVERSITY OF THE DISTRICT OF COLUMBIA, 621
UNIVERSITY OF THE SOUTH (SEWANEE), 621
UNIVERSITY OF THE VIRGIN ISLANDS, 621
UNIVERSITY OF TORONTO, 621
UNIVERSITY OF TULSA, 621
UNIVERSITY OF VERMONT EXTENSION, 621, 225
UNIVERSITY OF VERMONT, SCHOOL OF NATURAL RESOURCES, 622
UNIVERSITY OF WEST FLORIDA, 622
UNIVERSITY OF WISCONSIN, 622
UNIVERSITY OF WISCONSIN AT EAU CLAIRE, 622
UNIVERSITY OF WISCONSIN AT GREEN BAY
   Natural and Applied Sciences Department, 622
UNIVERSITY OF WISCONSIN AT LA CROSSE, 623
UNIVERSITY OF WISCONSIN AT MADISON, 623
UNIVERSITY OF WISCONSIN AT STEVENS POINT, 623
UNIVERSITY OF WISCONSIN-MADISON, 623
UNIVERSITY OF WYOMING, 623
   William D. Ruckelshaus Institute and the School of Environment and Natural Resources, 624
UPPER CHATTAHOOCHEE RIVERKEEPER, 527
UPPER COLORADO RIVER COMMISSION, 130
UPPER MISSISSIPPI RIVER CONSERVATION COMMITTEE, 527
UPPER SKAGIT BALD EAGLE FESTIVAL, 527
URBAN HABITAT PROGRAM, 527
URBAN WASTE MANAGEMENT & RESEARCH CENTER, 624
URBAN WILDLIFE RESOURCES, 527
USAID/TANZANIA, 131

USDA FOREST PRODUCTS LABORATORY, 131
UTAH ASSOCIATION OF CONSERVATION DISTRICTS, 528
UTAH BASS FEDERATION, 528
UTAH DEPARTMENT OF AGRICULTURE, 225
UTAH DEPARTMENT OF HEALTH, 225
UTAH DEPARTMENT OF NATURAL RESOURCES
   Division of Utah State Parks and Recreation, 225
   Division of Wildlife Resources, 225
UTAH FORESTRY, FIRE AND STATE LANDS, 225
UTAH GEOLOGICAL SURVEY, 225
UTAH NATIVE PLANT SOCIETY, 528
UTAH NATURE STUDY SOCIETY, 528
UTAH STATE DEPARTMENT OF NATURAL RESOURCES, 225
   Division of Water Resources, 226
   Division of Wildlife Resources, 226
   Utah Energy Office, 226
UTAH STATE SOIL CONSERVATION COMMISSION, 226
UTAH STATE UNIVERSITY
   Berryman Institute for Wildlife Damage Management, 624
   College of Natural Resources, 624
UTAH WILDERNESS COALITION, 528
UTAH WILDLIFE FEDERATION, 528
UTAH WOODLAND OWNERS COUNCIL, 528

V

VANDERBILT CENTER FOR ENVIRONMENTAL MANAGEMENT (VCEMS), 625
VANDERBILT UNIVERSITY, 625
VENICE AREA BEAUTIFICATION, INC, 529
VERMONT AGENCY OF AGRICULTURE, FOOD, AND MARKETS, 226
VERMONT AGENCY OF NATURAL RESOURCES, 226
   Department of Environmental Conservation, 226
   Department of Fish and Wildlife, 227
   Department of Forests, Parks, and Recreation, 227
   Vermont Geological Survey, 227
VERMONT ASSOCIATION OF CONSERVATION DISTRICTS, 529
VERMONT BASS FEDERATION, 529
VERMONT DEPARTMENT OF AGRICULTURE, FOOD, AND MARKETS, 227
   State Conservation Commission, 227
VERMONT DEPARTMENT OF HEALTH, 227
VERMONT ENVIRONMENTAL BOARD, 227
VERMONT INSTITUTE OF NATURAL SCIENCE, 529
VERMONT LAND TRUST, 529
VERMONT LAW SCHOOL, 625
VERMONT NATURAL RESOURCES COUNCIL, 529
VERMONT STATE-WIDE ENVIRONMENTAL EDUCATION PROGRAMS (SWEEP), 530
VERMONT WOODLANDS ASSOCIATION, 530
VERNAL POOL SOCIETY, THE, 530
VIDEO PROJECT, THE, 571
VINEYARD CONSERVATION SOCIETY, 530
VIRGIN ISLANDS CONSERVATION DISTRICT, 530
VIRGIN ISLANDS CONSERVATION SOCIETY, INC., 530
VIRGIN ISLANDS COOPERATIVE EXTENSION SERVICE, 228
VIRGIN ISLANDS SOIL AND WATER CONSERVATION DIVISION, 228
VIRGINIA ASSOCIATION FOR PARKS, 531
VIRGINIA ASSOCIATION OF CONSERVATION DISTRICTS, 531
VIRGINIA BASS FEDERATION, 531
VIRGINIA CONSERVATION NETWORK, 531
VIRGINIA COOPERATIVE EXTENSION, 228
VIRGINIA COOPERATIVE FISH AND WILDLIFE RESEARCH UNIT (USDI), 228
VIRGINIA DEPARTMENT OF AGRICULTURE AND CONSUMER SERVICES, 228
VIRGINIA DEPARTMENT OF CONSERVATION AND RECREATION, 228
   Board of Conservation and Recreation, 229
   Breaks Interstate Park Commission, 229
   Chippokes Plantation Farm Foundation, 229
   Conservation and Development of Public Beaches Board, 229
   Division of Administration, 229
   Division of Dam Safety, 229
   Division of Natural Heritage, 229
   Division of Soil and Water Conservation, 229
   Division of State Parks, 229
   Virginia Cave Board, 230
VIRGINIA DEPARTMENT OF ENVIRONMENTAL QUALITY, 230
VIRGINIA DEPARTMENT OF FORESTRY, 230
VIRGINIA DEPARTMENT OF GAME AND INLAND FISHERIES, 230
   Region II (Lynchburg), 230
   Region III, 231
   Region IV (Staunton), 231

VIRGINIA DEPARTMENT OF HEALTH, 231
VIRGINIA DEPARTMENT OF MINES, MINERALS AND ENERGY, 231
   Division of Energy, 231
   Division of Gas and Oil, 231
   Division of Mined Land Reclamation, 231
   Division of Mineral Mining, 231
VIRGINIA FORESTRY ASSOCIATION, 531
VIRGINIA MARINE RESOURCES COMMISSION, 232
VIRGINIA MUSEUM OF NATURAL HISTORY, 232
VIRGINIA NATIVE PLANT SOCIETY, 531
VIRGINIA OUTDOORS FOUNDATION, 232
VIRGINIA POLYTECHNIC INSTITUTE
   Fish and Wildlife Information Exchange, 625
VIRGINIA POLYTECHNIC INSTITUTE AND STATE UNIVERSITY
   College of Natural Resources, 625
VIRGINIA RESOURCE-USE EDUCATION COUNCIL, 532
VIRGINIA SOCIETY OF ORNITHOLOGY, 532
VIRGINIA SOIL AND CONSERVATION BOARD, 232
VIRGINIA TECH
   Department of Fisheries and Wildlife Sciences, 625
VIRGINIA TECH UNIVERSITY
   College of Natural Resources, 625

W

WABASH RIVER HERITAGE CORRIDOR COMMISSION, 232
WALKABOUT PRODUCTIONS, INC., 571
WARREN COUNTY CONSERVATION BOARD, 532
WASHINGTON ASSOCIATION OF CONSERVATION DISTRICTS, 533
WASHINGTON BASS FEDERATION, 533
WASHINGTON DEPARTMENT OF AGRICULTURE, 232
WASHINGTON DEPARTMENT OF ECOLOGY, 233
   Central Regional Office, 233
   Eastern Regional Office, 233
   Northwest Regional Office, 233
   Southwest Regional Office, 233
WASHINGTON DEPARTMENT OF FISH AND WILDLIFE
   Washington Fish and Wildlife Commission, 233
WASHINGTON ENVIRONMENTAL COUNCIL, 533
WASHINGTON FARM FORESTRY ASSOCIATION, 533
WASHINGTON FOUNDATION FOR THE ENVIRONMENT, 533
WASHINGTON NATIVE PLANT SOCIETY, 533
WASHINGTON NATURAL HERITAGE PROGRAM, 233
WASHINGTON RECREATION AND PARK ASSOCIATION, 533
WASHINGTON STATE CONSERVATION COMMISSION, 234
WASHINGTON STATE DEPARTMENT OF ECOLOGY, 234
WASHINGTON STATE DEPARTMENT OF NATURAL RESOURCES
   Olympic Region, 234
WASHINGTON STATE EXTENSION, 234
WASHINGTON STATE OFFICE OF ENVIRONMENTAL EDUCATION, 234
WASHINGTON STATE PARKS AND RECREATION COMMISSION, 234
   Eastern Region Headquarters, 235
   Northwest Region, 235
   Southwest Region, 235
WASHINGTON STATE SOCIETY OF AMERICAN FORESTERS, 534
WASHINGTON STATE UNIVERSITY, 626
WASHINGTON TOXICS COALITION, 534
WASHINGTON TRAILS ASSOCIATION, 534
WASHINGTON UNIVERSITY, 626
WASHINGTON WILDERNESS COALITION, 534
WASHINGTON WILDLIFE AND RECREATION COALITION, 534
WASHINGTON WILDLIFE FEDERATION, 534
WATER EDUCATION FOUNDATION, 535
WATER ENVIRONMENT FEDERATION, 535
WATER RESOURCES ASSOCIATION OF THE DELAWARE RIVER BASIN, 535
WATERLOO-WELLINGTON WILDFLOWER SOCIETY, 535
WATERMAN CONSERVATION EDUCATION CENTER, 535
WATERSHED MANAGEMENT COUNCIL, 535
WAYNE STATE UNIVERSITY DEPARTMENT OF BIOLOGICAL SCIENCES, 626
WELDER WILDLIFE FOUNDATION, 535
WELLSPRING INTERNATIONAL, INC., 571
WEST MICHIGAN ENVIRONMENTAL ACTION COUNCIL, 536
WEST VIRGINIA ASSOCIATION OF CONSERVATION DISTRICT SUPERVISORS ASSOCIATION, INC., 536
WEST VIRGINIA BASS FEDERATION, 536
WEST VIRGINIA COOPERATIVE FISH AND WILDLIFE RESEARCH UNIT
   Division of Forestry, 235
WEST VIRGINIA DEPARTMENT OF AGRICULTURE, 235
WEST VIRGINIA DEPARTMENT OF ENVIRONMENTAL PROTECTION, 235

ORGANIZATION NAME INDEX – W

WEST VIRGINIA DIVISION OF NATURAL RESOURCES, 236
WEST VIRGINIA GEOLOGICAL AND ECONOMIC SURVEY, 236
WEST VIRGINIA HIGHLANDS CONSERVANCY, 536
WEST VIRGINIA RAPTOR REHABILITATION CENTER, 536
WEST VIRGINIA SOIL CONSERVATION AGENCY, 236
WEST VIRGINIA UNIVERSITY, 626
   Extension Service, 236
WEST VIRGINIA WILDLIFE FEDERATION, INC., 536
WESTERN ASSOCIATION OF FISH AND WILDLIFE AGENCIES, 537
WESTERN ENVIRONMENTAL LAW CENTER, 537
WESTERN FORESTRY AND CONSERVATION ASSOCIATION, 537
WESTERN HEMISPHERE SHOREBIRD RESERVE NETWORK (WHSRN), 537
WESTERN ILLINOIS UNIVERSITY, 626
WESTERN MICHIGAN UNIVERSITY, 626
WESTERN PACIFIC REGIONAL FISHERY MANAGEMENT COUNCIL, 131
WESTERN PENNSYLVANIA CONSERVANCY, 537
WESTERN SNOWY PLOVER WORKING TEAM, 131
WESTERN WASHINGTON UNIVERSITY, 627
WESTERN WATERSHEDS PROJECT, 538
WETLAND HABITAT ALLIANCE OF TEXAS, 538
WETLANDS ACTION NETWORK, 538
WETLANDS INTERNATIONAL, 538
WHALE AND DOLPHIN CONSERVATION SOCIETY, 538
WHITE CLAY WATERSHED ASSOCIATION, 538
WHITETAILS UNLIMITED, INC., 539
WHOOPING CRANE CONSERVATION ASSOCIATION INC., 539
WIDENER UNIVERSITY, 627
WILD CANID SURVIVAL AND RESEARCH CENTER, 539
WILD DOG FOUNDATION, THE, 539
WILD FOUNDATION, THE, 539
WILD HORSE ORGANIZED ASSISTANCE, INC. (WHOA), 540
WILD ONES NATURAL LANDSCAPERS, LTD, 540
WILDCOAST, 540
WILDERNESS EDUCATION ASSOCIATION, 540
WILDERNESS LAND TRUST, THE, 540
WILDERNESS SOCIETY, THE, 541
WILDERNESS WATCH, 541
WILDFLOWER ASSOCIATION OF MICHIGAN, 541
WILDFOWL TRUST OF NORTH AMERICA, INC., THE, 541
WILDFUTURES, 542
WILDLANDS CONSERVANCY, 542
WILDLANDS PROJECT, 542
WILDLIFE ACTION, INC., 542
WILDLIFE CENTER OF VIRGINIA, THE, 542
WILDLIFE CONSERVATION ENFORCEMENT FUND, INC., 543
WILDLIFE CONSERVATION SOCIETY, 543
WILDLIFE DAMAGE REVIEW (WDR), 543
WILDLIFE DISEASE ASSOCIATION, 543
WILDLIFE EDUCATION PROGRAM AND DESIGN, 543
WILDLIFE FEDERATION OF ALASKA, 543
WILDLIFE FOREVER, 544
WILDLIFE FOUNDATION OF FLORIDA, INC., 544
WILDLIFE HABITAT CANADA, 544
WILDLIFE HABITAT COUNCIL, 544
WILDLIFE HERITAGE FOUNDATION OF WYOMING (WHFW), 544
WILDLIFE INFORMATION CENTER, INC., 545
WILDLIFE MANAGEMENT INSTITUTE, 545
WILDLIFE ORPHANAGE, INC., THE, 545
WILDLIFE PRESERVATION TRUST CANADA, 545
WILDLIFE SOCIETY, 545
   Alabama Chapter, 546
   Alaska Chapter, 546
   Alberta Chapter, 546
   Arizona Chapter, 546
   Arkansas Chapter, 546
   California Central Coast Chapter, 546
   California North Coast Chapter, 547
   Colorado Chapter, 547
   Florida Chapter, 547
   Georgia Chapter, 547
   Hawaii Chapter, 547
   Idaho Chapter, 547
   Illinois Chapter, 547
   Indiana Chapter, 548
   Iowa Chapter, 548
   Kansas Chapter, 548
   Kentucky Chapter, 548
   Louisiana Chapter, 548
   Maine Chapter, 548
   Manitoba Chapter, 549
   Maryland-Delaware Chapter, 549
   Michigan Chapter, 549
   Minnesota Chapter, 549
   Mississippi Chapter, 549
   Missouri Chapter, 550
   Montana Chapter, 550
   National Capital Chapter, 550
   Nebraska Chapter, 550
   Nevada Chapter, 550
   New England Chapter, 550
   New Jersey Chapter, 550
   New Mexico Chapter, 551
   New York Chapter, 551
   North Carolina Chapter, 551
   North Dakota Chapter, 551
   Ohio Chapter, 551
   Oklahoma Chapter, 551
   Oregon Chapter, 552
   Pennsylvania Chapter, 552
   Sacramento-Shasta Chapter, 552
   San Francisco Bay Area Chapter, 552
   San Joaquin Valley Chapter, 552
   South Carolina Chapter, 552
   South Dakota Chapter, 552
   Southern California Chapter, 553
   Tennessee Chapter, 553
   Texas Chapter, 553
   Utah Chapter, 553
   Virginia Chapter, 553
   Washington Chapter, 553
   West Virginia Chapter, 554
   Wisconsin Chapter, 554
   Wyoming Chapter, 554
WILDLIFE TRUST
   Wildlife Preservation Trust International, 554
WILDLIFE WAYSTATION, 554
WILKES UNIVERSITY, 627
WILLIAMS COLLEGE, 627
WILLOW MIXED MEDIA INC., 627
WILSON ORNITHOLOGICAL SOCIETY, 555
WINCHESTER NILO FARMS, 555
WINDSTAR FOUNDATION, THE, 555
WINDSTAR WILDLIFE INSTITUTE, 555
WISCONSIN ASSOCIATION FOR ENVIRONMENTAL EDUCATION, INC. (WAEE), 555
WISCONSIN ASSOCIATION OF LAKES (WAL), 555
WISCONSIN BASS FEDERATION, 556
WISCONSIN COOPERATIVE FISHERY RESEARCH UNIT USGS, 237
WISCONSIN COOPERATIVE WILDLIFE RESEARCH UNIT (USDI), 237
WISCONSIN DEPARTMENT OF AGRICULTURE TRADE AND CONSUMER PROTECTION, 237
WISCONSIN DEPARTMENT OF NATURAL RESOURCES, 237, 556
WISCONSIN DEPARTMENT OF PUBLIC INSTRUCTION, 238
WISCONSIN ENVIRONMENTAL EDUCATION BOARD (WEEB), 238
WISCONSIN GEOLOGICAL AND NATURAL HISTORY SURVEY, 238
WISCONSIN LAND AND WATER CONSERVATION ASSOCIATION, 556
WISCONSIN PARK AND RECREATION ASSOCIATION, 556
WISCONSIN SOCIETY FOR ORNITHOLOGY, INC., THE, 556
WISCONSIN STATE EXTENSION SERVICES, 238
WISCONSIN WATERFOWL ASSOCIATION, INC., 556
WISCONSIN WILDLIFE FEDERATION, 557
WISCONSIN WOODLAND OWNERS ASSOCIATION, 557
WOLF EDUCATION AND RESEARCH CENTER, 557
WOLF GROUP, THE, 557
WOLF HAVEN INTERNATIONAL, 557
WOMEN'S ENVIRONMENT AND DEVELOPMENT ORGANIZATION (WEDO), 557
WOMEN'S SHOOTING SPORTS FOUNDATION, 558
WOODLAND OWNERS ASSOCIATION OF WEST VIRGINIA, 558
WORLD ASSOCIATION OF GIRL GUIDES AND GIRL SCOUTS (WAGGGS), 558
WORLD BIRD SANCTUARY (WBS), 558
WORLD CONSERVATION UNION, 558
WORLD FORESTRY CENTER, 558
WORLD PARKS ENDOWMENT INC., 559
WORLD PHEASANT ASSOCIATION, 559
WORLD RESOURCES INSTITUTE, 559
WORLD SOCIETY FOR THE PROTECTION OF ANIMALS (WSPA), 559
WORLD WILDLIFE FUND, 559
   Gulf of California Regional Office, 560
   Peru Program Office, 560
WORLDWATCH INSTITUTE, 560
WWF JAPAN (WORLD WIDE FUND FOR NATURE JAPAN), 560
WWW.ACTIONBIOSCIENCE.ORG, 560

WYOMING ASSOCIATION OF CONSERVATION DISTRICTS, 560
WYOMING BASS FEDERATION, 560
WYOMING COOPERATIVE EXTENSION SERVICES, 238
WYOMING COOPERATIVE FISH AND WILDLIFE RESEARCH UNIT (USDI), 238
WYOMING DEPARTMENT OF AGRICULTURE, 239
WYOMING DEPARTMENT OF ENVIRONMENTAL QUALITY, 239
WYOMING GAME AND FISH DEPARTMENT, 239
WYOMING NATIVE PLANT SOCIETY, 561
WYOMING NATURAL DIVERSITY DATABASE, 571
WYOMING OUTDOOR COUNCIL, 561
WYOMING STATE BOARD OF LAND COMMISSIONERS, 239
WYOMING STATE FORESTRY DIVISION, 240
WYOMING STATE GEOLOGICAL SURVEY, 240
WYOMING STATE PARKS AND CULTURAL RESOURCES, 240
WYOMING WILDLIFE FEDERATION, 561

X

XERCES SOCIETY, THE, 561

Y

YALE LAW SCHOOL, 627
YALE UNIVERSITY
  School of Forestry and Environmental Studies, 628
YELL COUNTY WILDLIFE FEDERATION, 561
YMCA NATURE AND COMMUNITY CENTER, 562
YORK UNIVERSITY
  Faculty of Environmental Studies, 628
YOSEMITE RESTORATION TRUST, 562
YOUNG ENTOMOLOGISTS SOCIETY, INC., 562
YUKON DEPARTMENT OF RENEWABLE RESOURCES, 240
YUKON FISH AND GAME ASSOCIATION, 562

Z

ZERO, 562
ZUNGARO COCHA RESEARCH CENTER
  Exploration Educational Expeditions, 562

KEYWORD INDEX

AGRICULTURE/FARMING

20/20 VISION, 241
ABUNDANT LIFE SEED FOUNDATION, 241
ACADEMY FOR EDUCATIONAL DEVELOPMENT, 241
AFRICAN AMERICAN ENVIRONMENTALIST ASSOCIATION, 243
ALABAMA DEPARTMENT OF AGRICULTURE AND INDUSTRIES, 132
ALABAMA DEPARTMENT OF CONSERVATION AND NATURAL RESOURCES, 132
ALABAMA ENVIRONMENTAL COUNCIL, 244
ALASKA HEALTH PROJECT, 134
ALASKA RAINFOREST CAMPAIGN, 246
AMERICA THE BEAUTIFUL FUND, 248
AMERICAN BIRD CONSERVANCY, 249
AMERICAN FARMLAND TRUST, 251
AMERICAN LIVESTOCK BREEDS CONSERVANCY, 263
AMERICAN PLANNING ASSOCIATION, 264
APPALACHIAN TRAIL CONFERENCE, 270
APROVECHO RESEARCH CENTER, 270
ARCHBOLD BIOLOGICAL STATION, 270
ARIZONA STATE ENVIROTHON, INC., 271
ARKANSAS COOPERATIVE RESEARCH UNIT, 137
ARKANSAS NATURAL HERITAGE COMMISSION, 138
ARKANSAS WATERSHED ADVISORY GROUP (AWAG), 272
ATLANTIC CENTER FOR THE ENVIRONMENT
 Quebec-Labrador Foundation, 275
ATLANTIC SALMON FEDERATION, 275
ATLANTIC STATES LEGAL FOUNDATION, 275
AUBURN UNIVERSITY
 College of Agriculture, 579
AUDUBON INTERNATIONAL, 276
AUSTRALIA DEPARTMENT FOR ENVIRONMENT AND HERITAGE, 139
BAMA BACKPADDLERS ASSOCIATION, 276
BAT CONSERVATION INTERNATIONAL, 277
BEAR SPRINGS BLOSSOM NATURE CONSERVATION GROUP INC., 277
BERKSHIRE-LITCHFIELD ENVIRONMENTAL COUNCIL, INC., 277
BEYOND PESTICIDES, 277
BIG BEND NATURAL HISTORY ASSOCIATION, 277
BIOINTEGRAL RESOURCE CENTER, 278
BOARD OF MINERALS AND ENVIRONMENT, 139
BOONE AND CROCKETT FOUNDATION, 279
BUN-CA, 281
BUSINESS PUBLISHERS, INC., 564
CALIFORNIA COOPERATIVE FISHERY RESEARCH UNIT (USGS), 16
CALIFORNIA ENERGY COMMISSION
 Environmental Department, 143
CANADIAN FEDERATION OF HUMANE SOCIETIES, 286
CANON ENVIROTHON, 288
CARRYING CAPACITY NETWORK, 288
CATSKILL CENTER FOR CONSERVATION AND DEVELOPMENT, INC., THE, 289
CENTER FOR ENVIRONMENT AND POPULATION (CEP), 290
CENTER FOR ENVIRONMENT, COMMERCE & ENERGY, 290
CENTER FOR RESOURCE ECONOMICS/ISLAND PRESS, 293
CENTER FOR SCIENCE IN THE PUBLIC INTEREST, 293
CHARLES A. AND ANNE MORROW LINDBERGH FOUNDATION, THE, 294
CHESAPEAKE BAY FOUNDATION, INC.
 Maryland Office, 295
CHESAPEAKE FARMS, 564
CHESAPEAKE WILDLIFE HERITAGE (CWH), 295
CHIHUAHUAN DESERT RESEARCH INSTITUTE, 296
CIRCUMPOLAR CONSERVATION UNION, 297
CJE ASSOCIATES, 565
CLARK UNIVERSITY, 576
COLORADO DEPARTMENT OF AGRICULTURE, 146
COLORADO DEPARTMENT OF NATURAL RESOURCES
 Division of Parks and Outdoor Recreation, 146
COLORADO GOVERNOR'S OFFICE OF ENERGY MANAGEMENT AND CONSERVATION, 147
COLORADO TRAPPERS ASSOCIATION, 302
COMMUNITY ENVIRONMENTAL COUNCIL (CEC), 303
COMMUNITY RIGHTS COUNSEL, 303
CONNECTICUT BOTANICAL SOCIETY, 304
CONSERVATION FEDERATION OF MARYLAND/ F.A.R.M., 306
CONSERVATION LAW FOUNDATION, INC. (CLF), 307
CONSERVATION TECHNOLOGY INFORMATION CENTER, 308
COOK INLET KEEPER, 308
COTTONWOOD FOUNDATION, 309
COUNCIL FOR PLANNING AND CONSERVATION, 310
D ACRES, 311
DELAWARE ASSOCIATION OF CONSERVATION DISTRICTS, 312
DELAWARE COOPERATIVE EXTENSION SERVICES, 150

DELAWARE DEPARTMENT OF NATURAL RESOURCES AND ENVIRONMENTAL CONTROL
 Division of Soil and Water Conservation, 150
DELAWARE NATURE SOCIETY, 312
DELTA WILDLIFE INC., 313
DESCHUTES BASIN LAND TRUST, 313
DISTRICT OF COLUMBIA DEPARTMENT OF HEALTH
 Environmental Health Administration, Watershed Protection Division, 152
DUKE UNIVERSITY - ORGANIZATION FOR TROPICAL STUDIES, 580
EAGLE NATURE FOUNDATION, LTD., 316
EARTH POLICY INSTITUTE, 317
EARTHJUSTICE
 International Program, 319
 Oakland Office, 319
 Tallahassee Office, 320
EARTHSCAN, 320
ECODEFENSE, 321
ECOLOGY CENTER, 321
ECONOVA INC., 565
ENTOMOLOGICAL SOCIETY OF AMERICA, 323
ENVIRONMENT COUNCIL OF RHODE ISLAND, 323
ENVIRONMENTAL CONCERN INC., 324
ENVIRONMENTAL DEFENSE
 Headquarters, 324
ENVIRONMENTAL DEFENSE CENTER, 325
ENVIRONMENTAL ENTERPRISES ASSISTANCE FUND, INC., 326
ENVIRONMENTAL LAW INSTITUTE, THE, 327
ENVIRONMENTAL PROTECTION AGENCY
 Region 5 (IL, IN, MI, NM, OH, WI), 19
ENVIRONMENTAL RESOURCE CENTER (ERC), 328
EQUESTRIAN LAND CONSERVATION RESOURCE, 328
FEDERATION OF ENVIRONMENTAL EDUCATION IN ST. PETERSBURG, 329
FERRUM COLLEGE, 581
FLORIDA COOPERATIVE EXTENSION SERVICE, 582
FLORIDA DEPARTMENT OF ENVIRONMENTAL PROTECTION
 Division of Resource Assessment and Management, 154
FOOD AND AGRICULTURE ORGANIZATION OF THE UNITED NATIONS, 333
FOOD SUPPLY / HUMAN POPULATION EXPLOSION CONNECTION, 333
FOREST SOCIETY OF MAINE, 335
FOREST WATCH, 335
FRIENDS OF ANIMALS INC., 337
GARDEN CLUB OF AMERICA, THE, 340
GEORGE MIKSCH SUTTON AVIAN RESEARCH CENTER INC., 340
GEORGIA COOPERATIVE FISH AND WILDLIFE RESEARCH UNIT (USDI), 20
GEORGIA STATE EXTENSION SERVICE, 157
GEORGIA TRUST FOR HISTORIC PRESERVATION, 342
GOOD NATURE PUBLISHING CO., 566
GRANT TECH CONSULTING AND CONSERVATION SERVICES, 567
GREAT PLAINS NATIVE PLANT SOCIETY, 345
GREEN BALKANS FEDERATION OF NATURE CONSERVATION NGOS, 346
GREEN SPHERE INC., 347
GULF STATES MARINE FISHERIES COMMISSION, 20
HARBOR BRANCH OCEANOGRAPHIC INSTITUTION, 348
HELPING OUR PENINSULA'S ENVIRONMENT, 350
HENRY A. WALLACE INSTITUTE FOR ALTERNATIVE AGRICULTURE (HAWIAA), 350
HOLDEN ARBORETUM, THE, 351
HUMANE SOCIETY OF THE UNITED STATES, THE, 352
HUNTSMAN MARINE SCIENCE CENTRE, 353
IDAHO DEPARTMENT OF ENVIRONMENTAL QUALITY, 160
IDAHO DEPARTMENT OF PARKS AND RECREATION, 160
IDAHO DEPARTMENT OF WATER RESOURCES
 Water Awareness Week, 161
ILLINOIS DEPARTMENT OF TRANSPORTATION, 162
ILLINOIS ENVIRONMENTAL COUNCIL, 355
ILLINOIS ENVIRONMENTAL PROTECTION AGENCY, 162
INSTITUTE FOR AGRICULTURE AND TRADE POLICY, 358
INSTITUTE FOR TROPICAL ECOLOGY AND CONSERVATION (ITEC), 358
INTERNATIONAL ACADEMY, 567
INTERNATIONAL ASSOCIATION OF FISH AND WILDLIFE AGENCIES, 360
INTERNATIONAL EROSION CONTROL ASSOCIATION (IECA), 363
INTERNATIONAL JOINT COMMISSION
 Great Lakes Regional Office, 22
INTERNATIONAL PLANT PROPAGATORS SOCIETY, INC., 365
INTERNATIONAL UNION FOR CONSERVATION OF NATURE AND NATURAL RESOURCES (IUCN) THE WORLD CONSERVATION UNION
 Canada Office, 368
 Regional Office for Europe, 369

IOWA DEPARTMENT OF AGRICULTURE AND LAND STEWARDSHIP
   Bureau of Financial Incentive Program, 165
IOWA ENVIRONMENTAL COUNCIL, 372
IOWA STATE EXTENSION SERVICES
   Extension Wildlife Programs, 166
IOWA STATE UNIVERSITY
   College of Agriculture, 584
ISLESBORO ISLANDS TRUST, 375
IZAAK WALTON LEAGUE OF AMERICA, INC., THE
   MINNESOTA DIVISION, 377
IZAAK WALTON LEAGUE OF AMERICA, INC., THE
   Owatonna Minnesota Chapter, 377
J.N. (DING) DARLING FOUNDATION, 379
JACK MINER MIGRATORY BIRD FOUNDATION, INC., 379
JACKSON HOLE LAND TRUST, 379
JOHNS HOPKINS UNIVERSITY
   CENTER FOR A LIVABLE FUTURE, 584
JOHNSON STATE COLLEGE, 585
KANSAS BIOLOGICAL SURVEY, 166
KANSAS DEPARTMENT OF WILDLIFE AND PARKS
   Office of the Secretary, 167
   Operations Office, 167
   Region 1, 167
   Region 2, 168
   Region 3, 168
KANSAS ORNITHOLOGICAL SOCIETY, 381
KANSAS STATE CONSERVATION COMMISSION, 168
KANSAS STATE UNIVERSITY
   College of Agriculture, 585
   Department of Landscape Architecture / Regional and Community Planning, 585
KENTUCKY DEPARTMENT OF AGRICULTURE, 169
KENTUCKY DEPARTMENT OF FISH AND WILDLIFE RESOURCES, 169
KENTUCKY NATURAL RESOURCES AND ENVIRONMENTAL PROTECTION CABINET, 170
LAND CONSERVANCY OF WEST MICHIGAN, 386
LAST WIZARDS, THE, 568
LEGACY LAND TRUST, 388
LITERACY FOR ENVIRONMENTAL JUSTICE, 389
LIVING RIVERS, 390
LUMMI ISLAND HERITAGE TRUST, 568
MACOMB LAND CONSERVANCY, 391
MANOMET CENTER FOR CONSERVATION SCIENCES, 393
MARINE LABORATORY (FLORIDA), 176
MARYLAND ASSOCIATION OF CONSERVATION DISTRICTS, 395
MARYLAND DEPARTMENT OF AGRICULTURE, 176
MARYLAND FORESTS ASSOCIATION, 395
MASSACHUSETTS COOPERATIVE FISH AND WILDLIFE RESEARCH UNIT (USDI), 178
MASSACHUSETTS EXECUTIVE OFFICE OF ENVIRONMENTAL AFFAIRS
   Office of Technical Assistance for Toxic Use Reduction, 179
MCGILL UNIVERSITY, 587
MICHIGAN DEPARTMENT OF AGRICULTURE, 180
MICHIGAN DEPARTMENT OF ENVIRONMENTAL QUALITY, 180
MIDDLE TENNESSEE STATE UNIVERSITY, 588
MIDLAND CONSERVATION DISTRICT, 181
MINNESOTA POLLUTION CONTROL AGENCY
   Rochester, MN, 183
MISSISSIPPI STATE UNIVERSITY
   Forest and Wildlife Research Center, 588
MISSOURI DEPARTMENT OF AGRICULTURE, 185
MONTANA BASS FEDERATION, 403
MONTANA DEPARTMENT OF NATURAL RESOURCES AND CONSERVATION, 187
MONTANA ENVIRONMENTAL QUALITY COUNCIL, 187
MONTANA STATE UNIVERSITY
   College of Agriculture, 589
MONTANA WILDERNESS ASSOCIATION, 403
MOTE MARINE LABORATORY, 404
MOUNTAIN CONSERVATION TRUST OF GEORGIA, INC., 405
MOUNTAINEERS, THE, 405
MURRAY STATE UNIVERSITY, 589
NATIONAL AGRICULTURAL LIBRARY, 24
NATIONAL ASSOCIATION OF CONSERVATION DISTRICTS, 407
NATIONAL ASSOCIATION OF SERVICE AND CONSERVATION CORPS (NASCC), 408
NATIONAL ASSOCIATION OF STATE DEPARTMENTS OF AGRICULTURE, 408
NATIONAL AUDUBON SOCIETY
   Audubon Maryland-DC, 410
   Audubon of Kansas, 410
   Louisiana Audubon Council, 414
   Maine Audubon, 414
   Montana Audubon, 415
   New Jersey Chapter, 415
   Public Policy Office, 415
   Seattle Audubon Society, 416
NATIONAL BOWHUNTER EDUCATION FOUNDATION (NBEF), 417
NATIONAL CAUCUS OF ENVIRONMENTAL LEGISLATORS (NCEL), 417
NATIONAL CENTER FOR APPROPRIATE TECHNOLOGY, 417
NATIONAL FARMERS UNION, 419
NATIONAL FFA ORGANIZATION, 419
NATIONAL GARDEN CLUBS, INC., 420
NATIONAL GARDENING ASSOCIATION, 420
NATIONAL GRANGE, THE, 421
NATIONAL RECREATION AND PARK ASSOCIATION, 423
NATIONAL WATER RESOURCES ASSOCIATION, 426
NATIONAL WATERSHED COALITION, 426
NATIONAL WILDLIFE FEDERATION
   Headquarters, 427
NATIONAL WOODLAND OWNERS ASSOCIATION, 430
NATURE CONSERVANCY, THE
   Colorado Chapter, 434
   Iowa Chapter, 435
   Pennsylvania Chapter, 439
   Texas Chapter, 439
NAVAJO NATION DEPARTMENT OF FISH AND WILDLIFE, 188
NEBRASKA DEPARTMENT OF NATURAL RESOURCES, 188
NEBRASKA GAME AND PARKS COMMISSION
   OMAHA OFFICE, 189
NEBRASKA WILDLIFE FEDERATION, INC., 442
NEVADA ASSOCIATION OF CONSERVATION DISTRICTS, 442
NEW BRUNSWICK DEPARTMENT OF NATURAL RESOURCES, 189
NEW ENGLAND COALITION FOR SUSTAINABLE POPULATION (NECSP), 443
NEW ENGLAND WILD FLOWER SOCIETY, INC., 443
NEW HAMPSHIRE ASSOCIATION OF CONSERVATION DISTRICTS, 444
NEW HAMPSHIRE COUNCIL ON RESOURCES AND DEVELOPMENT, 190
NEW HAMPSHIRE DEPARTMENT OF AGRICULTURE, MARKETS, AND FOOD
   State Conservation Committee, 190
NEW HAMPSHIRE FISH AND GAME DEPARTMENT, 190
NEW JERSEY ASSOCIATION OF CONSERVATION DISTRICTS, 445
NEW JERSEY BASS FEDERATION, 445
NEW JERSEY DEPARTMENT OF AGRICULTURE
   Division of Rural Resources, 191
NEW JERSEY ENVIRONMENTAL LOBBY, 445
NEW MEXICO ASSOCIATION OF CONSERVATION DISTRICTS, 445
NEW MEXICO ENERGY, MINERALS, AND NATURAL RESOURCES DEPARTMENT
   Oil Conservation Division, 195
NEW MEXICO STATE UNIVERSITY
   College of Agriculture and Home Economics, 589
NEW YORK OFFICE OF ENERGY EFFICIENCY AND ENVIRONMENT, 197
NOLTE ASSOCIATES, INC., 569
NORTH AMERICAN BUTTERFLY ASSOCIATION, 448
NORTH CAROLINA DEPARTMENT OF AGRICULTURE AND CONSUMER SERVICES, 200
NORTH CAROLINA DIVISION OF SOIL AND WATER, 200
NORTH CAROLINA STATE UNIVERSITY, 590
NORTH DAKOTA DEPARTMENT OF AGRICULTURE, 201
NORTH DAKOTA STATE UNIVERSITY, 590
NORTHERN PLAINS RESOURCE COUNCIL, 453
NORTHWEST RESOURCE INFORMATION CENTER, 454
NORTHWEST TERRITORIES DEPARTMENT OF RESOURCES, WILDLIFE AND ECONOMIC DEVELOPMENT, 202
NOVA SCOTIA DEPARTMENT OF NATURAL RESOURCES, 203
OHIO DEPARTMENT OF NATURAL RESOURCES, 204
OHIO ENVIRONMENTAL REVIEW APPEALS COMMISSION, 205
OHIO FEDERATION OF SOIL AND WATER CONSERVATION DISTRICTS, 457
OHIO FORESTRY ASSOCIATION, INC., 457
OHIO STATE UNIVERSITY, 592
OKLAHOMA DEPARTMENT OF ENVIRONMENTAL QUALITY, 206
OKLAHOMA GEOLOGICAL SURVEY, 206
OKLAHOMA STATE EXTENSION SERVICES, 206
ONTARIO FEDERATION OF ANGLERS AND HUNTERS, 459
ONTARIO MINISTRY OF NATURAL RESOURCES
   South Central Region, 208
ORGANIZATION FOR BAT CONSERVATION, 461
PACIFIC RIVERS COUNCIL, 464
PENNSYLVANIA FISH AND BOAT COMMISSION
   Bureau of Law Enforcement
      Northcentral Region, 212

KEYWORD INDEX – A

PLAYA LAKES JOINT VENTURE, 469
PURPLE MARTIN CONSERVATION ASSOCIATION, 475
QUEBEC DEPARTMENT OF ENVIRONMENT AND WILDLIFE, 214
RACHEL CARSON COUNCIL, INC., 476
RAINFOREST RELIEF, 477
RAINFOREST TRUST, 477
RENEWABLE NATURAL RESOURCES FOUNDATION, 478
RHODE ISLAND WILD PLANT SOCIETY, 480
ROCKY MOUNTAIN BIRD OBSERVATORY, 482
ROGER WILLIAMS UNIVERSITY, 594
RUTGERS COOPERATIVE EXTENSION, 215
SAN DIEGUITO RIVER PARK JOINT POWERS AUTHORITY, 215
SAND CREEK WATERSHED PROJECT, THE, 215
SEACOAST ANTI-POLLUTION LEAGUE, 489
SIERRA CLUB
  Alaska Field Office, 490
  Cascade Chapter, 491
  Connecticut Chapter, 491
  Kansas Chapter, 493
  Lone Star Chapter, 493
  Mississippi Chapter, 494
  Nebraska Chapter, 494
  New Jersey Chapter, 495
  Northwest Office, 495
  Rio Grande Chapter (New Mexico/West Texas), 496
  Washington, DC Office, 499
  West Virginia Chapter, 499
SIERRA CLUB CALIFORNIA, 499
SIERRA CLUB FOUNDATION, THE, 499
SIERRA CLUB OF CANADA
  Atlantic Canada Chapter, 500
SLIPPERY ROCK UNIVERSITY, 595
SMITHSONIAN INSTITUTION, 501
SOCIETY FOR RANGE MANAGEMENT, 503
SOCIETY FOR THE PROTECTION OF NEW HAMPSHIRE FORESTS, 503
SOIL AND WATER CONSERVATION SOCIETY, 504
SOUTH DAKOTA ASSOCIATION OF CONSERVATION DISTRICTS, 506
SOUTH DAKOTA COOPERATIVE FISH AND WILDLIFE RESEARCH UNIT (USDI-USGS), 29
SOUTH DAKOTA DEPARTMENT OF GAME, FISH, AND PARKS, 219
SOUTH DAKOTA ORNITHOLOGISTS UNION, 507
SOUTH DAKOTA RESOURCES COALITION, 507
SOUTHEASTERN ASSOCIATION OF FISH AND WILDLIFE AGENCIES, 508
SOUTHEASTERN COOPERATIVE WILDLIFE DISEASE STUDY, 508
SOUTHERN ENVIRONMENTAL LAW CENTER, 509
SOUTHERN ILLINOIS UNIVERSITY CARBONDALE, 596
SOUTHWEST CENTER FOR ENVIRONMENTAL RESEARCH AND POLICY (SCERP), 596
SOUTHWEST CONSERVATION DISTRICT, 510
SOUTHWESTERN HERPETOLOGISTS SOCIETY, 510
STATE ENVIRONMENTAL RESOURCE CENTER (SERC), 512
STERLING COLLEGE, 508
SUSTAIN, 514
SUSTAINABLE ENERGY INSTITUTE
  Culture Change, 514
  Culture Change magazine, 514
  Food Not Lawns, 514
  Pedal Power Produce, 514
TENNESSEE DEPARTMENT OF AGRICULTURE, 221
TENNESSEE DEPARTMENT OF ENVIRONMENT AND CONSERVATION, 221
TEXAS A AND M UNIVERSITY AT KINGSVILLE
  Caesar Kleberg Wildlife Research Institute, 599
TEXAS COOPERATIVE FISH AND WILDLIFE RESEARCH UNIT, 30
TEXAS DEPARTMENT OF AGRICULTURE, 222
TEXAS DEPARTMENT OF HEALTH, 222
TEXAS FOREST SERVICE, 222
TEXAS RIPARIAN ASSOCIATION, 517
TREES FOR THE FUTURE, INC., 519
TROUT UNLIMITED
  Pennsylvania Council, 522
TRUST FOR WILDLIFE, INC., 524
TUG HILL TOMORROW LAND TRUST, 524
TULANE ENVIRONMENTAL LAW CLINIC, 600
TURTLE CREEK WATERSHED ASSOCIATION, INC., 525
TWO WHITE WOLVES SANCTUARY, 525
UNION OF CONCERNED SCIENTISTS, 525
UNITED STATES CHAMBER OF COMMERCE
  Environment, Technology and Regulatory Affairs, 526
UNITED STATES COMMITTEE FOR THE UNITED NATIONS ENVIRONMENT PROGRAMME, THE (U.S. AND UNEP), 526

UNITED STATES DEPARTMENT OF AGRICULTURE
  Economic Research Center, 33
  Forest Service
    Crooked River National Grassland, 37
    Pawnee National Grassland, 42
    Siuslaw National Forest, 45
UNITED STATES DEPARTMENT OF COMMERCE
  National Oceanic and Atmospheric Administration
    Sea Grant Program - Illinois-Indiana, 55
    Sea Grant Program - Massachusetts, 56
    Sea Grant Program - New York, 58
    Sea Grant Program - North Carolina, 58
    Sea Grant Program - Ohio, 58
    Sea Grant Program - South Carolina, 59
    Sea Grant Program - Texas, 59
    Wells National Estuarine Research Reserve, 60
UNITED STATES DEPARTMENT OF DEFENSE
  Air Force Major Air Commands
    Andrews AFB, MD, 61
    USAF Academy, 62
  Army Materiel Command, 72
  Navy, 74
UNITED STATES DEPARTMENT OF HOMELAND SECURITY
  Customs and Border Protection
    New York CMC, 76
UNITED STATES DEPARTMENT OF THE INTERIOR
  Bureau of Land Management
    Malta Field Office, 83
    Rawlins Field Office, 85
    Safford Field Office, 86
  Bureau of Reclamation, 89
  Fish and Wildlife Service
    Alligator River/Pea Island National Wildlife Refuge, 91
    Arrowwood National Wildlife Refuge Complex, 91
    Carolina Sandhills National Wildlife Refuge, 95
    Eastern Massachusetts National Wildlife Refuge Complex, 97
    Lacassine National Wildlife Refuge, 102
    Mattamuskeet National Wildlife Refuge, 104
    Morris Wetland Management District, 106
    Noxubee National Wildlife Refuge, 108
    Pocosin Lakes National Wildlife Refuge, 110
    San Francisco Bay National Wildlife Refuge Complex, 113
    White River National Wildlife Refuge, 118
    Willapa/Lewis and Clark National Wildlife Refuge, 118
  Montana State Extension Services, 119
  United States Geological Survey
    New Mexico Cooperative Fish and Wildlife Research Unit, 127
    Western Region, 127
  Washington Cooperative Fish and Wildlife Research Unit
    School of Aquatic and Fishery Sciences, 128
UNITED STATES INSTITUTE FOR ENVIRONMENTAL CONFLICT RESOLUTION, 130
UNITY COLLEGE, 601
UNIVERSITE LAVAL, 601
UNIVERSITY OF CONNECTICUT COOPERATIVE EXTENSION, 608
UNIVERSITY OF DAR ES SALAAM, 608
UNIVERSITY OF FLORIDA
  School of Forest Resources and Conservation, 609
UNIVERSITY OF FLORIDA INSTITUTE OF FOOD AND AGRICULTURAL SCIENCES, 609
UNIVERSITY OF GEORGIA
  Daniel B. Warnell School of Forest Resources, 609
UNIVERSITY OF HAWAII COOPERATIVE EXTENSION PROGRAM, 224
UNIVERSITY OF MAINE, 612
UNIVERSITY OF MAINE COOPERATIVE EXTENSION, 612
UNIVERSITY OF MARYLAND - AT COLLEGE PARK, 613
UNIVERSITY OF MARYLAND BALTIMORE COUNTY, 613
UNIVERSITY OF MICHIGAN, 614
UNIVERSITY OF MINNESOTA AT ST. PAUL, 615
UNIVERSITY OF NEW HAMPSHIRE COOPERATIVE EXTENSION, 617
UNIVERSITY OF NORTH DAKOTA, 618
UNIVERSITY OF SASKATCHEWAN, 620
UNIVERSITY OF SOUTHERN MISSISSIPPI, 620
UNIVERSITY OF THE DISTRICT OF COLUMBIA, 621
UNIVERSITY OF VERMONT EXTENSION, 225
UNIVERSITY OF WISCONSIN AT MADISON, 623
UTAH BASS FEDERATION, 528
UTAH STATE DEPARTMENT OF NATURAL RESOURCES
  Division of Water Resources, 226
UTAH WILDERNESS COALITION, 528
VERMONT AGENCY OF NATURAL RESOURCES
  Department of Environmental Conservation, 226
VERMONT LAND TRUST, 529

660 KEYWORD INDEX – A

VERMONT STATE-WIDE ENVIRONMENTAL EDUCATION PROGRAMS (SWEEP), 530
VERMONT WOODLANDS ASSOCIATION, 530
VINEYARD CONSERVATION SOCIETY, 530
VIRGINIA FORESTRY ASSOCIATION, 531
VIRGINIA MUSEUM OF NATURAL HISTORY, 232
VIRGINIA OUTDOORS FOUNDATION, 232
VIRGINIA SOCIETY OF ORNITHOLOGY, 532
VIRGINIA TECH
  Department of Fisheries and Wildlife Sciences, 625
VIRGINIA TECH UNIVERSITY
  College of Natural Resources, 625
WASHINGTON DEPARTMENT OF ECOLOGY
  Central Regional Office, 233
WASHINGTON STATE PARKS AND RECREATION COMMISSION
  Southwest Region, 235
WATERLOO-WELLINGTON WILDFLOWER SOCIETY, 535
WEST VIRGINIA DEPARTMENT OF AGRICULTURE, 235
WEST VIRGINIA DIVISION OF NATURAL RESOURCES, 236
WETLAND HABITAT ALLIANCE OF TEXAS, 538
WILD ONES NATURAL LANDSCAPERS, LTD, 540
WILDLIFE DAMAGE REVIEW (WDR), 543
WILDLIFE FEDERATION OF ALASKA, 543
WILDLIFE HABITAT CANADA, 544
WILDLIFE SOCIETY
  Arizona Chapter, 546
  Colorado Chapter, 547
  Illinois Chapter, 547
  Michigan Chapter, 549
  National Capital Chapter, 550
  Southern California Chapter, 553
WINDSTAR WILDLIFE INSTITUTE, 555
WISCONSIN PARK AND RECREATION ASSOCIATION, 556
WISCONSIN SOCIETY FOR ORNITHOLOGY, INC., THE, 556
WOLF GROUP, THE, 557
WORLDWATCH INSTITUTE, 560
WWW.ACTIONBIOSCIENCE.ORG, 560
WYOMING STATE BOARD OF LAND COMMISSIONERS, 239

AIR QUALITY/ATMOSPHERE

ACADEMY FOR EDUCATIONAL DEVELOPMENT, 241
ADIRONDACK COUNCIL, THE, 242
ADIRONDACK MOUNTAIN CLUB, INC., THE (ADK), 242
AFRICAN AMERICAN ENVIRONMENTALIST ASSOCIATION, 243
AIR & WASTE MANAGEMENT ASSOCIATION, 244
ALABAMA DEPARTMENT OF AGRICULTURE AND INDUSTRIES, 132
ALABAMA DEPARTMENT OF CONSERVATION AND NATURAL RESOURCES, 132
ALABAMA ENVIRONMENTAL COUNCIL, 244
ALASKA CONSERVATION ALLIANCE, 245, 246
ALASKA COOPERATIVE FISH AND WILDLIFE RESEARCH UNIT, 133
ALASKA DEPARTMENT OF ENVIRONMENTAL CONSERVATION, 133
AMERICAN CONSERVATION ASSOCIATION, INC., 251
AMERICAN COUNCIL FOR THE UNITED NATIONS UNIVERSITY (ACUNU), 251
AMERICAN LUNG ASSOCIATION, 263
APPALACHIAN MOUNTAIN CLUB, 269
APPALACHIAN TRAIL CONFERENCE, 270
APROVECHO RESEARCH CENTER, 270
ARENA CONSULTORES AMBIENTALES, 563
ARIZONA COOPERATIVE FISH AND WILDLIFE RESEARCH UNIT (USDI), 135
ARIZONA STATE UNIVERSITY
  Center for Environmental Studies, 573
AUSTRIALIA DEPARTMENT FOR ENVIRONMENT AND HERITAGE
  Environment Shop, The, 139
BEAR SPRINGS BLOSSOM NATURE CONSERVATION GROUP INC., 277
BEYOND PESTICIDES, 277
BORDER ECOLOGY PROJECT (BEP), 279
BRADLEY UNIVERSITY, 575
BROWN UNIVERSITY, 575
CALIFORNIA COOPERATIVE FISHERY RESEARCH UNIT (USGS), 16
CALIFORNIA DEPARTMENT OF PESTICIDE REGULATION, 143
CALIFORNIANS FOR POPULATION STABILIZATION (CAPS), 284
CAMP FIRE USA, 285
CAMPAIGN FOR AMERICA'S WILDERNESS, 285
CANADIAN ARCTIC RESOURCE COMMITTEE, INC., 285
CENTER FOR ENVIRONMENT AND POPULATION (CEP), 290
CENTER FOR ENVIRONMENT, COMMERCE & ENERGY, 290
CENTER FOR ENVIRONMENTAL HEALTH (CEH), 291
CENTER FOR ENVIRONMENTAL INFORMATION, 291
CENTER FOR ENVIRONMENTAL STUDY, 291

CENTER FOR RESOURCE ECONOMICS/ISLAND PRESS, 293
CHESAPEAKE BAY FOUNDATION, INC.
  Maryland Office, 295
  Pennsylvania Office, 295
CIRCUMPOLAR CONSERVATION UNION, 297
CITY UNIVERSITY OF NEW YORK
  College of Staten Island, 576
CJE ASSOCIATES, 565
CLARK UNIVERSITY, 576
CLEMSON UNIVERSITY
  School of the Environment, 577
COALITION FOR CLEAN AIR, 299
COLORADO MOUNTAIN COLLEGE, 577
COMMUNITIES FOR A BETTER ENVIRONMENT, 303
CONNECTICUT BOTANICAL SOCIETY, 304
CONNECTICUT FUND FOR THE ENVIRONMENT, 305
CONNECTICUT PUBLIC INTEREST RESEARCH GROUP (CONN PIRG), 305
CONSERVAMERICA, 305
CONSERVATION COUNCIL OF NORTH CAROLINA, 306
CONSERVATION LAW FOUNDATION, INC. (CLF)
  New England Region, 308
COUNCIL FOR PLANNING AND CONSERVATION, 310
DELAWARE NATURE SOCIETY, 312
DELTA COLLEGE, 579
EAGLE NATURE FOUNDATION, LTD., 316
EARTH POLICY INSTITUTE, 317
EARTHJUSTICE
  Environmental Law Clinic at the University of Denver, 318
  Headquarters, 318
  International Program, 319
  Oakland Office, 319
  Washington, DC, Office, 320
EARTHSCAN, 320
ECOLOGICAL SOCIETY OF AMERICA, THE, 321
ENVIRONMENT COUNCIL OF RHODE ISLAND, 323
ENVIRONMENTAL DEFENSE
  Headquarters, 324
ENVIRONMENTAL DEFENSE CENTER, 325
ENVIRONMENTAL EDUCATORS OF NORTH CAROLINA (EENC), 326
ENVIRONMENTAL LAW INSTITUTE, THE, 327
ENVIRONMENTAL LEAGUE OF MASSACHUSETTS, 327
ENVIRONMENTAL POLICY CENTER, THE, 327
ENVIRONMENTAL PROTECTION AGENCY
  Region 1 (CT, ME, MA, NH, RI, VT), 18
  Region 5 (IL, IN, MI, NM, OH, WI), 19
FEDERATION OF ENVIRONMENTAL EDUCATION IN ST. PETERSBURG, 329
FLAGSTAFF DARK SKIES COALITION (FDSC), 330
FLORIDA DEPARTMENT OF ENVIRONMENTAL PROTECTION
  Bureau of Beaches and Wetland Resources, 153
  Coastal and Aquatic Managed Areas, 153
FLORIDA FEDERATION OF GARDEN CLUBS, INC., 331
FOOD SUPPLY / HUMAN POPULATION EXPLOSION CONNECTION, 333
FOREST SOCIETY OF MAINE, 335
FRIENDS OF ACADIA, 336
FRIENDS OF THE BOUNDARY WATERS WILDERNESS, 337
FRIENDS OF THE EARTH, 337
GEORGIA CONSERVANCY, INC., THE, 341
GEORGIA DEPARTMENT OF NATURAL RESOURCES
  Environmental Protection Division
    Coastal Division, 156
GEORGIANS FOR CLEAN ENERGY, 342
GRAND CANYON TRUST, 344
GREEN SEAL, 347
GREEN SPHERE INC., 347
HELPING OUR PENINSULA'S ENVIRONMENT, 350
HOOSIER ENVIRONMENTAL COUNCIL, 352
HOUSE COMMITTEE ON RULES, 22
HUMAN ECOLOGY ACTION LEAGUE, INC., THE (HEAL), 352
HUNTSMAN MARINE SCIENCE CENTRE, 353
IDAHO DEPARTMENT OF WATER RESOURCES, 161
ILLINOIS DEPARTMENT OF NATURAL RESOURCES, 162
ILLINOIS ENVIRONMENTAL COUNCIL, 355
INFORM, INC., 357
INSTITUTE FOR ECOLOGICAL STUDIES UNIVERSITY OF NORTH DAKOTA, 164
INSTITUTO NACIONAL DE BIODIVERSIDAD (INBIO), 22
INTERNATIONAL ASSOCIATION OF FISH AND WILDLIFE AGENCIES, 360
INTERNATIONAL ASSOCIATION OF NATURAL RESOURCE PILOTS, 360
INTERNATIONAL EROSION CONTROL ASSOCIATION (IECA), 363
INTERNATIONAL JOINT COMMISSION
  Great Lakes Regional Office, 22

KEYWORD INDEX – A

INTERNATIONAL UNION FOR CONSERVATION OF NATURE AND NATURAL RESOURCES (IUCN) THE WORLD CONSERVATION UNION
  Environmental Law Centre, 368
IOWA DEPARTMENT OF NATURAL RESOURCES
  Fish and Wildlife Division, 166
IOWA PRAIRIE NETWORK, 373
IOWA STATE UNIVERSITY
  College of Agriculture, 584
IZAAK WALTON LEAGUE OF AMERICA ENDOWMENT, 375
IZAAK WALTON LEAGUE OF AMERICA, INC., THE, 375
  Alaska Division, 376
  Minnesota Division, 377
JOHNSON STATE COLLEGE, 585
KANSAS WATER OFFICE, 169
KENTUCKY DEPARTMENT OF AGRICULTURE, 169
KIDS FOR SAVING EARTH WORLDWIDE, 384
LAKEHEAD UNIVERSITY, 586
LEAGUE OF OHIO SPORTSMEN, 387
LEAGUE OF WOMEN VOTERS OF WASHINGTON, 388
LEGAL ENVIRONMENTAL ASSISTANCE FOUNDATION INC. (LEAF), 388
LITERACY FOR ENVIRONMENTAL JUSTICE, 389
LOUISIANA DEPARTMENT OF NATURAL RESOURCES, 172
LUMMI ISLAND HERITAGE TRUST, 568
MAINE DEPARTMENT OF CONSERVATION
  Land Use Regulation Commission, 175
MARYLAND DEPARTMENT OF NATURAL RESOURCES, 177
MASSACHUSETTS BASS FEDERATION, 396
MIAMI UNIVERSITY, 587
MICHIGAN FORESTS ASSOCIATION, 397
MICHIGAN TECHNOLOGICAL UNIVERSITY, SCHOOL OF FORESTRY AND WOOD PRODUCTS, 588
MIDDLE TENNESSEE STATE UNIVERSITY, 588
MINNESOTA FORESTRY ASSOCIATION, 399
MONTANA FOREST OWNERS ASSOCIATION, 403
MONTANA LAND RELIANCE, 403
MONTANA WILDLIFE FEDERATION, 404
MOUNT GRACE LAND CONSERVATION TRUST, 405
NATIONAL ASSOCIATION OF ENVIRONMENTAL PROFESSIONALS, THE, 408
NATIONAL ASSOCIATION OF SERVICE AND CONSERVATION CORPS (NASCC), 408
NATIONAL AUDUBON SOCIETY
  Audubon Society of Rhode Island, 412
  Connecticut Audubon Society, 412
  Louisiana Audubon Council, 414
  Michigan Audubon Society, 414
NATIONAL CAUCUS OF ENVIRONMENTAL LEGISLATORS (NCEL), 417
NATIONAL ENVIRONMENTAL HEALTH ASSOCIATION, 418
NATIONAL GRANGE, THE, 421
NATIONAL PARKS CONSERVATION ASSOCIATION (NPCA), 422
  Sun Coast Regional Office, 423
NATIONAL WATERWAYS CONFERENCE INC., 426
NATIONAL WILDLIFE FEDERATION
  Great Lakes Natural Resource Center, 427
NATURE CONSERVANCY, THE
  New York City Office, 437
NEBRASKA DEPARTMENT OF NATURAL RESOURCES, 188
NEGATIVE POPULATION GROWTH (NPG), 442
NEW HAMPSHIRE COUNCIL ON RESOURCES AND DEVELOPMENT, 190
NEW JERSEY FORESTRY ASSOCIATION, 445
NEW YORK STATE DEPARTMENT OF AGRICULTURE AND MARKETS, 197
NORTH AMERICAN DEVELOPMENT BANK, 24
NORTH AMERICAN WETLANDS CONSERVATION COUNCIL, 24
NORTH ATLANTIC SALMON CONSERVATION ORGANIZATION, 449
NORTH CAROLINA BASS FEDERATION, 450
NORTH CAROLINA COASTAL FEDERATION, INC., 450
NORTH CAROLINA CONSERVATION NETWORK, 450
NORTH CAROLINA COOPERATIVE FISH AND WILDLIFE RESEARCH UNIT (USDI), 200
NORTH CAROLINA STATE UNIVERSITY, 590
NORTH CAROLINA WILD FLOWER PRESERVATION SOCIETY, 451
NORTHERN PLAINS RESOURCE COUNCIL, 453
NORTHLAND COLLEGE, 591
NORTHWEST COALITION FOR ALTERNATIVES TO PESTICIDES, 453
NORTHWEST ENVIRONMENT WATCH, 454
NOVA SCOTIA DEPARTMENT OF NATURAL RESOURCES, 203
OHIO DEPARTMENT OF NATURAL RESOURCES, 204
OHIO FORESTRY ASSOCIATION, INC., 457
OKLAHOMA COOPERATIVE FISH AND WILDLIFE RESEARCH UNIT (USDI), 206
ONTARIO FEDERATION OF ANGLERS AND HUNTERS, 459

OREGON DEPARTMENT OF TRANSPORTATION, 209
OREGON ENVIRONMENTAL COUNCIL, 460
OREGON NATURAL RESOURCES COUNCIL, 460
OZONE ACTION, 463
PACIFIC INSTITUTE FOR STUDIES IN DEVELOPMENT, ENVIRONMENT, AND SECURITY, 463
PENNSYLVANIA ASSOCIATION OF CONSERVATION DISTRICTS, INC., 465
PENNSYLVANIA DEPARTMENT OF AGRICULTURE
  Region VII, 211
PEOPLE FOR PUGET SOUND
  South Sound Office, 467
PHEASANTS FOREVER, INC., 468
PIEDMONT ENVIRONMENTAL COUNCIL, 469
PINE BLUFF COOPERATIVE FISHERY RESEARCH PROJECT, 213
POCONO ENVIRONMENTAL EDUCATION CENTER, 470
POLLUTION PROBE, 470
POPULATION-ENVIRONMENT BALANCE, INC., 471
PROTECTED AREAS ASSOCIATION OF NEWFOUNDLAND AND LABRADOR, 474
PS ENTERPRISES, 570
PUBLIC EMPLOYEES FOR ENVIRONMENTAL RESPONSIBILITY (PEER), 474
PUERTO RICO SOIL CONSERVATION COMMITTEE, 213
PURPLE MARTIN CONSERVATION ASSOCIATION, 475
RENEWABLE NATURAL RESOURCES FOUNDATION, 478
RESOURCES FOR THE FUTURE, 479
RUTGERS UNIVERSITY, COOK COLLEGE, 594
SAVE THE DUNES COUNCIL, 485
SEACOAST ANTI-POLLUTION LEAGUE, 489
SIERRA CLUB
  Alaska Field Office, 490
  Connecticut Chapter, 491
  Hawaii Chapter, 492
  Lone Star Chapter, 493
  Mackinac Chapter, 493
  Maryland Chapter, 493
  Mississippi Chapter, 494
  Nebraska Chapter, 494
  New Jersey Chapter, 495
  Northwest Office, 495
  Pennsylvania Chapter, 496
  Rio Grande Chapter (New Mexico/West Texas), 496
  San francisco Bay Chapter, 497
  Washington, DC Office, 499
  West Virginia Chapter, 499
SIERRA CLUB CALIFORNIA, 499
SIERRA CLUB FOUNDATION, THE, 499
SIERRA CLUB OF CANADA
  Atlantic Canada Chapter, 500
SINAPU, 500
SOCIETY FOR THE PROTECTION OF NEW HAMPSHIRE FORESTS, 503
SOUTH CAROLINA DEPARTMENT OF AGRICULTURE, 217
SOUTH DAKOTA ASSOCIATION OF CONSERVATION DISTRICTS, 506
SOUTH DAKOTA DEPARTMENT OF AGRICULTURE
  Division of Resource Conservation and Forestry, 218
SOUTH DAKOTA DEPARTMENT OF ENVIRONMENT AND NATURAL RESOURCES, 219
SOUTH DAKOTA ORNITHOLOGISTS UNION, 507
SOUTHERN ENVIRONMENTAL LAW CENTER, 509
SOUTHWEST CENTER FOR ENVIRONMENTAL RESEARCH AND POLICY (SCERP), 506
SOUTHWESTERN HERPETOLOGISTS SOCIETY, 510
STATE AND TERRITORIAL AIR POLLUTION PROGRAM ADMINISTRATORS AND THE ASSOCIATION OF LOCAL AIR POLLUTION CONTROL OFFICIALS, 512
STATE ENVIRONMENTAL RESOURCE CENTER (SERC), 512
STATE UNIVERSITY OF NEW YORK AT STONY BROOK, 597
SUSTAIN, 514
SUSTAINABLE ENERGY INSTITUTE
  Culture Change, 514
  Culture Change magazine, 514
  Food Not Lawns, 514
  Pedal Power Produce, 514
TAHOE REGIONAL PLANNING AGENCY, 220
TALLAHASSEE MUSEUM OF HISTORY AND NATURAL SCIENCE, 515
TENNESSEE DEPARTMENT OF ENVIRONMENT AND CONSERVATION, 221
TENNESSEE FORESTRY ASSOCIATION, 516
TENNESSEE VALLEY AUTHORITY
  Muscle Shoals Technical Library, 30
TEXAS CHRISTIAN UNIVERSITY, 599
TREES FOR THE FUTURE, INC., 519

KEYWORD INDEX – A

TULANE ENVIRONMENTAL LAW CLINIC, 600
TWO WHITE WOLVES SANCTUARY, 525
UNITED NATIONS ENVIRONMENT PROGRAMME, 525
UNITED STATES CHAMBER OF COMMERCE
   Environment, Technology and Regulatory Affairs, 526
UNITED STATES DEPARTMENT OF AGRICULTURE
   Economic Research Center, 33
   Forest Service
      Gila National Forest, 38
      Green Mountain National Forest, 38
      Region 02 (Rocky Mountain), 43
      Siuslaw National Forest, 45
UNITED STATES DEPARTMENT OF COMMERCE
   National Oceanic and Atmospheric Administration
      National Marine Fisheries Service, 52
      Sea Grant Program - California, 54
      Sea Grant Program - DelAware, 54
      Sea Grant Program - Maryland, 56
      Sea Grant Program - Massachusetts, 56
      Sea Grant Program - Michigan, 57
      Sea Grant Program - Ohio, 58
      Sea Grant Program - Rhode Island, 59
UNITED STATES DEPARTMENT OF DEFENSE
   Air Force Major U.S. Installations
      Luke AFB (and the Barry M. Goldwater AFR), AZ, 65
      Randolph AFB, TX, 66
   Army Materiel Command, 72
   Navy, 74
UNITED STATES DEPARTMENT OF EDUCATION, 75
UNITED STATES DEPARTMENT OF THE INTERIOR
   Bureau of Land Management
      Northern Field Office, 84
      Rawlins Field Office, 85
      Safford Field Office, 86
   Fish and Wildlife Service
      Arthur R. Marshall Loxahatchee/Hope Sound National Wildlife Refuge, 91
      Mattamuskeet National Wildlife Refuge, 104
      Selawik National Wildlife Refuge, 114
   Montana Cooperative Fishery Research Unit, 119
   National Park Service
      Chihuahuan Desert Network, 121
      Mammoth Cave National Park, 124
      Mesa Verde National Park, 124
      Mount Rainier National Park, 124
      Sonoran Desert Network, 125
      Theodore Roosevelt National Park, 125
      Yellowstone National Park, 126
   United States Geological Survey
      New Mexico Cooperative Fish and Wildlife Research Unit, 127
      Western Region, 127
UNITED STATES DEPARTMENT OF TRANSPORTATION
   FEDERAL AVIATION ADMINISTRATION, 128
UNITED STATES ENVIRONMENTAL PROTECTION AGENCY
   Administration and Resources Management, 129
UNITED STATES INSTITUTE FOR ENVIRONMENTAL CONFLICT RESOLUTION, 130
UNITED STATES PUBLIC INTEREST RESEARCH GROUP
   U.S. PIRG, 526
UNIVERSITE LAVAL, 601
UNIVERSITY OF CALIFORNIA AT SAN DIEGO, 607
UNIVERSITY OF CONNECTICUT COOPERATIVE EXTENSION, 608
UNIVERSITY OF FLORIDA
   School of Forest Resources and Conservation, 609
UNIVERSITY OF FLORIDA INSTITUTE OF FOOD AND AGRICULTURAL SCIENCES, 609
UNIVERSITY OF GEORGIA
   Daniel B. Warnell School of Forest Resources, 609
UNIVERSITY OF MAINE, 612
UNIVERSITY OF MARYLAND - AT COLLEGE PARK, 613
UNIVERSITY OF MICHIGAN, 614
UNIVERSITY OF MISSOURI, 615
UNIVERSITY OF NEW BRUNSWICK, 616
UNIVERSITY OF NORTH CAROLINA AT ASHEVILLE, 617
UNIVERSITY OF SASKATCHEWAN, 620
UNIVERSITY OF TENNESSEE - AT KNOXVILLE, 621
UNIVERSITY OF WISCONSIN, 622
UNIVERSITY OF WISCONSIN-MADISON, 623
UNIVERSITY OF WYOMING
   William D. Ruckelshaus Institute and the School of Environment and Natural Resources, 624
URBAN WASTE MANAGEMENT & RESEARCH CENTER, 624
VERMONT DEPARTMENT OF AGRICULTURE, FOOD, AND MARKETS, 227
VERMONT ENVIRONMENTAL BOARD, 227
VERMONT STATE-WIDE ENVIRONMENTAL EDUCATION PROGRAMS (SWEEP), 530
VINEYARD CONSERVATION SOCIETY, 530
VIRGINIA CONSERVATION NETWORK, 531
VIRGINIA FORESTRY ASSOCIATION, 531
VIRGINIA SOIL AND CONSERVATION BOARD, 232
WARREN COUNTY CONSERVATION BOARD, 532
WASHINGTON STATE PARKS AND RECREATION COMMISSION
   Southwest Region, 235
WEST VIRGINIA RAPTOR REHABILITATION CENTER, 536
WILDLIFE ACTION, INC., 542
WISCONSIN COOPERATIVE FISHERY RESEARCH UNIT USGS, 237
WORLD RESOURCES INSTITUTE, 559
WWW.ACTIONBIOSCIENCE.ORG, 560
WYOMING OUTDOOR COUNCIL, 561

CLIMATE CHANGE

AFRICAN AMERICAN ENVIRONMENTALIST ASSOCIATION, 243
AIR & WASTE MANAGEMENT ASSOCIATION, 244
ALASKA CONSERVATION FOUNDATION, 246
AMERICAN ASSOCIATION FOR THE ADVANCEMENT OF SCIENCE, 249
AMERICAN BIRD CONSERVANCY, 249
AMERICAN COUNCIL FOR THE UNITED NATIONS UNIVERSITY (ACUNU), 251
AMERICAN FORESTS, 260
AMERICAN GEOGRAPHICAL SOCIETY, 260
ANTARCTICA PROJECT, THE, 269
APROVECHO RESEARCH CENTER, 270
ARIZONA STATE UNIVERSITY
   Center for Environmental Studies, 573
ASSOCIATION OF AMERICAN GEOGRAPHERS, 273
ATLANTIC SALMON FEDERATION, 275
AUSTRIALIA DEPARTMENT FOR ENVIRONMENT AND HERITAGE
   Environment Shop, The, 139
BEAR SPRINGS BLOSSOM NATURE CONSERVATION GROUP INC., 277
BROWN UNIVERSITY, 575
BUN-CA, 281
CALIFORNIA DEPARTMENT OF PESTICIDE REGULATION, 143
CENTER FOR ENVIRONMENT AND POPULATION (CEP), 290
CENTER FOR ENVIRONMENT, COMMERCE & ENERGY, 290
CENTER FOR ENVIRONMENTAL INFORMATION, 291
CENTER FOR INTERNATIONAL ENVIRONMENTAL LAW (CIEL), 292
CENTER FOR RESOURCE ECONOMICS/ISLAND PRESS, 293
CETACEAN SOCIETY INTERNATIONAL, 294
CHIHUAHUAN DESERT RESEARCH INSTITUTE, 296
CIRCUMPOLAR CONSERVATION UNION, 297
CITY UNIVERSITY OF NEW YORK
   College of Staten Island, 576
CJE ASSOCIATES, 565
COLORADO MOUNTAIN COLLEGE, 577
CONNECTICUT BOTANICAL SOCIETY, 304
CONSERVAMERICA, 305
CONSERVATION LAW FOUNDATION, INC. (CLF), 307
COUNCIL FOR PLANNING AND CONSERVATION, 310
DUKE UNIVERSITY - ORGANIZATION FOR TROPICAL STUDIES, 580
EARTH DAY NEW YORK, 316
EARTH POLICY INSTITUTE, 317
EARTHSCAN, 320
ECOLOGICAL SOCIETY OF AMERICA, THE, 321
ECOSEA, 322
ENVIRONMENT COUNCIL OF RHODE ISLAND, 323
ENVIRONMENTAL AND ENERGY STUDY INSTITUTE (EESI), 323
ENVIRONMENTAL DEFENSE
   Headquarters, 324
ENVIRONMENTAL PROTECTION AGENCY
   Region 1 (CT, ME, MA, NH, RI, VT), 18
EUROPARC FEDERATION, 328
FERRUM COLLEGE, 581
FLORIDA DEFENDERS OF THE ENVIRONMENT, INC., 331
FOOD SUPPLY / HUMAN POPULATION EXPLOSION CONNECTION, 333
FRIENDS OF THE EARTH, 337
GOOD NATURE PUBLISHING CO., 566
GRAND CANYON TRUST, 344
GREEN SPHERE INC., 347
GREENPEACE, INC., 347
GROWLING, 348
HUNTSMAN MARINE SCIENCE CENTRE, 353
INSTITUTE FOR TROPICAL ECOLOGY AND CONSERVATION (ITEC), 358
INTERNATIONAL CHILDREN'S CONFERENCE ON THE ENVIRONMENT, 362
INTERNATIONAL INSTITUTE FOR ENERGY CONSERVATION, 364

KEYWORD INDEX – C

INTERNATIONAL JOINT COMMISSION
  Great Lakes Regional Office, 22
INTERNATIONAL MARITIME ORGANIZATION, 364
INTERNATIONAL MIRE CONSERVATION GROUP, 365
INTERNATIONAL SOCIETY FOR THE PRESERVATION OF THE TROPICAL RAINFOREST, THE, 367
INTERNATIONAL UNION FOR CONSERVATION OF NATURE AND NATURAL RESOURCES (IUCN) THE WORLD CONSERVATION UNION
  Canada Office, 368
  Environmental Law Centre, 368
IOWA STATE UNIVERSITY
  College of Agriculture, 584
ISLAND RESOURCES FOUNDATION, 375
J.N. (DING) DARLING FOUNDATION, 379
JAGRATA JUBA SHANGHA (JJS), 568
JOHNSON STATE COLLEGE, 585
LIFE OF THE LAND, 389
LUMMI ISLAND HERITAGE TRUST, 568
MIAMI UNIVERSITY, 587
MICHIGAN TECHNOLOGICAL UNIVERSITY; SCHOOL OF FORESTRY AND WOOD PRODUCTS, 588
MONTANA FOREST OWNERS ASSOCIATION, 403
MONTANA LAND RELIANCE, 403
MUNDO AZUL, 406
NATIONAL AGRICULTURAL LIBRARY, 24
NATIONAL ASSOCIATION OF SERVICE AND CONSERVATION CORPS (NASCC), 408
NATIONAL AUDUBON SOCIETY
  Audubon Alaska, 409
  Audubon of Florida, 410
  Louisiana Audubon Council, 414
NATIONAL CAUCUS OF ENVIRONMENTAL LEGISLATORS (NCEL), 417
NATIONAL CENTER FOR APPROPRIATE TECHNOLOGY, 417
NATIONAL WILDLIFE FEDERATION
  Headquarters, 427
NATIONAL WILDLIFE PRODUCTIONS, INC., 429
NATURE CONSERVANCY, THE
  New York City Office, 437
  Rhode Island Chapter, 439
NEBRASKA DEPARTMENT OF NATURAL RESOURCES, 188
NEW HAMPSHIRE COUNCIL ON RESOURCES AND DEVELOPMENT, 190
NEW JERSEY DEPARTMENT OF ENVIRONMENTAL PROTECTION
  Division of Solid and Hazardous Waste, 192
NEW YORK STATE TUG HILL COMMISSION, 199
NORTH AMERICAN WETLANDS CONSERVATION COUNCIL, 24
NORTH ATLANTIC SALMON CONSERVATION ORGANIZATION, 449
NORTHERN ARIZONA UNIVERSITY
  Department of Geography, Planning, and Recreation, 591
NORTHWEST ENVIRONMENT WATCH, 454
NOVA SCOTIA DEPARTMENT OF NATURAL RESOURCES, 203
OHIO DEPARTMENT OF NATURAL RESOURCES, 204
OHIO ENVIRONMENTAL REVIEW APPEALS COMMISSION, 205
OKLAHOMA STATE UNIVERSITY, 592
ONTARIO FEDERATION OF ANGLERS AND HUNTERS, 459
ONTARIO MINISTRY OF NATURAL RESOURCES
  South Central Region, 208
OREGON NATURAL RESOURCES COUNCIL, 460
OZONE ACTION, 463
PACIFIC INSTITUTE FOR STUDIES IN DEVELOPMENT, ENVIRONMENT, AND SECURITY, 463
PEOPLE FOR PUGET SOUND
  South Sound Office, 467
POLLUTION PROBE, 470
PROTECTED AREAS ASSOCIATION OF NEWFOUNDLAND AND LABRADOR, 474
PS ENTERPRISES, 570
PURPLE MARTIN CONSERVATION ASSOCIATION, 475
RAINFOREST RELIEF, 477
RENEWABLE NATURAL RESOURCES FOUNDATION, 478
RETURNED PEACE CORPS VOLUNTEERS FOR ENVIRONMENT AND DEVELOPMENT (RPCVS-ED), 480
ROCKY MOUNTAIN BIOLOGICAL LABORATORY, THE, 482
RUTGERS UNIVERSITY, COOK COLLEGE, 594
SIERRA CLUB
  Alaska Field Office, 490
  Lone Star Chapter, 493
  Mackinac Chapter, 493
  Mississippi Chapter, 494
  Nebraska Chapter, 494
  New Jersey Chapter, 495
  Northwest Office, 495
  Washington, DC Office, 499
  West Virginia Chapter, 499

SIERRA CLUB CALIFORNIA, 499
SIERRA CLUB OF CANADA
  Atlantic Canada Chapter, 500
SIERRA STUDENT COALITION, 500
SOIL AND WATER CONSERVATION SOCIETY, 504
SOUTH CAROLINA DEPARTMENT OF PARKS, RECREATION AND TOURISM, 218
SOUTH CAROLINA NATIVE PLANT SOCIETY, 506
SOUTH DAKOTA ASSOCIATION OF CONSERVATION DISTRICTS, 506
SOUTHWEST CENTER FOR ENVIRONMENTAL RESEARCH AND POLICY (SCERP), 596
SOUTHWESTERN HERPETOLOGISTS SOCIETY, 510
STATE AND TERRITORIAL AIR POLLUTION PROGRAM ADMINISTRATORS AND THE ASSOCIATION OF LOCAL AIR POLLUTION CONTROL OFFICIALS, 512
STEPHEN F. AUSTIN STATE UNIVERSITY ARTHUR TEMPLE COLLEGE OF FORESTRY, 598
STROUD WATER RESEARCH CENTER, 512
STUDENT ENVIRONMENTAL ACTION COALITION (SEAC), 513
SUSTAIN, 514
SUSTAINABLE ENERGY INSTITUTE
  Culture Change, 514
  Culture Change magazine, 514
  Food Not Lawns, 514
  Pedal Power Produce, 514
TREES FOR THE FUTURE, INC., 519
UNION OF CONCERNED SCIENTISTS, 525
UNITED STATES CHAMBER OF COMMERCE
  Environment, Technology and Regulatory Affairs, 526
UNITED STATES COMMITTEE FOR THE UNITED NATIONS ENVIRONMENT PROGRAMME, THE (U.S. AND UNEP), 526
UNITED STATES DEPARTMENT OF AGRICULTURE
  Economic Research Center, 33
  Forest Service
    Region 02 (Rocky Mountain), 43
    Region 09 (Eastern), 43
UNITED STATES DEPARTMENT OF COMMERCE
  National Oceanic and Atmospheric Administration
    National Marine Fisheries Service, 52
    Sea Grant Program - Massachusetts, 56
    Wells National Estuarine Research Reserve, 60
UNITED STATES DEPARTMENT OF DEFENSE
  Army Corps of Engineers
    Walla Walla Engineer District, 72
  Navy, 74
UNITED STATES DEPARTMENT OF EDUCATION, 75
UNITED STATES DEPARTMENT OF THE INTERIOR
  Fish and Wildlife Service
    Pocosin Lakes National Wildlife Refuge, 110
  National Park Service
    Chihuahuan Desert Network, 121
  United States Geological Survey
    New Mexico Cooperative Fish and Wildlife Research Unit, 127
    Western Region, 127
UNITED STATES DEPARTMENT OF TRANSPORTATION
  Federal Aviation Administration, 128
UNITED STATES ENVIRONMENTAL PROTECTION AGENCY
  Administration and Resources Management, 129
UNITED STATES PUBLIC INTEREST RESEARCH GROUP, 526
UNIVERSITE LAVAL, 601
UNIVERSITY OF CALIFORNIA AT SAN DIEGO, 607
UNIVERSITY OF CONNECTICUT COOPERATIVE EXTENSION, 608
UNIVERSITY OF FLORIDA
  School of Forest Resources and Conservation, 609
UNIVERSITY OF FLORIDA INSTITUTE OF FOOD AND AGRICULTURAL SCIENCES, 609
UNIVERSITY OF GEORGIA
  Daniel B. Warnell School of Forest Resources, 609
UNIVERSITY OF MICHIGAN, 614
UNIVERSITY OF MINNESOTA AT ST. PAUL, 615
UNIVERSITY OF MISSOURI, 615
UNIVERSITY OF NEW BRUNSWICK, 616
UNIVERSITY OF NORTH CAROLINA AT ASHEVILLE, 617
UNIVERSITY OF NORTH DAKOTA, 618
UNIVERSITY OF NORTHERN BRITISH COLUMBIA, 618
UNIVERSITY OF RHODE ISLAND
  Department of Natural Resources Science, 619
UNIVERSITY OF SASKATCHEWAN, 620
UNIVERSITY OF WISCONSIN-MADISON, 623
UTAH STATE UNIVERSITY
  College of Natural Resources, 624
VERMONT STATE-WIDE ENVIRONMENTAL EDUCATION PROGRAMS (SWEEP), 530

VINEYARD CONSERVATION SOCIETY, 530
WARREN COUNTY CONSERVATION BOARD, 532
WISCONSIN COOPERATIVE FISHERY RESEARCH UNIT USGS, 237
WORLD RESOURCES INSTITUTE, 559
WORLDWATCH INSTITUTE, 560
WWW.ACTIONBIOSCIENCE.ORG, 560

DEVELOPMENT/DEVELOPING COUNTRIES

ADIRONDACK COUNCIL, THE, 242
AFRICA VISION TRUST, 243
AFRICAN AMERICAN ENVIRONMENTALIST ASSOCIATION, 243
AFRICAN CONSERVATION FOUNDATION, THE, 243
AFRICAN WILDLIFE FOUNDATION, 243
ALASKA CONSERVATION ALLIANCE, 245, 246
ALASKA DEPARTMENT OF FISH AND GAME, 134
ALASKA NATURAL HISTORY ASSOCIATION, 246
ALDEANATURAL.COM, 563
ALLIANCE FOR THE CHESAPEAKE BAY, 247
AMANAKAA AMAZON NETWORK, 248
AMERICAN BIRD CONSERVANCY, 249
AMERICAN COUNCIL FOR THE UNITED NATIONS UNIVERSITY (ACUNU), 251
AMERICAN GEOGRAPHICAL SOCIETY, 260
AMERICAN LIVESTOCK BREEDS CONSERVANCY, 263
AMERICAN PLANNING ASSOCIATION, 264
AMERICAN SPORTFISHING ASSOCIATION, 266
APROVECHO RESEARCH CENTER, 270
ARIZONA GEOLOGICAL SURVEY, 136
ARIZONA-SONORA DESERT MUSEUM, 271
ARKANSAS TECH UNIVERSITY
  Department of Parks, Recreation, and Hospitality Administration, 573
ASSOCIATION FOR THE PROTECTION OF THE ADIRONDACKS, THE, 273
ASSOCIATION OF AMERICAN GEOGRAPHERS, 273
ASSOCIATION OF NEW JERSEY ENVIRONMENTAL COMMISSIONS (ANJEC), 274
ATLANTIC CENTER FOR THE ENVIRONMENT
  Quebec-Labrador Foundation, 275
ATLANTIC STATES LEGAL FOUNDATION, 275
AUDUBON INTERNATIONAL, 276
AUDUBON NATURALIST SOCIETY OF THE CENTRAL ATLANTIC STATES, 276
AUSTRALIA DEPARTMENT FOR ENVIRONMENT AND HERITAGE, 139
BOONE AND CROCKETT FOUNDATION, 279
BUILDINGGREEN, INC., 564
BUN-CA, 281
CARIBBEAN NATURAL RESOURCES INSTITUTE, 288
CARRYING CAPACITY NETWORK, 288
CATSKILL CENTER FOR CONSERVATION AND DEVELOPMENT, INC., THE, 289
CATSKILL FOREST ASSOCIATION, 289
CENTER FOR A SUSTAINABLE COAST, 289
CENTER FOR ENVIRONMENT AND POPULATION (CEP), 290
CENTER FOR ENVIRONMENT, COMMERCE & ENERGY, 290
CENTER FOR RESOURCE ECONOMICS/ISLAND PRESS, 293
CENTER FOR WATERSHED PROTECTION, 293
CETACEAN SOCIETY INTERNATIONAL, 294
CIRCUMPOLAR CONSERVATION UNION, 297
CJE ASSOCIATES, 565
CLARK UNIVERSITY, 576
CLIMATE INSTITUTE, 299
COAST ALLIANCE, 300
COASTAL RESOURCE MANAGEMENT PROJECT, 146
COASTAL SOCIETY, THE, 301
COLORADO DEPARTMENT OF AGRICULTURE, 146
COLORADO MOUNTAIN COLLEGE, 577
COMMUNITY CONSERVATION /HOWLERS FOREVER, INC., 303
COMMUNITY ENVIRONMENTAL COUNCIL (CEC), 303
CONCERN, INC., 304
CONNECTICUT BOTANICAL SOCIETY, 304
CONSERVATION FEDERATION OF MARYLAND/ F.A.R.M., 306
CONSERVATION TREATY SUPPORT FUND, 308
COTTONWOOD FOUNDATION, 309
CRANSTON CONSERVATION COMMISSION, 150
DELAWARE GREENWAYS, INC., 312
DELAWARE NATURE SOCIETY, 312
DESERT FISHES COUNCIL, 314
DESERT RESEARCH FOUNDATION OF NAMIBIA, THE, 314
DUKE UNIVERSITY - ORGANIZATION FOR TROPICAL STUDIES, 580
EAGLE NATURE FOUNDATION, LTD., 316
EARTH ISLAND INSTITUTE, 317
EARTH POLICY INSTITUTE, 317
EARTHJUSTICE
  Headquarters, 318
  International Program, 319
EARTHSCAN, 320
ECONOVA INC., 565
ECOSEA, 322
ENVIRONMENTAL DEFENSE
  Headquarters, 324
ENVIRONMENTAL ENTERPRISES ASSISTANCE FUND, INC., 326
ENVIRONMENTAL LAW INSTITUTE, THE, 327
ENVIRONMENTAL LEAGUE OF MASSACHUSETTS, 327
ENVIRONMENTAL POLICY CENTER, THE, 327
EUROPARC FEDERATION, 328
FEDERATION OF ENVIRONMENTAL EDUCATION IN ST. PETERSBURG, 329
FOOD SUPPLY / HUMAN POPULATION EXPLOSION CONNECTION, 333
FOREST MANAGEMENT TRUST, 334
FOREST TRUST, 335
FRIENDS OF ANIMALS INC., 337
FUTURE GENERATIONS, 339
GEORGIA DEPARTMENT OF EDUCATION, 156
GEORGIA ENVIRONMENTAL ORGANIZATION, INC. (GEO), 341
GEORGIA FORESTRY COMMISSION, 157
GEORGIANS FOR CLEAN ENERGY, 342
GLOBAL ENVIRONMENTAL MANAGEMENT INITIATIVE (GEMI), 343
GREEN BALKANS FEDERATION OF NATURE CONSERVATION NGOS, 346
GREEN SEAL, 347
GREEN SPHERE INC., 347
HELPING OUR PENINSULA'S ENVIRONMENT, 350
HILTON POND CENTER FOR PIEDMONT NATURAL HISTORY, 351
HUMANE SOCIETY OF THE UNITED STATES, THE, 352
ILLINOIS WALNUT COUNCIL, 356
ILOVEPARKS.COM, 567
INDO-PACIFIC CONSERVATION ALLIANCE, 357
INSTITUTE FOR TROPICAL ECOLOGY AND CONSERVATION (ITEC), 358
INTERFAITH COUNCIL FOR THE PROTECTION OF ANIMALS AND NATURE INC. (ICPAN), 359
INTERNATIONAL ACADEMY, 567
INTERNATIONAL ASSOCIATION FOR ENVIRONMENTAL HYDROLOGY (IAEH), 359
INTERNATIONAL BICYCLE FUND, 361
INTERNATIONAL BOUNDARY AND WATER COMMISSION, UNITED STATES AND MEXICO, 22
INTERNATIONAL CENTRE FOR CONSERVATION EDUCATION, 361
INTERNATIONAL CHILDREN'S CONFERENCE ON THE ENVIRONMENT, 362
INTERNATIONAL ECOTOURISM SOCIETY, THE, 362
INTERNATIONAL EROSION CONTROL ASSOCIATION (IECA), 363
INTERNATIONAL INSTITUTE FOR ENERGY CONSERVATION, 364
INTERNATIONAL MARITIME ORGANIZATION, 364
INTERNATIONAL MIRE CONSERVATION GROUP, 365
INTERNATIONAL RIVERS NETWORK (IRN), 366
INTERNATIONAL SOCIETY FOR ECOLOGICAL ECONOMICS (ISEE), 366
INTERNATIONAL SOCIETY FOR ENDANGERED CATS, 366
INTERNATIONAL SONORAN DESERT ALLIANCE, 367
INTERNATIONAL UNION FOR CONSERVATION OF NATURE AND NATURAL RESOURCES (IUCN) THE WORLD CONSERVATION UNION
  Canada Office, 368
  Environmental Law Centre, 368
  Headquarters, 367
INTERTRIBAL BISON COOPERATIVE (ITBC), 372
IOWA ASSOCIATION OF NATURALISTS, 372
ISLAND INSTITUTE, THE, 374
ISLAND RESOURCES FOUNDATION, 375
IZAAK WALTON LEAGUE OF AMERICA, INC., THE
  Minnesota Division, 377
KANSAS FOREST SERVICE, 168
LAKEHEAD UNIVERSITY, 586
LAKENET, 385
LEAGUE OF ENVIRONMENTAL JOURNALISTS, 387
LEGACY INTERNATIONAL, 388
LOUISIANA DEPARTMENT OF AGRICULTURE AND FORESTRY, 172
MCGILL UNIVERSITY, 587
MICHIGAN DEPARTMENT OF NATURAL RESOURCES, 180
MICHIGAN TECHNOLOGICAL UNIVERSITY; SCHOOL OF FORESTRY AND WOOD PRODUCTS, 588
MINNESOTA ENVIRONMENTAL QUALITY BOARD, 182
MINNESOTA POLLUTION CONTROL AGENCY
  Rochester, MN, 183
MONTANA LAND RELIANCE, 403
MUNDO AZUL, 406

KEYWORD INDEX – E

NATIONAL 4-H COUNCIL, 406
NATIONAL AGRICULTURAL LIBRARY, 24
NATIONAL ASSOCIATION OF SERVICE AND CONSERVATION CORPS (NASCC), 408
NATIONAL AUDUBON SOCIETY
  Audubon Society of Portland, 411
  Fairfax Audubon Society, 413
  New Jersey Chapter, 415
NATIONAL COUNCIL FOR SCIENCE AND THE ENVIRONMENT, THE, 418
NATIONAL PARKS CONSERVATION ASSOCIATION (NPCA)
  Sun Coast Regional Office, 423
NATIONAL TRAPPERS ASSOCIATION, INC., 425
NATIONAL WATERSHED COALITION, 426
NATIONAL WILDLIFE FEDERATION
  Headquarters, 427
NATURE CONSERVANCY, THE
  Iowa Chapter, 435
  New York City Office, 437
  Oregon Chapter, 439
  Pennsylvania Chapter, 439
  Rhode Island Chapter, 439
  Texas Chapter, 439
NEVIS HISTORICAL AND CONSERVATION SOCIETY, 442
NEW HAMPSHIRE DEPARTMENT OF AGRICULTURE, MARKETS, AND FOOD
  State Conservation Committee, 190
NEW JERSEY ASSOCIATION OF CONSERVATION DISTRICTS, 445
NEW JERSEY DEPARTMENT OF ENVIRONMENTAL PROTECTION, 191
NEW JERSEY ENVIRONMENTAL LOBBY, 445
NEW JERSEY FORESTRY ASSOCIATION, 445
NEWFOUNDLAND DEPARTMENT OF FOREST RESOURCES AND AGRIFOODS
  Regional Offices, 199
NOLTE ASSOCIATES, INC., 569
NORTH AMERICAN DEVELOPMENT BANK, 24
OCEAN VOICE INTERNATIONAL, 455
OHIO DEPARTMENT OF NATURAL RESOURCES, 204
OHIO FORESTRY ASSOCIATION, INC., 457
ORANGUTAN FOUNDATION INTERNATIONAL, 460
ORGANIZATION FOR BAT CONSERVATION, 461
OZARKS RESOURCE CENTER, 463
PACIFIC INSTITUTE FOR STUDIES IN DEVELOPMENT, ENVIRONMENT, AND SECURITY, 463
PANOS INSTITUTE, THE, 464
PENNSYLVANIA FORESTRY ASSOCIATION, THE, 466
POPULATION ACTION INTERNATIONAL, 470
POPULATION CONNECTION, 471
POPULATION INSTITUTE, THE, 471
POPULATION REFERENCE BUREAU, INC., 471
PRIORITIES INSTITUTE, THE, 473
PROJECT SEAHORSE, 473
RAINBOW PUSH COALITION, 476
RAINFOREST ALLIANCE, 477
RESIDENTS FOR A MORE BEAUTIFUL PORT WASHINGTON, 479
RESOURCE RENEWAL INSTITUTE, THE, 479
RESOURCES FOR THE FUTURE, 470
RETURNED PEACE CORPS VOLUNTEERS FOR ENVIRONMENT AND DEVELOPMENT (RPCVS-ED), 480
SAVE AMERICA'S FORESTS, 485
SIERRA CLUB
  Alaska Chapter, 490
  Alaska Field Office, 490
  Connecticut Chapter, 491
SOCIETY FOR CONSERVATION BIOLOGY, 502
SOUTH CAROLINA COOPERATIVE FISH AND WILDLIFE RESEARCH UNIT, 217
SOUTHERN UTAH WILDERNESS ALLIANCE
  Moab Office, 510
SOUTHFACE ENERGY INSTITUTE, 510
SOUTHWEST CENTER FOR ENVIRONMENTAL RESEARCH AND POLICY (SCERP), 596
SOUTHWEST CONSERVATION DISTRICT, 510
STUDENTS PARTNERSHIP WORLDWIDE, 513
SUSTAINABLE ENERGY INSTITUTE
  Culture Change, 514
  Food Not Lawns, 514
  Pedal Power Produce, 514
TENNESSEE FORESTRY ASSOCIATION, 516
TERRA PENINSULAR, 516
TEXAS COOPERATIVE FISH AND WILDLIFE RESEARCH UNIT, 30
TEXAS WILDLIFE ASSOCIATION, 517
TOGETHER FOUNDATION, THE, 518

TREES FOR THE FUTURE, INC., 519
UNEP WORLD CONSERVATION MONITORING CENTRE, 525
UNION OF CONCERNED SCIENTISTS, 525
UNITED STATES DEPARTMENT OF AGRICULTURE
  Forest Service
    Green Mountain National Forest, 38
    Region 09 (Eastern), 43
UNITED STATES DEPARTMENT OF COMMERCE
  National Oceanic and Atmospheric Administration
    Sea Grant Program - Massachusetts, 56
UNITED STATES DEPARTMENT OF DEFENSE
  Army Corps of Engineers
    North Atlantic Engineer District, 70
  Assistant Chief of Staff for Installation Management, Office of the Director of Environmental Programs, and Conservation Team, 74
UNITED STATES DEPARTMENT OF THE INTERIOR
  Bureau of Land Management
    Eugene District Office, 81
  National Park Service
    Chihuahuan Desert Network, 121
UNITED STATES ENVIRONMENTAL PROTECTION AGENCY
  Administration and Resources Management, 129
UNIVERSITE LAVAL, 601
UNIVERSITY OF ARIZONA
  School of Renewable Natural Resources, 605
UNIVERSITY OF CONNECTICUT COOPERATIVE EXTENSION, 608
UNIVERSITY OF DAR ES SALAAM, 608
UNIVERSITY OF FLORIDA
  School of Forest Resources and Conservation, 609
UNIVERSITY OF MARYLAND - AT COLLEGE PARK, 613
UNIVERSITY OF MICHIGAN, 614
UNIVERSITY OF MINNESOTA AT ST. PAUL, 615
UNIVERSITY OF NEW HAVEN DEPT. OF BIOLOGY AND ENVIRONMENTAL SCIENCES, 617
UNIVERSITY OF NORTH CAROLINA AT ASHEVILLE, 617
UNIVERSITY OF SASKATCHEWAN, 620
UNIVERSITY OF WISCONSIN-MADISON, 623
URBAN WASTE MANAGEMENT & RESEARCH CENTER, 624
UTAH STATE DEPARTMENT OF NATURAL RESOURCES
  Division of Water Resources, 226
VIRGINIA RESOURCE-USE EDUCATION COUNCIL, 532
VIRGINIA TECH
  Department of Fisheries and Wildlife Sciences, 625
VIRGINIA TECH UNIVERSITY
  College of Natural Resources, 625
WABASH RIVER HERITAGE CORRIDOR COMMISSION, 232
WASHINGTON FARM FORESTRY ASSOCIATION, 533
WASHINGTON STATE OFFICE OF ENVIRONMENTAL EDUCATION, 234
WILD FOUNDATION, THE, 539
WILDLIFE ACTION, INC., 542
WILDLIFE DAMAGE REVIEW (WDR), 543
WILDLIFE HABITAT COUNCIL, 544
WORLD ASSOCIATION OF GIRL GUIDES AND GIRL SCOUTS (WAGGGS), 558
WORLD RESOURCES INSTITUTE, 559
WORLDWATCH INSTITUTE, 560
WWW.ACTIONBIOSCIENCE.ORG, 560
WYOMING STATE BOARD OF LAND COMMISSIONERS, 239

ECOSYSTEMS (PRECIOUS)

A CRITICAL DECISION, 241
AFRICAN AMERICAN ENVIRONMENTALIST ASSOCIATION, 243
AFRICAN CONSERVATION FOUNDATION, THE, 243
ALABAMA ENVIRONMENTAL COUNCIL, 244
ALABAMA WATERFOWL ASSOCIATION (AWA), 244
ALASKA CENTER FOR THE ENVIRONMENT, 245
ALASKA CONSERVATION ALLIANCE, 245, 246
ALASKA CONSERVATION FOUNDATION, 246
ALBERTA DEPARTMENT OF ENVIRONMENTAL PROTECTION
  Natural Resources Service, 135
ALDEANATURAL.COM, 563
AMERICAN ASSOCIATION OF FIELD BOTANISTS, 249
AMERICAN BIRD CONSERVANCY, 249
AMERICAN EAGLE FOUNDATION, 251
AMERICAN FISHERIES SOCIETY
  Minnesota Chapter, 256
AMERICAN RIVERS
  Nebraska Field Office, 265
AMERICAN RIVERS
  Voyage of Recovery, 265
ANACOSTIA WATERSHED SOCIETY, 268
ANTARCTICA PROJECT, THE, 269

KEYWORD INDEX – E

APPALACHIAN REGIONAL COMMISSION, 16
APPALACHIAN TRAIL CONFERENCE, 270
ARCTIC INSTITUTE OF NORTH AMERICA, 271
ARIZONA STATE ENVIROTHON, INC., 271
ARIZONA STATE UNIVERSITY
   Center for Environmental Studies, 573
ARIZONA-SONORA DESERT MUSEUM, 271
ARKANSAS GAME AND FISH COMMISSION, 137
ARKANSAS STATE PLANT BOARD, 138
ARKANSAS TECH UNIVERSITY
   Fisheries and Wildlife Biology Program, 573
ARKANSAS WATERSHED ADVISORY GROUP (AWAG), 272
ASSOCIATION OF AMERICAN GEOGRAPHERS, 273
ATLANTIC CENTER FOR THE ENVIRONMENT
   Quebec-Labrador Foundation, 275
ATLANTIC SALMON FEDERATION, 275
ATLANTIC STATES LEGAL FOUNDATION, 275
AUDUBON INTERNATIONAL, 276
AUSTRIALIA DEPARTMENT FOR ENVIRONMENT AND HERITAGE
   Environment Shop, The, 139
BAMA BACKPADDLERS ASSOCIATION, 276
BAT CONSERVATION INTERNATIONAL, 277
BEAR SPRINGS BLOSSOM NATURE CONSERVATION GROUP INC., 277
BIODIVERSITY CONSERVATION ALLIANCE, 278
BRADLEY UNIVERSITY, 575
BRITISH COLUMBIA MINISTRY OF WATER, LAND AND AIR PROTECTION, 140
BUILDINGGREEN, INC., 564
BYRON FOREST PRESERVE, 140
CALIFORNIA DEPARTMENT OF FISH AND GAME
   Elkhorn Slough National Estuarine Research Reserve, 141
   Office of Spill Prevention and Response, 141
CALIFORNIA ENERGY COMMISSION
   Environmental Department, 143
CALIFORNIA WILDERNESS COALITION, 284
CAMPAIGN FOR AMERICA'S WILDERNESS, 285
CANADA GOOSE PROJECT, 285
CANADIAN ARCTIC RESOURCE COMMITTEE, INC., 285
CARIBBEAN CONSERVATION CORPORATION, 288
CAVE RESEARCH FOUNDATION, 289
CENTER FOR ENVIRONMENT AND POPULATION (CEP), 290
CENTER FOR ENVIRONMENT, COMMERCE & ENERGY, 290
CENTER FOR NATIVE ECOSYSTEMS
   Front Range Office, 292
   West Slope Office, 292
CENTER FOR RESOURCE ECONOMICS/ISLAND PRESS, 293
CETACEAN SOCIETY INTERNATIONAL, 294
CHESAPEAKE WILDLIFE HERITAGE (CWH), 295
CHICAGO PARK DISTRICT, 296
CHICAGO REGION BIODIVERSITY COUNCIL, 296
CIRCUMPOLAR CONSERVATION UNION, 297
CITY UNIVERSITY OF NEW YORK
   College of Staten Island, 576
CJE ASSOCIATES, 565
CLEAR CREEK ENVIRONMENTAL FOUNDATION, 299
CLEMSON UNIVERSITY
   School of the Environment, 577
CLINTON RIVER WATERSHED COUNCIL (CRWC), 299
COASTAL AMERICA FOUNDATION, 300
COASTAL RESOURCE MANAGEMENT PROJECT, 146
COLORADO DEPARTMENT OF NATURAL RESOURCES
   Oil and Gas Conservation Commission, 147
COLORADO MOUNTAIN COLLEGE, 577
COMMUNITY CONSERVATION /HOWLERS FOREVER, INC., 303
CONNECTICUT BOTANICAL SOCIETY, 304
CONNECTICUT RIVER WATERSHED COUNCIL INC., 305
CONSERVATION ALLIANCE OF ST. LUCIE CO., 306
CONSERVATION LAW FOUNDATION, INC. (CLF), 307
CONSERVATION TREATY SUPPORT FUND, 308
COOK INLET KEEPER, 308
COTTONWOOD FOUNDATION, 309
COUNTY OF SAN DIEGO, 149
CRITICAL ECOSYSTEM PARTNERSHIP FUND, 311
DELAWARE MUSEUM OF NATURAL HISTORY, 312
DELAWARE NATURE SOCIETY, 312
DELAWARE RIVERKEEPER NETWORK, 313
DELTA WILDLIFE INC., 313
DEPARTAMENTO DE RECURSOS NATURALES Y AMBIENTALES, 151
DEPAUL UNIVERSITY
   Environmental Science Program, 579
DESCHUTES BASIN LAND TRUST, 313
DESERT FISHES COUNCIL, 314
DESERT TORTOISE PRESERVE COMMITTEE, INC., 314

DISTRICT OF COLUMBIA DEPARTMENT OF HEALTH
   Environmental Health Administration, Watershed Protection Division, 152
DUCKS UNLIMITED CANADA
   Saskatchewan Office, 315
DUKE UNIVERSITY - ORGANIZATION FOR TROPICAL STUDIES, 580
EAGLE NATURE FOUNDATION, LTD., 316
EARTH FRIENDS WILDLIFE FOUNDATION, 317
EARTH POLICY INSTITUTE, 317
EARTHJUSTICE
   Denver Office, 318
   Environmental Law Clinic at the University of Denver, 318
   Headquarters, 318
   Seattle Office, 320
ECOLOGICAL SOCIETY OF AMERICA, THE, 321
ECOSEA, 322
ENVIRONMENT AND ENERGY PUBLISHING, LLC, 566
ENVIRONMENT COUNCIL OF RHODE ISLAND, 323
ENVIRONMENTAL ALLIANCE FOR SENIOR INVOLVEMENT (EASI), 323
ENVIRONMENTAL DEFENSE
   Headquarters, 324
ENVIRONMENTAL DEFENSE CENTER, 325
ENVIRONMENTAL LAW INSTITUTE, THE, 327
ENVIRONMENTAL PROTECTION AGENCY
   Region 1 (CT, ME, MA, NH, RI, VT), 18
   Region 5 (IL, IN, MI, NM, OH, WI), 19
EUROPARC FEDERATION, 328
EVERGLADES COORDINATING COUNCIL (ECC), 329
FERRUM COLLEGE, 581
FLORIDA COOPERATIVE EXTENSION SERVICE, 582
FLORIDA DEPARTMENT OF ENVIRONMENTAL PROTECTION
   Coastal and Aquatic Managed Areas, 153
   Division of Resource Assessment and Management, 154
   Florida State Parks AmeriCorps, 154
FLORIDA FEDERATION OF GARDEN CLUBS, INC., 331
FLORIDA FISH AND WILDLIFE CONSERVATION COMMISSION, 154
FLORIDA NATIVE PLANT SOCIETY, 332
FLORIDA NATURAL AREAS INVENTORY, 332
FOOD SUPPLY / HUMAN POPULATION EXPLOSION CONNECTION, 333
FOREST MANAGEMENT TRUST, 334
FOREST SERVICE EMPLOYEES FOR ENVIRONMENTAL ETHICS (FSEEE), 334
FOUR CORNERS INSTITUTE, THE, 336
FRIENDS OF SUNKHAZE MEADOWS NATIONAL WILDLIFE REFUGE, 337
FRIENDS OF THE CARR REFUGE, 337
FRIENDS OF THE SEA OTTER, 338
FUTURE GENERATIONS, 339
GAME CONSERVANCY U.S.A., 339
GEORGE MIKSCH SUTTON AVIAN RESEARCH CENTER INC., 340
GEORGIA ENVIRONMENTAL POLICY INSTITUTE, 342
GEORGIA TRUST FOR HISTORIC PRESERVATION, 342
GLEN CANYON INSTITUTE, 343
GOOD NATURE PUBLISHING CO., 566
GRAND CANYON TRUST, 344
GRANT TECH CONSULTING AND CONSERVATION SERVICES, 567
GREATER YELLOWSTONE COALITION, 346
GREEN BALKANS FEDERATION OF NATURE CONSERVATION NGOS, 346
GREEN GUIDES, 346
GREEN MOUNTAIN CLUB INC., THE, 346
GREEN SPHERE INC., 347
GROWLING, 348
GULF STATES MARINE FISHERIES COMMISSION, 20
HAMLINE UNIVERSITY, 583
HARBOR BRANCH OCEANOGRAPHIC INSTITUTION, 348
HAWAIIAN BOTANICAL SOCIETY, 349
HEADLANDS INSTITUTE, 350
HELPING OUR PENINSULA'S ENVIRONMENT, 350
HILTON POND CENTER FOR PIEDMONT NATURAL HISTORY, 351
HIMALAYAN WILDLIFE FOUNDATION, 351
HOLDEN ARBORETUM, THE, 351
HOLLOW OAK LAND TRUST, 351
HUMANE SOCIETY OF THE UNITED STATES, THE, 352
HUNTSMAN MARINE SCIENCE CENTRE, 353
IDAHO DEPARTMENT OF WATER RESOURCES, 161
   Water Awareness Week, 161
IDAHO STATE SOIL CONSERVATION COMMISSION, 161
ILLINOIS NATURE PRESERVES COMMISSION (INPC), 163
ILOVEPARKS.COM, 567
INDO-PACIFIC CONSERVATION ALLIANCE, 357
INSTITUTE FOR GLOBAL COMMUNICATIONS, 567
INSTITUTE FOR TROPICAL ECOLOGY AND CONSERVATION (ITEC), 358
INSTITUTO NACIONAL DE BIODIVERSIDAD (INBIO), 22
INTERNATIONAL ACADEMY, 567

KEYWORD INDEX – E

INTERNATIONAL CHILDREN'S CONFERENCE ON THE ENVIRONMENT, 362
INTERNATIONAL ECOTOURISM SOCIETY, THE, 362
INTERNATIONAL MIRE CONSERVATION GROUP, 365
INTERNATIONAL UNION FOR CONSERVATION OF NATURE AND NATURAL RESOURCES (IUCN) THE WORLD CONSERVATION UNION
   Canada Office, 368
   Environmental Law Centre, 368
   Regional Office for Europe, 369
INTERNATIONAL WHALING COMMISSION, 23
INTERTRIBAL BISON COOPERATIVE (ITBC), 372
IOWA ASSOCIATION OF NATURALISTS, 372
IOWA STATE UNIVERSITY
   College of Agriculture, 584
ISLAND INSTITUTE, THE, 374
ISLAND RESOURCES FOUNDATION, 375
ISLESBORO ISLANDS TRUST, 375
IZAAK WALTON LEAGUE OF AMERICA, INC., THE
   Minnesota Division, 377
   Owatonna Minnesota Chapter, 377
J.N. (DING) DARLING FOUNDATION, 379
JACKSON HOLE CONSERVATION ALLIANCE, 379
JAPAN WILDLIFE RESEARCH CENTER (JWRC), 380
JOHN GRAY HIGH SCHOOL, GRAND CAYMAN, 584
JOHNS HOPKINS UNIVERSITY
   CENTER FOR A LIVABLE FUTURE, 584
JOHNSON STATE COLLEGE, 585
KANSAS COOPERATIVE FISH AND WILDLIFE RESEARCH UNIT, 167
KANSAS DEPARTMENT OF WILDLIFE AND PARKS
   Region 4, 168
KANSAS STATE UNIVERSITY
   Department of Landscape Architecture / Regional and Community Planning, 585
KANSAS WILDFLOWER SOCIETY, 381
KENTUCKY DEPARTMENT OF AGRICULTURE, 169
KIDS ON THE BAYOU, 384
LA JOLLA FRIENDS OF THE SEALS (LJFS), 384
LAKE SUPERIOR STATE UNIVERSITY, 586
LAKEHEAD UNIVERSITY, 586
LAKENET, 385
LAND AND WATER FUND OF THE ROCKIES, 386
LAND CONSERVANCY OF WEST MICHIGAN, 386
LAST WIZARDS, THE, 568
LEAGUE OF OHIO SPORTSMEN, 387
LEAGUE TO SAVE LAKE TAHOE, 388
LEGACY LAND TRUST, 388
LITERACY FOR ENVIRONMENTAL JUSTICE, 389
LIVING RIVERS, 300
LOUISIANA DEPARTMENT OF AGRICULTURE AND FORESTRY
   Office of Soil and Water Conservation, State Soil and Water Conservation Committee, 172
LOUISIANA STATE UNIVERSITY SCHOOL OF FORESTRY, WILDLIFE AND FISHERIES, 586
MACOMB LAND CONSERVANCY, 391
MANOMET CENTER FOR CONSERVATION SCIENCES, 393
MANTA MEXICO, 393
MARIE SELBY BOTANICAL GARDENS, THE, 393
MARYLAND DEPARTMENT OF AGRICULTURE, 176
MASSACHUSETTS BASS FEDERATION, 396
MASSACHUSETTS COOPERATIVE FISH AND WILDLIFE RESEARCH UNIT (USDI), 178
MASSACHUSETTS DIVISION OF FISHERIES AND WILDLIFE
   MassWildlife, 178
MASSACHUSETTS EXECUTIVE OFFICE OF ENVIRONMENTAL AFFAIRS, 178
   Office of Technical Assistance for Toxic Use Reduction, 179
MCGILL UNIVERSITY, 587
MIAMI UNIVERSITY, 587
MICHIGAN TECHNOLOGICAL UNIVERSITY; SCHOOL OF FORESTRY AND WOOD PRODUCTS, 588
MICHIGAN UNITED CONSERVATION CLUBS, INC., 398
MIDDLE TENNESSEE STATE UNIVERSITY, 588
MISSISSIPPI STATE UNIVERSITY
   Forest and Wildlife Research Center, 588
MISSOURI ASSOCIATION OF SOIL AND WATER CONSERVATION DISTRICTS, 402
MISSOURI DEPARTMENT OF AGRICULTURE, 185
MONTANA BASS FEDERATION, 403
MONTANA LAND RELIANCE, 403
MONTANA NATURAL HERITAGE PROGRAM, 187
MONTANA WILDLIFE FEDERATION, 404
MOTE MARINE LABORATORY, 404
MOUNTAINEERS, THE, 405

MUNDO AZUL, 406
MURRAY STATE UNIVERSITY, 589
NATIONAL AGRICULTURAL LIBRARY, 24
NATIONAL AUDUBON SOCIETY
   Audubon of Florida, 410
   Audubon of Kansas, 410
   Audubon Society of Portland, 411
   Audubon Society of Western Pennsylvania, 412
   Connecticut Audubon Society, 412
   Delaware Audubon Society, 413
   Fairfax Audubon Society, 413
   Louisiana Audubon Council, 414
   Maricopa Audubon Society, 414
   New Jersey Chapter, 415
   Public Policy Office, 415
   San Diego Chapter, 416
   Seattle Audubon Society, 416
   Tucson Audubon Society, 416
NATIONAL PARKS CONSERVATION ASSOCIATION (NPCA), 422
   Sun Coast Regional Office, 423
NATIONAL WATERSHED COALITION, 426
NATIONAL WILDLIFE FEDERATION
   Great Lakes Natural Resource Center, 427
   Headquarters, 427
NATIONAL WILDLIFE PRODUCTIONS, INC., 429
NATIONAL WOODLAND OWNERS ASSOCIATION, 430
NATURAL HISTORY SOCIETY OF MARYLAND, INC., THE, 431
NATURE CONSERVANCY, THE
   Arkansas Field Office, 434
   Canada Chapter, 434
   Eastern New York Chapter, 435
   Illinois Chapter, 435
   Iowa Chapter, 435
   Maryland/District of Columbia Chapter, 436
   New York City Chapter, 438
   New York City Office, 437
   Oklahoma Chapter, 439
   Oregon Chapter, 439
   Pennsylvania Chapter, 439
   Rhode Island Chapter, 439
   Texas Chapter, 439
   Washington Chapter, 440
NAVAJO NATION DEPARTMENT OF FISH AND WILDLIFE, 188
NEBRASKA DEPARTMENT OF ENVIRONMENTAL QUALITY, 188
NEBRASKA DEPARTMENT OF NATURAL RESOURCES, 188
NEGATIVE POPULATION GROWTH (NPG), 442
NEVADA ASSOCIATION OF CONSERVATION DISTRICTS, 442
NEW HAMPSHIRE COUNCIL ON RESOURCES AND DEVELOPMENT, 190
NEW HAMPSHIRE DEPARTMENT OF RESOURCES AND ECONOMIC DEVELOPMENT, 190
NEW MEXICO ENERGY, MINERALS, AND NATURAL RESOURCES DEPARTMENT
   Oil Conservation Division, 195
NEW MEXICO STATE UNIVERSITY
   College of Agriculture and Home Economics, 589
NOLTE ASSOCIATES, INC., 569
NORTH AMERICAN WETLANDS CONSERVATION COUNCIL, 24
NORTH AMERICAN WOLF ASSOCIATION, 449
NORTH CAROLINA BASS FEDERATION, 450
NORTH CAROLINA DEPARTMENT OF AGRICULTURE AND CONSUMER SERVICES, 200
NORTH CAROLINA STATE UNIVERSITY, 590
NORTHEASTERN UNIVERSITY, 590
NORTHERN ALASKA ENVIRONMENTAL CENTER, 453
NORTHERN ARIZONA UNIVERSITY
   Department of Geography, Planning, and Recreation, 591
NORTHLAND COLLEGE, 591
NORTHWEST ECOSYSTEM ALLIANCE, 453
NORTHWEST ENVIRONMENT WATCH, 454
NORTHWEST RESOURCE INFORMATION CENTER, 454
NOVA SCOTIA AGRICULTURE & FISHERIES, 203
NOVA SCOTIA DEPARTMENT OF NATURAL RESOURCES, 203
NOVA SCOTIA FORESTRY ASSOCIATION, 454
OCEANIC SOCIETY, 456
OHIO DEPARTMENT OF AGRICULTURE, 203
OHIO DEPARTMENT OF NATURAL RESOURCES, 204
OHIO ENERGY PROJECT, 456
OHIO STATE UNIVERSITY, 592
OKLAHOMA STATE UNIVERSITY, 592
ONEWILDWORLD, 459
ONTARIO FEDERATION OF ANGLERS AND HUNTERS, 459
ORANGUTAN FOUNDATION INTERNATIONAL, 460

OREGON SMALL WOODLANDS ASSOCIATION, 461
OTTER PROJECT, THE, 462
PACIFIC MARINE CONSERVATION COUNCIL, 464
PACIFIC RIVERS COUNCIL, 464
PARTNERS IN AMPHIBIAN AND REPTILE CONSERVATION (PARC), 465
PARTNERS IN PARKS, 465
PENNSYLVANIA ORGANIZATION FOR WATERSHEDS AND RIVERS (POWR), 466
PLAYA LAKES JOINT VENTURE, 469
PRAIRIE WILDLIFE RESEARCH, 472
PREDATOR CONSERVATION ALLIANCE, 472
PROGRESSIVE ANIMAL WELFARE SOCIETY, 473
PROJECT SEAHORSE, 473
PROTECTED AREAS ASSOCIATION OF NEWFOUNDLAND AND LABRADOR, 474
PUBLIC EMPLOYEES FOR ENVIRONMENTAL RESPONSIBILITY (PEER), 474
PURPLE MARTIN CONSERVATION ASSOCIATION, 475
RAINFOREST RELIEF, 477
RAINFOREST TRUST, 477
RAPTOR EDUCATION FOUNDATION, INC., 477
RARE CENTER FOR TROPICAL CONSERVATION, 478
REEF RELIEF, 478
RENEWABLE NATURAL RESOURCES FOUNDATION, 478
RHODE ISLAND STATE CONSERVATION COMMITTEE, 480
RIVER PROJECT, THE, 481
ROCKY MOUNTAIN BIRD OBSERVATORY, 482
ROCKY MOUNTAIN ELK FOUNDATION, 482
SAN DIEGO NATURAL HISTORY MUSEUM, 484
SAN DIEGUITO RIVER PARK JOINT POWERS AUTHORITY, 215
SAN ELIJO LAGOON CONSERVANCY, 484
SAN JUAN PRESERVATION TRUST, THE, 484
SANTA CLARA COMMUNITY ACTION PROGRAM, 594
SASKATCHEWAN WILDLIFE FEDERATION, 484
SAVE THE DUNES CONSERVATION FUND, 485
SAVE THE HARBOR/SAVE THE BAY, 486
SAVE THE SOUND, INC., 486
SAVE WETLANDS AND BAYS, 486
SAVE-THE-REDWOODS LEAGUE, 487
SEA SHEPHERD CONSERVATION SOCIETY
  Netherlands, 488
SEA TURTLE PRESERVATION SOCIETY, 489
SHELBURNE FARMS, 490
SHEPHERD COLLEGE, 595
SIERRA CLUB
  Alaska Field Office, 490
  Hawaii Chapter, 492
  Mackinac Chapter, 493
  Maryland Chapter, 493
  Mississippi Chapter, 494
  Nebraska Chapter, 494
  Northwest Office, 495
  Pennsylvania Chapter, 496
  Virginia Chapter, 499
  West Virginia Chapter, 499
SIERRA CLUB CALIFORNIA, 499
SIERRA CLUB FOUNDATION, THE, 499
SIERRA CLUB OF CANADA
  Atlantic Canada Chapter, 500
SLIPPERY ROCK UNIVERSITY, 595
SOCIEDAD AMBIENTE MARINO, 502
SOCIETY FOR RANGE MANAGEMENT, 503
SOCIETY FOR THE PRESERVATION OF BIRDS OF PREY, 503
SOIL AND WATER CONSERVATION SOCIETY, 504
SOUTH CAROLINA NATIVE PLANT SOCIETY, 506
SOUTH DAKOTA ASSOCIATION OF CONSERVATION DISTRICTS, 506
SOUTHEASTERN ASSOCIATION OF FISH AND WILDLIFE AGENCIES, 508
SOUTHERN APPALACHIAN BOTANICAL SOCIETY, 508
SOUTHERN ILLINOIS UNIVERSITY CARBONDALE, 596
SOUTHWEST CENTER FOR ENVIRONMENTAL RESEARCH AND POLICY (SCERP), 596
SOUTHWEST FLORIDA WATER MANAGEMENT DISTRICT (SWFWMD), 220
ST. LAWRENCE UNIVERSITY, 597
STATE ENVIRONMENTAL RESOURCE CENTER (SERC), 512
STEPHEN F. AUSTIN STATE UNIVERSITY ARTHUR TEMPLE COLLEGE OF FORESTRY, 598
STERLING COLLEGE, 598
STROUD WATER RESEARCH CENTER, 512
STUDENT CONSERVATION ASSOCIATION, INC., 512
STUDENTS PARTNERSHIP WORLDWIDE, 513
STURGEON FOR TOMORROW, 514

SUSTAIN, 514
TALL TIMBERS RESEARCH STATION (TTRS), 515
TERRA NATURE FUND, 516
TEXAS A AND M UNIVERSITY AT KINGSVILLE
  Caesar Kleberg Wildlife Research Institute, 599
TEXAS CHRISTIAN UNIVERSITY, 599
TEXAS COOPERATIVE FISH AND WILDLIFE RESEARCH UNIT, 30
TEXAS DISCOVERY GARDENS, 517
TEXAS FOREST SERVICE, 222
TEXAS ORGANIZATION FOR ENDANGERED SPECIES, 517
TEXAS RIPARIAN ASSOCIATION, 517
THEODORE PAYNE FOUNDATION FOR WILDFLOWERS AND NATIVE PLANTS, INC., 518
TROUT UNLIMITED
  Alaska Council, 520
  Pennsylvania Council, 522
TULANE UNIVERSITY
  Department of Ecology and Evolutionary Biology, 600
TURNER ENDANGERED SPECIES FUND, 571
TURTLE CREEK WATERSHED ASSOCIATION, INC., 525
TWO WHITE WOLVES SANCTUARY, 525
UNION OF CONCERNED SCIENTISTS, 525
UNITED STATES DEPARTMENT OF AGRICULTURE
  Economic Research Center, 33
  Forest Service
    Allegheny National Forest, 34
    Angelina, Davy Crockett, Sabine and Sam Houston National Forest, 34
    Crooked River National Grassland, 37
    Gila National Forest, 38
    Green Mountain National Forest, 38
    Los Padres National Forest, 40
    Nez Perce National Forest, 41
    Pawnee National Grassland, 42
    Region 02 (Rocky Mountain), 43
    Siuslaw National Forest, 45
UNITED STATES DEPARTMENT OF COMMERCE
  National Oceanic and Atmospheric Administration
    Chesapeake Bay National Estuarine Research Reserve
      Virginia Office, 50
    Delaware National Estuarine Research Reserve, 50
    Flower Garden Banks National Marine Sanctuary, 50
    Gray's Reef National Marine Sanctuary, 50
    Gulf of Farallones National Marine Sanctuary, 50
    Padilla Bay National Estuarine Research Reserve, 53
    Rookery Bay National Estuarine Research Reserve, 53
    Sea Grant Program - Massachusetts, 56
    Sea Grant Program - Rhode Island, 59
    Sea Grant Program - Texas, 59
    Stellwagen Bank National Marine Sanctuary, 60
    Wells National Estuarine Research Reserve, 60
UNITED STATES DEPARTMENT OF DEFENSE
  Air Force Major Air Commands
    Andrews AFB, MD, 61
    USAF Academy, 62
  Air Force Major U.S. Installations
    Eglin Air Force Base, 63
    Luke AFB (and the Barry M. Goldwater AFR), AZ, 65
    Randolph AFB, TX, 66
  Army Corps of Engineers
    BALTIMORE Engineer DISTRICT, 67
    Fort Worth Engineer District, 68
    Norfolk Engineer District, 70
    Pacific Ocean Engineer District, 70
    Philadelphia District, 70
    Walla Walla Engineer District, 72
  Army Materiel Command, 72
  HQ PACAF/CEVQ, 74
  Navy, 74
UNITED STATES DEPARTMENT OF THE INTERIOR
  Bureau of Land Management
    Bakersfield Field Office, 79
    Malta Field Office, 83
    Northern Field Office, 84
    Safford Field Office, 86
  Bureau of Reclamation
    Pacific Northwest Region, 89
  Fish & Wildlife Service, 90
    ACE Basin National Wildlife Refuge, 90
    Alligator River/Pea Island National Wildlife Refuge, 91
    Archie Carr National Wildlife Refuge, 91
    Arthur R. Marshall Loxahatchee/Hope Sound National Wildlife Refuge, 91
    California-Nevada Operations, 94
    Canaan Valley National Wildlife Refuge, 94

KEYWORD INDEX – E

Carolina Sandhills National Wildlife Refuge, 95
Eastern Massachusetts National Wildlife Refuge Complex, 97
Great Dismal Swamp/Nansemond National Wildlife Refuge, 98
Guadalupe-Nipomo Dunes National Wildlife Refuge, 99
Hobe Sound National Wildlife Refuge, 99
Kern/Pixley National Wildlife Refuge, 101
Kofa National Wildlife Refuge, 102
Lacassine National Wildlife Refuge, 102
Lake Andes/Karl E. Mundt National Wildlife Refuge, 102
Long Island National Wildlife Refuge Complex, 103
Long Lake National Wildlife Refuge, 103
Morris Wetland Management District, 106
Neal Smith National Wildlife Refuge, 107
Necedah National Wildlife Refuge, 107
Okefenokee (Banks Lake) National Wildlife Refuge, 108
Pelican Island National Wildlife Refuge, 109
Pocosin Lakes National Wildlife Refuge, 110
Red Rock Lakes National Wildlife Refuge, 111
region 1, Pacific Regional Office, 111
region 4, Southeast Regional office, 112
Ridgefield National Wildlife Refuge, 112
San Francisco Bay National Wildlife Refuge Complex, 113
Sandy Point National Wildlife Refuge, 114
Selawik National Wildlife Refuge, 114
Southeast Louisiana Complex National Wildlife Refuge, 115
Squaw Creek National Wildlife Refuge, 115
St. Catherine Creek National Wildlife Refuge, 115
St. Marks National Wildlife Refuge, 115
Wapanocca National Wildlife Refuge, 117
White River National Wildlife Refuge, 118
National Park Service
  Chihuahuan Desert Network, 121
  Grand Teton National Park, 122
  Mammoth Cave National Park, 124
  Mesa Verde National Park, 124
  Mount Rainier National Park, 124
  Sonoran Desert Network, 125
  Yellowstone National Park, 126
United States Geological Survey
  Western Region, 127
UNITED STATES DEPARTMENT OF TRANSPORTATION
  Federal Aviation Administration, 128
UNITED STATES ENVIRONMENTAL PROTECTION AGENCY
  Administration and Resources Management, 129
UNITED STATES INSTITUTE FOR ENVIRONMENTAL CONFLICT RESOLUTION, 130
UNITED STATES PUBLIC INTEREST RESEARCH GROUP, 526
UNITY COLLEGE, 601
UNIVERSITE LAVAL, 601
UNIVERSITY OF ARIZONA
  Department of Hydrology and Water Resources, 605
UNIVERSITY OF CALIFORNIA AT DAVIS
  School of Veterinary Medicine, 606
UNIVERSITY OF CALIFORNIA AT SAN DIEGO, 607
UNIVERSITY OF CONNECTICUT COOPERATIVE EXTENSION, 608
UNIVERSITY OF FLORIDA INSTITUTE OF FOOD AND AGRICULTURAL SCIENCES, 609
UNIVERSITY OF GEORGIA
  Daniel B. Warnell School of Forest Resources, 609
UNIVERSITY OF IDAHO
  College of Natural Resources
    Department of Fish and Wildlife Resources, 610
UNIVERSITY OF LOUISVILLE, 612
UNIVERSITY OF MAINE, 612
UNIVERSITY OF MANITOBA, 613
UNIVERSITY OF MARYLAND - AT COLLEGE PARK, 613
UNIVERSITY OF MICHIGAN, 614
UNIVERSITY OF MINNESOTA AT ST. PAUL, 615
UNIVERSITY OF NEW BRUNSWICK, 616
UNIVERSITY OF NORTH CAROLINA AT ASHEVILLE, 617
UNIVERSITY OF NORTH DAKOTA, 618
UNIVERSITY OF NORTH TEXAS, 618
UNIVERSITY OF NORTHERN BRITISH COLUMBIA, 618
UNIVERSITY OF OREGON
  School of Law, 618
UNIVERSITY OF PITTSBURGH
  Biology Department, 619
UNIVERSITY OF RHODE ISLAND
  Department of Natural Resources Science, 619
UNIVERSITY OF SASKATCHEWAN, 620
UNIVERSITY OF SOUTH CAROLINA
  Baruch Marine Field Laboratory, 620
UNIVERSITY OF SOUTH CAROLINA BEAUFORT, 620
UNIVERSITY OF SOUTHERN MISSISSIPPI, 620
UNIVERSITY OF TENNESSEE - AT KNOXVILLE, 621
UNIVERSITY OF THE DISTRICT OF COLUMBIA, 621
UNIVERSITY OF WISCONSIN AT LA CROSSE, 623
UNIVERSITY OF WISCONSIN AT MADISON, 623
UNIVERSITY OF WISCONSIN-MADISON, 623
UPPER MISSISSIPPI RIVER CONSERVATION COMMITTEE, 527
UTAH BASS FEDERATION, 528
UTAH STATE UNIVERSITY
  College of Natural Resources, 624
VERMONT STATE-WIDE ENVIRONMENTAL EDUCATION PROGRAMS (SWEEP), 530
VERMONT WOODLANDS ASSOCIATION, 530
VERNAL POOL SOCIETY, THE, 530
VINEYARD CONSERVATION SOCIETY, 530
VIRGINIA DEPARTMENT OF CONSERVATION AND RECREATION
  Division of Dam Safety, 229
VIRGINIA MUSEUM OF NATURAL HISTORY, 232
VIRGINIA TECH
  Department of Fisheries and Wildlife Sciences, 625
VIRGINIA TECH UNIVERSITY
  College of Natural Resources, 625
WARREN COUNTY CONSERVATION BOARD, 532
WASHINGTON DEPARTMENT OF ECOLOGY, 233
WASHINGTON RECREATION AND PARK ASSOCIATION, 533
WASHINGTON STATE CONSERVATION COMMISSION, 234
WASHINGTON STATE DEPARTMENT OF NATURAL RESOURCES
  Olympic Region, 234
WATERLOO-WELLINGTON WILDFLOWER SOCIETY, 535
WATERMAN CONSERVATION EDUCATION CENTER, 535
WEST VIRGINIA RAPTOR REHABILITATION CENTER, 536
WESTERN HEMISPHERE SHOREBIRD RESERVE NETWORK (WHSRN), 537
WESTERN ILLINOIS UNIVERSITY, 626
WESTERN PACIFIC REGIONAL FISHERY MANAGEMENT COUNCIL, 131
WESTERN SNOWY PLOVER WORKING TEAM, 131
WESTERN WATERSHEDS PROJECT, 538
WETLANDS ACTION NETWORK, 538
WILD FOUNDATION, THE, 539
WILD ONES NATURAL LANDSCAPERS, LTD, 540
WILDCOAST, 540
WILDERNESS SOCIETY, THE, 541
WILDERNESS WATCH, 541
WILDLIFE ACTION, INC., 542
WILDLIFE DAMAGE REVIEW (WDR), 543
WILDLIFE HABITAT COUNCIL, 544
WILDLIFE INFORMATION CENTER, INC., 545
WILDLIFE SOCIETY
  Arizona Chapter, 546
  Colorado Chapter, 547
  Illinois Chapter, 547
  National Capital Chapter, 550
  Southern California Chapter, 553
  Wildlife Preservation Trust International, 554

ECOSYSTEMS (PRECIOUS)

WISCONSIN COOPERATIVE FISHERY RESEARCH UNIT USGS, 237
WOLF GROUP, THE, 557
WOODLAND OWNERS ASSOCIATION OF WEST VIRGINIA, 558
WORLD RESOURCES INSTITUTE, 559
WORLDWATCH INSTITUTE, 560
WWW.ACTIONBIOSCIENCE.ORG, 560
WYOMING OUTDOOR COUNCIL, 561
YELL COUNTY WILDLIFE FEDERATION, 561
YMCA NATURE AND COMMUNITY CENTER, 562

ENERGY

AFRICAN AMERICAN ENVIRONMENTALIST ASSOCIATION, 243
ALABAMA DEPARTMENT OF CONSERVATION AND NATURAL RESOURCES, 132
ALABAMA ENVIRONMENTAL COUNCIL, 244
ALASKA CONSERVATION ALLIANCE, 246
ALASKA CONSERVATION FOUNDATION, 246
ALDO LEOPOLD FOUNDATION, 247
AMERICAN COUNCIL FOR AN ENERGY-EFFICIENT ECONOMY, 251
AMERICAN COUNCIL FOR THE UNITED NATIONS UNIVERSITY (ACUNU), 251
AMERICAN PLANNING ASSOCIATION, 264
AMERICAN RIVERS
  Voyage of Recovery, 265
APROVECHO RESEARCH CENTER, 270

ARENA CONSULTORES AMBIENTALES, 563
ARIZONA GAME AND FISH DEPARTMENT, 136
ASSOCIATION OF AMERICAN GEOGRAPHERS, 273
ATLANTIC CENTER FOR THE ENVIRONMENT
   Quebec-Labrador Foundation, 275
ATLANTIC SALMON FEDERATION, 275
AUDUBON INTERNATIONAL, 276
AUSTRIALIA DEPARTMENT FOR ENVIRONMENT AND HERITAGE
   Environment Shop, The, 139
BEAR SPRINGS BLOSSOM NATURE CONSERVATION GROUP INC., 277
BIODIVERSITY CONSERVATION ALLIANCE, 278
BUN-CA, 281
CALIFORNIA DEPARTMENT OF FOOD AND AGRICULTURE, 142
CALIFORNIA DEPARTMENT OF PESTICIDE REGULATION, 143
CALIFORNIA TROUT, INC., 283
CALIFORNIANS FOR POPULATION STABILIZATION (CAPS), 284
CATSKILL FOREST ASSOCIATION, 289
CENTER FOR BIOLOGICAL DIVERSITY, 290
CENTER FOR ENVIRONMENT AND POPULATION (CEP), 290
CENTER FOR ENVIRONMENT, COMMERCE & ENERGY, 290
CENTER FOR ENVIRONMENTAL INFORMATION, 291
CENTER FOR NATIVE ECOSYSTEMS
   Front Range Office, 292
   West Slope Office, 292
CENTER FOR RESOURCE ECONOMICS/ISLAND PRESS, 293
CHESAPEAKE BAY FOUNDATION, INC.
   Maryland Office, 295
   Pennsylvania Office, 295
CHICAGO PARK DISTRICT, 296
CITIZENS' NUCLEAR INFORMATION CENTER, 298
CITY OF BELDING, 145
CJE ASSOCIATES, 565
CLEMSON UNIVERSITY EXTENSION SERVICE, 145
CLIMATE INSTITUTE, 299
COASTAL AMERICA FOUNDATION, 300
COLORADO DEPARTMENT OF NATURAL RESOURCES
   Division of Minerals and Geology, 146
   Oil and Gas Conservation Commission, 147
COLORADO STATE UNIVERSITY
   Department of Fishery and Wildlife Biology, 578
CONNECTICUT BOTANICAL SOCIETY, 304
CONNECTICUT FUND FOR THE ENVIRONMENT, 305
CONSERVAMERICA, 305
CONSERVATION COUNCIL OF NORTH CAROLINA, 306
CONSERVATION LAW FOUNDATION, INC. (CLF)
   New England Region, 308
COOSA RIVER BASIN INITIATIVE, 309
COTTONWOOD FOUNDATION, 309
COUNCIL FOR PLANNING AND CONSERVATION, 310
D ACRES, 311
DELAWARE DEPARTMENT OF NATURAL RESOURCES AND
   ENVIRONMENTAL CONTROL
   Division of Soil and Water Conservation, 150
DESERT RESEARCH FOUNDATION OF NAMIBIA, THE, 314
EARTH DAY NEW YORK, 316
EARTH POLICY INSTITUTE, 317
EARTHJUSTICE
   Denver Office, 318
   Environmental Law Clinic at the University of Denver, 318
   Headquarters, 318
   International Program, 319
   Juneau Office, 319
   Policy and Legislation, 319
ECODEFENSE, 321
ECOSEA, 322
ENVIRONMENTAL COUNCIL OF RHODE ISLAND, 323
ENVIRONMENTAL AND ENERGY STUDY INSTITUTE (EESI), 323
ENVIRONMENTAL DEFENSE
   Headquarters, 324
ENVIRONMENTAL DEFENSE CENTER, 325
ENVIRONMENTAL ENTERPRISES ASSISTANCE FUND, INC., 326
ENVIRONMENTAL POLICY CENTER, THE, 327
ENVIRONMENTAL RESOURCE CENTER (ERC), 328
FERRUM COLLEGE, 581
FLORIDA DEFENDERS OF THE ENVIRONMENT, INC., 331
FLORIDA FEDERATION OF GARDEN CLUBS, INC., 331
FLORIDA NATURAL AREAS INVENTORY, 332
FOOD SUPPLY / HUMAN POPULATION EXPLOSION CONNECTION, 333
FRIENDS OF THE EARTH, 337
GENERAL FEDERATION OF WOMEN'S CLUBS, 340
GEORGIANS FOR CLEAN ENERGY, 342
GLEN CANYON INSTITUTE, 343
GOOD NATURE PUBLISHING CO., 566

GRAND CANYON TRUST, 344
GREEN SEAL, 347
GREEN SPHERE INC., 347
GREENPEACE, INC., 347
GUADALUPE-BLANCO RIVER AUTHORITY, 157
GULF COAST ENVIRONMENTAL DEFENSE, 348
HAMLINE UNIVERSITY, 583
HAWAII DEPARTMENT OF HEALTH
   Office of Environmental Quality Control, 159
HOUSE COMMITTEE ON RULES, 22
IDAHO DEPARTMENT OF WATER RESOURCES
   Water Awareness Week, 161
ILLINOIS ENVIRONMENTAL COUNCIL, 355
ILLINOIS NATURE PRESERVES COMMISSION (INPC), 163
INDIANA DEPARTMENT OF NATURAL RESOURCES, 163
INFORM, INC., 357
INITIATIVE FOR SOCIAL ACTION AND RENEWAL IN EURASIA, 357
INTERNATIONAL CHILDREN'S CONFERENCE ON THE
   ENVIRONMENT, 362
INTERNATIONAL INSTITUTE FOR ENERGY CONSERVATION, 364
INTERNATIONAL MIRE CONSERVATION GROUP, 365
INTERNATIONAL UNION FOR CONSERVATION OF NATURE AND
   NATURAL RESOURCES (IUCN) THE WORLD CONSERVATION UNION
   Environmental Law Centre, 368
IOWA DEPARTMENT OF NATURAL RESOURCES
   Fish and Wildlife Division, 166
   Parks, 166
IOWA PRAIRIE NETWORK, 373
IZAAK WALTON LEAGUE OF AMERICA, INC., THE
   Alaska Division, 376
   Minnesota Division, 377
J.N. (DING) DARLING FOUNDATION, 379
JACK MINER MIGRATORY BIRD FOUNDATION, INC., 379
JACKSON HOLE CONSERVATION ALLIANCE, 379
JAGRATA JUBA SHANGHA (JJS), 568
JOHNSON STATE COLLEGE, 585
KANSAS DEPARTMENT OF HEALTH AND ENVIRONMENT, 167
KANSAS ORNITHOLOGICAL SOCIETY, 381
KENTUCKY DEPARTMENT OF AGRICULTURE, 169
KEYSTONE CENTER, THE, 384
KIDS FOR SAVING EARTH WORLDWIDE, 384
LEAGUE OF ENVIRONMENTAL JOURNALISTS, 387
LEAGUE OF WOMEN VOTERS OF THE U.S., 387
LEAGUE OF WOMEN VOTERS OF WASHINGTON, 388
LIFE OF THE LAND, 389
LITERACY FOR ENVIRONMENTAL JUSTICE, 389
LIVING RIVERS, 390
LOUISIANA DEPARTMENT OF NATURAL RESOURCES, 172
   Office of Conservation, 172
LOUISIANA OFFICE OF STATE PARKS, DEPARTMENT OF CULTURE,
   RECREATION, AND TOURISM, 173
LUMMI ISLAND HERITAGE TRUST, 568
MANITOBA NATURALISTS SOCIETY, 393
MASSACHUSETTS EXECUTIVE OFFICE OF ENVIRONMENTAL AFFAIRS
   Office of Technical Assistance for Toxic Use Reduction, 179
MCGILL UNIVERSITY, 587
MIAMI UNIVERSITY, 587
MIDDLE TENNESSEE STATE UNIVERSITY, 588
MINNESOTA ENVIRONMENTAL QUALITY BOARD, 182
MINNESOTA LAND TRUST, 400
MISSOURI DEPARTMENT OF CONSERVATION
   Forestry Division, 185
MISSOURI DEPARTMENT OF NATURAL RESOURCES, 186
MONTANA BASS FEDERATION, 403
MONTANA ENVIRONMENTAL QUALITY COUNCIL, 187
MONTANA FOREST OWNERS ASSOCIATION, 403
MONTANA LAND RELIANCE, 403
NATIONAL 4-H COUNCIL, 406
NATIONAL ASSOCIATION OF ENVIRONMENTAL PROFESSIONALS,
   THE, 408
NATIONAL ASSOCIATION OF SERVICE AND CONSERVATION CORPS
   (NASCC), 408
NATIONAL AUDUBON SOCIETY
   Delaware Audubon Society, 413
   Louisiana Audubon Council, 414
   Maricopa Audubon Society, 414
   Michigan Audubon Society, 414
NATIONAL CAUCUS OF ENVIRONMENTAL LEGISLATORS (NCEL), 417
NATIONAL CENTER FOR APPROPRIATE TECHNOLOGY, 417
   CENTER FOR RESOURCEFUL BUILDING TECHNOLOGY, 417
NATIONAL ENVIRONMENTAL EDUCATION AND TRAINING
   FOUNDATION, 418
NATIONAL GRANGE, THE, 421

KEYWORD INDEX – E

NATIONAL TRANSPORTATION SAFETY BOARD, 24
NATIONAL WATERWAYS CONFERENCE INC., 426
NATIONAL WILDLIFE PRODUCTIONS, INC., 429
NEVADA ASSOCIATION OF CONSERVATION DISTRICTS, 442
NEW HAMPSHIRE COUNCIL ON RESOURCES AND DEVELOPMENT, 190
NEW JERSEY FORESTRY ASSOCIATION, 445
NEW MEXICO ASSOCIATION OF CONSERVATION DISTRICTS, 445
NEW MEXICO BUREAU OF GEOLOGY AND MINERAL RESOURCES
  Geological Information Center Library, 193
NEW MEXICO ENVIRONMENT DEPARTMENT, 195
NEW YORK DEPARTMENT OF AGRICULTURE AND MARKETS, 196
NEW YORK STATE DEPARTMENT OF AGRICULTURE AND MARKETS, 197
NOLTE ASSOCIATES, INC., 569
NORTH AMERICAN DEVELOPMENT BANK, 24
NORTH CAROLINA CONSERVATION NETWORK, 450
NORTH CAROLINA WATERSHED COALITION, INC., 451
NORTH DAKOTA STATE SOIL CONSERVATION COMMITTEE, 202
NORTHEAST SUSTAINABLE ENERGY ASSOCIATION, 452
NORTHERN PLAINS RESOURCE COUNCIL, 453
NORTHWEST COALITION FOR ALTERNATIVES TO PESTICIDES, 453
NORTHWEST ENVIRONMENT WATCH, 454
NORTHWEST RESOURCE INFORMATION CENTER, 454
NORTHWEST TERRITORIES DEPARTMENT OF RESOURCES, WILDLIFE AND ECONOMIC DEVELOPMENT, 202
NOVA SCOTIA DEPARTMENT OF NATURAL RESOURCES, 203
NW ENERGY COALITION, 454
OHIO DEPARTMENT OF AGRICULTURE, 203
OHIO DEPARTMENT OF NATURAL RESOURCES, 204
OHIO FORESTRY ASSOCIATION, INC., 457
OKLAHOMA BIOLOGICAL SURVEY, 205
OLYMPIC PARK INSTITUTE, 459
ONTARIO FEDERATION OF ANGLERS AND HUNTERS, 459
PEOPLE FOR PUGET SOUND
  South Sound Office, 467
PHYSICIANS FOR SOCIAL RESPONSIBILITY, 468
PIEDMONT ENVIRONMENTAL COUNCIL, 469
POCONO ENVIRONMENTAL EDUCATION CENTER, 470
POLLUTION PROBE, 470
POPULATION-ENVIRONMENT BALANCE, INC., 471
PS ENTERPRISES, 570
RESIDENTS FOR A MORE BEAUTIFUL PORT WASHINGTON, 479
RESOURCES FOR THE FUTURE, 479
RETURNED PEACE CORPS VOLUNTEERS FOR ENVIRONMENT AND DEVELOPMENT (RPCVS-ED), 480
ROCKY MOUNTAIN BIGHORN SOCIETY, 482
SANTA CLARA COMMUNITY ACTION PROGRAM, 594
SIERRA CLUB
  Alaska Chapter, 490
  Alaska Field Office, 490
  Cascade Chapter, 491
  Connecticut Chapter, 491
  Hawaii Chapter, 492
  Lone Star Chapter, 493
  Mackinac Chapter, 493
  Mississippi Chapter, 494
  Nebraska Chapter, 494
  New Jersey Chapter, 495
  Northwest Office, 495
  Pennsylvania Chapter, 496
  Rio Grande Chapter (New Mexico/West Texas), 496
  San Francisco Bay Chapter, 497
  Washington, DC Office, 499
  West Virginia Chapter, 499
  Wyoming Chapter, 499
SIERRA CLUB CALIFORNIA, 499
SIERRA CLUB FOUNDATION, THE, 499
SIERRA CLUB OF CANADA
  Atlantic Canada Chapter, 500
SIERRA STUDENT COALITION, 500
SOCIETY FOR THE PROTECTION OF NEW HAMPSHIRE FORESTS, 503
SOUTH DAKOTA ORNITHOLOGISTS UNION, 507
SOUTH DAKOTA RESOURCES COALITION, 507
SOUTHFACE ENERGY INSTITUTE, 510
SOUTHWEST CENTER FOR ENVIRONMENTAL RESEARCH AND POLICY (SCERP), 596
SOUTHWESTERN HERPETOLOGISTS SOCIETY, 510
STATE ENVIRONMENTAL RESOURCE CENTER (SERC), 512
STEPHEN F. AUSTIN STATE UNIVERSITY ARTHUR TEMPLE COLLEGE OF FORESTRY, 598
STERLING COLLEGE, 598

STUDENT ENVIRONMENTAL ACTION COALITION (SEAC), 513
STUDENT PUGWASH USA, 513
SUSTAIN, 514
SUSTAINABLE ENERGY INSTITUTE
  Culture Change, 514
  Culture Change magazine, 514
  Food Not Lawns, 514
  Pedal Power Produce, 514
TANZANIA COASTAL MANAGEMENT PARTNERSHIP, 30
TENNESSEE VALLEY AUTHORITY
  Muscle Shoals Technical Library, 30
TEXAS FOREST SERVICE, 222
TEXAS GENERAL LAND OFFICE, 222
TREES FOR THE FUTURE, INC., 519
TRUSTEES FOR ALASKA, 524
TWO WHITE WOLVES SANCTUARY, 525
UNION OF CONCERNED SCIENTISTS, 525
UNITED STATES CHAMBER OF COMMERCE
  Environment, Technology and Regulatory Affairs, 526
UNITED STATES DEPARTMENT OF AGRICULTURE
  Economic Research Center, 33
  Forest Service
    Los Padres National Forest, 40
    Pawnee National Grassland, 42
    Region 09 (Eastern), 43
UNITED STATES DEPARTMENT OF COMMERCE
  National Oceanic and Atmospheric Administration
    Sea Grant Program - California, 54
    Sea Grant Program - Massachusetts, 56
    Sea Grant Program - Texas, 59
UNITED STATES DEPARTMENT OF DEFENSE
  Army Corps of Engineers
    Nashville Engineer District, 69
    Norfolk Engineer District, 70
    North Atlantic Engineer District, 70
  Assistant Chief of Staff for Installation Management, Office of the Director of Environmental Programs, and Conservation Team, 74
UNITED STATES DEPARTMENT OF THE INTERIOR
  Bureau of Land Management
    Bakersfield Field Office, 79
    Malta Field Office, 83
    Northern Field Office, 84
    Rawlins Field Office, 85
    Renewable Energy, 86
    Safford Field Office, 86
  Bureau of Reclamation, 89
  United States Geological Survey
    New Mexico Cooperative Fish and Wildlife Research Unit, 127
    Western Region, 127
UNITED STATES ENVIRONMENTAL PROTECTION AGENCY
  Administration and Resources Management, 129
UNITED STATES INSTITUTE FOR ENVIRONMENTAL CONFLICT RESOLUTION, 130
UNITED STATES PUBLIC INTEREST RESEARCH GROUP, 526
UNIVERSITE LAVAL, 601
UNIVERSITY OF FLORIDA
  School of Forest Resources and Conservation, 600
UNIVERSITY OF FLORIDA INSTITUTE OF FOOD AND AGRICULTURAL SCIENCES, 609
UNIVERSITY OF GEORGIA
  Daniel B. Warnell School of Forest Resources, 609
UNIVERSITY OF MARYLAND - AT COLLEGE PARK, 613
UNIVERSITY OF MICHIGAN, 614
UNIVERSITY OF NORTH CAROLINA AT ASHEVILLE, 617
UNIVERSITY OF NORTH DAKOTA, 618
UNIVERSITY OF SASKATCHEWAN, 620
UNIVERSITY OF THE DISTRICT OF COLUMBIA, 621
UNIVERSITY OF WISCONSIN-MADISON, 623
UTAH BASS FEDERATION, 528
UTAH DEPARTMENT OF NATURAL RESOURCES
  Division of Wildlife Resources, 225
UTAH STATE DEPARTMENT OF NATURAL RESOURCES
  Division of Wildlife Resources, 226
VERMONT AGENCY OF NATURAL RESOURCES
  Department of Fish and Wildlife, 227
VERMONT STATE-WIDE ENVIRONMENTAL EDUCATION PROGRAMS (SWEEP), 530
VINEYARD CONSERVATION SOCIETY, 530
WARREN COUNTY CONSERVATION BOARD, 532
WASHINGTON WILDERNESS COALITION, 534
WELLSPRING INTERNATIONAL, INC., 571
WEST MICHIGAN ENVIRONMENTAL ACTION COUNCIL, 536
WEST VIRGINIA RAPTOR REHABILITATION CENTER, 536

WILDERNESS SOCIETY, THE, 541
WILDLIFE ACTION, INC., 542
WILDLIFE SOCIETY
  Michigan Chapter, 549
WISCONSIN COOPERATIVE WILDLIFE RESEARCH UNIT (USDI), 237
WORLD RESOURCES INSTITUTE, 559
WORLDWATCH INSTITUTE, 560
WYOMING COOPERATIVE FISH AND WILDLIFE RESEARCH UNIT (USDI), 238
WYOMING OUTDOOR COUNCIL, 561

ETHICS/ENVIRONMENTAL JUSTICE

ACADEMY FOR EDUCATIONAL DEVELOPMENT, 241
ADVOCATES OF THE COMMON WEALTH, INC., 243
AFRICAN AMERICAN ENVIRONMENTALIST ASSOCIATION, 243
ALABAMA ENVIRONMENTAL COUNCIL, 244
AMANAKAA AMAZON NETWORK, 248
AMERICA THE BEAUTIFUL FUND, 248
AMERICAN CANAL SOCIETY, INC., 250
AMERICAN COUNCIL FOR THE UNITED NATIONS UNIVERSITY (ACUNU), 251
AMERICAN PIE (PUBLIC INFORMATION ON THE ENVIRONMENT), 264
ANACOSTIA WATERSHED SOCIETY, 268
ARCHAEOLOGICAL CONSERVANCY, 270
ARIZONA STATE LAND DEPARTMENT, 136
ARKANSAS STATE EXTENSION SERVICES
  Four H Center, 138
ASSOCIATION FOR NATURAL RESOURCES ENFORCEMENT TRAINING, 273
ASSOCIATION OF AMERICAN GEOGRAPHERS, 273
ATLANTIC STATES LEGAL FOUNDATION, 275
BROWN UNIVERSITY, 575
BUILDINGGREEN, INC., 564
CALIFORNIA DEPARTMENT OF PESTICIDE REGULATION, 143
CALIFORNIA TRAPPERS ASSOCIATION, 283
CALIFORNIA UNIVERSITY OF PENNSYLVANIA, 576
CENTER FOR ENVIRONMENT, COMMERCE & ENERGY, 290
CENTER FOR ENVIRONMENTAL HEALTH (CEH), 291
CENTER FOR ENVIRONMENTAL PHILOSOPHY, 291
CENTER FOR HEALTH, ENVIRONMENT, AND JUSTICE, 291
CENTER FOR RESOURCE ECONOMICS/ISLAND PRESS, 293
CENTER FOR WATERSHED PROTECTION, 293
CENTRO DE INFORMACION, INVESTIGACION Y EDUCACION SOCIAL (CIIES), 294
CHESAPEAKE BAY FOUNDATION, INC.
  Maryland Office, 295
CHICAGO PARK DISTRICT, 296
CIRCUMPOLAR CONSERVATION UNION, 297
CITY UNIVERSITY OF NEW YORK
  College of Staten Island, 576
CJE ASSOCIATES, 565
CLARK UNIVERSITY, 576
COALITION FOR EDUCATION IN THE OUTDOORS, 299
COASTAL AMERICA FOUNDATION, 300
COASTAL RESOURCE MANAGEMENT PROJECT, 146
COLORADO MOUNTAIN COLLEGE, 577
COLORADO STATE FOREST SERVICE, 148
COMMUNITIES FOR A BETTER ENVIRONMENT, 303
CONFEDERATED SALISH AND KOOTENAI TRIBES, 304
CONNECTICUT BOTANICAL SOCIETY, 304
CONNECTICUT FUND FOR THE ENVIRONMENT, 305
CONSERVATION FEDERATION OF MARYLAND/ F.A.R.M., 306
CONSERVATION FORCE, 307
COTTONWOOD FOUNDATION, 309
COUNCIL FOR PLANNING AND CONSERVATION, 310
DELAWARE GREENWAYS, INC., 312
DELAWARE RIVERKEEPER NETWORK, 313
DESERT FISHES COUNCIL, 314
EAGLE NATURE FOUNDATION, LTD., 316
EARTHJUSTICE
  Headquarters, 318
  International Program, 319
EARTHSCAN, 320
ECOLOGICAL SOCIETY OF AMERICA, THE, 321
ECOLOGY CENTER, 321
ENVIRONMENT COUNCIL OF RHODE ISLAND, 323
ENVIRONMENTAL CAREERS ORGANIZATION, INC., THE, 324
ENVIRONMENTAL DEFENSE
  Headquarters, 324
  Rocky Mountain Office, 324
  Texas Office, 325
ENVIRONMENTAL DEFENSE CENTER, 325
ENVIRONMENTAL EDUCATORS OF NORTH CAROLINA (EENC), 326
ENVIRONMENTAL LAW INSTITUTE, THE, 327
ENVIRONMENTAL PROTECTION AGENCY
  Region 1 (CT, ME, MA, NH, RI, VT), 18
  Region 5 (IL, IN, MI, NM, OH, WI), 19
EUROPARC FEDERATION, 328
FEDERAL WILDLIFE OFFICERS ASSOCIATION, 329
FLINTSTEEL RESTORATION ASSOCIATION, INC., 330
FOOD SUPPLY / HUMAN POPULATION EXPLOSION CONNECTION, 333
FOREST SERVICE EMPLOYEES FOR ENVIRONMENTAL ETHICS (FSEEE), 334
FOREST SOCIETY OF MAINE, 335
FOREST STEWARDS GUILD, 335
FRIENDS OF THE EARTH, 337
FRIENDS OF THE REEDY RIVER, 338
FRIENDS OF THE SEA OTTER, 338
GEORGIA DEPARTMENT OF NATURAL RESOURCES
  Environmental Protection Division
    Coastal Division, 156
GEORGIA TRUST FOR HISTORIC PRESERVATION, 342
GIRL SCOUTS OF THE USA, 343
GLEN CANYON INSTITUTE, 343
GREAT LAKES UNITED
  CANADA OFFICE, 345
GREAT PLAINS NATIVE PLANT SOCIETY, 345
GREEN BALKANS FEDERATION OF NATURE CONSERVATION NGOS, 346
GREEN PARTNERS, 347
GREEN SPHERE INC., 347
GROWLING, 348
HIGH DESERT MUSEUM, THE, 351
IDAHO DEPARTMENT OF WATER RESOURCES, 161
  Water Awareness Week, 161
ILLINOIS ASSOCIATION OF CONSERVATION DISTRICTS, 354
ILOVEPARKS.COM, 567
INITIATIVE FOR SOCIAL ACTION AND RENEWAL IN EURASIA, 357
INTERAGENCY COMMITTEE FOR OUTDOOR RECREATION (IAC), 164
INTERNATIONAL MIRE CONSERVATION GROUP, 365
INTERNATIONAL SOCIETY FOR THE PRESERVATION OF THE TROPICAL RAINFOREST, THE, 367
INTERNATIONAL SONORAN DESERT ALLIANCE, 367
INTERNATIONAL UNION FOR CONSERVATION OF NATURE AND NATURAL RESOURCES (IUCN) THE WORLD CONSERVATION UNION
  Environmental Law Centre, 368
IOWA ACADEMY OF SCIENCE, 372
IOWA DEPARTMENT OF AGRICULTURE AND LAND STEWARDSHIP
  Bureau of Financial Incentive Program, 165
ISLAND RESOURCES FOUNDATION, 375
ISLESBORO ISLANDS TRUST, 375
IZAAK WALTON LEAGUE OF AMERICA, INC., THE, 375
  Minnesota Division, 377
  Owatonna Minnesota Chapter, 377
J.N. (DING) DARLING FOUNDATION, 379
JOHNSON STATE COLLEGE, 585
KANSAS STATE UNIVERSITY
  Department of Landscape Architecture / Regional and Community Planning, 585
KEEP FLORIDA BEAUTIFUL, INC., 382
KENTUCKY DEPARTMENT OF AGRICULTURE, 169
LAKEHEAD UNIVERSITY, 586
LAND BETWEEN THE LAKES ASSOCIATION, 386
LEAGUE OF OHIO SPORTSMEN, 387
LEARNING FOR ENVIRONMENTAL ACTION PROGRAMME (LEAP), 388
LEGAL ENVIRONMENTAL ASSISTANCE FOUNDATION INC. (LEAF), 388
LEWIS AND CLARK COLLEGE
  Law School, 586
LITERACY FOR ENVIRONMENTAL JUSTICE, 389
LIVING RIVERS, 390
LOUISIANA DEPARTMENT OF AGRICULTURE AND FORESTRY
  Office of Soil and Water Conservation, State Soil and Water Conservation Committee, 172
LOUISIANA WILDLIFE REHABILITATORS ASSOCIATION, 391
LUMMI ISLAND HERITAGE TRUST, 568
LVIV REGIONAL INSTITUTE OF EDUCATION, 391
MARYLAND DEPARTMENT OF NATURAL RESOURCES, 177
MASSACHUSETTS EXECUTIVE OFFICE OF ENVIRONMENTAL AFFAIRS, 178
MIAMI UNIVERSITY, 587
MICHIGAN UNITED CONSERVATION CLUBS, INC., 398
MIDDLE TENNESSEE STATE UNIVERSITY, 588
MISSISSIPPI RIVER BASIN ALLIANCE, 401
MOUNT GRACE LAND CONSERVATION TRUST, 405
NATIONAL ASSOCIATION OF SERVICE AND CONSERVATION CORPS (NASCC), 408

KEYWORD INDEX – E

NATIONAL AUDUBON SOCIETY
  Louisiana Audubon Council, 414
  Michigan Audubon Society, 414
NATIONAL CAUCUS OF ENVIRONMENTAL LEGISLATORS (NCEL), 417
NATIONAL PARK FOUNDATION, 422
NATIONAL PARKS CONSERVATION ASSOCIATION (NPCA), 422
NATIONAL WHISTLEBLOWER LEGAL DEFENSE & EDUCATION FUND, 426
NATIONAL WILDLIFE FEDERATION
  Great Lakes Natural Resource Center, 427
  Northern Rockies Natural Resource Center, 428
NATIONAL WILDLIFE PRODUCTIONS, INC., 429
NATIONAL WOODLAND OWNERS ASSOCIATION, 430
NATURE CONSERVANCY, THE
  Arkansas Field Office, 434
NATURESERVE, 441
NEVIS HISTORICAL AND CONSERVATION SOCIETY, 442
NEW HAMPSHIRE COUNCIL ON RESOURCES AND DEVELOPMENT, 190
NEW HAMPSHIRE DEPARTMENT OF AGRICULTURE, MARKETS, AND FOOD
  State Conservation Committee, 190
NEW MEXICO ENERGY, MINERALS, AND NATURAL RESOURCES DEPARTMENT
  Oil Conservation Division, 195
NEW YORK PUBLIC INTEREST RESEARCH GROUP (NYPIRG), 446
NEW YORK STATE FISH AND WILDLIFE MANAGEMENT BOARD
  Region 6, 198
NORTH AMERICAN WOLF ASSOCIATION, 449
NORTH CAROLINA COASTAL FEDERATION, INC., 450
NORTH CAROLINA CONSERVATION NETWORK, 450
NORTH CAROLINA COOPERATIVE FISH AND WILDLIFE RESEARCH UNIT (USDI), 200
NORTHEASTERN UNIVERSITY, 590
NORTHERN ARIZONA UNIVERSITY
  Department of Geography, Planning, and Recreation, 591
NORTHWEST INTERPRETIVE ASSOCIATION, 454
NORTHWEST RESOURCE INFORMATION CENTER, 454
NOVA SCOTIA FORESTRY ASSOCIATION, 454
OCEANIC SOCIETY, 456
OHIO ENERGY PROJECT, 456
OHIO FORESTRY ASSOCIATION, INC., 457
OHIO NATIVE PLANT SOCIETY, 457
OLYMPIC PARK INSTITUTE, 459
ONTARIO FORESTRY ASSOCIATION, 459
OREGON DEPARTMENT OF GEOLOGY AND MINERAL INDUSTRIES, 209
OREGON NATURAL RESOURCES COUNCIL, 460
OUTDOOR WRITERS ASSOCIATION OF AMERICA, INC., 462
OZARKS RESOURCE CENTER, 463
PACIFIC MARINE CONSERVATION COUNCIL, 464
PENNSYLVANIA DEPARTMENT OF ENVIRONMENTAL PROTECTION, 211
POLLUTION PROBE, 470
PS ENTERPRISES, 570
PUBLIC EMPLOYEES FOR ENVIRONMENTAL RESPONSIBILITY (PEER), 474
PURPLE MARTIN CONSERVATION ASSOCIATION, 476
QUALITY DEER MANAGEMENT ASSOCIATION, 476
RAINFOREST RELIEF, 477
RAPTOR EDUCATION FOUNDATION, INC., 477
RIVER PROJECT, THE, 481
SANTA CLARA COMMUNITY ACTION PROGRAM, 594
SAVE THE SOUND, INC., 486
SIERRA CLUB
  Alaska Field Office, 490
  Connecticut Chapter, 491
  Hawaii Chapter, 492
  Lone Star Chapter, 493
  Mississippi Chapter, 494
  Nebraska Chapter, 494
  New York City Office, 495
  Northwest Office, 495
  Washington, DC Office, 499
  West Virginia Chapter, 499
  Wyoming Chapter, 499
SIERRA CLUB CALIFORNIA, 499
SIERRA CLUB FOUNDATION, THE, 499
SIERRA CLUB OF CANADA
  Atlantic Canada Chapter, 500
SMITHSONIAN INSTITUTION, 501
SOIL AND WATER CONSERVATION SOCIETY, 504
SOUTH CAROLINA WILDLIFE FEDERATION, 506
SOUTHWEST CENTER FOR ENVIRONMENTAL RESEARCH AND POLICY (SCERP), 596
SOUTHWEST RESEARCH AND INFORMATION CENTER, 510
STATE ENVIRONMENTAL RESOURCE CENTER (SERC), 512
STUDENT ENVIRONMENTAL ACTION COALITION (SEAC), 513
STUDENTS PARTNERSHIP WORLDWIDE, 513
SUSTAIN, 514
TENNESSEE FORESTRY ASSOCIATION, 516
TEXAS DEPARTMENT OF AGRICULTURE, 222
THREE CIRCLES CENTER FOR MULTICULTURAL ENVIRONMENTAL EDUCATION, 518
TREES FOR TOMORROW, NATURAL RESOURCES EDUCATION CENTER, 519
TROUT UNLIMITED
  Pennsylvania Council, 522
TULANE ENVIRONMENTAL LAW CLINIC, 600
TWO WHITE WOLVES SANCTUARY, 525
UNITED NATIONS ENVIRONMENT PROGRAMME, 525
UNITED STATES CHAMBER OF COMMERCE
  Environment, Technology and Regulatory Affairs, 526
UNITED STATES DEPARTMENT OF COMMERCE
  National Oceanic and Atmospheric Administration
    Sea Grant Program - Massachusetts, 56
    Sea Grant Program - Rhode Island, 59
UNITED STATES DEPARTMENT OF DEFENSE
  Air Force Major U.S. Installations
    Luke AFB (and the Barry M. Goldwater AFR), AZ, 65
  Norfolk Engineer District, 70
UNITED STATES DEPARTMENT OF THE INTERIOR
  Bureau of Land Management
    Northern Field Office, 84
  Fish and Wildlife Service
    Eastern Massachusetts National Wildlife Refuge Complex, 97
UNITED STATES ENVIRONMENTAL PROTECTION AGENCY
  Administration and Resources Management, 129
UNITED STATES INSTITUTE FOR ENVIRONMENTAL CONFLICT RESOLUTION, 130
UNIVERSITE LAVAL, 601
UNIVERSITY OF COLORADO, 608
UNIVERSITY OF FLORIDA INSTITUTE OF FOOD AND AGRICULTURAL SCIENCES, 609
UNIVERSITY OF GEORGIA
  Daniel B. Warnell School of Forest Resources, 609
UNIVERSITY OF IDAHO
  College of Natural Resources
    Idaho Cooperative Fish and Wildlife Research Unit, 610
UNIVERSITY OF MARYLAND - AT COLLEGE PARK, 613
UNIVERSITY OF MARYLAND BALTIMORE COUNTY, 613
UNIVERSITY OF MICHIGAN, 614
UNIVERSITY OF NORTH CAROLINA AT ASHEVILLE, 617
UNIVERSITY OF NORTHERN BRITISH COLUMBIA, 618
UNIVERSITY OF WISCONSIN AT LA CROSSE, 623
UNIVERSITY OF WISCONSIN-MADISON, 623
URBAN HABITAT PROGRAM, 527
URBAN WASTE MANAGEMENT & RESEARCH CENTER, 624
UTAH BASS FEDERATION, 520
VERNAL POOL SOCIETY, THE, 530
WARREN COUNTY CONSERVATION BOARD, 532
WASHINGTON TRAILS ASSOCIATION, 534
WESTERN WATERSHEDS PROJECT, 538
WETLANDS ACTION NETWORK, 538
WHITE CLAY WATERSHED ASSOCIATION, 538
WILD ONES NATURAL LANDSCAPERS, LTD, 540
WILDLIFE ACTION, INC., 542
WILDLIFE MANAGEMENT INSTITUTE, 545
WOLF EDUCATION AND RESEARCH CENTER, 557
WOMEN'S SHOOTING SPORTS FOUNDATION, 558
WORLD ASSOCIATION OF GIRL GUIDES AND GIRL SCOUTS (WAGGGS), 558
WORLDWATCH INSTITUTE, 560
WWW.ACTIONBIOSCIENCE.ORG, 560
WYOMING OUTDOOR COUNCIL, 561
ZUNGARO COCHA RESEARCH CENTER
  Exploration Educational Expeditions, 562

EXECUTIVE/LEGISLATIVE/JUDICIAL REFORM

ADVOCATES OF THE COMMON WEALTH, INC., 243
AFRICAN AMERICAN ENVIRONMENTALIST ASSOCIATION, 243
ALASKA CONSERVATION ALLIANCE, 246
ALBERTA DEPARTMENT OF ENVIRONMENTAL PROTECTION
  Natural Resources Service, 135
AMERICAN BIRD CONSERVANCY, 249
AMERICAN RIVERS
  Nebraska Field Office, 265

ANIMALS ASIA FOUNDATION, 269
BASS DIVISION OF ESPN PRODUCTIONS INC, 564
BEYOND PESTICIDES, 277
BIODIVERSITY CONSERVATION ALLIANCE, 278
CALIFORNIA STATE LANDS COMMISSION, 145
CALIFORNIANS FOR POPULATION STABILIZATION (CAPS), 284
CENTER FOR ENVIRONMENT, COMMERCE & ENERGY, 290
CENTER FOR HEALTH, ENVIRONMENT, AND JUSTICE, 291
CENTER FOR NATIVE ECOSYSTEMS
   Front Range Office, 292
   West Slope Office, 292
CHESAPEAKE BAY FOUNDATION, INC.
   Maryland Office, 295
CITY UNIVERSITY OF NEW YORK
   College of Staten Island, 576
CJE ASSOCIATES, 565
COAST ALLIANCE, 300
COASTAL RESOURCE MANAGEMENT PROJECT, 146
COLORADO DEPARTMENT OF NATURAL RESOURCES
   Oil and Gas Conservation Commission, 147
CONSERVATION ALLIANCE OF ST. LUCIE CO., 306
DELAWARE NATURE SOCIETY, 312
EARTHJUSTICE
   Headquarters, 318
   Policy and Legislation, 319
ENVIRONMENT COUNCIL OF RHODE ISLAND, 323
ENVIRONMENTAL DEFENSE
   Rocky Mountain Office, 324
   Texas Office, 325
FOOD SUPPLY / HUMAN POPULATION EXPLOSION CONNECTION, 333
FOREST SERVICE EMPLOYEES FOR ENVIRONMENTAL ETHICS (FSEEE), 334
FOREST SOCIETY OF MAINE, 335
FRIENDS OF THE EARTH, 337
FRIENDS OF THE SEA OTTER, 338
GREEN BALKANS FEDERATION OF NATURE CONSERVATION NGOS, 346
GREEN MOUNTAIN CLUB INC., THE, 346
GULF STATES MARINE FISHERIES COMMISSION, 20
HUMANE SOCIETY OF THE UNITED STATES, THE, 352
ILOVEPARKS.COM, 567
IZAAK WALTON LEAGUE OF AMERICA, INC., THE
   Minnesota Division, 377
   Owatonna Minnesota Chapter, 377
KANSAS DEPTARTMENT OF WILDLIFE AND PARKS, 381
LAKEHEAD UNIVERSITY, 586
LIVING RIVERS, 390
LUMMI ISLAND HERITAGE TRUST, 568
MONTANA DEPARTMENT OF NATURAL RESOURCES AND CONSERVATION, 187
MOUNTAINEERS, THE, 405
NATIONAL AUDUBON SOCIETY
   Connecticut Audubon Society, 412
   Louisiana Audubon Council, 414
NATIONAL MILITARY FISH AND WILDLIFE ASSOCIATION, 421
NATIONAL WILDLIFE FEDERATION
   Great Lakes Natural Resource Center, 427
   Headquarters, 427
   Northern Rockies Natural Resource Center, 428
NATIONAL WOODLAND OWNERS ASSOCIATION, 430
NATURE CONSERVANCY, THE
   Colorado Chapter, 434
   Texas Chapter, 439
NEBRASKA DEPARTMENT OF ENVIRONMENTAL QUALITY, 188
NEBRASKA WILDLIFE FEDERATION, INC., 442
NEVADA ASSOCIATION OF CONSERVATION DISTRICTS, 442
NEW JERSEY ENVIRONMENTAL LOBBY, 445
NORTH CAROLINA WILDLIFE RESOURCES COMMISSION, 201
NORTHWEST RESOURCE INFORMATION CENTER, 454
NOVA SCOTIA DEPARTMENT OF NATURAL RESOURCES, 203
NOVA SCOTIA FORESTRY ASSOCIATION, 454
ONTARIO FEDERATION OF ANGLERS AND HUNTERS, 459
PACIFIC MARINE CONSERVATION COUNCIL, 464
PACIFIC RIVERS COUNCIL, 464
PENNSYLVANIA ORGANIZATION FOR WATERSHEDS AND RIVERS (POWR), 466
PS ENTERPRISES, 570
RESOURCE RENEWAL INSTITUTE, THE, 479
SAN DIEGUITO RIVER PARK JOINT POWERS AUTHORITY, 215
SAVE THE HARBOR/SAVE THE BAY, 486
SAVE WETLANDS AND BAYS, 486
SIERRA CLUB
   Alaska Field Office, 490
   Connecticut Chapter, 491
   Hawaii Chapter, 492
   New Jersey Chapter, 495
   West Virginia Chapter, 499
SIERRA CLUB CALIFORNIA, 499
SOUTH DAKOTA DEPARTMENT OF GAME, FISH, AND PARKS, 219
SOUTH DAKOTA RESOURCES COALITION, 507
SOUTHEASTERN ASSOCIATION OF FISH AND WILDLIFE AGENCIES, 508
SOUTHERN ENVIRONMENTAL LAW CENTER, 509
SOUTHWEST CENTER FOR ENVIRONMENTAL RESEARCH AND POLICY (SCERP), 596
SUSTAIN, 514
TEXAS BASS FEDERATION, 517
TWO WHITE WOLVES SANCTUARY, 525
UNITED STATES CHAMBER OF COMMERCE, 56
   Environment, Technology and Regulatory Affairs, 526
UNITED STATES DEPARTMENT OF COMMERCE
   National Oceanic and Atmospheric Administration
      Sea Grant Program - Massachusetts
UNITED STATES INSTITUTE FOR ENVIRONMENTAL CONFLICT RESOLUTION, 130
UNITY COLLEGE, 601
UNIVERSITE LAVAL, 601
UNIVERSITY OF COLORADO, 608
UNIVERSITY OF MICHIGAN, 614
URBAN WASTE MANAGEMENT & RESEARCH CENTER, 624
UTAH BASS FEDERATION, 528
VERMONT STATE-WIDE ENVIRONMENTAL EDUCATION PROGRAMS (SWEEP), 530
WETLANDS ACTION NETWORK, 538
WILDLIFE ACTION, INC., 542
WILDLIFE SOCIETY
   Illinois Chapter, 547
YELL COUNTY WILDLIFE FEDERATION, 561

FINANCE/BANKING/TRADE

ADVOCATES OF THE COMMON WEALTH, INC., 243
AFRICAN AMERICAN ENVIRONMENTALIST ASSOCIATION, 243
AMERICAN COUNCIL FOR THE UNITED NATIONS UNIVERSITY (ACUNU), 251
AMERICAN SOCIETY OF INTERNATIONAL LAW/WILDLIFE INTEREST GROUP, 266
CALIFORNIA STATE LANDS COMMISSION, 145
CENTER FOR ENVIRONMENT, COMMERCE & ENERGY, 290
CENTER FOR INTERNATIONAL ENVIRONMENTAL LAW (CIEL), 292
CINCINNATI NATURE CENTER, 297
CJE ASSOCIATES, 565
COLORADO WILDLIFE HERITAGE FOUNDATION, 302
EARTH POLICY INSTITUTE, 317
EARTHJUSTICE
   Headquarters, 318
EARTHSCAN, 320
ENVIRONMENTAL DEFENSE
   Headquarters, 324
FOOD SUPPLY / HUMAN POPULATION EXPLOSION CONNECTION, 333
HUMANE SOCIETY OF THE UNITED STATES, THE, 352
ISLESBORO ISLANDS TRUST, 375
J.N. (DING) DARLING FOUNDATION, 379
LAST WIZARDS, THE, 568
LEAGUE OF ENVIRONMENTAL JOURNALISTS, 387
NATIONAL WILDLIFE FEDERATION
   Headquarters, 427
NEVADA ASSOCIATION OF CONSERVATION DISTRICTS, 442
NORTH AMERICAN DEVELOPMENT BANK, 24
NOVA SCOTIA AGRICULTURE & FISHERIES, 203
RESTORE HETCH HETCHY, 479
SIERRA CLUB
   Connecticut Chapter, 491
   Northwest Office, 495
   West Virginia Chapter, 499
SOUTHWEST CENTER FOR ENVIRONMENTAL RESEARCH AND POLICY (SCERP), 596
SUSTAIN, 514
SUSTAINABLE ENERGY INSTITUTE
   Culture Change, 514
   Food Not Lawns, 514
   Pedal Power Produce, 514
UNITED STATES CHAMBER OF COMMERCE
   Environment, Technology and Regulatory Affairs, 526
UNITED STATES PUBLIC INTEREST RESEARCH GROUP, 526
UNIVERSITE LAVAL, 601
UNIVERSITY OF FLORIDA
   School of Forest Resources and Conservation, 609

KEYWORD INDEX – F

UNIVERSITY OF MICHIGAN, 614
WORLDWATCH INSTITUTE, 560

FORESTS/FORESTRY

ADIRONDACK MOUNTAIN CLUB, INC., THE (ADK), 242
AFRICAN AMERICAN ENVIRONMENTALIST ASSOCIATION, 243
AFRICAN CONSERVATION FOUNDATION, THE, 243
ALABAMA DEPARTMENT OF AGRICULTURE AND INDUSTRIES, 132
ALABAMA DEPARTMENT OF CONSERVATION AND NATURAL
   RESOURCES, 132
ALABAMA ENVIRONMENTAL COUNCIL, 244
ALASKA CENTER FOR THE ENVIRONMENT, 245
ALASKA CONSERVATION ALLIANCE, 245, 246
ALASKA CONSERVATION FOUNDATION, 246
ALASKA DEPARTMENT OF FISH AND GAME, 134
ALASKA HEALTH PROJECT, 134
ALBERTA WILDERNESS ASSOCIATION, 247
AMANAKAA AMAZON NETWORK, 248
AMERICAN ASSOCIATION OF FIELD BOTANISTS, 249
AMERICAN CHESTNUT FOUNDATION, THE, 250
AMERICAN FOREST FOUNDATION, 260
AMERICAN FORESTS, 260
AMERICAN HIKING SOCIETY, 261
AMERICAN LAND CONSERVANCY, 262
AMERICAN LANDS, 262
AMERICAN RESOURCES GROUP, 264
AMERICAN WILDLANDS, 267
ANCIENT FOREST INTERNATIONAL, 268
APPALACHIAN TRAIL CONFERENCE, 270
APROVECHO RESEARCH CENTER, 270
ARIZONA STATE ENVIROTHON, INC., 271
ARIZONA-SONORA DESERT MUSEUM, 271
ARKANSAS COOPERATIVE RESEARCH UNIT, 137
ARKANSAS DEPARTMENT OF ENVIRONMENTAL QUALITY, 137
ARKANSAS STATE PLANT BOARD, 138
ARKANSAS TECH UNIVERSITY
   Fisheries and Wildlife Biology Program, 573
ARKANSAS WATERSHED ADVISORY GROUP (AWAG), 272
ASSOCIATION OF CONSULTING FORESTERS OF AMERICA, 273
ATLANTIC CENTER FOR THE ENVIRONMENT
   Quebec-Labrador Foundation, 275
ATLANTIC SALMON FEDERATION, 275
AUBURN UNIVERSITY
   School of Forestry and Wildlife Sciences, 574
AUSTRALIA DEPARTMENT FOR ENVIRONMENT AND HERITAGE, 139
BAT CONSERVATION INTERNATIONAL, 277
BIODIVERSITY CONSERVATION ALLIANCE, 278
BOTANICAL CLUB OF WISCONSIN, 280
BRADLEY UNIVERSITY, 575
BROWN UNIVERSITY, 575
CALIFORNIA TROUT, INC., 283
CALIFORNIA UNIVERSITY OF PENNSYLVANIA, 576
CALIFORNIA WILDERNESS COALITION, 284
CAMP FIRE CLUB OF AMERICA, 284
CANADIAN FORESTRY ASSOCIATION, 286
CANADIAN INSTITUTE OF FORESTRY/INSTITUTE FORESTIER DU
   CANADA, 287
CANON ENVIROTHON, 288
CARIBBEAN NATURAL RESOURCES INSTITUTE, 288
CATSKILL FOREST ASSOCIATION, 289
CENTER FOR A SUSTAINABLE COAST, 289
CENTER FOR ENVIRONMENT AND POPULATION (CEP), 290
CENTER FOR ENVIRONMENT, COMMERCE & ENERGY, 290
CENTER FOR NATIVE ECOSYSTEMS
   Front Range Office, 292
   West Slope Office, 292
CENTER FOR RESOURCE ECONOMICS/ISLAND PRESS, 293
CENTER FOR SIERRA NEVADA CONSERVATION, 293
CENTER FOR WATERSHED PROTECTION, 293
CHESAPEAKE BAY FOUNDATION, INC.
   Maryland Office, 295
CHICAGO PARK DISTRICT, 296
CJE ASSOCIATES, 565
CLARK UNIVERSITY, 576
CLIMATE INSTITUTE, 299
COLORADO DEPARTMENT OF NATURAL RESOURCES
   Oil and Gas Conservation Commission, 147
COLORADO FORESTRY ASSOCIATION, 301
COLORADO MOUNTAIN CLUB, 302
COLORADO WATER CONSERVATION BOARD
   Water Conservation Board, 148
COLUMBIA RIVER INTER-TRIBAL FISH COMMISSION, 17
COMITE DESPERTAR CIDRENO, 148
CONNECTICUT BOTANICAL SOCIETY, 304
CONNECTICUT RIVER WATERSHED COUNCIL INC., 305
CONSERVAMERICA, 305
CONSERVATION ALLIANCE OF ST. LUCIE CO., 306
CONSERVATION COUNCIL OF NORTH CAROLINA, 306
CONSERVATION FUND, THE, 307
CONSERVATION INTERNATIONAL, 307
CONSERVATION LAW FOUNDATION, INC. (CLF), 307
   New England Region, 308
COOK INLET KEEPER, 308
COTTONWOOD FOUNDATION, 309
COUNCIL FOR PLANNING AND CONSERVATION, 310
D ACRES, 311
DEEP-PORTAGE CONSERVATION RESERVE, 311
DELAWARE COOPERATIVE EXTENSION SERVICES, 150
DELAWARE DEPARTMENT OF AGRICULTURE, 150
DELAWARE DEPARTMENT OF NATURAL RESOURCES AND
   ENVIRONMENTAL CONTROL
   Division of Air & Waste Management, 150
   Division of Soil and Water Conservation, 150
DELAWARE NATURE SOCIETY, 312
DELTA WILDLIFE INC., 313
DEPAUL UNIVERSITY
   Environmental Science Program, 579
DESCHUTES BASIN LAND TRUST, 313
DUCKS UNLIMITED CANADA
   Saskatchewan Office, 315
DUKE UNIVERSITY - ORGANIZATION FOR TROPICAL STUDIES, 580
EAGLE NATURE FOUNDATION, LTD., 316
EARTH FOUNDATION, 317
EARTH POLICY INSTITUTE, 317
EARTHJUSTICE
   Environmental Law Clinic at the University of Denver, 318
   Headquarters, 318
   Juneau Office, 319
   Oakland Office, 319
   Policy and Legislation, 319
   Seattle Office, 320
EARTHSCAN, 320
ECOLOGICAL SOCIETY OF AMERICA, THE, 321
ECOLOGY CENTER, 321
ELM RESEARCH INSTITUTE, 322
ENTOMOLOGICAL SOCIETY OF AMERICA, 323
ENVIRONMENT COUNCIL OF RHODE ISLAND, 323
ENVIRONMENTAL ALLIANCE FOR SENIOR INVOLVEMENT (EASI), 323
ENVIRONMENTAL DEFENSE
   Headquarters, 324
ENVIRONMENTAL DEFENSE CENTER, 325
ENVIRONMENTAL EDUCATION ASSOCIATES, 325
ENVIRONMENTAL LAW AND POLICY CENTER OF THE MIDWEST, 327
ENVIRONMENTAL MEDIA CORPORATION, 566
ENVIRONMENTAL POLICY CENTER, THE, 327
ENVIRONMENTAL PROTECTION AGENCY
   Region 1 (CT, ME, MA, NH, RI, VT), 18
   Region 5 (IL, IN, MI, NM, OH, WI), 19
EP EDUCATION SERVICES, INC., 328
EUROPARC FEDERATION, 328
FEDERATION OF FLY FISHERS (NCCFFF), 329
FEDERATION OF WESTERN OUTDOOR CLUBS, 330
FERRUM COLLEGE, 581
FLORIDA DEPARTMENT OF AGRICULTURE AND CONSUMER
   SERVICES
   Soil and Water Conservation Council, 153
FLORIDA DEPARTMENT OF ENVIRONMENTAL PROTECTION
   Division of Resource Assessment and Management, 154
   Florida State Parks AmeriCorps, 154
FLORIDA FEDERATION OF GARDEN CLUBS, INC., 331
FLORIDA FORESTRY ASSOCIATION, 331
FLORIDA NATIVE PLANT SOCIETY, 332
FOOD AND AGRICULTURE ORGANIZATION OF THE UNITED
   NATIONS, 333
FOOD SUPPLY / HUMAN POPULATION EXPLOSION CONNECTION, 333
FOREST HISTORY SOCIETY, INC., 334
FOREST LANDOWNERS ASSOCIATION, INC., 334
FOREST LANDOWNERS OF CALIFORNIA, 334
FOREST MANAGEMENT TRUST, 334
FOREST SERVICE EMPLOYEES FOR ENVIRONMENTAL ETHICS
   (FSEEE), 334
FOREST SOCIETY OF MAINE, 335
FOREST STEWARDS GUILD, 335
   Northwest Regional Chapter (GuildNW), 335
FOREST TRUST, 335

FOUR CORNERS INSTITUTE, THE, 336
FRIENDS OF THE BOUNDARY WATERS WILDERNESS, 337
FUTURE GENERATIONS, 339
GALIANO CONSERVANCY ASSOCIATION, 339
GEORGIA CONSERVANCY, INC., THE, 341
GEORGIA ENVIRONMENTAL ORGANIZATION, INC. (GEO), 341
GEORGIA ENVIRONMENTAL POLICY INSTITUTE, 342
GEORGIA FEDERATION OF FOREST OWNERS, 342
GEORGIA FORESTRY ASSOCIATION, INC., 342
GEORGIA TRUST FOR HISTORIC PRESERVATION, 342
GOOD NATURE PUBLISHING CO., 566
GRAND CANYON TRUST, 344
GREATER YELLOWSTONE COALITION, 346
GREEN BALKANS FEDERATION OF NATURE CONSERVATION NGOS, 346
GREEN MEDIA TOOLSHED, 346
GREEN SPHERE INC., 347
GUAM COASTAL MANAGEMENT PROGRAM, 158
GULF COAST RESEARCH LABORATORY, 158
HARDWOOD FOREST FOUNDATION, 348
HAWAII NATURE CENTER, 349
HAWAIIAN BOTANICAL SOCIETY, 349
HEADLANDS INSTITUTE, 350
HELPING OUR PENINSULA'S ENVIRONMENT, 350
HOLDEN ARBORETUM, THE, 351
HOLLOW OAK LAND TRUST, 351
IDAHO CONSERVATION LEAGUE, 354
IDAHO DEPARTMENT OF WATER RESOURCES
　Water Awareness Week, 161
ILLINOIS NATURE PRESERVES COMMISSION (INPC), 163
ILLINOIS WALNUT COUNCIL, 356
ILOVEPARKS.COM, 567
INDIANA DEPARTMENT OF ENVIRONMENTAL MANAGEMENT, 163
INDIANA NATIVE PLANT AND WILDFLOWER SOCIETY, 356
INDO-PACIFIC CONSERVATION ALLIANCE, 357
INSTITUTE FOR AGRICULTURE AND TRADE POLICY, 358
INSTITUTE FOR TROPICAL ECOLOGY AND CONSERVATION (ITEC), 358
INTERNATIONAL ACADEMY, 567
INTERNATIONAL ASSOCIATION OF FISH AND WILDLIFE AGENCIES, 360
INTERNATIONAL ASSOCIATION OF NATURAL RESOURCE PILOTS, 360
INTERNATIONAL ASSOCIATION OF WILDLAND FIRE, 361
INTERNATIONAL CHILDREN'S CONFERENCE ON THE ENVIRONMENT, 362
INTERNATIONAL EROSION CONTROL ASSOCIATION (IECA), 363
INTERNATIONAL MIRE CONSERVATION GROUP, 365
INTERNATIONAL PLANT PROPAGATORS SOCIETY, INC., 365
INTERNATIONAL PRIMATE PROTECTION LEAGUE, 365
INTERNATIONAL SOCIETY OF TROPICAL FORESTERS, INC., 367
INTERNATIONAL UNION FOR CONSERVATION OF NATURE AND NATURAL RESOURCES (IUCN) THE WORLD CONSERVATION UNION
　Canada Office, 368
　Environmental Law Centre, 368
　Regional Office for Europe, 369
IOWA PRAIRIE NETWORK, 373
IOWA STATE UNIVERSITY
　College of Agriculture, 584
ISLESBORO ISLANDS TRUST, 375
ISSAQUAH ALPS TRAILS CLUB (I.A.T.C.), 375
IZAAK WALTON LEAGUE OF AMERICA, INC., THE
　California State IWLA, 376
　Minnesota Division, 377
　Owatonna Minnesota Chapter, 377
J.N. (DING) DARLING FOUNDATION, 379
JACKSON HOLE CONSERVATION ALLIANCE, 379
JAGRATA JUBA SHANGHA (JJS), 568
JANE GOODALL INSTITUTE, THE, 380
JOHNSON STATE COLLEGE, 585
KANSAS ACADEMY OF SCIENCE, 380
KANSAS COOPERATIVE FISH AND WILDLIFE RESEARCH UNIT, 167
KANSAS DEPARTMENT OF WILDLIFE AND PARKS
　Region 4, 168
　Region 5, 168
KANSAS STATE UNIVERSITY
　Department of Landscape Architecture / Regional and Community Planning, 585
KANSAS WILDFLOWER SOCIETY, 381
KENTUCKY DEPARTMENT OF AGRICULTURE, 169
KENTUCKY NATURAL LANDS TRUST, 383
LAKE SUPERIOR STATE UNIVERSITY, 586
LAKEHEAD UNIVERSITY, 586
LAND TRUST ALLIANCE, THE, 386
LAST WIZARDS, THE, 568
LEAGUE OF KENTUCKY SPORTSMEN, INC., 387

LEAGUE OF OHIO SPORTSMEN, 387
LEAGUE TO SAVE LAKE TAHOE, 388
LEGACY LAND TRUST, 388
LIFE OF THE LAND, 389
LIGHTHAWK, 389
LIVING RIVERS, 390
LOUISIANA WILDLIFE FEDERATION, INC., 391
LOWER MERION CONSERVANCY, 391
LUMMI ISLAND HERITAGE TRUST, 568
MACOMB LAND CONSERVANCY, 391
MAINE BASS FEDERATION, 392
MANOMET CENTER FOR CONSERVATION SCIENCES, 393
MARYLAND ORNITHOLOGICAL SOCIETY, INC., 395
MASSACHUSETTS DIVISION OF FISHERIES AND WILDLIFE
　MassWildlife, 178
MASSACHUSETTS EXECUTIVE OFFICE OF ENVIRONMENTAL AFFAIRS
　Office of Technical Assistance for Toxic Use Reduction, 179
　Wetlands and Waterways Program, 179
MASSACHUSETTS TRAPPERS ASSOCIATION, INC., 396
MCGILL UNIVERSITY, 587
MICHIGAN DEPARTMENT OF AGRICULTURE, 180
MICHIGAN LAND USE INSTITUTE, 397
MICHIGAN NATURAL AREAS COUNCIL, 398
MICHIGAN STATE UNIVERSITY EXTENSION, 181
MICHIGAN TECHNOLOGICAL UNIVERSITY; SCHOOL OF FORESTRY AND WOOD PRODUCTS, 588
MICHIGAN UNITED CONSERVATION CLUBS, INC., 398
MIDDLE TENNESSEE STATE UNIVERSITY, 588
MIDLAND CONSERVATION DISTRICT, 181
MINNESOTA GROUND WATER ASSOCIATION, 400
MISSISSIPPI STATE UNIVERSITY
　College of Forest Resources, 588
　Forest and Wildlife Research Center, 588
MISSOURI DEPARTMENT OF AGRICULTURE, 185
MONO LAKE COMMITTEE, 402
MONTANA BASS FEDERATION, 403
MONTANA BUREAU OF MINES AND GEOLOGY, 186
MONTANA ENVIRONMENTAL QUALITY COUNCIL, 187
MONTANA FOREST OWNERS ASSOCIATION, 403
MONTANA NATURAL HERITAGE PROGRAM, 187
MONTANA WILDERNESS ASSOCIATION, 403
MONTANA WILDLIFE FEDERATION, 404
MOUNT GRACE LAND CONSERVATION TRUST, 405
MOUNT UNION COLLEGE, 589
NATIONAL AGRICULTURAL LIBRARY, 24
NATIONAL ARBOR DAY FOUNDATION, 406
NATIONAL ASSOCIATION OF SERVICE AND CONSERVATION CORPS (NASCC), 408
NATIONAL ASSOCIATION OF STATE FORESTERS, 408
NATIONAL AUDUBON SOCIETY
　Audubon Alaska, 409
　Audubon Maryland-DC, 410
　Audubon of Florida, 410
　Audubon Society of Portland, 411
　Kentucky Audubon Council, 413
　Louisiana Audubon Council, 414
　Maine Audubon, 414
　Maricopa Audubon Society, 414
　Montana Audubon, 415
　Public Policy Office, 415
　Seattle Audubon Society, 416
NATIONAL BOWHUNTER EDUCATION FOUNDATION (NBEF), 417
NATIONAL FOREST FOUNDATION, 420
NATIONAL FORESTRY ASSOCIATION, 420
NATIONAL NETWORK OF FOREST PRACTITIONERS, 422
NATIONAL TREE TRUST, 425
NATIONAL WATERSHED COALITION, 426
NATIONAL WILD TURKEY FEDERATION, INC., THE, 427
NATIONAL WILDLIFE FEDERATION
　Great Lakes Natural Resource Center, 427
　Headquarters, 427
NATIONAL WILDLIFE PRODUCTIONS, INC., 429
NATIONAL WOODLAND OWNERS ASSOCIATION, 430
NATIVE PLANT SOCIETY OF NORTHEASTERN OHIO, 430
NATIVE PLANT SOCIETY OF TEXAS, 431
NATIVE PRAIRIES ASSOCIATION OF TEXAS, 431
NATURAL HISTORY SOCIETY OF MARYLAND, INC., THE, 431
NATURE CONSERVANCY, THE
　Arkansas Field Office, 434
　Colorado Chapter, 434
　Eastern New York Chapter, 435
　Illinois Chapter, 435
　Iowa Chapter, 435

KEYWORD INDEX – F

Maryland/District of Columbia Chapter, 436
New York City Chapter, 438
New York City Office, 437
Oklahoma Chapter, 439
Oregon Chapter, 439
Pennsylvania Chapter, 439
Rhode Island Chapter, 439
NAVAJO NATION DEPARTMENT OF FISH AND WILDLIFE, 188
NEBRASKA DEPARTMENT OF ENVIRONMENTAL QUALITY, 188
NEBRASKA DEPARTMENT OF NATURAL RESOURCES, 188
NEBRASKA GAME AND PARKS COMMISSION
  OMAHA OFFICE, 189
NEBRASKA WILDLIFE FEDERATION, INC., 442
NEGATIVE POPULATION GROWTH (NPG), 442
NEW ENGLAND COALITION FOR SUSTAINABLE POPULATION (NECSP), 443
NEW HAMPSHIRE ASSOCIATION OF CONSERVATION COMMISSIONS, 443
NEW HAMPSHIRE ASSOCIATION OF CONSERVATION DISTRICTS, 444
NEW HAMPSHIRE DEPARTMENT OF RESOURCES AND ECONOMIC DEVELOPMENT, 190
NEW HAMPSHIRE LAKES ASSOCIATION, 444
NEW HAMPSHIRE TIMBERLAND OWNERS ASSOCIATION, 444
NEW JERSEY ASSOCIATION OF CONSERVATION DISTRICTS, 445
NEW JERSEY ENVIRONMENTAL LOBBY, 445
NEW MEXICO ASSOCIATION OF CONSERVATION DISTRICTS, 445
NEW MEXICO ENERGY, MINERALS, AND NATURAL RESOURCES DEPARTMENT
  Oil Conservation Division, 195
NEW MEXICO STATE UNIVERSITY
  College of Agriculture and Home Economics, 589, 590
  Department of Fishery and Wildlife Sciences
NEW YORK FOREST OWNERS ASSOCIATION, INC., 446
NEW YORK OFFICE OF ENERGY EFFICIENCY AND ENVIRONMENT, 197
NORTH AMERICAN WETLANDS CONSERVATION COUNCIL, 24
NORTH CAROLINA BASS FEDERATION, 450
NORTH CAROLINA COASTAL FEDERATION, INC., 450
NORTH CAROLINA CONSERVATION NETWORK, 450
NORTH CAROLINA DEPARTMENT OF AGRICULTURE AND CONSUMER SERVICES, 200
NORTH CAROLINA FORESTRY ASSOCIATION (NCFA), 450
NORTH CAROLINA STATE UNIVERSITY, 590
NORTH DAKOTA WATER COMMISSION, 202
NORTHLAND COLLEGE, 591
NORTHWEST COALITION FOR ALTERNATIVES TO PESTICIDES, 453
NORTHWEST ECOSYSTEM ALLIANCE, 453
NORTHWEST ENVIRONMENT WATCH, 454
NORTHWEST TERRITORIES DEPARTMENT OF RESOURCES, WILDLIFE AND ECONOMIC DEVELOPMENT, 202
NORTHWESTERN STATE UNIVERSITY OF LOUISIANA, 591
NOVA SCOTIA AGRICULTURE & FISHERIES, 203
NOVA SCOTIA DEPARTMENT OF NATURAL RESOURCES, 203
NOVA SCOTIA FEDERATION OF ANGLERS AND HUNTERS, 454
NOVA SCOTIA FORESTRY ASSOCIATION, 454
OHIO DEPARTMENT OF AGRICULTURE, 203
OHIO DEPARTMENT OF NATURAL RESOURCES, 204
OHIO FEDERATION OF SOIL AND WATER CONSERVATION DISTRICTS, 457
OKLAHOMA STATE EXTENSION SERVICES, 206
OKLAHOMA STATE UNIVERSITY, 592
OKLAHOMA WATER RESOURCES BOARD, 207
OLYMPIC PARK ASSOCIATES, 459
OLYMPIC PARK INSTITUTE, 459
ONTARIO FEDERATION OF ANGLERS AND HUNTERS, 459
OPENLANDS PROJECT, 460
ORANGUTAN FOUNDATION INTERNATIONAL, 460
OREGON DEPARTMENT OF GEOLOGY AND MINERAL INDUSTRIES, 209
OREGON SMALL WOODLANDS ASSOCIATION, 461
OREGON SOCIETY OF AMERICAN FORESTERS, 461
OREGON TROUT, 461
OUTDOOR RECREATION COUNCIL OF BRITISH COLUMBIA, 462
PACIFIC RIVERS COUNCIL, 464
PARTNERSHIP FOR SUSTAINABLE FORESTRY, 465
PENNSYLVANIA DEPARTMENT OF AGRICULTURE
  State Conservation Commission, 211
PENNSYLVANIA DEPARTMENT OF ENVIRONMENTAL PROTECTION, 211
PENNSYLVANIA ORGANIZATION FOR WATERSHEDS AND RIVERS (POWR), 466
PENNSYLVANIA RECREATION AND PARK SOCIETY, INC., 467
PENNSYLVANIA RESOURCES COUNCIL, INC., 467
PEOPLE FOR PUGET SOUND
  South Sound Office, 467
PINCHOT INSTITUTE FOR CONSERVATION, 469

POCONO ENVIRONMENTAL EDUCATION CENTER, 470
POPULATION-ENVIRONMENT BALANCE, INC., 471
POULSBO MARINE SCIENCE CENTER, 471
PROGRESSIVE ANIMAL WELFARE SOCIETY, 473
PROTECTED AREAS ASSOCIATION OF NEWFOUNDLAND AND LABRADOR, 474
PROVINCE OF QUEBEC SOCIETY FOR THE PROTECTION OF BIRDS, INC., 474
PUBLIC EMPLOYEES FOR ENVIRONMENTAL RESPONSIBILITY (PEER), 474
QUALITY DEER MANAGEMENT ASSOCIATION, 476
RAINFOREST ACTION NETWORK, 476
RAINFOREST ALLIANCE, 477
RAINFOREST RELIEF, 477
RAINFOREST TRUST, 477
RENEWABLE NATURAL RESOURCES FOUNDATION, 478
RESOURCES FOR THE FUTURE, 479
RHODE ISLAND WILD PLANT SOCIETY, 480
ROCKY MOUNTAIN BIRD OBSERVATORY, 482
ROCKY MOUNTAIN ELK FOUNDATION, 482
RUFFED GROUSE SOCIETY, THE, 482
RUFFNER MOUNTAIN NATURE COALITION, INC., 483
SAND CREEK WATERSHED PROJECT, THE, 215
SASKATCHEWAN WILDLIFE FEDERATION, 484
SAVE AMERICA'S FORESTS, 485
SAVE-THE-REDWOODS LEAGUE, 487
SCENIC AMERICA
  Scenic California, 487
SHELBURNE FARMS, 490
SIERRA CLUB
  Alaska Field Office, 490
  Connecticut Chapter, 491
  Hawaii Chapter, 492
  Lone Star Chapter, 493
  Mackinac Chapter, 493
  Maryland Chapter, 493
  Mississippi Chapter, 494
  New Jersey Chapter, 495
  Northwest Office, 495
  Pennsylvania Chapter, 496
  Rio Grande Chapter (New Mexico/West Texas), 496
  Washington, DC Office, 499
  West Virginia Chapter, 499
SIERRA CLUB CALIFORNIA, 499
SIERRA CLUB FOUNDATION, THE, 499
SIERRA CLUB OF CANADA
  Atlantic Canada Chapter, 500
SIERRA STUDENT COALITION, 500
SINAPU, 500
SLIPPERY ROCK UNIVERSITY, 595
SMALL WOODLAND OWNERS ASSOCIATION OF MAINE, 501
SMITHSONIAN INSTITUTION, 501
SOCIETY FOR RANGE MANAGEMENT, 503
SOCIETY OF AMERICAN FORESTERS, 503
SOIL AND WATER CONSERVATION SOCIETY, 504
SOUTH CAROLINA BASS FEDERATION, 506
SOUTH CAROLINA ENERGY OFFICE, 218
SOUTH CAROLINA NATIVE PLANT SOCIETY, 506
SOUTH CAROLINA WILDLIFE FEDERATION, 506
SOUTH DAKOTA ASSOCIATION OF CONSERVATION DISTRICTS, 506
SOUTH DAKOTA COOPERATIVE FISH AND WILDLIFE RESEARCH UNIT (USDI-USGS), 29
SOUTH DAKOTA DEPARTMENT OF GAME, FISH, AND PARKS, 219
SOUTHEAST ALASKA CONSERVATION COUNCIL (SEACC), 507
SOUTHEASTERN ASSOCIATION OF FISH AND WILDLIFE AGENCIES, 508
SOUTHERN APPALACHIAN BOTANICAL SOCIETY, 508
SOUTHERN ENVIRONMENTAL LAW CENTER, 509
SOUTHERN ILLINOIS UNIVERSITY CARBONDALE, 596
SOUTHERN NEW ENGLAND FOREST CONSORTIUM, INC. (SNEFCI), 509
SOUTHERN RHODE ISLAND STATE ASSOCIATION OF CONSERVATION DISTRICTS, 509
SOUTHERN UTAH WILDERNESS ALLIANCE
  Moab Office, 510
SOUTHWEST CENTER FOR ENVIRONMENTAL RESEARCH AND POLICY (SCERP), 596
SOUTHWEST CONSERVATION DISTRICT, 510
SOUTHWESTERN HERPETOLOGISTS SOCIETY, 510
STATE ENVIRONMENTAL RESOURCE CENTER (SERC), 512
STEPHEN F. AUSTIN STATE UNIVERSITY ARTHUR TEMPLE COLLEGE OF FORESTRY, 598
STERLING COLLEGE, 598

STUDENT CONSERVATION ASSOCIATION, INC., 512
STUDENT ENVIRONMENTAL ACTION COALITION (SEAC), 513
STUDENTS PARTNERSHIP WORLDWIDE, 513
SUSTAIN, 514
TAHOE REGIONAL PLANNING AGENCY, 220
TALL TIMBERS RESEARCH STATION (TTRS), 515
TENNESSEE CONSERVATION LEAGUE, 516
TENNESSEE DEPARTMENT OF ENVIRONMENT AND CONSERVATION, 221
TENNESSEE FORESTRY ASSOCIATION, 516
TENNESSEE VALLEY AUTHORITY
   Muscle Shoals Technical Library, 30
TERRA NATURE FUND, 516
TEXAS A AND M UNIVERSITY AT KINGSVILLE
   Caesar Kleberg Wildlife Research Institute, 599
TEXAS BASS FEDERATION, 517
TEXAS COMMITTEE ON NATURAL RESOURCES, 517
TEXAS COOPERATIVE FISH AND WILDLIFE RESEARCH UNIT, 30
TEXAS ORGANIZATION FOR ENDANGERED SPECIES, 517
TEXAS RIPARIAN ASSOCIATION, 517
TEXAS WATER DEVELOPMENT BOARD, 223
TREEPEOPLE, 519
TROUT UNLIMITED
   Alaska Council, 520
   Pennsylvania Council, 522
TRUST FOR PUBLIC LAND, THE, 523
TRUST FOR WILDLIFE, INC., 524
TRUSTEES FOR ALASKA, 524
TUG HILL TOMORROW LAND TRUST, 524
TULANE UNIVERSITY
   Department of Ecology and Evolutionary Biology, 600
TURTLE CREEK WATERSHED ASSOCIATION, INC., 525
TWO WHITE WOLVES SANCTUARY, 525
UNEP WORLD CONSERVATION MONITORING CENTRE, 525
UNION OF CONCERNED SCIENTISTS, 525
UNITED STATES CHAMBER OF COMMERCE
   Environment, Technology and Regulatory Affairs, 526
UNITED STATES DEPARTMENT OF AGRICULTURE
   Forest Service
      Allegheny National Forest, 34
      Angelina, Davy Crockett, Sabine and Sam Houston National Forest, 34
      Crooked River National Grassland, 37
      Finger Lakes National Forest, 37
      Gila National Forest, 38
      Green Mountain National Forest, 38
      Nez Perce National Forest, 41
      Pawnee National Grassland, 42
      Prescott National Forest, 42
      Region 02 (Rocky Mountain), 43
      Region 09 (Eastern), 43
      Siuslaw National Forest, 45
UNITED STATES DEPARTMENT OF COMMERCE
   National Oceanic and Atmospheric Administration
      Rookery Bay National Estuarine Research Reserve, 53
      Sea Grant Program - Louisiana, 56
      Sea Grant Program - Massachusetts, 56
      Sea Grant Program - North Carolina, 58
      Sea Grant Program - Rhode Island, 59
UNITED STATES DEPARTMENT OF DEFENSE
   Air Force Major Air Commands
      Andrews AFB, MD, 61
      USAF Academy, 62
   Air Force Major U.S. Installations
      Eglin Air Force Base, 63
   Army Materiel Command, 72
   HQ PACAF/CEVQ, 74
   Navy, 74
UNITED STATES DEPARTMENT OF THE INTERIOR
   Bureau of Land Management
      Bakersfield Field Office, 79
      Eugene District Office, 81
      Malta Field Office, 83
      Northern Field Office, 84
      Rawlins Field Office, 85
   Fish and Wildlife Service
      Alligator River/Pea Island National Wildlife Refuge, 91
      Carolina Sandhills National Wildlife Refuge, 95
      Chickasaw National Wildlife Refuge, 95
      Great Dismal Swamp/Nansemond National Wildlife Refuge, 98
      Hobe Sound National Wildlife Refuge, 99
      Necedah National Wildlife Refuge, 107
      Noxubee National Wildlife Refuge, 108
      Okefenokee (Banks Lake) National Wildlife Refuge, 108
      Patoka River National Wetlands Project National Wildlife Refuge, 109
      Ridgefield National Wildlife Refuge, 112
      Sandy Point National Wildlife Refuge, 114
      Selawik National Wildlife Refuge, 114
      St. Marks National Wildlife Refuge, 115
      White River National Wildlife Refuge, 118
      Wichita Mountains National Wildlife Refuge, 118
      Willapa/Lewis and Clark National Wildlife Refuge, 118
   Montana State Extension Services, 119
   National Park Service
      Chihuahuan Desert Network, 121
      Mammoth Cave National Park, 124
      Mesa Verde National Park, 124
      Mount Rainier National Park, 124
      Yellowstone National Park, 126
   Oregon Cooperative Fish and Wildlife Research Unit, 126
   United States Geological Survey
      New Mexico Cooperative Fish and Wildlife Research Unit, 127
      Western Region, 127
UNITED STATES INSTITUTE FOR ENVIRONMENTAL CONFLICT RESOLUTION, 130
UNITED STATES PUBLIC INTEREST RESEARCH GROUP, 526
UNITED STATES TOURIST COUNCIL, 527
UNITY COLLEGE, 601
UNIVERSITE LAVAL, 601
UNIVERSITY OF COLORADO, 608
UNIVERSITY OF DAR ES SALAAM, 608
UNIVERSITY OF FLORIDA
   School of Forest Resources and Conservation, 609
UNIVERSITY OF FLORIDA INSTITUTE OF FOOD AND AGRICULTURAL SCIENCES, 609
UNIVERSITY OF GEORGIA
   Daniel B. Warnell School of Forest Resources, 609
UNIVERSITY OF IDAHO
   College of Natural Resources
      Department of Fish and Wildlife Resources, 610
UNIVERSITY OF LOUISVILLE, 612
UNIVERSITY OF MAINE, 612
UNIVERSITY OF MAINE AT FORT KENT, 612
UNIVERSITY OF MARYLAND - AT COLLEGE PARK, 613
UNIVERSITY OF MARYLAND COOPERATIVE EXTENSION, 224
UNIVERSITY OF MICHIGAN, 614
UNIVERSITY OF MINNESOTA AT ST. PAUL, 615
UNIVERSITY OF MISSOURI, 615
UNIVERSITY OF NEW BRUNSWICK, 616
UNIVERSITY OF NORTH CAROLINA AT ASHEVILLE, 617
UNIVERSITY OF NORTHERN BRITISH COLUMBIA, 618
UNIVERSITY OF RHODE ISLAND
   Department of Natural Resources Science, 619
UNIVERSITY OF SASKATCHEWAN, 620
UNIVERSITY OF TENNESSEE - AT KNOXVILLE, 621
UNIVERSITY OF WISCONSIN, 622
UNIVERSITY OF WISCONSIN AT MADISON, 623
UPPER MISSISSIPPI RIVER CONSERVATION COMMITTEE, 527
URBAN WILDLIFE RESOURCES, 527
UTAH BASS FEDERATION, 528
UTAH DEPARTMENT OF NATURAL RESOURCES
   Division of Wildlife Resources, 225
VERMONT AGENCY OF NATURAL RESOURCES
   Department of Environmental Conservation, 226
VERMONT BASS FEDERATION, 529
VERMONT LAND TRUST, 529
VERMONT STATE-WIDE ENVIRONMENTAL EDUCATION PROGRAMS (SWEEP), 530
VERMONT WOODLANDS ASSOCIATION, 530
VIRGIN ISLANDS CONSERVATION DISTRICT, 530
VIRGINIA BASS FEDERATION, 531
VIRGINIA DEPARTMENT OF GAME AND INLAND FISHERIES
   Region IV (Staunton), 231
VIRGINIA TECH
   Department of Fisheries and Wildlife Sciences, 625
VIRGINIA TECH UNIVERSITY
   College of Natural Resources, 625
WARREN COUNTY CONSERVATION BOARD, 532
WASHINGTON DEPARTMENT OF ECOLOGY, 233
WASHINGTON FARM FORESTRY ASSOCIATION, 533
WASHINGTON FOUNDATION FOR THE ENVIRONMENT, 533
WASHINGTON RECREATION AND PARK ASSOCIATION, 533
WASHINGTON STATE DEPARTMENT OF NATURAL RESOURCES
   Olympic Region, 234
WASHINGTON STATE PARKS AND RECREATION COMMISSION
   Southwest Region, 235
WATERSHED MANAGEMENT COUNCIL, 535

KEYWORD INDEX – L

WEST VIRGINIA ASSOCIATION OF CONSERVATION DISTRICT SUPERVISORS ASSOCIATION, INC., 536
WEST VIRGINIA BASS FEDERATION, 536
WEST VIRGINIA DEPARTMENT OF AGRICULTURE, 235
WEST VIRGINIA HIGHLANDS CONSERVANCY, 536
WEST VIRGINIA RAPTOR REHABILITATION CENTER, 536
WESTERN FORESTRY AND CONSERVATION ASSOCIATION, 537
WETLAND HABITAT ALLIANCE OF TEXAS, 538
WHALE AND DOLPHIN CONSERVATION SOCIETY, 538
WILD FOUNDATION, THE, 539
WILD ONES NATURAL LANDSCAPERS, LTD, 540
WILDERNESS SOCIETY, THE, 541
WILDLIFE ACTION, INC., 542
WILDLIFE DAMAGE REVIEW (WDR), 543
WILDLIFE HABITAT CANADA, 544
WILDLIFE HABITAT COUNCIL, 544
WILDLIFE MANAGEMENT INSTITUTE, 545
WILDLIFE SOCIETY
  Arizona Chapter, 546
  Colorado Chapter, 547
  Illinois Chapter, 547
  Michigan Chapter, 549
  National Capital Chapter, 550
WINDSTAR WILDLIFE INSTITUTE, 555
WISCONSIN COOPERATIVE WILDLIFE RESEARCH UNIT (USDI), 237
WOODLAND OWNERS ASSOCIATION OF WEST VIRGINIA, 558
WORLD FORESTRY CENTER, 558
WORLD PARKS ENDOWMENT INC., 559
WORLD RESOURCES INSTITUTE, 559
WORLDWATCH INSTITUTE, 560
WWW.ACTIONBIOSCIENCE.ORG, 560
WYOMING DEPARTMENT OF ENVIRONMENTAL QUALITY, 239
WYOMING OUTDOOR COUNCIL, 561
YELL COUNTY WILDLIFE FEDERATION, 561
YMCA NATURE AND COMMUNITY CENTER, 562

LAND ISSUES

ACRES LAND TRUST, 241
ADIRONDACK COUNCIL, THE, 242
ADIRONDACK MOUNTAIN CLUB, INC., THE (ADK), 242
ADKINS ARBORETUM, 242
ADOPT-A-STREAM FOUNDATION, THE, 242
ADVOCATES OF THE COMMON WEALTH, INC., 243
AFRICA VISION TRUST, 243
AFRICAN AMERICAN ENVIRONMENTALIST ASSOCIATION, 243
AFRICAN CONSERVATION FOUNDATION, THE, 243
ALABAMA ENVIRONMENTAL COUNCIL, 244
ALASKA CENTER FOR THE ENVIRONMENT, 245
ALASKA CONSERVATION ALLIANCE, 245, 246
ALASKA HEALTH PROJECT, 134
ALASKA RAINFOREST CAMPAIGN, 246
ALBERTA DEPARTMENT OF ENVIRONMENTAL PROTECTION
  Natural Resources Service, 135
ALBERTA WILDERNESS ASSOCIATION, 247
ALDEANATURAL.COM, 563
ALDO LEOPOLD FOUNDATION, 247
AMERICAN ASSOCIATION OF FIELD BOTANISTS, 249
AMERICAN BIRD CONSERVANCY, 249
AMERICAN CAVE CONSERVATION ASSOCIATION, 250
AMERICAN FARMLAND TRUST, 251
AMERICAN FEDERATION OF MINERALOGICAL SOCIETIES (AFMS), 252
AMERICAN GEOGRAPHICAL SOCIETY, 260
AMERICAN GEOLOGICAL INSTITUTE, 260
AMERICAN HIKING SOCIETY, 261
AMERICAN HORSE PROTECTION ASSOCIATION, 261
AMERICAN LAND CONSERVANCY, 262
AMERICAN PLANNING ASSOCIATION, 264
AMERICAN SOCIETY OF LANDSCAPE ARCHITECTS, 266
AMERICAN SPORTFISHING ASSOCIATION, 266
AMERICAN WHITEWATER, 267
AMERICAN WILDERNESS COALITION, 267
AMERICAN WILDLANDS, 267
ANTARCTICA PROJECT, THE, 269
APPALACHIAN TRAIL CONFERENCE, 270
ARCHBOLD BIOLOGICAL STATION, 270
ARIZONA GAME AND FISH DEPARTMENT, 136
ARIZONA GEOLOGICAL SURVEY, 136
ARIZONA STATE ENVIROTHON, INC., 271
ARIZONA STATE UNIVERSITY
  Center for Environmental Studies, 573
ARIZONA-SONORA DESERT MUSEUM, 271

ARKANSAS STATE EXTENSION SERVICES
  Four H Center, 138
ARKANSAS WATERSHED ADVISORY GROUP (AWAG), 272
ARLINGTON OUTDOOR EDUCATION ASSOCIATION, INC. (AOEA), 272
ASSOCIATION FOR THE PROTECTION OF THE ADIRONDACKS, THE, 273
ASSOCIATION OF AMERICAN GEOGRAPHERS, 273
ASSOCIATION OF NEW JERSEY ENVIRONMENTAL COMMISSIONS (ANJEC), 274
ATLANTIC CENTER FOR THE ENVIRONMENT
  Quebec-Labrador Foundation, 275
ATLANTIC SALMON FEDERATION, 275
ATLANTIC STATES LEGAL FOUNDATION, 275
AUDUBON INTERNATIONAL, 276
AUSTRALIA DEPARTMENT FOR ENVIRONMENT AND HERITAGE, 139
  Environment Shop, The, 139
AUSTRALIAN MINERAL FOUNDATION, 563
BARRIER ISLAND TRUST, INC., 276
BASS DIVISION OF ESPN PRODUCTIONS INC, 564
BERKSHIRE-LITCHFIELD ENVIRONMENTAL COUNCIL, INC., 277
BIODIVERSITY CONSERVATION ALLIANCE, 278
BIRDLIFE INTERNATIONAL, 279
BOONE AND CROCKETT CLUB, 279
BOONE AND CROCKETT FOUNDATION, 279
BRADLEY UNIVERSITY, 575
BRANDYWINE CONSERVANCY INC., 280
BROWN UNIVERSITY, 575
BUN-CA, 281
BYRON FOREST PRESERVE, 140
CALIFORNIA DEPARTMENT OF FISH AND GAME
  Elkhorn Slough National Estuarine Research Reserve, 141
CALIFORNIA DEPARTMENT OF FOOD AND AGRICULTURE, 142
CALIFORNIA DEPARTMENT OF WATER RESOURCES, 143
CALIFORNIA ENERGY COMMISSION
  Environmental Department, 143
CALIFORNIA NATIVE PLANT SOCIETY, THE, 283
CALIFORNIA TRAPPERS ASSOCIATION, 283
CALIFORNIA WILDERNESS COALITION, 284
CALIFORNIANS FOR POPULATION STABILIZATION (CAPS), 284
CANADA GOOSE PROJECT, 285
CANADIAN PARKS AND WILDERNESS SOCIETY, 287
CANON ENVIROTHON, 288
CARRYING CAPACITY NETWORK, 288
CATSKILL CENTER FOR CONSERVATION AND DEVELOPMENT, INC., THE, 289
CATSKILL FOREST ASSOCIATION, 289
CAVE RESEARCH FOUNDATION, 289
CENTER FOR A SUSTAINABLE COAST, 289
CENTER FOR ENVIRONMENT AND POPULATION (CEP), 290
CENTER FOR ENVIRONMENT, COMMERCE & ENERGY, 290
CENTER FOR ENVIRONMENTAL PHILOSOPHY, 291
CENTER FOR NATIVE ECOSYSTEMS
  Front Range Office, 292
  West Slope Office, 292
CENTER FOR PLANT CONSERVATION, 292
CENTER FOR RESOURCE ECONOMICS/ISLAND PRESS, 293
CHESAPEAKE BAY FOUNDATION, INC.
  Maryland Office, 295
CHICAGO REGION BIODIVERSITY COUNCIL, 296
CHIHUAHUAN DESERT RESEARCH INSTITUTE, 296
CITY OF BELDING, 145
CITY UNIVERSITY OF NEW YORK
  College of Staten Island, 576
CJE ASSOCIATES, 565
CLARK UNIVERSITY, 576
CLINTON RIVER WATERSHED COUNCIL (CRWC), 299
COALITION FOR EDUCATION IN THE OUTDOORS, 299
COAST ALLIANCE, 300
COASTAL AMERICA FOUNDATION, 300
COASTAL RESOURCE MANAGEMENT PROJECT, 146
COLORADO DEPARTMENT OF NATURAL RESOURCES
  Division of Parks and Outdoor Recreation, 146
  Oil and Gas Conservation Commission, 147
COLORADO ENVIRONMENTAL COALITION, 301
COLORADO MOUNTAIN CLUB, 302
COLORADO MOUNTAIN COLLEGE, 577
COLORADO NATURAL HERITAGE PROGRAM, 302
COLORADO WATER CONSERVATION BOARD
  Water Conservation Board, 148
COLUMBIA RIVER INTER-TRIBAL FISH COMMISSION, 17
COMMUNITY CONSERVATION /HOWLERS FOREVER, INC., 303
COMMUNITY ENVIRONMENTAL COUNCIL (CEC), 303
CONFEDERATED SALISH AND KOOTENAI TRIBES, 304

CONNECTICUT BOTANICAL SOCIETY, 304
CONNECTICUT FUND FOR THE ENVIRONMENT, 305
CONNECTICUT RIVER WATERSHED COUNCIL INC., 305
CONSERVAMERICA, 305
CONSERVANCY OF SOUTHWEST FLORIDA, THE, 305
CONSERVATION ALLIANCE OF ST. LUCIE CO., 306
CONSERVATION COUNCIL OF NORTH CAROLINA, 306
CONSERVATION FEDERATION OF MARYLAND/ F.A.R.M., 306
CONSERVATION FUND, THE, 307
CONSERVATION LAW FOUNDATION, INC. (CLF), 307
   New England Region, 308
CONSERVATION TRUST OF PUERTO RICO, 308
COOK INLET KEEPER, 308
COTTONWOOD FOUNDATION, 309
COUNCIL FOR PLANNING AND CONSERVATION, 310
COUNTY OF SAN DIEGO, 149
CRANSTON CONSERVATION COMMISSION, 150
DELAWARE ASSOCIATION OF CONSERVATION DISTRICTS, 312
DELAWARE COOPERATIVE EXTENSION SERVICES, 150
DELAWARE DEPARTMENT OF NATURAL RESOURCES AND ENVIRONMENTAL CONTROL
   Division of Soil and Water Conservation, 150
DELAWARE GREENWAYS, INC., 312
DELAWARE NATURE SOCIETY, 312
DELAWARE RIVERKEEPER NETWORK, 313
DELAWARE WILD LANDS, INC., 313
DESCHUTES BASIN LAND TRUST, 313
DESERT FISHES COUNCIL, 314
DESERT RESEARCH FOUNDATION OF NAMIBIA, THE, 314
DESERT TORTOISE COUNCIL, 314
DESERT TORTOISE PRESERVE COMMITTEE, INC., 314
DRAGONFLY SOCIETY OF THE AMERICAS, THE, 314
DUCKS UNLIMITED CANADA
   Nova Scotia Office, 315
DUCKS UNLIMITED CANADA
   Saskatchewan Office, 315
EAGLE NATURE FOUNDATION, LTD., 316
EARTH FORCE
   GREEN (Global Rivers Environmental Education Network), 317
EARTH FOUNDATION, 317
EARTH POLICY INSTITUTE, 317
EARTHJUSTICE
   Denver Office, 318
   Environmental Law Clinic at the University of Denver, 318
   Headquarters, 318
   Juneau Office, 319
   Oakland Office, 319
   Policy and Legislation, 319
   Seattle Office, 320
   Tallahassee Office, 320
   Washington, DC, Office, 320
EARTHSCAN, 320
EASTERN SHORE LAND CONSERVANCY (ESLC), 321
ECOLOGICAL SOCIETY OF AMERICA, THE, 321
ECOLOGY CENTER, 321
ENVIRONMENT COUNCIL OF RHODE ISLAND, 323
ENVIRONMENTAL ALLIANCE FOR SENIOR INVOLVEMENT (EASI), 323
ENVIRONMENTAL DEFENSE CENTER, 325
ENVIRONMENTAL LAW INSTITUTE, THE, 327
ENVIRONMENTAL LEAGUE OF MASSACHUSETTS, 327
ENVIRONMENTAL POLICY CENTER, THE, 327
EQUESTRIAN LAND CONSERVATION RESOURCE, 328
EUROPARC FEDERATION, 328
EUROPEAN CETACEAN SOCIETY, 328
FEDERATION OF FLY FISHERS, 329
FEDERATION OF FLY FISHERS (NCCFFF), 329
FEDERATION OF WESTERN OUTDOOR CLUBS, 330
FERRUM COLLEGE, 581
FLINTSTEEL RESTORATION ASSOCIATION, INC., 330
FLORIDA DEFENDERS OF THE ENVIRONMENT, INC., 331
FLORIDA DEPARTMENT OF ENVIRONMENTAL PROTECTION
   Coastal and Aquatic Managed Areas, 153
   Division of Resource Assessment and Management, 154
FLORIDA EXOTIC PEST PLANT COUNCIL, 331
FLORIDA FEDERATION OF GARDEN CLUBS, INC., 331
FLORIDA FISH AND WILDLIFE CONSERVATION COMMISSION, 154
FLORIDA NATIVE PLANT SOCIETY, 332
FLORIDA PANTHER SOCIETY, INC., THE, 332
FLORIDA SPORTSMEN'S CONSERVATION ASSOCIATION, 333
FOOD SUPPLY / HUMAN POPULATION EXPLOSION CONNECTION, 333
FOREST FIRE LOOKOUT ASSOCIATION, 334
FOREST HISTORY SOCIETY, INC., 334
FOREST MANAGEMENT TRUST, 334

FOREST SERVICE EMPLOYEES FOR ENVIRONMENTAL ETHICS (FSEEE), 334
FOREST STEWARDS GUILD, 335
FOREST TRUST, 335
FOREST WATCH, 335
FORESTRY COMMISSION (SOUTH CAROLINA), 155
FRIENDS OF DISCOVERY PARK, 337
FRIENDS OF SUNKHAZE MEADOWS NATIONAL WILDLIFE REFUGE, 337
FRIENDS OF THE BOUNDARY WATERS WILDERNESS, 337
FRIENDS OF THE EARTH, 337
FRIENDS OF THE REEDY RIVER, 338
GALIANO CONSERVANCY ASSOCIATION, 339
GAME CONSERVANCY U.S.A., 339
GENERAL FEDERATION OF WOMEN'S CLUBS, 340
GEORGE MIKSCH SUTTON AVIAN RESEARCH CENTER INC., 340
GEORGE WRIGHT SOCIETY, THE, 341
GEORGIA CONSERVANCY, INC., THE, 341
GEORGIA DEPARTMENT OF NATURAL RESOURCES
   Environmental Protection Division
      Coastal Division, 156
GEORGIA ENVIRONMENTAL ORGANIZATION, INC. (GEO), 341
GEORGIA ENVIRONMENTAL POLICY INSTITUTE, 342
GEORGIA STATE EXTENSION SERVICE, 157
GEORGIA TRUST FOR HISTORIC PRESERVATION, 342
GRAND CANYON TRUST, 344
GRANT TECH CONSULTING AND CONSERVATION SERVICES, 567
GREAT LAKES UNITED, 345
GREAT PLAINS NATIVE PLANT SOCIETY, 345
GREATER YELLOWSTONE COALITION, 346
GREEN BALKANS FEDERATION OF NATURE CONSERVATION NGOS, 346
GREEN GUIDES, 346
GREEN MOUNTAIN CLUB INC., THE, 346
GREEN SPHERE INC., 347
GROWLING, 348
GULF STATES MARINE FISHERIES COMMISSION, 20
GWINNETT OPEN LAND TRUST, INC., 348
HARDWOOD FOREST FOUNDATION, 348
HAWAII NATURE CENTER, 349
HAWK MOUNTAIN SANCTUARY ASSOCIATION, VISITOR CENTER, 349
HAWKWATCH INTERNATIONAL, 350
HEADLANDS INSTITUTE, 350
HELPING OUR PENINSULA'S ENVIRONMENT, 350
HIGH DESERT MUSEUM, THE, 351
HOLDEN ARBORETUM, THE, 351
HOLLOW OAK LAND TRUST, 351
HOUSE COMMITTEE ON RULES, 22
IDAHO CONSERVATION LEAGUE, 354
IDAHO DEPARTMENT OF ENVIRONMENTAL QUALITY, 160
IDAHO DEPARTMENT OF PARKS AND RECREATION, 160
IDAHO DEPARTMENT OF WATER RESOURCES, 161
   Water Awareness Week, 161
IDAHO FISH AND WILDLIFE FOUNDATION, 161
IDAHO STATE SOIL CONSERVATION COMMISSION, 161
ILLINOIS ASSOCIATION OF CONSERVATION DISTRICTS, 354
ILLINOIS DEPARTMENT OF AGRICULTURE
   Bureau of Land and Water Resources, 162
ILLINOIS DEPARTMENT OF NATURAL RESOURCES, 162
ILLINOIS DEPARTMENT OF TRANSPORTATION, 162
ILLINOIS ENVIRONMENTAL COUNCIL, 355
ILLINOIS ENVIRONMENTAL PROTECTION AGENCY, 162
ILLINOIS NATIVE PLANT SOCIETY, 355
ILLINOIS NATURE PRESERVES COMMISSION (INPC), 163
ILLINOIS PRAIRIE PATH, 355
ILLINOIS WALNUT COUNCIL, 356
ILOVEPARKS.COM, 567
INDIAN CREEK NATURE CENTER, 356
INDIANA ASSOCIATION OF SOIL AND WATER CONSERVATION DISTRICTS, INC., 356
INDIANA STATE DEPARTMENT OF HEALTH, 164
INDUSTRIAL COMMISSION OF NORTH DAKOTA, 164
INSTITUTE FOR GLOBAL COMMUNICATIONS, 567
INSTITUTE FOR TROPICAL ECOLOGY AND CONSERVATION (ITEC), 358
INSTITUTO NACIONAL DE BIODIVERSIDAD (INBIO), 22
INTERNATIONAL ACADEMY, 567
INTERNATIONAL ASSOCIATION FOR BEAR RESEARCH AND MANAGEMENT, 359
INTERNATIONAL ASSOCIATION OF FISH AND WILDLIFE AGENCIES, 360
INTERNATIONAL ASSOCIATION OF NATURAL RESOURCE PILOTS, 360
INTERNATIONAL ASSOCIATION OF WILDLAND FIRE, 361
INTERNATIONAL BICYCLE FUND, 361
INTERNATIONAL CHILDREN'S CONFERENCE ON THE ENVIRONMENT, 362

KEYWORD INDEX – L

INTERNATIONAL ECOTOURISM SOCIETY, THE, 362
INTERNATIONAL EROSION CONTROL ASSOCIATION (IECA), 363
INTERNATIONAL MIRE CONSERVATION GROUP, 365
INTERNATIONAL SOCIETY FOR THE PRESERVATION OF THE
  TROPICAL RAINFOREST, THE, 367
INTERNATIONAL SONORAN DESERT ALLIANCE, 367
INTERNATIONAL UNION FOR CONSERVATION OF NATURE AND
  NATURAL RESOURCES (IUCN) THE WORLD CONSERVATION UNION
  Canada Office, 368
  Environmental Law Centre, 368
IOWA ASSOCIATION OF NATURALISTS, 372
IOWA DEPARTMENT OF AGRICULTURE AND LAND STEWARDSHIP
  Bureau of Financial Incentive Program, 165
IOWA NATIVE PLANT SOCIETY, 373
IOWA PRAIRIE NETWORK, 373
IOWA STATE UNIVERSITY
  College of Agriculture, 584
IOWA WILDLIFE FEDERATION, 374
IOWA WOMEN IN NATURAL RESOURCES, 374
ISLAND RESOURCES FOUNDATION, 375
ISLESBORO ISLANDS TRUST, 375
IZAAK WALTON LEAGUE OF AMERICA, INC., THE
  California State IWLA, 376
  Minnesota Division, 377
  Owatonna Minnesota Chapter, 377
  South Dakota Division, 378
J.N. (DING) DARLING FOUNDATION, 379
JACKSON HOLE CONSERVATION ALLIANCE, 379
JACKSON HOLE LAND TRUST, 379
JOHNSON STATE COLLEGE, 585
KANSAS ASSOCIATION FOR CONSERVATION AND ENVIRONMENTAL
  EDUCATION, KACEE, 380
KANSAS BASS FEDERATION, 381
KANSAS COOPERATIVE FISH AND WILDLIFE RESEARCH UNIT, 167
KANSAS DEPARTMENT OF WILDLIFE AND PARKS
  Region 4, 168
KANSAS GEOLOGICAL SURVEY, 168
KANSAS ORNITHOLOGICAL SOCIETY, 381
KANSAS STATE EXTENSION SERVICES, 169
KANSAS STATE UNIVERSITY
  College of Agriculture, 585
  Department of Landscape Architecture / Regional and Community
    Planning, 585
KEEP AMERICA BEAUTIFUL, INC., 382
KEEP FLORIDA BEAUTIFUL, INC., 382
KENTUCKY ACADEMY OF SCIENCE, 382
KENTUCKY DEPARTMENT OF AGRICULTURE, 169
KENTUCKY DEPARTMENT OF FISH AND WILDLIFE RESOURCES, 169
KENTUCKY NATURAL LANDS TRUST, 383
KENTUCKY NATURAL RESOURCES AND ENVIRONMENTAL
  PROTECTION CABINET, 170
  Environmental Quality Commission, 170
KIDS FOR SAVING EARTH WORLDWIDE, 384
LADY BIRD JOHNSON WILDFLOWER CENTER, 385
LAKEHEAD UNIVERSITY, 586
LAKENET, 385
LAND AND WATER FUND OF THE ROCKIES, 386
LAND BETWEEN THE LAKES ASSOCIATION, 386
LAND CONSERVANCY OF WEST MICHIGAN, 386
LAND TRUST ALLIANCE, THE, 386
LEAGUE OF OHIO SPORTSMEN, 387
LEAGUE OF WOMEN VOTERS OF WASHINGTON, 388
LEAGUE TO SAVE LAKE TAHOE, 388
LEGACY LAND TRUST, 388
LIFE OF THE LAND, 389
LIGHTHAWK, 389
  New England Region, 389
LIVING RIVERS, 390
LOUISIANA DEPARTMENT OF AGRICULTURE AND FORESTRY
  Office of Soil and Water Conservation, State Soil and Water
    Conservation Committee, 172
LOUISIANA STATE UNIVERSITY SCHOOL OF FORESTRY, WILDLIFE
  AND FISHERIES, 586
LOWER MERION CONSERVANCY, 391
LOWER MISSISSIPPI RIVER CONSERVATION COMMITTEE, 391
LUMMI ISLAND HERITAGE TRUST, 568
MACOMB LAND CONSERVANCY, 391
MAINE ASSOCIATION OF CONSERVATION COMMISSIONS (MACC), 392
MAINE ASSOCIATION OF CONSERVATION DISTRICTS, 392
MANOMET CENTER FOR CONSERVATION SCIENCES, 393
MARIE SELBY BOTANICAL GARDENS, THE, 393
MARYLAND ASSOCIATION OF CONSERVATION DISTRICTS, 395
MARYLAND BASS FEDERATION, 395

MARYLAND DEPARTMENT OF AGRICULTURE, 176
MASSACHUSETTS ASSOCIATION OF CONSERVATION DISTRICTS, 396
MASSACHUSETTS BASS FEDERATION, 396
MASSACHUSETTS DIVISION OF FISHERIES AND WILDLIFE
  MassWildlife, 178
MASSACHUSETTS EXECUTIVE OFFICE OF ENVIRONMENTAL AFFAIRS
  Office of Technical Assistance for Toxic Use Reduction, 179
MASSACHUSETTS TRAPPERS ASSOCIATION, INC., 396
MAX MCGRAW WILDLIFE FOUNDATION, 396
MIAMI UNIVERSITY, 587
MICHIGAN BASS FEDERATION, 397
MICHIGAN DEPARTMENT OF AGRICULTURE, 180
MICHIGAN DEPARTMENT OF ENVIRONMENTAL QUALITY, 180
MICHIGAN FORESTS ASSOCIATION, 397
MICHIGAN LAND USE INSTITUTE, 397
MICHIGAN NATURE ASSOCIATION, 398
MICHIGAN TECHNOLOGICAL UNIVERSITY; SCHOOL OF FORESTRY
  AND WOOD PRODUCTS, 588
MICHIGAN UNITED CONSERVATION CLUBS, INC., 398
MID-ATLANTIC COUNCIL OF WATERSHED ASSOCIATIONS, 398
MIDDLE TENNESSEE STATE UNIVERSITY, 588
MINERAL POLICY CENTER, 399
MINNESOTA ASSOCIATION OF SOIL AND WATER CONSERVATION
  DISTRICTS, 399
MINNESOTA BASS FEDERATION, 399
MINNESOTA HERPETOLOGICAL SOCIETY, 400
MINNESOTA ORNITHOLOGISTS' UNION, 400
MISSISSIPPI STATE UNIVERSITY
  Forest and Wildlife Research Center, 588
MISSOURI ASSOCIATION OF SOIL AND WATER CONSERVATION
  DISTRICTS, 402
MISSOURI DEPARTMENT OF CONSERVATION
  Forestry Division, 185
MISSOURI FOREST PRODUCTS ASSOCIATION, 402
MISSOURI PRAIRIE FOUNDATION, 402
MONTANA BASS FEDERATION, 403
MONTANA BUREAU OF MINES AND GEOLOGY, 186
MONTANA ENVIRONMENTAL QUALITY COUNCIL, 187
MONTANA FOREST OWNERS ASSOCIATION, 403
MONTANA LAND RELIANCE, 403
MONTANA NATURAL HERITAGE PROGRAM, 187
MONTANA STATE UNIVERSITY
  College of Agriculture, 589
MONTANA WILDERNESS ASSOCIATION, 403
MONTANA WILDLIFE FEDERATION, 404
MOUNT GRACE LAND CONSERVATION TRUST, 405
MOUNT UNION COLLEGE, 589
MOUNTAINEERS, THE, 405
NATIONAL ARBOR DAY FOUNDATION, 406
NATIONAL ASSOCIATION OF CONSERVATION DISTRICTS, 407
NATIONAL ASSOCIATION OF RECREATION RESOURCE PLANNERS, 408
NATIONAL ASSOCIATION OF STATE PARK DIRECTORS, 409
NATIONAL AUDUBON SOCIETY
  ATLANTA AUDUBON SOCIETY, 409
  Audubon Alaska, 409
  Audubon Council of Illinois, 410
  Audubon Missouri, 410
  Audubon of Florida, 410
  Audubon Society of Omaha, 411
  Audubon Society of Portland, 411
  Audubon Society of Rhode Island, 412
  Audubon Vermont, 412
  Connecticut Audubon Society, 412
  Fairfax Audubon Society, 413
  Hawaii Audubon Society, 413
  Illinois Audubon Society, 413
  Louisiana Audubon Council, 414
  Michigan Audubon Society, 414
  Montana Audubon, 415
  New Jersey Chapter, 415
  Public Policy Office, 415
  San Diego Chapter, 416
  Seattle Audubon Society, 416
  Tucson Audubon Society, 416
NATIONAL BOWHUNTER EDUCATION FOUNDATION (NBEF), 417
NATIONAL CAUCUS OF ENVIRONMENTAL LEGISLATORS (NCEL), 417
NATIONAL CENTER FOR APPROPRIATE TECHNOLOGY, 417
NATIONAL FARMERS UNION, 419
NATIONAL GRANGE, THE, 421
NATIONAL MILITARY FISH AND WILDLIFE ASSOCIATION, 421
NATIONAL NETWORK OF FOREST PRACTITIONERS, 422
NATIONAL PARK TRUST, 422
NATIONAL PARKS CONSERVATION ASSOCIATION (NPCA), 422

NATIONAL SPELEOLOGICAL SOCIETY, INC., 424
NATIONAL TRUST FOR HISTORIC PRESERVATION, 425
NATIONAL WATERSHED COALITION, 426
NATIONAL WILDLIFE FEDERATION
   Great Lakes Natural Resource Center, 427
   Headquarters, 427
   Northern Rockies Natural Resource Center, 428
   Rocky Mountain Natural Resource Center, 428
NATIONAL WILDLIFE PRODUCTIONS, INC., 429
NATIONAL WILDLIFE REFUGE ASSOCIATION, 429
NATIONAL WOODLAND OWNERS ASSOCIATION, 430
NATIVE PLANT SOCIETY OF NORTHEASTERN OHIO, 430
NATIVE PLANT SOCIETY OF TEXAS, 431
NATIVE PRAIRIES ASSOCIATION OF TEXAS, 431
NATURAL AREAS ASSOCIATION, 431
NATURAL LAND INSTITUTE, 431
NATURE CONSERVANCY, THE
   Adirondack Chapter, 433
   Alabama Chapter, 433
   Arkansas Field Office, 434
   Canada Chapter, 434
   Colorado Chapter, 434
   Eastern New York Chapter, 435
   Iowa Chapter, 435
   Kansas Chapter, 436
   Maryland/District of Columbia Chapter, 436
   New York City Chapter, 438
   New York City Office, 437
   Oklahoma Chapter, 439
   Oregon Chapter, 439
   Pennsylvania Chapter, 439
   Rhode Island Chapter, 439
   Texas Chapter, 439
NEBRASKA DEPARTMENT OF ENVIRONMENTAL QUALITY, 188
NEBRASKA DEPARTMENT OF NATURAL RESOURCES, 188
NEBRASKA GAME AND PARKS COMMISSION
   Omaha Office, 189
NEBRASKA WILDLIFE FEDERATION, INC., 442
NEGATIVE POPULATION GROWTH (NPG), 442
NEVADA ASSOCIATION OF CONSERVATION DISTRICTS, 442
NEW ENGLAND COALITION FOR SUSTAINABLE POPULATION
   (NECSP), 443
NEW ENGLAND WILD FLOWER SOCIETY, INC., 443
NEW HAMPSHIRE ASSOCIATION OF CONSERVATION COMMISSIONS,
   443
NEW HAMPSHIRE ASSOCIATION OF CONSERVATION DISTRICTS, 444
NEW HAMPSHIRE COUNCIL ON RESOURCES AND DEVELOPMENT,
   190
NEW HAMPSHIRE DEPARTMENT OF AGRICULTURE, MARKETS, AND
   FOOD
   State Conservation Committee, 190
NEW HAMPSHIRE DEPARTMENT OF RESOURCES AND ECONOMIC
   DEVELOPMENT, 190
NEW JERSEY ASSOCIATION OF CONSERVATION DISTRICTS, 445
NEW JERSEY DEPARTMENT OF ENVIRONMENTAL PROTECTION
   Division of Solid and Hazardous Waste, 192
   Green Acres Program, 192
NEW JERSEY ENVIRONMENTAL LOBBY, 445
NEW JERSEY FORESTRY ASSOCIATION, 445
NEW MEXICO BUREAU OF GEOLOGY AND MINERAL RESOURCES, 193
NEW MEXICO ENERGY, MINERALS, AND NATURAL RESOURCES
   DEPARTMENT
   Oil Conservation Division, 195
NEW MEXICO ENVIRONMENT DEPARTMENT, 195
NEW MEXICO STATE UNIVERSITY
   College of Agriculture and Home Economics
      Department of Fishery and Wildlife Sciences, 590
NEW YORK DEPARTMENT OF AGRICULTURE AND MARKETS, 196
NEW YORK GEOLOGICAL SURVEY AND STATE MUSEUM, 197
NEW YORK STATE DEPARTMENT OF AGRICULTURE AND MARKETS, 197
NEW YORK STATE FISH AND WILDLIFE MANAGEMENT BOARD
   Region 6, 198
   Region 8, 198
NEW YORK-NEW JERSEY TRAIL CONFERENCE INC., 446
NOLTE ASSOCIATES, INC., 569
NORTH CAROLINA BASS FEDERATION, 450
NORTH CAROLINA CONSERVATION NETWORK, 450
NORTH CAROLINA DEPARTMENT OF AGRICULTURE AND
   CONSUMER SERVICES, 200
NORTH CAROLINA DIVISION OF SOIL AND WATER, 200
NORTH CAROLINA RECREATION AND PARK SOCIETY, INC., 451
NORTH DAKOTA DEPARTMENT OF AGRICULTURE, 201
NORTH DAKOTA NATURAL SCIENCE SOCIETY, 452

NORTH DAKOTA STATE SOIL CONSERVATION COMMITTEE, 202
NORTHERN ALASKA ENVIRONMENTAL CENTER, 453
NORTHERN ARIZONA UNIVERSITY
   Department of Geography, Planning, and Recreation, 591
NORTHERN PLAINS RESOURCE COUNCIL, 453
NORTHLAND COLLEGE, 591
NORTHWEST COALITION FOR ALTERNATIVES TO PESTICIDES, 453
NORTHWEST ENVIRONMENT WATCH, 454
NORTHWEST INTERPRETIVE ASSOCIATION, 454
NORTHWEST RESOURCE INFORMATION CENTER, 454
NORTHWEST TERRITORIES DEPARTMENT OF RESOURCES,
   WILDLIFE AND ECONOMIC DEVELOPMENT, 202
NOVA SCOTIA AGRICULTURE & FISHERIES, 203
NOVA SCOTIA DEPARTMENT OF NATURAL RESOURCES, 203
NOVA SCOTIA FEDERATION OF ANGLERS AND HUNTERS, 454
NOVA SCOTIA FORESTRY ASSOCIATION, 454
OHIO ACADEMY OF SCIENCE, THE, 456
OHIO DEPARTMENT OF AGRICULTURE, 203
OHIO DEPARTMENT OF NATURAL RESOURCES, 204
OHIO ENERGY PROJECT, 456
OHIO STREAM PRESERVATION, 457
OKLAHOMA BIOLOGICAL SURVEY, 205
OKLAHOMA DEPARTMENT OF ENVIRONMENTAL QUALITY, 206
OKLAHOMA GEOLOGICAL SURVEY, 206
OKLAHOMA NATIVE PLANT SOCIETY, 458
ONTARIO FEDERATION OF ANGLERS AND HUNTERS, 459
ONTARIO FORESTRY ASSOCIATION, 459
ORANGUTAN FOUNDATION INTERNATIONAL, 460
OREGON ENVIRONMENTAL COUNCIL, 460
OREGON SMALL WOODLANDS ASSOCIATION, 461
OREGON SOCIETY OF AMERICAN FORESTERS, 461
OUTDOOR RECREATION COUNCIL OF BRITISH COLUMBIA, 462
OZARK SOCIETY, THE, 463
OZARKS RESOURCE CENTER, 463
PACIFIC BASIN ASSOCIATION OF SOIL AND WATER CONSERVATION
   DISTRICTS, 463
PACIFIC RIVERS COUNCIL, 464
PARTNERS IN AMPHIBIAN AND REPTILE CONSERVATION (PARC), 465
PARTNERS IN PARKS, 465
PENNSYLVANIA DEPARTMENT OF AGRICULTURE
   Region VII, 211
   State Conservation Commission, 211
PENNSYLVANIA DEPARTMENT OF ENVIRONMENTAL PROTECTION, 211
PENNSYLVANIA FISH AND BOAT COMMISSION
   Bureau of Law Enforcement
      Northcentral Region, 212
PENNSYLVANIA ORGANIZATION FOR WATERSHEDS AND RIVERS
   (POWR), 466
PENNSYLVANIA RESOURCES COUNCIL, INC.,, 467
PEOPLE FOR PUGET SOUND
   South Sound Office, 467
PIEDMONT ENVIRONMENTAL COUNCIL, 469
PLAYA LAKES JOINT VENTURE, 469
POPULATION-ENVIRONMENT BALANCE, INC., 471
POULSBO MARINE SCIENCE CENTER, 471
PRAIRIE CLUB, THE, 472
PRAIRIE GROUSE TECHNICAL COUNCIL, 472
PREDATOR CONSERVATION ALLIANCE, 472
PRIORITIES INSTITUTE, THE, 473
PROGRESSIVE ANIMAL WELFARE SOCIETY, 473
PROTECTED AREAS ASSOCIATION OF NEWFOUNDLAND AND
   LABRADOR, 474
PROVINCE OF QUEBEC SOCIETY FOR THE PROTECTION OF BIRDS,
   INC., 474
PS ENTERPRISES, 570
PUBLIC EMPLOYEES FOR ENVIRONMENTAL RESPONSIBILITY
   (PEER), 474
PUBLIC LANDS FOUNDATION, 474
PUERTO RICO CONSERVATION FOUNDATION, THE (PRCF), 475
PURPLE MARTIN CONSERVATION ASSOCIATION, 475
RACHEL CARSON COUNCIL, INC., 476
RAPTOR EDUCATION FOUNDATION, INC., 477
RED BUFFALO, LLC, 570
RENEWABLE NATURAL RESOURCES FOUNDATION, 478
RESIDENTS FOR A MORE BEAUTIFUL PORT WASHINGTON, 479
RESOURCES FOR THE FUTURE, 479
RHODE ISLAND DEPARTMENT OF TRANSPORTATION, 214
RHODE ISLAND FOREST CONSERVATOR'S ORGANIZATION, INC., 480
RHODE ISLAND WILD PLANT SOCIETY, 480
RIVER ALLIANCE OF WISCONSIN, 480
RIVER PROJECT, THE, 481
ROCK RIVER HEADWATERS, INC., 481
ROCKY MOUNTAIN BIRD OBSERVATORY, 482

ROCKY MOUNTAIN ELK FOUNDATION, 482
RUTGERS COOPERATIVE EXTENSION, 215
SACRED PASSAGE AND THE WAY OF NATURE, 483
SAN DIEGUITO RIVER PARK JOINT POWERS AUTHORITY, 215
SAN ELIJO LAGOON CONSERVANCY, 484
SAN JUAN PRESERVATION TRUST, THE, 484
SAND CREEK WATERSHED PROJECT, THE, 215
SANTA CLARA COMMUNITY ACTION PROGRAM, 594
SASKATCHEWAN WILDLIFE FEDERATION, 484
SAVE THE DUNES COUNCIL, 485
SAVE THE SOUND, INC., 486
SCENIC AMERICA, 487
   Scenic California, 487
SEACOAST ANTI-POLLUTION LEAGUE, 489
SIERRA CLUB
   Alaska Field Office, 490
   Connecticut Chapter, 491
   Hawaii Chapter, 492
   Lone Star Chapter, 493
   Maryland Chapter, 493
   Mississippi Chapter, 494
   Nebraska Chapter, 494
   Northwest Office, 495
   Pennsylvania Chapter, 496
   Rio Grande Chapter (New Mexico/West Texas), 496
   Tehipite Chapter (Northern California), 498
   Virginia Chapter, 499
   Washington, DC Office, 499
   West Virginia Chapter, 499
SIERRA CLUB CALIFORNIA, 499
SIERRA CLUB FOUNDATION, THE, 499
SIERRA CLUB OF CANADA
   Atlantic Canada Chapter, 500
SIERRA STUDENT COALITION, 500
SILK CITY NATURE ASSOCIATION, 500
SLIPPERY ROCK UNIVERSITY, 595
SMALL WOODLAND OWNERS ASSOCIATION OF MAINE, 501
SOCIETY FOR RANGE MANAGEMENT, 503
SOCIETY FOR THE PROTECTION OF NEW HAMPSHIRE FORESTS, 503
SOCIETY OF AMERICAN FORESTERS, 503
SOCIETY OF TYMPANUCHUS CUPIDO PINNATUS LTD., 504
SOIL AND WATER CONSERVATION SOCIETY, 504
SONORAN DESERT NATIONAL PARK FRIENDS, 504
SONORAN INSTITUTE, 505
SOUTH CAROLINA BASS FEDERATION, 506
SOUTH CAROLINA DEPARTMENT OF HEALTH AND ENVIRONMENTAL CONTROL, 217
SOUTH CAROLINA DEPARTMENT OF PARKS, RECREATION AND TOURISM, 218
SOUTH CAROLINA WILDLIFE FEDERATION, 506
SOUTH DAKOTA ASSOCIATION OF CONSERVATION DISTRICTS, 506
SOUTH DAKOTA COOPERATIVE EXTENSION SERVICE, 218
SOUTH DAKOTA COOPERATIVE FISH AND WILDLIFE RESEARCH UNIT (USDI-USGS), 29
SOUTH DAKOTA DEPARTMENT OF AGRICULTURE
   Division of Resource Conservation and Forestry, 218
SOUTH DAKOTA DEPARTMENT OF ENVIRONMENT AND NATURAL RESOURCES, 219
SOUTH DAKOTA DEPARTMENT OF GAME, FISH, AND PARKS, 219
SOUTHEASTERN ASSOCIATION OF FISH AND WILDLIFE AGENCIES, 508
SOUTHERN APPALACHIAN BOTANICAL SOCIETY, 508
SOUTHERN ILLINOIS UNIVERSITY CARBONDALE, 596
SOUTHERN UTAH WILDERNESS ALLIANCE
   Moab Office, 510
SOUTHWEST CENTER FOR ENVIRONMENTAL RESEARCH AND POLICY (SCERP), 596
SOUTHWEST CONSERVATION DISTRICT, 510
SOUTHWEST RESEARCH AND INFORMATION CENTER, 510
SOUTHWESTERN HERPETOLOGISTS SOCIETY, 510
SPORTSMEN'S NATIONAL LAND TRUST, THE, 511
STANFORD ENVIRONMENTAL LAW SOCIETY, 511
STATE ENVIRONMENTAL RESOURCE CENTER (SERC), 512
STEPHEN F. AUSTIN STATE UNIVERSITY ARTHUR TEMPLE COLLEGE OF FORESTRY, 598
STOP, 512
STROUD WATER RESEARCH CENTER, 512
STUDENT CONSERVATION ASSOCIATION, INC., 512
SUSTAIN, 514
SUSTAINABLE ENERGY INSTITUTE
   Culture Change, 514
   Food Not Lawns, 514
   Pedal Power Produce, 514

TAHOE REGIONAL PLANNING AGENCY, 220
TALL TIMBERS RESEARCH STATION (TTRS), 515
TENNESSEE CONSERVATION LEAGUE, 516
TENNESSEE DEPARTMENT OF AGRICULTURE, 221
TENNESSEE DEPARTMENT OF ENVIRONMENT AND CONSERVATION, 221
TENNESSEE VALLEY AUTHORITY
   Muscle Shoals Technical Library, 30
TERRA NATURE FUND, 516
TERRA PENINSULAR, 516
TEXAS A AND M UNIVERSITY AT KINGSVILLE
   Caesar Kleberg Wildlife Research Institute, 599
TEXAS BASS FEDERATION, 517
TEXAS COMMITTEE ON NATURAL RESOURCES, 517
TEXAS COOPERATIVE FISH AND WILDLIFE RESEARCH UNIT, 30
TEXAS DEPARTMENT OF AGRICULTURE, 222
TEXAS DEPARTMENT OF HEALTH, 222
TEXAS FOREST SERVICE, 222
TEXAS RIPARIAN ASSOCIATION, 517
TEXAS STATE SOIL AND WATER CONSERVATION BOARD, 223
TREAD LIGHTLY! INC, 518
TREES ATLANTA, 519
TREES FOR THE FUTURE, INC., 519
TREES FOR TOMORROW, NATURAL RESOURCES EDUCATION CENTER, 519
TRIANGLE RAILS-TO-TRAILS CONSERVANCY, 520
TROUT UNLIMITED
   Missouri Council, 522
   Pennsylvania Council, 522
TRUST FOR PUBLIC LAND, THE, 523
TRUSTEES FOR ALASKA, 524
TUG HILL TOMORROW LAND TRUST, 524
TULANE ENVIRONMENTAL LAW CLINIC, 600
TULANE UNIVERSITY
   Department of Ecology and Evolutionary Biology, 600
TURTLE CREEK WATERSHED ASSOCIATION, INC., 525
TWO WHITE WOLVES SANCTUARY, 525
UNEP WORLD CONSERVATION MONITORING CENTRE, 525
UNITED STATES CHAMBER OF COMMERCE
   Environment, Technology and Regulatory Affairs, 526
UNITED STATES DEPARTMENT OF AGRICULTURE
   Forest Service
      Crooked River National Grassland, 37
      Gila National Forest, 38
      Green Mountain National Forest, 38
      Nez Perce National Forest, 41
      Pawnee National Grassland, 42
      Region 02 (Rocky Mountain), 43
      Siuslaw National Forest, 45
UNITED STATES DEPARTMENT OF COMMERCE
   National Oceanic and Atmospheric Administration
      Delaware National Estuarine Research Reserve, 50
      Rookery Bay National Estuarine Research Reserve, 53
      Sea Grant Program - DelAware, 54
      Sea Grant Program - Georgia, 55
      Sea Grant Program - Illinois-Indiana, 55
      Sea Grant Program - Massachusetts, 56
      Sea Grant Program - Michigan, 57
      Sea Grant Program - Minnesota, 57
      Sea Grant Program - New York, 58
      Sea Grant Program - North Carolina, 58
      Sea Grant Program - Ohio, 58
      Sea Grant Program - Texas, 59
      Wells National Estuarine Research Reserve, 60
UNITED STATES DEPARTMENT OF DEFENSE
   Air Force Major Air Commands
      Andrews AFB, MD, 61
      USAF Academy, 62
   Air Force Major U.S. Installations
      Randolph AFB, TX, 66
   Army Corps of Engineers
      Nashville Engineer District, 69
      Norfolk Engineer District, 70
   Army Materiel Command, 72
   Navy, 74
UNITED STATES DEPARTMENT OF HOUSING AND URBAN DEVELOPMENT, 77
UNITED STATES DEPARTMENT OF THE INTERIOR
   Bureau of Land Management
      Bakersfield Field Office, 79
      Eugene District Office, 81
      Malta Field Office, 83
      Northern Field Office, 84

UNITED STATES DEPARTMENT OF THE INTERIOR (continued)
  Bureau of Land Management (continued)
    Rawlins Field Office, 85
    Safford Field Office, 86
    Tucson Field Office, 88
  Bureau of Reclamation, 89
  Fish and Wildlife Service, 90
    Archie Carr National Wildlife Refuge, 91
    Arthur R. Marshall Loxahatchee/Hope Sound National Wildlife Refuge, 91
    Ash Meadows National Wildlife Refuge, 92
    Benton Lake National Wildlife Refuge, 92
    California-Nevada Operations, 94
    Chickasaw National Wildlife Refuge, 95
    Eastern Massachusetts National Wildlife Refuge Complex, 97
    Great Dismal Swamp/Nansemond National Wildlife Refuge, 98
    Lacassine National Wildlife Refuge, 102
    Lake Andes/Karl E. Mundt National Wildlife Refuge, 102
    Long Lake National Wildlife Refuge, 103
    Morris Wetland Management District, 106
    Necedah National Wildlife Refuge, 107
    Patoka River National Wetlands Project National Wildlife Refuge, 109
    Pocosin Lakes National Wildlife Refuge, 110
    region 4, Southeast Regional office, 112
    Ridgefield National Wildlife Refuge, 112
    San Francisco Bay National Wildlife Refuge Complex, 113
    Sandy Point National Wildlife Refuge, 114
    Southeast Louisiana Complex National Wildlife Refuge, 115
    St. Marks National Wildlife Refuge, 115
    Wichita Mountains National Wildlife Refuge, 118
    Willapa/Lewis and Clark National Wildlife Refuge, 118
  Montana Cooperative Fishery Research Unit, 119
  National Park Service
    Mount Rainier National Park, 124
    Theodore Roosevelt National Park, 125
    Yellowstone National Park, 126
  North Dakota State University Extension Service, 126
  United States Geological Survey
    Western Region, 127
  Washington Cooperative Fish and Wildlife Research Unit
    School of Aquatic and Fishery Sciences, 128
UNITED STATES DEPARTMENT OF TRANSPORTATION
  Federal Aviation Administration, 128
UNITED STATES DEPARTMENT OF TREASURY, 129
UNITED STATES INSTITUTE FOR ENVIRONMENTAL CONFLICT RESOLUTION, 130
UNITED STATES PUBLIC INTEREST RESEARCH GROUP, 526
UNIVERSITE LAVAL, 601
UNIVERSITY OF CALIFORNIA AT DAVIS
  School of Veterinary Medicine, 606
UNIVERSITY OF COLORADO, 608
UNIVERSITY OF CONNECTICUT COOPERATIVE EXTENSION, 608
UNIVERSITY OF DAR ES SALAAM, 608
UNIVERSITY OF FLORIDA
  School of Forest Resources and Conservation, 609
UNIVERSITY OF FLORIDA INSTITUTE OF FOOD AND AGRICULTURAL SCIENCES, 609
UNIVERSITY OF GEORGIA
  Daniel B. Warnell School of Forest Resources, 609
UNIVERSITY OF HAWAII AT MANOA, 610
UNIVERSITY OF HAWAII COOPERATIVE EXTENSION PROGRAM, 224
UNIVERSITY OF IDAHO
  College of Natural Resources
    Department of Fish and Wildlife Resources, 610
UNIVERSITY OF IDAHO
  College of Natural Resources
    Idaho Cooperative Fish and Wildlife Research Unit, 610
UNIVERSITY OF LOUISVILLE, 612
UNIVERSITY OF MAINE, 612
UNIVERSITY OF MARYLAND - AT COLLEGE PARK, 613
UNIVERSITY OF MARYLAND COOPERATIVE EXTENSION, 224
UNIVERSITY OF MICHIGAN, 614
UNIVERSITY OF MINNESOTA AT ST. PAUL, 615
UNIVERSITY OF NEVADA COOPERATIVE EXTENSION, 616
UNIVERSITY OF NEW BRUNSWICK, 616
UNIVERSITY OF NEW HAMPSHIRE COOPERATIVE EXTENSION, 617
UNIVERSITY OF NEW HAVEN DEPT. OF BIOLOGY AND ENVIRONMENTAL SCIENCES, 617
UNIVERSITY OF NORTH CAROLINA AT ASHEVILLE, 617
UNIVERSITY OF NORTH DAKOTA, 618
UNIVERSITY OF NORTHERN BRITISH COLUMBIA, 618
UNIVERSITY OF SASKATCHEWAN, 620
UNIVERSITY OF TENNESSEE - AT KNOXVILLE, 621
UNIVERSITY OF VERMONT EXTENSION, 225

UNIVERSITY OF WISCONSIN, 622
UNIVERSITY OF WISCONSIN AT MADISON, 623
URBAN HABITAT PROGRAM, 527
USAID/TANZANIA, 131
UTAH ASSOCIATION OF CONSERVATION DISTRICTS, 528
UTAH BASS FEDERATION, 528
UTAH DEPARTMENT OF NATURAL RESOURCES
  Division of Wildlife Resources, 225
UTAH STATE DEPARTMENT OF NATURAL RESOURCES
  Division of Water Resources, 226
UTAH STATE UNIVERSITY
  College of Natural Resources, 624
UTAH WILDLIFE FEDERATION, 528
VERMONT AGENCY OF NATURAL RESOURCES
  Department of Environmental Conservation, 226
  Department of Fish and Wildlife, 227
VERMONT LAND TRUST, 529
VERMONT NATURAL RESOURCES COUNCIL, 529
VERMONT STATE-WIDE ENVIRONMENTAL EDUCATION PROGRAMS (SWEEP), 530
VERNAL POOL SOCIETY, THE, 530
VINEYARD CONSERVATION SOCIETY, 530
VIRGIN ISLANDS CONSERVATION DISTRICT, 530
VIRGINIA CONSERVATION NETWORK, 531
VIRGINIA DEPARTMENT OF CONSERVATION AND RECREATION
  Division of Dam Safety, 229
VIRGINIA DEPARTMENT OF HEALTH, 231
VIRGINIA FORESTRY ASSOCIATION, 531
VIRGINIA MUSEUM OF NATURAL HISTORY, 232
VIRGINIA SOCIETY OF ORNITHOLOGY, 532
VIRGINIA TECH
  Department of Fisheries and Wildlife Sciences, 625
VIRGINIA TECH UNIVERSITY
  College of Natural Resources, 625
WARREN COUNTY CONSERVATION BOARD, 532
WASHINGTON ASSOCIATION OF CONSERVATION DISTRICTS, 533
WASHINGTON DEPARTMENT OF AGRICULTURE, 232
WASHINGTON DEPARTMENT OF FISH AND WILDLIFE
  WASHINGTON FISH AND WILDLIFE COMMISSION, 233
WASHINGTON STATE CONSERVATION COMMISSION, 234
WASHINGTON WILDERNESS COALITION, 534
WASHINGTON WILDLIFE AND RECREATION COALITION, 534
WATERSHED MANAGEMENT COUNCIL, 535
WEST MICHIGAN ENVIRONMENTAL ACTION COUNCIL, 536
WEST VIRGINIA ASSOCIATION OF CONSERVATION DISTRICT SUPERVISORS ASSOCIATION, INC., 536
WEST VIRGINIA DIVISION OF NATURAL RESOURCES, 236
WEST VIRGINIA HIGHLANDS CONSERVANCY, 536
WETLAND HABITAT ALLIANCE OF TEXAS, 538
WETLANDS ACTION NETWORK, 538
WILD FOUNDATION, THE, 539
WILD ONES NATURAL LANDSCAPERS, LTD, 540
WILDCOAST, 540
WILDERNESS EDUCATION ASSOCIATION, 540
WILDERNESS LAND TRUST, THE, 540
WILDERNESS SOCIETY, THE, 541
WILDERNESS WATCH, 541
WILDFLOWER ASSOCIATION OF MICHIGAN, 541
WILDLANDS PROJECT, 542
WILDLIFE ACTION, INC., 542
WILDLIFE DAMAGE REVIEW (WDR), 543
WILDLIFE HABITAT COUNCIL, 544
WILDLIFE INFORMATION CENTER, INC., 545
WILDLIFE SOCIETY
  Arizona Chapter, 546
  Colorado Chapter, 547
  Illinois Chapter, 547
  Michigan Chapter, 549
  National Capital Chapter, 550
  New York Chapter, 551
  Southern California Chapter, 553
WISCONSIN COOPERATIVE FISHERY RESEARCH UNIT USGS, 237
WISCONSIN ENVIRONMENTAL EDUCATION BOARD (WEEB), 238
WISCONSIN LAND AND WATER CONSERVATION ASSOCIATION, 556
WISCONSIN STATE EXTENSION SERVICES, 238
WOLF GROUP, THE, 557
WOODLAND OWNERS ASSOCIATION OF WEST VIRGINIA, 558
WORLD PARKS ENDOWMENT INC., 559
WWW.ACTIONBIOSCIENCE.ORG, 560
WYOMING COOPERATIVE FISH AND WILDLIFE RESEARCH UNIT (USDI), 238
WYOMING DEPARTMENT OF AGRICULTURE, 239
WYOMING STATE GEOLOGICAL SURVEY, 240

KEYWORD INDEX – O

YALE LAW SCHOOL, 627
YELL COUNTY WILDLIFE FEDERATION, 561
YOSEMITE RESTORATION TRUST, 562
ZUNGARO COCHA RESEARCH CENTER
   Exploration Educational Expeditions, 562

OCEANS/COASTS/BEACHES

ADVOCATES OF THE COMMON WEALTH, INC., 243
AFRICA VISION TRUST, 243
AFRICAN CONSERVATION FOUNDATION, THE, 243
ALABAMA DEPARTMENT OF AGRICULTURE AND INDUSTRIES, 132
ALABAMA ENVIRONMENTAL COUNCIL, 244
ALASKA CENTER FOR THE ENVIRONMENT, 245
ALASKA CONSERVATION FOUNDATION, 246
ALASKA DEPARTMENT OF ENVIRONMENTAL CONSERVATION, 133
ALASKA NATURAL HISTORY ASSOCIATION, 246
ALLIANCE FOR THE CHESAPEAKE BAY, 247
AMERICAN BIRD CONSERVANCY, 249
AMERICAN CONSERVATION ASSOCIATION, INC., 251
AMERICAN LAND CONSERVANCY, 262
AMERICAN LITTORAL SOCIETY, 262
   Northeast Region, 262
AMERICAN SOCIETY OF LIMNOLOGY AND OCEANOGRAPHY, 266
AMERICAN ZOO AND AQUARIUM ASSOCIATION (AZA), 268
APPALACHIAN REGIONAL COMMISSION, 16
ARENA CONSULTORES AMBIENTALES, 563
ARIZONA COOPERATIVE FISH AND WILDLIFE RESEARCH UNIT (USDI), 135
ARIZONA-SONORA DESERT MUSEUM, 271
ASSOCIATION OF AMERICAN GEOGRAPHERS, 273
ATLANTIC CENTER FOR THE ENVIRONMENT
   Quebec-Labrador Foundation, 275
ATLANTIC SALMON FEDERATION, 275
ATLANTIC STATES LEGAL FOUNDATION, 275
AUSTRIALIA DEPARTMENT FOR ENVIRONMENT AND HERITAGE
   Environment Shop, The, 139
BARRIER ISLAND TRUST, INC., 276
BASS DIVISION OF ESPN PRODUCTIONS INC, 564
BORN FREE FOUNDATION, 280
BROTHERHOOD OF THE JUNGLE COCK, INC., THE, 281
BROWN UNIVERSITY, 575
BUSINESS PUBLISHERS, INC., 564
CALIFORNIA ACADEMY OF SCIENCES, 282
CALIFORNIA DEPARTMENT OF FISH AND GAME
   Elkhorn Slough National Estuarine Research Reserve, 141
   Office of Spill Prevention and Response, 141
CALIFORNIA DEPARTMENT OF FOOD AND AGRICULTURE, 142
CALIFORNIA ENERGY COMMISSION
   Environmental Department, 143
CALIFORNIA ENVIRONMENTAL PROTECTION AGENCY
   State Water Resources Control Board, 144
CALIFORNIA STATE LANDS COMMISSION, 145
CARIBBEAN CONSERVATION CORPORATION, 288
CASCADIA RESEARCH, 288
CENTER FOR ENVIRONMENT AND POPULATION (CEP), 290
CENTER FOR RESOURCE ECONOMICS/ISLAND PRESS, 293
CETACEAN SOCIETY INTERNATIONAL, 294
CHICAGO PARK DISTRICT, 296
CHINA REGION LAKES ALLIANCE, 296
CHLORINE-FREE PAPER CONSORTIUM, 297
CIRCUMPOLAR CONSERVATION UNION, 297
CITY UNIVERSITY OF NEW YORK
   College of Staten Island, 576
CJE ASSOCIATES, 565
CLEAN OCEAN ACTION
   Main Office, 298
   Mid-Coast Office, 298
   South Jersey Office, 298
CLIMATE INSTITUTE, 299
COAST ALLIANCE, 300
COASTAL AMERICA FOUNDATION, 300
COASTAL CONSERVATION AND EDUCATION FOUNDATION, INC., 565
COASTAL RESOURCE MANAGEMENT PROJECT, 146
COASTAL SOCIETY, THE, 301
COLORADO MOUNTAIN COLLEGE, 577
COLUMBIA RIVER INTER-TRIBAL FISH COMMISSION, 17
COMMUNITIES FOR A BETTER ENVIRONMENT, 303
COMMUNITY CONSERVATION /HOWLERS FOREVER, INC., 303
CONNECTICUT BOTANICAL SOCIETY, 304
CONNECTICUT FUND FOR THE ENVIRONMENT, 305
CONNECTICUT RIVER WATERSHED COUNCIL INC., 305
CONSERVAMERICA, 305

CONSERVATION ALLIANCE OF ST. LUCIE CO., 306
CONSERVATION COUNCIL OF NORTH CAROLINA, 306
CONSERVATION LAW FOUNDATION, INC. (CLF), 307
   New England Region, 308
CORAL REEF ALLIANCE, THE (CORAL), 309
COTTONWOOD FOUNDATION, 309
COUNCIL FOR PLANNING AND CONSERVATION, 310
COUSTEAU SOCIETY, INC., THE, 310
DELAWARE NATURE SOCIETY, 312
DELAWARE WILD LANDS, INC., 313
DELTA COLLEGE, 579
DISTRICT OF COLUMBIA DEPARTMENT OF HEALTH
   Environmental Health Administration, Watershed Protection Division, 152
DUKE UNIVERSITY - ORGANIZATION FOR TROPICAL STUDIES, 580
EARTH FORCE
   GREEN (Global Rivers Environmental Education Network)), 317
EARTH POLICY INSTITUTE, 317
EARTHJUSTICE
   Headquarters, 318
   Juneau Office, 319
   Tallahassee Office, 320
   Washington, DC, Office, 320
EARTHSCAN, 320
ECODEFENSE, 321
ECOLOGICAL SOCIETY OF AMERICA, THE, 321
ENVIRONMENT AND ENERGY PUBLISHING, LLC, 566
ENVIRONMENT COUNCIL OF RHODE ISLAND, 323
ENVIRONMENTAL ALLIANCE FOR SENIOR INVOLVEMENT (EASI), 323
ENVIRONMENTAL CONCERN INC., 324
ENVIRONMENTAL DEFENSE
   Headquarters, 324
ENVIRONMENTAL DEFENSE CENTER, 325
ENVIRONMENTAL ENTERPRISES ASSISTANCE FUND, INC., 326
ENVIRONMENTAL LEAGUE OF MASSACHUSETTS, 327
ENVIRONMENTAL MEDIA CORPORATION, 566
ENVIRONMENTAL PROTECTION AGENCY
   Region 1 (CT, ME, MA, NH, RI, VT), 18
   Region 5 (IL, IN, MI, NM, OH, WI), 19
EUROPARC FEDERATION, 328
FEDERATION OF FLY FISHERS (NCCFFF), 329
FERRUM COLLEGE, 581
FISHAMERICA FOUNDATION, 330
FLINTSTEEL RESTORATION ASSOCIATION, INC., 330
FLORIDA COOPERATIVE EXTENSION SERVICE, 582
FLORIDA DEPARTMENT OF ENVIRONMENTAL PROTECTION
   Coastal and Aquatic Managed Areas, 153
   Florida State Parks AmeriCorps, 154
FLORIDA EXOTIC PEST PLANT COUNCIL, 331
FLORIDA FEDERATION OF GARDEN CLUBS, INC., 331
FLORIDA FISH AND WILDLIFE CONSERVATION COMMISSION, 154
FOOD SUPPLY / HUMAN POPULATION EXPLOSION CONNECTION, 333
FOREST FIRE LOOKOUT ASSOCIATION, 334
FRIENDS OF THE CARR REFUGE, 337
FRIENDS OF THE SEA OTTER, 338
GALIANO CONSERVANCY ASSOCIATION, 339
GEORGIA CONSERVANCY, INC., THE, 341
GEORGIA DEPARTMENT OF AGRICULTURE, 155
GEORGIA DEPARTMENT OF EDUCATION, 156
GEORGIA DEPARTMENT OF NATURAL RESOURCES
   Environmental Protection Division
      Coastal Division, 156
GEORGIA FORESTRY COMMISSION, 157
GEORGIA TRUST FOR HISTORIC PRESERVATION, 342
GOOD NATURE PUBLISHING CO., 566
GREAT LAKES UNITED
   Canada Office, 345
GREEN BALKANS FEDERATION OF NATURE CONSERVATION NGOS, 346
GREEN SPHERE INC., 347
GULF STATES MARINE FISHERIES COMMISSION, 20
H. JOHN HEINZ III CENTER FOR SCIENCE, ECONOMICS, AND THE ENVIRONMENT, 348
HARBOR BRANCH OCEANOGRAPHIC INSTITUTION, 348
HAWAII DEPARTMENT OF HEALTH
   Office of Environmental Quality Control, 159
HAWAII DEPARTMENT OF LAND AND NATURAL RESOURCES
   Division of Water Resource Management, 159
HAWAII NATURE CENTER, 349
HEADLANDS INSTITUTE, 350
HELPING OUR PENINSULA'S ENVIRONMENT, 350
HOUSE COMMITTEE ON RULES, 22
HUMANE SOCIETY OF THE UNITED STATES, THE, 352
HUNTSMAN MARINE SCIENCE CENTRE, 353
IDAHO DEPARTMENT OF PARKS AND RECREATION, 160

ILLINOIS DEPARTMENT OF NATURAL RESOURCES, 162
ILOVEPARKS.COM, 567
INDIANA STATE DEPARTMENT OF HEALTH, 164
INDO-PACIFIC CONSERVATION ALLIANCE, 357
INITIATIVE FOR SOCIAL ACTION AND RENEWAL IN EURASIA, 357
INSTITUTE FOR TROPICAL ECOLOGY AND CONSERVATION (ITEC), 358
INSTITUTO NACIONAL DE BIODIVERSIDAD (INBIO), 22
INTERNATIONAL ACADEMY, 567
INTERNATIONAL ASSOCIATION FOR ENVIRONMENTAL HYDROLOGY (IAEH), 359
INTERNATIONAL CHILDREN'S CONFERENCE ON THE ENVIRONMENT, 362
INTERNATIONAL ECOTOURISM SOCIETY, THE, 362
INTERNATIONAL EROSION CONTROL ASSOCIATION (IECA), 363
INTERNATIONAL JOINT COMMISSION
  Great Lakes Regional Office, 22
  United States Section, 23
INTERNATIONAL MARINE MAMMAL PROJECT, THE, 364
INTERNATIONAL OCEANOGRAPHIC FOUNDATION, 365
INTERNATIONAL UNION FOR CONSERVATION OF NATURE AND NATURAL RESOURCES (IUCN) THE WORLD CONSERVATION UNION
  Canada Office, 368
  Environmental Law Centre, 368
INTERNATIONAL WHALING COMMISSION, 23
ISLAND CONSERVATION EFFORT, 374
ISLAND INSTITUTE, THE, 374
ISLAND RESOURCES FOUNDATION, 375
ISLESBORO ISLANDS TRUST, 375
IZAAK WALTON LEAGUE OF AMERICA, INC., THE
  California State IWLA, 376
  Minnesota Division, 377
  Owatonna Minnesota Chapter, 377
JACKSON HOLE CONSERVATION ALLIANCE, 379
JAGRATA JUBA SHANGHA (JJS), 568
JOHN GRAY HIGH SCHOOL, GRAND CAYMAN, 584
JOHNSON STATE COLLEGE, 585
KANSAS DEPARTMENT OF HEALTH AND ENVIRONMENT, 167
KANSAS GEOLOGICAL SURVEY, 168
LA JOLLA FRIENDS OF THE SEALS (LJFS), 384
LAKE ERIE CLEAN-UP COMMITTEE, INC., 385
LAKE MICHIGAN FEDERATION, 385
LAKE SUPERIOR STATE UNIVERSITY, 586
LAKENET, 385
LAND CONSERVANCY OF WEST MICHIGAN, 386
LANDOWNER PLANNING CENTER, 386
LEE COUNTY PARKS AND RECREATION, 171
LIGHTHAWK, 389
LITERACY FOR ENVIRONMENTAL JUSTICE, 389
LIVING RIVERS, 390
LOUISIANA DEPARTMENT OF AGRICULTURE AND FORESTRY, 172
LOUISIANA DEPARTMENT OF NATURAL RESOURCES
  Office of Conservation, 172
LOUISIANA OFFICE OF STATE PARKS, DEPARTMENT OF CULTURE, RECREATION, AND TOURISM, 173
LUMMI ISLAND HERITAGE TRUST, 568
MACBRIDE RAPTOR PROJECT, 391
MACOMB LAND CONSERVANCY, 391
MAINE ASSOCIATION OF CONSERVATION COMMISSIONS (MACC), 392
MAINE ASSOCIATION OF CONSERVATION DISTRICTS, 392
MAINE BASS FEDERATION, 392
MAINE DEPARTMENT OF INLAND FISHERIES AND WILDLIFE, 175
MANITOBA CONSERVATION
  Western Region, 176
MANOMET CENTER FOR CONSERVATION SCIENCES, 393
MANTA MEXICO, 393
MARINE CONSERVATION BIOLOGY INSTITUTE, 394
MARINE MAMMAL CENTER, THE, 394
MARINE SCIENCE INSTITUTE, 394
MARINE TECHNOLOGY SOCIETY, 395
MASSACHUSETTS COOPERATIVE FISH AND WILDLIFE RESEARCH UNIT (USDI), 178
MASSACHUSETTS EXECUTIVE OFFICE OF ENVIRONMENTAL AFFAIRS, 178
  Office of Technical Assistance for Toxic Use Reduction, 179
MICHIGAN DEPARTMENT OF AGRICULTURE, 180
MICHIGAN DEPARTMENT OF NATURAL RESOURCES, 180
MICHIGAN UNITED CONSERVATION CLUBS, INC., 398
MID-ATLANTIC COUNCIL OF WATERSHED ASSOCIATIONS, 398
MID-ATLANTIC FISHERY MANAGEMENT COUNCIL, 398
MIDDLE TENNESSEE STATE UNIVERSITY, 588
MINERAL POLICY CENTER, 399
MINNESOTA POLLUTION CONTROL AGENCY
  Rochester, MN, 183

MINNESOTA-WISCONSIN BOUNDARY AREA COMMISSION, 24
MISSISSIPPI STATE UNIVERSITY
  Forest and Wildlife Research Center, 588
MOTE MARINE LABORATORY, 404
MUNDO AZUL, 406
NATIONAL AGRICULTURAL LIBRARY, 24
NATIONAL ASSOCIATION OF CONSERVATION DISTRICTS, 407
NATIONAL ASSOCIATION OF SERVICE AND CONSERVATION CORPS (NASCC), 408
NATIONAL ASSOCIATION OF STATE DEPARTMENTS OF AGRICULTURE, 408
NATIONAL AUDUBON SOCIETY
  Audubon Alaska, 409
  Audubon of Florida, 410
  Audubon Society of Portland, 411
  Audubon Society of Rhode Island, 412
  Connecticut Audubon Society, 412
  Delaware Audubon Society, 413
  Living Oceans Program, 414
  Louisiana Audubon Council, 414
  New Jersey Chapter, 415
  Public Policy Office, 415
  San Diego Chapter, 416
  Seattle Audubon Society, 416
NATIONAL BOATING FEDERATION, 417
NATIONAL COALITION FOR MARINE CONSERVATION, 417
NATIONAL ENVIRONMENTAL HEALTH ASSOCIATION, 418
NATIONAL GEOGRAPHIC SOCIETY, 421
NATIONAL GROUND WATER ASSOCIATION, THE, 421
NATIONAL PARKS CONSERVATION ASSOCIATION (NPCA)
  Sun Coast Regional Office, 423
NATIONAL WATER RESOURCES ASSOCIATION, 426
NATIONAL WATERSHED COALITION, 426
NATIONAL WATERWAYS CONFERENCE INC., 426
NATIONAL WILDLIFE FEDERATION
  Great Lakes Natural Resource Center, 427
NATIONAL WILDLIFE PRODUCTIONS, INC., 429
NATURE CONSERVANCY, THE
  Colorado Chapter, 434
  Eastern New York Chapter, 435
  New York City Office, 437
  Oklahoma Chapter, 439
  Rhode Island Chapter, 439
NEGATIVE POPULATION GROWTH (NPG), 442
NEVIS HISTORICAL AND CONSERVATION SOCIETY, 442
NEW BRUNSWICK DEPARTMENT OF NATURAL RESOURCES, 189
NEW HAMPSHIRE ASSOCIATION OF CONSERVATION DISTRICTS, 444
NEW HAMPSHIRE COUNCIL ON RESOURCES AND DEVELOPMENT, 190
NEW JERSEY DEPARTMENT OF ENVIRONMENTAL PROTECTION
  Division of Solid and Hazardous Waste, 192
  Geological Survey, 192
NEW YORK DEPARTMENT OF AGRICULTURE AND MARKETS, 196
NEW YORK STATE TUG HILL COMMISSION, 199
NEWFOUNDLAND DEPARTMENT OF FOREST RESOURCES AND AGRIFOODS
  Regional Offices, 199
NORTH CAROLINA BEACH BUGGY ASSOCIATION, INC., 450
NORTH CAROLINA CONSERVATION NETWORK, 450
NORTH CAROLINA DEPARTMENT OF AGRICULTURE AND CONSUMER SERVICES, 200
NORTH CAROLINA WILD FLOWER PRESERVATION SOCIETY, 451
NORTH DAKOTA GAME AND FISH DEPARTMENT, 201
NORTH DAKOTA STATE SOIL CONSERVATION COMMITTEE, 202
NORTHERN ALASKA ENVIRONMENTAL CENTER, 453
NORTHWEST ATLANTIC FISHERIES ORGANIZATION (NAFO), 453
NORTHWEST RESOURCE INFORMATION CENTER, 454
NOVA SCOTIA AGRICULTURE & FISHERIES, 203
NOVA SCOTIA FORESTRY ASSOCIATION, 454
OCEAN CONSERVANCY, THE, 455
OCEAN PROJECT, THE, 455
OCEANIA, 455
OCEANIC SOCIETY, 456
OHIO DEPARTMENT OF AGRICULTURE, 203
OHIO DEPARTMENT OF NATURAL RESOURCES, 204
OHIO ENVIRONMENTAL REVIEW APPEALS COMMISSION, 205
OHIO NATIVE PLANT SOCIETY, 457
OHIO STATE UNIVERSITY, 592
OLYMPIC PARK INSTITUTE, 459
ONEWILDWORLD, 459
OREGON DEPARTMENT OF AGRICULTURE, 208
OREGON STATE MARINE BOARD, 210
OTTER PROJECT, THE, 462

KEYWORD INDEX – O

PACIFIC MARINE CONSERVATION COUNCIL, 464
PEOPLE FOR PUGET SOUND, 467
  North Sound Office, 467
PINE BLUFF COOPERATIVE FISHERY RESEARCH PROJECT, 213
POCONO ENVIRONMENTAL EDUCATION CENTER, 470
POINT TO POINT COMMUNICATIONS, 569
PROJECT SEAHORSE, 473
PROTECTED AREAS ASSOCIATION OF NEWFOUNDLAND AND LABRADOR, 474
PS ENTERPRISES, 570
PUBLIC EMPLOYEES FOR ENVIRONMENTAL RESPONSIBILITY (PEER), 474
PUERTO RICO DEPARTMENT OF AGRICULTURE, 213
QUEBEC WILDLIFE FEDERATION, 476
REEF RELIEF, 478
RENEWABLE NATURAL RESOURCES FOUNDATION, 478
RESIDENTS FOR A MORE BEAUTIFUL PORT WASHINGTON, 479
RESOURCE CENTER FOR ENVIRONMENTAL EDUCATION, THE, 479
RHODE ISLAND STATE CONSERVATION COMMITTEE, 480
RIVER PROJECT, THE, 481
ROCKY MOUNTAIN BIGHORN SOCIETY, 482
ROGER WILLIAMS UNIVERSITY, 594
RUTGERS COOPERATIVE EXTENSION, 215
SAN DIEGUITO RIVER PARK JOINT POWERS AUTHORITY, 215
SAN ELIJO LAGOON CONSERVANCY, 484
SASKATCHEWAN WILDLIFE FEDERATION, 484
SAVE SAN FRANCISCO BAY ASSOCIATION, 485
SAVE THE DUNES COUNCIL, 485
SAVE THE SOUND, INC., 486
SCIENTISTS CENTER FOR ANIMAL WELFARE, 488
SEA SHEPHERD CONSERVATION SOCIETY
  Netherlands, 488
SEA TURTLE PRESERVATION SOCIETY, 489
SEACAMP ASSOCIATION, INC., 489
SEAPLANE PILOTS ASSOCIATION, 489
SHEPHERD COLLEGE, 595
SIERRA CLUB
  Alaska Field Office, 490
  Hawaii Chapter, 492
  Mackinac Chapter, 493
  Maryland Chapter, 493
  Northwest Office, 495
  Tehipite Chapter (Northern California), 498
  West Virginia Chapter, 499
SIERRA CLUB CALIFORNIA, 499
SIERRA CLUB FOUNDATION, THE, 499
SIERRA CLUB OF CANADA
  Atlantic Canada Chapter, 500
SOCIEDAD AMBIENTE MARINO, 502
SOIL AND WATER CONSERVATION SOCIETY, 504
SOUTH ATLANTIC FISHERY MANAGEMENT COUNCIL, 29
SOUTH CAROLINA COOPERATIVE FISH AND WILDLIFE RESEARCH UNIT, 217
SOUTH CAROLINA DEPARTMENT OF HEALTH AND ENVIRONMENTAL CONTROL, 217
SOUTH CAROLINA DEPARTMENT OF PARKS, RECREATION AND TOURISM, 218
SOUTH CAROLINA WILDLIFE FEDERATION, 506
SOUTHEASTERN ASSOCIATION OF FISH AND WILDLIFE AGENCIES, 508
SOUTHERN ENVIRONMENTAL LAW CENTER, 509
SOUTHERN UTAH WILDERNESS ALLIANCE
  Moab Office, 510
SOUTHWEST CENTER FOR ENVIRONMENTAL RESEARCH AND POLICY (SCERP), 596
SOUTHWEST CONSERVATION DISTRICT, 510
STATE UNIVERSITY OF NEW YORK AT STONY BROOK, 597
STERLING COLLEGE, 598
STUDENT CONSERVATION ASSOCIATION, INC., 512
STUDENTS PARTNERSHIP WORLDWIDE, 513
SUNCOAST SEABIRD SANCTUARY INC., 514
SUSTAIN, 514
SUSTAINABLE ENERGY INSTITUTE
  Culture Change magazine, 514
TALLAHASSEE MUSEUM OF HISTORY AND NATURAL SCIENCE, 515
TENNESSEE AGRICULTURAL EXTENSION SERVICE, 220
TERRA NATURE FUND, 516
TEXAS CHRISTIAN UNIVERSITY, 599
TEXAS COOPERATIVE FISH AND WILDLIFE RESEARCH UNIT, 30
TEXAS DEPARTMENT OF AGRICULTURE, 222
TEXAS ORGANIZATION FOR ENDANGERED SPECIES, 517
TROUT UNLIMITED
  New York Council, 522
TULANE ENVIRONMENTAL LAW CLINIC, 600
TULANE UNIVERSITY
  Department of Ecology and Evolutionary Biology, 600
TURNER ENDANGERED SPECIES FUND, 571
TURTLE CREEK WATERSHED ASSOCIATION, INC., 525
UNEP WORLD CONSERVATION MONITORING CENTRE, 525
UNITED NATIONS ENVIRONMENT PROGRAMME, 525
UNITED STATES CHAMBER OF COMMERCE
  Environment, Technology and Regulatory Affairs, 526
UNITED STATES DEPARTMENT OF AGRICULTURE
  Forest Service
    Los Padres National Forest, 40
    Siuslaw National Forest, 45
UNITED STATES DEPARTMENT OF COMMERCE
  National Oceanic and Atmospheric Administration
    Chesapeake Bay National Estuarine Research Reserve
      Virginia Office, 50
    Delaware National Estuarine Research Reserve, 50
    Flower Garden Banks National Marine Sanctuary, 50
    Gray's Reef National Marine Sanctuary, 50
    Gulf of Farallones National Marine Sanctuary, 50
    Padilla Bay National Estuarine Research Reserve, 53
    Rookery Bay National Estuarine Research Reserve, 53
    Sea Grant Program - Alabama, 53
    Sea Grant Program - Maryland, 56
    Sea Grant Program - Massachusetts, 56
    Sea Grant Program - Michigan, 57
    Sea Grant Program - New Jersey, 57
    Sea Grant Program - North Carolina, 58
    Sea Grant Program - Ohio, 58
    Stellwagen Bank National Marine Sanctuary, 60
    Wells National Estuarine Research Reserve, 60
UNITED STATES DEPARTMENT OF DEFENSE
  Air Force Major Air Commands
    Andrews AFB, MD, 61
    USAF Academy, 62
  Army Corps of Engineers
    Baltimore Engineer District, 67
    Fort Worth Engineer District, 68
    North Atlantic Engineer District, 70
    Pacific Ocean Engineer District, 70
    Walla Walla Engineer District, 72
  Assistant Chief of Staff for Installation Management, Office of the Director of Environmental Programs, and Conservation Team, 74
  Navy, 74
UNITED STATES DEPARTMENT OF THE INTERIOR
  Bureau of Land Management
    Bakersfield Field Office, 79
    Northern Field Office, 84
  Fish & Wildlife Service
    Alligator River/Pea Island National Wildlife Refuge, 91
    Archie Carr National Wildlife Refuge, 91
    California-Nevada Operations, 94
    Guadalupe-Nipomo Dunes National Wildlife Refuge, 99
    Hobe Sound National Wildlife Refuge, 99
    Southeast Louisiana Complex National Wildlife Refuge, 115
    St. Marks National Wildlife Refuge, 115
    Upper Mississippi River National Wildlife and fish refuge, 117
    Washington Maritime National Wildlife Refuge Complex, 118
    Willapa/Lewis and Clark National Wildlife Refuge, 118
  United States Geological Survey
    Western Region, 127
UNITED STATES DEPARTMENT OF TRANSPORTATION
  Federal Aviation Administration, 128
UNITED STATES INSTITUTE FOR ENVIRONMENTAL CONFLICT RESOLUTION, 130
UNITED STATES PUBLIC INTEREST RESEARCH GROUP, 526
UNIVERSITE LAVAL, 601
UNIVERSITY OF CALIFORNIA AT DAVIS
  School of Veterinary Medicine, 606
UNIVERSITY OF CALIFORNIA AT SAN DIEGO, 607
UNIVERSITY OF CONNECTICUT COOPERATIVE EXTENSION, 608
UNIVERSITY OF FLORIDA INSTITUTE OF FOOD AND AGRICULTURAL SCIENCES, 609
UNIVERSITY OF ILLINOIS EXTENSION, 611
UNIVERSITY OF MAINE, 612
UNIVERSITY OF MARYLAND - AT COLLEGE PARK, 613
UNIVERSITY OF MARYLAND COOPERATIVE EXTENSION, 224
UNIVERSITY OF MICHIGAN, 614
UNIVERSITY OF NEW HAVEN DEPT. OF BIOLOGY AND ENVIRONMENTAL SCIENCES, 617
UNIVERSITY OF NORTH CAROLINA AT ASHEVILLE, 617
UNIVERSITY OF OREGON
  School of Law, 618

UNIVERSITY OF RHODE ISLAND
  Department of Natural Resources Science, 619
UNIVERSITY OF SOUTH CAROLINA
  Baruch Marine Field Laboratory, 620
UNIVERSITY OF SOUTH CAROLINA BEAUFORT, 620
UNIVERSITY OF SOUTHERN MISSISSIPPI, 620
UNIVERSITY OF THE DISTRICT OF COLUMBIA, 621
UNIVERSITY OF VERMONT EXTENSION, 225
UPPER COLORADO RIVER COMMISSION, 130
UTAH STATE UNIVERSITY
  College of Natural Resources, 624
VINEYARD CONSERVATION SOCIETY, 530
VIRGINIA DEPARTMENT OF ENVIRONMENTAL QUALITY, 230
VIRGINIA TECH
  Department of Fisheries and Wildlife Sciences, 625
VIRGINIA TECH UNIVERSITY
  College of Natural Resources, 625
WASHINGTON DEPARTMENT OF ECOLOGY, 233
WASHINGTON FARM FORESTRY ASSOCIATION, 533
WASHINGTON STATE CONSERVATION COMMISSION, 234
WASHINGTON STATE OFFICE OF ENVIRONMENTAL EDUCATION, 234
WATER RESOURCES ASSOCIATION OF THE DELAWARE RIVER BASIN, 535
WESTERN ENVIRONMENTAL LAW CENTER, 537
WESTERN HEMISPHERE SHOREBIRD RESERVE NETWORK (WHSRN), 537
WESTERN PACIFIC REGIONAL FISHERY MANAGEMENT COUNCIL, 131
WESTERN SNOWY PLOVER WORKING TEAM, 131
WETLANDS ACTION NETWORK, 538
WILDCOAST, 540
WILDERNESS WATCH, 541
WILDLIFE ACTION, INC., 542
WILDLIFE CONSERVATION SOCIETY, 543
WILDLIFE SOCIETY
  Colorado Chapter, 547
  New York Chapter, 551
WILDLIFE TRUST
  Wildlife Preservation Trust International, 554
WISCONSIN COOPERATIVE FISHERY RESEARCH UNIT USGS, 237
WORLD RESOURCES INSTITUTE, 559
WORLDWATCH INSTITUTE, 560
WWW.ACTIONBIOSCIENCE.ORG, 560
ZERO, 562

POLLUTION (GENERAL)

20/20 VISION, 241
ADVOCATES OF THE COMMON WEALTH, INC., 243
AFRICAN AMERICAN ENVIRONMENTALIST ASSOCIATION, 243
ALABAMA ENVIRONMENTAL COUNCIL, 244
ALASKA CENTER FOR THE ENVIRONMENT, 245
ALASKA CONSERVATION ALLIANCE, 245, 246
ALLIANCE FOR THE CHESAPEAKE BAY, 247
AMERICAN COUNCIL FOR AN ENERGY-EFFICIENT ECONOMY, 251
AMERICAN LITTORAL SOCIETY
  Northeast Region, 262
AMERICAN PIE (PUBLIC INFORMATION ON THE ENVIRONMENT), 264
AMERICAN WATER WORKS ASSOCIATION (AWWA), 267
ANACOSTIA WATERSHED SOCIETY, 268
ANGLERS FOR CLEAN WATER, 268
APROVECHO RESEARCH CENTER, 270
ARENA CONSULTORES AMBIENTALES, 563
ARIZONA COOPERATIVE FISH AND WILDLIFE RESEARCH UNIT (USDI), 135
ARIZONA STATE UNIVERSITY
  Center for Environmental Studies, 573
ARKANSAS WATERSHED ADVISORY GROUP (AWAG), 272
ASSOCIATION OF NEW JERSEY ENVIRONMENTAL COMMISSIONS (ANJEC), 274
ATLANTIC CENTER FOR THE ENVIRONMENT
  Quebec-Labrador Foundation, 275
ATLANTIC SALMON FEDERATION, 275
ATLANTIC STATES LEGAL FOUNDATION, 275
AUDUBON INTERNATIONAL, 276
AUSTRIALIA DEPARTMENT FOR ENVIRONMENT AND HERITAGE
  Environment Shop, The, 139
BASS DIVISION OF ESPN PRODUCTIONS INC, 564
BEAR SPRINGS BLOSSOM NATURE CONSERVATION GROUP INC., 277
BEYOND PESTICIDES, 277
BIOINTEGRAL RESOURCE CENTER, 278
BOARD OF MINERALS AND ENVIRONMENT, 139
BORDER ECOLOGY PROJECT (BEP), 279
BRANDYWINE CONSERVANCY INC., 280
CALIFORNIA COOPERATIVE FISHERY RESEARCH UNIT (USGS), 16
CALIFORNIA DEPARTMENT OF FISH AND GAME
  Office of Spill Prevention and Response, 141
CALIFORNIA DEPARTMENT OF PESTICIDE REGULATION, 143
CALIFORNIA UNIVERSITY OF PENNSYLVANIA, 576
CAMPAIGN FOR AMERICA'S WILDERNESS, 285
CARIBBEAN CONSERVATION CORPORATION, 288
CENTER FOR ENVIRONMENT AND POPULATION (CEP), 290
CENTER FOR ENVIRONMENT, COMMERCE & ENERGY, 290
CENTER FOR ENVIRONMENTAL HEALTH (CEH), 291
CENTER FOR HEALTH, ENVIRONMENT, AND JUSTICE, 291
CENTER FOR RESOURCE ECONOMICS/ISLAND PRESS, 293
CENTER FOR SCIENCE IN THE PUBLIC INTEREST, 293
CENTRO DE INFORMACION, INVESTIGACION Y EDUCACION SOCIAL (CIIES), 294
CHESAPEAKE BAY FOUNDATION, INC.
  Maryland Office, 295
CHICAGO PARK DISTRICT, 296
CHINA REGION LAKES ALLIANCE, 296
CINCINNATI NATURE CENTER, 297
CIRCUMPOLAR CONSERVATION UNION, 297
CITY UNIVERSITY OF NEW YORK
  College of Staten Island, 576
CJE ASSOCIATES, 565
CLARK UNIVERSITY, 576
CLEAN OCEAN ACTION
  Main Office, 298
  Mid-Coast Office, 298
  South Jersey Office, 298
CLEMSON UNIVERSITY
  School of the Environment, 577
CLINTON RIVER WATERSHED COUNCIL (CRWC), 299
COALITION FOR CLEAN AIR, 299
COAST ALLIANCE, 300
COASTAL AMERICA FOUNDATION, 300
COASTAL GEORGIA LAND TRUST INC., 300
COLORADO DEPARTMENT OF AGRICULTURE, 146
COLORADO DEPARTMENT OF NATURAL RESOURCES
  Division of Parks and Outdoor Recreation, 146
  Oil and Gas Conservation Commission, 147
COLORADO GOVERNOR'S OFFICE OF ENERGY MANAGEMENT AND CONSERVATION, 147
COLORADO MOUNTAIN COLLEGE, 577
COLORADO STATE FOREST SERVICE, 148
COLUMBIA RIVER INTER-TRIBAL FISH COMMISSION, 17
COMMUNITY ENVIRONMENTAL COUNCIL (CEC), 303
CONCERN, INC., 304
CONNECTICUT BOTANICAL SOCIETY, 304
CONNECTICUT FUND FOR THE ENVIRONMENT, 305
CONNECTICUT PUBLIC INTEREST RESEARCH GROUP (CONN PIRG), 305
CONNECTICUT RIVER WATERSHED COUNCIL INC., 305
CONSERVAMERICA, 305
CONSERVATION ALLIANCE OF ST. LUCIE CO., 306
CONSERVATION COUNCIL OF NORTH CAROLINA, 306
CONSERVATION LAW FOUNDATION, INC. (CLF)
  New England Region, 308
COTTONWOOD FOUNDATION, 309
DELAWARE COOPERATIVE EXTENSION SERVICES, 150
DELAWARE DEPARTMENT OF NATURAL RESOURCES AND ENVIRONMENTAL CONTROL
  Division of Parks and Recreation, 150
  Division of Soil and Water Conservation, 150
DELAWARE NATURE SOCIETY, 312
DELAWARE RIVERKEEPER NETWORK, 313
DELTA COLLEGE, 579
DELTA WILDLIFE INC., 313
DISTRICT OF COLUMBIA DEPARTMENT OF HEALTH
  Environmental Health Administration, Watershed Protection Division, 152
EAGLE NATURE FOUNDATION, LTD., 316
EARTH DAY NEW YORK, 316
EARTH FORCE
  GREEN (Global Rivers Environmental Education Network)), 317
EARTHJUSTICE
  Headquarters, 318
  International Program, 319
  Oakland Office, 319
  Seattle Office, 320
  Tallahassee Office, 320
  Washington, DC, Office, 320
EARTHSCAN, 320

KEYWORD INDEX – P

ECOLOGICAL SOCIETY OF AMERICA, THE, 321
ECOLOGY CENTER, 321
ECONOVA INC., 565
ENVIRONMENT COUNCIL OF RHODE ISLAND, 323
ENVIRONMENTAL ALLIANCE FOR SENIOR INVOLVEMENT (EASI), 323
ENVIRONMENTAL DEFENSE
  Headquarters, 324
ENVIRONMENTAL DEFENSE CENTER, 325
ENVIRONMENTAL EDUCATION ASSOCIATES, 325
ENVIRONMENTAL ENTERPRISES ASSISTANCE FUND, INC., 326
ENVIRONMENTAL LAW INSTITUTE, THE, 327
ENVIRONMENTAL LEAGUE OF MASSACHUSETTS, 327
ENVIRONMENTAL POLICY CENTER, THE, 327
ENVIRONMENTAL PROTECTION AGENCY
  Region 1 (CT, ME, MA, NH, RI, VT), 18
  Region 5 (IL, IN, MI, NM, OH, WI), 19
EP EDUCATION SERVICES, INC., 328
FEDERAL WILDLIFE OFFICERS ASSOCIATION, 329
FEDERATION OF FLY FISHERS (NCCFFF), 329
FERRUM COLLEGE, 581
FISHAMERICA FOUNDATION, 330
FLORIDA COOPERATIVE FISH AND WILDLIFE RESEARCH UNIT (USDI), 152
FLORIDA DEPARTMENT OF ENVIRONMENTAL PROTECTION
  Coastal and Aquatic Managed Areas, 153
FLORIDA EXOTIC PEST PLANT COUNCIL, 331
FLORIDA FEDERATION OF GARDEN CLUBS, INC., 331
FOOD SUPPLY / HUMAN POPULATION EXPLOSION CONNECTION, 333
FRIENDS OF THE EARTH, 337
FRIENDS OF THE SEA OTTER, 338
GALIANO CONSERVANCY ASSOCIATION, 339
GEORGIA CONSERVANCY, INC., THE, 341
GEORGIA COOPERATIVE FISH AND WILDLIFE RESEARCH UNIT (USDI), 20
GEORGIA DEPARTMENT OF NATURAL RESOURCES
  Environmental Protection Division
    Coastal Division, 156
GEORGIA ENVIRONMENTAL ORGANIZATION, INC. (GEO), 341
GLEN CANYON INSTITUTE, 343
GREAT LAKES UNITED
  CANADA OFFICE, 345
GREEN BALKANS FEDERATION OF NATURE CONSERVATION NGOS, 346
GREEN PARTNERS, 347
GREEN SPHERE INC., 347
GREENPEACE, INC., 347
GROUNDWATER FOUNDATION, THE, 347
GROWLING, 348
GUADALUPE-BLANCO RIVER AUTHORITY, 157
GULF STATES MARINE FISHERIES COMMISSION, 20
HAMLINE UNIVERSITY, 583
HAWAII DEPARTMENT OF HEALTH
  Office of Environmental Quality Control, 159
HAWAII NATURE CENTER, 349
HAWKWATCH INTERNATIONAL, 350
HEADLANDS INSTITUTE, 350
HELPING OUR PENINSULA'S ENVIRONMENT, 350
HOLLOW OAK LAND TRUST, 351
HOUSE COMMITTEE ON RULES, 22
HUMAN ECOLOGY ACTION LEAGUE, INC., THE (HEAL), 352
HUMMINGBIRD SOCIETY, THE, 353
HUNTSMAN MARINE SCIENCE CENTRE, 353
IDAHO DEPARTMENT OF PARKS AND RECREATION, 160
IDAHO DEPARTMENT OF WATER RESOURCES, 161
  Water Awareness Week, 161
ILLINOIS DEPARTMENT OF NATURAL RESOURCES, 162
ILLINOIS ENVIRONMENTAL COUNCIL, 355
ILLINOIS ENVIRONMENTAL PROTECTION AGENCY, 162
ILLINOIS NATURE PRESERVES COMMISSION (INPC), 163
ILLINOIS WALNUT COUNCIL, 356
ILOVEPARKS.COM, 567
INDIANA DEPARTMENT OF NATURAL RESOURCES, 163
INDIANA STATE DEPARTMENT OF HEALTH, 164
INFORM, INC., 357
INSTITUTE FOR ECOLOGICAL STUDIES UNIVERSITY OF NORTH DAKOTA, 164
INSTITUTO NACIONAL DE BIODIVERSIDAD (INBIO), 22
INTERNATIONAL ASSOCIATION FOR ENVIRONMENTAL HYDROLOGY (IAEH), 359
INTERNATIONAL ASSOCIATION OF NATURAL RESOURCE PILOTS, 360
INTERNATIONAL CHILDREN'S CONFERENCE ON THE ENVIRONMENT, 362
INTERNATIONAL JOINT COMMISSION
  Great Lakes Regional Office, 22

IOWA DEPARTMENT OF AGRICULTURE AND LAND STEWARDSHIP
  Bureau of Financial Incentive Program, 165
IOWA DEPARTMENT OF NATURAL RESOURCES
  Fish and Wildlife Division, 166
IOWA ENVIRONMENTAL COUNCIL, 372
IOWA PRAIRIE NETWORK, 373
IOWA STATE UNIVERSITY
  College of Agriculture, 584
ISLAND RESOURCES FOUNDATION, 375
ISLESBORO ISLANDS TRUST, 375
IZAAK WALTON LEAGUE OF AMERICA, INC., THE
  Minnesota Division, 377
  Owatonna Minnesota Chapter, 377
J.N. (DING) DARLING FOUNDATION, 379
JACKSON HOLE CONSERVATION ALLIANCE, 379
JOHNSON STATE COLLEGE, 585
KANSAS STATE UNIVERSITY
  Department of Landscape Architecture / Regional and Community Planning, 585
KANSAS WATER OFFICE, 169
KENTUCKY DEPARTMENT OF AGRICULTURE, 169
KENTUCKY DEPARTMENT OF FISH AND WILDLIFE RESOURCES, 169
KENTUCKY NATURAL RESOURCES AND ENVIRONMENTAL PROTECTION CABINET, 170
KENTUCKY WOODLAND OWNERS ASSOCIATION, 383
KIDS FOR SAVING EARTH WORLDWIDE, 384
KIDS ON THE BAYOU, 384
LAKE MICHIGAN FEDERATION, 385
LAKE SUPERIOR GREENS, 385
LAKE SUPERIOR STATE UNIVERSITY, 586
LAKENET, 385
LAST WIZARDS, THE, 568
LEAGUE OF OHIO SPORTSMEN, 387
LEAGUE OF WOMEN VOTERS OF WASHINGTON, 388
LEGAL ENVIRONMENTAL ASSISTANCE FOUNDATION INC. (LEAF), 388
LOWER MERION CONSERVANCY, 391
LUMMI ISLAND HERITAGE TRUST, 568
MAINE ASSOCIATION OF CONSERVATION DISTRICTS, 392
MAINE DEPARTMENT OF CONSERVATION
  Land Use Regulation Commission, 175
MANITOBA NATURALISTS SOCIETY, 393
MANOMET CENTER FOR CONSERVATION SCIENCES, 393
MANTA MEXICO, 393
MARYLAND DEPARTMENT OF AGRICULTURE, 176
MARYLAND DEPARTMENT OF NATURAL RESOURCES, 177
MASSACHUSETTS EXECUTIVE OFFICE OF ENVIRONMENTAL AFFAIRS, 178
  Office of Technical Assistance for Toxic Use Reduction, 179
MCGILL UNIVERSITY, 587
MIAMI UNIVERSITY, 587
MICHIGAN DEPARTMENT OF AGRICULTURE, 180
MICHIGAN DEPARTMENT OF ENVIRONMENTAL QUALITY, 100
MIDDLE TENNESSEE STATE UNIVERSITY, 588
MINERAL POLICY CENTER, 399
MINNESOTA BOARD OF WATER AND SOIL RESOURCES, 181
MINNESOTA FORESTRY ASSOCIATION, 399
MINNESOTA POLLUTION CONTROL AGENCY
  Rochester, MN, 183
MINNESOTA-WISCONSIN BOUNDARY AREA COMMISSION, 24
MISSISSIPPI STATE UNIVERSITY
  Forest and Wildlife Research Center, 588
MONTANA DEPARTMENT OF NATURAL RESOURCES AND CONSERVATION, 187
MONTANA LAND RELIANCE, 403
MOUNT GRACE LAND CONSERVATION TRUST, 405
MUNDO AZUL, 406
NATIONAL 4-H COUNCIL, 406
NATIONAL AGRICULTURAL LIBRARY, 24
NATIONAL ASSOCIATION OF STATE DEPARTMENTS OF AGRICULTURE, 408
NATIONAL AUDUBON SOCIETY
  Connecticut Audubon Society, 412
  Delaware Audubon Society, 413
  Louisiana Audubon Council, 414
NATIONAL CAUCUS OF ENVIRONMENTAL LEGISLATORS (NCEL), 417
NATIONAL ENVIRONMENTAL EDUCATION AND TRAINING FOUNDATION, 418
NATIONAL ENVIRONMENTAL HEALTH ASSOCIATION, 418
NATIONAL WATER RESOURCES ASSOCIATION, 426
NATIONAL WATERSHED COALITION, 426
NATIONAL WILDLIFE PRODUCTIONS, INC., 429
NATURE CONSERVANCY, THE
  Arkansas Field Office, 434

NEBRASKA WILDLIFE FEDERATION, INC., 442
NEGATIVE POPULATION GROWTH (NPG), 442
NEW HAMPSHIRE ASSOCIATION OF CONSERVATION DISTRICTS, 444
NEW HAMPSHIRE COUNCIL ON RESOURCES AND DEVELOPMENT, 190
NEW HAMPSHIRE FISH AND GAME DEPARTMENT, 190
NEW JERSEY DEPARTMENT OF ENVIRONMENTAL PROTECTION
   Division of Solid and Hazardous Waste, 192
NEW MEXICO BUREAU OF GEOLOGY AND MINERAL RESOURCES, 193
NEW YORK PUBLIC INTEREST RESEARCH GROUP (NYPIRG), 446
NORTH AMERICAN DEVELOPMENT BANK, 24
NORTH CAROLINA BASS FEDERATION, 450
NORTH CAROLINA CONSERVATION NETWORK, 450
NORTH CAROLINA COOPERATIVE FISH AND WILDLIFE RESEARCH UNIT (USDI), 200
NORTH CAROLINA DIVISION OF SOIL AND WATER, 200
NORTH CAROLINA STATE UNIVERSITY, 590
NORTH CAROLINA WILD FLOWER PRESERVATION SOCIETY, 451
NORTH DAKOTA DEPARTMENT OF AGRICULTURE, 201
NORTHWEST COALITION FOR ALTERNATIVES TO PESTICIDES, 453
NORTHWEST ENVIRONMENT WATCH, 454
NOVA SCOTIA DEPARTMENT OF NATURAL RESOURCES, 203
NOVA SCOTIA FORESTRY ASSOCIATION, 454
OCEANIA, 455
OHIO ACADEMY OF SCIENCE, THE, 456
OHIO DEPARTMENT OF AGRICULTURE, 203
OHIO DEPARTMENT OF NATURAL RESOURCES, 204
OHIO ENVIRONMENTAL REVIEW APPEALS COMMISSION, 205
OHIO FEDERATION OF SOIL AND WATER CONSERVATION DISTRICTS, 457
OHIO FORESTRY ASSOCIATION, INC., 457
OHIO NATIVE PLANT SOCIETY, 457
OHIO STATE UNIVERSITY, 592
OKLAHOMA COOPERATIVE FISH AND WILDLIFE RESEARCH UNIT (USDI), 206
OKLAHOMA DEPARTMENT OF ENVIRONMENTAL QUALITY, 206
OKLAHOMA GEOLOGICAL SURVEY, 206
OKLAHOMA STATE EXTENSION SERVICES, 206
ONEWILDWORLD, 459
ONTARIO FEDERATION OF ANGLERS AND HUNTERS, 459
ONTARIO FORESTRY ASSOCIATION, 459
OREGON DEPARTMENT OF TRANSPORTATION, 209
OREGON NATURAL RESOURCES COUNCIL, 460
OTTER PROJECT, THE, 462
PACIFIC RIVERS COUNCIL, 464
PACIFIC STATES MARINE FISHERIES COMMISSION, 27
PENNSYLVANIA DEPARTMENT OF AGRICULTURE
   REGION VII, 211
PENNSYLVANIA FEDERATION OF SPORTSMENS CLUBS, 466
PENNSYLVANIA ORGANIZATION FOR WATERSHEDS AND RIVERS (POWR), 466
PENNSYLVANIA RESOURCES COUNCIL, INC.., 467
PEOPLE FOR PUGET SOUND, 467
   North Sound Office, 467
   South Sound Office, 467
PHYSICIANS FOR SOCIAL RESPONSIBILITY, 468
POLLUTION PROBE, 470
POPULATION-ENVIRONMENT BALANCE, INC., 471
PS ENTERPRISES, 570
PUGET SOUNDKEEPER ALLIANCE, 475
PURPLE MARTIN CONSERVATION ASSOCIATION, 475
QUEBEC DEPARTMENT OF ENVIRONMENT AND WILDLIFE, 214
RACHEL CARSON COUNCIL, INC., 476
RAINBOW PUSH COALITION, 476
RAINFOREST RELIEF, 477
REEF RELIEF, 478
RENEWABLE NATURAL RESOURCES FOUNDATION, 478
RESIDENTS FOR A MORE BEAUTIFUL PORT WASHINGTON, 479
RIVER PROJECT, THE, 481
RUTGERS COOPERATIVE EXTENSION, 215
RUTGERS UNIVERSITY, COOK COLLEGE, 594
SAN DIEGUITO RIVER PARK JOINT POWERS AUTHORITY, 215
SAN ELIJO LAGOON CONSERVANCY, 484
SAND CREEK WATERSHED PROJECT, THE, 215
SANTA CLARA COMMUNITY ACTION PROGRAM, 594
SAVE THE HARBOR/SAVE THE BAY, 486
SAVE THE SOUND, INC., 486
SAVE WETLANDS AND BAYS, 486
SEACOAST ANTI-POLLUTION LEAGUE, 489
SIERRA CLUB
   Alaska Field Office, 490
   Connecticut Chapter, 491
   Hawaii Chapter, 492
   Lone Star Chapter, 493
   Mackinac Chapter, 493
   Maryland Chapter, 493
   Nebraska Chapter, 494
   New Jersey Chapter, 495
   Northwest Office, 495
   Pennsylvania Chapter, 496
   Rio Grande Chapter (New Mexico/West Texas), 496
   San francisco Bay Chapter, 497
   Washington, DC Office, 499
   West Virginia Chapter, 499
SIERRA CLUB CALIFORNIA, 499
SIERRA CLUB FOUNDATION, THE, 499
SIERRA CLUB OF CANADA
   Atlantic Canada Chapter, 500
SOCIETY FOR THE PROTECTION OF NEW HAMPSHIRE FORESTS, 503
SOUTH CAROLINA DEPARTMENT OF AGRICULTURE, 217
SOUTH CAROLINA NATIVE PLANT SOCIETY, 506
SOUTH DAKOTA ASSOCIATION OF CONSERVATION DISTRICTS, 506
SOUTH DAKOTA DEPARTMENT OF AGRICULTURE
   Division of Resource Conservation and Forestry, 218
SOUTH DAKOTA DEPARTMENT OF ENVIRONMENT AND NATURAL RESOURCES, 219
SOUTH DAKOTA RESOURCES COALITION, 507
SOUTHEASTERN ASSOCIATION OF FISH AND WILDLIFE AGENCIES, 508
SOUTHERN ENVIRONMENTAL LAW CENTER, 509
SOUTHERN UTAH WILDERNESS ALLIANCE
   Moab Office, 510
SOUTHFACE ENERGY INSTITUTE, 510
SOUTHWEST CENTER FOR ENVIRONMENTAL RESEARCH AND POLICY (SCERP), 596
SOUTHWEST CONSERVATION DISTRICT, 510
SOUTHWEST RESEARCH AND INFORMATION CENTER, 510
STATE AND TERRITORIAL AIR POLLUTION PROGRAM ADMINISTRATORS AND THE ASSOCIATION OF LOCAL AIR POLLUTION CONTROL OFFICIALS, 512
STATE ENVIRONMENTAL RESOURCE CENTER (SERC), 512
STEPHEN F. AUSTIN STATE UNIVERSITY ARTHUR TEMPLE COLLEGE OF FORESTRY, 598
STUDENT CONSERVATION ASSOCIATION, INC., 512
STUDENT ENVIRONMENTAL ACTION COALITION (SEAC), 513
SUSTAIN, 514
TALLAHASSEE MUSEUM OF HISTORY AND NATURAL SCIENCE, 515
TANZANIA COASTAL MANAGEMENT PARTNERSHIP, 30
TENNESSEE DEPARTMENT OF AGRICULTURE, 221
TENNESSEE FORESTRY ASSOCIATION, 516
TENNESSEE VALLEY AUTHORITY
   Muscle Shoals Technical Library, 30
TEXAS BASS FEDERATION, 517
TEXAS ORGANIZATION FOR ENDANGERED SPECIES, 517
TREES FOR THE FUTURE, INC., 519
TRI-STATE BIRD RESCUE AND RESEARCH, INC., 520
TROUT UNLIMITED
   New York Council, 522
TULANE ENVIRONMENTAL LAW CLINIC, 600
TULANE UNIVERSITY
   Department of Ecology and Evolutionary Biology, 600
TURNER ENDANGERED SPECIES FUND, 571
TWO WHITE WOLVES SANCTUARY, 525
UNITED NATIONS ENVIRONMENT PROGRAMME, 525
UNITED STATES CHAMBER OF COMMERCE
   Environment, Technology and Regulatory Affairs, 526
UNITED STATES DEPARTMENT OF AGRICULTURE
   Forest Service
      Green Mountain National Forest, 38
      Region 02 (Rocky Mountain), 43
      Region 09 (Eastern), 43
UNITED STATES DEPARTMENT OF COMMERCE
   National Oceanic and Atmospheric Administration
      Sea Grant Program - California, 54
      Sea Grant Program - Maryland, 56
      Sea Grant Program - Massachusetts, 56
      Sea Grant Program - Michigan, 57
      Sea Grant Program - New York, 58
      Sea Grant Program - Ohio, 58
      Sea Grant Program - Rhode Island, 59
      Sea Grant Program - Texas, 59
      Wells National Estuarine Research Reserve, 60
UNITED STATES DEPARTMENT OF DEFENSE
   Air Force Major Air Commands
      Andrews AFB, MD, 61

KEYWORD INDEX – P

Air Force Major U.S. Installations
  Luke AFB (and the Barry M. Goldwater AFR), AZ, 65
  Randolph AFB, TX, 66
Army Corps of Engineers
  Norfolk Engineer District, 70
  North Atlantic Engineer District, 70
Army Materiel Command, 72
Assistant Chief of Staff for Installation Management, Office of the Director of Environmental Programs, and Conservation Team, 74
Navy, 74
UNITED STATES DEPARTMENT OF THE INTERIOR
  Bureau of Land Management
    Northern Field Office, 84
    Safford Field Office, 86
  Fish and Wildlife Service
    Arthur R. Marshall Loxahatchee/Hope Sound National Wildlife Refuge, 91
    Benton Lake National Wildlife Refuge, 92
    Patoka River National Wetlands Project National Wildlife Refuge, 109
    Southeast Louisiana Complex National Wildlife Refuge, 115
    Washington Maritime National Wildlife Refuge Complex, 118
  National Park Service
    Chihuahuan Desert Network, 121
    Yellowstone National Park, 126
  United States Geological Survey
    New Mexico Cooperative Fish and Wildlife Research Unit, 127
    Utah Cooperative Fish and Wildlife Research Unit, 128
    Washington Cooperative Fish and Wildlife Research Unit
      School of Aquatic and Fishery Sciences, 128
UNITED STATES DEPARTMENT OF TRANSPORTATION
  Federal Aviation Administration, 128
UNITED STATES DEPARTMENT OF TREASURY, 129
UNITED STATES ENVIRONMENTAL PROTECTION AGENCY
  Administration and Resources Management, 129
UNITED STATES INSTITUTE FOR ENVIRONMENTAL CONFLICT RESOLUTION, 130
UNITED STATES PUBLIC INTEREST RESEARCH GROUP, 526
UNIVERSITY OF CALIFORNIA AT DAVIS
  School of Veterinary Medicine, 606
UNIVERSITY OF CALIFORNIA AT SAN DIEGO, 607
UNIVERSITY OF CONNECTICUT COOPERATIVE EXTENSION, 608
UNIVERSITY OF FLORIDA INSTITUTE OF FOOD AND AGRICULTURAL SCIENCES, 609
UNIVERSITY OF GEORGIA
  Daniel B. Warnell School of Forest Resources, 609
UNIVERSITY OF HAWAII COOPERATIVE EXTENSION PROGRAM, 224
UNIVERSITY OF IDAHO
  College of Natural Resources
    Department of Fish and Wildlife Resources, 610
UNIVERSITY OF LOUISVILLE, 612
UNIVERSITY OF MAINE, 612
UNIVERSITY OF MARYLAND - AT COLLEGE PARK, 613
UNIVERSITY OF MICHIGAN, 614
UNIVERSITY OF MISSOURI, 615
UNIVERSITY OF NORTH CAROLINA AT ASHEVILLE, 617
UNIVERSITY OF NORTHERN BRITISH COLUMBIA, 618
UNIVERSITY OF RHODE ISLAND
  Department of Natural Resources Science, 619
UNIVERSITY OF SASKATCHEWAN, 620
UNIVERSITY OF THE DISTRICT OF COLUMBIA, 621
UNIVERSITY OF WISCONSIN AT LA CROSSE, 623
UNIVERSITY OF WISCONSIN-MADISON, 623
UTAH BASS FEDERATION, 528
UTAH STATE UNIVERSITY
  College of Natural Resources, 624
VERMONT AGENCY OF NATURAL RESOURCES
  Department of Fish and Wildlife, 227
VERMONT ASSOCIATION OF CONSERVATION DISTRICTS, 529
VERMONT DEPARTMENT OF AGRICULTURE, FOOD, AND MARKETS, 227
VERMONT STATE-WIDE ENVIRONMENTAL EDUCATION PROGRAMS (SWEEP), 530
VINEYARD CONSERVATION SOCIETY, 530
VIRGIN ISLANDS CONSERVATION DISTRICT, 530
VIRGIN ISLANDS SOIL AND WATER CONSERVATION DIVISION, 228
VIRGINIA OUTDOORS FOUNDATION, 232
VIRGINIA SOCIETY OF ORNITHOLOGY, 532
WARREN COUNTY CONSERVATION BOARD, 532
WASHINGTON DEPARTMENT OF ECOLOGY
  Central Regional Office, 233
WASHINGTON STATE CONSERVATION COMMISSION, 234
WASHINGTON STATE PARKS AND RECREATION COMMISSION
  NORTHWEST REGION, 235
WASHINGTON TRAILS ASSOCIATION, 534
WATER ENVIRONMENT FEDERATION, 535
WEST MICHIGAN ENVIRONMENTAL ACTION COUNCIL, 536
WEST VIRGINIA DEPARTMENT OF AGRICULTURE, 235
WEST VIRGINIA DIVISION OF NATURAL RESOURCES, 236
WIDENER UNIVERSITY, 627
WILDFLOWER ASSOCIATION OF MICHIGAN, 541
WILDLIFE ACTION, INC., 542
WILDLIFE DAMAGE REVIEW (WDR), 543
WILDLIFE FEDERATION OF ALASKA, 543
WILDLIFE SOCIETY
  Colorado Chapter, 547
  Illinois Chapter, 547
WISCONSIN COOPERATIVE FISHERY RESEARCH UNIT USGS, 237
WISCONSIN LAND AND WATER CONSERVATION ASSOCIATION, 556
WISCONSIN SOCIETY FOR ORNITHOLOGY, INC., THE, 556
WORLDWATCH INSTITUTE, 560
WWW.ACTIONBIOSCIENCE.ORG, 560
WYOMING OUTDOOR COUNCIL, 561
YELL COUNTY WILDLIFE FEDERATION, 561
YMCA NATURE AND COMMUNITY CENTER, 562

POPULATION

A CRITICAL DECISION, 241
AFRICA VISION TRUST, 243
ALLIANCE FOR THE CHESAPEAKE BAY, 247
AMERICAN ASSOCIATION FOR THE ADVANCEMENT OF SCIENCE, 249
ARIZONA STATE UNIVERSITY
  Center for Environmental Studies, 573
ARKANSAS NATURAL HERITAGE COMMISSION, 130
ARKANSAS WATERSHED ADVISORY GROUP (AWAG), 272
ASSOCIATION OF AMERICAN GEOGRAPHERS, 273
CALIFORNIANS FOR POPULATION STABILIZATION (CAPS), 284
CARRYING CAPACITY NETWORK, 288
CENTER FOR ENVIRONMENT AND POPULATION (CEP), 290
CHARLES A. AND ANNE MORROW LINDBERGH FOUNDATION, THE, 294
CHICAGO PARK DISTRICT, 296
CITY UNIVERSITY OF NEW YORK
  College of Staten Island, 576
CJE ASSOCIATES, 565
CLARK UNIVERSITY, 576
COASTAL CONSERVATION AND EDUCATION FOUNDATION, INC., 565
COLORADO MOUNTAIN COLLEGE, 577
CONNECTICUT BOTANICAL SOCIETY, 304
EAGLE NATURE FOUNDATION, LTD., 316
EARTH POLICY INSTITUTE, 317
EARTHSCAN, 320
ECOSEA, 322
EDUCATIONAL COMMUNICATIONS, 322
ENGENDERHEALTH, 322
ENVIRONMENT COUNCIL OF RHODE ISLAND, 323
ENVIRONMENTAL ALLIANCE FOR SENIOR INVOLVEMENT (EASI), 323
FOOD SUPPLY / HUMAN POPULATION EXPLOSION CONNECTION, 333
GREEN BALKANS FEDERATION OF NATURE CONSERVATION NGOS, 346
GREEN SPHERE INC., 347
GROWLING, 348
HEADLANDS INSTITUTE, 350
HELPING OUR PENINSULA'S ENVIRONMENT, 350
ILOVEPARKS.COM, 567
INTERNATIONAL CHILDREN'S CONFERENCE ON THE ENVIRONMENT, 362
INTERNATIONAL ECOTOURISM SOCIETY, THE, 362
IZAAK WALTON LEAGUE OF AMERICA, INC., THE
  Minnesota Division, 377
J.N. (DING) DARLING FOUNDATION, 379
JAGRATA JUBA SHANGHA (JJS), 568
JOHNSON STATE COLLEGE, 585
KANSAS STATE UNIVERSITY
  Department of Landscape Architecture / Regional and Community Planning, 585
LANDWATCH MONTEREY COUNTY, 386
LUMMI ISLAND HERITAGE TRUST, 568
MIDDLE TENNESSEE STATE UNIVERSITY, 588
NATIONAL AGRICULTURAL LIBRARY, 24
NATIONAL AUDUBON SOCIETY
  Audubon of Florida, 410
  Public Policy Office, 415
NATIONAL WILDLIFE FEDERATION
  Headquarters, 427
NATIONAL WILDLIFE PRODUCTIONS, INC., 429
NATURE CONSERVANCY, THE
  Texas Chapter, 439
NEGATIVE POPULATION GROWTH (NPG), 442

NEVADA ASSOCIATION OF CONSERVATION DISTRICTS, 442
NEW YORK DEPARTMENT OF ENVIRONMENTAL CONSERVATION
   Division of Solid and Hazardous Materials, 196
NORTHWEST ENVIRONMENT WATCH, 454
PANOS INSTITUTE, THE, 464
PLANNED PARENTHOOD FEDERATION OF AMERICA, INC., 469
POPULATION ACTION INTERNATIONAL, 470
POPULATION COMMUNICATIONS INTERNATIONAL, 470
POPULATION CONNECTION, 471
POPULATION INSTITUTE, THE, 471
POPULATION REFERENCE BUREAU, INC., 471
POPULATION-ENVIRONMENT BALANCE, INC., 471
PURPLE MARTIN CONSERVATION ASSOCIATION, 475
RARE CENTER FOR TROPICAL CONSERVATION, 478
RENEWABLE NATURAL RESOURCES FOUNDATION, 478
SAND CREEK WATERSHED PROJECT, THE, 215
SIERRA CLUB
   Alaska Field Office, 490
   Connecticut Chapter, 491
   Lone Star Chapter, 493
   Mackinac Chapter, 493
   Maryland Chapter, 493
   Northwest Office, 495
   Pennsylvania Chapter, 496
   Washington, DC Office, 499
   West Virginia Chapter, 499
SIERRA CLUB CALIFORNIA, 499
SIERRA CLUB FOUNDATION, THE, 499
SOUTHWEST CENTER FOR ENVIRONMENTAL RESEARCH AND
   POLICY (SCERP), 596
SUSTAINABLE ENERGY INSTITUTE
   Culture Change, 514
   Culture Change magazine, 514
   Food Not Lawns, 514
   Pedal Power Produce, 514
TEXAS BASS FEDERATION, 517
TULANE UNIVERSITY
   Department of Ecology and Evolutionary Biology, 600
TWO WHITE WOLVES SANCTUARY, 525
UNITED STATES DEPARTMENT OF THE INTERIOR
   United States Geological Survey
      Western Region, 127
UNIVERSITY OF MARYLAND - AT COLLEGE PARK, 613
UNIVERSITY OF MARYLAND BALTIMORE COUNTY, 613
UNIVERSITY OF MICHIGAN, 614
UNIVERSITY OF NORTH CAROLINA AT ASHEVILLE, 617
UNIVERSITY OF NORTH DAKOTA, 618
VERMONT WOODLANDS ASSOCIATION, 530
WASHINGTON STATE CONSERVATION COMMISSION, 234
WILDLIFE ACTION, INC., 542
WILDLIFE SOCIETY
   Colorado Chapter, 547
WOMEN'S ENVIRONMENT AND DEVELOPMENT ORGANIZATION
   (WEDO), 557
WORLDWATCH INSTITUTE, 560
WWW.ACTIONBIOSCIENCE.ORG, 560

PUBLIC HEALTH

20/20 VISION, 241
ADVOCATES OF THE COMMON WEALTH, INC., 243
AFRICAN AMERICAN ENVIRONMENTALIST ASSOCIATION, 243
ALABAMA DEPARTMENT OF AGRICULTURE AND INDUSTRIES, 132
ALABAMA DEPARTMENT OF CONSERVATION AND NATURAL
   RESOURCES, 132
ALABAMA ENVIRONMENTAL COUNCIL, 244
ALASKA COOPERATIVE FISH AND WILDLIFE RESEARCH UNIT, 133
AMERICA THE BEAUTIFUL FUND, 248
AMERICAN CAMPING ASSOCIATION, INC., 250
AMERICAN PLANNING ASSOCIATION, 264
AMERICAN WATER WORKS ASSOCIATION (AWWA), 267
APROVECHO RESEARCH CENTER, 270
ARKANSAS WATERSHED ADVISORY GROUP (AWAG), 272
ASSOCIATION OF AMERICAN GEOGRAPHERS, 273
ASSOCIATION OF STATE AND TERRITORIAL HEALTH OFFICIALS, 274
ATLANTIC STATES LEGAL FOUNDATION, 275
BAT CONSERVATION INTERNATIONAL, 277
BEYOND PESTICIDES, 277
BROWN UNIVERSITY, 575
BUSINESS PUBLISHERS, INC., 564
CALIFORNIA DEPARTMENT OF PESTICIDE REGULATION, 143
CAMP FIRE USA, 285
CENTER FOR ENVIRONMENT AND POPULATION (CEP), 290

CENTER FOR ENVIRONMENT, COMMERCE & ENERGY, 290
CENTER FOR ENVIRONMENTAL HEALTH (CEH), 291
CENTER FOR HEALTH, ENVIRONMENT, AND JUSTICE, 291
CENTER FOR SCIENCE IN THE PUBLIC INTEREST, 293
CHARLES A. AND ANNE MORROW LINDBERGH FOUNDATION, THE, 294
CHICAGO PARK DISTRICT, 296
CINCINNATI NATURE CENTER, 297
CIRCUMPOLAR CONSERVATION UNION, 297
CITY UNIVERSITY OF NEW YORK
   College of Staten Island, 576
CJE ASSOCIATES, 565
CLARK UNIVERSITY, 576
COLORADO DEPARTMENT OF AGRICULTURE, 146
CONNECTICUT BOTANICAL SOCIETY, 304
CONSERVATION LAW FOUNDATION, INC. (CLF), 307
CONSERVATION LAW FOUNDATION, INC. (CLF)
   New England Region, 308
COTTONWOOD FOUNDATION, 309
COUNCIL FOR PLANNING AND CONSERVATION, 310
DELAWARE DEPARTMENT OF NATURAL RESOURCES AND
   ENVIRONMENTAL CONTROL
   Division of Air & Waste Management, 150
   Division of Soil and Water Conservation, 150
   Division of Water Resources, 151
DESERT TORTOISE COUNCIL, 314
EARTHJUSTICE
   Headquarters, 318
   Oakland Office, 319
   Seattle Office, 320
   Tallahassee Office, 320
   Washington, DC, Office, 320
ENGENDERHEALTH, 322
ENTOMOLOGICAL SOCIETY OF AMERICA, 323
ENVIRONMENT COUNCIL OF RHODE ISLAND, 323
ENVIRONMENTAL DEFENSE
   Headquarters, 324
ENVIRONMENTAL DEFENSE CENTER, 325
ENVIRONMENTAL PROTECTION AGENCY
   Region 1 (CT, ME, MA, NH, RI, VT), 18
   Region 5 (IL, IN, MI, NM, OH, WI), 19
EUROPARC FEDERATION, 328
FLORIDA COOPERATIVE FISH AND WILDLIFE RESEARCH UNIT
   (USDI), 152
FOOD AND AGRICULTURE ORGANIZATION OF THE UNITED
   NATIONS, 333
FOOD SUPPLY / HUMAN POPULATION EXPLOSION CONNECTION, 333
FUTURE GENERATIONS, 339
GEORGIA COOPERATIVE FISH AND WILDLIFE RESEARCH UNIT
   (USDI), 20
GLEN CANYON INSTITUTE, 343
GREEN SPHERE INC., 347
GUADALUPE-BLANCO RIVER AUTHORITY, 157
HAWAII DEPARTMENT OF HEALTH
   Office of Environmental Quality Control, 159
HELPING OUR PENINSULA'S ENVIRONMENT, 350
HUMAN ECOLOGY ACTION LEAGUE, INC., THE (HEAL), 352
IDAHO DEPARTMENT OF PARKS AND RECREATION, 160
IDAHO DEPARTMENT OF WATER RESOURCES, 161
   Water Awareness Week, 161
ILLINOIS DEPARTMENT OF TRANSPORTATION, 162
ILLINOIS ENVIRONMENTAL COUNCIL, 355
INDIANA DEPARTMENT OF NATURAL RESOURCES, 163
INDIANA STATE DEPARTMENT OF HEALTH, 164
INITIATIVE FOR SOCIAL ACTION AND RENEWAL IN EURASIA, 357
INTERNATIONAL JOINT COMMISSION
   Great Lakes Regional Office, 22
IOWA ENVIRONMENTAL COUNCIL, 372
IOWA PRAIRIE NETWORK, 373
ISLESBORO ISLANDS TRUST, 375
J.N. (DING) DARLING FOUNDATION, 379
JACKSON HOLE CONSERVATION ALLIANCE, 379
JOHNS HOPKINS UNIVERSITY
   CENTER FOR A LIVABLE FUTURE, 584
JOHNSON STATE COLLEGE, 585
KANSAS STATE UNIVERSITY
   Department of Landscape Architecture / Regional and Community
      Planning, 585
KANSAS WATER OFFICE, 169
KEEP FLORIDA BEAUTIFUL, INC., 382
KENTUCKY DEPARTMENT OF AGRICULTURE, 169
KEYSTONE CENTER, THE, 384
LAKENET, 385
LAST WIZARDS, THE, 568

KEYWORD INDEX – P

LEGAL ENVIRONMENTAL ASSISTANCE FOUNDATION INC. (LEAF), 388
LIVING RIVERS, 390
LOUISIANA DEPARTMENT OF NATURAL RESOURCES, 172
LUMMI ISLAND HERITAGE TRUST, 568
MACOMB LAND CONSERVANCY, 391
MAINE DEPARTMENT OF ENVIRONMENTAL PROTECTION, 175
MANITOBA CONSERVATION
  Western Region, 176
MASSACHUSETTS EXECUTIVE OFFICE OF ENVIRONMENTAL AFFAIRS
  Office of Technical Assistance for Toxic Use Reduction, 179
MICHIGAN DEPARTMENT OF AGRICULTURE, 180
MICHIGAN DEPARTMENT OF NATURAL RESOURCES, 180
MOTE MARINE LABORATORY, 404
NATIONAL 4-H COUNCIL, 406
NATIONAL AGRICULTURAL LIBRARY, 24
NATIONAL ASSOCIATION OF BIOLOGY TEACHERS, 407
NATIONAL ASSOCIATION OF STATE DEPARTMENTS OF AGRICULTURE, 408
NATIONAL AUDUBON SOCIETY
  Maine Audubon, 414
  Michigan Audubon Society, 414
NATIONAL CAUCUS OF ENVIRONMENTAL LEGISLATORS (NCEL), 417
NATIONAL ENVIRONMENTAL HEALTH ASSOCIATION, 418
NATIONAL FARMERS UNION, 419
NATIONAL FFA ORGANIZATION, 419
NATIONAL WILDLIFE FEDERATION
  Great Lakes Natural Resource Center, 427
NEBRASKA DEPARTMENT OF NATURAL RESOURCES, 188
NEBRASKA WILDLIFE FEDERATION, INC., 442
NEW HAMPSHIRE COUNCIL ON RESOURCES AND DEVELOPMENT, 190
NEW YORK DEPARTMENT OF ENVIRONMENTAL CONSERVATION
  Division of Solid and Hazardous Materials, 196
NORTH AMERICAN DEVELOPMENT BANK, 24
NORTH CAROLINA CONSERVATION NETWORK, 450
NORTH CAROLINA COOPERATIVE FISH AND WILDLIFE RESEARCH UNIT (USDI), 200
NORTH CAROLINA DIVISION OF SOIL AND WATER, 200
NORTHWEST ENVIRONMENT WATCH, 454
OCEANIA, 455
OHIO DEPARTMENT OF NATURAL RESOURCES, 204
OHIO STATE UNIVERSITY, 592
ONTARIO FEDERATION OF ANGLERS AND HUNTERS, 459
ONTARIO FORESTRY ASSOCIATION, 459
OREGON DEPARTMENT OF AGRICULTURE, 208
OREGON NATURAL RESOURCES COUNCIL, 460
ORGANIZATION FOR BAT CONSERVATION, 461
PENNSYLVANIA DEPARTMENT OF AGRICULTURE
  REGION VII, 211
PENNSYLVANIA FEDERATION OF SPORTSMENS CLUBS, 466
PENNSYLVANIA RESOURCES COUNCIL, INC., 467
PEOPLE FOR PUGET SOUND
  South Sound Office, 467
PLANNED PARENTHOOD FEDERATION OF AMERICA, INC., 469
POCONO ENVIRONMENTAL EDUCATION CENTER, 470
POPULATION ACTION INTERNATIONAL, 470
POPULATION COMMUNICATIONS INTERNATIONAL, 470
POPULATION CONNECTION, 471
PROTECTED AREAS ASSOCIATION OF NEWFOUNDLAND AND LABRADOR, 474
PS ENTERPRISES, 570
RACHEL CARSON COUNCIL, INC., 476
RHODE ISLAND DEPARTMENT OF TRANSPORTATION, 214
RIVER PROJECT, THE, 481
RUTGERS UNIVERSITY, COOK COLLEGE, 594
SAN DIEGUITO RIVER PARK JOINT POWERS AUTHORITY, 215
SAND CREEK WATERSHED PROJECT, THE, 215
SANTA CLARA COMMUNITY ACTION PROGRAM, 594
SAVE THE SOUND, INC., 486
SCIENTISTS CENTER FOR ANIMAL WELFARE, 488
SIERRA CLUB
  Connecticut Chapter, 491
  Nebraska Chapter, 494
  Rio Grande Chapter (New Mexico/West Texas), 496
  West Virginia Chapter, 499
SIERRA CLUB CALIFORNIA, 499
SIERRA CLUB FOUNDATION, THE, 499
SIERRA CLUB OF CANADA
  Atlantic Canada Chapter, 500
SOUTH CAROLINA DEPARTMENT OF AGRICULTURE, 217
SOUTH CAROLINA NATIVE PLANT SOCIETY, 506
SOUTH DAKOTA DEPARTMENT OF ENVIRONMENT AND NATURAL RESOURCES, 219

SOUTHEASTERN COOPERATIVE WILDLIFE DISEASE STUDY, 508
SOUTHWEST CENTER FOR ENVIRONMENTAL RESEARCH AND POLICY (SCERP), 596
SOUTHWEST RESEARCH AND INFORMATION CENTER, 510
STATE ENVIRONMENTAL RESOURCE CENTER (SERC), 512
STUDENT ENVIRONMENTAL ACTION COALITION (SEAC), 513
STUDENT PUGWASH USA, 513
SUSTAIN, 514
TENNESSEE FORESTRY ASSOCIATION, 516
TROUT UNLIMITED
  Pennsylvania Council, 522
TWO WHITE WOLVES SANCTUARY, 525
UNC-CH ENVIRONMENTAL RESOURCE PROGRAM, 601
UNION OF CONCERNED SCIENTISTS, 525
UNITED NATIONS ENVIRONMENT PROGRAMME, 525
UNITED STATES DEPARTMENT OF AGRICULTURE
  Forest Service
    Region 09 (Eastern), 43
UNITED STATES DEPARTMENT OF COMMERCE
  National Oceanic and Atmospheric Administration
    Sea Grant Program - Massachusetts, 56
    Sea Grant Program - New York, 58
    Sea Grant Program - North Carolina, 58
    Sea Grant Program - Texas, 59
    Wells National Estuarine Research Reserve, 60
UNITED STATES DEPARTMENT OF DEFENSE
  Air Force Major U.S. Installations
    Randolph AFB, TX, 66
  Army Corps of Engineers
    North Atlantic Engineer District, 70
  Assistant Chief of Staff for Installation Management, Office of the Director of Environmental Programs, and Conservation Team, 74
UNITED STATES DEPARTMENT OF THE INTERIOR
  Fish and Wildlife Service
    Ash Meadows National Wildlife Refuge, 92
  Utah Cooperative Fish and Wildlife Research Unit, 128
UNITED STATES DEPARTMENT OF TREASURY, 129
UNITED STATES ENVIRONMENTAL PROTECTION AGENCY
  Administration and Resources Management, 129
UNITED STATES PUBLIC INTEREST RESEARCH GROUP, 526
UNITY COLLEGE, 601
UNIVERSITE LAVAL, 601
UNIVERSITY OF CONNECTICUT COOPERATIVE EXTENSION, 608
UNIVERSITY OF HAWAII COOPERATIVE EXTENSION PROGRAM, 224
UNIVERSITY OF MARYLAND BALTIMORE COUNTY, 613
UNIVERSITY OF MICHIGAN, 614
UNIVERSITY OF NORTH CAROLINA AT ASHEVILLE, 617
UNIVERSITY OF RHODE ISLAND
  Department of Natural Resources Science, 619
URBAN WASTE MANAGEMENT & RESEARCH CENTER, 624
VERMONT DEPARTMENT OF AGRICULTURE, FOOD, AND MARKETS, 227
WASHINGTON STATE OFFICE OF ENVIRONMENTAL EDUCATION, 234
WEST VIRGINIA DIVISION OF NATURAL RESOURCES, 236
WILDLIFE ACTION, INC., 542
WILDLIFE DISEASE ASSOCIATION, 543
WILDLIFE TRUST
  Wildlife Preservation Trust International, 554
WISCONSIN COOPERATIVE FISHERY RESEARCH UNIT USGS, 237
WISCONSIN SOCIETY FOR ORNITHOLOGY, INC., THE, 556
WOMEN'S ENVIRONMENT AND DEVELOPMENT ORGANIZATION (WEDO), 557
WORLD ASSOCIATION OF GIRL GUIDES AND GIRL SCOUTS (WAGGGS), 558
WORLDWATCH INSTITUTE, 560
WWW.ACTIONBIOSCIENCE.ORG, 560
WYOMING DEPARTMENT OF ENVIRONMENTAL QUALITY, 239

PUBLIC LANDS/GREENSPACE

ADIRONDACK COUNCIL, THE, 242
ADIRONDACK MOUNTAIN CLUB, INC., THE (ADK), 242
ADOPT-A-STREAM FOUNDATION, THE, 242
AFRICA VISION TRUST, 243
AFRICAN AMERICAN ENVIRONMENTALIST ASSOCIATION, 243
AFRICAN CONSERVATION FOUNDATION, THE, 243
ALABAMA DEPARTMENT OF AGRICULTURE AND INDUSTRIES, 132
ALABAMA DEPARTMENT OF CONSERVATION AND NATURAL RESOURCES, 132
ALABAMA ENVIRONMENTAL COUNCIL, 244
ALASKA CENTER FOR THE ENVIRONMENT, 245
ALASKA CONSERVATION FOUNDATION, 246
ALASKA HEALTH PROJECT, 134

ALBERTA WILDERNESS ASSOCIATION, 247
AMERICAN ASSOCIATION OF BOTANICAL GARDENS AND ARBORETA, 249
AMERICAN ASSOCIATION OF FIELD BOTANISTS, 249
AMERICAN FEDERATION OF MINERALOGICAL SOCIETIES (AFMS), 252
AMERICAN FORESTS, 260
AMERICAN HIKING SOCIETY, 261
AMERICAN HORSE PROTECTION ASSOCIATION, 261
AMERICAN LAND CONSERVANCY, 262
AMERICAN LANDS, 262
AMERICAN PLANNING ASSOCIATION, 264
AMERICAN RESOURCES GROUP, 264
AMERICAN SOCIETY FOR ENVIRONMENTAL HISTORY, 265
AMERICAN SOCIETY OF LANDSCAPE ARCHITECTS, 266
AMERICAN SPORTFISHING ASSOCIATION, 266
AMERICAN WILDLANDS, 267
ANACOSTIA WATERSHED SOCIETY, 268
ANIMAL PROTECTION INSTITUTE, 268
APPALACHIAN MOUNTAIN CLUB, 269
APPALACHIAN TRAIL CONFERENCE, 270
ARIZONA GEOLOGICAL SURVEY, 136
ARIZONA STATE UNIVERSITY
  Center for Environmental Studies, 573
ARIZONA-SONORA DESERT MUSEUM, 271
ARKANSAS ENVIRONMENTAL EDUCATION ASSOCIATION, 272
ARKANSAS TECH UNIVERSITY
  Department of Parks, Recreation, and Hospitality Administration, 573
  Fisheries and Wildlife Biology Program, 573
ARKANSAS WATERSHED ADVISORY GROUP (AWAG), 272
ASSOCIATION FOR THE PROTECTION OF THE ADIRONDACKS, THE, 273
ASSOCIATION OF AMERICAN GEOGRAPHERS, 273
ASSOCIATION OF NEW JERSEY ENVIRONMENTAL COMMISSIONS (ANJEC), 274
ASSOCIATION OF PARTNERS FOR PUBLIC LANDS, 274
ATLANTIC CENTER FOR THE ENVIRONMENT
  Quebec-Labrador Foundation, 275
AUDUBON INTERNATIONAL, 276
AUDUBON NATURALIST SOCIETY OF THE CENTRAL ATLANTIC STATES, 276
BIG BEND NATURAL HISTORY ASSOCIATION, 277
BIODIVERSITY CONSERVATION ALLIANCE, 278
BIRDLIFE INTERNATIONAL, 279
BLUE GOOSE ALLIANCE, 279
BOONE AND CROCKETT FOUNDATION, 279
BOTANICAL SOCIETY OF WESTERN PENNSYLVANIA, 280
BROOKS BIRD CLUB INC., THE, 281
BYRON FOREST PRESERVE, 140
CALIFORNIA ACADEMY OF SCIENCES, 282
CALIFORNIA DEPARTMENT OF FOOD AND AGRICULTURE, 142
CALIFORNIA ENERGY COMMISSION
  Environmental Department, 143
CALIFORNIA WILDERNESS COALITION, 284
CALIFORNIANS FOR POPULATION STABILIZATION (CAPS), 284
CANADA GOOSE PROJECT, 285
CANADIAN PARKS AND WILDERNESS SOCIETY, 287
CANON ENVIROTHON, 288
CAVE RESEARCH FOUNDATION, 289
CENTER FOR A SUSTAINABLE COAST, 289
CENTER FOR ENVIRONMENT AND POPULATION (CEP), 290
CENTER FOR ENVIRONMENT, COMMERCE & ENERGY, 290
CENTER FOR NATIVE ECOSYSTEMS
  Front Range Office, 292
  West Slope Office, 292
CENTER FOR RESOURCE ECONOMICS/ISLAND PRESS, 293
CHESAPEAKE BAY FOUNDATION, INC.
  Maryland Office, 295
CHESAPEAKE BAY FOUNDATION, INC.
  Virginia Office, 295
CHICAGO PARK DISTRICT, 296
CHICAGO REGION BIODIVERSITY COUNCIL, 296
CITY OF BELDING, 145
CITY UNIVERSITY OF NEW YORK
  College of Staten Island, 576
CJE ASSOCIATES, 565
CLINTON RIVER WATERSHED COUNCIL (CRWC), 299
COALITION FOR EDUCATION IN THE OUTDOORS, 299
COASTAL AMERICA FOUNDATION, 300
COLORADO DEPARTMENT OF NATURAL RESOURCES
  Oil and Gas Conservation Commission, 147
COLORADO ENVIRONMENTAL COALITION, 301
COLORADO GOVERNOR'S OFFICE OF ENERGY MANAGEMENT AND CONSERVATION, 147

COLORADO MOUNTAIN CLUB, 302
COLORADO STATE UNIVERSITY COOPERATIVE EXTENSION, 148
COLUMBIA RIVER INTER-TRIBAL FISH COMMISSION, 17
COMMUNITY CONSERVATION /HOWLERS FOREVER, INC., 303
CONNECTICUT FUND FOR THE ENVIRONMENT, 305
CONSERVAMERICA, 305
CONSERVATION ALLIANCE OF ST. LUCIE CO., 306
CONSERVATION FUND, THE, 307
CONSERVATION LAW FOUNDATION, INC. (CLF), 307
  New England Region, 308
COTTONWOOD FOUNDATION, 309
COUNCIL FOR PLANNING AND CONSERVATION, 310
COUNTY OF SAN DIEGO, 149
CRANSTON CONSERVATION COMMISSION, 150
DELAWARE DEPARTMENT OF NATURAL RESOURCES AND ENVIRONMENTAL CONTROL
  Division of Air & Waste Management, 150
DELAWARE NATURE SOCIETY, 312
DELAWARE RIVERKEEPER NETWORK, 313
DELTA WILDLIFE INC., 313
DESCHUTES BASIN LAND TRUST, 313
DESERT TORTOISE COUNCIL, 314
DESERT TORTOISE PRESERVE COMMITTEE, INC., 314
DUCKS UNLIMITED CANADA
  Saskatchewan Office, 315
EAGLE NATURE FOUNDATION, LTD., 316
EARTHJUSTICE
  Denver Office, 318
  Environmental Law Clinic at the University of Denver, 318
  Headquarters, 318
  Policy and Legislation, 319
  Seattle Office, 320
EASTERN SHORE LAND CONSERVANCY (ESLC), 321
ECODEFENSE, 321
ECOLOGICAL SOCIETY OF AMERICA, THE, 321
ECOLOGY CENTER, 321
ENVIRONMENT COUNCIL OF RHODE ISLAND, 323
ENVIRONMENTAL ALLIANCE FOR SENIOR INVOLVEMENT (EASI), 323
ENVIRONMENTAL DEFENSE
  Headquarters, 324
ENVIRONMENTAL DEFENSE CENTER, 325
ENVIRONMENTAL EDUCATION ASSOCIATES, 325
ENVIRONMENTAL LAW AND POLICY CENTER OF THE MIDWEST, 327
ENVIRONMENTAL LEAGUE OF MASSACHUSETTS, 327
ENVIRONMENTAL POLICY CENTER, THE, 327
EQUESTRIAN LAND CONSERVATION RESOURCE, 328
FEDERATION OF ALBERTA NATURALISTS, 329
FEDERATION OF FLY FISHERS (NCCFFF), 329
FERRUM COLLEGE, 581
FLINTSTEEL RESTORATION ASSOCIATION, INC., 330
FLORIDA DEPARTMENT OF ENVIRONMENTAL PROTECTION
  Coastal and Aquatic Managed Areas, 153
  Division of Resource Assessment and Management, 154
  Florida State Parks AmeriCorps, 154
FLORIDA EXOTIC PEST PLANT COUNCIL, 331
FLORIDA FEDERATION OF GARDEN CLUBS, INC., 331
FLORIDA FISH AND WILDLIFE CONSERVATION COMMISSION, 154
FLORIDA NATIVE PLANT SOCIETY, 332
FLORIDA SPORTSMEN'S CONSERVATION ASSOCIATION, 333
FOOD SUPPLY / HUMAN POPULATION EXPLOSION CONNECTION, 333
FOREST HISTORY SOCIETY, INC., 334
FOREST SERVICE EMPLOYEES FOR ENVIRONMENTAL ETHICS (FSEEE), 334
FRIENDS OF ACADIA, 336
FRIENDS OF DISCOVERY PARK, 337
FRIENDS OF THE CARR REFUGE, 337
FRIENDS OF THE EARTH, 337
FRIENDS OF THE REEDY RIVER, 338
GENERAL FEDERATION OF WOMEN'S CLUBS, 340
GEORGIA CONSERVANCY, INC., THE, 341
GEORGIA DEPARTMENT OF NATURAL RESOURCES
  Environmental Protection Division
    Coastal Division, 156
GEORGIA ENVIRONMENTAL ORGANIZATION, INC. (GEO), 341
GEORGIA TRUST FOR HISTORIC PRESERVATION, 342
GLEN CANYON INSTITUTE, 343
GOOD NATURE PUBLISHING CO., 566
GRAND CANYON TRUST, 344
GRANT TECH CONSULTING AND CONSERVATION SERVICES, 567
GRASSLAND HERITAGE FOUNDATION, 344
GREAT BEAR FOUNDATION, 344
GREAT PLAINS NATIVE PLANT SOCIETY, 345
GREAT SMOKY MOUNTAINS INSTITUTE AT TREMONT, 345

GREATER YELLOWSTONE COALITION, 346
GREEN BALKANS FEDERATION OF NATURE CONSERVATION NGOS, 346
GREEN MEDIA TOOLSHED, 346
GREEN SPHERE INC., 347
GROWLING, 348
GUAM DEPARTMENT OF AGRICULTURE, 158
GULF COAST RESEARCH LABORATORY, 158
HAWAIIAN BOTANICAL SOCIETY, 349
HAWKWATCH INTERNATIONAL, 350
HELPING OUR PENINSULA'S ENVIRONMENT, 350
HIMALAYAN WILDLIFE FOUNDATION, 351
HOLDEN ARBORETUM, THE, 351
HOLLOW OAK LAND TRUST, 351
HUMANE SOCIETY OF THE UNITED STATES, THE, 352
IDAHO CONSERVATION LEAGUE, 354
ILLINOIS ENVIRONMENTAL COUNCIL, 355
ILLINOIS PRAIRIE PATH, 355
ILOVEPARKS.COM, 567
INDIANA ASSOCIATION OF SOIL AND WATER CONSERVATION
    DISTRICTS, INC., 356
INDIANA STATE DEPARTMENT OF HEALTH, 164
INDUSTRIAL COMMISSION OF NORTH DAKOTA, 164
INSTITUTE FOR GLOBAL COMMUNICATIONS, 567
INTERAGENCY COMMITTEE FOR OUTDOOR RECREATION (IAC), 164
INTERNATIONAL ACADEMY, 567
INTERNATIONAL ASSOCIATION FOR BEAR RESEARCH AND
    MANAGEMENT, 359
INTERNATIONAL ASSOCIATION OF FISH AND WILDLIFE AGENCIES, 360
INTERNATIONAL CHILDREN'S CONFERENCE ON THE
    ENVIRONMENT, 362
INTERNATIONAL MARINE MAMMAL PROJECT, THE, 364
IOWA ASSOCIATION OF NATURALISTS, 372
IOWA STATE UNIVERSITY
    College of Agriculture, 584
IOWA WILDLIFE FEDERATION, 374
IOWA WOMEN IN NATURAL RESOURCES, 374
ISLESBORO ISLANDS TRUST, 375
IZAAK WALTON LEAGUE OF AMERICA, INC., THE, 376
    Minnesota Division, 377
    Owatonna Minnesota Chapter, 377
J.N. (DING) DARLING FOUNDATION, 379
JACKSON HOLE CONSERVATION ALLIANCE, 379
JACKSON HOLE LAND TRUST, 379
JOHNSON STATE COLLEGE, 585
KANSAS BIOLOGICAL SURVEY, 166
KANSAS COOPERATIVE FISH AND WILDLIFE RESEARCH UNIT, 167
KANSAS DEPARTMENT OF WILDLIFE AND PARKS
    Office of the Secretary, 167
    Operations Office, 167
    Region 1, 167
    Region 2, 168
    Region 3, 168
    Region 4, 168
KANSAS STATE CONSERVATION COMMISSION, 168
KANSAS STATE UNIVERSITY
    College of Agriculture, 585
KANSAS STATE UNIVERSITY
    Department of Landscape Architecture / Regional and Community
        Planning, 585
KANSAS WILDFLOWER SOCIETY, 381
KEEP AMERICA BEAUTIFUL, INC., 382
KENTUCKY DEPARTMENT OF AGRICULTURE, 169
KENTUCKY NATURAL LANDS TRUST, 383
KENTUCKY NATURAL RESOURCES AND ENVIRONMENTAL
    PROTECTION CABINET
    Environmental Quality Commission, 170
KENTUCKY STATE NATURE PRESERVES COMMISSION, 171
KIDS FOR SAVING EARTH WORLDWIDE, 384
LAKE SUPERIOR STATE UNIVERSITY, 586
LAKEHEAD UNIVERSITY, 586
LAND BETWEEN THE LAKES ASSOCIATION, 386
LAND CONSERVANCY OF WEST MICHIGAN, 386
LEAGUE TO SAVE LAKE TAHOE, 388
LIFE OF THE LAND, 389
LIVING RIVERS, 390
LOUISIANA DEPARTMENT OF AGRICULTURE AND FORESTRY
    Office of Soil and Water Conservation, State Soil and Water
        Conservation Committee, 172
LOUISIANA STATE UNIVERSITY SCHOOL OF FORESTRY, WILDLIFE
    AND FISHERIES, 586
LOWER MERION CONSERVANCY, 391
LUMMI ISLAND HERITAGE TRUST, 568
MACOMB LAND CONSERVANCY, 391

MAINE ASSOCIATION OF CONSERVATION COMMISSIONS (MACC), 392
MAINE ASSOCIATION OF CONSERVATION DISTRICTS, 392
MAINE DEPARTMENT OF CONSERVATION
    Bureau of Geology and Natural Areas, 174
MARIE SELBY BOTANICAL GARDENS, THE, 393
MARYLAND ASSOCIATION OF CONSERVATION DISTRICTS, 395
MASSACHUSETTS ASSOCIATION OF CONSERVATION DISTRICTS,
    396
MASSACHUSETTS DIVISION OF FISHERIES AND WILDLIFE
    MassWildlife, 178
MASSACHUSETTS EXECUTIVE OFFICE OF ENVIRONMENTAL AFFAIRS
    Office of Technical Assistance for Toxic Use Reduction, 179
MAX MCGRAW WILDLIFE FOUNDATION, 396
MCGILL UNIVERSITY, 587
MECKLENBURG COUNTY PARK AND RECREATION DEPARTMENT, 179
MIAMI UNIVERSITY, 587
MICHIGAN DEPARTMENT OF AGRICULTURE, 180
MICHIGAN LAND USE INSTITUTE, 397
MICHIGAN NATURE ASSOCIATION, 398
MICHIGAN STATE UNIVERSITY EXTENSION, 181
MICHIGAN UNITED CONSERVATION CLUBS, INC., 398
MIDLAND CONSERVATION DISTRICT, 181
MINERAL POLICY CENTER, 399
MINNESOTA ASSOCIATION OF SOIL AND WATER CONSERVATION
    DISTRICTS, 399
MINNESOTA CENTER FOR ENVIRONMENTAL ADVOCACY (MCEA), 399
MINNESOTA NATIVE PLANT SOCIETY, 400
MISSISSIPPI RIVER BASIN ALLIANCE, 401
MISSISSIPPI STATE UNIVERSITY
    Forest and Wildlife Research Center, 588
MISSOURI ASSOCIATION OF SOIL AND WATER CONSERVATION
    DISTRICTS, 402
MISSOURI DEPARTMENT OF CONSERVATION
    Forestry Division, 185
MONTANA STATE UNIVERSITY
    College of Agriculture, 589
MONTANA WILDERNESS ASSOCIATION, 403
MONTANA WILDLIFE FEDERATION, 404
MOUNTAINEERS, THE, 405
NATIONAL ASSOCIATION OF RECREATION RESOURCE PLANNERS,
    408
NATIONAL ASSOCIATION OF SERVICE AND CONSERVATION CORPS
    (NASCC), 408
NATIONAL ASSOCIATION OF STATE DEPARTMENTS OF
    AGRICULTURE, 408
NATIONAL ASSOCIATION OF STATE PARK DIRECTORS, 409
NATIONAL AUDUBON SOCIETY
    Audubon Alaska, 409
    Audubon of Florida, 410
    Audubon Society of Portland, 411
    Audubon Society of Rhode Island, 412
    Connecticut Audubon Society, 412
    Fairfax Audubon Society, 413
    Hawaii Audubon Society, 413
    Maricopa Audubon Society, 414
    Michigan Audubon Society, 414
    Montana Audubon, 415
    New Jersey Chapter, 415
    Public Policy Office, 415
    San Diego Chapter, 416
    Seattle Audubon Society, 416
NATIONAL ENVIRONMENTAL EDUCATION AND TRAINING
    FOUNDATION, 418
NATIONAL FOREST FOUNDATION, 420
NATIONAL GEOGRAPHIC SOCIETY, 421
NATIONAL NETWORK OF FOREST PRACTITIONERS, 422
NATIONAL PARK FOUNDATION, 422
NATIONAL PARK TRUST, 422
NATIONAL PARKS CONSERVATION ASSOCIATION (NPCA), 422
    Sun Coast Regional Office, 423
NATIONAL TREE TRUST, 425
NATIONAL WATERSHED COALITION, 426
NATIONAL WILD TURKEY FEDERATION, INC., THE, 427
NATIONAL WILDLIFE FEDERATION
    Headquarters, 427
    Rocky Mountain Natural Resource Center, 428
NATIONAL WILDLIFE PRODUCTIONS, INC., 429
NATIONAL WILDLIFE REFUGE ASSOCIATION, 429
NATIONAL WOODLAND OWNERS ASSOCIATION, 430
NATIVE PLANT SOCIETY OF NORTHEASTERN OHIO, 430
NATIVE PLANT SOCIETY OF TEXAS, 431
NATURAL AREAS ASSOCIATION, 431
NATURAL HISTORY SOCIETY OF MARYLAND, INC., THE, 431

KEYWORD INDEX – P

NATURE CONSERVANCY, THE
   Alabama Chapter, 433
   Arkansas Field Office, 434
   Colorado Chapter, 434
   Eastern New York Chapter, 435
   Iowa Chapter, 435
   Kansas Chapter, 436
   Maryland/District of Columbia Chapter, 436
   Oklahoma Chapter, 439
   Pennsylvania Chapter, 439
   Texas Chapter, 439
NEBRASKA DEPARTMENT OF ENVIRONMENTAL QUALITY, 188
NEBRASKA GAME AND PARKS COMMISSION
   OMAHA OFFICE, 189
NEGATIVE POPULATION GROWTH (NPG), 442
NEVADA ASSOCIATION OF CONSERVATION DISTRICTS, 442
NEVIS HISTORICAL AND CONSERVATION SOCIETY, 442
NEW ENGLAND WILD FLOWER SOCIETY, INC., 443
NEW HAMPSHIRE ASSOCIATION OF CONSERVATION COMMISSIONS, 443
NEW HAMPSHIRE ASSOCIATION OF CONSERVATION DISTRICTS, 444
NEW HAMPSHIRE DEPARTMENT OF RESOURCES AND ECONOMIC DEVELOPMENT, 190
NEW JERSEY ASSOCIATION OF CONSERVATION DISTRICTS, 445
NEW JERSEY DEPARTMENT OF ENVIRONMENTAL PROTECTION, 191
   Division of Parks and Forestry, 192
   Division of Solid and Hazardous Waste, 192
NEW MEXICO ENERGY, MINERALS, AND NATURAL RESOURCES DEPARTMENT
   Oil Conservation Division, 195
NEW MEXICO STATE UNIVERSITY
   College of Agriculture and Home Economics, 589
NEW YORK STATE COOPERATIVE EXTENSION, 197
NEW YORK-NEW JERSEY TRAIL CONFERENCE INC., 446
NORTH CAROLINA BASS FEDERATION, 450
NORTH CAROLINA CONSERVATION NETWORK, 450
NORTH CAROLINA DEPARTMENT OF AGRICULTURE AND CONSUMER SERVICES, 200
NORTH CAROLINA RECREATION AND PARK SOCIETY, INC., 451
NORTH DAKOTA WATER COMMISSION, 202
NORTHERN ARIZONA UNIVERSITY
   Department of Geography, Planning, and Recreation, 591
NORTHWEST COALITION FOR ALTERNATIVES TO PESTICIDES, 453
NORTHWEST ECOSYSTEM ALLIANCE, 453
NORTHWEST RESOURCE INFORMATION CENTER, 454
NOVA SCOTIA AGRICULTURE & FISHERIES, 203
NOVA SCOTIA DEPARTMENT OF NATURAL RESOURCES, 203
NOVA SCOTIA FEDERATION OF ANGLERS AND HUNTERS, 454
OHIO DEPARTMENT OF AGRICULTURE, 203
OHIO DEPARTMENT OF NATURAL RESOURCES, 204
OHIO ENVIRONMENTAL COUNCIL, INC., 457
OHIO ENVIRONMENTAL REVIEW APPEALS COMMISSION, 205
OKLAHOMA DEPARTMENT OF AGRICULTURE, 205
OKLAHOMA NATIVE PLANT SOCIETY, 458
OLYMPIC PARK INSTITUTE, 459
ONTARIO FEDERATION OF ANGLERS AND HUNTERS, 459
OREGON SMALL WOODLANDS ASSOCIATION, 461
OREGON SOCIETY OF AMERICAN FORESTERS, 461
OUTDOOR RECREATION COUNCIL OF BRITISH COLUMBIA, 462
OZARK SOCIETY, THE, 463
PACIFIC NORTHWEST TRAIL ASSOCIATION, 464
PACIFIC RIVERS COUNCIL, 464
PARTNERS IN PARKS, 465
PARTNERSHIP FOR SUSTAINABLE FORESTRY, 465
PENNSYLVANIA DEPARTMENT OF AGRICULTURE
   State Conservation Commission, 211
PENNSYLVANIA DEPARTMENT OF ENVIRONMENTAL PROTECTION, 211
PENNSYLVANIA FORESTRY ASSOCIATION, THE, 466
PENNSYLVANIA ORGANIZATION FOR WATERSHEDS AND RIVERS (POWR), 466
PENNSYLVANIA RECREATION AND PARK SOCIETY, INC., 467
PENNSYLVANIA RESOURCES COUNCIL, INC.,, 467
PEOPLE FOR PUGET SOUND
   South Sound Office, 467
PINCHOT INSTITUTE FOR CONSERVATION, 469
POCONO ENVIRONMENTAL EDUCATION CENTER, 470
PREDATOR CONSERVATION ALLIANCE, 472
PROGRESSIVE ANIMAL WELFARE SOCIETY, 473
PROTECTED AREAS ASSOCIATION OF NEWFOUNDLAND AND LABRADOR, 474
PS ENTERPRISES, 570
PUBLIC EMPLOYEES FOR ENVIRONMENTAL RESPONSIBILITY (PEER), 474

PUBLIC LANDS FOUNDATION, 474
PURPLE MARTIN CONSERVATION ASSOCIATION, 475
RARE CENTER FOR TROPICAL CONSERVATION, 478
RENEWABLE NATURAL RESOURCES FOUNDATION, 478
RESIDENTS FOR A MORE BEAUTIFUL PORT WASHINGTON, 479
RESTORE HETCH HETCHY, 479
RHODE ISLAND FOREST CONSERVATOR'S ORGANIZATION, INC., 480
RHODE ISLAND STATE CONSERVATION COMMITTEE, 480
RIVER PROJECT, THE, 481
ROCKY MOUNTAIN ELK FOUNDATION, 482
RUFFNER MOUNTAIN NATURE COALITION, INC., 483
SAN DIEGUITO RIVER PARK JOINT POWERS AUTHORITY, 215
SAND CREEK WATERSHED PROJECT, THE, 215
SAVE AMERICA'S FORESTS, 485
SAVE THE DUNES COUNCIL, 485
SAVE THE HARBOR/SAVE THE BAY, 486
SAVE THE SOUND, INC., 486
SAVE WETLANDS AND BAYS, 486
SAVE-THE-REDWOODS LEAGUE, 487
SCENIC AMERICA, 487
SCENIC AMERICA
   Scenic Texas, 487
SEACOAST ANTI-POLLUTION LEAGUE, 489
SHELBURNE FARMS, 490
SHEPHERD COLLEGE, 595
SIERRA CLUB
   Alaska Field Office, 490
   Connecticut Chapter, 491
   Hawaii Chapter, 492
   Lone Star Chapter, 493
   Mackinac Chapter, 493
   Maryland Chapter, 493
   Nebraska Chapter, 494
   New Jersey Chapter, 495
   Northwest Office, 495
   Pennsylvania Chapter, 496
   San francisco Bay Chapter, 497
   Tehipite Chapter (Northern California), 498
   Washington, DC Office, 499
   West Virginia Chapter, 499
   Wyoming Chapter, 499
SIERRA CLUB CALIFORNIA, 499
SIERRA CLUB FOUNDATION, THE, 499
SIERRA STUDENT COALITION, 500
SILK CITY NATURE ASSOCIATION, 500
SINAPU, 500
SMALL WOODLAND OWNERS ASSOCIATION OF MAINE, 501
SOCIETY FOR RANGE MANAGEMENT, 503
SOCIETY OF AMERICAN FORESTERS, 503
SONORAN DESERT NATIONAL PARK FRIENDS, 504
SONORAN INSTITUTE, 505
SOUTH CAROLINA WILDLIFE FEDERATION, 506
SOUTH DAKOTA ASSOCIATION OF CONSERVATION DISTRICTS, 506
SOUTH DAKOTA COOPERATIVE EXTENSION SERVICE, 218
SOUTH DAKOTA COOPERATIVE FISH AND WILDLIFE RESEARCH UNIT (USDI-USGS), 29
SOUTH DAKOTA DEPARTMENT OF GAME, FISH, AND PARKS, 219
SOUTHEASTERN ASSOCIATION OF FISH AND WILDLIFE AGENCIES, 508
SOUTHERN APPALACHIAN BOTANICAL SOCIETY, 508
SOUTHERN ILLINOIS UNIVERSITY CARBONDALE, 596
SOUTHERN UTAH WILDERNESS ALLIANCE
   Moab Office, 510
SOUTHWEST CENTER FOR ENVIRONMENTAL RESEARCH AND POLICY (SCERP), 596
SOUTHWEST CONSERVATION DISTRICT, 510
SOUTHWESTERN HERPETOLOGISTS SOCIETY, 510
SPORTSMEN'S NATIONAL LAND TRUST, THE, 511
STANFORD ENVIRONMENTAL LAW SOCIETY, 511
STATE ENVIRONMENTAL RESOURCE CENTER (SERC), 512
STEPHEN F. AUSTIN STATE UNIVERSITY ARTHUR TEMPLE COLLEGE OF FORESTRY, 598
STUDENT CONSERVATION ASSOCIATION, INC., 512
SUSTAIN, 514
TENNESSEE AGRICULTURAL EXTENSION SERVICE, 220
TENNESSEE CONSERVATION LEAGUE, 516
TERRA NATURE FUND, 516
TERRA PENINSULAR, 516
TEXAS A AND M UNIVERSITY AT KINGSVILLE
   Caesar Kleberg Wildlife Research Institute, 599
TEXAS BASS FEDERATION, 517
TEXAS DISCOVERY GARDENS, 517
TEXAS FOREST SERVICE, 222

KEYWORD INDEX – P

TEXAS ORGANIZATION FOR ENDANGERED SPECIES, 517
TEXAS RIPARIAN ASSOCIATION, 517
TEXAS WATER DEVELOPMENT BOARD, 223
TROUT UNLIMITED
   Pennsylvania Council, 522
TRUST FOR PUBLIC LAND, THE, 523
TRUST FOR WILDLIFE, INC., 524
TRUSTEES FOR ALASKA, 524
TUG HILL TOMORROW LAND TRUST, 524
TULANE UNIVERSITY
   Department of Ecology and Evolutionary Biology, 600
TURTLE CREEK WATERSHED ASSOCIATION, INC., 525
TWO WHITE WOLVES SANCTUARY, 525
UNITED STATES CHAMBER OF COMMERCE
   Environment, Technology and Regulatory Affairs, 526
UNITED STATES DEPARTMENT OF AGRICULTURE
   Forest Service
      Gila National Forest, 38
      Green Mountain National Forest, 38
      Nez Perce National Forest, 41
      Pawnee National Grassland, 42
      Region 02 (Rocky Mountain), 43
UNITED STATES DEPARTMENT OF COMMERCE
   National Oceanic and Atmospheric Administration
      Delaware National Estuarine Research Reserve, 50
      Rookery Bay National Estuarine Research Reserve, 53
      Sea Grant Program - Massachusetts, 56
      Sea Grant Program - North Carolina, 58
UNITED STATES DEPARTMENT OF DEFENSE
   Air Force Major Air Commands
      Andrews AFB, MD, 61
      USAF Academy, 62
   Air Force Major U.S. Installations
      Eglin Air Force Base, 63
   Army Corps of Engineers
      Nashville Engineer District, 69
      Norfolk Engineer District, 70
      North Atlantic Engineer District, 70
   Army Materiel Command, 72
   Assistant Chief of Staff for Installation Management, Office of the Director of Environmental Programs, and Conservation Team, 74
   Navy, 74
UNITED STATES DEPARTMENT OF THE INTERIOR
   Bureau of Land Management
      Amarillo Field Office, 78
      Bakersfield Field Office, 79
      Malta Field Office, 83
      Northern Field Office, 84
      Rawlins Field Office, 85
      Safford Field Office, 86
   Fish and Wildlife Service, 90
      Archie Carr National Wildlife Refuge, 91
      Arthur R. Marshall Loxahatchee/Hope Sound National Wildlife Refuge, 91
      Balcones Canyonlands National Wildlife Refuge, 92
      Bombay Hook National Wildlife Refuge, 93
      California-Nevada Operations, 94
      Canaan Valley National Wildlife Refuge, 94
      Eastern Massachusetts National Wildlife Refuge Complex, 97
      Huron WMD National Wildlife Refuge, 100
      Kofa National Wildlife Refuge, 102
      Lacassine National Wildlife Refuge, 102
      Lake Andes/Karl E. Mundt National Wildlife Refuge, 102
      Mattamuskeet National Wildlife Refuge, 104
      Minnesota Valley National Wildlife Refuge, 105
      Morris Wetland Management District, 106
      Necedah National Wildlife Refuge, 107
      Noxubee National Wildlife Refuge, 108
      Patoka River National Wetlands Project National Wildlife Refuge, 109
      Pelican Island National Wildlife Refuge, 109
      Pocosin Lakes National Wildlife Refuge, 110
      Ridgefield National Wildlife Refuge, 112
      San Francisco Bay National Wildlife Refuge Complex, 113
      Sandy Point National Wildlife Refuge, 114
      Southeast Louisiana Complex National Wildlife Refuge, 115
      St. Catherine Creek National Wildlife Refuge, 115
      St. Marks National Wildlife Refuge, 115
      Wallkill River National Wildlife Refuge, 117
      Windom WMD National Wildlife Refuge, 119
   National Park Service
      Grand Teton National Park, 122
      Mammoth Cave National Park, 124
      Mount Rainier National Park, 124
      Sonoran Desert Network, 125

   United States Geological Survey
      Western Region, 127
UNITED STATES INSTITUTE FOR ENVIRONMENTAL CONFLICT RESOLUTION, 130
UNITED STATES PUBLIC INTEREST RESEARCH GROUP, 526
UNITY COLLEGE, 601
UNIVERSITE LAVAL, 601
UNIVERSITY OF COLORADO, 608
UNIVERSITY OF FLORIDA
   School of Forest Resources and Conservation, 609
UNIVERSITY OF FLORIDA INSTITUTE OF FOOD AND AGRICULTURAL SCIENCES, 609
UNIVERSITY OF GEORGIA
   Daniel B. Warnell School of Forest Resources, 609
UNIVERSITY OF IDAHO
   College of Natural Resources
      Department of Fish and Wildlife Resources, 610
      Idaho Cooperative Fish and Wildlife Research Unit, 610
UNIVERSITY OF MARYLAND COOPERATIVE EXTENSION, 224
UNIVERSITY OF MICHIGAN, 614
UNIVERSITY OF MISSOURI, 615
UNIVERSITY OF NEVADA COOPERATIVE EXTENSION, 616
UNIVERSITY OF NEW BRUNSWICK, 616
UNIVERSITY OF NEW HAVEN DEPT. OF BIOLOGY AND ENVIRONMENTAL SCIENCES, 617
UNIVERSITY OF NORTH DAKOTA, 618
UNIVERSITY OF PENNSYLVANIA, 619
UNIVERSITY OF SASKATCHEWAN, 620
UNIVERSITY OF TENNESSEE - AT KNOXVILLE, 621
UNIVERSITY OF WISCONSIN AT LA CROSSE, 623
UPPER CHATTAHOOCHEE RIVERKEEPER, 527
UPPER COLORADO RIVER COMMISSION, 130
URBAN WILDLIFE RESOURCES, 527
USAID/TANZANIA, 131
UTAH ASSOCIATION OF CONSERVATION DISTRICTS, 528
UTAH BASS FEDERATION, 528
UTAH DEPARTMENT OF NATURAL RESOURCES
   Division of Wildlife Resources, 225
UTAH NATURE STUDY SOCIETY, 528
UTAH STATE DEPARTMENT OF NATURAL RESOURCES, 225
UTAH WILDLIFE FEDERATION, 528
VERMONT STATE-WIDE ENVIRONMENTAL EDUCATION PROGRAMS (SWEEP), 530
VERNAL POOL SOCIETY, THE, 530
VINEYARD CONSERVATION SOCIETY, 530
VIRGINIA DEPARTMENT OF CONSERVATION AND RECREATION
   Division of Dam Safety, 229
VIRGINIA DEPARTMENT OF GAME AND INLAND FISHERIES
   Region IV (Staunton), 231
VIRGINIA MUSEUM OF NATURAL HISTORY, 232
VIRGINIA RESOURCE-USE EDUCATION COUNCIL, 532
WARREN COUNTY CONSERVATION BOARD, 532
WASHINGTON DEPARTMENT OF ECOLOGY, 233
WASHINGTON DEPARTMENT OF FISH AND WILDLIFE
   WASHINGTON FISH AND WILDLIFE COMMISSION, 233
WASHINGTON RECREATION AND PARK ASSOCIATION, 533
WASHINGTON TRAILS ASSOCIATION, 534
WASHINGTON WILDLIFE FEDERATION, 534
WATERLOO-WELLINGTON WILDFLOWER SOCIETY, 535
WATERSHED MANAGEMENT COUNCIL, 535
WEST VIRGINIA HIGHLANDS CONSERVANCY, 536
WESTERN HEMISPHERE SHOREBIRD RESERVE NETWORK (WHSRN), 537
WESTERN ILLINOIS UNIVERSITY, 626
WESTERN PENNSYLVANIA CONSERVANCY, 537
WESTERN WATERSHEDS PROJECT, 538
WETLAND HABITAT ALLIANCE OF TEXAS, 538
WHITE CLAY WATERSHED ASSOCIATION, 538
WILD ONES NATURAL LANDSCAPERS, LTD, 540
WILDERNESS SOCIETY, THE, 541
WILDERNESS WATCH, 541
WILDLIFE ACTION, INC., 542
WILDLIFE DAMAGE REVIEW (WDR), 543
WILDLIFE FOREVER, 544
WILDLIFE HABITAT COUNCIL, 544
WILDLIFE SOCIETY
   Colorado Chapter, 547
   Illinois Chapter, 547
   National Capital Chapter, 550
   New York Chapter, 551
   Southern California Chapter, 553
WINDSTAR WILDLIFE INSTITUTE, 555
WISCONSIN SOCIETY FOR ORNITHOLOGY, INC., THE, 556

WOLF EDUCATION AND RESEARCH CENTER, 557
WWW.ACTIONBIOSCIENCE.ORG, 560
WYOMING DEPARTMENT OF AGRICULTURE, 239
WYOMING OUTDOOR COUNCIL, 561
WYOMING STATE GEOLOGICAL SURVEY, 240
YALE LAW SCHOOL, 627
YELL COUNTY WILDLIFE FEDERATION, 561
YOSEMITE RESTORATION TRUST, 562

RECREATION/ECOTOURISM

A.E. HOWELL WILDLIFE CONSERVATION CENTER INC., 241
ACADEMY FOR EDUCATIONAL DEVELOPMENT, 241
ADIRONDACK MOUNTAIN CLUB, INC., THE (ADK), 242
AFRICA VISION TRUST, 243
AFRICAN AMERICAN ENVIRONMENTALIST ASSOCIATION, 243
AFRICAN CONSERVATION FOUNDATION, THE, 243
ALABAMA DEPARTMENT OF AGRICULTURE AND INDUSTRIES, 132
ALABAMA DEPARTMENT OF CONSERVATION AND NATURAL RESOURCES, 132
ALABAMA ENVIRONMENTAL COUNCIL, 244
ALABAMA WATERFOWL ASSOCIATION, INC. (AWA), 245
ALASKA DEPARTMENT OF PUBLIC SAFETY
   Alaska State Troopers, 134
ALASKA NATURAL HISTORY ASSOCIATION, 246
ALBERTA DEPARTMENT OF ENVIRONMENTAL PROTECTION
   Natural Resources Service, 135
ALDEANATURAL.COM, 563
ALDO LEOPOLD FOUNDATION, 247
AMERICAN ASSOCIATION FOR LEISURE AND RECREATION - AALR, 248
AMERICAN ASSOCIATION OF BOTANICAL GARDENS AND ARBORETA, 249
AMERICAN BIRD CONSERVANCY, 249
AMERICAN BIRDING ASSOCIATION (ABA), 250
AMERICAN CAMPING ASSOCIATION, INC., 250
AMERICAN CAVE CONSERVATION ASSOCIATION, 250
AMERICAN CONSERVATION ASSOCIATION, INC., 251
AMERICAN FORESTS, 260
AMERICAN HIKING SOCIETY, 261
AMERICAN LEAGUE OF ANGLERS AND BOATERS, 262
AMERICAN NATURE STUDY SOCIETY, 263
AMERICAN RIVERS
   Nebraska Field Office, 265
   Voyage of Recovery, 265
ANGLERS FOR CLEAN WATER, 268
ANIMAL PROTECTION INSTITUTE, 268
ANTARCTICA PROJECT, THE, 269
APPALACHIAN MOUNTAIN CLUB, 269
APPALACHIAN TRAIL CONFERENCE, 270
ARCHERY TRADE ASSOCIATION (ATA), 270
ARIZONA COOPERATIVE STATE EXTENSION SERVICES, 135
ARIZONA STATE LAND DEPARTMENT, 136
ARIZONA-SONORA DESERT MUSEUM, 271
ARKANSAS STATE EXTENSION SERVICES
   Four H Center, 138
ARKANSAS STATE PLANT BOARD, 138
ARKANSAS TECH UNIVERSITY
   Department of Parks, Recreation, and Hospitality Administration, 573
ARKANSAS WATERSHED ADVISORY GROUP (AWAG), 272
ASSOCIATION OF AMERICAN GEOGRAPHERS, 273
ASSOCIATION OF PARTNERS FOR PUBLIC LANDS, 274
ATLANTIC CENTER FOR THE ENVIRONMENT
   Quebec Labrador Foundation, 275
ATLANTIC SALMON FEDERATION, 275
ATLANTIC STATES LEGAL FOUNDATION, 275
AUDUBON INTERNATIONAL, 276
AUSTRIALIA DEPARTMENT FOR ENVIRONMENT AND HERITAGE
   Environment Shop, The, 139
BAMA BACKPADDLERS ASSOCIATION, 276
BASS DIVISION OF ESPN PRODUCTIONS INC, 564
BAT CONSERVATION INTERNATIONAL, 277
BEAR SPRINGS BLOSSOM NATURE CONSERVATION GROUP INC., 277
BILLFISH FOUNDATION, THE, 278
BIOSPHERE EXPEDITIONS, 278
BOONE AND CROCKETT CLUB, 279
BOONE AND CROCKETT FOUNDATION, 279
BORN FREE FOUNDATION, 280
BOY SCOUTS OF AMERICA, 280
BUILDINGGREEN, INC., 564
BYRON FOREST PRESERVE, 140
C.A.S.T. FOR KIDS FOUNDATION, 281

CALIFORNIA DEPARTMENT OF FISH AND GAME
   Elkhorn Slough National Estuarine Research Reserve, 141
CALIFORNIA DEPARTMENT OF PARKS AND RECREATION, 142
CALIFORNIA ENERGY COMMISSION
   Environmental Department, 143
CALIFORNIA RESOURCES AGENCY, THE, 145
CALIFORNIA STATE LANDS COMMISSION, 145
CALIFORNIA STATE UNIVERSITY AT CHICO, 575
CALIFORNIA TROUT, INC., 283
CALIFORNIA WATERFOWL ASSOCIATION, 283
CALIFORNIA WILDLIFE FEDERATION, 284
CAMP FIRE CLUB OF AMERICA, 284
CAMP FIRE USA, 285
CANADIAN NATIONAL SPORTSMENS SHOWS, 287
CATSKILL CENTER FOR CONSERVATION AND DEVELOPMENT, INC., THE, 289
CATSKILL FOREST ASSOCIATION, 289
CENTER FOR RESOURCE ECONOMICS/ISLAND PRESS, 293
CENTER FOR SIERRA NEVADA CONSERVATION, 293
CENTRAL OHIO ANGLERS AND HUNTERS CLUB, 294
CETACEAN SOCIETY INTERNATIONAL, 294
CHICAGO PARK DISTRICT, 296
CITY OF BELDING, 145
CJE ASSOCIATES, 565
CLARK UNIVERSITY, 576
CLINTON RIVER WATERSHED COUNCIL (CRWC), 299
COALITION FOR EDUCATION IN THE OUTDOORS, 299
COASTAL AMERICA FOUNDATION, 300
COASTAL RESOURCE MANAGEMENT PROJECT, 146
COLORADO DEPARTMENT OF AGRICULTURE, 146
COLORADO DEPARTMENT OF NATURAL RESOURCES, 146
   Oil and Gas Conservation Commission, 147
COLORADO MOUNTAIN CLUB, 302
COLORADO MOUNTAIN COLLEGE, 577
COLORADO STATE UNIVERSITY COOPERATIVE EXTENSION, 148
COLORADO TRAPPERS ASSOCIATION, 302
COLUMBIA RIVER INTER-TRIBAL FISH COMMISSION, 17
COMMUNITY CONSERVATION /HOWLERS FOREVER, INC., 303
CONNECTICUT BOTANICAL SOCIETY, 304
CONSERVATION FORCE, 307
COTTONWOOD FOUNDATION, 309
D ACRES, 311
DELAWARE DEPARTMENT OF NATURAL RESOURCES AND ENVIRONMENTAL CONTROL
   Division of Air & Waste Management, 150
DELAWARE NATURE SOCIETY, 312
DELAWARE RIVERKEEPER NETWORK, 313
DISTRICT OF COLUMBIA DEPARTMENT OF HEALTH
   Environmental Health Administration, Watershed Protection Division, 152
DUCKS UNLIMITED CANADA
   Nova Scotia Office, 315
EAGLE NATURE FOUNDATION, LTD., 316
EARTHSCAN, 320
ECODEFENSE, 321
EDUCATIONAL COMMUNICATIONS, 322
ENVIRONMENT COUNCIL OF RHODE ISLAND, 323
ENVIRONMENTAL DEFENSE CENTER, 325
ENVIRONMENTAL PROTECTION ASSOCIATION OF GHANA, 327
EQUESTRIAN LAND CONSERVATION RESOURCE, 328
EUROPARC FEDERATION, 328
EVERGLADES COORDINATING COUNCIL (ECC), 329
FEDERAL CARTRIDGE COMPANY, 329
FEDERAL WILDLIFE OFFICERS ASSOCIATION, 329
FEDERATION OF ENVIRONMENTAL EDUCATION IN ST. PETERSBURG, 329
FEDERATION OF FLY FISHERS, 329
FEDERATION OF FLY FISHERS (NCCFFF), 329
FEDERATION OF WESTERN OUTDOOR CLUBS, 330
FERRUM COLLEGE, 581
FISHAMERICA FOUNDATION, 330
FLORIDA DEPARTMENT OF ENVIRONMENTAL PROTECTION
   Coastal and Aquatic Managed Areas, 153
   Florida State Parks AmeriCorps, 154
   Waste Management Division, 154
FLORIDA EXOTIC PEST PLANT COUNCIL, 331
FLORIDA FISH AND WILDLIFE CONSERVATION COMMISSION, 154
FLORIDA NATIVE PLANT SOCIETY, 332
FLORIDA SPORTSMEN'S CONSERVATION ASSOCIATION, 333
FLORIDA TRAIL ASSOCIATION, INC., 333
FOOD SUPPLY / HUMAN POPULATION EXPLOSION CONNECTION, 333
FOREST FIRE LOOKOUT ASSOCIATION, 334
FORESTRY COMMISSION (SOUTH CAROLINA), 155
FOUNDATION FOR NORTH AMERICAN BIG GAME, 336

KEYWORD INDEX – R

FRIENDS OF ACADIA, 336
FRIENDS OF ANIMALS INC., 337
FRIENDS OF SUNKHAZE MEADOWS NATIONAL WILDLIFE REFUGE, 337
FRIENDS OF THE REEDY RIVER, 338
FRIENDS OF THE SEA OTTER, 338
FUTURE FISHERMAN FOUNDATION, 339
GEORGIA DEPARTMENT OF NATURAL RESOURCES
   Environmental Protection Division
      Coastal Division, 156
GEORGIA ENVIRONMENTAL ORGANIZATION, INC. (GEO), 341
GIRL SCOUTS OF THE USA, 343
GLEN CANYON INSTITUTE, 343
GOOD NATURE PUBLISHING CO., 566
GRANT TECH CONSULTING AND CONSERVATION SERVICES, 567
GREAT LAKES SPORT FISHING COUNCIL, 344
GREEN BALKANS FEDERATION OF NATURE CONSERVATION NGOS, 346
GREEN MOUNTAIN CLUB INC., THE, 346
GROWLING, 348
GUAM DEPARTMENT OF AGRICULTURE, 158
HELPING OUR PENINSULA'S ENVIRONMENT, 350
HUNTSMAN MARINE SCIENCE CENTRE, 353
IDAHO DEPARTMENT OF WATER RESOURCES
   Water Awareness Week, 161
IDAHO FISH AND WILDLIFE FOUNDATION, 161
ILLINOIS NATURE PRESERVES COMMISSION (INPC), 163
ILLINOIS PRAIRIE PATH, 355
ILOVEPARKS.COM, 567
INDIANA DEPARTMENT OF ENVIRONMENTAL MANAGEMENT, 163
INDO-PACIFIC CONSERVATION ALLIANCE, 357
INSTITUTE FOR ECOLOGICAL STUDIES UNIVERSITY OF NORTH DAKOTA, 164
INSTITUTE FOR TROPICAL ECOLOGY AND CONSERVATION (ITEC), 358
INSTITUTO NACIONAL DE BIODIVERSIDAD (INBIO), 22
INTERAGENCY COMMITTEE FOR OUTDOOR RECREATION (IAC), 164
INTERNATIONAL ACADEMY, 567
INTERNATIONAL ASSOCIATION OF FISH AND WILDLIFE AGENCIES, 360
INTERNATIONAL ASSOCIATION OF NATURAL RESOURCE PILOTS, 360
INTERNATIONAL BOUNDARY AND WATER COMMISSION, UNITED STATES AND MEXICO, 22
INTERNATIONAL ECOTOURISM SOCIETY, THE, 362
INTERNATIONAL GAME FISH ASSOCIATION, 364
INTERNATIONAL HUNTER EDUCATION ASSOCIATION, 364
INTERNATIONAL OCEANOGRAPHIC FOUNDATION, 365
IOWA ASSOCIATION OF NATURALISTS, 372
IOWA DEPARTMENT OF AGRICULTURE AND LAND STEWARDSHIP
   Bureau of Field Services, 165
IOWA DEPARTMENT OF NATURAL RESOURCES
   Fish and Wildlife Division, 166
IOWA STATE UNIVERSITY
   College of Agriculture, 584
IOWA TRAILS COUNCIL, 373
IOWA WILDLIFE FEDERATION, 374
ISLAND RESOURCES FOUNDATION, 375
ISLESBORO ISLANDS TRUST, 375
IZAAK WALTON LEAGUE OF AMERICA ENDOWMENT, 375
IZAAK WALTON LEAGUE OF AMERICA, INC., THE, 375
   Minnesota Division, 377
   Owatonna Minnesota Chapter, 377
JAPAN WILDLIFE RESEARCH CENTER (JWRC), 380
JOHNSON STATE COLLEGE, 585
KANSAS BIOLOGICAL SURVEY, 166
KANSAS COOPERATIVE FISH AND WILDLIFE RESEARCH UNIT, 167
KANSAS DEPARTMENT OF AGRICULTURE, 167
KANSAS DEPARTMENT OF WILDLIFE AND PARKS
   Office of the Secretary, 167
   Operations Office, 167
   Region 1, 167
   Region 2, 168
   Region 3, 168
   Region 4, 168
KANSAS STATE CONSERVATION COMMISSION, 168
KANSAS STATE UNIVERSITY
   Department of Landscape Architecture / Regional and Community Planning, 585
KEEP FLORIDA BEAUTIFUL, INC., 382
KENTUCKY DEPARTMENT OF AGRICULTURE, 169
KENTUCKY NATURAL RESOURCES AND ENVIRONMENTAL PROTECTION CABINET
   Environmental Quality Commission, 170
KIDS ON THE BAYOU, 384
LA JOLLA FRIENDS OF THE SEALS (LJFS), 384
LAKEHEAD UNIVERSITY, 586

LAKENET, 385
LAND AND WATER FUND OF THE ROCKIES, 386
LAND CONSERVANCY OF WEST MICHIGAN, 386
LEAGUE OF OHIO SPORTSMEN, 387
LEAGUE TO SAVE LAKE TAHOE, 388
LIVING RIVERS, 390
LOUISIANA DEPARTMENT OF AGRICULTURE AND FORESTRY, 172
   Office of Soil and Water Conservation, State Soil and Water Conservation Committee, 172
LOWER MERION CONSERVANCY, 391
LUMMI ISLAND HERITAGE TRUST, 568
MACBRIDE RAPTOR PROJECT, 391
MAINE ASSOCIATION OF CONSERVATION DISTRICTS, 392
MAINE DEPARTMENT OF CONSERVATION
   Bureau of Geology and Natural Areas, 174
MAINE DEPARTMENT OF MARINE RESOURCES, 175
MANITOBA WILDLIFE FEDERATION, 393
MANTA MEXICO, 393
MARIE SELBY BOTANICAL GARDENS, THE, 393
MARINE SCIENCE INSTITUTE, 394
MASSACHUSETTS DIVISION OF FISHERIES AND WILDLIFE
   MassWildlife, 170
MASSACHUSETTS EXECUTIVE OFFICE OF ENVIRONMENTAL AFFAIRS
   Office of Technical Assistance for Toxic Use Reduction, 179
MAX MCGRAW WILDLIFE FOUNDATION, 396
MCGILL UNIVERSITY, 587
MECKLENBURG COUNTY PARK AND RECREATION DEPARTMENT, 179
MICHIGAN DEPARTMENT OF AGRICULTURE, 180
MICHIGAN STATE UNIVERSITY EXTENSION, 181
MINNESOTA ASSOCIATION OF SOIL AND WATER CONSERVATION DISTRICTS, 399
MISSISSIPPI COOPERATIVE FISH AND WILDLIFE RESEARCH UNIT, 183
MISSISSIPPI INTERSTATE COOPERATIVE RESOURCE ASSOCIATION, 401
MISSISSIPPI SOIL AND WATER CONSERVATION COMMISSION, 184
MISSISSIPPI STATE UNIVERSITY
   College of Forest Resources, 588
   Forest and Wildlife Research Center, 588
MISSOURI ASSOCIATION OF SOIL AND WATER CONSERVATION DISTRICTS, 402
MISSOURI DEPARTMENT OF AGRICULTURE, 185
MISSOURI DEPARTMENT OF CONSERVATION
   Forestry Division, 185
MONTANA BASS FEDERATION, 403
MONTANA COOPERATIVE WILDLIFE RESEARCH UNIT (USGS/BRD), 186
MONTANA LAND RELIANCE, 403
MOUNTAINEERS, THE, 405
MULE DEER FOUNDATION, 405
MUNDO AZUL, 406
MUSKIES, INC., 406
NATIONAL ASSOCIATION OF RECREATION RESOURCE PLANNERS, 408
NATIONAL ASSOCIATION OF SERVICE AND CONSERVATION CORPS (NASCC), 408
NATIONAL ASSOCIATION OF STATE PARK DIRECTORS, 409
NATIONAL AUDUBON SOCIETY
   Audubon Alaska, 409
   Audubon Maryland-DC, 410
   Audubon Pennsylvania, 411
   Audubon Society of Portland, 411
   Connecticut Audubon Society, 412
   Fairfax Audubon Society, 413
   Louisiana Audubon Council, 414
   New Jersey Chapter, 415
   San Diego Chapter, 416
   Seattle Audubon Society, 416
   Tucson Audubon Society, 416
NATIONAL BOATING FEDERATION, 417
NATIONAL COALITION FOR MARINE CONSERVATION, 417
NATIONAL FIELD ARCHERY ASSOCIATION, 419
NATIONAL FOREST FOUNDATION, 420
NATIONAL HUNTERS ASSOCIATION, INC., 421
NATIONAL NETWORK OF FOREST PRACTITIONERS, 422
NATIONAL PARK FOUNDATION, 422
NATIONAL PARKS CONSERVATION ASSOCIATION (NPCA)
   Sun Coast Regional Office, 423
NATIONAL RECREATION AND PARK ASSOCIATION, 423
NATIONAL RIFLE ASSOCIATION OF AMERICA, 424
NATIONAL RIFLE ASSOCIATION WEST VIRGINIA
   White Horse Firearms and Outdoor Education Center, Inc., 424
NATIONAL SHOOTING SPORTS FOUNDATION, INC., 424
NATIONAL WATERSHED COALITION, 426
NATIONAL WILD TURKEY FEDERATION, CANADA, INC., THE, 426

KEYWORD INDEX – R

NATIONAL WILD TURKEY FEDERATION, INC., THE, 427
NATIONAL WILDLIFE FEDERATION
   Headquarters, 427
NATIONAL WILDLIFE PRODUCTIONS, INC., 429
NATIVE PLANT SOCIETY OF NORTHEASTERN OHIO, 430
NATURAL SCIENCE FOR YOUTH FOUNDATION, 432
NATURE CONSERVANCY, THE
   Arkansas Field Office, 434
   Colorado Chapter, 434
   New York City Chapter, 438
   New York City Office, 437
   Texas Chapter, 439
NATURESAVERS, 441
NAVAJO NATION DEPARTMENT OF FISH AND WILDLIFE, 188
NEBRASKA DEPARTMENT OF ENVIRONMENTAL QUALITY, 188
NEBRASKA DEPARTMENT OF NATURAL RESOURCES, 188
NEBRASKA WILDLIFE FEDERATION, INC., 442
NEVIS HISTORICAL AND CONSERVATION SOCIETY, 442
NEW BRUNSWICK DEPARTMENT OF NATURAL RESOURCES, 189
NEW ENGLAND COALITION FOR SUSTAINABLE POPULATION (NECSP), 443
NEW HAMPSHIRE ASSOCIATION OF CONSERVATION DISTRICTS, 444
NEW HAMPSHIRE DEPARTMENT OF ENVIRONMENTAL SERVICES, 190
NEW JERSEY DEPARTMENT OF ENVIRONMENTAL PROTECTION
   Division of Parks and Forestry, 192
NEW MEXICO ENVIRONMENT DEPARTMENT, 195
NEW MEXICO STATE UNIVERSITY
   College of Agriculture and Home Economics, 589
NEW YORK STATE COOPERATIVE EXTENSION, 197
NEW YORK STATE FISH AND WILDLIFE MANAGEMENT BOARD
   Region 6, 198
NEW YORK STATE TUG HILL COMMISSION, 199
NEW YORK-NEW JERSEY TRAIL CONFERENCE INC., 446
NEWFOUNDLAND DEPARTMENT OF FOREST RESOURCES AND AGRIFOODS
   Regional Offices, 199
NORTH AMERICAN BUTTERFLY ASSOCIATION, 448
NORTH AMERICAN FALCONERS ASSOCIATION, 448
NORTH AMERICAN GAMEBIRD ASSOCIATION, INC., 448
NORTH CAROLINA BEACH BUGGY ASSOCIATION, INC., 450
NORTH CAROLINA DEPARTMENT OF AGRICULTURE AND CONSUMER SERVICES, 200
NORTH CAROLINA RECREATION AND PARK SOCIETY, INC., 451
NORTHCOAST ENVIRONMENTAL CENTER, 452
NORTHERN ARIZONA UNIVERSITY
   Department of Geography, Planning, and Recreation, 591
NORTHWEST INTERPRETIVE ASSOCIATION, 454
NORTHWEST TERRITORIES DEPARTMENT OF RESOURCES, WILDLIFE AND ECONOMIC DEVELOPMENT, 202
NOVA SCOTIA AGRICULTURE & FISHERIES, 203
NOVA SCOTIA DEPARTMENT OF NATURAL RESOURCES, 203
NOVA SCOTIA FORESTRY ASSOCIATION, 454
OCEAN CONSERVANCY, THE, 455
OCEANIC SOCIETY, 456
OHIO DEPARTMENT OF AGRICULTURE, 203
OHIO DEPARTMENT OF NATURAL RESOURCES, 204
OHIO ENVIRONMENTAL REVIEW APPEALS COMMISSION, 205
OHIO FEDERATION OF SOIL AND WATER CONSERVATION DISTRICTS, 457
OHIO STATE UNIVERSITY, 592
OKLAHOMA CONSERVATION COMMISSION, 205
OKLAHOMA DEPARTMENT OF AGRICULTURE, 205
ONEWILDWORLD, 459
ONTARIO FEDERATION OF ANGLERS AND HUNTERS, 459
ONTARIO FORESTRY ASSOCIATION, 459
ORANGUTAN FOUNDATION INTERNATIONAL, 460
OREGON DEPARTMENT OF FISH AND WILDLIFE (ODFW), 208
OREGON SOCIETY OF AMERICAN FORESTERS, 461
OREGON STATE EXTENSION SERVICES, 209
OREGON STATE MARINE BOARD, 210
ORGANIZATION FOR BAT CONSERVATION, 461
OUTDOOR WRITERS ASSOCIATION OF AMERICA, INC., 462
OZARK SOCIETY, THE, 463
PACIFIC FISHERY MANAGEMENT COUNCIL, 463
PACIFIC NORTHWEST TRAIL ASSOCIATION, 464
PACIFIC STATES MARINE FISHERIES COMMISSION, 27
PENNSYLVANIA COOPERATIVE FISH AND WILDLIFE RESEARCH UNIT, 210
PENNSYLVANIA DEPARTMENT OF AGRICULTURE
   State Conservation Commission, 211
PENNSYLVANIA DEPARTMENT OF ENVIRONMENTAL PROTECTION, 211

PENNSYLVANIA FEDERATION OF SPORTSMENS CLUBS, 466
PENNSYLVANIA ORGANIZATION FOR WATERSHEDS AND RIVERS (POWR), 466
PENNSYLVANIA RECREATION AND PARK SOCIETY, INC., 467
PENNSYLVANIA RESOURCES COUNCIL, INC.,, 467
PLAYA LAKES JOINT VENTURE, 469
POINT TO POINT COMMUNICATIONS, 569
POWDER RIVER BASIN RESOURCE COUNCIL, 472
PRAIRIE CLUB, THE, 472
PUBLIC EMPLOYEES FOR ENVIRONMENTAL RESPONSIBILITY (PEER), 474
PUGET SOUNDKEEPER ALLIANCE, 475
PURPLE MARTIN CONSERVATION ASSOCIATION, 475
RAINFOREST TRUST, 477
RARE CENTER FOR TROPICAL CONSERVATION, 478
REEF RELIEF, 478
RENEWABLE NATURAL RESOURCES FOUNDATION, 478
RESOURCE CENTER FOR ENVIRONMENTAL EDUCATION, THE, 479
RIVER PROJECT, THE, 481
RIVERS COUNCIL OF WASHINGTON, 481
ROBERT ROADS ILLINOIS DEPARTMENT OF NATURAL RESOURCES, 481
ROCKY MOUNTAIN ELK FOUNDATION, 482
ROGER TORY PETERSON INSTITUTE OF NATURAL HISTORY, 482
RUFFNER MOUNTAIN NATURE COALITION, INC., 483
SAFARI CLUB INTERNATIONAL
   International Headquarters, 483
SAN DIEGO NATURAL HISTORY MUSEUM, 484
SAN DIEGUITO RIVER PARK JOINT POWERS AUTHORITY, 215
SAN ELIJO LAGOON CONSERVANCY, 484
SAND CREEK WATERSHED PROJECT, THE, 215
SAVE THE DUNES COUNCIL, 485
SAVE THE SOUND, INC., 486
SEACAMP ASSOCIATION, INC., 489
SEAPLANE PILOTS ASSOCIATION, 489
SHEPHERD COLLEGE, 595
SIERRA CLUB
   Alaska Field Office, 490
   Mackinac Chapter, 493
   Mississippi Chapter, 494
   Nebraska Chapter, 494
   Northwest Office, 495
   Pennsylvania Chapter, 496
   West Virginia Chapter, 499
SIERRA CLUB CALIFORNIA, 499
SOCIEDAD AMBIENTE MARINO, 502
SOCIETY FOR RANGE MANAGEMENT, 503
SOIL AND WATER CONSERVATION SOCIETY, 504
SONORAN DESERT NATIONAL PARK FRIENDS, 504
SONORAN INSTITUTE, 505
SOUND EXPERIENCE, 505
SOUTH CAROLINA DEPARTMENT OF PARKS, RECREATION AND TOURISM, 218
SOUTH DAKOTA ASSOCIATION OF CONSERVATION DISTRICTS, 506
SOUTH DAKOTA COOPERATIVE EXTENSION SERVICE, 218
SOUTHEASTERN ASSOCIATION OF FISH AND WILDLIFE AGENCIES, 508
SOUTHERN ILLINOIS UNIVERSITY CARBONDALE, 596
SOUTHERN UTAH WILDERNESS ALLIANCE
   Moab Office, 510
SOUTHWEST CENTER FOR ENVIRONMENTAL RESEARCH AND POLICY (SCERP), 596
SPORTSMEN'S NATIONAL LAND TRUST, THE, 511
STANFORD ENVIRONMENTAL LAW SOCIETY, 511
STEPHEN F. AUSTIN STATE UNIVERSITY ARTHUR TEMPLE COLLEGE OF FORESTRY, 598
STUDENT CONSERVATION ASSOCIATION, INC., 512
STURGEON FOR TOMORROW, 514
TENNESSEE BASS FEDERATION, 515
TENNESSEE COOPERATIVE FISHERY RESEARCH UNIT (USDI), 220
TENNESSEE DEPARTMENT OF ENVIRONMENT AND CONSERVATION, 221
TENNESSEE VALLEY AUTHORITY
   Muscle Shoals Technical Library, 30
TERRA PENINSULAR, 516
TEXAS BASS FEDERATION, 517
TEXAS DISCOVERY GARDENS, 517
TEXAS FOREST SERVICE, 222
TEXAS RIPARIAN ASSOCIATION, 517
TEXAS STATE SOIL AND WATER CONSERVATION BOARD, 223
TEXAS WILDLIFE ASSOCIATION, 517
THORNE ECOLOGICAL INSTITUTE, 518
TREAD LIGHTLY! INC, 518

KEYWORD INDEX – R

TREES FOR TOMORROW, NATURAL RESOURCES EDUCATION CENTER, 519
TRIANGLE RAILS-TO-TRAILS CONSERVANCY, 520
TROUT UNLIMITED
  Alaska Council, 520
  Pennsylvania Council, 522
TRUSTEES FOR ALASKA, 524
TUG HILL TOMORROW LAND TRUST, 524
TURTLE CREEK WATERSHED ASSOCIATION, INC., 525
UNITED STATES DEPARTMENT OF AGRICULTURE
  Forest Service
    Crooked River National Grassland, 37
    Gila National Forest, 38
    Los Padres National Forest, 40
    Nez Perce National Forest, 41
    Pawnee National Grassland, 42
    Region 02 (Rocky Mountain), 43
    Siuslaw National Forest, 45
UNITED STATES DEPARTMENT OF COMMERCE
  National Oceanic and Atmospheric Administration
    Delaware National Estuarine Research Reserve, 50
    Gulf of Farallones National Marine Sanctuary, 50
    Rookery Bay National Estuarine Research Reserve, 53
    Sea Grant Program - Louisiana, 56
    Sea Grant Program - Massachusetts, 56
    Sea Grant Program - North Carolina, 58
    Stellwagen Bank National Marine Sanctuary, 60
    Wells National Estuarine Research Reserve, 60
UNITED STATES DEPARTMENT OF DEFENSE
  Air Force Major Air Commands
    Andrews AFB, MD, 61
    USAF Academy, 62
  Air Force Major U.S. Installations
    Eglin Air Force Base, 63
    Randolph AFB, TX, 66
  Army Corps of Engineers
    BALTIMORE Engineer DISTRICT, 67
    Fort Worth Engineer District, 68
    Nashville Engineer District, 69
    Norfolk Engineer District, 70
    North Atlantic Engineer District, 70
    Pacific Ocean Engineer District, 70
    Philadelphia District, 70
  Army Materiel Command, 72
  Assistant Chief of Staff for Installation Management, Office of the Director of Environmental Programs, and Conservation Team, 74
  Navy, 74
UNITED STATES DEPARTMENT OF THE INTERIOR
  Bureau of Land Management
    Bakersfield Field Office, 79
    Eugene District Office, 81
    Malta Field Office, 83
    Northern Field Office, 84
    Rawlins Field Office, 85
    Safford Field Office, 86
  Bureau of Reclamation, 89
  Fish & Wildlife Service, 90
    Alligator River/Pea Island National Wildlife Refuge, 91
    Archie Carr National Wildlife Refuge, 91
    Arrowwood National Wildlife Refuge Complex, 91
    Arthur R. Marshall Loxahatchee/Hope Sound National Wildlife Refuge, 91
    Ash Meadows National Wildlife Refuge, 92
    Benton Lake National Wildlife Refuge, 92
    Bombay Hook National Wildlife Refuge, 93
    Browns Park National Wildlife Refuge, 94
    California-Nevada Operations, 94
    Carolina Sandhills National Wildlife Refuge, 95
    Chickasaw National Wildlife Refuge, 95
    Chincoteague/Wallops Island National Wildlife Refuge, 95
    Columbia National Wildlife Refuge, 96
    Eastern Massachusetts National Wildlife Refuge Complex, 97
    Edwin B. Forsythe National Wildlife Refuge, 97
    Great Dismal Swamp/Nansemond National Wildlife Refuge, 98
    Guadalupe-Nipomo Dunes National Wildlife Refuge, 99
    Hobe Sound National Wildlife Refuge, 99
    Kern/Pixley National Wildlife Refuge, 101
    Kofa National Wildlife Refuge, 102
    Lacassine National Wildlife Refuge, 102
    Long Island National Wildlife Refuge Complex, 103
    Long Lake National Wildlife Refuge, 103
    Mattamuskeet National Wildlife Refuge, 104
    Minnesota Valley National Wildlife Refuge, 105
    Morris Wetland Management District, 106
    Necedah National Wildlife Refuge, 107
    Noxubee National Wildlife Refuge, 108
    Okefenokee (Banks Lake) National Wildlife Refuge, 108
    Patoka River National Wetlands Project National Wildlife Refuge, 109
    Patuxent Research Refuge, 109
    Pelican Island National Wildlife Refuge, 109
    Piedmont National Wildlife Refuge, 110
    Pocosin Lakes National Wildlife Refuge, 110
    San Francisco Bay National Wildlife Refuge Complex, 113
    Selawik National Wildlife Refuge, 114
    Southeast Louisiana Complex National Wildlife Refuge, 115
    St. Marks National Wildlife Refuge, 115
    Sunkhaze Meadows National Wildlife Refuge/Carlton Pond Waterfowl Production Area, 116
    Wallkill River National Wildlife Refuge, 117
    Wapanocca National Wildlife Refuge, 117
    White River National Wildlife Refuge, 118
    Willapa/Lewis and Clark National Wildlife Refuge, 118
  Montana State Extension Services, 119
  National Park Service
    Chihuahuan Desert Network, 121
    Grand Teton National Park, 122
    Mammoth Cave National Park, 124
    Mesa Verde National Park, 124
    Mount Rainier National Park, 124
    Theodore Roosevelt National Park, 125
    Yellowstone National Park, 126
  United States Geological Survey
    Western Region, 127
UNITED STATES DEPARTMENT OF TRANSPORTATION
  Federal Aviation Administration, 128
UNITED STATES INSTITUTE FOR ENVIRONMENTAL CONFLICT RESOLUTION, 130
UNITED STATES SPORTSMEN'S ALLIANCE AND UNITED STATES SPORTSMEN'S ALLIANCE FOUNDATION, 526
UNITY COLLEGE, 601
UNIVERSITY OF ALASKA FAIRBANKS
  COOPERATIVE EXTENSION SERVICE College of Rural Alaska, 149
UNIVERSITY OF DAR ES SALAAM, 608
UNIVERSITY OF FLORIDA
  School of Forest Resources and Conservation, 609
UNIVERSITY OF FLORIDA INSTITUTE OF FOOD AND AGRICULTURAL SCIENCES, 609
UNIVERSITY OF GEORGIA
  Daniel B. Warnell School of Forest Resources, 609
UNIVERSITY OF IDAHO
  College of Natural Resources
    Idaho Cooperative Fish and Wildlife Research Unit, 610
UNIVERSITY OF MAINE, 612
UNIVERSITY OF MARYLAND - AT COLLEGE PARK, 613
UNIVERSITY OF MARYLAND COOPERATIVE EXTENSION, 224
UNIVERSITY OF MICHIGAN, 614
UNIVERSITY OF MISSOURI, 615
UNIVERSITY OF NEW BRUNSWICK, 618
UNIVERSITY OF TENNESSEE - AT KNOXVILLE, 621
UNIVERSITY OF WISCONSIN, 622
UNIVERSITY OF WISCONSIN AT MADISON, 623
UPPER CHATTAHOOCHEE RIVERKEEPER, 527
UTAH BASS FEDERATION, 528
UTAH DEPARTMENT OF NATURAL RESOURCES
  Division of Wildlife Resources, 225
UTAH STATE DEPARTMENT OF NATURAL RESOURCES, 225
UTAH WILDLIFE FEDERATION, 528
VERMONT AGENCY OF NATURAL RESOURCES
  Department of Environmental Conservation, 229
VERMONT ASSOCIATION OF CONSERVATION DISTRICTS, 529
VERNAL POOL SOCIETY, THE, 530
VIRGINIA DEPARTMENT OF FORESTRY, 230
VIRGINIA DEPARTMENT OF GAME AND INLAND FISHERIES
  Region IV (Staunton), 231
VIRGINIA DEPARTMENT OF HEALTH, 231
VIRGINIA RESOURCE-USE EDUCATION COUNCIL, 532
VIRGINIA TECH
  Department of Fisheries and Wildlife Sciences, 625
VIRGINIA TECH UNIVERSITY
  College of Natural Resources, 625
WABASH RIVER HERITAGE CORRIDOR COMMISSION, 232
WARREN COUNTY CONSERVATION BOARD, 532
WASHINGTON DEPARTMENT OF AGRICULTURE, 232
WASHINGTON DEPARTMENT OF ECOLOGY, 233
WASHINGTON DEPARTMENT OF FISH AND WILDLIFE
  WASHINGTON FISH AND WILDLIFE COMMISSION, 233
WASHINGTON RECREATION AND PARK ASSOCIATION, 533

WASHINGTON STATE CONSERVATION COMMISSION, 234
WASHINGTON STATE DEPARTMENT OF NATURAL RESOURCES
　Olympic Region, 234
WASHINGTON TOXICS COALITION, 534
WASHINGTON TRAILS ASSOCIATION, 534
WASHINGTON WILDLIFE FEDERATION, 534
WATERMAN CONSERVATION EDUCATION CENTER, 535
WEST VIRGINIA DEPARTMENT OF ENVIRONMENTAL PROTECTION, 235
WESTERN HEMISPHERE SHOREBIRD RESERVE NETWORK (WHSRN), 537
WESTERN PACIFIC REGIONAL FISHERY MANAGEMENT COUNCIL, 131
WESTERN PENNSYLVANIA CONSERVANCY, 537
WHITETAILS UNLIMITED, INC., 539
WILD FOUNDATION, THE, 539
WILDERNESS EDUCATION ASSOCIATION, 540
WILDLIFE ACTION, INC., 542
WILDLIFE DAMAGE REVIEW (WDR), 543
WILDLIFE FOREVER, 544
WILDLIFE HABITAT COUNCIL, 544
WILDLIFE INFORMATION CENTER, INC., 545
WILDLIFE SOCIETY
　Colorado Chapter, 547
　Illinois Chapter, 547
　Southern California Chapter, 553
WISCONSIN BASS FEDERATION, 556
WISCONSIN COOPERATIVE FISHERY RESEARCH UNIT USGS, 237
WISCONSIN GEOLOGICAL AND NATURAL HISTORY SURVEY, 238
WISCONSIN PARK AND RECREATION ASSOCIATION, 556
WOLF EDUCATION AND RESEARCH CENTER, 557
WOMEN'S SHOOTING SPORTS FOUNDATION, 558
WORLDWATCH INSTITUTE, 560
WYOMING STATE GEOLOGICAL SURVEY, 240
WYOMING STATE PARKS AND CULTURAL RESOURCES, 240
YALE LAW SCHOOL, 627
YELL COUNTY WILDLIFE FEDERATION, 561
YMCA NATURE AND COMMUNITY CENTER, 562
YOSEMITE RESTORATION TRUST, 562
YOUNG ENTOMOLOGISTS SOCIETY, INC., 562
ZERO, 562

REDUCE/REUSE/RECYCLE

A CRITICAL DECISION, 241
ACADEMY FOR EDUCATIONAL DEVELOPMENT, 241
ADIRONDACK MOUNTAIN CLUB, INC., THE (ADK), 242
ADKINS ARBORETUM, 242
ADOPT-A-STREAM FOUNDATION, THE, 242
ADVOCATES OF THE COMMON WEALTH, INC., 243
AFRICAN AMERICAN ENVIRONMENTALIST ASSOCIATION, 243
AFRICAN WILDLIFE FOUNDATION, 243
AIR & WASTE MANAGEMENT ASSOCIATION, 244
ALABAMA DEPARTMENT OF CONSERVATION AND NATURAL RESOURCES, 132
ALABAMA ENVIRONMENTAL COUNCIL, 244
ALABAMA FORESTRY COMMISSION, 133
ALABAMA WILDFLOWER SOCIETY, THE, 245
ALASKA CENTER FOR THE ENVIRONMENT, 245
ALASKA COOPERATIVE FISH AND WILDLIFE RESEARCH UNIT, 133
ALASKA DEPARTMENT OF ENVIRONMENTAL CONSERVATION, 133
ALASKA DEPARTMENT OF FISH AND GAME, 134
ALASKA HEALTH PROJECT, 134
ALASKA NATURAL HISTORY ASSOCIATION, 246
ALBERTA WILDERNESS ASSOCIATION, 247
AMERICA THE BEAUTIFUL FUND, 248
AMERICAN ASSOCIATION OF ZOO KEEPERS, INC., 249
AMERICAN BIRD CONSERVANCY, 249
AMERICAN CONSERVATION ASSOCIATION, INC., 251
AMERICAN FOREST FOUNDATION, 260
AMERICAN GEOGRAPHICAL SOCIETY, 260
AMERICAN INSTITUTE OF FISHERY RESEARCH BIOLOGISTS, 262
AMERICAN NATURE STUDY SOCIETY, 263
AMERICAN RESOURCES GROUP, 264
AMERICAN RIVERS
　Voyage of Recovery, 265
AMERICAN SOCIETY OF LANDSCAPE ARCHITECTS, 266
AMERICAN SPORTFISHING ASSOCIATION, 266
AMERICAN WATER RESOURCES ASSOCIATION, 267
AMERICAN WHITEWATER, 267
ANACOSTIA WATERSHED SOCIETY, 268
ANTARCTICA PROJECT, THE, 269
ARIZONA COOPERATIVE FISH AND WILDLIFE RESEARCH UNIT (USDI), 135

ARIZONA GEOLOGICAL SURVEY, 136
ARKANSAS COOPERATIVE RESEARCH UNIT, 137
ARKANSAS ENVIRONMENTAL EDUCATION ASSOCIATION, 272
ASSOCIATION OF CONSULTING FORESTERS OF AMERICA, 273
ATLANTIC CENTER FOR THE ENVIRONMENT
　Quebec-Labrador Foundation, 275
ATLANTIC SALMON FEDERATION, 275
ATLANTIC STATES LEGAL FOUNDATION, 275
AUDUBON INTERNATIONAL, 276
AUSTRALIA DEPARTMENT FOR ENVIRONMENT AND HERITAGE, 139
　Environment Shop, The, 139
BAMA BACKPADDLERS ASSOCIATION, 276
BASS DIVISION OF ESPN PRODUCTIONS INC, 564
BEAR SPRINGS BLOSSOM NATURE CONSERVATION GROUP INC., 277
BIOINTEGRAL RESOURCE CENTER, 278
BIRDLIFE INTERNATIONAL, 279
BOARD OF MINERALS AND ENVIRONMENT, 139
BOONE AND CROCKETT FOUNDATION, 279
BORDER ECOLOGY PROJECT (BEP), 279
BROWN UNIVERSITY, 575
BYRON FOREST PRESERVE, 140
CALCASIEU PARISH ANIMAL CONTROL AND PROTECTION DEPARTMENT, 282
CALIFORNIA TRAPPERS ASSOCIATION, 283
CANADIAN ARCTIC RESOURCE COMMITTEE, INC., 285
CANVASBACK SOCIETY, 288
CARRYING CAPACITY NETWORK, 288
CENTER FOR BIOLOGICAL DIVERSITY, 290
CENTER FOR ENVIRONMENT, COMMERCE & ENERGY, 290
CENTER FOR RESOURCE ECONOMICS/ISLAND PRESS, 293
CENTRAL OHIO ANGLERS AND HUNTERS CLUB, 294
CHARLES A. AND ANNE MORROW LINDBERGH FOUNDATION, THE, 294
CHESAPEAKE BAY FOUNDATION, INC.
　Maryland Office, 295
　Pennsylvania Office, 295
CHLORINE-FREE PAPER CONSORTIUM, 297
CJE ASSOCIATES, 565
CLARK UNIVERSITY, 576
CLEMSON UNIVERSITY
　School of the Environment, 577
CLEMSON UNIVERSITY EXTENSION SERVICE, 145
COASTAL AMERICA FOUNDATION, 300
COLORADO DEPARTMENT OF AGRICULTURE, 146
COLORADO MOUNTAIN COLLEGE, 577
COLORADO STATE FOREST SERVICE, 148
COLORADO STATE UNIVERSITY
　Department of Fishery and Wildlife Biology, 578
COMMUNITY ENVIRONMENTAL COUNCIL (CEC), 303
COMMUNITY RIGHTS COUNSEL, 303
CONCERN, INC., 304
CONFEDERATED SALISH AND KOOTENAI TRIBES, 304
CONNECTICUT BOTANICAL SOCIETY, 304
CONNECTICUT PUBLIC INTEREST RESEARCH GROUP (CONN PIRG), 305
CONSERVATION ALLIANCE OF ST. LUCIE CO., 306
CONSERVATION COUNCIL OF NORTH CAROLINA, 306
CONSERVATION FEDERATION OF MARYLAND/ F.A.R.M., 306
CONSERVATION FORCE, 307
CORAL REEF ALLIANCE, THE (CORAL), 309
COTTONWOOD FOUNDATION, 309
COUNCIL FOR ENVIRONMENTAL EDUCATION, 309
CROSBY ARBORETUM, THE, 311
DELAWARE ASSOCIATION OF CONSERVATION DISTRICTS, 312
DELAWARE DEPARTMENT OF NATURAL RESOURCES AND ENVIRONMENTAL CONTROL
　Division of Parks and Recreation, 150
　Division of Water Resources, 151
DELTA COLLEGE, 579
DESERT FISHES COUNCIL, 314
DESERT TORTOISE COUNCIL, 314
EAGLE NATURE FOUNDATION, LTD., 316
EAGLES 4 KIDS, 565
EARTH FORCE
　GREEN (Global Rivers Environmental Education Network)), 317
EARTH FRIENDS WILDLIFE FOUNDATION, 317
EARTH ISLAND INSTITUTE, 317
EARTHSCAN, 320
ECOLOGY CENTER, 321
ECONOVA INC., 565
ENVIRONMENT COUNCIL OF RHODE ISLAND, 323
ENVIRONMENTAL ALLIANCE FOR SENIOR INVOLVEMENT (EASI), 323
ENVIRONMENTAL DEFENSE
　Headquarters, 324

KEYWORD INDEX – R

ENVIRONMENTAL DEFENSE CENTER, 325
ENVIRONMENTAL EDUCATION ASSOCIATION OF ILLINOIS, 325
ENVIRONMENTAL EDUCATORS OF NORTH CAROLINA (EENC), 326
ENVIRONMENTAL ENTERPRISES ASSISTANCE FUND, INC., 326
ENVIRONMENTAL LAW INSTITUTE, THE, 327
ENVIRONMENTAL POLICY CENTER, THE, 327
ENVIRONMENTAL PROTECTION AGENCY
  Region 1 (CT, ME, MA, NH, RI, VT), 18
  Region 5 (IL, IN, MI, NM, OH, WI), 19
ENVIRONMENTAL PROTECTION MASSACHUSETTS, 152
ENVIRONMENTAL RESOURCE CENTER (ERC), 328
ENVIROSOUTH, INC., 328
FEDERATION OF FLY FISHERS (NCCFFF), 329
FERRUM COLLEGE, 581
FLORIDA DEPARTMENT OF ENVIRONMENTAL PROTECTION
  Coastal and Aquatic Managed Areas, 153
  Division of Water Resource Management, 154
FLORIDA FEDERATION OF GARDEN CLUBS, INC., 331
FLORIDA FISH AND WILDLIFE CONSERVATION COMMISSION, 154
FOOD SUPPLY / HUMAN POPULATION EXPLOSION CONNECTION, 333
FOREST HISTORY SOCIETY, INC., 334
FOREST LANDOWNERS ASSOCIATION, INC., 334
FOREST SOCIETY OF MAINE, 335
FRANKFURT ZOOLOGICAL SOCIETY-HELP FOR THREATENED WILDLIFE, 336
FRIENDS OF THE EARTH, 337
FRIENDS OF THE REEDY RIVER, 338
FUNDACION NATURA COLOMBIA, 339
GALIANO CONSERVANCY ASSOCIATION, 339
GENERAL FEDERATION OF WOMEN'S CLUBS, 340
GEORGIA DEPARTMENT OF EDUCATION, 156
GEORGIA DEPARTMENT OF NATURAL RESOURCES
  Environmental Protection Division
    Coastal Division, 156
GEORGIA ENVIRONMENTAL POLICY INSTITUTE, 342
GEORGIA STATE EXTENSION SERVICE, 157
GEORGIA TRUST FOR HISTORIC PRESERVATION, 342
GIRL SCOUTS OF THE USA, 343
GLACIER INSTITUTE, THE, 343
GOOD NATURE PUBLISHING CO., 566
GREAT LAKES UNITED
  Canada Office, 345
GREAT OUTDOORS CONSERVANCY, THE, 345
GREEN PARTNERS, 347
GREEN SEAL, 347
GREEN SPHERE INC., 347
GROWLING, 348
GULF COAST RESEARCH LABORATORY, 158
HAMLINE UNIVERSITY, 583
HARDWOOD FOREST FOUNDATION, 348
HAWAII NATURE CENTER, 349
HEADLANDS INSTITUTE, 350
HENRY STIFEL SCHRADER ENVIRONMENTAL EDUCATION CENTER, 350
HOLDEN ARBORETUM, THE, 351
HOLLOW OAK LAND TRUST, 351
HOOSIER ENVIRONMENTAL COUNCIL, 352
HUMAN ECOLOGY ACTION LEAGUE, INC., THE (HEAL), 352
HUNTSMAN MARINE SCIENCE CENTRE, 353
IDAHO DEPARTMENT OF ENVIRONMENTAL QUALITY, 160
IDAHO DEPARTMENT OF PARKS AND RECREATION, 160
IDAHO DEPARTMENT OF WATER RESOURCES, 161
ILLINOIS ENVIRONMENTAL PROTECTION AGENCY, 162
ILLINOIS NATIVE PLANT SOCIETY, 355
ILLINOIS NATURE PRESERVES COMMISSION (INPC), 163
ILLINOIS WALNUT COUNCIL, 356
INDIANA AUDUBON SOCIETY, INC., 356
INFORM, INC., 357
INSTITUTE FOR TROPICAL ECOLOGY AND CONSERVATION (ITEC), 358
INSTITUTO NACIONAL DE BIODIVERSIDAD (INBIO), 22
INTERNATIONAL ASSOCIATION OF NATURAL RESOURCE PILOTS, 360
INTERNATIONAL CHILDREN'S CONFERENCE ON THE ENVIRONMENT, 362
INTERNATIONAL PLANT PROPAGATORS SOCIETY, INC., 365
INTERNATIONAL SOCIETY OF TROPICAL FORESTERS, INC., 367
INTERNATIONAL UNION FOR CONSERVATION OF NATURE AND NATURAL RESOURCES (IUCN) THE WORLD CONSERVATION UNION
  Headquarters, 367
IOWA ASSOCIATION OF NATURALISTS, 372
IOWA DEPARTMENT OF NATURAL RESOURCES
  Fish and Wildlife Division, 166
  Parks, 166
IOWA NATIVE PLANT SOCIETY, 373

IOWA PRAIRIE NETWORK, 373
IOWA STATE EXTENSION SERVICES
  Extension Wildlife Programs, 166
IOWA STATE UNIVERSITY
  College of Agriculture, 584
IZAAK WALTON LEAGUE OF AMERICA, INC., THE
  Alaska Division, 376
  Minnesota Division, 377
  Owatonna Minnesota Chapter, 377
JACK MINER MIGRATORY BIRD FOUNDATION, INC., 379
JAGRATA JUBA SHANGHA (JJS), 568
JOHN INSKEEP ENVIRONMENTAL LEARNING CENTER, 380
JOHNS HOPKINS UNIVERSITY
  CENTER FOR A LIVABLE FUTURE, 584
JOHNSON STATE COLLEGE, 585
KANSAS ASSOCIATION FOR CONSERVATION AND ENVIRONMENTAL EDUCATION, KACEE, 380
KANSAS BASS FEDERATION, 381
KANSAS BIOLOGICAL SURVEY, 166
KANSAS DEPARTMENT OF WILDLIFE AND PARKS
  Office of the Secretary, 167
  Operations Office, 167
  Region 1, 167
  Region 2, 168
  Region 3, 168
  Region 5, 168
KANSAS STATE CONSERVATION COMMISSION, 168
KANSAS STATE UNIVERSITY
  Department of Landscape Architecture / Regional and Community Planning, 585
KANSAS WATER OFFICE, 169
KEEP AMERICA BEAUTIFUL, INC., 382
KEEP FLORIDA BEAUTIFUL, INC., 382
KENTUCKY ACADEMY OF SCIENCE, 382
KENTUCKY DEPARTMENT OF AGRICULTURE, 169
KIDS FOR SAVING EARTH WORLDWIDE, 384
LAKE SUPERIOR STATE UNIVERSITY, 586
LANDWATCH MONTEREY COUNTY, 386
LEAGUE OF CONSERVATION VOTERS, 387
LEAGUE OF ENVIRONMENTAL JOURNALISTS, 387
LEAGUE OF OHIO SPORTSMEN, 387
LEAGUE OF WOMEN VOTERS OF WASHINGTON, 388
LEARNING FOR ENVIRONMENTAL ACTION PROGRAMME (LEAP), 388
LIGHTHAWK, 389
LITERACY FOR ENVIRONMENTAL JUSTICE, 389
LOUISIANA DEPARTMENT OF AGRICULTURE AND FORESTRY, 172
LOUISIANA DEPARTMENT OF NATURAL RESOURCES, 172
LOWER MERION CONSERVANCY, 391
LUMMI ISLAND HERITAGE TRUST, 568
MAINE ASSOCIATION OF CONSERVATION DISTRICTS, 392
MAINE DEPARTMENT OF CONSERVATION
  Land Use Regulation Commission, 175
MARYLAND DEPARTMENT OF NATURAL RESOURCES, 177
MARYLAND ORNITHOLOGICAL SOCIETY, INC., 395
MASSACHUSETTS EXECUTIVE OFFICE OF ENVIRONMENTAL AFFAIRS
  Wetlands and Waterways Program, 179
MIAMI UNIVERSITY, 587
MICHIGAN FORESTS ASSOCIATION, 397
MICHIGAN LAND USE INSTITUTE, 397
MIDDLE TENNESSEE STATE UNIVERSITY, 588
MINERAL POLICY CENTER, 399
MINNESOTA BASS FEDERATION, 399
MINNESOTA LAND TRUST, 400
MISSISSIPPI STATE UNIVERSITY
  Forest and Wildlife Research Center, 588
MISSOURI ASSOCIATION OF SOIL AND WATER CONSERVATION DISTRICTS, 402
MONTANA LAND RELIANCE, 403
MUNDO AZUL, 406
NATIONAL 4-H COUNCIL, 406
NATIONAL ASSOCIATION OF CONSERVATION DISTRICTS, 407
NATIONAL ASSOCIATION OF ENVIRONMENTAL PROFESSIONALS, THE, 408
NATIONAL ASSOCIATION OF SERVICE AND CONSERVATION CORPS (NASCC), 408
NATIONAL ASSOCIATION OF STATE DEPARTMENTS OF AGRICULTURE, 408
NATIONAL AUDUBON SOCIETY
  Audubon Maryland-DC, 410
  Audubon of Florida, 410
  Audubon Society of Omaha, 411
  Audubon Society of Portland, 411
  Audubon Society of Rhode Island, 412

NATIONAL AUDUBON SOCIETY (continued)
   Audubon Vermont, 412
   Connecticut Audubon Society, 412
   Hawaii Audubon Society, 413
   Kentucky Audubon Council, 413
   Louisiana Audubon Council, 414
NATIONAL AVIARY, 568
NATIONAL BIRD-FEEDING SOCIETY, 416
NATIONAL CAUCUS OF ENVIRONMENTAL LEGISLATORS (NCEL), 417
NATIONAL CENTER FOR APPROPRIATE TECHNOLOGY
   Center for Resourceful Building Technology, 417
NATIONAL ENVIRONMENTAL HEALTH ASSOCIATION, 418
NATIONAL FARMERS UNION, 419
NATIONAL FFA ORGANIZATION, 419
NATIONAL SHOOTING SPORTS FOUNDATION, INC., 424
NATIONAL TRAPPERS ASSOCIATION, INC., 425
NATIONAL TRUST FOR HISTORIC PRESERVATION, 425
NATIONAL WILDLIFE PRODUCTIONS, INC., 429
NATIONAL WOODLAND OWNERS ASSOCIATION, 430
NATIVE PLANT SOCIETY OF NORTHEASTERN OHIO, 430
NATIVE PLANT SOCIETY OF OREGON, 430
NATURAL AREAS ASSOCIATION, 431
NATURE CONSERVANCY, THE
   Alabama Chapter, 433
NATURESAVERS, 441
NEBRASKA DEPARTMENT OF NATURAL RESOURCES, 188
NEBRASKA WILDLIFE FEDERATION, INC., 442
NEVIS HISTORICAL AND CONSERVATION SOCIETY, 442
NEW ENGLAND NATURAL RESOURCES CENTER, 443
NEW HAMPSHIRE COUNCIL ON RESOURCES AND DEVELOPMENT, 190
NEW HAMPSHIRE FISH AND GAME DEPARTMENT, 190
NEW MEXICO ENVIRONMENT DEPARTMENT, 195
NEW YORK OFFICE OF ENERGY EFFICIENCY AND ENVIRONMENT, 197
NEW YORK PUBLIC INTEREST RESEARCH GROUP (NYPIRG), 446
NEW YORK STATE DEPARTMENT OF AGRICULTURE AND MARKETS, 197
NEWFOUNDLAND DEPARTMENT OF FOREST RESOURCES AND AGRIFOODS
   Regional Offices, 199
NOLTE ASSOCIATES, INC., 569
NORTH AMERICAN ASSOCIATION FOR ENVIRONMENTAL EDUCATION, 447
NORTH AMERICAN BUTTERFLY ASSOCIATION, 448
NORTH AMERICAN COALITION ON RELIGION AND ECOLOGY (NACRE), 448
NORTH AMERICAN DEVELOPMENT BANK, 24
NORTH AMERICAN FALCONERS ASSOCIATION, 448
NORTH AMERICAN MEMBERSHIP GROUP, 449
NORTH CAROLINA BASS FEDERATION, 450
NORTH CAROLINA COASTAL FEDERATION, INC., 450
NORTH CAROLINA COOPERATIVE FISH AND WILDLIFE RESEARCH UNIT (USDI), 200
NORTH CAROLINA WILD FLOWER PRESERVATION SOCIETY, 451
NORTHERN ARIZONA UNIVERSITY
   Department of Geography, Planning, and Recreation, 591
NORTHERN PLAINS RESOURCE COUNCIL, 453
NOVA SCOTIA DEPARTMENT OF NATURAL RESOURCES, 203
NW ENERGY COALITION, 454
OHIO DEPARTMENT OF AGRICULTURE, 203
OHIO DEPARTMENT OF NATURAL RESOURCES, 204
OHIO ENVIRONMENTAL REVIEW APPEALS COMMISSION, 205
OHIO NATIVE PLANT SOCIETY, 457
OHIO STATE UNIVERSITY EXTENSION, 205
OKLAHOMA COOPERATIVE FISH AND WILDLIFE RESEARCH UNIT (USDI), 206
OKLAHOMA NATIVE PLANT SOCIETY, 458
OKLAHOMA ORNITHOLOGICAL SOCIETY, 458
OKLAHOMA STATE EXTENSION SERVICES, 206
OLYMPIC PARK INSTITUTE, 459
ONTARIO FEDERATION OF ANGLERS AND HUNTERS, 459
ONTARIO FORESTRY ASSOCIATION, 459
OREGON DEPARTMENT OF TRANSPORTATION, 209
OREGON SMALL WOODLANDS ASSOCIATION, 461
OREGON SOCIETY OF AMERICAN FORESTERS, 461
OREGON TROUT, 461
ORGANIZATION FOR BAT CONSERVATION, 461
OZARK SOCIETY, THE, 463
PACIFIC FISHERY MANAGEMENT COUNCIL, 463
PACIFIC INSTITUTE FOR STUDIES IN DEVELOPMENT, ENVIRONMENT, AND SECURITY, 463
PENNSYLVANIA ASSOCIATION OF CONSERVATION DISTRICTS, INC., 465

PENNSYLVANIA DEPARTMENT OF AGRICULTURE
   State Conservation Commission, 211
PENNSYLVANIA FEDERATION OF SPORTSMENS CLUBS, 466
PINE BLUFF COOPERATIVE FISHERY RESEARCH PROJECT, 213
POCONO ENVIRONMENTAL EDUCATION CENTER, 470
POPULATION ACTION INTERNATIONAL, 470
POPULATION CONNECTION, 471
POPULATION-ENVIRONMENT BALANCE, INC., 471
PRIORITIES INSTITUTE, THE, 473
PS ENTERPRISES, 570
PUBLIC LANDS FOUNDATION, 474
PUBLIC LANDS INTERPRETIVE ASSOCIATION, 570
PUERTO RICO ASSOCIATION OF SOIL AND WATER CONSERVATION DISTRICTS, 474
PUERTO RICO SOIL CONSERVATION COMMITTEE, 213
RAINBOW PUSH COALITION, 476
RAINFOREST RELIEF, 477
RAINFOREST TRUST, 477
RENEWABLE NATURAL RESOURCES FOUNDATION, 478
RESIDENTS FOR A MORE BEAUTIFUL PORT WASHINGTON, 479
RESOURCES FOR THE FUTURE, 479
RHODE ISLAND DEPARTMENT OF TRANSPORTATION, 214
RIVER PROJECT, THE, 481
RUTGERS COOPERATIVE EXTENSION, 215
RUTGERS UNIVERSITY, COOK COLLEGE, 594
SAND CREEK WATERSHED PROJECT, THE, 215
SANIBEL-CAPTIVA CONSERVATION FOUNDATION, INC., 484
SANTA CLARA COMMUNITY ACTION PROGRAM, 594
SAVE THE SOUND, INC., 486
SCENIC AMERICA, 487
SIERRA CLUB
   Alaska Field Office, 490
   Connecticut Chapter, 491
   Hawaii Chapter, 492
   Lone Star Chapter, 493
   Maryland Chapter, 493
   Nebraska Chapter, 494
   Northwest Office, 495
   Rio Grande Chapter (New Mexico/West Texas), 496
   West Virginia Chapter, 499
SIERRA CLUB CALIFORNIA, 499
SIERRA CLUB FOUNDATION, THE, 499
SOCIETY FOR ECOLOGICAL RESTORATION, 502
SOCIETY FOR THE PROTECTION OF NEW HAMPSHIRE FORESTS, 503
SOCIETY OF AMERICAN FORESTERS, 503
SONORAN INSTITUTE, 505
SOUTH CAROLINA DEPARTMENT OF AGRICULTURE, 217
SOUTH CAROLINA WILDLIFE FEDERATION, 506
SOUTH DAKOTA ASSOCIATION OF CONSERVATION DISTRICTS, 506
SOUTH DAKOTA COOPERATIVE FISH AND WILDLIFE RESEARCH UNIT (USDI-USGS), 29
SOUTH DAKOTA DEPARTMENT OF ENVIRONMENT AND NATURAL RESOURCES, 219
SOUTH DAKOTA DEPARTMENT OF GAME, FISH, AND PARKS, 219
SOUTH DAKOTA ORNITHOLOGISTS UNION, 507
SOUTH DAKOTA WILDLIFE FEDERATION, 507
SOUTHEASTERN FISHES COUNCIL, 508
SOUTHERN APPALACHIAN BOTANICAL SOCIETY, 508
SOUTHERN UTAH WILDERNESS ALLIANCE
   Moab Office, 510
SOUTHFACE ENERGY INSTITUTE, 510
SOUTHWEST CENTER FOR ENVIRONMENTAL RESEARCH AND POLICY (SCERP), 596
SOUTHWESTERN HERPETOLOGISTS SOCIETY, 510
STATE ENVIRONMENTAL RESOURCE CENTER (SERC), 512
STUDENT CONSERVATION ASSOCIATION, INC., 512
STUDENTS PARTNERSHIP WORLDWIDE, 513
SUSTAIN, 514
SUSTAINABLE ENERGY INSTITUTE
   Culture Change, 514
   Food Not Lawns, 514
   Pedal Power Produce, 514
TALLAHASSEE MUSEUM OF HISTORY AND NATURAL SCIENCE, 515
TENNESSEE DEPARTMENT OF ENVIRONMENT AND CONSERVATION, 221
TENNESSEE FORESTRY ASSOCIATION, 516
TEXAS DEPARTMENT OF AGRICULTURE, 222
TEXAS DEPARTMENT OF HEALTH, 222
TEXAS DISCOVERY GARDENS, 517
TEXAS ORGANIZATION FOR ENDANGERED SPECIES, 517
TEXAS STATE SOIL AND WATER CONSERVATION BOARD, 223
TEXAS WATER DEVELOPMENT BOARD, 223
TREEPEOPLE, 519

KEYWORD INDEX – S

TREES ATLANTA, 519
TREES FOR THE FUTURE, INC., 519
TROUT UNLIMITED
  New York Council, 522
TRUST FOR PUBLIC LAND, THE, 523
TRUSTEES FOR ALASKA, 524
TURNER ENDANGERED SPECIES FUND, 571
TWO WHITE WOLVES SANCTUARY, 525
UNEP WORLD CONSERVATION MONITORING CENTRE, 525
UNION OF CONCERNED SCIENTISTS, 525
UNITED NATIONS ENVIRONMENT PROGRAMME, 525
UNITED STATES DEPARTMENT OF AGRICULTURE
  Forest Service
    Green Mountain National Forest, 38
    Region 09 (Eastern), 43
UNITED STATES DEPARTMENT OF COMMERCE
  National Oceanic and Atmospheric Administration
    Sea Grant Program - California, 54
    Sea Grant Program - Louisiana, 56
    Sea Grant Program - Maryland, 56
    Sea Grant Program - Massachusetts, 56
    Sea Grant Program - Michigan, 57
    Sea Grant Program - North Carolina, 58
    Sea Grant Program - Ohio, 58
    Sea Grant Program - Texas, 59
UNITED STATES DEPARTMENT OF DEFENSE
  Air Force Major U.S. Installations
    Luke AFB (and the Barry M. Goldwater AFR), AZ, 65
    Randolph AFB, TX, 00
  Army Corps of Engineers
    North Atlantic Engineer District, 70
  Army Materiel Command, 72
  Assistant Chief of Staff for Installation Management, Office of the
    Director of Environmental Programs, and Conservation Team, 74
  Navy, 74
UNITED STATES DEPARTMENT OF THE INTERIOR
  Fish and Wildlife Service
    Arrowwood National Wildlife Refuge Complex, 91
    Kofa National Wildlife Refuge, 102
    Lacassine National Wildlife Refuge, 102
    Ridgefield National Wildlife Refuge, 112
  National Park Service
    Mammoth Cave National Park, 124
    Mount Rainier National Park, 124
    Yellowstone National Park, 126
  United States Geological Survey
    New Mexico Cooperative Fish and Wildlife Research Unit, 127
UNITED STATES DEPARTMENT OF TRANSPORTATION
  Federal Aviation Administration, 128
UNITED STATES DEPARTMENT OF TREASURY, 129
UNIVERSITY OF ALASKA FAIRBANKS
  COOPERATIVE EXTENSION SERVICE College of Rural Alaska, 149
UNIVERSITY OF DAR ES SALAAM, 608
UNIVERSITY OF FLORIDA INSTITUTE OF FOOD AND AGRICULTURAL
  SCIENCES, 609
UNIVERSITY OF GEORGIA
  Daniel B. Warnell School of Forest Resources, 609
UNIVERSITY OF HAWAII COOPERATIVE EXTENSION PROGRAM, 224
UNIVERSITY OF MICHIGAN, 614
UNIVERSITY OF WISCONSIN, 622
URBAN HABITAT PROGRAM, 527
URBAN WASTE MANAGEMENT & RESEARCH CENTER, 624
URBAN WILDLIFE RESOURCES, 527
UTAH BASS FEDERATION, 528
UTAH STATE DEPARTMENT OF NATURAL RESOURCES
  Division of Water Resources, 228
VERMONT ENVIRONMENTAL BOARD, 227
VERMONT STATE-WIDE ENVIRONMENTAL EDUCATION PROGRAMS
  (SWEEP), 530
VERMONT WOODLANDS ASSOCIATION, 530
VINEYARD CONSERVATION SOCIETY, 530
VIRGINIA DEPARTMENT OF ENVIRONMENTAL QUALITY, 230
VIRGINIA MUSEUM OF NATURAL HISTORY, 232
VIRGINIA RESOURCE-USE EDUCATION COUNCIL, 532
VIRGINIA SOIL AND CONSERVATION BOARD, 232
WARREN COUNTY CONSERVATION BOARD, 532
WASHINGTON DEPARTMENT OF ECOLOGY
  Eastern Regional Office, 233
  Southwest Regional Office, 233
WASHINGTON STATE PARKS AND RECREATION COMMISSION
  Southwest Region, 235
WASHINGTON WILDERNESS COALITION, 534
WATERSHED MANAGEMENT COUNCIL, 535
WELLSPRING INTERNATIONAL, INC., 571
WEST MICHIGAN ENVIRONMENTAL ACTION COUNCIL, 536
WEST VIRGINIA DEPARTMENT OF AGRICULTURE, 235
WETLAND HABITAT ALLIANCE OF TEXAS, 538
WIDENER UNIVERSITY, 627
WILD DOG FOUNDATION, THE, 539
WILD ONES NATURAL LANDSCAPERS, LTD, 540
WILDERNESS LAND TRUST, THE, 540
WILDLANDS PROJECT, 542
WILDLIFE ACTION, INC., 542
WILDLIFE DAMAGE REVIEW (WDR), 543
WILDLIFE SOCIETY
  National Capital Chapter, 550
WISCONSIN SOCIETY FOR ORNITHOLOGY, INC., THE, 556
WISCONSIN WILDLIFE FEDERATION, 557
WISCONSIN WOODLAND OWNERS ASSOCIATION, 557
WOMEN'S ENVIRONMENT AND DEVELOPMENT ORGANIZATION
  (WEDO), 557
WORLD FORESTRY CENTER, 558
WORLD RESOURCES INSTITUTE, 559
WORLD WILDLIFE FUND, 559
WORLDWATCH INSTITUTE, 560
WYOMING DEPARTMENT OF AGRICULTURE, 239
WYOMING DEPARTMENT OF ENVIRONMENTAL QUALITY, 239
WYOMING OUTDOOR COUNCIL, 561
YMCA NATURE AND COMMUNITY CENTER, 562

SPRAWL/URBAN PLANNING

AFRICAN AMERICAN ENVIRONMENTALIST ASSOCIATION, 243
ALABAMA DEPARTMENT OF CONSERVATION AND NATURAL
  RESOURCES, 132
ALABAMA ENVIRONMENTAL COUNCIL, 244
ALASKA CENTER FOR THE ENVIRONMENT, 245
AMERICAN FARMLAND TRUST, 251
AMERICAN PLANNING ASSOCIATION, 264
AMERICAN RIVERS
  Voyage of Recovery, 265
AMERICAN SOCIETY OF LANDSCAPE ARCHITECTS, 266
ANACOSTIA WATERSHED SOCIETY, 268
ARIZONA STATE UNIVERSITY
  Center for Environmental Studies, 573
ARIZONA-SONORA DESERT MUSEUM, 271
ARKANSAS WATERSHED ADVISORY GROUP (AWAG), 272
ASSOCIATION OF AMERICAN GEOGRAPHERS, 273
ASSOCIATION OF NEW JERSEY ENVIRONMENTAL COMMISSIONS
  (ANJEC), 274
ATLANTIC CENTER FOR THE ENVIRONMENT
  Quebec-Labrador Foundation, 275
AUDUBON INTERNATIONAL, 276
AUSTRALIA DEPARTMENT FOR ENVIRONMENT AND HERITAGE, 139
BROWN UNIVERSITY, 575
CALIFORNIA DEPARTMENT OF PESTICIDE REGULATION, 143
CALIFORNIA DEPARTMENT OF WATER RESOURCES, 143
CALIFORNIA WILDERNESS COALITION, 284
CALIFORNIA WILDLIFE DEFENDERS, 284
CALIFORNIANS FOR POPULATION STABILIZATION (CAPS), 284
CANADA GOOSE PROJECT, 285
CARIBBEAN NATURAL RESOURCES INSTITUTE, 288
CARRYING CAPACITY NETWORK, 288
CATSKILL CENTER FOR CONSERVATION AND DEVELOPMENT, INC.,
  THE, 289
CENTER FOR ENVIRONMENT AND POPULATION (CEP), 290
CENTER FOR ENVIRONMENT, COMMERCE & ENERGY, 290
CENTER FOR NATIVE ECOSYSTEMS
  Front Range Office, 292
  West Slope Office, 292
CENTER FOR RESOURCE ECONOMICS/ISLAND PRESS, 293
CENTER FOR WATERSHED PROTECTION, 293
CHESAPEAKE BAY FOUNDATION, INC.
  Maryland Office, 295
CHICAGO REGION BIODIVERSITY COUNCIL, 296
CITY OF BELDING, 145
CITY UNIVERSITY OF NEW YORK
  College of Staten Island, 576
CJE ASSOCIATES, 565
CLARK UNIVERSITY, 576
COASTAL AMERICA FOUNDATION, 300
COLORADO DEPARTMENT OF AGRICULTURE, 146
CONNECTICUT BOTANICAL SOCIETY, 304
CONNECTICUT FUND FOR THE ENVIRONMENT, 305
CONSERVATION ALLIANCE OF ST. LUCIE CO., 306
CONSERVATION COUNCIL OF NORTH CAROLINA, 306

CONSERVATION FUND, THE, 307
CONSERVATION LAW FOUNDATION, INC. (CLF), 307
  New England Region, 308
COUNCIL FOR PLANNING AND CONSERVATION, 310
DELAWARE NATURE SOCIETY, 312
DELAWARE RIVERKEEPER NETWORK, 313
EARTH DAY NEW YORK, 316
EARTHSCAN, 320
EASTERN SHORE LAND CONSERVANCY (ESLC), 321
ENTOMOLOGICAL SOCIETY OF AMERICA, 323
ENVIRONMENT COUNCIL OF RHODE ISLAND, 323
ENVIRONMENTAL ALLIANCE FOR SENIOR INVOLVEMENT (EASI), 323
ENVIRONMENTAL DEFENSE
  Headquarters, 324
ENVIRONMENTAL DEFENSE CENTER, 325
ENVIRONMENTAL LAW INSTITUTE, THE, 327
EQUESTRIAN LAND CONSERVATION RESOURCE, 328
FLORIDA COOPERATIVE EXTENSION SERVICE, 582
FLORIDA DEPARTMENT OF ENVIRONMENTAL PROTECTION
  Division of Resource Assessment and Management, 154
FLORIDA NATIVE PLANT SOCIETY, 332
FOOD AND AGRICULTURE ORGANIZATION OF THE UNITED NATIONS, 333
FOOD SUPPLY / HUMAN POPULATION EXPLOSION CONNECTION, 333
FRIENDS OF THE EARTH, 337
FRIENDS OF THE REEDY RIVER, 338
GEORGIA CONSERVANCY, INC., THE, 341
GEORGIA ENVIRONMENTAL ORGANIZATION, INC. (GEO), 341
GOOD NATURE PUBLISHING CO., 566
GRAND CANYON TRUST, 344
GREAT PLAINS NATIVE PLANT SOCIETY, 345
GREEN BALKANS FEDERATION OF NATURE CONSERVATION NGOS, 346
GREEN SPHERE INC., 347
GROWLING, 348
HELPING OUR PENINSULA'S ENVIRONMENT, 350
HOLDEN ARBORETUM, THE, 351
HOLLOW OAK LAND TRUST, 351
HOUSE COMMITTEE ON RULES, 22
HUMANE SOCIETY OF THE UNITED STATES, THE, 352
IDAHO DEPARTMENT OF WATER RESOURCES
  Water Awareness Week, 161
ILLINOIS DEPARTMENT OF TRANSPORTATION, 162
ILLINOIS ENVIRONMENTAL COUNCIL, 355
ILLINOIS NATURE PRESERVES COMMISSION (INPC), 163
ILOVEPARKS.COM, 567
INDIANA STATE DEPARTMENT OF HEALTH, 164
INTERNATIONAL JOINT COMMISSION
  Great Lakes Regional Office, 22
IOWA ASSOCIATION OF NATURALISTS, 372
IOWA PRAIRIE NETWORK, 373
IOWA WOMEN IN NATURAL RESOURCES, 374
ISLAND INSTITUTE, THE, 374
ISLESBORO ISLANDS TRUST, 375
IZAAK WALTON LEAGUE OF AMERICA, INC., THE
  Minnesota Division, 377
  Owatonna Minnesota Chapter, 377
JACKSON HOLE CONSERVATION ALLIANCE, 379
JOHNSON STATE COLLEGE, 585
KANSAS STATE UNIVERSITY
  Department of Landscape Architecture / Regional and Community Planning, 585
KENTUCKY DEPARTMENT OF AGRICULTURE, 169
KENTUCKY DEPARTMENT OF FISH AND WILDLIFE RESOURCES, 169
KIDS ON THE BAYOU, 384
LAKEHEAD UNIVERSITY, 586
LEAGUE TO SAVE LAKE TAHOE, 388
LEGACY LAND TRUST, 388
LOUISIANA DEPARTMENT OF NATURAL RESOURCES, 172
LOWER MERION CONSERVANCY, 391
LUMMI ISLAND HERITAGE TRUST, 568
MACOMB LAND CONSERVANCY, 391
MAINE ASSOCIATION OF CONSERVATION DISTRICTS, 392
MARIE SELBY BOTANICAL GARDENS, THE, 393
MASSACHUSETTS EXECUTIVE OFFICE OF ENVIRONMENTAL AFFAIRS
  Office of Technical Assistance for Toxic Use Reduction, 179
MIAMI UNIVERSITY, 587
MICHIGAN DEPARTMENT OF AGRICULTURE, 180
MICHIGAN UNITED CONSERVATION CLUBS, INC., 398
MINNESOTA LAND TRUST, 400
MISSISSIPPI STATE UNIVERSITY
  Forest and Wildlife Research Center, 588
MONTANA FOREST OWNERS ASSOCIATION, 403

MOUNTAINEERS, THE, 405
MUNDO AZUL, 406
NATIONAL ASSOCIATION OF STATE DEPARTMENTS OF AGRICULTURE, 408
NATIONAL AUDUBON SOCIETY
  Audubon of Florida, 410
  Audubon Society of Portland, 411
  Fairfax Audubon Society, 413
  Louisiana Audubon Council, 414
  Maine Audubon, 414
  Maricopa Audubon Society, 414
  New Jersey Chapter, 415
  San Diego Chapter, 416
  Seattle Audubon Society, 416
  Tucson Audubon Society, 416
NATIONAL CAUCUS OF ENVIRONMENTAL LEGISLATORS (NCEL), 417
NATIONAL ENVIRONMENTAL EDUCATION AND TRAINING FOUNDATION, 418
NATIONAL WILDLIFE FEDERATION
  Headquarters, 427
NATIONAL WILDLIFE PRODUCTIONS, INC., 429
NATIONAL WOODLAND OWNERS ASSOCIATION, 430
NATIVE PLANT SOCIETY OF TEXAS, 431
NATURE CONSERVANCY, THE
  Maryland/District of Columbia Chapter, 436
  Pennsylvania Chapter, 439
  Texas Chapter, 439
NEBRASKA DEPARTMENT OF NATURAL RESOURCES, 188
NEBRASKA WILDLIFE FEDERATION, INC., 442
NEGATIVE POPULATION GROWTH (NPG), 442
NEVADA ASSOCIATION OF CONSERVATION DISTRICTS, 442
NEW HAMPSHIRE ASSOCIATION OF CONSERVATION COMMISSIONS, 443
NEW HAMPSHIRE ASSOCIATION OF CONSERVATION DISTRICTS, 444
NEW HAMPSHIRE COUNCIL ON RESOURCES AND DEVELOPMENT, 190
NEW HAMPSHIRE DEPARTMENT OF AGRICULTURE, MARKETS, AND FOOD
  State Conservation Committee, 190
NEW JERSEY ASSOCIATION OF CONSERVATION DISTRICTS, 445
NEW JERSEY DEPARTMENT OF ENVIRONMENTAL PROTECTION
  Division of Solid and Hazardous Waste, 192
NEW MEXICO ENERGY, MINERALS, AND NATURAL RESOURCES DEPARTMENT
  Oil Conservation Division, 195
NEW YORK STATE TUG HILL COMMISSION, 199
NORTH CAROLINA CONSERVATION NETWORK, 450
NORTHEAST SUSTAINABLE ENERGY ASSOCIATION, 452
NORTHERN ARIZONA UNIVERSITY
  Department of Geography, Planning, and Recreation, 591
NORTHWEST ENVIRONMENT WATCH, 454
NORTHWEST TERRITORIES DEPARTMENT OF RESOURCES, WILDLIFE AND ECONOMIC DEVELOPMENT, 202
OHIO DEPARTMENT OF NATURAL RESOURCES, 204
OHIO ENVIRONMENTAL REVIEW APPEALS COMMISSION, 205
OHIO FEDERATION OF SOIL AND WATER CONSERVATION DISTRICTS, 457
OKLAHOMA NATIVE PLANT SOCIETY, 458
ONTARIO FEDERATION OF ANGLERS AND HUNTERS, 459
ONTARIO FORESTRY ASSOCIATION, 459
OREGON DEPARTMENT OF GEOLOGY AND MINERAL INDUSTRIES, 209
OREGON SOCIETY OF AMERICAN FORESTERS, 461
ORGANIZATION FOR BAT CONSERVATION, 461
OZARKS RESOURCE CENTER, 463
PENNSYLVANIA DEPARTMENT OF ENVIRONMENTAL PROTECTION, 211
PEOPLE FOR PUGET SOUND
  South Sound Office, 467
PIEDMONT ENVIRONMENTAL COUNCIL, 469
PLAYA LAKES JOINT VENTURE, 469
POINT TO POINT COMMUNICATIONS, 569
POPULATION-ENVIRONMENT BALANCE, INC., 471
PS ENTERPRISES, 570
PURPLE MARTIN CONSERVATION ASSOCIATION, 475
RENEWABLE NATURAL RESOURCES FOUNDATION, 478
RESIDENTS FOR A MORE BEAUTIFUL PORT WASHINGTON, 479
RHODE ISLAND STATE CONSERVATION COMMITTEE, 480
RIVER PROJECT, THE, 481
SAND CREEK WATERSHED PROJECT, THE, 215
SANTA CLARA COMMUNITY ACTION PROGRAM, 594
SAVE THE HARBOR/SAVE THE BAY, 486
SAVE THE SOUND, INC., 486

KEYWORD INDEX – T

SAVE WETLANDS AND BAYS, 486
SCENIC AMERICA
  Scenic California, 487
  Scenic Texas, 487
SEACOAST ANTI-POLLUTION LEAGUE, 489
SHEPHERD COLLEGE, 595
SIERRA CLUB
  Alaska Field Office, 490
  Connecticut Chapter, 491
  Hawaii Chapter, 492
  Lone Star Chapter, 493
  Mackinac Chapter, 493
  Maryland Chapter, 493
  Mississippi Chapter, 494
  Nebraska Chapter, 494
  New Jersey Chapter, 495
  Northwest Office, 495
  Pennsylvania Chapter, 496
  Rio Grande Chapter (New Mexico/West Texas), 496
  Tehipite Chapter (Northern California), 498
  Virginia Chapter, 499
  Washington, DC Office, 400
  West Virginia Chapter, 499
SIERRA CLUB CALIFORNIA, 499
SIERRA CLUB FOUNDATION, THE, 499
SIERRA CLUB OF CANADA
  Atlantic Canada Chapter, 500
SILK CITY NATURE ASSOCIATION, 500
SOCIETY OF AMERICAN FORESTERS, 503
SOIL AND WATER CONSERVATION SOCIETY, 504
SONORAN INSTITUTE, 505
SOUTH CAROLINA ENERGY OFFICE, 218
SOUTH CAROLINA NATIVE PLANT SOCIETY, 506
SOUTH DAKOTA COOPERATIVE FISH AND WILDLIFE RESEARCH UNIT (USDI-USGS), 29
SOUTH DAKOTA DEPARTMENT OF GAME, FISH, AND PARKS, 219
SOUTHERN ENVIRONMENTAL LAW CENTER, 509
SOUTHFACE ENERGY INSTITUTE, 510
SOUTHWEST CENTER FOR ENVIRONMENTAL RESEARCH AND POLICY (SCERP), 596
SOUTHWEST RESEARCH AND INFORMATION CENTER, 510
SOUTHWESTERN HERPETOLOGISTS SOCIETY, 510
SPORTSMEN'S NATIONAL LAND TRUST, THE, 511
STATE ENVIRONMENTAL RESOURCE CENTER (SERC), 512
STUDENTS PARTNERSHIP WORLDWIDE, 513
SUSTAIN, 514
SUSTAINABLE ENERGY INSTITUTE
  Culture Change magazine, 514
TALL TIMBERS RESEARCH STATION (TTRS), 515
TEMPLE UNIVERSITY, 599
TERRA PENINSULAR, 516
TEXAS BASS FEDERATION, 517
TEXAS COOPERATIVE FISH AND WILDLIFE RESEARCH UNIT, 30
TEXAS DISCOVERY GARDENS, 517
TEXAS RIPARIAN ASSOCIATION, 517
TREES FOR THE FUTURE, INC., 519
TRIANGLE RAILS-TO-TRAILS CONSERVANCY, 520
TROUT UNLIMITED
  Pennsylvania Council, 522
UNITED STATES CHAMBER OF COMMERCE
  Environment, Technology and Regulatory Affairs, 526
UNITED STATES DEPARTMENT OF COMMERCE
  National Oceanic and Atmospheric Administration
    Delaware National Estuarine Research Reserve, 50
    Sea Grant Program - Massachusetts, 56
    Sea Grant Program - North Carolina, 58
    Sea Grant Program - Texas, 59
    Wells National Estuarine Research Reserve, 60
UNITED STATES DEPARTMENT OF DEFENSE
  Air Force Major Air Commands
    USAF Academy, 62
  Army Materiel Command, 72
  Navy, 74
UNITED STATES DEPARTMENT OF THE INTERIOR
  Fish and Wildlife Service
    San Francisco Bay National Wildlife Refuge Complex, 113
UNITED STATES INSTITUTE FOR ENVIRONMENTAL CONFLICT RESOLUTION, 130
UNIVERSITE LAVAL, 601
UNIVERSITY OF CONNECTICUT COOPERATIVE EXTENSION, 608
UNIVERSITY OF DAR ES SALAAM, 608
UNIVERSITY OF FLORIDA
  School of Forest Resources and Conservation, 609
UNIVERSITY OF FLORIDA INSTITUTE OF FOOD AND AGRICULTURAL SCIENCES, 609
UNIVERSITY OF MARYLAND - AT COLLEGE PARK, 613
UNIVERSITY OF MARYLAND COOPERATIVE EXTENSION, 224
UNIVERSITY OF MICHIGAN, 614
UNIVERSITY OF MINNESOTA AT ST. PAUL, 615
UNIVERSITY OF NORTH CAROLINA AT ASHEVILLE, 617
UNIVERSITY OF RHODE ISLAND
  Department of Natural Resources Science, 619
UNIVERSITY OF THE DISTRICT OF COLUMBIA, 621
UNIVERSITY OF WISCONSIN AT MADISON, 623
URBAN WASTE MANAGEMENT & RESEARCH CENTER, 624
UTAH STATE UNIVERSITY
  College of Natural Resources, 624
VERMONT STATE-WIDE ENVIRONMENTAL EDUCATION PROGRAMS (SWEEP), 530
VERNAL POOL SOCIETY, THE, 530
VINEYARD CONSERVATION SOCIETY, 530
VIRGIN ISLANDS CONSERVATION DISTRICT, 530
VIRGINIA FORESTRY ASSOCIATION, 531
VIRGINIA TECH
  Department of Fisheries and Wildlife Sciences, 625
VIRGINIA TECH UNIVERSITY
  College of Natural Resources, 625
WARREN COUNTY CONSERVATION BOARD, 532
WILDLIFE ACTION, INC., 542
WILDLIFE DAMAGE REVIEW (WDR), 543
WILDLIFE SOCIETY
  Illinois Chapter, 547
  National Capital Chapter, 550
WISCONSIN COOPERATIVE FISHERY RESEARCH UNIT USGS, 237
WISCONSIN STATE EXTENSION SERVICES, 238
WORLDWATCH INSTITUTE, 560
YOSEMITE RESTORATION TRUST, 562

TRANSPORTATION

ADIRONDACK MOUNTAIN CLUB, INC., THE (ADK), 242
AFRICAN AMERICAN ENVIRONMENTALIST ASSOCIATION, 243
ALASKA CONSERVATION FOUNDATION, 246
AMERICAN COUNCIL FOR AN ENERGY-EFFICIENT ECONOMY, 251
AMERICAN PLANNING ASSOCIATION, 264
AMERICAN RIVERS
  Voyage of Recovery, 265
ARIZONA STATE UNIVERSITY
  Center for Environmental Studies, 573
ASSOCIATION OF AMERICAN GEOGRAPHERS, 273
ATLANTIC CENTER FOR THE ENVIRONMENT
  Quebec-Labrador Foundation, 275
CALIFORNIA DEPARTMENT OF FISH AND GAME
  Office of Spill Prevention and Response, 141
CALIFORNIA DEPARTMENT OF PESTICIDE REGULATION, 143
CALIFORNIA STATE LANDS COMMISSION, 145
CENTER FOR ENVIRONMENT AND POPULATION (CEP), 290
CENTER FOR ENVIRONMENT, COMMERCE & ENERGY, 290
CENTER FOR RESOURCE ECONOMICS/ISLAND PRESS, 293
CHESAPEAKE BAY FOUNDATION, INC.
  Maryland Office, 295
  Pennsylvania Office, 295
CITY OF BELDING, 145
CJE ASSOCIATES, 565
CLEMSON UNIVERSITY EXTENSION SERVICE, 145
COASTAL AMERICA FOUNDATION, 300
COLUMBIA RIVER INTER-TRIBAL FISH COMMISSION, 17
CONNECTICUT BOTANICAL SOCIETY, 304
CONNECTICUT FUND FOR THE ENVIRONMENT, 305
CONSERVATION COUNCIL OF NORTH CAROLINA, 306
CONSERVATION LAW FOUNDATION, INC. (CLF), 307
  New England Region, 308
COOSA RIVER BASIN INITIATIVE, 309
COTTONWOOD FOUNDATION, 309
COUNCIL FOR PLANNING AND CONSERVATION, 310
DELAWARE DEPARTMENT OF NATURAL RESOURCES AND ENVIRONMENTAL CONTROL
  Division of Parks and Recreation, 150
DELAWARE GREENWAYS, INC., 312
DISTRICT OF COLUMBIA DEPARTMENT OF HEALTH
  Environmental Health Administration, Watershed Protection Division, 152
EARTH POLICY INSTITUTE, 317
EARTHJUSTICE
  Headquarters, 318
  Oakland Office, 319
EARTHSCAN, 320

ENVIRONMENT COUNCIL OF RHODE ISLAND, 323
ENVIRONMENTAL AND ENERGY STUDY INSTITUTE (EESI), 323
ENVIRONMENTAL DEFENSE
   Headquarters, 324
ENVIRONMENTAL DEFENSE CENTER, 325
ENVIRONMENTAL POLICY CENTER, THE, 327
FLORIDA NATURAL AREAS INVENTORY, 332
FLORIDA TRAIL ASSOCIATION, INC., 333
FOOD SUPPLY / HUMAN POPULATION EXPLOSION CONNECTION, 333
FRIENDS OF ACADIA, 336
FRIENDS OF THE EARTH, 337
FRIENDS OF THE REEDY RIVER, 338
GEORGIA CONSERVANCY, INC., THE, 341
GEORGIA FORESTRY ASSOCIATION, INC., 342
GOOD NATURE PUBLISHING CO., 566
GREAT PLAINS NATIVE PLANT SOCIETY, 345
GREEN SPHERE INC., 347
GROWLING, 348
GULF STATES MARINE FISHERIES COMMISSION, 20
HELPING OUR PENINSULA'S ENVIRONMENT, 350
HOUSE COMMITTEE ON RULES, 22
ILLINOIS DEPARTMENT OF AGRICULTURE, 162
ILLINOIS ENVIRONMENTAL COUNCIL, 355
ILLINOIS PRAIRIE PATH, 355
INFORM, INC., 357
INTERNATIONAL ASSOCIATION OF NATURAL RESOURCE PILOTS, 360
INTERNATIONAL BICYCLE FUND, 361
INTERNATIONAL INSTITUTE FOR ENERGY CONSERVATION, 364
INTERNATIONAL MARITIME ORGANIZATION, 364
IOWA WILDLIFE FEDERATION, 374
IZAAK WALTON LEAGUE OF AMERICA, INC., THE
   Minnesota Division, 377
J.N. (DING) DARLING FOUNDATION, 379
JACKSON HOLE CONSERVATION ALLIANCE, 379
JAGRATA JUBA SHANGHA (JJS), 568
KANSAS STATE UNIVERSITY
   Department of Landscape Architecture / Regional and Community Planning, 585
LEAGUE TO SAVE LAKE TAHOE, 388
LIFE OF THE LAND, 389
LOUISIANA DEPARTMENT OF NATURAL RESOURCES, 172
LUMMI ISLAND HERITAGE TRUST, 568
MARYLAND DEPARTMENT OF NATURAL RESOURCES, 177
MINNESOTA ASSOCIATION OF SOIL AND WATER CONSERVATION DISTRICTS, 399
MONTANA FOREST OWNERS ASSOCIATION, 403
MONTANA LAND RELIANCE, 403
NATIONAL 4-H COUNCIL, 406
NATIONAL ASSOCIATION OF SERVICE AND CONSERVATION CORPS (NASCC), 408
NATIONAL AUDUBON SOCIETY
   Louisiana Audubon Council, 414
   Maine Audubon, 414
   San Diego Chapter, 416
NATIONAL CAUCUS OF ENVIRONMENTAL LEGISLATORS (NCEL), 417
NATIONAL GRANGE, THE, 421
NATIONAL PARKS CONSERVATION ASSOCIATION (NPCA), 422
NATIONAL WATERWAYS CONFERENCE INC., 426
NATIONAL WILDLIFE PRODUCTIONS, INC., 429
NATURE CONSERVANCY, THE
   Texas Chapter, 439
NEW HAMPSHIRE COUNCIL ON RESOURCES AND DEVELOPMENT, 190
NEW JERSEY FORESTRY ASSOCIATION, 445
NEW YORK PUBLIC INTEREST RESEARCH GROUP (NYPIRG), 446
NOLTE ASSOCIATES, INC., 569
NORTH CAROLINA CONSERVATION NETWORK, 450
NORTHEAST SUSTAINABLE ENERGY ASSOCIATION, 452
NORTHWEST ENVIRONMENT WATCH, 454
ONTARIO FEDERATION OF ANGLERS AND HUNTERS, 459
OREGON DEPARTMENT OF GEOLOGY AND MINERAL INDUSTRIES, 209
OREGON ENVIRONMENTAL COUNCIL, 460
OREGON NATURAL RESOURCES COUNCIL, 460
PACIFIC NORTHWEST TRAIL ASSOCIATION, 464
PIEDMONT ENVIRONMENTAL COUNCIL, 469
POCONO ENVIRONMENTAL EDUCATION CENTER, 470
POPULATION-ENVIRONMENT BALANCE, INC., 471
PREDATOR CONSERVATION ALLIANCE, 472
PRIORITIES INSTITUTE, THE, 473
RENEWABLE NATURAL RESOURCES FOUNDATION, 478
RESIDENTS FOR A MORE BEAUTIFUL PORT WASHINGTON, 479
RESOURCES FOR THE FUTURE, 479

RHODE ISLAND COOPERATIVE EXTENSION SERVICE, 214
SAN DIEGUITO RIVER PARK JOINT POWERS AUTHORITY, 215
SANTA CLARA COMMUNITY ACTION PROGRAM, 594
SAVE THE SOUND, INC., 486
SCENIC AMERICA
   Scenic Texas, 487
SEAPLANE PILOTS ASSOCIATION, 489
SIERRA CLUB
   Alaska Field Office, 490
   Connecticut Chapter, 491
   Hawaii Chapter, 492
   Lone Star Chapter, 493
   Maryland Chapter, 493
   Mississippi Chapter, 494
   Nebraska Chapter, 494
   New Jersey Chapter, 495
   Northwest Office, 495
   Pennsylvania Chapter, 496
   Rio Grande Chapter (New Mexico/West Texas), 496
   West Virginia Chapter, 499
SIERRA CLUB CALIFORNIA, 499
SIERRA CLUB FOUNDATION, THE, 499
SOUTH CAROLINA BASS FEDERATION, 506
SOUTHERN ENVIRONMENTAL LAW CENTER, 509
SOUTHERN UTAH WILDERNESS ALLIANCE
   Moab Office, 510
SOUTHFACE ENERGY INSTITUTE, 510
SOUTHWEST CENTER FOR ENVIRONMENTAL RESEARCH AND POLICY (SCERP), 596
SOUTHWESTERN HERPETOLOGISTS SOCIETY, 510
STATE ENVIRONMENTAL RESOURCE CENTER (SERC), 512
SUSTAIN, 514
SUSTAINABLE ENERGY INSTITUTE
   Culture Change, 514
   Culture Change magazine, 514
   Food Not Lawns, 514
   Pedal Power Produce, 514
TAHOE REGIONAL PLANNING AGENCY, 220
TALLAHASSEE MUSEUM OF HISTORY AND NATURAL SCIENCE, 515
TANZANIA COASTAL MANAGEMENT PARTNERSHIP, 30
TEXAS BASS FEDERATION, 517
TRIANGLE RAILS-TO-TRAILS CONSERVANCY, 520
UNION OF CONCERNED SCIENTISTS, 525
UNITED STATES DEPARTMENT OF COMMERCE
   National Oceanic and Atmospheric Administration
      Sea Grant Program - Massachusetts, 56
UNITED STATES DEPARTMENT OF DEFENSE
   Army Corps of Engineers
      North Atlantic Engineer District, 70
      Pacific Ocean Engineer District, 70
      Philadelphia District, 70
   Assistant Chief of Staff for Installation Management, Office of the Director of Environmental Programs, and Conservation Team, 74
UNITED STATES DEPARTMENT OF THE INTERIOR
   Bureau of Land Management
      Malta Field Office, 83
      Northern Field Office, 84
      Safford Field Office, 86
   National Park Service
      Grand Teton National Park, 122
      Yellowstone National Park, 126
   United States Geological Survey
      New Mexico Cooperative Fish and Wildlife Research Unit, 127
UNITED STATES DEPARTMENT OF TRANSPORTATION
   Federal Aviation Administration, 128
   Federal Railroad Administration, 129
UNITED STATES ENVIRONMENTAL PROTECTION AGENCY
   Administration and Resources Management, 129
UNITED STATES INSTITUTE FOR ENVIRONMENTAL CONFLICT RESOLUTION, 130
UNIVERSITY OF MICHIGAN, 614
UNIVERSITY OF WISCONSIN-MADISON, 623
URBAN HABITAT PROGRAM, 527
VANDERBILT CENTER FOR ENVIRONMENTAL MANAGEMENT (VCEMS), 625
VERMONT STATE-WIDE ENVIRONMENTAL EDUCATION PROGRAMS (SWEEP), 530
VINEYARD CONSERVATION SOCIETY, 530
VIRGINIA FORESTRY ASSOCIATION, 531
VIRGINIA TECH UNIVERSITY
   College of Natural Resources, 625
WASHINGTON TRAILS ASSOCIATION, 534
WILDLIFE ACTION, INC., 542

KEYWORD INDEX – W

WILDLIFE SOCIETY
  Michigan Chapter, 549
  New York Chapter, 551
WISCONSIN COOPERATIVE FISHERY RESEARCH UNIT USGS, 237
WORLD RESOURCES INSTITUTE, 559
WORLDWATCH INSTITUTE, 560
YOSEMITE RESTORATION TRUST, 562

WATER HABITATS & QUALITY

20/20 VISION, 241
A.E. HOWELL WILDLIFE CONSERVATION CENTER INC., 241
ACADEMY FOR EDUCATIONAL DEVELOPMENT, 241
ACRES LAND TRUST, 241
ADKINS ARBORETUM, 242
ADOPT-A-STREAM FOUNDATION, THE, 242
ADVOCATES OF THE COMMON WEALTH, INC., 243
AFRICA VISION TRUST, 243
AFRICAN AMERICAN ENVIRONMENTALIST ASSOCIATION, 243
AFRICAN CONSERVATION FOUNDATION, THE, 243
ALABAMA COOPERATIVE FISH AND WILDLIFE RESEARCH UNIT (USDI), 132
ALABAMA DEPARTMENT OF AGRICULTURE AND INDUSTRIES, 132
ALABAMA DEPARTMENT OF CONSERVATION AND NATURAL RESOURCES, 132
ALABAMA WATERFOWL ASSOCIATION, INC. (AWA), 245
ALASKA CONSERVATION ALLIANCE, 245, 246
ALASKA CONSERVATION FOUNDATION, 246
ALASKA COOPERATIVE FISH AND WILDLIFE RESEARCH UNIT, 133
ALASKA DEPARTMENT OF ENVIRONMENTAL CONSERVATION, 133
ALASKA NATURAL HISTORY ASSOCIATION, 246
ALBERTA DEPARTMENT OF ENVIRONMENTAL PROTECTION
  Natural Resources Service, 135
ALBERTA WILDERNESS ASSOCIATION, 247
ALDO LEOPOLD FOUNDATION, 247
ALLIANCE FOR THE CHESAPEAKE BAY, 247
AMERICAN AQUATICS, INC, 563
AMERICAN CETACEAN SOCIETY, 250
AMERICAN COUNCIL FOR THE UNITED NATIONS UNIVERSITY (ACUNU), 251
AMERICAN FARMLAND TRUST, 251
AMERICAN FISHERIES SOCIETY
  Minnesota Chapter, 256
AMERICAN GROUND WATER TRUST, 261
AMERICAN INSTITUTE OF FISHERY RESEARCH BIOLOGISTS, 262
AMERICAN LANDS, 262
AMERICAN LITTORAL SOCIETY, 262
  Northeast Region, 262
AMERICAN RIVERS
  Nebraska Field Office, 265
  Northwest Regional Office, 265
  Voyage of Recovery, 265
AMERICAN SOCIETY OF ICHTHYOLOGISTS AND HERPETOLOGISTS, 265
AMERICAN SOCIETY OF LIMNOLOGY AND OCEANOGRAPHY, 266
AMERICAN SPORTFISHING ASSOCIATION, 266
AMERICAN WATER RESOURCES ASSOCIATION, 267
AMERICAN WATER WORKS ASSOCIATION (AWWA), 267
AMERICAN WHITEWATER, 267
ANACOSTIA WATERSHED SOCIETY, 268
ANGLERS FOR CLEAN WATER, 268
APPALACHIAN MOUNTAIN CLUB, 269
APPALACHIAN REGIONAL COMMISSION, 16
ARIZONA COOPERATIVE FISH AND WILDLIFE RESEARCH UNIT (USDI), 135
ARIZONA STATE ENVIROTHON, INC., 271
ARIZONA STATE PARKS BOARD, 137
ARIZONA STATE UNIVERSITY
  Center for Environmental Studies, 573
ARIZONA-SONORA DESERT MUSEUM, 271
ARKANSAS COOPERATIVE RESEARCH UNIT, 137
ARKANSAS ENVIRONMENTAL EDUCATION ASSOCIATION, 272
ARKANSAS TECH UNIVERSITY
  Fisheries and Wildlife Biology Program, 573
ARKANSAS WATERSHED ADVISORY GROUP (AWAG), 272
ARLINGTON OUTDOOR EDUCATION ASSOCIATION, INC. (AOEA), 272
ASSOCIATION FOR THE PROTECTION OF THE ADIRONDACKS, THE, 273
ASSOCIATION OF AMERICAN GEOGRAPHERS, 273
ASSOCIATION OF NEW JERSEY ENVIRONMENTAL COMMISSIONS (ANJEC), 274
ATLANTIC CENTER FOR THE ENVIRONMENT
  Quebec-Labrador Foundation, 275
ATLANTIC SALMON FEDERATION, 275
ATLANTIC STATES LEGAL FOUNDATION, 275
AUDUBON INTERNATIONAL, 276
AUDUBON NATURALIST SOCIETY OF THE CENTRAL ATLANTIC STATES, 276
AUSTRALIAN MINERAL FOUNDATION, 563
AUSTRIALIA DEPARTMENT FOR ENVIRONMENT AND HERITAGE
  Environment Shop, The, 139
BASS DIVISION OF ESPN PRODUCTIONS INC, 564
BIODIVERSITY CONSERVATION ALLIANCE, 278
BORDER ECOLOGY PROJECT (BEP), 279
BRANDYWINE CONSERVANCY INC., 280
BRITISH COLUMBIA MINISTRY OF WATER, LAND AND AIR PROTECTION, 140
BROWN UNIVERSITY, 575
BUILDINGGREEN, INC., 564
BUSINESS PUBLISHERS, INC., 564
CADDO LAKE INSTITUTE, INC., 282
CALIFORNIA CONSERVATION CORPS, 140
CALIFORNIA DEPARTMENT OF FISH AND GAME
  Elkhorn Slough National Estuarine Research Reserve, 141
  Office of Spill Prevention and Response, 141
CALIFORNIA ENERGY COMMISSION
  Environmental Department, 143
CALIFORNIA ENVIRONMENTAL PROTECTION AGENCY
  State Water Resources Control Board, 144
CALIFORNIA NATIVE PLANT SOCIETY, THE, 283
CALIFORNIA STATE LANDS COMMISSION, 145
CALIFORNIA TRAPPERS ASSOCIATION, 283
CALIFORNIA TROUT, INC., 283
CALIFORNIA WATERFOWL ASSOCIATION, 283
CALIFORNIA WILD HERITAGE CAMPAIGN, 284
CAMPAIGN FOR AMERICA'S WILDERNESS, 285
CANADA GOOSE PROJECT, 285
CANON ENVIROTHON, 288
CANVASBACK SOCIETY, 288
CARIBBEAN NATURAL RESOURCES INSTITUTE, 288
CATSKILL FOREST ASSOCIATION, 289
CENTER FOR A SUSTAINABLE COAST, 289
CENTER FOR CHESAPEAKE COMMUNITIES, 290
CENTER FOR ENVIRONMENT AND POPULATION (CEP), 290
CENTER FOR ENVIRONMENT, COMMERCE & ENERGY, 290
CENTER FOR ENVIRONMENTAL STUDY, 291
CENTER FOR HEALTH, ENVIRONMENT, AND JUSTICE, 291
CENTER FOR RESOURCE ECONOMICS/ISLAND PRESS, 293
CENTER FOR THE STUDY OF TROPICAL BIRDS, INC.
  Administrative Office, 293
CHESAPEAKE BAY FOUNDATION, INC., 295
  Maryland Office, 295
  Virginia Office, 295
CHESAPEAKE WILDLIFE HERITAGE (CWH), 295
CHICAGO PARK DISTRICT, 296
CHICAGO REGION BIODIVERSITY COUNCIL, 296
CHINA REGION LAKES ALLIANCE, 296
CHLORINE-FREE PAPER CONSORTIUM, 297
CHRISTINA CONSERVANCY, INC., 297
CINCINNATI NATURE CENTER, 297
CITY OF BELDING, 145
CITY UNIVERSITY OF NEW YORK
  College of Staten Island, 576
CJE ASSOCIATES, 565
CLARK UNIVERSITY, 576
CLEAN WATER NETWORK, THE, 298
CLEMSON UNIVERSITY
  School of the Environment, 577
CLINTON RIVER WATERSHED COUNCIL (CRWC), 299
COAST ALLIANCE, 300
COASTAL AMERICA FOUNDATION, 300
COASTAL CONSERVATION AND EDUCATION FOUNDATION, INC., 565
COASTAL GEORGIA LAND TRUST INC., 300
COASTAL RESOURCE MANAGEMENT PROJECT, 146
COASTAL SOCIETY, THE, 301
COLORADO DEPARTMENT OF NATURAL RESOURCES, 146
  Oil and Gas Conservation Commission, 147
COLORADO MOUNTAIN COLLEGE, 577
COLORADO STATE UNIVERSITY
  Department of Fishery and Wildlife Biology, 578
COLORADO WILDLIFE HERITAGE FOUNDATION, 302
COLUMBIA RIVER INTER-TRIBAL FISH COMMISSION, 17
CONNECTICUT BOTANICAL SOCIETY, 304
CONNECTICUT FUND FOR THE ENVIRONMENT, 305
CONNECTICUT PUBLIC INTEREST RESEARCH GROUP (CONN PIRG), 305

CONNECTICUT RIVER WATERSHED COUNCIL INC., 305
CONNECTICUT WATERFOWL ASSOCIATION, INC., 305
CONSERVAMERICA, 305
CONSERVATION ALLIANCE OF ST. LUCIE CO., 306
CONSERVATION COUNCIL OF NORTH CAROLINA, 306
CONSERVATION FUND, THE, 307
CONSERVATION LAW FOUNDATION, INC. (CLF), 307
   New England Region, 308
CONSERVATION TECHNOLOGY INFORMATION CENTER, 308
COTTONWOOD FOUNDATION, 309
COUNCIL FOR PLANNING AND CONSERVATION, 310
CRAIGHEAD ENVIRONMENTAL RESEARCH INSTITUTE, 310
CRANSTON CONSERVATION COMMISSION, 150
DEFENDERS OF WILDLIFE, 311
DELAWARE ASSOCIATION OF CONSERVATION DISTRICTS, 312
DELAWARE DEPARTMENT OF NATURAL RESOURCES AND ENVIRONMENTAL CONTROL
   Division of Air & Waste Management, 150
DELAWARE NATURE SOCIETY, 312
DELAWARE RIVERKEEPER NETWORK, 313
DELAWARE WILD LANDS, INC., 313
DELTA WATERFOWL FOUNDATION, 313
DELTA WILDLIFE INC., 313
DEPAUL UNIVERSITY
   Environmental Science Program, 579
DESCHUTES BASIN LAND TRUST, 313
DESERT FISHES COUNCIL, 314
DESERT RESEARCH FOUNDATION OF NAMIBIA, THE, 314
DISTRICT OF COLUMBIA DEPARTMENT OF HEALTH
   Environmental Health Administration, Watershed Protection Division, 152
DRAGONFLY SOCIETY OF THE AMERICAS, THE, 314
DUCKS UNLIMITED CANADA
   Nova Scotia Office, 315
   Saskatchewan Office, 315
DUCKS UNLIMITED, INC., 315
EAGLE NATURE FOUNDATION, LTD., 316
EARTH FORCE, 316
   GREEN (Global Rivers Environmental Education Network)), 317
EARTHJUSTICE
   Environmental Law Clinic at the University of Denver, 318
   Headquarters, 318
   Tallahassee Office, 320
   Washington, DC, Office, 320
EARTHWATCH INSTITUTE, 321
ECOLOGICAL SOCIETY OF AMERICA, THE, 321
ECONOVA INC., 565
ENVIRONMENT AND ENERGY PUBLISHING, LLC, 566
ENVIRONMENT COUNCIL OF RHODE ISLAND, 323
ENVIRONMENTAL ALLIANCE FOR SENIOR INVOLVEMENT (EASI), 323
ENVIRONMENTAL CONCERN INC., 324
ENVIRONMENTAL DEFENSE
   Headquarters, 324
ENVIRONMENTAL DEFENSE CENTER, 325
ENVIRONMENTAL EDUCATION ASSOCIATES, 325
ENVIRONMENTAL EDUCATION ASSOCIATION OF ILLINOIS, 325
ENVIRONMENTAL EDUCATORS OF NORTH CAROLINA (EENC), 326
ENVIRONMENTAL LAW INSTITUTE, THE, 327
ENVIRONMENTAL LEAGUE OF MASSACHUSETTS, 327
ENVIRONMENTAL MEDIA CORPORATION, 566
ENVIRONMENTAL POLICY CENTER, THE, 327
ENVIRONMENTAL PROTECTION AGENCY
   Region 1 (CT, ME, MA, NH, RI, VT), 18
   Region 5 (IL, IN, MI, NM, OH, WI), 19
ENVIRONMENTAL PROTECTION ASSOCIATION OF GHANA, 327
ENVIRONMENTAL RESOURCE CENTER (ERC), 328
EUROPARC FEDERATION, 328
EUROPEAN ASSOCIATION FOR AQUATIC MAMMALS, 328
EVERGLADES COORDINATING COUNCIL (ECC), 329
FEDERATION OF FLY FISHERS, 329
FEDERATION OF FLY FISHERS (NCCFFF), 329
FERRUM COLLEGE, 581
FISHAMERICA FOUNDATION, 330
FLINTSTEEL RESTORATION ASSOCIATION, INC., 330
FLORIDA COOPERATIVE EXTENSION SERVICE, 582
FLORIDA DEFENDERS OF THE ENVIRONMENT, INC., 331
FLORIDA DEPARTMENT OF AGRICULTURE AND CONSUMER SERVICES
   Soil and Water Conservation Council, 153
FLORIDA DEPARTMENT OF ENVIRONMENTAL PROTECTION
   Coastal and Aquatic Managed Areas, 153
   Division of Water Resource Management, 154
   Florida State Parks AmeriCorps, 154
   Waste Management Division, 154

FLORIDA EXOTIC PEST PLANT COUNCIL, 331
FLORIDA FEDERATION OF GARDEN CLUBS, INC., 331
FLORIDA FISH AND WILDLIFE CONSERVATION COMMISSION, 154
FOOD SUPPLY / HUMAN POPULATION EXPLOSION CONNECTION, 333
FOREST FIRE LOOKOUT ASSOCIATION, 334
FOREST SOCIETY OF MAINE, 335
FORESTRY COMMISSION (SOUTH CAROLINA), 155
FRIENDS OF DISCOVERY PARK, 337
FRIENDS OF FAMOSA SLOUGH, 337
FRIENDS OF SUNKHAZE MEADOWS NATIONAL WILDLIFE REFUGE, 337
FRIENDS OF THE BOUNDARY WATERS WILDERNESS, 337
FRIENDS OF THE EARTH, 337
FRIENDS OF THE SEA OTTER, 338
FUTURE FISHERMAN FOUNDATION, 339
GALIANO CONSERVANCY ASSOCIATION, 339
GAME CONSERVANCY U.S.A., 339
GEORGIA CONSERVANCY, INC., THE, 341
GEORGIA DEPARTMENT OF NATURAL RESOURCES
   Environmental Protection Division
      Coastal Division, 156
GEORGIA ENVIRONMENTAL ORGANIZATION, INC. (GEO), 341
GEORGIA STATE EXTENSION SERVICE, 157
GEORGIA TRUST FOR HISTORIC PRESERVATION, 342
GLACIER INSTITUTE, THE, 343
GLEN CANYON INSTITUTE, 343
GRAND CANYON TRUST, 344
GRANT TECH CONSULTING AND CONSERVATION SERVICES, 567
GREAT LAKES SPORT FISHING COUNCIL, 344
GREAT LAKES UNITED
   CANADA OFFICE, 345
GREATER YELLOWSTONE COALITION, 346
GREEN BALKANS FEDERATION OF NATURE CONSERVATION NGOS, 346
GREEN GUIDES, 346
GREEN SPHERE INC., 347
GROUNDWATER FOUNDATION, THE, 347
GROWLING, 348
GULF COAST ENVIRONMENTAL DEFENSE, 348
GULF STATES MARINE FISHERIES COMMISSION, 20
HAMLINE UNIVERSITY, 583
HARBOR BRANCH OCEANOGRAPHIC INSTITUTION, 348
HAWAII DEPARTMENT OF HEALTH
   Office of Environmental Quality Control, 159
HAWAII DEPARTMENT OF LAND AND NATURAL RESOURCES
   Division of Boating and Ocean Recreation, 159
   Division of Water Resource Management, 159
HAWAII NATURE CENTER, 349
HEADLANDS INSTITUTE, 350
HELPING OUR PENINSULA'S ENVIRONMENT, 350
HENRY STIFEL SCHRADER ENVIRONMENTAL EDUCATION CENTER, 350
HOLDEN ARBORETUM, THE, 351
HOLLOW OAK LAND TRUST, 351
HOOSIER ENVIRONMENTAL COUNCIL, 352
HOUSE COMMITTEE ON RULES, 22
HUDSONIA LIMITED, 352
HUMANE SOCIETY OF THE UNITED STATES, THE, 352
HUMBOLT FIELD RESEARCH INSTITUTE, 353
HUMMINGBIRD SOCIETY, THE, 353
HUNTSMAN MARINE SCIENCE CENTRE, 353
HYDE CREEK WATERSHED SOCIETY, 353
IDAHO CONSERVATION LEAGUE, 354
IDAHO DEPARTMENT OF PARKS AND RECREATION, 160
IDAHO DEPARTMENT OF WATER RESOURCES, 161
   Water Awareness Week, 161
IDAHO FISH AND WILDLIFE FOUNDATION, 161
ILLINOIS DEPARTMENT OF TRANSPORTATION, 162
ILLINOIS ENVIRONMENTAL COUNCIL, 355
ILLINOIS NATIVE PLANT SOCIETY, 355
ILLINOIS NATURE PRESERVES COMMISSION (INPC), 163
ILLINOIS WALNUT COUNCIL, 356
ILOVEPARKS.COM, 567
INITIATIVE FOR SOCIAL ACTION AND RENEWAL IN EURASIA, 357
INSTITUTE FOR TROPICAL ECOLOGY AND CONSERVATION (ITEC), 358
INSTITUTO NACIONAL DE BIODIVERSIDAD (INBIO), 22
INTERNATIONAL ACADEMY, 567
INTERNATIONAL ASSOCIATION OF FISH AND WILDLIFE AGENCIES, 360
INTERNATIONAL ASSOCIATION OF NATURAL RESOURCE PILOTS, 360
INTERNATIONAL BOUNDARY AND WATER COMMISSION, UNITED STATES AND MEXICO, 22
INTERNATIONAL CHILDREN'S CONFERENCE ON THE ENVIRONMENT, 362
INTERNATIONAL CRANE FOUNDATION, 362

KEYWORD INDEX – W

INTERNATIONAL EROSION CONTROL ASSOCIATION (IECA), 363
INTERNATIONAL JOINT COMMISSION
   Great Lakes Regional Office, 22
INTERNATIONAL MARINE MAMMAL PROJECT, THE, 364
INTERNATIONAL MARITIME ORGANIZATION, 364
INTERNATIONAL RIVERS NETWORK (IRN), 366
INTERNATIONAL UNION FOR CONSERVATION OF NATURE AND
   NATURAL RESOURCES (IUCN) THE WORLD CONSERVATION UNION
   Canada Office, 368
IOWA ASSOCIATION OF COUNTY CONSERVATION BOARDS, 164
IOWA ASSOCIATION OF NATURALISTS, 372
IOWA DEPARTMENT OF AGRICULTURE AND LAND STEWARDSHIP
   Bureau of Financial Incentive Program, 165
IOWA DEPARTMENT OF NATURAL RESOURCES
   Fish and Wildlife Division, 166
IOWA ENVIRONMENTAL COUNCIL, 372
IOWA NATIVE PLANT SOCIETY, 373
IOWA PRAIRIE NETWORK, 373
IOWA STATE EXTENSION SERVICES
   Extension Wildlife Programs, 166
IOWA STATE UNIVERSITY
   College of Agriculture, 584
ISLAND INSTITUTE, THE, 374
ISLAND RESOURCES FOUNDATION, 375
ISLESBORO ISLANDS TRUST, 375
IZAAK WALTON LEAGUE OF AMERICA, INC., THE, 375
   Alaska Division, 376
   California State IWLA, 376
   Minnesota Division, 377
   Owatonna Minnesota Chapter, 377
   South Dakota Division, 378
   Wyoming Division, 378
J.N. (DING) DARLING FOUNDATION, 379
JACKSON HOLE CONSERVATION ALLIANCE, 379
JOHN INSKEEP ENVIRONMENTAL LEARNING CENTER, 380
JOHNSON STATE COLLEGE, 585
KANSAS BIOLOGICAL SURVEY, 166
KANSAS COOPERATIVE FISH AND WILDLIFE RESEARCH UNIT, 167
KANSAS DEPARTMENT OF AGRICULTURE, 167
KANSAS DEPARTMENT OF WILDLIFE AND PARKS
   Office of the Secretary, 167
   Operations Office, 167
   Region 1, 167
   Region 2, 168
   Region 4, 168
   Region 5, 168
KANSAS FOREST SERVICE, 168
KANSAS GEOLOGICAL SURVEY, 168
KANSAS ORNITHOLOGICAL SOCIETY, 381
KANSAS STATE CONSERVATION COMMISSION, 168
KANSAS STATE EXTENSION SERVICES, 169
KANSAS STATE UNIVERSITY
   Department of Landscape Architecture / Regional and Community
   Planning, 585
KANSAS WATER OFFICE, 169
KEEP FLORIDA BEAUTIFUL, INC., 382
KENTUCKY ACADEMY OF SCIENCE, 382
KENTUCKY DEPARTMENT OF AGRICULTURE, 169
KENTUCKY NATURAL RESOURCES AND ENVIRONMENTAL
   PROTECTION CABINET, 170
KENTUCKY STATE NATURE PRESERVES COMMISSION, 171
KENTUCKY WOODLAND OWNERS ASSOCIATION, 383
KIDS FOR SAVING EARTH WORLDWIDE, 384
KIDS ON THE BAYOU, 384
LA JOLLA FRIENDS OF THE SEALS (LJFS), 384
LAKE ERIE CLEAN-UP COMMITTEE, INC., 385
LAKE MICHIGAN FEDERATION, 385
LAKE SUPERIOR GREENS, 385
LAKE SUPERIOR STATE UNIVERSITY, 586
LAKEHEAD UNIVERSITY, 586
LAKENET, 385
LAND BETWEEN THE LAKES ASSOCIATION, 386
LAND CONSERVANCY OF WEST MICHIGAN, 386
LEAGUE OF ENVIRONMENTAL JOURNALISTS, 387
LEAGUE OF OHIO SPORTSMEN, 387
LEAGUE OF WOMEN VOTERS OF WASHINGTON, 388
LEAGUE TO SAVE LAKE TAHOE, 388
LEE COUNTY PARKS AND RECREATION, 171
LEGAL ENVIRONMENTAL ASSISTANCE FOUNDATION INC. (LEAF), 388
LIFE OF THE LAND, 389
LIGHTHAWK, 389
LITERACY FOR ENVIRONMENTAL JUSTICE, 389
LIVING RIVERS, 390

LOUISIANA BASS FEDERATION, 390
LOUISIANA DEPARTMENT OF AGRICULTURE AND FORESTRY, 172
LOUISIANA OFFICE OF STATE PARKS, DEPARTMENT OF CULTURE,
   RECREATION, AND TOURISM, 173
LOUISIANA STATE UNIVERSITY SCHOOL OF FORESTRY, WILDLIFE
   AND FISHERIES, 586
LOWER MERION CONSERVANCY, 391
LOWER MISSISSIPPI RIVER CONSERVATION COMMITTEE, 391
LUMMI ISLAND HERITAGE TRUST, 568
LVIV REGIONAL INSTITUTE OF EDUCATION, 391
MACBRIDE RAPTOR PROJECT, 391
MACOMB LAND CONSERVANCY, 391
MAINE ASSOCIATION OF CONSERVATION DISTRICTS, 392
MAINE ATLANTIC SALMON COMMISSION, 173
MAINE DEPARTMENT OF CONSERVATION
   Land Use Regulation Commission, 175
MAINE DEPARTMENT OF ENVIRONMENTAL PROTECTION, 175
MAINE DEPARTMENT OF INLAND FISHERIES AND WILDLIFE, 175
MAINE DEPARTMENT OF MARINE RESOURCES, 175
MANITOBA CONSERVATION
   Western Region, 176
MARINE SCIENCE INSTITUTE, 394
MARYLAND DEPARTMENT OF AGRICULTURE, 176
MARYLAND DEPARTMENT OF NATURAL RESOURCES, 177
MASSACHUSETTS ASSOCIATION OF CONSERVATION DISTRICTS, 396
MASSACHUSETTS DIVISION OF FISHERIES AND WILDLIFE
   MassWildlife, 178
MASSACHUSETTS EXECUTIVE OFFICE OF ENVIRONMENTAL
   AFFAIRS, 178
   Office of Technical Assistance for Toxic Use Reduction, 179
MCGILL UNIVERSITY, 587
MECKLENBURG COUNTY PARK AND RECREATION DEPARTMENT, 179
MERCK FOREST AND FARMLAND CENTER, 397
MIAMI UNIVERSITY, 587
MICHIGAN DEPARTMENT OF NATURAL RESOURCES, 180
MICHIGAN LAND USE INSTITUTE, 397
MICHIGAN TECHNOLOGICAL UNIVERSITY; SCHOOL OF FORESTRY
   AND WOOD PRODUCTS, 588
MICHIGAN UNITED CONSERVATION CLUBS, INC., 398
MID-ATLANTIC COUNCIL OF WATERSHED ASSOCIATIONS, 398
MID-ATLANTIC FISHERY MANAGEMENT COUNCIL, 398
MIDDLE TENNESSEE STATE UNIVERSITY, 588
MIDLAND CONSERVATION DISTRICT, 181
MINNESOTA BASS FEDERATION, 399
MINNESOTA BOARD OF WATER AND SOIL RESOURCES, 181
MINNESOTA CENTER FOR ENVIRONMENTAL ADVOCACY (MCEA), 399
MINNESOTA FORESTRY ASSOCIATION, 399
MINNESOTA HERPETOLOGICAL SOCIETY, 400
MINNESOTA-WISCONSIN BOUNDARY AREA COMMISSION, 24
MISSISSIPPI BASS FEDERATION, 401
MISSISSIPPI COOPERATIVE FISH AND WILDLIFE RESEARCH UNIT, 183
MISSISSIPPI INTERSTATE COOPERATIVE RESOURCE ASSOCIATION,
   401
MISSISSIPPI RIVER BASIN ALLIANCE, 401
MISSISSIPPI SOIL AND WATER CONSERVATION COMMISSION, 184
MISSISSIPPI STATE UNIVERSITY
   College of Forest Resources, 588
   Forest and Wildlife Research Center, 588
MISSOURI DEPARTMENT OF AGRICULTURE, 185
MISSOURI FOREST PRODUCTS ASSOCIATION, 402
MISSOURI STATE EXTENSION SERVICES, 186
MONTANA BASS FEDERATION, 403
MONTANA BUREAU OF MINES AND GEOLOGY, 186
MONTANA COOPERATIVE WILDLIFE RESEARCH UNIT (USGS/BRD),
   186
MONTANA DEPARTMENT OF NATURAL RESOURCES AND
   CONSERVATION, 187
MONTANA FOREST OWNERS ASSOCIATION, 403
MONTANA LAND RELIANCE, 403
MONTANA STATE UNIVERSITY
   College of Agriculture, 589
MONTANA WILDERNESS ASSOCIATION, 403
MONTANA WILDLIFE FEDERATION, 404
MOUNT GRACE LAND CONSERVATION TRUST, 405
MOUNT UNION COLLEGE, 589
MOUNTAINEERS, THE, 405
MRFC FISH CONSERVATION, 405
MUNDO AZUL, 406
MURRAY STATE UNIVERSITY, 589
MUSKIES, INC., 406
NATIONAL AGRICULTURAL LIBRARY, 24
NATIONAL ASSOCIATION OF SERVICE AND CONSERVATION CORPS
   (NASCC), 408

NATIONAL ASSOCIATION OF STATE DEPARTMENTS OF AGRICULTURE, 408
NATIONAL AUDUBON SOCIETY
  Audubon Alaska, 409
  Audubon Council of Illinois, 410
  Audubon Maryland-DC, 410
  Audubon of Florida, 410
  Audubon of Kansas, 410
  Audubon Pennsylvania, 411
  Audubon Society of Omaha, 411
  Audubon Society of Portland, 411
  Connecticut Audubon Society, 412
  Delaware Audubon Society, 413
  Fairfax Audubon Society, 413
  Hawaii Audubon Society, 413
  Louisiana Audubon Council, 414
  Maine Audubon, 414
  Maricopa Audubon Society, 414
  New Jersey Chapter, 415
  Public Policy Office, 415
  San Diego Chapter, 416
  Seattle Audubon Society, 416
NATIONAL BOATING FEDERATION, 417
NATIONAL CAUCUS OF ENVIRONMENTAL LEGISLATORS (NCEL), 417
NATIONAL COALITION FOR MARINE CONSERVATION, 417
NATIONAL ENVIRONMENTAL EDUCATION AND TRAINING FOUNDATION, 418
NATIONAL FOREST FOUNDATION, 420
NATIONAL NETWORK OF FOREST PRACTITIONERS, 422
NATIONAL PARKS CONSERVATION ASSOCIATION (NPCA), 422
  Sun Coast Regional Office, 423
NATIONAL WATER RESOURCES ASSOCIATION, 426
NATIONAL WATERSHED COALITION, 426
NATIONAL WATERWAYS CONFERENCE INC., 426
NATIONAL WILDLIFE FEDERATION
  Great Lakes Natural Resource Center, 427
  Gulf States Natural Resource Center, 428
  Headquarters, 427
  Rocky Mountain Natural Resource Center, 428
NATIONAL WILDLIFE PRODUCTIONS, INC., 429
NATIONAL WILDLIFE REFUGE ASSOCIATION, 429
NATIONAL WOODLAND OWNERS ASSOCIATION, 430
NATIVE PLANT SOCIETY OF NORTHEASTERN OHIO, 430
NATIVE PLANT SOCIETY OF TEXAS, 431
NATURE CONSERVANCY, THE
  Arkansas Field Office, 434
  Colorado Chapter, 434
  Eastern New York Chapter, 435
  Illinois Chapter, 435
  Kansas Chapter, 436
  Maryland/District of Columbia Chapter, 436
  New York City Chapter, 438
  New York City Office, 437
  Oklahoma Chapter, 439
  Oregon Chapter, 439
  Pennsylvania Chapter, 439
  Rhode Island Chapter, 439
  Texas Chapter, 439
  Washington Chapter, 440
NEBRASKA DEPARTMENT OF ENVIRONMENTAL QUALITY, 188
NEBRASKA DEPARTMENT OF NATURAL RESOURCES, 188
NEBRASKA GAME AND PARKS COMMISSION
  OMAHA OFFICE, 189
NEBRASKA WILDLIFE FEDERATION, INC., 442
NEGATIVE POPULATION GROWTH (NPG), 442
NEVADA ASSOCIATION OF CONSERVATION DISTRICTS, 442
NEW BRUNSWICK DEPARTMENT OF NATURAL RESOURCES, 189
NEW ENGLAND COALITION FOR SUSTAINABLE POPULATION (NECSP), 443
NEW HAMPSHIRE ASSOCIATION OF CONSERVATION COMMISSIONS, 443
NEW HAMPSHIRE ASSOCIATION OF CONSERVATION DISTRICTS, 444
NEW HAMPSHIRE COUNCIL ON RESOURCES AND DEVELOPMENT, 190
NEW HAMPSHIRE DEPARTMENT OF RESOURCES AND ECONOMIC DEVELOPMENT, 190
NEW JERSEY ASSOCIATION OF CONSERVATION DISTRICTS, 445
NEW JERSEY DEPARTMENT OF ENVIRONMENTAL PROTECTION
  Division of Solid and Hazardous Waste, 192
  Geological Survey, 192
NEW MEXICO BUREAU OF GEOLOGY AND MINERAL RESOURCES, 193
NEW MEXICO DEPARTMENT OF AGRICULTURE, 193

NEW MEXICO ENERGY, MINERALS, AND NATURAL RESOURCES DEPARTMENT
  Oil Conservation Division, 195
NEW MEXICO STATE UNIVERSITY
  College of Agriculture and Home Economics, 589
NEW MEXICO STATE UNIVERSITY
  College of Agriculture and Home Economics
    Department of Fishery and Wildlife Sciences, 590
NEW YORK DEPARTMENT OF ENVIRONMENTAL CONSERVATION
  Division of Solid and Hazardous Materials, 196
NEW YORK OFFICE OF ENERGY EFFICIENCY AND ENVIRONMENT, 197
NEW YORK STATE FISH AND WILDLIFE MANAGEMENT BOARD
  Region 8, 198
NEW YORK STATE TUG HILL COMMISSION, 199
NEWFOUNDLAND DEPARTMENT OF FOREST RESOURCES AND AGRIFOODS
  Regional Offices, 199
NOLTE ASSOCIATES, INC., 569
NORTH AMERICAN BENTHOLOGICAL SOCIETY, 447
NORTH AMERICAN CRANE WORKING GROUP, 448
NORTH AMERICAN DEVELOPMENT BANK, 24
NORTH AMERICAN LOON FUND, 448
NORTH AMERICAN NATIVE FISHES ASSOCIATION, 449
NORTH AMERICAN WETLANDS CONSERVATION COUNCIL, 24
NORTH CAROLINA BASS FEDERATION, 450
NORTH CAROLINA COASTAL FEDERATION, INC., 450
NORTH CAROLINA CONSERVATION NETWORK, 450
NORTH CAROLINA COOPERATIVE FISH AND WILDLIFE RESEARCH UNIT (USDI), 200
NORTH CAROLINA DEPARTMENT OF AGRICULTURE AND CONSUMER SERVICES, 200
NORTH CAROLINA STATE UNIVERSITY, 590
NORTH CAROLINA WILD FLOWER PRESERVATION SOCIETY, 451
NORTH DAKOTA DEPARTMENT OF AGRICULTURE, 201
NORTH DAKOTA DEPARTMENT OF HEALTH, 201
NORTH DAKOTA GAME AND FISH DEPARTMENT, 201
NORTH DAKOTA STATE UNIVERSITY, 590
NORTHERN ALASKA ENVIRONMENTAL CENTER, 453
NORTHERN PLAINS RESOURCE COUNCIL, 453
NORTHLAND COLLEGE, 591
NORTHWEST RESOURCE INFORMATION CENTER, 454
NORTHWEST TERRITORIES DEPARTMENT OF RESOURCES, WILDLIFE AND ECONOMIC DEVELOPMENT, 202
NOVA SCOTIA AGRICULTURE & FISHERIES, 203
NOVA SCOTIA FEDERATION OF ANGLERS AND HUNTERS, 454
NOVA SCOTIA FORESTRY ASSOCIATION, 454
OCEAN CONSERVANCY, THE, 455
OCEAN PROJECT, THE, 455
OCEAN VOICE INTERNATIONAL, 455
OCEANIA, 455
OHIO ACADEMY OF SCIENCE, THE, 456
OHIO BIOLOGICAL SURVEY, 456
OHIO DEPARTMENT OF AGRICULTURE, 203
OHIO DEPARTMENT OF NATURAL RESOURCES, 204
OHIO ENVIRONMENTAL REVIEW APPEALS COMMISSION, 205
OHIO FEDERATION OF SOIL AND WATER CONSERVATION DISTRICTS, 457
OHIO FORESTRY ASSOCIATION, INC., 457
OHIO NATIVE PLANT SOCIETY, 457
OHIO STATE UNIVERSITY, 592
OHIO STREAM PRESERVATION, 457
OKLAHOMA CONSERVATION COMMISSION, 205
OKLAHOMA COOPERATIVE FISH AND WILDLIFE RESEARCH UNIT (USDI), 206
OKLAHOMA DEPARTMENT OF ENVIRONMENTAL QUALITY, 206
OKLAHOMA GEOLOGICAL SURVEY, 206
OKLAHOMA NATIVE PLANT SOCIETY, 458
OKLAHOMA STATE UNIVERSITY, 592
OKLAHOMA WATER RESOURCES BOARD, 207
ONEWILDWORLD, 459
ONTARIO FEDERATION OF ANGLERS AND HUNTERS, 459
ONTARIO MINISTRY OF NATURAL RESOURCES
  South Central Region, 208
ORANGUTAN FOUNDATION INTERNATIONAL, 460
OREGON DEPARTMENT OF FISH AND WILDLIFE (ODFW), 208
OREGON DEPARTMENT OF GEOLOGY AND MINERAL INDUSTRIES, 209
OREGON DEPARTMENT OF TRANSPORTATION, 209
OREGON ENVIRONMENTAL COUNCIL, 460
OREGON NATURAL RESOURCES COUNCIL, 460
OREGON SMALL WOODLANDS ASSOCIATION, 461
OREGON SOCIETY OF AMERICAN FORESTERS, 461
OREGON STATE MARINE BOARD, 210

KEYWORD INDEX – W

OREGON WATER RESOURCES DEPARTMENT, 210
ORGANIZATION FOR BAT CONSERVATION, 461
OTTER PROJECT, THE, 462
OZARK SOCIETY, THE, 463
PACIFIC FISHERY MANAGEMENT COUNCIL, 463
PACIFIC INSTITUTE FOR STUDIES IN DEVELOPMENT, ENVIRONMENT, AND SECURITY, 463
PACIFIC MARINE CONSERVATION COUNCIL, 464
PACIFIC RIVERS COUNCIL, 464
PACIFIC STATES MARINE FISHERIES COMMISSION, 27
PACIFIC WHALE FOUNDATION, 464
PARTNERS IN AMPHIBIAN AND REPTILE CONSERVATION (PARC), 465
PARTNERS IN PARKS, 465
PENNSYLVANIA COOPERATIVE FISH AND WILDLIFE RESEARCH UNIT, 210
PENNSYLVANIA DEPARTMENT OF ENVIRONMENTAL PROTECTION, 211
PENNSYLVANIA FORESTRY ASSOCIATION, THE, 466
PENNSYLVANIA ORGANIZATION FOR WATERSHEDS AND RIVERS (POWR), 466
PENNSYLVANIA STATE EXTENSION SERVICES, 592
PEOPLE FOR PUGET SOUND, 467
   North Sound Office, 467
   South Sound Office, 467
PHEASANTS FOREVER, INC., 468
PIEDMONT ENVIRONMENTAL COUNCIL, 469
PLAYA LAKES JOINT VENTURE, 469
POCONO ENVIRONMENTAL EDUCATION CENTER, 470
POINT TO POINT COMMUNICATIONS, 569
POLLUTION PROBE, 470
POPULATION-ENVIRONMENT BALANCE, INC., 471
PRAIRIE RIVERS NETWORK, 472
PROTECTED AREAS ASSOCIATION OF NEWFOUNDLAND AND LABRADOR, 474
PS ENTERPRISES, 570
PUBLIC EMPLOYEES FOR ENVIRONMENTAL RESPONSIBILITY (PEER), 474
PUERTO RICO DEPARTMENT OF AGRICULTURE, 213
PUERTO RICO SOIL CONSERVATION COMMITTEE, 213
PUGET SOUNDKEEPER ALLIANCE, 475
PURPLE MARTIN CONSERVATION ASSOCIATION, 475
QUEBEC DEPARTMENT OF ENVIRONMENT AND WILDLIFE, 214
QUEBEC WILDLIFE FEDERATION, 476
RACHEL CARSON COUNCIL, INC., 476
REEF RELIEF, 478
RENEWABLE NATURAL RESOURCES FOUNDATION, 478
RESTORE HETCH HETCHY, 479
RHODE ISLAND DEPARTMENT OF TRANSPORTATION, 214
RHODE ISLAND STATE CONSERVATION COMMITTEE, 480
RIVER NETWORK, 480
   Eastern Office, 481
RIVER OTTER ALLIANCE, THE, 481
RIVER PROJECT, THE, 481
RIVERS COUNCIL OF WASHINGTON, 481
ROCK RIVER HEADWATERS, INC., 481
ROCKY MOUNTAIN BIGHORN SOCIETY, 482
RUTGERS COOPERATIVE EXTENSION, 215
RUTGERS UNIVERSITY, COOK COLLEGE, 594
SALTON SEA AUTHORITY, 215
SAN DIEGUITO RIVER PARK JOINT POWERS AUTHORITY, 215
SAN JUAN PRESERVATION TRUST, THE, 484
SAND CREEK WATERSHED PROJECT, THE, 215
SASKATCHEWAN WILDLIFE FEDERATION, 484
SAVE SAN FRANCISCO BAY ASSOCIATION, 485
SAVE THE DUNES CONSERVATION FUND, 485
SAVE THE HARBOR/SAVE THE BAY, 486
SAVE THE SOUND, INC., 486
SAVE WETLANDS AND BAYS, 486
SEA TURTLE PRESERVATION SOCIETY, 489
SEACAMP ASSOCIATION, INC., 489
SEACOAST ANTI-POLLUTION LEAGUE, 489
SEAPLANE PILOTS ASSOCIATION, 489
SHEPHERD COLLEGE, 595
SIERRA CLUB
   Alaska Field Office, 490
   Connecticut Chapter, 491
   Hawaii Chapter, 492
   Kansas Chapter, 493
   Lone Star Chapter, 493
   Mackinac Chapter, 493
   Maryland Chapter, 493
   Mississippi Chapter, 494
   Nebraska Chapter, 494
   Northwest Office, 495
   Pennsylvania Chapter, 496
   Rio Grande Chapter (New Mexico/West Texas), 496
   Washington, DC Office, 499
   West Virginia Chapter, 499
SIERRA CLUB CALIFORNIA, 499
SIERRA CLUB FOUNDATION, THE, 499
SILK CITY NATURE ASSOCIATION, 500
SINAPU, 500
SLIPPERY ROCK UNIVERSITY, 595
SMITHSONIAN INSTITUTION, 501
SOCIEDAD AMBIENTE MARINO, 502
SOCIETY FOR RANGE MANAGEMENT, 503
SOCIETY OF WETLAND SCIENTISTS, 504
SOIL AND WATER CONSERVATION SOCIETY, 504
SONORAN INSTITUTE, 505
SOUTH CAROLINA BASS FEDERATION, 506
SOUTH CAROLINA COOPERATIVE FISH AND WILDLIFE RESEARCH UNIT, 217
SOUTH CAROLINA DEPARTMENT OF HEALTH AND ENVIRONMENTAL CONTROL, 217
SOUTH CAROLINA DEPARTMENT OF PARKS, RECREATION AND TOURISM, 218
SOUTH CAROLINA ENERGY OFFICE, 218
SOUTH CAROLINA WILDLIFE FEDERATION, 506
SOUTH DAKOTA ASSOCIATION OF CONSERVATION DISTRICTS, 506
SOUTH DAKOTA COOPERATIVE EXTENSION SERVICE, 218
SOUTH DAKOTA COOPERATIVE FISH AND WILDLIFE RESEARCH UNIT (USDI-USGS), 29
SOUTH DAKOTA DEPARTMENT OF ENVIRONMENT AND NATURAL RESOURCES, 219
SOUTH DAKOTA DEPARTMENT OF GAME, FISH, AND PARKS, 219
SOUTH DAKOTA RESOURCES COALITION, 507
SOUTH DAKOTA WILDLIFE FEDERATION, 507
SOUTH FLORIDA WATER MANAGEMENT DISTRICT, 219
SOUTHEASTERN ASSOCIATION OF FISH AND WILDLIFE AGENCIES, 508
SOUTHEASTERN FISHES COUNCIL, 508
SOUTHERN APPALACHIAN BOTANICAL SOCIETY, 508
SOUTHERN ENVIRONMENTAL LAW CENTER, 509
SOUTHERN ILLINOIS UNIVERSITY CARBONDALE, 596
SOUTHERN UTAH WILDERNESS ALLIANCE
   Moab Office, 510
SOUTHFACE ENERGY INSTITUTE, 510
SOUTHWEST CENTER FOR ENVIRONMENTAL RESEARCH AND POLICY (SCERP), 596
SOUTHWEST CONSERVATION DISTRICT, 510
SOUTHWEST FLORIDA WATER MANAGEMENT DISTRICT (SWFWMD), 220
SOUTHWESTERN HERPETOLOGISTS SOCIETY, 510
STANFORD ENVIRONMENTAL LAW SOCIETY, 511
STATE ENVIRONMENTAL RESOURCE CENTER (SERC), 512
STATE UNIVERSITY OF NEW YORK AT STONY BROOK, 597
STEPHEN F. AUSTIN STATE UNIVERSITY ARTHUR TEMPLE COLLEGE OF FORESTRY, 598
STERLING COLLEGE, 598
STROUD WATER RESEARCH CENTER, 512
STUDENT CONSERVATION ASSOCIATION, INC., 512
STURGEON FOR TOMORROW, 514
SUSTAIN, 514
SUSTAINABLE ENERGY INSTITUTE
   Culture Change, 514
   Food Not Lawns, 514
   Pedal Power Produce, 514
TAHOE REGIONAL PLANNING AGENCY, 220
TANZANIA COASTAL MANAGEMENT PARTNERSHIP, 30
TENNESSEE CITIZENS FOR WILDERNESS PLANNING, 515
TENNESSEE CONSERVATION LEAGUE, 516
TENNESSEE DEPARTMENT OF AGRICULTURE, 221
TENNESSEE DEPARTMENT OF ENVIRONMENT AND CONSERVATION, 221
TENNESSEE VALLEY AUTHORITY
   Muscle Shoals Technical Library, 30
TEXAS A AND M UNIVERSITY AT KINGSVILLE
   Caesar Kleberg Wildlife Research Institute, 599
TEXAS A AND M UNIVERSITY SYSTEM
   Texas Cooperative Extension, 599
TEXAS BASS FEDERATION, 517
TEXAS CHRISTIAN UNIVERSITY, 599
TEXAS COMMITTEE ON NATURAL RESOURCES, 517
TEXAS COOPERATIVE FISH AND WILDLIFE RESEARCH UNIT, 30
TEXAS DEPARTMENT OF AGRICULTURE, 222
TEXAS DISCOVERY GARDENS, 517
TEXAS FOREST SERVICE, 222

KEYWORD INDEX – W

TEXAS ORGANIZATION FOR ENDANGERED SPECIES, 517
TEXAS RIPARIAN ASSOCIATION, 517
TEXAS STATE SOIL AND WATER CONSERVATION BOARD, 223
TEXAS WATER DEVELOPMENT BOARD, 223
THORNE ECOLOGICAL INSTITUTE, 518
TREES FOR TOMORROW, NATURAL RESOURCES EDUCATION CENTER, 519
TROUT UNLIMITED
  Alaska Council, 520
  Arizona Council, 521
  Missouri Council, 522
  New York Council, 522
  Pennsylvania Council, 522
TRUMPETER SWAN SOCIETY, THE, 523
TRUST FOR PUBLIC LAND, THE, 523
TRUST FOR WILDLIFE, INC., 524
TRUSTEES FOR ALASKA, 524
TULANE ENVIRONMENTAL LAW CLINIC, 600
TULANE UNIVERSITY
  Department of Ecology and Evolutionary Biology, 600
TURNER ENDANGERED SPECIES FUND, 571
TURTLE CREEK WATERSHED ASSOCIATION, INC., 525
UNEP WORLD CONSERVATION MONITORING CENTRE, 525
UNITED STATES CHAMBER OF COMMERCE
  Environment, Technology and Regulatory Affairs, 526
UNITED STATES DEPARTMENT OF AGRICULTURE
  Economic Research Center, 33
  Forest Service
    Angelina, Davy Crockett, Sabine and Sam Houston National Forest, 34
    Crooked River National Grassland, 37
    Gila National Forest, 38
    Green Mountain National Forest, 38
    Los Padres National Forest, 40
    Nez Perce National Forest, 41
    Pawnee National Grassland, 42
    Region 02 (Rocky Mountain), 43
    Region 09 (Eastern), 43
    Siuslaw National Forest, 45
UNITED STATES DEPARTMENT OF COMMERCE
  National Oceanic and Atmospheric Administration
    Chesapeake Bay National Estuarine Research Reserve
      Virginia Office, 50
    Delaware National Estuarine Research Reserve, 50
    Gray's Reef National Marine Sanctuary, 50
    Gulf of Farallones National Marine Sanctuary, 50
    Padilla Bay National Estuarine Research Reserve, 53
    Rookery Bay National Estuarine Research Reserve, 53
    Sea Grant Program - California, 54
    Sea Grant Program - DelAware, 54
    Sea Grant Program - Georgia, 55
    Sea Grant Program - Illinois-Indiana, 55
    Sea Grant Program - Massachusetts, 56
    Sea Grant Program - Michigan, 57
    Sea Grant Program - Minnesota, 57
    Sea Grant Program - New Jersey, 57
    Sea Grant Program - North Carolina, 58
    Sea Grant Program - Ohio, 58
    Sea Grant Program - Rhode Island, 59
    Sea Grant Program - South Carolina, 59
    Wells National Estuarine Research Reserve, 60
UNITED STATES DEPARTMENT OF DEFENSE
  Air Force Major Air Commands
    Andrews AFB, MD, 61
    USAF Academy, 62
  Air Force Major U.S. Installations
    Eglin Air Force Base, 63
    Luke AFB (and the Barry M. Goldwater AFR), AZ, 65
    Randolph AFB, TX, 66
  Army Corps of Engineers
    Baltimore Engineer District, 67
    Fort Worth Engineer District, 68
    Norfolk Engineer District, 70
    North Atlantic Engineer District, 70
    Pacific Ocean Engineer District, 70
    Philadelphia District, 70
    Walla Walla Engineer District, 72
  Army Materiel Command, 72
  Assistant Chief of Staff for Installation Management, Office of the Director of Environmental Programs, and Conservation Team, 74
  HQ PACAF/CEVQ, 74
  Navy, 74
UNITED STATES DEPARTMENT OF HOUSING AND URBAN DEVELOPMENT, 77

UNITED STATES DEPARTMENT OF THE INTERIOR
  Bureau of Land Management
    Bakersfield Field Office, 79
    Eugene District Office, 81
    Malta Field Office, 83
    Northern Field Office, 84
    Rawlins Field Office, 85
    Safford Field Office, 86
    Tucson Field Office, 88
  Fish and Wildlife Service, 90
    Arrowwood National Wildlife Refuge Complex, 91
    Arthur R. Marshall Loxahatchee/Hope Sound National Wildlife Refuge, 91
    Benton Lake National Wildlife Refuge, 92
    California-Nevada Operations, 94
    Canaan Valley National Wildlife Refuge, 94
    Carolina Sandhills National Wildlife Refuge, 95
    Chickasaw National Wildlife Refuge, 95
    Columbia National Wildlife Refuge, 96
    Eastern Massachusetts National Wildlife Refuge Complex, 97
    Hobe Sound National Wildlife Refuge, 99
    Kofa National Wildlife Refuge, 102
    Lacassine National Wildlife Refuge, 102
    Long Island National Wildlife Refuge Complex, 103
    Long Lake National Wildlife Refuge, 103
    Mattamuskeet National Wildlife Refuge, 104
    Mingo National Wildlife Refuge, 105
    Morris Wetland Management District, 106
    Necedah National Wildlife Refuge, 107
    Noxubee National Wildlife Refuge, 108
    Okefenokee (Banks Lake) National Wildlife Refuge, 108
    Patoka River National Wetlands Project National Wildlife Refuge, 109
    Rainwater Basin WMD National Wildlife Refuge, 111
    region 4, Southeast Regional office, 112
    San Francisco Bay National Wildlife Refuge Complex, 113
    Sandy Point National Wildlife Refuge, 114
    Southeast Louisiana Complex National Wildlife Refuge, 115
    Upper Mississippi River National Wildlife and fish refuge, 117
    White River National Wildlife Refuge, 118
    Willapa/Lewis and Clark National Wildlife Refuge, 118
  Montana Cooperative Fishery Research Unit, 119
  Montana State Extension Services, 119
  National Park Service
    Grand Teton National Park, 122
    Mammoth Cave National Park, 124
    Mesa Verde National Park, 124
    Mount Rainier National Park, 124
    Sonoran Desert Network, 125
    Yellowstone National Park, 126
  North Dakota State University Extension Service, 126
  United States Geological Survey
    New Mexico Cooperative Fish and Wildlife Research Unit, 127
    Western Region, 127
  Washington Cooperative Fish and Wildlife Research Unit
    School of Aquatic and Fishery Sciences, 128
UNITED STATES DEPARTMENT OF TRANSPORTATION
  Federal Aviation Administration, 128
UNITED STATES INSTITUTE FOR ENVIRONMENTAL CONFLICT RESOLUTION, 130
UNITED STATES PUBLIC INTEREST RESEARCH GROUP, 526
UNITED STATES TOURIST COUNCIL, 527
UNITY COLLEGE, 601
UNIVERSITE LAVAL, 601
UNIVERSITY OF ARIZONA
  Department of Hydrology and Water Resources, 605
UNIVERSITY OF CALIFORNIA AT DAVIS
  School of Veterinary Medicine, 606
UNIVERSITY OF CALIFORNIA AT SAN DIEGO, 607
UNIVERSITY OF CONNECTICUT COOPERATIVE EXTENSION, 608
UNIVERSITY OF FLORIDA
  School of Forest Resources and Conservation, 609
UNIVERSITY OF FLORIDA INSTITUTE OF FOOD AND AGRICULTURAL SCIENCES, 609
UNIVERSITY OF GEORGIA
  Daniel B. Warnell School of Forest Resources, 609
UNIVERSITY OF IDAHO
  College of Natural Resources
    Department of Fish and Wildlife Resources, 610
  Idaho Cooperative Fish and Wildlife Research Unit, 610
UNIVERSITY OF LOUISVILLE, 612
UNIVERSITY OF MAINE COOPERATIVE EXTENSION, 612
UNIVERSITY OF MARYLAND - AT COLLEGE PARK, 613
UNIVERSITY OF MARYLAND BALTIMORE COUNTY, 613
UNIVERSITY OF MARYLAND COOPERATIVE EXTENSION, 224

KEYWORD INDEX – W

UNIVERSITY OF MICHIGAN, 614
UNIVERSITY OF MINNESOTA AT ST. PAUL, 615
UNIVERSITY OF NEW BRUNSWICK, 616
UNIVERSITY OF NEW HAMPSHIRE COOPERATIVE EXTENSION, 617
UNIVERSITY OF NEW HAVEN DEPT. OF BIOLOGY AND ENVIRONMENTAL SCIENCES, 617
UNIVERSITY OF NORTH CAROLINA AT ASHEVILLE, 617
UNIVERSITY OF NORTH DAKOTA, 618
UNIVERSITY OF NORTH TEXAS, 618
UNIVERSITY OF RHODE ISLAND
   Department of Natural Resources Science, 619
UNIVERSITY OF SASKATCHEWAN, 620
UNIVERSITY OF SOUTH CAROLINA
   Baruch Marine Field Laboratory, 620
UNIVERSITY OF TENNESSEE - AT KNOXVILLE, 621
UNIVERSITY OF WISCONSIN AT LA CROSSE, 623
UNIVERSITY OF WISCONSIN-MADISON, 623
UPPER COLORADO RIVER COMMISSION, 130
UPPER MISSISSIPPI RIVER CONSERVATION COMMITTEE, 527
URBAN WASTE MANAGEMENT & RESEARCH CENTER, 624
UTAH BASS FEDERATION, 528
UTAH DEPARTMENT OF NATURAL RESOURCES
   Division of Wildlife Resources, 225
UTAH STATE UNIVERSITY
   College of Natural Resources, 624
VERMONT ASSOCIATION OF CONSERVATION DISTRICTS, 529
VERMONT DEPARTMENT OF AGRICULTURE, FOOD, AND MARKETS
   State Conservation Commission, 227
VERMONT STATE-WIDE ENVIRONMENTAL EDUCATION PROGRAMS (SWEEP), 530
VERMONT WOODLANDS ASSOCIATION, 530
VERNAL POOL SOCIETY, THE, 530
VINEYARD CONSERVATION SOCIETY, 530
VIRGIN ISLANDS CONSERVATION DISTRICT, 530
VIRGIN ISLANDS SOIL AND WATER CONSERVATION DIVISION, 228
VIRGINIA CONSERVATION NETWORK, 531
VIRGINIA DEPARTMENT OF AGRICULTURE AND CONSUMER SERVICES, 228
VIRGINIA DEPARTMENT OF CONSERVATION AND RECREATION
   Conservation and Development of Public Beaches Board, 229
   Virginia Cave Board, 230
VIRGINIA DEPARTMENT OF ENVIRONMENTAL QUALITY, 230
VIRGINIA DEPARTMENT OF FORESTRY, 230
VIRGINIA DEPARTMENT OF GAME AND INLAND FISHERIES
   Region IV (Staunton), 231
VIRGINIA FORESTRY ASSOCIATION, 531
VIRGINIA TECH
   Department of Fisheries and Wildlife Sciences, 625
VIRGINIA TECH UNIVERSITY
   College of Natural Resources, 625
WABASH RIVER HERITAGE CORRIDOR COMMISSION, 232
WARREN COUNTY CONSERVATION BOARD, 532
WASHINGTON DEPARTMENT OF ECOLOGY
   Eastern Regional Office, 233
   Southwest Regional Office, 233
WASHINGTON FARM FORESTRY ASSOCIATION, 533
WASHINGTON RECREATION AND PARK ASSOCIATION, 533
WASHINGTON STATE CONSERVATION COMMISSION, 234
WASHINGTON STATE OFFICE OF ENVIRONMENTAL EDUCATION, 234
WASHINGTON STATE PARKS AND RECREATION COMMISSION
NORTHWEST REGION, 235
WASHINGTON WILDLIFE AND RECREATION COALITION, 534
WATER ENVIRONMENT FEDERATION, 535
WATER RESOURCES ASSOCIATION OF THE DELAWARE RIVER BASIN, 535
WATERMAN CONSERVATION EDUCATION CENTER, 535
WELLSPRING INTERNATIONAL, INC., 571
WEST VIRGINIA DEPARTMENT OF ENVIRONMENTAL PROTECTION, 235
WEST VIRGINIA HIGHLANDS CONSERVANCY, 536
WEST VIRGINIA RAPTOR REHABILITATION CENTER, 536
WESTERN HEMISPHERE SHOREBIRD RESERVE NETWORK (WHSRN), 537
WESTERN ILLINOIS UNIVERSITY, 626
WESTERN WATERSHEDS PROJECT, 538
WETLANDS ACTION NETWORK, 538
WHITE CLAY WATERSHED ASSOCIATION, 538
WHOOPING CRANE CONSERVATION ASSOCIATION INC., 539
WILD ONES NATURAL LANDSCAPERS, LTD, 540
WILDERNESS WATCH, 541
WILDFLOWER ASSOCIATION OF MICHIGAN, 541
WILDFOWL TRUST OF NORTH AMERICA, INC., THE, 541
WILDLANDS CONSERVANCY, 542
WILDLIFE ACTION, INC., 542
WILDLIFE DAMAGE REVIEW (WDR), 543
WILDLIFE FOREVER, 544
WILDLIFE HABITAT CANADA, 544
WILDLIFE HABITAT COUNCIL, 544
WILDLIFE SOCIETY
   Colorado Chapter, 547
   Illinois Chapter, 547
   Michigan Chapter, 549
   Southern California Chapter, 553
WINDSTAR WILDLIFE INSTITUTE, 555
WISCONSIN ASSOCIATION OF LAKES (WAL), 555
WISCONSIN COOPERATIVE FISHERY RESEARCH UNIT USGS, 237
WISCONSIN GEOLOGICAL AND NATURAL HISTORY SURVEY, 238
WISCONSIN LAND AND WATER CONSERVATION ASSOCIATION, 556
WISCONSIN SOCIETY FOR ORNITHOLOGY, INC., THE, 556
WISCONSIN STATE EXTENSION SERVICES, 238
WISCONSIN WILDLIFE FEDERATION, 557
WISCONSIN WOODLAND OWNERS ASSOCIATION, 557
WORLDWATCH INSTITUTE, 560
WWW.ACTIONBIOSCIENCE.ORG, 560
WYOMING BASS FEDERATION, 560
WYOMING OUTDOOR COUNCIL, 561
YELL COUNTY WILDLIFE FEDERATION, 561
YMCA NATURE AND COMMUNITY CENTER, 562

WILDLIFE & SPECIES

A CRITICAL DECISION, 241
A.E. HOWELL WILDLIFE CONSERVATION CENTER INC., 241
ABUNDANT LIFE SEED FOUNDATION, 241
ACADEMY FOR EDUCATIONAL DEVELOPMENT, 241
ACRES LAND TRUST, 241
ADIRONDACK MOUNTAIN CLUB, INC., THE (ADK), 242
ADKINS ARBORETUM, 242
ADOPT-A-STREAM FOUNDATION, THE, 242
AFRICA VISION TRUST, 243
AFRICAN AMERICAN ENVIRONMENTALIST ASSOCIATION, 243
AFRICAN CONSERVATION FOUNDATION, THE, 243
AFRICAN WILDLIFE FOUNDATION, 243
ALABAMA COOPERATIVE EXTENSION SYSTEM, 132
ALABAMA COOPERATIVE FISH AND WILDLIFE RESEARCH UNIT (USDI), 132
ALABAMA DEPARTMENT OF AGRICULTURE AND INDUSTRIES, 132
ALABAMA DEPARTMENT OF CONSERVATION AND NATURAL RESOURCES, 132
ALABAMA WATERFOWL ASSOCIATION, INC. (AWA), 245
ALABAMA WILDFLOWER SOCIETY, THE, 245
ALASKA CENTER FOR THE ENVIRONMENT, 245
ALASKA CONSERVATION ALLIANCE, 245, 246
ALASKA CONSERVATION FOUNDATION, 246
ALASKA RAINFOREST CAMPAIGN, 246
ALASKA WILDLIFE ALLIANCE, THE, 246
ALBERTA DEPARTMENT OF ENVIRONMENTAL PROTECTION
   Natural Resources Service, 135
ALBERTA FISH AND GAME ASSOCIATION, 247
ALBERTA WILDERNESS ASSOCIATION, 247
ALDEANATURAL.COM, 563
ALLIANCE FOR THE CHESAPEAKE BAY, 247
AMERICA THE BEAUTIFUL FUND, 248
AMERICAN AQUATICS, INC, 563
AMERICAN ASSOCIATION FOR THE ADVANCEMENT OF SCIENCE, 249
AMERICAN ASSOCIATION OF BOTANICAL GARDENS AND ARBORETA, 249
AMERICAN ASSOCIATION OF FIELD BOTANISTS, 249
AMERICAN ASSOCIATION OF ZOO KEEPERS, INC., 249
AMERICAN BIRD CONSERVANCY, 249
AMERICAN BIRDING ASSOCIATION (ABA), 250
AMERICAN CAVE CONSERVATION ASSOCIATION, 250
AMERICAN CETACEAN SOCIETY, 250
AMERICAN CHESTNUT FOUNDATION, THE, 250
AMERICAN EAGLE FOUNDATION, 251
AMERICAN FORESTS, 260
AMERICAN HORSE PROTECTION ASSOCIATION, 261
AMERICAN INSTITUTE OF FISHERY RESEARCH BIOLOGISTS, 262
AMERICAN LAND CONSERVANCY, 262
AMERICAN LITTORAL SOCIETY, 262
AMERICAN LIVESTOCK BREEDS CONSERVANCY, 263
AMERICAN MUSEUM OF NATURAL HISTORY, 263
AMERICAN ORNITHOLOGISTS UNION, 263
AMERICAN RESOURCES GROUP, 264

KEYWORD INDEX – W

AMERICAN RIVERS
  Nebraska Field Office, 265
  Northwest Regional Office, 265
  Voyage of Recovery, 265
AMERICAN SOCIETY OF ICHTHYOLOGISTS AND HERPETOLOGISTS, 265
AMERICAN SOCIETY OF INTERNATIONAL LAW/WILDLIFE INTEREST GROUP, 266
AMERICAN SOCIETY OF MAMMALOGISTS, 266
AMERICAN SPORTFISHING ASSOCIATION, 266
AMERICAN WILDLANDS, 267
AMERICAN ZOO AND AQUARIUM ASSOCIATION (AZA), 268
ANCIENT FOREST INTERNATIONAL, 268
ANGLERS FOR CLEAN WATER, 268
ANIMAL PROTECTION INSTITUTE, 268
ANIMAL WELFARE INSTITUTE, 269
ANIMALS ASIA FOUNDATION, 269
ANTARCTICA PROJECT, THE, 269
APPALACHIAN TRAIL CONFERENCE, 270
ARCHAEOLOGICAL CONSERVANCY, 270
ARCHBOLD BIOLOGICAL STATION, 270
ARIZONA COOPERATIVE STATE EXTENSION SERVICES, 135
ARIZONA STATE ENVIROTHON, INC., 271
ARIZONA STATE LAND DEPARTMENT, 136
ARIZONA STATE PARKS BOARD, 137
ARIZONA STATE UNIVERSITY
  Center for Environmental Studies, 573
ARIZONA WILDLIFE FEDERATION, 271
ARIZONA-SONORA DESERT MUSEUM, 271
ARKANSAS COOPERATIVE RESEARCH UNIT, 137
ARKANSAS ENVIRONMENTAL EDUCATION ASSOCIATION, 272
ARKANSAS GAME AND FISH COMMISSION, 137
ARKANSAS NATURAL HERITAGE COMMISSION, 138
ARKANSAS STATE PLANT BOARD, 138
ARKANSAS TECH UNIVERSITY
  Fisheries and Wildlife Biology Program, 573
ARLINGTON OUTDOOR EDUCATION ASSOCIATION, INC. (AOEA), 272
ASSOCIATION FOR THE PROTECTION OF THE ADIRONDACKS, THE, 273
ASSOCIATION OF AVIAN VETERINARIANS, 273
ASSOCIATION OF FIELD ORNITHOLOGISTS, 274
ATLANTIC CENTER FOR THE ENVIRONMENT
  Quebec-Labrador Foundation, 275
ATLANTIC SALMON FEDERATION, 275
ATLANTIC STATES MARINE FISHERIES COMMISSION, 139
AUBURN UNIVERSITY
  School of Forestry and Wildlife Sciences, 574
AUDUBON INTERNATIONAL, 276
AUDUBON NATURALIST SOCIETY OF THE CENTRAL ATLANTIC STATES, 276
AUSTRALIA DEPARTMENT FOR ENVIRONMENT AND HERITAGE, 139
  Environment Shop, The, 139
BAMA BACKPADDLERS ASSOCIATION, 276
BASS DIVISION OF ESPN PRODUCTIONS INC, 564
BAT CONSERVATION INTERNATIONAL, 277
BERKSHIRE-LITCHFIELD ENVIRONMENTAL COUNCIL, INC., 277
BEYOND PESTICIDES, 277
BIG BEND NATURAL HISTORY ASSOCIATION, 277
BILLFISH FOUNDATION, THE, 278
BIODIVERSITY CONSERVATION ALLIANCE, 278
BIOINTEGRAL RESOURCE CENTER, 278
BIOSPHERE EXPEDITIONS, 278
BIRDLIFE INTERNATIONAL, 279
BIRDS PROTECTION AND STUDY SOCIETY OF VOJVODINA, 279
BOONE AND CROCKETT CLUB, 279
BORN FREE FOUNDATION, 280
BOTANICAL SOCIETY OF WESTERN PENNSYLVANIA, 280
BOUNTY INFORMATION SERVICE, 280
BRITISH COLUMBIA FIELD ORNITHOLOGISTS, 281
BROOKS BIRD CLUB INC., THE, 281
BROTHERHOOD OF THE JUNGLE COCK, INC., THE, 281
BUILDINGGREEN, INC., 564
BUN-CA, 281
BUSINESS PUBLISHERS, INC., 564
BYRON FOREST PRESERVE, 140
CALCASIEU PARISH ANIMAL CONTROL AND PROTECTION DEPARTMENT, 282
CALIFORNIA ACADEMY OF SCIENCES, 282
CALIFORNIA CONSERVATION CORPS, 140
CALIFORNIA DEPARTMENT OF FISH AND GAME
  Elkhorn Slough National Estuarine Research Reserve, 141
  Office of Spill Prevention and Response, 141

CALIFORNIA ENERGY COMMISSION
  Environmental Department, 143
CALIFORNIA NATIVE PLANT SOCIETY, THE, 283
CALIFORNIA TRAPPERS ASSOCIATION, 283
CALIFORNIA TROUT, INC., 283
CALIFORNIA UNIVERSITY OF PENNSYLVANIA, 576
CALIFORNIA WATERFOWL ASSOCIATION, 283
CALIFORNIA WILDERNESS COALITION, 284
CALIFORNIA WILDLIFE DEFENDERS, 284
CALIFORNIA WILDLIFE FEDERATION, 284
CAM VALLEY WILDLIFE GROUP, 284
CAMP FIRE CONSERVATION FUND, 285
CAMP FIRE USA, 285
CAMPAIGN FOR AMERICA'S WILDERNESS, 285
CANADA GOOSE PROJECT, 285
CANADIAN ARCTIC RESOURCE COMMITTEE, INC., 285
CANADIAN COOPERATIVE WILDLIFE HEALTH CENTRE, 286
CANADIAN FEDERATION OF HUMANE SOCIETIES, 286
CANADIAN SOCIETY OF ENVIRONMENTAL BIOLOGISTS, 287
CANON ENVIROTHON, 288
CANVASBACK SOCIETY, 288
CARIBBEAN CONSERVATION CORPORATION, 288
CAROLINA BIRD CLUB, INC., 288
CASCADIA RESEARCH, 288
CATSKILL FOREST ASSOCIATION, 289
CENTER FOR A SUSTAINABLE COAST, 289
CENTER FOR ENVIRONMENT AND POPULATION (CEP), 290
CENTER FOR ENVIRONMENT, COMMERCE & ENERGY, 290
CENTER FOR INTERNATIONAL ENVIRONMENTAL LAW (CIEL), 292
CENTER FOR NATIVE ECOSYSTEMS
  Front Range Office, 292
  West Slope Office, 292
CENTER FOR PLANT CONSERVATION, 292
CENTER FOR RESOURCE ECONOMICS/ISLAND PRESS, 293
CENTER FOR THE STUDY OF TROPICAL BIRDS, INC.
  Administrative Office, 293
CENTRO DE INFORMACION, INVESTIGACION Y EDUCACION SOCIAL (CIIES), 294
CETACEAN SOCIETY INTERNATIONAL, 294
CHESAPEAKE BAY FOUNDATION, INC.
  Virginia Office, 295
CHESAPEAKE WILDLIFE HERITAGE (CWH), 295
CHICAGO HERPETOLOGICAL SOCIETY, 295
CHICAGO PARK DISTRICT, 296
CHICAGO REGION BIODIVERSITY COUNCIL, 296
CHIHUAHUAN DESERT RESEARCH INSTITUTE, 296
CHISHOLM WOLF FOUNDATION, INC., 296
CHLORINE-FREE PAPER CONSORTIUM, 297
CIRCUMPOLAR CONSERVATION UNION, 297
CJE ASSOCIATES, 565
CLEMSON UNIVERSITY
  School of the Environment, 577
CLINTON RIVER WATERSHED COUNCIL (CRWC), 299
COASTAL AMERICA FOUNDATION, 300
COASTAL RESOURCE MANAGEMENT PROJECT, 146
COLORADO DEPARTMENT OF NATURAL RESOURCES, 146
  Division of Parks and Outdoor Recreation, 146
  Oil and Gas Conservation Commission, 147
COLORADO DEPARTMENT OF PUBLIC HEALTH AND ENVIRONMENT, 147
COLORADO MOUNTAIN COLLEGE, 577
COLORADO NATURAL HERITAGE PROGRAM, 302
COLORADO TRAPPERS ASSOCIATION, 302
COLORADO WILDLIFE HERITAGE FOUNDATION, 302
COLUMBIA BASIN FISH AND WILDLIFE AUTHORITY, 303
COLUMBIA RIVER INTER-TRIBAL FISH COMMISSION, 17
COMITE DESPERTAR CIDRENO, 148
COMMITTEE FOR NATIONAL ARBOR DAY, 303
COMMUNITY CONSERVATION /HOWLERS FOREVER, INC., 303
COMMUNITY RIGHTS COUNSEL, 303
CONNECTICUT BOTANICAL SOCIETY, 304
CONNECTICUT PUBLIC INTEREST RESEARCH GROUP (CONN PIRG), 305
CONNECTICUT WATERFOWL ASSOCIATION, INC., 305
CONSERVAMERICA, 305
CONSERVANCY OF SOUTHWEST FLORIDA, THE, 305
CONSERVATION ALLIANCE OF ST. LUCIE CO., 306
CONSERVATION FORCE, 306
CONSERVATION FUND, THE, 307
CONSERVATION INTERNATIONAL, 307
CONSERVATION LAW FOUNDATION, INC. (CLF), 307
CONSERVATION TREATY SUPPORT FUND, 308
CORNELL LAB OF ORNITHOLOGY, 309

KEYWORD INDEX – W

COTTONWOOD FOUNDATION, 309
COUNCIL FOR PLANNING AND CONSERVATION, 310
COUNTY OF SAN DIEGO, 149
COUSTEAU SOCIETY, INC., THE, 310
CRAIGHEAD ENVIRONMENTAL RESEARCH INSTITUTE, 310
CRAIGHEAD WILDLIFE-WILDLANDS INSTITUTE, 310
CRANSTON CONSERVATION COMMISSION, 150
CROSBY ARBORETUM, THE, 311
DAWES ARBORETUM, THE, 311
DEFENDERS OF WILDLIFE, 311
DELAWARE DEPARTMENT OF NATURAL RESOURCES AND ENVIRONMENTAL CONTROL
   Division of Air & Waste Management, 150
   Division of Soil and Water Conservation, 150
DELAWARE MUSEUM OF NATURAL HISTORY, 312
DELAWARE NATURE SOCIETY, 312
DELAWARE RIVERKEEPER NETWORK, 313
DELAWARE WILD LANDS, INC., 313
DELTA WATERFOWL FOUNDATION, 313
DELTA WILDLIFE INC., 313
DEPARTAMENTO DE RECURSOS NATURALES Y AMBIENTALES, 151
DESCHUTES BASIN LAND TRUST, 313
DESERT FISHES COUNCIL, 314
DESERT RESEARCH FOUNDATION OF NAMIBIA, THE, 314
DESERT TORTOISE COUNCIL, 314
DESERT TORTOISE PRESERVE COMMITTEE, INC., 314
DISTRICT OF COLUMBIA DEPARTMENT OF HEALTH
   Environmental Health Administration, Watershed Protection Division, 152
DRAGONFLY SOCIETY OF THE AMERICAS, THE, 314
DUCKS UNLIMITED CANADA
   Nova Scotia Office, 315
   Saskatchewan Office, 315
DUCKS UNLIMITED, INC., 315
EAGLE NATURE FOUNDATION, LTD., 316
EAGLES 4 KIDS, 565
EARTH FORCE
   GREEN (Global Rivers Environmental Education Network)), 317
EARTH FOUNDATION, 317
EARTH FRIENDS WILDLIFE FOUNDATION, 317
EARTH ISLAND INSTITUTE, 317
EARTHJUSTICE
   Environmental Law Clinic at the University of Denver, 318
   Headquarters, 318
   Juneau Office, 319
   Oakland Office, 319
   Policy and Legislation, 319
   Seattle Office, 320
   Tallahassee Office, 320
   Washington, DC, Office, 320
EARTHSCAN, 320
EARTHTRUST, 320
EARTHWATCH INSTITUTE, 321
ECOLOGICAL SOCIETY OF AMERICA, THE, 321
ECOLOGY CENTER, 321
ELM RESEARCH INSTITUTE, 322
ENDANGERED SPECIES AND WETLANDS REPORT, 566
ENDANGERED SPECIES COALITION, 322
ENTOMOLOGICAL SOCIETY OF AMERICA, 323
ENVIRONMENT AND ENERGY PUBLISHING, LLC, 566
ENVIRONMENT COUNCIL OF RHODE ISLAND, 323
ENVIRONMENTAL ALLIANCE FOR SENIOR INVOLVEMENT (EASI), 323
ENVIRONMENTAL CONCERN INC., 324
ENVIRONMENTAL DEFENSE
   Headquarters, 324
ENVIRONMENTAL DEFENSE CENTER, 325
ENVIRONMENTAL EDUCATION ASSOCIATION OF ILLINOIS, 325
ENVIRONMENTAL EDUCATORS OF NORTH CAROLINA (EENC), 326
ENVIRONMENTAL ENTERPRISES ASSISTANCE FUND, INC., 326
ENVIRONMENTAL LAW AND POLICY CENTER OF THE MIDWEST, 327
ENVIRONMENTAL LAW INSTITUTE, THE, 327
ENVIRONMENTAL MEDIA CORPORATION, 566
ENVIRONMENTAL PROTECTION ASSOCIATION OF GHANA, 327
EUROPARC FEDERATION, 328
EUROPEAN ASSOCIATION FOR AQUATIC MAMMALS, 328
EUROPEAN CETACEAN SOCIETY, 328
FEDERAL WILDLIFE OFFICERS ASSOCIATION, 329
FEDERATION OF ALBERTA NATURALISTS, 329
FEDERATION OF FLY FISHERS, 329
FEDERATION OF FLY FISHERS (NCCFFF), 329
FEDERATION OF NEW YORK STATE BIRD CLUBS, INC., 330
FERRUM COLLEGE, 581
FLORIDA DEFENDERS OF THE ENVIRONMENT, INC., 331

FLORIDA DEPARTMENT OF AGRICULTURE AND CONSUMER SERVICES
   Soil and Water Conservation Council, 153
FLORIDA DEPARTMENT OF ENVIRONMENTAL PROTECTION
   Division of Resource Assessment and Management, 154
   Florida State Parks AmeriCorps, 154
   Waste Management Division, 154
FLORIDA FEDERATION OF GARDEN CLUBS, INC., 331
FLORIDA FISH AND WILDLIFE CONSERVATION COMMISSION, 154
FLORIDA NATIVE PLANT SOCIETY, 332
FLORIDA NATURAL AREAS INVENTORY, 332
FLORIDA ORNITHOLOGICAL SOCIETY, 332
FLORIDA PANTHER PROJECT, INC., THE, 332
FLORIDA PANTHER SOCIETY, INC., THE, 332
FOOD AND AGRICULTURE ORGANIZATION OF THE UNITED NATIONS, 333
FOOD SUPPLY / HUMAN POPULATION EXPLOSION CONNECTION, 333
FOREST FIRE LOOKOUT ASSOCIATION, 334
FOREST MANAGEMENT TRUST, 334
FOREST SERVICE EMPLOYEES FOR ENVIRONMENTAL ETHICS (FSEEE), 334
FOREST SOCIETY OF MAINE, 335
FOREST STEWARDS GUILD
   Northwest Regional Chapter (GuildNW), 335
FOREST WATCH, 335
FORESTRY COMMISSION (ARKANSAS), 155
FORESTRY COMMISSION (SOUTH CAROLINA), 155
FOSSIL RIM WILDLIFE CENTER, 336
FOUNDATION FOR NORTH AMERICAN BIG GAME, 336
FOUNDATION FOR NORTH AMERICAN WILD SHEEP, 336
FRIENDS OF ANIMALS INC., 337
FRIENDS OF DISCOVERY PARK, 337
FRIENDS OF FAMOSA SLOUGH, 337
FRIENDS OF SUNKHAZE MEADOWS NATIONAL WILDLIFE REFUGE, 337
FRIENDS OF THE BOUNDARY WATERS WILDERNESS, 337
FRIENDS OF THE CARR REFUGE, 337
FRIENDS OF THE LITTLE PEND OREILLE NATIONAL WILDLIFE REFUGE, THE, 338
FRIENDS OF THE SEA OTTER, 338
FUNDACION NATURA COLOMBIA, 339
FUTURE GENERATIONS, 339
GALIANO CONSERVANCY ASSOCIATION, 339
GAME CONSERVANCY U.S.A., 339
GAME CONSERVATION INTERNATIONAL (GAME COIN), 339
GARDEN CLUB OF AMERICA, THE, 340
GEORGE MIKSCH SUTTON AVIAN RESEARCH CENTER INC., 340
GEORGE WRIGHT SOCIETY, THE, 341
GEORGIA DEPARTMENT OF NATURAL RESOURCES
   Environmental Protection Division
      Coastal Division, 156
GEORGIA ENVIRONMENTAL ORGANIZATION, INC. (GEO), 341
GEORGIA ENVIRONMENTAL POLICY INSTITUTE, 342
GEORGIA TRUST FOR HISTORIC PRESERVATION, 342
GLEN CANYON INSTITUTE, 343
GOPHER TORTOISE COUNCIL, 344
GRAND CANYON TRUST, 344
GRANT TECH CONSULTING AND CONSERVATION SERVICES, 567
GREAT BEAR FOUNDATION, 344
GREAT LAKES SPORT FISHING COUNCIL, 344
GREAT LAKES UNITED, 345
   CANADA OFFICE, 345
GREAT OUTDOORS CONSERVANCY, THE, 345
GREAT PLAINS NATIVE PLANT SOCIETY, 345
GREATER YELLOWSTONE COALITION, 346
GREEN BALKANS FEDERATION OF NATURE CONSERVATION NGOS, 346
GREEN SPHERE INC., 347
GREENPEACE, INC., 347
GROWLING, 348
GULF OF MEXICO FISHERY MANAGEMENT COUNCIL, 348
GULF STATES MARINE FISHERIES COMMISSION, 20
H. JOHN HEINZ III CENTER FOR SCIENCE, ECONOMICS, AND THE ENVIRONMENT, 348
HARBOR BRANCH OCEANOGRAPHIC INSTITUTION, 348
HAWAII DEPARTMENT OF LAND AND NATURAL RESOURCES
   Division of Water Resource Management, 159
HAWAII NATURE CENTER, 349
HAWK AND OWL TRUST, THE, 349
HAWK MIGRATION ASSOCIATION OF NORTH AMERICA, 349
HAWK MOUNTAIN SANCTUARY ASSOCIATION, VISITOR CENTER, 349
HAWKWATCH INTERNATIONAL, 350
HEADLANDS INSTITUTE, 350
HELPING OUR PENINSULA'S ENVIRONMENT, 350

HENRY STIFEL SCHRADER ENVIRONMENTAL EDUCATION CENTER, 350
HERPDIGEST, 350
HILTON POND CENTER FOR PIEDMONT NATURAL HISTORY, 351
HIMALAYAN WILDLIFE FOUNDATION, 351
HOLDEN ARBORETUM, THE, 351
HOLLOW OAK LAND TRUST, 351
HOOSIER ENVIRONMENTAL COUNCIL, 352
HUDSONIA LIMITED, 352
HUMANE SOCIETY OF THE UNITED STATES, THE, 352
HUMBOLT FIELD RESEARCH INSTITUTE, 353
HUNTSMAN MARINE SCIENCE CENTRE, 353
HYDE CREEK WATERSHED SOCIETY, 353
IDAHO CONSERVATION LEAGUE, 354
IDAHO DEPARTMENT OF PARKS AND RECREATION, 160
IDAHO FISH AND WILDLIFE FOUNDATION, 161
IDAHO STATE DEPARTMENT OF AGRICULTURE, 161
IDAHO STATE SOIL CONSERVATION COMMISSION, 161
ILLINOIS ASSOCIATION OF CONSERVATION DISTRICTS, 354
ILLINOIS NATIVE PLANT SOCIETY, 355
ILLINOIS NATURE PRESERVES COMMISSION (INPC), 163
ILLINOIS RAPTOR CENTER, 355
ILLINOIS WALNUT COUNCIL, 356
ILOVEPARKS.COM, 567
INDIANA ASSOCIATION OF SOIL AND WATER CONSERVATION DISTRICTS, INC., 356
INDIANA AUDUBON SOCIETY, INC., 356
INDO-PACIFIC CONSERVATION ALLIANCE, 357
INDUSTRIAL COMMISSION OF NORTH DAKOTA, 164
INSTITUTE FOR ECOLOGICAL STUDIES UNIVERSITY OF NORTH DAKOTA, 164
INSTITUTE FOR GLOBAL COMMUNICATIONS, 567
INSTITUTE FOR TROPICAL ECOLOGY AND CONSERVATION (ITEC), 358
INSTITUTO NACIONAL DE BIODIVERSIDAD (INBIO), 22
INTERFAITH COUNCIL FOR THE PROTECTION OF ANIMALS AND NATURE INC. (ICPAN), 359
INTERNATIONAL ACADEMY, 567
INTERNATIONAL ASSOCIATION FOR BEAR RESEARCH AND MANAGEMENT, 359
INTERNATIONAL ASSOCIATION OF FISH AND WILDLIFE AGENCIES, 360
INTERNATIONAL ASSOCIATION OF NATURAL RESOURCE PILOTS, 360
INTERNATIONAL ASSOCIATION OF WILDLAND FIRE, 361
INTERNATIONAL CENTRE FOR CONSERVATION EDUCATION, 361
INTERNATIONAL CHILDREN'S CONFERENCE ON THE ENVIRONMENT, 362
INTERNATIONAL CRANE FOUNDATION, 362
INTERNATIONAL ECOLOGY SOCIETY (IES), 362
INTERNATIONAL ECOTOURISM SOCIETY, THE, 362
INTERNATIONAL GAME FISH ASSOCIATION, 364
INTERNATIONAL MARINE MAMMAL PROJECT, THE, 364
INTERNATIONAL MIRE CONSERVATION GROUP, 365
INTERNATIONAL OCEANOGRAPHIC FOUNDATION, 365
INTERNATIONAL OSPREY FOUNDATION INC., THE, 365
INTERNATIONAL PLANT PROPAGATORS SOCIETY, INC., 365
INTERNATIONAL PRIMATE PROTECTION LEAGUE, 365
INTERNATIONAL SNOW LEOPARD TRUST, 366
INTERNATIONAL SOCIETY FOR ECOLOGICAL ECONOMICS (ISEE), 366
INTERNATIONAL SOCIETY FOR ENDANGERED CATS, 366
INTERNATIONAL SOCIETY FOR ENDANGERED CATS (ISEC), 366
INTERNATIONAL SOCIETY FOR THE PRESERVATION OF THE TROPICAL RAINFOREST, THE, 367
INTERNATIONAL SOCIETY OF TROPICAL FORESTERS, INC., 367
INTERNATIONAL UNION FOR CONSERVATION OF NATURE AND NATURAL RESOURCES (IUCN) THE WORLD CONSERVATION UNION
  Environmental Law Centre, 368
  Regional Office for Europe, 369
INTERNATIONAL WHALING COMMISSION, 23
INTERNATIONAL WILD WATERFOWL ASSOCIATION, 371
INTERNATIONAL WILDLIFE COALITION (IWC) AND THE WHALE ADOPTION PROJECT, 371
INTERNATIONAL WILDLIFE REHABILITATION COUNCIL, 371
INTERNATIONAL WOLF CENTER, 371
INTERTRIBAL BISON COOPERATIVE (ITBC), 372
IOWA ASSOCIATION OF COUNTY CONSERVATION BOARDS, 164
IOWA ASSOCIATION OF NATURALISTS, 372
IOWA BASS FEDERATION, 372
IOWA DEPARTMENT OF AGRICULTURE AND LAND STEWARDSHIP
  Bureau of Field Services, 165
IOWA DEPARTMENT OF NATURAL RESOURCES
  Fish and Wildlife Division, 166
IOWA ENVIRONMENTAL COUNCIL, 372
IOWA NATIVE PLANT SOCIETY, 373
IOWA PRAIRIE NETWORK, 373

IOWA STATE UNIVERSITY
  College of Agriculture, 584
IOWA WOMEN IN NATURAL RESOURCES, 374
ISLAND CONSERVATION EFFORT, 374
ISLAND RESOURCES FOUNDATION, 375
ISLESBORO ISLANDS TRUST, 375
IZAAK WALTON LEAGUE OF AMERICA ENDOWMENT, 375
IZAAK WALTON LEAGUE OF AMERICA, INC., THE
  California State IWLA, 376
  Minnesota Division, 377
  Owatonna Minnesota Chapter, 377
  South Dakota Division, 378
J.N. (DING) DARLING FOUNDATION, 379
JACKSON HOLE CONSERVATION ALLIANCE, 379
JACKSON HOLE LAND TRUST, 379
JAGRATA JUBA SHANGHA (JJS), 568
JANE GOODALL INSTITUTE, THE, 380
JAPAN WILDLIFE RESEARCH CENTER (JWRC), 380
JOHNSON STATE COLLEGE, 585
KANSAS ASSOCIATION FOR CONSERVATION AND ENVIRONMENTAL EDUCATION, KACEE, 380
KANSAS BASS FEDERATION, 381
KANSAS BIOLOGICAL SURVEY, 166
KANSAS COOPERATIVE FISH AND WILDLIFE RESEARCH UNIT, 167
KANSAS DEPARTMENT OF AGRICULTURE, 167
KANSAS DEPARTMENT OF WILDLIFE AND PARKS
  Office of the Secretary, 167
  Operations Office, 167
  Region 1, 167
  Region 2, 168
  Region 3, 168
  Region 4, 168
KANSAS NATURAL RESOURCE COUNCIL, 381
KANSAS STATE CONSERVATION COMMISSION, 168
KANSAS STATE EXTENSION SERVICES, 169
KANSAS STATE UNIVERSITY
  Department of Landscape Architecture / Regional and Community Planning, 585
KANSAS WILDFLOWER SOCIETY, 381
KANSAS WILDLIFE FEDERATION, 382
KEEP FLORIDA BEAUTIFUL, INC., 382
KENTUCKY DEPARTMENT OF AGRICULTURE, 169
KENTUCKY GEOLOGICAL SURVEY, 170
KENTUCKY NATURAL LANDS TRUST, 383
KENTUCKY STATE NATURE PRESERVES COMMISSION, 171
KIDS FOR SAVING EARTH WORLDWIDE, 384
KODIAK BROWN BEAR TRUST, 384
LA JOLLA FRIENDS OF THE SEALS (LJFS), 384
LADY BIRD JOHNSON WILDFLOWER CENTER, 385
LAKE ERIE CLEAN-UP COMMITTEE, INC., 385
LAKE SUPERIOR STATE UNIVERSITY, 586
LAKEHEAD UNIVERSITY, 586
LAKENET, 385
LAND AND WATER FUND OF THE ROCKIES, 386
LAND CONSERVANCY OF WEST MICHIGAN, 386
LAND TRUST ALLIANCE, THE, 386
LAST WIZARDS, THE, 568
LEAGUE OF ENVIRONMENTAL JOURNALISTS, 387
LEAGUE OF OHIO SPORTSMEN, 387
LEAGUE TO SAVE LAKE TAHOE, 388
LEE COUNTY PARKS AND RECREATION, 171
LEGACY LAND TRUST, 388
LIGHTHAWK, 389
LIVING RIVERS, 390
LONG LIVE THE KINGS, 390
LOUISIANA BASS FEDERATION, 390
LOUISIANA DEPARTMENT OF AGRICULTURE AND FORESTRY
  Office of Soil and Water Conservation, State Soil and Water Conservation Committee, 172
LOUISIANA STATE UNIVERSITY SCHOOL OF FORESTRY, WILDLIFE AND FISHERIES, 586
LOUISIANA WILDLIFE REHABILITATORS ASSOCIATION, 391
LOWER MERION CONSERVANCY, 391
LOWER MISSISSIPPI RIVER CONSERVATION COMMITTEE, 391
LSU AGCENTER - LOUISIANA COOPERATIVE EXTENSION SERVICE, 173
LUMMI ISLAND HERITAGE TRUST, 568
MACBRIDE RAPTOR PROJECT, 391
MACOMB LAND CONSERVANCY, 391
MAGIC, 392
MAINE ASSOCIATION OF CONSERVATION DISTRICTS, 392
MAINE ATLANTIC SALMON COMMISSION, 173
MAINE BASS FEDERATION, 392

KEYWORD INDEX – W

MAINE DEPARTMENT OF CONSERVATION
  Bureau of Geology and Natural Areas, 174
MAINE DEPARTMENT OF ENVIRONMENTAL PROTECTION, 175
MAINE DEPARTMENT OF INLAND FISHERIES AND WILDLIFE, 175
MAINE DEPARTMENT OF MARINE RESOURCES, 175
MANITOBA CONSERVATION
  Western REGION, 176
MANITOBA NATURALISTS SOCIETY, 393
MANOMET CENTER FOR CONSERVATION SCIENCES, 393
MANTA MEXICO, 393
MARINE CONSERVATION BIOLOGY INSTITUTE, 394
MARINE ENVIRONMENTAL RESEARCH INSTITUTE (MERI), 394
MARINE SCIENCE INSTITUTE, 394
MARYLAND BASS FEDERATION, 395
MARYLAND DEPARTMENT OF AGRICULTURE, 176
MASSACHUSETTS ASSOCIATION OF CONSERVATION DISTRICTS, 396
MASSACHUSETTS BASS FEDERATION, 396
MASSACHUSETTS COOPERATIVE FISH AND WILDLIFE RESEARCH UNIT (USDI), 178
MASSACHUSETTS DIVISION OF FISHERIES AND WILDLIFE
  MassWildlife, 178
MASSACHUSETTS EXECUTIVE OFFICE OF ENVIRONMENTAL AFFAIRS, 178
  Office of Technical Assistance for Toxic Use Reduction, 179
  Wetlands and Waterways Program, 179
MAX MCGRAW WILDLIFE FOUNDATION, 396
MCGILL UNIVERSITY, 587
MECKLENBURG COUNTY PARK AND RECREATION DEPARTMENT, 179
MERCK FOREST AND FARMLAND CENTER, 397
MIAMI UNIVERSITY, 587
MICHIGAN BASS FEDERATION, 397
MICHIGAN DEPARTMENT OF AGRICULTURE, 180
MICHIGAN DEPARTMENT OF ENVIRONMENTAL QUALITY, 180
MICHIGAN DEPARTMENT OF NATURAL RESOURCES, 180
MICHIGAN LAND USE INSTITUTE, 397
MICHIGAN NATURE ASSOCIATION, 398
MICHIGAN STATE UNIVERSITY EXTENSION, 181
MICHIGAN TECHNOLOGICAL UNIVERSITY, SCHOOL OF FORESTRY AND WOOD PRODUCTS, 588
MICHIGAN UNITED CONSERVATION CLUBS, INC., 398
MID-ATLANTIC FISHERY MANAGEMENT COUNCIL, 398
MIDDLE TENNESSEE STATE UNIVERSITY, 588
MIDLAND CONSERVATION DISTRICT, 181
MINNESOTA ASSOCIATION OF SOIL AND WATER CONSERVATION DISTRICTS, 399
MINNESOTA BOARD OF WATER AND SOIL RESOURCES, 181
MINNESOTA NATIVE PLANT SOCIETY, 400
MINNESOTA ORNITHOLOGISTS' UNION, 400
MINNESOTA POLLUTION CONTROL AGENCY
  Rochester, MN, 183
MISSISSIPPI BASS FEDERATION, 401
MISSISSIPPI COOPERATIVE FISH AND WILDLIFE RESEARCH UNIT, 183
MISSISSIPPI INTERSTATE COOPERATIVE RESOURCE ASSOCIATION, 401
MISSISSIPPI SOIL AND WATER CONSERVATION COMMISSION, 184
MISSISSIPPI STATE UNIVERSITY
  College of Forest Resources, 588
  Forest and Wildlife Research Center, 588
MISSOURI ASSOCIATION OF SOIL AND WATER CONSERVATION DISTRICTS, 402
MISSOURI DEPARTMENT OF AGRICULTURE, 185
MISSOURI PRAIRIE FOUNDATION, 402
MISSOURI STATE EXTENSION SERVICES, 186
MONTANA BASS FEDERATION, 403
MONTANA BUREAU OF MINES AND GEOLOGY, 186
MONTANA COOPERATIVE WILDLIFE RESEARCH UNIT (USGS/BRD), 186
MONTANA DEPARTMENT OF NATURAL RESOURCES AND CONSERVATION, 187
MONTANA LAND RELIANCE, 403
MONTANA NATURAL HERITAGE PROGRAM, 187
MONTANA STATE UNIVERSITY
  College of Agriculture, 589
MONTANA WILDERNESS ASSOCIATION, 403
MONTANA WILDLIFE FEDERATION, 404
MORONGO BASIN WILDLIFE REHAB STATION, 404
MOTE MARINE LABORATORY, 404
MOUNTAIN CONSERVATION TRUST OF GEORGIA, INC., 405
MOUNTAINEERS, THE, 405
MRFC FISH CONSERVATION, 405
MULE DEER FOUNDATION, 405
MUNDO AZUL, 406
MURRAY STATE UNIVERSITY, 589

NATIONAL AGRICULTURAL LIBRARY, 24
NATIONAL ARBOR DAY FOUNDATION, 406
NATIONAL ASSOCIATION OF BIOLOGY TEACHERS, 407
NATIONAL ASSOCIATION OF STATE PARK DIRECTORS, 409
NATIONAL ASSOCIATION OF UNIVERSITY FISHERIES AND WILDLIFE PROGRAMS, 409
NATIONAL AUDUBON SOCIETY, 409
  Audubon Alaska, 409
  Audubon Council of Connecticut, 409
  Audubon Council of Illinois, 410
  Audubon Maryland-DC, 410
  Audubon Missouri, 410
  Audubon of Florida, 410
  Audubon of Kansas, 410
  Audubon Pennsylvania, 411
  Audubon Society of Missouri, 411
  Audubon Society of Omaha, 411
  Audubon Society of Portland, 411
  Audubon Society of Rhode Island, 412
  Audubon Society of Western Pennsylvania, 412
  Audubon Vermont, 412
  Connecticut Audubon Society, 412
  Delaware Audubon Society, 413
  Fairfax Audubon Society, 413
  Hawaii Audubon Society, 413
  Illinois Audubon Society, 413
  Louisiana Audubon Council, 414
  Maricopa Audubon Society, 414
  Massachusetts Audubon Society, 414
  Montana Audubon, 415
  New Jersey Chapter, 415
  Public Policy Office, 415
  San Diego Chapter, 416
  Seattle Audubon Society, 416
  Tucson Audubon Society, 416
NATIONAL AVIARY, 568
NATIONAL BIRD-FEEDING SOCIETY, 416
NATIONAL BOWHUNTER EDUCATION FOUNDATION (NBEF), 417
NATIONAL COALITION FOR MARINE CONSERVATION, 417
NATIONAL FISH AND WILDLIFE FOUNDATION, 419
NATIONAL FOREST FOUNDATION, 420
NATIONAL GARDENING ASSOCIATION, 420
NATIONAL MILITARY FISH AND WILDLIFE ASSOCIATION, 421
NATIONAL NETWORK OF FOREST PRACTITIONERS, 422
NATIONAL PARK TRUST, 422
NATIONAL PARKS CONSERVATION ASSOCIATION (NPCA), 422
  Sun Coast Regional Office, 423
NATIONAL RECREATION AND PARK ASSOCIATION, 423
NATIONAL RIFLE ASSOCIATION WEST VIRGINIA
  White Horse Firearms and Outdoor Education Center, Inc., 424
NATIONAL SPELEOLOGICAL SOCIETY, INC., 424
NATIONAL WATER RESOURCES ASSOCIATION, 426
NATIONAL WATERSHED COALITION, 426
NATIONAL WATERWAYS CONFERENCE INC., 426
NATIONAL WILD TURKEY FEDERATION, CANADA, INC., THE, 426
NATIONAL WILD TURKEY FEDERATION, INC., THE, 427
NATIONAL WILDLIFE FEDERATION
  Great Lakes Natural Resource Center, 427
  Headquarters, 427
  Northern Rockies Natural Resource Center, 428
  Rocky Mountain Natural Resource Center, 428
NATIONAL WILDLIFE PRODUCTIONS, INC., 429
NATIONAL WILDLIFE REFUGE ASSOCIATION, 429
NATIONAL WILDLIFE REHABILITATORS ASSOCIATION, 429
NATIONAL WOODLAND OWNERS ASSOCIATION, 430
NATIVE PLANT SOCIETY OF NORTHEASTERN OHIO, 430
NATIVE PLANT SOCIETY OF OREGON, 430
NATIVE PLANT SOCIETY OF TEXAS, 431
NATURAL AREAS ASSOCIATION, 431
NATURAL HISTORY SOCIETY OF MARYLAND, INC., THE, 431
NATURAL LAND INSTITUTE, 431
NATURAL LANDS TRUST, 431
NATURAL RESOURCES COUNCIL OF MAINE, 432
NATURE CONSERVANCY, THE
  Alabama Chapter, 433
  Arkansas Field Office, 434
  Colorado Chapter, 434
  Eastern New York Chapter, 435
  Illinois Chapter, 435
  Kansas Chapter, 436
  Maryland/District of Columbia Chapter, 436
  New York City Chapter, 438
  New York City Office, 437

NATURE CONSERVANCY, THE (continued)
  Northwest and Hawaii Division Office, 438
  Oklahoma Chapter, 439
  Oregon Chapter, 439
  Pennsylvania Chapter, 439
  Rhode Island Chapter, 439
  Texas Chapter, 439
  Washington Chapter, 440
NAVAJO NATION DEPARTMENT OF FISH AND WILDLIFE, 188
NEBRASKA ASSOCIATION OF RESOURCE DISTRICTS, 441
NEBRASKA DEPARTMENT OF ENVIRONMENTAL QUALITY, 188
NEBRASKA DEPARTMENT OF NATURAL RESOURCES, 188
NEBRASKA WILDLIFE FEDERATION, INC., 442
NEGATIVE POPULATION GROWTH (NPG), 442
NEVADA ASSOCIATION OF CONSERVATION DISTRICTS, 442
NEW BRUNSWICK DEPARTMENT OF NATURAL RESOURCES, 189
NEW ENGLAND WILD FLOWER SOCIETY, INC., 443
NEW HAMPSHIRE ASSOCIATION OF CONSERVATION COMMISSIONS, 443
NEW HAMPSHIRE ASSOCIATION OF CONSERVATION DISTRICTS, 444
NEW HAMPSHIRE DEPARTMENT OF ENVIRONMENTAL SERVICES, 190
NEW HAMPSHIRE DEPARTMENT OF RESOURCES AND ECONOMIC DEVELOPMENT, 190
NEW HAMPSHIRE LAKES ASSOCIATION, 444
NEW HAMPSHIRE NATURAL HERITAGE BUREAU, 191
NEW JERSEY AGRICULTURAL SOCIETY, 444
NEW JERSEY ASSOCIATION OF CONSERVATION DISTRICTS, 445
NEW MEXICO BUREAU OF GEOLOGY AND MINERAL RESOURCES, 193
NEW MEXICO DEPARTMENT OF AGRICULTURE, 193
NEW MEXICO ENERGY, MINERALS, AND NATURAL RESOURCES DEPARTMENT
  Oil Conservation Division, 195
NEW MEXICO STATE UNIVERSITY
  College of Agriculture and Home Economics, 589
  Department of Fishery and Wildlife Sciences, 590
NEW YORK OFFICE OF ENERGY EFFICIENCY AND ENVIRONMENT, 197
NEW YORK STATE TUG HILL COMMISSION, 199
NEW YORK TURTLE AND TORTOISE SOCIETY, 446
NEWFOUNDLAND DEPARTMENT OF FOREST RESOURCES AND AGRIFOODS
  Regional Offices, 199
NORTH AMERICAN BENTHOLOGICAL SOCIETY, 447
NORTH AMERICAN BLUEBIRD SOCIETY, 447
NORTH AMERICAN BUTTERFLY ASSOCIATION, 448
NORTH AMERICAN COALITION ON RELIGION AND ECOLOGY (NACRE), 448
NORTH AMERICAN CRANE WORKING GROUP, 448
NORTH AMERICAN FALCONERS ASSOCIATION, 448
NORTH AMERICAN GAMEBIRD ASSOCIATION, INC., 448
NORTH AMERICAN LOON FUND, 448
NORTH AMERICAN NATIVE FISHES ASSOCIATION, 449
NORTH AMERICAN WETLANDS CONSERVATION COUNCIL, 24
NORTH AMERICAN WILDLIFE PARK FOUNDATION, INC., 449
NORTH AMERICAN WOLF ASSOCIATION, 449
NORTH ATLANTIC SALMON CONSERVATION ORGANIZATION, 449
NORTH CAROLINA BEACH BUGGY ASSOCIATION, INC., 450
NORTH CAROLINA COASTAL FEDERATION, INC., 450
NORTH CAROLINA CONSERVATION NETWORK, 450
NORTH CAROLINA DEPARTMENT OF AGRICULTURE AND CONSUMER SERVICES, 200
NORTH CAROLINA MUSEUM OF NATURAL SCIENCES, 450
NORTH CAROLINA STATE UNIVERSITY, 590
NORTH CASCADES CONSERVATION COUNCIL, 451
NORTH DAKOTA DEPARTMENT OF HEALTH, 201
NORTH DAKOTA NATURAL SCIENCE SOCIETY, 452
NORTH DAKOTA STATE UNIVERSITY, 590
NORTH DAKOTA WATER COMMISSION, 202
NORTHEASTERN UNIVERSITY, 590
NORTHLAND COLLEGE, 591
NORTHWEST ATLANTIC FISHERIES ORGANIZATION (NAFO), 453
NORTHWEST COALITION FOR ALTERNATIVES TO PESTICIDES, 453
NORTHWEST ECOSYSTEM ALLIANCE, 453
NORTHWEST RESOURCE INFORMATION CENTER, 454
NORTHWESTERN STATE UNIVERSITY OF LOUISIANA, 591
NOVA SCOTIA AGRICULTURE & FISHERIES, 203
NOVA SCOTIA DEPARTMENT OF NATURAL RESOURCES, 203
NOVA SCOTIA FEDERATION OF ANGLERS AND HUNTERS, 454
NOVA SCOTIA FORESTRY ASSOCIATION, 454
NW ENERGY COALITION, 454
OCEAN CONSERVANCY, THE, 455
OCEAN PROJECT, THE, 455
OCEAN VOICE INTERNATIONAL, 455
OCEANIA, 455
OCEANIC SOCIETY, 456
OHIO BIOLOGICAL SURVEY, 456
OHIO DEPARTMENT OF AGRICULTURE, 203
OHIO DEPARTMENT OF NATURAL RESOURCES, 204
OHIO ENERGY PROJECT, 456
OHIO ENVIRONMENTAL COUNCIL, INC., 457
OHIO ENVIRONMENTAL REVIEW APPEALS COMMISSION, 205
OHIO STATE UNIVERSITY, 592
OHIO STATE UNIVERSITY EXTENSION, 205
OHIO STREAM PRESERVATION, 457
OKLAHOMA CONSERVATION COMMISSION, 205
OKLAHOMA DEPARTMENT OF AGRICULTURE, 205
OKLAHOMA DEPARTMENT OF WILDLIFE CONSERVATION, 206
OKLAHOMA NATIVE PLANT SOCIETY, 458
OKLAHOMA STATE UNIVERSITY, 592
OKLAHOMA WATER RESOURCES BOARD, 207
OLYMPIC PARK INSTITUTE, 459
ONEWILDWORLD, 459
ONTARIO FEDERATION OF ANGLERS AND HUNTERS, 459
ONTARIO FORESTRY ASSOCIATION, 459
OPERATION MIGRATION, 460
ORANGUTAN FOUNDATION INTERNATIONAL, 460
OREGON DEPARTMENT OF AGRICULTURE, 208
OREGON DEPARTMENT OF GEOLOGY AND MINERAL INDUSTRIES, 209
OREGON SMALL WOODLANDS ASSOCIATION, 461
OREGON SOCIETY OF AMERICAN FORESTERS, 461
OREGON STATE EXTENSION SERVICES, 209
OREGON WATER RESOURCES DEPARTMENT, 210
ORGANIZATION FOR BAT CONSERVATION, 461
ORNITHOLOGICAL COUNCIL, 462
OTTER PROJECT, THE, 462
OUTDOOR RECREATION COUNCIL OF BRITISH COLUMBIA, 462
PACIFIC FISHERY MANAGEMENT COUNCIL, 463
PACIFIC MARINE CONSERVATION COUNCIL, 464
PACIFIC RIVERS COUNCIL, 464
PACIFIC SEABIRD GROUP, 464
PACIFIC WHALE FOUNDATION, 464
PARKS AND TRAILS COUNCIL OF MINNESOTA, 465
PARTNERS IN AMPHIBIAN AND REPTILE CONSERVATION (PARC), 465
PARTNERS IN PARKS, 465
PENNSYLVANIA COOPERATIVE FISH AND WILDLIFE RESEARCH UNIT, 210
PENNSYLVANIA DEPARTMENT OF AGRICULTURE
  State Conservation Commission, 211
PENNSYLVANIA DEPARTMENT OF ENVIRONMENTAL PROTECTION, 211
PEOPLE FOR PUGET SOUND, 467
  North Sound Office, 467
  South Sound Office, 467
PEREGRINE FUND, THE, 467
PHEASANTS FOREVER, INC., 468
PLAYA LAKES JOINT VENTURE, 469
POCONO WILDLIFE REHABILITATION CENTER, 470
POINT TO POINT COMMUNICATIONS, 569
PRAIRIE CLUB, THE, 472
PRAIRIE GROUSE TECHNICAL COUNCIL, 472
PRAIRIE WILDLIFE RESEARCH, 472
PREDATOR CONSERVATION ALLIANCE, 472
PROGRESSIVE ANIMAL WELFARE SOCIETY, 473
PROJECT SEAHORSE, 473
PROTECTED AREAS ASSOCIATION OF NEWFOUNDLAND AND LABRADOR, 474
PROVINCE OF QUEBEC SOCIETY FOR THE PROTECTION OF BIRDS, INC., 474
PTARMIGANS, THE, 474
PUBLIC EMPLOYEES FOR ENVIRONMENTAL RESPONSIBILITY (PEER), 474
PUBLIC LANDS INTERPRETIVE ASSOCIATION, 570
PUERTO RICO ASSOCIATION OF SOIL AND WATER CONSERVATION DISTRICTS, 474
PUERTO RICO CONSERVATION FOUNDATION, THE (PRCF), 475
PUERTO RICO DEPARTMENT OF AGRICULTURE, 213
PUERTO RICO SOIL CONSERVATION COMMITTEE, 213
PURPLE MARTIN CONSERVATION ASSOCIATION, 475
QUAIL UNLIMITED, INC., 475
QUALITY DEER MANAGEMENT ASSOCIATION, 476
QUEBEC WILDLIFE FEDERATION, 476
RACHEL CARSON COUNCIL, INC., 476
RAINFOREST ACTION NETWORK, 476
RAINFOREST ALLIANCE, 477
RAINFOREST RELIEF, 477
RAINFOREST TRUST, 477
RAPTOR CENTER, THE, 593

KEYWORD INDEX – W

RAPTOR EDUCATION FOUNDATION, INC., 477
RAPTOR RESEARCH FOUNDATION, INC., 477
RARE CENTER FOR TROPICAL CONSERVATION, 478
RED BUFFALO, LLC, 570
REEF RELIEF, 478
RENEWABLE NATURAL RESOURCES FOUNDATION, 478
RESOURCES FOR THE FUTURE, 479
RHODE ISLAND FOREST CONSERVATOR'S ORGANIZATION, INC., 480
RHODE ISLAND STATE CONSERVATION COMMITTEE, 480
RIVER ALLIANCE OF WISCONSIN, 480
RIVER OTTER ALLIANCE, THE, 481
RIVER PROJECT, THE, 481
RIVERSIDE COUNTY CONSERVATION AGENCY, 215
ROCKY MOUNTAIN BIGHORN SOCIETY, 482
ROCKY MOUNTAIN BIOLOGICAL LABORATORY, THE, 482
ROCKY MOUNTAIN BIRD OBSERVATORY, 482
ROCKY MOUNTAIN ELK FOUNDATION, 482
RUFFED GROUSE SOCIETY, THE, 482
RUFFNER MOUNTAIN NATURE COALITION, INC., 483
SAFARI CLUB INTERNATIONAL
   International Headquarters, 483
SAN DIEGO NATURAL HISTORY MUSEUM, 484
SAN DIEGUITO RIVER PARK JOINT POWERS AUTHORITY, 215
SAN ELIJO LAGOON CONSERVANCY, 484
SAND CREEK WATERSHED PROJECT, THE, 215
SASKATCHEWAN ENVIRONMENT AND RESOURCE MANAGEMENT
   Corporate Services, 216
SASKATCHEWAN WILDLIFE FEDERATION, 484
SAVE AMERICA'S FORESTS, 485
SAVE THE DUNES CONSERVATION FUND, 485
SAVE THE MANATEE CLUB, 486
SAVE THE SOUND, INC., 486
SAVE-THE-REDWOODS LEAGUE, 487
SCIENTISTS CENTER FOR ANIMAL WELFARE, 488
SEA SHEPHERD CONSERVATION SOCIETY
   International headquarters, 488
   Netherlands, 488
SEA TURTLE PRESERVATION SOCIETY, 489
SHELBURNE FARMS, 490
SHEPHERD COLLEGE, 595
SIERRA CLUB
   Alaska Field Office, 490
   Connecticut Chapter, 491
   Hawaii Chapter, 492
   Mackinac Chapter, 493
   Maryland Chapter, 493
   Mississippi Chapter, 494
   Nebraska Chapter, 494
   Northwest Office, 495
   Pennsylvania Chapter, 496
   Rio Grande Chapter (New Mexico/West Texas), 496
   Washington, DC Office, 499
   West Virginia Chapter, 499
SIERRA CLUB CALIFORNIA, 499
SIERRA CLUB FOUNDATION, THE, 499
SIERRA CLUB OF CANADA
   Atlantic Canada Chapter, 500
SIERRA STUDENT COALITION, 500
SINAPU, 500
SLIPPERY ROCK UNIVERSITY, 595
SMALL WOODLAND OWNERS ASSOCIATION OF MAINE, 501
SMITHSONIAN INSTITUTION, 501
SOCIETY FOR ANIMAL PROTECTIVE LEGISLATION, 502
SOCIETY FOR CONSERVATION BIOLOGY, 502
SOCIETY FOR INTEGRATIVE AND COMPARATIVE BIOLOGY, 502
SOCIETY FOR MARINE MAMMALOGY, THE, 503
SOCIETY FOR RANGE MANAGEMENT, 503
SOCIETY FOR THE PRESERVATION OF BIRDS OF PREY, 503
SOCIETY OF AMERICAN FORESTERS, 503
SOCIETY OF TYMPANUCHUS CUPIDO PINNATUS LTD., 504
SOIL AND WATER CONSERVATION SOCIETY, 504
SONORAN DESERT NATIONAL PARK FRIENDS, 504
SONORAN INSTITUTE, 505
SOUTH ATLANTIC FISHERY MANAGEMENT COUNCIL, 29
SOUTH CAROLINA COOPERATIVE FISH AND WILDLIFE RESEARCH
   UNIT, 217
SOUTH CAROLINA DEPARTMENT OF PARKS, RECREATION AND
   TOURISM, 218
SOUTH CAROLINA ENVIRONMENTAL LAW PROJECT, 506
SOUTH CAROLINA NATIVE PLANT SOCIETY, 506
SOUTH CAROLINA WILDLIFE FEDERATION, 506
SOUTH DAKOTA ASSOCIATION OF CONSERVATION DISTRICTS, 506
SOUTH DAKOTA BASS FEDERATION, 507

SOUTH DAKOTA COOPERATIVE EXTENSION SERVICE, 218
SOUTH DAKOTA DEPARTMENT OF AGRICULTURE, 218
SOUTH DAKOTA DEPARTMENT OF GAME, FISH, AND PARKS, 219
SOUTH DAKOTA WILDLIFE FEDERATION, 507
SOUTH FLORIDA WATER MANAGEMENT DISTRICT, 219
SOUTHEASTERN ASSOCIATION OF FISH AND WILDLIFE AGENCIES, 508
SOUTHEASTERN FISHES COUNCIL, 508
SOUTHERN APPALACHIAN BOTANICAL SOCIETY, 508
SOUTHERN ENVIRONMENTAL LAW CENTER, 509
SOUTHERN ILLINOIS UNIVERSITY CARBONDALE, 596
SOUTHERN UTAH WILDERNESS ALLIANCE
   Moab Office, 510
SOUTHWEST CENTER FOR ENVIRONMENTAL RESEARCH AND
   POLICY (SCERP), 596
SOUTHWEST CONSERVATION DISTRICT, 510
SOUTHWESTERN HERPETOLOGISTS SOCIETY, 510
SPORTSMAN NETWORK, INC., THE, 510
SPORTSMEN'S NATIONAL LAND TRUST, THE, 511
ST. FRANCIS WILDLIFE ASSOCIATION, 511
STANFORD ENVIRONMENTAL LAW SOCIETY, 511
STATE ENVIRONMENTAL RESOURCE CENTER (SERC), 512
STEAMBOATERS, THE, 512
STEPHEN F. AUSTIN STATE UNIVERSITY ARTHUR TEMPLE COLLEGE
   OF FORESTRY, 598
STERLING COLLEGE, 598
STROUD WATER RESEARCH CENTER, 512
STUDENT CONSERVATION ASSOCIATION, INC., 512
STURGEON FOR TOMORROW, 514
SUNCOAST SEABIRD SANCTUARY INC., 514
SUSTAIN, 514
TAHOE REGIONAL PLANNING AGENCY, 220
TALL TIMBERS RESEARCH STATION (TTRS), 515
TEMPLE UNIVERSITY, 599
TENNESSEE BASS FEDERATION, 515
TENNESSEE CITIZENS FOR WILDERNESS PLANNING, 515
TENNESSEE CONSERVATION LEAGUE, 516
TENNESSEE COOPERATIVE FISHERY RESEARCH UNIT (USDI), 220
TENNESSEE DEPARTMENT OF ENVIRONMENT AND CONSERVATION, 221
TENNESSEE VALLEY AUTHORITY
   Muscle Shoals Technical Library, 30
TERRA NATURE FUND, 516
TEXAS A AND M UNIVERSITY AT KINGSVILLE
   Caesar Kleberg Wildlife Research Institute, 599
TEXAS BASS FEDERATION, 517
TEXAS COOPERATIVE FISH AND WILDLIFE RESEARCH UNIT, 30
TEXAS DEPARTMENT OF AGRICULTURE, 222
TEXAS DISCOVERY GARDENS, 517
TEXAS ORGANIZATION FOR ENDANGERED SPECIES, 517
TEXAS RIPARIAN ASSOCIATION, 517
TEXAS STATE SOIL AND WATER CONSERVATION BOARD, 223
TEXAS WATER DEVELOPMENT BOARD, 223
TRAFFIC NORTH AMERICA, 518
TREEPEOPLE, 519
TREES ATLANTA, 519
TREES FOR THE FUTURE, INC., 519
TREES FOR TOMORROW, NATURAL RESOURCES EDUCATION
   CENTER, 519
TRI-STATE BIRD RESCUE AND RESEARCH, INC., 520
TROUT UNLIMITED
   Alaska Council, 520
   New York Council, 522
TRUMPETER SWAN SOCIETY, THE, 523
TRUST FOR PUBLIC LAND, THE, 523
TRUST FOR WILDLIFE, INC., 524
TRUSTEES FOR ALASKA, 524
TULANE ENVIRONMENTAL LAW CLINIC, 600
TULANE UNIVERSITY
   Department of Ecology and Evolutionary Biology, 600
TURNER ENDANGERED SPECIES FUND, 571
TURTLE CREEK WATERSHED ASSOCIATION, INC., 525
TWO WHITE WOLVES SANCTUARY, 525
UNEP WORLD CONSERVATION MONITORING CENTRE, 525
UNION OF CONCERNED SCIENTISTS, 525
UNITED NATIONS ENVIRONMENT PROGRAMME, 525
UNITED STATES COMMITTEE FOR THE UNITED NATIONS
   ENVIRONMENT PROGRAMME, THE (U.S. AND UNEP), 526
UNITED STATES DEPARTMENT OF AGRICULTURE
   Economic Research Center, 33
   Forest Service
      Angelina, Davy Crockett, Sabine and Sam Houston National Forest, 34
      Crooked River National Grassland, 37
      Gila National Forest, 38

UNITED STATES DEPARTMENT OF AGRICULTURE (continued)
  Forest Service (continued)
    Los Padres National Forest, 40
    Nez Perce National Forest, 41
    Pawnee National Grassland, 42
    Region 02 (Rocky Mountain), 43
    Siuslaw National Forest, 45
UNITED STATES DEPARTMENT OF COMMERCE
  National Oceanic and Atmospheric Administration
    Delaware National Estuarine Research Reserve, 50
    Gray's Reef National Marine Sanctuary, 50
    Gulf of Farallones National Marine Sanctuary, 50
    Rookery Bay National Estuarine Research Reserve, 53
    Sea Grant Program - Alabama, 53
    Sea Grant Program - California, 54
    Sea Grant Program - Georgia, 55
    Sea Grant Program - Massachusetts, 56
    Sea Grant Program - New York, 58
    Sea Grant Program - North Carolina, 58
    Sea Grant Program - Rhode Island, 59
    Sea Grant Program - Texas, 59
    Wells National Estuarine Research Reserve, 60
UNITED STATES DEPARTMENT OF DEFENSE
  Air Force Major Air Commands
    Andrews AFB, MD, 61
    USAF Academy, 62
  Air Force Major U.S. Installations
    Eglin Air Force Base, 63
    Luke AFB (and the Barry M. Goldwater AFR), AZ, 65
    Randolph AFB, TX, 66
  Army Corps of Engineers
    Fort Worth Engineer District, 68
    Norfolk Engineer District, 70
    North Atlantic Engineer District, 70
    Pacific Ocean Engineer District, 70
    Philadelphia District, 70
    Walla Walla Engineer District, 72
  Army Materiel Command, 72
  Assistant Chief of Staff for Installation Management, Office of the Director of Environmental Programs, and Conservation Team, 74
  HQ PACAF/CEVQ, 74
  Navy, 74
UNITED STATES DEPARTMENT OF HOMELAND SECURITY
  Customs and Border Protection
    Mid-America CMC, 76
UNITED STATES DEPARTMENT OF HOUSING AND URBAN DEVELOPMENT, 77
UNITED STATES DEPARTMENT OF THE INTERIOR
  Bureau of Land Management
    Bakersfield Field Office, 79
    Eugene District Office, 81
    Malta Field Office, 83
    Northern Field Office, 84
    Rawlins Field Office, 85
    Safford Field Office, 86
    Tucson Field Office, 88
  Bureau of Reclamation, 89
    Pacific Northwest Region, 89
  Fish & Wildlife Service, 90
    Alligator River/Pea Island National Wildlife Refuge, 91
    Archie Carr National Wildlife Refuge, 91
    Arrowwood National Wildlife Refuge Complex, 91
    Arthur R. Marshall Loxahatchee/Hope Sound National Wildlife Refuge, 91
    Ash Meadows National Wildlife Refuge, 92
    Balcones Canyonlands National Wildlife Refuge, 92
    Bombay Hook National Wildlife Refuge, 93
    Browns Park National Wildlife Refuge, 94
    California-Nevada Operations, 94
    Canaan Valley National Wildlife Refuge, 94
    Carolina Sandhills National Wildlife Refuge, 95
    Chickasaw National Wildlife Refuge, 95
    Chincoteague/Wallops Island National Wildlife Refuge, 95
    Columbia National Wildlife Refuge, 96
    Eastern Massachusetts National Wildlife Refuge Complex, 97
    Edwin B. Forsythe National Wildlife Refuge, 97
    Great Dismal Swamp/Nansemond National Wildlife Refuge, 98
    Guadalupe-Nipomo Dunes National Wildlife Refuge, 99
    Hobe Sound National Wildlife Refuge, 99
    Huron WMD National Wildlife Refuge, 100
    Kern/Pixley National Wildlife Refuge, 101
    Kofa National Wildlife Refuge, 102
    Lacassine National Wildlife Refuge, 102
    Lake Andes/Karl E. Mundt National Wildlife Refuge, 102
    Long Island National Wildlife Refuge Complex, 103
    Long Lake National Wildlife Refuge, 103
    Mattamuskeet National Wildlife Refuge, 104
    Mingo National Wildlife Refuge, 105
    Minnesota Valley National Wildlife Refuge, 105
    Moapa Valley National Wildlife Refuge, 106
    Morris Wetland Management District, 106
    Necedah National Wildlife Refuge, 107
    Noxubee National Wildlife Refuge, 108
    Okefenokee (Banks Lake) National Wildlife Refuge, 108
    Patoka River National Wetlands Project National Wildlife Refuge, 109
    Patuxent Research Refuge, 109
    Pelican Island National Wildlife Refuge, 109
    Piedmont National Wildlife Refuge, 110
    Pocosin Lakes National Wildlife Refuge, 110
    Rainwater Basin WMD National Wildlife Refuge, 111
    Red Rock Lakes National Wildlife Refuge, 111
    region 1, Pacific Regional Office, 111
    region 4, Southeast Regional office, 112
    Ridgefield National Wildlife Refuge, 112
    San Francisco Bay National Wildlife Refuge Complex, 113
    Sandy Point National Wildlife Refuge, 114
    Selawik National Wildlife Refuge, 114
    Southeast Louisiana Complex National Wildlife Refuge, 115
    St. Catherine Creek National Wildlife Refuge, 115
    St. Marks National Wildlife Refuge, 115
    Sunkhaze Meadows National Wildlife Refuge/Carlton Pond Waterfowl Production Area, 116
    Upper Souris National Wildlife Refuge, 117
    Wallkill River National Wildlife Refuge, 117
    Wapanocca National Wildlife Refuge, 117
    Washington Maritime National Wildlife Refuge Complex, 118
    White River National Wildlife Refuge, 118
    Wichita Mountains National Wildlife Refuge, 118
    Willapa/Lewis and Clark National Wildlife Refuge, 118
    Windom WMD National Wildlife Refuge, 119
  Montana State Extension Services, 119
  National Park Service
    Chihuahuan Desert Network, 121
    Grand Teton National Park, 122
    Mammoth Cave National Park, 124
    Mesa Verde National Park, 124
    Mount Rainier National Park, 124
    Sonoran Desert Network, 125
    Theodore Roosevelt National Park, 125
    Yellowstone National Park, 126
  Oregon Cooperative Fish and Wildlife Research Unit, 126
  United States Geological Survey
    Western Region, 127
UNITED STATES DEPARTMENT OF TRANSPORTATION
  Federal Aviation Administration, 128
UNITED STATES INSTITUTE FOR ENVIRONMENTAL CONFLICT RESOLUTION, 130
UNITED STATES PUBLIC INTEREST RESEARCH GROUP, 526
UNITY COLLEGE, 601
UNIVERSITY OF ALASKA FAIRBANKS
  COOPERATIVE EXTENSION SERVICE College of Rural Alaska, 149
UNIVERSITY OF CALIFORNIA AT DAVIS
  School of Veterinary Medicine, 606
UNIVERSITY OF CALIFORNIA AT SAN DIEGO, 607
UNIVERSITY OF CONNECTICUT COOPERATIVE EXTENSION, 608
UNIVERSITY OF DAR ES SALAAM, 608
UNIVERSITY OF FLORIDA
  School of Forest Resources and Conservation, 609
UNIVERSITY OF FLORIDA INSTITUTE OF FOOD AND AGRICULTURAL SCIENCES, 609
UNIVERSITY OF GEORGIA
  Daniel B. Warnell School of Forest Resources, 609
UNIVERSITY OF HAWAII AT MANOA, 610
UNIVERSITY OF HAWAII COOPERATIVE EXTENSION PROGRAM, 224
UNIVERSITY OF IDAHO
  College of Natural Resources
    Department of Fish and Wildlife Resources, 610
UNIVERSITY OF IDAHO EXTENSION, 611
UNIVERSITY OF LOUISVILLE, 612
UNIVERSITY OF MAINE, 612
UNIVERSITY OF MANITOBA, 613
UNIVERSITY OF MARYLAND - AT COLLEGE PARK, 613
UNIVERSITY OF MARYLAND BALTIMORE COUNTY, 613
UNIVERSITY OF MARYLAND COOPERATIVE EXTENSION, 224
UNIVERSITY OF MASSACHUSETTS EXTENSION, 224
UNIVERSITY OF MICHIGAN, 614

KEYWORD INDEX – W

UNIVERSITY OF MINNESOTA AT ST. PAUL, 615
UNIVERSITY OF MISSOURI, 615
UNIVERSITY OF NEW BRUNSWICK, 616
UNIVERSITY OF NORTH CAROLINA AT ASHEVILLE, 617
UNIVERSITY OF NORTH DAKOTA, 618
UNIVERSITY OF NORTH TEXAS, 618
UNIVERSITY OF NORTHERN BRITISH COLUMBIA, 618
UNIVERSITY OF RHODE ISLAND
  Department of Natural Resources Science, 619
UNIVERSITY OF SASKATCHEWAN, 620
UNIVERSITY OF SOUTH CAROLINA
  Baruch Marine Field Laboratory, 620
UNIVERSITY OF TENNESSEE - AT KNOXVILLE, 621
UNIVERSITY OF THE DISTRICT OF COLUMBIA, 621
UNIVERSITY OF TULSA, 621
UNIVERSITY OF WISCONSIN AT MADISON, 623
UPPER COLORADO RIVER COMMISSION, 130
UPPER MISSISSIPPI RIVER CONSERVATION COMMITTEE, 527
UPPER SKAGIT BALD EAGLE FESTIVAL, 527
USAID/TANZANIA, 131
UTAH ASSOCIATION OF CONSERVATION DISTRICTS, 528
UTAH BASS FEDERATION, 528
UTAH DEPARTMENT OF NATURAL RESOURCES
  Division of Wildlife Resources, 225
UTAH GEOLOGICAL SURVEY, 225
UTAH NATURE STUDY SOCIETY, 528
UTAH STATE UNIVERSITY
  College of Natural Resources, 624
VERMONT ASSOCIATION OF CONSERVATION DISTRICTS, 529
VERMONT ENVIRONMENTAL BOARD, 227
VERMONT STATE-WIDE ENVIRONMENTAL EDUCATION PROGRAMS (SWEEP), 530
VERMONT WOODLANDS ASSOCIATION, 530
VERNAL POOL SOCIETY, THE, 530
VIRGIN ISLANDS CONSERVATION DISTRICT, 530
VIRGIN ISLANDS COOPERATIVE EXTENSION SERVICE, 228
VIRGIN ISLANDS SOIL AND WATER CONSERVATION DIVISION, 228
VIRGINIA ASSOCIATION OF CONSERVATION DISTRICTS, 531
VIRGINIA DEPARTMENT OF AGRICULTURE AND CONSUMER SERVICES, 228
VIRGINIA DEPARTMENT OF CONSERVATION AND RECREATION
  Division of Dam Safety, 229
  Virginia Cave Board, 230
VIRGINIA DEPARTMENT OF FORESTRY, 230
VIRGINIA DEPARTMENT OF GAME AND INLAND FISHERIES
  Region IV (Staunton), 231
VIRGINIA DEPARTMENT OF HEALTH, 231
VIRGINIA OUTDOORS FOUNDATION, 232
VIRGINIA RESOURCE-USE EDUCATION COUNCIL, 532
VIRGINIA TECH
  Department of Fisheries and Wildlife Sciences, 625
VIRGINIA TECH UNIVERSITY
  College of Natural Resources, 625
WARREN COUNTY CONSERVATION BOARD, 532
WASHINGTON ASSOCIATION OF CONSERVATION DISTRICTS, 533
WASHINGTON DEPARTMENT OF ECOLOGY, 233
WASHINGTON DEPARTMENT OF FISH AND WILDLIFE
  WASHINGTON FISH AND WILDLIFE COMMISSION, 233
WASHINGTON FARM FORESTRY ASSOCIATION, 533
WASHINGTON RECREATION AND PARK ASSOCIATION, 533
WASHINGTON STATE CONSERVATION COMMISSION, 234
WASHINGTON STATE DEPARTMENT OF NATURAL RESOURCES
  Olympic Region, 234
WASHINGTON STATE OFFICE OF ENVIRONMENTAL EDUCATION, 234
WASHINGTON STATE PARKS AND RECREATION COMMISSION
  NORTHWEST REGION, 235
WASHINGTON WILDLIFE AND RECREATION COALITION, 534
WATERLOO-WELLINGTON WILDFLOWER SOCIETY, 535
WATERMAN CONSERVATION EDUCATION CENTER, 535
WATERSHED MANAGEMENT COUNCIL, 535
WELDER WILDLIFE FOUNDATION, 535
WEST VIRGINIA DEPARTMENT OF ENVIRONMENTAL PROTECTION, 235
WEST VIRGINIA RAPTOR REHABILITATION CENTER, 536
WEST VIRGINIA SOIL CONSERVATION AGENCY, 236
WESTERN ASSOCIATION OF FISH AND WILDLIFE AGENCIES, 537
WESTERN HEMISPHERE SHOREBIRD RESERVE NETWORK (WHSRN), 537
WESTERN ILLINOIS UNIVERSITY, 626
WESTERN PACIFIC REGIONAL FISHERY MANAGEMENT COUNCIL, 131
WESTERN PENNSYLVANIA CONSERVANCY, 537
WESTERN SNOWY PLOVER WORKING TEAM, 131
WESTERN WATERSHEDS PROJECT, 538

WETLAND HABITAT ALLIANCE OF TEXAS, 538
WETLANDS ACTION NETWORK, 538
WHOOPING CRANE CONSERVATION ASSOCIATION INC., 539
WILD CANID SURVIVAL AND RESEARCH CENTER, 539
WILD DOG FOUNDATION, THE, 539
WILD FOUNDATION, THE, 539
WILD HORSE ORGANIZED ASSISTANCE, INC. (WHOA), 540
WILD ONES NATURAL LANDSCAPERS, LTD, 540
WILDERNESS LAND TRUST, THE, 540
WILDERNESS SOCIETY, THE, 541
WILDERNESS WATCH, 541
WILDFOWL TRUST OF NORTH AMERICA, INC., THE, 541
WILDFUTURES, 542
WILDLANDS PROJECT, 542
WILDLIFE ACTION, INC., 542
WILDLIFE CENTER OF VIRGINIA, THE, 542
WILDLIFE CONSERVATION SOCIETY, 543
WILDLIFE DAMAGE REVIEW (WDR), 543
WILDLIFE DISEASE ASSOCIATION, 543
WILDLIFE FEDERATION OF ALASKA, 543
WILDLIFE FOREVER, 544
WILDLIFE HABITAT CANADA, 544
WILDLIFE HABITAT COUNCIL, 544
WILDLIFE HERITAGE FOUNDATION OF WYOMING (WHFW), 544
WILDLIFE INFORMATION CENTER, INC., 545
WILDLIFE MANAGEMENT INSTITUTE, 545
WILDLIFE ORPHANAGE, INC., THE, 545
WILDLIFE PRESERVATION TRUST CANADA, 545
WILDLIFE SOCIETY
  Arizona Chapter, 546
  Colorado Chapter, 547
  Illinois Chapter, 547
  Michigan Chapter, 549
  National Capital Chapter, 550
  New York Chapter, 551
WILDLIFE TRUST
  Wildlife Preservation Trust International, 554
WILDLIFE WAYSTATION, 554
WILSON ORNITHOLOGICAL SOCIETY, 555
WINDSTAR WILDLIFE INSTITUTE, 555
WISCONSIN BASS FEDERATION, 556
WISCONSIN COOPERATIVE FISHERY RESEARCH UNIT USGS, 237
WISCONSIN GEOLOGICAL AND NATURAL HISTORY SURVEY, 238
WISCONSIN PARK AND RECREATION ASSOCIATION, 556
WISCONSIN SOCIETY FOR ORNITHOLOGY, INC., THE, 556
WISCONSIN WILDLIFE FEDERATION, 557
WISCONSIN WOODLAND OWNERS ASSOCIATION, 557
WOLF EDUCATION AND RESEARCH CENTER, 557
WOLF GROUP, THE, 557
WOLF HAVEN INTERNATIONAL, 557
WOMEN'S SHOOTING SPORTS FOUNDATION, 558
WORLD BIRD SANCTUARY (WBS), 558
WORLD PARKS ENDOWMENT INC., 559
WORLD SOCIETY FOR THE PROTECTION OF ANIMALS (WSPA), 559
WORLD WILDLIFE FUND, 559
WORLDWATCH INSTITUTE, 560
WWW.ACTIONBIOSCIENCE.ORG, 560
WYOMING BASS FEDERATION, 560
WYOMING DEPARTMENT OF ENVIRONMENTAL QUALITY, 239
WYOMING STATE FORESTRY DIVISION, 240
WYOMING STATE PARKS AND CULTURAL RESOURCES, 240
XERCES SOCIETY, THE, 561
YALE LAW SCHOOL, 561
YELL COUNTY WILDLIFE FEDERATION, 561
YMCA NATURE AND COMMUNITY CENTER, 562
YOUNG ENTOMOLOGISTS SOCIETY, INC., 562
ZERO, 562
ZUNGARO COCHA RESEARCH CENTER
  Exploration Educational Expeditions, 562

STAFF NAME INDEX

A

Aasheim, Ron, 186
Aasness, Perry, 182
Abbey, Jim, 483
Abbey, Robert, 84
Abbott, George, 139
Abbott, Mary, 354
Abe, Elaine, 159
Abel, Ed, 206
Abent, Rob, 180
Aber, James, 380
Aber, John, 616
Abercrombie, Neil, 4
Aberle, Elton, 623
Abernethy, Virginia, 288, 471
Abkowitz, Mark, 625
Abrams, Sheldon, 262
Abromaitis, Sieglinde, 564
Acevedo, Miguel, 618
Acevedo-Vila, Anibal, 15
Acfalle, Joseph, 152
Achitoff, Paul, 319
Ackelson, Mark, 373
Ackerly, Margaret, 559
Ackerman, Gary L., 10
Ackerman, Sybil, 412
Ackermann, Michelle, 541
Acosta, Carlos, 562
Adair, Janice, 133
Adams, Audrey, 77
Adams, Betsy, 75
Adams, Bob, 388
Adams, Charles, 252
Adams, Charlotte, 129
Adams, Culver, 399
Adams, D., 267
Adams, Edward, 234
Adams, Glenn, 37
Adams, James, 230
Adams, Jamie, 167
Adams, John, 27, 432, 587
Adams, Kevin, 90
Adams, L., 60
Adams, Larry, 170
Adams, Louie, 473
Adams, Lowell, 528
Adams, Lucinda, 248
Adams, Pamela, 149
Adams, Richard, 83, 412
Adams, Ron, 334
Adams, Stan, 376
Adams, Stanford, 200
Adams, Steve, 57
Adams, Tim, 155
Adams-Wiley, Mary, 503
Adcock, Steve, 184
Addis, James, 237
Addison, Paul, 16
Adebayo, Marsha, 326
Adelaja, Adesoji, 594
Adelman, Ira, 252, 615
Adelmann, Gerald, 460
Aderholt, Robert B., 1
Adhikari, Ambika, 369
Adolf-Whipp, Stacy, 91
Adornato, John, 423
Afton, Alan, 172
Agner, Pat, 387
Agosta, Karin, 484
Aguilar, Varinka, 563
Ahern, Catherine, 264
Ahern, John, 459
Ahkeah, Robert, 271
Ahlm, Lief, 194
Ahmad, Mujahid, 351
Ahmed, A., 418
Ahmed, Saifuddin, 568
Ahrabi, Sajjad, 312
Ahrndt, Rodney, 106
Aiken, Patricia, 519
Akaka, Daniel K., 4
Akans, George, 221
Akers, John, 169

Akin, Todd, 8
Akishino, Prince, 560
Alaimo, Ellen, 466
Albers, Mark, 265
Albersworth, Dave, 541
Alberts, Bruce, 424
Albrecht, John, 204
Albright, Craig, 549
Albright, Larry, 295
Albright, Lorine, 520
Albright, Mel, 252
Albrink, Anne, 510
Albro, Dean, 214
Alderson, Jeanie, 453
Aldrich, Dorrie, 129
Aldrich, James, 436
Aldrich, Winthrop, 198
Alesii, Bruno, 308
Alexander, Craig, 77
Alexander, Don, 138
Alexander, Donna, 383
Alexander, Gerald, 169
Alexander, Glen, 409
Alexander, H., 150
Alexander, H. Lloyd, Jr., 150
Alexander, Lamar, 13
Alexander, Lloyd, 165
Alexander, Mike, 20
Alexander, Peter, 395
Alexander, Rodney, 6
Alexander, Vera, 604
Alexeev, Sergei, 329
Alford, Anne, 37
Alie, Ronald, 452
Alipio, Mel, 363
Allan, J., 226
Allanson, Karli, 554
Allar, Christy, 555
Allard, Guy, 602
Allard, Wayne, 3
Allee, A., 172
Alleman, Orville, 460
Allen, Alan, 517
Allen, Bruce, 193
Allen, Christopher, 349
Allen, Craig, 217
Allen, Dennis, 620
Allen, Gary, 290
Allen, Gary, 465
Allen, George, 14
Allen, Irma, 30
Allen, J., 157
Allen, Jeff, 460
Allen, Jerry, 475
Allen, John, 224
Allen, Priscilla, 366
Allen, Robin, 359
Allen, Thomas H., 6
Allen, Tim, 586
Allen, W., 524
Aller, Chuck, 153
Alley, Jamie, 139
Allgood, David, 299
Allinger, Steve, 323
Allis, Richard, 225
Allison, Chris, 195
Allison, David, 330
Allison, K., 209
Allison, M., 168
Allread, Jill, 163
Allred, C., 160
Allsbrook, Dixie, 616
Alovera, Rose, 437
Altadonna, Leigh, 411
Alter, Theodore, 592
Altman, Ellie, 242
Alula, Brian, 208
Alvarez, Eric, 90
Alvey, Ken, 204
Amack, Rex, 188, 360
Amaratunga, T., 453
Amato, George, 543
Ambrock, Ken, 537

Ambs, Todd, 480
Ament, Don, 146
Ames, Gregory, 186
Ames, Oakes, 323
Amidon, Thomas, 598
Amin, Adnan, 526
Amon, Lawrence J., 427, 429
Amos, Shelia, 65
Amy, Brian, 185
Anable, Michael, 137
Anane, Mike, 387
Andelt, William, 148
Anders, Kristie, 379, 484
Andersen, David, 181, 615
Andersen, Mark, 119
Anderson, Becky, 351
Anderson, Bob, 73
Anderson, Bruce, 448
Anderson, D., 226, 322
Anderson, Damon, 211
Anderson, Dave, 31
Anderson, David, 18, 179, 578
Anderson, Deborah, 181
Anderson, Delia, 594
Anderson, Ders, 460
Anderson, Dorothy, 615
Anderson, Eric, 623
Anderson, Fletcher, 422
Anderson, Hal, 161
Anderson, Harold, 184
Anderson, James, 554
Anderson, John, 364, 459
Anderson, Jon, 227
Anderson, Karl, 415
Anderson, Ken, 219
Anderson, Lloyd, 472
Anderson, Lynn, 261
Anderson, Mark, 612
Anderson, Mary, 61
Anderson, Paul, 56
Anderson, Phil, 233
Anderson, Renae, 47
Anderson, Robert, 74, 158
Anderson, Sally, 532
Anderson, Scott, 439
Anderson, Sharon, 126
Anderson, Stan, 554
Anderson, Stanley, 239, 623
Anderson, Steve, 334
Anderson, Susan, 248
Anderson, Thomas, 485, 486
Anderson, William, 329
Anderton, Kate, 487
Ando, Rodolfo, 152
Andrea, Richard, 333
Andreas, Terry, 574
Andren, Anders, 622
Andrew, Chris, 252
Andrew, Jerry, 578
Andrews, Alice, 463
Andrews, Bill, 141, 310
Andrews, David, 470
Andrews, Emilie, 149
Andrews, John, 233
Andrews, Katherine, 153
Andrews, Oakley, 288
Andrews, Robert E., 9
Andrews, Scott, 481
Andrick, Jill, 417
Andriguetto, Jose, 601
Angell, Debbie, 125
Angell, Jim, 318
Angell, Tony, 234
Angelle, Pedro, 172
Angers, Jeff, 300
Anglin, Ron, 209
Ankner, William, 214
Annderson, Sally, 532
Annelli, Joseph, 32
Ansah, Elliot, 387
Anthony, Carl, 527
Anthony, Mark, 203
Anthony, Robert, 126, 592

Antista, James, 155
Antoine, Jim, 203
Antwi, Kwabena, 328
Apel, Justin, 441
App, Leon, 229
Apple, Bob, 272
Apple, Mike, 221
Applegate, David, 260
Applegate, Michael, 61
Apsley, Dave, 73
Araiza, Robert, 155
Arambula, Tracy, 493
Arb, Sandra, 547
Arballo, Joe, 533
Arbour, Maurice, 602
Archer, Hugh, 170
Archibald, George, 362
Archie, Anne, 35
Areen, Judith, 582
Arena, Christine, 520
Arent, Lori, 593
Arganbright, Donald, 591
Argent, David, 576
Argo, Gene, 382
Argow, Keith, 264, 334, 420, 430
Argust, Marcia, 266, 285
Armandarez, Ava, 269
Armas, Lupe, 74
Armer, Walter, 137
Armitage, Brian, 456
Armour, Karyn, 240
Armstrong, Donald, 626
Armstrong, Eva, 154
Armstrong, James, 132, 546, 626
Arnberger, Rob, 120
Arnett, Edward, 552
Arnett, Stuart, 190
Arney, Ken, 43
Arnoff, Samuel, 357
Arnold, Abby, 299
Arnold, Ron, 239
Arnold, Susan, 270
Aronoff, Marcia, 324
Arrington, Bob, 232
Arriola, Vincent, 158
Arsenault, Bill, 461
Arsenault, George, 214
Artero, Victor, 158
Arthur, Bill, 495
Arthur, Gregg, 239
Artley, Don, 187
Asbell, G., 470
Asbury, Donna, 274
Ashbaugh, Bill, 377
Ashbaugh, David, 484
Asher, Kay, 288
Asher, Rick, 180
Ashley, Ken, 301
Ashley, Sharon, 27
Ashmeade-Hawkins, Brett, 477
Ashmeade-Hawkins, Mark, 477
Ashworth, Robert, 90
Aslin, Raymond, 168
Asmussen, Dennis, 182
Asner, Edward, 312, 367, 371
Asseltine, Craig, 176
Atchison, Robert, 168
Aterno, Kathleen, 298
Atkin, John, 486
Atkins, Lew, 233
Atkins, Van, 256
Atkinson, Nancy, 47
Atkinson, Samuel, 618
Atkinson, Thomas, 189
Atkinson, Tom, 246
Atwood, Tim, 419
Augulis, Richard, 52
Augustine, Gene, 66
Aus, Rebecca, 45
Austermuhle, Stefan, 406
Austin, Alice, 397
Austin, Jim, 196
Austin, Miriam, 538

STAFF NAME INDEX – B

Auyong, Jan, 58
Avalos, Edward, 193
Avary, Katherine, 236
Avery, David, 164
Axline, Michael, 537, 619
Axline, Michael, 619
Axon, James, 169
Ayer, Claire, 529
Ayers, Joseph, 590
Ayers, Kenneth, 214
Aylward, Kevin, 152
Ayres, Ed, 560
Ayres, Henry, 285
Ayres, Janet, 213
Azeez, Michael, 389

B

Baas, John, 552
Babb, John, 76
Babich, Adam, 600
Baca, Joe, 2
Bacca, Denise, 562
Bacchus, Tania, 585
Baccus, John, 296
Bach, Catherine, 581
Bach, Maryanne, 119
Bache, Maryanne, 484
Bachert, Russel, 489
Bachman, Peter, 399
Bachus, Spencer, 1
Bacik, Ginny, 451
Bacinski, Pete, 115
Back, Dale, 357
Bacle, Jean Pierre, 375
Bacon, Bob, 59
Bacon, Lawrence, 264
Bacone, John, 163
Bacsujlaky, Mara, 453
Badger, Ruthe, 237
Badgley, Anne, 91, 111
Badura, Laurel, 550
Baer, Richard, 579
Baer, Sara, 596
Baesler, Larry, 561
Baez, Albert, 242
Baggett, Arthur, 144
Bahali, Cosmas, 608
Baicich, Paul, 250
Bailey, Alan, 301
Bailey, Cameron, 31
Bailey, Craig, 552
Bailey, Dick, 210
Bailey, Donna, 256
Bailey, Geneva, 434
Bailey, James, 72
Bailey, Jared, 476
Bailey, Jim, 421
Bailey, Mark, 344
Bailey, Robert, 203
Bailey, Ron, 157
Bailey, Vicky, 75
Baird, Brian, 14
Baird, Dennis, 354
Baird, Philip, 614
Baird, Timothy, 330
Baird, Warren, 356
Bakamjian, Lynn, 322
Baker, Alan, 423
Baker, Bruce, 238
Baker, Dale, 58
Baker, Dayton, 568
Baker, Denise, 352
Baker, Edgar, 256
Baker, Elaine, 361
Baker, Everard, 184
Baker, Heather, 273
Baker, J., 23
Baker, John, 328
Baker, Michael, 204
Baker, Richard H., 6
Baker, Tom, 169
Baker, Vickie, 561
Baker, Victor, 605

Baker, William, 295
Bakker, Joe, 154
Bakunas, Edward, 61
Balaam, Robert, 191
Balcom, Nancy, 54
Bald, George, 190
Baldi, Josh, 533
Baldridge, Paul, 204
Baldwin, Mark, 482
Baldwin, Pat, 532
Baldwin, Tammy, 15
Bale, Charles, 169
Bales, Wade, 258
Balfour, David, 20, 180
Bali, Theodora, 608
Balkenbush, Paul, 458
Ball, I., 186
Ball, Joe, 384
Ball, Lindsay, 208, 209
Ball, Louise, 617
Ballance, Frank W., Jr., 10
Ballantyne, Chris, 495
Ballantyne, Dotty, 346
Ballantyne, Joe, 240
Ballard, Bill, 415
Ballard, Denny, 307
Ballard, Karin, 302
Ballenger, Cass, 10
Ballentine, Jane, 268
Balliet, Kris, 455
Balsillie, D., 621
Balton, David, 78
Balygatti, Wilhelmina, 599
Bambery, Carol, 180
Ban, Hideyuki, 298
Bancroft, David, 247, 248
Bancroft, G., 541
Bane, Sandra, 542
Bangart, Richard, 26
Bangert, Suzanne, 237
Banker, Harry, 303
Banker, Mark, 483
Banks, Alison, 482
Banks, David, 434
Banning, Kathleen, 150
Bansley, Marcia, 519
Banta, John, 132
Baquero, Jaime, 455
Baquet, Charles, 28
Barasch, Douglas, 432
Barash, Jean, 379
Barbaccia, Annette, 193
Barbaro, Henry, 179
Barbeau, Claude, 603
Barber, Edna, 73
Barber, Harry, 553
Barber, Patricia, 150
Barber, Rick, 487
Barber, Robert, 506
Barber, Syd, 216
Barberis, David, 570
Barcinas, Jeff, 158
Barclay, John, 608
Bard, John, 382
Barden, Alvin, 557
Bardsley, Marc, 452
Bareiss, Robert, 332
Barger, Don, 423
Baril, Marcel, 603
Barish, Jean, 242
Barker, David, 385
Barker, I., 286
Barker, Richard, 192
Barker, Roy, 62
Barkley, Robert, 577
Barkow, Lee, 04
Barla, Philippe, 603
Barlow, Roger, 183
Barna, David, 120
Barnes, Brian, 604
Barnes, Brooke, 175
Barnes, Deborah, 144
Barnes, Donald, 18

Barnes, Jackie, 343
Barnes, Jim, 269
Barnes, John, 381
Barnes, Petra, 47
Barnes, Phillip, 578
Barnes, Thomas, 171
Barnes-Cloth, Rhonda, 26
Barnett, Timothy, 433
Barnette, James, 21
Barney, Patricia, 178
Barney, Robert, 382
Barnhart, Gerald, 420
Barnhart, Gerry, 360
Baron, David, 320
Barram, David, 20
Barre, David, 347
Barrera, Juan, 560
Barresi, James, 192
Barret, Morley, 135
Barrett, J., 228
Barrett, J. Gresham, 12
Barrett, Lonice, 156
Barrett-O'Leary, Marilyn, 56
Barricklow, Deanna, 356
Barritt, David, 363
Barron, Edwin, 222
Barron, Tom, 515
Barros, Nelio, 404
Barrow, Willie, 476
Barry, Craig, 328
Barry, Cynthia, 111
Barry, Donald, 541
Barry, Larisa, 440
Barry, Robert, 65
Barry, William, 353
Barsamian, Loretta, 144
Barstow, Robbins, 294
Bartelt, Gerald, 554
Barth, Ellen, 449
Barth, Erik, 232
Barth, Sara, 541
Bartholomay, Keith, 202
Bartholomew, Jerri, 254
Bartlett, Chris, 56
Bartlett, Edmund, 513
Bartlett, Roscoe, 7
Bartlett, Terri, 470
Bartlett, William, Jr., 191
Barton, Bob, 287
Barton, Gerald, 212
Barton, Joe, 13
Barton, Louise, 242
Barton, Stephen, 160
Barton, Thomas, 163
Bartz, Bob, 204
Barzen, Jeb, 362
Basco, Pamela, 364
Basden, Thomas, 237
Basman, Cem, 596
Bass, Charles, 9
Bass, Edward, 559
Bass, Neil, 66
Bassett, Karen, 211
Bassi, Richard, 241
Bastable, Clare, 302
Basu, Rathin, 581
Bateni, Naser, 143
Bates, Bob, 66
Bates, Christine, 317
Bates, David, 280
Bates, Jack, 281
Bates, Jennifer, 278
Bates, Mike, 137
Bates, Rick, 215
Bates, Robert, 169
Bates, Sylvia, 411
Bathke, John, 399
Batker, Carol, 201
Batky, Bob, 90
Batt, Al, 400
Batt, Bruce, 316
Battocchi, Ron, 24
Batty, Sandy, 274

Bauchman, Ann, 187
Baucus, Max, 8
Bauer, Jeffrey, 595
Bauer, Jennifer, 296
Bauer, Tom, 112
Bauerle, Keith, 318
Baugh, Donald, 295
Baugh, Scotty, 168
Baughman, Jeffrey, 556
Baughman, John, 360
Baughman, Melvin, 183
Baughman, William, 546, 552
Bauknight, Amanda, 506
Baum, Ellen, 432
Baum, Kent, 90
Baumann, Rebecca, 556
Baumgartner, David, 234
Baumgartner, Sue, 607
Baust, Joe, 383
Bauthman, William, 334
Bay, Crandall, 608
Bay, Michael, 168
Baydack, Richard, 613
Bayer, Robin, 392
Bayersdorfer, Alan, 409
Bayh, Evan, 5
Bayles, David, 464
Bayliff, William, 359
Baz, Leila, 388
Bazzell, Darrell, 238, 556
Beach, Gary, 239
Beahrs, Dick, 407
Beal, Art, 353
Beal, Katherine, 552
Beal, Ken, 241
Beale, Ed, 601
Beane, Jeff, 451
Beane, Marjorie, 559
Bear, Dinah, 31
Beard, Dan, 416
Beard, Daniel, 409
Beard, Patti, 69
Beardsley, Timothy, 261
Bearzi, James, 195
Beasley, R., 598
Beattie, Ted, 268
Beatty, Robert, 275
Beauchamp, Claude, 603
Beauchamp, David, 128
Beaudet, Thérèse, 368
Beaudette, Paul, 323
Beauduy, Thomas, 30
Beaulieu, John, 209
Beauprez, Bob, 3
Beauvais, Gary, 571
Bebak, Daniel, 404
Becerra, Xavier, 2
Beck, Chris, 581
Beck, Fred, 478
Beck, Gregory, 330
Beck, Kim, 290
Beck, Ray, 187
Beckemeyer, Hoy, 315
Becker, Charlie, 382
Becker, Dennis, 456
Becker, Laurence, 227
Becker, Mimi, 616
Becker, Nancy, 355
Becker, Ronald, 56
Becker, S., 512
Beckett, David, 620
Beckman, Dave, 240
Beckman, Karen, 182
Beckner, John, 393
Beckstrom, Stanley, 553
Bedford, Charles, 434
Bednarz, James, 477
Bednarz, Robert, 418
Bedrin, Michael, 211
Beecher, William, 25
Beegle, Robert, 282
Beelman, Joyce, 73
Beem, Marley, 206

STAFF NAME INDEX – B

Beemer, James, 73, 421
Beeson, M., 542
Beetham, Mary Beth, 312
Beggs, Gail, 187
Begin, Paul, 214
Bégin, Yves, 603
Behling, Mary, 236
Beich, Dennis, 233
Beinecke, Frances, 432
Beissinger, Steven, 264
Belensky, Brenda, 549
Belfit, Scott, 73
Belknap, Daniel, 612
Bell, Chris, 14
Bell, Dick, 560
Bell, Elizabeth, 400
Bell, Hubert, 26
Bell, Jadee, 64
Bell, James, 514, 568
Bell, Jon, 474
Bell, Ken, 304
Bell, Larry, 193
Bell, Morris, 147
Bell, Ronald, 115
Bell, Susan, 460
Bell, Thomas, 93
Bell, William, 392
Bellafiore, Vincent, 611
Bellden, Allen, 532
Bellinger, John, 67
Bellon, Jim, 63
Belowski, Cynthia, 411
Belson, Jerry, 120
Belt, Jami, 343
Beltran-Burgos, Luis, 213
Beltz, Dennis, 397
Ben-David, Merav, 623
Bender, Bob, 170
Bender, Dave, 162
Bender, Hugh, 223
Bender, Louis, 127
Bender, Marjorie, 263
Bender, Norman, 608
Bendler, Thomas, 422
Benedetto, Debra, 396
Benedick, Richard, 418
Benedick, Robert, 439
Benedict, Les, 511
Benedict, Michelle, 471, 483
Benedict, Philip, 227
Benefield, Gary, 245
Beneka, Lee, 258
Benforado, Jay, 18
Benjamin, Thomas (Tom), 323
Benner, J., 552
Bennett, Albert, 503
Bennett, Betsy, 200
Bennett, C., 169
Bennett, Chuck, 137
Bennett, Colin, 533
Bennett, D., 262
Bennett, David, 157
Bennett, Dery, 298, 300
Bennett, Earl, 161
Bennett, James, 280
Bennett, Jim, 150
Bennett, Karen, 617
Bennett, Maratha, 148
Bennett, Richard, 112
Bennett, Robert, 14
Bennett, Thomas, 360
Bennett, Tony, 161, 506
Benson, Bob, 277
Benson, Carl, 271
Benson, Delwin, 148
Benson, Laura, 268
Benson, Ralph, 485
Benson, Susan, 174
Benson, Thomas, 180
Bentley, William, 598
Benton, Dempsey, 200
Benton, Jo, 242
Bentz, John, 301

Bentzmen, Michael, 471
Benz, Justin, 410
Berardi, Gigi, 627
Berdoll, Chris, 296
Berendsen, Pieter, 380
Bereuter, Doug, 8
Berg, Eric, 168
Berg, Karlyn, 543
Berg, Norman, 504
Berg, Thomas, 201, 204
Bergen, Roger, 321
Berger, Alan, 269
Berger, J., 606
Berger, Tommie, 382
Bergeron, Robert, 27
Bergersen, Eric, 578
Bergey, Hans, 509
Berghaier, Robert, 539
Bergin, Patrick, 244
Bergman, Harold, 624
Bergquist, Sarah, 376
Bergstrom, Mark, 283
Beringer, Peter, 174
Berkley, Shelley, 9
Berkovits, Annette, 543
Berkowitz, Alan, 358
Berkowitz, Francine, 501
Berlin, Kenneth, 327
Berlin, Linda, 622
Berman, Bruce, 486
Berman, Howard L., 2
Bernard, Steve, 178
Bernatchez, Heather, 545
Bernatchez, Louis, 603
Bernier, Louis, 604
Bernstein, Carol, 549
Berrios, Olga Rodriguez, 148
Berry, Bill, 152
Berry, Charles, 29, 596
Berry, Clinton, 245
Berry, Jim, 482
Berry, John, 25, 419
Berry, Joyce, 578
Berry, Kristen, 416
Berry, Marion, 1
Berry, Patrick, 529
Bertera, William, 535
Berthelsen, Peter, 468
Berthiaume, Luc, 214
Bertsch, Paul, 610
Berwald, Daphne, 78
Berzuh, Rudy, 65
Beske, John, 514
Besougloff, Jeff, 130
Besse, Dan, 306
Besse, Mark, 354
Best, Troy, 266
Bethea, Sally, 527
Bethel, Margaret, 181
Bethell, Helen, 396
Betit, Rod, 225
Betschart, A., 48
Bettas, George, 279
Bettinger, Mark, 495
Bettridge, Kristin, 234
Betts, Lynn, 47
Bevacqua, Frank, 23
Bevand, Hanni, 269
Bever, Chuck, 256
Bevis, Kenneth, 554
Beyer, Sally, 144
Bezan, David, 20
Bezanson, Janice, 517
Bhalta, Bishnu, 513
Bhumbla, D., 237
Biaggi, Allen, 189
Biaggi, Roberto, 475
Bianchi, Stephanie, 24
Bibler, Bart, 155
Bickford, James, 170
Biddle, Joel, 478
Biden, Joseph R., Jr., 3
Bider, Bill, 167

Bidwell, Dennis, 252
Bieker, Chris, 47
Bier, James, 581
Bierma, Thomas, 583
Bierwirth, John, 455
Biesinger, Esther, 128
Biesiot, Patricia, 620
Bifera, Frank, 196
Biggerstaff, Patricia, 539
Biggert, Judy, 5
Biggs, James, 551
Bignell, Guy, 339
Bilberry, Grady, 33
Bilbrey, Ellen, 137
Bildstein, Keith, 349, 477
Biles, Larry, 33
Bilirakis, Michael, 3
Billick, Ian, 482
Billing, Vesta, 175
Billings, Leon, 417
Bilodeau, Gilbert, 175
Bilski, Nanine, 248
Binder, Daniel, 457
Bingaman, Bob, 497, 499
Bingaman, Jeff, 9
Bingham, Alfred, 223
Bingham, Derek, 559
Bingham, W., 282
Birch, Clare, 213
Birch, Daniel, 302
Birch, Gayle, 209
Bird, Darin, 226
Bird, David, 587
Bird, Paul, 25
Bird, W. Jackson, 201
Bires, Fran, 358
Birkeland, Charles, 158
Birkhauser, Mark, 364
Birney, Claire, 512
Biro, Edina, 369
Bischoff, Donald, 129
Bish, Terry, 47
Bishop, Charles, 132
Bishop, Jim, 283
Bishop, Keith, 576, 606
Bishop, Richard, 165, 166, 419
Bishop, Rob, 14
Bishop, Robert, 289
Bishop, Sarah, 465
Bishop, Tim, 9
Bishop,, Sanford, Jr., 4
Bishton, Timothy, 229
Bissell, James, 299
Bissex, Glyn, 572
Bisson, Alain, 476
Bisson, Henri, 84, 85
Bissonette, John, 128
Bivens, Sandy, 323
Bivings, Albert, 72
Bixby, Donald, 263
Bixby, Martin, 533
Bjork, Bruce, 233
Black, David, 396
Black, Lindy, 457
Black, Scott Hoffman, 561
Black, Susan, 237
Blackburn, Gary, 167
Blackburn, Marsha, 13
Blackburn, Michel, 601
Blackburn, Theresa, 374
Blackburn, Wilbert, 48
Blackmore, Mary, 410
Blackwelder, Brent, 338
Blackwell, Bill, 364
Blackwell, Linda, 59
Blackwell, Raymond, 280
Blackwell, Sharon, 78
Blades, Michael, 478
Blaha, Kathy, 524
Blaine, Mark, 335
Blair, Aaron, 476
Blair, Amy, 570
Blair, Bowen, 524

Blair, Charles, 114
Blair, Jan, 420
Blais, Aurele, 476
Blais, Claudette, 214
Blake, Gloria, 331
Blake, J., 199
Blake, William, 544
Blakemore, Keith, 561
Blakeslee, George, 609
Blalock, Edwina, 230
Blanche, Catalino, 33
Blanco, José Ma., 281
Bland, Douglas, 195
Blaney, Karen, 513
Blankenship, Terry, 536, 553
Blanton, Mike, 200
Blauer, Mark, 349
Blauvelt, Mark, 522
Bledsoe, Paul, 89
Bleichner, Doug, 356
Bleier, Will, 590
Blem, Charles, 555
Blessington, Jacque, 249
Blevins, Heather, 374
Blevins, John, 150
Blevins, Matt, 460
Blex, C. Doug, 168
Blick, Larry, 47
Block, Rance, 482
Blockstein, David, 462
Blodgett, Putnam W., 530
Blodgett, Sarah, 407
Blomquist, Jim, 498
Blood, Brad, 553
Blood, Marcus, 64
Bloom, Arnold, 606
Bloome, Peter, 209
Bloomquist, Frank, 554
Blossom, Mary Helen, 313
Blot, Kim, 197
Bloyd, Barry, 205
Blue, Karen, 306
Bluemle, John, 164
Blum, Cristine, 384
Blum, Gordie, 131
Blumberg, Fred, 157
Blume, Ted, 188
Blumenauer, Earl, 12
Blumenfeld, Myron, 479
Blumstein, Carl, 251
Blundo, John, 179
Blunt, Roy, 8
Boal, Clint, 30
Board, Tempra, 520
Boatwright, Mike, 169
Boaz, Trish, 149
Bobertz, Dick, 215
Bobzien, Steven, 552
Bochenek, Eleanor, 58
Bock, Walter, 521
Boddicker, Maj., 302
Bode, Scott, 519
Bodie, Walt, 468
Bodin, Mark, 513
Bodman, Sam, 49
Boehlert, Sherwood L., 10
Boehm, David, 576
Boehm, Eric, 567
Boehner, John, 21
Boehner, John A., 11
Boehringer, Bo, 173
Boenning, Dickson, 412
Boergers, David, 75
Boesch, Donald, 613
Boettcher, Kelcy, 556
Boezi, Louis, 52
Bogar, Debra, 407
Bogard, Carol, 397
Bogenschutz, Todd, 548
Boger, Bruce, 25
Boggus, Tom, 222
Bogle, Andrea, 354
Bogner, Gary, 483

STAFF NAME INDEX – B

Bogner, Terry, 354
Boham, Russel, 583
Bohan, Carolyn, 111
Bohle, Ed, 376
Bohm, Shirley, 181
Bohmfalk, Erwin, 542
Bolduc, Herve, 214
Bolen, Patrick, 270
Bolenbaugh, Alan, 356
Boles, Jeffrey, 599
Boliver, Bruce, 595
Bollinger, Don, 534
Bollinger, Trent, 286
Bolster, Carl, Jr., 616
Bolton, Hannibal, 90, 257
Bolton, Yvonne, 149
Bonar, Scott, 135, 605
Bond, Christopher S. Kit, 8
Bond, Monica, 290
Bondi, Melissa, 432
Bondrup-Nielsen, Soren, 572
Bononborgor, Peter, 277
Boner, Rex, 307
Bongolan, Dixie, 464
Bonilla, Henry, 14
Bonilla, Hilda, 475
Bonk, Paula, 591
Bonner, Jo, 1
Bonner, Robert, 76
Bonney, Forrest, 253
Bonney, Rick, 309
Bono, Mary, 2
Bonomo, Jacquelyn, 537
Booker, John, 489
Boone, Robert, 268
Booth, Hank, 382
Boozman, John, 1
Borbely, Andy, 355
Bordallo, Madeleine Z., 15
Borden, David, 481
Bordogna, Joseph, 24
Boren, Jon, 195
Boren, Mike, 278
Borg, Elizabeth, 471
Borkowski, Francis, 573
Born, Stephen, 520
Borner, Markus, 336
Borre, Lisa, 385
Bortone, Steve, 306, 484
Boruff, Chet, 162
Boruff, Scott, 222
Borzeueri, Bob, 143
Bosma, Barbara, 318
Bosman, Corrie, 246, 290
Boss, Michael, 554
Bosted, Peter, 289
Bostic, James, 341
Bostick, William, 544
Boswell, Leonard L., 6
Boswell, Ted, 434
Bosworth, Dale, 33
Bosworth, Rob, 434
Bosworth, Robert, 134
Boteler, Frank, 235
Both, Mel, 345
Bott, Dave, 523
Botzojorns, Lars, 382
Bouc, Ken, 188
Bouchard, J., 328
Boucher, Rick, 14
Boucher, Stephanie, 476
Boullion, Thomas, 552
Boulton, Mark, 361
Bounds, Dixie, 614
Bourque, Herb, 47
Bourque, Peter, 175
Bouwer, Edward, 585
Bowen, Bonnie, 309
Bowen, John, 334
Bowen, Pamela, 332
Bowers, Jeffrey, 236
Bowers, Robert, 386
Bowie, David, 520

Bowler, Tom, 372
Bowman, Margaret, 265
Bowman, Marlene, 174
Bowman, Phil, 173
Bowman, Steven, 232
Boxer, Barbara, 1
Boxrucker, Jeff, 254
Boyce, Timothy, 133
Boyce, Walter, 606
Boyd, Bruce, 435
Boyd, F. Allen, Jr., 3
Boyd, Jim, 316
Boyd, Kenneth, 73
Boyd, Milton, 583
Boyd, Susan, 304
Boyd, Tom, 441
Boydstun, L., 142
Boyer, Jeff, 572
Boyer, Tom, 235
Boykin, Bill, 155
Boykin, Esther, 414
Boyle, Barbara, 491
Boyle, Harvey, 176
Boyle, Mike, 537
Boyle, Stewart, 364
Boyle, Sue, 191
Boyles, Kristen, 320
Boyles, Robert, 301
Boyleston, Larry, 217
Bozek, Michael, 237, 623
Bozek, Nancy, 557
Brabander, Jerry, 551
Brack, Andy, 506
Brackett, David, 17, 368
Bradberry, Terry, 231
Bradbury, Michael, 552
Bradford, Derek, 593
Bradford, Gary, 282
Bradley, Curt, 290
Bradley, Darby, 529
Bradley, Jeb, 9
Bradley, John, 524
Bradley, Ruth, 352
Bradstreet, Michael, 279
Bradt-Barnhart, Judy, 430
Brady, Amy, 219
Brady, Kat, 389
Brady, Kevin P., 13
Brady, Robert A., 12
Brady, Sheila, 487
Braibanti, Ralph, 78
Brainerd, Lyman, 322
Bramblett, Cheryl, 519
Branca, Barbara, 58
Brand, Chuck, 489
Brandenburg, Brooke, 341
Brandon, Clark, 63
Brandrup, Mike, 166
Brandson, Norm, 176
Brandt, Paul, 296
Brandup, Mike, 166
Brannan, Mark, 74
Brantly, Robert, 508, 544
Brassard, Bill, 424
Braswell, Allen, 73
Braswell, Alvin, 451
Bratsch, Gene, 294
Braudis, Brian, 93
Brauer, Richard, 564
Braun, Kevin, 566
Braunworth, William, 209
Braus, Judy, 447
Brawn, Jeff, 264
Braxton, Nancy, 578
Bray, Harvey, 475
Bray, Shirley, 247
Brazelton, Don, 164
Brazil, J., 199
Breakell, John, 304
Brean, Ron, 152
Breathitt, Linda, 75
Breau, Kasha, 412
Breaux, John B., 6

Breazeale, Daniel, 217
Brecher, Alan, 389
Breckenridge, Roy, 161
Breckenridge, Russ, 162
Breeding, Ron, 312
Breedlove, Buzz, 141
Breen, Barry, 130
Brehm, Laura, 524
Breitburg, Denise, 266
Breitmeyer, Richard, 142
Bremer, Linda, 544
Bremer, Steve, 189
Bremer, Walter, 575
Bremicker, Tim, 182
Brennan, Barry, 224
Brenneman, Russell, 443
Brenner, Dave, 57
Brenner, Robert, 18
Breslin, Vincent, 596
Bressor, James, 226
Breunig, Robert, 385
Brewer, Sherri, 296
Brewster, Paul, 37
Brewster, Paul, 38
Brewton, Charles, 221
Brian, Anderson, 162
Brice, William, 182
Brickell, Todd, 482
Brickley, David, 229
Bridle, Ken, 451
Brienich, Anna, 466
Brienzo, Gary, 407
Brière, Denis, 602
Briggs, Roger, 144
Brigham, Mark, 619
Bright, Ann, 223
Bright, Patricia, 250
Brill, Kenneth, 78
Brim, Greg, 296
Brinker, Richard, 574
Brinkley, Jessie A., 427
Briscoe, Robbie, 185
Briskey, Lisa, 542
Bristah, Cheryl, 460
Bristol, Jennifer, 438
Britt, Bruce, 333
Brittell, Dave, 233
Britting, Sue, 280
Brittingham, M., 592
Britton, Susan, 319
Britz, Kevin, 351
Bro, Kenneth, 591
Broadway, Michael, 591
Brobeck, Rod, 461
Brochu, Lisa, 407
Brock, Dennis, 20
Brock, Jenny, 333
Brock, Mike, 520
Brock, Richard, 55, 224
Brockman, Connie, 297
Brockman, Sue, 466
Broderick, Brian, 180
Broderick, Stephen, 608
Broderick, Thomas, 179
Brodie, W., 453
Brogan, Mike, 302
Brogie, Mark, 442
Brohman, Mark, 188
Brokaw, Howard, 250
Bromley, Peter, 200
Bronski, Peter, 276
Bronson, Charles, 152
Bronston, David, 242
Brook, Dan, 193
Brooke, Carl, 447
Brookerson, Bill, 232
Brooks, Christopher, 218
Brooks, Connie, 226
Brooks, James, 175
Brooks, Jerry, 154
Brooks, John, 486
Brooks, Kevin, 134
Brooks, Lila, 284

Brooks, Stuart, 365
Brooks, William, 217
Brooner, Roger, 382
Broughton, Jodi, 454
Brouha, Paul, 33
Broussard, Amy, 59
Browder, Hal, 562
Brown, Alex, 461
Brown, Alfred, 574
Brown, Anita, 47
Brown, Art, 235
Brown, Arthur, 444
Brown, Beth, 374, 599
Brown, Carl, 427
Brown, Carol, 208, 558
Brown, Charles, 458
Brown, Chris, 450
Brown, Corrine, 3
Brown, David, 621
Brown, Donald, 483
Brown, Eric, 289
Brown, Frank, 169
Brown, Gregory, 625
Brown, Henry E., Jr., 12
Brown, Hugh, 574
Brown, James, 209, 483
Brown, Jeanette, 18
Brown, Jessica, 275
Brown, John, 158
Brown, K., 586
Brown, Karen, 18
Brown, Karl, 211
Brown, Kirby, 517, 553
Brown, Kirk, 162
Brown, Larry, 211, 259
Brown, Lester, 317
Brown, Lewis, 586
Brown, Linfield, 600
Brown, Lori, 560
Brown, Lynn, 234
Brown, Marlene, 544
Brown, Mary, 444
Brown, Michael, 596
Brown, Michele, 133
Brown, Otis, 365, 614
Brown, Patrick, 611
Brown, Perry, 615
Brown, Portia, 540
Brown, Randall, 143
Brown, Robert, 546
Brown, Roger, 417
Brown, Russ, 259
Brown, Scott, 193
Brown, Sherrod, 11
Brown, Sibylla, 373
Brown, Steve, 197
Brown, Timothy, 71
Brown, Tom, 154
Brown, Tommy, 197
Brown, Torrey, 542
Brown, Vicki, 627
Brown-Waite, Ginny, 3
Brownback, Sam, 6, 29
Browne, Bob, 385
Browne, Brooks, 326
Brownell, William, 422
Browning, Dennis, 550
Browning, James, 114
Broz, Gordon, 179
Brubaker, Kevin, 327
Bruce, Ann, 515
Bruce, James, 504
Bruce, Jim, 532
Brucker, James, 525
Brucker, Thomas, 452
Bruderly, David, 331
Bruell, Harry, 408
Bruffy, Robert, 77
Bruner, Clark, 133
Bruns, Dale, 627
Brunsvold, Joal, 162
Brus, Keith, 468
Brusca, Richard, 272

STAFF NAME INDEX – B

Brusendorff, Anne, 21
Brush, Grace, 585
Bry, Jonathan, 491
Bryan, Charles, 172, 586
Bryan, Rorke, 621
Bryant, Bunyan, 614
Bryant, Darla, 138
Bryant, David, 55, 119
Bryant, Dirk, 433
Bryant, Douglas, 217
Bryant, Fred, 599
Bryant, Harold, 47
Bryant, Laura, 342
Bryant, Shari, 257
Bryant, Sherman, 356
Bryant, Tracey, 54
Bryce, Philip, 190
Bryne, Donald, 229
Bryson, Carolyn, 357
Brzuszek, Bob, 311, 401
Buchanan, Gale, 157
Buchanan, Stuart, 197
Buchert, Al, 360
Buchert, Beverly, 595
Buchner, Jay, 523
Buchner, Kathy, 520, 523
Buchsbaum, Andrew, 428
Buck, John, 404
Buck, LeAnn, 399
Buck, Michael, 159
Buck, Paige, 47
Buckheit, Kelly, 340
Buckhorn, Monica, 292
Buckhouse, John, 33
Buckingham, Melanie, 200
Buckley, Robert, 223
Bucklin, Ann, 57
Buckman, Arthur, 74
Buckner, Eldon Buck, 279
Budd, William, 626
Budney, Gregory, 309
Buechler, Dennis, 302
Buehler, David, 553
Buffett, Jimmy, 486
Buffington, John, 127, 128
Buford, Lori, 145
Buhler, Andy, 281
Buhler, Marilyn, 281
Buis, Tom, 419
Bujold, Guy, 27
Bull, Milan, 412
Bullock, Jimmy, 401
Bullock, Steve, 311
Bullock, Thomas, 445
Bulman, Jim, 166
Bulman, Lesley, 558
Bulson, Jennifer, 563
Bump, C., 483
Bump, Jerry, 168
Bundy, Susan, 214
Bunn, Barry, 218
Bunning, Jim, 6
Bunting, Bruce, 559
Bunuri, Tariq, 368
Burani, Matteo, 529
Burchfield, James, 615
Burckhardt, Jason, 259
Burde, John, 596
Burdette, John, 536
Burdick, Neal, 242
Burek, Tom, 245
Burger, Brian, 212
Burger, D., 606
Burger, Kristen, 141
Burgess, Harriet, 262
Burgess, Jay, 488
Burgess, Jim, 555
Burgess, Michael C., 14
Burgess, Van, 225
Burget, Mark, 434
Burgett, Meg, 245
Burgoyne, George, 180
Burgum, Barbara, 465

Burhenne, Wolfgang, 362
Burke, Alberta, 284
Burke, Gordon, 77
Burke, John, 187
Burke, Kevin, 294
Burke, Mark, 558
Burkert, Ronald, 483
Burkhart, Harold, 625
Burkholder, Melody, 168
Burks, Dennis, 137
Burley, Jeffery, 367
Burlington, D., 75
Burnett, Collin, 397
Burnett, Grove, 537
Burnette, Jim, 200
Burney, Daryl, 401
Burnham, Kenneth, 578
Burnham, William, 468
Burnley, Robert, 230
Burns, Amy Martin, 519
Burns, Clay, 288
Burns, Conrad, 8
Burns, Jennifer, 435
Burns, Karen, 404
Burns, Max, 4
Burns, Stephen, 26
Burns, William, 72, 266
Burpee, Robert, 52
Burr, Brooks, 266
Burr, Richard, 10
Burrell, Cole, 532
Burreson, E., 577
Burrough, Eric, 391
Burrows, Victoria, 320
Burt, Laurie, 270
Burt, Will, 147
Burtnett, Daryl, 437
Burton, Dan, 5
Burton, John, 616
Burton, Nelson, 376
Burton, Robert, 72
Busbice, Bill, 173
Busby, Fee, 624
Busby, Frank (Fee), 624
Busch, Rick, 230, 231
Bush, C., 334
Bush, Charles, 169
Bush, Donna, 539
Bushey, Thomas, 227
Bushway, Rodney, 612
Buskirk, Steve, 623
Bussert, Ellen, 206
Bussey, Bill, 520
Bustamante, Cruz, 145
Bustamante, Rosi, 516
Buthman, Mark, 66
Butler, C., 199
Butler, Eileen, 313
Butler, Mac, 590
Butler, Sydney, 268
Butler, Virginia, 77
Butterfield, Bruce, 420
Butterworth, Scott, 551
Buttrick, Sherry, 232
Butts, Greg, 137
Buxton, Dwayne, 31
Buyer, Steve, 5
Buzby, Brian, 450
Buzicky, Greg, 182
Byer, Linda, 548
Byer, Tim, 554
Byers, C. Randall, 470
Byers, John, 208
Byers, Kurt, 54
Byford, Jim, 621
Byford, Ron, 195
Byram, Emily, 416
Byrd, George, 581
Byrd, Jim, 404
Byrd, Robert, 28
Byrd, Robert C., 15
Byrne, James, 531
Byrne, Robert, 70, 545

Byrnes, Bridgett, 486
Byrum, Larry, 206

C

Cabasso, Israel, 598
Cabela, Richard, 527
Cable, Ted, 585
Cables, Rick, 43
Cabot, Charles, 308
Caccamise, Donald, 590
Caccese, Albert, 198
Cackette, Tom, 143
Cade, Tracy, 413
Caeser, Delane, 222
Caffey, Rex, 173
Cahill, M., 199
Cahill, Russ, 233
Cahill-Aylward, Susan, 266
Cain, Al, 134
Cain, Nancy, 578
Cain, Nick, 464
Cairns, Barbara, 390
Cairns, John, 625
Calambokidis, John, 289
Calcagno, Joan, 130
Calderwood, Louise, 227
Caldwell, Colleen, 127
Caldwell, Jack, 172
Caldwell, Larry, 549
Caldwell, Martyn, 624
Calfee, Alan, 397
Callaghan, Michael, 235
Callaghan-Chapell, Sara, 490
Callahan, Deb, 387
Callan, Leonard, 26
Callaway, Will, 516
Callery, Tom, 221
Callicott, J., 291
Callicott, J., 367
Callow, Nora, 386
Calpone, Jan, 298
Calumpong, Hilconida, 595
Calverley, Brett, 315
Calvert, Ken, 2
Calvert, William, 66
Calvin, Elizabeth, 558
Calvo, Patrick, 463
Camara, Andre, 245
Camardese, Mike, 66
Camenzind, Franz, 379
Cameron, Bob, 176
Camhi, Merry, 414
Camiré, Claude, 602
Camp, Dave, 7
Camp, Megan, 490
Camp, Paul, 90
Camp, Samuel, 159
Campa, Henry, 597
Campbell, Ben Nighthorse, 3
Campbell, Carl, 170
Campbell, Carter, 185
Campbell, Cecil, 155
Campbell, Christopher, 612
Campbell, Faith, 308, 532
Campbell, Fred, 273
Campbell, James, 398
Campbell, Lee, 301
Campbell, Lurlie, 377
Campbell, Marilyn, 413
Campbell, Mora, 628
Campbell, Peter, 551
Campbell, Todd, 299
Campen, Donald, 229
Campion, Dennis, 611
Canada, Mike, 113
Cancilla, Jodeane, 391
Canfield, Veronica, 560
Canham, Charles, 358
Cannaley, Paul, 289
Cannon, Chris, 14
Cannon, Ed, 450
Cannon, Shelton, 75
Cannon, Stuart, 72

Canny, M., 23
Cantin, Danielle, 368
Canton, Steve, 447
Cantor, Eric I., 14
Cantor, Ray, 191
Cantu, Celeste, 144
Cantu, Reynaldo, 367
Cantwell, Jean, 395
Cantwell, Maria, 14
Canzano, Pasquale, 151
Capito, Charles, 236
Capito, Shelley Moore, 15
Caporale, Walter, 363
Capotosto, Paul, 305
Capp, Wayne, 473
Cappel, Alise, 291
Capps, Lois, 2
Capuano, Michael, 7
Caputo, Guy, 25
Caputo, Paul, 407
Caraco, Nina, 358
Caravetta, John, 136
Carbee, Hunter, 444
Carbonell, Montserrat, 316
Card, Beth, 443
Cardin, Benjamin L., 7
Cardinal, Mike, 135
Cardoza, Dennis, 2
Carette, Jacques, 16
Carey, Daniel, 426
Carey, David, 149
Carey, Henry, 335
Carey, Karen, 229
Carey, Robert, 552
Carey, Shelley, 424
Carey, Tobe, 627
Cargile, R., 137
Carignan, George, 57
Carley, Wayne, 407
Carline, Robert, 210, 592
Carlisle, Martha, 335
Carlone, John, 445
Carlough, Yola, 336
Carlson, Chuck, 415
Carlson, Conrad, 452
Carlson, Frederick, 211
Carlson, Merlyn, 188
Carlson, Mike, 245
Carlson, Richard, 69
Carlson, Stephan, 183
Carlson, Steven, 583
Carlstrom, Terry, 120
Carlton, Gary, 144
Carlton, Ginny, 238
Carly, Keith, 283
Carman, Neil, 493
Carmichael, Tim, 299
Carnean, Kathy, 242
Carnevale, Ellen, 471
Carney, James, 188
Carney, Jan, 227
Carney, John, 379
Carno, John, 415
Caro, Angela, 335
Carolan, Lee, 169
Caron, Karen, 323
Carothers, Leslie, 327
Carothers, Sarah, 524
Carpenter, Elizabeth, 193
Carpenter, Glenn, 87
Carpenter, Jesse, 509
Carpenter, Kathy, 47
Carpenter, Len, 545
Carpenter, Phil, 150
Carper, Eric, 539
Carper, Thomas R., 3
Carpio, CeCe, 389
Carr, Bruce, 268
Carr, Michael, 433, 438
Carr, Timothy, 168
Carraway, Mike, 551
Carreon, Marco, 146
Carreto, Alberto, 516

STAFF NAME INDEX – C

Carrier, David, 264, 406
Carrier, Michael, 209
Carrierre, Murdoch, 216
Carrington, Patricia, 362
Carroll, David, 544
Carroll, Harold, 203
Carroll, Mike, 182
Carrow, Cynthia, 537
Carruthers, Thomas, 244
Carsalade, H., 333
Carson, Brad, 11
Carson, Brownie, 432
Carson, C., 155
Carson, Gene, 272
Carson, Jack, 205
Carson, Julia M., 5
Carson, Paul, 483
Carter, Allen, 445
Carter, Billy, 183
Carter, Colin, 606
Carter, Curt, 325
Carter, David, 419
Carter, Ed, 221
Carter, Jimmy, 200, 246
Carter, John, 538
Carter, John R., 14
Carter, Larry, 356
Carter, Lisa, 462
Carter, Marcia, 248
Carter, Michael, 470
Carter, Mike, 482
Carter, Ronald, 218
Carter, Thomas, 376
Carter, Virginia, 504
Carthy, Raymond, 152
Cartin, Anita, 446
Cartlidge, Robert, 458
Carutel, Amanda, 474
Caruso, Michael, 379
Carver, Andrew, 596
Casadevall, Thomas, 127
Case, Boyd, 16
Case, Ed, 4
Case, James, 240
Case, Larry, 419
Case, Marilyn, 541
Case, Marshal, 251, 524
Casey, Charles, 103
Casey, Lloyd, 466
Cash, Paige, 334
Cassada, Dawn, 149
Cassani, John, 255
Cassat, Richard, 137
Casselman, Tracy, 114
Cassidy, Shannon, 199
Castellano, Rick, 557
Castillan, Chris, 147
Castle, Megan, 147
Castle, Michael, 3
Castler, John, 192
Castles, Tom, 403
Castongue, Martin, 253
Castro, Alex, 488
Castro, Bernadette, 198
Castro, Dan, 296
Catanese, Carol, 539
Catania, Michael, 437
Cate, Nancy, 276
Cate, Tracy, 445
Cato, James, 55
Catoe, Mitchell, 341
Caton, Patti, 575
Cattany, Ronald, 146
Cauthen, Stephen, 133
Cavalier, Claudine, 339
Cavanaugh, Peggy, 288
Cavanaugh-Grant, Deborah, 504
Caves, H.A., 206
Cecere, Al, 251
Cecil, Maria, 312
Cederstav, Anna, 319
Cenarrusa, Pete, 160
Cerino, Harry, 349

Ceruti, Fiorella, 560
Cessna, Stella, 184
Cestero, Barb, 505
Chabot, Steve, 11
Chabot, Warner, 455, 456
Chacko, A., 601
Chadwick, Chris, 194
Chafee, Lincoln D., 12
Chalmers-Watson, Nicola, 559
Chamberlain, William, 446
Chamblee, Cary, 218
Chamblin, Mike, 243
Chambliss, Saxby, 4
Chamipagne, Alice, 527
Champeau, Randy, 623
Champness, Jessica, 327
Chamut, P., 453
Chamut, Pat, 20
Chan, Susan, 249
Chancellor, Richard, 239
Chanda, David, 192
Chandler, Allan, 354
Chandler, C., 274
Chandler, Frank, 272
Chandler, Harry, 530
Chandler, James, 506
Chandler, Paul, 574
Chandler, Val, 182
Chandler, William, 394
Chaney, Ed, 454
Chang, David, 592
Chang, Mingteh, 598
Chanhalbrandt, Catherine, 610
Chantry, Christine, 407
Chapco, William, 619
Chape, Stuart, 369
Chapin, Jim, 334
Chapman, Deb, 325
Chapman, Mary, 335
Chappell, Michelle, 113
Chapple, Tom, 133
Charland, Dave, 329
Charlebois, Patrice, 55
Charles, Cheryl, 555
Charles, Lalora, 510
Charles, Patricia, 288
Charlson, Evelyn, 557
Chase, Helen, 209
Chase, Jayni, 291
Chase, Robert, 418
Chateauneuf, Russell, 214
Chatham, Daphne, 614
Chaudhuri, Sumita, 177
Chavarria, Gaby, 427
Chavez-Quiroga, Amparo, 213
Chavies, Elmer, Jr., 511, 570
Chazin, Daniel, 447
Chekay, D., 315
Chelecki, Gene, 153
Chen, Paul, 33
Chénevert, Robert, 603
Cheng, Li, 603
Chenoweth, Michael, 376
Chepel, Leonard, 453
Cherel, Donna, 433
Chernick, Michael, 347
Cherry, Marion, 550
Chesemore, Ronald, 76
Chesky, David, 362
Chesney, Norma, 340
Chevalier, Susan, 554
Chezem, Linda, 213
Chiappetta, Florence, 545
Child, Betsy, 220
Child, Dennis, 578
Child, William, 162
Childress, Don, 165
Childress, Don, 187
Childs, Starling, 277
Chinchilli, Jolene, 295
Ching, Patrick, 73
Chipley, Robert, 250
Chipman, Richard, 551

Chipponeri, L., 143
Chipps, Steven, 29, 596
Chisholm, Vivian, 296
Chism, John, 383
Chittenden, Jessica, 197
Chocola, Chris, 5
Choksi, Kashyap, 406
Cholvin, Valerie, 337
Chonguica, Ebenizario, 369
Chrisman, Mike, 144
Chrisotomo, David, 158
Christensen, Douglass, 557
Christensen, James, 225
Christensen, Norman, 580
Christensen, Thomas, 202
Christensen, Todd, 87
Christensen, Walter, 31
Christenson, James, 135
Christian-Christensen,
  Donna M., 15
Christiansen, Liz, 165, 166
Christianson, Jay, 225
Christianson, Ward, 393
Christie, Nancy, 444
Christie, Rhiannon, 549
Christman, Russell, 617
Christopherson, Kristen, 63
Chrouch, Leigh Ann, 137
Chryssostomidis, Chrys, 56
Chu, Dan, 427
Chudleigh, Ted, 187
Chura, Mark, 150
Church, Lisa, 553
Church, Philip, 498
Churchwell, Stew, 538
Chute, Lionel, 191
Cilek, Jeffrey, 468
Cinq-Mars, Jean, 544
Cipriano, Renee, 162
Cirmo, Christopher, 597
Cisneros, Ella, 518
Citsay, Mark, 400
Citta, Joe, 441
Claeys, Thomas, 201
Clambey, Gary, 590
Clamen, Murray, 23
Clapp, Eugene, 308
Clark, Beth, 209
Clark, Christopher, 309
Clark, Edward, 371, 542
Clark, Eugenie, 404
Clark, Gary, 162
Clark, Greg, 381
Clark, James, 535
Clark, Jean, 415
Clark, Jeffrey, 77
Clark, Jerry, 419
Clark, Joe, 359
Clark, John, 218, 283
Clark, Mark, 590
Clark, Nancy, 137
Clark, Randy, 168
Clark, Renee, 278
Clark, Richard, 311
Clark, Ross, 580
Clark, Sandy, 119
Clark, Sharon, 182
Clark, Tom, 400
Clark, Walter, 301
Clarke, Nancy, 330
Clauson, Sam, 497
Clay, Bob, 315
Clay, L., 288
Clay, William L., Jr., 8
Clayton, Charles, 378
Clayton, Chuck, 376, 507
Clayton, Gary, 414
Clayton, Pat, 329
Cleary, D., 209
Cleary, Mike, 142
Cleary, Paul, 210
Cleaver, Jerry, 61
Clem, John, 360

Clement, Jessica, 578
Clement, Kent, 578
Clement, Stephanie, 336
Clemmer, Glenn, 189
Cleveland, Theodore, 610
Clewell, Richard, 72
Clifford, Janine, 416
Clift, Edward, 140
Clinch, Bud, 187
Cline, Dave, 384
Cline, Mike, 392
Cline, Tim, 471
Clingan, Chris, 373
Clinton, Hillary Rodham, 9
Close, David, 596
Clotworthy, Christopher, 479
Clough, Noreen, 279
Clouse, Bob, 421
Cloutier, Ron, 396
Cloutier, Terry, 406
Clover, Darlene, 388
Cludray, Patti, 596
Clugston, Richard, 352
Clumpner, Curtiss, 430
Clurman, Andrew, 519
Clusen, Charles, 251
Clyburn, James, 13
Coan, Gene, 197
Coates, Bob, 513
Cobb, Anthony, 305
Cobb, Britt, 200
Cobb, Coralie, 421
Cobb, David, 201
Cobb, James, 170
Cobb, Janet, 562
Cobb, Jonathon, 293
Cobb, Junior, 313
Cobble, Bill, 346
Coble, Daniel, 254
Coble, Howard, 10
Coble, Kim, 295
Cobourn, John, 616
Coburn, David, 161
Coburn, Nancy, 424
Cochara, Kelly, 511
Cochran, Carroll, 334
Cochran, Donald, 177
Cochran, Steve, 324
Cochran, Thad, 8
Cochrane, Gail, 269
Cockrell, David, 540
Cockrell, James, 134
Code, Aimee, 453
Coder, Kim, 367
Coderre, Sonja, 47
Coe, Lee, 181
Coe, Mike, 442
Coen, Amy, 470
Coffeen, Mike, 314
Coffey, Clarence, 221
Coffey, Dan, 134
Coffin, Barbara, 615
Coffman, Charles, 235
Coffman, Dave, 534
Coghlan, Stephen, 254
Cogliano, John, 179
Cohen, Barbara, 263
Cohen, Dave, 271
Cohen, Jules, 480
Cohen, Maria, 242
Cohen, Mark, 625
Cohen, Michelle, 552
Cohn, Stan, 579
Coit, Elizabeth, 541
Coker, Sam, 506
Colbert, K., 199
Colclasure, Chris, 138
Cole, Gary, 133
Cole, Jeff, 188
Cole, Jonathan, 358
Cole, Leslie, 171
Cole, Patrick, 188
Cole, Tom, 11

STAFF NAME INDEX – C

Coleman, Bob, 73
Coleman, Bruce, 204
Coleman, Catherine, 73
Coleman, James, 152
Coleman, Lewis, 282
Coleman, Mark, 206
Coleman, Norm, 8
Coleman, Ruth, 142, 152
Coleman, Stephen, 171
Coleman, Steve, 170
Coleman, Terry, 163
Coleman, Tom, 72
Colette, Martine, 554
Colgrove, Gary, 32
Colker, Ryan, 478
College, Melody, 429
Collier, Carol, 17
Collignon, Rick, 160
Collins, Alan, 626
Collins, Carole, 218
Collins, Ken, 357
Collins, Leroy, 277
Collins, Linda, 71
Collins, Mark, 525
Collins, Martha, 113
Collins, Mary, 439
Collins, Michael Mac, 4
Collins, Nancy, 371
Collins, Noelle, 276
Collins, Ralph, 170
Collins, Richard, 177
Collins, Sally, 33
Collins, Samuel, 26
Collins, Scott, 267
Collins, Susan M., 6
Collins, Vaughn, 90
Collopy, Michael, 616
Coloma-Agaran, Gilbert, 159
Colon, Norberto, 475
Colona, Robert, 425
Colton, Eldon, 373
Columna, Josie, 468
Colvin, Gordon, 196
Colwell, Rita, 24
Combest, Larry, 13, 21
Combs, Daniel, 599
Combs, Susan, 222
Combs, Terry, 302
Comeau, Roxanne, 287
Comerford, Jeanne, 47
Comoss, Eugene, 211
Compton, Glenn, 393
Compton, John, 390
Compton, Shane, 90
Compton, Steven, 251
Comus, Steve, 483
Conda, Judy, 332
Conder, Grace, 342
Cone, Joseph, 58
Congalton, Russell, 617
Congel, Frank, 25
Congleton, James, 611
Conkey, Alice, 423
Conkle, Tammy, 421
Conklin, Charles, 247
Conklin, Edwin, 154
Conkling, Philip, 374
Conley, Jan, 385
Conley, Richard, 445
Connaughton, Jim, 31
Connell, Jim, 240
Connelly, Kenneth, 280
Conner, Mark, 565
Connolly, James, 268
Connor, Michael, 314
Conover, Marion, 166
Conover, Michael, 624
Conrad, Eric, 211
Conrad, Kent, 11
Conroy, Donald, 448
Conroy, Michael, 20
Consolvo, Charles, 375
Conte, Marc, 496

Conti, Frank, 143
Conway, Kevin, 225, 226
Conway, Michael, 211
Conway, Mike, 133
Conway, Stuart, 520
Conyers, John, Jr., 7
Cooch, Edward, Jr., 297
Cook, David, 552
Cook, Diane, 365
Cook, Ernest, 524
Cook, Gary, 221
Cook, George, 152
Cook, Joe, 309
Cook, John, 324, 438
Cook, Lance, 240
Cook, Lynda, 239
Cook, Michael, 130
Cook, Monica, 309
Cook, Robert, 184, 222, 543
Cook, S., 127
Cook, Susan, 60
Cook, Wayne, 131
Cook, Wendy, 330, 339
Cook, William, 466
Cooke, Gregg, 19
Cooke, Trey, 313
Cookendorfer, Paul, 511, 570
Cooksey, Sarah, 151
Cooksie, Carolyn, 33
Cool, Donald, 25
Cool, K., 180
Coomer, Chuck, 157
Coon, John, 463
Coon, Maggie, 433
Coon, Thomas, 587
Cooney, Philip, 31
Cooper, Aziza, 510
Cooper, Faye, 232
Cooper, George, 49
Cooper, Gordon, 447
Cooper, James, 183
Cooper, Jim, 13
Cooper, John, 25, 219, 360
Cooper, Kathy, 286
Cooper, Kevin, 547
Cooper, Lori, 500
Cooper, Mike, 484
Cooper, Rita, 235
Cooper, Romain, 500
Cope, Grant, 320
Copeland, C., 343
Copeland, Jim, 421
Copping, Andrea, 60
Coppinger, Paul, 76
Coran, Laurie, 544
Corbett, Carl, 207
Corcoran, Bill, 490
Cordes, John, 25
Cordiviola, Steven, 170
Cordova, Robert, 301
Cordulack, Jeff, 505
Core, John, 153
Corey, Susan, 202
Coriel, Paul, 173
Corkery, Cathy, 495
Corlett, William, 466
Cormier, Yvon, 602
Cornelius, Mike, 62
Cornelius, Steve, 505
Cornell, Pat Appel, 265
Corner, James, 619
Cornyn, John, 13
Corral, Thais, 558
Correll, David, 501
Corson, Angela, 66
Cortelyou, Charlie, 234
Corven, Jim, 537
Corzine, Jon, 9
Cosby, Jeanne, 404
Cossette, Alain, 476
Cost, Richard, 612
Costa, Charles, 580
Costa-Pierce, Barry, 59

Costello, Jerry F., 5
Costello, John, 163
Costello, Mark, 353
Costie, Steve, 405
Cote, Diana, 134
Cote, Lawrence, 237
Cotnoir, Liliane, 345
Cotsworth, Elizabeth, 18, 19
Cotter, B., 26
Cottingham, David, 23, 247
Cottingham, Susan, 187
Cottle, Amelia Miner, 487
Cottle, Curt, 218
Cottrell, Marie, 73
Coughlin, Paul, 219, 553
Coulam, Nancy, 89
Coulon, Christina, 47
Coulter, Jane, 49
Coumbe, Louise, 298
Counts, Tommy, 546
Courson, Bud, 172
Courter, J., 228
Courtney, Elizabeth, 529
Courtney, Will, 390
Courville, Mary, 539
Cousteau, Francine, 310
Couston, Tom, 345
Coutts, John, 466
Covell, Darrel, 617
Covington, Rick, 513
Cowan, Doug, 260
Cowdery, John, 568
Cowen, Raymond, 196
Cowling, Terri, 218
Cox, Caroline, 453
Cox, Chad, 458
Cox, Christopher, 3
Cox, Craig, 504
Cox, Gregory, 396
Cox, Linda, 229
Cox, Patricia, 509
Coyle, Kevin, 418
Cozens, Toby, 252
Craft, Robert, 232
Crago, Tracey, 57
Craig, Jon, 206
Craig, Larry E., 4
Craig, Phil, 516
Craighead, April, 310
Craighead, Charles, 310
Craighead, Frank, 310
Craighead, John, 310
Cramer, Mark, 548
Cramer, Robert E. Bud, Jr., 1
Crandall, Derrick, 262, 264
Crandall, Doug, 420
Crane, Neil, 392
Crane, Philip M., 5
Craner, Lori, 446
Cranford, Gerald, 25
Cranney, Steve, 406
Crapa, Joseph, 18
Crapo, Michael D., 4
Crate, Susan, 587
Craven, Bill, 491
Craven, Scott, 238
Craves, Julie, 415
Crawford, Don, 221
Crawford, Gregory, 583
Crawford, Jamie, 184
Crawford, Kenneth, 383
Crawford, Richard, 164, 618
Crawford, Susan, 313
Crawford, Walter, Jr., 558
Crawforth, Terry, 189, 360
Creech, Dennis, 510
Creed, Lewie, 213
Creedon, Lesli, 479
Crenshaw, Ander, 3
Crenshaw, David, 599
Crenshaw, Teresa, 151
Cresci, Sharon, 276
Crick, Meribeth, 245

Crickenberger, Roger, 200
Crider, Kay, 335
Criner, George, 612
Crisell, Rob, 270
Crisp, James, 87
Crispin, Susan, 187
Crist, Larry, 227
Criste, Tim, 28
Cristini, Angela, 262
Crockett, Bonnie, 204
Crockett, Lee, 394
Croes, Bart, 143
Croke, L., 199
Cronin, John, 327
Cronin, Leslie, 276
Cronk, Edye, 511
Crooks, Joan, 533
Crooks, Tim, 40
Crosby, Greg, 33
Crosby, Susan, 261
Cross, Gerald, 228
Crossley, Alan, 554
Crossley, Joan, 296
Crossman, Marian, 411
Crotty, Erin, 196
Crouch, Barth, 468
Crouch, Roger, 245
Croucher, Bruce, 421
Crouse, Becky, 277
Crow, Rick, 63
Crowell, Howard, 404
Crowley, Becky, 402
Crowley, Chris, 301
Crowley, Joseph, 10
Crudele, Julie, 347
Cruden, John, 77
Crum, Matthew, 235
Cubbage, James, 289
Cubin, Barbara, 15
Cuellar, Yvonne, 366
Cuff, Courtney, 423
Cuillerier, Paul, 27
Culberson, John A., 13
Cullen, J., 190
Cullens, Michelle, 405
Cully, Jack, 119, 167
Culp, Carson, 85
Culter, James, 404
Culter, Ray, 433
Cumberland, Carol, 410
Cumberlidge, Neil, 591
Cumbie, Richard, 133
Cummings, Bob, 392
Cummings, Brendan, 290
Cummings, Elijah, 7
Cummins, David, 300
Cummins, James, 23
Cummins, Kenneth, 16
Cummins, Rick, 160
Cunniff, Peggy, 406
Cunningham, James, 409
Cunningham, Randy Duke, 3
Cunningham, Wayne, 146
Cunningham, William, 268
Cuomo, Carmela, 617
Curl, Sam, 206
Curley, Rosemary, 213
Curnew, K., 199
Curnow, Richard, 32
Curran, William, 132
Curren, Cathy, 211
Currey, Steve, 42
Currid, Peggy, 367
Currie, Leigh, 399
Currie, Patricia, 366
Currier, Mary, 185
Curry, Bob, 257
Curry, Neil, 138
Curtis, Henry, 389
Curtis, Jan, 293
Curtis, Jeff, 522
Curtis, Marc, 401
Curtis, Paul, 197

STAFF NAME INDEX – D

Curtis, Tom, 267
Curtiss, Bill, 318
Curtner, Kathryn, 237
Cusenza, Anthony, 145
Cushman, John, 280
Cushman, Robert, 75
Cusick, Penny, 233
Cusson, Charles, 275
Custer, Adrie, 33
Cuthbert, Francesca, 615
Cutler, Ruth, 305
Cutright, Noel, 556
Cutter, Susan, 273
Cutting, Lisa, 403
Cypher, Brian, 552
Cyr, Karen, 26
Czaplewski, Mark, 550
Czek, Rita, 624
Czinski, Ben, 581

D

Dabney, Walt, 223
Daggemart, Renee, 218
Daggett, Susan, 318
Daigle, J.J., 315
Dailey, Fred, 203
Daily, F.R., 279
Dale, Bob, 335
Dale, Boleyn, 532
Dale, Chip, 208
Dale, Martha, 534
Dalena, Cindy, 424
Daley, Anita, 309
Daley, Bill, 146, 303
Daley, James, 551
Daley, John, 232
Daley, Wayne, 253
Dalpra, Curtis, 23
Dalton, Richard, 192
Daly, Lisa, 466
Damron, Jack, 74
Dando, Muriel, 352
Danello, Mary, 75
Danford, R., 567
Daniel, David, 611
Daniel, Glenda, 460
Daniel, William, 236
Daniell, Rob, 170
Daniell, Robert, 170
Daniels, Elizabeth, 251
Daniels, George, 64
Daniels, Harry, 200
Daniels, James, 376
Daniels, Jane, 447
Daniels, Joyce, 57
Daniels, Kevin, 300
Dannenmaier, Eric, 600
Danson, Ted, 456
Danvir, Rick, 226
Daoust, Pierre Yves, 286
Darbe, Eric, 444
Darin, Jack, 492
Darnell, Tim, 185
Darrow, Robert, 530
Darveau-Fournier, Lise, 601
Daschle, Thomas A., 13
Dasher, Doug, 73
Dastrup, B., 226
Dates, Geoff, 481
Datres, Dana, 211
Daubendiek, Bertha, 308
Daugharty, David, 616
Daukas, Jimmy, 252
Dauray, Charles, 376
Davenport, Bobby, 272
David, Robert, 417
Davidson, Al, 302
Davidson, Alan, 484
Davidson, Charles, 307
Davidson, Dennis, 192
Davidson, Matt, 246
Davidson, Susan, 420
Davies, J., 479

Davies, John, 170
Davies, Loretta, 472
Davies, Milt, 472
Davies, Richard, 137
Davies, Russ, 427
Davies, Simon, 558
Davila-Casanova, Daniel, 151, 213
Davin, Bill, 309
Davis, Al, 136
Davis, Artur, 1
Davis, Charles, 431
Davis, Clark, 25
Davis, Danny K., 5
Davis, David, 189
Davis, Donald, 553
Davis, Gary, 448
Davis, Jerry, 244, 245
Davis, Jim, 4
Davis, Jo Ann S., 14
Davis, John, 27, 163
Davis, Loccio, 430
Davis, Lincoln, 13
Davis, Lori, 519
Davis, Lynn, 205
Davis, Mark, 474
Davis, Meighan, 500
Davis, Miki, 343
Davis, Paul, 221, 323
Davis, R. Laurence, 617
Davis, Ray, 230
Davis, Raymond, 230
Davis, Robert, 424
Davis, Rod, 140
Davis, Roger, 205
Davis, Scott, 439
Davis, Shannon, 136
Davis, Susan, 313
Davis, Susan A., 3
Davis, Thomas M., III, 14
Davis, William, 170, 555
Davis-Hilton, S., 538
Davison, Jason, 616
Davison, Robert, 545
Davit, Carol, 402
Daws, Russell, 515
Dawson, Robert, 215
Day, Brian, 241
Day, Jennifer, 22, 23
Day, M., 281
Day, Mark, 129
Day, Rich, 106
Day, Robert, 478
Day, Steve, 354
Dayrles, Rebecca, 600
Dayton, Mark, 8
De Dardel, Claes, 368
De Garmo, Jennifer, 496
De Ghetaldi, Evelyn, 242
de la Rocha, Rosamelia, 75
de Launay, David, 208
de Leon, Roy Olsen, 595
De Meyer, Kalli, 309
Deal, Edmond, 186
Deal, Nathan, 4
Dealters, Joseph, 214
Dean, Caroline, 245
Dean, Ellen, 606
Dean, Henry, 219
Dean, Jack, 176
Dean, Kama, 473
Dean, Norman, 338
Dean, Tommy, 475
Dean, Tracey, 353
Dearborn, Ronald, 54
Deason, Wayne, 89, 282
Deatherage, Karen, 247
Deaton, Linda, 515
Deaton, Roger, 218
Debevoise, Nancy, 561
Debiase, Ann Marie, 177
Debruin, Rodney, 240
Decamp, William, 298

DeCarlo, Anjanette, 362
Decker, Barbara, 405
Decker, Bob, 73, 74, 404
Decker, Daniel, 546
Decker, Jeff, 230
DeCock, John, 500
Dedrick, Allen, 31
Deeble, Ben, 428
DeFazio, Peter A., 12
Deford, Mac, 432
Degarmo, Glen, 73
Degenhardt, Arya, 403
DeGette, Diana L., 3
Degraaf, Richard, 614
Degrauwe, Beth, 484
DeGroff, Johanna, 267, 330
Degrosky, Mike, 361
Dehaven, W., 31
Dehayes, Donald, 622
Deiger, Gary, 212
Deisner, Vicki, 457
Deisting, Gus, 247
deJonge, Rhoda, 386
Dekker-Fiala, Emily, 341
Deklinski, Karen, 211
Del Frate, Gino, 546
Del Giudice, Paula, 428
Del Vecchio, Mark, 50
Delahunt, William, 7
Delamar, Nancy, 434
Delaney, Denise, 385
Delaney, Richard, 614
Delano, Everett, 303
Delany, Billy, 587
DeLauro, Rosa, 3
DeLay, Tom, 13
Deleers, Lawrence, Jr., 504
Delehanty, Steve, 100
Delfino, Kimberley, 312
Delisle, Dan, 398
Dellaria, Janet, 306
Deller, Nancy, 143
Deller-Jacobs, Amy, 549
Delong, Paul, 237
Delpizzo, Matthew, 413
DeMatteo, Jenell, 505
Demers, Chris, 241
DeMint, Jim, 12
Dempsey, Bernard, 313
Denke, Lynn, 506
Denker, Terry, 167
Denkhaus, Rob, 449
Dennerlein, Catherine, 409
Denney, Steve, 208
Dennin, Steve, 437
Dennis, Jane, 556
Dennio, Michael, 25
Dennis, Mike, 433
Denowski, Paul, 555
Denoyelles, Frank, 167
Dente, Chuck, 551
Denton, Joan, 144
Deopscine, Sarah, 389
DePeralta, Jennifer, 327
Deperry, Gerald, 20
Depolo, Michael, 398
Depp-Nestlerode, Mary Jo, 592
Deppner, Dave, 519
Depuit, Edward, 626
Derksen, Arthur, 256
Derner, David, 529
Derosa, Sheri, 57
Derr, Charles, 250
Derr, Rex, 235
Derry, Amy, 320
Derry, Clark Williams, 454
Derry, James, 523
Derty, Chantal, 363
Deruiter, Darla, 540
Des Clers, Bertrand, 307
Deschenes, Joe, 73
DeScherer, Chris, 308
Dessecker, Dan, 483

Dest, Paul, 60
Destefano, Steve, 178
Detoy, Anthony, 38
Detwiler, Stephanie, 335
Deutsch, Peter, 4
Deutz, Andrew, 368
Deutscher, Arlene, 47
Devane, Ben, 76
Devany, John, 509
Devault, Kevin, 539
Devick, William, 151
Devier-Heemey, Carol, 63
Devillars, John, 18
Devine, James, 127
Devine, Rita, 446
Devitt, R., 343
DeVivo, Laura, 200
Devoe, M., 59
Dew, Aloma, 171
Dew, Stephanie, 383
Dewald, Sandra, 485
Dewalle, Wendy, 374
DeWan, Deborah, 488
Dewey, Robert, 311
Dewhurst, David, 222
DeWine, Mike, 11
Dexter, David, 300
Deyrup, Nancy, 270
Dezern, Pat, 499
Deziel, Gary, 622
Dhaliwal, Herb, 26
Di Domenico, Dennis, 394
Di Giulio, Richard, 580
Diamond, Natacha, 536
Diana, James, 614
Dias, Nelson, 368
Diaz-Balart, Lincoln, 4
Diaz-Balart, Mario, 4
Diaz-Stero, Hilda, 33
Dibblee, Randall, 213
Dibona, Pamela, 327
Dickerson, Bev, 550
Dickerson, Bill, 200
Dickerson, Dennis, 144
Dickerson, Maria, 528
Dickerson, Mark, 61
Dickey, Elbert, 224
Dickinson, Kelley, 100
Dicks, Norman D., 15
Dickson, Andrew, 559
Dickson, James, 587
Dickson, Jan, 291, 618
Dickson, Jenny, 550
Dickson, Kelly, 337
Dickson, Kenneth, 618
Dickson, Tom, 187
Dickson, Billy, 195
Didion, Julie, 283
Didrickson, Betsy, 362
Diefenbach, Duane, 210
Diehl, Kathleen, 38
Diehl, Robert, 516
Diehn, Sonya, 290
Dierks, Wayne, 316
Diersing, Vic, 74
Diessner, Gretchen, 372
Dietrick, Larry, 133
Dietz, Lou Ann, 559
Difazio, Faye, 230
Difley, Jane, 503
Diggins, Molly, 495
Diggs, Daniel, 111
Diguer, Christine, 275
Dillard, Jim, 221
Dillen, Abigail, 318
Diller, Tom, 475
Dillon, Dave, 185
Dimase, Joseph, 276
Dimitre, Tom, 500
Dimmitt, Mark, 272
Dimoff, Keith, 457
Dineen, John, 565
Dingell, John D., 7

STAFF NAME INDEX – D

Dinger, James, 170
Dinkins, Gerry, 508
Dinkins, Matt, 344
Dinwiddie, Candace, 516
Dionne, Michele, 60
Diouf, Jacques, 333
Dipaolo, Tony, 395
DiPeso, Jim, 479
Dipolvere, Edward, 445
Dippel, Joseph, 149
Dirus, Greta, 26
Dishner, O., 231
Disilva, A., 444
Diskerud, Clayton, 274
Disner, Dan, 497
Disrud, Lowell, 202
DiStefano, Bob, 257
Ditto, Rose, 340
Dix, David, 402
Dixon, Brian, 471
Dixon, David, 455
Dixon, Freddie, 621
Dixon, John, 531
Dixon, Keri, 290
Dixon, L., 404
Dixon, Trudy, 296
Dlippinger, Joan, 211
Doak, Gary, 180
Doak, Tom, 174
Doan, Doug, 203
Dobb, Mike, 534
Dobkin, David, 309
Dobratz, Tod, 524
Dobson, Mary Lynn, 515
Docherty, Molly, 174
Dockry, Michael, 37
Dodd, Christopher, 29
Dodd, Christopher J., 3
Dodd, Hudson, 454
Dodds, Jane, 33
Doden, Darcie, 527
Dodier, Jose, 516
Dodson, Jerome, 242
Doerr, John, 613
Doggett, Lloyd, 13
Doggett, Marjorie, 365
Doherty, Douglas, 483
Dohm, Suzanne, 446
Dolan, John, 385
Dolan, Peter, 277
Dold, Jack, 357
Dole, Elizabeth, 10
Doliner, J., 326
Doll, Jim, 457
Dolliver, Sharon, 157
Dolloff, C., 625
Dolnack, Chris, 424
Dombeck, Mike, 623
Dombroski, Mark, 333
Dombrowski, Dan, 451
Domenici, Pete V., 9
Dominguez, Larry, 193
Dominitz, Sid, 452
Domke, Lorna, 185
Donahoe, Jeffery, 24
Donahue, John, 142
Donaldson, Graham, 242
Donaldson, Peter, 471
Donaldson, Walt, 226
Donalson, Teri, 153
Donarski, Dan, 274
Donelin, Dan, 585
Donheffner, Paul, 210
Donna, David, 401
Donnelly, Kevin, 151
Donnelly, Lloyd, 25
Donnelly, Maureen, 266
Donnelly, T.W., 315
Donnelly, Thomas, 426
Donoghue, Linda, 41
Donohue, Kenneth, Sr., 77
Donohue, Mary, 55
Donovan, Michael, 586

Donovan, Richard, 517
Donzella, Carol, 47
Doody, Allan, 76
Dooley, Calvin, 2
Dooley, Marlen, 191
Doolittle, Guerry, 334
Doolittle, John T., 1
Doolittle, Warren, 367
Doom, Chuck, 507
Doran, Jeff, 332
Doran, Terry, 235
Dore, Linda, 353
Dorfman, Mark, 330
Dorgan, Byron L., 11
Dorka, John, 204
Dormody, Sheila, 323
Dornfeld, Susan, 411
Dorrance, Michael, 546
Dorworth, Leslie, 55
Doscher, Paul, 503
Doss, Jim, 456
Dotson, Thomas, 236
Dott, Don, 171
Dott, Donald, 171
Doucette, Christine, 565
Doucette, Robert, 407
Dougal, Edward, 598
Dougherty, Cynthia, 130
Dougherty, Dean, 484
Dougherty, Nina, 498
Douglas, Donald, 313
Douglas, James, 188
Douglas, Jean, 248
Douglas, Karen, 469
Douglas, Melissa, 286
Douglas, Peter, 140
Douglass, Gus, 235
Dovichin, Erin, 434
Dow, Bob, 64
Dow, Jocelyn, 558
Dowdle, Bill, 136
Dowdle, Elizabeth, 307
Dowler, Bernard, 236
Dowling, David, 229
Dowling, Richard, 71
Dowling, Timothy, 304
Downes, Aczedine, 363
Downes, Patrick, 409
Downey, Laura, 380
Downey, Mortimer, 128
Downey, Rebecca, 409
Downey, Tim, 129
Downs, Joan, 543
Doxtater, Gary, 163
Doyle, Becky, 162
Doyle, Bob, 85
Doyle, Brian, 58
Doyle, Frances, 74
Doyle, Kevin, 570
Doyle, Mike, 12
Doyle, Pat, 287
Doyle, Robert, 618
Doyle, Samuel, 190
Doyle, Wayne, 167
Doyle, William, 260
Dozier, Alan, 157
Dragicevich, Rodney, 397
Drahovzal, James, 170
Drake, David, 215
Drake, Tricia, 625
Draper, Ray, 348
Draughon, David, 221
Drawe, D., 536
Drayton, William, 343
Drea, Stephanie, 455
Dreher, Karl, 161
Dreier, David, 2
Drew, Mimi, 154
Drew, Steve, 375
Drew, Timothy, 190
Drexler, Kenneth, 394
Dreyer, Glenn, 578
Drickamer, Lee, 590

Drier, David, 22
Drobney, Pauline, 107
Drobney, Ronald, 119
Droste, Chris, 525
Drucker, Harry, 163
Drummond, Boyce, 302
Drury, Richard, 303
Dryburgh, Jeanne, 441
Dryden, Doug, 140
Dryden, Ron, 335
Duane, Tim, 394
Dubé, Claude, 602
Dubick, Denise, 539
Dubitsky, Debbie, 412
Dubois, Frank, 193
Dubord, Daniel, 296
Ducey, Mark, 617
Duchesne, Josée, 603
Duck, Tim, 314
Ducmanis, Annie, 366
Duda, Mark, 570
Dudley, Joe, 74
Dueser, Raymond, 624
Dufault, Arthur, 225
Duff, Don, 520
Duff, James, 280
Duff, John, 301
Duffendack, Paul, 422
Duffy, Amy, 218
Duffy, Greg, 206
Duffy, Kevin, 134
Duffy, Robert, 578
Duffy, Walter, 16, 583
Dufour, Jean-Claude, 604
Dugan, Patrick, 368
Duggan, Joseph, 468
Duguay, Jeffery, 598
Duguay, Linda, 54, 620
Duinker, Peter, 579
Duker, Laurie, 385
Dulik, Karen, 552
Dulong, David, 70
Dumelie, Mike, 216
Dunagan, Rob, 278
Dunbar, Lynn, 270
Dunbar, Tim, 405
Duncan, B., 573
Duncan, Bob, 230
Duncan, Doug, 546
Duncan, Jeffrey, 77
Duncan, John J., Jr., 13
Duncan, Judy, 206
Duncan, Peter, 196
Duncan, Robert, 230
Dunham, Todd, 433
Dunkle, Richard, 32
Dunkle, S.W., 315
Dunmyer, James W., 177
Dunn, Allen, 145
Dunn, Chris, 73
Dunn, Cindy, 411
Dunn, Dianna, 562
Dunn, Gary, 562, 570
Dunn, Gregory, 349
Dunn, Jennifer, 15
Dunn, Michael, 173
Dunn, Renee, 588
Dunnagan, Robert, 354
Dunnam, Sylvia, 333
Dunne, Peter, 415
Dunning, Rick, 533
Dunning, Sandy, 586
Dunstan, Thomas, 626
Dunwell, Fran, 196
Dupaul, William, 59, 577
Dupree, Thomas, 214
Dupree, Thomas, 509
Dupuis, Yves, 27
Dupuy, Charles, 390
Duran, Lydia, 193
Duran, Patrick, 477
Durand, Amelia, 293
Durand, Bob, 178

Durand, Pierre, 602
Durant, John, 600
Durbin, Richard J., 5
Durham, David, 288
Duriancik, Lisa, 33
Durnell, Peter, 333
Durning, Alan, 454
Durocher, Phil, 223
Durr, Debbie, 569
Durst, Douglas, 316
Durst, John, 218
Duttenhefner, Kathy, 202
Dutton, Mark, 73
Duvall, Fern, 547
Duyvejonck, Jon, 527
Duzan, Steve, 272
Dwyer, Peggy, 175
Dyck, Rod, 247
Dye, Paul, 371
Dyer, A., 578
Dyer, Polly, 459
Dykes, John, 167
Dykstra, Dennis, 559
Dziubek, Dan, 595
Dziubek, Dan, 595
Dzus, Elston, 546

E

Eades, Glenn, 405
Eagan, Lloyd, 237
Eager, Barbara, 447
Eagle, Tim, 221
Eakins, Doug, 294
Eames, Cliff, 245
Earle, Pamela, 423
Early, Beth, 564
East, Wayne, 302
Easter, Becky, 283
Easterly, James, 162
Easterson, Brad, 264
Easterson, Toni, 264
Easterwood, Mark, 132
Eastham, Kyle, 206
Easton, Dan, 133
Eaton, Amy, 403
Eaton, Michael, 283
Eaton, Pamela, 541
Eav, Bob, 41
Ebeid, Nadia, 18
Eberlein, Charlotte, 611
Ebersbach, Paul, 63
Ebert, Mary, 391
Ebneter, Stewart, 26
Echols, Alex, 419
Echols, Louie, 60
Eckenfelder, Margaret, 140
Ecker, James, 549
Ecker, Michael, 311
Eckert, Al, 137
Eckert, Donald, 205
Eckl, Eric, 265
Eckman, Jan, 303
Edelson, Naomi, 360
Edgar, Cecilia, 201
Edgar, William, 145
Edge, Daniel, 592
Edge, W., 210
Edgerton, Wayne, 182
Edison, Robert, 272
Edminster, Carl, 605
Edmison, Lawrence, 205
Edmonds, Marion, 218
Edmonds, Robert, 617
Edrich, Liz, 354
Edson, David, 264
Edson, Dean, 441
Edward, Rob, 500
Edwards, Andy, 468
Edwards, Chet, 13
Edwards, Chiquita, 358
Edwards, Gordon, 315
Edwards, John R., 10
Edwards, Robert, 154

STAFF NAME INDEX – F

Edwards, Sandra, 321
Edwards,, Thomas, 128
Edwins, Diane, 506
Eflin, James, 574
Egar, D., 203
Egbert, Allan, 154, 544
Eger, Rebecca, 393
Egger, Keith, 618
Eggers, Doris, 202
Egol, Lew, 539
Ehlers, Angela, 507
Ehlers, Vernon, 7
Ehlert, Charles, 452
Ehm, William, 165
Ehresman, Marlene, 373, 374
Ehret, Heidi, 457
Ehret, Paul, 163
Ehrett, Mary, 586
Ehrhardt, Barbara, 587
Ehrlich, Paul, 597
Eichbaum, William, 559
Eichorn, Ellen, 511
Eiken, Douglas, 186
Eisele, Timothy, 557
Eisenmenger, Robert, 443
Eiserer, Elaine, 565
Eisma, Rose-Liza, 565
Eisner, Thomas, 561
Eithiear, Jack, 293
Ek, Alan, 615
Ekdahl, James, 180
Ekey, Robert, 541
Elam, Dayton, 516
Elbert, Stephen A., 544
Elbow, Gary, 418
Elder, Don, 481
Elder, James, 447
Elder, Jim, 458
Eldredge, Linda, 227
Eldridge, Charles, 375
Eldridge, Sharon Kingston, 442
Elfner, Lynn, 456
Elfner, Mary, 301
Eli, Sandra, 195
Eliason, Julie, 421
Elisens, Wayne, 205
Elkins, Bruce, 249
Elkind, Ken, 112
Elkins, Scott, 495
Elle, Steve, 255
Elliker, Robert, 378
Elliot, Charles, 548
Elliot, Statia, 176
Elliot-Fisk, Deborah, 606
Elliott, Catherine, 613
Elliott, Charles, 580
Elliott, James, 179
Elliott, Joni, 444
Elliott, Marilyn, 133
Elliott, Valerie, 65
Ellis, Anthony, 198
Ellis, Libby, 440
Ellis, Tom, 200
Ellison, Dan, 187
Ellison, Ken, 235
Elliston, Penny, 371
Ellsworth, David, 353
Elmore, Dave, 289
Elowe, Kenneth, 175
Elrod, Lewis F., 252
Elstad, Scott, 254
Elton, Joseph, 229
Elwart, David, 218
Elworth, Robert, 402
Ely, Craig, 208
Ely, Dean, 210
Elzerman, Alan, 577
Elzey, Sara, 453
Emanuel, Rahm, 5
Embrey, Montey, 424
Emerson, Jo Ann H., 8
Emerson, Melanie, 130
Emery, Steven, 193

Emmerson, Glyn, 347
Emmi, Jeremy, 398
Emmons, Terrell, 120
Emo, Kyra, 474
Emory, Dianna, 337
Emory, William, 504
Empson, G., 382
Emrick, Scott, 281
Endter-Wada, Joanna, 624
Eng, Michael, 130
Engbeck, Joe, 485
Engel, David, 472
Engel, Eliot, 10
Engelbart, Russell, 372
Engelman, David, 412
Engelman, Robert, 470
Engelsma, Frans, 328
Engesaeter, Sigmund, 25
Engfeldt, Christina, 333
England, Gordon, 74
Engle, David, 592
English, Pandy, 588
English, Philip S., 12
Engstrom, Cathy, 373
Engvall, Susanna, 295
Enk, Michael, 257
Enloe, Molly, 65
Ennis, Elizabeth, 250
Ensign, John, 9
Entz, Mich, 458
Enzi, Michael B., 15
Epifanio, John, 255
Erb, James, 211
Erdmann, Richard, 307
Erickson, Dave, 185
Erickson, David, 185
Erickson, Donna, 614
Erickson, Ed, 303
Erickson, Glenn, 187
Erickson, Kim, 206
Erickson, May, 37
Erickson, Mick, 95
Erickson, Ron, 216
Erickson, Teresa, 453
Ernst, Gerald, 378
Erskine, Andrea, 175
Ertmer, Susan, 316
Erttor, Robert S., 427
Ervin, David, 350
Erwin, Jeff, 207
Eschenbach, Beth, 583
Escobar, Elsa, 339
Escoe, Wayne, 156
Eshbaugh, Jeff, 283
Eshoo, Anna, 2
Espinoza, Virginia, 577
Esposito, David, 130
Espy, James, 392
Esson, John, 74, 566
Estabrook, E., 175
Estacion, Janet, 595
Estevez, Ernest, 404
Etgen, Robert, 321
Ethelston, Sally, 470
Etheridge, Bob, 10
Ethridge, Tom, 342
Ettema, Robert, 611
Evanich, David, 559
Evans, Brock, 322, 330
Evans, Donald, 49
Evans, Greg, 531
Evans, Joseph, 475
Evans, Joyce, 561
Evans, Lane, 5
Evans, Lemuel, 394
Evans, Peter, 329
Evans, Rhys, 421
Evans, Richard, 621
Evensen, Nancy, 449
Everage, Cynthia, 317
Everett, Douglas, 353
Everett, Lauren, 567
Everett, Terry, 1

Everitt, Bob, 233
Eversmyer, Deanne, 532
Everts, Todd, 187
Ewart, John, 150
Ewert, D., 197
Exter, Randee, 52

F

Faber, Daryl, 534
Fabian, Nelson, 418
Faesy, Nancy, 305
Fage, Ernest, 203
Fagely, Erin, 461
Fahey, Timothy, 579
Fahlgren, John, 83
Fahlund, Andrew, 265
Fahrnkopf, Kindi, 500
Fairbank, Bob, 401
Fairchild, Laurie, 543
Fairfield, Carol, 503
Fairleigh, Larry, 235
Fajardo, Kathya, 281
Fakir, Saliem, 370
Fakundiny, Robert, 197
Falco, Carl, 200
Falender, Andrew, 270
Faleomavaega, Eni F.H., 15
Falk, Donald, 502
Falk, James, 54
Falkenheiner, Doris, 414
Faltelsek, Jan, 400
Falvey, James, 401
Falwell, Jerome, 385
Fan, Weihong, 594
Fanta, Edith, 601
Farber, Laurie, 358
Fardoe, Gordon, 393
Farland, William, 130
Farley, Dennis, 211
Farling, Bruce, 522
Farmer, Barb, 238
Farmer, David, 620
Farmer, Don, 271
Farmer, W. Paul, 264
Farmer, Walt, 607
Farnsworth, Larry, 601
Farr, Sam, 2
Farrant, Greg, 450
Farrar, Patricia, 389
Farrar, Roy, 557
Farrar, Sally, 557
Farrell, Debra, 567
Farrell, Dolores, 141
Farrell, James, 459
Farrell, John, 257
Farrell, Patrick, 551
Farrell, Thomas, 248
Farris, Allen, 166
Farris, Jerry, 573
Farris, Robert, 157
Farrish, Kenneth, 598
Farro, Anthony, 192
Fascione, Nina, 312
Fassbind, Kevin, 556
Fast, Don, 16
Fatima, Kaniz, 568
Fattah, Chaka, 12
Fatz, Raymond, 67
Faulk, Ken, 461
Faulkner, Annie, 443
Faulkner, Dave, 27
Fauske, Glenda, 201
Fauske, Russell, 202
Faust, Ralph, 140
Faust, Richard, 336
Fauth, Laura, 476
Fazio, James, 407
Fedewa, Dennis, 180
Fedor, Karen, 260
Fedorenko, Vladimir, 25
Fedorko, Nick, 236
Fedullo, Charles, 133
Fee, Everett, 266

Fee, Scott, 424
Feeney, Tom, 4
Fehring, Michelle, 373
Feingold, Russ, 15
Feinstein, Dianne, 1
Feiro, Thomas, 615
Feit, Darrell, 339
Feldman, Jay, 277
Feldman, Marcus, 597
Feldt, Gloria, 469
Fellows, Larry, 136
Felt, Steve, 356
Felton, Michael, 375
Fenech, Robert A., 544
Fenn, Dennis, 127
Fenstemacher, Ron, 349
Fenton, Gary, 202
Fenwick, George, 249
Feral, Priscilla, 337
Ferenstein, Jennifer, 497
Ferguson, David, 162, 189
Ferguson, James, 201
Ferguson, John, 137
Ferguson, Michael A., 9
Ferguson-Southard, Denise, 177
Fernandez, Bobby, 76
Fernandez, Erik, 461
Fernandez, Ivan, 612
Fernandez, Nuria, 129
Fernholm, Bo, 23
Ferrante, Gretchen, 415
Ferreira, James, 196
Ferrell, Steve, 136
Ferretti, Will, 489
Ferring, Reid, 618
Ferrio, Maria, 420
Ferris, Shirley, 149
Ferriter, Amy, 331
Ferrulo, Mark, 333
Ferry, Miles, 225, 226
Fertig, Walter, 561
Fessenden, Joseph, 175
Fewin, Robert, 222
Fewless, Dennis, 201
Feyerherm, Jennifer, 494
Fiala, Charles, 67
Fiala, Holly, 426
Fickes, Roger, 211
Fickies, Robert, 197
Fidel, Jamey, 530
Field, David, 612
Fielder, John, 540
Fielder, Nick, 221
Fielder, Paul, 554
Fields, James, 236
Fields, Jim, 312
Fields, Mary, 220
Fields, Timothy, 19
Fifield, Shirley, 245
Figert, Dan, 548
Figueroa, Frank, 76
Fijalkowski, Dennis, 398
Filion, Bernard, 315
Filner, Bob, 3
Finch, Jamie, 24
Finch, Johnny, 531
Finck, Elmer, 452, 548
Findlay, Stuart, 358
Finfer, Larry, 85
Fingerman, Milton, 503
Finley, David, 239
Finn, Susan, 362
Finney, Dana, 72
Finney, George, 18
Finney, Tal, 145
Fiore, Nick, 557
Fischel, Helen, 313
Fischer, Burnell, 163
Fischer, Edward, 525
Fischer, Hank, 428
Fischer, John, 508
Fischer, Larry, 473
Fischer, R. Montgomery, 427

STAFF NAME INDEX – F

Fischer, Robert, 580
Fish, Ernest, 600
Fish, Ruth, 305, 479
Fisher, Corrine, 354
Fisher, Eddy, 162
Fisher, Frank, 594
Fisher, George, 313
Fisher, Jack, 354
Fisher, Janet, 235
Fisher, John, 576, 606
Fisher, Larry, 130
Fisher, Linda, 18
Fisher, Lyndal, 64
Fisher, Nicholas, 597
Fisher, Randy, 27
Fisher, Robbie, 436
Fisher, Wayne, 175
Fisher, William, 206, 576
Fiske, Ken, 354
Fitch, Larry, 227
Fitchett, Roger, 531
Fitts, Daniel, 132
Fitz, Chris, 386
Fitzgerald, Anne, 151
Fitzgerald, Martha, 294
Fitzgerald, Peter G., 5
Fitzgerald, Robert, 177, 395
FitzGerald, Tom, 383
Fitzgibbon, John, 610
Fitzpatrick, Jim, 477
Fitzpatrick, John, 263, 309
Fitzpatrick, Mary, 453
Fitzpatrick, Neal, 276
Fitzpatrick, Scott, 411
Fitzsimmons, Kevin, 135
Fitzsimmons, Sara, 251
Fitzwater, Steve, 425
Fitzwilliams, Kate, 362
Fjeld, Pam, 577
Flack, Deblyn, 413
Flake, Jeff, 1
Flake, Lester, 596
Flanagan, Ilsa, 514
Flanders, P., 227
Flanigan, David, 450
Flattery, Tom, 162
Flavin, Christopher, 560
Fleckenstein, Leonard, 130
Fleeger, Thomas, 70
Fleming, Emily, 236
Fleming, Gene, 142
Fleming, Richard, 313
Fleming, Roger, 308
Flemming, Jeff, 90
Fletcher, Douglas, 138
Fletcher, Ernest Lee, 6
Fletcher, Kathy, 467
Fletcher, Kevin, 276
Fletcher, Robert, 143
Fletcher, Roderick, 211
Flick, George, 228
Flick, Pamela, 284
Flicker, John, 409
Flickinger, Steve, 254
Fliczuck, Jim, 281
Flint, Peter, 312
Flood, James, 316
Flores, Michael, 144
Flory, Doyle, 357
Flowers, Kevin, 377
Flowers, Lisa, 279
Floyd, Martin, 548
Floyd, Ted, 250
Floyd, Veronica, 262
Floyd-Hanna, Lisa, 593
Flynn, Andy, 132
Focazio, Paul, 58
Fogel, Danielle, 386
Fogerty, Daniel, 163
Foley, Mark, 4
Foley, Patricia, 486
Folger, Sara, 472
Folks, John, 153

Fondren, Walter, 300
Fong, D., 199
Fong, David, 199
Fontaine, Colette, 176
Fontaine, Jan, 403
Fontenot, Bennie, 173
Foote, Edward, 365
Foote, Jerris, 404
Foote, Karen, 173
Forand, Liseanne, 27
Forbes, John, 433
Forbes, Randy, 14
Force, Lisa, 390
Ford, Arthur, 90
Ford, Britt, 424
Ford, Charles, 73
Ford, Cynthia, 381
Ford, Harold E., Jr., 13
Ford, Harvey, 331
Ford, Richard, 576
Ford, Thomas, 212
Ford, Tim, 331
Fordham, Jimmy, 530
Foreman, Dave, 542
Forest, Ben, 298
Forestell, Paul, 464
Forgey, William, 540
Forkan, Patricia, 352
Formica, Sandi, 272
Formica, Sandy, 137
Fornos, Werner, 471
Forrest, Clayton, 287
Forrest, Rosemary, 610
Forsgren, Harvey, 43
Forsgren, Ted, 300
Forsing, John, 52
Forsius, Kaj, 21
Forslof, Ed, 535
Fortier, Louis, 603
Fortin, Josée, 602
Fortuna, Roger, 26
Forward, Paul, 43
Fosburgh, Whit, 520
Fossella, Vito, 10
Fossum, Bob, 403
Foster, Barbara, 170
Foster, David, 206, 250
Foster, Herb, 230
Foster, Kent, 353
Foster, Lee, 74
Foster, Lorraine, 494
Foster, Nancy, 78
Foti, Tom, 138
Foulkrod, Tom, 289
Fountain, Michael, 598
Foushee, Rodney, 201
Foust, Allen, 446
Foust, Brady, 622
Fouts, Mark, 483
Fowler, Edward, 242
Fowler, John, 16
Fowler, Rod, 315
Fowler, Ron, 219
Fowler, Tim, 396
Fox, Carole, 427
Fox, Doug, 601
Fox, Howard, 320
Fox, J. Charles, 177
Fox, Jim, 164
Fox, John, 364, 367
Fox, Marvin, 556
Fox, Mike, 430
Fox, Mitzi, 442
Fox, Richard, 520
Fox, Ron, 221
Fox, Wayne, 316
Fox-Przeworski, Joanne, 574
Foy, Douglas, 308
Frailey, Kevin, 398
Fraley, George, 458
Fraley, Robert, 387
Frame, Bruce, 129
Frampton, John, 218

France, Thomas, 428
Francis, John, 112
Francis, Michael, 541
Francis, Ron, 407
Francis, Ronald, 408
Francisco, Gene, 237
Franck, Valerie, 55
Franco, Roberto, 370, 433
Frank, Barbara, 133
Frank, Barney, 7
Frank, Bobbie, 560
Frank, Jeff, 414
Frank, Michael, 524
Frank, Steve, 162
Franklin, Thomas, 546
Franks, Al, 204
Franks, Jim, 257
Franks, Trent, 1
Frase, Barbara, 575
Fraser, Celeste, 418
Frasier, John, 538
Frasier, Stan, 404
Fraticelli, Becky, 47
Frawley, Mark, 199
Fraysier, Michael, 227
Frazer, Gary, 90
Frazer, Nat, 582
Frazer, Scott, 552
Frazier, Frederick, 396
Frazier, Judy, 373
Frazier, Roger, 162
Frederick, David, 133
Frederick, Robert, 580
Fredericks, Todd, 179
Frederickson, David, 419
Fredin, Tracy, 583
Fredrick, David, 544
Fredriksson, Kurt, 133
Free, Stuart, 268
Freedgood, Julia, 252
Freedman, David, 156
Freel, Maeton, 40, 546
Freeland, Al, 73
Freeland, Kathy Stiles, 433
Freeman, Brenda, 226
Freeman, Carol, 221
Freeman, Charles, 205
Freeman, Craig, 381
Freeman, Gary, 402
Freeman, Helen, 366
Freemyer, Allen, 22
Fregonara, Jim, 554
Frehner, Sylvia, 17
Freilich, Larry, 498
Freimark, Robert, 541
Freimund, Wayne, 615
Frelinghuysen, Rodney, 9
French, Jim, 235
Fresco, Nancy, 453
Fresh, Kurt, 258
Fresques, Tom, 82
Fretz, Thomas, 224, 613
Frey, J., 489
Frey, Merritt, 299
Frey, Paul, 172
Frey, Serita, 617
Freyer, Mary Anne, 333
Freziers, John, 301
Fri, Robert, 501
Frick, Linda, 196
Fried, Michelle, 527
Friede, John, 248
Friedland, Andrew, 579
Friedland, Kevin, 614
Friedman, Linda, 204
Friedman, Mitch, 454
Friedman, Robert, 348
Frierson, Joseph, 340
Friese, Daniel, 61
Friesen, Cheryl, 552
Frink, Dale, 202
Frinsko, Paul, 174
Frist, Bill, 13, 29

Fristoe, Brad, 73
Fritsch, Elicia, 318
Fritz, Matthew, 149
Fritz, Susan, 225
Fritzell, Erik, 409
Fritzell, Peter, 548
Frizzell, Bruce, 74
Frizzell, Tim, 444
Froelich, Adrienne, 261
Froman, Sandra, 424
Front, Alan, 524
Frost, Cecil, 200
Frost, Dan, 469
Frost, Martin, 14
Frost, Peter, 537
Frumkies, Joan, 446
Fry, Glenda, 402
Frye, C.W., 379
Frye, E., 374
Frye, Ed, 308
Frye, Jack, 232
Frykman, Amy, 453
Fu, Melissa, 457
Fuad, Tara, 276
Fuentes, Lorrae, 283
Fuentes, Pedro, 474
Fuentes-Jones, Mari, 564
Fugimoto, Michael, 151
Fuhrman, Roger, 160
Fujita, Marty, 389
Fulgham, Tom, 316
Fuller, Cheri, 284
Fuller, James, 188
Fuller, Joseph, 222
Fuller, Kathryn, 559
Fuller, Manley, 333
Fuller, Marji, 541
Fullwood, Charles, 201
Fullwood, Keith, 570
Fullwood,, Charles, 200
Fulmer, Carol, 217
Fulton, David, 181
Fulton, M. E., 620
Fulton, Scott, 18
Fults, Jason, 513
Funches, Jesse, 26
Furlong, Daniel, 399
Furness, George, 308
Furnish, Jim, 34
Furr, Jonathon, 162
Futter, Ellen, 263
Fzykitka, Kirsten, 241

G

Gab, Robert, 219
Gabel, Caroline, 312
Gabelhouse, Don, 188
Gabliks, Maris, 192
Gabrey, Steven, 591
Gabriel, Larry, 218
Gabriel, Nancy, 334
Gabriele, Larry, 239
Gadbery, Earl, 270
Gadd, Colleen, 302
Gaddy, Joy, 433
Gaddy, Joy, 441
Gades, Victor, 106
Gadula, Charles, 27
Gaetano, Fioravante, 63
Gage, Robert, 137
Gagen, Charlie, 573
Gagliano, Drew, 566, 567
Gagner, David, 407
Gagnon, Alain, 476
Gagnon, Ronald, 214
Gailor, Allen, 169
Gainer, Carl, 236
Gaines, Bill, 283
Gala, Rob, 455
Galanti, Geri-Ann, 361
Galat, David, 119
Galbreagh, Dodd, 221
Gale, Margaret, 588

STAFF NAME INDEX – G

Gale, Marjorie, 227
Galehause, Jennifer, 145
Gales, Lawrence, 206
Gall, Leslie, 138
Gallagher, Andy, 235
Gallagher, Dawn, 174
Gallagher, Frank, 192
Gallagher, James, 544
Gallagher, John, 191
Gallagher, Suzanne, 24
Gallagher, Tim, 309
Gallegly, Elton, 2
Galloway, Rob, 208
Galvez-Cloutier, Rosa, 603
Galvin, Bonnie, 541
Galvin, Denis, 120
Galvin, Peter, 290
Gambell, R., 23
Gamez, Rodrigo, 22
Gammill, Stewart, 311
Gamon, John, 233
Gangemi, John, 267
Gangloff, Deborah, 260
Gann, George, 502
Gansberg, Bill, 235
Gansell, Stuart, 211
Gantz, Richard, 163
Ganzlin, Bill, 615
Garavelli, Ron, 184
Garbisch, Edgar, 324
Garbisch, Jon, 609
Garces, Francisco, 28
Garces, Grace, 158
Garcia, Emil, 376
Garcia, Juanita, 148
Garcia, Kwame, 228
Garcia, Lupo, 386
Garcias, Jorge, 24
Gard, Matt, 458
Gardere, John, 538
Gardill, Walter, 280
Gardner, Carol, 531, 532
Gardner, Charles, 200
Gardner, Dennis, 482
Gardner, Gary, 560
Gardner, Judy, 157
Gardner, Mike, 591
Gardner, Paul, 270
Gardner, Tim, 365
Garibaldi, Louis, 543
Garland, Bill, 73
Garland, L., 221
Garlick, Michael, 579
Garner, James, 230
Garner, Patrick, 396
Garner, William, 132
Garnham, Darlene, 393
Garnier, Denise, 185
Garrett, Christy, 246
Garrett, Jeremy, 362
Garrett, Linda, 525
Garrett, Scott, 9
Garrison, Lynn, 169
Garrison, Samuel, 191
Garstang, Mimi, 186
Gartlan, Joseph, 247
Gartside, Michael, 293
Garvey, Jane, 128
Gaska, Jeff, 468
Gasperi, Enrico, 530
Gast, Beau, 391
Gatchell, John, 404
Gates, Bill, 73
Gates, Bryan, 281
Gates, Jessica, 284
Gates, Keith, 55
Gates, Rick, 208
Gaubert, Kevin, 390
Gaume, Norman, 220
Gaunitz, Deb, 106
Gaunt, Carol, 458
Gause, Kathy, 33
Gauthier, Reed, 247

Gauvin, Charles, 520
Gaw, Hershel, 73
Gaynor, Michelle, 274
Geatz, Ron, 433
Geballe, Gordon, 628
Gebhardt, Allen, 221
Gebhardt, Karl, 457
Geck, Jason, 246
Geer, William, 462
Gehring, Janet, 575
Gehrke, Craig, 541
Geiger, Raymond, 153
Geiger, Roy, 323
Geiger, Sharon, 353
Geiger, Tom, 533
Geisler, George, 212
Gelfand, Julie, 287
Gell, Robert, 353
Geller, Marvin, 597
Genter, Robert, 585
Gentle, Bill, 240
Georgakokos, Aris, 583
George, Clinton, 228
George, Louis, 483
George, Luke, 583
George, Paul, 235
George, Russell, 147
Goorgo, Sarah, 266
Gephardt, Richard A., 8
Gerber, Carole, 93
Gerber, John, 224, 295
Gerdela, Joe, 446
Geringer, Jim, 239
Gerkin, Steve, 350
Gerl, Janet, 539
Gerl, Peter, 539
Gerl, William, 539
Gerlach, Jim, 12
Gerlitz, Wendy, 422
Germida, Jim, 620
Gerosa, Alix, 488
Gerrein, David, 171
Gerson, Leslie, 78
Gesner, Susan, 286
Geyer, Chris, 204
Ghai, Dharam, 31
Gian, Diane, 214
Gibbons, James A., 9
Gibbons, Mary Anne, 532
Gibbons, Robert, 32
Gibbons, Whit, 610
Gibbs, Joanne, 293
Gibbs, Lois, 292
Gibbs, Trey, 341
Giberson, Donna, 447
Gibson, David, 273
Gibson, Doug, 484
Gibson, John, 404
Gibson, Mike, 138
Gibson, Nancy, 605
Gibson, Rick, 209
Gibson, Wendy, 198
Gielty, Cathy, 350
Gieselman, Wayne, 166
Giesen, Kenneth, 472
Giesfeldt, Mark, 237
Gifford, Amy, 420
Gigstad, Orval, 441
Gilber, Bruce, 77
Gilbert, Brian, 203, 430
Gilbert, Dave, 209
Gilbert, Jonathan, 554
Gilbert, Reg, 345
Gilchrest, Wayne, 6
Gill, Deborah, 446
Gill, Frank, 409
Gillan, Chester, 213
Gillespie, Brian, 175, 176
Gillespie, Francis, 25
Gillespie, James, 165
Gillespie, Jim, 165
Gilley, Susan, 532
Gilliam, James, 590

Gilliam, Jay, 531
Gillies, Arch, 375
Gillihan, Scott, 482
Gillis, Jim, 157
Gillmor, Paul E., 11
Gilmore, Eve, 515
Gilmore, Robert, 550
Gilmore, Thomas, 415
Gilroy, John, 285
Gilson, James, 137
Gingras, Stephane, 345
Gingrey, Phil, 4
Gipson, Philip, 119, 167
Gipson, Rob, 254
Giroux, Eric, 320
Giroux, Lorne, 602
Girton, Donald, 430
Glaser, Barbara, 242
Glaser, Luis, 365
Glassberg, Jeffrey, 448
Glasscock, Selma, 536
Glatt, L. David, 201
Glaze, William, 617
Gleiber, John, 502
Gleick, Peter, 464
Glenn, Michael, 226
Glick, Anne, 267, 339
Glick, Dennis, 505
Glissman, Inge, 365
Glisson, Scott, 261
Glock, James, 463
Gloden, Teresa, 181
Gloutney, Mark, 315
Glover, Edward, 280
Glueck, Tom, 73
Glyde, Mark, 455
Gnam, Rosemarie, 374
Goad, David, 138
Gobin, Ann, 149
Godbout, Claude, 601
Godby, David, 169
Goddard, Chris, 20
Goddard, Jim, 302
Goddard, Ken, 107
Godfrey, Christine, 70
Godfrey, David, 288
Godfrey, Ted, 521
Godish, Thad, 574
Godwin, K., 549
Godwin, Kristina, 549
Goedecke, Peter, 340
Goergen, Glenn, 504
Goerl, Vincette, 34
Goessman, Doug, 320
Goettel, Beth, 115
Goettel, Robin, 56
Goetz, Ray, 202
Goff, Benny, 401
Goff, Debbie, 185
Goff, Deborah, 185
Goff, Gary, 197
Going, Tony, 445
Gold, Art, 214
Gold, Loretta, 415
Gold, Lou, 500
Gold, Mark, 350
Gold, Paula, 308
Gold, Rick, 89
Golden, Jennifer, 515
Golden, Raymond, 429
Golden, William, 249
Goldentyer, Elizabeth, 31
Goldman, Amy, 344
Goldman, Jeffrey, 261
Goldman, Jonathan, 355
Goldman, Patti, 320
Goldsworthy, Patrick, 452
Gole, Rudy, 307
Goll, Betsy, 490
Gollin, Jim, 476
Gomes, James, 327
Gomez, Luis, 580
Gonzalez, Charles A., 13

Gonzalez, Eugenio, 580
Gonzalez, Ignacio, 291
Gonzalez, Manuel, 367
Good, Alicia, 214
Good, Mary, 249
Good, Ron, 480
Goode, Andrew, 275
Goode, Virgil H., Jr., 14
Goodhart, Jim, 138
Goodheart, Jim, 398
Goodlatte, Bob, 14
Goodlet, Karen, 612
Goodlett, Tracy, 314
Goodman, Bethany, 487
Goodman, David, 607
Goodman, Jim, 170
Goodman, Nancy, 327
Goodman, Roy, 491
Goodnight, Bill, 354
Goodpaster, Gary, 316
Goodrich, Robert, 444
Goodrich, Shirley, 334
Goodson, Ralph, 342
Goodwin, Daniel, 501
Goodwin, Gary, 315
Goodwin, Ross, 271
Goodwin, Vickie, 472
Gordon, Bart, 13
Gordon, Gayle, 85
Gordon, Guy, 180
Gordon, John, 252
Gordon, Kathy, 89
Gordon, Ken, 511
Gordon, Suzanne, 442
Gordon, Theodore, 314
Gore, Bob, 232
Gore, Ron, 133
Gorham, Debbie, 208
Gorham, Shelly, 549
Gorman, Bill, 377
Gorman, Robert, 149
Gorton, Candace, 70
Gorzelany, Jay, 404
Gosliner, Michael, 23
Goss, Porter J., 4
Gossweiler, William, 73
Gosting, Diane, 433
Goswami, D., 609
Gothard, Tim, 245
Gott, Edwin, 483
Gottfried, Kurt, 525
Gottstein, Ruth, 242
Gough, Mary, 356
Gough, Stephen, 576, 606
Goulard, Cary, 575
Gould, Rowan, 111, 112
Gould, Stephen, 249
Gover, Charles, 236
Gover, Chuck, 236
Goverts, Irene, 313
Gowan, Charles, 259
Gowdey, Dave, 271
Grabb, Robert, 232
Graber, Clyde, 167
Graber, Steve, 356
Grace, Ami, 299
Grace, James, 211, 213
Graci, Joseph, 211
Grady, Sue, 238
Graebner, Joan, 411
Grafe, Vicki, 102
Graff, Walter, 270
Grafton, William, 237
Graham, Bob, 3, 208
Graham, Christopher, 398
Graham, Ed, 247
Graham, Lindsey O., 12
Graham, Peter, 366
Graham, Wendy, 609
Grams, Rod, 29
Gran, Lynn, 434
Grand, James, 132
Grandy, John, 352

STAFF NAME INDEX – G

Granger, Kay, 13
Granger, S., 243
Granillo, Isabel, 367
Grann, Douglas, 544
Grannan, Ted, 297
Granquist, Deborah, 529
Grant, Albert, 478
Grant, James, 155
Grant, Malcolm, 214
Grant, R., 76
Grant, Sue, 507
Grant, William, 590
Granter, Clyde, 152
Grassley, Charles E., 5
Grau, E. Gordon, 55
Grauer, Cheri, 373
Graves, Diane, 373
Graves, Donald, 612
Graves, J., 577
Graves, Leon, 227
Graves, Randy, 316
Graves, Samuel B., 8
Grawe, Robin, 24
Gray, Brian, 315
Gray, David, 517
Gray, Gerald, 260
Gray, Herb, 23
Gray, Jeffrey, 191
Gray, Kathleen, 601
Gray, Katie, 544
Gray, Mary, 148
Gray, P., 439
Gray, Pamela, 307
Gray, Paul, 190
Gray, Rachel, 328
Gray, Sarah, 447
Gray, Steve, 204
Gray, Steven, 575
Gray, Terrence, 214
Graybeal, James, 150
Graybill, Lowell, 466
Grayson, Leslie, 232
Greathead, R., 251
Green, Arlene, 138
Green, Bill, 384
Green, Daniel, 345
Green, Emily, 494
Green, Emory, 198
Green, Evon, 239
Green, Frank, 347
Green, Gary, 32
Green, Gene, 14
Green, George, 223
Green, Jay, 399
Green, Kelly, 584
Green, Lane, 515
Green, Mark, 15
Green, Mary, 494
Green, Michael, 291
Green, Norma, 533
Green, Orville, 160
Green, Paul, 250
Green, Ruth, 357
Green, Sara, 506
Green, Terry, 225
Greenberg, Jerry, 541
Greenberg, Jonathan, 285
Greene, Brian, 445
Greene, Dale, 342
Greene, Harry, 266
Greene, Thomas, 452
Greene, Wade, 387
Greenfield, Tony, 281
Greenhalgh, Randy, 528
Greenlee, Jack, 73
Greenlee, Jason, 361
Greenlees, Adrianne, 560
Greenwald, Noah, 290
Greenwood, Cary, 209
Greenwood, Jim, 12
Greenwood, Steve, 208
Greer, Jack, 56
Greeves, John, 25

Gregg, A., 340
Gregg, George, 210
Gregg, Judd, 9, 29
Gregg, William, 127
Gregory, Gary, 145
Gregory, John, 221
Gregory, Tommy, 183
Gregory, Wayne, 221
Grella, Rebecca, 244
Gresczyk, Bruce, 149
Grese, Robert, 398
Grey, Mike, 611
Grguric, Gordan, 594
Grice, Rick, 147
Griebling, Richard, 147
Grier, Norma, 453
Gries, Daniel, 557
Griffen, Philip, 196
Griffin, B.J., 394
Griffin, Brenda, 155
Griffin, Hollis, 223
Griffin, Robert, 404
Griffin, Stan, 520, 521
Griffin-Jones, Mary, 242
Griffith, Brad, 133
Griffith, Gary, 353
Griffith, Gwen, 516
Griffith, Robert, 467
Griggs, James, 132
Griggs, Lisa, 402
Grijalva, Raul, 1
Grilley, Dorian, 465
Grillot, Chris, 374
Grimes, Brian, 25
Grimes, Ray, Jr., 334
Grimes, Roy, 169, 548
Grimes, Stanley, 444
Grimm, Eric, 155
Grimm, Nancy, 447, 573
Grindal, Bruce, 582
Grishaw, Letitia, 77
Grisses, F. (Bud), 592
Grist, Joanna, 534
Griswold, Andrew, 412
Grizzard, Kent, 184
Grizzle, John, 573
Groat, Charles, 127
Groffman, Peter, 358
Groninger, John, 596
Gronowski, Robert, 189
Grosboll, Carolyn, 163
Groshek, Jessica, 453
Groskin, Robert, 273
Gross, David, 197
Gross, Howard, 350
Gross, Kitty, 375
Gross, Porter, 22
Grossi, Ralph, 252
Grossman, Dennis, 441
Grosswiler, Ed, 561
Grotewiel, Ken, 169
Groton, Jimmy, 515
Groty, Keith, 398
Grover, Kate, 380
Grover, Tony, 233
Groves, Desiree Sorenson, 416
Groves, Tom, 443
Grubbs, Geoffery, 130
Gruber, Alan, 270
Gruber, Elliot, 455
Grubinger, Vern, 622
Grue, Christian, 128
Gruebel, Ralph, 195
Gruenberg, Phil, 144
Grumbach, Antonia, 379
Grumbly, Tom, 384
Gryder, R., 134
Gryniewski, James, 182
Guaraldi, Sharon, 444
Guay, Louis, 603
Guay, Roger, 602
Guay, Tony, 498
Gudes, Scott, 49

Guenther, John, 182
Guertin, Annie, 476
Guertin, D., 605
Guest, David, 320
Gueuvara, Ana, 22
Guggenheim, David, 455
Guimond, Richard, 344
Guinn, Gary, 419
Guion, Ann, 412
Guise, Dennis, 212
Guisinger, Allen, 429
Gullestad, P., 453
Gullifer, Joanne, 554
Gulliver, R., 199
Gunderson, Jeffrey, 183
Gunlogson, Laura, 316
Gunn, Dick, 458
Gunn, Sue, 541
Gunn, Susan Adams, 209
Guntenspergen, Glenn, 504
Gunter, Dale, 138
Gunton, Russell, 210
Gupta, Gian, 613
Guritz, Dave, 325
Gusella, Mary, 22
Gustafson, Cole, 126
Guth, Candice, 430
Guthertz, Judith, 131
Guthrie, James, 476
Guthrie, Randy, 475
Gutierrez, Anne Marie, 207
Gutierrez, Franklin, 158
Gutierrez, Luis V., 5
Gutknecht, Gil, 8
Gutowski, Carolyn, 448
Guttier, Ann-Marie, 187
Guy, Christopher, 167
Guymon, Jim, 226
Guzman, Frank, 40
Guzman, Louann, 152
Guzzo, Dorothy, 192
Gwyn, Thomas, 562
Gwynn, Jack, 553
Gwyther, Chelsea, 290
Gyan, Isabella, 387

H

Haaf, Terry, 444
Haag, Kim, 447
Haas, Glenn, 179
Haas, Nina, 561
Haase, Bill, 614
Habel, Simon, 518
Haberman, Bob, 533
Haberman, Steve, 489
Habhab, Mimi, 373
Hack, Don, 73
Hacking, Elisabeth, 606
Hacking, Elisabeth Barratt, 576
Haddad, Kenneth, 360
Haddix, C., 144
Haddow, Kim, 497
Hadley, Ann, 304
Hadley, Kathleen, 417
Hadley, Kathy, 404
Haefner, Ken, 271
Haeger, Scott, 243
Haehl, Jana, 394
Haertel, Kandee, 328
Haffner, Marlene, 75
Hafker, John, 65
Hafner, Cindy, 204
Hagan, Mark, 64
Hagan, Sarah, 61
Hagebro, Claus, 21
Hagel, Chuck, 8, 29
Hagele, F., 317
Hageman, Susan, 596
Hagemeyer, Richard, 52
Hagenbuch, Steve, 530
Hagener, Jeff, 186
Hageniers, Marilyn, 379
Hagenstein, Perry, 443

Hagenstein, Randy, 434
Hager, Bryan, 492
Hager, Worth, 426
Haggie, Michael, 295
Hagley, Cynthia, 183
Hagood, R. Flip, 513
Hahn, Marianne, 410
Hahn, Roger, 556
Haight, Karen, 204
Haines, Dan, 548
Haire, David, 342
Hajny, Bryan, 40
Halcomb, Monty, 516
Haldeman, Dick, 475
Hale, Barry, 193
Hale, Ken, 570
Hale, Kenneth, 511
Hale, Pam, 333
Hales, David, 78
Haley, Wendell, 375
Halfhill, Michele, 234
Halfor, Sid, 627
Halfpenny, Geoff, 312
Halko, Eileen, 349
Hall, Barbara, 349
Hall, Ben, 387
Hall, Beverley, 200
Hall, Cathy, 307
Hall, Dale, 111
Hall, Doug, 260
Hall, Douglass, 547
Hall, George, 396
Hall, Heather, 473
Hall, J., 53
Hall, Jeff, 412
Hall, Jeremy, 461
Hall, John, 227
Hall, Judy, 538
Hall, Noah, 428
Hall, Patricia, 477
Hall, Pinky, 153
Hall, Ralph M., 13
Hall, Robert, 244
Hall, Steve, 364
Hall, Steven, 214
Hallett, Barbara, 535
Hallett, Diana, 545
Halley, Michelle, 428
Halliburton, Bobby, 251
Hallinan, Jacqueline, 536
Hallock, Stephanie, 208
Hallum, Alan, 156
Hallward, Clare, 294
Halman, Edward, 25
Halman, Robert, 177
Halpenny, Liza, 112
Halstead, Pete, 356
Halverson, Diane, 269
Halverson, Mark, 28
Halvorson, Christine, 248
Halvorson, Christine, 248
Halvorson, William, 502
Halvorson, William, 605
Ham, Michael, 158
Ham, Susan, 158
Hamann, Richard, 331
Hamas, Michael, 576
Hambley, Mark, 78
Hamilton, Bruce, 497
Hamilton, Chris, 392
Hamilton, Dawn, 300
Hamilton, Jim, 207
Hamilton, Joan, 497
Hamilton, John, 401
Hamilton, Kevin, 513
Hamilton, Larry, 84
Hamilton, Milton, 221
Hamilton, Richard, 201
Hamilton, Sam, 112
Hamlen, Devens, 375
Hamlett, Shelby, 340
Hamlin, Linda, 303
Hamm, Mike, 182

STAFF NAME INDEX – H

Hammaker, John, 433
Hammer, Matthias, 278
Hammer, R., 615
Hammerschmidt, Ron, 167
Hammett, Edwin, 204
Hammond, Brad, 162
Hammond, Carol, 414
Hammond, Keith, 510
Hammond, Stephen, 196
Hamrick, Ed, 236
Hancock, Don, 510
Hancock, J., 199
Hand, Edward, 479
Hand, Vincent, 587
Handl, Gunther, 600
Handley, Barbara, 349
Handley, Joy, 561
Handly, Herb, 346
Hands, Helen, 548
Haneline, Ellen, 581
Hanoy, Bernie, 446
Hanitin, Bridget, 180
Hankin, David, 583
Hanley, Donald, 234
Hanna, Carolyn, 591
Hanna, Robert, 598
Hanna, Stephanie, 128
Hanna, Todd, 255
Hannah, Judith, 578
Hannah, Richard, 235
Hannigan, Thomas, 143
Hannon, Bruce, 472
Hansch, Susan, 140
Hansel, John, 322
Hanselka, C., 599
Hanselmann, David, 204
Hancon, Dave, 203
Hansen, David, 373
Hansen, Doug, 219
Hansen, Ed, 249
Hansen, James, 22
Hansen, Jess, 162
Hansen, Katy, 480
Hansen, Paul, 376
Hansen, Peder, 151
Hanson, James, 224
Hanson, Jesse, 202
Hanson, Kim, 91
Hanson, Linda, 166
Hanson, Lynn, 481
Hanson, Martin, 101
Hanson, Michael, 547
Hanson, Nels, 420, 430
Hanson, Paul, 468
Hanson, Robert, 279
Hanson, Roseann, 505
Hanson, Suzanne, 183
Happe, Deb, 504
Harasewych, Oleh, 391
Harcharik, D., 333
Harcombe, Andrew, 139
Hard, Joel, 134
Hardage, James, 458
Harder, Jack, 305
Harder, Les, 143
Harder, Michael, 149
Hardin, Timothy, 258
Harding, Ben, 422
Harding, Marcy, 227
Harding, Russell, 180
Hardisky, Thomas, 552
Hardt, David, 101
Hardy, Fred, 392
Hardy, George, 275
Hardy, Gerald, 133
Hardy, John, 627
Hardy, Yvan, 17
Hare, Dan, 468
Harelson, Thomas, 237
Haresign, Tim, 594
Harger, Chuck, 515
Harger, Trisha, 412
Hargett, Dave, 338

Hargrave, Nancy, 261
Hargrove, Eugene, 291, 618
Hargrove, Karen, 588
Harizanoff, Larry, 230
Harizanoff, Larry, 230
Harkin, Tom, 5, 28
Harkins, Joe, 169
Harkins, P., 184
Harland, Jim, 225
Harlow, Henry, 623
Harlow, Trudy, 127
Harlowe, Anna, 322
Harman, Jane F., 2
Harmet, Joan, 448
Harmon, David, 341
Harmsen, Allen, 589
Harnack, Ronald, 181
Haro, Roger, 623
Haroldson, Brian, 549
Harper, Anne, 319
Harper, Anne, 505
Harper, Craig, 220
Harper, Herbert, 221
Harper, Jake, 244
Harper, Judy, 412
Harper, Larry, 606
Harper, Robert, 172
Harper, Sallyanne, 18
Harps, Shannon, 496
Harriman, Bettie, 556
Harrington, Brian, 537
Harrington, Cate, 440
Harrington, Michelle, 290
Harrington, Shirl, 335
Harrington, Steve, 335
Harrington, Steven, 335
Harris, Betty, 310
Harris, Bobby, 155
Harris, C., 419
Harris, Catherine, 501
Harris, Daniel, 204
Harris, Donny, 138
Harris, Elizabeth, 397
Harris, Ellen, 310
Harris, Fred, 201, 252
Harris, Gerald, 181
Harris, Glenn, 597
Harris, Hallett, 622
Harris, Jack, 402
Harris, James, 362
Harris, Jim, 235
Harris, John, 259
Harris, Katherine, 4
Harris, Mary, 420
Harris, Michael, 142
Harris, Mike, 157
Harris, Pat, 402
Harris, Ray, 240
Harris, Raymond, 392
Harris, Teresa, 430
Harris, Will, 174
Harrison, Autumn-Lynn, 502
Harrison, Ben, 309
Harrison, Betty, 276
Harrison, Charles, 218
Harrison, Dan, 612
Harrison, John, 224
Harrison, Kyle, 353
Harrison, Mark, 205
Harrison, Ross, 165
Harrison, Tom, 217
Harrison, Verna E., 177
Harrison, William, 168, 193
Harrod, Leigh, 400
Harsdorf, James, 237
Hart, Larry, 230, 231
Hart, Marjorie, 488
Hart, Melissa A., 12
Hart, T., 136
Hart, Tina, 449
Harte, Edward, 252
Harter, Paul, 367
Hartfield, Libby, 184
Hartke, Jan, 385

Hartley, Mitschka, 549
Hartman, Brad, 154
Hartman, Herb, 174
Hartman, Scott, 425
Hartnett, David, 586
Hartshorn, Gary, 261
Hartshorn, Gary, 580
Hartwell, David, 386, 465
Hartwell, Meredith, 290
Hartwig, William, 90, 112
Hartzell, Kenneth, 293
Harun, Kevin, 246
Harvey, Dave, 216
Harvey, Holger, 313
Harvey, M., 23
Harvey, Rose, 524
Harwood, Debbie, 429
Harwood, Terry, 247
Haseltine, Susan, 127
Hasenyager, Robert, 226
Haslett, Billye, 72
Hassel, Harry, 52
Hassell, Carol, 341, 348
Hassell, John, 308
Hassett, James, 598
Hassett, John, 598
Hassink, Ulrike, 21
Haslert, J. Dennis, 5
Hastings, Alcee L., 4
Hastings, Doc, 15
Hastings, Robert, 433
Hatakeyama, Hisako, 560
Hatch, Christopher, 476
Hatch, Ellis, 191
Hatch, Orrin G., 14
Hatch, Sue, 375
Hatch, Whitney, 524
Hatcher, Richard, 206
Hatfield, Nina, 85
Hatt, Royd, 448
Haub, Carl, 471
Haub, Tim, 510
Hauck, Ross, 168
Hauge, Thomas, 237
Haugen, Darrell, 106
Haughland, Gary, 447
Haughwout, Mark, 334
Haugland, Gary, 447
Haugrud, Jack, 77
Haun, Les, 221
Haurez, Carrie, 547
Hausel, W., 240
Hausrath, Alan, 354
Haverland, Pam, 303
Haviland, Jim, 403
Havlin, John, 590
Hawk, Debra, 552
Hawkes, Janet, 263
Hawkes, Mike, 27
Hawkey, David, 539
Hawkins, H., 353
Hawkins, Joyce, 47
Hawkins, Richard, 135
Hawkins, Steven, 68
Hawkins, T., 477
Hawley, Cliff, 195
Hawley, Kyle, 353
Haws, Jeanne, 322
Hawthorne, Josetta, 310
Hay, Anne, 484
Hayakawa, Mitsutoshi, 297
Hayashi, Stuart, 73
Hayden, Dana, 140
Hayden, Donald, 480
Hayden, Elizabeth, 26
Hayden, J. Michael, 167
Hayden, Kit, 532
Hayden, Marty, 319
Hayden, Mike, 266
Hayes, Bob, 249
Hayes, Helen, 385
Hayes, Irene, 396
Hayes, James, 342

Hayes, Justin, 354
Hayes, Randall, 476
Hayes, Robin, 10
Hayes, Roy, 194
Hayes, Sam, 211
Hayes, Tom, 396
Hayes, Yvonne, 377
Haynes, Ducote, 272
Haynes, Jane, 456
Haynes, Jim, 221
Hayning, John, 266
Hays, Bill, 194
Hayter, Virginia, 355
Hayward, Don, 404
Hayward, Winchell, 330
Haywood, Carlton, 23
Haywood, Mary, 280
Hayworth, J.D., 1
Hazard, Nancy, 452, 453
Hazell, Stephen, 287
Hazelwood, Susan, 411
Head, Carroll, 331
Head, Clifford, 447
Head, Shawn, 554
Healey, Burke, 205
Healey, Keith, 152
Healey, M., 606
Heape, Toye, 221
Hearn, Shelley, 585
Hearne, Naette, 222
Heaslip, Nancy, 551
Heath, Alison, 426
Heath, Becki, 38
Heath, Ralph, Jr., 514
Heath, Scott, 519
Heaton, Louis, 172
Heaton, Raymond, 226
Heatwole, Charles, 576
Heavers, Debra, 250
Heber, Sharon, 155
Hebert, Michele, 149
Hechinger, Deborah, 559
Hechter, Michael, 261
Heckclay, Marion, 326
Heckenlaible, Mark, 468
Hedden, Bill, 344
Hedges, Anne, 403
Hedrich, Anne, 432
Hedrick, Lee, 459
Heemstra, Theodore, 241
Hefferan, Colien, 49
Heffernan, Laurel, 575
Heflebower, Craig, 114
Hefley, Joel, 3
Heft, David, 87
Hegel, Craig, 521
Hegemann, Ingeborg, 396
Hegge, William, 587
Hegstad, Spence, 187
Heide, Cheryl, 182
Heideman, Mike, 167
Heider, William, 417
Heldorn, Randy, 163
Heidt, Gary, 605
Heidy, Bonnie, 411
Heiken, Doug, 460
Heil, Gerald, 182
Heilig, Dan, 561
Heimericks, Gary, 186
Heimermann, Dale, 182
Hein, Lisa, 373
Heinekamp, Neil, 272
Heinemann, Gene, 431
Heinemann, Thomas, 489
Heinicke, Ray, 373
Heins, David, 600
Heise, Colleen, 344
Heissenbuttel, Anne, 408
Heitman, J., 563
Held, Andy, 481
Held, Rodney, 271
Helfrich, Louis, 228, 259
Helinski, Ronald, 545

STAFF NAME INDEX – H

Hellem, Steven, 344
Heller, Victor, 154
Hellested, Leo, 214
Helliker, Paul, 143
Hellman, Ame, 437
Hellman, Richard, 526
Hellwig, Ray, 233
Helmig, Mary, 388
Hemenway, John, 530
Hemmer, Dennis, 239
Hemond, John, 392
Hempel, Monty, 283
Hendee, John, 540
Hendershott, Myrl, 607
Henderson, Brian, 66
Henderson, Cheryl, 270
Henderson, Cliff, 135
Henderson, K., 169
Henderson, Minuet, 57
Henderson, Patrick, 383
Henderson, R., 138
Henderson, Stuart, 483
Henderson, Wayne, 106
Henderson, William, 129
Hendricks, Scott, 341
Hendrickson, Dean, 314
Henkin, David, 319
Henne, Paul, 90
Henning, Eric, 468
Henning, Jimmy, 171
Hennings, Ronald, 238
Henningsgaard, Steve, 384
Henry, Don, 142
Henry, Jenny, 162
Henry, Leigh, 518
Henry, Michael, 404
Henry, Robert, 151
Henry, Steve, 194
Henry, Susanna, 102
Hensarling, Jeb, 13
Henschel, Kira, 298
Hensel, Mary, 489
Hensler, Ronald, 623
Hensley, Doug, 169
Henson, Paul, 111
Hepler, Kelly, 134
Herb, William, 73
Herbert, Curtis, 75
Herbert, Paul, 451
Herbst, David, 163
Herger, Wally, 1
Herlihy, Thomas, 75
Herman, Alexis, 77
Herman, Kim, 431
Herman, Lynn, 150
Herman, Tom, 572
Hermann, Elizabeth, 593
Hermann, Sharon, 344
Hernandez, Fidel, 553
Hernandez-Serrano, Carmen, 213
Herner, Brian, 410
Herpel, Rachael, 347
Herpen, Lori, 495
Herrera, Alfred, 349
Herrera, Marcareo, 271
Herrgesell, Perry, 142
Herrick, Theresa, 573
Herricks, Rosetta, 24
Herrighty, Lawrence, 192
Herring, Jennifer, 543
Herrman, Kandy, 302
Hersey, Rita, 297
Hersley, Ann, 235
Hertzel, Anthony, 400
Herwig, Mark, 468
Herzberg, Mark, 445
Herzfelder, Ellen Roy, 178
Hesla, Chris, 507
Hess, Gene, 312
Hess, Myron, 428
Hesselink, Fritz, 368
Hession, Jack, 490
Hession, Paul, 27

Hester, Carol, 204
Heston, Charlton, 424
Hettinger, Edward, 367
Hewings, Adrianna, 48
Hewlett, Elizabeth, 178
Hibbard, Don, 159
Hicken, Curt, 274
Hickle, Rodney, 452
Hickman, Tim, 162
Hickox, Winston, 144
Hicks, Anna, 224
Hicks, John, 197
Hiemenz, Greg, 551
Hiemenz, Kenneth, 399
Hier, Ross, 615
Higby, Sue, 336
Higgins, Joseph, 334
Higgins, Kenneth, 29, 596
Higgins, Wesley, 393
Higgs, Eric, 502
Highsmith, R., 556
Hight, Robert, 142
Higman, Phyllis, 398
Hildebrand, Cindy, 373
Hildebrand, Dean, 202, 381, 537
Hildreth, John, 426
Hill, Baron, 5
Hill, Barry, 130
Hill, Brian, 466
Hill, Carlton, 229
Hill, Harvey, 113
Hill, Isabel, 218
Hill, Jack, 473
Hill, James, 475
Hill, John, 164
Hill, Karen, 332
Hill, Ken, 155
Hill, Murray, 203
Hill, Spencer, 374
Hill, Tessa, 384
Hill, Thomas, 157, 220
Hill, William, 150
Hillard, Anne, 47
Hillberry, Gary, 76
Hillebrand, Kimberly, 462
Hillebrecht, Peter, 376
Hilliard, Marion, 331
Hillman, Bob, 161
Hills, Davie, 489
Hilly, James, 511
Hilton, Bill, 351
Hilton, Richard, 503
Hilts, Stu, 610
Himlan, Ed, 396
Hinchey, Maurice, 10
Hines, Ayelet, 498
Hines, Diane, 333
Hines, Mike, 162
Hinesley, Phillip, 132
Hiney, Jim, 59
Hinkley, Bill, 154
Hinman, Ken, 418
Hinman, Lani, 293
Hinojosa, Ruben E., 13
Hinschberger, Mark, 554
Hinshaw, Jeffrey, 200
Hinton, Karen, 616
Hippensteel, Peter, 164
Hirai, Lawrence, 73
Hiraiwa, Gaishi, 344
Hird, Bruce, 343
Hires, Brian, 477
Hirrel, Suzanne, 272
Hirsch, Octavio Telles, 563
Hirsch, Robert, 127
Hirsche, Evan, 429
Hirsh, Heidi, 63
Hirsh, Nancy, 455
Hirst, Eric, 515
Hirth, David, 622
Hisey, Kevin, 470
Hitch, Kenneth, 206
Hitchcock, Loren, 138

Hitchingham, Richard, 398
Hiteshue, Mindy, 450
Hitz, Russell, 557
Hixon, Karen, 468
Hluchy, Michele, 572
Hoachlander, Shayne, 552
Hoagland, Bruce, 205
Hoagland, Roy, 295
Hoare, John, 543
Hobbs, Alma, 49
Hobbs, Douglas, 550
Hobbs, Tim, 418
Hobson, David, 11
Hobson, Joan, 333
Hochhalter, Scott, 202
Hochmuth, Jay, 238
Hocker, Jean, 25
Hocog, Estanislao, 463
Hocutt, Charles, 613
Hodanbosi, Robert, 204
Hodgdon, Harry, 546
Hodges, Cathleen, 547
Hodges, Jeff, 475
Hodges, M., 25
Hodges, Mike, 374
Hodges, Theresa, 167
Hodsdon, John, 444
Hodson, Ronald, 58, 199
Hoecker, James, 75
Hoefer, Phil, 148, 301
Hoeffel, Joseph M., III, 12
Hoeffliger, Mary, 413
Hoeflich, Russell, 439
Hoekstra, Peter, 7
Hoerner, Gaia, 298
Hoese, Scott, 399
Hofer, Doug, 219
Hoff, Denna, 453
Hoffbuhr, Jack, 267
Hoffman, Douglas, 547
Hoffman, Joseph, 23
Hoffman, Judie, 387
Hoffmann, Thomas, 448
Hoffner, Brandon, 468
Hofherr, Peter, 185
Hogan, David, 290
Hogan, Eileen, 445
Hoganson, Edward, 189
Hogarth, William, 52
Hogg, Sonja, 271
Hohensee, Jeff, 519
Hohimer, Don, 276
Hohman, Tom, 163
Hohmann, Kathryn, 494
Hohmann, Stephen, 170
Hoistad, Harris, 100
Holahan, Gary, 26
Holbrook, Todd, 157
Holck, Alan, 62
Holcomb, Noel, 157
Holcomb, Sue, 344
Holden, Nelda, 507
Holden, Tim, 12
Holderman, Reed, 524
Holenstein, Julian, 345
Holford, Matt, 522
Holimon, Bill, 138
Hollabaugh, Paul, 356
Holland, Bruce, 63
Holland, Elise, 253
Holland, Matthew, 468
Holle, Deborah, 93, 517
Holley, Amy, 127
Holley, Robert, 513
Hollings, Ernest F., 12
Hollings, Fritz, 28
Hollingsworth, Carol, 47
Hollis, Sue, 402
Holloway, Anne, 259
Holloway, Roger, 558
Holloway, Thomas, 305
Hollums, Don, 146
Holm, Tom, 376

Holmer, Steve, 262
Holmes, Alan, 139
Holmes, Charles, 244
Holmes, Glen, 176
Holmes, Jerry, 390
Holmes, John, 510
Holmes, Robert, 66
Holmes, Steve, 530
Holmes, Susan, 319
Holmgren, Patricia Heaton, 367
Holmstead, Jeffrey, 18
Holperin, Jim, 519
Holsinger, Shawn, 74
Holst, Bruce, 393
Holston, Sharon, 76
Holt, Harvey, 367
Holt, Jasa, 138
Holt, Nicole, 498
Holt, Rush, 9
Holt, Sidney, 242
Holter, Richard, 399
Homann, Rich, 148
Homer, Peggy, 517
Homziak, Jurij, 622
Honda, Michael M., 2
Honne, Syozaburo, 344
Honnold, Douglas, 318
Hood, Peter, 255
Hooks, Clegg, 153
Hooley, Darlene, 12
Hooper, Irene, 489
Hooper, Jon, 575
Hoopes, Rickalon, 212
Hoopes, Robert, 545
Hoot, Lynne, 395
Hooten, Charles, 236
Hoover, Craig, 518
Hoover, Ed, 162
Hopkins, Suzanne, 394
Hopper, George, 220, 621
Hopper, Hilary, 260
Hopper, Steve, 402
Hoppie, Robert, 161
Hopple, William, 297
Horan, James, 235
Hord, Patrick, 384
Horiuchi, Cindy, 146
Horn, Charles, 133, 232, 509
Horn, Christine, 552
Horn, Floyd, 31
Horn, Thomas, 275
Horn, William, 527
Hornback, John, 170
Horne, Ellen, 309
Horner, Wesley, 281
Horrigan, Jim, 489
Horton, Alison, 397, 494
Horton, Chris, 564
Horton, Diana, 373
Horton, Jesse, 72
Horton, P., 146
Horton, Rick, 483
Horton, Scott, 234
Horton, Terry, 272
Horvath, Bill, 407
Horwich, Rob, 303
Horwitz, Robert, 195
Horzepa, George, 191
Hosenfeld, Robert, 127
Hoshino, Makoto, 560
Hoskins, David, 455
Hoskins, John, 185
Hoskins, Sherm, 226
Hossain, Atm, 568
Hostettler, John N., 5
Hotaling, A., 280
Hotaling, Leslie, 152
Hottle, Dan, 163
Houck, Oliver, 600
Hough-Stein, Judith, 609
Houghton, Amory, Jr., 10
Houglum, Lyla, 209

STAFF NAME INDEX – J

Houk, Julie, 279
Houpe, Lori, 204
Hourcle, Laurent, 582
Houser, Elizabeth, 142
Houska, Thomas, 151
Houston, James, 72
Hovanec, Sarah, 457
Hovanic, Catherine, 533
Hovencamp, Marian, 579
Hover, Jerold, 167
Hovorka, Duane, 442
Howard, Alice, 74
Howard, Bob, 542
Howard, Bruce, 487
Howard, Connie, 261
Howard, Dennis, 205
Howard, James, 583
Howard, Jim, 244
Howard, Marilyn, 160
Howard, Richard, 559
Howard, Robert, 101
Howard, William, 544
Howe, Paul, 531
Howe, Robert, 622
Howell, A. Eric, 241
Howell, David, 475
Howell, Liz, 495, 499
Howell, Lynn, 47
Howell, Steve, 433
Howerth, Elizabeth, 543
Howerton, Lorraine, 419
Howett, Ciannat, 509
Howman, Keith, 559
Hoyer, Steny H., 7
Hoyle, John, 26
Hoyle, Joyce, 221
Hoyt, Cathryn, 296
Hoyt, John, 359
Hristovski, Victoria, 132
Hubbard, Andy, 125
Hubbard, Daniel, 596
Hubbard, James, 148
Hubbard, William, 70
Hubbell, Stephen, 418
Huber, Michael, 262
Huber, Patrick, 181
Huber, Phil, 67
Hubert, Ed, 240
Hubert, Martin, 222
Hubert, Wayne, 239
Huckabey, Shawna, 406
Hudson, Bailey, 367
Hudson, Jay, 490
Hudson, John, 195
Hudson, Mike, 73
Hudson, Pamela, 501
Hueble, Tom, 506
Huebner, Erwing, 613
Huebner, Martin, 330
Hueckel, Greg, 233
Huelman, Patrick, 183
Huerta, Sergio, 151
Hueter, Robert, 404
Huffaker, Buddy, 247
Huffaker, Steve, 160
Huffaker, Steven, 537
Huffines, Eleanor, 541
Huffman, Randy, 235
Huffman, Rick, 506
Huggins, Joe, 364
Hughes, Daniel, 313
Hughes, Debbie, 445
Hughes, Gary, 180
Hughes, John, 151
Hughes, Julie, 554
Hughes, Layla, 319
Hughes, Robert, 141, 259
Hughes, Steven, 614
Hugo, Nancy, 532
Hugoson, Gene, 182
Huhta, Dean, 112
Hull, Diana, 284
Hull, James, 222

Hull, Peter, 404
Hull, William, 396
Hulme, Diana, 624
Hulsey, Brett, 494
Hulshof, Kenny C., 8
Hultine, Sarah, 247
Humburg, Dale, 185
Hume, Bob, 70
Humpert, Mark, 550
Humphrey, Beth, 42
Humphrey, Gilbert, 527
Humphrey, Rachael, 382
Humphrey, Stephen, 502
Humphreys, David, 264
Humphries, Rebecca, 181
Humrickhouse, Scott, 237
Huncke, John, 310
Hunsaker, J., 209
Hunst, Mike, 182
Hunt, Fran, 541
Hunt, Gary, 200
Hunt, Hugh, 210
Hunt, Jack, 223
Hunt, Janice, 524
Hunt, Suzelle, 268
Hunter, Bruce, 618
Hunter, Chris, 187
Hunter, David, 292
Hunter, Duncan, 3
Hunter, Malcolm, 502
Hunter, Norman, 613
Hunter, Richard, 155
Hunter, Tim, 66
Hunter, Tom, 16
Huntsman, Gene, 262
Huntzinger, Tom, 167
Huppert, George, 623
Hurd, David, 372
Hurley, Frederick, 175
Hurley, James, 622
Hurst, Daniel, 297
Hurwich, Evelyn, 297
Husband, Thomas, 619
Huse, Brian, 309
Huss, Joe, 240
Hussain, Mohammed, 370
Hussey, Arthur, 453
Hussey, Stephanie, 550
Hussmann, William, 178
Hust, George, 521
Husted, Lisa, 181
Hutchens, Thomas, 313
Hutcheon, Richard, 52
Hutcherson, Lucy, 296
Hutchins, Michael, 268
Hutchinson, Alan, 335
Hutchinson, Rick, 459
Hutchison, Alice, 343
Hutchison, Fred, 269
Hutchison, Kay Bailey, 13
Hutchison, Lynne, 269
Huth, Laura, 355
Hutson, Mary Pope, 386
Hutto, Ellen, 288
Huxmann, Jeffery, 297
Hyatt, Leedrue, 445
Hyatt, William, 149
Hyde, Arnout, 236
Hyde, Henry, 22
Hyde, Henry J., 5
Hyde, Les, 613
Hygnstrom, Scott, 225
Hymes, Jacqueline, 204
Hypes, Rene, 229
Hyzer, Maureen, 42

I

Iani, L., 19
Ibach, Greg, 188
Ikehara, Walter, 255
Iles, Jeff, 584
Imamura, Koji, 25
Imlay, Marc, 395

Imlay, Mark, 73
Imus, Brian, 397
Incerpi, Angelo, 227
Inch, Tony, 304
Ingle, Don, 397
Inglis, Jim, 468
Ingman, Dan, 235
Ingram, Dewayne, 612
Ingram, Otis, 334
Ingram, Terrence, 316
Inhofe, James, 29
Inhofe, James M., 11
Inkley, Doug, 427
Inman, Rich, 38
Inman, Roger, 155
Inouye, Daniel K., 4
Inouye, Ted, 507
Inslee, Jay, 14
Intino, Frank, 149
Irby, Lynn, 589
Ireland, John, 281
Ireland, Kate, 515
Ireland-Smith, Adair, 208
Irons, David, 464
Irvin, Tommy, 155
Irving, Martin, 202
Irwin, Elise, 132
Irwin, Paul, 352, 359, 361
Isaacson, M., 606
Isakson, Johnny, 4
Isely, J., 217
Isenberg, Henry, 334
Isham, Dell, 497
Iskra, Andy, 78
Islam, Anwarul, 368
Isom, Noelyn, 189
Ison, Jeanne, 26
Israel, Steve J., 9
Issa, Darrell, 3
Istoma, Elena, 489
Istook, Ernest, Jr., 11
Iturregui, Miguel, 475
Iuri, Maria, 368
Iverson, Dave, 335
Iverson, Paul, 189
Ives, Susan, 524
Ivey, Gary, 523
Iwama, George, 258

J

Jablonski, John, 294
Jacangelo, Dominic, 198
Jack, Jeff, 612
Jackson, Alvin, 210
Jackson, Darla, 302
Jackson, Jeffery, 157
Jackson, Jen, 485
Jackson, Jerome, 274, 332
Jackson, Jesse, 476
Jackson, Jesse L., Jr., 5
Jackson, John, 307, 345
Jackson, Ken, 171
Jackson, Kristina, 331
Jackson, Lee, 519
Jackson, Lois, 47
Jackson, Marion, 584
Jackson, Paul, 434
Jackson, Scott, 224
Jackson, Shirley, 26
Jackson, William, 558
Jacobs, Bruce, 444
Jacobs, Jerrold, 193
Jacobs, Kristi, 351
Jacobs, Mark, 183
Jacobs, Robert, 43
Jacobs, Ruth, 127
Jacobson, K., 226
Jacobson, Michael, 293
Jacobson, Robert, 507
Jacques, Jean-Claude, 369
Jacquez, Albert, 129
Jacquot, Raymond, 378
Jacqz, Christian, 179

Jaeger, Al, 346
Jaffe, Martin, 55
Jaffe, Mary Anne, 495
Jager, Matthew, 527
Jager, Sherrie, 113
Jagnandan, Sally, 166
Jagnow, David, 424
Jahn, Larry, 626
Jahnke, Jeff, 134
Jaindl, Ray, 208
James, Frances, 332
James, R., 345
James, Stanley, 530
James, Wendy, 299
James-Griffin, Brenda, 155
Jamison, Daphne, 531
Janecka, Rick, 193
Janes, Lamar, 303
Janes, Stewart, 596
Janeway, Katherine, 561
Janik, Phil, 33
Janklow, William J., 13
Jann, Beatrice, 329
Janowiak, John, 592
Jansen, Ruud, 368
Jansen, Val, 168
Janssen, Len, 512
Jantuah, F., 328
Januszewski, Robyn, 547
Jarrett, Jeffrey, 211
Jarvis, R., 199
Jarvis, T., 423
Jaussi, Andrea, 343
Jawetz, Pincas, 515
Jayne, Jerry, 354
Jeanneret, Doug, 527
Jeans, Rick, 458
Jeffers-Fabro, Atilano, 349
Jefferson, William J., 6
Jeffords, James M., 14
Jeffords, Jim, 29
Jeffress, James, 550
Jeffries, Kevin, 383
Jeffries, Michael, 360
Jelinski, David, 237
Jen, Joseph, 48
Jenkins, Carolyn, 388
Jenkins, James, 173, 508
Jenkins, Neal, 538
Jenkins, Olivia, 133
Jenkins, Ronald, 230
Jenkins, Sean, 626
Jenkins, Steve, 133
Jenkins, Teresa, 155
Jenkins, William L., 13
Jenks, Brett, 478
Jenks, Johnathan, 452
Jenks, Jonathan, 596
Jenne, Alan, 550
Jennings, Cecil, 20
Jennings, Gerry, 403
Jonny, J., 168
Jensen, Allan, 177
Jensen, Christopher, 90
Jensen, Deborah, 433
Jensen, Doug, 57
Jensen, Jim, 403
Jensen, John, 574
Jensen, Marvin, 168
Jensen, Mia, 379
Jeppson, Phil, 160
Jernigan, Alex, 300
Jerome, Laura, 339
Jesernig, Jim, 232
Jesperson, Michelle, 423
Jesse, Jeanne, 347
Jessen, Julie, 246, 568
Jessop, Justin (Judge), 507
Jessup, Steven, 500
Jewett, Joan, 111
Jezowski, Terrence, 322
Jimenez, Jorge, 580
Jimerfield, Shane, 290

Jiskra, Richard, 188
Jobst, Heather, 373
Jock, Ken, 511
Jody, Williams, 434
Joeres, Erhard, 623
Joerger, Sue, 475
Joffe, Paul, 428
Johannes, Jim, 119
Johansen, Paul, 236, 461
John, Bonnie, 410
John, Chacko, 173
John, Chris, 6
John, Romuli, 608
Johndrown, Wayne, 73
Johns, David, 500, 542
Johns, Mark, 551
Johns, Ruthie, 484
Johnsen, Peter, 457
Johnson, Barbara, 375
Johnson, Becky, 592
Johnson, Bern, 326
Johnson, Bob, 89
Johnson, Bruce, 358
Johnson, Carl, 196
Johnson, Carter, 301
Johnson, Charles, 626
Johnson, Dale, 616
Johnson, David, 28, 141, 581
Johnson, Dennis, 264
Johnson, Derek, 329
Johnson, Earl, 189
Johnson, Eddie Bernice, 14
Johnson, Eileen
    Morgan, 427, 429
Johnson, Elaine, 182
Johnson, Eric, 430
Johnson, George, 362
Johnson, Gerald, 64
Johnson, Greg, 589
Johnson, Huey, 242
Johnson, Huey, 479
Johnson, James, 228
Johnson, Jay, 116
Johnson, Jon, 511
Johnson, Judy, 235
Johnson, K., 520
Johnson, Kathryn, 541
Johnson, Kelly, 77
Johnson, Lady Bird, 385
Johnson, Larry, 528
Johnson, Laura, 161, 164, 414
Johnson, Lee, 304
Johnson, Leslie, 540
Johnson, Marsha, 376
Johnson, Meg, 338
Johnson, Michael, 605
Johnson, Mike, 271
Johnson, Nancy L., 3
Johnson, Nels, 439
Johnson, Nolton, 156
Johnson, Pam, 467
Johnson, Patricia, 218
Johnson, Paul, 478
Johnson, Paulette, 465, 595
Johnson, Phyllis, 48
Johnson, Ralph, 329
Johnson, Ray, 415
Johnson, Rick, 354
Johnson, Robert, 64, 544
Johnson, Roger, 201
Johnson, Ron, 225
Johnson, Ross, 142
Johnson, Russell, 540
Johnson, Sam, 13
Johnson, Sarah, 520
Johnson, Shirley, 412
Johnson, Stanley, 363
Johnson, Stephen, 130
Johnson, Steve, 543
Johnson, Tim, 13
Johnson, Timothy V., 5
Johnson, Todd, 227
Johnson, Tom, 489, 533
Johnson, Trudye, 177
Johnson, Tullie, 288
Johnson, Twig, 559
Johnson, Warren, 85
Johnson, Wendy, 413
Johnson, Wes, 523
Johnston, Gail, 619
Johnston, Tom, 161
Johnston, Tracy, 481
Johnstone, Scott, 226
Joichi, Jean, 572
Jolley, Jeffrey, 253
Jolly, Bill, 235
Jolly, William, 235
Jonas, Jill, 237
Jonasson, Harley, 175
Jones, Alvin, 347
Jones, Andrew, 627
Jones, Carol, 77
Jones, Christopher, 204
Jones, Clive, 358
Jones, David, 200
Jones, Donald, 352
Jones, Donna, 463
Jones, Doug, 154
Jones, Edwin, 199
Jones, Elise, 301
Jones, Gord, 175
Jones, Gwilym, 590
Jones, Jack, 615
Jones, Jeff, 323
Jones, Jerry, 162
Jones, Jim, 191
Jones, Kevin, 138, 167
Jones, Leslie, 541
Jones, Lloyd, 203, 313
Jones, Marshall, 90
Jones, Melinda, 367
Jones, Mike, 515
Jones, Paul, 552
Jones, Peg, 485
Jones, Peter, 455
Jones, Phil, 386
Jones, Pierce, 582
Jones, Richard, 240, 381
Jones, Robert, 73, 312
Jones, Roger, 435, 555
Jones, Sandra, 381
Jones, Sheldon, 135, 136
Jones, Sonja, 75
Jones, Stephanie Tubbs, 11
Jones, Todd, 107
Jones, W., 150
Jones, Walter, Jr., 10
Jones-Schulz, Jane, 138
Jonkel, Charles, 344
Jontz, Jim, 262
Jooss, Judy, 555
Joosten, Hans, 365
Jordan, Carl, 380
Jordan, Edward, 26
Jordan, J. Ralph, 431
Jordan, Jason, 264
Jordan, Lewis, 285
Jordan, Robert, 151
Jorgensen, Eric, 319, 551
Jorns, Byron, 69
Joseph, Carla, 531
Joseph, Jim, 192
Josey, Clint, 431
Josiah, Timothy, 128
Joslin, Lowell, 166
Joslin, Paul, 247
Joubert, Betty, 47
Joy, James, 217
Ju Ju, Jiann-Wen, 607
Judziewicz, Emmet, 280
Jue, Dean, 332
Jules, Erik, 500
Jules, Tysha, 531
Julian, Richard, 412
Julve, Philippe, 365
Jurries, James, 483
Jurzykowski, M., 336
Just, Sally, 211

K

Kabraji, Aban, 369
Kaderka, Susan, 428
Kaduck, Jennifer, 156
Kagan, Neil, 428
Kahn, Jordan, 220
Kaia, Joloyce, 507
Kaiser, Marshall, 247
Kakabadse, Yolanda, 368
Kakabadse-Navarro, Yolanda, 558
Kakakhel, Shafqat, 526
Kalayjian, Vasken, 483
Kalb, Dan, 493
Kales, Matt, 527
Kam, Alan, 55
Kam, Wendell, 159
Kamalpour, Hamid, 63
Kambesis, Pat, 289
Kamens, Richard, 617
Kamerzel, Thomas, 212, 452
Kaminsky, Leib, 513
Kammeyer, Francine, 142
Kamp, Dick, 280
Kamp, Marty, 458
Kanat, Leslie, 585
Kandle, Jay, 445
Kane, Abdoulaye, 370
Kane, Charles, 524
Kane, Dan, 354
Kane, William, 26
Kane-Synal, Lesley, 524
Kania, Gary, 419
Kanjorski, Paul E., 12
Kaparoff, Laura, 311
Kaplan, Lori, 163
Kaplan, Martin, 554
Kappe, Karl, 225
Kaptur, Marcy, 11
Kapuscinski, Anne, 615
Karch, Thomas, 201
Karczmarczyk, Paul, 483
Karels, James, 153
Karian, Michael, 597
Karp, Peter, 46
Karpanty, Sarah, 244
Karr, Bob, 588
Karson, Jeffrey, 580
Karwatowski, Chester, 522
Kasenow, Michael, 581
Kashgarian, Michael, 305
Kasimu-Graham, Jawara, 340
Kasowski, Kevin, 460
Kastl, Mike, 205
Katerere, Yemi, 370, 562
Katona, Steven, 577
Katsouros, Mary, 348
Katz, Daniel, 477, 559
Katz, Richard, 144
Katzke, John, 356
Kau, Brian, 159
Kauffman, Reah Janise, 317
Kauffman, Vanessa, 544
Kaufman, Barbara, 215
Kaufman, Gregory, 464
Kaul, N., 196
Kavanaugh, Stephanie, 469
Kawamura, Mitsugu, 560
Kawelo, Janet, 159
Kay, Aaryn, 326
Kay, Beryl, 242
Kaya, Harry, 606
Kays, Jonathan, 224
Kazlauskas, Joseph, 488
Kazmierczak, Ron, 237
Kea, Phil, 155
Keane, Christopher, 260
Keane, Kathleen, 553
Kearney, Marsha, 41
Kearney, Steve, 176
Kearns, Harold, 257
Kearns, Martin, 346
Kearns, Ron, 102
Kearsley, Steven, 366
Keasling, Phil, 85
Keating, Patti, 141
Keating, Tim, 477
Keck, Rob, 427
Kee, Tom, 459
Keefer, Chloe, 358
Keefer, Donald, 396
Keefover-Ring, Wendy, 500
Keel, Ralph, 553
Keen, Rob, 459
Keene, W., 450
Keese, William, 143
Keeter, Vyrl, 206
Keeton, Donnie, 383
Kefer, Jennifer, 320
Keiser, Terry, 456
Keith, Bill, 230
Keith, Edward, 503
Keith, Jeff, 216
Keithley, C., 585
Keliher, Pat, 300
Kellar, Bryan, 137
Keller, Bea, 265
Keller, Charles, 356
Keller, Henrietta, 421
Keller, J., 584
Keller, Janet, 214
Keller, Jay, 471
Keller, Ric, 3
Keller, Sue, 54
Kelley, Mike, 204
Kelley, Nancy, 438
Kelley, Peter, 265
Kellogg, Bob, 206
Kellsey, Donna, 216
Kelly, Butch, 532
Kelly, Eamon, 24
Kelly, J., 584
Kelly, Jack, 193
Kelly, John, 52, 196
Kelly, Kathy, 143
Kelly, Kelly, 270
Kelly, Marcy, 28
Kelly, Padgett, 588
Kelly, Sue W., 10
Kelly, Thomas, 130, 196
Kelsch, Steven, 618
Kelsch, Tom, 419
Kelsey, Valerie, 420
Kemerman, Linda, 187
Kemp, Neville, 357
Kempf, Jeff, 374
Kemple, Megan, 453
Kempthorne, Dirk, 160
Kendal, Art, 254
Kendall, Andy, 524
Kendall, Douglas, 304
Kendall, Kim, 530
Kennamer, James, 427
Kennay, Jill, 431
Kennedy, Caroline, 312
Kennedy, Donald, 249
Kennedy, Donna, 402
Kennedy, Edward F., 7
Kennedy, James, 618
Kennedy, Jim, 202
Kennedy, Kathryn, 292
Kennedy, Mark R., 8
Kennedy, Patrick J., 12
Kennedy, Ted, 29
Kennel, Charles, 607
Kennelly, John, 70, 605
Kenney, Brigid, 247
Kenny, Alexandra, 420
Kenny, Jane, 18
Kenrick, John, 207
Kent, Dan, 484
Kent, Fred, 316
Kent, Robert, 58, 273
Kent, Sherman, 529

STAFF NAME INDEX – K

Kentula, Mary, 504
Kenyon, Stephanie, 569
Keogh, Becky, 137
Keough, Dorothy, 73
Kephart, Jackie, 546
Kepler, David, 542
Kepner, John, 277
Kern, Carole, 373
Kern, Penny, 241
Kern, Wayne, 201
Kerns, Junior, 72
Kerr, Loralee, 181
Kerr, Patsy, 64
Kerr, Robert, 156
Kerry, John F., 7
Kershaw, John, 616
Kershner, Dave, 568
Kerton, Allan, 397
Kessen, Ann, 400
Kessler, Winifred, 546
Kessner, Burnett, 138
Keszler, Eric, 316
Ketcham, Stevie, 531
Ketcheson, Doug, 16
Keto, Stephan, 541
Kettering, Jana, 225
Kettle, W., 612
Keularts, Jozef, 228
Key, Patty, 427
Key, Tommy, 342
Keyes, Dale, 130
Keyser, Emmett, 219
Khadr, Nirvana, 18
Khanna, Davinder, 422, 531
Khanna, Mamta, 291
Khatun, Khadiza, 568
Kiariro, N., 525
Kidd, Claren, 206
Kidd, Susan, 341
Kidd, Virginia, 205
Kidwell, Birtrun, 378
Kie, Marti, 546
Kieckhefer, Tom, 338
Kiefer, John, 170
Kieffer, Cheryl, 387
Kiegelmayer, Kim, 422
Kiernan, Michael, 16
Kieser, Walter, 562
Kilbourne, James, 77
Kildee, Dale E., 7
Kiley, Michael, 163
Kilgore, Mike, 615
Kilishek, Martha, 557
Killam, Gayle, 481
Killingsworth, Charles, 248
Kilpatrick, Barbara, 294
Kilpatrick, Carolyn C., 7
Kilroy, Ken, 76
Kim, Margaret, 145
Kim, Mikyoung, 593
Kimball, Gordon, 408
Kimball, John, 226
Kimball, Kenneth, 270
Kimball, Suzzette, 127
Kimball-Smith, Pam, 405
Kimbell, Kim, 303
Kimble, Christy, 458
Kimble, Melinda, 78
Kime, P., 508
Kimmel, William, 576
Kimura, Kotaro, 344
Kincannon, Linn, 354
Kind, Ron J., 15
Kinder, Tupper, 411
Kindler, Roger, 352
Kindrachuk, Robert, 315
King, Albert, 176
King, Brian, 270
King, Duane, 112
King, Edgar, 48
King, Gary, 513
King, Joyce, 332
King, Karmen, 578

King, Kenneth, 352
King, Linda, 249
King, Lori, 296
King, Matthew, 27
King, Peter, 9
King, Robert, 73
King, Steve, 6
King, Susan Studer, 457
King, Wade, 254
Kingsolver, Robert, 382
Kingston, Jack, 4
Kinney, Marlene, 451
Kinney, Stephanie, 78
Kinsch, Michelle, 534
Kinsella, John, 32
Kircheis, Frederick, 174
Kirchhoff, Richard, 408
Kirchoff, Sue, 593
Kirk, John, 219
Kirk, Mark S., 5
Kirk, Richard, 221
Kirkland, Gordon, 266
Kirkpatrick, Barbara, 404
Kirkpatrick, Gary, 404
Kirkpatrick, Jason, 65
Kirkpatrick, Martha, 175
Kirkwood, John, 263
Kirn, Don, 336
Kirouac, Gilles, 601
Kirsch, Eileen, 309
Kirsch, Katya, 508
Kirschenmann, Thomas, 468
Kiseda, John, 171
Kiser, Sarah, 180
Kisner, Brenda, 473
Kissinger, Will, 186
Kist, Roger, 556
Kiswardy, Matt, 405
Kitchens, Wiley, 152
Kitterman, R., 458
Kitts, David, 110
Kiviat, Erik, 352
Kjerfve, Bjorn, 620
Klaphake, Clem, 442
Klarquist, Kenneth, 461
Klataske, Ron, 410
Klebnikov, Peter, 324
Kleczka, Jerry, 15
Klefos, Lauri, 190
Klein, Carla, 496
Klein, Curtiss, 202
Klein, Mary, 441
Klein, Rick, 268
Klein, Robert, 440
Klein, William, 483
Kleiner, Donald, 175
Kleintjes, Paula, 622
Klement, Judd, 416
Klimek, Larry, 96
Kline, Don, 255
Kline, Jim, 395
Kline, John, 8
Klineburger, Bert, 307
Kling, Jeanne, 378
Klinger, Pamela, 73
Klinghammer, Erich, 449
Klingman, Bruce, 538
Klippenstein, Murray, 287
Klopfenstein, Norm, 47
Klose, Eliza, 357
Klunder, Richard, 605
Knapp, Malcolm, 26
Knapp, Mary, 129, 255
Knapp, Pat, 494
Knapp, Peggy, 583
Knapp, Ron, 406
Knauf, Lisa, 205
Kneeland, Jason, 416
Kneipp, Sara, 282
Knickerbocker, Dennis, 398
Knight, David, 495
Knight, Elaine, 59
Knight, Jim, 119

Knight, Kathryn, 318
Knight, Peggy, 323
Knight, Richard, 465
Knighton, Raymond, 33
Knipling, Edward, 31
Knobbe, Edward, 592
Knoerr, Ken, 580
Knoll, Ralph, 174
Knollenberg, Joseph, 7
Knotek, George, 372
Knotts, Brent, 239
Knotts, David, 364
Knouf, Ken, 72
Knowles, Carol, 162
Knowles, Don, 421
Knowles, Donald, 52
Knowles, Tommy, 223
Knowlton, Terri, 497
Knox, John, 317
Knudsen, Brad, 109
Knudsen, Eric, 260
Knuth, Barbara, 252, 670
Koberstein, Ingrid, 336
Koch, Mindy, 181
Koch, Roy, 593
Koch-Weser, Marietta, 368
Kochert, Michael, 477
Kochevar, Richard, 193
Kociolek, Patrick, 282
Koehler, Bart, 508, 541
Koenig, Robert, 356
Koenings, Jeff, 233, 360, 537
Koenke, Anne, 372
Koepsel, Kirk, 495
Koerth, Richard, 167
Koester, Kevin, 353
Koford, Rolf, 127
Kogon, D., 475
Kohl, Herbert H., 15
Kohlenberg, A., 412
Kohler, Chris, 252
Kohm, Kathy, 502
Kohn, Barbara, 456
Kojis, Barbara, 224
Kok, C., 209
Kolaz, Dave, 162
Kolb, Peter, 403
Kolbash, Ron, 204
Kolbe, Jim, 1
Kolbenschlag, Pete, 301
Kolenberg, Dale, 251
Kolesnik, Kris, 426
Koll, Laurence, 400
Koncelik, Joseph, 204
Kondo, Ed, 16
Kondrashova, Lilia, 479
Koning, Thomas, 69
Konsis, Ken, 354, 355
Koontz, Fred, 554
Kooser, Jaime, 140
Kopecky, Keet, 496
Kopecky, Mary, 238
Kopf, Virgil, 230, 231
Kopitske, Virgil, 557
Kopp, John, 452
Kopp, Rick, 582
Koranda, Mike, 195
Korcak, Ronald, 48
Kordek, Walt, 236
Korolera, Alexandra, 321
Kortan, Ken, 406
Koss, Bill, 235
Koss, Christopher, 379
Kossler, Raymond, 378
Kosson, David, 555
Kostakow-Kampe, Ritva, 21
Kostmayer, Peter, 471
Kostroun, David, 222
Kotchman, Larry, 201
Koteff, Steve, 524
Kott, Russ, 444
Kotz, Nancy, 274
Kouda, Michel, 368

Koukol, David, 442
Kovacs, Cathie, 545
Kovacs, William, 526
Kovalick, Walter, 19
Koven, Anne, 459
Koven, Joan, 394
Kowal, Don, 27
Koziel, Rick, 238
Krabacher, Tom, 575
Kraft, Paul, 203
Kramb, Andrew, 519
Kramer, Brit, 534
Kramer, Dan, 357
Kramer, Donald, 54
Kramer, Joe, 167, 381
Kramer, John, 465
Kramer, Jonathan, 56
Kramer, Katie, 106
Kramer, Ken, 493
Kramer, R., 362
Kramer, Randall, 580
Kramer, Stuart, 215
Krantzberg, Gail, 23
Krantzberg, Jeff, 187
Krasny, Marianne, 197
Kraus, Janine, 309
Kraus, Joe, 289
Kraus, Mark, 410
Krause, Tom, 425
Krauthamer, Judith, 395
Kreager, Tim, 86
Kreamer, David, 616
Kreider, Karin, 477
Kreil, Randy, 202
Krementz, David, 137
Kremer, Roxanne, 367
Krepps, Bob, 185
Kresek, Ray, 264
Kress, Emily, 163
Kress, Stephen, 415
Kretzer, Jen, 242
Krier, Megan, 382
Krindle, Jackie, 287
Kris, Mary, 196
Krishna, Chandru, 478
Krishnarayan, Vijay, 288
Krishnaswamy, Ajit, 422
Kriss, Patricia, 412
Kroening, Nancy, 330
Krohn, William, 174, 612
Kroll, James, 598
Kroll, Wendi, 47
Kronrad, Gary, 598
Kropp, Jim, 187
Kroshus, James, 485
Kruckenberg, Larry, 239
Krueger, Hal, 555
Krueger, William, 182
Krug, Kelly, 142
Kruger, Fred, 360
Kruidenier, Bill, 407
Krukoski, Brian, 102
Krulisch, Lee, 488
Krull, John, 576
Krumperman, Chris, 412
Krumwiede, Louis, 321
Krupnick, Alan, 479
Krupovage, John, 66
Krupp, Fred, 324, 325
Krus, Glenn, 472
Kruse, Karl, 487
Kruse, Kipp, 580
Kruzansky, Charles, 323
Kubly, Dennis, 89
Kucinich, Dennis J., 11
Kuehl, Aaron, 468
Kuehl, S., 577
Kugler, Dan, 33
Kuharich, Rod, 148, 302
Kuhlmann, Michael, 158
Kuhn, Roger, 189
Kulhavy, David, 598
Kumabe, Elizabeth, 55

Kunimoto, Sandra, 159
Kunkel, Kyran, 571
Kunkel, Peter, 412
Kunkel, Tom, 196
Kunkle, Dan, 545
Kunstel, Marcia, 379
Kunz, Michael, 515
Kunz, Tom, 266
Kuperus, Charles, 191
Kurcinka, Joe, 182
Kuzila, Mark, 188
Kuznick, Katrina, 283
Kuzvart, Milos, 17
Kwak, Tom, 200, 257
Kwetz, Barbara, 152
Kwon, Hye, 293
Kyanka, George, 598
Kyl, Jon L., 1
Kyle, Rebecca, 490
Kyler, David, 290

L

La Vine, Kristen, 550
Laarveld, B., 620
LaBar, George, 610
Labonte, Serge, 27
LaBorde, Sara, 233
Labrecque, Jean, 330
Lacave, Geraldine, 328
Lachapelle, Diane, 601
Lackey, Jeanine, 550
Lacoss, Dennis, 250
Lacy, Gary, 422
Lacy, James, 383
Ladd, David K., 180
Ladner, Rob, 168
Lafleur, Donna, 414
Laforest, Jean-Paul, 602
Laframboise, Roy, 201
Lafranchi, Tim, 152
Lafreniere, Normand, 16
Lahmann, Enrique, 370
LaHood, Ray, 5
Lahser, Carl, 62
Lai, Chun K., 367
Laird, Jimmy, 184
Laist, David, 23
Lake, Barry, 221
Lalo, Julie, 537
Lamair, Mike, 373
Lamar, Agnes, 33
Lamb, Eugene, 407
Lamb, George, 285
Lamb, Randy, 271
Lamberson, Tom, 188
Lambert, Donald, 396
Lambert, Paul, 318
Lambert, William, 184
Lamborn, Katy, 50
LaMee, Bill, 345, 511
Lammers, Owen, 390
Lammert, Warren, 402
Lamont, Gil, 269
LaMontagne, Kris, 90
Lampson, Nicholas V., 13
Lampton, Mason, 527
Lamson, Dot, 392
Lamson, Susan, 424
Lance, Alan, 160
Lance, Linda, 541
Lancia, Richard, 545
Lanctot, Randy, 391
Land, Edward, 424
Land, Stephen, 357
Landes, Steven, 467
Landherr, Larry, 183
Landis, Paula, 143
Landis, Wayne, 627
Landreneau, Dwight, 173
Landrieu, Mary, 6
Lane, Margaret, 444
Lane, Peter, 358
Lane, S., 209

Lang, Chuck, 460
Lang, Mac, 364
Lange, Bob, 362
Langeland, Ken, 331
Langevin, James R., 12
Langford, Lynda, 217
Langlois, Luc, 602
Langlois, Susan, 550
Laning, Brent, 166
Lanphear, Kathleen, 214
Lanphear, Lauren, 367
Lantagne, Douglas, 622
Lantos, Tom, 2
Lantz, Don, 106
Lanza, Dana, 389
Lanza, Guy, 614
Lapayere, Megan, 586
Lapaz, Lourdes, 365
Lapeyre, Megan, 172
Lapham, Burks, 304
Lapierre, Wayne, 424
Lapoint, Thomas, 618
Lapoint, Tom, 618
Lapointe, George, 174, 175
Laporte, Elizabeth, 57
Lappin, Bert, 540
Lappin, Dawn, 540
Laret, Greg, 142
Larkins, John, 26
Larmer, Jeff, 268
Laroche, Yazmime, 28
Larock, Richard, 193
LaRouche, Grant, 358
Larsen, Doug, 546
Larsen, Elyse, 57
Larsen, Mike, 507
Larsen, Rick R., 14
Larson, Douglas, 469
Larson, John, 282
Larson, John B., 3
Larson, L., 334
Larson, Loren, 264
Larson, Lynn, 136
Larson, Reed, 182
Larson, Steve, 143
Larson, Vickie, 431
Larue, Ed, 314
Lasalle, Rodolphe, 476
Lash, Jonathan, 559
Lashbrook, C. Wayne, 457
Lassoie, James, 579
Latham, Tom, 6
Lathlin, Oscar, 176
Latimer, Jody, 137
LaTourette, Steven C., 11
Latta, Martha, 296
Lattimore, Leslie, 391
Lattis, Richard, 543
Lauer, Charlie, 207, 208
Lauer, Victor, 482
Lauffer, Laura, 306
Laun, H., 280
Laurent, Laurence, 303
Laurenzi, Andy, 505
Laurin, Nicholas, 287
Lauriski, Dave, 77
Laursen, Steven Daley, 183
Laustalot, Tom, 283
Lautenberg, Frank R., 9
Lautman, Kay, 248
LaVergne, Marie, 143
Laverty, Lyle, 147
Lavin, Johnny, 271
Lavkulich, L., 606
Lavoie, Marc, 603
Law, Steve, 180
Lawaetz, Hans, 530
Lawall, Lina, 328
Lawhern, Tim, 364
Lawley, M., 132
Lawrence, Louise, 177
Lawrence, Robert, 584
Lawrie, Barbara, 269

Lawson, Danielle, 474
Lawson, Jay, 239
Lawson, Katherine, 545
Lawson, Marvin, 228
Lawson, Mitch, 309
Lawson, Sean, 382
Laxton, William, 129
Layzer, James, 220
Lazenby, William, 157
Lea, George, 474
Leach, Dan, 356
Leach, Jim, 6
Leach, Larry, 397
Leach, Michael, 398
Leadon, Mark, 153
Leahy, P., 127
Leahy, Patrick J., 14
Leaman, Bruce, 23
Leander, Alan, 320
Leape, James, 559
Leaper, Eric, 422
Leaphart, Malcolm, 523
Learner, Howard, 327
Leary, Bill, 31
Leary, Ed, 227
Leary, John, 534
Leath, Mary, 137
Leavitt, Marcy, 195
Leavitt, Peter, 619
Lebard, Linda, 474
Lebarron, Sandy, 197
Lebel, Luc, 602
Leber, Kenneth, 404
Leblanc, Gerald, 590
Leblanc, Raymond, 601
Leblanc, Tim, 284
Leboubon, D., 199
Lecavalier, John, 380
Lechner, Larry, 217
Leckie, Fred, 230, 231
Lecount, Albert, 583
Ledbetter, Brownie, 558
Ledbetter, Jeri, 343
Ledbetter, Nancy, 138
Leddy, Linda, 393
Ledgerwood, Ray, 407
Lee, Amy, 353
Lee, Barbara, 2
Lee, Charles, 169
Lee, Dwayne, 245
Lee, Gregory, 65
Lee, Kai, 627
Lee, Karole, 404
Lee, Mercedes, 414
Lee, Mike, 350
Lee, Nelson, 524
Lee, Randy, 450
Lee, Raymond, 336
Lee, Ruth, 557
Lee, Sheila Jackson, 13
Lee, Shelley, 238
Lee, Thomas, 617
Leech, Michael, 364
Leeman, Wayne, 175
Leete, Jeanette, 400
Lefebvre, Richard, 132
Lefever, Susan, 497
Leff, David, 149
Leffler, John, 581
Legate, Shari, 558
Legault-Alaurent, Micheline, 368
Legg, Michael, 598
Leggett, Dale, 69
Leggett, Donna, 427
Leghorn, Ken, 246
LeGore, Steve, 404
Lehmann, Jill, 440
Lehmkuhl, John, 554
Lehner, Peter, 223
Leib, Jonathan, 418
Leiden, Yale, 475
Leigh, Alisha, 530
Leigh, Stan, 355

Leightley, Liam, 588
Leighton, F., 286
Lein, Gregory, 252
Lein, M., 264
Leitholf, Kurt, 211
Leitman, Steve, 331
Lejeune, Cyril, 172
Lemaster, Dennis, 593
Lemche, E., 25
Lemieux, Pierre, 602
Lemkay, David, 286
Lemke, David, 517
Lemke, Dean, 165
Lemke, Dean, 165
Lemmerman, James, 399
Lemmert, Bruce, 553
Lemmon, Carol, 304
Lemon, John, 107
Lemons, Peggy, 402
Lempa, Chris, 355
Lempicki, Edward, 192
Lemus, Judy, 54
Lenahan, Tim, 204
Lenette, David, 175
Lengauer, Allison, 479
Lenhardt, Roy, 412
Lenhart, Cynthia, 349
Lennon, George, 33
Lennon, Jennifer, 483
Lent, Rebecca, 52
Lenzini, Paul, 360
Leon, Warren, 452
Leonard, John, 221
Leonard, Tina, 518
Leonard, Tom, 536
Leong, Joann, 160
Leopold, Bruce, 588
Leopold, Estella, 247
Lepo, Joe, 622
LeppSnen, Juha-Markku, 21
LePrieur, Gerry, 202
Lequire, Roger, 201
Lerner, Joel, 178
Lerup, Lars, 594
Leschner, Becky, 182
Leschner, Lora, 464
Lesesne, Joab, 218
Leslie, David, 206, 592
Leslie, Gretchen, 211
Lester, Stephen, 292
Letellier, Sylvie, 16
Lettice, Paula, 323
Leukering, Tony, 482
LeValley, Ron, 464
LeVasseur, Doug, 448
Levin, Arnold, 26
Levin, Carl, 7
Levin, Chuck, 405
Levin, Debbie, 327
Levin, Sander M., 7
Levine, Alfred, 576
Levine, Greg, 519
LeVine, Michael, 319
Levine, Neil, 319
Levitt, Joseph, 75
Levitt, Michael, 364
Levy, Ron, 73
Lew, Alan, 591
Lewis, A., 606
Lewis, Brian, 358
Lewis, Cedrick, 530
Lewis, Cyndi, 534
Lewis, Darrell, 67
Lewis, David, 485
Lewis, Donald, 620
Lewis, Ed, 147
Lewis, George, 157
Lewis, Greg, 195
Lewis, James, 76
Lewis, Jeff, 183
Lewis, Jerry, 2
Lewis, John, 4
Lewis, Larry, 341

STAFF NAME INDEX – M

Lewis, Leslie, 322, 385
Lewis, Peter, 260
Lewis, Robert, 34
Lewis, Ron, 6
Lewis, Steve, 521
Lewis, Suzanne, 126
Lewis, W., 316
Lewis, William, 266
Ley, Diane, 159
Li, Hiram, 126
Li, Shiyou, 598
Liau, Frances, 518
Liberty, David, 17
Libonati, James, 143
Lichtman, Pamela, 379
Lick, Roland, 329
Lidholm, Elaine, 228
Lieb, Marilyn, 387
Lieberman, David, 365
Lieberman, Irene, 47
Lieberman, James, 26
Lieberman, Joseph I., 3
Liebow, Paul, 432
Liechti, Paul, 167
Liechty, Karen, 403
Liechty, Thorn, 403
Liffmann, Michael, 56
Light, Charles, 567
Ligon, Bill, 519
Ligon, David, 205
Likens, Gene, 358
Liles, F., 157
Liles, Richard, 132
Lillebo, Tim, 461
Lilley, Charles, 461
Liming, Robert, 218
Limtiaco, David, 152
Linam, Lee Ann, 517
Linck, Leanne Klyza, 542
Linck, Madeleine, 523
Lincoln, Blanche L., 1
Lind, Kevin, 472
Lind, Pollyanna, 453
Lindahl, Lasse, 613
Lindbergh, Kristina, 294
Lindbergh, Reeve, 294
Lindblad, Erick, 484
Lindekugel, Buck, 508
Linder, Don, 458
Linder, John, 4
Linder, Michael, 188
Linder, Sandra, 282
Lindgren, Cory, 549
Lindgren, Richard, 286
Lindheim, Leonard, 76
Lindsay, Don, 307
Lindsay, Melissa, 337
Lindsey, S., 129
Lindsey, Sue, 539
Lindsey, Trudy, 614
Lindzey, Fred, 239, 623
Lino, Loc, 524
Linehan, John, 26
Linglebach, Jenepher, 529
Linn, Robert, 341
Linthecum, Ginnie, 259
Linton, Gordon, 129
Lintott, Lloyd, 393
Linville, Rex, 321
Lipar, Leah, 563
Lipford, Michael, 440
Lipinski, William O., 5
Lipkis, Andy, 519
Lipkowski, Nick, 267
Lipman, Zoe, 428
Lippe, Pamela, 316
Lipphardt, Georgia, 142
Lipton, Doug, 224
Lis, Mary, 149
Lisa, Gwen, 63
Liss, Cathy, 269
Liss, Lauren, 152
List, Hank, 170

Little, Darryl, 138
Little, Edward, 281
Little, George W. (Bill), 414
Little, Irene, 26
Little, James, 33
Little, Jim, 334
Little, Joe, 331
Little, Ron, 168
Littler, Chris, 618
Litvaitis, John, 617
Liu, Michael, 77
Liverett, James, 163
Livermore, David, 440
Livingston, Christine, 486
Livingston, Cindy, 167
Livingston, Edwin, 143
Livingston, Gil, 529
Livingston, William, 612
Livingstone, Susan, 74
Llewelyn, Michael, 208
Lloveras, Fernando, 308
Lloyd, Alan, 143
Lloyd, Sarah, 247
Loarie, Greg, 319
LoBiondo, Frank A., 9
Lochmann, Steve, 213, 253
Locke, Paul, 585
Lockett, Peter, 175
Lookward, Ivan, 213
Lockwood, Dan, 451
Lockwood, Jeffrey, 477
Lockyer, Christina, 329
Loeb, Michael, 499
Loeb, Stanford, 611
Loeffler, Bob, 134
Loegering, John, 615
Loehr, Charles, 177
Loesch, Martin, 534
Loewen, James, 73
Lofgren, Zoe, 2
Loftin, Cynthia, 174
Logan, Brian, 404
Logan, Kathleen, 243, 291
Logan, Patrick, 214
Logan, Robert, 170
Lohaus, Paul, 26
Lohnes, Robin, 261
Lohrer, Fred, 270
Loiselle, Bette, 301
Lokkesmoe, Kent, 182
Lombard, Ernest, 160
Lombardo, Les, 142
Long, Alan, 609
Long, Becky, 453
Long, Burl, 252
Long, David, 133
Long, Jack, 201
Long, Mike, 153
Long, Nancy, 134
Longini, Rose, 339
Lonzarich, David, 260
Loo, Leona, 462
Loomis, Kay, 442
Lopez, Arthur, 129
Lopez, Glenn, 597
Lopez, Leah, 486
Lorensen, Ted, 209
Lorenz, Jerry, 416
Lorrain, Janice, 463
Lorson, Rick, 212
Loscutoff, William, 143
Losordo, Thomas, 200
Lott, Trent, 8
Lotze, Joerg-Henner, 353
Loucks, Andrea Bedell, 469
Louis, Rachel, 627
Lounds, John, 434
Louys, Robert, 183
Lovaglio, Ronald, 174
Lovan, Ike, 307
Love, David, 193
Love, Fulton, 29
Love, Jane, 193
Lovejoy, Thomas, 308

Lovelady, Gregory, 164
Loveless, Brad, 380
Loveless, David, 169
Lovell, Stewart, 151
Lovern, Rob, 154
Lovett, Gary, 358
Lovvorn, James, 623
Lowe, Lori, 272
Lowe, William, 371
Lowery, Mark, 551
Lowey, Nita M., 10
Lowman, Margaret, 393
Lowrance, Dan, 426
Lowrey, Kathy, 394
Lowry, Edwin, 143
Lowry, Kelly, 529
Loyd, Herb, 384
Loyd, Jo, 458
Lozeau, Michael, 318
Lubelczyk, Laura, 60
Luber, Gaye, 386
Lucas, Frank D., 11
Lucas, Ken R., 6
Lucas, Steven, 163
Lucas, Terri, 66
Lucchesi, John, 581
Luce, Ray, 156
Lucero, Dale, 194
Luckett, Mitch, 412
Ludder, David, 389
Ludke, J., 127
Luecke, Chris, 624
Lueckenhoff, William, 185
Luer, Carl, 404
Lueshen, Wiletta, 357
Luftig, Stephen, 19
Lugar, Richard, 28
Lugar, Richard G., 5
Luhikula, G., 30
Lukas, Debbie, 515
Lukas, William, 128
Lukascyk, Joseph, 316
Lukasik, Lynda, 345
Lukens, Ronald, 21
Lukens, Scott, 412
Lukowski, Paul, 73
Lum, Starlet, 488
Lundberg, Jan, 515
Lundin, Clifford, 385, 445
Lundy, James, 400
Lunney, Elizabeth, 534
Lupardus, April, 245
Luquer, Heidi, 537
Luscher, Katherine, 481
Luse, Keith, 28
Lusk, Virginia, 245
Lustigman, Bonnie, 589
Luther, Harry, 393
Luttrell, Allen, 170
Lutz, Charles, 173
Lutz, Judy, 340
Lux, Jim, 233
Lux, Joe, 345
Lyle, Steve, 142
Lyles, Etta, 177
Lyman, Robert, 240
Lymn, Nadine, 321
Lynch, Daniel, 191
Lynch, Dave, 207
Lynch, George, 387
Lynch, Jim, 204
Lynch, Kathy, 283
Lynch, Kenneth, 197
Lynch, Larry, 532
Lynch, Mo, 301
Lynch, Robert, 145
Lynch, Stephen F., 7
Lynn, Frances, 601
Lyon, David, 373
Lyon, Jim, 428
Lyon, Timothy, 574
Lyons, Johanna, 489
Lyons, John, 170

Lyons, Mike, 482
Lyons, William, 142

M

Maas, Richard, 617
Maassen, Steve, 540
Maassen, Zaiga, 298
Maatac, Celso, 519
Mabe, David, 160
Mac, Monica, 382
Mac'Kie, Pamela, 219
Macaulay, Ed, 203
Macaulay, Steve, 143
Macauley, Lydia, 431
MacCallum, Wayne, 25, 178
MacCannell, Dean, 606
MacCarter, Don, 193
MacColl, E. Kimbark, 461
MacDermott, Frances, 320
MacDonald, Alphonse, 293
Macdonald, Bill, 89
Macdonald, Carol, 85
Macdonald, Charles, 415
Macdonald, Greg, 242
Macdonald, Jim, 606
Macdonald, Larry, 392
MacDonald, Laurie, 312
MacDonald, Scott, 535
MacDonald, Shelagh, 286
MacDougall, Gerald, 213
Macera, John, 480
Macfarlane, Lewis, 366
MacGowan, Brian, 548
Machek, Richard, 153
Machol, Ben, 158
Maciejewski, Paul, 520
MacIntyre, Donald, 187
Mack, Cameron, 207, 208, 360
Mack, Gene, 111
Mack, Kevin, 473
Mack, Wayne, 217
Mackay, Jean, 276
Macke, Brian, 147
Mackereth, Rob, 258
Mackey, David, 204
Macklin, Amy, 343
Maclaren, Fergus, 362
MacLauchlan, Donald, 300
Maclean, Anita, 411
Maclean, David, 616
Macoun, M., 243
Macpherson, Seonaid, 217
Macravey, Richard, 302
MacSwords, Leah, 170
Macurak, Marty, 136
Macy, Sydney, 307
Madden, Kevin, 75
Madden, Roy, 74
Madden, Wales, 223
Maddy, Deborah, 209
Maddy, James, 422
Madera, Ignacio, 223
Madewell, Terry, 66
Madigan, Patricia, 204
Madin, Katherine, 57
Madison, Elizabeth, 307
Madsen, Lisa, 570
Mady, James, 400
Magee, John, 532
Maggiore, Pete, 195
Maghini, Mark, 103
Magin, Debbie, 157
Magnussen, Stephen, 89
Magoulick, Dan, 137
Magrane, David, 589
Maguire, Meg, 487
Mahadevan, Kumar, 404
Mahan, Carolyn, 552
Mahayni, Riad, 584
Maher, Dana, 557
Maher, Ron, 315
Mahern, Jim, 163
Mahler, Roy, 272

Mahon, Jim, 345
Mahon, Paul, 212
Mahoney, Ronald, 611
Mahoney, S., 199
Mahood, Robert, 29
Maier, Andrew, 536
Main, Kevan, 404
Mainella, Fran, 120
Maitland, Julie, 195
Majette, Denise L., 4
Majkut, Stephen, 214
Major, Marla, 337
Majors, Doyle, 332
Majot, Juliette, 366
Makemson, Jeff, 546
Makkonen, Hannu, 598
Makoedov, Anatoly, 25
Makris, James, 19
Malcolmson, Patricia, 188
Maldonado, Walter, 528
Malecki, Richard, 196
Malhadas, Ziole, 601
Malick, Buck, 24
Malinowski, Karyn, 215
Mallon, Tim, 332
Mallory, Bill, 275
Mallory, Dave, 227
Malloy, Timon, 316
Malmberg, Paul, 235
Malmquist, A., 457
Malmsheimer, Mary, 446
Maloney, Carolyn, 10
Maloney, Patie, 327
Maloney, Rick, 205
Maloney, Tim, 352
Malouf, Robert, 58
Malsawma, Zuali, 471
Malsch, Martin, 26
Maltby, Edward, 368
Maltese, Marie, 539
Maluia, Philo, 135
Mamane, M., 369
Manes, Rob, 545
Manfredo, Michael, 578
Mangun, Jean, 596
Manier, Heather, 407
Manilla, Steve, 204
Mankin, Charles, 206
Mann, Debora, 401
Mann, James, 425
Mannausa, Leonard, 385
Manner, Mark, 323
Manning, Al, 374
Manning, Brent, 360
Manning, Harvey, 375
Manning, Jay, 533
Manning, Kristy, 293
Manning, Robert, 622
Mansfield, Anne, 625
Mansfield, Terry, 160
Mansius, Don, 175
Manspeaker, Barbara, 249
Manthey, Rebecca, 296
Mantler, Fran, 420
Mantoni, Lisa, 486
Mantras, Carlos, 475
Manz, Bill, 204
Manzi, Ron, 305
Manzullo, Donald A., 5
Maraldo, Dave, 207
Marcaccio, Melanie, 214
Marcantel, David, 282
Marchand, Betsy, 145
Marcum, Larry, 221
Marcus, Felicia, 524
Marcus, Nancy, 176
Marcy, Julie, 549
Mardon, Russell, 155
Marek, Kris, 207
Marenzana, Jim, 304
Marghescu, Tamas, 369
Margolin, Allan, 324
Margraf, F., 133

Margraf, Joe, 604
Mariaca, Sharon, 395
Marin, Jeremy, 327
Marina, Marty, 516
Marino, Michael, 247
Marinoske, Stan, 240
Markarian, Michael, 338
Markee, W., 209
Marker, Nancy, 150
Markey, Edward J., 7
Markley, Jeff, 457
Marks, Elliot, 438
Marks, Eugenia, 276
Marks,, Martha, 479
Marlett, Patricia, 410
Maroon, Joseph, 228, 295
Marquart, Susan Fox, 465
Marquis-Borng, Elaine, 84
Marrero, Brenda, 213
Mars, Virginia, 554
Marsden, Jennifer, 500
Marsden, Steve, 500
Marsh, Kenneth, 445
Marsh, Langdon, 208
Marsh, Paul, 314
Marsh, Scott, 181
Marshall, Anne, 531
Marshall, David, 200
Marshall, Eve, 474
Marshall, Gary, 551
Marshall, Gregory, 192
Marshall, Jim, 4
Marshall, John, 220
Marshall, Michael, 225
Marshall, Patricia, 335
Marshall, S., 610
Marshall, Sue, 488
Marsollier, Elizabeth, 27
Marston, Maggie, 42
Martel, Andre, 214
Martel, Gary, 230, 231
Martens, Christopher, 617
Martens, Tom, 363
Marti, Monte, 533
Martian, Thomas, 26
Martin, Angelia, 65
Martin, Bob, 448
Martin, Chester, 421
Martin, Chip, 475
Martin, Donald, 550
Martin, Gale, 401
Martin, Jack, 76
Martin, Jerry, 143
Martin, Jim, 608
Martin, John, 20, 72
Martin, Keith, 458
Martin, Ken, 237
Martin, Ray, 466
Martin, Robert, 389
Martin, Sandra, 611
Martin, Stephanie, 232, 531
Martin, Stephen, 123
Martin, Thomas, 186, 317
Martin, Vance, 540
Martin, William, 580
Martin-MCormic, Linda, 268
Martineau, Daniel, 286
Martinez, Aida, 151
Martinez, Eluid, 89
Martinez, Frank, 271
Martinez, Mel, 77
Martinez, Neftali, 294
Martinez, Ricardo, 129
Martinez, Robert, 412
Martinez, Toby, 194
Martinez, Wilda, 48
Martinez-Medina, Aida, 213
Martini-Lamb, Jessica, 552
Martinko, Edward, 167, 612
Martinson, Richard, 346
Marvel, Jon, 538
Marventano, Dave, 21
Marvinney, Robert, 174

Marxer, Dale, 403
Masaki, Carl, 159
Mashuda, Steve, 320
Masica, Sue, 120
Mason, Chris, 452
Mason, Garland, 42
Mason, Lawrence, 308
Mason, Robert, 599
Mason, Timothy, 311
Masonis, Rob, 265
Massawe, V., 525
Massey, William, 75
Massman, Carole, 187
Masso, Tom, 182
Massucci, Stefanie, 58
Massue, Rogasian, 608
Mast, Gary, 407
Masters, A., 199
Masters, Ronald, 515
Masters, Sandy, 421, 569
Mastrup, Sonke, 142
Mata, Eric, 22
Matamorros, Vanessa, 22
Matera, Jaime, 300
Mather, Annie, 269
Mather, Martha, 178, 614
Mather, Richard, 211
Mather, Sandra, 418
Matherne, Charles, 172
Matheson, Jim, 14
Mathews, Bob, 167
Mathews, Kate, 311
Mathis, Maxine, 408
Mathis, Suzanne, 423
Matlack, Glenn, 621
Matlock, Robert, 580
Matowanyika, Joseph, 562
Matsui, Connie, 343
Matsui, Robert T., 1
Matsuura, Renee, 225
Matt, Fred, 304
Mattes, Lisa, 481
Mattfeld, George, 551
Matthews, Amy, 274
Matthews, Dexter, 200
Matthews, Doug, 203
Matthews, George, 544
Matthews, Michael, 551
Matthews, Robert, 450
Matthews, Robin, 627
Matthews, Scott, 143
Mattice, Jack, 58
Mattison, Clyde, 414
Mattison, Jim, 140
Mattson, Leslie, 379
Matyas, Jaime, 427
Matz, Mike, 285
Mauermann, Sue, 233
Maughan, Ralph, 354
Maulson, Tom, 20
Maurer, Rick, 171
Maurer, Stephen, 570
Maurier, Joe, 147
Mauro, Andrew, 484
Mauro, Flo, 263
Mauro, Florence, 263, 470
Mawyer, Bobby, 230
Maxfield, Lonnie, 515
Maxino, Mikhail, 595
Maxwell, Colin, 287
May, Carol, 409
May, Dale, 149
May, Elizabeth, 500
May, James, 68
May, Jeanine, 47
May, John, 236
Mayayi, Filos, 608
Maycroft, Kathleen, 105
Mayer, Mike, 320, 358
Mayer, Patrick, 548
Mayeux, L., 316
Mayeux, L. J., 316
Mayfield, Paul, 272

Maynard, Charles, 153
Maynes, Frank, 131
Maynes, Gretchen, 465
Mayo, R., 453
Maze, Dick, 136
Mazet, Jonna, 606
Mazik, Patricia, 235
Mazmanian, Daniel, 283, 614
Mazza, David, 467
McAfee, Robert, 272
McAllister, Dave, 208
McAllister, Ed, 506
McAninch, Jay, 270
McArthur, Johnny, 401
McAteer, J., 77
McBride, Don, 155
McBride, Gregory, 129
McBride, Jim, 500
McBride, Patrick, 282
Mcburney, Mary, 524
McCabe, Dick, 452
McCabe, Janet, 163
McCabe, John, 260
McCabe, Richard, 545
McCaffrey, James, 494
McCain, John, 1
McCain, John, 28
McCall, Jerry, 52
McCallie, Grady, 450
McCance, Elizabeth, 296
McCarren, David, 54
McCarron, Mary, 457
McCarter, Katherine, 321
McCarthy, Ann, 544
McCarthy, Bea, 187
McCarthy, Carolyn, 9
McCarthy, John, 354
McCarthy, Karen, 8
McCarthy, Laura, 335
McCarthy, Patricia, 342
McCarthy, Tom, 366
McCarty, Colleen, 327
McCarty, Gene, 223
McCarty, Jeanne, 380
McCawley, Paul, 611
McClain, Russ, 274
McClaren, Mitchel, 605
McClatchy, Ken, 521
McClaugherty, Charles, 589
McClaugherty, Chuck, 326
McClellan, Robin, 345
McClelland, Steven, 236
McClelland, William, 200
McCloy, Tom, 192
McClung, Don, 378
McClure, Beth, 218
McCollum, Betty, 8
McCollum, Jeff, 245
McCollum, Jerry, 342
McComb, William, 614
McConkey, Pam, 235
McConnaughay, Kelly, 575
McConnell, Jennifer, 420
McConnell, Mary, 435
McConnell, Mitch, 6
McCormick, Robert, 55
McCormick, Steve, 433
McCotter, Thaddeus G., 7
McCoy, Casey, 168
McCracken, Carrie, 477
McCracken, Helen, 364
McCracken, James, 73
McCrae, John, 524
McCray, Kevin, 421
McCrea, Dave, 219
McCrery, Jim, 6
McCue, Cathryn, 509
McCuean, Tavia, 435
McCullough, Brian, 315
McCullough, Fred, 281
McCullough, Karen, 271
McCully, Patrick, 366
McCurdy, Kevin, 73

STAFF NAME INDEX – M

McCutcheon, Gloria, 237
McDaniel, Perry, 235
McDermid, Mark, 238
McDermott, James, 26
McDermott, Jim, 15, 62
McDiarmid, Emly, 628
McDonald, David, 443, 623
McDonald, John, 550
McDonald, Mary, 264
McDonald, Norris, 243, 291
McDonald, Norris, 326
McDonnell, Dierdre, 319
McDougall, Daniel, 27
McDowell, Diana, 337
McDowell, Judith, 57
McDowell, Michael, 465
McDowell, Robert, 192
McDowell, William, 617
McElroy, Robert, 410
McElroy, William, 535
McElwaine, Andrew, 466
McEuen, Arohie, 312
McEvoy, Kathleen, 450
McEvoy, Thom, 622
McFadden, Jack, 207
McFall, Don, 163
McFarlane, Barrington, 541
McFarlane, Betsy, 474
Mcfate, R., 467
McGarland, Albert, 130
McGarth, David, 476
McGarvey, Jason, 376
McGaughey, James, 580
McGeorge, Leslie, 191
Mcghee, Steve, 475
McGill, Bill, 165
McGill, William, 165
McGinity, Jim, 555
McGinn, Debbie, 324
McGinty, Kathleen, 211
McGlashan, Charles, 394
Mcglauflin, Kathy, 260, 310
McGlenn, Ronni, 378
Mcgonigle, James, 512
McGorty, Kevin, 515
Mcgovern, Donald, 214
McGovern, James P., 7
McGovern, Joe, 373
McGovern, Michael, 47
McGowan, R., 218
McGrane, Pat, 47
McGrath, Dennis, 434
Mcgrath, M., 199
McGraw, Jack, 19
McGreal, Shirley, 365
McGregor, Bonnie, 127
McGregor, Emma, 495
McGregor, Pat, 533
McGrew, Cheryl, 434
McGruther, Faith, 430
Mcguire, A., 133
McGuire, Christina, 340
Mcguire, Robert, 73
McGuire, Thomas F., 427
McGuire, Walter, 327
Mcgurrin, Joseph, 520
McHugh, John, 10, 187
McHugh, Martin, 192
McIlnay, Dave, 83
McInnis, Martha, 328
McInnis, Scott, 3
McInnis-Leek, Nancy, 203
McIntosh, Alan, 622
McIntosh, Henry, 244
McIntosh, Patricia, 341
McIntosh, Shane, 382
McIntosh, Winsome, 312, 387
McIntyre, A.J., 267
McIntyre, Gary, 431
McIntyre, Jim, 240
McIntyre, Mike, 10
McIntyre, Robert, 524
McIsaac, Donald, 463

McKalip, Katie, 462
McKay, Jennifer, 311
McKay, Tim, 452
McKeag, Michael, 430
McKeating, Gerald, 16
McKee, Des, 207
McKee, Larry, 206
McKenna, Mike, 202
McKenzie, Donald, 545
McKenzie, Karen, 180
McKenzie, Shawn, 584
McKeon, Howard Buck, 2
McKeon, John, 196
McKeown, W., 543
McKim, Rob, 436
McKim, Robert, 435
McKinley, Craig, 206, 592
McKinley, William, 527
McKinney, David, 221
McKinney, Dennis, 474
McKinney, Kim, 539
McKinney, Larry, 223
Mckinnon, Joe, 396
McKnelly, Phil, 200, 409
McKnight, Betty, 263
McKnight, Keith, 316
McKown, Bette, 545
McLandress, Robert, 283
McLane, Adam, 403
McLaren, Brian, 396
McLaughlan, Betty, 412
McLaughlin, Sherry Lynn, 285
McLaughlin, Wayne, 235
McLavey, Robert, 146
McLead, Mary, 78
McLean, Bob, 165
McLean, Brian, 18
McLean, J., 606
McLean, Wallace, 227
McLellan, Anne, 17
McLellan, Jim, 401
Mclemore, Julia, 183
Mclenaghan, Theresa, 286
McLennan, Alan, 213
McLennan, Dan, 252
McLeod, David, 200
McLeod, Richard, 190
McLeod, Robert, 203
McLoskey, Jean, 17
McMahon, Edward, 307
McMahon, John, 152
McManis, Kenneth, 624
McManus, Brian, 188
McManus, Maureen, 273
McMurray, Dennis, 162
McNagny, Carolyn, 242
McNamara, Carole, 409
McNamara, Donna, 337
McNamara, Timothy, 72
McNaught, Scott, 576
McNaughton, Steve, 377
McNeel, Joseph, 235, 626
McNeely, Jeffrey, 368
McNeill, Pete, 384
McNelly, Jan, 387
McNichol, Laura, 407
McNicholl, Martin, 281
McNitt, Brian, 246
McNulty, Michael R., 10
McNulty, Tim, 459
McNulty-Huffman, Dan, 547
McNussen, John, 472
McNutt, Lester, 466
McOlvanine, Richard, 357
McPherson, Alexandra, 345
McPherson, Ronald, 52
McQuaid, Susan, 564
McQueen, Mike, 307
McQuilkin, Geoffrey, 402
McQuinn, Mary, 47
McShane, Lisa, 286, 454
McSharry, Joe, 431
McSweeney, Kevin, 623

Mctavish, Blair, 175
McTeer, William, 218
McVay, Laura, 373
McWilliams, Sue, 351
Mead, Robert, 232
Meadows, B., 287
Meadows, Chuck, 320
Meadows, Jim, 183
Meadows, Vicker, 77
Meadows, William, 541
Mecom, Doug, 134
Medd, Ken, 545
Medwid, Walter, 372
Meehan, Marty, 7
Meehan, Pat, 141
Meehan, Rosa, 543
Meek, Kendrick B., 4
Meek, Lance, 458
Meek, Royce, 458
Meeks, Gregory W., 10
Meffe, Gary, 502
Megorden, Karen, 282
Mehan, Tracy, 130
Mehl, Molly, 108
Meiburg, Stanley, 19
Meier, David, 238
Meier, Marvin, 557
Meiklejohn, Douglas, 446
Melcher, Duane, 464
Melcher, Steve, 263
Meldrum, John, 259
Meldrum, Vince, 317
Melewski, Bernard, 242
Melius, Thomas, 90
Melli, Frank, 347
Mellon, Dianne, 277
Mellon, Knox, 152
Mellon, S., 483
Melton, Michael, 207
Mendelson, Frank, 593
Mendenhall, Vivian, 464
Mendes, Valerie, 507
Mendez, Kenneth, 520
Menendez, Robert, 9
Mengak, Kathy, 581
Mengel, David, 585
Mensinger, Joanne, 374
Menzel, Bruce, 33, 109
Menzer, James, 458
Meral, Gerald, 469
Mercer, Linda, 175
Merchant, Carolyn, 265
Merchant, Henry, 582
Merchant, James, 611
Meredith, William, 150
Merget, Astrid, 584
Merker, Bjorn, 301
Merner, Kathy, 354
Merrell, William, 348
Merriam, Anne, 396
Merriam, Chip, 219
Merriam, Gene, 182
Merrill, Sam, 490
Merriman, Tim, 407
Merritt, Clifton, 268
Merritt, Peter, 332
Merritt, Regna, 460
Mersky, Ronald, 627
Meserve, Richard, 26
Meshach, Jeffery, 558
Mess, Walter, 202
Messenger, Deborah, 325
Messer, Susan, 472
Messerle, Kerry, 212
Messick, Ann, 532
Messics, Dave, 482
Messinger, Luke, 311
Messman, Hubert, 176
Metcalf, Mary, 489
Metcalfe, Ed, 524
Metheney, Twila, 236
Methier, Ron, 156
Method, Timothy, 163

Mettenbrink, Roger, 377
Metter, Jeff, 395
Metty, Julie, 487
Metz, Lorraine, 175
Metz, Mark, 558
Metz, Tim, 268
Meulengracht, Bob, 406
Meyer, Dan, 474
Meyer, George, 238
Meyer, Gerald, 75
Meyer, Gordy, 399
Meyer, Jeff, 260
Meyer, Joseph, 623
Meyer, L., 586
Meyer, Robert, 244
Meyer, Steven, 234
Meyer, Susan, 528
Meyer, Therese, 528
Meyers, Carmen, 251
Meyers, Lee, 155
Meyers, Roger, 73
Meyers, Tom, 472
Meysenburg, Arnold, 307
Mezainis, Valdis, 34
Mfugale, Robert, 599
Mica, John, 3
Michael, Ed, 345
Michael, Jerry, 446
Michaels, Arthur, 212
Michaels, Keith, 137
Michaud, Michael H., 6
Michaud, Nathan, 375
Michel, Mark, 270
Micheli, Ron, 239
Micka, Richard, 385
Middaugh, Daniel, 134
Middleberg, Maurice, 322
Middleton, Donnie, 506
Middleton, Frederick, 509
Miecoch, Colleen, 182
Mielke, Paula, 452
Mies, Rob, 461
Miget, Russell, 59
Mighetto, Lisa, 265
Miglarese, John, 218
Mihalo, Mark, 486
Mihlbachler, Brian, 62
Mijares, Marie, 141
Mikesell, John, 584
Mikics, Denise, 191
Miklaski, Sheri, 484
Mikol, Gerald, 197
Mikota, Mike, 187
Mikula, Charles, 63
Mikulski, Barbara A., 6
Mila, Bogdan, 358
Milburn, Cindy, 361
Milburn, Philip, 519
Miles, Bob, 136
Miles, Bob, 360
Miles, Denny, 461
Miles, Susan, 404
Milhoan, James, 26
Milius, Pauline, 77
Millard, Ken, 339
Millenbah, Kelly, 549
Millender-McDonald, Juanita, 2
Miller, Allan, 576
Miller, Amy, 376
Miller, Bartshe, 403
Miller, Benjamin, 552
Miller, Beth, 555
Miller, Brad, 11
Miller, Brian, 56, 213
Miller, Candice, 7
Miller, Chris, 531
Miller, Christopher, 469
Miller, Craig, 312
Miller, Darren, 549
Miller, David, 413
Miller, Deborah, 326
Miller, Dorothy, 299
Miller, Erica, 430

STAFF NAME INDEX – M

Miller, G. William, 348
Miller, Gary G., 2
Miller, George, 2
Miller, Glen, 117
Miller, Glenn, 214, 616
Miller, Gordon, 16
Miller, Henry, 75
Miller, Hubert, 26
Miller, Jack, 352
Miller, Jacquelin, 224
Miller, Jane, 356
Miller, Jeff, 3, 290
Miller, Jennifer, 453
Miller, Jerry, 163
Miller, John, 73, 404
Miller, Julie, 290
Miller, Karin, 395
Miller, Marc, 472
Miller, Marion, 606
Miller, Marvin, 302
Miller, Mike, 167
Miller, Randall, 184
Miller, Robert, 367
Miller, Roy, 150
Miller, Sarah, 286
Miller, Stephan, 422
Miller, Stephen, 375
Miller, Sterling, 359, 428
Miller, Steve, 25
Miller, Steven, 179, 238
Miller, Todd, 300, 450
Miller, Velma, 382
Miller, Watkins, 616
Miller, Zell B., 4
Millhon, Jerry, 336
Milling, Marcus, 261
Mills, Ann, 265
Mills, Bob, 332
Mills, Darrel, 373
Mills, Edward, 579
Mills, Jennifer, 307
Mills, Marquesa, 503
Mills, W., 593
Mills, Wayne, 295
Millsap, Brian, 90
Milmoe, Dolores, 306
Milne, David, 236
Milner, Kelsey, 615
Milton, John, 483
Mims, Robert, 316
Minaeva, Tatiana, 365
Minaya, Theresa, 374
Miner, Charles, 191
Miner, Edna, 379
Miner, Greg, 509
Miner, Kirk, 379
Miner, Tom, 305
Mineta, Norm, 128
Minja, Z. Kristos, 131
Minton, Jonas, 143
Minton, R. Vernon, 132
Mioff, Stephanie, 466
Miraglia, Frank, 26
Miranda, L., 183
Mirande, Claire, 362
Mirelson, Robert, 67
Mirzakhalili, Ali, 150
Mishrigi, Fadia, 207
Misseldine, Carol, 397
Mister, Hagner, 177
Mitchell, Anne, 287
Mitchell, Anne, 365
Mitchell, Becky, 524
Mitchell, Brad, 178
Mitchell, Brent, 275
Mitchell, Charles, 424
Mitchell, Charles, 515
Mitchell, Frank, 617
Mitchell, John, 414
Mitchell, Julie, 338
Mitchell, Larry, 33, 387
Mitchell, Leanne, 560
Mitchell, Michael, 132

Mitchell, Nora, 121
Mitchell, Robert, 345
Mitchell, Stacy, 47
Mitchelll, Kathy, 626
Mitchelson, William, 417
Mitsos, Mary, 420
Mitten, Sue, 216
Mittermeier, Russell, 307
Mitton, Linda, 275
Mitton-Walker, Cynthia, 259
Mmari, D., 243
Moats, L., 315
Mochnacz, Neil, 549
Mock, George, 274
Mode, Richard, 451
Model, Robert, 279
Modisette, Christopher, 509
Moe, Richard, 425
Moehl, Thomas, 356
Moehle, Carm, 521
Moehle, Mark, 458
Moen, Sharon, 57
Moffatt, Tom, 511
Moffitt, Christine, 611
Moffitt, Donna, 200
Mohiuddin, Khaza, 568
Mokarebin, Mesbahul, 568
Moler, Paul, 547
Moles, Kendall, 546
Molina, Suki, 354
Molines, Karyn, 395
Moll, Gary, 260
Moll, Russell, 54
Mollo, Marcello, 319
Mollohan, Alan B., 15
Moltzen, Roberta, 43
Monahan, Edward, 54
Moncrief, Aliki, 320
Moncur, James, 224, 610
Money, Charles, 246
Monger, Doug, 187
Moniz, Gary, 159
Monk, Jan, 273
Monostory, Les, 377
Monson, John, 444
Montague, Chris, 440
Montague, Christopher, 403
Montague, Deaderick, 509
Montalbano, Frank, 154
Montgomery, Edward, 77
Montgomery, Joe, 341
Montgomery, Steve, 382
Montgomery, Steven, 306
Montoya, David, 89
Montoya, Eddie, 302
Monz, Chris, 598
Mood, Doug, 187
Moody, Brandon, 341
Moody, Howard, 424
Moody, J., 204
Moody, Michael, 173
Moon, Melissa, 473
Moon, Thomas, 576
Mooney, Marianne, 532
Moore, Adam, 305
Moore, Alan, 522
Moore, Andrea, 162
Moore, Andrew, 408
Moore, Bob, 156
Moore, Brad, 182
Moore, D. Martin, 449
Moore, David, 220
Moore, Dennis, 6
Moore, Gary, 212
Moore, Jennifer, 28
Moore, Jim, 133
Moore, Joan, 399
Moore, John, 519
Moore, Julia, 24
Moore, Mike, 130
Moore, Paul, 512
Moore, Portia, 339
Moore, Randy, 407

Moore, Richard, 411
Moore, Robert, 472
Moore, Ronald, 73
Moore, Steve, 218
Moore, Virgil, 160
Moore, Wendy, 200
Mooring, Jean, 355
Mooring, Paul, 355
Moorman, Chris, 200, 551
Moorman, Randall, 319
Moos, Kenton, 106
Mootnick, Alan, 361
Moquin, Gabriel, 149
Moran, James P., 14
Moran, Jerry, 6
Moran, Katy, 478
Moran, Leticia, 76
Moran, Marc, 197
Morasch, A., 247
Morast, Daniel, 371
Moravcik, Philip, 610
Morden, Clifford, 349
Mordica, James, 184
Morehouse, Doug, 343
Morehouse, W., 412
Moreland, Debbie, 272
Moresi, Robert, 267
Moretti, Miles, 226
Morey, Sandra, 142
Morgan, Don, 336
Morgan, Donald, 470
Morgan, Ellen, 184
Morgan, Max, 226
Morgan, Robert, 226
Morgan, Robin, 150
Morgenweck, Ralph, 112
Morgereth, Edward, 549
Morigeau, Sandra, 304
Morijah, Heather, 497
Moring, John, 174
Morini, Lucy, 530
Moriwake, Isaac, 319
Morrell, Shelly, 482
Morrill, Valerie, 72
Morrill, William, 277
Morris, Bill, 26
Morris, Don, 64
Morris, Ed, 137
Morris, Frederick, 308
Morris, James, 259
Morris, Jan, 364
Morris, John, 200
Morris, Lawrence, 275
Morris, Lisa, 204
Morris, Sara, 555
Morris, Sherri, 575
Morrison, Bart, 475
Morrison, David, 26
Morrison, James, 281
Morrison, Jill, 472
Morrison, Merrie, 249
Morrison, Nadine, 513
Morrison, Ron, 203
Morrison, William, 145
Morrissey, Bill, 182
Morrissey, Tom, 149
Morrow, Dave, 225
Morrow, Marilyn, 583
Morrow, Patrick, 72
Morry, Chris, 368
Morse, Charlie, 366
Morse, Dana, 56
Morse, Herbert, 511
Morse, Steve, 182
Morse, Susan, 382
Morton, David, 582
Morton, Laura, 47
Morton, Robert, 548
Morton, Wayne, 402
Moscariello, Orysia, 141
Moser, Don, 501
Moser, Kathy, 435
Moser, Michael, 167

Moses, John, 424
Mosher, Jim, 376
Mosher, Katie, 58
Mosher, Peter, 174
Moshkalo, Vladimir, 370
Moskowitz, Brad, 585
Moss, Bill, 400
Moss, Heather, 326
Moss, Julie, 164
Mossier, Jere, 568
Motoyoshi, Chris, 520
Mott, Bill, 455
Mott, Paul, 342
Mouchet, Rhett, 301
Moulton, Kirk, 349
Moulton, Norm, 392
Moulton-Patterson, Linda, 144
Mount, Pam, 444
Mount, Paul, 145
Mountain, Bruce, 373
Mouradjian, Larry, 214
Mouton, Edmond, 548
Mowry, Kenneth, 210
Moy, Tracy, 138
Moyer, Bruce, 210
Moyer, Edwin, 154
Moyer, Paula, 515
Moyer, Steven, 520
Moyer, William, 151
Moyer-Angus, Maria, 317
Moyo, Sam, 562
Mozer, David, 361
Mozley, Samuel, 590
Mroz, Glenn, 588
Mrutu, Ernest, 599
Mtelits, Michael, 78
Muckenfuss, Ed, 155
Muddle, Krista, 274
Mueldener, Karl, 167
Mueller, Erich, 404
Mueller, Peter, 68
Mueller, Stephanie, 530
Mueller, Terry, 337
Muessig, Karl, 192
Muhweezi, Alex, 370
Muise, Leo, 203
Mulala, Sally, 371
Muldoon, Paul, 286
Mulford, Jon, 540
Mulhern, Joan, 319
Mulkey, Marcia, 130
Mull, David, 274
Mullane, Neil, 208
Mullen, P., 191
Muller, Gretchen, 429
Muller, Lisa, 553
Mullican, Bill, 223
Mullikin, Linda, 472
Mullins, Gary, 205, 592
Mullins, Tom, 601
Mullins, William, 537
Mulvihill, John, 481
Mumma, Tracy, 417
Mumme, Ronald, 546
Mundheim, Marie, 47
Mungari, Robert, 197
Munoz, Jean, 284
Munoz, Miguel, 213
Munson, Fred, 454
Munson, Mary, 423
Murack, Ron, 304
Muraro, Joan, 162
Murdoch, Tom, 243
Murkowski, Frank, 29
Murkowski, Lisa, 1
Murphey, Duane, 507
Murphree, Rick, 516
Murphy, Bob, 517
Murphy, Brian, 476
Murphy, Dave, 550
Murphy, Hoy, 236
Murphy, James, 73
Murphy, John, Jr., 340

STAFF NAME INDEX – O

Murphy, Patricia, 137
Murphy, Robert, 203
Murphy, Thomas, 579
Murphy, Timothy F., 12
Murray, A., 191
Murray, Alan, 155
Murray, Bennie, 72
Murray, Brian, 222
Murray, Bruce, 76
Murray, Connie, 458
Murray, Greg, 465
Murray, John, 539
Murray, Joyce, 139, 140
Murray, Patty, 14
Murrell, Zack, 451, 509
Murriner, Edward, 558
Murtha, John P., 12
Murzin, Richard, 199
Muschaweck, Julius, 379
Musgrave, Marilyn, 3
Musgrave, Ruth, 294
Musil, Robert, 468
Musser, Philip, 77
Musso, Jim, 591
Mustico, Lisa, 350
Musumeci, Jo Ann, 182
Muszynski, William, 18
Mutel, Connie, 373
Mutsigwa, J., 562
Myers, Eric, 246
Myers, Gary, 221
Myers, Gordon, 201
Myers, Jan, 356
Myers, Katie, 506
Myers, Larry, 187
Myers, Mark, 134
Myers, Marvin, 73
Myers-Jones, Holly, 574
Myrick, Paul, 184
Myrick, Sue, 10
Myron, Jim, 461

N

Nabors, Johnsie, 74
Nachtigall, Paul, 503
Nadarajah, Ramani, 286
Nadel, Steve, 251
Nadler, Jerrold, 10
Naftzger, Roy, 364
Nagel, Carlos, 367
Nagy, Lewis, 198
Nakazawa, Anthony, 149
Nalbone, Jennifer, 345
Nance, Jim, 221
Nance, Larry, 155
Nance, Toni, 218
Nania, Jeff, 556
Nanney, Eddie, 221
Nannini, Edward, 336
Napolitano, Grace F., 2
Napton, Luanne, 507
Narang, Karl, 48
Nardozzi, Charlie, 420
Nash, Arthur, 180
Nash, Claude, 184
Nash, Daryl, 581
Nason, Rochelle, 388
Nassar, Ron, 391
Nates, Larry, 505
Naughton, Nell, 269
Navarro-Monzo, Julio, 519
Naydol, Allan, 66
Naze, Kevin, 539
Ndinga, Assitou, 369
Neal, Benjamin, 375
Neal, Michael, 367
Neal, Richard E., 7
Neale, David, 269
Nedd, Mike, 84
Neel, Leah Doney, 304
Neel, Linda, 407
Neelis, Duane, 273
Neely, Robert, 581

Neenan, Tom, 373
Nehrig, R., 210
Neighbor, Bruce, 318
Neil, Helen, 616
Neill, Kim, 491
Nelson, Ben, 8
Nelson, Bill, 3
Nelson, Courtland, 225
Nelson, D., 468
Nelson, Dave, 441
Nelson, Eric, 149
Nelson, Garland, 157
Nelson, Gaylord, 541
Nelson, Harvey, 523
Nelson, James, 549
Nelson, Jim, 601
Nelson, John, 139, 191
Nelson, Kirk, 189
Nelson, Larry, 146
Nelson, Leo, 472
Nelson, Michael J., 177
Nelson, Mike, 276
Nelson, Patt, 459
Nelson, Paul, 289
Nelson, Ryan, 63
Nemeth, Richard, 621
Nerrie, Brian, 228
Nesbitt, William, 336
Nesbitt, Wm., 360
Nesmith, Martin, 300
Nessel, Laurie, 414
Nestor, Robert, 212
Nethercutt, George R., Jr., 15
Neubacher, Don, 125
Neuhauser, Hans, 342
Neustadt, Debbie, 373
Nevendorf, Klaus, 209
Neves, Richard, 625
Nevins, Christopher, 412
New Breast, Ira, 430
Newbold, John, 450
Newbold, Michael, 305
Newbold, Sharon, 450
Newcomb, Leonard, 593
Newell, Mike, 475
Newhouse, Bruce, 430
Newland, Leo, 600
Newman, Arnold, 367
Newman, Robert, 618
Newport, Bruce, 516
Newton, Carlton, 622
Newton, Eileen, 566
Newton, Steve, 334
Ney, Bob, 11
Ng'itu, Jerome, 599
Niblett, Gregory, 241
Nicholas, Mary, 145
Nicholas, Nick, 324
Nicholas, Wendy, 425
Nichols, Allison, 571
Nichols, Henry, 174
Nichols, James, 129
Nichols, Lacy, 150
Nichols, Leonard, 561
Nichols, Marvin, 99
Nicholson, Al, 160
Nicholson, Allen, 626
Nicholson, Beth, 486
Nicholson, Richard, 249
Nickas, George, 541
Nickens, Eddie, 451
Nickerson, Diane, 430
Nickerson, Norma, 615
Nickles, Don, 11
Nickum, David, 520, 521
Nicodemus, Terri, 250
Nicolescu, Jerry, 161
Nicoll, Jill, 422
Niederer, Thomas, 445
Nielsen, Craig, 177
Nieman, Doug, 258
Niering, William, 502
Nieswiadomy, Mike, 618

Nieuwenhuis, Richard, 444
Nightingale, Stuart, 76
Nikides, Harry, 164
Niland, Gary, 211
Niles, Larry, 192
Nimry, Basil, 166
Nishi, Yuji, 297
Nishida, Jane, 177
Nishioka, Linnel, 159
Nix, Shauni, 457
Nixon, Annie, 318
Nixon, Scott, 620
Noble, Lisa, 467
Nock, Laurie, 17
Noem, Rollie, 219
Nolan, Elizabeth, 560
Nolan, Pat, 340
Nolin, Michael, 190
Nolte, George, 313
Nolte, Richard, 260
Nomsen, David, 25, 468
Noonan, Patrick, 307
Norbriga, David, 507
Nordgren, John, 393
Nordlie, Frank, 331
Nordstrom, Carl, 192
Norgarrd, Richard, 366
Norland, Eric, 33
Norman, Charles, 220
Norman, Gayle, 47
Norman, Julie, 500
Norman, Philip, 549
Normoyle, Debra, 27
Norris, Barry, 210
Norris, Sharon, 47
Norry, Patricia, 26
Norse, Elliott, 394
North, Doug, 481
North, Elizabeth, 423
North, Gary, 380
Northcutt, Ben, 363
Northrup, Molly, 437
Northup, Anne M., 6
Northup, Jim, 336
Norton, James, 522
Norton, Jane, 147
Norton, Jeanne, 377
Norton, W., 540
Nortrup, Megan, 273
Norwood, Charles, 4
Novosat-Gradert, Lisa, 456
Novotny, Lawrence, 507
Nowak, Mariette, 540
Nowak, Matt, 73
Nowicki, Brian, 290
Nuechterlein, Gary, 590
Nunes, Devin, 2
Nunes, Toni, 277
Nunnari, Barbara, 340
Nuquist, Andrew, 347
Nussle, Jim, 5
Nussman, Michael, 266
Nussman, Mike, 267
Nuszbaum, Joyce, 348
Nutt, Jennifer, 321
Nuzzo, Jacques, 355
Nvitez, Norma, 560
Nyahay, Richard, 197
Nystrom, Erik, 280

O

O'Brian, Patrick, 489
O'Brien, Donal, 149, 409
O'Brien, Donald, 275
O'Brien, Philip, 190
O'Brien, Tim, 261
O'Clair, Terry, 201
O'Connell, James, 57
O'Conner, Kevin, 552
O'Connor, Carl, 238
O'Connor, David, 129
O'Connor, Joe, 175
O'Connor, Judy, 285

O'Connor, Matthew, 468
O'Connor, Roy, 403
O'Connor, Tony, 27
O'Day, Jodi, 307
O'Dell, John, 138
O'Donnell, Cathy, 413
O'Donnell, Eleanor, 442
O'Donnell, Gary, 64
O'Donnell, Patty, 345
O'Gara, Anita, 373
O'Gorman, Denis, 140
O'Grady, Richard, 261
O'Hara, James, 76
O'Neil, William, 364
O'Neill, James, 150
O'Neill, Mary, 182
O'Neill, Melissa, 60
O'Neill, Michael, 33
O'Neill, Richard, 75
O'Neill, Suzanne, 302
O'Neill, Tracy, 516
O'Regan, Fred, 363
O'Rourke, Timothy, 71
O'Shea, John, 139
O'Sullivan, Patrick, 582
O'Toole, Anne, 27
Oakes, Cheryl, 334
Oakes, David, 601
Oakes, Joy, 494
Oakleaf, Barbara, 561
Oakley, Dan, 200
Oates, William, 222
Obara, Linda, 449
Oberstar, James L., 8
Obey, David R., 15
Obrein, Eric, 294
Ochs, Joan, 331
Ockenfels, Alfred, 511
Odato, Gene, 213
Odell, Daniel, 503
Odom, Bob, 172
Oelschlaeger, Max, 291
Offield, Paxson, 278, 468
Offutt, Susan, 33
Ofterdahl, Lenora, 17
Oge, Margo, 18
Ogilvie, Ken, 470
Ogle, Charlie, 497
Ogle, Norma, 346
Oglesby, Donna, 106
Oglesby, Gene, 442
Oglesby, Rob, 143
Ogunleye, Bisi, 558
Ohmstede, Will, 300
Okoh, Joseph, 613
Olah, Otto, 203
Oldham, Mike, 96
Olin, Paul, 54
Olinde, Mike, 548
Oliphant, Bill, 346
Oliva, Frank, 70
Oliveira, Rafael, 518
Oliver, John, 52
Oliver, John, 211
Oliver, Terry, 364
Olivier, Alain, 602
Olivier, W., 508
Olmstead, Francis, 280
Olmstead, William, 26
Olmsted, Edwin, 301
Olsen, Erik, 241
Olsen, George, 403
Olson, Christyann, 247
Olson, Dan, 239
Olson, Glenn, 409
Olson, Howard, 465
Olson, Jeff, 540
Olson, Jeffrey, 465
Olson, Judith, 24
Olson, Kim, 221
Olson, Leonard, 223
Olson, Norval, 481
Olson, Rebecca, 431

Olson, Robert, 326
Olson, Roger, 177
Olson, W., 336
Oltmann, Julie, 142
Olver, John W., 7
Oman, Maryellen, 490
Omans, Jim, 74
Onate, Pilar, 152
Ontiveros, Lucy, 79
Opliger, Robert, 429
Oppenlander, John, 42
Oppert, Brenda, 380
Oram, John, 301
Orasin, Charles, 311
Orbach, Michael, 580
Oren, Carrie, 306
Orenstein, Ronald, 371
Organ, John, 546
Orlick, Steve, 595
Orr, David, 390, 591
Orr, Gary, 304
Orr, Patricia, 130
Orsello, Bill, 404
Ort, Jon, 200
Orth, Donald, 625
Orthmeyer, Dennis, 283
Ortiz, Mary, 372
Ortiz, Solomon P., 14
Orvillian, Larae, 558
Osborn, Nic, 277
Osborne, Cindy, 138
Osborne, Na`taki, 343
Osborne, Patrick, 361
Osborne, Tom, 8
Osburn, Hal, 223
Osburn, Jane, 395
Ose, Doug, 1
Oskay, Clare, 356
Osleeb, Jeffery, 576
Ostby, Frederick, 52
Oster, Walter, 287
Osterby, Bruce, 623
Ostermann, Thomas, 240
Ostervich, Joseph, 279
Ostfeld, Richard, 358
Oswald, Brian, 598
Oswald, Fatima, 405
Oswald, Nancy, 513
Otey, Kirk, 520
Othberg, Kurt, 161
Otis, David, 127
Ott, Marty, 126
Ott, Rae Evening Earth, 449
Otter, C.L. Butch, 5
Otter, Richard, 487
Ottinger, Mary, 503
Ottinger, Richard, 324
Otto, Betsy, 265
Otuski, E., 453
Ouchley, Keith, 436
Outlaw, Brenda, 450
Overcash, Jesse, 553
Owen, Dana, 508
Owen, Jon, 534
Owen, Luther, 73
Owen, Sandy, 437
Owen, T., 578
Owens, Cameron, 385
Owens, Jim, 282
Owens, Kagan, 277
Owens, Major R., 10
Owens, Margie, 609
Owens, Steve, 169
Owings, Raymond, 129
Owsley, Amy, 321
Owusu, F., 328
Owusu, John, 328
Oxenhandler, Sally, 185
Oxford, Richard, 136
Oxley, Flo, 385
Oxley, Michael G., 11

P

Pabst, D., 503
Pace, Michael, 359
Pacelle, Wayne, 352
Pacheco, Elaine, 220
Pacheco, Peggy, 396
Paddon, Robert, 364
Pagac, Gerald, 163
Paganelli, Linda, 453
Page, Larry, 266
Page, Peter, 191
Page, Steve, 18
Pagnard, David, 204
Pahl, Barbara, 425
Paige, Roderick, 75
Pail, Joellen, 461
Painter, Doug, 424
Painter, Mary, 532
Palazzo, Jose, 371
Palin, Bruce, 163
Pallone, Frank, Jr., 9
Palma, Juan, 220
Palmer, Christopher, 427, 429
Palmer, Eric, 227
Palmer, Ira, 360
Palmer, Jeffrey, 507
Palmer, Jerry, 74
Palmer, Larry, 182
Palmer, Roy, 457
Palmer, Ruth, 436
Palmer, Sarah, 130
Palmer, William, 482, 535
Palmquist, Julie, 557
Palola, Eric, 428
Palumbo, Nancy, 198
Pampush, Geoff, 435
Pandini, Cindy, 420
Panio, John, 364
Paperiello, Carl, 26
Papouchis, Christopher, 405
Paquin, Emery, 203
Pardo, Nina, 406
Pardue, Dan, 356
Pardue, Len, 288
Parent, Tom, 175
Parenteau, Al, 216
Parise, Frank, 212
Parish, Elizabeth, 502
Park, Greg, 350
Park, James, 162
Park, Joey, 223
Parker, Brian, 329
Parker, Buck, 318
Parker, Edward, 149, 360
Parker, John, 195
Parker, Julie, 494
Parker, Kathy, 561
Parker, Kip, 473
Parker, Mamie, 90
Parker, Mike, 468
Parker, Nick, 30
Parker, Randy, 225
Parker, Ron, 195
Parker, Sara, 186
Parker, Warren, 336
Parkes, Mike, 456
Parkhurst, James, 228
Parks, Roger, 584
Parlee, Rodney, 565
Parmer, Delarie, 73
Parr, Mike, 250
Parran, Wilson H., 177
Parrella, Michael, 606
Parrish, Crystal, 406
Parrish, James, 158
Parrish, Jay, 211
Parrish, John, 395
Parry, Chris, 140
Parry, Susan, 466
Parsons, Brian, 351, 483
Parsons, Jessica, 485
Parsons, Richard, 483
Parton, Web, 271

Paschall, Sue, 459
Pascrell, Bill, Jr., 9
Paseka, Janice, 442
Pashley, David, 250
Pasicznyk, David, 192
Pasquier, Roger, 559
Passmore, Mike, 422
Pastor, Ed, 1
Pate, Kim, 355
Pate, Preston, 139, 200
Patino, Reynaldo, 30
Patlan, Mary Ann, 68
Patnude, Sue, 233
Patrick, Steve, 221
Patrick, Thomas, 555
Patt, Olney, Jr., 17
Patte, David, 111
Patten, Michael, 340
Pattengale, Darwin, 195
Patterson, Connie, 186
Patterson, Daniel, 290
Patterson, Gary, 592
Patterson, Rich, 356
Patterson, Robert, 483
Pattison, Hoyt, 220
Patton, Gary, 386
Patton, James, 173
Patton, Paul, 16
Patton, Sara, 455
Patton-Mallory, Marcia, 44
Paul, Edward, 594
Paul, Ellen, 462
Paul, Pat, 47
Paul, Ron E., 13
Paul, Tom, 210
Paul, Valerie, 502
Paulin, Kathleen, 553
Pauline, Rob, 544
Paulson, Brian, 576
Paulson, Jerry, 431
Paxson, Don, 381
Paxton, Gregory, 342
Payer, Ron, 182
Payne, Donald M., 9
Payne, Richard, 250
Pazenti, Catherine, 64
Peabody, Mary, 622
Peabody, Timothy, 175
Peace, Steve, 145
Pearce, Ron, 74
Pearce, Steve, 9
Pearl, Mary, 554
Pearlman, Nancy, 322
Pearse, John, 282
Pearson, Deborah, 401
Pearson, Patricia, 333
Pearson, William, 612
Pease, James, 166
Pease, Joshua, 168
Peay, Ted, 570
Peberdy, Blair, 459
Pechmann, John, 201
Peck, Larry, 233
Peck, W., 186
Pecor, Sally, 563
Peddicord, Carol, 545
Pedersen, Amanda, 76
Pedersen, Jordan, 226
Pederson, Clay, 419
Pederson, Ronald, 446
Peebles, Roger, 359
Peek, Mottell, 285
Peel, Ellen, 278
Peet, Steve, 419
Pekins, Peter, 617
Pelikan, Matt, 250
Pell, Clark, 198
Pellegrino, Robert, 149
Pellerin, Joanna, 190
Pelletier, Elizabeth, 368
Pelletiere, Danilo, 499
Pelosi, Nancy, 2
Pelren, Eric, 553

Pence, Daniel, 543
Pence, Mike, 5
Pendergraft, Bill, 566
Penfound, Rosalind, 203
Pennaz, Steve, 449
Penney, Gary, 454
Pennington, Margaret, 496
Pennington, Stephen, 166
Pennington, Steve, 166
Penny, Dale, 513
Penrod, Ken, 395
Pentis, Al, 530
Pentis, Mary Anne, 530
Peoples, Alan, 206
Pepper, Terry, 312
Percival, Dean, 396
Percival, H., 152
Perea, P.J., 274
Pereira, Christy, 33
Pereira, Grant, 488
Perez, Benito, 111
Perez-Gea, Armando, 24
Perkins, Calvin, 444
Perkins, Logan, 473
Perkins, Mitchell, 531
Perkins, Nathan, 610
Perkins, Robin, 318
Perkinson, Mike, 271
Perko, Daniel, 240
Permetti, Joseph, 519
Pernell, Robert, 143
Perock, Wayne, 189
Perrigo, Terri, 187
Perrin, William, 503
Perry, Earl, 422
Perry, Jim, 615
Perry, Lee, 174, 175, 360
Perry, Randall, 157
Perry, Stephen, 191
Pesenti, Chris, 473
Pete, Mary, 134
Peter, Maria, 592
Peterman, Frank, 541
Peterman, Larry, 186
Peteroy, Alain, 405
Peters, Christopher, 262
Peters, Cindy, 580
Petersen, Mark, 544
Petersen, Susan, 517
Peterson, Anne, 231
Peterson, Arlene, 539
Peterson, Bill, 135
Peterson, Carol, 481
Peterson, Christina, 416
Peterson, Collin, 8
Peterson, Curt, 618
Peterson, Douglas, 576
Peterson, Jack, 136
Peterson, James, 20, 418
Peterson, Jesse, 556
Peterson, John, 426
Peterson, John E., 12
Peterson, Mark, 423
Peterson, Mike, 534
Peterson, Nancy, 609
Peterson, Randall, 89
Peterson, Susan, 518
Petrachenko, Donna, 27
Petri, Thomas E., 15
Petrichenko, Paul, 47
Petrick, Carl, 422
Petritz, David, 213
Petrongolo, Tony, 192
Petrucci, Bryan, 252
Petsonk, Annie, 324
Petterson, Elizabeth, 394
Petzal, David, 285
Petzing, Kim, 325
Pew, Jim, 320
Pezold, Frank, 508
Pfaender, Frederic, 617
Pfannmuller, Lee, 182
Pfeiffer, Donald, 548

STAFF NAME INDEX – R

Pfeiffer, Michael, 334
Pfeiffer, Peter, 169
Pfister, Robert, 615
Phalen, Tim, 551
Phelan, Michael, 267
Phelps, John, 596
Phelps, Robert, 137
Phenneger, Sharon, 252
Philip, James, 613
Phillips, Abe, 307
Phillips, Adrian, 368
Phillips, Christine, 494
Phillips, Dave, 217
Phillips, David, 307, 317, 364
Phillips, Dwain, 47
Phillips, Howard, 110
Phillips, Jennifer, 574
Phillips, Patricia, 184
Phillips, Randy, 33
Phillips, Richard, 227
Phillips, Victor, 623
Phillips, William, 000
Phillips, Wilson, 424
Phinney, Cheyrl, 472
Phinney, Jonathan, 266
Phipps, Tim, 626
Piacentini, Richard, 249
Piché, Christiane, 601
Pichler, Susan, 469
Pichtel, John, 574
Pickerd, Howard, 240
Pickering, Charles Chip, Jr., 8
Pickett, Frank, 550
Pickett, Steward, 359
Pidgeon, Walter, 527
Piegat, James, 400
Pierce, Clay, 127
Pierce, Jacquelyn, 340
Pierce, Jim, 298, 299
Pierce, Judy, 224
Pierce, Richard, 404
Piergrossi, Monica, 301
Pierson, Robert, 43
Pierson, Scott, 379
Pietz, Curtis, 182
Pigeon, Michel, 601
Pike, Cara, 318
Pike, Doug, 300
Pike, Gary, 269
Pike, Stephen, 232
Pileggi, Martha, 312
Pincetl, Stephanie, 303
Pinchot, Nancy, 469
Pinchot, Peter, 469
Pindar, Georgine, 433
Pine, Rachael, 322
Pinney, Michele, 404
Pinnix, Cleve, 235
Piotrow, Phyllis, 470
Pipas, James, 619
Piret, Fern, 177
Pirner, Steven, 139, 219
Pister, Edwin, 314
Pitelka, Louis, 613
Pitman, J.L., 138
Pitre, John, 548
Pittenger-Slear, Suzanne, 324
Pittman, William, 73
Pitts, Alexandra, 90
Pitts, Don, 422
Pitts, Joseph R., 12
Piva, Alfio, 22
Pizzini, Manuel Valdes, 59
Pizzuto, Ernest, 443
Placer, Jose, 301
Plageman, Tim, 551
Plante, Patrick, 315
Plasencia, Doug, 444
Plasket, Elizabeth, 373
Plaskett, Dean, 223
Plater, Brent, 290
Plath, Rob, 283
Platt, David, 375

Platt, Dorothy, 528
Platt, Dwight, 381
Platts, Todd R., 12
Playfair, Bob, 533
Playne, Jack, 427
Plemmons, Tim, 312
Pletscher, Daniel, 409, 615
Plonski, John, 211
Poague, Terry, 244
Pocius, E., 336
Pockman, Mary, 532
Podolsky, W., 175
Pohl, Russ, 157
Pohlad, Bob, 581
Pohle, Gerhard, 353
Pohlman, John, 162
Poindexter, Alfred, 469
Pokrywka, Gregory, 396
Polis, Gary, 606
Polischuk, Wasyl, 212
Pollack, Amy, 322
Pollack, Lana, 607
Pollan, Gayden, 313
Pollard, Ben, 205
Polles, Sam, 184
Polli, Rudolph, 227
Pollock, Glenn, 373
Pollom, Alan, 436
Polls, Irwin, 543
Polo, Barbara, 456
Polo, Richard, 68
Poltak, Ronald, 443
Pombo, Richard, 2
Pomerance, Rafe, 78
Pomeroy, Earl, 11
Pomeroy, Paul, 26
Pomeroy, Walt, 466
Pomroy, Walter, 347
Pongratz, Eva, 328
Pontti, Michael, 352
Pool, Michael, 84
Poole, Anne, 445
Poole, John, 133
Poole, Kerry, 176
Poole, William, 424
Poor, Bancroft, 414
Poor, Deborah, 480
Pope, Carl, 497
Pope, David, 167
Pope, J. R., 236
Popham, James, 65
Popkin, Rodger, 250
Poppino, John, 461
Poppe, Steven, 667
Porath, Mark, 257
Porteck, Kevin, 61
Porter, Andres, 246
Porter, Bill, 168
Porter, Jon C., 9
Porter, Mary, 76
Porter, Michael, 254, 551
Porter, Sandra, 154
Porter, William, 598
Portman, Rob J., 11
Portner, Linda, 26
Portney, Paul, 479
Porvaznik, Richard, 470
Possiel, William, 420
Post, Diana, 476
Post, Roger, 546
Potter, Bruce, 375
Potter, Dave, 601
Potter, Eric, 140
Potter, Jerry, 489
Potter, Maryanne, 340
Potter, Thomas, 52
Pottie, James, 72
Pottinger, Lori, 366
Potts, Gary, 546
Potts, Robert, 439
Potucek, Dorothy, 486
Poulsen, Dorothy, 415
Pouncy, Keith, 184

Pourchot, Pat, 134
Powelka, Joe, 540
Powell, Abby, 133
Powell, Ann, 524
Powell, Barbara, 329
Powell, Brad, 43
Powell, Bradley, 43
Powell, Carrie, 534
Powell, Colin, 77
Powell, David, 287
Powell, James, 554
Powell, Jason, 582
Powell, Keri, 320
Powell, Laura, 204
Powell, Royden, 177
Power, Donna, 317
Powers, Bradley, 177
Powers, John, 301
Powers, Kirsten, 460
Powers, Paul, 197
Powless, Douglas, 386
Poynter, Ken, 400
Pranis, Eve, 420
Prather, Kerry, 256
Pratson, Lincoln, 580
Pratt, H., 141
Pratt, Jeff, 170
Pratt, Jerome, 539
Pray, Roger, 480
Prchal, Douglas, 202
Preble, Jeff, 349
Prendergast, Gregory, 179
Prescott, Heidi, 338
Preso, Tim, 318
Preston, Bret, 236
Prevado, Glenna, 43
Prevost, Yves, 586
Prewitt, Hal, 278
Prey, Dave, 441
Price, Anne, 477
Price, David E., 10
Price, Harry, 236
Price, Hugh, 400
Price, Jim, 498
Price, Jonathan, 189
Price, Rae, 419
Price, Scott, 476
Price, Steve, 168
Price, Thomas, 279
Price, Will, 469
Price, William, 229
Prichard, Michael, 465
Prichett, Rebecca, 245
Priekett, Tommy, 173
Prince, Bernadine, 252
Prindle, Barb, 399
Pristash, Sherri, 54
Pritchard, John, 339
Pritchard, Mary, 442
Pritchard, Paul, 422
Pritchard, Phil, 251
Probasco, Irene, 450
Proctor, Lezlin, 184
Prokopowich, Ruth, 453
Propst, Luther, 505
Prosser, Kathy, 306
Prosser, Norville, 266
Proudman, Robert, 270
Prouse, C., 176
Prouty, Jordan, 449
Prowse, Harold, 415
Pruit, Philip, 62, 64
Pruitt, Kenneth, 396
Pruitt, William, 232
Pruss, Mike, 468
Pryce, Deborah, 11
Pryor, Joan, 331
Pryor, Mark, 1
Puent, Sally, 208
Puffinberger, Charles, 177
Pugh, Corky, 132
Pugh, M.N. Corky, 360
Pugh, Michelle, 374

Puhalski, Jon, 304
Pulins, Benita, 350
Pulkki, Reino, 586
Pulliam, David, 550
Pulsipher, Sue, 256
Punter, David, 613
Pupke, Andi, 295
Pupke, Chris, 295
Puppe, Gary, 452
Purnell, Til, 486
Pusateri, Francie, 547
Putnam, Adam, 4
Putnam, Mike, 362

Q

Quackenbush, Lanny, 209
Quackenbush, Mary, 454
Quakenbush, Lori, 134
Qualley, George, 143
Quan, Felix, 463
Quarles, William, 278
Quatrano, Ralph, 626
Quayle, Frederick, 229
Quayle, Moura, 606
Queral, Alejandro, 498
Quesnel, Louise, 603
Quevedo-Bonilla, Vicente, 213
Quick, Betty, 347
Quigley, Mike, 163
Quill, Stephen, 400
Quink, Thomas, 396
Quinn, Catherine, 528
Quinn, Dan, 159, 479
Quinn, Jack, 10
Quinn, Randy, 72
Quinn, Robert, 199
Quinnell, Tony, 403
Quinney, Terry, 459
Quirk, Bill, 73
Quirk, Thomas, 285
Quirolo, Craig, 478
Quirolo, DeeVon, 478
Quirós, Kattia, 281
Quisenberry, Bill, 184
Quy, Laurence, 393
Qzbal, Hafiz, 611

R

Rabbon, Peter, 145
Rabeni, Charles, 119, 615
Rabin, Philip, 312
Rabinovitch, Paul, 438
Rabolli, Charles, 342
Rackiewicz, Joe, 304
Radford, Ginny, 558
Radomski, Paul, 256
Radosevich, Steven, 592
Rael, Wilfred, 510
Raeside, Robert, 572
Raether, Keith, 538
Raettig, Karla, 600
Raffaele, Herbert, 90
Raganit, Larry, 354
Ragen, Timothy, 23
Raglin, Kenneth, 26
Ragouzina, Galina, 321
Ragsdale, Austin, 300
Ragsdale, Duncan, 384
Rahall, Nick J., II, 15
Rahder, Barbara, 628
Rahm, Jennifer, 545
Rahman, Anis, 351
Rainey, C., 544
Rainey, John, 429
Rainford, Sylvia, 47
Rains, Michael, 33
Rainwater, Bill, 272
Rait, Ken, 285
Raitter, James, 354
Rakestraw, Dariel, 312
Rakocy, James, 228
Raley, Catherine, 554
Ralston, Patrick, 163

STAFF NAME INDEX – R

Ralston, Peter, 375
Ramaswamy, Shri, 615
Ramey, Barbara, 581
Ramsay, Scott, 174
Ramsey, Charles, 155
Ramsey, Ron, 439
Ramstad, Jim, 8
Rana, Naureen, 469
Randolph, J., 584
Randolph, Scott, 389
Randovich, George P., 2
Rands, Tim, 317
Raney, Jay, 140
Rangel, Charles B., 10
Rankel, Gary, 78
Ranney, Sally, 268
Ransom, Michel, 585
Rapier, Kenny, 170
Rapp, Jim, 411
Rappa, Peter, 55
Rappold, John, 279
Rasker, Ray, 505
Rasmussen, Fred, 520
Rasmussen, Jay, 59
Rasmussen, Thomas, 83
Rasor, Annie, 457
Rasor, Lori, 461, 533, 534
Rassam, Gus, 241, 252
Ratcliff, Doug, 140
Ratcliff, Sheila, 625
Rathbone, Cindy, 471
Rathbun, Dennis, 26
Rathner, Todd, 406
Ratner, Jonathan, 538
Ratz, Margaret, 539
Raudzens, Adriana, 497
Rauscher, Ken, 180
Rawlins, Wayne, 208
Rawson, Mac, 55
Ray, Mike, 21
Rayburn, Richard, 152
Raymond, Janis, 203
Raymond, Sal, 162
Raymond, Stephanie, 467
Rea, Phil, 451
Read, Charlotte, 486
Read, Edith, 502
Read, Jennifer, 57
Reader, Michael, 459
Reagor, Karen, 383
Reaka, Marjorie, 503
Reames, Clark, 73
Reames, Deborah, 319
Rebach, Steve, 58, 613
Recht, Philip, 129
Reck, Ruth, 606
Reckhow, Kenneth, 580
Record, Richard, 175
Redding, Al, 244
Redding, Bill, 494
Redett, Robert B., 457
Redig, Patrick, 593
Redman, Charles, 573
Redmond, Dennis, 356
Reeb, Mary, 622
Reece, Gary, 405
Reed, A., 210
Reed, Bill, 536
Reed, Charles, 149
Reed, Cynthia, 345
Reed, Danny, 170
Reed, Donald, 173
Reed, Jack, 12
Reed, Leonard, 223
Reed, Valerie, 541
Reed, Wendy, 520, 590
Reed-Smith, Jan, 249
Reed-Wise, Dana, 163
Reel, Christine, 556
Rees, Sandy, 235
Rees-Webbe, Robin, 349
Reese, Brandon, 346
Reese, Peg, 47
Reeser, Rondalyn, 352
Reeves, Bill, 222, 401
Reeves, Reggie, 221
Regan, Ann, 230
Regan, Ron, 227
Regelin, Wayne, 134
Regenstein, Lewis, 359
Register, Richard, 515
Regn, Ann, 532
Rego, Paul, 550
Regula, Ralph, 11
Rehberg, Dennis, 8
Reheis, Harold, 156
Reiber, Carl, 616
Reice, Seth, 618
Reich, Dennis, 202
Reich, Richard, 200
Reich, Tim, 407
Reichert, Gerald, 438
Reichert, Melissa, 38
Reid, Alan, 576, 606
Reid, Bob, 333
Reid, C. P., 605
Reid, Harry, 9
Reid, Kenneth, 267
Reid, Sharon, 271
Reiff, Cheryl, 497
Reifsnyder, Daniel, 78
Reilly, Margaret, 198
Reilly, Patrick, 129
Reilly, Sharon, 413
Reilly, William, 252
Reimer, Monica, 320
Reinhardt, Viktor, 269
Reinhart, Rachel, 244
Reinthal, Victoria, 538
Reis, Kathryn, 545
Reisdorf, Thomas, 523
Reiser, Hildy, 64, 421
Reiss, Warren, 488
Reiswig, Barry, 107
Reitsma, Jan, 214
Rempel, Ron, 142
Remus, Kurt, Jr., 504
Remus, Laurel, 196
Renaud, Patty, 432
Rene, Gaurab, 513
Reneau, Jack, 279
Renner, Robert, 267
Renner, Tracy, 561
Renzi, Rick, 1
Reshetniak, Peter, 477
Rettig, Virginia, 548
Reuter, Don, 200
Reutter, Jeffrey, 58
Revier, Paul, 485
Rewerts, Milan, 148
Rexroad, Caird, 31
Reyes, Carmen, 251, 379
Reyes, Luis, 26
Reyes, Silvestre, 13
Reynolds, Bob, 433
Reynolds, Harry, 359
Reynolds, Jim, 162
Reynolds, John, 120, 404
Reynolds, Marjorie, 500
Reynolds, Stephen, 312, 316
Reynolds, Thomas, 10
Reynolds, Tom, 304
Rezac, Don, 381
Rheinhardt, George, 155
Rhoades, Kevin, 462
Rhodes, Olin, 548
Rhorer, Skip, 172
Rhubart, Pam, 584
Ribe, Robert, 619
Ribic, Christine, 237
Ricart, Juan, 475
Ricci, Hugh, 189
Ricciardelli, Laura, 542
Rice, Chuck, 451
Rice, David, 189
Rice, Gary, 192
Rice, James, 200
Rice, Joe, 137
Rice, Ronald, 20
Rice, William, 19
Rich, James, 169
Richard, Paul, 179
Richards, Anne, 256
Richards, Carl, 57
Richards, Douglas, 588
Richards, William, 244
Richardson, Curtis, 580
Richardson, Douglas, 273
Richardson, Fred, 493
Richardson, Jill, 579
Richardson, Joan, 444
Richardson, Judith, 412
Richardson, Kermit, 421
Richardson, Kory, 117
Richardson, Nancy, 276
Richardson, Roger, 312
Richardson, Russ, 558
Richardson, Sonny, 222
Richardson, Steven, 89
Richardson, Tim, 384
Richbourg, Joe, 155
Richerson, Pat, 61
Richey, Jacki, 460
Richmond, Alan, 64
Richmond, Milo, 196
Richter, Daniel, 580
Richter, Jean, 113
Rickard, Patricia, 589
Rickards, William, 59
Rickenbach, Mark, 238
Rico, Richard, 136
Ridenburg, John, 68
Ridenhour, Cory, 402
Ridgeway, Lori, 27
Ridlon, Jerri, 591
Rieff, Susan, 427
Riemer, Jim, 162
Rienhardt, James, 470
Riepe, Don, 263
Riesenberg, Lou, 611
Riester, Andrew, 426
Rigby, Jerry, 161
Rigby, William, 528
Riggs, Kimberly, 500
Riggs, Sara, 476
Rike, Kay, 217
Riker, Beverly, 133
Riley, Dennis, 153
Riley, Larry, 253
Riley, Terry, 545
Riley, Wilson, 471
Riley-West, Erin, 488
Rillero, Anne, 464
Rimmer, Christopher, 529
Rimmer, Jennifer, 479
Rinaldo, Paul, 249
Rineer, Robert, 395
Rinehart, Claire, 383
Ring, Bettina, 230
Ring, Dick, 120
Ring, Ginette, 419
Ringe, Jim, 504
Ringenberg, Jay, 188
Ringler, Neil, 598
Ringo, Jerome, 427
Rinker, H. Bruce, 393
Rioba, Ayub, 599
Ripley, Arlene, 448
Ripley, Bob, 221
Ripley, J., 286
Ris, Howard, 525
Risbrudt, Chris, 131
Risdon, Karla, 415
Risk, Paul, 598
Riska, Mike, 312, 403
Risnes, Phillip, 507
Ristow, Mark, 509
Ritchie, Ian, 587
Ritchie, J., 460
Rittenour, Charles, 244
Rittschof, Dan, 580
Riutor, Raul, 514
Rivera, Betty, 194
Rivera, Dennis, 476
Rivera, Oscar, 516
Rivera-Lucena, Eliu, 213
Rivero, Machela, 569
Rivero-Blanco, Carlos, 563, 569
Rizzio, Tony, 73
Roach, Greg, 203
Roads, Bob, 162
Roads, Robert, 481
Roady, Steve, 320
Robb, Laura, 319
Robbins, Brad, 404
Robbins, Chandler, 395
Robbins, Michelle, 260
Robbins, Russell, 184
Roberson, Donnis, 184
Roberts, Adam, 269
Roberts, Christopher, 17
Roberts, David, 624
Roberts, Dick, 140
Roberts, Eric, 513
Roberts, Jamie, 259
Roberts, Jay, 212
Roberts, Kenneth, 173
Roberts, M., 577
Roberts, Michele, 292
Roberts, Pat, 6
Roberts, Pierce, 176
Roberts, Terry, 145
Roberts, Thomas, 582
Robertson, George, 133, 244
Robertson, Gordon, 267
Robertson, James, 238
Robertson, Jason, 267
Robertson, Jessica, 244
Robertson, Jim, 63
Robertson, Mark, 439
Robertson, Steve, 412
Robertus, John, 144
Robinette, Randall, 578
Robinson, Bina, 362
Robinson, David, 442
Robinson, Felicia, 163
Robinson, Jill, 269, 363
Robinson, John, 392, 543
Robinson, Jon, 493
Robinson, Kayne, 424
Robinson, Michael, 290
Robinson, Muriel, 276
Robinson, Nicholas, 368
Robinson, Scott, 611
Robinson, Steve, 189
Robinson, Sumner, 461
Robison, Margaret, 518
Roby, Dan, 464
Roby, Daniel, 126
Rocha, Robert, 136
Roche, Jean, 430
Rochefort, Line, 602
Rock, Robert, 37
Rockefeller, David, 246
Rockefeller, John D., 15
Rockefeller, Laurance, 251
Rockefeller, Winthrop, 278
Rockers, Phil, 550
Rockey, Sally, 49
Rocque, Arthur, 149
Roczicka, Greg, 134
Rodd, Judy, 536
Rodefeld, Nels, 206
Rodemacher, Gus, 173
Roden, Robert, 238
Rodgers, A.J. (Tony), 454
Rodgers, Forrest, 351
Rodgers, John, 577
Rodgers, Kirk, 89, 334
Rodrigues, Vera, 359
Rodriguez, Ciro D., 14
Rodriguez, Migdalia, 475

STAFF NAME INDEX – S

Rodriguez, Raul, 24
Roe, Susie, 290
Roehrich, Kenneth, 445
Roekel, Dennis, 418
Rogers, Dan, 66
Rogers, Erin, 493
Rogers, Harold, 6
Rogers, Janel, 241
Rogers, Karel, 536
Rogers, Kathleen, 316
Rogers, Kenneth, 26
Rogers, Marihelen, 419
Rogers, Michael D., 1
Rogers, Michael J., 7
Rogers, Owen, 366
Rogers, Raymond, 628
Rogers, Richard, 200
Rogers, Ross, 403
Rogers, Sam, 195
Rogers, Stanley, 62
Rogers, Will, 524
Rohall, Ron, 465
Rohe, Debbie, 487
Rohrabacher, Dana, 2
Rohrback, Donald, 549
Rohwer, Frank, 548
Rojas, Esther, 475
Rojas, Sonia, 22
Rold, Robert, 413
Rolfe, Gary, 611
Rolfsmeyer, Chuck, 556
Rolls, Alice, 318
Roloson, Randy, 427
Rolston, Dennis, 606
Rom, Becky, 541
Romain, Robert, 604
Roman, Michael, 613
Romaniuk, Nestor, 287
Romano, Gregory, 191
Romano, Kathie, 545
Romans, John, 383
Rome, Adam, 334
Romero, Kate, 308
Romic, Bob, 71
Romine, Richard, 178
Rominger, Eric, 551
Romo, John, 469
Roncoli, Mark, 68
Ronnerud, James, 316
Roope, Bruce, 392
Roosevelt, Theodore, 387
Ros-Lehtinen, Ileana, 4
Rosapepe, John, 497
Rose, Ben, 347
Rose, Charles, 597
Rose, Chris, 524
Rose, Helen, 320
Rose, Jerry, 430
Rose, Lu, 260
Rose, Maureen, 285
Rose, Pandora, 405
Rose, Paul, 69
Rosen, Ron, 383
Rosenberg, David, 447
Rosenberg, Larry, 70
Rosenberg, Steve, 488
Rosenfeld, Art, 143
Rosenkranz, Herbert, 619
Rosenlieb, Dick, 427
Rosenow, John, 407
Rosenquist, Eric, 438
Rosevear, William, 467
Ross, Albert, 364
Ross, Bill, 200
Ross, Brad, 457
Ross, Carl, 485
Ross, David, 250
Ross, Denwood, 26
Ross, Gale, 174
Ross, Kelly, 478
Ross, Mike, 1
Ross, S., 209
Ross, Stephen, 508, 621

Ross, William, 207
Rosselet, Dale, 415
Rossi, C., 26
Rossi, Jim, 301
Rossi, Michael, 617
Rossi, Mwajabu, 599
Rossi, Patrizia, 328
Rossiter, William, 294
Roster, Tom, 165
Rostvet, Roger, 202
Roswal, Glenn, 248
Rotella, Jay, 589
Rotenberry, John, 309
Roth, Chuck, 335
Roth, Paul, 596
Roth, Peter, 17
Roth, Roland, 299, 609
Rothe, Ann, 524
Rothman, Hal, 265
Rothman, Steven R., 9
Roudna, Milena, 17
Roussel, John, 173
Row, Greg, 433
Rowan, Gloria, 236
Rowdabaugh, Kirk, 136
Rowland, Paul, 591
Rowland, Ruth, 474
Rowley, Rex, 81
Rowman, Richard, 521
Rowntree, Lester, 594
Roxburgh, Scottey, 273
Roybal-Allard, Lucille, 2
Royce, Bob, 160
Royce, Edward, 2
Roza, Ralph, 70
Rozum, Mary, 33
Rubenstein, Paul, 67
Rubin, Robert, 270
Rubingh, Jim, 146
Ruch, Jeffrey, 474
Ruddell, John, 154
Rudgers, Nathan, 197
Rudy, Carol, 357
Rue, Frank, 134
Rueger, Walter, 419
Rufe, Roger, 455
Ruff, Margaret, 458
Ruffner, Charles, 596
Rufsvold, Coleen, 36
Ruiz, Rick, 570
Rukeyser, William, 144
Rummel, Vicky, 500
Rump, Jack, 145
Rumsey, Kay, 453
Rundquist, Eric, 381
Runnels, Bruce, 439
Running, Steven, 615
Running-Grass, , 518
Runyan, James, 198
Ruppersberger, C.A. Dutch, 7
Rush, Bobby L., 5
Rushing, Amy, 567
Rusmore, Barbara, 358
Rusnak, Terry, 272
Russell, Aubrey, 516
Russell, Bobbi, 346
Russell, Dean, 511
Russell, Dianne, 358
Russell, Ed, 265
Russell, Jeanne, 326
Russell, John, 600
Russell, Keith, 288
Russell, Robert, 375
Russo, Rosemarie, 578
Russo, Todd, 413
Rust, Marie, 120
Rust, Sheila, 286
Rustay, Christopher, 470
Ruta, Gwen, 324
Ruth, Terry, 72
Ruther, Paul, 292
Rutherford, Brad, 366
Rutherford, Brent, 628

Rutherford, Jay, 227
Rutherford, Jeff, 394
Rutherford, Nelson, 461
Rutishauser, Matt, 338
Rutledge, Wallace, 209
Rutter, Allan, 129
Ruwaldt, Matt, 557
Ruyle, George, 135, 605
Ruzifka, Ron, 137
Ryan, Barbara, 127
Ryan, Christopher, 554
Ryan, Paul D., 15
Ryan, Tim, 11
Ryan, W., 18
Ryden, Hope, 539
Ryder, Thomas, 546
Rylander, Jason, 304
Ryun, Jim R., 6

S

Saavedra, Paul, 220
Sabatoso, William, 212
Sabean, Barry, 203
Sabella, Susan, 347
Sabins, Dugan, 391
Sablan, Joseph, 158
Sabo, Chris, 566
Sabo, Martin Olav, 8
Sack, Karen, 269
Sackett, Bruce, 189
Sadler, Kim, 588
Sadler, Lynn, 405
Sadler, William, 539
Sadley, Jim, 191
Sadusky, Nancy, 486
Saer, Anne, 307
Safina, Carl, 414, 416
Sage, Don, 198
Sage, Samuel, 276
Sage, Shellie, 477
Sager, Scott, 609
Sagoff, Mark, 367
Sahaj, Janet, 129
Sakal, Suzanne, 514
Sakaria, Regina, 276
Sakofs, Mitchell, 540
Sakuma, Tomoko, 467
Salari, Ahmad, 225
Salas, Salvador, 213
Salazar, Rodolfo, 367
Salazar-Henry, Roberta, 193
Saldana, Lydia, 223
Saleh, Farida, 618
Saley, Jeff, 40
Salgado, Brenda, 389
Salinger, Gerhard, 471
Salisbury, Jennifer, 193
Salkin, Charles, 150
Sallee, Dan, 527
Sallee, R., 255
Salley, Mark, 73
Salmonson, Genevieve, 150
Salmony, Steven, 334
Salter, Laura, 559
Saltzman, Charles, 460
Salwasser, Harold, 592
Salzberg, Allen, 351
Sammon, Robert, 408
Samor, Chris, 305
Sample, V., 469
Samples, Ernie, 570
Samples, Peter, 511, 570
Sampliner, Tom, 430
Sampson, Carol, 75
Sampson, David, 49
Sams, M., 215
Samuel, Joseph, 530
Samuels, William, 332
San Nicholas, Clarissa, 158
Sanchez, Linda T., 2
Sanchez, Loretta L., 2
Sandberg, Nicole, 455
Sandeen, Bill, 65

Sandell, Roberta, 483
Sanders, Bernard, 14
Sanders, Dwight, 145
Sanders, Joe, 221
Sanders, Reed, 169
Sanders, Rodney, 184
Sanders, William, 130
Sanderson, Richard, 130
Sanderson, Steven, 543
Sandheinrich, Mark, 623
Sandifer, Paul, 508
Sandler, Craig, 424
Sandlin, Max A., Jr., 13
Sandoval, J., 160
Sands, Diane T., 282
Sandstrom, David, 483
Saner, Theo, 245
Sanjanwala, Umesh, 184
Sankovitch, Nina, 486
Sansonetti, Thomas, 77
Sant, Roger, 559
Santacania, Carmen, 111
Santiago, Roberto Quero, 563
Santiago, Vivian, 148
Santorum, Rick, 12
Santos, Blanca, 308
Santucci, Michael, 201
Sapp, Tammy Bristow, 427
Sarbanes, Paul S., 6
Sarro, James, 142
Sarty, Jim, 203
Sasowsky, Ira, 604
Sass, Ronald, 594
Saterson, Kathryn, 280
Sato, Ken, 17, 18
Sato, Miko, 467
Sattler, Polly, 318
Satz, Jay, 513
Saunders, Gerry, 618
Saunders, Lloyd, 67
Saunders, Norm, 395
Saunders, Richard, 528
Saunders, Stuart, 244
Saundry, Peter, 418
Saurez, Richard, 257
Sausville, Lisa, 553
Sauvain, Terry, 28
Savage, Leslie, 413
Savage, Michael, 204
Savard, Michel, 476
Saville, Dave, 536
Savioe, Brandt, 173
Savitt, Charles, 293
Sawatzky, Tammy, 426
Saxton, Jim, 9
Saxton, L., 161
Sayre, Dan, 293
Scaggs, Susan, 428
Scalet, Charles, 596
Scalf, Anna, 374
Scallion, Mark, 410
Scamehorn, Eileen, 415
Scanlon, John, 368
Scanlon, Kelly, 453
Scarborough, Robert, 50
Scarth, Jonathan, 313
Scarth, Linda, 373
Schade, Duffy, 412
Schadewald, Paul, 202
Schaefer, Joesph, 582
Schaefer, Joyce, 340
Schaefer, Larry, 328
Schaefer, Mark, 441
Schaefer, Michael, 328
Schaefer, Richard, 262
Schaefer, Rick, 557
Schaffer, Corliss, 463
Schaffer, Eric, 130
Schaffer, Mary, 47
Schaffer, Rebecca, 75
Schakowsky, Janice D., 5
Schallert, Russell, 504
Schane, Demian, 319

STAFF NAME INDEX – S

Scharpf, Stephanie, 449
Schassler, Steve, 197
Schatz, Daniel, 215
Schatz, Kurt, 214
Scheberle, Denise, 622
Schechter, Claudia, 422
Scheibelhut, Becky, 357
Scheibelhut, Rebecca, 427
Scheible, Michael, 143
Scheman, Carol, 76
Schemenauer, Joe, 485
Schenck, John, 73
Schenck, Robb, 507
Schenk, Kathryn, 70
Schenk, William, 120
Scheppner, Jerry, 195
Scherch, Jonathan, 572
Scherr, Paulette, 91
Schickedanz, Jerry, 195, 590
Schiff, Adam, 2
Schiff, David, 543
Schimel, Barry, 422
Schinkten, Jeffrey, 539
Schisler, John, 217
Schisler, Lee, 276
Schlageter, Martin, 490
Schlender, James, 20
Schlenk, Cornelia, 58
Schlesinger, William, 580
Schlickeisen, Rodger, 311
Schloss, Alice, 352
Schloss, Jeffrey, 617
Schlosser, Issac, 618
Schlueter, Chuck, 219
Schmidt, Bob, 274, 345
Schmidt, Christina, 554
Schmidt, Christine, 535
Schmidt, Jeff, 496
Schmidt, Jen, 285
Schmidt, Lou, 520
Schmidt, Penny, 72
Schmidt, Walter, 154
Schmidt, Wayne, 427
Schmoetzer, Lisa, 271
Schneider, Daniel, 248
Schneider, Jim, 587
Schneider, Joan, 165
Schneider, John, 151
Schneider, Keith, 398
Schneider, Pat, 298
Schneider, Rebecca, 197
Schock, Andrew, 429
Schoen, John, 409
Schoen, Michael, 571
Schoenfelder, Jack, 296
Schoenrock, Linda, 316
Scholl, Steve, 140
Scholle, Peter, 193
Schollenberg, Shirley, 245
Scholtz, April, 386
Schoolmaster, Andy, 618
Schoonmaker, Peter, 539
Schoonover, Royl, 425
Schornack, Dennis, 23
Schrader, Mark, 152
Schrader, Sue, 246, 508
Schram, Gus, 300
Schramel, John, 282
Schramm, Harold, 183
Schramm, Mary Jane, 51
Schraufnagel, John, 385
Schreck, Carl, 126, 592
Schreuder, Jack, 176
Schrock, Edward L., 14
Schroder, Ron, 198
Schroeder, Dan, 498
Schroeder, David, 608
Schroeder, Mari, 553
Schrom, David, 392
Schronce, Arty, 155
Schubert, Paul, 20
Schuchat, Sam, 140
Schueler, Thomas, 293

Schueller, Harry, 144
Schuerch, Kate, 306
Schuerg, Alvin, 157
Schuett, Lowen, 181
Schukman, John, 381
Schulke, Todd, 290
Schuller, Reid, 431
Schultz, Caroline, 279, 287
Schultz, Tom, 187
Schultze, Gordon, 415
Schulz, John, 551
Schulze, Miles, 459
Schumacher, Martha, 312
Schumacher, Milton, 480
Schumer, Charles E., 9
Schuster, Henry, 228
Schuster, Marc, 549
Schuurmans, Robert, 219
Schwartz, Jim, 239
Schwartz, John, 57
Schwartz, Malia, 59
Schwartz, Nancy, 372
Schwartz, Sam, 241
Schwartz, Susan, 481
Schwartz, Suzanne, 223
Schwartz, Tom, 468
Schwarzschild, B. Shimon, 242
Schwegman, John, 163
Schweig, Eric, 449
Schweiger, Larry, 537
Schweitzer, Sara, 547
Schwerd, William, 268
Schwetz, Bernard, 75
Schwolert, Phil, 148
Sciasca, James, 550
Sciascia, Jim, 192
Sciuto, Frank, 276
Scobel, Matt, 481
Scoles, Graham, 620
Scorby, R., 209
Scott, Anita, 273
Scott, Bob, 134, 247
Scott, Bobby, 14
Scott, David, 4
Scott, Don, 199
Scott, Doug, 285
Scott, J., 610, 611
Scott, Kathy, 220
Scott, Lauren, 532
Scott, Lori, 294
Scott, Lorne, 215
Scott, Michael, 346
Scott, Nadine, 282
Scott, Robert, 190, 506
Scott, Steve, 155
Scott, Sue, 275
Scott, William, 576, 605
Scribner, Tom, 454
Scroggie, Adrienne, 242
Scroggie, Alan, 242
Scroggins, Ronald, 26
Scully, R., 78
Scully, William, 69
Scuse, Michael, 151
Seaborn, Eric, 73
Seacrest, Susan, 347
Seager, Ann, 471
Seale, Robert, 26
Seales, Frank, 129
Seaman, William, 55
Searle, Colgate, 593
Searock, Teresa, 247
Sears, Mark, 610
Sease, Debbie, 499
Sease, Stephen, 226
Seaton, Dick, 410
Sebert, Dan, 205, 426
Sebesta, Dawn, 350
Sebren, Ray, 138
Seck, Kathryn, 285
Seckler, Thomas, 192
Secord, Jane, 291
Sedgwick, Walter, 515

Sedinger, James, 616
Sedivec, Kevin, 126
Seeber, Glenn, 611
Seegars, Wes, 201
Seek, George, 185
Seeley, Rod, 583
Seeling, Marty, 153
Seeling, Mike, 274
Seely, Mary, 314
Seemann, Jeffrey, 214
Sefton, Donna, 555
Segee, Brian, 290
Seger, James, 463
Seibel, John, 555
Seibert, Tom, 557
Seideman, David, 409
Seifert, Tim, 484
Seith, William, 162
Seitz, Jane, 355
Sekscienski, Steve, 73
Selditch, Diane, 505
Seligman, Ann, 554
Seligmann, Peter, 307
Selin, Steve, 626
Sellers, Stephen, 163
Sellstrom, Gail, 452
Selmon, Michelle, 552
Selva, Steven, 612
Selvidge, Maggie, 414
Selzer, Lawrence, 307
Selzer, Lawrence A., 544
Semenchuk, Glen, 329
Senatore, Michael, 312
Seng, Phil, 548
Senn, Mike, 136
Senner, Stanley, 409
Sensenbrenner, F. James, Jr., 15
Septoff, Alan, 399
Septon, Gregory, 504
Sepulveda, Jose, 294
Seput, Gary, 283
Seriff, Don, 180
Seriff, Donald, 551
Serodes, Jean, 603
Sérodes, Jean-Baptiste, 603
Serold, Bryan, 157
Serrano, Jose E., 10
Serrano, Linda, 500
Serynek, Thomas, 486
Sessions, Jeff, 1
Sessions, Pete, 14
Seth, Susen, 389
Sethi, Gautam, 574
Setser, Jim, 156
Settergren, Carl, 615
Settle, Patrick, 560
Seward, Roy, 228
Sexson, Keith, 167
Sexson, Mark, 168, 548
Sexton, Karen, 304
Sexton, Robert, 527
Sexton, Terry, 242
Seymour, Carl, 446
Seymour, Ingrid, 269
Seymour, Rosie, 385
Sflnchez, Carlos Peynador, 563
Sgro, Leslie, 162
Shackleton, D., 606
Shaddox, Bill, 120
Shadegg, John B., 1
Shadel, William, 486
Shafer, Thomas, 73
Shafer, Tracy, 543
Shaffer, Diana, 136
Shaffer, El, 225
Shaffer, Mark, 312
Shaffer, Martha, 378
Shaffer, William, 379
Shafroth, Will, 386
Shakely, William, 211
Shallenberger, Mary, 469
Shane, John, 622
Shaner, Jack, 457

Shank, Dawn, 532
Shank, Fred, 75
Shank, Rich, 439
Shannon, John, 155
Shannon, Kathy, 374
Shannon-Beaver, Linda, 471
Shanteau, Cherie, 130
Shao, Lawrence, 26
Shapiro, Carl, 127
Sharik, Terry, 624
Sharp, Diane, 33
Sharp, Gregory, 524
Sharp, Mike, 205
Sharp, Warren, 471
Sharpe, Craig, 404
Shattuck, William, 219
Shauri, Vincent, 243
Shavelson, Bob, 308
Shaver, Stephen, 621
Shaw, E. Clay, Jr., 4
Shaw, James, 551, 592
Shaw, R., 217
Shaw, Roger, 606
Shaw, Susan, 394, 413
Shaw, William, 605
Shawyer, Colin, 349
Shay, Vince, 437
Shays, Christopher, 3
Shea, Allen, 238
Shea, Ernest, 407
Shea, Kathie, 162
Shea, Ruth, 523
Sheaffer, Amy, 574
Sheaffer, C., 120
Shedlock, Marlo, 246
Sheehan, Francis, 196
Sheehan, Linda, 455
Sheehan, Sean, 289
Sheeran, Lori, 361
Sheffield, Emilyn, 575
Sheffield, Jim, 189
Shelby, Janet, 69
Shelby, Luke, 194
Shelby, Richard, 1
Shell, Jim, 137
Shell, Ronnie, 110
Shelley, Beverly, 218
Shelley, Peter, 308
Shellman, Dwight, 282
Sheltmire, Jack, 597
Shelton, A., 158
Shelton, Bonnie, 447
Shelton, Jo-Ann, 607
Shelton, Kevin, 249
Shelton, L., 129
Shepard, Bob, 276
Shepard, John, 505
Shepherd, Matthew, 561
Sher, Sarah, 483
Sherby, Louise, 576
Sheridan, Lori, 562
Sheridan, Neil, 305
Sherman, Brad, 2
Sherman, Bruce, 149
Sherman, Roma, 532
Sheroan, Donald, 73
Sheron, Brian, 26
Sherrod, C., 517
Sherrod, Steve, 205, 340
Sherwood, Don, 12
Sherwood, John, 589
Sherwood, Mike, 319
Shetler, Stanwyn, 532
Shewmangal, Nanda, 422
Shiek, Abdul, 72
Shields, David, 281
Shimada, Alan, 262
Shimalla, Thomas, 470
Shimek, Steve, 462
Shimkus, John M., 5
Shimoda, Risa, 267
Shingleton, Michael, 236, 259
Shinn, Robert, 191

STAFF NAME INDEX – S

Shipley, Sara, 267
Shipley, Sheryl, 363
Shipley, Shiray, 491
Shipman, Clyde, 150
Shipman, Susan, 139, 156
Shipp, Carol, 191
Shiralipour, Aziz, 609
Shire, Gavin, 250
Shirey, Ruth, 418
Shively, Paul, 496
Shoesmith, Merlin, 176
Shon, Frederick, 26
Shore, Debra, 296
Shostal, H., 289
Shoun, Gary, 146
Showalter, Robert, 155
Shriner, Ernie, 340
Shropshire, Cathy, 401
Shropshire, Tommy, 184
Shrouds, James, 128
Shroufe, Duane, 25, 156
Shuffield, Bob, 73
Shugrue, Edward, 339
Shuler, Scott, 255
Shull, Gary, 451
Shultz, Michael, 295
Shupe, Todd, 173
Shupp, Bruce, 268, 564
Shuster, Bill, 12
Shuster, Guenter, 581
Shute, Peggy, 508
Shy, Marilyn, 397
Siar, Charles, 376
Siart, Leeanne, 461
Sibley, John, 341
Sicard, Raymond, 383
Sicking, Joe, 442
Sidell, Bruce, 612
Siegel, Kassie, 290
Siegenthaler, Kim, 573
Siegrist, Gary, 415
Siembieda, William, 575
Siener, Joseph, 163
Sievers, Don, 306
Sievers, Donald, 548
Sievert, Paul, 178
Siewert, Fred, 574
Siewert, Rachel, 17
Sigman, William, 356
Silberhorn, Gene, 577
Silberman, Katherine, 291
Sillick, Darlene, 448
Silva, Peter, 144
Silva, Ralph, 179
Silva, Teresa Cristina, 347
Silver, Christopher, 611
Silver, Robin, 290
Silverberg, Alan, 136
Silverstone, Martin, 275
Simino, Larry, 227
Simmonds, Mark, 538
Simmons, John, 212
Simmons, Robert R., 3
Simmons, Roderick, 395
Simms, Herman, 129
Simms, William, 281
Simon, Carol, 518
Simon, Jack, 271
Simonds, Kitty, 131
Simonik, Michael, 306
Simons, Bob, 331
Simonsen, Charlie, 76
Simonton, Hugh, 221
Simpson, Bill, 366
Simpson, Hal, 147
Simpson, John, 163
Simpson, Kevin, 395
Simpson, Larry, 21
Simpson, Mike, 5
Simpson, Nancy, 163
Simpson, Oscar, 305
Simpson, Robert, 260
Simpson, Tommy, 542

Sims, Olin, 560
Sinclair, Ellery, 277
Sinclair, Steven, 227
Singer, Harold, 144
Singer, Jodie, 391
Singer, John, 612
Singer, Philip, 618
Singer, Roger, 495
Singh, Susan, 480
Singhaus, Barbara, 469
Singhurst, Jason, 517
Sinton, Diana, 572
Siska, Peter, 598
Sissenwine, Michael, 52
Sistare, Yvette, 218
Sitzes, Lester, 138
Sivas, Debbie, 318
Siver, Peter, 578
Skager, Cameo, 452
Skeele, Thomas, 472
Skeen, John, 551
Skelton, Ike, 8
Skillin, Rick, 493
Skinner, Alex, 68
Skinner, Katherine, 436, 438
Skinner, Peter, 223
Skinner, Richard, 174
Skinner, Steve, 204
Skinner, Thomas, 19
Skinner, Tom, 178, 179
Skousen, Jeffrey, 237
Skovron, David, 242
Skowronski, Bill, 204
Slama, Jim, 514
Slater, Carl, 281
Slater, Joe, 397
Slater, Scott, 261
Slatterly, Mark, 166
Slaughter, Louise McIntosh, 10
Slayden, Jocelyn, 532
Sledd, Charles, 230, 231
Sledge, James, 184
Sleeman, Jonathan, 542
Sliter, Deborah, 418
Sliva, Jan, 365
Slivken, Susan, 420
Sloan, Mary Margaret, 261
Sloan, Ted, 169
Slobe, Debbie, 470
Slocum, Bob, 450
Slotpe, Elizabeth, 31
Slusher, John, 186
Slutz, Jim, 163
Small, Connie, 000
Small, Eugene, 316
Small, Gregg, 534
Small, Lawrence, 501
Smallidge, Peter, 197
Smallwood, John, 555
Smardon, Richard, 598
Smart, Miles, 276
Smith, Adam, 15
Smith, Adele, 182
Smith, Al, 564
Smith, Andrew, 47
Smith, April, 184
Smith, Arthur, 213, 553
Smith, Billy, 169
Smith, Brad, 484
Smith, Bradley, 627
Smith, C., 357
Smith, Carl, 236
Smith, Chad, 265
Smith, Charles, 532, 579
Smith, Christian, 186
Smith, Christopher H., 9
Smith, Clay, 558
Smith, Connie, 206, 447
Smith, Daniel, 146
Smith, David, 25, 615
Smith, Dawn, 204
Smith, Del, 134
Smith, Dena, 404

Smith, Donald, 149, 509
Smith, Donna, 407
Smith, Douglas, 75
Smith, Duane, 207
Smith, Ed, 616
Smith, Edward, 551
Smith, Eric, 149
Smith, Ernest, 222
Smith, George, 511
Smith, Gordon, 11
Smith, Greg, 204
Smith, Guy, 277
Smith, H., 266
Smith, J., 407
Smith, Jack, 473
Smith, Jackie, 331
Smith, Jane, 185
Smith, Janelle, 512
Smith, Jeff, 350
Smith, Jennifer, 309
Smith, John, 157, 165, 185
Smith, Julia, 230, 231
Smith, Karen, 136, 138
Smith, Keith, 205
Smith, Kelley, 181
Smith, Ken, 195, 397
Smith, Kevin, 333
Smith, Kimberly, 264
Smith, Kitty, 33
Smith, Lamar S., 13
Smith, Larry, 375, 426
Smith, Laura, 41
Smith, Lawrence, 230
Smith, Leslie, 356
Smith, Lora L., 344
Smith, Marek, 180
Smith, Mark, 156, 259, 406
Smith, Mary Grace, 138
Smith, Matt, 548
Smith, McClain, 397
Smith, Michael, 261
Smith, Mike, 313
Smith, Mitchell, 277
Smith, Nancy, 289, 352
Smith, Nick, 7
Smith, Paula, 163
Smith, Peg, 250
Smith, R., 197
Smith, Ray, 520
Smith, Rich, 457
Smith, Rob, 498
Smith, Robert, 387
Smith, Robin, 200
Smith, Roger, 73
Smith, Sarah, 617
Smith, Scott, 421, 493
Smith, Stewart, 285
Smith, Tat, 599
Smith, Thomas, 229
Smith, Tim, 225, 233
Smith, Tin, 60
Smith, Walter, 471
Smith, Wayne, 458
Smith, William, 238, 241
Smith, Winston, 266
Smith, Zane, 260
Smith-Walters, Cindi, 588
Smitherman, John, 523
Smithers, F., 524
Smoak, Cameron, 155
Smoot, Bob, 225
Smulian, Robert, 341
Snape, William, 312
Snedeker, Mark, 564
Snider, Christine, 204
Sniffen, James, 526
Snitkin, Barry, 500
Snobelen, John, 188
Snodgrass, Jerry, 354
Snook, John, 281
Snovell, Christine, 418
Snow, Kerry, 471
Snowe, Olympia J., 6

Snyder, Deborah, 611
Snyder, Ed, 595
Snyder, Ellen, 617
Snyder, Erin, 210
Snyder, Gregory, 130
Snyder, Katharine, 77
Snyder, Keith, 364
Snyder, Steve, 218
Snyder, Vic, 1
Sobeck, Eileen, 77
Sobel, David, 291
Sobel, Jack, 455
Sobel, Kelli, 181
Sochasky, Lee, 511
Soest, Sally, 459
Sokolov, V., 25
Solberg, Trygve, 238
Soldwedel, Robert, 192
Sole, Michael, 153
Soles, Roger, 78
Solis, Hilda L., 2
Soliva, Delmina, 152
Sollman, Dave, 425
Solomon, Steve, 414
Solt, Ronald, 352
Somerville, Nancy, 266
Sommer, George, 528
Sommers, Larry, 420
Sondermeyer, Gary, 191
Sons, Gregg, 207
Soots, Robert, 67
Sorensen, Ann, 252
Sorensen, Troy, 546
Sosa, Ricardo, 526
Sosnowski, Susan, 480
Sotirin, Barbara, 68
Soto, Tom, 570
Soucy, David, 174
Souder, Mark, 5
Souers, Amy, 265
Soukup, Michael, 120
Soule, Jeff, 264
Southard, Lou, 230
Southwick, Rob, 339
Sowers, Raymond, 218, 219
Sowka, Patti, 344
Spagnolo, Lori, 312
Spalding, H., 485
Spalthoff, Yvonne, 322
Spang, Ed, 474
Spangenberg, N., 267
Spangler, Conrad, 232
Spangler, Kathy, 423
Spangler, Scott, 170
Sparkman, Chris, 184
Sparks, Jack, 261
Sparks, James, 427
Sparks, Julie, 165
Sparrowe, Rollin, 545
Spayd, Philip, 76
Speaker, Bob, 72
Spear, Bob, 204
Spear, Frank, 593
Spear, Robert, 174
Speck, Samuel, 204
Specter, Arlen, 12
Spector, Paul, 263
Speedy, Loree, 280
Speir, Edwin, 342
Speis, Themis, 26
Spelce, Allen, 222
Spell, Lester, 184
Spelliscy, Sandra, 469
Spelman, Lucy, 502
Spence, Don, 332
Spence, John, 605
Spence, Lawrence, 384
Spencer, Don, 474
Spencer, John, 129
Spencer, Marcus, 550
Spevacek, Jo Ann, 531
Spicer, Bradley, 172
Spicklemier, Steve, 354

753

Staff Name Index

STAFF NAME INDEX – S

Spickler, Donald, 395
Spinosa, Salvatore, 226
Spitler, Ron, 397
Spivak, Randi, 262
Spivey, Helen, 486
Spivey, Joseph, 251
Spivy-Weber, Francis, 402
Sponenberg, Phillip, 263
Sponsler, Mike, 163, 204
Spooner, Brian, 586
Spooner, Charlie, 512
Spraggins, Leslee, 435
Sprague, Ann, 554
Spranger, Michael, 55
Spratling, Boyd, 189
Spratt, John M., Jr., 12
Sprenkle, Richard, 211
Springborg, Denise, 443
Springer, Jim, 448
Springer, Michael, 26
Springuel, Natalie, 56
Sprinkmann, Jeff, 65
Sproat, Kapua, 319, 389
Sprout, Paul, 20
Spruance, Halsey, 281
Spruill, Vikki, 489
Sprunger-Allworth, Amy, 106
Sprynczynatyk, David, 426
Spurger, Steve, 618
Spurlock, Thad, 172
Squier, Anne, 148
Sramek, Jenn, 389
St-Arnaud, Pierre, 603
St. George, Paul, 315
St. John, Joann, 567
St. John, Judith, 31
St. Pierre, Bob, 468
Staats, Jessica, 362
Stabb, Jo, 606
Stabeno, Debra, 222
Stabenow, Debbie A., 7
Staber, Lorie, 242
Stables, Andrew, 576, 605
Stacey, Greg, 360
Stacey, Pamela, 394
Stadler, G., 175
Stafford, Susan, 578
Stafford, Susan, 615
Staggs, Michael, 238, 254
Stahl, Andy, 335
Stahl, Jane, 149
Staley, Dorothy, 47
Stalling, Dick, 591
Stallsmith, Bruce, 449
Stallwood, Kim, 563
Stallworth, Marla, 405
Stamats, Maria, 423
Stanfield, Richard, 395
Stang, Douglas, 258
Stangel, Peter, 419
Stankiewicz, Steve, 167
Stanley, Derrek, 287
Stanley, Erica, 285
Stanley, Patricia, 381
Stanley, Roya, 166
Stanley, Shelley, 148
Stansell, Ken, 90
Stanton, Gina, 391
Stanton, Nancy, 623
Stanton, Robert, 422
Staples-Bortner, Sandra, 546
Stapleton, Carl, 605
Stapleton, Michael, 595
Stapleton, Shirley, 573
Stapp, Katherine, 344
Starbard, Howard, 134
Stark, Daniel, 249
Stark, Fortney H. Pete, 2
Stark, J. Alan, 168
Stark, Robert, 539
Starke, Barry, 478
Starnes, Melanie, 401
Starr, C., 284

Starr, D. Curtis, 346
Starr, James, 230
Starr, Patrick, 466
Starrs, Paul, 260
Startzell, David, 270
Staudinger, Jeff, 326
Staunton, Nicky, 532
Stearns, Cliff, 3
Stebbins, Cynthia, 554
Steele, Jim, 142
Steele, Robert, 310
Steele, Sally, 450
Steele, Terry, 511
Steenstra, Norm, 536
Stefanski, Mary, 105, 112
Steffen, Chuck, 548
Steffes, Laurel, 238
Steffey, Kevin, 323
Stegmier, Robert, 377
Stehsel, Donald, 283
Steiger, Gretchen, 289
Steimle, Frank, 262
Stein, Bernie, 301
Stein, Bruce, 441
Stein, Kalman, 318
Stein, Roland, 167
Steinauer, Garry, 550
Steinberg, Alan, 312
Steinberg, Burt, 266
Steindler, Curt, 510
Steindler, Martin, 26
Steiner, Achim, 558
Steiner, Bruce, 311
Steiner, Linda, 466
Steiner, Mary, 462
Steinwand, Terry, 202
Stengler, Jim, 64
Stenholm, Charles W., 13
Stenmetz, John, 164
Stephens, Barry, 221
Stephens, Keith, 138
Stephens, Kyle, 225
Stephenson, John, 553
Stephenson, Robert, 33
Sterling, Pamela, 130
Sterner, Robert, 615
Stessman, Neal, 89
Stetson, Deborah, 207
Stetson, Paul, 304
Stettner, Karen, 106
Steuber, John, 205
Steury, Paul, 325
Stevens, Christine, 269
Stevens, Gretchen, 352
Stevens, Josh, 269
Stevens, Mary, 184
Stevens, Norman, 311
Stevens, Ted, 1
Stevens, V., 31
Stevens, William, 329
Stevenson, Barbara, 287
Stevenson, Karen, 385
Stevenson, Kate, 120
Stevenson, Tod, 194
Stevenson, Tom, 483
Steward, Dennis, 185
Stewart, Allan, 208
Stewart, Andrea, 103
Stewart, Christin, 489
Stewart, Connie, 452
Stewart, David, 522
Stewart, Don, 572
Stewart, Doug, 203
Stewart, Gary, 315
Stewart, George, 262, 622
Stewart, Harry, 190
Stewart, Janet, 205
Stewart, Jon, 381
Stewart, Margaret, 266
Stewart, Patrick, 287
Stewart, Richard, 458
Stewart, Teri, 538
Stewart-Kent, Deborah, 333

Sticht, Nancy, 67
Stickler, Richard, 211
Stickles, Van, 218
Stickney, Robert, 59
Stieglitz, Ronald, 623
Stiehler, Joyce, 206
Stiles, David, 572
Stiles, Eric, 415
Stiller-Rikleen, Lauren, 327
Stine, Bob, 615
Stine, Jeffrey, 265
Stinebaugh, Jim, 223
Stitzhal, David, 534
Stock, Jasen, 444
Stockdale, Deborah, 65
Stocker, Randall, 609
Stockwell, Craig, 590
Stoeckel, Joseph, 573
Stoever, Henry, 568
Stoffle, Carla, 605
Stoflet, Roger, 72
Stogner, Joseph, 582
Stoiber, Carlton, 26
Stokes, Donald, 417
Stokes, John, 193
Stokes, Judy, 191, 273
Stokes, Julia, 198
Stokes, Phil, 532
Stokes, Robert, 192
Stokes, Rodney, 181
Stokowski, Patricia, 622
Stolgitis, John, 214
Stoll, Mary Ellen, 208
Stoltz, Michael, 209
Stolz, Gary, 101
Stolz, Robert, 621
Stone, Alan, 585
Stone, Alexander, 478
Stone, Andrew, 261
Stone, Ann, 250
Stone, Charlie, 209
Stone, Chris, 354
Stone, Lee, 431
Stone, M., 227
Stone, Mike, 239
Stone, Roger, 288
Stone, Sheridan, 73
Stonecipher, Harlan, 206
Stoneman, Julie, 386
Storey, Richard, 407
Stormo, Jack, 74
Stortz, Peter, 149
Story, Rick, 527
Stossel, Robert, 333
Stout, Gene, 74
Stoutamire, Jim, 153
Strahl, Stuart, 410
Strait, Donald, 305
Stranges, Mike, 457
Strasser, Virginia, 75
Stratman, Omar, 245
Stratton, Jim, 134
Straughan, Baird, 358
Strauss, Charles, 592
Strauss, Hanna, 510
Strawberry, Barbara, 483
Strayer, David, 359
Strayer, Nancy, 204
Street, Bill, 427
Streeter, Tracy, 169
Streich, John, 206
Strickland, Genie, 492
Strickland, Rennard, 619
Strickland, Ted, 11
Strickler, John, 380
Stringer, Bill, 506
Stringer, Jeff, 504
Stroeder, Celina, 203
Strojan, Carl, 610
Strom, Peter, 594
Stroman, Michael, 179
Strommen, Sarah, 337
Strong, Dave, 466

Strong, Janice, 142
Strother, Jessica, 532
Stroud, Chris, 538
Struble, Dave, 175
Struhs, David, 153
Stuart, David, 582
Stuart, John, 583
Stubbs, Mitiz, 184
Stucky, Norm, 185, 401
Stucky, Norman, 185
Studders, Karen, 183
Studebaker, Stacy, 246
Studer, Marie, 321
Studt, John, 67
Stuhr, Michael, 568
Stults, Jack, 187
Stumbough, Grant, 239
Stupak, Bart, 7
Sturdy, Jerry, 74
Sturgeon, Walter, 371
Sturges, Wilton, 582
Sturgess-Streich, Melinda, 206
Sturm, Charles, 298
Sturm, Robert, 28
Sturm, Russell, 364
Sturtevant, Bob, 148
Stushnoff, Brian, 311
Stutler, Denver, 153
Stutzman, Roger, 353
Stymmes, Ric, 330
Sublette, Dick, 155
Suckling, Kieran, 290
Sugal, Cheri, 559
Sugameli, Glenn, 319
Sugarbaker, Larry, 441
Suleiman, Samuel, 502
Sullivan, Beth, 387
Sullivan, Blake, 342
Sullivan, Brian, 470
Sullivan, Jeremiah, 76
Sullivan, John, 11
Sullivan, Kate, 481
Sullivan, Larry, 135
Sullivan, Michael, 182, 189
Sullivan, Ned, 488
Sullivan, Susan, 443
Sullivan, Tade, 33
Sullivan, Terry, 439
Sullivan, Tim, 401
Summers, Jim, 519, 536
Summers, Robert, 177
Summers, William, 61
Sumners, Barry, 222
Sundberg, Marshall, 581
Sunderland, Larry, 411
Sundstrom, Lori, 209
Sununu, John E., 9
Suphatranand, Tanya, 544
Surber, Laura, 532
Surkin, Elliot, 524
Sussman, Adam, 210
Suter, Stacy, 511
Sutherland, David, 307
Sutherlin, John, 624
Suto, Barbara, 430, 514
Suttles, John, 600
Suttles, Ron, 206
Sutton, Elizabeth, 383
Sutton, Keith, 138
Sutton, Robert, 214
Svedarsky, Daniel, 615
Sveikauskas, Geddy, 289
Svensen, Gene, 66
Svetahor, Emil, 212
Swackhamer, Deb, 615
Swain, Hilary, 270
Swan, Christopher, 600
Swan, Tom, 168
Swaney, Rhonda, 304
Swann, Ladon, 57
Swanson, D., 453
Swanson, David, 507
Swanson, Merv, 217

STAFF NAME INDEX – T

Swanson, Robert, 509
Swanson, Sherman, 616
Swanstrom, Florence, 554
Swartz, Paul, 30
Swartz, Steven, 503
Swayer, Michael, 532
Swayne, Cheryl, 167
Sweatman, Michael, 540
Swedburg, Randy, 248
Sweeney, Bernard, 512
Sweeney, Debra, 555
Sweeney, James, 609
Sweeney, John, 146, 577
Sweeney, John E., 10
Sweeney, Kevin, 463
Sweeney, Michael, 145
Sweetland, Helen, 497
Sweetwood, Sage, 469
Sweitzer, Richard, 618
Swenarchuk, Michelle, 286
Swengel, Ann, 448
Swenson, Guy, 448
Swenson, Jim, 189
Swenson, Paul, 182
Swenson, Steve, 247
Swift, Byron, 559
Swihart, Robert, 593
Swinehart, Bonnie, 466
Swingle, Wayne, 348
Switkes, Glenn, 366
Swope, Marjory, 443
Swormstead, Geraldine, 491
Sybert, Brian, 493
Sykes, Jack, 229
Sylvester, Susan, 238
Szaro, Robert, 42
Szczytko, Stan, 623
Szelc, Gary, 274
Szlosberg, Nina, 306
Szramoski, Matthew, 424

T

Taal, B., 367
Tabor, Lance, 236
Taborsky, Theresea, 627
Taff, Steven, 183
Taft, John, 361
Taft, Lawrence, 276
Taft, Melody, 361
Taft, Ned, 253
Taggart, Bruce, 168
Taggert, Peter, 453
Tahirkheli, Sharon, 261
Taillon, Andre, 214
Taintor, Jacob, 384
Tak, Jetty, 363
Takasugi, Patrick, 161
Taki, Yasuhiko, 380
Talbot, Martha, 476
Talbot, Serge, 601
Talent, Jim, 8
Talkington, Mike, 205
Talley, John, 151
Tallman, Dan, 507
Taluto, Susan, 190
Tamaru, Clyde, 55
Tamayose, Joy, 547
Tan, Betsy, 595
Tancredo, Thomas G., 3
Tanner, Gregg, 189
Tanner, John S., 13
Tanner, Paul, 79
Tansill, Linda, 506
Tanton, Mary, 487
Tapia, Alvaro, 293
Tarantino, Helen, 231
Taranto, Steve, 334
Tarkington, Ken, 222
Tarnopol, Joe, 74
Tart, Carl, 200
Tart, Libby, 497
Tate, David, 355
Tate, Nancy, 388

Tate, Robert, 594
Taubert, Bruce, 136
Tauer, Jonathon, 452
Tauscher, Ellen O., 2
Tauzin, Billy, 21
Tauzin, W.J. Billy, 6
Tavolga, William, 404
Tayer, Jeff, 233
Taylor, Anne, 200
Taylor, Betsy, 289
Taylor, Bill, 275
Taylor, Caroline, 306
Taylor, Charles, 572
Taylor, Charles H., 10
Taylor, Curtis, 236, 360
Taylor, Daisan, 72
Taylor, E. Louise, 306
Taylor, Gary, 360
Taylor, Gene, 8
Taylor, Helen, 436
Taylor, J., 163
Taylor, James, 20
Taylor, Janice, 313, 424
Taylor, Jeffrey, 190
Taylor, Jennifer, 276
Taylor, Ken, 134
Taylor, Kent, 221, 411
Taylor, Marcy, 568
Taylor, Marsh, 235
Taylor, Martin, 290
Taylor, Meghan, 277
Taylor, Michael, 76
Taylor, Robert, 589
Taylor, Ron, 175
Taylor, Stephen, 190
Taylor, Sylvia, 398
Taylor, William, 57, 587
Taylor-Ide, Daniel, 339
Teague, Wade, 475
Teal, John, 308
Tederko, Zenon, 370
Teel, Julie, 290
Teer, James, 307
Teich, Susan, 487
Teichert, Kurt, 575
Teig, Donald, 74
Teigen, Dan, 453
Teillon, H., 227
Temes, Peter, 572
Tempero, James, 525
Templeton, Billy, 424
Templeton, David, 219
Templeton, Derek, 404
Tomploton, Susan, 383
Teneyck, Elizabeth, 26
Tennis, Michael, 453
Tennison, Harry, 340
Tennyson, Janet, 267
Tenore, Kenneth, 613
Terrell, Karen, 163
Terrell, Sandra, 618
Terry, Gordon, 097
Terry, Lee, 8
Terry, Lynn, 143
Tesarik, Susan, 555
Tesitor, Carlos, 531
Teske, Richard, 75
Tess, Mike, 589
Teven, Mercy, 468
Thacker, Randall, 553
Thadani, Ashok, 26
Thain, David, 189
Tham, Phil, 222
Thayer, Dan, 331
Thayer, Paul, 145
Theisen-Watt, Lee, 371
Theodore, Karen, 346
Theodorson, Lisa, 465
Thériault, Marius, 604
Theriot, Edwin, 72
Therkelsen, Robert, 143
Thiaw, Ibrahim, 370
Thibeault, Gerald, 144

Thibedeau, Richard, 179
Thiel, Dan, 316
Thiele, Amy, 138
Thiele, Tim, 315
Thielke, Rose, 506
Thigpen, Drew, 223
Thigpen, Jack, 58
Thill, Marvin, 316
Thom, Derrick, 624
Thomann, Judy, 163
Thomas, Carolyn, 582
Thomas, Christine, 623
Thomas, Craig, 15, 284
Thomas, Dan, 345
Thomas, Diane, 352
Thomas, Donna, 282
Thomas, Doug, 169
Thomas, Edward, 129
Thomas, Emy, 531
Thomas, Jack, 279, 615
Thomas, Judy, 277
Thomas, Matthew, 266
Thomas, Sandra, 375
Thomas, Sandy, 452
Thomas, Steve, 209, 495
Thomas, William M., 2
Thomas-Slayter, Barbara, 576
Thomashow, Cindy, 291
Thomason, Bill, 184
Thomason, Chris, 258
Thomasson, Brenda, 161
Thomasson, Kevin, 374
Thomlison, Bryan, 347
Thompson, Bennie G., 8
Thompson, Bridgett, 479
Thompson, Bruce, 127
Thompson, Charles, 332
Thompson, Clyde, 34
Thompson, Derek, 140
Thompson, Dianne, 76
Thompson, Doug, 374
Thompson, Edward, 252
Thompson, Elizabeth, 324
Thompson, Garland, 157
Thompson, Gloria, 52
Thompson, Hugh, 26, 226
Thompson, Jeff, 548
Thompson, Jim, 387
Thompson, John, 327, 397
Thompson, Larry, 157
Thompson, Mark, 170
Thompson, Mike, 1
Thompson, Paul, 27
Thompson, Rudi, 618
Thompson, Stephen, 524
Thompson, Steve, 94, 111, 556
Thompson, Steven, 206
Thompson, Terrie, 605
Thompson, Tommy, 75
Thompson, Warren, 588
Thompson, William, 137
Thomson, David, 287
Thomson, Kirk, 534
Thong, Nguyen, 371
Thorn, Colin, 611
Thornberry, William Mac, 13
Thorne, Janet, 351
Thorne, Oakleigh, 518, 520
Thorne, Steven, 399
Thorne, Tom, 239
Thornhill, Alan, 502
Thornton, Robert, 245
Thoroughgood, Carolyn, 54
Thorp, Lynn, 347
Thorp, Tom, 451
Thorpe, Doris, 276
Thorpe, Greg, 200
Thorpe, Kenneth, 474
Thorson, Jerry, 271
Thorvig, Lisa, 183
Thraikill, Jim, 552
Thralls, Mike, 205
Thrasher, Barbara, 532

Thrune, Elaine, 430
Thurman, Steve, 74
Thurstrom, Sam, 31
Tiahrt, Todd, 6
Tiberi, Patrick J., 11
Tichenor, Carey, 170
Tidemann, Larry, 218
Tiemann, Larry, 168
Tierney, John F., 7
Tierney, Tim, 242
Tierney, Vanyla, 467
Tiersch, Terry, 256
Tigner, Timothy, 230
Tilford, Monique, 289
Tillotson, Virginia, 430
Tillson, John, 184
Tilt, Whitney, 419, 505
Timmel, Bertha, 414
Timmerman, James, 218
Timmons, Tom, 589
Timony, Sheila, 351
Tindal, D., 217
Tindall, Barry, 423
Tinjum, Dale, 452
Tinker, Scott, 140
Tinnemore, Rod, 234
Tinsley, Nikki, 18
Tintera, Marcy, 615
Tippett, Russell, 583
Tipps, Christine, 248
Tipton, W., 85
Tischler, Bonni, 76
Titman, Rodger, 587
Titmann, Rodger, 474
Tittel, Erin, 530
Tittel, Jeff, 405
Tittlebaum, Marty, 624
Titus, Elizabeth, 513
Tjaden, Bob, 224
Tobin, Rich, 40
Tobin, Richard, 385
Toborg, Barbara, 263
Todd, Arlen, 546
Todd, Clyde, 390
Todd, Laura, 552
Todd, Murray, 271
Toepfer, Karen, 381
Toepfer, Klaus, 526
Toews, Don, 240
Tokas, Ed, 451
Tokue, Michiaki, 447
Tolentino, Amado, 362
Tollefsrud, Tim, 219
Tollentino, Scott, 253
Toman, Michael, 479
Tomassi, Wayne, 446
Tomera, Patsy, 442
Tomke, John, 316
Tomlinson, Charles, 334
Tomlinson, Jeanie, 555
Tomoney, Thomas, 382
Tompkins, David, 217
Tongate, Butch, 195
Tonsor, Stephen, 619
Toohey, Mary, 232
Tooker, Leisa, 259
Toole, Robert, 407
Toombs, Ted, 482
Toomey, Pat, 12
Toor, Will, 608
Topham, Gordon, 225
Toplisek, Timothy, 67
Topping, John, 299
Topping, Steven, 176
Torbit, Stephen, 429
Torgerson, Ollie, 381
Toridis, Theodore, 582
Torley, Coral, 377
Tormey, Brian, 166
Tormey, Edmund, 204
Torok, Laurance, 550
Torrence, Jim, 454
Torres, Alfonso, 32

Totah, Anthony, 298
Totin, Elissa, 465
Totman, Lori, 311
Totten, Debbie, 454
Totten, Scott, 186
Tougaard, O., 25
Tourtelotte, Marilyn, 174
Tout, Sue, 367
Tow, Kenneth, 165
Towery, Dan, 308
Towle, Edward, 375
Towle, Judith, 375
Towns, Edolphus, 10
Towns, Eleanor, 43
Townsend, Blaine, 389
Townsend, Christopher, 467
Townsend, Dave, 612
Townsend, Georgia, 376, 377
Townsend, Jerry, 403
Townsend, Laird, 322
Townsend, Peter, 572
Tramblay, Albin, 28
Tramell, Thomas, 154
Trammontano, Ronald, 197
Trantham, Kathi, 463
Traore, Moctar, 369
Trask, R., 199
Traub, Pat, 539
Travelstead, Jack, 232
Travers, Will, 280
Travers, William, 26
Travis, Will, 215
Travous, Kenneth, 137
Treanor, Robert, 144
Treanor, Steven, 152
Tremblay, Germain, 602
Tremblay, Marc, 480
Tremblay, Michele, 444
Tremble, Elaine, 47
Tremoulet, Kristen, 534
Trenchik, Melissa, 66
Trent, Tracey, 160
Trew, Leslie, 232
Trianosky, Paul, 440
Triff, Michael, 524
Trimberger, E. John, 377
Trine, Cheryl, 264
Tripp, James, 325
Tripp, Jim, 316
Tritaik, Paul, 91, 109
Trollan, Marla, 399
Trosow, Esther, 338
Trotta, Lee, 400
Trottier, Tim, 217
Troutman, Wade, 533
Troxell, Pam, 591
Troyer, Jack, 43
Trudeau, Maurice, 215
True, Todd, 320
Trueblood, Jack, 160
Truesdell, Robert, 405
Trujillo, Tom, 195
Truland, Mary, 295
Truland, Robert, 295
Trusso, Samara, 360
Tryon, Craig, 198
Trzyna, Ted, 283
Tschogl, Kathleen, 143
Tseng, Florina, 430
Tsuneyoshi, Raynor, 141
Tubbs, Dennis, 212
Tuck, Al, 184
Tucker, Arianne, 386
Tucker, Judy, 301
Tucker, Robert, 174
Tucker, Thurman, 400
Tuftey, James, 196
Tuggle, Benjamin, 90
Tukahirwa, Eldad, 369
Tulang, Mike, 507
Tull, J., 582
Tullbane, Joseph, 597
Tullius, Mary, 225

Tulloch, Dave, 216
Tulloch, Lynn, 216
Tunberg, Gail, 551
Tupper, Doug, 135
Turcotte, Jacques, 603
Turissini, Dani, 505
Turnbow, Robert, 74
Turner, Alan, 235
Turner, Daniel, 352
Turner, Jim, 13
Turner, John, 438
Turner, Larry, 171
Turner, Lisa, 483
Turner, Michael, 11
Turner, Paul, 257
Turner, Ronald, 146, 186
Turney, Thomas, 220
Turnipseed, R. Michael, 189
Turpin, Barbara, 594
Turrini, Tony, 427
Tutchton, Jay, 290, 319
Tuttle, Andrea, 142
Tuttle, Anita, 532
Tuttle, Merlin, 277
Twarkins, Martha, 37
Tween, Gordon, 32
Twichell, Sophia, 385
Twiggs, Stacy, 517
Tyas, Jim, 376
Tyler, Bob, 184
Tyler, Breck, 464
Tyler, R., 620
Tymeson, Christopher, 364
Tyndall, Patricia Earnhardt, 256
Tyser, Robin, 623
Tyson, Tony, 157

U

Ubbelohde, Kurt, 70
Ucelli, Loretta, 18
Udall, Mark, 3
Udall, Tom, 9
Udell, Bert, 430
Ueber, Edward, 51
Uecker, Cheryl, 539
Uerz, Jeff, 230
Uerz, Jeffrey, 231
Ugalde, Jesus, 22
Ugarenko, Len, 360
Uhazy, Leslie, 543
Uhlendorf, Karen, 585
Uhlenhuth, Karen, 410
Uhmann, Tanys, 549
Uhrie, Larry, 415
Uihlein, Pam, 344
Ulliam, Barbara, 500
Ulman, Suzanne, 284
Ulrich, David, 19
Ultee, Casper, 304
Umaña, Leonel, 281
Umansky, David, 501
Umstead, Geralyn, 211
Undercoffer, Ken, 522
Underwood, Don, 184
Underwood, H., 598
Underwood, Joanna, 357
Underwood, Peter, 203
Unfried, Stephen, 346
Unger, Daniel, 598
Unger, Lorraine, 493
Unkenholz, Dennis, 219
Upshaw, Grace, 489
Upton, Fred, 7
Uram, Eric, 494
Urban, Matt, 491
Urrutia, Al, 63
Uttech, Mary, 556
Uttecht, Jan, 442
Utzinger, Con, 554
Uyeda, Craig, 138
Uzzell, James, 239

V

Vacek, Sara, 106
Valdez, Lori, 48
Valencic, Cynthia, 389
Valenta, Jodi, 424
Valentine, Al, 357
Valentine, Gary, 517
Valentine, Gayle, 161
Valentine, Jane, 267
Valentine, Michael, 142
Valentinetti, Richard, 227
Vallee, Judith, 486
Vallender, Leonard, 285
Vallet, Rudy, 198
Van Abbemg, Jim, 446
Van Aken, Alan, 158
van de Hoek, Robert Roy, 538
Van Deelen, Tim, 547
Van der Zel, D., 508
Van Dyke, Gerald, 590
Van Gilder, David, 241
Van Gilder, Gail, 312
Van Hollen, Chris, Jr., 7
Van Lockwood, Peter, 298
van Manen, Frank, 359
Van Matre, Steve, 358
Van Ningen, Paul, 103
Van Noppen, Trip, 509
Van Norman, Kelli, 430
Van Patten, Peg, 54
Van Raalte, Gerrit, 17
Van Roeckel, Joel, 532
Van Rossum, Maya, 313
Van Schoik, D., 596
Van Thull, Traci, 284
Van Tongerloo, Robert, 286
Van Tussenbrook, Lee, 233
van Tuyn, Peter, 524
Van Waus, David, 468
Van Wie, David, 175
van Zwoll, Wayne, 406
Vanaller, Robert, 158
Vanblaricom, Glenn, 128, 503
VanBuecken, Donna, 540
Vance, Grace, 433
Vance, Tamara, 232
Vandel, George, 165, 219, 420
Vandenberg, Thomas, 278
Vanderhoop, Matthew, 430
Vandermark, Peter, 489
Vandersteen, Charles, 390
Vandiver, Ruth, 65
Vandrey, Don, 176
Vang, Alfred, 218
Vangyeek, Richard, 379
Vanicek, C., 575
Vaniman, Mark, 91
Vanlopik, Jack, 56
Vansant, Coleen, 133
Vanyo, Theresa, 488
Vanzyll de Jong, M., 199
Vargas, Martha, 518
Vargo, Anthony, 420
Vargo, George, 357
Varner, Dennis, 181
Varner, Mark, 613
Vasquez, Sarita, 303
Vasuki, N., 151
Vaughan, Katherine, 172
Vaughn, Caryn, 205
Vaughn, Denise, 463
Veeman, Michele, 605
Vehrs, Kristin, 268
Velazquez, Nydia, 10
Veneman, Ann, 31
Ventola, Anne Marie, 437
Ventura, Aldrina, 462
Venturini, Peter, 143
Verardo, Denzil, 152
Verbon, Ivor, 488
Verdoliva, Fran, 196
Veres, Susan, 513
Vergara, Napoleon, 367

Verigin, Steve, 143
Vernachio, Brian, 415
Verner, Abbey, 273
Verploeg, Alan, 240
Vetter, Mary, 619
Veverka, Mary, 76
Vezina, Guy, 476
Vibert, Joan, 381
Vice, David, 164
Vicente, Ralph, 278
Vick, Chris, 538
Vickerman, Sara, 312
Vickers, John, 71
Vicory, Alan, 26
Victor, Robert, 294
Vidrine, Winton, 173
Vigil, Alfredo, 469
Vigil, Eddie, 445
Vilakati, J., 30
Vilardo, Frank, 584
Vilches, Maria, 294
Vilella, Francisco, 183
Viljoen, C., 508
Villafane, Awilda, 76
Villanueva, L., 93
Vincent, Amanda, 473
Vincent, Frederick, 214
Vincent, Howard, 468
Vincent, Matt, 268
Vincent, Randall, 431
Vincenti, Frank, 539
Vinebrooke, Rolf, 619
Vines, Susan, 424
Viney, Angela, 506
Viney, Michelle, 272
Virden, Terry, 78
Virgin, Randy, 245
Visclosky, Peter J., 5
Visson, Rita, 529
Vitter, David, 6
Vlahovich, Stjepan, 204
Vodak, Mark, 215
Voecks, Larry, 189
Voeks, Robert, 575
Voeltz, Barbara, 189
Voeltz, Barbara, 432
Vogel, David, 200, 201, 450
Vogel, Harry, 411
Vogel, Richard, 600
Vogt, Albert, 615
Vohres, Courte, 195
Voinovich, George V., 11
Vokaty, Chris, 399
Volk, John, 149
Volk, Michael, 489
Vollmer, Katrina, 420
Volp, Jeannot, 189
Von Finger, Kevin, 74
Von Rueden, Gerald, 64
Vondracek, Bruce, 181
Vonk, Jeffrey, 165, 166
Voorhis, Ken, 346
Vorac, Tom, 72
Vorland, Jeanine, 549
Vornberg, Catherine, 66
Voronkov, Victor, 292
Vorontsova, Masha, 363
Voss, Hans, 398
Vota, Andrew, 336
Votteler, Todd, 157
Vreeland, Justin, 547

W

Waddill, Christine, 582
Wade, Edge, 411
Wade, James, 224
Wade, Jeptha, 393
Wade, Jerry, 411
Wade, Karen, 120
Wadick, Ashley, 222
Wadsworth, Frank, 367
Wagener, Joel, 261
Wagener, Karl, 149

STAFF NAME INDEX – W

Waggoner, Lynda, 537
Wagner, Barbara, 529
Wagner, Curtis, 75
Wagner, Denise, 249
Wagner, Kristen, 518
Wagner, Martin, 319
Wagner, Philip, 163
Wagner, Robert, 252
Wainman, Barbara, 127
Wait, Paul, 374
Waite, G., 353
Waito, Barry, 286
Wajda, Becky, 259
Wakimoto, Roger, 606
Walcher, Greg, 146
Walden, Greg, 12
Waldman, Bill, 438
Waldman, Doug, 325
Waldo, Thomas, 319
Waldon, Jefferson, 553, 626
Walke, Ted, 212
Walker, Barbara, 212
Walker, Bill, 16
Walker, Charles, 163
Walker, David, 360
Walker, Don, 169
Walker, Donald, 578
Walker, Hiram, 129
Walker, James, 270
Walker, Jennifer, 493
Walker, Jim, 140, 184
Walker, John, 321
Walker, Judy, 288
Walker, Lee, 230, 231
Walker, Mark, 616
Walker, Mason, 73
Walker, Polly, 584
Walker, Randy, 55, 284
Walker, Randy, 393
Walker, Richard, 242, 315
Walker, Roger, 616
Walker, Viola, 61
Walker, William, 158
Walkowiak, John, 166
Wall, Diana, 578
Wall, Steve, 306
Wallace, Alice, 353
Wallace, Charles, 612
Wallace, Don, 145
Wallace, Jim, 386
Wallace, Kathleen, 182
Wallace, Peter, 208
Waller, David, 157
Waller, William, 618
Wallis, Cliff, 247
Walsh, Barry, 393
Walsh, Bob, 89
Walsh, James T., 10
Walsh, John, 559
Walsh, Kathleen, 143
Walsh, Kevin, 179
Walsh, Patrick, 238
Walsh, William, 129
Walsh-McGehee, Martha, 374
Walters, Clara, 442
Walters, Debra, 258
Walters, Diane, 365
Waltman, Jim, 541
Walton, Becky, 217
Walton, Bill, 57
Walton, Bruce, 151
Walton, Dean, 532
Walton, Lynn, 157
Waltz, Robert, 163
Waltzer, Kurt, 457
Walz, Stephen, 231
Wamp, Zach, 13
Wampler, Glen, 74
Wampler, Steve, 73
Wang, Deane, 622
Wanha, Jeffrey, 292
Wannamaker, Katherine, 512
Warburton, Janet, 246

Ward, Bruce, 253
Ward, C., 594
Ward, Charles, 168
Ward, Harold, 575
Ward, J., 223
Ward, Jay, 460
Ward, Michael, 305
Ward, Milton, 280
Ward, Nathalie, 340
Ward, Sara, 204
Ward, Vivian, 407
Ward, Wesley, 524
Wardwell, Bob, 73
Ware, James, 316
Warham, Bill, 490
Waring, Linda, 232
Warkentine, Barbara, 262
Warlen, Stan, 451
Warman, Tim, 252
Warner, Barry, 504
Warner, Glenn, 608
Warner, James, 100
Warner, Janett, 528
Warner, Jerry, 382
Warner, John W., 14
Warner, Joseph, 359
Warner, Liz, 48
Warner, Richard, 55
Warner, Robert, 515
Warner, Susan, 144
Warner, Thomas, 585
Warr, Edward, 553
Warr, James, 133
Warren, Bob, 74
Warren, Charles, 302
Warren, David, 206
Warren, L., 315
Warren, Louise, 512
Warren, Melvin, 508
Warren, Robert, 545
Warrender, Virginia, 480
Warriner, Michael, 138
Wartenberg, Charles, 371
Warwick, John, 267
Wary, Sharon, 470
Washburn, Randy, 307
Washburn, W., 402
Washington, Val, 323
Washkuhn, Robert, 556
Wasley, Bill, 34
Wasserman, Pamela, 471
Watanabe, Steve, 141
Watchman, Laura, 312
Waters, Alicia, 551
Waters, Chuck, 547
Waters, Jim, 289
Waters, Maxine, 2
Waters, Mike, 451
Waters, Tim, 233
Watkins, Carolyn, 204
Watkins, Hardy, 207
Watkins, Joyce, 40
Watkins, Richard, 31
Watson, Alan, 610
Watson, Alexander, 433
Watson, Carolyn V., 177
Watson, Dennis, 169
Watson, Diane, 2
Watson, Jack, 592
Watson, Jim, 184, 612
Watson, John, 192
Watson, Kelley, 505
Watson, Leroy, 421
Watson, Melyssa, 267
Watson, Paul, 488
Watson, Ray, 152
Watt, Doris, 555
Watt, Melvin L., 11
Watters, Kathleen, 357
Watts, David, 184
Watts, Myles, 589
Watwood, Mary, 583
Waugh, Gary, 76, 229

Waxman, Henry A., 2
Waycott, Russ, 454
Wayland, Robert, 130
Weary, Robert, 440
Weathers, Don, 111
Weathers, Kathleen, 359
Weaver, Burton, 172
Weaver, Dennis, 225
Weaver, Kathy, 161
Weaver, Keith, 115
Weaver, Reg, 418
Weaver, Ron, 155
Weaver, Scott, 513
Weaver, Susan, 155
Webb, Alexander, 490
Webb, Brad, 358
Webb, Dan, 142
Webb, Donald, 447
Webb, Mark, 329
Webb, Robert, 169
Webber, Joe, 76
Webber, Matt, 377
Webber, Peter, 179
Weber, Barbara, 34
Weber, Gary, 334
Weber, John, 561
Weber, Ken, 276
Weber, Mike, 361
Weber, Steven, 191
Weber, Susan, 143
Weber, Will, 349
Weber, William, 375
Webster, Mike, 333
Wecker, Kendra, 551
Weddle, Tom, 174
Weedon, Ronald, 345
Week, Larry, 142
Weekes, David, 440
Weeks, Bill, 433
Weerts, Burt, 156
Wege, Peter, 291
Wegwart, Gordon, 183
Wehle, Carol, 220
Wehri, Tom, 282
Weicher, John, 77
Weidenhaft, Ray, 240
Weihing, Wayne, 508
Weikert, Bill, 480
Weil, Jeffrey, 349
Weil, Michael, 622
Weilbacher, Mike, 391
Weiler, Bill, 358
Weiler, Jeff, 413
Wein, Howard, 467
Weinberg, Peggy, 539
Weinberg, Philip, 289
Weiner, Anthony D., 10
Weingarden, Karen, 398
Weinstein, Kenneth, 129
Weinstein, Michael, 58
Weiringo, Pam, 532
Weishan, James, 557
Weisheit, John, 390
Weismiller, Richard, 613
Weiss, Dennis, 594
Weiss, Josh, 233
Weiss, Richard, 137
Weiss, Zeze, 248
Weisser, Pete, 143
Weissman, Arthur, 347
Welch, Alison, 203
Welch, Lane, 297
Welch, Patricia, 581
Welch, Susan, 193
Welch, Thomas, 186
Weldon, Curt, 12
Weldon, Daniel, 334
Weldon, Dave, 4
Welle, Patrick, 574
Weller, Candace, 332
Weller, Gene, 189
Weller, Jerry, 5
Weller, Marcia, 467

Wellford, L., 620
Wellings, Linda, 490
Wellings, Linda, 530
Wells, Doug, 549
Wells, Randall, 404
Wells, Rob, 134
Wells, Roger, 475
Wells, Sue, 417
Wells, Thomas, 192
Wells-Harley, Mary, 178
Welsch, David, 157
Welsh, Donald, 19
Welsh, James, 172
Welsh, Stuart, 235
Welton, Richard, 300
Welty, Claire, 580
Wendland, Mike, 403
Wendy, Stanton, 110
Wenker, Ron, 83
Wennberg, Jeffrey, 227
Wentworth, Rand, 386
Wentz, Chris, 104
Wentz, W., 25, 316
Wenzler, Mark, 499
Wenzlick, John, 522
Werden, Wendy Erica, 505
Werndli, Phillip, 154
Werner, Carol, 324
Werner, Mark, 316
Werthen, Ione, 411
Wesley, David, 111
Woccon, Jim, 232
West, B., 422
West, Dan, 204
West, Gary, 193
West, Lisa, 451
West, Mary, 78
West, Richard, 445
West, Stanford, 527
West, Timothy, 127
West, W., 157
West, William, 376
Westbrook, Christopher, 598
Westbrook, Corry, 416
Westcott, Mal, 589
Westcott, Marisa, 278
Westerholt, Duane, 189
Westley, Laurie, 343
Westly, Steve, 145
Weston, Al, 561
Weston, Judy, 155
Westra, Laura, 367
Westworth, Frank, 487
Wetzel, Dana, 404
Wetzel, Richard, 577
Wex, Richard, 27
Wexler, Robert I., 4
Weymouth, George, 281
Whalen, Sidney, 217
Whalen, William, 242
Whaley, Jane, 110
Whatley, Carolyn, 132
Whealan, Iensie, 477
Wheatley, Clara, 171
Wheatley, Henry, 375
Wheaton, Chris, 208
Wheeler, Dan, 221
Wheeler, Gerald, 424
Wheeler, Leslie, 333
Wheeler, Mindy, 528
Whellan, Leah, 376
Wherley, Sean, 337
Whinnery, Ellie, 230
Whipkey, Bob, 558
Whippen, William, 398
Whipple, Craig, 227
Whipple, Glen, 238
Whiston, Steve, 223
Whitaker, Mary Beth, 354
Whitaker, Scott, 300
Whitaker-Hoagland, Jullianne, 552
White, Alan, 146
White, Beatrice, 516

STAFF NAME INDEX – W

White, Ben, 269
White, Charles, 143
White, David, 58, 455, 589
White, Donald, 321
White, Gwen, 254
White, Howard, 375
White, Jacques, 467
White, Jean, 528
White, Jeffrey, 584
White, Jesse, 16
White, Jim, 74, 313
White, John, 134
White, Karen M., 177
White, Kevin, 546
White, Lyn, 269
White, Marlene, 294
White, Nina, 321
White, Rhett, 200
White, Ron, 482
White, Ronald, 193
White, Stephen, 589
White, Tina, 425
White, Tom, 189
White,, Alan, 565
Whiteford, Cynthia, 524
Whitehouse, Richard, 305
Whitehurst, David, 230, 231
Whiteman, Howard, 589
Whitfield, Edward, 6
Whiting, R., 598
Whiting-Grant, Kristen, 56
Whitmore, Robert, 626
Whitmore, Susan, 285
Whitney, Mark, 547
Whitney, Marsha, 529
Whitson, Bob, 599
Whittemore, Don, 168
Whitten, R., 199
Whitworth, Jack, 124
Whitworth, Joe, 461
Whoriskey, Frederick, 275
Wichers, Bill, 239
Wichers, William, 419
Wicker, Roger F., 8
Wickersham, Jay, 178, 179
Widell, Dave, 152
Wideman, Jo, 284
Widen, Jeff, 301
Wiebers, David, 353
Wiedemer, Steve, 525
Wiedenfeld, David, 264
Wiersma, Bruce, 612
Wiessner, Andy, 540
Wiggins, Winston, 160
Wilchorek, Paul, 524
Wilcox, Pamela, 189
Wilcoxson, Catherine, 407
Wild, Cari, 191
Wildeman, John, 196
Wilder, George, 430
Wildes, Emerson, 509
Wilensky, Myra, 429
Wiles, Kirk, 222
Wiley, James, 614
Wiley, Joseph, 549
Wilford, John, 260
Wilhelmi, Debra, 164
Wilhoite, Sarah, 319
Wilk, Peter, 468
Wilkenloh, Amy, 337
Wilkenson, Rip, 423
Wilkes, Lorna, 561
Wilkes, Samuel, 138
Wilkin, Tracy, 294
Wilkins, David, 460
Wilkins, Doak, 113
Wilkins, Jane, 345
Wilkins, Neal, 553, 599
Wilkinson, Bob, 317
Wilkinson, Joe, 374
Wilkoff, Leslie, 408
Will, Daniel, III, 340
Willard, Steve, 74

Willcox, Michelle, 102
Willeke, Gene, 587
Willett, Monica, 496
Willhite, Marcia, 163
Williams, Bruce, 200, 336
Williams, Darryl, 243
Williams, Deborah, 246
Williams, Evan, 586
Williams, Gene, 102
Williams, Ginger, 201
Williams, Gordy, 134
Williams, Hans, 598
Williams, J., 160
Williams, Jamie, 437
Williams, Jean, 77
Williams, Jim, 400, 448
Williams, John, 175, 334
Williams, Kim, 461
Williams, Linda, 582
Williams, Mark, 221
Williams, Mike, 39
Williams, Nat, 436
Williams, Nick, 331
Williams, Robert, 599
Williams, Roy, 162, 280
Williams, Stephen, 332
Williams, Steve, 25, 90
Williams, Sybil, 395
Williams, Ted, 542
Williamson, David, 433
Williamson, Jerry, 74
Williamson, John, 598
Williamson, Karla Jessen, 271
Williamson, Larry, 211
Williamson, Scot, 545
Williard, Karl, 596
Willis, Darshoel, 243, 291
Willis, Dave, 500
Willis, David, 596
Willis, Jack, 520
Willis, Michele, 204
Willsey, Bill, 316
Wilmore, Sandra, 485
Wilmore, Sandra, 486
Wilshire, Howard, 474
Wilson, Billy, 407, 458
Wilson, Bob, 231, 412
Wilson, Brian, 27
Wilson, Bud, 483
Wilson, Cynthia, 269
Wilson, Edward, 321
Wilson, Everett, 90
Wilson, G., 225
Wilson, Gregory, 164
Wilson, Heather A., 9
Wilson, J., 621
Wilson, James, 342
Wilson, Jim, 409
Wilson, Joe, 12
Wilson, John, 418
Wilson, Jonathan, 320
Wilson, Kelpie, 500
Wilson, Kevin, 482
Wilson, Laurie, 321
Wilson, Lynn, 274
Wilson, Mike, 138
Wilson, P., 333
Wilson, Patricia, 425
Wilson, Paul, 20, 499
Wilson, Robert, 395
Wilson, Ron, 202
Wilson, Ruth, 238
Wilson, Sally, 363
Wilson, Scott, 619
Wilson, Stephen, 138, 185
Wilson, Susan, 466
Wilson, Ted, 509
Wilson, Wendy, 481
Wiltse, Milton, 134
Wiltshire, Bob, 329
Wilzbach, Margaret, 16
Winchcombe, Raymond, 359
Windish, Dorothy, 151

Windler, Peter, 62
Windsor, Dave, 273
Windsor, M.I., 449
Windus, Walter, 489
Winegrad, Gerald, 250
Winer, Rachel, 354
Wingerter, Eric, 474
Wingfield, Martha, 531
Wingo, W., 229
Wingrove, Ted, 353
Winistorfer, Paul, 625
Wink, Judy, 542
Winkel, Rob, 192
Winkleman, Dana, 206
Winkler, Karl, 143
Winland, Mark, 561
Winn, Chester, 143
Winn, Richard, 489
Winslow, Christine, 413
Winsor, Dean, 198
Winsor, Don, 444
Winstead, Jack, 401
Winston, Judy, 232
Winston, Tom, 204
Winter, A. Jay, 306
Winter, Edward, 453
Winter, Linda, 250
Winter, Michael, 129
Winter, Wayne, 219
Winter, William, 598
Winterer, Patricia, 242
Winters, Owen, 433
Winterwood, Charlie, 492
Winton, Kyle, 535
Wirth, Barry, 89
Wirtz, Christina, 150
Wise, W., 597
Wisely, Sally, 84, 88
Wiseman, Earl, 20
Wiseman, Laurence, 260
Wisenbaugh, John, 508
Wishart, Bruce, 467
Wishart, Rick, 315
Wisiol, Klaus, 540
Wite, Seth, 259
Withee, Gregory, 52
Withers, Mike, 236
Witherspoon, Catherine, 143
Witley, Joe, 433
Witsell, Theo, 138
Witt, Peter, 599
Witte, Doug, 245
Witte, Jeff, 193
Wittman, Stephen, 622
Wobeser, G., 286
Wodder, Rebecca, 264, 265
Woehr, James, 545
Woelfle-Erskine, Cleo, 389
Woerner, Alice, 457
Wogan, Terri, 340
Wohl, Jim, 315
Woiwode, Anne, 493
Wolch, Jennifer, 273
Wolcott, James, 67
Wolf, Annett, 456
Wolf, Frank R., 14
Wolf, Hazel, 330
Wolf, Richie, 140
Wolfe, Bill, 495
Wolfe, Marcia, 552
Wolfe, Matt, 486
Wolfe, Roger, 168
Wolfe, Sheldon, 394
Wolgast, Timothy, 129
Wolkonowski, Chris, 475
Wolman, M., 585
Wolthausen, Doug, 544
Woltman, Sandy, 430
Womack, Mona, 107
Woo, Roy, 209
Wood, Alison, 538
Wood, Anthony, 386
Wood, Bob, 288

Wood, C., 527
Wood, Diane, 559
Wood, George, 245
Wood, Jim, 272
Wood, Jonathan, 227
Wood, June, 420
Wood, Mary, 537
Wood, Megan, 362
Wood, Mike, 145
Wood, Petra, 235
Wood, Robert, 75, 222
Wood, Van, 305
Wood, Wendell, 461
Woodall, David, 604
Woodbury, Dan, 564
Woodfin, Bill, 230
Woodfork, Larry, 236
Woodhouse, Graeme, 516
Woodring, George, 465
Woodruff, Amy Jo, 273
Woodruff, Diane Moore, 562
Woodruff, Paden, 153
Woodruff, Tom, 374
Woods, Bill, 533
Woods, Cathy, 627
Woods, Erin, 533
Woods, Jean, 312
Woods, Susanne, 382
Woods, Terry, 250
Woods-Bloom, Becky, 379
Woods-Hussey, Sharon, 343
Woodson, Bill, 74
Woodsum, Harold, 392
Woodsum, Karen, 493
Woodward, Dave, 222
Woodward, John, 390
Woodwell, Davitt, 466
Woodworth, Neil, 242
Woody, Carol Ann, 252
Woolaway, Christine, 55
Woolbright, Lawrence, 276
Wooley, James, 468
Woolley, Ted, 225
Woolsey, Lynn, 2
Woolsey, Suzanne, 424
Wooster, Margaret, 345
Wooster, Wayne, 148
Wooten, John, 337
Wooton, Windel, 386
Word, David, 156
Word, Thomas, 483
Worden, Nick, 505
Worden, Randy, 157
Worley, Ian, 622
Wormser, Julie, 541
Worth, Edwin, 62
Worthen, J., 354
Worthington, David, 415
Wott, John, 365
Wouters, Wayne, 26
Woy-Hazleton, Sandra, 587
Wraith, Jon, 589
Wray, Galen, 442
Wray, Pat, 209
Wray, Paul, 166
Wrazen, John, 585
Wright, Al, 142
Wright, Alvin, 218
Wright, Bishop, 329, 333
Wright, Bosley, 281
Wright, Bruce, 176
Wright, Gerry, 431
Wright, John, 256
Wright, Katherine, 229
Wright, L., 577
Wright, Lisa, 227
Wright, Lloyd, 583
Wright, R., 244, 611
Wright, Sandra, 246
Wright, Scott, 543
Wristen, Karen, 286
Wrona, Nancy, 136
Wrotenberry, Lori, 195

STAFF NAME INDEX – Z

Wu, David, 11
Wuebker, Pete, 544
Wurfel, Bradley, 180
Wyant, Dan, 180
Wyatt, James, 349
Wyatt, Maggie, 84
Wyatt, Rodney, 151
Wyden, Ron, 11
Wyerman, James, 241
Wykoff, Randolph, 75
Wyland, Eileen, 333
Wyman, Dody, 371
Wynn, Albert, 7
Wynn, G., 606
Wynne, Carol, 569
Wyss, Hansjorg, 509
Wyss, John, 32

Y

Yackulic, Corrie, 537
Yada, l larry, 160
Yager, Jill, 572
Yager, Mary, 407
Yamamura, Tsunetoshi, 297
Yamase, Kazuhiro, 380
Yandow, Heather, 450
Yang, Xiusheng, 608
Yank, Andrea, 402
Yanke, Ronald, 468
Yaple, Charles, 299
Yarrow, Greg, 146
Yasaratne, Shiranee, 370
Yates, Scott, 522
Yatskievych, George, 402
Yeadon, Geoffrey, 20
Yeager, Paula, 357
Yeany, Judith, 102
Yeates, William, 469

Yee, Lane, 140
Yelton, Charles, 180
Yen, A., 129
Yerger, Dale, 311
Yoder, Melvin, 457
Yokoyama, Kevin, 159
York, Don, 387
York, Elaine, 440
Yoshida, Masahito, 441
Yoshida, Tomio, 560
Yoshii, Laura, 19
Yoshinaga, Alvin, 349
Young, Barbara, 302
Young, Bill, 21
Young, Bobby, 222
Young, C.W. Bill, 3
Young, Chip, 577, 620
Young, D., 316
Young, Daniel, 550
Young, Darryl, 141
Young, Deborah, 135
Young, Don, 1, 22
Young, Dona, 352
Young, Frank, 536
Young, Gene, 381
Young, James, 212, 590
Young, Jim, 495
Young, John, 186
Young, Larry, 509
Young, Lily, 594
Young, Linda, 299, 313
Young, Mason, 159
Young, Nina, 455
Young, Rick, 468
Young, Sharon, 112
Young, Stanley, 145
Young, Thomas, 169
Youngberg, Garth, 350

Youngblood, Leigh, 405
Youngren, Jim, 390
Younker, Gordon, 528
Yurgosky, Patrick, 437

Z

Zabel, Richard, 537
Zaber, John, 598
Zachmann, Kate, 465
Zaczek, James, 596
Zaelke, Durwood, 292
Zahrt, David, 373
Zajac, Roman, 617
Zalen, Pien, 369
Zalesky, Phil, 452
Zalesky, Philip, 459
Zamora, Natalia, 22
Zanabria, Karla, 22
Zanpaglione, Tracy, 306
Zaremba, Renee, 516
Zarillo, Kim, 332
Zastrow, Michelle, 106
Zaw-Mon, Merrylin, 177
Zawadowski, Joe, 451
Zawadzki, Alice, 451
Zebroski, Robert, 148
Zeh, Joellen, 276
Zohm, Polly, 233
Zehnder, Larry, 423
Zeitlin, June, 558
Zekor, Dan, 550
Zelazny, Julian, 411
Zellar, Ron, 186
Zenn, Rick, 559
Zeph, Paul, 413
Zepp, Andrew, 386
Zevin, Susan, 52
Zicot, Jude, 289

Ziehmer, Robert, 185
Zielinski, Elaine, 84
Ziemer, Robert, 583
Zierenberg, Nancy, 543
Zierold, John, 283
Zietlow, John, 374
Zimmer, Bill, 216
Zimmer, Gary, 483, 554
Zimmerman, Eric, 607
Zimmerman, Gerald, 148
Zimmerman, Gregory, 586
Zimmerman, Richard, 237
Zimmerman, Roy, 26
Zinn, Jan, 466
Zipf, Cindy, 298
Zipperer, Wayne, 598
Zirkle, Ernest, 191
Zody, Scott, 204
Zokovitch, Jeanne, 389
Zollers, William, 211
Zonk, Jeffrey, 165
Zoon, Kathryn, 70
Zuckerman, Karen, 325
Zuke, Stephen, 30
Zukoski, Ted, 318
Zukowsky, Ron, 217
Zullinger, Melody, 466
Zuniga, Rody, 526
Zurawski, Ron, 221
Zuther, Carol, 202
Zuuring, Hans, 615
Zwarts, Patty, 144
Zwick, David, 298
Zwolinski, Malcom, 605
Zygmut, Ed, 466

GEOGRAPHIC INDEX

ANDORRA
ONTARIO MINISTRY OF NATURAL RESOURCES
  Algonquin Forestry Authority, 207

ANTIGUA BARBUDA
ISLAND RESOURCES FOUNDATION
  Eastern Caribbean Biodiversity Program Office, 375

AUSTRALIA
AUSTRALIA DEPARTMENT FOR ENVIRONMENT AND HERITAGE, 139
AUSTRALIAN MINERAL FOUNDATION, 563
AUSTRIALIA DEPARTMENT FOR ENVIRONMENT AND HERITAGE
  Environment Shop, The, 139
CONSERVATION COUNCIL OF WESTERN AUSTRALIA, INC., 17
GROWLING, 348
INTERNATIONAL FUND FOR ANIMAL WELFARE
  Asia/Pacific, 363
SEA SHEPHERD CONSERVATION SOCIETY
  Australia Office, 488

BANGLADESH
INTERNATIONAL UNION FOR CONSERVATION OF NATURE AND NATURAL RESOURCES (IUCN) THE WORLD CONSERVATION UNION
  Bangladesh Country Office, 368
JAGRATA JUBA SHANGHA (JJS), 568

BELGIUM
EUROPEAN CETACEAN SOCIETY, 328
INTERNATIONAL FUND FOR ANIMAL WELFARE
  European Union, 363
INTERNATIONAL UNION FOR CONSERVATION OF NATURE AND NATURAL RESOURCES (IUCN) THE WORLD CONSERVATION UNION
  Regional Office for Europe, 369

BOTSWANA
INTERNATIONAL UNION FOR CONSERVATION OF NATURE AND NATURAL RESOURCES (IUCN) THE WORLD CONSERVATION UNION
  Botswana Country Office, 368

BRAZIL
INSTITUTO BRASIL DE EDUCACAO AMBIENTAL, 359
SEA SHEPHERD CONSERVATION SOCIETY
  Brazil-Instituto Sea Shepherd Brasil, 488
UNIVERSIDADE FEDERAL DO PARANA, 601, 601

BULGARIA
GREEN BALKANS FEDERATION OF NATURE CONSERVATION NGOS, 346

BURKINA FASO
INTERNATIONAL UNION FOR CONSERVATION OF NATURE AND NATURAL RESOURCES (IUCN) THE WORLD CONSERVATION UNION
  Burkina Country Faso Office, 368
  Regional Office for West Africa, 370

CAMEROON
INTERNATIONAL UNION FOR CONSERVATION OF NATURE AND NATURAL RESOURCES (IUCN) THE WORLD CONSERVATION UNION
  Regional Office for Central Africa, 369

CANADA
FEDERATION OF ALBERTA NATURALISTS, 329
ONTARIO MINISTRY OF NATURAL RESOURCES
  Field Services Division, 207

ALBERTA
ALBERTA DEPARTMENT OF ENVIRONMENTAL PROTECTION
  Communications Division, 134
  Environmental Service, 134
  Land and Forest Service, 135
  Natural Resources Service, 135
ALBERTA DEPARTMENT OF SUSTAINABLE RESOURCE DEVELOPMENT
  Fish and Wildlife Division, 135
ALBERTA ENVIRONMENTAL CONSERVATION SERVICE, 16
ALBERTA FISH AND GAME ASSOCIATION, 247
ALBERTA TRAPPERS ASSOCIATION, 247
ALBERTA WILDERNESS ASSOCIATION, 247
ARCTIC INSTITUTE OF NORTH AMERICA, 271
DUCKS UNLIMITED CANADA
  ALBERTA OFFICE, 315
INTERNATIONAL SOCIETY FOR ENDANGERED CATS, 366
INTERPRETATION CANADA, 372
SIERRA CLUB
  Prairie Chapter (AB, MB, SK), 496
UNIVERSITY OF ALBERTA, 604
WILDLIFE SOCIETY
  Alberta Chapter, 546

BRITISH COLUMBIA
AMERICAN FISHERIES SOCIETY
  Canadian Aquatic Resources Section, 253
  Physiology Section, 258
BRITISH COLUMBIA CONSERVATION DATA CENTRE
  Ministry of Sustainable Resource Management, 139
BRITISH COLUMBIA ENVIRONMENTAL CONSERVATION SERVICE, 16
BRITISH COLUMBIA FIELD ORNITHOLOGISTS, 281
BRITISH COLUMBIA MINISTRY OF AGRICULTURE FOOD AND FISHERIES
  British Columbia Fisheries, 139
BRITISH COLUMBIA MINISTRY OF COMMUNITY ABORIGINAL AND WOMEN SERVICES, 139
BRITISH COLUMBIA MINISTRY OF WATER, LAND AND AIR PROTECTION, 140
BRITISH COLUMBIA WATERFOWL SOCIETY, THE, 281
CANADIAN FOREST SERVICE NATURAL RESOURCES CANADA, 16
CRESTON VALLEY WILDLIFE MANAGEMENT AREA, 310
GALIANO CONSERVANCY ASSOCIATION, 339
HYDE CREEK WATERSHED SOCIETY, 353
LEARNING FOR ENVIRONMENTAL ACTION PROGRAMME (LEAP), 388
NORTH PACIFIC ANADROMOUS FISH COMMISSION, 25
OUTDOOR RECREATION COUNCIL OF BRITISH COLUMBIA, 462
PACIFIC SALMON COMMISSION, 27
PROJECT SEAHORSE, 473
SEA SHEPHERD CONSERVATION SOCIETY
  Canada Office, 488
SIERRA CLUB
  British Columbia Chapter, 490
UNIVERSITY OF BRITISH COLUMBIA, 606
UNIVERSITY OF NORTHERN BRITISH COLUMBIA, 618

MANITOBA
AMERICAN FISHERIES SOCIETY
  Mid-Canada Chapter, 256
DELTA WATERFOWL FOUNDATION, 313
DUCKS UNLIMITED CANADA
  MANITOBA OFFICE, 315
MANITOBA CONSERVATION, 175
  Central Region, 176
  Eastern Region, 176
  Northeastern Region, 176
  Northwestern Region, 176
  Western Region, 176
MANITOBA CONSERVATION DATA CENTRE
  Wildlife And Ecosystem Protection Branch, 176
MANITOBA DEPARTMENT OF CULTURE, HERITAGE, AND TOURISM, 176
MANITOBA NATURALISTS SOCIETY, 393
MANITOBA WILDLIFE FEDERATION, 393
UNIVERSITY OF MANITOBA, 613
WILDLIFE SOCIETY
  Manitoba Chapter, 549

NEW BRUNSWICK
ATLANTIC SALMON FEDERATION, 275
ENVIRONMENTAL CONSERVATION SERVICE
  Atlantic Region Environment Canada, 18
HUNTSMAN MARINE SCIENCE CENTRE, 353
NEW BRUNSWICK DEPARTMENT OF NATURAL RESOURCES, 189
NEW BRUNSWICK WILDLIFE FEDERATION, 442
UNIVERSITY OF NEW BRUNSWICK, 616

NEWFOUNDLAND
DEPARTMENT OF TOURISM, CULTURE AND RECREATION, 152
NEWFOUNDLAND DEPARTMENT OF FOREST RESOURCES AND AGRIFOODS
  Ecosystem Health Division, 199
  Inland Fish and Wildlife Division, 199
  Legislation and Compliance Division, 199
  Regional Offices, 199
NEWFOUNDLAND LABRADOR WILDLIFE FEDERATION, 447
PROTECTED AREAS ASSOCIATION OF NEWFOUNDLAND AND LABRADOR, 474

NORTHWEST TERRITORIES
NORTHWEST TERRITORIES DEPARTMENT OF RESOURCES, WILDLIFE AND ECONOMIC DEVELOPMENT, 202
NORTHWEST TERRITORIES ENVIRONMENTAL PROTECTION SERVICE, 203

GEOGRAPHIC INDEX – C

NOVA SCOTIA
ACADIA UNIVERSITY, 572
DALHOUSIE UNIVERSITY, 579
DUCKS UNLIMITED CANADA
  Nova Scotia Office, 315
NORTHWEST ATLANTIC FISHERIES ORGANIZATION (NAFO), 453
NOVA SCOTIA AGRICULTURE & FISHERIES, 203
NOVA SCOTIA DEPARTMENT OF NATURAL RESOURCES, 203
NOVA SCOTIA FEDERATION OF ANGLERS AND HUNTERS, 454
NOVA SCOTIA FORESTRY ASSOCIATION, 454
SIERRA CLUB OF CANADA
  Atlantic Canada Chapter, 500

ONTARIO
AMERICAN FISHERIES SOCIETY
  Northwestern Ontario Chapter, 258
  Southern Ontario Chapter, 259
BIRDLIFE INTERNATIONAL, 279
CANADIAN ARCTIC RESOURCE COMMITTEE, INC., 285
CANADIAN ENVIRONMENTAL LAW ASSOCIATION, 286
CANADIAN FEDERATION OF HUMANE SOCIETIES, 286
CANADIAN FORESTRY ASSOCIATION, 286
CANADIAN INSTITUTE FOR ENVIRONMENTAL LAW AND POLICY (CIELAP), 286
CANADIAN INSTITUTE OF FORESTRY/INSTITUTE FORESTIER DU CANADA, 287
CANADIAN NATIONAL SPORTSMENS SHOWS, 287
CANADIAN NATURE FEDERATION, 287
CANADIAN PARKS AND WILDERNESS SOCIETY, 287
CANADIAN SOCIETY OF ENVIRONMENTAL BIOLOGISTS, 287
CANADIAN WILDLIFE FEDERATION, 287
CANADIAN WILDLIFE SERVICE, 17
DUCKS UNLIMITED CANADA
  ONTARIO OFFICE, 315
FEDERATION OF ONTARIO NATURALISTS, 330
FISHERIES AND OCEANS CANADA
  Communications Directorate, 20
  Fisheries and Management, 20
INTERNATIONAL JOINT COMMISSION
  Canadian Section, 22
  Great Lakes Regional Office, 22
INTERNATIONAL SOCIETY FOR ENVIRONMENTAL ETHICS, 366
JACK MINER MIGRATORY BIRD FOUNDATION, INC., 379
LAKEHEAD UNIVERSITY, 586
NATIONAL WILD TURKEY FEDERATION, CANADA, INC., THE, 426
NATURAL RESOURCES CANADA
  Ontario, 187
NATURE CONSERVANCY, THE
  Canada Chapter, 434
NIAGARA ESCARPMENT COMMISSION, 199
OCEAN VOICE INTERNATIONAL, 455
ONTARIO DEPARTMENT OF FISHERIES AND OCEANS
  Canada Division, 26
  Canadian Coast Guard, 26
  Corporate Services, 27
  Legal Services, 27
  Oceans, 27
  Policy, 27
  Science, 27
ONTARIO FEDERATION OF ANGLERS AND HUNTERS, 459
ONTARIO FORESTRY ASSOCIATION, 459
ONTARIO MINISTRY OF NATURAL RESOURCES, 207
  Corporate Services Division, 207
  Fish and Wildlife Branch, 207
  Natural Resource Management Division, 208
  Northeast Region, 208
  Northwest Region, 208
  South Central Region, 208
OPERATION MIGRATION, 460
POLLUTION PROBE, 470
SIERRA CLUB
  Eastern Canada Chapter, 491
SIERRA CLUB OF CANADA, 500
UNIVERSITY OF GUELPH, 610
UNIVERSITY OF TORONTO, 621
WATERLOO-WELLINGTON WILDFLOWER SOCIETY, 535
WILDLIFE HABITAT CANADA, 544
WILDLIFE PRESERVATION TRUST CANADA, 545
YORK UNIVERSITY
  Faculty of Environmental Studies, 628

PRINCE EDWARD ISLAND
PRINCE EDWARD ISLAND DEPARTMENT OF FISHERIES, AQUACULTURE AND ENVIRONMENT, 213

QUEBEC
ATLANTIC CENTER FOR THE ENVIRONMENT
  Quebec-Labrador Foundation, 275
CANADIAN WILDLIFE SERVICE, 17
DUCKS UNLIMITED CANADA
  Quebec Office, 315
ENVIRONMENT CANADA, 18
ENVIRONMENTAL CONSERVATION SERVICE, 18
GREAT LAKES UNITED
  CANADA OFFICE, 345
INTERNATIONAL UNION FOR CONSERVATION OF NATURE AND NATURAL RESOURCES (IUCN) THE WORLD CONSERVATION UNION
  Canada Office, 368
MCGILL UNIVERSITY, 587
PROVINCE OF QUEBEC SOCIETY FOR THE PROTECTION OF BIRDS, INC., 474
QUEBEC DEPARTMENT OF CANADIAN HERITAGE, 28
QUEBEC DEPARTMENT OF ENVIRONMENT AND WILDLIFE, 214
QUEBEC ENVIRONMENTAL CONSERVATION SERVICE
  Ecosystem and Environmental Resources Directorate, 28
  Quebec Region Environment Canada, 28
QUEBEC WILDLIFE FEDERATION, 476
STOP, 512
UNIVERSITE LAVAL, 601
  Center for Research in Economics of Agri-Food (CREA), 604
  Faculty of Agricultural and Food Sciences, 602, 604
  Faculty of Architecture, Planning and Visual Arts, 602
  Faculty of Forestry and Geomatics, 602
  Faculty of Law, 602
  Faculty of Medicine, 602
  Faculty of Philosophy, 602
  Faculty of Sciences and Engineering, 603
  Faculty of Social Sciences, 603
  Forest Biology Research Center (CRBF), 604
  Group for Research on Energy, Environment and Natural Resource Economics (GREEN), 603
  Nordic Studies Center (CEN), 603
  Quebec-Ocean, 603
  Research Center for Planning and Regional Development (CRAD), 604

SASKATCHEWAN
CANADIAN COOPERATIVE WILDLIFE HEALTH CENTRE, 286
DUCKS UNLIMITED CANADA
  Saskatchewan Office, 315
NATURE SASKATCHEWAN, 441
SASKATCHEWAN ENVIRONMENT AND RESOURCE MANAGEMENT, 215
  Corporate Services, 216
  East Boreal EcoRegion, 216
  Enforcement and Compliance Branch, 216
  Fire Management and Forest Protection Branch, 216
  Fish and Wildlife Branch
    Director, 216
    Saskatchewan Conservation Data Centre (SKCDC), 216
  Grassland EcoRegion, 216
  Operations, 216
  Parkland EcoRegion, 217
  Policy and Assessment, 217
  Shield EcoRegion, 217
  West Boreal EcoRegion, 217
SASKATCHEWAN WILDLIFE FEDERATION, 484
UNIVERSITY OF REGINA, 619
UNIVERSITY OF SASKATCHEWAN, 620

YUKON
YUKON DEPARTMENT OF RENEWABLE RESOURCES, 240
YUKON FISH AND GAME ASSOCIATION, 562

COLOMBIA
FUNDACION NATURA COLOMBIA, 339

COSTA RICA
BUN-CA, 281
INSTITUTO NACIONAL DE BIODIVERSIDAD (INBIO), 22
INTERNATIONAL UNION FOR CONSERVATION OF NATURE AND NATURAL RESOURCES (IUCN) THE WORLD CONSERVATION UNION
  Regional Office for MesoAmerica, 370

CZECH REP
CZECH REPUBLIC MINISTRY OF THE ENVIRONMENT, 17

ECUADOR
INTERNATIONAL UNION FOR CONSERVATION OF NATURE AND NATURAL RESOURCES (IUCN) THE WORLD CONSERVATION UNION
  Regional Office for South America, 370

NATURE AND NATURAL RESOURCES (IUCN), 433
PEACE CORPS
  Ecuador, 28

EGYPT
EGYPTIAN ENVIRONMENTAL AFFAIRS AGENCY, 18

FINLAND
HELSINKI COMMISSION/ BALTIC MARINE ENVIRONMENT PROTECTION COMMISSION, 21

FRANCE
COUSTEAU SOCIETY, INC., THE
  France Office, 310
INTERNATIONAL FUND FOR ANIMAL WELFARE
  French Office, 363

GERMANY
EUROPARC FEDERATION, 328
FRANKFURT ZOOLOGICAL SOCIETY-HELP FOR THREATENED WILDLIFE, 336
INTERNATIONAL COUNCIL OF ENVIRONMENTAL LAW, 362
INTERNATIONAL FUND FOR ANIMAL WELFARE
  German Office, 363
INTERNATIONAL MIRE CONSERVATION GROUP, 365
INTERNATIONAL UNION FOR CONSERVATION OF NATURE AND NATURAL RESOURCES (IUCN) THE WORLD CONSERVATION UNION
  Environmental Law Centre, 368
UNITED STATES DEPARTMENT OF DEFENSE
  Air Force Major Air Commands
    Germany AFB, 62

GHANA
ENVIRONMENTAL PROTECTION ASSOCIATION OF GHANA, 327
LEAGUE OF ENVIRONMENTAL JOURNALISTS, 387

GUINEA BISSAU
INTERNATIONAL UNION FOR CONSERVATION OF NATURE AND NATURAL RESOURCES (IUCN) THE WORLD CONSERVATION UNION
  Guinea-Bissau Country Office, 368

HONG KONG
ANIMALS ASIA FOUNDATION, 269
INTERNATIONAL FUND FOR ANIMAL WELFARE
  Hong Kong Office, 363

ITALY
FOOD AND AGRICULTURE ORGANIZATION OF THE UNITED NATIONS, 333
INTERNATIONAL FUND FOR ANIMAL WELFARE
  Italian Office, 363

JAPAN
CITIZENS ALLIANCE FOR SAVING THE ATMOSPHERE AND THE EARTH (CASA), 297
CITIZENS' NUCLEAR INFORMATION CENTER, 298
GLOBAL INDUSTRIAL AND SOCIAL PROGRESS RESEARCH INSTITUTE (GISPRI), 344
JAPAN WILDLIFE RESEARCH CENTER (JWRC), 380
MUSASHI INSTITUTE OF TECHNOLOGY, 589
NATURE CONSERVATION SOCIETY OF JAPAN, THE (NACS-J), 440
NIPPON ECOLOGY NETWORK, 447
PEOPLE'S FORUM 2001, JAPAN, 467
UNITED STATES DEPARTMENT OF AGRICULTURE
  ANIMAL AND PLANT HEALTH INSPECTION SERVICE
    International Services Asia and Pacific Office, 32
WWF JAPAN (WORLD WIDE FUND FOR NATURE JAPAN), 560

KENYA
INTERNATIONAL UNION FOR CONSERVATION OF NATURE AND NATURAL RESOURCES (IUCN) THE WORLD CONSERVATION UNION
  Regional Office for Eastern Africa, 369
UNITED NATIONS ENVIRONMENT PROGRAMME, 525

LAOS
INTERNATIONAL UNION FOR CONSERVATION OF NATURE AND NATURAL RESOURCES (IUCN) THE WORLD CONSERVATION UNION
  Lao People's Democratic Republic Country Office, 369

MALI
INTERNATIONAL UNION FOR CONSERVATION OF NATURE AND NATURAL RESOURCES (IUCN) THE WORLD CONSERVATION UNION
  Mali Country Office, 369

MEXICO
ARENA CONSULTORES AMBIENTALES, 563
CENTER FOR THE STUDY OF TROPICAL BIRDS, INC.
  Field Office, 293
JOURNALISM TO RAISE ENVIRONMENTAL AWARENESS, 380
TERRA PENINSULAR, 516
UNITED NATIONS ENVIRONMENT PROGRAMME, 526
  LATIN AMERICAN AND CARIBBEAN, 526
WORLD WILDLIFE FUND
  Gulf of California Regional Office, 560

MOZAMBIQUE
INTERNATIONAL UNION FOR CONSERVATION OF NATURE AND NATURAL RESOURCES (IUCN) THE WORLD CONSERVATION UNION
  IUCN Beira Project Office, 369

NAMIBIA
DESERT RESEARCH FOUNDATION OF NAMIBIA, THE, 314

NEPAL
INTERNATIONAL UNION FOR CONSERVATION OF NATURE AND NATURAL RESOURCES (IUCN) THE WORLD CONSERVATION UNION
  Nepal Country Office, 369
STUDENTS PARTNERSHIP WORLDWIDE, 513

NETHERLANDS
EUROPEAN ASSOCIATION FOR AQUATIC MAMMALS, 328
INTERNATIONAL FUND FOR ANIMAL WELFARE
  Holland Office, 363
SEA SHEPHERD CONSERVATION SOCIETY
  European Community/Netherlands, 488
WETLANDS INTERNATIONAL, 538

NIGER
INTERNATIONAL UNION FOR CONSERVATION OF NATURE AND NATURAL RESOURCES (IUCN) THE WORLD CONSERVATION UNION
  Niger Country Office, 369

PAKISTAN
HIMALAYAN WILDLIFE FOUNDATION, 351
INTERNATIONAL UNION FOR CONSERVATION OF NATURE AND NATURAL RESOURCES (IUCN) THE WORLD CONSERVATION UNION
  Pakistan Country Office, 369
UNIVERSITY OF ITO PUNJAB, 611

PERU
MUNDO AZUL, 406
WORLD WILDLIFE FUND
  Peru Program Office, 560

PHILIPPINES
COASTAL CONSERVATION AND EDUCATION FOUNDATION, INC., 565
COASTAL RESOURCE MANAGEMENT PROJECT, 146
INTERNATIONAL FUND FOR ANIMAL WELFARE
  Philippines Office, 363
PHILIPPINES ENVIRONMENT AND NATURAL RESOURCES MANAGEMENT DIVISION, 468
SILLMAN UNIVERSITY, 595

POLAND
INTERNATIONAL UNION FOR CONSERVATION OF NATURE AND NATURAL RESOURCES (IUCN) THE WORLD CONSERVATION UNION
  Subregional Office for Central Europe, 370

PUERTO RICO
CONSERVATION TRUST OF PUERTO RICO, 308
DEPARTAMENTO DE RECURSOS NATURALES Y AMBIENTALES, 151
PUERTO RICO DIVISION DE PATRIMONIO NATURAL, 213

RUSSIA
CENTER FOR INDEPENDENT SOCIAL RESEARCH, 292
ECODEFENSE, 321
FEDERATION OF ENVIRONMENTAL EDUCATION IN ST. PETERSBURG, 329
INSTITUTE FOR CIVIC INITIATIVES SUPPORT, 358
INTERNATIONAL FUND FOR ANIMAL WELFARE
  Russian Office, 363
INTERNATIONAL UNION FOR CONSERVATION OF NATURE AND NATURAL RESOURCES (IUCN) THE WORLD CONSERVATION UNION
  Subregional Office for the Commonwealth of Independent States, 370
RESOURCE CENTER FOR ENVIRONMENTAL EDUCATION, THE, 479

GEOGRAPHIC INDEX – U

SENEGAL
INTERNATIONAL UNION FOR CONSERVATION OF NATURE AND NATURAL RESOURCES (IUCN) THE WORLD CONSERVATION UNION
   Senegal Country Office, 370

SINGAPORE
SEA SHEPHERD CONSERVATION SOCIETY
   Singapore/Asia, 488

SOUTH AFRICA
INTERNATIONAL FUND FOR ANIMAL WELFARE
   South African Office, 363
INTERNATIONAL PROFESSIONAL HUNTERS' ASSOCIATION, 365
INTERNATIONAL UNION FOR CONSERVATION OF NATURE AND NATURAL RESOURCES (IUCN) THE WORLD CONSERVATION UNION
   South Africa Country Office, 370
SAFARI CLUB INTERNATIONAL
   South Africa Office, 484
SOUTHERN AFRICAN INSTITUTE OF FORESTRY, 508

SRI LANKA
INTERNATIONAL UNION FOR CONSERVATION OF NATURE AND NATURAL RESOURCES (IUCN) THE WORLD CONSERVATION UNION
   Sri Lanka Country Office, 370

ST KITTS AND NEVIS
NEVIS HISTORICAL AND CONSERVATION SOCIETY, 442

SWAZILAND
SWAZILAND ENVIRONMENT AUTHORITY (SEA), 30

SWITZERLAND
INTERNATIONAL UNION FOR CONSERVATION OF NATURE AND NATURAL RESOURCES (IUCN) THE WORLD CONSERVATION UNION
   Headquarters, 367
UNITED NATIONS RESEARCH INSTITUTE FOR SOCIAL DEVELOPMENT (UNRISD), 30
WORLD CONSERVATION UNION, 558

TANZANIA
AFRICA VISION TRUST, 243
TANZANIA COASTAL MANAGEMENT PARTNERSHIP, 30
TANZANIA SCHOOL OF JOURNALISM, 598
TUMAINI ENVIRONMENTAL CONSERVATION GROUP, 525
UNIVERSITY OF DAR ES SALAAM, 608
USAID/TANZANIA, 131

THAILAND
INTERNATIONAL UNION FOR CONSERVATION OF NATURE AND NATURAL RESOURCES (IUCN) THE WORLD CONSERVATION UNION
   Regional Office of South and Southeast Asia, 370

TRINIDAD AND TOBAGO
CARIBBEAN NATURAL RESOURCES INSTITUTE, 288

UGANDA
INTERNATIONAL UNION FOR CONSERVATION OF NATURE AND NATURAL RESOURCES (IUCN) THE WORLD CONSERVATION UNION
   Uganda Country Office, 370

UKRAINE
LVIV REGIONAL INSTITUTE OF EDUCATION, 391

UNITED KINGDOM
AFRICAN CONSERVATION FOUNDATION, THE, 243
BIOSPHERE EXPEDITIONS, 278
BORN FREE FOUNDATION, 280
CAM VALLEY WILDLIFE GROUP, 284
CENTRE FOR RESEARCH IN EDUCATION AND THE ENVIRONMENT, THE, 576
EARTHSCAN, 320
HAWK AND OWL TRUST, THE, 349
INTERNATIONAL CENTRE FOR CONSERVATION EDUCATION, 361
INTERNATIONAL FUND FOR ANIMAL WELFARE
   United Kingdom, 364
INTERNATIONAL MARITIME ORGANIZATION, 364
INTERNATIONAL WHALING COMMISSION, 23
JOHN GRAY HIGH SCHOOL, GRAND CAYMAN, 584
NORTH ATLANTIC SALMON CONSERVATION ORGANIZATION, 449
NORTHEAST ATLANTIC FISHERIES COMMISSION, 25
SEA SHEPHERD CONSERVATION SOCIETY
   United Kingdom, 488
UNEP WORLD CONSERVATION MONITORING CENTRE, 525
UNIVERSITY OF BATH, 605
WHALE AND DOLPHIN CONSERVATION SOCIETY, 538
WORLD ASSOCIATION OF GIRL GUIDES AND GIRL SCOUTS (WAGGGS), 558
WORLD PHEASANT ASSOCIATION, 559

UNITED STATES
UNITED STATES DEPARTMENT OF AGRICULTURE
   Animal and Plant Health Inspection Service
      International Services Central America, Caribbean and Panama Office, 32
      International Services Europe, Africa, Russia, Near East Office, 32
UNITED STATES DEPARTMENT OF DEFENSE
   Marine Corps Installations, United States, 74
UNITED STATES ENVIRONMENTAL PROTECTION AGENCY
   Water, United States, 130

ALABAMA
ALABAMA ASSOCIATION OF SOIL AND WATER CONSERVATION DISTRICTS, 244
ALABAMA BASS FEDERATION, 244
ALABAMA COOPERATIVE EXTENSION SYSTEM, 132
ALABAMA COOPERATIVE FISH AND WILDLIFE RESEARCH UNIT (USDI), 132
ALABAMA DEPARTMENT OF AGRICULTURE AND INDUSTRIES, 132
ALABAMA DEPARTMENT OF CONSERVATION AND NATURAL RESOURCES, 132
ALABAMA DEPARTMENT OF ENVIRONMENTAL MANAGEMENT, 133
ALABAMA ENVIRONMENTAL COUNCIL, 244
ALABAMA FORESTRY COMMISSION, 133
ALABAMA SOIL AND WATER CONSERVATION COMMITTEE, 133
ALABAMA WATERFOWL ASSOCIATION (AWA), 244
ALABAMA WATERFOWL ASSOCIATION, INC. (AWA), 245
ALABAMA WILDFLOWER SOCIETY, THE, 245
ALABAMA WILDLIFE FEDERATION, 245
AMERICAN FISHERIES SOCIETY
   Alabama Chapter, 252
   Auburn University Chapter, 253
ANGLERS FOR CLEAN WATER, 268
AUBURN UNIVERSITY
   College of Agriculture, 573
   College of Sciences and Mathematics, 574
   School of Forestry and Wildlife Sciences, 574
BAMA BACKPADDLERS ASSOCIATION, 276
BASS DIVISION OF ESPN PRODUCTIONS INC, 564
ENVIROSOUTH, INC., 328
NATIONAL SPELEOLOGICAL SOCIETY, INC., 424
NATURE CONSERVANCY, THE
   Alabama Chapter, 433
   Alabama Operating Unit, 433
RUFFNER MOUNTAIN NATURE COALITION, INC., 483
SIERRA CLUB
   Alabama Chapter, 490
   Southeast Office, 498
TENNESSEE VALLEY AUTHORITY
   Muscle Shoals Technical Library, 30
UNITED STATES DEPARTMENT OF AGRICULTURE
   Forest Service
      National Forests in Alabama, 41
UNITED STATES DEPARTMENT OF COMMERCE
   National Oceanic and Atmospheric Administration
      Weeks Bay National Estuarine Research Reserve, 60
UNITED STATES DEPARTMENT OF DEFENSE
   Air Force Major U.S. Installations
      Maxwell AFB, AL, 65
   Army Corps of Engineers
      Mobile Engineer District, 69
UNITED STATES DEPARTMENT OF THE INTERIOR
   Fish and Wildlife Service
      Bon Secour National Wildlife Refuge, 93
      Choctaw National Wildlife Refuge, 95
      Eufaula National Wildlife Refuge, 98
      Wheeler National Wildlife Refuge, 118
WILDLIFE SOCIETY
   Alabama Chapter, 546

ALASKA
ALASKA ASSOCIATION OF SOIL AND WATER CONSERVATION DISTRICTS, 245
ALASKA CENTER FOR THE ENVIRONMENT, 245
ALASKA CONSERVATION ALLIANCE, 245, 246
ALASKA CONSERVATION FOUNDATION, 246
ALASKA COOPERATIVE FISH AND WILDLIFE RESEARCH UNIT, 133
ALASKA DEPARTMENT OF ENVIRONMENTAL CONSERVATION, 133

ALASKA DEPARTMENT OF FISH AND GAME, 134
ALASKA DEPARTMENT OF NATURAL RESOURCES, 134
ALASKA DEPARTMENT OF PUBLIC SAFETY, 134
   Alaska State Troopers, 134
ALASKA HEALTH PROJECT, 134
ALASKA NATURAL HISTORY ASSOCIATION, 246
ALASKA NATURAL RESOURCE AND OUTDOOR EDUCATION ASSOCIATION, 246
ALASKA RAINFOREST CAMPAIGN, 246
ALASKA WILDLIFE ALLIANCE, THE, 246
AMERICAN FISHERIES SOCIETY
   Alaska Chapter, 252
   Western Division, 260
COOK INLET KEEPER, 308
EARTHJUSTICE
   Juneau Office, 319
IZAAK WALTON LEAGUE OF AMERICA, INC., THE
   Alaska Division, 376
KODIAK BROWN BEAR TRUST, 384
NATIONAL AUDUBON SOCIETY
   Audubon Alaska, 409
NATIONAL PARKS CONSERVATION ASSOCIATION (NPCA)
   Alaska Regional Office, 423
NATIONAL WILDLIFE FEDERATION
   Alaska Natural Resource Center, 427
NATURE CONSERVANCY, THE
   Alaska Chapter, 434
NORTHERN ALASKA ENVIRONMENTAL CENTER, 453
SIERRA CLUB
   Alaska Chapter, 490
   Alaska Field Office, 490
SOUTHEAST ALASKA CONSERVATION COUNCIL (SEACC), 507
TROUT UNLIMITED
   Alaska Council, 520
TRUSTEES FOR ALASKA, 524
UNITED STATES DEPARTMENT OF AGRICULTURE
   Forest Service
      Chugach National Forest, 36
      Region 10 (Alaska), 43
      Tongass National Forest, 45
      Tongass-Ketchikan Area National Forest, 45
      Tongass-Petersburg Office National Forest, 45
UNITED STATES DEPARTMENT OF COMMERCE
   National Oceanic and Atmospheric Administration
      Kachemak Bay National Estuarine Research Reserve, 51
      Sea Grant Program - Alaska, 53
UNITED STATES DEPARTMENT OF DEFENSE
   Air Force Major U.S. Installations
      Eielson AFB, AK, 64
      Elmendorf AFB, AK, 64
      Remote Sites (611 Support Group), AK, 66
   Army Corps of Engineers
      Alaska Engineer District, 67
UNITED STATES DEPARTMENT OF THE INTERIOR
   Bureau of Land Management
      Anchorage District, 79
      Glennallen District, 82
      Northern Field Office, 84
   Fish and Wildlife Service
      Alaska Maritime National Wildlife Refuge, 90
      Alaska Peninsula/Becharof National Wildlife Refuge, 90
      Arctic National Wildlife Refuge, 91
      Innoko National Wildlife Refuge, 100
      Izembek National Wildlife Refuge, 100
      Kanuti National Wildlife Refuge, 101
      Kenai National Wildlife Refuge, 101
      Kodiak National Wildlife Refuge, 102
      Nowitna/Koyukuk National Wildlife Refuge, 108
      Region 6, Mountain-Prairie Regional Office, 112
      Seedskadee/Cokeville Meadows National Wildlife Refuge, 114
      Tetlin National Wildlife Refuge, 116
      Togiak National Wildlife Refuge, 116
      Yukon Delta National Wildlife Refuge, 119
      Yukon Flats National Wildlife Refuge, 119
   National Park Service
      Denali National Park, 122
      Gates of the Arctic National Park, 122
      Glacier Bay National Park, 122
      Katmai National Park, 123
      Kenai Fjords National Park, 123
      Kobuk Valley National Park, 124
      Lake Clark National Park, 124
      Wrangell-St. Elias National Park, 126

UNIVERSITY OF ALASKA AT FAIRBANKS
   College of Science, Engineering and Mathematics, 604
   Cooperative Extension Service College of Rural Alaska, 149
   School of Fisheries and Ocean Sciences, 604
WILDLIFE FEDERATION OF ALASKA, 543
WILDLIFE SOCIETY
   Alaska Chapter, 546

AMERICA SAMOA
AMERICAN SAMOA DEPARTMENT OF AGRICULTURE, 135
UNITED STATES DEPARTMENT OF THE INTERIOR
   National Park Service
      National Park of American Samoa, 124

ARIZONA
AMERICAN FISHERIES SOCIETY
   Arizona-New Mexico Chapter, 252
ARIZONA ASSOCIATION OF CONSERVATION DISTRICTS, 271
ARIZONA BASS FEDERATION, 271
ARIZONA COOPERATIVE FISH AND WILDLIFE RESEARCH UNIT (USDI), 135
ARIZONA COOPERATIVE STATE EXTENSION SERVICES, 135
ARIZONA DEPARTMENT OF AGRICULTURE, 135
   Animal Services Division, 135
   Environmental Services Division, 136
ARIZONA DEPARTMENT OF AGRICULTURE PLANT SERVICES DIVISION, 136
ARIZONA DEPARTMENT OF ENVIRONMENTAL QUALITY, 136
ARIZONA GAME AND FISH DEPARTMENT, 136
ARIZONA GEOLOGICAL SURVEY, 136
ARIZONA STATE ENVIROTHON, INC., 271
ARIZONA STATE LAND DEPARTMENT, 136
ARIZONA STATE PARKS BOARD, 137
ARIZONA STATE UNIVERSITY
   Center for Environmental Studies, 573
ARIZONA WILDLIFE FEDERATION, 271
ARIZONA-SONORA DESERT MUSEUM, 271
BORDER ECOLOGY PROJECT (BEP), 279
CAVE RESEARCH FOUNDATION, 289
CENTER FOR BIOLOGICAL DIVERSITY, 290
ELEMENTAL TECHNOLOGY, LLC, 566
FLAGSTAFF DARK SKIES COALITION (FDSC), 330
GRAND CANYON TRUST, 344
HIGHLANDS CENTER FOR NATURAL HISTORY, 351
INTERNATIONAL SONORAN DESERT ALLIANCE, 367
NATIONAL ASSOCIATION OF STATE PARK DIRECTORS, 409
NATIONAL AUDUBON SOCIETY
   Maricopa Audubon Society, 414
   Tucson Audubon Society, 416
NAVAJO NATION DEPARTMENT OF FISH AND WILDLIFE, 188
NORTHERN ARIZONA UNIVERSITY
   College of Arts and Sciences, 590
   College of Ecosystem Science and Management, 590
   Department of Geography, Planning, and Recreation, 591
   Northern Arizona Environmental Education Resources Center, 591
PRESCOTT COLLEGE, LIBERAL ARTS AND THE ENVIRONMENTAL STUDIES PROGRAM, 593
SACRED PASSAGE AND THE WAY OF NATURE, 483
SAFARI CLUB INTERNATIONAL
   International Headquarters, 483
SIERRA CLUB
   Grand Canyon Chapter, 492
   Southwest Office, 498
SOCIETY FOR ECOLOGICAL RESTORATION, 502
SONORAN DESERT NATIONAL PARK FRIENDS, 504
SONORAN INSTITUTE, 505
TROUT UNLIMITED
   Arizona Council, 521
UNITED STATES DEPARTMENT OF AGRICULTURE
   Forest Service
      Apache-Sitgreaves National Forest, 34
      Coconino National Forest, 36
      Coronado National Forest, 36
      Kaibab National Forest, 39
      Prescott National Forest, 42
      Tonto National Forest, 46
UNITED STATES DEPARTMENT OF DEFENSE
   Air Force Major U.S. Installations
      Davis-Monthan AFB, AZ, 63
      Luke AFB (and the Barry M. Goldwater AFR), AZ, 65
UNITED STATES DEPARTMENT OF THE INTERIOR
   Bureau of Land Management
      Arizona State Office, 79
      Kingman Field Office, 82

GEOGRAPHIC INDEX – U

    Lake Havasu Field Office, 82
    National Training Center, 84
    Phoenix Field Office, 85
    Safford Field Office, 86
    San Pedro Project Office, 87
    Tucson Field Office, 88
    Yuma Field Office, 89
  Fish and Wildlife Service
    Buenos Aires National Wildlife Refuge, 94
    Cabeza Prieta National Wildlife Refuge, 94
    Imperial National Wildlife Refuge, 100
    Kofa National Wildlife Refuge, 102
    Lower Colorado River Complex National Wildlife Refuge, 104
    San Andres National Wildlife Refuge, 113
  National Park Service
    Grand Canyon National Park, 122
    Petrified Forest National Park, 125
    Sonoran Desert Network, 125
UNITED STATES INSTITUTE FOR ENVIRONMENTAL CONFLICT RESOLUTION, 130
UNIVERSITY OF ARIZONA
  Department of Hydrology and Water Resources, 605
  School of Renewable Natural Resources, 605
WILDLIFE DAMAGE REVIEW (WDR), 543
WILDLIFE SOCIETY
  Arizona Chapter, 546

ARKANSAS

AMERICAN FISHERIES SOCIETY
  Arkansas Chapter, 253
ARKANSAS ASSOCIATION OF CONSERVATION DISTRICTS, 272
ARKANSAS BASS FEDERATION, 272
ARKANSAS COOPERATIVE RESEARCH UNIT, 137
ARKANSAS DEPARTMENT OF ENVIRONMENTAL QUALITY, 137
ARKANSAS DEPARTMENT OF PARKS AND TOURISM, 137
ARKANSAS ENVIRONMENTAL EDUCATION ASSOCIATION, 272
ARKANSAS GAME AND FISH COMMISSION, 137
ARKANSAS NATURAL HERITAGE COMMISSION, 138
ARKANSAS STATE EXTENSION SERVICES
  Four H Center, 138
ARKANSAS STATE PLANT BOARD, 138
ARKANSAS STATE UNIVERSITY
  Department of Biological Science, 573
ARKANSAS TECH UNIVERSITY
  Department of Parks, Recreation, and Hospitality Administration, 573
  Fisheries and Wildlife Biology Program, 573
ARKANSAS WATERSHED ADVISORY GROUP (AWAG), 272
ARKANSAS WILDLIFE FEDERATION, 272
FORESTRY COMMISSION (ARKANSAS), 155
NATIONAL BOWHUNTER EDUCATION FOUNDATION (NBEF), 417
NATURE CONSERVANCY, THE
  Arkansas Field Office, 434
OZARK SOCIETY, THE, 463
PINE BLUFF COOPERATIVE FISHERY RESEARCH PROJECT, 213
UNITED STATES DEPARTMENT OF AGRICULTURE
  FOREST SERVICE
    Ouachita National Forest, 42
    Ozark-St. Francis National Forest, 42
UNITED STATES DEPARTMENT OF DEFENSE
  Air Force Major U.S. Installations
    Little Rock AFB, AR, 65
  Army Corps of Engineers
    Little Rock Engineer District, 69
UNITED STATES DEPARTMENT OF THE INTERIOR
  Fish and Wildlife Service
    Bald Knob National Wildlife Refuge, 92
    Big Lake National Wildlife Refuge, 93
    Cache River National Wildlife Refuge, 94
    Felsenthal National Wildlife Refuge, 98
    Holla Bend/Logan Cave National Wildlife Refuge, 100
    Overflow National Wildlife Refuge, 109
    Pond Creek National Wildlife Refuge, 110
    Wapanocca National Wildlife Refuge, 117
    White River National Wildlife Refuge, 118
  National Park Service
    Hot Springs National Park, 123
UNIVERSITY OF ARKANSAS AT LITTLE ROCK, 605
UNIVERSITY OF ARKANSAS AT MONTICELLO, 605
WILDLIFE SOCIETY
  Arkansas Chapter, 546
YELL COUNTY WILDLIFE FEDERATION, 561

CALIFORNIA

ACTION FOR NATURE, INC., 242
AMERICAN CETACEAN SOCIETY, 250
AMERICAN FISHERIES SOCIETY
  California-Nevada Chapter, 253
  Fish Health Section, 254
  Humboldt Chapter, 255
  Water Quality Section, 259
AMERICAN INSTITUTE OF FISHERY RESEARCH BIOLOGISTS, 262
AMERICAN LAND CONSERVANCY, 262
AMERICAN SOCIETY OF INTERNATIONAL LAW/WILDLIFE INTEREST GROUP, 266
AMERICAN SOCIETY OF MAMMALOGISTS, 266
ANCIENT FOREST INTERNATIONAL, 268
ANIMAL PROTECTION INSTITUTE, 268
BACK COUNTRY LAND TRUST, 276
BIOINTEGRAL RESOURCE CENTER, 278
C.A.R.E (CITIZENS AGAINST RACCOON EXTERMINATION), 564
CALIFORNIA ACADEMY OF SCIENCES, 282
CALIFORNIA ACADEMY OF SCIENCES LIBRARY, 282
CALIFORNIA ASSOCIATION OF RESOURCE CONSERVATION DISTRICTS, 282
CALIFORNIA BASS FEDERATION, 282
CALIFORNIA COASTAL COMMISSION, 140
CALIFORNIA COASTAL CONSERVANCY, 140
CALIFORNIA CONSERVATION CORPS, 140
CALIFORNIA COOPERATIVE FISHERY RESEARCH UNIT (USGS), 16
CALIFORNIA DEPARTMENT OF BOATING AND WATERWAYS, 141
CALIFORNIA DEPARTMENT OF CONSERVATION, 141
CALIFORNIA DEPARTMENT OF EDUCATION
  Office of Environmental Education, 141
CALIFORNIA DEPARTMENT OF FISH AND GAME
  Elkhorn Slough National Estuarine Research Reserve, 141
  Office of Spill Prevention and Response, 141
  Resources Agency, The, 141
    Wildlife Conservation Board, 142
CALIFORNIA DEPARTMENT OF FOOD AND AGRICULTURE, 142
CALIFORNIA DEPARTMENT OF FORESTRY AND FIRE PROTECTION, 142
CALIFORNIA DEPARTMENT OF PARKS AND RECREATION, 142
CALIFORNIA DEPARTMENT OF PESTICIDE REGULATION, 143
CALIFORNIA DEPARTMENT OF WATER RESOURCES, 143
CALIFORNIA ENERGY COMMISSION
  Environmental Department, 143
CALIFORNIA ENVIRONMENTAL PROTECTION AGENCY
  California Air Resources Board, 143
  Department of Toxic Substances Control, 143
  Integrated Waste Management Board, IWMB, 144
  Office of Environmental Health Hazard Assessment, 144
  Office of the Secretary, 144
  State Water Resources Control Board, 144
CALIFORNIA FISH AND GAME COMMISSION, 144
CALIFORNIA GOVERNORS OFFICE OF PLANNING AND RESEARCH
  State Clearinghouse, 144
CALIFORNIA INSTITUTE OF PUBLIC AFFAIRS, 283
CALIFORNIA NATIVE PLANT SOCIETY, THE, 283
CALIFORNIA POLYTECHNIC STATE UNIVERSITY, 575
CALIFORNIA RECLAMATION BOARD, 145
CALIFORNIA RESOURCES AGENCY, THE, 145
CALIFORNIA STATE LANDS COMMISSION, 145
CALIFORNIA STATE UNIVERSITY AT CHICO, 575
CALIFORNIA STATE UNIVERSITY AT FULLERTON, 575
CALIFORNIA STATE UNIVERSITY AT SACRAMENTO, 575
CALIFORNIA TRAPPERS ASSOCIATION, 283
CALIFORNIA TROUT, INC., 283
CALIFORNIA WATER COMMISSION, 145
CALIFORNIA WATERFOWL ASSOCIATION, 283
CALIFORNIA WILD HERITAGE CAMPAIGN, 284
CALIFORNIA WILDERNESS COALITION, 284
CALIFORNIA WILDLIFE DEFENDERS, 284
CALIFORNIA WILDLIFE FEDERATION, 284
CALIFORNIANS FOR POPULATION STABILIZATION (CAPS), 284
CANADA GOOSE PROJECT, 285
CENTER FOR ENVIRONMENTAL HEALTH (CEH), 291
CENTER FOR SIERRA NEVADA CONSERVATION, 293
COALITION FOR CLEAN AIR, 299
COLORADO RIVER BOARD OF CALIFORNIA, 147
COMMUNITIES FOR A BETTER ENVIRONMENT, 303
COMMUNITY ENVIRONMENTAL COUNCIL (CEC), 303
CORAL REEF ALLIANCE, THE (CORAL), 309
COUNCIL FOR PLANNING AND CONSERVATION, 310
COUNTY OF SAN DIEGO, 149
DEPARTMENT OF PARKS AND RECREATION, 151
DESERT PROTECTIVE COUNCIL, 314
DESERT TORTOISE COUNCIL, 314
DESERT TORTOISE PRESERVE COMMITTEE, INC., 314

DONALD BREN SCHOOL OF ENVIRONMENTAL SCIENCE AND MANAGEMENT, 579
EARTH ISLAND INSTITUTE, 317
EARTHJUSTICE
   Environmental Law Clinic at Stanford University, 318
   Headquarters, 318
   International Program, 319
   Oakland Office, 319
ECOLOGY CENTER, 321
ECOROOMMATES.COM, 566
EDUCATIONAL COMMUNICATIONS, 322
ENDANGERED HABITATS LEAGUE, 322
ENVIRONMENTAL DEFENSE
   West Coast Office, 325
ENVIRONMENTAL DEFENSE CENTER, 325
ENVIRONMENTAL FRONTLINES, 326
ENVIRONMENTAL MEDIA ASSOCIATION, 327
ENVIRONMENTAL POLICY CENTER, THE, 327
ENVIRONMENTAL PROTECTION AGENCY
   Region 9 (GU, AS, NV, HI, CA, AZ), 19
FEDERATION OF FLY FISHERS (NCCFFF), 329
FOREST LANDOWNERS OF CALIFORNIA, 334
FRIENDS OF FAMOSA SLOUGH, 337
FRIENDS OF THE RIVER, 338
FRIENDS OF THE SEA OTTER, 338
GREEN TV, 347
HEADLANDS INSTITUTE, 350
HEAL THE BAY, 350
HELPING OUR PENINSULA'S ENVIRONMENT, 350
HUMBOLDT STATE UNIVERSITY, 583
INSTITUTE FOR GLOBAL COMMUNICATIONS, 567
INTERAMERICAN TROPICAL TUNA COMMISSION, 359
INTERNATIONAL ACADEMY, 567
INTERNATIONAL CENTER FOR EARTH CONCERNS, 361
INTERNATIONAL CENTER FOR GIBBON STUDIES, 361
INTERNATIONAL MARINE MAMMAL PROJECT, THE, 364
INTERNATIONAL RIVERS NETWORK (IRN), 366
INTERNATIONAL SOCIETY FOR THE PRESERVATION OF THE TROPICAL RAINFOREST, THE, 367
INTERNATIONAL WILDLIFE REHABILITATION COUNCIL, 371
IZAAK WALTON LEAGUE OF AMERICA, INC., THE
   California Division, 376
   California State IWLA, 376
JONES AND STOKES, 568
LA JOLLA FRIENDS OF THE SEALS (LJFS), 384
LANDWATCH MONTEREY COUNTY, 386
LEAGUE TO SAVE LAKE TAHOE, 388
LITERACY FOR ENVIRONMENTAL JUSTICE, 389
LOS ANGELES AND SAN GABRIEL RIVERS WATERSHED COUNCIL, THE, 390
MAGIC, 392
MANTA MEXICO, 393
MARIN CONSERVATION LEAGUE, 394
MARINE MAMMAL CENTER, THE, 394
MARINE SCIENCE INSTITUTE, 394
MONO LAKE COMMITTEE, 402
MORONGO BASIN WILDLIFE REHAB STATION, 404
MOUNTAIN DEFENSE LEAGUE, 405
MOUNTAIN LION FOUNDATION, 405
NATIONAL AUDUBON SOCIETY
   San Diego Chapter, 416
NATIONAL FIELD ARCHERY ASSOCIATION, 419
NATIONAL PARKS CONSERVATION ASSOCIATION (NPCA)
   Pacific Regional Office, 423
NATIONAL TRUST FOR HISTORIC PRESERVATION
   Western, 426
NATIONAL WILDLIFE FEDERATION
   Western Natural Resource Center, 429
NATIVE AMERICAN HERITAGE COMMISSION, 187
NATURE CONSERVANCY, THE
   California Chapter, 434
NOLTE ASSOCIATES, INC., 569
NORTHCOAST ENVIRONMENTAL CENTER, 452
OCEANIC SOCIETY, 456
ORANGUTAN FOUNDATION INTERNATIONAL, 460
OTTER PROJECT, THE, 462
PACIFIC INSTITUTE FOR STUDIES IN DEVELOPMENT, ENVIRONMENT, AND SECURITY, 463
PLANNING AND CONSERVATION LEAGUE, 469
PRO PENINSULA, 473
PS ENTERPRISES, 570
RAINFOREST ACTION NETWORK, 476
RESOURCE RENEWAL INSTITUTE, THE, 479

RESTORE HETCH HETCHY, 479
RIVER PROJECT, THE, 481
RIVERSIDE COUNTY CONSERVATION AGENCY, 215
SALTON SEA AUTHORITY, 215
SAN DIEGO NATURAL HISTORY MUSEUM, 484
SAN DIEGUITO RIVER PARK JOINT POWERS AUTHORITY, 215
SAN ELIJO LAGOON CONSERVANCY, 484
SAN FRANCISCO BAY CONSERVATION AND DEVELOPMENT COMMISSION, 215
SAN JOSE STATE UNIVERSITY, 594
SANTA CLARA COMMUNITY ACTION PROGRAM, 594
SAVE SAN FRANCISCO BAY ASSOCIATION, 485
SAVE-THE-REDWOODS LEAGUE, 487
SCENIC AMERICA
   Scenic California, 487
SEA SHEPHERD CONSERVATION SOCIETY
   USA Regional-SSCS Monterey, 489
SHARING NATURE FOUNDATION, 570
SIERRA CLUB
   Angeles Chapter, 490
   Bay Area Field Office, 490
   California/Nevada/Hawaii Office and California Legislative Office, 490
   Kern-Kaweah Chapter, 493
   Loma Prieta Chapter, 493
   Los Padres Chapter, 493
   Mother Lode Chapter, 494
   Redwood Chapter (Northern California), 496
   San Diego Chapter (Southern California), 497
   San francisco Bay Chapter, 497
   San Gorgonio Chapter (Southern California), 497
   Santa Lucia Chapter, 497
   Southern California/Nevada Field Office, 498
   Tehipite Chapter (Northern California), 498
   Ventana Chapter (Northern California), 498
SIERRA CLUB CALIFORNIA, 499
SIERRA CLUB FOUNDATION, THE, 499
SOCIETY FOR THE PRESERVATION OF BIRDS OF PREY, 503
SONOMA STATE UNIVERSITY
   Department of Environmental Studies and Planning, 595
      Environmental Technology Center, 595
SOUTHWEST CENTER FOR ENVIRONMENTAL RESEARCH AND POLICY (SCERP), 596
SOUTHWESTERN HERPETOLOGISTS SOCIETY, 510
STANFORD ENVIRONMENTAL LAW SOCIETY, 511
STANFORD UNIVERSITY
   Department of Biological Sciences, 597
   Morrison Institute for Population and Resource Studies, 597
STUDENT CONSERVATION ASSOCIATION, INC.
   California Southwest Regional Office, 513
SUSTAINABLE ENERGY INSTITUTE
   Culture Change, 514
   Food Not Lawns, 514
   Pedal Power Produce, 514
TERRA NATURE FUND, 516
THEODORE PAYNE FOUNDATION FOR WILDFLOWERS AND NATIVE PLANTS, INC., 518
THREE CIRCLES CENTER FOR MULTICULTURAL ENVIRONMENTAL EDUCATION, 518
TREEPEOPLE, 519
TROUT UNLIMITED
   California Council, 521
TRUST FOR PUBLIC LAND, THE, 523
TWO WHITE WOLVES SANCTUARY, 525
UNITED STATES DEPARTMENT OF AGRICULTURE
   ANIMAL AND PLANT HEALTH INSPECTION SERVICE
      Animal Care Western Regional Office, 32
   Forest Service
      Angeles National Forests, 34
      Butte Valley National Grassland, 35
      Cleveland National Forest, 36
      Eldorado National Forest, 37
      Inyo National Forest, 39
      Klamath National Forest, 39
      Lake Tahoe Basin Management Unit, 39
      Los Padres National Forest, 40
      Mendocino National Forest, 40
      Modoc National Forest, 41
      Pacific Southwest Research Station, 42
      Plumas National Forest, 42
      Region 05 (Pacific Southwest), 43
      San Bernardino National Forest, 44
      Sequoia National Forest, 44
      Shasta-Trinity National Forest, 44
      Sierra National Forest, 45

GEOGRAPHIC INDEX – U

  Six Rivers National Forest, 45
  Stanislaus National Forest, 45
  Tahoe National Forest, 45
 Research Education and Economics
  ARS Pacific West Area, 48
UNITED STATES DEPARTMENT OF COMMERCE
 National Oceanic and Atmospheric Administration
  Channel Islands National Marine Sanctuary, 49
  Cordell Bank National Marine Sanctuary, 50
  Gulf of Farallones National Marine Sanctuary, 50
  Monterey Bay National Marine Sanctuary, 51
  Sea Grant Program - California, 54
  Tijuana River National Estuarine Research Reserve, 60
UNITED STATES DEPARTMENT OF DEFENSE
 Air Force Major U.S. Installations
  Beale AFB, CA, 63
  Edwards AFB, CA, 63
  McClellan AFB, CA, 65
  Travis AFB, CA, 66
  Vandenberg AFB, CA, 66
 Army Corps of Engineers
  Los Angeles Engineer District, 69
  Sacramento Engineer District, 71
  San Francisco Engineer District, 71
  South Pacific Engineer District, 71
UNITED STATES DEPARTMENT OF HOMELAND SECURITY
 Customs and Border Protection
  South Pacific CMC, 77
UNITED STATES DEPARTMENT OF THE INTERIOR
 Bureau of Land Management
  Alturas Field Office, 78
  Arcata Field Office, 79
  Bakersfield Field Office, 79
  Barstow Field Office, 79
  Bishop Field Office, 79
  Eagle Lake Field Office, 81
  El Centro Field Office, 81
  Folsom Field Office, 81
  Hollister Field Office, 82
  Needles Field Office, 84
  Palm Springs / South Coast Field Office, 85
  Redding Field Office, 85
  Ridgecrest Field Office, 86
  State Office for CA, 87
  Surprise Field Office, 88
  Ukiah Field Office, 88
 Bureau of Reclamation
  Mid Pacific Region, 89
 Fish & Wildlife Service
  Guadalupe-Nipomo Dunes National Wildlife Refuge, 99
  Antioch Dunes National Wildlife Refuge, 91
  Bitter Creek National Wildlife Refuge, 93
  Blue Ridge National Wildlife Refuge, 93
  California Nevada Operations, 94
  Hopper Mountain Complex National Wildlife Refuge, 100
  Humboldt Bay National Wildlife Refuge, 100
  Kern/Pixley National Wildlife Refuge, 101
  Keterson National Wildlife Refuge, 101
  Klamath Basin Complex National Wildlife Refuge, 102
  Modoc National Wildlife Refuge, 106
  Sabine National Wildlife Refuge, 113
  San Bernardino/Leslie Canyon National Wildlife Refuge, 113
  San Francisco Bay National Wildlife Refuge Complex, 113
  Silvio O. Conte National Wildlife and Fish Refuge, 114
  Stone Lakes National Wildlife Refuge, 116
 National Park Service
  Channel Islands National Park, 121
  Death Valley National Park, 122
  Joshua Tree National Park, 123
  Lassen Volcanic National Park, 124
  Point Reyes National Seashore, 125
  Redwood National Park, 125
  Sequoia and Kings Canyon National Park, 125
  Yosemite National Park, 126
UNIVERSITY OF CALIFORNIA AT DAVIS
 College of Agriculture and Environmental Science, 606
 Herbarium, 606
 School of Veterinary Medicine, 606
UNIVERSITY OF CALIFORNIA AT LOS ANGELES
 College Letters and Science, 606
 School of Engineering and Applied Science, 607
UNIVERSITY OF CALIFORNIA AT RIVERSIDE
 Department of Environmental Science, 607
 Graduate School of Environmental Science and Engineering, 607

UNIVERSITY OF CALIFORNIA AT SAN DIEGO, 607
UNIVERSITY OF CALIFORNIA AT SANTA BARBARA, 607
UNIVERSITY OF CALIFORNIA AT SANTA CRUZ, 607
UNIVERSITY OF CALIFORNIA, BERKELEY, 607
UNIVERSITY OF CALIFORNIA, SANTA BARBARA, 607
UNIVERSITY OF SOUTHERN CALIFORNIA
 Department of Civil and Environmental Engineering, 620
 Environmental Studies Program, 620
URBAN HABITAT PROGRAM, 527
VERNAL POOL SOCIETY, THE, 530
VIDEO PROJECT, THE, 571
WATER EDUCATION FOUNDATION, 535
WATERSHED MANAGEMENT COUNCIL, 535
WETLANDS ACTION NETWORK, 538
WILD FOUNDATION, THE, 539
WILDCOAST, 540
WILDLIFE SOCIETY
 California Central Coast Chapter, 546
 California North Coast Chapter, 547
 Sacramento-Shasta Chapter, 552
 San Francisco Bay Area Chapter, 552
 San Joaquin Valley Chapter, 552
 Southern California Chapter, 553
WILDLIFE WAYSTATION, 554
YOSEMITE RESTORATION TRUST, 562

COLORADO
AMERICAN BIRDING ASSOCIATION (ABA), 250
AMERICAN HUMANE, 261
AMERICAN WATER WORKS ASSOCIATION (AWWA), 267
CADDO LAKE INSTITUTE, INC., 282
CAMPAIGN FOR AMERICA'S WILDERNESS, 285
CENTER FOR NATIVE ECOSYSTEMS
 Front Range Office, 292
CENTER FOR NATIVE ECOSYSTEMS
 West Slope Office, 292
COLORADO ASSOCIATION OF SOIL CONSERVATION DISTRICTS, 301
COLORADO BASS FEDERATION, 301
COLORADO DEPARTMENT OF AGRICULTURE, 146
COLORADO DEPARTMENT OF EDUCATION, 146
COLORADO DEPARTMENT OF NATURAL RESOURCES, 146
 Colorado Geologic Survey, 146
 Division of Minerals and Geology, 146
 Division of Parks and Outdoor Recreation, 146
 Division of Water Resources, 147
 Division of Wildlife, 147
 Oil and Gas Conservation Commission, 147
 State Board of Land Commissioners, 147
COLORADO DEPARTMENT OF PUBLIC HEALTH AND ENVIRONMENT, 147
COLORADO ENVIRONMENTAL COALITION, 301
COLORADO FORESTRY ASSOCIATION, 301
COLORADO GOVERNOR'S OFFICE OF ENERGY MANAGEMENT AND CONSERVATION, 147
COLORADO MOUNTAIN CLUB, 302
COLORADO MOUNTAIN COLLEGE, 577
COLORADO NATURAL HERITAGE PROGRAM, 302
COLORADO STATE CONSERVATION BOARD
 Colorado Department of Agriculture, 148
COLORADO STATE FOREST SERVICE, 148
COLORADO STATE UNIVERSITY
 College of Natural Resources, 578
 Department of Fishery and Wildlife Biology, 578
 Department of Political Science, 578
COLORADO STATE UNIVERSITY COOPERATIVE EXTENSION, 148
COLORADO TRAPPERS ASSOCIATION, 302
COLORADO WATER CONGRESS, 302
COLORADO WATER CONSERVATION BOARD
 Water Conservation Board, 148
COLORADO WILDLIFE FEDERATION, 302
COLORADO WILDLIFE HERITAGE FOUNDATION, 302
EARTHJUSTICE
 Denver Office, 318
 Environmental Law Clinic at the University of Denver, 318
ENVIRONMENTAL DEFENSE
 Rocky Mountain Office, 324
ENVIRONMENTAL PROTECTION AGENCY
 Region 8 (CO, MT, ND, SD, UT, WY), 19
INTERNATIONAL EROSION CONTROL ASSOCIATION (IECA), 363
INTERNATIONAL HUNTER EDUCATION ASSOCIATION, 364
IZAAK WALTON LEAGUE OF AMERICA, INC., THE
 Colorado Division, 376
KEYSTONE CENTER, THE, 384
LAND AND WATER FUND OF THE ROCKIES, 386

LEGACY LAND TRUST, 388
NATIONAL ASSOCIATION FOR INTERPRETATION, 407
NATIONAL BISON ASSOCIATION, 417
NATIONAL ENVIRONMENTAL HEALTH ASSOCIATION, 418
NATIONAL FARMERS UNION, 419
NATIONAL ORGANIZATION FOR RIVERS (NORS), 422
NATIONAL PARKS CONSERVATION ASSOCIATION (NPCA)
   State of the Parks Program Office, 423
NATIONAL TRUST FOR HISTORIC PRESERVATION
   Mountains - Plains Office, 425
NATIONAL WILDLIFE FEDERATION
   Rocky Mountain Natural Resource Center, 428
NATIVE AMERICAN FISH AND WILDLIFE SOCIETY (NAFWS), 430
NATURE CONSERVANCY, THE
   Colorado Chapter, 434
   Rocky Mountain Division Office, 439
PARTNERS IN PARKS, 465
PLAYA LAKES JOINT VENTURE, 469
PRIORITIES INSTITUTE, THE, 473
RAPTOR EDUCATION FOUNDATION, INC., 477
RIVER OTTER ALLIANCE, THE, 481
ROCKY MOUNTAIN BIGHORN SOCIETY, 482
ROCKY MOUNTAIN BIOLOGICAL LABORATORY, THE, 482
ROCKY MOUNTAIN BIRD OBSERVATORY, 482
SIERRA CLUB
   Colorado Field Office, 491
   Rocky Mountain Chapter (Colorado), 497
SINAPU, 500
SOCIETY FOR RANGE MANAGEMENT, 503
THORNE ECOLOGICAL INSTITUTE, 518
TREES, WATER, AND PEOPLE, 519
TROUT UNLIMITED
   Colorado Council, 521
UNITED STATES DEPARTMENT OF AGRICULTURE
   ANIMAL AND PLANT HEALTH INSPECTION SERVICE
     National Wildlife Research Center, 32
   Forest Service
     Arapaho and Roosevelt National Forests, 34
     Comanche National Grassland, 36
     Grand Mesa, Uncompahgre and Gunnison National Forests, 38
     Pawnee National Grassland, 42
     Pike and San Isabel National Forests, 42
     Region 02 (Rocky Mountain), 43
     Rio Grande National Forest, 44
     Rocky Mountain Research Station, 44
     Routt National Forest, 44
     San Juan National Forest, 44
     White River National Forest, 46
   Research Education and Economics
     ARS Northern Plains Area Office, 48
UNITED STATES DEPARTMENT OF DEFENSE
   Air Force Major Air Commands
     Peterson AFB, CO, 62
     USAF Academy, 62
   Air Force Major U.S. Installations
     Peterson AFB, CO, 66
     Shriever AFB, CO, 66
UNITED STATES DEPARTMENT OF THE INTERIOR
   Bureau of Land Management
     Anasazi Heritage Center, 79
     Colorado State Office, 80
     Glenwood Springs Field Office, 82
     Grand Junction Field Office/Western Slope Center, 82
     Gunnison Field Office, 82
     Kremmling Field Office, 82
     La Jara Field Office, 82
     Little Snake Field Office, 83
     Royal Gorge Field Office/Front Range Center, 86
     Saguache Field Office, 86
     San Juan Field Office, 87
     Uncompahgre Field Office/Southwest Center, 88
     White River Field Office, 88
   BUREAU OF RECLAMATION
     Denver Office, 89
   Fish and Wildlife Service
     Alamosa/Monte Vista National Wildlife Refuge, 90
     Arapaho National Wildlife Refuge, 91
     Browns Park National Wildlife Refuge, 94
     Region 5, Northeast Regional Office, 112
     Two Ponds, C/O Rocky Mountain Arsenal National Wildlife Refuge, 117
   National Park Service
     Mesa Verde National Park, 124
     Rocky Mountain National Park, 125

UNIVERSITY OF COLORADO, 608
UNIVERSITY OF COLORADO AT BOULDER, 608
UNIVERSITY OF NORTHERN COLORADO, 618
WILDLIFE SOCIETY
   Colorado Chapter, 547
WINDSTAR FOUNDATION, THE, 555
WOMEN'S SHOOTING SPORTS FOUNDATION, 558

CONNECTICUT
BERKSHIRE-LITCHFIELD ENVIRONMENTAL COUNCIL, INC., 277
CETACEAN SOCIETY INTERNATIONAL, 294
CONNECTICUT ASSOCIATION OF CONSERVATION DISTRICTS, INC., 304
CONNECTICUT BASS FEDERATION, 304
CONNECTICUT BOTANICAL SOCIETY, 304
CONNECTICUT CARIBOU CLAN, 565
CONNECTICUT COLLEGE, 578
CONNECTICUT COUNCIL ON ENVIRONMENTAL QUALITY, 148
CONNECTICUT DEPARTMENT OF AGRICULTURE, 149
CONNECTICUT DEPARTMENT OF ENVIRONMENTAL PROTECTION, 149
CONNECTICUT FOREST AND PARK ASSOCIATION, 304
CONNECTICUT FUND FOR THE ENVIRONMENT, 305
CONNECTICUT PUBLIC INTEREST RESEARCH GROUP (CONN PIRG), 305
CONNECTICUT WATERFOWL ASSOCIATION, INC., 305
EP EDUCATION SERVICES, INC., 328
FRIENDS OF ANIMALS INC., 337
GAME CONSERVANCY U.S.A., 339
INTERNATIONAL CHILDREN'S CONFERENCE ON THE ENVIRONMENT, 362
KEEP AMERICA BEAUTIFUL, INC., 382
NATIONAL AUDUBON SOCIETY
   Audubon Council of Connection, 409
   Connecticut Audubon Society, 412
NATIONAL SHOOTING SPORTS FOUNDATION, INC., 424
NATURE CONSERVANCY, THE
   Connecticut Chapter, 434
SAVE THE SOUND, INC., 486
SIERRA CLUB
   Connecticut Chapter, 491
SOUNDWATERS, 505
SOUTHERN CONNECTICUT STATE UNIVERSITY, 596
SOUTHWEST CONSERVATION DISTRICT, 510
TROUT UNLIMITED
   Connecticut Council, 521
UNITED STATES DEPARTMENT OF COMMERCE
   National Oceanic and Atmospheric Administration
     Sea Grant Program - Connecticut, 54
UNIVERSITY OF CONNECTICUT, 608
UNIVERSITY OF CONNECTICUT COOPERATIVE EXTENSION, 608
UNIVERSITY OF NEW HAVEN DEPT. OF BIOLOGY AND ENVIRONMENTAL SCIENCES, 617
WILDLIFE ORPHANAGE, INC., THE, 545
YALE LAW SCHOOL, 627
YALE UNIVERSITY
   School of Forestry and Environmental Studies, 628

DELAWARE
AMERICAN ASSOCIATION OF BOTANICAL GARDENS AND ARBORETA, 249
AMERICAN FISHERIES SOCIETY
   Mid-Atlantic Chapter, 256
CHRISTINA CONSERVANCY, INC., 297
COALITION FOR NATURAL STREAM VALLEYS, INC., 299
DELAWARE ASSOCIATION OF CONSERVATION DISTRICTS, 312
DELAWARE BASS FEDERATION, 312
DELAWARE COOPERATIVE EXTENSION SERVICES, 150
DELAWARE DEPARTMENT OF AGRICULTURE, 150
DELAWARE DEPARTMENT OF NATURAL RESOURCES AND ENVIRONMENTAL CONTROL
   Division of Air & Waste Management, 150
   Division of Fish and Wildlife, 150
   Division of Parks and Recreation, 150
   Division of Soil and Water Conservation, 150
   Division of Water Resources, 151
DELAWARE FOREST SERVICE, 151
DELAWARE GEOLOGICAL SURVEY, 151
DELAWARE GREENWAYS, INC., 312
DELAWARE MUSEUM OF NATURAL HISTORY, 312
DELAWARE NATURE SOCIETY, 312
DELAWARE SOLID WASTE AUTHORITY, 151
DELAWARE WILD LANDS, INC., 313
DELMARVA ORNITHOLOGICAL SOCIETY, 313

GEOGRAPHIC INDEX – U

HUMMINGBIRD SOCIETY, THE, 353
MID-ATLANTIC FISHERY MANAGEMENT COUNCIL, 398
NATIONAL AUDUBON SOCIETY
   Delaware Audubon Society, 413
NATURE CONSERVANCY, THE
   Delaware Chapter, 434
SAVE WETLANDS AND BAYS, 486
SIERRA CLUB
   Delaware Chapter, 491
TRI-STATE BIRD RESCUE AND RESEARCH, INC., 520
UNITED STATES DEPARTMENT OF COMMERCE
   National Oceanic and Atmospheric Administration
      Delaware National Estuarine Research Reserve, 50
      Sea Grant Program - Delaware, 54
UNITED STATES DEPARTMENT OF DEFENSE
   Air Force Major U.S. Installations
      Dover AFB, DE, 63
UNITED STATES DEPARTMENT OF THE INTERIOR
   Fish and Wildlife Service
      Bombay Hook National Wildlife Refuge, 93
      Delaware Bay Estuary Project, 97
      Prime Hook National Wildlife Refuge, 110
UNIVERSITY OF DELAWARE, 608

DISTRICT OF COLUMBIA
20/20 VISION, 241
ACADEMY FOR EDUCATIONAL DEVELOPMENT, 241
ADVISORY COUNCIL ON HISTORIC PRESERVATION, 16
AFRICAN WILDLIFE FOUNDATION, 243
AMERICA THE BEAUTIFUL FUND, 248
AMERICAN ASSOCIATION FOR THE ADVANCEMENT OF SCIENCE, 249
AMERICAN CHEMICAL SOCIETY, 563
AMERICAN CONSERVATION ASSOCIATION, INC., 251
AMERICAN COUNCIL FOR AN ENERGY-EFFICIENT ECONOMY, 251
AMERICAN COUNCIL FOR THE UNITED NATIONS UNIVERSITY (ACUNU), 251
AMERICAN FARMLAND TRUST, 251
AMERICAN FISHERIES SOCIETY
   Potomac Chapter, 258
AMERICAN FOREST FOUNDATION, 260
AMERICAN FORESTS, 260
AMERICAN HORSE PROTECTION ASSOCIATION, 261
AMERICAN INSTITUTE OF BIOLOGICAL SCIENCES, 261
AMERICAN LANDS, 262
AMERICAN LEAGUE OF ANGLERS AND BOATERS, 262
AMERICAN ORNITHOLOGISTS UNION, 263
AMERICAN PLANNING ASSOCIATION, 264
AMERICAN RECREATION COALITION, 264
AMERICAN RIVERS, 264
   Voyage of Recovery, 265
AMERICAN SOCIETY OF LANDSCAPE ARCHITECTS, 266
AMERICAN WILDERNESS COALITION, 267
ANIMAL WELFARE INSTITUTE, 269
ANTARCTICA PROJECT, THE, 269
APPALACHIAN REGIONAL COMMISSION, 16
ASSOCIATION OF AMERICAN GEOGRAPHERS, 273
ASSOCIATION OF STATE AND TERRITORIAL HEALTH OFFICIALS, 274
ATLANTIC STATES MARINE FISHERIES COMMISSION, 139
BEYOND PESTICIDES, 277
CARRYING CAPACITY NETWORK, 288
CENTER FOR INTERNATIONAL ENVIRONMENTAL LAW (CIEL), 292
CENTER FOR RESOURCE ECONOMICS/ISLAND PRESS, 293
CENTER FOR SCIENCE IN THE PUBLIC INTEREST, 293
CIRCUMPOLAR CONSERVATION UNION, 297
CLEAN WATER ACTION, 298
CLEAN WATER FUND, 298
CLEAN WATER NETWORK, THE, 298
CLIMATE INSTITUTE, 299
COAST ALLIANCE, 300
COMMUNITY RIGHTS COUNSEL, 303
CONCERN, INC., 304
CONGRESSIONAL GREEN SHEETS, INC., 565
CONSERVATION INTERNATIONAL, 307
CRITICAL ECOSYSTEM PARTNERSHIP FUND, 311
DEFENDERS OF WILDLIFE, 311
DISTRICT OF COLUMBIA DEPARTMENT OF HEALTH
   Environmental Health Administration, Watershed Protection Division, 152
DISTRICT OF COLUMBIA DEPARTMENT OF PUBLIC WORKS, 152
DISTRICT OF COLUMBIA SOIL AND WATER CONSERVATION - DISTRICT, 314
EARTH DAY NETWORK, 316
EARTH POLICY INSTITUTE, 317

EARTHJUSTICE
   Policy and Legislation, 319
   Washington, DC, Office, 320
ECOLOGICAL SOCIETY OF AMERICA, THE, 321
ENDANGERED SPECIES COALITION, 322
ENVIRONMENT AND ENERGY PUBLISHING, LLC, 566
ENVIRONMENTAL AND ENERGY STUDY INSTITUTE (EESI), 323
ENVIRONMENTAL DEFENSE
   Capital Office, 324
ENVIRONMENTAL LAW INSTITUTE, THE, 327
ENVIRONMENTAL PROTECTION AGENCY, 18
   Air and Radiation, 18
   Solid Waste and Emergency Response, 19
FRIENDS OF THE EARTH, 337
GENERAL FEDERATION OF WOMEN'S CLUBS, 340
GENERAL SERVICES ADMINISTRATION, 20
GEORGE WASHINGTON CARVER OUTDOOR SCHOOL, INC., THE, 340
GEORGE WASHINGTON UNIVERSITY, 582
   Law School, 582
GEORGETOWN ENVIRONMENTAL LAW & POLICY INSTITUTE, 582
GLOBAL ENVIRONMENTAL MANAGEMENT INITIATIVE (GEMI), 343
GREEN MEDIA TOOLSHED, 346
GREEN SEAL, 347
GREENPEACE, INC., 347
GREENWIRE, 567
H. JOHN HEINZ III CENTER FOR SCIENCE, ECONOMICS, AND THE ENVIRONMENT, 348
HOUSE COMMITTEE ON AGRICULTURE, 21
HOUSE COMMITTEE ON APPROPRIATIONS, 21
HOUSE COMMITTEE ON EDUCATION AND THE WORKFORCE, 21
HOUSE COMMITTEE ON ENERGY AND COMMERCE, 21
HOUSE COMMITTEE ON INTERNATIONAL RELATIONS, 21
HOUSE COMMITTEE ON RESOURCES, 22
HOUSE COMMITTEE ON RULES, 22
HOUSE COMMITTEE ON TRANSPORTATION AND INFRASTRUCTURE, 22
HUMANE SOCIETY OF THE UNITED STATES, THE, 352
INDO-PACIFIC CONSERVATION ALLIANCE, 357
INITIATIVE FOR SOCIAL ACTION AND RENEWAL IN EURASIA, 357
INTERNATIONAL ASSOCIATION OF FISH AND WILDLIFE AGENCIES, 360
INTERNATIONAL ECOTOURISM SOCIETY, THE, 362
INTERNATIONAL INSTITUTE FOR ENERGY CONSERVATION, 364
INTERNATIONAL JOINT COMMISSION
   United States Section, 23
INTERNATIONAL UNION FOR CONSERVATION OF NATURE AND NATURAL RESOURCES (IUCN) THE WORLD CONSERVATION UNION
   United States Office, Washington, DC, 371
LAND TRUST ALLIANCE, THE, 386
LEAGUE OF CONSERVATION VOTERS, 387
LEAGUE OF WOMEN VOTERS OF THE U.S., 387
MARINE FISH CONSERVATION NETWORK, 394
MIGRATORY BIRD CONSERVATION COMMISSION, 23
MINERAL POLICY CENTER, 399
NATIONAL ASSOCIATION OF CONSERVATION DISTRICTS, 407
NATIONAL ASSOCIATION OF SERVICE AND CONSERVATION CORPS (NASCC), 408
NATIONAL ASSOCIATION OF STATE DEPARTMENTS OF AGRICULTURE, 408
NATIONAL ASSOCIATION OF STATE FORESTERS, 408
NATIONAL AUDUBON SOCIETY
   Public Policy Office, 415
   Washington, D.C. Office, 416
NATIONAL CAUCUS OF ENVIRONMENTAL LEGISLATORS (NCEL), 417
NATIONAL COUNCIL FOR SCIENCE AND THE ENVIRONMENT, THE, 418
NATIONAL EDUCATION ASSOCIATION, 418
NATIONAL ENVIRONMENTAL EDUCATION AND TRAINING FOUNDATION, 418
NATIONAL FISH AND WILDLIFE FOUNDATION, 419
NATIONAL GEOGRAPHIC SOCIETY, 421
NATIONAL GRANGE, THE, 421
NATIONAL PARK FOUNDATION, 422
NATIONAL PARK TRUST, 422
NATIONAL PARKS CONSERVATION ASSOCIATION (NPCA), 422
NATIONAL RESEARCH COUNCIL, 423
NATIONAL TRANSPORTATION SAFETY BOARD, 24
NATIONAL TREE TRUST, 425
NATIONAL TRUST FOR HISTORIC PRESERVATION, 425
NATIONAL WATERWAYS CONFERENCE INC., 426
NATIONAL WHISTLEBLOWER LEGAL DEFENSE & EDUCATION FUND, 426
NATIONAL WILDLIFE FEDERATION
   International Affairs, 428
   Office of Congressional and Federal Affairs, 428

NATIONAL WILDLIFE REFUGE ASSOCIATION, 429
NATURAL RESOURCES COUNCIL OF AMERICA, 432
NORTH AMERICAN COALITION ON RELIGION AND ECOLOGY
 (NACRE), 448
NUCLEAR REGULATORY COMMISSION, 25
OCEAN CONSERVANCY, THE, 455
OCEANIA, 455
ORNITHOLOGICAL COUNCIL, 462
OZONE ACTION, 463
PANOS INSTITUTE, THE, 464
PEACE CORPS, 27
PHYSICIANS FOR SOCIAL RESPONSIBILITY, 468
PINCHOT INSTITUTE FOR CONSERVATION, 469
POPULATION ACTION INTERNATIONAL, 470
POPULATION CONNECTION, 471
POPULATION INSTITUTE, THE, 471
POPULATION REFERENCE BUREAU, INC., 471
POPULATION-ENVIRONMENT BALANCE, INC., 471
PUBLIC EMPLOYEES FOR ENVIRONMENTAL RESPONSIBILITY
 (PEER), 474
RAINBOW PUSH COALITION, 476
RENEW THE EARTH, 478
RENEWABLE ENERGY POLICY PROJECT (REPP), 478
RESOURCES FOR THE FUTURE, 479
RIVER NETWORK
 Eastern Office, 481
SAFARI CLUB INTERNATIONAL
 Washington, DC Office, 484
SAVE AMERICA'S FORESTS, 485
SCENIC AMERICA, 487
SEAWEB, 489
SENATE COMMITTEE ON AGRICULTURE, NUTRITION, AND
 FORESTRY, 28
SENATE COMMITTEE ON APPROPRIATIONS, 28
SENATE COMMITTEE ON COMMERCE, SCIENCE, AND
 TRANSPORTATION, 28
SENATE COMMITTEE ON ENERGY AND NATURAL RESOURCES, 29
SENATE COMMITTEE ON ENVIRONMENT AND PUBLIC WORKS, 29
SENATE COMMITTEE ON FOREIGN RELATIONS, 29
SENATE COMMITTEE ON HEALTH, EDUCATION, LABOR, AND
 PENSIONS, 29
SIERRA CLUB
 Washington, DC Chapter, 499
 Washington, DC Office, 499
SIERRA STUDENT COALITION, 500
SMITHSONIAN INSTITUTION, 501
 National Museum of Natural History, 501
 Office of Fellowships, 501
 Office of International Relations, 501
 Smithsonian Institution Press, 501
SMITHSONIAN INSTITUTION NATIONAL ZOOLOGICAL PARK, 501
SOCIETY FOR ANIMAL PROTECTIVE LEGISLATION, 502
SOUTHERN UTAH WILDERNESS ALLIANCE
 Washington, DC Office, 510
STATE AND TERRITORIAL AIR POLLUTION PROGRAM
 ADMINISTRATORS AND THE ASSOCIATION OF LOCAL AIR
 POLLUTION CONTROL OFFICIALS, 512
STUDENT PUGWASH USA, 513
THEODORE ROOSEVELT CONSERVATION PARTNERSHIP, 518
TRAFFIC NORTH AMERICA, 518
UNITED STATES CHAMBER OF COMMERCE
 Environment, Technology and Regulatory Affairs, 526
UNITED STATES COMMITTEE FOR THE UNITED NATIONS
 ENVIRONMENT PROGRAMME, THE (U.S. AND UNEP), 526
UNITED STATES COUNCIL ON ENVIRONMENTAL QUALITY, 31
UNITED STATES DEPARTMENT OF AGRICULTURE, 31
 Agricultural Research Service, 31
 Animal and Plant Health Inspection Service
  Plant Protection and Quarantine, 32
 Cooperative State Research, Education, Extension Service (CSREES), 33
 Economic Research Center, 33
 Farm Service Agency (FSA), 33
 Forest Service, 33
 Natural Resources Conservation Service, 46
 Research Education and Economics, 48
  Cooperative State Research, Education, and Extension Service, 49
UNITED STATES DEPARTMENT OF COMMERCE, 49
 Economic Development Administration, 49
 National Oceanic and Atmospheric Administration, 49
UNITED STATES DEPARTMENT OF DEFENSE, 61
 Air Force Major Air Commands
  Bolling AFB, DC, 61
  USAF/ILEV Headquarters, 62

 Air Force Major U.S. Installations
  Bolling AFB, DC, 63
 Army, 67
 Army Corps of Engineers
  Headquarters, 67
 Assistant Chief of Staff for Installation Management, Office of the
  Director of Environmental Programs, and Conservation Team, 74
 Marine Corps, 74
 Navy, 74
 Office of the Civil Engineer, 74
UNITED STATES DEPARTMENT OF EDUCATION, 75
UNITED STATES DEPARTMENT OF ENERGY, 75
 Federal Energy Regulatory Commission, 75
UNITED STATES DEPARTMENT OF HEALTH AND HUMAN SERVICES, 75
UNITED STATES DEPARTMENT OF HOMELAND SECURITY
 Customs and Border Protection
  Office of Public Affairs, 76
UNITED STATES DEPARTMENT OF HOUSING AND URBAN
 DEVELOPMENT, 77
UNITED STATES DEPARTMENT OF JUSTICE, 77
UNITED STATES DEPARTMENT OF LABOR, 77
 Job Corps, 77
UNITED STATES DEPARTMENT OF STATE, 77
 Bureau of Oceans and International Environmental and Scientific Affairs,
  78
 United States Man and the Biosphere Program (U.S. MAB), 78
UNITED STATES DEPARTMENT OF THE INTERIOR, 78
 Bureau of Indian Affairs, 78
 Bureau of Land Management
  National Applied Resource Center, 84
  Public Affairs, 85
 Bureau of Reclamation, 89
 Fish and Wildlife Service, 90
  Washington Office, 118
 National Park Service, 120
 Office of Surface Mining Reclamation and Enforcement, 126
UNITED STATES DEPARTMENT OF TRANSPORTATION, 128
 Coast Guard, 128
 Federal Aviation Administration, 128
 Federal Highway Administration, 128
 Federal Railroad Administration, 129
 Federal Transit Administration, 129
 National Highway Traffic Safety Administration, 129
 Saint Lawrence Seaway Development Corporation, 129
UNITED STATES DEPARTMENT OF TREASURY, 129
UNITED STATES ENVIRONMENTAL PROTECTION AGENCY
 Administration and Resources Management, 129
 Enforcement and Compliance, 129
 Office of Research and Development, 130
 Prevention, Pesticides, and Toxic Substances, 130
 Science Policy, 130
UNITED STATES PUBLIC INTEREST RESEARCH GROUP, 526
UNITED STATES TOURIST COUNCIL, 527
UNIVERSITY OF THE DISTRICT OF COLUMBIA, 621
WILDERNESS SOCIETY, THE, 541
WILDLIFE MANAGEMENT INSTITUTE, 545
WORLD PARKS ENDOWMENT INC., 559
WORLD RESOURCES INSTITUTE, 559
WORLD WILDLIFE FUND, 559
WORLDWATCH INSTITUTE, 560

FLORIDA
AMERICAN FISHERIES SOCIETY
 Agriculture Economics Section, 252
 Florida Chapter, 254
AMERICAN SOCIETY OF ICHTHYOLOGISTS AND HERPETOLOGISTS,
 265
ARCHBOLD BIOLOGICAL STATION, 270
ASSOCIATION OF AVIAN VETERINARIANS, 273
BARRIER ISLAND TRUST, INC., 276
BILLFISH FOUNDATION, THE, 278
BLUE GOOSE ALLIANCE, 279
CARIBBEAN CONSERVATION CORPORATION, 288
CHELONIA INSTITUTE, 295
CITIZENS FOR A SCENIC FLORIDA, INC., 297
CONSERVANCY OF SOUTHWEST FLORIDA, THE, 305
CONSERVATION ALLIANCE OF ST. LUCIE CO., 306
EARTHJUSTICE
 Tallahassee Office, 320
EVERGLADES COORDINATING COUNCIL (ECC), 329
FAU PINE JOG ENVIROMENTAL EDUCATION CENTER, 581
FLORIDA ASSOCIATION OF SOIL AND WATER CONSERVATION
 DISTRICTS, 331
FLORIDA BASS CHAPTER FEDERATION, 331

GEOGRAPHIC INDEX – U

FLORIDA COOPERATIVE EXTENSION SERVICE, 582
FLORIDA COOPERATIVE FISH AND WILDLIFE RESEARCH UNIT (USDI), 152
FLORIDA DEFENDERS OF THE ENVIRONMENT, INC., 331
FLORIDA DEPARTMENT OF AGRICULTURE AND CONSUMER SERVICES, 152
   Division of Forestry, 153
   Office of Agricultural Water Policy, 153
   Soil and Water Conservation Council, 153
FLORIDA DEPARTMENT OF ENVIRONMENTAL PROTECTION, 153
   Air Resources Management Division, 153
   Bureau of Beaches and Wetland Resources, 153
   Coastal and Aquatic Managed Areas, 153
   Division of Law Enforcement, 153
   Division of Resource Assessment and Management, 154
   Division of State Lands, 154
   Division of Water Resource Management, 154
   Florida State Parks AmeriCorps, 154
   Recreation and Parks Division, 154
   Waste Management Division, 154
FLORIDA EXOTIC PEST PLANT COUNCIL, 331
FLORIDA FEDERATION OF GARDEN CLUBS, INC., 331
FLORIDA FISH AND WILDLIFE CONSERVATION COMMISSION, 154
FLORIDA FORESTRY ASSOCIATION, 331
FLORIDA NATIVE PLANT SOCIETY, 332
FLORIDA NATURAL AREAS INVENTORY, 332
FLORIDA ORNITHOLOGICAL SOCIETY, 332
FLORIDA PANTHER PROJECT, INC., THE, 332
FLORIDA PANTHER SOCIETY, INC., THE, 332
FLORIDA PUBLIC INTEREST RESEARCH GROUP (FLORIDA PIRG), 332
FLORIDA SPORTSMEN'S CONSERVATION ASSOCIATION, 333
FLORIDA STATE DEPARTMENT OF HEALTH, 155
FLORIDA STATE UNIVERSITY, 582
FLORIDA TRAIL ASSOCIATION, INC., 333
FLORIDA WILDLIFE FEDERATION, 333
FOREST MANAGEMENT TRUST, 334
FRIENDS OF THE CARR REFUGE, 337
GOPHER TORTOISE COUNCIL, 344
GREAT OUTDOORS CONSERVANCY, THE, 345
GREEN PARTNERS, 347
GULF COAST ENVIRONMENTAL DEFENSE, 348
GULF OF MEXICO FISHERY MANAGEMENT COUNCIL, 348
HARBOR BRANCH OCEANOGRAPHIC INSTITUTION, 348
INSTITUTE FOR TROPICAL ECOLOGY AND CONSERVATION (ITEC), 358
INTERNATIONAL GAME FISH ASSOCIATION, 364
INTERNATIONAL OCEANOGRAPHIC FOUNDATION, 365
INTERNATIONAL OSPREY FOUNDATION INC., THE, 365
ISLAND CONSERVATION EFFORT, 374
IZAAK WALTON LEAGUE OF AMERICA, INC., THE
   Florida Division, 376
J.N. (DING) DARLING FOUNDATION, 379
KEEP FLORIDA BEAUTIFUL, INC., 382
LEE COUNTY PARKS AND RECREATION, 171
LEGAL ENVIRONMENTAL ASSISTANCE FOUNDATION INC. (LEAF), 388
MANASOTA-88, 393
MARIE SELBY BOTANICAL GARDENS, THE, 393
MARINE LABORATORY (FLORIDA), 176
MOTE MARINE LABORATORY, 404
NATIONAL AUDUBON SOCIETY
   Audubon of Florida, 410
   Tavernier Science Center, 416
NATIONAL PARKS CONSERVATION ASSOCIATION (NPCA)
   Sun Coast Regional Office, 423
NATURE CONSERVANCY, THE
   Florida Chapter, 435
   Southeast Division Office, 439
NOAH'S NOTES, INC., 569
ONEWILDWORLD, 459
RAINFOREST TRUST, 477
REEF RELIEF, 478
REEFGUARDIAN INTERNATIONAL, 478
SANIBEL CAPTIVA CONSERVATION FOUNDATION, INC., 484
SAVE THE MANATEE CLUB, 486
SEA TURTLE PRESERVATION SOCIETY, 489
SEACAMP ASSOCIATION, INC., 489
SEAPLANE PILOTS ASSOCIATION, 489
SIERRA CLUB
   Florida (South) Field Office, 492
   Florida Chapter, 491
   Florida Regional Field Office, 491
SMITHSONIAN INSTITUTION
   Smithsonian Tropical Research Institute, 501
SMITHSONIAN MARINE STATION AT FORT PIERCE, 502
SOUTH FLORIDA WATER MANAGEMENT DISTRICT, 219
SOUTHEASTERN ASSOCIATION OF FISH AND WILDLIFE AGENCIES, 508
SOUTHWEST FLORIDA WATER MANAGEMENT DISTRICT (SWFWMD), 220
SPORTSMEN'S NATIONAL LAND TRUST, THE, 511
ST. FRANCIS WILDLIFE ASSOCIATION, 511
SUNCOAST SEABIRD SANCTUARY INC., 514
TALL TIMBERS RESEARCH STATION (TTRS), 515
TALLAHASSEE MUSEUM OF HISTORY AND NATURAL SCIENCE, 515
UNITED STATES DEPARTMENT OF AGRICULTURE
   Forest Service
      National Forests in FLorida, 41
UNITED STATES DEPARTMENT OF COMMERCE
   National Oceanic and Atmospheric Administration
      Apalachicola National Estuarine Research Reserve, 49
      Florida Keys National Marine Sanctuary, 50
      Rookery Bay National Estuarine Research Reserve, 53
      Sea Grant Program - Florida, 55
UNITED STATES DEPARTMENT OF DEFENSE
   Air Force Major Air Commands
      AFSOC/EV Headquarters, 61
      Special Operations Command, 62
   Air Force Major U.S. Installations
      Avon Park AFB, FL, 63
      Eglin Air Force Base, 63
      Hurlburt Field, FL, 64
      MacDill AFB, FL, 65
      Patrick AFB, FL, 66
      Tyndall AFB, FL, 66
   Army Corps of Engineers
      Jacksonville Engineer District, 68
UNITED STATES DEPARTMENT OF HOMELAND SECURITY
   CUSTOMS AND BORDER PROTECTION
      South Florida CMC, 76
UNITED STATES DEPARTMENT OF THE INTERIOR
   Fish and Wildlife Service
      Archie Carr National Wildlife Refuge, 91
      Arthur R. Marshall Loxahatchee/Hope Sound National Wildlife Refuge, 91
      Chassahowitzka National Wildlife Refuge, 95
      Crocodile Lake National Wildlife Refuge, 96
      Florida Panther/Ten Thousand Island National Wildlife Refuge, 98
      Hobe Sound National Wildlife Refuge, 99
      J.N. "Ding" Darling National Wildlife Refuge, 101
      Lake Woodruff National Wildlife Refuge, 103
      Lower Suwannee/Cedar Keys National Wildlife Refuge, 104
      Merritt Island National Wildlife Refuge, 105
      National Key Deer Wildlife Refuge, 107
      Pelican Island National Wildlife Refuge, 109
      St. Marks National Wildlife Refuge, 115
      St. Vincent National Wildlife Refuge, 115
   National Park Service
      Biscayne National Park, 120
      Canaveral National Seashore, 121
      Dry Tortugas National Park, 122
      Everglades National Park, 122
      Gulf Islands National Seashore, 123
UNIVERSITY OF FLORIDA
   School of Forest Resources and Conservation, 609
   Solar Energy and Energy Conversion Laboratories, 609
UNIVERSITY OF FLORIDA INSTITUTE OF FOOD AND AGRICULTURAL SCIENCES, 609
UNIVERSITY OF MIAMI, 614
UNIVERSITY OF WEST FLORIDA, 622
VENICE AREA BEAUTIFICATION, INC, 529
WILDLIFE FOUNDATION OF FLORIDA, INC., 544
WILDLIFE SOCIETY
   Florida Chapter, 547
WWW.ACTIONBIOSCIENCE.ORG, 560

GEORGIA
AMERICAN FISHERIES SOCIETY
   Georgia Chapter, 255
CENTER FOR A SUSTAINABLE COAST, 289
COASTAL CONSERVATION ASSOCIATION GEORGIA, 300
COASTAL GEORGIA LAND TRUST INC., 300
COOSA RIVER BASIN INITIATIVE, 309
EARTH SHARE OF GEORGIA, 318
EMORY UNIVERSITY, 581
ENVIRONMENTAL PROTECTION AGENCY
   Region 4 (AL, FL, GA, KY, MS, NC, SC, TN), 19
FOREST LANDOWNERS ASSOCIATION, INC., 334
GEORGIA ASSOCIATION OF CONSERVATION DISTRICT SUPERVISORS, 341

GEORGIA BASS FEDERATION, 341
GEORGIA CONSERVANCY, INC., THE, 341
GEORGIA COOPERATIVE FISH AND WILDLIFE RESEARCH UNIT (USDI), 20
GEORGIA DEPARTMENT OF AGRICULTURE, 155
GEORGIA DEPARTMENT OF EDUCATION, 156
GEORGIA DEPARTMENT OF NATURAL RESOURCES, 156
  Coastal Resources Division, 156
  Environmental Protection Division, 156
    Coastal Division, 156
  Historic Preservation Division, 156
  Parks, Recreation and Historic Sites Division, 156
  Pollution Prevention Assistance Division, 156
  Wildlife Resources Division, 157
GEORGIA ENVIRONMENTAL COUNCIL, INC., 341
GEORGIA ENVIRONMENTAL ORGANIZATION, INC. (GEO), 341
GEORGIA ENVIRONMENTAL POLICY INSTITUTE, 342
GEORGIA FEDERATION OF FOREST OWNERS, 342
GEORGIA FORESTRY ASSOCIATION, INC., 342
GEORGIA FORESTRY COMMISSION, 157
GEORGIA INSTITUTE OF TECHNOLOGY, 583
GEORGIA STATE EXTENSION SERVICE, 157
GEORGIA STATE SOIL AND WATER CONSERVATION COMMISSION, 157
GEORGIA TRAPPERS ASSOCIATION, 342
GEORGIA TRUST FOR HISTORIC PRESERVATION, 342
GEORGIA WILDLIFE FEDERATION, 342
GEORGIANS FOR CLEAN ENERGY, 342
GWINNETT OPEN LAND TRUST, INC., 348
HUMAN ECOLOGY ACTION LEAGUE, INC., THE (HEAL), 352
INTERFAITH COUNCIL FOR THE PROTECTION OF ANIMALS AND NATURE INC. (ICPAN), 359
MOUNTAIN CONSERVATION TRUST OF GEORGIA, INC., 405
NATIONAL AUDUBON SOCIETY
  Atlanta Audubon Society, 409
NATIONAL WILDLIFE FEDERATION
  Southeastern National Resource Center, 429
NATURAL SCIENCE FOR YOUTH FOUNDATION, 432
NATURE CONSERVANCY, THE
  Georgia Chapter, 435
NORTH AMERICAN ASSOCIATION FOR ENVIRONMENTAL EDUCATION, 447
  Conference, Publications and Membership Office, 447
QUALITY DEER MANAGEMENT ASSOCIATION, 476
SIERRA CLUB
  Georgia Chapter, 492
  Georgia Field Office/Louisiana and Alabama Field Office, 492
SOUTHEASTERN COOPERATIVE WILDLIFE DISEASE STUDY, 508
SOUTHFACE ENERGY INSTITUTE, 510
TREES ATLANTA, 519
TROUT UNLIMITED
  Georgia Council, 521
UNITED STATES DEPARTMENT OF AGRICULTURE
  Forest Service
    Chattahoochee and Oconee National Forests, 35
    Region 08 (Southern), 43
  Research Education and Economics
    ARS South Atlantic Office, 48
UNITED STATES DEPARTMENT OF COMMERCE
  National Oceanic and Atmospheric Administration
    Gray's Reef National Marine Sanctuary, 50
    Sapelo Island National Estuarine Research Reserve, 53
    Sea Grant Program - Georgia, 55
UNITED STATES DEPARTMENT OF DEFENSE
  Air Force Major Air Commands
    Robins AFB, GA, 62
  Air Force Major U.S. Installations
    Moody AFB, GA, 65
  Army Corps of Engineers
    South Atlantic Engineer District, 71
  ARMY FORCES COMMAND, 72
UNITED STATES DEPARTMENT OF THE INTERIOR
  Fish and Wildlife Service
    Okefenokee (Banks Lake) National Wildlife Refuge, 108
    Piedmont National Wildlife Refuge, 110
    Region 3, Great Lakes-Big Rivers Regional Office, 111
    Sandy Point National Wildlife Refuge, 114
  National Park Service
    Cumberland Island National Seashore, 122
UNIVERSITY OF GEORGIA
  Daniel B. Warnell School of Forest Resources, 609
  Marine Institute, 609
UPPER CHATTAHOOCHEE RIVERKEEPER, 527
WILDLIFE SOCIETY
  Georgia Chapter, 547

GUAM
DIVISION OF FORESTRY AND SOIL RESOURCES OF GUAM, 152
GUAM COASTAL MANAGEMENT PROGRAM, 158
GUAM COOPERATIVE EXTENSION SERVICE, 158
GUAM DEPARTMENT OF AGRICULTURE, 158
  Division of Aquatic and Wildlife Resources, 158
GUAM DEPARTMENT OF PARKS AND RECREATION, 158
GUAM ENVIRONMENTAL PROTECTION AGENCY, 158
PACIFIC BASIN ASSOCIATION OF SOIL AND WATER CONSERVATION DISTRICTS, 463
UNITED STATES DEPARTMENT OF DEFENSE
  Air Force Major U.S. Installations
    Anderson AFB, Guam, 63
UNITED STATES DEPARTMENT OF THE INTERIOR
  Fish and Wildlife Service
    Guam National Wildlife Refuge, 99

HAWAII
AMERICAN FISHERIES SOCIETY
  Hawaii Chapter, 255
CONSERVATION COUNCIL FOR HAWAII, 306
DEPARTMENT OF LAND AND NATURAL RESOURCES (HAWAII), 151
EARTHJUSTICE
  Honolulu Office, 319
EARTHTRUST, 320
HAWAII COOPERATIVE FISHERY RESEARCH UNIT (USDI), 158
HAWAII DEPARTMENT OF AGRICULTURE, 158
HAWAII DEPARTMENT OF HEALTH
  Office of Environmental Quality Control, 159
HAWAII DEPARTMENT OF LAND AND NATURAL RESOURCES, 159
  Division of Boating and Ocean Recreation, 159
  Division of Conservation and Resources Enforcement, 159
  Division of Forestry and Wildlife, 159
  Division of State Parks, 159
  Division of Water Resource Management, 159
  Land Division, 160
HAWAII INSTITUTE OF MARINE BIOLOGY, 160
HAWAII NATURE CENTER, 349
HAWAIIAN BOTANICAL SOCIETY, 349
LIFE OF THE LAND, 389
NATIONAL AUDUBON SOCIETY
  Hawaii AUDUBON SOCIETY, 413
NATURE CONSERVANCY, THE
  Asia/Pacific Program, 434
  Hawaii Chapter, 435
OUTDOOR CIRCLE, THE, 462
PACIFIC WHALE FOUNDATION, 464
SIERRA CLUB
  Hawaii Chapter, 492
SOCIETY FOR MARINE MAMMALOGY, THE, 503
SOUTH OAHU SOIL AND WATER CONSERVATION DISTRICT, 507
UNITED STATES DEPARTMENT OF COMMERCE
  National Oceanic and Atmospheric Administration
    Hawaiian Islands Humpback Whale National Sanctuary, 51
    Sea Grant Program - Hawaii, 55
UNITED STATES DEPARTMENT OF DEFENSE
  Air Force Major U.S. Installations
    Hickam AFB, HI, 64
  Army Corps of Engineers
    Honolulu Engineer District, 68
    Pacific Ocean Engineer District, 70
  HQ PACAF/CEVQ, 74
UNITED STATES DEPARTMENT OF THE INTERIOR
  Fish and Wildlife Service
    Hakalau Forest National Wildlife Refuge, 99
    Hawaiian and Pacific Islands National Wildlife Refuge Complex, 99
    Johnston Island National Wildlife Refuge, 101
    Kealia Pond National Wildlife Refuge, 101
    Kilauea Point (Hanalei, Huleia) National Wildlife Refuge, 101
    Midway Atoll National Wildlife Refuge, 105
    Oahu National Wildlife Refuge Complex, 108
    Pacific/Remote Islands Complex (Hawaiian Islands, Baker Island, Howland Island, Jarvis Island, Rose Atoll) National Wildlife Refuge, 109
  National Park Service
    Haleakala National Park, 123
    Hawaii Volcanoes National Park, 123
UNIVERSITY OF HAWAII, 610
  Environmental Center, 224
UNIVERSITY OF HAWAII AT MANOA, 610
UNIVERSITY OF HAWAII COOPERATIVE EXTENSION PROGRAM, 224
WESTERN PACIFIC REGIONAL FISHERY MANAGEMENT COUNCIL, 131
WILDLIFE SOCIETY
  Hawaii Chapter, 547

GEOGRAPHIC INDEX – U

IDAHO
ABSEARCH, INC., 563
AMERICAN FISHERIES SOCIETY
  Idaho Chapter, 255
ENVIRONMENTAL RESOURCE CENTER (ERC), 328
IDAHO ASSOCIATION OF SOIL CONSERVATION DISTRICTS, 353
IDAHO BASS FEDERATION, 353
IDAHO CONSERVATION LEAGUE, 354
IDAHO DEPARTMENT OF ENVIRONMENTAL QUALITY, 160
IDAHO DEPARTMENT OF FISH AND GAME, 160
IDAHO DEPARTMENT OF LANDS, 160
IDAHO DEPARTMENT OF PARKS AND RECREATION, 160
IDAHO DEPARTMENT OF WATER RESOURCES, 161
  Water Awareness Week, 161
IDAHO ENVIRONMENTAL COUNCIL, 354
IDAHO FISH AND WILDLIFE FOUNDATION, 161
IDAHO GEOLOGICAL SURVEY, 161
IDAHO STATE DEPARTMENT OF AGRICULTURE, 161
IDAHO STATE SOIL CONSERVATION COMMISSION, 161
IDAHO STATE UNIVERSITY, 583
IDAHO TROUT LIMITED, 354
IDAHO WILDLIFE FEDERATION, 354
JERE MOSSIER PRODUCTIONS/ UNDERWATER IMAGES, 568
NATURE CONSERVANCY, THE
  Idaho Chapter, 435
NORTHWEST RESOURCE INFORMATION CENTER, 454
PEREGRINE FUND, THE, 467
RAPTOR RESEARCH FOUNDATION, INC., 477
SIERRA CLUB
  Northern Rockies Chapter (Idaho/Washington), 495
UNITED STATES DEPARTMENT OF AGRICULTURE
  Forest Service
    Boise National Forest, 35
    Caribou-Targhee National Forest, 35
    Clearwater national Forest, 36
    Curlew National Grassland, 37
    Idaho Panhandle National Forests, 39
    Nez Perce National Forest, 41
    Payette National Forest, 42
    Salmon-Challis National Forest, 44
    Sawtooth National Forest, 44
UNITED STATES DEPARTMENT OF DEFENSE
  Air Force Major U.S. Installations
    Mountain Home AFB, ID 83648, 65
UNITED STATES DEPARTMENT OF THE INTERIOR
  Bureau of Land Management
    Bruneau Field Office, 79
    Burley Field Office, 80
    Challis Field Office, 80
    Coeur d'Alene Field Office, 80
    Cottonwood Field Office, 80
    Four Rivers Field Office, 81
    Idaho Falls Field Office, 82
    Jarbridge Field Office, 82
    Malad Field Office, 83
    National Interagency Fire Center, 84
    Owyhee Field Office, 85
    Pocatello Field Office, 85
    Salmon Field Office, 86
    Shoshone Field Office, 87
    State Office for ID, 87
  Bureau of Reclamation
    Pacific Northwest Region, 89
  Fish and Wildlife Service
    Bear Lake National Wildlife Refuge, 92
    Camas National Wildlife Refuge, 94
    Deer Flat National Wildlife Refuge, 97
    Grays Lake National Wildlife Refuge, 98
    Kootenai National Wildlife Refuge, 102
    Minidoka National Wildlife Refuge, 105
    Oxford Slough WPA National Wildlife Refuge Complex, 109
UNIVERSITY OF IDAHO
  College of Natural Resources
    Department of Fish and Wildlife Resources, 610
    Idaho Cooperative Fish and Wildlife Research Unit, 610
  Women in Natural Resources, 611
UNIVERSITY OF IDAHO EXTENSION, 611
WESTERN WATERSHEDS PROJECT, 538
WILDLIFE SOCIETY
  Idaho Chapter, 547
WOLF EDUCATION AND RESEARCH CENTER, 557

ILLINOIS
AMERICAN FISHERIES SOCIETY
  Illinois Chapter, 255
ASSOCIATION OF GREAT LAKES OUTDOOR WRITERS (AGLOW), 274
BRADLEY UNIVERSITY, 575
BYRON FOREST PRESERVE, 140
CHICAGO HERPETOLOGICAL SOCIETY, 295
CHICAGO PARK DISTRICT, 296
CHICAGO REGION BIODIVERSITY COUNCIL, 296
CORLANDS, 309
DEPAUL UNIVERSITY
  Biological Sciences, 579
  Environmental Science Program, 579
EAGLE NATURE FOUNDATION, LTD., 316
EAST CENTRAL ILLINOIS FUR TAKERS, 321
EASTERN ILLINOIS UNIVERSITY, 580
ENVIRONMENTAL EDUCATION ASSOCIATION OF ILLINOIS, 325
ENVIRONMENTAL LAW AND POLICY CENTER OF THE MIDWEST, 327
ENVIRONMENTAL PROTECTION AGENCY
  Region 5 (IL, IN, MI, NM, OH, WI), 19
EQUESTRIAN LAND CONSERVATION RESOURCE, 328
GREAT LAKES SPORT FISHING COUNCIL, 344
ILLINOIS ASSOCIATION OF CONSERVATION DISTRICTS, 354
ILLINOIS ASSOCIATION OF SOIL AND WATER CONSERVATION
  DISTRICTS, 354
ILLINOIS BASS FEDERATION, 355
ILLINOIS DEPARTMENT OF AGRICULTURE, 162
  Bureau of Land and Water Resources, 162
ILLINOIS DEPARTMENT OF NATURAL RESOURCES, 162
ILLINOIS DEPARTMENT OF TRANSPORTATION, 162
ILLINOIS ENVIRONMENTAL COUNCIL, 355
ILLINOIS ENVIRONMENTAL PROTECTION AGENCY, 162
ILLINOIS NATIVE PLANT SOCIETY, 355
ILLINOIS NATURE PRESERVES COMMISSION (INPC), 163
ILLINOIS PRAIRIE PATH, 355
ILLINOIS RAPTOR CENTER, 355
ILLINOIS STATE UNIVERSITY, 583
ILLINOIS STUDENT ENVIRONMENTAL NETWORK, 355
ILLINOIS WALNUT COUNCIL, 356
INTERNATIONAL SOCIETY OF ARBORICULTURE, 367
IZAAK WALTON LEAGUE OF AMERICA, INC., THE
  Illinois Division, 376
LAKE MICHIGAN FEDERATION, 385
LAST WIZARDS, THE, 568
MAX MCGRAW WILDLIFE FOUNDATION, 396
NATIONAL ANTI-VIVISECTION SOCIETY, 406
NATIONAL AUDUBON SOCIETY
  Audubon Council of Illinois, 410
  Illinois Audubon Society, 413
NATIONAL BIRD-FEEDING SOCIETY, 416
NATIONAL TRUST FOR HISTORIC PRESERVATION
  Midwest Office, 425
NATURAL LAND INSTITUTE, 431
NATURE CONSERVANCY, THE
  Illinois Chapter, 435
OPENLANDS PROJECT, 460
PRAIRIE CLUB, THE, 472
PRAIRIE RIVERS NETWORK, 472
ROBERT ROADS ILLINOIS DEPARTMENT OF NATURAL RESOURCES, 481
SIERRA CLUB
  Illinois Chapter, 492
SOUTHERN ILLINOIS UNIVERSITY CARBONDALE, 506
SUSTAIN, 514
TROUT UNLIMITED
  Illinois Council, 521
UNITED STATES DEPARTMENT OF AGRICULTURE
  Forest Service
    Shawnee National Forest, 44
  Research Education and Economics
    ARS Midwest Office, 48
UNITED STATES DEPARTMENT OF COMMERCE
  National Oceanic and Atmospheric Administration
    Sea Grant Program - Illinois-Indiana, 55
UNITED STATES DEPARTMENT OF DEFENSE
  Air Force Major Air Commands
    Air Mobility Command (AMC), 61
  Air Force Major U.S. Installations
    Scott AFB, IL, 66
  Army Corps of Engineers
    Champaign Engineer District, 67
    Chicago Engineer District, 68
    Rock Island Engineer District, 71
  Army Engineer Research and Development Center, 72

UNITED STATES DEPARTMENT OF HOMELAND SECURITY
  Customs and Border Protection
    Mid-America CMC, 76
UNITED STATES DEPARTMENT OF THE INTERIOR
  Fish and Wildlife Service
    Crab Orchard National Wildlife Refuge, 96
    Cypress Creek National Wildlife Refuge, 96
    Illinois River National Wildlife and Fish Refuge (Chautauqua, Emiquon, Meredosia), 100
    Mark Twain National Wildlife Refuge, 104
    Mark Twain/Brussels District National Wildlife Refuge, 104
UNIVERSITY OF ILLINOIS AT URBANA-CHAMPAIGN, 611
UNIVERSITY OF ILLINOIS EXTENSION, 611
UPPER MISSISSIPPI RIVER CONSERVATION COMMITTEE, 527
WESTERN ILLINOIS UNIVERSITY, 626
WILDLIFE SOCIETY
  Illinois Chapter, 547
WINCHESTER NILO FARMS, 555

INDIANA
ACRES LAND TRUST, 241
AMERICAN CAMPING ASSOCIATION, INC., 250
AMERICAN FISHERIES SOCIETY
  Indiana Chapter, 255
BALL STATE UNIVERSITY, 574
CONSERVATION TECHNOLOGY INFORMATION CENTER, 308
ENVIRONMENTAL EDUCATION ASSOCIATION OF INDIANA, 325
HOOSIER ENVIRONMENTAL COUNCIL, 352
INDIANA ASSOCIATION OF SOIL AND WATER CONSERVATION DISTRICTS, INC., 356
INDIANA AUDUBON SOCIETY, INC., 356
INDIANA BASS FEDERATION, 356
INDIANA DEPARTMENT OF ENVIRONMENTAL MANAGEMENT, 163
INDIANA DEPARTMENT OF NATURAL RESOURCES, 163
  DIVISION OF SOIL CONSERVATION, 164
INDIANA FORESTRY AND WOODLAND OWNERS ASSOCIATION, 356
INDIANA GEOLOGICAL SURVEY, 164
INDIANA NATIVE PLANT AND WILDFLOWER SOCIETY, 356
INDIANA STATE DEPARTMENT OF HEALTH, 164
INDIANA STATE TRAPPERS ASSOCIATION, INC., 357
INDIANA STATE UNIVERSITY, 583
INDIANA UNIVERSITY, 584
INDIANA WILDLIFE FEDERATION, 357
IZAAK WALTON LEAGUE OF AMERICA, INC., THE
  Indiana Division, 376
MANCHESTER COLLEGE, 587
NATIONAL FFA ORGANIZATION, 419
NATURE CONSERVANCY, THE
  Indiana Chapter, 435
NORTH AMERICAN WILDLIFE PARK FOUNDATION, INC., 449
PURDUE UNIVERSITY, 593
PURDUE UNIVERSITY EXTENSION SERVICES, 213
SAND CREEK WATERSHED PROJECT, THE, 215
SAVE THE DUNES CONSERVATION FUND, 485
SAVE THE DUNES COUNCIL, 485
SIERRA CLUB
  Hoosier Chapter, 492
UNITED STATES DEPARTMENT OF AGRICULTURE
  Forest Service
    Hoosier National Forest, 39
UNITED STATES DEPARTMENT OF THE INTERIOR
  Fish and Wildlife Service
    Muscatatuck National Wildlife Refuge, 107
    Patoka River National Wetlands Project National Wildlife Refuge, 109
WABASH RIVER HERITAGE CORRIDOR COMMISSION, 232
WILDERNESS EDUCATION ASSOCIATION, 540
WILDLIFE SOCIETY
  Indiana Chapter, 548

IOWA
AMERICAN FISHERIES SOCIETY
  Iowa Chapter, 255
CONSERVATION EDUCATION CENTER, THE, 306
INDIAN CREEK NATURE CENTER, 356
IOWA ACADEMY OF SCIENCE, 372
IOWA ASSOCIATION OF COUNTY CONSERVATION BOARDS, 164
IOWA ASSOCIATION OF NATURALISTS, 372
IOWA BASS FEDERATION, 372
IOWA DEPARTMENT OF AGRICULTURE AND LAND STEWARDSHIP
  Bureau of Field Services, 165
  Bureau of Financial Incentive Program, 165
  Bureau of Water Resources, 165
  Division of Soil Conservation, 165

IOWA DEPARTMENT OF NATURAL RESOURCES, 165
  Cooperative North American Shotgunning Education Program, 165
  Energy and Waste Management Bureau, 165
  Environmental Protection Division, 166
  Fish and Wildlife Division, 166
  Forests and Prairies Division, 166
  Management Services Division, 166
  Parks, 166
  Waste Management Division, 166
IOWA ENVIRONMENTAL COUNCIL, 372
IOWA NATIVE PLANT SOCIETY, 373
IOWA NATURAL HERITAGE FOUNDATION, 373
IOWA PRAIRIE NETWORK, 373
IOWA STATE EXTENSION SERVICES
  Extension Wildlife Programs, 166
IOWA STATE UNIVERSITY
  College of Agriculture, 584
  College of Design, 584
IOWA TRAILS COUNCIL, 373
IOWA TRAPPERS ASSOCIATION, INC., 373
IOWA WILDLIFE FEDERATION, 374
IOWA WILDLIFE REHABILITATORS ASSOCIATION, 374
IOWA WOMEN IN NATURAL RESOURCES, 374
IOWA WOODLAND OWNERS ASSOCIATION, 374
IZAAK WALTON LEAGUE OF AMERICA ENDOWMENT, 375
IZAAK WALTON LEAGUE OF AMERICA, INC., THE
  Iowa Division, 376
LEAGUE OF WOMEN VOTERS OF IOWA, 387
MACBRIDE RAPTOR PROJECT, 391
NATIONAL ASSOCIATION OF UNIVERSITY FISHERIES AND WILDLIFE PROGRAMS, 409
NATIONAL AUDUBON SOCIETY
  Iowa Audubon, 413
NATURE CONSERVANCY, THE
  Iowa Chapter, 435
RETURNED PEACE CORPS VOLUNTEERS FOR ENVIRONMENT AND DEVELOPMENT (RPCVS-ED), 480
SIERRA CLUB
  Iowa Chapter, 492
SOIL AND WATER CONSERVATION SOCIETY, 504
UNITED STATES DEPARTMENT OF THE INTERIOR
  Fish and Wildlife Service
    De Soto (Boyer Chute National Wildlife Refuge), 96
    Neal Smith National Wildlife Refuge, 107
    Port Louisa National Wildlife Refuge, 110
    Union Slough (Iowa WMD) National Wildlife Refuge, 117
  United States Geological Survey
    Iowa Cooperative Fish and Wildlife Research Unit, 127
UNIVERSITY OF IOWA, 611
WARREN COUNTY CONSERVATION BOARD, 532
WILDLIFE SOCIETY
  Iowa Chapter, 548

KANSAS
AMERICAN ASSOCIATION OF ZOO KEEPERS, INC., 249
AMERICAN FISHERIES SOCIETY
  Kansas Chapter, 256
COOPER ORNITHOLOGICAL SOCIETY, 308
EMPORIA STATE UNIVERSITY, 581
ENVIRONMENTAL PROTECTION AGENCY
  Region 7 (KS, MO, NE), 19
GRANT TECH CONSULTING AND CONSERVATION SERVICES, 567
GRASSLAND HERITAGE FOUNDATION, 344
KANSAS ACADEMY OF SCIENCE, 380
KANSAS ASSOCIATION FOR CONSERVATION AND ENVIRONMENTAL EDUCATION, KACEE, 380
KANSAS ASSOCIATION OF CONSERVATION DISTRICTS, 380
KANSAS BIOLOGICAL SURVEY, 166
KANSAS COOPERATIVE FISH AND WILDLIFE RESEARCH UNIT, 167
KANSAS DEPARTMENT OF AGRICULTURE, 167
KANSAS DEPARTMENT OF HEALTH AND ENVIRONMENT, 167
KANSAS DEPARTMENT OF WILDLIFE AND PARKS
  Office of the Secretary, 167
  Operations Office, 167
  Region 1, 167
  Region 2, 168
  Region 3, 168
  Region 4, 168
  Region 5, 168
KANSAS FOREST SERVICE, 168
KANSAS GEOLOGICAL SURVEY, 168
KANSAS HERPETOLOGICAL SOCIETY, 381
KANSAS NATURAL RESOURCE COUNCIL, 381

KANSAS ORNITHOLOGICAL SOCIETY, 381
KANSAS SCHOOL NATURALIST, 585
KANSAS STATE CONSERVATION COMMISSION, 168
KANSAS STATE EXTENSION SERVICES, 169
KANSAS STATE UNIVERSITY
  College of Agriculture, 585
  Department of Landscape Architecture / Regional and Community Planning, 585
  Division of Biology, 586
KANSAS WATER OFFICE, 169
KANSAS WILDFLOWER SOCIETY, 381
KANSAS WILDLIFE FEDERATION, 382
KANSAS WILDSCAPE FOUNDATION, 382
NATIONAL AUDUBON SOCIETY
  Audubon of Kansas, 410
NATURE CONSERVANCY, THE
  Kansas Chapter, 436
NORTH AMERICAN BENTHOLOGICAL SOCIETY, 447
NORTH DAKOTA NATURAL SCIENCE SOCIETY, 452
SIERRA CLUB
  Kansas Chapter, 493
UNITED STATES DEPARTMENT OF AGRICULTURE
  Forest Service
    Cimarron National Grassland, 36
UNITED STATES DEPARTMENT OF DEFENSE
  Air Force Major U.S. Installations
    McConnell AFB, KS, 65
UNITED STATES DEPARTMENT OF THE INTERIOR
  Fish and Wildlife Service
    Flint Hills (Marais des Cygnes) National Wildlife Refuge, 98
    Kirwin National Wildlife Refuge, 101
    Quivira National Wildlife Refuge, 110
  Kansas State Cooperative Fish and Wildlife Research Unit, 119
UNIVERSITY OF KANSAS, 611
UNIVERSITY OF KANSAS FIELD STATION AND ECOLOGICAL RESERVES, 612
WILDLIFE SOCIETY
  Kansas Chapter, 548

KENTUCKY
AMERICAN CAVE CONSERVATION ASSOCIATION, 250
AMERICAN FISHERIES SOCIETY
  Kentucky Chapter, 256
EASTERN KENTUCKY UNIVERSITY, 580
GEORGETOWN COLLEGE, 582
KENTUCKY ACADEMY OF SCIENCE, 382
KENTUCKY ASSOCIATION FOR ENVIRONMENTAL EDUCATION (KAEE), 383
KENTUCKY ASSOCIATION OF CONSERVATION DISTRICTS, 383
KENTUCKY BASS FEDERATION, 383
KENTUCKY DEPARTMENT OF AGRICULTURE, 169
KENTUCKY DEPARTMENT OF FISH AND WILDLIFE RESOURCES, 169
KENTUCKY DEPARTMENT OF PARKS, 169
KENTUCKY GEOLOGICAL SURVEY, 170
KENTUCKY NATURAL LANDS TRUST, 383
KENTUCKY NATURAL RESOURCES AND ENVIRONMENTAL PROTECTION CABINET, 170
  Department for Environmental Protection, 170
  Department for Natural Resources, 170
  Environmental Quality Commission, 170
  Kentucky State Nature Preserves Commission, 171
KENTUCKY RESOURCES COUNCIL, 383
KENTUCKY SOIL AND WATER CONSERVATION COMMISSION, 171
KENTUCKY STATE COOPERATIVE EXTENSION SERVICES, 171
KENTUCKY STATE NATURE PRESERVES COMMISSION, 171
KENTUCKY WOODLAND OWNERS ASSOCIATION, 383
KIDS FOR A BETTER ENVIRONMENT, 384
LAND BETWEEN THE LAKES ASSOCIATION, 386
LEAGUE OF KENTUCKY SPORTSMEN, INC., 387
MOREHEAD STATE UNIVERSITY, 589
MURRAY STATE UNIVERSITY, 589
NATIONAL AUDUBON SOCIETY
  Daviess County Audubon Society, 413
  Kentucky Audubon Council, 413
NATURE CONSERVANCY, THE
  Kentucky Chapter, 436
SIERRA CLUB
  Cumberland Chapter, 491
SOCIETY OF AMERICAN FORESTERS
  UNIVERSITY OF KENTUCKY, 504
SPORTSMAN NETWORK, INC., THE, 510
SPORTSMANS NETWORK, INC., THE, 570

UNITED STATES DEPARTMENT OF AGRICULTURE
  Forest Service
    Daniel Boone National Forest, 37
UNITED STATES DEPARTMENT OF DEFENSE
  Army Corps of Engineers
    Louisville Engineer District, 69
UNITED STATES DEPARTMENT OF THE INTERIOR
  Fish and Wildlife Service
    Clarks River National Wildlife Refuge, 95
  National Park Service
    Mammoth Cave National Park, 124
UNIVERSITY OF KENTUCKY, 612
UNIVERSITY OF LOUISVILLE, 612
WILDLIFE SOCIETY
  Kentucky Chapter, 548

LOUISIANA
AMERICAN FISHERIES SOCIETY
  Louisiana Chapter, 256
CALCASIEU PARISH ANIMAL CONTROL AND PROTECTION DEPARTMENT, 282
CONSERVATION FORCE, 307
LOUISIANA ASSOCIATION OF CONSERVATION DISTRICTS, 300
LOUISIANA BASS FEDERATION, 390
LOUISIANA COOPERATIVE FISH AND WILDLIFE RESEARCH UNIT (USDI), 172
LOUISIANA DEPARTMENT OF AGRICULTURE AND FORESTRY, 172
  Office of Forestry, 172
  Office of Soil and Water Conservation. State Soil and Water Conservation Committee, 172
LOUISIANA DEPARTMENT OF NATURAL RESOURCES, 172
  Office of Conservation, 172
  Office of Mineral Resources, 172
LOUISIANA DEPARTMENT OF WILDLIFE AND FISHERIES, 173
LOUISIANA FORESTRY ASSOCIATION, 390
LOUISIANA GEOLOGICAL SURVEY, 173
LOUISIANA OFFICE OF STATE PARKS, DEPARTMENT OF CULTURE, RECREATION, AND TOURISM, 173
LOUISIANA STATE UNIVERSITY SCHOOL OF FORESTRY, WILDLIFE AND FISHERIES, 586
LOUISIANA TECH UNIVERSITY, 587
LOUISIANA WILDLIFE FEDERATION, INC., 391
LOUISIANA WILDLIFE REHABILITATORS ASSOCIATION, 391
LSU AGCENTER - LOUISIANA COOPERATIVE EXTENSION SERVICE, 173
MCNEESE STATE UNIVERSITY, 587
NATIONAL AUDUBON SOCIETY
  LOUISIANA AUDUBON COUNCIL, 414
NATURE CONSERVANCY, THE
  Louisiana Chapter, 436
NORTHWESTERN STATE UNIVERSITY OF LOUISIANA, 591
SIERRA CLUB
  Delta Chapter, 491
TULANE ENVIRONMENTAL LAW CLINIC, 600
TULANE INSTITUTE FOR ENVIRONMENTAL LAW AND POLICY, 600
TULANE UNIVERSITY
  Department of Ecology and Evolutionary Biology, 600
  Tulane Law School, 600
UNITED STATES DEPARTMENT OF AGRICULTURE
  FOREST SERVICE
    Kisatchie National Forest, 39
UNITED STATES DEPARTMENT OF COMMERCE
  National Oceanic and Atmospheric Administration
    Sea Grant Program - Louisiana, 56
UNITED STATES DEPARTMENT OF DEFENSE
  Air Force Major U.S. Installations
    Barksdale AFB, LA, 63
  Army Corps of Engineers
    New Orleans Engineer District, 70
UNITED STATES DEPARTMENT OF HOMELAND SECURITY
  CUSTOMS AND BORDER PROTECTION
    Gulf CMC, 76
UNITED STATES DEPARTMENT OF THE INTERIOR
  Fish and Wildlife Service
    Bayou Cocodrie National Wildlife Refuge, 92
    Cameron Prairie National Wildlife Refuge, 94
    Catahoula National Wildlife Refuge, 95
    Lacassine National Wildlife Refuge, 102
    Louisiana WMD/Handy Brake National Wildlife Refuge, 103
    North Louisiana Complex National Wildlife Refuge, 108
    Ruby Lake National Wildlife Refuge, 113
    Sonny Bono Salton Sea National Wildlife Refuge, 115
    Tensas River National Wildlife Refuge, 116

URBAN WASTE MANAGEMENT & RESEARCH CENTER, 624
WHOOPING CRANE CONSERVATION ASSOCIATION INC., 539
WILDLIFE SOCIETY
  Louisiana Chapter, 548

MAINE

A.E. HOWELL WILDLIFE CONSERVATION CENTER INC., 241
AMERICAN FISHERIES SOCIETY
  Atlantic International Chapter, 253
CHINA REGION LAKES ALLIANCE, 296
COLLEGE OF THE ATLANTIC, 577
CONSERVATION LAW FOUNDATION, INC. (CLF), 307
FOREST SOCIETY OF MAINE, 335
FRIENDS OF ACADIA, 336
FRIENDS OF SUNKHAZE MEADOWS NATIONAL WILDLIFE REFUGE, 337
HUMBOLT FIELD RESEARCH INSTITUTE, 353
INTERNATIONAL ASSOCIATION OF FISH AND WILDLIFE AGENCIES, 360
ISLAND INSTITUTE, THE, 374
ISLESBORO ISLANDS TRUST, 375
LAUDHOLM TRUST, 386
MAINE ASSOCIATION OF CONSERVATION COMMISSIONS (MACC), 392
MAINE ASSOCIATION OF CONSERVATION DISTRICTS, 392
MAINE ATLANTIC SALMON COMMISSION, 173
MAINE BASS FEDERATION, 392
MAINE COAST HERITAGE TRUST, 392
MAINE COOPERATIVE FISH AND WILDLIFE RESEARCH UNIT (USDI), 174
MAINE DEPARTMENT OF AGRICULTURE, FOOD, AND RURAL RESOURCES, 174
MAINE DEPARTMENT OF CONSERVATION, 174
  Bureau of Geology and Natural Areas, 174
  Bureau of Parks and Lands, 174
  Forest Service, 174
  Land Use Regulation Commission, 175
MAINE DEPARTMENT OF ENVIRONMENTAL PROTECTION, 175
MAINE DEPARTMENT OF INLAND FISHERIES AND WILDLIFE, 175
MAINE DEPARTMENT OF MARINE RESOURCES, 175
MAINE ENVIRONMENTAL EDUCATION ASSOCIATION, 392
NATIONAL AUDUBON SOCIETY
  Maine Audubon, 414
NATURAL RESOURCES COUNCIL OF MAINE, 432
NATURE CONSERVANCY, THE
  Maine Chapter, 436
SHEEPSCOT VALLEY CONSERVATION ASSOCIATION, THE, 489
SIERRA CLUB
  Maine Chapter, 493
SMALL WOODLAND OWNERS ASSOCIATION OF MAINE, 501
SPORTSMANS ALLIANCE OF MAINE, 511
ST. CROIX INTERNATIONAL WATERWAY COMMISSION, 511
UNITED STATES DEPARTMENT OF COMMERCE
  National Oceanic and Atmospheric Administration
    Sea Grant Program - Maine, 56
    Wells National Estuarine Research Reserve, 60
UNITED STATES DEPARTMENT OF THE INTERIOR
  Fish and Wildlife Service
    Moosehorn National Wildlife Refuge, 106
    Petit Manan National Wildlife Refuge, 110
    Rachel Carson National Wildlife Refuge, 111
    Sunkhaze Meadows National Wildlife Refuge/Carlton Pond Waterfowl Production Area, 116
  National Park Service
    Acadia National Park, 120
UNITY COLLEGE, 601
UNIVERSITY OF MAINE, 612
UNIVERSITY OF MAINE AT FORT KENT, 612
UNIVERSITY OF MAINE AT ORONO, 612
UNIVERSITY OF MAINE COOPERATIVE EXTENSION, 612
WILDLIFE SOCIETY
  Maine Chapter, 548

MARYLAND

ADKINS ARBORETUM, 242
AFRICAN AMERICAN ENVIRONMENTALIST ASSOCIATION, 243
ALLIANCE FOR THE CHESAPEAKE BAY, 247
AMERICAN FISHERIES SOCIETY, 252
  Fisheries Administrators Section, 254
  Genetics Section, 255
AMERICAN HIKING SOCIETY, 261
AMERICAN WHITEWATER, 267
AMERICAN ZOO AND AQUARIUM ASSOCIATION (AZA), 268
ANACOSTIA WATERSHED SOCIETY, 268
ANIMALS AGENDA, 563

ASSOCIATION OF PARTNERS FOR PUBLIC LANDS, 274
AUDUBON NATURALIST SOCIETY OF THE CENTRAL ATLANTIC STATES, 276
BROTHERHOOD OF THE JUNGLE COCK, INC., THE, 281
BUSINESS PUBLISHERS, INC., 564
C AND O CANAL NATIONAL HISTORICAL PARK, 16
CENTER FOR A NEW AMERICAN DREAM, THE, 289
CENTER FOR CHESAPEAKE COMMUNITIES, 290
CENTER FOR ENVIRONMENT, COMMERCE & ENERGY, 290
CENTER FOR WATERSHED PROTECTION, 293
CHESAPEAKE BAY FOUNDATION, INC., 295
  Maryland Office, 295
CHESAPEAKE FARMS, 564
CHESAPEAKE WILDLIFE HERITAGE (CWH), 295
CONSERVATION FEDERATION OF MARYLAND/ F.A.R.M., 306
CONSERVATION TREATY SUPPORT FUND, 308
EARTH SHARE, 317
EASTERN SHORE LAND CONSERVANCY (ESLC), 321
ENDANGERED SPECIES AND WETLANDS REPORT, 566
ENTOMOLOGICAL SOCIETY OF AMERICA, 323
ENVIRONMENTAL CONCERN INC., 324
ENVIRONMENTAL JUSTICE COALITION, 326
FISH AND WILDLIFE REFERENCE SERVICE, 19
FROSTBURG STATE UNIVERSITY (UNIVERSITY OF MARYLAND), 582
FUND FOR ANIMALS, 338
HENRY A. WALLACE INSTITUTE FOR ALTERNATIVE AGRICULTURE (HAWIAA), 350
HOLLY SOCIETY OF AMERICA, INC., 352
INSTITUTE FOR CONSERVATION LEADERSHIP, 358
INTERNATIONAL SOCIETY OF TROPICAL FORESTERS, INC., 367
INTERSTATE COMMISSION ON THE POTOMAC RIVER BASIN, 23
IZAAK WALTON LEAGUE OF AMERICA, INC., THE, 375
  Maryland Division, 377
JANE GOODALL INSTITUTE, THE, 380
JOHNS HOPKINS UNIVERSITY
  CENTER FOR A LIVABLE FUTURE, 584
  Department of Geography and Environmental Engineering, 584
  School of Public Health, 585
LAKENET, 385
LEXIS/NEXIS ACADEMIC AND LIBRARY SOLUTIONS, 568
MARINE MAMMAL COMMISSION, 23
MARINE TECHNOLOGY SOCIETY, 395
MARYLAND ASSOCIATION OF CONSERVATION DISTRICTS, 395
MARYLAND BASS FEDERATION, 395
MARYLAND DEPARTMENT OF AGRICULTURE, 176
  State Soil Conservation Committee, 177
MARYLAND DEPARTMENT OF NATURAL RESOURCES, 177
MARYLAND DEPARTMENT OF THE ENVIRONMENT, 177
MARYLAND FORESTS ASSOCIATION, 395
MARYLAND NATIVE PLANT SOCIETY, 395
MARYLAND ORNITHOLOGICAL SOCIETY, INC., 395
MARYLAND-NATIONAL CAPITAL PARK AND PLANNING COMMISSION, 177
MATTS (MID-ATLANTIC TURTLE AND TORTOISE SOCIETY, INC.), 396
NATIONAL 4-H COUNCIL, 406
NATIONAL AGRICULTURAL LIBRARY, 24
NATIONAL ASSOCIATION OF ENVIRONMENTAL PROFESSIONALS, THE, 408
NATIONAL AUDUBON SOCIETY
  Audubon Maryland-DC, 410
NATIONAL BOATING FEDERATION, 417
NATIONAL MARINE FISHERIES SERVICE, 421
NATIONAL MILITARY FISH AND WILDLIFE ASSOCIATION, 421
NATURAL HISTORY SOCIETY OF MARYLAND, INC., THE, 431
NATURE CONSERVANCY, THE
  Maryland/District of Columbia Chapter, 436
NISC (NATIONAL INFORMATION SERVICES CORPORATION), 569
NORTH AMERICAN NATIVE FISHES ASSOCIATION, 449
PARTNERSHIP FOR SUSTAINABLE FORESTRY, 465
RACHEL CARSON COUNCIL, INC., 476
RENEWABLE NATURAL RESOURCES FOUNDATION, 478
SCIENTISTS CENTER FOR ANIMAL WELFARE, 488
SIERRA CLUB
  Maryland Chapter, 493
SOCIETY OF AMERICAN FORESTERS, 503
TREES FOR THE FUTURE, INC., 519
TROUT UNLIMITED
  Maryland Council, Mid-Atlantic, 521
UNITED STATES DEPARTMENT OF AGRICULTURE
  Animal and Plant Health Inspection Service
    Animal Care, 31
    Veterinary Services, 32
  Research Education and Economics
    ARS Beltsville Area, 48

GEOGRAPHIC INDEX – U

UNITED STATES DEPARTMENT OF COMMERCE
  National Oceanic and Atmospheric Administration
    Chesapeake Bay National Estuarine Research Reserve
      Maryland Office, 49
    National Environmental Satellite, Data, and Information Service, 52
    National Marine Fisheries Service, 52
    National Weather Service, 52
    Office of Global Program, 53
    Office of Oceanic and Atmospheric Research, 53
    Sea Grant Program - Maryland, 56
UNITED STATES DEPARTMENT OF DEFENSE
  Air Force Major Air Commands
    Andrews AFB, MD, 61
  Air Force Major U.S. Installations
    Andrews AFB, MD, 63
  Army Corps of Engineers
    Baltimore Engineer District, 67
UNITED STATES DEPARTMENT OF HEALTH AND HUMAN SERVICES
  Food and Drug Administration, 75
UNITED STATES DEPARTMENT OF THE INTERIOR
  Fish and Wildlife Service
    Blackwater National Wildlife Refuge, 93
    Eastern Neck National Wildlife Refuge, 97
    Patuxent Research Refuge, 109
  National Park Service
    Assateague Island National Seashore, 120
UNIVERSITY OF MARYLAND - AT COLLEGE PARK, 613
UNIVERSITY OF MARYLAND AT EASTERN SHORE, 613
UNIVERSITY OF MARYLAND BALTIMORE COUNTY, 613
UNIVERSITY OF MARYLAND CENTER FOR ENVIRONMENTAL SCIENCE, 613
UNIVERSITY OF MARYLAND COOPERATIVE EXTENSION, 224
UNIVERSITY OF MARYLAND EASTERN SHORE, 614
UNIVERSITY OF MARYLAND, COLLEGE PARK
  Graduate School, 614
URBAN WILDLIFE RESOURCES, 527
WALKABOUT PRODUCTIONS, INC., 571
WILDFOWL TRUST OF NORTH AMERICA, INC., THE, 541
WILDLIFE CONSERVATION ENFORCEMENT FUND, INC., 543
WILDLIFE HABITAT COUNCIL, 544
WILDLIFE SOCIETY, 545
  Maryland-Delaware Chapter, 549
WINDSTAR WILDLIFE INSTITUTE, 555

MASSACHUSETTS
AMERICAN FISHERIES SOCIETY
  Marine Fisheries Section, 256
  Northeastern Division, 258
APPALACHIAN MOUNTAIN CLUB, 269
ATLANTIC CENTER FOR THE ENVIRONMENT
  Quebec-Labrador Foundation, 275
BOSTON UNIVERSITY, 574
CLARK UNIVERSITY, 576
COASTAL AMERICA FOUNDATION, 300
CONNECTICUT RIVER WATERSHED COUNCIL INC., 305
CONSERVATION LAW FOUNDATION, INC. (CLF)
  New England Region, 308
CONWAY SCHOOL OF LANDSCAPE DESIGN, 578
CUTTER INFORMATION CORPORATION, 565
EARTHWATCH INSTITUTE, 321
ENVIRONMENTAL CAREERS ORGANIZATION, INC., THE, 324
ENVIRONMENTAL DEFENSE
  Alliance for Environmental Innovation, 324
ENVIRONMENTAL LEAGUE OF MASSACHUSETTS, 327
ENVIRONMENTAL PROTECTION AGENCY
  Region 1 (CT, ME, MA, NH, RI, VT), 10
ENVIRONMENTAL PROTECTION MASSACHUSETTS, 152
GECKO PRODUCTIONS, INC., 340
GREEN MOUNTAIN POST FILMS, 567
INTERNATIONAL FUND FOR ANIMAL WELFARE, 363
INTERNATIONAL WILDLIFE COALITION (IWC) AND THE WHALE ADOPTION PROJECT, 371
LANDOWNER PLANNING CENTER, 386
MANOMET CENTER FOR CONSERVATION SCIENCES, 393
MASSACHUSETTS ASSOCIATION OF CONSERVATION COMMISSIONS (MACC), 396
MASSACHUSETTS ASSOCIATION OF CONSERVATION DISTRICTS, 396
MASSACHUSETTS BASS FEDERATION, 396
MASSACHUSETTS COOPERATIVE FISH AND WILDLIFE RESEARCH UNIT (USDI), 178
MASSACHUSETTS DIVISION OF FISHERIES AND WILDLIFE
  MassWildlife, 178
MASSACHUSETTS EXECUTIVE OFFICE OF ENVIRONMENTAL AFFAIRS, 178
  Bureau of Pesticides, 178
  Department of Agricultural Resources, 178
  Department of Conservation and Recreation, 178
  Division of Conservation Services, 179
  Geographic Information System, 179
  Massachusetts Coastal Zone Management, 179
  Massachusetts Environmental Policy Act., 179
  Massachusetts Environmental Trust, 179
  Office of Technical Assistance for Toxic Use Reduction, 179
  Wetlands and Waterways Program, 179
MASSACHUSETTS FORESTRY ASSOCIATION, 396
MASSACHUSETTS HIGHWAY DEPARTMENT, 179
MASSACHUSETTS TRAPPERS ASSOCIATION, INC., 396
METROPOLITAN DISTRICT COMMISSION, 180
MOUNT GRACE LAND CONSERVATION TRUST, 405
NATIONAL AUDUBON SOCIETY
  Massachusetts Audubon Society, 414
NATIONAL TRUST FOR HISTORIC PRESERVATION
  Northeast Office, 425
NATURE CONSERVANCY, THE
  Massachusetts Chapter, 436
NEW ENGLAND ASSOCIATION OF ENVIRONMENTAL BIOLOGISTS (NEAEB), 443
NEW ENGLAND COALITION FOR SUSTAINABLE POPULATION (NECSP), 443
NEW ENGLAND INTERSTATE WATER POLLUTION CONTROL COMMISSION, 443
NEW ENGLAND NATURAL RESOURCES CENTER, 443
NEW ENGLAND WILD FLOWER SOCIETY, INC., 443
NORTH AMERICAN FALCONERS ASSOCIATION, 448
NORTHEAST SUSTAINABLE ENERGY ASSOCIATION, 452
NORTHEASTERN UNIVERSITY, 590
ORION SOCIETY, THE, 462
SAVE THE HARBOR/SAVE THE BAY, 486
SIERRA CLUB
  Massachusetts Chapter, 493
SUDBURY VALLEY TRUSTEES, 514
TRUSTEES OF RESERVATIONS, THE, 524
TUFTS UNIVERSITY CIVIL ENGINEERING, 600
UNION OF CONCERNED SCIENTISTS, 525
UNITED STATES DEPARTMENT OF COMMERCE
  National Oceanic and Atmospheric Administration
    Sea Grant Program - Massachusetts, 56, 56
    Stellwagen Bank National Marine Sanctuary, 60
    Waquoit Bay National Estuarine Research Reserve, 60
UNITED STATES DEPARTMENT OF DEFENSE
  Air Force Major U.S. Installations
    Hanscom AFB, MA, 64
  Army Corps of Engineers
    New England District, 69
UNITED STATES DEPARTMENT OF HOMELAND SECURITY
  CUSTOMS AND BORDER PROTECTION
    North Atlantic CMC, 76
UNITED STATES DEPARTMENT OF THE INTERIOR
  Fish and Wildlife Service
    Eastern Massachusetts National Wildlife Refuge Complex, 97
    Monomoy National Wildlife Refuge, 106
    Parker River/Thatcher Island National Wildlife Refuge, 109
    region 4, Southeast Regional office, 112
    Shiawassee National Wildlife Refuge, 114
  National Park Service
    Cape Cod National Seashore, 121
UNIVERSITY OF MASSACHUSETTS
  Department of Natural Resources Conservation, 614
  Urban Harbors Institute, 614
UNIVERSITY OF MASSACHUSETTS EXTENSION, 224
VINEYARD CONSERVATION SOCIETY, 530
WESTERN HEMISPHERE SHOREBIRD RESERVE NETWORK (WHSRN), 537
WILLIAMS COLLEGE, 627
WORLD SOCIETY FOR THE PROTECTION OF ANIMALS (WSPA), 559

MICHIGAN
AMERICAN FISHERIES SOCIETY
  Equal Opportunities Section, 254
  Introduced Fish Section, 255
  Michigan Chapter, 256
BERLET FILMS AND VIDEOS, 564
BRAUER PRODUCTIONS, 564
CENTER FOR ENVIRONMENTAL STUDY, 291
CENTRAL MICHIGAN UNIVERSITY, 576
CITY OF BELDING, 145
CLINTON RIVER WATERSHED COUNCIL (CRWC), 299

DELTA COLLEGE, 579
EASTERN MICHIGAN UNIVERSITY, 581
FERRIS STATE UNIVERSITY, 581
FLINTSTEEL RESTORATION ASSOCIATION, INC., 330
GEORGE WRIGHT SOCIETY, THE, 341
GREAT LAKES FISHERY COMMISSION, 20
IZAAK WALTON LEAGUE OF AMERICA, INC., THE
   Michigan Division, 377
LAKE ERIE CLEAN-UP COMMITTEE, INC., 385
LAKE SUPERIOR STATE UNIVERSITY, 586
LAND CONSERVANCY OF WEST MICHIGAN, 386
MACOMB LAND CONSERVANCY, 391
MICHIGAN ASSOCIATION OF CONSERVATION DISTRICTS, 397
MICHIGAN BASS FEDERATION, 397
MICHIGAN DEPARTMENT OF AGRICULTURE, 180
MICHIGAN DEPARTMENT OF ENVIRONMENTAL QUALITY, 180
MICHIGAN DEPARTMENT OF NATURAL RESOURCES, 180
MICHIGAN ENVIRONMENTAL COUNCIL, 397
MICHIGAN FORESTS ASSOCIATION, 397
MICHIGAN LAND USE INSTITUTE, 397
MICHIGAN NATURAL AREAS COUNCIL, 398
MICHIGAN NATURE ASSOCIATION, 398
MICHIGAN STATE UNIVERSITY, 587
MICHIGAN STATE UNIVERSITY EXTENSION, 181
MICHIGAN TECHNOLOGICAL UNIVERSITY; SCHOOL OF FORESTRY AND WOOD PRODUCTS, 588
MICHIGAN UNITED CONSERVATION CLUBS, INC., 398
MICHIGAN WILDLIFE CONSERVANCY, 398
MIDLAND CONSERVATION DISTRICT, 181
NATIONAL AUDUBON SOCIETY
   Michigan Audubon Society, 414
NATIONAL WILDLIFE FEDERATION
   Great Lakes Natural Resource Center, 427
NATURE CONSERVANCY, THE
   Michigan Chapter, 436
NORTHERN MICHIGAN UNIVERSITY
   Biology, 591
ORGANIZATION FOR BAT CONSERVATION, 461
SCENIC AMERICA
   Scenic Michigan, 487
SIERRA CLUB
   Mackinac Chapter, 493
SIERRA CLUB
   MIDWEST OFFICE
      Traverse City Office, 494
SILK CITY NATURE ASSOCIATION, 500
STURGEON FOR TOMORROW, 514
TROUT UNLIMITED
   Michigan Council, 521
UNITED STATES DEPARTMENT OF AGRICULTURE
   Forest Service
      Hiawatha National Forest, 39
      Huron-Manistee National Forest, 39
      Ottawa National Forest, 42
UNITED STATES DEPARTMENT OF COMMERCE
   National Oceanic and Atmospheric Administration
      Sea Grant Program - Michigan, 57
UNITED STATES DEPARTMENT OF DEFENSE
   Army Corps of Engineers
      Detroit Engineer District, 68
UNITED STATES DEPARTMENT OF THE INTERIOR
   Fish and Wildlife Service
      Michigan WMD National Wildlife Refuge, 105
      Selawik National Wildlife Refuge, 114
      Sherburne/Crane Meadows National Wildlife Refuge, 114
   National Park Service
      Isle Royale National Park, 123
UNIVERSITY OF MICHIGAN, 614
WAYNE STATE UNIVERSITY DEPARTMENT OF BIOLOGICAL SCIENCES, 626
WEST MICHIGAN ENVIRONMENTAL ACTION COUNCIL, 536
WESTERN MICHIGAN UNIVERSITY, 626
WILDFLOWER ASSOCIATION OF MICHIGAN, 541
WILDLIFE SOCIETY
   Michigan Chapter, 549
WILSON ORNITHOLOGICAL SOCIETY, 555
YOUNG ENTOMOLOGISTS SOCIETY, INC., 562

MINNESOTA
AMERICAN FISHERIES SOCIETY
   Minnesota Chapter, 256
AMERICAN PIE (PUBLIC INFORMATION ON THE ENVIRONMENT), 264
ARCHERY TRADE ASSOCIATION (ATA), 270
BEMIDJI STATE UNIVERSITY, 574
CHARLES A. AND ANNE MORROW LINDBERGH FOUNDATION, THE, 294
COTTONWOOD FOUNDATION, 309
DEEP-PORTAGE CONSERVATION RESERVE, 311
FEDERAL CARTRIDGE COMPANY, 329
FRIENDS OF THE BOUNDARY WATERS WILDERNESS, 337
HAMLINE UNIVERSITY, 583
INSTITUTE FOR AGRICULTURE AND TRADE POLICY, 358
INTERNATIONAL ECOLOGY SOCIETY (IES), 362
INTERNATIONAL RESEARCH AND EVALUATION, 567
INTERNATIONAL WOLF CENTER, 371
   Administrative Offices, 372
IZAAK WALTON LEAGUE OF AMERICA, INC., THE
   Minnesota Division, 377
   Owatonna Minnesota Chapter, 377
KIDS FOR SAVING EARTH WORLDWIDE, 384
MINNESOTA ASSOCIATION OF SOIL AND WATER CONSERVATION DISTRICTS, 399
MINNESOTA BASS FEDERATION, 399
MINNESOTA BOARD OF WATER AND SOIL RESOURCES, 181
MINNESOTA CENTER FOR ENVIRONMENTAL ADVOCACY (MCEA), 399
MINNESOTA CONSERVATION FEDERATION, 399
MINNESOTA COOPERATIVE FISH AND WILDLIFE RESEARCH UNIT, 181
MINNESOTA DEPARTMENT OF AGRICULTURE, 181
MINNESOTA DEPARTMENT OF NATURAL RESOURCES, 182
MINNESOTA ENVIRONMENTAL QUALITY BOARD, 182
MINNESOTA FORESTRY ASSOCIATION, 399
MINNESOTA GEOLOGICAL SURVEY, 182
MINNESOTA GROUND WATER ASSOCIATION, 400
MINNESOTA HERPETOLOGICAL SOCIETY, 400
MINNESOTA LAND TRUST, 400
MINNESOTA NATIVE PLANT SOCIETY, 400
MINNESOTA ORNITHOLOGISTS' UNION, 400
MINNESOTA POLLUTION CONTROL AGENCY
   Baxter, MN, 182
   Detroit Lakes, MN, 183
   Duluth, MN, 183
   Marshall, MN, 183
   Rochester, MN, 183
   St. Paul, MN, 183
MINNESOTA STATE EXTENSION SERVICES, 183
MINNESOTA WILDLIFE HERITAGE FOUNDATION, INC., 400
MINNESOTA WINGS SOCIETY, INC., 400
MISSISSIPPI RIVER BASIN ALLIANCE, 401
MUSKIES, INC., 406
NATIONAL WILDLIFE REHABILITATORS ASSOCIATION, 429
NATURE CONSERVANCY, THE
   Great Plains Division, 435
   Minnesota Chapter, 436
NORTH AMERICAN MEMBERSHIP GROUP, 449
PARKS AND TRAILS COUNCIL OF MINNESOTA, 465
PHEASANTS FOREVER, INC., 468
POPE AND YOUNG CLUB, 470
RAPTOR CENTER, THE, 593
SIERRA CLUB
   North Star Chapter (Minnesota), 495
ST. CLOUD STATE UNIVERSITY, 597
TROUT UNLIMITED
   Minnesota Council, 521
TRUMPETER SWAN SOCIETY, THE, 523
UNITED STATES DEPARTMENT OF AGRICULTURE
   Forest Service
      Chippewa National Forest, 36
      North Central Research Station, 41
      Superior National Forest, 45
UNITED STATES DEPARTMENT OF COMMERCE
   National Oceanic and Atmospheric Administration
      Sea Grant Program - Minnesota, 57
UNITED STATES DEPARTMENT OF DEFENSE
   Army Corps of Engineers
      St. Paul Engineer District, 71
UNITED STATES DEPARTMENT OF THE INTERIOR
   FISH AND WILDLIFE SERVICE
      Agassiz National Wildlife Refuge, 90
      Big Stone National Wildlife Refuge, 93
      Detroit Lakes WMD, 97
      Fergus Falls WMD National Wildlife Refuge, 98
      Litchfield WMD, 103
      Mille Lacs National Wildlife Refuge, 105
      Minnesota Valley National Wildlife Refuge, 105
      Morris Wetland Management District, 106
      Region 2, Southwest Regional Office, 111
      Sheldon/Hart Mountain National Wildlife Refuge, 114

GEOGRAPHIC INDEX – U

   Tamarac National Wildlife Refuge, 116
   Upper Mississippi River National Wildlife and fish refuge, 117
   Windom WMD National Wildlife Refuge, 119
  National Park Service
   Voyageurs National Park, 125
UNIVERSITY OF MINNESOTA AT CROOKSTON, 614
UNIVERSITY OF MINNESOTA AT ST. PAUL, 615
WILDLIFE EDUCATION PROGRAM AND DESIGN, 543
WILDLIFE FOREVER, 544
WILDLIFE SOCIETY
  Minnesota Chapter, 549

MISSISSIPPI
AMERICAN FISHERIES SOCIETY
  Computer User Section, 254
  Fish Culture Section, 254
  Mississippi Chapter, 257
CROSBY ARBORETUM, THE, 311
DELTA WILDLIFE INC., 313
GULF COAST RESEARCH LABORATORY, 158
GULF STATES MARINE FISHERIES COMMISSION, 20
LOWER MISSISSIPPI RIVER CONSERVATION COMMITTEE, 301
MADISON COUNTY SOIL & WATER CONSERVATION DISTRICT
  Soil & Water Conservation District, 173
MISSISSIPPI ASSOCIATION OF CONSERVATION DISTRICTS, INC., 401
MISSISSIPPI BASS FEDERATION, 401
MISSISSIPPI COOPERATIVE FISH AND WILDLIFE RESEARCH UNIT, 183
MISSISSIPPI DEPARTMENT OF AGRICULTURE AND COMMERCE, 183
MISSISSIPPI DEPARTMENT OF ENVIRONMENTAL QUALITY
  Office of Land and Water Resources, 184
  Office of Pollution Control, 184
MISSISSIPPI DEPARTMENT OF WILDLIFE, FISHERIES, AND PARKS, 184
MISSISSIPPI FORESTRY COMMISSION, 184
MISSISSIPPI NATIVE PLANT SOCIETY, 401
MISSISSIPPI SOIL AND WATER CONSERVATION COMMISSION, 184
MISSISSIPPI STATE DEPARTMENT OF HEALTH, 185
MISSISSIPPI STATE UNIVERSITY
  College of Forest Resources, 588
  Forest and Wildlife Research Center, 588
MISSISSIPPI WILDLIFE FEDERATION, 401
NATURE CONSERVANCY, THE
  Mississippi Chapter, 436
SIERRA CLUB
  Mississippi Chapter, 494
SOUTHEASTERN FISHES COUNCIL, 508
UNITED STATES DEPARTMENT OF AGRICULTURE
  Forest Service
   Bienville, Delta, Desoto, Holly Springs, Homochitto, and Tombigbee National Forests, 34
  Research Education and Economics
   ARS Mid South Office, 48
UNITED STATES DEPARTMENT OF COMMERCE
  National Oceanic and Atmospheric Administration
   Sea Grant Program - Alabama, 53
   Sea Grant Program - Mississippi-Alabama Consortium, 57
UNITED STATES DEPARTMENT OF DEFENSE
  Air Force Major U.S. Installations
   Columbus AFB, MS, 63
   Keesler AFB, MS, 64
  Army Corps of Engineers
   Mississippi Valley Engineer Division, 60
   Vicksburg Engineer District, 72
UNITED STATES DEPARTMENT OF THE INTERIOR
  Bureau of Land Management
   Jackson Field Office, 82
  Fish and Wildlife Service
   Hillside National Wildlife Refuge, 99
   Mississippi Sandhill Crane/Grand Bay National Wildlife Refuge, 106
   Mississippi WMD National Wildlife Refuge, 106
   Noxubee National Wildlife Refuge, 108
   Panther Swamp National Wildlife Refuge, 109
   St. Catherine Creek National Wildlife Refuge, 115
   Yazoo National Wildlife Refuge, 119
UNIVERSITY OF SOUTHERN MISSISSIPPI, 620
WILDLIFE SOCIETY
  Mississippi Chapter, 549

MISSOURI
AMERICAN FISHERIES SOCIETY
  Missouri Chapter, 257
ASSOCIATION FOR NATURAL RESOURCES ENFORCEMENT TRAINING, 273
BOUNTY INFORMATION SERVICE, 280

CAMP FIRE USA, 285
CENTER FOR PLANT CONSERVATION, 292
COLUMBIA ENVIRONMENTAL RESEARCH CENTER, 303
CONSERVATION FEDERATION OF MISSOURI, 307
INTERNATIONAL CENTER FOR TROPICAL ECOLOGY, 361
KANSAS BASS FEDERATION, 381
MISSOURI ASSOCIATION OF SOIL AND WATER CONSERVATION DISTRICTS, 402
MISSOURI BASS FEDERATION, 402
MISSOURI DEPARTMENT OF AGRICULTURE, 185
MISSOURI DEPARTMENT OF CONSERVATION, 185
  Design and Development Division, 185
  Fisheries Division, 185
  Forestry Division, 185
  Human Resources Section, 185
  Outreach and Education Division, 185
  Protection Division, 185
  Wildlife Division, 185
MISSOURI DEPARTMENT OF NATURAL RESOURCES, 186
MISSOURI FOREST PRODUCTS ASSOCIATION, 402
MISSOURI NATIVE PLANT SOCIETY, 402
MISSOURI PRAIRIE FOUNDATION, 402
MISSOURI STATE EXTENSION SERVICES, 186
NATIONAL AUDUBON SOCIETY
  Audubon Missouri, 410
  Audubon Society of Missouri, 411
NATIONAL GARDEN CLUBS, INC., 420
NATURE CONSERVANCY, THE
  Missouri Chapter, 436
OZARKS RESOURCE CENTER, 463
SCENIC AMERICA
  Scenic Missouri, 487
SIERRA CLUB
  Ozark Chapter (Missouri), 496
TROUT UNLIMITED
  Missouri Council, 522
UNITED STATES DEPARTMENT OF AGRICULTURE
  Forest Service
   Mark Twain National Forest, 40
UNITED STATES DEPARTMENT OF DEFENSE
  Air Force Major U.S. Installations
   Whiteman AFB, MO, 66
  Army Corps of Engineers
   Kansas City Engineer District, 69
   St. Louis Engineer District, 71
UNITED STATES DEPARTMENT OF THE INTERIOR
  Fish and Wildlife Service
   Big Muddy National Fish & Wildlife Refuge, 93
   Great River National Wildife Refuge, 98
   Mingo National Wildlife Refuge, 105
   Squaw Creek National Wildlife Refuge, 115
   Swan Lake National Wildlife Refuge, 116
  Missouri Cooperative Fish and Wildlife Research Unit, 119
UNIVERSITY OF MISSOURI, 615
WASHINGTON UNIVERSITY, 626
WILD CANID SURVIVAL AND RESEARCH CENTER, 539
WILDLIFE SOCIETY
  Missouri Chapter, 550
WORLD BIRD SANCTUARY (WBS), 558

MONTANA
AMERICAN FISHERIES SOCIETY
  Montana Chapter, 257
AMERICAN RIVERS
  Montana Field Office, 265
AMERICAN WILDLANDS, 267
BOONE AND CROCKETT CLUB, 279
BOONE AND CROCKETT FOUNDATION, 279
CONFEDERATED SALISH AND KOOTENAI TRIBES, 304
CRAIGHEAD ENVIRONMENTAL RESEARCH INSTITUTE, 310
CRAIGHEAD WILDLIFE-WILDLANDS INSTITUTE, 310
EARTHJUSTICE
  Bozeman Office, 318
FEDERATION OF FLY FISHERS, 329
GLACIER INSTITUTE, THE, 343
GREAT BEAR FOUNDATION, 344
GREATER YELLOWSTONE COALITION, 346
LIGHTHAWK
  Northern Rocky Mountain Field Office, 389
MONTANA ASSOCIATION OF CONSERVATION DISTRICTS, 403
MONTANA BASS FEDERATION, 403
MONTANA BUREAU OF MINES AND GEOLOGY, 186
MONTANA COOPERATIVE WILDLIFE RESEARCH UNIT (USGS/BRD), 186

MONTANA DEPARTMENT OF AGRICULTURE, 186
MONTANA DEPARTMENT OF FISH, WILDLIFE, AND PARKS, 186
MONTANA DEPARTMENT OF NATURAL RESOURCES AND
    CONSERVATION, 187
MONTANA ENVIRONMENTAL INFORMATION CENTER, 403
MONTANA ENVIRONMENTAL QUALITY COUNCIL, 187
MONTANA FOREST OWNERS ASSOCIATION, 403
MONTANA LAND RELIANCE, 403
MONTANA NATURAL HERITAGE PROGRAM, 187
MONTANA STATE UNIVERSITY
    College of Agriculture, 589
MONTANA STATE UNIVERSITY
    Department of Ecology, 589
MONTANA WILDERNESS ASSOCIATION, 403
MONTANA WILDLIFE FEDERATION, 404
NATIONAL AUDUBON SOCIETY
    Montana Audubon, 415
NATIONAL CENTER FOR APPROPRIATE TECHNOLOGY, 417
    CENTER FOR RESOURCEFUL BUILDING TECHNOLOGY, 417
NATIONAL FOREST FOUNDATION, 420
NATIONAL WILDLIFE FEDERATION
    Northern Rockies Natural Resource Center, 428
NATURE CONSERVANCY, THE
    Montana Chapter, 437
NORTH AMERICAN BEAR FEDERATION, 447
NORTHERN PLAINS RESOURCE COUNCIL, 453
OUTDOOR WRITERS ASSOCIATION OF AMERICA, INC., 462
PREDATOR CONSERVATION ALLIANCE, 472
ROCKY MOUNTAIN ELK FOUNDATION, 482
SIERRA CLUB
    Montana Chapter, 494
    Montana Field Office, 494
TROUT UNLIMITED
    Montana Council, 522
TURNER ENDANGERED SPECIES FUND, 571
UNITED STATES DEPARTMENT OF AGRICULTURE
    Forest Service
        Beaverhead-Deerlodge National Forest, 34
        Bitterroot National Forest, 34
        Custer National Forest, 37
        Flathead National Forest, 37
        Gallatin National Forest, 38
        Helena National Forest, 38
        Kootenai National Forest, 39
        Lewis and Clark National Forest, 39
        Lolo National Forest, 40
        Region 01 (Northern), 43
UNITED STATES DEPARTMENT OF DEFENSE
    Air Force Major U.S. Installations
        Malmstrom AFB, MT, 65
UNITED STATES DEPARTMENT OF THE INTERIOR
    Bureau of Land Management
        Billings Field Office, 79
        Butte Field Office, 80
        Dillon Field Office, 81
        Lewistown Field Office, 83
        Malta Field Office, 83
        Miles City Field Office, 83
        Missoula Field Office, 84
        State Office for MT, ND and SD, 87
    Fish and Wildlife Service
        Benton Lake National Wildlife Refuge, 92
        Bowdoin National Wildlife Refuge, 94
        Charles M. Russell National Wildlife Refuge, 95
        Lee Metcalf National Wildlife Refuge, 103
        Medicine Lake National Wildlife Refuge Complex, 105
        National Bison Range National Wildlife Refuge, 107
        Red Rock Lakes National Wildlife Refuge, 111
    Great Plains Region, 119
    Montana Cooperative Fishery Research Unit, 119
    Montana State Extension Services, 119
    National Park Service
        Glacier National Park, 122
UNIVERSITY OF MONTANA, 615
UNIVERSITY OF MONTANA SCHOOL OF FORESTRY, 615
WILDERNESS WATCH, 541
WILDLIFE SOCIETY
    Montana Chapter, 550

NEBRASKA
AMERICAN FISHERIES SOCIETY
    Nebraska Chapter, 257
AMERICAN RIVERS
    Nebraska Field Office, 265
GAME AND PARKS COMMISSION-NEBRASKA, 339
GROUNDWATER FOUNDATION, THE, 347
IZAAK WALTON LEAGUE OF AMERICA, INC., THE
    Nebraska Division, 377
NATIONAL ARBOR DAY FOUNDATION, 406
NATIONAL AUDUBON SOCIETY
    Audubon Society of Omaha, 411
NATURE CONSERVANCY, THE
    Nebraska Chapter, 437
NEBRASKA ASSOCIATION OF RESOURCE DISTRICTS, 441
NEBRASKA BASS FEDERATION, 441
NEBRASKA CONSERVATION AND SURVEY DIVISION, 188
NEBRASKA DEPARTMENT OF AGRICULTURE, 188
NEBRASKA DEPARTMENT OF ENVIRONMENTAL QUALITY, 188
NEBRASKA DEPARTMENT OF NATURAL RESOURCES, 188
NEBRASKA GAME AND PARKS COMMISSION, 188
    Omaha Office, 189
NEBRASKA ORNITHOLOGISTS UNION, INC., 441
NEBRASKA WILDLIFE FEDERATION, INC., 442
SIERRA CLUB
    Nebraska Chapter, 494
UNITED STATES DEPARTMENT OF AGRICULTURE
    Forest Service
        Nebraska National Forest, 41
        Oglala National Grassland, 41
UNITED STATES DEPARTMENT OF DEFENSE
    Air Force Major U.S. Installations
        Offut AFB, NE, 66
    Army Corps of Engineers
        Omaha Engineer District, 70
UNITED STATES DEPARTMENT OF THE INTERIOR
    Fish and Wildlife Service
        Crescent Lake National Wildlife Refuge, 96
        Crescent Lake/North Platte Complex National Wildlife Refuge, 96
        Fort Niobrara/Valentine National Wildlife Refuge, 98
        Rainwater Basin WMD National Wildlife Refuge, 111
UNIVERSITY OF NEBRASKA, 615
UNIVERSITY OF NEBRASKA COOPERATIVE EXTENSION, 224
WILDLIFE SOCIETY
    Nebraska Chapter, 550

NEVADA
MULE DEER FOUNDATION, 405
NATURE CONSERVANCY, THE
    Nevada Chapter, 437
NEVADA ASSOCIATION OF CONSERVATION DISTRICTS, 442
NEVADA BUREAU OF MINES AND GEOLOGY, 189
NEVADA DEPARTMENT OF AGRICULTURE, 189
NEVADA DEPARTMENT OF CONSERVATION AND NATURAL
    RESOURCES, 189
NEVADA DEPARTMENT OF WILDLIFE, 189
NEVADA NATURAL HERITAGE PROGRAM, 189
NEVADA WILDLIFE FEDERATION, INC., 442
SIERRA CLUB
    Toiyabe Chapter (Nevada/Eastern California), 498
TAHOE REGIONAL PLANNING AGENCY, 220
TROUT UNLIMITED
    Nevada Council, 522
UNITED STATES DEPARTMENT OF AGRICULTURE
    Forest Service
        Humboldt-Toiyabe National Forest, 39
UNITED STATES DEPARTMENT OF DEFENSE
    Air Force Major U.S. Installations
        Nellis AFB, NV, 65
UNITED STATES DEPARTMENT OF THE INTERIOR
    Bureau of Land Management
        Battle Mountain Field Office, 79
        Carson City Field Office, 80
        Elko Field Office, 81
        Ely Field Office, 81
        Las Vegas Field Office, 83
        State Office for NV, 87
        Winnemucca Field Office, 89
    Bureau of Reclamation
        Lower Colorado Region, 89
    Desert National Wildlife Range, 90
    Fish and Wildlife Service
        Ash Meadows National Wildlife Refuge, 92
        Moapa Valley National Wildlife Refuge, 106
        Pahranagat National Wildlife Refuge, 109
        Roanoke River National Wildlife Refuge, 112
        Stillwater National Wildlife Refuge Complex, 115
    National Park Service
        Great Basin National Park, 123

GEOGRAPHIC INDEX – U

UNIVERSITY OF NEVADA - AT RENO, 616
UNIVERSITY OF NEVADA AT LAS VEGAS
   Environmental Science Program, 616
   Water Resources Program, 616
UNIVERSITY OF NEVADA COOPERATIVE EXTENSION, 616
WILD HORSE ORGANIZED ASSISTANCE, INC. (WHOA), 540
WILDLIFE SOCIETY
   Nevada Chapter, 550

NEW HAMPSHIRE
AMERICAN GROUND WATER TRUST, 261
ANTIOCH NEW ENGLAND GRADUATE SCHOOL, 572
ANTIOCH NEW ENGLAND GRADUATE SCHOOL, ENVIRONMENTAL STUDIES, 572
ASSOCIATION FOR CONSERVATION INFORMATION, INC., 273
CENTER FOR ENVIRONMENT AND POPULATION (CEP), 290
CENTER FOR ENVIRONMENTAL EDUCATION, 291
D ACRES, 311
DARTMOUTH COLLEGE, 579
ELM RESEARCH INSTITUTE, 322
KEENE STATE COLLEGE, 586
NATIONAL AUDUBON SOCIETY
   Audubon Society of New Hampshire, 411
NATURE CONSERVANCY, THE
   New Hampshire Chapter, 437
NEW HAMPSHIRE ASSOCIATION OF CONSERVATION COMMISSIONS, 443
NEW HAMPSHIRE ASSOCIATION OF CONSERVATION DISTRICTS, 444
NEW HAMPSHIRE BASS FEDERATION, 444
NEW HAMPSHIRE COUNCIL ON RESOURCES AND DEVELOPMENT, 190
NEW HAMPSHIRE DEPARTMENT OF AGRICULTURE, MARKETS, AND FOOD, 190
   State Conservation Committee, 190
NEW HAMPSHIRE DEPARTMENT OF ENVIRONMENTAL SERVICES, 190
NEW HAMPSHIRE DEPARTMENT OF RESOURCES AND ECONOMIC DEVELOPMENT, 190
NEW HAMPSHIRE FISH AND GAME DEPARTMENT, 190
NEW HAMPSHIRE LAKES ASSOCIATION, 444
NEW HAMPSHIRE NATURAL HERITAGE BUREAU, 191
NEW HAMPSHIRE TIMBERLAND OWNERS ASSOCIATION, 444
NEW HAMPSHIRE WILDLIFE FEDERATION, 444
NORTH AMERICAN LOON FUND, 448
NORTHEASTERN FOREST FIRE PROTECTION COMMISSION, 25
SEACOAST ANTI-POLLUTION LEAGUE, 489
SIERRA CLUB
   New Hampshire Chapter, 494
SOCIETY FOR THE PROTECTION OF NEW HAMPSHIRE FORESTS, 503
STATEWIDE PROGRAM OF ACTION TO CONSERVE OUR ENVIRONMENT (SPACE), 512
STUDENT CONSERVATION ASSOCIATION, INC., 512
TROUT UNLIMITED
   New Hampshire Council, 522
UNITED STATES DEPARTMENT OF AGRICULTURE
   Forest Service
      White Mountain National Forest, 46
UNITED STATES DEPARTMENT OF COMMERCE
   National Oceanic and Atmospheric Administration
      Great Bay National Estuarine Research Reserve, 50
      Sea Grant Program - New Hampshire, 57
UNITED STATES DEPARTMENT OF DEFENSE
   Army Corps of Engineers
      Hanover Engineer District, 68
UNITED STATES DEPARTMENT OF THE INTERIOR
   Fish and Wildlife Service
      Lake Umbagog National Wildlife Refuge, 102
UNIVERSITY OF NEW HAMPSHIRE, 616
UNIVERSITY OF NEW HAMPSHIRE COOPERATIVE EXTENSION, 617

NEW JERSEY
AMERICAN B.A.S.S. ASSOCIATION OF EASTERN PENNSYLVANIA/ NEW JERSEY, THE, 249
AMERICAN LITTORAL SOCIETY, 262
ASSOCIATION OF NEW JERSEY ENVIRONMENTAL COMMISSIONS (ANJEC), 274
CLEAN OCEAN ACTION
   Main Office, 298
   Mid-Coast Office, 298
   South Jersey Office, 298
COMMITTEE FOR NATIONAL ARBOR DAY, 303
DELAWARE RIVER BASIN COMMISSION, 17
HAWK MIGRATION ASSOCIATION OF NORTH AMERICA, 349
LAKE HOPATCONG PROTECTIVE ASSOCIATION, 385
MONTCLAIR STATE UNIVERSITY, 589
NATIONAL AUDUBON SOCIETY
   New Jersey Chapter, 415
NATURE CONSERVANCY, THE
   New Jersey Chapter, 437
NEW JERSEY AGRICULTURAL SOCIETY, 444
NEW JERSEY ASSOCIATION OF CONSERVATION DISTRICTS, 445
NEW JERSEY BASS FEDERATION, 445
NEW JERSEY CONSERVATION FOUNDATION, 445
NEW JERSEY DEPARTMENT OF AGRICULTURE, 191
   Division of Rural Resources, 191
NEW JERSEY DEPARTMENT OF ENVIRONMENTAL PROTECTION, 191
   Division of Fish and Wildlife, 191
   Division of Parks and Forestry, 192
   Division of Publicly Funded Site Remediation, 192
   Division of Solid and Hazardous Waste, 192
   Geological Survey, 192
   Green Acres Program, 192
NEW JERSEY ENVIRONMENTAL LOBBY, 445
NEW JERSEY FORESTRY ASSOCIATION, 445
NEW JERSEY PINELANDS COMMISSION, 193
NEW YORK TURTLE AND TORTOISE SOCIETY, 446
NEW YORK-NEW JERSEY TRAIL CONFERENCE INC., 446
NORTH AMERICAN BUTTERFLY ASSOCIATION, 448
PINES ROWAN UNIVERSITY, 592
RICHARD STOCKTON COLLEGE, 594
RUTGERS COOPERATIVE EXTENSION, 215
RUTGERS UNIVERSITY, COOK COLLEGE, 594
SIERRA CLUB
   New Jersey Chapter, 495
UNITED STATES DEPARTMENT OF COMMERCE
   National Oceanic and Atmospheric Administration
      Jacques Cousteau National Estuarine Research Reserve Institute of Marine and Coastal Sciences, 51
      Sea Grant Program - New Jersey, 57
UNITED STATES DEPARTMENT OF DEFENSE
   Air Force Major U.S. Installations
      McGuire AFB, NJ, 65
UNITED STATES DEPARTMENT OF THE INTERIOR
   Fish and Wildlife Service
      Cape May National Wildlife Refuge, 94
      Edwin B. Forsythe National Wildlife Refuge, 97
      Great Swamp National Wildlife Refuge, 98
      Supawna Meadows National Wildlife Refuge, 116
      Wallkill River National Wildlife Refuge, 117
WELL SPRING INTERNATIONAL, INC., 571
WILDLIFE SOCIETY
   New Jersey Chapter, 550

NEW MEXICO
AMERICAN FISHERIES SOCIETY
   New Mexico State University Student Chapter, 257
ARCHAEOLOGICAL CONSERVANCY, 270
CENTER FOR WILDLIFE LAW, 293
CONSERVAMERICA, 305
CROWNPOINT INSTITUTE OF TECHNOLOGY, 565
FOREST STEWARDS GUILD, 335
FOREST TRUST, 335
FOUR CORNERS INSTITUTE, THE, 336
NATURE CONSERVANCY, THE
   New Mexico Chapter, 437
NEW MEXICO ASSOCIATION OF CONSERVATION DISTRICTS, 445
NEW MEXICO BUREAU OF GEOLOGY AND MINERAL RESOURCES, 193
   Geological Information Center Library, 193
NEW MEXICO DEPARTMENT OF AGRICULTURE, 193
NEW MEXICO DEPARTMENT OF GAME AND FISH, 193
   Albuquerque NM Office, 194
   Raton NM Office, 194
   Roswell NM Office, 194
   SW Area Operations, 194
NEW MEXICO ENERGY, MINERALS, AND NATURAL RESOURCES DEPARTMENT, 194
   Administrative Services Division, 194
   Energy Conservation and Management Division, 194
   Forestry Division, 194
   Mining and Minerals Division, 195
   Oil Conservation Division, 195
   State Parks and Recreation Division, 195
NEW MEXICO ENVIRONMENT DEPARTMENT, 195
NEW MEXICO ENVIRONMENTAL LAW CENTER, 445
NEW MEXICO SOIL AND WATER CONSERVATION COMMISSION, 195

NEW MEXICO STATE UNIVERSITY
   College of Agriculture and Home Economics, 589
      Department of Fishery and Wildlife Sciences, 590
   Cooperative Extension Services, 195
PUBLIC LANDS INTERPRETIVE ASSOCIATION, 570
REP AMERICA, 479
SIERRA CLUB
   Rio Grande Chapter (New Mexico/West Texas), 496
SOUTHWEST RESEARCH AND INFORMATION CENTER, 510
STATE ENGINEER OFFICE/INTERSTATE STREAM COMMISSION, 220
UNITED STATES DEPARTMENT OF AGRICULTURE
   Forest Service
      Carson National Forest, 35
      Cibola National Forest, 36
      Gila National Forest, 38
      Kiow / Rita Blanca National Grassland, 39
      Lincoln National Forest, 39
      Region 03 (Southwestern), 43
      Santa Fe National Forest, 44
UNITED STATES DEPARTMENT OF DEFENSE
   Air Force Major Air Commands
      Kirtland AFB, NM, 62
   Air Force Major U.S. Installations
      Cannon AFB, NM, 63
      Holloman AFB, NM, 64
      Kirtland AFB, NM, 64
   Army Corps of Engineers
      Albuquerque Engineer District, 67
UNITED STATES DEPARTMENT OF THE INTERIOR
   Bureau of Land Management
      Albuquerque Field Office, 78
      Carlsbad Field Office, 80
      Las Cruces District, 83
      Renewable Energy, 86
      Roswell District, 86
      Socorro Field Office, 87
      State Office for NM, TX, OK and KS, 87
      Taos Field Office, 88
   Fish and Wildlife Service
      Bitter Lake National Wildlife Refuge, 93
      Bosque de Apache National Wildlife Refuge, 93
      Las Vegas National Wildlife Refuge, 103
      Maxwell National Wildlife Refuge, 104
      Salt Plains National Wildlife Refuge, 113
      Sequoyah/Ozark Plateau National Wildlife Refuge, 114
      Southeast Louisiana Complex National Wildlife Refuge, 115
   National Park Service
      Carlsbad Caverns National Park, 121
   United States Geological Survey
      New Mexico Cooperative Fish and Wildlife Research Unit, 127
ZUNGARO COCHA RESEARCH CENTER
   Exploration Educational Expeditions, 562

NEW YORK
ADIRONDACK COUNCIL, THE, 242
ADIRONDACK MOUNTAIN CLUB, INC., THE (ADK), 242
ADIRONDACK PARK AGENCY, 132
AIZA BIBY, 244
ALFRED UNIVERSITY, 572
AMANAKAA AMAZON NETWORK, 248
AMERICAN CONSERVATION ASSOCIATION, INC.
   New York Office, 251
AMERICAN FISHERIES SOCIETY
   College of Environmental Science and Forestry Chapter, 253
   New York Chapter, 257
AMERICAN GEOGRAPHICAL SOCIETY, 260
AMERICAN LITTORAL SOCIETY
   Northeast Region, 262
AMERICAN LUNG ASSOCIATION, 263
AMERICAN MUSEUM OF NATURAL HISTORY, 263
AMERICAN WILDLIFE RESEARCH FOUNDATION, INC., 268
ASSOCIATION FOR THE PROTECTION OF THE ADIRONDACKS, THE, 273
ASSOCIATION OF FIELD ORNITHOLOGISTS, 274
ATLANTIC STATES LEGAL FOUNDATION, 275
AUDUBON INTERNATIONAL, 276
BARD COLLEGE, 574
BROOKVIEW PRESS, 564
CAMP FIRE CLUB OF AMERICA, 284
CAMP FIRE CONSERVATION FUND, 285
CATSKILL CENTER FOR CONSERVATION AND DEVELOPMENT, INC., THE, 289
CATSKILL FOREST ASSOCIATION, 289
CENTER FOR ENVIRONMENTAL INFORMATION, 291
CHAUTAUQUA WATERSHED CONSERVANCY, 294
CITY UNIVERSITY OF NEW YORK
   College of Staten Island, 576
CITY UNIVERSITY OF NEW YORK
   Hunter College, 576
COALITION FOR EDUCATION IN THE OUTDOORS, 299
CORNELL LAB OF ORNITHOLOGY, 309
CORNELL UNIVERSITY, 578
DRAGONFLY SOCIETY OF THE AMERICAS, THE, 314
EARTH DAY NEW YORK, 316
ECOSEA, 322
ENGENDERHEALTH, 322
ENVIRONMENTAL ADVOCATES OF NEW YORK, 323
ENVIRONMENTAL DEFENSE
   Headquarters, 324
ENVIRONMENTAL EDUCATION ASSOCIATES, 325
ENVIRONMENTAL PROTECTION AGENCY
   Region 2 (NJ, NY, PR, VI), 18
FEDERATION OF NEW YORK STATE BIRD CLUBS, INC., 330
GARDEN CLUB OF AMERICA, THE, 340
GIRL SCOUTS OF THE USA, 343
GLOBAL INFORMATION NETWORK, 344
GREAT LAKES UNITED, 345
GREEN SPHERE INC., 347
HERPDIGEST, 350
HUDSONIA LIMITED, 352
INFORM, INC., 357
INSTITUTE OF ECOSYSTEM STUDIES, 358
IZAAK WALTON LEAGUE OF AMERICA, INC., THE
   New York State Division, 377
JACKSON HOLE PRESERVE, INC., 379
MARINE ENVIRONMENTAL RESEARCH INSTITUTE (MERI), 394
NATIONAL AUDUBON SOCIETY, 409
   Audubon Society of New York 411
   Living Oceans Program, 414
   Project Puffin, 415
   Scully Science Center, 416
NATURAL RESOURCES DEFENSE COUNCIL, INC., 432
NATURE CONSERVANCY, THE
   Adirondack Chapter, 433
   Eastern New York Chapter, 435
   New York Adirondack Chapter, 438
   New York Central/Western Chapter, 438
   New York City Chapter, 438
   New York City Office, 437
   New York Long Island Chapter, 438
   New York South Fork/ Shelter Island Chapter, 438
NEW YORK ASSOCIATION OF CONSERVATION DISTRICTS, INC., 446
NEW YORK BASS FEDERATION, 446
NEW YORK COOPERATIVE FISH AND WILDLIFE RESEARCH UNIT, 196
NEW YORK DEPARTMENT OF AGRICULTURE AND MARKETS, 196
NEW YORK DEPARTMENT OF ENVIRONMENTAL CONSERVATION, 196
   Division of Public Affairs and Education, 196
   Division of Solid and Hazardous Materials, 196
   Division of Water, 196
NEW YORK DEPARTMENT OF HEALTH, 197
NEW YORK FOREST OWNERS ASSOCIATION, INC., 446
NEW YORK GEOLOGICAL SURVEY AND STATE MUSEUM, 197
NEW YORK OFFICE OF ENERGY EFFICIENCY AND ENVIRONMENT, 197
NEW YORK PUBLIC INTEREST RESEARCH GROUP (NYPIRG), 446
NEW YORK STATE COOPERATIVE EXTENSION, 197
NEW YORK STATE DEPARTMENT OF AGRICULTURE AND MARKETS, 197
NEW YORK STATE FISH AND WILDLIFE MANAGEMENT BOARD, 198
   Region 3, 198
   Region 4, 198
   Region 5, 198
   Region 6, 198
   Region 7, 198
   Region 8, 198
NEW YORK STATE OFFICE OF PARKS, RECREATION AND HISTORIC PRESERVATION, 198
NEW YORK STATE TUG HILL COMMISSION, 199
PLANNED PARENTHOOD FEDERATION OF AMERICA, INC., 469
POLYTECHNIC UNIVERSITY OF NEW YORK, 592
POPULATION COMMUNICATIONS INTERNATIONAL, 470
RAINFOREST ALLIANCE, 477
RAINFOREST RELIEF, 477
RENSSELAER POLYTECHNIC INSTITUTE
   Department of Earth and Environmental Sciences, 593
   Lally School of Management and Technology, 593
RESIDENTS FOR A MORE BEAUTIFUL PORT WASHINGTON, 479

GEOGRAPHIC INDEX – U

ROGER TORY PETERSON INSTITUTE OF NATURAL HISTORY, 482
SCENIC HUDSON, INC., 488
SIERRA CLUB
   Atlantic Chapter, 490
   New York City Office, 495
   Northeast Regional Field Office, 495
ST. LAWRENCE UNIVERSITY, 597
ST. REGIS MOHAWK TRIBE, 511
STATE UNIVERSITY OF NEW YORK AT CORTLAND, 597
STATE UNIVERSITY OF NEW YORK AT STONY BROOK, 597
STATE UNIVERSITY OF NEW YORK COLLEGE OF ENVIRONMENTAL SCIENCE AND FORESTRY, 598
TOGETHER FOUNDATION, THE, 518
TROUT UNLIMITED
   New York Council, 522
TUG HILL TOMORROW LAND TRUST, 524
UNITED NATIONS ENVIRONMENT PROGRAMME
   New York Office, 526
UNITED STATES DEPARTMENT OF AGRICULTURE
   ANIMAL AND PLANT HEALTH INSPECTION SERVICE
      International Services South America Office: USDA/APHIS, 32
   Forest Service
      Finger Lakes National Forest, 37
UNITED STATES DEPARTMENT OF COMMERCE
   National Oceanic and Atmospheric Administration
      Hudson River National Estuarine Research Reserve, 51
      Sea Grant Program - New York, 58
UNITED STATES DEPARTMENT OF DEFENSE
   Army Corps of Engineers
      Buffalo Engineer District, 67
      New York Engineer District., 70
      North Atlantic Engineer District, 70
   Army Military Academy, 73
UNITED STATES DEPARTMENT OF HOMELAND SECURITY
   Customs and Border Protection
      New York CMC, 76
UNITED STATES DEPARTMENT OF THE INTERIOR
   Fish and Wildlife Service
      Iroquois National Wildlife Refuge, 100
      Long Island National Wildlife Refuge Complex, 103
      Montezuma National Wildlife Refuge, 106
      St. Lawrence National Wildlife Refuge, 115
   National Park Service
      Fire Island National Seashore, 122
UNITED STATES ENVIRONMENTAL PROTECTION BUREAU, 223
WATERMAN CONSERVATION EDUCATION CENTER, 535
WILD DOG FOUNDATION, THE, 539
WILDLIFE CONSERVATION SOCIETY, 543
WILDLIFE SOCIETY
   New York Chapter, 551
WILDLIFE TRUST
   Wildlife Preservation Trust International, 554
WILLOW MIXED MEDIA INC., 627
WOMEN'S ENVIRONMENT AND DEVELOPMENT ORGANIZATION (WEDO), 557

NORTH CAROLINA
AMERICAN FISHERIES SOCIETY
   Early Life History, 254
   North Carolina Chapter, 257
   Tidewater Chapter, 259
AMERICAN LIVESTOCK BREEDS CONSERVANCY, 263
AMERICAN SOCIETY FOR ENVIRONMENTAL HISTORY, 265
APPALACHIAN STATE UNIVERSITY, 572
ASSOCIATION FOR THE STUDY OF LITERATURE AND ENVIRONMENT (ASLE), 573
CAROLINA BIRD CLUB, INC., 288
CONSERVATION COUNCIL OF NORTH CAROLINA, 306
DUKE UNIVERSITY, 580
DUKE UNIVERSITY - ORGANIZATION FOR TROPICAL STUDIES, 580
EARTH SCHOOL, 565
ENVIRONMENTAL DEFENSE
   North Carolina Office, 324
ENVIRONMENTAL EDUCATORS OF NORTH CAROLINA (EENC), 326
FOOD SUPPLY / HUMAN POPULATION EXPLOSION CONNECTION, 333
FOREST HISTORY SOCIETY, INC., 334
MECKLENBURG COUNTY PARK AND RECREATION DEPARTMENT, 179
NATIONAL HUNTERS ASSOCIATION, INC., 421
NATURE CONSERVANCY, THE
   Mid-Atlantic Division Office, 436
   North Carolina Chapter, 438
NORTH AMERICAN GAMEBIRD ASSOCIATION, INC., 448
NORTH CAROLINA ASSOCIATION OF SOIL AND WATER CONSERVATION DISTRICTS, 450
NORTH CAROLINA BASS FEDERATION, 450
NORTH CAROLINA BEACH BUGGY ASSOCIATION, INC., 450
NORTH CAROLINA COASTAL FEDERATION, INC., 450
NORTH CAROLINA CONSERVATION NETWORK, 450
NORTH CAROLINA COOPERATIVE EXTENSION SERVICE, 199
NORTH CAROLINA COOPERATIVE FISH AND WILDLIFE RESEARCH UNIT (USDI), 200
NORTH CAROLINA DEPARTMENT OF AGRICULTURE AND CONSUMER SERVICES, 200
NORTH CAROLINA DEPARTMENT OF ENVIRONMENT AND NATURAL RESOURCES, 200
NORTH CAROLINA DIVISION OF SOIL AND WATER, 200
NORTH CAROLINA FORESTRY ASSOCIATION (NCFA), 450
NORTH CAROLINA MUSEUM OF NATURAL SCIENCES, 450
NORTH CAROLINA RECREATION AND PARK SOCIETY, INC., 451
NORTH CAROLINA STATE UNIVERSITY, 590
NORTH CAROLINA WATERSHED COALITION, INC., 451
NORTH CAROLINA WILD FLOWER PRESERVATION SOCIETY, 451
NORTH CAROLINA WILDLIFE FEDERATION, 451
NORTH CAROLINA WILDLIFE RESOURCES COMMISSION, 201
PROFESSIONAL BOWHUNTERS SOCIETY, 473
SAVE OUR RIVERS, INC., 485
SIERRA CLUB
   North Carolina Chapter, 495
SOUTHERN ENVIRONMENTAL LAW CENTER
   North Carolina Office, 509
TRIANGLE RAILS-TO-TRAILS CONSERVANCY, 520
TROUT UNLIMITED
   North Carolina council, 522
UNC-CH ENVIRONMENTAL RESOURCE PROGRAM, 601
UNITED STATES DEPARTMENT OF AGRICULTURE
   Animal and Plant Health Inspection Service
      Animal Care Eastern Regional Office, 31
   Forest Service
      Croatan, Nantahala, Pisgah and Uwharrie National Forests, 36
      Southern Research Station, 45
UNITED STATES DEPARTMENT OF COMMERCE
   National Oceanic and Atmospheric Administration
      North Carolina National Estuarine Research Reserve, 52
      Sea Grant Program - North Carolina, 58
UNITED STATES DEPARTMENT OF DEFENSE
   Air Force
      Pope AFB, NC, 61
   Air Force Major U.S. Installations
      Seymour Johnson AFB (and Dare County AFR), NC, 66
   Army Corps of Engineers
      Wilmington Engineer District, 72
UNITED STATES DEPARTMENT OF THE INTERIOR
   Fish and Wildlife Service
      Alligator River/Pea Island National Wildlife Refuge, 91
      Mackay Island/Currituck National Wildlife Refuge, 104
      Mattamuskeet National Wildlife Refuge, 104
      Pee Dee National Wildlife Refuge, 109
      Pocosin Lakes National Wildlife Refuge, 110
      Ridgefield National Wildlife Refuge, 112
   National Park Service
      Cape Hatteras National Seashore, 121
      Cape Lookout National Seashore, 121
UNIVERSITY OF NORTH CAROLINA AT ASHEVILLE, 617
UNIVERSITY OF NORTH CAROLINA AT CHAPEL HILL, 617
WILDLIFE SOCIETY
   North Carolina Chapter, 551

NORTH DAKOTA
AMERICAN FISHERIES SOCIETY
   Dakota Chapter, 254
INDUSTRIAL COMMISSION OF NORTH DAKOTA, 164
INSTITUTE FOR ECOLOGICAL STUDIES UNIVERSITY OF NORTH DAKOTA, 164
NATIONAL FLYWAY COUNCIL
   North Dakota Game and Fish Department, 419
NATURE CONSERVANCY, THE
   North Dakota Chapter, 438
NORTH DAKOTA ASSOCIATION OF SOIL CONSERVATION DISTRICTS, 452
NORTH DAKOTA DEPARTMENT OF AGRICULTURE, 201
NORTH DAKOTA DEPARTMENT OF HEALTH, 201
NORTH DAKOTA FOREST SERVICE, 201
NORTH DAKOTA GAME AND FISH DEPARTMENT, 201
NORTH DAKOTA PARKS AND RECREATION DEPARTMENT, 202
NORTH DAKOTA STATE SOIL CONSERVATION COMMITTEE, 202
NORTH DAKOTA STATE UNIVERSITY, 590

NORTH DAKOTA WATER COMMISSION, 202
NORTH DAKOTA WILDLIFE FEDERATION, 452
SIERRA CLUB
   Dacotah Chapter, 491
UNITED STATES DEPARTMENT OF AGRICULTURE
   Forest Service
      Cheyenne National Grassland, 36
      Little Missouri National Forest, McKenzie Ranger District, 40
      Little Missouri National Grasslands, Medora Ranger District, 40
UNITED STATES DEPARTMENT OF DEFENSE
   Air Force Major U.S. Installations
      Grand Forks AFB, ND, 64
UNITED STATES DEPARTMENT OF THE INTERIOR
   Bureau of Land Management
      North Dakota Field Office, 84
   Fish and Wildlife Service
      Arrowwood National Wildlife Refuge Complex, 91
      Audubon National Wildlife Refuge, 92
      Chase Lake National Wildlife Refuge, 95
      Crosby WMD/Lake Zahl National Wildlife Refuge, 96
      Des Lacs National Wildlife Refuge, 97
      Devils Lake WMD National Wildlife Refuge, 97
      J. Clark Salyer National Wildlife Refuge, 100
      Kulm WMD National Wildlife Refuge, 102
      Long Lake National Wildlife Refuge, 103
      Tewaukon National Wildlife Refuge, 116
      Upper Souris National Wildlife Refuge, 117
      Valley City Wetland Management District, 117
   National Park Service
      Theodore Roosevelt National Park, 125
   North Dakota State University Extension Service, 126
UNIVERSITY OF NORTH DAKOTA, 618
WILDLIFE SOCIETY
   North Dakota Chapter, 551

OHIO
A CRITICAL DECISION, 241
AMERICAN FISHERIES SOCIETY
   Ohio Chapter, 258
ANTIOCH COLLEGE, 572
BOWLING GREEN STATE UNIVERSITY, 574
CANVASBACK SOCIETY, 288
CENTRAL OHIO ANGLERS AND HUNTERS CLUB, 294
CINCINNATI NATURE CENTER, 297
CLEVELAND MUSEUM OF NATURAL HISTORY, THE, 299
DAWES ARBORETUM, THE, 311
EAGLES 4 KIDS, 565
ENVIRONMENTAL EDUCATION COUNCIL OF OHIO, 326
HOCKING COLLEGE, 583
HOLDEN ARBORETUM, THE, 351
INLAND BIRD BANDING ASSOCIATION, 357
INTERNATIONAL ASSOCIATION OF NATURAL RESOURCE PILOTS, 360
INTERNATIONAL SOCIETY FOR ENDANGERED CATS (ISEC), 366
INTERNATIONAL WILD WATERFOWL ASSOCIATION, 371
IZAAK WALTON LEAGUE OF AMERICA, INC., THE
   OHIO DIVISION, 377
LEAGUE OF OHIO SPORTSMEN, 387
MIAMI UNIVERSITY, 587
MOUNT UNION COLLEGE, 589
NATIONAL AUDUBON SOCIETY
   Audubon Ohio, 410
NATIONAL GROUND WATER ASSOCIATION, THE, 421
NATIONAL GROUND WATER INFORMATION CENTER, 568
NATIVE PLANT SOCIETY OF NORTHEASTERN OHIO, 430
NATURE CONSERVANCY, THE
   Ohio Chapter, 438
NORTH AMERICAN BLUEBIRD SOCIETY, 447
OBERLIN COLLEGE, 591
OHIO ACADEMY OF SCIENCE, THE, 456
OHIO ALLIANCE FOR THE ENVIRONMENT, 456
OHIO BASS FEDERATION, 456
OHIO BIOLOGICAL SURVEY, 456
OHIO DEPARTMENT OF AGRICULTURE, 203
OHIO DEPARTMENT OF DEVELOPMENT, 203
OHIO DEPARTMENT OF NATURAL RESOURCES, 204
OHIO ENERGY PROJECT, 456
OHIO ENVIRONMENTAL COUNCIL, INC., 457
OHIO ENVIRONMENTAL PROTECTION AGENCY, 204
OHIO ENVIRONMENTAL REVIEW APPEALS COMMISSION, 205
OHIO FEDERATION OF SOIL AND WATER CONSERVATION DISTRICTS, 457
OHIO FORESTRY ASSOCIATION, INC., 457
OHIO NATIVE PLANT SOCIETY, 457

OHIO RIVER VALLEY WATER SANITATION COMMISSION, 26
OHIO STATE UNIVERSITY, 592
OHIO STATE UNIVERSITY EXTENSION, 205
OHIO STREAM PRESERVATION, 457
SHAWNEE STATE UNIVERSITY, 595
SIERRA CLUB
   Ohio Chapter, 496
TROUT UNLIMITED
   Ohio Council, 522
UNITED STATES DEPARTMENT OF AGRICULTURE
   Forest Service
      Wayne National Forest, 46
UNITED STATES DEPARTMENT OF COMMERCE
   National Oceanic and Atmospheric Administration
      Old Woman Creek National Estuarine Research Reserve, 53
      Sea Grant Program - Ohio, 58
UNITED STATES DEPARTMENT OF DEFENSE
   Air Force Major Air Commands
      Wright Patterson AFB, OH, 62
   Army Corps of Engineers
      Great Lakes and Ohio Engineer District, 68
UNITED STATES DEPARTMENT OF THE INTERIOR
   Fish and Wildlife Service
      Ottawa National Wildlife Refuge, 108
UNITED STATES SPORTSMEN'S ALLIANCE AND UNITED STATES SPORTSMEN'S ALLIANCE FOUNDATION, 526
UNIVERSITY OF AKRON, 604
WILDLIFE SOCIETY
   Ohio Chapter, 551

OKLAHOMA
AMERICAN FISHERIES SOCIETY
   Fisheries Management Section, 254
GEORGE MIKSCH SUTTON AVIAN RESEARCH CENTER INC., 340
NATIONAL AUDUBON SOCIETY
   Oklahoma Audubon Council, 415
NATURE CONSERVANCY, THE
   Oklahoma Chapter, 439
OKLAHOMA ASSOCIATION OF CONSERVATION DISTRICTS, 458
OKLAHOMA BASS FEDERATION, 458
OKLAHOMA BIOLOGICAL SURVEY, 205
OKLAHOMA CONSERVATION COMMISSION, 205
OKLAHOMA COOPERATIVE FISH AND WILDLIFE RESEARCH UNIT (USDI), 206
OKLAHOMA DEPARTMENT OF AGRICULTURE, 205
OKLAHOMA DEPARTMENT OF ENVIRONMENTAL QUALITY, 206
OKLAHOMA DEPARTMENT OF WILDLIFE CONSERVATION, 458, 206
OKLAHOMA GEOLOGICAL SURVEY, 206
OKLAHOMA NATIVE PLANT SOCIETY, 458
OKLAHOMA ORNITHOLOGICAL SOCIETY, 458
OKLAHOMA STATE EXTENSION SERVICES, 206
OKLAHOMA STATE UNIVERSITY, 592
OKLAHOMA TOURISM AND RECREATION DEPARTMENT, 207
OKLAHOMA WATER RESOURCES BOARD, 207
OKLAHOMA WILDLIFE FEDERATION, 458
OKLAHOMA WOODLAND OWNERS ASSOCIATION (OWOA), 458
SIERRA CLUB
   Oklahoma Chapter, 496
UNITED STATES DEPARTMENT OF AGRICULTURE
   Forest Service
      McClellan Creek/Black Kettle National Grassland, 40
UNITED STATES DEPARTMENT OF DEFENSE
   Air Force Major U.S. Installations
      Altus AFB, OK, 63
      Tinker AFB, OK, 66
      Vance AFB, OK, 66
   Army Corps of Engineers
      Tulsa Engineer District, 71
UNITED STATES DEPARTMENT OF THE INTERIOR
   Bureau of Land Management
      Oklahoma Field Office-TuLSa #101, 85
   Fish and Wildlife Service
      Deep Fork National Wildlife Refuge, 96
      Little River/Little Sandy National Wildlife Refuge, 103
      Sacramento National Wildlife Refuge, 113
      Seney National Wildlife Refuge, 114
      Tishomingo National Wildlife Refuge, 116
      Washita/Optima National Wildlife Refuge, 118
      Wichita Mountains National Wildlife Refuge, 118
UNIVERSITY OF TULSA, 621
WILDLIFE SOCIETY
   Oklahoma Chapter, 551

GEOGRAPHIC INDEX – U

OREGON
AMERICAN FISHERIES SOCIETY
  Greater Portland, OR Chapter, 255
  Oregon Chapter, 258
APROVECHO RESEARCH CENTER, 270
COLUMBIA BASIN FISH AND WILDLIFE AUTHORITY, 303
COLUMBIA RIVER INTER-TRIBAL FISH COMMISSION, 17
CONSERVATION BIOLOGY INSTITUTE, 306
DESCHUTES BASIN LAND TRUST, 313
ENVIRONMENTAL LAW ALLIANCE WORLDWIDE, U.S. (E-LAW U.S.), 326
FOREST SERVICE EMPLOYEES FOR ENVIRONMENTAL ETHICS (FSEEE), 334
GREEN GUIDES, 346
HIGH DESERT MUSEUM, THE, 351
IZAAK WALTON LEAGUE OF AMERICA, INC., THE
  Oregon Divison, 377
JOHN INSKEEP ENVIRONMENTAL LEARNING CENTER, 380
LEWIS AND CLARK COLLEGE
  College of Arts and Sciences, 586
  Law School, 586
NATIONAL AUDUBON SOCIETY
  AUDUBON SOCIETY OF PORTLAND, 411
NATIVE PLANT SOCIETY OF OREGON, 430
NATURAL AREAS ASSOCIATION, 431
NATURAL RESOURCES INFORMATION COUNCIL, 432
NATURE CONSERVANCY, THE
  Oregon Chapter, 439
NORTHWEST COALITION FOR ALTERNATIVES TO PESTICIDES, 453
OREGON BASS FEDERATION, 460
OREGON DEPARTMENT OF AGRICULTURE, 208
OREGON DEPARTMENT OF ENVIRONMENTAL QUALITY (DEQ), 208
OREGON DEPARTMENT OF FISH AND WILDLIFE (ODFW), 208
OREGON DEPARTMENT OF FORESTRY, 209
OREGON DEPARTMENT OF GEOLOGY AND MINERAL INDUSTRIES, 209
OREGON DEPARTMENT OF TRANSPORTATION, 209
OREGON ENVIRONMENTAL COUNCIL, 460
OREGON FISH AND WILDLIFE DIVISION/DEPARTMENT OF STATE POLICE, 209
OREGON NATURAL RESOURCES COUNCIL, 460
OREGON PARKS AND RECREATION DEPARTMENT, 209
OREGON SMALL WOODLANDS ASSOCIATION, 461
OREGON SOCIETY OF AMERICAN FORESTERS, 461
OREGON STATE EXTENSION SERVICES, 209
OREGON STATE MARINE BOARD, 210
OREGON STATE UNIVERSITY DEPT OF FISHERIES AND WILDLIFE, 592
OREGON TROUT, 461
OREGON WATER RESOURCES DEPARTMENT, 210
OREGON WILDLIFE HERITAGE FOUNDATION, 461
PACIFIC FISHERY MANAGEMENT COUNCIL, 463
PACIFIC MARINE CONSERVATION COUNCIL, 464
PACIFIC RIVERS COUNCIL, 464
PACIFIC STATES MARINE FISHERIES COMMISSION, 27
PORTLAND STATE UNIVERSITY, 593
RIVER NETWORK, 480
SALMON-SAFE, 484
SIERRA CLUB
  Oregon Chapter, 496
SISKIYOU PROJECT, 500
SISKIYOU REGIONAL EDUCATION PROJECT, 500
SOUTHERN OREGON UNIVERSITY, 596
STEAMBOATERS, THE, 512
TREASURE VALLEY COMMUNITY COLLEGE, 600
TROUT UNLIMITED
  Oregon Council, 522
UNITED STATES DEPARTMENT OF AGRICULTURE
  Forest Service
    Crooked River National Grassland, 37
    Deschutes National Forest, 37
    Fremont National Forest, 38
    Malheur National Forest, 40
    Mt. Hood National Forest, 41
    Ochoco National Forest, 41
    Pacific Northwest Research Station, 42
    Region 06 (Pacific Northwest), 43
    Rogue River National Forest, 44
    Siskiyou National Forest, 45
    Siuslaw National Forest, 45
    Umatilla National Forest, 46
    Umpqua National Forest, 46
    Wallowa Whitman National Forests, 46
    Willamette National Forest, 46
    Winema National Forest, 46
UNITED STATES DEPARTMENT OF COMMERCE
  National Oceanic and Atmospheric Administration
    Sea Grant Program - Oregon, 58
    South Slough National Estuarine Research Reserve, 60
UNITED STATES DEPARTMENT OF DEFENSE
  Army Corps of Engineers
    Northwestern Division, 70
    Portland Engineer District, 71
UNITED STATES DEPARTMENT OF THE INTERIOR
  Bureau of Land Management
    Burns District, 80
    Coos Bay Field Office, 80
    Eugene District Office, 81
    Eugene Field Office, 81
    Lakeview District, 83
    Lakeview Resource Area, 83
    Medford District Office, 83
    Prineville District Field Office, 85
    Roseburg District, 86
    Salem District Office, 86
    State Office for OR and WA, 88
    Vale District, 88
  Fish and Wildlife Service
    Ankeny National Wildlife Refuge, 91
    Hart Mountain National Antelope Refuge National Wildlife Refuge, 99
    Malheur National Wildlife Refuge, 101
    National Fish and Wildlife Forensics Laboratory, 107
    Oregon Coast National Wildlife Refuge Complex, 108
    region 1, Pacific Regional Office, 111
    Sevilleta National Wildlife Refuge, 114
    Tualatin River National Wildlife Refuge, 117
    Western Oregon National Wildlife Refuge Complex, 118
  National Park Service
    Crater Lake National Park, 122
  Oregon Cooperative Fish and Wildlife Research Unit, 126
  United States Geological Survey
    Forest and Rangeland Ecosystem Science Center, 127
UNIVERSITY OF OREGON, 619
  Institute for a Sustainable Environment, 619
  School of Law, 618
WASHINGTON STATE SOCIETY OF AMERICAN FORESTERS, 534
WESTERN ENVIRONMENTAL LAW CENTER, 537
WESTERN FORESTRY AND CONSERVATION ASSOCIATION, 537
WESTERN SNOWY PLOVER WORKING TEAM, 131
WILDERNESS LAND TRUST, THE, 540
WILDLIFE SOCIETY
  Oregon Chapter, 552
WORLD FORESTRY CENTER, 558
XERCES SOCIETY, THE, 561

PENNSYLVANIA
AIR & WASTE MANAGEMENT ASSOCIATION, 244
ALLIANCE FOR THE CHESAPEAKE BAY
  Harrisburg Office, 248
AMERICAN FISHERIES SOCIETY
  Pennsylvania Chapter, 258
AMERICAN NATURE STUDY SOCIETY, 263
BIOSIS, 278
BOTANICAL SOCIETY OF WESTERN PENNSYLVANIA, 280
BRANDYWINE CONSERVANCY INC., 280
BULLFROG FILMS, 564
CALIFORNIA UNIVERSITY OF PENNSYLVANIA, 576
CHESAPEAKE BAY FOUNDATION, INC.
  Pennsylvania Office, 295
DELAWARE RIVERKEEPER NETWORK, 313
DREXEL UNIVERSITY, 579
ENVIRONMENTAL PROTECTION AGENCY
  Region 3 (DE, DC, MD, PA, VA, WV), 19
FEDERAL WILDLIFE OFFICERS ASSOCIATION, 329
HAWK MOUNTAIN SANCTUARY ASSOCIATION, VISITOR CENTER, 349
HOLLOW OAK LAND TRUST, 351
IZAAK WALTON LEAGUE OF AMERICA, INC., THE
  Pennsylvania Division, 378
  York Chapter #57, 378
LITTLE JUNIATA RIVER CHAPTER, 390
LOWER MERION CONSERVANCY, 391
MID-ATLANTIC COUNCIL OF WATERSHED ASSOCIATIONS, 398
MRFC FISH CONSERVATION, 405
NATIONAL AUDUBON SOCIETY
  Audubon Pennsylvania, 411
  Audubon Society of Western Pennsylvania, 412

NATIONAL AVIARY, 568
NATIONAL COUNCIL FOR GEOGRAPHIC EDUCATION, 418
NATIONAL TRUST FOR HISTORIC PRESERVATION
 Mid Atlantic, 425
NATURAL LANDS TRUST, 431
NATURE CONSERVANCY, THE
 Pennsylvania Chapter, 439
PA CLEANWAYS, 463
PENNSYLVANIA ASSOCIATION OF CONSERVATION DISTRICTS, INC., 465
PENNSYLVANIA CENTER FOR ENVIRONMENTAL EDUCATION (PCEE), 465
PENNSYLVANIA CITIZENS ADVISORY COUNCIL TO DEPARTMENT OF ENVIRONMENTAL PROTECTION, 466
PENNSYLVANIA COOPERATIVE FISH AND WILDLIFE RESEARCH UNIT, 210
PENNSYLVANIA DEPARTMENT OF AGRICULTURE
 Region I, 210
 Region II, 210
 Region III, 210
 Region IV, 210
 Region V, 210
 Region VI, 211
 Region VII, 211
 State Conservation Commission, 211
PENNSYLVANIA DEPARTMENT OF CONSERVATION AND NATURAL RESOURCES, 211
PENNSYLVANIA DEPARTMENT OF ENVIRONMENTAL PROTECTION, 211
PENNSYLVANIA ENVIRONMENTAL COUNCIL, INC. (PEC), 466
PENNSYLVANIA FEDERATION OF SPORTSMENS CLUBS, 466
PENNSYLVANIA FISH AND BOAT COMMISSION, 212
 Bureau of Law Enforcement
  Northcentral Region, 212
  Northeast Region, 212
  Northwest Region, 212
  SouthCentral Region, 212
  Southeast Region, 212
  Southwest Region, 212
PENNSYLVANIA FOREST STEWARDSHIP PROGRAM, 212
PENNSYLVANIA FORESTRY ASSOCIATION, THE, 466
PENNSYLVANIA ORGANIZATION FOR WATERSHEDS AND RIVERS (POWR), 466
PENNSYLVANIA RECREATION AND PARK SOCIETY, INC., 467
PENNSYLVANIA RESOURCES COUNCIL, INC.,, 467
PENNSYLVANIA STATE EXTENSION SERVICES, 592
PENNSYLVANIA STATE UNIVERSITY, 592
POCONO ENVIRONMENTAL EDUCATION CENTER, 470
POCONO WILDLIFE REHABILITATION CENTER, 470
PURPLE MARTIN CONSERVATION ASSOCIATION, 475
RUFFED GROUSE SOCIETY, THE, 482
SIERRA CLUB
 Pennsylvania Chapter, 496
SLIPPERY ROCK UNIVERSITY, 595
STROUD WATER RESEARCH CENTER, 512
STUDENT ENVIRONMENTAL ACTION COALITION (SEAC), 513
SUSQUEHANNA RIVER BASIN COMMISSION, 29
TEMPLE UNIVERSITY, 599
TROUT UNLIMITED
 Pennsylvania Council, 522
TURTLE CREEK WATERSHED ASSOCIATION, INC., 525
UNITED STATES DEPARTMENT OF AGRICULTURE
 Forest Service
  Allegheny National Forest, 34
  Northeastern Research Station, 41
 Research Education and Economics
  ARS North Atlantic Office, 48
UNITED STATES DEPARTMENT OF DEFENSE
 Army Corps of Engineers
  Philadelphia District, 70
  Pittsburgh Engineer District, 71
UNITED STATES DEPARTMENT OF THE INTERIOR
 Fish and Wildlife Service
  Erie National Wildlife Refuge, 98
  John Heinz National Wildlife Refuge at Tinicum, 101
UNIVERSITY OF PENNSYLVANIA, 619
UNIVERSITY OF PITTSBURGH
 Biology Department, 619
 Graduate School of Public Health
  Department of Environmental and Occupational Health, 619
WATER RESOURCES ASSOCIATION OF THE DELAWARE RIVER BASIN, 535
WESTERN PENNSYLVANIA CONSERVANCY, 537
WHITE CLAY WATERSHED ASSOCIATION, 538
WIDENER UNIVERSITY, 627
WILDLANDS CONSERVANCY, 542
WILDLIFE INFORMATION CENTER, INC., 545
WILDLIFE SOCIETY
 Pennsylvania Chapter, 552
WILKES UNIVERSITY, 627

PUERTO RICO
CENTRO DE INFORMACION, INVESTIGACION Y EDUCACION SOCIAL (CIIES), 294
COMITE DESPERTAR CIDRENO, 148
PUERTO RICO ASSOCIATION OF SOIL AND WATER CONSERVATION DISTRICTS, 474
PUERTO RICO CONSERVATION FOUNDATION, THE (PRCF), 475
PUERTO RICO DEPARTMENT OF AGRICULTURE, 213
PUERTO RICO DEPARTMENT OF NATURAL AND ENVIRONMENTAL RESOURCES, 213
PUERTO RICO SOIL CONSERVATION COMMITTEE, 213
SOCIEDAD AMBIENTE MARINO, 502
UNITED STATES DEPARTMENT OF AGRICULTURE
 Forest Service
  Caribbean National Forest, 35
UNITED STATES DEPARTMENT OF COMMERCE
 National Oceanic and Atmospheric Administration
  Jobos Bay National Estuarine Research Reserve, 51
  Sea Grant Program - Puerto Rico, 59
UNITED STATES DEPARTMENT OF THE INTERIOR
 Fish and Wildlife Service
  Caribbean Islands National Wildlife Refuge, 95
  Culebra National Wildlife Refuge, 96

RHODE ISLAND
AMERICAN FISHERIES SOCIETY
 South New England Chapter, 259
BROWN UNIVERSITY, 575
COASTAL RESOURCES CENTER, 577
CRANSTON CONSERVATION COMMISSION, 150
ENVIRONMENT COUNCIL OF RHODE ISLAND, 323
NATIONAL AUDUBON SOCIETY
 Audubon Society of Rhode Island, 412
NATIONAL NETWORK OF FOREST PRACTITIONERS, 422
NATURE CONSERVANCY, THE
 Northeast/ Caribbean Division Office, 438
 Rhode Island Chapter, 439
NORTHEAST CONSERVATION LAW ENFORCEMENT CHIEFS' ASSOCIATION (CLECA), 452
OCEAN PROJECT, THE, 455
RHODE ISLAND BASS FEDERATION, 480
RHODE ISLAND COOPERATIVE EXTENSION SERVICE, 214
RHODE ISLAND DEPARTMENT OF ENVIRONMENTAL MANAGEMENT, 214
RHODE ISLAND DEPARTMENT OF TRANSPORTATION, 214
RHODE ISLAND FOREST CONSERVATOR'S ORGANIZATION, INC., 480
RHODE ISLAND SCHOOL OF DESIGN, 593
RHODE ISLAND STATE CONSERVATION COMMITTEE, 480
RHODE ISLAND STATE WATER RESOURCES BOARD, 214
RHODE ISLAND WILD PLANT SOCIETY, 480
ROGER WILLIAMS UNIVERSITY, 594
SAVE THE BAY - PEOPLE FOR NARRAGANSETT BAY, 485
SIERRA CLUB
 Rhode Island Chapter, 496
SOUTHERN NEW ENGLAND FOREST CONSORTIUM, INC. (SNEFCI), 509
SOUTHERN RHODE ISLAND STATE ASSOCIATION OF CONSERVATION DISTRICTS, 509
UNITED STATES DEPARTMENT OF COMMERCE
 National Oceanic and Atmospheric Administration
  Narragansett Bay National Estuarine Research Reserve, 51
  Sea Grant Program - Rhode Island, 59
UNITED STATES DEPARTMENT OF THE INTERIOR
 Fish and Wildlife Service
  Rhode Island National Wildlife Refuge Complex, 112
UNIVERSITY OF RHODE ISLAND
 Department of Natural Resources Science, 619
 Graduate School of Oceanography and Coastal Resources Center, 619

SOUTH CAROLINA
AMERICAN FISHERIES SOCIETY
 South Carolina Chapter, 258
CLEMSON UNIVERSITY
 Forestry and Natural Resources, 577
 School of the Environment, 577
CLEMSON UNIVERSITY EXTENSION SERVICE, 145

GEOGRAPHIC INDEX – U

ENVIRONMENTAL MEDIA CORPORATION, 566
FORESTRY COMMISSION (SOUTH CAROLINA), 155
FRIENDS OF THE REEDY RIVER, 338
HILTON POND CENTER FOR PIEDMONT NATURAL HISTORY, 351
INTERNATIONAL PRIMATE PROTECTION LEAGUE, 365
NATIONAL TRUST FOR HISTORIC PRESERVATION
   Southern Office, 425
NATIONAL WILD TURKEY FEDERATION, INC., THE, 427
NATURE CONSERVANCY, THE
   South Carolina Chapter, 439
NATURESAVERS, 441
PARTNERS IN AMPHIBIAN AND REPTILE CONSERVATION (PARC), 465
QUAIL UNLIMITED, INC., 475
SIERRA CLUB
   South Carolina Chapter, 497
SOUTH ATLANTIC FISHERY MANAGEMENT COUNCIL, 29
SOUTH CAROLINA ASSOCIATION OF CONSERVATION DISTRICTS, 505
SOUTH CAROLINA BASS FEDERATION, 506
SOUTH CAROLINA COOPERATIVE FISH AND WILDLIFE RESEARCH UNIT, 217
SOUTH CAROLINA DEPARTMENT OF AGRICULTURE, 217
SOUTH CAROLINA DEPARTMENT OF HEALTH AND ENVIRONMENTAL CONTROL, 217
   Office of Ocean and Coastal Resource Management (OCRM), 217
SOUTH CAROLINA DEPARTMENT OF NATURAL RESOURCES, 218
SOUTH CAROLINA DEPARTMENT OF PARKS, RECREATION AND TOURISM, 218
SOUTH CAROLINA ENERGY OFFICE, 218
SOUTH CAROLINA ENVIRONMENTAL LAW PROJECT, 506
SOUTH CAROLINA FORESTRY ASSOCIATION, 506
SOUTH CAROLINA NATIVE PLANT SOCIETY, 506
SOUTH CAROLINA WILDLIFE FEDERATION, 506
SOUTHERN APPALACHIAN BOTANICAL SOCIETY, 508
TROUT UNLIMITED
   South Carolina COUNCIL, 522
UNITED STATES DEPARTMENT OF AGRICULTURE
   Forest Service
      Francis Marion and Sumter National Forest, 38
UNITED STATES DEPARTMENT OF COMMERCE
   National Oceanic and Atmospheric Administration
      ACE Basin National Estuarine Research Reserve, 49
      National Ocean Service, 52
      North Inlet National Estuarine Research Reserve, 52
      Sea Grant Program - South Carolina, 59
UNITED STATES DEPARTMENT OF DEFENSE
   Air Force Major U.S. Installations
      Charleston AFB, SC, 63
      Shaw AFB, SC, 66
   Army Corps of Engineers
      Charleston Engineer District, 68
UNITED STATES DEPARTMENT OF THE INTERIOR
   Fish and Wildlife Service
      ACE Basin National Wildlife Refuge, 90
      Cape Romain/Santee National Wildlife Refuge, 95
      Carolina Sandhills National Wildlife Refuge, 95
UNIVERSITY OF GEORGIA
   Savannah River Ecology Laboratory, 609
UNIVERSITY OF SOUTH CAROLINA
   Baruch Marine Field Laboratory, 620
   Marine Science Program, 620
UNIVERSITY OF SOUTH CAROLINA BEAUFORT, 620
WILDLIFE ACTION, INC., 542
WILDLIFE SOCIETY
   South Carolina Chapter, 552
YMCA NATURE AND COMMUNITY CENTER, 562

SOUTH DAKOTA
BOARD OF MINERALS AND ENVIRONMENT, 139
GREAT PLAINS NATIVE PLANT SOCIETY, 345
INTERTRIBAL BISON COOPERATIVE (ITBC), 372
IZAAK WALTON LEAGUE OF AMERICA, INC., THE
   South Dakota Division, 378
NATIONAL FLYWAY COUNCIL
   South Dakota Game, Fish and Parks, 420
PRAIRIE WILDLIFE RESEARCH, 472
SIERRA CLUB
   South Dakota Chapter, 497
SOUTH DAKOTA ASSOCIATION OF CONSERVATION DISTRICTS, 506
SOUTH DAKOTA BASS FEDERATION, 507
SOUTH DAKOTA COOPERATIVE EXTENSION SERVICE, 218
SOUTH DAKOTA COOPERATIVE FISH AND WILDLIFE RESEARCH UNIT (USDI-USGS), 29

SOUTH DAKOTA DEPARTMENT OF AGRICULTURE, 218
   Division of Resource Conservation and Forestry, 218
   State Conservation Commission, 219
SOUTH DAKOTA DEPARTMENT OF ENVIRONMENT AND NATURAL RESOURCES, 219
SOUTH DAKOTA DEPARTMENT OF GAME, FISH, AND PARKS, 219
SOUTH DAKOTA ORNITHOLOGISTS UNION, 507
SOUTH DAKOTA RESOURCES COALITION, 507
SOUTH DAKOTA STATE UNIVERSITY, 595
SOUTH DAKOTA WILDLIFE FEDERATION, 507
UNITED STATES DEPARTMENT OF AGRICULTURE
   Forest Service
      Black Hills National Forest, 34
      Buffalo Gap National Grassland, 35
      Buffalo Gap National Grassland, Fall River Ranger District, 35
      Cedar River / Grand River National Grassland, 35
      Fort Pierre National Grassland, 38
UNITED STATES DEPARTMENT OF DEFENSE
   Air Force Major U.S. Installations
      Ellsworth AFB, SD, 64
UNITED STATES DEPARTMENT OF THE INTERIOR
   Bureau of Land Management
      South Dakota Field Office, 87
   Fish and Wildlife Service
      Huron WMD National Wildlife Refuge, 100
      Lacreek/Bear Butte National Wildlife Refuge, 102
      Lake Andes/Karl E. Mundt National Wildlife Refuge, 102
      Madison WMD National Wildlife Refuge, 104
      San Luis National Wildlife Refuge Complex, 113
      Waubay National Wildlife Refuge, 118
   National Park Service
      Badlands National Park, 120
      Wind Cave National Park, 126
WILDLIFE SOCIETY
   South Dakota Chapter, 552

TENNESSEE
AMERICAN AQUATICS, INC, 563
AMERICAN ASSOCIATION OF FIELD BOTANISTS, 249
AMERICAN CANAL SOCIETY, INC., 250
AMERICAN EAGLE FOUNDATION, 251
AMERICAN FEDERATION OF MINERALOGICAL SOCIETIES (AFMS), 252
DUCKS UNLIMITED, INC., 315
   Wetlands America Trust, Inc. Office, 316
ENVIRONMENTAL ACTION FUND (EAF), 323
GREAT SMOKY MOUNTAINS INSTITUTE AT TREMONT, 345
HARDWOOD FOREST FOUNDATION, 348
INTERNATIONAL ASSOCIATION FOR BEAR RESEARCH AND MANAGEMENT, 359
MIDDLE TENNESSEE STATE UNIVERSITY, 588
NATIONAL PARKS CONSERVATION ASSOCIATION (NPCA)
   Southeast Regional Office, 423
NATURE CONSERVANCY, THE
   Tennessee Chapter, 439
NEAL COMMUNICATIONS, 569
SIERRA CLUB
   Tennessee Chapter, 498
TENEESSEE DEPARTMENT OF ENVIRONMENT & CONSERVATION, 220
TENNESSEE AGRICULTURAL EXTENSION SERVICE, 220
TENNESSEE BASS FEDERATION, 515
TENNESSEE CITIZENS FOR WILDERNESS PLANNING, 515
TENNESSEE CONSERVATION LEAGUE, 516
TENNESSEE COOPERATIVE FISHERY RESEARCH UNIT (USDI), 220
TENNESSEE DEPARTMENT OF AGRICULTURE, 221
   State Soil Conservation Committee, 221
TENNESSEE DEPARTMENT OF ENVIRONMENT AND CONSERVATION, 221
TENNESSEE ENVIRONMENTAL COUNCIL, 516
TENNESSEE FORESTRY ASSOCIATION, 516
TENNESSEE TECHNOLOGICAL UNIVERSITY, 599
TENNESSEE VALLEY AUTHORITY, 30
   Research Library, Knoxville and Chattanooga, 30
TENNESSEE WILDLIFE RESOURCES AGENCY, 221
TROUT UNLIMITED
   Tennessee Council, 523
UNITED STATES DEPARTMENT OF AGRICULTURE
   Forest Service
      Cherokee National Forest, 35
UNITED STATES DEPARTMENT OF DEFENSE
   Air Force Major U.S. Installations
      Arnold AFB, TN, 63

GEOGRAPHIC INDEX – U

UNITED STATES DEPARTMENT OF DEFENSE (continued)
  Army Corps of Engineers
    Memphis Engineer District, 69
    Nashville Engineer District, 69
UNITED STATES DEPARTMENT OF ENERGY
  Carbon Dioxide Information Analysis Center, 75
UNITED STATES DEPARTMENT OF THE INTERIOR
  Fish and Wildlife Service
    Chickasaw National Wildlife Refuge, 95
    Cross Creeks National Wildlife Refuge, 96
    Hatchie National Wildlife Refuge, 99
    Lower Hatchie National Wildlife Refuge, 104
    Tennessee National Wildlife Refuge, 116
    West Tennessee Refuges, 118
  National Park Service
    Great Smoky Mountains National Park, 123
UNIVERSITY OF TENNESSEE - AT KNOXVILLE, 621
UNIVERSITY OF TENNESSEE AT MARTIN, 621
UNIVERSITY OF THE SOUTH (SEWANEE), 621
VANDERBILT CENTER FOR ENVIRONMENTAL MANAGEMENT (VCEMS), 625
VANDERBILT UNIVERSITY, 625
WILDLIFE SOCIETY
  Tennessee Chapter, 553

TEXAS

AMERICAN FISHERIES SOCIETY
  Texas A and M Chapter, 259
AMERICAN SOCIETY OF LIMNOLOGY AND OCEANOGRAPHY, 266
BAT CONSERVATION INTERNATIONAL, 277
BEAR SPRINGS BLOSSOM NATURE CONSERVATION GROUP INC., 277
BIG BEND NATURAL HISTORY ASSOCIATION, 277
BOY SCOUTS OF AMERICA, 280
BUREAU OF ECONOMIC GEOLOGY, 140
CANON ENVIROTHON, 288
CENTER FOR ENVIRONMENTAL PHILOSOPHY, 291
CENTER FOR THE STUDY OF TROPICAL BIRDS, INC.
  Administrative Office, 293
CHIHUAHUAN DESERT RESEARCH INSTITUTE, 296
CHISHOLM WOLF FOUNDATION, INC., 296
CLEAR CREEK ENVIRONMENTAL FOUNDATION, 299
COASTAL CONSERVATION ASSOCIATION, 300
COUNCIL FOR ENVIRONMENTAL EDUCATION, 309
DESERT FISHES COUNCIL, 314
EARTH FOUNDATION, 317
ENVIRONMENTAL DEFENSE
  Texas Office, 325
ENVIRONMENTAL PROTECTION AGENCY
  Region 6 (AR, LA, NM, OK, TX), 19
FOSSIL RIM WILDLIFE CENTER, 336
GAME CONSERVATION INTERNATIONAL (GAME COIN), 339
GUADALUPE-BLANCO RIVER AUTHORITY, 157
ILOVEPARKS.COM, 567
INTERNATIONAL ASSOCIATION FOR ENVIRONMENTAL HYDROLOGY (IAEH), 359
INTERNATIONAL BOUNDARY AND WATER COMMISSION, UNITED STATES AND MEXICO, 22
KIDS ON THE BAYOU, 384
LADY BIRD JOHNSON WILDFLOWER CENTER, 385
NATIONAL ASSOCIATION OF CONSERVATION DISTRICTS
  League City Office, 408
NATIONAL ASSOCIATION OF RECREATION RESOURCE PLANNERS, 408
NATIONAL TRAPPERS ASSOCIATION, INC., 425
NATIONAL TRUST FOR HISTORIC PRESERVATION
  SOUTHWEST OFFICE, 426
NATIONAL WILDLIFE FEDERATION
  Gulf States Natural Resource Center, 428
NATIVE PLANT SOCIETY OF TEXAS, 431
NATIVE PRAIRIES ASSOCIATION OF TEXAS, 431
NATURE CONSERVANCY, THE
  Texas Chapter, 439
NORTH AMERICAN DEVELOPMENT BANK, 24
NORTH AMERICAN WOLF ASSOCIATION, 449
PRAIRIE GROUSE TECHNICAL COUNCIL, 472
PRESERVATION SOCIETY FOR SPRING CREEK FOREST, 473
RED BUFFALO, LLC, 570
RICE UNIVERSITY, 594
  Rice School of Architecture, 594
SCENIC AMERICA
  Scenic Texas, 487
SIERRA CLUB
  Lone Star Chapter, 493
  Southern Plains National Field Office, 498
STEPHEN F. AUSTIN STATE UNIVERSITY ARTHUR TEMPLE COLLEGE OF FORESTRY, 598
TEXAS A AND M UNIVERSITY AT COLLEGE STATION
  College of Agriculture and Life Sciences, 599
TEXAS A AND M UNIVERSITY AT COMMERCE
  Department of Agricultural Sciences, 599
TEXAS A AND M UNIVERSITY AT KINGSVILLE
  Caesar Kleberg Wildlife Research Institute, 599
TEXAS A AND M UNIVERSITY SYSTEM
  Texas Cooperative Extension, 599
TEXAS ASSOCIATION OF SOIL AND WATER CONSERVATION DISTRICTS, 516
TEXAS BASS FEDERATION, 517
TEXAS CHRISTIAN UNIVERSITY, 599
TEXAS COMMITTEE ON NATURAL RESOURCES, 517
TEXAS COOPERATIVE FISH AND WILDLIFE RESEARCH UNIT, 30
TEXAS DEPARTMENT OF AGRICULTURE, 222
TEXAS DEPARTMENT OF HEALTH, 222
TEXAS DISCOVERY GARDENS, 517
TEXAS FOREST SERVICE, 222
TEXAS GENERAL LAND OFFICE, 222
TEXAS ORGANIZATION FOR ENDANGERED SPECIES, 517
TEXAS PARKS AND WILDLIFE DEPARTMENT, 222
TEXAS RIPARIAN ASSOCIATION, 517
TEXAS STATE SOIL AND WATER CONSERVATION BOARD, 223
TEXAS TECH UNIVERSITY, 600
TEXAS WATER DEVELOPMENT BOARD, 223
TEXAS WILDLIFE ASSOCIATION, 517
UNITED STATES DEPARTMENT OF AGRICULTURE
  Animal and Plant Health Inspection Service
    Animal Care Central Regional Office, 31
    International Services Mexico Office, 32
    International Services Screwworm Eradication Program Office, 32
  Forest Service
    Angelina National Forest, 34
    Angelina, Davy Crockett, Sabine and Sam Houston National Forest, 34
    Lyndon B. Johnson / Caddo National Forest, 40
  Research Education and Economics
    ARS Southern Plains Office, 48
UNITED STATES DEPARTMENT OF COMMERCE
  National Oceanic and Atmospheric Administration
    Flower Garden Banks National Marine Sanctuary, 50
    Sea Grant Program - Texas, 59
UNITED STATES DEPARTMENT OF DEFENSE
  Air Force
    Center For Environmental Excellence, 61
  Air Force Major Air Commands
    Randolph AFB, TX, 62
  Air Force Major U.S. Installations
    Brooks AFB, TX, 63
    Dyess AFB, TX, 63
    Goodfellow AFB, TX, 64
    Lackland AFB, TX, 64
    Laughlin AFB, TX, 64
    Randolph AFB, TX, 66
    Sheppard AFB, TX, 66
  Army Corps of Engineers
    Fort Worth Engineer District, 68
    Galveston Engineer District, 68
    Southwestern Engineer District, 71
UNITED STATES DEPARTMENT OF HOMELAND SECURITY
  Customs and Border Protection
    East Texas CMC, 76
UNITED STATES DEPARTMENT OF THE INTERIOR
  Bureau of Land Management
    Amarillo Field Office, 78
  Fish and Wildlife Service
    Anahuac National Wildlife Refuge, 91
    Arkansas National Wildlife Refuge, 91
    Attwater Prairie Chicken National Wildlife Refuge, 92
    Balcones Canyonlands National Wildlife Refuge, 92
    Brazoria National Wildlife Refuge, 94
    Buffalo Lake National Wildlife Refuge, 94
    Hagerman National Wildlife Refuge, 99
    Laguna Atascosa National Wildlife Refuge, 102
    Lower Rio Grande/Santa Anna Complex National Wildlife Refuge, 104
    Muleshoe/Grulla National Wildlife Refuge, 107
    Trinity River National Wildlife Refuge, 116
  National Park Service
    Big Bend National Park, 120
    Chihuahuan Desert Network, 121
    Guadalupe Mountains National Park, 123
    Padre Island National Seashore, 124

GEOGRAPHIC INDEX – U

UNIVERSITY OF HOUSTON, 610
UNIVERSITY OF NORTH TEXAS, 618
WELDER WILDLIFE FOUNDATION, 535
WETLAND HABITAT ALLIANCE OF TEXAS, 538
WILDLIFE SOCIETY
   Texas Chapter, 553
WOLF GROUP, THE, 557

UTAH
ADVOCATES OF THE COMMON WEALTH, INC., 243
AMERICAN FISHERIES SOCIETY
   Bonneville Chapter, 253
ECONOVA INC., 565
GLEN CANYON INSTITUTE, 343
HAWKWATCH INTERNATIONAL, 350
JACK H. BERRYMAN INSTITUTE FOR WILDLIFE DAMAGE MANAGEMENT, 379
LIVING RIVERS, 390
NATURE CONSERVANCY, THE
   Utah Chapter, 440
SIERRA CLUB
   Utah Chapter, 498
   Utah Field Office, 498
SOUTHERN UTAH WILDERNESS ALLIANCE, 509
   Moab Office, 510
   St. George Office, 510
TREAD LIGHTLY! INC, 518
TROUT UNLIMITED
   Utah Council, 523
UNITED STATES DEPARTMENT OF AGRICULTURE
   Forest Service
      Ashley National Forest, 34
      Dixie National Forest, 37
      Fishlake National Forest, 37
      Manti-LaSal National Forest, 40
      Region 04 (Intermountain), 43
      Uinta National Forest, 46
      Wasatch-Cache National Forest, 48
UNITED STATES DEPARTMENT OF DEFENSE
   Air Force Major U.S. Installations
      Hill AFB, UT, 64
UNITED STATES DEPARTMENT OF THE INTERIOR
   Bureau of Land Management
      Arizona Strip Field Office, 79
      Cedar City District Field Office, 80
      Fillmore Field Office, 81
      Kanab, 82
      Moab District Field Office, 84
      Monticello Field Office, 84
      Richfield District Field Office, 86
      Salt Lake Field Office, 86
      St. George Field Office, 87
      State Office FOR UT, 88
      Vernal District, 88
   Bureau of Reclamation
      Upper Colorado Region, 89
   Fish and Wildlife Service
      Bear River Migratory Bird National Wildlife Refuge, 92
      Fish Springs National Wildlife Refuge, 98
      Ouray National Wildlife Refuge, 108
   National Park Service
      Arches National Park, 120
      Bryce Canyon National Park, 120
      Canyonlands National Park, 121
      Capitol Reef National Park, 121
      Zion National Park, 120
   Utah Cooperative Fish and Wildlife Research Unit, 128
UPPER COLORADO RIVER COMMISSION, 130
UTAH ASSOCIATION OF CONSERVATION DISTRICTS, 528
UTAH BASS FEDERATION, 528
UTAH DEPARTMENT OF AGRICULTURE, 225
UTAH DEPARTMENT OF HEALTH, 225
UTAH DEPARTMENT OF NATURAL RESOURCES
   Division of Utah State Parks and Recreation, 225
   Division of Wildlife Resources, 225
UTAH FORESTRY, FIRE AND STATE LANDS, 225
UTAH GEOLOGICAL SURVEY, 225
UTAH NATIVE PLANT SOCIETY, 528
UTAH NATURE STUDY SOCIETY, 528
UTAH STATE DEPARTMENT OF NATURAL RESOURCES, 225
   Division of Water Resources, 226
   Division of Wildlife Resources, 226
   Utah Energy Office, 226
UTAH STATE SOIL CONSERVATION COMMISSION, 226

UTAH STATE UNIVERSITY
   Berryman Institute for Wildlife Damage Management, 624
   College of Natural Resources, 624
UTAH WILDERNESS COALITION, 528
UTAH WILDLIFE FEDERATION, 528
UTAH WOODLAND OWNERS COUNCIL, 528
WILDLIFE SOCIETY
   Utah Chapter, 553

VERMONT
AMERICAN CHESTNUT FOUNDATION, THE, 250
ATLANTIC CENTER FOR THE ENVIRONMENT
   New England Office, 275
BUILDINGGREEN, INC., 564
FOREST WATCH, 335
FRIENDS OF MISSISQUOI NATIONAL WILDLIFE REFUGE, INC., 337
GREEN MOUNTAIN CLUB INC., THE, 346
JOHNSON STATE COLLEGE, 585
KEEPING TRACK, INC, 382
LIGHTHAWK
   New England Region, 389
MERCK FOREST AND FARMLAND CENTER, 397
NATIONAL AUDUBON SOCIETY
   Audubon Vermont, 412
NATIONAL GARDENING ASSOCIATION, 420
NATIONAL WILDLIFE FEDERATION
   Northeast Natural Resource Center, 428
NATURE CONSERVANCY, THE
   Vermont Chapter, 440
SHELBURNE FARMS, 490
SIERRA CLUB
   Vermont Chapter, 498
STERLING COLLEGE, 598
TRUST FOR WILDLIFE, INC., 524
UNITED STATES DEPARTMENT OF AGRICULTURE
   Forest Service
      Green Mountain National Forest, 38
UNITED STATES DEPARTMENT OF THE INTERIOR
   Fish and Wildlife Service
      Missisquoi National Wildlife Refuge, 106
   National Park Service
      Conservation Study Institute, 121
UNIVERSITY OF VERMONT EXTENSION, 621, 225
UNIVERSITY OF VERMONT, SCHOOL OF NATURAL RESOURCES, 622
VERMONT AGENCY OF AGRICULTURE, FOOD, AND MARKETS, 226
VERMONT AGENCY OF NATURAL RESOURCES, 226
   Department of Environmental Conservation, 226
   Department of Fish and Wildlife, 227
   Department of Forests, Parks, and Recreation, 227
   Vermont Geological Survey, 227
VERMONT ASSOCIATION OF CONSERVATION DISTRICTS, 529
VERMONT BASS FEDERATION, 529
VERMONT DEPARTMENT OF AGRICULTURE, FOOD, AND MARKETS, 227
   State Conservation Commission, 227
VERMONT DEPARTMENT OF HEALTH, 227
VERMONT ENVIRONMENTAL BOARD, 227
VERMONT INSTITUTE OF NATURAL SCIENCE, 529
VERMONT LAND TRUST, 529
VERMONT LAW SCHOOL, 625
VERMONT NATURAL RESOURCES COUNCIL, 529
VERMONT STATE-WIDE ENVIRONMENTAL EDUCATION PROGRAMS (SWEEP), 530
VERMONT WOODLANDS ASSOCIATION, 530
WILDLANDS PROJECT, 542

VIRGIN ISLANDS
ISLAND RESOURCES FOUNDATION, 375
NATURE CONSERVANCY, THE
   Virgin Islands Chapter, 440
UNITED STATES DEPARTMENT OF THE INTERIOR
   Fish and Wildlife Service
      Sand Lake National Wildlife Refuge, 113
   National Park Service
      Virgin Islands National Park, 125
UNITED STATES VIRGIN ISLANDS DEPARTMENT OF PLANNING AND NATURAL RESOURCES
   Division of Environmental Protection, 223
   Division of Fish and Wildlife, 224
UNIVERSITY OF THE VIRGIN ISLANDS, 621
VIRGIN ISLANDS CONSERVATION DISTRICT, 530
VIRGIN ISLANDS CONSERVATION SOCIETY, INC., 530
VIRGIN ISLANDS COOPERATIVE EXTENSION SERVICE, 228
VIRGIN ISLANDS SOIL AND WATER CONSERVATION DIVISION, 228

VIRGINIA
ALLIANCE FOR THE CHESAPEAKE BAY
  Richmond, VA Office, 248
AMERICAN ALLIANCE FOR HEALTH, PHYSICAL EDUCATION AND RECREATION AND DANCE, 248
AMERICAN ASSOCIATION FOR LEISURE AND RECREATION - AALR, 248
AMERICAN BIRD CONSERVANCY, 249
AMERICAN FISHERIES SOCIETY
  Native People Fisheries Section, 257
  Virginia Chapter, 259
  Virginia Tech Chapter, 259
AMERICAN GEOLOGICAL INSTITUTE, 260
AMERICAN RESOURCES GROUP, 264
AMERICAN SPORTFISHING ASSOCIATION, 266, 267
AMERICAN WATER RESOURCES ASSOCIATION, 267
ARLINGTON OUTDOOR EDUCATION ASSOCIATION, INC. (AOEA), 272
ASSOCIATION OF CONSULTING FORESTERS OF AMERICA, 273
CENTER FOR HEALTH, ENVIRONMENT, AND JUSTICE, 291
CHESAPEAKE BAY FOUNDATION, INC.
  Virginia Office, 295
CJE ASSOCIATES, 565
COASTAL SOCIETY, THE, 301
COLLEGE OF WILLIAM AND MARY, 577
CONSERVATION FUND, THE, 307
COUSTEAU SOCIETY, INC., THE, 310
EARTH FORCE, 316
EARTH FORCE
  GREEN (Global Rivers Environmental Education Network), 317
ENVIRONMENTAL ALLIANCE FOR SENIOR INVOLVEMENT (EASI), 323
ENVIRONMENTAL CAREER CENTER, 566
ENVIRONMENTAL ENTERPRISES ASSISTANCE FUND, INC., 326
ENVIROSCAPE, 566
FERRUM COLLEGE, 581
FISH FOREVER, 330
FISHAMERICA FOUNDATION, 330
FOREST FIRE LOOKOUT ASSOCIATION, 334
FOUNDATION FOR NORTH AMERICAN BIG GAME, 336
FUTURE FISHERMAN FOUNDATION, 339
GET AMERICA WORKING!, 343
INTERNATIONAL SOCIETY FOR ECOLOGICAL ECONOMICS (ISEE), 366
IZAAK WALTON LEAGUE OF AMERICA, INC., THE
  Virginia Division, 378
LEGACY INTERNATIONAL, 388
NATIONAL ASSOCIATION OF BIOLOGY TEACHERS, 407
NATIONAL AUDUBON SOCIETY
  FAIRFAX AUDUBON SOCIETY, 413
NATIONAL COALITION FOR MARINE CONSERVATION, 417
NATIONAL FORESTRY ASSOCIATION, 420
NATIONAL RECREATION AND PARK ASSOCIATION, 423
NATIONAL RIFLE ASSOCIATION OF AMERICA, 424
NATIONAL SCIENCE FOUNDATION, 24
NATIONAL SCIENCE TEACHERS ASSOCIATION, 424
NATIONAL WATER RESOURCES ASSOCIATION, 426
NATIONAL WATERSHED COALITION, 426
NATIONAL WILDLIFE FEDERATION
  Headquarters, 427
NATIONAL WILDLIFE FEDERATION ENDOWMENT, INC., 429
NATIONAL WILDLIFE PRODUCTIONS, INC., 429
NATIONAL WOODLAND OWNERS ASSOCIATION, 430
NATURE CONSERVANCY, THE, 433
  Virginia Program, 440
NATURESERVE, 441
NEGATIVE POPULATION GROWTH (NPG), 442
NORTH AMERICAN WETLANDS CONSERVATION COUNCIL, 24
NORTHERN VIRGINIA REGIONAL PARK AUTHORITY, 202
PIEDMONT ENVIRONMENTAL COUNCIL, 469
POINT TO POINT COMMUNICATIONS, 569
POTOMAC APPALACHIAN TRAIL CLUB, 471
PUBLIC LANDS FOUNDATION, 474
RARE CENTER FOR TROPICAL CONSERVATION, 478
RESPONSIVE MANAGEMENT, 570
SIERRA CLUB
  Mid-Atlantic Regional Office, 494
  Virginia Chapter, 499
SOCIETY FOR CONSERVATION BIOLOGY, 502
SOCIETY FOR INTEGRATIVE AND COMPARATIVE BIOLOGY, 502
SOCIETY OF WETLAND SCIENTISTS, 504
SOUTHERN ENVIRONMENTAL LAW CENTER, 509
STUDENT CONSERVATION ASSOCIATION, INC.
  Office of the National Capital Region
    Mid-Atlantic/Southeast Regional Office, 513
TROUT UNLIMITED
  National Headquarters, 520
  Virginia Council, 523
UNITED STATES DEPARTMENT OF AGRICULTURE
  Forest Service
    George Washington and Jefferson National Forests, 38
UNITED STATES DEPARTMENT OF COMMERCE
  National Oceanic and Atmospheric Administration
    Chesapeake Bay National Estuarine Research Reserve
      Virginia Office, 50
    Monitor National Marine Sanctuary, 51
    Sea Grant Program - Virginia, 59
UNITED STATES DEPARTMENT OF DEFENSE
  Air Force Major Air Commands
    AFBCA/EV Headquarters, 61
    Langley AFB, VA, 62
  Air Force Major U.S. Installations
    Langley AFB, VA, 64
  Army Corps of Engineers
    Alexandria Engineer District, 67
    Alexandria Engineer District, 67
    Norfolk Engineer District, 70
  Army Materiel Command, 72
  Army Training and Doctrine Command, 73, 74
UNITED STATES DEPARTMENT OF LABOR
  Mine Safety and Health Administration, 77
UNITED STATES DEPARTMENT OF THE INTERIOR
  Bureau of Land Management
    Eastern States Office, 81
  Fish and Wildlife Service
    Back Bay/Plum Tree Island National Wildlife Refuge, 92
    Chincoteague/Wallops Island National Wildlife Refuge, 95
    Eastern Shore of VA/Fisherman Island National Wildlife Refuge, 97
    Great Dismal Swamp/Nansemond National Wildlife Refuge, 98
    Potomac River Complex National Wildlife Refuge, 110
    Rappahannock River Valley National Wildlife Refuge, 111
  National Park Service
    Shenandoah National Park, 125
  United States Geological Survey, 126
    Biological Resources Division, 127
VIRGINIA ASSOCIATION FOR PARKS, 531
VIRGINIA ASSOCIATION OF CONSERVATION DISTRICTS, 531
VIRGINIA BASS FEDERATION, 531
VIRGINIA CONSERVATION NETWORK, 531
VIRGINIA COOPERATIVE EXTENSION, 228
VIRGINIA COOPERATIVE FISH AND WILDLIFE RESEARCH UNIT (USDI), 228
VIRGINIA DEPARTMENT OF AGRICULTURE AND CONSUMER SERVICES, 228
VIRGINIA DEPARTMENT OF CONSERVATION AND RECREATION, 228
  Board of Conservation and Recreation, 229
  Breaks Interstate Park Commission, 229
  Chippokes Plantation Farm Foundation, 229
  Conservation and Development of Public Beaches Board, 229
  Division of Administration, 229
  Division of Dam Safety, 229
  Division of Natural Heritage, 229
  Division of Soil and Water Conservation, 229
  Division of State Parks, 229
  Virginia Cave Board, 230
VIRGINIA DEPARTMENT OF ENVIRONMENTAL QUALITY, 230
VIRGINIA DEPARTMENT OF FORESTRY, 230
VIRGINIA DEPARTMENT OF GAME AND INLAND FISHERIES, 230
  Region II (Lynchburg), 230
  Region III, 231
  Region IV (Staunton), 231
VIRGINIA DEPARTMENT OF HEALTH, 231
VIRGINIA DEPARTMENT OF MINES, MINERALS AND ENERGY, 231
  Division of Gas and Oil, 231
  Division of Mined Land Reclamation, 231
  Division of Mineral Mining, 231
VIRGINIA FORESTRY ASSOCIATION, 531
VIRGINIA MARINE RESOURCES COMMISSION, 232
VIRGINIA MUSEUM OF NATURAL HISTORY, 232
VIRGINIA NATIVE PLANT SOCIETY, 531
VIRGINIA OUTDOORS FOUNDATION, 232
VIRGINIA POLYTECHNIC INSTITUTE
  Fish and Wildlife Information Exchange, 625
VIRGINIA POLYTECHNIC INSTITUTE AND STATE UNIVERSITY
  College of Natural Resources, 625
VIRGINIA RESOURCE-USE EDUCATION COUNCIL, 532
VIRGINIA SOCIETY OF ORNITHOLOGY, 532
VIRGINIA SOIL AND CONSERVATION BOARD, 232

GEOGRAPHIC INDEX – U

VIRGINIA TECH
   Department of Fisheries and Wildlife Sciences, 625
VIRGINIA TECH UNIVERSITY
   College of Natural Resources, 625
WATER ENVIRONMENT FEDERATION, 535
WILDLIFE CENTER OF VIRGINIA, THE, 542
WILDLIFE SOCIETY
   National Capital Chapter, 550
   Virginia Chapter, 553

WASHINGTON
ABUNDANT LIFE SEED FOUNDATION, 241
ADOPT-A-STREAM FOUNDATION, THE, 242
AMERICAN FISHERIES SOCIETY
   Bioengineering Section, 253
   North Pacific International Chapter, 258
AMERICAN RIVERS
   Northwest Regional Office, 265
ANTIOCH UNIVERSITY SEATTLE, 572
BIODIVERSITY NORTHWEST, 278
C.A.S.T. FOR KIDS FOUNDATION, 281
CASCADIA RESEARCH, 200
COEREBA SOCIETY, 301
COLUMBIA RIVER GORGE COMMISSION, 148
EARTHJUSTICE
   Seattle Office, 320
EARTHSTEWARDS NETWORK, 320
ENVIRONMENTAL EDUCATION ASSOCIATION OF WASHINGTON, 325
ENVIRONMENTAL PROTECTION AGENCY
   Region 10 (WA, OR, ID, AK), 19
FEDERATION OF WESTERN OUTDOOR CLUBS, 330
FOREST STEWARDS GUILD
   Northwest Regional Chapter (GuildNW), 335
FRIENDS OF DISCOVERY PARK, 337
FRIENDS OF THE LITTLE PEND OREILLE NATIONAL WILDLIFE REFUGE, THE, 338
FRIENDS OF THE SAN JUANS, 338
GOOD NATURE PUBLISHING CO., 566
INTERAGENCY COMMITTEE FOR OUTDOOR RECREATION (IAC), 164
INTERNATIONAL ASSOCIATION OF WILDLAND FIRE, 361
INTERNATIONAL BICYCLE FUND, 361
INTERNATIONAL PACIFIC HALIBUT COMMISSION, 23
INTERNATIONAL PLANT PROPAGATORS SOCIETY, INC., 365
INTERNATIONAL SNOW LEOPARD TRUST, 366
ISSAQUAH ALPS TRAILS CLUB (I.A.T.C.), 375
IZAAK WALTON LEAGUE OF AMERICA, INC., THE
   Washington Division, 378
LEAGUE OF WOMEN VOTERS OF WASHINGTON, 388
LIGHTHAWK
   Northwest Field Office, 389
LONG LIVE THE KINGS, 390
LUMMI ISLAND HERITAGE TRUST, 568
MARINE CONSERVATION BIOLOGY INSTITUTE, 394
MOUNTAINEERS, THE, 405
NATIONAL AUDUBON SOCIETY
   Seattle Audubon Society, 416
NATIONAL WILDLIFE FEDERATION
   Northwestern Natural Resource Center, 428
NATURE CONSERVANCY, THE
   Northwest and Hawaii Division Office, 438
   Washington Chapter, 440
NORTH AMERICAN CRANE WORKING GROUP, 448
NORTH CASCADES CONSERVATION COUNCIL, 451
NORTHWEST ECOSYSTEM ALLIANCE, 453
NORTHWEST ENVIRONMENT WATCH, 454
NORTHWEST INTERPRETIVE ASSOCIATION, 454
NW ENERGY COALITION, 454
OLYMPIC PARK ASSOCIATES, 459
OLYMPIC PARK INSTITUTE, 459
PACIFIC NORTHWEST TRAIL ASSOCIATION, 464
PACIFIC SEABIRD GROUP, 464
PEOPLE FOR PUGET SOUND, 467
   North Sound Office, 467
   South Sound Office, 467
POULSBO MARINE SCIENCE CENTER, 471
PROGRESSIVE ANIMAL WELFARE SOCIETY, 473
PTARMIGANS, THE, 474
PUGET SOUNDKEEPER ALLIANCE, 475
RIVERS COUNCIL OF WASHINGTON, 481
SAN JUAN PRESERVATION TRUST, THE, 484
SEA SHEPHERD CONSERVATION SOCIETY
   International Headquarters, 488

SIERRA CLUB
   Cascade Chapter, 491
   Columbia Basin Office, 491
   Northwest Office, 495
SOUND EXPERIENCE, 505
STUDENT CONSERVATION ASSOCIATION, INC.
   Northwest Office, 513
TEENS FOR RECREATION AND ENVIRONMENTAL CONSERVATION (TREC), 515
TROUT UNLIMITED
   Washington Council, 523
UNITED STATES DEPARTMENT OF AGRICULTURE
   Forest Service
      Colville National Forest, 36
      Gifford Pinchot National Forest, 38
      Okanogan National Forest, 41
      Olympic National Forest, 42
      Wenatchee National Forest, 46
UNITED STATES DEPARTMENT OF COMMERCE
   National Oceanic and Atmospheric Administration
      Olympic Coast National Marine Sanctuary, 53
      Padilla Bay National Estuarine Research Reserve, 56
      Sea Grant Program - Washington, 59
UNITED STATES DEPARTMENT OF DEFENSE
   Air Force Major U.S. Installations
      Fairchild AFB, WA, 64
      McChord AFB, WA, 65
   Army Corps of Engineers
      Seattle Engineer District, 71
      Walla Walla Engineer District, 72
UNITED STATES DEPARTMENT OF THE INTERIOR
   Bureau of Land Management
      Spokane District, 87
   Fish and Wildlife Service
      Columbia National Wildlife Refuge, 96
      Conboy Lake National Wildlife Refuge, 96
      Hanford Complex/Saddle Mountain National Wildlife Refuge, 99
      Julia Butler Hansen Refuge for the Columbia White-tailed Deer National Wildlife Refuge, 101
      Little Pend Oreille National Wildlife Refuge, 103
      Mid-Columbia River National Wildlife Refuge Complex, 105
      Nisqually/Grays Harbor National Wildlife Refuge, 108
      Pierce National Wildlife Refuge, 110
      Rice Lake National Wildlife Refuge, 112
      Turnbull National Wildlife Refuge, 117
      Washington Maritime National Wildlife Refuge Complex, 118
      Willapa/Lewis and Clark National Wildlife Refuge, 118
   National Park Service
      Mount Rainier National Park, 124
      North Cascades National Park, 124
      Olympic National Park, 124
   Uunited States Geological Survey
      Western Region, 127
   Washington Cooperative Fish and Wildlife Research Unit
      School of Aquatic and Fishery Sciences, 128
UPPER SKAGIT BALD EAGLE FESTIVAL, 527
WASHINGTON ASSOCIATION OF CONSERVATION DISTRICTS, 533
WASHINGTON BASS FEDERATION, 533
WASHINGTON DEPARTMENT OF AGRICULTURE, 232
WASHINGTON DEPARTMENT OF ECOLOGY
   Eastern Regional Office, 233
   Central Regional Office, 233
   Northwest Regional Office, 233
   Southwest Regional Office, 233
WASHINGTON DEPARTMENT OF FISH AND WILDLIFE
   Washington Fish and Wildlife Commission, 233
WASHINGTON ENVIRONMENTAL COUNCIL, 533
WASHINGTON FARM FORESTRY ASSOCIATION, 533
WASHINGTON FOUNDATION FOR THE ENVIRONMENT, 533
WASHINGTON NATIVE PLANT SOCIETY, 533
WASHINGTON NATURAL HERITAGE PROGRAM, 233
WASHINGTON RECREATION AND PARK ASSOCIATION, 533
WASHINGTON STATE CONSERVATION COMMISSION, 234
WASHINGTON STATE DEPARTMENT OF ECOLOGY, 234
WASHINGTON STATE DEPARTMENT OF NATURAL RESOURCES
   Olympic Region, 234
WASHINGTON STATE EXTENSION, 234
WASHINGTON STATE OFFICE OF ENVIRONMENTAL EDUCATION, 234
WASHINGTON STATE PARKS AND RECREATION COMMISSION, 234
   Eastern Region Headquarters, 235
   Northwest Region, 235
   Southwest Region, 235
WASHINGTON STATE UNIVERSITY, 626

WASHINGTON TOXICS COALITION, 534
WASHINGTON TRAILS ASSOCIATION, 534
WASHINGTON WILDERNESS COALITION, 534
WASHINGTON WILDLIFE AND RECREATION COALITION, 534
WASHINGTON WILDLIFE FEDERATION, 534
WESTERN WASHINGTON UNIVERSITY, 627
WILDFUTURES, 542
WILDLIFE SOCIETY
   Washington Chapter, 553
WOLF HAVEN INTERNATIONAL, 557

WEST VIRGINIA
AMERICAN FISHERIES SOCIETY
   West Virginia, 259
APPALACHIAN TRAIL CONFERENCE, 270
BROOKS BIRD CLUB INC., THE, 281
FUTURE GENERATIONS, 339
HENRY STIFEL SCHRADER ENVIRONMENTAL EDUCATION CENTER, 350
INSTITUTE FOR EARTH EDUCATION, THE, 358
IZAAK WALTON LEAGUE OF AMERICA, INC., THE
   West Virginia Division, 378
NATIONAL RIFLE ASSOCIATION WEST VIRGINIA
   White Horse Firearms and Outdoor Education Center, Inc., 424
NATURE CONSERVANCY, THE
   West Virginia Chapter, 440
ORGANIZATION OF WILDLIFE PLANNERS, 461
SHEPHERD COLLEGE, 595
SIERRA CLUB
   West Virginia Chapter, 499
TROUT UNLIMITED
   West Virginia Council, 523
UNITED STATES DEPARTMENT OF AGRICULTURE
   Forest Service
      Monongahela National Forest, 41
UNITED STATES DEPARTMENT OF DEFENSE
   Army Corps of Engineers
      Huntington Engineer District, 68
UNITED STATES DEPARTMENT OF THE INTERIOR
   Fish and Wildlife Service
      Canaan Valley National Wildlife Refuge, 94
      National Conservation Training Center, 107
      Ohio River Islands National Wildlife Refuge, 108
WEST VIRGINIA ASSOCIATION OF CONSERVATION DISTRICT SUPERVISORS ASSOCIATION, INC., 536
WEST VIRGINIA BASS FEDERATION, 536
WEST VIRGINIA COOPERATIVE FISH AND WILDLIFE RESEARCH UNIT
   Division of Forestry, 235
WEST VIRGINIA DEPARTMENT OF AGRICULTURE, 235
WEST VIRGINIA DEPARTMENT OF ENVIRONMENTAL PROTECTION, 235
WEST VIRGINIA DIVISION OF NATURAL RESOURCES, 236
WEST VIRGINIA GEOLOGICAL AND ECONOMIC SURVEY, 236
WEST VIRGINIA HIGHLANDS CONSERVANCY, 536
WEST VIRGINIA RAPTOR REHABILITATION CENTER, 536
WEST VIRGINIA SOIL CONSERVATION AGENCY, 236
WEST VIRGINIA UNIVERSITY, 626
WEST VIRGINIA UNIVERSITY
   Extension Service, 236
WEST VIRGINIA WILDLIFE FEDERATION, INC., 536
WILDLIFE SOCIETY
   West Virginia Chapter, 554
WOODLAND OWNERS ASSOCIATION OF WEST VIRGINIA, 558

WISCONSIN
ALDO LEOPOLD FOUNDATION, 247
AMERICAN FISHERIES SOCIETY
   Fisheries History Section, 254
   Wisconsin Chapter, 260
BOTANICAL CLUB OF WISCONSIN, 280
CHLORINE-FREE PAPER CONSORTIUM, 297
CITIZENS NATURAL RESOURCES ASSOCIATION OF WISCONSIN, INC., 297
COMMUNITY CONSERVATION /HOWLERS FOREVER, INC., 303
GREAT LAKES INDIAN FISH AND WILDLIFE COMMISSION, 20
INTERNATIONAL CRANE FOUNDATION, 362
IZAAK WALTON LEAGUE OF AMERICA, INC., THE
   Wisconsin Division, 378
LAKE SUPERIOR GREENS, 385
MINNESOTA-WISCONSIN BOUNDARY AREA COMMISSION, 24
NATURAL RESOURCES FOUNDATION OF WISCONSIN, 432
NATURE CONSERVANCY, THE
   Wisconsin Chapter, 440
NAVARINO NATURE CENTER, 441
NORTHLAND COLLEGE, 591
PROPERTY CARETAKING OPPORTUNITIES WORLDWIDE, 569
RIVER ALLIANCE OF WISCONSIN, 480
ROCK RIVER HEADWATERS, INC., 481
SIERRA CLUB
   John Muir Chapter, 492
SIERRA CLUB
   Midwest Office
      Madison Office, 494
SOCIETY OF TYMPANUCHUS CUPIDO PINNATUS LTD., 504
ST. NORBERT COLLEGE, 597
STATE ENVIRONMENTAL RESOURCE CENTER (SERC), 512
TREES FOR TOMORROW, NATURAL RESOURCES EDUCATION CENTER, 519
UNITED STATES DEPARTMENT OF AGRICULTURE
   Forest Service
      Chequamegon-Nicolet National Forest, 35
      Region 09 (Eastern), 43
UNITED STATES DEPARTMENT OF THE INTERIOR
   Bureau of Land Management
      Milwaukee Field Office, 83
   Fish and Wildlife Service
      Horicon Complex National Wildlife Refuge, 100
      Leopold National Wildlife Refuge, 103
      Necedah National Wildlife Refuge, 107
      St. Croix Wetland Management District, 115
      Trempealeau National Wildlife Refuge, 116
UNIVERSITY OF WISCONSIN, 622
UNIVERSITY OF WISCONSIN AT EAU CLAIRE, 622
UNIVERSITY OF WISCONSIN AT GREEN BAY
   Natural and Applied Sciences Department, 622
UNIVERSITY OF WISCONSIN AT LA CROSSE, 623
UNIVERSITY OF WISCONSIN AT MADISON, 623
UNIVERSITY OF WISCONSIN AT STEVENS POINT, 623
UNIVERSITY OF WISCONSIN-MADISON, 623
USDA FOREST PRODUCTS LABORATORY, 131
WHITETAILS UNLIMITED, INC., 539
WILD ONES NATURAL LANDSCAPERS, LTD, 540
WILDLIFE DISEASE ASSOCIATION, 543
WILDLIFE SOCIETY
   Wisconsin Chapter, 554
WISCONSIN ASSOCIATION FOR ENVIRONMENTAL EDUCATION, INC. (WAEE), 555
WISCONSIN ASSOCIATION OF LAKES (WAL), 555
WISCONSIN BASS FEDERATION, 556
WISCONSIN COOPERATIVE FISHERY RESEARCH UNIT USGS, 237
WISCONSIN COOPERATIVE WILDLIFE RESEARCH UNIT (USDI), 237
WISCONSIN DEPARTMENT OF AGRICULTURE TRADE AND CONSUMER PROTECTION, 237
WISCONSIN DEPARTMENT OF NATURAL RESOURCES, 556, 237
WISCONSIN DEPARTMENT OF PUBLIC INSTRUCTION, 238
WISCONSIN ENVIRONMENTAL EDUCATION BOARD (WEEB), 238
WISCONSIN GEOLOGICAL AND NATURAL HISTORY SURVEY, 238
WISCONSIN LAND AND WATER CONSERVATION ASSOCIATION, 556
WISCONSIN PARK AND RECREATION ASSOCIATION, 556
WISCONSIN SOCIETY FOR ORNITHOLOGY, INC., THE, 556
WISCONSIN STATE EXTENSION SERVICES, 238
WISCONSIN WATERFOWL ASSOCIATION, INC.. 556
WISCONSIN WILDLIFE FEDERATION, 557
WISCONSIN WOODLAND OWNERS ASSOCIATION, 557

WYOMING
AMERICAN FISHERIES SOCIETY
   Colorado-Wyoming Chapter, 253
   University of Wyoming Student Chapter, 259
BIODIVERSITY CONSERVATION ALLIANCE, 278
EARTH FRIENDS WILDLIFE FOUNDATION, 317
FOUNDATION FOR NORTH AMERICAN WILD SHEEP, 336
IZAAK WALTON LEAGUE OF AMERICA, INC., THE
   Wyoming Division, 378
JACKSON HOLE CONSERVATION ALLIANCE, 379
JACKSON HOLE LAND TRUST, 379
LIGHTHAWK, 389
NATIONAL FLYWAY COUNCIL
   Central Flyway Office, 419
NATURE CONSERVANCY, THE
   Wyoming Chapter, 440
POWDER RIVER BASIN RESOURCE COUNCIL, 472
SIERRA CLUB
   Northern Plains Region, 495
   Wyoming Chapter, 499
TROUT UNLIMITED
   Wyoming Council, 523

GEOGRAPHIC INDEX – Z

UNITED STATES DEPARTMENT OF AGRICULTURE
  Forest Service
    Bighorn National Forest, 34
    Bridger-Teton National Forest, 35
    Medicine Bow-Routt National Forest, 40
    Shoshone National Forest, 44
    Thunder Basin National Grasslands, 45
UNITED STATES DEPARTMENT OF DEFENSE
  Air Force Major U.S. Installations
    F.E. Warren AFB, WY, 64
UNITED STATES DEPARTMENT OF THE INTERIOR
  Bureau of Land Management
    Buffalo Field Office, 80
    Casper District, 80
    Cody Field Office, 80
    Kemmerer Field Office, 82
    Lander Field Office, 83
    Newcastle Field Office, 84
    Pinedale Field Office, 85
    Rawlins Field Office, 85
    Rock Springs Field Office, 86
    State Office for WY and NE, 88
    Worland Field Office, 89
  Fish and Wildlife Service
    National Elk Refuge, 107
    Savannah Coastal Refuges, 114
  National Park Service
    Grand Teton National Park, 122
    Yellowstone National Park, 126
UNIVERSITY OF WYOMING, 623
  William D. Ruckelshaus Institute and the School of Environment and Natural Resources, 624
WESTERN ASSOCIATION OF FISH AND WILDLIFE AGENCIES, 537
WILDLIFE HERITAGE FOUNDATION OF WYOMING (WHFW), 544
WILDLIFE SOCIETY
  Wyoming Chapter, 554
WYOMING ASSOCIATION OF CONSERVATION DISTRICTS, 560
WYOMING BASS FEDERATION, 560
WYOMING COOPERATIVE EXTENSION SERVICES, 238
WYOMING COOPERATIVE FISH AND WILDLIFE RESEARCH UNIT (USDI), 238
WYOMING DEPARTMENT OF AGRICULTURE, 239
WYOMING DEPARTMENT OF ENVIRONMENTAL QUALITY, 239
WYOMING GAME AND FISH DEPARTMENT, 239
WYOMING NATIVE PLANT SOCIETY, 561
WYOMING NATURAL DIVERSITY DATABASE, 571
WYOMING OUTDOOR COUNCIL, 561
WYOMING STATE BOARD OF LAND COMMISSIONERS, 239
WYOMING STATE FORESTRY DIVISION, 240
WYOMING STATE GEOLOGICAL SURVEY, 240
WYOMING STATE PARKS AND CULTURAL RESOURCES, 240
WYOMING WILDLIFE FEDERATION, 561

VENEZUELA
ALDEANATURAL.COM, 563
PARQUE NACIONAL SIERRA NEVADA, 569

VIETNAM
INTERNATIONAL UNION FOR CONSERVATION OF NATURE AND NATURAL RESOURCES (IUCN) THE WORLD CONSERVATION UNION
  Vietnam Country Office, 371

YUGOSLAVIA
BIRDS PROTECTION AND STUDY SOCIETY OF VOJVODINA, 279

ZAMBIA
INTERNATIONAL UNION FOR CONSERVATION OF NATURE AND NATURAL RESOURCES (IUCN) THE WORLD CONSERVATION UNION
  Zambia Country Office, 371

ZIMBABWE
INTERNATIONAL UNION FOR CONSERVATION OF NATURE AND NATURAL RESOURCES (IUCN) THE WORLD CONSERVATION UNION
  Regional Office for Southern Africa (ROSA), 370
ZERO, 562

UPDATE YOUR LISTING/CHANGE OF ADDRESS

Please help us keep the information in the directory up to date. Use this form to let us know of changes to your listing such as a new address or a new e-mail.

Please type or print clearly.

ORGANIZATION NAME _____

ADDRESS: STREET _____

CITY _____ STATE _____ ZIP _____ - _____

COUNTRY _____ E-MAIL _____

WEB SITE _____

PHONE NUMBER _____ FAX NUMBER _____

PAGE NUMBER IN 2004 DIRECTORY _____

CHANGES TO YOUR DESCRIPTION _____

_____

_____

_____

ADD CONTACT PERSON _____

REMOVE CONTACT PERSON _____

Please give us a contact name for the person we can obtain updates from.

NAME _____ PHONE _____ - _____ - _____

Further updating materials will be sent to all organizations listed in the *2004 Conservation Directory* when updating begins for the *2005 Conservation Directory*.

Please mail form to:

NATIONAL WILDLIFE FEDERATION
ATTN: CONSERVATION DIRECTORY
11100 WILDLIFE CENTER DRIVE
RESTON, VA 20190-5362
PHONE: 703-438-6000
FAX: 703-438-6061

Information may be submitted on photocopies of this form.

Visit the *Conservation Directory* online at www.nwf.org to update your organization's information automatically at any time.

APPLICATION REQUEST

If you would like your organization to be listed in the *Conservation Directory* or you have a suggestion of an organization that should be listed in the directory, please let us know. An electronic version of this form is available at www.nwf.org/printandfilm/publications/consdir/infoform.html.

Please type or print clearly.

❏ Request for Listing ❏ Suggested New Organization

ORGANIZATION NAME _____

ADDRESS: STREET _____

CITY _____ STATE _____ ZIP _____ - _____

COUNTRY _____ E-MAIL _____

WEB SITE _____

PHONE NUMBER _____ FAX NUMBER _____

CONTACT PERSON _____

Please mail form to:

NATIONAL WILDLIFE FEDERATION
ATTN: CONSERVATION DIRECTORY
11100 WILDLIFE CENTER DRIVE
RESTON, VA 20190-5362
PHONE: 703-438-6000
FAX: 703-438-6061

Information may be submitted on photocopies of this form.

Visit the *Conservation Directory* online at www.nwf.org to add a listing automatically at any time.

NATIONAL WILDLIFE FEDERATION
Conservation Directory 2004

The National Wildlife Federation's *Conservation Directory* is also available online. Groups listed in the *Conservation Directory* can update their organization's record automatically and immediately. New groups can apply online for inclusion in the *Directory*. To view the online version or to find out more about it, visit **www.nwf.org/conservationdirectory**.

ORDER FORM

Yes, I would like to order the National Wildlife Federation *Conservation Directory 2004*

_____ **Paperback copies @ $75.00 each**
(ISBN: 1-55963-415-4)

_____ **Total Book Price**

_____ **Sales Tax** *(CA 7.25%; DC 5.75%)*

Shipping & Handling
❏ **Via UPS**
$9.75 for the first book, $6.00 for each additional

❏ **Via USPS Media Mail (Book Rate)**
$7.75 for the first book, $4.00 for each additional

_____ **TOTAL**

To place a standing order for future editions of the *Conservation Directory* at a 20% discount, please contact the Island Press customer service department at **1-800-828-1302** or by email at **service@islandpress.org**

Receive useful information from Island Press via email

❏ Please send me your electronic newsletter, *Eco-Compass*

❏ I would like to receive subject-specific new-title release notifications for the following subject areas:

  ❏ Ecosystem Studies
  ❏ Human Health & Environment
  ❏ Land Use, Planning, & Environmental Design
  ❏ Global Issues
  ❏ Economics, Policy, & Law
  ❏ General Interest

My email address is:
_____

To sign up for Eco-Compass *or new-title release*

Name / Address / City / State / Zip
_____
_____
_____
_____

❏ **Enclosed is my purchase order**
(universities, public libraries, and government agencies only)

Purchase Order #: _____
The Island Press Federal ID Number is 94-2578166

❏ **Enclosed is my check.**

Please charge to my: ❏ Visa   ❏ American Express
                     ❏ Discover ❏ MasterCard

Card #: _____
Expiration Date: _____
Signature: _____
Phone #: _____
E-mail: _____
(in case we have a question about your order)

For fastest service, order online at
www.islandpress.org/nwf04
or call **1-800-828-1302**
(Mon.–Fri., 8:00 A.M.–5:00 P.M., Pacific Coast Time)
Outside of the U.S., call **707-983-6432**
Fax orders to **707-983-6414**
Send inquiries to **service@islandpress.org**

Mail orders to:
ISLAND PRESS, PO Box 7, Covelo, CA 95428

The largest member-supported conservation education and advocacy group in the United States, the National Wildlife Federation unites people from all walks of life to protect nature, wildlife and the world we all share. The Federation has educated and inspired families to uphold America's conservation tradition since 1936.